OSL

OFFICIAL SCRABBLE® LISTS

OSL

OFFICIAL SCRABBLE® LISTS

Comprehensive lists, with hints and strategies

Second edition

Compiled by
Allan Simmons and Darryl Francis

Chambers

CHAMBERS
An imprint of Chambers Harrap Publishers Ltd
7 Hopetoun Crescent
Edinburgh EH7 4AY

This edition first published by Chambers 1996
Reprinted 1997, 1998
First edition by W & R Chambers Ltd 1991

A CIP catalogue record for this book is available from the British Library

ISBN 0 550 19046 5

Managing editor Catherine Schwarz
Computer compilation Peter Schwarz

Typeset by In Production Ltd, Edinburgh
Printed and bound in Great Britain by
Caledonian International Book Manufacturing Ltd, Glasgow

Preface to second edition

This new edition of *Official Scrabble® Lists* is a vast collection of lists of words, specifically structured to aid Scrabble playing. Based on *Official Scrabble® Words,* and ultimately on *The Chambers Dictionary,* this useful book helps Scrabble players to improve their game by adding to their word knowledge, their skills and their strategies.

As well as the lists, many of them new for this edition, there are informative introductions to each section, explaining the importance of the lists and how to make best use of them. There are also the hints, on such subtleties as Rack Balancing, Managing the Big Four and Looking at Hooks; these and many others add to the Scrabble player's enjoyment of and advantages in the game.

I am sure that OSL, along with its companion OSW, will inspire you to make the most of every game of Scrabble.

Philip Nelkon
J W Spear and Sons PLC
Manager – National Scrabble Clubs

Contents

Hints

Introduction

Official Scrabble® Lists (OSL) is the perfect companion to *Official Scrabble® Words* (OSW), which is itself hailed as the definitive authority for all Scrabble players. OSL is a unique and thorough collection derived from the wealth of words within OSW, and is organized into useful sections by Allan Simmons and Darryl Francis, two of the UK's top Scrabble players. Whether you are a casual or regular player, the lists are an invaluable aid, acting as a convenient vocabulary-building guide for the newcomer and a specialist reference for the more experienced.

This new edition of OSL reflects the changes in OSW (3rd edition) resulting from the publication of the latest *Chambers Dictionary*. In OSL (2nd edition) there are also new and improved lists, making the book even more valuable than before. The starter section serves as a quick introduction to an armoury of essential vocabulary, giving all the valid two-, three- and four-letter words, plus lists of words containing the high-scoring letters.

There are lists to help players get out of difficult situations: words with many vowels; words with many consonants; words containing two B's, two C's, two F's, etc. There is also a section which concentrates on word-endings, and another featuring 250 specially-selected combinations of letters particularly fruitful in Scrabble playing, yielding thousands of likely seven- and eight-letter 'bonus-scoring' words. In addition to these sets, there are further lists of high probability 'bonus words' worth learning.

And then there's the specialist 'hooks and blockers' section. The hook lists detail every possible single-letter extension of words of from two to seven letters to form valid longer words. As well as everyday examples such as ARSON to PARSON and ABLE to TABLE, there are fascinating novelties to be unearthed, such as HOMELY to HOMELYN and READING to AREADING, and common but often unthought-of extensions such as FLAMING to FLAMINGO and UNFAIR to FUNFAIR. These lists now also include the more unusual extensions of eight-letter words, some of which are quite delightful, such as MELINITE to GMELINITE – especially if you get to play them! If you're in a mean mood, then the blocker lists will help make life difficult for your opponent.

Of course, no Scrabble book is complete without anagrams. OSL lists every valid seven- and eight-letter word according to its constituent letters in alphabetical order. Here are thousands of anagrams at your fingertips, from the exotic KURSAAL/RUSALKA to the surprising HAPPIEST/EPITAPHS, and ready solutions for jumbles of letters such as AAAGMNR – what else but ANAGRAM!

What more could the Scrabble player want? How about advice on learning words and tips on strategic play? OSL provides the answer here too, with over 25 hints offering sound advice to help improve your vocabulary and revealing strategic secrets of success.

Official Scrabble® Lists certainly helped me on the road to winning the World Scrabble Championship and I recommend this new updated edition as the ultimate single-volume Scrabble players' ready-reckoner.

Mark Nyman
World Scrabble Champion 1993

SECTION ONE

STARTER LISTS

Introduction

This section contains a variety of so-called 'starter lists'. There are the basic words – a complete listing of all valid two-letter, three-letter and four-letter words. There are lists of words with many vowels and words with many consonants – ammunition for helping you discard disproportionate numbers of vowels or consonants. There are lists of words with multiple numbers of the same vowel or same consonant – the awkward vowel dumps and the awkward consonant dumps. There are lists of words up to five letters long with a K or V. And there are complete lists of words up to eight letters long with a J, Q, X or Z. Each of the various lists is described in more detail in its accompanying introductory text.

BASIC WORDS

The following lists contain all the valid two-letter, three-letter and four-letter words. There are just over 6000 words in these three lists, and while it is not essential to know all of them, it will certainly help your game to know as many as possible.

There are 109 two-letter words listed here. Two-letter words can be considered as the backbone words of any Scrabble game. They are very important, not necessarily for the scores which they themselves achieve, but also for the scores of other words whose play they facilitate, either at the same time or later in a game.

The two-letter words provide a means of playing words parallel to other words already on the board, resolving surplus vowel problems (for example, AA, EE and OO), squeezing scores out of tight board situations, or opening the board for future scoring opportunities. Many of the two-letter words can have letters added before or after them, in order to make valid three-letter words – see the Hooks section for these.

Make a list of the two-letter words that you are not familiar with and try to introduce them into your games. You might find it additionally helpful to know what your words mean. This really can help to cement the words into your mind. But you will have to check *The Chambers Dictionary* or the Appendix of *Official Scrabble® Words* (3rd edition) for meanings. Top-flight Scrabble players will know all 109 of these words, and will also be able to define most of them!

There are over 1100 three-letter words listed here. These are important as they provide a means of discarding unwanted letters, a means of squeezing scores out of difficult board situations, and a means of playing higher-scoring words (perhaps bonuses) by turning two-letter words into three-letter words. Try to familiarize yourself with some of those which are unknown to you, and see if you can play them in your games. Leading Scrabble players will be aware of most of the three-letter words and will be able to call on them when they are needed. But most of the top players will occasionally be uncertain of a three-letter specimen. For example, a Scrabble player may well recall FAY and FEY, but will be unsure of FOY, a player might know HAH and HOH, but will be uncertain about HEH and HUH. Again, meanings can be helpful, and are easily found in *The Chambers Dictionary* or OSW (3rd edition).

There are almost 4800 four-letter words here. Their importance is less than that of the two- and three-letter words, but they do still provide a useful pool of words to dip into for scoring or rack balancing purposes.

2-LETTER WORDS

AA	AX	EA	FY	IO	ME	OD	OW	SO	US
AD	AY	EE	GI	IS	MI	OE	OX	ST	UT
AE	BA	EF	GO	IT	MO	OF	OY	TA	WE
AH	BE	EH	GU	JO	MU	OH	PA	TE	WO
AI	BI	EL	HA	KA	MY	OI	PH	TI	XI
AM	BO	EM	HE	KO	NA	OM	PI	TO	XU
AN	BY	EN	HI	KY	NE	ON	PO	UG	YE
AR	CH	ER	HO	LA	NO	OO	QI	UM	YO
AS	DA	ES	ID	LI	NU	OR	RE	UN	YU
AT	DI	EX	IF	LO	NY	OS	SH	UP	ZO
AW	DO	FA	IN	MA	OB	OU	SI	UR	

HINT

Two's Company

There are 109 two-letter words and they are all fundamental to the game. The importance of knowing all the two-letter words can't be emphasized enough. They are vital for parallel word play and maximizing scoring on tight boards and should be learnt off by heart. Write out the complete list over and over again. Play a few solo games allowing yourself to 'cheat' by referring to the list, but don't rely on the lists for too long. If you don't exercise your memory you won't recall them during actual play.

HINT

Score or Strategy?

The highest-scoring move is not always the best play. Always consider lower-scoring alternatives that might be better for your strategy. A lower-scoring move might not give so many points away to your opponent, or might leave you with a better balance of letters on your rack, or might enable you to set yourself up for a good score the next turn. Losing 10 points one turn may provide an extra 20 points the following turn or, if your emphasis had been on rack balance rather than score, it may even yield a 50-point bonus play.

3-LETTER WORDS

AAS
ABA
ABB
ABY
ACE
ACH
ACT
ADD
ADO
ADS
ADZ
AFT
AGA
AGE
AGO
AHA
AHS
AIA
AID
AIL
AIM
AIN
AIR
AIS
AIT
AKE
ALA
ALB
ALE
ALL
ALP
ALS
ALT
AMI
AMP
ANA
AND
ANE
ANI
ANN
ANT
ANY
APE
APT
ARB
ARC
ARD
ARE
ARK
ARM
ARS
ART
ARY
ASH
ASK
ASP
ASS
ATE
AUF
AUK
AVA
AVE
AWA
AWE
AWL
AWN
AXE
AYE
AYS
AYU

BAA
BAD
BAG
BAH
BAM
BAN
BAP
BAR
BAS
BAT
BAY
BED
BEE
BEG
BEL
BEN
BET
BEY
BEZ
BIB
BID
BIG
BIN
BIO
BIS
BIT
BIZ
BOA
BOB
BOD
BOG
BOH
BOK
BON
BOO
BOP
BOR
BOS
BOT
BOW
BOX
BOY
BRA
BRO
BUB
BUD
BUG
BUM
BUN
BUR
BUS
BUT
BUY
BYE
BYS

CAB
CAD
CAM
CAN
CAP
CAR
CAT
CAW
CAY
CEE
CEL
CEP
CHA
CHE
CHI
CID
CIG
CIT
CLY
COB
COD
COG
COL
CON
COO
COP
COR
COS
COT
COW
COX
COY
COZ
CRU
CRY
CUB
CUD
CUE
CUM
CUP
CUR
CUT
CUZ
CWM

DAB
DAD
DAE
DAG
DAH
DAK
DAL
DAM
DAN
DAP
DAS
DAW
DAY
DEB
DEE
DEF
DEI
DEL
DEN
DEW
DEY
DIB
DID
DIE
DIG
DIM
DIN
DIP
DIT
DIV
DOB
DOC
DOD
DOE
DOG
DOH
DON
DOO
DOP
DOR
DOS
DOT
DOW
DRY
DSO
DUB
DUD
DUE
DUG
DUN
DUO
DUP
DUX
DYE
DZO

EAN
EAR
EAS
EAT
EAU
EBB
ECH
ECO
ECU
EDH
EEK
EEL
EEN
EFF
EFS
EFT
EGG
EGO
EHS
EIK
EKE
ELD
ELF
ELK
ELL
ELM
ELS
ELT
EME
EMS
EMU
END
ENE
ENG
ENS
EON
ERA
ERE
ERF
ERG
ERK
ERN
ERR
ERS
ESS
EST
ETA
ETH
EUK
EVE
EWE
EWK
EWT
EYE

FAB
FAD
FAG
FAH
FAN
FAP
FAR
FAS
FAT
FAW
FAX
FAY
FED
FEE
FEN
FET
FEU
FEW
FEY
FEZ
FIB
FID
FIE
FIG
FIL
FIN
FIR
FIT
FIX
FIZ
FLU
FLY
FOB
FOE
FOG
FOH
FON
FOP
FOR
FOU
FOX
FOY
FRA
FRO
FRY
FUB
FUD
FUG
FUM
FUN
FUR

GAB
GAD
GAE
GAG
GAL
GAM
GAN
GAP
GAR
GAS
GAT
GAU
GAY
GED
GEE
GEL
GEM
GEN
GEO
GET
GEY
GHI
GIB
GID
GIE
GIF
GIG
GIN
GIO
GIP
GIS
GIT
GJU
GNU
GOA
GOB
GOD
GOE
GON
GOO
GOS
GOT
GOV
GOY
GUB
GUE
GUM
GUN
GUP
GUR
GUS
GUT
GUV
GUY
GYM
GYP

HAD
HAE
HAG
HAH
HAJ
HAM
HAN
HAP
HAS
HAT
HAW
HAY
HEM
HEN
HEP
HER
HES
HET
HEW
HEX
HEY
HIC
HID
HIE
HIM
HIN
HIP
HIS
HIT
HOA
HOB
HOC
HOD
HOE
HOG
HOH
HOI
HON
HOO
HOP
HOS
HOT
HOW
HOX
HOY
HUB
HUE
HUG
HUH
HUI
HUM
HUP
HUT
HYE
HYP

ICE
ICH
ICY
IDE
IDS
IFF
IFS
ILK
ILL
IMP
INK
INN
INS
ION
IOS
IRE
IRK
ISH
ISM
ISO
ITA
ITS
IVY

JAB
JAG
JAK
JAM
JAP
JAR
JAW
JAY
JEE
JET
JEU
JEW
JIB
JIG
JIZ
JOB
JOE
JOG
JOR
JOT
JOW
JOY
JUD
JUG
JUS
JUT

KAE
KAI
KAM
KAS
KAT
KAW
KAY
KEA
KEB
KED
KEF
KEG
KEN
KEP
KET
KEX
KEY
KID
KIF
KIN
KIP
KIR
KIT
KOA
KOB
KON
KOP
KOS
KOW
KYE
KYU

LAB
LAC
LAD
LAG
LAH
LAM
LAP
LAR
LAS
LAT
LAV
LAW
LAX
LAY
LEA
LED
LEE
LEG
LEI
LEK
LEP
LES
LET
LEU
LEV
LEW
LEX
LEY
LEZ
LIB
LID
LIE
LIG
LIN
LIP
LIS
LIT
LOB
LOG
LOO
LOP
LOR
LOS
LOT
LOW
LOX
LOY
LUD
LUG
LUM
LUR
LUV
LUX
LUZ
LYE
LYM

MAA
MAC
MAD
MAE
MAG
MAK
MAL
MAM
MAN
MAP
MAR
MAS
MAT
MAW
MAX
MAY
MEG
MEL
MEN
MES
MET
MEU
MEW
MHO
MID
MIL
MIM
MIR
MIS
MIX
MIZ
MNA
MOA
MOB
MOD
MOE
MOG
MOI
MOM
MON
MOO
MOP
MOR
MOT
MOU
MOW
MOY
MOZ
MUD
MUG
MUM
MUN
MUS
MUX

NAB
NAE
NAG
NAM
NAN
NAP
NAS
NAT
NAY
NEB
NED
NEE
NEF
NEK
NEP
NET
NEW
NIB
NID
NIE
NIL
NIM
NIP
NIS
NIT
NIX
NOB

NOD
NOG
NOH
NOM
NON
NOR
NOS
NOT
NOW
NOX
NOY
NTH
NUB
NUN
NUR
NUS
NUT
NYE
NYS

OAF
OAK
OAR
OAT
OBA
OBI
OBO
OBS
OCA
OCH
ODA
ODD
ODE
ODS
OES
OFF
OFT
OHM
OHO
OIK
OIL
OKE
OLD
OLE
OLM
OMS
ONE
ONS
OOF
OOH
OOM
OON
OOP
OOR
OOS
OPE
OPT
ORB
ORC
ORD
ORE
ORF
ORS
ORT
OUK
OUP
OUR
OUT
OVA
OWE
OWL
OWN
OWT
OYE
OYS

PAD
PAH
PAL
PAM
PAN
PAP
PAR
PAS
PAT
PAW
PAX
PAY
PEA
PEC
PED
PEE
PEG
PEN
PEP
PER
PET
PEW
PHI
PHO
PHS
PIA
PIC
PIE
PIG
PIN
PIP
PIR
PIS
PIT
PIU
PIX
PLY
POA
POD
POH
POI
POM
POO
POP
POS
POT
POW
POX
POZ
PRE
PRO
PRY
PSI
PST
PUB
PUD
PUG
PUH
PUN
PUP
PUR
PUS
PUT
PUY
PYE
PYX

QAT
QIS
QUA

RAD
RAG
RAH
RAI
RAJ
RAM
RAN
RAP
RAS
RAT
RAW
RAX
RAY
REC
RED
REE
REF
REH
REM
REN
REP
RES
RET
REV
REW
REX
REZ
RHO
RHY
RIA
RIB
RID
RIG
RIM
RIN
RIP
RIT
RIZ
ROB
ROC
ROD
ROE
ROK
ROM
ROO
ROT
ROW
RUB
RUC
RUD
RUE
RUG
RUM
RUN
RUT
RYA
RYE

SAB
SAC
SAD
SAE
SAG
SAI
SAL
SAM
SAN
SAP
SAR
SAT
SAW
SAX
SAY
SAZ
SEA
SEC
SED
SEE
SEG
SEI
SEL
SEN
SET
SEW
SEX
SEY
SEZ
SHE
SHY
SIB
SIC
SIM
SIN
SIP
SIR
SIS
SIT
SIX
SKA
SKI
SKY
SLY
SMA
SNY
SOB
SOC
SOD
SOG
SOH
SOL
SON
SOP
SOS
SOT
SOU
SOV
SOW
SOX
SOY
SPA
SPY
STY
SUB
SUD
SUE
SUI
SUK
SUM
SUN
SUP
SUQ
SUR
SUS
SWY
SYE

TAB
TAD
TAE
TAG
TAI
TAJ
TAK
TAM
TAN
TAP
TAR
TAT
TAU
TAW
TAX
TAY
TEA
TED
TEE
TEF
TEG
TEL
TEN
TES
TEW
THE
THO
THY
TIC
TID
TIE
TIG
TIL
TIN
TIP
TIS
TIT
TOC
TOD
TOE
TOG
TOM
TON
TOO
TOP
TOR
TOT
TOW
TOY
TRY
TUB
TUG
TUI
TUM
TUN
TUP
TUT
TUX
TWA
TWO
TWP
TYE
TYG

UDO
UDS
UEY
UFO
UGH
UGS
UKE
ULE
UNI
UNS
UPS
URD
URE
URN
USE
UTE
UTS
UTU
UVA

VAC
VAE
VAN
VAS
VAT
VAU
VEE
VEG
VET
VEX
VIA
VID
VIE
VIM
VIN
VIS
VLY
VOE
VOL
VOR
VOW
VOX
VUG
VUM

WAD
WAE
WAG
WAN
WAP
WAR
WAS
WAT
WAW
WAX
WAY
WEB
WED
WEE
WEM
WEN
WET
WEX
WEY
WHA
WHO
WHY
WIG
WIN
WIS
WIT
WOE
WOG
WOK
WON
WOO
WOP
WOS
WOT
WOW
WOX
WRY
WUD
WUS
WYE
WYN

XIS

YAH
YAK
YAM
YAP
YAW
YEA
YEN
YEP
YES
YET
YEW
YEX
YGO
YIN
YIP
YOB
YOD
YOK
YON
YOS
YOU
YOW
YUG
YUK
YUP
YUS

ZAG
ZAP
ZAX
ZEA
ZED
ZEE
ZEK
ZEL
ZEX
ZHO
ZIG
ZIP
ZIT
ZIZ
ZOA
ZOO
ZOS
ZUZ

HINT

Tackling the Threes

To the uninitiated the number of allowable three-letter words is quite daunting. However, if you ignore the everyday words the lists begin to become a little more manageable. Pay particular attention to those that can be made by extending two-letter words (see the Hooks section) and those containing tiles worth three points or more. Write out those you don't know. Many players also find it helpful to know the definitions. These you will find in *The Chambers Dictionary* or in the Appendix of *Official Scrabble Words* (3rd edition).

HINT

Open Play

Most people play Scrabble to win, which is natural and should not be discouraged. However, if you are keen to improve your scoring power and vocabulary, try playing the occasional more open game. This will enable you to concentrate on strengthening your rack-balancing, bonus-spotting and hook-word skills. Here are a few tips on open play:

- Try to ensure vowels are next to premium squares to provide scoring opportunities for high-scoring consonants.
- Experiment with playing the first word to the left of the board to enable easier access to the otherwise awkward top left.
- Play conservatively and consider points per tile gained each move rather than points per move.
- Don't be afraid to open up the triple-word squares and equally don't think you have to take a triple-word square as soon as it is available.
- Change tiles if your rack gets imbalanced and the only moves available block the openings on the board.
- Whenever you get the opportunity start a game with a three-letter word consisting of vowel-consonant-vowel played centrally to open up all four areas of the board, eg ADO, EGO, IRE, OCA, UDO etc.

HINT

Fours Feeding

Very few top players are actually familiar with all the four-letter words. The ones they tend to concentrate on are those that are formed from three-letter words (see the Hooks section), those that contain the higher-scoring consonants, and those that are useful for sorting out those vowel problems. Work through the four-letter list and highlight those you don't know then play a solo game restricting yourself to just four-letter words as far as you are able. Initially consult the list whilst playing but also try to play from memory. After a while oddities such as BAPU, COFT, DHAL and EUOI become second nature to your game, and impress your opponents!

4-LETTER WORDS

ABAC
ABAS
ABBA
ABBE
ABBS
ABED
ABET
ABID
ABLE
ABLY
ABUT
ABYE
ACED
ACER
ACES
ACHE
ACHY
ACID
ACME
ACNE
ACRE
ACTA
ACTS
ACYL
ADAW
ADDS
ADIT
ADOS
ADRY
ADZE
AEON
AERO
AERY
AESC
AFAR
AFFY
AFRO
AGAR
AGAS
AGED
AGEE
AGEN
AGES
AGHA
AGIN
AGIO
AGMA
AGOG
AGON
AGUE
AHED
AHEM
AHOY
AIAS
AIDE
AIDS
AILS
AIMS
AINE
AIRN
AIRS
AIRT
AIRY
AITS
AITU
AJAR
AJEE
AKED
AKEE
AKES
AKIN
ALAE
ALAP
ALAR
ALAS
ALAY
ALBE
ALBS
ALEE
ALES
ALEW
ALFA
ALGA
ALIT
ALKY
ALLS
ALLY
ALMA
ALME
ALMS
ALOD
ALOE
ALOW
ALPS
ALSO
ALTO
ALTS
ALUM
AMAH
AMBO
AMEN
AMID
AMIE
AMIR
AMIS
AMLA
AMMO
AMOK
AMPS
AMYL
ANAL
ANAN
ANAS
ANCE
ANDS
ANES
ANEW
ANIL
ANIS
ANKH
ANNA
ANNO
ANNS
ANOA
ANON
ANOW
ANTA
ANTE
ANTI
ANTS
ANUS
APAY
APED
APES
APEX
APOD
APSE
APTS
AQUA
ARAK
ARAR
ARBA
ARBS
ARCH
ARCO
ARCS
ARDS
AREA
ARED
AREG
ARES
ARET
AREW
ARIA
ARID
ARIL
ARIS
ARKS
ARLE
ARMS
ARMY
ARNA
AROW
ARSE
ARTS
ARTY
ARUM
ARVO
ARYL
ASAR
ASCI
ASHY
ASKS
ASPS
ATAP
ATOC
ATOK
ATOM
ATOP
AUFS
AUKS
AULA
AULD
AUNE
AUNT
AURA
AUTO
AVAL
AVAS
AVER
AVES
AVID
AVOW
AWAY
AWDL
AWED
AWES
AWLS
AWNS
AWNY
AWRY
AXED
AXEL
AXES
AXIL
AXIS
AXLE
AXON
AYAH
AYES
AYRE
AYUS
AZAN
AZYM

BAAS
BABA
BABE
BABU
BABY
BACH
BACK
BADE
BADS
BAEL
BAFF
BAFT
BAGS
BAHT
BAIL
BAIT
BAJU
BAKE
BALD
BALE
BALK
BALL
BALM
BALU
BAMS
BANC
BAND
BANE
BANG
BANI
BANK
BANS
BANT
BAPS
BAPU
BARB
BARD
BARE
BARF
BARK
BARM
BARN
BARP
BARS
BASE
BASH
BASK
BASS
BAST
BATE
BATH
BATS
BATT
BAUD
BAUK
BAUR
BAWD
BAWL
BAWN
BAWR
BAYE
BAYS
BAYT
BEAD
BEAK
BEAM
BEAN
BEAR
BEAT
BEAU
BECK
BEDE
BEDS
BEEF
BEEN
BEEP
BEER
BEES
BEET
BEGO
BEGS
BEIN
BELL
BELS
BELT
BEMA
BEND
BENE
BENI
BENJ
BENS
BENT
BERE
BERG
BERK
BERM
BEST
BETA
BETE
BETH
BETS
BEVY
BEYS
BHEL
BIAS
BIBS
BICE
BIDE
BIDS
BIEN
BIER
BIFF
BIGA
BIGG
BIGS
BIKE
BILE
BILK
BILL
BIND
BINE
BING
BINK
BINS
BINT
BIOG
BIOS
BIRD
BIRK
BIRL
BIRR
BISE
BISH
BISK
BITE
BITO
BITS
BITT
BLAB
BLAD
BLAE
BLAG
BLAH
BLAT
BLAY
BLEB
BLED
BLEE
BLET
BLEW
BLEY
BLIN
BLIP
BLOB
BLOC
BLOT
BLOW
BLUB
BLUE
BLUR
BOAK
BOAR
BOAS
BOAT
BOBA
BOBS
BOCK
BODE
BODS
BODY
BOFF
BOGS
BOGY
BOHS
BOIL
BOKE
BOKO
BOKS
BOLD
BOLE
BOLL
BOLO
BOLT
BOMA
BOMB
BONA
BOND
BONE
BONG
BONK
BONY
BOOB
BOOH
BOOK
BOOL
BOOM
BOON
BOOR
BOOS
BOOT
BOPS
BORA
BORD
BORE
BORN
BORS
BORT
BOSH
BOSK
BOSS
BOTH
BOTS
BOTT
BOUK
BOUN
BOUT
BOWL
BOWR
BOWS
BOXY
BOYG
BOYO
BOYS
BOZO
BRAD
BRAE
BRAG
BRAN
BRAS
BRAT
BRAW
BRAY
BRED
BREE
BREN
BRER
BREW
BRIG
BRIM
BRIO
BRIT
BROD
BROG
BROO
BROS
BROW
BRRR
BRUT
BUAT
BUBA
BUBO
BUBS
BUCK
BUDO
BUDS
BUFF
BUFO
BUGS
BUHL
BUIK
BUKE
BULB
BULK
BULL
BUMF
BUMP
BUMS
BUNA
BUND
BUNG
BUNK
BUNS
BUNT
BUOY
BURD
BURG
BURK
BURL
BURN
BURP
BURR
BURS
BURY
BUSH
BUSK
BUSS
BUST
BUSY
BUTE
BUTS
BUTT
BUYS
BUZZ
BYES
BYKE
BYRE
BYTE

CABA
CABS
CADE
CADI
CADS
CAFE
CAFF
CAGE
CAGY
CAIN
CAKE
CAKY
CALF
CALK
CALL
CALM
CALP
CALX
CAME
CAMP
CAMS
CANE
CANG
CANN
CANS
CANT
CANY
CAPA
CAPE
CAPI
CAPO
CAPS
CARB
CARD
CARE
CARK
CARL
CARP
CARR
CARS
CART
CASA
CASE
CASH
CASK
CAST
CATE
CATS
CAUF
CAUK
CAUL
CAUM
CAUP
CAVE
CAVY
CAWK
CAWS
CAYS
CEAS
CECA
CEDE
CEDI
CEES
CEIL
CELL
CELS
CELT
CENS
CENT
CEPS
CERE
CERT
CESS
CETE
CHAD
CHAI
CHAL
CHAM
CHAP
CHAR
CHAS
CHAT
CHAW
CHAY
CHEF
CHER
CHEW
CHEZ
CHIC
CHID
CHIK
CHIN
CHIP
CHIS
CHIT
CHIV
CHIZ
CHOC
CHON
CHOP
CHOU
CHOW
CHUB
CHUG
CHUM
CHUT
CIAO
CIDS
CIEL
CIGS
CILL
CION
CIRE
CIRL
CIST
CITE
CITO
CITS
CITY
CIVE
CLAD
CLAG
CLAM
CLAN
CLAP
CLAT
CLAW
CLAY
CLEF
CLEG
CLEM
CLEW
CLIP
CLOD
CLOG
CLOP
CLOT
CLOU
CLOW
CLOY
CLUB
CLUE
COAL
COAT
COAX
COBB
COBS
COCA
COCK
COCO
CODA
CODE
CODS
COED
COFF
COFT
COGS

COHO	CREE	DAPS	DIBS	DOOL	DUEL	EELS	ETHE	FAVE	FITT
COIF	CREW	DARE	DICE	DOOM	DUES	EELY	ETHS	FAWN	FIVE
COIL	CRIB	DARG	DICH	DOOR	DUET	EERY	ETNA	FAWS	FIZZ
COIN	CRIM	DARI	DICK	DOOS	DUFF	EEVN	ETUI	FAYS	FLAB
COIR	CRIT	DARK	DICT	DOPA	DUGS	EFFS	EUGE	FAZE	FLAG
COIT	CROC	DARN	DIDO	DOPE	DUKE	EFTS	EUGH	FEAL	FLAK
COKE	CROP	DART	DIEB	DOPS	DULE	EGAD	EUKS	FEAR	FLAM
COKY	CROW	DASH	DIED	DOPY	DULL	EGAL	EUOI	FEAT	FLAN
COLA	CRUD	DATA	DIES	DORK	DULY	EGER	EURO	FECK	FLAP
COLD	CRUS	DATE	DIET	DORM	DUMA	EGGS	EVEN	FEDS	FLAT
COLE	CRUX	DAUB	DIGS	DORP	DUMB	EGGY	EVER	FEED	FLAW
COLL	CUBE	DAUD	DIKA	DORR	DUMP	EGIS	EVES	FEEL	FLAX
COLS	CUBS	DAUR	DIKE	DORS	DUNE	EGMA	EVET	FEER	FLAY
COLT	CUDS	DAUT	DILL	DORT	DUNG	EGOS	EVIL	FEES	FLEA
COMA	CUED	DAWD	DIME	DORY	DUNK	EHED	EVOE	FEET	FLED
COMB	CUES	DAWK	DIMS	DOSE	DUNS	EIKS	EWER	FEGS	FLEE
COME	CUFF	DAWN	DINE	DOSH	DUNT	EILD	EWES	FEHM	FLEG
COMP	CUIF	DAWS	DING	DOSS	DUOS	EINE	EWKS	FEIS	FLEW
COMS	CUIT	DAWT	DINK	DOST	DUPE	EKED	EWTS	FELL	FLEX
COND	CULL	DAYS	DINS	DOTE	DUPS	EKES	EXAM	FELT	FLEY
CONE	CULM	DAZE	DINT	DOTH	DURA	EKKA	EXES	FEME	FLIC
CONK	CULT	DEAD	DIPS	DOTS	DURE	ELAN	EXIT	FEND	FLIP
CONN	CUNT	DEAF	DIRE	DOTY	DURN	ELDS	EXON	FENI	FLIT
CONS	CUPS	DEAL	DIRK	DOUC	DURO	ELFS	EXPO	FENS	FLIX
CONY	CURB	DEAN	DIRL	DOUP	DUSH	ELKS	EXUL	FENT	FLOE
COOF	CURD	DEAR	DIRT	DOUR	DUSK	ELLS	EYAS	FEOD	FLOG
COOK	CURE	DEAW	DISA	DOUT	DUST	ELMS	EYED	FERE	FLOP
COOL	CURL	DEBS	DISC	DOVE	DUTY	ELMY	EYES	FERM	FLOR
COOM	CURN	DEBT	DISH	DOWD	DWAM	ELSE	EYNE	FERN	FLOW
COON	CURR	DECK	DISK	DOWF	DYAD	ELTS	EYOT	FESS	FLUB
COOP	CURS	DECO	DISS	DOWL	DYED	EMES	EYRA	FEST	FLUE
COOS	CURT	DEED	DITA	DOWN	DYER	EMEU	EYRE	FETA	FLUS
COOT	CUSH	DEEK	DITE	DOWP	DYES	EMIR	EYRY	FETE	FLUX
COPE	CUSK	DEEM	DITS	DOWS	DYKE	EMIT		FETS	FOAL
COPS	CUSP	DEEN	DITT	DOWT	DYNE	EMMA	FACE	FETT	FOAM
COPY	CUSS	DEEP	DIVA	DOXY	DZHO	EMUS	FACT	FEUD	FOBS
CORD	CUTE	DEER	DIVE	DOZE	DZOS	EMYS	FADE	FEUS	FOCI
CORE	CUTS	DEES	DIVI	DOZY		ENDS	FADO	FEYS	FOEN
CORF	CWMS	DEEV	DIVS	DRAB	EACH	ENES	FADS	FIAR	FOES
CORK	CYAN	DEFT	DIXI	DRAD	EALE	ENEW	FADY	FIAT	FOGS
CORM	CYMA	DEFY	DIXY	DRAG	EANS	ENGS	FAFF	FIBS	FOGY
CORN	CYME	DEID	DOAB	DRAM	EARD	ENOW	FAGS	FICO	FOHN
CORS	CYST	DEIL	DOAT	DRAP	EARL	ENVY	FAHS	FIDS	FOHS
CORY	CZAR	DELE	DOBS	DRAT	EARN	EOAN	FAIK	FIEF	FOID
COSE		DELF	DOCK	DRAW	EARS	EONS	FAIL	FIFE	FOIL
COSH	DABS	DELI	DOCS	DRAY	EASE	EORL	FAIN	FIGO	FOIN
COSS	DACE	DELL	DODO	DREE	EAST	EPEE	FAIR	FIGS	FOLD
COST	DADO	DELS	DODS	DREG	EASY	EPHA	FAIX	FIKE	FOLK
COSY	DADS	DELT	DOEK	DREK	EATH	EPIC	FAKE	FIKY	FOND
COTE	DAES	DEME	DOEN	DREW	EATS	EPOS	FALL	FILE	FONE
COTH	DAFF	DEMO	DOER	DREY	EAUS	ERAS	FALX	FILL	FONS
COTS	DAFT	DEMY	DOES	DRIB	EAUX	ERED	FAME	FILM	FONT
COTT	DAGO	DENE	DOFF	DRIP	EBBS	ERES	FAND	FILO	FOOD
COUP	DAGS	DENS	DOGE	DROP	EBON	ERGO	FANE	FILS	FOOL
COUR	DAHL	DENT	DOGS	DROW	ECAD	ERGS	FANG	FIND	FOOT
COVE	DAHS	DENY	DOGY	DRUB	ECCE	ERIC	FANK	FINE	FOPS
COWL	DAIS	DERE	DOHS	DRUG	ECCO	ERKS	FANS	FINI	FORA
COWP	DAKS	DERM	DOIT	DRUM	ECHE	ERNE	FARD	FINK	FORB
COWS	DALE	DERN	DOJO	DSOS	ECHO	ERNS	FARE	FINO	FORD
COXA	DALI	DERV	DOLE	DUAD	ECHT	ERRS	FARL	FINS	FORE
COXY	DALS	DESK	DOLL	DUAL	ECOD	ERST	FARM	FIRE	FORK
COZE	DALT	DEUS	DOLT	DUAN	ECRU	ESKY	FARO	FIRK	FORM
COZY	DAME	DEVA	DOME	DUAR	ECUS	ESNE	FARS	FIRM	FORT
CRAB	DAMN	DEWS	DOMY	DUBS	EDDO	ESPY	FART	FIRN	FOSS
CRAG	DAMP	DEWY	DONA	DUCE	EDDY	ESSE	FASH	FIRS	FOUD
CRAM	DAMS	DEYS	DONE	DUCK	EDGE	ESTS	FAST	FISC	FOUL
CRAN	DANG	DHAK	DONG	DUCT	EDGY	ETAS	FATE	FISH	FOUR
CRAP	DANK	DHAL	DONS	DUDE	EDHS	ETAT	FATS	FISK	FOUS
CRAW	DANS	DHOW	DOOB	DUDS	EDIT	ETCH	FAUN	FIST	FOWL
CRED	DANT	DIAL	DOOK	DUED	EECH	ETEN	FAUX	FITS	FOXY

FOYS FOZY FRAB FRAE FRAG FRAP FRAS FRAU FRAY FREE FRET FRIG FRIS FRIT FRIZ FROG FROM FROW FUBS FUCI FUCK FUDS FUEL FUFF FUGS FULL FUME FUMS FUMY FUND FUNG FUNK FUNS FURL FURR FURS FURY FUSC FUSE FUSS FUST FUZE FUZZ FYKE FYLE FYRD

GABS GABY GADE GADI GADS GAED GAES GAFF GAGA GAGE GAGS GAID GAIN GAIR GAIT GAJO GALA GALE GALL GALS GAMB GAME GAMP

GAMS GAMY GANE GANG GANT GAOL GAPE GAPO GAPS GARB GARE GARS GART GASH GASP GAST GATE GATH GATS GAUD GAUM GAUN GAUP GAUR GAUS GAVE GAWD GAWK GAWP GAYS GAZE GAZY GEAL GEAN GEAR GEAT GECK GEDS GEED GEEK GEEP GEES GEIT GELD GELS GELT GEMS GENA GENE GENS GENT GENU GEOS GERE GERM GEST GETA GETS GEUM GHAT GHEE GHIS GIBE GIBS GIDS GIED GIEN GIES GIFT GIGA

GIGS GILA GILD GILL GILT GIMP GING GINK GINN GINS GIOS GIPS GIRD GIRL GIRN GIRO GIRR GIRT GISM GIST GITE GITS GIVE GIZZ GJUS GLAD GLAM GLED GLEE GLEG GLEI GLEN GLEY GLIA GLIB GLID GLIM GLIT GLOB GLOM GLOP GLOW GLUE GLUG GLUM GLUT GNAR GNAT GNAW GNUS GOAD GOAF GOAL GOAS GOAT GOBO GOBS GOBY GODS GOEL GOER GOES GOEY GOFF GOGO GOLD GOLE GOLF GOLP GONE

GONG GONK GONS GOOD GOOF GOOK GOOL GOON GOOP GOOR GOOS GORE GORM GORP GORY GOSH GOUK GOUT GOVS GOWD GOWF GOWK GOWL GOWN GOYS GRAB GRAD GRAM GRAN GRAT GRAY GREE GREN GREW GREY GRID GRIG GRIM GRIN GRIP GRIS GRIT GROG GROT GROW GRUB GRUE GRUM GUAN GUAR GUBS GUCK GUDE GUES GUFF GUGA GUID GULA GULE GULF GULL GULP GULY GUMP GUMS GUNK GUNS GUPS GURL GURN

GURS GURU GUSH GUST GUTS GUVS GUYS GYAL GYBE GYMP GYMS GYNY GYPS GYRE GYRI GYRO GYTE GYVE

HAAF HAAR HACK HADE HADJ HADS HAEM HAET HAFF HAFT HAGG HAGS HAIK HAIL HAIN HAIR HAJI HAJJ HAKA HAKE HALE HALF HALL HALM HALO HALT HAME HAMS HAND HANG HANK HAPS HARD HARE HARK HARL HARM HARN HARO HARP HART HASH HASK HASP HAST HATE HATH HATS HAUD HAUL HAUT

HAVE HAWK HAWM HAWS HAYS HAZE HAZY HEAD HEAL HEAP HEAR HEAT HEBE HECH HECK HEED HEEL HEFT HEID HEIL HEIR HELD HELE HELL HELM HELP HEME HEMP HEMS HEND HENS HENT HEPS HEPT HERB HERD HERE HERL HERM HERN HERO HERS HERY HESP HEST HETE HETS HEWN HEWS HEYS HICK HIDE HIED HIES HIGH HIKE HILA HILD HILI HILL HILT HIND HING HINS HINT HIPS HIPT HIRE HISH HISN

HISS HIST HITS HIVE HIYA HIZZ HOAR HOAS HOAX HOBO HOBS HOCK HODS HOED HOER HOES HOGG HOGH HOGS HOHS HOIK HOKE HOKI HOLD HOLE HOLM HOLP HOLS HOLT HOLY HOME HOMO HOMY HOND HONE HONG HONK HONS HOOD HOOF HOOK HOON HOOP HOOT HOPE HOPS HORE HORN HORS HOSE HOSS HOST HOTE HOTS HOUF HOUR HOUT HOVE HOWE HOWF HOWK HOWL HOWS HOYA HOYS HUBS HUCK HUED HUER HUES

HUFF HUGE HUGS HUGY HUIA HUIS HULA HULE HULK HULL HUMA HUMF HUMP HUMS HUNG HUNK HUNT HUPS HURL HURT HUSH HUSK HUSO HUSS HUTS HWYL HYED HYEN HYES HYKE HYLE HYMN HYPE HYPO HYPS

IAMB IBEX IBIS ICED ICER ICES ICKY ICON IDEA IDEE IDEM IDES IDLE IDLY IDOL IDYL IFFY IGAD IKAT IKON ILEA ILEX ILIA ILKA ILKS ILLS ILLY IMAM IMPI IMPS INBY INCH INFO INGO

INIA INKS INKY INLY INNS INRO INTI INTO IONS IOTA IRES IRID IRIS IRKS IRON ISLE ISMS ISOS ITAS ITCH ITEM IURE IWIS IXIA

JABS JACK JADE JAGS JAIL JAKE JAKS JAMB JAMS JANE JANN JAPE JAPS JARK JARL JARS JASP JASS JASY JATO JAUP JAWS JAYS JAZY JAZZ JEAN JEAT JEED JEEL JEER JEES JEFF JELL JERK JESS JEST JETE JETS JEUX JEWS JIAO JIBE JIBS JIFF JIGS

JILL JILT JIMP JINK JINN JINX JIRD JISM JIVE JIZZ JOBE JOBS JOCK JOCO JOES JOEY JOGS JOHN JOIN JOKE JOKY JOLE JOLL JOLT JOMO JOOK JORS JOSH JOSS JOTA JOTS JOUK JOUR JOWL JOWS JOYS JUBA JUBE JUDO JUDS JUDY JUGA JUGS JUJU JUKE JUMP JUNK JURA JURE JURY JUST JUTE JUTS JUVE JYNX

KADE KADI KAED KAES KAGO KAID KAIE KAIF KAIL KAIM KAIN KAIS KAKA KAKI

KALE
KALI
KAMA
KAME
KAMI
KANA
KANG
KANS
KANT
KAON
KARA
KART
KATA
KATI
KATS
KAVA
KAWS
KAYO
KAYS
KAZI
KEAS
KEBS
KECK
KEDS
KEEK
KEEL
KEEN
KEEP
KEFS
KEGS
KEIR
KELL
KELP
KELT
KEMB
KEMP
KENO
KENS
KENT
KEPI
KEPS
KEPT
KERB
KERF
KERN
KESH
KEST
KETA
KETS
KEYS
KHAN
KHAT
KHOR
KHUD
KIBE
KICK
KIDS
KIER
KIFS
KIKE
KILD
KILL
KILN
KILO
KILP
KILT
KINA
KIND
KINE
KING

KINK
KINO
KINS
KIPE
KIPP
KIPS
KIRK
KIRN
KIRS
KISH
KISS
KIST
KITE
KITH
KITS
KIVA
KIWI
KNAG
KNAP
KNAR
KNEE
KNEW
KNIT
KNOB
KNOP
KNOT
KNOW
KNUB
KNUR
KNUT
KOAN
KOAS
KOBS
KOFF
KOHL
KOLA
KOLO
KOND
KONK
KONS
KOOK
KOPH
KOPS
KORA
KORE
KOSS
KOTO
KOWS
KRAB
KRIS
KSAR
KUDU
KUKU
KURI
KURU
KYAT
KYLE
KYND
KYNE
KYTE
KYUS

LABS
LACE
LACK
LACS
LACY
LADE
LADS
LADY

LAER
LAGS
LAHS
LAIC
LAID
LAIK
LAIN
LAIR
LAKE
LAKH
LAKY
LAMA
LAMB
LAME
LAMP
LAMS
LANA
LAND
LANE
LANG
LANK
LANT
LANX
LAPS
LARD
LARE
LARK
LARN
LASE
LASH
LASS
LAST
LATE
LATH
LATS
LAUD
LAUF
LAVA
LAVE
LAVS
LAWK
LAWN
LAWS
LAYS
LAZE
LAZO
LAZY
LEAD
LEAF
LEAK
LEAL
LEAM
LEAN
LEAP
LEAR
LEAS
LEAT
LECH
LEED
LEEK
LEEP
LEER
LEES
LEET
LEFT
LEGS
LEHR
LEIR
LEIS
LEKE

LEKS
LEME
LEND
LENG
LENO
LENS
LENT
LEPS
LERE
LERP
LESS
LEST
LETS
LEVA
LEVE
LEVY
LEWD
LEYS
LEZZ
LIAR
LIBS
LICE
LICH
LICK
LIDO
LIDS
LIED
LIEF
LIEN
LIER
LIES
LIEU
LIFE
LIFT
LIGS
LIKE
LILL
LILO
LILT
LILY
LIMA
LIMB
LIME
LIMN
LIMO
LIMP
LIMY
LIND
LINE
LING
LINK
LINN
LINO
LINS
LINT
LINY
LION
LIPS
LIRA
LIRE
LIRK
LISK
LISP
LIST
LITE
LITH
LIVE
LOAD
LOAF
LOAM

LOAN
LOBE
LOBI
LOBO
LOBS
LOCH
LOCI
LOCK
LOCO
LODE
LOFT
LOGE
LOGO
LOGS
LOGY
LOID
LOIN
LOIR
LOKE
LOLL
LOMA
LOME
LONE
LONG
LOOF
LOOK
LOOM
LOON
LOOP
LOOR
LOOS
LOOT
LOPE
LOPS
LORD
LORE
LORN
LORY
LOSE
LOSH
LOSS
LOST
LOTA
LOTE
LOTH
LOTO
LOTS
LOUD
LOUN
LOUP
LOUR
LOUT
LOVE
LOWE
LOWN
LOWS
LOWT
LOYS
LUAU
LUCE
LUCK
LUDO
LUDS
LUES
LUFF
LUGE
LUGS
LUIT
LUKE
LULL

LULU
LUMP
LUMS
LUNA
LUNE
LUNG
LUNT
LURE
LURK
LURS
LUSH
LUSK
LUST
LUTE
LUTZ
LUVS
LUXE
LYAM
LYES
LYME
LYMS
LYNE
LYNX
LYRE
LYSE
LYTE

MAAR
MAAS
MACE
MACK
MACS
MADE
MADS
MAGE
MAGG
MAGI
MAGS
MAID
MAIK
MAIL
MAIM
MAIN
MAIR
MAKE
MAKO
MAKS
MALE
MALI
MALL
MALM
MALS
MALT
MAMA
MAMS
MANA
MAND
MANE
MANG
MANI
MANO
MANS
MANY
MAPS
MARA
MARC
MARD
MARE
MARG
MARK

MARL
MARM
MARS
MART
MARY
MASA
MASE
MASH
MASK
MASS
MAST
MASU
MATE
MATH
MATS
MATT
MATY
MAUD
MAUL
MAUN
MAWK
MAWR
MAWS
MAXI
MAYA
MAYS
MAZE
MAZY
MEAD
MEAL
MEAN
MEAT
MEED
MEEK
MEER
MEET
MEGA
MEGS
MEIN
MELA
MELD
MELL
MELS
MELT
MEMO
MEND
MENE
MENG
MENT
MENU
MEOW
MERC
MERE
MERI
MERK
MERL
MESA
MESE
MESH
MESS
METE
METS
MEUS
MEVE
MEWL
MEWS
MEZE
MHOS
MICA
MICE

MICK
MICO
MIDI
MIDS
MIEN
MIFF
MIKE
MILD
MILE
MILK
MILL
MILO
MILS
MILT
MIME
MINA
MIND
MINE
MING
MINI
MINK
MINO
MINT
MINX
MINY
MIRE
MIRI
MIRK
MIRS
MIRV
MIRY
MISE
MISO
MISS
MIST
MITE
MITT
MITY
MIXT
MIXY
MIZZ
MNAS
MOAN
MOAS
MOAT
MOBS
MOCH
MOCK
MODE
MODI
MODS
MOES
MOGS
MOHR
MOIL
MOIT
MOJO
MOKE
MOKI
MOKO
MOLA
MOLD
MOLE
MOLL
MOLT
MOLY
MOME
MOMS
MONA
MONG

MONK
MONO
MONY
MOOD
MOOI
MOOK
MOOL
MOON
MOOP
MOOR
MOOS
MOOT
MOPE
MOPS
MOPY
MORA
MORE
MORN
MORS
MORT
MOSE
MOSS
MOST
MOTE
MOTH
MOTS
MOTT
MOTU
MOUE
MOUP
MOUS
MOVE
MOWA
MOWN
MOWS
MOXA
MOYA
MOYL
MOYS
MOZE
MOZZ
MUCH
MUCK
MUDS
MUFF
MUGS
MUID
MUIL
MUIR
MULE
MULL
MUMM
MUMP
MUMS
MUNT
MUON
MURE
MURK
MURL
MUSE
MUSH
MUSK
MUSO
MUSS
MUST
MUTE
MUTI
MUTT
MYAL
MYNA

MYTH
MZEE

NAAM
NAAN
NABK
NABS
NACH
NADA
NAFF
NAGA
NAGS
NAIF
NAIK
NAIL
NAIN
NALA
NAME
NAMS
NANA
NANS
NAOI
NAOS
NAPA
NAPE
NAPS
NARC
NARD
NARE
NARK
NARY
NATS
NAVE
NAVY
NAYS
NAZE
NEAL
NEAP
NEAR
NEAT
NEBS
NECK
NEDS
NEED
NEEM
NEEP
NEFS
NEIF
NEKS
NEMN
NENE
NEON
NEPS
NERD
NERK
NESH
NESS
NEST
NETE
NETS
NETT
NEUK
NEUM
NEVE
NEVI
NEWS
NEWT
NEXT
NIBS
NICE

NICK
NIDE
NIDI
NIDS
NIED
NIEF
NIES
NIFE
NIFF
NIGH
NILL
NILS
NIMB
NIMS
NINE
NIPA
NIPS
NIRL
NISI
NITE
NITS
NIXY
NOBS
NOCK
NODE
NODI
NODS
NOEL
NOES
NOGG
NOGS
NOIL
NOLE
NOLL
NOMA
NOME
NOMS
NONE
NONG
NOOK
NOON
NOOP
NOPE
NORI
NORK
NORM
NOSE
NOSH
NOSY
NOTA
NOTE
NOTT
NOUL
NOUN
NOUP
NOUS
NOUT
NOVA
NOWL
NOWN
NOWS
NOWT
NOWY
NOYS
NUBS
NUDE
NUFF
NUKE
NULL
NUMB

NUNS
NURD
NURL
NURR
NURS
NUTS
NYAS
NYED
NYES

OAFS
OAKS
OAKY
OARS
OARY
OAST
OATH
OATS
OBAS
OBEY
OBIA
OBIS
OBIT
OBOE
OBOL
OBOS
OCAS
OCHE
OCTA
ODAL
ODAS
ODDS
ODEA
ODES
ODIC
ODOR
ODSO
ODYL
OFAY
OFFS
OGAM
OGEE
OGLE
OGRE
OHMS
OHOS
OIKS
OILS
OILY
OINK
OINT
OKAY
OKES
OKRA
OKTA
OLDS
OLDY
OLEO
OLID
OLIO
OLLA
OLMS
OLPE
OMBU
OMEN
OMER
OMIT
ONCE
ONER
ONES

ONLY
ONST
ONTO
ONUS
ONYX
OOFS
OOHS
OOMS
OONS
OONT
OOPS
OOSE
OOSY
OOZE
OOZY
OPAH
OPAL
OPED
OPEN
OPES
OPTS
OPUS
ORAL
ORBS
ORBY
ORCA
ORCS
ORDS
ORES
ORFE
ORFS
ORGY
ORLE
ORRA
ORTS
ORYX
OSSA
OTIC
OTTO
OUCH
OUKS
OULD
OULK
OUPH
OUPS
OURN
OURS
OUST
OUTS
OUZO
OVAL
OVEN
OVER
OVUM
OWED
OWER
OWES
OWLS
OWLY
OWNS
OWRE
OWTS
OXEN
OXER
OYER
OYES
OYEZ

PACA
PACE

PACK
PACO
PACT
PACY
PADS
PAGE
PAHS
PAID
PAIK
PAIL
PAIN
PAIR
PAIS
PALE
PALL
PALM
PALP
PALS
PALY
PAMS
PAND
PANE
PANG
PANS
PANT
PAPA
PAPE
PAPS
PARA
PARD
PARE
PARK
PARP
PARR
PARS
PART
PASH
PASS
PAST
PATE
PATH
PATS
PAUA
PAUL
PAVE
PAWA
PAWK
PAWL
PAWN
PAWS
PAYS
PEAG
PEAK
PEAL
PEAN
PEAR
PEAS
PEAT
PEBA
PECH
PECK
PECS
PEDS
PEED
PEEK
PEEL
PEEN
PEEP
PEER
PEES

PEGH
PEGS
PEIN
PEKE
PELA
PELE
PELF
PELL
PELT
PEND
PENE
PENI
PENK
PENS
PENT
PEON
PEPO
PEPS
PERE
PERI
PERK
PERM
PERN
PERT
PERV
PESO
PEST
PETS
PEWS
PHEW
PHIS
PHIZ
PHOH
PHON
PHOS
PHOT
PHUT
PIAS
PICA
PICE
PICK
PICS
PIED
PIER
PIES
PIET
PIGS
PIKA
PIKE
PILA
PILE
PILI
PILL
PIMP
PINA
PINE
PING
PINK
PINS
PINT
PINY
PION
PIOY
PIPA
PIPE
PIPI
PIPS
PIPY
PIRL
PIRN

PIRS
PISE
PISH
PISS
PITA
PITH
PITS
PITY
PIUM
PIXY
PIZE
PLAN
PLAP
PLAT
PLAY
PLEA
PLEB
PLED
PLIE
PLIM
PLOD
PLOP
PLOT
PLOW
PLOY
PLUG
PLUM
PLUS
POAS
POCK
POCO
PODS
POEM
POET
POGO
POIS
POKE
POKY
POLE
POLK
POLL
POLO
POLT
POLY
POME
POMP
POMS
POND
PONE
PONG
PONK
PONS
PONT
PONY
POOD
POOF
POOH
POOK
POOL
POON
POOP
POOR
POOS
POOT
POPE
POPS
PORE
PORK
PORN
PORT

PORY
POSE
POSH
POSS
POST
POSY
POTE
POTS
POTT
POUF
POUK
POUR
POUT
POWN
POWS
POXY
POZZ
PRAD
PRAM
PRAT
PRAU
PRAY
PREE
PREP
PREX
PREY
PRIG
PRIM
PROA
PROB
PROD
PROF
PROG
PROM
PROO
PROP
PROS
PROW
PRUH
PRYS
PSIS
PSST
PUBS
PUCE
PUCK
PUDS
PUDU
PUER
PUFF
PUGH
PUGS
PUIR
PUJA
PUKE
PUKU
PULA
PULE
PULK
PULL
PULP
PULU
PULY
PUMA
PUMP
PUMY
PUNA
PUNK
PUNS
PUNT
PUNY

PUPA
PUPS
PURE
PURI
PURL
PURR
PURS
PUSH
PUSS
PUTS
PUTT
PUTZ
PUYS
PYAT
PYES
PYET
PYNE
PYOT
PYRE
PYRO

QADI
QATS
QOPH
QUAD
QUAG
QUAT
QUAY
QUEP
QUEY
QUID
QUIM
QUIN
QUIP
QUIT
QUIZ
QUOD
QUOP

RABI
RACA
RACE
RACH
RACK
RACY
RADE
RADS
RAFF
RAFT
RAGA
RAGE
RAGG
RAGI
RAGS
RAHS
RAID
RAIK
RAIL
RAIN
RAIS
RAIT
RAJA
RAKE
RAKI
RAKU
RALE
RAMI
RAMP
RAMS
RANA

RAND
RANG
RANI
RANK
RANT
RAPE
RAPS
RAPT
RARE
RASE
RASH
RASP
RAST
RATA
RATE
RATH
RATS
RATU
RAUN
RAVE
RAWN
RAWS
RAYS
RAZE
RAZZ
READ
REAK
REAL
REAM
REAN
REAP
REAR
RECK
RECS
REDD
REDE
REDO
REDS
REED
REEF
REEK
REEL
REEN
REES
REFS
REFT
REGO
REHS
REIF
REIK
REIN
REIS
REKE
RELY
REMS
REND
RENS
RENT
RENY
REPO
REPP
REPS
REST
RETE
RETS
REVS
REWS
RHEA
RHOS
RHUS

RIAL
RIAS
RIBS
RICE
RICH
RICK
RICY
RIDE
RIDS
RIEL
RIEM
RIFE
RIFF
RIFT
RIGG
RIGS
RILE
RILL
RIMA
RIME
RIMS
RIMU
RIMY
RIND
RINE
RING
RINK
RINS
RIOT
RIPE
RIPP
RIPS
RIPT
RISE
RISK
RISP
RITE
RITS
RITT
RIVA
RIVE
RIVO
RIZA
ROAD
ROAM
ROAN
ROAR
ROBE
ROBS
ROCH
ROCK
ROCS
RODE
RODS
ROED
ROES
ROIL
ROIN
ROJI
ROKE
ROKS
ROKY
ROLE
ROLL
ROMA
ROMP
RONE
RONG
RONT
ROOD

ROOF ROOK ROOM ROON ROOP ROOS ROOT ROPE ROPY RORE RORT RORY ROSE ROST ROSY ROTA ROTE ROTI ROTL ROTS ROUE ROUL ROUM ROUP ROUT ROUX ROVE ROWS ROWT RUBE RUBS RUBY RUCK RUCS RUDD RUDE RUDS RUED RUES RUFF RUGS RUIN RUKH RULE RULY RUME RUMP RUMS RUND RUNE RUNG RUNS RUNT RURP RURU RUSA RUSE RUSH RUSK RUST RUTH RUTS RYAL RYAS RYES RYFE RYKE RYND RYOT RYPE

SABS SACK SACS SADE SAFE SAGA SAGE SAGO SAGS SAGY SAIC SAID SAIL SAIM SAIN SAIR SAIS SAKE SAKI SALE SALP SALS SALT SAMA SAME SAMP SAND SANE SANG SANK SANS SANT SAPS SARD SARI SARK SARS SASH SASS SATE SATI SAUL SAUT SAVE SAWN SAWS SAYS SCAB SCAD SCAG SCAM SCAN SCAR SCAT SCAW SCOG SCOP SCOT SCOW SCRY SCUD SCUG SCUL SCUM SCUP SCUR SCUT SCYE SEAL

SEAM SEAN SEAR SEAS SEAT SECO SECS SECT SEED SEEK SEEL SEEM SEEN SEEP SEER SEES SEGO SEGS SEIF SEIK SEIL SEIR SEIS SEKT SELD SELE SELF SELL SELS SEME SEMI SENA SEND SENS SENT SEPS SEPT SERA SERE SERF SERK SERR SESE SESS SETA SETS SETT SEWN SEWS SEXT SEXY SEYS SHAD SHAG SHAH SHAM SHAN SHAT SHAW SHAY SHEA SHED SHES SHET SHEW SHIM SHIN SHIP SHIR SHIT

SHIV SHMO SHOD SHOE SHOG SHOO SHOP SHOT SHOW SHUL SHUN SHUT SHWA SIAL SIBB SIBS SICE SICH SICK SICS SIDA SIDE SIEN SIFT SIGH SIGN SIJO SIKA SIKE SILD SILE SILK SILL SILO SILT SIMA SIMI SIMP SIMS SIND SINE SING SINK SINS SIPE SIPS SIRE SIRI SIRS SISS SIST SITE SITH SITS SIZE SIZY SKAG SKAS SKAT SKAW SKEG SKEO SKEP SKER SKEW SKID SKIM SKIN SKIO SKIP

SKIS SKIT SKOL SKRY SKUA SKUG SKYR SLAB SLAE SLAG SLAM SLAP SLAT SLAW SLAY SLED SLEE SLEW SLEY SLID SLIM SLIP SLIT SLOB SLOE SLOG SLOP SLOT SLOW SLUB SLUE SLUG SLUM SLUR SLUT SMEE SMEW SMIR SMIT SMOG SMUG SMUR SMUT SNAB SNAG SNAP SNAR SNEB SNED SNEE SNIB SNIG SNIP SNOB SNOD SNOG SNOT SNOW SNUB SNUG SNYE SOAK SOAP SOAR SOBS SOCA SOCK SOCS SODA SODS

SOFA SOFT SOGS SOHO SOHS SOIL SOJA SOKE SOLA SOLD SOLE SOLI SOLO SOLS SOMA SOME SONE SONG SONS SOOK SOOM SOON SOOP SOOT SOPH SOPS SORA SORB SORD SORE SORI SORN SORT SOSS SOTS SOUK SOUL SOUM SOUP SOUR SOUS SOUT SOVS SOWF SOWL SOWM SOWN SOWP SOWS SOYA SOYS SPAE SPAG SPAN SPAR SPAS SPAT SPAW SPAY SPEC SPED SPEK SPET SPEW SPIC SPIE SPIK SPIN SPIT SPIV

SPOT SPRY SPUD SPUE SPUN SPUR STAB STAG STAP STAR STAW STAY STED STEM STEN STEP STET STEW STEY STIE STIR STOA STOB STOP STOT STOW STUB STUD STUM STUN STYE SUBS SUCH SUCK SUDD SUDS SUED SUER SUES SUET SUID SUIT SUKH SUKS SULK SULU SUMO SUMP SUMS SUNG SUNK SUNN SUNS SUPE SUPS SUQS SURA SURD SURE SURF SUSS SWAB SWAD SWAG SWAM SWAN SWAP SWAT SWAY SWEE

SWEY SWIG SWIM SWIZ SWOB SWOP SWOT SWUM SYBO SYCE SYED SYEN SYES SYKE SYNC SYND SYNE SYPE

TABI TABS TABU TACE TACH TACK TACO TACT TADS TAED TAEL TAES TAGS TAHA TAHR TAIL TAIS TAIT TAKA TAKE TAKI TAKS TAKY TALA TALC TALE TALI TALK TALL TAME TAMP TAMS TANA TANE TANG TANH TANK TANS TAPA TAPE TAPS TAPU TARA TARE TARN TARO TARP TARS TART TASH TASK

TASS TATE TATH TATS TATT TATU TAUS TAUT TAVA TAWA TAWS TAWT TAXA TAXI TAYS TEAD TEAK TEAL TEAM TEAR TEAS TEAT TECH TEDS TEDY TEED TEEL TEEM TEEN TEER TEES TEFF TEFS TEGG TEGS TEGU TEHR TEIL TELA TELD TELL TELS TELT TEME TEMP TEMS TEND TENE TENS TENT TERF TERM TERN TEST TETE TEWS TEXT THAE THAN THAR THAT THAW THEE THEM THEN THEW THEY THIG THIN THIR

THIS THON THOU THRO THRU THUD THUG THUS TIAR TICE TICH TICK TICS TIDE TIDS TIDY TIED TIER TIES TIFF TIFT TIGE TIGS TIKA TIKE TIKI TILE TILL TILS TILT TIME TIND TINE TING TINK TINS TINT TINY TIPI TIPS TIPT TIRE TIRL TIRO TIRR TITE TITI TITS TIZZ TOAD TOBY TOCK TOCO TOCS TODS TODY TOEA TOED TOES TOEY TOFF TOFT TOFU TOGA TOGE TOGS TOHO TOIL TOKE TOKO

TOLA
TOLD
TOLE
TOLL
TOLT
TOLU
TOMB
TOME
TOMS
TONE
TONG
TONK
TONS
TONY
TOOK
TOOL
TOOM
TOON
TOOT
TOPE
TOPI
TOPS
TORC
TORE
TORI
TORN
TORR
TORS
TORT
TOSA
TOSE
TOSH
TOSS
TOST
TOTE
TOTS
TOUK
TOUN
TOUR
TOUT
TOWN
TOWS
TOWT
TOWY
TOYS
TOZE
TRAD
TRAM
TRAP
TRAT
TRAY
TREE
TREF
TREK
TRES
TRET
TREW
TREY
TREZ
TRIE
TRIG
TRIM
TRIN
TRIO
TRIP
TROD
TROG
TRON
TROT
TROW
TROY
TRUE
TRUG
TRYE
TRYP
TSAR
TUAN
TUBA
TUBE
TUBS
TUCK
TUFA
TUFF
TUFT
TUGS
TUIS
TULE
TUMP
TUMS
TUNA
TUND
TUNE
TUNS
TUNY
TUPS
TURD
TURF
TURM
TURN
TUSH
TUSK
TUTS
TUTU
TUZZ
TWAE
TWAL
TWAS
TWAT
TWAY
TWEE
TWIG
TWIN
TWIT
TWOS
TYDE
TYED
TYES
TYGS
TYKE
TYMP
TYND
TYNE
TYPE
TYPO
TYRE
TYRO
TYTE
TZAR

UDAL
UDOS
UEYS
UFOS
UGHS
UGLI
UGLY
UKES
ULES
ULEX
ULNA
ULVA
UMBO
UMPH
UNAU
UNBE
UNCE
UNCI
UNCO
UNDE
UNDO
UNIS
UNIT
UNTO
UPAS
UPBY
UPGO
UPON
UPSY
URAO
URDE
URDS
URDY
UREA
URES
URGE
URIC
URNS
URUS
URVA
USED
USER
USES
UTAS
UTES
UTIS
UTUS
UVAE
UVAS
UVEA

VACS
VADE
VAES
VAGI
VAIL
VAIN
VAIR
VALE
VALI
VAMP
VANE
VANG
VANS
VANT
VARA
VARE
VARY
VASA
VASE
VAST
VATS
VATU
VAUS
VAUT
VEAL
VEEP
VEER
VEES
VEGA
VEHM
VEIL
VEIN
VELA
VELD
VELE
VELL
VENA
VEND
VENT
VERB
VERS
VERT
VERY
VEST
VETO
VETS
VEXT
VIAE
VIAL
VIAS
VIBS
VICE
VIDE
VIDS
VIED
VIER
VIES
VIEW
VILD
VILE
VILL
VIMS
VINA
VINE
VINO
VINS
VINT
VINY
VIOL
VIRE
VIRL
VISA
VISE
VITA
VITE
VIVA
VIVE
VIVO
VIZY
VLEI
VOAR
VOES
VOID
VOLA
VOLE
VOLK
VOLS
VOLT
VORS
VOTE
VOWS
VRIL
VROW
VUGS
VULN
VUMS

WACK
WADD
WADE
WADI
WADS
WADT
WADY
WAES
WAFF
WAFT
WAGE
WAGS
WAID
WAIF
WAIL
WAIN
WAIT
WAKA
WAKE
WAKF
WALD
WALE
WALI
WALK
WALL
WALY
WAME
WAND
WANE
WANG
WANK
WANS
WANT
WANY
WAPS
WAQF
WARD
WARE
WARK
WARM
WARN
WARP
WARS
WART
WARY
WASE
WASH
WASM
WASP
WAST
WATE
WATS
WATT
WAUK
WAUL
WAUR
WAVE
WAVY
WAWE
WAWL
WAWS
WAXY
WAYS
WEAK
WEAL
WEAN
WEAR
WEBS
WEDS
WEED
WEEK
WEEL
WEEM
WEEN
WEEP
WEER
WEES
WEET
WEFT
WEID
WEIL
WEIR
WEKA
WELD
WELK
WELL
WELT
WEMB
WEMS
WEND
WENS
WENT
WEPT
WERE
WERT
WEST
WETA
WETS
WEXE
WEYS
WHAM
WHAP
WHAT
WHEE
WHEN
WHET
WHEW
WHEY
WHID
WHIG
WHIM
WHIN
WHIP
WHIR
WHIT
WHIZ
WHOA
WHOM
WHOP
WHOT
WHOW
WICE
WICH
WICK
WIDE
WIEL
WIFE
WIGS
WILD
WILE
WILI
WILL
WILT
WILY
WIMP
WIND
WINE
WING
WINK
WINN
WINO
WINS
WINY
WIPE
WIRE
WIRY
WISE
WISH
WISP
WIST
WITE
WITH
WITS
WIVE
WOAD
WOCK
WOES
WOGS
WOKE
WOKS
WOLD
WOLF
WOMB
WONS
WONT
WOOD
WOOF
WOOL
WOON
WOOS
WOOT
WOPS
WORD
WORE
WORK
WORM
WORN
WORT
WOST
WOTS
WOVE
WOWF
WOWS
WRAP
WREN
WRIT
WUDS
WULL
WUSS
WYCH
WYES
WYND
WYNN
WYNS
WYTE

XYST

YACK
YAFF
YAHS
YAKS
YALD
YALE
YAMS
YANG
YANK
YAPP
YAPS
YARD
YARE
YARN
YARR
YATE
YAUD
YAUP
YAWL
YAWN
YAWP
YAWS
YAWY
YBET
YEAD
YEAH
YEAN
YEAR
YEAS
YECH
YEDE
YEED
YEGG
YELD
YELK
YELL
YELM
YELP
YELT
YENS
YEPS
YERD
YERK
YESK
YEST
YETI
YETT
YEUK
YEVE
YEWS
YGOE
YIKE
YILL
YINS
YIPS
YIRD
YIRK
YITE
YLEM
YLKE
YMPE
YMPT
YOBS
YOCK
YODE
YOGA
YOGH
YOGI
YOKE
YOKS
YOLD
YOLK
YOMP
YOND
YONI
YONT
YOOF
YOOP
YORE
YORK
YOUK
YOUR
YOWE
YOWL
YOWS
YUAN
YUCA
YUCK
YUFT
YUGA
YUGS
YUKE
YUKO
YUKS
YUKY
YULE
YUMP
YUNX
YUPS
YURT
YWIS

ZACK
ZAGS
ZANY
ZAPS
ZARF
ZATI
ZEAL
ZEAS
ZEBU
ZEDS
ZEES
ZEIN
ZEKS
ZELS
ZERO
ZEST
ZETA
ZEZE
ZHOS
ZIFF
ZIGS
ZILA
ZIMB
ZINC
ZING
ZIPS
ZITE
ZITI
ZITS
ZIZZ
ZOBO
ZOBU
ZOEA
ZOIC
ZONA
ZONE
ZONK
ZOOM
ZOON
ZOOS
ZOPP
ZOUK
ZULU
ZUPA
ZURF
ZYGA
ZYME

HINT

Practising with Plates

A convenient way to practise Scrabble vocabulary whilst travelling by car is to find words from car number plates. There are a number of Scrabble games playable (if you're not the driver!):

- Find the shortest word containing the three letters of the number plate (ignoring the letter denoting the year).
- Look for seven-letter words by converting the numerals to letters thus (1=I, 2=Z, 3=E, 4=A, 5=S, 6=G, 7=T, 8=B, 9=G, 0=O)
  eg DGF 105H makes DOGFISH!
- Look for seven-letter words by taking the four letters and adding the letters A E I, or I E S, or similar, to give a good 'rack'.

HINT

Suspicious Minds

Don't be suspicious of all your opponent's moves. It is often better to play to the strength of your own rack and think about your scoring potential than worry too much about whether your opponent's play is a set-up for a good score next turn. Even amongst top players there are few occasions when there is a deliberate setup play.

HINT

Tile Turnover

An additional consideration when deciding upon the best move is the number of tiles you use. Although other factors such as the score, the balance of the letters left on your rack, and the openness of the move, are just as important, the basic philosophy that using more tiles than your opponent increases your chances of getting any of the good tiles remaining in the bag cannot be completely ignored.

When faced with a choice of moves with a poor rack, more often than not the play using most tiles is the one to favour. The exception is when the only tiles remaining are the awkward tiles that you would rather avoid (eg the Q and the V's). Keeping track of the tiles played is advantageous in judging the value of a high turnover play but ultimately you are at the mercy of your own discretion.

LIGHT AND HEAVY WORDS

Light words are those with many vowels, excluding Y's. Light words are useful for discarding excessive vowels from your rack, in an attempt to return to a more balanced rack. The numbers of vowels for words of varying lengths in these lists are given here:

2-letter words, 2 vowels (eg AE, OI)
3-letter words, 3 vowels (AIA, EAU)
4-letter words, 3 vowels or more (eg EUOI, IOTA)
5-letter words, 4 vowels (eg AUDIO, QUEUE)
6-letter words, 4 vowels or more (eg COOKIE, LEAGUE)
7-letter words, 5 vowels or more (eg ANAEMIA, EVACUEE)
8-letter words, 5 vowels or more (eg ALIENATE, ORATORIO)

Words of four or more letters are listed by the vowel groups they contain. For example, ANEMIA and AVIATE are both listed in the group of 6-letter words having the vowels AAEI. This will help you learn and recall words with many vowels.

Heavy words are those with many consonants. These are useful for discarding excessive consonants from your rack, again in an attempt to return to a more balanced rack. The numbers of vowels for words of varying lengths in these lists are given here:

2-letter words, no vowels except Y (eg MY, SH)
3-letter words, no vowels except Y (eg FRY, NTH)
4-letter words, no vowels except Y (eg HYMN, YMPT)
5-letter words, no vowels except Y (eg CRWTH, NYMPH)
6-letter words, 1 vowel (eg CHINTZ, RHYTHM)

To avoid these lists ballooning in size, inflections ending in -S have been omitted. In trying to recall words with many consonants, try to home in on words with frequently-occurring clumps of letters – for example, CH, GHT, NCH, PH, SCH, SCR, TCH and TH. Of course, there are many others apart from these.

LIGHT WORDS (Many Vowels)

2-letter words - 2 vowels

AA AE AI EA EE IO OE OI OO OU

3-letter words - 3 vowels

AIA EAU

4-letter words - 3 vowels or more (by vowel content)

AAE ALAE AREA
AAI AIAS ARIA
AAO ANOA
AAU AQUA AULA AURA PAUA
AEE AGEE AJEE AKEE ALEE EALE EASE
AEI AIDE AINE AMIE IDEA ILEA KAIE VIAE
AEO AEON AERO ALOE EOAN ODEA TOEA ZOEA
AEU AGUE AUNE BEAU EAUS EAUX UREA UVAE UVEA
AII ILIA INIA IXIA
AIO AGIO CIAO IOTA JIAO NAOI OBIA
AIU AITU HUIA
AOU AUTO URAO
AUU LUAU UNAU
EEE EPEE
EEI EINE IDEE
EEO EVOE OGEE
EEU EMEU EUGE
EIOU EUOI
EIU ETUI IURE LIEU
EOO OBOE OLEO OOSE OOZE
EOU EURO MOUE ROUE
IOO MOOI OLIO
OOU OUZO

5-letter words - 4 vowels or more (by vowel content)

AAEI AECIA
AAEU AQUAE AURAE
AEEI AERIE AINEE
AEEO ZOEAE
AEIU ADIEU AUREI URAEI
AEOO ZOOEA
AIIO AIDOI AIOLI OIDIA
AIOU AUDIO AULOI OUIJA
EEEI EERIE
EEOO COOEE
EEUU QUEUE
EIOO OORIE
EIOU OURIE

6-letter words - 4 vowels or more (by vowel content)

AAAE AGAPAE AZALEA
AAAI ACACIA ALALIA ARALIA ATAXIA TAIAHA
AAAU UJAMAA
AAEE AERATE AMEBAE EATAGE GALEAE PALEAE PERAEA TALEAE
AAEI ABELIA ACEDIA AERIAL ALEXIA AMELIA ANEMIA ARAISE AVAILE AVIATE LAMIAE REALIA TAENIA
AAEO AMOEBA AORTAE APNOEA AREOLA OARAGE OZAENA
AAEU ALULAE AUBADE AURATE BATEAU BAUERA CADEAU CAUSAE FAUNAE GATEAU NAUSEA
AAII HAIKAI KAIKAI
AAIO ADAGIO AIKONA ALOGIA ANOXIA APORIA ATOCIA COAITA ORARIA ZOARIA
AAIU ABULIA ANURIA AUMAIL IGUANA QUALIA UAKARI
AAOO MANOAO
AAOU ACAJOU AGOUTA AMADOU AOUDAD AURORA
AAUU AUCUBA
AEEI AEDILE AERIER AERIES APIECE BAILEE BEANIE DEARIE DEAWIE EASIER EPEIRA FAERIE HEARIE IDEATE KEAVIE LAESIE MEALIE MEANIE MEDIAE PEREIA REDIAE SEMEIA TENIAE
AEEO AEROBE APOGEE AREOLE COATEE EVOVAE FOVEAE GOATEE OCREAE OEDEMA OLEATE
AEEOO ZOOEAE
AEEOUU EUOUAE
AEEU AEMULE AVENUE ELUATE EPAULE EQUATE EUREKA FEAGUE HEAUME LEAGUE QUAERE QUELEA RESEAU UNEASE
AEII AIRIER BAILIE LIAISE SAIKEI TIBIAE
AEIO ANOMIE AZIONE BOATIE EIDOLA EPIZOA FEIJOA GOALIE IODATE LEIPOA OAKIER OARIER OPIATE ROADIE ROARIE SOAPIE
AEIU ACULEI ADIEUS ADIEUX AECIUM AGUISE AGUIZE AUDILE AUGITE AUNTIE CAIQUE CURIAE DAUTIE ELUVIA EUCAIN GAUCIE GUINEA HAIQUE SAIQUE SAULIE TAUPIE UREDIA UREMIA
AEOO AMOOVE ZOOEAL ZOOEAS
AEOU AROUSE AVOURE COTEAU DOUANE OPAQUE OUTAGE OUTATE OUTEAT
AEUU AUREUS AUTEUR BUREAU URAEUS UVULAE
AIIO AIKIDO AIOLIS ARIOSI DAIMIO
AIOO ARIOSO OOIDAL OOMIAC OOMIAK OORIAL
AIOU AGOUTI AUDIOS BAGUIO GIAOUR OUIJAS OURALI OURARI QUINOA SOUARI UTOPIA
AOOU VAUDOO
AOUU AUROUS
EEEE PEEWEE TEEPEE
EEEI DEEPIE EELIER EERIER FEERIE HEEZIE JEELIE KEELIE MEEMIE PEERIE REEKIE WEEPIE
EEEO EPOPEE
EEEU EKUELE EMEUTE
EEII KIERIE MEINIE WIENIE
EEIO ETOILE OREIDE SOIREE TOEIER VOIDEE
EEIU ECURIE EPUISE EQUINE EQUIPE UREIDE
EEOO BOOTEE COOEED COOEES SOOGEE TOETOE
EEOU COULEE COUPEE EVOLUE

OEUVRE TOUPEE
EEUU QUEUED QUEUES
EIIO IODIDE IODINE IODISE IODIZE IOLITE IONISE IONIZE OILIER
EIIU EURIPI MILIEU QUINIE
EIOO BOODIE BOOGIE BOOKIE COOKIE COOLIE COOTIE DOOLIE FOODIE FOOTIE GOOIER GOOLIE HOODIE IONONE KOOKIE LOONIE NOOKIE OOLITE OORIER OOSIER OOZIER ORIOLE OROIDE OTIOSE ROOKIE ROOMIE SOOGIE TOORIE WOODIE
EIOU BOUGIE MOUSIE OUGLIE OUREBI OURIER OUTLIE OUTVIE POURIE TOURIE TOUTIE
EIUU UBIQUE UNIQUE
EOOO HOOPOE
EOOU QUOOKE
EOUU UVEOUS
IIOO OPIOID TOITOI
IIOU IONIUM OIDIUM
IIUU PIUPIU
IOOU IODOUS KOUROI ODIOUS
OOOO BOOBOO GOOROO HOODOO HOOROO KOODOO VOODOO ZOOZOO
OOUU ROUCOU VOUDOU

7-letter words - 5 vowels or more (by vowel content)

AAAEI ANAEMIA
AAAIU AQUARIA
AAEEI TAENIAE
AAEEO AMOEBAE AREOLAE
AAEEU AUREATE
AAEII AECIDIA
AAEIO AEOLIAN AEONIAN OLEARIA
AAEIU AURELIA CAMAIEU URAEMIA
AAEOU AUREOLA AURORAE
AAIOU ABOULIA OUABAIN OUAKARI RAOULIA SAOUARI
AEEEI ALIENEE
AEEEU EVACUEE
AEEII AIERIES
AEEIO ETAERIO
AEEIU EUCAINE EUGENIA EUTEXIA EXUVIAE
AEEOU AENEOUS AUREOLE
AEEOUU EUOUAES
AEIIU EQUINIA
AEIOO IPOMOEA ZOOECIA
AEIOU DOULEIA EULOGIA MOINEAU SEQUOIA
AEOUU AQUEOUS AUTOCUE NOUVEAU ROULEAU
AIOOO OOGONIA
EEEIU EPUISEE QUEENIE

8-letter words - 5 vowels or more (by vowel content)

AAAAI ARAPAIMA ATARAXIA
AAAEI ACADEMIA ACHAENIA ANAEMIAS ASSEGAAI
AAAEO PARANOEA
AAAEU ACAUDATE AGUACATE AQUACADE
AAAII APIARIAN RADIALIA
AAAIO PARANOIA
AAAIU ADULARIA AQUARIAN AULARIAN AVIFAUNA SAPUCAIA
AAAOU AUTOMATA
AAAUU AQUANAUT
AAEEE HETAERAE
AAEEI ACIERAGE ACIERATE AGACERIE ALIENAGE ALIENATE AWEARIED EMACIATE ENCAENIA EPIGAEAL EPIGAEAN ERADIATE FACETIAE HAEREMAI TAENIATE
AAEEO ANAEROBE AREOLATE OEDEMATA
AAEEU ACULEATE ADEQUATE CAESURAE ECAUDATE EVACUATE EVALUATE LAUREATE NAUSEATE PAENULAE SEAQUAKE
AAEII ACTINIAE AKINESIA APIARIES AVIARIES HETAIRAI HETAIRIA LACINIAE VIRAEMIA
AAEIO AERATION AGIOTAGE ALOPECIA ANOREXIA APOGAEIC CAPOEIRA EGOMANIA METANOIA OLEARIAS PAROEMIA TOXAEMIA ZABAIONE
AAEIOU ABOIDEAU ABOITEAU
AAEIU ACAULINE ALLELUIA AUBRETIA AUBRIETA AUMAILED AURELIAN AURELIAS CAMAIEUX DIAPAUSE INAURATE MAUVAISE PERIAGUA URAEMIAS
AAEOU ACAULOSE AERONAUT ANALOGUE ARACEOUS ARANEOUS AUREOLAS AUROREAN AUTOCADE AUTOMATE OCEANAUT
AAIII MILIARIA NIRAMIAI
AAIIO APOSITIA AVIATION MAIOLICA ZOIATRIA
AAIIU AUXILIAR BAUHINIA UNIAXIAL
AAIOO APOLOGIA
AAIOU ABOULIAS AUTACOID AUTOPSIA AZOTURIA CARIACOU OUABAINS OUAKARIS PAROUSIA RAOULIAS SAOUARIS
AAIUU AQUARIUM AURICULA GUAIACUM
AEEEE RELEASEE
AEEEI ALIENEES DETAINEE EARPIECE EATERIES EXAMINEE
AEEEU EMERAUDE EVACUEES SEQUELAE
AEEII AEGIRINE AEGIRITE ASEITIES EPICEDIA GAIETIES IDEALISE IDEALIZE IDEATIVE INFERIAE METAIRIE
AEEIO ACOEMETI AEROLITE AMEIOSES ETAERIOS ETIOLATE FOEDARIE OEILLADE PAEONIES
AEEIOO EPOPOEIA
AEEIU AUDIENCE BANLIEUE BEAUTIED BEAUTIES BEAUXITE CAUSERIE DECIDUAE EQUALISE EQUALIZE EQUIPAGE EQUISETA EUCAINES EUGENIAS EUPEPSIA EUTAXIES EUTAXITE EUTEXIAS EXEQUIAL EXUVIATE LEUKEMIA MAUVEINE QUEASIER QUEAZIER UNEASIER
AEEOO FOVEOLAE PAHOEHOE PEEKABOO
AEEOU AEGLOGUE ALEURONE AUREOLED AUREOLES FEATEOUS JEALOUSE OUTEATEN REAROUSE
AEEUU URAEUSES
AEIII INITIATE RETIARII
AEIIO AMEIOSIS HEMIOLIA HEMIOPIA IDEATION TAENIOID
AEIIU ACUITIES AECIDIUM AIGUILLE AQUILINE AUDITIVE AURIFIED AURIFIES EQUINIAS INDUCIAE INDUVIAE MAIEUTIC MINUTIAE UINTAITE

	UREDINIA	AEIUU	AUGURIES		ORAGIOUS	EEIIU	EQUITIES		UNIONIZE
AEIOO	AEROFOIL		AUTUNITE		OVARIOUS		QUIETIVE	EIOOO	FORHOOIE
	AMOEBOID		FAUTEUIL	AIOUU	CAUTIOUS		UBIETIES		OOLOGIES
	COENOBIA	AEOOO	ZOOGLOEA		SUBAUDIO	EEIOO	COOEEING	EIOOU	ISOLOGUE
	IPOMOEAS	AEOOU	APOLOGUE	AOOOU	OOGAMOUS		OOGENIES		OUTVOICE
	OOGAMIES		AUTOSOME	AOOUU	ANOUROUS	EEIOU	BOUDERIE		ZOOECIUM
	OVARIOLE		POACEOUS	EEEEU	SQUEEGEE		EPIGEOUS	EIOUU	BOUTIQUE
AEIOU	AGOUTIES	AEOUU	AUTOCUES	EEEIO	EOLIENNE		EPILOGUE		EULOGIUM
	CAESIOUS		FEATUOUS	EEEIU	EUXENITE		EQUIVOKE		EUROPIUM
	DIALOGUE		HUAQUERO		EXEQUIES		ETOURDIE		EXIGUOUS
	DOUANIER		NAUSEOUS		MEUNIERE		EULOGIES		TENUIOUS
	DOULEIAS		OUTVALUE		QUEENIER		EULOGISE	EOOOO	HOODOOED
	EDACIOUS		ROULEAUS		QUEENIES		EULOGIZE		VOODOOED
	EQUATION		ROULEAUX		QUEENITE		OBSEQUIE	EOOUU	DUOLOGUE
	EUPHOBIA	AIIIO	OITICICA	EEIIO	EBIONISE		OUVRIERE		OUTHOUSE
	EUPHONIA	AIIIU	DAIQUIRI		EBIONIZE	EEIUU	EUPHUISE		VOUDOUED
	EUPHORIA	AIIOO	AVOISION		EGOITIES		EUPHUIZE	IIIOU	OUISTITI
	JALOUSIE	AIIOU	AUDITION		EOLIPILE		QUEUEING	IOOOU	OOGONIUM
	MOINEAUS		OLIGURIA		ERIONITE		QUIETUDE	IOOUU	BOUZOUKI
	ODALIQUE	AIOOO	OOGONIAL		MEIONITE	EIIIO	IDIOCIES		UXORIOUS
	POULAINE		ORATORIO		MOIETIES	EIIOU	EXIMIOUS	IOUUU	USURIOUS
	SEQUOIAS		ZOONOMIA		OILERIES		FILIOQUE		
	THIOUREA	AIOOU	AUTOGIRO		OSIERIES		UNIONISE		

HINT

Vowel Advice

Once you have more than two of any vowel on your rack (except perhaps E's) it is all too easy to accumulate more because of the difficulty in sorting out the initial problem. Try the following exercise to become more familiar with those words that solve your multiple vowel imbalance.

Select three A's and then repeatedly pick up any four consonants and see how many A-words you can think of for the first move. Try to find the highest scoring first move and then consult the Awkward Vowel lists for added inspiration. Do not actually play words on the board but treat each fresh rack as if it were the first move. Repeat the exercise with the O's, I's and U's.

HINT

Triple Tactics

Every player recognizes the need to avoid giving the opponent easy access to the triple-word squares. However it is important not to be obsessive about giving away triple-word scores. Playing a word out to the edge of the board such that the word covers the double-letter square between two triple-word squares with a low-scoring tile, does not make it that easy for the opponent to score highly from the triple-word square. In fact, it may force the opponent to use his best tiles to block your use of the triple-word square next turn.

HINT

Valuing the S and Blank

The blank and the S are the most valuable tiles in the Scrabble set. Treat them as if they are worth a potential 50 points each. They are the ingredients of most seven and eight-letter bonus plays and as such should be used wisely. It is rarely worth playing an S for just a few extra points unless the move is essential for blocking the opponent in a game where winning is all important. A blank retained on the rack, even if not utilized in a bonus play, will provide that extra degree of flexibility of choice for endgame strategy.

HINT

ING Addiction

Every Scrabble player has retained ING on their rack at some time or another in the hope of getting an -ING bonus word. The usefulness of this strategy is frequently overrated amongst less experienced players. Although it is a common ending, unless you have the fortune to pick up the right letters for an -ING seven-letter word you will find the G more of a hindrance. Furthermore, if you religiously cling on to the ING you are severely limiting your choice of play for each move and are effectively playing with only four tiles. The advice is to avoid any ING addiction and concentrate on just keeping any subset of the letters RETAIN that you may have. This will be more fruitful.

HINT

Looking at Hooks

The two, three and four-letter hook words are probably the most important of the hook words. Try to learn a few useful ones at a time and attempt to introduce them into your game. An interesting exercise to assist is as follows:

Take each letter of the alphabet and find a two, three and four-letter word that takes that letter before or after as a hook to make a longer word. There may be none for some of the more awkward letters. This will give you a balanced variety of some 100 hook words to study.

Note that, for ruthless blocking strategies, the three and four-letter words that do not take hook letters before or after are just as important.

HEAVY WORDS (Many Consonants) except -S inflections

2-letter words - no vowels except Y

BY	CH	FY	KY	MY	NY	PH	SH	ST

3-letter words - no vowels except Y

CLY	FLY	HYP	PLY	RHY	SNY	THY	VLY
CRY	FRY	LYM	PRY	SHY	SPY	TRY	WHY
CWM	GYM	NTH	PST	SKY	STY	TWP	WRY
DRY	GYP	NYS	PYX	SLY	SWY	TYG	WYN

4-letter words - no vowels except Y

BRRR	GYMP	HYMN	LYNX	PSST	SKRY	SYNC	TYMP	WYND	YMPT
CYST	GYNY	JYNX	MYTH	RYND	SKYR	SYND	TYND	WYNN	
FYRD	HWYL	KYND	PRYS	SCRY	SPRY	TRYP	WYCH	XYST	

5-letter words - no vowels except Y

CHYND	DRYLY	GRYPT	GYPSY	LYNCH	PSYCH	SLYLY	SYNTH	WRYLY
CRWTH	GHYLL	GYNNY	KYDST	MYRRH	PYGMY	SYLPH	THYMY	XYLYL
CRYPT	GLYPH	GYPPY	LYMPH	NYMPH	SHYLY	SYNCH	TRYST	

6-letter words - one vowel

BLANCH	CRANCH	FROWST	PLONGD	SCRAWL	SHROWD	SPARTH	STANCK	STROWN	THRONG
BLENCH	CRANTS	GLITCH	PRANCK	SCRAWM	SHRUNK	SPERST	STARCH	STRUCK	THROWN
BLIGHT	CRATCH	GLUMPS	PROMPT	SCRIMP	SHTCHI	SPETCH	STENCH	STRUNG	THRUSH
BLINTZ	CROTCH	GROWTH	PUTSCH	SCRIPT	SHTETL	SPHINX	STITCH	STRUNT	THRUST
BLOTCH	CRUNCH	GRUMPH	RHYTHM	SCROLL	SHTICK	SPIGHT	STOWND	SWARTH	THWACK
BORSCH	CRUTCH	GRUTCH	SCARPH	SCROWL	SHTUCK	SPILTH	STRAFF	SWATCH	THWART
BRANCH	CULTCH	HIGHTH	SCARTH	SCRUFF	SHTUMM	SPLASH	STRAMP	SWITCH	TRENCH
BRIGHT	DIRNDL	KIRSCH	SCATCH	SCRUMP	SKARTH	SPLIFF	STRAND	SWOWND	TROGGS
BROWST	DRACHM	KITSCH	SCHELM	SCRUNT	SKETCH	SPLINT	STRASS	TCHICK	TWIGHT
BRUNCH	DRENCH	KLEPHT	SCHISM	SCULPT	SKLENT	SPLOSH	STRATH	THATCH	TWITCH
CATCHT	FLANCH	KNICKS	SCHIST	SCUTCH	SKLIFF	SPRACK	STRAWN	THETCH	WARMTH
CHINCH	FLENCH	KNIGHT	SCHLEP	SHLOCK	SKRIMP	SPRANG	STRESS	THIRST	WHILST
CHINTZ	FLETCH	KNITCH	SCHORL	SHMOCK	SKRUMP	SPRAWL	STREWN	THRALL	WHISHT
CHRISM	FLIGHT	KRANTZ	SCHTIK	SHMUCK	SLATCH	SPREDD	STRICH	THRANG	WRENCH
CHURCH	FLINCH	KVETCH	SCHUSS	SHRANK	SLIGHT	SPRENT	STRICT	THRASH	WRETCH
CLASTS	FLITCH	LENGTH	SCLAFF	SHREWD	SMATCH	SPRING	STRIFT	THRAWN	WRIGHT
CLATCH	FLYSCH	MENSCH	SCLIFF	SHRIFT	SMIGHT	SPRINT	STRING	THRESH	
CLENCH	FRATCH	PHLEGM	SCORCH	SHRILL	SMIRCH	SPRONG	STROLL	THRIFT	
CLINCH	FRENCH	PLANCH	SCOTCH	SHRIMP	SMUTCH	SPRUNG	STROMB	THRILL	
CLUNCH	FRICHT	PLIGHT	SCOWTH	SHRINK	SNATCH	SPRUSH	STROND	THRIPS	
CLUTCH	FRIGHT	PLINTH	SCRAMB	SHROFF	SNITCH	STANCH	STRONG	THRIST	

HINT

Fishing

It is rarely worth holding on to a set of letters hoping to pick up that one tile that will transform your rack into a wonderful high-scoring bonus word. However, if the six letters you are holding on to are likely to yield a bonus play with *many* of the tiles that you are likely to pick up (see Bonus Word Sets section) then 'fishing' could be strategically beneficial. Always consider the chances of actually getting the tile or tiles you hope for and balance this against any alternative scoring plays. Knowledge of the letter distribution and the most fruitful six-letter combinations is mandatory for timely 'fishing'.

HINT

Mind Your Changing

Since it is permissible to change any number of your letters instead of a turn during a game (unless there are fewer than seven tiles in the bag), it can be a wise decision to change some or all of your letters even if you can find a word to play on the board. You should consider changing when:

- You have an imbalance of vowels and consonants and the available dump words do not solve your rack problems, score very little, or provide too many scoring opportunities for your opponent.
- There are no scoring opportunities on the board and you don't wish to block your opponent with a low-scoring play.
- You have a Q with no U and none of the U-less Q words are playable. Note that the existence of QI makes the Q less of a problem, and it may be worth forgoing changing if you can score well with your other letters and there are still I's left.
- You have a promising six-letter combination that combines well with many other letters to make a seven-letter word – but not with the seventh letter on your rack. Changing the odd letter in this situation is often not the best strategic move but the time for such a change may be ripe if you desperately need the bonus to catch up or there are no other worthwhile alternatives.

HINT

Bonus Hunting

Faced with a rack of seven letters in any order it is not always easy to spot even common seven-letter words. Moving the tiles around will often enable an otherwise hidden seven-letter word to come to light. But rather than frantic shuffling and reshuffling in the hope of inspiration a more organized approach is recommended. Form beginnings and endings with the letters on your rack and check the remaining tiles to see if they form a word with that beginning or ending. For example, with the rack EEFGLOR making the prefix FORE will lead you to FORELEG. With ACEORTV, the prefix OVER will inspire OVERACT. Similarly with the racks AINOORT, AGEINOS and AEFHLTU it may only be by forming the endings -TION, -ISE and -FUL that you will stumble across ORATION, AGONISE and HATEFUL respectively. Also, splitting your rack into two shorter words may enable you to spot an allowable compound word. For example, the unlikely ADEEESW yields SEA and WEED (SEAWEED) and AADORWY makes ROAD and WAY (ROADWAY).

AWKWARD VOWEL DUMPS

It is often a problem when you are faced with two of the same vowel on your rack, except perhaps when they are two E's; it can be a nightmare when you are confronted with more than two, especially if they are I's or U's. Playing just one of the multiple vowels does not always resolve the problem, and you can be faced with the same problem on subsequent turns. This of course does not help your game, so ideally the problem needs to be resolved in one turn. You should find that the following lists of words containing multiple A's, E's, I's, O's or U's will greatly assist you in such situations.

The words in these lists can be summarized as follows:

A words:	3 letters, 2 A's (eg ABA, BAA)
	4 letters, 2 A's (eg AWAY, LAVA)
	5 letters, 3 A's (eg ABACA, KAAMA)
	6 letters, 3 A's (eg BANANA, BAZAAR)
E words:	4 letters, 3 E's (EPEE)
	5 letters, 3 E's (eg GEESE, MELEE)
	6 letters, 4 E's (eg PEEWEE, TEEPEE)
I words:	4 letters, 2 I's (eg IRIS, KIWI)
	5 letters, 2 I's (eg ICING, RIGID)
	6 letters, 3 I's (eg BIKINI, IRITIC)
O words:	5 letters, 3 O's (OVOLO)
	6 letters, 3 O's or more (eg COCOON, VOODOO)
U words:	3 letters, 2 U's (UTU)
	4 letters, 2 U's (eg GURU, LUAU)
	5 letters, 2 U's or more (eg AUGUR, QUEUE)
	6 letters, 3 U's (eg MUTUUM, UHURUS)

(Note that there is no list of four-letter words with 2 O's – it is not too difficult to play a couple of O's in a four-letter word. Think of all the words with a double-O in them to begin with. Three-letter words with 2 E's or 2 O's are also not difficult; there are no three-letter words with 2 I's.)

AWKWARD VOWEL DUMPS - A's

3-letter words - 2 A's

AAS AGA AIA ANA AWA MAA
ABA AHA ALA AVA BAA

4-letter words - 2 A's

ABAC AGHA ALAY ANAS ARBA AVAL CAPA KAKA LAVA NAAM
ABAS AGMA ALFA ANNA AREA AVAS CASA KAMA MAAR NAAN
ABBA AIAS ALGA ANOA ARIA AWAY DATA KANA MAAS NADA
ACTA AJAR ALMA ANTA ARNA AYAH GAGA KARA MAMA NAGA
ADAW ALAE AMAH APAY ASAR AZAN GALA KATA MANA NALA
AFAR ALAP AMLA AQUA ATAP BAAS HAAF KAVA MARA NANA
AGAR ALAR ANAL ARAK AULA BABA HAAR LAMA MASA NAPA
AGAS ALAS ANAN ARAR AURA CABA HAKA LANA MAYA PACA

PAPA PAWA RAJA SAGA TAKA TAPA TAWA VASA
PARA RACA RANA SAMA TALA TARA TAXA WAKA
PAUA RAGA RATA TAHA TANA TAVA VARA

5-letter words - 3 A's

ABACA ABAYA AFARA ALAAP ALAPA ANANA ARABA ASANA KAAMA

6-letter words - 3 A's

ABACAS ABAYAS ACACIA AFARAS AGAPAE ALAAPS ALALIA
ALAPAS ALBATA ALPACA ANABAS ANANAS ANATTA ANTARA
ARABAS ARALIA ARCANA ARGALA ARMADA ASANAS ATABAL
ATAMAN ATAXIA AVATAR AZALEA BAHADA BAJADA BALATA
BANANA BARAZA BATATA BAZAAR CABALA CABANA CANADA
DAGABA JACANA JATAKA KAAMAS KABALA KABAYA KAMALA
KANAKA KARAKA KATANA LABARA MANANA MARACA NAGANA
PALAMA PANADA PANAMA PAPAYA PATACA SALAAM SAMAAN
SAMARA SATARA TAIAHA TAMARA UJAMAA ZAPATA

AWKWARD VOWEL DUMPS - E's

4-letter words - 3 E's

EPEE

5-letter words - 3 E's

BELEE BESEE DEERE DEEVE
EERIE EEVEN ELPEE EMCEE
EMEER EPEES ETWEE EXEEM
EXEME FEESE FEEZE GEESE
HEEZE KEEVE LEESE LEVEE
MELEE NEELE NEESE NEEZE
PEECE PEEPE PEEVE REEDE
REEVE SEMEE TEENE TEPEE
WEEKE WEETE

6-letter words - 4 E's

PEEWEE TEEPEE

AWKWARD VOWEL DUMPS - I's

4-letter words - 2 I's

DIVI DIXI FINI
HILI IBIS ILIA
IMPI INIA INTI
IRID IRIS IWIS
IXIA KIWI MIDI
MINI MIRI NIDI
NISI PILI PIPI
SIMI SIRI TIKI
TIPI TITI WILI
ZITI

5-letter words - 2 I's

ACINI AIDOI AIOLI ALIBI BIFID BIKIE BIVIA BLINI CEILI CHILI CILIA CIPPI
CIRRI CIVIC CIVIL DIGIT DILLI DINIC DIVIS DIXIE FINIS GENII IAMBI ICIER
ICILY ICING ICTIC IDIOM IDIOT ILIAC ILIUM IMARI IMIDE IMINE IMMIT IMMIX
IMPIS IMSHI INDIE INDRI INFIX INION INTIL INTIS INWIT IODIC IONIC IRIDS
ISSEI IVIED IVIES IXIAS JINNI KIKOI KILIM KININ KIRRI KIWIS LICHI LICIT
LIKIN LIMIT LININ LIPID LIVID MEDII MIDIS MIMIC MINIM MINIS MIRIN MODII
NIHIL NIMBI NISEI NITID NIXIE OBIIT OIDIA ORIBI PILEI PILIS PIPIS PIPIT
PIRAI PIXIE RADII RICIN RIGID RISHI SIGIL SIMIS SIRIH SIRIS TIBIA TIKIS
TIMID TIPIS TITIS TORII VIGIA VIGIL VILLI VIRID VISIE VISIT VIVID VIZIR
WIFIE WILIS ZIMBI

6-letter words - 3 I's

BIKINI IMIDIC IRIDIC IRITIC IRITIS MIRITI

AWKWARD VOWEL DUMPS - O's

5-letter words - 3 O's

OVOLO POTOO

6-letter words - 3 O's or more

BOOBOO COMODO DOOCOT GOOGOL HOODOO HOOROO OOLOGY POTOOS ROTOLO ZOOZOO
COCOON COROZO FORHOO GOOROO HOOPOE KOODOO OOLONG ROCOCO VOODOO

AWKWARD VOWEL DUMPS - U's

3-letter words - 2 U's

UTU

4-letter words - 2 U's

GURU KUDU KURU LULU PUKU RURU TUTU URUS ZULU
JUJU KUKU LUAU PUDU PULU SULU UNAU UTUS

5-letter words - 2 U's or more

AUGUR DURUM JUGUM KURUS MUNTU QUIPU TUTUS UNDUE USUAL VOULU
BUCHU FUCUS JUJUS LUAUS PUDUS RURUS UHURU UNDUG USURE WUSHU
BUCKU FUGUE KUDUS LULUS PUKUS SULUS UNAUS UNGUM USURP ZULUS
BUNDU GURUS KUDZU LUPUS PULUS SUNUP UNCUS UPRUN USURY
BUSSU HUMUS KUKUS MUCUS QUEUE TUQUE UNCUT URUBU UVULA

6-letter words - 3 U's

MUTUUM UHURUS URUBUS

HINT

Flashcards

A popular way of testing Scrabble vocabulary is a system called flashcards. Small index cards are used which have 'questions' on one side and the 'answer words' on the reverse. For example if you were using flashcards to learn two-letter words you may have on one card A=13, with the 13 two-letter words beginning with A on the reverse. On another card B=5, and another C=1, would reveal BA BE BI BO BY and CH on the reverse respectively. Whenever you get a moment you can quickly flick through the cards and test yourself. The system can be used for many categories such as five-vowelled seven-letter words, words containing J Q X Z, and so on. A good use of flashcards is to log every seven-letter word played against you that you didn't know, thus naturally building up your personal testing library.

HINT

Fighting Back

Don't trade off catching up with poor rack retention. A more balanced rack will enable a greater choice of strategic plays in subsequent turns. Initially concentrate on not slipping any further behind and be wary of scoring opportunities open only to yourself. Perhaps you have the last S or the last A for an (A)JAR hook, and so on. Try to keep the board open unless you can block and catch up in a single play. If your opponent is in front it is likely their rack is worsening whilst they are blocking. Keeping the board open and maintaining your rack balance will keep your hopes alive whereas playing too defensively will only assist your opponent to keep their lead.

HINT

Passing Thoughts

It is allowable to pass in Scrabble, that is, to not play a word or change any tiles. This is in effect what a player does at the end of the game if stuck with any unplayable tiles. However, it is rarely worth passing during the game in the hope that the opponent will give you that vital opening or letter you need.

An example of an occasion where passing may be of advantage is if you have a good rack such as TAILEND and it is your play first, or your opponent has just changed letters instead of playing first. Since TAILEND combines with one of the four vowels (A E O U) to make an eight-letter word (DENTALIA, ENTAILED or LINEATED, DELATION, UNTAILED), it is likely your opponent may give you a bonus play next turn.

HINT

Learn As You Play

Always have a scrap of paper with you other than the scoresheet. Jot down any promising racks you find yourself with, seven-letter words you played that might have anagrams, and any words you think of playing but are unsure of. After the game spend a few minutes with *Official Scrabble Lists* and check out your words and racks, noting any new discoveries. Going through this exercise after every game will gradually strengthen your vocabulary without too much effort.

AWKWARD CONSONANT DUMPS

The best way to describe the words in the following lists is this: words of three to five letters that contain at least two of any one of the following consonants – B, C, F, H, V, W and Y. (Purists should note that Y is referred to here as a consonant, regardless of whether it is acting as a vowel or a consonant in any individual word.) It is usually not too difficult to dump a single F or an H in an attempt to achieve a reasonable score and balance your rack. It is more of a problem to dump two F's, two H's, and so on. These lists should help with your awkward consonant racks.

The lists are arranged so that all the B words come together, then the C words, and so on. The three-letter B words come before the four-letter B words, which come before the five-letter words. Similarly for the other awkward consonants. Do note that there are no three-letter lists here for the letters C, V and Y, as there are no three-letter words having two C's, two V's or two Y's.

AWKWARD CONSONANT DUMPS - B's

3-letter words - 2 B's

ABB BIB BOB BUB EBB

4-letter words - 2 B's

ABBA BABA BABY BLAB BLUB BOMB BUBO COBB
ABBE BABE BARB BLEB BOBA BOOB BUBS EBBS
ABBS BABU BIBS BLOB BOBS BUBA BULB SIBB

5-letter words - 2 B's or more

ABBAS BABUL BIMBO BOBAS BUBAL COBBS FUBBY KEBAB REBBE WEBBY
ABBES BABUS BLABS BOBBY BUBAS COBBY GABBY KEBOB RIBBY YABBY
ABBEY BARBE BLEBS BOMBE BUBBY CUBBY GOBBI LOBBY SIBBS YOBBO
ABBOT BARBS BLOBS BOMBO BULBS CUBEB GOBBO MOBBY SLUBB ZEBUB
BABAS BEBOP BLUBS BOMBS BUMBO DEBBY HOBBY NABOB SUBBY
BABEL BEROB BLURB BOOBS BUSBY DIBBS HUBBY NOBBY SYBBE
BABES BIBLE BOBAC BOOBY CABBY DOBBY KABAB NUBBY TABBY
BABOO BILBO BOBAK BRIBE CABOB EBBED KABOB RABBI TUBBY

AWKWARD CONSONANT DUMPS - C's

4-letter words - 2 C's

CECA CHIC CHOC COCA COCK COCO CROC ECCE ECCO

5-letter words - 2 C's or more

ACCOY CACHE CHACE CHOCK CIVIC COCCI CONIC CULCH ICTIC TICCA
ACOCK CACTI CHACK CHOCO CLACK COCCO COSEC CUMEC OCCAM WICCA
BACCA CAECA CHACO CHOCS CLECK COCKS COUCH CURCH OCCUR YACCA
BACCO CASCO CHECK CHUCK CLICK COCKY CRACK CUSEC PICCY YUCCA
BACCY CATCH CHICA CINCH CLOCK COCOA CRICK CUTCH RECCE ZOCCO
BICCY CECAL CHICH CINCT CLUCK COCOS CROCK CYCAD RECCO
BOCCA CECUM CHICK CIRCA COACH COLIC CROCS CYCLE RECCY
CABOC CERCI CHICO CIRCS COACT COMIC CRUCK CYCLO SECCO
CACAO CERIC CHICS CISCO COCAS CONCH CUBIC CYNIC SUCCI

AWKWARD CONSONANT DUMPS - F's

3-letter words - 2 F's

EFF	IFF	OFF

4-letter words - 2 F's or more

AFFY	CAFF	DUFF	FUFF	HUFF	LUFF	NUFF	RUFF	WAFF
BAFF	COFF	EFFS	GAFF	IFFY	MIFF	OFFS	TEFF	YAFF
BIFF	CUFF	FAFF	GOFF	JEFF	MUFF	PUFF	TIFF	ZIFF
BOFF	DAFF	FIEF	GUFF	JIFF	NAFF	RAFF	TOFF	
BUFF	DOFF	FIFE	HAFF	KOFF	NIFF	RIFF	TUFF	

5-letter words - 2 F's or more

AFFIX	CAFFS	DRAFF	FLAFF	GUFFS	LUFFS	OFFER	SCAFF	STUFF	WHIFF
BAFFS	CHAFF	DUFFS	FLUFF	HAFFS	MIFFS	PLUFF	SCOFF	TAFFY	YAFFS
BAFFY	CHUFF	EFFED	FUFFS	HOUFF	MIFFY	PUFFS	SCUFF	TEFFS	ZIFFS
BIFFS	CLIFF	FAFFS	FUFFY	HOWFF	MUFFS	PUFFY	SKIFF	TIFFS	
BLUFF	CLOFF	FEOFF	GAFFE	HUFFS	NAFFS	QUAFF	SKOFF	TOFFS	
BOFFS	COFFS	FIEFS	GAFFS	HUFFY	NIFFS	QUIFF	SNIFF	TOFFY	
BUFFA	CUFFO	FIFED	GLIFF	JEFFS	NIFFY	RAFFS	SNUFF	TRIFF	
BUFFE	CUFFS	FIFER	GOFFS	JIFFS	NUFFS	REFFO	SOWFF	TUFFE	
BUFFI	DAFFS	FIFES	GRAFF	JIFFY	NYAFF	RIFFS	SPIFF	TUFFS	
BUFFO	DAFFY	FIFTH	GRIFF	KOFFS	OFFAL	RUFFE	STAFF	WAFFS	
BUFFS	DOFFS	FIFTY	GRUFF	LUFFA	OFFED	RUFFS	STIFF	WAUFF	

AWKWARD CONSONANT DUMPS - H's

3-letter words - 2 H's

HAH	HOH	HUH

4-letter words - 2 H's

HASH	HATH	HECH	HIGH	HISH	HOGH	HOHS	HUSH	PHOH	SHAH

5-letter words - 2 H's

AHIGH	HANCH	HAUGH	HEUCH	HIGHT	HOGHS	HOTCH	HUSHY	PHOHS	SHUSH
CHICH	HARSH	HEATH	HEUGH	HILCH	HOHED	HOUGH	HUTCH	SHAHS	THIGH
EPHAH	HASHY	HECHT	HEWGH	HITCH	HOOCH	HUMPH	HYPHA	SHASH	WHICH
HAITH	HATCH	HEIGH	HIGHS	HITHE	HOOSH	HUNCH	HYTHE	SHCHI	WHISH

AWKWARD CONSONANT DUMPS - V's

4-letter words - 2 V's

VIVA	VIVE	VIVO

5-letter words - 2 V's

BEVVY	CIVVY	NAVVY	VALVE	VERVE	VIVAT	VIVER	VIVID	VOLVE
BIVVY	DIVVY	SAVVY	VARVE	VIVAS	VIVDA	VIVES	VOLVA	VULVA

AWKWARD CONSONANT DUMPS - W's

3-letter words - 2 W's

WAW	WOW

4-letter words - 2 W's

WAWE	WAWL	WAWS	WHEW	WHOW	WOWF	WOWS

5-letter words - 2 W's

EWHOW PAWAW WAWES WAWLS WHEWS WIDOW WOWED WOWEE WRAWL

AWKWARD CONSONANT DUMPS - Y's

4-letter words - 2 Y's

EYRY GYNY YAWY YUKY

5-letter words - 2 Y's

AZYGY DOYLY GYNNY PYGMY SLYLY XYLYL YAWEY YIPPY YUKKY
BYWAY DRYLY GYPPY SHYLY THYMY YABBY YAWNY YOLKY YUMMY
COYLY DYKEY GYPSY SKYEY WRYLY YAPPY YESTY YUCKY YUPPY

HINT

Rack Balancing

Always try to keep a balanced rack of vowels and consonants. The more balanced your rack the more choice of words you will have each turn and the more chance you will have of being able to play a bonus-scoring seven-letter word. It helps to be aware that there are 42 vowels to 56 consonants (and 2 blanks) in the Scrabble set. That's three vowels for every four consonants. Counting how many vowels and consonants already played at any stage of a game will serve as a useful guide as to the vowel/consonant distribution remaining in the bag. If there is a surplus of consonants left you might wish to counteract your likely consonant pickup by retaining vowels on your rack when you play, or vice versa.

See the Awkward Vowel Dumps list and the Light and Heavy Words list for some words that will help you keep a balanced rack.

HINT

Edging the Endgame

In a tight game where the scores are close there is an advantage in being the player to be the first to play out and finish the game, thus gaining any points remaining on the opponent's rack and depriving him of another scoring opportunity. Playing out first is often the difference between winning and losing. A handy tip, whenever you have the opportunity or choice near the end of a game, is to ensure there is a single tile in the bag after your turn. This means that, next turn, you have the first opportunity to play with no tiles remaining in the bag thus giving you an advantage in planning a two-move finish. There is further advantage if you have been keeping track of the tiles since you can then have the benefit of the endgame initiative knowing your opponent's exact tiles.

HINT

Combination Management

If you have one of the promising six-letter combinations given under the Bonus Sets section but unfortunately do not have an appropriate seventh letter to make a bonus word, or the bonus word you have does not fit on the board, then it is wiser not to be overly concerned about holding on to your useful six-letter combinations. Rather than just playing the one letter and hoping for a playable bonus word next turn, play two or three tiles. This will probably enable you to score more whilst still retaining the makings of a bonus word. The skill is in making sure you play off the right letters.

For example, with OILERS and an F on your rack there is no bonus word. Rather than just play the F, in the hope of picking a B for BOILERS or a U for LOUSIER perhaps, it is better to play IF or OF. The retention of OLERS or ILERS with a vowel pickup next turn is likely to produce another good six-letter combination such as AILERS, OILERS or RELIES, and hopefully an obliging seventh letter to make a bonus play. If it doesn't, well at least you've scored some points meanwhile.

HINT

Unusual Clues

In browsing through the Anagram section you will find an abundance of unusual seven and eight-letter words. Some of these are more useful than others depending on their constituent letters. Those consisting of just the one and two-point Scrabble tiles (ie A D E G I L N O R S T U) are more likely to appear on your rack and are the ones to concentrate on. A good way to remember these words is by making up a non-existent anagram that you are more likely to form on your rack and that will act as an aide-mémoire. For example, the likely rack ELNOSTU yields the bonus word LENTOUS which may best be recalled as the anagram of the non-existent OUTLENS. Similarly, SEERING makes GREISEN and LOOTIER makes TROOLIE. Both SEERING and LOOTIER are not actual words but merely the clues to GREISEN and TROOLIE. Where there is a more common anagram of an unusual word then this naturally serves as a clue, eg OUTLINE gives ELUTION and AGAINST gives GITANAS.

K AND V WORDS

The following lists contain all the words of length two to five letters which contain either a K or a V. Words having two K's or two V's are also included. These words can be particularly useful for scoring perhaps 40 or so points, while offloading otherwise awkward letters.

If a word contains a K and a V, it will appear in both the K and V lists.

K-WORDS

K - 2-letter words

KA	KO	KY

K - 3-letter words

AKE	EIK	INK	KAT	KEG	KIF	KON	MAK	SKA	YAK
ARK	EKE	IRK	KAW	KEN	KIN	KOP	NEK	SKI	YOK
ASK	ELK	JAK	KAY	KEP	KIP	KOS	OAK	SKY	YUK
AUK	ERK	KAE	KEA	KET	KIR	KOW	OIK	SUK	ZEK
BOK	EUK	KAI	KEB	KEX	KIT	KYE	OKE	TAK	
DAK	EWK	KAM	KED	KEY	KOA	KYU	OUK	UKE	
EEK	ILK	KAS	KEF	KID	KOB	LEK	ROK	WOK	

K - 4-letter words

AKED	BUKE	DORK	GOWK	JERK	KAVA	KHUD	KNEW	KYTE	MILK
AKEE	BULK	DREK	GUCK	JINK	KAWS	KIBE	KNIT	KYUS	MINK
AKES	BUNK	DUCK	GUNK	JOCK	KAYO	KICK	KNOB	LACK	MIRK
AKIN	BURK	DUKE	HACK	JOKE	KAYS	KIDS	KNOP	LAIK	MOCK
ALKY	BUSK	DUNK	HAIK	JOKY	KAZI	KIER	KNOT	LAKE	MOKE
AMOK	BYKE	DUSK	HAKA	JOOK	KEAS	KIFS	KNOW	LAKH	MOKI
ANKH	CAKE	DYKE	HAKE	JOUK	KEBS	KIKE	KNUB	LAKY	MOKO
ARAK	CAKY	EIKS	HANK	JUKE	KECK	KILD	KNUR	LANK	MONK
ARKS	CALK	EKED	HARK	JUNK	KEDS	KILL	KNUT	LARK	MOOK
ASKS	CARK	EKES	HASK	KADE	KEEK	KILN	KOAN	LAWK	MUCK
ATOK	CASK	EKKA	HAWK	KADI	KEEL	KILO	KOAS	LEAK	MURK
AUKS	CAUK	ELKS	HECK	KAED	KEEN	KILP	KOBS	LEEK	MUSK
BACK	CAWK	ERKS	HICK	KAES	KEEP	KILT	KOFF	LEKE	NABK
BAKE	CHIK	ESKY	HIKE	KAGO	KEFS	KINA	KOHL	LEKS	NAIK
BALK	COCK	EUKS	HOCK	KAID	KEGS	KIND	KOLA	LICK	NARK
BANK	COKE	EWKS	HOIK	KAIE	KEIR	KINE	KOLO	LIKE	NECK
BARK	COKY	FAIK	HOKE	KAIF	KELL	KING	KOND	LINK	NEKS
BASK	CONK	FAKE	HOKI	KAIL	KELP	KINK	KONK	LIRK	NERK
BAUK	COOK	FANK	HONK	KAIM	KELT	KINO	KONS	LISK	NEUK
BEAK	CORK	FECK	HOOK	KAIN	KEMB	KINS	KOOK	LOCK	NICK
BECK	CUSK	FIKE	HOWK	KAIS	KEMP	KIPE	KOPH	LOKE	NOCK
BERK	DAKS	FIKY	HUCK	KAKA	KENO	KIPP	KOPS	LOOK	NOOK
BIKE	DANK	FINK	HULK	KAKI	KENS	KIPS	KORA	LUCK	NORK
BILK	DARK	FIRK	HUNK	KALE	KENT	KIRK	KORE	LUKE	NUKE
BINK	DAWK	FISK	HUSK	KALI	KEPI	KIRN	KOSS	LURK	OAKS
BIRK	DECK	FLAK	HYKE	KAMA	KEPS	KIRS	KOTO	LUSK	OAKY
BISK	DEEK	FOLK	ICKY	KAME	KEPT	KISH	KOWS	MACK	OIKS
BOAK	DESK	FORK	IKAT	KAMI	KERB	KISS	KRAB	MAIK	OINK
BOCK	DHAK	FUCK	IKON	KANA	KERF	KIST	KRIS	MAKE	OKAY
BOKE	DICK	FUNK	ILKA	KANG	KERN	KITE	KSAR	MAKO	OKES
BOKO	DIKA	FYKE	ILKS	KANS	KESH	KITH	KUDU	MAKS	OKRA
BOKS	DIKE	GAWK	INKS	KANT	KEST	KITS	KUKU	MARK	OKTA
BONK	DINK	GECK	INKY	KAON	KETA	KIVA	KURI	MASK	OUKS
BOOK	DIRK	GEEK	IRKS	KARA	KETS	KIWI	KURU	MAWK	OULK
BOSK	DISK	GINK	JACK	KART	KEYS	KNAG	KYAT	MEEK	PACK
BOUK	DOCK	GONK	JAKE	KATA	KHAN	KNAP	KYLE	MERK	PAIK
BUCK	DOEK	GOOK	JAKS	KATI	KHAT	KNAR	KYND	MICK	PARK
BUIK	DOOK	GOUK	JARK	KATS	KHOR	KNEE	KYNE	MIKE	PAWK

PEAK
PECK
PEEK
PEKE
PENK
PERK
PICK
PIKA
PIKE
PINK
POCK
POKE
POKY
POLK
PONK
POOK
PORK

POUK
PUCK
PUKE
PUKU
PULK
PUNK
RACK
RAIK
RAKE
RAKI
RAKU
RANK
REAK
RECK
REEK
REIK
REKE

RICK
RINK
RISK
ROCK
ROKE
ROKS
ROKY
ROOK
RUCK
RUKH
RUSK
RYKE
SACK
SAKE
SAKI
SANK
SARK

SEEK
SEIK
SEKT
SERK
SICK
SIKA
SIKE
SILK
SINK
SKAG
SKAS
SKAT
SKAW
SKEG
SKEO
SKEP
SKER

SKEW
SKID
SKIM
SKIN
SKIO
SKIP
SKIS
SKIT
SKOL
SKRY
SKUA
SKUG
SKYR
SOAK
SOCK
SOKE
SOOK

SOUK
SPEK
SPIK
SUCK
SUKH
SUKS
SULK
SUNK
SYKE
TACK
TAKA
TAKE
TAKI
TAKS
TAKY
TALK
TANK

TASK
TEAK
TICK
TIKA
TIKE
TIKI
TINK
TOCK
TOKE
TOKO
TONK
TOOK
TOUK
TREK
TUCK
TUSK
TYKE

UKES
VOLK
WACK
WAKA
WAKE
WAKF
WALK
WANK
WARK
WAUK
WEAK
WEEK
WEKA
WELK
WICK
WINK
WOCK

WOKE
WOKS
WORK
YACK
YAKS
YANK
YELK
YERK
YESK
YEUK
YIKE
YIRK
YLKE
YOCK
YOKE
YOKS
YOLK

YORK
YOUK
YUCK
YUKE
YUKO
YUKS
YUKY
ZACK
ZEKS
ZONK
ZOUK

K - 5-letter words

ABACK
ABASK
ACKEE
ACOCK
AKEES
AKENE
AKING
AKKAS
ALACK
ALIKE
ALKIE
ALKYD
ALKYL
AMUCK
ANKER
ANKHS
ANKLE
ANKUS
APEAK
APEEK
ARAKS
ARKED
ASKED
ASKER
ASKEW
ATOKE
ATOKS
AWAKE
AWOKE
AWORK
BACKS
BAKED
BAKEN
BAKER
BAKES
BALKS
BALKY
BANKS
BARKS
BARKY
BASKS
BATIK
BAUKS
BAULK
BEAKS
BEAKY
BECKE
BECKS
BEKAH
BERKS

BIKED
BIKER
BIKES
BIKIE
BILKS
BINKS
BIRKS
BISKS
BLACK
BLANK
BLEAK
BLINK
BLOCK
BLOKE
BLUNK
BOAKS
BOBAK
BOCKS
BOINK
BOKED
BOKES
BOKOS
BONKS
BOOKS
BOOKY
BORAK
BOSKS
BOSKY
BOUKS
BRACK
BRAKE
BRAKY
BRANK
BREAK
BRICK
BRINK
BRISK
BROCK
BROKE
BROOK
BUCKO
BUCKS
BUCKU
BUIKS
BUKES
BULKS
BULKY
BUNKO
BUNKS
BURKA

BURKE
BURKS
BUSKS
BUSKY
BYKED
BYKES
CAKED
CAKES
CAKEY
CALKS
CARKS
CASKS
CAUKS
CAULK
CAWKS
CHACK
CHALK
CHANK
CHARK
CHECK
CHEEK
CHEKA
CHICK
CHIKS
CHINK
CHIRK
CHOCK
CHOKE
CHOKO
CHOKY
CHOOK
CHUCK
CHUNK
CLACK
CLANK
CLECK
CLEEK
CLERK
CLICK
CLINK
CLOAK
CLOCK
CLOKE
CLONK
CLUCK
CLUNK
COCKS
COCKY
COKED
COKES

CONKS
CONKY
COOKS
COOKY
CORKS
CORKY
CRACK
CRAKE
CRANK
CREAK
CREEK
CRICK
CROAK
CROCK
CRONK
CROOK
CRUCK
CUSKS
DAKER
DANKS
DARKS
DARKY
DAWKS
DECKO
DECKS
DEKKO
DESKS
DHAKS
DICKS
DICKY
DIKAS
DIKED
DIKER
DIKES
DIKEY
DINKS
DINKY
DIRKE
DIRKS
DISKS
DOCKS
DOEKS
DOOKS
DORKS
DORKY
DRAKE
DRANK
DRECK
DREKS
DRINK

DROOK
DROUK
DRUNK
DUCKS
DUCKY
DUKED
DUKES
DUMKA
DUMKY
DUNKS
DUSKS
DUSKY
DYKED
DYKES
DYKEY
EIKED
EIKON
EKING
EKKAS
ENOKI
ENSKY
ERICK
ESKAR
ESKER
EUKED
EVOKE
EWKED
FAIKS
FAKED
FAKER
FAKES
FAKIR
FANKS
FECKS
FENKS
FIKED
FIKES
FINKS
FIRKS
FISKS
FLACK
FLAKE
FLAKS
FLAKY
FLANK
FLASK
FLECK
FLICK
FLISK
FLOCK

FLUKE
FLUKY
FLUNK
FOLKS
FORKS
FORKY
FRACK
FRANK
FREAK
FRISK
FROCK
FUCKS
FUNKS
FUNKY
FYKED
FYKES
GAWKS
GAWKY
GECKO
GECKS
GEEKS
GEEKY
GINKS
GLAIK
GLEEK
GLIKE
GLISK
GONKS
GOOKS
GOPAK
GOUKS
GOWKS
GRIKE
GRYKE
GUCKS
GUCKY
GUNKS
HACEK
HACKS
HAICK
HAIKS
HAIKU
HAKAM
HAKAS
HAKES
HAKIM
HANKS
HANKY
HARKS
HASKS

HAWKS
HECKS
HICKS
HIKED
HIKER
HIKES
HOCKS
HOICK
HOIKS
HOKED
HOKES
HOKEY
HOKIS
HOKKU
HOKUM
HONKS
HONKY
HOOKA
HOOKS
HOOKY
HOWKS
HUCKS
HULKS
HULKY
HUNKS
HUNKY
HUSKS
HUSKY
HYKES
ICKER
IKATS
IKONS
INKED
INKER
INKLE
IRKED
IROKO
JACKS
JAKES
JARKS
JERKS
JERKY
JINKS
JOCKO
JOCKS
JOKED
JOKER
JOKES
JOKEY
JOKOL

JOOKS
JOUKS
JUKED
JUKES
JUNKS
JUNKY
KAAMA
KABAB
KABOB
KACHA
KADES
KADIS
KAGOS
KAHAL
KAIAK
KAIDS
KAIES
KAIFS
KAILS
KAIMS
KAING
KAINS
KAKAS
KAKIS
KALES
KALIF
KALIS
KALPA
KAMAS
KAMES
KAMIK
KAMIS
KAMME
KANAS
KANDY
KANEH
KANGA
KANGS
KANJI
KANTS
KANZU
KAONS
KAPOK
KAPPA
KAPUT
KARAS
KARAT
KARMA
KARRI
KARST

KARSY
KARTS
KARZY
KASHA
KATAS
KATIS
KATTI
KAUGH
KAURI
KAVAS
KAWED
KAYAK
KAYLE
KAYOS
KAZIS
KAZOO
KEBAB
KEBOB
KECKS
KEDGE
KEDGY
KEECH
KEEKS
KEELS
KEENS
KEEPS
KEEVE
KEFIR
KEIRS
KELIM
KELLS
KELLY
KELPS
KELPY
KELTS
KELTY
KEMBO
KEMBS
KEMPS
KEMPT
KENAF
KENDO
KENOS
KENTS
KEPIS
KERBS
KERFS
KERNE
KERNS
KERVE

KESAR
KESTS
KETAS
KETCH
KEVEL
KEXES
KEYED
KHADI
KHAKI
KHANS
KHATS
KHAYA
KHEDA
KHOJA
KHORS
KHUDS
KIANG
KIBES
KICKS
KIDDO
KIDDY
KIDEL
KIDGE
KIERS
KIEVE
KIGHT
KIKES
KIKOI
KILEY
KILIM
KILLS
KILNS
KILOS
KILPS
KILTS
KILTY
KIMBO
KINAS
KINDA
KINDS
KINDY
KINGS
KININ
KINKS
KINKY
KINOS
KIOSK
KIPES
KIPPA
KIPPS

KIRKS
KIRNS
KIRRI
KISAN
KISTS
KITED
KITES
KITHE
KITHS
KITTY
KIVAS
KIWIS
KLANG
KLOOF
KLUTZ
KNACK
KNAGS
KNAPS
KNARL
KNARS
KNAVE
KNEAD
KNEED
KNEEL
KNEES
KNELL
KNELT
KNIFE
KNISH
KNITS
KNIVE
KNOBS
KNOCK
KNOLL
KNOPS
KNOSP
KNOTS
KNOUT
KNOWE
KNOWN
KNOWS
KNUBS
KNURL
KNURR
KNURS
KNUTS
KOALA
KOANS
KOBAN
KOFFS
KOFTA
KOHLS
KOINE
KOKER
KOKRA
KOKUM
KOLAS
KOLOS
KOMBU
KONKS
KOOKS
KOOKY
KOORI
KOPHS
KOPJE

KOPPA
KORAS
KORES
KORMA
KOSES
KOTOS
KOTOW
KRAAL
KRABS
KRAFT
KRAIT
KRANG
KRANS
KRANZ
KRAUT
KRENG
KRILL
KRONA
KRONE
KSARS
KUDOS
KUDUS
KUDZU
KUKRI
KUKUS
KULAK
KULAN
KURIS
KURRE
KURTA
KURUS
KUTCH
KVASS
KWELA
KYANG
KYATS
KYDST
KYLES
KYLIE
KYLIN
KYLIX
KYLOE
KYNDE
KYNDS
KYTES
KYTHE
LACKS
LAIKA
LAIKS
LAKED
LAKER
LAKES
LAKHS
LAKIN
LANKS
LANKY
LARKS
LARKY
LATKE
LAWKS
LEAKS
LEAKY
LEEKS
LICKS
LIKED

LIKEN
LIKER
LIKES
LIKIN
LINKS
LIRKS
LISKS
LOCKS
LOKES
LOOKS
LUCKS
LUCKY
LURKS
LUSKS
MACKS
MAIKO
MAIKS
MAKAR
MAKER
MAKES
MAKOS
MALIK
MANKY
MARKS
MASKS
MAWKS
MAWKY
MELIK
MERKS
MICKS
MICKY
MIKES
MIKRA
MILKO
MILKS
MILKY
MINKE
MINKS
MIRKS
MOCKS
MOKES
MOKIS
MOKOS
MONKS
MOOKS
MUCKS
MUCKY
MUJIK
MURKS
MURKY
MUSKS
MUSKY
NABKS
NAIKS
NAKED
NAKER
NARKS
NARKY
NEBEK
NECKS
NERKA
NERKS
NEUKS
NICKS
NIKAU

NOCKS
NOOKS
NOOKY
NORKS
NUKED
NUKES
OAKEN
OAKER
OAKUM
OCKER
OINKS
OKAPI
OKAYS
OKRAS
OKTAS
ONKUS
OULKS
OZEKI
PACKS
PAIKS
PAKKA
PALKI
PARKA
PARKI
PARKS
PARKY
PAWKS
PAWKY
PEAKS
PEAKY
PECKE
PECKS
PEEKS
PEKAN
PEKES
PEKOE
PENKS
PERKS
PERKY
PESKY
PICKS
PICKY
PIKAS
PIKED
PIKER
PIKES
PIKUL
PINKO
PINKS
PINKY
PISKY
PLACK
PLANK
PLINK
PLONK
PLOOK
PLOUK
PLUCK
PLUNK
POAKA
POAKE
POCKS
POCKY
POKAL
POKED

POKER
POKES
POKEY
POLKA
POLKS
PONKS
POOKA
POOKS
PORKS
PORKY
POUKE
POUKS
PRANK
PRICK
PRINK
PROKE
PRONK
PUCKA
PUCKS
PUKED
PUKER
PUKES
PUKKA
PUKUS
PULKA
PULKS
PUNKA
PUNKS
QUACK
QUAKE
QUAKY
QUARK
QUICK
QUIRK
QUONK
RACKS
RAIKS
RAKED
RAKEE
RAKER
RAKES
RAKIS
RAKUS
RANKE
RANKS
REAKS
RECKS
REEKS
REEKY
REIKS
REKED
REKES
RICKS
RINKS
RISKS
RISKY
ROCKS
ROCKY
ROKED
ROKER
ROKES
ROOKS
ROOKY
RUCKS
RUKHS

RUSKS
RYKED
RYKES
SACKS
SAICK
SAKER
SAKES
SAKIA
SAKIS
SANKO
SARKS
SARKY
SCULK
SEEKS
SEKOS
SEKTS
SERKS
SHACK
SHAKE
SHAKO
SHAKT
SHAKY
SHANK
SHARK
SHEIK
SHIRK
SHMEK
SHOCK
SHOOK
SHUCK
SICKO
SICKS
SIKAS
SIKES
SILKS
SILKY
SINKS
SINKY
SKAGS
SKAIL
SKALD
SKANK
SKART
SKATE
SKATS
SKATT
SKAWS
SKEAN
SKEAR
SKEER
SKEET
SKEGG
SKEGS
SKEIN
SKELF
SKELL
SKELM
SKELP
SKENE
SKEOS
SKEPS
SKERS
SKEWS
SKIDS
SKIED

SKIER
SKIES
SKIEY
SKIFF
SKILL
SKIMP
SKIMS
SKINK
SKINS
SKINT
SKIOS
SKIPS
SKIRL
SKIRR
SKIRT
SKITE
SKITS
SKIVE
SKIVY
SKLIM
SKOAL
SKOFF
SKRAN
SKRIK
SKUAS
SKUGS
SKULK
SKULL
SKUNK
SKYER
SKYEY
SKYRE
SKYRS
SKYTE
SLACK
SLAKE
SLEEK
SLICK
SLINK
SLUNK
SMACK
SMAIK
SMEEK
SMIRK
SMOCK
SMOKE
SMOKO
SMOKY
SNACK
SNAKE
SNAKY
SNARK
SNEAK
SNECK
SNICK
SNOEK
SNOKE
SNOOK
SNOWK
SNUCK
SOAKS
SOCKO
SOCKS
SOKAH
SOKEN

SOKES
SOOKS
SOUKS
SPAKE
SPANK
SPARK
SPEAK
SPECK
SPEKS
SPELK
SPICK
SPIKE
SPIKS
SPIKY
SPINK
SPOKE
SPOOK
SPUNK
STACK
STAKE
STALK
STANK
STARK
STEAK
STEEK
STICK
STINK
STIRK
STOCK
STOKE
STONK
STOOK
STORK
STUCK
STUNK
SUCKS
SUKHS
SULKS
SULKY
SUNKS
SWACK
SWANK
SWINK
SYKER
SYKES
TACKS
TACKY
TAKAS
TAKEN
TAKER
TAKES
TAKHI
TAKIN
TAKIS
TALAK
TALKS
TALKY
TALUK
TANKA
TANKS
TANKY
TAROK
TASKS
TEAKS
TEREK

THACK
THANK
THEEK
THICK
THILK
THINK
TICKS
TICKY
TIKAS
TIKES
TIKIS
TIKKA
TINKS
TOCKS
TOKAY
TOKED
TOKEN
TOKES
TOKOS
TONKS
TOPEK
TORSK
TOUKS
TRACK
TRAIK
TRECK
TREKS
TRICK
TRIKE
TROCK
TROKE
TRUCK
TRUNK
TUCKS
TUPEK
TUPIK
TUSKS
TUSKY
TWANK
TWEAK
TWINK
TYKES
UKASE
UMIAK
UNKED
UNKET
UNKID
UPTAK
VAKIL
VODKA
VOLKS
WACKE
WACKO
WACKS
WACKY
WAKAS
WAKED
WAKEN
WAKER
WAKES
WAKFS
WALKS
WANKS
WANKY
WARKS

WAUKS
WAULK
WEEKE
WEEKS
WEKAS
WELKE
WELKS
WELKT
WHACK
WHELK
WHILK
WHISK
WICKS
WICKY
WINKS
WOCKS
WOKEN
WONKY
WORKS
WRACK
WREAK
WRECK
WRICK
WROKE
YACKS
YAKKA
YAKOW
YANKS
YAPOK
YELKS
YERKS
YESKS
YEUKS
YIKES
YIRKS
YLIKE
YLKES
YOCKS
YOICK
YOKED
YOKEL
YOKES
YOKUL
YOLKS
YOLKY
YONKS
YORKS
YOUKS
YUCKS
YUCKY
YUKED
YUKES
YUKKY
YUKOS
ZACKS
ZAKAT
ZINKE
ZINKY
ZONKS
ZOOKS
ZOUKS

V-WORDS

V - 3-letter words

AVA	GOV	LEV	SOV	VAN	VEE	VIA	VIN	VOL	VUG
AVE	GUV	LUV	UVA	VAS	VEG	VID	VIS	VOR	VUM
DIV	IVY	OVA	VAC	VAT	VET	VIE	VLY	VOW	
EVE	LAV	REV	VAE	VAU	VEX	VIM	VOE	VOX	

V - 4-letter words

ARVO	DIVS	HOVE	NEVE	TAVA	VANT	VELA	VICE	VIRL	VOTE
AVAL	DOVE	JIVE	NEVI	ULVA	VARA	VELD	VIDE	VISA	VOWS
AVAS	EEVN	JUVE	NOVA	URVA	VARE	VELE	VIDS	VISE	VRIL
AVER	ENVY	KAVA	OVAL	UVAE	VARY	VELL	VIED	VITA	VROW
AVES	EVEN	KIVA	OVEN	UVAS	VASA	VENA	VIER	VITE	VUGS
AVID	EVER	LAVA	OVER	UVEA	VASE	VEND	VIES	VIVA	VULN
AVOW	EVES	LAVE	OVUM	VACS	VAST	VENT	VIEW	VIVE	VUMS
BEVY	EVET	LAVS	PAVE	VADE	VATS	VERB	VILD	VIVO	WAVE
CAVE	EVIL	LEVA	PERV	VAES	VATU	VERS	VILE	VIZY	WAVY
CAVY	EVOE	LEVE	RAVE	VAGI	VAUS	VERT	VILL	VLEI	WIVE
CHIV	FAVE	LEVY	REVS	VAIL	VAUT	VERY	VIMS	VOAR	WOVE
CIVE	FIVE	LIVE	RIVA	VAIN	VEAL	VEST	VINA	VOES	YEVE
COVE	GAVE	LOVE	RIVE	VAIR	VEEP	VETO	VINE	VOID	
DEEV	GIVE	LUVS	RIVO	VALE	VEER	VETS	VINO	VOLA	
DERV	GOVS	MEVE	ROVE	VALI	VEES	VEXT	VINS	VOLE	
DEVA	GUVS	MIRV	SAVE	VAMP	VEGA	VIAE	VINT	VOLK	
DIVA	GYVE	MOVE	SHIV	VANE	VEHM	VIAL	VINY	VOLS	
DIVE	HAVE	NAVE	SOVS	VANG	VEIL	VIAS	VIOL	VOLT	
DIVI	HIVE	NAVY	SPIV	VANS	VEIN	VIBS	VIRE	VORS	

V - 5-letter words

ABOVE	BRAVE	CURVE	EMOVE	GYVES	KVASS	MIRVS	OVATE	REIVE	SHIVE
ADVEW	BRAVI	CURVY	ENVOI	HALVA	LARVA	MOOVE	OVENS	REVEL	SHIVS
AGAVE	BRAVO	CUVEE	ENVOY	HALVE	LAVAS	MOVED	OVERS	REVET	SHOVE
ALIVE	BREVE	DAVEN	ERVEN	HAVEN	LAVED	MOVER	OVERT	REVIE	SIEVE
AMOVE	CALVE	DAVIT	EVADE	HAVER	LAVER	MOVES	OVINE	REVUE	SILVA
ANVIL	CARVE	DEAVE	EVENS	HAVES	LAVES	MOVIE	OVIST	RIEVE	SIVER
ARVAL	CARVY	DEEVE	EVENT	HAVOC	LAVRA	MURVA	OVOID	RIVAL	SKIVE
ARVOS	CAVED	DEEVS	EVERT	HEAVE	LEAVE	MVULE	OVOLI	RIVAS	SKIVY
AVAIL	CAVEL	DELVE	EVERY	HEAVY	LEAVY	NAEVE	OVOLO	RIVED	SLAVE
AVALE	CAVER	DERVS	EVETS	HELVE	LEVEE	NAEVI	OVULE	RIVEL	SLIVE
AVANT	CAVES	DEVAS	EVHOE	HEVEA	LEVEL	NAIVE	PAVAN	RIVEN	SLOVE
AVAST	CAVIE	DEVEL	EVICT	HIVED	LEVER	NAVAL	PAVED	RIVER	SOLVE
AVENS	CAVIL	DEVIL	EVILS	HIVER	LEVIN	NAVEL	PAVEN	RIVES	SPIVS
AVERS	CHAVE	DEVOT	EVITE	HIVES	LEVIS	NAVES	PAVER	RIVET	STAVE
AVERT	CHEVY	DIVAN	EVOHE	HOOVE	LIEVE	NAVEW	PAVES	RIVOS	STIVE
AVGAS	CHIVE	DIVAS	EVOKE	HOVED	LIVED	NAVVY	PAVID	ROVED	STIVY
AVIAN	CHIVS	DIVED	FAVEL	HOVEL	LIVEN	NEIVE	PAVIN	ROVER	STOVE
AVINE	CHIVY	DIVER	FAVER	HOVEN	LIVER	NERVE	PAVIS	ROVES	SUAVE
AVION	CIVES	DIVES	FAVOR	HOVER	LIVES	NERVY	PEAVY	SALVE	SWIVE
AVISE	CIVET	DIVIS	FAVUS	HOVES	LIVID	NEVEL	PEEVE	SALVO	SYLVA
AVISO	CIVIC	DIVOT	FEVER	IVIED	LIVOR	NEVER	PERVE	SAVED	SYVER
AVIZE	CIVIL	DIVVY	FIVER	IVIES	LIVRE	NEVES	PERVS	SAVER	TAVAH
AVOID	CIVVY	DOVED	FIVES	IVORY	LOAVE	NEVUS	PIVOT	SAVES	TAVAS
AVOWS	CLAVE	DOVER	FOVEA	JAVEL	LOVAT	NIEVE	POOVE	SAVEY	TAVER
AVYZE	CLEVE	DOVES	GAVEL	JIVED	LOVED	NIVAL	POOVY	SAVIN	TRAVE
AWAVE	CLOVE	DOVIE	GIVED	JIVER	LOVER	NOVAE	PREVE	SAVOR	ULVAS
BAVIN	CONVO	DRAVE	GIVEN	JIVES	LOVES	NOVAS	PRIVY	SAVOY	URVAS
BEVEL	COVED	DRIVE	GIVER	JUVES	LOVEY	NOVEL	PROVE	SAVVY	UVEAL
BEVER	COVEN	DROVE	GIVES	KAVAS	MALVA	NOVUM	RAVED	SELVA	UVEAS
BEVUE	COVER	DUVET	GLOVE	KEEVE	MAUVE	OAVES	RAVEL	SENVY	UVULA
BEVVY	COVES	EAVES	GRAVE	KERVE	MAVEN	OGIVE	RAVEN	SERVE	VACUA
BIVIA	COVET	EEVEN	GRAVY	KEVEL	MAVIN	OLIVE	RAVER	SERVO	VADED
BIVVY	COVEY	EEVNS	GREVE	KIEVE	MAVIS	OLLAV	RAVES	SEVEN	VADES
BLIVE	COVIN	ELVAN	GROVE	KIVAS	MEVED	ORVAL	RAVIN	SEVER	VAGAL
BOVID	CRAVE	ELVER	GUAVA	KNAVE	MEVES	OVALS	REAVE	SHAVE	VAGUE
BRAVA	CRUVE	ELVES	GYVED	KNIVE	MIEVE	OVARY	REEVE	SHEVA	VAGUS

VAILS	VARDY	VEEPS	VENGE	VEZIR	VINAL	VIRTU	VIVID	VOLKS	VROWS
VAIRE	VAREC	VEERS	VENIN	VIALS	VINAS	VIRUS	VIXEN	VOLTA	VUGGY
VAIRS	VARES	VEERY	VENOM	VIAND	VINCA	VISAS	VIZIR	VOLTE	VULGO
VAIRY	VARIX	VEGAN	VENTS	VIBES	VINED	VISED	VIZOR	VOLTS	VULNS
VAKIL	VARNA	VEGAS	VENUE	VIBEX	VINER	VISES	VLEIS	VOLVA	VULVA
VALES	VARUS	VEGES	VENUS	VICAR	VINES	VISIE	VLIES	VOLVE	VYING
VALET	VARVE	VEGIE	VERBS	VICED	VINEW	VISIT	VOARS	VOMER	WAIVE
VALID	VASAL	VEHME	VERGE	VICES	VINOS	VISNE	VOCAB	VOMIT	WAVED
VALIS	VASES	VEILS	VERRY	VICHY	VINTS	VISON	VOCAL	VOTED	WAVER
VALOR	VASTS	VEILY	VERSE	VIDEO	VINYL	VISOR	VOCES	VOTER	WAVES
VALSE	VASTY	VEINS	VERSO	VIERS	VIOLA	VISTA	VODKA	VOTES	WAVEY
VALUE	VATIC	VEINY	VERST	VIEWS	VIOLD	VISTO	VOGIE	VOUCH	WEAVE
VALVE	VATUS	VELAR	VERTS	VIEWY	VIOLS	VITAE	VOGUE	VOUGE	WIVED
VAMPS	VAULT	VELDS	VERTU	VIFDA	VIPER	VITAL	VOICE	VOULU	WIVES
VANED	VAUNT	VELDT	VERVE	VIGIA	VIRAL	VITAS	VOIDS	VOWED	WOLVE
VANES	VAUTE	VELES	VESPA	VIGIL	VIRED	VITEX	VOILA	VOWEL	WOVEN
VANGS	VAUTS	VELLS	VESTA	VIGOR	VIREO	VITTA	VOILE	VOWER	YEVEN
VANTS	VAWTE	VELUM	VESTS	VILDE	VIRES	VIVAS	VOLAE	VOZHD	YEVES
VAPID	VEALE	VENAE	VETCH	VILER	VIRGA	VIVAT	VOLAR	VRAIC	YRIVD
VAPOR	VEALS	VENAL	VEXED	VILLA	VIRGE	VIVDA	VOLED	VRILS	
VARAN	VEALY	VENDS	VEXER	VILLI	VIRID	VIVER	VOLES	VROOM	
VARAS	VEENA	VENEY	VEXES	VILLS	VIRLS	VIVES	VOLET	VROUW	

HINT

Q But No U

If you are not familiar with *Official Scrabble Words* you may be unaware that there are quite a few words that contain Q with no U. These are all to be found in the Q lists but it is worth highlighting them separately. You should certainly write down and learn the shorter ones. They are so vital in situations that would otherwise necessitate a change.

QI, QAT, QADI, QOPH, WAQF, QANAT, QIBLA, TALAQ,
QASIDA, QIGONG, QINTAR, QWERTY, YAQONA,
INQILAB, QABALAH, TSADDIQ, TZADDIQ,
MBAQANGA, QAIMAQAM, QALAMDAN,
TSADDIQIM, TZADDIQIM.

Note that -S plural forms are all allowed except for TSADDIQIM and TZADDIQIM which are already plural. QWERTY has the plural QWERTIES as well as QWERTYS.

Also note that the following Q words and their corresponding -S plural forms have a U, but not after the Q.

BURQA, MUQADDAM, QIVIUT, QINGHAOSU, SUQ.

HIGH SCORERS

The following lists contain all the words of length two to eight letters which contain any of the four high-scoring letters J, Q, X and Z. While most Scrabble players know the obvious words, such as JUDGE, QUEEN, EXALT and ZEROS, how many know the more obscure POOJA, SQUEG, SIXTE and NIZAM?

Knowing these words will enable you to be more adventurous when it comes to grabbing the odd triple-word-score square for 50-odd points – or perhaps playing a bonus word with six single-point letters and a high-scoring letter, such as NAARTJE, LASQUES, ANOXIAS and LAIRIZE, or even playing a bonus word using a letter on the board with words such as REJONEOS, EQUITANT, XENURINE and LAZURITE.

If a word contains two of these four high-scoring letters (such as JAZZY, JYNX, QUIZ and ZOOTAXY), then it will appear in two places.

J-WORDS

J - 2-letter words

JO

J - 3-letter words

GJU	JAG	JAP	JAY	JEU	JIG	JOE	JOT	JUD	JUT
HAJ	JAK	JAR	JEE	JEW	JIZ	JOG	JOW	JUG	RAJ
JAB	JAM	JAW	JET	JIB	JOB	JOR	JOY	JUS	TAJ

J - 4-letter words

AJAR	JADE	JARL	JEAT	JEUX	JINX	JOHN	JOTA	JUGA	JUVE
AJEE	JAGS	JARS	JEED	JEWS	JIRD	JOIN	JOTS	JUGS	JYNX
BAJU	JAIL	JASP	JEEL	JIAO	JISM	JOKE	JOUK	JUJU	MOJO
BENJ	JAKE	JASS	JEER	JIBE	JIVE	JOKY	JOUR	JUKE	PUJA
DOJO	JAKS	JASY	JEES	JIBS	JIZZ	JOLE	JOWL	JUMP	RAJA
GAJO	JAMB	JATO	JEFF	JIFF	JOBE	JOLL	JOWS	JUNK	ROJI
GJUS	JAMS	JAUP	JELL	JIGS	JOBS	JOLT	JOYS	JURA	SIJO
HADJ	JANE	JAWS	JERK	JILL	JOCK	JOMO	JUBA	JURE	SOJA
HAJI	JANN	JAYS	JESS	JILT	JOCO	JOOK	JUBE	JURY	
HAJJ	JAPE	JAZY	JEST	JIMP	JOES	JORS	JUDO	JUST	
JABS	JAPS	JAZZ	JETE	JINK	JOEY	JOSH	JUDS	JUTE	
JACK	JARK	JEAN	JETS	JINN	JOGS	JOSS	JUDY	JUTS	

J - 5-letter words

AFLAJ	FALAJ	JABOT	JAMMY	JATOS	JELAB	JEUNE	JIMPY	JOCKS	JOLLY
AJWAN	FJORD	JACKS	JANES	JAUNT	JELLO	JEWED	JINGO	JODEL	JOLTS
BAJAN	GADJE	JADED	JANNS	JAUPS	JELLS	JEWEL	JINKS	JOEYS	JOLTY
BAJRA	GAJOS	JADES	JANTY	JAVEL	JELLY	JHALA	JINNI	JOHNS	JOMOS
BAJRI	GANJA	JAGER	JAPAN	JAWAN	JEMMY	JIAOS	JINNS	JOINS	JONTY
BAJUS	GAUJE	JAGGY	JAPED	JAWED	JENNY	JIBED	JIRDS	JOINT	JOOKS
BANJO	HADJI	JAGIR	JAPER	JAZZY	JERID	JIBER	JIRGA	JOIST	JORAM
BIJOU	HAJES	JAILS	JAPES	JEANS	JERKS	JIBES	JISMS	JOKED	JORUM
BUNJE	HAJIS	JAKES	JARKS	JEATS	JERKY	JIFFS	JIVED	JOKER	JOTAS
BUNJY	HAJJI	JALAP	JARLS	JEBEL	JERRY	JIFFY	JIVER	JOKES	JOTUN
CAJUN	HEJAB	JAMBE	JARTA	JEELS	JESTS	JIGOT	JIVES	JOKEY	JOUAL
DJINN	HEJRA	JAMBO	JARUL	JEELY	JESUS	JIHAD	JNANA	JOKOL	JOUGS
DOJOS	HIJAB	JAMBS	JASEY	JEERS	JETES	JILLS	JOBED	JOLED	JOUKS
EJECT	HIJRA	JAMBU	JASPE	JEFFS	JETON	JILTS	JOBES	JOLES	JOULE
ENJOY	HODJA	JAMES	JASPS	JEHAD	JETTY	JIMMY	JOCKO	JOLLS	JOURS

JOUST	JUBES	JUICY	JUMBY	JUNTO	JUTTY	MOJOS	PUJAS	SAJOU	UPJET
JOWAR	JUDAS	JUJUS	JUMPS	JUPON	JUVES	MUJIK	RAJAH	SHOJI	WILJA
JOWED	JUDGE	JUKED	JUMPY	JURAL	KANJI	NINJA	RAJAS	SIJOS	YOJAN
JOWLS	JUDOS	JUKES	JUNCO	JURAT	KHOJA	OBJET	RAJES	SOJAS	ZANJA
JOWLY	JUGAL	JULEP	JUNKS	JUROR	KOPJE	OJIME	REJIG	SUJEE	
JOYED	JUGUM	JUMAR	JUNKY	JUSTS	LAPJE	OUIJA	REJON	TAJES	
JUBAS	JUICE	JUMBO	JUNTA	JUTES	MAJOR	POOJA	ROJIS	THUJA	

J - 6-letter words

ABJECT	FINJAN	JACKSY	JARGON	JELABS	JIGJIG	JOGGER	JOVIAL	JUNCUS	OBJECT
ABJURE	FJORDS	JADERY	JAROOL	JELLED	JIGOTS	JOGGLE	JOWARI	JUNGLE	OBJETS
ACAJOU	FRIJOL	JADING	JARRAH	JELLOS	JIGSAW	JOHNNY	JOWARS	JUNGLI	OBJURE
ADJOIN	GADJES	JADISH	JARRED	JEMIMA	JIHADS	JOINED	JOWING	JUNGLY	OJIMES
ADJURE	GAIJIN	JAEGER	JARTAS	JENNET	JILGIE	JOINER	JOWLED	JUNIOR	OUIJAS
ADJUST	GANJAS	JAGERS	JARULS	JERBIL	JILLET	JOINTS	JOWLER	JUNKED	OUTJET
AJOWAN	GARJAN	JAGGED	JARVEY	JERBOA	JILTED	JOISTS	JOYFUL	JUNKER	OUTJUT
AJWANS	GAUJES	JAGGER	JARVIE	JEREED	JIMINY	JOJOBA	JOYING	JUNKET	PAJOCK
BAJADA	GIDJEE	JAGHIR	JASEYS	JERIDS	JIMJAM	JOKERS	JOYOUS	JUNKIE	POOJAH
BAJANS	GURJUN	JAGIRS	JASIES	JERKED	JIMPER	JOKIER	JUBATE	JUNTAS	POOJAS
BAJRAS	HADJES	JAGUAR	JASPER	JERKER	JIMPLY	JOKING	JUBBAH	JUNTOS	POPJOY
BAJREE	HADJIS	JAILED	JASPES	JERKIN	JINGAL	JOLING	JUDDER	JUPATI	RAJAHS
BAJRIS	HAJJES	JAILER	JASPIS	JERQUE	JINGLE	JOLLED	JUDGED	JUPONS	RAMJET
BANJAX	HAJJIS	JAILOR	JASSES	JERSEY	JINGLY	JOLLEY	JUDGES	JURANT	REJECT
BANJOS	HANJAR	JALAPS	JATAKA	JESSED	JINKED	JOLTED	JUDIES	JURATS	REJIGS
BEJADE	HEJABS	JALOPY	JAUNCE	JESSES	JINKER	JOLTER	JUDOGI	JURIES	REJOIN
BEJANT	HEJIRA	JAMBEE	JAUNSE	JESSIE	JINNEE	JOOKED	JUDOKA	JURIST	SAJOUS
BENJES	HEJRAS	JAMBER	JAUNTS	JESTED	JINXED	JORAMS	JUGALS	JURORS	SANJAK
BHAJAN	HIJABS	JAMBES	JAUNTY	JESTEE	JINXES	JORDAN	JUGATE	JUSTED	SEJANT
BHAJEE	HIJACK	JAMBOK	JAUPED	JESTER	JIRBLE	JORUMS	JUGFUL	JUSTER	SHOJIS
BIJOUX	HIJRAH	JAMBOS	JAVELS	JETONS	JIRGAS	JOSEPH	JUGGED	JUSTLE	SOOJEY
BUNJEE	HIJRAS	JAMBUL	JAWANS	JETSAM	JISSOM	JOSHED	JUGGLE	JUSTLY	SUJEES
BUNJES	HOBJOB	JAMBUS	JAWARI	JETSOM	JITNEY	JOSHER	JUGLET	JUTTED	SWARAJ
BUNJIE	HODJAS	JAMJAR	JAWBOX	JETSON	JITTER	JOSHES	JUICED	JYMOLD	TAJINE
CAJOLE	INJECT	JAMMED	JAWING	JETTED	JIVERS	JOSKIN	JUICER	JYNXES	THUJAS
COJOIN	INJERA	JAMMER	JAZIES	JETTON	JIVING	JOSSER	JUICES	KANJIS	TINAJA
CONJEE	INJURE	JAMPAN	JAZZED	JEWELS	JIZZES	JOSSES	JUJUBE	KHODJA	UJAMAA
DEEJAY	INJURY	JAMPOT	JAZZER	JEWING	JNANAS	JOSTLE	JUKING	KHOJAS	UNJUST
DEJECT	JABBED	JANDAL	JAZZES	JEZAIL	JOANNA	JOTTED	JULEPS	KOPJES	UPJETS
DJEBEL	JABBER	JANGLE	JEBELS	JHALAS	JOBBED	JOTTER	JUMARS	LAPJES	WILJAS
DJINNI	JABBLE	JANGLY	JEEING	JIBBAH	JOBBER	JOTUNN	JUMART	MAJLIS	WILTJA
DONJON	JABERS	JANKER	JEELED	JIBBED	JOBBIE	JOTUNS	JUMBAL	MAJORS	YOJANA
EJECTA	JABIRU	JANSKY	JEELIE	JIBBER	JOBING	JOUALS	JUMBIE	MASJID	YOJANS
EJECTS	JABOTS	JANTEE	JEERED	JIBERS	JOCKEY	JOUKED	JUMBLE	MATJES	ZANJAS
ENJAMB	JACANA	JAPANS	JEERER	JIBING	JOCKOS	JOULED	JUMBLY	MEJLIS	
ENJOIN	JACENT	JAPERS	JEFFED	JIGGED	JOCOSE	JOULES	JUMBOS	MOJOES	
ENJOYS	JACKAL	JAPING	JEHADS	JIGGER	JOCUND	JOUNCE	JUMPED	MOUJIK	
EVEJAR	JACKED	JAPPED	JEJUNA	JIGGLE	JODELS	JOURNO	JUMPER	MUJIKS	
FEIJOA	JACKET	JARFUL	JEJUNE	JIGGLY	JOGGED	JOUSTS	JUNCOS	NINJAS	

J - 7-letter words

ABJECTS	BAJADAS	CAJOLES	DJIBBAH	HANJARS	JABBLES	JACONET	JALOPPY	JAMMING
ABJOINT	BAJREES	CAJUPUT	DONJONS	HEJIRAS	JABIRUS	JACUZZI	JALOUSE	JAMPANI
ABJURED	BANJOES	COJOINS	EJECTED	HIJACKS	JACAMAR	JADEDLY	JAMADAR	JAMPANS
ABJURER	BASENJI	COJONES	EJECTOR	HIJINKS	JACANAS	JADEITE	JAMBEAU	JAMPOTS
ABJURES	BEJADED	CONJECT	ENJAMBS	HIJRAHS	JACCHUS	JAEGERS	JAMBEES	JANDALS
ACAJOUS	BEJADES	CONJEED	ENJOINS	HOBJOBS	JACINTH	JAGGERS	JAMBERS	JANGLED
ADJOINS	BEJANTS	CONJEES	ENJOYED	IJTIHAD	JACKALS	JAGGERY	JAMBEUX	JANGLER
ADJOINT	BEJEWEL	CONJOIN	ENJOYER	INJECTS	JACKASS	JAGGIER	JAMBIER	JANGLES
ADJOURN	BHAJANS	CONJURE	EVEJARS	INJELLY	JACKDAW	JAGGING	JAMBIYA	JANITOR
ADJUDGE	BHAJEES	CONJURY	FAJITAS	INJERAS	JACKEEN	JAGHIRE	JAMBOKS	JANIZAR
ADJUNCT	BLOWJOB	DEEJAYS	FEIJOAS	INJOINT	JACKETS	JAGHIRS	JAMBONE	JANKERS
ADJURED	BONJOUR	DEJECTA	FINJANS	INJUNCT	JACKING	JAGUARS	JAMBOOL	JANNOCK
ADJURES	BRINJAL	DEJECTS	FRIJOLE	INJURED	JACKMAN	JAILERS	JAMBULS	JANSKYS
ADJUSTS	BUNJEES	DEJEUNE	GARJANS	INJURER	JACKMEN	JAILING	JAMDANI	JANTIER
AJOWANS	BUNJIES	DISJECT	GIDJEES	INJURES	JACKPOT	JAILORS	JAMESES	JANTIES
AJUTAGE	CAJEPUT	DISJOIN	GOUJONS	JABBERS	JACKSIE	JAKESES	JAMJARS	JAPINGS
ALFORJA	CAJOLED	DISJUNE	GURJUNS	JABBING	JACOBIN	JALAPIC	JAMMERS	JAPPING
AZULEJO	CAJOLER	DJEBELS	HANDJAR	JABBLED	JACOBUS	JALAPIN	JAMMIER	JARFULS

JARGONS	JEELING	JESSIES	JIMPEST	JOINING	JOUNCED	JUMBIES	JUTTIED	POPJOYS
JARGOON	JEEPERS	JESTEES	JIMPIER	JOINTED	JOUNCES	JUMBLED	JUTTIES	PREJINK
JARKMAN	JEEPNEY	JESTERS	JINGALS	JOINTER	JOURNAL	JUMBLER	JUTTING	PROJECT
JARKMEN	JEERERS	JESTFUL	JINGLED	JOINTLY	JOURNEY	JUMBLES	JUVENAL	PYJAMAS
JAROOLS	JEERING	JESTING	JINGLER	JOISTED	JOURNOS	JUMBUCK	KAJAWAH	RAMJETS
JARRAHS	JEFFING	JETFOIL	JINGLES	JOJOBAS	JOUSTED	JUMELLE	KHANJAR	REJECTS
JARRING	JEJUNUM	JETSAMS	JINGLET	JOKIEST	JOUSTER	JUMPERS	KHODJAS	REJOICE
JARVEYS	JELLABA	JETSOMS	JINGOES	JOLLEYS	JOWARIS	JUMPIER	KILLJOY	REJOINS
JARVIES	JELLIED	JETSONS	JINJILI	JOLLIED	JOWLERS	JUMPILY	LOCKJAW	REJONEO
JASMINE	JELLIES	JETTIED	JINKERS	JOLLIER	JOWLIER	JUMPING	MAATJES	REJONES
JASPERS	JELLIFY	JETTIER	JINKING	JOLLIES	JOWLING	JUNCATE	MAJESTY	REJOURN
JASPERY	JELLING	JETTIES	JINXING	JOLLIFY	JOYANCE	JUNCOES	MAJORAT	REJUDGE
JATAKAS	JEMADAR	JETTING	JIPYAPA	JOLLILY	JOYLESS	JUNGLES	MAJORED	SANJAKS
JAUNCED	JEMIDAR	JETTONS	JIRBLED	JOLLING	JUBBAHS	JUNGLIS	MANJACK	SAPAJOU
JAUNCES	JEMIMAS	JEWELRY	JIRBLES	JOLLITY	JUBILEE	JUNIORS	MASJIDS	SEJEANT
JAUNSED	JEMMIED	JEWFISH	JISSOMS	JOLLYER	JUDASES	JUNIPER	MISJOIN	SJAMBOK
JAUNSES	JEMMIER	JEZAILS	JITNEYS	JOLTERS	JUDDERS	JUNKERS	MOUJIKS	SKYJACK
JAUNTED	JEMMIES	JIBBAHS	JITTERS	JOLTIER	JUDGING	JUNKETS	MUDEJAR	SOJOURN
JAUNTEE	JENNETS	JIBBERS	JITTERY	JOLTING	JUDOGIS	JUNKIER	MUNTJAC	SOOJEYS
JAUNTIE	JENNIES	JIBBING	JOANNAS	JONQUIL	JUDOIST	JUNKIES	MUNTJAK	SUBJECT
JAUPING	JEOFAIL	JIFFIES	JOANNES	JONTIES	JUDOKAS	JUNKING	NAARTJE	SUBJOIN
JAVELIN	JEOPARD	JIGAJIG	JOBBERS	JOOKERY	JUGFULS	JUNKMAN	NARTJIE	TAJINES
JAWARIS	JERBILS	JIGAJOG	JOBBERY	JOOKING	JUGGING	JUNKMEN	OBJECTS	TINAJAS
JAWBONE	JERBOAS	JIGGERS	JOBBIES	JORDANS	JUGGINS	JUPATIS	OBJURED	TRAJECT
JAWFALL	JEREEDS	JIGGING	JOBBING	JOSEPHS	JUGGLED	JURALLY	OBJURES	UJAMAAS
JAWHOLE	JERKERS	JIGGISH	JOBLESS	JOSHERS	JUGGLER	JURANTS	OUTJEST	UNJADED
JAWINGS	JERKIER	JIGGLED	JOCKEYS	JOSHING	JUGGLES	JURIDIC	OUTJETS	UNJOINT
JAYWALK	JERKIES	JIGGLES	JOCULAR	JOSKINS	JUGHEAD	JURISTS	OUTJUMP	WILTJAS
JAZZERS	JERKING	JIGJIGS	JOGGERS	JOSSERS	JUGLETS	JURYMAN	OUTJUTS	YOJANAS
JAZZIER	JERKINS	JIGSAWS	JOGGING	JOSTLED	JUGULAR	JURYMEN	OVERJOY	ZANJERO
JAZZILY	JERQUED	JILGIES	JOGGLED	JOSTLES	JUICERS	JUSSIVE	PAJAMAS	
JAZZING	JERQUER	JILLETS	JOGGLES	JOTTERS	JUICIER	JUSTEST	PAJOCKE	
JAZZMAN	JERQUES	JILLION	JOGTROT	JOTTING	JUICING	JUSTICE	PAJOCKS	
JAZZMEN	JERRIES	JILTING	JOHNNIE	JOTUNNS	JUJUBES	JUSTIFY	PERJINK	
JEALOUS	JERSEYS	JIMJAMS	JOINDER	JOUKERY	JUKSKEI	JUSTING	PERJURE	
JEELIED	JESSAMY	JIMMIED	JOINERS	JOUKING	JUMARTS	JUSTLED	PERJURY	
JEELIES	JESSANT	JIMMIES	JOINERY	JOULING	JUMBALS	JUSTLES	POOJAHS	

J - 8-letter words

ABJECTED	BENJAMIN	DISJOINT	INJURING	JAMADARS	JARRINGS	JEMADARS	JIGGERED
ABJECTLY	BIJWONER	DISJUNCT	JABBERED	JAMBEAUX	JASMINES	JEMIDARS	JIGGINGS
ABJOINTS	BLOWJOBS	DISJUNES	JABBERER	JAMBIERS	JASPISES	JEMMIEST	JIGGLIER
ABJURERS	BRINJALS	DJELLABA	JABBLING	JAMBIYAH	JAUNCING	JEMMYING	JIGGLING
ABJURING	CAJEPUTS	DJIBBAHS	JACAMARS	JAMBIYAS	JAUNDICE	JEOFAILS	JIGSAWED
ADJACENT	CAJOLERS	EJECTING	JACINTHS	JAMBOLAN	JAUNSING	JEOPARDS	JILLAROO
ADJOINED	CAJOLERY	EJECTION	JACKAROO	JAMBONES	JAUNTIER	JEOPARDY	JILLIONS
ADJOINTS	CAJOLING	EJECTIVE	JACKBOOT	JAMBOOLS	JAUNTIES	JEREMIAD	JIMCRACK
ADJOURNS	CAJUPUTS	EJECTORS	JACKDAWS	JAMBOREE	JAUNTILY	JERKIEST	JIMMYING
ADJUDGED	CARCAJOU	ENJAMBED	JACKEENS	JAMDANIS	JAUNTING	JERKINGS	JIMPIEST
ADJUDGES	CARJACOU	ENJOINED	JACKEROO	JAMMIEST	JAVELINS	JEROBOAM	JIMPNESS
ADJUNCTS	COJOINED	ENJOINER	JACKETED	JAMPANEE	JAWBONED	JERQUERS	JINGBANG
ADJURING	CONJECTS	ENJOYERS	JACKPOTS	JAMPANIS	JAWBONES	JERQUING	JINGLERS
ADJUSTED	CONJOINS	ENJOYING	JACKSIES	JANGLERS	JAWBOXES	JERRICAN	JINGLETS
ADJUSTER	CONJOINT	FLAPJACK	JACOBINS	JANGLIER	JAWFALLS	JERRYCAN	JINGLIER
ADJUSTOR	CONJUGAL	FORJUDGE	JACONETS	JANGLING	JAWHOLES	JESTBOOK	JINGLING
ADJUTAGE	CONJUNCT	FRABJOUS	JACQUARD	JANITORS	JAYWALKS	JESTINGS	JINGOISH
ADJUTANT	CONJURED	FRIJOLES	JACULATE	JANITRIX	JAZERANT	JETFOILS	JINGOISM
ADJUVANT	CONJURER	GOUJEERS	JACUZZIS	JANIZARS	JAZZIEST	JETLINER	JINGOIST
AJUTAGES	CONJURES	HANDJARS	JADEITES	JANIZARY	JEALOUSE	JETPLANE	JINJILIS
ALFORJAS	CONJUROR	HIGHJACK	JADERIES	JANNOCKS	JEALOUSY	JETTIEST	JIPYAPAS
AZULEJOS	CRACKJAW	HIJACKED	JAGGEDLY	JANTIEST	JEANETTE	JETTISON	JIRBLING
BANJAXED	CUNJEVOI	HIJACKER	JAGGIEST	JAPANNED	JEELYING	JETTYING	JIRKINET
BANJAXES	DEEJAYED	IJTIHADS	JAGHIRES	JAPANNER	JEEPNEYS	JEWELLED	JITTERED
BANJOIST	DEJECTED	INJECTED	JALAPENO	JAPONICA	JEERINGS	JEWELLER	JOBATION
BASENJIS	DEJEUNER	INJECTOR	JALAPINS	JARARACA	JEJUNELY	JIBBERED	JOBBINGS
BEJABERS	DEJEUNES	INJOINTS	JALOPIES	JARARAKA	JEJUNITY	JIBBINGS	JOBSHARE
BEJADING	DEMIJOHN	INJUNCTS	JALOUSED	JARGONED	JELLABAS	JICKAJOG	JOCKETTE
BEJESUIT	DISJECTS	INJURERS	JALOUSES	JARGOONS	JELLYING	JIGAJIGS	JOCKEYED
BEJEWELS	DISJOINS	INJURIES	JALOUSIE	JAROSITE	JELUTONG	JIGAJOGS	JOCOSELY

JOCOSITY	JOLTHEAD	JUDGMENT	JUMPIEST	KAJAWAHS	NARTJIES	PULSOJET	SKYJACKS
JOCUNDLY	JOLTIEST	JUDICIAL	JUNCATES	KHANJARS	NIGHTJAR	PYJAMAED	SLAPJACK
JODELLED	JONCANOE	JUDOISTS	JUNCTION	KILLJOYS	NINJITSU	RAJASHIP	SOJOURNS
JODHPURS	JONGLEUR	JUGGINGS	JUNCTURE	KINKAJOU	NINJUTSU	READJUST	STICKJAW
JOGGINGS	JONQUILS	JUGGLERS	JUNCUSES	KOMITAJI	NONJUROR	REJECTED	SUBJECTS
JOGGLING	JORDELOO	JUGGLERY	JUNGLIER	LOCKJAWS	OBJECTED	REJECTER	SUBJOINS
JOGPANTS	JOSTLING	JUGGLING	JUNIPERS	LOGJUICE	OBJECTOR	REJECTOR	SUCURUJU
JOGTROTS	JOTTINGS	JUGHEADS	JUNKANOO	MAHARAJA	OBJURING	REJIGGED	SUPERJET
JOHANNES	JOUNCING	JUGULARS	JUNKETED	MAJESTIC	OUTJESTS	REJIGGER	SWARAJES
JOHNNIES	JOURNALS	JUGULATE	JUNKIEST	MAJLISES	OUTJUMPS	REJOICED	TJANTING
JOINDERS	JOURNEYS	JUICIEST	JURATORY	MAJOLICA	OVERJOYS	REJOICER	TRAJECTS
JOININGS	JOUSTERS	JUKSKEIS	JURISTIC	MAJORATS	OVERJUMP	REJOICES	TURBOJET
JOINTERS	JOUSTING	JULIENNE	JURYMAST	MAJORING	PAJOCKES	REJOINED	UNJOINTS
JOINTING	JOVIALLY	JUMARRED	JUSSIVES	MAJORITY	PEJORATE	REJONEOS	UNJOYFUL
JOINTURE	JOWLIEST	JUMBLERS	JUSTICER	MANJACKS	PERJURED	REJOURNS	UNJOYOUS
JOISTING	JOYANCES	JUMBLIER	JUSTICES	MARJORAM	PERJURER	REJUDGED	UNJUSTER
JOKESOME	JOYFULLY	JUMBLING	JUSTLING	MEJLISES	PERJURES	REJUDGES	UNJUSTLY
JOKINGLY	JOYOUSLY	JUMBOISE	JUSTNESS	MISJOINS	POPINJAY	SAPAJOUS	UPJETTED
JOLLEYER	JUBILANT	JUMBOIZE	JUTTYING	MISJUDGE	POPJOYED	SCRAMJET	VERJUICE
JOLLIEST	JUBILATE	JUMBUCKS	JUVENALS	MUNTJACS	PREJUDGE	SERJEANT	WHIPJACK
JOLLYERS	JUBILEES	JUMELLES	JUVENILE	MUNTJAKS	PROJECTS	SJAMBOKS	ZANJEROS
JOLLYING	JUDDERED	JUMPABLE	KABELJOU	NAARTJES	PULSEJET	SKIPJACK	

Q-WORDS

Q - 2-letter words

QI

Q - 3-letter words

QAT QIS QUA SUQ

Q - 4-letter words

AQUA	QATS	QUAD	QUAT	QUEP	QUID	QUIN	QUIT	QUOD	SUQS
QADI	QOPH	QUAG	QUAY	QUEY	QUIM	QUIP	QUIZ	QUOP	WAQF

Q - 5-letter words

AQUAE	QANAT	QUAKE	QUASI	QUENA	QUIDS	QUINT	QUITS	QUOTA	SQUEG
AQUAS	QIBLA	QUAKY	QUATS	QUERN	QUIET	QUIPO	QUOAD	QUOTE	SQUIB
BURQA	QOPHS	QUALE	QUAYD	QUERY	QUIFF	QUIPS	QUODS	QUOTH	SQUID
EQUAL	QUACK	QUALM	QUAYS	QUEST	QUILL	QUIPU	QUOIF	QUYTE	SQUIT
EQUID	QUADS	QUANT	QUEAN	QUEUE	QUILT	QUIRE	QUOIN	ROQUE	SQUIZ
EQUIP	QUAFF	QUARE	QUEEN	QUEYN	QUIMS	QUIRK	QUOIT	SQUAB	TALAQ
MAQUI	QUAGS	QUARK	QUEER	QUEYS	QUINA	QUIRT	QUOLL	SQUAD	TOQUE
PIQUE	QUAIL	QUART	QUELL	QUICH	QUINE	QUIST	QUONK	SQUAT	TUQUE
QADIS	QUAIR	QUASH	QUEME	QUICK	QUINS	QUITE	QUOPS	SQUAW	WAQFS

Q - 6-letter words

ACQUIT	COQUET	MANQUE	QUACKS	QUANGO	QUEENS	QUEUES	QUINSY	QUOIFS	QWERTY
ASQUAT	EQUALS	MAQUIS	QUAERE	QUANTA	QUEENY	QUEYNS	QUINTA	QUOINS	REQUIT
BARQUE	EQUANT	MARQUE	QUAFFS	QUANTS	QUEERS	QUICHE	QUINTE	QUOIST	RISQUE
BASQUE	EQUATE	MASQUE	QUAGGA	QUARER	QUEEST	QUICKS	QUINTS	QUOITS	ROQUES
BISQUE	EQUIDS	MOSQUE	QUAGGY	QUARKS	QUEINT	QUIDAM	QUINZE	QUOKKA	ROQUET
BURQAS	EQUINE	OPAQUE	QUAHOG	QUARRY	QUELCH	QUIETS	QUIPOS	QUOLLS	SACQUE
CAIQUE	EQUIPE	PIQUED	QUAICH	QUARTE	QUELEA	QUIFFS	QUIPUS	QUONKS	SAIQUE
CALQUE	EQUIPS	PIQUES	QUAIGH	QUARTO	QUELLS	QUIGHT	QUIRED	QUOOKE	SEQUEL
CASQUE	EQUITY	PIQUET	QUAILS	QUARTS	QUEMED	QUILLS	QUIRES	QUORUM	SEQUIN
CHEQUE	EXEQUY	PLAQUE	QUAINT	QUARTZ	QUEMES	QUILTS	QUIRKS	QUOTAS	SQUABS
CHEQUY	FAQUIR	PULQUE	QUAIRS	QUASAR	QUENAS	QUINAS	QUIRKY	QUOTED	SQUADS
CINQUE	HAIQUE	QANATS	QUAKED	QUATCH	QUENCH	QUINCE	QUIRTS	QUOTER	SQUAIL
CIRQUE	JERQUE	QASIDA	QUAKER	QUAVER	QUERNS	QUINES	QUISTS	QUOTES	SQUALL
CLAQUE	LASQUE	QIBLAS	QUAKES	QUEACH	QUESTS	QUINIC	QUITCH	QUOTHA	SQUAMA
CLIQUE	LIQUID	QIGONG	QUALIA	QUEANS	QUETCH	QUINIE	QUITED	QUOTUM	SQUAME
CLIQUY	LIQUOR	QINTAR	QUALMS	QUEASY	QUETHE	QUINOA	QUITES	QUYTED	SQUARE
CLOQUE	LOQUAT	QIVIUT	QUALMY	QUEAZY	QUEUED	QUINOL	QUIVER	QUYTES	SQUASH

SQUATS	SQUEAK	SQUIBS	SQUIFF	SQUINY	SQUIRR	SQUITS	TORQUE	UNIQUE
SQUAWK	SQUEAL	SQUIDS	SQUILL	SQUIRE	SQUIRT	TALAQS	TUQUES	YANQUI
SQUAWS	SQUEGS	SQUIER	SQUINT	SQUIRM	SQUISH	TOQUES	UBIQUE	YAQONA

Q - 7-letter words

ACQUEST	CIRQUES	JERQUED	QABALAH	QUARTIC	QUICHES	QUIPPED	REQUITE	SQUIDGE
ACQUIRE	CLAQUES	JERQUER	QASIDAS	QUARTOS	QUICKEN	QUIRING	REQUITS	SQUIDGY
ACQUIST	CLIQUES	JERQUES	QIGONGS	QUARTZY	QUICKER	QUIRKED	REQUOTE	SQUIERS
ACQUITE	CLIQUEY	JONQUIL	QINTARS	QUASARS	QUICKIE	QUIRTED	RISQUES	SQUIFFY
ACQUITS	CLOQUES	KUMQUAT	QIVIUTS	QUASHED	QUICKLY	QUITING	ROCQUET	SQUILLA
ALFAQUI	COEQUAL	LACQUER	QUACKED	QUASHEE	QUIDAMS	QUITTAL	ROQUETS	SQUILLS
ALIQUOT	CONQUER	LACQUEY	QUACKER	QUASHES	QUIDDIT	QUITTED	RORQUAL	SQUINCH
ANTIQUE	COQUETS	LASQUES	QUACKLE	QUASHIE	QUIDDLE	QUITTER	SACQUES	SQUINNY
AQUAFER	COQUINA	LIQUATE	QUADDED	QUASSIA	QUIESCE	QUITTOR	SAIQUES	SQUINTS
AQUARIA	COQUITO	LIQUEFY	QUADRAT	QUAVERS	QUIETED	QUIVERS	SEQUELA	SQUIRED
AQUATIC	CROQUET	LIQUEUR	QUADRIC	QUAVERY	QUIETEN	QUIVERY	SEQUELS	SQUIRES
AQUAVIT	CROQUIS	LIQUIDS	QUAERED	QUAYAGE	QUIETER	QUIZZED	SEQUENT	SQUIRMS
AQUEOUS	CUMQUAT	LIQUORS	QUAERES	QUEACHY	QUIETLY	QUIZZER	SEQUINS	SQUIRMY
AQUIFER	DAQUIRI	LOQUATS	QUAFFED	QUEECHY	QUIETUS	QUIZZES	SEQUOIA	SQUIRRS
AQUILON	DOCQUET	MACAQUE	QUAFFER	QUEENED	QUIGHTS	QUODDED	SILIQUA	SQUIRTS
AQUIVER	ENQUIRE	MADOQUA	QUAGGAS	QUEENIE	QUILLAI	QUODLIN	SILIQUE	SQUISHY
ASQUINT	ENQUIRY	MARQUEE	QUAHAUG	QUEENLY	QUILLED	QUOIFED	SQUABBY	SQUITCH
BANQUET	EQUABLE	MARQUES	QUAHOGS	QUEERED	QUILLET	QUOINED	SQUACCO	SUBAQUA
BAROQUE	EQUABLY	MARQUIS	QUAICHS	QUEERER	QUILLON	QUOISTS	SQUADDY	TEQUILA
BARQUES	EQUALLY	MASQUER	QUAIGHS	QUEERLY	QUILTED	QUOITED	SQUAILS	TORQUED
BASQUED	EQUANTS	MASQUES	QUAILED	QUEESTS	QUILTER	QUOITER	SQUALID	TORQUES
BASQUES	EQUATED	MESQUIN	QUAKERS	QUELEAS	QUINARY	QUOKKAS	SQUALLS	TSADDIQ
BEQUEST	EQUATES	MESQUIT	QUAKIER	QUELLED	QUINATE	QUONDAM	SQUALLY	TZADDIQ
BEZIQUE	EQUATOR	MOSQUES	QUAKING	QUELLER	QUINCES	QUONKED	SQUALOR	UNEQUAL
BISQUES	EQUERRY	OBLIQUE	QUALIFY	QUEMING	QUINCHE	QUOPPED	SQUAMAE	UNIQUER
BOSQUET	EQUINAL	OBLOQUY	QUALITY	QUERIED	QUINIES	QUORATE	SQUAMES	UNIQUES
BOUQUET	EQUINIA	OBSEQUY	QUAMASH	QUERIES	QUININE	QUORUMS	SQUARED	UNQUEEN
BRIQUET	EQUINOX	OPAQUED	QUANGOS	QUERIST	QUINNAT	QUOTERS	SQUARER	UNQUIET
BRUSQUE	EQUIPES	OPAQUER	QUANNET	QUESTED	QUINOAS	QUOTING	SQUARES	UNQUOTE
CACIQUE	ESQUIRE	OPAQUES	QUANTAL	QUESTER	QUINOID	QUOTUMS	SQUASHY	VAQUERO
CAIQUES	FAQUIRS	PARQUET	QUANTED	QUESTOR	QUINOLS	QUYTING	SQUATTY	YANQUIS
CALQUED	GRECQUE	PERIQUE	QUANTIC	QUETHES	QUINONE	QWERTYS	SQUAWKS	YAQONAS
CALQUES	HAIQUES	PICQUET	QUANTUM	QUETSCH	QUINTAL	RACQUET	SQUAWKY	
CASQUES	INQILAB	PIQUANT	QUAREST	QUETZAL	QUINTAN	RELIQUE	SQUEAKS	
CAZIQUE	INQUERE	PIQUETS	QUARREL	QUEUING	QUINTAS	REPIQUE	SQUEAKY	
CHARQUI	INQUEST	PIQUING	QUARTAN	QUEYNIE	QUINTES	REQUERE	SQUEALS	
CHEQUER	INQUIET	PLAQUES	QUARTER	QUIBBLE	QUINTET	REQUEST	SQUEEZE	
CHEQUES	INQUIRE	PREQUEL	QUARTES	QUIBLIN	QUINTIC	REQUIEM	SQUEEZY	
CINQUES	INQUIRY	PULQUES	QUARTET	QUICHED	QUINZES	REQUIRE	SQUELCH	

Q - 8-letter words

ACQUAINT	AQUATICS	CACIQUES	COTQUEAN	EQUINITY	INQILABS	LIQUORED	OBLIQUED
ACQUESTS	AQUATINT	CALQUING	CRITIQUE	EQUIPAGE	INQUERED	LOQUITUR	OBLIQUER
ACQUIGHT	AQUAVITS	CAZIQUES	CROQUETS	EQUIPPED	INQUERES	LUSTIQUE	OBLIQUES
ACQUIRAL	AQUEDUCT	CHARQUIS	CUMQUATS	EQUISETA	INQUESTS	MACAQUES	OBLIQUID
ACQUIRED	AQUIFERS	CHEQUERS	DAIQUIRI	EQUITANT	INQUIETS	MADOQUAS	OBSEQUIE
ACQUIRES	AQUILINE	CINQUAIN	DAQUIRIS	EQUITIES	INQUIRED	MAQUETTE	ODALIQUE
ACQUISTS	AQUILONS	CLAQUEUR	DETRAQUE	EQUIVOKE	INQUIRER	MAROQUIN	OLDSQUAW
ACQUITES	ARQUEBUS	CLINIQUE	DISQUIET	ESQUIRES	INQUIRES	MARQUEES	OPAQUELY
ADEQUACY	BANQUETS	CLIQUIER	DOCQUETS	ESQUISSE	JACQUARD	MARQUESS	OPAQUEST
ADEQUATE	BARBEQUE	CLIQUISH	ELOQUENT	EXEQUIAL	JERQUERS	MARQUISE	OPAQUING
ALFAQUIS	BAROQUES	CLIQUISM	EMBUSQUE	EXEQUIES	JERQUING	MASQUERS	PARAQUAT
ALIQUANT	BASQUINE	COEQUALS	ENQUIRED	FILIOQUE	JONQUILS	MBAQANGA	PAROQUET
ANTIQUED	BEQUEATH	COLLOQUE	ENQUIRER	FREQUENT	KUMQUATS	MESQUINE	PARQUETS
ANTIQUES	BEQUESTS	COLLOQUY	ENQUIRES	GRECQUES	LACQUERS	MESQUITE	PERIQUES
APPLIQUE	BEZIQUES	CONQUERS	EQUALISE	HAQUETON	LACQUEYS	MESQUITS	PERRUQUE
AQUACADE	BLANQUET	CONQUEST	EQUALITY	HENEQUEN	LIQUABLE	MISQUOTE	PETANQUE
AQUAFERS	BOSQUETS	COQUETRY	EQUALIZE	HENEQUIN	LIQUATED	MOQUETTE	PHYSIQUE
AQUALUNG	BOUQUETS	COQUETTE	EQUALLED	HENIQUIN	LIQUATES	MOSQUITO	PICQUETS
AQUANAUT	BOUTIQUE	COQUILLA	EQUATING	HUAQUERO	LIQUESCE	MUQADDAM	PIQUANCY
AQUARIAN	BRELOQUE	COQUILLE	EQUATION	ILLIQUID	LIQUEURS	MUSQUASH	PIQUETED
AQUARIST	BRIQUETS	COQUINAS	EQUATORS	INEQUITY	LIQUIDLY	MYSTIQUE	PRATIQUE
AQUARIUM	BRUSQUER	COQUITOS	EQUINIAS	INIQUITY	LIQUIDUS	NARQUOIS	PREQUELS

QABALAHS	QUANTIZE	QUEERISH	QUIESCED	QUIRKISH	REQUIRER	SQUANDER	SQUINTED
QAIMAQAM	QUANTONG	QUEERITY	QUIESCES	QUIRTING	REQUIRES	SQUARELY	SQUINTER
QALAMDAN	QUARRELS	QUELCHED	QUIETENS	QUISLING	REQUITAL	SQUARERS	SQUIRAGE
QUACKERS	QUARRIED	QUELCHES	QUIETERS	QUITCHED	REQUITED	SQUAREST	SQUIREEN
QUACKERY	QUARRIER	QUELLERS	QUIETEST	QUITCHES	REQUITER	SQUARIAL	SQUIRELY
QUACKING	QUARRIES	QUELLING	QUIETING	QUITTALS	REQUITES	SQUARING	SQUIRESS
QUACKLED	QUARTANS	QUENCHED	QUIETISM	QUITTERS	REQUOTED	SQUARISH	SQUIRING
QUACKLES	QUARTERN	QUENCHER	QUIETIST	QUITTING	REQUOTES	SQUARSON	SQUIRMED
QUADDING	QUARTERS	QUENCHES	QUIETIVE	QUITTORS	REQUOYLE	SQUASHED	SQUIRRED
QUADRANS	QUARTETS	QUENELLE	QUIETUDE	QUIVERED	ROCQUETS	SQUASHER	SQUIRREL
QUADRANT	QUARTETT	QUERISTS	QUIGHTED	QUIXOTIC	ROQUETED	SQUASHES	SQUIRTED
QUADRATE	QUARTICS	QUERYING	QUILLAIS	QUIXOTRY	ROQUETTE	SQUATTED	SQUIRTER
QUADRATS	QUARTIER	QUESTANT	QUILLETS	QUIZZERS	RORQUALS	SQUATTER	SQUISHED
QUADRICS	QUARTILE	QUESTERS	QUILLING	QUIZZERY	SEAQUAKE	SQUATTLE	SQUISHES
QUADRIGA	QUARTZES	QUESTING	QUILLMAN	QUIZZIFY	SEQUELAE	SQUAWKED	SQUIZZES
QUADROON	QUASHEES	QUESTION	QUILLMEN	QUIZZING	SEQUENCE	SQUAWKER	SUBEQUAL
QUAESTOR	QUASHIES	QUESTORS	QUILLONS	QUODDING	SEQUENTS	SQUAWMAN	SURQUEDY
QUAFFERS	QUASHING	QUETCHED	QUILTERS	QUODLINS	SEQUINED	SQUAWMEN	TEQUILAS
QUAFFING	QUASSIAS	QUETCHES	QUILTING	QUOIFING	SEQUOIAS	SQUEAKED	TEQUILLA
QUAGGIER	QUATCHED	QUETHING	QUINCHED	QUOINING	SILIQUAS	SQUEAKER	TOQUILLA
QUAGMIRE	QUATCHES	QUETZALS	QUINCHES	QUOITERS	SILIQUES	SQUEALED	TORQUATE
QUAGMIRY	QUATORZE	QUEUEING	QUINCUNX	QUOITING	SQUABASH	SQUEALER	TRANQUIL
QUAHAUGS	QUATRAIN	QUEUINGS	QUINELLA	QUONKING	SQUABBED	SQUEEGEE	TRUQUAGE
QUAILING	QUAVERED	QUEYNIES	QUININES	QUOPPING	SQUABBER	SQUEEZED	TRUQUEUR
QUAINTER	QUAVERER	QUIBBLED	QUINNATS	QUOTABLE	SQUABBLE	SQUEEZER	TSADDIQS
QUAINTLY	QUAYAGES	QUIBBLER	QUINOIDS	QUOTABLY	SQUACCOS	SQUEEZES	TZADDIQS
QUAKIEST	QUAYSIDE	QUIBBLES	QUINONES	QUOTIENT	SQUADDIE	SQUEGGED	UBIQUITY
QUAKINGS	QUEACHES	QUIBLINS	QUINSIED	QWERTIES	SQUADRON	SQUEGGER	UMQUHILE
QUALMIER	QUEASIER	QUICHING	QUINSIES	RACQUETS	SQUAILED	SQUELCHY	UNEQUALS
QUALMING	QUEASILY	QUICKENS	QUINTAIN	RAMEQUIN	SQUAILER	SQUIBBED	UNIQUELY
QUALMISH	QUEAZIER	QUICKEST	QUINTALS	RELIQUES	SQUALENE	SQUIDDED	UNIQUEST
QUANDANG	QUEENDOM	QUICKIES	QUINTETS	REMARQUE	SQUALLED	SQUIDGED	UNQUEENS
QUANDARY	QUEENIER	QUICKSET	QUINTETT	REPIQUED	SQUALLER	SQUIDGES	UNQUIETS
QUANDONG	QUEENIES	QUIDDANY	QUINTILE	REPIQUES	SQUALOID	SQUIFFER	UNQUOTED
QUANNETS	QUEENING	QUIDDITS	QUIPPING	REQUERED	SQUALORS	SQUIGGLE	UNQUOTES
QUANTICS	QUEENITE	QUIDDITY	QUIPPISH	REQUERES	SQUAMATE	SQUIGGLY	VANQUISH
QUANTIFY	QUEENLET	QUIDDLED	QUIPSTER	REQUESTS	SQUAMOSE	SQUILGEE	VAQUEROS
QUANTING	QUEERDOM	QUIDDLER	QUIRKIER	REQUIEMS	SQUAMOUS	SQUILLAS	VEHMIQUE
QUANTISE	QUEEREST	QUIDDLES	QUIRKILY	REQUIGHT	SQUAMULA	SQUINIED	VERQUERE
QUANTITY	QUEERING	QUIDNUNC	QUIRKING	REQUIRED	SQUAMULE	SQUINIES	VERQUIRE

X-WORDS

X - 2-letter words

AX	EX	OX	XI	XU

X - 3-letter words

AXE	FAX	HOX	LOX	MUX	PIX	REX	SOX	VOX	XIS
BOX	FIX	KEX	LUX	NIX	POX	SAX	TAX	WAX	YEX
COX	FOX	LAX	MAX	NOX	PYX	SEX	TUX	WEX	ZAX
DUX	HEX	LEX	MIX	PAX	RAX	SIX	VEX	WOX	ZEX

X - 4-letter words

APEX	AXON	DIXI	EXON	FLEX	IXIA	MAXI	ONYX	ROUX	VEXT
AXED	BOXY	DIXY	EXPO	FLIX	JEUX	MINX	ORYX	SEXT	WAXY
AXEL	CALX	DOXY	EXUL	FLUX	JINX	MIXT	OXEN	SEXY	WEXE
AXES	COAX	EAUX	FAIX	FOXY	JYNX	MIXY	OXER	TAXA	XYST
AXIL	COXA	EXAM	FALX	HOAX	LANX	MOXA	PIXY	TAXI	YUNX
AXIS	COXY	EXES	FAUX	IBEX	LUXE	NEXT	POXY	TEXT	
AXLE	CRUX	EXIT	FLAX	ILEX	LYNX	NIXY	PREX	ULEX	

X - 5-letter words

ADDAX	ANNEX	AXELS	AXILS	AXLES	AXOID	BOLIX	BOXEN	BRAXY	CALYX
ADMIX	ATAXY	AXIAL	AXING	AXMAN	AXONS	BORAX	BOXER	BUXOM	CAREX
AFFIX	AUXIN	AXILE	AXIOM	AXMEN	BEAUX	BOXED	BOXES	CALIX	CAXON

CHOUX	EXALT	EXTRA	HOXES	MALAX	NOXAL	PYXED	SIXES	UNBOX	XEBEC
CIMEX	EXAMS	EXUDE	HYRAX	MAXES	NOXES	PYXES	SIXTE	UNFIX	XENIA
CODEX	EXCEL	EXULS	IMMIX	MAXIM	OXERS	PYXIS	SIXTH	UNSEX	XENON
COXAE	EXEAT	EXULT	INDEX	MAXIS	OXIDE	RADIX	SIXTY	UNTAX	XERIC
COXAL	EXEEM	EXURB	INFIX	MIXED	OXIME	RAXED	SOREX	VARIX	XOANA
COXED	EXEME	FAXED	IXIAS	MIXEN	OXLIP	RAXES	TAXED	VEXED	XYLEM
COXES	EXERT	FAXES	IXTLE	MIXER	OXTER	REDOX	TAXER	VEXER	XYLIC
CULEX	EXIES	FIXED	KEXES	MIXES	PANAX	RELAX	TAXES	VEXES	XYLOL
CYLIX	EXILE	FIXER	KYLIX	MOXAS	PAXES	REMEX	TAXIS	VIBEX	XYLYL
DESEX	EXINE	FIXES	LATEX	MOXIE	PHLOX	REMIX	TAXOL	VITEX	XYSTI
DETOX	EXIST	FLAXY	LAXER	MUREX	PIXEL	SALIX	TAXON	VIXEN	XYSTS
DIXIE	EXITS	FOXED	LAXES	MUXED	PIXES	SAXES	TAXOR	WAXED	YEXED
DRUXY	EXODE	FOXES	LAXLY	MUXES	PIXIE	SEXED	TELEX	WAXEN	YEXES
DUXES	EXONS	HELIX	LEXES	NEXTS	PODEX	SEXER	TEXAS	WAXER	ZAXES
EMBOX	EXPAT	HEXAD	LEXIS	NEXUS	POXED	SEXES	TEXTS	WAXES	ZEXES
ENFIX	EXPEL	HEXED	LIMAX	NIXED	POXES	SEXTS	TOXIC	WEXED	
EPOXY	EXPOS	HEXES	LOXES	NIXES	PREXY	SILEX	TOXIN	WEXES	
EXACT	EXTOL	HOXED	LUXES	NIXIE	PROXY	SIXER	TUXES	WOXEN	

X - 6-letter words

ADIEUX	CALXES	EFFLUX	EXODES	EXUDES	HOAXED	MIXENS	PIXIES	SIXAIN	VOLVOX
AFFLUX	CARFAX	ELIXIR	EXODIC	EXULTS	HOAXER	MIXERS	PLEXOR	SIXERS	VORTEX
ALEXIA	CARFOX	EUTAXY	EXODUS	EXURBS	HOAXES	MIXIER	PLEXUS	SIXTES	WAXERS
ALEXIC	CAUDEX	EXACTS	EXOGEN	FAXING	HOXING	MIXING	POLLEX	SIXTHS	WAXIER
ALEXIN	CAXONS	EXALTS	EXOMIS	FIXATE	IBEXES	MOXIES	POXIER	SMILAX	WAXILY
ANNEXE	CERVIX	EXAMEN	EXONIC	FIXERS	ICEBOX	MUXING	POXING	SPADIX	WAXING
ANOXIA	CHENIX	EXARCH	EXONYM	FIXING	ILEXES	MYXOMA	PRAXES	SPHINX	WEXING
ANOXIC	CLIMAX	EXCAMB	EXOPOD	FIXITY	IMBREX	NEXTLY	PRAXIS	STORAX	WRAXLE
APEXES	COAXED	EXCEED	EXOTIC	FIXIVE	IMPLEX	NIXIES	PREFIX	STYRAX	XEBECS
ATAXIA	COAXER	EXCELS	EXPAND	FIXURE	INFLUX	NIXING	PREMIX	SUFFIX	XENIAL
ATAXIC	COAXES	EXCEPT	EXPATS	FLAXEN	IXTLES	ONYXES	PREXES	SURTAX	XENIAS
ATWIXT	COCCYX	EXCESS	EXPECT	FLAXES	JAWBOX	OREXIS	PROLIX	SYNTAX	XENIUM
AUXINS	COMMIX	EXCIDE	EXPELS	FLEXED	JINXED	ORIFEX	PTYXES	SYRINX	XENONS
AXEMAN	CONFIX	EXCISE	EXPEND	FLEXES	JINXES	ORYXES	PTYXIS	TAXERS	XEROMA
AXEMEN	CONVEX	EXCITE	EXPERT	FLEXOR	JYNXES	OUTBOX	PYXING	TAXIED	XOANON
AXILLA	CORTEX	EXCUSE	EXPIRE	FLIXED	KLAXON	OUTFOX	RAXING	TAXIES	XYLEMS
AXIOMS	COWPOX	EXEATS	EXPIRY	FLIXES	LARNAX	OXALIC	REFLEX	TAXING	XYLENE
AXISES	COXIER	EXEDRA	EXPORT	FLUXED	LARYNX	OXALIS	REFLUX	TAXMAN	XYLOID
AXOIDS	COXING	EXEEMS	EXPOSE	FLUXES	LAXEST	OXFORD	RHEXES	TAXMEN	XYLOLS
BANJAX	CRUXES	EXEMED	EXPUGN	FORFEX	LAXISM	OXGANG	RHEXIS	TAXOLS	XYLOMA
BAXTER	DEFLEX	EXEMES	EXSECT	FORNIX	LAXIST	OXGATE	SAXAUL	TAXORS	XYLOSE
BEMBEX	DEIXES	EXEMPT	EXSERT	FOXIER	LAXITY	OXHEAD	SAXONY	TETTIX	XYLYLS
BEMBIX	DEIXIS	EXEQUY	EXTANT	FOXING	LEXEME	OXIDES	SCOLEX	THORAX	XYSTER
BIAXAL	DENTEX	EXERTS	EXTASY	FRUTEX	LUMMOX	OXIMES	SEXERS	TOXINS	XYSTOI
BIJOUX	DEXTER	EXEUNT	EXTEND	GALAXY	LUXATE	OXLAND	SEXFID	TOXOID	XYSTOS
BOLLIX	DIAXON	EXHALE	EXTENT	HALLUX	LUXURY	OXLIPS	SEXIER	TUTRIX	XYSTUS
BOMBAX	DIOXAN	EXHORT	EXTERN	HATBOX	LYNXES	OXSLIP	SEXING	TUXEDO	YEXING
BONXIE	DIOXIN	EXHUME	EXTINE	HAYBOX	MAGNOX	OXTAIL	SEXISM	ULEXES	YUNXES
BOXCAR	DIPLEX	EXILED	EXTIRP	HEXACT	MATRIX	OXTERS	SEXIST	UNISEX	
BOXERS	DIXIES	EXILES	EXTOLD	HEXADS	MAXIMA	OXYGEN	SEXPOT	URTEXT	
BOXFUL	DOGFOX	EXILIC	EXTOLS	HEXANE	MAXIMS	OXYMEL	SEXTAN	VERTEX	
BOXIER	DOXIES	EXINES	EXTORT	HEXENE	MAXIXE	PAXWAX	SEXTET	VEXERS	
BOXING	DUPLEX	EXISTS	EXTRAS	HEXING	MENINX	PINXIT	SEXTON	VEXING	
BOYAUX	EARWAX	EXITED	EXUDED	HEXOSE	MINXES	PIXELS	SEXUAL	VIXENS	

X - 7-letter words

ABAXIAL	ANNEXES	ATARAXY	BAUXITE	BOXIEST	COAXERS	DETOXED	ELIXIRS	EXACTER
ABRAXAS	ANOREXY	ATAXIAS	BAXTERS	BOXINGS	COAXIAL	DETOXES	EMBOXED	EXACTLY
ADAXIAL	ANOXIAS	ATAXIES	BEESWAX	BOXROOM	COAXING	DEXTERS	EMBOXES	EXACTOR
ADDAXES	ANTEFIX	AUXESES	BETWIXT	BOXWOOD	COEXIST	DEXTRAL	ENFIXED	EXALTED
ADMIXED	ANTHRAX	AUXESIS	BIAXIAL	BRAXIES	COMPLEX	DEXTRAN	ENFIXES	EXAMENS
ADMIXES	ANXIETY	AUXETIC	BOLIXED	BRUXISM	CONFLUX	DEXTRIN	EPAXIAL	EXAMINE
AFFIXED	ANXIOUS	AXIALLY	BOLIXES	BUREAUX	CONTEXT	DIAXONS	EPITAXY	EXAMPLE
AFFIXES	APOPLEX	AXILLAE	BONXIES	BUXOMER	COTEAUX	DIOXANE	EPOXIDE	EXARATE
ALEXIAS	APRAXIA	AXILLAR	BORAXES	CACHEXY	COXCOMB	DIOXANS	EPOXIES	EXARCHS
ALEXINS	APTERYX	AXINITE	BOSTRYX	CADEAUX	COXIEST	DIOXIDE	EQUINOX	EXARCHY
ANAXIAL	ASEXUAL	AXOLOTL	BOXCARS	CALYXES	DESEXED	DIOXINS	EUTEXIA	EXCAMBS
ANNEXED	ASPHYXY	BATEAUX	BOXFULS	CHOENIX	DESEXES	DRUXIER	EXACTED	EXCEEDS

EXCEPTS	EXIGENT	EXPURGE	FLUXING	LATEXES	OXHEADS	RELAXED	TAXABLE	VEXEDLY
EXCERPT	EXILIAN	EXSCIND	FLUXION	LAXATOR	OXIDANT	RELAXES	TAXABLY	VEXILLA
EXCHEAT	EXILING	EXSECTS	FLUXIVE	LAXISMS	OXIDASE	RELAXIN	TAXICAB	VEXINGS
EXCIDED	EXILITY	EXSERTS	FOXHOLE	LAXISTS	OXIDATE	REMIXED	TAXIING	VICTRIX
EXCIDES	EXISTED	EXTATIC	FOXIEST	LAXNESS	OXIDISE	REMIXES	TAXIMAN	VITEXES
EXCISED	EXITING	EXTENDS	FOXINGS	LEXEMES	OXIDIZE	RESEAUX	TAXIMEN	VITRAUX
EXCISES	EXOCARP	EXTENSE	FOXSHIP	LEXICAL	OXLANDS	SALPINX	TAXINGS	VIXENLY
EXCITED	EXODERM	EXTENTS	FOXTROT	LEXICON	OXONIUM	SALTBOX	TAXIWAY	WAXBILL
EXCITER	EXODIST	EXTERNE	GATEAUX	LEXISES	OXSLIPS	SANDBOX	TAXLESS	WAXIEST
EXCITES	EXOGAMY	EXTERNS	GEARBOX	LIXIVIA	OXTAILS	SAXAULS	TAXYING	WAXINGS
EXCITON	EXOGENS	EXTINCT	GRAVLAX	LOXYGEN	OXTERED	SAXHORN	TECTRIX	WAXWING
EXCITOR	EXOMION	EXTINES	HELIXES	LUXATED	OXYGENS	SEALWAX	TELEFAX	WAXWORK
EXCLAIM	EXONYMS	EXTIRPS	HEXACTS	LUXATES	OXYMELS	SEEDBOX	TELETEX	WOODWAX
EXCLAVE	EXOPODS	EXTORTS	HEXADIC	MAILBOX	OXYTONE	SEXFOIL	TELEXED	WORKBOX
EXCLUDE	EXORDIA	EXTRACT	HEXAGON	MALAXED	PANAXES	SEXIEST	TELEXES	WRAXLED
EXCRETA	EXOTICA	EXTRAIT	HEXANES	MALAXES	PANCHAX	SEXISMS	TEXASES	WRAXLES
EXCRETE	EXOTICS	EXTREAT	HEXAPLA	MARTEXT	PARADOX	SEXISTS	TEXTILE	XANTHAM
EXCUDIT	EXPANDS	EXTREME	HEXAPOD	MAXILLA	PAXIUBA	SEXLESS	TEXTUAL	XANTHAN
EXCURSE	EXPANSE	EXTRUDE	HEXARCH	MAXIMAL	PERPLEX	SEXPERT	TEXTURE	XANTHIC
EXCUSAL	EXPECTS	EXUDATE	HEXENES	MAXIMIN	PHALANX	SEXPOTS	TOOLBOX	XANTHIN
EXCUSED	EXPENDS	EXUDING	HEXINGS	MAXIMUM	PHARYNX	SEXTANS	TORTRIX	XERAFIN
EXCUSER	EXPENSE	EXULTED	HEXOSES	MAXIXES	PHLOXES	SEXTANT	TOXEMIA	XERARCH
EXCUSES	EXPERTS	EXURBAN	HOAXERS	MAXWELL	PHOENIX	SEXTETS	TOXEMIC	XERASIA
EXECUTE	EXPIATE	EXURBIA	HOAXING	MILIEUX	PICKAXE	SEXTETT	TOXICAL	XEROMAS
EXEDRAE	EXPIRED	EXUVIAE	HYDROXY	MINIMAX	PLANXTY	SEXTILE	TOXOIDS	XEROSES
EXEEMED	EXPIRES	EXUVIAL	HYPOXIA	MIXABLE	PLEXORS	SEXTONS	TRIAXON	XEROSIS
EXEGETE	EXPLAIN	FIREBOX	HYPOXIC	MIXEDLY	PLEXURE	SEXTUOR	TRIPLEX	XEROTES
EXEMING	EXPLANT	FIXABLE	HYRAXES	MIXIEST	PODEXES	SHOWBOX	TUBIFEX	XEROTIC
EXEMPLA	EXPLODE	FIXATED	IMMIXED	MIXTION	POSTBOX	SILEXES	TUXEDOS	XIPHOID
EXEMPLE	EXPLOIT	FIXATES	IMMIXES	MIXTURE	POSTFIX	SIMPLEX	UNBOXED	XYLENES
EXEMPTS	EXPLORE	FIXEDLY	INDEXAL	MONAXON	POXIEST	SIXAINE	UNBOXES	XYLENOL
EXERGUE	EXPORTS	FIXINGS	INDEXED	MUREXES	PRETEXT	SIXAINS	UNFIXED	XYLITOL
EXERTED	EXPOSAL	FIXTURE	INDEXER	NARTHEX	PREXIES	SIXFOLD	UNFIXES	XYLOGEN
EXHALED	EXPOSED	FIXURES	INDEXES	NOXIOUS	PRINCOX	SIXTEEN	UNMIXED	XYLOMAS
EXHALES	EXPOSER	FLAXIER	INDOXYL	ORATRIX	PROXIES	SIXTHLY	UNSEXED	XYLONIC
EXHAUST	EXPOSES	FLEXILE	INEXACT	OVERTAX	PROXIMO	SIXTIES	UNSEXES	XYLOSES
EXHEDRA	EXPOUND	FLEXING	INFIXED	OXALATE	PYREXIA	SOAPBOX	UNTAXED	XYSTERS
EXHIBIT	EXPRESS	FLEXION	INFIXES	OXAZINE	PYREXIC	SOREXES	UNTAXES	ZEUXITE
EXHORTS	EXPUGNS	FLEXORS	INVEXED	OXBLOOD	PYXIDES	SPANDEX	UNVEXED	ZOOTAXY
EXHUMED	EXPULSE	FLEXURE	JAMBEUX	OXFORDS	PYXIDIA	SUBTEXT	URTEXTS	
EXHUMER	EXPUNCT	FLIXING	JINXING	OXGANGS	REANNEX	SYNAXES	UXORIAL	
EXHUMES	EXPUNGE	FLUMMOX	KLAXONS	OXGATES	RECTRIX	SYNAXIS	VAUDOUX	

X - 8-letter words

ADMIXING	AXINITES	BUXOMEST	COMMIXES	DEXTROSE	EUTEXIAS	EXCESSES	EXCUSALS
AFFIXING	AXIOLOGY	CACHEXIA	CONFIXED	DEXTROUS	EUXENITE	EXCHANGE	EXCUSERS
AFFLUXES	AXOLOTLS	CACODOXY	CONFIXES	DIOXANES	EXACTERS	EXCHEATS	EXCUSING
AMPLEXUS	AXOPLASM	CACOMIXL	CONTEXTS	DIOXIDES	EXACTEST	EXCIDING	EXCUSIVE
ANNEXING	BANDEAUX	CAMAIEUX	CONVEXED	DISANNEX	EXACTING	EXCISING	EXECRATE
ANNEXION	BANJAXED	CARBOXYL	CONVEXES	DOGFOXES	EXACTION	EXCISION	EXECUTED
ANNEXURE	BANJAXES	CARFAXES	CONVEXLY	DOXOLOGY	EXACTORS	EXCITANT	EXECUTER
ANOREXIA	BANXRING	CARFOXES	CORTEXES	DRUXIEST	EXALTING	EXCITERS	EXECUTES
ANOREXIC	BAUXITES	CARNIFEX	COWPOXES	DUPLEXER	EXAMINED	EXCITING	EXECUTOR
ANTEFIXA	BAUXITIC	CATHEXES	COXALGIA	DUPLEXES	EXAMINEE	EXCITONS	EXECUTRY
ANTHELIX	BEAUXITE	CATHEXIS	COXCOMBS	DUXELLES	EXAMINER	EXCITORS	EXEEMING
APOMIXES	BEMBEXES	CAUDEXES	COXINESS	DYSLEXIA	EXAMINES	EXCLAIMS	EXEGESES
APOMIXIS	BEMBIXES	CERVIXES	COXSWAIN	DYSLEXIC	EXAMPLAR	EXCLAVES	EXEGESIS
APOPLEXY	BERCEAUX	CHAPEAUX	CREATRIX	EARTHWAX	EXAMPLED	EXCLUDED	EXEGETES
APPENDIX	BICONVEX	CHATEAUX	CRUCIFIX	EARWAXES	EXAMPLES	EXCLUDEE	EXEGETIC
APRAXIAS	BISEXUAL	CHENIXES	CURATRIX	ECOTOXIC	EXANTHEM	EXCLUDER	EXEMPLAR
APYREXIA	BOLIXING	CICATRIX	DEFLEXED	EFFLUXES	EXARCHAL	EXCLUDES	EXEMPLES
ASPHYXIA	BOLLIXED	CINEPLEX	DEFLEXES	EMBOXING	EXCAMBED	EXCRETAL	EXEMPLUM
ATARAXIA	BOLLIXES	CLACKBOX	DENTEXES	ENDEIXES	EXCAVATE	EXCRETED	EXEMPTED
ATARAXIC	BOMBAXES	CLANGBOX	DESEXING	ENDEIXIS	EXCEEDED	EXCRETER	EXEQUIAL
AUXETICS	BOXINESS	CLIMAXED	DETOXIFY	ENFIXING	EXCELLED	EXCRETES	EXEQUIES
AUXILIAR	BOXROOMS	CLIMAXES	DETOXING	EPICALYX	EXCEPTED	EXCUBANT	EXERCISE
AVIATRIX	BOXWOODS	COEXISTS	DEXTRANS	EPOXIDES	EXCEPTOR	EXCURSED	EXERGUAL
AXIALITY	BRAINBOX	COEXTEND	DEXTRINE	EUTAXIES	EXCERPTA	EXCURSES	EXERGUES
AXILLARY	BRUXISMS	COMMIXED	DEXTRINS	EUTAXITE	EXCERPTS	EXCURSUS	EXERTING

EXERTION EXERTIVE EXHALANT EXHALING EXHAUSTS EXHEDRAE EXHIBITS EXHORTED EXHORTER EXHUMATE EXHUMERS EXHUMING EXIGEANT EXIGENCE EXIGENCY EXIGENTS EXIGIBLE EXIGUITY EXIGUOUS EXIMIOUS EXISTENT EXISTING EXITANCE EXOCARPS EXOCRINE EXODERMS EXODISTS EXODUSES EXOERGIC EXOGAMIC EXOMIONS EXOMISES EXOPHAGY EXOPLASM EXORABLE EXORCISE EXORCISM EXORCIST EXORCIZE EXORDIAL EXORDIUM EXOSMOSE EXOSPORE EXOTERIC EXOTOXIC EXOTOXIN EXPANDED EXPANDER EXPANDOR EXPANSES EXPECTED EXPECTER EXPEDITE EXPELLED EXPELLEE EXPENDED

EXPENDER EXPENSES EXPERTED EXPERTLY EXPIABLE EXPIATED EXPIATES EXPIATOR EXPIRANT EXPIRIES EXPIRING EXPLAINS EXPLANTS EXPLICIT EXPLODED EXPLODER EXPLODES EXPLOITS EXPLORED EXPLORER EXPLORES EXPONENT EXPORTED EXPORTER EXPOSALS EXPOSERS EXPOSING EXPOSURE EXPOUNDS EXPRESSO EXPUGNED EXPULSED EXPULSES EXPUNCTS EXPUNGED EXPUNGER EXPUNGES EXPURGED EXPURGES EXSCINDS EXSECTED EXSERTED EXTASIES EXTENDED EXTENDER EXTENSOR EXTERIOR EXTERNAL EXTERNAT EXTERNES EXTIRPED EXTOLLED EXTOLLER EXTORTED EXTRACTS EXTRADOS

EXTRAITS EXTREATS EXTREMER EXTREMES EXTRORSE EXTRUDED EXTRUDER EXTRUDES EXUDATES EXULTANT EXULTING EXURBIAS EXUVIATE FABLIAUX FIXATING FIXATION FIXATIVE FIXATURE FIXITIES FIXTURES FLAXIEST FLEXIBLE FLEXIBLY FLEXIONS FLEXUOSE FLEXUOUS FLEXURAL FLEXURES FLUXIONS FORFEXES FOXBERRY FOXGLOVE FOXHOLES FOXHOUND FOXINESS FOXSHARK FOXSHIPS FOXTROTS GALAXIES GENETRIX GENITRIX GEOTAXES GEOTAXIS GIAMBEUX GLOXINIA HARUSPEX HATBOXES HAYBOXES HERITRIX HEXAFOIL HEXAGLOT HEXAGONS HEXAGRAM HEXAPLAR HEXAPLAS HEXAPODS

HEXAPODY HEXYLENE HOMEOBOX HYDROXYL HYPOXIAS ICEBOXES IMMIXING IMPLEXES INDEXERS INDEXING INDOXYLS INEXPERT INFIXING INFLEXED INFLUXES INTERMIX INTERREX INTERSEX JAMBEAUX JANITRIX JAWBOXES KLAXONED LARYNXES LAXATIVE LAXATORS LAXITIES LEXICONS LEXIGRAM LIVEAXLE LIXIVIAL LIXIVIUM LOXYGENS LUMMOXES LUXATING LUXATION LUXMETER LUXURIES LUXURIST MAGNOXES MALAXAGE MALAXATE MALAXING MANTEAUX MARTEXTS MATCHBOX MATRIXES MAXILLAE MAXIMINS MAXIMISE MAXIMIST MAXIMIZE MAXWELLS MIREPOIX MIXTIONS MIXTURES MONAXIAL

MONAXONS MONOXIDE MORCEAUX MYXEDEMA MYXOMATA NALOXONE NEOTOXIN NEXTNESS NITROXYL OPOPANAX OREXISES ORIFEXES ORTHODOX OUTBOXED OUTBOXES OUTFOXED OUTFOXES OXALATES OXALISES OXAZINES OXBLOODS OXIDANTS OXIDASES OXIDATED OXIDATES OXIDISED OXIDISER OXIDISES OXIDIZED OXIDIZER OXIDIZES OXIMETER OXONIUMS OXTERING OXYMORON OXYTOCIC OXYTOCIN OXYTONES PANMIXIA PANMIXIS PARADOXY PARALLAX PAROXYSM PAXIUBAS PAXWAXES PEROXIDE PHORMINX PICKAXES PLATEAUX PLEXURES PLEXUSES POLYAXON PONCEAUX PONTIFEX POXVIRUS PREFIXED

PREFIXES PREMIXED PREMIXES PRETEXTS PROLIXLY PROXIMAL PTYXISES PYREXIAL PYREXIAS PYROXENE PYROXYLE PYXIDIUM QUINCUNX QUIXOTIC QUIXOTRY REFLEXED REFLEXES REFLEXLY REFLUXED REFLUXES RELAXANT RELAXING RELAXINS REMIXING RHEXISES RONDEAUX ROULEAUX SARDONYX SAUCEBOX SAXATILE SAXHORNS SAXONIES SAXONITE SCRUMPOX SEXFOILS SEXINESS SEXOLOGY SEXPERTS SEXTANTS SEXTETTE SEXTETTS SEXTILES SEXTOLET SEXTUORS SEXTUPLE SEXUALLY SIXAINES SIXPENCE SIXPENNY SIXSCORE SIXTEENS SIXTIETH SMALLPOX SMILAXES SNUFFBOX SPARAXIS

SPHINXES SPINIFEX SPINTEXT STORAXES STYRAXES SUBOXIDE SUBTEXTS SUFFIXAL SUFFIXED SUFFIXES SUPERTAX SURTAXED SURTAXES SYNTAXES SYNTEXIS SYRINXES TABLEAUX TAXATION TAXATIVE TAXIARCH TAXICABS TAXIWAYS TAXONOMY TEGUEXIN TELETEXT TELEXING TETRAXON TETTIXES TEXTBOOK TEXTILES TEXTLESS TEXTUARY TEXTURAL TEXTURED TEXTURES THORAXES THYROXIN TOADFLAX TONNEAUX TOXAEMIA TOXAEMIC TOXEMIAS TOXICANT TOXICITY TOXOCARA TRACTRIX TRANSFIX TRIAXIAL TRIAXONS TRIOXIDE TRUMEAUX TUTRIXES TUXEDOES UNBOXING UNFIXING UNFIXITY

UNIAXIAL UNSEXING UNSEXIST UNSEXUAL UNTAXING UXORIOUS VERTEXES VEXATION VEXATORY VEXILLUM VEXINGLY VIDEOTEX VIXENISH VOLVOXES VORTEXES WATCHBOX WATERPOX WAXBERRY WAXBILLS WAXCLOTH WAXINESS WAXWINGS WAXWORKS WRAXLING XANTHAMS XANTHANS XANTHATE XANTHEIN XANTHENE XANTHINE XANTHINS XANTHOMA XANTHOUS XENOGAMY XENOLITH XENOPHYA XENOTIME XENURINE XERAFINS XERANSES XERANSIS XERANTIC XERAPHIM XERASIAS XEROMATA XYLENOLS XYLITOLS XYLOCARP XYLOGENS XYLOIDIN XYLOLOGY XYLOMATA XYLONITE ZELATRIX ZEUXITES ZOOTOXIN

Z-WORDS

Z - 2-letter words

ZO

Z - 3-letter words

ADZ BEZ BIZ COZ CUZ DZO FEZ FIZ JIZ LEZ LUZ MIZ MOZ POZ REZ RIZ SAZ SEZ ZAG ZAP ZAX ZEA ZED ZEE ZEK ZEL ZEX ZHO ZIG ZIP ZIT ZIZ ZOA ZOO ZOS ZUZ

Z - 4-letter words

ADZE	DOZY	HAZE	MAZE	PHIZ	TOZE	ZEAL	ZHOS	ZOBO	ZULU
AZAN	DZHO	HAZY	MAZY	PIZE	TREZ	ZEAS	ZIFF	ZOBU	ZUPA
AZYM	DZOS	HIZZ	MEZE	POZZ	TUZZ	ZEBU	ZIGS	ZOEA	ZURF
BOZO	FAZE	JAZY	MIZZ	PUTZ	TZAR	ZEDS	ZILA	ZOIC	ZYGA
BUZZ	FIZZ	JAZZ	MOZE	QUIZ	VIZY	ZEES	ZIMB	ZONA	ZYME
CHEZ	FOZY	JIZZ	MOZZ	RAZE	WHIZ	ZEIN	ZINC	ZONE	
CHIZ	FRIZ	KAZI	MZEE	RAZZ	ZACK	ZEKS	ZING	ZONK	
COZE	FUZE	LAZE	NAZE	RIZA	ZAGS	ZELS	ZIPS	ZOOM	
COZY	FUZZ	LAZO	OOZE	SIZE	ZANY	ZERO	ZITE	ZOON	
CZAR	GAZE	LAZY	OOZY	SIZY	ZAPS	ZEST	ZITI	ZOOS	
DAZE	GAZY	LEZZ	OUZO	SWIZ	ZARF	ZETA	ZITS	ZOPP	
DOZE	GIZZ	LUTZ	OYEZ	TIZZ	ZATI	ZEZE	ZIZZ	ZOUK	

Z - 5-letter words

ABUZZ	BOZOS	DOZER	GLOZE	LAZZO	OUZOS	SIZED	WEIZE	ZESTY	ZOEAS
ADZES	BRAZE	DOZES	GONZO	LEAZE	OZEKI	SIZEL	WHIZZ	ZETAS	ZOISM
AGAZE	BRIZE	DZHOS	GRAZE	LEZES	OZONE	SIZER	WINZE	ZEXES	ZOIST
AIZLE	BUAZE	FAZED	GRIZE	LEZZY	PEAZE	SIZES	WIZEN	ZEZES	ZOMBI
AMAZE	BUZZY	FAZES	HAMZA	LOZEN	PEIZE	SPITZ	WOOTZ	ZHOMO	ZONAE
AVIZE	BWAZI	FEEZE	HAZED	MAIZE	PIEZO	SQUIZ	WOOZY	ZIBET	ZONAL
AVYZE	CAPIZ	FEZES	HAZEL	MATZA	PIZES	TAZZA	ZABRA	ZIFFS	ZONDA
AZANS	CEAZE	FIZZY	HAZER	MATZO	PIZZA	TAZZE	ZACKS	ZIGAN	ZONED
AZIDE	CHIZZ	FRIZE	HAZES	MAZED	PLAZA	TEAZE	ZAIRE	ZILAS	ZONES
AZINE	CLOZE	FRIZZ	HEEZE	MAZER	POZZY	TIZZY	ZAKAT	ZILCH	ZONKS
AZOIC	COBZA	FROZE	HERTZ	MAZES	PRIZE	TOAZE	ZAMAN	ZIMBI	ZOOEA
AZOTE	COLZA	FURZE	HIZEN	MAZUT	PUZEL	TOPAZ	ZAMBO	ZIMBS	ZOOID
AZOTH	COZED	FURZY	HUZZA	MEZES	PZAZZ	TOUZE	ZAMIA	ZINCO	ZOOKS
AZURE	COZEN	FUZEE	HUZZY	MEZZE	RAZED	TOUZY	ZANJA	ZINCS	ZOOMS
AZURN	COZES	FUZES	IZARD	MEZZO	RAZEE	TOWZE	ZANTE	ZINCY	ZOONS
AZURY	CRAZE	FUZZY	IZZAT	MILTZ	RAZES	TOWZY	ZANZE	ZINEB	ZOPPO
AZYGY	CRAZY	GAUZE	JAZZY	MIZEN	RAZOO	TOZED	ZAPPY	ZINGS	ZORIL
AZYME	CROZE	GAUZY	KANZU	MOTZA	RAZOR	TOZES	ZARFS	ZINGY	ZORRO
AZYMS	CZARS	GAZAL	KARZY	MOZED	RITZY	TOZIE	ZATIS	ZINKE	ZOUKS
BAIZE	DARZI	GAZED	KAZIS	MOZES	RIZAS	TZARS	ZAXES	ZINKY	ZOWIE
BAZAR	DAZED	GAZER	KAZOO	MUZZY	ROZET	ULZIE	ZEALS	ZIPPO	ZULUS
BEZEL	DAZER	GAZES	KLUTZ	MZEES	ROZIT	UNZIP	ZEBEC	ZIPPY	ZUPAN
BEZES	DAZES	GAZON	KRANZ	NAZES	SADZA	VEZIR	ZEBRA	ZIZEL	ZUPAS
BLAZE	DIAZO	GAZOO	KUDZU	NAZIR	SAZES	VIZIR	ZEBUB	ZLOTY	ZURFS
BLITZ	DITZY	GHAZI	LAZAR	NEEZE	SCUZZ	VIZOR	ZEBUS	ZOBOS	ZUZIM
BONZA	DIZEN	GIZMO	LAZED	NIZAM	SEAZE	VOZHD	ZEINS	ZOBUS	ZYGAL
BONZE	DIZZY	GLAZE	LAZES	OOZED	SEIZE	WALTZ	ZERDA	ZOCCO	ZYGON
BOOZE	DOZED	GLAZY	LAZOS	OOZES	SENZA	WANZE	ZEROS	ZOEAE	ZYMES
BOOZY	DOZEN	GLITZ	LAZZI	OUZEL	SIZAR	WAZIR	ZESTS	ZOEAL	ZYMIC

Z - 6-letter words

ABLAZE	AZIONE	BENZYL	BOOZES	CEAZES	DEFUZE	FEEZED	FROZEN	GIZZEN	HAZERS
ABRAZO	AZOLLA	BEZANT	BOOZEY	CHAZAN	DIAZOS	FEEZES	FURZES	GIZZES	HAZIER
AGAZED	AZONAL	BEZAZZ	BORZOI	CHINTZ	DIZAIN	FEZZED	FUZEES	GLAZED	HAZILY
AGNIZE	AZONIC	BEZELS	BRAIZE	COBZAS	DIZENS	FEZZES	FUZZED	GLAZEN	HAZING
AGRIZE	AZOTES	BEZOAR	BRAZED	COLZAS	DONZEL	FIZGIG	FUZZES	GLAZER	HEEZED
AGRYZE	AZOTHS	BEZZLE	BRAZEN	COROZO	DORIZE	FIZZED	FUZZLE	GLAZES	HEEZES
AGUIZE	AZOTIC	BIZAZZ	BRAZES	CORYZA	DOZENS	FIZZEN	GAUZES	GLITZY	HEEZIE
AIZLES	AZURES	BIZONE	BRAZIL	COZENS	DOZERS	FIZZER	GAZALS	GLOZED	HIZENS
ALTEZA	AZYGOS	BIZZES	BREEZE	COZIER	DOZIER	FIZZES	GAZEBO	GLOZES	HIZZED
AMAZED	AZYMES	BLAIZE	BREEZY	COZIES	DOZING	FIZZLE	GAZERS	GOZZAN	HIZZES
AMAZES	BAIZED	BLAZED	BRIZES	COZING	DRAZEL	FLOOZY	GAZIER	GRAZED	HOWZAT
AMAZON	BAIZES	BLAZER	BRONZE	COZZES	DZEREN	FOOZLE	GAZING	GRAZER	HUZOOR
APOZEM	BANZAI	BLAZES	BRONZY	CRAZED	ECZEMA	FOZIER	GAZONS	GRAZES	HUZZAS
ASSIZE	BARAZA	BLAZON	BROUZE	CRAZES	ENTREZ	FRANZY	GAZOON	GRIZES	IODIZE
AVIZED	BAZAAR	BLINTZ	BUAZES	CROZES	ENZIAN	FRAZIL	GAZOOS	GUIZER	IONIZE
AVIZES	BAZARS	BLOWZE	BUZZED	CUZZES	ENZONE	FREEZE	GAZUMP	GUTZER	IZARDS
AVYZED	BAZAZZ	BLOWZY	BUZZER	CZAPKA	ENZYME	FRENZY	GEEZER	GUZZLE	IZZARD
AVYZES	BEDAZE	BONZER	BUZZES	DARZIS	EPIZOA	FRIEZE	GHAZAL	HAMZAH	IZZATS
AZALEA	BENZAL	BONZES	BWAZIS	DAZERS	ERSATZ	FRIZES	GHAZEL	HAMZAS	JAZIES
AZIDES	BENZIL	BOOZED	BYZANT	DAZING	EVZONE	FRIZZY	GHAZIS	HAZARD	JAZZED
AZINES	BENZOL	BOOZER	CEAZED	DAZZLE	FAZING	FROWZY	GIZMOS	HAZELS	JAZZER

JAZZES
JEZAIL
JIZZES
KAMEEZ
KANZUS
KAZOOS
KIBITZ
KRANTZ
KUDZUS
KWANZA
LAZARS
LAZIER
LAZILY
LAZING
LAZOED
LAZOES
LEAZES
LEZZES
LIZARD
LOZELL
LOZENS
LUTZES
LUZERN
LUZZES
MAHZOR
MAIZES
MAMZER
MATZAH
MATZAS
MATZOH
MATZOS
MATZOT
MAZARD
MAZERS
MAZHBI
MAZIER
MAZILY
MAZING
MAZOUT
MAZUMA
MAZUTS
MEAZEL
MEZAIL
MEZUZA
MEZZES
MEZZOS
MIZENS
MIZZEN
MIZZES
MIZZLE
MIZZLY
MOMZER
MOTZAS
MOZING
MOZZES
MOZZIE
MOZZLE
MUZAKY
MUZHIK
MUZZLE
MZUNGU
NAZIRS
NEEZED
NEEZES
NIZAMS
NOZZER
NOZZLE
NUZZER
NUZZLE
NYANZA
OOZIER
OOZILY
OOZING
OUZELS
OYEZES
OZAENA
OZEKIS
OZONES
PANZER
PATZER
PAZAZZ
PEAZED
PEAZES
PEIZED
PEIZES
PEZANT
PHEEZE
PHIZOG
PIAZZA
PIZAZZ
PIZZAS
PIZZLE
PLAZAS
PODZOL
PRIZED
PRIZER
PRIZES
PUTZES
PUZELS
PUZZEL
PUZZLE
QUARTZ
QUEAZY
QUINZE
RANZEL
RAZEED
RAZEES
RAZING
RAZOOS
RAZORS
RAZURE
RAZZED
RAZZES
RAZZIA
RAZZLE
REZONE
REZZES
RHIZIC
RIZARD
RIZZAR
RIZZER
RIZZOR
ROZETS
ROZITS
ROZZER
SADZAS
SAZHEN
SAZZES
SCAZON
SCHIZO
SCRUZE
SCUZZY
SEAZED
SEAZES
SEIZED
SEIZER
SEIZES
SEIZIN
SIZARS
SIZELS
SIZERS
SIZIER
SIZING
SIZISM
SIZIST
SIZZLE
SLEAZE
SLEAZY
SLEEZY
SNAZZY
SNEEZE
SNEEZY
SNOOZE
SNOOZY
SOZZLE
SOZZLY
STANZA
STANZE
STANZO
SUIVEZ
SYZYGY
TAZZAS
TEAZED
TEAZEL
TEAZES
TEAZLE
TENZON
TIZWAS
TIZZES
TOAZED
TOAZES
TOLZEY
TOUZED
TOUZES
TOUZLE
TOWZED
TOWZES
TOZIES
TOZING
TREZES
TUZZES
TWEEZE
TZETSE
ULZIES
UNZIPS
UPGAZE
VEZIRS
VIZARD
VIZIED
VIZIER
VIZIES
VIZIRS
VIZORS
VIZSLA
VIZZIE
VOZHDS
WANZED
WANZES
WAZIRS
WEAZEN
WEIZED
WEIZES
WEZAND
WHEEZE
WHEEZY
WINZES
WIZARD
WIZENS
WIZIER
WUZZLE
YAKUZA
ZABETA
ZABRAS
ZADDIK
ZAFFER
ZAFFRE
ZAGGED
ZAKATS
ZAMANG
ZAMANS
ZAMBOS
ZAMBUK
ZAMIAS
ZANDER
ZANIED
ZANIER
ZANIES
ZANJAS
ZANTES
ZANZES
ZAPATA
ZAPPED
ZAPPER
ZARAPE
ZAREBA
ZARIBA
ZARNEC
ZEALOT
ZEBECK
ZEBECS
ZEBRAS
ZEBUBS
ZELANT
ZELOSO
ZENANA
ZENDIK
ZENITH
ZEPHYR
ZERDAS
ZEREBA
ZERIBA
ZEROED
ZEROTH
ZESTED
ZESTER
ZEUGMA
ZHOMOS
ZIBETS
ZIGANS
ZIGGED
ZIGZAG
ZILLAH
ZIMBIS
ZIMMER
ZINCED
ZINCKY
ZINCOS
ZINEBS
ZINGED
ZINGEL
ZINGER
ZINKED
ZINKES
ZINNIA
ZIPPED
ZIPPER
ZIPPOS
ZIPTOP
ZIRCON
ZITHER
ZIZELS
ZIZZED
ZIZZES
ZLOTYS
ZOARIA
ZOCCOS
ZODIAC
ZOETIC
ZOISMS
ZOISTS
ZOMBIE
ZOMBIS
ZONARY
ZONATE
ZONDAS
ZONING
ZONKED
ZONOID
ZONULA
ZONULE
ZONURE
ZOOEAE
ZOOEAL
ZOOEAS
ZOOIDS
ZOOMED
ZOONAL
ZOONIC
ZOOZOO
ZORILS
ZORINO
ZORROS
ZOSTER
ZOUNDS
ZUFOLI
ZUFOLO
ZUPANS
ZYGOMA
ZYGOSE
ZYGOTE
ZYMASE
ZYMITE
ZYMOID
ZYMOME
ZYTHUM

Z - 7-letter words

ABRAZOS
ADONIZE
AGNIZED
AGNIZES
AGONIZE
AGRIZED
AGRIZES
AGRYZED
AGRYZES
AGUIZED
AGUIZES
ALCAZAR
ALCORZA
ALFEREZ
ALIZARI
ALTEZAS
ALTEZZA
AMAZING
AMAZONS
ANALYZE
ANODIZE
ANZIANI
APOZEMS
APPRIZE
ARABIZE
ASSIZED
ASSIZER
ASSIZES
ATHEIZE
ATOMIZE
AVIZING
AVYZING
AZALEAS
AZIMUTH
AZIONES
AZOLLAS
AZOTISE
AZOTIZE
AZOTOUS
AZULEJO
AZUREAN
AZURINE
AZURITE
AZYGIES
AZYGOUS
AZYMITE
AZYMOUS
BAIZING
BANZAIS
BAPTIZE
BARAZAS
BAZAARS
BAZOOKA
BAZOUKI
BEDAZED
BEDAZES
BEDIZEN
BEMAZED
BENZALS
BENZENE
BENZILS
BENZINE
BENZOIC
BENZOIN
BENZOLE
BENZOLS
BENZOYL
BENZYLS
BEZANTS
BEZIQUE
BEZOARS
BEZZLED
BEZZLES
BIZARRE
BIZONAL
BIZONES
BLAZERS
BLAZING
BLAZONS
BLINTZE
BLITZED
BLITZES
BLOWZED
BLOWZES
BONANZA
BOOZERS
BOOZIER
BOOZILY
BOOZING
BORAZON
BORZOIS
BRAIZES
BRAZENS
BRAZIER
BRAZILS
BRAZING
BREEZED
BREEZES
BRITZKA
BRONZED
BRONZEN
BRONZER
BRONZES
BROUZES
BRULZIE
BUMBAZE
BUZZARD
BUZZERS
BUZZIER
BUZZING
BYZANTS
CADENZA
CALZONE
CALZONI
CANZONA
CANZONE
CANZONI
CAPIZES
CAPSIZE
CAZIQUE
CEAZING
CHALAZA
CHALUTZ
CHAZANS
CHINTZY
CHIZZED
CHIZZES
CHORIZO
CITIZEN
COALIZE
COGNIZE
COROZOS
CORYZAS
COZENED
COZENER
COZIERS
COZIEST
CRAZIER
CRAZIES
CRAZILY
CRAZING
CROZIER
CRUZADO
CYANIZE
CZAPKAS
CZARDAS
CZARDOM
CZARINA
CZARISM
CZARIST
DAMOZEL
DAZEDLY
DAZZLED
DAZZLER
DAZZLES
DEFROZE
DEFUZED
DEFUZES
DENIZEN
DIALYZE
DIARIZE
DIAZOES
DITZIER
DIZAINS
DIZENED
DIZZARD
DIZZIED
DIZZIER
DIZZIES
DIZZILY
DOCKIZE
DONZELS
DORIZED
DORIZES
DOZENED
DOZENTH
DOZIEST
DOZINGS
DRAZELS
DRIZZLE
DRIZZLY
DZERENS
EBONIZE
ECHOIZE
ECTOZOA
ECZEMAS
EGOTIZE
ELEGIZE
EMBLAZE
ENDOZOA
ENFROZE
ENTOZOA
ENZIANS
ENZONED
ENZONES
ENZYMES
ENZYMIC
EPIZOAN
EPIZOIC
EPIZOON
EVZONES
FAHLERZ
FANZINE
FAZENDA
FEEZING
FILAZER
FIZGIGS
FIZZENS
FIZZERS
FIZZGIG
FIZZIER
FIZZING
FIZZLED
FIZZLES
FLOOZIE
FOOZLED
FOOZLER
FOOZLES
FORZATI
FORZATO
FOZIEST
FRAZILS
FRAZZLE
FREEZER
FREEZES
FRIEZED
FRIEZES
FRIZING
FRIZZED
FRIZZES
FRIZZLE
FRIZZLY
FURZIER
FUZZIER
FUZZILY
FUZZING
FUZZLED
FUZZLES
GALLIZE
GAUZIER
GAZANIA
GAZEBOS
GAZEFUL
GAZELLE
GAZETTE
GAZIEST
GAZOOKA
GAZOONS
GAZUMPS
GEEZERS
GENIZAH
GHAZALS
GHAZELS
GIZZARD
GIZZENS
GLAZERS
GLAZIER
GLAZING
GLITZES
GLOZING
GOZZANS
GRAZERS
GRAZIER
GRAZING
GRECIZE
GRIZZLE
GRIZZLY
GUEREZA
GUIZERS
GUTZERS
GUZZLED
GUZZLER
GUZZLES
HAMZAHS
HAZARDS
HAZELLY
HAZIEST
HAZINGS
HEEZIES
HEEZING
HEROIZE
HERTZES
HIZZING
HOATZIN
HORIZON
HUMBUZZ
HUTZPAH
HUZOORS
HUZZAED
HUZZIES
ICONIZE
IDOLIZE
IODIZED
IODIZES
IONIZED
IONIZER
IONIZES
IRIDIZE
IRONIZE
ITEMIZE
IZZARDS
JACUZZI
JANIZAR
JAZZERS
JAZZIER
JAZZILY

JAZZING
JAZZMAN
JAZZMEN
JEZAILS
KARZIES
KIBBUTZ
KLUTZES
KOLKHOZ
KRANZES
KUNZITE
KWANZAS
KYANIZE
LAICIZE
LAIRIZE
LAZARET
LAZIEST
LAZOING
LEZZIES
LIONIZE
LIZARDS
LOZELLS
LOZENGE
LOZENGY
LUZERNS
MACHZOR
MADZOON
MAMZERS
MATZAHS
MATZOON
MATZOTH
MAZARDS
MAZEFUL
MAZHBIS
MAZIEST
MAZOUTS
MAZUMAS
MAZURKA
MAZZARD
MEAZELS
MESTIZA
MESTIZO
METAZOA
MEZAILS
MEZUZAH
MIDSIZE
MILTZES
MITZVAH
MIZMAZE
MIZZENS
MIZZLED
MIZZLES
MOMZERS
MOZETTA
MOZZIES
MOZZLES
MUEZZIN
MUZHIKS
MUZZIER
MUZZILY
MUZZLED
MUZZLER
MUZZLES
MYTHIZE
MZUNGUS
NEEZING
NOZZERS
NOZZLES
NUZZERS
NUZZLED
NUZZLES
NYANZAS
OBELIZE
ODZOOKS
OOZIEST
ORGANZA
OUTSIZE
OXAZINE
OXIDIZE
OZAENAS
OZONISE
OZONIZE
PALAZZI
PALAZZO
PANZERS
PARAZOA
PATZERS
PEAZING
PECTIZE
PEIZING
PEPTIZE
PEZANTS
PHEAZAR
PHEEZED
PHEEZES
PHIZOGS
PHIZZES
PIAZZAS
PIZZLES
PODZOLS
POETIZE
POLYZOA
POZZIES
PRENZIE
PRETZEL
PREZZIE
PRIZERS
PRIZING
PUZZELS
PUZZLED
PUZZLER
PUZZLES
PZAZZES
QUARTZY
QUETZAL
QUINZES
QUIZZED
QUIZZER
QUIZZES
RANZELS
RAZURES
RAZZIAS
RAZZING
RAZZLES
REALIZE
REFROZE
REPRIZE
RESEIZE
REZONED
REZONES
RHIZINE
RHIZOID
RHIZOME
RHIZOPI
RIOTIZE
RITZIER
RIZARDS
RIZZARS
RIZZART
RIZZERS
RIZZORS
ROZELLE
ROZETED
ROZITED
ROZZERS
SAZERAC
SAZHENS
SCAZONS
SCHANZE
SCHERZI
SCHERZO
SCHIZOS
SCHMELZ
SCHMOOZ
SCRUZED
SCRUZES
SCUZZES
SEAZING
SEIZERS
SEIZING
SEIZINS
SEIZURE
SELTZER
SHIATZU
SHMALTZ
SHMOOZE
SHOWBIZ
SIAMEZE
SIZABLE
SIZEISM
SIZEIST
SIZIEST
SIZINGS
SIZISMS
SIZISTS
SIZZLED
SIZZLER
SIZZLES
SLEAZES
SNEEZED
SNEEZER
SNEEZES
SNOOZED
SNOOZER
SNOOZES
SNOOZLE
SNUZZLE
SOZZLED
SOZZLES
SPITZES
SPREAZE
SPREEZE
SPULZIE
SQUEEZE
SQUEEZY
STANZAS
STANZES
STANZOS
STARETZ
STYLIZE
SUBZERO
SUBZONE
SWAZZLE
SWIZZED
SWIZZES
SWIZZLE
SWOZZLE
TAILZIE
TEAZELS
TEAZING
TEAZLED
TEAZLES
TENDENZ
TENZONS
TIZZIES
TOAZING
TOLZEYS
TOPAZES
TOUZIER
TOUZING
TOUZLED
TOUZLES
TOWZIER
TOWZING
TRAPEZE
TRIZONE
TUILZIE
TWEEZED
TWEEZES
TWIZZLE
TZADDIK
TZADDIQ
TZETSES
TZIGANY
TZIMMES
UNFAZED
UNFROZE
UNITIZE
UNSIZED
UNZONED
UPGAZED
UPGAZES
UTILIZE
VIZARDS
VIZIERS
VIZORED
VIZSLAS
VIZYING
VIZZIED
VIZZIES
WALTZED
WALTZER
WALTZES
WANZING
WEAZAND
WEAZENS
WEIZING
WEZANDS
WHAIZLE
WHEEZED
WHEEZES
WHEEZLE
WHIZZED
WHIZZER
WHIZZES
WIZARDS
WIZENED
WIZIERS
WOOTZES
WOOZIER
WOOZILY
WRIZLED
WUZZLED
WUZZLES
ZABETAS
ZABTIEH
ZADDIKS
ZAFFERS
ZAFFRES
ZAGGING
ZAKUSKA
ZAKUSKI
ZAMANGS
ZAMARRA
ZAMARRO
ZAMBUCK
ZAMBUKS
ZAMOUSE
ZAMPONE
ZAMPONI
ZANDERS
ZANELLA
ZANIEST
ZANJERO
ZANYING
ZANYISM
ZAPPERS
ZAPPIER
ZAPPING
ZAPTIAH
ZAPTIEH
ZARAPES
ZAREBAS
ZAREEBA
ZARIBAS
ZARNECS
ZARNICH
ZEALANT
ZEALFUL
ZEALOTS
ZEALOUS
ZEBECKS
ZEBRASS
ZEBRINA
ZEBRINE
ZEBROID
ZEBRULA
ZEBRULE
ZEDOARY
ZELANTS
ZELATOR
ZEMSTVA
ZEMSTVO
ZENANAS
ZENDIKS
ZENITHS
ZEOLITE
ZEPHYRS
ZEREBAS
ZERIBAS
ZEROING
ZESTERS
ZESTFUL
ZESTIER
ZESTING
ZETETIC
ZEUGMAS
ZEUXITE
ZIFFIUS
ZIGANKA
ZIGGING
ZIGZAGS
ZILCHES
ZILLAHS
ZILLION
ZIMMERS
ZIMOCCA
ZINCIER
ZINCIFY
ZINCING
ZINCITE
ZINCKED
ZINCODE
ZINCOID
ZINCOUS
ZINGELS
ZINGERS
ZINGIER
ZINGING
ZINKIER
ZINKIFY
ZINKING
ZINNIAS
ZIPLOCK
ZIPPERS
ZIPPIER
ZIPPING
ZIRCONS
ZITHERN
ZITHERS
ZIZANIA
ZIZZING
ZOARIUM
ZOCCOLO
ZODIACS
ZOEFORM
ZOISITE
ZOMBIES
ZOMBIFY
ZONATED
ZONINGS
ZONKING
ZONULAE
ZONULAR
ZONULAS
ZONULES
ZONULET
ZONURES
ZOOECIA
ZOOGAMY
ZOOGENY
ZOOGONY
ZOOIDAL
ZOOLITE
ZOOLITH
ZOOLOGY
ZOOMING
ZOONITE
ZOONOMY
ZOOPERY
ZOOTAXY
ZOOTOMY
ZOOTYPE
ZOOZOOS
ZORGITE
ZORILLE
ZORILLO
ZORINOS
ZOSTERS
ZUFFOLI
ZUFFOLO
ZYGOMAS
ZYGOSES
ZYGOSIS
ZYGOTES
ZYGOTIC
ZYMASES
ZYMITES
ZYMOGEN
ZYMOMES
ZYMOSES
ZYMOSIS
ZYMOTIC
ZYMURGY
ZYTHUMS

Z - 8-letter words

ADONIZED
ADONIZES
AGNIZING
AGONIZED
AGONIZES
AGRIZING
AGRYZING
AGUIZING
ALBITIZE
ALCAZARS
ALCORZAS
ALGUAZIL
ALIZARIN
ALIZARIS
ALKALIZE
ALTEZZAS
AMAZEDLY
AMORTIZE
ANALYZED
ANALYZER
ANALYZES
ANNALIZE
ANODIZED
ANODIZES
ANTICIZE
APHETIZE
APHORIZE
APPETIZE
APPRIZED
APPRIZER
APPRIZES
ARABIZED
ARABIZES
ARCHAIZE
ARMOZEEN
ARMOZINE
ASSIZERS
ASSIZING
ATHEIZED
ATHEIZES
ATHETIZE
ATMOLYZE
ATOMIZED
ATOMIZER
ATOMIZES
ATRAZINE
AUTOLYZE
AZIMUTHS
AZOTISED
AZOTISES
AZOTIZED
AZOTIZES
AZOTURIA
AZULEJOS
AZURINES
AZURITES
AZYGOSES
AZYMITES
BANALIZE
BAPTIZED
BAPTIZES
BAROMETZ
BARTIZAN
BAZAZZES
BAZOOKAS
BAZOUKIS
BEDAZING
BEDAZZLE
BEDIZENS
BENZENES
BENZINES
BENZOATE
BENZOINS
BENZOLES
BENZOYLS
BEZAZZES
BEZIQUES
BEZONIAN
BEZZLING
BIZAZZES
BIZCACHA
BLAZERED
BLAZONED
BLAZONER
BLAZONRY
BLINTZES
BLITZING
BLIZZARD
BLOWZIER
BONANZAS
BOOZIEST
BORAZONS
BOTANIZE
BOUZOUKI
BOZZETTI
BOZZETTO
BRAZENED
BRAZENLY
BRAZENRY
BRAZIERS
BRAZILIN
BREEZIER
BREEZILY
BREEZING
BRITZKAS
BRITZSKA
BRONZERS
BRONZIER
BRONZIFY
BRONZING
BRONZITE
BRUILZIE
BRULZIES
BULLDOZE
BUMBAZED
BUMBAZES
BUZZARDS
BUZZIEST
BUZZINGS
BUZZWORD
CADENZAS
CALZONES
CANALIZE
CANONIZE
CANZONAS
CANZONET
CAPONIZE
CAPSIZAL
CAPSIZED
CAPSIZES
CATALYZE
CAZIQUES
CHALAZAE
CHALAZAS
CHALAZIA
CHINTZES
CHIZZING
CHORIZOS
CHUTZPAH
CITIZENS
CIVILIZE
COALIZED
COALIZES
COENZYME
COGNIZED
COGNIZES
COLONIZE
COZENAGE
COZENERS
COZENING
CRAZIEST
CREDENZA

CREUTZER
CROZIERS
CRUZADOS
CRUZEIRO
CURARIZE
CUTINIZE
CYANIZED
CYANIZES
CZARDOMS
CZAREVNA
CZARINAS
CZARISMS
CZARISTS
CZARITSA
DAMOZELS
DAZZLERS
DAZZLING
DEFREEZE
DEFROZEN
DEFUZING
DEMONIZE
DENAZIFY
DENIZENS
DEPUTIZE
DIALYZED
DIALYZER
DIALYZES
DIARIZED
DIARIZES
DIAZEPAM
DIGITIZE
DIMERIZE
DIPLOZOA
DISPRIZE
DISSEIZE
DITZIEST
DIVINIZE
DIZENING
DIZZARDS
DIZZIEST
DIZZYING
DOCKIZED
DOCKIZES
DORIZING
DOUZEPER
DOWNSIZE
DOZENING
DOZENTHS
DOZINESS
DRIZZLED
DRIZZLES
DYNAMIZE
EBENEZER
EBIONIZE
EBONIZED
EBONIZES
ECHOIZED
ECHOIZES
ECTOZOAN
ECTOZOIC
ECTOZOON
EGOTIZED
EGOTIZES
ELEGIZED
ELEGIZES
EMBEZZLE
EMBLAZED
EMBLAZES
EMBLAZON
EMPERIZE
ENDOZOIC
ENDOZOON
ENERGIZE
ENFREEZE
ENFROZEN
ENTOZOAL
ENTOZOIC
ENTOZOON
ENZONING
ENZOOTIC
EPIZOANS
EQUALIZE
ERGOTIZE
ERSATZES
ETERNIZE
ETHERIZE
ETHICIZE
EULOGIZE
EUPHUIZE
EXORCIZE
FABULIZE
FANZINES
FARADIZE
FAZENDAS
FEMINIZE
FILAZERS
FINALIZE
FIZZGIGS
FIZZIEST
FIZZINGS
FIZZLING
FLOOZIES
FLUIDIZE
FOCALIZE
FOOZLERS
FOOZLING
FORZANDI
FORZANDO
FORZATOS
FOZINESS
FRANZIER
FRAZZLED
FRAZZLES
FREEZERS
FREEZING
FRENZIED
FRENZIES
FRIEZING
FRIZZIER
FRIZZING
FRIZZLED
FRIZZLES
FROWZIER
FURZIEST
FUZZIEST
FUZZLING
GADZOOKS
GALLIZED
GALLIZES
GARBANZO
GAUZIEST
GAZANIAS
GAZEBOES
GAZELLES
GAZEMENT
GAZETTED
GAZETTES
GAZOGENE
GAZOOKAS
GAZPACHO
GAZUMPED
GAZUNDER
GENIZAHS
GIZZARDS
GIZZENED
GLAZIERS
GLAZIEST
GLAZINGS
GLITZIER
GLITZILY
GLOZINGS
GOLDSIZE
GRAZIERS
GRAZINGS
GRAZIOSO
GRECIZED
GRECIZES
GRIZZLED
GRIZZLER
GRIZZLES
GUEREZAS
GUZZLERS
GUZZLING
HAZARDED
HAZARDRY
HAZELNUT
HAZINESS
HEPATIZE
HEROIZED
HEROIZES
HOACTZIN
HOATZINS
HOLOZOIC
HORIZONS
HOWITZER
HUMANIZE
HUTZPAHS
HUZZAING
HYDROZOA
ICONIZED
ICONIZES
IDEALIZE
IDOLIZED
IDOLIZER
IDOLIZES
IMMUNIZE
INFAMIZE
IODIZING
IONIZERS
IONIZING
IRIDIZED
IRIDIZES
IRONIZED
IRONIZES
ITEMIZED
ITEMIZES
IZVESTIA
JACUZZIS
JANIZARS
JANIZARY
JAZERANT
JAZZIEST
JUMBOIZE
KAMEEZES
KAMIKAZE
KAZATZKA
KIBITZED
KIBITZER
KIBITZES
KRANTZES
KREUTZER
KUNZITES
KYANIZED
KYANIZES
LAICIZED
LAICIZES
LAIRIZED
LAIRIZES
LAZARETS
LAZINESS
LAZULITE
LAZURITE
LEGALIZE
LIONIZED
LIONIZES
LOCALIZE
LOGICIZE
LOZENGED
LOZENGES
LYSOZYME
MACARIZE
MADERIZE
MADZOONS
MAGAZINE
MAHZORIM
MAMZERIM
MANZELLO
MARZIPAN
MATZOONS
MAXIMIZE
MAZARINE
MAZELTOV
MAZEMENT
MAZINESS
MAZURKAS
MAZZARDS
MELODIZE
MEMORIZE
MESPRIZE
MESTIZAS
MESTIZOS
METALIZE
METAZOAN
METAZOIC
METAZOON
MEZEREON
MEZEREUM
MEZUZAHS
MEZUZOTH
MINIMIZE
MISPRIZE
MITZVAHS
MITZVOTH
MIZMAZES
MIZZLIER
MIZZLING
MOBILIZE
MOMZERIM
MONAZITE
MONETIZE
MORALIZE
MOTORIZE
MOZETTAS
MOZZETTA
MUEZZINS
MUZZIEST
MUZZLERS
MUZZLING
MYTHIZED
MYTHIZES
NASALIZE
NEBULIZE
NODALIZE
NOMADIZE
NOTARIZE
NOVELIZE
NUZZLING
OBELIZED
OBELIZES
OOZINESS
OPALIZED
OPTIMIZE
ORGANIZE
ORGANZAS
OUTPRIZE
OUTSIZED
OUTSIZES
OVERSIZE
OXAZINES
OXIDIZED
OXIDIZER
OXIDIZES
OZONISED
OZONISER
OZONISES
OZONIZED
OZONIZER
OZONIZES
PAGANIZE
PAPALIZE
PARALYZE
PARAZOAN
PARAZOON
PARTIZAN
PAZAZZES
PECTIZED
PECTIZES
PENALIZE
PEPTIZED
PEPTIZES
PETUNTZE
PEZIZOID
PHEAZARS
PHEEZING
PIAZZIAN
PIROZHKI
PIZAZZES
PIZZERIA
POETIZED
POETIZES
POLARIZE
POLEMIZE
POLONIZE
POLYZOAN
POLYZOIC
POLYZOON
PRETZELS
PREZZIES
PRIZABLE
PRIZEMAN
PRIZEMEN
PROTOZOA
PTYALIZE
PUZZLERS
PUZZLING
PYRITIZE
PYROLYZE
QUANTIZE
QUARTZES
QUATORZE
QUEAZIER
QUETZALS
QUIZZERS
QUIZZERY
QUIZZIFY
QUIZZING
RACEMIZE
RAZEEING
RAZMATAZ
REALIZED
REALIZER
REALIZES
REFREEZE
REFROZEN
REGULIZE
RENDZINA
REPRIZED
REPRIZES
RESEIZED
RESEIZES
RESINIZE
REZONING
RHIZINES
RHIZOBIA
RHIZOIDS
RHIZOMES
RHIZOPOD
RHIZOPUS
RIBOZYME
RIGIDIZE
RIOTIZES
RITZIEST
RIVALIZE
RIZZARED
RIZZARTS
RIZZERED
RIZZORED
ROBOTIZE
ROYALIZE
ROZELLES
ROZETING
ROZITING
RURALIZE
SAMIZDAT
SANITIZE
SARRAZIN
SATIRIZE
SAZERACS
SCHANTZE
SCHANZES
SCHERZOS
SCHIZOID
SCHIZONT
SCHMALTZ
SCHMOOZE
SCRUZING
SCUZZIER
SEIZABLE
SEIZINGS
SEIZURES
SELTZERS
SFORZATI
SFORZATO
SHIATZUS
SHMALTZY
SHMOOZED
SHMOOZES
SIAMEZED
SIAMEZES
SIMAZINE
SIMILIZE
SINICIZE
SIRENIZE
SIZEABLE
SIZEISMS
SIZEISTS
SIZINESS
SIZZLERS
SIZZLING
SLEAZIER
SLEAZILY
SLEEZIER
SMORZATO
SNAZZIER
SNEEZERS
SNEEZIER
SNEEZING
SNOOZERS
SNOOZIER
SNOOZING
SNOOZLED
SNOOZLES
SNUZZLED
SNUZZLES
SOBERIZE
SODOMIZE
SOLARIZE
SOLECIZE
SOLONETZ
SORORIZE
SOZZLIER
SOZZLING
SPETSNAZ
SPETZNAZ
SPREAZED
SPREAZES
SPREEZED
SPREEZES
SPRITZER
SPRITZIG
SPUILZIE
SPULZIED
SPULZIES
SQUEEZED
SQUEEZER
SQUEEZES
SQUIZZES
STANZAIC
STANZOES
STRELITZ
STYLIZED
STYLIZES
SUBERIZE
SUBITIZE
SUBSIZAR
SUBZONAL
SUBZONES
SUZERAIN
SWAZZLES
SWIZZING
SWIZZLED
SWIZZLES
SWOZZLES
SYZYGIAL
SYZYGIES
TAILZIES
TEAZELED
TEAZLING
TERRAZZO
TERZETTA
TERZETTI
TERZETTO
TETANIZE
THEORIZE
THIAZIDE
THIAZINE
TIZWASES
TOPAZINE
TOTALIZE
TOUZIEST
TOUZLING
TOWZIEST
TRAPEZED
TRAPEZES
TRAPEZIA
TRAPEZII
TRIZONAL
TRIZONES
TUILZIED
TUILZIES
TUTORIZE
TWEEZERS
TWEEZING
TWIZZLED
TWIZZLES
TZADDIKS
TZADDIQS
TZATZIKI
UNAMAZED
UNDAZZLE
UNFREEZE
UNFROZEN
UNGLAZED
UNGRAZED
UNIONIZE
UNITIZED
UNITIZES
UNMUZZLE
UNPRIZED
UNSEIZED
UNVIZARD
UNZIPPED
UPGAZING
URBANIZE
UTILIZED
UTILIZER
UTILIZES
VALORIZE
VAPORIZE
VELARIZE
VITALIZE
VIZAMENT
VIZARDED
VIZCACHA
VIZIRATE
VIZIRIAL
VIZORING
VOCALIZE
VOWELIZE
WALTZERS
WALTZING
WEAZANDS
WEAZENED
WHAIZLED
WHAIZLES
WHEEZIER
WHEEZILY
WHEEZING
WHEEZLED
WHEEZLES

WHIZBANG
WHIZZERS
WHIZZING
WIZARDLY
WIZARDRY
WIZENING
WOMANIZE
WOOZIEST
WURTZITE
WUZZLING
YOKOZUNA
ZABAIONE
ZABTIEHS
ZADDIKIM
ZAMARRAS
ZAMARROS
ZAMBOMBA
ZAMBUCKS
ZAMINDAR
ZAMOUSES
ZAMPOGNA
ZANELLAS
ZANINESS
ZANJEROS
ZANYISMS
ZAPPIEST
ZAPTIAHS
ZAPTIEHS
ZARATITE
ZAREEBAS
ZARNICHS
ZARZUELA
ZASTRUGA
ZASTRUGI
ZEALANTS
ZEALLESS
ZEALOTRY
ZEBRINAS
ZEBRINNY
ZEBRULAS
ZEBRULES
ZECCHINE
ZECCHINI
ZECCHINO
ZELATORS
ZELATRIX
ZEMINDAR
ZEMSTVOS
ZENITHAL
ZEOLITES
ZEOLITIC
ZEPPELIN
ZERUMBET
ZESTIEST
ZETETICS
ZEUXITES
ZIBELINE
ZIGANKAS
ZIGGURAT
ZIGZAGGY
ZIKKURAT
ZILLIONS
ZIMOCCAS
ZINCIEST
ZINCITES
ZINCKIER
ZINCKIFY
ZINCKING
ZINCODES
ZINGIBER
ZINGIEST
ZINKIEST
ZIPPERED
ZIPPIEST
ZIRCALOY
ZIRCONIA
ZIRCONIC
ZITHERNS
ZIZANIAS
ZIZYPHUS
ZOCCOLOS
ZODIACAL
ZOETROPE
ZOIATRIA
ZOISITES
ZOMBIISM
ZOMBORUK
ZONATION
ZONELESS
ZONULETS
ZOOBLAST
ZOOCHORE
ZOOCHORY
ZOOCYTIA
ZOOECIUM
ZOOGENIC
ZOOGLOEA
ZOOGRAFT
ZOOLATER
ZOOLATRY
ZOOLITES
ZOOLITHS
ZOOLITIC
ZOOMANCY
ZOOMETRY
ZOOMORPH
ZOONITES
ZOONITIC
ZOONOMIA
ZOONOMIC
ZOONOSES
ZOONOSIS
ZOONOTIC
ZOOPATHY
ZOOPERAL
ZOOPHAGY
ZOOPHILE
ZOOPHILY
ZOOPHORI
ZOOPHYTE
ZOOSCOPY
ZOOSPERM
ZOOSPORE
ZOOTHOME
ZOOTOMIC
ZOOTOXIN
ZOOTROPE
ZOOTYPES
ZOOTYPIC
ZOPILOTE
ZORGITES
ZORILLES
ZORILLOS
ZUCCHINI
ZUCHETTA
ZUCHETTO
ZUGZWANG
ZYGAENID
ZYGANTRA
ZYGODONT
ZYGOMATA
ZYLONITE
ZYMOGENS
ZYMOLOGY
ZYMOTICS

HINT

Managing the Big Four

It is rarely worth holding on to the J Q X or Z in the hope of a very high score later in the game unless you are aware of the letters you are likely to pick up and you are not sacrificing scores in the process. Generally, keeping the high score letters back will hinder future opportunities and rack balance. It is often wiser to score what you can rather than wait for something better. But if you are to hold on to any of the big four the X is probably the safest and most flexible simply because of the two-letter words playable. It is also the one your opponent is most likely to unwittingly provide a scoring opportunity for.

HINT

Knowing Non-Words

Much time can be wasted in a game when you have a promising-looking set of seven letters on your rack but can't remember whether they make a seven-letter word or not. Therefore it is also beneficial to be familiar with those common sets of seven letters that *don't* make a seven-letter word. Some examples are: ENRAISE, IRELAND, and TAILEND. Note that by forming 'non-words' with these racks they can be more easily recognized during play. Having armed yourself with a selection of non-words the next task is to learn the possible eight-letter plays so that you can be aware of possible bonus plays using available letters on the board. The IRELAND set makes eight-letter words with the letters B F G H N S. These words and those of the other non-words mentioned above can be readily unearthed from the Eight-Letter Anagram lists.

HINT

Learning the J Q X Z Words

If you have trouble remembering those useful words containg the J Q X or Z then try the following solo game as a learning exercise. Take the J X Z Q and one U out of the letter bag and put to one side. Take six letters at random from the letter bag and place on your rack. Then give yourself a couple of minutes with each of J Q X and Z to see how many different words you can make by combining them with the six letters on your rack. When playing with the Q, if you haven't also picked a U, utilize the U you you've put to one side. Make a note of the highest scoring play you found with each of J Q X and Z and then check with the lists in this book to see if there was anything you missed. Having completed the exercise with the first rack, play any word from your six letters on the board, keeping the J Q X Z and U to one side, and return any remaining letters to the bag. Select another six letters at random for the second turn. repeat the exercise with the fresh rack and so on.

HINT

Do-It-Yourself Six-Letter Sets

The 250 six-letter combinations (stems) in this book represent those most useful to the Scrabble player. There are many more stems that are useful to study and, as is nearly always the case, compiling lists yourself not only helps you memorize the words but is also more interesting than simply learning from those readily provided. Try deriving your own six-letter stem lists based on names (SHEILA, DANIEL, etc) or fictitious words (INCORE, POSIER, etc) as mnemonics. The Anagram section will be your ideal hunting-ground for this exercise.

HINT

Tile-Tracking

It is acceptable in tournament Scrabble to have a note of the letter distribution and to use it during play as a checklist of what letters are still to come. Most top players use this method to enable them to work out what tiles their opponents have at the end of the game. Such a checklist, when used skilfully, can also provide mid-game information about likely pickups and enable the right combination of tiles to be kept on the rack to give the greatest possibility of playing a bonus word. If you practise tile-tracking whilst playing you will soon find you are more aware of the letter distribution which in turn will assist you to maintain a balanced rack. Even if you don't track all the tiles, keeping a note of the vowels, the S's and blanks, the J Q X Z and the awkward consonants C V and K, will help improve your rack management.

SECTION TWO

ENDINGS

Introduction

Scrabble players naturally think about beginnings of words when they are looking for a play. Can I find a word beginning with BE- or DIS- or QU- or RE- or UN-? As a player becomes more adept, he or she will consider the more obvious endings, such as -ED and -ER and -IER and -ING, and even the humble -S.

The following lists offer a variety of words arranged according to their endings rather than their beginnings. The first set of lists covers useful suffixes, and the second set of lists addresses words ending with the vowels A, I, O and U.

USEFUL SUFFIXES

The following lists offer seven- and eight-letter words ending with these suffixes:

-ABLE	-ISE	-MEN
-AGE	-ISH	-OID
-EST	-ISM	-OR
-FUL	-IST	-OUS
-IBLE	-LY	-TION
-INGS	-MAN	

Those ending with -INGS, -LY and -EST should be especially useful. There are many times that Scrabble players ponder questions such as:

'I know HOSTING is a word, but does it take an S?'
'I know SULTRY is all right, but what about SULTRILY?'
'I know the adjective OARY, but is the superlative OARIEST acceptable?'

Familiarity with the lists here should provide instant answers to these and similar questions. In the case of the -EST words, where these are superlatives, it can be implied that the corresponding comparatives ending in -ER are also acceptable, eg OARIER.

Chambers Back-Words, which shows all words according to alphabetical sequence of endings, can be used as a pointer to other endings, but note that it is *not* based on *Official Scrabble Words*.

WORDS ENDING IN -ABLE

7-letter words -ABLE

ACCABLE	CITABLE	EATABLE	FRIABLE	MIRABLE	PARABLE	ROWABLE	SUEABLE	UNHABLE
ACTABLE	CURABLE	EFFABLE	HATABLE	MIXABLE	PAYABLE	RULABLE	TAKABLE	VATABLE
AFFABLE	DATABLE	EQUABLE	HIRABLE	MOVABLE	PLIABLE	SALABLE	TAMABLE	VOCABLE
AMIABLE	DISABLE	ERRABLE	LIKABLE	MUTABLE	POTABLE	SAVABLE	TAXABLE	VOLABLE
ASTABLE	DOWABLE	FADABLE	LIVABLE	NAMABLE	RATABLE	SAYABLE	TENABLE	
BATABLE	DUPABLE	FINABLE	LOSABLE	NOTABLE	RETABLE	SEEABLE	TOWABLE	
BUYABLE	DURABLE	FIXABLE	LOVABLE	PACABLE	RIDABLE	SIZABLE	TRIABLE	
CAPABLE	DYEABLE	FLYABLE	MAKABLE	PAPABLE	ROPABLE	SKIABLE	TUNABLE	

8-letter words -ABLE

ABATABLE	BISTABLE	DISHABLE	FILMABLE	HANGABLE	JUMPABLE	LIVEABLE	OPENABLE
ADORABLE	BLAMABLE	DRAWABLE	FISHABLE	HATEABLE	KICKABLE	LOANABLE	OPERABLE
AMENABLE	BOOKABLE	DRIVABLE	FOLDABLE	HEALABLE	KISSABLE	LOCKABLE	OPINABLE
AMICABLE	CHEWABLE	DUTIABLE	FORDABLE	HELPABLE	KNOWABLE	LOVEABLE	PALPABLE
AMUSABLE	CITEABLE	EDUCABLE	FORMABLE	HIREABLE	LAPSABLE	LUGGABLE	PANTABLE
ARGUABLE	CLUBABLE	ENVIABLE	FUNDABLE	HUGGABLE	LAUDABLE	MAILABLE	PASSABLE
AVOWABLE	COOKABLE	ERASABLE	GAINABLE	HUMMABLE	LEASABLE	MAKEABLE	PECCABLE
BAILABLE	CULPABLE	EVADABLE	GETTABLE	IMITABLE	LETTABLE	MISSABLE	PINTABLE
BANKABLE	CURBABLE	EVITABLE	GRADABLE	INARABLE	LEVIABLE	MOCKABLE	PITIABLE
BEARABLE	DAMNABLE	EVOCABLE	GROWABLE	INSTABLE	LIFTABLE	MOOTABLE	PLACABLE
BEATABLE	DATEABLE	EXORABLE	GUIDABLE	INVIABLE	LIKEABLE	MOVEABLE	PLAYABLE
BEDDABLE	DENIABLE	EXPIABLE	GULLABLE	ISOLABLE	LINKABLE	NAMEABLE	PORTABLE
BIDDABLE	DIGGABLE	FELLABLE	GUSTABLE	ISSUABLE	LIQUABLE	OATHABLE	POSEABLE

POURABLE REUSABLE SATIABLE SOCIABLE TAMEABLE TIPPABLE VIEWABLE WILLABLE
PRIZABLE RIDEABLE SCALABLE SOLVABLE TANNABLE TITHABLE VIOLABLE WINNABLE
PROBABLE RINSABLE SEIZABLE SORTABLE TAPEABLE TOLLABLE VITIABLE WORKABLE
PROVABLE ROLLABLE SELLABLE SPARABLE TAPPABLE TRADABLE VOIDABLE WRITABLE
QUOTABLE ROPEABLE SHAKABLE STATABLE TASTABLE TUNEABLE WALKABLE
RAISABLE RUINABLE SHAMABLE STORABLE TEARABLE UNSTABLE WARHABLE
RATEABLE RUNNABLE SHAPABLE SUITABLE TELLABLE UNUSABLE WASHABLE
READABLE SAILABLE SINGABLE SYLLABLE TESTABLE UNVIABLE WASTABLE
RELIABLE SALEABLE SIZEABLE TAKEABLE TILLABLE VALUABLE WEARABLE
RENTABLE SALVABLE SMOKABLE TALKABLE TILTABLE VARIABLE WELDABLE

WORDS ENDING IN -AGE

7-letter words -AGE

ABUSAGE BROCAGE CRANAGE HAULAGE MILEAGE PLUSAGE SALVAGE TANNAGE VOLTAGE
ACREAGE BROKAGE DISCAGE HEADAGE MINTAGE PONDAGE SAUSAGE TEENAGE WAFTAGE
AJUTAGE BUOYAGE DOCKAGE HERBAGE MOCKAGE PONTAGE SCAVAGE TENTAGE WAINAGE
AMENAGE BURGAGE DRAYAGE HIREAGE MONTAGE PORTAGE SCUTAGE THANAGE WANTAGE
APANAGE CABBAGE DUNNAGE HOSTAGE MOORAGE POSTAGE SEEPAGE TILLAGE WASTAGE
ARRIAGE CARNAGE ESCUAGE KEELAGE MOULAGE POTTAGE SELVAGE TOLLAGE WATTAGE
ASSUAGE CARTAGE ETALAGE KIPPAGE OUTRAGE PRESAGE SERFAGE TONNAGE WEFTAGE
ASSWAGE CENTAGE FALDAGE LAIRAGE OUVRAGE PRIMAGE SIGNAGE TRUCAGE WINDAGE
AULNAGE COINAGE FARDAGE LASTAGE OVERAGE PRISAGE SINKAGE TUNNAGE WORDAGE
AVERAGE COLLAGE FLOTAGE LEAFAGE PACKAGE PROPAGE SOAKAGE UMBRAGE YARDAGE
BAGGAGE COMPAGE FLOWAGE LEAKAGE PANNAGE QUAYAGE SOCCAGE UPSTAGE
BANDAGE CORDAGE FOGGAGE LIGNAGE PASSAGE RAMPAGE SOILAGE VANTAGE
BARRAGE CORKAGE FOLIAGE LINEAGE PAYSAGE REMUAGE SONDAGE VENDAGE
BEERAGE CORNAGE FOOTAGE LINKAGE PEERAGE RESTAGE STORAGE VENTAGE
BONDAGE CORSAGE FULLAGE LOCKAGE PEONAGE RIBCAGE STOWAGE VIDUAGE
BOSCAGE COTTAGE GARBAGE LUGGAGE PIERAGE ROOTAGE SULLAGE VILLAGE
BOSKAGE COURAGE GUIDAGE MASSAGE PILLAGE RUMMAGE TALLAGE VINTAGE
BREWAGE COWHAGE GUNNAGE MESSAGE PLUMAGE SACKAGE TANKAGE VITRAGE

8-letter words -AGE

ACCORAGE BLOCKAGE DIALLAGE FRONDAGE MALAXAGE PUCELAGE STEARAGE TUTELAGE
ACIERAGE BREAKAGE DISUSAGE FRONTAGE MARITAGE PUPILAGE STEERAGE TUTORAGE
ADJUTAGE BROCKAGE DRAINAGE FROTTAGE MARRIAGE ROUGHAGE STERNAGE UMPIRAGE
AGIOTAGE CABOTAGE DRESSAGE FRUITAGE MESSUAGE SABOTAGE STILLAGE VAULTAGE
ALIENAGE CARRIAGE DRIFTAGE FUSELAGE METAYAGE SEWERAGE STOPPAGE VAUNTAGE
ALTARAGE CARUCAGE ENALLAGE GRAINAGE MISUSAGE SHORTAGE STREWAGE VERBIAGE
AMPERAGE CHANTAGE ENDAMAGE GRILLAGE MORTGAGE SLIPPAGE STUMPAGE VICARAGE
APPANAGE CHUMMAGE ENSILAGE GROUPAGE MUCILAGE SMALLAGE SUBSTAGE VICINAGE
BADINAGE CLEARAGE ENVISAGE GUARDAGE OVERPAGE SPILLAGE SUFFRAGE WAGONAGE
BARONAGE CLEAVAGE EQUIPAGE HELOTAGE PILOTAGE SPOILAGE TASSWAGE WATERAGE
BERTHAGE CLOUDAGE FERRIAGE HERITAGE PLANTAGE SPOUSAGE THIRLAGE WEIGHAGE
BEVERAGE COVERAGE FLOATAGE LANGRAGE PLUSSAGE SQUIRAGE TRACKAGE WHARFAGE
BIRDCAGE COZENAGE FOOTPAGE LANGUAGE POUNDAGE STAFFAGE TRUCKAGE WRAPPAGE
BLINDAGE CRIBBAGE FRAUTAGE LEVERAGE PROPHAGE STALLAGE TRUQUAGE WRECKAGE

WORDS ENDING IN -EST

7-letter words -EST

ACHIEST ASHIEST BOLDEST CHICEST DAFTEST DEWIEST DOWIEST EERIEST FIRMEST
ACIDEST AULDEST BONIEST CLOSEST DAMPEST DICIEST DOZIEST EGGIEST FITTEST
ACQUEST AVIDEST BOSSEST COKIEST DANKEST DIKIEST DROLEST ELMIEST FLUIEST
ACUTEST AWAREST BOXIEST COLDEST DARKEST DIMMEST DUFFEST EVENEST FONDEST
ADDREST AWNIEST BRAVEST CONFEST DEADEST DINKEST DULLEST FABBEST FOULEST
AERIEST BABIEST BRAWEST CONGEST DEAFEST DISGEST DUMBEST FADIEST FOXIEST
AGILEST BALDEST BUSIEST CONTEST DEAREST DISNEST DUNNEST FAINEST FOZIEST
AIRIEST BARGEST CAGIEST COOLEST DEEDEST DOMIEST DUSKEST FAIREST FULLEST
AMPLEST BASSEST CAKIEST COSIEST DEEPEST DOPIEST DYKIEST FALSEST FUMIEST
ANAPEST BEQUEST CALMEST COXIEST DEFFEST DOTIEST EARNEST FASTEST GABFEST
ARCHEST BIGGEST CAMPEST COZIEST DEFTEST DOUCEST EASIEST FATTEST GAINEST
ARIDEST BLATEST CANIEST CRUDEST DEIDEST DOUREST EDGIEST FELLEST GAMIEST
ARTIEST BLUIEST CANTEST CURTEST DENSEST DOVIEST EELIEST FIKIEST GAZIEST

GLUIEST	INQUEST	LONGEST	MOPIEST	OURIEST	RACIEST	SALTEST	TARTEST	WANIEST
GOLDEST	IRATEST	LOOSEST	MOTIEST	OUTJEST	RADGEST	SAMIEST	TAUTEST	WANNEST
GOOIEST	JIMPEST	LOTHEST	MURKEST	OWLIEST	RANKEST	SEAREST	TEDIEST	WARIEST
GORIEST	JOKIEST	LOUDEST	NAIFEST	OWRIEST	RASHEST	SEIKEST	TEMPEST	WARMEST
GOWDEST	JUSTEST	LOWSEST	NAIVEST	PACIEST	RATHEST	SEXIEST	TENSEST	WATTEST
GRAVEST	KEENEST	LUSHEST	NEAREST	PALIEST	REALEST	SICKEST	TERSEST	WAVIEST
GRAYEST	KINDEST	MADDEST	NEATEST	PERTEST	REDDEST	SIZIEST	TIDIEST	WAXIEST
GREYEST	LACIEST	MAINEST	NESHEST	PINIEST	REQUEST	SKEWEST	TINIEST	WEAKEST
HARDEST	LAKIEST	MATIEST	NIGHEST	PINKEST	RICHEST	SKYIEST	TOEIEST	WEETEST
HARVEST	LANGEST	MAUVEST	NOBLEST	PIPIEST	RICIEST	SLOWEST	TONIEST	WETTEST
HAZIEST	LANKEST	MAZIEST	NOSIEST	POKIEST	RILIEST	SNIDEST	TOOMEST	WHITEST
HEPPEST	LARGEST	MEANEST	NUMBEST	POOREST	RIMIEST	SOFTEST	TOWIEST	WILDEST
HIGHEST	LAZIEST	MEEKEST	OAKIEST	PORIEST	ROKIEST	SOONEST	TRITEST	WILIEST
HIPPEST	LEANEST	MEETEST	OARIEST	POSHEST	ROPIEST	SOUREST	TUNIEST	WILLEST
HOKIEST	LENGEST	MIDDEST	OBESEST	POSIEST	RORIEST	SPAREST	UGLIEST	WINIEST
HOLIEST	LEWDEST	MILDEST	OILIEST	POXIEST	ROSIEST	SPRYEST	UNBLEST	WIRIEST
HOMIEST	LIEFEST	MIMMEST	ONLIEST	PRETEST	RUBIEST	STALEST	VAGUEST	WOTTEST
HOTTEST	LIEVEST	MINIEST	OORIEST	PRONEST	RULIEST	STEYEST	VAINEST	WOWFEST
ICKIEST	LIMIEST	MIRIEST	OOSIEST	PROTEST	RUMMEST	SUAVEST	VASTEST	YUKIEST
IFFIEST	LIMPEST	MIRKEST	OOZIEST	PUIREST	SADDEST	SUGGEST	VERIEST	ZANIEST
IMPREST	LINIEST	MITIEST	OPENEST	PULIEST	SAGIEST	TAKIEST	VINIEST	
INANEST	LITHEST	MIXIEST	ORBIEST	PUNIEST	SAIDEST	TALLEST	VOGIEST	
INKIEST	LOGIEST	MOOTEST	OULDEST	QUAREST	SAIREST	TANNEST	WALIEST	

8-letter words -EST

ACERBEST	BLOWIEST	CAULDEST	DAUBIEST	DUNNIEST	FLUKIEST	GIDDIEST	HAIRIEST
ACRIDEST	BLUDIEST	CHARIEST	DEBBIEST	DURGIEST	FLUSHEST	GIMPIEST	HAMMIEST
ADEPTEST	BLUFFEST	CHASTEST	DEEDIEST	DUSKIEST	FLUTIEST	GINNIEST	HANDIEST
AFFOREST	BLUNTEST	CHEAPEST	DEFOREST	DUSTIEST	FOAMIEST	GIRNIEST	HANGNEST
ALCAHEST	BODGIEST	CHEWIEST	DEMUREST	EAGEREST	FOGGIEST	GLADDEST	HAPPIEST
ALERTEST	BOGGIEST	CHIEFEST	DICKIEST	EARLIEST	FOOTIEST	GLADIEST	HARDIEST
ALKAHEST	BONNIEST	CHILLEST	DICTIEST	EMONGEST	FOOTREST	GLARIEST	HARSHEST
ANAPAEST	BOOKIEST	CHOICEST	DIDDIEST	EMPTIEST	FORKIEST	GLAZIEST	HASHIEST
ANGRIEST	BOOKREST	CHOKIEST	DILLIEST	ENFOREST	FRAILEST	GLEGGEST	HASTIEST
ARBALEST	BOOZIEST	CISSIEST	DINGIEST	EVILLEST	FRANKEST	GLIBBEST	HEADIEST
ARTSIEST	BOSKIEST	CLAYIEST	DINKIEST	EXACTEST	FRESHEST	GLIDDEST	HEADREST
ASTUTEST	BOSSIEST	CLEANEST	DIPPIEST	FADDIEST	FROWIEST	GLUMMEST	HEAPIEST
BAGGIEST	BOUSIEST	CLEAREST	DIRTIEST	FAINTEST	FUBBIEST	GOATIEST	HEAVIEST
BALKIEST	BRAIDEST	COALIEST	DISHIEST	FANCIEST	FUBSIEST	GODLIEST	HEDGIEST
BALMIEST	BRAKIEST	COARSEST	DITSIEST	FARTHEST	FUFFIEST	GOLDIEST	HEFTIEST
BANALEST	BRASHEST	COBBIEST	DITZIEST	FATTIEST	FUGGIEST	GOODIEST	HEMPIEST
BANDIEST	BRENTEST	COCKIEST	DIVINEST	FEEBLEST	FUNKIEST	GOOFIEST	HENNIEST
BARDIEST	BRIEFEST	COMBIEST	DIZZIEST	FEINTEST	FUNNIEST	GOOPIEST	HERBIEST
BARGHEST	BRILLEST	COMFIEST	DOCILEST	FELTIEST	FURRIEST	GOOSIEST	HILLIEST
BARKIEST	BRINIEST	CONQUEST	DODDIEST	FENDIEST	FURTHEST	GORMIEST	HIPPIEST
BARMIEST	BRISKEST	COOMIEST	DODGIEST	FENNIEST	FURZIEST	GORSIEST	HOARIEST
BASSIEST	BROADEST	COPSIEST	DOGGIEST	FERLIEST	FUSSIEST	GOUTIEST	HOARSEST
BATTIEST	BROWNEST	CORKIEST	DOILTEST	FERNIEST	FUSTIEST	GRANDEST	HOOKIEST
BAWDIEST	BUDDIEST	CORNIEST	DONSIEST	FETIDEST	FUTILEST	GRAPIEST	HOOLIEST
BEADIEST	BUGGIEST	COUTHEST	DOOMIEST	FICKLEST	FUZZIEST	GREATEST	HOPPIEST
BEAKIEST	BULGIEST	CRAPIEST	DORKIEST	FIERCEST	GABBIEST	GREENEST	HORNIEST
BEAMIEST	BULKIEST	CRASSEST	DORTIEST	FIERIEST	GAMMIEST	GRIMIEST	HORSIEST
BEEFIEST	BULLIEST	CRAZIEST	DOTTIEST	FILMIEST	GAPPIEST	GRIMMEST	HUFFIEST
BEERIEST	BUMPIEST	CREPIEST	DOTTLEST	FINNIEST	GASPIEST	GRITTEST	HULKIEST
BENDIEST	BUNTIEST	CRISPEST	DOWDIEST	FIRRIEST	GASSIEST	GRODIEST	HULLIEST
BENTIEST	BURLIEST	CRONKEST	DOWNIEST	FISHIEST	GAUCHEST	GROSSEST	HUMANEST
BILGIEST	BURRIEST	CROOKEST	DRABBEST	FISTIEST	GAUCIEST	GROUSEST	HUMBLEST
BIRKIEST	BUSHIEST	CROSSEST	DREAREST	FITLIEST	GAUDIEST	GRUFFEST	HUMIDEST
BIRSIEST	BUSTIEST	CRUMPEST	DROLLEST	FIZZIEST	GAUMIEST	GRUMMEST	HUMPIEST
BITSIEST	BUTCHEST	CURDIEST	DRONIEST	FLAKIEST	GAUNTEST	GUCKIEST	HUNKIEST
BITTIEST	BUXOMEST	CURLIEST	DRUNKEST	FLAMIEST	GAUZIEST	GULFIEST	HUSHIEST
BLACKEST	BUZZIEST	CURNIEST	DRUSIEST	FLARIEST	GAWCIEST	GUMMIEST	HUSKIEST
BLANDEST	CADGIEST	CURVIEST	DRUXIEST	FLASHEST	GAWKIEST	GUNGIEST	IMMODEST
BLANKEST	CALMIEST	CUSHIEST	DUCKIEST	FLATTEST	GAWSIEST	GURLIEST	IMPUREST
BLEAKEST	CAMPIEST	CUTTIEST	DUDDIEST	FLAWIEST	GEEKIEST	GUSHIEST	INDIGEST
BLEAREST	CANNIEST	DAFFIEST	DULLIEST	FLAXIEST	GELIDEST	GUSTIEST	INEPTEST
BLINDEST	CANTIEST	DAGGIEST	DUMMIEST	FLEETEST	GEMMIEST	GUTSIEST	INERTEST
BLITHEST	CARNIEST	DAMPIEST	DUMPIEST	FLIPPEST	GENTIEST	GUTTIEST	INSANEST
BLONDEST	CATTIEST	DANDIEST	DUNGIEST	FLORIEST	GENTLEST	HAILIEST	INTEREST

ITCHIEST
JAGGIEST
JAMMIEST
JANTIEST
JAZZIEST
JEMMIEST
JERKIEST
JETTIEST
JIMPIEST
JOLLIEST
JOLTIEST
JOWLIEST
JUICIEST
JUMPIEST
JUNKIEST
KEDGIEST
KIDGIEST
KINKIEST
KITTLEST
KOOKIEST
LAIGHEST
LAIRIEST
LANKIEST
LARDIEST
LARKIEST
LATHIEST
LAWNIEST
LEADIEST
LEAFIEST
LEAKIEST
LEARIEST
LEAVIEST
LEDGIEST
LEERIEST
LEGGIEST
LEISHEST
LICHTEST
LIGHTEST
LINGIEST
LINTIEST
LIPPIEST
LITTLEST
LIVIDEST
LOAMIEST
LOATHEST
LOFTIEST
LOOBIEST
LOONIEST
LOOPIEST
LOSSIEST
LOURIEST
LOUSIEST
LOWLIEST
LUCIDEST
LUCKIEST
LUMMIEST
LUMPIEST
LURIDEST
LUSHIEST
LUSTIEST
MALTIEST
MANGIEST
MANIFEST
MANKIEST
MANLIEST
MARDIEST
MARLIEST
MASHIEST
MASSIEST
MASTIEST
MATUREST
MAWKIEST
MEAGREST
MEALIEST
MEATIEST
MERRIEST
MESHIEST
MESSIEST
MIFFIEST
MIGHTEST
MILKIEST
MIMSIEST
MINGIEST
MINTIEST
MINUTEST
MIRLIEST
MISSIEST
MISTIEST
MOCHIEST
MOISTEST
MOODIEST
MOONIEST
MOORIEST
MOPPIEST
MOROSEST
MOSSIEST
MOTHIEST
MOTLIEST
MOTTIEST
MOUSIEST
MUCKIEST
MUDDIEST
MUGGIEST
MUMSIEST
MURKIEST
MURLIEST
MUSHIEST
MUSKIEST
MUSSIEST
MUSTIEST
MUZZIEST
NAGGIEST
NAKEDEST
NAPPIEST
NARKIEST
NASTIEST
NATTIEST
NEEDIEST
NERDIEST
NERVIEST
NETTIEST
NEWSIEST
NIFFIEST
NIFTIEST
NIMBLEST
NIPPIEST
NIRLIEST
NITTIEST
NOBBIEST
NOISIEST
NOOKIEST
NOUNIEST
NUBBIEST
NUTTIEST
OBTUSEST
OFTENEST
OPAQUEST
ORANGEST
ORNATEST
OUTWREST
OVERKEST
PALLIEST
PALMIEST
PALSIEST
PAPPIEST
PARKIEST
PASTIEST
PAWKIEST
PEAKIEST
PEATIEST
PEERIEST
PEPPIEST
PERKIEST
PESKIEST
PETTIEST
PHONIEST
PICKIEST
PIGGIEST
PINKIEST
PIPPIEST
PITHIEST
PLAINEST
PLATIEST
PLUMIEST
PLUMPEST
PLUSHEST
POCKIEST
PODDIEST
PODGIEST
POLITEST
PONCIEST
PONGIEST
POOFIEST
POOVIEST
POPPIEST
PORKIEST
PORTIEST
POTTIEST
POUTIEST
PRICIEST
PRIMMEST
PRIVIEST
PROSIEST
PROUDEST
PUDGIEST
PUDSIEST
PUFFIEST
PUGGIEST
PULPIEST
PURPLEST
PURSIEST
PURTIEST
PUSHIEST
QUAKIEST
QUEEREST
QUICKEST
QUIETEST
RABIDEST
RAGGIEST
RAINIEST
RANDIEST
RANGIEST
RAPIDEST
RASPIEST
RATTIEST
RAUCLEST
READIEST
REAMIEST
REARREST
REDDIEST
REEDIEST
REEKIEST
REFOREST
REINVEST
REMOTEST
RESTIEST
RIBBIEST
RICHTEST
RIDGIEST
RIFTIEST
RIGHTEST
RIGIDEST
RINDIEST
RISKIEST
RITZIEST
ROARIEST
ROCKIEST
ROILIEST
ROOFIEST
ROOMIEST
ROOPIEST
ROOTIEST
RORTIEST
ROUGHEST
ROUNDEST
ROUPIEST
ROWDIEST
RUDDIEST
RUGGIEST
RUMMIEST
RUNNIEST
RUNTIEST
RUSHIEST
RUSTIEST
RUTTIEST
SAGGIEST
SALTIEST
SANDIEST
SAPPIEST
SARKIEST
SASSIEST
SAUCIEST
SAVAGEST
SCALIEST
SCANTEST
SCARCEST
SCARIEST
SEAMIEST
SECUREST
SEDATEST
SEDGIEST
SEEDIEST
SEELIEST
SEEPIEST
SEMPLEST
SERENEST
SEVEREST
SHADIEST
SHAKIEST
SHALIEST
SHARPEST
SHEEREST
SHINIEST
SHOALEST
SHORTEST
SHOWIEST
SILKIEST
SILLIEST
SILTIEST
SIMPLEST
SINKIEST
SISSIEST
SKIEYEST
SKINTEST
SKIVIEST
SLACKEST
SLATIEST
SLEEKEST
SLICKEST
SLIMIEST
SLIMMEST
SLOPIEST
SLUGFEST
SMALLEST
SMARTEST
SMOKIEST
SMUGGEST
SNAKIEST
SNARIEST
SNELLEST
SNIPIEST
SNODDEST
SNOWIEST
SNUGGEST
SOAPIEST
SOBEREST
SODDIEST
SOGGIEST
SOILIEST
SOLIDEST
SOMBREST
SONGFEST
SONSIEST
SOOTHEST
SOOTIEST
SOPPIEST
SORRIEST
SOUNDEST
SOUPIEST
SPACIEST
SPARSEST
SPEWIEST
SPICIEST
SPICKEST
SPIKIEST
SPINIEST
SPIRIEST
SPRUCEST
SPUMIEST
SQUAREST
STABLEST
STAGIEST
STAIDEST
STARKEST
STEEPEST
STEEVEST
STERNEST
STEWIEST
STIEVEST
STIFFEST
STILLEST
STIVIEST
STONIEST
STOUTEST
SUBTLEST
SUDSIEST
SUETIEST
SULKIEST
SUNNIEST
SUPPLEST
SURFIEST
SURGIEST
SURLIEST
SVELTEST
SWALIEST
SWANKEST
SWEETEST
SWELLEST
SWIFTEST
SWIPIEST
SWISHEST
TACKIEST
TAGGIEST
TALCIEST
TALKFEST
TALKIEST
TANGIEST
TARDIEST
TARRIEST
TARTIEST
TASTIEST
TATTIEST
TAWNIEST
TAWTIEST
TEARIEST
TECHIEST
TEENIEST
TENTIEST
TEPIDEST
TESTIEST
TEUCHEST
TEUGHEST
THAWIEST
THEWIEST
THICKEST
THINNEST
THYMIEST
TICHIEST
TIDDIEST
TIGHTEST
TILLIEST
TIMIDEST
TINNIEST
TINTIEST
TIPPIEST
TIPSIEST
TIREDEST
TOFFIEST
TOSHIEST
TOSSIEST
TOTTIEST
TOUGHEST
TOUSIEST
TOUTIEST
TOUZIEST
TOWNIEST
TOWSIEST
TOWZIEST
TRIFFEST
TRIGGEST
TRIMMEST
TRIPIEST
TUBBIEST
TUFTIEST
TUMPIEST
TURFIEST
TUSKIEST
TWINIEST
UNHONEST
UNIQUEST
UNPRIEST
UNRIPEST
UNSAFEST
UNSUREST
UNTRUEST
UNWISEST
URBANEST
UTTEREST
VAIRIEST
VALIDEST
VAPIDEST
VASTIEST
VEALIEST
VEILIEST
VEINIEST
VIEWIEST
VIVIDEST
VOGUIEST
VUGGIEST
WACKIEST
WALLIEST
WALTIEST
WANKIEST
WARBIEST
WARTIEST
WASHIEST
WASPIEST
WASPNEST
WEARIEST
WEBBIEST
WEDGIEST
WEEDIEST
WEENIEST
WEEPIEST
WEIRDEST
WENNIEST
WERSHEST
WHEYIEST
WHINIEST
WHITIEST
WIMPIEST
WINDIEST
WINGIEST
WISPIEST
WITHIEST
WITTIEST
WONKIEST
WOODIEST
WOOFIEST
WOOZIEST
WORDIEST
WORMIEST
WRONGEST
YAPPIEST
YAWNIEST
YOLKIEST
YOUNGEST
YUCKIEST
YUKKIEST
YUMMIEST
ZAPPIEST
ZESTIEST
ZINCIEST
ZINGIEST
ZINKIEST
ZIPPIEST

WORDS ENDING IN -FUL

7-letter words -FUL

BALEFUL
BANEFUL
BASHFUL
BODEFUL
BOOKFUL
BOWLFUL
BRIMFUL
CAREFUL
CROPFUL
DAREFUL
DEEDFUL
DERNFUL
DIREFUL
DISHFUL
DOLEFUL
DOOMFUL
DUREFUL
DUTIFUL
EASEFUL
FATEFUL
FEARFUL
FISHFUL
FISTFUL
FOODFUL
FORKFUL
FRETFUL
GAINFUL

GASHFUL HEEDFUL LOOFFUL NEEDFUL PLAYFUL RUTHFUL SOULFUL TUBEFUL WISTFUL
GAZEFUL HELPFUL LUNGFUL NESTFUL PLOTFUL SACKFUL TACTFUL TUNEFUL WORKFUL
GLADFUL HOPEFUL LUSTFUL PAILFUL POKEFUL SHIPFUL TALEFUL VIALFUL ZEALFUL
GLEEFUL HORNFUL MASTFUL PAINFUL PREYFUL SHOPFUL TANKFUL WAILFUL ZESTFUL
GUSTFUL HURTFUL MAZEFUL PALMFUL PUSHFUL SIGHFUL TEARFUL WAKEFUL
GUTSFUL JESTFUL MINDFUL PESTFUL RAGEFUL SKEPFUL TEEMFUL WAMEFUL
HANDFUL LIFEFUL MISTFUL PIPEFUL RESTFUL SKILFUL TENTFUL WILEFUL
HARMFUL LISTFUL MOANFUL PITHFUL RISKFUL SKINFUL TOILFUL WILLFUL
HATEFUL LOCKFUL MUSEFUL PITIFUL ROOMFUL SONGFUL TRAYFUL WISHFUL

8-letter words -FUL

APRONFUL DREADFUL GLOOMFUL MOURNFUL RIGHTFUL SPITEFUL TROUTFUL WATCHFUL
AVAILFUL DREAMFUL GRACEFUL MOUTHFUL SCENTFUL SPOILFUL TRUNKFUL WEARIFUL
BASINFUL EVENTFUL GRATEFUL NIEVEFUL SCOOPFUL SPOONFUL TRUSTFUL WORTHFUL
BELLYFUL FAITHFUL GRIEFFUL NOISEFUL SCORNFUL SPORTFUL TRUTHFUL WRACKFUL
BLAMEFUL FANCIFUL GROANFUL PAUSEFUL SENSEFUL STARTFUL UDDERFUL WRATHFUL
BLISSFUL FAULTFUL GUILEFUL PEACEFUL SHAMEFUL STICKFUL UNARTFUL WREAKFUL
BLUSHFUL FEASTFUL HOUSEFUL PLAINFUL SHELLFUL STORMFUL UNJOYFUL WRECKFUL
BOASTFUL FORCEFUL LADLEFUL PLATEFUL SKILLFUL SURGEFUL UNLAWFUL WRONGFUL
CHARMFUL FOUNTFUL LAUGHFUL POUCHFUL SLOTHFUL TABLEFUL UNUSEFUL YOUTHFUL
CHEERFUL FRAUDFUL LIGHTFUL POWERFUL SMILEFUL TASTEFUL UNWILFUL
CHESTFUL FREAKFUL LOATHFUL PRANKFUL SNOOTFUL THANKFUL VAUNTFUL
CRIMEFUL FRISKFUL MENSEFUL PRESSFUL SOOTHFUL TOOTHFUL VENGEFUL
DEARNFUL FRUITFUL MERCIFUL PRIDEFUL SPADEFUL TRADEFUL VOICEFUL
DEATHFUL GHASTFUL MIGHTFUL PROUDFUL SPEEDFUL TRISTFUL WAGONFUL
DOUBTFUL GLASSFUL MIRTHFUL PURSEFUL SPELLFUL TROTHFUL WASTEFUL

WORDS ENDING IN -IBLE

7-letter words -IBLE

AUDIBLE DELIBLE DOCIBLE FUSIBLE LEGIBLE PATIBLE RIBIBLE RISIBLE VISIBLE

8-letter words -IBLE

CREDIBLE ELUDIBLE FALLIBLE FORCIBLE MANDIBLE POSSIBLE SUASIBLE THURIBLE
CRUCIBLE ERODIBLE FEASIBLE GULLIBLE MISCIBLE RINSIBLE TANGIBLE VENDIBLE
EDUCIBLE EVASIBLE FENCIBLE HORRIBLE PARTIBLE RUNCIBLE TENSIBLE VINCIBLE
ELIGIBLE EXIGIBLE FLEXIBLE INEDIBLE PASSIBLE SENSIBLE TERRIBLE

WORDS ENDING IN -INGS

7-letter words -INGS

ACHINGS CAKINGS DYEINGS GIVINGS LIKINGS OGLINGS RIDINGS SPYINGS UNKINGS
ACTINGS CANINGS EARINGS GORINGS LIMINGS ONDINGS RISINGS STRINGS UPPINGS
AGEINGS CASINGS EATINGS HAVINGS LININGS OUTINGS ROBINGS TAKINGS URGINGS
AIRINGS CAVINGS EDGINGS HAYINGS LIVINGS PAGINGS RODINGS TAMINGS URNINGS
ANTINGS CAWINGS ELDINGS HAZINGS LOBINGS PALINGS ROPINGS TARINGS VEXINGS
ARCINGS CODINGS ENDINGS HEWINGS LORINGS PARINGS ROVINGS TAWINGS VIKINGS
AWNINGS COMINGS ENRINGS HEXINGS LOSINGS PAVINGS ROWINGS TAXINGS WADINGS
BAAINGS COOINGS ERRINGS HIDINGS LOVINGS PAYINGS RUBINGS TIDINGS WAKINGS
BAKINGS COPINGS FACINGS HIRINGS LOWINGS PILINGS RULINGS TILINGS WANINGS
BESINGS COVINGS FADINGS HOLINGS LUGINGS PIPINGS SAVINGS TIMINGS WAVINGS
BIDINGS CRYINGS FILINGS HOMINGS LUTINGS POLINGS SAWINGS TIRINGS WAXINGS
BIKINGS DARINGS FININGS INNINGS MAKINGS POSINGS SAYINGS TOLINGS WIPINGS
BITINGS DATINGS FIRINGS JAPINGS MAYINGS PRYINGS SEEINGS TONINGS WIRINGS
BLUINGS DICINGS FIXINGS JAWINGS MININGS PULINGS SEWINGS TOWINGS WONINGS
BODINGS DIVINGS FLYINGS KITINGS MOWINGS RACINGS SIDINGS TOYINGS WOOINGS
BONINGS DONINGS FOXINGS LACINGS MUSINGS RAGINGS SIZINGS TRYINGS YOKINGS
BORINGS DOPINGS FRYINGS LADINGS NAMINGS RAKINGS SKIINGS TUBINGS ZONINGS
BOWINGS DOTINGS GAMINGS LASINGS NIDINGS RATINGS SOWINGS TUNINGS
BOXINGS DOZINGS GAPINGS LAWINGS NOSINGS RAVINGS SPAINGS TYPINGS
BUSINGS DRYINGS GATINGS LAYINGS OFFINGS RAWINGS SPRINGS ULLINGS

8-letter words -INGS

ABIDINGS
AISLINGS
AMBLINGS
ANGLINGS
ARCKINGS
AWAKINGS
BACKINGS
BAGGINGS
BAITINGS
BALKINGS
BALLINGS
BANDINGS
BANGINGS
BANKINGS
BANTINGS
BARRINGS
BASHINGS
BASTINGS
BATTINGS
BAWLINGS
BEADINGS
BEAMINGS
BEARINGS
BEATINGS
BEDDINGS
BEGGINGS
BELTINGS
BENDINGS
BETTINGS
BIASINGS
BIDDINGS
BILLINGS
BINDINGS
BIRDINGS
BIRLINGS
BLUEINGS
BOATINGS
BOILINGS
BOLTINGS
BONDINGS
BOOKINGS
BOOMINGS
BOWLINGS
BREWINGS
BRIMINGS
BROKINGS
BRUTINGS
BUCKINGS
BUDDINGS
BUFFINGS
BUGGINGS
BULLINGS
BUMPINGS
BUNTINGS
BURNINGS
BUSHINGS
BUSKINGS
BUSSINGS
BUSTINGS
BUZZINGS
CABLINGS
CALLINGS
CANTINGS
CAPPINGS
CARLINGS
CARPINGS
CARVINGS
CASTINGS

CATLINGS
CEASINGS
CEILINGS
CHASINGS
CHIDINGS
CIELINGS
CLOSINGS
COAMINGS
COATINGS
CODLINGS
COGGINGS
COININGS
COLLINGS
COMBINGS
COMPINGS
CONNINGS
CORDINGS
COWLINGS
CRAVINGS
CUBBINGS
CULLINGS
CUNNINGS
CUPPINGS
CURLINGS
CURSINGS
CUTTINGS
CYCLINGS
DAFFINGS
DAGGINGS
DAMPINGS
DANCINGS
DARLINGS
DARNINGS
DAUBINGS
DAWNINGS
DEALINGS
DECKINGS
DEVLINGS
DIGGINGS
DILLINGS
DIPPINGS
DISHINGS
DOATINGS
DOCKINGS
DODGINGS
DOGGINGS
DOPPINGS
DRAWINGS
DROVINGS
DUBBINGS
DUCKINGS
DUFFINGS
DUNNINGS
EANLINGS
EARNINGS
EARRINGS
EASTINGS
EEVNINGS
EILDINGS
ENVYINGS
ETCHINGS
EVENINGS
FABLINGS
FAGGINGS
FAILINGS
FAIRINGS
FALLINGS
FANNINGS

FARCINGS
FARDINGS
FARMINGS
FASTINGS
FATLINGS
FAWNINGS
FEEDINGS
FEELINGS
FEERINGS
FELTINGS
FENCINGS
FERNINGS
FEUDINGS
FILLINGS
FINDINGS
FIRRINGS
FISHINGS
FITTINGS
FIZZINGS
FLUTINGS
FLYTINGS
FOAMINGS
FOILINGS
FOLDINGS
FOOLINGS
FOOTINGS
FOPLINGS
FORGINGS
FORMINGS
FOWLINGS
FRAMINGS
FRAYINGS
FUCKINGS
FUNDINGS
FURRINGS
GADLINGS
GAFFINGS
GAININGS
GANGINGS
GASPINGS
GASSINGS
GAUGINGS
GEARINGS
GELDINGS
GETTINGS
GILDINGS
GIRDINGS
GLAZINGS
GLIDINGS
GLOVINGS
GLOZINGS
GODLINGS
GOLFINGS
GOSLINGS
GRATINGS
GRAVINGS
GRAZINGS
GREYINGS
GRICINGS
GROWINGS
GUIDINGS
GUISINGS
GUMMINGS
GUNNINGS
HACKINGS
HAININGS
HALLINGS
HALTINGS

HANGINGS
HARLINGS
HARPINGS
HASTINGS
HATTINGS
HAWKINGS
HEADINGS
HEALINGS
HEARINGS
HEATINGS
HEAVINGS
HEDGINGS
HEELINGS
HELPINGS
HERLINGS
HERRINGS
HIDLINGS
HILDINGS
HIPPINGS
HIRLINGS
HISSINGS
HOGGINGS
HOLDINGS
HOPPINGS
HORNINGS
HORSINGS
HOSTINGS
HOTTINGS
HOUSINGS
HOUTINGS
HOWLINGS
HUMMINGS
HUNTINGS
HURLINGS
HUSKINGS
HUSTINGS
HUTTINGS
HYLDINGS
IMAGINGS
INBEINGS
INBRINGS
INGOINGS
INKLINGS
INSWINGS
IRONINGS
JARRINGS
JEERINGS
JERKINGS
JESTINGS
JIBBINGS
JIGGINGS
JOBBINGS
JOGGINGS
JOININGS
JOTTINGS
JUGGINGS
KARTINGS
KAYOINGS
KEELINGS
KEENINGS
KEEPINGS
KEMPINGS
KENNINGS
KERNINGS
KIDLINGS
KILLINGS
KIRKINGS
KITLINGS

KNIFINGS
LAGGINGS
LALLINGS
LAMMINGS
LAMPINGS
LANDINGS
LAPPINGS
LAPWINGS
LASHINGS
LASTINGS
LATHINGS
LEADINGS
LEANINGS
LEASINGS
LEAVINGS
LEERINGS
LEGGINGS
LEKKINGS
LEMMINGS
LENDINGS
LETTINGS
LICKINGS
LIGGINGS
LIMPINGS
LISPINGS
LISTINGS
LOADINGS
LOAFINGS
LOANINGS
LODGINGS
LOGGINGS
LONGINGS
LOONINGS
LOOPINGS
LOOTINGS
LOPPINGS
LORDINGS
LOURINGS
LUGEINGS
LURKINGS
MADLINGS
MAILINGS
MAIMINGS
MALTINGS
MAPPINGS
MARKINGS
MARLINGS
MASHINGS
MATTINGS
MEANINGS
MEETINGS
MELTINGS
MENDINGS
MERLINGS
MESHINGS
MICHINGS
MILKINGS
MILLINGS
MINCINGS
MINDINGS
MISTINGS
MOBBINGS
MOCKINGS
MOORINGS
MOOTINGS
MORLINGS
MORNINGS
MOSHINGS

MOSLINGS
MOUSINGS
MUGGINGS
MUMMINGS
MUNTINGS
NAILINGS
NECKINGS
NESTINGS
NETTINGS
NITHINGS
NODDINGS
NOGGINGS
NOONINGS
NOTHINGS
NULLINGS
NURSINGS
NUTTINGS
OAKLINGS
ONGOINGS
OPENINGS
OUTWINGS
PACKINGS
PADDINGS
PAIRINGS
PANNINGS
PANTINGS
PARKINGS
PARSINGS
PARTINGS
PASSINGS
PASTINGS
PAUSINGS
PECKINGS
PEELINGS
PEGGINGS
PELTINGS
PETTINGS
PICKINGS
PIGGINGS
PIGLINGS
PILLINGS
PINKINGS
PINNINGS
PIONINGS
PITTINGS
PLACINGS
PLATINGS
POLLINGS
POSTINGS
POURINGS
POUTINGS
PRATINGS
PRAYINGS
PRIMINGS
PROSINGS
PROVINGS
PRUNINGS
PUDDINGS
PUFFINGS
PUGGINGS
PUNNINGS
PURGINGS
PURLINGS
PURRINGS
PUTTINGS
PYONINGS
QUAKINGS
QUEUINGS

RACKINGS
RAGGINGS
RAILINGS
RAISINGS
RAMPINGS
RANKINGS
RANTINGS
RAPPINGS
RASPINGS
RATLINGS
RATTINGS
READINGS
REDDINGS
REDWINGS
REEDINGS
REEFINGS
REELINGS
RENNINGS
REPPINGS
RESTINGS
RIBBINGS
RIDGINGS
RIFLINGS
RIGGINGS
RIGLINGS
RIMMINGS
RINGINGS
RINSINGS
RIOTINGS
RISPINGS
ROADINGS
ROAMINGS
ROARINGS
ROCKINGS
RODDINGS
ROLFINGS
ROLLINGS
ROOFINGS
ROOTINGS
ROUMINGS
ROUTINGS
RUBBINGS
RUCHINGS
RUGGINGS
RUININGS
RUNNINGS
RUSTINGS
RUTTINGS
SACKINGS
SACRINGS
SAGGINGS
SAILINGS
SALTINGS
SALVINGS
SANDINGS
SAPLINGS
SARKINGS
SCALINGS
SCORINGS
SCRYINGS
SEALINGS
SEARINGS
SEATINGS
SEEDINGS
SEELINGS
SEEMINGS
SEININGS
SEIZINGS

SELFINGS
SENDINGS
SENSINGS
SERVINGS
SETTINGS
SHADINGS
SHAKINGS
SHAPINGS
SHARINGS
SHAVINGS
SHOEINGS
SHORINGS
SHOWINGS
SIBLINGS
SIFTINGS
SIGNINGS
SINDINGS
SINGINGS
SINKINGS
SITTINGS
SKATINGS
SKIVINGS
SLATINGS
SLICINGS
SLIDINGS
SLOWINGS
SMILINGS
SMOKINGS
SNARINGS
SNIPINGS
SNORINGS
SOAKINGS
SOARINGS
SOBBINGS
SOGGINGS
SOILINGS
SOOPINGS
SOPPINGS
SORNINGS
SORTINGS
SOSSINGS
SOTTINGS
SOUMINGS
SOURINGS
SOUSINGS
SPACINGS
SPILINGS
STAGINGS
STARINGS
STEWINGS
STONINGS
STOPINGS
STOVINGS
STOWINGS
SUBBINGS
SUBRINGS
SUCKINGS
SUGGINGS
SUITINGS
SUMMINGS
SURFINGS
SURGINGS
SWALINGS
SWAYINGS
SYNDINGS
TABLINGS
TACKINGS
TAGGINGS

TAILINGS
TALKINGS
TAMPINGS
TANKINGS
TANLINGS
TANNINGS
TAPPINGS
TARRINGS
TASKINGS
TASTINGS
TATTINGS
TEAMINGS
TEASINGS
TELLINGS
TENTINGS
TESTINGS
THAWINGS
TICKINGS
TIFFINGS
TILLINGS
TILTINGS
TINNINGS
TINTINGS
TIPPINGS
TITHINGS
TITLINGS
TOILINGS
TOLLINGS
TOOLINGS
TOPPINGS
TOSSINGS
TOTTINGS
TOURINGS
TOUSINGS
TRACINGS
TRADINGS
TUBBINGS
TUFTINGS
TUGGINGS
TUNNINGS
TURFINGS
TURNINGS
TUSKINGS
TUTTINGS
TWININGS
UNBEINGS
UNDOINGS
UNITINGS
UNSLINGS
UNTYINGS
UPBRINGS
UPGOINGS
UPSWINGS
VAMPINGS
VANNINGS
VARYINGS
VEERINGS
VEILINGS
VEININGS
VENTINGS
VERSINGS
VESTINGS
VIEWINGS
VOGUINGS
VOICINGS
VOIDINGS
WADDINGS
WAFTINGS
WAILINGS
WAITINGS
WALKINGS
WALLINGS
WANTINGS
WARDINGS
WARLINGS
WARMINGS
WARNINGS
WARPINGS
WASHINGS
WASTINGS
WAULINGS
WAWLINGS
WAXWINGS
WEARINGS
WEAVINGS
WEBBINGS
WEDDINGS
WEDGINGS
WEEDINGS
WEEPINGS
WELDINGS
WELLINGS
WESTINGS
WHALINGS
WHININGS
WHITINGS
WIGGINGS
WILDINGS
WINCINGS
WINDINGS
WINKINGS
WINNINGS
WISHINGS
WITLINGS
WITTINGS
WOLFINGS
WOLVINGS
WONNINGS
WORDINGS
WORKINGS
WRITINGS
YAWNINGS
YELLINGS
YELPINGS
YOWLINGS

WORDS ENDING IN -ISE

7-letter words -ISE

ABSCISE
ADONISE
AGONISE
ANODISE
ANYWISE
APPRISE
ARABISE
ATHEISE
ATOMISE
AZOTISE
BAPTISE
CHAMISE
CHEMISE
COALISE
COGNISE
CONCISE
COTTISE
CYANISE
DESPISE
DIARISE
DOCKISE
EBONISE
ECHOISE
EGOTISE
ELEGISE
EMPRISE
ENDWISE
FADAISE
GALLISE
GRECISE
HEROISE
ICONISE
IDOLISE
IRIDISE
IRONISE
ITEMISE
KYANISE
LAICISE
LAIRISE
LIONISE
MALAISE
MAPWISE
MORTISE
MYTHISE
OBELISE
OXIDISE
OZONISE
PARVISE
PECTISE
PENTISE
PEPTISE
POETISE
PRECISE
PREMISE
PREVISE
PROMISE
REALISE
REARISE
REPRISE
RIOTISE
SOUBISE
STYLISE
SUCCISE
SUNRISE
SUNWISE
SURMISE
TRENISE
UNITISE
UPRAISE
UTILISE

8-letter words -ISE

ALBITISE
ALKALISE
AMORTISE
ANNALISE
APHETISE
APHORISE
APPETISE
APPRAISE
ARCHAISE
ARCHWISE
ATHETISE
BANALISE
BENDWISE
BEPRAISE
BOTANISE
BRANDISE
CANALISE
CANONISE
CAPONISE
CHASTISE
CIVILISE
COLONISE
COMBWISE
COMPRISE
COVETISE
CRABWISE
CURARISE
CUTINISE
DEMONISE
DEPUTISE
DIGITISE
DIMERISE
DISGUISE
DISSEISE
DIVINISE
DROPWISE
DYNAMISE
EBIONISE
EDGEWISE
ELSEWISE
EMPERISE
ENERGISE
EQUALISE
ERGOTISE
ETERNISE
ETHERISE
ETHICISE
EULOGISE
EUPHUISE
EXERCISE
EXORCISE
FABULISE
FARADISE
FEMINISE
FINALISE
FLATWISE
FLUIDISE
FOCALISE
HEPATISE
HUMANISE
IDEALISE
IMMUNISE
INFAMISE
JUMBOISE
LEGALISE
LIKEWISE
LOCALISE
LOGICISE
LONGWISE
MACARISE
MADERISE
MARQUISE
MAUVAISE
MAXIMISE
MELODISE
MEMORISE
MESPRISE
MINIMISE
MISPRISE
MOBILISE
MONETISE
MOONRISE
MORALISE
MOTORISE
NASALISE
NEBULISE
NODALISE
NOMADISE
NOTARISE
NOVELISE
OPTIMISE
ORGANISE
OVERWISE
PAGANISE
PAIRWISE
PALEWISE
PAPALISE
PARADISE
PENALISE
POLARISE
POLEMISE
POLONISE
PORPOISE
PORTOISE
PRACTISE
PTYALISE
PYRITISE
QUANTISE
RACEMISE
READVISE
REGULISE
REREVISE
RESINISE
RIGIDISE
RINGWISE
RIVALISE
ROBOTISE
ROYALISE
RURALISE
SANITISE
SATIRISE
SIDEWISE
SIMILISE
SINICISE
SIRENISE
SOBERISE
SODOMISE
SOLARISE
SOLECISE
SOMEWISE
SORORISE
STEPWISE
SUBERISE
SUBITISE
SUCHWISE
SURPRISE
TEAMWISE
TELEVISE
TENTWISE
TETANISE
THEORISE
THUSWISE
TORTOISE
TOTALISE
TREATISE
TUTORISE
UNIONISE
UNPRAISE
URBANISE
VALORISE
VAPORISE
VELARISE
VITALISE
VOCALISE
VOWELISE
WOMANISE

WORDS ENDING IN -ISH

7-letter words -ISH

ABOLISH
ALUMISH
ANGUISH
BABYISH
BADDISH
BALDISH
BATFISH
BEAMISH
BEARISH
BEAUISH
BIGGISH
BLEMISH
BOARISH
BOBBISH
BOOKISH
BOORISH
BRINISH
BRUTISH
BUCKISH
BULLISH
BURNISH
CADDISH
CARLISH
CATFISH
CATTISH
CHERISH
CLAYISH
CODFISH
COLDISH
COLTISH
COOLISH
COWFISH
CUBBISH
CULTISH
CURRISH
DAMPISH
DANKISH
DARKISH
DERVISH
DIMMISH
DOGFISH
DOGGISH
DOLLISH
DOLTISH
DONNISH
DOVEISH
DRONISH
DULLISH
DUMPISH
DUNNISH
DUSKISH
EVANISH
FADDISH
FAIRISH
FALSISH
FASTISH
FATTISH
FENNISH
FILMISH
FINEISH
FLEMISH
FOGYISH
FOOLISH
FOPPISH
FULLISH
FURBISH
FURNISH
GAMPISH
GARFISH
GARNISH
GEMFISH
GIRLISH
GNOMISH
GOATISH
GOLDISH
GOODISH
GREYISH
GUARISH
GULLISH
HAGFISH
HAGGISH
HARDISH
HASHISH
HAWKISH
HELLISH
HIGHISH
HIPPISH
HOBBISH
HOGGISH
HORNISH
HOTTISH
HUFFISH
JEWFISH
JIGGISH
KERNISH
KNAVISH
LADYISH
LARGISH
LARKISH
LEFTISH
LOMPISH
LONGISH
LOUDISH
LOUTISH
LUBFISH
LUMPISH
LUSKISH
MAIDISH

MANNISH	MUMPISH	PETTISH	PUCKISH	ROINISH	SELFISH	SUNFISH	TUBFISH	WETTISH
MAWKISH	MURKISH	PIEDISH	PUGGISH	ROMPISH	SERFISH	SWINISH	VAMPISH	WHEYISH
MISSISH	NEBBISH	PIGGISH	PUPFISH	ROOKISH	SICKISH	TALLISH	VARNISH	WHITISH
MOBBISH	NICEISH	PINFISH	RAFFISH	ROYNISH	SLAVISH	TARNISH	VOGUISH	WHORISH
MONKISH	NOURISH	PINKISH	RAMMISH	RUBBISH	SLOWISH	TARTISH	WAGGISH	WILDISH
MOONISH	NUNNISH	PLANISH	RATTISH	RUMMISH	SNAKISH	TIGRISH	WAMPISH	WIMPISH
MOORISH	OGREISH	PLENISH	REDDISH	RUNTISH	SNOWISH	TITTISH	WANNISH	WOLFISH
MOREISH	OOFTISH	POORISH	REDFISH	RUTTISH	SOFTISH	TOFFISH	WARMISH	WOLVISH
MUDFISH	PARKISH	POPPISH	RELLISH	SADDISH	SOTTISH	TONNISH	WASPISH	WORDISH
MUFFISH	PECKISH	PRUDISH	RIGGISH	SALTISH	SOURISH	TOWNISH	WEARISH	YOBBISH
MUGGISH	PEEVISH	PUBLISH	ROGUISH	SAWFISH	STYLISH	TUBBISH	WENNISH	

8-letter words -ISH

ADMONISH	CHILDISH	DROLLISH	GLUMPISH	PLUMPISH	SCOMFISH	SPOOKISH	TINGLISH
ASTONISH	CHURLISH	DROOGISH	GOATFISH	POKERISH	SCUMFISH	SQUARISH	TOADFISH
BABELISH	CLANNISH	DRUMFISH	GOLDFISH	PRANKISH	SHARPISH	STABLISH	TOADYISH
BAITFISH	CLAPDISH	DWARFISH	GREENISH	PRIGGISH	SHEEPISH	STANDISH	TOLLDISH
BLACKISH	CLERKISH	EMPERISH	GRUFFISH	PROUDISH	SHORTISH	STARFISH	TOUGHISH
BLANDISH	CLIQUISH	ENRAVISH	IDIOTISH	PSEUDISH	SHREWISH	STARTISH	TOVARISH
BLIMPISH	CLODDISH	ESSAYISH	JINGOISH	PUPPYISH	SKIRMISH	STEEPISH	TRAMPISH
BLOCKISH	CLOWNISH	FAINTISH	KINGFISH	PURPLISH	SKITTISH	STIFFISH	TRICKISH
BLOKEISH	CLUBBISH	FEEBLISH	KNACKISH	QUALMISH	SLANGISH	STILTISH	UNMODISH
BLOWFISH	COALFISH	FEVERISH	LANGUISH	QUEERISH	SLIMMISH	STOUTISH	UNPOLISH
BLUEFISH	COARSISH	FIENDISH	LIGHTISH	QUIPPISH	SLOBBISH	SUMPHISH	VAGARISH
BLUNTISH	COMPLISH	FIFTYISH	LIVERISH	QUIRKISH	SLUGGISH	SURFFISH	VANQUISH
BOARFISH	CRAWFISH	FLATFISH	LUMPFISH	RIGHTISH	SLUTTISH	SWAINISH	VIGORISH
BOOBYISH	CRAYFISH	FLATTISH	MILKFISH	ROCKFISH	SMALLISH	SWEETISH	VIPERISH
BRACKISH	CROSSISH	FLIRTISH	MONKFISH	ROSEFISH	SMARTISH	SWELLISH	VIXENISH
BRAINISH	DANDYISH	FLOURISH	NANNYISH	ROUGHISH	SNAPPISH	SYLPHISH	WALLFISH
BRANDISH	DEALFISH	FOGEYISH	NOHOWISH	ROUNDISH	SNEAKISH	THICKISH	WATERISH
BRATTISH	DEMOLISH	FORTYISH	NOVELISH	ROWDYISH	SNOBBISH	THIEVISH	WEAKFISH
BRISKISH	DEVILISH	FRAILISH	NYMPHISH	SAILFISH	SNUBBISH	THINNISH	WOMANISH
BROADISH	DIMINISH	FREAKISH	OVERFISH	SAINTISH	SOLIDISH	TICKLISH	YOKELISH
BROGUISH	DOWDYISH	FRESHISH	PAGANISH	SALTFISH	SORRYISH	TIGERISH	YOUNGISH
BROWNISH	DRABBISH	FRUMPISH	PIPEFISH	SCAMPISH	SPARKISH	TIGHTISH	
CAMELISH	DRAFFISH	GHOULISH	PLAINISH	SCARFISH	SPOFFISH	TILEFISH	

WORDS ENDING IN -ISM

7-letter words -ISM

AMORISM	BROMISM	CRETISM	ENTRISM	FOODISM	LADYISM	ODYLISM	REALISM	TROPISM
ANIMISM	BRUXISM	CULTISM	EPICISM	GURUISM	LEFTISM	ONANISM	SELFISM	TSARISM
ASTEISM	CAMBISM	CZARISM	EROTISM	HEROISM	LEGGISM	ORALISM	SENSISM	TYCHISM
ATAVISM	CHARISM	DIORISM	ETACISM	HEURISM	LIONISM	PEONISM	SIZEISM	URANISM
ATHEISM	CHEMISM	DONNISM	FADDISM	HOBOISM	LOOKISM	PHAEISM	SOPHISM	UTOPISM
ATOMISM	CHORISM	DUALISM	FALSISM	IDOLISM	MAIDISM	PHOBISM	STATISM	WHOLISM
BABUISM	CLADISM	ECHOISM	FASCISM	IMAGISM	MYALISM	PHOTISM	TACHISM	YOBBISM
BAPTISM	COPYISM	EGOTISM	FIDEISM	ITACISM	MYTHISM	PIANISM	TACTISM	ZANYISM
BOGYISM	COSMISM	ELITISM	FOGYISM	KARAISM	NEURISM	PIETISM	TOURISM	

8-letter words -ISM

ACOSMISM	ATROPISM	CRONYISM	DYNAMISM	FAKIRISM	IDEALISM	MODALISM	OPTIMISM
ACROTISM	BABELISM	CULLYISM	EBIONISM	FAMILISM	IDIOTISM	MONADISM	ORGANISM
ACTINISM	BATHMISM	CYNICISM	EMBOLISM	FARADISM	INCIVISM	MORALISM	PACIFISM
ACTIVISM	BETACISM	DANDYISM	ENDEMISM	FATALISM	INTIMISM	NATIVISM	PAGANISM
ALARMISM	BOGEYISM	DEMONISM	ENTRYISM	FEMINISM	JINGOISM	NATURISM	PALUDISM
ALBINISM	BOOBYISM	DEVILISM	ERETHISM	FINALISM	LACONISM	NAVALISM	PAPALISM
ALGORISM	BOTULISM	DIMERISM	ERGOTISM	FOGEYISM	LEGALISM	NEGROISM	PARTYISM
ALIENISM	BULLYISM	DIOECISM	ESCAPISM	FUTURISM	LOCALISM	NEPOTISM	PELORISM
ALPINISM	CABALISM	DIRIGISM	ETHERISM	GIANTISM	LOGICISM	NIHILISM	PETALISM
ALTRUISM	CAFFEISM	DITHEISM	ETHICISM	GYPSYISM	LYRICISM	NIMBYISM	PEYOTISM
ANEURISM	CENTRISM	DONATISM	EUGENISM	HEDONISM	MACARISM	NOMADISM	PHALLISM
APHORISM	CHARTISM	DOWDYISM	EUMERISM	HELOTISM	MELANISM	NOVELISM	PHRENISM
APTERISM	CLASSISM	DRUDGISM	EUPHUISM	HOBBYISM	MERYCISM	OBEAHISM	PLUMBISM
ARCHAISM	CLIQUISM	DRUIDISM	EXORCISM	HUMANISM	METOPISM	OCKERISM	POLONISM
ASTERISM	CLUBBISM	DWARFISM	FAIRYISM	HYLICISM	MINIMISM	OPIUMISM	POPULISM

PRIAPISM PUGILISM ROYALISM SCRIBISM SOLIDISM THUGGISM TROILISM VIRILISM
PRIGGISM PUPPYISM RURALISM SEISMISM SOMATISM TIGERISM TUTORISM VITALISM
PROSAISM QUIETISM SAINTISM SIMPLISM STOICISM TITANISM ULTRAISM VOCALISM
PSELLISM RACEMISM SAPPHISM SINAPISM STRABISM TOADYISM UNDINISM VOLTAISM
PSEPHISM REGALISM SATANISM SNOBBISM SWINGISM TOKENISM UNIONISM ZOMBIISM
PSYCHISM RIGORISM SAVAGISM SOLARISM SYBOTISM TOTEMISM UNTRUISM
PTYALISM ROWDYISM SCIOLISM SOLECISM TERATISM TRIALISM VEGANISM

WORDS ENDING IN -IST

7-letter words -IST

ACQUIST CASUIST CULTIST ELEGIST FLORIST IMAGIST ONANIST REALIST TACHIST
AGONIST CELLIST CYCLIST ELITIST FLUTIST INTWIST PALMIST RHYMIST TOURIST
AMORIST CHEKIST CZARIST ELOGIST FUGUIST IRONIST PERSIST SACRIST TROPIST
ANGLIST CHEMIST DENTIST ENTRIST GAMBIST IVORIST PHOBIST SELFIST TSARIST
ANIMIST CHORIST DIALIST ENTWIST GNOMIST JUDOIST PIANIST SENSIST UNALIST
ATHEIST CHUTIST DIARIST EPICIST HARPIST LEFTIST PIARIST SIZEIST UNTWIST
ATOMIST CLADIST DIETIST EXODIST HERBIST MAPPIST PIETIST SOLOIST UPHOIST
ATTRIST COEXIST DUALIST FADDIST HORNIST METRIST PLENIST SOPHIST UTOPIST
BAPTIST CONSIST DUMAIST FASCIST HYLOIST MYTHIST PLUMIST STATIST VACUIST
BASSIST COPYIST EBONIST FAUNIST HYMNIST NAIVIST POLOIST STYLIST VIOLIST
BIBLIST CORNIST ECHOIST FEUDIST IAMBIST OCULIST PROTIST SUBSIST WHOLIST
CAMBIST COSMIST EGOTIST FIDEIST IDOLIST OLIGIST QUERIST SUMMIST

8-letter words -IST

ACOSMIST BOTANIST DRUGGIST FUTURIST LOYALIST NIELLIST REGALIST TANGOIST
ACTIVIST BURINIST DUELLIST GARAGIST LUMINIST NIHILIST REVERIST TENORIST
ALARMIST CABALIST DUETTIST GROUPIST LUNARIST NOVELIST RIGHTIST THEORIST
ALIENIST CALORIST DYNAMIST HANDLIST LUTANIST ODONTIST RIGORIST TOTEMIST
ALPINIST CANOEIST ENTRYIST HEDONIST LUTENIST OOLOGIST ROYALIST TRIADIST
ALTRUIST CANONIST ERRORIST HOBBYIST LUXURIST OPTIMIST RURALIST TRIALIST
ANNALIST CENTOIST ESCAPIST HOMILIST LYRICIST ORGANIST SAFARIST TROILIST
APHORIST CENTRIST ESSAYIST HUMANIST MAXIMIST PACIFIST SAPPHIST ULTRAIST
APIARIST CERAMIST ETHERIST HUMORIST MEDALIST PAPALIST SATIRIST UNIONIST
AQUARIST CHARTIST ETHICIST HYLICIST MELODIST PARODIST SCIOLIST UNSEXIST
ARBALIST CIVILIST EUGENIST HYPOCIST METALIST PEYOTIST SHOOTIST VISAGIST
ARBORIST CLASSIST EULOGIST IDEALIST MINIMIST POLEMIST SILURIST VITALIST
ARCANIST CLUBBIST EUPHUIST IDYLLIST MODALIST POPULIST SIMONIST VOCALIST
ARCHAIST COLONIST EXORCIST INTIMIST MONODIST PROSAIST SIMPLIST VOLUMIST
ARMORIST CONTRIST FABULIST JINGOIST MORALIST PSALMIST SOLARIST VOTARIST
ARSONIST CREOLIST FATALIST LEGALIST MOTORIST PSYCHIST SOLECIST
AVIARIST DEMONIST FEMINIST LINGUIST MURALIST PUCKFIST SOLIDIST
BACKLIST DEMOTIST FIGURIST LOBBYIST NATIVIST PUGILIST SOMATIST
BANJOIST DIGAMIST FINALIST LOCALIST NATURIST QUIETIST STOCKIST
BIGAMIST DITHEIST FLAUTIST LOGICIST NEPOTIST RALLYIST SUBTRIST

WORDS ENDING IN -LY

7-letter words -LY

ACUTELY AWFULLY BLUNTLY CAVALLY CRAZILY DOUCELY EQUABLY FLESHLY GALLFLY
ADEPTLY AXIALLY BONNILY CHARILY CRINKLY DOWDILY EQUALLY FOAMILY GAUDILY
AFFABLY BAGGILY BOOZILY CHEAPLY CRISPLY DREADLY ERECTLY FOCALLY GAUNTLY
AGILELY BAIRNLY BOSSILY CHEERLY CROSSLY DRIBBLY EXACTLY FOGGILY GELIDLY
ALERTLY BALMILY BRAMBLY CHIEFLY CRUDELY DRIZZLY FADEDLY FRAILLY GHASTLY
ALONELY BANALLY BRAVELY CHILDLY CRUELLY DROPFLY FAINTLY FRANKLY GHOSTLY
ALOOFLY BAWDILY BRIEFLY CIVILLY CRUMBLY DUCALLY FAIRILY FRECKLY GIANTLY
AMIABLY BEAMILY BRISKLY CLEANLY DANDILY DUOPOLY FALSELY FRESHLY GIDDILY
ANGERLY BEASTLY BRISTLY CLEARLY DAZEDLY DURABLY FATALLY FRIARLY GODLILY
ANGRILY BLACKLY BRITTLY CLERKLY DEARNLY DUSKILY FIERILY FRITFLY GOOFILY
ANOMALY BLANDLY BROADLY CLOSELY DEATHLY DUSTILY FIFTHLY FRIZZLY GOUTFLY
APETALY BLANKLY BUIRDLY COCKILY DEEDILY DYINGLY FINALLY FUGALLY GRADELY
APHYLLY BLEAKLY BULKILY CORNFLY DENSELY EAGERLY FIREFLY FUNNILY GRANDLY
APISHLY BLINDLY BUMPILY COURTLY DIRTILY EARTHLY FIRSTLY FUSSILY GRAVELY
AUDIBLY BLOWFLY CANNILY CRACKLY DISALLY ELDERLY FIXEDLY FUSTILY GRAYFLY
AURALLY BLUFFLY CATTILY CRASSLY DIZZILY EMPTILY FLEETLY FUZZILY GREATLY

GREENLY
GREISLY
GRIESLY
GRIMILY
GRISELY
GRISTLY
GRIZZLY
GROSSLY
GRUFFLY
GRUMBLY
GRYESLY
GRYSELY
GYRALLY
HAMMILY
HANDILY
HAPPILY
HARDILY
HARSHLY
HARTELY
HASTILY
HAZELLY
HEADILY
HEARTLY
HEAVILY
HEFTILY
HOARILY
HUFFILY
HUMANLY
HUMIDLY
HUSKILY
IDEALLY
IGNOBLY
INANELY
INAPTLY
INEPTLY

INERTLY
INJELLY
IRATELY
JADEDLY
JAZZILY
JOINTLY
JOLLILY
JUMPILY
JURALLY
KNOBBLY
KNUBBLY
KNUCKLY
LADYFLY
LANKILY
LARGELY
LEGALLY
LEGIBLY
LICHTLY
LICITLY
LIGHTLY
LITHELY
LIVIDLY
LOATHLY
LOCALLY
LOFTILY
LOOBILY
LOOSELY
LOUSILY
LOVERLY
LOWLILY
LOYALLY
LUCIDLY
LUCKILY
LUMPILY
LURIDLY

LUSTILY
LYINGLY
MASCULY
MEATILY
MERRILY
MESALLY
MESSILY
METALLY
MIFFILY
MILKILY
MISALLY
MISERLY
MISTILY
MIXEDLY
MODALLY
MOISTLY
MONTHLY
MOODILY
MORALLY
MOVABLY
MUDDILY
MURKILY
MUSHILY
MUSKILY
MUSTILY
MUTABLY
MUZZILY
NAIVELY
NAKEDLY
NARGILY
NASALLY
NASTILY
NATTILY
NEEDILY
NERVILY

NIFTILY
NIGHTLY
NINTHLY
NIPPILY
NOBBILY
NODALLY
NOISILY
NOTABLY
NOTEDLY
NUTTILY
NYMPHLY
ORDERLY
OVERFLY
OVERPLY
OVERTLY
PANOPLY
PAPALLY
PAWKILY
PEARTLY
PENALLY
PERKILY
PESKILY
PETTILY
PIOUSLY
PITHILY
PLAINLY
PLIABLY
PLUMPLY
PRICKLY
PRIMELY
PRIVILY
PRONELY
PROSILY
PROUDLY
PUFFILY

PULPILY
QUEENLY
QUEERLY
QUICKLY
QUIETLY
RABIDLY
RAPIDLY
RATABLY
READILY
REAPPLY
REGALLY
RIGHTLY
RIGIDLY
RISKILY
ROCKILY
ROOMILY
ROUGHLY
ROUNDLY
ROWDILY
ROYALLY
RUDDILY
RUMMILY
RURALLY
RUSTILY
SAINTLY
SALABLY
SALTILY
SANDFLY
SAUCILY
SCANTLY
SCRAWLY
SEEDILY
SHADILY
SHAKILY
SHAMBLY

SHAPELY
SHARPLY
SHEERLY
SHINGLY
SHOGGLY
SHOOFLY
SHOOGLY
SHORTLY
SHOWILY
SHRILLY
SIGHTLY
SILKILY
SILLILY
SIXTHLY
SLACKLY
SLANTLY
SLEEKLY
SLICKLY
SLIMILY
SMARTLY
SMICKLY
SMOKILY
SNAKILY
SNIDELY
SNOWILY
SNUFFLY
SOAPILY
SOBERLY
SOGGILY
SOLIDLY
SOOTHLY
SOOTILY
SOPPILY
SORRILY
SOUNDLY

SPANGLY
SPARELY
SPARKLY
SPICILY
SPIKILY
SPINDLY
SPRAWLY
SQUALLY
STAGILY
STAIDLY
STALELY
STARKLY
STARTLY
STATELY
STEEPLY
STERNLY
STIFFLY
STONILY
STOUTLY
STUBBLY
STUMBLY
SUAVELY
SULKILY
SUNNILY
SURLILY
SWEETLY
SWIFTLY
TACITLY
TACKILY
TARDILY
TASTILY
TATTILY
TAXABLY
TECHILY
TENSELY

TENTHLY
TEPIDLY
TERSELY
TESTILY
THICKLY
THIRDLY
THISTLY
THRILLY
TIGERLY
TIGHTLY
TIMIDLY
TIPSILY
TIREDLY
TONALLY
TOSSILY
TOTALLY
TOUGHLY
TREACLY
TREMBLY
TRICKLY
TRIFOLY
TRITELY
TUMIDLY
TUNABLY
TWADDLY
TWIDDLY
UNAPTLY
UNFITLY
UNGODLY
UNMANLY
UNTRULY
USUALLY
UTTERLY
VAGUELY
VALIDLY

VAPIDLY
VENALLY
VERMILY
VEXEDLY
VISIBLY
VITALLY
VIVIDLY
VIXENLY
VOCALLY
VOLUBLY
VOWELLY
VYINGLY
WEARILY
WEEVILY
WEIRDLY
WHITELY
WIGHTLY
WINDILY
WITTILY
WOFULLY
WOMANLY
WOOZILY
WORDILY
WORLDLY
WRIGGLY
WRINKLY
WRONGLY
YOUNGLY
YOUTHLY

8-letter words -LY

ABJECTLY
ABRUPTLY
ABSENTLY
ABSURDLY
ACHINGLY
ACTIVELY
ACTUALLY
ADORABLY
ADROITLY
AERIALLY
AGUISHLY
AMAZEDLY
AMENABLY
AMICABLY
AMUSEDLY
ANIMALLY
ANNUALLY
APICALLY
ARCANELY
ARDENTLY
ARGUABLY
ARGUTELY
ARRANTLY
ARTFULLY
ASSEMBLY
ASTUTELY
AUGUSTLY
AVERSELY
AVOWEDLY
BADGERLY
BANKERLY
BEARABLY

BEASTILY
BEGGARLY
BEHOVELY
BENIGNLY
BESEEMLY
BITCHILY
BITTERLY
BLAMABLY
BLITHELY
BLOODILY
BORINGLY
BOUNCILY
BOVINELY
BOYISHLY
BRASSILY
BRAZENLY
BREEZILY
BRIGHTLY
BROKENLY
BRUTALLY
CANDIDLY
CARNALLY
CASUALLY
CATCHFLY
CAUSALLY
CHASTELY
CHEEKILY
CHEERILY
CHILLILY
CHIRPILY
CHOICELY
CHORALLY

CHURCHLY
CLAMMILY
CLEVERLY
CLONALLY
CLOUDILY
CLUMSILY
COARSELY
COGENTLY
COMMONLY
CONVEXLY
COOINGLY
COUSINLY
COVERTLY
COWARDLY
CRABBILY
CRAFTILY
CRANEFLY
CRANKILY
CRAVENLY
CREAKILY
CREDIBLY
CROAKILY
CROUSELY
CRUSTILY
CULPABLY
CURSEDLY
DAINTILY
DAMNABLY
DAPPERLY
DARINGLY
DECENTLY
DEMISSLY

DEMURELY
DENIABLY
DEUCEDLY
DEVOUTLY
DIRECTLY
DISAPPLY
DISMALLY
DISTALLY
DIVERSLY
DIVINELY
DOCTORLY
DOGGEDLY
DOOLALLY
DORSALLY
DOTINGLY
DREAMILY
DREARILY
DROOPILY
DROWSILY
EASTERLY
EFFETELY
EIGHTHLY
ELATEDLY
ELIGIBLY
ENTIRELY
ENVIABLY
EPICALLY
ERRANTLY
ERRINGLY
EVANGELY
EXPERTLY
FACIALLY

FACILELY
FALLIBLY
FAMOUSLY
FATHERLY
FAULTILY
FEASIBLY
FELLOWLY
FERVIDLY
FESTALLY
FEUDALLY
FIERCELY
FILIALLY
FILTHILY
FINITELY
FISCALLY
FITFULLY
FLABBILY
FLASHILY
FLEXIBLY
FLIMSILY
FLINTILY
FLOPPILY
FLORALLY
FLORIDLY
FLUENTLY
FORCEDLY
FORCIBLY
FORKEDLY
FORMALLY
FORMERLY
FOURTHLY
FRIENDLY

FRIGIDLY
FRISKILY
FROSTILY
FROTHILY
FRUGALLY
FUTILELY
GAPINGLY
GARISHLY
GENIALLY
GIBINGLY
GIFTEDLY
GINGELLY
GINGERLY
GLASSILY
GLITZILY
GLOBALLY
GLOOMILY
GLOSSILY
GOLDENLY
GRAITHLY
GRAVELLY
GREASILY
GREEDILY
GREENFLY
GRUMPILY
GUILTILY
HEARTILY
HEAVENLY
HECTORLY
HEROICLY
HIDDENLY
HITCHILY

HOARSELY
HOLLOWLY
HOMELILY
HONESTLY
HOPINGLY
HORRIBLY
HORRIDLY
HORSEFLY
HOUSEFLY
HUMANELY
HUNGERLY
HUNGRILY
IMMANELY
IMPISHLY
IMPURELY
INFIRMLY
INNATELY
INSANELY
INTENTLY
INWARDLY
IREFULLY
ISSUABLY
JAGGEDLY
JAUNTILY
JEJUNELY
JOCOSELY
JOCUNDLY
JOKINGLY
JOVIALLY
JOYFULLY
JOYOUSLY
KERNELLY

KINDLILY
KNIGHTLY
LABIALLY
LATENTLY
LATTERLY
LAUDABLY
LAVISHLY
LAWFULLY
LAWYERLY
LEADENLY
LETHALLY
LIMPIDLY
LINEALLY
LINEARLY
LIQUIDLY
LISSOMLY
LITHERLY
LIVELILY
LOBLOLLY
LOSINGLY
LOUCHELY
LOVELILY
LOVINGLY
LUBBERLY
LUMBERLY
LUMPENLY
MAIDENLY
MALIGNLY
MANFULLY
MANNERLY
MANUALLY
MARKEDLY

MASTERLY
MATRONLY
MATURELY
MEAGRELY
MEDIALLY
MELLOWLY
MENTALLY
MESIALLY
MIGHTILY
MINUTELY
MISAPPLY
MODERNLY
MODESTLY
MODISHLY
MOLTENLY
MOMENTLY
MONOPOLY
MOPINGLY
MOPISHLY
MORBIDLY
MOROSELY
MORTALLY
MOTHERLY
MOVEABLY
MOVINGLY
MULISHLY
MULTIPLY
MUSINGLY
MUTUALLY
NARGHILY
NARGILLY
NARROWLY
NATIVELY
NEURALLY
NEWISHLY
NOCENTLY
NORMALLY
OBTUSELY
OCCULTLY
OCULARLY
ODIOUSLY
ONWARDLY
OPAQUELY
ORNATELY
PALLIDLY
PALPABLY
PALTRILY
PANDERLY
PASSABLY
PASSIBLY
PASTORLY
PATCHILY
PATENTLY
PEDATELY
PETTEDLY
PITIABLY
PLACABLY
PLACIDLY
PLAGUILY
PLIANTLY
PLUCKILY
PLURALLY
POLITELY
POPISHLY
PORTERLY
POSINGLY
POSSIBLY
POSTALLY
POTENTLY
PREPPILY
PRETTILY
PRIESTLY
PRIMALLY
PRINCELY
PROBABLY
PROLIXLY
PROMPTLY
PROPERLY
PROVABLY
PRYINGLY
PUBLICLY
PULINGLY
PUTRIDLY
QUAINTLY
QUEASILY
QUIRKILY
QUOTABLY
RACIALLY
RADIALLY
RAGGEDLY
RAGINGLY
RAKISHLY
RANDOMLY
RASCALLY
RATEABLY
RAVINGLY
READABLY
RECENTLY
RECTALLY
REDBELLY
REFLEXLY
RELIABLY
REMISSLY
REMOTELY
RETRALLY
RITUALLY
ROBUSTLY
ROOTEDLY
ROTTENLY
ROTUNDLY
ROVINGLY
RUEFULLY
RUGGEDLY
RUGOSELY
SACREDLY
SAILORLY
SALEABLY
SAVAGELY
SAVINGLY
SAVOURLY
SCANTILY
SCARCELY
SCRAGGLY
SCRIBBLY
SCRIGGLY
SCRIMPLY
SCURVILY
SEAMANLY
SECANTLY
SECONDLY
SECRETLY
SECURELY
SEDATELY
SENILELY
SENSIBLY
SERENELY
SERIALLY
SEVERELY
SEXUALLY
SHABBILY
SHAGGILY
SHAUCHLY
SHIFTILY
SHIRTILY
SHODDILY
SHREWDLY
SICKERLY
SICKLILY
SIGNALLY
SILENTLY
SILVERLY
SINFULLY
SISTERLY
SKIMPILY
SLANGILY
SLEAZILY
SLEEPILY
SLIGHTLY
SLOPPILY
SLOVENLY
SMALMILY
SMARMILY
SMEARILY
SMOOTHLY
SMUDGILY
SMUTTILY
SNAPPILY
SNEAKILY
SNIFFILY
SNIVELLY
SNOOTILY
SNOTTILY
SOCIABLY
SOCIALLY
SOLEMNLY
SOMBRELY
SORDIDLY
SOUTERLY
SOVRANLY
SPARSELY
SPEEDILY
SPIRALLY
SPONGILY
SPOOKILY
SPOONILY
SPORTILY
SPOTTILY
SPRITELY
SPRUCELY
SQUARELY
SQUIGGLY
SQUIRELY
STARRILY
STATEDLY
STEADILY
STEAMILY
STEEVELY
STICKILY
STIEVELY
STINGILY
STOCKILY
STODGILY
STOLIDLY
STONEFLY
STORMILY
STRAGGLY
STRAITLY
STRICTLY
STRONGLY
STUFFILY
STUMPILY
STUPIDLY
STURDILY
SUDDENLY
SUITABLY
SULLENLY
SULTRILY
SUMMERLY
SUPERBLY
SUPINELY
SUPPLELY
SYMPHILY
TAKINGLY
TANGIBLY
TARNALLY
TARTARLY
TASSELLY
TAWDRILY
TENDERLY
TERRIBLY
TETCHILY
THWARTLY
TIMOUSLY
TINSELLY
TONISHLY
TOOTHILY
TORPIDLY
TORRIDLY
TOUCHILY
TOWARDLY
TOYISHLY
TRASHILY
TRENDILY
TREVALLY
TRIBALLY
TRICKILY
TRUSTILY
TRYINGLY
TUNBELLY
TURBIDLY
TURGIDLY
UNCOMELY
UNCOSTLY
UNEASILY
UNEVENLY
UNFAIRLY
UNGAINLY
UNGENTLY
UNHOLILY
UNHOMELY
UNIQUELY
UNITEDLY
UNJUSTLY
UNKINDLY
UNKINGLY
UNLIKELY
UNLIVELY
UNLORDLY
UNLOVELY
UNMEETLY
UNREALLY
UNSAFELY
UNSEEMLY
UNTIDILY
UNTIMELY
UNUSABLY
UNWARELY
UNWARILY
UNWIFELY
UNWISELY
UPPISHLY
UPWARDLY
URBANELY
URGENTLY
USEFULLY
UVULARLY
VACANTLY
VALUABLY
VARIABLY
VARIEDLY
VENDIBLY
VENIALLY
VERBALLY
VERNALLY
VEXINGLY
VIOLABLY
VIRGINLY
VISUALLY
VULGARLY
WANTONLY
WEASELLY
WEEVILLY
WESTERLY
WHEEZILY
WHIMSILY
WHITEFLY
WICKEDLY
WILFULLY
WINGEDLY
WINTERLY
WITTOLLY
WIZARDLY
WOEFULLY
WOODENLY
WOOINGLY
WORTHILY
WOUNDILY
WRATHILY
WRITERLY
YEOMANLY
YONDERLY
YONGTHLY
ZOOPHILY

WORDS ENDING IN -MAN

7-letter words -MAN

ARTSMAN
BASEMAN
BATSMAN
BEADMAN
BEDEMAN
BELLMAN
BELTMAN
BILLMAN
BIRDMAN
BOATMAN
BONDMAN
BOOKMAN
BUSHMAN
BYREMAN
CASEMAN
CAVEMAN
CHAPMAN
CLUBMAN
COALMAN
DAYSMAN
DECUMAN
DRAYMAN
DUSTMAN
FACEMAN
FIREMAN
FOOTMAN
FOREMAN
FREEMAN
FROGMAN
GADSMAN
GATEMAN
GLEEMAN
GOODMAN
GOWNMAN
GUDEMAN
HANGMAN
HANUMAN
HEADMAN
HELIMAN
HERDMAN
HIGHMAN
HOODMAN
HOSEMAN
INHUMAN
ISLEMAN
JACKMAN
JARKMAN
JAZZMAN
JUNKMAN
JURYMAN
KEELMAN
KINSMAN
LANDMAN
LENSMAN
LINEMAN
LINKMAN
LOCKMAN
LOCOMAN
MAGSMAN
MAILMAN
MALTMAN
MARKMAN
MASHMAN
MILKMAN
MOBSMAN
MOORMAN
MOOTMAN
NEWSMAN
OARSMAN
ODDSMAN
OTTOMAN
OVERMAN
PACKMAN
PASSMAN
PEATMAN
PIKEMAN
POLLMAN
PORTMAN
POSTMAN
RAFTMAN
RAILMAN
REELMAN
REPOMAN
RINGMAN
ROADMAN
RODSMAN
SAGAMAN
SANDMAN
SHIPMAN
SHOPMAN
SHOWMAN
SIDEMAN
SNOWMAN
SOKEMAN
SONGMAN
SPAEMAN
SURFMAN
SWAGMAN
TAPSMAN
TAXIMAN
TOLLMAN
TOOLMAN
TOPSMAN
TRUEMAN
TURFMAN
UNHUMAN
UNWOMAN
WAKEMAN
WIREMAN
WOODMAN
WOOLMAN
WORKMAN
YARDMAN
YEGGMAN

8-letter words -MAN

AIRWOMAN
ALDERMAN
BAILSMAN
BANDSMAN
BANDYMAN
BANKSMAN
BARGEMAN
BATWOMAN
BEADSMAN
BEDESMAN
BONDSMAN
BOTHYMAN
BRAKEMAN
BRIDEMAN
BRINKMAN
BUTTYMAN
CHAINMAN
CHAIRMAN
CHESSMAN
CHOIRMAN
CLANSMAN
CLASSMAN
COACHMAN
CRAGSMAN
DAIRYMAN
DALESMAN
DOOMSMAN
DOORSMAN
DRAGOMAN
DRAGSMAN
EARTHMAN
EVERYMAN
FERRYMAN
FORGEMAN
FREEDMAN
FRESHMAN
FRONTMAN
FUGLEMAN
GANGSMAN
GAVELMAN
GLASSMAN
GOADSMAN
GOWNSMAN
HANDYMAN
HEADSMAN
HELMSMAN
HENCHMAN
HERDSMAN
HIELAMAN
HOASTMAN
HOISTMAN
HORSEMAN
HOUSEMAN
HUNTSMAN
ISLESMAN
LANDSMAN

LAYWOMAN LEADSMAN LIEGEMAN LINESMAN LOCKSMAN LODESMAN MADWOMAN MARCHMAN MARKSMAN MERESMAN MERRYMAN
MONEYMAN MOTORMAN NOBLEMAN OVERSMAN PENWOMAN PETERMAN PILOTMAN PITCHMAN PLACEMAN PLAIDMAN PLATEMAN
PREHUMAN PRESSMAN PRIZEMAN PROSEMAN PUNTSMAN QUILLMAN RAFTSMAN RAMPSMAN RANCHMAN REINSMAN RIFLEMAN
RIVERMAN ROADSMAN ROUTEMAN SALESMAN SCENEMAN SEAWOMAN SEEDSMAN SHAREMAN SHEARMAN SHIREMAN SHOREMAN
SIDESMAN SOUNDMAN SPACEMAN SPADEMAN SPEARMAN SQUAWMAN STALLMAN STEELMAN STOCKMAN STOREMAN STUNTMAN
SUBHUMAN SUPERMAN SWAGSMAN SWORDMAN TACKSMAN TALESMAN TALISMAN TALLYMAN TIDESMAN TOWNSMAN TOYWOMAN
TRACKMAN TRASHMAN TREWSMAN TRIPEMAN TRUCHMAN TRUCKMAN UNDERMAN WATCHMAN WATERMAN WEALSMAN WHALEMAN
WHEELMAN WIDOWMAN WINCHMAN WOODSMAN YARRAMAN

WORDS ENDING IN -MEN

7-letter words -MEN

ABDOMEN AGNOMEN ALBUMEN ARTSMEN BASEMEN BATSMEN BEADMEN BEDEMEN BELLMEN BELTMEN BILLMEN BIRDMEN BITUMEN BOATMEN
BONDMEN BOOKMEN BUSHMEN BYREMEN CASEMEN CAVEMEN CERUMEN CHAPMEN CLUBMEN COALMEN DAYSMEN DRAYMEN DURAMEN DUSTMEN
FACEMEN FIREMEN FOOTMEN FORAMEN FOREMEN FREEMEN FROGMEN GADSMEN GATEMEN GLEEMEN GOODMEN GOWNMEN GUDEMEN HANGMEN
HEADMEN HELIMEN HERDMEN HIGHMEN HILLMEN HOODMEN HOSEMEN ISLEMEN JACKMEN JARKMEN JAZZMEN JUNKMEN JURYMEN KEELMEN
KINSMEN LANDMEN LENSMEN LINEMEN LINKMEN LOCKMEN LOCOMEN MAGSMEN MAILMEN MALTMEN MARKMEN MASHMEN MILKMEN MOBSMEN
MOLIMEN MOORMEN MOOTMEN NEWSMEN OARSMEN ODDSMEN OVERMEN PACKMEN PASSMEN PEATMEN PIKEMEN POLLMEN PORTMEN POSTMEN
PUTAMEN RAFTMEN RAILMEN REELMEN REGIMEN REPOMEN RINGMEN ROADMEN RODSMEN SAGAMEN SANDMEN SHIPMEN SHOPMEN SHOWMEN
SIDEMEN SNOWMEN SOKEMEN SONGMEN SPAEMEN SUDAMEN SURFMEN SWAGMEN TAPSMEN TAXIMEN TOLLMEN TOOLMEN TOPSMEN TRUEMEN
TURFMEN VELAMEN WAKEMEN WIREMEN WOODMEN WOOLMEN WORKMEN YARDMEN YEGGMEN

8-letter words -MEN

AIRWOMEN ALDERMEN BAILSMEN BANDSMEN BANDYMEN BANKSMEN BARGEMEN BATWOMEN BEADSMEN BEDESMEN BONDSMEN BOTHYMEN BRAKEMEN BRIDEMEN BRINKMEN BUTTYMEN CHAINMEN CHAIRMEN
CHESSMEN CHOIRMEN CLANSMEN CLASSMEN CLINAMEN COACHMEN COGNOMEN CRAGSMEN CYCLAMEN DAIRYMEN DALESMEN DOOMSMEN DOORSMEN DRAGSMEN EARTHMEN EVERYMEN FERRYMEN FORGEMEN
FREEDMEN FRESHMEN FRONTMEN FUGLEMEN GANGSMEN GAVELMEN GLASSMEN GOADSMEN GOWNSMEN GRAVAMEN HANDYMEN HEADSMEN HELMSMEN HENCHMEN HERDSMEN HOASTMEN HOISTMEN HORSEMEN
HOUSEMEN HUNTSMEN ISLESMEN LANDSMEN LAYWOMEN LEADSMEN LIEGEMEN LINESMEN LOCKSMEN LODESMEN MADWOMEN MARCHMEN MARKSMEN MERESMEN MERRYMEN MONEYMEN MOTORMEN NOBLEMEN
OVERSMEN PENWOMEN PETERMEN PILOTMEN PITCHMEN PLACEMEN PLAIDMEN PLATEMEN PRESSMEN PRIZEMEN PROSEMEN PUNTSMEN QUILLMEN RAFTSMEN RAMPSMEN RANCHMEN REINSMEN RIFLEMEN
RIVERMEN ROADSMEN ROUTEMEN SALESMEN SCENEMEN SEAWOMEN SEEDSMEN SHAREMEN SHEARMEN SHIREMEN SHOREMEN SIDESMEN SOUNDMEN SPACEMEN SPADEMEN SPEARMEN SPECIMEN SQUAWMEN
STALLMEN STEELMEN STOCKMEN STOREMEN STUNTMEN SUPERMEN SWAGSMEN SWORDMEN TACKSMEN TALESMEN TALLYMEN TIDESMEN TOWNSMEN TOYWOMEN TRACKMEN TRASHMEN TREWSMEN TRIPEMEN
TRUCHMEN TRUCKMEN UNDERMEN WATCHMEN WATERMEN WEALSMEN WHALEMEN WHEELMEN WIDOWMEN WINCHMEN WOODSMEN

WORDS ENDING IN -OID

7-letter words -OID

ACAROID ADENOID AGAMOID AMBROID AMYLOID ANDROID ANEROID ANTHOID ARCTOID ASTROID
BYSSOID CESTOID CHELOID CHOROID CIRSOID CISSOID COCCOID COLLOID COTTOID CRICOID
CRINOID CTENOID CYCLOID CYSTOID DELTOID DENTOID DERMOID DESMOID DIPLOID DISCOID
ERICOID ETHMOID FACTOID FIBROID FUNGOID GLENOID GLOBOID GOBIOID HAPLOID HELCOID
HISTOID HYALOID HYDROID HYPNOID LABROID LENTOID LIANOID LITHOID MASTOID MATTOID
MUSCOID MYELOID NAEVOID NEGROID OBOVOID OCELOID OCHROID OSTEOID PERCOID PHACOID
PIGMOID PLACOID PYGMOID QUINOID RHIZOID SARCOID SAUROID SIALOID SIGMOID SPAROID
SPIROID STEROID STYLOID TABLOID TENIOID THEROID THYROID TIGROID TURDOID TYPHOID
VESPOID XIPHOID ZEBROID ZINCOID

8-letter words -OID

ACTINOID CANCROID ECHINOID HYRACOID PARANOID RESINOID SOLENOID THYREOID
ALKALOID CARDIOID EMBRYOID KERATOID PETALOID RETINOID SORICOID THYRSOID
AMBEROID CENTROID EMULSOID LAMBDOID PEZIZOID RHABDOID SPHENOID TRICHOID
AMMONOID CERATOID ERGATOID LEMUROID PHALLOID RHOMBOID SPHEROID TRIPLOID
AMOEBOID CHORIOID GABBROID LIGULOID PHELLOID SCAPHOID SPONGOID TROCHOID
ARILLOID CICHLOID GALENOID LYMPHOID PHYLLOID SCHIZOID SQUALOID VOLUTOID
ASTEROID CLUPEOID GEOMYOID MEDUSOID PINACOID SCINCOID STURNOID YPSILOID
ATHETOID CONCHOID HELICOID MYTILOID PINAKOID SCIUROID TAENIOID
AUTACOID CORACOID HISTIOID NEMATOID PITYROID SCLEROID TAPIROID
BLASTOID CORONOID HOMALOID NEPHROID POLYPOID SEPALOID TARSIOID
BOTRYOID COTYLOID HOMINOID ODONTOID PRISMOID SESAMOID TERATOID
CALYCOID DENDROID HUMANOID OMOHYOID PSYCHOID SILUROID TETANOID
CAMELOID DORIDOID HYDATOID ONISCOID PYRENOID SINUSOID THALLOID

WORDS ENDING IN -OR

7-letter words -OR

ABACTOR BIOPHOR DILATOR EVERTOR LANGUOR OFFEROR QUITTOR SIGNIOR VENATOR
ABETTOR CAMPHOR DILUTOR EVICTOR LAXATOR OUTDOOR REACTOR SIMILOR VISITOR
ABLATOR CHADDOR DIVISOR EXACTOR LEGATOR PANDOOR REALTOR SPONSOR WARRIOR
ADAPTOR CHANTOR DONATOR EXCITOR LEVATOR PARADOR RELATOR SQUALOR ZELATOR
ADVISOR CHIKHOR EDUCTOR FEOFFOR MACHZOR PARITOR REVISOR STENTOR
AERATOR CLANGOR EJECTOR GENITOR MAORMOR PICADOR REVIVOR STRIDOR
AGISTOR CREATOR ELECTOR GRANTOR MARKHOR PLEDGOR ROTATOR TANDOOR
ALIENOR CURATOR EMPEROR HERITOR MATADOR PLESSOR SCISSOR TEMBLOR
ATHANOR DEBITOR EMULSOR HUMIDOR MIRADOR PRAETOR SENATOR TRACTOR
AUDITOR DECOLOR ENACTOR INCISOR MONITOR PRESSOR SEPTUOR TRAITOR
AVIATOR DELATOR EQUATOR ISOCHOR MORMAOR PROCTOR SETTLOR TWISTOR
BELABOR DEVISOR ERECTOR JANITOR OBLIGOR QUESTOR SEXTUOR UNVISOR

8-letter words -OR

ABDUCTOR BEHAVIOR DETECTOR EXPIATOR ISOLATOR PREDATOR REMITTOR TRADITOR
ACCENTOR BISECTOR DEVIATOR EXTENSOR KURVEYOR PRODITOR RESISTOR TRAPDOOR
ACCEPTOR CANEPHOR DICTATOR EXTERIOR LICENSOR PROMISOR RONCADOR TRICOLOR
ACTUATOR CHELATOR DIRECTOR GILLYVOR MAINDOOR PROMOTOR SCULPTOR ULTERIOR
ADDUCTOR COFACTOR DISCOLOR GOVERNOR MANDATOR PRONATOR SECTATOR UNANCHOR
ADJUSTOR COLLATOR DISFAVOR HELIODOR MEDIATOR PROVEDOR SEDUCTOR UNICOLOR
ADULATOR CONCOLOR DISHONOR IMITATOR METAPHOR PROVIDOR SEIGNIOR URINATOR
AGITATOR CONJUROR EDUCATOR IMPOSTOR MIGRATOR PROVISOR SELECTOR VALUATOR
ANCESTOR CONVENOR EFFECTOR INCENSOR MISCOLOR PULSATOR SERVITOR VARACTOR
ANIMATOR CONVEYOR ELEVATOR INCEPTOR NARRATOR PUNDONOR SPLENDOR VARISTOR
ANTERIOR CORRIDOR ELICITOR INDUCTOR NEIGHBOR PURVEYOR STRESSOR VERDEROR
ARRESTOR CREDITOR EMBRASOR INFECTOR NONJUROR QUAESTOR SUBFLOOR VIBRATOR
ASSENTOR CREMATOR EMULATOR INFERIOR OBJECTOR RADIATOR SUBPRIOR VIOLATOR
ASSERTOR CURSITOR ENDEAVOR INFLATOR OCCLUSOR RECAPTOR SUPERIOR VITIATOR
ASSESSOR CUSPIDOR EPILATOR INJECTOR OPERATOR RECEPTOR SURVEYOR WHEREFOR
ASSIGNOR DEFECTOR EVOCATOR INTERIOR PATENTOR REDACTOR SURVIVOR
ATTESTOR DEFLATOR EXCEPTOR INVENTOR PHOSPHOR REGRATOR TESTATOR
BACHELOR DEMEANOR EXECUTOR INVERTOR PISCATOR REJECTOR THEREFOR
BARRATOR DEPICTOR EXPANDOR INVESTOR PLEDGEOR RELEASOR TOREADOR

WORDS ENDING IN -OUS

7-letter words -OUS

ACAJOUS ANXIOUS BADIOUS CASEOUS CUPROUS FEATOUS GIBBOUS HYDROUS NACROUS
ACEROUS APODOUS BILIOUS CEREOUS CURIOUS FERROUS GLEBOUS IGNEOUS NERVOUS
ACETOUS AQUEOUS BIVIOUS CHYMOUS DEVIOUS FIBROUS GLOBOUS IMPIOUS NIMIOUS
ACINOUS ARDUOUS BRUMOUS CIRROUS DUBIOUS FULVOUS GRUMOUS INVIOUS NIOBOUS
AENEOUS ATHEOUS BULBOUS CITROUS DUTEOUS FUNGOUS GUMMOUS JEALOUS NITROUS
AGAMOUS ATOKOUS BURNOUS CONGOUS EMULOUS FURIOUS HEINOUS LENTOUS NIVEOUS
AMADOUS AZOTOUS CACHOUS COPIOUS ENVIOUS FUSCOUS HERBOUS LEPROUS NOCUOUS
AMOROUS AZYGOUS CALLOUS CORIOUS ESTROUS GASEOUS HIDEOUS LIMBOUS NOXIOUS
ANUROUS AZYMOUS CARIOUS CORMOUS FATUOUS GEALOUS HUGEOUS LUTEOUS OBVIOUS

OCHROUS	OSSEOUS	PITEOUS	RHODOUS	SARCOUS	SUCCOUS	UMBROUS	VEINOUS	ZINCOUS
ODOROUS	PAPPOUS	PLUMOUS	RIOTOUS	SERIOUS	TALCOUS	URANOUS	VICIOUS	
OMINOUS	PARLOUS	POMPOUS	ROUCOUS	SIMIOUS	TEDIOUS	URINOUS	VIDUOUS	
ONEROUS	PERLOUS	PORTOUS	ROUTOUS	SINUOUS	TENUOUS	USUROUS	VILLOUS	
ONYMOUS	PETROUS	PULPOUS	RUBIOUS	SOUKOUS	TIMEOUS	VACUOUS	VISCOUS	
OPACOUS	PICEOUS	RAMEOUS	RUINOUS	SPINOUS	TYPHOUS	VALGOUS	VOUDOUS	
OSMIOUS	PILEOUS	RAUCOUS	SANIOUS	SPUMOUS	UBEROUS	VARIOUS	ZEALOUS	

8-letter words -OUS

ACARPOUS	CERNUOUS	EXIGUOUS	GRISEOUS	NIDOROUS	PRECIOUS	SONOROUS	ULCEROUS
ADUNCOUS	CHLOROUS	EXIMIOUS	GYPSEOUS	NODULOUS	PREVIOUS	SOPOROUS	UNCTUOUS
AMBEROUS	CITREOUS	FABULOUS	HALITOUS	NUBILOUS	PYRITOUS	SPACIOUS	UNDULOUS
ANOUROUS	CORNEOUS	FACTIOUS	HUMOROUS	NUMEROUS	PYRRHOUS	SPECIOUS	UNJOYOUS
ANTICOUS	COUSCOUS	FASHIOUS	ICHOROUS	NUMINOUS	RAMULOUS	SPERMOUS	USURIOUS
APHONOUS	COVETOUS	FASTUOUS	INCUBOUS	OCHEROUS	RAVENOUS	SPURIOUS	UXORIOUS
APHTHOUS	COVINOUS	FEATEOUS	INERMOUS	OCHREOUS	RESINOUS	SQUAMOUS	VALOROUS
APTEROUS	CRIBROUS	FEATUOUS	INFAMOUS	OESTROUS	RIGOROUS	STANNOUS	VANADOUS
ARACEOUS	CROCEOUS	FELONOUS	KOUSKOUS	OOGAMOUS	RUMOROUS	STOCIOUS	VAPOROUS
ARANEOUS	CROUPOUS	FERREOUS	LACTEOUS	ORAGIOUS	SABULOUS	STOTIOUS	VENOMOUS
ARBOROUS	CUMBROUS	FEVEROUS	LEAPROUS	ORDUROUS	SAPAJOUS	STRATOUS	VENTROUS
ASPEROUS	CUPREOUS	FIDDIOUS	LIBELOUS	ORGULOUS	SAPOROUS	STRUMOUS	VERTUOUS
ASTOMOUS	DARTROUS	FLATUOUS	LIGNEOUS	OVARIOUS	SAVOROUS	STUDIOUS	VIGOROUS
ATROPOUS	DECOROUS	FLEXUOUS	LUMINOUS	PABULOUS	SCABIOUS	SUBEROUS	VIPEROUS
BIBULOUS	DESIROUS	FRABJOUS	LUSCIOUS	PALUDOUS	SCABROUS	SUDOROUS	VIRTUOUS
BIGAMOUS	DEXTROUS	GEMINOUS	LUSTROUS	PAPULOUS	SCARIOUS	TEMEROUS	VITREOUS
BIMANOUS	DIDYMOUS	GEMMEOUS	MANITOUS	PATULOUS	SCIOLOUS	TENUIOUS	WAVEROUS
BIPAROUS	DIGAMOUS	GENEROUS	MARABOUS	PERILOUS	SCLEROUS	THALLOUS	WONDROUS
BIRAMOUS	DIGYNOUS	GLABROUS	MELANOUS	PERVIOUS	SCORIOUS	TIMOROUS	WRONGOUS
CADUCOUS	DIMEROUS	GLAREOUS	MIASMOUS	PETALOUS	SEDULOUS	TINAMOUS	XANTHOUS
CAESIOUS	DIPNOOUS	GLAUCOUS	MUTICOUS	PLUMBOUS	SELENOUS	TITANOUS	YTTRIOUS
CANOROUS	DITOKOUS	GLORIOUS	MUTINOUS	PLUVIOUS	SENSUOUS	TORTIOUS	
CAPTIOUS	DOLOROUS	GOITROUS	NACREOUS	POACEOUS	SEPALOUS	TORTUOUS	
CARIBOUS	EDACIOUS	GORGEOUS	NAUSEOUS	POLYPOUS	SETULOUS	TUBEROUS	
CARNEOUS	ENORMOUS	GRACIOUS	NEBULOUS	POPULOUS	SIBILOUS	TUBULOUS	
CAUTIOUS	EPIGEOUS	GRIEVOUS	NEMOROUS	PORTEOUS	SOMBROUS	TUMOROUS	

WORDS ENDING IN -TION

7-letter words -TION

AMATION	CAPTION	DICTION	EMOTION	FICTION	MIXTION	PORTION	STATION	UNCTION
AUCTION	CAUTION	EDITION	EMPTION	LECTION	ORATION	RECTION	SUCTION	UNITION
BASTION	COCTION	ELATION	ENATION	MENTION	OVATION	RUCTION	TACTION	
CANTION	COITION	ELUTION	FACTION	MICTION	PACTION	SECTION	TUITION	

8-letter words -TION

ABLATION	COACTION	EJECTION	FRUITION	LEGATION	NIDATION	REACTION	TAXATION
ABLUTION	CONATION	ELECTION	FUNCTION	LENITION	NODATION	RELATION	TRACTION
ABORTION	CREATION	EMICTION	GELATION	LIBATION	NOLITION	REMOTION	VACATION
ADAPTION	DELATION	ENACTION	GUMPTION	LIGATION	NOTATION	ROGATION	VENATION
ADDITION	DELETION	EQUATION	GYRATION	LIMATION	NOVATION	ROTATION	VEXATION
ADNATION	DEMOTION	ERECTION	HALATION	LOBATION	NUDATION	SANCTION	VOCATION
ADOPTION	DERATION	ERUPTION	HIMATION	LOCATION	NUTATION	SCONTION	VOLITION
AERATION	DEVOTION	EVECTION	IDEATION	LOCUTION	OBLATION	SEDATION	VOLUTION
AGNATION	DILATION	EVICTION	IGNITION	LUNATION	PACATION	SEDITION	ZONATION
AMBITION	DILUTION	EXACTION	ILLATION	LUXATION	PETITION	SOLATION	
AUDITION	DONATION	EXERTION	INACTION	MONITION	POSITION	SOLUTION	
AVIATION	DOTATION	FIXATION	INUSTION	MUNITION	POTATION	SORPTION	
BIBATION	DURATION	FLECTION	JOBATION	MUTATION	PUNITION	STICTION	
CIBATION	EDUCTION	FRACTION	JUNCTION	NATATION	PUPATION	SUDATION	
CITATION	EGESTION	FRICTION	LAVATION	NEGATION	QUESTION	SWAPTION	

UNUSUAL VOWEL ENDINGS

Even when Scrabble players are thinking about the endings of words, they are likely to concentrate on the 'obvious' endings – like -ATE, -ISE, -URE, -ED, -ER and -ENT. These tend to end with a fairly restricted group of letters – usually D, E, R, S and T. Players do not naturally think of words ending with unusual letters. It takes some effort to start thinking about words ending in A, I, O and U. Yet these four letters make up 30% of the tiles in a Scrabble set. They will frequently appear on your rack, but familiarity with everyday English does not encourage you to think of these letters at the end of words. They can be very useful for linking on to other letters on the board, making two-letter words which begin or end with A, I, O or U.

The following lists are ammunition for correcting that rather limiting view of word endings. Here are lists of all valid words of lengths two to eight letters which end with A, I, O or U.

WORDS ENDING IN -A

2-letter words ending in -A

AA	DA	FA	KA	MA	PA
BA	EA	HA	LA	NA	TA

3-letter words ending in -A

ABA	ANA	BRA	GOA	LEA	OCA	POA	SKA	UVA	ZOA
AGA	AVA	CHA	HOA	MAA	ODA	QUA	SMA	VIA	
AHA	AWA	ERA	ITA	MNA	OVA	RIA	SPA	WHA	
AIA	BAA	ETA	KEA	MOA	PEA	RYA	TEA	YEA	
ALA	BOA	FRA	KOA	OBA	PIA	SEA	TWA	ZEA	

4-letter words ending in -A

ABBA	BONA	EGMA	HUMA	LANA	MYNA	PEBA	ROMA	TAHA	VASA
ACTA	BORA	EKKA	IDEA	LAVA	NADA	PELA	ROTA	TAKA	VEGA
AGHA	BUBA	EMMA	ILEA	LEVA	NAGA	PICA	RUSA	TALA	VELA
AGMA	BUNA	EPHA	ILIA	LIMA	NALA	PIKA	SAGA	TANA	VENA
ALFA	CABA	ETNA	ILKA	LIRA	NANA	PILA	SAMA	TAPA	VINA
ALGA	CAPA	EYRA	INIA	LOMA	NAPA	PINA	SENA	TARA	VISA
ALMA	CASA	FETA	IOTA	LOTA	NIPA	PIPA	SERA	TAVA	VITA
AMLA	CECA	FLEA	IXIA	LUNA	NOMA	PITA	SETA	TAWA	VIVA
ANNA	COCA	FORA	JOTA	MAMA	NOTA	PLEA	SHEA	TAXA	VOLA
ANOA	CODA	GAGA	JUBA	MANA	NOVA	PROA	SHWA	TELA	WAKA
ANTA	COLA	GALA	JUGA	MARA	OBIA	PUJA	SIDA	TIKA	WEKA
AQUA	COMA	GENA	JURA	MASA	OCTA	PULA	SIKA	TOEA	WETA
ARBA	COXA	GETA	KAKA	MAYA	ODEA	PUMA	SIMA	TOGA	WHOA
AREA	CYMA	GIGA	KAMA	MEGA	OKRA	PUNA	SKUA	TOLA	YOGA
ARIA	DATA	GILA	KANA	MELA	OKTA	PUPA	SOCA	TOSA	YUCA
ARNA	DEVA	GLIA	KARA	MESA	OLLA	RACA	SODA	TUBA	YUGA
AULA	DIKA	GUGA	KATA	MICA	ORCA	RAGA	SOFA	TUFA	ZETA
AURA	DISA	GULA	KAVA	MINA	ORRA	RAJA	SOJA	TUNA	ZILA
BABA	DITA	HAKA	KETA	MOLA	OSSA	RANA	SOLA	ULNA	ZOEA
BEMA	DIVA	HILA	KINA	MONA	PACA	RATA	SOMA	ULVA	ZONA
BETA	DONA	HIYA	KIVA	MORA	PAPA	RHEA	SORA	UREA	ZUPA
BIGA	DOPA	HOYA	KOLA	MOWA	PARA	RIMA	SOYA	URVA	ZYGA
BOBA	DUMA	HUIA	KORA	MOXA	PAUA	RIVA	STOA	UVEA	
BOMA	DURA	HULA	LAMA	MOYA	PAWA	RIZA	SURA	VARA	

5-letter words ending in -A

ABACA ABAYA ABUNA ADYTA AECIA AFARA AGILA AGORA ALAPA ALDEA ALIYA ALOHA ALPHA ALULA AMEBA AMNIA ANANA ANIMA ANTRA AORTA APNEA ARABA ARECA ARENA AROBA AROMA ASANA ATRIA BACCA BAJRA BALSA BANDA BANIA BARCA BASTA BATTA BELGA BIGHA BIOTA BIVIA BOCCA BOHEA BONZA BRAVA BUFFA BULLA BUNIA BUNYA BURKA

BURQA BURSA BWANA CAECA CALLA CALPA CANNA CARTA CAUSA CELLA CERIA CHARA CHAYA CHEKA CHELA CHICA CHINA CHOTA CHUFA CILIA CIRCA CNIDA COBIA COBRA COBZA COCOA COLZA COMMA CONGA CONIA COPRA CORIA COSTA COTTA CRENA CUPPA CURIA DACHA DAGGA DARGA DELTA DERMA DICTA DIOTA DOGMA DOLIA DOLMA DONGA DOONA

DORSA DOUMA DOURA DOWNA DRAMA DULIA DUMKA DURRA EDEMA ENEMA ENTIA ERBIA ERICA ETYMA EXTRA FACIA FATWA FAUNA FELLA FESTA FETTA FETWA FLORA FLOTA FOLIA FONDA FOSSA FOVEA FRENA GALEA GAMBA GAMMA GANJA GARDA GEMMA GENOA GOMPA GONIA GONNA GOTTA GOURA GRAMA GROMA GUANA GUAVA GUMMA GUSLA GUTTA HALFA

HALMA HALVA HAMZA HAOMA HASTA HEJRA HENNA HERMA HEVEA HIJRA HODJA HOLLA HOOKA HOSTA HURRA HUTIA HUZZA HYDRA HYENA HYPHA HYPNA IDOLA INFRA INTRA INULA JARTA JHALA JIRGA JNANA JUNTA KAAMA KACHA KALPA KANGA KAPPA KARMA KASHA KHAYA KHEDA KHOJA KINDA KIPPA KOALA KOFTA KOKRA KOPPA KORMA KRONA KURTA

KWELA LABDA LABIA LABRA LAIKA LAMIA LARVA LAURA LAVRA LEMMA LEPRA LEPTA LIANA LIBRA LIMMA LINGA LLAMA LOGIA LONGA LOOFA LUBRA LUFFA LYSSA LYTTA MAFIA MAGMA MAHUA MAHWA MALVA MAMBA MAMMA MANGA MANIA MANNA MANTA MARIA MASSA MATZA MBIRA MEDIA MENTA MICRA MIKRA MISSA MOCHA MOLLA MOMMA MOOLA MORIA

MORRA MOTZA MOWRA MUDRA MULGA MURRA MURVA MUSHA MYOMA NABLA NAIRA NALLA NANNA NAPPA NERKA NGANA NINJA NORIA NORMA NUBIA NUCHA NULLA NYALA NYSSA OCREA OIDIA OMASA OMEGA OPERA ORGIA OSSIA OSTIA OUIJA PACHA PACTA PADMA PAISA PAKKA PALEA PALLA PAMPA PANDA PANGA PARKA PASHA PASTA PELMA PELTA PENNA

PEPLA PHOCA PHYLA PICRA PIETA PILEA PINNA PINTA PITTA PIZZA PLAYA PLAZA PLENA PLICA POAKA PODIA POLKA PONGA POOJA POOKA POPPA PORTA PRANA PRESA PRIMA PSORA PUCKA PUKKA PULKA PUNGA PUNKA QIBLA QUENA QUINA QUOTA RAITA RASTA REATA RECTA REDIA REGMA RENGA REPLA RHYTA RIATA ROOSA RUANA RUMBA RUPIA

RUSMA SABRA SACRA SADZA SAIGA SAKIA SALPA SALSA SAMBA SANSA SAUBA SAUNA SCALA SCAPA SCENA SCHWA SCOPA SCUBA SCUTA SELLA SELVA SENNA SENSA SENZA SEPIA SEPTA SERRA SESSA SHAMA SHAYA SHEVA SHOLA SHURA SIDHA SIGLA SIGMA SILVA SOFTA SOPRA SORDA SORRA SPICA SPINA SPUTA STELA STIPA STOMA STRIA STUPA

SULFA SUMMA SURRA SUTRA SYLVA TABLA TAFIA TAGMA TAIGA TAIRA TALEA TALMA TALPA TANGA TANKA TANNA TAPPA TAYRA TAZZA TECTA TELIA TENIA TERGA TERRA TESLA TESTA TETRA THANA THECA THEMA THETA THUJA THUYA TIARA TIBIA TICCA TIKKA TINEA TOMIA TONGA TREFA TREMA TRONA TSUBA TUGRA ULEMA ULTRA UMBRA URENA

USNEA UVULA VACUA VARNA VEENA VESPA VESTA VIFDA VIGIA VILLA VINCA VIOLA VIRGA VISTA VITTA VIVDA VODKA VOILA VOLTA VOLVA VULVA WALLA WANNA WICCA WILGA WILJA WINNA WONGA XENIA XOANA YACCA YAKKA YARFA YARTA YENTA YERBA YUCCA ZABRA ZAMIA ZANJA ZEBRA ZERDA ZONDA ZOOEA

6-letter words ending in -A

ABELIA ABOLLA ABULIA ACACIA ACEDIA AGENDA AGOUTA AHIMSA AIKONA ALALIA ALBATA ALEXIA ALISMA ALOGIA ALPACA ALTEZA

ALTHEA ALUMNA AMELIA AMENTA AMOEBA AMRITA ANATTA ANCORA ANEMIA ANGINA ANGOLA ANGORA ANOXIA ANTARA ANTLIA ANURIA

APHTHA APNOEA APORIA ARALIA ARCANA AREOLA ARGALA ARISTA ARMADA ARNICA AROLLA ARROBA ASTHMA ATAXIA ATOCIA AUCUBA

AURORA AXILLA AZALEA AZOLLA BACKRA BACULA BAHADA BAJADA BALATA BALBOA BANANA BARAZA BARYTA BATATA BAUERA BEFANA

BELUGA BEMATA BERTHA BODEGA BOORKA BOSHTA BREGMA BROLGA BUCKRA BUDDHA BUNNIA CABALA CABANA CAFILA CALIMA CALTHA

CAMBIA CAMERA CANADA CANULA CAPITA CARINA CASSIA CATENA CEDULA CEMBRA CENTRA CESURA CHACMA CHAETA CHAKRA CHAPKA

CHARKA CHARTA CHATTA CHICHA CHOANA CHOKRA CHORDA CHOREA CHORIA CHROMA CHUKKA CICADA CICALA CICUTA CINEMA CLIVIA

CLOACA CLUSIA COAITA CONCHA CONIMA CONTRA COPITA COPULA CORNEA CORNUA CORONA CORYZA COSMEA COWPEA CRANIA CRISSA

CRISTA CRUSTA CUBICA CUESTA CUPOLA CURARA CUTCHA CZAPKA DAGABA DAGOBA DAHLIA DATURA DHARMA DHARNA DHURRA DOLINA

DUENNA ECZEMA EGESTA EIDOLA EJECTA ELUVIA ELYTRA EMPUSA ENIGMA ENTERA EPEIRA EPIZOA EPOCHA ERRATA ESPADA EUREKA

EXEDRA FACULA FARINA FASCIA FATSIA FAVELA FECULA FEDORA FEIJOA FEMORA FERULA FIBULA FIESTA FOOTRA FOUSSA FOUTRA FRAENA FRISKA FRUSTA FULCRA FUNKIA GALENA GARRYA GARUDA GEISHA GELADA GENERA GENEVA GITANA GLIOMA GLORIA GLOSSA GOANNA GOONDA GOPURA GORGIA GRAMMA GRAPPA

GUINEA HALLOA HEBONA HEGIRA HEJIRA HEMINA HERNIA HOLLOA HOLMIA HYAENA HYDRIA IGUANA IMPALA INDABA INDUNA INFULA INJERA INSULA INTIMA INYALA ISCHIA JACANA JATAKA JEJUNA JEMIMA JERBOA JOANNA JOJOBA JUDOKA KABALA KABAYA KACCHA KAFILA KALMIA KAMALA KAMELA KAMILA KANAKA

KANGHA KANTHA KARAKA KATANA KENTIA KERRIA KGOTLA KHANGA KHODJA KHURTA KINEMA KORORA KORUNA KUMARA KUTCHA KWACHA KWANZA LABARA LACUNA LAGENA LAMBDA LAMINA LATRIA LEIPOA LIGULA LINGUA LIPOMA LITHIA LOCHIA LOGGIA LORCHA LORICA LUCUMA LUMINA LUNULA LUSTRA MACOYA MACULA

MAFFIA MALTHA MANANA MANILA MANTRA MANTUA MANUKA MARACA MARINA MARKKA MASHUA MASULA MAUNNA MAXIMA MAZUMA MEDAKA MEDINA MEDUSA MEGARA MESETA MEZUZA MGANGA MIASMA MIMOSA MINIMA MODENA MONERA MOORVA MORULA MOTUCA MUCOSA MUMMIA MURENA MURRHA MUTUCA MYOPIA MYXOMA NAGANA

NATURA NAUSEA NEBULA NEPETA NOCTUA NOMINA NOVENA NUMINA NUTRIA NYANZA OCHREA OEDEMA OMENTA OMERTA ONYCHA OPTIMA ORARIA ORBITA ORGANA OSCULA OTTAVA OZAENA PAELLA PAGODA PAKEHA PAKORA PALAMA PALLIA PANADA PANAMA PAPAYA PAPULA PATACA PATERA PATINA PAYOLA PELOTA PERAEA

PEREIA PESETA PESEWA PESHWA PETARA PHOBIA PIAZZA PILULA PINATA PINETA PIRANA PIRAYA PITARA PLANTA PLASMA PLEURA PNEUMA POSADA PREMIA PROTEA PRUINA PSYLLA PTERIA PULKHA PUNCTA PYEMIA PYURIA QASIDA QUAGGA QUALIA QUANTA QUELEA QUINOA QUINTA QUOKKA QUOTHA RADULA RAFFIA

RANULA RAPHIA RAZZIA REALIA REDOWA REGINA REGULA REMORA REMUDA RESEDA RETAMA RETINA RHUMBA ROSTRA ROSULA ROTULA RUCOLA RUMINA RUSSIA SABKHA SAHIBA SALINA SALIVA SALVIA SAMARA SAMOSA SANCTA SAPOTA SATARA SATYRA SCARPA SCHEMA SCILLA SCLERA SCOLIA SCORIA SCOTIA SCROTA

SEMEIA SENEGA SEROSA SHAMBA SHARIA SHEILA SHERIA SHERPA SHIKSA SHIRRA SIDDHA SIENNA SIERRA SIESTA SIFAKA SILICA SISTRA SITULA SKOLIA SMEGMA SOLERA SOMATA SONATA SPIREA SQUAMA STADDA STADIA STANZA STATUA STEMMA STERNA STIGMA STIRRA STRATA STRIGA STROMA STRUMA SUBSEA

SULPHA SUNDRA SYLVIA TABULA TAENIA TAFFIA TAHINA TAIAHA TALUKA TAMARA TANKIA TANTRA TAPETA TARSIA TEGULA TELEGA TEPHRA TERATA TEREFA TERTIA THANNA THORIA THULIA TINAJA TIPULA TORANA TORULA TOTARA TRAUMA TRIVIA TROIKA TSAMBA TUGHRA TUNDRA UJAMAA ULTIMA UNGULA UREDIA

UREMIA URTICA UTOPIA VAGINA VALETA VALUTA VARROA VEDUTA VELETA VESICA VICUNA VIHARA VIMANA VIZSLA VOMICA WHATNA WILTJA WOMERA XEROMA XYLOMA YAKUZA YAQONA YARPHA YOJANA YTTRIA YUKATA ZABETA ZAPATA ZAREBA ZARIBA ZENANA ZEREBA ZERIBA ZEUGMA ZINNIA ZOARIA ZONULA ZYGOMA

7-letter words ending in -A

ABOMASA ABOULIA ACANTHA ACAPNIA ACHARYA ACHENIA ACROMIA ACTINIA ACUSHLA ADDENDA ADENOMA ADHARMA AECIDIA AGNOSIA AGRAPHA ALAMEDA ALCHERA ALCORZA ALFALFA ALFORJA ALGEBRA ALGESIA ALLUVIA ALTEZZA ALTHAEA ALUMINA AMANITA AMENTIA AMMONIA

AMNESIA AMOROSA AMPHORA AMPULLA ANAEMIA ANALOGA ANCILIA ANESTRA ANGIOMA ANNATTA ANONYMA ANOSMIA ANTENNA APADANA APEPSIA APHAGIA APHASIA APHELIA APHONIA APLASIA APRAXIA APTERIA AQUARIA ARABICA ARAROBA ARGYRIA ARIETTA ARMILLA ARUGULA

ASCIDIA ASHRAMA ASPIDIA ASTERIA ATALAYA ATHLETA ATRESIA ATROPIA AURELIA AUREOLA BACCARA BACLAVA BAKLAVA BALISTA BANDANA BANDORA BANDURA BANKSIA BARBOLA BARILLA BASIDIA BATTUTA BAZOOKA BEFFANA BEGONIA BEGORRA BERGAMA BHANGRA BIDARKA

BIODATA BIRETTA BOMBORA BONAMIA BONANZA BORONIA BOTTEGA BOURKHA BRACCIA BRACHIA BRAVURA BRECCIA BRITSKA BRITZKA BRUHAHA BUBINGA BUCCINA BULIMIA CABBALA CADENZA CAESURA CAFFILA CALDERA CALLUNA CALUMBA CAMORRA CAMPANA CANASTA CANDELA

CANDIDA CANELLA CANNULA CANTALA CANTATA CANTINA CANZONA CAPUERA CARAMBA CARANNA CARAUNA CARIAMA CARIOCA CASCARA CASSATA CASSAVA CATALPA CATASTA CATAWBA CAVALLA CEDILLA CELESTA CEMENTA CEREBRA CHALAZA CHARKHA CHECHIA CHIASMA CHICANA

CHIKARA CHIMERA CHOLERA CIBORIA CIMELIA CINEREA CINGULA CITHARA CLARKIA COAGULA COCHLEA CODETTA CODILLA COMITIA CONARIA CONIDIA COPAIBA COPAIVA COQUINA CORALLA CORDOBA CORELLA COROLLA CORPORA CORRIDA COTINGA CREMONA CRIMINA CROTALA

CURACOA CURCUMA CURIOSA CURTANA CYMATIA CYPSELA CZARINA DATARIA DAVIDIA DECIDUA DECURIA DEJECTA DELENDA DELIRIA DIGAMMA DIHEDRA DILEMMA DILUVIA DIORAMA DIPLOMA DIPTERA DOMATIA DOPATTA DOULEIA DRACHMA DROSERA DUODENA DUPATTA DVANDVA

DYSPNEA DYSURIA ECHIDNA ECTHYMA ECTOPIA ECTOZOA EDEMATA EMBLEMA EMPORIA EMPYEMA ENCOMIA ENDOZOA ENEMATA ENTOZOA EPHEDRA EQUINIA EROTEMA EROTICA EUGENIA EULOGIA EUTEXIA EXCRETA EXEMPLA EXHEDRA EXORDIA EXOTICA EXURBIA FALBALA FALCULA

FARRUCA FAZENDA FELICIA FELUCCA FERMATA FIBROMA FILARIA FIMBRIA FISTULA FLUTINA FORLANA FORMULA FOSSULA FOVEOLA FREESIA FRENULA FUCHSIA FURCULA FURLANA GALABEA GALABIA GALANGA GALATEA GANGLIA GAZANIA GAZOOKA GENISTA GERBERA GERTCHA

GLUCINA
GOBURRA
GODETIA
GONDOLA
GONIDIA
GORILLA
GRANDMA
GRANDPA
GRANITA
GRANOLA
GUARANA
GUEREZA
GUMMATA
GUNNERA
GYNECIA
HARMALA
HELLOVA
HELLUVA
HEMIOLA
HETAERA
HETAIRA
HEUREKA
HEXAPLA
HIDALGA
HIMATIA
HOSANNA
HYMENIA
HYPOGEA
HYPOXIA
IKEBANA
ILLUVIA
IMPERIA
IMPRESA
INDICIA
INDUSIA
INERTIA
INFANTA
INGESTA
INOCULA
INTRADA
IPOMOEA
ISODICA
ISODOMA
JAMBIYA
JELLABA
JIPYAPA
KABBALA
KACHCHA
KACHINA
KANTELA
KATORGA
KEITLOA
KERYGMA
KHALIFA
KHEDIVA
KIBITKA
KITHARA
KUCHCHA
LABELLA
LACINIA
LAMBADA
LAMELLA
LAMPUKA
LANGAHA
LANTANA
LASAGNA
LAVOLTA
LEMMATA
LEMPIRA
LEUCOMA
LEWISIA
LINGULA
LIXIVIA
LOBELIA
LOCUSTA
LOGANIA
LOMENTA
MADOQUA
MADRASA
MADRONA
MAGENTA
MAGMATA
MAHATMA
MAHONIA
MALACIA
MALARIA
MAMILLA
MANCALA
MANDALA
MANDIRA
MANDOLA
MANDORA
MANILLA
MANUMEA
MANYATA
MAREMMA
MARGOSA
MARIMBA
MARKKAA
MASCARA
MASTABA
MAXILLA
MAZURKA
MEDACCA
MEDULLA
MELISMA
MESHUGA
MESTIZA
METAZOA
MICELLA
MILITIA
MINEOLA
MINUTIA
MOMENTA
MONARDA
MONILIA
MORPHIA
MORRHUA
MOUSAKA
MOZETTA
MUDIRIA
MULATTA
MURAENA
MUTANDA
MYALGIA
MYCELIA
MYELOMA
MYOMATA
MYRINGA
NAPHTHA
NEMESIA
NEUROMA
NIGELLA
NIHONGA
NIRVANA
NORTENA
NOTANDA
NOTITIA
NOUMENA
NOVALIA
NOVELLA
OCARINA
OCTAPLA
OLEARIA
OMMATEA
OMNIANA
ONDATRA
ONYCHIA
OOGONIA
OPHIURA
OPUNTIA
ORGANZA
OROPESA
OSMUNDA
OSTEOMA
OSTRACA
OSTRAKA
OTALGIA
OVERSEA
PADELLA
PAENULA
PALABRA
PALMYRA
PALOOKA
PANACEA
PANDORA
PANDURA
PANOCHA
PAPILLA
PAPRIKA
PARATHA
PARAZOA
PAREIRA
PARELLA
PARERGA
PARGANA
PARTITA
PATAGIA
PATELLA
PAVLOVA
PAXIUBA
PECULIA
PEISHWA
PELORIA
PENTHIA
PEREIRA
PERGOLA
PERIDIA
PERINEA
PERSONA
PESSIMA
PETUNIA
PINNULA
PIRAGUA
PIRANHA
PISCINA
PITUITA
PLACITA
PLANULA
PLATINA
PLECTRA
PLEROMA
PLUMULA
PODAGRA
PODESTA
POLACCA
POLENTA
POLYNIA
POLYNYA
POLYOMA
POLYZOA
POTASSA
PRECAVA
PRIMULA
PRONOTA
PROPYLA
PTERYLA
PUDENDA
PUNALUA
PUPARIA
PUPUNHA
PURPURA
PYAEMIA
PYGIDIA
PYREXIA
PYXIDIA
QUASSIA
RABANNA
RADIATA
RAMENTA
RAOULIA
RATAFIA
REFUGIA
REGALIA
REGATTA
REGMATA
REPLICA
RESIDUA
RETSINA
RHODORA
RHYTINA
RICKSHA
RICOTTA
RIVIERA
ROBINIA
ROBUSTA
ROMAIKA
ROMNEYA
ROSACEA
ROSALIA
ROSELLA
ROSEOLA
ROTUNDA
RUBELLA
RUBEOLA
RUELLIA
RUFIYAA
RUSALKA
SABELLA
SABURRA
SACELLA
SAGITTA
SAMBUCA
SAMSARA
SANGOMA
SANGRIA
SAPHENA
SARCOMA
SARDANA
SATSUMA
SAVANNA
SCAGLIA
SCAPULA
SCHISMA
SCHOLIA
SCOPULA
SCOTOMA
SCYBALA
SECRETA
SEDILIA
SEQUELA
SEQUOIA
SERIEMA
SERINGA
SERPULA
SESTINA
SEVRUGA
SHASTRA
SHEHITA
SHEIKHA
SHICKSA
SIGNORA
SILESIA
SILIQUA
SILPHIA
SINOPIA
SKIMMIA
SOLARIA
SOLATIA
SOREDIA
SPATULA
SPECTRA
SPECULA
SPICULA
SPIRAEA
SPLENIA
SQUILLA
SRADDHA
STAMINA
STASIMA
STOMATA
STRETTA
STRIATA
SUBAQUA
SUBAREA
SUCCUBA
SUDARIA
SULTANA
SUMATRA
SYCONIA
SYNOVIA
SYRINGA
TAFFETA
TAGMATA
TALARIA
TALOOKA
TAMASHA
TAMBURA
TANAGRA
TANIWHA
TANTARA
TAPIOCA
TARTANA
TAVERNA
TEDESCA
TEGMINA
TEMPERA
TEMPURA
TEQUILA
TEREBRA
TESSERA
THEMATA
THRIMSA
THRYMSA
TILAPIA
TOCCATA
TOHEROA
TOHUNGA
TOMBOLA
TOMENTA
TORMINA
TOSTADA
TOXEMIA
TRACHEA
TREHALA
TRISULA
TSARINA
TUATARA
TUTANIA
TYMPANA
ULNARIA
URAEMIA
URETHRA
VALONEA
VALONIA
VALVULA
VANESSA
VANILLA
VARIOLA
VASCULA
VEDALIA
VELARIA
VENTANA
VERANDA
VERBENA
VERRUCA
VERRUGA
VETTURA
VEXILLA
VIATICA
VIDENDA
VIHUELA
VINCULA
VIRANDA
VISCERA
VIVARIA
VIVERRA
VOLUSPA
WALLABA
WEIGELA
WOODSIA
WOOMERA
WOORARA
XERASIA
YAMULKA
YESHIVA
ZAKUSKA
ZAMARRA
ZANELLA
ZAREEBA
ZEBRINA
ZEBRULA
ZEMSTVA
ZIGANKA
ZIMOCCA
ZIZANIA
ZOOECIA

8-letter words ending in -A

ABDOMINA
ABSCISSA
ACADEMIA
ACHAENIA
ACHILLEA
ADESPOTA
ADULARIA
ADYNAMIA
AGNOMINA
AGRAPHIA
AKINESIA
ALGAROBA
ALIGARTA
ALLELUIA
ALOPECIA
AMBROSIA
AMYGDALA
ANACONDA
ANALECTA
ANALEMMA
ANAPHORA
ANASARCA
ANATHEMA
ANGELICA
ANOESTRA
ANOREXIA
ANTEFIXA
ANTHELIA
ANTHEMIA
ANTISERA
APOLOGIA
APOSITIA
APYREXIA
ARAPAIMA
ARAPONGA
ARAPUNGA
ARBORETA
ASPHYXIA
ASTHENIA
ASTIGMIA
ATARAXIA
ATHEROMA
AUBRETIA
AUBRIETA
AURICULA
AUTOMATA
AUTOPSIA
AVIFAUNA
AZOTURIA
BABIRUSA
BABUSHKA
BACTERIA
BALLISTA
BANDANNA
BARATHEA
BARRANCA
BASILICA
BATTALIA
BAUHINIA
BERGENIA
BERYLLIA
BETHESDA
BIGNONIA
BISCACHA
BIZCACHA
BLASTEMA
BLASTULA
BONSELLA
BRANCHIA
BRASSICA
BREGMATA
BRITZSKA
BROMELIA
BRONCHIA
BROUHAHA
BUDDLEIA
BURLETTA
CAATINGA
CABRETTA
CACHEXIA
CACHUCHA
CALATHEA
CALCANEA
CALCARIA
CALDARIA
CALISAYA
CALVARIA
CALYPTRA
CAMELLIA
CAMPAGNA
CAPITULA
CAPOEIRA
CAPYBARA
CARACARA
CARNAUBA
CASTELLA
CATHEDRA
CATHISMA
CATTLEYA
CAVATINA
CECROPIA
CERCARIA
CHALAZIA
CHARISMA
CHICKPEA
CHILLADA
CHIMAERA
CHINAMPA
CHINKARA
CHIRAGRA
CHLOASMA
CHOLEMIA
CHURINGA
CHYLURIA
CINCHONA
CISTERNA
CLAUSTRA
CLAUSULA
CLITELLA
COCCIDIA
COENOBIA
COLCHICA
COLLEGIA
COLLYRIA
COLOBOMA
CONFERVA
CONSULTA
CONTAGIA
CONTESSA
CONTINUA
CONURBIA
COPROSMA
COQUILLA
CORMIDIA
COXALGIA
CREDENDA
CREDENZA
CRIBELLA
CRITERIA
CROMORNA
CUNABULA
CYMBIDIA
CZAREVNA
CZARITSA
DECENNIA
DEMENTIA
DEMERARA
DENTALIA
DENTARIA
DIARRHEA
DIASPORA
DIASTEMA
DICENTRA
DICHASIA
DIELYTRA
DIPLEGIA
DIPLOPIA
DIPLOZOA
DJELLABA
DULCIANA
DYSCHROA
DYSLEXIA
DYSMELIA
DYSPNOEA
DYSTOCIA
DYSTONIA
DYSTOPIA
ECCLESIA

EFFLUVIA	GLIOMATA	LAVATERA	MYCETOMA	POLYGALA	SEMICOMA	SYNAPHEA	VAGINULA
EGOMANIA	GLORIOSA	LECANORA	MYOTONIA	POLYURIA	SEMOLINA	SYNCYTIA	VALLONIA
ENCAENIA	GLOSSINA	LEUKEMIA	MYXEDEMA	POSTCAVA	SEMUNCIA	SYNECHIA	VELAMINA
ENDOSTEA	GLOXINIA	LIPOMATA	MYXOMATA	PRAECAVA	SENSILLA	SYNEDRIA	VELATURA
ENGRAMMA	GLUMELLA	LISTERIA	NAVICULA	PREDELLA	SENSORIA	SYNTAGMA	VENDETTA
EPHEMERA	GLYCERIA	LODICULA	NUBECULA	PRESCUTA	SEPARATA	SYSSITIA	VERONICA
EPICEDIA	GOLFIANA	LONICERA	NYMPHAEA	PRESIDIA	SEPTARIA	TAKAMAKA	VERTEBRA
EPITHEMA	GUERILLA	LYMPHOMA	ODONTOMA	PROFORMA	SEPTLEVA	TAMANDUA	VESICULA
EPOPOEIA	GURDWARA	MACAHUBA	OEDEMATA	PROGERIA	SERENATA	TAMBOURA	VESTIGIA
EQUISETA	GYMKHANA	MADRASSA	OITICICA	PROTOZOA	SHAMIANA	TAPADERA	VIBRISSA
ERYTHEMA	GYMNASIA	MAGNESIA	OLIGURIA	PRUNELLA	SHECHITA	TEGMENTA	VICTORIA
ESTANCIA	GYNAECIA	MAGNOLIA	OMBRELLA	PRYTANEA	SHIGELLA	TENACULA	VIEWDATA
ESTHESIA	GYNOECIA	MAHARAJA	OPERCULA	PTERYGIA	SHRADDHA	TENTORIA	VIRAEMIA
ETCETERA	HABANERA	MAIOLICA	OPERETTA	PUTAMINA	SIDALCEA	TEQUILLA	VIRTUOSA
EUPEPSIA	HACIENDA	MAJOLICA	OPUSCULA	PYCNIDIA	SIGNORIA	TERATOMA	VISCACHA
EUPHOBIA	HAMARTIA	MALVASIA	ORCHELLA	QUADRIGA	SILICULA	TERRARIA	VITICETA
EUPHONIA	HEARTPEA	MAMMILLA	ORCHILLA	QUINELLA	SIMARUBA	TERRELLA	VIZCACHA
EUPHORIA	HEMIOLIA	MANDIOCA	PALESTRA	RACHILLA	SINFONIA	TERZETTA	VULSELLA
EXCERPTA	HEMIOPIA	MANDORLA	PANDEMIA	RADIALIA	SONATINA	TESSELLA	WISTARIA
FALDETTA	HERBARIA	MANTILLA	PANMIXIA	RAKSHASA	SORBARIA	TETRAPLA	WISTERIA
FANTASIA	HETAIRIA	MANTISSA	PANORAMA	RAPHANIA	SPIRILLA	THERIACA	XANTHOMA
FASCIOLA	HIRAGANA	MANUBRIA	PARABEMA	REDDENDA	SPORIDIA	THIOUREA	XENOPHYA
FASCISTA	HOSPITIA	MANYATTA	PARABOLA	RENDZINA	SQUAMULA	TOQUILLA	XEROMATA
FENESTRA	HYDREMIA	MARCELLA	PARANOEA	RESINATA	STAPELIA	TORMENTA	XYLOMATA
FIBRILLA	HYDROZOA	MARCHESA	PARANOIA	RESPONSA	STAROSTA	TORTILLA	YAKIMONA
FISTIANA	HYPALGIA	MARINERA	PARHELIA	RETINULA	STEATOMA	TOXAEMIA	YARMULKA
FLABELLA	HYPOGAEA	MARIPOSA	PAROEMIA	REWAREWA	STEMMATA	TOXOCARA	YERSINIA
FLAGELLA	HYSTERIA	MARSUPIA	PAROUSIA	RHIZOBIA	STERIGMA	TRACHOMA	YOKOZUNA
FLOTILLA	IMPLUVIA	MARTYRIA	PASHMINA	RUTABAGA	STIGMATA	TRAPEZIA	YTTERBIA
FORAMINA	INSIGNIA	MASSOOLA	PELLAGRA	SACRARIA	STOCCATA	TRAUMATA	ZAMBOMBA
FUGHETTA	INSOMNIA	MATADORA	PENUMBRA	SALICETA	STOTINKA	TRICHINA	ZAMPOGNA
GALLABEA	INTARSIA	MATAMATA	PERFECTA	SAPUCAIA	STROBILA	TRIDACNA	ZARZUELA
GALLABIA	INTIFADA	MBAQANGA	PERIAGUA	SARMENTA	STROMATA	TRIFECTA	ZASTRUGA
GALLERIA	ISABELLA	MELANOMA	PETECHIA	SASARARA	STRONTIA	TRIFORIA	ZIRCONIA
GALTONIA	ISCHEMIA	MELODICA	PHACELIA	SASTRUGA	SUBCOSTA	TRILEMMA	ZOIATRIA
GAMBETTA	ISCHURIA	MENSTRUA	PHOTINIA	SAYONARA	SUBPHYLA	TRIPUDIA	ZOOCYTIA
GAMMADIA	IZVESTIA	MESHUGGA	PHOTOPIA	SCHAPSKA	SUBPOENA	TRITONIA	ZOOGLOEA
GAMMATIA	JAPONICA	METANOIA	PHYSALIA	SCHEMATA	SUBTOPIA	TROCHLEA	ZOONOMIA
GARCINIA	JARARACA	MIASMATA	PIASSABA	SCIATICA	SUBUCULA	TROPARIA	ZUCHETTA
GARDENIA	JARARAKA	MILIARIA	PIASSAVA	SCLEREMA	SUBURBIA	TSAREVNA	ZYGANTRA
GASTRAEA	KALYPTRA	MILTONIA	PIZZERIA	SCLEROMA	SUDAMINA	TSARITSA	ZYGOMATA
GASTRULA	KARATEKA	MINNEOLA	PLACENTA	SCOLIOMA	SVASTIKA	ULTIMATA	
GEMATRIA	KATAKANA	MONSTERA	PLANURIA	SCOTOMIA	SWASTIKA	UMBRELLA	
GEROPIGA	KAZATZKA	MONTARIA	PLATANNA	SCOTOPIA	SWEETPEA	UNDERSEA	
GESNERIA	KHANSAMA	MOUSSAKA	PLATYSMA	SCROFULA	SYMPODIA	UREDINIA	
GLABELLA	KINAKINA	MOZZETTA	PLETHORA	SCUTELLA	SYMPOSIA	UROPYGIA	
GLAUCOMA	KRAMERIA	MRIDANGA	POLLINIA	SEMANTRA	SYNANGIA	VACCINIA	

WORDS ENDING IN -I

2-letter words ending in -I

AI	DI	HI	MI	PI	SI	XI
BI	GI	LI	OI	QI	TI	

3-letter words ending in -I

AMI	DEI	HUI	MOI	POI	SAI	SUI	UNI
ANI	GHI	KAI	OBI	PSI	SEI	TAI	
CHI	HOI	LEI	PHI	RAI	SKI	TUI	

4-letter words ending in -I

ANTI	CEDI	DIXI	FUCI	HOKI	KAMI	LOBI	MERI	MOOI	NODI
ASCI	CHAI	ETUI	GADI	IMPI	KATI	LOCI	MIDI	MUTI	NORI
BANI	DALI	EUOI	GLEI	INTI	KAZI	MAGI	MINI	NAOI	PENI
BENI	DARI	FENI	GYRI	KADI	KEPI	MALI	MIRI	NEVI	PERI
CADI	DELI	FINI	HAJI	KAKI	KIWI	MANI	MODI	NIDI	PILI
CAPI	DIVI	FOCI	HILI	KALI	KURI	MAXI	MOKI	NISI	PIPI

PURI	RAKI	ROTI	SEMI	SORI	TAXI	TOPI	VAGI	WALI	YONI
QADI	RAMI	SAKI	SIMI	TABI	TIKI	TORI	VALI	WILI	ZATI
RABI	RANI	SARI	SIRI	TAKI	TIPI	UGLI	VLEI	YETI	ZITI
RAGI	ROJI	SATI	SOLI	TALI	TITI	UNCI	WADI	YOGI	

5-letter words ending in -I

ABACI	BLINI	CORGI	FRATI	JINNI	LURGI	OZEKI	RISHI	SWAMI	URAEI
ACARI	BRAVI	CORNI	FUNDI	KANJI	MAQUI	PAGRI	RUBAI	TAKHI	URALI
ACINI	BUFFI	CURSI	FUNGI	KARRI	MEDII	PALKI	SALMI	TANGI	URARI
AGAMI	BWAZI	DARZI	GARNI	KATTI	MODII	PALPI	SAMPI	TANTI	UTERI
AGGRI	BYSSI	DHOBI	GENII	KAURI	MOOLI	PAOLI	SCAPI	TARSI	VILLI
AGUTI	CACTI	DHOTI	GHAZI	KHADI	MUFTI	PARDI	SCUDI	TEMPI	WONGI
AIDOI	CARDI	DILLI	GOBBI	KHAKI	MYTHI	PARKI	SERAI	TERAI	XYSTI
AIOLI	CARPI	DUOMI	GUSLI	KIKOI	NAEVI	PARTI	SHCHI	THAGI	ZIMBI
ALIBI	CEILI	ELCHI	HADJI	KIRRI	NIMBI	PERAI	SHOGI	THOLI	ZOMBI
APPUI	CERCI	ELEMI	HAJJI	KOORI	NISEI	PILEI	SHOJI	THYMI	
ARDRI	CESTI	ENNUI	HONGI	KUKRI	NOMOI	PIRAI	SOLDI	TONDI	
ASSAI	CHILI	ENOKI	HOURI	LASSI	OBELI	POORI	SPAHI	TOPHI	
AULOI	CHOLI	ENVOI	IAMBI	LATHI	OBOLI	PUTTI	STOAI	TOPOI	
AUREI	CIPPI	FARCI	IMARI	LAZZI	OCULI	QUASI	STYLI	TORII	
BAJRI	CIRRI	FASCI	IMSHI	LENTI	OKAPI	RABBI	SUCCI	TORSI	
BASSI	COATI	FASTI	INDRI	LICHI	ORIBI	RADII	SULCI	TRAGI	
BENNI	COCCI	FERMI	ISSEI	LUNGI	OVOLI	RECTI	SUSHI	TUTTI	

6-letter words ending in -I

ACULEI	BINGHI	CUMULI	GEMINI	KABUKI	MODULI	PAPYRI	SAMITI	SOUARI	UAKARI
AGOUTI	BOLETI	CURARI	GHARRI	KAIKAI	MOPANI	PERITI	SANCAI	STRATI	UNCINI
ALKALI	BONSAI	CYATHI	GILGAI	KIMCHI	MUESLI	PHALLI	SANDHI	SUNDRI	URACHI
ALUMNI	BORZOI	CYTISI	GLUTEI	KOUROI	MUNSHI	PITHOI	SANSEI	TAHINI	WAKIKI
ANNULI	BUKSHI	DECANI	GOMUTI	KOWHAI	MYTHOI	PITURI	SATORI	TAMARI	WAPITI
ARCHEI	BURITI	DEWANI	GRIGRI	KUMARI	NAGARI	POLYPI	SBIRRI	TAPETI	XYSTOI
ARGALI	CALAMI	DHOOTI	GURAMI	LIMULI	NEROLI	PUTELI	SCAMPI	TATAMI	YANQUI
ARGULI	CANTHI	DJINNI	HAIKAI	LITCHI	NIELLI	RAGINI	SCYPHI	THALLI	YOGINI
ARILLI	CAROLI	DROMOI	HAMULI	LOBULI	NILGAI	RAMULI	SESELI	THOLOI	ZUFOLI
ARIOSI	CESTUI	DUETTI	HUMERI	LOCULI	NOSTOI	RENVOI	SHALLI	THYRSI	
ASKARI	CHATTI	ECHINI	ILLUPI	MALLEI	NUCLEI	RHOMBI	SHTCHI	TIFOSI	
AVANTI	CHICHI	ELTCHI	INCAVI	MANATI	OCELLI	RUBATI	SHUFTI	TITOKI	
BAILLI	CHILLI	EMBOLI	INCUBI	MAULVI	OCTOPI	SACCOI	SIDDHI	TOITOI	
BANZAI	CHOKRI	EPHEBI	JAWARI	MAZHBI	OCTROI	SAFARI	SILENI	TORULI	
BHAKTI	CHOWRI	EURIPI	JOWARI	MEISHI	OURALI	SAIKEI	SIMPAI	TROCHI	
BHINDI	CLYPEI	FLOCCI	JUDOGI	MILADI	OURARI	SAKKOI	SMALTI	TROPHI	
BHISTI	COLOBI	GARDAI	JUNGLI	MIRITI	OUREBI	SALAMI	SOLIDI	TSOTSI	
BIKINI	CONGII	GELATI	JUPATI	MISHMI	PALAGI	SALUKI	SONERI	TUMULI	

7-letter words ending in -I

ABOMASI	BIRYANI	COENURI	ETOURDI	JUKSKEI	NAUTILI	RAVIOLI	SECONDI	THALAMI
ACOUCHI	BOUILLI	COLIBRI	FAGOTTI	KABADDI	NONETTI	REMBLAI	SENARII	THROMBI
ALFAQUI	BRONCHI	COLOSSI	FLOKATI	KACHERI	NUCELLI	REVERSI	SERKALI	TIMPANI
ALIZARI	CADUCEI	CORTILI	FORZATI	KAHAWAI	NURAGHI	RHIZOPI	SERRATI	TONDINI
ALVEOLI	CALATHI	CRIMINI	FUMETTI	KAMICHI	ORIGAMI	RHOMBOI	SHIKARI	TORTONI
AMORINI	CALCULI	DAKOITI	FUSILLI	LAMPUKI	OUAKARI	RHONCHI	SIGNORI	TRIPOLI
ANESTRI	CALZONI	DAQUIRI	GHILGAI	LAPILLI	OUSTITI	RHYTHMI	SONDELI	TSUNAMI
ANZIANI	CANZONI	DASHEKI	GINGILI	LECYTHI	PACHISI	RIKISHI	SOPRANI	TYMPANI
APPALTI	CAVETTI	DASHIKI	GLUTAEI	MACRAMI	PADRONI	RILIEVI	SORDINI	URCEOLI
ARCHAEI	CEMBALI	DEMENTI	GNOCCHI	MAESTRI	PALAZZI	RIPIENI	SPLENII	VENTURI
ASSAGAI	CHAPATI	DENARII	GOURAMI	MAFIOSI	PECCAVI	SACCULI	STAMNOI	VITELLI
ASSEGAI	CHARQUI	DIDAKAI	GRADINI	MARCONI	PENUCHI	SAIMIRI	STICHOI	VOLVULI
ASTATKI	CHIASMI	DIDAKEI	GUARANI	MARTINI	PINDARI	SAMADHI	STIMULI	WISTITI
BACCHII	CHILIOI	DIDICOI	HALLALI	MATSURI	PRELUDI	SAMURAI	STRETTI	WOORALI
BACILLI	CHONDRI	DOCHMII	HIBACHI	MENISCI	PRONAOI	SAOUARI	SUCCUBI	WOURALI
BAMBINI	CHORAGI	EFFENDI	JACUZZI	MODELLI	PULVINI	SARANGI	SUNDARI	ZAKUSKI
BASENJI	CHOREGI	ELENCHI	JAMDANI	MODIOLI	QUILLAI	SASHIMI	SURCULI	ZAMPONI
BAZOUKI	CHUPATI	EMERITI	JAMPANI	MOLOSSI	RABBONI	SCALENI	SYLLABI	ZUFFOLI
BILIMBI	CLARINI	EPIGONI	JINJILI	NAUPLII	RANGOLI	SCHERZI	TERMINI	

8-letter words ending in -I

ACOEMETI	CALCANEI	CUNJEVOI	GLADIOLI	MARAVEDI	PERIBOLI	SHERWANI	THESAURI
ALBERGHI	CALYCULI	DAIQUIRI	GRAFFITI	MARCHESI	PERRADII	SIGISBEI	TRAPEZII
AMORETTI	CANCELLI	DECUBITI	HAEREMAI	MARIACHI	PIROSHKI	SOFFIONI	TZATZIKI
ANOESTRI	CANTHARI	DIADOCHI	HALLOUMI	MENOMINI	PIROZHKI	SOLFEGGI	UMBILICI
ANTENATI	CAPITANI	DIPTEROI	HETAIRAI	MORBILLI	POSTNATI	SOUVLAKI	URANISCI
ASSEGAAI	CAPRICCI	DIVIDIVI	HYDROSKI	NANNYGAI	PRODROMI	STAPEDII	UTRICULI
BANDITTI	CASTRATI	DRACHMAI	KACHAHRI	NARCISSI	PULVILLI	STOTINKI	VIRTUOSI
BERIBERI	CHAPATTI	DUPONDII	KOFTGARI	NENNIGAI	RENMINBI	STROBILI	YAKITORI
BIMBASHI	CHUPATTI	DURUKULI	KOHLRABI	NIRAMIAI	RETIARII	SUKIYAKI	ZASTRUGI
BIRIYANI	CICERONI	DUUMVIRI	KOMITAJI	NUCLEOLI	RIGATONI	SUMOTORI	ZECCHINI
BONAMANI	CICISBEI	ESOPHAGI	LEKYTHOI	OBLIGATI	RISPETTI	TAGLIONI	ZOOPHORI
BOSTANGI	CONCEPTI	FASCISMI	LIBRETTI	OUISTITI	RYOTWARI	TANDOORI	ZUCCHINI
BOUZOUKI	CONCERTI	FASCISTI	LINGUINI	PARCHESI	SANNYASI	TARAKIHI	
BOZZETTI	CONCETTI	FEDELINI	LITERATI	PASTICCI	SARTORII	TEDESCHI	
BRINDISI	CONDUCTI	FLOCCULI	LUMBRICI	PASTRAMI	SASTRUGI	TEOCALLI	
BROCCOLI	CONFETTI	FORZANDI	MACARONI	PEDICULI	SCALDINI	TERAKIHI	
BUMALOTI	CORNETTI	FUNICULI	MAHARANI	PEPERONI	SFORZATI	TERIYAKI	
CALAMARI	COTHURNI	GINGLYMI	MALLEOLI	PERFECTI	SHANGHAI	TERZETTI	

WORDS ENDING IN -O

2-letter words ending in -O

BO	GO	IO	KO	MO	OO	SO	WO	ZO
DO	HO	JO	LO	NO	PO	TO	YO	

3-letter words ending in -O

ADO	BRO	DUO	FRO	HOO	MOO	POO	THO	UFO	ZHO
AGO	COO	DZO	GEO	ISO	OBO	PRO	TOO	WHO	ZOO
BIO	DOO	ECO	GIO	LOO	OHO	RHO	TWO	WOO	
BOO	DSO	EGO	GOO	MHO	PHO	ROO	UDO	YGO	

4-letter words ending in -O

AERO	BOZO	DODO	GAJO	INTO	LILO	MOKO	PYRO	SUMO	UPGO
AFRO	BRIO	DOJO	GAPO	JATO	LIMO	MONO	REDO	SYBO	URAO
AGIO	BROO	DURO	GIRO	JIAO	LINO	MUSO	REGO	TACO	VETO
ALSO	BUBO	DZHO	GOBO	JOCO	LOBO	ODSO	REPO	TARO	VINO
ALTO	BUDO	ECCO	GOGO	JOMO	LOCO	OLEO	RIVO	THRO	VIVO
AMBO	BUFO	ECHO	GYRO	JUDO	LOGO	OLIO	SAGO	TIRO	WINO
AMMO	CAPO	EDDO	HALO	KAGO	LOTO	ONTO	SECO	TOCO	YUKO
ANNO	CIAO	ERGO	HARO	KAYO	LUDO	OTTO	SEGO	TOHO	ZERO
ARCO	CITO	EURO	HERO	KENO	MAKO	OUZO	SHMO	TOKO	ZOBO
ARVO	COCO	EXPO	HOBO	KILO	MANO	PACO	SHOO	TRIO	
AUTO	COHO	FADO	HOMO	KINO	MEMO	PEPO	SIJO	TYPO	
BEGO	DADO	FARO	HUSO	KOLO	MICO	PESO	SILO	TYRO	
BITO	DAGO	FICO	HYPO	KOTO	MILO	POCO	SKEO	UMBO	
BOKO	DECO	FIGO	INFO	LAZO	MINO	POGO	SKIO	UNCO	
BOLO	DEMO	FILO	INGO	LENO	MISO	POLO	SOHO	UNDO	
BOYO	DIDO	FINO	INRO	LIDO	MOJO	PROO	SOLO	UNTO	

5-letter words ending in -O

ADDIO	BASTO	BUROO	CHINO	CORSO	DITTO	FORGO	GONZO	HULLO	KAZOO
AGGRO	BEANO	BURRO	CHOCO	CREDO	DOGGO	FUERO	GREGO	HYDRO	KEMBO
AMIGO	BILBO	CACAO	CHOKO	CUFFO	DOHYO	GADSO	GUACO	IGAPO	KENDO
AUDIO	BIMBO	CAMEO	CISCO	CURIO	DSOBO	GAMBO	GUANO	IGLOO	KIDDO
AVISO	BINGO	CAMPO	CLARO	CUTTO	DSOMO	GARBO	GUIRO	IMAGO	KIMBO
AWETO	BOMBO	CANTO	COCCO	CYCLO	DUMBO	GAZOO	GUMBO	INTRO	LARGO
BABOO	BONGO	CARGO	COMBO	DANIO	DUNNO	GECKO	GUSTO	IROKO	LASSO
BACCO	BORGO	CASCO	COMMO	DECKO	DUOMO	GESSO	GYPPO	JAMBO	LAZZO
BALOO	BRAVO	CELLO	COMPO	DEKKO	ESTRO	GIPPO	HALLO	JELLO	LENTO
BANCO	BUCKO	CENTO	CONDO	DIAZO	FANGO	GISMO	HELLO	JINGO	LESBO
BANJO	BUFFO	CHACO	CONGO	DILDO	FATSO	GIZMO	HILLO	JOCKO	LIMBO
BARDO	BUMBO	CHIAO	CONTO	DINGO	FIBRO	GOBBO	HIPPO	JUMBO	LINGO
BASHO	BUNCO	CHICO	CONVO	DIPSO	FOLIO	GODSO	HOLLO	JUNCO	LITHO
BASSO	BUNKO	CHIMO	CORNO	DISCO	FORDO	GOMBO	HOWSO	JUNTO	LLANO

LOTTO MICRO NEGRO PHOTO PROSO REGGO SCHMO STYLO VERSO ZINCO
MACHO MILKO NGAIO PIANO PULMO REPRO SCUDO TABOO VIDEO ZIPPO
MACRO MISDO ORTHO PIEZO PUNTO RETRO SECCO TACHO VIREO ZOCCO
MAIKO MISGO OUTDO PINGO PUTTO RHINO SEGNO TANGO VISTO ZOPPO
MAMBO MOLTO OUTGO PINKO QUIPO RODEO SERVO TANTO VULGO ZORRO
MANGO MONDO OVOLO PINTO RADIO RONDO SHAKO TEMPO WACKO
MANTO MORRO PANTO POLIO RATIO RONEO SICKO TENNO WAHOO
MATLO MOTTO PAOLO PONGO RATOO RUMBO SMOKO TIMBO WHOSO
MATZO MUCRO PAREO PORNO RAZOO SALTO SOCKO TONDO YAHOO
MENTO MUNGO PASEO POTOO REALO SALVO SOLDO TORSO YARTO
MESTO NACHO PATIO POTTO RECCO SAMBO SORDO TURBO YOBBO
METRO NAPOO PEDRO PRIMO RECTO SANKO SORGO TYPTO ZAMBO
MEZZO NARCO PESTO PROMO REFFO SARGO SPADO UREDO ZHOMO

6-letter words ending in -O

ABRAZO BONITO DAIMIO GABBRO HERETO MANITO PHYLLO ROCOCO STEREO VAUDOO
ADAGIO BOOBOO DAYGLO GALAGO HETERO MANOAO PHYSIO ROTOLO STINGO VIBRIO
AIKIDO BRONCO DOMINO GAUCHO HONCHO MATICO POMATO RUBATO STINKO VIGORO
AKIMBO BUMALO DORADO GAZEBO HOODOO MEDICO POMELO SAMFOO STUCCO VIRAGO
ALBEDO BURGOO DRONGO GELATO HOOROO MELANO PONCHO SANCHO STUDIO VIRINO
ALBINO CALICO DUELLO GENTOO IGNARO MERINO POTATO SAPEGO SUBITO VOMITO
ALBUGO CALIGO DUETTO GHERAO INCAVO MIKADO PRESTO SBIRRO TATTOO VOODOO
ANATTO CAMSHO DYNAMO GHETTO INDIGO MIOMBO PRONTO SCHIZO TECHNO VORAGO
ANGICO CASINO EMBRYO GIGOLO JOURNO MODULO PSEUDO SCRUTO TENUTO WANDOO
APOLLO CATALO ENHALO GINGKO KAKAPO MORPHO PSYCHO SHACKO TERCIO WEIRDO
ARIOSO CHEAPO ERINGO GINKGO KATIPO NANDOO PUEBLO SHEEPO TEREDO WHACKO
ARISTO CHOCHO ERYNGO GITANO KIMONO NARDOO PUKEKO SHIPPO THICKO WHAMMO
ARROYO CHOCKO ESCUDO GIUSTO KOODOO NIELLO PUMELO SHIVOO THUGGO WHATSO
BABACO CHROMO FASCIO GOMBRO KORERO NUNCIO PUNCTO SISSOO TIFOSO ZELOSO
BAGNIO CICERO FIASCO GOMUTO LANUGO NYMPHO QUANGO SKIDOO TOMATO ZOOZOO
BAGUIO COLUGO FINSKO GOOROO LAVABO OCTAVO QUARTO SMALTO TORERO ZORINO
BAMBOO COMEDO FOREGO GORGIO LEGATO OVERDO RABATO SOLANO TRILLO ZUFOLO
BARRIO COMODO FORHOO GRINGO LIBERO OVERGO RANCHO SOLITO TROPPO
BISTRO COROZO FRANCO GROTTO LIBIDO PALOLO REBATO SORGHO TUPELO
BLANCO CRAMBO FRESCO GUANGO LOLIGO PARAMO REGULO SPEEDO TURACO
BLOTTO CRYPTO FUGATO HAIRDO LUCUMO PEDALO RIGHTO STALKO TUXEDO
BOLERO CUCKOO FUMADO HALLOO MACACO PEPINO ROBALO STANZO ULTIMO

7-letter words ending in -O

AGITATO BRONCHO CONCEDO GESTAPO MODELLO PEDRERO REVERSO SORDINO UNDERDO
AILANTO BUDGERO COQUITO GIOCOSO MONTERO PEEKABO RIDOTTO SQUACCO UNDERGO
ALBERGO BUFFALO CORANTO GRADINO MORELLO PERSICO RILIEVO STRETTO VAQUERO
ALLEGRO BUGABOO CORNUTO GUANACO MORENDO PIANINO RIPIENO SUBZERO VERISMO
AMORINO BUMMALO CRIOLLO HIDALGO MORISCO PICCOLO RISOTTO SUPREMO VERTIGO
AMOROSO BURRITO CRUSADO HISTRIO MOROCCO PIFFERO RONDINO SYNCHRO VIBRATO
ANNATTO BUSHIDO CRUZADO HORNITO MULATTO PIMENTO ROSOLIO TAMARAO VILIACO
APPALTO CALANDO CURACAO HUANACO NATHEMO PINTADO SAGUARO TANGELO VILIAGO
ARNOTTO CALYPSO CYMBALO IMPASTO NAVARHO PLACEBO SALTATO TEDESCO VIRANDO
ARRIERO CANTICO DIABOLO INFERNO NELUMBO PLENIPO SAMSHOO TENTIGO VOLCANO
ASINICO CARABAO EIGHTVO LENTIGO NITROSO POINADO SAPSAGO TESTUDO VOLPINO
ATISHOO CASSINO ELECTRO LLANERO NONETTO POMPANO SCALADO THEORBO WENDIGO
AVOCADO CATTALO EMBARGO LUMBAGO NORTENO POMPELO SCHERZO THERETO WHERESO
AZULEJO CAVETTO ESPARTO MADRONO OKIMONO PORRIGO SCIOLTO TIMPANO WHERETO
BAMBINO CEMBALO ETAERIO MAESTRO OLOROSO PORTICO SECONDO TOBACCO WINDIGO
BAROCCO CENTAVO FAGOTTO MAFIOSO OREGANO POTOROO SENECIO TOMBOLO ZAMARRO
BARRICO CENTIMO FARRAGO MAGNETO PAISANO PRIMERO SERPIGO TONDINO ZANJERO
BATTERO CHAMISO FERRUGO MALICHO PAKAPOO PRIVADO SFUMATO TORNADO ZEMSTVO
BEEFALO CHEERIO FINNSKO MARCATO PALAZZO PROVISO SHAKUDO TORPEDO ZOCCOLO
BOTARGO CHICANO FORZATO MEMENTO PAMPERO PROXIMO SHAMPOO TOURACO ZORILLO
BRACCIO CHORIZO FUMETTO MESTIZO PAPILIO PRURIGO SIROCCO TREMOLO ZUFFOLO
BRASERO CLARINO FURIOSO MISTICO PASSADO REJONEO SOLDADO TROMINO
BRAVADO COMMODO GAMBADO MOCKADO PATRICO RELIEVO SOPRANO TYMPANO

8-letter words ending in -O

ALFRESCO ARMIGERO AUTOGIRO BARBASCO BESOGNIO BORDELLO BUCKAYRO CAMISADO
AMARETTO ARPEGGIO AUTOGYRO BARGELLO BONAMANO BOZZETTO BUCKEROO CAPITANO
AMORETTO ASSIENTO BALLYHOO BARRANCO BORACHIO BUCKAROO CACAFOGO CASTRATO

CAUDILLO CHARANGO CHARNECO CHECHAKO CICISBEO COCKATOO COMMANDO CONCERTO CONCETTO CONTANGO CONTINUO CONTORNO CORAGGIO CORNETTO COROCORO CRUZEIRO CURCULIO DOLOROSO DUETTINO ENCIERRO ESCALADO
ESCAPADO ESPRESSO ESPUMOSO EXPRESSO FALSETTO FANDANGO FASCISMO FELLATIO FINNESKO FINOCHIO FLAMENCO FLAMINGO FORZANDO GALAPAGO GARBANZO GARDYLOO GAZPACHO GILLAROO GRACIOSO GRAFFITO GRAZIOSO
GUACHARO HALLALOO HEREUNTO HITHERTO HUAQUERO HUBBUBOO IMPETIGO INNUENDO INTAGLIO INTONACO JACKAROO JACKEROO JALAPENO JILLAROO JORDELOO JUNKANOO KAKEMONO KANGAROO LENTANDO LIBECCIO LIBRETTO
LITERATO LOCOFOCO MACHISMO MAESTOSO MAKIMONO MALGRADO MALLECHO MAMELUCO MANCANDO MANZELLO MARTELLO MODERATO MONTANTO MOSQUITO NEUTRINO NOCTILIO OBLIGATO OCOTILLO ORATORIO OSTINATO OTTAVINO
PACHINKO PADERERO PALAMINO PALISADO PALMETTO PALOMINO PARLANDO PATERERO PEDERERO PEEKABOO PEPERINO PERDENDO PERFECTO PIMIENTO PLUMBAGO POIGNADO POLITICO PRELUDIO PRESIDIO PRUNELLO PULVILIO
RANCHERO REDDENDO RENEGADO RISOLUTO RISPETTO RITENUTO ROSOGLIO SALTANDO SARGASSO SCALDINO SCENARIO SCIROCCO SCORDATO SEICENTO SERAGLIO SESTETTO SFORZATO SIGISBEO SMORZATO SOLIDAGO SOMBRERO
SPADILLO SPICCATO STACCATO STAMPEDO STICCADO STICCATO STILETTO STOCCADO SUBAUDIO SUBIMAGO SUPEREGO SUPERLOO SUPPEAGO TAPACOLO TAPACULO TAPADERO TENEBRIO TERRAZZO TERZETTO TRAPUNTO TRECENTO
TUCOTUCO TUCUTUCO TWELVEMO UMBRELLO VARGUENO VARLETTO VERDELHO VILLAGIO VILLIAGO VINDALOO VIRTUOSO VITILIGO WALLAROO WANDEROO ZECCHINO ZUCHETTO

WORDS ENDING IN -U

2-letter words ending in -U

GU MU NU OU XU YU

3-letter words ending in -U

AYU CRU EAU
ECU EMU FEU
FLU FOU GAU
GJU GNU JEU
KYU LEU MEU
MOU PIU SOU
TAU UTU VAU
YOU

4-letter words ending in -U

AITU BABU BAJU BALU BAPU
BEAU CHOU CLOU ECRU EMEU
FRAU GENU GURU JUJU KUDU
KUKU KURU LIEU LUAU LULU
MASU MENU MOTU OMBU PRAU
PUDU PUKU PULU RAKU RATU
RIMU RURU SULU TABU TAPU
TATU TEGU THOU THRU TOFU
TOLU TUTU UNAU VATU ZEBU
ZOBU ZULU

5-letter words ending in -U

ADIEU BANTU BAYOU BIJOU BOYAU
BUCHU BUCKU BUNDU BUSSU CORNU
COYPU FICHU HAIKU HOKKU JAMBU
KANZU KOMBU KUDZU LASSU MUNTU
NANDU NIKAU NOYAU PAREU PERDU
PILAU POILU PRAHU QUIPU SADHU
SAJOU SAMFU SHOYU SNAFU TATOU
UHURU URUBU VERTU VIRTU VOULU
WUSHU

6-letter words ending in -U

ABATTU ACAJOU AMADOU APERCU
BATEAU BUREAU CACHOU CADEAU
CONGOU COTEAU DETENU EPERDU
GAGAKU GATEAU GOMOKU INGENU
JABIRU KIKUYU LANDAU MILIEU
MZUNGU NHANDU NILGAU NOGAKU
ORMOLU PILLAU PIUPIU RESEAU
ROUCOU SADDHU SAMSHU SUBFEU
TAMANU TELEDU VOUDOU YNAMBU

7-letter words ending in -U

BABASSU BANDEAU BEBEERU BERCEAU BUNRAKU
CAMAIEU CARDECU CARIBOU CATECHU CATTABU
CHANOYU CHAPEAU CHATEAU CORBEAU FABLIAU
INCONNU JAMBEAU MANITOU MANTEAU MARABOU
MOINEAU MORCEAU NOUVEAU NYLGHAU PARVENU
PLATEAU PONCEAU PURLIEU ROKKAKU RONDEAU
ROULEAU SAPAJOU SEPPUKU SHIATSU SHIATZU
TABLEAU TAMANDU TAMARAU TIMARAU TINAMOU
TONNEAU TRUMEAU

8-letter words ending in -U

ABOIDEAU ABOITEAU CARCAJOU
CARIACOU CARJACOU FELDGRAU
FLAMBEAU HAUSFRAU KABELJOU
KINKAJOU MINSHUKU NINJITSU
NINJUTSU NUNCHAKU PIRARUCU
PYENGADU SUCURUJU SURUCUCU
THANKYOU TIRAMISU TSUTSUMU

SECTION THREE

BONUS WORD LISTS

Introduction

Since there is a 50-point bonus for playing all seven tiles at one turn, seven-letter words are an essential part of the Scrabble player's vocabulary. As seven tiles can also be played around an existing letter on the board, eight-letter words are also a key part of the Scrabble player's word knowledge. Any words which use all seven of the letters on your rack are called bonus words, or just plain bonuses. Bonuses usually have seven or eight letters, but could have more. (In the USA and some other parts of the world, words which score a 50-point bonus are called 'bingos'.)

6-plus-1 sets

Some seven-letter words are more useful than others, simply because they are more likely to occur, given the distribution of letters in the Scrabble set. For this reason, it is an unnecessary task (and a painstakingly lengthy one!) to attempt to learn all of the seven-letter words. There are over 26 000 seven-letter words, yet it is much more worthwhile (and a lot easier!) to concentrate on some of the 20-25% that are going to be the most useful to you. Such seven-letter words can be arranged conveniently according to common six-letter groups of letters (stems). Each stem yields a set of seven-letter words that can be made by the addition of a single seventh letter. These are the '6-plus-1 sets' – six letters plus another one letter to make a variety of seven-letter words. The more different letters of the alphabet that a stem goes with, the higher its utility to the Scrabble player.

6-plus-2 sets

Similar considerations also apply to the 8-letter words, the '6-plus-2 sets'. There will be many occasions when the seven tiles on your rack can be added to a single letter already on the board, to make an eight-letter word.

Perhaps the seven letters on your rack do not make a bonus word by themselves. Even if they do, perhaps the bonus word won't fit in on the board anywhere. These are the occasions when you may need to think bigger – eight-letter words! Of course, the seven-letter word on your rack may go down on the board, but the eight-letter word might score quite a few more points. Sometimes an eight-letter word will score a lot more points, if it covers two triple-word-score squares – this is the 'nine-timer' that Scrabble players strive for.

The 6-letter stems

The 250 6-letter stems used as the basis for the 6-plus-1 and 6-plus-2 sets represent the 250 most likely and most fruitful stems, based on an algorithm of the probability of the six letters occurring and the number of different letters the stem combines with.

A list of these stems is shown before the 6-plus-1 sets, with the letters in the stems in alphabetical order and – in turn – the stems listed in alphabetical order. Alongside each stem is shown its respective position (or 'ranking') in the top 250, as well as a mnemonic of the stem as an aide-mémoire. For example, AEINRT has a ranking of 1 and the mnemonic RETAIN, while AAEMNT has a ranking of 229 and the mnemonic MANATE. Note that not all the mnemonics are real words, but it is nevertheless easier to recall that MANATE plus an I makes ANIMATE, rather than that AAEMNT plus an I does.

These six-letter stems simplify learning and should assist recollection during an actual game. If the concept is new to you, then just concentrate on two or three of the most fertile stems, such as AEINRT, AENRST and EGINRS. When the seven- or eight-letter words associated with these become familiar, move on and tackle other six-letter stems.

Alphabetic list of all the words in the bonus sets

Following the 6-plus-1 sets is a straightforward alphabetical listing of all the seven-letter words appearing in the 6-plus-1 sets. All duplicates have been removed. Similarly, an alphabetic list of the eight-letter words follows the 6-plus-2 sets.

Additional high probability bonus words

Many worthwhile seven- and eight-letter words don't appear in the 6-plus-1 and 6-plus-2 sets, even though they have combinations of letters which are quite likely to occur. More about these later on.

SUMMARY OF 6-LETTER STEMS
in alphabetical order, showing ranking and mnemonic

Stem	Rank	Mnemonic
AAEMNT	229	MANATE
ABDEIR	134	ABRIDE
ABEILS	188	ISABEL
ABELRT	207	ALBERT
ABEORS	144	ABORES
ABERST	122	BREAST
ACDERS	240	SACRED
ACEILR	121	LACIER
ACEINR	65	CANIER
ACEINS	119	INCASE
ACELST	243	CASTLE
ACENRS	175	CANERS
ACENRT	96	CANTER
ACENST	149	STANCE
ACEORS	103	ORACES
ACEOST	146	ACTOSE
ACERST	141	CATERS
ACIRST	245	ARTICS
ADEERS	70	SEARED
ADEEST	85	SEATED
ADEGLN	197	DANGLE
ADEGNR	126	DANGER
ADEGRS	221	GRADES
ADEILR	19	RAILED
ADEILS	33	LADIES
ADEINR	4	RAINED
ADEINS	22	SANDIE
ADEIRS	12	RAISED
ADEIST	26	IDATES
ADELNR	79	LANDER
ADELNS	137	ANDLES
ADELRS	88	ALDERS
ADELST	110	SALTED
ADEMNS	246	AMENDS
ADENRS	62	ANDERS
ADENRU	64	AUNDER
ADENST	36	STANED
ADEORS	48	ADORES
ADEPRT	228	PRATED
ADERRS	235	ARDERS
ADERST	49	DATERS
ADGINR	135	RADING
ADINRS	105	DRAINS
AEELRS	72	EALERS
AEEMRS	238	SEAMER
AEEPRT	142	REPEAT
AEERRS	162	ERASER
AEERST	20	EATERS
AEGILN	55	EALING
AEGINR	15	EARING
AEGLNR	91	ANGLER
AEGLNS	170	ANGLES
AEGLNT	118	TANGLE
AEGLRS	167	LAGERS
AEGLST	187	GLATES
AEGNRS	86	ANGERS
AEGNRT	54	GANTER
AEGNST	115	TANGES
AEGRST	80	GATERS
AEHLRT	212	LATHER
AEHRST	169	HATERS
AEILMN	133	MALINE
AEILNT	11	ENTAIL
AEILRS	16	SAILER
AEILRT	10	RETAIL
AEILSS	248	LASSIE
AEILST	24	ALITES
AEIMNR	61	REMAIN
AEIMNS	98	MANIES
AEIMNT	53	INMATE
AEIMRS	112	ARMIES
AEIMST	95	MATIES
AEINRS	6	SARNIE
AEINRT	1	RETAIN
AEINST	2	SATINE
AEIPRS	75	PRAISE
AEIRST	3	SATIRE
AEIRTT	29	ATTIRE
AEISTT	83	TASTIE
AELMNT	211	LAMENT
AELNRS	63	LANERS
AELNRT	28	ANTLER
AELNST	34	ANTLES
AELORS	42	ALORES
AELOST	46	SOLATE
AELPRS	231	PALERS
AELPRT	206	PLATER
AELRST	38	ALTERS
AEMNST	168	STAMEN
AEMRST	124	MATERS
AENNST	152	ANNETS
AENPST	185	PATENS
AENRRT	87	RANTER
AENRSS	223	SANERS
AENRST	9	ANTERS
AENRTT	71	NATTER
AENSTT	116	ATTENS
AEORST	13	ORATES
AEPRST	129	PATERS
AERRST	138	RATERS
AERSST	220	ASSERT
AERSTT	97	TASTER
AERSTW	194	WATERS
AGILNR	199	RALING
AGILNS	219	SIGNAL
AGILNT	174	LATING
AGINRS	123	GRAINS
AGINRT	69	RATING
AGINST	108	SATING
AINRST	40	TRAINS
AINSTT	213	TANIST
ANORST	60	RATONS
BDEIRS	242	BRIDES
BEILRS	205	LIBERS
BEIRST	184	TRIBES
BEORST	225	STROBE
CEINOS	109	CONIES
CEINRS	183	INCERS
CEINST	196	INSECT
CEIORS	156	COSIER
CEIRST	166	CITERS
CENORS	172	CONERS
CENOST	224	CONEST
CEORST	234	CORSET
DEEINR	43	DENIER
DEEIRS	58	RESIDE
DEELNS	239	ENDLES
DEENRS	92	ENDERS
DEENST	111	NESTED
DEERST	151	RESTED
DEGILN	164	DINGLE
DEGINR	82	RINGED
DEGINS	154	SINGED
DEGIRS	210	GRIDES
DEILNS	120	INDLES
DEILRT	73	TRIDLE
DEINOS	41	ONSIDE
DEINRS	51	DINERS
DEINRU	52	RUINED
DEINST	32	SINTED
DEIORS	27	ORIDES
DEIOST	35	ODITES
DEIPRT	215	PRITED
DEIRST	57	STRIDE
DEIRSU	143	URDIES
DELNOS	181	OLDENS
DELORS	145	OLDERS
DELORT	100	DOLTER
DENORU	99	UNDOER
DENOST	74	STONED
DENRSU	179	UNDERS
DENSTU	217	UNSTED
DEORST	50	SORTED
DEOSTU	180	OUSTED
DERSTU	244	RUSTED
DGINOR	209	ORDING
EEFIRS	241	FERIES
EEGNRS	237	GREENS
EEILRS	90	RELIES
EEILRV	232	RELIVE
EEILST	89	ELITES
EEIMNS	192	EMINES
EEIMRS	202	MISERE
EEINRT	8	ENTIRE
EEIRRS	182	ERRIES
EEIRST	31	ESTIER
EEIRSV	222	REVISE
EELNST	161	NESTLE
EELRST	157	ELTERS
EENRST	56	ENTERS
EEORSV	247	REVOSE
EERRST	236	RESTER
EERSTT	200	ETTERS
EFIRST	191	STRIFE
EGHINT	250	ETHING
EGILNR	125	LINGER
EGILNS	117	SINGLE
EGILNT	66	TINGLE
EGILOS	132	LOGIES
EGILRS	159	LIGERS
EGILST	190	LEGIST
EGINNR	178	GINNER
EGINOS	78	INGOES
EGINRS	68	SINGER
EGINRT	39	TINGER
EGINST	107	ESTING
EGNORS	155	ONGERS
EHINRS	227	SHRINE
EHIRST	153	ITHERS
EHORST	189	OTHERS
EIILST	139	TILIES
EIINRT	30	INTIRE
EILNOS	47	OLINES
EILNRS	77	LINERS
EILNST	45	INTLES

Stem	No.	Word
EILORS	37	OILERS
EILORT	18	LOITER
EILOST	21	OILETS
EILRST	44	LITERS
EILSTU	136	UTILES
EIMNOS	131	MONIES
EIMNRS	177	MINERS
EIMNST	201	MINEST
EIMOST	150	SOMITE
EIMRST	140	MITERS
EINNST	113	SINNET
EINOPS	130	PONIES
EINORS	7	SENIOR
EINOSS	204	SONSIE
EINOST	14	TONIES
EINPRS	158	PINERS
EINPST	148	INSTEP
EINRSS	249	RESINS
EINRST	17	INTERS
EINRSV	226	VINERS
EINRTT	76	TINTER
EINRTU	25	TUNIER
EINSST	218	INSETS
EINSTT	160	INTEST
EINSTU	81	UNITES
EIOPST	101	SOPITE
EIORSS	214	SORIES
EIORST	5	TORIES
EIORSV	127	VIROSE
EIOSTT	93	OTTIES
EIPRST	147	STRIPE
EIRRST	165	TRIERS
EIRSTT	104	SITTER
EIRSTV	163	STRIVE
ELNSTU	216	LUNETS
ELORST	67	TOLERS
ELOSTU	173	TOUSLE
ELRSTU	208	RUSTLE
EMNORS	230	SERMON
EMNOST	186	MONETS
EMORST	198	MOTERS
ENOPRS	203	PERSON
ENORST	23	TONERS
ENOSTT	195	ONTEST
ENOSTU	94	OUTENS
ENRSTU	84	TUNERS
EOPRST	193	POSTER
EORRST	106	SORTER
EORSTT	114	OTTERS
GIINRT	233	TIRING
GILNOT	171	TOLING
GINORS	128	SIGNOR
GINORT	102	ROTING
GINOST	176	OSTING
INORST	59	TRIONS

7-LETTER SETS
from the top 250 6-letter stems

AAEMNT 229
(MANATE)
D MANDATE
E EMANATE
ENEMATA
MANATEE
G GATEMAN
MAGENTA
MAGNATE
I AMENTIA
ANIMATE
L AMENTAL
N EMANANT
P PEATMAN
R RAMENTA
S NAMASTE
U MANTEAU

ABDEIR 134
(ABRIDE)
C CARBIDE
D BRAIDED
E BEADIER
BEARDIE
G ABRIDGE
BRIGADE
L BRAILED
RAILBED
RIDABLE
M EMBRAID
N BANDIER
BRAINED
R BARDIER
BRAIDER
BRIARED
RABIDER
S BRAISED
DARBIES
SEABIRD
SIDEBAR
T TRIBADE
U DAUBIER
W BAWDIER

ABEILS 188
(ISABEL)
A ABELIAS
D BALDIES
DIABLES
DISABLE
E BAILEES
F FAIBLES
I BAILIES
K SKIABLE
M EMBAILS
LAMBIES
N LESBIAN
R BAILERS
S ABSEILS
ISABELS
LABISES
T ALBITES
ASTILBE
BESTIAL
LIBATES
STABILE
W BEWAILS
Y BAILEYS
Z SIZABLE

ABELRT 207
(ALBERT)
A RATABLE
E BLEATER
RETABLE
H BLATHER
HALBERT
I LIBRATE
TABLIER
TRIABLE
M LAMBERT
N BRANTLE
O BLOATER
S ALBERTS
BATLERS
BLASTER
LABRETS
STABLER
T BATTLER
BLATTER
BRATTLE
W BLEWART

ABEORS 144
(ABORES)
B EARBOBS
E AEROBES
G BORAGES
I ISOBARE
J JERBOAS
L LABROSE
N BORANES
P SAPROBE
R ARBORES
BRASERO
T BOASTER
BOATERS
BORATES
SORBATE
U AEROBUS
V BRAVOES
X BORAXES
Y ROSEBAY
Z BEZOARS

ABERST 122
(BREAST)
A ABREAST
B BARBETS
RABBETS
STABBER
D DABSTER
TABERDS
E BEATERS
BERATES
REBATES
G BARGEST
H BATHERS
BERTHAS
BREATHS
I BAITERS
BARITES
L ALBERTS
BATLERS
BLASTER
LABRETS
STABLER
M TAMBERS
N BANTERS
O BOASTER
BOATERS
BORATES
SORBATE
R BARRETS
BARTERS
S BASTERS
BESTARS
BRASSET
BREASTS
T BATTERS
TABRETS
U ARBUTES
SURBATE
V BRAVEST
W BRAWEST
WABSTER
X BAXTERS
Y BARYTES
BETRAYS

ACDERS 240
(SACRED)
A ARCADES
B DECARBS
E CREASED
DECARES
SEARCED
F SCARFED
G CADGERS
H CRASHED
I CARDIES
DARCIES
RADICES
SIDECAR
K DACKERS
L CRADLES
SCALDER
N DANCERS
O SARCODE
P REDCAPS
SCARPED
SCRAPED
R CARDERS
SCARRED
T REDACTS
SCARTED
U CRUSADE
SCAURED

ACEILR 121
(LACIER)
B CALIBER
CALIBRE
D DECRIAL
RADICEL
RADICLE
F FILACER
G GLACIER
GRACILE
H CHARLIE
M CALMIER
CLAIMER
MIRACLE
RECLAIM
N CARLINE
O CALORIE
CARIOLE
COALIER
LORICAE
P CALIPER
REPLICA
R CERRIAL
S CLARIES
ECLAIRS
SCALIER
T ARTICLE
RECITAL
TALCIER
U AURICLE
V CALIVER
CLAVIER
VELARIC
Y CLAYIER

ACEINR 65
(CANIER)
A ACARINE
CARINAE
B CARBINE
D CAIRNED
CARNIED
E CINEREA
F FANCIER
G GRECIAN
L CARLINE
M CARMINE
N CANNIER
P CAPRINE
R CARNIER
S ARSENIC
CARNIES
CERASIN
T CANTIER
CERTAIN
CREATIN
CRINATE
NACRITE

ACEINS 119
(INCASE)
D CANDIES
INCASED
F FANCIES
FASCINE
FIANCES
G CEASING
INCAGES
H CHAINES
INCHASE
L INLACES
SANICLE
SCALENI
M AMNESIC
CINEMAS
N CANINES
NANCIES
O ACINOSE
P INSCAPE
PINCASE
R ARSENIC
CARNIES
CERASIN
S CASEINS
INCASES
T CANIEST
CINEAST
U EUCAINS
V INCAVES
Y CYANISE

ACELST 243
(CASTLE)
A ACETALS
LACTASE
B CABLETS
D CASTLED
SCLATED
E CELESTA
H CHALETS
LATCHES
SATCHEL
I ASTELIC
ELASTIC
LACIEST
LATICES
SALICET
K TACKLES
L CALLETS
M CALMEST
CAMLETS
N CANTLES
CENTALS
LANCETS
SCANTLE
O ALECOST
LACTOSE
LOCATES
SCATOLE
TALCOSE
P CAPLETS
PLACETS
R CARTELS
CLARETS
SCARLET
TARCELS
S CASTLES
SCLATES
U CAUTELS
SULCATE
Y ACETYLS
SCYTALE

ACENRS 175
(CANERS)
C CANCERS
D DANCERS
E CAREENS
CASERNE
ENRACES
H CHENARS
RANCHES
I ARSENIC
CARNIES
CERASIN
K CANKERS
L LANCERS
RANCELS
N CANNERS
SCANNER
O CARNOSE
COARSEN
CORNEAS
EARCONS
P PRANCES
S ANCRESS
CASERNS
T CANTERS
CARNETS
NECTARS
RECANTS
SCANTER
TANRECS
TRANCES
U SURANCE
V CAVERNS
CRAVENS
Y CARNEYS
SCENARY
Z ZARNECS

ACENRT 96
(CANTER)
A CATERAN
D CANTRED
TRANCED
E CENTARE
CRENATE
F CANTREF
H CHANTER
TRANCHE
I CANTIER
CERTAIN
CREATIN
CRINATE
NACRITE
L CENTRAL
O ENACTOR
S CANTERS
CARNETS
NECTARS
RECANTS
SCANTER
TANRECS
TRANCES
T TRANECT
U CENTAUR
UNCRATE
UNTRACE
Y ENCRATY
NECTARY

ACENST 149
(STANCE)
A CATENAS
C ACCENTS
D DECANTS
DESCANT
SCANTED
E CETANES
TENACES
H CHASTEN
NATCHES
I CANIEST
CINEAST
K NACKETS
L CANTLES
CENTALS
LANCETS
SCANTLE
N NASCENT
O COSTEAN
OCTANES
P CATNEPS
R CANTERS
CARNETS
NECTARS
RECANTS
SCANTER
TANRECS
TRANCES
S ASCENTS
SECANTS
STANCES
T CANTEST
U NUTCASE
I SOCIATE
L ALECOST
LACTOSE
LOCATES
SCATOLE
TALCOSE
M CAMOTES
COMATES
N COSTEAN
OCTANES
P CAPOTES
SCOPATE
TOECAPS
R COASTER
COATERS
T COSTATE
U ACETOUS
V AVOCETS
OCTAVES

ACEORS 103
(ORACES)
A ROSACEA
D SARCODE
E ACEROSE
G CARGOES
CORSAGE
SOCAGER
H CHOREAS
ORACHES
ROACHES
I ORACIES
SCORIAE
L CLAROES
COALERS
ESCOLAR
ORACLES
M AMORCES
N CARNOSE
COARSEN
CORNEAS
EARCONS
R COARSER
S ROSACES
T COASTER
COATERS
U ACEROUS
CAROUSE
X COAXERS

ACEOST 146
(ACTOSE)
D COASTED
E ACETOSE
COATEES

ACERST 141
(CATERS)
A ACATERS
D REDACTS
SCARTED
E CERATES
CREATES
ECARTES
SECRETA
H ARCHEST
CHARETS
CHASTER
RATCHES
I CRISTAE
RACIEST
STEARIC
K RACKETS
STACKER
TACKERS
L CARTELS
CLARETS
SCARLET
TARCELS
M MERCATS
N CANTERS
CARNETS
NECTARS
RECANTS
SCANTER
TANRECS
TRANCES
O COASTER
COATERS
P CARPETS
PRECAST
SPECTRA
R CARTERS
CRATERS
TRACERS
S ACTRESS
CASTERS
RECASTS
T SCATTER
U ACTURES
CAUTERS
CRUSTAE
CURATES
Y SECTARY

ACIRST 245
(ARTICS)
A CARITAS
B CABRITS
C ARCTICS
D DRASTIC
E CRISTAE
RACIEST
STEARIC
G GASTRIC
I SATIRIC
K KARSTIC
M MATRICS
R TRICARS
S RACISTS
SACRIST
T ASTRICT
U URTICAS
W TWISCAR
Y SATYRIC
Z CZARIST

ADEERS 70
(SEARED)
B DEBASER
SABERED
C CREASED
DECARES
SEARCED
D DEADERS
G DRAGEES
GREASED
H ADHERES
HEADERS
HEARSED
SHEARED
I DEARIES
READIES
K SKEARED
L DEALERS
LEADERS
REDEALS
M REMADES
REMEADS
SMEARED
N DEANERS
ENDEARS
O OREADES
P PREASED
SPEARED
R DREARES
READERS
REDSEAR
REREADS
S RESEDAS
T DEAREST
DERATES
ESTRADE
REASTED
REDATES
SEDATER
STEARED
TASERED
V ADVERSE
EVADERS
W DRAWEES

ADEEST 85
(SEATED)
B BESTEAD
DEBATES
C TEDESCA
D DEADEST
SEDATED
STEADED
F DEAFEST
DEFASTE
DEFEATS
FEASTED
H HEADSET
I IDEATES
L DELATES
STEALED
M STEAMED
N STANDEE
STEANED
R DEAREST
DERATES
ESTRADE
REASTED
REDATES
SEDATER
STEARED
TASERED
S SEDATES
T ESTATED
U SAUTEED
W SWEATED
Y YEASTED

ADEGLN 197
(DANGLE)
B BANGLED
C CANGLED
CLANGED
GLANCED
D DANGLED
GLADDEN
E GLEANED
F FANGLED
FLANGED
I ALIGNED
DEALING
LEADING
J JANGLED
M MANGLED
N ENDLANG
R DANGLER
GNARLED
S DANGLES
GLANDES
SLANGED
T TANGLED
U LANGUED
W WANGLED

ADEGNR 126
(DANGER)
E ANGERED
DERANGE
ENRAGED
GRANDEE
GRENADE
I AREDING
DEARING
DERAIGN
EARDING
GRADINE
GRAINED
READING
L DANGLER
GNARLED
O GROANED
P PRANGED
R GNARRED
GRANDER
S DANGERS
GANDERS
GARDENS
T DRAGNET
GRANTED
U ENGUARD
RAUNGED

ADEGRS 221
(GRADES)
B BADGERS
C CADGERS
D GADDERS
E DRAGEES
GREASED
G DAGGERS
I AGRISED
L DARGLES
N DANGERS
GANDERS
GARDENS
P GRASPED
SPADGER
SPARGED
R GRADERS
REGARDS
S GRASSED
T RADGEST
U SUGARED

ADEILR 19
(RAILED)
A RADIALE
B BRAILED
RAILBED
RIDABLE
C DECRIAL
RADICEL
RADICLE
D DIEDRAL
DRAILED
E LEADIER
G GLADIER
GLAIRED
I DELIRIA
IRIDEAL
L DALLIER
DIALLER
RALLIED
O DARIOLE
P PEDRAIL
PREDIAL
R LARDIER
S DERAILS
REDIALS
SIDERAL
T DILATER
TRAILED
V VALIDER
Y READILY

ADEILS 33
(LADIES)
B BALDIES
DIABLES
DISABLE
C SCAILED
D DAIDLES
LADDIES
E AEDILES
DEISEAL
F DISLEAF
G SILAGED
H HALIDES
I DAILIES
LIAISED
SEDILIA
K SKAILED
L DALLIES
DISLEAL
LALDIES
SALLIED
M MAELIDS
MEDIALS
MISDEAL
MISLEAD
N DENIALS
SNAILED
O DEASOIL
P ALIPEDS
PAIDLES
PALSIED
R DERAILS
REDIALS
SIDERAL
S AIDLESS
DEASILS
T DETAILS
DILATES
U AUDILES
DEASIUL
V DEVISAL
Y DIALYSE
EYLIADS

ADEINR 4
(RAINED)
A ARANEID
B BANDIER
BRAINED
C CAIRNED
CARNIED
D DANDIER
DRAINED
F FRIANDE
G AREDING
DEARING
DERAIGN
EARDING
GRADINE
GRAINED
READING
H HANDIER
I DENARII
M ADERMIN
INARMED
O ANEROID
P PARDINE
R DRAINER
RANDIER
S RANDIES
SANDIER
SARDINE
T DETRAIN

TRAINED
U UNAIRED
URANIDE
V INVADER
RAVINED

ADEINS 22
(SANDIE)
A NAIADES
B BANDIES
C CANDIES
INCASED
D DANDIES
SDAINED
E ANISEED
G AGNISED
K KANDIES
L DENIALS
SNAILED
M DEMAINS
MAIDENS
MEDIANS
MEDINAS
SIDEMAN
O ADONISE
ANODISE
SODAINE
P PANDIES
PANSIED
SPAINED
R RANDIES
SANDIER
SARDINE
S SDAINES
T DETAINS
INSTEAD
SAINTED
SATINED
STAINED
V INVADES
W DEWANIS

ADEIRS 12
(RAISED)
A ARAISED
B BRAISED
DARBIES
SEABIRD
SIDEBAR
C CARDIES
DARCIES
RADICES
SIDECAR
E DEARIES
READIES
F FRAISED
G AGRISED
H SHADIER
I AIRSIDE
DAIRIES
DIARIES
DIARISE
K DAIKERS
DARKIES
L DERAILS
REDIALS
SIDERAL
M ADMIRES
MARDIES
MISREAD
SIDEARM
N RANDIES
SANDIER
SARDINE
O ROADIES
SOREDIA
P ASPIRED
DESPAIR
DIAPERS
PRAISED
R ARRIDES
RAIDERS
T ARIDEST
ASTERID
ASTRIDE
DIASTER
DISRATE
STAIDER
STAIRED
TARDIES
TIRADES
U RESIDUA
V ADVISER
VARDIES

ADEIST 26
(IDATES)
B BASTIDE
C ACIDEST
DACITES
D TADDIES
E IDEATES
F DAFTIES
FADIEST
G AGISTED
L DETAILS
DILATES
M MISDATE
N DETAINS
INSTEAD
SAINTED
SATINED
STAINED
O IODATES
TOADIES
R ARIDEST
ASTERID
ASTRIDE
DIASTER
DISRATE
STAIDER
STAIRED
TARDIES
TIRADES
S DISSEAT
SAIDEST
U DAUTIES
V AVIDEST
DATIVES
VISTAED
W DAWTIES
WAISTED

ADELNR 79
(LANDER)
A ADRENAL
B BLANDER
D DANDLER
E LEARNED
G DANGLER
GNARLED
H HANDLER
K RANKLED
L LANDLER
M MANDREL
O LADRONE
S DARNELS
ENLARDS
LANDERS
SLANDER
SNARLED
U LAUNDER
LURDANE
RUNDALE
Y DEARNLY

ADELNS 137
(ANDLES)
C CALENDS
CANDLES
D DANDLES
E LEADENS
G DANGLES
GLANDES
SLANGED
H HANDLES
HANDSEL
I DENIALS
SNAILED
K KALENDS
O LOADENS
R DARNELS
ENLARDS
LANDERS
SLANDER
SNARLED
S SENDALS
T DENTALS
SLANTED
U UNLADES
UNLEADS

ADELRS 88
(ALDERS)
B BEDRALS
C CRADLES
SCALDER
D LADDERS
RADDLES
SADDLER
E DEALERS
LEADERS
REDEALS
F FARDELS
G DARGLES
H HARELDS
HERALDS
I DERAILS
REDIALS
SIDERAL
K DARKLES
M MEDLARS
N DARNELS
ENLARDS
LANDERS
SLANDER
SNARLED
O LOADERS
ORDEALS
RELOADS
P PEDLARS
R LARDERS
S SARDELS
T DARTLES
U LAUDERS
W WARSLED
Z DRAZELS

ADELST 110
(SALTED)
B BALDEST
BLASTED
STABLED
C CASTLED
SCLATED
D STADDLE
E DELATES
STEALED
I DETAILS
DILATES
K SKLATED
STALKED
L STALLED
N DENTALS
SLANTED
O SALTOED
P SPALTED
STAPLED
R DARTLES
S DESALTS
T SLATTED
U AULDEST
SALUTED

ADEMNS 246
(AMENDS)
A ANADEMS
MAENADS
D DEMANDS
MADDENS
E AMENDES
DEMEANS
G GADSMEN
I DEMAINS
MAIDENS
MEDIANS
MEDINAS
SIDEMAN
N SANDMEN
O DAEMONS
MASONED
MODENAS
MONADES
NOMADES
P DAMPENS
R MANREDS
RANDEMS
REMANDS
S DESMANS
MADNESS
T TANDEMS
U MEDUSAN
SUDAMEN
Y DAYSMEN

ADENRS 62
(ANDERS)
C DANCERS
D DANDERS
E DEANERS
ENDEARS
F FARDENS
G DANGERS
GANDERS
GARDENS
H HANDERS
HARDENS
I RANDIES
SANDIER
SARDINE
K DARKENS
L DARNELS
ENLARDS
LANDERS
SLANDER
SNARLED
M MANREDS
RANDEMS
REMANDS
P PANDERS
R DARNERS
ERRANDS
SNARRED
S SANDERS
SARSDEN
T ENDARTS
STANDER
STARNED
U ASUNDER
DANSEUR
DAUNERS
W DAWNERS
WANDERS
WARDENS
Z ZANDERS

ADENRU 64
(AUNDER)
B UNBARED
C DURANCE
UNRACED
D DAUNDER
E UNEARED
G ENGUARD
RAUNGED
H UNHEARD
I UNAIRED
URANIDE
K UNRAKED
L LAUNDER
LURDANE
RUNDALE
M DURAMEN
MANURED
MAUNDER
UNARMED
O RONDEAU
P UNPARED
S ASUNDER
DANSEUR
DAUNERS
T DAUNTER
NATURED
UNRATED
UNTREAD
Y UNREADY

ADENST 36
(STANED)
A ANSATED
C DECANTS
DESCANT
SCANTED
E STANDEE
STEANED
G STANGED
H HANDSET
I DETAINS
INSTEAD
SAINTED
SATINED
STAINED
K DANKEST
L DENTALS
SLANTED
M TANDEMS
N STANDEN
O ASTONED
DONATES
ONSTEAD
P PEDANTS
PENTADS
R ENDARTS
STANDER
STARNED
T ATTENDS
U SAUNTED
UNSATED
V ADVENTS
Y STAYNED

ADEORS 48
(ADORES)
C SARCODE
D DEODARS
E OREADES
F FEDORAS
I ROADIES
SOREDIA
L LOADERS
ORDEALS
RELOADS
M RADOMES
R ADORERS
DROSERA
T DOATERS
ROASTED
TORSADE
TROADES
U AROUSED
V SAVORED
W REDOWAS

ADEPRT 228
(PRATED)
A ADAPTER
READAPT
E ADEPTER
PREDATE
TAPERED
I DIPTERA
PARTIED
PIRATED
M TRAMPED
O ADOPTER
READOPT
P TRAPPED
S DEPARTS
DRAPETS
PETARDS

T PRATTED
U UPRATED

ADERRS 235
(ARDERS)
A ARRASED
C CARDERS
SCARRED
E DREARES
READERS
REDSEAR
REREADS
G GRADERS
REGARDS
I ARRIDES
RAIDERS
L LARDERS
N DARNERS
ERRANDS
SNARRED
O ADORERS
DROSERA
P DRAPERS
SPARRED
T DARTERS
DARTRES
RETARDS
STARRED
TRADERS
W DRAWERS
REDRAWS
REWARDS
WARDERS

ADERST 49
(DATERS)
B DABSTER
TABERDS
C REDACTS
SCARTED
D ADDREST
E DEAREST
DERATES
ESTRADE
REASTED
REDATES
SEDATER
STEARED
TASERED
F STRAFED
G RADGEST
H DEARTHS
HARDEST
HATREDS
THREADS
TRASHED
I ARIDEST
ASTERID
ASTRIDE
DIASTER
DISRATE
STAIDER
STAIRED
TARDIES
TIRADES
K DARKEST
STARKED
L DARTLES
M SMARTED
N ENDARTS
STANDER
STARNED
O DOATERS
ROASTED
TORSADE
TROADES
P DEPARTS
DRAPETS
PETARDS
R DARTERS
DARTRES
RETARDS
STARRED
TRADERS
T STARTED
TETRADS
V ADVERTS
STARVED
W STEWARD
STRAWED
WRASTED
Y STRAYED

ADGINR 135
(RADING)
B BARDING
BRIGAND
C CARDING
E AREDING
DEARING
DERAIGN
EARDING
GRADINE
GRAINED
READING
F FARDING
G GRADING
NIGGARD
I GRADINI
RAIDING
L DARLING
LARDING
M MRIDANG
N DARNING
NARDING
RANDING
O ADORING
GRADINO
ROADING
P DRAPING
R DARRING
S DARINGS
GRADINS
T DARTING
TRADING
U DAURING
W DRAWING
WARDING
Y YARDING

ADINRS 105
(DRAINS)
A RADIANS
B RIBANDS
E RANDIES
SANDIER
SARDINE
F FRIANDS
G DARINGS
GRADINS
K DISRANK
L ALDRINS
M MANDIRS
N INNARDS
O INROADS
ORDAINS
SADIRON
T INDARTS
U DURIANS
SUNDARI
W INWARDS

AEELRS 72
(EALERS)
C ALERCES
CEREALS
RESCALE
D DEALERS
LEADERS
REDEALS
E RELEASE
G GALERES
REGALES
H HEALERS
I EARLIES
REALISE
K LEAKERS
M MEALERS
O AREOLES
P LEAPERS
PLEASER
RELAPSE
REPEALS
S EARLESS
LEASERS
RESALES
RESEALS
SEALERS
T ELATERS
REALEST
RELATES
STEALER
U LEASURE
V LAVEERS
LEAVERS
REVEALS
SEVERAL
VEALERS
X RELAXES
Y SEALERY

AEEMRS 238
(SEAMER)
B BEAMERS
BESMEAR
C AMERCES
CAREMES
RACEMES
D REMADES
REMEADS
SMEARED
G MEAGRES
H HAREEMS
MAHSEER
I SEAMIER
SERIEMA
K REMAKES
L MEALERS
N RENAMES
P AMPERES
EMPARES
R REAMERS
S SEAMERS
T STEAMER
TEAMERS
U MEASURE

AEEPRT 142
(REPEAT)
A PATERAE
D ADEPTER
PREDATE
TAPERED
H PREHEAT
I PEATIER
K PERTAKE
L PLEATER
PRELATE
M TEMPERA
O OPERATE
R TAPERER
S REPEATS
U EPURATE
Y PEATERY
Z TRAPEZE

AEERRS 162
(ERASER)
B BEARERS
BREARES
C CAREERS
CREASER
D DREARES
READERS
REDSEAR
REREADS
G GREASER
H HEARERS
REHEARS
SHEARER
I REARISE
M REAMERS
N EARNERS
O REAROSE
P REAPERS
R REARERS
S ERASERS
T SERRATE
TEARERS
U ERASURE
V REAVERS
W SWEARER
WEARERS

AEERST 20
(EATERS)
A AERATES
B BEATERS
BERATES
REBATES
C CERATES
CREATES
ECARTES
SECRETA
D DEAREST
DERATES
ESTRADE
REASTED
REDATES
SEDATER
STEARED
TASERED
F AFREETS
FEASTER
G ERGATES
RESTAGE
H AETHERS
HEATERS
REHEATS
I AERIEST
SERIATE
K RETAKES
SAKERET
L ELATERS
REALEST
RELATES
STEALER
M STEAMER
TEAMERS
N EARNEST
EASTERN
NEAREST
O ROSEATE
P REPEATS
R SERRATE
TEARERS
S RESEATS
SAETERS
SEAREST
SEATERS
STEARES
TEASERS
TESSERA
T ESTREAT
RESTATE
U AUSTERE
W SWEATER

AEGILN 55
(EALING)
C ANGELIC
ANGLICE
D ALIGNED
DEALING
LEADING
E LINEAGE
F FEALING
FINAGLE
LEAFING
G GEALING
LIGNAGE
H HEALING
K LEAKING
LINKAGE
L NIGELLA
M LEAMING
MEALING
N ANELING
EANLING
LEANING
NEALING
P LEAPING
PEALING
PLEAING
R ENGRAIL
LAERING
LEARING
NARGILE
REALIGN
REGINAL
S LEASING
LINAGES
SEALING
T ATINGLE
ELATING
GELATIN
GENITAL
U LINGUAE
V LEAVING
Y ALEYING

AEGINR 15
(EARING)
B BEARING
C GRECIAN
D AREDING
DEARING
DERAIGN
EARDING
GRADINE
GRAINED
READING
E REGINAE
F FEARING
G GEARING
NAGGIER
H HEARING
K REAKING
L ENGRAIL
LAERING
LEARING
NARGILE
REALIGN
REGINAL
M GERMAIN
MANGIER
MEARING
REAMING
N AGINNER
EARNING
ENGRAIN
GRANNIE
NEARING
O ORIGANE
P REAPING
R ANGRIER
EARRING
GRAINER
RANGIER
REARING
S ANGRIES
EARINGS
ERASING
GAINERS
GRAINES
REGAINS
REGINAS
SEARING
SERINGA
T GRANITE
GRATINE
INGRATE
TANGIER
TEARING
V REAVING
VINEGAR
W WEARING

AEGLNR 91
(ANGLER)
A ALNAGER
B BRANGLE
C CLANGER
D DANGLER
GNARLED
E ENLARGE
GENERAL
GLEANER
G GANGREL
I ENGRAIL
LAERING
LEARING
NARGILE
REALIGN
REGINAL
J JANGLER
L LANGREL
M MANGLER
P GRAPNEL
S ANGLERS
LARGENS
SLANGER
T TANGLER
TRANGLE
U GRANULE
W WANGLER
WRANGLE
Y ANGERLY

AEGLNS 170
(ANGLES)
A ALNAGES
ANLAGES
GALENAS
LAGENAS
LASAGNE
B BANGLES
C CANGLES
GLANCES
D DANGLES
GLANDES
SLANGED
F FANGLES
FLANGES
G LAGGENS
I LEASING
LINAGES
SEALING
J JANGLES
L LEGLANS
M MANGELS
MANGLES
O ENGAOLS
P SPANGLE
R ANGLERS
LARGENS
SLANGER
S GLASSEN
T LANGEST
TANGLES
U ANGELUS
LAGUNES
LANGUES
W WANGLES
Y LYNAGES

AEGLNT 118
(TANGLE)
D TANGLED
E ELEGANT
H ALENGTH
I ATINGLE
ELATING
GELATIN
GENITAL
O TANGELO
R TANGLER
TRANGLE
S LANGEST
TANGLES
T GANTLET
U LANGUET
W TWANGLE

AEGLRS 167
(LAGERS)
A ALEGARS
LAAGERS
B GARBLES
D DARGLES
E GALERES
REGALES
F REFLAGS
G GARGLES
LAGGERS
RAGGLES
I GRAILES
K GRAKLES
M MALGRES
N ANGLERS
LARGENS
SLANGER
O GAOLERS
P GRAPLES
S LARGESS
T LARGEST
V GRAVELS
VERGLAS
Y ARGYLES
GRAYLES
Z GLAZERS

AEGLST 187
(GLATES)
A AGELAST
ALGATES
LASTAGE
B GABLETS
E EAGLETS
LEGATES
TEAGLES
TELEGAS
H HAGLETS
I AGILEST
AIGLETS
LIGATES
TAIGLES
L GALLETS
N LANGEST
TANGLES
O LEGATOS
R LARGEST
T GESTALT
W TALWEGS

AEGNRS 86
(ANGERS)
B BANGERS
GRABENS
D DANGERS
GANDERS
GARDENS
E ENRAGES
G GANGERS
GRANGES
NAGGERS
H GNASHER
HANGERS
REHANGS
I ANGRIES
EARINGS
ERASING
GAINERS
GRAINES
REGAINS
REGINAS
SEARING
SERINGA
L ANGLERS
LARGENS
SLANGER
M ENGRAMS
GERMANS
MANGERS
O ONAGERS
ORANGES
P ENGRASP
R GARNERS
RANGERS
S SERANGS
T ARGENTS
GARNETS
STRANGE
U RAUNGES
UNGEARS
W GNAWERS

AEGNRT 54
(GANTER)
A TANAGER
D DRAGNET
GRANTED
E GRANTEE
GREATEN
REAGENT
F ENGRAFT
I GRANITE
GRATINE
INGRATE
TANGIER
TEARING
L TANGLER
TRANGLE
M GARMENT
MARGENT
RAGMENT
N REGNANT
P TREPANG
R GRANTER
REGRANT
S ARGENTS
GARNETS
STRANGE
U GAUNTER

AEGNST 115
(TANGES)
A AGNATES
D STANGED
E NEGATES
H STENGAH
I EASTING
EATINGS
GAINEST
GENISTA
INGATES
INGESTA
SEATING
TANGIES
TEASING
TSIGANE
L LANGEST
TANGLES
M MAGNETS
N GANNETS
R ARGENTS
GARNETS
STRANGE
T GESTANT

AEGRST 80
(GATERS)
A AGRASTE
B BARGEST
D RADGEST
E ERGATES
RESTAGE
G GAGSTER
GARGETS
STAGGER
TAGGERS
H GATHERS
I AGISTER
GAITERS
STAGIER
STRIGAE
TRIAGES
L LARGEST
N ARGENTS
GARNETS
STRANGE
O ORGEATS
STORAGE
TOERAGS
P PARGETS
R GARRETS
GARTERS
GRATERS
S GASTERS
STAGERS
T TARGETS
V GRAVEST
Y GRAYEST
GYRATES
STAGERY

AEHLRT 212
(LATHER)
A TREHALA
B BLATHER
HALBERT
C ARCHLET
E LEATHER
F FARTHEL
I LATHIER
M THERMAL
N ENTHRAL
O LOATHER
S HALTERS
HARSLET
LATHERS
SLATHER
THALERS
Y EARTHLY
HARTELY
HEARTLY
LATHERY

AEHRST 169
(HATERS)
B BATHERS
BERTHAS
BREATHS
C ARCHEST
CHARETS
CHASTER
RATCHES
D DEARTHS
HARDEST
HATREDS
THREADS
TRASHED
E AETHERS
HEATERS
REHEATS
F FATHERS
SHAFTER
G GATHERS
H HEARTHS
I HASTIER
SHERIAT
L HALTERS
HARSLET
LATHERS
SLATHER
THALERS
M HAMSTER
N ANTHERS
HARTENS
THENARS
O ASTHORE
EARSHOT
HAROSET
P SPARTHE
TEPHRAS
THREAPS
S RASHEST
SHASTER
TRASHES
T HATTERS
RATHEST
SHATTER
THREATS
V HARVEST
THRAVES
W THAWERS
WREATHS

AEILMN 133
(MALINE)
A LAMINAE
C CNEMIAL
MELANIC
F FEMINAL
INFLAME
G LEAMING
MEALING
H HELIMAN
L MANILLE
M MAILMEN
N LINEMAN
MELANIN
O MINEOLA
P IMPANEL
MANIPLE
R MANLIER
MARLINE
MINERAL
RAILMEN
S ISLEMAN
MENIALS
SEMINAL
T AILMENT
ALIMENT

AEILNT 11
(ENTAIL)
A ANTLIAE
E LINEATE
F INFLATE
G ATINGLE
ELATING
GELATIN
GENITAL
M AILMENT
ALIMENT
O ELATION
TOENAIL
P PANTILE
R ENTRAIL
LATRINE
RATLINE
RELIANT
RETINAL
TRENAIL
S EASTLIN
ELASTIN
ENTAILS
SALIENT
SLAINTE
STANIEL
TENAILS
U ALUNITE
V VENTAIL

AEILRS 16
(SAILER)
A AERIALS
B BAILERS
C CLARIES
ECLAIRS
SCALIER
D DERAILS
REDIALS
SIDERAL
E EARLIES
REALISE
G GRAILES
H HAILERS
SHALIER
I LAIRISE
J JAILERS
K LAIKERS
SERKALI
L RALLIES

M MAILERS
REALISM
N NAILERS
P PALSIER
PARLIES
R RAILERS
RERAILS
S AIRLESS
SAILERS
SERAILS
SERIALS
T REALIST
RETAILS
SALTIER
SALTIRE
SLATIER
V REVISAL
W SWALIER
WAILERS

AEILRT 10
(RETAIL)
B LIBRATE
TABLIER
TRIABLE
C ARTICLE
RECITAL
TALCIER
D DILATER
TRAILED
E ATELIER
REALTIE
H LATHIER
K TALKIER
L LITERAL
TALLIER
M LAMITER
MALTIER
N ENTRAIL
LATRINE
RATLINE
RELIANT
RETINAL
TRENAIL
P PLAITER
PLATIER
R RETIRAL
RETRIAL
TRAILER
S REALIST
RETAILS
SALTIER
SALTIRE
SLATIER
T TERTIAL
U URALITE
W WALTIER
Y IRATELY
REALITY

AEILSS 248
(LASSIE)
A ALIASES
B ABSEILS
ISABELS
LABISES
C SALICES
D AIDLESS
DEASILS
F FALSIES
FILASSE
G ALGESIS
LIGASES
SILAGES
H SHEILAS
I LIAISES
SILESIA
K ALSIKES
L ALLISES
SALLIES
M AIMLESS
MESAILS
SAMIELS
SEISMAL
N SALINES
SILANES
P ESPIALS
LAPISES
LIPASES
PALSIES
R AIRLESS
SAILERS
SERAILS
SERIALS
S LAISSES
LASSIES
U SAULIES
V VALISES
VESSAIL
W WALISES

AEILST 24
(ALITES)
B ALBITES
ASTILBE
BESTIAL
LIBATES
STABILE
C ASTELIC
ELASTIC
LACIEST
LATICES
SALICET
D DETAILS
DILATES
G AGILEST
AIGLETS
LIGATES
TAIGLES
H HALITES
I LAITIES
K LAKIEST
TALKIES
L TAILLES
TALLIES
N EASTLIN
ELASTIN
ENTAILS
SALIENT
SLAINTE
STANIEL
TENAILS
O ISOLATE
P APLITES
PALIEST
TALIPES
R REALIST
RETAILS
SALTIER
SALTIRE
SLATIER
U SITULAE
V ESTIVAL
W WALIEST
Y TAILYES
Z LAZIEST

AEIMNR 61
(REMAIN)
B MIRBANE
C CARMINE
D ADERMIN
INARMED
E REMANIE
F FIREMAN
G GERMAIN
MANGIER
MEARING
REAMING
H HARMINE
K MANKIER
RAMEKIN
L MANLIER
MARLINE
MINERAL
RAILMEN
O MORAINE
R MARINER
S MARINES
REMAINS
SEMINAR
SIRNAME
T MINARET
RAIMENT
V VERMIAN
W WIREMAN

AEIMNS 98
(MANIES)
A AMNESIA
ANEMIAS
C AMNESIC
CINEMAS
D DEMAINS
MAIDENS
MEDIANS
MEDINAS
SIDEMAN
E MEANIES
NEMESIA
F FAMINES
INFAMES
G ENIGMAS
GAMINES
MEASING
SEAMING
H HAEMINS
HEMINAS
J JASMINE
K KINEMAS
L ISLEMAN
MENIALS
SEMINAL
M MISNAME
O ANOMIES
R MARINES
REMAINS
SEMINAR
SIRNAME
S INSEAMS
SAMISEN
T INMATES
MAINEST
MANTIES
TAMINES

AEIMNT 53
(INMATE)
A AMENTIA
ANIMATE
B AMBIENT
C EMICANT
NEMATIC
D MEDIANT
E MATINEE
G MINTAGE
TEAMING
TEGMINA
I INTIMAE
MINIATE
L AILMENT
ALIMENT
N MANNITE
R MINARET
RAIMENT
S INMATES
MAINEST
MANTIES
TAMINES
X TAXIMEN
Y AMENITY
ANYTIME

AEIMRS 112
(ARMIES)
B AMBRIES
D ADMIRES
MARDIES
MISREAD
SIDEARM
E SEAMIER
SERIEMA
F MISFARE
G GISARME
MAIGRES
MIRAGES
H MASHIER
MISHEAR
L MAILERS
REALISM
M RAMMIES
N MARINES
REMAINS
SEMINAR
SIRNAME
P IMPRESA
SAMPIRE
R MARRIES
SIMARRE
S MASSIER
T IMARETS
MAESTRI
MAISTER
MASTIER
MISRATE
SEMITAR
SMARTIE
U UREMIAS
W AWMRIES

AEIMST 95
(MATIES)
C ACMITES
ETACISM
MICATES
SEMATIC
D MISDATE
E STEAMIE
G GAMIEST
SIGMATE
H ATHEISM
I AMITIES
ATIMIES
K MISTAKE
M MISMATE
TAMMIES
N INMATES
MAINEST
MANTIES
TAMINES
O AMOSITE
ATOMIES
ATOMISE
OSMIATE
P IMPASTE
PASTIME
R IMARETS
MAESTRI
MAISTER
MASTIER
MISRATE
SEMITAR
SMARTIE
S ASTEISM
SAMIEST
SAMITES
TAMISES
T MATIEST
MATTIES
Z MAZIEST
MESTIZA

AEINRS 6
(SARNIE)
C ARSENIC
CARNIES
CERASIN
D RANDIES
SANDIER
SARDINE
F INFARES
SERAFIN
G ANGRIES
EARINGS
ERASING
GAINERS
GRAINES
REGAINS
REGINAS
SEARING
SERINGA
H ARSHINE
HERNIAS
I SENARII
J INJERAS
K SNAKIER
L NAILERS
M MARINES
REMAINS
SEMINAR
SIRNAME
N INSANER
INSNARE
O ERASION
P RAPINES
R SIERRAN
SNARIER
S ARSINES
SARNIES
T ANESTRI
NASTIER
RATINES
RESIANT
RETAINS
RETINAS
RETSINA
STAINER
STARNIE
STEARIN
V AVENIRS
RAVINES

AEINRT 1
(RETAIN)
B ATEBRIN
C CANTIER
CERTAIN
CREATIN
CRINATE
NACRITE
D DETRAIN
TRAINED
E RETINAE
TRAINEE
F FAINTER
FENITAR
G GRANITE
GRATINE
INGRATE
TANGIER
TEARING
H HAIRNET
INEARTH
THERIAN
I INERTIA
J JANTIER
NARTJIE
K KERATIN
L ENTRAIL
LATRINE
RATLINE
RELIANT
RETINAL
TRENAIL
M MINARET
RAIMENT
N ENTRAIN
TRANNIE
O OTARINE
P PAINTER
PERTAIN
REPAINT
R RETRAIN
TERRAIN
TRAINER
S ANESTRI
NASTIER
RATINES
RESIANT
RETAINS

RETINAS
RETSINA
STAINER
STARNIE
STEARIN
T INTREAT
ITERANT
NATTIER
NITRATE
TARTINE
TERTIAN
U RUINATE
TAURINE
URANITE
URINATE
W TAWNIER
TINWARE

AEINST 2
(SATINE)
A TAENIAS
B BASINET
BESAINT
BESTAIN
C CANIEST
CINEAST
D DETAINS
INSTEAD
SAINTED
SATINED
STAINED
E ETESIAN
F FAINEST
NAIFEST
G EASTING
EATINGS
GAINEST
GENISTA
INGATES
INGESTA
SEATING
TANGIES
TEASING
TSIGANE
I ISATINE
J JANTIES
TAJINES
K INTAKES
KENTIAS
TANKIES
L EASTLIN
ELASTIN
ENTAILS
SALIENT
SLAINTE
STANIEL
TENAILS
M INMATES
MAINEST
MANTIES
TAMINES
N INANEST
O ATONIES
P PANTIES
PATINES
SAPIENT
SPINATE
R ANESTRI
NASTIER
RATINES
RESIANT
RETAINS
RETINAS
RETSINA
STAINER
STARNIE
STEARIN
S ENTASIS
NASTIES
SESTINA
TANSIES
TISANES
T INSTATE
SATINET
U AUNTIES
SINUATE
V NAIVEST
NATIVES
VAINEST
W AWNIEST
TAWNIES
WANIEST
WANTIES
Z ZANIEST

AEIPRS 75
(PRAISE)
A SPIRAEA
C EPACRIS
SCRAPIE
SPACIER
D ASPIRED
DESPAIR
DIAPERS
PRAISED
E APERIES
EPEIRAS
G GASPIER
PRISAGE
SPAIRGE
H HARPIES
SHARPIE
K PARKIES
SPARKIE
L PALSIER
PARLIES
M IMPRESA
SAMPIRE
N RAPINES
O SOAPIER
P APPRISE
SAPPIER
R PARRIES
PRAISER
RAPIERS
RASPIER
REPAIRS
S ASPIRES
PARESIS
PRAISES
SPIREAS
T PARTIES
PASTIER
PIASTRE
PIRATES
PRATIES
TRAIPSE
U SPURIAE
UPRAISE
V PARVISE
W WASPIER

AEIRST 3
(SATIRE)
A ARISTAE
ASTERIA
ATRESIA
B BAITERS
BARITES
C CRISTAE
RACIEST
STEARIC
D ARIDEST
ASTERID
ASTRIDE
DIASTER
DISRATE
STAIDER
STAIRED
TARDIES
TIRADES
E AERIEST
SERIATE
F FAIREST
G AGISTER
GAITERS
STAGIER
STRIGAE
TRIAGES
H HASTIER
SHERIAT
I AIRIEST
IRISATE
K ARKITES
KARITES
L REALIST
RETAILS
SALTIER
SALTIRE
SLATIER
M IMARETS
MAESTRI
MAISTER
MASTIER
MISRATE
SEMITAR
SMARTIE
N ANESTRI
NASTIER
RATINES
RESIANT
RETAINS
RETINAS
RETSINA
STAINER
STARNIE
STEARIN
O OARIEST
OTARIES
P PARTIES
PASTIER
PIASTRE
PIRATES
PRATIES
TRAIPSE
R ARTSIER
SERRATI
TARRIES
TARSIER
S ARTSIES
SAIREST
SATIRES
TIRASSE
T ARTIEST
ARTISTE
ATTIRES
IRATEST
STRIATE
TASTIER
TERTIAS
V TAIVERS
VASTIER
W WAISTER
WAITERS
WARIEST

AEIRTT 29
(ATTIRE)
A ARIETTA
B BATTIER
BIRETTA
C CATTIER
CITRATE
D ATTIRED
E ARIETTE
ITERATE
F FATTIER
L TERTIAL
N INTREAT
ITERANT
NATTIER
NITRATE
TARTINE
TERTIAN
P PARTITE
R RATTIER
RETRAIT
TARTIER
S ARTIEST
ARTISTE
ATTIRES
IRATEST
STRIATE
TASTIER
TERTIAS
T ATTRITE
TATTIER
TITRATE
V TAIVERT
W TAWTIER
X EXTRAIT

AEISTT 83
(TASTIE)
A SATIATE
B BATISTE
C CATTIES
STATICE
TIETACS
F FATTIES
H ATHEIST
STAITHE
K TAKIEST
M MATIEST
MATTIES
N INSTATE
SATINET
O OSTIATE
TOASTIE
P PATTIES
TAPETIS
R ARTIEST
ARTISTE
ATTIRES
IRATEST
STRIATE
TASTIER
TERTIAS
T TATTIES
U SITUATE
V STATIVE
W TWAITES
Y SATIETY

AELMNT 211
(LAMENT)
A AMENTAL
B BELTMAN
LAMBENT
D MANTLED
E MANTEEL
I AILMENT
ALIMENT
M MALTMEN
O LOMENTA
OMENTAL
TELAMON
S LAMENTS
MANTELS
MANTLES
T MANTLET
U NUTMEAL

AELNRS 63
(LANERS)
A ARSENAL
B BRANLES
BRANSLE
C LANCERS
RANCELS
D DARNELS
ENLARDS
LANDERS
SLANDER
SNARLED
F SALFERN
G ANGLERS
LARGENS
SLANGER
I NAILERS
K RANKLES
N ENSNARL
LANNERS
O ORLEANS
P PLANERS
REPLANS
R SNARLER
S RANSELS
T ANTLERS
RENTALS
SALTERN
STERNAL
Z RANZELS

AELNRT 28
(ANTLER)
B BRANTLE
C CENTRAL
E ALTERNE
ENTERAL
ETERNAL
G TANGLER
TRANGLE
H ENTHRAL
I ENTRAIL
LATRINE
RATLINE
RELIANT
RETINAL
TRENAIL
L ENTRALL
N LANTERN
P PANTLER
PLANTER
REPLANT
S ANTLERS
RENTALS
SALTERN
STERNAL
T TRENTAL
U NEUTRAL
V VENTRAL

AELNST 34
(ANTLES)
A SEALANT
C CANTLES
CENTALS
LANCETS
SCANTLE
D DENTALS
SLANTED
E ELANETS
LATEENS
LEANEST
G LANGEST
TANGLES
H HANTLES
I EASTLIN
ELASTIN
ENTAILS
SALIENT
SLAINTE
STANIEL
TENAILS
K ANKLETS
ASKLENT
LANKEST
M LAMENTS
MANTELS
MANTLES
N STANNEL
O ETALONS
P PLANETS
PLATENS
R ANTLERS
RENTALS
SALTERN
STERNAL
T LATTENS
TALENTS
U ELUANTS
UNLASTE
V LEVANTS
Y STANYEL
Z ZELANTS

AELORS 42
(ALORES)
B LABROSE

C CLAROES
COALERS
ESCOLAR
ORACLES
D LOADERS
ORDEALS
RELOADS
E AREOLES
F LOAFERS
SAFROLE
G GAOLERS
H SHOALER
L ROSELLA
M MORALES
N ORLEANS
O AEROSOL
ROSEOLA
P PAROLES
REPOSAL
S OARLESS
SOLERAS
T OESTRAL

AELOST 46
(SOLATE)
B BOATELS
OBLATES
C ALECOST
LACTOSE
LOCATES
SCATOLE
TALCOSE
D SALTOED
E OLEATES
F FOLATES
G LEGATOS
H LOATHES
I ISOLATE
K SKATOLE
M MALTOSE
N ETALONS
P APOSTLE
PELOTAS
R OESTRAL
V SOLVATE
Z ZEALOTS

AELPRS 231
(PALERS)
A EARLAPS
C CARPELS
CLASPER
CRAPLES
PARCELS
PLACERS
SCALPER
D PEDLARS
E LEAPERS
PLEASER
RELAPSE
REPEALS
F FELSPAR
G GRAPLES
H SPHERAL
I PALSIER
PARLIES
K SPARKLE
M EMPARLS
LAMPERS
PALMERS
SAMPLER
N PLANERS
REPLANS
O PAROLES
REPOSAL
P LAPPERS
RAPPELS
SLAPPER
R PARRELS
T PALTERS
PLASTER
PLATERS
PSALTER
STAPLER
U PERUSAL
SERPULA
W PRAWLES
Y PARLEYS
PARSLEY
PLAYERS
REPLAYS
SPARELY

AELPRT 206
(PLATER)
A APTERAL
C PLECTRA
E PLEATER
PRELATE
I PLAITER
PLATIER
M TEMPLAR
TRAMPLE
N PANTLER
PLANTER
REPLANT
O PROLATE
S PALTERS
PLASTER
PLATERS
PSALTER
STAPLER
T PARTLET
PLATTER
PRATTLE
Y PEARTLY
PRELATY
PTERYLA

AELRST 38
(ALTERS)
B ALBERTS
BATLERS
BLASTER
LABRETS
STABLER
C CARTELS
CLARETS
SCARLET
TARCELS
D DARTLES
E ELATERS
REALEST
RELATES
STEALER
F FALTERS
G LARGEST
H HALTERS
HARSLET
LATHERS
SLATHER
THALERS
I REALIST
RETAILS
SALTIER
SALTIRE
SLATIER
K STALKER
TALKERS
L STELLAR
TELLARS
M ARMLETS
MARTELS
N ANTLERS
RENTALS
SALTERN
STERNAL
O OESTRAL
P PALTERS
PLASTER
PLATERS
PSALTER
STAPLER
S ARTLESS
LASTERS
SALTERS
SLATERS
TARSELS
T RATTLES
SLATTER
STARLET
STARTLE
TATLERS
U SALUTER
V TRAVELS
VARLETS
VESTRAL
W WASTREL
Y RAYLETS

AEMNST 168
(STAMEN)
A NAMASTE
B BATSMEN
D TANDEMS
E ENTAMES
MEANEST
G MAGNETS
H ANTHEMS
HETMANS
I INMATES
MAINEST
MANTIES
TAMINES
L LAMENTS
MANTELS
MANTLES
O MANTOES
P ENSTAMP
TAPSMEN
R ARTSMEN
MARTENS
SARMENT
SMARTEN
S STAMENS
U UNTAMES
UNTEAMS
Y AMNESTY

AEMRST 124
(MATERS)
A AMEARST
RETAMAS
B TAMBERS
C MERCATS
D SMARTED
E STEAMER
TEAMERS
H HAMSTER
I IMARETS
MAESTRI
MAISTER
MASTIER
MISRATE
SEMITAR
SMARTIE
J RAMJETS
K MARKETS
L ARMLETS
MARTELS
M STAMMER
N ARTSMEN
MARTENS
SARMENT
SMARTEN
O AMORETS
MAESTRO
OMERTAS
P EMPARTS
STAMPER
TAMPERS
R SMARTER
S MASTERS
STREAMS
T MATTERS
SMATTER
U MATURES
STRUMAE
W WARMEST
Y MASTERY
MAYSTER
STREAMY

AENNST 152
(ANNETS)
A ANNATES
C NASCENT
D STANDEN
E NEATENS
F ENFANTS
G GANNETS
I INANEST
K KANTENS
L STANNEL
R TANNERS
T TANNEST
TENANTS
W WANNEST

AENPST 185
(PATENS)
A ANAPEST
PEASANT
C CATNEPS
D PEDANTS
PENTADS
E NEPETAS
PENATES
PESANTE
H HAPTENS
I PANTIES
PATINES
SAPIENT
SPINATE
L PLANETS
PLATENS
M ENSTAMP
TAPSMEN
R ARPENTS
ENTRAPS
PANTERS
PARENTS
PASTERN
PERSANT
TREPANS
S APTNESS
PATNESS
PESANTS
T PATENTS
PATTENS
U PEANUTS
PESAUNT
W STEWPAN
Y SYNAPTE
Z PEZANTS

AENRRT 87
(RANTER)
A NARRATE
E TERRANE
G GRANTER
REGRANT
I RETRAIN
TERRAIN
TRAINER
O ORNATER
P PARTNER
S ERRANTS
RANTERS
T TRANTER
Y TERNARY

AENRSS 223
(SANERS)
A NARASES
C ANCRESS
CASERNS
D SANDERS
SARSDEN
E ENSEARS
F FARNESS
G SERANGS
H HARNESS
I ARSINES
SARNIES
K KRANSES
L RANSELS
O REASONS
R SERRANS
SNARERS
S SARSENS
T SARSNET
TRANSES
W ANSWERS
RAWNESS
Y SARNEYS

AENRST 9
(ANTERS)
A ANESTRA
B BANTERS
C CANTERS
CARNETS
NECTARS
RECANTS
SCANTER
TANRECS
TRANCES
D ENDARTS
STANDER
STARNED
E EARNEST
EASTERN
NEAREST
G ARGENTS
GARNETS
STRANGE
H ANTHERS
HARTENS
THENARS
I ANESTRI
NASTIER
RATINES
RESIANT
RETAINS
RETINAS
RETSINA
STAINER
STARNIE
STEARIN
K RANKEST
STARKEN
TANKERS
L ANTLERS
RENTALS
SALTERN
STERNAL
M ARTSMEN
MARTENS
SARMENT
SMARTEN
N TANNERS
O ATONERS
SENATOR
TREASON
P ARPENTS
ENTRAPS
PANTERS
PARENTS
PASTERN
PERSANT
TREPANS
R ERRANTS
RANTERS
S SARSNET
TRANSES
T NATTERS
RATTENS
U AUNTERS
NATURES
SAUNTER
V SERVANT
TAVERNS
VERSANT
W STRAWEN
WANTERS
Y TRAYNES

AENRTT 71
(NATTER)
A TARTANE
C TRANECT
D TRANTED
E ENTREAT
RATTEEN
TERNATE
I INTREAT
ITERANT
NATTIER
NITRATE
TARTINE
TERTIAN
L TRENTAL
N ENTRANT
P PATTERN
REPTANT
R TRANTER
S NATTERS
RATTENS
U TAUNTER
Y NATTERY

AENSTT 116
(ATTENS)
B BATTENS
C CANTEST
D ATTENDS
E NEATEST
F FATTENS
G GESTANT
I INSTATE
SATINET
L LATTENS
TALENTS
N TANNEST
TENANTS
O ATTONES
NOTATES
P PATENTS
PATTENS
R NATTERS
RATTENS
T ATTENTS
U ATTUNES
NUTATES
TAUTENS
TETANUS
UNSTATE
X SEXTANT

AEORST 13
(ORATES)
B BOASTER
BOATERS
BORATES
SORBATE
C COASTER
COATERS
D DOATERS
ROASTED
TORSADE
TROADES
E ROSEATE
G ORGEATS
STORAGE
TOERAGS
H ASTHORE
EARSHOT
HAROSET
I OARIEST
OTARIES
L OESTRAL
M AMORETS
MAESTRO
OMERTAS
N ATONERS
SENATOR
TREASON
P ESPARTO
PROTEAS
SEAPORT
R ROASTER
T ROTATES
TOASTER

AEPRST 129
(PATERS)
A PETARAS
C CARPETS
PRECAST
SPECTRA
D DEPARTS
DRAPETS
PETARDS
E REPEATS
G PARGETS
H SPARTHE
TEPHRAS
THREAPS
I PARTIES
PASTIER
PIASTRE
PIRATES
PRATIES
TRAIPSE
L PALTERS
PLASTER
PLATERS
PSALTER
STAPLER
M EMPARTS
STAMPER
TAMPERS
N ARPENTS
ENTRAPS
PANTERS
PARENTS
PASTERN
PERSANT
TREPANS
O ESPARTO
PROTEAS
SEAPORT
P TAPPERS
R PARTERS
PRATERS
S PASTERS
REPASTS
SPAREST
T PATTERS
SPATTER
TAPSTER
U PASTURE
UPRATES
UPSTARE
UPTEARS
Y YAPSTER
Z PATZERS

AERRST 138
(RATERS)
B BARRETS
BARTERS
C CARTERS
CRATERS
TRACERS
D DARTERS
DARTRES
RETARDS
STARRED
TRADERS
E SERRATE
TEARERS
F FRATERS
RAFTERS
G GARRETS
GARTERS
GRATERS
I ARTSIER
SERRATI
TARRIES
TARSIER
K KARTERS
KRATERS
STARKER
M SMARTER
N ERRANTS
RANTERS
O ROASTER
P PARTERS
PRATERS
S ARRESTS
RASTERS
STARERS
T RATTERS
RESTART
STARTER
Y STRAYER

AERSST 220
(ASSERT)
A SEARATS
B BASTERS
BESTARS
BRASSET
BREASTS
C ACTRESS
CASTERS
RECASTS
E RESEATS
SAETERS
SEAREST
SEATERS
STEARES
TEASERS
TESSERA
F FASTERS
STRAFES
G GASTERS
STAGERS
H RASHEST
SHASTER
TRASHES
I ARTSIES
SAIREST
SATIRES
TIRASSE
K SKATERS
STRAKES
STREAKS
TASKERS
L ARTLESS
LASTERS
SALTERS
SLATERS
TARSELS
M MASTERS
STREAMS
N SARSNET
TRANSES
P PASTERS
REPASTS
SPAREST
R ARRESTS
RASTERS
STARERS
S ASSERTS
TRASSES
T ASTERTS
STARETS
STATERS
TASTERS
V STARVES
W WASTERS
Y ESTRAYS
STAYERS
STAYRES

AERSTT 97
(TASTER)
B BATTERS
TABRETS
C SCATTER
D STARTED
TETRADS
E ESTREAT
RESTATE
G TARGETS
H HATTERS
RATHEST
SHATTER
THREATS
I ARTIEST
ARTISTE
ATTIRES
IRATEST
STRIATE
TASTIER
TERTIAS
L RATTLES
SLATTER
STARLET
STARTLE
TATLERS
M MATTERS
SMATTER
N NATTERS
RATTENS
O ROTATES
TOASTER
P PATTERS
SPATTER
TAPSTER
R RATTERS
RESTART
STARTER
S ASTERTS
STARETS
STATERS
TASTERS
T STRETTA
TARTEST
TATTERS
U ASTUTER
STATURE
V VATTERS
W SWATTER
TEWARTS
Y YATTERS
Z STARETZ

AERSTW 194
(WATERS)
A AWAREST
B BRAWEST
WABSTER
D STEWARD
STRAWED
WRASTED
E SWEATER
F FRETSAW
WAFTERS
H THAWERS
WREATHS
I WAISTER
WAITERS
WARIEST
L WASTREL
M WARMEST
N STRAWEN
WANTERS
S WASTERS
T SWATTER
TEWARTS
Y WASTERY

AGILNR 199
(RALING)
B BLARING
C CARLING
D DARLING
LARDING
E ENGRAIL
LAERING
LEARING
NARGILE
REALIGN
REGINAL
F FLARING
G GLARING
H HARLING
I GLAIRIN
LAIRING
RAILING
K LARKING
M MARLING
N LARNING
O RANGOLI
P PARLING
T RATLING
W WARLING
Y ANGRILY
NARGILY
RAYLING

AGILNS 219
(SIGNAL)
A AGNAILS
B SABLING
C LACINGS
SCALING
D LADINGS
LIGANDS
E LEASING
LINAGES
SEALING
F FALSING
G GINGALS
LAGGINS
H HALSING
LASHING
SHALING
I AISLING
NILGAIS
SAILING
J JINGALS
K SLAKING
M LINGAMS
MALIGNS
N LINSANG
P LAPSING
PALINGS
SAPLING
S LASINGS
SIGNALS
T ANGLIST
LASTING
SALTING
SLATING
STALING
U LINGUAS
NILGAUS
SALUING
V SALVING
SLAVING
VALSING
W LAWINGS
SWALING
Y LAYINGS
SLAYING

AGILNT 174
(LATING)
B TABLING
C CATLING
TALCING
E ATINGLE
ELATING
GELATIN
GENITAL
F FATLING
H HALTING
LATHING
I TAILING
K TALKING
M MALTING
N TANLING
O ANTILOG
P PLATING
R RATLING
S ANGLIST
LASTING
SALTING
SLATING
STALING
Y GIANTLY

AGINRS 123
(GRAINS)
A NAGARIS
SANGRIA
SARANGI
B SABRING
C ARCINGS
RACINGS
SACRING
SCARING
D DARINGS
GRADINS
E ANGRIES
EARINGS
ERASING
GAINERS
GRAINES
REGAINS
REGINAS
SEARING
SERINGA
F FARSING
G RAGINGS
SIRGANG
H GARNISH
RASHING
SHARING
I AIRINGS
ARISING
RAGINIS
RAISING
SAIRING
K RAKINGS
SARKING
M MARGINS
N SNARING
O IGNAROS
ORIGANS
SIGNORA
SOARING
P PARINGS
PARSING
RASPING
SPARING
T GASTRIN
GRATINS
RATINGS
STARING
TARINGS
V RAVINGS
W RAWINGS
Y SIGNARY
SYRINGA

AGINRT 69
(RATING)
A GRANITA
C CARTING
CRATING
TRACING
D DARTING
TRADING
E GRANITE
GRATINE
INGRATE
TANGIER
TEARING
F FARTING
INGRAFT
RAFTING
G GRATING
TARGING
I AIRTING
RAITING
K KARTING
L RATLING
M MARTING
MIGRANT
N RANTING
O ORATING
ROATING
P PARTING
PRATING
TRAPING
R TARRING
S GASTRIN
GRATINS
RATINGS
STARING
TARINGS
T RATTING
Y GIANTRY

AGINST 108
(SATING)
A AGAINST
GITANAS
B BASTING
C ACTINGS
CASTING
D DATINGS
E EASTING
EATINGS
GAINEST
GENISTA
INGATES
INGESTA
SEATING
TANGIES
TEASING
TSIGANE
F FASTING
G GASTING
GATINGS
STAGING
H HASTING
TASHING
K SKATING
STAKING
TAKINGS
TASKING
L ANGLIST
LASTING
SALTING
SLATING
STALING
M MASTING
TAMINGS
N ANTINGS
STANING
O AGONIST
GITANOS
P PASTING
R GASTRIN
GRATINS
RATINGS
STARING
TARINGS
T STATING
TASTING
U SAUTING
V STAVING
W STAWING
TAWINGS
WASTING
X TAXINGS
Y STAYING

AINRST 40
(TRAINS)
A ANTIARS
ARTISAN
TSARINA
D INDARTS
E ANESTRI
NASTIER
RATINES
RESIANT
RETAINS
RETINAS
RETSINA
STAINER
STARNIE
STEARIN
G GASTRIN
GRATINS
RATINGS
STARING
TARINGS
H TARNISH
L RATLINS
M MARTINS
O AROINTS
RATIONS
P SPIRANT
SPRAINT
Q QINTARS
S INSTARS
SANTIRS
STRAINS
T STRAINT
TRANSIT
U NUTRIAS

AINSTT 213
(TANIST)
A ATTAINS
D DISTANT
E INSTATE
SATINET
G STATING
TASTING
I TITANIS
TITIANS
M MATTINS
N INSTANT
O STATION
R STRAINT
TRANSIT
S TANISTS

ANORST 60
(RATONS)
A TORANAS
B BARTONS
C CANTORS
CARTONS
CONTRAS
CRATONS
E ATONERS
SENATOR
TREASON
I AROINTS
RATIONS
L LATRONS
M MATRONS
TRANSOM
N NATRONS
O RATOONS
P PARTONS
PATRONS
TARPONS
T ATTORNS
RATTONS
ROTTANS
U ROUSANT
SANTOUR
Y AROYNTS

BDEIRS 242
(BRIDES)
A BRAISED
DARBIES
SEABIRD
SIDEBAR
B DIBBERS
C SCRIBED
D BIDDERS
E DERBIES
G BEGIRDS
BRIDGES
I BIRDIES
BRIDIES
K BRISKED
L BIRSLED
BRIDLES
N BINDERS
REBINDS
O BORIDES
DISROBE
R BIRDERS
T BESTRID
BISTRED
U BRUISED
BURDIES
V VERBIDS

BEILRS 205
(LIBERS)
A BAILERS
B LIBBERS
D BIRSLED
BRIDLES
E BELIERS
G GERBILS
I RISIBLE
J JERBILS
JIRBLES
K BILKERS
M LIMBERS
N BERLINS
O BOILERS
LIBEROS
REBOILS
R BIRLERS
S BIRSLES
RIBLESS
T BLISTER
BRISTLE
RIBLETS

BEIRST 184
(TRIBES)
A BAITERS
BARITES
D BESTRID
BISTRED
E REBITES
F FIBSTER
H HERBIST
I BITSIER
K BRISKET
L BLISTER
BRISTLE
RIBLETS
M BETRIMS
TIMBERS
TIMBRES
O ORBIEST
SORBITE
S BESTIRS
BISTERS
BISTRES
T BITTERS
U BUSTIER
RUBIEST

BEORST 225
(STROBE)
A BOASTER
BOATERS
BORATES
SORBATE
D DEBTORS
H BOSHTER
BOTHERS
I ORBIEST
SORBITE
L BOLSTER
BOLTERS
LOBSTER
M BESTORM
MOBSTER
N BRETONS
SORBENT
O BOOSTER
P BESPORT
S BESORTS
SORBETS
STROBES
T BETTORS
U OBTUSER
V OBVERTS

CEINOS 109
(CONIES)
A ACINOSE
C CONCISE
D CONDIES
SECONDI
E SENECIO
G COGNISE
COIGNES
I ICONISE
L CINEOLS
CONSEIL
INCLOSE
M INCOMES
MESONIC
N CONINES
R COINERS
CRINOSE
CRONIES
ORCEINS
ORCINES
RECOINS
SERICON
S CESSION
COSINES
T NOTICES
SECTION
V NOVICES

CEINRS 183
(INCERS)
A ARSENIC
CARNIES
CERASIN
D CINDERS
DISCERN
RESCIND
E CERESIN
SCRIENE
SINCERE
G CRINGES
H NICHERS
RICHENS
I IRENICS
SERICIN
SIRENIC
K NICKERS
SNICKER
M CREMSIN
MINCERS
O COINERS
CRINOSE
CRONIES
ORCEINS
ORCINES
RECOINS
SERICON
P PINCERS
PRINCES
S SCRINES
T CISTERN
CRETINS
V CRIVENS
W WINCERS

CEINST 196
(INSECT)
A CANIEST
CINEAST
E ENTICES
F INFECTS
H ETHNICS
STHENIC
I INCITES
J INJECTS
K SNICKET
TICKENS
L CLIENTS
LECTINS
STENCIL
O NOTICES
SECTION
P INCEPTS
INSPECT
PECTINS
PEINCTS
R CISTERN

CRETINS
S INCESTS
INSECTS
Y CYSTINE

CEIORS 156
(COSIER)
A ORACIES
SCORIAE
B CORBIES
C CICEROS
D DISCOER
H COHEIRS
HEROICS
L RECOILS
N COINERS
CRINOSE
CRONIES
ORCEINS
ORCINES
RECOINS
SERICON
P COPIERS
COPSIER
PERSICO
R CIRROSE
CORRIES
CROSIER
S COSIERS
T EROTICS
TERCIOS
U SCOURIE
V CORSIVE
VOICERS
W COWRIES
SCOWRIE
Z COZIERS

CEIRST 166
(CITERS)
A CRISTAE
RACIEST
STEARIC
C CRETICS
D CREDITS
DIRECTS
E CERITES
RECITES
TIERCES
H CITHERS
ESTRICH
RICHEST
I ERISTIC
RICIEST
K RICKETS
STICKER
TICKERS
L RELICTS
M CRETISM
METRICS
N CISTERN
CRETINS
O EROTICS
TERCIOS
P TRICEPS
T TRISECT
U CUITERS
CURIETS
ICTERUS
W TWICERS

CENORS 172
(CONERS)
A CARNOSE
COARSEN
CORNEAS
EARCONS
D CONDERS
CORSNED
SCORNED
E ENCORES
NECROSE
F CONFERS
G CONGERS
I COINERS
CRINOSE
CRONIES
ORCEINS
ORCINES
RECOINS
SERICON
K CONKERS
RECKONS
L CORNELS
N CONNERS
O CEROONS
P CREPONS
R CORNERS
SCORNER
S CENSORS
T CONSTER
CORNETS
CRESTON
CRONETS
U CONURES
ROUNCES

CENOST 224
(CONEST)
A COSTEAN
OCTANES
D DOCENTS
E CENOTES
F CONFEST
G CONGEST
H NOTCHES
TECHNOS
I NOTICES
SECTION
K NOCKETS
N CONSENT
NOCENTS
R CONSTER
CORNETS
CRESTON
CRONETS
T CONTEST
U CONTUSE
ECONUTS
V COVENTS

CEORST 234
(CORSET)
A COASTER
COATERS
H HECTORS
ROCHETS
ROTCHES
TOCHERS
TORCHES
TROCHES
I EROTICS
TERCIOS
K RESTOCK
ROCKETS
STOCKER
L COLTERS
CORSLET
COSTREL
LECTORS
N CONSTER
CORNETS
CRESTON
CRONETS
O SCOOTER
P COPTERS
R RECTORS
S CORSETS
COSTERS
ESCORTS
SCOTERS
SECTORS
T COTTERS
U COUTERS
CROUTES
SCOUTER
V CORVETS
COVERTS
VECTORS

DEEINR 43
(DENIER)
B BENDIER
INBREED
C CEDRINE
E NEEDIER
F DEFINER
ENFIRED
FENDIER
REFINED
G DREEING
ENERGID
GREINED
REEDING
REIGNED
H INHERED
L RELINED
M ERMINED
O ORDINEE
P REPINED
RIPENED
R DERNIER
NERDIER
S DENIERS
NEREIDS
RESINED
U UREDINE
W WIDENER
X INDEXER

DEEIRS 58
(RESIDE)
A DEARIES
READIES
B DERBIES
C DECRIES
D DERIDES
DESIRED
DIEDRES
RESIDED
E SEEDIER
F DEFIERS
G SEDGIER
L RESILED
M REMEIDS
REMISED
N DENIERS
NEREIDS
RESINED
O OREIDES
OSIERED
P PREDIES
PRESIDE
SPEIRED
R DERRIES
DESIRER
RESIDER
SERRIED
S DESIRES
RESIDES
T DIETERS
REISTED
U RESIDUE
UREIDES
V DERIVES
DEVISER
DIVERSE
REVISED

DEELNS 239
(ENDLES)
A LEADENS
B BLENDES
D LEDDENS
E NEEDLES
F FLENSED
G LEGENDS
I ENISLED
ENSILED
LINSEED
L SNELLED
R LENDERS
SLENDER
S ENDLESS
T DENTELS
NESTLED
W WEDELNS
Y DENSELY

DEENRS 92
(ENDERS)
A DEANERS
ENDEARS
B BENDERS
C DECERNS
SCERNED
D REDDENS
E NEEDERS
SERENED
SNEERED
F FENDERS
G GENDERS
H HERDENS
I DENIERS
NEREIDS
RESINED
-L LENDERS
SLENDER
M MENDERS
O ENDORSE
P SPENDER
R RENDERS
S REDNESS
SENDERS
T STERNED
TENDERS
TENDRES
U ENDURES
ENSURED
V VENDERS
Z DZERENS

DEENST 111
(NESTED)
A STANDEE
STEANED
C DESCENT
SCENTED
D STENDED
E STEENED
I DESTINE
ENDITES
STEINED
L DENTELS
NESTLED
M DEMENTS
N DENNETS
STENNED
O DENOTES
R STERNED
TENDERS
TENDRES
S DENSEST
T DETENTS
STENTED
U DETENUS
DETUNES
X EXTENDS

DEERST 151
(RESTED)
A DEAREST
DERATES
ESTRADE
REASTED
REDATES
SEDATER
STEARED
TASERED
C CRESTED
D REDDEST
TEDDERS
E REESTED
STEERED
I DIETERS
REISTED
N STERNED
TENDERS
TENDRES
O OERSTED
ROSETED
TEREDOS
P PRESTED
S DESERTS
DESSERT
TRESSED
V STERVED
VERDETS
W STREWED
WRESTED
X DEXTERS
Y DYESTER

DEGILN 164
(DINGLE)
A ALIGNED
DEALING
LEADING
B BINGLED
E DELEING
G GELDING
NIGGLED
H HINDLEG
I EILDING
ELIDING
J JINGLED
M MEDLING
MELDING
MINGLED
N LENDING
O GLENOID
P PINGLED
S DINGLES
ELDINGS
ENGILDS
SINGLED
T GLINTED
TINGLED
U ELUDING
INDULGE
V DELVING
DEVLING
W WELDING

DEGINR 82
(RINGED)
A AREDING
DEARING
DERAIGN
EARDING
GRADINE
GRAINED
READING
B BREDING
C CRINGED
D GRINDED
REDDING
E DREEING
ENERGID
GREINED
REEDING
REIGNED
F FRINGED
H HERDING
I DINGIER
N GRINNED
RENDING
O ERODING
GROINED
IGNORED
NEGROID
REDOING
R GRINDER
REGRIND
S DINGERS
ENGIRDS
U DUNGIER
W REDWING
WRINGED
Y YERDING

DEGINS 154
(SINGED)
A AGNISED
E SDEIGNE
SEEDING
G EDGINGS
SNIGGED
I DINGIES
L DINGLES
ELDINGS
ENGILDS
SINGLED
M SMIDGEN
N ENDINGS
SENDING
O DINGOES
R DINGERS
ENGIRDS
S DESIGNS
SDEIGNS
T NIDGETS
STEDING
STINGED
U GUNDIES
SUEDING
W SWINDGE
SWINGED
Y DINGEYS
DYEINGS

DEGIRS 210
(GRIDES)
A AGRISED
B BEGIRDS
BRIDGES
E SEDGIER
F FRIDGES
G DIGGERS
I DIRIGES
L GILDERS
GIRDLES
GLIDERS
GRISLED
LIDGERS
RIDGELS
N DINGERS
ENGIRDS
R GIRDERS
RIDGERS
S DIGRESS
U GUIDERS

DEILNS 120
(INDLES)
A DENIALS
SNAILED
D DINDLES
SLIDDEN
E ENISLED
ENSILED
LINSEED
G DINGLES
ELDINGS
ENGILDS
SINGLED
I INISLED
K KINDLES
M MILDENS
N DINNLES
LINDENS
O DOLINES
INDOLES
SONDELI
P SPELDIN
SPINDLE
SPLINED
T DENTILS
W SWINDLE
WINDLES
Y SNIDELY

DEILRT 73
(TRIDLE)
A DILATER
TRAILED
B DRIBLET
D TIDDLER
E RETILED
F FLIRTED
TRIFLED
H THIRLED
K KIRTLED
L TRILLED
N TENDRIL
TRINDLE
O DOILTER
P TRIPLED
U DILUTER
W TWIRLED
Y TIREDLY

DEINOS 41
(ONSIDE)
A ADONISE
ANODISE
SODAINE
C CONDIES
SECONDI
D NODDIES
G DINGOES
H HOIDENS
I IODINES
IONISED
L DOLINES
INDOLES
SONDELI
M MISDONE
N ONDINES
P DISPONE
SPINODE
R DONSIER
INDORSE
ROSINED
S ONSIDES
T DITONES
STONIED

DEINRS 51
(DINERS)
A RANDIES
SANDIER
SARDINE
B BINDERS
REBINDS
C CINDERS
DISCERN
RESCIND
E DENIERS
NEREIDS
RESINED
F FINDERS
FRIENDS
G DINGERS
ENGIRDS
H HINDERS
SHRINED
I INSIDER
K KINDERS
KINREDS
REDSKIN
M MINDERS
REMINDS
N DINNERS
O DONSIER
INDORSE
ROSINED
P PINDERS
T TINDERS
U INSURED
V VERDINS
W REWINDS
WINDERS

DEINRU 52
(RUINED)
A UNAIRED
URANIDE
C INDUCER
D UNDRIED
E UREDINE
F UNFIRED
G DUNGIER
H UNHIRED
I URIDINE
J INJURED
M UNRIMED
N DUNNIER
INURNED
O DOURINE
S INSURED
T INTRUDE
TURDINE
UNTIRED
UNTRIDE
UNTRIED
W UNWIRED

DEINST 32
(SINTED)
A DETAINS
INSTEAD
SAINTED
SATINED
STAINED
B BIDENTS
D DISTEND
E DESTINE
ENDITES
STEINED
F SNIFTED
G NIDGETS
STEDING
STINGED
I INDITES
TINEIDS
K DINKEST
KINDEST
L DENTILS
M MINDSET
N DENTINS
INDENTS
INTENDS
O DITONES
STONIED
P STIPEND
R TINDERS
S DISNEST
DISSENT
SNIDEST
T DENTIST
DISTENT
STINTED
U DISTUNE
DUNITES
Y DENSITY
DESTINY

DEIORS 27
(ORIDES)
A ROADIES
SOREDIA
B BORIDES
DISROBE
C DISCOER
D DORISED
SODDIER
E OREIDES
OSIERED
H RHODIES
L SOLDIER
SOLIDER
M MISDOER
MOIDERS
N DONSIER
INDORSE
ROSINED
O OROIDES
P PERIODS
S DORISES
DOSSIER
T EDITORS
ROISTED
ROSITED
SORTIED
STEROID
STORIED
TIERODS
TRIODES
V DEVISOR
DEVOIRS
VISORED
VOIDERS
W DOWRIES
ROWDIES
WEIRDOS
Z DORIZES

DEIOST 35
(ODITES)
A IODATES
TOADIES
C CESTOID
COTISED
D TODDIES
F FOISTED
H HOISTED
J JOISTED
M DOMIEST
MODISTE
MOISTED
N DITONES
STONIED
O OSTEOID
P DEPOSIT
DOPIEST
PODITES
POSITED
SOPITED
TOPSIDE
R EDITORS
ROISTED
ROSITED
SORTIED
STEROID
STORIED
TIERODS
TRIODES
T DOTIEST
STOITED
U OUTSIDE
TEDIOUS
V DOVIEST
W DOWIEST
X EXODIST
Z DOZIEST

DEIPRT 215
(PRITED)
A DIPTERA
PARTIED
PIRATED
C PREDICT
E TEPIDER
I RIPTIDE
L TRIPLED
M DIREMPT
N PRINTED
O DIOPTER
DIOPTRE
PERIDOT
PROTEID
P TRIPPED
S SPIRTED
STRIPED

DEIRST 57
(STRIDE)
A ARIDEST
ASTERID
ASTRIDE
DIASTER
DISRATE
STAIDER
STAIRED
TARDIES
TIRADES
B BESTRID
BISTRED
C CREDITS
DIRECTS
E DIETERS
REISTED
F FRISTED
H DITHERS
SHIRTED
I DIRTIES
DITSIER
K SKIRTED
N TINDERS
O EDITORS
ROISTED
ROSITED
SORTIED
STEROID
STORIED
TIERODS
TRIODES
P SPIRTED
STRIPED
R STIRRED
S DISSERT
STRIDES
U DUSTIER
REDUITS
STUDIER
V DIVERTS
STRIVED
VERDITS

DEIRSU 143
(URDIES)
A RESIDUA
B BRUISED
BURDIES
C CRUISED
DISCURE
D RUDDIES
E RESIDUE
UREIDES
G GUIDERS
H HURDIES
K DUIKERS
DUSKIER
N INSURED
P PUDSIER
SIRUPED
Q SQUIRED
R DRUSIER
DURRIES
S DISEURS
SUDSIER
T DUSTIER
REDUITS
STUDIER

DELNOS 181
(OLDENS)
A LOADENS
B BLONDES
BOLDENS
D NODDLES
F ENFOLDS
FONDLES
G DONGLES
GOLDENS
I DOLINES
INDOLES
SONDELI
M DOLMENS
O NOODLES
SNOOLED
R RONDELS
S OLDNESS
U LOUDENS
NODULES
NOUSLED
W DOWLNES
Z DONZELS

DELORS 145
(OLDERS)
A LOADERS
ORDEALS
RELOADS
B BORDELS
C SCOLDER
E RESOLED
F FOLDERS
G LODGERS
H HOLDERS
I SOLDIER
SOLIDER
M SMOLDER
N RONDELS
P POLDERS
S DORSELS
RODLESS
SOLDERS
T DROLEST
OLDSTER
STRODLE
W WELDORS
Y YODLERS

DELORT 100
(DOLTER)
A DELATOR
LEOTARD
D TODDLER
I DOILTER
L TROLLED
N ENTROLD
O ROOTLED
P DROPLET
S DROLEST
OLDSTER
STRODLE
T DOTTLER
DOTTREL
U TROULED

DENORU 99
(UNDOER)
A RONDEAU
B BOUNDER
REBOUND
UNROBED
D REDOUND
ROUNDED
UNDERDO
F FOUNDER
REFOUND
G GUERDON
UNDERGO
UNGORED
I DOURINE
L LOUNDER
ROUNDEL
ROUNDLE
M MOURNED
N ENROUND
P POUNDER
UNROPED
R RONDURE
ROUNDER
UNORDER
S RESOUND
SOUNDER
UNDOERS
W REWOUND
WOUNDER

DENOST 74
(STONED)
A ASTONED
DONATES
ONSTEAD
B OBTENDS
C DOCENTS
E DENOTES
F FONDEST
I DITONES
STONIED
M ENDMOST
N STONNED
TENDONS
O SNOOTED
STOODEN
R RODENTS
SNORTED
T SNOTTED
U DEUTONS
SNOUTED

DENRSU 179
(UNDERS)
A ASUNDER
DANSEUR
DAUNERS
B BURDENS
D DUNDERS
E ENDURES
ENSURED
F FUNDERS
REFUNDS
G GERUNDS
NUDGERS
H HURDENS
I INSURED
K DUNKERS
L LURDENS
NURDLES
NURSLED
RUNDLES
N UNDERNS
O RESOUND
SOUNDER
UNDOERS
P SPURNED
S SUNDERS
UNDRESS
T RETUNDS
U UNSURED

DENSTU 217
(UNSTED)
A SAUNTED
UNSATED
B SUBTEND
D STUDDEN
E DETENUS
DETUNES
H SHUNTED
I DISTUNE
DUNITES
M DUSTMEN
N DUNNEST
STUNNED
O DEUTONS
SNOUTED
R RETUNDS
T STUDENT
STUNTED

DEORST 50
(SORTED)
A DOATERS
ROASTED
TORSADE
TROADES
B DEBTORS
E OERSTED
ROSETED
TEREDOS
F DEFROST
FROSTED
G STODGER
H DEHORTS
SHORTED
I EDITORS
ROISTED
ROSITED
SORTIED
STEROID
STORIED
TIERODS
TRIODES
K STROKED
L DROLEST
OLDSTER
STRODLE
M STORMED
N RODENTS
SNORTED
O ROOSTED
P DEPORTS
REDTOPS
SPORTED
R DORTERS
RODSTER
T DETORTS
U DETOURS
DOUREST
DOUTERS
OUTREDS
ROUSTED
W STROWED
WORSTED
Y DESTROY
ROYSTED
STROYED

DEOSTU 180
(OUSTED)
C DOUCEST
DOUCETS
SCOUTED
G DEGOUTS
H SHOUTED
SOUTHED
I OUTSIDE
TEDIOUS
J JOUSTED
L LOUDEST
OULDEST
TOUSLED
M MOUSTED
SMOUTED
N DEUTONS
SNOUTED
O OUTDOES
P SPOUTED
R DETOURS
DOUREST
DOUTERS
OUTREDS
ROUSTED
T DUETTOS
TESTUDO
U DUTEOUS
X TUXEDOS

DERSTU 244
(RUSTED)
B BURSTED
C CRUDEST
CRUSTED
G TRUDGES
I DUSTIER
REDUITS
STUDIER
L LUSTRED
RUSTLED
STRUDEL
N RETUNDS
O DETOURS
DOUREST
DOUTERS
OUTREDS
ROUSTED
P SPURTED
R RUSTRED
S DUSTERS
TRUSSED
T STURTED
TRUSTED
U SUTURED

DGINOR 209
(ORDING)
A ADORING
GRADINO
ROADING
C CORDING
D RODDING
E ERODING
GROINED
IGNORED
NEGROID
REDOING
F FORDING
H HORDING
L GIRLOND
LORDING
N DRONING
R DORRING
S RODINGS
T DORTING
V DROVING
W WORDING

EEFIRS 241
(FERIES)
A AREFIES
FAERIES
FREESIA
D DEFIERS
E FEERIES
F EFFEIRS
H HEIFERS
I REIFIES
L FERLIES
RELIEFS
N ENFIRES
FEERINS
FINEERS
REFINES
P PREIFES
PRIEFES
R FERRIES
S FRISEES
Z FRIEZES

EEGNRS 237
(GREENS)
A ENRAGES
D GENDERS
E RENEGES
I GREISEN
M GERMENS
O ENGORES
NEGROES
S NEGRESS
T GERENTS
REGENTS
V VENGERS

EEILRS 90
(RELIES)
A EARLIES
REALISE
B BELIERS
D RESILED
E SEELIER
F FERLIES
RELIEFS
G LEIGERS
LIEGERS
H LEISHER
L LEISLER
N LIERNES
RELINES
P REPLIES
SPIELER
R RELIERS
S RESILES
T LEISTER
RETILES
STERILE
U LEISURE
V RELIVES
REVILES
SERVILE

EEILRV 232
(RELIVE)
A LEAVIER
VEALIER
D DELIVER
RELIVED
REVILED
E RELIEVE
G VELIGER
I VEILIER
L EVILLER
M VERMEIL
N LIVENER
O OVERLIE
RELIEVO
R RELIVER
REVILER
S RELIVES
REVILES
SERVILE

EEILST 89
(ELITES)
C SECTILE
E EELIEST
F FELSITE
LEFTIES
LIEFEST
G ELEGIST
ELEGITS
H SHELTIE
K KELTIES
SLEEKIT
L TELLIES
M ELMIEST
N SETLINE
TENSILE
O ESTOILE
ETOILES
P EPISTLE
PELITES
R LEISTER
RETILES
STERILE
S TELESIS
TIELESS
V LEVITES
LIEVEST
X SEXTILE

EEIMNS 192
(EMINES)
A MEANIES
NEMESIA
D DESMINE
SIDEMEN
E ENEMIES
G SEEMING
I MEINIES
L ISLEMEN
M IMMENSE
O SEMEION
R ERMINES
S INSEEMS
MISSEEN
NEMESIS
SIEMENS
T EMETINS
W MISWEEN
Y MEINEYS
MENYIES

EEIMRS 202
(MISERE)
A SEAMIER
SERIEMA
B BEMIRES
BIREMES
C MERCIES
D REMEIDS
REMISED
E EMERIES
G EMIGRES
REGIMES
REMIGES

H MESHIER
M IMMERSE
N ERMINES
O ISOMERE
P EMPIRES
EMPRISE
EPIMERS
IMPRESE
PREMIES
PREMISE
SPIREME
R MERRIES
S MESSIER
MISERES
REMISES
T METIERS
RETIMES
TREMIES
TRISEME
X REMIXES

EEINRT 8
(ENTIRE)
A RETINAE
TRAINEE
B BENTIER
C ENTERIC
ENTICER
E TEENIER
F FEINTER
G GENTIER
INTEGER
TEERING
TREEING
H NEITHER
THEREIN
I ERINITE
NITERIE
K KERNITE
N INTERNE
P INEPTER
R INERTER
REINTER
RENTIER
TERRINE
S ENTIRES
ENTRIES
NERITES
TRENISE
T NETTIER
TENTIER
U NEURITE
RETINUE
REUNITE
UTERINE

EEIRRS 182
(ERRIES)
A REARISE
B BERRIES
D DERRIES
DESIRER
RESIDER
SERRIED
F FERRIES
H HERRIES
J JERRIES
L RELIERS
M MERRIES
N RESINER

O ROSIERE
P PERRIES
REPRISE
RESPIRE
S SERRIES
SIRREES
T ETRIERS
REITERS
RESTIER
RETIRES
RETRIES
TERRIES
V REIVERS
REVERSI
REVISER
RIEVERS
W REWIRES

EEIRST 31
(ESTIER)
A AERIEST
SERIATE
B REBITES
C CERITES
RECITES
TIERCES
D DIETERS
REISTED
E EERIEST
H HEISTER
K KEISTER
L LEISTER
RETILES
STERILE
M METIERS
RETIMES
TREMIES
TRISEME
N ENTIRES
ENTRIES
NERITES
TRENISE
P RESPITE
R ETRIERS
REITERS
RESTIER
RETIRES
RETRIES
TERRIES
T TESTIER
U SUETIER
V RESTIVE
SIEVERT
STIEVER
VERIEST
W STEWIER
Z ZESTIER

EEIRSV 222
(REVISE)
C SCRIEVE
SERVICE
D DERIVES
DEVISER
DIVERSE
REVISED
E VEERIES
G GRIEVES
REGIVES
H SHRIEVE

L RELIVES
REVILES
SERVILE
N ENVIERS
INVERSE
VENIRES
VERSINE
O EROSIVE
P PREVISE
PRIEVES
R REIVERS
REVERSI
REVISER
RIEVERS
S IVRESSE
REVISES
T RESTIVE
SIEVERT
STIEVER
VERIEST
V REVIVES
W REVIEWS
VIEWERS

EELNST 161
(NESTLE)
A ELANETS
LATEENS
LEANEST
D DENTELS
NESTLED
E STELENE
G GENTLES
LENGEST
I SETLINE
TENSILE
L TELLENS
P PENTELS
R RELENTS
SLENTER
S NESTLES
T NETTLES
U ELUENTS
UNSTEEL
Y ENSTYLE
TENSELY

EELRST 157
(ELTERS)
A ELATERS
REALEST
RELATES
STEALER
B BELTERS
TREBLES
C TERCELS
F FELTERS
REFLETS
TELFERS
G REGLETS
H SHELTER
I LEISTER
RETILES
STERILE
K KELTERS
KESTREL
SKELTER
L RETELLS
TELLERS
M SMELTER

N RELENTS
SLENTER
P PELTERS
PETRELS
RESPELT
SPELTER
S STREELS
TRESSEL
T LETTERS
LETTRES
SETTLER
STERLET
TRESTLE
V SVELTER
W SWELTER
WELTERS
WRESTLE
Y RESTYLE
TERSELY
Z SELTZER

EENRST 56
(ENTERS)
A EARNEST
EASTERN
NEAREST
C CENTERS
CENTRES
TENRECS
D STERNED
TENDERS
TENDRES
E ENTREES
RETENES
G GERENTS
REGENTS
H THRENES
I ENTIRES
ENTRIES
NERITES
TRENISE
L RELENTS
SLENTER
N RENNETS
TENNERS
P PRESENT
REPENTS
SERPENT
R RENTERS
STERNER
S NESTERS
RESENTS
STRENES
T TENTERS
TESTERN
U NEUTERS
RETUNES
TENURES
TUREENS
V VENTERS
VENTRES
W WESTERN
X EXTERNS
Y STYRENE
YESTERN

EEORSV 247
(REVOSE)
A OVERSEA
B OBSERVE

OBVERSE
VERBOSE
C CORVEES
E OVERSEE
I EROSIVE
K EVOKERS
REVOKES
L RESOLVE
M REMOVES
R REVERSO
T ESTOVER
OVERSET
U OEUVRES
OVERUSE
W OVERSEW

EERRST 236
(RESTER)
A SERRATE
TEARERS
B BERRETS
E RETREES
STEERER
F FERRETS
G REGRETS
I ETRIERS
REITERS
RESTIER
RETIRES
RETRIES
TERRIES
M TERMERS
N RENTERS
STERNER
O RESTORE
S RESTERS
T TERRETS
U URETERS
V REVERTS
W STREWER
WRESTER

EERSTT 200
(ETTERS)
A ESTREAT
RESTATE
B BETTERS
C TERCETS
E TEETERS
TERETES
F FETTERS
G GETTERS
H TETHERS
I TESTIER
L LETTERS
LETTRES
SETTLER
STERLET
TRESTLE
N TENTERS
TESTERN
O ROSETTE
P PERTEST
PETTERS
PRETEST
R TERRETS
S SETTERS
STREETS
TERSEST
TESTERS

T STRETTE
TETTERS
U TRUSTEE
Y STREETY

EFIRST 191
(STRIFE)
A FAIREST
B FIBSTER
D FRISTED
F RESTIFF
STIFFER
H SHIFTER
I FISTIER
K FRISKET
L FILTERS
LIFTERS
STIFLER
TRIFLES
M FIRMEST
FREMITS
N SNIFTER
O FOISTER
FORTIES
S SIFTERS
STRIFES
T FITTERS
TITFERS
U FUSTIER
SURFEIT
W SWIFTER

EGHINT 250
(ETHING)
A GAHNITE
HEATING
B BENIGHT
C ETCHING
D NIGHTED
E THEEING
F HEFTING
I NIGHTIE
L ENLIGHT
LIGHTEN
M THEMING
N HENTING
R RIGHTEN
S NIGHEST
T TIGHTEN

EGILNR 125
(LINGER)
A ENGRAIL
LAERING
LEARING
NARGILE
REALIGN
REGINAL
C CLINGER
CRINGLE
E LEERING
REELING
F FLINGER
G NIGGLER
H HERLING
I LEIRING
LINGIER
J JINGLER
M GREMLIN
MERLING

MINGLER
P PINGLER
S GIRNELS
LINGERS
SLINGER
T RINGLET
TINGLER
TRINGLE
Y RELYING

EGILNS 117
(SINGLE)
A LEASING
LINAGES
SEALING
B BINGLES
D DINGLES
ELDINGS
ENGILDS
SINGLED
E LEESING
SEELING
F SELFING
G GINGLES
NIGGLES
SNIGGLE
H SHINGLE
I SEILING
J JINGLES
K KINGLES
L LEGLINS
LINGELS
LINGLES
SELLING
M MINGLES
N GINNELS
O ELOIGNS
LEGIONS
LIGNOSE
LINGOES
P PINGLES
SPIGNEL
R GIRNELS
LINGERS
SLINGER
S SINGLES
T GLISTEN
LESTING
SINGLET
TINGLES
U LUNGIES
SLUEING
W SLEWING
SWINGLE
Z ZINGELS

EGILNT 66
(TINGLE)
A ATINGLE
ELATING
GELATIN
GENITAL
B BELTING
D GLINTED
TINGLED
E GENTILE
F FELTING
H ENLIGHT
LIGHTEN
I LIGNITE
J JINGLET
K KINGLET
L TELLING
M MELTING
O LENTIGO
P PELTING
R RINGLET
TINGLER
TRINGLE
S GLISTEN
LESTING
SINGLET
TINGLES
T ETTLING
LETTING
U ELUTING
W WELTING
WINGLET

EGILOS 132
(LOGIES)
A GOALIES
SOILAGE
B OBLIGES
E ELOGIES
L GOLLIES
N ELOIGNS
LEGIONS
LIGNOSE
LINGOES
O GOOLIES
OLOGIES
P EPILOGS
R GLOIRES
GLORIES
S GLIOSES
T ELOGIST
LOGIEST
U OUGLIES

EGILRS 159
(LIGERS)
A GRAILES
B GERBILS
D GILDERS
GIRDLES
GLIDERS
GRISLED
LIDGERS
RIDGELS
E LEIGERS
LIEGERS
G LIGGERS
I GIRLIES
K KILERGS
L GRILLES
N GIRNELS
LINGERS
SLINGER
O GLOIRES
GLORIES
S GRILSES
T GLISTER
GRISTLE
U GUILERS
LIGURES
LURGIES
Y GREISLY
GRIESLY
GRISELY

EGILST 190
(LEGIST)
A AGILEST
AIGLETS
LIGATES
TAIGLES
B GIBLETS
E ELEGIST
ELEGITS
G GIGLETS
H SLEIGHT
L GILLETS
M GIMLETS
N GLISTEN
LESTING
SINGLET
TINGLES
O ELOGIST
LOGIEST
P PIGLETS
R GLISTER
GRISTLE
S LEGISTS
U GLUIEST
UGLIEST
Z GLITZES

EGINNR 178
(GINNER)
A AGINNER
EARNING
ENGRAIN
GRANNIE
NEARING
C CERNING
D GRINNED
RENDING
E ENGINER
INGENER
F FERNING
G GERNING
I GINNIER
REINING
K KERNING
M RINGMEN
N RENNING
R GRINNER
S ENRINGS
GINNERS
T RENTING
RINGENT
TERNING
U ENURING
V NERVING
Y GINNERY
RENYING

EGINOS 78
(INGOES)
A AGONIES
AGONISE
B BIOGENS
C COGNISE
COIGNES
D DINGOES
E SOIGNEE
H SHOEING
J JINGOES
L ELOIGNS
LEGIONS
LIGNOSE
LINGOES
M MISGONE
P EPIGONS
PIGEONS
PINGOES
R ERINGOS
IGNORES
REGIONS
SIGNORE
U IGNEOUS
W WIGEONS
Y ISOGENY

EGINRS 68
(SINGER)
A ANGRIES
EARINGS
ERASING
GAINERS
GRAINES
REGAINS
REGINAS
SEARING
SERINGA
B BINGERS
C CRINGES
D DINGERS
ENGIRDS
E GREISEN
F FINGERS
FRINGES
G GINGERS
NIGGERS
SNIGGER
L GIRNELS
LINGERS
SLINGER
M GERMINS
N ENRINGS
GINNERS
O ERINGOS
IGNORES
REGIONS
SIGNORE
P PERSING
PINGERS
SPRINGE
R ERRINGS
GIRNERS
RINGERS
SERRING
S INGRESS
RESIGNS
SIGNERS
SINGERS
T RESTING
STINGER
U REUSING
RUEINGS
SIGNEUR
V SERVING
VERSING
W SWINGER
WINGERS
Y SYRINGE
Z ZINGERS

EGINRT 39
(TINGER)
A GRANITE
GRATINE
INGRATE
TANGIER
TEARING
E GENTIER
INTEGER
TEERING
TREEING
H RIGHTEN
I IGNITER
TIERING
TIGRINE
L RINGLET
TINGLER
TRINGLE
M METRING
TERMING
N RENTING
RINGENT
TERNING
O GENITOR
S RESTING
STINGER
T GITTERN
RETTING
U TRUEING
V VERTING
Y RETYING

EGINST 107
(ESTING)
A EASTING
EATINGS
GAINEST
GENISTA
INGATES
INGESTA
SEATING
TANGIES
TEASING
TSIGANE
B BESTING
D NIDGETS
STEDING
STINGED
H NIGHEST
I IGNITES
J JESTING
K KESTING
L GLISTEN
LESTING
SINGLET
TINGLES
M STEMING
TEMSING
N NESTING
SENTING
TENSING
R RESTING
STINGER
S INGESTS
SIGNETS
T SETTING
TESTING
U GUNITES
V VESTING
W STEWING
TWINGES
WESTING
Z ZESTING

EGNORS 155
(ONGERS)
A ONAGERS
ORANGES
C CONGERS
E ENGORES
NEGROES
I ERINGOS
IGNORES
REGIONS
SIGNORE
M MONGERS
MORGENS
O ORGONES
OROGENS
P SPONGER
S ENGROSS
U SURGEON
V GOVERNS
Y ERYNGOS
GROYNES

EHINRS 227
(SHRINE)
A ARSHINE
HERNIAS
C NICHERS
RICHENS
D HINDERS
SHRINED
E HENRIES
INHERES
I SHINIER
K KERNISH
M MENHIRS
O HEROINS
INSHORE
S SHINERS
SHRINES
V SHRIVEN
W WHINERS

EHIRST 153
(ITHERS)
A HASTIER
SHERIAT
B HERBIST
C CITHERS
ESTRICH
RICHEST
D DITHERS
SHIRTED
E HEISTER
F SHIFTER
G SIGHTER
H HITHERS
I HIRSTIE
L SLITHER
M HERMITS
MITHERS
O HERIOTS
HOISTER
SHORTIE
TOSHIER
P HIPSTER
T HITTERS

TITHERS
U HIRSUTE
V THRIVES
W SWITHER
WITHERS
WRITHES
Z ZITHERS

EHORST 189
(OTHERS)
A ASTHORE
EARSHOT
HAROSET
B BOSHTER
BOTHERS
C HECTORS
ROCHETS
ROTCHES
TOCHERS
TORCHES
TROCHES
D DEHORTS
SHORTED
E HETEROS
F FOTHERS
I HERIOTS
HOISTER
SHORTIE
TOSHIER
L HOLSTER
HOSTLER
M MOTHERS
SMOTHER
N HORNETS
SHORTEN
THRENOS
THRONES
O HOOTERS
SHOOTER
SOOTHER
P POTHERS
STROPHE
THORPES
R RHETORS
ROTHERS
SHORTER
S TOSHERS
T HOTTERS
U SHOUTER
SOUTHER
W THROWES
X EXHORTS

EIILST 139
(TILIES)
A LAITIES
C ELICITS
I ILEITIS
K KILTIES
L ILLITES
M ELITISM
LIMIEST
LIMITES
N LINIEST
LINTIES
O IOLITES
OILIEST
P SPILITE
R RILIEST
SILTIER
T ELITIST
U UTILISE
W WILIEST

EIINRT 30
(INTIRE)
A INERTIA
C CITRINE
CRINITE
INCITER
NERITIC
D INDITER
NITRIDE
E ERINITE
NITERIE
F NIFTIER
G IGNITER
TIERING
TIGRINE
H INHERIT
L LINTIER
NITRILE
M INTERIM
MINTIER
TERMINI
N TINNIER
T NITRITE
NITTIER
TINTIER
V INVITER
VITRINE
W TWINIER

EILNOS 47
(OLINES)
C CINEOLS
CONSEIL
INCLOSE
D DOLINES
INDOLES
SONDELI
F OLEFINS
G ELOIGNS
LEGIONS
LIGNOSE
LINGOES
I ELISION
ISOLINE
LIONISE
L LIONELS
NIELLOS
M MOLINES
O LOONIES
P EPSILON
PINOLES
R NEROLIS
S ESLOINS
INSOLES
LESIONS
LIONESS
T ENTOILS
LIONETS
ONLIEST
U ELUSION

EILNRS 77
(LINERS)
A NAILERS
B BERLINS
E LIERNES
RELINES
G GIRNELS
LINGERS
SLINGER
I INLIERS
K LINKERS
SLINKER
M LIMNERS
MERLINS
O NEROLIS
P PILSNER
T LINTERS
SLINTER
SNIRTLE
V SILVERN

EILNST 45
(INTLES)
A EASTLIN
ELASTIN
ENTAILS
SALIENT
SLAINTE
STANIEL
TENAILS
C CLIENTS
LECTINS
STENCIL
D DENTILS
E SETLINE
TENSILE
G GLISTEN
LESTING
SINGLET
TINGLES
I LINIEST
LINTIES
K LENTISK
TINKLES
L LENTILS
LINTELS
TELLINS
N LINNETS
O ENTOILS
LIONETS
ONLIEST
P PINTLES
PLENIST
R LINTERS
SLINTER
SNIRTLE
S ENLISTS
LISTENS
SILENTS
TINSELS
U LUTEINS
UNTILES
UTENSIL
V VENTILS
W WESTLIN
WINTLES

EILORS 37
(OILERS)
B BOILERS
LIBEROS
REBOILS
C RECOILS
D SOLDIER
SOLIDER
G GLOIRES
GLORIES
I SOILIER
M MOILERS
N NEROLIS
O ORIOLES
P SLOPIER
SPOILER
R LORRIES
S LORISES
LOSSIER
RISSOLE
T LOITERS
TOILERS
U LOUSIER
SOILURE
V OLIVERS
VIOLERS

EILORT 10
(LOITER)
B TRILOBE
C CORTILE
D DOILTER
E TROELIE
F LOFTIER
TREFOIL
J JOLTIER
M MOTLIER
N RETINOL
O TROOLIE
P POITREL
POLITER
S LOITERS
TOILERS
T TORTILE
TRIOLET
U OUTLIER

EILOST 21
(OILETS)
A ISOLATE
B BETOILS
C CITOLES
E ESTOILE
ETOILES
G ELOGIST
LOGIEST
H EOLITHS
HOLIEST
HOSTILE
I IOLITES
OILIEST
L OILLETS
M MOTILES
N ENTOILS
LIONETS
ONLIEST
O OOLITES
OSTIOLE
STOOLIE
P PIOLETS
PISTOLE
R LOITERS
TOILERS
T LITOTES
TOILETS
U OUTLIES
V OLIVETS
VIOLETS
W OWLIEST

EILRST 44
(LITERS)
A REALIST
RETAILS
SALTIER
SALTIRE
SLATIER
B BLISTER
BRISTLE
RIBLETS
C RELICTS
E LEISTER
RETILES
STERILE
F FILTERS
LIFTERS
STIFLER
TRIFLES
G GLISTER
GRISTLE
H SLITHER
I RILIEST
SILTIER
K KILTERS
KIRTLES
L RILLETS
STILLER
TILLERS
TRELLIS
M MILTERS
N LINTERS
SLINTER
SNIRTLE
O LOITERS
TOILERS
P SPIRTLE
TRIPLES
S LISTERS
T LITTERS
SLITTER
STILTER
TESTRIL
TILTERS
TITLERS
U LUSTIER
RULIEST
RUTILES

EILSTU 136
(UTILES)
A SITULAE
B BLUIEST
SUBTILE
D DILUTES
F FLUIEST
SULFITE
G GLUIEST
UGLIEST
I UTILISE
L TUILLES
N LUTEINS
UNTILES
UTENSIL
O OUTLIES
P PULIEST
PUTELIS
STIPULE
R LUSTIER
RULIEST
RUTILES
T TITULES

EIMNOS 131
(MONIES)
A ANOMIES
C INCOMES
MESONIC
D MISDONE
E SEMEION
G MISGONE
L MOLINES
O MOONIES
NOISOME
P IMPONES
PEONISM
R MERINOS
MERSION
S EONISMS
T MOISTEN
W WINSOME

EIMNRS 177
(MINERS)
A MARINES
REMAINS
SEMINAR
SIRNAME
C CREMSIN
MINCERS
D MINDERS
REMINDS
E ERMINES
G GERMINS
H MENHIRS
K MERKINS
L LIMNERS
MERLINS
M NIMMERS
O MERINOS
MERSION
T ENTRISM
MINSTER
MINTERS
REMINTS
U MURINES
NEURISM
V VERMINS

EIMNST 201
(MINEST)
A INMATES
MAINEST
MANTIES
TAMINES
D MINDSET
E EMETINS
G STEMING
TEMSING
I MINIEST
K MISKENT
O MOISTEN
P PIMENTS
R ENTRISM
MINSTER
MINTERS
REMINTS
S MISSENT
T MITTENS

SMITTEN
U MINUETS
MINUTES
MISTUNE
MUNITES
MUTINES
W MISWENT

EIMOST 150
(SOMITE)
A AMOSITE
ATOMIES
ATOMISE
OSMIATE
D DOMIEST
MODISTE
MOISTED
F FOMITES
G EGOTISM
H HOMIEST
L MOTILES
M TOMMIES
N MOISTEN
P MOPIEST
OPTIMES
R EROTISM
MOISTER
MORTISE
TRISOME
S MITOSES
SOMITES
T MOTIEST
TITMOSE
U TIMEOUS
V MOTIVES
Z MESTIZO

EIMRST 140
(MITERS)
A IMARETS
MAESTRI
MAISTER
MASTIER
MISRATE
SEMITAR
SMARTIE
B BETRIMS
TIMBERS
TIMBRES
C CRETISM
METRICS
E METIERS
RETIMES
TREMIES
TRISEME
F FIRMEST
FREMITS
H HERMITS
MITHERS
I MIRIEST
MISTIER
RIMIEST
K MIRKEST
L MILTERS
M MISTERM
N ENTRISM
MINSTER
MINTERS
REMINTS
O EROTISM
MOISTER
MORTISE
TRISOME
P IMPREST
PERMITS
R RETRIMS
TRIMERS
S MISTERS
SMITERS
T METRIST
U MUSTIER
Y MISTERY
SMYTRIE

EINNST 113
(SINNET)
A INANEST
D DENTINS
INDENTS
INTENDS
E INTENSE
TENNIES
G NESTING
SENTING
TENSING
I INTINES
TINNIES
L LINNETS
O INTONES
TENSION
P PINNETS
SPINNET
TENPINS
R INTERNS
TINNERS
S SENNITS
SINNETS
T INTENTS
U TUNNIES
V INVENTS

EINOPS 130
(PONIES)
D DISPONE
SPINODE
E PEONIES
G EPIGONS
PIGEONS
PINGOES
H PHONIES
I PIONIES
K PINKOES
L EPSILON
PINOLES
M IMPONES
PEONISM
N PENSION
P PEPINOS
R ORPINES
PIONERS
PROINES
S SPINOSE
T POINTES
PONTIES
W POWNIES
Y PIONEYS

EINORS 7
(SENIOR)
A ERASION
C COINERS
CRINOSE
CRONIES
ORCEINS
ORCINES
RECOINS
SERICON
D DONSIER
INDORSE
ROSINED
G ERINGOS
IGNORES
REGIONS
SIGNORE
H HEROINS
INSHORE
I IONISER
IRONIES
IRONISE
NOISIER
J JOINERS
REJOINS
L NEROLIS
M MERINOS
MERSION
O EROSION
P ORPINES
PIONERS
PROINES
R IRONERS
S ORNISES
SENIORS
SONERIS
SONSIER
T NORITES
ORIENTS
STONIER
TERSION
TRIONES
U URINOSE
V RENVOIS
VERSION
W SNOWIER

EINOSS 204
(SONSIE)
A ANOESIS
B BESOINS
C CESSION
COSINES
D ONSIDES
I IONISES
K KENOSIS
L ESLOINS
INSOLES
LESIONS
LIONESS
M EONISMS
N SONNIES
P SPINOSE
R ORNISES
SENIORS
SONERIS
SONSIER
S ESSOINS
OSSEINS
SESSION
T NOSIEST
SONTIES
STONIES
U SINUOSE

EINOST 14
(TONIES)
A ATONIES
B BONIEST
EBONIST
C NOTICES
SECTION
D DITONES
STONIED
H HISTONE
J JONTIES
L ENTOILS
LIONETS
ONLIEST
M MOISTEN
N INTONES
TENSION
O ISOTONE
P POINTES
PONTIES
R NORITES
ORIENTS
STONIER
TERSION
TRIONES
S NOSIEST
SONTIES
STONIES
T SNOTTIE
TONIEST
TONITES
W TOWNIES

EINPRS 158
(PINERS)
A RAPINES
C PINCERS
PRINCES
D PINDERS
E EREPSIN
REPINES
G PERSING
PINGERS
SPRINGE
I INSPIRE
PIRNIES
SNIPIER
SPINIER
K PERKINS
L PILSNER
N PINNERS
SPINNER
O ORPINES
PIONERS
PROINES
P NIPPERS
SNIPPER
S SNIPERS
T NIPTERS
PTERINS
U PRUINES
PURINES
UPRISEN

EINPST 148
(INSTEP)
A PANTIES
PATINES
SAPIENT
SPINATE
C INCEPTS
INSPECT
PECTINS
PEINCTS
D STIPEND
E PENTISE
I PINIEST
PINITES
TIEPINS
K PINKEST
L PINTLES
PLENIST
M PIMENTS
N PINNETS
SPINNET
TENPINS
O POINTES
PONTIES
P SNIPPET
R NIPTERS
PTERINS
S INSTEPS
SPINETS
T SPITTEN
U PUNIEST
PUNTIES

EINRSS 249
(RESINS)
A ARSINES
SARNIES
C SCRINES
E SEINERS
SEREINS
SERINES
G INGRESS
RESIGNS
SIGNERS
SINGERS
H SHINERS
SHRINES
K SINKERS
N SINNERS
O ORNISES
SENIORS
SONERIS
SONSIER
P SNIPERS
R RINSERS
T INSERTS
SINTERS
U INSURES
SUNRISE
V VERSINS

EINRST 17
(INTERS)
A ANESTRI
NASTIER
RATINES
RESIANT
RETAINS
RETINAS
RETSINA
STAINER
STARNIE
STEARIN
C CISTERN
CRETINS
D TINDERS
E ENTIRES
ENTRIES
NERITES
TRENISE
F SNIFTER
G RESTING
STINGER
K SKINTER
STINKER
TINKERS
L LINTERS
SLINTER
SNIRTLE
M ENTRISM
MINSTER
MINTERS
REMINTS
N INTERNS
TINNERS
O NORITES
ORIENTS
STONIER
TERSION
TRIONES
P NIPTERS
PTERINS
S INSERTS
SINTERS
T ENTRIST
STINTER
TINTERS
U TRIUNES
UNITERS
V INVERTS
STRIVEN
W TWINERS
WINTERS
Y SINTERY

EINRSV 226
(VINERS)
A AVENIRS
RAVINES
C CRIVENS
D VERDINS
E ENVIERS
INVERSE
VENIRES
VERSINE
G SERVING
VERSING
H SHRIVEN
L SILVERN
M VERMINS
O RENVOIS
VERSION
S VERSINS
T INVERTS
STRIVEN
W WIVERNS

EINRTT 76
(TINTER)
A INTREAT
ITERANT
NATTIER
NITRATE
TARTINE

TERTIAN
B BITTERN
C CITTERN
D TRIDENT
E NETTIER
TENTIER
G GITTERN
RETTING
I NITRITE
NITTIER
TINTIER
K KNITTER
TRINKET
O TRITONE
S ENTRIST
STINTER
TINTERS
U NUTTIER
W TWINTER
WRITTEN

EINRTU 25
(TUNIER)
A RUINATE
TAURINE
URANITE
URINATE
B BUNTIER
TRIBUNE
TURBINE
D INTRUDE
TURDINE
UNTIRED
UNTRIDE
UNTRIED
E NEURITE
RETINUE
REUNITE
UTERINE
G TRUEING
M MINUTER
O ROUTINE
P REPUNIT
R RUNTIER
S TRIUNES
UNITERS
T NUTTIER
V UNRIVET
VENTURI
W UNWRITE

EINSST 218
(INSETS)
A ENTASIS
NASTIES
SESTINA
TANSIES
TISANES
C INCESTS
INSECTS
D DISNEST
DISSENT
SNIDEST
E SEITENS
SESTINE
F FITNESS
INFESTS
G INGESTS
SIGNETS
H SITHENS
L ENLISTS
LISTENS
SILENTS
TINSELS
M MISSENT
N SENNITS
SINNETS
O NOSIEST
SONTIES
STONIES
P INSTEPS
SPINETS
R INSERTS
SINTERS
S SENSIST
U INTUSES
V INVESTS
W WISENTS
WITNESS
Y TINSEYS

EINSTT 160
(INTEST)
A INSTATE
SATINET
D DENTIST
DISTENT
STINTED
G SETTING
TESTING
I SITTINE
TINIEST
K KITTENS
M MITTENS
SMITTEN
N INTENTS
O SNOTTIE
TONIEST
TONITES
P SPITTEN
R ENTRIST
STINTER
TINTERS
U TUNIEST
W ENTWIST
TWINSET
Y TENSITY

EINSTU 81
(UNITES)
A AUNTIES
SINUATE
D DISTUNE
DUNITES
G GUNITES
I UNITIES
UNITISE
L LUTEINS
UNTILES
UTENSIL
M MINUETS
MINUTES
MISTUNE
MUNITES
MUTINES
N TUNNIES
P PUNIEST
PUNTIES
Q INQUEST
QUINTES
R TRIUNES
UNITERS
S INTUSES
T TUNIEST

EIOPST 101
(SOPITE)
A ATOPIES
OPIATES
C POETICS
D DEPOSIT
DOPIEST
PODITES
POSITED
SOPITED
TOPSIDE
E POETISE
H ETHIOPS
OPHITES
K POKIEST
L PIOLETS
PISTOLE
M MOPIEST
OPTIMES
N POINTES
PONTIES
O ISOTOPE
R PERIOST
PORIEST
REPOSIT
RIPOSTE
ROPIEST
S POSIEST
POSTIES
SEPIOST
SOPITES
T POTTIES
TIPTOES
U PITEOUS
X POXIEST
Y ISOTYPE

EIORSS 214
(SORIES)
B BOSSIER
RIBOSES
C COSIERS
D DORISES
DOSSIER
E SOIREES
F FROISES
H HOSIERS
L LORISES
LOSSIER
RISSOLE
M ISOMERS
MOISERS
MOSSIER
N ORNISES
SENIORS
SONERIS
SONSIER
P POISERS
R ORRISES
ROSIERS
T ROSIEST
SORITES
SORTIES
STORIES
TOSSIER
U SERIOUS
V VIROSES
X XEROSIS

EIORST 5
(TORIES)
A OARIEST
OTARIES
B ORBIEST
SORBITE
C EROTICS
TERCIOS
D EDITORS
ROISTED
ROSITED
SORTIED
STEROID
STORIED
TIERODS
TRIODES
F FOISTER
FORTIES
G GOITERS
GOITRES
GORIEST
H HERIOTS
HOISTER
SHORTIE
TOSHIER
I RIOTISE
K ROKIEST
L LOITERS
TOILERS
M EROTISM
MOISTER
MORTISE
TRISOME
N NORITES
ORIENTS
STONIER
TERSION
TRIONES
O OORIEST
ROOTIES
SOOTIER
TOORIES
P PERIOST
PORIEST
REPOSIT
RIPOSTE
ROPIEST
R RIOTERS
ROISTER
RORIEST
S ROSIEST
SORITES
SORTIES
STORIES
TOSSIER
T STOITER
U OURIEST
TOURIES
TOUSIER
V TORSIVE
W OWRIEST
TOWSIER

EIORSV 127
(VIROSE)
A OVARIES
C CORSIVE
VOICERS
D DEVISOR
DEVOIRS
VISORED
VOIDERS
E EROSIVE
I IVORIES
L OLIVERS
VIOLERS
M VERISMO
N RENVOIS
VERSION
R REVISOR
S VIROSES
T TORSIVE

EIOSTT 93
(OTTIES)
A OSTIATE
TOASTIE
B BOTTIES
C COTTISE
D DOTIEST
STOITED
E TOEIEST
G EGOTIST
H HOTTIES
L LITOTES
TOILETS
M MOTIEST
TITMOSE
N SNOTTIE
TONIEST
TONITES
O TOOTSIE
P POTTIES
TIPTOES
R STOITER
T TOTTIES
U TOUSTIE
W TOWIEST

EIPRST 147
(STRIPE)
A PARTIES
PASTIER
PIASTRE
PIRATES
PRATIES
TRAIPSE
C TRICEPS
D SPIRTED
STRIPED
E RESPITE
H HIPSTER
I PITIERS
TIPSIER
L SPIRTLE
TRIPLES
M IMPREST
PERMITS
N NIPTERS
PTERINS
O PERIOST
PORIEST
REPOSIT
RIPOSTE
ROPIEST
P TIPPERS
S ESPRITS
PERSIST
PRIESTS
SITREPS
SPRITES
STIRPES
STRIPES
TRIPSES
T PITTERS
SPITTER
TIPSTER
U PERITUS
PUIREST
V PRIVETS
X EXTIRPS
Y PYRITES
STRIPEY

EIRRST 165
(TRIERS)
A ARTSIER
SERRATI
TARRIES
TARSIER
D STIRRED
E ETRIERS
REITERS
RESTIER
RETIRES
RETRIES
TERRIES
K SKIRRET
SKIRTER
STRIKER
M RETRIMS
TRIMERS
O RIOTERS
ROISTER
RORIEST
R STIRRER
S STIRRES
T RITTERS
TERRITS
U RUSTIER
V STRIVER
W WRITERS

EIRSTT 104
(SITTER)
A ARTIEST
ARTISTE
ATTIRES
IRATEST
STRIATE
TASTIER
TERTIAS
B BITTERS
C TRISECT
E TESTIER
F FITTERS
TITFERS
H HITTERS
TITHERS
J JITTERS
K SKITTER
L LITTERS
SLITTER
STILTER
TESTRIL
TILTERS

TITLERS
M METRIST
N ENTRIST
STINTER
TINTERS
O STOITER
P PITTERS
SPITTER
TIPSTER
R RITTERS
TERRITS
S SITTERS
T STRETTI
TITTERS
TRITEST
U TERTIUS
V TRIVETS
W TWISTER
WITTERS

EIRSTV 163
(STRIVE)
A TAIVERS
VASTIER
D DIVERTS
STRIVED
VERDITS
E RESTIVE
SIEVERT
STIEVER
VERIEST
G GRIVETS
H THRIVES
I REVISIT
STIVIER
VISITER
N INVERTS
STRIVEN
O TORSIVE
P PRIVETS
R STRIVER
S STIVERS
STRIVES
TREVISS
VERISTS
T TRIVETS
U VIRTUES

ELNSTU 216
(LUNETS)
A ELUANTS
UNLASTE
B SUNBELT
UNBELTS
UNBLEST
E ELUENTS
UNSTEEL
F FLUENTS
NESTFUL
NETFULS
G ENGLUTS
GLUTENS
I LUTEINS
UNTILES
UTENSIL
N TUNNELS
O LENTOUS
P PENULTS
R RUNLETS
T NUTLETS

ELORST 67
(TOLERS)
A OESTRAL
B BOLSTER
BOLTERS
LOBSTER
C COLTERS
CORSLET
COSTREL
LECTORS
D DROLEST
OLDSTER
STRODLE
F FLORETS
LOFTERS
H HOLSTER
HOSTLER
I LOITERS
TOILERS
J JOLTERS
L TOLLERS
N LENTORS
O LOOTERS
RETOOLS
ROOTLES
TOOLERS
P PETROLS
S OSTLERS
STEROLS
TORSELS
T SETTLOR
SLOTTER
TOLTERS
U ELUTORS
OUTLERS
TROULES
V REVOLTS
W TROWELS
WORTLES

ELOSTU 173
(TOUSLE)
B BOLETUS
D LOUDEST
OULDEST
TOUSLED
F FOULEST
I OUTLIES
L OUTSELL
N LENTOUS
O OUTSOLE
P TUPELOS
R ELUTORS
OUTLERS
TROULES
S LOTUSES
SOLUTES
TOUSLES
T OUTLETS
U LUTEOUS
V VOLUTES
Z TOUZLES

ELRSTU 208
(RUSTLE)
A SALUTER
B BLUSTER
BUSTLER
BUTLERS
SUBTLER
C CLUSTER
CULTERS
CUSTREL
CUTLERS
RELUCTS
D LUSTRED
RUSTLED
STRUDEL
F FLUSTER
FLUTERS
RESTFUL
G GURLETS
H HURTLES
HUSTLER
I LUSTIER
RULIEST
RUTILES
N RUNLETS
O ELUTORS
OUTLERS
TROULES
P SPURTLE
R RUSTLER
S LUSTERS
LUSTRES
RESULTS
RUSTLES
SUTLERS
ULSTERS
T TURTLES
Y SUTLERY

EMNORS 230
(SERMON)
A ENAMORS
MOANERS
OARSMEN
D MODERNS
RODSMEN
E MOREENS
F ENFORMS
G MONGERS
MORGENS
I MERINOS
MERSION
L MERLONS
O MOONERS
S SERMONS
T MENTORS
MONSTER
MONTRES

EMNOST 186
(MONETS)
A MANTOES
B ENTOMBS
D ENDMOST
E TEMENOS
TONEMES
F FOMENTS
G EMONGST
H MONETHS
I MOISTEN
L LOMENTS
MELTONS
M MOMENTS
MONTEMS
O MOONSET
P POSTMEN
TOPSMEN
R MENTORS
MONSTER
MONTRES
S STEMSON
U UNSMOTE
Y ETYMONS

EMORST 198
(MOTERS)
A AMORETS
MAESTRO
OMERTAS
B BESTORM
MOBSTER
D STORMED
E METEORS
REMOTES
G GROMETS
H MOTHERS
SMOTHER
I EROTISM
MOISTER
MORTISE
TRISOME
N MENTORS
MONSTER
MONTRES
O MOOTERS
P STOMPER
TROMPES
R TERMORS
TREMORS
S MOTSERS
U MOUTERS
OESTRUM

ENOPRS 203
(PERSON)
A PERSONA
C CREPONS
D PONDERS
RESPOND
E OPENERS
PERONES
REOPENS
REPONES
G SPONGER
H PHONERS
I ORPINES
PIONERS
PROINES
O OPERONS
SNOOPER
R PERRONS
S PERSONS
T POSTERN
PRONEST
U UNROPES
Y PROYNES
PYONERS

ENORST 23
(TONERS)
A ATONERS
SENATOR
TREASON
B BRETONS
SORBENT
C CONSTER
CORNETS
CRESTON
CRONETS
D RODENTS
SNORTED
H HORNETS
SHORTEN
THRENOS
THRONES
I NORITES
ORIENTS
STONIER
TERSION
TRIONES
K STONKER
STROKEN
TONKERS
L LENTORS
M MENTORS
MONSTER
MONTRES
N STONERN
O ENROOTS
P POSTERN
PRONEST
R SNORTER
S STONERS
TENSORS
T ROTTENS
SNOTTER
STENTOR
U TENOURS
TONSURE
Y TYRONES

ENOSTT 195
(ONTEST)
A ATTONES
NOTATES
C CONTEST
D SNOTTED
H SHOTTEN
I SNOTTIE
TONIEST
TONITES
J JETTONS
L TONLETS
O TESTOON
P POTENTS
R ROTTENS
SNOTTER
STENTOR
S OSTENTS
TESTONS
U STOUTEN
TENUTOS

ENOSTU 94
(OUTENS)
A SOUTANE
C CONTUSE
ECONUTS
D DEUTONS
SNOUTED
G TONGUES
L LENTOUS
M UNSMOTE
N NEUSTON
O UNSOOTE
R TENOURS
TONSURE
S OUTNESS
TONUSES
T STOUTEN
TENUTOS
U TENUOUS

ENRSTU 84
(TUNERS)
A AUNTERS
NATURES
SAUNTER
B BRUNETS
BUNTERS
BURNETS
BURSTEN
C ENCRUST
D RETUNDS
E NEUTERS
RETUNES
TENURES
TUREENS
F FUNSTER
G GUNTERS
GURNETS
SURGENT
H HUNTERS
SHUNTER
UNHERST
I TRIUNES
UNITERS
L RUNLETS
M MUNSTER
STERNUM
N RUNNETS
STUNNER
O TENOURS
TONSURE
P PUNSTER
PUNTERS
R RETURNS
TURNERS
S UNRESTS
T ENTRUST
NUTTERS

EOPRST 193
(POSTER)
A ESPARTO
PROTEAS
SEAPORT
B BESPORT
C COPTERS
D DEPORTS
REDTOPS
SPORTED
F FORPETS
H POTHERS
STROPHE
THORPES
I PERIOST
PORIEST
REPOSIT
RIPOSTE
ROPIEST
L PETROLS
M STOMPER
TROMPES
N POSTERN
PRONEST
O POOREST

POOTERS
STOOPER
P STOPPER
TOPPERS
R PORTERS
PRETORS
REPORTS
SPORTER
S PORTESS
POSTERS
PRESTOS
REPOSTS
T POTTERS
PROTEST
SPOTTER
U PETROUS
POSTURE
POUTERS
PROTEUS
SEPTUOR
SPOUTER
TROUPES
W POWTERS
X EXPORTS

EORRST 106
(SORTER)
A ROASTER
C RECTORS
D DORTERS
RODSTER
E RESTORE
G GROSERT
H RHETORS
ROTHERS
SHORTER
I RIOTERS
ROISTER
RORIEST
K STROKER
M TERMORS
TREMORS
N SNORTER
O ROOSTER
ROOTERS
TOREROS
P PORTERS
PRETORS
REPORTS
SPORTER
R RORTERS
TERRORS
S RESORTS
ROSTERS
SORTERS
STORERS
T RETORTS
ROTTERS
TORRETS
U RETOURS
ROUSTER
ROUTERS
TOURERS
TROUSER
V TROVERS
W STROWER
Y ROYSTER

EORSTT 114
(OTTERS)
A ROTATES
TOASTER
B BETTORS
C COTTERS
D DETORTS
E ROSETTE
H HOTTERS
I STOITER
J JOTTERS
L SETTLOR
SLOTTER
TOLTERS
N ROTTENS
SNOTTER
STENTOR
O TOOTERS
P POTTERS
PROTEST
SPOTTER
R RETORTS
ROTTERS
TORRETS
T STOTTER
STRETTO
TOTTERS
U STOUTER
TOUTERS
W SWOTTER
X EXTORTS
Y ROSETTY

GIINRT 233
(TIRING)
A AIRTING
RAITING
B RINGBIT
C TRICING
D DIRTING
E IGNITER
TIERING
TIGRINE
F RIFTING
G GIRTING
RINGGIT
K TRIKING
L TIRLING
M MITRING
N TRINING
O RIOTING
R TIRRING
S STIRING
TIRINGS
T RITTING
W TWIRING
WRITING

GILNOT 171
(TOLING)
A ANTILOG
B BILTONG
BOLTING
C COLTING
E LENTIGO
F LOFTING
H THOLING
I TOILING
J JOLTING
L TOLLING
M MOLTING
O LOOTING
TOOLING
P POLTING
S LINGOTS
TIGLONS
TOLINGS
T LOTTING
U LOUTING
W LOWTING

GINORS 128
(SIGNOR)
A IGNAROS
ORIGANS
SIGNORA
SOARING
B BORINGS
ROBINGS
SORBING
C SCORING
D RODINGS
E ERINGOS
IGNORES
REGIONS
SIGNORE
G GORINGS
GRINGOS
H HORSING
SHORING
I ORIGINS
SIGNIOR
SIGNORI
L LORINGS
M SMORING
N SNORING
SORNING
O ROOSING
P PROIGNS
PROSING
ROPINGS
S GRISONS
INGROSS
SIGNORS
T ROSTING
SORTING
STORING
TRIGONS
U ROUSING
SOURING
V ROVINGS
W ROWINGS
WORSING
Y ROSYING
SIGNORY

GINORT 102
(ROTING)
A ORATING
ROATING
D DORTING
E GENITOR
F FORTING
I RIOTING
K TROKING
O ROOTING
P PORTING
TROPING
R RORTING
S ROSTING
SORTING
STORING
TRIGONS
T ROTTING
U ROUTING
TOURING
W ROWTING
TROWING

GINOST 176
(OSTING)
A AGONIST
GITANOS
C COSTING
GNOSTIC
D DOTINGS
F SOFTING
H HOSTING
TOSHING
K STOKING
L LINGOTS
TIGLONS
TOLINGS
M GNOMIST
N STONING
TONINGS
O SOOTING
P POSTING
STOPING
R ROSTING
SORTING
STORING
TRIGONS
S STINGOS
TOSSING
T SOTTING
U OUSTING
OUTINGS
TOUSING
V STOVING
W STOWING
TOWINGS
TOWSING
Y TOYINGS

INORST 59
(TRIONS)
A AROINTS
RATIONS
B RIBSTON
C CISTRON
CITRONS
CORNIST
E NORITES
ORIENTS
STONIER
TERSION
TRIONES
F FORINTS
G ROSTING
SORTING
STORING
TRIGONS
H HORNIST
I IRONIST
L NOSTRIL
N INTRONS
O ISOTRON
NITROSO
TORSION
T TRITONS
U NITROUS
TURIONS

7-LETTER SETS LIST

alphabetical list of all words appearing in 7-Letter Sets

ABELIAS
ABREAST
ABRIDGE
ABSEILS
ACARINE
ACATERS
ACCENTS
ACEROSE
ACEROUS
ACETALS
ACETOSE
ACETOUS
ACETYLS
ACIDEST
ACINOSE
ACMITES
ACTINGS
ACTRESS
ACTURES
ADAPTER
ADDREST
ADEPTER
ADERMIN
ADHERES
ADMIRES
ADONISE
ADOPTER
ADORERS
ADORING
ADRENAL
ADVENTS
ADVERSE
ADVERTS
ADVISER
AEDILES
AERATES
AERIALS
AERIEST
AEROBES
AEROBUS
AEROSOL
AETHERS
AFREETS
AGAINST
AGELAST
AGILEST
AGINNER
AGISTED
AGISTER
AGNAILS
AGNATES
AGNISED
AGONIES
AGONISE
AGONIST
AGRASTE
AGRISED
AIDLESS
AIGLETS
AILMENT
AIMLESS
AIRIEST
AIRINGS
AIRLESS
AIRSIDE
AIRTING
AISLING
ALBERTS
ALBITES
ALDRINS
ALECOST
ALEGARS
ALENGTH
ALERCES
ALEYING
ALGATES
ALGESIS
ALIASES
ALIGNED
ALIMENT
ALIPEDS
ALLISES
ALNAGER
ALNAGES
ALSIKES
ALTERNE
ALUNITE
AMBIENT
AMBRIES
AMEARST
AMENDES
AMENITY
AMENTAL
AMENTIA
AMERCES
AMITIES
AMNESIA
AMNESIC
AMNESTY
AMORCES
AMORETS
AMOSITE
AMPERES
ANADEMS
ANAPEST
ANCRESS
ANELING
ANEMIAS
ANEROID
ANESTRA
ANESTRI
ANGELIC
ANGELUS
ANGERED
ANGERLY
ANGLERS
ANGLICE
ANGLIST
ANGRIER
ANGRIES
ANGRILY
ANIMATE
ANISEED
ANKLETS
ANLAGES
ANNATES
ANODISE
ANOESIS
ANOMIES
ANSATED
ANSWERS
ANTHEMS
ANTHERS
ANTIARS
ANTILOG
ANTINGS
ANTLERS
ANTLIAE
ANYTIME
APERIES
APLITES
APOSTLE
APPRISE
APTERAL
APTNESS
ARAISED
ARANEID
ARBORES
ARBUTES
ARCADES
ARCHEST
ARCHLET
ARCINGS
ARCTICS
AREDING
AREFIES
AREOLES
ARGENTS
ARGYLES
ARIDEST
ARIETTA
ARIETTE
ARISING
ARISTAE
ARKITES
ARMLETS
AROINTS
AROUSED
AROYNTS
ARPENTS
ARRASED
ARRESTS
ARRIDES
ARSENAL
ARSENIC
ARSHINE
ARSINES
ARTICLE
ARTIEST
ARTISAN
ARTISTE
ARTLESS
ARTSIER
ARTSIES
ARTSMEN
ASCENTS
ASKLENT
ASPIRED
ASPIRES
ASSERTS
ASTEISM
ASTELIC
ASTERIA
ASTERID
ASTERTS
ASTHORE
ASTILBE
ASTONED
ASTRICT
ASTRIDE
ASTUTER
ASUNDER
ATEBRIN
ATELIER
ATHEISM
ATHEIST
ATIMIES
ATINGLE
ATOMIES
ATOMISE
ATONERS
ATONIES
ATOPIES
ATRESIA
ATTAINS
ATTENDS
ATTENTS
ATTIRED
ATTIRES
ATTONES
ATTORNS
ATTRITE
ATTUNES
AUDILES
AULDEST
AUNTERS
AUNTIES
AURICLE
AUSTERE
AVENIRS
AVIDEST
AVOCETS
AWAREST
AWMRIES
AWNIEST
BADGERS
BAILEES
BAILERS
BAILEYS
BAILIES
BAITERS
BALDEST
BALDIES
BANDIER
BANDIES
BANGERS
BANGLED
BANGLES
BANTERS
BARBETS
BARDIER
BARDING
BARGEST
BARITES
BARRETS
BARTERS
BARTONS
BARYTES
BASINET
BASTERS
BASTIDE
BASTING
BATHERS
BATISTE
BATLERS
BATSMEN
BATTENS
BATTERS
BATTIER
BATTLER
BAWDIER
BAXTERS
BEADIER
BEAMERS
BEARDIE
BEARERS
BEARING
BEATERS
BEDRALS
BEGIRDS
BELIERS
BELTERS
BELTING
BELTMAN
BEMIRES
BENDERS
BENDIER
BENIGHT
BENTIER
BERATES
BERLINS
BERRETS
BERRIES
BERTHAS
BESAINT
BESMEAR
BESOINS
BESORTS
BESPORT
BESTAIN
BESTARS
BESTEAD
BESTIAL
BESTING
BESTIRS
BESTORM
BESTRID
BETOILS
BETRAYS
BETRIMS
BETTERS
BETTORS
BEWAILS
BEZOARS
BIDDERS
BIDENTS
BILKERS
BILTONG
BINDERS
BINGERS
BINGLED
BINGLES
BIOGENS
BIRDERS
BIRDIES
BIREMES
BIRETTA
BIRLERS
BIRSLED
BIRSLES
BISTERS
BISTRED
BISTRES
BITSIER
BITTERN
BITTERS
BLANDER
BLARING
BLASTED
BLASTER
BLATHER
BLATTER
BLEATER
BLENDES
BLEWART
BLISTER
BLOATER
BLONDES
BLUIEST
BLUSTER
BOASTER
BOATELS
BOATERS
BOILERS
BOLDENS
BOLETUS
BOLSTER
BOLTERS
BOLTING
BONIEST
BOOSTER
BORAGES
BORANES
BORATES
BORAXES
BORDELS
BORIDES
BORINGS
BOSHTER
BOSSIER
BOTHERS
BOTTIES
BOUNDER
BRAIDED
BRAIDER
BRAILED
BRAINED
BRAISED
BRANGLE
BRANLES
BRANSLE
BRANTLE
BRASERO
BRASSET
BRATTLE
BRAVEST
BRAVOES
BRAWEST
BREARES
BREASTS
BREATHS
BREDING
BRETONS
BRIARED
BRIDGES
BRIDIES
BRIDLES
BRIGADE
BRIGAND
BRISKED
BRISKET
BRISTLE
BRUISED
BRUNETS
BUNTERS
BUNTIER
BURDENS
BURDIES
BURNETS
BURSTED
BURSTEN
BUSTIER
BUSTLER
BUTLERS
CABLETS
CABRITS
CADGERS
CAIRNED
CALENDS
CALIBER
CALIBRE
CALIPER
CALIVER
CALLETS
CALMEST
CALMIER
CALORIE
CAMLETS
CAMOTES
CANCERS
CANDIES
CANDLES
CANGLED
CANGLES
CANIEST
CANINES
CANKERS
CANNERS
CANNIER
CANTERS
CANTEST
CANTIER
CANTLES
CANTORS
CANTRED
CANTREF
CAPLETS
CAPOTES
CAPRINE
CARBIDE
CARBINE
CARDERS
CARDIES
CARDING
CAREENS
CAREERS
CAREMES
CARGOES
CARINAE
CARIOLE
CARITAS
CARLINE
CARLING
CARMINE
CARNETS
CARNEYS
CARNIED
CARNIER
CARNIES
CARNOSE
CAROUSE
CARPELS
CARPETS
CARTELS
CARTERS
CARTING
CARTONS
CASEINS
CASERNE
CASERNS
CASTERS
CASTING
CASTLED
CASTLES
CATENAS
CATERAN
CATLING
CATNEPS
CATTIER
CATTIES
CAUTELS
CAUTERS
CAVERNS
CEASING
CEDRINE
CELESTA
CENOTES
CENSORS
CENTALS
CENTARE
CENTAUR
CENTERS
CENTRAL
CENTRES
CERASIN
CERATES
CEREALS
CERESIN
CERITES
CERNING
CEROONS
CERRIAL
CERTAIN
CESSION
CESTOID
CETANES
CHAINES
CHALETS
CHANTER
CHARETS
CHARLIE
CHASTEN
CHASTER
CHENARS
CHOREAS
CICEROS
CINDERS
CINEAST
CINEMAS
CINEOLS
CINEREA
CIRROSE
CISTERN
CISTRON
CITHERS
CITOLES
CITRATE
CITRINE
CITRONS
CITTERN
CLAIMER
CLANGED
CLANGER
CLARETS
CLARIES
CLAROES
CLASPER
CLAVIER
CLAYIER
CLIENTS
CLINGER
CLUSTER
CNEMIAL
COALERS
COALIER
COARSEN
COARSER
COASTED
COASTER
COATEES
COATERS
COAXERS
COGNISE
COHEIRS
COIGNES
COINERS
COLTERS
COLTING
COMATES
CONCISE
CONDERS
CONDIES
CONFERS
CONFEST
CONGERS
CONGEST
CONINES
CONKERS
CONNERS
CONSEIL
CONSENT
CONSTER
CONTEST
CONTRAS
CONTUSE

CONURES
COPIERS
COPSIER
COPTERS
CORBIES
CORDING
CORNEAS
CORNELS
CORNERS
CORNETS
CORNIST
CORRIES
CORSAGE
CORSETS
CORSIVE
CORSLET
CORSNED
CORTILE
CORVEES
CORVETS
COSIERS
COSINES
COSTATE
COSTEAN
COSTERS
COSTING
COSTREL
COTISED
COTTERS
COTTISE
COUTERS
COVENTS
COVERTS
COWRIES
COZIERS
CRADLES
CRAPLES
CRASHED
CRATERS
CRATING
CRATONS
CRAVENS
CREASED
CREASER
CREATES
CREATIN
CREDITS
CREMSIN
CRENATE
CREPONS
CRESTED
CRESTON
CRETICS
CRETINS
CRETISM
CRINATE
CRINGED
CRINGES
CRINGLE
CRINITE
CRINOSE
CRISTAE
CRIVENS
CRONETS
CRONIES
CROSIER
CROUTES
CRUDEST
CRUISED
CRUSADE

CRUSTAE
CRUSTED
CUITERS
CULTERS
CURATES
CURIETS
CUSTREL
CUTLERS
CYANISE
CYSTINE
CZARIST
DABSTER
DACITES
DACKERS
DAEMONS
DAFTIES
DAGGERS
DAIDLES
DAIKERS
DAILIES
DAIRIES
DALLIER
DALLIES
DAMPENS
DANCERS
DANDERS
DANDIER
DANDIES
DANDLER
DANDLES
DANGERS
DANGLED
DANGLER
DANGLES
DANKEST
DANSEUR
DARBIES
DARCIES
DARGLES
DARINGS
DARIOLE
DARKENS
DARKEST
DARKIES
DARKLES
DARLING
DARNELS
DARNERS
DARNING
DARRING
DARTERS
DARTING
DARTLES
DARTRES
DATINGS
DATIVES
DAUBIER
DAUNDER
DAUNERS
DAUNTER
DAURING
DAUTIES
DAWNERS
DAWTIES
DAYSMEN
DEADERS
DEADEST
DEAFEST
DEALERS
DEALING

DEANERS
DEAREST
DEARIES
DEARING
DEARNLY
DEARTHS
DEASILS
DEASIUL
DEASOIL
DEBASER
DEBATES
DEBTORS
DECANTS
DECARBS
DECARES
DECERNS
DECRIAL
DECRIES
DEFASTE
DEFEATS
DEFIERS
DEFINER
DEFROST
DEGOUTS
DEHORTS
DEISEAL
DELATES
DELATOR
DELEING
DELIRIA
DELIVER
DELVING
DEMAINS
DEMANDS
DEMEANS
DEMENTS
DENARII
DENIALS
DENIERS
DENNETS
DENOTES
DENSELY
DENSEST
DENSITY
DENTALS
DENTELS
DENTILS
DENTINS
DENTIST
DEODARS
DEPARTS
DEPORTS
DEPOSIT
DERAIGN
DERAILS
DERANGE
DERATES
DERBIES
DERIDES
DERIVES
DERNIER
DERRIES
DESALTS
DESCANT
DESCENT
DESERTS
DESIGNS
DESIRED
DESIRER
DESIRES

DESMANS
DESMINE
DESPAIR
DESSERT
DESTINE
DESTINY
DESTROY
DETAILS
DETAINS
DETENTS
DETENUS
DETORTS
DETOURS
DETRAIN
DETUNES
DEUTONS
DEVISAL
DEVISER
DEVISOR
DEVLING
DEVOIRS
DEWANIS
DEXTERS
DIABLES
DIALLER
DIALYSE
DIAPERS
DIARIES
DIARISE
DIASTER
DIBBERS
DIEDRAL
DIEDRES
DIETERS
DIGGERS
DIGRESS
DILATER
DILATES
DILUTER
DILUTES
DINDLES
DINGERS
DINGEYS
DINGIER
DINGIES
DINGLES
DINGOES
DINKEST
DINNERS
DINNLES
DIOPTER
DIOPTRE
DIPTERA
DIRECTS
DIREMPT
DIRIGES
DIRTIES
DIRTING
DISABLE
DISCERN
DISCOER
DISCURE
DISEURS
DISLEAF
DISLEAL
DISNEST
DISPONE
DISRANK
DISRATE
DISROBE

DISSEAT
DISSENT
DISSERT
DISTANT
DISTEND
DISTENT
DISTUNE
DITHERS
DITONES
DITSIER
DIVERSE
DIVERTS
DOATERS
DOCENTS
DOILTER
DOLINES
DOLMENS
DOMIEST
DONATES
DONGLES
DONSIER
DONZELS
DOPIEST
DORISED
DORISES
DORIZES
DORRING
DORSELS
DORTERS
DORTING
DOSSIER
DOTIEST
DOTINGS
DOTTLER
DOTTREL
DOUCEST
DOUCETS
DOUREST
DOURINE
DOUTERS
DOVIEST
DOWIEST
DOWLNES
DOWRIES
DOZIEST
DRAGEES
DRAGNET
DRAILED
DRAINED
DRAINER
DRAPERS
DRAPETS
DRAPING
DRASTIC
DRAWEES
DRAWERS
DRAWING
DRAZELS
DREARES
DREEING
DRIBLET
DROLEST
DRONING
DROPLET
DROSERA
DROVING
DRUSIER
DUETTOS
DUIKERS
DUNDERS

DUNGIER
DUNITES
DUNKERS
DUNNEST
DUNNIER
DURAMEN
DURANCE
DURIANS
DURRIES
DUSKIER
DUSTERS
DUSTIER
DUSTMEN
DUTEOUS
DYEINGS
DYESTER
DZERENS
EAGLETS
EANLING
EARBOBS
EARCONS
EARDING
EARINGS
EARLAPS
EARLESS
EARLIES
EARNERS
EARNEST
EARNING
EARRING
EARSHOT
EARTHLY
EASTERN
EASTING
EASTLIN
EATINGS
EBONIST
ECARTES
ECLAIRS
ECONUTS
EDGINGS
EDITORS
EELIEST
EERIEST
EFFEIRS
EGOTISM
EGOTIST
EILDING
ELANETS
ELASTIC
ELASTIN
ELATERS
ELATING
ELATION
ELDINGS
ELEGANT
ELEGIST
ELEGITS
ELICITS
ELIDING
ELISION
ELITISM
ELITIST
ELMIEST
ELOGIES
ELOGIST
ELOIGNS
ELUANTS
ELUDING
ELUENTS

ELUSION
ELUTING
ELUTORS
EMANANT
EMANATE
EMBAILS
EMBRAID
EMERIES
EMETINS
EMICANT
EMIGRES
EMONGST
EMPARES
EMPARLS
EMPARTS
EMPIRES
EMPRISE
ENACTOR
ENAMORS
ENCORES
ENCRATY
ENCRUST
ENDARTS
ENDEARS
ENDINGS
ENDITES
ENDLANG
ENDLESS
ENDMOST
ENDORSE
ENDURES
ENEMATA
ENEMIES
ENERGID
ENFANTS
ENFIRED
ENFIRES
ENFOLDS
ENFORMS
ENGAOLS
ENGILDS
ENGINER
ENGIRDS
ENGLUTS
ENGORES
ENGRAFT
ENGRAIL
ENGRAIN
ENGRAMS
ENGRASP
ENGROSS
ENGUARD
ENIGMAS
ENISLED
ENLARDS
ENLARGE
ENLIGHT
ENLISTS
ENRACES
ENRAGED
ENRAGES
ENRINGS
ENROOTS
ENROUND
ENSEARS
ENSILED
ENSNARL
ENSTAMP
ENSTYLE
ENSURED

ENTAILS
ENTAMES
ENTASIS
ENTERAL
ENTERIC
ENTHRAL
ENTICER
ENTICES
ENTIRES
ENTOILS
ENTOMBS
ENTRAIL
ENTRAIN
ENTRALL
ENTRANT
ENTRAPS
ENTREAT
ENTREES
ENTRIES
ENTRISM
ENTRIST
ENTROLD
ENTRUST
ENTWIST
ENURING
ENVIERS
EOLITHS
EONISMS
EPACRIS
EPEIRAS
EPIGONS
EPILOGS
EPIMERS
EPISTLE
EPSILON
EPURATE
ERASERS
ERASING
ERASION
ERASURE
EREPSIN
ERGATES
ERINGOS
ERINITE
ERISTIC
ERMINED
ERMINES
ERODING
EROSION
EROSIVE
EROTICS
EROTISM
ERRANDS
ERRANTS
ERRINGS
ERYNGOS
ESCOLAR
ESCORTS
ESLOINS
ESPARTO
ESPIALS
ESPRITS
ESSOINS
ESTATED
ESTIVAL
ESTOILE
ESTOVER
ESTRADE
ESTRAYS
ESTREAT

ESTRICH
ETACISM
ETALONS
ETCHING
ETERNAL
ETESIAN
ETHIOPS
ETHNICS
ETOILES
ETRIERS
ETTLING
ETYMONS
EUCAINS
EVADERS
EVILLER
EVOKERS
EXHORTS
EXODIST
EXPORTS
EXTENDS
EXTERNS
EXTIRPS
EXTORTS
EXTRAIT
EYLIADS
FADIEST
FAERIES
FAIBLES
FAINEST
FAINTER
FAIREST
FALSIES
FALSING
FALTERS
FAMINES
FANCIER
FANCIES
FANGLED
FANGLES
FARDELS
FARDENS
FARDING
FARNESS
FARSING
FARTHEL
FARTING
FASCINE
FASTERS
FASTING
FATHERS
FATLING
FATTENS
FATTIER
FATTIES
FEALING
FEARING
FEASTED
FEASTER
FEDORAS
FEERIES
FEERINS
FEINTER
FELSITE
FELSPAR
FELTERS
FELTING
FEMINAL
FENDERS
FENDIER
FENITAR

FERLIES
FERNING
FERRETS
FERRIES
FETTERS
FIANCES
FIBSTER
FILACER
FILASSE
FILTERS
FINAGLE
FINDERS
FINEERS
FINGERS
FIREMAN
FIRMEST
FISTIER
FITNESS
FITTERS
FLANGED
FLANGES
FLARING
FLENSED
FLINGER
FLIRTED
FLORETS
FLUENTS
FLUIEST
FLUSTER
FLUTERS
FOISTED
FOISTER
FOLATES
FOLDERS
FOMENTS
FOMITES
FONDEST
FONDLES
FORDING
FORINTS
FORPETS
FORTIES
FORTING
FOTHERS
FOULEST
FOUNDER
FRAISED
FRATERS
FREESIA
FREMITS
FRETSAW
FRIANDE
FRIANDS
FRIDGES
FRIENDS
FRIEZES
FRINGED
FRINGES
FRISEES
FRISKET
FRISTED
FROISES
FROSTED
FUNDERS
FUNSTER
FUSTIER
GABLETS
GADDERS
GADSMEN
GAGSTER
GAHNITE
GAINERS
GAINEST
GAITERS
GALENAS
GALERES
GALLETS
GAMIEST
GAMINES
GANDERS
GANGERS
GANGREL
GANNETS
GANTLET
GAOLERS
GARBLES
GARDENS
GARGETS
GARGLES
GARMENT
GARNERS
GARNETS
GARNISH
GARRETS
GARTERS
GASPIER
GASTERS
GASTING
GASTRIC
GASTRIN
GATEMAN
GATHERS
GATINGS
GAUNTER
GEALING
GEARING
GELATIN
GELDING
GENDERS
GENERAL
GENISTA
GENITAL
GENITOR
GENTIER
GENTILE
GENTLES
GERBILS
GERENTS
GERMAIN
GERMANS
GERMENS
GERMINS
GERNING
GERUNDS
GESTALT
GESTANT
GETTERS
GIANTLY
GIANTRY
GIBLETS
GIGLETS
GILDERS
GILLETS
GIMLETS
GINGALS
GINGERS
GINGLES
GINNELS
GINNERS
GINNERY
GINNIER
GIRDERS
GIRDLES
GIRLIES
GIRLOND
GIRNELS
GIRNERS
GIRTING
GISARME
GITANAS
GITANOS
GITTERN
GLACIER
GLADDEN
GLADIER
GLAIRED
GLAIRIN
GLANCED
GLANCES
GLANDES
GLARING
GLASSEN
GLAZERS
GLEANED
GLEANER
GLENOID
GLIDERS
GLINTED
GLIOSES
GLISTEN
GLISTER
GLITZES
GLOIRES
GLORIES
GLUIEST
GLUTENS
GNARLED
GNARRED
GNASHER
GNAWERS
GNOMIST
GNOSTIC
GOALIES
GOITERS
GOITRES
GOLDENS
GOLLIES
GOOLIES
GORIEST
GORINGS
GOVERNS
GRABENS
GRACILE
GRADERS
GRADINE
GRADING
GRADINI
GRADINO
GRADINS
GRAILES
GRAINED
GRAINER
GRAINES
GRAKLES
GRANDEE
GRANDER
GRANGES
GRANITA
GRANITE
GRANNIE
GRANTED
GRANTEE
GRANTER
GRANULE
GRAPLES
GRAPNEL
GRASPED
GRASSED
GRATERS
GRATINE
GRATING
GRATINS
GRAVELS
GRAVEST
GRAYEST
GRAYLES
GREASED
GREASER
GREATEN
GRECIAN
GREINED
GREISEN
GREISLY
GREMLIN
GRENADE
GRIESLY
GRIEVES
GRILLES
GRILSES
GRINDED
GRINDER
GRINGOS
GRINNED
GRINNER
GRISELY
GRISLED
GRISONS
GRISTLE
GRIVETS
GROANED
GROINED
GROMETS
GROSERT
GROYNES
GUERDON
GUIDERS
GUILERS
GUNDIES
GUNITES
GUNTERS
GURLETS
GURNETS
GYRATES
HAEMINS
HAGLETS
HAILERS
HAIRNET
HALBERT
HALIDES
HALITES
HALSING
HALTERS
HALTING
HAMSTER
HANDERS
HANDIER
HANDLER
HANDLES
HANDSEL
HANDSET
HANGERS
HANTLES
HAPTENS
HARDENS
HARDEST
HAREEMS
HARELDS
HARLING
HARMINE
HARNESS
HAROSET
HARPIES
HARSLET
HARTELY
HARTENS
HARVEST
HASTIER
HASTING
HATREDS
HATTERS
HEADERS
HEADSET
HEALERS
HEALING
HEARERS
HEARING
HEARSED
HEARTHS
HEARTLY
HEATERS
HEATING
HECTORS
HEFTING
HEIFERS
HEISTER
HELIMAN
HEMINAS
HENRIES
HENTING
HERALDS
HERBIST
HERDENS
HERDING
HERIOTS
HERLING
HERMITS
HERNIAS
HEROICS
HEROINS
HERRIES
HETEROS
HETMANS
HINDERS
HINDLEG
HIPSTER
HIRSTIE
HIRSUTE
HISTONE
HITHERS
HITTERS
HOIDENS
HOISTED
HOISTER
HOLDERS
HOLIEST
HOLSTER
HOMIEST
HOOTERS
HORDING
HORNETS
HORNIST
HORSING
HOSIERS
HOSTILE
HOSTING
HOSTLER
HOTTERS
HOTTIES
HUNTERS
HURDENS
HURDIES
HURTLES
HUSTLER
ICONISE
ICTERUS
IDEATES
IGNAROS
IGNEOUS
IGNITER
IGNITES
IGNORED
IGNORES
ILEITIS
ILLITES
IMARETS
IMMENSE
IMMERSE
IMPANEL
IMPASTE
IMPONES
IMPRESA
IMPRESE
IMPREST
INANEST
INARMED
INBREED
INCAGES
INCASED
INCASES
INCAVES
INCEPTS
INCESTS
INCHASE
INCITER
INCITES
INCLOSE
INCOMES
INDARTS
INDENTS
INDEXER
INDITER
INDITES
INDOLES
INDORSE
INDUCER
INDULGE
INEARTH
INEPTER
INERTER
INERTIA
INFAMES
INFARES
INFECTS
INFESTS
INFLAME
INFLATE
INGATES
INGENER
INGESTA
INGESTS
INGRAFT
INGRATE
INGRESS
INGROSS
INHERED
INHERES
INHERIT
INISLED
INJECTS
INJERAS
INJURED
INLACES
INLIERS
INMATES
INNARDS
INQUEST
INROADS
INSANER
INSCAPE
INSEAMS
INSECTS
INSEEMS
INSERTS
INSHORE
INSIDER
INSNARE
INSOLES
INSPECT
INSPIRE
INSTANT
INSTARS
INSTATE
INSTEAD
INSTEPS
INSURED
INSURES
INTAKES
INTEGER
INTENDS
INTENSE
INTENTS
INTERIM
INTERNE
INTERNS
INTIMAE
INTINES
INTONES
INTREAT
INTRONS
INTRUDE
INTUSES
INURNED
INVADER
INVADES
INVENTS
INVERSE
INVERTS
INVESTS
INVITER
INWARDS
IODATES
IODINES
IOLITES
IONISED
IONISER
IONISES
IRATELY
IRATEST
IRENICS
IRIDEAL
IRISATE
IRONERS
IRONIES
IRONISE
IRONIST
ISABELS
ISATINE
ISLEMAN
ISLEMEN
ISOBARE
ISOGENY
ISOLATE
ISOLINE
ISOMERE
ISOMERS
ISOTONE
ISOTOPE
ISOTRON
ISOTYPE
ITERANT
ITERATE
IVORIES
IVRESSE
JAILERS
JANGLED
JANGLER
JANGLES
JANTIER
JANTIES
JASMINE
JERBILS
JERBOAS
JERRIES
JESTING
JETTONS
JINGALS
JINGLED
JINGLER
JINGLES
JINGLET
JINGOES
JIRBLES
JITTERS
JOINERS
JOISTED
JOLTERS
JOLTIER
JOLTING
JONTIES
JOTTERS
JOUSTED
KALENDS
KANDIES
KANTENS
KARITES
KARSTIC
KARTERS
KARTING
KEISTER
KELTERS
KELTIES
KENOSIS
KENTIAS
KERATIN
KERNING
KERNISH
KERNITE
KESTING
KESTREL
KILERGS
KILTERS
KILTIES
KINDERS
KINDEST
KINDLES
KINEMAS
KINGLES
KINGLET
KINREDS
KIRTLED
KIRTLES
KITTENS
KNITTER
KRANSES
KRATERS
LAAGERS
LABISES
LABRETS
LABROSE
LACIEST
LACINGS
LACTASE
LACTOSE
LADDERS
LADDIES
LADINGS
LADRONE
LAERING
LAGENAS
LAGGENS
LAGGERS
LAGGINS
LAGUNES
LAIKERS
LAIRING
LAIRISE
LAISSES
LAITIES
LAKIEST
LALDIES
LAMBENT
LAMBERT
LAMBIES
LAMENTS
LAMINAE
LAMITER
LAMPERS
LANCERS
LANCETS
LANDERS
LANDLER
LANGEST
LANGREL
LANGUED
LANGUES
LANGUET
LANKEST
LANNERS
LANTERN
LAPISES
LAPPERS
LAPSING
LARDERS
LARDIER
LARDING
LARGENS
LARGESS
LARGEST
LARKING
LARNING

LASAGNE
LASHING
LASINGS
LASSIES
LASTAGE
LASTERS
LASTING
LATCHES
LATEENS
LATHERS
LATHERY
LATHIER
LATHING
LATICES
LATRINE
LATRONS
LATTENS
LAUDERS
LAUNDER
LAVEERS
LAWINGS
LAYINGS
LAZIEST
LEADENS
LEADERS
LEADIER
LEADING
LEAFING
LEAKERS
LEAKING
LEAMING
LEANEST
LEANING
LEAPERS
LEAPING
LEARING
LEARNED
LEASERS
LEASING
LEASURE
LEATHER
LEAVERS
LEAVIER
LEAVING
LECTINS
LECTORS
LEDDENS
LEERING
LEESING
LEFTIES
LEGATES
LEGATOS
LEGENDS
LEGIONS
LEGISTS
LEGLANS
LEGLINS
LEIGERS
LEIRING
LEISHER
LEISLER
LEISTER
LEISURE
LENDERS
LENDING
LENGEST
LENTIGO
LENTILS
LENTISK
LENTORS
LENTOUS
LEOTARD
LESBIAN
LESIONS
LESTING
LETTERS
LETTING
LETTRES
LEVANTS
LEVITES
LIAISED
LIAISES
LIBATES
LIBBERS
LIBEROS
LIBRATE
LIDGERS
LIEFEST
LIEGERS
LIERNES
LIEVEST
LIFTERS
LIGANDS
LIGASES
LIGATES
LIGGERS
LIGHTEN
LIGNAGE
LIGNITE
LIGNOSE
LIGURES
LIMBERS
LIMIEST
LIMITES
LIMNERS
LINAGES
LINDENS
LINEAGE
LINEATE
LINEMAN
LINGAMS
LINGELS
LINGERS
LINGIER
LINGLES
LINGOES
LINGOTS
LINGUAE
LINGUAS
LINIEST
LINKAGE
LINKERS
LINNETS
LINSANG
LINSEED
LINTELS
LINTERS
LINTIER
LINTIES
LIONELS
LIONESS
LIONETS
LIONISE
LIPASES
LISTENS
LISTERS
LITERAL
LITOTES
LITTERS
LIVENER
LOADENS
LOADERS
LOAFERS
LOATHER
LOATHES
LOBSTER
LOCATES
LODGERS
LOFTERS
LOFTIER
LOFTING
LOGIEST
LOITERS
LOMENTA
LOMENTS
LOONIES
LOOTERS
LOOTING
LORDING
LORICAE
LORINGS
LORISES
LORRIES
LOSSIER
LOTTING
LOTUSES
LOUDENS
LOUDEST
LOUNDER
LOUSIER
LOUTING
LOWTING
LUNGIES
LURDANE
LURDENS
LURGIES
LUSTERS
LUSTIER
LUSTRED
LUSTRES
LUTEINS
LUTEOUS
LYNAGES
MADDENS
MADNESS
MAELIDS
MAENADS
MAESTRI
MAESTRO
MAGENTA
MAGNATE
MAGNETS
MAHSEER
MAIDENS
MAIGRES
MAILERS
MAILMEN
MAINEST
MAISTER
MALGRES
MALIGNS
MALTIER
MALTING
MALTMEN
MALTOSE
MANATEE
MANDATE
MANDIRS
MANDREL
MANGELS
MANGERS
MANGIER
MANGLED
MANGLER
MANGLES
MANILLE
MANIPLE
MANKIER
MANLIER
MANNITE
MANREDS
MANTEAU
MANTEEL
MANTELS
MANTIES
MANTLED
MANTLES
MANTLET
MANTOES
MANURED
MARDIES
MARGENT
MARGINS
MARINER
MARINES
MARKETS
MARLINE
MARLING
MARRIES
MARTELS
MARTENS
MARTING
MARTINS
MASHIER
MASONED
MASSIER
MASTERS
MASTERY
MASTIER
MASTING
MATIEST
MATINEE
MATRICS
MATRONS
MATTERS
MATTIES
MATTINS
MATURES
MAUNDER
MAYSTER
MAZIEST
MEAGRES
MEALERS
MEALING
MEANEST
MEANIES
MEARING
MEASING
MEASURE
MEDIALS
MEDIANS
MEDIANT
MEDINAS
MEDLARS
MEDLING
MEDUSAN
MEINEYS
MEINIES
MELANIC
MELANIN
MELDING
MELTING
MELTONS
MENDERS
MENHIRS
MENIALS
MENTORS
MENYIES
MERCATS
MERCIES
MERINOS
MERKINS
MERLING
MERLINS
MERLONS
MERRIES
MERSION
MESAILS
MESHIER
MESONIC
MESSIER
MESTIZA
MESTIZO
METEORS
METIERS
METRICS
METRING
METRIST
MICATES
MIGRANT
MILDENS
MILTERS
MINARET
MINCERS
MINDERS
MINDSET
MINEOLA
MINERAL
MINGLED
MINGLER
MINGLES
MINIATE
MINIEST
MINSTER
MINTAGE
MINTERS
MINTIER
MINUETS
MINUTER
MINUTES
MIRACLE
MIRAGES
MIRBANE
MIRIEST
MIRKEST
MISDATE
MISDEAL
MISDOER
MISDONE
MISERES
MISFARE
MISGONE
MISHEAR
MISKENT
MISLEAD
MISMATE
MISNAME
MISRATE
MISREAD
MISSEEN
MISSENT
MISTAKE
MISTERM
MISTERS
MISTERY
MISTIER
MISTUNE
MISWEEN
MISWENT
MITHERS
MITOSES
MITRING
MITTENS
MOANERS
MOBSTER
MODENAS
MODERNS
MODISTE
MOIDERS
MOILERS
MOISERS
MOISTED
MOISTEN
MOISTER
MOLINES
MOLTING
MOMENTS
MONADES
MONETHS
MONGERS
MONSTER
MONTEMS
MONTRES
MOONERS
MOONIES
MOONSET
MOOTERS
MOPIEST
MORAINE
MORALES
MOREENS
MORGENS
MORTISE
MOSSIER
MOTHERS
MOTIEST
MOTILES
MOTIVES
MOTLIER
MOTSERS
MOURNED
MOUSTED
MOUTERS
MRIDANG
MUNITES
MUNSTER
MURINES
MUSTIER
MUTINES
NACKETS
NACRITE
NAGARIS
NAGGERS
NAGGIER
NAIADES
NAIFEST
NAILERS
NAIVEST
NAMASTE
NANCIES
NARASES
NARDING
NARGILE
NARGILY
NARRATE
NARTJIE
NASCENT
NASTIER
NASTIES
NATCHES
NATIVES
NATRONS
NATTERS
NATTERY
NATTIER
NATURED
NATURES
NEALING
NEAREST
NEARING
NEATENS
NEATEST
NECROSE
NECTARS
NECTARY
NEEDERS
NEEDIER
NEEDLES
NEGATES
NEGRESS
NEGROES
NEGROID
NEITHER
NEMATIC
NEMESIA
NEMESIS
NEPETAS
NERDIER
NEREIDS
NERITES
NERITIC
NEROLIS
NERVING
NESTERS
NESTFUL
NESTING
NESTLED
NESTLES
NETFULS
NETTIER
NETTLES
NEURISM
NEURITE
NEUSTON
NEUTERS
NEUTRAL
NICHERS
NICKERS
NIDGETS
NIELLOS
NIFTIER
NIGELLA
NIGGARD
NIGGERS
NIGGLED
NIGGLER
NIGGLES
NIGHEST
NIGHTED
NIGHTIE
NILGAIS
NILGAUS
NIMMERS
NIPPERS
NIPTERS
NITERIE
NITRATE
NITRIDE
NITRILE
NITRITE
NITROSO
NITROUS
NITTIER
NOCENTS
NOCKETS
NODDIES
NODDLES
NODULES
NOISIER
NOISOME
NOMADES
NOODLES
NORITES
NOSIEST
NOSTRIL
NOTATES
NOTCHES
NOTICES
NOUSLED
NOVICES
NUDGERS
NURDLES
NURSLED
NUTATES
NUTCASE
NUTLETS
NUTMEAL
NUTRIAS
NUTTERS
NUTTIER
OARIEST
OARLESS
OARSMEN
OBLATES
OBLIGES
OBSERVE
OBTENDS
OBTUSER
OBVERSE
OBVERTS
OCTANES
OCTAVES
OERSTED
OESTRAL
OESTRUM
OEUVRES
OILIEST
OILLETS
OLDNESS
OLDSTER
OLEATES
OLEFINS
OLIVERS
OLIVETS
OLOGIES
OMENTAL
OMERTAS
ONAGERS
ONDINES
ONLIEST
ONSIDES
ONSTEAD
OOLITES
OORIEST
OPENERS
OPERATE
OPERONS
OPHITES
OPIATES
OPTIMES
ORACHES
ORACIES
ORACLES
ORANGES
ORATING
ORBIEST
ORCEINS
ORCINES
ORDAINS
ORDEALS
ORDINEE
OREADES
OREIDES
ORGEATS
ORGONES
ORIENTS
ORIGANE
ORIGANS
ORIGINS
ORIOLES
ORLEANS
ORNATER
ORNISES
OROGENS
OROIDES
ORPINES
ORRISES
OSIERED
OSMIATE
OSSEINS
OSTENTS
OSTEOID
OSTIATE
OSTIOLE
OSTLERS
OTARIES
OTARINE
OUGLIES
OULDEST
OURIEST
OUSTING
OUTDOES
OUTINGS
OUTLERS
OUTLETS
OUTLIER
OUTLIES
OUTNESS
OUTREDS
OUTSELL
OUTSIDE
OUTSOLE
OVARIES
OVERLIE
OVERSEA
OVERSEE
OVERSET
OVERSEW
OVERUSE
OWLIEST

OWRIEST
PAIDLES
PAINTER
PALIEST
PALINGS
PALMERS
PALSIED
PALSIER
PALSIES
PALTERS
PANDERS
PANDIES
PANSIED
PANTERS
PANTIES
PANTILE
PANTLER
PARCELS
PARDINE
PARENTS
PARESIS
PARGETS
PARINGS
PARKIES
PARLEYS
PARLIES
PARLING
PAROLES
PARRELS
PARRIES
PARSING
PARSLEY
PARTERS
PARTIED
PARTIES
PARTING
PARTITE
PARTLET
PARTNER
PARTONS
PARVISE
PASTERN
PASTERS
PASTIER
PASTIME
PASTING
PASTURE
PATENTS
PATERAE
PATINES
PATNESS
PATRONS
PATTENS
PATTERN
PATTERS
PATTIES
PATZERS
PEALING
PEANUTS
PEARTLY
PEASANT
PEATERY
PEATIER
PEATMAN
PECTINS
PEDANTS
PEDLARS
PEDRAIL
PEINCTS
PELITES

PELOTAS
PELTERS
PELTING
PENATES
PENSION
PENTADS
PENTELS
PENTISE
PENULTS
PEONIES
PEONISM
PEPINOS
PERIDOT
PERIODS
PERIOST
PERITUS
PERKINS
PERMITS
PERONES
PERRIES
PERRONS
PERSANT
PERSICO
PERSING
PERSIST
PERSONA
PERSONS
PERTAIN
PERTAKE
PERTEST
PERUSAL
PESANTE
PESANTS
PESAUNT
PETARAS
PETARDS
PETRELS
PETROLS
PETROUS
PETTERS
PEZANTS
PHONERS
PHONIES
PIASTRE
PIGEONS
PIGLETS
PILSNER
PIMENTS
PINCASE
PINCERS
PINDERS
PINGERS
PINGLED
PINGLER
PINGLES
PINGOES
PINIEST
PINITES
PINKEST
PINKOES
PINNERS
PINNETS
PINOLES
PINTLES
PIOLETS
PIONERS
PIONEYS
PIONIES
PIRATED
PIRATES

PIRNIES
PISTOLE
PITEOUS
PITIERS
PITTERS
PLACERS
PLACETS
PLAITER
PLANERS
PLANETS
PLANTER
PLASTER
PLATENS
PLATERS
PLATIER
PLATING
PLATTER
PLAYERS
PLEAING
PLEASER
PLEATER
PLECTRA
PLENIST
PODITES
POETICS
POETISE
POINTES
POISERS
POITREL
POKIEST
POLDERS
POLITER
POLTING
PONDERS
PONTIES
POOREST
POOTERS
PORIEST
PORTERS
PORTESS
PORTING
POSIEST
POSITED
POSTERN
POSTERS
POSTIES
POSTING
POSTMEN
POSTURE
POTENTS
POTHERS
POTTERS
POTTIES
POUNDER
POUTERS
POWNIES
POWTERS
POXIEST
PRAISED
PRAISER
PRAISES
PRANCES
PRANGED
PRATERS
PRATIES
PRATING
PRATTED
PRATTLE
PRAWLES
PREASED

PRECAST
PREDATE
PREDIAL
PREDICT
PREDIES
PREHEAT
PREIFES
PRELATE
PRELATY
PREMIES
PREMISE
PRESENT
PRESIDE
PRESTED
PRESTOS
PRETEST
PRETORS
PREVISE
PRIEFES
PRIESTS
PRIEVES
PRINCES
PRINTED
PRISAGE
PRIVETS
PROIGNS
PROINES
PROLATE
PRONEST
PROSING
PROTEAS
PROTEID
PROTEST
PROTEUS
PROYNES
PRUINES
PSALTER
PTERINS
PTERYLA
PUDSIER
PUIREST
PULIEST
PUNIEST
PUNSTER
PUNTERS
PUNTIES
PURINES
PUTELIS
PYONERS
PYRITES
QINTARS
QUINTES
RABBETS
RABIDER
RACEMES
RACIEST
RACINGS
RACISTS
RACKETS
RADDLES
RADGEST
RADIALE
RADIANS
RADICEL
RADICES
RADICLE
RADOMES
RAFTERS
RAFTING
RAGGLES

RAGINGS
RAGINIS
RAGMENT
RAIDERS
RAIDING
RAILBED
RAILERS
RAILING
RAILMEN
RAIMENT
RAISING
RAITING
RAKINGS
RALLIED
RALLIES
RAMEKIN
RAMENTA
RAMJETS
RAMMIES
RANCELS
RANCHES
RANDEMS
RANDIER
RANDIES
RANDING
RANGERS
RANGIER
RANGOLI
RANKEST
RANKLED
RANKLES
RANSELS
RANTERS
RANTING
RANZELS
RAPIERS
RAPINES
RAPPELS
RASHEST
RASHING
RASPIER
RASPING
RASTERS
RATABLE
RATCHES
RATHEST
RATINES
RATINGS
RATIONS
RATLINE
RATLING
RATLINS
RATOONS
RATTEEN
RATTENS
RATTERS
RATTIER
RATTING
RATTLES
RATTONS
RAUNGED
RAUNGES
RAVINED
RAVINES
RAVINGS
RAWINGS
RAWNESS
RAYLETS
RAYLING
READAPT

READERS
READIES
READILY
READING
READOPT
REAGENT
REAKING
REALEST
REALIGN
REALISE
REALISM
REALIST
REALITY
REALTIE
REAMERS
REAMING
REAPERS
REAPING
REARERS
REARING
REARISE
REAROSE
REASONS
REASTED
REAVERS
REAVING
REBATES
REBINDS
REBITES
REBOILS
REBOUND
RECANTS
RECASTS
RECITAL
RECITES
RECKONS
RECLAIM
RECOILS
RECOINS
RECTORS
REDACTS
REDATES
REDCAPS
REDDENS
REDDEST
REDDING
REDEALS
REDIALS
REDNESS
REDOING
REDOUND
REDOWAS
REDRAWS
REDSEAR
REDSKIN
REDTOPS
REDUITS
REDWING
REEDING
REELING
REESTED
REFINED
REFINES
REFLAGS
REFLETS
REFOUND
REFUNDS
REGAINS
REGALES
REGARDS

REGENTS
REGIMES
REGINAE
REGINAL
REGINAS
REGIONS
REGIVES
REGLETS
REGNANT
REGRANT
REGRETS
REGRIND
REHANGS
REHEARS
REHEATS
REIFIES
REIGNED
REINING
REINTER
REISTED
REITERS
REIVERS
REJOINS
RELAPSE
RELATES
RELAXES
RELEASE
RELENTS
RELIANT
RELICTS
RELIEFS
RELIERS
RELIEVE
RELIEVO
RELINED
RELINES
RELIVED
RELIVER
RELIVES
RELOADS
RELUCTS
RELYING
REMADES
REMAINS
REMAKES
REMANDS
REMANIE
REMEADS
REMEIDS
REMIGES
REMINDS
REMINTS
REMISED
REMISES
REMIXES
REMOTES
REMOVES
RENAMES
RENDERS
RENDING
RENEGES
RENNETS
RENNING
RENTALS
RENTERS
RENTIER
RENTING
RENVOIS
RENYING
REOPENS

REPAINT
REPAIRS
REPASTS
REPEALS
REPEATS
REPENTS
REPINED
REPINES
REPLANS
REPLANT
REPLAYS
REPLICA
REPLIES
REPONES
REPORTS
REPOSAL
REPOSIT
REPOSTS
REPRISE
REPTANT
REPUNIT
RERAILS
REREADS
RESALES
RESCALE
RESCIND
RESEALS
RESEATS
RESEDAS
RESENTS
RESIANT
RESIDED
RESIDER
RESIDES
RESIDUA
RESIDUE
RESIGNS
RESILED
RESILES
RESINED
RESINER
RESOLED
RESOLVE
RESORTS
RESOUND
RESPELT
RESPIRE
RESPITE
RESPOND
RESTAGE
RESTART
RESTATE
RESTERS
RESTFUL
RESTIER
RESTIFF
RESTING
RESTIVE
RESTOCK
RESTORE
RESTYLE
RESULTS
RETABLE
RETAILS
RETAINS
RETAKES
RETAMAS
RETARDS
RETELLS
RETENES

RETILED
RETILES
RETIMES
RETINAE
RETINAL
RETINAS
RETINOL
RETINUE
RETIRAL
RETIRES
RETOOLS
RETORTS
RETOURS
RETRAIN
RETRAIT
RETREES
RETRIAL
RETRIES
RETRIMS
RETSINA
RETTING
RETUNDS
RETUNES
RETURNS
RETYING
REUNITE
REUSING
REVEALS
REVERSI
REVERSO
REVERTS
REVIEWS
REVILED
REVILER
REVILES
REVISAL
REVISED
REVISER
REVISES
REVISIT
REVISOR
REVIVES
REVOKES
REVOLTS
REWARDS
REWINDS
REWIRES
REWOUND
RHETORS
RHODIES
RIBANDS
RIBLESS
RIBLETS
RIBOSES
RIBSTON
RICHENS
RICHEST
RICIEST
RICKETS
RIDABLE
RIDGELS
RIDGERS
RIEVERS
RIFTING
RIGHTEN
RILIEST
RILLETS
RIMIEST
RINGBIT
RINGENT

RINGERS
RINGGIT
RINGLET
RINGMEN
RINSERS
RIOTERS
RIOTING
RIOTISE
RIPENED
RIPOSTE
RIPTIDE
RISIBLE
RISSOLE
RITTERS
RITTING
ROACHES
ROADIES
ROADING
ROASTED
ROASTER
ROATING
ROBINGS
ROCHETS
ROCKETS
RODDING
RODENTS
RODINGS
RODLESS
RODSMEN
RODSTER
ROISTED
ROISTER
ROKIEST
RONDEAU
RONDELS
RONDURE
ROOSING
ROOSTED
ROOSTER
ROOTERS
ROOTIES
ROOTING
ROOTLED
ROOTLES
ROPIEST
ROPINGS
RORIEST
RORTERS
RORTING
ROSACEA
ROSACES
ROSEATE
ROSEBAY
ROSELLA
ROSEOLA
ROSETED
ROSETTE
ROSETTY
ROSIERE
ROSIERS
ROSIEST
ROSINED
ROSITED
ROSTERS
ROSTING
ROSYING
ROTATES
ROTCHES
ROTHERS
ROTTANS
ROTTENS
ROTTERS
ROTTING
ROUNCES
ROUNDED
ROUNDEL
ROUNDER
ROUNDLE
ROUSANT
ROUSING
ROUSTED
ROUSTER
ROUTERS
ROUTINE
ROUTING
ROVINGS
ROWDIES
ROWINGS
ROWTING
ROYSTED
ROYSTER
RUBIEST
RUDDIES
RUEINGS
RUINATE
RULIEST
RUNDALE
RUNDLES
RUNLETS
RUNNETS
RUNTIER
RUSTIER
RUSTLED
RUSTLER
RUSTLES
RUSTRED
RUTILES
SABERED
SABLING
SABRING
SACRING
SACRIST
SADDLER
SADIRON
SAETERS
SAFROLE
SAIDEST
SAILERS
SAILING
SAINTED
SAIREST
SAIRING
SAKERET
SALFERN
SALICES
SALICET
SALIENT
SALINES
SALLIED
SALLIES
SALTERN
SALTERS
SALTIER
SALTING
SALTIRE
SALTOED
SALUING
SALUTED
SALUTER
SALVING
SAMIELS
SAMIEST
SAMISEN
SAMITES
SAMPIRE
SAMPLER
SANDERS
SANDIER
SANDMEN
SANGRIA
SANICLE
SANTIRS
SANTOUR
SAPIENT
SAPLING
SAPPIER
SAPROBE
SARANGI
SARCODE
SARDELS
SARDINE
SARKING
SARMENT
SARNEYS
SARNIES
SARSDEN
SARSENS
SARSNET
SATCHEL
SATIATE
SATIETY
SATINED
SATINET
SATIRES
SATIRIC
SATYRIC
SAULIES
SAUNTED
SAUNTER
SAUTEED
SAUTING
SAVORED
SCAILED
SCALDER
SCALENI
SCALIER
SCALING
SCALPER
SCANNER
SCANTED
SCANTER
SCANTLE
SCARFED
SCARING
SCARLET
SCARPED
SCARRED
SCARTED
SCATOLE
SCATTER
SCAURED
SCENARY
SCENTED
SCERNED
SCLATED
SCLATES
SCOLDER
SCOOTER
SCOPATE
SCORIAE
SCORING
SCORNED
SCORNER
SCOTERS
SCOURIE
SCOUTED
SCOUTER
SCOWRIE
SCRAPED
SCRAPIE
SCRIBED
SCRIENE
SCRIEVE
SCRINES
SCYTALE
SDAINED
SDAINES
SDEIGNE
SDEIGNS
SEABIRD
SEALANT
SEALERS
SEALERY
SEALING
SEAMERS
SEAMIER
SEAMING
SEAPORT
SEARATS
SEARCED
SEAREST
SEARING
SEATERS
SEATING
SECANTS
SECONDI
SECRETA
SECTARY
SECTILE
SECTION
SECTORS
SEDATED
SEDATER
SEDATES
SEDGIER
SEDILIA
SEEDIER
SEEDING
SEELIER
SEELING
SEEMING
SEILING
SEINERS
SEISMAL
SEITENS
SELFING
SELLING
SELTZER
SEMATIC
SEMEION
SEMINAL
SEMINAR
SEMITAR
SENARII
SENATOR
SENDALS
SENDERS
SENDING
SENECIO
SENIORS
SENNITS
SENSIST
SENTING
SEPIOST
SEPTUOR
SERAFIN
SERAILS
SERANGS
SEREINS
SERENED
SERIALS
SERIATE
SERICIN
SERICON
SERIEMA
SERINES
SERINGA
SERIOUS
SERKALI
SERMONS
SERPENT
SERPULA
SERRANS
SERRATE
SERRATI
SERRIED
SERRIES
SERRING
SERVANT
SERVICE
SERVILE
SERVING
SESSION
SESTINA
SESTINE
SETLINE
SETTERS
SETTING
SETTLER
SETTLOR
SEVERAL
SEXTANT
SEXTILE
SHADIER
SHAFTER
SHALIER
SHALING
SHARING
SHARPIE
SHASTER
SHATTER
SHEARED
SHEARER
SHEILAS
SHELTER
SHELTIE
SHERIAT
SHIFTER
SHINERS
SHINGLE
SHINIER
SHIRTED
SHOALER
SHOEING
SHOOTER
SHORING
SHORTED
SHORTEN
SHORTER
SHORTIE
SHOTTEN
SHOUTED
SHOUTER
SHRIEVE
SHRINED
SHRINES
SHRIVEN
SHUNTED
SHUNTER
SIDEARM
SIDEBAR
SIDECAR
SIDEMAN
SIDEMEN
SIDERAL
SIEMENS
SIERRAN
SIEVERT
SIFTERS
SIGHTER
SIGMATE
SIGNALS
SIGNARY
SIGNERS
SIGNETS
SIGNEUR
SIGNIOR
SIGNORA
SIGNORE
SIGNORI
SIGNORS
SIGNORY
SILAGED
SILAGES
SILANES
SILENTS
SILESIA
SILTIER
SILVERN
SIMARRE
SINCERE
SINGERS
SINGLED
SINGLES
SINGLET
SINKERS
SINNERS
SINNETS
SINTERS
SINTERY
SINUATE
SINUOSE
SIRENIC
SIRGANG
SIRNAME
SIRREES
SIRUPED
SITHENS
SITREPS
SITTERS
SITTINE
SITUATE
SITULAE
SIZABLE
SKAILED
SKATERS
SKATING
SKATOLE
SKEARED
SKELTER
SKIABLE
SKINTER
SKIRRET
SKIRTED
SKIRTER
SKITTER
SKLATED
SLAINTE
SLAKING
SLANDER
SLANGED
SLANGER
SLANTED
SLAPPER
SLATERS
SLATHER
SLATIER
SLATING
SLATTED
SLATTER
SLAVING
SLAYING
SLEEKIT
SLEIGHT
SLENDER
SLENTER
SLEWING
SLIDDEN
SLINGER
SLINKER
SLINTER
SLITHER
SLITTER
SLOPIER
SLOTTER
SLUEING
SMARTED
SMARTEN
SMARTER
SMARTIE
SMATTER
SMEARED
SMELTER
SMIDGEN
SMITERS
SMITTEN
SMOLDER
SMORING
SMOTHER
SMOUTED
SMYTRIE
SNAILED
SNAKIER
SNARERS
SNARIER
SNARING
SNARLED
SNARLER
SNARRED
SNEERED
SNELLED
SNICKER
SNICKET
SNIDELY
SNIDEST
SNIFTED
SNIFTER
SNIGGED
SNIGGER
SNIGGLE
SNIPERS
SNIPIER
SNIPPER
SNIPPET
SNIRTLE
SNOOLED
SNOOPER
SNOOTED
SNORING
SNORTED
SNORTER
SNOTTED
SNOTTER
SNOTTIE
SNOUTED
SNOWIER
SOAPIER
SOARING
SOCAGER
SOCIATE
SODAINE
SODDIER
SOFTING
SOIGNEE
SOILAGE
SOILIER
SOILURE
SOIREES
SOLDERS
SOLDIER
SOLERAS
SOLIDER
SOLUTES
SOLVATE
SOMITES
SONDELI
SONERIS
SONNIES
SONSIER
SONTIES
SOOTHER
SOOTIER
SOOTING
SOPITED
SOPITES
SORBATE
SORBENT
SORBETS
SORBING
SORBITE
SOREDIA
SORITES
SORNING
SORTERS
SORTIED
SORTIES
SORTING
SOTTING
SOUNDER
SOURING
SOUTANE
SOUTHED
SOUTHER
SPACIER
SPADGER
SPAINED
SPAIRGE
SPALTED
SPANGLE
SPARELY
SPAREST
SPARGED
SPARING
SPARKIE
SPARKLE
SPARRED
SPARTHE
SPATTER
SPEARED
SPECTRA
SPEIRED
SPELDIN
SPELTER
SPENDER
SPHERAL
SPIELER
SPIGNEL
SPILITE
SPINATE
SPINDLE
SPINETS
SPINIER
SPINNER
SPINNET
SPINODE
SPINOSE
SPIRAEA
SPIRANT
SPIREAS
SPIREME
SPIRTED
SPIRTLE
SPITTEN
SPITTER
SPLINED
SPOILER
SPONGER
SPORTED
SPORTER
SPOTTER
SPOUTED
SPOUTER
SPRAINT
SPRINGE
SPRITES
SPURIAE
SPURNED
SPURTED
SPURTLE
SQUIRED
STABBER
STABILE
STABLED
STABLER
STACKER
STADDLE
STAGERS
STAGERY
STAGGER
STAGIER
STAGING
STAIDER
STAINED
STAINER
STAIRED
STAITHE
STAKING
STALING
STALKED
STALKER

STALLED
STAMENS
STAMMER
STAMPER
STANCES
STANDEE
STANDEN
STANDER
STANGED
STANIEL
STANING
STANNEL
STANYEL
STAPLED
STAPLER
STARERS
STARETS
STARETZ
STARING
STARKED
STARKEN
STARKER
STARLET
STARNED
STARNIE
STARRED
STARTED
STARTER
STARTLE
STARVED
STARVES
STATERS
STATICE
STATING
STATION
STATIVE
STATURE
STAVING
STAWING
STAYERS
STAYING
STAYNED
STAYRES
STEADED
STEALED
STEALER
STEAMED
STEAMER
STEAMIE
STEANED
STEARED
STEARES
STEARIC
STEARIN
STEDING
STEENED
STEERED
STEERER
STEINED
STELENE
STELLAR
STEMING
STEMSON
STENCIL
STENDED
STENGAH
STENNED
STENTED
STENTOR
STERILE

STERLET
STERNAL
STERNED
STERNER
STERNUM
STEROID
STEROLS
STERVED
STEWARD
STEWIER
STEWING
STEWPAN
STHENIC
STICKER
STIEVER
STIFFER
STIFLER
STILLER
STILTER
STINGED
STINGER
STINGOS
STINKER
STINTED
STINTER
STIPEND
STIPULE
STIRING
STIRPES
STIRRED
STIRRER
STIRRES
STIVERS
STIVIER
STOCKER
STODGER
STOITED
STOITER
STOKING
STOMPER
STONERN
STONERS
STONIED
STONIER
STONIES
STONING
STONKER
STONNED
STOODEN
STOOLIE
STOOPER
STOPING
STOPPER
STORAGE
STORERS
STORIED
STORIES
STORING
STORMED
STOTTER
STOUTEN
STOUTER
STOVING
STOWING
STRAFED
STRAFES
STRAINS
STRAINT
STRAKES
STRANGE

STRAWED
STRAWEN
STRAYED
STRAYER
STREAKS
STREAMS
STREAMY
STREELS
STREETS
STREETY
STRENES
STRETTA
STRETTE
STRETTI
STRETTO
STREWED
STREWER
STRIATE
STRIDES
STRIFES
STRIGAE
STRIKER
STRIPED
STRIPES
STRIPEY
STRIVED
STRIVEN
STRIVER
STRIVES
STROBES
STRODLE
STROKED
STROKEN
STROKER
STROPHE
STROWED
STROWER
STROYED
STRUDEL
STRUMAE
STUDDEN
STUDENT
STUDIER
STUNNED
STUNNER
STUNTED
STURTED
STYRENE
SUBTEND
SUBTILE
SUBTLER
SUDAMEN
SUDSIER
SUEDING
SUETIER
SUGARED
SULCATE
SULFITE
SUNBELT
SUNDARI
SUNDERS
SUNRISE
SURANCE
SURBATE
SURFEIT
SURGENT
SURGEON
SUTLERS
SUTLERY
SUTURED

SVELTER
SWALIER
SWALING
SWATTER
SWEARER
SWEATED
SWEATER
SWELTER
SWIFTER
SWINDGE
SWINDLE
SWINGED
SWINGER
SWINGLE
SWITHER
SWOTTER
SYNAPTE
SYRINGA
SYRINGE
TABERDS
TABLIER
TABLING
TABRETS
TACKERS
TACKLES
TADDIES
TAENIAS
TAGGERS
TAIGLES
TAILING
TAILLES
TAILYES
TAIVERS
TAIVERT
TAJINES
TAKIEST
TAKINGS
TALCIER
TALCING
TALCOSE
TALENTS
TALIPES
TALKERS
TALKIER
TALKIES
TALKING
TALLIER
TALLIES
TALWEGS
TAMBERS
TAMINES
TAMINGS
TAMISES
TAMMIES
TAMPERS
TANAGER
TANDEMS
TANGELO
TANGIER
TANGIES
TANGLED
TANGLER
TANGLES
TANISTS
TANKERS
TANKIES
TANLING
TANNERS
TANNEST
TANRECS

TANSIES
TAPERED
TAPERER
TAPETIS
TAPPERS
TAPSMEN
TAPSTER
TARCELS
TARDIES
TARGETS
TARGING
TARINGS
TARNISH
TARPONS
TARRIES
TARRING
TARSELS
TARSIER
TARTANE
TARTEST
TARTIER
TARTINE
TASERED
TASHING
TASKERS
TASKING
TASTERS
TASTIER
TASTING
TATLERS
TATTERS
TATTIER
TATTIES
TAUNTER
TAURINE
TAUTENS
TAVERNS
TAWINGS
TAWNIER
TAWNIES
TAWTIER
TAXIMEN
TAXINGS
TEAGLES
TEAMERS
TEAMING
TEARERS
TEARING
TEASERS
TEASING
TECHNOS
TEDDERS
TEDESCA
TEDIOUS
TEENIER
TEERING
TEETERS
TEGMINA
TELAMON
TELEGAS
TELESIS
TELFERS
TELLARS
TELLENS
TELLERS
TELLIES
TELLING
TELLINS
TEMENOS
TEMPERA

TEMPLAR
TEMSING
TENACES
TENAILS
TENANTS
TENDERS
TENDONS
TENDRES
TENDRIL
TENNERS
TENNIES
TENOURS
TENPINS
TENRECS
TENSELY
TENSILE
TENSING
TENSION
TENSITY
TENSORS
TENTERS
TENTIER
TENUOUS
TENURES
TENUTOS
TEPHRAS
TEPIDER
TERCELS
TERCETS
TERCIOS
TEREDOS
TERETES
TERMERS
TERMING
TERMINI
TERMORS
TERNARY
TERNATE
TERNING
TERRAIN
TERRANE
TERRETS
TERRIES
TERRINE
TERRITS
TERRORS
TERSELY
TERSEST
TERSION
TERTIAL
TERTIAN
TERTIAS
TERTIUS
TESSERA
TESTERN
TESTERS
TESTIER
TESTING
TESTONS
TESTOON
TESTRIL
TESTUDO
TETANUS
TETHERS
TETRADS
TETTERS
TEWARTS
THALERS
THAWERS
THEEING

THEMING
THENARS
THEREIN
THERIAN
THERMAL
THIRLED
THOLING
THORPES
THRAVES
THREADS
THREAPS
THREATS
THRENES
THRENOS
THRIVES
THRONES
THROWES
TICKENS
TICKERS
TIDDLER
TIELESS
TIEPINS
TIERCES
TIERING
TIERODS
TIETACS
TIGHTEN
TIGLONS
TIGRINE
TILLERS
TILTERS
TIMBERS
TIMBRES
TIMEOUS
TINDERS
TINEIDS
TINGLED
TINGLER
TINGLES
TINIEST
TINKERS
TINKLES
TINNERS
TINNIER
TINNIES
TINSELS
TINSEYS
TINTERS
TINTIER
TINWARE
TIPPERS
TIPSIER
TIPSTER
TIPTOES
TIRADES
TIRASSE
TIREDLY
TIRINGS
TIRLING
TIRRING
TISANES
TITANIS
TITFERS
TITHERS
TITIANS
TITLERS
TITMOSE
TITRATE
TITTERS
TITULES

TOADIES
TOASTER
TOASTIE
TOCHERS
TODDIES
TODDLER
TOECAPS
TOEIEST
TOENAIL
TOERAGS
TOILERS
TOILETS
TOILING
TOLINGS
TOLLERS
TOLLING
TOLTERS
TOMMIES
TONEMES
TONGUES
TONIEST
TONINGS
TONITES
TONKERS
TONLETS
TONSURE
TONUSES
TOOLERS
TOOLING
TOORIES
TOOTERS
TOOTSIE
TOPPERS
TOPSIDE
TOPSMEN
TORANAS
TORCHES
TOREROS
TORRETS
TORSADE
TORSELS
TORSION
TORSIVE
TORTILE
TOSHERS
TOSHIER
TOSHING
TOSSIER
TOSSING
TOTTERS
TOTTIES
TOURERS
TOURIES
TOURING
TOUSIER
TOUSING
TOUSLED
TOUSLES
TOUSTIE
TOUTERS
TOUZLES
TOWIEST
TOWINGS
TOWNIES
TOWSIER
TOWSING
TOYINGS
TRACERS
TRACING
TRADERS

TRADING
TRAILED
TRAILER
TRAINED
TRAINEE
TRAINER
TRAIPSE
TRAMPED
TRAMPLE
TRANCED
TRANCES
TRANCHE
TRANECT
TRANGLE
TRANNIE
TRANSES
TRANSIT
TRANSOM
TRANTED
TRANTER
TRAPEZE
TRAPING
TRAPPED
TRASHED
TRASHES
TRASSES
TRAVELS
TRAYNES
TREASON
TREBLES
TREEING
TREFOIL
TREHALA
TRELLIS
TREMIES
TREMORS
TRENAIL
TRENISE
TRENTAL
TREPANG
TREPANS
TRESSED
TRESSEL
TRESTLE
TREVISS
TRIABLE
TRIAGES
TRIBADE
TRIBUNE
TRICARS
TRICEPS
TRICING
TRIDENT
TRIFLED
TRIFLES
TRIGONS
TRIKING
TRILLED
TRILOBE
TRIMERS
TRINDLE
TRINGLE
TRINING
TRINKET
TRIODES
TRIOLET
TRIONES
TRIPLED
TRIPLES
TRIPPED

TRIPSES
TRISECT
TRISEME
TRISOME
TRITEST
TRITONE
TRITONS
TRIUNES
TRIVETS
TROADES
TROCHES
TROELIE
TROKING
TROLLED
TROMPES
TROOLIE
TROPING
TROULED
TROULES
TROUPES
TROUSER
TROVERS
TROWELS
TROWING
TRUDGES
TRUEING
TRUSSED
TRUSTED
TRUSTEE
TSARINA
TSIGANE
TUILLES
TUNIEST
TUNNELS
TUNNIES
TUPELOS
TURBINE
TURDINE
TUREENS
TURIONS
TURNERS
TURTLES
TUXEDOS
TWAITES
TWANGLE
TWICERS
TWINERS
TWINGES
TWINIER
TWINSET
TWINTER
TWIRING
TWIRLED
TWISCAR
TWISTER
TYRONES
UGLIEST
ULSTERS
UNAIRED
UNARMED
UNBARED
UNBELTS
UNBLEST
UNCRATE
UNDERDO
UNDERGO
UNDERNS
UNDOERS
UNDRESS
UNDRIED
UNEARED
UNFIRED
UNGEARS
UNGORED
UNHEARD
UNHERST
UNHIRED
UNITERS
UNITIES
UNITISE
UNLADES
UNLASTE
UNLEADS
UNORDER
UNPARED
UNRACED
UNRAKED
UNRATED
UNREADY
UNRESTS
UNRIMED
UNRIVET
UNROBED
UNROPED
UNROPES
UNSATED
UNSMOTE
UNSOOTE
UNSTATE
UNSTEEL
UNSURED
UNTAMES
UNTEAMS
UNTILES
UNTIRED
UNTRACE
UNTREAD
UNTRIDE
UNTRIED
UNWIRED
UNWRITE
UPRAISE
UPRATED
UPRATES
UPRISEN
UPSTARE
UPTEARS
URALITE
URANIDE
URANITE
UREDINE
UREIDES
UREMIAS
URETERS
URIDINE
URINATE
URINOSE
URTICAS
UTENSIL
UTERINE
UTILISE
VAINEST
VALIDER
VALISES
VALSING
VARDIES
VARLETS
VASTIER
VATTERS
VEALERS
VEALIER
VECTORS
VEERIES
VEILIER
VELARIC
VELIGER
VENDERS
VENGERS
VENIRES
VENTAIL
VENTERS
VENTILS
VENTRAL
VENTRES
VENTURI
VERBIDS
VERBOSE
VERDETS
VERDINS
VERDITS
VERGLAS
VERIEST
VERISMO
VERISTS
VERMEIL
VERMIAN
VERMINS
VERSANT
VERSINE
VERSING
VERSINS
VERSION
VERTING
VESSAIL
VESTING
VESTRAL
VIEWERS
VINEGAR
VIOLERS
VIOLETS
VIROSES
VIRTUES
VISITER
VISORED
VISTAED
VITRINE
VOICERS
VOIDERS
VOLUTES
WABSTER
WAFTERS
WAILERS
WAISTED
WAISTER
WAITERS
WALIEST
WALISES
WALTIER
WANDERS
WANGLED
WANGLER
WANGLES
WANIEST
WANNEST
WANTERS
WANTIES
WARDENS
WARDERS
WARDING
WARIEST
WARLING
WARMEST
WARSLED
WASPIER
WASTERS
WASTERY
WASTING
WASTREL
WEARERS
WEARING
WEDELNS
WEIRDOS
WELDING
WELDORS
WELTERS
WELTING
WESTERN
WESTING
WESTLIN
WHINERS
WIDENER
WIGEONS
WILIEST
WINCERS
WINDERS
WINDLES
WINGERS
WINGLET
WINSOME
WINTERS
WINTLES
WIREMAN
WISENTS
WITHERS
WITNESS
WITTERS
WIVERNS
WORDING
WORSING
WORSTED
WORTLES
WOUNDER
WRANGLE
WRASTED
WREATHS
WRESTED
WRESTER
WRESTLE
WRINGED
WRITERS
WRITHES
WRITING
WRITTEN
XEROSIS
YAPSTER
YARDING
YATTERS
YEASTED
YERDING
YESTERN
YODLERS
ZANDERS
ZANIEST
ZARNECS
ZEALOTS
ZELANTS
ZESTIER
ZESTING
ZINGELS
ZINGERS
ZITHERS

8-LETTER SETS
from the top 250 6-letter stems

AAEMNT 229
(MANATE)
AH ANATHEMA
CS CAMSTANE
DD MANDATED
DE EMANATED
DI ANIMATED
DIAMANTE
DS MANDATES
EP NAMETAPE
ES EMANATES
MANATEES
GS MAGENTAS
MAGNATES
HI ANTHEMIA
HAEMATIN
HL METHANAL
HR EARTHMAN
IL ALAIMENT
LAMINATE
IO METANOIA
IP IMPANATE
IR ANIMATER
MARINATE
IS AMENTIAS
ANIMATES
LO MALONATE
LP PLATEMAN
LR MATERNAL
LS TALESMAN
MR ARMAMENT
OZ METAZOAN
PR PARAMENT
RS SARMENTA
SEMANTRA
RT ATRAMENT
RW WATERMAN
SS NAMASTES
SU MANTEAUS
UX MANTEAUX

ABDEIR 134
(ABRIDE)
AD ABRAIDED
AG BIGARADE
AS ARABISED
AZ ARABIZED
BR DRABBIER
BT RABBITED
CG BIRDCAGE
CAGEBIRD
CL CALIBRED
CS ASCRIBED
CARBIDES
DG ABRIDGED
BRIGADED
DN BRANDIED
DR BRAIRDED
EL RIDEABLE
ES BEARDIES
ET EBRIATED
GN BEARDING
BREADING
GR ABRIDGER
GS ABRIDGES
BRIGADES
IT DIATRIBE
KM IMBARKED
LN BILANDER
LS RAILBEDS
LT LIBRATED
LV DRIVABLE
LY DIABLERY
MN BRIDEMAN
MO AMBEROID
MR IMBARRED
MS EMBRAIDS
NO DEBONAIR
NS BRANDIES
BRANDISE
SS SEABIRDS
SIDEBARS
ST BARDIEST
BRAIDEST
RABIDEST
TRIBADES
SW BAWDRIES
DAWBRIES
TV VIBRATED

ABEILS 188
(ISABEL)
AL ISABELLA
SAILABLE
AN BANALISE
AR RAISABLE
AT BALISTAE
LABIATES
SATIABLE
BH BABELISH
BM BABELISM
BR SLABBIER
BT BISTABLE
CL ICEBALLS
CM ALEMBICS
CO SOCIABLE
CR CALIBERS
CALIBRES
DD DISABLED
DE ABSEILED
DH DISHABLE
DP PIEBALDS
DR RAILBEDS
DS DISABLES
DU AUDIBLES
EF FEASIBLE
EM BELAMIES
ET SEABLITE
EV EVASIBLE
EZ SEIZABLE
SIZEABLE
FG FILABEGS
FH FISHABLE
FR BARFLIES
FU FABULISE
FY FEASIBLY
GN SINGABLE
HR BLASHIER
IL BAILLIES
IR BISERIAL
IT ALBITISE
SIBILATE
KN BLANKIES
KS KISSABLE
KT BALKIEST
LO ISOLABLE
LOBELIAS
LR BALLSIER
LIBERALS
LT BASTILLE
MN BAILSMEN
MR REMBLAIS
MS MISSABLE
MT BALMIEST
TIMBALES
NP BIPLANES
NR RINSABLE
NS ALBINESS
LESBIANS
NT INSTABLE
NU SABULINE
PS PASSIBLE
PT EPIBLAST
RT LIBRATES
TABLIERS
ST ASTILBES
BESTIALS
STABILES
SU ISSUABLE
SUASIBLE
TU SUITABLE
TY BEASTILY
UX BISEXUAL
VV BIVALVES

ABELRT 207
(ALBERT)
AC BRACTEAL
AD TRADABLE
AE RATEABLE
TEARABLE
AG GLABRATE
AS ARBALEST
AY BETRAYAL
RATEABLY
CE BRACELET
CO BROCATEL
CT BRACTLET
DI LIBRATED
DT BRATTLED
EI LIBERATE
EM ATREMBLE
EN RENTABLE
ES BLEAREST
BLEATERS
RETABLES
ET BATTELER
EU BATELEUR
BLEUATRE
HL BETHRALL
HS BLATHERS
HALBERTS
IP PARTIBLE
IS LIBRATES
TABLIERS
IW WRITABLE
MS LAMBERTS
NS BRANTLES
OP PORTABLE
OS BLOATERS
SORTABLE
STORABLE
PU PUBERTAL
RU BARRULET
SS BLASTERS
STABLERS
ST BATTLERS
BLATTERS
BRATTLES
SU BALUSTER
SW BLEWARTS
TU BURLETTA
REBUTTAL

ABEORS 144
(ABORES)
AD SEABOARD
AT RABATOES
BD ABSORBED
BL BELABORS
BR ABSORBER
REABSORB
CD BROCADES
CG BROCAGES
CH BROACHES
CI AEROBICS
CM CRAMBOES
CN BACONERS
CU CORBEAUS
DD ADSORBED
DN BANDORES
BROADENS
DR BOARDERS
DT BROADEST
DW SOWBREAD
EL EARLOBES
EN SEABORNE
ET REBATOES
FR FORBEARS
GK BROKAGES
GROSBEAK
GO BARGOOSE
HJ JOBSHARE
HT BATHORSE
IN BARONIES
IS ISOBARES
IT SABOTIER
KO ABROOKES
LT BLOATERS
SORTABLE
STORABLE
LU RUBEOLAS
LV ABSOLVER
MR EMBRASOR
MT BROMATES
MU AMBEROUS
NN BARONNES
NS BARONESS
NT BARONETS
PS SAPROBES
PT PROBATES
QU BAROQUES
RS BRASEROS
RT ARBORETS
TABORERS
ST BOASTERS
SORBATES
SY ROSEBAYS
TT ABETTORS
BATTEROS
TABORETS
TU SABOTEUR

ABERST 122
(BREAST)
AC ABREACTS
CABARETS
AL ARBALEST
AN ANTBEARS
RATSBANE
AO RABATOES
AT RABATTES
TABARETS
AU ABATURES
BD DRABBEST
DRABBETS
BS STABBERS
CE ACERBEST
CH BRACHETS
CK BRACKETS
DE BETREADS
BREASTED
DEBATERS
DH BREADTHS
DI BARDIEST
BRAIDEST
RABIDEST
TRIBADES
DN BANDSTER
DO BROADEST
DS DABSTERS
DU SURBATED
DW BEDSTRAW
DY DRYBEATS
EG ABSTERGE
EH BREATHES
HARTBEES
EK BESTREAK
EL BLEAREST
BLEATERS
RETABLES
EO REBATOES
ER REBATERS
TABRERES
TEREBRAS
ET ABETTERS
EU SUBERATE
GH BARGHEST
GN BANGSTER
GS BARGESTS
HL BLATHERS
HALBERTS
HO BATHORSE
HS BRASHEST
IK BARKIEST
BRAKIEST
BREASKIT
IL LIBRATES
TABLIERS
IM BARMIEST
IN ATEBRINS
BANISTER
IO SABOTIER
IR ARBITERS
RAREBITS
IT BIRETTAS
IV VIBRATES
IW WARBIEST
IY BESTIARY
SYBARITE
KY BASKETRY
LM LAMBERTS
LN BRANTLES
LO BLOATERS
SORTABLE
STORABLE
LS BLASTERS
STABLERS
LT BATTLERS
BLATTERS
BRATTLES
LU BALUSTER
LW BLEWARTS
MO BROMATES
NO BARONETS
NU UNBRASTE
URBANEST
OP PROBATES
OR ARBORETS
TABORERS
OS BOASTERS
SORBATES
OT ABETTORS
BATTEROS
TABORETS
OU SABOTEUR
SS BRASSETS
SU ABSTRUSE
SURBATES
SW WABSTERS
TU ABUTTERS

ACDERS 240
(SACRED)
AC CARCASED
AH CHARADES
AL CALDERAS
AP SCARPAED
AT CADASTRE
AV CADAVERS
BB SCRABBED
BI ASCRIBED
CARBIDES
BK REDBACKS
BM SCRAMBED
BO BROCADES
BU CUDBEARS
CE ACCEDERS
CU ACCURSED
CARDECUS

DL CLADDERS
DU ADDUCERS
CRUSADED
EE DECREASE
EF DEFACERS
FRESCADE
EH SEARCHED
EI DECIARES
EK SCREAKED
EL DECLARES
RESCALED
EM SCREAMED
EN ASCENDER
REASCEND
EP ESCARPED
ER SCAREDER
ES CARESSED
ET CEDRATES
FU SURFACED
GG SCRAGGED
GI DISGRACE
GO CORDAGES
HI RACHIDES
HL CHALDERS
HP SCARPHED
HT STARCHED
IL DECRIALS
RADICELS
RADICLES
IO IDOCRASE
IP EPACRIDS
IS SIDECARS
IT ACRIDEST
IU DECURIAS
LS SCALDERS
LW SCRAWLED
LY SACREDLY
MM SCRAMMED
MO COMRADES
MW SCRAWMED
NO DRACONES
ENDOSARC
NT CANTREDS
NU DURANCES
OR CORRADES
OS SARCODES
OT REDCOATS
OU CAROUSED
PP SCRAPPED
RU CRUSADER
SU CRUSADES
TT DETRACTS
SCRATTED
TU TRADUCES

ACEILR 121
(LACIER)
AT TAILRACE
AV CAVALIER
BB BARBICEL
BD CALIBRED
BK CRABLIKE
BL CRIBELLA
BO ALBICORE
CABRIOLE
BS CALIBERS
CALIBRES
CE CELERIAC
CL CLERICAL
CV CERVICAL
DF FRICADEL
DH HERALDIC
DP PLACIDER
DS DECRIALS
RADICELS
RADICLES
DT ARTICLED
DU AURICLED
RADICULE
EH LEACHIER
EN CINEREAL
RELIANCE
ES ESCALIER
EV RECEIVAL
FS FILACERS
GG CLAGGIER
GL ALLERGIC
GN CLEARING
GS GLACIERS
GV CLAVIGER
GY GLYCERIA
HK CHALKIER
HACKLIER
HO HALICORE
HEROICAL
HP PARHELIC
HS CHARLIES
IN IRENICAL
KT TALCKIER
KY CREAKILY
LM MICELLAR
MILLRACE
LO ROCAILLE
LP CALLIPER
LV CAVILLER
MM CLAMMIER
MS CLAIMERS
MIRACLES
RECLAIMS
MT METRICAL
NN ENCRINAL
NO ACROLEIN
CREOLIAN
LONICERA
NS CARLINES
NT CLARINET
OP CAPRIOLE
OR CARRIOLE
OS CALORIES
CARIOLES
OT EROTICAL
LORICATE
OV ARVICOLE
PS CALIPERS
REPLICAS
SPIRACLE
PT PARTICLE
PRELATIC
PU PECULIAR
RT CLARTIER
RW CRAWLIER
SS CLASSIER
ST ALTRICES
ARTICLES
RECITALS
SELICTAR
SU AURICLES
SV CALIVERS
CLAVIERS
VISCERAL
TT TRACTILE
TV VERTICAL
TY LITERACY

ACEINR 65
(CANIER)
AB CARABINE
AD CANARIED
RADIANCE
AG CANAIGRE
AS CANARIES
AT CARINATE
AV VARIANCE
BS CARBINES
CH CHANCIER
CHICANER
CN CANCRINE
DD CANDIDER
RIDDANCE
DE DERACINE
DH INARCHED
DI ACRIDINE
DN CRANNIED
DR RANCIDER
DT CRINATED
DICENTRA
EL CINEREAL
RELIANCE
EN NARCEINE
ES CINEREAS
INCREASE
RESIANCE
ET CENTIARE
CREATINE
INCREATE
ITERANCE
FG REFACING
FS FANCIERS
FX CARNIFEX
GH REACHING
GK CREAKING
GL CLEARING
GM AMERCING
CREAMING
GN ENRACING
GP CAPERING
PEARCING
PREACING
GS CREASING
GRECIANS
SEARCING
GT CATERING
CITRANGE
CREATING
REACTING
HM CHAIRMEN
HS INARCHES
HV VACHERIN
IL IRENICAL
IS RIANCIES
JR JERRICAN
KK KNACKIER
KR CRANKIER
LN ENCRINAL
LO ACROLEIN
CREOLIAN
LONICERA
LS CARLINES
LT CLARINET
MO CORAMINE
MS CARMINES
MU MANICURE
NS CRANNIES
OP APOCRINE
CAPONIER
PROCAINE
OS SCENARIO
OT ANORETIC
CREATION
REACTION
OV VERONICA
OX ANOREXIC
RU CURARINE
RY CINERARY
SS ARSENICS
CERASINS
RACINESS
ST CANISTER
CARNIEST
CISTERNA
CREATINS
NACRITES
SCANTIER
TT INTERACT
TV NAVICERT
TX XERANTIC
VY VICENARY

ACEINS 119
(INCASE)
AD AIDANCES
AL CANALISE
AM AMNESIAC
AR CANARIES
AT ESTANCIA
BR CARBINES
BT CABINETS
CG ACCINGES
CH CHICANES
CL CALCINES
SCENICAL
CO COCAINES
CV VACCINES
DH ECHIDNAS
INCHASED
DI SCIAENID
DO DIOCESAN
OCEANIDS
DS ACIDNESS
DT DISTANCE
DY CYANIDES
CYANISED
EF FAIENCES
FIANCEES
EG AGENCIES
EL SALIENCE
EP SAPIENCE
ER CINEREAS
INCREASE
RESIANCE
ET CINEASTE
EU EUCAINES
FF CAFFEINS
FN FINANCES
FR FANCIERS
FS FASCINES
FT FANCIEST
GN ENCASING
GO COINAGES
GP ESCAPING
GR CREASING
GRECIANS
SEARCING
GS CAGINESS
CEASINGS
HH HAINCHES
HM MACHINES
HN ENCHAINS
HR INARCHES
HS INCHASES
HT ASTHENIC
CHANTIES
HY HYACINES
SYNECHIA
IL SALICINE
IP PISCINAE
IR RIANCIES
IT CANITIES
KP CAPESKIN
LM MESCALIN
LP CAPELINS
PANICLES
PELICANS
LR CARLINES
LS SANICLES
LU AESCULIN
LUNACIES
LY SALIENCY
MP PEMICANS
MR CARMINES
MS AMNESICS
MT SEMANTIC
MU SEMUNCIA
MY SYCAMINE
NO CANONISE
NP PINNACES
NR CRANNIES
NT ANCIENTS
CANNIEST
INSTANCE
NU NUISANCE
NY CYANINES
OP CANOPIES
CAPONISE
PAEONICS
OR SCENARIO
OT ACONITES
CANOEIST
PS INSCAPES
PINCASES
RS ARSENICS
CERASINS
RACINESS
RT CANISTER
CARNIEST
CISTERNA
CREATINS
NACRITES
SCANTIER
ST CINEASTS
SCANTIES
SU ISSUANCE
SY CYANISES
TT CANTIEST
NICTATES
TETANICS
TV CISTVAEN
VESICANT
TY CYANITES
YZ CYANIZES

ACELST 243
(CASTLE)
AA CATALASE
AE ESCALATE
AH ALCAHEST
AI SALICETA
AL CASTELLA
LACTEALS
AN ANALECTS
AO CATALOES
AP PLACATES
AS LACTASES
AT LACTATES
AY CATALYSE
BK BLACKEST
BO OBSTACLE
CH CLATCHES
CI CALCITES
CO CACOLETS
DI CITADELS
DIALECTS
DN SCANTLED
DU CAULDEST
SULCATED
EH CHELATES
EN CLEANEST
LATENCES
EP CAPELETS
ER CLEAREST
SCELERAT
TREACLES
ES CELESTAS
ET TELECAST
FK FLACKETS
GI GELASTIC
GO CATELOGS
HH HATCHELS
HI ETHICALS
HK HACKLETS
HM CHAMLETS
HN STANCHEL
HO CATHOLES
ESCHALOT
HP CHAPLETS
HR ARCHLETS
HS SATCHELS
SLATCHES
HT CHATTELS
LATCHETS
HY CHASTELY
II CILIATES
SILICATE
IM CALMIEST
CLEMATIS
CLIMATES
METICALS
IO ALOETICS
COALIEST
SOCIETAL
IP PLICATES
IR ALTRICES
ARTICLES
RECITALS
SELICTAR
IS ELASTICS
SALICETS
SCALIEST
IT LATTICES
TALCIEST
IY CLAYIEST

KP PLACKETS
KR TACKLERS
KS SLACKEST
LO COLLATES
LU SCUTELLA
MO CAMELOTS
MOLECAST
MU CALUMETS
MUSCATEL
NO LACTONES
NP CLAPNETS
NS SCANTLES
NT CANTLETS
NY SECANTLY
OP POLECATS
OR SECTORAL
OS ALECOSTS
COATLESS
LACTOSES
SCATOLES
OT CALOTTES
OU LACTEOUS
LOCUSTAE
OSCULATE
OY ACOLYTES
PR SCEPTRAL
SPECTRAL
RS SCARLETS
RT CLATTERS
SCRATTLE
RU RAUCLEST
ST TACTLESS
SY SCYTALES

ACENRS 175
(CANERS)
AG CARNAGES
CRANAGES
AI CANARIES
AP PANCREAS
AT CANASTER
CATERANS
BH BRANCHES
BI CARBINES
BK BRACKENS
BO BACONERS
BU UNBRACES
CE CREANCES
CH CHANCERS
CHANCRES
CRANCHES
CO CONACRES
DE ASCENDER
REASCEND
DO DRACONES
ENDOSARC
DT CANTREDS
DU DURANCES
EE ENCREASE
EG ENGRACES
EH ENARCHES
EI CINEREAS
INCREASE
RESIANCE
EL CLEANERS
CLEANSER
EM MENACERS
EN NARCEENS
ES CASERNES
ET CENTARES
REASCENT
SARCENET
FI FANCIERS
FT CANTREFS
FU FURNACES
GH CHANGERS
GI CREASING
GRECIANS
SEARCING
GL CLANGERS
GM CRAGSMEN
GO ACROGENS
CORNAGES
HI INARCHES
HL CHARNELS
HM ENCHARMS
HN CHANNERS
HR RANCHERS
HS ARCHNESS
HT CHANTERS
SNATCHER
STANCHER
TRANCHES
HU RAUNCHES
II RIANCIES
IL CARLINES
IM CARMINES
IN CRANNIES
IO SCENARIO
IS ARSENICS
CERASINS
RACINESS
IT CANISTER
CARNIEST
CISTERNA
CREATINS
NACRITES
SCANTIER
KK KNACKERS
KL CRANKLES
KP PRANCKES
LN SCRANNEL
LU LUCARNES
MO CREMONAS
ROMANCES
NS SCANNERS
OS COARSENS
NARCOSES
OT ANCESTOR
ENACTORS
SORTANCE
OU CARNEOUS
NACREOUS
PR PRANCERS
PU ENCARPUS
PRAUNCES
ST CRANTSES
SU SURANCES
TT TRANECTS
TRANSECT
TU CENTAURS
RECUSANT
UNCRATES
UNTRACES
TY ANCESTRY

ACENRT 96
(CANTER)
AC CARCANET
AI CARINATE
AL LACERANT
AS CANASTER
CATERANS
AT REACTANT
AY CATENARY
BE CABERNET
CO ACCENTOR
DE CANTERED
CRENATED
DECANTER
NECTARED
RECANTED
DI CRINATED
DICENTRA
DO CARTONED
DS CANTREDS
DU UNCARTED
UNCRATED
UNDERACT
UNTRACED
EI CENTIARE
CREATINE
INCREATE
ITERANCE
EN ENTRANCE
EO CAROTENE
EP PERCEANT
ER RECANTER
RECREANT
ES CENTARES
REASCENT
SARCENET
EU ENACTURE
UNCREATE
FP PENCRAFT
FS CANTREFS
GI CATERING
CITRANGE
CREATING
REACTING
HH ETHNARCH
HM MERCHANT
HO ANCHORET
HP PENTARCH
HS CHANTERS
SNATCHER
STANCHER
TRANCHES
HT TRANCHET
HU CHAUNTER
IL CLARINET
IO ANORETIC
CREATION
REACTION
IS CANISTER
CARNIEST
CISTERNA
CREATINS
NACRITES
SCANTIER
IT INTERACT
IV NAVICERT
IX XERANTIC
KM TRACKMEN
OO CORONATE
OP PORTANCE
OS ANCESTOR
ENACTORS
SORTANCE
OT CONTRATE
OU COURANTE
OUTRANCE
SS CRANTSES
ST TRANECTS
TRANSECT
SU CENTAURS
RECUSANT
UNCRATES
UNTRACES
SY ANCESTRY
TU TRUNCATE
UY CENTAURY
CYANURET

ACENST 149
(STANCE)
AI ESTANCIA
AL ANALECTS
AM CAMSTANE
AP PASTANCE
AR CANASTER
CATERANS
AT CANTATES
CASTANET
AY CYANATES
BI CABINETS
CE ACESCENT
CO COSECANT
DH SNATCHED
STANCHED
DI DISTANCE
DL SCANTLED
DN SCANDENT
DP PANDECTS
DR CANTREDS
DS DESCANTS
EG CENTAGES
EI CINEASTE
EL CLEANEST
LATENCES
EM CASEMENT
EN CANTEENS
EO ACETONES
NOTECASE
ER CENTARES
REASCENT
SARCENET
FI FANCIEST
FR CANTREFS
GO COGNATES
HI ASTHENIC
CHANTIES
HL STANCHEL
HM MANCHETS
HN ENCHANTS
HR CHANTERS
SNATCHER
STANCHER
TRANCHES
HS CHASTENS
SNATCHES
STANCHES
HT ETCHANTS
HU NAUTCHES
UNCHASTE
HY CHANTEYS
HZ SCHANTZE
II CANITIES
IM SEMANTIC
IN ANCIENTS
CANNIEST
INSTANCE
IO ACONITES
CANOEIST
IR CANISTER
CARNIEST
CISTERNA
CREATINS
NACRITES
SCANTIER
IS CINEASTS
SCANTIES
IT CANTIEST
NICTATES
TETANICS
IV CISTVAEN
VESICANT
IY CYANITES
JO JACONETS
JU JUNCATES
KM TACKSMEN
LO LACTONES
LP CLAPNETS
LS SCANTLES
LT CANTLETS
LY SECANTLY
MO CAMSTONE
OP CAPSTONE
OR ANCESTOR
ENACTORS
SORTANCE
OS CONTESSA
COSTEANS
OT CONSTATE
OV CENTAVOS
PT PENTACTS
RS CRANTSES
RT TRANECTS
TRANSECT
RU CENTAURS
RECUSANT
UNCRATES
UNTRACES
RY ANCESTRY
ST SCANTEST
SU NUTCASES
SW NEWSCAST

ACEORS 103
(ORACES)
AS ROSACEAS
AU ARACEOUS
BD BROCADES
BG BROCAGES
BH BROACHES
BI AEROBICS
BM CRAMBOES
BN BACONERS
BU CORBEAUS
CH CAROCHES
COACHERS
CL CORACLES
CN CONACRES
CS ARCCOSES
CT ECTOSARC
DG CORDAGES
DI IDOCRASE
DM COMRADES
DN DRACONES
ENDOSARC
DR CORRADES
DS SARCODES
DT REDCOATS
DU CAROUSED
EL ESCAROLE
EM RACEMOSE
ET CREASOTE
FF AFFORCES
FL ALFRESCO
FR FORECARS
FT FORECAST
FX CARFOXES
GK CORKAGES
GM SCARMOGE
GN ACROGENS
CORNAGES
GO CARGOOSE
GS CORSAGES
SOCAGERS
GT ESCARGOT
GU COURAGES
HL CHOLERAS
CHORALES
HP POACHERS
HR HORSECAR
HT CHAROSET
THORACES
IL CALORIES
CARIOLES
IN SCENARIO
IV COVARIES
VARICOSE
JL CAJOLERS
KL EARLOCKS
KR CROAKERS
KW CASEWORK
LL CORELLAS
LM CAROMELS
SCLEROMA
LP PARCLOSE
POLACRES
LS ESCOLARS
LACROSSE
LT SECTORAL
LU CAROUSEL
LY CALOYERS
COARSELY
MN CREMONAS
ROMANCES
MO ACROSOME
MP COMPARES
COMPEARS
MESOCARP
MY SYCAMORE
NS COARSENS
NARCOSES
NT ANCESTOR
ENACTORS
SORTANCE
NU CARNEOUS
NACREOUS
PP COPPERAS
PX EXOCARPS
RT ACROTERS
CREATORS
REACTORS
RU CAROUSER
ST COARSEST
COASTERS
SU CAROUSES

TT SECTATOR
TU OUTRACES
TV OVERACTS
OVERCAST
TX EXACTORS

ACEOST 146
(ACTOSE)
AK OATCAKES
AL CATALOES
AS SEACOAST
BI ICEBOATS
BL OBSTACLE
CD ACCOSTED
CL CACOLETS
CN COSECANT
CR ECTOSARC
DH CATHODES
DK STOCKADE
DR REDCOATS
DT CODETTAS
COSTATED
EN ACETONES
NOTECASE
ER CREASOTE
ET ECOSTATE
EV EVOCATES
FG GEOFACTS
FP POSTFACE
FR FORECAST
FU OUTFACES
GL CATELOGS
GN COGNATES
GR ESCARGOT
GT COTTAGES
HI TOISEACH
HL CATHOLES
ESCHALOT
HR CHAROSET
THORACES
HU CATHOUSE
SOUTACHE
HY CHAYOTES
IL ALOETICS
COALIEST
SOCIETAL
IN ACONITES
CANOEIST
IP ECTOPIAS
IS SOCIATES
IT OSCITATE
JN JACONETS
LL COLLATES
LM CAMELOTS
MOLECAST
LN LACTONES
LP POLECATS
LR SECTORAL
LS ALECOSTS
COATLESS
LACTOSES
SCATOLES
LT CALOTTES
LU LACTEOUS
LOCUSTAE
OSCULATE
LY ACOLYTES
MN CAMSTONE
MO COMATOSE
NP CAPSTONE
NR ANCESTOR
ENACTORS
SORTANCE
NS CONTESSA
COSTEANS
NT CONSTATE
NV CENTAVOS
PU OUTPACES
RR ACROTERS
CREATORS
REACTORS
RS COARSEST
COASTERS
RT SECTATOR
RU OUTRACES
RV OVERACTS
OVERCAST
RX EXACTORS
TU OUTCASTE
UU AUTOCUES

ACERST 141
(CATERS)
AB ABREACTS
CABARETS
AD CADASTRE
AF SEACRAFT
AG CARTAGES
AN CANASTER
CATERANS
AP CAPRATES
AT CASTRATE
BE ACERBEST
BH BRACHETS
BK BRACKETS
CE ACCRETES
CH CATCHERS
CRATCHES
CO ECTOSARC
CR CARRECTS
CS SCARCEST
DE CEDRATES
DH STARCHED
DI ACRIDEST
DN CANTREDS
DO REDCOATS
DT DETRACTS
SCRATTED
DU TRADUCES
EH CHEATERS
HECTARES
RECHATES
RECHEATS
TEACHERS
EL CLEAREST
SCELERAT
TREACLES
EM CREMATES
MEERCATS
EN CENTARES
REASCENT
SARCENET
EO CREASOTE
ER CATERERS
RETRACES
TERRACES
ES CATERESS
CERASTES
EX EXACTERS
FH FRATCHES
FN CANTREFS
FO FORECAST
FR REFRACTS
FU FACTURES
GI AGRESTIC
GO ESCARGOT
GU TRUCAGES
HH HATCHERS
HI CHARIEST
THERIACS
HL ARCHLETS
HM MATCHERS
HN CHANTERS
SNATCHER
STANCHER
TRANCHES
HO CHAROSET
THORACES
HP CHAPTERS
PATCHERS
HR CHARTERS
RECHARTS
STARCHER
HS STARCHES
HT CHATTERS
RATCHETS
HW WATCHERS
HY YACHTERS
IL ALTRICES
ARTICLES
RECITALS
SELICTAR
IM CERAMIST
MATRICES
IN CANISTER
CARNIEST
CISTERNA
CREATINS
NACRITES
SCANTIER
IP CRAPIEST
CRISPATE
PICRATES
PRACTISE
IR ERRATICS
IS SCARIEST
IT CITRATES
CRISTATE
SCATTIER
IU SURICATE
IZ CRAZIEST
JM SCRAMJET
JT TRAJECTS
KL TACKLERS
KR TRACKERS
KS STACKERS
KT RACKETTS
KU RUCKSEAT
LO SECTORAL
LP SCEPTRAL
SPECTRAL
LS SCARLETS
LT CLATTERS
SCRATTLE
LU RAUCLEST
MP CRAMPETS
NO ANCESTOR
ENACTORS
SORTANCE
NS CRANTSES
NT TRANECTS
TRANSECT
NU CENTAURS
RECUSANT
UNCRATES
UNTRACES
NY ANCESTRY
OR ACROTERS
CREATORS
REACTORS
OS COARSEST
COASTERS
OT SECTATOR
OU OUTRACES
OV OVERACTS
OVERCAST
OX EXACTORS
PU CAPTURES
PRESCUTA
QU RACQUETS
RT RETRACTS
SS CRASSEST
ST SCATTERS
TT TETRACTS
TU CRUSTATE
TX EXTRACTS
TY SCATTERY

ACIRST 245
(ARTICS)
AH ARCHAIST
CITHARAS
AN ARCANIST
AT CASTRATI
AZ CZARITSA
BD CATBIRDS
BI TRIBASIC
BT ABSTRICT
CO ACROSTIC
CP PRACTICS
CY SCARCITY
DE ACRIDEST
DI ARCTIIDS
CARDITIS
DP ADSCRIPT
DS DRASTICS
DT DISTRACT
EG AGRESTIC
EH CHARIEST
THERIACS
EL ALTRICES
ARTICLES
RECITALS
SELICTAR
EM CERAMIST
MATRICES
EN CANISTER
CARNIEST
CISTERNA
CREATINS
NACRITES
SCANTIER
EP CRAPIEST
CRISPATE
PICRATES
PRACTISE
ER ERRATICS
ES SCARIEST
ET CITRATES
CRISTATE
SCATTIER
EU SURICATE
EZ CRAZIEST
FF TRAFFICS
FN INFARCTS
INFRACTS
GN SCARTING
TRACINGS
GO ORGASTIC
HI RACHITIS
HM CHARTISM
HO CHARIOTS
HARICOTS
HR TRIARCHS
HT CHARTIST
STRAICHT
HU HAIRCUTS
IM SCIMITAR
IO AORISTIC
IT ARTISTIC
TRIATICS
KP PATRICKS
LO CALORIST
LU CURTAILS
RUSTICAL
MO ACROTISM
MP CRAMPITS
PTARMICS
NO CANTORIS
CAROTINS
NP CANTRIPS
NU CURTAINS
SATURNIC
TURACINS
OP APRICOTS
PISCATOR
OT RICOTTAS
QU QUARTICS
SS SACRISTS
ST ASTRICTS
SW TWISCARS
SY SACRISTY
SZ CZARISTS

ADEERS 70
(SEARED)
AP PASEARED
BI BEARDIES
BL BEDERALS
BM EMBREADS
BP BESPREAD
BS DEBASERS
BT BETREADS
BREASTED
DEBATERS
CC ACCEDERS
CE DECREASE
CF DEFACERS
FRESCADE
CH SEARCHED
CI DECIARES
CK SCREAKED
CL DECLARES
RESCALED
CM SCREAMED
CN ASCENDER
REASCEND
CP ESCARPED
CR SCAREDER
CS CARESSED
CT CEDRATES
DG DEGRADES
DH REDHEADS
DR DREADERS
DW SAWDERED
EG DEGREASE
EL RELEASED
RESEALED
EN ENSEARED
SERENADE
EP RAPESEED
ER ARREEDES
ET RESEATED
FI FEDARIES
FL FEDERALS
FP PREFADES
FT DRAFTEES
GI DISAGREE
GN DERANGES
GRANDEES
GRENADES
GP ASPERGED
PRESAGED
GR REGRADES
GS DRESSAGE
GT RESTAGED
GU GUARDEES
GW RAGWEEDS
HH REHASHED
HL ASHLERED
HO SOREHEAD
HP EPHEDRAS
RESHAPED
HR ADHERERS
REDSHARE
HT HEADREST
HW WASHERED
IJ JADERIES
IL REALISED
SIDEREAL
IM MADERISE
IN ARSENIDE
DENARIES
DRAISENE
NEARSIDE
IP AIRSPEED
IT READIEST
SERIATED
SIDERATE
STEADIER
IV READVISE
KN KNEADERS
KT STREAKED
LL SARDELLE
LM DEMERSAL
EMERALDS
LP PLEADERS
RELAPSED
LT TREADLES
LV SLAVERED
LW LEEWARDS
LY DELAYERS
MN AMENDERS
MEANDERS
REAMENDS
MO SEADROME
MR DREAMERS
MT MASTERED
STREAMED
MU MEASURED

NN ENSNARED
NO REASONED
NS DEARNESS
NU UNDERSEA
NW ANSWERED
OW OARWEEDS
PR SPREADER
PS ASPERSED
PREASSED
REPASSED
PT PEDERAST
PREDATES
REPASTED
TRAPESED
PU PERSUADE
PV DEPRAVES
PERVADES
PW PERSWADE
PZ SPREAZED
RT ARRESTED
DREAREST
RETREADS
SERRATED
TREADERS
RV ADVERSER
ST ASSERTED
ESTRADES
TT ASTERTED
RESTATED
TW DEWATERS
TARWEEDS
WASTERED
TY ESTRAYED

ADEEST 85
(SEATED)
AC ESTACADE
BD BEDSTEAD
BESTADDE
BH BETHESDA
BI BEADIEST
DIABETES
BN ABSENTED
BR BETREADS
BREASTED
DEBATERS
BS BASSETED
BESTEADS
CH DETACHES
CP ASPECTED
CR CEDRATES
CU EDUCATES
DI STEADIED
DL DESALTED
DO DEODATES
EL TEASELED
ER RESEATED
FL DEFLATES
FN FASTENED
FR DRAFTEES
GO DOGEATES
GR RESTAGED
GT GESTATED
HH SHEATHED
HI ATHEISED
HEADIEST
HN HASTENED
HR HEADREST
HS HEADSETS
IJ JADEITES
IL LEADIEST
IM MEDIATES
IN ANDESITE
IR READIEST
SERIATED
SIDERATE
STEADIER
IS STEADIES
IV DEVIATES
SEDATIVE
KN NAKEDEST
KR STREAKED
LM MEDALETS
LO DESOLATE
LP PEDESTAL
LR TREADLES
LS DATELESS
TASSELED
LY SEDATELY
MN STAMENED
MP STAMPEDE
STEPDAME
MR MASTERED
STREAMED
MW MATWEEDS
NO ENDOSTEA
NS ASSENTED
STANDEES
NU UNSEATED
PR PEDERAST
PREDATES
REPASTED
TRAPESED
PS STAPEDES
PT ADEPTEST
RR ARRESTED
DREAREST
RETREADS
SERRATED
TREADERS
RS ASSERTED
ESTRADES
RT ASTERTED
RESTATED
RW DEWATERS
TARWEEDS
WASTERED
RY ESTRAYED
ST SEDATEST
TT ATTESTED
UX EXUDATES

ADEGLN 197
(DANGLE)
AH DANELAGH
AM MAGDALEN
AS SELADANG
BI BLINDAGE
BR BRANGLED
DE DANEGELD
DS GLADDENS
EO ENGAOLED
ER ENLARGED
LARGENED
ET DANEGELT
FI FINAGLED
HI HEALDING
HO HEADLONG
II GLIADINE
IM MALIGNED
MEDALING
IO GALENOID
IP PEDALING
PLEADING
IR DANGLIER
DEARLING
DRAGLINE
IS DEALINGS
LEADINGS
SIGNALED
IT DELATING
IY DELAYING
LU GLANDULE
UNGALLED
OY GONDELAY
PS SPANGLED
RS DANGLERS
GLANDERS
RW WRANGLED
SS GLADNESS
TW TWANGLED
UZ UNGLAZED

ADEGNR 126
(DANGER)
AI AREADING
DRAINAGE
GARDENIA
AR ARRANGED
BI BEARDING
BREADING
BL BRANGLED
BO BONDAGER
CE ENGRACED
CU UNGRACED
DE DANGERED
DERANGED
GARDENED
DI DREADING
DU UNGRADED
EE RENEGADE
EI REGAINED
EL ENLARGED
LARGENED
EM GENDARME
EN ENDANGER
ENRANGED
EO RENEGADO
ER GARDENER
GARNERED
ES DERANGES
GRANDEES
GRENADES
EU DUNGAREE
RENAGUED
UNGEARED
EV ENGRAVED
FO FRONDAGE
HI ADHERING
HEADRING
HT THRANGED
IK DAKERING
IL DANGLIER
DEARLING
DRAGLINE
IM DREAMING
MARGINED
IN GRANNIED
IO ORGANDIE
IR DREARING
IS DERAIGNS
GRADINES
READINGS
IT DERATING
GRADIENT
REDATING
TREADING
IY DERAYING
READYING
YEARDING
JO JARGONED
LS DANGLERS
GLANDERS
LW WRANGLED
MS DRAGSMEN
NO ANDROGEN
DRAGONNE
OT DRAGONET
RU GRANDEUR
ST DRAGNETS
GRANDEST
SU ENGUARDS
UU UNARGUED
UZ GAZUNDER
UNGRAZED

ADEGRS 221
(GRADES)
AF FARDAGES
AG AGGRADES
AH RAGHEADS
RHAGADES
AM MEGARADS
AT GRADATES
AV SAVEGARD
AY DRAYAGES
YARDAGES
BH BEGHARDS
BI ABRIDGES
BRIGADES
BL BELGARDS
BU SUBGRADE
CG SCRAGGED
CI DISGRACE
CO CORDAGES
DE DEGRADES
DI DISGRADE
EE DEGREASE
EI DISAGREE
EN DERANGES
GRANDEES
GRENADES
EP ASPERGED
PRESAGED
ER REGRADES
ES DRESSAGE
ET RESTAGED
EU GUARDEES
EW RAGWEEDS
GL DRAGGLES
GP SPRAGGED
HI GARISHED
HEADRIGS
IL SLAIRGED
IN DERAIGNS
GRADINES
READINGS
IP SPAIRGED
LN DANGLERS
GLANDERS
MN DRAGSMEN
MO ORGASMED
NT DRAGNETS
GRANDEST
NU ENGUARDS
OT GOADSTER
OW DOWAGERS
WORDAGES
PS SPADGERS
PU UPGRADES
RT DRAGSTER
SU GRADUSES

ADEILR 19
(RAILED)
AH HEADRAIL
RAILHEAD
AP PRAEDIAL
AS SALARIED
BC CALIBRED
BE RIDEABLE
BN BILANDER
BS RAILBEDS
BT LIBRATED
BV DRIVABLE
BY DIABLERY
CF FRICADEL
CH HERALDIC
CP PLACIDER
CS DECRIALS
RADICELS
RADICLES
CT ARTICLED
CU AURICLED
RADICULE
DE DEADLIER
DERAILED
REDIALED
DH DIHEDRAL
DS DIEDRALS
EL REALLIED
EM REMEDIAL
EP PEDALIER
ER DERAILER
RERAILED
ES REALISED
SIDEREAL
ET RETAILED
EZ REALIZED
FI AIRFIELD
FN FILANDER
FO FORELAID
GL GRILLADE
GN DANGLIER
DEARLING
DRAGLINE
GS SLAIRGED
HN HARDLINE
IP PERIDIAL
IS LAIRISED
IZ LAIRIZED
LO ARILLODE
LP PALLIDER
LS DALLIERS
DIALLERS
LT TRIALLED
LV RIVALLED
MP IMPARLED
MY DREAMILY
NN INLANDER
NS ISLANDER
OS DARIOLES
SOLIDARE
SOREDIAL
OT IDOLATER
TAILORED
OV OVERLAID
OX EXORDIAL
PS PEDRAILS
PREDIALS
PT DIPTERAL
TRIPEDAL
PU EPIDURAL
PV DEPRIVAL
RY DREARILY
ST DILATERS
LARDIEST
SU RESIDUAL
SY DIALYSER
TT DETRITAL
TY DIELYTRA
VY VARIEDLY
YZ DIALYZER

ADEILS 33
(LADIES)
AC ALCAIDES
SIDALCEA
AD ALIDADES
AM MALADIES
AP PALISADE
AR SALARIED
AS ASSAILED
AV VEDALIAS
BD DISABLED
BE ABSEILED
BH DISHABLE
BP PIEBALDS
BR RAILBEDS
BS DISABLES
BU AUDIBLES
CI LAICISED
CL CEDILLAS
CM CAMELIDS
DECIMALS
DECLAIMS
MEDICALS
CO COALISED
CP DISPLACE
CR DECRIALS
RADICELS
RADICLES
CT CITADELS
DIALECTS
DG GLADDIES
DN ISLANDED
LANDSIDE
DR DIEDRALS
DY DIALYSED
EH DEISHEAL
EI IDEALISE
EK LAKESIDE
EM LIMEADES
EN DELAINES
ER REALISED
SIDEREAL
ES DEISEALS
ET LEADIEST
EV DISLEAVE
EY EYELIADS

FG GADFLIES
GASFIELD
FH DEALFISH
FI LADIFIES
SALIFIED
FS DISLEAFS
FY LADYFIES
GL GALLISED
GN DEALINGS
LEADINGS
SIGNALED
GO GOLIASED
GR SLAIRGED
GS GLISSADE
GT GLADIEST
GV DISGAVEL
HP HELIPADS
HV LAVISHED
HW WHAISLED
IM IDEALISM
MILADIES
IR LAIRISED
IT IDEALIST
KW SIDEWALK
LP ILLAPSED
SPADILLE
LR DALLIERS
DIALLERS
LW SIDEWALL
MM DILEMMAS
MO DAMOISEL
MP IMPLEADS
MISPLEAD
MS MAIDLESS
MISDEALS
MISLEADS
MT MEDALIST
MISDEALT
MY DYSMELIA
NN ANNELIDS
LINDANES
NO NODALISE
NR ISLANDER
NU UNSAILED
NV ANDVILES
OP EPISODAL
OPALISED
SEPALOID
OR DARIOLES
SOLIDARE
SOREDIAL
OS ASSOILED
DEASOILS
OT DIASTOLE
ISOLATED
SODALITE
SOLIDATE
OU DOULEIAS
PR PEDRAILS
PREDIALS
PS DESPISAL
PT TALIPEDS
QU SQUAILED
RT DILATERS
LARDIEST
RU RESIDUAL
RY DIALYSER
SU DEASIULS
SV DEVISALS
SY DIALYSES
TV VALIDEST
TY DIASTYLE
STEADILY
UV DISVALUE
XY DYSLEXIA
YZ DIALYZES

ADEINR 4
(RAINED)

AC CANARIED
RADIANCE
AG AREADING
DRAINAGE
GARDENIA
AM MARINADE
AR DARRAINE
AS ARANEIDS
AT DENTARIA
RAINDATE
BD BRANDIED
BG BEARDING
BREADING
BL BILANDER
BM BRIDEMAN
BO DEBONAIR
BS BRANDIES
BRANDISE
CD CANDIDER
RIDDANCE
CE DERACINE
CH INARCHED
CI ACRIDINE
CN CRANNIED
CR RANCIDER
CT CRINATED
DICENTRA
DG DREADING
DO ORDAINED
DT INDARTED
EF FREDAINE
EG REGAINED
EM REMAINED
EP PINDAREE
ES ARSENIDE
DENARIES
DRAISENE
NEARSIDE
ET DETAINER
RETAINED
FL FILANDER
FR INFRARED
FS FRIANDES
FU UNFAIRED
GH ADHERING
HEADRING
GK DAKERING
GL DANGLIER
DEARLING
DRAGLINE
GM DREAMING
MARGINED
GN GRANNIED
GO ORGANDIE
GR DREARING
GS DERAIGNS
GRADINES
READINGS
GT DERATING
GRADIENT
REDATING
TREADING
GY DERAYING
READYING
YEARDING
HL HARDLINE
HU UNHAIRED
IM MERIDIAN
IS DRAISINE
IT DAINTIER
IU UREDINIA
LN INLANDER
LS ISLANDER
MR MANRIDER
MS ADERMINS
SIRNAMED
MY DAIRYMEN
MZ ZEMINDAR
NS INSNARED
NZ RENDZINA
OR ORDAINER
REORDAIN
OS ANEROIDS
DONARIES
OT AROINTED
DERATION
ORDINATE
RATIONED
OU DOUANIER
PS SPRAINED
PT DIPTERAN
PU UNPAIRED
UNREPAID
RS DRAINERS
SERRANID
SS ARIDNESS
SARDINES
ST DETRAINS
RANDIEST
STRAINED
SU DENARIUS
UNRAISED
URANIDES
SV INVADERS
SANDIVER
SY SYNEDRIA
TT NITRATED
TU DATURINE
INDURATE
RUINATED
URINATED
UV UNVARIED
VY VINEYARD

ADEINS 22
(SANDIE)

AC AIDANCES
AR ARANEIDS
BD SIDEBAND
BG BEADINGS
DEBASING
BH BANISHED
BR BRANDIES
BRANDISE
BT BANDIEST
BU UNBIASED
BW BEDAWINS
CH ECHIDNAS
INCHASED
CI SCIAENID
CO DIOCESAN
OCEANIDS
CS ACIDNESS
CT DISTANCE
CY CYANIDES
CYANISED
DL ISLANDED
LANDSIDE
DO ADENOIDS
ADONISED
ANODISED
DT DANDIEST
EL DELAINES
EM DEMAINES
INSEAMED
EN ADENINES
ANDESINE
ER ARSENIDE
DENARIES
DRAISENE
NEARSIDE
ES ANISEEDS
ET ANDESITE
FI SANIFIED
FR FRIANDES
GH HEADINGS
SHEADING
GL DEALINGS
LEADINGS
SIGNALED
GO AGONISED
DIAGNOSE
GR DERAIGNS
GRADINES
READINGS
GS ASSIGNED
GT SEDATING
STEADING
GW WINDAGES
HK SKINHEAD
HO ADHESION
HP DEANSHIP
PINHEADS
HS SHANDIES
HT HANDIEST
HV VANISHED
IN SANIDINE
IR DRAISINE
IT ADENITIS
DAINTIES
KY KYANISED
LN ANNELIDS
LINDANES
LO NODALISE
LR ISLANDER
LU UNSAILED
LV ANDVILES
MM MISNAMED
MO NOMADIES
NOMADISE
MR ADERMINS
SIRNAMED
MS SIDESMAN
MT MEDIANTS
TIDESMAN
MU MAUNDIES
MY DYNAMISE
NN NANDINES
NR INSNARED
NU UNSAINED
NX DISANNEX
OR ANEROIDS
DONARIES
OS ADONISES
ANODISES
OT ASTONIED
SEDATION
OX DIOXANES
OZ ADONIZES
ANODIZES
PR SPRAINED
PT DEPAINTS
PV SPAVINED
RR DRAINERS
SERRANID
RS ARIDNESS
SARDINES
RT DETRAINS
RANDIEST
STRAINED
RU DENARIUS
UNRAISED
URANIDES
RV INVADERS
SANDIVER
RY SYNEDRIA
ST SANDIEST
SV AVIDNESS
SW WINDASES
TT INSTATED
TU AUDIENTS
SINUATED
TV DEVIANTS
TY DESYATIN

ADEIRS 12
(RAISED)

AB ARABISED
AF FARADISE
SAFARIED
AH AIRHEADS
AL SALARIED
AN ARANEIDS
AP PARADISE
AT DATARIES
RADIATES
BC ASCRIBED
CARBIDES
BE BEARDIES
BG ABRIDGES
BRIGADES
BL RAILBEDS
BM EMBRAIDS
BN BRANDIES
BRANDISE
BS SEABIRDS
SIDEBARS
BT BARDIEST
BRAIDEST
RABIDEST
TRIBADES
BW BAWDRIES
DAWBRIES
CE DECIARES
CG DISGRACE
CH RACHIDES
CL DECRIALS
RADICELS
RADICLES
CO IDOCRASE
CP EPACRIDS
CS SIDECARS
CT ACRIDEST
CU DECURIAS
DG DISGRADE
DI DIARISED
DL DIEDRALS
DM DISARMED
MISDREAD
DO ROADSIDE
SIDEROAD
DP DISPREAD
DT DISRATED
DW SIDEWARD
EF FEDARIES
EG DISAGREE
EJ JADERIES
EL REALISED
SIDEREAL
EM MADERISE
EN ARSENIDE
DENARIES
DRAISENE
NEARSIDE
EP AIRSPEED
ET READIEST
SERIATED
SIDERATE
STEADIER
EV READVISE
FM MISFARED
FN FRIANDES
FO FORESAID
GH GARISHED
HEADRIGS
GL SLAIRGED
GN DERAIGNS
GRADINES
READINGS
GP SPAIRGED
HM MISHEARD
HP RAPHIDES
HS RADISHES
HT HAIRSTED
HARDIEST
HV RAVISHED
HW RAWHIDES
HY HAYRIDES
IL LAIRISED
IN DRAISINE
IP PRESIDIA
IS AIRSIDES
DIARISES
IT IRISATED
IZ DIARIZES
JM JEMIDARS
KT STRAIKED
LL DALLIERS
DIALLERS
LN ISLANDER
LO DARIOLES
SOLIDARE
SOREDIAL
LP PEDRAILS
PREDIALS
LT DILATERS
LARDIEST
LU RESIDUAL
LY DIALYSER
MM MERMAIDS
MN ADERMINS

SIRNAMED
MR ADMIRERS
DISARMER
MS MISREADS
SIDEARMS
MT MARDIEST
MISRATED
READMITS
NN INSNARED
NO ANEROIDS
DONARIES
NP SPRAINED
NR DRAINERS
SERRANID
NS ARIDNESS
SARDINES
NT DETRAINS
RANDIEST
STRAINED
NU DENARIUS
UNRAISED
URANIDES
NV INVADERS
SANDIVER
NY SYNEDRIA
OP DIASPORE
PARODIES
OT ASTEROID
PP APPRISED
DRAPPIES
PR DRAPIERS
PS DESPAIRS
PT DIPTERAS
RAPIDEST
SPIRATED
TARSIPED
TRAIPSED
PU UPRAISED
RW SWARDIER
ST ASTERIDS
DIASTERS
DISASTER
DISRATES
SU RADIUSES
SUDARIES
SV ADVISERS
TT STRAITED
STRIATED
TARDIEST
TW TAWDRIES

ADEIST 26
(IDATES)
AM DIASTEMA
AR DATARIES
RADIATES
AS DIASTASE
AT SATIATED
BE BEADIEST
DIABETES
BN BANDIEST
BP BAPTISED
BR BARDIEST
BRAIDEST
RABIDEST
TRIBADES
BS BASTIDES
BU DAUBIEST
BW BAWDIEST
CG CADGIEST
CH SCAITHED
CL CITADELS
DIALECTS
CN DISTANCE
CP SPICATED
CR ACRIDEST
CT DICTATES
DE STEADIED
DF FADDIEST
DM MISDATED
DN DANDIEST
DR DISRATED
EH ATHEISED
HEADIEST
EJ JADEITES
EL LEADIEST
EM MEDIATES
EN ANDESITE
ER READIEST
SERIATED
SIDERATE
STEADIER
ES STEADIES
EV DEVIATES
SEDATIVE
FF DAFFIEST
GG DAGGIEST
GL GLADIEST
GM SIGMATED
GN SEDATING
STEADING
GO GODETIAS
GU GAUDIEST
HH SHITHEAD
HK SKAITHED
HN HANDIEST
HP PITHEADS
SIDEPATH
HR HAIRSTED
HARDIEST
HS SHADIEST
IL IDEALIST
IN ADENITIS
DAINTIES
IP STAPEDII
IR IRISATED
KR STRAIKED
LM MEDALIST
MISDEALT
LO DIASTOLE
ISOLATED
SODALITE
SOLIDATE
LP TALIPEDS
LR DILATERS
LARDIEST
LV VALIDEST
LY DIASTYLE
STEADILY
MM MISMATED
MN MEDIANTS
TIDESMAN
MO ATOMISED
MP DAMPIEST
IMPASTED
MR MARDIEST
MISRATED
READMITS
MS MISDATES
MU TAEDIUMS
MY DAYTIMES
NO ASTONIED
SEDATION
NP DEPAINTS
NR DETRAINS
RANDIEST
STRAINED
NS SANDIEST
NT INSTATED
NU AUDIENTS
SINUATED
NV DEVIANTS
NY DESYATIN
OP DIOPTASE
OR ASTEROID
OX OXIDATES
OZ AZOTISED
PR DIPTERAS
RAPIDEST
SPIRATED
TARSIPED
TRAIPSED
PV VAPIDEST
RS ASTERIDS
DIASTERS
DISASTER
DISRATES
RT STRAITED
STRIATED
TARDIEST
RW TAWDRIES
SS ASSISTED
DISSEATS
ST DISTASTE
STAIDEST
TU SITUATED
WY TIDEWAYS

ADELNR 79
(LANDER)
AC CALENDAR
LANDRACE
AH ANHEDRAL
AK KALENDAR
AM ALDERMAN
MALANDER
AS ADRENALS
BG BRANGLED
BI BILANDER
BO BANDEROL
BY BYLANDER
CE CALENDER
ENCRADLE
CH CHANDLER
CK CRANKLED
CO COLANDER
CY CALENDRY
DE ENLARDED
DS DANDLERS
EG ENLARGED
LARGENED
EH REHANDLE
EM ALDERMEN
EO OLEANDER
ET ANTLERED
EV LAVENDER
FI FILANDER
FO FORELAND
FU DEARNFUL
GI DANGLIER
DEARLING
DRAGLINE
GS DANGLERS
GLANDERS
GW WRANGLED
HI HARDLINE
HS HANDLERS
IN INLANDER
IS ISLANDER
KP PRANKLED
LS LANDLERS
MS MANDRELS
OP PONDERAL
OS LADRONES
SOLANDER
OU UNLOADER
URODELAN
OV OVERLAND
RONDAVEL
PS SPANDREL
PU PENDULAR
UNDERLAP
UPLANDER
PY PANDERLY
SS SLANDERS
SU LAUNDERS
LURDANES
RUNDALES
TY ARDENTLY
UY UNDERLAY

ADELNS 137
(ANDLES)
AC CANDELAS
AG SELADANG
AM DALESMAN
LEADSMAN
AR ADRENALS
AT EASTLAND
AW DANELAWS
AY ANALYSED
BB SNABBLED
BS BALDNESS
BT BLANDEST
CE CLEANSED
CO CELADONS
CT SCANTLED
CU UNSCALED
DG GLADDENS
DI ISLANDED
LANDSIDE
DR DANDLERS
DU UNSADDLE
EE ENSEALED
EI DELAINES
EM DALESMEN
EMENDALS
LEADSMEN
EP DEPLANES
EU UNLEASED
UNSEALED
EV ENSLAVED
FF SNAFFLED
FL ELFLANDS
FN FENLANDS
GI DEALINGS
LEADINGS
SIGNALED
GP SPANGLED
GR DANGLERS
GLANDERS
GS GLADNESS
HR HANDLERS
HS HANDLESS
HANDSELS
HT SHETLAND
HU UNHALSED
UNLASHED
UNSHALED
IN ANNELIDS
LINDANES
IO NODALISE
IR ISLANDER
IU UNSAILED
IV ANDVILES
KU UNSLAKED
LP SPENDALL
LR LANDLERS
LS LANDLESS
LW ELLWANDS
WALLSEND
MN LANDSMEN
MO LODESMAN
MR MANDRELS
OR LADRONES
SOLANDER
OY YEALDONS
PR SPANDREL
PY DYSPNEAL
RS SLANDERS
RU LAUNDERS
LURDANES
RUNDALES
TU UNSALTED
TW WETLANDS

ADELRS 88
(ALDERS)
AB BASELARD
AC CALDERAS
AH ASHLARED
AI SALARIED
AN ADRENALS
AP PARDALES
AY SALEYARD
BB DABBLERS
DRABBLES
BD BLADDERS
BE BEDERALS
BG BELGARDS
BH HALBERDS
BI RAILBEDS
BR DRABLERS
BU DURABLES
CD CLADDERS
CE DECLARES
RESCALED
CH CHALDERS
CI DECRIALS
RADICELS
RADICLES
CS SCALDERS
CW SCRAWLED
CY SACREDLY
DI DIEDRALS
DN DANDLERS
DP PADDLERS
DS SADDLERS
DT STRADDLE
DW DAWDLERS
SWADDLER
WADDLERS
DY SADDLERY
EE RELEASED
RESEALED
EF FEDERALS
EH ASHLERED
EI REALISED
SIDEREAL
EL SARDELLE
EM DEMERSAL
EMERALDS
EP PLEADERS
RELAPSED
ET TREADLES
EV SLAVERED
EW LEEWARDS
EY DELAYERS
FP FELDSPAR
GG DRAGGLES
GI SLAIRGED
GN DANGLERS
GLANDERS
HN HANDLERS
II LAIRISED
IL DALLIERS
DIALLERS
IN ISLANDER
IO DARIOLES
SOLIDARE
SOREDIAL
IP PEDRAILS
PREDIALS
IT DILATERS
LARDIEST
IU RESIDUAL
IY DIALYSER
KP SPARKLED
LN LANDLERS
LO ODALLERS
LU UDALLERS
MN MANDRELS
MO EARLDOMS
NO LADRONES
SOLANDER
NP SPANDREL
NS SLANDERS
NU LAUNDERS
LURDANES
RUNDALES
OP LEOPARDS
OS ROADLESS
OT DELATORS
LEOTARDS
LODESTAR
OU ROULADES
PW SPRAWLED
RU RUDERALS
RW DRAWLERS
TT STARTLED
ZZ DAZZLERS

ADELST 110
(SALTED)
AN EASTLAND
AT SALTATED
AU ADULATES
AY DAYTALES
BF FLATBEDS
BN BLANDEST

BU SUBLATED
CI CITADELS
DIALECTS
CN SCANTLED
CU CAULDEST
SULCATED
DE DESALTED
DG GLADDEST
DR STRADDLE
DS STADDLES
DW TWADDLES
EE TEASELED
EF DEFLATES
EI LEADIEST
EM MEDALETS
EO DESOLATE
EP PEDESTAL
ER TREADLES
ES DATELESS
TASSELED
EY SEDATELY
FU DEFAULTS
SULFATED
GI GLADIEST
HN SHETLAND
II IDEALIST
IM MEDALIST
MISDEALT
IO DIASTOLE
ISOLATED
SODALITE
SOLIDATE
IP TALIPEDS
IR DILATERS
LARDIEST
IV VALIDEST
IY DIASTYLE
STEADILY
NU UNSALTED
NW WETLANDS
OP TADPOLES
OR DELATORS
LEOTARDS
LODESTAR
OV SOLVATED
PT SPLATTED
PU PULSATED
RT STARTLED
TY STATEDLY

ADEMNS 246
(AMENDS)
AB BEADSMAN
AH HEADSMAN
AL DALESMAN
LEADSMAN
AO ADENOMAS
AP SPADEMAN
AT MANDATES
BE BEADSMEN
BEDESMAN
BN BANDSMEN
BO ABDOMENS
CU DECUMANS
EE DEMEANES
ENSEAMED
EG ENDGAMES
EH HEADSMEN
EI DEMAINES
INSEAMED
EL DALESMEN
EMENDALS
LEADSMEN
EP SPADEMEN
ER AMENDERS
MEANDERS
REAMENDS
ES SEEDSMAN
ET STAMENED
EU UNSEAMED
EY DEMAYNES
GO GOADSMEN
GR DRAGSMEN
HO HANDSOME
HR HERDSMAN
HU UNSHAMED
IM MISNAMED
IO NOMADIES
NOMADISE
IR ADERMINS
SIRNAMED
IS SIDESMAN
IT MEDIANTS
TIDESMAN
IU MAUNDIES
IY DYNAMISE
KU UNMASKED
LN LANDSMEN
LO LODESMAN
LR MANDRELS
OR MADRONES
RANSOMED
ROADSMEN
PS DAMPNESS
RU DURAMENS
MAUNDERS
SURNAMED
SU MEDUSANS
UU UNAMUSED

ADENRS 62
(ANDERS)
AI ARANEIDS
AL ADRENALS
AV VERANDAS
BI BRANDIES
BRANDISE
BO BANDORES
BROADENS
BR BRANDERS
BS DRABNESS
BT BANDSTER
CE ASCENDER
REASCEND
CO DRACONES
ENDOSARC
CT CANTREDS
CU DURANCES
DL DANDLERS
DT STRANDED
DU DAUNDERS
EE ENSEARED
SERENADE
EG DERANGES
GRANDEES
GRENADES
EI ARSENIDE
DENARIES
DRAISENE
NEARSIDE
EK KNEADERS
EM AMENDERS
MEANDERS
REAMENDS
EN ENSNARED
EO REASONED
ES DEARNESS
EU UNDERSEA
EW ANSWERED
FI FRIANDES
GI DERAIGNS
GRADINES
READINGS
GL DANGLERS
GLANDERS
GM DRAGSMEN
GT DRAGNETS
GRANDEST
GU ENGUARDS
HK REDSHANK
HL HANDLERS
HM HERDSMAN
HS HARDNESS
HU UNSHARED
HW SWANHERD
II DRAISINE
IL ISLANDER
IM ADERMINS
SIRNAMED
IN INSNARED
IO ANEROIDS
DONARIES
IP SPRAINED
IR DRAINERS
SERRANID
IS ARIDNESS
SARDINES
IT DETRAINS
RANDIEST
STRAINED
IU DENARIUS
UNRAISED
URANIDES
IV INVADERS
SANDIVER
IY SYNEDRIA
KS DARKNESS
LL LANDLERS
LM MANDRELS
LO LADRONES
SOLANDER
LP SPANDREL
LS SLANDERS
LU LAUNDERS
LURDANES
RUNDALES
MO MADRONES
RANSOMED
ROADSMEN
MU DURAMENS
MAUNDERS
SURNAMED
OP OPERANDS
PANDORES
OT TORNADES
PP PARPENDS
PR PARDNERS
PU UNSPARED
PW PREDAWNS
QU SQUANDER
RY REYNARDS
SS SARSDENS
ST STANDERS
SU DANSEURS
TU DAUNTERS
TRANSUDE
UNTREADS
TX DEXTRANS
UY UNDERSAY

ADENRU 64
(AUNDER)
BB UNBARBED
BC UNBRACED
BF FABURDEN
BK UNBARKED
BR UNBARRED
BT BREADNUT
TURBANED
CF FURNACED
CG UNGRACED
CH RAUNCHED
CK UNRACKED
CP PRAUNCED
CS DURANCES
CT UNCARTED
UNCRATED
UNDERACT
UNTRACED
DD DEUDDARN
DE DAUNERED
DG UNGRADED
DO UNADORED
DP UNDRAPED
DS DAUNDERS
DT DRAUNTED
UNTRADED
DW UNWARDED
EF UNFEARED
EG DUNGAREE
RENAGUED
UNGEARED
EN UNEARNED
EP UNREAPED
ES UNDERSEA
ET DENATURE
EV UNREAVED
FI UNFAIRED
FL DEARNFUL
FM UNFRAMED
GR GRANDEUR
GS ENGUARDS
GU UNARGUED
GZ GAZUNDER
UNGRAZED
HI UNHAIRED
HM UNHARMED
HS UNSHARED
HT UNTHREAD
II UREDINIA
IO DOUANIER
IP UNPAIRED
UNREPAID
IS DENARIUS
UNRAISED
URANIDES
IT DATURINE
INDURATE
RUINATED
URINATED
IV UNVARIED
KM UNMARKED
LO UNLOADER
URODELAN
LP PENDULAR
UNDERLAP
UPLANDER
LS LAUNDERS
LURDANES
RUNDALES
LY UNDERLAY
MN MUNDANER
UNDERMAN
MR UNDERARM
UNMARRED
MS DURAMENS
MAUNDERS
SURNAMED
MT UNDREAMT
MW UNWARMED
NR UNDERRAN
NW UNWARNED
OX RONDEAUX
PS UNSPARED
PT DEPURANT
PW UNWARPED
PY UNDERPAY
UNPRAYED
QS SQUANDER
RT UNTARRED
SS DANSEURS
ST DAUNTERS
TRANSUDE
UNTREADS
SY UNDERSAY
TT TRUANTED
WY UNDERWAY

ADENST 36
(STANED)
AK ASKANTED
AL EASTLAND
AM MANDATES
AN ANDANTES
BE ABSENTED
BI BANDIEST
BL BLANDEST
BR BANDSTER
CH SNATCHED
STANCHED
CI DISTANCE
CL SCANTLED
CN SCANDENT
CP PANDECTS
CR CANTREDS
CS DESCANTS
DI DANDIEST
DR STRANDED
EF FASTENED
EH HASTENED
EI ANDESITE
EK NAKEDEST
EM STAMENED
EO ENDOSTEA
ES ASSENTED
STANDEES
EU UNSEATED
FS DAFTNESS
GI SEDATING
STEADING
GR DRAGNETS
GRANDEST
HI HANDIEST
HL SHETLAND
HS HANDSETS
II ADENITIS
DAINTIES
IM MEDIANTS
TIDESMAN
IO ASTONIED
SEDATION
IP DEPAINTS
IR DETRAINS
RANDIEST
STRAINED
IS SANDIEST
IT INSTATED
IU AUDIENTS
SINUATED
IV DEVIANTS
IY DESYATIN
LU UNSALTED
LW WETLANDS
NP PENDANTS
NU ASTUNNED
OP TONEPADS
OR TORNADES
OS ONSTEADS
RS STANDERS
RU DAUNTERS
TRANSUDE
UNTREADS
RX DEXTRANS
TU UNSTATED
UNTASTED
UW UNWASTED
UY UNSTAYED
UNSTEADY

ADEORS 48
(ADORES)
AB SEABOARD
BB ABSORBED
BC BROCADES
BD ADSORBED
BN BANDORES
BROADENS
BR BOARDERS
BT BROADEST
BW SOWBREAD
CG CORDAGES
CI IDOCRASE
CM COMRADES
CN DRACONES
ENDOSARC
CR CORRADES
CS SARCODES
CT REDCOATS
CU CAROUSED
DD ADDORSED
DI ROADSIDE
SIDEROAD
EH SOREHEAD
EM SEADROME
EN REASONED
EW OARWEEDS
FI FORESAID
GM ORGASMED
GT GOADSTER
GW DOWAGERS

WORDAGES
HK HARDOKES
HM HADROMES
HP RHAPSODE
HR HOARDERS
HW SHADOWER
IL DARIOLES
SOLIDARE
SOREDIAL
IN ANEROIDS
DONARIES
IP DIASPORE
PARODIES
IT ASTEROID
JP JEOPARDS
KM DARKSOME
LL ODALLERS
LM EARLDOMS
LN LADRONES
SOLANDER
LP LEOPARDS
LS ROADLESS
LT DELATORS
LEOTARDS
LODESTAR
LU ROULADES
MN MADRONES
RANSOMED
ROADSMEN
MT STROAMED
NP OPERANDS
PANDORES
NT TORNADES
PR EARDROPS
PT ADOPTERS
ASPORTED
READOPTS
RS DROSERAS
RT ROADSTER
ST ASSORTED
TORSADES
TU OUTDARES
TX EXTRADOS
UV SAVOURED
WY RODEWAYS

ADEPRT 228
(PRATED)
AA TAPADERA
AO TAPADERO
AS ADAPTERS
READAPTS
BO PROBATED
CE CARPETED
CU CAPTURED
DE DEPARTED
PREDATED
EE REPEATED
EG PARGETED
EL PALTERED
EM EMPARTED
TAMPERED
EN PARENTED
EO OPERATED
ER DEPARTER
ES PEDERAST
PREDATES
REPASTED
TRAPESED
ET PATTERED
EU DEPURATE
EPURATED
EZ TRAPEZED
IL DIPTERAL
TRIPEDAL
IM IMPARTED
IN DIPTERAN
IS DIPTERAS
RAPIDEST
SPIRATED
TARSIPED
TRAIPSED
IU EUPATRID
LM TRAMPLED
LO PROLATED
LT PRATTLED
MS STRAMPED
NO PRONATED
NU DEPURANT
NY PEDANTRY
OR PARROTED
PREDATOR
PRORATED
OS ADOPTERS
ASPORTED
READOPTS
OT TETRAPOD
PS STRAPPED
RU RAPTURED
SU PASTURED
UPSTARED

ADERRS 235
(ARDERS)
BB DRABBERS
BL DRABLERS
BN BRANDERS
BO BOARDERS
BU ABSURDER
CE SCAREDER
CO CORRADES
CU CRUSADER
DE DREADERS
EE ARREEDES
EG REGRADES
EH ADHERERS
REDSHARE
EM DREAMERS
EP SPREADER
ET ARRESTED
DREAREST
RETREADS
SERRATED
TREADERS
EV ADVERSER
FT DRAFTERS
REDRAFTS
GT DRAGSTER
HO HOARDERS
IM ADMIRERS
DISARMER
IN DRAINERS
SERRANID
IP DRAPIERS
IW SWARDIER
LU RUDERALS
LW DRAWLERS
MU EARDRUMS
NP PARDNERS
NY REYNARDS
OP EARDROPS
OS DROSERAS
OT ROADSTER
SW WARDRESS
TT REDSTART

ADERST 49
(DATERS)
AC CADASTRE
AG GRADATES
AI DATARIES
RADIATES
AP ADAPTERS
READAPTS
AS ASSARTED
AT ASTARTED
AW EASTWARD
RADWASTE
BB DRABBEST
DRABBETS
BE BETREADS
BREASTED
DEBATERS
BH BREADTHS
BI BARDIEST
BRAIDEST
RABIDEST
TRIBADES
BN BANDSTER
BO BROADEST
BS DABSTERS
BU SURBATED
BW BEDSTRAW
BY DRYBEATS
CE CEDRATES
CH STARCHED
CI ACRIDEST
CN CANTREDS
CO REDCOATS
CT DETRACTS
SCRATTED
CU TRADUCES
DI DISRATED
DL STRADDLE
DN STRANDED
EE RESEATED
EF DRAFTEES
EG RESTAGED
EH HEADREST
EI READIEST
SERIATED
SIDERATE
STEADIER
EK STREAKED
EL TREADLES
EM MASTERED
STREAMED
EP PEDERAST
PREDATES
REPASTED
TRAPESED
ER ARRESTED
DREAREST
RETREADS
SERRATED
TREADERS
ES ASSERTED
ESTRADES
ET ASTERTED
RESTATED
EW DEWATERS
TARWEEDS
WASTERED
EY ESTRAYED
FF STRAFFED
FR DRAFTERS
REDRAFTS
GN DRAGNETS
GRANDEST
GO GOADSTER
GR DRAGSTER
HH THRASHED
HI HAIRSTED
HARDIEST
HY HYDRATES
II IRISATED
IK STRAIKED
IL DILATERS
LARDIEST
IM MARDIEST
MISRATED
READMITS
IN DETRAINS
RANDIEST
STRAINED
IO ASTEROID
IP DIPTERAS
RAPIDEST
SPIRATED
TARSIPED
TRAIPSED
IS ASTERIDS
DIASTERS
DISASTER
DISRATES
IT STRAITED
STRIATED
TARDIEST
IW TAWDRIES
JU ADJUSTER
READJUST
LO DELATORS
LEOTARDS
LODESTAR
LT STARTLED
MO STROAMED
MP STRAMPED
NO TORNADES
NS STANDERS
NU DAUNTERS
TRANSUDE
UNTREADS
NX DEXTRANS
OP ADOPTERS
ASPORTED
READOPTS
OR ROADSTER
OS ASSORTED
TORSADES
OU OUTDARES
OX EXTRADOS
PP STRAPPED
PU PASTURED
UPSTARED
RT REDSTART
SW STEWARDS
TU STATURED
UX SURTAXED
WW WESTWARD

ADGINR 135
(RADING)
AB ABRADING
AC ARCADING
CARANGID
CARDIGAN
AE AREADING
DRAINAGE
GARDENIA
AM MRIDANGA
AP PARADING
AR DARRAIGN
AU GUARDIAN
AW AWARDING
BB DRABBING
BE BEARDING
BREADING
BH HANGBIRD
BI BRAIDING
BL BARDLING
BN BRANDING
BO ABORDING
BOARDING
BS BRIGANDS
CL CRADLING
DE DREADING
DL RADDLING
EE REGAINED
EH ADHERING
HEADRING
EK DAKERING
EL DANGLIER
DEARLING
DRAGLINE
EM DREAMING
MARGINED
EN GRANNIED
EO ORGANDIE
ER DREARING
ES DERAIGNS
GRADINES
READINGS
ET DERATING
GRADIENT
REDATING
TREADING
EY DERAYING
READYING
YEARDING
FS FARDINGS
FT DRAFTING
FW DWARFING
GG DRAGGING
GS NIGGARDS
GU GUARDING
HO HOARDING
HP HANDGRIP
IL DRAILING
IM ADMIRING
IN DRAINING
IO RADIOING
IR ARRIDING
IY DAIRYING
JU ADJURING
KL DARKLING
LS DARLINGS
LT DARTLING
LW DRAWLING
LY DARINGLY
MM DRAMMING
MS MRIDANGS
MY MARDYING
NO ADORNING
NS DARNINGS
NT DRANTING
OO RIGADOON
OS ROADINGS
PP DRAPPING
ST TRADINGS
SW DRAWINGS
SWARDING
WARDINGS
TY TARDYING

ADINRS 105
(DRAINS)
AE ARANEIDS
AL LANIARDS
AM MANDIRAS
AR DARRAINS
AT INTRADAS
RADIANTS
AV VIRANDAS
BB RIBBANDS
BE BRANDIES
BRANDISE
BG BRIGANDS
BH BRANDISH
BT ANTBIRDS
CI ACRIDINS
CO SARDONIC
DO ANDROIDS
DISADORN
EE ARSENIDE
DENARIES
DRAISENE
NEARSIDE
EF FRIANDES
EG DERAIGNS
GRADINES
READINGS
EI DRAISINE
EL ISLANDER
EM ADERMINS
SIRNAMED
EN INSNARED
EO ANEROIDS
DONARIES
EP SPRAINED
ER DRAINERS
SERRANID
ES ARIDNESS
SARDINES
ET DETRAINS
RANDIEST
STRAINED
EU DENARIUS
UNRAISED
URANIDES
EV INVADERS
SANDIVER
EY SYNEDRIA
FG FARDINGS
FM FINDRAMS
FT INDRAFTS
GG NIGGARDS
GL DARLINGS
GM MRIDANGS
GN DARNINGS
GO ROADINGS

GT TRADINGS
GW DRAWINGS
SWARDING
WARDINGS
IP PINDARIS
IT DISTRAIN
KS DISRANKS
KT STINKARD
LM MANDRILS
LO ORDINALS
LP SPANDRIL
LU DIURNALS
MW MISDRAWN
MY MISANDRY
NO ANDIRONS
NY INNYARDS
OP PONIARDS
OR ORDINARS
OS SADIRONS
OT INTRADOS
OU DINOSAUR
OV VIRANDOS
RT TRIDARNS
SU SUNDARIS
TU UNITARDS

AEELRS 72
(EALERS)
AB ERASABLE
AT LAETARES
BD BEDERALS
BG BEAGLERS
BN ENABLERS
BO EARLOBES
BP BEPEARLS
BT BLEAREST
BLEATERS
RETABLES
BU REUSABLE
BV BESLAVER
CD DECLARES
RESCALED
CH RELACHES
CI ESCALIER
CM RECLAMES
SCLEREMA
CN CLEANERS
CLEANSER
CO ESCAROLE
CP PERCALES
REPLACES
CR CLEARERS
CS CARELESS
RESCALES
CT CLEAREST
SCELERAT
TREACLES
CV CLEAVERS
DE RELEASED
RESEALED
DF FEDERALS
DH ASHLERED
DI REALISED
SIDEREAL
DL SARDELLE
DM DEMERSAL
EMERALDS
DP PLEADERS
RELAPSED
DT TREADLES
DV SLAVERED
DW LEEWARDS
DY DELAYERS
EE RELEASEE
EF EELFARES
ER RELEASER
ES RELEASES
ET TEASELER
EW WEASELER
FI SERAFILE
FS FEARLESS
FT REFLATES
FW WELFARES
GG GREGALES
GH SHEARLEG
GI GASELIER
GL ALLEGERS
GN ENLARGES
GENERALS
GLEANERS
GP PEREGALS
GS EELGRASS
GEARLESS
LARGESSE
GU LEAGUERS
GW LEGWEARS
HI SHIRALEE
HO ARSEHOLE
HT HALTERES
LEATHERS
HV HAVERELS
IL REALLIES
IM ALMERIES
MEASLIER
IP ESPALIER
PEARLIES
IR REALISER
IS REALISES
IT ATELIERS
EARLIEST
LEARIEST
REALTIES
IV VELARISE
IY YEARLIES
IZ REALIZES
SLEAZIER
LP PARELLES
MT LAMETERS
NR LEARNERS
NS REALNESS
NT ALTERNES
NV ENSLAVER
NW RENEWALS
OP PAROLEES
OR RELEASOR
OT OLEASTER
OU AUREOLES
PR PEARLERS
RELAPSER
PS PLEASERS
RELAPSES
PT PLEATERS
PRELATES
PU PLEASURE
SERPULAE
PV VESPERAL
QU SQUEALER
RT RELATERS
RV REVERSAL
SLAVERER
ST STEALERS
TEARLESS
TESSERAL
SU LEASURES
SV SEVERALS
SW WARELESS
TT ALERTEST
TU RESALUTE
TY EASTERLY
UV REVALUES
VY AVERSELY

AEEMRS 238
(SEAMER)
AP PARAMESE
BC EMBRACES
BD EMBREADS
BS BESMEARS
BV EMBRAVES
CD SCREAMED
CH CASHMERE
MACHREES
MARCHESE
CI CASIMERE
RACEMISE
CL RECLAMES
SCLEREMA
CN MENACERS
CO RACEMOSE
CR CREAMERS
SCREAMER
CT CREMATES
MEERCATS
DI MADERISE
DL DEMERSAL
EMERALDS
DN AMENDERS
MEANDERS
REAMENDS
DO SEADROME
DR DREAMERS
DT MASTERED
STREAMED
DU MEASURED
EP PERMEASE
FN ENFRAMES
FO FEARSOME
FR REFRAMES
GI GAMESIER
GN AGREMENS
GT GAMESTER
MEAGREST
GU REMUAGES
HN SHAREMEN
SHEARMEN
HS MAHSEERS
HT ERATHEMS
IL ALMERIES
MEASLIER
IN REMANIES
IP EMPAIRES
IR SMEARIER
IS SERIEMAS
IT EMIRATES
REAMIEST
STEAMIER
KT MEERKATS
LT LAMETERS
MN MERESMAN
MT AMMETERS
METAMERS
NP SPEARMEN
NT REMANETS
NW MENSWEAR
OT EROTEMAS
PT TEMPERAS
QU MARQUEES
RT REMASTER
STREAMER
RU MEASURER
ST MASSETER
SEAMSTER
STEAMERS
SU MEASURES
REASSUME
TT TEAMSTER
TY METAYERS

AEEPRT 142
(REPEAT)
AH HEARTPEA
AK PARAKEET
AN PARANETE
AS ASPERATE
SEPARATE
CC ACCEPTER
CD CARPETED
CF PERFECTA
PRAEFECT
CH ETHERCAP
CN PERCEANT
CT ETTERCAP
CU PERACUTE
CX EXCERPTA
DD DEPARTED
PREDATED
DE REPEATED
DG PARGETED
DL PALTERED
DM EMPARTED
TAMPERED
DN PARENTED
DO OPERATED
DR DEPARTER
DS PEDERAST
PREDATES
REPASTED
TRAPESED
DT PATTERED
DU DEPURATE
EPURATED
DZ TRAPEZED
EM PERMEATE
ER REPARTEE
REPEATER
GR PARGETER
HS PREHEATS
SPREATHE
IL PEARLITE
IN APERIENT
IS PETARIES
IV PERVIATE
JO PEJORATE
KN PERTAKEN
KS PERTAKES
LR PALTERER
LS PLEATERS
PRELATES
LY PTERYLAE
MN PETERMAN
MR TAMPERER
MS TEMPERAS
MT ATTEMPER
OR PATERERO
PERORATE
OS OPERATES
PROTEASE
OT OPERETTA
RR PARTERRE
RS TAPERERS
RT PATTERER
RU APERTURE
SS TRAPESES
SU EPURATES
SUPERATE
SZ TRAPEZES

AEERRS 162
(ERASER)
AF SEAFARER
AN ARRASENE
BC REBRACES
BG GERBERAS
BK BREAKERS
BT REBATERS
TABRERES
TEREBRAS
CD SCAREDER
CH REACHERS
RESEARCH
SEARCHER
CI CARIERES
CREASIER
CL CLEARERS
CM CREAMERS
SCREAMER
CP CAPERERS
CS CREASERS
CT CATERERS
RETRACES
TERRACES
CU ECRASEUR
DD DREADERS
DE ARREEDES
DG REGRADES
DH ADHERERS
REDSHARE
DM DREAMERS
DP SPREADER
DT ARRESTED
DREAREST
RETREADS
SERRATED
TREADERS
DV ADVERSER
EH REHEARSE
EL RELEASER
ET ARRESTEE
FI RAREFIES
FM REFRAMES
FT FERRATES
GI GREASIER
GP ASPERGER
PRESAGER
GS GREASERS
GT REGRATES
GW WAGERERS
HI HEARSIER
HP REPHRASE
HS SHEARERS
IK RAKERIES
SKEARIER
IL REALISER
IM SMEARIER
IN REARISEN
IP PEREIRAS
SPEARIER
IS REARISES
IT ARTERIES
REASTIER
KT RETAKERS
STREAKER
KW WREAKERS
LN LEARNERS
LO RELEASOR
LP PEARLERS
RELAPSER
LT RELATERS
LV REVERSAL
SLAVERER
MT REMASTER
STREAMER
MU MEASURER
NO REASONER
NS RARENESS
NT TERRANES
NV RAVENERS
NW ANSWERER
REANSWER
NY YEARNERS
OU REAROUSE
OW SOWARREE
PP PAPERERS
PREPARES
REPAPERS
PT TAPERERS
RT ARRESTER
REARREST
ST ASSERTER
REASSERT
SERRATES
TERRASES
SU ERASURES
REASSURE
SW SWEARERS
TT RETRATES
RETREATS
TREATERS
TU AUSTERER
TREASURE
TV TRAVERSE
TW WATERERS
VW WAVERERS

AEERST 20
(EATERS)
AG STEARAGE
AL LAETARES
AN ARSENATE
SERENATA
AP ASPERATE
SEPARATE
AT STEARATE
AW SEAWATER
BC ACERBEST
BD BETREADS
BREASTED
DEBATERS
BG ABSTERGE
BH BREATHES

HARTBEES
BK BESTREAK
BL BLEAREST
BLEATERS
RETABLES
BO REBATOES
BR REBATERS
TABRERES
TEREBRAS
BT ABETTERS
BU SUBERATE
CC ACCRETES
CD CEDRATES
CH CHEATERS
HECTARES
RECHATES
RECHEATS
TEACHERS
CL CLEAREST
SCELERAT
TREACLES
CM CREMATES
MEERCATS
CN CENTARES
REASCENT
SARCENET
CO CREASOTE
CR CATERERS
RETRACES
TERRACES
CS CATERESS
CERASTES
CX EXACTERS
DE RESEATED
DF DRAFTEES
DG RESTAGED
DH HEADREST
DI READIEST
SERIATED
SIDERATE
STEADIER
DK STREAKED
DL TREADLES
DM MASTERED
STREAMED
DP PEDERAST
PREDATES
REPASTED
TRAPESED
DR ARRESTED
DREAREST
RETREADS
SERRATED
TREADERS
DS ASSERTED
ESTRADES
DT ASTERTED
RESTATED
DW DEWATERS
TARWEEDS
WASTERED
DY ESTRAYED
EG EAGEREST
ETAGERES
STEERAGE
EI EATERIES
EL TEASELER
EN SERENATE
ER ARRESTEE
ES TESSERAE

FH FEATHERS
FL REFLATES
FN FASTENER
FENESTRA
FR FERRATES
FS FEASTERS
FU FEATURES
GM GAMESTER
MEAGREST
GN ESTRANGE
GRANTEES
GREATENS
REAGENTS
SEGREANT
SERGEANT
STERNAGE
GR REGRATES
GS RESTAGES
GT GREATEST
GU TREAGUES
GW STREWAGE
HH HEATHERS
HI HEARTIES
HL HALTERES
LEATHERS
HM ERATHEMS
HN HASTENER
HEARTENS
HP PREHEATS
SPREATHE
HT THEATERS
THEATRES
HV THREAVES
HW WEATHERS
WREATHES
IL ATELIERS
EARLIEST
LEARIEST
REALTIES
IM EMIRATES
REAMIEST
STEAMIER
IN ARSENITE
RESINATE
STEARINE
TRAINEES
IO ETAERIOS
IP PETARIES
IR ARTERIES
REASTIER
IS SERIATES
IT ARIETTES
ITERATES
TEARIEST
TREATIES
TREATISE
IV EVIRATES
IW SWEATIER
TAWERIES
WEARIEST
IY YEASTIER
JN SERJEANT
KM MEERKATS
KO KERATOSE
KREASOTE
KP PERTAKES
KR RETAKERS
STREAKER
KS SAKERETS
LM LAMETERS

LN ALTERNES
LO OLEASTER
LP PLEATERS
PRELATES
LR RELATERS
LS STEALERS
TEARLESS
TESSERAL
LT ALERTEST
LU RESALUTE
LY EASTERLY
MM AMMETERS
METAMERS
MN REMANETS
MO EROTEMAS
MP TEMPERAS
MR REMASTER
STREAMER
MS MASSETER
SEAMSTER
STEAMERS
MT TEAMSTER
MY METAYERS
NO RESONATE
NR TERRANES
NS ASSENTER
EARNESTS
SARSENET
NT ENTREATS
RATTEENS
NV AVENTRES
VETERANS
OP OPERATES
PROTEASE
OV OVEREATS
PR TAPERERS
PS TRAPESES
PU EPURATES
SUPERATE
PZ TRAPEZES
RR ARRESTER
REARREST
RS ASSERTER
REASSERT
SERRATES
TERRASES
RT RETRATES
RETREATS
TREATERS
RU AUSTERER
TREASURE
RV TRAVERSE
RW WATERERS
ST ESTREATS
RESTATES
SW SWEATERS
SZ ERSATZES
TT ATTESTER
TX EXTREATS
WW WETWARES

AEGILN 55
(EALING)
AB GAINABLE
AC ANGELICA
AE ALIENAGE
AP PELAGIAN
AR REGALIAN
AT AGENTIAL
ALGINATE

BC BELACING
BD BLINDAGE
BG BEAGLING
BM EMBALING
BN ENABLING
BR BLEARING
BS SINGABLE
BT BELATING
BLEATING
TANGIBLE
BY BELAYING
CG CAGELING
GLACEING
CH LEACHING
CN CLEANING
ELANCING
ENLACING
CR CLEARING
CT CLEATING
CV CLEAVING
CW LACEWING
DF FINAGLED
DH HEALDING
DI GLIADINE
DM MALIGNED
MEDALING
DO GALENOID
DP PEDALING
PLEADING
DR DANGLIER
DEARLING
DRAGLINE
DS DEALINGS
LEADINGS
SIGNALED
DT DELATING
DY DELAYING
EM LIEGEMAN
ER ALGERINE
ES ENSILAGE
LINEAGES
ET GALENITE
GELATINE
LEGATINE
EV INVEAGLE
FS FINAGLES
GG ALEGGING
GL ALLEGING
GM GLEAMING
GN GLEANING
GR GANGLIER
REGALING
GS LIGNAGES
GT TEAGLING
GU LEAGUING
HR NARGHILE
NARGILEH
HS HEALINGS
LEASHING
SHEALING
HT ATHELING
HX EXHALING
IN ALIENING
IR GAINLIER
JR JANGLIER
KS LINKAGES
KW WEAKLING
LS NIGELLAS
LU LINGULAE
LY GENIALLY

MP EMPALING
MR GERMINAL
MALIGNER
MALINGER
MS MEASLING
MT LIGAMENT
METALING
MU AEMULING
MY YEALMING
NR LEARNING
NS EANLINGS
LEANINGS
NT GANTLINE
LATENING
NU UNGENIAL
NW WEANLING
NY YEANLING
OR GERANIOL
REGIONAL
OS GASOLINE
OT GELATION
LEGATION
PR PEARLING
PS ELAPSING
PLEASING
PT PLEATING
RR GNARLIER
RS ENGRAILS
NARGILES
REALIGNS
SALERING
SANGLIER
SIGNALER
SLANGIER
RT ALERTING
ALTERING
INTEGRAL
RELATING
TANGLIER
TRIANGLE
RX RELAXING
RY LAYERING
RELAYING
YEARLING
SS GAINLESS
GLASSINE
LEASINGS
SEALINGS
ST EASTLING
GELATINS
GENITALS
STEALING
SV LEAVINGS
SLEAVING
SW SWEALING
TV VALETING
TX EXALTING
TZ TEAZLING
UV VAGINULE

AEGINR 15
(EARING)
AB ABEARING
AC CANAIGRE
AD AREADING
DRAINAGE
GARDENIA
AF AFEARING
AG GRAINAGE
AL REGALIAN

AN ANEARING
AS ANGARIES
AT AERATING
BD BEARDING
BREADING
BE BAREGINE
BERGENIA
BK BREAKING
BL BLEARING
BM BREAMING
BO ABORIGEN
BS BEARINGS
SABERING
BT BERATING
REBATING
BW BEWARING
BY BERAYING
CF REFACING
CH REACHING
CK CREAKING
CL CLEARING
CM AMERCING
CREAMING
CN ENRACING
CP CAPERING
PEARCING
PREACING
CS CREASING
GRECIANS
SEARCING
CT CATERING
CITRANGE
CREATING
REACTING
DD DREADING
DE REGAINED
DH ADHERING
HEADRING
DK DAKERING
DL DANGLIER
DEARLING
DRAGLINE
DM DREAMING
MARGINED
DN GRANNIED
DO ORGANDIE
DR DREARING
DS DERAIGNS
GRADINES
READINGS
DT DERATING
GRADIENT
REDATING
TREADING
DY DERAYING
READYING
YEARDING
EG AGREEING
EI AEGIRINE
EL ALGERINE
EM GERMAINE
EP PERIGEAN
ER REGAINER
ES GESNERIA
ET GRATINEE
EZ RAZEEING
FH HANGFIRE
FK FREAKING
FW WAFERING
FY AREFYING

GK KNAGGIER
GL GANGLIER
REGALING
GN ANGERING
ENRAGING
GS GEARINGS
GREASING
SNAGGIER
GV GREAVING
GW WAGERING
HL NARGHILE
NARGILEH
HS HEARINGS
HEARSING
SHEARING
HT EARTHING
HEARTING
INGATHER
HV HAVERING
IL GAINLIER
IM IMAGINER
MIGRAINE
IN ARGININE
IR GRAINIER
JL JANGLIER
KM REMAKING
KS SKEARING
KT RETAKING
KW WREAKING
LM GERMINAL
MALIGNER
MALINGER
LN LEARNING
LO GERANIOL
REGIONAL
LP PEARLING
LR GNARLIER
LS ENGRAILS
NARGILES
REALIGNS
SALERING
SANGLIER
SIGNALER
SLANGIER
LT ALERTING
ALTERING
INTEGRAL
RELATING
TANGLIER
TRIANGLE
LX RELAXING
LY LAYERING
RELAYING
YEARLING
MN ENARMING
RENAMING
MP EMPARING
MR REARMING
MS GERMAINS
SMEARING
MT EMIGRANT
MU GERANIUM
MAUNGIER
NS AGINNERS
EARNINGS
ENGRAINS
GRANNIES
NV RAVENING
NY RENAYING
YEARNING

OS IGNAROES
ORGANISE
ORIGANES
OZ ORGANIZE
PP PAPERING
PS PREASING
SPEARING
PT TAPERING
PY REPAYING
RS EARRINGS
GRAINERS
RV AVERRING
SS REASSIGN
SEARINGS
SERINGAS
ST ANGRIEST
ASTRINGE
GANISTER
GANTRIES
GRANITES
INGRATES
RANGIEST
REASTING
STEARING
TASERING
SV VINEGARS
SW SWEARING
WEARINGS
SY RESAYING
TT ARETTING
TREATING
TV AVERTING
TAVERING
VINTAGER
TW TWANGIER
WATERING
VW WAVERING
VY VINEGARY
WY WEARYING

AEGLNR 91
(ANGLER)

AG LANGRAGE
AI REGALIAN
AS ALNAGERS
AU AULNAGER
BD BRANGLED
BI BLEARING
BS BRANGLES
CI CLEARING
CS CLANGERS
DE ENLARGED
LARGENED
DI DANGLIER
DEARLING
DRAGLINE
DS DANGLERS
GLANDERS
DW WRANGLED
EE GENERALE
EI ALGERINE
EL ALLERGEN
EN ENLARGEN
ER ENLARGER
ES ENLARGES
GENERALS
GLEANERS
GI GANGLIER
REGALING
GS GANGRELS
HI NARGHILE
NARGILEH
II GAINLIER
IJ JANGLIER
IM GERMINAL
MALIGNER
MALINGER
IN LEARNING
IO GERANIOL
REGIONAL
IP PEARLING
IR GNARLIER
IS ENGRAILS
NARGILES
REALIGNS
SALERING
SANGLIER
SIGNALER
SLANGIER
IT ALERTING
ALTERING
INTEGRAL
RELATING
TANGLIER
TRIANGLE
IX RELAXING
IY LAYERING
RELAYING
YEARLING
JS JANGLERS
LS LANGRELS
MS MANGLERS
OY YEARLONG
PS GRAPNELS
SPANGLER
SPRANGLE
RW WRANGLER
SS SLANGERS
ST STRANGLE
TANGLERS
TRANGLES
SU GRANULES
SW WANGLERS
WRANGLES
SY LARYNGES
UY GUNLAYER

AEGLNS 170
(ANGLES)

AD SELADANG
AM GAMELANS
AR ALNAGERS
AS LASAGNES
AU AULNAGES
BI SINGABLE
BR BRANGLES
CO CONGEALS
CR CLANGERS
DD GLADDENS
DI DEALINGS
LEADINGS
SIGNALED
DP SPANGLED
DR DANGLERS
GLANDERS
DS GLADNESS
EI ENSILAGE
LINEAGES
EM MELANGES
EO GASOLENE
ER ENLARGES
GENERALS
GLEANERS
EV EVANGELS
FI FINAGLES
FS FANGLESS
GI LIGNAGES
GR GANGRELS
HI HEALINGS
LEASHING
SHEALING
HO HALOGENS
IK LINKAGES
IL NIGELLAS
IM MEASLING
IN EANLINGS
LEANINGS
IO GASOLINE
IP ELAPSING
PLEASING
IR ENGRAILS
NARGILES
REALIGNS
SALERING
SANGLIER
SIGNALER
SLANGIER
IS GAINLESS
GLASSINE
LEASINGS
SEALINGS
IT EASTLING
GELATINS
GENITALS
STEALING
IV LEAVINGS
SLEAVING
IW SWEALING
JR JANGLERS
LO ALLONGES
GALLEONS
LP LANGSPEL
LR LANGRELS
MR MANGLERS
MS GLASSMEN
OT TANGELOS
PR GRAPNELS
SPANGLER
SPRANGLE
PS PANGLESS
SPANGLES
PT SPANGLET
RS SLANGERS
RT STRANGLE
TANGLERS
TRANGLES
RU GRANULES
RW WANGLERS
WRANGLES
RY LARYNGES
TT GANTLETS
TU LANGUETS
TW TWANGLES
UW GUNWALES

AEGLNT 118
(TANGLE)

AI AGENTIAL
ALGINATE
AP PLANTAGE
AU ANGULATE
BI BELATING
BLEATING
TANGIBLE
CI CLEATING
DE DANEGELT
DI DELATING
DW TWANGLED
EI GALENITE
GELATINE
LEGATINE
EN ENTANGLE
EO ELONGATE
GI TEAGLING
HI ATHELING
IM LIGAMENT
METALING
IN GANTLINE
LATENING
IO GELATION
LEGATION
IP PLEATING
IR ALERTING
ALTERING
INTEGRAL
RELATING
TANGLIER
TRIANGLE
IS EASTLING
GELATINS
GENITALS
STEALING
IV VALETING
IX EXALTING
IZ TEAZLING
MU GUNMETAL
NP PLANGENT
NU UNTANGLE
OP GANTLOPE
OS TANGELOS
PS SPANGLET
RS STRANGLE
TANGLERS
TRANGLES
ST GANTLETS
SU LANGUETS
SW TWANGLES
TU GAUNTLET
UU UNGULATE

AEGLRS 167
(LAGERS)

AB ALGEBRAS
AI GASALIER
LAIRAGES
REGALIAS
AN ALNAGERS
AR REALGARS
RESALGAR
AT AGRESTAL
BB GABBLERS
GRABBLES
BD BELGARDS
BE BEAGLERS
BG BLAGGERS
BM GAMBLERS
GAMBRELS
BN BRANGLES
BR GARBLERS
CH SCHLAGER
CI GLACIERS
CK GRACKLES
CN CLANGERS
DG DRAGGLES
DI SLAIRGED
DN DANGLERS
GLANDERS
EG GREGALES
EH SHEARLEG
EI GASELIER
EL ALLEGERS
EN ENLARGES
GENERALS
GLEANERS
EP PEREGALS
ES EELGRASS
GEARLESS
LARGESSE
EU LEAGUERS
EW LEGWEARS
GH HAGGLERS
GI SLAGGIER
GN GANGRELS
GT STRAGGLE
HU LAUGHERS
IM GREMIALS
LAMIGERS
REGALISM
IN ENGRAILS
NARGILES
REALIGNS
SALERING
SANGLIER
SIGNALER
SLANGIER
IO GASOLIER
GIRASOLE
SERAGLIO
IS GLASSIER
IT GLARIEST
REGALIST
IY GREASILY
IZ GLAZIERS
JN JANGLERS
LN LANGRELS
LO ALLEGROS
MN MANGLERS
MO GOMERALS
MU MAULGRES
NP GRAPNELS
SPANGLER
SPRANGLE
NS SLANGERS
NT STRANGLE
TANGLERS
TRANGLES
NU GRANULES
NW WANGLERS
WRANGLES
NY LARYNGES
OP PERGOLAS
OT GLOATERS
LEGATORS
OU GLAREOUS
PP GRAPPLES
PU EARPLUGS
GRAUPELS
RU REGULARS
TU GAULTERS
GESTURAL

TRAGULES

AEGLST 187
(GLATES)
AA GALATEAS
AE ETALAGES
AL GALLATES
STALLAGE
TALLAGES
AR AGRESTAL
AS AGELASTS
LASTAGES
BU GUSTABLE
CI GELASTIC
CO CATELOGS
DD GLADDEST
DI GLADIEST
EE LEGATEES
EI ELEGIAST
EO SEGOLATE
ES GATELESS
ET GALETTES
EV VEGETALS
FO FLOTAGES
GR STRAGGLE
HI LAIGHEST
HW THALWEGS
IL LEGALIST
STILLAGE
TILLAGES
IN EASTLING
GELATINS
GENITALS
STEALING
IO OTALGIES
IR GLARIEST
REGALIST
IZ GLAZIEST
LO TOLLAGES
NO TANGELOS
NP SPANGLET
NR STRANGLE
TANGLERS
TRANGLES
NT GANTLETS
NU LANGUETS
NW TWANGLES
OR GLOATERS
LEGATORS
OV VOLTAGES
RU GAULTERS
GESTURAL
TRAGULES
ST GESTALTS
UU GLUTAEUS
UV VULGATES

AEGNRS 86
(ANGERS)
AC CARNAGES
CRANAGES
AE SANGAREE
AI ANGARIES
AL ALNAGERS
AM MANAGERS
AR ARRANGES
AT STARAGEN
TANAGERS
BI BEARINGS
SABERING
BL BRANGLES
BT BANGSTER
CE ENGRACES
CH CHANGERS
CI CREASING
GRECIANS
SEARCING
CL CLANGERS
CM CRAGSMEN
CO ACROGENS
CORNAGES
DE DERANGES
GRANDEES
GRENADES
DI DERAIGNS
GRADINES
READINGS
DL DANGLERS
GLANDERS
DM DRAGSMEN
DT DRAGNETS
GRANDEST
DU ENGUARDS
EG ENGAGERS
EH SHAGREEN
EI GESNERIA
EL ENLARGES
GENERALS
GLEANERS
EM AGREMENS
EN ENRANGES
ET ESTRANGE
GRANTEES
GREATENS
REAGENTS
SEGREANT
SERGEANT
STERNAGE
EU RENAGUES
EV AVENGERS
ENGRAVES
FF ENGRAFFS
FR GRANFERS
FT ENGRAFTS
GI GEARINGS
GREASING
SNAGGIER
GL GANGRELS
GR GRANGERS
GT GANGSTER
HI HEARINGS
HEARSING
SHEARING
HS GNASHERS
IK SKEARING
IL ENGRAILS
NARGILES
REALIGNS
SALERING
SANGLIER
SIGNALER
SLANGIER
IM GERMAINS
SMEARING
IN AGINNERS
EARNINGS
ENGRAINS
GRANNIES
IO IGNAROES
ORGANISE
ORIGANES
IP PREASING
SPEARING
IR EARRINGS
GRAINERS
IS REASSIGN
SEARINGS
SERINGAS
IT ANGRIEST
ASTRINGE
GANISTER
GANTRIES
GRANITES
INGRATES
RANGIEST
REASTING
STEARING
TASERING
IV VINEGARS
IW SWEARING
WEARINGS
IY RESAYING
JL JANGLERS
LL LANGRELS
LM MANGLERS
LP GRAPNELS
SPANGLER
SPRANGLE
LS SLANGERS
LT STRANGLE
TANGLERS
TRANGLES
LU GRANULES
LW WANGLERS
WRANGLES
LY LARYNGES
MO MEGARONS
MT GARMENTS
MARGENTS
RAGMENTS
NU GUNNERAS
OO OREGANOS
OR GROANERS
OT ORANGEST
RAGSTONE
STONERAG
OW WAGONERS
PS ENGRASPS
PT TREPANGS
RT GRANTERS
REGRANTS
STRANGER
TU STRAUNGE
YY ASYNERGY

AEGNRT 54
(GANTER)
AI AERATING
AS STARAGEN
TANAGERS
AU RUNAGATE
BI BERATING
REBATING
BS BANGSTER
BU BURGANET
CI CATERING
CITRANGE
CREATING
REACTING
DH THRANGED
DI DERATING
GRADIENT
REDATING
TREADING
DO DRAGONET
DS DRAGNETS
GRANDEST
EE GENERATE
RENEGATE
TEENAGER
EI GRATINEE
EM AGREMENT
EN GENERANT
ER ETRANGER
ES ESTRANGE
GRANTEES
GREATENS
REAGENTS
SEGREANT
SERGEANT
STERNAGE
EU GAUNTREE
FM FRAGMENT
FO FRONTAGE
FS ENGRAFTS
GS GANGSTER
HI EARTHING
HEARTING
INGATHER
IK RETAKING
IL ALERTING
ALTERING
INTEGRAL
RELATING
TANGLIER
TRIANGLE
IM EMIGRANT
IP TAPERING
IS ANGRIEST
ASTRINGE
GANISTER
GANTRIES
GRANITES
INGRATES
RANGIEST
REASTING
STEARING
TASERING
IT ARETTING
TREATING
IV AVERTING
TAVERING
VINTAGER
IW TWANGIER
WATERING
LS STRANGLE
TANGLERS
TRANGLES
MS GARMENTS
MARGENTS
RAGMENTS
MU ARGUMENT
NO NEGATRON
NP PREGNANT
NY GANNETRY
OS ORANGEST
RAGSTONE
STONERAG
OT TETRAGON
OY NEGATORY
PS TREPANGS
RS GRANTERS
REGRANTS
STRANGER
SU STRAUNGE

AEGNST 115
(TANGES)
AH THANAGES
AI SAGINATE
AK TANKAGES
AM MAGENTAS
MAGNATES
AN TANNAGES
AP PAGEANTS
AR STARAGEN
TANAGERS
AT STAGNATE
AV VANTAGES
AW WANTAGES
BI BEATINGS
BN BANTENGS
BR BANGSTER
BU SUBAGENT
CE CENTAGES
CO COGNATES
DI SEDATING
STEADING
DR DRAGNETS
GRANDEST
EF FANTEEGS
EI SAGENITE
ER ESTRANGE
GRANTEES
GREATENS
REAGENTS
SEGREANT
SERGEANT
STERNAGE
ET TENTAGES
EV VENTAGES
FI FEASTING
FR ENGRAFTS
GI NAGGIEST
GR GANGSTER
HI GAHNITES
HEATINGS
HN HANGNEST
HS STENGAHS
IL EASTLING
GELATINS
GENITALS
STEALING
IM MANGIEST
MINTAGES
STEAMING
TEAMINGS
IN ANTIGENS
GENTIANS
STEANING
IR ANGRIEST
ASTRINGE
GANISTER
GANTRIES
GRANITES
INGRATES
RANGIEST
REASTING
STEARING
TASERING
IS EASTINGS
GENISTAS
GIANTESS
SEATINGS
TEASINGS
TSIGANES
IT ESTATING
TANGIEST
IU SAUTEING
IV VINTAGES
IW SWEATING
IY YEASTING
LO TANGELOS
LP SPANGLET
LR STRANGLE
TANGLERS
TRANGLES
LT GANTLETS
LU LANGUETS
LW TWANGLES
MO GEOMANTS
MAGNETOS
MEGATONS
MONTAGES
MR GARMENTS
MARGENTS
RAGMENTS
MU AUGMENTS
MUTAGENS
NO TONNAGES
NT TANGENTS
NU TUNNAGES
OP PONTAGES
OR ORANGEST
RAGSTONE
STONERAG
PR TREPANGS
RR GRANTERS
REGRANTS
STRANGER
RU STRAUNGE
SS GASTNESS
TU GAUNTEST
TUTENAGS

AEGRST 80
(GATERS)
AA GASTRAEA
AC CARTAGES
AD GRADATES
AE STEARAGE
AG AGGRATES
AL AGRESTAL
AN STARAGEN
TANAGERS
AT REGATTAS
BE ABSTERGE
BH BARGHEST
BN BANGSTER
BS BARGESTS
CI AGRESTIC
CO ESCARGOT
CU TRUCAGES
DE RESTAGED
DN DRAGNETS
GRANDEST
DO GOADSTER
DR DRAGSTER
EE EAGEREST
ETAGERES

STEERAGE
EM GAMESTER
MEAGREST
EN ESTRANGE
GRANTEES
GREATENS
REAGENTS
SEGREANT
SERGEANT
STERNAGE
ER REGRATES
ES RESTAGES
ET GREATEST
EU TREAGUES
EW STREWAGE
FI FRIGATES
FN ENGRAFTS
FR GRAFTERS
GI RAGGIEST
GL STRAGGLE
GN GANGSTER
GS GAGSTERS
STAGGERS
HO SHORTAGE
IL GLARIEST
REGALIST
IM MAGISTER
MIGRATES
RAGTIMES
STERIGMA
IN ANGRIEST
ASTRINGE
GANISTER
GANTRIES
GRANITES
INGRATES
RANGIEST
REASTING
STEARING
TASERING
IP GRAPIEST
IS AGISTERS
IT STRIGATE
IV VIRGATES
VITRAGES
LN STRANGLE
TANGLERS
TRANGLES
LO GLOATERS
LEGATORS
LU GAULTERS
GESTURAL
TRAGULES
MN GARMENTS
MARGENTS
RAGMENTS
NO ORANGEST
RAGSTONE
STONERAG
NP TREPANGS
NR GRANTERS
REGRANTS
STRANGER
NU STRAUNGE
OO ROOTAGES
OP PORTAGES
POTAGERS
OR GARROTES
OS STORAGES
OT GAROTTES
OU OUTRAGES
TY STRATEGY
UU AUGUSTER

AEHLRT 212
(LATHER)
AC TRACHEAL
AS TREHALAS
AT THEATRAL
BL BETHRALL
BS BLATHERS
HALBERTS
CO CHELATOR
CHLORATE
TROCHLEA
CP CHAPTREL
CS ARCHLETS
CU ARCHLUTE
TRAUCHLE
DE HALTERED
LATHERED
DL THRALLED
EE ETHEREAL
EI ETHERIAL
EN LEATHERN
ES HALTERES
LEATHERS
ET HEARTLET
EY LEATHERY
FS FARTHELS
FY FATHERLY
GI LITHARGE
THIRLAGE
GU LAUGHTER
GY LETHARGY
IO AEROLITH
LOATHIER
IY HEARTILY
LN ENTHRALL
MS THERMALS
NS ENTHRALS
OP PLETHORA
OS LOATHERS
PP THRAPPLE
RU URETHRAL
SS HARSLETS
SLATHERS

AEHRST 169
(HATERS)
AI HETAIRAS
AL TREHALAS
BC BRACHETS
BD BREADTHS
BE BREATHES
HARTBEES
BG BARGHEST
BL BLATHERS
HALBERTS
BO BATHORSE
BS BRASHEST
CC CATCHERS
CRATCHES
CD STARCHED
CE CHEATERS
HECTARES
RECHATES
RECHEATS
TEACHERS
CF FRATCHES
CH HATCHERS
CI CHARIEST
THERIACS
CL ARCHLETS
CM MATCHERS
CN CHANTERS
SNATCHER
STANCHER
TRANCHES
CO CHAROSET
THORACES
CP CHAPTERS
PATCHERS
CR CHARTERS
RECHARTS
STARCHER
CS STARCHES
CT CHATTERS
RATCHETS
CW WATCHERS
CY YACHTERS
DE HEADREST
DH THRASHED
DI HAIRSTED
HARDIEST
DY HYDRATES
EF FEATHERS
EH HEATHERS
EI HEARTIES
EL HALTERES
LEATHERS
EM ERATHEMS
EN HASTENER
HEARTENS
EP PREHEATS
SPREATHE
ET THEATERS
THEATRES
EV THREAVES
EW WEATHERS
WREATHES
FL FARTHELS
FS SHAFTERS
FT FARTHEST
GO SHORTAGE
HO HAROSETH
HR THRASHER
HS HARSHEST
THRASHES
II HAIRIEST
IN HAIRNETS
INEARTHS
THERIANS
IO HOARIEST
IR TRASHIER
IS SHERIATS
IU THESAURI
IW SWATHIER
WATERISH
IY HYSTERIA
KN THANKERS
LM THERMALS
LN ENTHRALS
LO LOATHERS
LS HARSLETS
SLATHERS
MN TRASHMEN
MP HAMPSTER
MS HAMSTERS
MU MAUTHERS
MW MAWTHERS
NP PANTHERS
NU HAUNTERS
UNEARTHS
UNHEARTS
URETHANS
OO TOHEROAS
OP POTSHARE
OS ASTHORES
EARSHOTS
HAROSETS
HOARSEST
OT RHEOSTAT
OX THORAXES
PS SHARPEST
SPARTHES
RU URETHRAS
RY TRASHERY
SS SHASTERS
ST SHATTERS
SV HARVESTS
TY SHATTERY
UU HAUTEURS

AEILMN 133
(MALINE)
AC ANALCIME
CALAMINE
AH HIELAMAN
AT ALAIMENT
LAMINATE
AV VELAMINA
BD MANDIBLE
BG EMBALING
BS BAILSMEN
BT BAILMENT
CE CAMELINE
CH INCHMEAL
CI LIMACINE
CN CLINAMEN
CO COALMINE
CP MANCIPLE
CS MESCALIN
DE ENDEMIAL
DF INFLAMED
DG MALIGNED
MEDALING
DI LIMNAEID
DP PLAIDMEN
DU UNMAILED
DY MAIDENLY
EF FILENAME
EG LIEGEMAN
EM MELAMINE
ET MELANITE
FR INFLAMER
RIFLEMAN
FS FLAMINES
INFLAMES
MISFALNE
FT FILAMENT
GG GLEAMING
GP EMPALING
GR GERMINAL
MALIGNER
MALINGER
GS MEASLING
GT LIGAMENT
METALING
GU AEMULING
GY YEALMING
HY HYMENIAL
IN MAINLINE
IS ALIENISM
LS MANILLES
MS MELANISM
MY IMMANELY
NO MINNEOLA
NP IMPANNEL
NS LINESMAN
MELANINS
OS LAMINOSE
MINEOLAS
SEMOLINA
PS IMPANELS
MANIPLES
RS MARLINES
MINERALS
RT TERMINAL
TRAMLINE
RU LEMURIAN
SS ISLESMAN
ST AILMENTS
ALIMENTS
MANLIEST

AEILNT 11
(ENTAIL)
AC ANALCITE
LAITANCE
AD DENTALIA
AE ALIENATE
AG AGENTIAL
ALGINATE
AH ANTHELIA
AM ALAIMENT
LAMINATE
AP PALATINE
AT ANTLIATE
AV AVENTAIL
BD BIDENTAL
BG BELATING
BLEATING
TANGIBLE
BL LIBELANT
BM BAILMENT
BP PINTABLE
BS INSTABLE
BV BIVALENT
CC CANTICLE
CG CLEATING
CH CHAINLET
CHATLINE
ETHNICAL
CL CLIENTAL
CP PECTINAL
PLANETIC
CR CLARINET
DD TIDELAND
DE ENTAILED
LINEATED
DF INFLATED
DG DELATING
DO DELATION
DP PANTILED
DU UNTAILED
DV DIVALENT
EG GALENITE
GELATINE
LEGATINE
EL TENAILLE
EM MELANITE
EP PETALINE
TAPELINE
ER ELATERIN
ENTAILER
TREENAIL
EV ELVANITE
VENTAILE
FM FILAMENT
FO OLEFIANT
FS INFLATES
GG TEAGLING
GH ATHELING
GM LIGAMENT
METALING
GN GANTLINE
LATENING
GO GELATION
LEGATION
GP PLEATING
GR ALERTING
ALTERING
INTEGRAL
RELATING
TANGLIER
TRIANGLE
GS EASTLING
GELATINS
GENITALS
STEALING
GV VALETING
GX EXALTING
GZ TEAZLING
HL THALLINE
HX ANTHELIX
HZ ZENITHAL
IK KALINITE
IR INERTIAL
IS ALIENIST
LITANIES
KS LANKIEST
MR TERMINAL
TRAMLINE
MS AILMENTS
ALIMENTS
MANLIEST
NR INTERNAL
NY INNATELY
OP ANTIPOLE
OR ORIENTAL
RELATION
TAILERON
OS ELATIONS
INSOLATE
TOENAILS
OT TONALITE
PR TRIPLANE
PS PANTILES
PLAINEST
PT TINPLATE
RS ENTRAILS
LATRINES
RATLINES
TRENAILS
RT RATTLINE
RU AUNTLIER
RETINULA
TENURIAL
RV INTERVAL

RY INTERLAY
SS EASTLINS
ELASTINS
SALIENTS
STANIELS
SU ALUNITES
INSULATE
SV VENTAILS
SW LAWNIEST
VY NATIVELY
VENALITY

AEILRS 16
(SAILER)
AB RAISABLE
AD SALARIED
AG GASALIER
LAIRAGES
REGALIAS
AO OLEARIAS
AS ASSAILER
SALARIES
AU AURELIAS
BB SLABBIER
BC CALIBERS
CALIBRES
BD RAILBEDS
BF BARFLIES
BH BLASHIER
BI BISERIAL
BL BALLSIER
LIBERALS
BM REMBLAIS
BN RINSABLE
BT LIBRATES
TABLIERS
CD DECRIALS
RADICELS
RADICLES
CE ESCALIER
CF FILACERS
CG GLACIERS
CH CHARLIES
CM CLAIMERS
MIRACLES
RECLAIMS
CN CARLINES
CO CALORIES
CARIOLES
CP CALIPERS
REPLICAS
SPIRACLE
CS CLASSIER
CT ALTRICES
ARTICLES
RECITALS
SELICTAR
CU AURICLES
CV CALIVERS
CLAVIERS
VISCERAL
DD DIEDRALS
DE REALISED
SIDEREAL
DG SLAIRGED
DI LAIRISED
DL DALLIERS
DIALLERS
DN ISLANDER
DO DARIOLES
SOLIDARE
SOREDIAL
DP PEDRAILS
PREDIALS
DT DILATERS
LARDIEST
DU RESIDUAL
DY DIALYSER
EF SERAFILE
EG GASELIER
EH SHIRALEE
EL REALLIES
EM ALMERIES
MEASLIER
EP ESPALIER
PEARLIES
ER REALISER
ES REALISES
ET ATELIERS
EARLIEST
LEARIEST
REALTIES
EV VELARISE
EY YEARLIES
EZ REALIZES
SLEAZIER
FH FLASHIER
FO FORESAIL
FT FLARIEST
FRAILEST
FU FAILURES
FV FAVRILES
FZ FILAZERS
GG SLAGGIER
GM GREMIALS
LAMIGERS
REGALISM
GN ENGRAILS
NARGILES
REALIGNS
SALERING
SANGLIER
SIGNALER
SLANGIER
GO GASOLIER
GIRASOLE
SERAGLIO
GS GLASSIER
GT GLARIEST
REGALIST
GY GREASILY
GZ GLAZIERS
HN INHALERS
HO AIRHOLES
SHOALIER
HP PLASHIER
HS HAIRLESS
HU HAULIERS
HV LAVISHER
SHRIEVAL
IL RAILLIES
IN AIRLINES
SNAILIER
IS LAIRISES
IT LAIRIEST
LISTERIA
IV RIVALISE
IZ LAIRIZES
KS SERKALIS
KT LARKIEST
STALKIER
STARLIKE
KV KLAVIERS
LR RALLIERS
LS RAILLESS
LT LITERALS
TALLIERS
LU RUELLIAS
LY SERIALLY
MN MARLINES
MINERALS
MO MORALISE
MP IMPEARLS
LEMPIRAS
MR LARMIERS
MS REALISMS
MT LAMITERS
MARLIEST
MY SMEARILY
NO AILERONS
ALERIONS
ALIENORS
NP PEARLINS
PRALINES
NR SNARLIER
NS RAINLESS
NT ENTRAILS
LATRINES
RATLINES
TRENAILS
NU LUNARIES
NV RAVELINS
NX RELAXINS
NY INLAYERS
SNAILERY
OP PELORIAS
POLARISE
OS SOLARISE
OT SOTERIAL
OV OVERSAIL
VALORISE
VARIOLES
VOLARIES
OY ROYALISE
OZ SOLARIZE
PP APPERILS
APPLIERS
PR REPRISAL
PT PILASTER
PLAISTER
PLAITERS
PV PREVAILS
PW SLIPWARE
QU SQUAILER
RT RETIRALS
RETRIALS
TRAILERS
RU RURALISE
ST REALISTS
SALTIERS
SALTIRES
SLAISTER
SV REVISALS
RIVALESS
TT TERTIALS
TU URALITES
VV REVIVALS
VY VIRELAYS

AEILRT 10
(RETAIL)
AC TAILRACE
AL ARILLATE
AM MATERIAL
AP PARIETAL
AR ARTERIAL
AV VARIETAL
BD LIBRATED
BE LIBERATE
BP PARTIBLE
BS LIBRATES
TABLIERS
BW WRITABLE
CD ARTICLED
CK TALCKIER
CM METRICAL
CN CLARINET
CO EROTICAL
LORICATE
CP PARTICLE
PRELATIC
CR CLARTIER
CS ALTRICES
ARTICLES
RECITALS
SELICTAR
CT TRACTILE
CV VERTICAL
CY LITERACY
DE RETAILED
DL TRIALLED
DO IDOLATER
TAILORED
DP DIPTERAL
TRIPEDAL
DS DILATERS
LARDIEST
DT DETRITAL
DY DIELYTRA
EF FRAILTEE
EH ETHERIAL
EM EREMITAL
MATERIEL
REALTIME
EN ELATERIN
ENTAILER
TREENAIL
EO AEROLITE
EP PEARLITE
ER RETAILER
ES ATELIERS
EARLIEST
LEARIEST
REALTIES
ET LATERITE
LITERATE
EV LEVIRATE
RELATIVE
FO FLOATIER
FS FLARIEST
FRAILEST
FT FILTRATE
FU FAULTIER
FILATURE
GH LITHARGE
THIRLAGE
GN ALERTING
ALTERING
INTEGRAL
RELATING
TANGLIER
TRIANGLE
GS GLARIEST
REGALIST
GT AGLITTER
GU LIGATURE
GY REGALITY
HO AEROLITH
LOATHIER
HY HEARTILY
IN INERTIAL
IP LIPARITE
IS LAIRIEST
LISTERIA
IT LITERATI
KP TRAPLIKE
KS LARKIEST
STALKIER
STARLIKE
KW WARTLIKE
LS LITERALS
TALLIERS
LU TAILLEUR
MM TRILEMMA
MN TERMINAL
TRAMLINE
MS LAMITERS
MARLIEST
MT REMITTAL
NN INTERNAL
NO ORIENTAL
RELATION
TAILERON
NP TRIPLANE
NS ENTRAILS
LATRINES
RATLINES
TRENAILS
NT RATTLINE
NU AUNTLIER
RETINULA
TENURIAL
NV INTERVAL
NY INTERLAY
OP EPILATOR
PETIOLAR
OS SOTERIAL
OT LITERATO
OV VIOLATER
PR PALTRIER
PS PILASTER
PLAISTER
PLAITERS
QU QUARTILE
REQUITAL
RS RETIRALS
RETRIALS
TRAILERS
RT RATTLIER
RY LITERARY
SS REALISTS
SALTIERS
SALTIRES
SLAISTER
ST TERTIALS
SU URALITES
TY ALTERITY
UZ LAZURITE
VV TRIVALVE
XZ ZELATRIX

AEILSS 248
(LASSIE)
AD ASSAILED
AG ALGESIAS
AM MALAISES
AN NASALISE
AR ASSAILER
SALARIES
BD DISABLES
BK KISSABLE
BM MISSABLE
BN ALBINESS
LESBIANS
BP PASSIBLE
BT ASTILBES
BESTIALS
STABILES
BU ISSUABLE
SUASIBLE
CG GLACISES
CI LAICISES
CN SANICLES
CO COALISES
CP SLIPCASE
SPECIALS
CR CLASSIER
CT ELASTICS
SALICETS
SCALIEST
DE DEISEALS
DF DISLEAFS
DG GLISSADE
DM MAIDLESS
MISDEALS
MISLEADS
DO ASSOILED
DEASOILS
DP DESPISAL
DU DEASIULS
DV DEVISALS
DY DIALYSES
EN SEALINES
ER REALISES
ET ASTELIES
FI SALIFIES
FS FILASSES
GL GALLISES
GN GAINLESS
GLASSINE
LEASINGS
SEALINGS
GO GOLIASES
SOILAGES
GR GLASSIER
HR HAIRLESS
HT SHALIEST
HV LAVISHES
HW SHAWLIES
WHAISLES
IR LAIRISES
IS SILESIAS
IW LEWISIAS
JM MAJLISES
KL KILLASES
KN SEALSKIN
KP KALPISES
KR SERKALIS
KS SAIKLESS

LN NAILLESS
SENSILLA
LP ILLAPSES
LR RAILLESS
LS SAILLESS
LT TAILLESS
MM MELISMAS
MN ISLESMAN
MP PESSIMAL
MR REALISMS
MX SMILAXES
NP PAINLESS
SPANIELS
NR RAINLESS
NT EASTLINS
ELASTINS
SALIENTS
STANIELS
NU INULASES
NZ LAZINESS
OR SOLARISE
OT ISOLATES
OX OXALISES
PT PALSIEST
PY PAISLEYS
RT REALISTS
SALTIERS
SALTIRES
SLAISTER
RV REVISALS
RIVALESS
SV VESSAILS
TT SALTIEST
SLATIEST
TW SWALIEST

AEILST 24
(ALITES)

AB BALISTAE
LABIATES
SATIABLE
AC SALICETA
AP STAPELIA
AV AESTIVAL
SALIVATE
AX SAXATILE
BB BISTABLE
BE SEABLITE
BI ALBITISE
SIBILATE
BK BALKIEST
BL BASTILLE
BM BALMIEST
TIMBALES
BN INSTABLE
BP EPIBLAST
BR LIBRATES
TABLIERS
BS ASTILBES
BESTIALS
STABILES
BU SUITABLE
BY BEASTILY
CC CALCITES
CD CITADELS
DIALECTS
CG GELASTIC
CH ETHICALS
CI CILIATES
SILICATE
CM CALMIEST
CLEMATIS
CLIMATES
METICALS
CO ALOETICS
COALIEST
SOCIETAL
CP PLICATES
CR ALTRICES
ARTICLES
RECITALS
SELICTAR
CS ELASTICS
SALICETS
SCALIEST
CT LATTICES
TALCIEST
CY CLAYIEST
DE LEADIEST
DG GLADIEST
DI IDEALIST
DM MEDALIST
MISDEALT
DO DIASTOLE
ISOLATED
SODALITE
SOLIDATE
DP TALIPEDS
DR DILATERS
LARDIEST
DV VALIDEST
DY DIASTYLE
STEADILY
EF FEALTIES
LEAFIEST
EG ELEGIAST
EK LEAKIEST
EL LEALTIES
EM MEALIEST
EP EPILATES
ER ATELIERS
EARLIEST
LEARIEST
REALTIES
ES ASTELIES
ET AILETTES
EV ELATIVES
LEAVIEST
VEALIEST
FI FILIATES
FK FLAKIEST
FM FLAMIEST
FN INFLATES
FO FOLIATES
FP FLEAPITS
FR FLARIEST
FRAILEST
FU FISTULAE
FV FESTIVAL
FW FLATWISE
FLAWIEST
FX FLAXIEST
GH LAIGHEST
GL LEGALIST
STILLAGE
TILLAGES
GN EASTLING
GELATINS
GENITALS
STEALING
GO OTALGIES
GR GLARIEST
REGALIST
GZ GLAZIEST
HI HAILIEST
HS SHALIEST
HT LATHIEST
LITHATES
HY HYALITES
IL TAILLIES
IN ALIENIST
LITANIES
IR LAIRIEST
LISTERIA
IV VITALISE
IX LAXITIES
IZ TAILZIES
KN LANKIEST
KO KEITLOAS
KR LARKIEST
STALKIER
STARLIKE
KT TALKIEST
LP PALLIEST
PASTILLE
LR LITERALS
TALLIERS
LS TAILLESS
LW WALLIEST
MN AILMENTS
ALIMENTS
MANLIEST
MO LOAMIEST
MP IMPLATES
PALMIEST
PALMIETS
PETALISM
SEPTIMAL
MR LAMITERS
MARLIEST
MT MALTIEST
METALIST
SMALTITE
MU SIMULATE
MY LAYTIMES
STEAMILY
NO ELATIONS
INSOLATE
TOENAILS
NP PANTILES
PLAINEST
NR ENTRAILS
LATRINES
RATLINES
TRENAILS
NS EASTLINS
ELASTINS
SALIENTS
STANIELS
NU ALUNITES
INSULATE
NV VENTAILS
NW LAWNIEST
OP SPOLIATE
OR SOTERIAL
OS ISOLATES
OT TOTALISE
OV VIOLATES
PR PILASTER
PLAISTER
PLAITERS
PS PALSIEST
PT PLATIEST
PY PTYALISE
QU LIQUATES
TEQUILAS
RR RETIRALS
RETRIALS
TRAILERS
RS REALISTS
SALTIERS
SALTIRES
SLAISTER
RT TERTIALS
RU URALITES
ST SALTIEST
SLATIEST
SW SWALIEST
TW WALTIEST
VY VILAYETS

AEIMNR 61
(REMAIN)

AD MARINADE
AP PEARMAIN
AR MARINERA
AT ANIMATER
MARINATE
AZ MAZARINE
BD BRIDEMAN
BG BREAMING
BS MIRBANES
CG AMERCING
CREAMING
CH CHAIRMEN
CO CORAMINE
CS CARMINES
CU MANICURE
DE REMAINED
DG DREAMING
MARGINED
DI MERIDIAN
DR MANRIDER
DS ADERMINS
SIRNAMED
DY DAIRYMEN
DZ ZEMINDAR
EG GERMAINE
ES REMANIES
EX EXAMINER
FL INFLAMER
RIFLEMAN
GI IMAGINER
MIGRAINE
GK REMAKING
GL GERMINAL
MALIGNER
MALINGER
GN ENARMING
RENAMING
GP EMPARING
GR REARMING
GS GERMAINS
SMEARING
GT EMIGRANT
GU GERANIUM
MAUNGIER
HS HARMINES
SHIREMAN
KS RAMEKINS
LS MARLINES
MINERALS
LT TERMINAL
TRAMLINE
LU LEMURIAN
NS REINSMAN
OS MORAINES
OW AIRWOMEN
OZ ARMOZINE
PT TRIPEMAN
PZ PRIZEMAN
QU RAMEQUIN
RS MARINERS
RV RIVERMAN
SS SEMINARS
SIRNAMES
ST MINARETS
RAIMENTS
SU ANEURISM
SY SEMINARY
TT MARTINET
TU RUMINATE
TW WARIMENT
TY TYRAMINE

AEIMNS 98
(MANIES)

AA ANAEMIAS
AC AMNESIAC
AG MAGNESIA
AS AMNESIAS
AT AMENTIAS
ANIMATES
BG BEAMINGS
EMBASING
BL BAILSMEN
BR MIRBANES
BT AMBIENTS
CH MACHINES
CL MESCALIN
CP PEMICANS
CR CARMINES
CS AMNESICS
CT SEMANTIC
CU SEMUNCIA
CY SYCAMINE
DE DEMAINES
INSEAMED
DM MISNAMED
DO NOMADIES
NOMADISE
DR ADERMINS
SIRNAMED
DS SIDESMAN
DT MEDIANTS
TIDESMAN
DU MAUNDIES
DY DYNAMISE
ER REMANIES
ES NEMESIAS
ET MATINEES
SEMINATE
EX EXAMINES
FI INFAMIES
INFAMISE
FL FLAMINES
INFLAMES
MISFALNE
FT MANIFEST
GI IMAGINES
GL MEASLING
GN MEANINGS
GR GERMAINS
SMEARING
GS GAMINESS
GT MANGIEST
MINTAGES
STEAMING
TEAMINGS
GV VEGANISM
HR HARMINES
SHIREMAN
HS SHAMISEN
HU HUMANISE
IL ALIENISM
IT MINIATES
IZ SIMAZINE
JS JASMINES
KR RAMEKINS
KT MANKIEST
MISTAKEN
LL MANILLES
LM MELANISM
LN LINESMAN
MELANINS
LO LAMINOSE
MINEOLAS
SEMOLINA
LP IMPANELS
MANIPLES
LR MARLINES
MINERALS
LS ISLESMAN
LT AILMENTS
ALIMENTS
MANLIEST
MS MISNAMES
NR REINSMAN
NT MANNITES
OR MORAINES
OT SOMNIATE
OU MOINEAUS
OW WOMANISE
RR MARINERS
RS SEMINARS
SIRNAMES
RT MINARETS
RAIMENTS
RU ANEURISM
RY SEMINARY
SS SAMISENS
ST MANTISES
MATINESS
SU ANIMUSES
SZ MAZINESS
UV MAUVEINS
MAUVINES

AEIMNT 53
(INMATE)

AD ANIMATED
DIAMANTE
AH ANTHEMIA
HAEMATIN
AL ALAIMENT
LAMINATE
AO METANOIA
AP IMPANATE
AR ANIMATER
MARINATE

AS AMENTIAS
ANIMATES
BL BAILMENT
BS AMBIENTS
CG MAGNETIC
CS SEMANTIC
DE DEMENTIA
DI MINIATED
DO DOMINATE
NEMATOID
DS MEDIANTS
TIDESMAN
DY DYNAMITE
EG GEMINATE
EK KETAMINE
EL MELANITE
EM MEANTIME
ES MATINEES
SEMINATE
FL FILAMENT
FS MANIFEST
GL LIGAMENT
METALING
GN ENTAMING
GR EMIGRANT
GS MANGIEST
MINTAGES
STEAMING
TEAMINGS
HI THIAMINE
HU INHUMATE
IS MINIATES
IT INTIMATE
IU MINUTIAE
IV VITAMINE
KS MANKIEST
MISTAKEN
LR TERMINAL
TRAMLINE
LS AILMENTS
ALIMENTS
MANLIEST
MN IMMANENT
MO AMMONITE
NO NOMINATE
NS MANNITES
OP PTOMAINE
OS SOMNIATE
OZ MONAZITE
PR TRIPEMAN
RS MINARETS
RAIMENTS
RT MARTINET
RU RUMINATE
RW WARIMENT
RY TYRAMINE
SS MANTISES
MATINESS
TU MATUTINE
VZ VIZAMENT

AEIMRS 112
(ARMIES)
AC MACARISE
MESARAIC
AU URAEMIAS
BD EMBRAIDS
BG GAMBIERS
BJ JAMBIERS
BL REMBLAIS
BN MIRBANES
BT BARMIEST
BU AUMBRIES
CC CERAMICS
CE CASIMERE
RACEMISE
CG GRIMACES
CH CHASMIER
CHIMERAS
MARCHESI
CL CLAIMERS
MIRACLES
RECLAIMS
CM RACEMISM
CN CARMINES
CT CERAMIST
MATRICES
DD DISARMED
MISDREAD
DE MADERISE
DF MISFARED
DH MISHEARD
DJ JEMIDARS
DM MERMAIDS
DN ADERMINS
SIRNAMED
DR ADMIRERS
DISARMER
DS MISREADS
SIDEARMS
DT MARDIEST
MISRATED
READMITS
EG GAMESIER
EL ALMERIES
MEASLIER
EN REMANIES
EP EMPAIRES
ER SMEARIER
ES SERIEMAS
ET EMIRATES
REAMIEST
STEAMIER
FI RAMIFIES
FR FIREARMS
FS MISFARES
GL GREMIALS
LAMIGERS
REGALISM
GN GERMAINS
SMEARING
GO GORAMIES
GP EPIGRAMS
PRIMAGES
GR ARMIGERS
GS GISARMES
GT MAGISTER
MIGRATES
RAGTIMES
STERIGMA
HN HARMINES
SHIREMAN
HP SAMPHIRE
SERAPHIM
HR MARSHIER
HS MARISHES
MISHEARS
IT AIRTIMES
SERIATIM
KN RAMEKINS
KP RAMPIKES
LN MARLINES
MINERALS
LO MORALISE
LP IMPEARLS
LEMPIRAS
LR LARMIERS
LS REALISMS
LT LAMITERS
MARLIEST
LY SMEARILY
MP SPAMMIER
MR SMARMIER
MT MARMITES
NN REINSMAN
NO MORAINES
NR MARINERS
NS SEMINARS
SIRNAMES
NT MINARETS
RAIMENTS
NU ANEURISM
NY SEMINARY
OR ARMOIRES
ARMORIES
OT AMORTISE
ATOMISER
PR RAMPIRES
PS IMPRESAS
SAMPIRES
PT APTERISM
PRIMATES
PV VAMPIRES
PW SWAMPIER
QU MARQUISE
RR MARRIERS
RS SIMARRES
ST ASTERISM
MAISTERS
MISRATES
SEMITARS
SMARTIES
SY EMISSARY
TT MISTREAT
TERATISM
TU MURIATES
SEMITAUR
TW WARTIMES
TX MATRIXES
TY SYMITARE
WW SWIMWEAR

AEIMST 95
(MATIES)
AD DIASTEMA
AM IMAMATES
AN AMENTIAS
ANIMATES
BC BETACISM
BE BEAMIEST
BG MEGABITS
BH IMBATHES
BL BALMIEST
TIMBALES
BN AMBIENTS
BR BARMIEST
CE EMICATES
CH MISTEACH
TACHISME
CJ MAJESTIC
CL CALMIEST
CLEMATIS
CLIMATES
METICALS
CN SEMANTIC
CP CAMPIEST
CAMPSITE
CR CERAMIST
MATRICES
CS ETACISMS
DD MISDATED
DE MEDIATES
DG SIGMATED
DL MEDALIST
MISDEALT
DM MISMATED
DN MEDIANTS
TIDESMAN
DO ATOMISED
DP DAMPIEST
IMPASTED
DR MARDIEST
MISRATED
READMITS
DS MISDATES
DU TAEDIUMS
DY DAYTIMES
EL MEALIEST
EN MATINEES
SEMINATE
ER EMIRATES
REAMIEST
STEAMIER
ES SEAMIEST
STEAMIES
ET ESTIMATE
ETATISME
MEATIEST
TEATIMES
EW TEAMWISE
FL FLAMIEST
FN MANIFEST
FO FOAMIEST
GM GAMMIEST
GN MANGIEST
MINTAGES
STEAMING
TEAMINGS
GP PIGMEATS
GR MAGISTER
MIGRATES
RAGTIMES
STERIGMA
GS SIGMATES
GU GAUMIEST
HM HAMMIEST
HP MATESHIP
SHIPMATE
HS ATHEISMS
MASHIEST
MATHESIS
IN MINIATES
IR AIRTIMES
SERIATIM
IT IMITATES
JM JAMMIEST
KN MANKIEST
MISTAKEN
KS MISTAKES
KW MAWKIEST
LN AILMENTS
ALIMENTS
MANLIEST
LO LOAMIEST
LP IMPLATES
PALMIEST
PALMIETS
PETALISM
SEPTIMAL
LR LAMITERS
MARLIEST
LT MALTIEST
METALIST
SMALTITE
LU SIMULATE
LY LAYTIMES
STEAMILY
MP PSAMMITE
MR MARMITES
MS MISMATES
NN MANNITES
NO SOMNIATE
NR MINARETS
RAIMENTS
NS MANTISES
MATINESS
OR AMORTISE
ATOMISER
OS AMITOSES
AMOSITES
ATOMISES
OSMIATES
OX TOXEMIAS
OZ ATOMIZES
PR APTERISM
PRIMATES
PS IMPASTES
PASTIMES
RS ASTERISM
MAISTERS
MISRATES
SEMITARS
SMARTIES
RT MISTREAT
TERATISM
RU MURIATES
SEMITAUR
RW WARTIMES
RX MATRIXES
RY SYMITARE
SS ASTEISMS
MASSIEST
ST MASTIEST
MISSTATE
SZ MESTIZAS
YZ AZYMITES

AEINRS 6
(SARNIE)
AC CANARIES
AD ARANEIDS
AG ANGARIES
AP PANARIES
AT ANTISERA
ARTESIAN
RESINATA
BC CARBINES
BD BRANDIES
BRANDISE
BG BEARINGS
SABERING
BI BINARIES
BK BEARSKIN
INBREAKS
BL RINSABLE
BM MIRBANES
BO BARONIES
BT ATEBRINS
BANISTER
BU ANBURIES
URBANISE
BZ ZEBRINAS
CE CINEREAS
INCREASE
RESIANCE
CF FANCIERS
CG CREASING
GRECIANS
SEARCING
CH INARCHES
CI RIANCIES
CL CARLINES
CM CARMINES
CN CRANNIES
CO SCENARIO
CS ARSENICS
CERASINS
RACINESS
CT CANISTER
CARNIEST
CISTERNA
CREATINS
NACRITES
SCANTIER
DE ARSENIDE
DENARIES
DRAISENE
NEARSIDE
DF FRIANDES
DG DERAIGNS
GRADINES
READINGS
DI DRAISINE
DL ISLANDER
DM ADERMINS
SIRNAMED
DN INSNARED
DO ANEROIDS
DONARIES
DP SPRAINED
DR DRAINERS
SERRANID
DS ARIDNESS
SARDINES
DT DETRAINS
RANDIEST
STRAINED
DU DENARIUS
UNRAISED
URANIDES
DV INVADERS
SANDIVER
DY SYNEDRIA
EG GESNERIA
EH INHEARSE
EK SNEAKIER
EM REMANIES
EN ANSERINE
EP NAPERIES
ER REARISEN

ES SENARIES
ET ARSENITE
RESINATE
STEARINE
TRAINEES
EU UNEASIER
FO FARINOSE
FP FIREPANS
FR REFRAINS
FS FAIRNESS
SANSERIF
SERAFINS
FT FENITARS
FX XERAFINS
GG GEARINGS
GREASING
SNAGGIER
GH HEARINGS
HEARSING
SHEARING
GK SKEARING
GL ENGRAILS
NARGILES
REALIGNS
SALERING
SANGLIER
SIGNALER
SLANGIER
GM GERMAINS
SMEARING
GN AGINNERS
EARNINGS
ENGRAINS
GRANNIES
GO IGNAROES
ORGANISE
ORIGANES
GP PREASING
SPEARING
GR EARRINGS
GRAINERS
GS REASSIGN
SEARINGS
SERINGAS
GT ANGRIEST
ASTRINGE
GANISTER
GANTRIES
GRANITES
INGRATES
RANGIEST
REASTING
STEARING
TASERING
GV VINEGARS
GW SWEARING
WEARINGS
GY RESAYING
HL INHALERS
HM HARMINES
SHIREMAN
HP HEPARINS
PARISHEN
SERAPHIN
HR SHARNIER
HS ARSHINES
HT HAIRNETS
INEARTHS
THERIANS
HV ENRAVISH

VANISHER
HW SHERWANI
IK KAISERIN
IL AIRLINES
SNAILIER
IN SIRENIAN
IS AIRINESS
IT INERTIAS
RAINIEST
IY YERSINIA
JT NARTJIES
KM RAMEKINS
KT KERATINS
NARKIEST
KW SWANKIER
LM MARLINES
MINERALS
LO AILERONS
ALERIONS
ALIENORS
LP PEARLINS
PRALINES
LR SNARLIER
LS RAINLESS
LT ENTRAILS
LATRINES
RATLINES
TRENAILS
LU LUNARIES
LV RAVELINS
LX RELAXINS
LY INLAYERS
SNAILERY
MN REINSMAN
MO MORAINES
MR MARINERS
MS SEMINARS
SIRNAMES
MT MINARETS
RAIMENTS
MU ANEURISM
MY SEMINARY
NO RAISONNE
NP PANNIERS
NS INSNARES
NT ENTRAINS
TRANNIES
NU ANEURINS
UNARISEN
NW SWANNIER
OS ERASIONS
SENSORIA
OT ANOESTRI
ARSONITE
NOTARIES
NOTARISE
ROSINATE
OV AVERSION
PP SNAPPIER
PT PAINTERS
PANTRIES
PERTAINS
PINASTER
PRISTANE
REPAINTS
PU UNPRAISE
PW SPAWNIER
RT RESTRAIN
RETRAINS
STRAINER

TERRAINS
TRAINERS
TRANSIRE
ST ARTINESS
RESIANTS
RETSINAS
SNARIEST
STAINERS
STARNIES
STEARINS
SU SENARIUS
SW WARINESS
SX XERANSIS
TT INTREATS
NITRATES
STRAITEN
TARTINES
TERTIANS
TU RUINATES
TAURINES
URANITES
URINATES
TW TINWARES
UV VAURIENS
UZ AZURINES
SUZERAIN
VV VERVAINS
ZZ SNAZZIER

AEINRT 1
(RETAIN)
AB RABATINE
AC CARINATE
AD DENTARIA
RAINDATE
AG AERATING
AM ANIMATER
MARINATE
AO AERATION
AS ANTISERA
ARTESIAN
RESINATA
AT REATTAIN
AU INAURATE
AZ ATRAZINE
BG BERATING
REBATING
BO BARITONE
OBTAINER
BS ATEBRINS
BANISTER
BU BRAUNITE
URBANITE
CD CRINATED
DICENTRA
CE CENTIARE
CREATINE
INCREATE
ITERANCE
CG CATERING
CITRANGE
CREATING
REACTING
CL CLARINET
CO ANORETIC
CREATION
REACTION
CS CANISTER
CARNIEST
CISTERNA

CREATINS
NACRITES
SCANTIER
CT INTERACT
CV NAVICERT
CX XERANTIC
DD INDARTED
DE DETAINER
RETAINED
DG DERATING
GRADIENT
REDATING
TREADING
DI DAINTIER
DO AROINTED
DERATION
ORDINATE
RATIONED
DP DIPTERAN
DS DETRAINS
RANDIEST
STRAINED
DT NITRATED
DU DATURINE
INDURATE
RUINATED
URINATED
EG GRATINEE
EH ATHERINE
EK ANKERITE
KREATINE
EL ELATERIN
ENTAILER
TREENAIL
EP APERIENT
ER RETAINER
ES ARSENITE
RESINATE
STEARINE
TRAINEES
FI FAINTIER
FS FENITARS
GH EARTHING
HEARTING
INGATHER
GK RETAKING
GL ALERTING
ALTERING
INTEGRAL
RELATING
TANGLIER
TRIANGLE
GM EMIGRANT
GP TAPERING
GS ANGRIEST
ASTRINGE
GANISTER
GANTRIES
GRANITES
INGRATES
RANGIEST
REASTING
STEARING
TASERING
GT ARETTING
TREATING
GV AVERTING
TAVERING
VINTAGER
GW TWANGIER

WATERING
HP PERIANTH
HS HAIRNETS
INEARTHS
THERIANS
HU HAURIENT
HW TARWHINE
IL INERTIAL
IP PAINTIER
IS INERTIAS
RAINIEST
JS NARTJIES
JU JAUNTIER
KS KERATINS
NARKIEST
KW KNITWEAR
LM TERMINAL
TRAMLINE
LN INTERNAL
LO ORIENTAL
RELATION
TAILERON
LP TRIPLANE
LS ENTRAILS
LATRINES
RATLINES
TRENAILS
LT RATTLINE
LU AUNTLIER
RETINULA
TENURIAL
LV INTERVAL
LY INTERLAY
MP TRIPEMAN
MS MINARETS
RAIMENTS
MT MARTINET
MU RUMINATE
MW WARIMENT
MY TYRAMINE
NO ANOINTER
INORNATE
NR INERRANT
NS ENTRAINS
TRANNIES
OP ATROPINE
OR ANTERIOR
OS ANOESTRI
ARSONITE
NOTARIES
NOTARISE
ROSINATE
OT TENTORIA
OZ NOTARIZE
PR TERRAPIN
PS PAINTERS
PANTRIES
PERTAINS
PINASTER
PRISTANE
REPAINTS
PT TRIPTANE
PU PAINTURE
PX EXPIRANT
QU QUAINTER
RS RESTRAIN
RETRAINS
STRAINER
TERRAINS
TRAINERS

TRANSIRE
RV VERATRIN
RW INTERWAR
SS ARTINESS
RESIANTS
RETSINAS
SNARIEST
STAINERS
STARNIES
STEARINS
ST INTREATS
NITRATES
STRAITEN
TARTINES
TERTIANS
SU RUINATES
TAURINES
URANITES
URINATES
SW TINWARES
TU TAINTURE
UV VAUNTIER

AEINST 2
(SATINE)
AB BASANITE
AC ESTANCIA
AG SAGINATE
AH ASTHENIA
AM AMENTIAS
ANIMATES
AR ANTISERA
ARTESIAN
RESINATA
AT ASTATINE
SANITATE
TANAISTE
AV SANATIVE
BC CABINETS
BD BANDIEST
BE BETAINES
BG BEATINGS
BH ABSINTHE
BI BAINITES
BK BEATNIKS
BL INSTABLE
BM AMBIENTS
BO BOTANIES
BOTANISE
NIOBATES
OBEISANT
BP BEPAINTS
BR ATEBRINS
BANISTER
BS BASINETS
BASSINET
BESAINTS
BESTAINS
BT TABINETS
CD DISTANCE
CE CINEASTE
CF FANCIEST
CH ASTHENIC
CHANTIES
CI CANITIES
CM SEMANTIC
CN ANCIENTS
CANNIEST
INSTANCE
CO ACONITES

CANOEIST
CR CANISTER
CARNIEST
CISTERNA
CREATINS
NACRITES
SCANTIER
CS CINEASTS
SCANTIES
CT CANTIEST
NICTATES
TETANICS
CV CISTVAEN
VESICANT
CY CYANITES
DD DANDIEST
DE ANDESITE
DG SEDATING
STEADING
DH HANDIEST
DI ADENITIS
DAINTIES
DM MEDIANTS
TIDESMAN
DO ASTONIED
SEDATION
DP DEPAINTS
DR DETRAINS
RANDIEST
STRAINED
DS SANDIEST
DT INSTATED
DU AUDIENTS
SINUATED
DV DEVIANTS
DY DESYATIN
EG SAGENITE
EM MATINEES
SEMINATE
ER ARSENITE
RESINATE
STEARINE
TRAINEES
ET ANISETTE
TETANIES
TETANISE
EV NAIVETES
FG FEASTING
FI FAINITES
FL INFLATES
FM MANIFEST
FN INFANTES
FR FENITARS
FT FAINTEST
GG NAGGIEST
GH GAHNITES
HEATINGS
GL EASTLING
GELATINS
GENITALS
STEALING
GM MANGIEST
MINTAGES
STEAMING
TEAMINGS
GN ANTIGENS
GENTIANS
STEANING
GR ANGRIEST
ASTRINGE

GANISTER
GANTRIES
GRANITES
INGRATES
RANGIEST
REASTING
STEARING
TASERING
GS EASTINGS
GENISTAS
GIANTESS
SEATINGS
TEASINGS
TSIGANES
GT ESTATING
TANGIEST
GU SAUTEING
GV VINTAGES
GW SWEATING
GY YEASTING
HP PENTHIAS
THESPIAN
HR HAIRNETS
INEARTHS
THERIANS
HS ANTHESIS
SHANTIES
HT HESITANT
HW INSWATHE
IK KAINITES
IL ALIENIST
LITANIES
IM MINIATES
IP PIANISTE
IR INERTIAS
RAINIEST
IS ISATINES
SANITIES
SANITISE
IV VANITIES
IX AXINITES
IZ SANITIZE
JR NARTJIES
JT JANTIEST
JU JAUNTIES
KL LANKIEST
KM MANKIEST
MISTAKEN
KR KERATINS
NARKIEST
KS SNAKIEST
KV KISTVAEN
KW WANKIEST
KY KYANITES
LM AILMENTS
ALIMENTS
MANLIEST
LO ELATIONS
INSOLATE
TOENAILS
LP PANTILES
PLAINEST
LR ENTRAILS
LATRINES
RATLINES
TRENAILS
LS EASTLINS
ELASTINS
SALIENTS
STANIELS

LU ALUNITES
INSULATE
LV VENTAILS
LW LAWNIEST
MN MANNITES
MO SOMNIATE
MR MINARETS
RAIMENTS
MS MANTISES
MATINESS
NO ENATIONS
NP PANTINES
NR ENTRAINS
TRANNIES
NS INSANEST
NT ANTIENTS
STANNITE
OP SAPONITE
OR ANOESTRI
ARSONITE
NOTARIES
NOTARISE
ROSINATE
OS ASSIENTO
ASTONIES
OV STOVAINE
OX SAXONITE
PP NAPPIEST
PR PAINTERS
PANTRIES
PERTAINS
PINASTER
PRISTANE
REPAINTS
PS STEAPSIN
PT PATIENTS
PU PETUNIAS
SUPINATE
PY EPINASTY
QU ANTIQUES
QUANTISE
RR RESTRAIN
RETRAINS
STRAINER
TERRAINS
TRAINERS
TRANSIRE
RS ARTINESS
RESIANTS
RETSINAS
SNARIEST
STAINERS
STARNIES
STEARINS
RT INTREATS
NITRATES
STRAITEN
TARTINES
TERTIANS
RU RUINATES
TAURINES
URANITES
URINATES
RW TINWARES
SS SAINTESS
SESTINAS
ST INSTATES
NASTIEST
SATINETS
TITANESS

TT NATTIEST
TV TASTEVIN
TW TAWNIEST
UV SUIVANTE
WY YAWNIEST

AEIPRS 75
(PRAISE)
AC AIRSPACE
AD PARADISE
AG IGARAPES
AI APIARIES
AN PANARIES
AP APPRAISE
AR PAREIRAS
AS SPIRAEAS
AT ASPIRATE
PARASITE
SEPTARIA
BE BEPRAISE
CC CAPRICES
CD EPACRIDS
CG SPAGERIC
CH ASPHERIC
CHARPIES
PARCHESI
SERAPHIC
CI PIRACIES
CK EARPICKS
CL CALIPERS
REPLICAS
SPIRACLE
CP EPICARPS
CR PERISARC
CS SCRAPIES
CT CRAPIEST
CRISPATE
PICRATES
PRACTISE
DD DISPREAD
DE AIRSPEED
DG SPAIRGED
DH RAPHIDES
DI PRESIDIA
DL PEDRAILS
PREDIALS
DN SPRAINED
DO DIASPORE
PARODIES
DP APPRISED
DRAPPIES
DR DRAPIERS
DS DESPAIRS
DT DIPTERAS
RAPIDEST
SPIRATED
TARSIPED
TRAIPSED
DU UPRAISED
EG PIERAGES
EL ESPALIER
PEARLIES
EM EMPAIRES
EN NAPERIES
ER PEREIRAS
SPEARIER
ET PETARIES
FF PIAFFERS
FN FIREPANS
GK GARPIKES

GM EPIGRAMS
PRIMAGES
GN PREASING
SPEARING
GS PRISAGES
SPAIRGES
GT GRAPIEST
HL PLASHIER
HM SAMPHIRE
SERAPHIM
HN HEPARINS
PARISHEN
SERAPHIN
HO APHORISE
HP PAPISHER
SAPPHIRE
HR PHRASIER
HS PARISHES
SHARPIES
IR PRAIRIES
IT PARITIES
IW PAIRWISE
KM RAMPIKES
KR SPARKIER
KS SPARKIES
KT PARKIEST
LM IMPEARLS
LEMPIRAS
LN PEARLINS
PRALINES
LO PELORIAS
POLARISE
LP APPERILS
APPLIERS
LR REPRISAL
LT PILASTER
PLAISTER
PLAITERS
LV PREVAILS
LW SLIPWARE
MM SPAMMIER
MR RAMPIRES
MS IMPRESAS
SAMPIRES
MT APTERISM
PRIMATES
MV VAMPIRES
MW SWAMPIER
NN PANNIERS
NP SNAPPIER
NT PAINTERS
PANTRIES
PERTAINS
PINASTER
PRISTANE
REPAINTS
NU UNPRAISE
NW SPAWNIER
OV VAPORISE
PR APPRISER
PS APPRISES
PT PERIAPTS
PZ APPRIZES
RR SPARRIER
RS PRAISERS
RY SPRAYIER
ST PASTRIES
PIASTRES
RASPIEST
TRAIPSES

SU UPRAISES
SV PARVISES
TV PRIVATES
TW WIRETAPS
TY ASPERITY
VY VESPIARY
XY PYREXIAS

AEIRST 3
(SATIRE)
AD DATARIES
RADIATES
AH HETAIRAS
AN ANTISERA
ARTESIAN
RESINATA
AP ASPIRATE
PARASITE
SEPTARIA
AS ASTERIAS
ATRESIAS
AT ARIETTAS
ARISTATE
AV VARIATES
BD BARDIEST
BRAIDEST
RABIDEST
TRIBADES
BK BARKIEST
BRAKIEST
BREASKIT
BL LIBRATES
TABLIERS
BM BARMIEST
BN ATEBRINS
BANISTER
BO SABOTIER
BR ARBITERS
RAREBITS
BT BIRETTAS
BV VIBRATES
BW WARBIEST
BY BESTIARY
SYBARITE
CD ACRIDEST
CG AGRESTIC
CH CHARIEST
THERIACS
CL ALTRICES
ARTICLES
RECITALS
SELICTAR
CM CERAMIST
MATRICES
CN CANISTER
CARNIEST
CISTERNA
CREATINS
NACRITES
SCANTIER
CP CRAPIEST
CRISPATE
PICRATES
PRACTISE
CR ERRATICS
CS SCARIEST
CT CITRATES
CRISTATE
SCATTIER
CU SURICATE

CZ CRAZIEST
DD DISRATED
DE READIEST
SERIATED
SIDERATE
STEADIER
DH HAIRSTED
HARDIEST
DI IRISATED
DK STRAIKED
DL DILATERS
LARDIEST
DM MARDIEST
MISRATED
READMITS
DN DETRAINS
RANDIEST
STRAINED
DO ASTEROID
DP DIPTERAS
RAPIDEST
SPIRATED
TARSIPED
TRAIPSED
DS ASTERIDS
DIASTERS
DISASTER
DISRATES
DT STRAITED
STRIATED
TARDIEST
DW TAWDRIES
EE EATERIES
EH HEARTIES
EL ATELIERS
EARLIEST
LEARIEST
REALTIES
EM EMIRATES
REAMIEST
STEAMIER
EN ARSENITE
RESINATE
STEARINE
TRAINEES
EO ETAERIOS
EP PETARIES
ER ARTERIES
REASTIER
ES SERIATES
ET ARIETTES
ITERATES
TEARIEST
TREATIES
TREATISE
EV EVIRATES
EW SWEATIER
TAWERIES
WEARIEST
EY YEASTIER
FG FRIGATES
FI RATIFIES
FL FLARIEST
FRAILEST
FN FENITARS
FR FRATRIES
FW WASTRIFE
GG RAGGIEST
GL GLARIEST
REGALIST
GM MAGISTER
MIGRATES
RAGTIMES
STERIGMA
GN ANGRIEST
ASTRINGE
GANISTER
GANTRIES
GRANITES
INGRATES
RANGIEST
REASTING
STEARING
TASERING
GP GRAPIEST
GS AGISTERS
GT STRIGATE
GV VIRGATES
VITRAGES
HI HAIRIEST
HN HAIRNETS
INEARTHS
THERIANS
HO HOARIEST
HR TRASHIER
HS SHERIATS
HU THESAURI
HW SWATHIER
WATERISH
HY HYSTERIA
IL LAIRIEST
LISTERIA
IM AIRTIMES
SERIATIM
IN INERTIAS
RAINIEST
IP PARITIES
IR RARITIES
IS IRISATES
SATIRISE
IV VAIRIEST
IW WISTERIA
IZ SATIRIZE
JN NARTJIES
JO JAROSITE
KL LARKIEST
STALKIER
STARLIKE
KN KERATINS
NARKIEST
KP PARKIEST
KS ASTERISK
SARKIEST
LL LITERALS
TALLIERS
LM LAMITERS
MARLIEST
LN ENTRAILS
LATRINES
RATLINES
TRENAILS
LO SOTERIAL
LP PILASTER
PLAISTER
PLAITERS
LR RETIRALS
RETRIALS
TRAILERS
LS REALISTS
SALTIERS
SALTIRES
SLAISTER
LT TERTIALS
LU URALITES
MM MARMITES
MN MINARETS
RAIMENTS
MO AMORTISE
ATOMISER
MP APTERISM
PRIMATES
MS ASTERISM
MAISTERS
MISRATES
SEMITARS
SMARTIES
MT MISTREAT
TERATISM
MU MURIATES
SEMITAUR
MW WARTIMES
MX MATRIXES
MY SYMITARE
NN ENTRAINS
TRANNIES
NO ANOESTRI
ARSONITE
NOTARIES
NOTARISE
ROSINATE
NP PAINTERS
PANTRIES
PERTAINS
PINASTER
PRISTANE
REPAINTS
NR RESTRAIN
RETRAINS
STRAINER
TERRAINS
TRAINERS
TRANSIRE
NS ARTINESS
RESIANTS
RETSINAS
SNARIEST
STAINERS
STARNIES
STEARINS
NT INTREATS
NITRATES
STRAITEN
TARTINES
TERTIANS
NU RUINATES
TAURINES
URANITES
URINATES
NW TINWARES
OR ROARIEST
ROTARIES
OV VOTARIES
PP PERIAPTS
PS PASTRIES
PIASTRES
RASPIEST
TRAIPSES
PV PRIVATES
PW WIRETAPS
PY ASPERITY
RR STARRIER
TARRIERS
RS TARSIERS
RT RETRAITS
STRAITER
TARRIEST
RW STRAWIER
SS TIRASSES
ST ARTISTES
ARTSIEST
STRIATES
SV TRAVISES
SW WAISTERS
WAITRESS
WASTRIES
TT ATTRITES
RATTIEST
TARTIEST
TITRATES
TW WARTIEST
TX EXTRAITS
UZ AZURITES
VY VESTIARY

AEIRTT 29
(ATTIRE)

AN REATTAIN
AP PATRIATE
AS ARIETTAS
ARISTATE
AZ ZARATITE
BC BRATTICE
BE BATTERIE
BR BRATTIER
BS BIRETTAS
BY YTTERBIA
CD TETRACID
TETRADIC
CF TRIFECTA
CH CHATTIER
THEATRIC
CL TRACTILE
CM TREMATIC
CN INTERACT
CR RETRAICT
CS CITRATES
CRISTATE
SCATTIER
CU URTICATE
CV TRACTIVE
DE ITERATED
DL DETRITAL
DN NITRATED
DO TERATOID
DS STRAITED
STRIATED
TARDIEST
DT ATTRITED
TITRATED
EG AIGRETTE
EL LATERITE
LITERATE
ER RETRAITE
ES ARIETTES
ITERATES
TEARIEST
TREATIES
TREATISE
FL FILTRATE
GL AGLITTER
GN ARETTING
TREATING
GS STRIGATE
HP THREAPIT
IL LITERATI
IR IRRITATE
IT TRITIATE
LM REMITTAL
LN RATTLINE
LO LITERATO
LR RATTLIER
LS TERTIALS
LY ALTERITY
MN MARTINET
MO AMORETTI
MS MISTREAT
TERATISM
NO TENTORIA
NP TRIPTANE
NS INTREATS
NITRATES
STRAITEN
TARTINES
TERTIANS
NU TAINTURE
OV ROTATIVE
RS RETRAITS
STRAITER
TARRIEST
RT RETRAITT
RY TERTIARY
SS ARTISTES
ARTSIEST
STRIATES
ST ATTRITES
RATTIEST
TARTIEST
TITRATES
SW WARTIEST
SX EXTRAITS
TW ATWITTER

AEISTT 83
(TASTIE)

AD SATIATED
AG AGITATES
AN ASTATINE
SANITATE
TANAISTE
AP APATITES
AR ARIETTAS
ARISTATE
AS SATIATES
BC TABETICS
BN TABINETS
BR BIRETTAS
BS BATISTES
BT BATTIEST
CC ECSTATIC
CD DICTATES
CH CHATTIES
TACHISTE
CK TACKIEST
TIETACKS
CL LATTICES
TALCIEST
CN CANTIEST
NICTATES
TETANICS
CO OSCITATE
CR CITRATES
CRISTATE
SCATTIER
CS STATICES
CT CATTIEST
CU EUSTATIC
CW SCAWTITE
DN INSTATED
DR STRAITED
STRIATED
TARDIEST
DS DISTASTE
STAIDEST
DU SITUATED
EH ATHETISE
HESITATE
EL AILETTES
EM ESTIMATE
ETATISME
MEATIEST
TEATIMES
EN ANISETTE
TETANIES
TETANISE
EP PEATIEST
ER ARIETTES
ITERATES
TEARIEST
TREATIES
TREATISE
ET ETATISTE
STEATITE
EV AVIETTES
ESTIVATE
EVITATES
FN FAINTEST
FT FATTIEST
GG TAGGIEST
GN ESTATING
TANGIEST
GO GOATIEST
GR STRIGATE
GS STAGIEST
HL LATHIEST
LITHATES
HN HESITANT
HS ATHEISTS
HASTIEST
STAITHES
HW THAWIEST
THWAITES
IM IMITATES
IV VITIATES
JN JANTIEST
KL TALKIEST
LM MALTIEST
METALIST
SMALTITE
LO TOTALISE
LP PLATIEST
LR TERTIALS
LS SALTIEST
SLATIEST
LW WALTIEST
MR MISTREAT
TERATISM
MS MASTIEST
MISSTATE
NN ANTIENTS
STANNITE

NP PATIENTS
NR INTREATS
NITRATES
STRAITEN
TARTINES
TERTIANS
NS INSTATES
NASTIEST
SATINETS
TITANESS
NT NATTIEST
NV TASTEVIN
NW TAWNIEST
OS TOASTIES
PS PASTIEST
RR RETRAITS
STRAITER
TARRIEST
RS ARTISTES
ARTSIEST
STRIATES
RT ATTRITES
RATTIEST
TARTIEST
TITRATES
RW WARTIEST
RX EXTRAITS
ST TASTIEST
SU SITUATES
SV VASTIEST
TT TATTIEST
TU ATTUITES
TW TAWTIEST

AELMNT 211
(LAMENT)
AH METHANAL
AI ALAIMENT
LAMINATE
AO MALONATE
AP PLATEMAN
AR MATERNAL
AS TALESMAN
BI BAILMENT
BS SEMBLANT
DE LAMENTED
EI MELANITE
EP PLATEMEN
ES MANTEELS
STEELMAN
TALESMEN
ET MANTELET
EV LAVEMENT
FI FILAMENT
FO MATFELON
GI LIGAMENT
METALING
GU GUNMETAL
HO METHANOL
IR TERMINAL
TRAMLINE
IS AILMENTS
ALIMENTS
MANLIEST
LS STALLMEN
LY MENTALLY
TALLYMEN
NU UNMANTLE
OS SALMONET
ST MANTLETS
SU NUTMEALS

AELNRS 63
(LANERS)
AD ADRENALS
AG ALNAGERS
AK LARNAKES
AP PRENASAL
AS ARSENALS
AY ANALYSER
BE ENABLERS
BG BRANGLES
BI RINSABLE
BS BRANSLES
BT BRANTLES
BY BLARNEYS
CE CLEANERS
CLEANSER
CG CLANGERS
CH CHARNELS
CI CARLINES
CK CRANKLES
CN SCRANNEL
CU LUCARNES
DD DANDLERS
DG DANGLERS
GLANDERS
DH HANDLERS
DI ISLANDER
DL LANDLERS
DM MANDRELS
DO LADRONES
SOLANDER
DP SPANDREL
DS SLANDERS
DU LAUNDERS
LURDANES
RUNDALES
EG ENLARGES
GENERALS
GLEANERS
ER LEARNERS
ES REALNESS
ET ALTERNES
EV ENSLAVER
EW RENEWALS
FK FLANKERS
FO FARNESOL
FS SALFERNS
FU FLANEURS
FUNERALS
GG GANGRELS
GI ENGRAILS
NARGILES
REALIGNS
SALERING
SANGLIER
SIGNALER
SLANGIER
GJ JANGLERS
GL LANGRELS
GM MANGLERS
GP GRAPNELS
SPANGLER
SPRANGLE
GS SLANGERS
GT STRANGLE
TANGLERS
TRANGLES
GU GRANULES
GW WANGLERS
WRANGLES
GY LARYNGES
HI INHALERS
HP SHRAPNEL
HT ENTHRALS
II AIRLINES
SNAILIER
IM MARLINES
MINERALS
IO AILERONS
ALERIONS
ALIENORS
IP PEARLINS
PRALINES
IR SNARLIER
IS RAINLESS
IT ENTRAILS
LATRINES
RATLINES
TRENAILS
IU LUNARIES
IV RAVELINS
IX RELAXINS
IY INLAYERS
SNAILERY
KP PRANKLES
LO LLANEROS
MO ALMONERS
MP LAMPERNS
MU MENSURAL
NUMERALS
NP PLANNERS
NS ENSNARLS
NT LANTERNS
NU UNLEARNS
OP PERSONAL
PSORALEN
OU ALEURONS
OV VERONALS
PT PANTLERS
PLANTERS
REPLANTS
PU PURSLANE
SUPERNAL
RS SNARLERS
ST SALTERNS
TT SLATTERN
TRENTALS
TU NEUTRALS
TV VENTRALS
UV UNRAVELS
VY SYLVANER
XY LARYNXES

AELNRT 28
(ANTLER)
AC LACERANT
AM MATERNAL
AP PARENTAL
PATERNAL
PRENATAL
AT ALTERANT
ALTERNAT
AX RELAXANT
BE RENTABLE
BS BRANTLES
CI CLARINET
DE ANTLERED
DY ARDENTLY
EH LEATHERN
EI ELATERIN
ENTAILER
TREENAIL
EN LANNERET
ES ALTERNES
EV LEVANTER
RELEVANT
EX EXTERNAL
FU FLAUNTER
GI ALERTING
ALTERING
INTEGRAL
RELATING
TANGLIER
TRIANGLE
GS STRANGLE
TANGLERS
TRANGLES
HL ENTHRALL
HS ENTHRALS
II INERTIAL
IM TERMINAL
TRAMLINE
IN INTERNAL
IO ORIENTAL
RELATION
TAILERON
IP TRIPLANE
IS ENTRAILS
LATRINES
RATLINES
TRENAILS
IT RATTLINE
IU AUNTLIER
RETINULA
TENURIAL
IV INTERVAL
IY INTERLAY
NS LANTERNS
NU UNLEARNT
OT TETRONAL
TOLERANT
OU OUTLEARN
OY ORNATELY
PS PANTLERS
PLANTERS
REPLANTS
PY PLENARTY
RY ERRANTLY
SS SALTERNS
ST SLATTERN
TRENTALS
SU NEUTRALS
SV VENTRALS

AELNST 34
(ANTLES)
AB BANALEST
AC ANALECTS
AD EASTLAND
AK ALKANETS
KANTELAS
AM TALESMAN
AP PLATANES
PLEASANT
AS SEALANTS
AZ ZEALANTS
BD BLANDEST
BI INSTABLE
BK BLANKEST
BLANKETS
BL NETBALLS
BM SEMBLANT
BO NEOBLAST
NOTABLES
BR BRANTLES
BU UNSTABLE
BY ABSENTLY
CD SCANTLED
CE CLEANEST
LATENCES
CH STANCHEL
CO LACTONES
CP CLAPNETS
CS SCANTLES
CT CANTLETS
CY SECANTLY
DH SHETLAND
DU UNSALTED
DW WETLANDS
EE SELENATE
EK KANTELES
EM MANTEELS
STEELMAN
TALESMEN
ER ALTERNES
ES LATENESS
EY ENTAYLES
FI INFLATES
FS FLATNESS
FT FLATTENS
GI EASTLING
GELATINS
GENITALS
STEALING
GO TANGELOS
GP SPANGLET
GR STRANGLE
TANGLERS
TRANGLES
GT GANTLETS
GU LANGUETS
GW TWANGLES
HO ETHANOLS
HR ENTHRALS
HS NATHLESS
HY NAYTHLES
II ALIENIST
LITANIES
IK LANKIEST
IM AILMENTS
ALIMENTS
MANLIEST
IO ELATIONS
INSOLATE
TOENAILS
IP PANTILES
PLAINEST
IR ENTRAILS
LATRINES
RATLINES
TRENAILS
IS EASTLINS
ELASTINS
SALIENTS
STANIELS
IU ALUNITES
INSULATE
IV VENTAILS
IW LAWNIEST
LM STALLMEN
LS TALLNESS
LT TALLENTS
MO SALMONET
MT MANTLETS
MU NUTMEALS
NR LANTERNS
NS STANNELS
NU ANNULETS
OP LAPSTONE
PLEONAST
POLENTAS
OV VOLANTES
PR PANTLERS
PLANTERS
REPLANTS
PX EXPLANTS
RS SALTERNS
RT SLATTERN
TRENTALS
RU NEUTRALS
RV VENTRALS
SS SALTNESS
SY STANYELS
UV ENVAULTS

AELORS 42
(ALORES)
AI OLEARIAS
AU AUREOLAS
BB BELABORS
BE EARLOBES
BT BLOATERS
SORTABLE
STORABLE
BU RUBEOLAS
BV ABSOLVER
CC CORACLES
CE ESCAROLE
CF ALFRESCO
CH CHOLERAS
CHORALES
CI CALORIES
CARIOLES
CJ CAJOLERS
CK EARLOCKS
CL CORELLAS
CM CAROMELS
SCLEROMA
CP PARCLOSE
POLACRES
CS ESCOLARS
LACROSSE
CT SECTORAL
CU CAROUSEL
CY CALOYERS
COARSELY
DI DARIOLES
SOLIDARE
SOREDIAL
DL ODALLERS
DM EARLDOMS
DN LADRONES
SOLANDER
DP LEOPARDS
DS ROADLESS
DT DELATORS
LEOTARDS
LODESTAR

DU ROULADES
EH ARSEHOLE
EP PAROLEES
ER RELEASOR
ET OLEASTER
EU AUREOLES
FH FAHLORES
FI FORESAIL
FN FARNESOL
FS SAFROLES
FT FLOATERS
FORESTAL
REFLOATS
FU FUSAROLE
FY FORELAYS
GI GASOLIER
GIRASOLE
SERAGLIO
GL ALLEGROS
GM GOMERALS
GP PERGOLAS
GT GLOATERS
LEGATORS
GU GLAREOUS
HI AIRHOLES
SHOALIER
HM ARMHOLES
HT LOATHERS
HY HOARSELY
IM MORALISE
IN AILERONS
ALERIONS
ALIENORS
IP PELORIAS
POLARISE
IS SOLARISE
IT SOTERIAL
IV OVERSAIL
VALORISE
VARIOLES
VOLARIES
IY ROYALISE
IZ SOLARIZE
KY ROKELAYS
LN LLANEROS
LP REPOSALL
LS ROSELLAS
LT REALLOTS
LV OVERALLS
LW SALLOWER
MN ALMONERS
MO SALEROOM
MP PLEROMAS
MT MOLERATS
MU RAMULOSE
MV REMOVALS
NP PERSONAL
PSORALEN
NU ALEURONS
NV VERONALS
OS AEROSOLS
ROSEOLAS
PP PROLAPSE
PROPALES
SAPROPEL
PS REPOSALS
PT PETROSAL
PROLATES
PU LEAPROUS
PV OVERLAPS
RT REALTORS
RELATORS
TU ROSULATE
TV LEVATORS
TY ROYALETS
TZ ZELATORS
UU ROULEAUS
VY OVERLAYS
WY OWRELAYS

AELOST 46
(SOLATE)
AC CATALOES
AM OATMEALS
AX OXALATES
BC OBSTACLE
BN NEOBLAST
NOTABLES
BP POTABLES
BR BLOATERS
SORTABLE
STORABLE
BU ABSOLUTE
BW BESTOWAL
CC CACOLETS
CG CATELOGS
CH CATHOLES
ESCHALOT
CI ALOETICS
COALIEST
SOCIETAL
CL COLLATES
CM CAMELOTS
MOLECAST
CN LACTONES
CP POLECATS
CR SECTORAL
CS ALECOSTS
COATLESS
LACTOSES
SCATOLES
CT CALOTTES
CU LACTEOUS
LOCUSTAE
OSCULATE
CY ACOLYTES
DE DESOLATE
DI DIASTOLE
ISOLATED
SODALITE
SOLIDATE
DP TADPOLES
DR DELATORS
LEOTARDS
LODESTAR
DV SOLVATED
EG SEGOLATE
ER OLEASTER
FG FLOTAGES
FI FOLIATES
FL FLOATELS
FR FLOATERS
FORESTAL
REFLOATS
FT FALSETTO
GI OTALGIES
GL TOLLAGES
GN TANGELOS
GR GLOATERS
LEGATORS
GV VOLTAGES
HN ETHANOLS
HR LOATHERS
HS SHOALEST
HT LOATHEST
IK KEITLOAS
IM LOAMIEST
IN ELATIONS
INSOLATE
TOENAILS
IP SPOLIATE
IR SOTERIAL
IS ISOLATES
IT TOTALISE
IV VIOLATES
KS SKATOLES
STALKOES
LR REALLOTS
MN SALMONET
MR MOLERATS
MS MALTOSES
MT MATELOTS
MY ATMOLYSE
NP LAPSTONE
PLEONAST
POLENTAS
NV VOLANTES
PR PETROSAL
PROLATES
PS APOSTLES
PT PALETOTS
PU OUTLEAPS
PETALOUS
RR REALTORS
RELATORS
RU ROSULATE
RV LEVATORS
RY ROYALETS
RZ ZELATORS
SV SOLVATES
SY ASYSTOLE
TU TOLUATES
TW WASTELOT
UV OVULATES
UY AUTOLYSE

AELPRS 231
(PALERS)
AB PARABLES
SPARABLE
AD PARDALES
AF EARFLAPS
PARAFLES
AL PARELLAS
AN PRENASAL
AP APPARELS
AT PALESTRA
AV PALAVERS
AY PARALYSE
BB PRABBLES
BE BEPEARLS
CE PERCALES
REPLACES
CI CALIPERS
REPLICAS
SPIRACLE
CK SPRACKLE
CM CLAMPERS
CO PARCLOSE
POLACRES
CP CLAPPERS
SCRAPPLE
CS CLASPERS
SCALPERS
CT SCEPTRAL
SPECTRAL
CU SPECULAR
DD PADDLERS
DE PLEADERS
RELAPSED
DF FELDSPAR
DI PEDRAILS
PREDIALS
DK SPARKLED
DN SPANDREL
DO LEOPARDS
DW SPRAWLED
EG PEREGALS
EI ESPALIER
PEARLIES
EL PARELLES
EO PAROLEES
ER PEARLERS
RELAPSER
ES PLEASERS
RELAPSES
ET PLEATERS
PRELATES
EU PLEASURE
SERPULAE
EV VESPERAL
FP FLAPPERS
FS FELSPARS
FY PALFREYS
GN GRAPNELS
SPANGLER
SPRANGLE
GO PERGOLAS
GP GRAPPLES
GU EARPLUGS
GRAUPELS
HI PLASHIER
HN SHRAPNEL
HS SPLASHER
IM IMPEARLS
LEMPIRAS
IN PEARLINS
PRALINES
IO PELORIAS
POLARISE
IP APPERILS
APPLIERS
IR REPRISAL
IT PILASTER
PLAISTER
PLAITERS
IV PREVAILS
IW SLIPWARE
KN PRANKLES
KR SPARKLER
KS SPARKLES
KT SPARKLET
LO REPOSALL
MN LAMPERNS
MO PLEROMAS
MS SAMPLERS
MT TEMPLARS
TRAMPLES
MY LAMPREYS
SAMPLERY
NN PLANNERS
NO PERSONAL
PSORALEN
NT PANTLERS
PLANTERS
REPLANTS
NU PURSLANE
SUPERNAL
OP PROLAPSE
PROPALES
SAPROPEL
OS REPOSALS
OT PETROSAL
PROLATES
OU LEAPROUS
OV OVERLAPS
PS SLAPPERS
RW SPRAWLER
ST PLASTERS
PSALTERS
STAPLERS
SU PERUSALS
SY PARSLEYS
SPARSELY
TT PARTLETS
PLATTERS
PRATTLES
SPLATTER
SPRATTLE
TU APLUSTRE
TY PLASTERY
PSALTERY

AELPRT 206
(PLATER)
AI PARIETAL
AL PATELLAR
AM MALAPERT
AN PARENTAL
PATERNAL
PRENATAL
AS PALESTRA
AT TETRAPLA
BI PARTIBLE
BO PORTABLE
BU PUBERTAL
CH CHAPTREL
CI PARTICLE
PRELATIC
CO PECTORAL
CS SCEPTRAL
SPECTRAL
DE PALTERED
DI DIPTERAL
TRIPEDAL
DM TRAMPLED
DO PROLATED
DT PRATTLED
EI PEARLITE
ER PALTERER
ES PLEATERS
PRELATES
EY PTERYLAE
FL PRATFELL
FO TERAFLOP
HO PLETHORA
HP THRAPPLE
II LIPARITE
IK TRAPLIKE
IN TRIPLANE
IO EPILATOR
PETIOLAR
IR PALTRIER
IS PILASTER
PLAISTER
PLAITERS
KS SPARKLET
MO PROMETAL
TEMPORAL
MR TRAMPLER
MS TEMPLARS
TRAMPLES
NS PANTLERS
PLANTERS
REPLANTS
NY PLENARTY
OS PETROSAL
PROLATES
RT PRATTLER
SS PLASTERS
PSALTERS
STAPLERS
ST PARTLETS
PLATTERS
PRATTLES
SPLATTER
SPRATTLE
SU APLUSTRE
SY PLASTERY
PSALTERY

AELRST 38
(ALTERS)
AB ARBALEST
AE LAETARES
AG AGRESTAL
AH TREHALAS
AL LATERALS
AP PALESTRA
AZ LAZARETS
BE BLEAREST
BLEATERS
RETABLES
BH BLATHERS
HALBERTS
BI LIBRATES
TABLIERS
BM LAMBERTS
BN BRANTLES
BO BLOATERS
SORTABLE
STORABLE
BS BLASTERS
STABLERS
BT BATTLERS
BLATTERS
BRATTLES
BU BALUSTER
BW BLEWARTS
CE CLEAREST
SCELERAT
TREACLES
CH ARCHLETS
CI ALTRICES
ARTICLES
RECITALS
SELICTAR
CK TACKLERS
CO SECTORAL
CP SCEPTRAL

SPECTRAL
CS SCARLETS
CT CLATTERS
SCRATTLE
CU RAUCLEST
DD STRADDLE
DE TREADLES
DI DILATERS
LARDIEST
DO DELATORS
LEOTARDS
LODESTAR
DT STARTLED
EE TEASELER
EF REFLATES
EH HALTERES
LEATHERS
EI ATELIERS
EARLIEST
LEARIEST
REALTIES
EM LAMETERS
EN ALTERNES
EO OLEASTER
EP PLEATERS
PRELATES
ER RELATERS
ES STEALERS
TEARLESS
TESSERAL
ET ALERTEST
EU RESALUTE
EY EASTERLY
FH FARTHELS
FI FLARIEST
FRAILEST
FK FARTLEKS
FO FLOATERS
FORESTAL
REFLOATS
FT FATTRELS
FLATTERS
FU REFUTALS
GG STRAGGLE
GI GLARIEST
REGALIST
GN STRANGLE
TANGLERS
TRANGLES
GO GLOATERS
LEGATORS
GU GAULTERS
GESTURAL
TRAGULES
HM THERMALS
HN ENTHRALS
HO LOATHERS
HS HARSLETS
SLATHERS
II LAIRIEST
LISTERIA
IK LARKIEST
STALKIER
STARLIKE
IL LITERALS
TALLIERS
IM LAMITERS
MARLIEST
IN ENTRAILS
LATRINES

RATLINES
TRENAILS
IO SOTERIAL
IP PILASTER
PLAISTER
PLAITERS
IR RETIRALS
RETRIALS
TRAILERS
IS REALISTS
SALTIERS
SALTIRES
SLAISTER
IT TERTIALS
IU URALITES
KP SPARKLET
KS STALKERS
LO REALLOTS
MM STRAMMEL
TRAMMELS
MO MOLERATS
MP TEMPLARS
TRAMPLES
MT MALTSTER
MARTLETS
MY MASTERLY
NN LANTERNS
NP PANTLERS
PLANTERS
REPLANTS
NS SALTERNS
NT SLATTERN
TRENTALS
NU NEUTRALS
NV VENTRALS
OP PETROSAL
PROLATES
OR REALTORS
RELATORS
OU ROSULATE
OV LEVATORS
OY ROYALETS
OZ ZELATORS
PS PLASTERS
PSALTERS
STAPLERS
PT PARTLETS
PLATTERS
PRATTLES
SPLATTER
SPRATTLE
PU APLUSTRE
PY PLASTERY
PSALTERY
RT RATTLERS
STARTLER
RW TRAWLERS
SS STARLESS
ST SLATTERS
STARLETS
STARTLES
SU SALUTERS
SW WARTLESS
WASTRELS
TT TARTLETS
TATTLERS
TU LUSTRATE
TUTELARS
TY SLATTERY
UV VAULTERS

VESTURAL
WZ WALTZERS

AEMNST 168
(STAMEN)
AC CAMSTANE
AD MANDATES
AE EMANATES
MANATEES
AG MAGENTAS
MAGNATES
AI AMENTIAS
ANIMATES
AL TALESMAN
AR SARMENTA
SEMANTRA
AS NAMASTES
AU MANTEAUS
BE BASEMENT
BI AMBIENTS
BL SEMBLANT
CE CASEMENT
CH MANCHETS
CI SEMANTIC
CK TACKSMEN
CO CAMSTONE
DE STAMENED
DI MEDIANTS
TIDESMAN
EE EASEMENT
EH METHANES
EI MATINEES
SEMINATE
EL MANTEELS
STEELMAN
TALESMEN
ER REMANETS
ES TAMENESS
EU MANSUETE
FI MANIFEST
FR RAFTSMEN
GI MANGIEST
MINTAGES
STEAMING
TEAMINGS
GO GEOMANTS
MAGNETOS
MEGATONS
MONTAGES
GR GARMENTS
MARGENTS
RAGMENTS
GU AUGMENTS
MUTAGENS
HO HOASTMEN
HR TRASHMEN
HU HUMANEST
II MINIATES
IK MANKIEST
MISTAKEN
IL AILMENTS
ALIMENTS
MANLIEST
IN MANNITES
IO SOMNIATE
IR MINARETS
RAIMENTS
IS MANTISES
MATINESS
LL STALLMEN

LO SALMONET
LT MANTLETS
LU NUTMEALS
NR MANRENTS
REMNANTS
OR MONSTERA
STOREMAN
OU NOTAEUMS
OUTNAMES
SEAMOUNT
PS ENSTAMPS
PASSMENT
PY PAYMENTS
RS SARMENTS
SMARTENS
RU ANESTRUM
MENSTRUA
TRANSUME
RV VARMENTS
RW TRANSMEW
TREWSMAN
WY WAYMENTS

AEMRST 124
(MATERS)
AF FERMATAS
AN SARMENTA
SEMANTRA
AU AMATEURS
BI BARMIEST
BL LAMBERTS
BO BROMATES
CE CREMATES
MEERCATS
CH MATCHERS
CI CERAMIST
MATRICES
CJ SCRAMJET
CP CRAMPETS
DE MASTERED
STREAMED
DI MARDIEST
MISRATED
READMITS
DO STROAMED
DP STRAMPED
EG GAMESTER
MEAGREST
EH ERATHEMS
EI EMIRATES
REAMIEST
STEAMIER
EK MEERKATS
EL LAMETERS
EM AMMETERS
METAMERS
EN REMANETS
EO EROTEMAS
EP TEMPERAS
ER REMASTER
STREAMER
ES MASSETER
SEAMSTER
STEAMERS
ET TEAMSTER
EY METAYERS
FN RAFTSMEN
FO FOREMAST
FORMATES
GI MAGISTER

MIGRATES
RAGTIMES
STERIGMA
GN GARMENTS
MARGENTS
RAGMENTS
HL THERMALS
HN TRASHMEN
HP HAMPSTER
HS HAMSTERS
HU MAUTHERS
HW MAWTHERS
II AIRTIMES
SERIATIM
IL LAMITERS
MARLIEST
IM MARMITES
IN MINARETS
RAIMENTS
IO AMORTISE
ATOMISER
IP APTERISM
PRIMATES
IS ASTERISM
MAISTERS
MISRATES
SEMITARS
SMARTIES
IT MISTREAT
TERATISM
IU MURIATES
SEMITAUR
IW WARTIMES
IX MATRIXES
IY SYMITARE
LM STRAMMEL
TRAMMELS
LO MOLERATS
LP TEMPLARS
TRAMPLES
LT MALTSTER
MARTLETS
LY MASTERLY
MO MARMOSET
MS STAMMERS
NN MANRENTS
REMNANTS
NO MONSTERA
STOREMAN
NS SARMENTS
SMARTENS
NU ANESTRUM
MENSTRUA
TRANSUME
NV VARMENTS
NW TRANSMEW
TREWSMAN
OR REARMOST
OS MAESTROS
OV OVERMAST
PR TRAMPERS
PS STAMPERS
PT TRAMPETS
PU TEMPURAS
UPSTREAM
ST MATTRESS
SMARTEST
SMATTERS
SY MAYSTERS
TU MATUREST

TESTAMUR
TX MARTEXTS

AENNST 152
(ANNETS)
AD ANDANTES
AG TANNAGES
AN ANTENNAS
AT STANNATE
TANNATES
AU NAUSEANT
AV VENTANAS
BG BANTENGS
CD SCANDENT
CE CANTEENS
CH ENCHANTS
CI ANCIENTS
CANNIEST
INSTANCE
DP PENDANTS
DU ASTUNNED
EO NEONATES
EP PENTANES
ES NEATNESS
FI INFANTES
FU UNFASTEN
GH HANGNEST
GI ANTIGENS
GENTIANS
STEANING
GO TONNAGES
GT TANGENTS
GU TUNNAGES
IM MANNITES
IO ENATIONS
IP PANTINES
IR ENTRAINS
TRANNIES
IS INSANEST
IT ANTIENTS
STANNITE
LR LANTERNS
LS STANNELS
LU ANNULETS
MR MANRENTS
REMNANTS
NP PENNANTS
OP PENTOSAN
OR NORTENAS
RESONANT
OU TONNEAUS
QU QUANNETS
RT ENTRANTS
RY TYRANNES

AENPST 185
(PATENS)
AA ANAPAEST
AC PASTANCE
AG PAGEANTS
AH PHEASANT
AL PLATANES
PLEASANT
AS ANAPESTS
PEASANTS
AT ANTEPAST
AY PEASANTY
BI BEPAINTS
CD PANDECTS
CL CLAPNETS

CO CAPSTONE
CT PENTACTS
DI DEPAINTS
DN PENDANTS
DO TONEPADS
EH HEPTANES
PHENATES
STEPHANE
EN PENTANES
GL SPANGLET
GO PONTAGES
GR TREPANGS
HI PENTHIAS
THESPIAN
HO PHAETONS
PHONATES
STANHOPE
HR PANTHERS
II PIANISTE
IL PANTILES
PLAINEST
IN PANTINES
IO SAPONITE
IP NAPPIEST
IR PAINTERS
PANTRIES
PERTAINS
PINASTER
PRISTANE
REPAINTS
IS STEAPSIN
IT PATIENTS
IU PETUNIAS
SUPINATE
IY EPINASTY
LO LAPSTONE
PLEONAST
POLENTAS
LR PANTLERS
PLANTERS
REPLANTS
LX EXPLANTS
MS ENSTAMPS
PASSMENT
MY PAYMENTS
NN PENNANTS
NO PENTOSAN
OO TEASPOON
OR OPERANTS
PRONATES
PR PARPENTS
RR PARTNERS
RS PASTERNS
RT PATTERNS
TRANSEPT
RU PERSAUNT
SU PESAUNTS
SW STEWPANS
WASPNEST
SY SYNAPTES
SZ SPETSNAZ
ZZ SPETZNAZ

AENRRT 87
(RANTER)
AB ABERRANT
AD NARRATED
AS NARRATES
BE BANTERER
CE RECANTER
RECREANT
DU UNTARRED
EG ETRANGER
EI RETAINER
ES TERRANES
ET NATTERER
EV TAVERNER
FS TRANSFER
GS GRANTERS
REGRANTS
STRANGER
IN INERRANT
IO ANTERIOR
IP TERRAPIN
IS RESTRAIN
RETRAINS
STRAINER
TERRAINS
TRAINERS
TRANSIRE
IV VERATRIN
IW INTERWAR
LY ERRANTLY
OO RATOONER
OS ANTRORSE
PS PARTNERS
QU QUARTERN
RY ERRANTRY
ST TRANTERS

AENRSS 223
(SANERS)
AL ARSENALS
AR NARRASES
BD DRABNESS
BE BARENESS
BL BRANSLES
BO BARONESS
CE CASERNES
CH ARCHNESS
CI ARSENICS
CERASINS
RACINESS
CN SCANNERS
CO COARSENS
NARCOSES
CT CRANTSES
CU SURANCES
DE DEARNESS
DH HARDNESS
DI ARIDNESS
SARDINES
DK DARKNESS
DL SLANDERS
DS SARSDENS
DT STANDERS
DU DANSEURS
EH ARSHEENS
EI SENARIES
EK SNEAKERS
EL REALNESS
EN ENSNARES
NEARNESS
EO SEASONER
ER RARENESS
ES SEARNESS
ET ASSENTER
EARNESTS
SARSENET
EX XERANSES
FI FAIRNESS
SANSERIF
SERAFINS
FL SALFERNS
GH GNASHERS
GI REASSIGN
SEARINGS
SERINGAS
GL SLANGERS
GP ENGRASPS
HH HARSHENS
HI ARSHINES
HO HOARSENS
HP SHARPENS
HS RASHNESS
II AIRINESS
IL RAINLESS
IM SEMINARS
SIRNAMES
IN INSNARES
IO ERASIONS
SENSORIA
IT ARTINESS
RESIANTS
RETSINAS
SNARIEST
STAINERS
STARNIES
STEARINS
IU SENARIUS
IW WARINESS
IX XERANSIS
KN RANKNESS
KP SPANKERS
KT STARKENS
KW SWANKERS
LN ENSNARLS
LR SNARLERS
LT SALTERNS
MP PRESSMAN
MT SARMENTS
SMARTENS
MU SURNAMES
MW WARMNESS
NP SPANNERS
OP PERSONAS
RESPONSA
OT ASSENTOR
SENATORS
TREASONS
PP PARSNEPS
SNAPPERS
PT PASTERNS
PW SPAWNERS
ST SARSNETS
TT TARTNESS
TU ANESTRUS
SAUNTERS
TV SERVANTS
VERSANTS
UW UNSWEARS

AENRST 9
(ANTERS)
AB ANTBEARS
RATSBANE
AC CANASTER
CATERANS
AE ARSENATE
SERENATA
AG STARAGEN
TANAGERS
AI ANTISERA
ARTESIAN
RESINATA
AJ NAARTJES
AM SARMENTA
SEMANTRA
AO ANOESTRA
AR NARRATES
AT TARTANES
AV TAVERNAS
TSAREVNA
BD BANDSTER
BG BANGSTER
BI ATEBRINS
BANISTER
BL BRANTLES
BO BARONETS
BU UNBRASTE
URBANEST
CD CANTREDS
CE CENTARES
REASCENT
SARCENET
CF CANTREFS
CH CHANTERS
SNATCHER
STANCHER
TRANCHES
CI CANISTER
CARNIEST
CISTERNA
CREATINS
NACRITES
SCANTIER
CO ANCESTOR
ENACTORS
SORTANCE
CS CRANTSES
CT TRANECTS
TRANSECT
CU CENTAURS
RECUSANT
UNCRATES
UNTRACES
CY ANCESTRY
DD STRANDED
DG DRAGNETS
GRANDEST
DI DETRAINS
RANDIEST
STRAINED
DO TORNADES
DS STANDERS
DU DAUNTERS
TRANSUDE
UNTREADS
DX DEXTRANS
EE SERENATE
EF FASTENER
FENESTRA
EG ESTRANGE
GRANTEES
GREATENS
REAGENTS
SEGREANT
SERGEANT
STERNAGE
EH HASTENER
HEARTENS
EI ARSENITE
RESINATE
STEARINE
TRAINEES
EJ SERJEANT
EL ALTERNES
EM REMANETS
EO RESONATE
ER TERRANES
ES ASSENTER
EARNESTS
SARSENET
ET ENTREATS
RATTEENS
EV AVENTRES
VETERANS
FG ENGRAFTS
FI FENITARS
FK FRANKEST
FM RAFTSMEN
FO SEAFRONT
FR TRANSFER
GG GANGSTER
GI ANGRIEST
ASTRINGE
GANISTER
GANTRIES
GRANITES
INGRATES
RANGIEST
REASTING
STEARING
TASERING
GL STRANGLE
TANGLERS
TRANGLES
GM GARMENTS
MARGENTS
RAGMENTS
GO ORANGEST
RAGSTONE
STONERAG
GP TREPANGS
GR GRANTERS
REGRANTS
STRANGER
GU STRAUNGE
HI HAIRNETS
INEARTHS
THERIANS
HK THANKERS
HL ENTHRALS
HM TRASHMEN
HP PANTHERS
HU HAUNTERS
UNEARTHS
UNHEARTS
URETHANS
II INERTIAS
RAINIEST
IJ NARTJIES
IK KERATINS
NARKIEST
IL ENTRAILS
LATRINES
RATLINES
TRENAILS
IM MINARETS
RAIMENTS
IN ENTRAINS
TRANNIES
IO ANOESTRI
ARSONITE
NOTARIES
NOTARISE
ROSINATE
IP PAINTERS
PANTRIES
PERTAINS
PINASTER
PRISTANE
REPAINTS
IR RESTRAIN
RETRAINS
STRAINER
TERRAINS
TRAINERS
TRANSIRE
IS ARTINESS
RESIANTS
RETSINAS
SNARIEST
STAINERS
STARNIES
STEARINS
IT INTREATS
NITRATES
STRAITEN
TARTINES
TERTIANS
IU RUINATES
TAURINES
URANITES
URINATES
IW TINWARES
KS STARKENS
KZ KRANTZES
LN LANTERNS
LP PANTLERS
PLANTERS
REPLANTS
LS SALTERNS
LT SLATTERN
TRENTALS
LU NEUTRALS
LV VENTRALS
MN MANRENTS
REMNANTS
MO MONSTERA
STOREMAN
MS SARMENTS
SMARTENS
MU ANESTRUM
MENSTRUA
TRANSUME
MV VARMENTS
MW TRANSMEW
TREWSMAN
NO NORTENAS
RESONANT
NT ENTRANTS
NY TYRANNES
OP OPERANTS
PRONATES
OR ANTRORSE
OS ASSENTOR
SENATORS
TREASONS
OT ORNATEST

OV VENATORS
OW STONERAW
PP PARPENTS
PR PARTNERS
PS PASTERNS
PT PATTERNS
TRANSEPT
PU PERSAUNT
RT TRANTERS
SS SARSNETS
ST TARTNESS
SU ANESTRUS
SAUNTERS
SV SERVANTS
VERSANTS
TU TAUNTERS
UV VAUNTERS
UW UNWATERS
WY STERNWAY

AENRTT 71
(NATTER)
AC REACTANT
AD TARTANED
AE ANTEATER
AI REATTAIN
AL ALTERANT
ALTERNAT
AM ATRAMENT
AS TARTANES
BO BETATRON
CH TRANCHET
CI INTERACT
CO CONTRATE
CS TRANECTS
TRANSECT
CU TRUNCATE
DE ATTENDER
NATTERED
RATTENED
DI NITRATED
DO ATTORNED
DU TRUANTED
DY TYRANTED
EE ENTERATE
EF FATTENER
EH HATERENT
THREATEN
ER NATTERER
ES ENTREATS
RATTEENS
EV ANTEVERT
EX EXTERNAT
EY ENTREATY
GI ARETTING
TREATING
GO TETRAGON
IL RATTLINE
IM MARTINET
IO TENTORIA
IP TRIPTANE
IS INTREATS
NITRATES
STRAITEN
TARTINES
TERTIANS
IU TAINTURE
LO TETRONAL
TOLERANT
LS SLATTERN
TRENTALS
MO TORMENTA
NS ENTRANTS
NY TENANTRY
OP PATENTOR
OS ORNATEST
OX TETRAXON
OY ATTORNEY
PS PATTERNS
TRANSEPT
RS TRANTERS
SS TARTNESS
SU TAUNTERS

AENSTT 116
(ATTENS)
AC CANTATES
CASTANET
AG STAGNATE
AI ASTATINE
SANITATE
TANAISTE
AN STANNATE
TANNATES
AP ANTEPAST
AR TARTANES
BI TABINETS
CH ETCHANTS
CI CANTIEST
NICTATES
TETANICS
CL CANTLETS
CO CONSTATE
CP PENTACTS
CR TRANECTS
TRANSECT
CS SCANTEST
DI INSTATED
DU UNSTATED
UNTASTED
EG TENTAGES
EI ANISETTE
TETANIES
TETANISE
ER ENTREATS
RATTEENS
EV NAVETTES
FI FAINTEST
FL FLATTENS
GI ESTATING
TANGIEST
GL GANTLETS
GN TANGENTS
GU GAUNTEST
TUTENAGS
HI HESITANT
HS THATNESS
IJ JANTIEST
IN ANTIENTS
STANNITE
IP PATIENTS
IR INTREATS
NITRATES
STRAITEN
TARTINES
TERTIANS
IS INSTATES
NASTIEST
SATINETS
TITANESS
IT NATTIEST
IV TASTEVIN
IW TAWNIEST
LL TALLENTS
LM MANTLETS
LR SLATTERN
TRENTALS
NR ENTRANTS
OR ORNATEST
PR PATTERNS
TRANSEPT
QU QUESTANT
RR TRANTERS
RS TARTNESS
RU TAUNTERS
SU TAUTNESS
UNSTATES
SX SEXTANTS

AEORST 13
(ORATES)
AB RABATOES
AN ANOESTRA
AR AERATORS
AT AEROSTAT
BD BROADEST
BE REBATOES
BH BATHORSE
BI SABOTIER
BL BLOATERS
SORTABLE
STORABLE
BM BROMATES
BN BARONETS
BP PROBATES
BR ARBORETS
TABORERS
BS BOASTERS
SORBATES
BT ABETTORS
BATTEROS
TABORETS
BU SABOTEUR
CC ECTOSARC
CD REDCOATS
CE CREASOTE
CF FORECAST
CG ESCARGOT
CH CHAROSET
THORACES
CL SECTORAL
CN ANCESTOR
ENACTORS
SORTANCE
CR ACROTERS
CREATORS
REACTORS
CS COARSEST
COASTERS
CT SECTATOR
CU OUTRACES
CV OVERACTS
OVERCAST
CX EXACTORS
DG GOADSTER
DI ASTEROID
DL DELATORS
LEOTARDS
LODESTAR
DM STROAMED
DN TORNADES
DP ADOPTERS
ASPORTED
READOPTS
DR ROADSTER
DS ASSORTED
TORSADES
DU OUTDARES
DX EXTRADOS
EI ETAERIOS
EK KERATOSE
KREASOTE
EL OLEASTER
EM EROTEMAS
EN RESONATE
EP OPERATES
PROTEASE
EV OVEREATS
FF AFFOREST
FL FLOATERS
FORESTAL
REFLOATS
FM FOREMAST
FORMATES
FN SEAFRONT
FP FOREPAST
FW FORWASTE
SOFTWARE
FY FORESTAY
GH SHORTAGE
GL GLOATERS
LEGATORS
GN ORANGEST
RAGSTONE
STONERAG
GO ROOTAGES
GP PORTAGES
POTAGERS
GR GARROTES
GS STORAGES
GT GAROTTES
GU OUTRAGES
HH HAROSETH
HI HOARIEST
HL LOATHERS
HO TOHEROAS
HP POTSHARE
HS ASTHORES
EARSHOTS
HAROSETS
HOARSEST
HT RHEOSTAT
HX THORAXES
IJ JAROSITE
IL SOTERIAL
IM AMORTISE
ATOMISER
IN ANOESTRI
ARSONITE
NOTARIES
NOTARISE
ROSINATE
IR ROARIEST
ROTARIES
IV VOTARIES
KV OVERTASK
LL REALLOTS
LM MOLERATS
LP PETROSAL
PROLATES
LR REALTORS
RELATORS
LU ROSULATE
LV LEVATORS
LY ROYALETS
LZ ZELATORS
MM MARMOSET
MN MONSTERA
STOREMAN
MR REARMOST
MS MAESTROS
MV OVERMAST
NN NORTENAS
RESONANT
NP OPERANTS
PRONATES
NR ANTRORSE
NS ASSENTOR
SENATORS
TREASONS
NT ORNATEST
NV VENATORS
NW STONERAW
OR SORORATE
PR PRAETORS
PRORATES
PS ESPARTOS
PORTASES
PROTASES
SEAPORTS
PT PROSTATE
PU APTEROUS
PV OVERPAST
QU EQUATORS
QUAESTOR
RR ARRESTOR
RS ASSERTOR
ASSORTER
ORATRESS
ROASTERS
RT ROSTRATE
ST STRATOSE
TOASTERS
SV VOTARESS
SX STORAXES
TT ATTESTOR
TESTATOR
TU OUTRATES
OUTSTARE
UW OUTSWEAR
OUTWEARS
VY OVERSTAY

AEPRST 129
(PATERS)
AA SEPARATA
AC CAPRATES
AD ADAPTERS
READAPTS
AE ASPERATE
SEPARATE
AI ASPIRATE
PARASITE
SEPTARIA
AK PARTAKES
AL PALESTRA
AP PARAPETS
BO PROBATES
CH CHAPTERS
PATCHERS
CI CRAPIEST
CRISPATE
PICRATES
PRACTISE
CL SCEPTRAL
SPECTRAL
CM CRAMPETS
CU CAPTURES
PRESCUTA
DE PEDERAST
PREDATES
REPASTED
TRAPESED
DI DIPTERAS
RAPIDEST
SPIRATED
TARSIPED
TRAIPSED
DM STRAMPED
DO ADOPTERS
ASPORTED
READOPTS
DP STRAPPED
DU PASTURED
UPSTARED
EH PREHEATS
SPREATHE
EI PETARIES
EK PERTAKES
EL PLEATERS
PRELATES
EM TEMPERAS
EO OPERATES
PROTEASE
ER TAPERERS
ES TRAPESES
EU EPURATES
SUPERATE
EZ TRAPEZES
FO FOREPAST
FS PRESSFAT
GI GRAPIEST
GN TREPANGS
GO PORTAGES
POTAGERS
HM HAMPSTER
HN PANTHERS
HO POTSHARE
HS SHARPEST
SPARTHES
II PARITIES
IK PARKIEST
IL PILASTER
PLAISTER
PLAITERS
IM APTERISM
PRIMATES
IN PAINTERS
PANTRIES
PERTAINS
PINASTER
PRISTANE
REPAINTS
IP PERIAPTS
IS PASTRIES
PIASTRES
RASPIEST
TRAIPSES
IV PRIVATES
IW WIRETAPS

IY ASPERITY
KL SPARKLET
LM TEMPLARS
TRAMPLES
LN PANTLERS
PLANTERS
REPLANTS
LO PETROSAL
PROLATES
LS PLASTERS
PSALTERS
STAPLERS
LT PARTLETS
PLATTERS
PRATTLES
SPLATTER
SPRATTLE
LU APLUSTRE
LY PLASTERY
PSALTERY
MR TRAMPERS
MS STAMPERS
MT TRAMPETS
MU TEMPURAS
UPSTREAM
NO OPERANTS
PRONATES
NP PARPENTS
NR PARTNERS
NS PASTERNS
NT PATTERNS
TRANSEPT
NU PERSAUNT
OR PRAETORS
PRORATES
OS ESPARTOS
PORTASES
PROTASES
SEAPORTS
OT PROSTATE
OU APTEROUS
OV OVERPAST
PR STRAPPER
TRAPPERS
QU PARQUETS
RU PARTURES
RAPTURES
SS SPARSEST
TRESPASS
ST SPATTERS
TAPSTERS
SU PASTURES
UPSTARES
SY YAPSTERS
TU STUPRATE
TY TAPESTRY
UX SUPERTAX

AERRST 138
(RATERS)

AN NARRATES
AO AERATORS
AS TARRASES
AT TARTARES
BE REBATERS
TABRERES
TEREBRAS
BI ARBITERS
RAREBITS
BO ARBORETS
TABORERS
CC CARRECTS
CE CATERERS
RETRACES
TERRACES
CF REFRACTS
CH CHARTERS
RECHARTS
STARCHER
CI ERRATICS
CK TRACKERS
CO ACROTERS
CREATORS
REACTORS
CT RETRACTS
DE ARRESTED
DREAREST
RETREADS
SERRATED
TREADERS
DF DRAFTERS
REDRAFTS
DG DRAGSTER
DO ROADSTER
DT REDSTART
EE ARRESTEE
EF FERRATES
EG REGRATES
EI ARTERIES
REASTIER
EK RETAKERS
STREAKER
EL RELATERS
EM REMASTER
STREAMER
EN TERRANES
EP TAPERERS
ER ARRESTER
REARREST
ES ASSERTER
REASSERT
SERRATES
TERRASES
ET RETRATES
RETREATS
TREATERS
EU AUSTERER
TREASURE
EV TRAVERSE
EW WATERERS
FG GRAFTERS
FI FRATRIES
FN TRANSFER
GN GRANTERS
REGRANTS
STRANGER
GO GARROTES
HH THRASHER
HI TRASHIER
HU URETHRAS
HY TRASHERY
II RARITIES
IL RETIRALS
RETRIALS
TRAILERS
IN RESTRAIN
RETRAINS
STRAINER
TERRAINS
TRAINERS
TRANSIRE
IO ROARIEST
ROTARIES
IR STARRIER
TARRIERS
IS TARSIERS
IT RETRAITS
STRAITER
TARRIEST
IW STRAWIER
KS STARKERS
LO REALTORS
RELATORS
LT RATTLERS
STARTLER
LW TRAWLERS
MO REARMOST
MP TRAMPERS
NO ANTRORSE
NP PARTNERS
NT TRANTERS
OO SORORATE
OP PRAETORS
PRORATES
OR ARRESTOR
OS ASSERTOR
ASSORTER
ORATRESS
ROASTERS
OT ROSTRATE
PP STRAPPER
TRAPPERS
PU PARTURES
RAPTURES
QU QUARTERS
ST RESTARTS
STARTERS
SU SERRATUS
SY STRAYERS
UY TREASURY

AERSST 220
(ASSERT)

AD ASSARTED
AI ASTERIAS
ATRESIAS
AR TARRASES
BB STABBERS
BD DABSTERS
BG BARGESTS
BH BRASHEST
BL BLASTERS
STABLERS
BO BOASTERS
SORBATES
BS BRASSETS
BU ABSTRUSE
SURBATES
BW WABSTERS
CC SCARCEST
CE CATERESS
CERASTES
CH STARCHES
CI SCARIEST
CK STACKERS
CL SCARLETS
CN CRANTSES
CO COARSEST
COASTERS
CS CRASSEST
CT SCATTERS
DE ASSERTED
ESTRADES
DI ASTERIDS
DIASTERS
DISASTER
DISRATES
DN STANDERS
DO ASSORTED
TORSADES
DW STEWARDS
EE TESSERAE
EF FEASTERS
EG RESTAGES
EI SERIATES
EK SAKERETS
EL STEALERS
TEARLESS
TESSERAL
EM MASSETER
SEAMSTER
STEAMERS
EN ASSENTER
EARNESTS
SARSENET
EP TRAPESES
ER ASSERTER
REASSERT
SERRATES
TERRASES
ET ESTREATS
RESTATES
EW SWEATERS
EZ ERSATZES
FF RESTAFFS
STAFFERS
FH SHAFTERS
FP PRESSFAT
FW FRETSAWS
GG GAGSTERS
STAGGERS
GI AGISTERS
GO STORAGES
HH HARSHEST
THRASHES
HI SHERIATS
HL HARSLETS
SLATHERS
HM HAMSTERS
HO ASTHORES
EARSHOTS
HAROSETS
HOARSEST
HP SHARPEST
SPARTHES
HS SHASTERS
HT SHATTERS
HV HARVESTS
II IRISATES
SATIRISE
IK ASTERISK
SARKIEST
IL REALISTS
SALTIERS
SALTIRES
SLAISTER
IM ASTERISM
MAISTERS
MISRATES
SEMITARS
SMARTIES
IN ARTINESS
RESIANTS
RETSINAS
SNARIEST
STAINERS
STARNIES
STEARINS
IP PASTRIES
PIASTRES
RASPIEST
TRAIPSES
IR TARSIERS
IS TIRASSES
IT ARTISTES
ARTSIEST
STRIATES
IV TRAVISES
IW WAISTERS
WAITRESS
WASTRIES
KL STALKERS
KN STARKENS
KR STARKERS
KT STARKEST
LN SALTERNS
LP PLASTERS
PSALTERS
STAPLERS
LS STARLESS
LT SLATTERS
STARLETS
STARTLES
LU SALUTERS
LW WARTLESS
WASTRELS
MM STAMMERS
MN SARMENTS
SMARTENS
MO MAESTROS
MP STAMPERS
MT MATTRESS
SMARTEST
SMATTERS
MY MAYSTERS
NO ASSENTOR
SENATORS
TREASONS
NP PASTERNS
NS SARSNETS
NT TARTNESS
NU ANESTRUS
SAUNTERS
NV SERVANTS
VERSANTS
OP ESPARTOS
PORTASES
PROTASES
SEAPORTS
OR ASSERTOR
ASSORTER
ORATRESS
ROASTERS
OT STRATOSE
TOASTERS
OV VOTARESS
OX STORAXES
PS SPARSEST
TRESPASS
PT SPATTERS
TAPSTERS
PU PASTURES
UPSTARES
PY YAPSTERS
QU SQUAREST
RT RESTARTS
STARTERS
RU SERRATUS
RY STRAYERS
SS STRASSES
SY SATYRESS
TU STATURES
TW SWATTERS
UX SURTAXES
XY STYRAXES

AERSTT 97
(TASTER)

AB RABATTES
TABARETS
AC CASTRATE
AD ASTARTED
AE STEARATE
AG REGATTAS
AI ARIETTAS
ARISTATE
AN TARTANES
AO AEROSTAT
AR TARTARES
AU SATURATE
BE ABETTERS
BI BIRETTAS
BL BATTLERS
BLATTERS
BRATTLES
BO ABETTORS
BATTEROS
TABORETS
BU ABUTTERS
CD DETRACTS
SCRATTED
CH CHATTERS
RATCHETS
CI CITRATES
CRISTATE
SCATTIER
CJ TRAJECTS
CK RACKETTS
CL CLATTERS
SCRATTLE
CN TRANECTS
TRANSECT
CO SECTATOR
CR RETRACTS
CS SCATTERS
CT TETRACTS
CU CRUSTATE
CX EXTRACTS
CY SCATTERY
DE ASTERTED
RESTATED
DI STRAITED
STRIATED
TARDIEST
DL STARTLED
DR REDSTART
DU STATURED
EG GREATEST
EH THEATERS
THEATRES

EI ARIETTES
ITERATES
TEARIEST
TREATIES
TREATISE
EL ALERTEST
EM TEAMSTER
EN ENTREATS
RATTEENS
ER RETRATES
RETREATS
TREATERS
ES ESTREATS
RESTATES
ET ATTESTER
EX EXTREATS
FH FARTHEST
FL FATTRELS
FLATTERS
GI STRIGATE
GO GAROTTES
GY STRATEGY
HO RHEOSTAT
HS SHATTERS
HY SHATTERY
IL TERTIALS
IM MISTREAT
TERATISM
IN INTREATS
NITRATES
STRAITEN
TARTINES
TERTIANS
IR RETRAITS
STRAITER
TARRIEST
IS ARTISTES
ARTSIEST
STRIATES
IT ATTRITES
RATTIEST
TARTIEST
TITRATES
IW WARTIEST
IX EXTRAITS
KS STARKEST
LM MALTSTER
MARTLETS
LN SLATTERN
TRENTALS
LP PARTLETS
PLATTERS
PRATTLES
SPLATTER
SPRATTLE
LR RATTLERS
STARTLER
LS SLATTERS
STARLETS
STARTLES
LT TARTLETS
TATTLERS
LU LUSTRATE
TUTELARS
LY SLATTERY
MP TRAMPETS
MS MATTRESS
SMARTEST
SMATTERS
MU MATUREST

TESTAMUR
MX MARTEXTS
NN ENTRANTS
NO ORNATEST
NP PATTERNS
TRANSEPT
NR TRANTERS
NS TARTNESS
NU TAUNTERS
OP PROSTATE
OR ROSTRATE
OS STRATOSE
TOASTERS
OT ATTESTOR
TESTATOR
OU OUTRATES
OUTSTARE
PS SPATTERS
TAPSTERS
PU STUPRATE
PY TAPESTRY
QU QUARTETS
SQUATTER
RS RESTARTS
STARTERS
SU STATURES
SW SWATTERS
UV VETTURAS
VY TRAVESTY

AERSTW 194
(WATERS)
AD EASTWARD
RADWASTE
AE SEAWATER
BD BEDSTRAW
BI WARBIEST
BL BLEWARTS
BS WABSTERS
CH WATCHERS
DE DEWATERS
TARWEEDS
WASTERED
DI TAWDRIES
DS STEWARDS
DW WESTWARD
EG STREWAGE
EH WEATHERS
WREATHES
EI SWEATIER
TAWERIES
WEARIEST
ER WATERERS
ES SWEATERS
EW WETWARES
FI WASTRIFE
FO FORWASTE
SOFTWARE
FS FRETSAWS
FU WAFTURES
HI SWATHIER
WATERISH
HM MAWTHERS
II WISTERIA
IM WARTIMES
IN TINWARES
IP WIRETAPS
IR STRAWIER
IS WAISTERS
WAITRESS

WASTRIES
IT WARTIEST
LR TRAWLERS
LS WARTLESS
WASTRELS
LZ WALTZERS
MN TRANSMEW
TREWSMAN
NO STONERAW
NU UNWATERS
NY STERNWAY
OU OUTSWEAR
OUTWEARS
ST SWATTERS

AGILNR 199
(RALING)
AE REGALIAN
AG GANGLIAR
AK KRAALING
AM ALARMING
MARGINAL
AR LARRIGAN
BB RABBLING
BD BARDLING
BE BLEARING
BG GARBLING
BI BRAILING
BM MARBLING
RAMBLING
BO LABORING
BT BRATLING
BW BRAWLING
WARBLING
CD CRADLING
CE CLEARING
CO ORACLING
CS CARLINGS
CT CLARTING
CW CRAWLING
DD RADDLING
DE DANGLIER
DEARLING
DRAGLINE
DI DRAILING
DK DARKLING
DS DARLINGS
DT DARTLING
DW DRAWLING
DY DARINGLY
EE ALGERINE
EG GANGLIER
REGALING
EH NARGHILE
NARGILEH
EI GAINLIER
EJ JANGLIER
EM GERMINAL
MALIGNER
MALINGER
EN LEARNING
EO GERANIOL
REGIONAL
EP PEARLING
ER GNARLIER
ES ENGRAILS
NARGILES
REALIGNS
SALERING
SANGLIER

SIGNALER
SLANGIER
ET ALERTING
ALTERING
INTEGRAL
RELATING
TANGLIER
TRIANGLE
EX RELAXING
EY LAYERING
RELAYING
YEARLING
FF RAFFLING
GG GARGLING
RAGGLING
GI GLAIRING
GM MALGRING
GN GNARLING
GY GRAYLING
RAGINGLY
HS HARLINGS
RINGHALS
HY NARGHILY
IO ORIGINAL
IS GLAIRINS
RAILINGS
IT RINGTAIL
TRAILING
IV VIRGINAL
KN RANKLING
LU ALLURING
LINGULAR
LY NARGILLY
RALLYING
MS MARLINGS
NS SNARLING
OP PAROLING
OS RANGOLIS
OT TRIGONAL
PS SPARLING
SPRINGAL
ST RATLINGS
STARLING
SU SINGULAR
SW WARLINGS
WARSLING
TT RATTLING
TW TRAWLING
VY RAVINGLY
WW WRAWLING
WX WRAXLING

AGILNS 219
(SIGNAL)
AD SALADING
AI ALIASING
AK ASLAKING
AO LOGANIAS
AS SALSAING
BB SLABBING
BC CABLINGS
BE SINGABLE
BF FABLINGS
BI SAIBLING
BK BALKINGS
BL BALLINGS
BM AMBLINGS
BT BLASTING
STABLING
TABLINGS

BW BAWLINGS
CD SCALDING
CH CLASHING
CI SCAILING
CK SLACKING
CL CALLINGS
CO SOLACING
CP CLASPING
PLACINGS
SCALPING
CR CARLINGS
CS CLASSING
SCALINGS
CT CASTLING
CATLINGS
SCLATING
CU GLUCINAS
DD SADDLING
DE DEALINGS
LEADINGS
SIGNALED
DG GADLINGS
DI GLIADINS
DM MADLINGS
DN LANDINGS
SANDLING
DO LOADINGS
DR DARLINGS
EE ENSILAGE
LINEAGES
EF FINAGLES
EG LIGNAGES
EH HEALINGS
LEASHING
SHEALING
EK LINKAGES
EL NIGELLAS
EM MEASLING
EN EANLINGS
LEANINGS
EO GASOLINE
EP ELAPSING
PLEASING
ER ENGRAILS
NARGILES
REALIGNS
SALERING
SANGLIER
SIGNALER
SLANGIER
ES GAINLESS
GLASSINE
LEASINGS
SEALINGS
ET EASTLING
GELATINS
GENITALS
STEALING
EV LEAVINGS
SLEAVING
EW SWEALING
FH FLASHING
FI FAILINGS
FL FALLINGS
FO LOAFINGS
FT FATLINGS
GG LAGGINGS
SLAGGING
GI SILAGING
GL GINGALLS

GN ANGLINGS
SLANGING
GS GLASSING
GZ GLAZINGS
HL HALLINGS
HO SHOALING
HP PLASHING
HR HARLINGS
RINGHALS
HS HASSLING
LASHINGS
SLANGISH
SLASHING
HT HALTINGS
LATHINGS
HU LANGUISH
HW SHAWLING
WHALINGS
II LIAISING
IK SKAILING
IM MAILINGS
MISALIGN
IN NAILINGS
SNAILING
IR GLAIRINS
RAILINGS
IS AISLINGS
SAILINGS
IT TAILINGS
IW WAILINGS
KO OAKLINGS
KT SKLATING
STALKING
TALKINGS
KW WALKINGS
LL LALLINGS
LM SMALLING
LP SPALLING
LT STALLING
LU LINGULAS
LW WALLINGS
LY SALLYING
SIGNALLY
SLANGILY
MM LAMMINGS
SLAMMING
SMALMING
MP LAMPINGS
SAMPLING
MR MARLINGS
MT MALTINGS
NO LOANINGS
NR SNARLING
NS LINSANGS
NT SLANTING
TANLINGS
OO ISOGONAL
OP GALOPINS
OR RANGOLIS
OS GLOSSINA
LASSOING
OT ANTILOGS
SALTOING
PP LAPPINGS
SAPPLING
SLAPPING
PR SPARLING
SPRINGAL
PS SAPLINGS
PT PLATINGS

SPALTING
STAPLING
PW LAPWINGS
SPAWLING
PY PALSYING
SPLAYING
RT RATLINGS
STARLING
RU SINGULAR
RW WARLINGS
WARSLING
ST ANGLISTS
LASTINGS
SALTINGS
SLATINGS
SV SALVINGS
SW SWALINGS
TT SLATTING
TU SALUTING
UV AVULSING
UW WAULINGS
VY SAVINGLY
WW WAWLINGS
WY SWAYLING

AGILNT 174
(LATING)

AB ABLATING
AE AGENTIAL
ALGINATE
AO GALTONIA
AP PALATING
BE BELATING
BLEATING
TANGIBLE
BI LIBATING
BN BANTLING
BO BLOATING
OBLIGANT
BR BRATLING
BS BLASTING
STABLING
TABLINGS
BT BATTLING
BLATTING
BY TANGIBLY
CE CLEATING
CH LATCHING
CK TACKLING
TALCKING
CN CANTLING
CO LOCATING
CR CLARTING
CS CASTLING
CATLINGS
SCLATING
CT CLATTING
CU CLAUTING
DE DELATING
DI DILATING
DR DARTLING
EE GALENITE
GELATINE
LEGATINE
EG TEAGLING
EH ATHELING
EM LIGAMENT
METALING
EN GANTLINE
LATENING
EO GELATION
LEGATION
EP PLEATING
ER ALERTING
ALTERING
INTEGRAL
RELATING
TANGLIER
TRIANGLE
ES EASTLING
GELATINS
GENITALS
STEALING
EV VALETING
EX EXALTING
EZ TEAZLING
FH FANLIGHT
FL FLATLING
FO FLOATING
FS FATLINGS
FT FLATTING
FU FAULTING
GI LIGATING
TAIGLING
GN GNATLING
TANGLING
GO GLOATING
GOATLING
HL ALLNIGHT
HO LOATHING
HS HALTINGS
LATHINGS
IO INTAGLIO
LIGATION
TAGLIONI
IP PLAITING
IR RINGTAIL
TRAILING
IS TAILINGS
IT LITIGANT
IV VIGILANT
KS SKLATING
STALKING
TALKINGS
KY TAKINGLY
LS STALLING
LY TALLYING
MN MANTLING
MS MALTINGS
NP PLANTING
NS SLANTING
TANLINGS
OP PLOATING
OR TRIGONAL
OS ANTILOGS
SALTOING
OY ANTILOGY
PS PLATINGS
SPALTING
STAPLING
PT PLATTING
RS RATLINGS
STARLING
RT RATTLING
RW TRAWLING
SS ANGLISTS
LASTINGS
SALTINGS
SLATINGS
ST SLATTING
SU SALUTING
TT TATTLING
TW WATTLING
UV VAULTING
UX LUXATING
WZ WALTZING

AGINRS 123
(GRAINS)

AB BARGAINS
AE ANGARIES
AI ARAISING
AR ARRAIGNS
AS SANGRIAS
SARANGIS
AT GRANITAS
AU GUARANIS
AY ARAYSING
BD BRIGANDS
BE BEARINGS
SABERING
BH BRASHING
BI BRAISING
BR BARRINGS
BT BRASTING
CE CREASING
GRECIANS
SEARCING
CF FARCINGS
SCARFING
CH CHAGRINS
CRASHING
CK ARCKINGS
RACKINGS
CL CARLINGS
CP CARPINGS
SCARPING
SCRAPING
CR SCARRING
CS SACRINGS
CT SCARTING
TRACINGS
CU SCAURING
CV CARVINGS
CRAVINGS
DE DERAIGNS
GRADINES
READINGS
DF FARDINGS
DG NIGGARDS
DL DARLINGS
DM MRIDANGS
DN DARNINGS
DO ROADINGS
DT TRADINGS
DW DRAWINGS
SWARDING
WARDINGS
EE GESNERIA
EG GEARINGS
GREASING
SNAGGIER
EH HEARINGS
HEARSING
SHEARING
EK SKEARING
EL ENGRAILS
NARGILES
REALIGNS
SALERING
SANGLIER
SIGNALER
SLANGIER
EM GERMAINS
SMEARING
EN AGINNERS
EARNINGS
ENGRAINS
GRANNIES
EO IGNAROES
ORGANISE
ORIGANES
EP PREASING
SPEARING
ER EARRINGS
GRAINERS
ES REASSIGN
SEARINGS
SERINGAS
ET ANGRIEST
ASTRINGE
GANISTER
GANTRIES
GRANITES
INGRATES
RANGIEST
REASTING
STEARING
TASERING
EV VINEGARS
EW SWEARING
WEARINGS
EY RESAYING
FI FAIRINGS
FRAISING
FM FARMINGS
FRAMINGS
FT INGRAFTS
STRAFING
FW SWARFING
FY FRAYINGS
GG RAGGINGS
GI AGRISING
GP GRASPING
SPARGING
GS GRASSING
SIRGANGS
GT GRATINGS
GU SUGARING
GV GRAVINGS
GZ GRAZINGS
HK SHARKING
HL HARLINGS
RINGHALS
HP HARPINGS
PHRASING
SHARPING
HS SHARINGS
HT TRASHING
IL GLAIRINS
RAILINGS
IN INGRAINS
IO SIGNORIA
IP ASPIRING
PAIRINGS
PRAISING
IS RAISINGS
JR JARRINGS
KM MARKINGS
KN RANKINGS
KP PARKINGS
SPARKING
KS SARKINGS
KT KARTINGS
STARKING
LM MARLINGS
LN SNARLING
LO RANGOLIS
LP SPARLING
SPRINGAL
LT RATLINGS
STARLING
LU SINGULAR
LW WARLINGS
WARSLING
MM SMARMING
MO ORGANISM
ROAMINGS
MP RAMPINGS
MT MIGRANTS
SMARTING
MW SWARMING
WARMINGS
MY MYRINGAS
NR SNARRING
NS SNARINGS
NT RANTINGS
STARNING
NW WARNINGS
OR GARRISON
ROARINGS
OS ASSIGNOR
SOARINGS
OT ORGANIST
ROASTING
OU AROUSING
OV SAVORING
PP RAPPINGS
PR SPARRING
PS PARSINGS
RASPINGS
PT PARTINGS
PRATINGS
PW WARPINGS
PY PRAYINGS
SPRAYING
QU SQUARING
RT STARRING
TARRINGS
ST GASTRINS
STARINGS
SU ASSURING
SY SYRINGAS
TT RATTINGS
STARTING
TV STARVING
TW STRAWING
WRASTING
TY STRAYING
VW SWARVING
VY VARYINGS
WY RINGWAYS

AGINRT 69
(RATING)

AE AERATING
AS GRANITAS
BE BERATING
REBATING
BL BRATLING
BO ABORTING
TABORING
BS BRASTING
CE CATERING
CITRANGE
CREATING
REACTING
CF CRAFTING
FRACTING
CH CHARTING
RATCHING
CI GRANITIC
CK TRACKING
CL CLARTING
CN TRANCING
CS SCARTING
TRACINGS
CT TRACTING
CU CURATING
DE DERATING
GRADIENT
REDATING
TREADING
DF DRAFTING
DL DARTLING
DN DRANTING
DS TRADINGS
DY TARDYING
EE GRATINEE
EH EARTHING
HEARTING
INGATHER
EK RETAKING
EL ALERTING
ALTERING
INTEGRAL
RELATING
TANGLIER
TRIANGLE
EM EMIGRANT
EP TAPERING
ES ANGRIEST
ASTRINGE
GANISTER
GANTRIES
GRANITES
INGRATES
RANGIEST
REASTING
STEARING
TASERING
ET ARETTING
TREATING
EV AVERTING
TAVERING
VINTAGER
EW TWANGIER
WATERING
FG GRAFTING
FH FARTHING
FS INGRAFTS
STRAFING
FU FIGURANT
GN GRANTING
GS GRATINGS
GY GYRATING
HJ NIGHTJAR
HS TRASHING
HW THRAWING
WRATHING

IK TRAIKING
IL RINGTAIL
TRAILING
IN TRAINING
IO RIGATONI
IP PIRATING
IT ATTIRING
KS KARTINGS
STARKING
LO TRIGONAL
LS RATLINGS
STARLING
LT RATTLING
LW TRAWLING
MM TRAMMING
MP TRAMPING
MS MIGRANTS
SMARTING
MU MATURING
NO IGNORANT
NS RANTINGS
STARNING
NT TRANTING
NU NATURING
NY TRAYNING
TYRANING
OO ROGATION
OS ORGANIST
ROASTING
OT ROTATING
TROATING
OV GRAVITON
OY GYRATION
ORGANITY
PP TRAPPING
PS PARTINGS
PRATINGS
PT PRATTING
PU UPRATING
PY PARTYING
RS STARRING
TARRINGS
RY TARRYING
SS GASTRINS
STARINGS
ST RATTINGS
STARTING
SV STARVING
SW STRAWING
WRASTING
SY STRAYING

AGINST 108
(SATING)

AE SAGINATE
AR GRANITAS
AS ASSIGNAT
BB STABBING
BD DINGBATS
BE BEATINGS
BI BAITINGS
BL BLASTING
STABLING
TABLINGS
BN BANTINGS
BO BOASTING
BOATINGS
BOSTANGI
BR BRASTING
BS BASTINGS
BT BATTINGS
BW BATSWING
CH SCATHING
CK STACKING
TACKINGS
CL CASTLING
CATLINGS
SCLATING
CN CANTINGS
SCANTING
CO AGNOSTIC
COASTING
COATINGS
COTINGAS
CR SCARTING
TRACINGS
CS CASTINGS
CT SCATTING
DE SEDATING
STEADING
DN STANDING
DO DOATINGS
DR TRADINGS
DU ADUSTING
SUDATING
EE SAGENITE
EF FEASTING
EG NAGGIEST
EH GAHNITES
HEATINGS
EL EASTLING
GELATINS
GENITALS
STEALING
EM MANGIEST
MINTAGES
STEAMING
TEAMINGS
EN ANTIGENS
GENTIANS
STEANING
ER ANGRIEST
ASTRINGE
GANISTER
GANTRIES
GRANITES
INGRATES
RANGIEST
REASTING
STEARING
TASERING
ES EASTINGS
GENISTAS
GIANTESS
SEATINGS
TEASINGS
TSIGANES
ET ESTATING
TANGIEST
EU SAUTEING
EV VINTAGES
EW SWEATING
EY YEASTING
FF STAFFING
FH SHAFTING
FL FATLINGS
FR INGRAFTS
STRAFING
FS FASTINGS
FW WAFTINGS
GG STAGGING
TAGGINGS
GH GHASTING
GI AGISTING
GN STANGING
GR GRATINGS
GS STAGINGS
HL HALTINGS
LATHINGS
HN TANGHINS
HO HOASTING
HR TRASHING
HS HASTINGS
STASHING
HT HATTINGS
HW SWATHING
THAWINGS
IL TAILINGS
IM GIANTISM
IN SAINTING
SATINING
STAINING
IV VISTAING
IW WAITINGS
KL SKLATING
STALKING
TALKINGS
KN TANKINGS
KO GOATSKIN
KR KARTINGS
STARKING
KS SKATINGS
TASKINGS
LL STALLING
LM MALTINGS
LN SLANTING
TANLINGS
LO ANTILOGS
SALTOING
LP PLATINGS
SPALTING
STAPLING
LR RATLINGS
STARLING
LS ANGLISTS
LASTINGS
SALTINGS
SLATINGS
LT SLATTING
LU SALUTING
MP STAMPING
TAMPINGS
MR MIGRANTS
SMARTING
MT MATTINGS
NN TANNINGS
NO ASTONING
NP PANTINGS
NR RANTINGS
STARNING
NU SAUNTING
UNSATING
NW WANTINGS
NY STAYNING
OR ORGANIST
ROASTING
OS AGONISTS
OT TANGOIST
TOASTING
PP STAPPING
TAPPINGS
PR PARTINGS
PRATINGS
PS PASTINGS
PT SPATTING
RR STARRING
TARRINGS
RS GASTRINS
STARINGS
RT RATTINGS
STARTING
RV STARVING
RW STRAWING
WRASTING
RY STRAYING
ST TASTINGS
SW WASTINGS
TT TATTINGS
TW SWATTING

AINRST 40
(TRAINS)

AB ATABRINS
BARTISAN
AC ARCANIST
AD INTRADAS
RADIANTS
AE ANTISERA
ARTESIAN
RESINATA
AG GRANITAS
AI INTARSIA
AM TAMARINS
AP ASPIRANT
PARTISAN
AS ARTISANS
TSARINAS
AV VARIANTS
AY SANITARY
BD ANTBIRDS
BE ATEBRINS
BANISTER
BG BRASTING
BO TABORINS
CE CANISTER
CARNIEST
CISTERNA
CREATINS
NACRITES
SCANTIER
CF INFARCTS
INFRACTS
CG SCARTING
TRACINGS
CO CANTORIS
CAROTINS
CP CANTRIPS
CU CURTAINS
SATURNIC
TURACINS
DE DETRAINS
RANDIEST
STRAINED
DF INDRAFTS
DG TRADINGS
DI DISTRAIN
DK STINKARD
DO INTRADOS
DR TRIDARNS
DU UNITARDS
EE ARSENITE
RESINATE
STEARINE
TRAINEES
EF FENITARS
EG ANGRIEST
ASTRINGE
GANISTER
GANTRIES
GRANITES
INGRATES
RANGIEST
REASTING
STEARING
TASERING
EH HAIRNETS
INEARTHS
THERIANS
EI INERTIAS
RAINIEST
EJ NARTJIES
EK KERATINS
NARKIEST
EL ENTRAILS
LATRINES
RATLINES
TRENAILS
EM MINARETS
RAIMENTS
EN ENTRAINS
TRANNIES
EO ANOESTRI
ARSONITE
NOTARIES
NOTARISE
ROSINATE
EP PAINTERS
PANTRIES
PERTAINS
PINASTER
PRISTANE
REPAINTS
ER RESTRAIN
RETRAINS
STRAINER
TERRAINS
TRAINERS
TRANSIRE
ES ARTINESS
RESIANTS
RETSINAS
SNARIEST
STAINERS
STARNIES
STEARINS
ET INTREATS
NITRATES
STRAITEN
TARTINES
TERTIANS
EU RUINATES
TAURINES
URANITES
URINATES
EW TINWARES
FG INGRAFTS
STRAFING
FK RATFINKS
FX TRANSFIX
GG GRATINGS
GH TRASHING
GK KARTINGS
STARKING
GL RATLINGS
STARLING
GM MIGRANTS
SMARTING
GN RANTINGS
STARNING
GO ORGANIST
ROASTING
GP PARTINGS
PRATINGS
GR STARRING
TARRINGS
GS GASTRINS
STARINGS
GT RATTINGS
STARTING
GV STARVING
GW STRAWING
WRASTING
GY STRAYING
HL INTHRALS
HO TRAHISON
HP TRANSHIP
HY RHYTINAS
IM MARTINIS
IV VITRAINS
JO JANITORS
KO SKIATRON
LT RATTLINS
LU LUNARIST
MT TRANSMIT
MU NATRIUMS
NATURISM
MV VARMINTS
NT INTRANTS
NU INSURANT
NY TYRANNIS
OO ORATIONS
OP ATROPINS
OS ARSONIST
OT STRONTIA
OU SUTORIAN
OX TRIAXONS
PS SPIRANTS
SPRAINTS
PU PURITANS
UPTRAINS
ST STRAINTS
TRANSITS
TU ANTIRUST
NATURIST
TY TANISTRY

AINSTT 213
(TANIST)

AE ASTATINE
SANITATE
TANAISTE
AT ANTISTAT
ATTAINTS
AU TUTANIAS
AY SATANITY
BE TABINETS
BG BATTINGS
BO BOTANIST
CE CANTIEST
NICTATES

TETANICS
CG SCATTING
CK TINTACKS
CM CATMINTS
CO OSCITANT
TACTIONS
CY SANCTITY
SCANTITY
DE INSTATED
EE ANISETTE
TETANIES
TETANISE
EF FAINTEST
EG ESTATING
TANGIEST
EH HESITANT
EJ JANTIEST
EN ANTIENTS
STANNITE
EP PATIENTS
ER INTREATS
NITRATES
STRAITEN
TARTINES
TERTIANS
ES INSTATES
NASTIEST
SATINETS
TITANESS
ET NATTIEST
EV TASTEVIN
EW TAWNIEST
GH HATTINGS
GL SLATTING
GM MATTINGS
GO TANGOIST
TOASTING
GP SPATTING
GR RATTINGS
STARTING
GS TASTINGS
GT TATTINGS
GW SWATTING
IM IMITANTS
TITANISM
IO NOTITIAS
IV NATIVIST
VISITANT
KO STOTINKA
LR RATTLINS
LU LUTANIST
MR TRANSMIT
NR INTRANTS
NS INSTANTS
NY NYSTATIN
OO OSTINATO
OP POSTNATI
OR STRONTIA
OS STATIONS
OU TITANOUS
RS STRAINTS
TRANSITS
RU ANTIRUST
NATURIST
RY TANISTRY

ANORST 60
(RATONS)
AD ONDATRAS
AE ANOESTRA
AH ATHANORS
AY SANATORY
BE BARONETS
BI TABORINS
BY BARYTONS
CE ANCESTOR
ENACTORS
SORTANCE
CG CONGRATS
CH CHANTORS
CI CANTORIS
CAROTINS
CO CARTOONS
CORANTOS
OSTRACON
CT CONTRAST
CONTRATS
CU COURANTS
DE TORNADES
DI INTRADOS
DM DORMANTS
MORDANTS
DO DONATORS
ODORANTS
TANDOORS
TORNADOS
DU ROTUNDAS
DW SANDWORT
EE RESONATE
EF SEAFRONT
EG ORANGEST
RAGSTONE
STONERAG
EI ANOESTRI
ARSONITE
NOTARIES
NOTARISE
ROSINATE
EM MONSTERA
STOREMAN
EN NORTENAS
RESONANT
EP OPERANTS
PRONATES
ER ANTRORSE
ES ASSENTOR
SENATORS
TREASONS
ET ORNATEST
EV VENATORS
EW STONERAW
FF AFFRONTS
FL FRONTALS
FM FORMANTS
GI ORGANIST
ROASTING
GM ANGSTROM
GR GRANTORS
HI TRAHISON
HL ALTHORNS
IJ JANITORS
IK SKIATRON
IO ORATIONS
IP ATROPINS
IS ARSONIST
IT STRONTIA
IU SUTORIAN
IX TRIAXONS
KO OSTRAKON
KU OUTRANKS
LO ORTOLANS
LP PLASTRON
MS TRANSOMS
MU ROMAUNTS
NO SONORANT
OP PATROONS
OT ARNOTTOS
PU STROUPAN
SU SANTOURS
VY SOVRANTY

BDEIRS 242
(BRIDES)
AA ARABISED
AC ASCRIBED
CARBIDES
AE BEARDIES
AG ABRIDGES
BRIGADES
AL RAILBEDS
AM EMBRAIDS
AN BRANDIES
BRANDISE
AS SEABIRDS
SIDEBARS
AT BARDIEST
BRAIDEST
RABIDEST
TRIBADES
AW BAWDRIES
DAWBRIES
BL DIBBLERS
DRIBBLES
BR DRIBBERS
CE DESCRIBE
ESCRIBED
DE BIRDSEED
DEBRIDES
DO DISORBED
DISROBED
EF DEBRIEFS
EK KERBSIDE
EN INBREEDS
ET BESTRIDE
FL FILBERDS
FO FIBROSED
LN BLINDERS
BRINDLES
LR BRIDLERS
LT BRISTLED
DRIBLETS
LU BUILDERS
REBUILDS
MO BROMIDES
MU IMBURSED
NU BURNSIDE
OR BROIDERS
OS DISROBES
OT DEBITORS
OV OVERBIDS
SU DISBURSE

BEILRS 205
(LIBERS)
AA RAISABLE
AB SLABBIER
AC CALIBERS
CALIBRES
AD RAILBEDS
AF BARFLIES
AH BLASHIER
AI BISERIAL
AL BALLSIER
LIBERALS
AM REMBLAIS
AN RINSABLE
AT LIBRATES
TABLIERS
BC CRIBBLES
SCRIBBLE
BD DIBBLERS
DRIBBLES
BF FRIBBLES
BG GRIBBLES
BI RIBIBLES
BN NIBBLERS
BO SLOBBIER
BP PRIBBLES
BT STIBBLER
TRIBBLES
BU SLUBBIER
CM CLIMBERS
RECLIMBS
CO BRICOLES
CORBEILS
DF FILBERDS
DN BLINDERS
BRINDLES
DR BRIDLERS
DT BRISTLED
DRIBLETS
DU BUILDERS
REBUILDS
EF BELFRIES
EL LIBELERS
EN BERLINES
EU BLUESIER
FT FILBERTS
GT GILBERTS
HO BOLSHIER
HT BLITHERS
IN RINSIBLE
IT TRILBIES
KN BLINKERS
LO BROLLIES
LT BRILLEST
MO EMBROILS
MS BRIMLESS
MT TIMBRELS
MU SUBLIMER
MW WIMBRELS
OR BROILERS
OT STROBILE
TRILOBES
OW BLOWSIER
ST BLISTERS
BRISTLES
TT BRITTLES
TRIBLETS
TU BURLIEST
SUBTILER
TY BLISTERY
UY BRULYIES
UZ BRULZIES

BEIRST 184
(TRIBES)
AD BARDIEST
BRAIDEST
RABIDEST
TRIBADES
AK BARKIEST
BRAKIEST
BREASKIT
AL LIBRATES
TABLIERS
AM BARMIEST
AN ATEBRINS
BANISTER
AO SABOTIER
AR ARBITERS
RAREBITS
AT BIRETTAS
AV VIBRATES
AW WARBIEST
AY BESTIARY
SYBARITE
BI RIBBIEST
BL STIBBLER
TRIBBLES
BU STUBBIER
SUBTRIBE
CH BRITCHES
CO BISECTOR
CU BRUCITES
DE BESTRIDE
DL BRISTLED
DRIBLETS
DO DEBITORS
EE BEERIEST
EF BRIEFEST
EH HERBIEST
EU UBERTIES
FL FILBERTS
FS FIBSTERS
GL GILBERTS
HL BLITHERS
HR REBIRTHS
HS HERBISTS
IK BIRKIEST
IL TRILBIES
IN BRINIEST
IO ORBITIES
IS BIRSIEST
KS BRISKEST
BRISKETS
LL BRILLEST
LM TIMBRELS
LO STROBILE
TRILOBES
LS BLISTERS
BRISTLES
LT BRITTLES
TRIBLETS
LU BURLIEST
SUBTILER
LY BLISTERY
MU IMBRUTES
RESUBMIT
TERBIUMS
NO BORNITES
RIBSTONE
NT BITTERNS
NU TRIBUNES
TURBINES
OO ROBOTISE
OR ORBITERS
OS SORBITES
OY SOBRIETY
QU BRIQUETS
RU BURRIEST
SU BUSTIERS
TU TRIBUTES
TY TREYBITS

BEORST 225
(STROBE)
AA RABATOES
AD BROADEST
AE REBATOES
AH BATHORSE
AI SABOTIER
AL BLOATERS
SORTABLE
STORABLE
AM BROMATES
AN BARONETS
AP PROBATES
AR ARBORETS
TABORERS
AS BOASTERS
SORBATES
AT ABETTORS
BATTEROS
TABORETS
AU SABOTEUR
CH BOTCHERS
CI BISECTOR
CK BROCKETS
DE BESORTED
BESTRODE
DI DEBITORS
DU DOUBTERS
OBTRUDES
REDOUBTS
ES SOBEREST
EU TUBEROSE
EW BESTOWER
HL BROTHELS
HO THEORBOS
HR BROTHERS
HT BETROTHS
II ORBITIES
IL STROBILE
TRILOBES
IN BORNITES
RIBSTONE
IO ROBOTISE
IR ORBITERS
IS SORBITES
IY SOBRIETY
KO BOOKREST
LM TEMBLORS
LS BOLSTERS
LOBSTERS
LT BLOTTERS
BOTTLERS
LU BOULTERS
TROUBLES
MS BESTORMS
MOBSTERS
SOMBREST
NS SORBENTS
NU RUBSTONE
NW BESTROWN
BROWNEST
OS BOOSTERS
OY BOTRYOSE
PS BESPORTS
RU ROBUSTER

UU TUBEROUS

CEINOS 109
(CONIES)
AC COCAINES
AD DIOCESAN
OCEANIDS
AG COINAGES
AN CANONISE
AP CANOPIES
CAPONISE
PAEONICS
AR SCENARIO
AT ACONITES
CANOEIST
BL BINOCLES
BM COMBINES
BR BICORNES
CD CONCISED
CH CONCHIES
CN INSCONCE
CR CONCISER
CORNICES
CROCEINS
CS CONCISES
CT CONCEITS
DE CODEINES
DF CONFIDES
DG COGNISED
DH HEDONICS
DI DECISION
ICONISED
DL INCLOSED
DR CONSIDER
DT DEONTICS
DU DOUCINES
DZ ZINCODES
EL CINEOLES
ES SENECIOS
ET ICESTONE
SEICENTO
FN CONFINES
FR CONIFERS
FORENSIC
FORINSEC
FORNICES
INFORCES
FX CONFIXES
GL ECLOSING
GS COGNISES
GZ COGNIZES
HL CHOLINES
HELICONS
HO COHESION
HP CHOPINES
HR CHORINES
HY HYOSCINE
IL ISOCLINE
SILICONE
IN CONIINES
OSCININE
IP EPINOSIC
IR RECISION
SORICINE
IS ICONISES
IV INVOICES
IX EXCISION
IZ ICONIZES
LL LIONCELS
LO COLONIES
COLONISE
ECLOSION
LP PINOCLES
LR INCLOSER
LICENSOR
LS CONSEILS
INCLOSES
LT LECTIONS
LX LEXICONS
MN MECONINS
MR CREMOSIN
INCOMERS
SERMONIC
MT CENTIMOS
NR INCENSOR
NV CONNIVES
OT COONTIES
PR CONSPIRE
INCORPSE
PT PONCIEST
RR RESORCIN
RS NECROSIS
SERICONS
RT CORNIEST
RECTIONS
RU NOURICES
ROUNCIES
SS CESSIONS
COSINESS
ST SECTIONS
SX COXINESS
TT CENTOIST
STENOTIC
TU COUNTIES
TX EXCITONS
TY CYTOSINE
UV UNVOICES
VV CONVIVES

CEINRS 183
(INCERS)
AA CANARIES
AB CARBINES
AE CINEREAS
INCREASE
RESIANCE
AF FANCIERS
AG CREASING
GRECIANS
SEARCING
AH INARCHES
AI RIANCIES
AL CARLINES
AM CARMINES
AN CRANNIES
AO SCENARIO
AS ARSENICS
CERASINS
RACINESS
AT CANISTER
CARNIEST
CISTERNA
CREATINS
NACRITES
SCANTIER
BI INSCRIBE
BO BICORNES
BU BRUCINES
CO CONCISER
CORNICES
CROCEINS
DO CONSIDER
DP PRESCIND
DS DISCERNS
RESCINDS
DU INDUCERS
EE CERESINE
EG CREESING
GENERICS
EH ENRICHES
INHERCES
EK SICKENER
EL LICENSER
RECLINES
SILENCER
EN INCENSER
ER SINCERER
ES CERESINS
SCRIENES
ET CENTRIES
ENTERICS
ENTICERS
SCIENTER
SECRETIN
EU INSECURE
SINECURE
FO CONIFERS
FORENSIC
FORINSEC
FORNICES
INFORCES
GL CLINGERS
CRINGLES
GN SCERNING
GR CRINGERS
GT CRESTING
GU RECUSING
RESCUING
SCUNGIER
SECURING
GW SCREWING
GY SYNERGIC
HO CHORINES
HP PINCHERS
HS RICHNESS
HT CHRISTEN
CITHERNS
SNITCHER
IN CINERINS
IO RECISION
SORICINE
IS SERICINS
IT CITRINES
CRINITES
INCITERS
IU INCISURE
SCIURINE
KK KNICKERS
KL CLINKERS
CRINKLES
KS SNICKERS
KT STRICKEN
KU UNSICKER
LO INCLOSER
LICENSOR
MO CREMOSIN
INCOMERS
SERMONIC
MT CENTRISM
NO INCENSOR
OP CONSPIRE
INCORPSE
OR RESORCIN
OS NECROSIS
SERICONS
OT CORNIEST
RECTIONS
OU NOURICES
ROUNCIES
PS PRINCESS
ST CISTERNS
TT CENTRIST
CITTERNS
TU CURNIEST
UV INCURVES
VV CRIVVENS

CEINST 196
(INSECT)
AA ESTANCIA
AB CABINETS
AD DISTANCE
AE CINEASTE
AF FANCIEST
AH ASTHENIC
CHANTIES
AI CANITIES
AM SEMANTIC
AN ANCIENTS
CANNIEST
INSTANCE
AO ACONITES
CANOEIST
AR CANISTER
CARNIEST
CISTERNA
CREATINS
NACRITES
SCANTIER
AS CINEASTS
SCANTIES
AT CANTIEST
NICTATES
TETANICS
AV CISTVAEN
VESICANT
AY CYANITES
CH TECHNICS
CO CONCEITS
CY SYNECTIC
DH SNITCHED
DO DEONTICS
DY SYNDETIC
EG GENETICS
EH SITHENCE
EI NICETIES
EK NECKTIES
EM CENTIMES
EN NESCIENT
EO ICESTONE
SEICENTO
EP PECTINES
PENTICES
ER CENTRIES
ENTERICS
ENTICERS
SCIENTER
SECRETIN
ES CENTESIS
EY CYSTEINE
FL INFLECTS
GH CHESTING
ETCHINGS
GN SCENTING
GR CRESTING
HI ICHNITES
HK CHETNIKS
KITCHENS
KNITCHES
THICKENS
HL LINCHETS
TINCHELS
HR CHRISTEN
CITHERNS
SNITCHER
HS SNITCHES
HW WITCHENS
HZ CHINTZES
IK KINETICS
IN INSCIENT
IR CITRINES
CRINITES
INCITERS
IU CUTINISE
IY CYTISINE
SYENITIC
IZ CITIZENS
ZINCIEST
ZINCITES
KR STRICKEN
KS SNICKETS
LO LECTIONS
LS STENCILS
LU CUTLINES
TUNICLES
MO CENTIMOS
MR CENTRISM
OO COONTIES
OP PONCIEST
OR CORNIEST
RECTIONS
OS SECTIONS
OT CENTOIST
STENOTIC
OU COUNTIES
OX EXCITONS
OY CYTOSINE
PS INSPECTS
PY PYCNITES
RS CISTERNS
RT CENTRIST
CITTERNS
RU CURNIEST
SY CYSTINES

CEIORS 156
(COSIER)
AB AEROBICS
AD IDOCRASE
AL CALORIES
CARIOLES
AN SCENARIO
AV COVARIES
VARICOSE
BH BRIOCHES
BL BRICOLES
CORBEILS
BM CROMBIES
MICROBES
BN BICORNES
BR CRIBROSE
BT BISECTOR
CK COCKSIER
CN CONCISER
CORNICES
CROCEINS
CT CORTICES
DL SCLEROID
DN CONSIDER
DO CORODIES
DS DISCOERS
DT CORDITES
DU DISCOURE
DV DISCOVER
DIVORCES
DW CROWDIES
DY DECISORY
EH CHEERIOS
EJ REJOICES
ET COTERIES
ESOTERIC
EX EXORCISE
FF OFFICERS
FI ORIFICES
FN CONIFERS
FORENSIC
FORINSEC
FORNICES
INFORCES
FP FORCIPES
GG GEORGICS
SCROGGIE
HM MORICHES
HN CHORINES
HO CHOOSIER
ISOCHORE
HP SOPHERIC
HS CHORISES
ORCHESIS
ORCHISES
HT ROTCHIES
THEORICS
HW CHOWRIES
IM ISOMERIC
IN RECISION
SORICINE
IP IRISCOPE
KM OCKERISM
KR ROCKIERS
KT CORKIEST
ROCKIEST
STOCKIER
LL COLLIERS
ORSELLIC
LN INCLOSER
LICENSOR
LT CLOISTER
COISTREL
COSTLIER
CREOLIST
MN CREMOSIN
INCOMERS
SERMONIC
MP COMPRISE
MR MORRICES
MT MORTICES
MX EXORCISM
MY ISOCRYME
NN INCENSOR
NP CONSPIRE

INCORPSE
NR RESORCIN
NS NECROSIS
SERICONS
NT CORNIEST
RECTIONS
NU NOURICES
ROUNCIES
OP OPORICES
PP CROPPIES
PS PERSICOS
PT PERSICOT
PU PRECIOUS
RS CROSIERS
RU COURIERS
RZ CROZIERS
ST CROSSTIE
SU SCOURIES
SV CORSIVES
SW SCOWRIES
SX SIXSCORE
TT COTTIERS
TU CITREOUS
OUTCRIES
TV EVICTORS
VORTICES
TX EXCITORS
EXORCIST
VY VICEROYS

CEIRST 166
(CITERS)
AD ACRIDEST
AG AGRESTIC
AH CHARIEST
THERIACS
AL ALTRICES
ARTICLES
RECITALS
SELICTAR
AM CERAMIST
MATRICES
AN CANISTER
CARNIEST
CISTERNA
CREATINS
NACRITES
SCANTIER
AP CRAPIEST
CRISPATE
PICRATES
PRACTISE
AR ERRATICS
AS SCARIEST
AT CITRATES
CRISTATE
SCATTIER
AU SURICATE
AZ CRAZIEST
BH BRITCHES
BO BISECTOR
BU BRUCITES
CI ICTERICS
CK CRICKETS
CL CIRCLETS
CO CORTICES
DE DISCREET
DISCRETE
DH DITCHERS
DI ICTERIDS
DO CORDITES
DP PREDICTS
SCRIPTED
DU CRUDITES
CURDIEST
CURTSIED
DV VERDICTS
EF FIERCEST
EH CHESTIER
HERETICS
EI SERICITE
EL RETICLES
SCLERITE
TIERCELS
EN CENTRIES
ENTERICS
ENTICERS
SCIENTER
SECRETIN
EO COTERIES
ESOTERIC
EP CREPIEST
RECEIPTS
ER RECITERS
ET TIERCETS
EU CERUSITE
CUTESIER
EUCRITES
EV VERTICES
EX EXCITERS
FU FRUTICES
GN CRESTING
GU SCUTIGER
HH HITCHERS
HI CHRISTIE
HN CHRISTEN
CITHERNS
SNITCHER
HO ROTCHIES
THEORICS
HP PITCHERS
SPITCHER
HS STRICHES
HT CHITTERS
RICHTEST
STITCHER
HY HYSTERIC
IK STICKIER
IM MERISTIC
TRISEMIC
IN CITRINES
CRINITES
INCITERS
IP PICRITES
PRICIEST
IT RECTITIS
IV VERISTIC
JU JUSTICER
KL STICKLER
STRICKLE
TICKLERS
TRICKLES
KN STRICKEN
KO CORKIEST
ROCKIEST
STOCKIER
KP PRICKETS
KR TRICKERS
KS STICKERS
KU TRUCKIES
LO CLOISTER
COISTREL
COSTLIER
CREOLIST
LT CLITTERS
LU CURLIEST
UTRICLES
MN CENTRISM
MO MORTICES
MS CRETISMS
NO CORNIEST
RECTIONS
NS CISTERNS
NT CENTRIST
CITTERNS
NU CURNIEST
OP PERSICOT
OS CROSSTIE
OT COTTIERS
OU CITREOUS
OUTCRIES
OV EVICTORS
VORTICES
OX EXCITORS
EXORCIST
PR RESCRIPT
PS CRISPEST
PU CREPITUS
CUPRITES
PICTURES
PIECRUST
RT CRITTERS
RESTRICT
STRICTER
RU CRUSTIER
RECRUITS
ST TRISECTS
SU CITRUSES
CURTSIES
RICTUSES
SV VICTRESS
TU TUTRICES
UV CURVIEST
UY SECURITY

CENORS 172
(CONERS)
AB BACONERS
AC CONACRES
AD DRACONES
ENDOSARC
AG ACROGENS
CORNAGES
AI SCENARIO
AM CREMONAS
ROMANCES
AS COARSENS
NARCOSES
AT ANCESTOR
ENACTORS
SORTANCE
AU CARNEOUS
NACREOUS
BE OBSCENER
BI BICORNES
BU BOUNCERS
CI CONCISER
CORNICES
CROCEINS
CN CONCERNS
CT CONCERTS
CW CONCREWS
DE CENSORED
NECROSED
SECONDER
DH CHONDRES
DI CONSIDER
DS CORSNEDS
DW DECROWNS
EF ENFORCES
EG COGENERS
CONGREES
EL ENCLOSER
ES NECROSES
EV CONSERVE
CONVERSE
EZ COZENERS
FI CONIFERS
FORENSIC
FORINSEC
FORNICES
INFORCES
FU FROUNCES
GH GROSCHEN
GS CONGRESS
GU CONGRUES
SCROUNGE
GY CRYOGENS
HI CHORINES
HO COEHORNS
SCHOONER
HT NOTCHERS
HV CHEVRONS
II RECISION
SORICINE
IL INCLOSER
LICENSOR
IM CREMOSIN
INCOMERS
SERMONIC
IN INCENSOR
IP CONSPIRE
INCORPSE
IR RESORCIN
IS NECROSIS
SERICONS
IT CORNIEST
RECTIONS
IU NOURICES
ROUNCIES
JU CONJURES
KK KNOCKERS
KT CRONKEST
LO CONSOLER
MU CONSUMER
MUCRONES
OR CORONERS
CROONERS
OT CORONETS
OU CORNEOUS
PY NECROPSY
QU CONQUERS
RS SCORNERS
RW CROWNERS
ST CONSTERS
CRESTONS
TT CORNETTS
TU CONSTRUE
CORNUTES
COUNTERS
RECOUNTS
TROUNCES
TV CONVERTS
TW CROWNETS
UU CERNUOUS
COENURUS
UV UNCOVERS
UY CYNOSURE

CENOST 224
(CONEST)
AC COSECANT
AE ACETONES
NOTECASE
AG COGNATES
AI ACONITES
CANOEIST
AJ JACONETS
AL LACTONES
AM CAMSTONE
AP CAPSTONE
AR ANCESTOR
ENACTORS
SORTANCE
AS CONTESSA
COSTEANS
AT CONSTATE
AV CENTAVOS
CF CONFECTS
CI CONCEITS
CJ CONJECTS
CK CONTECKS
CN CONCENTS
CONNECTS
CP CONCEPTS
CR CONCERTS
DI DEONTICS
DN CONTENDS
DO SECODONT
DU CONTUSED
EI ICESTONE
SEICENTO
EN CENTONES
EP POTENCES
FU CONFUTES
GS CONGESTS
HL CHOLENTS
NOTCHELS
HR NOTCHERS
IL LECTIONS
IM CENTIMOS
IO COONTIES
IP PONCIEST
IR CORNIEST
RECTIONS
IS SECTIONS
IT CENTOIST
STENOTIC
IU COUNTIES
IX EXCITONS
IY CYTOSINE
KL STENLOCK
KM STOCKMEN
KP PENSTOCK
KR CRONKEST
KU UNSOCKET
LU NOCTULES
MM COMMENTS
MN CONTEMNS
NO CONNOTES
NS CONSENTS
NT CONTENTS
NV CONVENTS
OR CORONETS
PU POUNCETS
QU CONQUEST
RS CONSTERS
CRESTONS
RT CORNETTS
RU CONSTRUE
CORNUTES
COUNTERS
RECOUNTS
TROUNCES
RV CONVERTS
RW CROWNETS
ST CONTESTS
SU CONTUSES
COUNTESS
TX CONTEXTS

CEORST 234
(CORSET)
AC ECTOSARC
AD REDCOATS
AE CREASOTE
AF FORECAST
AG ESCARGOT
AH CHAROSET
THORACES
AL SECTORAL
AN ANCESTOR
ENACTORS
SORTANCE
AR ACROTERS
CREATORS
REACTORS
AS COARSEST
COASTERS
AT SECTATOR
AU OUTRACES
AV OVERACTS
OVERCAST
AX EXACTORS
BH BOTCHERS
BI BISECTOR
BK BROCKETS
CH CROCHETS
CROTCHES
CI CORTICES
CK CROCKETS
CN CONCERTS
CR CORRECTS
CU STUCCOER
CW TWOCCERS
DE CORSETED
ESCORTED
SECTORED
DI CORDITES
DS DOCTRESS
DU EDUCTORS
SEDUCTOR
EG CORTEGES
EH TROCHEES
EI COTERIES
ESOTERIC
EJ EJECTORS
EL CORSELET
ELECTORS
ELECTROS

SELECTOR
EO CREOSOTE
ER ERECTORS
EW COWTREES
EX CORTEXES
FF COFFRETS
FR CROFTERS
FU FRUCTOSE
HI ROTCHIES
THEORICS
HL CHORTLES
HN NOTCHERS
HO CHEROOTS
HP POTCHERS
HR TORCHERS
HU SCOUTHER
TOUCHERS
HW SCOWTHER
IK CORKIEST
ROCKIEST
STOCKIER
IL CLOISTER
COISTREL
COSTLIER
CREOLIST
IM MORTICES
IN CORNIEST
RECTIONS
IP PERSICOT
IS CROSSTIE
IT COTTIERS
IU CITREOUS
OUTCRIES
IV EVICTORS
VORTICES
IX EXCITORS
EXORCIST
JP PROJECTS
KN CRONKEST
KO CROOKEST
KP SPROCKET
KS RESTOCKS
STOCKERS
LS CORSLETS
COSTRELS
CROSSLET
LT CLOTTERS
CROTTLES
LU CLOTURES
CLOUTERS
COULTERS
LY COYSTREL
MP COMPTERS
MU COSTUMER
CUSTOMER
NO CORONETS
NS CONSTERS
CRESTONS
NT CORNETTS
NU CONSTRUE
CORNUTES
COUNTERS
RECOUNTS
TROUNCES
NV CONVERTS
NW CROWNETS
OS SCOOTERS
PP PROSPECT
PR PORRECTS
PT PROTECTS
PW SCREWTOP
QU CROQUETS
ROCQUETS
RY CORSETRY
SS CROSSEST
SU SCOUTERS
UU COUTURES
UV COUVERTS
UY COURTESY

DEEINR 43
(DENIER)
AC DERACINE
AF FREDAINE
AG REGAINED
AM REMAINED
AP PINDAREE
AS ARSENIDE
DENARIES
DRAISENE
NEARSIDE
AT DETAINER
RETAINED
BD REBIDDEN
BF BEFRIEND
BG BREEDING
BM BRIDEMEN
BS INBREEDS
CD CINDERED
CG RECEDING
CH ENRICHED
INHERCED
NICHERED
RICHENED
CK NICKERED
CL RECLINED
CM ENDERMIC
CO RECOINED
CP PINCERED
DF FRIENDED
DG ENRIDGED
DH HINDERED
DM REMINDED
DN DINNERED
DT DENDRITE
EF FINEERED
NEEDFIRE
REDEFINE
EL NEEDLIER
ER REINDEER
ES NEREIDES
FF NIFFERED
FG FINGERED
FR INFERRED
FS DEFINERS
FZ FRENZIED
GG GINGERED
NIGGERED
RENIGGED
GL ENGIRDLE
LINGERED
REEDLING
GM REMEDING
GN ENRINGED
GS DESIGNER
ENERGIDS
REDESIGN
REEDINGS
RESIGNED
HR HINDERER
HS DRISHEEN
JO REJOINED
KL REKINDLE
KS DEERSKIN
KT TINKERED
LU UNDERLIE
MO DOMINEER
MR REMINDER
MT REMINTED
MV VERMINED
NS SINNERED
NT INDENTER
INTENDER
INTERNED
NU UNREINED
NV INNERVED
OS ORDINEES
OT ORIENTED
PP NIPPERED
QU ENQUIRED
INQUERED
RT INTERRED
TRENDIER
RV REDRIVEN
ST INSERTED
NERDIEST
RESIDENT
SINTERED
TRENDIES
SU UREDINES
SW WIDENERS
SX INDEXERS
TU REUNITED
TV INVERTED
TW WINTERED
TX DEXTRINE

DEEIRS 58
(RESIDE)
AB BEARDIES
AC DECIARES
AF FEDARIES
AG DISAGREE
AJ JADERIES
AL REALISED
SIDEREAL
AM MADERISE
AN ARSENIDE
DENARIES
DRAISENE
NEARSIDE
AP AIRSPEED
AT READIEST
SERIATED
SIDERATE
STEADIER
AV READVISE
BC DESCRIBE
ESCRIBED
BD BIRDSEED
DEBRIDES
BF DEBRIEFS
BK KERBSIDE
BN INBREEDS
BT BESTRIDE
CD DECIDERS
DESCRIED
CG GRECISED
CL SCLEREID
CM MISCREED
CP PRECISED
CR DECRIERS
CS DESCRIES
CT DISCREET
DISCRETE
CU DECURIES
CV DESCRIVE
SCRIEVED
SERVICED
DP PRESIDED
DR DERIDERS
DT REDDIEST
DV DIVERSED
EM REMEDIES
EN NEREIDES
EP SPEEDIER
ES DIERESES
ET REEDIEST
EZ RESEIZED
FI DEIFIERS
EDIFIERS
FIRESIDE
FL DEFILERS
FIELDERS
FN DEFINERS
FO FORESIDE
GL LEIDGERS
GN DESIGNER
ENERGIDS
REDESIGN
REEDINGS
RESIGNED
GT DIGESTER
ESTRIDGE
GU GUDESIRE
GV DIVERGES
HK SHREIKED
SHRIEKED
HL RELISHED
SHIELDER
HN DRISHEEN
HO HEROISED
HP HESPERID
PERISHED
HR REDSHIRE
HV SHIVERED
SHRIEVED
HW SHREWDIE
IM DIMERISE
IP EPEIRIDS
IS DIERESIS
IT SIDERITE
IV DERISIVE
IW WEIRDIES
KN DEERSKIN
KU DUKERIES
KV SKIVERED
LU LEISURED
LV DELIVERS
DESILVER
SILVERED
SLIVERED
LW WIELDERS
LY YIELDERS
MM IMMERSED
SIMMERED
MP DEMIREPS
PREMISED
SIMPERED
MS DERMISES
MT DEMERITS
DEMISTER
DIMETERS
MISTERED
NN SINNERED
NO ORDINEES
NT INSERTED
NERDIEST
RESIDENT
SINTERED
TRENDIES
NU UREDINES
NW WIDENERS
NX INDEXERS
OV OVERSIDE
PR REPRISED
RESPIRED
PS DESPISER
DISPERSE
PRESIDES
PT PRIESTED
RESPITED
PU DUPERIES
PV DEPRIVES
PREVISED
RS DERRISES
DESIRERS
DRESSIER
RESIDERS
RT DESTRIER
RU RUDERIES
RV REDRIVES
ST EDITRESS
RESISTED
SISTERED
SU DIURESES
REISSUED
RESIDUES
SV DEVISERS
DISSERVE
DISSEVER
DIVERSES
TT TIREDEST
TU ERUDITES
SURETIED
TV VERDITES
TW WEIRDEST

DEELNS 239
(ENDLES)
AC CLEANSED
AE ENSEALED
AI DELAINES
AM DALESMEN
EMENDALS
LEADSMEN
AP DEPLANES
AU UNLEASED
UNSEALED
AV ENSLAVED
BR BLENDERS
BT BENDLETS
CI DECLINES
LICENSED
SILENCED
CO ENCLOSED
EI SELENIDE
ER NEEDLERS
ES LESSENED
NEEDLESS
SELDSEEN
EU UNSEELED
FU UNSELFED
GI SEEDLING
HI ENSHIELD
II SIDELINE
IK SILKENED
IO ESLOINED
IS IDLENESS
LINSEEDS
IT ENLISTED
LINTSEED
LISTENED
TINSELED
IY DYELINES
KO SLOKENED
KT SKLENTED
MO LODESMEN
OO LOOSENED
OS LESSONED
OU ENSOULED
OY ESLOYNED
PR RESPLEND
SW LEWDNESS
TY ENSTYLED

DEENRS 92
(ENDERS)
AC ASCENDER
REASCEND
AE ENSEARED
SERENADE
AG DERANGES
GRANDEES
GRENADES
AI ARSENIDE
DENARIES
DRAISENE
NEARSIDE
AK KNEADERS
AM AMENDERS
MEANDERS
REAMENDS
AN ENSNARED
AO REASONED
AS DEARNESS
AU UNDERSEA
AW ANSWERED
BI INBREEDS
BL BLENDERS
BP PREBENDS
CE RECENSED
SCREENED
SECERNED
CH DRENCHES
CK REDNECKS
CO CENSORED
NECROSED
SECONDER
CU CENSURED
DO ENDORSED
DP SPREDDEN
DU SUNDERED
EI NEREIDES
EL NEEDLERS
EO ENDORSEE
ET RESENTED
FI DEFINERS
GI DESIGNER
ENERGIDS

REDESIGN
REEDINGS
RESIGNED
HI DRISHEEN
HM HERDSMEN
HP PREHENDS
IK DEERSKIN
IN SINNERED
IO ORDINEES
IT INSERTED
NERDIEST
RESIDENT
SINTERED
TRENDIES
IU UREDINES
IW WIDENERS
IX INDEXERS
LP RESPLEND
MO SERMONED
NO ENDERONS
OR ENDORSER
OS ENDORSES
OT ERODENTS
OW ENDOWERS
WORSENED
PP PERPENDS
PS SPENDERS
PT PRETENDS
RU ENDURERS
SUNDERER
SU RUDENESS
TU DENTURES
SEDERUNT
UNDERSET
UNDESERT
UU UNDERUSE
UV UNVERSED

DEENST 111
(NESTED)
AB ABSENTED
AF FASTENED
AH HASTENED
AI ANDESITE
AK NAKEDEST
AM STAMENED
AO ENDOSTEA
AS ASSENTED
STANDEES
AU UNSEATED
BI BENDIEST
BL BENDLETS
CH STENCHED
CS DESCENTS
CY ENCYSTED
DI DESTINED
EF ENFESTED
EI NEEDIEST
ER RESENTED
ET DETENTES
EU DETENUES
EX DENTEXES
FI FENDIEST
INFESTED
FO SOFTENED
FS DEFTNESS
GI INGESTED
SIGNETED
STEEDING
HI DISTHENE
HU ENTHUSED
II DIETINES
IL ENLISTED
LINTSEED
LISTENED
TINSELED
IM DEMENTIS
SEDIMENT
TIDESMEN
IN DENTINES
DESINENT
IO SIDENOTE
IP PENTISED
IR INSERTED
NERDIEST
RESIDENT
SINTERED
TRENDIES
IS DESTINES
IT DINETTES
IU DETINUES
IV EVIDENTS
INVESTED
KL SKLENTED
LY ENSTYLED
NO SONNETED
NP PENDENTS
NU UNNESTED
OP PENTODES
OR ERODENTS
OS STENOSED
PR PRETENDS
RU DENTURES
SEDERUNT
UNDERSET
UNDESERT
TU UNTESTED

DEERST 151
(RESTED)
AB BETREADS
BREASTED
DEBATERS
AC CEDRATES
AE RESEATED
AF DRAFTEES
AG RESTAGED
AH HEADREST
AI READIEST
SERIATED
SIDERATE
STEADIER
AK STREAKED
AL TREADLES
AM MASTERED
STREAMED
AP PEDERAST
PREDATES
REPASTED
TRAPESED
AR ARRESTED
DREAREST
RETREADS
SERRATED
TREADERS
AS ASSERTED
ESTRADES
AT ASTERTED
RESTATED
AW DEWATERS
TARWEEDS
WASTERED
AY ESTRAYED
BI BESTRIDE
BO BESORTED
BESTRODE
CE DECREETS
RESECTED
SECRETED
CI DISCREET
DISCRETE
CO CORSETED
ESCORTED
SECTORED
CP SCEPTRED
DE DESERTED
DI REDDIEST
DL TREDDLES
DU DETRUDES
EF FESTERED
EG DETERGES
EI REEDIEST
EK STREEKED
EL DEERLETS
STREELED
EM DEEMSTER
EN RESENTED
EP ESTREPED
PESTERED
ER DESERTER
ET RESETTED
SETTERED
STREETED
EV REVESTED
EW WESTERED
EX EXSERTED
FO DEFOREST
FORESTED
FOSTERED
GI DIGESTER
ESTRIDGE
GU GESTURED
HH THRESHED
II SIDERITE
IM DEMERITS
DEMISTER
DIMETERS
MISTERED
IN INSERTED
NERDIEST
RESIDENT
SINTERED
TRENDIES
IP PRIESTED
RESPITED
IR DESTRIER
IS EDITRESS
RESISTED
SISTERED
IT TIREDEST
IU ERUDITES
SURETIED
IV VERDITES
IW WEIRDEST
LU LUSTERED
RESULTED
ULSTERED
LW LEWDSTER
WRESTLED
LY RESTYLED
MO MODESTER
MP DEMPSTER
MU DEMUREST
MUSTERED
NO ERODENTS
NP PRETENDS
NU DENTURES
SEDERUNT
UNDERSET
UNDESERT
OP POSTERED
REEDSTOP
REPOSTED
OR RESORTED
RESTORED
ROSTERED
OS OERSTEDS
OT ROSETTED
TETRODES
OX DEXTROSE
OY STOREYED
PU PERTUSED
SS DESSERTS
STRESSED
SU RUSSETED
SY DYESTERS
UV VESTURED
UX EXTRUDES

DEGILN 164
(DINGLE)
AB BLINDAGE
AF FINAGLED
AH HEALDING
AI GLIADINE
AM MALIGNED
MEDALING
AO GALENOID
AP PEDALING
PLEADING
AR DANGLIER
DEARLING
DRAGLINE
AS DEALINGS
LEADINGS
SIGNALED
AT DELATING
AY DELAYING
BE BLEEDING
BI BIELDING
BN BLENDING
BO INGLOBED
DE ENGILDED
DH HEDDLING
DM MEDDLING
DP PEDDLING
DR REDDLING
DS SLEDDING
DU DELUDING
INDULGED
UNGILDED
EN NEEDLING
EO ELOIGNED
LEGIONED
ER ENGIRDLE
LINGERED
REEDLING
ES SEEDLING
ET DELETING
FG FLEDGING
FI DEFILING
FIELDING
FU INGULFED
GG GLEDGING
GP PLEDGING
GS GELDINGS
SLEDGING
SNIGGLED
GU DELUGING
HS HINDLEGS
SHINGLED
IR GRIDELIN
IS EILDINGS
SIDELING
IT DILIGENT
IV DEVILING
IW WIELDING
IY YIELDING
KU DUKELING
LU DUELLING
LW DWELLING
MO MODELING
NO OLDENING
NS LENDINGS
OP DELOPING
DIPLOGEN
OS GLENOIDS
SIDELONG
PS SPELDING
RU INDULGER
RY YELDRING
SU INDULGES
SV DEVLINGS
SW SWINGLED
WELDINGS
WY WINGEDLY

DEGINR 82
(RINGED)
AA AREADING
DRAINAGE
GARDENIA
AB BEARDING
BREADING
AD DREADING
AE REGAINED
AH ADHERING
HEADRING
AK DAKERING
AL DANGLIER
DEARLING
DRAGLINE
AM DREAMING
MARGINED
AN GRANNIED
AO ORGANDIE
AR DREARING
AS DERAIGNS
GRADINES
READINGS
AT DERATING
GRADIENT
REDATING
TREADING
AY DERAYING
READYING
YEARDING
BE BREEDING
CE RECEDING
CO RECODING
CU REDUCING
CY DECRYING
DE ENRIDGED
DG DREDGING
DI DERIDING
DL REDDLING
DS REDDINGS
DU UNGIRDED
EF FINGERED
EG GINGERED
NIGGERED
RENIGGED
EL ENGIRDLE
LINGERED
REEDLING
EM REMEDING
EN ENRINGED
ES DESIGNER
ENERGIDS
REDESIGN
REEDINGS
RESIGNED
GU UNRIGGED
IL GRIDELIN
IN NIDERING
IS DESIRING
RESIDING
RINGSIDE
IT DIRIGENT
IV DERIVING
VIRGINED
IW WEIRDING
LU INDULGER
LY YELDRING
MU DEMURING
NT TRENDING
NU ENDURING
UNRINGED
OP PROIGNED
OR ORDERING
OS NEGROIDS
OU GUERIDON
OV DOVERING
OW DOWERING
PS SPRINGED
PY PREDYING
RS GRINDERS
REGRINDS
RY GRINDERY
SS DRESSING
ST STRINGED
SW REDWINGS
SY SYNERGID
SYRINGED

DEGINS 154
(SINGED)
AB BEADINGS
DEBASING
AH HEADINGS
SHEADING
AL DEALINGS
LEADINGS
SIGNALED
AO AGONISED
DIAGNOSE
AR DERAIGNS
GRADINES
READINGS
AS ASSIGNED

AT SEDATING
STEADING
AW WINDAGES
BD BEDDINGS
BN BENDINGS
BO OBSIGNED
CE SECEDING
CK DECKINGS
CN SCENDING
CO COGNISED
CU SEDUCING
CY DYSGENIC
DE DESIGNED
SDEIGNED
DH SHEDDING
DL SLEDDING
DN SNEDDING
DR REDDINGS
DT STEDDING
DW SWINDGED
WEDDINGS
EF FEEDINGS
EL SEEDLING
EN ENSIGNED
EP SPEEDING
ER DESIGNER
ENERGIDS
REDESIGN
REEDINGS
RESIGNED
ES DINGESES
EDGINESS
SDEIGNES
SEEDINGS
ET INGESTED
SIGNETED
STEEDING
EW WEEDINGS
EX DESEXING
FU DEFUSING
FEUDINGS
GH HEDGINGS
GL GELDINGS
SLEDGING
SNIGGLED
GW WEDGINGS
HI DINGHIES
HL HINDLEGS
SHINGLED
HN SHENDING
IL EILDINGS
SIDELING
IM DEMISING
IN DESINING
SDEINING
IO INDIGOES
IR DESIRING
RESIDING
RINGSIDE
IT DINGIEST
INDIGEST
IV DEVISING
LN LENDINGS
LO GLENOIDS
SIDELONG
LP SPELDING
LU INDULGES
LV DEVLINGS
LW SWINGLED
WELDINGS
MN MENDINGS
MO SMIDGEON
MS SMIDGENS
NP SPENDING
NS SENDINGS
NT STENDING
NU UNSIGNED
NY DESYNING
OP DEPOSING
DISPONGE
PIDGEONS
OR NEGROIDS
OW WENDIGOS
WIDGEONS
PR SPRINGED
PU DISPUNGE
RR GRINDERS
REGRINDS
RS DRESSING
RT STRINGED
RW REDWINGS
RY SYNERGID
SYRINGED
SU DINGUSES
SW SWINDGES
TU DUNGIEST

DEGIRS 210
(GRIDES)
AB ABRIDGES
BRIGADES
AC DISGRACE
AD DISGRADE
AE DISAGREE
AH GARISHED
HEADRIGS
AL SLAIRGED
AN DERAIGNS
GRADINES
READINGS
AP SPAIRGED
CE GRECISED
DL GRIDDLES
DN REDDINGS
DR GRIDDERS
EL LEIDGERS
EN DESIGNER
ENERGIDS
REDESIGN
REEDINGS
RESIGNED
ET DIGESTER
ESTRIDGE
EU GUDESIRE
EV DIVERGES
FO FIREDOGS
GO DISGORGE
GP SPRIGGED
GT STRIGGED
GU DRUGGIES
II RIGIDISE
IN DESIRING
RESIDING
RINGSIDE
IT RIDGIEST
RIGIDEST
LR GIRDLERS
LU GUILDERS
SLUDGIER
LW WERGILDS
MU SMUDGIER
NO NEGROIDS
NP SPRINGED
NR GRINDERS
REGRINDS
NS DRESSING
NT STRINGED
NW REDWINGS
NY SYNERGID
SYRINGED
OO GOODSIRE
OT GRODIEST
STODGIER
TU DURGIEST

DEILNS 120
(INDLES)
AD ISLANDED
LANDSIDE
AE DELAINES
AG DEALINGS
LEADINGS
SIGNALED
AN ANNELIDS
LINDANES
AO NODALISE
AR ISLANDER
AU UNSAILED
AV ANDVILES
BR BLINDERS
BRINDLES
BT BLINDEST
CE DECLINES
LICENSED
SILENCED
CO INCLOSED
CU INCLUDES
NUCLIDES
UNSLICED
DG SLEDDING
DP SPINDLED
SPLENDID
DW DWINDLES
SWINDLED
EE SELENIDE
EG SEEDLING
EH ENSHIELD
EI SIDELINE
EK SILKENED
EO ESLOINED
ES IDLENESS
LINSEEDS
ET ENLISTED
LINTSEED
LISTENED
TINSELED
EY DYELINES
FF SNIFFLED
FI INFIDELS
INFIELDS
FR FLINDERS
GG GELDINGS
SLEDGING
SNIGGLED
GH HINDLEGS
SHINGLED
GI EILDINGS
SIDELING
GN LENDINGS
GO GLENOIDS
SIDELONG
GP SPELDING
GU INDULGES
GV DEVLINGS
GW SWINGLED
WELDINGS
IK DISLIKEN
IO LIONISED
KR KINDLERS
KS KINDLESS
LW INDWELLS
MS MILDNESS
MINDLESS
MU MUSLINED
OO SOLENOID
OR DISENROL
OS SONDELIS
OU DELUSION
INSOULED
UNSOILED
PR SPELDRIN
PS SPELDINS
SPINDLES
PT SPLINTED
RS RINDLESS
RT SNIRTLED
TENDRILS
TRINDLES
RW SWINDLER
SV VILDNESS
SW SWINDLES
WILDNESS
WINDLESS
TU DILUENTS
INSULTED
UNLISTED

DEILRT 73
(TRIDLE)
AB LIBRATED
AC ARTICLED
AE RETAILED
AL TRIALLED
AO IDOLATER
TAILORED
AP DIPTERAL
TRIPEDAL
AS DILATERS
LARDIEST
AT DETRITAL
AY DIELYTRA
BB DRIBBLET
BO TRILOBED
BS BRISTLED
DRIBLETS
CE DERELICT
CH ELDRITCH
CK TRICKLED
CY DIRECTLY
DI TIDDLIER
DN TRINDLED
DS STRIDDLE
TIDDLERS
DW TWIDDLER
EF FILTERED
EL TILLERED
TREDILLE
EO DOLERITE
LOITERED
ET LITTERED
RETITLED
HL THRILLED
HW WRITHLED
IP TRIPLIED
IS REDISTIL
NS SNIRTLED
TENDRILS
TRINDLES
NY TRENDILY
OS STOLIDER
PP TRIPPLED
SU DILUTERS
LURIDEST
VY DEVILTRY

DEINOS 41
(ONSIDE)
AC DIOCESAN
OCEANIDS
AD ADENOIDS
ADONISED
ANODISED
AG AGONISED
DIAGNOSE
AH ADHESION
AL NODALISE
AM NOMADIES
NOMADISE
AR ANEROIDS
DONARIES
AS ADONISES
ANODISES
AT ASTONIED
SEDATION
AX DIOXANES
AZ ADONIZES
ANODIZES
BE EBONISED
BG OBSIGNED
BO NOBODIES
BU BEDOUINS
CC CONCISED
CE CODEINES
CF CONFIDES
CG COGNISED
CH HEDONICS
CI DECISION
ICONISED
CL INCLOSED
CR CONSIDER
CT DEONTICS
CU DOUCINES
CZ ZINCODES
DP DISPONED
DR INDORSED
DW DISENDOW
DISOWNED
DOWNSIDE
EL ESLOINED
EM DEMONISE
DOMINEES
EP DISPONEE
ER ORDINEES
ET SIDENOTE
EV NOSEDIVE
GI INDIGOES
GL GLENOIDS
SIDELONG
GM SMIDGEON
GP DEPOSING
DISPONGE
PIDGEONS
GR NEGROIDS
GW WENDIGOS
WIDGEONS
HM HEDONISM
HP DIPHONES
SIPHONED
SPHENOID
HR HORDEINS
HT HEDONIST
IL LIONISED
IM DOMINIES
IR DERISION
IRONISED
RESINOID
IT EDITIONS
SEDITION
IV VISIONED
JR JOINDERS
LO SOLENOID
LR DISENROL
LS SONDELIS
LU DELUSION
INSOULED
UNSOILED
MM DEMONISM
MN MISDONNE
MO DOMINOES
MONODIES
MT DEMONIST
NR ENDIRONS
OP POISONED
OZ OZONISED
PR DISPONER
POINDERS
PRISONED
PS DISPONES
DOPINESS
SPINODES
PU UNPOISED
RS INDORSES
RT DRONIEST
RU DOURINES
SOURDINE
RW DISOWNER
WINDORES
WINDROSE
ST DONSIEST
SV VOIDNESS
SZ DOZINESS
TW DOWNIEST
WZ DOWNSIZE

DEINRS 51
(DINERS)
AA ARANEIDS
AB BRANDIES
BRANDISE
AE ARSENIDE
DENARIES
DRAISENE
NEARSIDE
AF FRIANDES
AG DERAIGNS
GRADINES
READINGS
AI DRAISINE
AL ISLANDER
AM ADERMINS

SIRNAMED
AN INSNARED
AO ANEROIDS
DONARIES
AP SPRAINED
AR DRAINERS
SERRANID
AS ARIDNESS
SARDINES
AT DETRAINS
RANDIEST
STRAINED
AU DENARIUS
UNRAISED
URANIDES
AV INVADERS
SANDIVER
AY SYNEDRIA
BE INBREEDS
BL BLINDERS
BRINDLES
BU BURNSIDE
CO CONSIDER
CP PRESCIND
CS DISCERNS
RESCINDS
CU INDUCERS
DG REDDINGS
DK KINDREDS
DO INDORSED
DT STRIDDEN
EE NEREIDES
EF DEFINERS
EG DESIGNER
ENERGIDS
REDESIGN
REEDINGS
RESIGNED
EH DRISHEEN
EK DEERSKIN
EN SINNERED
EO ORDINEES
ET INSERTED
NERDIEST
RESIDENT
SINTERED
TRENDIES
EU UREDINES
EW WIDENERS
EX INDEXERS
FL FLINDERS
GI DESIRING
RESIDING
RINGSIDE
GO NEGROIDS
GP SPRINGED
GR GRINDERS
REGRINDS
GS DRESSING
GT STRINGED
GW REDWINGS
GY SYNERGID
SYRINGED
HO HORDEINS
IO DERISION
IRONISED
RESINOID
IP INSPIRED
IS INDRISES
INSIDERS
IT DISINTER
INDITERS
NITRIDES
RINDIEST
IU DISINURE
URIDINES
IV DIVINERS
JO JOINDERS
KL KINDLERS
KR DRINKERS
KS REDSKINS
LO DISENROL
LP SPELDRIN
LS RINDLESS
LT SNIRTLED
TENDRILS
TRINDLES
LW SWINDLER
NO ENDIRONS
OP DISPONER
POINDERS
PRISONED
OS INDORSES
OT DRONIEST
OU DOURINES
SOURDINE
OW DISOWNER
WINDORES
WINDROSE
PT SPRINTED
SU INSUREDS
SUNDRIES
TT STRIDENT
TRIDENTS
TU INTRUDES
TX DEXTRINS

DEINRU 52
(RUINED)
AF UNFAIRED
AH UNHAIRED
AI UREDINIA
AO DOUANIER
AP UNPAIRED
UNREPAID
AS DENARIUS
UNRAISED
URANIDES
AT DATURINE
INDURATE
RUINATED
URINATED
AV UNVARIED
BB UNRIBBED
BD UNDERBID
BL UNBRIDLE
BS BURNSIDE
BT TURBINED
UNDERBIT
BU UNBURIED
CG REDUCING
CO DECURION
CP UNPRICED
CR INCURRED
CS INDUCERS
CV INCURVED
DD UNDERDID
DG UNGIRDED
DL UNRIDDLE
DN UNRIDDEN
DT INTRUDED
EL UNDERLIE
EN UNREINED
EQ ENQUIRED
INQUERED
ES UREDINES
ET REUNITED
FL UNRIFLED
URNFIELD
FN REINFUND
UNFRIEND
GG UNRIGGED
GL INDULGER
GM DEMURING
GN ENDURING
UNRINGED
GO GUERIDON
IQ INQUIRED
IS DISINURE
URIDINES
IT UNTIDIER
KN UNKINDER
LP UNDERLIP
MP UNPRIMED
MT RUDIMENT
NO UNIRONED
NP UNDERPIN
NU UNINURED
NV UNDRIVEN
OS DOURINES
SOURDINE
PP UNRIPPED
PT TURNIPED
PZ UNPRIZED
RT INTRUDER
SS INSUREDS
SUNDRIES
ST INTRUDES
TW UNDERWIT

DEINST 32
(SINTED)
AB BANDIEST
AC DISTANCE
AD DANDIEST
AE ANDESITE
AG SEDATING
STEADING
AH HANDIEST
AI ADENITIS
DAINTIES
AM MEDIANTS
TIDESMAN
AO ASTONIED
SEDATION
AP DEPAINTS
AR DETRAINS
RANDIEST
STRAINED
AS SANDIEST
AT INSTATED
AU AUDIENTS
SINUATED
AV DEVIANTS
AY DESYATIN
BE BENDIEST
BL BLINDEST
CH SNITCHED
CO DEONTICS
CY SYNDETIC
DE DESTINED
DG STEDDING
DR STRIDDEN
DS DISTENDS
DU DISTUNED
EE NEEDIEST
EF FENDIEST
INFESTED
EG INGESTED
SIGNETED
STEEDING
EH DISTHENE
EI DIETINES
EL ENLISTED
LINTSEED
LISTENED
TINSELED
EM DEMENTIS
SEDIMENT
TIDESMEN
EN DENTINES
DESINENT
EO SIDENOTE
EP PENTISED
ER INSERTED
NERDIEST
RESIDENT
SINTERED
TRENDIES
ES DESTINES
ET DINETTES
EU DETINUES
EV EVIDENTS
INVESTED
FU UNSIFTED
GI DINGIEST
INDIGEST
GN STENDING
GR STRINGED
GU DUNGIEST
HO HEDONIST
IK DINKIEST
IO EDITIONS
SEDITION
IR DISINTER
INDITERS
NITRIDES
RINDIEST
IS INSISTED
TIDINESS
IU DISUNITE
NUDITIES
UNITISED
UNTIDIES
IV DIVINEST
IW WINDIEST
LP SPLINTED
LR SNIRTLED
TENDRILS
TRINDLES
LU DILUENTS
INSULTED
UNLISTED
MO DEMONIST
MS MINDSETS
MU MISTUNED
NU DUNNIEST
DUNNITES
OR DRONIEST
OS DONSIEST
OW DOWNIEST
PR SPRINTED
PS STIPENDS
QU SQUINTED
RT STRIDENT
TRIDENTS
RU INTRUDES
RX DEXTRINS
SS DISNESTS
DISSENTS
ST DENTISTS
SU DISTUNES
UU UNSUITED

DEIORS 27
(ORIDES)
AC IDOCRASE
AD ROADSIDE
SIDEROAD
AF FORESAID
AL DARIOLES
SOLIDARE
SOREDIAL
AN ANEROIDS
DONARIES
AP DIASPORE
PARODIES
AT ASTEROID
BD DISORBED
DISROBED
BF FIBROSED
BM BROMIDES
BR BROIDERS
BS DISROBES
BT DEBITORS
BV OVERBIDS
CL SCLEROID
CN CONSIDER
CO CORODIES
CS DISCOERS
CT CORDITES
CU DISCOURE
CV DISCOVER
DIVORCES
CW CROWDIES
CY DECISORY
DH SHODDIER
DM DERMOIDS
DN INDORSED
DP DROPSIED
DR DISORDER
SORDIDER
EF FORESIDE
EH HEROISED
EN ORDINEES
EV OVERSIDE
FF OFFSIDER
FG FIREDOGS
FU FOUDRIES
GG DISGORGE
GN NEGROIDS
GO GOODSIRE
GT GRODIEST
STODGIER
HM HEIRDOMS
HN HORDEINS
HP SPHEROID
HS DISHORSE
HIDROSES
IL IDOLISER
IN DERISION
IRONISED
RESINOID
IP PRESIDIO
IT DIORITES
IX OXIDISER
JN JOINDERS
KS DROSKIES
KT DORKIEST
LL DOLLIERS
LN DISENROL
LS SOLDIERS
LT STOLIDER
LU SOULDIER
LY SOLDIERY
MO MOIDORES
MP PROMISED
MR MISORDER
MORRISED
MS MISDOERS
MT MORTISED
MU DIMEROUS
ERODIUMS
SOREDIUM
NN ENDIRONS
NP DISPONER
POINDERS
PRISONED
NS INDORSES
NT DRONIEST
NU DOURINES
SOURDINE
NW DISOWNER
WINDORES
WINDROSE
OW WOODSIER
PS DISPOSER
DROPSIES
PT DIOPTERS
DIOPTRES
DIPTEROS
PERIDOTS
PROTEIDS
RIPOSTED
PV DISPROVE
PROVIDES
PW DROPWISE
RS DROSSIER
RW DROWSIER
RY DERISORY
SS DOSSIERS
ST STEROIDS
SU DESIROUS
SV DEVISORS
TT DORTIEST
TU IODURETS
OUTRIDES
OUTSIDER
SUITORED
TW ROWDIEST
WORDIEST
WW WIDOWERS

DEIOST 35
(ODITES)
AG GODETIAS
AL DIASTOLE
ISOLATED
SODALITE
SOLIDATE

AM ATOMISED
AN ASTONIED
SEDATION
AP DIOPTASE
AR ASTEROID
AX OXIDATES
AZ AZOTISED
BG BODGIEST
BR DEBITORS
CL DOCILEST
CM DOMESTIC
CN DEONTICS
CP DESPOTIC
CR CORDITES
CS CESTOIDS
CT COTTISED
DD DODDIEST
DG DODGIEST
DI ODDITIES
DL DELTOIDS
DP PODDIEST
DS SODDIEST
DW DOWDIEST
EG EGOTISED
EM TEDISOME
EN SIDENOTE
EP EPIDOTES
POETISED
GG DOGGIEST
GL GODLIEST
GOLDIEST
GO GOODIEST
GP PODGIEST
GR GRODIEST
STODGIER
HN HEDONIST
HU HIDEOUTS
IN EDITIONS
SEDITION
IR DIORITES
KR DORKIEST
LM MELODIST
LR STOLIDER
LS SOLIDEST
LT DOILTEST
LU SOLITUDE
MM IMMODEST
MN DEMONIST
MO DOOMIEST
MOODIEST
SODOMITE
MR MORTISED
MS MODISTES
MT DEMOTIST
NR DRONIEST
NS DONSIEST
NW DOWNIEST
OW WOODIEST
PR DIOPTERS
DIOPTRES
DIPTEROS
PERIDOTS
PROTEIDS
RIPOSTED
PS DEPOSITS
TOPSIDES
RS STEROIDS
RT DORTIEST
RU IODURETS
OUTRIDES
OUTSIDER
SUITORED
RW ROWDIEST
WORDIEST
SU OUTSIDES
SX EXODISTS
TT DOTTIEST
UZ OUTSIZED

DEIPRT 215
(PRITED)
AL DIPTERAL
TRIPEDAL
AM IMPARTED
AN DIPTERAN
AS DIPTERAS
RAPIDEST
SPIRATED
TARSIPED
TRAIPSED
AU EUPATRID
CE DECREPIT
DEPICTER
CO DEPICTOR
CS PREDICTS
SCRIPTED
CU PICTURED
EO PERIDOTE
ER TREPIDER
ES PRIESTED
RESPITED
ET PITTERED
PRETTIED
EX EXTIRPED
FO PROFITED
HO TROPHIED
IL TRIPLIED
IN INTREPID
IO DIPTEROI
IS RIPTIDES
SPIRITED
LP TRIPPLED
MO IMPORTED
MS DIREMPTS
NS SPRINTED
NU TURNIPED
OS DIOPTERS
DIOPTRES
DIPTEROS
PERIDOTS
PROTEIDS
RIPOSTED
PS STRIPPED
RU IRRUPTED
PUTRIDER
SU DISPUTER
STUPIDER

DEIRST 57
(STRIDE)
AA DATARIES
RADIATES
AB BARDIEST
BRAIDEST
RABIDEST
TRIBADES
AC ACRIDEST
AD DISRATED
AE READIEST
SERIATED
SIDERATE
STEADIER
AH HAIRSTED
HARDIEST
AI IRISATED
AK STRAIKED
AL DILATERS
LARDIEST
AM MARDIEST
MISRATED
READMITS
AN DETRAINS
RANDIEST
STRAINED
AO ASTEROID
AP DIPTERAS
RAPIDEST
SPIRATED
TARSIPED
TRAIPSED
AS ASTERIDS
DIASTERS
DISASTER
DISRATES
AT STRAITED
STRIATED
TARDIEST
AW TAWDRIES
BE BESTRIDE
BL BRISTLED
DRIBLETS
BO DEBITORS
CE DISCREET
DISCRETE
CH DITCHERS
CI ICTERIDS
CO CORDITES
CP PREDICTS
SCRIPTED
CU CRUDITES
CURDIEST
CURTSIED
CV VERDICTS
DE REDDIEST
DL STRIDDLE
TIDDLERS
DN STRIDDEN
DU RUDDIEST
STURDIED
EE REEDIEST
EG DIGESTER
ESTRIDGE
EI SIDERITE
EM DEMERITS
DEMISTER
DIMETERS
MISTERED
EN INSERTED
NERDIEST
RESIDENT
SINTERED
TRENDIES
EP PRIESTED
RESPITED
ER DESTRIER
ES EDITRESS
RESISTED
SISTERED
ET TIREDEST
EU ERUDITES
SURETIED
EV VERDITES
EW WEIRDEST
FR DRIFTERS
GG STRIGGED
GI RIDGIEST
RIGIDEST
GN STRINGED
GO GRODIEST
STODGIER
GU DURGIEST
HI DISHERIT
HT THIRSTED
THRISTED
IL REDISTIL
IN DISINTER
INDITERS
NITRIDES
RINDIEST
IO DIORITES
IP RIPTIDES
SPIRITED
IT DIRTIEST
TRITIDES
KO DORKIEST
LN SNIRTLED
TENDRILS
TRINDLES
LO STOLIDER
LU DILUTERS
LURIDEST
MM MIDTERMS
MO MORTISED
MP DIREMPTS
NO DRONIEST
NP SPRINTED
NT STRIDENT
TRIDENTS
NU INTRUDES
NX DEXTRINS
OP DIOPTERS
DIOPTRES
DIPTEROS
PERIDOTS
PROTEIDS
RIPOSTED
OS STEROIDS
OT DORTIEST
OU IODURETS
OUTRIDES
OUTSIDER
SUITORED
OW ROWDIEST
WORDIEST
PP STRIPPED
PU DISPUTER
STUPIDER
QU SQUIRTED
RU STURDIER
SS DISSERTS
DISTRESS
SU DIESTRUS
DRUSIEST
STUDIERS
STURDIES
TU DETRITUS
UX DRUXIEST

DEIRSU 143
(URDIES)
AC DECURIAS
AL RESIDUAL
AN DENARIUS
UNRAISED
URANIDES
AP UPRAISED
AS RADIUSES
SUDARIES
BL BUILDERS
REBUILDS
BM IMBURSED
BN BURNSIDE
BS DISBURSE
CD DISCURED
CE DECURIES
CN INDUCERS
CO DISCOURE
CR SCURRIED
CS DISCURES
CT CRUDITES
CURDIEST
CURTSIED
DP SPUDDIER
DS DRUIDESS
DT RUDDIEST
STURDIED
EG GUDESIRE
EK DUKERIES
EL LEISURED
EN UREDINES
EP DUPERIES
ER RUDERIES
ES DIURESES
REISSUED
RESIDUES
ET ERUDITES
SURETIED
FF DIFFUSER
FO FOUDRIES
FS FISSURED
GG DRUGGIES
GL GUILDERS
SLUDGIER
GM SMUDGIER
GT DURGIEST
HR DHURRIES
IN DISINURE
URIDINES
IS DIURESIS
KP PRUSIKED
SPRUIKED
KR SKURRIED
LM MISRULED
LO SOULDIER
LT DILUTERS
LURIDEST
MO DIMEROUS
ERODIUMS
SOREDIUM
MQ SQUIRMED
MS SURMISED
MU RESIDUUM
NO DOURINES
SOURDINE
NS INSUREDS
SUNDRIES
NT INTRUDES
OS DESIROUS
OT IODURETS
OUTRIDES
OUTSIDER
SUITORED
PS DISPURSE
SUSPIRED
PT DISPUTER
STUPIDER
QR SQUIRRED
QT SQUIRTED
RT STURDIER
ST DIESTRUS
DRUSIEST
STUDIERS
STURDIES
SY DYSURIES
TT DETRITUS
TX DRUXIEST
VV SURVIVED

DELNOS 181
(OLDENS)
AC CELADONS
AI NODALISE
AM LODESMAN
AR LADRONES
SOLANDER
AY YEALDONS
BS BOLDNESS
BT BLONDEST
CE ENCLOSED
CI INCLOSED
CO CONDOLES
CONSOLED
CS COLDNESS
CU ENCLOUDS
UNCLOSED
CY CONDYLES
SECONDLY
EI ESLOINED
EK SLOKENED
EM LODESMEN
EO LOOSENED
ES LESSONED
EU ENSOULED
EY ESLOYNED
FP PENFOLDS
FR FONDLERS
FORLENDS
GI GLENOIDS
SIDELONG
II LIONISED
IO SOLENOID
IR DISENROL
IS SONDELIS
IU DELUSION
INSOULED
UNSOILED
MU UNSELDOM
OU NODULOSE
UNLOOSED
OZ SNOOZLED
PR SPLENDOR
RU LOUNDERS
NOURSLED
ROUNDELS
ROUNDLES
UNSOLDER
SU LOUDNESS
UU UNDULOSE

UNSOULED
UV UNSOLVED

DELORS 145
(OLDERS)
AI DARIOLES
SOLIDARE
SOREDIAL
AL ODALLERS
AM EARLDOMS
AN LADRONES
SOLANDER
AP LEOPARDS
AS ROADLESS
AT DELATORS
LEOTARDS
LODESTAR
AU ROULADES
BU BOULDERS
DOUBLERS
BW BOWLDERS
CE RECLOSED
CI SCLEROID
CL SCROLLED
CO CROODLES
DECOLORS
CS CORDLESS
SCOLDERS
CU CLOSURED
CW CLOWDERS
SCROWLED
DE SOLDERED
DO DOODLERS
DP PLODDERS
DT STRODDLE
STRODLED
TODDLERS
EM MODELERS
REMODELS
EP DEPLORES
ER SOLDERER
EU URODELES
EV RESOLVED
FN FONDLERS
FORLENDS
FO FORSLOED
FU FOULDERS
GG DOGGRELS
GP PLEDGORS
HU SHOULDER
II IDOLISER
IL DOLLIERS
IN DISENROL
IS SOLDIERS
IT STOLIDER
IU SOULDIER
IY SOLDIERY
LP REDPOLLS
LS LORDLESS
LT DROLLEST
STROLLED
MS SMOLDERS
MU MOULDERS
REMOULDS
SMOULDER
NP SPLENDOR
NU LOUNDERS
NOURSLED
ROUNDELS
ROUNDLES
UNSOLDER
OS LORDOSES
OV OVERSOLD
OW WOOLDERS
PP DROPPLES
PT DROPLETS
PU POULDERS
POULDRES
ST OLDSTERS
STRODLES
SW WORDLESS
TT DOTTRELS
UY DELUSORY

DELORT 100
(DOLTER)
AF DEFLATOR
AI IDOLATER
TAILORED
AP PROLATED
AS DELATORS
LEOTARDS
LODESTAR
BI TRILOBED
BU TROUBLED
CH CHORTLED
CU CLOTURED
DS STRODDLE
STRODLED
TODDLERS
EI DOLERITE
LOITERED
EN REDOLENT
EO RETOOLED
ET DOTTEREL
TOLTERED
EV REVOLTED
EY DELETORY
FO FORETOLD
IS STOLIDER
LS DROLLEST
STROLLED
NU ROUNDLET
OY ROOTEDLY
PS DROPLETS
SS OLDSTERS
STRODLES
ST DOTTRELS

DENORU 99
(UNDOER)
AD UNADORED
AI DOUANIER
AL UNLOADER
URODELAN
AX RONDEAUX
BS BOUNDERS
REBOUNDS
SUBORNED
CD UNCORDED
CF FROUNCED
UNFORCED
CG CONGRUED
CI DECURION
CJ CONJURED
CK UNCORKED
CT CORNUTED
TROUNCED
DG GROUNDED
UNDERDOG
DL UNLORDED
DS REDOUNDS
DT ROTUNDED
DW UNWORDED
ET DEUTERON
FG UNFORGED
FL FLOUNDER
UNFOLDER
FM UNFORMED
FO UNROOFED
FR FRONDEUR
FS FOUNDERS
REFOUNDS
FT FORTUNED
FV OVERFUND
GG UNGORGED
GI GUERIDON
GN GROUNDEN
GR GROUNDER
REGROUND
GS GUERDONS
GT TRUDGEON
GU UNROUGED
HO HONOURED
HS ENSHROUD
UNHORSED
IN UNIRONED
IS DOURINES
SOURDINE
KW UNWORKED
LL UNROLLED
LS LOUNDERS
NOURSLED
ROUNDELS
ROUNDLES
UNSOLDER
LT ROUNDLET
MO UNMOORED
MW UNWORMED
NS ENROUNDS
OT UNROOTED
PS POUNDERS
PV UNPROVED
RS RONDURES
ROUNDERS
UNORDERS
RT ROTUNDER
RU ROUNDURE
SS DOURNESS
RESOUNDS
SOUNDERS
ST ROUNDEST
TONSURED
UNSORTED
SU UNROUSED
UNSOURED
SW WOUNDERS
TT UNROTTED
TW UNDERTOW

DENOST 74
(STONED)
AE ENDOSTEA
AI ASTONIED
SEDATION
AP TONEPADS
AR TORNADES
AS ONSTEADS
BL BLONDEST
CI DEONTICS
CN CONTENDS
CO SECODONT
CU CONTUSED
DM ODDMENTS
DS SNODDEST
DU STOUNDED
DW STOWNDED
EF SOFTENED
EI SIDENOTE
EN SONNETED
EP PENTODES
ER ERODENTS
ES STENOSED
GO STEGODON
HI HEDONIST
HZ DOZENTHS
II EDITIONS
SEDITION
IM DEMONIST
IR DRONIEST
IS DONSIEST
IW DOWNIEST
MR MORDENTS
MU DEMOUNTS
MUDSTONE
NR TENDRONS
OU DUOTONES
PR PORTENDS
PROTENDS
PU OUTSPEND
UNPOSTED
PW STEWPOND
RU ROUNDEST
TONSURED
UNSORTED
SU SOUNDEST
UW UNSTOWED

DENRSU 179
(UNDERS)
AC DURANCES
AD DAUNDERS
AE UNDERSEA
AG ENGUARDS
AH UNSHARED
AI DENARIUS
UNRAISED
URANIDES
AL LAUNDERS
LURDANES
RUNDALES
AM DURAMENS
MAUNDERS
SURNAMED
AP UNSPARED
AQ SQUANDER
AS DANSEURS
AT DAUNTERS
TRANSUDE
UNTREADS
AY UNDERSAY
BI BURNSIDE
BL BLUNDERS
BO BOUNDERS
REBOUNDS
SUBORNED
BU UNBRUSED
CE CENSURED
CH CHUNDERS
CI INDUCERS
CU UNCURSED
DE SUNDERED
DH HUNDREDS
DO REDOUNDS
EI UREDINES
ER ENDURERS
SUNDERER
ES RUDENESS
ET DENTURES
SEDERUNT
UNDERSET
UNDESERT
EU UNDERUSE
EV UNVERSED
FO FOUNDERS
REFOUNDS
GO GUERDONS
GT TRUDGENS
HO ENSHROUD
UNHORSED
HT THUNDERS
II DISINURE
URIDINES
IO DOURINES
SOURDINE
IS INSUREDS
SUNDRIES
IT INTRUDES
KT DRUNKEST
KY UNDERSKY
LO LOUNDERS
NOURSLED
ROUNDELS
ROUNDLES
UNSOLDER
LP PLUNDERS
LT RUNDLETS
TRUNDLES
NO ENROUNDS
OP POUNDERS
OR RONDURES
ROUNDERS
UNORDERS
OS DOURNESS
RESOUNDS
SOUNDERS
OT ROUNDEST
TONSURED
UNSORTED
OU UNROUSED
UNSOURED
OW WOUNDERS
PT UPTRENDS
PU UNPURSED
SS SUNDRESS
TT STRUNTED

DENSTU 217
(UNSTED)
AE UNSEATED
AI AUDIENTS
SINUATED
AL UNSALTED
AN ASTUNNED
AR DAUNTERS
TRANSUDE
UNTREADS
AT UNSTATED
UNTASTED
AW UNWASTED
AY UNSTAYED
UNSTEADY
BS SUBTENDS
CF DEFUNCTS
CO CONTUSED
DI DISTUNED
DO STOUNDED
DY SUDDENTY
EE DETENUES
EH ENTHUSED
EI DETINUES
EN UNNESTED
ER DENTURES
SEDERUNT
UNDERSET
UNDESERT
ET UNTESTED
FI UNSIFTED
GI DUNGIEST
GR TRUDGENS
HR THUNDERS
II DISUNITE
NUDITIES
UNITISED
UNTIDIES
IL DILUENTS
INSULTED
UNLISTED
IM MISTUNED
IN DUNNIEST
DUNNITES
IQ SQUINTED
IR INTRUDES
IS DISTUNES
IU UNSUITED
KR DRUNKEST
LR RUNDLETS
TRUNDLES
MO DEMOUNTS
MUDSTONE
OO DUOTONES
OP OUTSPEND
UNPOSTED
OR ROUNDEST
TONSURED
UNSORTED
OS SOUNDEST
OW UNSTOWED
PR UPTRENDS
RT STRUNTED
ST STUDENTS
VY DUVETYNS

DEORST 50
(SORTED)
AB BROADEST
AC REDCOATS
AG GOADSTER
AI ASTEROID
AL DELATORS
LEOTARDS
LODESTAR
AM STROAMED
AN TORNADES
AP ADOPTERS
ASPORTED
READOPTS
AR ROADSTER
AS ASSORTED
TORSADES

AU OUTDARES
AX EXTRADOS
BE BESORTED
BESTRODE
BI DEBITORS
BU DOUBTERS
OBTRUDES
REDOUBTS
CE CORSETED
ESCORTED
SECTORED
CI CORDITES
CS DOCTRESS
CU EDUCTORS
SEDUCTOR
DL STRODDLE
STRODLED
TODDLERS
EF DEFOREST
FORESTED
FOSTERED
EM MODESTER
EN ERODENTS
EP POSTERED
REEDSTOP
REPOSTED
ER RESORTED
RESTORED
ROSTERED
ES OERSTEDS
ET ROSETTED
TETRODES
EX DEXTROSE
EY STOREYED
FS DEFROSTS
FW FROWSTED
GI GRODIEST
STODGIER
GS STODGERS
GU DROGUETS
HP POTSHERD
HR REDSHORT
II DIORITES
IK DORKIEST
IL STOLIDER
IM MORTISED
IN DRONIEST
IP DIOPTERS
DIOPTRES
DIPTEROS
PERIDOTS
PROTEIDS
RIPOSTED
IS STEROIDS
IT DORTIEST
IU IODURETS
OUTRIDES
OUTSIDER
SUITORED
IW ROWDIEST
WORDIEST
LL DROLLEST
STROLLED
LP DROPLETS
LS OLDSTERS
STRODLES
LT DOTTRELS
MN MORDENTS
MO DOOMSTER
NN TENDRONS
NP PORTENDS
PROTENDS
NU ROUNDEST
TONSURED
UNSORTED
OP DOORSTEP
TORPEDOS
OR REDROOTS
PP STROPPED
PU POSTURED
PROUDEST
SPROUTED
RS RODSTERS
SW WORSTEDS
SY DESTROYS
TU STROUTED
UU OUTDURES
UV OVERDUST
UX DEXTROUS

DEOSTU 180
(OUSTED)
AB BOUTADES
AR OUTDARES
AT OUTDATES
BL DOUBLETS
BR DOUBTERS
OBTRUDES
REDOUBTS
CC STUCCOED
CL LOCUSTED
CM COSTUMED
CUSTOMED
CN CONTUSED
CQ DOCQUETS
CR EDUCTORS
SEDUCTOR
CS CUSTODES
DN STOUNDED
EG OUTEDGES
EW OUTWEEDS
EX TUXEDOES
GR DROGUETS
HI HIDEOUTS
HS STOUSHED
IL SOLITUDE
IR IODURETS
OUTRIDES
OUTSIDER
SUITORED
IS OUTSIDES
IZ OUTSIZED
LP POSTLUDE
MN DEMOUNTS
MUDSTONE
MO OUTMODES
NO DUOTONES
NP OUTSPEND
UNPOSTED
NR ROUNDEST
TONSURED
UNSORTED
NS SOUNDEST
NW UNSTOWED
PR POSTURED
PROUDEST
SPROUTED
RT STROUTED
RU OUTDURES
RV OVERDUST
RX DEXTROUS
ST TESTUDOS

DERSTU 244
(RUSTED)
AB SURBATED
AC TRADUCES
AJ ADJUSTER
READJUST
AN DAUNTERS
TRANSUDE
UNTREADS
AO OUTDARES
AP PASTURED
UPSTARED
AT STATURED
AX SURTAXED
BO DOUBTERS
OBTRUDES
REDOUBTS
BU SUBTRUDE
CI CRUDITES
CURDIEST
CURTSIED
CO EDUCTORS
SEDUCTOR
CT DESTRUCT
DE DETRUDES
DI RUDDIEST
STURDIED
EG GESTURED
EI ERUDITES
SURETIED
EL LUSTERED
RESULTED
ULSTERED
EM DEMUREST
MUSTERED
EN DENTURES
SEDERUNT
UNDERSET
UNDESERT
EP PERTUSED
ES RUSSETED
EV VESTURED
EX EXTRUDES
GG DRUGGETS
GI DURGIEST
GN TRUDGENS
GO DROGUETS
GR TRUDGERS
HN THUNDERS
HR DRUTHERS
HT THRUSTED
IL DILUTERS
LURIDEST
IN INTRUDES
IO IODURETS
OUTRIDES
OUTSIDER
SUITORED
IP DISPUTER
STUPIDER
IQ SQUIRTED
IR STURDIER
IS DIESTRUS
DRUSIEST
STUDIERS
STURDIES
IT DETRITUS
IX DRUXIEST
KN DRUNKEST
LN RUNDLETS
TRUNDLES
LS STRUDELS
MM STRUMMED
NO ROUNDEST
TONSURED
UNSORTED
NP UPTRENDS
NT STRUNTED
OP POSTURED
PROUDEST
SPROUTED
OT STROUTED
OU OUTDURES
OV OVERDUST
OX DEXTROUS
TT STRUTTED

DGINOR 209
(ORDING)
AB ABORDING
BOARDING
AE ORGANDIE
AH HOARDING
AI RADIOING
AN ADORNING
AO RIGADOON
AS ROADINGS
BD BRODDING
BO BROODING
BS BIRDSONG
SONGBIRD
BU OBDURING
CE RECODING
CH CHORDING
CS CORDINGS
CW CROWDING
DP PRODDING
DS RODDINGS
EP PROIGNED
ER ORDERING
ES NEGROIDS
EU GUERIDON
EV DOVERING
EW DOWERING
FO FORDOING
IL DROILING
IR GRIDIRON
IS DORISING
IZ DORIZING
KO DROOKING
KU DROUKING
LL DROLLING
LORDLING
LO DROOLING
LS GIRLONDS
LORDINGS
LY YOLDRING
NU ROUNDING
NW DROWNING
ROWNDING
OP DROOPING
PP DROPPING
SV DROVINGS
SW DROWSING
SWORDING
WORDINGS

EEFIRS 241
(FERIES)
AD FEDARIES
AG FEGARIES
AH SHEAFIER
AK FAKERIES
AL SERAFILE
AR RAREFIES
AS FREESIAS
BD DEBRIEFS
BE FREEBIES
BL BELFRIES
BT BRIEFEST
BU RUBEFIES
CT FIERCEST
DI DEIFIERS
EDIFIERS
FIRESIDE
DL DEFILERS
FIELDERS
DN DEFINERS
DO FORESIDE
GN FEERINGS
REEFINGS
HL FLESHIER
SHELFIER
HV FEVERISH
IK FIKERIES
IN FINERIES
IT FEISTIER
FERITIES
FIERIEST
IV VERIFIES
KL SERFLIKE
LO FORELIES
LS FIRELESS
LT FERLIEST
LU FUSILEER
MT FEMITERS
NR REFINERS
NS FINESSER
RIFENESS
NT FERNIEST
NU REINFUSE
NZ FRENZIES
OX ORIFEXES
PX PREFIXES
RT FERRITES
TT FRISETTE
TY ESTERIFY

EEGNRS 237
(GREENS)
AA SANGAREE
AC ENGRACES
AD DERANGES
GRANDEES
GRENADES
AG ENGAGERS
AH SHAGREEN
AI GESNERIA
AL ENLARGES
GENERALS
GLEANERS
AM AGREMENS
AN ENRANGES
AT ESTRANGE
GRANTEES
GREATENS
REAGENTS
SEGREANT
SERGEANT
STERNAGE
AU RENAGUES
AV AVENGERS
ENGRAVES
BI BIGENERS
BU SUBGENRE
CE REGENCES
CI CREESING
GENERICS
CO COGENERS
CONGREES
CU URGENCES
DI DESIGNER
ENERGIDS
REDESIGN
REEDINGS
RESIGNED
EI ENERGIES
ENERGISE
GREENIES
EN SENGREEN
EP EPERGNES
ER GREENERS
RENEGERS
ET GREENEST
EU RENEGUES
EV REVENGES
FI FEERINGS
REEFINGS
GI GREESING
GO ENGORGES
HI GREENISH
SHEERING
HT GREENTHS
HY GREYHENS
IJ JEERINGS
IK KREESING
SKEERING
IL LEERINGS
REELINGS
IM REGIMENS
IN ENGINERS
INGENERS
SERENING
SNEERING
IO ERINGOES
IP SPEERING
SPREEING
IR RESIGNER
IS GREISENS
IT GENTRIES
INTEGERS
REESTING
STEERING
STREIGNE
IU SEIGNEUR
IV SEVERING
VEERINGS
IW SEWERING
KO KEROGENS
KU GERENUKS
OT ESTROGEN
OU GENEROUS
OY ERYNGOES
SY GREYNESS
UY GUERNSEY

EEILRS 90
(RELIES)
AC ESCALIER
AD REALISED
SIDEREAL
AF SERAFILE
AG GASELIER
AH SHIRALEE
AL REALLIES
AM ALMERIES
MEASLIER
AP ESPALIER
PEARLIES
AR REALISER
AS REALISES
AT ATELIERS
EARLIEST
LEARIEST
REALTIES
AV VELARISE
AY YEARLIES
AZ REALIZES
SLEAZIER
BF BELFRIES
BL LIBELERS
BN BERLINES
BU BLUESIER
CD SCLEREID
CE CELERIES
CG CLERGIES
CN LICENSER
RECLINES
SILENCER
CT RETICLES
SCLERITE
TIERCELS
CU CISELEUR
CISELURE
RECUILES
CV VERSICLE
DF DEFILERS
FIELDERS
DG LEIDGERS
DH RELISHED
SHIELDER
DU LEISURED
DV DELIVERS
DESILVER
SILVERED
SLIVERED
DW WIELDERS
DY YIELDERS
EK SKEELIER
SLEEKIER
EM SEEMLIER
EP SLEEPIER
ET LEERIEST
SLEETIER
STEELIER
EV RELIEVES
EZ SLEEZIER
FH FLESHIER
SHELFIER
FK SERFLIKE
FO FORELIES
FS FIRELESS
FT FERLIEST
FU FUSILEER
GH SLEIGHER
GN LEERINGS
REELINGS
GU REGULISE
GV VELIGERS
HL HELLIERS
SHELLIER
HS HEIRLESS
RELISHES
HV SHELVIER
IO OILERIES
IT TILERIES
IV LIVERIES
KL SKELLIER
KO ROSELIKE
KT TRISKELE
LM SMELLIER
LO ORSEILLE
LS LEISLERS
LT TREILLES
MN ERMELINS
MT TERMLIES
MV VERMEILS
NO ELOINERS
NP PILSENER
NS REINLESS
NT LISTENER
SILENTER
NV LIVENERS
OP PELORIES
OT LITEROSE
TROELIES
OV OVERLIES
RELIEVOS
VOLERIES
OW OWLERIES
PR REPLIERS
PS SPIELERS
PT EPISTLER
PELTRIES
PERLITES
REPTILES
QU RELIQUES
RV RELIVERS
REVILERS
ST LEISTERS
RITELESS
TIRELESS
SU LEISURES
SV SERVILES
SW WIRELESS
TT RETITLES

EEILRV 232
(RELIVE)
AC RECEIVAL
AS VELARISE
AT LEVIRATE
RELATIVE
AW LIVEWARE
REVIEWAL
AZ VELARIZE
BE BELIEVER
CH CHEVERIL
CN VERNICLE
CS VERSICLE
DE RELIEVED
DI LIVERIED
DL RIVELLED
DS DELIVERS
DESILVER
SILVERED
SLIVERED
DY DELIVERY
EL REVEILLE
ER RELIEVER
ES RELIEVES
GN LEVERING
GS VELIGERS
GT VERLIGTE
HS SHELVIER
IL LIVELIER
IS LIVERIES
LO LOVELIER
MS VERMEILS
NP REPLEVIN
NS LIVENERS
NU UNVEILER
OR OVERLIER
OS OVERLIES
RELIEVOS
VOLERIES
OV OVERLIVE
OVERVEIL
RS RELIVERS
REVILERS
SS SERVILES

EEILST 89
(ELITES)
AB SEABLITE
AD LEADIEST
AF FEALTIES
LEAFIEST
AG ELEGIAST
AK LEAKIEST
AL LEALTIES
AM MEALIEST
AP EPILATES
AR ATELIERS
EARLIEST
LEARIEST
REALTIES
AS ASTELIES
AT AILETTES
AV ELATIVES
LEAVIEST
VEALIEST
BN STILBENE
TENSIBLE
BT BETITLES
CR RETICLES
SCLERITE
TIERCELS
CT TELESTIC
TESTICLE
CU LEUCITES
DG GELIDEST
LEDGIEST
DN ENLISTED
LINTSEED
LISTENED
TINSELED
DP EPISTLED
DS TIDELESS
DU DILUTEES
DV DEVILETS
EN SELENITE
ER LEERIEST
SLEETIER
STEELIER
ES SEELIEST
EV TELEVISE
FM FISTMELE
FR FERLIEST
FS FELSITES
FT FELTIEST
GG LEGGIEST
GN GENTILES
SLEETING
STEELING
GS ELEGISTS
HS LEISHEST
SHELTIES
IN LENITIES
IR TILERIES
IV LEVITIES
VEILIEST
IW LEWISITE
KN NESTLIKE
KP PIKELETS
SPIKELET
KR TRISKELE
LM MELLITES
LR TREILLES
LV EVILLEST
MO MESOLITE
MISLETOE
MP IMPLETES
MR TERMLIES
MS TIMELESS
NN LENIENTS
SENTINEL
NO NOSELITE
NP PLENTIES
NR LISTENER
SILENTER
NS SETLINES
NT ENTITLES
NV VEINLETS
OP PETIOLES
OR LITEROSE
TROELIES
OS ESTOILES
OW OWELTIES
OZ ZEOLITES
PR EPISTLER
PELTRIES
PERLITES
REPTILES
PS EPISTLES
PY EPISTYLE
RS LEISTERS
RITELESS
TIRELESS
RT RETITLES
SW WITELESS
SX SEXTILES
TX TEXTILES
VY STIEVELY

EEIMNS 192
(EMINES)
AD DEMAINES
INSEAMED
AR REMANIES
AS NEMESIAS
AT MATINEES
SEMINATE
AX EXAMINES
CD ENDEMICS
CG MISCEGEN
CP SPECIMEN
CT CENTIMES
DE INSEEMED
DH INMESHED
DM ENDEMISM
DO DEMONISE
DOMINEES
DS DESMINES
SIDESMEN
DT DEMENTIS
SEDIMENT
TIDESMEN
ET EMETINES
FI FEMINISE
GI GEMINIES
GK SMEEKING
GN MENINGES
GR REGIMENS
GS SEEMINGS
GT MEETINGS
STEEMING
GU EUGENISM
HO HEMIONES
HR SHIREMEN
HS INMESHES
IT ENMITIES
LN LINESMEN
LR ERMELINS
LS ISLESMEN
LU SELENIUM
SEMILUNE
MR IMMENSER
NO NOMINEES
NR REINSMEN
OP EPISEMON
OR EMERSION
OT MONETISE
SEMITONE
PT SEPIMENT
QU MESQUINE
RV MINEVERS
SW MISWEENS
TT MINETTES

EEIMRS 202
(MISERE)
AC CASIMERE
RACEMISE
AD MADERISE
AG GAMESIER
AL ALMERIES
MEASLIER
AN REMANIES
AP EMPAIRES
AR SMEARIER
AS SERIEMAS
AT EMIRATES
REAMIEST
STEAMIER
BG BEGRIMES
CD MISCREED
CH CHIMERES
CM MESMERIC
DE REMEDIES
DI DIMERISE
DM IMMERSED
SIMMERED
DP DEMIREPS
PREMISED
SIMPERED
DS DERMISES
DT DEMERITS
DEMISTER
DIMETERS
MISTERED
EL SEEMLIER
EP EMPERIES
EMPERISE
PREEMIES
ER MISERERE
ET EREMITES
FT FEMITERS
GM IMMERGES
GN REGIMENS
HN SHIREMEN
HP EMPERISH
HT ERETHISM
ETHERISM
IP RIEMPIES
IS MISERIES
KS KERMISES
LL SMELLIER
LN ERMELINS
LT TERMLIES
LV VERMEILS
MN IMMENSER
MO MEMORIES
MEMORISE
MS IMMERSES
MT MERISTEM
MIMESTER
MISMETRE
MU EUMERISM
NN REINSMEN
NO EMERSION
NV MINEVERS
OP PROMISEE
REIMPOSE
OS ISOMERES
OT TIRESOME
PP EPISPERM
PR PREMIERS
REPRIMES
SIMPERER
PS EMPRISES
IMPRESES
IMPRESSE
MESPRISE
PREMISES
SPIREMES
PT EMPTIERS
PX PREMIXES
PZ MESPRIZE
QU REQUIEMS
RT MERRIEST
TRIREMES
ST TRISEMES
TT EMITTERS
TERMITES
TU EMERITUS

EEINRT 8
(ENTIRE)
AC CENTIARE
CREATINE
INCREATE
ITERANCE
AD DETAINER
RETAINED
AG GRATINEE

AH ATHERINE
AK ANKERITE
KREATINE
AL ELATERIN
ENTAILER
TREENAIL
AP APERIENT
AR RETAINER
AS ARSENITE
RESINATE
STEARINE
TRAINEES
BI BENITIER
BO TENEBRIO
BT REBITTEN
CF FRENETIC
CG ERECTING
GENTRICE
CI ICTERINE
CN INCENTRE
CO ERECTION
NEOTERIC
CP PRENTICE
CS CENTRIES
ENTERICS
ENTICERS
SCIENTER
SECRETIN
CT RETICENT
CU CEINTURE
ENURETIC
DD DENDRITE
DK TINKERED
DM REMINTED
DN INDENTER
INTENDER
INTERNED
DO ORIENTED
DR INTERRED
TRENDIER
DS INSERTED
NERDIEST
RESIDENT
SINTERED
TRENDIES
DU REUNITED
DV INVERTED
DW WINTERED
DX DEXTRINE
EN INTERNEE
ES ETERNISE
TEENSIER
ET REINETTE
TEENTIER
EZ ETERNIZE
FS FERNIEST
GG GREETING
GM METERING
REGIMENT
GN ENTERING
GP PETERING
GS GENTRIES
INTEGERS
REESTING
STEERING
STREIGNE
GU GENITURE
GV EVERTING
GW TWEERING
GX EXERTING
GENETRIX
HN INHERENT
HO ETHERION
HP NEPHRITE
PREHNITE
TREPHINE
HT THIRTEEN
HW WHITENER
IO ERIONITE
IS ERINITES
NITERIES
IT INTERTIE
RETINITE
JL JETLINER
KR TINKERER
KS KERNITES
LS LISTENER
SILENTER
LT NETTLIER
LY ENTIRELY
LIENTERY
MO TIMONEER
MP TRIPEMEN
MR TERMINER
MU MUTINEER
MV VIREMENT
NS INTENSER
INTERNES
NT INTERNET
RENITENT
OR REORIENT
OS SEROTINE
OT TENORITE
OX EXERTION
PX INEXPERT
RS INSERTER
REINSERT
REINTERS
RENTIERS
TERRINES
RV INVERTER
RX INTERREX
SS INTERESS
SENTRIES
TRENISES
ST INERTEST
INTEREST
STERNITE
SU ESURIENT
NEURITES
RETINUES
REUNITES
SV NERVIEST
REINVEST
SERVIENT
SIRVENTE
SX INTERSEX
SY SERENITY
TY ENTIRETY
ETERNITY

EEIRRS 182
(ERRIES)

AC CARIERES
CREASIER
AF RAREFIES
AG GREASIER
AH HEARSIER
AK RAKERIES
SKEARIER
AL REALISER
AM SMEARIER
AN REARISEN
AP PEREIRAS
SPEARIER
AS REARISES
AT ARTERIES
REASTIER
BB BERBERIS
BU REBURIES
BV BREVIERS
CD DECRIERS
CH CHERRIES
CN SINCERER
CP PIERCERS
PRECISER
CS CERRISES
CT RECITERS
CW SCREWIER
DD DERIDERS
DH REDSHIRE
DP REPRISED
RESPIRED
DS DERRISES
DESIRERS
DRESSIER
RESIDERS
DT DESTRIER
DU RUDERIES
DV REDRIVES
EK SKEERIER
EM MISERERE
EN SNEERIER
ET REESTIER
RETIREES
EV REREVISE
REVERIES
FN REFINERS
FT FERRITES
GN RESIGNER
GT REGISTER
GV GRIEVERS
HK SHRIEKER
HN ERRHINES
HP PERISHER
SPHERIER
HS SHERRIES
HV SHIVERER
HW WHERRIES
IV RIVIERES
KS SKERRIES
LP REPLIERS
LV RELIVERS
REVILERS
MP PREMIERS
REPRIMES
SIMPERER
MT MERRIEST
TRIREMES
NP REPINERS
NS RESINERS
NT INSERTER
REINSERT
REINTERS
RENTIERS
TERRINES
NU REINSURE
NV VERNIERS
OP ROPERIES
OR ORRERIES
OS ROSERIES
ROSIERES
PP PERSPIRE
PR PERRIERS
PS REPRISES
RESPIRES
PV REPRIVES
PZ REPRIZES
QU REQUIRES
RT RETIRERS
TERRIERS
ST TRESSIER
SV REVERSIS
REVISERS
TV REVERIST
RIVERETS
RIVETERS
TW REWRITES
VV REVIVERS

EEIRST 31
(ESTIER)

AD READIEST
SERIATED
SIDERATE
STEADIER
AE EATERIES
AH HEARTIES
AL ATELIERS
EARLIEST
LEARIEST
REALTIES
AM EMIRATES
REAMIEST
STEAMIER
AN ARSENITE
RESINATE
STEARINE
TRAINEES
AO ETAERIOS
AP PETARIES
AR ARTERIES
REASTIER
AS SERIATES
AT ARIETTES
ITERATES
TEARIEST
TREATIES
TREATISE
AV EVIRATES
AW SWEATIER
TAWERIES
WEARIEST
AY YEASTIER
BD BESTRIDE
BE BEERIEST
BF BRIEFEST
BH HERBIEST
BU UBERTIES
CD DISCREET
DISCRETE
CF FIERCEST
CH CHESTIER
HERETICS
CI SERICITE
CL RETICLES
SCLERITE
TIERCELS
CN CENTRIES
ENTERICS
ENTICERS
SCIENTER
SECRETIN
CO COTERIES
ESOTERIC
CP CREPIEST
RECEIPTS
CR RECITERS
CT TIERCETS
CU CERUSITE
CUTESIER
EUCRITES
CV VERTICES
CX EXCITERS
DD REDDIEST
DE REEDIEST
DG DIGESTER
ESTRIDGE
DI SIDERITE
DM DEMERITS
DEMISTER
DIMETERS
MISTERED
DN INSERTED
NERDIEST
RESIDENT
SINTERED
TRENDIES
DP PRIESTED
RESPITED
DR DESTRIER
DS EDITRESS
RESISTED
SISTERED
DT TIREDEST
DU ERUDITES
SURETIED
DV VERDITES
DW WEIRDEST
EH ETHERISE
SHEETIER
EK REEKIEST
EL LEERIEST
SLEETIER
STEELIER
EM EREMITES
EN ETERNISE
TEENSIER
EP PEERIEST
STEEPIER
ER REESTIER
RETIREES
ES STEERIES
FI FEISTIER
FERITIES
FIERIEST
FL FERLIEST
FM FEMITERS
FN FERNIEST
FR FERRITES
FT FRISETTE
FY ESTERIFY
GN GENTRIES
INTEGERS
REESTING
STEERING
STREIGNE
GO ERGOTISE
GP PRESTIGE
GR REGISTER
GT GRISETTE
TERGITES
GU GUERITES
HM ERETHISM
ETHERISM
HO ISOTHERE
THEORIES
THEORISE
HP TREESHIP
HS HEISTERS
HT ETHERIST
IL TILERIES
IN ERINITES
NITERIES
IV VERITIES
JK JERKIEST
KL TRISKELE
KN KERNITES
KP PERKIEST
KS KEISTERS
LL TREILLES
LM TERMLIES
LN LISTENER
SILENTER
LO LITEROSE
TROELIES
LP EPISTLER
PELTRIES
PERLITES
REPTILES
LS LEISTERS
RITELESS
TIRELESS
LT RETITLES
MM MERISTEM
MIMESTER
MISMETRE
MO TIRESOME
MP EMPTIERS
MR MERRIEST
TRIREMES
MS TRISEMES
MT EMITTERS
TERMITES
MU EMERITUS
NN INTENSER
INTERNES
NO SEROTINE
NR INSERTER
REINSERT
REINTERS
RENTIERS
TERRINES
NS INTERESS
SENTRIES
TRENISES
NT INERTEST
INTEREST
STERNITE
NU ESURIENT
NEURITES
RETINUES
REUNITES
NV NERVIEST
REINVEST
SERVIENT
SIRVENTE
NX INTERSEX
NY SERENITY
OP POETRIES

OS EROTESIS
PS RESPITES
PT PRETTIES
PY PERSEITY
QU QUIETERS
REQUITES
QW QWERTIES
RR RETIRERS
TERRIERS
RS TRESSIER
RV REVERIST
RIVERETS
RIVETERS
RW REWRITES
ST RESTIEST
SU SURETIES
SV SIEVERTS
TREVISES
VESTRIES
VV VETIVERS
VY SEVERITY

EEIRSV 222
(REVISE)
AD READVISE
AH SHIVAREE
AL VELARISE
AT EVIRATES
AV AVERSIVE
BR BREVIERS
CC CERVICES
CRESCIVE
CREVICES
CD DESCRIVE
SCRIEVED
SERVICED
CE RECEIVES
CL VERSICLE
CS SCRIEVES
SERVICES
CT VERTICES
CX CERVIXES
DD DIVERSED
DG DIVERGES
DH SHIVERED
SHRIEVED
DI DERISIVE
DK SKIVERED
DL DELIVERS
DESILVER
SILVERED
SLIVERED
DO OVERSIDE
DP DEPRIVES
PREVISED
DR REDRIVES
DS DEVISERS
DISSERVE
DISSEVER
DIVERSES
DT VERDITES
EL RELIEVES
EN VENERIES
ER REREVISE
REVERIES
ES SEVERIES
FH FEVERISH
FI VERIFIES
GL VELIGERS
GN SEVERING
VEERINGS
GR GRIEVERS
HL SHELVIER
HR SHIVERER
HS SHRIEVES
IL LIVERIES
IN VINERIES
IR RIVIERES
IT VERITIES
LM VERMEILS
LN LIVENERS
LO OVERLIES
RELIEVOS
VOLERIES
LR RELIVERS
REVILERS
LS SERVILES
MN MINEVERS
NN INNERVES
NERVINES
NO EVERSION
NR VERNIERS
NS INVERSES
VERSINES
NT NERVIEST
REINVEST
SERVIENT
SIRVENTE
NU UNIVERSE
OW OVERWISE
OZ OVERSIZE
PR REPRIVES
PS PREVISES
PW PREVIEWS
RS REVERSIS
REVISERS
RT REVERIST
RIVERETS
RIVETERS
RV REVIVERS
SS IVRESSES
ST SIEVERTS
TREVISES
VESTRIES
TV VETIVERS
TY SEVERITY

EELNST 161
(NESTLE)
AC CLEANEST
LATENCES
AE SELENATE
AK KANTELES
AM MANTEELS
STEELMAN
TALESMEN
AR ALTERNES
AS LATENESS
AY ENTAYLES
BD BENDLETS
BI STILBENE
TENSIBLE
CG NEGLECTS
CK NECKLETS
CR LECTERNS
CU ESCULENT
DI ENLISTED
LINTSEED
LISTENED
TINSELED
DK SKLENTED
DY ENSTYLED
EI SELENITE
EM ELEMENTS
STEELMEN
FO FELSTONE
GI GENTILES
SLEETING
STEELING
GT GENTLEST
II LENITIES
IK NESTLIKE
IN LENIENTS
SENTINEL
IO NOSELITE
IP PLENTIES
IR LISTENER
SILENTER
IS SETLINES
IT ENTITLES
IV VEINLETS
KO SKELETON
LS SNELLEST
LU ENTELLUS
OR ENTRESOL
OS NOTELESS
TONELESS
OT NOTELETS
OU TOLUENES
RS SLENTERS
RT LETTERNS
ST TENTLESS
SU TUNELESS
UNSTEELS
SY ENSTYLES
TU LUNETTES
UNSETTLE

EELRST 157
(ELTERS)
AA LAETARES
AB BLEAREST
BLEATERS
RETABLES
AC CLEAREST
SCELERAT
TREACLES
AD TREADLES
AE TEASELER
AF REFLATES
AH HALTERES
LEATHERS
AI ATELIERS
EARLIEST
LEARIEST
REALTIES
AM LAMETERS
AN ALTERNES
AO OLEASTER
AP PLEATERS
PRELATES
AR RELATERS
AS STEALERS
TEARLESS
TESSERAL
AT ALERTEST
AU RESALUTE
AY EASTERLY
BH BLETHERS
HERBLETS
BM TREMBLES
CE RESELECT
CF REFLECTS
CI RETICLES
SCLERITE
TIERCELS
CN LECTERNS
CO CORSELET
ELECTORS
ELECTROS
SELECTOR
CP PLECTRES
PRELECTS
CS LECTRESS
CU LECTURES
CY SECRETLY
DD TREDDLES
DE DEERLETS
STREELED
DU LUSTERED
RESULTED
ULSTERED
DW LEWDSTER
WRESTLED
DY RESTYLED
EI LEERIEST
SLEETIER
STEELIER
EO SLOETREE
EP REPLETES
ES TREELESS
ET RESETTLE
EV LEVERETS
VERSELET
FI FERLIEST
FT FETTLERS
FU FLEURETS
HH THRESHEL
HO HOSTELER
HP TELPHERS
HS SHELTERS
HY SHELTERY
II TILERIES
IK TRISKELE
IL TREILLES
IM TERMLIES
IN LISTENER
SILENTER
IO LITEROSE
TROELIES
IP EPISTLER
PELTRIES
PERLITES
REPTILES
IS LEISTERS
RITELESS
TIRELESS
IT RETITLES
KS KESTRELS
SKELTERS
LO SOLLERET
MO MOLESTER
MS SMELTERS
TERMLESS
MY SMELTERY
NO ENTRESOL
NS SLENTERS
NT LETTERNS
OT LORETTES
OU RESOLUTE
PS SPELTERS
PZ PRETZELS
RW WRESTLER
SS RESTLESS
TRESSELS
ST SETTLERS
STERLETS
TRESTLES
SW SWELTERS
WRESTLES
SY RESTYLES
TYRELESS
SZ SELTZERS
WY WESTERLY

EENRST 56
(ENTERS)
AA ARSENATE
SERENATA
AC CENTARES
REASCENT
SARCENET
AE SERENATE
AF FASTENER
FENESTRA
AG ESTRANGE
GRANTEES
GREATENS
REAGENTS
SEGREANT
SERGEANT
STERNAGE
AH HASTENER
HEARTENS
AI ARSENITE
RESINATE
STEARINE
TRAINEES
AJ SERJEANT
AL ALTERNES
AM REMANETS
AO RESONATE
AR TERRANES
AS ASSENTER
EARNESTS
SARSENET
AT ENTREATS
RATTEENS
AV AVENTRES
VETERANS
BP BESPRENT
BT BRENTEST
BW BESTREWN
CC CRESCENT
CH TRENCHES
CI CENTRIES
ENTERICS
ENTICERS
SCIENTER
SECRETIN
CL LECTERNS
CN CENTNERS
CU UNSECRET
DE RESENTED
DI INSERTED
NERDIEST
RESIDENT
SINTERED
TRENDIES
DO ERODENTS
DP PRETENDS
DU DENTURES
SEDERUNT
UNDERSET
UNDESERT
EG GREENEST
EI ETERNISE
TEENSIER
EM ENTREMES
EN ETRENNES
EP PRETENSE
TERPENES
ER ENTERERS
RESENTER
TERREENS
TERRENES
ES SERENEST
EV EVENTERS
EX EXTERNES
EY YESTREEN
FI FERNIEST
FM FERMENTS
FO ENFOREST
SOFTENER
GH GREENTHS
GI GENTRIES
INTEGERS
REESTING
STEERING
STREIGNE
GO ESTROGEN
HO HONESTER
II ERINITES
NITERIES
IK KERNITES
IL LISTENER
SILENTER
IN INTENSER
INTERNES
IO SEROTINE
IR INSERTER
REINSERT
REINTERS
RENTIERS
TERRINES
IS INTERESS
SENTRIES
TRENISES
IT INERTEST
INTEREST
STERNITE
IU ESURIENT
NEURITES
RETINUES
REUNITES
IV NERVIEST
REINVEST
SERVIENT
SIRVENTE
IX INTERSEX
IY SERENITY
LO ENTRESOL
LS SLENTERS
LT LETTERNS
MO SERMONET
STOREMEN
MU MUENSTER
MW TREWSMEN
NO TENONERS
OO ROESTONE

OP PROTENSE
OT ONSETTER
OV OVERNETS
OX EXTENSOR
PP PERPENTS
PS PERTNESS
PRESENTS
SERPENTS
PT STREPENT
PV PREVENTS
RV RENVERST
ST STERNEST
TESTERNS
SU TRUENESS
SW WESTERNS
SY STYRENES
UV VENTURES

EEORSV 247
(REVOSE)
AG OVERAGES
AS OVERSEAS
AT OVEREATS
AW OVERAWES
BD OBSERVED
BR OBSERVER
VERBOSER
BS OBSERVES
OBVERSES
CN CONSERVE
CONVERSE
CR RECOVERS
DI OVERSIDE
DL RESOLVED
DO OVERDOES
OVERDOSE
DR OVERREDS
DU OVERUSED
DY OVERDYES
EN OVERSEEN
ER OVERSEER
ES OVERSEES
EY OVEREYES
FR FOREVERS
FU FEVEROUS
GO OVERGOES
GT OVERGETS
HL SHOVELER
HO OVERSHOE
HW WHOSEVER
IL OVERLIES
RELIEVOS
VOLERIES
IN EVERSION
IW OVERWISE
IZ OVERSIZE
KT OVERKEST
LL OVERSELL
LR RESOLVER
LS RESOLVES
LV EVOLVERS
REVOLVES
MN OVERSMEN
MP PREMOVES
MR REMOVERS
NR OVERRENS
NT OVERNETS
NW OVERSEWN
PR REPROVES
PT OVERSTEP
RS REVERSOS
RT EVERTORS
ST ESTOVERS
OVERSETS
SU OVERUSES
SW OVERSEWS
TX VORTEXES

EERRST 236
(RESTER)
AB REBATERS
TABRERES
TEREBRAS
AC CATERERS
RETRACES
TERRACES
AD ARRESTED
DREAREST
RETREADS
SERRATED
TREADERS
AE ARRESTEE
AF FERRATES
AG REGRATES
AI ARTERIES
REASTIER
AK RETAKERS
STREAKER
AL RELATERS
AM REMASTER
STREAMER
AN TERRANES
AP TAPERERS
AR ARRESTER
REARREST
AS ASSERTER
REASSERT
SERRATES
TERRASES
AT RETRATES
RETREATS
TREATERS
AU AUSTERER
TREASURE
AV TRAVERSE
AW WATERERS
BW BREWSTER
CE ERECTERS
CI RECITERS
CO ERECTORS
CS RECTRESS
DE DESERTER
DI DESTRIER
DO RESORTED
RESTORED
ROSTERED
EG GREETERS
REGREETS
EI REESTIER
RETIREES
EN ENTERERS
RESENTER
TERREENS
TERRENES
EP PESTERER
ES STEERERS
ET RESETTER
FI FERRITES
FO FORESTER
FOSTERER
REFOREST
FU REFUTERS
GI REGISTER
GO OSTREGER
HH THRESHER
HW WHERRETS
IM MERRIEST
TRIREMES
IN INSERTER
REINSERT
REINTERS
RENTIERS
TERRINES
IR RETIRERS
TERRIERS
IS TRESSIER
IV REVERIST
RIVERETS
RIVETERS
IW REWRITES
KK TREKKERS
LW WRESTLER
MU MUSTERER
NV RENVERST
OR RESORTER
RESTORER
RETRORSE
OS RESTORES
OU REROUTES
OV EVERTORS
OX EXTRORSE
PV PERVERTS
SU TRESSURE
SW STREWERS
WRESTERS
TU REUTTERS
UTTERERS
UV VESTURER
VY REVESTRY

EERSTT 200
(ETTERS)
AA STEARATE
AB ABETTERS
AD ASTERTED
RESTATED
AG GREATEST
AH THEATERS
THEATRES
AI ARIETTES
ITERATES
TEARIEST
TREATIES
TREATISE
AL ALERTEST
AM TEAMSTER
AN ENTREATS
RATTEENS
AR RETRATES
RETREATS
TREATERS
AS ESTREATS
RESTATES
AT ATTESTER
AX EXTREATS
BE BESETTER
BN BRENTEST
BU BURETTES
CI TIERCETS
CU CURETTES
DE RESETTED
SETTERED
STREETED
DI TIREDEST
DO ROSETTED
TETRODES
EL RESETTLE
ER RESETTER
EW TWEETERS
FI FRISETTE
FL FETTLERS
GI GRISETTE
TERGITES
HI ETHERIST
HW WHETTERS
IL RETITLES
IM EMITTERS
TERMITES
IN INERTEST
INTEREST
STERNITE
IP PRETTIES
IS RESTIEST
LN LETTERNS
LO LORETTES
LS SETTLERS
STERLETS
TRESTLES
MO REMOTEST
MP TEMPTERS
NO ONSETTER
NP STREPENT
NS STERNEST
TESTERNS
OP TREETOPS
OS ROSETTES
PS PRETESTS
PU UPSETTER
PX PRETEXTS
RU REUTTERS
UTTERERS
SU TRUSTEES
TU UTTEREST
UX TEXTURES

EFIRST 191
(STRIFE)
AG FRIGATES
AI RATIFIES
AL FLARIEST
FRAILEST
AN FENITARS
AR FRATRIES
AW WASTRIFE
BE BRIEFEST
BL FILBERTS
BS FIBSTERS
CE FIERCEST
CU FRUTICES
DR DRIFTERS
EI FEISTIER
FERITIES
FIERIEST
EL FERLIEST
EM FEMITERS
EN FERNIEST
ER FERRITES
ET FRISETTE
EY ESTERIFY
FO FORFEITS
FT TRIFFEST
FU STUFFIER
GH FIGHTERS
FREIGHTS
GR GRIFTERS
HI SHIFTIER
HS SHIFTERS
IN SNIFTIER
IP SPITFIRE
IR FIRRIEST
IT RIFTIEST
KO FORKIEST
KS FRISKETS
LO FLORIEST
TREFOILS
LR TRIFLERS
LS RIFTLESS
STIFLERS
LT FLITTERS
LW FEWTRILS
MO SETIFORM
MU FREMITUS
NS SNIFTERS
OO ROOFIEST
OP FIREPOTS
OR FROSTIER
ROTIFERS
OS FOISTERS
OU FOUSTIER
OW FROWIEST
RT FRITTERS
RU FRITURES
FRUITERS
FURRIEST
SU SURFEITS
SURFIEST
SW SWIFTERS
TU TURFIEST
TURFITES
UX FIXTURES
UZ FURZIEST

EGHINT 250
(ETHING)
AB BEATHING
AC CHEATING
TEACHING
AL ATHELING
AN NAETHING
AR EARTHING
HEARTING
INGATHER
AS GAHNITES
HEATINGS
AT GNATHITE
BO BEHOTING
BR BERTHING
BRIGHTEN
BS BENIGHTS
CF FECHTING
FETCHING
CH HECHTING
CK KETCHING
CL LETCHING
CR RETCHING
CS CHESTING
ETCHINGS
DK KNIGHTED
EE EIGHTEEN
EH HEIGHTEN
EK THEEKING
EP PHENGITE
ES SEETHING
SHEETING
ET TEETHING
FR FRIGHTEN
IR THINGIER
IS HEISTING
NIGHTIES
THINGIES
IV THIEVING
LP PENLIGHT
LS ENLIGHTS
LIGHTENS
NS SENNIGHT
OR THROEING
OS HISTOGEN
QU QUETHING
RS RIGHTENS
RW WRETHING
ST SHETTING
TIGHTENS
TW WHETTING

EGILNR 125
(LINGER)
AA REGALIAN
AB BLEARING
AC CLEARING
AD DANGLIER
DEARLING
DRAGLINE
AE ALGERINE
AG GANGLIER
REGALING
AH NARGHILE
NARGILEH
AI GAINLIER
AJ JANGLIER
AM GERMINAL
MALIGNER
MALINGER
AN LEARNING
AO GERANIOL
REGIONAL
AP PEARLING
AR GNARLIER
AS ENGRAILS
NARGILES
REALIGNS
SALERING
SANGLIER
SIGNALER
SLANGIER
AT ALERTING
ALTERING
INTEGRAL
RELATING
TANGLIER
TRIANGLE
AX RELAXING
AY LAYERING
RELAYING
YEARLING
BM REMBLING
BO IGNOBLER
BT TREBLING
CI CLINGIER
CK CLERKING
RECKLING

CS CLINGERS
CRINGLES
CU RECULING
ULCERING
CY GLYCERIN
DD REDDLING
DE ENGIRDLE
LINGERED
REEDLING
DI GRIDELIN
DU INDULGER
DY YELDRING
EF FLEERING
EG LEGERING
EI LINGERIE
EO ELOIGNER
ER LINGERER
ES LEERINGS
REELINGS
EU REGULINE
EV LEVERING
FO FLORIGEN
FS FLINGERS
FY FERLYING
GI NIGGLIER
GS NIGGLERS
SNIGGLER
GU GRUELING
GY GINGERLY
HI HIRELING
HS HERLINGS
SHINGLER
IJ JINGLIER
IK KINGLIER
IN RELINING
IO RELIGION
IS RESILING
IT GIRTLINE
RETILING
TINGLIER
TIRELING
IV RELIVING
REVILING
JS JINGLERS
JU JUNGLIER
MS GREMLINS
MERLINGS
MINGLERS
MU RELUMING
OS RESOLING
OW LOWERING
PS PINGLERS
SPERLING
SPRINGLE
PY REPLYING
RU RULERING
RY ERRINGLY
SS RINGLESS
SLINGERS
ST LINGSTER
RINGLETS
STERLING
TINGLERS
TRINGLES
SW NEWSGIRL
UV VELURING

EGILNS 117
(SINGLE)
AB SINGABLE
AD DEALINGS
LEADINGS
SIGNALED
AE ENSILAGE
LINEAGES
AF FINAGLES
AG LIGNAGES
AH HEALINGS
LEASHING
SHEALING
AK LINKAGES
AL NIGELLAS
AM MEASLING
AN EANLINGS
LEANINGS
AO GASOLINE
AP ELAPSING
PLEASING
AR ENGRAILS
NARGILES
REALIGNS
SALERING
SANGLIER
SIGNALER
SLANGIER
AS GAINLESS
GLASSINE
LEASINGS
SEALINGS
AT EASTLING
GELATINS
GENITALS
STEALING
AV LEAVINGS
SLEAVING
AW SWEALING
BM SEMBLING
BO INGLOBES
BS BLESSING
GLIBNESS
BT BELTINGS
BU BLUEINGS
BULGINES
CI CEILINGS
CIELINGS
CO ECLOSING
CR CLINGERS
CRINGLES
CU LUCIGENS
CY GLYCINES
DD SLEDDING
DE SEEDLING
DG GELDINGS
SLEDGING
SNIGGLED
DH HINDLEGS
SHINGLED
DI EILDINGS
SIDELING
DN LENDINGS
DO GLENOIDS
SIDELONG
DP SPELDING
DU INDULGES
DV DEVLINGS
DW SWINGLED
WELDINGS
EF FEELINGS
EG NEGLIGES
EH HEELINGS
SHEELING
EK KEELINGS
SLEEKING
EP PEELINGS
SLEEPING
SPEELING
ER LEERINGS
REELINGS
ES SEELINGS
ET GENTILES
SLEETING
STEELING
EV SLEEVING
EW SWEELING
FH FLESHING
SHELFING
FN FLENSING
FR FLINGERS
FS SELFINGS
FT FELTINGS
GG LEGGINGS
GR NIGGLERS
SNIGGLER
GS SNIGGLES
GU LUGEINGS
HI SHEILING
SHIELING
HL SHELLING
HP HELPINGS
HR HERLINGS
SHINGLER
HS SHINGLES
HT ENLIGHTS
LIGHTENS
HV SHELVING
HW WELSHING
IN ENISLING
ENSILING
IP SPIELING
IR RESILING
IT LIGNITES
LINGIEST
IV VEILINGS
IW WISELING
JR JINGLERS
JT JINGLETS
KK LEKKINGS
KO SONGLIKE
KP SKELPING
KS KINGLESS
KT KINGLETS
LM SMELLING
LN SNELLING
LO LOGLINES
LP SPELLING
LT STELLING
TELLINGS
LW SWELLING
WELLINGS
LY YELLINGS
MM LEMMINGS
MR GREMLINS
MERLINGS
MINGLERS
MT MELTINGS
SMELTING
MU LEGUMINS
NT NESTLING
OR RESOLING
OS LIGNOSES
OU LIGNEOUS
OW LONGWISE
PR PINGLERS
SPERLING
SPRINGLE
PS SPIGNELS
PT PELTINGS
PESTLING
PY YELPINGS
RS RINGLESS
SLINGERS
RT LINGSTER
RINGLETS
STERLING
TINGLERS
TRINGLES
RW NEWSGIRL
SS SIGNLESS
ST GLISTENS
SINGLETS
SU UGLINESS
SW SWINGLES
WINGLESS
TT LETTINGS
SETTLING
TW SWELTING
WINGLETS
UV EVULSING

EGILNT 66
(TINGLE)
AA AGENTIAL
ALGINATE
AB BELATING
BLEATING
TANGIBLE
AC CLEATING
AD DELATING
AE GALENITE
GELATINE
LEGATINE
AG TEAGLING
AH ATHELING
AM LIGAMENT
METALING
AN GANTLINE
LATENING
AO GELATION
LEGATION
AP PLEATING
AR ALERTING
ALTERING
INTEGRAL
RELATING
TANGLIER
TRIANGLE
AS EASTLING
GELATINS
GENITALS
STEALING
AV VALETING
AX EXALTING
AZ TEAZLING
BE BEETLING
BR TREBLING
BS BELTINGS
BT BLETTING
CE ELECTING
CH LETCHING
CI GENTILIC
CU CULTIGEN
DE DELETING
DI DILIGENT
EF FLEETING
EG GLEETING
ES GENTILES
SLEETING
STEELING
EW TWEELING
EX TELEXING
FS FELTINGS
FT FETTLING
GN GENTLING
GLENTING
HP PENLIGHT
HS ENLIGHTS
LIGHTENS
IR GIRTLINE
RETILING
TINGLIER
TIRELING
IS LIGNITES
LINGIEST
JS JINGLETS
KS KINGLETS
LS STELLING
TELLINGS
LU GLUTELIN
MS MELTINGS
SMELTING
NS NESTLING
NT NETTLING
OW TOWELING
PS PELTINGS
PESTLING
PT PETTLING
RS LINGSTER
RINGLETS
STERLING
TINGLERS
TRINGLES
SS GLISTENS
SINGLETS
ST LETTINGS
SETTLING
SW SWELTING
WINGLETS
UX EXULTING

EGILOS 132
(LOGIES)
AC CALIGOES
AD GOLIASED
AF FOLIAGES
AN GASOLINE
AP SPOILAGE
AR GASOLIER
GIRASOLE
SERAGLIO
AS GOLIASES
SOILAGES
AT OTALGIES
BE OBLIGEES
BN INGLOBES
CI LOGICISE
CN ECLOSING
DD DISLODGE
DN GLENOIDS
SIDELONG
DT GODLIEST
GOLDIEST
DZ GOLDSIZE
ES GELOSIES
EU EULOGIES
EULOGISE
FG SOLFEGGI
GO GOOGLIES
HU OUGHLIES
KN SONGLIKE
LN LOGLINES
MR GOMERILS
MU ELOGIUMS
NR RESOLING
NS LIGNOSES
NU LIGNEOUS
NW LONGWISE
OO OOLOGIES
OU ISOLOGUE
RS GLOSSIER
SS GLOSSIES
ST ELOGISTS
TU EULOGIST

EGILRS 159
(LIGERS)
AA GASALIER
LAIRAGES
REGALIAS
AC GLACIERS
AD SLAIRGED
AE GASELIER
AG SLAGGIER
AM GREMIALS
LAMIGERS
REGALISM
AN ENGRAILS
NARGILES
REALIGNS
SALERING
SANGLIER
SIGNALER
SLANGIER
AO GASOLIER
GIRASOLE
SERAGLIO
AS GLASSIER
AT GLARIEST
REGALIST
AY GREASILY
AZ GLAZIERS
BB GRIBBLES
BT GILBERTS
CE CLERGIES
CG SCRIGGLE
CN CLINGERS
CRINGLES
DD GRIDDLES
DE LEIDGERS
DR GIRDLERS
DU GUILDERS
SLUDGIER
DW WERGILDS
EH SLEIGHER
EN LEERINGS
REELINGS
EU REGULISE
EV VELIGERS
FN FLINGERS
GG GIGGLERS
GH HIGGLERS

GN NIGGLERS
SNIGGLER
GW WIGGLERS
WRIGGLES
HN HERLINGS
SHINGLER
HT LIGHTERS
RELIGHTS
SLIGHTER
IN RESILING
IR GRISLIER
JN JINGLERS
MM GLIMMERS
MN GREMLINS
MERLINGS
MINGLERS
MO GOMERILS
NO RESOLING
NP PINGLERS
SPERLING
SPRINGLE
NS RINGLESS
SLINGERS
NT LINGSTER
RINGLETS
STERLING
TINGLERS
TRINGLES
NW NEWSGIRL
OS GLOSSIER
PP GRIPPLES
ST GLISTERS
GRISTLES
TT GLITTERS
TU GURLIEST
UV VIRGULES
ZZ GRIZZLES

EGILST 190
(LEGIST)

AC GELASTIC
AD GLADIEST
AE ELEGIAST
AH LAIGHEST
AL LEGALIST
STILLAGE
TILLAGES
AN EASTLING
GELATINS
GENITALS
STEALING
AO OTALGIES
AR GLARIEST
REGALIST
AZ GLAZIEST
BB GLIBBEST
BI BILGIEST
BN BELTINGS
BR GILBERTS
BU BULGIEST
CH GLITCHES
DD GLIDDEST
DE GELIDEST
LEDGIEST
DH DELIGHTS
SLIGHTED
DO GODLIEST
GOLDIEST
EG LEGGIEST
EN GENTILES
SLEETING
STEELING
ES ELEGISTS
FN FELTINGS
FU GULFIEST
HN ENLIGHTS
LIGHTENS
HP PIGHTLES
HR LIGHTERS
RELIGHTS
SLIGHTER
HS SLEIGHTS
HT LIGHTEST
IM LEGITIMS
IN LIGNITES
LINGIEST
JN JINGLETS
KN KINGLETS
LN STELLING
TELLINGS
MN MELTINGS
SMELTING
NN NESTLING
NP PELTINGS
PESTLING
NR LINGSTER
RINGLETS
STERLING
TINGLERS
TRINGLES
NS GLISTENS
SINGLETS
NT LETTINGS
SETTLING
NW SWELTING
WINGLETS
OS ELOGISTS
OU EULOGIST
RS GLISTERS
GRISTLES
RT GLITTERS
RU GURLIEST

EGINNR 178
(GINNER)

AA ANEARING
AC ENRACING
AD GRANNIED
AG ANGERING
ENRAGING
AI ARGININE
AL LEARNING
AM ENARMING
RENAMING
AS AGINNERS
EARNINGS
ENGRAINS
GRANNIES
AV RAVENING
AY RENAYING
YEARNING
BE BEGINNER
BENIGNER
BN BRENNING
BO ENROBING
RINGBONE
CO ENCORING
CS SCERNING
CT CENTRING
DE ENRINGED
DI NIDERING
DT TRENDING
DU ENDURING
UNRINGED
EE ENGINEER
EG GREENING
RENEGING
EP PREENING
ES ENGINERS
INGENERS
SERENING
SNEERING
ET ENTERING
EV ENERVING
EW RENEWING
EY ENGINERY
RENEYING
FI ENFIRING
INFRINGE
REFINING
FS FERNINGS
GI GREINING
REIGNING
GN GRENNING
GO ENGORING
HI INHERING
IL RELINING
IP REPINING
RIPENING
IS RESINING
KS KERNINGS
NS RENNINGS
OO RONEOING
OP REPONING
OT NITROGEN
OV VIGNERON
OZ REZONING
PT PRENTING
RS GRINNERS
RU UNERRING
ST STERNING
SU ENSURING
TU RETUNING
TV VENTRING

EGINOS 78
(INGOES)

AB BEGONIAS
AC COINAGES
AD AGONISED
DIAGNOSE
AL GASOLINE
AN GANOINES
AR IGNAROES
ORGANISE
ORIGANES
AS AGONISES
AZ AGONIZES
BD OBSIGNED
BL INGLOBES
BM BESOMING
BO BESOGNIO
BR SOBERING
CD COGNISED
CL ECLOSING
CS COGNISES
CZ COGNIZES
DI INDIGOES
DL GLENOIDS
SIDELONG
DM SMIDGEON
DP DEPOSING
DISPONGE
PIDGEONS
DR NEGROIDS
DW WENDIGOS
WIDGEONS
EO OOGENIES
EP EPIGONES
ER ERINGOES
ET EGESTION
GK GINGKOES
GINKGOES
HS SHOEINGS
HT HISTOGEN
HU GINHOUSE
IM IGNOMIES
IR SEIGNIOR
KL SONGLIKE
LL LOGLINES
LR RESOLING
LS LIGNOSES
LU LIGNEOUS
LW LONGWISE
MR NEGROISM
MT MITOGENS
MU GEMINOUS
MY MOSEYING
NP OPENINGS
PR PERIGONS
REPOSING
SPONGIER
PT PONGIEST
PX EXPOSING
PY POESYING
RR IGNORERS
RS GORINESS
SIGNORES
RT GENITORS
ROSETING
RY SEIGNORY
TT TENTIGOS

EGINRS 68
(SINGER)

AA ANGARIES
AB BEARINGS
SABERING
AC CREASING
GRECIANS
SEARCING
AD DERAIGNS
GRADINES
READINGS
AE GESNERIA
AG GEARINGS
GREASING
SNAGGIER
AH HEARINGS
HEARSING
SHEARING
AK SKEARING
AL ENGRAILS
NARGILES
REALIGNS
SALERING
SANGLIER
SIGNALER
SLANGIER
AM GERMAINS
SMEARING
AN AGINNERS
EARNINGS
ENGRAINS
GRANNIES
AO IGNAROES
ORGANISE
ORIGANES
AP PREASING
SPEARING
AR EARRINGS
GRAINERS
AS REASSIGN
SEARINGS
SERINGAS
AT ANGRIEST
ASTRINGE
GANISTER
GANTRIES
GRANITES
INGRATES
RANGIEST
REASTING
STEARING
TASERING
AV VINEGARS
AW SWEARING
WEARINGS
AY RESAYING
BE BIGENERS
BO SOBERING
BR BRINGERS
BW BREWINGS
CE CREESING
GENERICS
CL CLINGERS
CRINGLES
CN SCERNING
CR CRINGERS
CT CRESTING
CU RECUSING
RESCUING
SCUNGIER
SECURING
CW SCREWING
CY SYNERGIC
DD REDDINGS
DE DESIGNER
ENERGIDS
REDESIGN
REEDINGS
RESIGNED
DI DESIRING
RESIDING
RINGSIDE
DO NEGROIDS
DP SPRINGED
DR GRINDERS
REGRINDS
DS DRESSING
DT STRINGED
DW REDWINGS
DY SYNERGID
SYRINGED
EE ENERGIES
ENERGISE
GREENIES
EF FEERINGS
REEFINGS
EG GREESING
EH GREENISH
SHEERING
EJ JEERINGS
EK KREESING
SKEERING
EL LEERINGS
REELINGS
EM REGIMENS
EN ENGINERS
INGENERS
SERENING
SNEERING
EO ERINGOES
EP SPEERING
SPREEING
ER RESIGNER
ES GREISENS
ET GENTRIES
INTEGERS
REESTING
STEERING
STREIGNE
EU SEIGNEUR
EV SEVERING
VEERINGS
EW SEWERING
FH FRESHING
FL FLINGERS
FN FERNINGS
FU GUNFIRES
REFUSING
FW SWERFING
GL NIGGLERS
SNIGGLER
GS GRESSING
SNIGGERS
GY GREYINGS
HK GHERKINS
HL HERLINGS
SHINGLER
HP SPHERING
HR HERRINGS
HT RIGHTENS
HU USHERING
HW SHREWING
WHINGERS
IL RESILING
IM REMISING
IN RESINING
IO SEIGNIOR
IP SPEIRING
IT GIRNIEST
IGNITERS
REISTING
STINGIER
STRIGINE
IU SIGNIEUR
IV REVISING
IW RINGWISE
SWINGIER
JK JERKINGS
JL JINGLERS
KN KERNINGS
KR SKERRING
KU RESKUING
LM GREMLINS
MERLINGS
MINGLERS
LO RESOLING
LP PINGLERS

SPERLING
SPRINGLE
LS RINGLESS
SLINGERS
LT LINGSTER
RINGLETS
STERLING
TINGLERS
TRINGLES
LW NEWSGIRL
MO NEGROISM
MP IMPREGNS
MS GRIMNESS
MU RESUMING
NN RENNINGS
NR GRINNERS
NT STERNING
NU ENSURING
OP PERIGONS
REPOSING
SPONGIER
OR IGNORERS
OS GORINESS
SIGNORES
OT GENITORS
ROSETING
OY SEIGNORY
PP REPPINGS
PR SPERRING
SPRINGER
PS PRESSING
SPERSING
SPRINGES
PT PRESTING
PU PERSUING
PERUSING
RT RESTRING
RINGSTER
STRINGER
RW WRINGERS
RY SERRYING
ST RESTINGS
STINGERS
TRESSING
TRIGNESS
SV SERVINGS
VERSINGS
SW SWINGERS
SY SYRINGES
TT GITTERNS
TV STERVING
TW STREWING
WRESTING
VW SWERVING

EGINRT 39
(TINGER)
AA AERATING
AB BERATING
REBATING
AC CATERING
CITRANGE
CREATING
REACTING
AD DERATING
GRADIENT
REDATING
TREADING
AE GRATINEE
AH EARTHING
HEARTING
INGATHER
AK RETAKING
AL ALERTING
ALTERING
INTEGRAL
RELATING
TANGLIER
TRIANGLE
AM EMIGRANT
AP TAPERING
AS ANGRIEST
ASTRINGE
GANISTER
GANTRIES
GRANITES
INGRATES
RANGIEST
REASTING
STEARING
TASERING
AT ARETTING
TREATING
AV AVERTING
TAVERING
VINTAGER
AW TWANGIER
WATERING
BH BERTHING
BRIGHTEN
BI REBITING
BL TREBLING
CE ERECTING
GENTRICE
CH RETCHING
CI RECITING
CK TRECKING
CN CENTRING
CO GERONTIC
CS CRESTING
CU ERUCTING
DI DIRIGENT
DN TRENDING
DS STRINGED
EG GREETING
EM METERING
REGIMENT
EN ENTERING
EP PETERING
ES GENTRIES
INTEGERS
REESTING
STEERING
STREIGNE
EU GENITURE
EV EVERTING
EW TWEERING
EX EXERTING
GENETRIX
FH FRIGHTEN
FT FRETTING
FU FEUTRING
REFUTING
FY GENTRIFY
HI THINGIER
HO THROEING
HS RIGHTENS
HW WRETHING
IL GIRTLINE
RETILING
TINGLIER
TIRELING
IM MERITING
MITERING
RETIMING
IR RETIRING
IS GIRNIEST
IGNITERS
REISTING
STINGIER
STRIGINE
IU INTRIGUE
IV RIVETING
IX GENITRIX
KK TREKKING
LS LINGSTER
RINGLETS
STERLING
TINGLERS
TRINGLES
NO NITROGEN
NP PRENTING
NS STERNING
NU RETUNING
NV VENTRING
OS GENITORS
ROSETING
OT OTTERING
OU OUTREIGN
ROUTEING
OW TOWERING
OX OXTERING
OZ ROZETING
PS PRESTING
PU ERUPTING
REPUTING
RS RESTRING
RINGSTER
STRINGER
RY RETRYING
SS RESTINGS
STINGERS
TRESSING
TRIGNESS
ST GITTERNS
SV STERVING
SW STREWING
WRESTING
TU UTTERING

EGINST 107
(ESTING)
AA SAGINATE
AB BEATINGS
AD SEDATING
STEADING
AE SAGENITE
AF FEASTING
AG NAGGIEST
AH GAHNITES
HEATINGS
AL EASTLING
GELATINS
GENITALS
STEALING
AM MANGIEST
MINTAGES
STEAMING
TEAMINGS
AN ANTIGENS
GENTIANS
STEANING
AR ANGRIEST
ASTRINGE
GANISTER
GANTRIES
GRANITES
INGRATES
RANGIEST
REASTING
STEARING
TASERING
AS EASTINGS
GENISTAS
GIANTESS
SEATINGS
TEASINGS
TSIGANES
AT ESTATING
TANGIEST
AU SAUTEING
AV VINTAGES
AW SWEATING
AY YEASTING
BE BEIGNETS
BH BENIGHTS
BL BELTINGS
BT BETTINGS
CE GENETICS
CH CHESTING
ETCHINGS
CN SCENTING
CR CRESTING
DD STEDDING
DE INGESTED
SIGNETED
STEEDING
DI DINGIEST
INDIGEST
DN STENDING
DR STRINGED
DU DUNGIEST
EG EGESTING
EH SEETHING
SHEETING
EK KITENGES
STEEKING
EL GENTILES
SLEETING
STEELING
EM MEETINGS
STEEMING
EN STEENING
EO EGESTION
EP STEEPING
ER GENTRIES
INTEGERS
REESTING
STEERING
STREIGNE
ET GENTIEST
EU EUGENIST
EV STEEVING
VENTIGES
EW SWEETING
EX EXIGENTS
FL FELTINGS
FM FIGMENTS
GT GETTINGS
GU GUESTING
GUNGIEST
HI HEISTING
NIGHTIES
THINGIES
HL ENLIGHTS
LIGHTENS
HN SENNIGHT
HO HISTOGEN
HR RIGHTENS
HT SHETTING
TIGHTENS
IL LIGNITES
LINGIEST
IM MINGIEST
IN GINNIEST
STEINING
IR GIRNIEST
IGNITERS
REISTING
STINGIER
STRIGINE
IW WINGIEST
IX EXISTING
IZ ZINGIEST
JL JINGLETS
JS JESTINGS
KL KINGLETS
LL STELLING
TELLINGS
LM MELTINGS
SMELTING
LN NESTLING
LP PELTINGS
PESTLING
LR LINGSTER
RINGLETS
STERLING
TINGLERS
TRINGLES
LS GLISTENS
SINGLETS
LT LETTINGS
SETTLING
LW SWELTING
WINGLETS
MM STEMMING
MO MITOGENS
MP PIGMENTS
NN STENNING
NR STERNING
NS NESTINGS
NT NETTINGS
STENTING
TENTINGS
NV VENTINGS
OP PONGIEST
OR GENITORS
ROSETING
OT TENTIGOS
PP STEPPING
PR PRESTING
PT PETTINGS
SPETTING
QU QUESTING
RR RESTRING
RINGSTER
STRINGER
RS RESTINGS
STINGERS
TRESSING
TRIGNESS
RT GITTERNS
RV STERVING
RW STREWING
WRESTING
ST SETTINGS
TESTINGS
SV VESTINGS
SW STEWINGS
WESTINGS
TT STETTING

EGNORS 155
(ONGERS)
AC ACROGENS
CORNAGES
AI IGNAROES
ORGANISE
ORIGANES
AM MEGARONS
AO OREGANOS
AR GROANERS
AT ORANGEST
RAGSTONE
STONERAG
AW WAGONERS
BI SOBERING
BU BURGEONS
CE COGENERS
CONGREES
CH GROSCHEN
CS CONGRESS
CU CONGRUES
SCROUNGE
CY CRYOGENS
DI NEGROIDS
DO DRONGOES
DU GUERDONS
EG ENGORGES
EI ERINGOES
EK KEROGENS
ET ESTROGEN
EU GENEROUS
EY ERYNGOES
GT GONGSTER
HL LEGHORNS
HM GEMSHORN
HU ENROUGHS
ROUGHENS
II SEIGNIOR
IL RESOLING
IM NEGROISM
IP PERIGONS
REPOSING
SPONGIER
IR IGNORERS
IS GORINESS
SIGNORES
IT GENITORS
ROSETING
IY SEIGNORY
LM MONGRELS
LU LOUNGERS
MU MURGEONS
NT RONTGENS
PS SPONGERS
PY PYROGENS
RT STRONGER
RW WRONGERS
ST SONGSTER

SU SURGEONS
TT TONGSTER
TU STURGEON
TW WRONGEST

EHINRS 227
(SHRINE)
AC INARCHES
AE INHEARSE
AG HEARINGS
HEARSING
SHEARING
AL INHALERS
AM HARMINES
SHIREMAN
AP HEPARINS
PARISHEN
SERAPHIN
AR SHARNIER
AS ARSHINES
AT HAIRNETS
INEARTHS
THERIANS
AV ENRAVISH
VANISHER
AW SHERWANI
CE ENRICHES
INHERCES
CO CHORINES
CP PINCHERS
CS RICHNESS
CT CHRISTEN
CITHERNS
SNITCHER
DE DRISHEEN
DO HORDEINS
EE SHEENIER
EG GREENISH
SHEERING
EM SHIREMEN
EN ENSHRINE
EO HEROINES
EP INSPHERE
ER ERRHINES
FG FRESHING
FI FINISHER
GK GHERKINS
GL HERLINGS
SHINGLER
GP SPHERING
GR HERRINGS
GT RIGHTENS
GU USHERING
GW SHREWING
WHINGERS
IN INSHRINE
IT INHERITS
IZ RHIZINES
KO SHONKIER
KR SHRINKER
KT RETHINKS
THINKERS
MP PHRENISM
MU INHUMERS
RHENIUMS
NT THINNERS
OS HERISSON
OT HORNIEST
PU PUNISHER
SU INRUSHES
TZ ZITHERNS

EHIRST 153
(ITHERS)
AA HETAIRAS
AC CHARIEST
THERIACS
AD HAIRSTED
HARDIEST
AE HEARTIES
AI HAIRIEST
AN HAIRNETS
INEARTHS
THERIANS
AO HOARIEST
AR TRASHIER
AS SHERIATS
AU THESAURI
AW SWATHIER
WATERISH
AY HYSTERIA
BC BRITCHES
BE HERBIEST
BL BLITHERS
BR REBIRTHS
BS HERBISTS
CD DITCHERS
CE CHESTIER
HERETICS
CH HITCHERS
CI CHRISTIE
CN CHRISTEN
CITHERNS
SNITCHER
CO ROTCHIES
THEORICS
CP PITCHERS
SPITCHER
CS STRICHES
CT CHITTERS
RICHTEST
STITCHER
CY HYSTERIC
DI DISHERIT
DT THIRSTED
THRISTED
EE ETHERISE
SHEETIER
EM ERETHISM
ETHERISM
EO ISOTHERE
THEORIES
THEORISE
EP TREESHIP
ES HEISTERS
ET ETHERIST
FG FIGHTERS
FREIGHTS
FI SHIFTIER
FS SHIFTERS
GG THIGGERS
GI TIGERISH
GL LIGHTERS
RELIGHTS
SLIGHTER
GN RIGHTENS
GO GHOSTIER
GR RIGHTERS
GS SIGHTERS
GT RIGHTEST
STREIGHT
HW WHITHERS
IN INHERITS
IR SHIRTIER
IT SHITTIER
THIRTIES
KN RETHINKS
THINKERS
LL THILLERS
LP PHILTERS
PHILTRES
LS SLITHERS
THRISSEL
LT THRISTLE
LU LUTHIERS
LW WHIRTLES
WHISTLER
LY SLITHERY
MO ISOTHERM
MOITHERS
MS SMITHERS
MY SMITHERY
NN THINNERS
NO HORNIEST
NZ ZITHERNS
OP TROPHIES
OR HERITORS
OS HOISTERS
HORSIEST
HOSTRIES
SHORTIES
OT THEORIST
THORITES
OU OUTHIRES
OV OVERHITS
OW WORTHIES
PS HIPSTERS
THRIPSES
PW WHIPSTER
RT THIRSTER
RV THRIVERS
RW WHIRRETS
SU RUSHIEST
SW SWITHERS
TW WHITRETS
WHITSTER
WHITTERS

EHORST 189
(OTHERS)
AB BATHORSE
AC CHAROSET
THORACES
AG SHORTAGE
AH HAROSETH
AI HOARIEST
AL LOATHERS
AO TOHEROAS
AP POTSHARE
AS ASTHORES
EARSHOTS
HAROSETS
HOARSEST
AT RHEOSTAT
AX THORAXES
BC BOTCHERS
BL BROTHELS
BO THEORBOS
BR BROTHERS
BT BETROTHS
CC CROCHETS
CROTCHES
CE TROCHEES
CI ROTCHIES
THEORICS
CL CHORTLES
CN NOTCHERS
CO CHEROOTS
CP POTCHERS
CR TORCHERS
CU SCOUTHER
TOUCHERS
CW SCOWTHER
DP POTSHERD
DR REDSHORT
EE SHOETREE
EI ISOTHERE
THEORIES
THEORISE
EL HOSTELER
EM THEOREMS
EN HONESTER
FN FORHENTS
GI GHOSTIER
GU ROUGHEST
HU SHOUTHER
IM ISOTHERM
MOITHERS
IN HORNIEST
IP TROPHIES
IR HERITORS
IS HOISTERS
HORSIEST
HOSTRIES
SHORTIES
IT THEORIST
THORITES
IU OUTHIRES
IV OVERHITS
IW WORTHIES
LN HORNLETS
LS HOLSTERS
HOSTLERS
LT THROSTLE
LY HOSTELRY
MO SMOOTHER
MS SMOTHERS
MU MOUTHERS
MY SMOTHERY
NR NORTHERS
NS SHORTENS
NT THORNSET
NU SOUTHERN
OS ORTHOSES
SHOOTERS
SOOTHERS
OV OVERSHOT
PP PROPHETS
PS STROPHES
PU POUTHERS
PY TROPHESY
RW THROWERS
ST SHORTEST
SU SHOUTERS
SOUTHERS
UY OUTHYRES

EIILST 139
(TILIES)
AB ALBITISE
SIBILATE
AC CILIATES
SILICATE
AD IDEALIST
AF FILIATES
AH HAILIEST
AL TAILLIES
AN ALIENIST
LITANIES
AR LAIRIEST
LISTERIA
AV VITALISE
AX LAXITIES
AZ TAILZIES
BG BILGIEST
BR TRILBIES
BT STILBITE
CC SCILICET
CF FELSITIC
DD TIDDLIES
DL DILLIEST
DM DELIMITS
LIMITEDS
DR REDISTIL
DU UTILISED
DV LIVIDEST
EN LENITIES
ER TILERIES
EV LEVITIES
VEILIEST
EW LEWISITE
FH TILEFISH
FM FILMIEST
FT FITLIEST
GM LEGITIMS
GN LIGNITES
LINGIEST
HL HILLIEST
HT LITHITES
KM MILKIEST
KS SILKIEST
LN NIELLIST
LR STILLIER
LS SILLIEST
LT TILLIEST
TILLITES
LW TWILLIES
MP LIMEPITS
MR LIMITERS
MIRLIEST
MS ELITISMS
SLIMIEST
MT MISTITLE
MY MYELITIS
NO ETIOLINS
NR NIRLIEST
NITRILES
NT LINTIEST
NY SENILITY
OP PISOLITE
POLITIES
OR ROILIEST
OS SOILIEST
PP LIPPIEST
PR TRIPLIES
PS PITILESS
SPILITES
PY PYELITIS
RT STILTIER
RU UTILISER
ST ELITISTS
SILTIEST
SU ULITISES
UTILISES
UY TUILYIES
UZ TUILZIES
UTILIZES

EIINRT 30
(INTIRE)
AD DAINTIER
AF FAINTIER
AL INERTIAL
AP PAINTIER
AS INERTIAS
RAINIEST
BE BENITIER
BG REBITING
BS BRINIEST
CD INDIRECT
CE ICTERINE
CG RECITING
CN INTRINCE
CS CITRINES
CRINITES
INCITERS
CU NEURITIC
DD NITRIDED
DG DIRIGENT
DM DIRIMENT
DO RETINOID
DP INTREPID
DS DISINTER
INDITERS
NITRIDES
RINDIEST
DU UNTIDIER
EO ERIONITE
ES ERINITES
NITERIES
ET INTERTIE
RETINITE
FL FLINTIER
FO NOTIFIER
FR FERRITIN
FS SNIFTIER
GH THINGIER
GL GIRTLINE
RETILING
TINGLIER
TIRELING
GM MERITING
MITERING
RETIMING
GR RETIRING
GS GIRNIEST
IGNITERS
REISTING
STINGIER
STRIGINE
GU INTRIGUE
GV RIVETING
GX GENITRIX
HR HIRRIENT
HS INHERITS
JK JIRKINET
KL TINKLIER
LS NIRLIEST
NITRILES
MS INTERIMS

MINISTER
MT INTERMIT
MX INTERMIX
NV INVERTIN
OP POINTIER
OR INTERIOR
PS PRISTINE
RW WINTRIER
SS SINISTER
ST NITRITES
STINTIER
SU NEURITIS
SV INVITERS
VINTRIES
VITRINES

EILNOS 47
(OLINES)
AD NODALISE
AG GASOLINE
AK KAOLINES
AM LAMINOSE
MINEOLAS
SEMOLINA
AN SOLANINE
AP OPALINES
AR AILERONS
ALERIONS
ALIENORS
AT ELATIONS
INSOLATE
TOENAILS
BC BINOCLES
BG INGLOBES
BO OBELIONS
BP BONSPIEL
BW BOWLINES
CD INCLOSED
CE CINEOLES
CG ECLOSING
CH CHOLINES
HELICONS
CI ISOCLINE
SILICONE
CL LIONCELS
CO COLONIES
COLONISE
ECLOSION
CP PINOCLES
CR INCLOSER
LICENSOR
CS CONSEILS
INCLOSES
CT LECTIONS
CX LEXICONS
DE ESLOINED
DG GLENOIDS
SIDELONG
DI LIONISED
DO SOLENOID
DR DISENROL
DS SONDELIS
DU DELUSION
INSOULED
UNSOILED
EF FELONIES
OLEFINES
ER ELOINERS
ET NOSELITE
EV NOVELISE
FU NOISEFUL
FX FLEXIONS
GK SONGLIKE
GL LOGLINES
GR RESOLING
GS LIGNOSES
GU LIGNEOUS
GW LONGWISE
HK SINKHOLE
HL HELLIONS
HP PINHOLES
HS HOLINESS
HT HOTLINES
NEOLITHS
HV NOVELISH
IS ELISIONS
ISOLINES
LIONISES
OILINESS
IT ETIOLINS
IV OLIVINES
IZ LIONIZES
KM MOLESKIN
KW SNOWLIKE
LT STELLION
MM MOLIMENS
MT MOLINETS
MU EMULSION
MV NOVELISM
NT INSOLENT
NW SNOWLINE
OP POLONIES
POLONISE
OT LOONIEST
OILSTONE
OV VIOLONES
PP PLENIPOS
PR PROLINES
PS EPSILONS
PT POINTELS
PONTILES
TOPLINES
RR LORINERS
RT RETINOLS
SU ELUSIONS
SW LEWISSON
TU ELUTIONS
OUTLINES
TV NOVELIST
VIOLENTS
TW TOWLINES
UV EVULSION
VV INVOLVES

EILNRS 77
(LINERS)
AB RINSABLE
AC CARLINES
AD ISLANDER
AG ENGRAILS
NARGILES
REALIGNS
SALERING
SANGLIER
SIGNALER
SLANGIER
AH INHALERS
AI AIRLINES
SNAILIER
AM MARLINES
MINERALS
AO AILERONS
ALERIONS
ALIENORS
AP PEARLINS
PRALINES
AR SNARLIER
AS RAINLESS
AT ENTRAILS
LATRINES
RATLINES
TRENAILS
AU LUNARIES
AV RAVELINS
AX RELAXINS
AY INLAYERS
SNAILERY
BB NIBBLERS
BD BLINDERS
BRINDLES
BE BERLINES
BI RINSIBLE
BK BLINKERS
CE LICENSER
RECLINES
SILENCER
CG CLINGERS
CRINGLES
CK CLINKERS
CRINKLES
CO INCLOSER
LICENSOR
DF FLINDERS
DK KINDLERS
DO DISENROL
DP SPELDRIN
DS RINDLESS
DT SNIRTLED
TENDRILS
TRINDLES
DW SWINDLER
EG LEERINGS
REELINGS
EM ERMELINS
EO ELOINERS
EP PILSENER
ES REINLESS
ET LISTENER
SILENTER
EV LIVENERS
FF SNIFFLER
FG FLINGERS
GG NIGGLERS
SNIGGLER
GH HERLINGS
SHINGLER
GI RESILING
GJ JINGLERS
GM GREMLINS
MERLINGS
MINGLERS
GO RESOLING
GP PINGLERS
SPERLING
SPRINGLE
GS RINGLESS
SLINGERS
GT LINGSTER
RINGLETS
STERLING
TINGLERS
TRINGLES
GW NEWSGIRL
IK SLINKIER
IT NIRLIEST
NITRILES
KK KLINKERS
KM KREMLINS
KP SPRINKLE
KS SLINKERS
KT LINKSTER
STRINKLE
TINKLERS
KW WINKLERS
WRINKLES
MT MINSTREL
OP PROLINES
OR LORINERS
OT RETINOLS
PS PILSNERS
PT SPLINTER
PU PURLINES
ST SLINTERS
SNIRTLES
TU INSULTER
LUSTRINE
TY TINSELRY

EILNST 45
(INTLES)
AB INSTABLE
AF INFLATES
AG EASTLING
GELATINS
GENITALS
STEALING
AI ALIENIST
LITANIES
AK LANKIEST
AM AILMENTS
ALIMENTS
MANLIEST
AO ELATIONS
INSOLATE
TOENAILS
AP PANTILES
PLAINEST
AR ENTRAILS
LATRINES
RATLINES
TRENAILS
AS EASTLINS
ELASTINS
SALIENTS
STANIELS
AU ALUNITES
INSULATE
AV VENTAILS
AW LAWNIEST
BD BLINDEST
BE STILBENE
TENSIBLE
BG BELTINGS
BM NIMBLEST
BZ BLINTZES
CF INFLECTS
CH LINCHETS
TINCHELS
CO LECTIONS
CS STENCILS
CU CUTLINES
TUNICLES
DE ENLISTED
LINTSEED
LISTENED
TINSELED
DP SPLINTED
DR SNIRTLED
TENDRILS
TRINDLES
DU DILUENTS
INSULTED
UNLISTED
EE SELENITE
EG GENTILES
SLEETING
STEELING
EI LENITIES
EK NESTLIKE
EN LENIENTS
SENTINEL
EO NOSELITE
EP PLENTIES
ER LISTENER
SILENTER
ES SETLINES
ET ENTITLES
EV VEINLETS
FG FELTINGS
GH ENLIGHTS
LIGHTENS
GI LIGNITES
LINGIEST
GJ JINGLETS
GK KINGLETS
GL STELLING
TELLINGS
GM MELTINGS
SMELTING
GN NESTLING
GP PELTINGS
PESTLING
GR LINGSTER
RINGLETS
STERLING
TINGLERS
TRINGLES
GS GLISTENS
SINGLETS
GT LETTINGS
SETTLING
GW SWELTING
WINGLETS
HO HOTLINES
NEOLITHS
IL NIELLIST
IO ETIOLINS
IR NIRLIEST
NITRILES
IT LINTIEST
IY SENILITY
KR LINKSTER
STRINKLE
TINKLERS
KS LENTISKS
KT KNITTLES
KW TWINKLES
LO STELLION
LY SILENTLY
TINSELLY
MO MOLINETS
MR MINSTREL
MU MUSLINET
NO INSOLENT
OO LOONIEST
OILSTONE
OP POINTELS
PONTILES
TOPLINES
OR RETINOLS
OU ELUTIONS
OUTLINES
OV NOVELIST
VIOLENTS
OW TOWLINES
PR SPLINTER
PS PLENISTS
RS SLINTERS
SNIRTLES
RU INSULTER
LUSTRINE
RY TINSELRY
ST TINTLESS
SU UTENSILS
SW WESTLINS
TU LUTENIST

EILORS 37
(OILERS)
AA OLEARIAS
AC CALORIES
CARIOLES
AD DARIOLES
SOLIDARE
SOREDIAL
AF FORESAIL
AG GASOLIER
GIRASOLE
SERAGLIO
AH AIRHOLES
SHOALIER
AM MORALISE
AN AILERONS
ALERIONS
ALIENORS
AP PELORIAS
POLARISE
AS SOLARISE
AT SOTERIAL
AV OVERSAIL
VALORISE
VARIOLES
VOLARIES
AY ROYALISE
AZ SOLARIZE
BB SLOBBIER
BC BRICOLES
CORBEILS
BH BOLSHIER
BL BROLLIES
BM EMBROILS
BR BROILERS
BT STROBILE
TRILOBES
BW BLOWSIER
CD SCLEROID
CL COLLIERS
ORSELLIC
CN INCLOSER
LICENSOR

CT CLOISTER
COISTREL
COSTLIER
CREOLIST
DI IDOLISER
DL DOLLIERS
DN DISENROL
DS SOLDIERS
DT STOLIDER
DU SOULDIER
DY SOLDIERY
EF FORELIES
EI OILERIES
EK ROSELIKE
EL ORSEILLE
EN ELOINERS
EP PELORIES
ET LITEROSE
TROELIES
EV OVERLIES
RELIEVOS
VOLERIES
EW OWLERIES
FJ FRIJOLES
FK FOLKSIER
FP PROFILES
FS FLOSSIER
FT FLORIEST
TREFOILS
GM GOMERILS
GN RESOLING
GS GLOSSIER
HP PILHORSE
POLISHER
HS SLOSHIER
IT ROILIEST
LT TRILLOES
TROLLIES
LU ROUILLES
LZ ZORILLES
MO SLOOMIER
MP IMPLORES
PELORISM
MR LORIMERS
NP PROLINES
NR LORINERS
NT RETINOLS
OT TROOLIES
PP SLOPPIER
PS SPOILERS
PT POITRELS
PU PERILOUS
PV OVERSLIP
SS RISSOLES
SU SOILURES
TT TRIOLETS
TU LOURIEST
OUTLIERS
ZZ SOZZLIER

EILORT 18
(LOITER)
AC EROTICAL
LORICATE
AD IDOLATER
TAILORED
AE AEROLITE
AF FLOATIER
AH AEROLITH
LOATHIER
AN ORIENTAL
RELATION
TAILERON
AP EPILATOR
PETIOLAR
AS SOTERIAL
AT LITERATO
AV VIOLATER
BD TRILOBED
BS STROBILE
TRILOBES
BT BLOTTIER
LIBRETTO
CH CHLORITE
CLOTHIER
CI ELICITOR
CP PETROLIC
CS CLOISTER
COISTREL
COSTLIER
CREOLIST
CT CLOTTIER
CY CRYOLITE
DE DOLERITE
LOITERED
DS STOLIDER
EH HOTELIER
EK LORIKEET
EM MOTELIER
ER LOITERER
ES LITEROSE
TROELIES
FF FORELIFT
FS FLORIEST
TREFOILS
FU FLUORITE
GH REGOLITH
GY GYROLITE
HP HELIPORT
HY RHYOLITE
IS ROILIEST
IT TROILITE
KO ROOTLIKE
LS TRILLOES
TROLLIES
NP TOPLINER
NR RITORNEL
NS RETINOLS
NT TROTLINE
NW TOWNLIER
OS TROOLIES
OV OVERTOIL
PR PORTLIER
PS POITRELS
PW PILEWORT
RU ULTERIOR
ST TRIOLETS
SU LOURIEST
OUTLIERS
TY TOILETRY

EILOST 21
(OILETS)
AC ALOETICS
COALIEST
SOCIETAL
AD DIASTOLE
ISOLATED
SODALITE
SOLIDATE
AF FOLIATES
AG OTALGIES
AK KEITLOAS
AM LOAMIEST
AN ELATIONS
INSOLATE
TOENAILS
AP SPOLIATE
AR SOTERIAL
AS ISOLATES
AT TOTALISE
AV VIOLATES
BB BIBELOTS
BF BOTFLIES
BO LOOBIEST
BR STROBILE
TRILOBES
BW BLOWIEST
CD DOCILEST
CN LECTIONS
CP TOECLIPS
CR CLOISTER
COISTREL
COSTLIER
CREOLIST
CS SOLECIST
SOLSTICE
CT COLETITS
DD DELTOIDS
DG GODLIEST
GOLDIEST
DM MELODIST
DR STOLIDER
DS SOLIDEST
DT DOILTEST
DU SOLITUDE
EM MESOLITE
MISLETOE
EN NOSELITE
EP PETIOLES
ER LITEROSE
TROELIES
ES ESTOILES
EW OWELTIES
EZ ZEOLITES
FJ JETFOILS
FM FILEMOTS
FR FLORIEST
TREFOILS
FT LOFTIEST
FU OUTFLIES
GS ELOGISTS
GU EULOGIST
HH SHITHOLE
HM HELOTISM
HN HOTLINES
NEOLITHS
HO HOOLIEST
HP HELISTOP
HOPLITES
ISOPLETH
IN ETIOLINS
IP PISOLITE
POLITIES
IR ROILIEST
IS SOILIEST
JL JOLLIEST
JT JOLTIEST
JW JOWLIEST
KY YOLKIEST
LM MELILOTS
LN STELLION
LR TRILLOES
TROLLIES
LS TOILLESS
LW LOWLIEST
MN MOLINETS
MO TOILSOME
MP POLEMIST
MT MOTLIEST
NN INSOLENT
NO LOONIEST
OILSTONE
NP POINTELS
PONTILES
TOPLINES
NR RETINOLS
NU ELUTIONS
OUTLINES
NV NOVELIST
VIOLENTS
NW TOWLINES
OP LOOPIEST
OR TROOLIES
OS OSTIOLES
STOOLIES
OZ ZOOLITES
PR POITRELS
PS PISTOLES
PTILOSES
SLOPIEST
PT PISTOLET
PLOTTIES
POLITEST
PX EXPLOITS
RT TRIOLETS
RU LOURIEST
OUTLIERS
SS LOSSIEST
SU LOUSIEST
TT STILETTO
UV OUTLIVES
SOLUTIVE

EILRST 44
(LITERS)
AB LIBRATES
TABLIERS
AC ALTRICES
ARTICLES
RECITALS
SELICTAR
AD DILATERS
LARDIEST
AE ATELIERS
EARLIEST
LEARIEST
REALTIES
AF FLARIEST
FRAILEST
AG GLARIEST
REGALIST
AI LAIRIEST
LISTERIA
AK LARKIEST
STALKIER
STARLIKE
AL LITERALS
TALLIERS
AM LAMITERS
MARLIEST
AN ENTRAILS
LATRINES
RATLINES
TRENAILS
AO SOTERIAL
AP PILASTER
PLAISTER
PLAITERS
AR RETIRALS
RETRIALS
TRAILERS
AS REALISTS
SALTIERS
SALTIRES
SLAISTER
AT TERTIALS
AU URALITES
BB STIBBLER
TRIBBLES
BD BRISTLED
DRIBLETS
BF FILBERTS
BG GILBERTS
BH BLITHERS
BI TRILBIES
BL BRILLEST
BM TIMBRELS
BO STROBILE
TRILOBES
BS BLISTERS
BRISTLES
BT BRITTLES
TRIBLETS
BU BURLIEST
SUBTILER
BY BLISTERY
CC CIRCLETS
CE RETICLES
SCLERITE
TIERCELS
CK STICKLER
STRICKLE
TICKLERS
TRICKLES
CO CLOISTER
COISTREL
COSTLIER
CREOLIST
CT CLITTERS
CU CURLIEST
UTRICLES
DD STRIDDLE
TIDDLERS
DI REDISTIL
DN SNIRTLED
TENDRILS
TRINDLES
DO STOLIDER
DU DILUTERS
LURIDEST
EE LEERIEST
SLEETIER
STEELIER
EF FERLIEST
EI TILERIES
EK TRISKELE
EL TREILLES
EM TERMLIES
EN LISTENER
SILENTER
EO LITEROSE
TROELIES
EP EPISTLER
PELTRIES
PERLITES
REPTILES
ES LEISTERS
RITELESS
TIRELESS
ET RETITLES
FO FLORIEST
TREFOILS
FR TRIFLERS
FS RIFTLESS
STIFLERS
FT FLITTERS
FW FEWTRILS
GH LIGHTERS
RELIGHTS
SLIGHTER
GN LINGSTER
RINGLETS
STERLING
TINGLERS
TRINGLES
GS GLISTERS
GRISTLES
GT GLITTERS
GU GURLIEST
HL THILLERS
HP PHILTERS
PHILTRES
HS SLITHERS
THRISSEL
HT THRISTLE
HU LUTHIERS
HW WHIRTLES
WHISTLER
HY SLITHERY
IL STILLIER
IM LIMITERS
MIRLIEST
IN NIRLIEST
NITRILES
IO ROILIEST
IP TRIPLIES
IT STILTIER
IU UTILISER
KN LINKSTER
STRINKLE
TINKLERS
LO TRILLOES
TROLLIES
LS STILLERS
LT TESTRILL
MN MINSTREL
MU MURLIEST
MY LYMITERS
NO RETINOLS
NP SPLINTER
NS SLINTERS
SNIRTLES
NU INSULTER
LUSTRINE
NY TINSELRY
OO TROOLIES
OP POITRELS
OT TRIOLETS
OU LOURIEST

OUTLIERS
PP RIPPLETS
STIPPLER
TIPPLERS
TRIPPLES
PS SPIRTLES
PT SPLITTER
TRIPLETS
PY PRIESTLY
SPRITELY
QU QUILTERS
RU SULTRIER
RW TWIRLERS
SS STIRLESS
ST SLITTERS
STILTERS
TESTRILS
SU SURLIEST
SY SISTERLY
TU SURTITLE
TW WRISTLET
TZ STRELITZ
UV RIVULETS

EILSTU 136
(UTILES)
AB SUITABLE
AF FISTULAE
AM SIMULATE
AN ALUNITES
INSULATE
AQ LIQUATES
TEQUILAS
AR URALITES
BD BLUDIEST
BG BULGIEST
BK BULKIEST
BL BULLIEST
BR BURLIEST
SUBTILER
BT SUBTITLE
CC CUTICLES
CD DULCITES
LUCIDEST
CE LEUCITES
CK LUCKIEST
CN CUTLINES
TUNICLES
CR CURLIEST
UTRICLES
CT CUITTLES
DE DILUTEES
DI UTILISED
DL DUELLIST
DULLIEST
DN DILUENTS
INSULTED
UNLISTED
DO SOLITUDE
DP STIPULED
DR DILUTERS
LURIDEST
DY SEDULITY
FG GULFIEST
FK FLUKIEST
FO OUTFLIES
FP SPITEFUL
FS SULFITES
FT FLUTIEST
FUTILEST
GO EULOGIST
GR GURLIEST
HK HULKIEST
HL HULLIEST
HP SULPHITE
HR LUTHIERS
HS LUSHIEST
HT THULITES
IR UTILISER
IS ULITISES
UTILISES
IY TUILYIES
IZ TUILZIES
UTILIZES
KS SULKIEST
LQ QUILLETS
LV VITELLUS
MM LUMMIEST
MN MUSLINET
MP LUMPIEST
PLUMIEST
MR MURLIEST
MS LITMUSES
NO ELUTIONS
OUTLINES
NR INSULTER
LUSTRINE
NS UTENSILS
NT LUTENIST
OR LOURIEST
OUTLIERS
OS LOUSIEST
OV OUTLIVES
SOLUTIVE
PP PULPIEST
PS STIPULES
QR QUILTERS
QU LUSTIQUE
RR SULTRIER
RS SURLIEST
RT SURTITLE
RV RIVULETS
ST LUSTIEST
SU LITUUSES

EIMNOS 131
(MONIES)
AD NOMADIES
NOMADISE
AL LAMINOSE
MINEOLAS
SEMOLINA
AR MORAINES
AT SOMNIATE
AU MOINEAUS
AW WOMANISE
BC COMBINES
BG BESOMING
BI EBIONISM
BR BROMINES
CN MECONINS
CR CREMOSIN
INCOMERS
SERMONIC
CT CENTIMOS
DE DEMONISE
DOMINEES
DG SMIDGEON
DH HEDONISM
DI DOMINIES
DM DEMONISM
DN MISDONNE
DO DOMINOES
MONODIES
DT DEMONIST
EH HEMIONES
EN NOMINEES
EP EPISEMON
ER EMERSION
ET MONETISE
SEMITONE
FI FISNOMIE
OMNIFIES
FR ENSIFORM
FERMIONS
GI IGNOMIES
GR NEGROISM
GT MITOGENS
GU GEMINOUS
GY MOSEYING
HI HOMINIES
HT HOISTMEN
HU HEMIONUS
IS EMISSION
SIMONIES
IV VISNOMIE
KL MOLESKIN
KR MONIKERS
KT TOKENISM
KU MOUSEKIN
LM MOLIMENS
LT MOLINETS
LU EMULSION
LV NOVELISM
MR MISNOMER
NT MENTIONS
OP EMPOISON
OR IONOMERS
MOONRISE
OS MONOSIES
OT EMOTIONS
MOONIEST
OX EXOMIONS
PS PEONISMS
PT EMPTIONS
NEPOTISM
PIMENTOS
RS MERSIONS
RU INERMOUS
MONSIEUR
RW WINSOMER
ST MOISTENS

EIMNRS 177
(MINERS)
AB MIRBANES
AC CARMINES
AD ADERMINS
SIRNAMED
AE REMANIES
AG GERMAINS
SMEARING
AH HARMINES
SHIREMAN
AK RAMEKINS
AL MARLINES
MINERALS
AN REINSMAN
AO MORAINES
AR MARINERS
AS SEMINARS
SIRNAMES
AT MINARETS
RAIMENTS
AU ANEURISM
AY SEMINARY
BO BROMINES
CO CREMOSIN
INCOMERS
SERMONIC
CT CENTRISM
EG REGIMENS
EH SHIREMEN
EL ERMELINS
EM IMMENSER
EN REINSMEN
EO EMERSION
EV MINEVERS
FO ENSIFORM
FERMIONS
FS FIRMNESS
GI REMISING
GL GREMLINS
MERLINGS
MINGLERS
GO NEGROISM
GP IMPREGNS
GS GRIMNESS
GU RESUMING
HP PHRENISM
HU INHUMERS
RHENIUMS
IP PRIMINES
IS MIRINESS
IT INTERIMS
MINISTER
IV MINIVERS
KL KREMLINS
KO MONIKERS
LT MINSTREL
MO MISNOMER
OO IONOMERS
MOONRISE
OS MERSIONS
OU INERMOUS
MONSIEUR
OW WINSOMER
PS PRIMNESS
ST ENTRISMS
MINSTERS
TRIMNESS
SU NEURISMS
TU TERMINUS
TY ENTRYISM
MISENTRY

EIMNST 201
(MINEST)
AA AMENTIAS
ANIMATES
AB AMBIENTS
AC SEMANTIC
AD MEDIANTS
TIDESMAN
AE MATINEES
SEMINATE
AF MANIFEST
AG MANGIEST
MINTAGES
STEAMING
TEAMINGS
AI MINIATES
AK MANKIEST
MISTAKEN
AL AILMENTS
ALIMENTS
MANLIEST
AN MANNITES
AO SOMNIATE
AR MINARETS
RAIMENTS
AS MANTISES
MATINESS
BL NIMBLEST
BU BITUMENS
CE CENTIMES
CO CENTIMOS
CR CENTRISM
DE DEMENTIS
SEDIMENT
TIDESMEN
DO DEMONIST
DS MINDSETS
DU MISTUNED
EE EMETINES
EG MEETINGS
STEEMING
EI ENMITIES
EO MONETISE
SEMITONE
EP SEPIMENT
ET MINETTES
FG FIGMENTS
FI FEMINIST
FT FITMENTS
GI MINGIEST
GL MELTINGS
SMELTING
GM STEMMING
GO MITOGENS
GP PIGMENTS
HK METHINKS
HO HOISTMEN
HP SHIPMENT
HY THYMINES
IR INTERIMS
MINISTER
IT MINTIEST
IU MUTINIES
IV MINIVETS
KO TOKENISM
LO MOLINETS
LR MINSTREL
LU MUSLINET
NO MENTIONS
OO EMOTIONS
MOONIEST
OP EMPTIONS
NEPOTISM
PIMENTOS
OS MOISTENS
PS MISSPENT
PU NUMPTIES
RS ENTRISMS
MINSTERS
TRIMNESS
RU TERMINUS
RY ENTRYISM
MISENTRY
SU MISTUNES
TU MINUTEST

EIMOST 150
(SOMITE)
AD ATOMISED
AF FOAMIEST
AL LOAMIEST
AN SOMNIATE
AR AMORTISE
ATOMISER
AS AMITOSES
AMOSITES
ATOMISES
OSMIATES
AX TOXEMIAS
AZ ATOMIZES
BB BOMBSITE
BC COMBIEST
BG MISBEGOT
CC COSMETIC
CD DOMESTIC
CF COMFIEST
CH MOCHIEST
CI COMITIES
SEMIOTIC
CN CENTIMOS
CO COOMIEST
CR MORTICES
CV VICOMTES
DE TEDISOME
DL MELODIST
DM IMMODEST
DN DEMONIST
DO DOOMIEST
MOODIEST
SODOMITE
DR MORTISED
DS MODISTES
DT DEMOTIST
EI MOIETIES
EL MESOLITE
MISLETOE
EM SOMETIME
EN MONETISE
SEMITONE
EP EPITOMES
EPSOMITE
ER TIRESOME
FL FILEMOTS
FR SETIFORM
FT OFTTIMES
GN MITOGENS
GR ERGOTISM
GORMIEST
GS EGOTISMS
GW TWIGSOME
HL HELOTISM
HN HOISTMEN
HO SMOOTHIE
HR ISOTHERM
MOITHERS
HT MOTHIEST
IP OPTIMISE
IY MOYITIES
KN TOKENISM
KS SMOKIEST
LL MELILOTS
LN MOLINETS
LO TOILSOME
LP POLEMIST

LT MOTLIEST
MP METOPISM
MT TOTEMISM
NN MENTIONS
NO EMOTIONS
MOONIEST
NP EMPTIONS
NEPOTISM
PIMENTOS
NS MOISTENS
OR MOORIEST
MOTORISE
ROOMIEST
PP MOPPIEST
PR IMPOSTER
PY PEYOTISM
QU MISQUOTE
RR MORTISER
STORMIER
RS EROTISMS
MORTISES
TRISOMES
RT OMITTERS
RU MISROUTE
MOISTURE
RW MISWROTE
WORMIEST
RY ISOMETRY
SS MOSSIEST
ST MOISTEST
SU MOUSIEST
SZ MESTIZOS
TT MOTTIEST
TOTEMIST
TU TITMOUSE

EIMRST 140
(MITERS)
AB BARMIEST
AC CERAMIST
MATRICES
AD MARDIEST
MISRATED
READMITS
AE EMIRATES
REAMIEST
STEAMIER
AG MAGISTER
MIGRATES
RAGTIMES
STERIGMA
AI AIRTIMES
SERIATIM
AL LAMITERS
MARLIEST
AM MARMITES
AN MINARETS
RAIMENTS
AO AMORTISE
ATOMISER
AP APTERISM
PRIMATES
AS ASTERISM
MAISTERS
MISRATES
SEMITARS
SMARTIES
AT MISTREAT
TERATISM
AU MURIATES
SEMITAUR
AW WARTIMES
AX MATRIXES
AY SYMITARE
BL TIMBRELS
BU IMBRUTES
RESUBMIT
TERBIUMS
CI MERISTIC
TRISEMIC
CN CENTRISM
CO MORTICES
CS CRETISMS
DE DEMERITS
DEMISTER
DIMETERS
MISTERED
DM MIDTERMS
DO MORTISED
DP DIREMPTS
EE EREMITES
EF FEMITERS
EH ERETHISM
ETHERISM
EL TERMLIES
EM MERISTEM
MIMESTER
MISMETRE
EO TIRESOME
EP EMPTIERS
ER MERRIEST
TRIREMES
ES TRISEMES
ET EMITTERS
TERMITES
EU EMERITUS
FO SETIFORM
FU FREMITUS
GI GRIMIEST
TIGERISM
GM GRIMMEST
GO ERGOTISM
GORMIEST
HO ISOTHERM
MOITHERS
HS SMITHERS
HY SMITHERY
IL LIMITERS
MIRLIEST
IN INTERIMS
MINISTER
IT METRITIS
IW MISWRITE
KU MURKIEST
LN MINSTREL
LU MURLIEST
LY LYMITERS
MP PRIMMEST
MR TRIMMERS
MS MISTERMS
MT TRIMMEST
MU RUMMIEST
NS ENTRISMS
MINSTERS
TRIMNESS
NU TERMINUS
NY ENTRYISM
MISENTRY
OO MOORIEST
MOTORISE
ROOMIEST
OP IMPOSTER
OR MORTISER
STORMIER
OS EROTISMS
MORTISES
TRISOMES
OT OMITTERS
OU MISROUTE
MOISTURE
OW MISWROTE
WORMIEST
OY ISOMETRY
PS IMPRESTS
PU IMPUREST
IMPUTERS
STUMPIER
SS MISTRESS
ST METRISTS
SY SMYTRIES
TU SMUTTIER
UV VITREUMS
UX MIXTURES

EINNST 113
(SINNET)
AC ANCIENTS
CANNIEST
INSTANCE
AF INFANTES
AG ANTIGENS
GENTIANS
STEANING
AM MANNITES
AO ENATIONS
AP PANTINES
AR ENTRAINS
TRANNIES
AS INSANEST
AT ANTIENTS
STANNITE
BO BONNIEST
CE NESCIENT
CG SCENTING
CI INSCIENT
DE DENTINES
DESINENT
DG STENDING
DU DUNNIEST
DUNNITES
EF FENNIEST
EG STEENING
EH HENNIEST
EI NINETIES
EL LENIENTS
SENTINEL
ER INTENSER
INTERNES
ES TENNISES
ET SENTIENT
EW ENTWINES
WENNIEST
FI FINNIEST
FU FUNNIEST
GH SENNIGHT
GI GINNIEST
STEINING
GL NESTLING
GN STENNING
GR STERNING
GS NESTINGS
GT NETTINGS
STENTING
TENTINGS
GV VENTINGS
HR THINNERS
HS THINNESS
HT THINNEST
IS TININESS
IT TINNIEST
IW INTWINES
KO INKSTONE
LO INSOLENT
MO MENTIONS
OR INTONERS
TERNIONS
OS TENSIONS
OT TINSTONE
TONTINES
OU NOUNIEST
PR ENPRINTS
PS SPINNETS
RU RUNNIEST
STURNINE
RV VINTNERS
SU SUNNIEST
UW UNTWINES

EINOPS 130
(PONIES)
AC CANOPIES
CAPONISE
PAEONICS
AE PAEONIES
AH APHONIES
AL OPALINES
AT SAPONITE
AZ EPIZOANS
BH HOPBINES
BL BONSPIEL
CH CHOPINES
CI EPINOSIC
CL PINOCLES
CR CONSPIRE
INCORPSE
CT PONCIEST
DD DISPONED
DE DISPONEE
DG DEPOSING
DISPONGE
PIDGEONS
DH DIPHONES
SIPHONED
SPHENOID
DO POISONED
DR DISPONER
POINDERS
PRISONED
DS DISPONES
DOPINESS
SPINODES
DU UNPOISED
EG EPIGONES
EM EPISEMON
ER ISOPRENE
PIONEERS
FR FORPINES
GN OPENINGS
GR PERIGONS
REPOSING
SPONGIER
GT PONGIEST
GX EXPOSING
GY POESYING
HL PINHOLES
HT PHONIEST
SIPHONET
IR RIPIENOS
IT SINOPITE
LO POLONIES
POLONISE
LP PLENIPOS
LR PROLINES
LS EPSILONS
LT POINTELS
PONTILES
TOPLINES
MO EMPOISON
MS PEONISMS
MT EMPTIONS
NEPOTISM
PIMENTOS
NS PENSIONS
OR POISONER
SNOOPIER
SPOONIER
OS SPOONIES
PR POPERINS
PROPINES
RR PRISONER
RS PORINESS
PRESSION
ROPINESS
RT POINTERS
PROTEINS
REPOINTS
RU PRUINOSE
RV OVERSPIN
PROVINES
TT NEPOTIST

EINORS 7
(SENIOR)
AB BARONIES
AC SCENARIO
AD ANEROIDS
DONARIES
AF FARINOSE
AG IGNAROES
ORGANISE
ORIGANES
AL AILERONS
ALERIONS
ALIENORS
AM MORAINES
AN RAISONNE
AS ERASIONS
SENSORIA
AT ANOESTRI
ARSONITE
NOTARIES
NOTARISE
ROSINATE
AV AVERSION
BB SNOBBIER
BC BICORNES
BF BONFIRES
BG SOBERING
BI BRIONIES
BM BROMINES
BT BORNITES
RIBSTONE
BW BROWNIES
BY BRYONIES
CC CONCISER
CORNICES
CROCEINS
CD CONSIDER
CF CONIFERS
FORENSIC
FORINSEC
FORNICES
INFORCES
CH CHORINES
CI RECISION
SORICINE
CL INCLOSER
LICENSOR
CM CREMOSIN
INCOMERS
SERMONIC
CN INCENSOR
CP CONSPIRE
INCORPSE
CR RESORCIN
CS NECROSIS
SERICONS
CT CORNIEST
RECTIONS
CU NOURICES
ROUNCIES
DD INDORSED
DE ORDINEES
DG NEGROIDS
DH HORDEINS
DI DERISION
IRONISED
RESINOID
DJ JOINDERS
DL DISENROL
DN ENDIRONS
DP DISPONER
POINDERS
PRISONED
DS INDORSES
DT DRONIEST
DU DOURINES
SOURDINE
DW DISOWNER
WINDORES
WINDROSE
EG ERINGOES
EH HEROINES
EK KEROSINE
EL ELOINERS
EM EMERSION
EP ISOPRENE
PIONEERS
ES ESSOINER
ET SEROTINE
EV EVERSION
FK FORESKIN
FM ENSIFORM
FERMIONS
FN INFERNOS
FP FORPINES
FU REFUSION
GI SEIGNIOR
GL RESOLING
GM NEGROISM

GP PERIGONS
REPOSING
SPONGIER
GR IGNORERS
GS GORINESS
SIGNORES
GT GENITORS
ROSETING
GY SEIGNORY
HK SHONKIER
HS HERISSON
HT HORNIEST
IP RIPIENOS
IS IONISERS
IRONISES
IV REVISION
VISIONER
IZ IONIZERS
IRONIZES
JT JOINTERS
KM MONIKERS
KO ROOINEKS
LP PROLINES
LR LORINERS
LT RETINOLS
MM MISNOMER
MO IONOMERS
MOONRISE
MS MERSIONS
MU INERMOUS
MONSIEUR
MW WINSOMER
NT INTONERS
TERNIONS
NU REUNIONS
NV ENVIRONS
OP POISONER
SNOOPIER
SPOONIER
OS EROSIONS
OT SNOOTIER
OZ OZONISER
SNOOZIER
PP POPERINS
PROPINES
PR PRISONER
PS PORINESS
PRESSION
ROPINESS
PT POINTERS
PROTEINS
REPOINTS
PU PRUINOSE
PV OVERSPIN
PROVINES
RT INTRORSE
SNORTIER
SS ROSINESS
ST TERSIONS
SU NEUROSIS
RESINOUS
SV VERSIONS
TT SNOTTIER
TENORIST
TRITONES
TU ROUTINES
SNOUTIER
TV INVESTOR
TY TYROSINE
TZ TRIZONES
UV SOUVENIR

EINOSS 204
(SONSIE)

AD ADONISES
ANODISES
AG AGONISES
AR ERASIONS
SENSORIA
AT ASSIENTO
ASTONIES
AV EVASIONS
AX SAXONIES
BE EBONISES
BN BENISONS
BONINESS
BT EBONISTS
BX BOXINESS
CC CONCISES
CE SENECIOS
CG COGNISES
CI ICONISES
CL CONSEILS
INCLOSES
CR NECROSIS
SERICONS
CS CESSIONS
COSINESS
CT SECTIONS
CX COXINESS
DL SONDELIS
DP DISPONES
DOPINESS
SPINODES
DR INDORSES
DT DONSIEST
DV VOIDNESS
DZ DOZINESS
ER ESSOINER
ET ESSONITE
FX FOXINESS
FZ FOZINESS
GH SHOEINGS
GL LIGNOSES
GR GORINESS
SIGNORES
HL HOLINESS
HR HERISSON
HT HISTONES
IL ELISIONS
ISOLINES
LIONISES
OILINESS
IM EMISSION
SIMONIES
IR IONISERS
IRONISES
IT NOISIEST
LP EPSILONS
LU ELUSIONS
LW LEWISSON
MO MONOSIES
MP PEONISMS
MR MERSIONS
MT MOISTENS
NP PENSIONS
NS NOSINESS
NT TENSIONS
NV VENISONS
OP SPOONIES
OR EROSIONS
OT ISOTONES
OZ OOZINESS
OZONISES
PR PORINESS
PRESSION
ROPINESS
RS ROSINESS
RT TERSIONS
RU NEUROSIS
RESINOUS
RV VERSIONS
SS SESSIONS
ST SONSIEST
STENOSIS
TT SNOTTIES
STONIEST
TW SNOWIEST

EINOST 14
(TONIES)

AB BOTANIES
BOTANISE
NIOBATES
OBEISANT
AC ACONITES
CANOEIST
AD ASTONIED
SEDATION
AL ELATIONS
INSOLATE
TOENAILS
AM SOMNIATE
AN ENATIONS
AP SAPONITE
AR ANOESTRI
ARSONITE
NOTARIES
NOTARISE
ROSINATE
AS ASSIENTO
ASTONIES
AV STOVAINE
AX SAXONITE
BB NOBBIEST
BE BETONIES
EBONITES
BI NIOBITES
BN BONNIEST
BR BORNITES
RIBSTONE
BS EBONISTS
BT BOTTINES
BU BOUNTIES
CC CONCEITS
CD DEONTICS
CE ICESTONE
SEICENTO
CL LECTIONS
CM CENTIMOS
CO COONTIES
CP PONCIEST
CR CORNIEST
RECTIONS
CS SECTIONS
CT CENTOIST
STENOTIC
CU COUNTIES
CX EXCITONS
CY CYTOSINE
DE SIDENOTE
DH HEDONIST
DI EDITIONS
SEDITION
DM DEMONIST
DR DRONIEST
DS DONSIEST
DW DOWNIEST
EG EGESTION
EL NOSELITE
EM MONETISE
SEMITONE
ER SEROTINE
ES ESSONITE
ET NOISETTE
TEOSINTE
FI NOTIFIES
GH HISTOGEN
GM MITOGENS
GP PONGIEST
GR GENITORS
ROSETING
GT TENTIGOS
HL HOTLINES
NEOLITHS
HM HOISTMEN
HP PHONIEST
SIPHONET
HR HORNIEST
HS HISTONES
HU OUTSHINE
IL ETIOLINS
IP SINOPITE
IS NOISIEST
IV NOVITIES
JR JOINTERS
JT JETTISON
KM TOKENISM
KN INKSTONE
KO NOOKIEST
KW WONKIEST
LL STELLION
LM MOLINETS
LN INSOLENT
LO LOONIEST
OILSTONE
LP POINTELS
PONTILES
TOPLINES
LR RETINOLS
LU ELUTIONS
OUTLINES
LV NOVELIST
VIOLENTS
LW TOWLINES
MN MENTIONS
MO EMOTIONS
MOONIEST
MP EMPTIONS
NEPOTISM
PIMENTOS
MS MOISTENS
NR INTONERS
TERNIONS
NS TENSIONS
NT TINSTONE
TONTINES
NU NOUNIEST
OR SNOOTIER
OS ISOTONES
OZ ZOONITES
PR POINTERS
PROTEINS
REPOINTS
PT NEPOTIST
QU QUESTION
RR INTRORSE
SNORTIER
RS TERSIONS
RT SNOTTIER
TENORIST
TRITONES
RU ROUTINES
SNOUTIER
RV INVESTOR
RY TYROSINE
RZ TRIZONES
SS SONSIEST
STENOSIS
ST SNOTTIES
STONIEST
SW SNOWIEST
TT TOTIENTS
TW TOWNIEST
UU TENUIOUS
VY VENOSITY

EINPRS 158
(PINERS)

AA PANARIES
AD SPRAINED
AE NAPERIES
AF FIREPANS
AG PREASING
SPEARING
AH HEPARINS
PARISHEN
SERAPHIN
AL PEARLINS
PRALINES
AN PANNIERS
AP SNAPPIER
AT PAINTERS
PANTRIES
PERTAINS
PINASTER
PRISTANE
REPAINTS
AU UNPRAISE
AW SPAWNIER
BE PEBRINES
CD PRESCIND
CH PINCHERS
CO CONSPIRE
INCORPSE
CS PRINCESS
DG SPRINGED
DI INSPIRED
DL SPELDRIN
DO DISPONER
POINDERS
PRISONED
DT SPRINTED
EG SPEERING
SPREEING
EH INSPHERE
EI PINERIES
EL PILSENER
EO ISOPRENE
PIONEERS
ER REPINERS
ES EREPSINS
RIPENESS
EU PENURIES
RESUPINE
FO FORPINES
GH SPHERING
GI SPEIRING
GL PINGLERS
SPERLING
SPRINGLE
GM IMPREGNS
GO PERIGONS
REPOSING
SPONGIER
GP REPPINGS
GR SPERRING
SPRINGER
GS PRESSING
SPERSING
SPRINGES
GT PRESTING
GU PERSUING
PERUSING
HM PHRENISM
HU PUNISHER
IM PRIMINES
IO RIPIENOS
IP SNIPPIER
IR INSPIRER
IS INSPIRES
IT PRISTINE
JU JUNIPERS
KL SPRINKLE
KU SPUNKIER
LO PROLINES
LS PILSNERS
LT SPLINTER
LU PURLINES
MS PRIMNESS
NS SPINNERS
NT ENPRINTS
NY SPINNERY
OO POISONER
SNOOPIER
SPOONIER
OP POPERINS
PROPINES
OR PRISONER
OS PORINESS
PRESSION
ROPINESS
OT POINTERS
PROTEINS
REPOINTS
OU PRUINOSE
OV OVERSPIN
PROVINES
PS SNIPPERS
RT PRINTERS
REPRINTS
SPRINTER
ST SPINSTER
TU REPUNITS
UNPRIEST
UNRIPEST

EINPST 148
(INSTEP)

AB BEPAINTS

AD DEPAINTS
AH PENTHIAS
THESPIAN
AI PIANISTE
AL PANTILES
PLAINEST
AN PANTINES
AO SAPONITE
AP NAPPIEST
AR PAINTERS
PANTRIES
PERTAINS
PINASTER
PRISTANE
REPAINTS
AS STEAPSIN
AT PATIENTS
AU PETUNIAS
SUPINATE
AY EPINASTY
CE PECTINES
PENTICES
CO PONCIEST
CS INSPECTS
CY PYCNITES
DE PENTISED
DL SPLINTED
DR SPRINTED
DS STIPENDS
EG STEEPING
EL PLENTIES
EM SEPIMENT
ES PENTISES
ET INEPTEST
SPINETTE
GL PELTINGS
PESTLING
GM PIGMENTS
GO PONGIEST
GP STEPPING
GR PRESTING
GT PETTINGS
SPETTING
HM SHIPMENT
HO PHONIEST
SIPHONET
IK PINKIEST
IO SINOPITE
IP NIPPIEST
IR PRISTINE
IS SNIPIEST
SPINIEST
LO POINTELS
PONTILES
TOPLINES
LR SPLINTER
LS PLENISTS
MO EMPTIONS
NEPOTISM
PIMENTOS
MS MISSPENT
MU NUMPTIES
NR ENPRINTS
NS SPINNETS
OR POINTERS
PROTEINS
REPOINTS
OT NEPOTIST
PS SNIPPETS
PY SNIPPETY
RR PRINTERS
REPRINTS
SPRINTER
RS SPINSTER
RU REPUNITS
UNPRIEST
UNRIPEST
TX SPINTEXT
TY TINTYPES

EINRSS 249
(RESINS)

AC ARSENICS
CERASINS
RACINESS
AD ARIDNESS
SARDINES
AE SENARIES
AF FAIRNESS
SANSERIF
SERAFINS
AG REASSIGN
SEARINGS
SERINGAS
AH ARSHINES
AI AIRINESS
AL RAINLESS
AM SEMINARS
SIRNAMES
AN INSNARES
AO ERASIONS
SENSORIA
AT ARTINESS
RESIANTS
RETSINAS
SNARIEST
STAINERS
STARNIES
STEARINS
AU SENARIUS
AW WARINESS
AX XERANSIS
BE NEBRISES
BK BRISKENS
BU SUBERINS
CD DISCERNS
RESCINDS
CE CERESINS
SCRIENES
CH RICHNESS
CI SERICINS
CK SNICKERS
CO NECROSIS
SERICONS
CP PRINCESS
CT CISTERNS
DG DRESSING
DI INDRISES
INSIDERS
DK REDSKINS
DL RINDLESS
DO INDORSES
DU INSUREDS
SUNDRIES
EE EERINESS
EF FINESSER
RIFENESS
EG GREISENS
EI RESINISE
SIRENISE
EL REINLESS
EO ESSOINER
EP EREPSINS
RIPENESS
ER RESINERS
ET INTERESS
SENTRIES
TRENISES
EU ENURESIS
EV INVERSES
VERSINES
FF SNIFFERS
FM FIRMNESS
FT SNIFTERS
FU INFUSERS
GG GRESSING
SNIGGERS
GL RINGLESS
SLINGERS
GM GRIMNESS
GO GORINESS
SIGNORES
GP PRESSING
SPERSING
SPRINGES
GT RESTINGS
STINGERS
TRESSING
TRIGNESS
GV SERVINGS
VERSINGS
GW SWINGERS
GY SYRINGES
HO HERISSON
HU INRUSHES
IM MIRINESS
IO IONISERS
IRONISES
IP INSPIRES
IT SINISTER
IW WIRINESS
KK SKINKERS
KL SLINKERS
KN SKINNERS
KT STINKERS
LP PILSNERS
LT SLINTERS
SNIRTLES
MO MERSIONS
MP PRIMNESS
MT ENTRISMS
MINSTERS
TRIMNESS
MU NEURISMS
NP SPINNERS
OO EROSIONS
OP PORINESS
PRESSION
ROPINESS
OS ROSINESS
OT TERSIONS
OU NEUROSIS
RESINOUS
OV VERSIONS
PP SNIPPERS
PT SPINSTER
RU INSURERS
ST INSTRESS
SU SUNRISES
TT ENTRISTS
STINTERS
XY SYRINXES

EINRST 17
(INTERS)

AA ANTISERA
ARTESIAN
RESINATA
AB ATEBRINS
BANISTER
AC CANISTER
CARNIEST
CISTERNA
CREATINS
NACRITES
SCANTIER
AD DETRAINS
RANDIEST
STRAINED
AE ARSENITE
RESINATE
STEARINE
TRAINEES
AF FENITARS
AG ANGRIEST
ASTRINGE
GANISTER
GANTRIES
GRANITES
INGRATES
RANGIEST
REASTING
STEARING
TASERING
AH HAIRNETS
INEARTHS
THERIANS
AI INERTIAS
RAINIEST
AJ NARTJIES
AK KERATINS
NARKIEST
AL ENTRAILS
LATRINES
RATLINES
TRENAILS
AM MINARETS
RAIMENTS
AN ENTRAINS
TRANNIES
AO ANOESTRI
ARSONITE
NOTARIES
NOTARISE
ROSINATE
AP PAINTERS
PANTRIES
PERTAINS
PINASTER
PRISTANE
REPAINTS
AR RESTRAIN
RETRAINS
STRAINER
TERRAINS
TRAINERS
TRANSIRE
AS ARTINESS
RESIANTS
RETSINAS
SNARIEST
STAINERS
STARNIES
STEARINS
AT INTREATS
NITRATES
STRAITEN
TARTINES
TERTIANS
AU RUINATES
TAURINES
URANITES
URINATES
AW TINWARES
BI BRINIEST
BO BORNITES
RIBSTONE
BT BITTERNS
BU TRIBUNES
TURBINES
CE CENTRIES
ENTERICS
ENTICERS
SCIENTER
SECRETIN
CG CRESTING
CH CHRISTEN
CITHERNS
SNITCHER
CI CITRINES
CRINITES
INCITERS
CK STRICKEN
CM CENTRISM
CO CORNIEST
RECTIONS
CS CISTERNS
CT CENTRIST
CITTERNS
CU CURNIEST
DD STRIDDEN
DE INSERTED
NERDIEST
RESIDENT
SINTERED
TRENDIES
DG STRINGED
DI DISINTER
INDITERS
NITRIDES
RINDIEST
DL SNIRTLED
TENDRILS
TRINDLES
DO DRONIEST
DP SPRINTED
DT STRIDENT
TRIDENTS
DU INTRUDES
DX DEXTRINS
EE ETERNISE
TEENSIER
EF FERNIEST
EG GENTRIES
INTEGERS
REESTING
STEERING
STREIGNE
EI ERINITES
NITERIES
EK KERNITES
EL LISTENER
SILENTER
EN INTENSER
INTERNES
EO SEROTINE
ER INSERTER
REINSERT
REINTERS
RENTIERS
TERRINES
ES INTERESS
SENTRIES
TRENISES
ET INERTEST
INTEREST
STERNITE
EU ESURIENT
NEURITES
RETINUES
REUNITES
EV NERVIEST
REINVEST
SERVIENT
SIRVENTE
EX INTERSEX
EY SERENITY
FI SNIFTIER
FS SNIFTERS
GH RIGHTENS
GI GIRNIEST
IGNITERS
REISTING
STINGIER
STRIGINE
GL LINGSTER
RINGLETS
STERLING
TINGLERS
TRINGLES
GN STERNING
GO GENITORS
ROSETING
GP PRESTING
GR RESTRING
RINGSTER
STRINGER
GS RESTINGS
STINGERS
TRESSING
TRIGNESS
GT GITTERNS
GV STERVING
GW STREWING
WRESTING
HI INHERITS
HK RETHINKS
THINKERS
HN THINNERS
HO HORNIEST
HZ ZITHERNS
IL NIRLIEST
NITRILES
IM INTERIMS
MINISTER
IP PRISTINE
IS SINISTER
IT NITRITES
STINTIER
IU NEURITIS

IV INVITERS
VINTRIES
VITRINES
JO JOINTERS
KL LINKSTER
STRINKLE
TINKLERS
KS STINKERS
KT KNITTERS
TRINKETS
LM MINSTREL
LO RETINOLS
LP SPLINTER
LS SLINTERS
SNIRTLES
LU INSULTER
LUSTRINE
LY TINSELRY
MS ENTRISMS
MINSTERS
TRIMNESS
MU TERMINUS
MY ENTRYISM
MISENTRY
NO INTONERS
TERNIONS
NP ENPRINTS
NU RUNNIEST
STURNINE
NV VINTNERS
OO SNOOTIER
OP POINTERS
PROTEINS
REPOINTS
OR INTRORSE
SNORTIER
OS TERSIONS
OT SNOTTIER
TENORIST
TRITONES
OU ROUTINES
SNOUTIER
OV INVESTOR
OY TYROSINE
OZ TRIZONES
PR PRINTERS
REPRINTS
SPRINTER
PS SPINSTER
PU REPUNITS
UNPRIEST
UNRIPEST
QU SQUINTER
SS INSTRESS
ST ENTRISTS
STINTERS
TU RUNTIEST
TW TWINTERS
TY ENTRYIST
UV UNRIVETS
VENTURIS
UW UNWRITES

EINRSV 226
(VINERS)
AD INVADERS
SANDIVER
AG VINEGARS
AH ENRAVISH
VANISHER
AL RAVELINS
AO AVERSION
AU VAURIENS
AV VERVAINS
CU INCURVES
CV CRIVVENS
DI DIVINERS
EE VENERIES
EG SEVERING
VEERINGS
EI VINERIES
EL LIVENERS
EM MINEVERS
EN INNERVES
NERVINES
EO EVERSION
ER VERNIERS
ES INVERSES
VERSINES
ET NERVIEST
REINVEST
SERVIENT
SIRVENTE
EU UNIVERSE
GI REVISING
GS SERVINGS
VERSINGS
GT STERVING
GW SWERVING
IM MINIVERS
IO REVISION
VISIONER
IT INVITERS
VINTRIES
VITRINES
NO ENVIRONS
NT VINTNERS
OP OVERSPIN
PROVINES
OS VERSIONS
OT INVESTOR
OU SOUVENIR
TU UNRIVETS
VENTURIS

EINRTT 76
(TINTER)
AA REATTAIN
AC INTERACT
AD NITRATED
AG ARETTING
TREATING
AL RATTLINE
AM MARTINET
AO TENTORIA
AP TRIPTANE
AS INTREATS
NITRATES
STRAITEN
TARTINES
TERTIANS
AU TAINTURE
BE REBITTEN
BS BITTERNS
CE RETICENT
CO CONTRITE
CORNETTI
CS CENTRIST
CITTERNS
CU INTERCUT
TINCTURE
DO INTORTED
DS STRIDENT
TRIDENTS
EE REINETTE
TEENTIER
EH THIRTEEN
EI INTERTIE
RETINITE
EL NETTLIER
EN INTERNET
RENITENT
EO TENORITE
ES INERTEST
INTEREST
STERNITE
EY ENTIRETY
ETERNITY
FG FRETTING
FL FLITTERN
FU UNFITTER
GO OTTERING
GS GITTERNS
GU UTTERING
IM INTERMIT
IS NITRITES
STINTIER
KO KNOTTIER
KS KNITTERS
TRINKETS
LO TROTLINE
NO TONTINER
NU NUTRIENT
OS SNOTTIER
TENORIST
TRITONES
OU RITENUTO
PU INPUTTER
SS ENTRISTS
STINTERS
SU RUNTIEST
SW TWINTERS
SY ENTRYIST

EINRTU 25
(TUNIER)
AA INAURATE
AB BRAUNITE
URBANITE
AD DATURINE
INDURATE
RUINATED
URINATED
AH HAURIENT
AJ JAUNTIER
AL AUNTLIER
RETINULA
TENURIAL
AM RUMINATE
AP PAINTURE
AQ QUAINTER
AS RUINATES
TAURINES
URANITES
URINATES
AT TAINTURE
AV VAUNTIER
BD TURBINED
UNDERBIT
BS TRIBUNES
TURBINES
CC CINCTURE
CE CEINTURE
ENURETIC
CG ERUCTING
CH RUTHENIC
CI NEURITIC
CL LINCTURE
CO NEUROTIC
CS CURNIEST
CT INTERCUT
TINCTURE
DD INTRUDED
DE REUNITED
DI UNTIDIER
DM RUDIMENT
DP TURNIPED
DR INTRUDER
DS INTRUDES
DW UNDERWIT
EG GENITURE
EM MUTINEER
ES ESURIENT
NEURITES
RETINUES
REUNITES
FG FEUTRING
REFUTING
FT UNFITTER
GI INTRIGUE
GN RETUNING
GO OUTREIGN
ROUTEING
GP ERUPTING
REPUTING
GT UTTERING
IS NEURITIS
JO JOINTURE
KP TURNPIKE
KR RETURNIK
LS INSULTER
LUSTRINE
LV VIRULENT
MS TERMINUS
NO NEUTRINO
NS RUNNIEST
STURNINE
NT NUTRIENT
OP ERUPTION
OS ROUTINES
SNOUTIER
OT RITENUTO
PR PRURIENT
PS REPUNITS
UNPRIEST
UNRIPEST
PT INPUTTER
QS SQUINTER
ST RUNTIEST
SV UNRIVETS
VENTURIS
SW UNWRITES
UV UNVIRTUE

EINSST 218
(INSETS)
AB BASINETS
BASSINET
BESAINTS
BESTAINS
AC CINEASTS
SCANTIES
AD SANDIEST
AG EASTINGS
GENISTAS
GIANTESS
SEATINGS
TEASINGS
TSIGANES
AH ANTHESIS
SHANTIES
AI ISATINES
SANITIES
SANITISE
AK SNAKIEST
AL EASTLINS
ELASTINS
SALIENTS
STANIELS
AM MANTISES
MATINESS
AN INSANEST
AO ASSIENTO
ASTONIES
AP STEAPSIN
AR ARTINESS
RESIANTS
RETSINAS
SNARIEST
STAINERS
STARNIES
STEARINS
AS SAINTESS
SESTINAS
AT INSTATES
NASTIEST
SATINETS
TITANESS
BI STIBINES
BO EBONISTS
CE CENTESIS
CH SNITCHES
CK SNICKETS
CL STENCILS
CO SECTIONS
CP INSPECTS
CR CISTERNS
CY CYSTINES
DD DISTENDS
DE DESTINES
DI INSISTED
TIDINESS
DM MINDSETS
DO DONSIEST
DP STIPENDS
DS DISNESTS
DISSENTS
DT DENTISTS
DU DISTUNES
EL SETLINES
EN TENNISES
EO ESSONITE
EP PENTISES
ER INTERESS
SENTRIES
TRENISES
ES SESTINES
EW NEWSIEST
EX SIXTEENS
EY SYENITES
FF STIFFENS
FR SNIFTERS
GJ JESTINGS
GL GLISTENS
SINGLETS
GN NESTINGS
GR RESTINGS
STINGERS
TRESSING
TRIGNESS
GT SETTINGS
TESTINGS
GV VESTINGS
GW STEWINGS
WESTINGS
HI SHINIEST
SHINTIES
HN THINNESS
HO HISTONES
HS THISNESS
IK SINKIEST
IN TININESS
IO NOISIEST
IP SNIPIEST
SPINIEST
IR SINISTER
IU UNITISES
KL LENTISKS
KR STINKERS
KT SKINTEST
LP PLENISTS
LR SLINTERS
SNIRTLES
LT TINTLESS
LU UTENSILS
LW WESTLINS
MO MOISTENS
MP MISSPENT
MR ENTRISMS
MINSTERS
TRIMNESS
MU MISTUNES
NO TENSIONS
NP SPINNETS
NU SUNNIEST
OO ISOTONES
OR TERSIONS
OS SONSIEST
STENOSIS
OT SNOTTIES
STONIEST
OW SNOWIEST
PP SNIPPETS
PR SPINSTER
QU INQUESTS
RS INSTRESS
RT ENTRISTS
STINTERS
SS SENSISTS
TW ENTWISTS
TWINSETS
UW UNWISEST
UX UNSEXIST
XY SYNTEXIS

EINSTT 160
(INTEST)
AA ASTATINE
SANITATE
TANAISTE

AB TABINETS
AC CANTIEST
NICTATES
TETANICS
AD INSTATED
AE ANISETTE
TETANIES
TETANISE
AF FAINTEST
AG ESTATING
TANGIEST
AH HESITANT
AJ JANTIEST
AN ANTIENTS
STANNITE
AP PATIENTS
AR INTREATS
NITRATES
STRAITEN
TARTINES
TERTIANS
AS INSTATES
NASTIEST
SATINETS
TITANESS
AT NATTIEST
AV TASTEVIN
AW TAWNIEST
BE BENTIEST
BG BETTINGS
BI STIBNITE
BO BOTTINES
BR BITTERNS
BU BUNTIEST
CO CENTOIST
STENOTIC
CR CENTRIST
CITTERNS
DE DINETTES
DR STRIDENT
TRIDENTS
DS DENTISTS
EE TEENIEST
EF FEINTEST
EG GENTIEST
EI ENTITIES
EL ENTITLES
EM MINETTES
EN SENTIENT
EO NOISETTE
TEOSINTE
EP INEPTEST
SPINETTE
ER INERTEST
INTEREST
STERNITE
ET NETTIEST
TENTIEST
EW TENTWISE
TWENTIES
EX EXISTENT
FI NIFTIEST
FM FITMENTS
GG GETTINGS
GH SHETTING
TIGHTENS
GL LETTINGS
SETTLING
GN NETTINGS
STENTING
TENTINGS
GO TENTIGOS
GP PETTINGS
SPETTING
GR GITTERNS
GS SETTINGS
TESTINGS
GT STETTING
HN THINNEST
IL LINTIEST
IM MINTIEST
IN TINNIEST
IR NITRITES
STINTIER
IT NITTIEST
TINTIEST
IW TWINIEST
JO JETTISON
KL KNITTLES
KR KNITTERS
TRINKETS
KS SKINTEST
LS TINTLESS
LU LUTENIST
MU MINUTEST
NO TINSTONE
TONTINES
OP NEPOTIST
OR SNOTTIER
TENORIST
TRITONES
OS SNOTTIES
STONIEST
OT TOTIENTS
OW TOWNIEST
PX SPINTEXT
PY TINTYPES
QU QUINTETS
RS ENTRISTS
STINTERS
RU RUNTIEST
RW TWINTERS
RY ENTRYIST
SW ENTWISTS
TWINSETS
TU NUTTIEST
TW TWITTENS

EINSTU 81
(UNITES)
AD AUDIENTS
SINUATED
AG SAUTEING
AJ JAUNTIES
AL ALUNITES
INSULATE
AP PETUNIAS
SUPINATE
AQ ANTIQUES
QUANTISE
AR RUINATES
TAURINES
URANITES
URINATES
AV SUIVANTE
BB NUBBIEST
BM BITUMENS
BO BOUNTIES
BR TRIBUNES
TURBINES
BT BUNTIEST
CI CUTINISE
CL CUTLINES
TUNICLES
CO COUNTIES
CR CURNIEST
DD DISTUNED
DE DETINUES
DF UNSIFTED
DG DUNGIEST
DI DISUNITE
NUDITIES
UNITISED
UNTIDIES
DL DILUENTS
INSULTED
UNLISTED
DM MISTUNED
DN DUNNIEST
DUNNITES
DQ SQUINTED
DR INTRUDES
DS DISTUNES
DU UNSUITED
EG EUGENIST
EQ QUIETENS
ER ESURIENT
NEURITES
RETINUES
REUNITES
FK FUNKIEST
FN FUNNIEST
GG GUESTING
GUNGIEST
GQ QUESTING
HK HUNKIEST
HO OUTSHINE
IM MUTINIES
IQ INQUIETS
IR NEURITIS
IS UNITISES
IZ UNITIZES
JK JUNKIEST
KZ KUNZITES
LM MUSLINET
LO ELUTIONS
OUTLINES
LR INSULTER
LUSTRINE
LS UTENSILS
LT LUTENIST
MP NUMPTIES
MR TERMINUS
MS MISTUNES
MT MINUTEST
NO NOUNIEST
NR RUNNIEST
STURNINE
NS SUNNIEST
NW UNTWINES
OQ QUESTION
OR ROUTINES
SNOUTIER
OU TENUIOUS
PR REPUNITS
UNPRIEST
UNRIPEST
QR SQUINTER
QS INQUESTS
QT QUINTETS
QU UNIQUEST
UNQUIETS
RT RUNTIEST
RV UNRIVETS
VENTURIS
RW UNWRITES
SW UNWISEST
SX UNSEXIST
TT NUTTIEST

EIOPST 101
(SOPITE)
AC ECTOPIAS
AD DIOPTASE
AL SPOLIATE
AN SAPONITE
AP APPOSITE
AS SOAPIEST
BY BIOTYPES
CD DESPOTIC
CE ECTOPIES
PICOTEES
CH POSTICHE
POTICHES
CK POCKIEST
CL TOECLIPS
CN PONCIEST
CR PERSICOT
CS COPSIEST
DD PODDIEST
DE EPIDOTES
POETISED
DG PODGIEST
DR DIOPTERS
DIOPTRES
DIPTEROS
PERIDOTS
PROTEIDS
RIPOSTED
DS DEPOSITS
TOPSIDES
EL PETIOLES
EM EPITOMES
EPSOMITE
EP EPITOPES
ER POETRIES
ES POETISES
EZ POETIZES
FO POOFIEST
FR FIREPOTS
GN PONGIEST
GO GOOPIEST
HL HELISTOP
HOPLITES
ISOPLETH
HN PHONIEST
SIPHONET
HP HOPPIEST
POETSHIP
HR TROPHIES
IL PISOLITE
POLITIES
IM OPTIMISE
IN SINOPITE
IV POSITIVE
KR PORKIEST
LM POLEMIST
LN POINTELS
PONTILES
TOPLINES
LO LOOPIEST
LR POITRELS
LS PISTOLES
PTILOSES
SLOPIEST
LT PISTOLET
PLOTTIES
POLITEST
LX EXPLOITS
MM METOPISM
MN EMPTIONS
NEPOTISM
PIMENTOS
MP MOPPIEST
MR IMPOSTER
MY PEYOTISM
NR POINTERS
PROTEINS
REPOINTS
NT NEPOTIST
OP OPPOSITE
OR PORTOISE
ROOPIEST
OS ISOTOPES
OV POOVIEST
PP POPPIEST
PS SOPPIEST
RR PIERROTS
SPORTIER
RS PERIOSTS
PROSIEST
REPOSITS
RIPOSTES
TRIPOSES
RT PORTIEST
RISPETTO
SPOTTIER
RU ROUPIEST
SPOUTIER
RV PIVOTERS
SPORTIVE
SS SEPIOSTS
SU SOUPIEST
SY ISOTYPES
TT POTTIEST
TU POUTIEST
TY PEYOTIST
UW WIPEOUTS

EIORSS 214
(SORIES)
AB ISOBARES
AG ARGOSIES
AL SOLARISE
AN ERASIONS
SENSORIA
AR ROSARIES
AV SAVORIES
BD DISROBES
BE SOBERISE
BF FIBROSES
BT SORBITES
CD DISCOERS
CH CHORISES
ORCHESIS
ORCHISES
CN NECROSIS
SERICONS
CP PERSICOS
CR CROSIERS
CT CROSSTIE
CU SCOURIES
CV CORSIVES
CW SCOWRIES
CX SIXSCORE
DH DISHORSE
HIDROSES
DK DROSKIES
DL SOLDIERS
DM MISDOERS
DN INDORSES
DP DISPOSER
DROPSIES
DR DROSSIER
DS DOSSIERS
DT STEROIDS
DU DESIROUS
DV DEVISORS
EH HEROISES
EI OSIERIES
EM ISOMERES
EN ESSOINER
ER ROSERIES
ROSIERES
ET EROTESIS
EX OREXISES
FH ROSEFISH
FL FLOSSIER
FT FOISTERS
GL GLOSSIER
GN GORINESS
SIGNORES
GT GORSIEST
STRIGOSE
GU GRISEOUS
HL SLOSHIER
HM HEROISMS
HN HERISSON
HP ROSEHIPS
SPOSHIER
HT HOISTERS
HORSIEST
HOSTRIES
SHORTIES
IN IONISERS
IRONISES
IT RIOTISES
LP SPOILERS
LS RISSOLES
LU SOILURES
MN MERSIONS
MP IMPOSERS
PROMISES
MR MORRISES
MT EROTISMS
MORTISES
TRISOMES
MV VERISMOS
NO EROSIONS
NP PORINESS
PRESSION
ROPINESS
NS ROSINESS
NT TERSIONS
NU NEUROSIS
RESINOUS
NV VERSIONS
OR SORORISE
PR PRIORESS
PT PERIOSTS

PROSIEST
REPOSITS
RIPOSTES
TRIPOSES
RT RESISTOR
ROISTERS
SORRIEST
RV REVISORS
TT STOITERS
TY SEROSITY

EIORST 5
(TORIES)
AB SABOTIER
AD ASTEROID
AE ETAERIOS
AH HOARIEST
AJ JAROSITE
AL SOTERIAL
AM AMORTISE
ATOMISER
AN ANOESTRI
ARSONITE
NOTARIES
NOTARISE
ROSINATE
AR ROARIEST
ROTARIES
AV VOTARIES
BC BISECTOR
BD DEBITORS
BI ORBITIES
BL STROBILE
TRILOBES
BN BORNITES
RIBSTONE
BO ROBOTISE
BR ORBITERS
BS SORBITES
BY SOBRIETY
CC CORTICES
CD CORDITES
CE COTERIES
ESOTERIC
CH ROTCHIES
THEORICS
CK CORKIEST
ROCKIEST
STOCKIER
CL CLOISTER
COISTREL
COSTLIER
CREOLIST
CM MORTICES
CN CORNIEST
RECTIONS
CP PERSICOT
CS CROSSTIE
CT COTTIERS
CU CITREOUS
OUTCRIES
CV EVICTORS
VORTICES
CX EXCITORS
EXORCIST
DG GRODIEST
STODGIER
DI DIORITES
DK DORKIEST
DL STOLIDER
DM MORTISED
DN DRONIEST
DP DIOPTERS
DIOPTRES
DIPTEROS
PERIDOTS
PROTEIDS
RIPOSTED
DS STEROIDS
DT DORTIEST
DU IODURETS
OUTRIDES
OUTSIDER
SUITORED
DW ROWDIEST
WORDIEST
EG ERGOTISE
EH ISOTHERE
THEORIES
THEORISE
EL LITEROSE
TROELIES
EM TIRESOME
EN SEROTINE
EP POETRIES
ES EROTESIS
FF FORFEITS
FK FORKIEST
FL FLORIEST
TREFOILS
FM SETIFORM
FO ROOFIEST
FP FIREPOTS
FR FROSTIER
ROTIFERS
FS FOISTERS
FU FOUSTIER
FW FROWIEST
GH GHOSTIER
GM ERGOTISM
GORMIEST
GN GENITORS
ROSETING
GS GORSIEST
STRIGOSE
GU GOUSTIER
GV VERTIGOS
GY OYSTRIGE
GZ ZORGITES
HM ISOTHERM
MOITHERS
HN HORNIEST
HP TROPHIES
HR HERITORS
HS HOISTERS
HORSIEST
HOSTRIES
SHORTIES
HT THEORIST
THORITES
HU OUTHIRES
HV OVERHITS
HW WORTHIES
IL ROILIEST
IR RIOTRIES
IS RIOTISES
IZ RIOTIZES
JN JOINTERS
KP PORKIEST
LL TRILLOES
TROLLIES
LN RETINOLS
LO TROOLIES
LP POITRELS
LT TRIOLETS
LU LOURIEST
OUTLIERS
MO MOORIEST
MOTORISE
ROOMIEST
MP IMPOSTER
MR MORTISER
STORMIER
MS EROTISMS
MORTISES
TRISOMES
MT OMITTERS
MU MISROUTE
MOISTURE
MW MISWROTE
WORMIEST
MY ISOMETRY
NN INTONERS
TERNIONS
NO SNOOTIER
NP POINTERS
PROTEINS
REPOINTS
NR INTRORSE
SNORTIER
NS TERSIONS
NT SNOTTIER
TENORIST
TRITONES
NU ROUTINES
SNOUTIER
NV INVESTOR
NY TYROSINE
NZ TRIZONES
OP PORTOISE
ROOPIEST
OR ROOTSIER
OT ROOTIEST
TORTOISE
PR PIERROTS
SPORTIER
PS PERIOSTS
PROSIEST
REPOSITS
RIPOSTES
TRIPOSES
PT PORTIEST
RISPETTO
SPOTTIER
PU ROUPIEST
SPOUTIER
PV PIVOTERS
SPORTIVE
QU QUOITERS
RR ERRORIST
RS RESISTOR
ROISTERS
SORRIEST
RT RORTIEST
RU STOURIER
RV SERVITOR
ST STOITERS
SY SEROSITY
TU TUTORISE
TV VIRETOTS
UV VIRTUOSE
VITREOUS
VOITURES

EIORSV 127
(VIROSE)
AC COVARIES
VARICOSE
AG VIRAGOES
AL OVERSAIL
VALORISE
VARIOLES
VOLARIES
AN AVERSION
AP VAPORISE
AS SAVORIES
AT VOTARIES
AW AVOWRIES
BD OVERBIDS
CD DISCOVER
DIVORCES
CS CORSIVES
CT EVICTORS
VORTICES
CY VICEROYS
DE OVERSIDE
DP DISPROVE
PROVIDES
DS DEVISORS
EL OVERLIES
RELIEVOS
VOLERIES
EN EVERSION
EW OVERWISE
EZ OVERSIZE
FG FORGIVES
FH OVERFISH
GT VERTIGOS
GU GRIEVOUS
HT OVERHITS
IN REVISION
VISIONER
KP OVERSKIP
LP OVERSLIP
MP IMPROVES
MS VERISMOS
MW OVERSWIM
NN ENVIRONS
NP OVERSPIN
PROVINES
NS VERSIONS
NT INVESTOR
NU SOUVENIR
PT PIVOTERS
SPORTIVE
PU PERVIOUS
PREVIOUS
VIPEROUS
RS REVISORS
RT SERVITOR
RU OUVRIERS
RV REVIVORS
RY REVISORY
TT VIRETOTS
TU VIRTUOSE
VITREOUS
VOITURES

EIOSTT 93
(OTTIES)
AC OSCITATE
AG GOATIEST
AL TOTALISE
AS TOASTIES
BI BIOTITES
BN BOTTINES
CD COTTISED
CL COLETITS
CN CENTOIST
STENOTIC
CR COTTIERS
CS COTTISES
DL DOILTEST
DM DEMOTIST
DR DORTIEST
DT DOTTIEST
EN NOISETTE
TEOSINTE
FF TOFFIEST
FL LOFTIEST
FM OFTTIMES
FO FOOTIEST
GH GOTHITES
GN TENTIGOS
GS EGOTISTS
GU GOUTIEST
HM MOTHIEST
HR THEORIST
THORITES
HS TOSHIEST
IS OSTEITIS
OTITISES
JL JOLTIEST
JN JETTISON
LM MOTLIEST
LP PISTOLET
PLOTTIES
POLITEST
LR TRIOLETS
LT STILETTO
MM TOTEMISM
MR OMITTERS
MS MOISTEST
MT MOTTIEST
TOTEMIST
MU TITMOUSE
NN TINSTONE
TONTINES
NP NEPOTIST
NR SNOTTIER
TENORIST
TRITONES
NS SNOTTIES
STONIEST
NT TOTIENTS
NW TOWNIEST
OR ROOTIEST
TORTOISE
OS SOOTIEST
TOOTSIES
PR PORTIEST
RISPETTO
SPOTTIER
PT POTTIEST
PU POUTIEST
PY PEYOTIST
RR RORTIEST
RS STOITERS
RU TUTORISE
RV VIRETOTS
SS TOSSIEST
SU TOUSIEST
SW TOWSIEST
TT TOTTIEST
TU TOUTIEST
UZ TOUZIEST
WZ TOWZIEST

EIPRST 147
(STRIPE)
AA ASPIRATE
PARASITE
SEPTARIA
AC CRAPIEST
CRISPATE
PICRATES
PRACTISE
AD DIPTERAS
RAPIDEST
SPIRATED
TARSIPED
TRAIPSED
AE PETARIES
AG GRAPIEST
AI PARITIES
AK PARKIEST
AL PILASTER
PLAISTER
PLAITERS
AM APTERISM
PRIMATES
AN PAINTERS
PANTRIES
PERTAINS
PINASTER
PRISTANE
REPAINTS
AP PERIAPTS
AS PASTRIES
PIASTRES
RASPIEST
TRAIPSES
AV PRIVATES
AW WIRETAPS
AY ASPERITY
CD PREDICTS
SCRIPTED
CE CREPIEST
RECEIPTS
CH PITCHERS
SPITCHER
CI PICRITES
PRICIEST
CK PRICKETS
CO PERSICOT
CR RESCRIPT
CS CRISPEST
CU CREPITUS
CUPRITES
PICTURES
PIECRUST
DE PRIESTED
RESPITED
DI RIPTIDES
SPIRITED
DM DIREMPTS
DN SPRINTED
DO DIOPTERS

DIOPTRES
DIPTEROS
PERIDOTS
PROTEIDS
RIPOSTED
DP STRIPPED
DU DISPUTER
STUPIDER
EE PEERIEST
STEEPIER
EG PRESTIGE
EH TREESHIP
EK PERKIEST
EL EPISTLER
PELTRIES
PERLITES
REPTILES
EM EMPTIERS
EO POETRIES
ES RESPITES
ET PRETTIES
EY PERSEITY
FI SPITFIRE
FO FIREPOTS
GN PRESTING
HL PHILTERS
PHILTRES
HO TROPHIES
HS HIPSTERS
THRIPSES
HW WHIPSTER
IL TRIPLIES
IN PRISTINE
IR STRIPIER
IS SPIRIEST
IT RISPETTI
TRIPIEST
IU PURITIES
IV PRIVIEST
IY PYRITISE
KO PORKIEST
LN SPLINTER
LO POITRELS
LP RIPPLETS
STIPPLER
TIPPLERS
TRIPPLES
LS SPIRTLES
LT SPLITTER
TRIPLETS
LY PRIESTLY
SPRITELY
MM PRIMMEST
MO IMPOSTER
MS IMPRESTS
MU IMPUREST
IMPUTERS
STUMPIER
NN ENPRINTS
NO POINTERS
PROTEINS
REPOINTS
NR PRINTERS
REPRINTS
SPRINTER
NS SPINSTER
NU REPUNITS
UNPRIEST
UNRIPEST
OO PORTOISE
ROOPIEST
OR PIERROTS
SPORTIER
OS PERIOSTS
PROSIEST
REPOSITS
RIPOSTES
TRIPOSES
OT PORTIEST
RISPETTO
SPOTTIER
OU ROUPIEST
SPOUTIER
OV PIVOTERS
SPORTIVE
PR STRIPPER
TRIPPERS
PT TRIPPETS
QU QUIPSTER
RZ SPRITZER
SS PERSISTS
ST SPITTERS
TIPSTERS
SU PURSIEST
TU PURTIEST
PUTTIERS

EIRRST 165
(TRIERS)
AB ARBITERS
RAREBITS
AC ERRATICS
AE ARTERIES
REASTIER
AF FRATRIES
AH TRASHIER
AI RARITIES
AL RETIRALS
RETRIALS
TRAILERS
AN RESTRAIN
RETRAINS
STRAINER
TERRAINS
TRAINERS
TRANSIRE
AO ROARIEST
ROTARIES
AR STARRIER
TARRIERS
AS TARSIERS
AT RETRAITS
STRAITER
TARRIEST
AW STRAWIER
BH REBIRTHS
BO ORBITERS
BU BURRIEST
CE RECITERS
CK TRICKERS
CP RESCRIPT
CT CRITTERS
RESTRICT
STRICTER
CU CRUSTIER
RECRUITS
DE DESTRIER
DF DRIFTERS
DU STURDIER
EE REESTIER
RETIREES
EF FERRITES
EG REGISTER
EM MERRIEST
TRIREMES
EN INSERTER
REINSERT
REINTERS
RENTIERS
TERRINES
ER RETIRERS
TERRIERS
ES TRESSIER
EV REVERIST
RIVERETS
RIVETERS
EW REWRITES
FG GRIFTERS
FI FIRRIEST
FL TRIFLERS
FO FROSTIER
ROTIFERS
FT FRITTERS
FU FRITURES
FRUITERS
FURRIEST
GG TRIGGERS
GH RIGHTERS
GN RESTRING
RINGSTER
STRINGER
GT GRITTERS
GY REGISTRY
HI SHIRTIER
HO HERITORS
HT THIRSTER
HV THRIVERS
HW WHIRRETS
IO RIOTRIES
IP STRIPIER
IW WRISTIER
KS SKIRRETS
SKIRTERS
STRIKERS
LU SULTRIER
LW TWIRLERS
MM TRIMMERS
MO MORTISER
STORMIER
NO INTRORSE
SNORTIER
NP PRINTERS
REPRINTS
SPRINTER
OO ROOTSIER
OP PIERROTS
SPORTIER
OR ERRORIST
OS RESISTOR
ROISTERS
SORRIEST
OT RORTIEST
OU STOURIER
OV SERVITOR
PP STRIPPER
TRIPPERS
PZ SPRITZER
QU SQUIRTER
RS STIRRERS
SV STRIVERS
TU TRUSTIER

EIRSTT 104
(SITTER)
AA ARIETTAS
ARISTATE
AB BIRETTAS
AC CITRATES
CRISTATE
SCATTIER
AD STRAITED
STRIATED
TARDIEST
AE ARIETTES
ITERATES
TEARIEST
TREATIES
TREATISE
AG STRIGATE
AL TERTIALS
AM MISTREAT
TERATISM
AN INTREATS
NITRATES
STRAITEN
TARTINES
TERTIANS
AR RETRAITS
STRAITER
TARRIEST
AS ARTISTES
ARTSIEST
STRIATES
AT ATTRITES
RATTIEST
TARTIEST
TITRATES
AW WARTIEST
AX EXTRAITS
BL BRITTLES
TRIBLETS
BN BITTERNS
BU TRIBUTES
BY TREYBITS
CE TIERCETS
CH CHITTERS
RICHTEST
STITCHER
CI RECTITIS
CL CLITTERS
CN CENTRIST
CITTERNS
CO COTTIERS
CR CRITTERS
RESTRICT
STRICTER
CS TRISECTS
CU TUTRICES
DE TIREDEST
DH THIRSTED
THRISTED
DI DIRTIEST
TRITIDES
DN STRIDENT
TRIDENTS
DO DORTIEST
DU DETRITUS
EF FRISETTE
EG GRISETTE
TERGITES
EH ETHERIST
EL RETITLES
EM EMITTERS
TERMITES
EN INERTEST
INTEREST
STERNITE
EP PRETTIES
ES RESTIEST
FF TRIFFEST
FI RIFTIEST
FL FLITTERS
FR FRITTERS
FU TURFIEST
TURFITES
GG TRIGGEST
GH RIGHTEST
STREIGHT
GL GLITTERS
GN GITTERNS
GR GRITTERS
GT GRITTEST
HI SHITTIER
THIRTIES
HL THRISTLE
HO THEORIST
THORITES
HR THIRSTER
HW WHITRETS
WHITSTER
WHITTERS
IL STILTIER
IM METRITIS
IN NITRITES
STINTIER
IP RISPETTI
TRIPIEST
IU UTERITIS
IW TWISTIER
IZ RITZIEST
KN KNITTERS
TRINKETS
KS SKITTERS
LL TESTRILL
LO TRIOLETS
LP SPLITTER
TRIPLETS
LS SLITTERS
STILTERS
TESTRILS
LU SURTITLE
LW WRISTLET
LZ STRELITZ
MM TRIMMEST
MO OMITTERS
MS METRISTS
MU SMUTTIER
NO SNOTTIER
TENORIST
TRITONES
NS ENTRISTS
STINTERS
NU RUNTIEST
NW TWINTERS
NY ENTRYIST
OO ROOTIEST
TORTOISE
OP PORTIEST
RISPETTO
SPOTTIER
OR RORTIEST
OS STOITERS
OU TUTORISE
OV VIRETOTS
PP TRIPPETS
PS SPITTERS
TIPSTERS
PU PURTIEST
PUTTIERS
QU QUITTERS
RU TRUSTIER
SU RUSTIEST
TRUSTIES
SW TWISTERS
TU RUTTIEST
TW TWITTERS
UX TUTRIXES

EIRSTV 163
(STRIVE)
AA VARIATES
AB VIBRATES
AE EVIRATES
AG VIRGATES
VITRAGES
AI VAIRIEST
AO VOTARIES
AP PRIVATES
AS TRAVISES
AY VESTIARY
CD VERDICTS
CE VERTICES
CI VERISTIC
CO EVICTORS
VORTICES
CS VICTRESS
CU CURVIEST
DE VERDITES
EI VERITIES
EN NERVIEST
REINVEST
SERVIENT
SIRVENTE
ER REVERIST
RIVERETS
RIVETERS
ES SIEVERTS
TREVISES
VESTRIES
EV VETIVERS
EY SEVERITY
GN STERVING
GO VERTIGOS
HO OVERHITS
HR THRIVERS
IN INVITERS
VINTRIES
VITRINES
IP PRIVIEST
IS REVISITS
VISITERS
LU RIVULETS
MU VITREUMS
NN VINTNERS
NO INVESTOR
NU UNRIVETS
VENTURIS
OP PIVOTERS
SPORTIVE
OR SERVITOR

OT VIRETOTS
OU VIRTUOSE
VITREOUS
VOITURES
RS STRIVERS

ELNSTU 216
(LUNETS)
AB UNSTABLE
AD UNSALTED
AG LANGUETS
AI ALUNITES
INSULATE
AM NUTMEALS
AN ANNULETS
AR NEUTRALS
AV ENVAULTS
BS SUNBELTS
BT BLUNTEST
BU UNSUBTLE
CE ESCULENT
CF SCENTFUL
CI CUTLINES
TUNICLES
CO NOCTULES
CR LECTURNS
DI DILUENTS
INSULTED
UNLISTED
DR RUNDLETS
TRUNDLES
EL ENTELLUS
EO TOLUENES
ES TUNELESS
UNSTEELS
ET LUNETTES
UNSETTLE
FS NESTFULS
FT TENTFULS
GR GRUNTLES
HL NUTSHELL
HR LUTHERNS
IM MUSLINET
IO ELUTIONS
OUTLINES
IR INSULTER
LUSTRINE
IS UTENSILS
IT LUTENIST
OR TURNSOLE
OZ ZONULETS

ELORST 67
(TOLERS)
AB BLOATERS
SORTABLE
STORABLE
AC SECTORAL
AD DELATORS
LEOTARDS
LODESTAR
AE OLEASTER
AF FLOATERS
FORESTAL
REFLOATS
AG GLOATERS
LEGATORS
AH LOATHERS
AI SOTERIAL
AL REALLOTS
AM MOLERATS
AP PETROSAL
PROLATES
AR REALTORS
RELATORS
AU ROSULATE
AV LEVATORS
AY ROYALETS
AZ ZELATORS
BH BROTHELS
BI STROBILE
TRILOBES
BM TEMBLORS
BS BOLSTERS
LOBSTERS
BT BLOTTERS
BOTTLERS
BU BOULTERS
TROUBLES
CE CORSELET
ELECTORS
ELECTROS
SELECTOR
CH CHORTLES
CI CLOISTER
COISTREL
COSTLIER
CREOLIST
CS CORSLETS
COSTRELS
CROSSLET
CT CLOTTERS
CROTTLES
CU CLOTURES
CLOUTERS
COULTERS
CY COYSTREL
DD STRODDLE
STRODLED
TODDLERS
DI STOLIDER
DL DROLLEST
STROLLED
DP DROPLETS
DS OLDSTERS
STRODLES
DT DOTTRELS
EE SLOETREE
EH HOSTELER
EI LITEROSE
TROELIES
EL SOLLERET
EM MOLESTER
EN ENTRESOL
ET LORETTES
EU RESOLUTE
FG FROGLETS
FI FLORIEST
TREFOILS
FT FORTLETS
FW FELWORTS
HN HORNLETS
HS HOLSTERS
HOSTLERS
HT THROSTLE
HY HOSTELRY
II ROILIEST
IL TRILLOES
TROLLIES
IN RETINOLS
IO TROOLIES
IP POITRELS
IT TRIOLETS
IU LOURIEST
OUTLIERS
LP POLLSTER
LR STROLLER
TROLLERS
LY TROLLEYS
MM TROMMELS
MO TREMOLOS
NU TURNSOLE
OS ROOTLESS
OT ROOTLETS
OU TORULOSE
PT PLOTTERS
PU PLOUTERS
POULTERS
PW PLOWTERS
PY PROSTYLE
PROTYLES
ST SETTLORS
SLOTTERS
UY SOUTERLY
UROSTYLE

ELOSTU 173
(TOUSLE)
AB ABSOLUTE
AC LACTEOUS
LOCUSTAE
OSCULATE
AP OUTLEAPS
PETALOUS
AR ROSULATE
AT TOLUATES
AV OVULATES
AY AUTOLYSE
BD DOUBLETS
BR BOULTERS
TROUBLES
BY OBTUSELY
CD LOCUSTED
CE ELOCUTES
CH SELCOUTH
CN NOCTULES
CP COUPLETS
OCTUPLES
CR CLOTURES
CLOUTERS
COULTERS
CT CULOTTES
DI SOLITUDE
DP POSTLUDE
EN TOLUENES
EP EELPOUTS
OUTSLEEP
ER RESOLUTE
ES SETULOSE
EV EVOLUTES
VELOUTES
FI OUTFLIES
GI EULOGIST
IN ELUTIONS
OUTLINES
IR LOURIEST
OUTLIERS
IS LOUSIEST
IV OUTLIVES
SOLUTIVE
JP PULSOJET
LP POLLUTES
LS OUTSELLS
LT OUTTELLS
LW OUTSWELL
OUTWELLS
NR TURNSOLE
NZ ZONULETS
OR TORULOSE
OS OUTSOLES
PR PLOUTERS
POULTERS
PT OUTSLEPT
RY SOUTERLY
UROSTYLE
SU SETULOUS

ELRSTU 208
(RUSTLE)
AB BALUSTER
AC RAUCLEST
AE RESALUTE
AF REFUTALS
AG GAULTERS
GESTURAL
TRAGULES
AI URALITES
AN NEUTRALS
AO ROSULATE
AP APLUSTRE
AS SALUTERS
AT LUSTRATE
TUTELARS
AV VAULTERS
VESTURAL
BI BURLIEST
SUBTILER
BM STUMBLER
TUMBLERS
TUMBRELS
BO BOULTERS
TROUBLES
BS BLUSTERS
BUSTLERS
BY BLUSTERY
CE LECTURES
CI CURLIEST
UTRICLES
CK TRUCKLES
CN LECTURNS
CO CLOTURES
CLOUTERS
COULTERS
CS CLUSTERS
CUSTRELS
CT CLUTTERS
SCUTTLER
CU CULTURES
CV CULVERTS
CY CLUSTERY
DE LUSTERED
RESULTED
ULSTERED
DI DILUTERS
LURIDEST
DN RUNDLETS
TRUNDLES
DS STRUDELS
EF FLEURETS
EO RESOLUTE
FF TRUFFLES
FS FLUSTERS
FT FLUTTERS
FU FRUSTULE
FY FLUSTERY
GG STRUGGLE
GI GURLIEST
GN GRUNTLES
HI LUTHIERS
HN LUTHERNS
HS HURTLESS
HUSTLERS
RUTHLESS
II UTILISER
IM MURLIEST
IN INSULTER
LUSTRINE
IO LOURIEST
OUTLIERS
IQ QUILTERS
IR SULTRIER
IS SURLIEST
IT SURTITLE
IV RIVULETS
MM STRUMMEL
MU MULTURES
NO TURNSOLE
OO TORULOSE
OP PLOUTERS
POULTERS
OY SOUTERLY
UROSTYLE
PP PURPLEST
PS SPURTLES
PT SPLUTTER
PU PULTURES
RS RUSTLERS
RT TURTLERS
SS RUSTLESS
TY SLUTTERY
UV VULTURES

EMNORS 230
(SERMON)
AC CREMONAS
ROMANCES
AD MADRONES
RANSOMED
ROADSMEN
AG MEGARONS
AH HORSEMAN
MENORAHS
SHOREMAN
AI MORAINES
AL ALMONERS
AP PROSEMAN
AR RANSOMER
AT MONSTERA
STOREMAN
AU ENAMOURS
NEUROMAS
AV OVERMANS
OVERSMAN
AY ROMNEYAS
BI BROMINES
BW EMBROWNS
BY EMBRYONS
CI CREMOSIN
INCOMERS
SERMONIC
CU CONSUMER
MUCRONES
DE SERMONED
DO DOORSMEN
DT MORDENTS
DW SWORDMEN
DY SYNDROME
EH HORSEMEN
SHOREMEN
EI EMERSION
EL SOLEMNER
EP PROSEMEN
ER SERMONER
ET SERMONET
STOREMEN
EU MOUNSEER
EV OVERSMEN
EY MONEYERS
FI ENSIFORM
FERMIONS
GH GEMSHORN
GI NEGROISM
GL MONGRELS
GU MURGEONS
HO HORMONES
MOORHENS
IK MONIKERS
IM MISNOMER
IO IONOMERS
MOONRISE
IS MERSIONS
IU INERMOUS
MONSIEUR
IW WINSOMER
MO MONOMERS
MU SUMMONER
MY MERONYMS
OT MESOTRON
MONTEROS
OU ENORMOUS
NEMOROUS
OW NEWSROOM
RU MOURNERS
ST MONSTERS
TT SORTMENT
TORMENTS
TU MONTURES
MOUNTERS
REMOUNTS
UU NUMEROUS

EMNOST 186
(MONETS)
AC CAMSTONE
AG GEOMANTS
MAGNETOS
MEGATONS
MONTAGES
AH HOASTMEN
AI SOMNIATE
AL SALMONET
AR MONSTERA
STOREMAN
AU NOTAEUMS
OUTNAMES
SEAMOUNT
CI CENTIMOS
CK STOCKMEN
CM COMMENTS
CN CONTEMNS

DD ODDMENTS
DI DEMONIST
DR MORDENTS
DU DEMOUNTS
MUDSTONE
EG EMONGEST
GEMSTONE
EI MONETISE
SEMITONE
EM MEMENTOS
ER SERMONET
STOREMEN
GI MITOGENS
HI HOISTMEN
HL MENTHOLS
HO SMOOTHEN
IK TOKENISM
IL MOLINETS
IN MENTIONS
IO EMOTIONS
MOONIEST
IP EMPTIONS
NEPOTISM
PIMENTOS
IS MOISTENS
LO MOONLETS
MY METONYMS
NW TOWNSMEN
OP METOPONS
OR MESOTRON
MONTEROS
OS MOONSETS
RS MONSTERS
RT SORTMENT
TORMENTS
RU MONTURES
MOUNTERS
REMOUNTS
SS STEMSONS

EMORST 198
(MOTERS)
AB BROMATES
AD STROAMED
AE EROTEMAS
AF FOREMAST
FORMATES
AI AMORTISE
ATOMISER
AL MOLERATS
AM MARMOSET
AN MONSTERA
STOREMAN
AR REARMOST
AS MAESTROS
AV OVERMAST
BL TEMBLORS
BS BESTORMS
MOBSTERS
SOMBREST
CI MORTICES
CP COMPTERS
CU COSTUMER
CUSTOMER
DE MODESTER
DI MORTISED
DN MORDENTS
DO DOOMSTER
EE EROTEMES
STEREOME
EH THEOREMS
EI TIRESOME
EL MOLESTER
EN SERMONET
STOREMEN
ES SOMERSET
ET REMOTEST
EU TEMEROUS
FI SETIFORM
FO FOREMOST
FP POMFRETS
GI ERGOTISM
GORMIEST
GM GROMMETS
GU GOURMETS
HI ISOTHERM
MOITHERS
HO SMOOTHER
HS SMOTHERS
HU MOUTHERS
HY SMOTHERY
IO MOORIEST
MOTORISE
ROOMIEST
IP IMPOSTER
IR MORTISER
STORMIER
IS EROTISMS
MORTISES
TRISOMES
IT OMITTERS
IU MISROUTE
MOISTURE
IW MISWROTE
WORMIEST
IY ISOMETRY
LM TROMMELS
LO TREMOLOS
NO MESOTRON
MONTEROS
NS MONSTERS
NT SORTMENT
TORMENTS
NU MONTURES
MOUNTERS
REMOUNTS
OP PROMOTES
OS MOROSEST
PS STOMPERS
SU OESTRUMS
STRUMOSE

ENOPRS 203
(PERSON)
AD OPERANDS
PANDORES
AE PERAEONS
PERSONAE
AF PROFANES
AL PERSONAL
PSORALEN
AM PROSEMAN
AP PROPANES
AS PERSONAS
RESPONSA
AT OPERANTS
PRONATES
CI CONSPIRE
INCORPSE
CY NECROPSY
DF FORSPEND
DI DISPONER
POINDERS
PRISONED
DL SPLENDOR
DO PRODNOSE
DP PROPENDS
DS RESPONDS
DT PORTENDS
PROTENDS
DU POUNDERS
DV PROVENDS
EI ISOPRENE
PIONEERS
EK RESPOKEN
EM PROSEMEN
EP PREPONES
PROPENES
PROPENSE
ES RESPONSE
ET PROTENSE
EU PERONEUS
FI FORPINES
FT FORSPENT
GI PERIGONS
REPOSING
SPONGIER
GS SPONGERS
GY PYROGENS
HN NEPHRONS
HY HYPERONS
II RIPIENOS
IL PROLINES
IO POISONER
SNOOPIER
SPOONIER
IP POPERINS
PROPINES
IR PRISONER
IS PORINESS
PRESSION
ROPINESS
IT POINTERS
PROTEINS
REPOINTS
IU PRUINOSE
IV OVERSPIN
PROVINES
KL PLONKERS
NU UNPERSON
OP PROPONES
OS POORNESS
SNOOPERS
RU PRONEURS
ST POSTERNS
TT PORTENTS

ENORST 23
(TONERS)
AA ANOESTRA
AB BARONETS
AC ANCESTOR
ENACTORS
SORTANCE
AD TORNADES
AE RESONATE
AF SEAFRONT
AG ORANGEST
RAGSTONE
STONERAG
AI ANOESTRI
ARSONITE
NOTARIES
NOTARISE
ROSINATE
AM MONSTERA
STOREMAN
AN NORTENAS
RESONANT
AP OPERANTS
PRONATES
AR ANTRORSE
AS ASSENTOR
SENATORS
TREASONS
AT ORNATEST
AV VENATORS
AW STONERAW
BI BORNITES
RIBSTONE
BS SORBENTS
BU RUBSTONE
BW BESTROWN
BROWNEST
CC CONCERTS
CH NOTCHERS
CI CORNIEST
RECTIONS
CK CRONKEST
CO CORONETS
CS CONSTERS
CRESTONS
CT CORNETTS
CU CONSTRUE
CORNUTES
COUNTERS
RECOUNTS
TROUNCES
CV CONVERTS
CW CROWNETS
DE ERODENTS
DI DRONIEST
DM MORDENTS
DN TENDRONS
DP PORTENDS
PROTENDS
DU ROUNDEST
TONSURED
UNSORTED
EF ENFOREST
SOFTENER
EG ESTROGEN
EH HONESTER
EI SEROTINE
EL ENTRESOL
EM SERMONET
STOREMEN
EN TENONERS
EO ROESTONE
EP PROTENSE
ET ONSETTER
EV OVERNETS
EX EXTENSOR
FH FORHENTS
FN FORNENST
FP FORSPENT
FR RENFORST
FU FORTUNES
GG GONGSTER
GI GENITORS
ROSETING
GN RONTGENS
GR STRONGER
GS SONGSTER
GT TONGSTER
GU STURGEON
GW WRONGEST
HI HORNIEST
HL HORNLETS
HR NORTHERS
HS SHORTENS
HT THORNSET
HU SOUTHERN
IJ JOINTERS
IL RETINOLS
IN INTONERS
TERNIONS
IO SNOOTIER
IP POINTERS
PROTEINS
REPOINTS
IR INTRORSE
SNORTIER
IS TERSIONS
IT SNOTTIER
TENORIST
TRITONES
IU ROUTINES
SNOUTIER
IV INVESTOR
IY TYROSINE
IZ TRIZONES
KO STROOKEN
KS STONKERS
KT KNOTTERS
KW NETWORKS
LU TURNSOLE
MO MESOTRON
MONTEROS
MS MONSTERS
MT SORTMENT
TORMENTS
MU MONTURES
MOUNTERS
REMOUNTS
NO NORTENOS
NS STERNSON
NU NEUTRONS
PS POSTERNS
PT PORTENTS
RS SNORTERS
RT TORRENTS
ST SNOTTERS
STENTORS
SU TONSURES
TU STENTOUR
TY SNOTTERY
UV VENTROUS
UY TOURNEYS

ENOSTT 195
(ONTEST)
AC CONSTATE
AR ORNATEST
BI BOTTINES
CI CENTOIST
STENOTIC
CN CONTENTS
CR CORNETTS
CS CONTESTS
CX CONTEXTS
EF OFTENEST
EI NOISETTE
TEOSINTE
EL NOTELETS
EN NONETTES
ER ONSETTER
FL FLETTONS
FONTLETS
GI TENTIGOS
GR TONGSTER
HR THORNSET
IJ JETTISON
IN TINSTONE
TONTINES
IP NEPOTIST
IR SNOTTIER
TENORIST
TRITONES
IS SNOTTIES
STONIEST
IT TOTIENTS
IW TOWNIEST
KR KNOTTERS
MR SORTMENT
TORMENTS
NO NONETTOS
OP POTSTONE
OS TESTOONS
PR PORTENTS
PU OUTSPENT
RR TORRENTS
RS SNOTTERS
STENTORS
RU STENTOUR
RY SNOTTERY
SU STOUTENS

ENOSTU 94
(OUTENS)
AM NOTAEUMS
OUTNAMES
SEAMOUNT
AN TONNEAUS
AS SOUTANES
BE TUBENOSE
BI BOUNTIES
BR RUBSTONE
CD CONTUSED
CF CONFUTES
CI COUNTIES
CK UNSOCKET
CL NOCTULES
CP POUNCETS
CQ CONQUEST
CR CONSTRUE
CORNUTES
COUNTERS
RECOUNTS
TROUNCES
CS CONTUSES
COUNTESS
DD STOUNDED
DM DEMOUNTS
MUDSTONE
DO DUOTONES
DP OUTSPEND
UNPOSTED
DR ROUNDEST
TONSURED

UNSORTED
DS SOUNDEST
DW UNSTOWED
EL TOLUENES
FR FORTUNES
GH TOUGHENS
GN GUNSTONE
GR STURGEON
GY YOUNGEST
HI OUTSHINE
HN UNHONEST
HO OUTSHONE
HR SOUTHERN
HU NUTHOUSE
IL ELUTIONS
OUTLINES
IN NOUNIEST
IQ QUESTION
IR ROUTINES
SNOUTIER
IU TENUIOUS
LR TURNSOLE
LZ ZONULETS
MR MONTURES
MOUNTERS
REMOUNTS
NR NEUTRONS
NS NEUSTONS
SUNSTONE
PT OUTSPENT
QU UNQUOTES
RS TONSURES
RT STENTOUR
RV VENTROUS
RY TOURNEYS
ST STOUTENS

ENRSTU 84
(TUNERS)
AB UNBRASTE
URBANEST
AC CENTAURS
RECUSANT
UNCRATES
UNTRACES
AD DAUNTERS
TRANSUDE
UNTREADS
AG STRAUNGE
AH HAUNTERS
UNEARTHS
UNHEARTS
URETHANS
AI RUINATES
TAURINES
URANITES
URINATES
AL NEUTRALS
AM ANESTRUM
MENSTRUA
TRANSUME
AP PERSAUNT
AS ANESTRUS
SAUNTERS
AT TAUNTERS
AV VAUNTERS
AW UNWATERS
BH BURTHENS
BI TRIBUNES
TURBINES
BO RUBSTONE
CE UNSECRET
CH CHUNTERS
CI CURNIEST
CL LECTURNS
CM CENTRUMS
CO CONSTRUE
CORNUTES
COUNTERS
RECOUNTS
TROUNCES
CR CURRENTS
CS CURTNESS
ENCRUSTS
DE DENTURES
SEDERUNT
UNDERSET
UNDESERT
DG TRUDGENS
DH THUNDERS
DI INTRUDES
DK DRUNKEST
DL RUNDLETS
TRUNDLES
DO ROUNDEST
TONSURED
UNSORTED
DP UPTRENDS
DT STRUNTED
EI ESURIENT
NEURITES
RETINUES
REUNITES
EM MUENSTER
ES TRUENESS
EV VENTURES
FO FORTUNES
FS FUNSTERS
GL GRUNTLES
GO STURGEON
GR GRUNTERS
RESTRUNG
HL LUTHERNS
HO SOUTHERN
HS HUNTRESS
SHUNTERS
II NEURITIS
IL INSULTER
LUSTRINE
IM TERMINUS
IN RUNNIEST
STURNINE
IO ROUTINES
SNOUTIER
IP REPUNITS
UNPRIEST
UNRIPEST
IQ SQUINTER
IT RUNTIEST
IV UNRIVETS
VENTURIS
IW UNWRITES
JU UNJUSTER
KY TURNKEYS
LO TURNSOLE
MO MONTURES
MOUNTERS
REMOUNTS
MS MUNSTERS
STERNUMS
NO NEUTRONS
NS STUNNERS
OS TONSURES
OT STENTOUR
OV VENTROUS
OY TOURNEYS
PS PUNSTERS
RU NURTURES
ST ENTRUSTS
SU UNSUREST
TU UNTRUEST

EOPRST 193
(POSTER)
AB PROBATES
AD ADOPTERS
ASPORTED
READOPTS
AE OPERATES
PROTEASE
AF FOREPAST
AG PORTAGES
POTAGERS
AH POTSHARE
AL PETROSAL
PROLATES
AN OPERANTS
PRONATES
AR PRAETORS
PRORATES
AS ESPARTOS
PORTASES
PROTASES
SEAPORTS
AT PROSTATE
AU APTEROUS
AV OVERPAST
BS BESPORTS
CH POTCHERS
CI PERSICOT
CJ PROJECTS
CK SPROCKET
CM COMPTERS
CP PROSPECT
CR PORRECTS
CT PROTECTS
CW SCREWTOP
DE POSTERED
REEDSTOP
REPOSTED
DH POTSHERD
DI DIOPTERS
DIOPTRES
DIPTEROS
PERIDOTS
PROTEIDS
RIPOSTED
DL DROPLETS
DN PORTENDS
PROTENDS
DO DOORSTEP
TORPEDOS
DP STROPPED
DU POSTURED
PROUDEST
SPROUTED
EG PROTEGES
EI POETRIES
EN PROTENSE
EO PROTEOSE
ES PORTESSE
ET TREETOPS
EU OUTPEERS
EV OVERSTEP
EY SEROTYPE
FI FIREPOTS
FM POMFRETS
FN FORSPENT
FO FORETOPS
POOFTERS
FU POUFTERS
HI TROPHIES
HP PROPHETS
HS STROPHES
HU POUTHERS
HY TROPHESY
IK PORKIEST
IL POITRELS
IM IMPOSTER
IN POINTERS
PROTEINS
REPOINTS
IO PORTOISE
ROOPIEST
IR PIERROTS
SPORTIER
IS PERIOSTS
PROSIEST
REPOSITS
RIPOSTES
TRIPOSES
IT PORTIEST
RISPETTO
SPOTTIER
IU ROUPIEST
SPOUTIER
IV PIVOTERS
SPORTIVE
KU UPSTROKE
LL POLLSTER
LT PLOTTERS
LU PLOUTERS
POULTERS
LW PLOWTERS
LY PROSTYLE
PROTYLES
MO PROMOTES
MS STOMPERS
NS POSTERNS
NT PORTENTS
OR PROTORES
TROOPERS
OS STOOPERS
OU OUTROPES
PORTEOUS
OV OVERPOST
OVERTOPS
STOPOVER
OW TOWROPES
PS STOPPERS
RS PORTRESS
SPORTERS
RU POSTURER
TROUPERS
ST PROTESTS
SPOTTERS
SU POSTURES
SEPTUORS
SPOUTERS

EORRST 106
(SORTER)
AA AERATORS
AB ARBORETS
TABORERS
AC ACROTERS
CREATORS
REACTORS
AD ROADSTER
AG GARROTES
AI ROARIEST
ROTARIES
AL REALTORS
RELATORS
AM REARMOST
AN ANTRORSE
AO SORORATE
AP PRAETORS
PRORATES
AR ARRESTOR
AS ASSERTOR
ASSORTER
ORATRESS
ROASTERS
AT ROSTRATE
BH BROTHERS
BI ORBITERS
BU ROBUSTER
CC CORRECTS
CE ERECTORS
CF CROFTERS
CH TORCHERS
CP PORRECTS
CY CORSETRY
DE RESORTED
RESTORED
ROSTERED
DH REDSHORT
DO REDROOTS
DS RODSTERS
EF FORESTER
FOSTERER
REFOREST
EG OSTREGER
ER RESORTER
RESTORER
RETRORSE
ES RESTORES
EU REROUTES
EV EVERTORS
EX EXTRORSE
FI FROSTIER
ROTIFERS
FN RENFORST
FS FORTRESS
FW FROWSTER
FY FORESTRY
GN STRONGER
GS GROSERTS
GU GROUTERS
HI HERITORS
HN NORTHERS
HW THROWERS
II RIOTRIES
IM MORTISER
STORMIER
IN INTRORSE
SNORTIER
IO ROOTSIER
IP PIERROTS
SPORTIER
IR ERRORIST
IS RESISTOR
ROISTERS
SORRIEST
IT RORTIEST
IU STOURIER
IV SERVITOR
KS STROKERS
LL STROLLER
TROLLERS
NS SNORTERS
NT TORRENTS
OP PROTORES
TROOPERS
OS ROOSTERS
PS PORTRESS
SPORTERS
PU POSTURER
TROUPERS
SS STRESSOR
TROSSERS
SU ROUSTERS
TROUSERS
SW STROWERS
TROWSERS
SY ROYSTERS
TT TROTTERS
TU TORTURES
TROUTERS

EORSTT 114
(OTTERS)
AA AEROSTAT
AB ABETTORS
BATTEROS
TABORETS
AC SECTATOR
AG GAROTTES
AH RHEOSTAT
AN ORNATEST
AP PROSTATE
AR ROSTRATE
AS STRATOSE
TOASTERS
AT ATTESTOR
TESTATOR
AU OUTRATES
OUTSTARE
BH BETROTHS
BL BLOTTERS
BOTTLERS
CI COTTIERS
CL CLOTTERS
CROTTLES
CN CORNETTS
CP PROTECTS
DE ROSETTED
TETRODES
DI DORTIEST
DL DOTTRELS
DU STROUTED
EL LORETTES
EM REMOTEST
EN ONSETTER
EP TREETOPS
ES ROSETTES
FL FORTLETS
FO FOOTREST
GN TONGSTER

GO GROTTOES
HI THEORIST
THORITES
HL THROSTLE
HN THORNSET
HS SHORTEST
IL TRIOLETS
IM OMITTERS
IN SNOTTIER
TENORIST
TRITONES
IO ROOTIEST
TORTOISE
IP PORTIEST
RISPETTO
SPOTTIER
IR RORTIEST
IS STOITERS
IU TUTORISE
IV VIRETOTS
KN KNOTTERS
LO ROOTLETS
LP PLOTTERS
LS SETTLORS
SLOTTERS
MN SORTMENT
TORMENTS
NP PORTENTS
NR TORRENTS
NS SNOTTERS
STENTORS
NU STENTOUR
NY SNOTTERY
PS PROTESTS
SPOTTERS
RT TROTTERS
RU TORTURES
TROUTERS
ST STOTTERS
SU TUTORESS
SW SWOTTERS
UW OUTWREST

GIINRT 233
(TIRING)
AC GRANITIC
AK TRAIKING
AL RINGTAIL
TRAILING
AN TRAINING
AO RIGATONI
AP PIRATING
AT ATTIRING
BE REBITING
BH BIRTHING
BO ORBITING
BS RINGBITS
BU BRUITING
CE RECITING
CH CHIRTING
RICHTING
CK TRICKING
CO TRIGONIC
DE DIRIGENT
DF DRIFTING
DH THIRDING
DS STRIDING
DY DIRTYING
EH THINGIER
EL GIRTLINE
RETILING
TINGLIER
TIRELING
EM MERITING
MITERING
RETIMING
ER RETIRING
ES GIRNIEST
IGNITERS
REISTING
STINGIER
STRIGINE
EU INTRIGUE
EV RIVETING
EX GENITRIX
FG GRIFTING
FL FLIRTING
TRIFLING
FS FRISTING
FT FRITTING
FU FRUITING
GG TRIGGING
GH GIRTHING
RIGHTING
GS RINGGITS
GT GRITTING
HL THIRLING
HS SHIRTING
HV THRIVING
HW WRITHING
KS SKIRTING
STRIKING
LL TRILLING
LP TRIPLING
LW TWIRLING
MM TRIMMING
NO IGNITRON
NP PRINTING
NU UNTIRING
OS RIOTINGS
ROISTING
ROSITING
OZ ROZITING
PP TRIPPING
PS SPIRTING
STRIPING
QU QUIRTING
RS STIRRING
SV STRIVING
SW WRITINGS

GILNOT 171
(TOLING)
AA GALTONIA
AB BLOATING
OBLIGANT
AC LOCATING
AE GELATION
LEGATION
AF FLOATING
AG GLOATING
GOATLING
AH LOATHING
AI INTAGLIO
LIGATION
TAGLIONI
AP PLOATING
AR TRIGONAL
AS ANTILOGS
SALTOING
AY ANTILOGY
BS BILTONGS
BOLTINGS
BT BLOTTING
BOTTLING
BU BOULTING
CH CLOTHING
CT CLOTTING
CU CLOUTING
DD TODDLING
DY DOTINGLY
EW TOWELING
FO FOOTLING
FS SOFTLING
FU FLOUTING
OUTFLING
GG TOGGLING
GU GLOUTING
HS SLOTHING
IP PILOTING
IS TOILINGS
JS JOSTLING
LR TROLLING
LS TOLLINGS
MR MORTLING
MT MOTTLING
MU MOULTING
NW TOWNLING
OR ROOTLING
OS LOOTINGS
STOOLING
TOOLINGS
OT TOOTLING
PP TOPPLING
PT PLOTTING
RU TROULING
ST SLOTTING
SU TOUSLING
UY OUTLYING
UZ TOUZLING

GINORS 128
(SIGNOR)
AD ROADINGS
AE IGNAROES
ORGANISE
ORIGANES
AI SIGNORIA
AL RANGOLIS
AM ORGANISM
ROAMINGS
AR GARRISON
ROARINGS
AS ASSIGNOR
SOARINGS
AT ORGANIST
ROASTING
AU AROUSING
AV SAVORING
BD BIRDSONG
SONGBIRD
BE SOBERING
BH BIGHORNS
BK BROKINGS
BM SOMBRING
BW BROWSING
CD CORDINGS
CK ROCKINGS
CN SCORNING
CP CORPSING
CS CROSSING
SCORINGS
SCORSING
CU COURSING
SCOURING
SOURCING
DD RODDINGS
DE NEGROIDS
DI DORISING
DL GIRLONDS
LORDINGS
DV DROVINGS
DW DROWSING
SWORDING
WORDINGS
EE ERINGOES
EI SEIGNIOR
EL RESOLING
EM NEGROISM
EP PERIGONS
REPOSING
SPONGIER
ER IGNORERS
ES GORINESS
SIGNORES
ET GENITORS
ROSETING
EY SEIGNORY
FF GRIFFONS
FG FORGINGS
FL ROLFINGS
FM FORMINGS
FO ROOFINGS
FT FROSTING
GP PROGGINS
GS GROSSING
GU GROUSING
GW GROWINGS
HN HORNINGS
HS HORSINGS
SHORINGS
HT SHORTING
HV SHROVING
HW SHROWING
IL LIGROINS
IN IRONINGS
NIGROSIN
ROSINING
IS SIGNIORS
IT RIOTINGS
ROISTING
ROSITING
IV VISORING
KT STROKING
KW WORKINGS
LL ROLLINGS
LM MORLINGS
LU LOURINGS
MN MORNINGS
MO MOORINGS
SMOORING
MT STORMING
MU ROUMINGS
NS SNORINGS
SORNINGS
NT SNORTING
NU GRUNIONS
OP SPOORING
OT ROOSTING
ROOTINGS
PS PROSINGS
PT SPORTING
PU INGROUPS
POURINGS
PV PROVINGS
ST SORTINGS
SU SOURINGS
TU ROUSTING
ROUTINGS
TOURINGS
TW STROWING
WORSTING
TY ROYSTING
STORYING
STROYING

GINORT 102
(ROTING)
AB ABORTING
TABORING
AI RIGATONI
AL TRIGONAL
AN IGNORANT
AO ROGATION
AS ORGANIST
ROASTING
AT ROTATING
TROATING
AV GRAVITON
AY GYRATION
ORGANITY
BI ORBITING
CE GERONTIC
CF CROFTING
CH TORCHING
CI TRIGONIC
CK TROCKING
CU COURTING
EH THROEING
EN NITROGEN
ES GENITORS
ROSETING
ET OTTERING
EU OUTREIGN
ROUTEING
EW TOWERING
EX OXTERING
EZ ROZETING
FH FROTHING
FN FRONTING
FS FROSTING
FU FOUTRING
GG TROGGING
GU GROUTING
HN NORTHING
THORNING
THRONING
HS SHORTING
HT TROTHING
HW INGROWTH
THROWING
WORTHING
IN IGNITRON
IS RIOTINGS
ROISTING
ROSITING
IZ ROZITING
KS STROKING
LL TROLLING
LM MORTLING
LO ROOTLING
LU TROULING
MO MOTORING
MP TROMPING
MS STORMING
NS SNORTING
OP TROOPING
OS ROOSTING
ROOTINGS
OW WROOTING
PS SPORTING
PU TROUPING
SS SORTINGS
SU ROUSTING
ROUTINGS
TOURINGS
SW STROWING
WORSTING
SY ROYSTING
STORYING
STROYING
TT TROTTING
TU TROUTING
TUTORING

GINOST 176
(OSTING)
AB BOASTING
BOATINGS
BOSTANGI
AC AGNOSTIC
COASTING
COATINGS
COTINGAS
AD DOATINGS
AH HOASTING
AK GOATSKIN
AL ANTILOGS
SALTOING
AN ASTONING
AR ORGANIST
ROASTING
AS AGONISTS
AT TANGOIST
TOASTING
BL BILTONGS
BOLTINGS
BO BOOSTING
CI COTISING
CK STOCKING
CO SCOOTING
CU SCOUTING
DG STODGING
EE EGESTION
EH HISTOGEN
EM MITOGENS
EP PONGIEST
ER GENITORS
ROSETING
ET TENTIGOS
FI FOISTING
FL SOFTLING
FO FOOTINGS
FR FROSTING
GH GHOSTING
GO STOOGING
HI HOISTING
HL SLOTHING
HN NOTHINGS
HO SHOOTING

SOOTHING
HR SHORTING
HS HOSTINGS
HT HOTTINGS
SHOTTING
TONIGHTS
HU HOUTINGS
SHOUTING
SOUTHING
HW SOWTHING
IJ JINGOIST
JOISTING
IL TOILINGS
IM MOISTING
IP POSITING
SOPITING
IR RIOTINGS
ROISTING
ROSITING
IT STOITING
JL JOSTLING
JT JOTTINGS
JU JOUSTING
KN STONKING
KO STOOKING
KP KINGPOST
KR STROKING
LL TOLLINGS
LO LOOTINGS
STOOLING
TOOLINGS
LT SLOTTING
LU TOUSLING
MO MOOTINGS
SMOOTING
MP STOMPING
MR STORMING
MS GNOMISTS
MU MOUSTING
SMOUTING
NN STONNING
NO SNOOTING
NR SNORTING
NS STONINGS
NT SNOTTING
NU SNOUTING
STOUNING
NY STONYING
OP STOOPING
OR ROOSTING
ROOTINGS
OT TOOTSING
PP STOPPING
TOPPINGS
PR SPORTING
PS POSTINGS
SIGNPOST
STOPINGS
PT SPOTTING
PU POUTINGS
SPOUTING
RS SORTINGS
RU ROUSTING
ROUTINGS
TOURINGS
RW STROWING
WORSTING
RY ROYSTING
STORYING
STROYING
SS TOSSINGS
ST SOTTINGS
SU TOUSINGS
SV STOVINGS
SW STOWINGS
TT STOTTING
TOTTINGS
TW SWOTTING
UW OUTSWING
OUTWINGS

INORST 59
(TRIONS)
AB TABORINS
AC CANTORIS
CAROTINS
AD INTRADOS
AE ANOESTRI
ARSONITE
NOTARIES
NOTARISE
ROSINATE
AG ORGANIST
ROASTING
AH TRAHISON
AJ JANITORS
AK SKIATRON
AO ORATIONS
AP ATROPINS
AS ARSONIST
AT STRONTIA
AU SUTORIAN
AX TRIAXONS
BE BORNITES
RIBSTONE
BO ISOBRONT
BS RIBSTONS
CE CORNIEST
RECTIONS
CR TRICORNS
CS CISTRONS
CORNISTS
CT CONTRIST
CU RUCTIONS
DE DRONIEST
DO TORDIONS
DU STURNOID
TURDIONS
EE SEROTINE
EG GENITORS
ROSETING
EH HORNIEST
EJ JOINTERS
EL RETINOLS
EN INTONERS
TERNIONS
EO SNOOTIER
EP POINTERS
PROTEINS
REPOINTS
ER INTRORSE
SNORTIER
ES TERSIONS
ET SNOTTIER
TENORIST
TRITONES
EU ROUTINES
SNOUTIER
EV INVESTOR
EY TYROSINE
EZ TRIZONES
FG FROSTING
GH SHORTING
GI RIOTINGS
ROISTING
ROSITING
GK STROKING
GM STORMING
GN SNORTING
GO ROOSTING
ROOTINGS
GP SPORTING
GS SORTINGS
GU ROUSTING
ROUTINGS
TOURINGS
GW STROWING
WORSTING
GY ROYSTING
STORYING
STROYING
HI HISTRION
HN TINHORNS
HO HORNITOS
HS HORNISTS
IS IRONISTS
IT INTROITS
KK KIRKTONS
LS NOSTRILS
LU TORULINS
LY NITROSYL
MO MONITORS
TROMINOS
MY TRIONYMS
NO NOTORNIS
OP PORTIONS
POSITRON
SORPTION
OS ISOTRONS
TORSIONS
OT TORTONIS
OY SONORITY

8-LETTER SETS LIST

alphabetical list of all words appearing in 8-Letter Sets

ABATURES
ABDOMENS
ABEARING
ABERRANT
ABETTERS
ABETTORS
ABLATING
ABORDING
ABORIGEN
ABORTING
ABRADING
ABRAIDED
ABREACTS
ABRIDGED
ABRIDGER
ABRIDGES
ABROOKES
ABSEILED
ABSENTED
ABSENTLY
ABSINTHE
ABSOLUTE
ABSOLVER
ABSORBED
ABSORBER
ABSTERGE
ABSTRICT
ABSTRUSE
ABSURDER
ABUTTERS
ACCEDERS
ACCENTOR
ACCEPTER
ACCINGES
ACCOSTED
ACCRETES
ACCURSED
ACERBEST
ACESCENT
ACETONES
ACIDNESS
ACOLYTES
ACONITES
ACRIDEST
ACRIDINE
ACRIDINS
ACROGENS
ACROLEIN
ACROSOME
ACROSTIC
ACROTERS
ACROTISM
ADAPTERS
ADDORSED
ADDUCERS
ADENINES
ADENITIS
ADENOIDS
ADENOMAS
ADEPTEST
ADERMINS
ADHERERS
ADHERING
ADHESION
ADJURING
ADJUSTER
ADMIRERS
ADMIRING
ADONISED
ADONISES
ADONIZES
ADOPTERS
ADORNING
ADRENALS
ADSCRIPT
ADSORBED
ADULATES
ADUSTING
ADVERSER
ADVISERS
AEGIRINE
AEMULING
AERATING
AERATION
AERATORS
AEROBICS
AEROLITE
AEROLITH
AEROSOLS
AEROSTAT
AESCULIN
AESTIVAL
AFEARING
AFFORCES
AFFOREST
AFFRONTS
AGELASTS
AGENCIES
AGENTIAL
AGGRADES
AGGRATES
AGINNERS
AGISTERS
AGISTING
AGITATES
AGLITTER
AGNOSTIC
AGONISED
AGONISES
AGONISTS
AGONIZES
AGREEING
AGREMENS
AGREMENT
AGRESTAL
AGRESTIC
AGRISING
AIDANCES
AIGRETTE
AILERONS
AILETTES
AILMENTS
AIRFIELD
AIRHEADS
AIRHOLES
AIRINESS
AIRLINES
AIRSIDES
AIRSPACE
AIRSPEED
AIRTIMES
AIRWOMEN
AISLINGS
ALAIMENT
ALARMING
ALBICORE
ALBINESS
ALBITISE
ALCAHEST
ALCAIDES
ALDERMAN
ALDERMEN
ALECOSTS
ALEGGING
ALEMBICS
ALERIONS
ALERTEST
ALERTING
ALEURONS
ALFRESCO
ALGEBRAS
ALGERINE
ALGESIAS
ALGINATE
ALIASING
ALIDADES
ALIENAGE
ALIENATE
ALIENING
ALIENISM
ALIENIST
ALIENORS
ALIMENTS
ALKANETS
ALLEGERS
ALLEGING
ALLEGROS
ALLERGEN
ALLERGIC
ALLNIGHT
ALLONGES
ALLURING
ALMERIES
ALMONERS
ALNAGERS
ALOETICS
ALTERANT
ALTERING
ALTERITY
ALTERNAT
ALTERNES
ALTHORNS
ALTRICES
ALUNITES
AMATEURS
AMBEROID
AMBEROUS
AMBIENTS
AMBLINGS
AMENDERS
AMENTIAS
AMERCING
AMITOSES
AMMETERS
AMMONITE
AMNESIAC
AMNESIAS
AMNESICS
AMORETTI
AMORTISE
AMOSITES
ANAEMIAS
ANALCIME
ANALCITE
ANALECTS
ANALYSED
ANALYSER
ANAPAEST
ANAPESTS
ANATHEMA
ANBURIES
ANCESTOR
ANCESTRY
ANCHORET
ANCIENTS
ANDANTES
ANDESINE
ANDESITE
ANDIRONS
ANDROGEN
ANDROIDS
ANDVILES
ANEARING
ANEROIDS
ANESTRUM
ANESTRUS
ANEURINS
ANEURISM
ANGARIES
ANGELICA
ANGERING
ANGLINGS
ANGLISTS
ANGRIEST
ANGSTROM
ANGULATE
ANHEDRAL
ANIMATED
ANIMATER
ANIMATES
ANIMUSES
ANISEEDS
ANISETTE
ANKERITE
ANNELIDS
ANNULETS
ANODISED
ANODISES
ANODIZES
ANOESTRA
ANOESTRI
ANOINTER
ANORETIC
ANOREXIC
ANSERINE
ANSWERED
ANSWERER
ANTBEARS
ANTBIRDS
ANTEATER
ANTENNAS
ANTEPAST
ANTERIOR
ANTEVERT
ANTHELIA
ANTHELIX
ANTHEMIA
ANTHESIS
ANTIENTS
ANTIGENS
ANTILOGS
ANTILOGY
ANTIPOLE
ANTIQUES
ANTIRUST
ANTISERA
ANTISTAT
ANTLERED
ANTLIATE
ANTRORSE
AORISTIC
APATITES
APERIENT
APERTURE
APHONIES
APHORISE
APIARIES
APLUSTRE
APOCRINE
APOSTLES
APPARELS
APPERILS
APPLIERS
APPOSITE
APPRAISE
APPRISED
APPRISER
APPRISES
APPRIZES
APRICOTS
APTERISM
APTEROUS
ARABISED
ARABIZED
ARACEOUS
ARAISING
ARANEIDS
ARAYSING
ARBALEST
ARBITERS
ARBORETS
ARCADING
ARCANIST
ARCCOSES
ARCHAIST
ARCHLETS
ARCHLUTE
ARCHNESS
ARCKINGS
ARCTIIDS
ARDENTLY
AREADING
AREFYING
ARETTING
ARGININE
ARGOSIES
ARGUMENT
ARIDNESS
ARIETTAS
ARIETTES
ARILLATE
ARILLODE
ARISTATE
ARMAMENT
ARMHOLES
ARMIGERS
ARMOIRES
ARMORIES
ARMOZINE
ARNOTTOS
AROINTED
AROUSING
ARRAIGNS
ARRANGED
ARRANGES
ARRASENE
ARREEDES
ARRESTED
ARRESTEE
ARRESTER
ARRESTOR
ARRIDING
ARSEHOLE
ARSENALS
ARSENATE
ARSENICS
ARSENIDE
ARSENITE
ARSHEENS
ARSHINES
ARSONIST
ARSONITE
ARTERIAL
ARTERIES
ARTESIAN
ARTICLED
ARTICLES
ARTINESS
ARTISANS
ARTISTES
ARTISTIC
ARTSIEST
ARVICOLE
ASCENDER
ASCRIBED
ASHLARED
ASHLERED
ASKANTED
ASLAKING
ASPECTED
ASPERATE
ASPERGED
ASPERGER
ASPERITY
ASPERSED
ASPHERIC
ASPIRANT
ASPIRATE
ASPIRING
ASPORTED
ASSAILED
ASSAILER
ASSARTED
ASSENTED
ASSENTER
ASSENTOR
ASSERTED
ASSERTER
ASSERTOR
ASSIENTO
ASSIGNAT
ASSIGNED
ASSIGNOR
ASSISTED
ASSOILED
ASSORTED
ASSORTER
ASSURING
ASTARTED
ASTATINE
ASTEISMS
ASTELIES
ASTERIAS
ASTERIDS
ASTERISK
ASTERISM
ASTEROID
ASTERTED
ASTHENIA
ASTHENIC
ASTHORES
ASTILBES
ASTONIED
ASTONIES
ASTONING
ASTRICTS
ASTRINGE
ASTUNNED
ASYNERGY
ASYSTOLE
ATABRINS
ATEBRINS
ATELIERS
ATHANORS
ATHEISED
ATHEISMS
ATHEISTS
ATHELING
ATHERINE
ATHETISE
ATMOLYSE
ATOMISED
ATOMISER
ATOMISES
ATOMIZES
ATRAMENT
ATRAZINE
ATREMBLE
ATRESIAS
ATROPINE
ATROPINS
ATTAINTS
ATTEMPER
ATTENDER
ATTESTED
ATTESTER
ATTESTOR
ATTIRING
ATTORNED
ATTORNEY
ATTRITED
ATTRITES
ATTUITES
ATWITTER
AUDIBLES
AUDIENTS
AUGMENTS
AUGUSTER
AULNAGER
AULNAGES
AUMBRIES
AUNTLIER
AURELIAS
AUREOLAS
AUREOLES
AURICLED
AURICLES
AUSTERER
AUTOCUES
AUTOLYSE
AVENGERS
AVENTAIL
AVENTRES
AVERRING
AVERSELY
AVERSION
AVERSIVE
AVERTING
AVIDNESS
AVIETTES
AVOWRIES
AVULSING
AWARDING
AXINITES
AZOTISED
AZURINES
AZURITES
AZYMITES
BABELISH
BABELISM
BACONERS
BAILLIES
BAILMENT
BAILSMEN
BAINITES
BAITINGS
BALDNESS
BALISTAE
BALKIEST
BALKINGS
BALLINGS
BALLSIER
BALMIEST
BALUSTER
BANALEST
BANALISE
BANDEROL
BANDIEST
BANDORES
BANDSMEN

BANDSTER
BANGSTER
BANISHED
BANISTER
BANTENGS
BANTERER
BANTINGS
BANTLING
BAPTISED
BARBICEL
BARDIEST
BARDLING
BAREGINE
BARENESS
BARFLIES
BARGAINS
BARGESTS
BARGHEST
BARGOOSE
BARITONE
BARKIEST
BARMIEST
BARONESS
BARONETS
BARONIES
BARONNES
BAROQUES
BARRINGS
BARRULET
BARTISAN
BARYTONS
BASANITE
BASELARD
BASEMENT
BASINETS
BASKETRY
BASSETED
BASSINET
BASTIDES
BASTILLE
BASTINGS
BATELEUR
BATHORSE
BATISTES
BATSWING
BATTELER
BATTERIE
BATTEROS
BATTIEST
BATTINGS
BATTLERS
BATTLING
BAWDIEST
BAWDRIES
BAWLINGS
BEADIEST
BEADINGS
BEADSMAN
BEADSMEN
BEAGLERS
BEAGLING
BEAMIEST
BEAMINGS
BEARDIES
BEARDING
BEARINGS
BEARSKIN
BEASTILY
BEATHING
BEATINGS
BEATNIKS
BEDAWINS
BEDDINGS
BEDERALS
BEDESMAN
BEDOUINS
BEDSTEAD
BEDSTRAW
BEERIEST
BEETLING
BEFRIEND
BEGHARDS
BEGINNER
BEGONIAS
BEGRIMES
BEHOTING
BEIGNETS
BELABORS
BELACING
BELAMIES
BELATING
BELAYING
BELFRIES
BELGARDS
BELIEVER
BELTINGS
BENDIEST
BENDINGS
BENDLETS
BENIGHTS
BENIGNER
BENISONS
BENITIER
BENTIEST
BEPAINTS
BEPEARLS
BEPRAISE
BERATING
BERAYING
BERBERIS
BERGENIA
BERLINES
BERTHING
BESAINTS
BESETTER
BESLAVER
BESMEARS
BESOGNIO
BESOMING
BESORTED
BESPORTS
BESPREAD
BESPRENT
BESTADDE
BESTAINS
BESTEADS
BESTIALS
BESTIARY
BESTORMS
BESTOWAL
BESTOWER
BESTREAK
BESTREWN
BESTRIDE
BESTRODE
BESTROWN
BETACISM
BETAINES
BETATRON
BETHESDA
BETHRALL
BETITLES
BETONIES
BETRAYAL
BETREADS
BETROTHS
BETTINGS
BEWARING
BIBELOTS
BICORNES
BIDENTAL
BIELDING
BIGARADE
BIGENERS
BIGHORNS
BILANDER
BILGIEST
BILTONGS
BINARIES
BINOCLES
BIOTITES
BIOTYPES
BIPLANES
BIRDCAGE
BIRDSEED
BIRDSONG
BIRETTAS
BIRKIEST
BIRSIEST
BIRTHING
BISECTOR
BISERIAL
BISEXUAL
BISTABLE
BITTERNS
BITUMENS
BIVALENT
BIVALVES
BLACKEST
BLADDERS
BLAGGERS
BLANDEST
BLANKEST
BLANKETS
BLANKIES
BLARNEYS
BLASHIER
BLASTERS
BLASTING
BLATHERS
BLATTERS
BLATTING
BLEAREST
BLEARING
BLEATERS
BLEATING
BLEEDING
BLENDERS
BLENDING
BLESSING
BLETHERS
BLETTING
BLEUATRE
BLEWARTS
BLINDAGE
BLINDERS
BLINDEST
BLINKERS
BLINTZES
BLISTERS
BLISTERY
BLITHERS
BLOATERS
BLOATING
BLONDEST
BLOTTERS
BLOTTIER
BLOTTING
BLOWIEST
BLOWSIER
BLUDIEST
BLUEINGS
BLUESIER
BLUNDERS
BLUNTEST
BLUSTERS
BLUSTERY
BOARDERS
BOARDING
BOASTERS
BOASTING
BOATINGS
BODGIEST
BOLDNESS
BOLSHIER
BOLSTERS
BOLTINGS
BOMBSITE
BONDAGER
BONFIRES
BONINESS
BONNIEST
BONSPIEL
BOOKREST
BOOSTERS
BOOSTING
BORNITES
BOSTANGI
BOTANIES
BOTANISE
BOTANIST
BOTCHERS
BOTFLIES
BOTRYOSE
BOTTINES
BOTTLERS
BOTTLING
BOULDERS
BOULTERS
BOULTING
BOUNCERS
BOUNDERS
BOUNTIES
BOUTADES
BOWLDERS
BOWLINES
BOXINESS
BRACELET
BRACHETS
BRACKENS
BRACKETS
BRACTEAL
BRACTLET
BRAIDEST
BRAIDING
BRAILING
BRAIRDED
BRAISING
BRAKIEST
BRANCHES
BRANDERS
BRANDIED
BRANDIES
BRANDING
BRANDISE
BRANDISH
BRANGLED
BRANGLES
BRANSLES
BRANTLES
BRASEROS
BRASHEST
BRASHING
BRASSETS
BRASTING
BRATLING
BRATTICE
BRATTIER
BRATTLED
BRATTLES
BRAUNITE
BRAWLING
BREADING
BREADNUT
BREADTHS
BREAKERS
BREAKING
BREAMING
BREASKIT
BREASTED
BREATHES
BREEDING
BRENNING
BRENTEST
BREVIERS
BREWINGS
BREWSTER
BRICOLES
BRIDEMAN
BRIDEMEN
BRIDLERS
BRIEFEST
BRIGADED
BRIGADES
BRIGANDS
BRIGHTEN
BRILLEST
BRIMLESS
BRINDLES
BRINGERS
BRINIEST
BRIOCHES
BRIONIES
BRIQUETS
BRISKENS
BRISKEST
BRISKETS
BRISTLED
BRISTLES
BRITCHES
BRITTLES
BROACHES
BROADENS
BROADEST
BROCADES
BROCAGES
BROCATEL
BROCKETS
BRODDING
BROIDERS
BROILERS
BROKAGES
BROKINGS
BROLLIES
BROMATES
BROMIDES
BROMINES
BROODING
BROTHELS
BROTHERS
BROWNEST
BROWNIES
BROWSING
BRUCINES
BRUCITES
BRUITING
BRULYIES
BRULZIES
BRYONIES
BUILDERS
BULGIEST
BULGINES
BULKIEST
BULLIEST
BUNTIEST
BURETTES
BURGANET
BURGEONS
BURLETTA
BURLIEST
BURNSIDE
BURRIEST
BURTHENS
BUSTIERS
BUSTLERS
BYLANDER
CABARETS
CABERNET
CABINETS
CABLINGS
CABRIOLE
CACOLETS
CADASTRE
CADAVERS
CADGIEST
CAFFEINS
CAGEBIRD
CAGELING
CAGINESS
CAJOLERS
CALAMINE
CALCINES
CALCITES
CALDERAS
CALENDAR
CALENDER
CALENDRY
CALIBERS
CALIBRED
CALIBRES
CALIGOES
CALIPERS
CALIVERS
CALLINGS
CALLIPER
CALMIEST
CALORIES
CALORIST
CALOTTES
CALOYERS
CALUMETS
CAMELIDS
CAMELINE
CAMELOTS
CAMPIEST
CAMPSITE
CAMSTANE
CAMSTONE
CANAIGRE
CANALISE
CANARIED
CANARIES
CANASTER
CANCRINE
CANDELAS
CANDIDER
CANISTER
CANITIES
CANNIEST
CANOEIST
CANONISE
CANOPIES
CANTATES
CANTEENS
CANTERED
CANTICLE
CANTIEST
CANTINGS
CANTLETS
CANTLING
CANTORIS
CANTREDS
CANTREFS
CANTRIPS
CAPELETS
CAPELINS
CAPERERS
CAPERING
CAPESKIN
CAPONIER
CAPONISE
CAPRATES
CAPRICES
CAPRIOLE
CAPSTONE
CAPTURED
CAPTURES
CARABINE
CARANGID
CARBIDES
CARBINES
CARCANET
CARCASED
CARDECUS
CARDIGAN
CARDITIS
CARELESS
CARESSED
CARFOXES
CARGOOSE
CARIERES
CARINATE
CARIOLES
CARLINES
CARLINGS
CARMINES
CARNAGES
CARNEOUS
CARNIEST
CARNIFEX
CAROCHES
CAROMELS
CAROTENE
CAROTINS
CAROUSED
CAROUSEL
CAROUSER
CAROUSES
CARPETED
CARPINGS
CARRECTS
CARRIOLE
CARTAGES
CARTONED
CARTOONS
CARVINGS
CASEMENT
CASERNES
CASEWORK
CASHMERE
CASIMERE
CASTANET
CASTELLA
CASTINGS
CASTLING
CASTRATE
CASTRATI
CATALASE
CATALOES
CATALYSE
CATBIRDS
CATCHERS
CATELOGS
CATENARY
CATERANS
CATERERS
CATERESS
CATERING
CATHODES
CATHOLES
CATHOUSE
CATLINGS
CATMINTS
CATTIEST
CAULDEST
CAVALIER
CAVILLER
CEASINGS
CEDILLAS
CEDRATES
CEILINGS
CEINTURE
CELADONS
CELERIAC
CELERIES
CELESTAS
CENSORED
CENSURED
CENTAGES
CENTARES
CENTAURS
CENTAURY
CENTAVOS
CENTESIS
CENTIARE
CENTIMES
CENTIMOS
CENTNERS
CENTOIST
CENTONES

CENTRIES
CENTRING
CENTRISM
CENTRIST
CENTRUMS
CERAMICS
CERAMIST
CERASINS
CERASTES
CERESINE
CERESINS
CERNUOUS
CERRISES
CERUSITE
CERVICAL
CERVICES
CERVIXES
CESSIONS
CESTOIDS
CHAGRINS
CHAINLET
CHAIRMEN
CHALDERS
CHALKIER
CHAMLETS
CHANCERS
CHANCIER
CHANCRES
CHANDLER
CHANGERS
CHANNERS
CHANTERS
CHANTEYS
CHANTIES
CHANTORS
CHAPLETS
CHAPTERS
CHAPTREL
CHARADES
CHARIEST
CHARIOTS
CHARLIES
CHARNELS
CHAROSET
CHARPIES
CHARTERS
CHARTING
CHARTISM
CHARTIST
CHASMIER
CHASTELY
CHASTENS
CHATLINE
CHATTELS
CHATTERS
CHATTIER
CHATTIES
CHAUNTER
CHAYOTES
CHEATERS
CHEATING
CHEERIOS
CHELATES
CHELATOR
CHEROOTS
CHERRIES
CHESTIER
CHESTING
CHETNIKS
CHEVERIL
CHEVRONS
CHICANER
CHICANES
CHIMERAS
CHIMERES
CHINTZES
CHIRTING
CHITTERS
CHLORATE
CHLORITE
CHOLENTS
CHOLERAS
CHOLINES
CHONDRES
CHOOSIER
CHOPINES
CHORALES
CHORDING
CHORINES
CHORISES
CHORTLED
CHORTLES
CHOWRIES
CHRISTEN
CHRISTIE
CHUNDERS
CHUNTERS
CIELINGS
CILIATES
CINCTURE
CINDERED
CINEASTE
CINEASTS
CINEOLES
CINERARY
CINEREAL
CINEREAS
CINERINS
CIRCLETS
CISELEUR
CISELURE
CISTERNA
CISTERNS
CISTRONS
CISTVAEN
CITADELS
CITHARAS
CITHERNS
CITIZENS
CITRANGE
CITRATES
CITREOUS
CITRINES
CITRUSES
CITTERNS
CLADDERS
CLAGGIER
CLAIMERS
CLAMMIER
CLAMPERS
CLANGERS
CLAPNETS
CLAPPERS
CLARINET
CLARTIER
CLARTING
CLASHING
CLASPERS
CLASPING
CLASSIER
CLASSING
CLATCHES
CLATTERS
CLATTING
CLAUTING
CLAVIERS
CLAVIGER
CLAYIEST
CLEANERS
CLEANEST
CLEANING
CLEANSED
CLEANSER
CLEARERS
CLEAREST
CLEARING
CLEATING
CLEAVERS
CLEAVING
CLEMATIS
CLERGIES
CLERICAL
CLERKING
CLIENTAL
CLIMATES
CLIMBERS
CLINAMEN
CLINGERS
CLINGIER
CLINKERS
CLITTERS
CLOISTER
CLOSURED
CLOTHIER
CLOTHING
CLOTTERS
CLOTTIER
CLOTTING
CLOTURED
CLOTURES
CLOUTERS
CLOUTING
CLOWDERS
CLUSTERS
CLUSTERY
CLUTTERS
COACHERS
COALIEST
COALISED
COALISES
COALMINE
COARSELY
COARSENS
COARSEST
COASTERS
COASTING
COATINGS
COATLESS
COCAINES
COCKSIER
CODEINES
CODETTAS
COEHORNS
COENURUS
COFFRETS
COGENERS
COGNATES
COGNISED
COGNISES
COGNIZES
COHESION
COINAGES
COISTREL
COLANDER
COLDNESS
COLETITS
COLLATES
COLLIERS
COLONIES
COLONISE
COMATOSE
COMBIEST
COMBINES
COMFIEST
COMITIES
COMMENTS
COMPARES
COMPEARS
COMPRISE
COMPTERS
COMRADES
CONACRES
CONCEITS
CONCENTS
CONCEPTS
CONCERNS
CONCERTS
CONCHIES
CONCISED
CONCISER
CONCISES
CONCREWS
CONDOLES
CONDYLES
CONFECTS
CONFIDES
CONFINES
CONFIXES
CONFUTES
CONGEALS
CONGESTS
CONGRATS
CONGREES
CONGRESS
CONGRUED
CONGRUES
CONIFERS
CONIINES
CONJECTS
CONJURED
CONJURES
CONNECTS
CONNIVES
CONNOTES
CONQUERS
CONQUEST
CONSEILS
CONSENTS
CONSERVE
CONSIDER
CONSOLED
CONSOLER
CONSPIRE
CONSTATE
CONSTERS
CONSTRUE
CONSUMER
CONTECKS
CONTEMNS
CONTENDS
CONTENTS
CONTESSA
CONTESTS
CONTEXTS
CONTRAST
CONTRATE
CONTRATS
CONTRIST
CONTRITE
CONTUSED
CONTUSES
CONVENTS
CONVERSE
CONVERTS
CONVIVES
COOMIEST
COONTIES
COPPERAS
COPSIEST
CORACLES
CORAMINE
CORANTOS
CORBEAUS
CORBEILS
CORDAGES
CORDINGS
CORDITES
CORDLESS
CORELLAS
CORKAGES
CORKIEST
CORNAGES
CORNEOUS
CORNETTI
CORNETTS
CORNICES
CORNIEST
CORNISTS
CORNUTED
CORNUTES
CORODIES
CORONATE
CORONERS
CORONETS
CORPSING
CORRADES
CORRECTS
CORSAGES
CORSELET
CORSETED
CORSETRY
CORSIVES
CORSLETS
CORSNEDS
CORTEGES
CORTEXES
CORTICES
COSECANT
COSINESS
COSMETIC
COSTATED
COSTEANS
COSTLIER
COSTRELS
COSTUMED
COSTUMER
COTERIES
COTINGAS
COTISING
COTTAGES
COTTIERS
COTTISED
COTTISES
COULTERS
COUNTERS
COUNTESS
COUNTIES
COUPLETS
COURAGES
COURANTE
COURANTS
COURIERS
COURSING
COURTESY
COURTING
COUTURES
COUVERTS
COVARIES
COWTREES
COXINESS
COYSTREL
COZENERS
CRABLIKE
CRADLING
CRAFTING
CRAGSMEN
CRAMBOES
CRAMPETS
CRAMPITS
CRANAGES
CRANCHES
CRANKIER
CRANKLED
CRANKLES
CRANNIED
CRANNIES
CRANTSES
CRAPIEST
CRASHING
CRASSEST
CRATCHES
CRAVINGS
CRAWLIER
CRAWLING
CRAZIEST
CREAKILY
CREAKING
CREAMERS
CREAMING
CREANCES
CREASERS
CREASIER
CREASING
CREASOTE
CREATINE
CREATING
CREATINS
CREATION
CREATORS
CREESING
CREMATES
CREMONAS
CREMOSIN
CRENATED
CREOLIAN
CREOLIST
CREOSOTE
CREPIEST
CREPITUS
CRESCENT
CRESCIVE
CRESTING
CRESTONS
CRETISMS
CREVICES
CRIBBLES
CRIBELLA
CRIBROSE
CRICKETS
CRINATED
CRINGERS
CRINGLES
CRINITES
CRINKLES
CRISPATE
CRISPEST
CRISTATE
CRITTERS
CRIVVENS
CROAKERS
CROCEINS
CROCHETS
CROCKETS
CROFTERS
CROFTING
CROMBIES
CRONKEST
CROODLES
CROOKEST
CROONERS
CROPPIES
CROQUETS
CROSIERS
CROSSEST
CROSSING
CROSSLET
CROSSTIE
CROTCHES
CROTTLES
CROWDIES
CROWDING
CROWNERS
CROWNETS
CROZIERS
CRUDITES
CRUSADED
CRUSADER
CRUSADES
CRUSTATE
CRUSTIER
CRYOGENS
CRYOLITE
CUDBEARS
CUITTLES
CULOTTES
CULTIGEN
CULTURES
CULVERTS
CUPRITES
CURARINE
CURATING
CURDIEST
CURETTES
CURLIEST
CURNIEST
CURRENTS
CURTAILS
CURTAINS
CURTNESS
CURTSIED
CURTSIES
CURVIEST
CUSTODES
CUSTOMED
CUSTOMER
CUSTRELS
CUTESIER
CUTICLES
CUTINISE
CUTLINES
CYANATES
CYANIDES
CYANINES
CYANISED
CYANISES
CYANITES
CYANIZES
CYANURET
CYNOSURE
CYSTEINE
CYSTINES
CYTISINE
CYTOSINE
CZARISTS
CZARITSA
DABBLERS
DABSTERS
DAFFIEST
DAFTNESS
DAGGIEST
DAINTIER
DAINTIES
DAIRYING
DAIRYMEN
DAKERING
DALESMAN
DALESMEN
DALLIERS
DAMOISEL
DAMPIEST
DAMPNESS
DANDIEST
DANDLERS
DANEGELD
DANEGELT
DANELAGH
DANELAWS
DANGERED
DANGLERS
DANGLIER
DANSEURS
DARINGLY
DARIOLES
DARKLING
DARKNESS
DARKSOME
DARLINGS
DARNINGS
DARRAIGN
DARRAINE
DARRAINS
DARTLING
DATARIES
DATELESS
DATURINE
DAUBIEST
DAUNDERS
DAUNERED
DAUNTERS
DAWBRIES

DAWDLERS
DAYTALES
DAYTIMES
DAZZLERS
DEADLIER
DEALFISH
DEALINGS
DEANSHIP
DEARLING
DEARNESS
DEARNFUL
DEASIULS
DEASOILS
DEBASERS
DEBASING
DEBATERS
DEBITORS
DEBONAIR
DEBRIDES
DEBRIEFS
DECANTER
DECIARES
DECIDERS
DECIMALS
DECISION
DECISORY
DECKINGS
DECLAIMS
DECLARES
DECLINES
DECOLORS
DECREASE
DECREETS
DECREPIT
DECRIALS
DECRIERS
DECROWNS
DECRYING
DECUMANS
DECURIAS
DECURIES
DECURION
DEEMSTER
DEERLETS
DEERSKIN
DEFACERS
DEFAULTS
DEFILERS
DEFILING
DEFINERS
DEFLATES
DEFLATOR
DEFOREST
DEFROSTS
DEFTNESS
DEFUNCTS
DEFUSING
DEGRADES
DEGREASE
DEIFIERS
DEISEALS
DEISHEAL
DELAINES
DELATING
DELATION
DELATORS
DELAYERS
DELAYING
DELETING
DELETORY

DELIGHTS
DELIMITS
DELIVERS
DELIVERY
DELOPING
DELTOIDS
DELUDING
DELUGING
DELUSION
DELUSORY
DEMAINES
DEMAYNES
DEMEANES
DEMENTIA
DEMENTIS
DEMERITS
DEMERSAL
DEMIREPS
DEMISING
DEMISTER
DEMONISE
DEMONISM
DEMONIST
DEMOTIST
DEMOUNTS
DEMPSTER
DEMUREST
DEMURING
DENARIES
DENARIUS
DENATURE
DENDRITE
DENTALIA
DENTARIA
DENTEXES
DENTINES
DENTISTS
DENTURES
DEODATES
DEONTICS
DEPAINTS
DEPARTED
DEPARTER
DEPICTER
DEPICTOR
DEPLANES
DEPLORES
DEPOSING
DEPOSITS
DEPRAVES
DEPRIVAL
DEPRIVES
DEPURANT
DEPURATE
DERACINE
DERAIGNS
DERAILED
DERAILER
DERANGED
DERANGES
DERATING
DERATION
DERAYING
DERELICT
DERIDERS
DERIDING
DERISION
DERISIVE
DERISORY
DERIVING

DERMISES
DERMOIDS
DERRISES
DESALTED
DESCANTS
DESCENTS
DESCRIBE
DESCRIED
DESCRIES
DESCRIVE
DESERTED
DESERTER
DESEXING
DESIGNED
DESIGNER
DESILVER
DESINENT
DESINING
DESIRERS
DESIRING
DESIROUS
DESMINES
DESOLATE
DESPAIRS
DESPISAL
DESPISER
DESPOTIC
DESSERTS
DESTINED
DESTINES
DESTRIER
DESTROYS
DESTRUCT
DESYATIN
DESYNING
DETACHES
DETAINER
DETENTES
DETENUES
DETERGES
DETINUES
DETRACTS
DETRAINS
DETRITAL
DETRITUS
DETRUDES
DEUDDARN
DEUTERON
DEVIANTS
DEVIATES
DEVILETS
DEVILING
DEVILTRY
DEVISALS
DEVISERS
DEVISING
DEVISORS
DEVLINGS
DEWATERS
DEXTRANS
DEXTRINE
DEXTRINS
DEXTROSE
DEXTROUS
DHURRIES
DIABETES
DIABLERY
DIAGNOSE
DIALECTS
DIALLERS

DIALYSED
DIALYSER
DIALYSES
DIALYZER
DIALYZES
DIAMANTE
DIARISED
DIARISES
DIARIZES
DIASPORE
DIASTASE
DIASTEMA
DIASTERS
DIASTOLE
DIASTYLE
DIATRIBE
DIBBLERS
DICENTRA
DICTATES
DIEDRALS
DIELYTRA
DIERESES
DIERESIS
DIESTRUS
DIETINES
DIFFUSER
DIGESTER
DIHEDRAL
DILATERS
DILATING
DILEMMAS
DILIGENT
DILLIEST
DILUENTS
DILUTEES
DILUTERS
DIMERISE
DIMEROUS
DIMETERS
DINETTES
DINGBATS
DINGESES
DINGHIES
DINGIEST
DINGUSES
DINKIEST
DINNERED
DINOSAUR
DIOCESAN
DIOPTASE
DIOPTERS
DIOPTRES
DIORITES
DIOXANES
DIPHONES
DIPLOGEN
DIPTERAL
DIPTERAN
DIPTERAS
DIPTEROI
DIPTEROS
DIRECTLY
DIREMPTS
DIRIGENT
DIRIMENT
DIRTIEST
DIRTYING
DISABLED
DISABLES
DISADORN

DISAGREE
DISANNEX
DISARMED
DISARMER
DISASTER
DISBURSE
DISCERNS
DISCOERS
DISCOURE
DISCOVER
DISCREET
DISCRETE
DISCURED
DISCURES
DISENDOW
DISENROL
DISGAVEL
DISGORGE
DISGRACE
DISGRADE
DISHABLE
DISHERIT
DISHORSE
DISINTER
DISINURE
DISLEAFS
DISLEAVE
DISLIKEN
DISLODGE
DISNESTS
DISORBED
DISORDER
DISOWNED
DISOWNER
DISPERSE
DISPLACE
DISPONED
DISPONEE
DISPONER
DISPONES
DISPONGE
DISPOSER
DISPREAD
DISPROVE
DISPUNGE
DISPURSE
DISPUTER
DISRANKS
DISRATED
DISRATES
DISROBED
DISROBES
DISSEATS
DISSENTS
DISSERTS
DISSERVE
DISSEVER
DISTANCE
DISTASTE
DISTENDS
DISTHENE
DISTRACT
DISTRAIN
DISTRESS
DISTUNED
DISTUNES
DISUNITE
DISVALUE
DITCHERS
DIURESES

DIURESIS
DIURNALS
DIVALENT
DIVERGES
DIVERSED
DIVERSES
DIVINERS
DIVINEST
DIVORCES
DOATINGS
DOCILEST
DOCQUETS
DOCTRESS
DODDIEST
DODGIEST
DOGEATES
DOGGIEST
DOGGRELS
DOILTEST
DOLERITE
DOLLIERS
DOMESTIC
DOMINATE
DOMINEER
DOMINEES
DOMINIES
DOMINOES
DONARIES
DONATORS
DONSIEST
DOODLERS
DOOMIEST
DOOMSTER
DOORSMEN
DOORSTEP
DOPINESS
DORISING
DORIZING
DORKIEST
DORMANTS
DORTIEST
DOSSIERS
DOTINGLY
DOTTEREL
DOTTIEST
DOTTRELS
DOUANIER
DOUBLERS
DOUBLETS
DOUBTERS
DOUCINES
DOULEIAS
DOURINES
DOURNESS
DOVERING
DOWAGERS
DOWDIEST
DOWERING
DOWNIEST
DOWNSIDE
DOWNSIZE
DOZENTHS
DOZINESS
DRABBERS
DRABBEST
DRABBETS
DRABBIER
DRABBING
DRABBLES
DRABLERS

DRABNESS
DRACONES
DRAFTEES
DRAFTERS
DRAFTING
DRAGGING
DRAGGLES
DRAGLINE
DRAGNETS
DRAGONET
DRAGONNE
DRAGSMEN
DRAGSTER
DRAILING
DRAINAGE
DRAINERS
DRAINING
DRAISENE
DRAISINE
DRAMMING
DRANTING
DRAPIERS
DRAPPIES
DRAPPING
DRASTICS
DRAUNTED
DRAWINGS
DRAWLERS
DRAWLING
DRAYAGES
DREADERS
DREADING
DREAMERS
DREAMILY
DREAMING
DREAREST
DREARILY
DREARING
DREDGING
DRENCHES
DRESSAGE
DRESSIER
DRESSING
DRIBBERS
DRIBBLES
DRIBBLET
DRIBLETS
DRIFTERS
DRIFTING
DRINKERS
DRISHEEN
DRIVABLE
DROGUETS
DROILING
DROLLEST
DROLLING
DRONGOES
DRONIEST
DROOKING
DROOLING
DROOPING
DROPLETS
DROPPING
DROPPLES
DROPSIED
DROPSIES
DROPWISE
DROSERAS
DROSKIES
DROSSIER

DROUKING
DROVINGS
DROWNING
DROWSIER
DROWSING
DRUGGETS
DRUGGIES
DRUIDESS
DRUNKEST
DRUSIEST
DRUTHERS
DRUXIEST
DRYBEATS
DUELLING
DUELLIST
DUKELING
DUKERIES
DULCITES
DULLIEST
DUNGAREE
DUNGIEST
DUNNIEST
DUNNITES
DUOTONES
DUPERIES
DURABLES
DURAMENS
DURANCES
DURGIEST
DUVETYNS
DWARFING
DWELLING
DWINDLES
DYELINES
DYESTERS
DYNAMISE
DYNAMITE
DYSGENIC
DYSLEXIA
DYSMELIA
DYSPNEAL
DYSURIES
EAGEREST
EANLINGS
EARDROPS
EARDRUMS
EARFLAPS
EARLDOMS
EARLIEST
EARLOBES
EARLOCKS
EARNESTS
EARNINGS
EARPICKS
EARPLUGS
EARRINGS
EARSHOTS
EARTHING
EARTHMAN
EASEMENT
EASTERLY
EASTINGS
EASTLAND
EASTLING
EASTLINS
EASTWARD
EATERIES
EBIONISM
EBONISED
EBONISES

EBONISTS
EBONITES
EBRIATED
ECHIDNAS
ECLOSING
ECLOSION
ECOSTATE
ECRASEUR
ECSTATIC
ECTOPIAS
ECTOPIES
ECTOSARC
EDGINESS
EDIFIERS
EDITIONS
EDITRESS
EDUCATES
EDUCTORS
EELFARES
EELGRASS
EELPOUTS
EERINESS
EGESTING
EGESTION
EGOTISED
EGOTISMS
EGOTISTS
EIGHTEEN
EILDINGS
EJECTORS
ELANCING
ELAPSING
ELASTICS
ELASTINS
ELATERIN
ELATIONS
ELATIVES
ELDRITCH
ELECTING
ELECTORS
ELECTROS
ELEGIAST
ELEGISTS
ELEMENTS
ELFLANDS
ELICITOR
ELISIONS
ELITISMS
ELITISTS
ELLWANDS
ELOCUTES
ELOGISTS
ELOGIUMS
ELOIGNED
ELOIGNER
ELOINERS
ELONGATE
ELUSIONS
ELUTIONS
ELVANITE
EMANATED
EMANATES
EMBALING
EMBASING
EMBRACES
EMBRAIDS
EMBRASOR
EMBRAVES
EMBREADS
EMBROILS

EMBROWNS
EMBRYONS
EMENDALS
EMERALDS
EMERITUS
EMERSION
EMETINES
EMICATES
EMIGRANT
EMIRATES
EMISSARY
EMISSION
EMITTERS
EMONGEST
EMOTIONS
EMPAIRES
EMPALING
EMPARING
EMPARTED
EMPERIES
EMPERISE
EMPERISH
EMPOISON
EMPRISES
EMPTIERS
EMPTIONS
EMULSION
ENABLERS
ENABLING
ENACTORS
ENACTURE
ENAMOURS
ENARCHES
ENARMING
ENATIONS
ENCARPUS
ENCASING
ENCHAINS
ENCHANTS
ENCHARMS
ENCLOSED
ENCLOSER
ENCLOUDS
ENCORING
ENCRADLE
ENCREASE
ENCRINAL
ENCRUSTS
ENCYSTED
ENDANGER
ENDEMIAL
ENDEMICS
ENDEMISM
ENDERMIC
ENDERONS
ENDGAMES
ENDIRONS
ENDORSED
ENDORSEE
ENDORSER
ENDORSES
ENDOSARC
ENDOSTEA
ENDOWERS
ENDURERS
ENDURING
ENERGIDS
ENERGIES
ENERGISE
ENERVING

ENFESTED
ENFIRING
ENFORCES
ENFOREST
ENFRAMES
ENGAGERS
ENGAOLED
ENGILDED
ENGINEER
ENGINERS
ENGINERY
ENGIRDLE
ENGORGES
ENGORING
ENGRACED
ENGRACES
ENGRAFFS
ENGRAFTS
ENGRAILS
ENGRAINS
ENGRASPS
ENGRAVED
ENGRAVES
ENGUARDS
ENISLING
ENLACING
ENLARDED
ENLARGED
ENLARGEN
ENLARGER
ENLARGES
ENLIGHTS
ENLISTED
ENMITIES
ENORMOUS
ENPRINTS
ENQUIRED
ENRACING
ENRAGING
ENRANGED
ENRANGES
ENRAVISH
ENRICHED
ENRICHES
ENRIDGED
ENRINGED
ENROBING
ENROUGHS
ENROUNDS
ENSEALED
ENSEAMED
ENSEARED
ENSHIELD
ENSHRINE
ENSHROUD
ENSIFORM
ENSIGNED
ENSILAGE
ENSILING
ENSLAVED
ENSLAVER
ENSNARED
ENSNARES
ENSNARLS
ENSOULED
ENSTAMPS
ENSTYLED
ENSTYLES
ENSURING
ENTAILED

ENTAILER
ENTAMING
ENTANGLE
ENTAYLES
ENTELLUS
ENTERATE
ENTERERS
ENTERICS
ENTERING
ENTHRALL
ENTHRALS
ENTHUSED
ENTICERS
ENTIRELY
ENTIRETY
ENTITIES
ENTITLES
ENTRAILS
ENTRAINS
ENTRANCE
ENTRANTS
ENTREATS
ENTREATY
ENTREMES
ENTRESOL
ENTRISMS
ENTRISTS
ENTRUSTS
ENTRYISM
ENTRYIST
ENTWINES
ENTWISTS
ENURESIS
ENURETIC
ENVAULTS
ENVIRONS
EPACRIDS
EPEIRIDS
EPERGNES
EPHEDRAS
EPIBLAST
EPICARPS
EPIDOTES
EPIDURAL
EPIGONES
EPIGRAMS
EPILATES
EPILATOR
EPINASTY
EPINOSIC
EPISEMON
EPISODAL
EPISPERM
EPISTLED
EPISTLER
EPISTLES
EPISTYLE
EPITOMES
EPITOPES
EPIZOANS
EPSILONS
EPSOMITE
EPURATED
EPURATES
EQUATORS
ERASABLE
ERASIONS
ERASURES
ERATHEMS
ERECTERS

ERECTING
ERECTION
ERECTORS
EREMITAL
EREMITES
EREPSINS
ERETHISM
ERGOTISE
ERGOTISM
ERINGOES
ERINITES
ERIONITE
ERMELINS
ERODENTS
ERODIUMS
EROSIONS
EROTEMAS
EROTEMES
EROTESIS
EROTICAL
EROTISMS
ERRANTLY
ERRANTRY
ERRATICS
ERRHINES
ERRINGLY
ERRORIST
ERSATZES
ERUCTING
ERUDITES
ERUPTING
ERUPTION
ERYNGOES
ESCALATE
ESCALIER
ESCAPING
ESCARGOT
ESCAROLE
ESCARPED
ESCHALOT
ESCOLARS
ESCORTED
ESCRIBED
ESCULENT
ESLOINED
ESLOYNED
ESOTERIC
ESPALIER
ESPARTOS
ESSOINER
ESSONITE
ESTACADE
ESTANCIA
ESTATING
ESTERIFY
ESTIMATE
ESTIVATE
ESTOILES
ESTOVERS
ESTRADES
ESTRANGE
ESTRAYED
ESTREATS
ESTREPED
ESTRIDGE
ESTROGEN
ESURIENT
ETACISMS
ETAERIOS
ETAGERES

ETALAGES
ETATISME
ETATISTE
ETCHANTS
ETCHINGS
ETERNISE
ETERNITY
ETERNIZE
ETHANOLS
ETHERCAP
ETHEREAL
ETHERIAL
ETHERION
ETHERISE
ETHERISM
ETHERIST
ETHICALS
ETHNARCH
ETHNICAL
ETIOLINS
ETRANGER
ETRENNES
ETTERCAP
EUCAINES
EUCRITES
EUGENISM
EUGENIST
EULOGIES
EULOGISE
EULOGIST
EUMERISM
EUPATRID
EUSTATIC
EVANGELS
EVASIBLE
EVASIONS
EVENTERS
EVERSION
EVERTING
EVERTORS
EVICTORS
EVIDENTS
EVILLEST
EVIRATES
EVITATES
EVOCATES
EVOLUTES
EVOLVERS
EVULSING
EVULSION
EXACTERS
EXACTORS
EXALTING
EXAMINER
EXAMINES
EXCERPTA
EXCISION
EXCITERS
EXCITONS
EXCITORS
EXERTING
EXERTION
EXHALING
EXIGENTS
EXISTENT
EXISTING
EXOCARPS
EXODISTS
EXOMIONS
EXORCISE

EXORCISM
EXORCIST
EXORDIAL
EXPIRANT
EXPLANTS
EXPLOITS
EXPOSING
EXSERTED
EXTENSOR
EXTERNAL
EXTERNAT
EXTERNES
EXTIRPED
EXTRACTS
EXTRADOS
EXTRAITS
EXTREATS
EXTRORSE
EXTRUDES
EXUDATES
EXULTING
EYELIADS
FABLINGS
FABULISE
FABURDEN
FACTURES
FADDIEST
FAHLORES
FAIENCES
FAILINGS
FAILURES
FAINITES
FAINTEST
FAINTIER
FAIRINGS
FAIRNESS
FAKERIES
FALLINGS
FALSETTO
FANCIERS
FANCIEST
FANGLESS
FANLIGHT
FANTEEGS
FARADISE
FARCINGS
FARDAGES
FARDINGS
FARINOSE
FARMINGS
FARNESOL
FARTHELS
FARTHEST
FARTHING
FARTLEKS
FASCINES
FASTENED
FASTENER
FASTINGS
FATHERLY
FATLINGS
FATTENER
FATTIEST
FATTRELS
FAULTIER
FAULTING
FAVRILES
FEALTIES
FEARLESS
FEARSOME

FEASIBLE
FEASIBLY
FEASTERS
FEASTING
FEATHERS
FEATURES
FECHTING
FEDARIES
FEDERALS
FEEDINGS
FEELINGS
FEERINGS
FEGARIES
FEINTEST
FEISTIER
FELDSPAR
FELONIES
FELSITES
FELSITIC
FELSPARS
FELSTONE
FELTIEST
FELTINGS
FELWORTS
FEMINISE
FEMINIST
FEMITERS
FENDIEST
FENESTRA
FENITARS
FENLANDS
FENNIEST
FERITIES
FERLIEST
FERLYING
FERMATAS
FERMENTS
FERMIONS
FERNIEST
FERNINGS
FERRATES
FERRITES
FERRITIN
FESTERED
FESTIVAL
FETCHING
FETTLERS
FETTLING
FEUDINGS
FEUTRING
FEVERISH
FEVEROUS
FEWTRILS
FIANCEES
FIBROSED
FIBROSES
FIBSTERS
FIELDERS
FIELDING
FIERCEST
FIERIEST
FIGHTERS
FIGMENTS
FIGURANT
FIKERIES
FILABEGS
FILACERS
FILAMENT
FILANDER
FILASSES

FILATURE
FILAZERS
FILBERDS
FILBERTS
FILEMOTS
FILENAME
FILIATES
FILMIEST
FILTERED
FILTRATE
FINAGLED
FINAGLES
FINANCES
FINDRAMS
FINEERED
FINERIES
FINESSER
FINGERED
FINISHER
FINNIEST
FIREARMS
FIREDOGS
FIRELESS
FIREPANS
FIREPOTS
FIRESIDE
FIRMNESS
FIRRIEST
FISHABLE
FISNOMIE
FISSURED
FISTMELE
FISTULAE
FITLIEST
FITMENTS
FIXTURES
FLACKETS
FLAKIEST
FLAMIEST
FLAMINES
FLANEURS
FLANKERS
FLAPPERS
FLARIEST
FLASHIER
FLASHING
FLATBEDS
FLATLING
FLATNESS
FLATTENS
FLATTERS
FLATTING
FLATWISE
FLAUNTER
FLAWIEST
FLAXIEST
FLEAPITS
FLEDGING
FLEERING
FLEETING
FLENSING
FLESHIER
FLESHING
FLETTONS
FLEURETS
FLEXIONS
FLINDERS
FLINGERS
FLINTIER
FLIRTING
FLITTERN
FLITTERS
FLOATELS
FLOATERS
FLOATIER
FLOATING
FLORIEST
FLORIGEN
FLOSSIER
FLOTAGES
FLOUNDER
FLOUTING
FLUKIEST
FLUORITE
FLUSTERS
FLUSTERY
FLUTIEST
FLUTTERS
FOAMIEST
FOISTERS
FOISTING
FOLIAGES
FOLIATES
FOLKSIER
FONDLERS
FONTLETS
FOOTIEST
FOOTINGS
FOOTLING
FOOTREST
FORBEARS
FORCIPES
FORDOING
FORECARS
FORECAST
FORELAID
FORELAND
FORELAYS
FORELIES
FORELIFT
FOREMAST
FOREMOST
FORENSIC
FOREPAST
FORESAID
FORESAIL
FORESIDE
FORESKIN
FORESTAL
FORESTAY
FORESTED
FORESTER
FORESTRY
FORETOLD
FORETOPS
FOREVERS
FORFEITS
FORGINGS
FORGIVES
FORHENTS
FORINSEC
FORKIEST
FORLENDS
FORMANTS
FORMATES
FORMINGS
FORNENST
FORNICES
FORPINES
FORSLOED
FORSPEND
FORSPENT
FORTLETS
FORTRESS
FORTUNED
FORTUNES
FORWASTE
FOSTERED
FOSTERER
FOUDRIES
FOULDERS
FOUNDERS
FOUSTIER
FOUTRING
FOXINESS
FOZINESS
FRACTING
FRAGMENT
FRAILEST
FRAILTEE
FRAISING
FRAMINGS
FRANKEST
FRATCHES
FRATRIES
FRAYINGS
FREAKING
FREDAINE
FREEBIES
FREESIAS
FREIGHTS
FREMITUS
FRENETIC
FRENZIED
FRENZIES
FRESCADE
FRESHING
FRETSAWS
FRETTING
FRIANDES
FRIBBLES
FRICADEL
FRIENDED
FRIGATES
FRIGHTEN
FRIJOLES
FRISETTE
FRISKETS
FRISTING
FRITTERS
FRITTING
FRITURES
FROGLETS
FRONDAGE
FRONDEUR
FRONTAGE
FRONTALS
FRONTING
FROSTIER
FROSTING
FROTHING
FROUNCED
FROUNCES
FROWIEST
FROWSTED
FROWSTER
FRUCTOSE
FRUITERS
FRUITING
FRUSTULE
FRUTICES
FUNERALS
FUNKIEST
FUNNIEST
FUNSTERS
FURNACED
FURNACES
FURRIEST
FURZIEST
FUSAROLE
FUSILEER
FUTILEST
GABBLERS
GADFLIES
GADLINGS
GAGSTERS
GAHNITES
GAINABLE
GAINLESS
GAINLIER
GALATEAS
GALENITE
GALENOID
GALETTES
GALLATES
GALLEONS
GALLISED
GALLISES
GALOPINS
GALTONIA
GAMBIERS
GAMBLERS
GAMBRELS
GAMELANS
GAMESIER
GAMESTER
GAMINESS
GAMMIEST
GANGLIAR
GANGLIER
GANGRELS
GANGSTER
GANISTER
GANNETRY
GANOINES
GANTLETS
GANTLINE
GANTLOPE
GANTRIES
GARBLERS
GARBLING
GARDENED
GARDENER
GARDENIA
GARGLING
GARISHED
GARMENTS
GARNERED
GAROTTES
GARPIKES
GARRISON
GARROTES
GASALIER
GASELIER
GASFIELD
GASOLENE
GASOLIER
GASOLINE
GASTNESS
GASTRAEA
GASTRINS
GATELESS
GAUDIEST
GAULTERS
GAUMIEST
GAUNTEST
GAUNTLET
GAUNTREE
GAZUNDER
GEARINGS
GEARLESS
GELASTIC
GELATINE
GELATINS
GELATION
GELDINGS
GELIDEST
GELOSIES
GEMINATE
GEMINIES
GEMINOUS
GEMSHORN
GEMSTONE
GENDARME
GENERALE
GENERALS
GENERANT
GENERATE
GENERICS
GENEROUS
GENETICS
GENETRIX
GENIALLY
GENISTAS
GENITALS
GENITORS
GENITRIX
GENITURE
GENTIANS
GENTIEST
GENTILES
GENTILIC
GENTLEST
GENTLING
GENTRICE
GENTRIES
GENTRIFY
GEOFACTS
GEOMANTS
GEORGICS
GERANIOL
GERANIUM
GERBERAS
GERENUKS
GERMAINE
GERMAINS
GERMINAL
GERONTIC
GESNERIA
GESTALTS
GESTATED
GESTURAL
GESTURED
GETTINGS
GHASTING
GHERKINS
GHOSTIER
GHOSTING
GIANTESS
GIANTISM
GIGGLERS
GILBERTS
GINGALLS
GINGERED
GINGERLY
GINGKOES
GINHOUSE
GINKGOES
GINNIEST
GIRASOLE
GIRDLERS
GIRLONDS
GIRNIEST
GIRTHING
GIRTLINE
GISARMES
GITTERNS
GLABRATE
GLACEING
GLACIERS
GLACISES
GLADDENS
GLADDEST
GLADDIES
GLADIEST
GLADNESS
GLAIRING
GLAIRINS
GLANDERS
GLANDULE
GLAREOUS
GLARIEST
GLASSIER
GLASSINE
GLASSING
GLASSMEN
GLAZIERS
GLAZIEST
GLAZINGS
GLEAMING
GLEANERS
GLEANING
GLEDGING
GLEETING
GLENOIDS
GLENTING
GLIADINE
GLIADINS
GLIBBEST
GLIBNESS
GLIDDEST
GLIMMERS
GLISSADE
GLISTENS
GLISTERS
GLITCHES
GLITTERS
GLOATERS
GLOATING
GLOSSIER
GLOSSIES
GLOSSINA
GLOUTING
GLUCINAS
GLUTAEUS
GLUTELIN
GLYCERIA
GLYCERIN
GLYCINES
GNARLIER
GNARLING
GNASHERS
GNATHITE
GNATLING
GNOMISTS
GOADSMEN
GOADSTER
GOATIEST
GOATLING
GOATSKIN
GODETIAS
GODLIEST
GOLDIEST
GOLDSIZE
GOLIASED
GOLIASES
GOMERALS
GOMERILS
GONDELAY
GONGSTER
GOODIEST
GOODSIRE
GOOGLIES
GOOPIEST
GORAMIES
GORINESS
GORMIEST
GORSIEST
GOTHITES
GOURMETS
GOUSTIER
GOUTIEST
GRABBLES
GRACKLES
GRADATES
GRADIENT
GRADINES
GRADUSES
GRAFTERS
GRAFTING
GRAINAGE
GRAINERS
GRAINIER
GRANDEES
GRANDEST
GRANDEUR
GRANFERS
GRANGERS
GRANITAS
GRANITES
GRANITIC
GRANNIED
GRANNIES
GRANTEES
GRANTERS
GRANTING
GRANTORS
GRANULES
GRAPIEST
GRAPNELS
GRAPPLES
GRASPING
GRASSING
GRATINEE
GRATINGS
GRAUPELS
GRAVINGS
GRAVITON
GRAYLING
GRAZINGS
GREASERS
GREASIER
GREASILY
GREASING
GREATENS
GREATEST
GREAVING
GRECIANS
GRECISED
GREENERS
GREENEST
GREENIES
GREENING
GREENISH
GREENTHS
GREESING
GREETERS
GREETING
GREGALES
GREINING
GREISENS
GREMIALS
GREMLINS
GRENADES
GRENNING
GRESSING
GREYHENS
GREYINGS
GREYNESS
GRIBBLES
GRIDDERS
GRIDDLES
GRIDELIN
GRIDIRON
GRIEVERS
GRIEVOUS
GRIFFONS
GRIFTERS
GRIFTING
GRILLADE
GRIMACES
GRIMIEST
GRIMMEST
GRIMNESS
GRINDERS
GRINDERY
GRINNERS
GRIPPLES
GRISEOUS
GRISETTE
GRISLIER
GRISTLES
GRITTERS
GRITTEST
GRITTING
GRIZZLES
GROANERS
GRODIEST
GROMMETS
GROSBEAK
GROSCHEN
GROSERTS
GROSSING
GROTTOES
GROUNDED
GROUNDEN
GROUNDER
GROUSING
GROUTERS
GROUTING

GROWINGS
GRUELING
GRUNIONS
GRUNTERS
GRUNTLES
GUARANIS
GUARDEES
GUARDIAN
GUARDING
GUDESIRE
GUERDONS
GUERIDON
GUERITES
GUERNSEY
GUESTING
GUILDERS
GULFIEST
GUNFIRES
GUNGIEST
GUNLAYER
GUNMETAL
GUNNERAS
GUNSTONE
GUNWALES
GURLIEST
GUSTABLE
GYRATING
GYRATION
GYROLITE
HACKLETS
HACKLIER
HADROMES
HAEMATIN
HAGGLERS
HAILIEST
HAINCHES
HAIRCUTS
HAIRIEST
HAIRLESS
HAIRNETS
HAIRSTED
HALBERDS
HALBERTS
HALICORE
HALLINGS
HALOGENS
HALTERED
HALTERES
HALTINGS
HAMMIEST
HAMPSTER
HAMSTERS
HANDGRIP
HANDIEST
HANDLERS
HANDLESS
HANDSELS
HANDSETS
HANDSOME
HANGBIRD
HANGFIRE
HANGNEST
HARDIEST
HARDLINE
HARDNESS
HARDOKES
HARICOTS
HARLINGS
HARMINES
HAROSETH
HAROSETS
HARPINGS
HARSHENS
HARSHEST
HARSLETS
HARTBEES
HARVESTS
HASSLING
HASTENED
HASTENER
HASTIEST
HASTINGS
HATCHELS
HATCHERS
HATERENT
HATTINGS
HAULIERS
HAUNTERS
HAURIENT
HAUTEURS
HAVERELS
HAVERING
HAYRIDES
HEADIEST
HEADINGS
HEADLONG
HEADRAIL
HEADREST
HEADRIGS
HEADRING
HEADSETS
HEADSMAN
HEADSMEN
HEALDING
HEALINGS
HEARINGS
HEARSIER
HEARSING
HEARTENS
HEARTIES
HEARTILY
HEARTING
HEARTLET
HEARTPEA
HEATHERS
HEATINGS
HECHTING
HECTARES
HEDDLING
HEDGINGS
HEDONICS
HEDONISM
HEDONIST
HEELINGS
HEIGHTEN
HEIRDOMS
HEIRLESS
HEISTERS
HEISTING
HELICONS
HELIPADS
HELIPORT
HELISTOP
HELLIERS
HELLIONS
HELOTISM
HELPINGS
HEMIONES
HEMIONUS
HENNIEST
HEPARINS
HEPTANES
HERALDIC
HERBIEST
HERBISTS
HERBLETS
HERDSMAN
HERDSMEN
HERETICS
HERISSON
HERITORS
HERLINGS
HEROICAL
HEROINES
HEROISED
HEROISES
HEROISMS
HERRINGS
HESITANT
HESITATE
HESPERID
HETAIRAS
HIDEOUTS
HIDROSES
HIELAMAN
HIGGLERS
HILLIEST
HINDERED
HINDERER
HINDLEGS
HIPSTERS
HIRELING
HIRRIENT
HISTOGEN
HISTONES
HISTRION
HITCHERS
HOARDERS
HOARDING
HOARIEST
HOARSELY
HOARSENS
HOARSEST
HOASTING
HOASTMEN
HOISTERS
HOISTING
HOISTMEN
HOLINESS
HOLSTERS
HOMINIES
HONESTER
HONOURED
HOOLIEST
HOPBINES
HOPLITES
HOPPIEST
HORDEINS
HORMONES
HORNIEST
HORNINGS
HORNISTS
HORNITOS
HORNLETS
HORSECAR
HORSEMAN
HORSEMEN
HORSIEST
HORSINGS
HOSTELER
HOSTELRY
HOSTINGS
HOSTLERS
HOSTRIES
HOTELIER
HOTLINES
HOTTINGS
HOUTINGS
HULKIEST
HULLIEST
HUMANEST
HUMANISE
HUNDREDS
HUNKIEST
HUNTRESS
HURTLESS
HUSTLERS
HYACINES
HYALITES
HYDRATES
HYMENIAL
HYOSCINE
HYPERONS
HYSTERIA
HYSTERIC
ICEBALLS
ICEBOATS
ICESTONE
ICHNITES
ICONISED
ICONISES
ICONIZES
ICTERICS
ICTERIDS
ICTERINE
IDEALISE
IDEALISM
IDEALIST
IDLENESS
IDOCRASE
IDOLATER
IDOLISER
IGARAPES
IGNAROES
IGNITERS
IGNITRON
IGNOBLER
IGNOMIES
IGNORANT
IGNORERS
ILLAPSED
ILLAPSES
IMAGINER
IMAGINES
IMAMATES
IMBARKED
IMBARRED
IMBATHES
IMBRUTES
IMBURSED
IMITANTS
IMITATES
IMMANELY
IMMANENT
IMMENSER
IMMERGES
IMMERSED
IMMERSES
IMMODEST
IMPANATE
IMPANELS
IMPANNEL
IMPARLED
IMPARTED
IMPASTED
IMPASTES
IMPEARLS
IMPLATES
IMPLEADS
IMPLETES
IMPLORES
IMPORTED
IMPOSERS
IMPOSTER
IMPREGNS
IMPRESAS
IMPRESES
IMPRESSE
IMPRESTS
IMPROVES
IMPUREST
IMPUTERS
INARCHED
INARCHES
INAURATE
INBREAKS
INBREEDS
INCENSER
INCENSOR
INCENTRE
INCHASED
INCHASES
INCHMEAL
INCISURE
INCITERS
INCLOSED
INCLOSER
INCLOSES
INCLUDES
INCOMERS
INCORPSE
INCREASE
INCREATE
INCURRED
INCURVED
INCURVES
INDARTED
INDENTER
INDEXERS
INDIGEST
INDIGOES
INDIRECT
INDITERS
INDORSED
INDORSES
INDRAFTS
INDRISES
INDUCERS
INDULGED
INDULGER
INDULGES
INDURATE
INDWELLS
INEARTHS
INEPTEST
INERMOUS
INERRANT
INERTEST
INERTIAL
INERTIAS
INEXPERT
INFAMIES
INFAMISE
INFANTES
INFARCTS
INFERNOS
INFERRED
INFESTED
INFIDELS
INFIELDS
INFLAMED
INFLAMER
INFLAMES
INFLATED
INFLATES
INFLECTS
INFORCES
INFRACTS
INFRARED
INFRINGE
INFUSERS
INGATHER
INGENERS
INGESTED
INGLOBED
INGLOBES
INGRAFTS
INGRAINS
INGRATES
INGROUPS
INGROWTH
INGULFED
INHALERS
INHEARSE
INHERCED
INHERCES
INHERENT
INHERING
INHERITS
INHUMATE
INHUMERS
INKSTONE
INLANDER
INLAYERS
INMESHED
INMESHES
INNATELY
INNERVED
INNERVES
INNYARDS
INORNATE
INPUTTER
INQUERED
INQUESTS
INQUIETS
INQUIRED
INRUSHES
INSANEST
INSCAPES
INSCIENT
INSCONCE
INSCRIBE
INSEAMED
INSECURE
INSEEMED
INSERTED
INSERTER
INSHRINE
INSIDERS
INSISTED
INSNARED
INSNARES
INSOLATE
INSOLENT
INSOULED
INSPECTS
INSPHERE
INSPIRED
INSPIRER
INSPIRES
INSTABLE
INSTANCE
INSTANTS
INSTATED
INSTATES
INSTRESS
INSULATE
INSULTED
INSULTER
INSURANT
INSUREDS
INSURERS
INSWATHE
INTAGLIO
INTARSIA
INTEGERS
INTEGRAL
INTENDER
INTENSER
INTERACT
INTERCUT
INTERESS
INTEREST
INTERIMS
INTERIOR
INTERLAY
INTERMIT
INTERMIX
INTERNAL
INTERNED
INTERNEE
INTERNES
INTERNET
INTERRED
INTERREX
INTERSEX
INTERTIE
INTERVAL
INTERWAR
INTHRALS
INTIMATE
INTONERS
INTORTED
INTRADAS
INTRADOS
INTRANTS
INTREATS
INTREPID
INTRIGUE
INTRINCE
INTROITS
INTRORSE
INTRUDED
INTRUDER
INTRUDES
INTWINES
INULASES
INVADERS
INVEAGLE
INVERSES
INVERTED
INVERTER
INVERTIN
INVESTED
INVESTOR
INVITERS
INVOICES
INVOLVES
IODURETS
IONISERS
IONIZERS
IONOMERS
IRENICAL
IRISATED
IRISATES
IRISCOPE
IRONINGS
IRONISED
IRONISES
IRONISTS
IRONIZES
IRRITATE
IRRUPTED
ISABELLA
ISATINES
ISLANDED
ISLANDER
ISLESMAN
ISLESMEN
ISOBARES
ISOBRONT
ISOCHORE
ISOCLINE
ISOCRYME
ISOGONAL
ISOLABLE
ISOLATED
ISOLATES
ISOLINES
ISOLOGUE
ISOMERES
ISOMERIC
ISOMETRY
ISOPLETH
ISOPRENE
ISOTHERE
ISOTHERM
ISOTONES
ISOTOPES
ISOTRONS
ISOTYPES
ISSUABLE
ISSUANCE
ITERANCE
ITERATED
ITERATES
IVRESSES
JACONETS
JADEITES
JADERIES
JAMBIERS
JAMMIEST
JANGLERS
JANGLIER
JANITORS
JANTIEST
JARGONED
JAROSITE
JARRINGS
JASMINES

JAUNTIER
JAUNTIES
JEERINGS
JEMIDARS
JEOPARDS
JERKIEST
JERKINGS
JERRICAN
JESTINGS
JETFOILS
JETLINER
JETTISON
JINGLERS
JINGLETS
JINGLIER
JINGOIST
JIRKINET
JOBSHARE
JOINDERS
JOINTERS
JOINTURE
JOISTING
JOLLIEST
JOLTIEST
JOSTLING
JOTTINGS
JOUSTING
JOWLIEST
JUNCATES
JUNGLIER
JUNIPERS
JUNKIEST
JUSTICER
KAINITES
KAISERIN
KALENDAR
KALINITE
KALPISES
KANTELAS
KANTELES
KAOLINES
KARTINGS
KEELINGS
KEISTERS
KEITLOAS
KERATINS
KERATOSE
KERBSIDE
KERMISES
KERNINGS
KERNITES
KEROGENS
KEROSINE
KESTRELS
KETAMINE
KETCHING
KILLASES
KINDLERS
KINDLESS
KINDREDS
KINETICS
KINGLESS
KINGLETS
KINGLIER
KINGPOST
KIRKTONS
KISSABLE
KISTVAEN
KITCHENS
KITENGES
KLAVIERS
KLINKERS
KNACKERS
KNACKIER
KNAGGIER
KNEADERS
KNICKERS
KNIGHTED
KNITCHES
KNITTERS
KNITTLES
KNITWEAR
KNOCKERS
KNOTTERS
KNOTTIER
KRAALING
KRANTZES
KREASOTE
KREATINE
KREESING
KREMLINS
KUNZITES
KYANISED
KYANITES
LABIATES
LABORING
LACERANT
LACEWING
LACROSSE
LACTASES
LACTATES
LACTEALS
LACTEOUS
LACTONES
LACTOSES
LADIFIES
LADRONES
LADYFIES
LAETARES
LAGGINGS
LAICISED
LAICISES
LAIGHEST
LAIRAGES
LAIRIEST
LAIRISED
LAIRISES
LAIRIZED
LAIRIZES
LAITANCE
LAKESIDE
LALLINGS
LAMBERTS
LAMENTED
LAMETERS
LAMIGERS
LAMINATE
LAMINOSE
LAMITERS
LAMMINGS
LAMPERNS
LAMPINGS
LAMPREYS
LANDINGS
LANDLERS
LANDLESS
LANDRACE
LANDSIDE
LANDSMEN
LANGRAGE
LANGRELS
LANGSPEL
LANGUETS
LANGUISH
LANIARDS
LANKIEST
LANNERET
LANTERNS
LAPPINGS
LAPSTONE
LAPWINGS
LARDIEST
LARGENED
LARGESSE
LARKIEST
LARMIERS
LARNAKES
LARRIGAN
LARYNGES
LARYNXES
LASAGNES
LASHINGS
LASSOING
LASTAGES
LASTINGS
LATCHETS
LATCHING
LATENCES
LATENESS
LATENING
LATERALS
LATERITE
LATHERED
LATHIEST
LATHINGS
LATRINES
LATTICES
LAUGHERS
LAUGHTER
LAUNDERS
LAVEMENT
LAVENDER
LAVISHED
LAVISHER
LAVISHES
LAWNIEST
LAXITIES
LAYERING
LAYTIMES
LAZARETS
LAZINESS
LAZURITE
LEACHIER
LEACHING
LEADIEST
LEADINGS
LEADSMAN
LEADSMEN
LEAFIEST
LEAGUERS
LEAGUING
LEAKIEST
LEALTIES
LEANINGS
LEAPROUS
LEARIEST
LEARNERS
LEARNING
LEASHING
LEASINGS
LEASURES
LEATHERN
LEATHERS
LEATHERY
LEAVIEST
LEAVINGS
LECTERNS
LECTIONS
LECTRESS
LECTURES
LECTURNS
LEDGIEST
LEERIEST
LEERINGS
LEEWARDS
LEGALIST
LEGATEES
LEGATINE
LEGATION
LEGATORS
LEGERING
LEGGIEST
LEGGINGS
LEGHORNS
LEGIONED
LEGITIMS
LEGUMINS
LEGWEARS
LEIDGERS
LEISHEST
LEISLERS
LEISTERS
LEISURED
LEISURES
LEKKINGS
LEMMINGS
LEMPIRAS
LEMURIAN
LENDINGS
LENIENTS
LENITIES
LENTISKS
LEOPARDS
LEOTARDS
LESBIANS
LESSENED
LESSONED
LETCHING
LETHARGY
LETTERNS
LETTINGS
LEUCITES
LEVANTER
LEVATORS
LEVERETS
LEVERING
LEVIRATE
LEVITIES
LEWDNESS
LEWDSTER
LEWISIAS
LEWISITE
LEWISSON
LEXICONS
LIAISING
LIBATING
LIBELANT
LIBELERS
LIBERALS
LIBERATE
LIBRATED
LIBRATES
LIBRETTO
LICENSED
LICENSER
LICENSOR
LIEGEMAN
LIENTERY
LIGAMENT
LIGATING
LIGATION
LIGATURE
LIGHTENS
LIGHTERS
LIGHTEST
LIGNAGES
LIGNEOUS
LIGNITES
LIGNOSES
LIGROINS
LIMACINE
LIMEADES
LIMEPITS
LIMITEDS
LIMITERS
LIMNAEID
LINCHETS
LINCTURE
LINDANES
LINEAGES
LINEATED
LINESMAN
LINESMEN
LINGERED
LINGERER
LINGERIE
LINGIEST
LINGSTER
LINGULAE
LINGULAR
LINGULAS
LINKAGES
LINKSTER
LINSANGS
LINSEEDS
LINTIEST
LINTSEED
LIONCELS
LIONISED
LIONISES
LIONIZES
LIPARITE
LIPPIEST
LIQUATES
LISTENED
LISTENER
LISTERIA
LITANIES
LITERACY
LITERALS
LITERARY
LITERATE
LITERATI
LITERATO
LITEROSE
LITHARGE
LITHATES
LITHITES
LITIGANT
LITMUSES
LITTERED
LITUUSES
LIVELIER
LIVENERS
LIVERIED
LIVERIES
LIVEWARE
LIVIDEST
LLANEROS
LOADINGS
LOAFINGS
LOAMIEST
LOANINGS
LOATHERS
LOATHEST
LOATHIER
LOATHING
LOBELIAS
LOBSTERS
LOCATING
LOCUSTAE
LOCUSTED
LODESMAN
LODESMEN
LODESTAR
LOFTIEST
LOGANIAS
LOGICISE
LOGLINES
LOITERED
LOITERER
LONGWISE
LONICERA
LOOBIEST
LOONIEST
LOOPIEST
LOOSENED
LOOTINGS
LORDINGS
LORDLESS
LORDLING
LORDOSES
LORETTES
LORICATE
LORIKEET
LORIMERS
LORINERS
LOSSIEST
LOUDNESS
LOUNDERS
LOUNGERS
LOURIEST
LOURINGS
LOUSIEST
LOVELIER
LOWERING
LOWLIEST
LUCARNES
LUCIDEST
LUCIGENS
LUCKIEST
LUGEINGS
LUMMIEST
LUMPIEST
LUNACIES
LUNARIES
LUNARIST
LUNETTES
LURDANES
LURIDEST
LUSHIEST
LUSTERED
LUSTIEST
LUSTIQUE
LUSTRATE
LUSTRINE
LUTANIST
LUTENIST
LUTHERNS
LUTHIERS
LUXATING
LYMITERS
MACARISE
MACHINES
MACHREES
MADERISE
MADLINGS
MADRONES
MAESTROS
MAGDALEN
MAGENTAS
MAGISTER
MAGNATES
MAGNESIA
MAGNETIC
MAGNETOS
MAHSEERS
MAIDENLY
MAIDLESS
MAILINGS
MAINLINE
MAISTERS
MAJESTIC
MAJLISES
MALADIES
MALAISES
MALANDER
MALAPERT
MALGRING
MALIGNED
MALIGNER
MALINGER
MALONATE
MALTIEST
MALTINGS
MALTOSES
MALTSTER
MANAGERS
MANATEES
MANCHETS
MANCIPLE
MANDATED
MANDATES
MANDIBLE
MANDIRAS
MANDRELS
MANDRILS
MANGIEST
MANGLERS
MANICURE
MANIFEST
MANILLES
MANIPLES
MANKIEST
MANLIEST
MANNITES
MANRENTS
MANRIDER
MANSUETE
MANTEAUS
MANTEAUX
MANTEELS
MANTELET
MANTISES
MANTLETS
MANTLING
MARBLING
MARCHESE
MARCHESI
MARDIEST
MARDYING
MARGENTS
MARGINAL
MARGINED
MARINADE
MARINATE
MARINERA
MARINERS
MARISHES
MARKINGS
MARLIEST
MARLINES
MARLINGS
MARMITES
MARMOSET
MARQUEES
MARQUISE
MARRIERS
MARSHIER
MARTEXTS
MARTINET
MARTINIS
MARTLETS
MASHIEST
MASSETER
MASSIEST
MASTERED
MASTERLY
MASTIEST
MATCHERS
MATELOTS
MATERIAL
MATERIEL
MATERNAL
MATESHIP
MATFELON
MATHESIS
MATINEES
MATINESS
MATRICES
MATRIXES
MATTINGS
MATTRESS
MATUREST
MATURING
MATUTINE
MATWEEDS
MAULGRES
MAUNDERS
MAUNDIES
MAUNGIER
MAUTHERS
MAUVEINS
MAUVINES
MAWKIEST
MAWTHERS
MAYSTERS
MAZARINE
MAZINESS
MEAGREST

MEALIEST
MEANDERS
MEANINGS
MEANTIME
MEASLIER
MEASLING
MEASURED
MEASURER
MEASURES
MEATIEST
MECONINS
MEDALETS
MEDALING
MEDALIST
MEDDLING
MEDIANTS
MEDIATES
MEDICALS
MEDUSANS
MEERCATS
MEERKATS
MEETINGS
MEGABITS
MEGARADS
MEGARONS
MEGATONS
MELAMINE
MELANGES
MELANINS
MELANISM
MELANITE
MELILOTS
MELISMAS
MELLITES
MELODIST
MELTINGS
MEMENTOS
MEMORIES
MEMORISE
MENACERS
MENDINGS
MENINGES
MENORAHS
MENSTRUA
MENSURAL
MENSWEAR
MENTALLY
MENTHOLS
MENTIONS
MERCHANT
MERESMAN
MERIDIAN
MERISTEM
MERISTIC
MERITING
MERLINGS
MERMAIDS
MERONYMS
MERRIEST
MERSIONS
MESARAIC
MESCALIN
MESMERIC
MESOCARP
MESOLITE
MESOTRON
MESPRISE
MESPRIZE
MESQUINE
MESTIZAS
MESTIZOS
METALING
METALIST
METAMERS
METANOIA
METAYERS
METAZOAN
METERING
METHANAL
METHANES
METHANOL
METHINKS
METICALS
METONYMS
METOPISM
METOPONS
METRICAL
METRISTS
METRITIS
MICELLAR
MICROBES
MIDTERMS
MIGRAINE
MIGRANTS
MIGRATES
MILADIES
MILDNESS
MILKIEST
MILLRACE
MIMESTER
MINARETS
MINDLESS
MINDSETS
MINEOLAS
MINERALS
MINETTES
MINEVERS
MINGIEST
MINGLERS
MINIATED
MINIATES
MINISTER
MINIVERS
MINIVETS
MINNEOLA
MINSTERS
MINSTREL
MINTAGES
MINTIEST
MINUTEST
MINUTIAE
MIRACLES
MIRBANES
MIRINESS
MIRLIEST
MISALIGN
MISANDRY
MISBEGOT
MISCEGEN
MISCREED
MISDATED
MISDATES
MISDEALS
MISDEALT
MISDOERS
MISDONNE
MISDRAWN
MISDREAD
MISENTRY
MISERERE
MISERIES
MISFALNE
MISFARED
MISFARES
MISHEARD
MISHEARS
MISLEADS
MISLETOE
MISMATED
MISMATES
MISMETRE
MISNAMED
MISNAMES
MISNOMER
MISORDER
MISPLEAD
MISQUOTE
MISRATED
MISRATES
MISREADS
MISROUTE
MISRULED
MISSABLE
MISSPENT
MISSTATE
MISTAKEN
MISTAKES
MISTEACH
MISTERED
MISTERMS
MISTITLE
MISTREAT
MISTRESS
MISTUNED
MISTUNES
MISWEENS
MISWRITE
MISWROTE
MITERING
MITOGENS
MIXTURES
MOBSTERS
MOCHIEST
MODELERS
MODELING
MODESTER
MODISTES
MOIDORES
MOIETIES
MOINEAUS
MOISTENS
MOISTEST
MOISTING
MOISTURE
MOITHERS
MOLECAST
MOLERATS
MOLESKIN
MOLESTER
MOLIMENS
MOLINETS
MONAZITE
MONETISE
MONEYERS
MONGRELS
MONIKERS
MONITORS
MONODIES
MONOMERS
MONOSIES
MONSIEUR
MONSTERA
MONSTERS
MONTAGES
MONTEROS
MONTURES
MOODIEST
MOONIEST
MOONLETS
MOONRISE
MOONSETS
MOORHENS
MOORIEST
MOORINGS
MOOTINGS
MOPPIEST
MORAINES
MORALISE
MORDANTS
MORDENTS
MORICHES
MORLINGS
MORNINGS
MOROSEST
MORRICES
MORRISED
MORRISES
MORTICES
MORTISED
MORTISER
MORTISES
MORTLING
MOSEYING
MOSSIEST
MOTELIER
MOTHIEST
MOTLIEST
MOTORING
MOTORISE
MOTTIEST
MOTTLING
MOULDERS
MOULTING
MOUNSEER
MOUNTERS
MOURNERS
MOUSEKIN
MOUSIEST
MOUSTING
MOUTHERS
MOYITIES
MRIDANGA
MRIDANGS
MUCRONES
MUDSTONE
MUENSTER
MULTURES
MUNDANER
MUNSTERS
MURGEONS
MURIATES
MURKIEST
MURLIEST
MUSCATEL
MUSLINED
MUSLINET
MUSTERED
MUSTERER
MUTAGENS
MUTINEER
MUTINIES
MYELITIS
MYRINGAS
NAARTJES
NACREOUS
NACRITES
NAETHING
NAGGIEST
NAILINGS
NAILLESS
NAIVETES
NAKEDEST
NAMASTES
NAMETAPE
NANDINES
NAPERIES
NAPPIEST
NARCEENS
NARCEINE
NARCOSES
NARGHILE
NARGHILY
NARGILEH
NARGILES
NARGILLY
NARKIEST
NARRASES
NARRATED
NARRATES
NARTJIES
NASALISE
NASTIEST
NATHLESS
NATIVELY
NATIVIST
NATRIUMS
NATTERED
NATTERER
NATTIEST
NATURING
NATURISM
NATURIST
NAUSEANT
NAUTCHES
NAVETTES
NAVICERT
NAYTHLES
NEARNESS
NEARSIDE
NEATNESS
NEBRISES
NECKLETS
NECKTIES
NECROPSY
NECROSED
NECROSES
NECROSIS
NECTARED
NEEDFIRE
NEEDIEST
NEEDLERS
NEEDLESS
NEEDLIER
NEEDLING
NEGATORY
NEGATRON
NEGLECTS
NEGLIGES
NEGROIDS
NEGROISM
NEMATOID
NEMESIAS
NEMOROUS
NEOBLAST
NEOLITHS
NEONATES
NEOTERIC
NEPHRITE
NEPHRONS
NEPOTISM
NEPOTIST
NERDIEST
NEREIDES
NERVIEST
NERVINES
NESCIENT
NESTFULS
NESTINGS
NESTLIKE
NESTLING
NETBALLS
NETTIEST
NETTINGS
NETTLIER
NETTLING
NETWORKS
NEURISMS
NEURITES
NEURITIC
NEURITIS
NEUROMAS
NEUROSIS
NEUROTIC
NEUSTONS
NEUTRALS
NEUTRINO
NEUTRONS
NEWSCAST
NEWSGIRL
NEWSIEST
NEWSROOM
NIBBLERS
NICETIES
NICHERED
NICKERED
NICTATES
NIDERING
NIELLIST
NIFFERED
NIFTIEST
NIGELLAS
NIGGARDS
NIGGERED
NIGGLERS
NIGGLIER
NIGHTIES
NIGHTJAR
NIGROSIN
NIMBLEST
NINETIES
NIOBATES
NIOBITES
NIPPERED
NIPPIEST
NIRLIEST
NITERIES
NITRATED
NITRATES
NITRIDED
NITRIDES
NITRILES
NITRITES
NITROGEN
NITROSYL
NITTIEST
NOBBIEST
NOBODIES
NOCTULES
NODALISE
NODULOSE
NOISEFUL
NOISETTE
NOISIEST
NOMADIES
NOMADISE
NOMINATE
NOMINEES
NONETTES
NONETTOS
NOOKIEST
NORTENAS
NORTENOS
NORTHERS
NORTHING
NOSEDIVE
NOSELITE
NOSINESS
NOSTRILS
NOTABLES
NOTAEUMS
NOTARIES
NOTARISE
NOTARIZE
NOTCHELS
NOTCHERS
NOTECASE
NOTELESS
NOTELETS
NOTHINGS
NOTIFIER
NOTIFIES
NOTITIAS
NOTORNIS
NOUNIEST
NOURICES
NOURSLED
NOVELISE
NOVELISH
NOVELISM
NOVELIST
NOVITIES
NUBBIEST
NUCLIDES
NUDITIES
NUISANCE
NUMERALS
NUMEROUS
NUMPTIES
NURTURES
NUTCASES
NUTHOUSE
NUTMEALS
NUTRIENT
NUTSHELL
NUTTIEST
NYSTATIN
OAKLINGS
OARWEEDS
OATCAKES
OATMEALS
OBDURING
OBEISANT
OBELIONS
OBLIGANT
OBLIGEES
OBSCENER
OBSERVED
OBSERVER
OBSERVES
OBSIGNED
OBSTACLE
OBTAINER
OBTRUDES
OBTUSELY
OBVERSES
OCEANIDS
OCKERISM
OCTUPLES
ODALLERS
ODDITIES
ODDMENTS
ODORANTS
OERSTEDS
OESTRUMS
OFFICERS
OFFSIDER
OFTENEST
OFTTIMES
OILERIES
OILINESS
OILSTONE
OLDENING
OLDSTERS
OLEANDER
OLEARIAS
OLEASTER
OLEFIANT
OLEFINES
OLIVINES
OMITTERS
OMNIFIES
ONDATRAS
ONSETTER
ONSTEADS
OOGENIES
OOLOGIES
OOZINESS
OPALINES
OPALISED
OPENINGS
OPERANDS
OPERANTS
OPERATED
OPERATES
OPERETTA
OPORICES
OPPOSITE
OPTIMISE
ORACLING
ORANGEST
ORATIONS
ORATRESS
ORBITERS
ORBITIES
ORBITING
ORCHESIS
ORCHISES
ORDAINED
ORDAINER
ORDERING

ORDINALS
ORDINARS
ORDINATE
ORDINEES
OREGANOS
OREXISES
ORGANDIE
ORGANISE
ORGANISM
ORGANIST
ORGANITY
ORGANIZE
ORGASMED
ORGASTIC
ORIENTAL
ORIENTED
ORIFEXES
ORIFICES
ORIGANES
ORIGINAL
ORNATELY
ORNATEST
ORRERIES
ORSEILLE
ORSELLIC
ORTHOSES
ORTOLANS
OSCININE
OSCITANT
OSCITATE
OSCULATE
OSIERIES
OSMIATES
OSTEITIS
OSTINATO
OSTIOLES
OSTRACON
OSTRAKON
OSTREGER
OTALGIES
OTITISES
OTTERING
OUGHLIES
OUTCASTE
OUTCRIES
OUTDARES
OUTDATES
OUTDURES
OUTEDGES
OUTFACES
OUTFLIES
OUTFLING
OUTHIRES
OUTHYRES
OUTLEAPS
OUTLEARN
OUTLIERS
OUTLINES
OUTLIVES
OUTLYING
OUTMODES
OUTNAMES
OUTPACES
OUTPEERS
OUTRACES
OUTRAGES
OUTRANCE
OUTRANKS
OUTRATES
OUTREIGN
OUTRIDES
OUTROPES
OUTSELLS
OUTSHINE
OUTSHONE
OUTSIDER
OUTSIDES
OUTSIZED
OUTSLEEP
OUTSLEPT
OUTSOLES
OUTSPEND
OUTSPENT
OUTSTARE
OUTSWEAR
OUTSWELL
OUTSWING
OUTTELLS
OUTWEARS
OUTWEEDS
OUTWELLS
OUTWINGS
OUTWREST
OUVRIERS
OVERACTS
OVERAGES
OVERALLS
OVERAWES
OVERBIDS
OVERCAST
OVERDOES
OVERDOSE
OVERDUST
OVERDYES
OVEREATS
OVEREYES
OVERFISH
OVERFUND
OVERGETS
OVERGOES
OVERHITS
OVERKEST
OVERLAID
OVERLAND
OVERLAPS
OVERLAYS
OVERLIER
OVERLIES
OVERLIVE
OVERMANS
OVERMAST
OVERNETS
OVERPAST
OVERPOST
OVERREDS
OVERRENS
OVERSAIL
OVERSEAS
OVERSEEN
OVERSEER
OVERSEES
OVERSELL
OVERSETS
OVERSEWN
OVERSEWS
OVERSHOE
OVERSHOT
OVERSIDE
OVERSIZE
OVERSKIP
OVERSLIP
OVERSMAN
OVERSMEN
OVERSOLD
OVERSPIN
OVERSTAY
OVERSTEP
OVERSWIM
OVERTASK
OVERTOIL
OVERTOPS
OVERUSED
OVERUSES
OVERVEIL
OVERWISE
OVULATES
OWELTIES
OWLERIES
OWRELAYS
OXALATES
OXALISES
OXIDATES
OXIDISER
OXTERING
OYSTRIGE
OZONISED
OZONISER
OZONISES
PADDLERS
PAEONICS
PAEONIES
PAGEANTS
PAINLESS
PAINTERS
PAINTIER
PAINTURE
PAIRINGS
PAIRWISE
PAISLEYS
PALATINE
PALATING
PALAVERS
PALESTRA
PALETOTS
PALFREYS
PALISADE
PALLIDER
PALLIEST
PALMIEST
PALMIETS
PALSIEST
PALSYING
PALTERED
PALTERER
PALTRIER
PANARIES
PANCREAS
PANDECTS
PANDERLY
PANDORES
PANGLESS
PANICLES
PANNIERS
PANTHERS
PANTILED
PANTILES
PANTINES
PANTINGS
PANTLERS
PANTRIES
PAPERERS
PAPERING
PAPISHER
PARABLES
PARADING
PARADISE
PARAFLES
PARAKEET
PARALYSE
PARAMENT
PARAMESE
PARANETE
PARAPETS
PARASITE
PARCHESI
PARCLOSE
PARDALES
PARDNERS
PAREIRAS
PARELLAS
PARELLES
PARENTAL
PARENTED
PARGETED
PARGETER
PARHELIC
PARIETAL
PARISHEN
PARISHES
PARITIES
PARKIEST
PARKINGS
PARODIES
PAROLEES
PAROLING
PARPENDS
PARPENTS
PARQUETS
PARROTED
PARSINGS
PARSLEYS
PARSNEPS
PARTAKES
PARTERRE
PARTIBLE
PARTICLE
PARTINGS
PARTISAN
PARTLETS
PARTNERS
PARTURES
PARTYING
PARVISES
PASEARED
PASSIBLE
PASSMENT
PASTANCE
PASTERNS
PASTIEST
PASTILLE
PASTIMES
PASTINGS
PASTRIES
PASTURED
PASTURES
PATCHERS
PATELLAR
PATENTOR
PATERERO
PATERNAL
PATIENTS
PATRIATE
PATRICKS
PATROONS
PATTERED
PATTERER
PATTERNS
PAYMENTS
PEARCING
PEARLERS
PEARLIES
PEARLING
PEARLINS
PEARLITE
PEARMAIN
PEASANTS
PEASANTY
PEATIEST
PEBRINES
PECTINAL
PECTINES
PECTORAL
PECULIAR
PEDALIER
PEDALING
PEDANTRY
PEDDLING
PEDERAST
PEDESTAL
PEDRAILS
PEELINGS
PEERIEST
PEJORATE
PELAGIAN
PELICANS
PELORIAS
PELORIES
PELORISM
PELTINGS
PELTRIES
PEMICANS
PENCRAFT
PENDANTS
PENDENTS
PENDULAR
PENFOLDS
PENLIGHT
PENNANTS
PENSIONS
PENSTOCK
PENTACTS
PENTANES
PENTARCH
PENTHIAS
PENTICES
PENTISED
PENTISES
PENTODES
PENTOSAN
PENURIES
PEONISMS
PERACUTE
PERAEONS
PERCALES
PERCEANT
PEREGALS
PEREIRAS
PERFECTA
PERGOLAS
PERIANTH
PERIAPTS
PERIDIAL
PERIDOTE
PERIDOTS
PERIGEAN
PERIGONS
PERILOUS
PERIOSTS
PERISARC
PERISHED
PERISHER
PERKIEST
PERLITES
PERMEASE
PERMEATE
PERONEUS
PERORATE
PERPENDS
PERPENTS
PERRIERS
PERSAUNT
PERSEITY
PERSICOS
PERSICOT
PERSISTS
PERSONAE
PERSONAL
PERSONAS
PERSPIRE
PERSUADE
PERSUING
PERSWADE
PERTAINS
PERTAKEN
PERTAKES
PERTNESS
PERTUSED
PERUSALS
PERUSING
PERVADES
PERVERTS
PERVIATE
PERVIOUS
PESAUNTS
PESSIMAL
PESTERED
PESTERER
PESTLING
PETALINE
PETALISM
PETALOUS
PETARIES
PETERING
PETERMAN
PETIOLAR
PETIOLES
PETROLIC
PETROSAL
PETTINGS
PETTLING
PETUNIAS
PEYOTISM
PEYOTIST
PHAETONS
PHEASANT
PHENATES
PHENGITE
PHILTERS
PHILTRES
PHONATES
PHONIEST
PHRASIER
PHRASING
PHRENISM
PIAFFERS
PIANISTE
PIASTRES
PICOTEES
PICRATES
PICRITES
PICTURED
PICTURES
PIDGEONS
PIEBALDS
PIECRUST
PIERAGES
PIERCERS
PIERROTS
PIGHTLES
PIGMEATS
PIGMENTS
PIKELETS
PILASTER
PILEWORT
PILHORSE
PILOTING
PILSENER
PILSNERS
PIMENTOS
PINASTER
PINCASES
PINCERED
PINCHERS
PINDAREE
PINDARIS
PINERIES
PINGLERS
PINHEADS
PINHOLES
PINKIEST
PINNACES
PINOCLES
PINTABLE
PIONEERS
PIRACIES
PIRATING
PISCATOR
PISCINAE
PISOLITE
PISTOLES
PISTOLET
PITCHERS
PITHEADS
PITILESS
PITTERED
PIVOTERS
PLACATES
PLACIDER
PLACINGS
PLACKETS
PLAIDMEN
PLAINEST
PLAISTER
PLAITERS
PLAITING
PLANETIC
PLANGENT
PLANNERS
PLANTAGE
PLANTERS
PLANTING
PLASHIER
PLASHING
PLASTERS
PLASTERY
PLASTRON
PLATANES
PLATEMAN
PLATEMEN
PLATIEST
PLATINGS
PLATTERS
PLATTING
PLEADERS
PLEADING
PLEASANT
PLEASERS
PLEASING
PLEASURE
PLEATERS
PLEATING
PLECTRES
PLEDGING
PLEDGORS
PLENARTY
PLENIPOS
PLENISTS
PLENTIES
PLEONAST
PLEROMAS
PLETHORA
PLICATES
PLOATING
PLODDERS
PLONKERS
PLOTTERS
PLOTTIES
PLOTTING
PLOUTERS
PLOWTERS
PLUMIEST
PLUNDERS
POACHERS
POCKIEST
PODDIEST
PODGIEST
POESYING
POETISED
POETISES
POETIZES
POETRIES
POETSHIP
POINDERS
POINTELS
POINTERS
POINTIER
POISONED
POISONER
POITRELS
POLACRES
POLARISE
POLECATS
POLEMIST
POLENTAS
POLISHER
POLITEST
POLITIES
POLLSTER
POLLUTES
POLONIES

POLONISE
POMFRETS
PONCIEST
PONDERAL
PONGIEST
PONIARDS
PONTAGES
PONTILES
POOFIEST
POOFTERS
POORNESS
POOVIEST
POPERINS
POPPIEST
PORINESS
PORKIEST
PORRECTS
PORTABLE
PORTAGES
PORTANCE
PORTASES
PORTENDS
PORTENTS
PORTEOUS
PORTESSE
PORTIEST
PORTIONS
PORTLIER
PORTOISE
PORTRESS
POSITING
POSITIVE
POSITRON
POSTERED
POSTERNS
POSTFACE
POSTICHE
POSTINGS
POSTLUDE
POSTNATI
POSTURED
POSTURER
POSTURES
POTABLES
POTAGERS
POTCHERS
POTENCES
POTICHES
POTSHARE
POTSHERD
POTSTONE
POTTIEST
POUFTERS
POULDERS
POULDRES
POULTERS
POUNCETS
POUNDERS
POURINGS
POUTHERS
POUTIEST
POUTINGS
PRABBLES
PRACTICS
PRACTISE
PRAEDIAL
PRAEFECT
PRAETORS
PRAIRIES
PRAISERS
PRAISING
PRALINES
PRANCERS
PRANCKES
PRANKLED
PRANKLES
PRATFELL
PRATINGS
PRATTING
PRATTLED
PRATTLER
PRATTLES
PRAUNCED
PRAUNCES
PRAYINGS
PREACING
PREASING
PREASSED
PREBENDS
PRECIOUS
PRECISED
PRECISER
PREDATED
PREDATES
PREDATOR
PREDAWNS
PREDIALS
PREDICTS
PREDYING
PREEMIES
PREENING
PREFADES
PREFIXES
PREGNANT
PREHEATS
PREHENDS
PREHNITE
PRELATES
PRELATIC
PRELECTS
PREMIERS
PREMISED
PREMISES
PREMIXES
PREMOVES
PRENASAL
PRENATAL
PRENTICE
PRENTING
PREPARES
PREPONES
PRESAGED
PRESAGER
PRESCIND
PRESCUTA
PRESENTS
PRESIDED
PRESIDES
PRESIDIA
PRESIDIO
PRESSFAT
PRESSING
PRESSION
PRESSMAN
PRESTIGE
PRESTING
PRETENDS
PRETENSE
PRETESTS
PRETEXTS
PRETTIED
PRETTIES
PRETZELS
PREVAILS
PREVENTS
PREVIEWS
PREVIOUS
PREVISED
PREVISES
PRIBBLES
PRICIEST
PRICKETS
PRIESTED
PRIESTLY
PRIMAGES
PRIMATES
PRIMINES
PRIMMEST
PRIMNESS
PRINCESS
PRINTERS
PRINTING
PRIORESS
PRISAGES
PRISONED
PRISONER
PRISTANE
PRISTINE
PRIVATES
PRIVIEST
PRIZEMAN
PROBATED
PROBATES
PROCAINE
PRODDING
PRODNOSE
PROFANES
PROFILES
PROFITED
PROGGINS
PROIGNED
PROJECTS
PROLAPSE
PROLATED
PROLATES
PROLINES
PROMETAL
PROMISED
PROMISEE
PROMISES
PROMOTES
PRONATED
PRONATES
PRONEURS
PROPALES
PROPANES
PROPENDS
PROPENES
PROPENSE
PROPHETS
PROPINES
PROPONES
PRORATED
PRORATES
PROSEMAN
PROSEMEN
PROSIEST
PROSINGS
PROSPECT
PROSTATE
PROSTYLE
PROTASES
PROTEASE
PROTECTS
PROTEGES
PROTEIDS
PROTEINS
PROTENDS
PROTENSE
PROTEOSE
PROTESTS
PROTORES
PROTYLES
PROUDEST
PROVENDS
PROVIDES
PROVINES
PROVINGS
PRUINOSE
PRURIENT
PRUSIKED
PSALTERS
PSALTERY
PSAMMITE
PSORALEN
PTARMICS
PTERYLAE
PTILOSES
PTOMAINE
PTYALISE
PUBERTAL
PULPIEST
PULSATED
PULSOJET
PULTURES
PUNISHER
PUNSTERS
PURITANS
PURITIES
PURLINES
PURPLEST
PURSIEST
PURSLANE
PURTIEST
PUTRIDER
PUTTIERS
PYCNITES
PYELITIS
PYREXIAS
PYRITISE
PYROGENS
QUAESTOR
QUAINTER
QUANNETS
QUANTISE
QUARTERN
QUARTERS
QUARTETS
QUARTICS
QUARTILE
QUESTANT
QUESTING
QUESTION
QUETHING
QUIETENS
QUIETERS
QUILLETS
QUILTERS
QUINTETS
QUIPSTER
QUIRTING
QUITTERS
QUOITERS
QWERTIES
RABATINE
RABATOES
RABATTES
RABBITED
RABBLING
RABIDEST
RACEMISE
RACEMISM
RACEMOSE
RACHIDES
RACHITIS
RACINESS
RACKETTS
RACKINGS
RACQUETS
RADDLING
RADIANCE
RADIANTS
RADIATES
RADICELS
RADICLES
RADICULE
RADIOING
RADISHES
RADIUSES
RADWASTE
RAFFLING
RAFTSMEN
RAGGIEST
RAGGINGS
RAGGLING
RAGHEADS
RAGINGLY
RAGMENTS
RAGSTONE
RAGTIMES
RAGWEEDS
RAILBEDS
RAILHEAD
RAILINGS
RAILLESS
RAILLIES
RAIMENTS
RAINDATE
RAINIEST
RAINLESS
RAISABLE
RAISINGS
RAISONNE
RAKERIES
RALLIERS
RALLYING
RAMBLING
RAMEKINS
RAMEQUIN
RAMIFIES
RAMPIKES
RAMPINGS
RAMPIRES
RAMULOSE
RANCHERS
RANCIDER
RANDIEST
RANGIEST
RANGOLIS
RANKINGS
RANKLING
RANKNESS
RANSOMED
RANSOMER
RANTINGS
RAPESEED
RAPHIDES
RAPIDEST
RAPPINGS
RAPTURED
RAPTURES
RAREBITS
RAREFIES
RARENESS
RARITIES
RASHNESS
RASPIEST
RASPINGS
RATCHETS
RATCHING
RATEABLE
RATEABLY
RATFINKS
RATIFIES
RATIONED
RATLINES
RATLINGS
RATOONER
RATSBANE
RATTEENS
RATTENED
RATTIEST
RATTINGS
RATTLERS
RATTLIER
RATTLINE
RATTLING
RATTLINS
RAUCLEST
RAUNCHED
RAUNCHES
RAVELINS
RAVENERS
RAVENING
RAVINGLY
RAVISHED
RAWHIDES
RAZEEING
REABSORB
REACHERS
REACHING
REACTANT
REACTING
REACTION
REACTORS
READAPTS
READIEST
READINGS
READJUST
READMITS
READOPTS
READVISE
READYING
REAGENTS
REALGARS
REALIGNS
REALISED
REALISER
REALISES
REALISMS
REALISTS
REALIZED
REALIZES
REALLIED
REALLIES
REALLOTS
REALNESS
REALTIES
REALTIME
REALTORS
REAMENDS
REAMIEST
REANSWER
REARISEN
REARISES
REARMING
REARMOST
REAROUSE
REARREST
REASCEND
REASCENT
REASONED
REASONER
REASSERT
REASSIGN
REASSUME
REASSURE
REASTIER
REASTING
REATTAIN
REBATERS
REBATING
REBATOES
REBIDDEN
REBIRTHS
REBITING
REBITTEN
REBOUNDS
REBRACES
REBUILDS
REBURIES
REBUTTAL
RECANTED
RECANTER
RECEDING
RECEIPTS
RECEIVAL
RECEIVES
RECENSED
RECHARTS
RECHATES
RECHEATS
RECISION
RECITALS
RECITERS
RECITING
RECKLING
RECLAIMS
RECLAMES
RECLIMBS
RECLINED
RECLINES
RECLOSED
RECODING
RECOINED
RECOUNTS
RECOVERS
RECREANT
RECRUITS
RECTIONS
RECTITIS
RECTRESS
RECUILES
RECULING
RECUSANT
RECUSING
REDATING
REDBACKS
REDCOATS
REDDIEST
REDDINGS
REDDLING
REDEFINE
REDESIGN
REDHEADS
REDIALED
REDISTIL
REDNECKS
REDOLENT
REDOUBTS
REDOUNDS
REDPOLLS
REDRAFTS
REDRIVEN
REDRIVES
REDROOTS
REDSHANK
REDSHARE
REDSHIRE
REDSHORT
REDSKINS
REDSTART
REDUCING
REDWINGS
REEDIEST
REEDINGS
REEDLING
REEDSTOP
REEFINGS
REEKIEST
REELINGS
REESTIER
REESTING
REFACING
REFINERS
REFINING
REFLATES
REFLECTS
REFLOATS
REFOREST
REFOUNDS
REFRACTS
REFRAINS
REFRAMES
REFUSING
REFUSION
REFUTALS
REFUTERS
REFUTING
REGAINED
REGAINER
REGALIAN
REGALIAS
REGALING
REGALISM
REGALIST
REGALITY
REGATTAS
REGENCES
REGIMENS

REGIMENT
REGIONAL
REGISTER
REGISTRY
REGOLITH
REGRADES
REGRANTS
REGRATES
REGREETS
REGRINDS
REGROUND
REGULARS
REGULINE
REGULISE
REHANDLE
REHASHED
REHEARSE
REIGNING
REIMPOSE
REINDEER
REINETTE
REINFUND
REINFUSE
REINLESS
REINSERT
REINSMAN
REINSMEN
REINSURE
REINTERS
REINVEST
REISSUED
REISTING
REJOICES
REJOINED
REKINDLE
RELACHES
RELAPSED
RELAPSER
RELAPSES
RELATERS
RELATING
RELATION
RELATIVE
RELATORS
RELAXANT
RELAXING
RELAXINS
RELAYING
RELEASED
RELEASEE
RELEASER
RELEASES
RELEASOR
RELEVANT
RELIANCE
RELIEVED
RELIEVER
RELIEVES
RELIEVOS
RELIGHTS
RELIGION
RELINING
RELIQUES
RELISHED
RELISHES
RELIVERS
RELIVING
RELUMING
REMAINED
REMAKING

REMANETS
REMANIES
REMASTER
REMBLAIS
REMBLING
REMEDIAL
REMEDIES
REMEDING
REMINDED
REMINDER
REMINTED
REMISING
REMITTAL
REMNANTS
REMODELS
REMOTEST
REMOULDS
REMOUNTS
REMOVALS
REMOVERS
REMUAGES
RENAGUED
RENAGUES
RENAMING
RENAYING
RENDZINA
RENEGADE
RENEGADO
RENEGATE
RENEGERS
RENEGING
RENEGUES
RENEWALS
RENEWING
RENEYING
RENFORST
RENIGGED
RENITENT
RENNINGS
RENTABLE
RENTIERS
RENVERST
REORDAIN
REORIENT
REPAINTS
REPAPERS
REPARTEE
REPASSED
REPASTED
REPAYING
REPEATED
REPEATER
REPHRASE
REPINERS
REPINING
REPLACES
REPLANTS
REPLETES
REPLEVIN
REPLICAS
REPLIERS
REPLYING
REPOINTS
REPONING
REPOSALL
REPOSALS
REPOSING
REPOSITS
REPOSTED
REPPINGS

REPRIMES
REPRINTS
REPRISAL
REPRISED
REPRISES
REPRIVES
REPRIZES
REPROVES
REPTILES
REPUNITS
REPUTING
REQUIEMS
REQUIRES
REQUITAL
REQUITES
RERAILED
REREVISE
REROUTES
RESALGAR
RESALUTE
RESAYING
RESCALED
RESCALES
RESCINDS
RESCRIPT
RESCUING
RESEALED
RESEARCH
RESEATED
RESECTED
RESEIZED
RESELECT
RESENTED
RESENTER
RESETTED
RESETTER
RESETTLE
RESHAPED
RESIANCE
RESIANTS
RESIDENT
RESIDERS
RESIDING
RESIDUAL
RESIDUES
RESIDUUM
RESIGNED
RESIGNER
RESILING
RESINATA
RESINATE
RESINERS
RESINING
RESINISE
RESINOID
RESINOUS
RESISTED
RESISTOR
RESKUING
RESOLING
RESOLUTE
RESOLVED
RESOLVER
RESOLVES
RESONANT
RESONATE
RESORCIN
RESORTED
RESORTER
RESOUNDS

RESPIRED
RESPIRES
RESPITED
RESPITES
RESPLEND
RESPOKEN
RESPONDS
RESPONSA
RESPONSE
RESTAFFS
RESTAGED
RESTAGES
RESTARTS
RESTATED
RESTATES
RESTIEST
RESTINGS
RESTLESS
RESTOCKS
RESTORED
RESTORER
RESTORES
RESTRAIN
RESTRICT
RESTRING
RESTRUNG
RESTYLED
RESTYLES
RESUBMIT
RESULTED
RESUMING
RESUPINE
RETABLES
RETAILED
RETAILER
RETAINED
RETAINER
RETAKERS
RETAKING
RETCHING
RETHINKS
RETICENT
RETICLES
RETILING
RETIMING
RETINITE
RETINOID
RETINOLS
RETINUES
RETINULA
RETIRALS
RETIREES
RETIRERS
RETIRING
RETITLED
RETITLES
RETOOLED
RETRACES
RETRACTS
RETRAICT
RETRAINS
RETRAITE
RETRAITS
RETRAITT
RETRATES
RETREADS
RETREATS
RETRIALS
RETRORSE
RETRYING

RETSINAS
RETUNING
RETURNIK
REUNIONS
REUNITED
REUNITES
REUSABLE
REUTTERS
REVALUES
REVEILLE
REVENGES
REVERIES
REVERIST
REVERSAL
REVERSIS
REVERSOS
REVESTED
REVESTRY
REVIEWAL
REVILERS
REVILING
REVISALS
REVISERS
REVISING
REVISION
REVISITS
REVISORS
REVISORY
REVIVALS
REVIVERS
REVIVORS
REVOLTED
REVOLVES
REWRITES
REYNARDS
REZONING
RHAGADES
RHAPSODE
RHENIUMS
RHEOSTAT
RHIZINES
RHYOLITE
RHYTINAS
RIANCIES
RIBBANDS
RIBBIEST
RIBIBLES
RIBSTONE
RIBSTONS
RICHENED
RICHNESS
RICHTEST
RICHTING
RICOTTAS
RICTUSES
RIDDANCE
RIDEABLE
RIDGIEST
RIEMPIES
RIFENESS
RIFLEMAN
RIFTIEST
RIFTLESS
RIGADOON
RIGATONI
RIGHTENS
RIGHTERS
RIGHTEST
RIGHTING
RIGIDEST

RIGIDISE
RINDIEST
RINDLESS
RINGBITS
RINGBONE
RINGGITS
RINGHALS
RINGLESS
RINGLETS
RINGSIDE
RINGSTER
RINGTAIL
RINGWAYS
RINGWISE
RINSABLE
RINSIBLE
RIOTINGS
RIOTISES
RIOTIZES
RIOTRIES
RIPENESS
RIPENING
RIPIENOS
RIPOSTED
RIPOSTES
RIPPLETS
RIPTIDES
RISPETTI
RISPETTO
RISSOLES
RITELESS
RITENUTO
RITORNEL
RITZIEST
RIVALESS
RIVALISE
RIVALLED
RIVELLED
RIVERETS
RIVERMAN
RIVETERS
RIVETING
RIVIERES
RIVULETS
ROADINGS
ROADLESS
ROADSIDE
ROADSMEN
ROADSTER
ROAMINGS
ROARIEST
ROARINGS
ROASTERS
ROASTING
ROBOTISE
ROBUSTER
ROCAILLE
ROCKIERS
ROCKIEST
ROCKINGS
ROCQUETS
RODDINGS
RODEWAYS
RODSTERS
ROESTONE
ROGATION
ROILIEST
ROISTERS
ROISTING
ROKELAYS

ROLFINGS
ROLLINGS
ROMANCES
ROMAUNTS
ROMNEYAS
RONDAVEL
RONDEAUX
RONDURES
RONEOING
RONTGENS
ROOFIEST
ROOFINGS
ROOINEKS
ROOMIEST
ROOPIEST
ROOSTERS
ROOSTING
ROOTAGES
ROOTEDLY
ROOTIEST
ROOTINGS
ROOTLESS
ROOTLETS
ROOTLIKE
ROOTLING
ROOTSIER
ROPERIES
ROPINESS
RORTIEST
ROSACEAS
ROSARIES
ROSEBAYS
ROSEFISH
ROSEHIPS
ROSELIKE
ROSELLAS
ROSEOLAS
ROSERIES
ROSETING
ROSETTED
ROSETTES
ROSIERES
ROSINATE
ROSINESS
ROSINING
ROSITING
ROSTERED
ROSTRATE
ROSULATE
ROTARIES
ROTATING
ROTATIVE
ROTCHIES
ROTIFERS
ROTUNDAS
ROTUNDED
ROTUNDER
ROUGHENS
ROUGHEST
ROUILLES
ROULADES
ROULEAUS
ROUMINGS
ROUNCIES
ROUNDELS
ROUNDERS
ROUNDEST
ROUNDING
ROUNDLES
ROUNDLET

ROUNDURE
ROUPIEST
ROUSTERS
ROUSTING
ROUTEING
ROUTINES
ROUTINGS
ROWDIEST
ROWNDING
ROYALETS
ROYALISE
ROYSTERS
ROYSTING
ROZETING
ROZITING
RUBEFIES
RUBEOLAS
RUBSTONE
RUCKSEAT
RUCTIONS
RUDDIEST
RUDENESS
RUDERALS
RUDERIES
RUDIMENT
RUELLIAS
RUINATED
RUINATES
RULERING
RUMINATE
RUMMIEST
RUNAGATE
RUNDALES
RUNDLETS
RUNNIEST
RUNTIEST
RURALISE
RUSHIEST
RUSSETED
RUSTICAL
RUSTIEST
RUSTLERS
RUSTLESS
RUTHENIC
RUTHLESS
RUTTIEST
SABERING
SABOTEUR
SABOTIER
SABULINE
SACREDLY
SACRINGS
SACRISTS
SACRISTY
SADDLERS
SADDLERY
SADDLING
SADIRONS
SAFARIED
SAFROLES
SAGENITE
SAGINATE
SAIBLING
SAIKLESS
SAILABLE
SAILINGS
SAILLESS
SAINTESS
SAINTING
SAKERETS

SALADING	SARKIEST	SCENDING	SCUTTLER	SEIZABLE	SERINGAS	SHEARLEG	SHRAPNEL
SALARIED	SARKINGS	SCENICAL	SCYTALES	SELADANG	SERJEANT	SHEARMEN	SHREIKED
SALARIES	SARMENTA	SCENTFUL	SDEIGNED	SELCOUTH	SERKALIS	SHEATHED	SHREWDIE
SALERING	SARMENTS	SCENTING	SDEIGNES	SELDSEEN	SERMONED	SHEDDING	SHREWING
SALEROOM	SARSDENS	SCEPTRAL	SDEINING	SELECTOR	SERMONER	SHEELING	SHRIEKED
SALEYARD	SARSENET	SCEPTRED	SEABIRDS	SELENATE	SERMONET	SHEENIER	SHRIEKER
SALFERNS	SARSNETS	SCERNING	SEABLITE	SELENIDE	SERMONIC	SHEERING	SHRIEVAL
SALICETA	SATANITY	SCHANTZE	SEABOARD	SELENITE	SEROSITY	SHEETIER	SHRIEVED
SALICETS	SATCHELS	SCHLAGER	SEABORNE	SELENIUM	SEROTINE	SHEETING	SHRIEVES
SALICINE	SATIABLE	SCHOONER	SEACOAST	SELFINGS	SEROTYPE	SHEILING	SHRINKER
SALIENCE	SATIATED	SCIAENID	SEACRAFT	SELICTAR	SERPENTS	SHELFIER	SHROVING
SALIENCY	SATIATES	SCIENTER	SEADROME	SELTZERS	SERPULAE	SHELFING	SHROWING
SALIENTS	SATINETS	SCILICET	SEAFARER	SEMANTIC	SERRANID	SHELLIER	SHUNTERS
SALIFIED	SATINING	SCIMITAR	SEAFRONT	SEMANTRA	SERRATED	SHELLING	SIBILATE
SALIFIES	SATIRISE	SCIURINE	SEALANTS	SEMBLANT	SERRATES	SHELTERS	SICKENER
SALIVATE	SATIRIZE	SCLATING	SEALINES	SEMBLING	SERRATUS	SHELTERY	SIDALCEA
SALLOWER	SATURATE	SCLEREID	SEALINGS	SEMILUNE	SERRYING	SHELTIES	SIDEARMS
SALLYING	SATURNIC	SCLEREMA	SEALSKIN	SEMINARS	SERVANTS	SHELVIER	SIDEBAND
SALMONET	SATYRESS	SCLERITE	SEAMIEST	SEMINARY	SERVICED	SHELVING	SIDEBARS
SALSAING	SAUNTERS	SCLEROID	SEAMOUNT	SEMINATE	SERVICES	SHENDING	SIDECARS
SALTATED	SAUNTING	SCLEROMA	SEAMSTER	SEMIOTIC	SERVIENT	SHERIATS	SIDELINE
SALTERNS	SAUTEING	SCOLDERS	SEAPORTS	SEMITARS	SERVILES	SHERRIES	SIDELING
SALTIERS	SAVEGARD	SCOOTERS	SEARCHED	SEMITAUR	SERVINGS	SHERWANI	SIDELONG
SALTIEST	SAVINGLY	SCOOTING	SEARCHER	SEMITONE	SERVITOR	SHETLAND	SIDENOTE
SALTINGS	SAVORIES	SCORINGS	SEARCING	SEMOLINA	SESSIONS	SHETTING	SIDEPATH
SALTIRES	SAVORING	SCORNERS	SEARINGS	SEMUNCIA	SESTINAS	SHIELDER	SIDERATE
SALTNESS	SAVOURED	SCORNING	SEARNESS	SENARIES	SESTINES	SHIELING	SIDEREAL
SALTOING	SAWDERED	SCORSING	SEASONER	SENARIUS	SETIFORM	SHIFTERS	SIDERITE
SALUTERS	SAXATILE	SCOURIES	SEATINGS	SENATORS	SETLINES	SHIFTIER	SIDEROAD
SALUTING	SAXONIES	SCOURING	SEAWATER	SENDINGS	SETTERED	SHINGLED	SIDESMAN
SALVINGS	SAXONITE	SCOUTERS	SECANTLY	SENECIOS	SETTINGS	SHINGLER	SIDESMEN
SAMISENS	SCAILING	SCOUTHER	SECEDING	SENGREEN	SETTLERS	SHINGLES	SIDEWALK
SAMPHIRE	SCAITHED	SCOUTING	SECERNED	SENILITY	SETTLING	SHINIEST	SIDEWALL
SAMPIRES	SCALDERS	SCOWRIES	SECODONT	SENNIGHT	SETTLORS	SHINTIES	SIDEWARD
SAMPLERS	SCALDING	SCOWTHER	SECONDER	SENSILLA	SETULOSE	SHIPMATE	SIEVERTS
SAMPLERY	SCALIEST	SCRABBED	SECONDLY	SENSISTS	SETULOUS	SHIPMENT	SIGHTERS
SAMPLING	SCALINGS	SCRAGGED	SECRETED	SENSORIA	SEVERALS	SHIRALEE	SIGMATED
SANATIVE	SCALPERS	SCRAMBED	SECRETIN	SENTIENT	SEVERIES	SHIREMAN	SIGMATES
SANATORY	SCALPING	SCRAMJET	SECRETLY	SENTINEL	SEVERING	SHIREMEN	SIGNALED
SANCTITY	SCANDENT	SCRAMMED	SECTATOR	SENTRIES	SEVERITY	SHIRTIER	SIGNALER
SANDIEST	SCANNERS	SCRANNEL	SECTIONS	SEPALOID	SEWERING	SHIRTING	SIGNALLY
SANDIVER	SCANTEST	SCRAPIES	SECTORAL	SEPARATA	SEXTANTS	SHITHEAD	SIGNETED
SANDLING	SCANTIER	SCRAPING	SECTORED	SEPARATE	SEXTILES	SHITHOLE	SIGNIEUR
SANDWORT	SCANTIES	SCRAPPED	SECURING	SEPIMENT	SHADIEST	SHITTIER	SIGNIORS
SANGAREE	SCANTING	SCRAPPLE	SECURITY	SEPIOSTS	SHADOWER	SHIVAREE	SIGNLESS
SANGLIER	SCANTITY	SCRATTED	SEDATELY	SEPTARIA	SHAFTERS	SHIVERED	SIGNORES
SANGRIAS	SCANTLED	SCRATTLE	SEDATEST	SEPTIMAL	SHAFTING	SHIVERER	SIGNORIA
SANICLES	SCANTLES	SCRAWLED	SEDATING	SEPTUORS	SHAGREEN	SHOALEST	SIGNPOST
SANIDINE	SCARCEST	SCRAWMED	SEDATION	SERAFILE	SHALIEST	SHOALIER	SILAGING
SANIFIED	SCARCITY	SCREAKED	SEDATIVE	SERAFINS	SHAMISEN	SHOALING	SILENCED
SANITARY	SCAREDER	SCREAMED	SEDERUNT	SERAGLIO	SHANDIES	SHODDIER	SILENCER
SANITATE	SCARFING	SCREAMER	SEDIMENT	SERAPHIC	SHANTIES	SHOEINGS	SILENTER
SANITIES	SCARIEST	SCREENED	SEDITION	SERAPHIM	SHAREMEN	SHOETREE	SILENTLY
SANITISE	SCARLETS	SCREWIER	SEDUCING	SERAPHIN	SHARINGS	SHONKIER	SILESIAS
SANITIZE	SCARMOGE	SCREWING	SEDUCTOR	SERENADE	SHARKING	SHOOTERS	SILICATE
SANSERIF	SCARPAED	SCREWTOP	SEDULITY	SERENATA	SHARNIER	SHOOTING	SILICONE
SANTOURS	SCARPHED	SCRIBBLE	SEEDINGS	SERENATE	SHARPENS	SHOREMAN	SILKENED
SAPIENCE	SCARPING	SCRIENES	SEEDLING	SERENEST	SHARPEST	SHOREMEN	SILKIEST
SAPLINGS	SCARRING	SCRIEVED	SEEDSMAN	SERENING	SHARPIES	SHORINGS	SILLIEST
SAPONITE	SCARTING	SCRIEVES	SEELIEST	SERENITY	SHARPING	SHORTAGE	SILTIEST
SAPPHIRE	SCATHING	SCRIGGLE	SEELINGS	SERFLIKE	SHASTERS	SHORTENS	SILVERED
SAPPLING	SCATOLES	SCRIPTED	SEEMINGS	SERGEANT	SHATTERS	SHORTEST	SIMARRES
SAPROBES	SCATTERS	SCROGGIE	SEEMLIER	SERIALLY	SHATTERY	SHORTIES	SIMAZINE
SAPROPEL	SCATTERY	SCROLLED	SEETHING	SERIATED	SHAWLIES	SHORTING	SIMMERED
SARANGIS	SCATTIER	SCROUNGE	SEGOLATE	SERIATES	SHAWLING	SHOTTING	SIMONIES
SARCENET	SCATTING	SCROWLED	SEGREANT	SERIATIM	SHEADING	SHOULDER	SIMPERED
SARCODES	SCAURING	SCUNGIER	SEICENTO	SERICINS	SHEAFIER	SHOUTERS	SIMPERER
SARDELLE	SCAWTITE	SCURRIED	SEIGNEUR	SERICITE	SHEALING	SHOUTHER	SIMULATE
SARDINES	SCELERAT	SCUTELLA	SEIGNIOR	SERICONS	SHEARERS	SHOUTING	SINCERER
SARDONIC	SCENARIO	SCUTIGER	SEIGNORY	SERIEMAS	SHEARING	SHOVELER	SINECURE

SINGABLE
SINGLETS
SINGULAR
SINISTER
SINKHOLE
SINKIEST
SINNERED
SINOPITE
SINTERED
SINUATED
SIPHONED
SIPHONET
SIRENIAN
SIRENISE
SIRGANGS
SIRNAMED
SIRNAMES
SIRVENTE
SISTERED
SISTERLY
SITHENCE
SITUATED
SITUATES
SIXSCORE
SIXTEENS
SIZEABLE
SKAILING
SKAITHED
SKATINGS
SKATOLES
SKEARIER
SKEARING
SKEELIER
SKEERIER
SKEERING
SKELETON
SKELLIER
SKELPING
SKELTERS
SKERRIES
SKERRING
SKIATRON
SKINHEAD
SKINKERS
SKINNERS
SKINTEST
SKIRRETS
SKIRTERS
SKIRTING
SKITTERS
SKIVERED
SKLATING
SKLENTED
SKURRIED
SLABBIER
SLABBING
SLACKEST
SLACKING
SLAGGIER
SLAGGING
SLAIRGED
SLAISTER
SLAMMING
SLANDERS
SLANGERS
SLANGIER
SLANGILY
SLANGING
SLANGISH
SLANTING
SLAPPERS
SLAPPING
SLASHING
SLATCHES
SLATHERS
SLATIEST
SLATINGS
SLATTERN
SLATTERS
SLATTERY
SLATTING
SLAVERED
SLAVERER
SLEAVING
SLEAZIER
SLEDDING
SLEDGING
SLEEKIER
SLEEKING
SLEEPIER
SLEEPING
SLEETIER
SLEETING
SLEEVING
SLEEZIER
SLEIGHER
SLEIGHTS
SLENTERS
SLIGHTED
SLIGHTER
SLIMIEST
SLINGERS
SLINKERS
SLINKIER
SLINTERS
SLIPCASE
SLIPWARE
SLITHERS
SLITHERY
SLITTERS
SLIVERED
SLOBBIER
SLOETREE
SLOKENED
SLOOMIER
SLOPIEST
SLOPPIER
SLOSHIER
SLOTHING
SLOTTERS
SLOTTING
SLUBBIER
SLUDGIER
SLUTTERY
SMALLING
SMALMING
SMALTITE
SMARMIER
SMARMING
SMARTENS
SMARTEST
SMARTIES
SMARTING
SMATTERS
SMEARIER
SMEARILY
SMEARING
SMEEKING
SMELLIER
SMELLING
SMELTERS
SMELTERY
SMELTING
SMIDGENS
SMIDGEON
SMILAXES
SMITHERS
SMITHERY
SMOKIEST
SMOLDERS
SMOORING
SMOOTHEN
SMOOTHER
SMOOTHIE
SMOOTING
SMOTHERS
SMOTHERY
SMOULDER
SMOUTING
SMUDGIER
SMUTTIER
SMYTRIES
SNABBLED
SNAFFLED
SNAGGIER
SNAILERY
SNAILIER
SNAILING
SNAKIEST
SNAPPERS
SNAPPIER
SNARIEST
SNARINGS
SNARLERS
SNARLIER
SNARLING
SNARRING
SNATCHED
SNATCHER
SNATCHES
SNAZZIER
SNEAKERS
SNEAKIER
SNEDDING
SNEERIER
SNEERING
SNELLEST
SNELLING
SNICKERS
SNICKETS
SNIFFERS
SNIFFLED
SNIFFLER
SNIFTERS
SNIFTIER
SNIGGERS
SNIGGLED
SNIGGLER
SNIGGLES
SNIPIEST
SNIPPERS
SNIPPETS
SNIPPETY
SNIPPIER
SNIRTLED
SNIRTLES
SNITCHED
SNITCHER
SNITCHES
SNOBBIER
SNODDEST
SNOOPERS
SNOOPIER
SNOOTIER
SNOOTING
SNOOZIER
SNOOZLED
SNORINGS
SNORTERS
SNORTIER
SNORTING
SNOTTERS
SNOTTERY
SNOTTIER
SNOTTIES
SNOTTING
SNOUTIER
SNOUTING
SNOWIEST
SNOWLIKE
SNOWLINE
SOAPIEST
SOARINGS
SOBEREST
SOBERING
SOBERISE
SOBRIETY
SOCAGERS
SOCIABLE
SOCIATES
SOCIETAL
SODALITE
SODDIEST
SODOMITE
SOFTENED
SOFTENER
SOFTLING
SOFTWARE
SOILAGES
SOILIEST
SOILURES
SOLACING
SOLANDER
SOLANINE
SOLARISE
SOLARIZE
SOLDERED
SOLDERER
SOLDIERS
SOLDIERY
SOLECIST
SOLEMNER
SOLENOID
SOLFEGGI
SOLIDARE
SOLIDATE
SOLIDEST
SOLITUDE
SOLLERET
SOLSTICE
SOLUTIVE
SOLVATED
SOLVATES
SOMBREST
SOMBRING
SOMERSET
SOMETIME
SOMNIATE
SONDELIS
SONGBIRD
SONGLIKE
SONGSTER
SONNETED
SONORANT
SONORITY
SONSIEST
SOOTHERS
SOOTHING
SOOTIEST
SOPHERIC
SOPITING
SOPPIEST
SORBATES
SORBENTS
SORBITES
SORDIDER
SOREDIAL
SOREDIUM
SOREHEAD
SORICINE
SORNINGS
SORORATE
SORORISE
SORPTION
SORRIEST
SORTABLE
SORTANCE
SORTINGS
SORTMENT
SOTERIAL
SOTTINGS
SOULDIER
SOUNDERS
SOUNDEST
SOUPIEST
SOURCING
SOURDINE
SOURINGS
SOUTACHE
SOUTANES
SOUTERLY
SOUTHERN
SOUTHERS
SOUTHING
SOUVENIR
SOVRANTY
SOWARREE
SOWBREAD
SOWTHING
SOZZLIER
SPADEMAN
SPADEMEN
SPADGERS
SPADILLE
SPAGERIC
SPAIRGED
SPAIRGES
SPALLING
SPALTING
SPAMMIER
SPANDREL
SPANDRIL
SPANGLED
SPANGLER
SPANGLES
SPANGLET
SPANIELS
SPANKERS
SPANNERS
SPARABLE
SPARGING
SPARKIER
SPARKIES
SPARKING
SPARKLED
SPARKLER
SPARKLES
SPARKLET
SPARLING
SPARRIER
SPARRING
SPARSELY
SPARSEST
SPARTHES
SPATTERS
SPATTING
SPAVINED
SPAWLING
SPAWNERS
SPAWNIER
SPEARIER
SPEARING
SPEARMEN
SPECIALS
SPECIMEN
SPECTRAL
SPECULAR
SPEEDIER
SPEEDING
SPEELING
SPEERING
SPEIRING
SPELDING
SPELDINS
SPELDRIN
SPELLING
SPELTERS
SPENDALL
SPENDERS
SPENDING
SPERLING
SPERRING
SPERSING
SPETSNAZ
SPETTING
SPETZNAZ
SPHENOID
SPHERIER
SPHERING
SPHEROID
SPICATED
SPIELERS
SPIELING
SPIGNELS
SPIKELET
SPILITES
SPINDLED
SPINDLES
SPINETTE
SPINIEST
SPINNERS
SPINNERY
SPINNETS
SPINODES
SPINSTER
SPINTEXT
SPIRACLE
SPIRAEAS
SPIRANTS
SPIRATED
SPIREMES
SPIRIEST
SPIRITED
SPIRTING
SPIRTLES
SPITCHER
SPITEFUL
SPITFIRE
SPITTERS
SPLASHER
SPLATTED
SPLATTER
SPLAYING
SPLENDID
SPLENDOR
SPLINTED
SPLINTER
SPLITTER
SPLUTTER
SPOILAGE
SPOILERS
SPOLIATE
SPONGERS
SPONGIER
SPOONIER
SPOONIES
SPOORING
SPORTERS
SPORTIER
SPORTING
SPORTIVE
SPOSHIER
SPOTTERS
SPOTTIER
SPOTTING
SPOUTERS
SPOUTIER
SPOUTING
SPRACKLE
SPRAGGED
SPRAINED
SPRAINTS
SPRANGLE
SPRATTLE
SPRAWLED
SPRAWLER
SPRAYIER
SPRAYING
SPREADER
SPREATHE
SPREAZED
SPREDDEN
SPREEING
SPRIGGED
SPRINGAL
SPRINGED
SPRINGER
SPRINGES
SPRINGLE
SPRINKLE
SPRINTED
SPRINTER
SPRITELY
SPRITZER
SPROCKET
SPROUTED
SPRUIKED
SPUDDIER
SPUNKIER
SPURTLES
SQUAILED
SQUAILER
SQUANDER
SQUAREST
SQUARING
SQUATTER
SQUEALER
SQUINTED
SQUINTER
SQUIRMED
SQUIRRED
SQUIRTED
SQUIRTER
STABBERS
STABBING
STABILES
STABLERS
STABLING
STACKERS
STACKING
STADDLES
STAFFERS
STAFFING
STAGGERS
STAGGING
STAGIEST
STAGINGS
STAGNATE
STAIDEST
STAINERS
STAINING
STAITHES
STALKERS
STALKIER
STALKING
STALKOES
STALLAGE
STALLING
STALLMEN
STAMENED
STAMMERS
STAMPEDE
STAMPERS
STAMPING
STANCHED
STANCHEL
STANCHER
STANCHES
STANDEES
STANDERS
STANDING
STANGING
STANHOPE
STANIELS
STANNATE
STANNELS
STANNITE
STANYELS
STAPEDES
STAPEDII
STAPELIA
STAPLERS
STAPLING
STAPPING
STARAGEN
STARCHED
STARCHER
STARCHES
STARINGS
STARKENS

STARKERS
STARKEST
STARKING
STARLESS
STARLETS
STARLIKE
STARLING
STARNIES
STARNING
STARRIER
STARRING
STARTERS
STARTING
STARTLED
STARTLER
STARTLES
STARVING
STASHING
STATEDLY
STATICES
STATIONS
STATURED
STATURES
STAYNING
STEADIED
STEADIER
STEADIES
STEADILY
STEADING
STEALERS
STEALING
STEAMERS
STEAMIER
STEAMIES
STEAMILY
STEAMING
STEANING
STEAPSIN
STEARAGE
STEARATE
STEARINE
STEARING
STEARINS
STEATITE
STEDDING
STEEDING
STEEKING
STEELIER
STEELING
STEELMAN
STEELMEN
STEEMING
STEENING
STEEPIER
STEEPING
STEERAGE
STEERERS
STEERIES
STEERING
STEEVING
STEGODON
STEINING
STELLING
STELLION
STEMMING
STEMSONS
STENCHED
STENCILS
STENDING
STENGAHS
STENLOCK
STENNING
STENOSED
STENOSIS
STENOTIC
STENTING
STENTORS
STENTOUR
STEPDAME
STEPHANE
STEPPING
STEREOME
STERIGMA
STERLETS
STERLING
STERNAGE
STERNEST
STERNING
STERNITE
STERNSON
STERNUMS
STERNWAY
STEROIDS
STERVING
STETTING
STEWARDS
STEWINGS
STEWPANS
STEWPOND
STIBBLER
STIBINES
STIBNITE
STICKERS
STICKIER
STICKLER
STIEVELY
STIFFENS
STIFLERS
STILBENE
STILBITE
STILETTO
STILLAGE
STILLERS
STILLIER
STILTERS
STILTIER
STINGERS
STINGIER
STINKARD
STINKERS
STINTERS
STINTIER
STIPENDS
STIPPLER
STIPULED
STIPULES
STIRLESS
STIRRERS
STIRRING
STITCHER
STOCKADE
STOCKERS
STOCKIER
STOCKING
STOCKMEN
STODGERS
STODGIER
STODGING
STOITERS
STOITING
STOLIDER
STOMPERS
STOMPING
STONERAG
STONERAW
STONIEST
STONINGS
STONKERS
STONKING
STONNING
STONYING
STOOGING
STOOKING
STOOLIES
STOOLING
STOOPERS
STOOPING
STOPINGS
STOPOVER
STOPPERS
STOPPING
STORABLE
STORAGES
STORAXES
STOREMAN
STOREMEN
STOREYED
STORMIER
STORMING
STORYING
STOTINKA
STOTTERS
STOTTING
STOUNDED
STOUNING
STOURIER
STOUSHED
STOUTENS
STOVAINE
STOVINGS
STOWINGS
STOWNDED
STRADDLE
STRAFFED
STRAFING
STRAGGLE
STRAICHT
STRAIKED
STRAINED
STRAINER
STRAINTS
STRAITED
STRAITEN
STRAITER
STRAMMEL
STRAMPED
STRANDED
STRANGER
STRANGLE
STRAPPED
STRAPPER
STRASSES
STRATEGY
STRATOSE
STRAUNGE
STRAWIER
STRAWING
STRAYERS
STRAYING
STREAKED
STREAKER
STREAMED
STREAMER
STREEKED
STREELED
STREETED
STREIGHT
STREIGNE
STRELITZ
STREPENT
STRESSED
STRESSOR
STREWAGE
STREWERS
STREWING
STRIATED
STRIATES
STRICHES
STRICKEN
STRICKLE
STRICTER
STRIDDEN
STRIDDLE
STRIDENT
STRIDING
STRIGATE
STRIGGED
STRIGINE
STRIGOSE
STRIKERS
STRIKING
STRINGED
STRINGER
STRINKLE
STRIPIER
STRIPING
STRIPPED
STRIPPER
STRIVERS
STRIVING
STROAMED
STROBILE
STRODDLE
STRODLED
STRODLES
STROKERS
STROKING
STROLLED
STROLLER
STRONGER
STRONTIA
STROOKEN
STROPHES
STROPPED
STROUPAN
STROUTED
STROWERS
STROWING
STROYING
STRUDELS
STRUGGLE
STRUMMED
STRUMMEL
STRUMOSE
STRUNTED
STRUTTED
STUBBIER
STUCCOED
STUCCOER
STUDENTS
STUDIERS
STUFFIER
STUMBLER
STUMPIER
STUNNERS
STUPIDER
STUPRATE
STURDIED
STURDIER
STURDIES
STURGEON
STURNINE
STURNOID
STYRAXES
STYRENES
SUASIBLE
SUBAGENT
SUBERATE
SUBERINS
SUBGENRE
SUBGRADE
SUBLATED
SUBLIMER
SUBORNED
SUBTENDS
SUBTILER
SUBTITLE
SUBTRIBE
SUBTRUDE
SUDARIES
SUDATING
SUDDENTY
SUGARING
SUITABLE
SUITORED
SUIVANTE
SULCATED
SULFATED
SULFITES
SULKIEST
SULPHITE
SULTRIER
SUMMONER
SUNBELTS
SUNDARIS
SUNDERED
SUNDERER
SUNDRESS
SUNDRIES
SUNNIEST
SUNRISES
SUNSTONE
SUPERATE
SUPERNAL
SUPERTAX
SUPINATE
SURANCES
SURBATED
SURBATES
SURETIED
SURETIES
SURFACED
SURFEITS
SURFIEST
SURGEONS
SURICATE
SURLIEST
SURMISED
SURNAMED
SURNAMES
SURTAXED
SURTAXES
SURTITLE
SURVIVED
SUSPIRED
SUTORIAN
SUZERAIN
SWADDLER
SWALIEST
SWALINGS
SWAMPIER
SWANHERD
SWANKERS
SWANKIER
SWANNIER
SWARDIER
SWARDING
SWARFING
SWARMING
SWARVING
SWATHIER
SWATHING
SWATTERS
SWATTING
SWAYLING
SWEALING
SWEARERS
SWEARING
SWEATERS
SWEATIER
SWEATING
SWEELING
SWEETING
SWELLING
SWELTERS
SWELTING
SWERFING
SWERVING
SWIFTERS
SWIMWEAR
SWINDGED
SWINDGES
SWINDLED
SWINDLER
SWINDLES
SWINGERS
SWINGIER
SWINGLED
SWINGLES
SWITHERS
SWORDING
SWORDMEN
SWOTTERS
SWOTTING
SYBARITE
SYCAMINE
SYCAMORE
SYENITES
SYENITIC
SYLVANER
SYMITARE
SYNAPTES
SYNDETIC
SYNDROME
SYNECHIA
SYNECTIC
SYNEDRIA
SYNERGIC
SYNERGID
SYNTEXIS
SYRINGAS
SYRINGED
SYRINGES
SYRINXES
TABARETS
TABETICS
TABINETS
TABLIERS
TABLINGS
TABORERS
TABORETS
TABORING
TABORINS
TABRERES
TACHISME
TACHISTE
TACKIEST
TACKINGS
TACKLERS
TACKLING
TACKSMEN
TACTIONS
TACTLESS
TADPOLES
TAEDIUMS
TAGGIEST
TAGGINGS
TAGLIONI
TAIGLING
TAILERON
TAILINGS
TAILLESS
TAILLEUR
TAILLIES
TAILORED
TAILRACE
TAILZIES
TAINTURE
TAKINGLY
TALCIEST
TALCKIER
TALCKING
TALESMAN
TALESMEN
TALIPEDS
TALKIEST
TALKINGS
TALLAGES
TALLENTS
TALLIERS
TALLNESS
TALLYING
TALLYMEN
TAMARINS
TAMENESS
TAMPERED
TAMPERER
TAMPINGS
TANAGERS
TANAISTE
TANDOORS
TANGELOS
TANGENTS
TANGHINS
TANGIBLE
TANGIBLY
TANGIEST
TANGLERS
TANGLIER
TANGLING
TANGOIST
TANISTRY
TANKAGES
TANKINGS
TANLINGS
TANNAGES
TANNATES
TANNINGS
TAPADERA
TAPADERO
TAPELINE
TAPERERS
TAPERING
TAPESTRY
TAPPINGS
TAPSTERS
TARDIEST
TARDYING
TARRASES
TARRIERS
TARRIEST
TARRINGS
TARRYING
TARSIERS
TARSIPED
TARTANED
TARTANES
TARTARES
TARTIEST
TARTINES
TARTLETS
TARTNESS
TARWEEDS
TARWHINE
TASERING
TASKINGS
TASSELED
TASTEVIN
TASTIEST
TASTINGS
TATTIEST
TATTINGS
TATTLERS
TATTLING
TAUNTERS
TAURINES
TAUTNESS
TAVERING
TAVERNAS
TAVERNER
TAWDRIES
TAWERIES
TAWNIEST
TAWTIEST
TEACHERS
TEACHING
TEAGLING
TEAMINGS
TEAMSTER
TEAMWISE
TEARABLE
TEARIEST
TEARLESS
TEASELED
TEASELER
TEASINGS
TEASPOON
TEATIMES
TEAZLING
TECHNICS

TEDISOME
TEENAGER
TEENIEST
TEENSIER
TEENTIER
TEETHING
TELECAST
TELESTIC
TELEVISE
TELEXING
TELLINGS
TELPHERS
TEMBLORS
TEMEROUS
TEMPERAS
TEMPLARS
TEMPORAL
TEMPTERS
TEMPURAS
TENAILLE
TENANTRY
TENDRILS
TENDRONS
TENEBRIO
TENNISES
TENONERS
TENORIST
TENORITE
TENSIBLE
TENSIONS
TENTAGES
TENTFULS
TENTIEST
TENTIGOS
TENTINGS
TENTLESS
TENTORIA
TENTWISE
TENUIOUS
TENURIAL
TEOSINTE
TEQUILAS
TERAFLOP
TERATISM
TERATOID
TERBIUMS
TEREBRAS
TERGITES
TERMINAL
TERMINER
TERMINUS
TERMITES
TERMLESS
TERMLIES
TERNIONS
TERPENES
TERRACES
TERRAINS
TERRANES
TERRAPIN
TERRASES
TERREENS
TERRENES
TERRIERS
TERRINES
TERSIONS
TERTIALS
TERTIANS
TERTIARY
TESSERAE
TESSERAL
TESTAMUR
TESTATOR
TESTERNS
TESTICLE
TESTINGS
TESTOONS
TESTRILL
TESTRILS
TESTUDOS
TETANICS
TETANIES
TETANISE
TETRACID
TETRACTS
TETRADIC
TETRAGON
TETRAPLA
TETRAPOD
TETRAXON
TETRODES
TETRONAL
TEXTILES
TEXTURES
THALLINE
THALWEGS
THANAGES
THANKERS
THATNESS
THAWIEST
THAWINGS
THEATERS
THEATRAL
THEATRES
THEATRIC
THEEKING
THEORBOS
THEOREMS
THEORICS
THEORIES
THEORISE
THEORIST
THERIACS
THERIANS
THERMALS
THESAURI
THESPIAN
THIAMINE
THICKENS
THIEVING
THIGGERS
THILLERS
THINGIER
THINGIES
THINKERS
THINNERS
THINNESS
THINNEST
THIRDING
THIRLAGE
THIRLING
THIRSTED
THIRSTER
THIRTEEN
THIRTIES
THISNESS
THORACES
THORAXES
THORITES
THORNING
THORNSET
THRALLED
THRANGED
THRAPPLE
THRASHED
THRASHER
THRASHES
THRAWING
THREAPIT
THREATEN
THREAVES
THRESHED
THRESHEL
THRESHER
THRILLED
THRIPSES
THRISSEL
THRISTED
THRISTLE
THRIVERS
THRIVING
THROEING
THRONING
THROSTLE
THROWERS
THROWING
THRUSTED
THULITES
THUNDERS
THWAITES
THYMINES
TICKLERS
TIDDLERS
TIDDLIER
TIDDLIES
TIDELAND
TIDELESS
TIDESMAN
TIDESMEN
TIDEWAYS
TIDINESS
TIERCELS
TIERCETS
TIETACKS
TIGERISH
TIGERISM
TIGHTENS
TILEFISH
TILERIES
TILLAGES
TILLERED
TILLIEST
TILLITES
TIMBALES
TIMBRELS
TIMELESS
TIMONEER
TINCHELS
TINCTURE
TINGLERS
TINGLIER
TINHORNS
TININESS
TINKERED
TINKERER
TINKLERS
TINKLIER
TINNIEST
TINPLATE
TINSELED
TINSELLY
TINSELRY
TINSTONE
TINTACKS
TINTIEST
TINTLESS
TINTYPES
TINWARES
TIPPLERS
TIPSTERS
TIRASSES
TIREDEST
TIRELESS
TIRELING
TIRESOME
TITANESS
TITANISM
TITANOUS
TITMOUSE
TITRATED
TITRATES
TOASTERS
TOASTIES
TOASTING
TODDLERS
TODDLING
TOECLIPS
TOENAILS
TOFFIEST
TOGGLING
TOHEROAS
TOILETRY
TOILINGS
TOILLESS
TOILSOME
TOISEACH
TOKENISM
TOLERANT
TOLLAGES
TOLLINGS
TOLTERED
TOLUATES
TOLUENES
TONALITE
TONELESS
TONEPADS
TONGSTER
TONIGHTS
TONNAGES
TONNEAUS
TONSURED
TONSURES
TONTINER
TONTINES
TOOLINGS
TOOTLING
TOOTSIES
TOOTSING
TOPLINER
TOPLINES
TOPPINGS
TOPPLING
TOPSIDES
TORCHERS
TORCHING
TORDIONS
TORMENTA
TORMENTS
TORNADES
TORNADOS
TORPEDOS
TORRENTS
TORSADES
TORSIONS
TORTOISE
TORTONIS
TORTURES
TORULINS
TORULOSE
TOSHIEST
TOSSIEST
TOSSINGS
TOTALISE
TOTEMISM
TOTEMIST
TOTIENTS
TOTTIEST
TOTTINGS
TOUCHERS
TOUGHENS
TOURINGS
TOURNEYS
TOUSIEST
TOUSINGS
TOUSLING
TOUTIEST
TOUZIEST
TOUZLING
TOWELING
TOWERING
TOWLINES
TOWNIEST
TOWNLIER
TOWNLING
TOWNSMEN
TOWROPES
TOWSIEST
TOWZIEST
TOXEMIAS
TRACHEAL
TRACINGS
TRACKERS
TRACKING
TRACKMEN
TRACTILE
TRACTING
TRACTIVE
TRADABLE
TRADINGS
TRADUCES
TRAFFICS
TRAGULES
TRAHISON
TRAIKING
TRAILERS
TRAILING
TRAINEES
TRAINERS
TRAINING
TRAIPSED
TRAIPSES
TRAJECTS
TRAMLINE
TRAMMELS
TRAMMING
TRAMPERS
TRAMPETS
TRAMPING
TRAMPLED
TRAMPLER
TRAMPLES
TRANCHES
TRANCHET
TRANCING
TRANECTS
TRANGLES
TRANNIES
TRANSECT
TRANSEPT
TRANSFER
TRANSFIX
TRANSHIP
TRANSIRE
TRANSITS
TRANSMEW
TRANSMIT
TRANSOMS
TRANSUDE
TRANSUME
TRANTERS
TRANTING
TRAPESED
TRAPESES
TRAPEZED
TRAPEZES
TRAPLIKE
TRAPPERS
TRAPPING
TRASHERY
TRASHIER
TRASHING
TRASHMEN
TRAUCHLE
TRAVERSE
TRAVESTY
TRAVISES
TRAWLERS
TRAWLING
TRAYNING
TREACLES
TREADERS
TREADING
TREADLES
TREAGUES
TREASONS
TREASURE
TREASURY
TREATERS
TREATIES
TREATING
TREATISE
TREBLING
TRECKING
TREDDLES
TREDILLE
TREELESS
TREENAIL
TREESHIP
TREETOPS
TREFOILS
TREHALAS
TREILLES
TREKKERS
TREKKING
TREMATIC
TREMBLES
TREMOLOS
TRENAILS
TRENCHES
TRENDIER
TRENDIES
TRENDILY
TRENDING
TRENISES
TRENTALS
TREPANGS
TREPHINE
TREPIDER
TRESPASS
TRESSELS
TRESSIER
TRESSING
TRESSURE
TRESTLES
TREVISES
TREWSMAN
TREWSMEN
TREYBITS
TRIALLED
TRIANGLE
TRIARCHS
TRIATICS
TRIAXONS
TRIBADES
TRIBASIC
TRIBBLES
TRIBLETS
TRIBUNES
TRIBUTES
TRICKERS
TRICKING
TRICKLED
TRICKLES
TRICORNS
TRIDARNS
TRIDENTS
TRIFECTA
TRIFFEST
TRIFLERS
TRIFLING
TRIGGERS
TRIGGEST
TRIGGING
TRIGNESS
TRIGONAL
TRIGONIC
TRILBIES
TRILEMMA
TRILLING
TRILLOES
TRILOBED
TRILOBES
TRIMMERS
TRIMMEST
TRIMMING
TRIMNESS
TRINDLED
TRINDLES
TRINGLES
TRINKETS
TRIOLETS
TRIONYMS
TRIPEDAL
TRIPEMAN
TRIPEMEN
TRIPIEST
TRIPLANE
TRIPLETS
TRIPLIED
TRIPLIES
TRIPLING
TRIPOSES
TRIPPERS
TRIPPETS
TRIPPING
TRIPPLED
TRIPPLES
TRIPTANE
TRIREMES
TRISECTS
TRISEMES
TRISEMIC
TRISKELE
TRISOMES
TRITIATE
TRITIDES
TRITONES
TRIVALVE
TRIZONES
TROATING
TROCHEES
TROCHLEA
TROCKING
TROELIES
TROGGING
TROILITE
TROLLERS
TROLLEYS
TROLLIES
TROLLING
TROMINOS
TROMMELS
TROMPING
TROOLIES
TROOPERS
TROOPING
TROPHESY
TROPHIED
TROPHIES
TROSSERS
TROTHING
TROTLINE
TROTTERS
TROTTING
TROUBLED
TROUBLES
TROULING
TROUNCED
TROUNCES
TROUPERS
TROUPING
TROUSERS
TROUTERS
TROUTING
TROWSERS
TRUANTED
TRUCAGES
TRUCKIES
TRUCKLES
TRUDGENS
TRUDGEON
TRUDGERS
TRUENESS
TRUFFLES
TRUNCATE
TRUNDLES
TRUSTEES
TRUSTIER
TRUSTIES
TSAREVNA

TSARINAS
TSIGANES
TUBENOSE
TUBEROSE
TUBEROUS
TUILYIES
TUILZIES
TUMBLERS
TUMBRELS
TUNELESS
TUNICLES
TUNNAGES
TURACINS
TURBANED
TURBINED
TURBINES
TURDIONS
TURFIEST
TURFITES
TURNIPED
TURNKEYS
TURNPIKE
TURNSOLE
TURTLERS
TUTANIAS
TUTELARS
TUTENAGS
TUTORESS
TUTORING
TUTORISE
TUTRICES
TUTRIXES
TUXEDOES
TWADDLES
TWANGIER
TWANGLED
TWANGLES
TWEELING
TWEERING
TWEETERS
TWENTIES
TWIDDLER
TWIGSOME
TWILLIES
TWINIEST
TWINKLES
TWINSETS
TWINTERS
TWIRLERS
TWIRLING
TWISCARS
TWISTERS
TWISTIER
TWITTENS
TWITTERS
TWOCCERS
TYRAMINE
TYRANING
TYRANNES
TYRANNIS
TYRANTED
TYRELESS
TYROSINE
UBERTIES
UDALLERS
UGLINESS
ULCERING
ULITISES
ULSTERED
ULTERIOR

UNADORED
UNAMUSED
UNARGUED
UNARISEN
UNBARBED
UNBARKED
UNBARRED
UNBIASED
UNBRACED
UNBRACES
UNBRASTE
UNBRIDLE
UNBRUSED
UNBURIED
UNCARTED
UNCHASTE
UNCLOSED
UNCORDED
UNCORKED
UNCOVERS
UNCRATED
UNCRATES
UNCREATE
UNCURSED
UNDERACT
UNDERARM
UNDERBID
UNDERBIT
UNDERDID
UNDERDOG
UNDERLAP
UNDERLAY
UNDERLIE
UNDERLIP
UNDERMAN
UNDERPAY
UNDERPIN
UNDERRAN
UNDERSAY
UNDERSEA
UNDERSET
UNDERSKY
UNDERTOW
UNDERUSE
UNDERWAY
UNDERWIT
UNDESERT
UNDRAPED
UNDREAMT
UNDRIVEN
UNDULOSE
UNEARNED
UNEARTHS
UNEASIER
UNERRING
UNFAIRED
UNFASTEN
UNFEARED
UNFITTER
UNFOLDER
UNFORCED
UNFORGED
UNFORMED
UNFRAMED
UNFRIEND
UNGALLED
UNGEARED
UNGENIAL
UNGILDED
UNGIRDED

UNGLAZED
UNGORGED
UNGRACED
UNGRADED
UNGRAZED
UNGULATE
UNHAIRED
UNHALSED
UNHARMED
UNHEARTS
UNHONEST
UNHORSED
UNINURED
UNIQUEST
UNIRONED
UNITARDS
UNITISED
UNITISES
UNITIZES
UNIVERSE
UNJUSTER
UNKINDER
UNLASHED
UNLEARNS
UNLEARNT
UNLEASED
UNLISTED
UNLOADER
UNLOOSED
UNLORDED
UNMAILED
UNMANTLE
UNMARKED
UNMARRED
UNMASKED
UNMOORED
UNNESTED
UNORDERS
UNPAIRED
UNPERSON
UNPOISED
UNPOSTED
UNPRAISE
UNPRAYED
UNPRICED
UNPRIEST
UNPRIMED
UNPRIZED
UNPROVED
UNPURSED
UNQUIETS
UNQUOTES
UNRACKED
UNRAISED
UNRAVELS
UNREAPED
UNREAVED
UNREINED
UNREPAID
UNRIBBED
UNRIDDEN
UNRIDDLE
UNRIFLED
UNRIGGED
UNRINGED
UNRIPEST
UNRIPPED
UNRIVETS
UNROLLED
UNROOFED

UNROOTED
UNROTTED
UNROUGED
UNROUSED
UNSADDLE
UNSAILED
UNSAINED
UNSALTED
UNSATING
UNSCALED
UNSEALED
UNSEAMED
UNSEATED
UNSECRET
UNSEELED
UNSELDOM
UNSELFED
UNSETTLE
UNSEXIST
UNSHALED
UNSHAMED
UNSHARED
UNSICKER
UNSIFTED
UNSIGNED
UNSLAKED
UNSLICED
UNSOCKET
UNSOILED
UNSOLDER
UNSOLVED
UNSORTED
UNSOULED
UNSOURED
UNSPARED
UNSTABLE
UNSTATED
UNSTATES
UNSTAYED
UNSTEADY
UNSTEELS
UNSTOWED
UNSUBTLE
UNSUITED
UNSUREST
UNSWEARS
UNTAILED
UNTANGLE
UNTARRED
UNTASTED
UNTESTED
UNTHREAD
UNTIDIER
UNTIDIES
UNTIRING
UNTRACED
UNTRACES
UNTRADED
UNTREADS
UNTRUEST
UNTWINES
UNVARIED
UNVEILER
UNVERSED
UNVIRTUE
UNVOICES
UNWARDED
UNWARMED
UNWARNED
UNWARPED

UNWASTED
UNWATERS
UNWISEST
UNWORDED
UNWORKED
UNWORMED
UNWRITES
UPGRADES
UPLANDER
UPRAISED
UPRAISES
UPRATING
UPSETTER
UPSTARED
UPSTARES
UPSTREAM
UPSTROKE
UPTRAINS
UPTRENDS
URAEMIAS
URALITES
URANIDES
URANITES
URBANEST
URBANISE
URBANITE
UREDINES
UREDINIA
URETHANS
URETHRAL
URETHRAS
URGENCES
URIDINES
URINATED
URINATES
URNFIELD
URODELAN
URODELES
UROSTYLE
URTICATE
USHERING
UTENSILS
UTERITIS
UTILISED
UTILISER
UTILISES
UTILIZES
UTRICLES
UTTERERS
UTTEREST
UTTERING
VACCINES
VACHERIN
VAGINULE
VAIRIEST
VALETING
VALIDEST
VALORISE
VAMPIRES
VANISHED
VANISHER
VANITIES
VANTAGES
VAPIDEST
VAPORISE
VARIANCE
VARIANTS
VARIATES
VARICOSE
VARIEDLY

VARIETAL
VARIOLES
VARMENTS
VARMINTS
VARYINGS
VASTIEST
VAULTERS
VAULTING
VAUNTERS
VAUNTIER
VAURIENS
VEALIEST
VEDALIAS
VEERINGS
VEGANISM
VEGETALS
VEILIEST
VEILINGS
VEINLETS
VELAMINA
VELARISE
VELARIZE
VELIGERS
VELOUTES
VELURING
VENALITY
VENATORS
VENERIES
VENISONS
VENOSITY
VENTAGES
VENTAILE
VENTAILS
VENTANAS
VENTIGES
VENTINGS
VENTRALS
VENTRING
VENTROUS
VENTURES
VENTURIS
VERANDAS
VERATRIN
VERBOSER
VERDICTS
VERDITES
VERIFIES
VERISMOS
VERISTIC
VERITIES
VERLIGTE
VERMEILS
VERMINED
VERNICLE
VERNIERS
VERONALS
VERONICA
VERSANTS
VERSELET
VERSICLE
VERSINES
VERSINGS
VERSIONS
VERTICAL
VERTICES
VERTIGOS
VERVAINS
VESICANT
VESPERAL
VESPIARY

VESSAILS
VESTIARY
VESTINGS
VESTRIES
VESTURAL
VESTURED
VESTURER
VETERANS
VETIVERS
VETTURAS
VIBRATED
VIBRATES
VICENARY
VICEROYS
VICOMTES
VICTRESS
VIGILANT
VIGNERON
VILAYETS
VILDNESS
VINEGARS
VINEGARY
VINERIES
VINEYARD
VINTAGER
VINTAGES
VINTNERS
VINTRIES
VIOLATER
VIOLATES
VIOLENTS
VIOLONES
VIPEROUS
VIRAGOES
VIRANDAS
VIRANDOS
VIRELAYS
VIREMENT
VIRETOTS
VIRGATES
VIRGINAL
VIRGINED
VIRGULES
VIRTUOSE
VIRULENT
VISCERAL
VISIONED
VISIONER
VISITANT
VISITERS
VISNOMIE
VISORING
VISTAING
VITALISE
VITAMINE
VITELLUS
VITIATES
VITRAGES
VITRAINS
VITREOUS
VITREUMS
VITRINES
VIZAMENT
VOIDNESS
VOITURES
VOLANTES
VOLARIES
VOLERIES
VOLTAGES
VORTEXES

VORTICES
VOTARESS
VOTARIES
VULGATES
VULTURES
WABSTERS
WADDLERS
WAFERING
WAFTINGS
WAFTURES
WAGERERS
WAGERING
WAGONERS
WAILINGS
WAISTERS
WAITINGS
WAITRESS
WALKINGS
WALLIEST
WALLINGS
WALLSEND
WALTIEST
WALTZERS
WALTZING
WANGLERS
WANKIEST
WANTAGES
WANTINGS
WARBIEST
WARBLING
WARDINGS
WARDRESS
WARELESS
WARIMENT
WARINESS
WARLINGS
WARMINGS
WARMNESS
WARNINGS
WARPINGS
WARSLING
WARTIEST
WARTIMES
WARTLESS
WARTLIKE
WASHERED
WASPNEST
WASTELOT
WASTERED
WASTINGS
WASTRELS
WASTRIES
WASTRIFE
WATCHERS
WATERERS
WATERING
WATERISH
WATERMAN
WATTLING
WAULINGS
WAVERERS
WAVERING
WAWLINGS
WAYMENTS
WEAKLING
WEANLING
WEARIEST
WEARINGS
WEARYING
WEASELER

WEATHERS
WEDDINGS
WEDGINGS
WEEDINGS
WEIRDEST
WEIRDIES
WEIRDING
WELDINGS
WELFARES
WELLINGS
WELSHING
WENDIGOS
WENNIEST
WERGILDS
WESTERED
WESTERLY
WESTERNS
WESTINGS
WESTLINS
WESTWARD
WETLANDS
WETWARES
WHAISLED
WHAISLES
WHALINGS
WHERRETS
WHERRIES
WHETTERS
WHETTING
WHINGERS
WHIPSTER
WHIRRETS
WHIRTLES
WHISTLER
WHITENER
WHITHERS
WHITRETS
WHITSTER
WHITTERS
WHOSEVER
WIDENERS
WIDGEONS
WIDOWERS
WIELDERS
WIELDING
WIGGLERS
WILDNESS
WIMBRELS
WINDAGES
WINDASES
WINDIEST
WINDLESS
WINDORES
WINDROSE
WINGEDLY
WINGIEST
WINGLESS
WINGLETS
WINKLERS
WINSOMER
WINTERED
WINTRIER
WIPEOUTS
WIRELESS
WIRETAPS
WIRINESS
WISELING
WISTERIA
WITCHENS
WITELESS
WOMANISE
WONKIEST
WOODIEST
WOODSIER
WOOLDERS
WORDAGES
WORDIEST
WORDINGS
WORDLESS
WORKINGS
WORMIEST
WORSENED
WORSTEDS
WORSTING
WORTHIES
WORTHING
WOUNDERS
WRANGLED
WRANGLER
WRANGLES
WRASTING
WRATHING
WRAWLING
WRAXLING
WREAKERS
WREAKING
WREATHES
WRESTERS
WRESTING
WRESTLED
WRESTLER
WRESTLES
WRETHING
WRIGGLES
WRINGERS
WRINKLES
WRISTIER
WRISTLET
WRITABLE
WRITHING
WRITHLED
WRITINGS
WRONGERS
WRONGEST
WROOTING
XERAFINS
XERANSES
XERANSIS
XERANTIC
YACHTERS
YAPSTERS
YARDAGES
YAWNIEST
YEALDONS
YEALMING
YEANLING
YEARDING
YEARLIES
YEARLING
YEARLONG
YEARNERS
YEARNING
YEASTIER
YEASTING
YELDRING
YELLINGS
YELPINGS
YERSINIA
YESTREEN
YIELDERS
YIELDING
YOLDRING
YOLKIEST
YOUNGEST
YTTERBIA
ZARATITE
ZEALANTS
ZEBRINAS
ZELATORS
ZELATRIX
ZEMINDAR
ZENITHAL
ZEOLITES
ZINCIEST
ZINCITES
ZINCODES
ZINGIEST
ZITHERNS
ZONULETS
ZOOLITES
ZOONITES
ZORGITES
ZORILLES

ADDITIONAL HIGH PROBABILITY WORDS

There are many seven- and eight-letter words using likely combinations of letters which don't appear in the 6-plus-1 and 6-plus-2 bonus sets. These are listed under the headings shown below, where the criteria for inclusion are also explained.

Additional words – 1- and 2-point tiles

This section contains two alphabetic listings, one of seven-letter words and one of eight-letter words. Criteria for inclusion are:

- words are not included in the 6-plus-1 and 6-plus-2 bonus sets;
- they contain only the 1- and 2-point tiles ADEGILNORSTU;
- they contain no duplicates, except for A (up to 2 allowed), E (up to 3), I (up to 2), and O (up to 2).

Note that multiple duplicate letters are allowed, as in DEITIES (2 E's and 2 I's) and GAINSAID (2 A's and 2 I's).

Additional words – 3- and 4-point tiles

This section contains two alphabetic listings, one of seven-letter words and one of eight-letter words. Criteria for inclusion are:

- words are not included in the 6-plus-1 and 6-plus-2 bonus sets;
- they contain any one of the 3- and 4-point tiles BCFHMPVWY;
- otherwise, they contain only the 1- and 2-point tiles ADEGILNORSTU;
- they contain no duplicates, except for A (up to 2 allowed), E (up to 3), I (up to 2), and O (up to 2).

Note that multiple duplicate letters are allowed, as in ABIGAIL (2 A's and 2 I's) and ABNEGATE (2 A's and 2 E's).

ADDITIONAL BONUS WORDS (1 and 2 point tiles only)

7-letter words (1 and 2 point tiles only)

ADAGIOS
ADULATE
AENEOUS
AEOLIAN
AERATED
AGENDAS
AGENTED
AGISTOR
AGNOSIA
AGOUTAS
AGOUTIS
AGROUND
AGUISED
AIERIES
AILANTO
AILERON
AIRLINE
ALERION
ALERTED
ALEURON
ALGESIA
ALIENED
ALIENEE
ALIENOR
ALIUNDE
ALOGIAS
ALONGST
ALSOONE
ALTERED
ANALOGS
ANEARED
ANGORAS
ANGULAR
ANURIAS
AREOLAE
ARGALIS
ARGANDS
AROUSAL
ASTOUND
ASTRAND
ASTROID
AUDIENT
AUDITOR
AUGITES
AULNAGE
AURATED
AURATES
AUREATE
AURELIA
AUREOLA
AUREOLE
AUSTRAL
DALTONS
DATURAS
DAUTING
DEERLET
DEGREES
DEITIES
DELAINE
DELETES
DELOUSE
DELUGES
DENGUES
DENTURE
DETENUE
DETERGE
DETINUE
DIALING
DIALIST
DIALOGS
DIARIAL
DIARIAN
DIARIST
DIETINE
DIETING
DIGITAL
DIGLOTS
DIGONAL
DILATOR
DILUENT
DILUTEE
DILUTOR
DIORITE
DIRLING
DISROOT
DISTAIN
DIURNAL
DOATING
DOGATES
DOGEATE
DOILIES
DOLINAS
DOLOURS
DONATOR
DOOLIES
DOTAGES
DOUANES
DOULEIA
DOUSING
DOUTING
DRAGONS
DRAGOON
DRAUNTS
DROGUES
DROGUET
DRONGOS
DUALINS
DUALIST
DUOTONE
DURANTS
DURGANS
DURIONS
DUSTING
EATAGES
EDENTAL
EDGIEST
EDITING
EDITION
EGESTED
EGOTISE
EIDOLON
ELEGIES
ELEGISE
ELOINED
ELOINER
ELUATES

ELUDERS
ELUTION
ENGORED
ENTERED
ERELONG
ERODENT
ERUDITE
ETAERIO
ETAGERE
ETALAGE
ETIOLIN
ETOURDI
EUGENIA
EUGENOL
EULOGIA
GADROON
GALEATE
GALIOTS
GALOOTS
GANOIDS
GARDANT
GARIALS
GARLAND
GARUDAS
GATEAUS
GAUDIER
GAUDIES
GAULTER
GAUNTED
GEALOUS
GELADAS
GELDERS
GELIDER
GENTEEL
GENTLED
GENTLER
GENTOOS
GEOIDAL
GESTURE
GIAOURS
GIRASOL
GIROSOL
GIUSTED
GLADIUS
GLEETED
GLENTED
GLIADIN
GLOATED
GLOATER
GLORIAS
GLORIED
GLOUTED
GLUTAEI
GOATEED
GOATEES
GOATIER
GODETIA
GODLIER
GOETIES
GOITRED
GOLDARN
GOLDEST
GOLDIER
GOLIARD
GONADAL
GONDOLA
GONIDIA
GOODIER
GOODIES
GOOIEST
GOONDAS
GOOSIER
GOURDES
GOUTIER
GRADATE
GRADUAL
GRANOLA
GREENED
GREENIE
GREETED
GREETES
GRIESIE
GROUNDS
GROUSED
GROUTED
GRUNTED
GRUNTLE
GUARANI
GUARDEE
GUERITE
GUESTED
GUESTEN
GUIDONS
GUILDER
GUINEAS
GUISARD
GUITARS
GULDENS
GUSTIER
GUTSIER
IDOLISE
IDOLIST
IGNITED
IGUANAS
IGUANID
INDIGOS
INDOORS
INDULTS
INDUSIA
INSULAE
INSULAR
INTRADA
INTROLD
INULASE
IODURET
ISODONT
LAETARE
LAGOONS
LAIDING
LAIRAGE
LANDAUS
LANGUID
LANGUOR
LANGURS
LANIARD
LANUGOS
LARDONS
LARDOON
LARIATS
LATENED
LATRIAS
LAUDING
LEAGUED
LEAGUER
LEAGUES
LEDGERS
LEDGIER
LEGATEE
LEGATOR
LEIDGER
LENTOID
LIAISON
LIANOID
LIGATED
LIGROIN
LISTING
LOADING
LOGANIA
LOIDING
LONGEST
LOONIER
LOOSING
LORIOTS
LOTIONS
LOUNGED
LOUNGER
LOUNGES
LOURING
LOUSING
LUNATED
LURDANS
LUSTING
LUTINGS
NARDOOS
NATURAE
NATURAL
NAUTILI
NEEDLER
NEGATED
NODULAR
NOUGATS
NOURSLE
OARAGES
ODORANT
ODORATE
OILNUTS
OLEARIA
OLIGIST
ONDATRA
ONEROUS
OODLINS
OORIALS
ORATION
ORDINAL
OREGANO
ORGIAST
OROTUND
ORTOLAN
OTALGIA
OUGLIED
OULONGS
OURALIS
OUTAGES
OUTDARE
OUTDONE
OUTEDGE
OUTGOER
OUTGOES
OUTGONE
OUTLAID
OUTLAIN
OUTLAND
OUTLIED
OUTLINE
OUTRAGE
OUTRIDE
OUTRODE
OUTSAIL
OUTSOAR
OUTSOLD
RADIALS
RADIANT
RADIATE
RADULAE
RAGLANS
RAGOUTS
RAGULED
RANULAS
RAOULIA
REDEALT
REDLEGS
REGALED
REGALIA
REGULAE
REGULOS
RELATED
RENAGUE
RENEGED
RENEGUE
RETUNED
RIDGILS
RIDINGS
RIGLINS
RIOTOUS
RITUALS
ROILING
RONEOED
ROOTAGE
ROSALIA
ROTULAS
ROTUNDA
ROTUNDS
ROULADE
RULINGS
RUNDLET
RUSTING
SAGOUIN
SAGUARO
SALIGOT
SAOUARI
SAURIAN
SAUROID
SAUTOIR
SEALINE
SETUALE
SIALOID
SIDLING
SILOING
SILTING
SILURID
SINGULT
SIRLOIN
SLADANG
SLEDGER
SLEETED
SLIDING
SOILING
SOLARIA
SOLATIA
SOLITON
SOLOING
SONDAGE
SOOGEED
SOOGIED
SOOLING
SORDINI
SORDINO
SOULDAN
STADIAL
STEELED
STILING
STOOGED
STOOLED
STRIGIL
SUDARIA
SUDORAL
SUIDIAN
SUITING
SULTANA
SUNDIAL
SURLOIN
TAENIAE
TAGUANS
TAIGLED
TAILARD
TAILORS
TALIONS
TALONED
TANDOOR
TANGOED
TARANDS
TAUREAN
TEAGLED
TEENAGE
TEGULAE
TEGULAR
TELEDUS
TENIOID
TENURED
TIARAED
TIDINGS
TIGROID
TILINGS
TINDALS
TOLUENE
TONGUED
TORDION
TORNADE
TORNADO
TOROIDS
TORULAE
TORULIN
TRAGULE
TREADLE
TREAGUE
TRIDUAN
TRISULA
TROGONS
TRUDGEN
TRUNDLE
TUNDRAS
TURDION
ULNARIA
ULTIONS
UNALIST
UNDEALT
UNEDGES
UNGILDS
UNGIRDS
UNIDEAL
UNITARD
UNLOADS
UNLOOSE
UNLORDS
UNOILED
UNREELS
UNROOST
UNROOTS
UNSOLID
UNSTAID
UNTILED
URINALS
URODELE

8-letter words (1 and 2 point tiles only)

ADULATOR
AEGIRITE
AERONAUT
AGOUTIES
AILANTOS
ALEURONE
ALIENEES
ANALOGUE
ARANEOUS
AREOLATE
ARGONAUT
AUDITING
AUDITION
AUDITORS
AURELIAN
AUREOLED
AUTOGIRO
DELEGATE
DELETION
DEROGATE
DETAINEE
DIAGONAL
DIALOGUE
DIGITALS
DILATION
DILATORS
DILUTING
DILUTION
DILUTORS
DISLOIGN
DISTRAIL
DOORNAIL
DRAGOONS
DURATION
EGLATERE
EGOITIES
ELEGISED
ENGOULED
ENROOTED
ENTOILED
ERADIATE
ERGATOID
ETOURDIE
EUGENIAS
EUGENOLS
GADROONS
GAIETIES
GAINSAID
GALEATED
GARDANTS
GARLANDS
GASTRULA
GLADIATE
GLEETIER
GLORIOSA
GLORIOUS
GOITROUS
GOLDENER
GOLIARDS
GONADIAL
GONDOLAS
GONIDIAL
GOODLIER
GRADUALS
GRADUATE
GRANOLAS
GREENLET
GRUNTLED
GUARDANT
GUILTIER
IDEATING
IDEATION
IGUANIDS
INDAGATE
INDUSIAL
INOSITOL
ISOLATOR
LAAGERED
LANGUORS
LARDOONS
LAUREATE
LINGUIST
LOADSTAR
LOOSENER
LUSTRING
NATURALS
NAUSEATE
NEUTERED
NIDOROUS
NOTARIAL
OLIGURIA
ORAGIOUS
ORDALIAN
OSTEOGEN
OTALGIAS
OUTDOING
OUTGLARE
OUTGOERS
OUTLANDS
OUTLINED
OUTRAGED
RADULATE
RAGOUTED
RAOULIAS
RATIONAL
RATOONED
REGELATE
REGULATE
RELEGATE
RELENTED
RENEGUED
RISOLUTO
RUSTLING
SALTANDO
SILUROID
SOLATION
SOLIDAGO
SOLUTION
SUDATION
SUTORIAL
TAENIOID
TAILARDS
TANDOORI
TARSIOID
TEENAGED
TOROIDAL
UNDERLET
UNELATED
UNREELED
UROSTEGE

ADDITIONAL BONUS WORDS (with one 3 or 4 point tile)

7-letter words (with one 3 or 4 point tile)

ABALONE
ABASING
ABATING
ABATORS
ABATURE
ABIDING
ABIGAIL
ABLATED
ABLATES
ABLATOR
ABLAUTS
ABODING
ABORTED
ABOULIA
ABOUNDS
ABRADES
ABRAIDS
ABREGES
ABROADS
ABSTAIN
ABULIAS
ABUSAGE
ABUSING
ABUSION
ACARIDS
ACAROID
ACATOUR
ACEDIAS
ACERATE
ACETONE
ACINOUS
ACONITE
ACORNED
ACREAGE
ACRIDIN
ACROGEN

ACTINAL
ACTINIA
ACTIONS
ADAPTOR
ADAWING
ADENOMA
ADIPOSE
ADMIRAL
ADVENES
ADVISOR
AECIDIA
AEFAULD
AEMULED
AEMULES
AFEARED
AGAMIDS
AGAMOID
AGAMOUS
AGARICS
AGILITY
AGNAMED
AGNAMES
AGNATIC
AIBLINS
AIDANCE
AIRBASE
AIRFOIL
AIRGAPS
AIRHEAD
AIRHOLE
AIRLIFT
AIRMAIL
AIRSTOP
AIRTIME
ALAMODE
ALAMORT
ALARMED
ALARUMS
ALAYING
ALBEDOS
ALBERGO
ALBINOS
ALBUGOS
ALCAIDE
ALEPINE
ALEVINS
ALGEBRA
ALGINIC
ALICANT
ALIGHTS
ALMAINS
ALMONDS
ALMONER
ALODIUM
ALOETIC
ALPEENS
ALPINES
ALREADY
ALRIGHT
ALTHEAS
ALTHORN
ALUMINA
ALUMNAE
AMADOUS
AMATEUR
AMATING
AMATION
AMATOLS
AMELIAS
AMENAGE

AMENDER
AMILDAR
AMONGST
AMORANT
AMORINI
AMORINO
AMORIST
AMOROSA
AMOROUS
AMOUNTS
AMRITAS
AMULETS
AMUSING
ANALOGY
ANALYSE
ANALYST
ANCILIA
ANDVILE
ANELACE
ANGICOS
ANGIOMA
ANGUISH
ANICUTS
ANILITY
ANIMALS
ANIMIST
ANLACES
ANOETIC
ANOSMIA
ANOTHER
ANTACID
ANTBEAR
ANTBIRD
ANTHOID
ANTIGAY
ANTIWAR
ANYROAD
APNOEAS
APODOUS
APOGEAL
APOGEAN
APOGEES
APORIAS
APOSTIL
APRONED
APSIDAL
APTERIA
ARABINS
ARABISE
ARAYSED
ARBLAST
ARCTANS
ARCTIID
ARCTOID
ARCUATE
AREFIED
ARGHANS
ARIDITY
ARNICAS
ARSHEEN
ARTSMAN
ASCARID
ASCAUNT
ASCIDIA
ASINICO
ASOCIAL
ASPERGE
ASPIDIA
ASPIRIN
ASPREAD

ASPROUT
ASTABLE
ASTYLAR
ATABEGS
ATABRIN
ATHANOR
ATHEISE
ATHEOUS
ATISHOO
ATOCIAS
ATRIUMS
ATROPIA
ATROPIN
AUBADES
AUBERGE
AUCTION
AUDIBLE
AUGITIC
AUGMENT
AUMAILS
AUREITY
AUTHORS
AUTOCAR
AVAILED
AVAILES
AVALING
AVAUNTS
AVENGED
AVENGER
AVENGES
AVENTRE
AVENUES
AVERAGE
AVERTED
AVIATED
AVIATES
AVIATOR
AVIDINS
AVISING
AVOURES
AVULSED
AWAITED
AWARNED
BAAINGS
BADIOUS
BAGNIOS
BAGUIOS
BAILING
BAILORS
BAINITE
BAITING
BALADIN
BALDING
BALEENS
BALISTA
BANALER
BANDAGE
BANDARS
BANDEAU
BANDITS
BANDOGS
BANDORA
BANDORE
BANDROL
BANDURA
BAREGES
BARGAIN
BARGEES
BARONET
BARONGS

BASIDIA
BASILAR
BASTARD
BASTION
BATONED
BATOONS
BAUERAS
BAUSOND
BEADING
BEADLES
BEAGLED
BEAGLER
BEAGLES
BEANIES
BEASTIE
BEATING
BEDERAL
BEDOUIN
BEDSORE
BEDUINS
BEDUNGS
BEELINE
BEERAGE
BEETING
BEETLED
BEETLES
BEGILDS
BEGONIA
BEGORED
BEGUILE
BEGUINE
BEGUINS
BEIGELS
BEIGNET
BELATED
BELATES
BELAUDS
BELGARD
BELONGS
BELUGAS
BENDLET
BERATED
BERLINE
BESIEGE
BETAINE
BETIDES
BETREAD
BIASING
BIDINGS
BIGENER
BIGOTED
BILGIER
BILIANS
BILIOUS
BINGIES
BIODATA
BIOTINS
BIRDING
BIRLING
BITINGS
BITONAL
BLAGUES
BLEARED
BLEATED
BLEEDER
BLENDER
BLINDER
BLOATED
BLONDER
BLOUSED

BLOUSON
BLUDGER
BLUDGES
BLUDIER
BLUEING
BLUINGS
BLUNDER
BLUNGED
BLUNGER
BLUNGES
BLUNTED
BLUNTER
BLURTED
BOASTED
BOATIES
BOATING
BODEGAS
BODGERS
BODGIER
BODGIES
BODINGS
BODRAGS
BOGLAND
BOILING
BOINGED
BOLDEST
BOLEROS
BOLIDES
BONDAGE
BONDERS
BONESET
BONITOS
BONSOIR
BOODIES
BOODLES
BOOGIED
BOOGIES
BOORDES
BOOSING
BOOSTED
BOOTEES
BOOTIES
BOOTING
BOOTLEG
BOREENS
BORNITE
BORONIA
BORSTAL
BOTARGO
BOUDOIR
BOUGETS
BOUGIES
BOULDER
BOULTED
BOULTER
BOURDON
BOURNES
BOUSIER
BOUSING
BOUTADE
BOUTONS
BRIDALS
BRIDING
BRIDOON
BRIGUED
BRIGUES
BRINDLE
BROADEN
BROGANS
BROGUES

BROILED
BROLGAS
BRUITED
BRUNTED
BRUTING
BUDGERO
BUDGERS
BUDGETS
BUDGIES
BUGLERS
BUGLETS
BUILDER
BUISTED
BULGERS
BULGIER
BULGINE
BUNDLES
BUNGEES
BUNGIES
BUNGLED
BUNGLER
BUNGLES
BUNTALS
BURGEES
BURGEON
BURGLED
BURGLES
BURGOOS
BURIALS
BURITIS
BURLING
BURTONS
BUSGIRL
BUSTARD
BUSTING
BUSTLED
BUTANES
BUTANOL
BUTENES
CADGIER
CADRANS
CAERULE
CAESURA
CAGIEST
CAGOULE
CAGOULS
CALANDO
CALDERA
CALDRON
CALIGOS
CANARDS
CANDELA
CANDORS
CANDOUR
CANGUES
CANTARS
CANTDOG
CANTLED
CANULAE
CANULAS
CARDOON
CARGOED
CARINAS
CARIOUS
CARLOAD
CARLOTS
CARNAGE
CARNALS
CAROLUS
CAROTID

CAROTIN
CARTAGE
CARTOON
CASTRAL
CATALOG
CATALOS
CATELOG
CATENAE
CATERED
CATIONS
CAUDATE
CAUDLES
CAUDRON
CAULDER
CAULINE
CAUSING
CAUTION
CEDRATE
CEDULAS
CEILING
CELADON
CELESTE
CENSUAL
CENSURE
CENTAGE
CENTRED
CERATED
CEREOUS
CESTODE
CESURAE
CESURAL
CIDARIS
CIELING
CIERGES
CILIATE
CINEOLE
CINGULA
CIRSOID
CITADEL
CITRINS
CITROUS
CLADIST
CLANGOR
CLARAIN
CLARINI
CLARINO
CLARION
CLARTED
CLAUTED
CLEANED
CLEANER
CLEANSE
CLEARED
CLEATED
CLOISON
CLOSING
CLOSURE
CLOTURE
CLOURED
CLOUTED
CLOUTER
CLUDGIE
CLUEING
COAGULA
COAITAS
COALING
COALISE
COALTAR
COASTAL
COATING

CODEINE
CODGERS
CODINGS
CODLING
CODLINS
COENURI
COGENER
COGNATE
COIGNED
COILING
COINAGE
COITION
COLDEST
COLITIS
COLOGNE
COLONES
COLORED
COLOURS
COLUGOS
COLURES
CONARIA
CONATUS
CONDOLE
CONDORS
CONDUIT
CONGAED
CONGEAL
CONGEED
CONGEES
CONGIUS
CONGOUS
CONGREE
CONGRUE
CONIDIA
CONOIDS
CONSOLE
CONSORT
CONSULT
CONTOUR
CONTROL
COOINGS
COOLANT
COOLERS
COOLEST
COOLIES
COOLING
COONTIE
COOTIES
CORANTO
CORDAGE
CORDATE
CORDIAL
CORDITE
CORDONS
CORIOUS
CORNAGE
CORNEAL
CORNUAL
CORNUTE
CORNUTO
CORONAE
CORONAL
CORONAS
CORONET
CORONIS
CORTEGE
CORTILI
COSTARD
COTERIE
COTIDAL

COTINGA
COTLAND
COUGARS
COULEES
COULOIR
COULTER
COUNSEL
COUNTED
COUNTER
COURAGE
COURANT
COURING
COURLAN
COURSED
COURTED
COUTILS
CRANAGE
CRANIAL
CREATED
CREDENT
CREEDAL
CREEING
CREESED
CRENELS
CREOLES
CREOSOL
CRINOID
CROODLE
CROONED
CROTALA
CROTALS
CROTONS
CROUTON
CRUISIE
CRUSADO
CRUSIAN
CRUSTAL
CTENOID
CUDGELS
CUISINE
CUNDIES
CUNEATE
CURATED
CURDING
CURDLES
CURIOSA
CURLING
CURSING
CURTAIL
CURTAIN
CURTALS
CURTANA
CUSTARD
CUTLINE
DACOITS
DAFTARS
DAGOBAS
DAHLIAS
DAIMIOS
DAIMONS
DAMAGES
DAMOSEL
DANELAW
DAPSONE
DAREFUL
DARSHAN
DASHEEN
DASHING
DASYURE
DATABLE

DATABUS
DATIVAL
DAUBERS
DAUBING
DAWTING
DAYLONG
DAYSTAR
DAYTALE
DEACONS
DEAFENS
DEANERY
DEAVING
DEBATER
DEBITOR
DEBTEES
DECAGON
DECANAL
DECANES
DECEASE
DECEITS
DECIARE
DECLARE
DECLINE
DECOLOR
DECREES
DECREET
DECURIA
DEEMING
DEEPENS
DEEPEST
DEEPIES
DEEVING
DEFAULT
DEFENSE
DEFIANT
DEFILER
DEFILES
DEFINES
DEFLATE
DEFOULS
DEHORNS
DEIFIER
DEIFIES
DEISTIC
DELAPSE
DELAYER
DELICES
DELICTS
DELIGHT
DELIMIT
DELOPES
DELTAIC
DELVERS
DEMAINE
DEMEANE
DEMENTI
DEMERGE
DEMERIT
DEMERSE
DEMESNE
DEMOTES
DEMOUNT
DEMURES
DENTARY
DEONTIC
DEPAINT
DEPLANE
DEPLETE
DEPLORE
DEPONES
DEPOSAL
DEPOSER
DEPUTES
DERNFUL
DESCALE
DESERVE
DESPITE
DESPOIL
DEVALUE
DEVIANT
DEVIATE
DEVILET
DEVIOUS
DEVISEE
DEVOTEE
DEVOTES
DEVOURS
DEWATER
DEWIEST
DHARNAS
DHOOTIS
DIABASE
DIABOLO
DIAGRAM
DIALECT
DIAPASE
DIAPIRS
DIATOMS
DICIEST
DICINGS
DICTIER
DICTING
DICTION
DIETARY
DIGNITY
DILUVIA
DIMETER
DINGBAT
DIOCESE
DIORAMA
DIORISM
DIPLOES
DIPLONS
DIPLONT
DIPOLAR
DIPOLES
DIREFUL
DIRTILY
DISCAGE
DISCANT
DISCING
DISGOWN
DISHIER
DISHING
DISHORN
DISLIMN
DISPART
DISPORT
DISPUTE
DISRUPT
DISTURB
DISTYLE
DIVERGE
DIVINER
DIVINES
DIVINGS
DIVISOR
DIVULGE
DOCILER
DOCTORS
DOGBANE
DOGBOLT
DOGCART
DOGHOLE
DOGTOWN
DOGVANE
DOLMANS
DOLTISH
DOMAINS
DOMATIA
DOMINEE
DOMINIE
DOMINOS
DOOMIER
DOOMING
DOORMAT
DOPANTS
DOPINGS
DORMANT
DOUBLER
DOUBLES
DOUBLET
DOUBTER
DOUCINE
DOVELET
DOWAGER
DOWNERS
DOWNIER
DOWSING
DOYLIES
DRACONE
DRAFTEE
DRAUGHT
DRAYAGE
DRIVELS
DRIVING
DROMONS
DRONISH
DROOMES
DROUGHT
DROUTHS
DRUMLIN
DRUPELS
DRYINGS
DUALISM
DUALITY
DUCTILE
DUCTING
DULCIAN
DULCITE
DULCOSE
DULOTIC
DUMAIST
DUPIONS
DUPLETS
DUPLIES
DURABLE
DURMAST
DUSHING
DUSTBIN
DUSTILY
DUSTMAN
DYELINE
DYSURIA
EAGERLY
EARFULS
EARLDOM
EARLOBE
EARPLUG
EARTHED
EARTHEN
EARWIGS
EASEFUL
EATABLE
EBONIES
EBONISE
EBONITE
EBRIATE
EBRIOSE
ECLOGUE
ECLOSED
ECURIES
EDEMATA
EDIBLES
EDICTAL
EDIFIER
EDIFIES
EDUCATE
EDUCING
EDUCTOR
EELFARE
EELPOUT
EGALITY
EGENCES
EIDETIC
EIRENIC
ELANCED
ELANCES
ELAPSED
ELATIVE
ELECTED
ELECTOR
ELECTRO
ELEGIAC
ELEMENT
ELEVATE
ELEVENS
ELEVONS
ELOCUTE
ELOGIUM
ELOPERS
ELOPING
ELUSIVE
ELUSORY
ELYTRON
EMERALD
EMERGED
EMERGES
EMERIED
EMERITI
EMERODS
EMERSED
EMETINE
EMEUTES
EMIRATE
EMONGES
EMOTING
EMOTION
EMULATE
EMULGED
EMULGES
EMULING
EMULSIN
EMULSOR
EMUNGED
EMUNGES
EMURING
ENABLED
ENABLER
ENABLES
ENACTED
ENAMELS
ENAMOUR
ENARMED
ENCAGED
ENCAGES
ENCASED
ENCLOSE
ENCLOUD
ENCODES
ENCORED
ENDGAME
ENDIVES
ENDOWER
ENDWISE
ENERGIC
ENERVED
ENERVES
ENFILED
ENFREED
ENFREES
ENGLOBE
ENGLOOM
ENGOBES
ENGRACE
ENGRAVE
ENGULFS
ENHALOS
ENLACED
ENLACES
ENOUGHS
ENRACED
ENROBED
ENROBES
ENROUGH
ENSEWED
ENSLAVE
ENSTEEP
ENTAMED
ENTAYLE
ENTHUSE
ENTICED
ENVAULT
ENVIOUS
EPAULES
EPAULET
EPEIRID
EPERDUE
EPERGNE
EPIDOTE
EPIGEAL
EPIGEAN
EPIGENE
EPIGONE
EPIGONI
EPILATE
EPISODE
EPUISEE
ERECTED
EREMITE
ERGODIC
ERICOID
ERMELIN
ERODIUM
EROTEMA
EROTEME
EROTICA
ERUCTED
ERUPTED
ESCUAGE
ESLOYNE
ESOTERY
ESTREPE
ESTUARY
ETHANES
ETHANOL
ETHENES
EUCAINE
EUCLASE
EUCRITE
EUGENIC
EUSTYLE
EVADING
EVANGEL
EVASION
EVENERS
EVENEST
EVENTED
EVENTER
EVERTED
EVIDENT
EVIRATE
EVITING
EVOLUES
EVOLUTE
EVULSED
EYALETS
EYELETS
EYELIAD
EYELIDS
EYESORE
FADAISE
FADEURS
FADINGS
FAGOTED
FAILING
FAILURE
FAINTED
FAIRIES
FAIRING
FAITORS
FAITOUR
FALDAGE
FANTADS
FANTAIL
FANTEEG
FANTODS
FARDAGE
FARINAS
FATIGUE
FAULTED
FAUNIST
FAUTORS
FEAGUED
FEAGUES
FEATING
FEATOUS
FEATURE
FEDARIE
FEDERAL
FEEDERS
FEEDING
FEEDLOT
FEELERS
FEELING
FEERING
FEESING
FEIGNED
FEINTED
FELINES
FELTIER
FERLIED
FERTILE
FERULAS
FERULES
FESTOON
FETIDER
FEUDING
FEUDIST
FEUTRED
FEUTRES
FIATING
FIAUNTS
FIDEIST
FIDGETS
FIELDER
FIGURAL
FIGURED
FIGURES
FILARIA
FILIATE
FILINGS
FINALES
FINIALS
FIORINS
FIREDOG
FIRINGS
FIRLOTS
FISTING
FISTULA
FITLIER
FLAGONS
FLANEUR
FLAUNES
FLAUNTS
FLEDGES
FLEEING
FLEERED
FLEETED
FLEETER
FLEURET
FLEURON
FLINDER
FLITING
FLOATED
FLOATER
FLOORED
FLOOSIE
FLOREAT
FLORINS
FLORIST
FLORUIT
FLOTAGE
FLOURED
FLOUSED
FLOUTED
FLUATES
FLUTIER
FLUTINA
FLUTING
FOALING
FOETORS
FOILING
FOLDING
FOLIAGE
FOLIATE
FOLIOED
FOLIOSE
FONDLER
FONDUES
FOODIES
FOOLING
FOOTAGE
FOOTERS
FOOTIER
FOOTIES
FOOTING
FOOTLED
FOOTLES
FOOTRAS
FORAGED
FORAGES
FORDOES
FORDONE
FOREGUT
FOREIGN
FORELEG
FORELIE
FORESEE
FORGETS
FORGOES
FORGONE
FORLANA
FORLEND
FORLENT
FORLESE
FORSAID
FORSLOE
FORTUNE
FOUDRIE
FOUGADE
FOULARD
FOULDER
FOULING
FOURGON
FOUTERS
FOUTRAS
FOUTRED
FOUTRES
FRAGILE
FREEING
FRENULA
FRESNEL
FRIGATE
FRIGOTS
FROGLET
FRONTAL
FRONTED
FRUITED
FUGATOS
FULGENT
FULGORS
FUNDIES
FUNERAL
FUNGOID
FURANES
FURIOSO
FURLANA
FURLING
FURLONG
FUROLES
FUSAROL
FUSTIAN
FUSTING
FUTILER
GABIONS
GADSMAN
GAINFUL
GAINSAY
GALIPOT
GALOPED
GALOPIN
GALUTHS
GAMELAN
GAMETAL
GAMETES
GARBLED
GARBOIL
GARCONS
GARLICS
GARVIES
GASAHOL
GASEITY
GASOHOL
GATEMEN
GAUCIER
GAUDERY
GAUDILY
GAUFERS
GAUFRES
GAUMIER
GAUNTLY
GAUNTRY
GAUPERS
GAVIALS
GAWSIER
GENERIC
GENETIC
GENEVAS
GENOMES
GEODESY
GEOMANT
GERMANE
GESTAPO
GHARIAL
GHASTED
GHERAOS
GHOSTED
GILBERT
GILPIES
GIPSIED
GIRLISH
GIRONIC
GIRTHED
GLACEED
GLAIVED
GLAIVES
GLAMORS
GLAMOUR
GLAUMED
GLEAMED
GLEAVES
GLEBOUS
GLEEMAN
GLEEMEN
GLIOMAS
GLOBATE
GLOBINS
GLOBOID
GLOBOSE
GLOBOUS
GLOOMED
GLOOPED
GLOVERS
GLOWERS
GLUCINA
GLUCOSE
GNASHED
GNATHAL
GOATISH

GOBIIDS
GOBIOID
GOBLETS
GOBLINS
GODOWNS
GODWITS
GOLDEYE
GOLDISH
GOLFERS
GOMERAL
GOMERIL
GOMUTIS
GOMUTOS
GONADIC
GONIDIC
GOOBERS
GOODISH
GOODMAN
GOODMEN
GOOFIER
GOOLEYS
GOONEYS
GOOPIER
GOOSERY
GOPURAS
GORMAND
GOULASH
GOURAMI
GOURMET
GOWANED
GOWDEST
GOWLAND
GOWLANS
GRADELY
GRAFTED
GRAITHS
GRANDAM
GRANDLY
GRANDMA
GRANDPA
GRAUPEL
GRAVIES
GREATLY
GREAVED
GREAVES
GRECISE
GREECES
GREENLY
GREENTH
GREMIAL
GREYEST
GRIECED
GRIECES
GRIEVED
GRIFTED
GRISTLY
GROOMED
GROOVED
GROOVES
GROUPED
GROUPIE
GROVELS
GROVETS
GROWLED
GRUFTED
GRUMOSE
GUANACO
GUARISH
GUDEMAN
GUDEMEN
GUILDRY
GULFIER
GULPERS
GUNBOAT
GUNFIRE
GUNPORT
GUNROOM
GUNSHOT
GUNWALE
GURAMIS
GURNEYS
GUSHIER
GUYLERS
GWINIAD
GYRATED
HADRONS
HAGDENS
HAGDONS
HAILIER
HAILING
HAIRDOS
HAIRING
HALITUS
HALOGEN
HALOIDS
HALOING
HANDOUT
HANGARS
HANGOUT
HARLOTS
HARTALS
HAUDING
HAULAGE
HAULERS
HAULIER
HAULING
HAUNTED
HAUNTER
HAUSING
HEADAGE
HEADIER
HEADING
HEADRIG
HEARTED
HEARTEN
HEDERAL
HEDGERS
HEDGIER
HEEDING
HEELERS
HEELING
HEGIRAS
HEINOUS
HEIRING
HEISTED
HERNIAL
HEROINE
HEROISE
HEROONS
HETAERA
HETAIRA
HIDAGES
HIDALGA
HIDALGO
HIDEOUS
HIDEOUT
HIDINGS
HIDLING
HIDLINS
HILDING
HILTING
HIRAGES
HIREAGE
HIRINGS
HIRLING
HIRSLED
HIRUDIN
HISTING
HISTOID
HISTRIO
HOARING
HOARSEN
HOASTED
HOGTIED
HOGTIES
HOISING
HOLDING
HOLINGS
HONORED
HONOURS
HOODIES
HOODING
HOOLIER
HOOTING
HORDEIN
HORNITO
HORNLET
HOSTAGE
HOTLINE
HOUDANS
HOUSING
HOUTING
HUITAIN
HUNGERS
HURDLES
HURLIES
HURLING
HURTING
HURTLED
HUSTLED
ICTERID
IDENTIC
IDOLISM
IGARAPE
IGNOBLE
ILIACUS
IMAGINE
IMAGIST
IMAGOES
INBOARD
INBURST
INCAGED
INCEDES
INCISED
INCISOR
INCITED
INCLUDE
INCRUST
INCUDES
INCUSED
INDABAS
INDICES
INDICTS
INDIUMS
INDRAFT
INDUCES
INDUCTS
INDWELT
INERTLY
INFAUST
INFIDEL
INFIELD
INFOLDS
INFULAE
INFUSED
INFUSER
INGLOBE
INGROUP
INGULFS
INHALED
INHALER
INHALES
INHAULS
INHAUST
INLACED
INLAYER
INOCULA
INORBED
INSIGHT
INSOOTH
INTHRAL
INVALID
INVIOUS
INVITED
INVITEE
INVITES
INYALAS
IONIUMS
IONOMER
IRACUND
ISODICA
ISODOMA
ISOGRAM
ITALICS
ITEMING
ITEMISE
IVORIED
IVORIST
LABIATE
LABORED
LABOURS
LABRIDS
LABROID
LACINIA
LACTONE
LACUNAE
LACUNAR
LADANUM
LAICISE
LAIGHER
LAMETER
LAMIGER
LAMINAR
LANIARY
LANYARD
LAPDOGS
LAPSANG
LARGISH
LARVATE
LATENCE
LATHEES
LAUGHED
LAUGHER
LAUNCED
LAUNCES
LAUNDRY
LAUWINE
LAVAGES
LAWNIER
LAWSUIT
LAYERED
LAYOUTS
LEAFAGE
LEAFIER
LEASHED
LEASOWE
LEAVENS
LECTERN
LECTION
LECTURE
LECTURN
LEEPING
LEEWARD
LEGHORN
LEGITIM
LEGROOM
LEGUMES
LEGUMIN
LEGWEAR
LEIPOAS
LEMONED
LEMURES
LENGTHS
LEOPARD
LEPROSE
LEPROUS
LEPTONS
LETHEAN
LETHEES
LETHIED
LEUCINE
LEUCINS
LEUCITE
LEUGHEN
LEVATOR
LEVERED
LEVERET
LEWDEST
LEWISIA
LIBATED
LIBIDOS
LICENSE
LICTORS
LIFTING
LIGHTED
LIGHTER
LIGNUMS
LIMEADE
LIMINGS
LIMITED
LIMITER
LINCTUS
LINOCUT
LIONISM
LIPIDES
LIPOIDS
LISPING
LISPUND
LITHIAS
LITHING
LITHOID
LITURGY
LIVENED
LIVIDER
LIVINGS
LOAFING
LOAMIER
LOAMING
LOATHED
LOAVING
LOBINGS
LOCATED
LOCUSTA
LONGISH
LOOBIER
LOOBIES
LOOMING
LOOPERS
LOOPIER
LOOPING
LOUDISH
LOUPING
LOUTISH
LOUVERS
LOUVRED
LOUVRES
LOVAGES
LOVERED
LOVINGS
LOWERED
LOWINGS
LOWSING
LUCARNE
LUCERNE
LUCERNS
LUCIDER
LUCIGEN
LUMINED
LUMINES
LUNATIC
LUNYIES
LUPINES
LUSHIER
LUSHING
LUTHERN
LUTHIER
LYRATED
MADLING
MADRONA
MADRONE
MADRONO
MAGIANS
MAGNETO
MAIDANS
MAIDING
MAILING
MAINORS
MAINOUR
MALAISE
MALATES
MALEATE
MALGRED
MALISON
MALTASE
MANAGED
MANAGER
MANAGES
MANATIS
MANDIRA
MANDOLA
MANDORA
MANDRIL
MANEGED
MANEGES
MANGALS
MANGOES
MANGOLD
MANILAS
MANITOS
MANITOU
MANOAOS
MANSARD
MANTIDS
MANTRAS
MANTUAS
MANUALS
MANURES
MARAUDS
MARGOSA
MARINAS
MARITAL
MARLINS
MAROONS
MARTIAL
MARTINI
MASTOID
MATADOR
MATINAL
MATSURI
MATURED
MAUDLIN
MAUGRED
MAUGRES
MAULERS
MAULGRE
MAULING
MEALIER
MEALIES
MEANDER
MEASLED
MEATIER
MEDALET
MEDIATE
MEDUSAE
MEERING
MEETING
MEGARAD
MEGARON
MEGATON
MELANGE
MELANOS
MELDERS
MENAGED
MENAGES
MENEERS
MENSUAL
MENTEES
MERITED
MESELED
METAGES
METALED
METERED
MEUSING
MIAULED
MIDAIRS
MIDGETS
MIDIRON
MIGRATE
MILADIS
MILAGES
MILDEST
MILEAGE
MILIEUS
MILITAR
MILORDS
MILREIS
MILTING
MINGIER
MINORED
MINUTED
MINUTIA
MISDIAL
MISDIET
MISLAID
MISRULE
MISTING
MISTLED
MISTOLD
MISTRAL
MITERED
MITOGEN
MOATING
MODELER
MODIOLI
MODULAR
MODULES
MOGULED
MOIDORE
MOILING
MOINEAU
MOLDING
MOLERAT
MOLINET
MONARDA
MONAULS
MONDIAL
MONGOLS
MONGREL
MONIALS
MONILIA
MONITOR
MONTAGE
MONTERO
MONTURE
MOODIER
MOODIES
MOOLIES
MOOLING
MOONIER
MOONLET
MOONLIT
MOORAGE
MOORING
MOOTING
MORDANT
MORDENT
MORENDO
MORGUES
MORIONS
MORLING
MORTALS
MORULAE
MOTIONS
MOTORED
MOULAGE
MOULDER
MOULINS
MOULTED
MOULTEN
MOUNTED
MOUNTER
MOUSIER
MOUSING
MOUSLED
MOUTANS
MOUTONS
MUDGERS
MUDIRIA
MUISTED
MUNITED
MURAENA
MURAGES
MURENAS
MURGEON
MURIATE
MURLAIN
MURLANS
MURLING
MURLINS
MUSTANG
MUSTARD
MUSTING
MUTAGEN
MUTANDA
MUTINED
NACROUS
NAEVOID
NAGAPIE
NAILERY
NAIVETE
NAIVIST
NAPOOED
NASTILY
NATRIUM
NAUGHTS
NAUPLII
NAUTICS
NAVAIDS
NEBULAE
NEBULAR
NEBULAS
NEBULES
NEEDFUL
NEEDILY
NEGLECT
NEIGHED
NEMORAL
NEOLITH
NEOLOGY
NERVATE
NERVOUS
NERVULE
NEUROMA
NEWSIER
NIMIOUS
NIOBATE
NIOBITE
NIOBOUS
NITRYLS
NIVEOUS
NOBLEST
NOCTUAS
NOCTUID
NOCTULE
NODICAL
NOISILY
NORMALS
NORTHED
NOSEBAG
NOSEGAY
NOSTRUM
NOTABLE
NOTAEUM
NOTEDLY
NOTICED
NOUGHTS
NOURICE
NOURISH
NOVALIA
NOYADES

NUCLEAR
NUCLIDE
NUMERAL
NUPTIAL
NURAGHE
NURAGHI
NURHAGS
NUTMEGS
NUTWOOD
OARSMAN
OARWEED
OATMEAL
OBDURES
OBELION
OBELISE
OBITUAL
OBLIGED
OBLIGEE
OBLIGOR
OBLONGS
OBTAINS
OBTRUDE
OBTUNDS
OCARINA
OCEANID
OCELOID
OCELOTS
OCREATE
OCTAGON
OCTROIS
OCTUORS
OCULARS
OCULATE
OCULIST
ODONTIC
OEDEMAS
OENOMEL
OFTENER
OGREISH
OILCANS
OLEFINE
OLITORY
OLIVINE
OMELETS
OMINOUS
ONBOARD
ONEFOLD
ONEIRIC
ONESELF
ONEYERS
ONEYRES
ONSHORE
ONWARDS
OOLITIC
OPALINE
OPENEST
OPERAND
OPERANT
OPEROSE
OPIATED
OPTIONS
OPULENT
OPUNTIA
ORACLED
ORALISM
ORALITY
ORANGEY
ORBITAL
ORBITAS
ORBITED
ORCINOL
OREWEED
ORGANIC
ORGANUM
ORIGAMI
ORMOLUS
OROGENY
OROPESA
ORTHIAN
OSCULAR
OSMUNDA
OSTEOMA
OSTIARY
OSTRACA
OUABAIN
OUREBIS
OURSELF
OUTBARS
OUTBIDS
OUTBRAG
OUTBRED
OUTGAVE
OUTGIVE
OUTGREW
OUTGROW
OUTHIRE
OUTLASH
OUTLAWS
OUTLAYS
OUTLEAP
OUTLIVE
OUTMANS
OUTMODE
OUTNAME
OUTPEER
OUTRACE
OUTROPE
OUTSPAN
OUTVIED
OUTVIES
OUTWARD
OUTWEAR
OUTWEED
OUTWIND
OUTWING
OUTWINS
OUTWORE
OUTWORN
OUVERTE
OUVRAGE
OVARIAN
OVATING
OVATION
OVATORS
OVERAGE
OVERATE
OVERDUE
OVEREAT
OVERGET
OVERGOT
OVERING
OVERNET
OVOIDAL
OVULATE
PADANGS
PADRONE
PADRONI
PAENULA
PAGEANT
PAGINAL
PAGODAS
PAGURID
PAIGLES
PAINTED
PAIRIAL
PAIRING
PAISANO
PALADIN
PALAGIS
PALATED
PALATES
PANDARS
PANDITS
PANDOOR
PANDORA
PANDORE
PANDOUR
PANDURA
PARADES
PARADOS
PARAGES
PARAGON
PARANGS
PARASOL
PARDALE
PARDALS
PARDONS
PARIALS
PARISON
PARLOUS
PAROLED
PAROLEE
PAROTID
PAROTIS
PARTANS
PARTIAL
PARULIS
PATINAS
PATINED
PATRIAL
PATROLS
PATROON
PATULIN
PAUSING
PEARLED
PEARLIN
PEASING
PEDALOS
PEELERS
PEELING
PEENGED
PEENGES
PEERAGE
PEERIES
PEERING
PEISING
PELAGES
PELOIDS
PELORIA
PELORUS
PENSILE
PENTODE
PENTOSE
PEONAGE
PERAEON
PERDUES
PEREGAL
PEREION
PERGOLA
PERIDIA
PERIGEE
PERIGON
PERINEA
PERLITE
PERLOUS
PERSUED
PERTUSE
PERUSED
PESTLED
PETERED
PETIOLE
PETUNIA
PIANIST
PIARIST
PIDGEON
PIDGINS
PIERAGE
PIERIDS
PIETIES
PIGNUTS
PIGSNIE
PIGTAIL
PILEATE
PILEOUS
PILINGS
PILOTED
PILOTIS
PINATAS
PINDARI
PINGUID
PINTADO
PINTAIL
PIONEER
PIRAGUA
PIRANAS
PIROGUE
PITARAS
PITURIS
PLAGUED
PLAGUES
PLAINED
PLAINER
PLAINTS
PLAITED
PLANTAR
PLANTAS
PLANTED
PLASTID
PLATANE
PLATANS
PLATEAU
PLATINA
PLATOON
PLAUDIT
PLEADER
PLEASED
PLEATED
PLEDGEE
PLEDGER
PLEDGES
PLEDGET
PLEDGOR
PLEURAE
PLEURON
PLOATED
PLONGED
PLONGES
PLOSION
PLOUTER
PLUNDER
PLUNGED
PLUNGER
PLUNGES
PLUSAGE
PLUSING
PLUTONS
PODAGRA
PODESTA
PODGIER
POESIED
POINADO
POINDER
POINTED
POINTEL
POINTER
POISING
POLARON
POLENTA
POLINGS
POLOIST
POLONIE
PONDAGE
PONGEES
PONGIDS
PONGIER
PONGOES
PONIARD
PONTAGE
PONTILE
PONTILS
POODLES
POOLING
POOTING
PORGIES
PORTAGE
PORTALS
PORTEND
PORTION
PORTOUS
POSAUNE
POSITON
POSTAGE
POSTEEN
POTAGER
POTAGES
POTEENS
POTGUNS
POTIONS
POUDERS
POUDRES
POULARD
POULDER
POULDRE
POULTER
POUNDAL
POURIES
POURING
POUTIER
POUTING
PRALINE
PREEING
PREENED
PRELUDE
PRELUDI
PRENTED
PRESAGE
PRETEND
PRIDIAN
PRIDING
PRISING
PROINED
PROLEGS
PROLINE
PROLING
PROLONG
PRONAOI
PRONAOS
PRONATE
PRONGED
PRONOTA
PROTEAN
PROTEGE
PROTEIN
PROTEND
PROTONS
PROULED
PRUDENT
PRUINAS
PRUNTED
PTERION
PUDGIER
PUERILE
PUERING
PULDRON
PULINGS
PULSATE
PULSING
PULTANS
PULTONS
PULTOON
PUNDITS
PUNTEES
PURITAN
PURLINE
PURLING
PURLINS
PURLOIN
PURSING
PUSLING
PUTEALS
PUTLOGS
RACOONS
RADICAL
RADIUMS
RAFALES
RAGBOLT
RAGEFUL
RAGHEAD
RAGMANS
RAGTIME
RAGTOPS
RAGWEED
RAILBUS
RAILMAN
RAIYATS
RAMEOUS
RANDOMS
RATBAGS
RAVAGED
RAVAGES
RAVELIN
RAVENED
RAVIOLI
REACTED
READMIT
REAMEND
REBATED
REBOANT
REBUILD
REBUILT
RECEDES
RECENSE
RECITED
RECLINE
RECLOSE
RECLUSE
RECODES
RECOUNT
RECTION
RECUILE
RECULED
RECULES
RECUSED
REDCOAT
REDEEMS
REDOUBT
REDUCES
REEFING
REELMAN
REELMEN
REEVING
REFLATE
REFLOAT
REFOOTS
REFUELS
REFUGED
REFUGEE
REFUGES
REFUGIA
REFUSAL
REFUSED
REFUTAL
REFUTED
REFUTES
REGENCE
REGIMEN
REGIVEN
REGMATA
REHEELS
REHOUSE
REIFIED
REIVING
RELAYED
RELIGHT
RELUMED
RELUMES
REMANET
REMEDES
REMODEL
REMOULD
REMOUNT
REMUAGE
REMUDAS
RENAMED
RENAYED
RENEWAL
RENEWED
RENEYED
REPLETE
REPLIED
REPOINT
REPONED
REPOSED
REPTILE
REPUGNS
REPULSE
REPUTED
REPUTES
RESCUED
RESUMED
RETICLE
RETIMED
REVALUE
REVENGE
REVENUE
REVEUSE
RHODOUS
RIBALDS
RIBAUDS
RIEVING
RIFLING
RIGHTED
RIGHTOS
RIGIDLY
RILIEVO
RIPIENO
RISPING
RIVAGES
RIVETED
RIVLINS
RIVULET
ROADMAN
ROADMEN
ROAMING
ROBALOS
ROBINIA
ROBUSTA
RODSMAN
ROGUISH
ROINISH
ROLFING
ROMAGES
ROMAUNT
ROOFING
ROOMIES
ROOMING
ROOPING
ROSEBUD
ROUBLES
ROUGHED
ROUGHEN
ROUGHIE
ROUMING
ROUNDLY
ROUPING
ROUTHIE
ROYALET
RUBATOS
RUBEOLA
RUBINES
RUCOLAS
RUCTION
RUGBIES
RUNFLAT
RUNTISH
RUSHING
RUSTILY
SABATON
SACATON
SAGAMEN
SAINTLY
SALAMON
SALBAND
SALICIN
SALPIAN
SALVAGE
SALVETE
SAMURAI
SANDBAG
SANDPIT
SANGOMA
SARCOID
SARONIC
SATANIC
SATYRAL
SATYRID
SAUCIER
SAUCING
SAVAGED
SAVAGER
SAVARIN
SAVIOUR
SCAGLIA
SCALADE
SCALADO
SCALENE
SCANDAL
SCEDULE
SCIARID
SCIOLTO
SCOLION
SCOOGED
SCOOTED
SCOUGED
SCOURED
SCOURGE
SCROOGE
SCROTAL
SCROUGE
SCUDLER
SCUNGED
SCUTAGE
SEAFOOD
SEAMAID
SEAWARD
SEAWARE
SEAWEED
SECEDER
SECLUDE
SECONDE
SECONDO
SECRETE
SECULAR
SECURED
SEDUCER
SEEABLE
SEEDILY
SEEDLIP
SEEPAGE
SEEPIER
SEEPING
SEETHED
SEETHER
SEEWING
SEGMENT
SELENIC
SELVAGE
SERFAGE
SERPIGO
SERUEWE
SEVERED
SEVRUGA
SEWERED
SHADING
SHAITAN
SHARIAT
SHEALED
SHEELED
SHEENED
SHEERED

SHEETED
SHIELED
SHINDIG
SHITING
SHOALED
SHOOGIE
SHOOGLE
SHOOING
SHOOLED
SHOTGUN
SHRINAL
SHULING
SIAMANG
SIBLING
SIEVING
SIFTING
SIGHTED
SIGMOID
SILENCE
SILICON
SIMILAR
SIMILOR
SIMITAR
SIMULAR
SINEWED
SINICAL
SINOPIA
SITHING
SLEAVED
SLEEPER
SLEEVED
SLEEVER
SLICING
SLIMIER
SLIMING
SLIVING
SLOOMED
SLOPING
SLOTHED
SLOWING
SLUICED
SLURPED
SMARAGD
SMELTED
SMIDGIN
SMILING
SMITING
SMOILED
SMOORED
SMOOTED
SMUDGER
SNEAPED
SNOOPED
SOAPING
SOBERED
SOLACED
SOLANUM
SOLFEGE
SOLICIT
SOLIDUM
SOLIPED
SOLVENT
SOLVING
SOMEONE
SOMITAL
SOMNIAL
SONGFUL
SOOMING
SOOPING
SOOTHED
SOOTILY
SOPRANI
SOPRANO
SOREHON
SORITIC
SOROBAN
SOUCING
SOUGHED
SOUMING
SOUNDLY
SOUPIER
SOUPLED
SOURCED
SOWLING
SPADING
SPAEING
SPANGED
SPANIEL
SPAROID
SPARTAN
SPATIAL
SPATULA
SPATULE
SPEANED
SPEEDER
SPEELED
SPEELER
SPEERED
SPELDER
SPELEAN
SPIELED
SPILING
SPINOUT
SPINULE
SPIRING
SPIROID
SPITING
SPLENIA
SPLENII
SPLODGE
SPLURGE
SPOILED
SPONDEE
SPONGED
SPOOLED
SPOOLER
SPOONED
SPOORED
SPORULE
SPUEING
STADIUM
STAGILY
STAIDLY
STAMINA
STAMNOI
STARDOM
STEEMED
STEEPED
STEEPEN
STEEPER
STEEPLE
STEEVED
STEEVER
STERNLY
STIBIAL
STIBINE
STIFLED
STIMIED
STIMING
STIMULI
STIVING
STOICAL
STONILY
STOOPED
STOWAGE
STRINGY
STUPING
STYLING
STYLOID
STYRING
SUBADAR
SUBAREA
SUBARID
SUBDEAN
SUBEDAR
SUBEDIT
SUBERIN
SUBGOAL
SUBLATE
SUBRING
SUBTEEN
SUCTION
SUEABLE
SUICIDE
SULFATE
SULFIDE
SULFONE
SUMATRA
SUNBEAT
SUNBIRD
SUNGLOW
SUNROOF
SUNTRAP
SUNWARD
SURAMIN
SURCOAT
SURDITY
SURFING
SURNAME
SWEALED
SWEEING
SWEELED
SWEERED
SWEETED
SWEETEN
SWEETER
SWEETIE
SWELTED
SWIRLED
SWOONED
SWOUNED
SYENITE
SYNODAL
TABANID
TABARDS
TABLEAU
TABLOID
TABOOED
TABORED
TABORIN
TABOURS
TABUING
TABULAE
TABULAR
TADPOLE
TAEDIUM
TAHINAS
TAHINIS
TAIPANS
TALCOUS
TALIPED
TALMUDS
TAMALES
TAMANDU
TAMANUS
TAMARIN
TAMARIS
TANGRAM
TANYARD
TAPUING
TARDILY
TARDIVE
TARPANS
TARWEED
TAUPIES
TAVERED
TAVERNA
TEARFUL
TEDESCO
TEDIUMS
TEEMERS
TEEMING
TELERGY
TENABLE
TENFOLD
TENSIVE
TERPENE
TEUGHER
THALIAN
THANAGE
THEINES
THEREON
THEROID
THONDER
THONGED
THORIAS
THORNED
THORONS
THOUING
THRANGS
THRONED
THRONGS
THULIAS
THUNDER
TIDYING
TIERCED
TIERCEL
TIGERLY
TIGRISH
TILAPIA
TIMARAU
TIMIDER
TIMINGS
TINAMOU
TINCALS
TINDERY
TINFOIL
TINFULS
TIPULAS
TOEHOLD
TOHEROA
TOHUNGA
TONEPAD
TOOLBAG
TOOLBAR
TOOLMAN
TOOLMEN
TOOMING
TOPLINE
TOPSAIL
TOPSOIL
TORMINA
TORPEDO
TORPIDS
TOUCANS
TOUGHEN
TOUGHER
TOUGHIE
TOUPEES
TOURACO
TOURISM
TOURNEY
TOWAGES
TOWARDS
TOWELED
TOWERED
TOWLINE
TOWNEES
TOWNIER
TRADUCE
TRAGEDY
TRANGAM
TRAPANS
TRAUMAS
TRAVAIL
TRAVOIS
TRAWLED
TRAYNED
TREACLE
TREBLED
TREMOLO
TRIACID
TRIADIC
TRILOGY
TRIPODS
TRIPOLI
TRIVIAL
TROMINO
TROOPED
TROUBLE
TROUGHS
TROUNCE
TROUPED
TRUCAGE
TRUCIAL
TRUEMAN
TRUEMEN
TRUNCAL
TRYINGS
TRYSAIL
TSARDOM
TSUNAMI
TUBAGES
TUBINGS
TUGHRAS
TUILYIE
TULBANS
TULWARS
TUNABLE
TUNICLE
TURACIN
TURACOS
TURBAND
TURBANS
TURBOND
TURFING
TURMOIL
TURNIPS
TUSHING
TUYERES
TWANGED
TWEEDLE
TWEELED
TWEERED
TWINGED
TYRANED
ULCERED
ULICONS
ULTIMAS
UNACTED
UNAIMED
UNALIVE
UNAWARE
UNBARES
UNBATED
UNBEARS
UNBEGET
UNBEGOT
UNBOLTS
UNBOOTS
UNCAGED
UNCAGES
UNCARTS
UNCASED
UNCIALS
UNCITED
UNCLEAR
UNCLOGS
UNCLOSE
UNCOILS
UNCOLTS
UNCORDS
UNDEAFS
UNDIGHT
UNDRAWS
UNEARTH
UNFAIRS
UNFILDE
UNFILED
UNFOLDS
UNFOOLS
UNFREED
UNGIRTH
UNGLOVE
UNGODLY
UNHAIRS
UNHEADS
UNHEALS
UNHEART
UNHELED
UNHELES
UNHOARD
UNHOODS
UNHORSE
UNIFIED
UNIFIER
UNIFIES
UNIPEDS
UNIPODS
UNITARY
UNITIVE
UNLACED
UNLACES
UNLAWED
UNLEASH
UNLIMED
UNLIMES
UNLIVED
UNLIVES
UNLOVED
UNLOVES
UNMATED
UNMETED
UNMOORS
UNMORAL
UNPAGED
UNPLAIT
UNPOSED
UNRAVEL
UNREAVE
UNREEVE
UNRIGHT
UNROBES
UNROOFS
UNROYAL
UNSAFER
UNSAVED
UNSCALE
UNSEWED
UNSHALE
UNSHOED
UNSHOOT
UNSIGHT
UNSMART
UNSPIDE
UNSPIED
UNSPILT
UNSTRAP
UNSTRIP
UNSWEAR
UNSWEET
UNSWORE
UNTAMED
UNTRIMS
UNVAILE
UNVAILS
UNVEILS
UNVISOR
UNVITAL
UNWAGED
UNWARES
UNWARIE
UNWATER
UNWEALS
UNWIRES
UNWISER
UNWOOED
UNWROTE
UPDATES
UPDRAGS
UPGRADE
UPLANDS
UPLEADS
UPLEANS
UPLEANT
UPRISAL
UPROOTS
UPSILON
UPSTAGE
UPSTAIR
UPSTAND
UPSTOOD
UPTRAIN
UPTREND
URACILS
URAEMIA
URANISM
URANYLS
URCEOLI
URETHAN
URGENCE
URICASE
UROLITH
UROLOGY
UROPODS
UROSOME
USHERED
UTOPIAN
UTOPIAS
UTRICLE
UVEITIS
VAGINAE
VAGINAL
VAGINAS
VAGITUS
VAGRANT
VAGUEST
VAILING
VALETAS
VALETED
VALETES
VALGOUS
VALIANT
VALINES
VALONEA
VALONIA
VALOURS
VALUATE
VALUERS
VALUING
VALUTAS
VANDALS
VANITAS
VANTAGE
VAREUSE
VARIANT
VARIATE
VARIOLA
VARIOLE
VARIOUS
VAUDOOS
VAULTED
VAULTER
VAUNTED
VAUNTER
VAURIEN
VAUTING
VEDALIA
VEERING
VEGETAL
VEILING
VEINIER
VEINLET
VEINOUS
VELARIA
VELATED
VELETAS
VELOURS
VELOUTE
VELURED
VELURES
VENATOR
VENDAGE
VENDEES
VENDORS
VENDUES
VENEERS
VENITES
VENTAGE
VENTIGE
VENTOSE
VENTRED
VENTURE
VENULES
VERANDA
VERDANT
VERDITE
VERONAL
VERSUTE
VERTIGO
VERTUES
VESTIGE
VESTURE
VETERAN
VETOING
VIATORS
VIDUAGE
VIGOROS
VIGOURS
VILIAGO
VINIEST
VINTAGE
VIOLATE
VIOLENT
VIOLINS
VIOLIST
VIOLONE
VIRAGOS
VIRANDA
VIRANDO
VIRGATE
VIRGINS
VIRGULE
VIRINOS
VIRIONS
VIROIDS
VIRTUAL
VISAGED
VISAING
VISEING
VISITED
VISITEE
VISITOR
VITRAGE
VITRAIL
VITRAIN
VITRIOL
VITULAR
VOGIEST
VOGUERS
VOGUIER
VOIDEES
VOIDING
VOITURE
VOLANTE
VOLTAGE
VOLUTED
VOLUTIN
VOTEENS
VOULGES
VULGARS
VULGATE
WADINGS
WAGERED
WAGONED
WAGONER
WAGTAIL
WAILING
WAINAGE
WAITING

WALNUTS
WANDOOS
WANTAGE
WARDOGS
WARISON
WASTAGE
WATERED
WAULING
WAURING
WEANELS
WEANERS
WEARIED
WEARIES
WEASAND
WEDGIER
WEDGIES
WEEDERS
WEEDIER
WEEDING
WEENIER
WEENIES
WEETING
WEIGELA
WEIRDIE
WEIRING
WEISING
WELDERS
WENDIGO
WERGILD
WETLAND
WIDGEON
WIDGETS
WIDGIES
WIELDER
WIENIES
WILDERS
WILDEST
WILDING
WILTING
WINDAGE
WINDIER
WINDIGO
WINDORE
WINGIER
WINIEST
WINTLED
WIRIEST
WIRINGS
WISTING
WITLING
WONDERS
WONGIED
WOODIER
WOODIES
WOODING
WOODSIA
WOOINGS
WOOLDER
WOOLENS
WOORALI
WORDAGE
WOULDST
WOURALI
WRONGED
WROOTED
WURLIES
YAOURTS
YARDAGE
YARDANG
YEADING
YEALDON
YEARNED
YEEDING
YIELDER
YIRDING
YODLING
YOGINIS
YOGURTS
YONDERS
YOUNGER

8-letter words (with one 3 or 4 point tile)

AASVOGEL
ABALONES
ABIDINGS
ABIGAILS
ABLATION
ABLATORS
ABLUTION
ABNEGATE
ABOIDEAU
ABOITEAU
ABORIGIN
ABORTION
ABOULIAS
ABRASION
ABROGATE
ABSENTEE
ABUTILON
ACATOURS
ACAULINE
ACAULOSE
ACIERAGE
ACIERATE
ACREAGES
ACTINIAE
ACTINIAS
ACTINIDE
ACTINOID
ACTIONED
ACUITIES
ACULEATE
ADAPTING
ADAPTION
ADAPTORS
ADEEMING
ADESPOTA
ADHERENT
ADMIRALS
ADOPTING
ADOPTION
ADORABLE
ADROITLY
ADULTERY
ADUNCATE
ADVISING
AERODYNE
AEROFOIL
AEROLOGY
AGACERIE
AGAMOIDS
AGENTIVE
AGERATUM
AIRFOILS
AIRLIFTS
AIRMAILS
AIRPLANE
ALAMODES
ALARMIST
ALARUMED
ALASTRIM
ALEATORY
ALEPINES
ALGICIDE
ALGIDITY
ALGORISM
ALICANTS
ALIGHTED
ALODIUMS
ALPINIST
ALTRUISM
ALUMINAS
ALVEATED
AMATIONS
AMENAGED
AMENAGES
AMIANTUS
AMILDARS
AMOUNTED
ANAEROBE
ANALOGIC
ANECDOTE
ANELACES
ANGIOMAS
ANGUIPED
ANIMATOR
ANTACIDS
ANTECEDE
ANTELOPE
ANTEROOM
ANTICOUS
ANTIPODE
APIARIST
APOLOGIA
APOLOGUE
APOSITIA
ARBALIST
ARCUATED
ARGEMONE
ARGUABLE
ARGUFIED
ARGUFIES
ARGUTELY
ARMGAUNT
AROYNTED
ASCIDIAN
ASTIGMIA
ATROPIAS
ATROPOUS
AUBERGES
AUBRETIA
AUBRIETA
AUCTIONS
AUDIENCE
AUDITIVE
AUDITORY
AUMAILED
AURIFIED
AURIFIES
AUTACOID
AUTHORED
AUTOCADE
AUTOCARS
AUTODYNE
AUTOGENY
AUTOGYRO
AUTOLOGY
AUTOPSIA
AUTOSOME
AVAILING
AVAUNTED
AVENTRED
AVENTURE
AVERAGED
AVERAGES
AVIARIES
AVIARIST
AVIATING
AVIATION
AVIATORS
AVOIDING
AVOISION
AVULSION
AWAITING
AWEARIED
BADINAGE
BALADINE
BALADINS
BANDAGES
BANDELET
BANDORAS
BANDROLS
BANDURAS
BANLIEUE
BANTERED
BARGEESE
BARONAGE
BARONIAL
BASIDIAL
BATOONED
BAUDRONS
BEAUTIED
BEAUTIES
BEDEGUAR
BEELINES
BEERAGES
BEGUILED
BEGUILER
BEGUILES
BEGUINES
BELEEING
BELONGED
BELONGER
BENISEED
BESEEING
BESIEGED
BESIEGER
BESOULED
BESUITED
BETIDING
BETOILED
BIELDIER
BINAURAL
BIRDINGS
BIRLINGS
BIRSLING
BLASTOID
BLAUDING
BLEEDERS
BLOODIER
BLOODIES
BLOODING
BLOUSING
BLUDGEON
BLUDGERS
BLUENOSE
BLUIDIER
BLUNGERS
BLURTING
BOGLANDS
BOILINGS
BONDAGES
BOOTLEGS
BORONIAS
BOTARGOS
BOUDERIE
BOUDOIRS
BOUNTREE
BOURDONS
BOURGEON
BRIDLING
BRIDOONS
BRISLING
BROILING
BRUISING
BRUSTING
BRUTINGS
BUDGEREE
BUDGEROS
BUILDING
BUISTING
BUNGLERS
BURGONET
BURINIST
BURSTING
BUSTLING
BUTANOLS
BUTLERED
CAESURAE
CAESURAL
CAGOULES
CALDRONS
CALUTRON
CANDOURS
CANOODLE
CANOROUS
CANTDOGS
CARDINAL
CARDOONS
CAREENED
CARGEESE
CARLOADS
CAROUSAL
CARTLOAD
CATALOGS
CAUDLING
CAUDRONS
CAULDRON
CAUSERIE
CAUTIONS
CENTERED
CENTRODE
CENTROID
CERATOID
CERULEAN
CERULEIN
CISLUNAR
CLANGORS
CLANGOUR
CLARAINS
CLARETED
CLARINOS
CLARIONS
CLAUSTRA
CLEARAGE
CLITORIS
CLOSETED
CLOUDAGE
CLOUDIER
CLOUDING
CLOURING
CLUDGIES
COALTARS
CODLINGS
COISTRIL
COITIONS
COLESEED
COLOGNES
COLONIST
COLORANT
COLORING
COLOURED
CONARIAL
CONDUITS
CONGREED
CONGREET
CONIDIAL
CONOIDAL
CONSULAR
CONSULTA
CONTAGIA
CONTOURS
CONTRAIL
CONTROLE
CONTROLS
CONTROUL
COOEEING
COOLANTS
CORDIALS
COREGENT
CORNUTOS
CORONALS
CORTISOL
COTELINE
COTLANDS
COULOIRS
COUNTROL
COURLANS
CREODONT
CRINOIDS
CROUTONS
CRUISING
CRUSTING
CUITERED
CURDLING
CURLINGS
CURTANAS
DAINTILY
DATEABLE
DAUBINGS
DAUGHTER
DAYTALER
DEALBATE
DEATHIER
DEBATING
DEBITING
DEBUTING
DECAGONS
DECENTER
DECOLOUR
DECORATE
DECOROUS
DECRETAL
DEFERENT
DEFINITE
DEFLATER
DEFLUENT
DELETIVE
DELIBATE
DELICATE
DELIRIUM
DELUSIVE
DEMEANOR
DEMERGES
DEMIURGE
DEMOTING
DEMOTION
DENIABLE
DENTICLE
DEPILATE
DEPLETES
DEPORTEE
DEPUTIES
DEPUTING
DEPUTISE
DERIVATE
DESELECT
DETHRONE
DEVALUES
DEVIATOR
DEVOTEES
DEVOTING
DEVOTION
DEVOUTER
DHOOLIES
DIABOLOS
DIACONAL
DIACTINE
DIAGRAMS
DIALOGIC
DIAMETER
DIANTHUS
DIAPASON
DIAPAUSE
DIAPENTE
DIASPORA
DIATONIC
DICTIONS
DIGAMIES
DIGAMIST
DIGAMOUS
DIGYNOUS
DILATIVE
DILATORY
DILUVIAN
DILUVION
DIORAMAS
DIPLEGIA
DIPLONTS
DIPNOOUS
DISCOING
DISCOLOR
DISCOUNT
DISHONOR
DISMOUNT
DISPLANT
DISPLING
DISUNITY
DIURETIC
DIVAGATE
DIVULGES
DOCTORAL
DOCTRINE
DOGBANES
DOGBOLTS
DOGCARTS
DOGHOLES
DOGSLEEP
DOGTOWNS
DOGVANES
DOLESOME
DOLOMITE
DOMAINAL
DOMANIAL
DONATARY
DONATISM
DONATIVE
DONATORY
DOORMATS
DOORSMAN
DORMIENT
DORMOUSE
DOUBLING
DOUBTING
DOUGHIER
DOVELETS
DOVETAIL
DRAGOMAN
DRAGSMAN
DRAUGHTS
DRIFTAGE
DROOGISH
DROUGHTS
DRUMLINS
DRUPELET
DUCATOON
DUELSOME
DULCIANA
DULCIANS
DUNGMERE
DUTIABLE
DUVETINE
DYSTONIA
EATABLES
EBENISTE
EBIONISE
ECAUDATE
ECLOGITE
ECLOGUES
EDACIOUS
EDGEBONE
EDGEWISE
EDUCATOR
EDUCTION
EGENCIES
EGESTIVE
EGOISTIC
EGOMANIA
EIDETICS
EIGHTIES
ELECTION
ELECTRON
ELEGANCE
ELEGIACS
ELEVATED
ELEVATES

ELEVATOR
ELICITED
ELOCUTED
EMENDATE
EMERAUDE
EMERGENT
EMIGRATE
EMULATED
EMULATES
EMULATOR
EMULGENT
EMULSOID
ENAMORED
ENCOLOUR
ENCOLURE
ENDAMAGE
ENDEAVOR
ENERVATE
ENFILADE
ENGLOBED
ENGLOBES
ENGLOOMS
ENGRIEVE
ENGROOVE
ENGULFED
ENHALOED
ENHALOES
ENHEARSE
ENTAYLED
ENTODERM
ENVEIGLE
ENVISAGE
EPANODOS
EPAULETS
EPIGAEAL
EPIGAEAN
EPIGEOUS
EPILATED
EPILOGUE
EPULIDES
ERECTILE
ERGATIVE
ERODIBLE
EROGENIC
ESCALADE
ESCALADO
ESPIEGLE
ETIOLOGY
EUGENICS
EVALUATE
EVENTIDE
EVENTUAL
EVIRATED
EVOLUTED
EVULGATE
EYELINER
FAITOURS
FALDAGES
FALTERED
FANTAILS
FANTIGUE
FATIGUED
FATIGUES
FAUSTIAN
FEATEOUS
FEATURED
FEDELINI
FEDERATE
FEEDLOTS
FEELGOOD
FELDGRAU
FELONOUS
FELTERED
FIGULINE
FIGURATE
FIGURINE
FIGURIST
FILAGREE
FILARIAS
FILIATED
FILIGREE
FINALISE
FINALIST
FINITUDE
FISTIANA
FISTULAR
FLAGRANT
FLANERIE
FLATIRON
FLAUNTED
FLEDGIER
FLEURONS
FLOATAGE
FLOODING
FLOORING
FLORUITS
FLOURING
FLOUSING
FLUIDISE
FLUORIDE
FLUORINE
FLUTINAS
FLUTINGS
FOEDARIE
FOETIDER
FOILINGS
FOLDINGS
FOLIAGED
FOLIATED
FOLIOING
FOOLINGS
FOOTAGES
FOOTGEAR
FOOTRULE
FOREDATE
FOREGOES
FOREGONE
FOREGUTS
FORELAIN
FORELEGS
FORELEND
FORELENT
FORESEEN
FORLANAS
FOUGADES
FOULARDS
FOURGONS
FOURTEEN
FOUTERED
FRAULEIN
FRAUTAGE
FREELOAD
FRONDOSE
FRUITAGE
FRUITION
FUNEREAL
FURLANAS
FURLONGS
FUSELAGE
FUSILIER
GABIONED
GADABOUT
GALIPOTS
GALOSHED
GAPESEED
GARBOILS
GARCINIA
GARDYLOO
GASIFIED
GASIFIER
GATEFOLD
GATHERED
GAUCIEST
GEALOUSY
GELIDITY
GEMATRIA
GENITIVE
GENOCIDE
GEODESIC
GEODETIC
GEOLATRY
GEOMETER
GHARIALS
GHERAOED
GILTWOOD
GIMLETED
GIRLHOOD
GLABROUS
GLACIATE
GLADSOME
GLAMORED
GLAMOURS
GLEAMIER
GLEESOME
GLIOMATA
GLOBATED
GLOBOIDS
GLOOMIER
GLOOPIER
GLOWERED
GOADSMAN
GOALPOST
GOATHERD
GOATWEED
GOLDEYES
GOLFIANA
GOLIARDY
GOLOSHED
GONIDIUM
GOODTIME
GOODYEAR
GOOFIEST
GORMANDS
GOSPODAR
GOURAMIS
GOURMAND
GOUTWEED
GOVERNED
GOWLANDS
GRACIOSO
GRACIOUS
GRADABLE
GRADATIM
GRAITHED
GRANDAMS
GRANDMAS
GRANDPAS
GRATEFUL
GRAVITAS
GREEDILY
GROANFUL
GROUPIES
GROUPIST
GROUPLET
GROVELED
GRUESOME
GUANACOS
GUARANTY
GUIDABLE
GUIDANCE
GULOSITY
GUNBOATS
GUNPORTS
GUNROOMS
GWINIADS
GYROIDAL
HAIRLINE
HALATION
HALIOTIS
HALITOUS
HANDLIST
HANDOUTS
HANDRAIL
HANGOUTS
HARANGUE
HARIGALS
HARTENED
HATGUARD
HAULAGES
HAURIANT
HEADAGES
HEADGEAR
HEADLINE
HEADNOTE
HEDGIEST
HELIODOR
HELOTAGE
HEREUNTO
HERITAGE
HETAERAE
HETAIRAI
HETAIRIA
HIDALGAS
HIDALGOS
HIDLINGS
HILDINGS
HIREAGES
HIRLINGS
HIRSLING
HIRUDINS
HOLDINGS
HOOLIGAN
HORNGELD
HORNTAIL
HOURLONG
HOUSLING
HUITAINS
HUNGERED
HURDLING
HURLINGS
HURTLING
HUSTLING
IDEALITY
IDEATIVE
IDEOGRAM
IDEOLOGY
IDIOLECT
IDOLATRY
ILMENITE
IMAGINAL
IMAGINED
INARABLE
INDICATE
INDICTEE
INDOCILE
INDUCIAE
INDUCTEE
INDUCTOR
INDUSTRY
INDUVIAE
INDUVIAL
INEDIBLE
INFERIAE
INFLATOR
INFLATUS
INGROOVE
INHAULER
INHOLDER
INTIFADA
INVALIDS
INVEIGLE
INVITEES
INVOLUTE
IODYRITE
IRONICAL
ISODICON
ISOGONIC
ISOPODAN
ISOTONIC
ITEMISED
LABOURED
LABROIDS
LACERATE
LACINIAE
LACUNARS
LACUNATE
LACUNOSE
LADANUMS
LANCETED
LANYARDS
LAPIDATE
LARVATED
LAUGHIER
LAUWINES
LAVATION
LAVEERED
LEAFAGES
LEASOWED
LEAVENED
LECANORA
LECTURED
LEGACIES
LEGATARY
LEGENDRY
LEGERITY
LEGROOMS
LEMONADE
LEMURINE
LEMUROID
LENIFIED
LENIFIES
LENITIVE
LEPIDOTE
LEPORINE
LEUCINES
LEVANTED
LEVEEING
LEVERAGE
LEVIGATE
LIBATION
LICENSEE
LIEGEDOM
LIEGEMEN
LIMATION
LIMONITE
LINOCUTS
LISPOUND
LITURGIC
LOBATION
LOCATION
LOCUTION
LODGMENT
LOGBOARD
LOGICIAN
LOGICIST
LOGISTIC
LONESOME
LONGBOAT
LONGSOME
LOOPINGS
LORDOTIC
LOUVERED
LUCERNES
LUMINIST
LUNATICS
LUNGWORT
MADRIGAL
MADRONAS
MADRONOS
MAGNOLIA
MAINDOOR
MAINOURS
MAINSAIL
MALEATES
MALGRADO
MALODOUR
MANDATOR
MANDOLAS
MANDORAS
MANDORLA
MANGOLDS
MANITOUS
MANORIAL
MANURIAL
MARIGOLD
MARITAGE
MAROONED
MARTAGON
MASTODON
MATADORE
MATADORS
MATRONAL
MAULGRED
MEDIATOR
MEGADOSE
MEIONITE
MELANOUS
MELINITE
MELODEON
MELODIES
MELODION
MELODISE
MERENGUE
MERINGUE
METAIRIE
MEUNIERE
MIAULING
MIDIRONS
MIGRATED
MILEAGES
MILTONIA
MIRLITON
MISDOING
MISGUIDE
MISTLING
MISTRIAL
MODALIST
MODERATE
MODERATO
MODIOLAR
MODIOLUS
MODULATE
MOLESTED
MONARDAS
MONAURAL
MONILIAS
MONODIST
MONORAIL
MONTAGED
MONTARIA
MOONSAIL
MOONSEED
MOORAGES
MOORLAND
MORAINAL
MORALIST
MOTIONAL
MOTIONED
MOTORAIL
MOTORIAL
MOULAGES
MOULDIER
MOULDING
MOULINET
MOUSLING
MOUTERED
MUDIRIAS
MUISTING
MULETEER
MUNGOOSE
MURAENAS
MURALIST
MURIATED
MURLAINS
MUTINIED
NAGAPIES
NASALITY
NAUTICAL
NAVIGATE
NEBULISE
NEGATIVE
NEMATODE
NEOLOGIC
NERVELET
NERVULES
NEUROPIL
NEWSREEL
NOCTILIO
NOCTUIDS
NODALITY
NODOSITY
NOTIFIED
NOVELESE
NUCLEASE
NUCLEATE
NUCLEIDE
NUGATORY
NUMERATE
NUPTIALS
NUTWOODS
OBDURATE
OBEDIENT
OBELISED
OBLATION
OBLIGATE
OBLIGATI
OBLIGATO
OBLIGORS
OBSIDIAN
OBSOLETE
OBTAINED
OCARINAS
OCEANAUT
OCTAGONS
OCULATED
ODIOUSLY
ODOMETER
OEDEMATA
OENOMELS
ONISCOID
OOGAMIES
OPIATING
OPTIONAL
OPUNTIAS
ORBITALS
ORCINOLS
ORDALIUM
OREWEEDS
ORIGAMIS
ORIGANUM
OROGENIC
OSCULANT
OSNABURG
OSTRACOD
OUABAINS
OUGHLIED
OUTBOARD
OUTBRAGS
OUTBREED
OUTCRIED
OUTDANCE
OUTDRIVE
OUTDROVE
OUTFIELD
OUTGIVEN
OUTGIVES
OUTGROWN
OUTGROWS
OUTHIRED
OUTLAWED
OUTLIVED
OUTNAMED
OUTRACED
OUTRIVAL
OUTSCOLD
OUTSCORN
OUTSWORE
OUTSWORN
OUTWARDS
OUTWINDS
OUVRAGES
OVARIOLE
OVARIOUS
OVARITIS
OVATIONS
OVERDONE
OVERGONE
OVERLADE
OVERLAIN
OVERLEND

OVERLENT
OVERLOAD
OVERLONG
OVERLOUD
OVERNEAT
OVERSOUL
OVERTONE
OVULATED
PAENULAE
PAENULAS
PAGANISE
PAGINATE
PAGURIAN
PAGURIDS
PAIRIALS
PALADINS
PALINODE
PALISADO
PALUDINE
PALUDOSE
PANDOORS
PANDORAS
PANDOURS
PANDURAS
PARAGONS
PARANOID
PARDALIS
PARLANDO
PARODIST
PAROTIDS
PAROUSIA
PARTIALS
PASTORAL
PASTURAL
PATRIALS
PATRONAL
PATULINS
PAULDRON
PEDALOES
PEDIGREE
PEERAGES
PEIGNOIR
PELERINE
PELTERED
PENALISE
PEONAGES
PERIAGUA
PERIGEAL
PERIGEES
PERIGONE
PERILUNE
PERINEAL
PERONEAL
PETALOID
PETIOLED
PETRONEL
PIGEONED
PIGTAILS
PILEATED
PILOTAGE
PINTADOS
PINTAILS
PIRAGUAS
PIROGUES
PLAGUIER
PLAIDING
PLANURIA
PLATEAUS
PLATINAS
PLATOONS
PLAUDITE
PLAUDITS
PLEDGEES
PLEDGEOR
PLEDGERS
PLEDGETS
PLIOSAUR
PLOIDIES
PLUNGERS
PLURISIE
PODAGRAL
PODAGRAS
PODARGUS
POIGNADO
POLARONS
PONDAGES
POOLSIDE
PORTAGUE
PORTIGUE
PORTLAND
PORTOLAN
PORTULAN
POSITION
POSTORAL
POSTURAL
POULAINE
POULARDS
POULDRON
POUNDAGE
POUNDALS
PRANDIAL
PRELUDES
PRELUDIO
PRODIGAL
PROLOGUE
PROLONGE
PROLONGS
PRONOTAL
PROTEGEE
PROULING
PUDGIEST
PUGILIST
PULDRONS
PULSATOR
PULSIDGE
PULTOONS
PUREEING
PURLINGS
PURLOINS
PURSLAIN
RADICALS
RADICANT
RADICATE
RAGBOLTS
RAINCOAT
RATIFIED
RAVENOUS
RAVIOLIS
READABLE
REBOILED
RECOILED
RECUILED
REDOUBLE
REFLATED
REFLUENT
REFOOTED
REFUGEES
REGICIDE
REHEATED
REHOUSED
RELOCATE
RELUCENT
RELUCTED
RELUMINE
REMEDIAT
REMIGATE
REMIGIAL
REMOTION
RENOVATE
REOPENED
REPEALED
REPENTED
REPETEND
REPLETED
REPUGNED
REPULSED
RETICULE
REVALUED
REVEALED
REVENGED
REVENUED
REVENUES
REVOLUTE
RIDICULE
RIFLINGS
ROADSMAN
ROBINIAS
ROTUNDLY
ROUGHIES
ROUNDISH
ROUTEMAN
ROUTEMEN
ROYALIST
RUGOSELY
RUGOSITY
RUINABLE
SABOTAGE
SAFRONAL
SAGAMORE
SAILROOM
SAINTDOM
SALINITY
SALMONID
SALOPIAN
SALUTARY
SALVAGED
SAUFGARD
SAUROPOD
SCALDINI
SCALDINO
SCAUDING
SCIUROID
SCOLDING
SCORDATO
SCOURGED
SCROOGED
SCROUGED
SEAHOUND
SEAPLANE
SECONDEE
SELECTED
SELVAGED
SELVAGEE
SELVEDGE
SEPALINE
SERENELY
SEROLOGY
SERUEWED
SEWERAGE
SHAGROON
SHEERLEG
SHOGUNAL
SHOOGIED
SHOOGLED
SHOOLING
SIBILANT
SIMULANT
SIRUPING
SITOLOGY
SLEIGHED
SLEUTHED
SLOOMING
SLOUGHED
SLUGHORN
SLUICIER
SLUICING
SLURPING
SMILODON
SMOILING
SNOOTFUL
SNOOTILY
SOAPLAND
SODALITY
SOLARIUM
SOLATIUM
SOLIDARY
SOLIDITY
SOLITARY
SOLPUGID
SOMEDEAL
SOMEDELE
SOMEGATE
SONOGRAM
SORBITOL
SORICOID
SOUPLING
SOUTHRON
SPADROON
SPATULAR
SPELAEAN
SPIRLING
SPLURGED
SPOILING
SPONGOID
SPOOLING
SPORIDIA
SPURLING
SPURTING
STEEPLED
STIFLING
STINGILY
STIPULAR
STODGILY
STRAVAIG
STROBILA
STROBILI
STRONGLY
STRONGYL
STUDYING
STURDILY
SUBTIDAL
SUDAMINA
SUDATORY
SUICIDAL
SULTANIC
SUMOTORI
SUNLIGHT
SUPEREGO
SUPERLOO
SURGICAL
SWIRLING
TABANIDS
TABLOIDS
TABOOING
TABOURED
TABOURIN
TAILSPIN
TAIVERED
TALAPOIN
TALIONIC
TALISMAN
TAMANDUS
TAMANOIR
TAMARIND
TANGRAMS
TANYARDS
TAPENADE
TAPIROID
TEABOARD
TELECINE
TELEGONY
TELEGRAM
TELERGIC
TELFERED
TELOMERE
TENACULA
TENDERLY
TENEBRAE
THIOUREA
THOUSAND
THREADEN
THRENODE
THRONGED
TILAPIAS
TIMARAUS
TIMELIER
TIMOROUS
TINAMOUS
TINFOILS
TINGLISH
TIRAMISU
TOADRUSH
TOADYING
TOEHOLDS
TOHUNGAS
TOLEWARE
TOOLBAGS
TOOLBARS
TOPLINED
TORMINAL
TORNADIC
TOUGHIES
TOURACOS
TRADEFUL
TRAGICAL
TRAGOPAN
TRANGAMS
TRAVAILS
TRAVELED
TRAVELOG
TREACLED
TRIALISM
TRIAPSAL
TRIBUNAL
TRIDACNA
TRIPLOID
TRIPODAL
TRIPOLIS
TRIPUDIA
TROILISM
TROOPIAL
TROUPIAL
TUILYIED
TUNEABLE
TURBANDS
TURBINAL
TURBONDS
TURFINGS
TURGIDLY
TURMOILS
TWEEDIER
TWEEDLER
TWEEDLES
TWEENIES
UBIETIES
UDOMETER
UGLIFIED
UGLIFIES
ULCERATE
ULTRAISM
UNABATED
UNAFRAID
UNAWARES
UNBAITED
UNBEGETS
UNBELTED
UNBOLTED
UNBOOTED
UNCOATED
UNCOILED
UNCOLTED
UNDIGHTS
UNEASILY
UNEATHES
UNESPIED
UNFOOLED
UNFOOTED
UNFORGOT
UNGIFTED
UNGIRTHS
UNGLOVED
UNGLOVES
UNHAILED
UNHEALED
UNHEARSE
UNHEATED
UNHOARDS
UNHOLIER
UNICOLOR
UNIFIERS
UNIFILAR
UNILOBAR
UNILOBED
UNIPOLAR
UNITEDLY
UNMELTED
UNPEELED
UNPEERED
UNPITIED
UNPLAITS
UNPOLITE
UNREAVES
UNREEVED
UNREEVES
UNRIGHTS
UNSOAPED
UNSOCIAL
UNSPOILT
UNTEAMED
UNTIDILY
UNTOWARD
UNVAILED
UNVAILES
UNVEILED
UPDATING
UPLEANED
UPRISING
UPROOTAL
UPROOTED
UPSTAGED
URALITIC
URANISCI
URANITIC
URETHANE
URGENTLY
UROLITHS
UROLOGIC
UTOPIANS
VAGARIES
VAGINATE
VAGINULA
VAGRANTS
VALERIAN
VALIANTS
VALIDATE
VALONEAS
VALONIAS
VALOROUS
VALUATED
VALUATES
VALUATOR
VANADOUS
VANGUARD
VANTAGED
VARGUENO
VARIATED
VARIOLAS
VAULTAGE
VAUNTAGE
VEINIEST
VELATURA
VENDAGES
VENDEUSE
VENERATE
VENEREAL
VENTURED
VESTIGIA
VIDEOING
VIDUAGES
VIGOROUS
VILIAGOS
VINDALOO
VINTAGED
VIOLATED
VIOLATOR
VIROGENE
VIRTUOSA
VIRTUOSI
VIRTUOSO
VISIONAL
VITRIOLS
VITULINE
VOGUIEST
VOIDINGS
VOLITION
VOLUTINS
VOLUTION
VOLUTOID
VORAGOES
WAGTAILS
WAINAGES
WANDEROO
WATERAGE
WATERLOG
WEASELED
WEDGIEST
WEEDIEST
WEENIEST
WEIGELAS
WELTERED
WEREGILD
WIELDIER
WILDINGS
WINDIGOS
WINDSAIL
WINERIES
WISTARIA
WITLINGS
WONDROUS
WOODENER
WOOLDING
WOORALIS
WOURALIS
WRONGOUS
YARDANGS
YGLAUNST
YULETIDE

AEIO BONUS WORDS

All seven- and eight-letter words which contain one each of the four vowels AEIO are given in the following lists. These lists may repeat words which appear in the 6-plus-1 and 6-plus-2 bonus sets. To assist learning, the words are grouped in accordance with the sequence of the four vowels – for example, AVOIDED, AGONISE and CALORIE all appear in the AOIE portion of the seven-letter list. Within a vowel grouping (such as AOIE), the words are listed in alphabetical order of the last 3 letters. (Thus, in the AOIE portion of the seven-letter list, AVOIDED occurs before AGONISE, since the sequence -DED alphabetically precedes -ISE.) Where there are several words with the same last three letters, they are listed alphabetically by the first four letters. (Thus, ADONISE precedes AGONISE.)

AEIO bonus words containing only these vowels are listed first, followed by lists of the few that also contain a U.

AEIO BONUS WORDS (no U)

7-letter AEIO words (no U)

AEIO ALERION

AEOI AEROBIC PAEONIC ADENOID ANEROID NAEVOID ALVEOLI

AIEO ARRIERO ALIENOR AILERON

AIOE PAIOCKE AZIONES VAIVODE WAIVODE WAIWODE RADIOED AIRHOLE CARIOLE DARIOLE VARIOLE ACINOSE ADIPOSE ABIOSES

AOEI AMOEBIC ANOESIS ALOETIC ANOETIC

AOIE AVOIDED CAMOGIE ACCOIED AGONIES ANOMIES ATOMIES ATONIES ATOPIES GANOINE KAOLINE ARMOIRE ADONISE AGONISE ANODISE ATOMISE AZOTISE ACONITE AMOSITE ADONIZE AGONIZE ANODIZE ATOMIZE AZOTIZE CALORIE

EAIO ELATION ENATION ERASION EVASION

EAOI DEASOIL

EIOA KEITLOA EPIZOAN FEIJOAS LEIPOAS HEMIOLA

EOAI JEOFAIL

EOIA GEOIDAL EXORDIA EROTICA EXOTICA ENCOMIA BEGONIA ECTOPIA EMPORIA PELORIA

IAOE DIAZOES IMAGOES ISAGOGE MIAOWED

IEOA ICEBOAT MINEOLA

IOAE DIOXANE ISOBARE ISOBASE ISOLATE NIOBATE VIOLATE IODATES

OAIE OAKIEST OARIEST TOADIED COALIER FOAMIER GOATIER HOARIER LOAMIER ROARIER SOAPIER BOATIES GOALIES ORACIES OTARIES OVARIES ROADIES SOAPIES TOADIES COCAINE MORAINE OPALINE OTARINE OXAZINE SODAINE COALISE COALIZE TOASTIE

OEAI TOENAIL OCEANIC OCEANID

OEIA SOREDIA COELIAC LOBELIA TOXEMIA GODETIA

OIAE COINAGE FOLIAGE SOILAGE ORIGANE OXIDASE FOLIATE OBVIATE OSMIATE OSTIATE OXIDATE SOCIATE LORICAE VOMICAE SCORIAE OPIATED OPIATES

8-letter AEIO words (no U)

AEIO ARPEGGIO
ADHESION
ALLERION
ANNEXION
APHELION
AVERSION
ANTERIOR
ALERIONS
AERIFORM
AEOI AEROBICS
PAEONICS
ADENOIDS
ANEROIDS
AEROLITH
DAEMONIC
ANECHOIC
AMBEROID
ASTEROID
ATHETOID
CAMELOID
GALENOID
MALLEOLI
AIEO ARMIGERO
KAKIEMON
ASSIENTO
AILERONS
ALIENORS
TAILERON
ARRIEROS
AIOE VAIVODES
WAIVODES
WAIWODES
PAIOCKES
AIRHOLES
CARIOLES
DARIOLES
VARIOLES
AIRWOMEN
ACTIONED
GABIONED
RATIONED
RAISONNE
ANTINODE
ANTIPODE
ARILLODE
PALINODE
CALICOES
CALIGOES
ANTIPOLE
ARVICOLE
CABRIOLE
CAMISOLE
CAPRIOLE
CARRIOLE
FASCIOLE
GLADIOLE
AIRDROME
BARITONE
ANTIPOPE
CALLIOPE
ALBICORE
HALICORE
FARINOSE
LAMINOSE
VARICOSE
ANTIDOTE
HALIMOTE
TAILORED
AIRBORNE
ACIDOSES
AMITOSES
AOEI ACROLEIN
ALOETICS
CANOEING
CANOEIST
ANORETIC
ANOESTRI
AMORETTI
ANOREXIC
AOIE ABORIGEN
ASTONIED
CANOPIED
PARODIED
CAPONIER
GASOLIER
SABOTIER
APHONIES
ARGOSIES
ARMORIES
ASTONIES
AVOWRIES
BARONIES
CALORIES
CAMOGIES
CANOPIES
JALOPIES
PARODIES
SAVORIES
SAXONIES
CAMOMILE
APOCRINE
ARMOZINE
ATROPINE
GASOLINE
LANOLINE
PAVONINE
WAGMOIRE
AMORTISE
APHORISE
CANONISE
CAPONISE
VALORISE
VAPORISE
AMMONITE
APPOSITE
ARSONITE
DATOLITE
FAVORITE
JAROSITE
SAPONITE
SAXONITE
TACONITE
ABORTIVE
ADOPTIVE
AMORTIZE
APHORIZE
CANONIZE
CAPONIZE
VALORIZE
VAPORIZE
ASSOILED
ADJOINED
GANOINES
KAOLINES
ARMOIRES
ADONISED
AGONISED
ANODISED
ATOMISED
AZOTISED
DAMOISEL
ATOMISER
ADONISES
AGONISES
ANODISES
ATOMISES
AZOTISES
ANOINTED
AROINTED
ADROITER
ANOINTER
ACONITES
AMOSITES
APOMIXES
ADONIZED
AGONIZED
ANODIZED
ATOMIZED
AZOTIZED
ATOMIZER
ADONIZES
AGONIZES
ANODIZES
ATOMIZES
AZOTIZES
EAIO GERANIOL
CREATION
DELATION
DERATION
ENACTION
EXACTION
GELATION
LEGATION
NEGATION
REACTION
RELATION
SEDATION
VENATION
VEXATION
BEHAVIOR
SERAGLIO
ELATIONS
ENATIONS
ERASIONS
EVASIONS
SCENARIO
FELLATIO
EAOI EPAGOGIC
DEASOILS
METAZOIC
CERATOID
ERGATOID
KERATOID
NEMATOID
PETALOID
SEPALOID
SESAMOID
TERATOID
TETANOID
HEXAFOIL
EIAO DEVIATOR
EPILATOR
EXPIATOR
MEDIATOR
EIOA EPIZOANS
EPIFOCAL
EPISODAL
PETIOLAR
HEMIOLAS
REGIONAL
KEITLOAS
SEMICOMA
EOAI ESOPHAGI
REORDAIN
DEBONAIR
JEOFAILS
TEOCALLI
EXOGAMIC
GEOTAXIS
EOIA EROTICAL
HEROICAL
KELOIDAL
DEMONIAC
EXORDIAL
MEMORIAL
BESONIAN
BEZONIAN
CREOLIAN
DEMONIAN
BEGONIAS
ECTOPIAS
PELORIAS
MELODICA
VERONICA
GEROPIGA
SEMOLINA
CECROPIA
SENSORIA
TENTORIA
IAOE ISAGOGES
FIASCOES
IGNAROES
VIRAGOES
DIASTOLE
GIRASOLE
DIAPHONE
DIASCOPE
DIASPORE
PINAFORE
DIAGNOSE
IEAO LITERATO
IEOA ICEBOATS
MINEOLAS
SIDEROAD
LIFEBOAT
MINNEOLA
IDEOGRAM
IOAE PILOTAGE
IRONWARE
DIOPTASE
IDOCRASE
BILOBATE
IMMOLATE
INCHOATE
INNOVATE
INORNATE
INSOLATE
INTONATE
PRIORATE
ISOLABLE
VIOLABLE
DIOXANES
ISOBARES
BIOGASES
ISOBASES
ISOLATED
VIOLATED
IDOLATER
VIOLATER
ISOLATES
NIOBATES
VIOLATES
IOEA DIOCESAN
OAEI TOXAEMIC
OAIE ORGANDIE
COALIEST
FOAMIEST
GOATIEST
HOARIEST
LOAMIEST
ROARIEST
SOAPIEST
ROADSIDE
SODAMIDE
COVARIED
CROAKIER
FLOATIER
LOATHIER
POACHIER
SHOALIER
BOTANIES
COACHIES
COVARIES
DONARIES
GORAMIES
NOMADIES
NOTARIES
OCCAMIES
OTALGIES
ROSARIES
ROTARIES
TOASTIES
VOLARIES
VOTARIES
FORHAILE
VOLATILE
COALMINE
CORAMINE
DOPAMINE
MONDAINE
PROCAINE
PTOMAINE
SOLANINE
STOVAINE
TOPAZINE
BOTANISE
FOCALISE
LOCALISE
MORALISE
NODALISE
NOMADISE
NOTARISE
ORGANISE
POLARISE
ROYALISE
SOLARISE
TOTALISE
VOCALISE
WOMANISE
BORACITE

MONAZITE
SODALITE
TONALITE
COACTIVE
CONATIVE
DONATIVE
LOCATIVE
OPTATIVE
ROTATIVE
VOCATIVE
BOTANIZE
FOCALIZE
LOCALIZE
MORALIZE
NODALIZE
NOMADIZE
NOTARIZE
ORGANIZE
POLARIZE
ROYALIZE
SOLARIZE
TOTALIZE
VOCALIZE
WOMANIZE
ROCAILLE
OBTAINED
ORDAINED
OBTAINER
ORDAINER
COCAINES
MORAINES
OPALINES
OXAZINES
COALISED
OPALISED
COALISES
OXALISES
COALIZED
OPALIZED
COALIZES
OEAI FORELAID
FORESAID
OVERLAID
OVERPAID
DOVETAIL
FORESAIL
OVERSAIL
FORELAIN
OVERLAIN
OVERHAIR
OCEANIDS
TOENAILS
OBEAHING
OBEAHISM
OPERATIC
POEMATIC
OEIA COELIACS
OBEISANT
OLEFIANT
POETICAL
GYNOECIA
COLLEGIA
PROEMIAL
SOREDIAL
SOTERIAL
COMEDIAN
GODETIAS
LOBELIAS
TOXEMIAS
BROMELIA
CHOLEMIA
PROGERIA
OIAE BONIFACE
SPOILAGE
SOLIDARE
COGITATE
DOMINATE
FORMIATE
LORICATE
MOTIVATE
NOMINATE
OBLIGATE
OPPILATE
OPTIMATE
ORDINATE
OSCITATE
ROSINATE
SOLIDATE
SOMNIATE
SPOLIATE
VOLITATE
OPINABLE
SOCIABLE
VOIDABLE
FOLIAGED
COINAGES
FOLIAGES
SOILAGES
VOIDANCE
ORIGANES
GOLIASED
GOLIASES
OXIDASES
FOLIATED
OBVIATED
OXIDATED
FOLIATES
OBVIATES
OSMIATES
OXIDATES
SOCIATES
OIEA TOISEACH
LONICERA
ORIENTAL
SOCIETAL

AEIO BONUS WORDS (with U)

7-letter AEIO words (with U)

EOIA EULOGIA
SEQUOIA
OEIA DOULEIA
OIEA MOINEAU

8-letter AEIO words (with U)

AEIO CAESIOUS
AOIE AGOUTIES
JALOUSIE
EAIO EQUATION
EDACIOUS
EOIA EUPHOBIA
SEQUOIAS
EUPHONIA
EUPHORIA
IAOE DIALOGUE
IOEA THIOUREA
OAIE DOUANIER
POULAINE
ODALIQUE
OEIA DOULEIAS
OIEA MOINEAUS

SECTION FOUR

HOOKS AND BLOCKERS

Introduction

Which two-letter words can be transformed into which three-letter words by the addition of a single letter at either the front or back end? An example is HI to CHI, GHI and PHI (by adding a letter at the front of HI), and HIC, HID, HIE, HIM, HIN, HIP, HIS and HIT (by adding a letter at the end). Words which can add a letter at the front or back are called hooks, as they provide places for other words to hook on to.

Conversely, words which cannot have a letter added at the front or back are called blockers.

HOOKS

The following lists of hooks show words of length two to eight letters which can have a letter added, either at the front or back, to create a longer word.

In actual play, it can be very useful to play a three-letter word (BAP, say), which has an obscure extension to four letters (BAPU, in this case). If the S's and blanks have already been played, the chances are that your opponent won't know BAPU, so the opening is likely to be safe until you want to put a U on the end of BAP.

It was felt that for learning purposes it would be valuable also to include in the two- and three-letter lists those words that *cannot* be extended (and are therefore blockers rather than hooks). These words are of course also listed in the Blockers section.

For eight-letter words, only a subset of the possible hooks is shown. All nine-letter words which are -S inflections of eight-letter words have been omitted – so, for example, the hook AARDVARK-S is not listed. However, where nine-letter words are non-plural -S hooks of eight-letter words already ending in -S (for example, NERVINES-S and TYRANNES-S), these have been retained in the lists.

2-LETTER WORD HOOKS: including all root words

AA	NAE	AIT	NAN	ARB	ASS	LAW	GAY	BAY	BON
BAA	SAE	**AM**	PAN	ARC	**AT**	MAW	HAY	**BE**	BOO
MAA	TAE	BAM	RAN	ARD	BAT	PAW	JAY	BED	BOP
AAS	VAE	CAM	SAN	ARE	CAT	RAW	KAY	BEE	BOR
AD	WAE	DAM	TAN	ARK	EAT	SAW	LAY	BEG	BOS
BAD	**AH**	GAM	VAN	ARM	FAT	TAW	MAY	BEL	BOT
CAD	BAH	HAM	WAN	ARS	GAT	WAW	NAY	BEN	BOW
DAD	DAH	JAM	ANA	ART	HAT	YAW	PAY	BET	BOX
FAD	FAH	KAM	AND	ARY	KAT	AWA	RAY	BEY	BOY
GAD	HAH	LAM	ANE	**AS**	LAT	AWE	SAY	BEZ	**BY**
HAD	LAH	MAM	ANI	AAS	MAT	AWL	TAY	**BI**	ABY
LAD	PAH	NAM	ANN	BAS	NAT	AWN	WAY	OBI	BYE
MAD	RAH	PAM	ANT	DAS	OAT	**AX**	AYE	BIB	BYS
PAD	YAH	RAM	ANY	EAS	PAT	FAX	AYS	BID	**CH**
RAD	AHA	SAM	**AR**	FAS	QAT	LAX	AYU	BIG	ACH
SAD	AHS	TAM	BAR	GAS	RAT	MAX	**BA**	BIN	ECH
TAD	**AI**	YAM	CAR	HAS	SAT	PAX	ABA	BIO	ICH
WAD	KAI	AMI	EAR	KAS	TAT	RAX	OBA	BIS	OCH
ADD	RAI	AMP	FAR	LAS	VAT	SAX	BAA	BIT	CHA
ADO	SAI	**AN**	GAR	MAS	WAT	TAX	BAD	BIZ	CHE
ADS	TAI	BAN	JAR	NAS	ATE	WAX	BAG	**BO**	CHI
ADZ	AIA	CAN	LAR	PAS	**AW**	ZAX	BAH	OBO	**DA**
AE	AID	DAN	MAR	RAS	CAW	AXE	BAM	BOA	ODA
DAE	AIL	EAN	OAR	VAS	DAW	**AY**	BAN	BOB	DAB
GAE	AIM	FAN	PAR	WAS	FAW	BAY	BAP	BOD	DAD
HAE	AIN	GAN	SAR	ASH	HAW	CAY	BAR	BOG	DAE
KAE	AIR	HAN	TAR	ASK	JAW	DAY	BAS	BOH	DAG
MAE	AIS	MAN	WAR	ASP	KAW	FAY	BAT	BOK	DAH

DAK
DAL
DAM
DAN
DAP
DAS
DAW
DAY
DI
DIB
DID
DIE
DIG
DIM
DIN
DIP
DIT
DIV
DO
ADO
UDO
DOB
DOC
DOD
DOE
DOG
DOH
DON
DOO
DOP
DOR
DOS
DOT
DOW
EA
KEA
LEA
PEA
SEA
TEA
YEA
ZEA
EAN
EAR
EAS
EAT
EAU
EE
BEE
CEE
DEE
FEE
GEE
JEE
LEE
NEE
PEE
REE
SEE
TEE
VEE
WEE
ZEE
EEK
EEL
EEN
EF
DEF
KEF
NEF

REF
TEF
EFF
EFS
EFT
EH
REH
EHS
EL
BEL
CEL
DEL
EEL
GEL
MEL
SEL
TEL
ZEL
ELD
ELF
ELK
ELL
ELM
ELS
ELT
EM
GEM
HEM
REM
WEM
EME
EMS
EMU
EN
BEN
DEN
EEN
FEN
GEN
HEN
KEN
MEN
PEN
REN
SEN
TEN
WEN
YEN
END
ENE
ENG
ENS
ER
HER
PER
ERA
ERE
ERF
ERG
ERK
ERN
ERR
ERS
ES
HES
LES
MES
OES
RES
TES

YES
ESS
EST
EX
HEX
KEX
LEX
REX
SEX
VEX
WEX
YEX
ZEX
FA
FAB
FAD
FAG
FAH
FAN
FAP
FAR
FAS
FAT
FAW
FAX
FAY
FY
GI
GIB
GID
GIE
GIF
GIG
GIN
GIO
GIP
GIS
GIT
GO
AGO
EGO
YGO
GOA
GOB
GOD
GOE
GON
GOO
GOS
GOT
GOV
GOY
GU
GUB
GUE
GUM
GUN
GUP
GUR
GUS
GUT
GUV
GUY
HA
AHA
CHA
WHA
HAD
HAE
HAG

HAH
HAJ
HAM
HAN
HAP
HAS
HAT
HAW
HAY
HE
CHE
SHE
THE
HEM
HEN
HEP
HER
HES
HET
HEW
HEX
HEY
HI
CHI
GHI
PHI
HIC
HID
HIE
HIM
HIN
HIP
HIS
HIT
HO
MHO
OHO
PHO
RHO
THO
WHO
ZHO
HOA
HOB
HOC
HOD
HOE
HOG
HOH
HOI
HON
HOO
HOP
HOS
HOT
HOW
HOX
HOY
ID
AID
BID
CID
DID
FID
GID
HID
KID
LID
MID
NID

RID
TID
VID
IDE
IDS
IF
GIF
KIF
IFF
IFS
IN
AIN
BIN
DIN
FIN
GIN
HIN
KIN
LIN
PIN
RIN
SIN
TIN
VIN
WIN
YIN
INK
INN
INS
IO
BIO
GIO
ION
IOS
IS
AIS
BIS
GIS
HIS
LIS
MIS
NIS
PIS
QIS
SIS
TIS
VIS
WIS
XIS
ISH
ISM
ISO
IT
AIT
BIT
CIT
DIT
FIT
GIT
HIT
KIT
LIT
NIT
PIT
RIT
SIT
TIT
WIT
ZIT
ITA

ITS
JO
JOB
JOE
JOG
JOR
JOT
JOW
JOY
KA
SKA
KAE
KAI
KAM
KAS
KAT
KAW
KAY
KO
KOA
KOB
KON
KOP
KOS
KOW
KY
SKY
KYE
KYU
LA
ALA
LAB
LAC
LAD
LAG
LAH
LAM
LAP
LAR
LAS
LAT
LAV
LAW
LAX
LAY
LI
LIB
LID
LIE
LIG
LIN
LIP
LIS
LIT
LO
LOB
LOG
LOO
LOP
LOR
LOS
LOT
LOW
LOX
LOY
MA
SMA
MAA
MAC
MAD

MAE
MAG
MAK
MAL
MAM
MAN
MAP
MAR
MAS
MAT
MAW
MAX
MAY
ME
EME
MEG
MEL
MEN
MES
MET
MEU
MEW
MI
AMI
MID
MIL
MIM
MIR
MIS
MIX
MIZ
MO
MOA
MOB
MOD
MOE
MOG
MOI
MOM
MON
MOO
MOP
MOR
MOT
MOU
MOW
MOY
MOZ
MU
EMU
MUD
MUG
MUM
MUN
MUS
MUX
MY
NA
ANA
MNA
NAB
NAE
NAG
NAM
NAN
NAP
NAS
NAT
NAY
NE

ANE
ENE
ONE
NEB
NED
NEE
NEF
NEK
NEP
NET
NEW
NO
NOB
NOD
NOG
NOH
NOM
NON
NOR
NOS
NOT
NOW
NOX
NOY
NU
GNU
NUB
NUN
NUR
NUS
NUT
NY
ANY
SNY
NYE
NYS
OB
BOB
COB
DOB
FOB
GOB
HOB
JOB
KOB
LOB
MOB
NOB
ROB
SOB
YOB
OBA
OBI
OBO
OBS
OD
BOD
COD
DOD
GOD
HOD
MOD
NOD
POD
ROD
SOD
TOD
YOD
ODA
ODD

ODE
ODS
OE
DOE
FOE
GOE
HOE
JOE
MOE
ROE
TOE
VOE
WOE
OES
OF
OOF
OFF
OFT
OH
BOH
DOH
FOH
HOH
NOH
OOH
POH
SOH
OHM
OHO
OI
HOI
MOI
POI
OIK
OIL
OM
MOM
NOM
OOM
POM
ROM
TOM
OMS
ON
BON
CON
DON
EON
FON
GON
HON
ION
KON
MON
NON
OON
SON
TON
WON
YON
ONE
ONS
OO
BOO
COO
DOO
GOO
HOO
LOO
MOO

POO
ROO
TOO
WOO
ZOO
OOF
OOH
OOM
OON
OOP
OOR
OOS
OR
BOR
COR
DOR
FOR
JOR
LOR
MOR
NOR
OOR
TOR
VOR
ORB
ORC
ORD
ORE
ORF
ORS
ORT
OS
BOS
COS
DOS
GOS
HOS
IOS
KOS
LOS
NOS
OOS
POS
SOS
WOS
YOS
ZOS
OU
FOU
MOU
SOU
YOU
OUK
OUP
OUR
OUT
OW
BOW
COW
DOW
HOW
JOW
KOW
LOW
MOW
NOW
POW
ROW
SOW
TOW

VOW	PAH	POS	SIB	TAD	TIS	HUM	GUR	AWE	OYE
WOW	PAL	POT	SIC	TAE	TIT	LUM	LUR	EWE	PYE
YOW	PAM	POW	SIM	TAG	**TO**	MUM	NUR	OWE	RYE
OWE	PAN	POX	SIN	TAI	TOC	RUM	OUR	WEB	SYE
OWL	PAP	POZ	SIP	TAJ	TOD	SUM	PUR	WED	TYE
OWN	PAR	**QI**	SIR	TAK	TOE	TUM	SUR	WEE	WYE
OWT	PAS	QIS	SIS	TAM	TOG	VUM	URD	WEM	YEA
OX	PAT	**RE**	SIT	TAN	TOM	**UN**	URE	WEN	YEN
BOX	PAW	ARE	SIX	TAP	TON	BUN	URN	WET	YEP
COX	PAX	ERE	**SO**	TAR	TOO	DUN	**US**	WEX	YES
FOX	PAY	IRE	DSO	TAT	TOP	FUN	BUS	WEY	YET
HOX	**PH**	ORE	ISO	TAU	TOR	GUN	GUS	**WO**	YEW
LOX	PHI	PRE	SOB	TAW	TOT	MUN	JUS	TWO	YEX
NOX	PHO	URE	SOC	TAX	TOW	NUN	MUS	WOE	**YO**
POX	PHS	REC	SOD	TAY	TOY	PUN	NUS	WOG	YOB
SOX	**PI**	RED	SOG	**TE**	**UG**	RUN	PUS	WOK	YOD
VOX	PIA	REE	SOH	ATE	BUG	SUN	SUS	WON	YOK
WOX	PIC	REF	SOL	UTE	DUG	TUN	WUS	WOO	YON
OY	PIE	REH	SON	TEA	FUG	UNI	YUS	WOP	YOS
BOY	PIG	REM	SOP	TED	HUG	UNS	USE	WOS	YOU
COY	PIN	REN	SOS	TEE	JUG	**UP**	**UT**	WOT	YOW
FOY	PIP	REP	SOT	TEF	LUG	CUP	BUT	WOW	**YU**
GOY	PIR	RES	SOU	TEG	MUG	DUP	CUT	WOX	AYU
HOY	PIS	RET	SOV	TEL	PUG	GUP	GUT	**XI**	KYU
JOY	PIT	REV	SOW	TEN	RUG	HUP	HUT	XIS	YUG
LOY	PIU	REW	SOX	TES	TUG	OUP	JUT	**XU**	YUK
MOY	PIX	REX	SOY	TEW	VUG	PUP	NUT	**YE**	YUP
NOY	**PO**	REZ	**ST**	**TI**	YUG	SUP	OUT	AYE	YUS
SOY	POA	**SH**	EST	TIC	UGH	TUP	PUT	BYE	**ZO**
TOY	POD	ASH	PST	TID	UGS	YUP	RUT	DYE	DZO
OYE	POH	ISH	STY	TIE	**UM**	UPS	TUT	EYE	ZOA
OYS	POI	SHE	**TA**	TIG	BUM	**UR**	UTE	HYE	ZOO
PA	POM	SHY	ETA	TIL	CUM	BUR	UTS	KYE	ZOS
SPA	POO	**SI**	ITA	TIN	FUM	CUR	UTU	LYE	
PAD	POP	PSI	TAB	TIP	GUM	FUR	**WE**	NYE	

3-LETTER WORD HOOKS: including all root words

AAS	EACH	RADS	AGES	**AIL**	PAIN	RAIT	**ALB**	TALL	AMIS
BAAS	NACH	TADS	**AGO**	BAIL	RAIN	TAIT	ALBE	WALL	**AMP**
MAAS	RACH	WADS	DAGO	FAIL	SAIN	WAIT	ALBS	ALLS	CAMP
ABA	TACH	**ADZ**	KAGO	HAIL	VAIN	AITS	**ALE**	ALLY	DAMP
BABA	ACHE	ADZE	SAGO	JAIL	WAIN	AITU	BALE	**ALP**	GAMP
CABA	ACHY	**AFT**	AGOG	KAIL	AINE	**AKE**	DALE	CALP	LAMP
ABAC	**ACT**	BAFT	AGON	MAIL	**AIR**	BAKE	EALE	PALP	RAMP
ABAS	FACT	DAFT	**AHA**	NAIL	FAIR	CAKE	GALE	SALP	SAMP
ABB	PACT	HAFT	TAHA	PAIL	GAIR	FAKE	HALE	ALPS	TAMP
ABBA	TACT	RAFT	**AHS**	RAIL	HAIR	HAKE	KALE	**ALS**	VAMP
ABBE	ACTA	WAFT	DAHS	SAIL	LAIR	JAKE	MALE	DALS	AMPS
ABBS	ACTS	**AGA**	FAHS	TAIL	MAIR	LAKE	PALE	GALS	**ANA**
ABY	**ADD**	GAGA	LAHS	VAIL	PAIR	MAKE	RALE	MALS	KANA
BABY	WADD	NAGA	PAHS	WAIL	SAIR	RAKE	SALE	PALS	LANA
GABY	ADDS	RAGA	RAHS	AILS	VAIR	SAKE	TALE	SALS	MANA
ABYE	**ADO**	SAGA	YAHS	**AIM**	AIRN	TAKE	VALE	ALSO	NANA
ACE	DADO	AGAR	**AIA**	KAIM	AIRS	WAKE	WALE	**ALT**	RANA
DACE	FADO	AGAS	AIAS	MAIM	AIRT	AKED	YALE	DALT	TANA
FACE	ADOS	**AGE**	**AID**	SAIM	AIRY	AKEE	ALEE	HALT	ANAL
LACE	**ADS**	CAGE	GAID	AIMS	**AIS**	AKES	ALES	MALT	ANAN
MACE	BADS	GAGE	KAID	**AIN**	DAIS	**ALA**	ALEW	SALT	ANAS
PACE	CADS	MAGE	LAID	CAIN	KAIS	GALA	**ALL**	ALTO	**AND**
RACE	DADS	PAGE	MAID	FAIN	PAIS	NALA	BALL	ALTS	BAND
TACE	FADS	RAGE	PAID	GAIN	RAIS	TALA	CALL	**AMI**	FAND
ACED	GADS	SAGE	RAID	HAIN	SAIS	ALAE	FALL	KAMI	HAND
ACER	HADS	WAGE	SAID	KAIN	TAIS	ALAP	GALL	RAMI	LAND
ACES	LADS	AGED	WAID	LAIN	**AIT**	ALAR	HALL	AMID	MAND
ACH	MADS	AGEE	AIDE	MAIN	BAIT	ALAS	MALL	AMIE	PAND
BACH	PADS	AGEN	AIDS	NAIN	GAIT	ALAY	PALL	AMIR	RAND

SAND
WAND
ANDS
ANE
BANE
CANE
FANE
GANE
JANE
LANE
MANE
PANE
SANE
TANE
VANE
WANE
ANES
ANEW
ANI
BANI
MANI
RANI
ANIL
ANIS
ANN
CANN
JANN
ANNA
ANNO
ANNS
ANT
BANT
CANT
DANT
GANT
KANT
LANT
PANT
RANT
SANT
VANT
WANT
ANTA
ANTE
ANTI
ANTS
ANY
CANY
MANY
WANY
ZANY
APE
CAPE
GAPE
JAPE
NAPE
PAPE
RAPE
TAPE
APED
APES
APEX
APT
RAPT
APTS
ARB
BARB
CARB
GARB
ARBA

ARBS
ARC
MARC
NARC
ARCH
ARCO
ARCS
ARD
BARD
CARD
EARD
FARD
HARD
LARD
MARD
NARD
PARD
SARD
WARD
YARD
ARDS
ARE
BARE
CARE
DARE
FARE
GARE
HARE
LARE
MARE
NARE
PARE
RARE
TARE
VARE
WARE
YARE
AREA
ARED
AREG
ARES
ARET
AREW
ARK
BARK
CARK
DARK
HARK
JARK
LARK
MARK
NARK
PARK
SARK
WARK
ARKS
ARM
BARM
FARM
HARM
MARM
WARM
ARMS
ARMY
ARS
BARS
CARS
EARS
FARS
GARS

JARS
MARS
OARS
PARS
SARS
TARS
WARS
ARSE
ART
CART
DART
FART
GART
HART
KART
MART
PART
TART
WART
ARTS
ARTY
ARY
MARY
NARY
OARY
VARY
WARY
ARYL
ASH
BASH
CASH
DASH
FASH
GASH
HASH
LASH
MASH
PASH
RASH
SASH
TASH
WASH
ASHY
ASK
BASK
CASK
HASK
MASK
TASK
ASKS
ASP
GASP
HASP
JASP
RASP
WASP
ASPS
ASS
BASS
JASS
LASS
MASS
PASS
SASS
TASS
ATE
BATE
CATE
DATE
FATE

GATE
HATE
LATE
MATE
PATE
RATE
SATE
TATE
WATE
YATE
AUF
CAUF
LAUF
AUFS
AUK
BAUK
CAUK
WAUK
AUKS
AVA
KAVA
LAVA
TAVA
AVAL
AVAS
AVE
CAVE
FAVE
GAVE
HAVE
LAVE
NAVE
PAVE
RAVE
SAVE
WAVE
AVER
AVES
AWA
PAWA
TAWA
AWAY
AWE
WAWE
AWED
AWES
AWL
BAWL
PAWL
WAWL
YAWL
AWLS
AWN
BAWN
DAWN
FAWN
LAWN
PAWN
RAWN
SAWN
YAWN
AWNS
AWNY
AXE
AXED
AXEL
AXES
AYE
BAYE
AYES

AYS
BAYS
CAYS
DAYS
FAYS
GAYS
HAYS
JAYS
KAYS
LAYS
MAYS
NAYS
PAYS
RAYS
SAYS
TAYS
WAYS
AYU
AYUS
BAA
BAAS
BAD
BADE
BADS
BAG
BAGS
BAH
BAHT
BAM
BAMS
BAN
BANC
BAND
BANE
BANG
BANI
BANK
BANS
BANT
BAP
BAPS
BAPU
BAR
BARB
BARD
BARE
BARF
BARK
BARM
BARN
BARP
BARS
BAS
ABAS
OBAS
BASE
BASH
BASK
BASS
BAST
BAT
BATE
BATH
BATS
BATT
BAY
BAYE
BAYS
BAYT
BED

ABED
BEDE
BEDS
BEE
BEEF
BEEN
BEEP
BEER
BEES
BEET
BEG
BEGO
BEGS
BEL
BELL
BELS
BELT
BEN
BEND
BENE
BENI
BENJ
BENS
BENT
BET
ABET
YBET
BETA
BETE
BETH
BETS
BEY
OBEY
BEYS
BEZ
BIB
BIBS
BID
ABID
BIDE
BIDS
BIG
BIGA
BIGG
BIGS
BIN
BIND
BINE
BING
BINK
BINS
BINT
BIO
BIOG
BIOS
BIS
IBIS
OBIS
BISE
BISH
BISK
BIT
OBIT
BITE
BITO
BITS
BITT
BIZ
BOA
BOAK

BOAR
BOAS
BOAT
BOB
BOBA
BOBS
BOD
BODE
BODS
BODY
BOG
BOGS
BOGY
BOH
BOHS
BOK
BOKE
BOKO
BOKS
BON
EBON
BONA
BOND
BONE
BONG
BONK
BONY
BOO
BOOB
BOOH
BOOK
BOOL
BOOM
BOON
BOOR
BOOS
BOOT
BOP
BOPS
BOR
BORA
BORD
BORE
BORN
BORS
BORT
BOS
OBOS
BOSH
BOSK
BOSS
BOT
BOTH
BOTS
BOTT
BOW
BOWL
BOWR
BOWS
BOX
BOXY
BOY
BOYG
BOYO
BOYS
BRA
BRAD
BRAE
BRAG
BRAN

BRAS
BRAT
BRAW
BRAY
BRO
BROD
BROG
BROO
BROS
BROW
BUB
BUBA
BUBO
BUBS
BUD
BUDO
BUDS
BUG
BUGS
BUM
BUMF
BUMP
BUMS
BUN
BUNA
BUND
BUNG
BUNK
BUNS
BUNT
BUR
BURD
BURG
BURK
BURL
BURN
BURP
BURR
BURS
BURY
BUS
BUSH
BUSK
BUSS
BUST
BUSY
BUT
ABUT
BUTE
BUTS
BUTT
BUY
BUYS
BYE
ABYE
BYES
BYS
CAB
SCAB
CABA
CABS
CAD
ECAD
SCAD
CADE
CADI
CADS
CAM
SCAM
CAME

CAMP
CAMS
CAN
SCAN
CANE
CANG
CANN
CANS
CANT
CANY
CAP
CAPA
CAPE
CAPI
CAPO
CAPS
CAR
SCAR
CARB
CARD
CARE
CARK
CARL
CARP
CARR
CARS
CART
CAT
SCAT
CATE
CATS
CAW
SCAW
CAWK
CAWS
CAY
CAYS
CEE
CEES
CEL
CELL
CELS
CELT
CEP
CEPS
CHA
CHAD
CHAI
CHAL
CHAM
CHAP
CHAR
CHAS
CHAT
CHAW
CHAY
CHE
ACHE
ECHE
OCHE
CHEF
CHER
CHEW
CHEZ
CHI
CHIC
CHID
CHIK
CHIN
CHIP

CHIS
CHIT
CHIV
CHIZ
CID
ACID
CIDS
CIG
CIGS
CIT
CITE
CITO
CITS
CITY
CLY
COB
COBB
COBS
COD
ECOD
CODA
CODE
CODS
COG
SCOG
COGS
COL
COLA
COLD
COLE
COLL
COLS
COLT
CON
ICON
COND
CONE
CONK
CONN
CONS
CONY
COO
COOF
COOK
COOL
COOM
COON
COOP
COOS
COOT
COP
SCOP
COPE
COPS
COPY
COR
CORD
CORE
CORF
CORK
CORM
CORN
CORS
CORY
COS
COSE
COSH
COSS
COST
COSY

COT
SCOT
COTE
COTH
COTS
COTT
COW
SCOW
COWL
COWP
COWS
COX
COXA
COXY
COY
COZ
COZE
COZY
CRU
ECRU
CRUD
CRUS
CRUX
CRY
SCRY
CUB
CUBE
CUBS
CUD
SCUD
CUDS
CUE
CUED
CUES
CUM
SCUM
CUP
SCUP
CUPS
CUR
SCUR
CURB
CURD
CURE
CURL
CURN
CURR
CURS
CURT
CUT
SCUT
CUTE
CUTS
CUZ
CWM
CWMS
DAB
DABS
DAD
DADO
DADS
DAE
DAES
DAG
DAGO
DAGS
DAH
DAHL
DAHS
DAK

DAKS
DAL
ODAL
UDAL
DALE
DALI
DALS
DALT
DAM
DAME
DAMN
DAMP
DAMS
DAN
DANG
DANK
DANS
DANT
DAP
DAPS
DAS
ODAS
DASH
DAW
ADAW
DAWD
DAWK
DAWN
DAWS
DAWT
DAY
DAYS
DEB
DEBS
DEBT
DEE
IDEE
DEED
DEEK
DEEM
DEEN
DEEP
DEER
DEES
DEEV
DEF
DEFT
DEFY
DEI
DEID
DEIL
DEL
DELE
DELF
DELI
DELL
DELS
DELT
DEN
DENE
DENS
DENT
DENY
DEW
DEWS
DEWY
DEY
DEYS
DIB
DIBS

DID
DIDO
DIE
DIEB
DIED
DIES
DIET
DIG
DIGS
DIM
DIME
DIMS
DIN
DINE
DING
DINK
DINS
DINT
DIP
DIPS
DIT
ADIT
EDIT
DITA
DITE
DITS
DITT
DIV
DIVA
DIVE
DIVI
DIVS
DOB
DOBS
DOC
DOCK
DOCS
DOD
DODO
DODS
DOE
DOEK
DOEN
DOER
DOES
DOG
DOGE
DOGS
DOGY
DOH
DOHS
DON
DONA
DONE
DONG
DONS
DOO
DOOB
DOOK
DOOL
DOOM
DOOR
DOOS
DOP
DOPA
DOPE
DOPS
DOPY
DOR
ODOR

DORK
DORM
DORP
DORR
DORS
DORT
DORY
DOS
ADOS
UDOS
DOSE
DOSH
DOSS
DOST
DOT
DOTE
DOTH
DOTS
DOTY
DOW
DOWD
DOWF
DOWL
DOWN
DOWP
DOWS
DOWT
DRY
ADRY
DSO
ODSO
DSOS
DUB
DUBS
DUD
DUDE
DUDS
DUE
DUED
DUEL
DUES
DUET
DUG
DUGS
DUN
DUNE
DUNG
DUNK
DUNS
DUNT
DUO
DUOS
DUP
DUPE
DUPS
DUX
DYE
DYED
DYER
DYES
DZO
DZOS
EAN
BEAN
DEAN
GEAN
JEAN
LEAN
MEAN
PEAN

REAN
SEAN
WEAN
YEAN
EANS
EAR
BEAR
DEAR
FEAR
GEAR
HEAR
LEAR
NEAR
PEAR
REAR
SEAR
TEAR
WEAR
YEAR
EARD
EARL
EARN
EARS
EAS
CEAS
KEAS
LEAS
PEAS
SEAS
TEAS
YEAS
ZEAS
EASE
EAST
EASY
EAT
BEAT
FEAT
GEAT
HEAT
JEAT
LEAT
MEAT
NEAT
PEAT
SEAT
TEAT
EATH
EATS
EAU
BEAU
EAUS
EAUX
EBB
EBBS
ECH
EECH
HECH
LECH
PECH
TECH
YECH
ECHE
ECHO
ECHT
ECO
DECO
SECO
ECOD
ECU

ECUS
EDH
EDHS
EEK
DEEK
GEEK
KEEK
LEEK
MEEK
PEEK
REEK
SEEK
WEEK
EEL
FEEL
HEEL
JEEL
KEEL
PEEL
REEL
SEEL
TEEL
WEEL
EELS
EELY
EEN
BEEN
DEEN
KEEN
PEEN
REEN
SEEN
TEEN
WEEN
EFF
JEFF
TEFF
EFFS
EFS
KEFS
NEFS
REFS
TEFS
EFT
DEFT
HEFT
LEFT
REFT
WEFT
EFTS
EGG
TEGG
YEGG
EGGS
EGGY
EGO
BEGO
REGO
SEGO
EGOS
EHS
REHS
EIK
REIK
SEIK
EIKS
EKE
LEKE
PEKE
REKE

EKED
EKES
ELD
GELD
HELD
MELD
SELD
TELD
VELD
WELD
YELD
ELDS
ELF
DELF
PELF
SELF
ELFS
ELK
WELK
YELK
ELKS
ELL
BELL
CELL
DELL
FELL
HELL
JELL
KELL
MELL
PELL
SELL
TELL
VELL
WELL
YELL
ELLS
ELM
HELM
YELM
ELMS
ELMY
ELS
BELS
CELS
DELS
EELS
GELS
MELS
SELS
TELS
ZELS
ELSE
ELT
BELT
CELT
DELT
FELT
GELT
KELT
MELT
PELT
TELT
WELT
YELT
ELTS
EME
DEME
FEME
HEME

LEME
SEME
TEME
EMES
EMEU
EMS
GEMS
HEMS
REMS
TEMS
WEMS
EMU
EMUS
END
BEND
FEND
HEND
LEND
MEND
PEND
REND
SEND
TEND
VEND
WEND
ENDS
ENE
BENE
DENE
GENE
MENE
NENE
PENE
TENE
ENES
ENEW
ENG
LENG
MENG
ENGS
ENS
BENS
CENS
DENS
FENS
GENS
HENS
KENS
LENS
PENS
RENS
SENS
TENS
WENS
YENS
EON
AEON
NEON
PEON
EONS
ERA
SERA
ERAS
ERE
BERE
CERE
DERE
FERE
GERE
HERE

LERE
MERE
PERE
SERE
WERE
ERED
ERES
ERF
KERF
SERF
TERF
ERG
BERG
ERGO
ERGS
ERK
BERK
JERK
MERK
NERK
PERK
SERK
YERK
ERKS
ERN
DERN
FERN
HERN
KERN
PERN
TERN
ERNE
ERNS
ERR
SERR
ERRS
ERS
HERS
VERS
ERST
ESS
CESS
FESS
JESS
LESS
MESS
NESS
SESS
ESSE
EST
BEST
FEST
GEST
HEST
JEST
KEST
LEST
NEST
PEST
REST
TEST
VEST
WEST
YEST
ZEST
ESTS
ETA
BETA
FETA
GETA

KETA
SETA
WETA
ZETA
ETAS
ETAT
ETH
BETH
ETHE
ETHS
EUK
NEUK
YEUK
EUKS
EVE
LEVE
MEVE
NEVE
YEVE
EVEN
EVER
EVES
EVET
EWE
EWER
EWES
EWK
EWKS
EWT
NEWT
EWTS
EYE
EYED
EYES
FAB
FAD
FADE
FADO
FADS
FADY
FAG
FAGS
FAH
FAHS
FAN
FAND
FANE
FANG
FANK
FANS
FAP
FAR
AFAR
FARD
FARE
FARL
FARM
FARO
FARS
FART
FAS
FASH
FAST
FAT
FATE
FATS
FAW
FAWN
FAWS
FAX

FAY
OFAY
FAYS
FED
FEDS
FEE
FEED
FEEL
FEER
FEES
FEET
FEN
FEND
FENI
FENS
FENT
FET
FETA
FETE
FETS
FETT
FEU
FEUD
FEUS
FEW
FEY
FEYS
FEZ
FIB
FIBS
FID
FIDS
FIE
FIEF
FIG
FIGO
FIGS
FIL
FILE
FILL
FILM
FILO
FILS
FIN
FIND
FINE
FINI
FINK
FINO
FINS
FIR
FIRE
FIRK
FIRM
FIRN
FIRS
FIT
FITS
FITT
FIX
FIZ
FIZZ
FLU
FLUB
FLUE
FLUS
FLUX
FLY
FOB
FOBS
FOE
FOEN
FOES
FOG
FOGS
FOGY
FOH
FOHN
FOHS
FON
FOND
FONE
FONS
FONT
FOP
FOPS
FOR
FORA
FORB
FORD
FORE
FORK
FORM
FORT
FOU
FOUD
FOUL
FOUR
FOUS
FOX
FOXY
FOY
FOYS
FRA
FRAB
FRAE
FRAG
FRAP
FRAS
FRAU
FRAY
FRO
AFRO
FROG
FROM
FROW
FRY
FUB
FUBS
FUD
FUDS
FUG
FUGS
FUM
FUME
FUMS
FUMY
FUN
FUND
FUNG
FUNK
FUNS
FUR
FURL
FURR
FURS
FURY
GAB
GABS
GABY
GAD
EGAD
IGAD
GADE
GADI
GADS
GAE
GAED
GAES
GAG
GAGA
GAGE
GAGS
GAL
EGAL
GALA
GALE
GALL
GALS
GAM
OGAM
GAMB
GAME
GAMP
GAMS
GAMY
GAN
GANE
GANG
GANT
GAP
GAPE
GAPO
GAPS
GAR
AGAR
GARB
GARE
GARS
GART
GAS
AGAS
GASH
GASP
GAST
GAT
GATE
GATH
GATS
GAU
GAUD
GAUM
GAUN
GAUP
GAUR
GAUS
GAY
GAYS
GED
AGED
GEDS
GEE
AGEE
OGEE
GEED
GEEK
GEEP
GEES
GEL
GELD
GELS
GELT
GEM
GEMS
GEN
AGEN
GENA
GENE
GENS
GENT
GENU
GEO
GEOS
GET
GETA
GETS
GEY
GHI
GHIS
GIB
GIBE
GIBS
GID
GIDS
GIE
GIED
GIEN
GIES
GIF
GIFT
GIG
GIGA
GIGS
GIN
AGIN
GING
GINK
GINN
GINS
GIO
AGIO
GIOS
GIP
GIPS
GIS
EGIS
GISM
GIST
GIT
GITE
GITS
GJU
GJUS
GNU
GNUS
GOA
GOAD
GOAF
GOAL
GOAS
GOAT
GOB
GOBO
GOBS
GOBY
GOD
GODS
GOE
YGOE
GOEL
GOER
GOES
GOEY
GON
AGON
GONE
GONG
GONK
GONS
GOO
GOOD
GOOF
GOOK
GOOL
GOON
GOOP
GOOR
GOOS
GOS
EGOS
GOSH
GOT
GOV
GOVS
GOY
GOYS
GUB
GUBS
GUE
AGUE
GUES
GUM
GUMP
GUMS
GUN
GUNK
GUNS
GUP
GUPS
GUR
GURL
GURN
GURS
GURU
GUS
GUSH
GUST
GUT
GUTS
GUV
GUVS
GUY
GUYS
GYM
GYMP
GYMS
GYP
GYPS
HAD
CHAD
SHAD
HADE
HADJ
HADS
HAE
THAE
HAEM
HAET
HAG
SHAG
HAGG
HAGS
HAH
SHAH
HAJ
HAJI
HAJJ
HAM
CHAM
SHAM
WHAM
HAME
HAMS
HAN
KHAN
SHAN
THAN
HAND
HANG
HANK
HAP
CHAP
WHAP
HAPS
HAS
CHAS
HASH
HASK
HASP
HAST
HAT
CHAT
GHAT
KHAT
SHAT
THAT
WHAT
HATE
HATH
HATS
HAW
CHAW
SHAW
THAW
HAWK
HAWM
HAWS
HAY
CHAY
SHAY
HAYS
HEM
AHEM
THEM
HEME
HEMP
HEMS
HEN
THEN
WHEN
HEND
HENS
HENT
HEP
HEPS
HEPT
HER
CHER
HERB
HERD
HERE
HERL
HERM
HERN
HERO
HERS
HERY
HES
SHES
HESP
HEST
HET
SHET
WHET
HETE
HETS
HEW
CHEW
PHEW
SHEW
THEW
WHEW
HEWN
HEWS
HEX
HEY
THEY
WHEY
HEYS
HIC
CHIC
HICK
HID
CHID
WHID
HIDE
HIE
HIED
HIES
HIM
SHIM
WHIM
HIN
CHIN
SHIN
THIN
WHIN
HIND
HING
HINS
HINT
HIP
CHIP
SHIP
WHIP
HIPS
HIPT
HIS
CHIS
GHIS
PHIS
THIS
HISH
HISN
HISS
HIST
HIT
CHIT
SHIT
WHIT
HITS
HOA
WHOA
HOAR
HOAS
HOAX
HOB
HOBO
HOBS
HOC
CHOC
HOCK
HOD
SHOD
HODS
HOE
SHOE
HOED
HOER
HOES
HOG
SHOG
HOGG
HOGH
HOGS
HOH
PHOH
HOHS
HOI
HOIK
HON
CHON
PHON
THON
HOND
HONE
HONG
HONK
HONS
HOO
SHOO
HOOD
HOOF
HOOK
HOON
HOOP
HOOT
HOP
CHOP
SHOP
WHOP
HOPE
HOPS
HOS
MHOS
OHOS
PHOS
RHOS
ZHOS
HOSE
HOSS
HOST
HOT
PHOT
SHOT
WHOT
HOTE
HOTS
HOW
CHOW
DHOW
SHOW
WHOW
HOWE
HOWF
HOWK
HOWL
HOWS
HOX
HOY
AHOY
HOYA
HOYS
HUB
CHUB
HUBS
HUE
HUED
HUER
HUES
HUG
CHUG
THUG
HUGE
HUGS
HUGY
HUH
HUI
HUIA
HUIS
HUM
CHUM
HUMA
HUMF
HUMP
HUMS
HUP
HUPS
HUT
CHUT
PHUT
SHUT
HUTS
HYE
HYED
HYEN
HYES
HYP
HYPE
HYPO
HYPS
ICE
BICE
DICE
LICE
MICE
NICE
PICE
RICE
SICE
TICE
VICE
WICE
ICED
ICER
ICES
ICH
DICH
LICH
RICH
SICH
TICH
WICH
ICY
RICY
IDE
AIDE
BIDE
HIDE
NIDE
RIDE
SIDE
TIDE
VIDE
WIDE
IDEA
IDEE
IDEM
IDES
IDS
AIDS
BIDS
CIDS
FIDS
GIDS
KIDS
LIDS
MIDS
NIDS
RIDS
TIDS
VIDS
IFF
BIFF
JIFF
MIFF
NIFF
RIFF
TIFF
ZIFF
IFFY
IFS
KIFS
ILK
BILK
MILK
SILK
ILKA
ILKS
ILL
BILL
CILL
DILL
FILL
GILL
HILL
JILL
KILL
LILL
MILL
NILL
PILL
RILL
SILL
TILL
VILL
WILL
YILL
ILLS
ILLY

IMP
GIMP
JIMP
LIMP
PIMP
SIMP
WIMP
IMPI
IMPS
INK
BINK
DINK
FINK
GINK
JINK
KINK
LINK
MINK
OINK
PINK
RINK
SINK
TINK
WINK
INKS
INKY
INN
GINN
JINN
LINN
WINN
INNS
INS
BINS
DINS
FINS
GINS
HINS
KINS
LINS
PINS
RINS
SINS
TINS
VINS
WINS
YINS
ION
CION
LION
PION
IONS
IOS
BIOS
GIOS
IRE
CIRE
DIRE
FIRE
HIRE
LIRE
MIRE
SIRE
TIRE
VIRE
WIRE
IRES
IRK
BIRK
DIRK

FIRK
KIRK
LIRK
MIRK
YIRK
IRKS
ISH
BISH
DISH
FISH
HISH
KISH
PISH
WISH
ISM
GISM
JISM
ISMS
ISO
MISO
ISOS
ITA
DITA
PITA
VITA
ITAS
ITS
AITS
BITS
CITS
DITS
FITS
GITS
HITS
KITS
NITS
PITS
RITS
SITS
TITS
WITS
ZITS
IVY
JAB
JABS
JAG
JAGS
JAK
JAKE
JAKS
JAM
JAMB
JAMS
JAP
JAPE
JAPS
JAR
AJAR
JARK
JARL
JARS
JAW
JAWS
JAY
JAYS
JEE
AJEE
JEED
JEEL
JEER

JEES
JET
JETE
JETS
JEU
JEUX
JEW
JEWS
JIB
JIBE
JIBS
JIG
JIGS
JIZ
JIZZ
JOB
JOBE
JOBS
JOE
JOES
JOEY
JOG
JOGS
JOR
JORS
JOT
JOTA
JOTS
JOW
JOWL
JOWS
JOY
JOYS
JUD
JUDO
JUDS
JUDY
JUG
JUGA
JUGS
JUS
GJUS
JUST
JUT
JUTE
JUTS
KAE
KAED
KAES
KAI
KAID
KAIE
KAIF
KAIL
KAIM
KAIN
KAIS
KAM
KAMA
KAME
KAMI
KAS
SKAS
KAT
IKAT
SKAT
KATA
KATI
KATS
KAW

SKAW
KAWS
KAY
OKAY
KAYO
KAYS
KEA
KEAS
KEB
KEBS
KED
AKED
EKED
KEDS
KEF
KEFS
KEG
SKEG
KEGS
KEN
KENO
KENS
KENT
KEP
SKEP
KEPI
KEPS
KEPT
KET
KETA
KETS
KEX
KEY
KEYS
KID
SKID
KIDS
KIF
KIFS
KIN
AKIN
SKIN
KINA
KIND
KINE
KING
KINK
KINO
KINS
KIP
SKIP
KIPE
KIPP
KIPS
KIR
KIRK
KIRN
KIRS
KIT
SKIT
KITE
KITH
KITS
KOA
KOAN
KOAS
KOB
KOBS
KON
IKON

KOND
KONK
KONS
KOP
KOPH
KOPS
KOS
KOSS
KOW
KOWS
KYE
KYU
KYUS
LAB
BLAB
FLAB
SLAB
LABS
LAC
LACE
LACK
LACS
LACY
LAD
BLAD
CLAD
GLAD
LADE
LADS
LADY
LAG
BLAG
CLAG
FLAG
SLAG
LAGS
LAH
BLAH
LAHS
LAM
CLAM
FLAM
GLAM
SLAM
LAMA
LAMB
LAME
LAMP
LAMS
LAP
ALAP
CLAP
FLAP
PLAP
SLAP
LAPS
LAR
ALAR
LARD
LARE
LARK
LARN
LAS
ALAS
LASE
LASH
LASS
LAST
LAT
BLAT

CLAT
FLAT
PLAT
SLAT
LATE
LATH
LATS
LAV
LAVA
LAVE
LAVS
LAW
CLAW
FLAW
SLAW
LAWK
LAWN
LAWS
LAX
FLAX
LAY
ALAY
BLAY
CLAY
FLAY
PLAY
SLAY
LAYS
LEA
FLEA
ILEA
PLEA
LEAD
LEAF
LEAK
LEAL
LEAM
LEAN
LEAP
LEAR
LEAS
LEAT
LED
BLED
FLED
GLED
PLED
SLED
LEE
ALEE
BLEE
FLEE
GLEE
SLEE
LEED
LEEK
LEEP
LEER
LEES
LEET
LEG
CLEG
FLEG
GLEG
LEGS
LEI
GLEI
VLEI
LEIR
LEIS

LEK
LEKE
LEKS
LEP
LEPS
LES
ALES
ULES
LESS
LEST
LET
BLET
LETS
LEU
LEV
LEVA
LEVE
LEVY
LEW
ALEW
BLEW
CLEW
FLEW
SLEW
LEWD
LEX
FLEX
ILEX
ULEX
LEY
BLEY
FLEY
GLEY
SLEY
LEYS
LEZ
LEZZ
LIB
GLIB
LIBS
LID
GLID
OLID
SLID
LIDO
LIDS
LIE
PLIE
LIED
LIEF
LIEN
LIER
LIES
LIEU
LIG
LIGS
LIN
BLIN
LIND
LINE
LING
LINK
LINN
LINO
LINS
LINT
LINY
LIP
BLIP
CLIP

FLIP
SLIP
LIPS
LIS
LISK
LISP
LIST
LIT
ALIT
FLIT
GLIT
SLIT
LITE
LITH
LOB
BLOB
GLOB
SLOB
LOBE
LOBI
LOBO
LOBS
LOG
CLOG
FLOG
SLOG
LOGE
LOGO
LOGS
LOGY
LOO
LOOF
LOOK
LOOM
LOON
LOOP
LOOR
LOOS
LOOT
LOP
CLOP
FLOP
GLOP
PLOP
SLOP
LOPE
LOPS
LOR
FLOR
LORD
LORE
LORN
LORY
LOS
LOSE
LOSH
LOSS
LOST
LOT
BLOT
CLOT
PLOT
SLOT
LOTA
LOTE
LOTH
LOTO
LOTS
LOW
ALOW

BLOW
CLOW
FLOW
GLOW
PLOW
SLOW
LOWE
LOWN
LOWS
LOWT
LOX
LOY
CLOY
PLOY
LOYS
LUD
LUDO
LUDS
LUG
GLUG
PLUG
SLUG
LUGE
LUGS
LUM
ALUM
GLUM
PLUM
SLUM
LUMP
LUMS
LUR
BLUR
SLUR
LURE
LURK
LURS
LUV
LUVS
LUX
FLUX
LUXE
LUZ
LYE
LYES
LYM
LYME
LYMS
MAA
MAAR
MAAS
MAC
MACE
MACK
MACS
MAD
MADE
MADS
MAE
MAG
MAGE
MAGG
MAGI
MAGS
MAK
MAKE
MAKO
MAKS
MAL
MALE

MALI
MALL
MALM
MALS
MALT
MAM
IMAM
MAMA
MAMS
MAN
MANA
MAND
MANE
MANG
MANI
MANO
MANS
MANY
MAP
MAPS
MAR
MARA
MARC
MARD
MARE
MARG
MARK
MARL
MARM
MARS
MART
MARY
MAS
MASA
MASE
MASH
MASK
MASS
MAST
MASU
MAT
MATE
MATH
MATS
MATT
MATY
MAW
MAWK
MAWR
MAWS
MAX
MAXI
MAY
MAYA
MAYS
MEG
MEGA
MEGS
MEL
MELA
MELD
MELL
MELS
MELT
MEN
AMEN
OMEN
MEND
MENE
MENG

MENT
MENU
MES
EMES
MESA
MESE
MESH
MESS
MET
METE
METS
MEU
EMEU
MEUS
MEW
SMEW
MEWL
MEWS
MHO
MHOS
MID
AMID
MIDI
MIDS
MIL
MILD
MILE
MILK
MILL
MILO
MILS
MILT
MIM
MIME
MIR
AMIR
EMIR
SMIR
MIRE
MIRI
MIRK
MIRS
MIRV
MIRY
MIS
AMIS
MISE
MISO
MISS
MIST
MIX
MIXT
MIXY
MIZ
MIZZ
MNA
MNAS
MOA
MOAN
MOAS
MOAT
MOB
MOBS
MOD
MODE
MODI
MODS
MOE
MOES
MOG

SMOG
MOGS
MOI
MOIL
MOIT
MOM
MOME
MOMS
MON
MONA
MONG
MONK
MONO
MONY
MOO
MOOD
MOOI
MOOK
MOOL
MOON
MOOP
MOOR
MOOS
MOOT
MOP
MOPE
MOPS
MOPY
MOR
MORA
MORE
MORN
MORS
MORT
MOT
MOTE
MOTH
MOTS
MOTT
MOTU
MOU
MOUE
MOUP
MOUS
MOW
MOWA
MOWN
MOWS
MOY
MOYA
MOYL
MOYS
MOZ
MOZE
MOZZ
MUD
MUDS
MUG
SMUG
MUGS
MUM
MUMM
MUMP
MUMS
MUN
MUNT
MUS
EMUS
MUSE
MUSH

MUSK
MUSO
MUSS
MUST
MUX
NAB
SNAB
NABK
NABS
NAE
NAG
KNAG
SNAG
NAGA
NAGS
NAM
NAME
NAMS
NAN
ANAN
NANA
NANS
NAP
KNAP
SNAP
NAPA
NAPE
NAPS
NAS
ANAS
MNAS
NAT
GNAT
NATS
NAY
NAYS
NEB
SNEB
NEBS
NED
SNED
NEDS
NEE
KNEE
SNEE
NEED
NEEM
NEEP
NEF
NEFS
NEK
NEKS
NEP
NEPS
NET
NETE
NETS
NETT
NEW
ANEW
ENEW
KNEW
NEWS
NEWT
NIB
SNIB
NIBS
NID
NIDE
NIDI

NIDS
NIE
NIED
NIEF
NIES
NIL
ANIL
NILL
NILS
NIM
NIMB
NIMS
NIP
SNIP
NIPA
NIPS
NIS
ANIS
UNIS
NISI
NIT
KNIT
UNIT
NITE
NITS
NIX
NIXY
NOB
KNOB
SNOB
NOBS
NOD
SNOD
NODE
NODI
NODS
NOG
SNOG
NOGG
NOGS
NOH
NOM
NOMA
NOME
NOMS
NON
ANON
NONE
NONG
NOR
NORI
NORK
NORM
NOS
NOSE
NOSH
NOSY
NOT
KNOT
SNOT
NOTA
NOTE
NOTT
NOW
ANOW
ENOW
KNOW
SNOW
NOWL
NOWN

NOWS
NOWT
NOWY
NOX
NOY
NOYS
NTH
NUB
KNUB
SNUB
NUBS
NUN
NUNS
NUR
KNUR
NURD
NURL
NURR
NURS
NUS
ANUS
GNUS
ONUS
NUT
KNUT
NUTS
NYE
SNYE
NYED
NYES
NYS
OAF
GOAF
LOAF
OAFS
OAK
BOAK
SOAK
OAKS
OAKY
OAR
BOAR
HOAR
ROAR
SOAR
VOAR
OARS
OARY
OAT
BOAT
COAT
DOAT
GOAT
MOAT
OATH
OATS
OBA
BOBA
OBAS
OBI
LOBI
OBIA
OBIS
OBIT
OBO
GOBO
HOBO
LOBO
ZOBO
OBOE

OBOL
OBOS
OBS
BOBS
COBS
DOBS
FOBS
GOBS
HOBS
JOBS
KOBS
LOBS
MOBS
NOBS
ROBS
SOBS
YOBS
OCA
COCA
SOCA
OCAS
OCH
LOCH
MOCH
ROCH
OCHE
ODA
CODA
SODA
ODAL
ODAS
ODD
ODDS
ODE
BODE
CODE
LODE
MODE
NODE
RODE
YODE
ODEA
ODES
ODS
BODS
CODS
DODS
GODS
HODS
MODS
NODS
PODS
RODS
SODS
TODS
ODSO
OES
DOES
FOES
GOES
HOES
JOES
MOES
NOES
ROES
TOES
VOES
WOES
OFF
BOFF

COFF
DOFF
GOFF
KOFF
TOFF
OFFS
OFT
COFT
LOFT
SOFT
TOFT
OHM
OHMS
OHO
COHO
SOHO
TOHO
OHOS
OIK
HOIK
OIKS
OIL
BOIL
COIL
FOIL
MOIL
NOIL
ROIL
SOIL
TOIL
OILS
OILY
OKE
BOKE
COKE
HOKE
JOKE
LOKE
MOKE
POKE
ROKE
SOKE
TOKE
WOKE
YOKE
OKES
OLD
BOLD
COLD
FOLD
GOLD
HOLD
MOLD
SOLD
TOLD
WOLD
YOLD
OLDS
OLDY
OLE
BOLE
COLE
DOLE
GOLE
HOLE
JOLE
MOLE
NOLE
POLE
ROLE

SOLE
TOLE
VOLE
OLEO
OLM
HOLM
OLMS
OMS
COMS
MOMS
NOMS
OOMS
POMS
TOMS
ONE
BONE
CONE
DONE
FONE
GONE
HONE
LONE
NONE
PONE
RONE
SONE
TONE
ZONE
ONER
ONES
ONS
CONS
DONS
EONS
FONS
GONS
HONS
IONS
KONS
OONS
PONS
SONS
TONS
WONS
ONST
OOF
COOF
GOOF
HOOF
LOOF
POOF
ROOF
WOOF
YOOF
OOFS
OOH
BOOH
POOH
OOHS
OOM
BOOM
COOM
DOOM
LOOM
ROOM
SOOM
TOOM
ZOOM
OOMS
OON

BOON
COON
GOON
HOON
LOON
MOON
NOON
POON
ROON
SOON
TOON
WOON
ZOON
OONS
OONT
OOP
COOP
GOOP
HOOP
LOOP
MOOP
NOOP
POOP
ROOP
SOOP
YOOP
OOPS
OOR
BOOR
DOOR
GOOR
LOOR
MOOR
POOR
OOS
BOOS
COOS
DOOS
GOOS
LOOS
MOOS
POOS
ROOS
WOOS
ZOOS
OOSE
OOSY
OPE
COPE
DOPE
HOPE
LOPE
MOPE
NOPE
POPE
ROPE
TOPE
OPED
OPEN
OPES
OPT
OPTS
ORB
FORB
SORB
ORBS
ORBY
ORC
TORC
ORCA

ORCS
ORD
BORD
CORD
FORD
LORD
SORD
WORD
ORDS
ORE
BORE
CORE
FORE
GORE
HORE
KORE
LORE
MORE
PORE
RORE
SORE
TORE
WORE
YORE
ORES
ORF
CORF
ORFE
ORFS
ORS
BORS
CORS
DORS
HORS
JORS
MORS
TORS
VORS
ORT
BORT
DORT
FORT
MORT
PORT
RORT
SORT
TORT
WORT
ORTS
OUK
BOUK
GOUK
JOUK
POUK
SOUK
TOUK
YOUK
ZOUK
OUKS
OUP
COUP
DOUP
LOUP
MOUP
NOUP
ROUP
SOUP
OUPH
OUPS
OUR

COUR
DOUR
FOUR
HOUR
JOUR
LOUR
POUR
SOUR
TOUR
YOUR
OURN
OURS
OUT
BOUT
DOUT
GOUT
HOUT
LOUT
NOUT
POUT
ROUT
SOUT
TOUT
OUTS
OVA
NOVA
OVAL
OWE
HOWE
LOWE
YOWE
OWED
OWER
OWES
OWL
BOWL
COWL
DOWL
FOWL
GOWL
HOWL
JOWL
NOWL
SOWL
YOWL
OWLS
OWLY
OWN
DOWN
GOWN
LOWN
MOWN
NOWN
POWN
SOWN
TOWN
OWNS
OWT
DOWT
LOWT
NOWT
ROWT
TOWT
OWTS
OYE
OYER
OYES
OYEZ
OYS
BOYS

FOYS
GOYS
HOYS
JOYS
LOYS
MOYS
NOYS
SOYS
TOYS
PAD
PADS
PAH
OPAH
PAHS
PAL
OPAL
PALE
PALL
PALM
PALP
PALS
PALY
PAM
PAMS
PAN
SPAN
PAND
PANE
PANG
PANS
PANT
PAP
PAPA
PAPE
PAPS
PAR
SPAR
PARA
PARD
PARE
PARK
PARP
PARR
PARS
PART
PAS
SPAS
UPAS
PASH
PASS
PAST
PAT
SPAT
PATE
PATH
PATS
PAW
SPAW
PAWA
PAWK
PAWL
PAWN
PAWS
PAX
PAY
APAY
SPAY
PAYS
PEA
PEAG

PEAK
PEAL
PEAN
PEAR
PEAS
PEAT
PEC
SPEC
PECH
PECK
PECS
PED
APED
OPED
SPED
PEDS
PEE
EPEE
PEED
PEEK
PEEL
PEEN
PEEP
PEER
PEES
PEG
PEGH
PEGS
PEN
OPEN
PEND
PENE
PENI
PENK
PENS
PENT
PEP
PEPO
PEPS
PER
PERE
PERI
PERK
PERM
PERN
PERT
PERV
PET
SPET
PETS
PEW
SPEW
PEWS
PHI
PHIS
PHIZ
PHO
PHOH
PHON
PHOS
PHOT
PHS
PIA
PIAS
PIC
EPIC
SPIC
PICA
PICE
PICK

PICS
PIE
SPIE
PIED
PIER
PIES
PIET
PIG
PIGS
PIN
SPIN
PINA
PINE
PING
PINK
PINS
PINT
PINY
PIP
PIPA
PIPE
PIPI
PIPS
PIPY
PIR
PIRL
PIRN
PIRS
PIS
PISE
PISH
PISS
PIT
SPIT
PITA
PITH
PITS
PITY
PIU
PIUM
PIX
PIXY
PLY
POA
POAS
POD
APOD
PODS
POH
POI
POIS
POM
POME
POMP
POMS
POO
POOD
POOF
POOH
POOK
POOL
POON
POOP
POOR
POOS
POOT
POP
POPE
POPS
POS

EPOS
POSE
POSH
POSS
POST
POSY
POT
SPOT
POTE
POTS
POTT
POW
POWN
POWS
POX
POXY
POZ
POZZ
PRE
PREE
PREP
PREX
PREY
PRO
PROA
PROB
PROD
PROF
PROG
PROM
PROO
PROP
PROS
PROW
PRY
SPRY
PRYS
PSI
PSIS
PST
PUB
PUBS
PUD
SPUD
PUDS
PUDU
PUG
PUGH
PUGS
PUH
PUN
SPUN
PUNA
PUNK
PUNS
PUNT
PUNY
PUP
PUPA
PUPS
PUR
SPUR
PURE
PURI
PURL
PURR
PURS
PUS
OPUS
PUSH

PUSS
PUT
PUTS
PUTT
PUTZ
PUY
PUYS
PYE
PYES
PYET
PYX
QAT
QATS
QIS
QUA
AQUA
QUAD
QUAG
QUAT
QUAY
RAD
BRAD
DRAD
GRAD
PRAD
TRAD
RADE
RADS
RAG
BRAG
CRAG
DRAG
FRAG
RAGA
RAGE
RAGG
RAGI
RAGS
RAH
RAHS
RAI
RAID
RAIK
RAIL
RAIN
RAIS
RAIT
RAJ
RAJA
RAM
CRAM
DRAM
GRAM
PRAM
TRAM
RAMI
RAMP
RAMS
RAN
BRAN
CRAN
GRAN
RANA
RAND
RANG
RANI
RANK
RANT
RAP
CRAP

DRAP
FRAP
TRAP
WRAP
RAPE
RAPS
RAPT
RAS
BRAS
ERAS
FRAS
RASE
RASH
RASP
RAST
RAT
BRAT
DRAT
GRAT
PRAT
TRAT
RATA
RATE
RATH
RATS
RATU
RAW
BRAW
CRAW
DRAW
RAWN
RAWS
RAX
RAY
BRAY
DRAY
FRAY
GRAY
PRAY
TRAY
RAYS
REC
RECK
RECS
RED
ARED
BRED
CRED
ERED
REDD
REDE
REDO
REDS
REE
BREE
CREE
DREE
FREE
GREE
PREE
TREE
REED
REEF
REEK
REEL
REEN
REES
REF
TREF
REFS

REFT
REH
REHS
REM
REMS
REN
BREN
GREN
WREN
REND
RENS
RENT
RENY
REP
PREP
REPO
REPP
REPS
RES
ARES
ERES
IRES
ORES
TRES
URES
REST
RET
ARET
FRET
TRET
RETE
RETS
REV
REVS
REW
AREW
BREW
CREW
DREW
GREW
TREW
REWS
REX
PREX
REZ
TREZ
RHO
RHOS
RHY
RIA
ARIA
RIAL
RIAS
RIB
CRIB
DRIB
RIBS
RID
ARID
GRID
IRID
RIDE
RIDS
RIG
BRIG
FRIG
GRIG
PRIG
TRIG
RIGG

RIGS
RIM
BRIM
CRIM
GRIM
PRIM
TRIM
RIMA
RIME
RIMS
RIMU
RIMY
RIN
GRIN
TRIN
RIND
RINE
RING
RINK
RINS
RIP
DRIP
GRIP
TRIP
RIPE
RIPP
RIPS
RIPT
RIT
BRIT
CRIT
FRIT
GRIT
WRIT
RITE
RITS
RITT
RIZ
FRIZ
RIZA
ROB
PROB
ROBE
ROBS
ROC
CROC
ROCH
ROCK
ROCS
ROD
BROD
PROD
TROD
RODE
RODS
ROE
ROED
ROES
ROK
ROKE
ROKS
ROKY
ROM
FROM
PROM
ROMA
ROMP
ROO
BROO
PROO

ROOD
ROOF
ROOK
ROOM
ROON
ROOP
ROOS
ROOT
ROT
GROT
TROT
ROTA
ROTE
ROTI
ROTL
ROTS
ROW
AROW
BROW
CROW
DROW
FROW
GROW
PROW
TROW
VROW
ROWS
ROWT
RUB
DRUB
GRUB
RUBE
RUBS
RUBY
RUC
RUCK
RUCS
RUD
CRUD
RUDD
RUDE
RUDS
RUE
GRUE
TRUE
RUED
RUES
RUG
DRUG
TRUG
RUGS
RUM
ARUM
DRUM
GRUM
RUME
RUMP
RUMS
RUN
RUND
RUNE
RUNG
RUNS
RUNT
RUT
BRUT
RUTH
RUTS
RYA
RYAL

RYAS
RYE
TRYE
RYES
SAB
SABS
SAC
SACK
SACS
SAD
SADE
SAE
SAG
SAGA
SAGE
SAGO
SAGS
SAGY
SAI
SAIC
SAID
SAIL
SAIM
SAIN
SAIR
SAIS
SAL
SALE
SALP
SALS
SALT
SAM
SAMA
SAME
SAMP
SAN
SAND
SANE
SANG
SANK
SANS
SANT
SAP
SAPS
SAR
ASAR
KSAR
TSAR
SARD
SARI
SARK
SARS
SAT
SATE
SATI
SAW
SAWN
SAWS
SAX
SAY
SAYS
SAZ
SEA
SEAL
SEAM
SEAN
SEAR
SEAS
SEAT
SEC
SECO
SECS
SECT
SED
USED
SEE
SEED
SEEK
SEEL
SEEM
SEEN
SEEP
SEER
SEES
SEG
SEGO
SEGS
SEI
SEIF
SEIK
SEIL
SEIR
SEIS
SEL
SELD
SELE
SELF
SELL
SELS
SEN
SENA
SEND
SENS
SENT
SET
SETA
SETS
SETT
SEW
SEWN
SEWS
SEX
SEXT
SEXY
SEY
SEYS
SEZ
SHE
SHEA
SHED
SHES
SHET
SHEW
SHY
ASHY
SIB
SIBB
SIBS
SIC
SICE
SICH
SICK
SICS
SIM
SIMA
SIMI
SIMP
SIMS
SIN
SIND
SINE
SING
SINK
SINS
SIP
SIPE
SIPS
SIR
SIRE
SIRI
SIRS
SIS
PSIS
SISS
SIST
SIT
SITE
SITH
SITS
SIX
SKA
SKAG
SKAS
SKAT
SKAW
SKI
SKID
SKIM
SKIN
SKIO
SKIP
SKIS
SKIT
SKY
ESKY
SKYR
SLY
SMA
SNY
SNYE
SOB
SOBS
SOC
SOCA
SOCK
SOCS
SOD
SODA
SODS
SOG
SOGS
SOH
SOHO
SOHS
SOL
SOLA
SOLD
SOLE
SOLI
SOLO
SOLS
SON
SONE
SONG
SONS
SOP
SOPH
SOPS
SOS
DSOS
ISOS
SOSS
SOT
SOTS
SOU
SOUK
SOUL
SOUM
SOUP
SOUR
SOUS
SOUT
SOV
SOVS
SOW
SOWF
SOWL
SOWM
SOWN
SOWP
SOWS
SOX
SOY
SOYA
SOYS
SPA
SPAE
SPAG
SPAN
SPAR
SPAS
SPAT
SPAW
SPAY
SPY
ESPY
STY
STYE
SUB
SUBS
SUD
SUDD
SUDS
SUE
SUED
SUER
SUES
SUET
SUI
SUID
SUIT
SUK
SUKH
SUKS
SUM
SUMO
SUMP
SUMS
SUN
SUNG
SUNK
SUNN
SUNS
SUP
SUPE
SUPS
SUQ
SUQS
SUR
SURA
SURD
SURE
SURF
SUS
SUSS
SWY
SYE
SYED
SYEN
SYES
TAB
STAB
TABI
TABS
TABU
TAD
TADS
TAE
TAED
TAEL
TAES
TAG
STAG
TAGS
TAI
TAIL
TAIS
TAIT
TAJ
TAK
TAKA
TAKE
TAKI
TAKS
TAKY
TAM
TAME
TAMP
TAMS
TAN
TANA
TANE
TANG
TANH
TANK
TANS
TAP
ATAP
STAP
TAPA
TAPE
TAPS
TAPU
TAR
STAR
TARA
TARE
TARN
TARO
TARP
TARS
TART
TAT
ETAT
TATE
TATH
TATS
TATT
TATU
TAU
TAUS
TAUT
TAW
STAW
TAWA
TAWS
TAWT
TAX
TAXA
TAXI
TAY
STAY
TAYS
TEA
TEAD
TEAK
TEAL
TEAM
TEAR
TEAS
TEAT
TED
STED
TEDS
TEDY
TEE
TEED
TEEL
TEEM
TEEN
TEER
TEES
TEF
TEFF
TEFS
TEG
TEGG
TEGS
TEGU
TEL
TELA
TELD
TELL
TELS
TELT
TEN
ETEN
STEN
TEND
TENE
TENS
TENT
TES
UTES
TEST
TEW
STEW
TEWS
THE
ETHE
THEE
THEM
THEN
THEW
THEY
THO
THON
THOU
THY
TIC
OTIC
TICE
TICH
TICK
TICS
TID
TIDE
TIDS
TIDY
TIE
STIE
TIED
TIER
TIES
TIG
TIGE
TIGS
TIL
TILE
TILL
TILS
TILT
TIN
TIND
TINE
TING
TINK
TINS
TINT
TINY
TIP
TIPI
TIPS
TIPT
TIS
UTIS
TIT
TITE
TITI
TITS
TOC
ATOC
TOCK
TOCO
TOCS
TOD
TODS
TODY
TOE
TOEA
TOED
TOES
TOEY
TOG
TOGA
TOGE
TOGS
TOM
ATOM
TOMB
TOME
TOMS
TON
TONE
TONG
TONK
TONS
TONY
TOO
TOOK
TOOL
TOOM
TOON
TOOT
TOP
ATOP
STOP
TOPE
TOPI
TOPS
TOR
TORC
TORE
TORI
TORN
TORR
TORS
TORT
TOT
STOT
TOTE
TOTS
TOW
STOW
TOWN
TOWS
TOWT
TOWY
TOY
TOYS
TRY
TRYE
TRYP
TUB
STUB
TUBA
TUBE
TUBS
TUG
TUGS
TUI
ETUI
TUIS
TUM
STUM
TUMP
TUMS
TUN
STUN
TUNA
TUND
TUNE
TUNS
TUNY
TUP
TUPS
TUT
TUTS
TUTU
TUX
TWA
TWAE
TWAL
TWAS
TWAT
TWAY
TWO
TWOS
TWP
TYE
STYE
TYED
TYES
TYG
TYGS
UDO
BUDO
JUDO
LUDO
UDOS
UDS
BUDS
CUDS
DUDS
FUDS
JUDS
LUDS
MUDS
PUDS
RUDS
SUDS
WUDS
UEY
QUEY
UEYS
UFO
BUFO
UFOS
UGH
EUGH
PUGH
UGHS
UGS
BUGS
DUGS
FUGS
HUGS
JUGS
LUGS
MUGS
PUGS
RUGS
TUGS
VUGS
YUGS
UKE
BUKE
DUKE
JUKE
LUKE
NUKE
PUKE
YUKE
UKES
ULE
DULE
GULE
HULE
MULE
PULE
RULE
TULE
YULE
ULES
ULEX
UNI
UNIS
UNIT
UNS
BUNS
DUNS
FUNS
GUNS
NUNS
PUNS
RUNS
SUNS
TUNS
UPS
CUPS
DUPS
GUPS
HUPS
OUPS
PUPS
SUPS
TUPS
YUPS
UPSY
URD
BURD
CURD
NURD
SURD
TURD
URDE
URDS
URDY
URE
CURE
DURE
IURE
JURE
LURE
MURE
PURE
SURE
UREA
URES
URN
BURN
CURN
DURN
GURN
OURN
TURN
URNS
USE
FUSE
MUSE
RUSE
USED
USER
USES
UTE
BUTE
CUTE
JUTE
LUTE
MUTE
UTES
UTS
BUTS
CUTS
GUTS
HUTS
JUTS
NUTS
OUTS
PUTS

RUTS
TUTS
UTU
TUTU
UTUS
UVA
UVAE
UVAS
VAC
VACS
VAE
UVAE
VAES
VAN
VANE
VANG
VANS
VANT
VAS
AVAS
UVAS
VASA
VASE
VAST
VAT
VATS
VATU
VAU
VAUS
VAUT
VEE
VEEP
VEER
VEES
VEG
VEGA
VET
EVET
VETO
VETS

VEX
VEXT
VIA
VIAE
VIAL
VIAS
VID
AVID
VIDE
VIDS
VIE
VIED
VIER
VIES
VIEW
VIM
VIMS
VIN
VINA
VINE
VINO
VINS
VINT
VINY
VIS
VISA
VISE
VLY
VOE
EVOE
VOES
VOL
VOLA
VOLE
VOLK
VOLS
VOLT
VOR
VORS
VOW

AVOW
VOWS
VOX
VUG
VUGS
VUM
OVUM
VUMS
WAD
SWAD
WADD
WADE
WADI
WADS
WADT
WADY
WAE
TWAE
WAES
WAG
SWAG
WAGE
WAGS
WAN
SWAN
WAND
WANE
WANG
WANK
WANS
WANT
WANY
WAP
SWAP
WAPS
WAR
WARD
WARE
WARK
WARM

WARN
WARP
WARS
WART
WARY
WAS
TWAS
WASE
WASH
WASM
WASP
WAST
WAT
SWAT
TWAT
WATE
WATS
WATT
WAW
WAWE
WAWL
WAWS
WAX
WAXY
WAY
AWAY
SWAY
TWAY
WAYS
WEB
WEBS
WED
AWED
OWED
WEDS
WEE
SWEE
TWEE
WEED
WEEK

WEEL
WEEM
WEEN
WEEP
WEER
WEES
WEET
WEM
WEMB
WEMS
WEN
WEND
WENS
WENT
WET
WETA
WETS
WEX
WEXE
WEY
SWEY
WEYS
WHA
WHAM
WHAP
WHAT
WHO
WHOA
WHOM
WHOP
WHOT
WHOW
WHY
WIG
SWIG
TWIG
WIGS
WIN
TWIN
WIND

WINE
WING
WINK
WINN
WINO
WINS
WINY
WIS
IWIS
YWIS
WISE
WISH
WISP
WIST
WIT
TWIT
WITE
WITH
WITS
WOE
WOES
WOG
WOGS
WOK
WOKE
WOKS
WON
WONS
WONT
WOO
WOOD
WOOF
WOOL
WOON
WOOS
WOOT
WOP
SWOP
WOPS
WOS

TWOS
WOST
WOT
SWOT
WOTS
WOW
WOWF
WOWS
WOX
WRY
AWRY
WUD
WUDS
WUS
WUSS
WYE
WYES
WYN
WYND
WYNN
WYNS
XIS
AXIS
YAH
AYAH
YAHS
YAK
YAKS
YAM
LYAM
YAMS
YAP
YAPP
YAPS
YAW
YAWL
YAWN
YAWP
YAWS
YAWY

YEA
YEAD
YEAH
YEAN
YEAR
YEAS
YEN
HYEN
SYEN
YENS
YEP
YEPS
YES
AYES
BYES
DYES
EYES
HYES
LYES
NYES
OYES
PYES
RYES
SYES
TYES
WYES
YESK
YEST
YET
PYET
YETI
YETT
YEW
YEWS
YEX
YGO
YGOE
YIN
YINS
YIP

YIPS
YOB
YOBS
YOD
YODE
YOK
YOKE
YOKS
YON
YOND
YONI
YONT
YOS
YOU
YOUK
YOUR
YOW
YOWE
YOWL
YOWS
YUG
YUGA
YUGS
YUK
YUKE
YUKO
YUKS
YUKY
YUP
YUPS
YUS
AYUS
KYUS
ZAG
ZAGS
ZAP
ZAPS
ZAX
ZEA
ZEAL

ZEAS
ZED
ZEDS
ZEE
MZEE
ZEES
ZEK
ZEKS
ZEL
ZELS
ZEX
ZHO
DZHO
ZHOS
ZIG
ZIGS
ZIP
ZIPS
ZIT
ZITE
ZITI
ZITS
ZIZ
ZIZZ
ZOA
ZOO
ZOOM
ZOON
ZOOS
ZOS
DZOS
ZUZ

4-LETTER WORD HOOKS: extensible words only

ABAC
ABACA
ABACI
ABACK
ABACS
ABAS
BABAS
CABAS
ABASE
ABASH
ABASK
ABBA
ABBAS
ABBE
ABBES
ABBEY
ABET
ABETS
ABID
RABID
TABID
ABIDE
ABLE
CABLE
FABLE
GABLE
HABLE
SABLE
TABLE
ABLED
ABLER
ABLES
ABLET
ABUT
ABUTS
ABYE
ABYES
ACED
FACED
LACED
MACED
PACED
RACED
ACER
FACER
MACER
PACER
RACER
ACERB
ACERS
ACES
DACES
FACES
LACES
MACES
PACES
RACES
TACES
ACHE
CACHE
NACHE
RACHE
TACHE
ACHED
ACHES

ACID
ACIDS
ACME
ACMES
ACNE
ACNES
ACRE
NACRE
ACRED
ACRES
ACTA
PACTA
ACTS
FACTS
PACTS
TACTS
ACYL
ACYLS
ADAW
ADAWS
ADDS
WADDS
ADIT
ADITS
ADOS
DADOS
FADOS
ADZE
ADZES
AEON
PAEON
AEONS
AERO
AEROS
AERY
FAERY
AFAR
AFARA
AFFY
BAFFY
DAFFY
TAFFY
AFRO
AFROS
AGAR
AGARS
AGAS
NAGAS
RAGAS
SAGAS
AGAST
AGED
CAGED
GAGED
PAGED
RAGED
WAGED
AGEE
RAGEE
AGEN
AGENE
AGENT
AGES
CAGES
GAGES

MAGES
PAGES
RAGES
SAGES
WAGES
AGHA
AGHAS
AGIN
AGING
AGIO
AGIOS
AGMA
MAGMA
TAGMA
AGMAS
AGOG
AGOGE
AGON
WAGON
AGONE
AGONS
AGONY
AGUE
VAGUE
AGUED
AGUES
AHED
RAHED
AIDE
WAIDE
AIDED
AIDER
AIDES
AIDS
GAIDS
KAIDS
LAIDS
MAIDS
RAIDS
SAIDS
AILS
BAILS
FAILS
HAILS
JAILS
KAILS
MAILS
NAILS
PAILS
RAILS
SAILS
TAILS
VAILS
WAILS
AIMS
KAIMS
MAIMS
SAIMS
AINE
DAINE
FAINE
RAINE
SAINE
AINEE
AIRN

BAIRN
CAIRN
AIRNS
AIRS
FAIRS
GAIRS
HAIRS
LAIRS
MAIRS
PAIRS
SAIRS
VAIRS
AIRT
AIRTS
AIRY
DAIRY
FAIRY
HAIRY
LAIRY
VAIRY
AITS
BAITS
GAITS
RAITS
TAITS
WAITS
AITU
AITUS
AKED
BAKED
CAKED
FAKED
LAKED
NAKED
RAKED
WAKED
AKEE
RAKEE
AKEES
AKES
BAKES
CAKES
FAKES
HAKES
JAKES
LAKES
MAKES
RAKES
SAKES
TAKES
WAKES
AKIN
LAKIN
TAKIN
AKING
ALAP
JALAP
ALAPA
ALAPS
ALAR
MALAR
TALAR
ALARM
ALARY
ALAS

BALAS
GALAS
NALAS
PALAS
TALAS
ALAY
PALAY
ALAYS
ALBE
ALBEE
ALES
BALES
DALES
EALES
GALES
HALES
KALES
MALES
PALES
RALES
SALES
TALES
VALES
WALES
YALES
ALEW
ALEWS
ALFA
HALFA
ALFAS
ALGA
ALGAE
ALGAL
ALKY
BALKY
TALKY
ALKYD
ALKYL
ALLS
BALLS
CALLS
FALLS
GALLS
HALLS
MALLS
PALLS
WALLS
ALLY
BALLY
DALLY
GALLY
PALLY
RALLY
SALLY
TALLY
WALLY
ALLYL
ALMA
HALMA
TALMA
ALMAH
ALMAS
ALME
ALMEH
ALMES

ALMS
BALMS
CALMS
HALMS
MALMS
PALMS
ALOD
ALODS
ALOE
ALOED
ALOES
ALOW
ALOWE
ALPS
CALPS
PALPS
SALPS
ALTO
SALTO
ALTOS
ALTS
DALTS
HALTS
MALTS
SALTS
ALUM
ALUMS
AMAH
AMAHS
AMBO
GAMBO
JAMBO
MAMBO
SAMBO
ZAMBO
AMBOS
AMEN
RAMEN
SAMEN
YAMEN
AMEND
AMENE
AMENS
AMENT
AMID
AMIDE
AMIE
RAMIE
AMIES
AMIR
AMIRS
AMIS
CAMIS
KAMIS
RAMIS
TAMIS
AMISS
AMLA
AMLAS
AMMO
AMMON
AMMOS
AMPS
CAMPS
DAMPS

GAMPS
LAMPS
RAMPS
SAMPS
TAMPS
VAMPS
AMYL
AMYLS
ANAL
BANAL
CANAL
FANAL
ANAN
ANANA
ANAS
KANAS
LANAS
MANAS
NANAS
RANAS
TANAS
ANCE
DANCE
HANCE
LANCE
NANCE
PANCE
RANCE
ANDS
BANDS
FANDS
HANDS
LANDS
PANDS
RANDS
SANDS
WANDS
ANES
BANES
CANES
FANES
JANES
LANES
MANES
PANES
VANES
WANES
ANIL
ANILE
ANILS
ANIS
MANIS
RANIS
ANISE
ANKH
ANKHS
ANNA
CANNA
MANNA
NANNA
TANNA
WANNA
ANNAL
ANNAS
ANNAT

ANNO
ANNOY
ANNS
BANNS
CANNS
JANNS
ANOA
ANOAS
ANON
CANON
FANON
ANTA
MANTA
ANTAE
ANTAR
ANTAS
ANTE
ZANTE
ANTED
ANTES
ANTI
TANTI
ANTIC
ANTIS
ANTS
BANTS
CANTS
DANTS
GANTS
KANTS
LANTS
PANTS
RANTS
SANTS
VANTS
WANTS
ANUS
MANUS
APAY
APAYD
APAYS
APED
CAPED
GAPED
JAPED
RAPED
TAPED
APES
CAPES
GAPES
JAPES
NAPES
PAPES
RAPES
TAPES
APOD
APODE
APODS
APSE
LAPSE
APSES
AQUA
AQUAE
AQUAS
ARAK

ARAKS
ARAR
ARARS
ARBA
ARBAS
ARBS
BARBS
CARBS
GARBS
ARCH
LARCH
MARCH
PARCH
ARCO
NARCO
ARCS
MARCS
NARCS
ARDS
BARDS
CARDS
EARDS
FARDS
HARDS
LARDS
NARDS
PARDS
SARDS
WARDS
YARDS
AREA
AREAD
AREAL
AREAR
AREAS
ARED
BARED
CARED
DARED
EARED
FARED
HARED
OARED
PARED
SARED
TARED
WARED
AREDD
AREDE
ARES
BARES
CARES
DARES
FARES
HARES
LARES
MARES
NARES
PARES
TARES
VARES
WARES
ARET
CARET
ARETE

ARETS
ARETT
ARIA
MARIA
ARIAS
ARID
MARID
ARIL
ARILS
ARIS
DARIS
SARIS
ARISE
ARISH
ARKS
BARKS
CARKS
DARKS
HARKS
JARKS
LARKS
MARKS
NARKS
PARKS
SARKS
WARKS
ARLE
FARLE
MARLE
PARLE
ARLED
ARLES
ARMS
BARMS
FARMS
HARMS
MARMS
WARMS
ARMY
BARMY
ARNA
VARNA
ARNAS
ARSE
CARSE
FARSE
PARSE
ARSES
ARTS
CARTS
DARTS
FARTS
HARTS
KARTS
MARTS
PARTS
TARTS
WARTS
ARTSY
ARTY
PARTY
TARTY
WARTY
ARUM
GARUM

LARUM
ARUMS
ARVO
ARVOS
ARYL
ARYLS
ASAR
TASAR
ASCI
FASCI
ASHY
HASHY
MASHY
WASHY
ASKS
BASKS
CASKS
HASKS
MASKS
TASKS
ASPS
GASPS
HASPS
JASPS
RASPS
WASPS
ATAP
WATAP
ATAPS
ATOC
ATOCS
ATOK
ATOKE
ATOKS
ATOM
ATOMS
ATOMY
ATOP
ATOPY
AUFS
LAUFS
AUKS
BAUKS
CAUKS
WAUKS
AULA
AULAS
AULD
CAULD
HAULD
TAULD
YAULD
AUNE
AUNES
AUNT
DAUNT
GAUNT
HAUNT
JAUNT
NAUNT
SAUNT
TAUNT
VAUNT
AUNTS
AUNTY
AURA
LAURA
AURAE
AURAL
AURAS
AUTO
AUTOS
AVAL
NAVAL
AVALE
AVAS
KAVAS
LAVAS
TAVAS
AVAST
AVER
CAVER
FAVER
HAVER
LAVER
PAVER
RAVER
SAVER
TAVER
WAVER
AVERS
AVERT
AVES
CAVES
EAVES
HAVES
LAVES
NAVES
OAVES
PAVES
RAVES
SAVES
WAVES
AVID
PAVID
AVOW
AVOWS
AWAY
AWAYS
AWDL
AWDLS
AWED
CAWED
DAWED
HAWED
JAWED
KAWED
LAWED
PAWED
SAWED
TAWED
YAWED
AWES
WAWES
AWLS
BAWLS
PAWLS
WAWLS
YAWLS
AWNS
BAWNS
DAWNS
FAWNS
LAWNS
PAWNS
RAWNS
YAWNS
AWNY
LAWNY
TAWNY
YAWNY
AXED
FAXED
RAXED
TAXED
WAXED
AXEL
AXELS
AXES
FAXES
LAXES
MAXES
PAXES
RAXES
SAXES
TAXES
WAXES
ZAXES
AXIL
AXILE
AXILS
AXIS
MAXIS
TAXIS
AXLE
AXLES
AXON
CAXON
TAXON
AXONS
AYAH
RAYAH
AYAHS
AYES
BAYES
AYRE
FAYRE
AYRES
AZAN
AZANS
AZYM
AZYME
AZYMS
BABA
BABAS
BABE
BABEL
BABES
BABU
BABUL
BABUS
BACH
BACHS
BACK
ABACK
BACKS
BAEL
BAELS
BAFF
BAFFS
BAFFY
BAFT
ABAFT
BAFTS
BAHT
BAHTS
BAIL
BAILS
BAIT
BAITS
BAJU
BAJUS
BAKE
BAKED
BAKEN
BAKER
BAKES
BALD
BALDY
BALE
BALED
BALER
BALES
BALK
BALKS
BALKY
BALL
BALLS
BALLY
BALM
BALMS
BALMY
BALU
BALUS
BANC
BANCO
BANCS
BAND
ABAND
BANDA
BANDS
BANDY
BANE
BANED
BANES
BANG
OBANG
BANGS
BANI
BANIA
BANK
BANKS
BANT
BANTS
BANTU
BAPU
BAPUS
BARB
BARBE
BARBS
BARD
BARDO
BARDS
BARDY
BARE
BARED
BARER
BARES
BARF
BARFS
BARK
BARKS
BARKY
BARM
BARMS
BARMY
BARN
BARNS
BARP
BARPS
BASE
ABASE
BASED
BASER
BASES
BASH
ABASH
BASHO
BASK
ABASK
BASKS
BASS
BASSE
BASSI
BASSO
BASSY
BAST
BASTA
BASTE
BASTO
BASTS
BATE
ABATE
BATED
BATES
BATH
BATHE
BATHS
BATT
BATTA
BATTS
BATTY
BAUD
BAUDS
BAUK
BAUKS
BAUR
BAURS
BAWD
BAWDS
BAWDY
BAWL
BAWLS
BAWN
BAWNS
BAWR
BAWRS
BAYE
BAYED
BAYES
BAYT
BAYTS
BEAD
BEADS
BEADY
BEAK
BEAKS
BEAKY
BEAM
ABEAM
BEAMS
BEAMY
BEAN
BEANO
BEANS
BEAR
ABEAR
BEARD
BEARE
BEARS
BEAT
BEATH
BEATS
BEAU
BEAUT
BEAUX
BECK
BECKE
BECKS
BEDE
BEDEL
BEDES
BEDEW
BEEF
BEEFS
BEEFY
BEEP
BEEPS
BEER
BEERS
BEERY
BEET
BEETS
BEGO
BEGOT
BEIN
BEING
BELL
BELLE
BELLS
BELLY
BELT
BELTS
BEMA
BEMAD
BEMAS
BEND
BENDS
BENDY
BENE
BENES
BENET
BENI
BENIS
BENT
BENTS
BENTY
BERE
BERES
BERET
BERG
BERGS
BERK
BERKS
BERM
BERMS
BEST
BESTS
BETA
BETAS
BETE
BETED
BETEL
BETES
BETH
BETHS
BETS
ABETS
BEYS
OBEYS
BHEL
BHELS
BIAS
OBIAS
BICE
BICES
BIDE
ABIDE
BIDED
BIDES
BIDET
BIER
BIERS
BIFF
BIFFS
BIGA
BIGAE
BIGG
BIGGS
BIGGY
BIKE
BIKED
BIKER
BIKES
BILE
BILES
BILK
BILKS
BILL
BILLS
BILLY
BIND
BINDS
BINE
BINES
BING
BINGE
BINGO
BINGS
BINGY
BINK
BINKS
BINT
BINTS
BIOG
BIOGS
BIRD
BIRDS
BIRK
BIRKS
BIRL
BIRLE
BIRLS
BIRR
BIRRS
BISE
BISES
BISK
BISKS
BITE
BITER
BITES
BITO
BITOS
BITS
OBITS
BITSY
BITT
BITTE
BITTS
BITTY
BLAB
BLABS
BLAD
BLADE
BLADS
BLAE
BLAER
BLAES
BLAG
BLAGS
BLAH
BLAHS
BLAT
BLATE
BLATS
BLATT
BLAY
BLAYS
BLEB
BLEBS
BLED
ABLED
BLEE
BLEED
BLEEP
BLEES
BLET
ABLET
BLETS
BLEY
BLEYS
BLIN
BLIND
BLINI
BLINK
BLINS
BLIP
BLIPS
BLOB
BLOBS
BLOC
BLOCK
BLOCS
BLOT
BLOTS
BLOW
ABLOW
BLOWN
BLOWS
BLOWY
BLUB
BLUBS
BLUE
BLUED
BLUER
BLUES
BLUEY
BLUR
BLURB
BLURS
BLURT
BOAK
BOAKS
BOAR
BOARD
BOARS
BOART
BOAS
BOAST
BOAT
BOATS
BOBA
BOBAC
BOBAK
BOBAS
BOCK
BOCKS
BODE
ABODE
BODED
BODES
BOFF
BOFFS
BOIL
ABOIL
BOILS
BOKE
BOKED
BOKES
BOKO
BOKOS
BOLD
BOLDS
BOLE
BOLES
BOLL
BOLLS
BOLO
BOLOS
BOLT
BOLTS
BOMA
BOMAS
BOMB
BOMBE
BOMBO
BOMBS
BOND
BONDS
BONE
BONED
BONER
BONES
BONG
BONGO
BONGS
BONK
BONKS
BONY
EBONY
BOOB
BOOBS
BOOBY
BOOH
BOOHS
BOOK
BOOKS
BOOKY
BOOL
BOOLS
BOOM
BOOMS
BOON
BOONG
BOONS
BOOR
BOORD
BOORS
BOOS
BOOSE
BOOST
BOOT
BOOTH
BOOTS
BOOTY
BORA
BORAK
BORAS
BORAX
BORD
ABORD
BORDE
BORDS
BORE
ABORE
YBORE
BORED
BOREE
BOREL
BORER
BORES
BORN
BORNE
BORT
ABORT
BORTS
BOSK
BOSKS
BOSKY
BOSS
BOSSY
BOTH
BOTHY
BOTT
BOTTE
BOTTS
BOTTY
BOUK
BOUKS
BOUN
BOUND
BOUNS
BOUT
ABOUT
BOUTS
BOWL
BOWLS
BOWR
BOWRS
BOWS
BOWSE
BOYG
BOYGS
BOYO
BOYOS
BOZO
BOZOS
BRAD
BRADS
BRAE
BRAES
BRAG
BRAGS
BRAN
BRAND
BRANK
BRANS
BRAS
BRASH

BRASS
BRAST
BRAT
BRATS
BRAW
BRAWL
BRAWN
BRAWS
BRAY
ABRAY
BRAYS
BRED
BREDE
BREE
BREED
BREEM
BREER
BREES
BREN
BRENS
BRENT
BRER
BRERE
BRERS
BREW
BREWS
BRIG
BRIGS
BRIM
ABRIM
BRIMS
BRIO
BRIOS
BRIT
BRITS
BROD
BRODS
BROG
BROGH
BROGS
BROO
BROOD
BROOK
BROOL
BROOM
BROOS
BROS
BROSE
BROW
BROWN
BROWS
BRUT
BRUTE
BUAT
BUATS
BUBA
BUBAL
BUBAS
BUCK
BUCKO
BUCKS
BUCKU
BUDO
BUDOS
BUFF
BUFFA
BUFFE
BUFFI
BUFFO
BUFFS

BUFO
BUFOS
BUHL
BUHLS
BUIK
BUIKS
BUKE
BUKES
BULB
BULBS
BULK
BULKS
BULKY
BULL
BULLA
BULLS
BULLY
BUMF
BUMFS
BUMP
BUMPH
BUMPS
BUMPY
BUNA
ABUNA
BUNAS
BUND
BUNDS
BUNDU
BUNG
BUNGS
BUNGY
BUNK
BUNKO
BUNKS
BUNT
BUNTS
BUNTY
BUOY
BUOYS
BURD
BURDS
BURG
BURGH
BURGS
BURK
BURKA
BURKE
BURKS
BURL
BURLS
BURLY
BURN
BURNS
BURNT
BURP
BURPS
BURR
BURRO
BURRS
BURRY
BURS
BURSA
BURSE
BURST
BUSH
BUSHY
BUSK
BUSKS
BUSKY

BUSS
BUSSU
BUST
BUSTS
BUSTY
BUTE
BUTES
BUTS
ABUTS
BUTT
BUTTE
BUTTS
BUTTY
BUZZ
ABUZZ
BUZZY
BYES
ABYES
BYKE
BYKED
BYKES
BYRE
BYRES
BYTE
BYTES
CABA
CABAL
CABAS
CABS
SCABS
CADE
CADEE
CADES
CADET
CADI
CADIE
CADIS
CADS
ECADS
SCADS
CAFE
CAFES
CAFF
SCAFF
CAFFS
CAGE
CAGED
CAGES
CAGEY
CAIN
CAINS
CAKE
CAKED
CAKES
CAKEY
CALF
CALFS
CALK
CALKS
CALL
SCALL
CALLA
CALLS
CALM
CALMS
CALMY
CALP
SCALP
CALPA
CALPS

CAME
CAMEL
CAMEO
CAMES
CAMP
SCAMP
CAMPO
CAMPS
CAMPY
CAMS
SCAMS
CANE
CANED
CANEH
CANES
CANG
CANGS
CANN
CANNA
CANNS
CANNY
CANS
SCANS
CANST
CANT
SCANT
CANTO
CANTS
CANTY
CAPA
SCAPA
CAPAS
CAPE
SCAPE
CAPED
CAPER
CAPES
CAPI
SCAPI
CAPIZ
CAPO
CAPON
CAPOS
CAPOT
CARB
CARBS
CARBY
CARD
CARDI
CARDS
CARDY
CARE
SCARE
CARED
CARER
CARES
CARET
CAREX
CARK
CARKS
CARL
CARLS
CARP
SCARP
CARPI
CARPS
CARR
CARRS
CARRY
CARS

SCARS
CARSE
CART
SCART
CARTA
CARTE
CARTS
CASA
CASAS
CASE
CASED
CASES
CASK
CASKS
CAST
CASTE
CASTS
CATE
CATER
CATES
CATS
SCATS
CAUK
CAUKS
CAUL
CAULD
CAULK
CAULS
CAUM
CAUMS
CAUP
SCAUP
CAUPS
CAVE
CAVED
CAVEL
CAVER
CAVES
CAWK
CAWKS
CAWS
SCAWS
CEAS
CEASE
CECA
CECAL
CEDE
CEDED
CEDES
CEDI
CEDIS
CEIL
CEILI
CEILS
CELL
CELLA
CELLO
CELLS
CELT
CELTS
CENS
CENSE
CENT
SCENT
CENTO
CENTS
CERE
CERED
CERES
CERT

CERTS
CESS
CESSE
CETE
CETES
CHAD
CHADS
CHAI
CHAIN
CHAIR
CHAIS
CHAL
CHALK
CHALS
CHAM
CHAMP
CHAMS
CHAP
CHAPE
CHAPS
CHAR
CHARA
CHARD
CHARE
CHARK
CHARM
CHARR
CHARS
CHART
CHARY
CHAS
CHASE
CHASM
CHAT
CHATS
CHAW
CHAWS
CHAY
CHAYA
CHAYS
CHEF
CHEFS
CHER
OCHER
CHERE
CHERT
CHEW
CHEWS
CHEWY
CHIC
CHICA
CHICH
CHICK
CHICO
CHICS
CHID
CHIDE
CHIK
CHIKS
CHIN
CHINA
CHINE
CHINK
CHINO
CHINS
CHIP
CHIPS
CHIT
CHITS
CHIV

CHIVE
CHIVS
CHIVY
CHIZ
CHIZZ
CHOC
CHOCK
CHOCO
CHOCS
CHON
CHONS
CHOP
CHOPS
CHOU
CHOUT
CHOUX
CHOW
CHOWS
CHUB
CHUBS
CHUG
CHUGS
CHUM
CHUMP
CHUMS
CHUT
CHUTE
CIAO
CIAOS
CIDS
ACIDS
CIEL
CIELS
CILL
CILLS
CION
SCION
CIONS
CIRE
CIRES
CIRL
CIRLS
CIST
CISTS
CITE
CITED
CITER
CITES
CIVE
CIVES
CIVET
CLAD
YCLAD
CLADE
CLADS
CLAG
CLAGS
CLAM
CLAME
CLAMP
CLAMS
CLAN
CLANG
CLANK
CLANS
CLAP
CLAPS
CLAT
ECLAT
CLATS

CLAW
CLAWS
CLAY
CLAYS
CLEF
CLEFS
CLEFT
CLEG
CLEGS
CLEM
CLEMS
CLEW
CLEWS
CLIP
CLIPE
CLIPS
CLIPT
CLOD
CLODS
CLOG
CLOGS
CLOP
CLOPS
CLOT
CLOTE
CLOTH
CLOTS
CLOU
CLOUD
CLOUR
CLOUS
CLOUT
CLOW
CLOWN
CLOWS
CLOY
CLOYS
CLUB
CLUBS
CLUE
CLUED
CLUES
COAL
COALS
COALY
COAT
COATE
COATI
COATS
COBB
COBBS
COBBY
COCA
COCAS
COCK
ACOCK
COCKS
COCKY
COCO
COCOA
COCOS
CODA
CODAS
CODE
CODED
CODES
CODEX
COED
COEDS
COFF

SCOFF
COFFS
COGS
SCOGS
COHO
COHOE
COHOG
COHOS
COIF
COIFS
COIL
COILS
COIN
COINS
COIR
COIRS
COIT
COITS
COKE
COKED
COKES
COLA
COLAS
COLD
ACOLD
SCOLD
COLDS
COLE
COLES
COLEY
COLL
COLLS
COLLY
COLT
COLTS
COMA
COMAE
COMAL
COMAS
COMB
COMBE
COMBO
COMBS
COMBY
COME
COMER
COMES
COMET
COMP
COMPO
COMPS
COMPT
COND
YCOND
CONDO
CONE
SCONE
CONED
CONES
CONEY
CONK
CONKS
CONKY
CONN
CONNE
CONNS
CONS
ICONS
COOF
COOFS

COOK
COOKS
COOKY
COOL
COOLS
COOLY
COOM
COOMB
COOMS
COOMY
COON
COONS
COOP
SCOOP
COOPS
COOPT
COOS
COOST
COOT
SCOOT
COOTS
COPE
SCOPE
COPED
COPER
COPES
COPS
COPSE
COPSY
CORD
CORDS
CORE
SCORE
CORED
CORER
CORES
COREY
CORK
CORKS
CORKY
CORM
CORMS
CORN
ACORN
SCORN
CORNI
CORNO
CORNS
CORNU
CORNY
CORS
CORSE
CORSO
COSE
COSEC
COSED
COSES
COSET
COST
COSTA
COSTE
COSTS
COTE
COTED
COTES
COTH
COTHS
COTS
SCOTS
COTT

COTTA COTTS **COUP** SCOUP COUPE COUPS **COUR** SCOUR COURB COURD COURE COURS COURT **COVE** COVED COVEN COVER COVES COVET COVEY **COWL** SCOWL COWLS **COWP** SCOWP COWPS **COWS** SCOWS **COXA** COXAE COXAL **COZE** COZED COZEN COZES **CRAB** SCRAB CRABS **CRAG** SCRAG CRAGS **CRAM** SCRAM CRAME CRAMP CRAMS **CRAN** SCRAN CRANE CRANK CRANS **CRAP** SCRAP CRAPE CRAPS CRAPY **CRAW** SCRAW CRAWL CRAWS **CRED** ACRED CREDO CREDS **CREE** SCREE CREED CREEK CREEL CREEP

CREES **CREW** SCREW CREWE CREWS **CRIB** CRIBS **CRIM** SCRIM CRIME CRIMP CRIMS **CRIT** CRITH CRITS **CROC** CROCK CROCS **CROP** CROPS **CROW** SCROW CROWD CROWN CROWS **CRUD** CRUDE CRUDS **CRUS** ECRUS CRUSE CRUSH CRUST CRUSY **CUBE** CUBEB CUBED CUBES **CUDS** SCUDS **CUFF** SCUFF CUFFO CUFFS **CUIF** CUIFS **CUIT** CUITS **CULL** SCULL CULLS CULLY **CULM** CULMS **CULT** CULTS **CUNT** CUNTS **CUPS** SCUPS **CURB** CURBS **CURD** CURDS CURDY **CURE** CURED CURER CURES **CURL**

CURLS CURLY **CURN** CURNS CURNY **CURR** CURRS CURRY **CURS** SCURS CURSE CURSI CURST **CUSH** CUSHY **CUSK** CUSKS **CUSP** CUSPS **CUTE** ACUTE SCUTE CUTER CUTES CUTEY **CUTS** SCUTS **CYAN** CYANS **CYMA** CYMAR CYMAS **CYME** CYMES **CYST** CYSTS **CZAR** CZARS **DACE** DACES **DADO** DADOS **DAFF** DAFFS DAFFY **DAGO** DAGOS **DAHL** DAHLS **DAIS** DAISY **DALE** DALES **DALI** DALIS **DALS** ODALS UDALS **DALT** DALTS **DAME** DAMES **DAMN** DAMNS **DAMP** DAMPS DAMPY **DANG** DANGS **DANK**

DANKS **DANT** DANTS **DARE** DARED DARES **DARG** DARGA DARGS **DARI** DARIC DARIS **DARK** DARKS DARKY **DARN** DARNS **DART** DARTS **DATA** DATAL **DATE** DATED DATER DATES **DAUB** DAUBE DAUBS DAUBY **DAUD** DAUDS **DAUR** DAURS **DAUT** DAUTS **DAWD** DAWDS **DAWK** DAWKS **DAWN** DAWNS **DAWS** ADAWS **DAWT** DAWTS **DAYS** ADAYS **DAZE** DAZED DAZER DAZES **DEAD** DEADS **DEAL** IDEAL DEALS DEALT **DEAN** DEANS **DEAR** DEARE DEARN DEARS DEARY **DEAW** DEAWS DEAWY **DEBT** DEBTS **DECK**

DECKO DECKS **DECO** DECOR DECOY **DEED** DEEDS DEEDY **DEEM** ADEEM DEEMS **DEEN** DEENS **DEEP** DEEPS **DEER** DEERE **DEES** IDEES **DEEV** DEEVE DEEVS **DEID** DEIDS **DEIL** DEILS **DELE** DELED DELES **DELF** DELFS DELFT **DELI** DELIS **DELL** DELLS **DELT** DELTA DELTS **DEME** DEMES **DEMO** DEMOB DEMON DEMOS **DENE** DENES **DENS** DENSE **DENT** DENTS **DERE** DERED DERES **DERM** DERMA DERMS **DERN** DERNS **DERV** DERVS **DESK** DESKS **DEVA** DEVAS **DHAK** DHAKS **DHAL** DHALS **DHOW**

DHOWS **DIAL** DIALS **DICE** DICED DICER DICES DICEY **DICH** DICHT **DICK** DICKS DICKY **DICT** EDICT DICTA DICTS DICTY **DIDO** DIDOS **DIEB** DIEBS **DIET** DIETS **DIKA** DIKAS **DIKE** DIKED DIKER DIKES DIKEY **DILL** DILLI DILLS DILLY **DIME** DIMER DIMES **DINE** DINED DINER DINES **DING** DINGE DINGO DINGS DINGY **DINK** DINKS DINKY **DINT** DINTS **DIPS** DIPSO **DIRE** DIRER **DIRK** DIRKE DIRKS **DIRL** DIRLS **DIRT** DIRTS DIRTY **DISA** DISAS **DISC** DISCO DISCS **DISH**

DISHY **DISK** DISKS **DITA** DITAL DITAS **DITE** DITED DITES **DITS** ADITS EDITS DITSY **DITT** DITTO DITTS DITTY **DIVA** DIVAN DIVAS **DIVE** DIVED DIVER DIVES **DIVI** DIVIS **DIXI** DIXIE **DOAB** DOABS **DOAT** DOATS **DOCK** DOCKS **DODO** DODOS **DOEK** DOEKS **DOER** DOERS **DOES** DOEST **DOFF** DOFFS **DOGE** DOGES **DOIT** DOITS **DOJO** DOJOS **DOLE** DOLED DOLES **DOLL** DOLLS DOLLY **DOLT** DOLTS **DOME** DOMED DOMES **DONA** DONAH DONAS **DONE** DONEE **DONG** DONGA DONGS **DOOB**

DOOBS **DOOK** DOOKS **DOOL** DOOLE DOOLS **DOOM** DOOMS DOOMY **DOOR** DOORN DOORS **DOPA** DOPAS **DOPE** DOPED DOPER DOPES DOPEY **DORK** DORKS DORKY **DORM** DORMS DORMY **DORP** DORPS **DORR** DORRS **DORS** ODORS DORSA DORSE **DORT** DORTS DORTY **DOSE** DOSED DOSEH DOSES **DOTE** DOTED DOTER DOTES **DOUC** DOUCE DOUCS **DOUP** DOUPS **DOUR** ODOUR DOURA **DOUT** DOUTS **DOVE** DOVED DOVER DOVES **DOWD** DOWDS DOWDY **DOWL** DOWLE DOWLS **DOWN** ADOWN DOWNA DOWNS DOWNY **DOWP**

DOWPS **DOWS** DOWSE **DOWT** DOWTS **DOZE** DOZED DOZEN DOZER DOZES **DRAB** DRABS **DRAD** ADRAD YDRAD **DRAG** DRAGS **DRAM** DRAMA DRAMS **DRAP** DRAPE DRAPS **DRAW** DRAWL DRAWN DRAWS **DRAY** DRAYS **DREE** DREED DREES **DREG** DREGS **DREK** DREKS **DREY** DREYS **DRIB** DRIBS **DRIP** DRIPS **DROP** DROPS **DROW** DROWN DROWS **DRUB** DRUBS **DRUG** DRUGS **DRUM** DRUMS **DSOS** ODSOS **DUAD** DUADS **DUAL** DUALS **DUAN** DUANS **DUAR** DUARS **DUCE** EDUCE DUCES **DUCK** DUCKS DUCKY **DUCT**

EDUCT DUCTS **DUDE** DUDES **DUEL** DUELS **DUET** DUETS DUETT **DUFF** DUFFS **DUKE** DUKED DUKES **DULE** DULES **DULL** DULLS DULLY **DUMA** DUMAS **DUMB** DUMBO DUMBS **DUMP** DUMPS DUMPY **DUNE** DUNES **DUNG** DUNGS DUNGY **DUNK** DUNKS **DUNS** DUNSH **DUNT** DUNTS **DUPE** DUPED DUPER DUPES **DURA** DURAL DURAS **DURE** DURED DURES **DURN** DURNS **DURO** DUROS DUROY **DUSK** DUSKS DUSKY **DUST** ADUST DUSTS DUSTY **DWAM** DWAMS **DYAD** DYADS **DYER** DYERS **DYKE** DYKED DYKES DYKEY

DYNE
DYNES
DZHO
DZHOS
EACH
BEACH
LEACH
PEACH
REACH
TEACH
EALE
VEALE
EALES
EANS
BEANS
DEANS
GEANS
JEANS
LEANS
MEANS
PEANS
REANS
SEANS
WEANS
YEANS
EARD
BEARD
HEARD
YEARD
EARDS
EARL
PEARL
EARLS
EARLY
EARN
DEARN
LEARN
YEARN
EARNS
EARS
BEARS
DEARS
FEARS
GEARS
HEARS
LEARS
NEARS
PEARS
REARS
SEARS
TEARS
WEARS
YEARS
EARST
EASE
CEASE
LEASE
MEASE
PEASE
SEASE
TEASE
EASED
EASEL
EASES
EAST
BEAST
FEAST
HEAST
LEAST
REAST

YEAST
EASTS
EATH
BEATH
DEATH
HEATH
MEATH
NEATH
EATHE
EATS
BEATS
FEATS
GEATS
HEATS
JEATS
LEATS
MEATS
PEATS
SEATS
TEATS
EAUX
BEAUX
EBON
EBONS
EBONY
ECAD
DECAD
ECADS
ECCE
RECCE
ECCO
RECCO
SECCO
ECHE
ECHED
ECHES
ECHT
FECHT
HECHT
WECHT
ECRU
ECRUS
EDDY
NEDDY
REDDY
TEDDY
EDGE
HEDGE
KEDGE
LEDGE
SEDGE
WEDGE
EDGED
EDGER
EDGES
EDGY
HEDGY
KEDGY
LEDGY
SEDGY
WEDGY
EDIT
EDITS
EECH
BEECH
KEECH
LEECH
REECH
EELS
FEELS

HEELS
JEELS
KEELS
PEELS
REELS
SEELS
TEELS
WEELS
EELY
JEELY
SEELY
EERY
BEERY
LEERY
PEERY
VEERY
EEVN
EEVNS
EFFS
JEFFS
TEFFS
EFTS
HEFTS
LEFTS
WEFTS
EGAD
BEGAD
EGAL
LEGAL
REGAL
EGER
LEGER
EGERS
EGGS
TEGGS
YEGGS
EGGY
LEGGY
PEGGY
EGIS
AEGIS
EGMA
REGMA
EGMAS
EGOS
REGOS
SEGOS
EIKS
REIKS
EILD
EILDS
EINE
SEINE
EKED
REKED
EKES
PEKES
REKES
EKKA
EKKAS
ELAN
ELAND
ELANS
ELDS
GELDS
MELDS
VELDS
WELDS
ELFS
DELFS

PELFS
SELFS
ELKS
WELKS
YELKS
ELLS
BELLS
CELLS
DELLS
FELLS
HELLS
JELLS
KELLS
MELLS
PELLS
SELLS
TELLS
VELLS
WELLS
YELLS
ELMS
HELMS
YELMS
ELTS
BELTS
CELTS
DELTS
FELTS
GELTS
KELTS
MELTS
PELTS
WELTS
YELTS
EMES
DEMES
FEMES
HEMES
LEMES
TEMES
EMEU
EMEUS
EMIR
EMIRS
EMIT
DEMIT
REMIT
EMITS
EMMA
GEMMA
LEMMA
EMMAS
ENDS
BENDS
FENDS
HENDS
LENDS
MENDS
PENDS
RENDS
SENDS
TENDS
VENDS
WENDS
ENES
BENES
DENES
GENES
LENES
MENES

NENES
PENES
TENES
ENEW
RENEW
ENEWS
ENGS
LENGS
MENGS
ENVY
SENVY
EONS
AEONS
NEONS
PEONS
EORL
CEORL
EORLS
EPEE
TEPEE
EPEES
EPHA
EPHAH
EPHAS
EPIC
EPICS
EPOS
PEPOS
REPOS
ERAS
TERAS
ERASE
ERED
CERED
DERED
LERED
MERED
SERED
ERES
BERES
CERES
DERES
FERES
GERES
LERES
MERES
PERES
SERES
TERES
ERGO
ERGON
ERGOT
ERGS
BERGS
ERIC
CERIC
SERIC
XERIC
ERICA
ERICK
ERICS
ERKS
BERKS
JERKS
MERKS
NERKS
PERKS
SERKS
YERKS
ERNE

CERNE
GERNE
KERNE
TERNE
ERNED
ERNES
ERNS
DERNS
FERNS
HERNS
KERNS
PERNS
TERNS
ERRS
SERRS
ERST
PERST
VERST
ESKY
PESKY
ESNE
MESNE
ESNES
ESSE
CESSE
DESSE
FESSE
GESSE
ESSES
ESTS
BESTS
FESTS
GESTS
HESTS
JESTS
KESTS
LESTS
NESTS
PESTS
RESTS
TESTS
VESTS
WESTS
YESTS
ZESTS
ETAS
BETAS
FETAS
GETAS
KETAS
WETAS
ZETAS
ETAT
ETATS
ETCH
FETCH
KETCH
LETCH
RETCH
VETCH
ETEN
ETENS
ETHE
ETHER
ETHS
BETHS
METHS
ETNA
ETNAS
ETUI

ETUIS
EUGH
HEUGH
LEUGH
TEUGH
EUGHS
EUKS
NEUKS
YEUKS
EURO
EUROS
EVEN
EEVEN
SEVEN
YEVEN
EVENS
EVENT
EVER
BEVER
FEVER
LEVER
NEVER
SEVER
EVERT
EVERY
EVES
MEVES
NEVES
YEVES
EVET
REVET
EVETS
EVIL
DEVIL
EVILS
EWER
FEWER
HEWER
NEWER
SEWER
EWERS
EWES
EWEST
EWTS
NEWTS
EXAM
EXAMS
EXES
HEXES
KEXES
LEXES
SEXES
VEXES
WEXES
YEXES
ZEXES
EXIT
EXITS
EXON
EXONS
EXPO
EXPOS
EXUL
EXULS
EXULT
EYED
FEYED
HEYED
KEYED
EYOT

EYOTS
EYRA
EYRAS
EYRE
EYRES
FACE
FACED
FACER
FACES
FACET
FACT
FACTS
FADE
FADED
FADER
FADES
FADO
FADOS
FAFF
FAFFS
FAIK
FAIKS
FAIL
FAILS
FAIN
FAINE
FAINS
FAINT
FAIR
FAIRS
FAIRY
FAKE
FAKED
FAKER
FAKES
FALL
FALLS
FAME
FAMED
FAMES
FAND
FANDS
FANE
FANES
FANG
FANGO
FANGS
FANK
FANKS
FARD
FARDS
FARE
FARED
FARES
FARL
FARLE
FARLS
FARM
FARMS
FARO
FAROS
FARS
FARSE
FART
FARTS
FAST
FASTI
FASTS
FATE
FATED

FATES
FATS
FATSO
FAUN
FAUNA
FAUNS
FAVE
FAVEL
FAVER
FAWN
FAWNS
FAYS
OFAYS
FAZE
FAZED
FAZES
FEAL
FEALS
FEAR
AFEAR
FEARE
FEARS
FEAT
FEATS
FECK
FECKS
FEED
FEEDS
FEEL
FEELS
FEER
FEERS
FEES
FEESE
FEHM
FEHME
FELL
FELLA
FELLS
FELLY
FELT
FELTS
FELTY
FEME
FEMES
FEND
FENDS
FENDY
FENI
FENIS
FENT
FENTS
FEOD
FEODS
FERE
YFERE
FERER
FERES
FERM
FERMI
FERMS
FERN
FERNS
FERNY
FESS
FESSE
FEST
FESTA
FESTS
FETA

FETAL
FETAS
FETE
FETED
FETES
FETT
FETTA
FETTS
FEUD
FEUDS
FIAR
FIARS
FIAT
FIATS
FICO
FICOS
FIEF
FIEFS
FIFE
FIFED
FIFER
FIFES
FIGO
FIGOS
FIKE
FIKED
FIKES
FILE
FILED
FILER
FILES
FILET
FILL
FILLE
FILLS
FILLY
FILM
FILMS
FILMY
FILO
FILOS
FIND
FINDS
FINE
FINED
FINER
FINES
FINI
FINIS
FINK
FINKS
FINO
FINOS
FIRE
AFIRE
FIRED
FIRER
FIRES
FIRK
FIRKS
FIRM
FIRMS
FIRN
FIRNS
FIRS
FIRST
FISC
FISCS
FISH
FISHY

FISK
FISKS
FIST
FISTS
FISTY
FITT
FITTE
FITTS
FIVE
FIVER
FIVES
FIZZ
FIZZY
FLAB
FLABS
FLAG
OFLAG
FLAGS
FLAK
FLAKE
FLAKS
FLAKY
FLAM
FLAME
FLAMM
FLAMS
FLAMY
FLAN
FLANK
FLANS
FLAP
FLAPS
FLAT
FLATS
FLAW
FLAWN
FLAWS
FLAWY
FLAX
FLAXY
FLAY
FLAYS
FLEA
FLEAM
FLEAS
FLEE
FLEER
FLEES
FLEET
FLEG
FLEGS
FLEW
FLEWS
FLEY
FLEYS
FLIC
FLICK
FLICS
FLIP
FLIPS
FLIT
FLITE
FLITS
FLITT
FLOE
FLOES
FLOG
FLOGS
FLOP
FLOPS
FLOR
FLORA
FLORS
FLORY
FLOW
FLOWN
FLOWS
FLUB
FLUBS
FLUE
FLUES
FLUEY
FLUS
FLUSH
FOAL
FOALS
FOAM
FOAMS
FOAMY
FOHN
FOHNS
FOID
FOIDS
FOIL
FOILS
FOIN
FOINS
FOLD
FOLDS
FOLK
FOLKS
FOND
FONDA
FONDS
FONT
FONTS
FOOD
FOODS
FOODY
FOOL
FOOLS
FOOT
AFOOT
FOOTS
FOOTY
FORA
FORAY
FORB
FORBS
FORBY
FORD
FORDO
FORDS
FORE
AFORE
FOREL
FORES
FORK
FORKS
FORKY
FORM
FORME
FORMS
FORT
FORTE
FORTH
FORTS
FORTY
FOSS
FOSSA
FOSSE
FOUD
FOUDS
FOUL
AFOUL
FOULE
FOULS
FOUR
FOURS
FOWL
FOWLS
FRAB
FRABS
FRAG
FRAGS
FRAP
FRAPS
FRAS
FRASS
FRAU
FRAUD
FRAUS
FRAY
FRAYS
FREE
FREED
FREER
FREES
FREET
FRET
FRETS
FRIG
FRIGS
FRIS
FRISK
FRIST
FRIT
AFRIT
FRITH
FRITS
FRIZ
FRIZE
FRIZZ
FROG
FROGS
FROW
FROWN
FROWS
FROWY
FUBS
FUBSY
FUCK
FUCKS
FUEL
FUELS
FUFF
FUFFS
FUFFY
FULL
FULLS
FULLY
FUME
FUMED
FUMES
FUMET
FUND
FUNDI
FUNDS
FUNDY
FUNG
FUNGI
FUNGS
FUNK
FUNKS
FUNKY
FURL
FURLS
FURR
FURRS
FURRY
FUSE
FUSED
FUSEE
FUSES
FUSS
FUSSY
FUST
FUSTS
FUSTY
FUZE
FUZEE
FUZES
FUZZ
FUZZY
FYKE
FYKED
FYKES
FYLE
FYLES
FYRD
FYRDS
GADE
GADES
GADI
GADIS
GADS
GADSO
GAFF
GAFFE
GAFFS
GAGE
GAGED
GAGES
GAID
GAIDS
GAIN
AGAIN
GAINS
GAIR
GAIRS
GAIT
GAITS
GAITT
GAJO
GAJOS
GALA
GALAH
GALAS
GALE
GALEA
GALES
GALL
GALLS
GALLY
GAMB
GAMBA
GAMBO
GAMBS
GAME
GAMED
GAMER
GAMES
GAMEY
GAMP
GAMPS
GAMS
OGAMS
GANG
GANGS
GANT
GANTS
GAOL
GAOLS
GAPE
AGAPE
GAPED
GAPER
GAPES
GAPO
IGAPO
GAPOS
GARB
GARBE
GARBO
GARBS
GARS
AGARS
GART
GARTH
GASP
GASPS
GASPY
GAST
AGAST
GASTS
GATE
AGATE
GATED
GATES
GATH
GATHS
GAUD
GAUDS
GAUDY
GAUM
GAUMS
GAUMY
GAUN
GAUNT
GAUP
GAUPS
GAUR
GAURS
GAUS
GAUSS
GAVE
AGAVE
GAVEL
GAWD
GAWDS
GAWK
GAWKS
GAWKY
GAWP
GAWPS
GAZE
AGAZE
GAZED
GAZER
GAZES
GEAL
GEALS
GEAN
GEANS
GEAR
GEARE
GEARS
GEAT
GEATS
GECK
GECKO
GECKS
GEEK
GEEKS
GEEKY
GEEP
GEEPS
GEES
OGEES
GEESE
GEIT
GEITS
GELD
GELDS
GELT
GELTS
GENA
GENAL
GENAS
GENE
AGENE
GENES
GENET
GENT
AGENT
GENTS
GENTY
GENU
GENUS
GERE
GERES
GERM
GERMS
GEST
EGEST
GESTE
GESTS
GETA
GETAS
GEUM
GEUMS
GHAT
GHATS
GHEE
GHEES
GIBE
GIBED
GIBEL
GIBER
GIBES
GIFT
GIFTS
GIGA
GIGAS
GILA
AGILA
GILAS
GILD
GILDS
GILL
GILLS
GILLY
GILT
GILTS
GIMP
GIMPS
GIMPY
GING
AGING
GINGS
GINK
GINKS
GINN
GINNY
GIOS
AGIOS
GIPS
GIPSY
GIRD
GIRDS
GIRL
GIRLS
GIRLY
GIRN
GIRNS
GIRO
GIRON
GIROS
GIRR
GIRRS
GIRT
GIRTH
GIRTS
GISM
GISMO
GISMS
GIST
AGIST
GISTS
GITE
GITES
GIVE
OGIVE
GIVED
GIVEN
GIVER
GIVES
GLAD
GLADE
GLADS
GLADY
GLAM
GLAMS
GLED
OGLED
GLEDE
GLEDS
GLEE
AGLEE
GLEED
GLEEK
GLEES
GLEET
GLEI
GLEIS
GLEN
GLENS
GLENT
GLEY
AGLEY
GLEYS
GLIA
GLIAL
GLIAS
GLIB
GLIBS
GLID
GLIDE
GLIM
GLIMS
GLIT
GLITS
GLITZ
GLOB
GLOBE
GLOBS
GLOBY
GLOM
GLOMS
GLOP
GLOPS
GLOW
AGLOW
GLOWS
GLUE
GLUED
GLUER
GLUES
GLUEY
GLUG
GLUGS
GLUM
GLUME
GLUT
GLUTS
GNAR
GNARL
GNARR
GNARS
GNAT
GNATS
GNAW
GNAWN
GNAWS
GOAD
GOADS
GOAF
GOAFS
GOAL
GOALS
GOAT
GOATS
GOATY
GOBO
GOBOS
GODS
GODSO
GOEL
GOELS
GOER
GOERS
GOFF
GOFFS
GOLD
GOLDS
GOLDY
GOLE
GOLEM
GOLES
GOLF
GOLFS
GOLP
GOLPE
GOLPS
GONE
AGONE
GONER
GONG
GONGS
GONK
GONKS
GONS
AGONS
GOOD
AGOOD
GOODS
GOODY
GOOF
GOOFS
GOOFY
GOOK
GOOKS
GOOL
GOOLD
GOOLS
GOOLY
GOON
GOONS
GOOP
GOOPS
GOOPY
GOOR
GOORS
GOOS
GOOSE
GOOSY
GORE
GORED
GORES
GORM
GORMS
GORMY
GORP
GORPS
GOSH
GOSHT
GOUK
GOUKS
GOUT
GOUTS
GOUTY
GOWD
GOWDS
GOWF
GOWFS
GOWK
GOWKS
GOWL
GOWLS
GOWN
GOWNS
GRAB
GRABS
GRAD
GRADE
GRADS
GRAM
GRAMA
GRAME
GRAMS
GRAN
GRAND
GRANS
GRANT
GRAT
GRATE
GRAY
GRAYS
GREE
AGREE
GREED
GREEN
GREES
GREET
GREN
GRENS
GREW
GREWS
GREY
GREYS
GRID
GRIDE
GRIDS
GRIG
GRIGS
GRIM
GRIME
GRIMY
GRIN
AGRIN
GRIND
GRINS
GRIP
GRIPE
GRIPS
GRIS
GRISE
GRIST
GRISY
GRIT
GRITH
GRITS
GROG
GROGS
GROT
GROTS
GROW
GROWL
GROWN
GROWS
GRUB
GRUBS
GRUE
GRUED
GRUEL
GRUES
GRUM
GRUME
GRUMP
GUAN
GUANA
GUANO
GUANS
GUAR
GUARD
GUARS
GUCK
GUCKS
GUCKY
GUDE

GUDES
GUES
AGUES
GUESS
GUEST
GUFF
GUFFS
GUGA
GUGAS
GUID
GUIDE
GUIDS
GULA
GULAG
GULAR
GULAS
GULE
GULES
GULF
GULFS
GULFY
GULL
GULLS
GULLY
GULP
GULPH
GULPS
GUMP
GUMPS
GUNK
GUNKS
GURL
GURLS
GURLY
GURN
GURNS
GURU
GURUS
GUSH
GUSHY
GUST
GUSTO
GUSTS
GUSTY
GUTS
GUTSY
GUYS
GUYSE
GYAL
GYALS
GYBE
GYBED
GYBES
GYMP
GYMPS
GYPS
GYPSY
GYRE
GYRED
GYRES
GYRO
GYRON
GYROS
GYTE
GYTES
GYVE
GYVED
GYVES
HAAF
HAAFS

HAAR
HAARS
HACK
CHACK
SHACK
THACK
WHACK
HACKS
HADE
SHADE
HADED
HADES
HADJ
HADJI
HADS
CHADS
SHADS
HADST
HAEM
HAEMS
HAET
HAETS
HAFF
CHAFF
HAFFS
HAFT
CHAFT
SHAFT
HAFTS
HAGG
HAGGS
HAGS
SHAGS
HAIK
HAIKS
HAIKU
HAIL
HAILS
HAILY
HAIN
CHAIN
HAINS
HAIR
CHAIR
HAIRS
HAIRY
HAJI
HAJIS
HAJJ
HAJJI
HAKA
HAKAM
HAKAS
HAKE
SHAKE
HAKES
HALE
SHALE
WHALE
HALED
HALER
HALES
HALF
HALFA
HALFS
HALL
SHALL
HALLO
HALLS
HALM

SHALM
HALMA
HALMS
HALO
HALON
HALOS
HALT
SHALT
HALTS
HAME
SHAME
HAMED
HAMES
HAMS
CHAMS
SHAMS
WHAMS
HAND
SHAND
HANDS
HANDY
HANG
BHANG
PHANG
WHANG
HANGS
HANK
CHANK
SHANK
THANK
HANKS
HANKY
HAPS
CHAPS
SHAPS
WHAPS
HARD
CHARD
SHARD
HARDS
HARDY
HARE
CHARE
PHARE
SHARE
WHARE
HARED
HAREM
HARES
HARK
CHARK
SHARK
HARKS
HARL
HARLS
HARM
CHARM
HARMS
HARN
SHARN
HARNS
HARO
HAROS
HARP
SHARP
HARPS
HARPY
HART
CHART
HARTS

HASH
SHASH
HASHY
HASK
HASKS
HASP
HASPS
HAST
GHAST
HASTA
HASTE
HASTY
HATE
HATED
HATER
HATES
HATS
CHATS
GHATS
KHATS
WHATS
HAUD
HAUDS
HAUL
HAULD
HAULM
HAULS
HAULT
HAUT
GHAUT
HAUTE
HAVE
CHAVE
SHAVE
HAVEN
HAVER
HAVES
HAWK
HAWKS
HAWM
SHAWM
HAWMS
HAWS
CHAWS
SHAWS
THAWS
HAWSE
HAYS
CHAYS
SHAYS
HAZE
HAZED
HAZEL
HAZER
HAZES
HEAD
AHEAD
HEADS
HEADY
HEAL
SHEAL
WHEAL
HEALD
HEALS
HEAP
AHEAP
CHEAP
HEAPS
HEAPY
HEAR

SHEAR
WHEAR
HEARD
HEARE
HEARS
HEART
HEAT
CHEAT
WHEAT
HEATH
HEATS
HEBE
HEBEN
HEBES
HECH
HECHT
HECK
CHECK
HECKS
HEED
THEED
HEEDS
HEEDY
HEEL
SHEEL
WHEEL
HEELS
HEFT
THEFT
WHEFT
HEFTE
HEFTS
HEFTY
HEID
HEIDS
HEIR
THEIR
HEIRS
HELE
HELED
HELES
HELL
SHELL
HELLO
HELLS
HELM
WHELM
HELMS
HELP
WHELP
HELPS
HEME
THEME
HEMES
HEMP
HEMPS
HEMPY
HEND
SHEND
HENDS
HENS
THENS
WHENS
HENT
AHENT
SHENT
HENTS
HERB
HERBS
HERBY

HERD
SHERD
HERDS
HERE
CHERE
SHERE
THERE
WHERE
HERL
HERLS
HERM
THERM
HERMA
HERMS
HERN
HERNS
HERO
HEROE
HERON
HERS
HERSE
HERY
HERYE
HESP
HESPS
HEST
CHEST
GHEST
HESTS
HETE
THETE
HETES
HETS
SHETS
WHETS
HEWN
SHEWN
HEWS
CHEWS
SHEWS
THEWS
WHEWS
HEYS
WHEYS
HICK
CHICK
THICK
HICKS
HIDE
CHIDE
HIDED
HIDER
HIDES
HIED
SHIED
HIES
RHIES
SHIES
HIGH
AHIGH
THIGH
HIGHS
HIGHT
HIKE
HIKED
HIKER
HIKES
HILA
HILAR
HILD

CHILD
HILI
CHILI
HILL
CHILL
SHILL
THILL
HILLO
HILLS
HILLY
HILT
HILTS
HIND
AHIND
HINDS
HING
AHING
EHING
THING
HINGE
HINGS
HINS
CHINS
SHINS
THINS
WHINS
HINT
AHINT
HINTS
HIPS
CHIPS
SHIPS
WHIPS
HIPT
WHIPT
HIRE
SHIRE
HIRED
HIRER
HIRES
HISH
WHISH
HISS
WHISS
HIST
WHIST
HISTS
HITS
CHITS
SHITS
WHITS
HIVE
CHIVE
SHIVE
HIVED
HIVER
HIVES
HIZZ
CHIZZ
WHIZZ
HOAR
HOARD
HOARS
HOARY
HOAS
HOAST
HOBO
HOBOS
HOCK
CHOCK

SHOCK
HOCKS
HOED
SHOED
HOER
SHOER
HOERS
HOES
SHOES
HOGG
HOGGS
HOGH
HOGHS
HOGS
SHOGS
HOHS
PHOHS
HOIK
HOIKS
HOKE
CHOKE
HOKED
HOKES
HOKEY
HOKI
HOKIS
HOLD
AHOLD
HOLDS
HOLE
DHOLE
THOLE
WHOLE
HOLED
HOLES
HOLEY
HOLM
HOLMS
HOLT
HOLTS
HOME
HOMED
HOMER
HOMES
HOMEY
HOMO
ZHOMO
HOMOS
HOND
HONDS
HONE
OHONE
PHONE
RHONE
SHONE
HONED
HONER
HONES
HONEY
HONG
THONG
HONGI
HONGS
HONK
HONKS
HONKY
HONS
CHONS
PHONS
HOOD

HOODS
HOOF
CHOOF
HOOFS
HOOK
CHOOK
SHOOK
HOOKA
HOOKS
HOOKY
HOON
SHOON
HOONS
HOOP
WHOOP
HOOPS
HOOT
SHOOT
WHOOT
HOOTS
HOPE
SHOPE
HOPED
HOPER
HOPES
HOPS
CHOPS
SHOPS
WHOPS
HORE
CHORE
SHORE
WHORE
HORN
SHORN
THORN
HORNS
HORNY
HORS
KHORS
HORSE
HORST
HORSY
HOSE
CHOSE
THOSE
WHOSE
HOSED
HOSEN
HOSES
HOST
GHOST
HOSTA
HOSTS
HOTE
SHOTE
HOTEL
HOTEN
HOTS
PHOTS
SHOTS
HOUF
HOUFF
HOUFS
HOUR
HOURI
HOURS
HOUT
CHOUT
SHOUT

HOUTS
HOVE
SHOVE
HOVED
HOVEL
HOVEN
HOVER
HOVES
HOWE
HOWES
HOWF
HOWFF
HOWFS
HOWK
HOWKS
HOWL
THOWL
HOWLS
HOWS
CHOWS
DHOWS
SHOWS
HOWSO
HOYA
HOYAS
HUBS
CHUBS
HUCK
CHUCK
SHUCK
HUCKS
HUER
HUERS
HUFF
CHUFF
HUFFS
HUFFY
HUGE
HUGER
HUGS
CHUGS
THUGS
HUIA
HUIAS
HULA
HULAS
HULE
SHULE
HULES
HULK
HULKS
HULKY
HULL
AHULL
HULLO
HULLS
HULLY
HUMA
HUMAN
HUMAS
HUMF
HUMFS
HUMP
CHUMP
THUMP
HUMPH
HUMPS
HUMPY
HUMS
CHUMS

HUNK
CHUNK
HUNKS
HUNKY
HUNT
SHUNT
HUNTS
HURL
CHURL
HURLS
HURLY
HURT
HURTS
HUSH
SHUSH
HUSHY
HUSK
HUSKS
HUSKY
HUSO
HUSOS
HUSS
HUSSY
HUTS
PHUTS
SHUTS
HWYL
HWYLS
HYEN
HYENA
HYENS
HYKE
HYKES
HYLE
CHYLE
PHYLE
HYLEG
HYLES
HYMN
HYMNS
HYPE
HYPED
HYPER
HYPES
HYPO
HYPOS
IAMB
IAMBI
IAMBS
IBEX
VIBEX
ICED
DICED
RICED
TICED
VICED
ICER
DICER
NICER
RICER
ICERS
ICES
BICES
DICES
RICES
SICES
TICES
VICES
ICKY
DICKY
MICKY
PICKY
TICKY
WICKY
ICON
ICONS
IDEA
IDEAL
IDEAS
IDEE
IDEES
IDES
AIDES
BIDES
HIDES
NIDES
RIDES
SIDES
TIDES
WIDES
IDLE
SIDLE
IDLED
IDLER
IDLES
IDOL
IDOLA
IDOLS
IDYL
IDYLL
IDYLS
IFFY
JIFFY
MIFFY
NIFFY
IKAT
IKATS
IKON
EIKON
IKONS
ILEA
PILEA
ILEAC
ILEX
SILEX
ILIA
CILIA
ILIAC
ILKS
BILKS
MILKS
SILKS
ILLS
BILLS
CILLS
DILLS
FILLS
GILLS
HILLS
JILLS
KILLS
LILLS
MILLS
NILLS
PILLS
RILLS
SILLS
TILLS
VILLS
WILLS
YILLS
ILLY
BILLY
DILLY
FILLY
GILLY
HILLY
SILLY
TILLY
WILLY
IMAM
IMAMS
IMPI
IMPIS
IMPS
GIMPS
LIMPS
PIMPS
SIMPS
TIMPS
WIMPS
INBY
INBYE
INCH
CINCH
FINCH
LINCH
PINCH
WINCH
INFO
INFOS
INGO
BINGO
DINGO
JINGO
LINGO
PINGO
INGOT
INKS
BINKS
DINKS
FINKS
GINKS
JINKS
KINKS
LINKS
MINKS
OINKS
PINKS
RINKS
SINKS
TINKS
WINKS
INKY
DINKY
KINKY
PINKY
SINKY
ZINKY
INNS
JINNS
LINNS
WINNS
INTI
INTIL
INTIS
INTO
PINTO
IONS
CIONS
LIONS
PIONS
IOTA
BIOTA
DIOTA
IOTAS
IRES
CIRES
FIRES
HIRES
MIRES
SIRES
TIRES
VIRES
WIRES
IRID
VIRID
IRIDS
IRIS
SIRIS
IRKS
BIRKS
DIRKS
FIRKS
KIRKS
LIRKS
MIRKS
YIRKS
IRON
GIRON
IRONS
IRONY
ISLE
AISLE
LISLE
ISLED
ISLES
ISLET
ISMS
GISMS
JISMS
ISOS
MISOS
ITAS
DITAS
PITAS
VITAS
ITCH
AITCH
BITCH
DITCH
FITCH
HITCH
MITCH
PITCH
TITCH
WITCH
ITCHY
ITEM
ITEMS
IWIS
KIWIS
IXIA
IXIAS
JACK
JACKS
JADE
JADED
JADES
JAIL
JAILS
JAKE
JAKES
JAMB
JAMBE
JAMBO
JAMBS
JAMBU
JANE
JANES
JANN
JANNS
JAPE
JAPED
JAPER
JAPES
JARK
JARKS
JARL
JARLS
JASP
JASPE
JASPS
JATO
JATOS
JAUP
JAUPS
JAZZ
JAZZY
JEAN
JEANS
JEAT
JEATS
JEEL
JEELS
JEELY
JEER
JEERS
JEFF
JEFFS
JELL
JELLO
JELLS
JELLY
JERK
JERKS
JERKY
JEST
JESTS
JETE
JETES
JIAO
JIAOS
JIBE
JIBED
JIBER
JIBES
JIFF
JIFFS
JIFFY
JILL
JILLS
JILT
JILTS
JIMP
JIMPY
JINK
JINKS
JINN
DJINN
JINNI
JINNS
JIRD
JIRDS
JISM
JISMS
JIVE
JIVED
JIVER
JIVES
JOBE
JOBED
JOBES
JOCK
JOCKO
JOCKS
JOEY
JOEYS
JOHN
JOHNS
JOIN
JOINS
JOINT
JOKE
JOKED
JOKER
JOKES
JOKEY
JOLE
JOLED
JOLES
JOLL
JOLLS
JOLLY
JOLT
JOLTS
JOLTY
JOMO
JOMOS
JOOK
JOOKS
JOTA
JOTAS
JOUK
JOUKS
JOUR
JOURS
JOWL
JOWLS
JOWLY
JUBA
JUBAS
JUBE
JUBES
JUDO
JUDOS
JUGA
JUGAL
JUJU
JUJUS
JUKE
JUKED
JUKES
JUMP
JUMPS
JUMPY
JUNK
JUNKS
JUNKY
JURA
JURAL
JURAT
JUST
JUSTS
JUTE
JUTES
JUVE
JUVES
KADE
KADES
KADI
KADIS
KAGO
KAGOS
KAID
KAIDS
KAIE
KAIES
KAIF
KAIFS
KAIL
SKAIL
KAILS
KAIM
KAIMS
KAIN
KAING
KAINS
KAKA
KAKAS
KAKI
KAKIS
KALE
KALES
KALI
KALIF
KALIS
KAMA
KAMAS
KAME
KAMES
KAMI
KAMIK
KAMIS
KANA
KANAS
KANG
KANGA
KANGS
KANT
KANTS
KAON
KAONS
KARA
KARAS
KARAT
KART
SKART
KARTS
KATA
KATAS
KATI
KATIS
KATS
IKATS
SKATS
KAVA
KAVAS
KAWS
SKAWS
KAYO
KAYOS
KAYS
OKAYS
KAZI
KAZIS
KECK
KECKS
KEEK
KEEKS
KEEL
KEELS
KEEN
KEENS
KEEP
KEEPS
KEGS
SKEGS
KEIR
KEIRS
KELL
SKELL
KELLS
KELLY
KELP
SKELP
KELPS
KELPY
KELT
KELTS
KELTY
KEMB
KEMBO
KEMBS
KEMP
KEMPS
KEMPT
KENO
KENOS
KENT
KENTS
KEPI
KEPIS
KEPS
SKEPS
KERB
KERBS
KERF
KERFS
KERN
KERNE
KERNS
KEST
KESTS
KETA
KETAS
KHAN
KHANS
KHAT
KHATS
KHOR
KHORS
KHUD
KHUDS
KIBE
KIBES
KICK
KICKS
KIDS
SKIDS
KIER
SKIER
KIERS
KIKE
KIKES
KILL
SKILL
KILLS
KILN
KILNS
KILO
KILOS
KILP
KILPS
KILT
KILTS
KILTY
KINA
KINAS
KIND
KINDA
KINDS
KINDY
KING
AKING
EKING
KINGS
KINK
SKINK
KINKS
KINKY
KINO
KINOS
KINS
SKINS
KIPE
KIPES
KIPP
KIPPA
KIPPS
KIPS
SKIPS
KIRK
KIRKS
KIRN
KIRNS
KIST
KISTS
KITE
SKITE
KITED
KITES
KITH
KITHE
KITHS
KITS
SKITS
KIVA
KIVAS
KIWI
KIWIS
KNAG
KNAGS
KNAP
KNAPS
KNAR
KNARL
KNARS
KNEE
KNEED
KNEEL
KNEES
KNIT
KNITS
KNOB
KNOBS
KNOP
KNOPS
KNOT
KNOTS
KNOW
KNOWE
KNOWN
KNOWS
KNUB
KNUBS
KNUR
KNURL
KNURR
KNURS
KNUT
KNUTS
KOAN
KOANS
KOFF
SKOFF
KOFFS
KOHL
KOHLS
KOLA
KOLAS
KOLO
KOLOS
KONK
KONKS
KONS
IKONS
KOOK
KOOKS
KOOKY
KOPH
KOPHS
KORA
KORAS
KORE
KORES
KOTO
KOTOS
KOTOW
KRAB
KRABS
KSAR
KSARS
KUDU
KUDUS
KUKU
KUKUS
KURI
KURIS
KURU
KURUS
KYAT
KYATS
KYLE
KYLES
KYND
KYNDE
KYNDS
KYTE
SKYTE

KYTES
LABS
BLABS
FLABS
SLABS
LACE
GLACE
PLACE
LACED
LACES
LACET
LACEY
LACK
ALACK
BLACK
CLACK
FLACK
PLACK
SLACK
LACKS
LADE
BLADE
CLADE
GLADE
SLADE
LADED
LADEN
LADES
LADS
BLADS
CLADS
GLADS
LADY
GLADY
LAER
BLAER
LAERS
LAGS
BLAGS
CLAGS
FLAGS
SLAGS
LAHS
BLAHS
LAIC
LAICS
LAID
PLAID
SLAID
LAIDS
LAIK
GLAIK
LAIKA
LAIKS
LAIN
BLAIN
PLAIN
SLAIN
LAIR
FLAIR
GLAIR
LAIRD
LAIRS
LAIRY
LAKE
FLAKE
SLAKE
LAKED
LAKER
LAKES

LAKH
LAKHS
LAKY
FLAKY
LAMA
LLAMA
LAMAS
LAMB
LAMBS
LAME
BLAME
CLAME
FLAME
LAMED
LAMER
LAMES
LAMP
CLAMP
LAMPS
LAMS
CLAMS
FLAMS
GLAMS
SLAMS
LANA
LANAS
LAND
ALAND
BLAND
ELAND
GLAND
LANDE
LANDS
LANE
PLANE
SLANE
LANES
LANG
ALANG
CLANG
KLANG
SLANG
LANK
BLANK
CLANK
FLANK
PLANK
LANKS
LANKY
LANT
PLANT
SLANT
LANTS
LAPS
ALAPS
CLAPS
FLAPS
PLAPS
SLAPS
LAPSE
LARD
LARDS
LARDY
LARE
BLARE
FLARE
GLARE
LARES
LARK
LARKS

LARKY
LARN
LARNS
LASE
BLASE
LASED
LASER
LASES
LASH
BLASH
CLASH
FLASH
PLASH
SLASH
LASS
CLASS
GLASS
LASSI
LASSO
LASSU
LAST
BLAST
PLAST
LASTS
LATE
ALATE
BLATE
ELATE
PLATE
SLATE
LATED
LATEN
LATER
LATEX
LATH
LATHE
LATHI
LATHS
LATHY
LATS
BLATS
CLATS
FLATS
PLATS
SLATS
LAUD
BLAUD
LAUDS
LAUF
LAUFS
LAVA
LAVAS
LAVE
CLAVE
SLAVE
LAVED
LAVER
LAVES
LAWK
LAWKS
LAWN
FLAWN
LAWNS
LAWNY
LAWS
CLAWS
FLAWS
SLAWS
LAYS
ALAYS

BLAYS
CLAYS
FLAYS
PLAYS
SLAYS
LAZE
BLAZE
GLAZE
LAZED
LAZES
LAZO
LAZOS
LAZY
GLAZY
LEAD
PLEAD
LEADS
LEADY
LEAF
LEAFS
LEAFY
LEAK
BLEAK
LEAKS
LEAKY
LEAM
FLEAM
GLEAM
LEAMS
LEAN
CLEAN
GLEAN
LEANS
LEANT
LEANY
LEAP
LEAPS
LEAPT
LEAR
BLEAR
CLEAR
LEARE
LEARN
LEARS
LEARY
LEAS
FLEAS
PLEAS
LEASE
LEASH
LEAST
LEAT
BLEAT
CLEAT
PLEAT
LEATS
LEED
BLEED
GLEED
LEEK
CLEEK
GLEEK
SLEEK
LEEKS
LEEP
BLEEP
CLEEP
SLEEP
LEEPS
LEER

FLEER
SLEER
LEERS
LEERY
LEES
BLEES
FLEES
GLEES
LEESE
LEET
FLEET
GLEET
SLEET
LEETS
LEFT
ALEFT
CLEFT
LEFTE
LEFTS
LEFTY
LEGS
CLEGS
FLEGS
LEHR
LEHRS
LEIR
LEIRS
LEIS
GLEIS
VLEIS
LEISH
LEME
FLEME
LEMED
LEMEL
LEMES
LEND
BLEND
LENDS
LENG
LENGS
LENO
LENOS
LENS
GLENS
LENT
BLENT
GLENT
OLENT
LENTI
LENTO
LERE
LERED
LERES
LERP
LERPS
LESS
BLESS
LEST
BLEST
LESTS
LETS
BLETS
LEVE
CLEVE
LEVEE
LEVEL
LEVER
LEYS
BLEYS

FLEYS
GLEYS
SLEYS
LEZZ
LEZZY
LIAR
LIARD
LIARS
LIART
LIBS
GLIBS
LICE
SLICE
LICH
LICHI
LICHT
LICK
CLICK
FLICK
SLICK
LICKS
LIDO
LIDOS
LIED
CLIED
PLIED
LIEF
LIEFS
LIEN
ALIEN
LIENS
LIER
FLIER
PLIER
SLIER
LIERS
LIES
CLIES
FLIES
PLIES
VLIES
LIEU
LIEUS
LIFE
LIFER
LIFT
CLIFT
GLIFT
LIFTS
LIKE
ALIKE
GLIKE
YLIKE
LIKED
LIKEN
LIKER
LIKES
LILL
LILLS
LILO
LILOS
LILT
LILTS
LILY
SLILY
LIMA
LIMAS
LIMAX
LIMB
CLIMB

LIMBO
LIMBS
LIME
CLIME
SLIME
LIMED
LIMEN
LIMES
LIMEY
LIMN
LIMNS
LIMO
LIMOS
LIMP
BLIMP
FLIMP
LIMPS
LIMY
BLIMY
SLIMY
LIND
BLIND
LINDS
LINE
ALINE
CLINE
LINED
LINEN
LINER
LINES
LINEY
LING
CLING
FLING
PLING
SLING
LINGA
LINGO
LINGS
LINGY
LINK
BLINK
CLINK
PLINK
SLINK
LINKS
LINN
LINNS
LINNY
LINO
LINOS
LINS
BLINS
LINT
CLINT
FLINT
GLINT
LINTS
LINTY
LION
LIONS
LIPS
BLIPS
CLIPS
FLIPS
SLIPS
LIRA
LIRAS
LIRK
LIRKS

LISK
FLISK
GLISK
LISKS
LISP
LISPS
LIST
BLIST
LISTS
LITE
BLITE
ELITE
FLITE
LITED
LITER
LITES
LITH
LITHE
LITHO
LITHS
LIVE
ALIVE
BLIVE
OLIVE
SLIVE
LIVED
LIVEN
LIVER
LIVES
LOAD
LOADS
LOAF
LOAFS
LOAM
CLOAM
LOAMS
LOAMY
LOAN
SLOAN
LOANS
LOBE
GLOBE
LOBED
LOBES
LOBO
LOBOS
LOBS
BLOBS
GLOBS
SLOBS
LOCH
LOCHS
LOCK
BLOCK
CLOCK
FLOCK
LOCKS
LOCO
LOCOS
LODE
GLODE
LODEN
LODES
LOFT
ALOFT
LOFTS
LOFTY
LOGE
ELOGE
LOGES

LOGO
LOGOS
LOGS
CLOGS
FLOGS
SLOGS
LOGY
ELOGY
OLOGY
LOID
SLOID
LOIDS
LOIN
ELOIN
LOINS
LOIR
LOIRS
LOKE
BLOKE
CLOKE
LOKES
LOLL
LOLLS
LOLLY
LOMA
LOMAS
LOME
LOMED
LOMES
LONE
ALONE
CLONE
LONER
LONG
ALONG
FLONG
PLONG
LONGA
LONGE
LONGS
LOOF
ALOOF
KLOOF
LOOFA
LOOFS
LOOK
PLOOK
LOOKS
LOOM
BLOOM
GLOOM
SLOOM
LOOMS
LOON
LOONS
LOONY
LOOP
BLOOP
CLOOP
GLOOP
SLOOP
LOOPS
LOOPY
LOOR
FLOOR
LOORD
LOOS
LOOSE
LOOT
CLOOT

SLOOT
LOOTS
LOPE
ELOPE
SLOPE
LOPED
LOPER
LOPES
LOPS
CLOPS
ELOPS
FLOPS
GLOPS
PLOPS
SLOPS
LORD
LORDS
LORDY
LORE
BLORE
LOREL
LORES
LORY
FLORY
GLORY
LOSE
CLOSE
LOSED
LOSEL
LOSEN
LOSER
LOSES
LOSH
FLOSH
SLOSH
LOSS
FLOSS
GLOSS
LOSSY
LOTA
FLOTA
LOTAH
LOTAS
LOTE
CLOTE
FLOTE
LOTES
LOTH
CLOTH
SLOTH
LOTO
LOTOS
LOTS
BLOTS
CLOTS
PLOTS
SLOTS
LOUD
ALOUD
CLOUD
LOUN
LOUND
LOUNS
LOUP
LOUPE
LOUPS
LOUR
CLOUR
FLOUR
LOURE

LOURS
LOURY
LOUT
CLOUT
FLOUT
GLOUT
LOUTS
LOVE
CLOVE
GLOVE
SLOVE
LOVED
LOVER
LOVES
LOVEY
LOWE
ALOWE
LOWED
LOWER
LOWES
LOWN
BLOWN
CLOWN
FLOWN
LOWND
LOWNE
LOWNS
LOWS
BLOWS
CLOWS
FLOWS
GLOWS
PLOWS
SLOWS
LOWSE
LOWT
LOWTS
LOYS
CLOYS
PLOYS
LUAU
LUAUS
LUCE
LUCES
LUCK
CLUCK
PLUCK
LUCKS
LUCKY
LUDO
LUDOS
LUES
BLUES
CLUES
FLUES
GLUES
SLUES
LUFF
BLUFF
FLUFF
PLUFF
LUFFA
LUFFS
LUGE
LUGED
LUGER
LUGES
LUGS
GLUGS
PLUGS
SLUGS
LUIT
SLUIT
LUKE
FLUKE
LULL
LULLS
LULU
LULUS
LUMP
CLUMP
FLUMP
PLUMP
SLUMP
LUMPS
LUMPY
LUMS
ALUMS
PLUMS
SLUMS
LUNA
LUNAR
LUNAS
LUNE
LUNES
LUNG
CLUNG
FLUNG
SLUNG
LUNGE
LUNGI
LUNGS
LUNT
BLUNT
LUNTS
LURE
ALURE
LURED
LURES
LURK
LURKS
LURS
BLURS
SLURS
LUSH
BLUSH
FLUSH
PLUSH
SLUSH
LUSHY
LUSK
LUSKS
LUST
LUSTS
LUSTY
LUTE
ELUTE
FLUTE
LUTED
LUTER
LUTES
LUTZ
KLUTZ
LUXE
LUXES
LYAM
LYAMS
LYME
LYMES
LYNE
LYNES
LYRE
LYRES
LYSE
LYSED
LYSES
LYTE
FLYTE
LYTED
LYTES
MAAR
MAARS
MACE
MACED
MACER
MACES
MACK
SMACK
MACKS
MAGE
IMAGE
MAGES
MAGG
MAGGS
MAGI
MAGIC
MAID
MAIDS
MAIK
SMAIK
MAIKO
MAIKS
MAIL
MAILE
MAILS
MAIM
MAIMS
MAIN
AMAIN
MAINS
MAIR
MAIRE
MAIRS
MAKE
MAKER
MAKES
MAKO
MAKOS
MALE
MALES
MALI
MALIC
MALIK
MALIS
MALL
SMALL
MALLS
MALM
SMALM
MALMS
MALT
SMALT
MALTS
MALTY
MAMA
MAMAS
MAMS
IMAMS
MANA
MANAS
MANE
MANED
MANEH
MANES
MANET
MANG
MANGA
MANGE
MANGO
MANGS
MANGY
MANI
MANIA
MANIC
MANIS
MANO
MANOR
MANOS
MANS
MANSE
MARA
MARAE
MARAH
MARAS
MARC
MARCH
MARCS
MARD
MARDY
MARE
MARES
MARG
MARGE
MARGS
MARK
MARKS
MARL
MARLE
MARLS
MARLY
MARM
SMARM
MARMS
MARS
MARSH
MART
SMART
MARTS
MASA
OMASA
MASAS
MASE
MASED
MASER
MASES
MASH
SMASH
MASHY
MASK
MASKS
MASS
AMASS
MASSA
MASSE
MASSY
MAST
MASTS
MASTY
MASU
MASUS
MATE
AMATE
MATED
MATER
MATES
MATEY
MATH
MATHS
MATT
MATTE
MAUD
MAUDS
MAUL
MAULS
MAUN
MAUND
MAWK
MAWKS
MAWKY
MAWR
MAWRS
MAXI
MAXIM
MAXIS
MAYA
MAYAS
MAYS
MAYST
MAZE
AMAZE
MAZED
MAZER
MAZES
MEAD
MEADS
MEAL
MEALS
MEALY
MEAN
MEANE
MEANS
MEANT
MEANY
MEAT
MEATH
MEATS
MEATY
MEED
MEEDS
MEEK
SMEEK
MEER
AMEER
EMEER
MEERS
MEET
MEETS
MEGA
OMEGA
MEIN
MEINS
MEINT
MEINY
MELA
MELAS
MELD
MELDS
MELL
SMELL
MELLS
MELT
SMELT
MELTS
MEMO
MEMOS
MEND
AMEND
EMEND
MENDS
MENE
AMENE
MENED
MENES
MENG
MENGE
MENGS
MENT
AMENT
MENTA
MENTO
MENU
MENUS
MEOW
MEOWS
MERC
MERCS
MERCY
MERE
MERED
MEREL
MERER
MERES
MERI
MERIL
MERIS
MERIT
MERK
MERKS
MERL
MERLE
MERLS
MESA
MESAL
MESAS
MESE
MESEL
MESES
MESH
MESHY
MESS
MESSY
METE
METED
METER
METES
MEUS
EMEUS
MEUSE
MEVE
MEVED
MEVES
MEWL
MEWLS
MEWS
SMEWS
MEZE
MEZES
MICA
MICAS
MICE
AMICE
MICK
MICKS
MICKY
MICO
MICOS
MIDI
MIDIS
MIDS
MIDST
MIEN
MIENS
MIFF
MIFFS
MIFFY
MIKE
MIKES
MILD
MILDS
MILE
SMILE
MILER
MILES
MILK
MILKO
MILKS
MILKY
MILL
MILLE
MILLS
MILO
MILOR
MILOS
MILT
MILTS
MILTZ
MIME
MIMED
MIMER
MIMES
MINA
MINAE
MINAR
MINAS
MIND
MINDS
MINE
AMINE
IMINE
MINED
MINER
MINES
MING
MINGE
MINGS
MINGY
MINI
MINIM
MINIS
MINK
MINKE
MINKS
MINO
MINOR
MINOS
MINT
MINTS
MINTY
MIRE
MIRED
MIRES
MIRI
MIRIN
MIRK
SMIRK
MIRKS
MIRS
AMIRS
EMIRS
SMIRS
MIRV
MIRVS
MISE
MISER
MISES
MISO
MISOS
MISS
AMISS
MISSA
MISSY
MIST
MISTS
MISTY
MITE
SMITE
MITER
MITES
MITT
MITTS
MITY
AMITY
MOAN
MOANS
MOAT
MOATS
MOCH
MOCHA
MOCHS
MOCHY
MOCK
SMOCK
MOCKS
MODE
MODEL
MODEM
MODER
MODES
MODI
MODII
MOGS
SMOGS
MOHR
MOHRS
MOIL
MOILS
MOIT
MOITS
MOJO
MOJOS
MOKE
SMOKE
MOKES
MOKI
MOKIS
MOKO
SMOKO
MOKOS
MOLA
MOLAL
MOLAR
MOLAS
MOLD
MOLDS
MOLE
MOLES
MOLL
MOLLA
MOLLS
MOLLY
MOLT
SMOLT
YMOLT
MOLTO
MOLTS
MOME
MOMES
MONA
MONAD
MONAL
MONAS
MONG
AMONG
EMONG
MONGS
MONK
MONKS
MONO
MONOS
MOOD
MOODS
MOODY
MOOK
MOOKS
MOOL
MOOLA
MOOLI
MOOLS
MOOLY
MOON
MOONS
MOONY
MOOP
MOOPS
MOOR
SMOOR
MOORS
MOORY
MOOS
MOOSE
MOOT
SMOOT
MOOTS
MOPE
MOPED
MOPER
MOPES
MOPEY
MOPS
MOPSY
MORA
MORAL
MORAS
MORAT
MORAY
MORE
SMORE
MOREL
MORES
MORN
MORNE
MORNS
MORS
MORSE
MORT
AMORT
MORTS
MOSE
MOSED
MOSES
MOSEY
MOSS
MOSSY
MOST
MOSTS
MOTE
EMOTE
SMOTE
MOTED
MOTEL
MOTEN
MOTES
MOTET
MOTEY
MOTH
MOTHS
MOTHY
MOTT
MOTTE
MOTTO
MOTTS
MOTTY
MOTU
MOTUS
MOUE
MOUES
MOUP
MOUPS
MOUS
MOUSE
MOUST
MOUSY
MOVE
AMOVE
EMOVE
MOVED
MOVER
MOVES
MOWA
MOWAS
MOXA
MOXAS
MOYA
MOYAS
MOYL
MOYLE
MOYLS
MOZE
MOZED
MOZES
MUCK
AMUCK
MUCKS
MUCKY
MUFF
MUFFS
MUGS
SMUGS
MUID
MUIDS

MUIL
MUILS
MUIR
MUIRS
MULE
EMULE
MULES
MULEY
MULL
MULLS
MUMM
MUMMS
MUMMY
MUMP
MUMPS
MUMS
MUMSY
MUNT
MUNTS
MUNTU
MUON
MUONS
MURE
EMURE
MURED
MURES
MUREX
MURK
MURKS
MURKY
MURL
MURLS
MURLY
MUSE
AMUSE
MUSED
MUSER
MUSES
MUSET
MUSH
MUSHA
MUSHY
MUSK
MUSKS
MUSKY
MUSO
MUSOS
MUSS
MUSSE
MUSSY
MUST
MUSTH
MUSTS
MUSTY
MUTE
MUTED
MUTER
MUTES
MUTI
MUTIS
MUTT
MUTTS
MYAL
MYALL
MYNA
MYNAH
MYNAS
MYTH
MYTHI
MYTHS

MZEE
MZEES
NAAM
NAAMS
NAAN
NAANS
NABK
NABKS
NABS
SNABS
NACH
NACHE
NACHO
NADA
NADAS
NAFF
NAFFS
NAGA
NAGAS
NAGS
KNAGS
SNAGS
NAIK
NAIKS
NAIL
SNAIL
NAILS
NALA
NALAS
NAME
NAMED
NAMER
NAMES
NANA
ANANA
JNANA
NANAS
NAPA
NAPAS
NAPE
NAPES
NAPS
KNAPS
SNAPS
NARC
NARCO
NARCS
NARD
NARDS
NARE
SNARE
NARES
NARK
SNARK
NARKS
NARKY
NARY
SNARY
NATS
GNATS
NAVE
KNAVE
NAVEL
NAVES
NAVEW
NAZE
NAZES
NEAL
NEALS
NEAP

SNEAP
NEAPS
NEAR
ANEAR
NEARS
NEAT
NEATH
NEBS
SNEBS
NECK
SNECK
NECKS
NEDS
SNEDS
NEED
KNEED
SNEED
NEEDS
NEEDY
NEEM
NEEMB
NEEMS
NEEP
NEEPS
NEIF
NEIFS
NEMN
NEMNS
NENE
NENES
NEON
NEONS
NERD
NERDS
NERDY
NERK
NERKA
NERKS
NEST
NESTS
NETE
NETES
NETT
NETTS
NETTY
NEUK
NEUKS
NEUM
NEUME
NEUMS
NEVE
NEVEL
NEVER
NEVES
NEWS
ENEWS
NEWSY
NEWT
NEWTS
NEXT
NEXTS
NIBS
SNIBS
NICE
NICER
NICK
SNICK
NICKS
NIDE
SNIDE

NIDES
NIEF
NIEFS
NIES
SNIES
NIFE
KNIFE
NIFES
NIFF
SNIFF
NIFFS
NIFFY
NIGH
ANIGH
NIGHS
NIGHT
NILL
NILLS
NILS
ANILS
NIMB
NIMBI
NIMBS
NINE
NINES
NIPA
NIPAS
NIPS
SNIPS
NIRL
NIRLS
NIRLY
NITE
UNITE
NITER
NITES
NITS
KNITS
UNITS
NOBS
KNOBS
SNOBS
NOCK
KNOCK
NOCKS
NODE
ANODE
NODES
NODS
SNODS
NOEL
NOELS
NOGG
NOGGS
NOGS
SNOGS
NOIL
NOILS
NOLE
NOLES
NOLL
KNOLL
NOLLS
NOMA
NOMAD
NOMAS
NOME
GNOME
NOMEN
NOMES

NONE
NONES
NONET
NONG
NONGS
NOOK
SNOOK
NOOKS
NOOKY
NOON
NOONS
NOOP
SNOOP
NOOPS
NORI
NORIA
NORIS
NORK
NORKS
NORM
ENORM
NORMA
NORMS
NOSE
NOSED
NOSER
NOSES
NOSEY
NOTA
NOTAL
NOTE
NOTED
NOTER
NOTES
NOUL
NOULD
NOULE
NOULS
NOUN
NOUNS
NOUNY
NOUP
NOUPS
NOUT
KNOUT
SNOUT
NOVA
NOVAE
NOVAS
NOWL
NOWLS
NOWN
KNOWN
NOWS
KNOWS
SNOWS
NOWT
NOWTS
NOWY
SNOWY
NUBS
KNUBS
SNUBS
NUDE
NUDER
NUDES
NUFF
SNUFF
NUFFS
NUKE

NUKED
NUKES
NULL
NULLA
NULLS
NUMB
NUMBS
NURD
NURDS
NURL
KNURL
NURLS
NURR
KNURR
NURRS
NURS
KNURS
NURSE
NUTS
KNUTS
NYES
SNYES
OAFS
GOAFS
LOAFS
OAKS
BOAKS
SOAKS
OARS
BOARS
HOARS
ROARS
SOARS
VOARS
OARY
GOARY
HOARY
ROARY
OAST
BOAST
COAST
HOAST
LOAST
ROAST
TOAST
OASTS
OATH
LOATH
OATHS
OATS
BOATS
COATS
DOATS
GOATS
MOATS
OBAS
BOBAS
OBEY
OBEYS
OBIA
COBIA
OBIAS
OBIT
OOBIT
OBITS
OBOE
OBOES
OBOL
OBOLI
OBOLS

OBOS
GOBOS
HOBOS
LOBOS
ZOBOS
OCAS
COCAS
SOCAS
OCHE
BOCHE
OCHER
OCHES
OCTA
OCTAD
OCTAL
OCTAS
ODAL
MODAL
NODAL
PODAL
ODALS
ODAS
CODAS
SODAS
ODES
BODES
CODES
LODES
MODES
NODES
RODES
ODIC
IODIC
SODIC
ODOR
ODORS
ODSO
GODSO
ODSOS
ODYL
ODYLE
ODYLS
OFAY
OFAYS
OFFS
BOFFS
COFFS
DOFFS
GOFFS
KOFFS
TOFFS
OGAM
OGAMS
OGEE
OGEES
OGLE
BOGLE
FOGLE
OGLED
OGLER
OGLES
OGRE
OGRES
OHOS
COHOS
TOHOS
OIKS
HOIKS
OILS
BOILS

COILS
FOILS
MOILS
NOILS
ROILS
SOILS
TOILS
OILY
DOILY
ROILY
SOILY
OINK
BOINK
OINKS
OINT
JOINT
NOINT
POINT
OINTS
OKAY
TOKAY
OKAYS
OKES
BOKES
COKES
HOKES
JOKES
LOKES
MOKES
POKES
ROKES
SOKES
TOKES
YOKES
OKRA
KOKRA
OKRAS
OKTA
OKTAS
OLDS
BOLDS
COLDS
FOLDS
GOLDS
HOLDS
MOLDS
SOLDS
WOLDS
OLDY
GOLDY
OLEO
OLEOS
OLID
SOLID
OLIO
FOLIO
POLIO
OLIOS
OLLA
HOLLA
MOLLA
OLLAS
OLLAV
OLMS
HOLMS
OLPE
GOLPE
OLPES
OMBU
KOMBU

OMBUS
OMEN
NOMEN
WOMEN
OMENS
OMER
COMER
HOMER
VOMER
OMERS
OMIT
VOMIT
OMITS
ONCE
BONCE
NONCE
PONCE
SONCE
ONCER
ONCES
ONER
BONER
GONER
HONER
LONER
MONER
TONER
ONERS
ONES
BONES
CONES
HONES
NONES
PONES
RONES
SONES
TONES
ZONES
ONLY
FONLY
ONTO
CONTO
ONUS
BONUS
TONUS
OOFS
COOFS
GOOFS
HOOFS
LOOFS
POOFS
ROOFS
WOOFS
YOOFS
OOHS
BOOHS
OOMS
BOOMS
COOMS
DOOMS
LOOMS
ROOMS
SOOMS
TOOMS
ZOOMS
OONS
BOONS
COONS
GOONS
HOONS

LOONS
MOONS
NOONS
POONS
ROONS
TOONS
WOONS
ZOONS
OONT
OONTS
OOPS
COOPS
GOOPS
HOOPS
LOOPS
MOOPS
NOOPS
POOPS
ROOPS
SOOPS
YOOPS
OOSE
BOOSE
GOOSE
LOOSE
MOOSE
NOOSE
ROOSE
OOSES
OOSY
GOOSY
OOZE
BOOZE
OOZED
OOZES
OOZY
BOOZY
WOOZY
OPAH
OPAHS
OPAL
COPAL
NOPAL
OPALS
OPED
COPED
DOPED
HOPED
LOPED
MOPED
OOPED
ROPED
TOPED
OPEN
OPENS
OPES
COPES
DOPES
HOPES
LOPES
MOPES
POPES
ROPES
TOPES
OPUS
MOPUS
ORAL
CORAL
GORAL
HORAL

LORAL MORAL PORAL RORAL SORAL ORALS **ORBS** FORBS SORBS **ORBY** FORBY **ORCA** ORCAS **ORCS** TORCS **ORDS** BORDS CORDS FORDS LORDS SORDS WORDS **ORES** BORES CORES FORES GORES KORES LORES MORES PORES RORES SORES TORES YORES **ORFE** ORFES **ORGY** PORGY **ORLE** ORLES **ORRA** MORRA SORRA **ORTS** BORTS DORTS FORTS MORTS PORTS RORTS SORTS TORTS WORTS **OSSA** FOSSA **OTIC** LOTIC **OTTO** LOTTO MOTTO POTTO OTTOS **OUCH** COUCH MOUCH POUCH TOUCH VOUCH OUCHT

OUKS BOUKS GOUKS JOUKS POUKS SOUKS TOUKS YOUKS ZOUKS **OULD** COULD MOULD NOULD WOULD **OULK** OULKS **OUPH** OUPHE OUPHS **OUPS** COUPS DOUPS LOUPS MOUPS NOUPS ROUPS SOUPS **OURN** BOURN MOURN YOURN **OURS** COURS FOURS HOURS JOURS LOURS POURS SOURS TOURS YOURS **OUST** JOUST MOUST ROUST OUSTS **OUTS** BOUTS DOUTS GOUTS HOUTS LOUTS POUTS ROUTS SOUTS TOUTS **OUZO** OUZOS **OVAL** OVALS **OVEN** COVEN HOVEN WOVEN OVENS **OVER** COVER DOVER HOVER LOVER

MOVER ROVER OVERS OVERT **OVUM** NOVUM **OWED** BOWED COWED DOWED JOWED LOWED MOWED NOWED ROWED SOWED TOWED VOWED WOWED **OWER** BOWER COWER DOWER LOWER MOWER POWER ROWER SOWER TOWER VOWER **OWES** BOWES HOWES LOWES YOWES **OWLS** BOWLS COWLS DOWLS FOWLS GOWLS HOWLS JOWLS NOWLS SOWLS YOWLS **OWLY** JOWLY LOWLY **OWNS** DOWNS GOWNS LOWNS POWNS TOWNS **OWRE** HOWRE POWRE OWRES **OWTS** DOWTS LOWTS NOWTS ROWTS TOWTS **OXEN** BOXEN WOXEN **OXER** BOXER

OXERS **OYER** COYER FOYER TOYER OYERS **OYES** NOYES **PACA** PACAS **PACE** APACE SPACE PACED PACER PACES PACEY **PACK** PACKS **PACO** PACOS **PACT** EPACT PACTA PACTS **PACY** SPACY **PAGE** APAGE PAGED PAGER PAGES **PAHS** OPAHS **PAID** APAID **PAIK** PAIKS **PAIL** PAILS **PAIN** SPAIN PAINS PAINT **PAIR** PAIRE PAIRS **PAIS** PAISA PAISE **PALE** SPALE PALEA PALED PALER PALES PALET **PALL** SPALL PALLA PALLS PALLY **PALM** PALMS PALMY **PALP** PALPI PALPS **PALS** OPALS

PALSY **PAND** PANDA PANDS PANDY **PANE** SPANE PANED PANEL PANES **PANG** SPANG PANGA PANGS **PANS** SPANS PANSY **PANT** PANTO PANTS **PAPA** PAPAL PAPAS PAPAW **PAPE** PAPER PAPES **PARA** PARAS **PARD** SPARD PARDI PARDS PARDY **PARE** SPARE PARED PAREO PARER PARES PAREU **PARK** SPARK PARKA PARKI PARKS PARKY **PARP** PARPS **PARR** PARRS PARRY **PARS** SPARS PARSE **PART** APART SPART PARTI PARTS PARTY **PASH** PASHA PASHM **PASS** PASSE **PAST** PASTA PASTE PASTS

PASTY **PATE** SPATE PATED PATEN PATER PATES **PATH** PATHS **PATS** SPATS PATSY **PAUA** PAUAS **PAUL** SPAUL PAULS **PAVE** PAVED PAVEN PAVER PAVES **PAWA** PAWAS PAWAW **PAWK** PAWKS PAWKY **PAWL** SPAWL PAWLS **PAWN** SPAWN PAWNS **PAWS** SPAWS **PAYS** APAYS SPAYS PAYSD **PEAG** PEAGS **PEAK** APEAK SPEAK PEAKS PEAKY **PEAL** SPEAL PEALS **PEAN** SPEAN PEANS **PEAR** SPEAR PEARE PEARL PEARS PEART **PEAS** PEASE **PEAT** SPEAT PEATS PEATY **PEBA** PEBAS **PECH** PECHS **PECK**

SPECK PECKE PECKS **PECS** SPECS **PEED** SPEED **PEEK** APEEK PEEKS **PEEL** SPEEL PEELS **PEEN** PEENS **PEEP** PEEPE PEEPS **PEER** SPEER PEERS PEERY **PEES** EPEES **PEGH** PEGHS **PEIN** PEINS **PEKE** PEKES **PELA** PELAS **PELE** PELES **PELF** PELFS **PELL** SPELL PELLS **PELT** SPELT PELTA PELTS **PEND** SPEND UPEND PENDS **PENE** PENED PENES **PENI** PENIE PENIS **PENK** PENKS **PENS** OPENS **PENT** SPENT PENTS **PEON** PEONS PEONY **PEPO** PEPOS **PERE** PERES **PERI** PERIL PERIS

PERK PERKS PERKY **PERM** SPERM PERMS **PERN** PERNS **PERT** APERT PERTS **PERV** PERVE PERVS **PESO** PESOS **PEST** PESTO PESTS **PETS** SPETS **PEWS** SPEWS **PHIS** APHIS **PHOH** PHOHS **PHON** PHONE PHONS PHONY **PHOT** PHOTO PHOTS **PHUT** PHUTS **PICA** SPICA PICAS **PICE** SPICE **PICK** SPICK PICKS PICKY **PICS** EPICS SPICS **PIED** SPIED **PIER** PIERS PIERT **PIES** SPIES **PIET** PIETA PIETS PIETY **PIKA** PIKAS **PIKE** SPIKE PIKED PIKER PIKES **PILA** PILAU PILAW **PILE**

SPILE PILEA PILED PILEI PILER PILES **PILI** PILIS **PILL** SPILL PILLS **PIMP** PIMPS **PINA** SPINA PINAS **PINE** OPINE SPINE PINED PINES PINEY **PING** APING OPING PINGO PINGS **PINK** SPINK PINKO PINKS PINKY **PINS** SPINS **PINT** PINTA PINTO PINTS **PINY** SPINY **PION** PIONS PIONY **PIOY** PIOYE PIOYS **PIPA** PIPAL PIPAS **PIPE** PIPED PIPER PIPES **PIPI** PIPIS PIPIT **PIRL** PIRLS **PIRN** PIRNS **PISE** PISES **PISH** APISH **PITA** PITAS **PITH** PITHS PITHY **PITS**

SPITS **PIUM** OPIUM PIUMS **PIZE** PIZES **PLAN** PLANE PLANK PLANS PLANT **PLAP** PLAPS **PLAT** SPLAT PLATE PLATS PLATY **PLAY** SPLAY UPLAY PLAYA PLAYS **PLEA** PLEAD PLEAS PLEAT **PLEB** PLEBS **PLED** UPLED **PLIE** PLIED PLIER PLIES **PLIM** PLIMS **PLOD** PLODS **PLOP** PLOPS **PLOT** PLOTS **PLOW** PLOWS **PLOY** PLOYS **PLUG** PLUGS **PLUM** PLUMB PLUME PLUMP PLUMS PLUMY **PLUS** PLUSH **POCK** POCKS POCKY **PODS** APODS **POEM** POEMS **POET** POETS **POGO** POGOS **POIS** POISE

POKE SPOKE POKED POKER POKES POKEY
POLE POLED POLER POLES POLEY
POLK POLKA POLKS
POLL POLLS POLLY
POLO POLOS
POLT POLTS
POLY POLYP POLYS
POME POMES
POMP POMPS
POND PONDS
PONE PONES PONEY
PONG PONGA PONGO PONGS PONGY
PONK PONKS
PONT PONTS PONTY
POOD POODS
POOF SPOOF POOFS POOFY
POOK SPOOK POOKA POOKS
POOL SPOOL POOLS
POON SPOON POONS
POOP APOOP POOPS
POOR SPOOR POORI POORT
POOT SPOOT POOTS
POPE POPES
POPS POPSY
PORE SPORE PORED PORER PORES
PORK PORKS PORKY
PORN PORNO PORNS
PORT APORT SPORT PORTA PORTS PORTY
POSE POSED POSER POSES POSEY
POSH SPOSH
POSS POSSE
POST POSTS
POTE POTED POTES
POTS SPOTS
POTT POTTO POTTS POTTY
POUF POUFS
POUK POUKE POUKS
POUR POURS
POUT SPOUT POUTS POUTY
POWN POWND POWNS POWNY
POXY EPOXY
POZZ POZZY
PRAD SPRAD PRADS
PRAM PRAMS
PRAT SPRAT PRATE PRATS PRATT PRATY
PRAU PRAUS
PRAY SPRAY PRAYS
PREE SPREE PREED PREEN PREES
PREP PREPS
PREX PREXY
PREY PREYS
PRIG SPRIG PRIGS
PRIM PRIMA PRIME PRIMO PRIMP PRIMS PRIMY
PROA PROAS
PROB PROBE PROBS
PROD SPROD PRODS
PROF PROFS
PROG SPROG PROGS
PROM EPROM PROMO PROMS
PROO PROOF
PROP PROPS
PROS PROSE PROSO PROSY
PROW PROWL PROWS
PRYS PRYSE
PSIS APSIS
PUCE PUCES
PUCK PUCKA PUCKS
PUDS SPUDS PUDSY
PUDU PUDUS
PUER PUERS
PUFF PUFFS PUFFY
PUJA PUJAS
PUKE PUKED PUKER PUKES
PUKU PUKUS
PULA PULAS
PULE SPULE PULED PULER PULES
PULK PULKA PULKS
PULL PULLS
PULP PULPS PULPY
PULU PULUS
PUMA PUMAS
PUMP PUMPS
PUMY SPUMY
PUNA PUNAS
PUNK SPUNK PUNKA PUNKS
PUNT PUNTO PUNTS PUNTY
PUPA PUPAE PUPAL PUPAS
PURE PURED PUREE PURER PURES
PURI PURIM PURIN PURIS
PURL PURLS
PURR PURRS
PURS SPURS PURSE PURSY
PUSH PUSHY
PUSS PUSSY
PUTT PUTTI PUTTO PUTTS PUTTY
PYAT PYATS
PYET PYETS
PYNE PYNED PYNES
PYOT PYOTS
PYRE SPYRE PYRES
PYRO PYROS
QADI QADIS
QOPH QOPHS
QUAD SQUAD QUADS
QUAG QUAGS
QUAT SQUAT QUATS
QUAY QUAYD QUAYS
QUEY QUEYN QUEYS
QUID EQUID SQUID QUIDS
QUIM QUIMS
QUIN QUINA QUINE QUINS QUINT
QUIP EQUIP QUIPO QUIPS QUIPU
QUIT SQUIT QUITE QUITS
QUIZ SQUIZ
QUOD QUODS
QUOP QUOPS
RABI RABIC RABID RABIS
RACE BRACE GRACE TRACE RACED RACER RACES
RACH BRACH ORACH RACHE
RACK BRACK CRACK FRACK TRACK WRACK RACKS
RACY ORACY
RADE GRADE IRADE TRADE
RADS BRADS GRADS PRADS TRADS
RAFF DRAFF GRAFF RAFFS
RAFT CRAFT DRAFT GRAFT KRAFT RAFTS
RAGA RAGAS
RAGE RAGED RAGEE RAGER RAGES
RAGG RAGGS RAGGY
RAGI TRAGI RAGIS
RAGS BRAGS CRAGS DRAGS FRAGS
RAID BRAID RAIDS
RAIK TRAIK RAIKS
RAIL BRAIL DRAIL FRAIL GRAIL TRAIL RAILE RAILS
RAIN BRAIN DRAIN GRAIN TRAIN RAINE RAINS RAINY
RAIS RAISE
RAIT KRAIT TRAIT RAITA RAITS
RAJA RAJAH RAJAS
RAKE BRAKE CRAKE DRAKE RAKED RAKEE RAKER RAKES
RAKI RAKIS
RAKU RAKUS
RALE RALES
RAMI RAMIE RAMIN RAMIS
RAMP CRAMP TRAMP RAMPS
RAMS CRAMS DRAMS GRAMS PRAMS TRAMS
RANA PRANA RANAS
RAND BRAND GRAND RANDS RANDY
RANG KRANG ORANG PRANG RANGE RANGY
RANI RANIS
RANK BRANK CRANK DRANK FRANK PRANK RANKE RANKS
RANT DRANT GRANT ORANT TRANT RANTS
RAPE CRAPE DRAPE GRAPE TRAPE RAPED RAPER RAPES
RAPS CRAPS DRAPS FRAPS TRAPS WRAPS
RAPT WRAPT YRAPT
RARE CRARE RARER
RASE ERASE PRASE RASED RASES
RASH BRASH CRASH TRASH
RASP GRASP RASPS RASPY
RAST BRAST WRAST RASTA
RATA RATAN RATAS
RATE CRATE FRATE GRATE IRATE ORATE PRATE URATE WRATE RATED RATEL RATER RATES
RATH WRATH RATHE RATHS
RATS BRATS PRATS TRATS
RATU RATUS
RAUN RAUNS
RAVE BRAVE CRAVE DRAVE GRAVE TRAVE RAVED RAVEL RAVEN RAVER RAVES
RAWN BRAWN DRAWN PRAWN RAWNS
RAWS BRAWS CRAWS DRAWS
RAYS BRAYS DRAYS FRAYS GRAYS PRAYS TRAYS
RAZE BRAZE CRAZE GRAZE RAZED RAZEE RAZES
READ AREAD BREAD DREAD OREAD TREAD READS READY
REAK BREAK CREAK FREAK WREAK REAKS
REAL AREAL UREAL REALM REALO REALS
REAM BREAM CREAM DREAM REAME REAMS REAMY
REAN REANS
REAP REAPS
REAR AREAR DREAR REARM REARS
RECK DRECK TRECK WRECK RECKS
REDD AREDD REDDS REDDY
REDE AREDE BREDE REDES
REDO CREDO UREDO REDOS REDOX
REDS CREDS
REED BREED CREED DREED FREED GREED PREED TREED REEDE REEDS REEDY
REEF REEFS
REEK CREEK REEKS REEKY
REEL CREEL REELS
REEN GREEN PREEN TREEN REENS
REES BREES CREES DREES FREES GREES PREES TREES REEST
REGO GREGO REGOS
REIF PREIF TREIF REIFS REIFY
REIK REIKS
REIN GREIN REINS
REIS REIST
REKE REKED REKES

REND
TREND
RENDS
RENS
BRENS
GRENS
WRENS
RENT
BRENT
DRENT
PRENT
URENT
YRENT
RENTE
RENTS
REPO
REPOS
REPOT
REPP
REPPS
REPS
PREPS
REST
CREST
DREST
PREST
TREST
WREST
RESTS
RESTY
RETE
ARETE
RETES
RETS
ARETS
FRETS
TRETS
REWS
BREWS
CREWS
GREWS
TREWS
RHEA
RHEAS
RIAL
PRIAL
TRIAL
URIAL
RIALS
RIAS
ARIAS
RIBS
CRIBS
DRIBS
RICE
GRICE
PRICE
TRICE
RICED
RICER
RICES
RICEY
RICH
RICHT
RICK
BRICK
CRICK
ERICK
PRICK
TRICK

WRICK
RICKS
RICY
PRICY
RIDE
BRIDE
GRIDE
PRIDE
TRIDE
RIDER
RIDES
RIDS
GRIDS
IRIDS
RIEL
ARIEL
ORIEL
RIELS
RIEM
RIEMS
RIFE
RIFER
RIFF
GRIFF
TRIFF
RIFFS
RIFT
DRIFT
GRIFT
RIFTE
RIFTS
RIFTY
RIGG
RIGGS
RIGS
BRIGS
FRIGS
GRIGS
PRIGS
TRIGS
RILE
RILED
RILES
RILEY
RILL
BRILL
DRILL
FRILL
GRILL
KRILL
PRILL
TRILL
RILLE
RILLS
RIMA
PRIMA
RIMAE
RIME
CRIME
GRIME
PRIME
RIMED
RIMER
RIMES
RIMS
BRIMS
CRIMS
PRIMS
TRIMS
RIMU

RIMUS
RIMY
GRIMY
PRIMY
RIND
GRIND
RINDS
RINDY
RINE
BRINE
CRINE
TRINE
URINE
RINES
RING
BRING
ERING
WRING
RINGS
RINK
BRINK
DRINK
PRINK
RINKS
RINS
GRINS
TRINS
RINSE
RIOT
ARIOT
GRIOT
RIOTS
RIPE
GRIPE
TRIPE
RIPED
RIPEN
RIPER
RIPES
RIPP
RIPPS
RIPS
DRIPS
GRIPS
TRIPS
RISE
ARISE
BRISE
CRISE
GRISE
PRISE
RISEN
RISER
RISES
RISK
BRISK
FRISK
RISKS
RISKY
RISP
CRISP
RISPS
RITE
TRITE
URITE
WRITE
RITES
RITS
BRITS
CRITS

FRITS
GRITS
WRITS
RITT
RITTS
RIVA
RIVAL
RIVAS
RIVE
DRIVE
RIVED
RIVEL
RIVEN
RIVER
RIVES
RIVET
RIVO
RIVOS
RIZA
RIZAS
ROAD
BROAD
TROAD
ROADS
ROAM
ROAMS
ROAN
GROAN
ROANS
ROAR
ROARS
ROARY
ROBE
PROBE
ROBED
ROBES
ROBS
PROBS
ROCH
BROCH
ROCK
BROCK
CROCK
FROCK
TROCK
ROCKS
ROCKY
ROCS
CROCS
RODE
ERODE
TRODE
RODED
RODEO
RODES
RODS
BRODS
PRODS
TRODS
ROIL
BROIL
DROIL
ROILS
ROILY
ROIN
GROIN
PROIN
ROINS
ROJI
ROJIS

ROKE
BROKE
PROKE
TROKE
WROKE
ROKED
ROKER
ROKES
ROLE
DROLE
PROLE
ROLES
ROLL
DROLL
PROLL
TROLL
ROLLS
ROMA
AROMA
GROMA
ROMAL
ROMAN
ROMAS
ROMP
TROMP
ROMPS
RONE
CRONE
DRONE
GRONE
KRONE
PRONE
TRONE
RONEO
RONES
RONG
PRONG
WRONG
RONT
FRONT
RONTE
RONTS
ROOD
BROOD
ROODS
ROOF
GROOF
PROOF
ROOFS
ROOFY
ROOK
BROOK
CROOK
DROOK
ROOKS
ROOKY
ROOM
BROOM
GROOM
VROOM
ROOMS
ROOMY
ROON
CROON
ROONS
ROOP
DROOP
TROOP
ROOPS
ROOPY

ROOS
BROOS
ROOSA
ROOSE
ROOST
ROOT
WROOT
ROOTS
ROOTY
ROPE
GROPE
TROPE
ROPED
ROPER
ROPES
ROPEY
RORE
CRORE
FRORE
PRORE
RORES
RORT
RORTS
RORTY
RORY
FRORY
ROSE
AROSE
BROSE
EROSE
PROSE
ROSED
ROSES
ROSET
ROST
FROST
ROSTS
ROSY
PROSY
ROTA
ROTAL
ROTAS
ROTE
WROTE
ROTED
ROTES
ROTI
ROTIS
ROTL
ROTLS
ROTS
GROTS
TROTS
ROUE
ROUES
ROUL
PROUL
ROULE
ROULS
ROUM
ROUMS
ROUP
CROUP
GROUP
ROUPS
ROUPY
ROUT
CROUT
GROUT
TROUT

ROUTE
ROUTH
ROUTS
ROVE
DROVE
GROVE
PROVE
ROVED
ROVER
ROVES
ROWS
BROWS
CROWS
DROWS
FROWS
GROWS
PROWS
TROWS
VROWS
ROWT
ROWTH
ROWTS
RUBE
RUBES
RUBS
DRUBS
GRUBS
RUCK
CRUCK
TRUCK
RUCKS
RUDD
RUDDS
RUDDY
RUDE
CRUDE
PRUDE
RUDER
RUDES
RUDS
CRUDS
RUED
GRUED
TRUED
RUES
GRUES
TRUES
RUFF
GRUFF
RUFFE
RUFFS
RUGS
DRUGS
TRUGS
RUIN
RUING
RUINS
RUKH
RUKHS
RULE
BRULE
RULED
RULER
RULES
RULY
TRULY
RUME
BRUME
GRUME
RUMEN

RUMES
RUMP
CRUMP
FRUMP
GRUMP
TRUMP
RUMPS
RUMPY
RUMS
ARUMS
DRUMS
RUND
RUNDS
RUNE
PRUNE
RUNED
RUNES
RUNG
WRUNG
RUNGS
RUNT
BRUNT
GRUNT
PRUNT
RUNTS
RUNTY
RURP
RURPS
RURU
RURUS
RUSA
RUSAS
RUSE
CRUSE
DRUSE
RUSES
RUSH
BRUSH
CRUSH
FRUSH
RUSHY
RUSK
RUSKS
RUST
BRUST
CRUST
FRUST
TRUST
RUSTS
RUSTY
RUTH
TRUTH
RUTHS
RYAL
RYALS
RYKE
GRYKE
RYKED
RYKES
RYND
RYNDS
RYOT
RYOTS
RYPE
GRYPE
RYPER
SACK
SACKS
SADE
SADES

SAFE
SAFED
SAFER
SAFES
SAGA
SAGAS
SAGE
USAGE
SAGER
SAGES
SAGO
SAGOS
SAIC
SAICE
SAICK
SAICS
SAID
SAIDS
SAIL
SAILS
SAIM
SAIMS
SAIN
SAINE
SAINS
SAINT
SAIR
SAIRS
SAIS
SAIST
SAKE
SAKER
SAKES
SAKI
SAKIA
SAKIS
SALE
SALEP
SALES
SALET
SALP
SALPA
SALPS
SALS
SALSA
SALSE
SALT
SALTO
SALTS
SALTY
SAMA
SAMAN
SAMAS
SAME
YSAME
SAMEL
SAMEN
SAMES
SAMEY
SAMP
SAMPI
SAMPS
SAND
SANDS
SANDY
SANE
SANER
SANG
SANGS
SANK

SANKO
SANS
SANSA
SANT
SANTS
SARD
SARDS
SARI
SARIN
SARIS
SARK
SARKS
SARKY
SARS
KSARS
TSARS
SASS
SASSE
SASSY
SATE
SATED
SATES
SATI
SATIN
SATIS
SAUL
SAULS
SAULT
SAUT
SAUTE
SAUTS
SAVE
SAVED
SAVER
SAVES
SAVEY
SAYS
SAYST
SCAB
SCABS
SCAD
SCADS
SCAG
SCAGS
SCAM
SCAMP
SCAMS
SCAN
SCAND
SCANS
SCANT
SCAR
SCARE
SCARF
SCARP
SCARS
SCART
SCARY
SCAT
SCATH
SCATS
SCATT
SCAW
SCAWS
SCOG
SCOGS
SCOP
SCOPA
SCOPE
SCOT

ASCOT
ESCOT
SCOTS
SCOW
SCOWL
SCOWP
SCOWS
SCUD
SCUDI
SCUDO
SCUDS
SCUG
SCUGS
SCUL
SCULK
SCULL
SCULP
SCULS
SCUM
SCUMS
SCUP
SCUPS
SCUR
SCURF
SCURS
SCUT
SCUTA
SCUTE
SCUTS
SCYE
SCYES
SEAL
SEALS
SEAM
SEAME
SEAMS
SEAMY
SEAN
SEANS
SEAR
SEARE
SEARS
SEAS
SEASE
SEAT
SEATS
SECT
SECTS
SEED
SEEDS
SEEDY
SEEK
SEEKS
SEEL
SEELD
SEELS
SEELY
SEEM
SEEMS
SEEP
SEEPS
SEEPY
SEER
SEERS
SEGO
SEGOL
SEGOS
SEIF
SEIFS
SEIL

SEILS
SEIR
SEIRS
SEIS
SEISE
SEISM
SEKT
SEKTS
SELE
SELES
SELF
SELFS
SELL
SELLA
SELLE
SELLS
SEME
SEMEE
SEMEN
SEMI
SEMIE
SEMIS
SENA
SENAS
SEND
SENDS
SENS
SENSA
SENSE
SENT
SENTS
SEPT
SEPTA
SEPTS
SERA
SERAC
SERAI
SERAL
SERE
SERED
SERER
SERES
SERF
SERFS
SERK
SERKS
SERR
SERRA
SERRE
SERRS
SERRY
SESE
SESEY
SESS
SESSA
SETA
SETAE
SETT
SETTS
SEXT
SEXTS
SHAD
SHADE
SHADS
SHADY
SHAG
SHAGS
SHAH
SHAHS
SHAM

SHAMA
SHAME
SHAMS
SHAN
SHAND
SHANK
SHANS
SHAW
PSHAW
SHAWL
SHAWM
SHAWS
SHAY
SHAYA
SHAYS
SHEA
SHEAF
SHEAL
SHEAR
SHEAS
SHED
SHEDS
SHES
ASHES
ISHES
SHET
ASHET
SHETS
SHEW
SHEWN
SHEWS
SHIM
SHIMS
SHIN
SHINE
SHINS
SHINY
SHIP
SHIPS
SHIR
SHIRE
SHIRK
SHIRR
SHIRS
SHIRT
SHIT
SHITE
SHITS
SHIV
SHIVE
SHIVS
SHMO
SHMOE
SHOE
SHOED
SHOER
SHOES
SHOG
SHOGI
SHOGS
SHOO
SHOOK
SHOOL
SHOON
SHOOS
SHOOT
SHOP
SHOPE
SHOPS
SHOT

SHOTE
SHOTS
SHOTT
SHOW
SHOWN
SHOWS
SHOWY
SHUL
SHULE
SHULN
SHULS
SHUN
SHUNS
SHUNT
SHUT
SHUTE
SHUTS
SHWA
SHWAS
SIAL
SIALS
SIBB
SIBBS
SICE
SICES
SICK
SICKO
SICKS
SIDA
SIDAS
SIDE
ASIDE
SIDED
SIDER
SIDES
SIEN
SIENS
SIENT
SIFT
SIFTS
SIGH
SIGHS
SIGHT
SIGN
SIGNS
SIJO
SIJOS
SIKA
SIKAS
SIKE
SIKES
SILD
SILDS
SILE
ESILE
SILED
SILEN
SILER
SILES
SILEX
SILK
SILKS
SILKY
SILL
SILLS
SILLY
SILO
SILOS
SILT
SILTS

SILTY
SIMA
SIMAR
SIMAS
SIMI
SIMIS
SIMP
SIMPS
SIND
SINDS
SINE
SINED
SINES
SINEW
SING
USING
SINGE
SINGS
SINK
SINKS
SINKY
SIPE
SIPED
SIPES
SIRE
SIRED
SIREN
SIRES
SIRI
SIRIH
SIRIS
SISS
SISSY
SIST
SISTS
SITE
SITED
SITES
SITH
SITHE
SIZE
SIZED
SIZEL
SIZER
SIZES
SKAG
SKAGS
SKAT
SKATE
SKATS
SKATT
SKAW
SKAWS
SKEG
SKEGG
SKEGS
SKEO
SKEOS
SKEP
SKEPS
SKER
ASKER
ESKER
SKERS
SKEW
ASKEW
SKEWS
SKID
SKIDS
SKIM

SKIMP
SKIMS
SKIN
SKINK
SKINS
SKINT
SKIO
SKIOS
SKIP
SKIPS
SKIT
SKITE
SKITS
SKUA
SKUAS
SKUG
SKUGS
SKYR
SKYRE
SKYRS
SLAB
SLABS
SLAE
SLAES
SLAG
SLAGS
SLAM
SLAMS
SLAP
SLAPS
SLAT
SLATE
SLATS
SLATY
SLAW
SLAWS
SLAY
SLAYS
SLED
ISLED
SLEDS
SLEE
SLEEK
SLEEP
SLEER
SLEET
SLEW
SLEWS
SLEY
SLEYS
SLID
SLIDE
SLIM
SLIME
SLIMS
SLIMY
SLIP
SLIPE
SLIPS
SLIPT
SLIT
SLITS
SLOB
SLOBS
SLOE
SLOES
SLOG
SLOGS
SLOP
SLOPE

SLOPS
SLOPY
SLOT
SLOTH
SLOTS
SLOW
SLOWS
SLUB
SLUBB
SLUBS
SLUE
SLUED
SLUES
SLUG
SLUGS
SLUM
SLUMP
SLUMS
SLUR
SLURB
SLURP
SLURS
SLUT
SLUTS
SMEE
SMEEK
SMEES
SMEW
SMEWS
SMIR
SMIRK
SMIRR
SMIRS
SMIT
SMITE
SMITH
SMITS
SMOG
SMOGS
SMUG
SMUGS
SMUR
SMURS
SMUT
SMUTS
SNAB
SNABS
SNAG
SNAGS
SNAP
SNAPS
SNAR
SNARE
SNARK
SNARL
SNARS
SNARY
SNEB
SNEBS
SNED
SNEDS
SNEE
SNEED
SNEER
SNEES
SNIB
SNIBS
SNIG
SNIGS
SNIP

SNIPE
SNIPS
SNIPY
SNOB
SNOBS
SNOD
SNODS
SNOG
SNOGS
SNOT
SNOTS
SNOW
SNOWK
SNOWS
SNOWY
SNUB
SNUBS
SNUG
SNUGS
SNYE
SNYES
SOAK
SOAKS
SOAP
SOAPS
SOAPY
SOAR
SOARE
SOARS
SOCA
SOCAS
SOCK
SOCKO
SOCKS
SODA
SODAS
SOFA
SOFAR
SOFAS
SOFT
SOFTA
SOFTS
SOFTY
SOIL
SOILS
SOILY
SOJA
SOJAS
SOKE
SOKEN
SOKES
SOLA
SOLAH
SOLAN
SOLAR
SOLAS
SOLD
SOLDE
SOLDI
SOLDO
SOLDS
SOLE
SOLED
SOLER
SOLES
SOLI
SOLID
SOLO
SOLOS
SOMA

SOMAN
SOMAS
SONE
SONES
SONG
SONGS
SONS
SONSE
SONSY
SOOK
SOOKS
SOOM
SOOMS
SOOP
SOOPS
SOOT
SOOTE
SOOTH
SOOTS
SOOTY
SOPH
SOPHS
SORA
PSORA
SORAL
SORAS
SORB
SORBS
SORD
SORDA
SORDO
SORDS
SORE
SORED
SOREE
SOREL
SORER
SORES
SOREX
SORN
SORNS
SORT
SORTS
SOUK
SOUKS
SOUL
SOULS
SOUM
SOUMS
SOUP
SOUPS
SOUPY
SOUR
SOURS
SOUS
SOUSE
SOUT
SOUTH
SOUTS
SOWF
SOWFF
SOWFS
SOWL
SOWLE
SOWLS
SOWM
SOWMS
SOWN
SOWND
SOWNE

SOWP
SOWPS
SOWS
SOWSE
SOYA
SOYAS
SPAE
SPAED
SPAER
SPAES
SPAG
SPAGS
SPAN
SPANE
SPANG
SPANK
SPANS
SPAR
SPARD
SPARE
SPARK
SPARS
SPART
SPAS
SPASM
SPAT
SPATE
SPATS
SPAW
SPAWL
SPAWN
SPAWS
SPAY
SPAYD
SPAYS
SPEC
SPECK
SPECS
SPEK
SPEKS
SPET
SPETS
SPEW
SPEWS
SPEWY
SPIC
ASPIC
SPICA
SPICE
SPICK
SPICS
SPICY
SPIE
SPIED
SPIEL
SPIES
SPIK
SPIKE
SPIKS
SPIKY
SPIN
SPINA
SPINE
SPINK
SPINS
SPINY
SPIT
SPITE
SPITS
SPITZ

SPIV	**STOP**	**SURD**	SYNDS	**TALL**	TASKS	TEENS	**TEXT**	STIES	**TIZZ**
SPIVS	ESTOP	SURDS	**SYNE**	STALL	**TASS**	TEENY	TEXTS	**TIFF**	TIZZY
SPOT	STOPE	**SURE**	SYNED	TALLY	TASSE	**TEER**	**THAN**	STIFF	**TOAD**
SPOTS	STOPS	USURE	SYNES	**TAME**	**TATE**	STEER	THANA	TIFFS	TOADS
SPUD	**STOT**	SURED	**SYPE**	TAMED	STATE	TEERS	THANE	**TIFT**	TOADY
SPUDS	STOTS	SURER	SYPED	TAMER	TATER	**TEFF**	THANK	TIFTS	**TOCK**
SPUE	**STOW**	SURES	SYPES	TAMES	TATES	TEFFS	THANS	**TIGE**	STOCK
SPUED	STOWN	**SURF**	**TABI**	**TAMP**	**TATH**	**TEGG**	**THAR**	TIGER	TOCKS
SPUES	STOWS	SURFS	TABID	STAMP	TATHS	TEGGS	THARS	TIGES	**TOCO**
SPUN	**STUB**	SURFY	TABIS	TAMPS	**TATS**	**TEGU**	**THAW**	**TIKA**	TOCOS
SPUNK	STUBS	**SWAB**	**TABS**	**TANA**	ETATS	TEGUS	THAWS	TIKAS	**TOCS**
SPUR	**STUD**	SWABS	STABS	TANAS	**TATT**	**TEHR**	THAWY	**TIKE**	ATOCS
SPURN	STUDS	**SWAD**	**TABU**	**TANE**	TATTS	TEHRS	**THEE**	TIKES	**TOEA**
SPURS	STUDY	SWADS	TABUN	STANE	TATTY	**TEIL**	THEED	**TIKI**	TOEAS
SPURT	**STUM**	**SWAG**	TABUS	**TANG**	**TATU**	STEIL	THEEK	TIKIS	**TOFF**
STAB	STUMM	SWAGE	**TACE**	STANG	TATUS	TEILS	THEES	**TILE**	TOFFS
STABS	STUMP	SWAGS	TACES	TANGA	**TAUT**	**TELA**	**THEM**	STILE	TOFFY
STAG	STUMS	**SWAM**	TACET	TANGI	TAUTS	STELA	THEMA	UTILE	**TOFT**
STAGE	**STUN**	SWAMI	**TACH**	TANGO	**TAVA**	TELAE	THEME	TILED	TOFTS
STAGS	ASTUN	SWAMP	TACHE	TANGS	TAVAH	**TELL**	**THEN**	TILER	**TOFU**
STAGY	STUNG	**SWAN**	TACHO	TANGY	TAVAS	STELL	THENS	TILES	TOFUS
STAP	STUNK	SWANG	**TACK**	**TANH**	**TAWA**	TELLS	**THEW**	**TILL**	**TOGA**
STAPH	STUNS	SWANK	STACK	TANHS	TAWAS	TELLY	THEWS	STILL	TOGAS
STAPS	STUNT	SWANS	TACKS	**TANK**	**TAWS**	**TEME**	THEWY	TILLS	**TOGE**
STAR	**STYE**	**SWAP**	TACKY	STANK	STAWS	STEME	**THIG**	TILLY	TOGED
STARE	STYED	SWAPS	**TACO**	TANKA	TAWSE	TEMED	THIGH	**TILT**	TOGES
STARK	STYES	SWAPT	TACOS	TANKS	**TAWT**	TEMES	THIGS	ATILT	**TOHO**
STARN	**SUCK**	**SWAT**	**TACT**	TANKY	TAWTS	**TEMP**	**THIN**	STILT	TOHOS
STARR	SUCKS	SWATH	TACTS	**TANS**	**TAXI**	TEMPI	THINE	TILTH	**TOIL**
STARS	**SUDD**	SWATS	**TAEL**	TANSY	TAXIS	TEMPO	THING	TILTS	TOILE
START	SUDDS	**SWAY**	TAELS	**TAPA**	**TAYS**	TEMPS	THINK	**TIME**	TOILS
STAW	**SUDS**	ASWAY	**TAGS**	TAPAS	STAYS	TEMPT	THINS	STIME	**TOKE**
STAWS	SUDSY	SWAYL	STAGS	**TAPE**	**TEAD**	**TEMS**	**THIR**	TIMED	ATOKE
STAY	**SUED**	SWAYS	**TAHA**	ETAPE	STEAD	ITEMS	THIRD	TIMER	STOKE
STAYS	SUEDE	**SWEE**	TAHAS	TAPED	TEADE	STEMS	THIRL	TIMES	TOKED
STED	**SUER**	SWEED	**TAHR**	TAPEN	TEADS	TEMSE	**THON**	**TIND**	TOKEN
STEDD	SUERS	SWEEL	TAHRS	TAPER	**TEAK**	**TEND**	THONG	TINDS	TOKES
STEDE	**SUET**	SWEEP	**TAIL**	TAPES	STEAK	STEND	**THOU**	**TINE**	**TOKO**
STEDS	SUETS	SWEER	TAILS	TAPET	TEAKS	TENDS	THOUS	TINEA	TOKOS
STEM	SUETY	SWEES	**TAIS**	**TAPS**	**TEAL**	**TENE**	**THRO**	TINED	**TOLA**
STEME	**SUID**	SWEET	TAISH	ATAPS	STEAL	CTENE	THROB	TINES	TOLAS
STEMS	SUIDS	**SWEY**	**TAIT**	STAPS	TEALS	TENES	THROE	**TING**	**TOLE**
STEN	**SUIT**	SWEYS	TAITS	**TAPU**	**TEAM**	TENET	THROW	STING	STOLE
STEND	SUITE	**SWIG**	**TAKA**	TAPUS	STEAM	**TENS**	**THRU**	TINGE	TOLED
STENS	SUITS	SWIGS	TAKAS	**TARA**	TEAMS	ETENS	THRUM	TINGS	TOLES
STENT	**SUKH**	**SWIM**	**TAKE**	TARAS	**TEAR**	STENS	**THUD**	**TINK**	**TOLL**
STEP	SUKHS	ASWIM	STAKE	**TARE**	STEAR	TENSE	THUDS	STINK	ATOLL
STEPS	**SULK**	SWIMS	TAKEN	STARE	TEARS	**TENT**	**THUG**	TINKS	TOLLS
STEPT	SULKS	**SWOB**	TAKER	TARED	TEARY	STENT	THUGS	**TINT**	**TOLT**
STET	SULKY	SWOBS	TAKES	TARES	**TEAS**	TENTH	**TIAR**	STINT	TOLTS
STETS	**SULU**	**SWOP**	**TAKI**	**TARN**	TEASE	TENTS	TIARA	TINTS	**TOLU**
STEW	SULUS	SWOPS	TAKIN	STARN	**TEAT**	TENTY	TIARS	TINTY	TOLUS
STEWS	**SUMO**	SWOPT	TAKIS	TARNS	TEATS	**TERF**	**TICE**	**TIPI**	**TOMB**
STEWY	SUMOS	**SWOT**	**TALA**	**TARO**	**TECH**	TERFE	TICED	TIPIS	TOMBS
STIE	**SUMP**	SWOTS	TALAK	TAROC	TECHS	TERFS	TICES	**TIPS**	**TOME**
STIED	SUMPH	**SYBO**	TALAQ	TAROK	TECHY	**TERM**	**TICH**	TIPSY	TOMES
STIES	SUMPS	SYBOE	TALAR	TAROS	**TEDS**	TERMS	STICH	**TIRE**	**TOMS**
STIR	**SUNK**	SYBOW	TALAS	TAROT	STEDS	**TERN**	TICHY	STIRE	ATOMS
ASTIR	SUNKS	**SYCE**	**TALC**	**TARP**	**TEED**	STERN	**TICK**	TIRED	**TONE**
STIRE	**SUNN**	SYCEE	TALCS	TARPS	STEED	TERNE	STICK	TIRES	ATONE
STIRK	SUNNS	SYCES	TALCY	**TARS**	**TEEL**	TERNS	TICKS	**TIRL**	STONE
STIRP	SUNNY	**SYEN**	**TALE**	STARS	STEEL	**TEST**	TICKY	TIRLS	TONED
STIRS	**SUPE**	SYENS	STALE	TARSI	TEELS	TESTA	**TIDE**	**TIRO**	TONER
STOA	SUPER	**SYKE**	TALEA	**TART**	**TEEM**	TESTE	TIDED	TIROS	TONES
STOAE	SUPES	SYKER	TALER	START	STEEM	TESTS	TIDES	**TIRR**	TONEY
STOAI	**SURA**	SYKES	TALES	TARTS	TEEMS	TESTY	**TIED**	TIRRS	**TONG**
STOAS	SURAH	**SYNC**	**TALK**	TARTY	**TEEN**	**TETE**	STIED	**TITE**	STONG
STOAT	SURAL	SYNCH	STALK	**TASH**	STEEN	TETES	**TIER**	TITER	TONGA
STOB	SURAS	SYNCS	TALKS	STASH	TEEND	**TEWS**	TIERS	**TITI**	TONGS
STOBS	SURAT	**SYND**	TALKY	**TASK**	TEENE	STEWS	**TIES**	TITIS	**TONK**

STONK
TONKS
TONY
ATONY
STONY
TOOK
STOOK
TOOL
STOOL
TOOLS
TOOM
TOOMS
TOON
TOONS
TOOT
TOOTH
TOOTS
TOPE
STOPE
TOPED
TOPEE
TOPEK
TOPER
TOPES
TOPI
TOPIC
TOPIS
TOPS
STOPS
TORC
TORCH
TORCS
TORE
STORE
TORES
TORI
TORIC
TORII
TORR
TORRS
TORS
TORSE
TORSI
TORSK
TORSO
TORT
TORTE
TORTS
TOSA
TOSAS
TOSE
TOSED
TOSES
TOSH
TOSHY
TOSS
STOSS
TOSSY
TOST
YTOST
TOTE
TOTED
TOTEM
TOTES
TOTS
STOTS
TOUK
TOUKS
TOUN
STOUN
TOUNS
TOUR
STOUR
TOURS
TOUT
STOUT
TOUTS
TOWN
STOWN
TOWNS
TOWNY
TOWS
STOWS
TOWSE
TOWSY
TOWT
TOWTS
TOZE
TOZED
TOZES
TRAD
STRAD
TRADE
TRADS
TRAM
TRAMP
TRAMS
TRAP
STRAP
TRAPE
TRAPS
TRAT
TRATS
TRATT
TRAY
STRAY
TRAYS
TREE
TREED
TREEN
TREES
TREF
TREFA
TREK
TREKS
TRES
TRESS
TREST
TRET
TRETS
TREW
STREW
TREWS
TREY
TREYS
TRIE
TRIED
TRIER
TRIES
TRIG
STRIG
TRIGS
TRIM
TRIMS
TRIN
TRINE
TRINS
TRIO
TRIOR
TRIOS
TRIP
ATRIP
STRIP
TRIPE
TRIPS
TRIPY
TROD
TRODE
TRODS
TROG
TROGS
TRON
TRONA
TRONC
TRONE
TRONS
TROT
TROTH
TROTS
TROW
STROW
TROWS
TROY
STROY
TROYS
TRUE
TRUED
TRUER
TRUES
TRUG
TRUGS
TRYE
TRYER
TRYP
TRYPS
TSAR
TSARS
TUAN
TUANS
TUBA
TUBAE
TUBAL
TUBAR
TUBAS
TUBE
TUBED
TUBER
TUBES
TUBS
STUBS
TUCK
STUCK
TUCKS
TUFA
TUFAS
TUFF
STUFF
TUFFE
TUFFS
TUFT
TUFTS
TUFTY
TUIS
ETUIS
TUISM
TULE
TULES
TUMP
STUMP
TUMPS
TUMPY
TUMS
STUMS
TUNA
TUNAS
TUND
TUNDS
TUNE
TUNED
TUNER
TUNES
TUNS
STUNS
TURD
TURDS
TURF
TURFS
TURFY
TURM
TURME
TURMS
TURN
TURNS
TUSH
TUSHY
TUSK
TUSKS
TUSKY
TUTU
TUTUS
TWAE
TWAES
TWAL
TWALS
TWAT
TWATS
TWAY
TWAYS
TWEE
ETWEE
TWEED
TWEEL
TWEER
TWEET
TWIG
TWIGS
TWIN
TWINE
TWINK
TWINS
TWINY
TWIT
TWITE
TWITS
TYED
STYED
TYES
STYES
TYKE
TYKES
TYMP
TYMPS
TYND
TYNDE
TYNE
TYNED
TYNES
TYPE
TYPED
TYPES
TYPO
TYPOS
TYRE
STYRE
TYRED
TYRES
TYRO
TYROS
TYTE
STYTE
TZAR
TZARS
UDAL
UDALS
UDOS
BUDOS
JUDOS
KUDOS
LUDOS
UEYS
QUEYS
UFOS
BUFOS
UGHS
EUGHS
UGLI
UGLIS
UKES
BUKES
DUKES
JUKES
NUKES
PUKES
YUKES
ULES
DULES
GULES
HULES
MULES
PULES
RULES
TULES
YULES
ULEX
CULEX
ULNA
ULNAE
ULNAR
ULVA
VULVA
ULVAS
UMBO
BUMBO
DUMBO
GUMBO
JUMBO
RUMBO
UMBOS
UMPH
BUMPH
HUMPH
SUMPH
UNAU
UNAUS
UNBE
UNBED
UNCE
BUNCE
DUNCE
OUNCE
PUNCE
UNCES
UNCO
BUNCO
JUNCO
UNCOS
UNDE
UNDEE
UNDER
UNIT
UNITE
UNITS
UNITY
UNTO
JUNTO
PUNTO
UPAS
PUPAS
ZUPAS
UPBY
UPBYE
UPON
JUPON
YUPON
URAO
URAOS
URDE
URDEE
URDS
BURDS
CURDS
HURDS
NURDS
SURDS
TURDS
URDY
CURDY
UREA
UREAL
UREAS
URES
CURES
DURES
LURES
MURES
PURES
SURES
URGE
GURGE
PURGE
SURGE
URGED
URGER
URGES
URIC
AURIC
URNS
BURNS
CURNS
DURNS
GURNS
TURNS
URUS
GURUS
KURUS
RURUS
URVA
MURVA
URVAS
USED
BUSED
FUSED
MUSED
USER
MUSER
USERS
USES
BUSES
FUSES
MUSES
PUSES
RUSES
SUSES
WUSES
UTES
BUTES
CUTES
JUTES
LUTES
MUTES
UTIS
CUTIS
MUTIS
UTUS
TUTUS
UVEA
UVEAL
UVEAS
VADE
EVADE
VADED
VADES
VAIL
AVAIL
VAILS
VAIR
VAIRE
VAIRS
VAIRY
VALE
AVALE
VALES
VALET
VALI
VALID
VALIS
VAMP
VAMPS
VANE
VANED
VANES
VANG
VANGS
VANT
AVANT
VANTS
VARA
VARAN
VARAS
VARE
VAREC
VARES
VARY
OVARY
VASA
VASAL
VASE
VASES
VAST
AVAST
VASTS
VASTY
VATU
VATUS
VAUT
VAUTE
VAUTS
VEAL
UVEAL
VEALE
VEALS
VEALY
VEEP
VEEPS
VEER
VEERS
VEERY
VEGA
VEGAN
VEGAS
VEHM
VEHME
VEIL
VEILS
VEILY
VEIN
VEINS
VEINY
VELA
VELAR
VELD
VELDS
VELDT
VELE
VELES
VELL
VELLS
VENA
VENAE
VENAL
VEND
VENDS
VENT
EVENT
VENTS
VERB
VERBS
VERS
AVERS
OVERS
VERSE
VERSO
VERST
VERT
AVERT
EVERT
OVERT
VERTS
VERTU
VERY
EVERY
VEST
VESTA
VESTS
VETS
EVETS
VIAL
VIALS
VICE
VICED
VICES
VIDE
VIDEO
VIED
IVIED
VIER
VIERS
VIES
IVIES
VIEW
VIEWS
VIEWY
VILD
VILDE
VILE
VILER
VILL
VILLA
VILLI
VILLS
VINA
VINAL
VINAS
VINE
AVINE
OVINE
VINED
VINER
VINES
VINEW
VINO
VINOS
VINT
VINTS
VINY
VINYL
VIOL
VIOLA
VIOLD
VIOLS
VIRE
VIRED
VIREO
VIRES
VIRL
VIRLS
VISA
VISAS
VISE
AVISE
VISED
VISES
VITA
VITAE
VITAL
VITAS
VITE
EVITE
VITEX
VIVA
VIVAS
VIVAT
VIVE
VIVER
VIVES
VLEI
VLEIS
VOAR
VOARS
VOID
AVOID
OVOID
VOIDS
VOLA
VOLAE
VOLAR
VOLE
VOLED
VOLES
VOLET
VOLK
VOLKS
VOLT
VOLTA
VOLTE
VOLTS
VOTE
VOTED
VOTER
VOTES
VOWS
AVOWS
VRIL
VRILS
VROW
VROWS
VULN
VULNS
WACK
SWACK
WACKE
WACKO
WACKS
WACKY
WADD
WADDS
WADDY
WADE
WADED
WADER
WADES
WADI
WADIS
WADS
SWADS
WADT
WADTS
WAES
TWAES
WAFF
WAFFS
WAFT
WAFTS
WAGE
SWAGE
WAGED
WAGER
WAGES
WAGS
SWAGS
WAID
WAIDE
WAIF
WAIFS
WAIFT
WAIL
WAILS
WAIN
SWAIN
TWAIN

WAINS
WAIT
AWAIT
WAITE
WAITS
WAKA
WAKAS
WAKE
AWAKE
WAKED
WAKEN
WAKER
WAKES
WAKF
WAKFS
WALD
WALDS
WALE
DWALE
SWALE
WALED
WALER
WALES
WALI
WALIS
WALK
WALKS
WALL
WALLA
WALLS
WALLY
WALY
SWALY
WAME
WAMED
WAMES
WAND
WANDS
WANE
WANED
WANES
WANEY
WANG
DWANG
SWANG
TWANG
WANGS
WANK
SWANK
TWANK
WANKS
WANKY
WANS
SWANS
WANT
WANTS
WANTY
WAPS
SWAPS
WAQF
WAQFS
WARD
AWARD
SWARD
WARDS
WARE
AWARE
SWARE
WARED

WARES
WARK
WARKS
WARM
SWARM
WARMS
WARN
AWARN
WARNS
WARP
WARPS
WARS
WARST
WART
SWART
WARTS
WARTY
WASE
WASES
WASH
AWASH
SWASH
WASHY
WASM
WASMS
WASP
WASPS
WASPY
WAST
WASTE
WASTS
WATE
WATER
WATS
SWATS
TWATS
WATT
WATTS
WAUK
WAUKS
WAUL
WAULK
WAULS
WAUR
WAURS
WAVE
AWAVE
WAVED
WAVER
WAVES
WAVEY
WAWE
WAWES
WAWL
WAWLS
WAYS
AWAYS
SWAYS
TWAYS
WEAK
TWEAK
WEAL
SWEAL
WEALD
WEALS
WEAN
WEANS
WEAR
SWEAR

WEARS
WEARY
WEED
SWEED
TWEED
WEEDS
WEEDY
WEEK
WEEKE
WEEKS
WEEL
AWEEL
SWEEL
TWEEL
WEELS
WEEM
WEEMS
WEEN
WEENS
WEENY
WEEP
SWEEP
WEEPS
WEEPY
WEER
SWEER
TWEER
WEES
SWEES
WEEST
WEET
SWEET
TWEET
WEETE
WEETS
WEFT
WEFTE
WEFTS
WEID
WEIDS
WEIL
WEILS
WEIR
SWEIR
WEIRD
WEIRS
WEKA
WEKAS
WELD
WELDS
WELK
WELKE
WELKS
WELKT
WELL
DWELL
SWELL
WELLS
WELLY
WELT
DWELT
SWELT
WELTS
WEMB
WEMBS
WEND
WENDS
WENT
WENTS

WEPT
SWEPT
WEST
EWEST
WESTS
WETA
WETAS
WEXE
WEXED
WEXES
WEYS
SWEYS
WHAM
WHAMS
WHAP
WHAPS
WHAT
WHATS
WHEE
WHEEL
WHEEN
WHEN
WHENS
WHET
WHETS
WHEW
WHEWS
WHEY
WHEYS
WHID
WHIDS
WHIG
WHIGS
WHIM
WHIMS
WHIN
WHINE
WHINS
WHINY
WHIP
WHIPS
WHIPT
WHIR
WHIRL
WHIRR
WHIRS
WHIT
WHITE
WHITS
WHITY
WHIZ
WHIZZ
WHOP
WHOPS
WHOW
EWHOW
WICE
TWICE
WICK
WICKS
WICKY
WIDE
WIDEN
WIDER
WIDES
WIEL
WIELD
WIELS
WIGS

SWIGS
TWIGS
WILD
WILDS
WILE
DWILE
WILED
WILES
WILI
WILIS
WILL
SWILL
TWILL
WILLS
WILLY
WILT
TWILT
WILTS
WIMP
WIMPS
WIMPY
WIND
WINDS
WINDY
WINE
DWINE
SWINE
TWINE
WINED
WINES
WINEY
WING
AWING
OWING
SWING
WINGE
WINGS
WINGY
WINK
SWINK
TWINK
WINKS
WINN
WINNA
WINNS
WINO
WINOS
WINS
TWINS
WINY
TWINY
WIPE
SWIPE
WIPED
WIPER
WIPES
WIRE
SWIRE
TWIRE
WIRED
WIRER
WIRES
WISE
WISED
WISER
WISES
WISH
SWISH
WISP

WISPS
WISPY
WIST
TWIST
WISTS
WITE
TWITE
WITED
WITES
WITH
SWITH
WITHE
WITHS
WITHY
WITS
SWITS
TWITS
WIVE
SWIVE
WIVED
WIVES
WOAD
WOADS
WOCK
WOCKS
WOKE
AWOKE
WOKEN
WOLD
WOLDS
WOLF
WOLFS
WOMB
WOMBS
WOMBY
WONT
WONTS
WOOD
WOODS
WOODY
WOOF
WOOFS
WOOFY
WOOL
WOOLD
WOOLS
WOON
SWOON
WOONS
WOOS
WOOSH
WOOT
WOOTZ
WOPS
SWOPS
WORD
SWORD
WORDS
WORDY
WORE
SWORE
WORK
AWORK
WORKS
WORM
WORMS
WORMY
WORN
SWORN

WORT
WORTH
WORTS
WOTS
SWOTS
WOVE
WOVEN
WRAP
WRAPS
WRAPT
WREN
WRENS
WRIT
WRITE
WRITS
WULL
WULLS
WYND
WYNDS
WYNN
WYNNS
WYTE
WYTED
WYTES
XYST
XYSTI
XYSTS
YACK
YACKS
YAFF
NYAFF
YAFFS
YAHS
AYAHS
YALE
YALES
YAMS
LYAMS
YANG
KYANG
YANGS
YANK
YANKS
YAPP
YAPPS
YAPPY
YARD
YARDS
YARE
YARER
YARN
YARNS
YARR
YARRS
YATE
YATES
YAUD
YAUDS
YAWL
YAWLS
YAWN
YAWNS
YAWNY
YAWP
YAWPS
YEAD
YEADS
YEAN
YEANS

YEAR
YEARD
YEARN
YEARS
YEAS
YEAST
YEDE
YEDES
YEED
YEEDS
YEGG
YEGGS
YELD
GYELD
YELK
YELKS
YELL
YELLS
YELM
YELMS
YELP
AYELP
YELPS
YELT
YELTS
YENS
HYENS
SYENS
YERD
YERDS
YERK
YERKS
YESK
YESKS
YEST
YESTS
YESTY
YETI
YETIS
YETT
YETTS
YEUK
YEUKS
YEVE
YEVEN
YEVES
YIKE
YIKES
YILL
YILLS
YIRD
YIRDS
YIRK
YIRKS
YITE
YITES
YLEM
XYLEM
YLEMS
YLKE
YLKES
YMPE
YMPES
YOCK
YOCKS
YODE
YODEL
YOGA
YOGAS

YOGH
YOGHS
YOGI
YOGIC
YOGIN
YOGIS
YOKE
YOKED
YOKEL
YOKES
YOLK
YOLKS
YOLKY
YOMP
YOMPS
YONI
YONIS
YONT
AYONT
YOOF
YOOFS
YOOP
YOOPS
YORE
YORES
YORK
YORKS
YOUK
YOUKS
YOUR
YOURN
YOURS
YOURT
YOWE
YOWES
YOWL
YOWLS
YUCA
YUCAS
YUCK
YUCKS
YUCKY
YUFT
YUFTS
YUGA
YUGAS
YUKE
YUKED
YUKES
YUKO
YUKOS
YULE
YULES
YUMP
YUMPS
YURT
YURTS
ZACK
ZACKS
ZARF
ZARFS
ZATI
ZATIS
ZEAL
ZEALS
ZEBU
ZEBUB
ZEBUS
ZEES

MZEES
ZEIN
ZEINS
ZERO
ZEROS
ZEST
ZESTS
ZESTY
ZETA
ZETAS
ZEZE
ZEZES
ZHOS
DZHOS
ZIFF
ZIFFS
ZILA
ZILAS
ZIMB
ZIMBI
ZIMBS
ZINC
ZINCO
ZINCS
ZINCY
ZING
ZINGS
ZINGY
ZOBO
ZOBOS
ZOBU
ZOBUS
ZOEA
ZOEAE
ZOEAL
ZOEAS
ZOIC
AZOIC
ZONA
ZONAE
ZONAL
ZONE
OZONE
ZONED
ZONES
ZONK
ZONKS
ZOOM
ZOOMS
ZOON
ZOONS
ZOPP
ZOPPO
ZOUK
ZOUKS
ZULU
ZULUS
ZUPA
ZUPAN
ZUPAS
ZURF
ZURFS
ZYGA
ZYGAL
ZYME
AZYME
ZYMES

5-LETTER WORD HOOKS: extensible words only

ABACA
ABACAS
ABAND
ABANDS
ABASE
ABASED
ABASES
ABATE
ABATED
ABATES
ABAYA
KABAYA
ABAYAS
ABBES
ABBESS
ABBEY
ABBEYS
ABBOT
ABBOTS
ABCEE
ABCEES
ABEAR
ABEARS
ABELE
KABELE
ABELES
ABHOR
ABHORS
ABIDE
ABIDED
ABIDES
ABIES
BABIES
GABIES
RABIES
ABLED
CABLED
FABLED
GABLED
SABLED
TABLED
ABLER
FABLER
ABLES
CABLES
FABLES
GABLES
SABLES
TABLES
ABLEST
ABLET
CABLET
GABLET
TABLET
ABLETS
ABODE
ABODED
ABODES
ABORD
ABORDS
ABORT
ABORTS
ABOUT
ABOUTS
ABRAY

ABRAYS
ABRIN
ABRINS
ABSEY
ABSEYS
ABSIT
ABSITS
ABUNA
ABUNAS
ABUSE
ABUSED
ABUSER
ABUSES
ABYSM
ABYSMS
ACARI
ACARID
ACCOY
ACCOYS
ACERS
FACERS
MACERS
PACERS
RACERS
ACHED
BACHED
CACHED
ACHES
BACHES
CACHES
LACHES
NACHES
RACHES
TACHES
ACING
FACING
LACING
MACING
PACING
RACING
ACKEE
HACKEE
ACKEES
ACORN
ACORNS
ACRED
NACRED
SACRED
ACRES
NACRES
ACTIN
ACTING
ACTINS
ACTON
ACTONS
ACTOR
FACTOR
ACTORS
ACUTE
ACUTER
ACUTES
ADAGE
ADAGES
ADAPT
ADAPTS

ADDED
DADDED
GADDED
MADDED
PADDED
WADDED
ADDER
GADDER
LADDER
MADDER
PADDER
SADDER
ADDERS
ADDIO
ADDIOS
ADDLE
DADDLE
FADDLE
PADDLE
RADDLE
SADDLE
WADDLE
ADDLED
ADDLES
ADEEM
ADEEMS
ADEPT
ADEPTS
ADIEU
ADIEUS
ADIEUX
ADIOS
RADIOS
ADMAN
BADMAN
MADMAN
ADMEN
BADMEN
MADMEN
ADMIN
ADMINS
ADMIT
ADMITS
ADOBE
ADOBES
ADOPT
ADOPTS
ADORE
ADORED
ADORER
ADORES
ADORN
ADORNS
ADULT
ADULTS
ADUST
ADUSTS
ADVEW
ADVEWS
AEONS
PAEONS
AERIE
FAERIE
AERIER
AERIES

AFARA
AFARAS
AFEAR
AFEARD
AFEARS
AFRIT
AFRITS
AFTER
DAFTER
RAFTER
WAFTER
AFTERS
AGAMI
AGAMIC
AGAMID
AGAMIS
AGATE
AGATES
AGAVE
AGAVES
AGAZE
AGAZED
AGENE
SAGENE
AGENES
AGENT
AGENTS
AGGER
DAGGER
GAGGER
JAGGER
LAGGER
NAGGER
SAGGER
TAGGER
YAGGER
AGGERS
AGGRO
AGGROS
AGHAS
AGHAST
AGILA
AGILAS
AGILE
VAGILE
AGILER
AGING
CAGING
GAGING
PAGING
RAGING
WAGING
AGINGS
AGIST
AGISTS
AGLET
EAGLET
HAGLET
AGLETS
AGMAS
MAGMAS
AGOGE
AGOGES
AGONS
WAGONS

AGORA
AGORAS
AGREE
AGREED
AGREES
AGUED
VAGUED
AGUES
VAGUES
AGUTI
AGUTIS
AHING
RAHING
AIDED
LAIDED
MAIDED
RAIDED
AIDER
RAIDER
AIDERS
AILED
BAILED
FAILED
HAILED
JAILED
MAILED
NAILED
RAILED
SAILED
TAILED
VAILED
WAILED
AIMED
MAIMED
AIOLI
AIOLIS
AIRED
FAIRED
HAIRED
LAIRED
PAIRED
SAIRED
AIRER
FAIRER
SAIRER
AIRERS
AIRNS
BAIRNS
CAIRNS
AISLE
AISLED
AISLES
AIZLE
AIZLES
AJWAN
AJWANS
AKEES
RAKEES
AKENE
AKENES
AKING
BAKING
CAKING
FAKING
LAKING

MAKING
RAKING
TAKING
WAKING
AKKAS
YAKKAS
ALAAP
ALAAPS
ALANG
LALANG
ALANGS
ALAPA
ALAPAS
ALAPS
JALAPS
ALARM
ALARMS
ALARY
SALARY
ALATE
MALATE
PALATE
ALATED
ALAYS
PALAYS
ALBUM
ALBUMS
ALDEA
ALDEAS
ALDER
BALDER
ALDERN
ALDERS
ALEPH
ALEPHS
ALERT
ALERTS
ALEYE
ALEYED
ALEYES
ALFAS
HALFAS
ALGIN
ALGINS
ALGUM
ALGUMS
ALIBI
ALIBIS
ALIEN
ALIENS
ALIGN
MALIGN
ALIGNS
ALINE
SALINE
VALINE
ALINED
ALINES
ALIYA
ALIYAH
ALIYAS
ALKIE
TALKIE
ALKIES
ALKYD

ALKYDS
ALKYL
ALKYLS
ALLAY
ALLAYS
ALLEE
MALLEE
SALLEE
ALLEES
ALLEL
ALLELE
ALLELS
ALLEY
GALLEY
VALLEY
ALLEYS
ALLOD
ALLODS
ALLOT
BALLOT
TALLOT
ALLOTS
ALLOW
BALLOW
CALLOW
FALLOW
GALLOW
HALLOW
MALLOW
SALLOW
TALLOW
WALLOW
ALLOWS
ALLOY
ALLOYS
ALLYL
ALLYLS
ALMAH
ALMAHS
ALMAS
HALMAS
TALMAS
ALMEH
ALMEHS
ALMUG
ALMUGS
ALOED
HALOED
ALOES
HALOES
ALONG
KALONG
ALPHA
ALPHAS
ALTAR
ALTARS
ALTER
FALTER
HALTER
PALTER
SALTER
ALTERN
ALTERS
ALTOS
SALTOS

ALULA
ALULAE
ALURE
ALURES
ALWAY
ALWAYS
AMASS
CAMASS
AMATE
HAMATE
RAMATE
AMATED
AMATES
AMAZE
AMAZED
AMAZES
AMBAN
AMBANS
AMBER
CAMBER
JAMBER
LAMBER
TAMBER
AMBERS
AMBERY
AMBIT
GAMBIT
AMBITS
AMBLE
GAMBLE
HAMBLE
RAMBLE
WAMBLE
AMBLED
AMBLER
AMBLES
AMBOS
GAMBOS
JAMBOS
MAMBOS
SAMBOS
ZAMBOS
AMEBA
AMEBAE
AMEBAS
AMEER
AMEERS
AMEND
AMENDE
AMENDS
AMENE
AMENED
AMENS
RAMENS
YAMENS
AMENT
LAMENT
AMENTA
AMENTS
AMICE
AMICES
AMIDE
AMIDES
AMIES
RAMIES

AMIGO
AMIGOS
AMINE
FAMINE
GAMINE
TAMINE
AMINES
AMMAN
AMMANS
AMMON
GAMMON
MAMMON
AMMONS
AMOUR
AMOURS
AMOVE
AMOVED
AMOVES
AMPLE
CAMPLE
SAMPLE
AMPLER
AMPLY
CAMPLY
DAMPLY
AMPUL
AMPULE
AMPULS
AMRIT
AMRITA
AMRITS
AMUSE
AMUSED
AMUSER
AMUSES
ANANA
BANANA
MANANA
ANANAS
ANCLE
ANCLES
ANEAR
ANEARS
ANELE
ANELED
ANELES
ANENT
MANENT
ANGEL
MANGEL
ANGELS
ANGER
BANGER
DANGER
GANGER
HANGER
LANGER
MANGER
RANGER
ANGERS
ANGLE
BANGLE
CANGLE
DANGLE
FANGLE

JANGLE
MANGLE
TANGLE
WANGLE
ANGLED
ANGLER
ANGLES
ANGST
ANGSTS
ANIGH
ANIGHT
ANIMA
ANIMAL
ANIMAS
ANIME
ANIMES
ANION
FANION
ANIONS
ANISE
ANISES
ANKER
BANKER
CANKER
DANKER
HANKER
JANKER
LANKER
RANKER
TANKER
WANKER
YANKER
ANKERS
ANKLE
FANKLE
RANKLE
WANKLE
ANKLED
ANKLES
ANKLET
ANNAL
ANNALS
ANNAS
CANNAS
MANNAS
NANNAS
TANNAS
ANNAT
ANNATS
ANNEX
ANNEXE
ANNOY
TANNOY
ANNOYS
ANNUL
ANNULI
ANNULS
ANODE
ANODES
ANTAR
CANTAR
KANTAR
ANTARA
ANTARS
ANTAS
MANTAS
ANTED
BANTED
CANTED
DANTED
GANTED
KANTED
PANTED
RANTED
WANTED
ANTES
ZANTES
ANTIC
MANTIC
ANTICK
ANTICS
ANTIS
MANTIS
ANTRA
MANTRA
TANTRA
ANTRE
ANTRES
ANVIL
ANVILS
AORTA
AORTAE
AORTAL
AORTAS
APERY
NAPERY
PAPERY
APHID
APHIDS
APHIS
RAPHIS
APING
CAPING
GAPING
JAPING
RAPING
TAPING
APIOL
APIOLS
APISH
PAPISH
APISM
PAPISM
APISMS
APNEA
APNEAS
APODE
APODES
APPAL
APPALS
APPAY
APPAYD
APPAYS
APPEL
LAPPEL
RAPPEL
APPELS
APPLE
DAPPLE
SAPPLE
APPLES
APPUI
APPUIS
APPUY
APPUYS
APRON
NAPRON
APRONS
APSES
LAPSES
APTLY
RAPTLY
ARABA
ARABAS
ARAME
ARAMES
ARBOR
HARBOR
ARBORS
ARCED
FARCED
ARDEB
ARDEBS
ARDOR
ARDORS
ARDRI
ARDRIS
AREAD
AREADS
ARECA
ARECAS
AREDE
AREDES
AREFY
RAREFY
ARENA
ARENAS
ARETE
ARETES
ARETS
CARETS
ARETT
ARETTS
ARGAL
ARGALA
ARGALI
ARGAN
ARGAND
ARGANS
ARGIL
ARGILS
ARGOL
ARGOLS
ARGON
JARGON
ARGONS
ARGOT
ARGOTS
ARGUE
ARGUED
ARGUER
ARGUES
ARGUS
SARGUS
ARIEL
ARIELS
ARISE
ARISEN
ARISES
ARISH
BARISH
GARISH
HARISH
MARISH
PARISH
ARKED
BARKED
CARKED
HARKED
LARKED
MARKED
NARKED
PARKED
ARLED
HARLED
MARLED
PARLED
ARLES
FARLES
MARLES
PARLES
ARMED
FARMED
HARMED
WARMED
ARMET
ARMETS
ARMIL
ARMILS
ARMOR
ARMORS
ARMORY
ARNAS
VARNAS
ARNUT
ARNUTS
AROBA
AROBAS
AROID
LAROID
AROIDS
AROMA
AROMAS
ARRAH
JARRAH
ARRAS
NARRAS
TARRAS
ARRAY
WARRAY
ARRAYS
ARRET
BARRET
GARRET
ARRETS
ARRIS
KARRIS
ARRISH
ARROW
BARROW
FARROW
HARROW
MARROW
NARROW
TARROW
YARROW
ARROWS
ARROWY
ARSES
CARSES
FARSES
PARSES
ARSON
PARSON
ARSONS
ARTAL
HARTAL
ARTEL
CARTEL
MARTEL
ARTELS
ARTIC
ARTICS
ARUMS
GARUMS
LARUMS
ARVAL
LARVAL
ASANA
ASANAS
ASCOT
MASCOT
ASCOTS
ASHEN
WASHEN
ASHES
BASHES
CASHES
DASHES
FASHES
GASHES
HASHES
LASHES
MASHES
PASHES
RASHES
SASHES
TASHES
WASHES
ASHET
ASHETS
ASIDE
ASIDES
ASKED
BASKED
CASKED
MASKED
TASKED
ASKER
MASKER
TASKER
ASKERS
ASPEN
ASPENS
ASPER
GASPER
JASPER
RASPER
ASPERS
ASPIC
ASPICK
ASPICS
ASSAI
ASSAIL
ASSAIS
ASSAY
ASSAYS
ASSES
BASSES
GASSES
JASSES
LASSES
MASSES
PASSES
RASSES
SASSES
TASSES
ASSESS
ASSET
BASSET
TASSET
ASSETS
ASSOT
ASSOTS
ASSOTT
ASTER
BASTER
CASTER
EASTER
FASTER
GASTER
LASTER
MASTER
PASTER
RASTER
TASTER
VASTER
WASTER
ASTERN
ASTERS
ASTERT
ASTUN
ASTUNS
ATAPS
WATAPS
ATMAN
BATMAN
VATMAN
ATMANS
ATOKE
MATOKE
ATOKES
ATOLL
ATOLLS
ATONE
ATONED
ATONER
ATONES
ATRIA
LATRIA
ATRIAL
ATTAP
ATTAPS
ATTAR
ATTARS
ATTIC
ATTICS
AUDIO
AUDIOS
AUDIT
AUDITS
AUGER
GAUGER
SAUGER
AUGERS
AUGHT
CAUGHT
HAUGHT
NAUGHT
RAUGHT
TAUGHT
WAUGHT
AUGHTS
AUGUR
AUGURS
AUGURY
AUMIL
AUMILS
AUNTS
DAUNTS
GAUNTS
HAUNTS
JAUNTS
NAUNTS
SAUNTS
TAUNTS
VAUNTS
AUNTY
JAUNTY
VAUNTY
AURAS
LAURAS
AURIC
TAURIC
AUXIN
AUXINS
AVAIL
AVAILE
AVAILS
AVALE
AVALED
AVALES
AVANT
SAVANT
AVANTI
AVENS
DAVENS
HAVENS
MAVENS
PAVENS
RAVENS
AVERS
CAVERS
HAVERS
LAVERS
PAVERS
RAVERS
SAVERS
TAVERS
WAVERS
AVERSE
AVERT
TAVERT
AVERTS
AVINE
RAVINE
SAVINE
AVION
AVIONS
AVISE
PAVISE
AVISED
AVISES
AVISO
AVISOS
AVIZE
AVIZED
AVIZES
AVOID
AVOIDS
AVYZE
AVYZED
AVYZES
AWAIT
AWAITS
AWAKE
AWAKED
AWAKEN
AWAKES
AWARD
VAWARD
AWARDS
AWARE
AWARER
AWARN
AWARNS
AWETO
AWETOS
AWFUL
LAWFUL
AWING
CAWING
DAWING
HAWING
JAWING
KAWING
LAWING
PAWING
RAWING
SAWING
TAWING
YAWING
AWNED
DAWNED
FAWNED
PAWNED
YAWNED
AWNER
DAWNER
FAWNER
PAWNER
AWNERS
AWOKE
AWOKEN
AXING
FAXING
RAXING
TAXING
WAXING
AXIOM
AXIOMS
AXMAN
TAXMAN
AXMEN
TAXMEN
AXOID
AXOIDS
AXONS
CAXONS
AYAHS
RAYAHS
AYRES
FAYRES
AYRIE
AYRIES
AZIDE
AZIDES
AZINE
AZINES
AZOTE
AZOTES
AZOTH
AZOTHS
AZURE
RAZURE
AZURES
AZYME
AZYMES
BABEL
BABELS
BABOO
BABOON
BABOOS
BABUL
BABULS
BACCA
BACCAE
BACCAS
BACCO
BACCOS
BACON
BACONS
BADGE
BADGED
BADGER
BADGES
BAGEL
BAGELS
BAHUT
BAHUTS
BAIRN
BAIRNS
BAIZE
BAIZED
BAIZES
BAJAN
BAJANS
BAJRA
BAJRAS
BAJRI
BAJRIS
BAKER
BAKERS
BAKERY
BALER
BALERS
BALLS
BALLSY
BALOO
BALOOS
BALSA
BALSAM
BALSAS
BANCO
BANCOS
BANDA
BANDAR
BANDAS
BANDS
ABANDS
BANGS
OBANGS
BANIA
BANIAN
BANIAS
BANJO
BANJOS
BANTU
BANTUS
BARBE
BARBED
BARBEL
BARBER
BARBES
BARBET
BARCA
BARCAS
BARDO
BARDOS
BARES

BAREST
BARGE
BARGED
BARGEE
BARGES
BARON
BARONG
BARONS
BARONY
BARRE
BARRED
BARREL
BARREN
BARRES
BARRET
BARYE
BARYES
BASAL
BASALT
BASAN
BASANS
BASED
ABASED
BASES
ABASES
BASEST
BASIC
BASICS
BASIL
BASILS
BASIN
BASING
BASINS
BASON
BASONS
BASSE
BASSED
BASSER
BASSES
BASSET
BASSO
BASSOS
BASTE
BASTED
BASTER
BASTES
BASTO
BASTOS
BATED
ABATED
BATES
ABATES
BATHE
BATHED
BATHER
BATHES
BATIK
BATIKS
BATON
BATONS
BATTA
BATTAS
BAULK
BAULKS
BAVIN
BAVINS
BAYLE
BAYLES
BAYOU
BAYOUS

BAZAR
BAZARS
BEACH
BEACHY
BEANO
BEANOS
BEARD
BEARDS
BEARE
BEARED
BEARER
BEARES
BEARS
ABEARS
BEAST
BEASTS
BEATH
BEATHS
BEAUT
BEAUTS
BEAUTY
BEBOP
BEBOPS
BECKE
BECKED
BECKES
BECKET
BEDEL
BEDELL
BEDELS
BEDEW
BEDEWS
BEDIM
BEDIMS
BEDYE
BEDYED
BEDYES
BEFIT
BEFITS
BEFOG
BEFOGS
BEGAR
BEGARS
BEGEM
BEGEMS
BEGET
BEGETS
BEGIN
BEGINS
BEGUM
BEGUMS
BEGUN
BEGUNK
BEIGE
BEIGEL
BEIGES
BEING
BEINGS
BEKAH
BEKAHS
BELAH
BELAHS
BELAY
BELAYS
BELEE
BELEED
BELEES
BELGA
BELGAS
BELIE

BELIED
BELIEF
BELIER
BELIES
BELLE
BELLED
BELLES
BEMAD
BEMADS
BEMUD
BEMUDS
BENET
BENETS
BENNE
BENNES
BENNET
BENNI
BENNIS
BEPAT
BEPATS
BERAY
BERAYS
BERET
BERETS
BEROB
BEROBS
BERTH
BERTHA
BERTHE
BERTHS
BERYL
BERYLS
BESEE
BESEEM
BESEEN
BESEES
BESET
BESETS
BESIT
BESITS
BESOM
BESOMS
BESOT
BESOTS
BETEL
BETELS
BETID
BETIDE
BETON
BETONS
BETONY
BEVEL
BEVELS
BEVER
BEVERS
BEVUE
BEVUES
BEWET
BEWETS
BEWIG
BEWIGS
BEZEL
BEZELS
BHANG
BHANGS
BIBLE
BIBLES
BICES
IBICES
BIDED

ABIDED
BIDES
ABIDES
BIDET
BIDETS
BIDON
BIDONS
BIELD
BIELDS
BIELDY
BIGHA
BIGHAS
BIGHT
BIGHTS
BIGOT
BIGOTS
BIJOU
BIJOUX
BIKER
BIKERS
BIKIE
BIKIES
BILBO
BILBOS
BILGE
BILGED
BILGES
BIMBO
BIMBOS
BINGE
BINGED
BINGER
BINGES
BINGO
BINGOS
BIOME
BIOMES
BIONT
BIONTS
BIOTA
BIOTAS
BIPED
BIPEDS
BIPOD
BIPODS
BIRLE
BIRLED
BIRLER
BIRLES
BIRSE
BIRSES
BIRTH
BIRTHS
BISES
IBISES
BISON
BISONS
BITCH
BITCHY
BITER
OBITER
BITERS
BITTE
BITTED
BITTEN
BITTER
BLACK
BLACKS
BLADE
BLADED

BLADES
BLAES
BLAEST
BLAIN
BLAINS
BLAME
BLAMED
BLAMES
BLAND
BLANDS
BLANK
BLANKS
BLANKY
BLARE
BLARED
BLARES
BLASH
BLASHY
BLAST
OBLAST
BLASTS
BLATE
ABLATE
OBLATE
BLATER
BLATT
BLATTS
BLAUD
BLAUDS
BLAZE
ABLAZE
BLAZED
BLAZER
BLAZES
BLEAK
BLEAKS
BLEAKY
BLEAR
BLEARS
BLEARY
BLEAT
BLEATS
BLEED
BLEEDS
BLEEP
BLEEPS
BLEND
BLENDE
BLENDS
BLENT
YBLENT
BLEST
ABLEST
BLETS
ABLETS
BLIMP
BLIMPS
BLIND
BLINDS
BLINI
BLINIS
BLINK
BLINKS
BLINS
ABLINS
BLITE
BLITES
BLOAT
BLOATS
BLOCK

BLOCKS
BLOCKY
BLOKE
BLOKES
BLOND
BLONDE
BLONDS
BLOOD
BLOODS
BLOODY
BLOOM
ABLOOM
BLOOMS
BLOOMY
BLOOP
BLOOPS
BLORE
BLORES
BLOWS
BLOWSE
BLOWSY
BLUDE
BLUDES
BLUES
BLUEST
BLUESY
BLUEY
BLUEYS
BLUFF
BLUFFS
BLUID
BLUIDS
BLUIDY
BLUNK
BLUNKS
BLUNT
BLUNTS
BLURB
BLURBS
BLURT
BLURTS
BLUSH
ABLUSH
BOARD
ABOARD
BOARDS
BOART
BOARTS
BOAST
BOASTS
BOBAC
BOBACS
BOBAK
BOBAKS
BOCCA
BOCCAS
BOCHE
BOCHES
BODED
ABODED
BODES
ABODES
BODGE
BODGED
BODGER
BODGES
BODLE
BODLES
BOGAN
BOGANS

BOGEY
BOGEYS
BOGIE
BOGIES
BOGLE
BOGLES
BOHEA
BOHEAS
BOING
BOINGS
BOINK
BOINKS
BOLUS
OBOLUS
BOMBE
BOMBED
BOMBER
BOMBES
BOMBO
BOMBOS
BONCE
BONCES
BONER
BONERS
BONGO
BONGOS
BONIE
BONIER
BONNE
BONNES
BONNET
BONZE
BONZER
BONZES
BOOKS
BOOKSY
BOONG
BOONGS
BOORD
BOORDE
BOORDS
BOOSE
BOOSED
BOOSES
BOOST
BOOSTS
BOOTH
BOOTHS
BOOZE
BOOZED
BOOZER
BOOZES
BOOZEY
BORAK
BORAKS
BORDE
BORDEL
BORDER
BORDES
BORDS
ABORDS
BOREE
BOREEN
BOREES
BORER
BORERS
BORGO
BORGOS
BORNE
ABORNE

BORON
BORONS
BORTS
ABORTS
BOSOM
BOSOMS
BOSOMY
BOSON
BOSONS
BOSUN
BOSUNS
BOTCH
BOTCHY
BOTEL
BOTELS
BOTTE
BOTTED
BOTTES
BOUGE
BOUGED
BOUGES
BOUGET
BOUGH
BOUGHS
BOUGHT
BOULE
BOULES
BOULT
BOULTS
BOUND
ABOUND
YBOUND
BOUNDS
BOURD
BOURDS
BOURG
BOURGS
BOURN
BOURNE
BOURNS
BOUSE
BOUSED
BOUSES
BOUTS
ABOUTS
BOVID
BOVIDS
BOWAT
BOWATS
BOWEL
BOWELS
BOWER
BOWERS
BOWERY
BOWET
BOWETS
BOWNE
BOWNED
BOWNES
BOWSE
BOWSED
BOWSER
BOWSES
BOXER
BOXERS
BOYAR
BOYARS
BOYAU
BOYAUX
BRACE

BRACED
BRACER
BRACES
BRACK
BRACKS
BRACT
BRACTS
BRAID
ABRAID
BRAIDE
BRAIDS
BRAIL
BRAILS
BRAIN
BRAINS
BRAINY
BRAKE
BRAKED
BRAKES
BRAME
BRAMES
BRAND
BRANDS
BRANDY
BRANK
BRANKS
BRANKY
BRASH
BRASHY
BRASS
BRASSY
BRAST
BRASTS
BRAVE
BRAVED
BRAVER
BRAVES
BRAVO
BRAVOS
BRAWL
BRAWLS
BRAWLY
BRAWN
BRAWNS
BRAWNY
BRAYS
ABRAYS
BRAZE
BRAZED
BRAZEN
BRAZES
BREAD
BREADS
BREAK
BREAKS
BREAM
BREAMS
BREDE
BREDED
BREDES
BREED
BREEDS
BREER
BREERS
BREES
BREESE
BRENT
YBRENT
BRERE
BRERES

BREVE
BREVES
BREVET
BRIAR
BRIARS
BRIBE
BRIBED
BRIBER
BRIBES
BRICK
BRICKS
BRICKY
BRIDE
BRIDED
BRIDES
BRIEF
BRIEFS
BRIER
BRIERS
BRIERY
BRILL
BRILLS
BRINE
BRINED
BRINES
BRING
BRINGS
BRINK
BRINKS
BRISE
BRISES
BRISK
BRISKS
BRISKY
BRIZE
BRIZES
BROAD
ABROAD
BROADS
BROCH
BROCHE
BROCHS
BROCK
BROCKS
BROGH
BROGHS
BROIL
BROILS
BROKE
BROKED
BROKEN
BROKER
BROKES
BROND
BRONDS
BROOD
BROODS
BROODY
BROOK
BROOKS
BROOL
BROOLS
BROOM
BROOMS
BROOMY
BROOS
BROOSE
BROSE
BROSES
BROTH

BROTHS
BROWN
BROWNS
BROWNY
BROWS
BROWSE
BROWST
BROWSY
BRUIT
BRUITS
BRUME
BRUMES
BRUNT
BRUNTS
BRUSH
BRUSHY
BRUST
BRUSTS
BRUTE
BRUTED
BRUTER
BRUTES
BUAZE
BUAZES
BUBAL
BUBALS
BUCHU
BUCHUS
BUCKU
BUCKUS
BUDGE
BUDGED
BUDGER
BUDGES
BUDGET
BUFFE
BUFFED
BUFFER
BUFFET
BUGLE
BUGLED
BUGLER
BUGLES
BUGLET
BUILD
BUILDS
BUIST
BUISTS
BULGE
BULGED
BULGER
BULGES
BULLA
BULLAE
BULSE
BULSES
BUMBO
BUMBOS
BUMPH
BUMPHS
BUNAS
ABUNAS
BUNCE
BUNCED
BUNCES
BUNCH
BUNCHY
BUNCO
BUNCOS
BUNDU

BUNDUS
BUNIA
BUNIAS
BUNJE
BUNJEE
BUNJES
BUNKO
BUNKOS
BUNYA
BUNYAS
BURAN
BURANS
BURET
BURETS
BURGH
BURGHS
BURIN
BURINS
BURKA
BURKAS
BURKE
BURKED
BURKES
BUROO
BUROOS
BURQA
BURQAS
BURRO
BURROS
BURROW
BURSA
BURSAE
BURSAL
BURSAR
BURSE
BURSES
BURST
ABURST
BURSTS
BUSED
ABUSED
BUSES
ABUSES
BUSSU
BUSSUS
BUTTE
BUTTED
BUTTER
BUTTES
BUTYL
BUTYLS
BUYER
BUYERS
BWANA
BWANAS
BWAZI
BWAZIS
BYLAW
BYLAWS
BYWAY
BYWAYS
CABAL
CABALA
CABALS
CABBY
SCABBY
CABER
CABERS
CABIN
CABINS

CABLE
CABLED
CABLES
CABLET
CABOB
CABOBS
CABOC
CABOCS
CACAO
CACAOS
CACHE
CACHED
CACHES
CACHET
CADEE
CADEES
CADET
CADETS
CADGE
CADGED
CADGER
CADGES
CADIE
CADIES
CADRE
CADRES
CAECA
CAECAL
CAFFS
SCAFFS
CAGOT
CAGOTS
CAIRD
CAIRDS
CAIRN
CAIRNS
CALIF
CALIFS
CALLA
CALLAN
CALLAS
CALLS
SCALLS
CALPA
CALPAC
CALPAS
CALPS
SCALPS
CALVE
CALVED
CALVER
CALVES
CAMAN
CAMANS
CAMAS
CAMASH
CAMASS
CAMEL
SCAMEL
CAMELS
CAMEO
CAMEOS
CAMES
CAMESE
CAMIS
CAMISE
CAMPO
CAMPOS
CAMPS
SCAMPS

CANAL
CANALS
CANEH
CANEHS
CANID
CANIDS
CANNA
CANNAE
CANNAS
CANOE
CANOED
CANOES
CANON
CANONS
CANTO
CANTON
CANTOR
CANTOS
CANTS
SCANTS
CANTY
SCANTY
CAPAS
SCAPAS
CAPED
SCAPED
CAPER
CAPERS
CAPES
SCAPES
CAPLE
CAPLES
CAPLET
CAPON
CAPONS
CAPOT
CAPOTE
CAPOTS
CAPUL
CAPULS
CARAP
CARAPS
CARAT
CARATS
CARDI
CARDIS
CARED
SCARED
CARER
SCARER
CARERS
CARES
SCARES
CARESS
CARET
CARETS
CAROB
CAROBS
CAROL
CAROLI
CAROLS
CAROM
CAROMS
CARPS
SCARPS
CARRY
SCARRY
CARSE
CARSES
CARSEY

CARTA
CARTAS
CARTE
ECARTE
CARTED
CARTEL
CARTER
CARTES
CARTS
SCARTS
CARVE
CARVED
CARVEL
CARVEN
CARVER
CARVES
CASCO
CASCOS
CASTE
CASTED
CASTER
CASTES
CATCH
SCATCH
CATCHT
CATCHY
CATER
ACATER
CATERS
CATES
ACATES
CATTY
SCATTY
CAULD
CAULDS
CAULK
CAULKS
CAUPS
SCAUPS
CAUSA
CAUSAE
CAUSAL
CAUSE
CAUSED
CAUSEN
CAUSER
CAUSES
CAUSEY
CAVEL
CAVELS
CAVER
CAVERN
CAVERS
CAVIE
CAVIES
CAVIL
CAVILS
CAXON
CAXONS
CEASE
CEASED
CEASES
CEAZE
CEAZED
CEAZES
CEDAR
CEDARN
CEDARS
CEILI
CEILIS

CELLA
CELLAE
CELLAR
CELLO
CELLOS
CELOM
CELOMS
CENSE
CENSED
CENSER
CENSES
CENTO
CENTOS
CENTS
SCENTS
CEORL
CEORLS
CERGE
CERGES
CERIA
CERIAS
CERNE
SCERNE
CERNED
CERNES
CESSE
CESSED
CESSER
CESSES
CETYL
ACETYL
CETYLS
CHACE
CHACED
CHACES
CHACK
CHACKS
CHACO
CHACOS
CHAFE
CHAFED
CHAFER
CHAFES
CHAFF
CHAFFS
CHAFT
CHAFTS
CHAIN
CHAINE
CHAINS
CHAIR
CHAIRS
CHAIS
CHAISE
CHALK
CHALKS
CHALKY
CHAMP
CHAMPS
CHANK
CHANKS
CHANT
CHANTS
CHANTY
CHAPE
CHAPEL
CHAPES
CHARA
CHARAS
CHARD

CHARDS
CHARE
CHARED
CHARES
CHARET
CHARK
CHARKA
CHARKS
CHARM
CHARMS
CHARR
CHARRS
CHARRY
CHART
CHARTA
CHARTS
CHASE
CHASED
CHASER
CHASES
CHASM
CHASMS
CHASMY
CHAYA
CHAYAS
CHEAP
CHEAPO
CHEAPS
CHEAPY
CHEAT
CHEATS
CHECK
CHECKS
CHECKY
CHEEK
CHEEKS
CHEEKY
CHEEP
CHEEPS
CHEER
CHEERS
CHEERY
CHEKA
CHEKAS
CHELA
CHELAE
CHELAS
CHERT
CHERTS
CHERTY
CHEST
CHESTS
CHESTY
CHICA
CHICAS
CHICH
CHICHA
CHICHI
CHICK
TCHICK
CHICKS
CHICO
CHICON
CHICOS
CHIDE
CHIDED
CHIDER
CHIDES
CHIEF
CHIEFS

CHIEL
CHIELD
CHIELS
CHILD
CHILDE
CHILDS
CHILE
CHILES
CHILI
CHILIS
CHILL
CHILLI
CHILLS
CHILLY
CHIMB
CHIMBS
CHIME
CHIMED
CHIMER
CHIMES
CHIMP
CHIMPS
CHINA
CHINAR
CHINAS
CHINE
CHINED
CHINES
CHINK
CHINKS
CHINKY
CHINO
CHINOS
CHIRK
CHIRKS
CHIRL
CHIRLS
CHIRM
CHIRMS
CHIRP
CHIRPS
CHIRPY
CHIRR
CHIRRE
CHIRRS
CHIRT
CHIRTS
CHIVE
CHIVED
CHIVES
CHOCK
CHOCKO
CHOCKS
CHOCO
CHOCOS
CHOIR
CHOIRS
CHOKE
CHOKED
CHOKER
CHOKES
CHOKEY
CHOKO
CHOKOS
CHOLI
CHOLIC
CHOLIS
CHOMP
CHOMPS
CHOOF

CHOOFS
CHOOK
CHOOKS
CHOOM
CHOOMS
CHORD
CHORDA
CHORDS
CHORE
CHOREA
CHOREE
CHORES
CHOSE
CHOSEN
CHOSES
CHOTT
CHOTTS
CHOUT
SCHOUT
CHOUTS
CHUCK
CHUCKS
CHUFA
CHUFAS
CHUFF
CHUFFS
CHUFFY
CHUMP
CHUMPS
CHUNK
CHUNKS
CHUNKY
CHURL
CHURLS
CHURN
CHURNS
CHURR
CHURRS
CHUSE
CHUSES
CHUTE
CHUTES
CHYLE
CHYLES
CHYME
CHYMES
CIBOL
CIBOLS
CIDER
ACIDER
CIDERS
CIDERY
CIGAR
CIGARS
CIMAR
CIMARS
CIONS
SCIONS
CIRCA
CIRCAR
CISCO
CISCOS
CITAL
CITALS
CITER
CITERS
CITES
CITESS
CIVET
CIVETS
CIVIC
CIVICS
CLACK
CLACKS
CLADE
CLADES
CLAIM
CLAIMS
CLAME
CLAMES
CLAMP
CLAMPS
CLANG
CLANGS
CLANK
CLANKS
CLARO
CLAROS
CLART
CLARTS
CLARTY
CLASP
CLASPS
CLASS
CLASSY
CLATS
ECLATS
CLAUT
CLAUTS
CLAVE
SCLAVE
CLAVER
CLAVES
CLEAN
CLEANS
CLEAR
CLEARS
CLEAT
CLEATS
CLECK
CLECKS
CLEEK
CLEEKS
CLEEP
CLEEPS
CLEFT
CLEFTS
CLEPE
CLEPED
CLEPES
CLERK
CLERKS
CLEVE
CLEVER
CLEVES
CLICK
CLICKS
CLIFF
SCLIFF
CLIFFS
CLIFFY
CLIFT
CLIFTS
CLIFTY
CLIMB
CLIMBS
CLIME
CLIMES
CLINE
CLINES
CLING
CLINGS
CLINGY
CLINK
CLINKS
CLINT
CLINTS
CLIPE
CLIPED
CLIPES
CLOAK
CLOAKS
CLOAM
CLOAMS
CLOCK
CLOCKS
CLOFF
CLOFFS
CLOKE
CLOKED
CLOKES
CLOMP
CLOMPS
CLONE
CLONED
CLONES
CLONK
CLONKS
CLOOP
CLOOPS
CLOOT
CLOOTS
CLOSE
ECLOSE
CLOSED
CLOSER
CLOSES
CLOSET
CLOTE
CLOTES
CLOTH
CLOTHE
CLOTHS
CLOUD
CLOUDS
CLOUDY
CLOUR
CLOURS
CLOUT
CLOUTS
CLOVE
CLOVEN
CLOVER
CLOVES
CLOWN
CLOWNS
CLUCK
CLUCKS
CLUCKY
CLUMP
CLUMPS
CLUMPY
CLUNK
CLUNKS
CLYPE
CLYPED
CLYPEI
CLYPES
CNIDA
CNIDAE
COACH
COACHY
COACT
COACTS
COAPT
COAPTS
COARB
COARBS
COAST
COASTS
COATE
COATED
COATEE
COATER
COATES
COATI
COATIS
COBIA
COBIAS
COBLE
COBLES
COBRA
COBRAS
COBZA
COBZAS
COCCI
COCCID
COCCO
COCCOS
COCKS
COCKSY
COCOA
COCOAS
CODON
CODONS
COFFS
SCOFFS
COGIE
COGIES
COGUE
COGUES
COHAB
COHABS
COHOE
COHOES
COHOG
COHOGS
COIGN
COIGNE
COIGNS
COLDS
SCOLDS
COLEY
COLEYS
COLIC
COLICS
COLIN
COLINS
COLON
COLONS
COLONY
COLOR
COLORS
COLZA
COLZAS
COMBE
COMBED
COMBER
COMBES
COMBO
COMBOS
COMER
COMERS
COMET
COMETS
COMIC
COMICE
COMICS
COMMA
COMMAS
COMMO
COMMON
COMMOS
COMMOT
COMPO
COMPOS
COMPOT
COMPT
COMPTS
CONCH
CONCHA
CONCHE
CONCHS
CONCHY
CONDO
CONDOM
CONDOR
CONDOS
CONES
SCONES
CONEY
CONEYS
CONGA
CONGAS
CONGE
CONGED
CONGEE
CONGER
CONGES
CONGO
CONGOS
CONGOU
CONIA
CONIAS
CONIC
ICONIC
CONICS
CONIN
CONINE
CONING
CONINS
CONNE
CONNED
CONNER
CONNES
CONTE
CONTES
CONTO
CONTOS
CONVO
CONVOS
CONVOY
COOEE
COOEED
COOEES
COOEY
COOEYS
COOMB
COOMBE
COOMBS
COOPS
SCOOPS
COOPT
COOPTS
COOTS
SCOOTS
COPAL
COPALS
COPED
SCOPED
COPER
COPERS
COPES
SCOPES
COPRA
COPRAS
COPSE
COPSED
COPSES
CORAL
CORALS
CORBE
CORBEL
CORBES
CORED
SCORED
CORER
SCORER
CORERS
CORES
SCORES
COREY
COREYS
CORGI
CORGIS
CORIA
SCORIA
CORNS
ACORNS
SCORNS
CORNU
CORNUA
CORPS
CORPSE
CORSE
SCORSE
CORSES
CORSET
CORSO
CORSOS
COSEC
COSECH
COSECS
COSET
COSETS
COSTA
COSTAE
COSTAL
COSTE
COSTED
COSTER
COSTES
COTTA
COTTAR
COTTAS
COUCH
COUCHE
COUGH
COUGHS
COUNT
COUNTS
COUNTY
COUPE
COUPED
COUPEE
COUPER
COUPES
COUPS
SCOUPS
COURB
COURBS
COURE
COURED
COURES
COURS
SCOURS
COURSE
COURT
COURTS
COUTH
SCOUTH
COUTHY
COVEN
COVENS
COVENT
COVER
COVERS
COVERT
COVET
COVETS
COVEY
COVEYS
COVIN
COVING
COVINS
COWAL
COWALS
COWAN
COWANS
COWER
COWERS
COWLS
SCOWLS
COWPS
SCOWPS
COYPU
COYPUS
COZEN
COZENS
CRABS
SCRABS
CRACK
CRACKS
CRAFT
CRAFTS
CRAFTY
CRAGS
SCRAGS
CRAIG
CRAIGS
CRAKE
CRAKED
CRAKES
CRAME
CRAMES
CRAMP
CRAMPS
CRAMPY
CRAMS
SCRAMS
CRANE
CRANED
CRANES
CRANK
CRANKS
CRANKY
CRANS
SCRANS
CRAPE
SCRAPE
CRAPES
CRAPS
SCRAPS
CRARE
CRARES
CRATE
CRATED
CRATER
CRATES
CRAVE
CRAVED
CRAVEN
CRAVER
CRAVES
CRAWL
ACRAWL
SCRAWL
CRAWLS
CRAWLY
CRAWS
SCRAWS
CRAZE
CRAZED
CRAZES
CREAK
SCREAK
CREAKS
CREAKY
CREAM
SCREAM
CREAMS
CREAMY
CREDO
CREDOS
CREED
SCREED
CREEDS
CREEK
CREEKS
CREEKY
CREEL
CREELS
CREEP
CREEPS
CREEPY
CREES
SCREES
CREESE
CREESH
CREME
CREMES
CRENA
CRENAS
CREPE
CREPES
CREPEY
CREST
CRESTS
CREWE
CREWED
CREWEL
CREWES
CREWS
SCREWS
CRICK
CRICKS
CRICKY
CRIED
SCRIED
CRIER
CRIERS
CRIES
SCRIES
CRIME
CRIMED
CRIMEN
CRIMES
CRIMP
SCRIMP
CRIMPS
CRIMPY
CRIMS
SCRIMS
CRINE
SCRINE
CRINED
CRINES
CRISE
CRISES
CRISP
CRISPS
CRISPY
CRITH
CRITHS
CROAK
CROAKS
CROAKY
CROCK
CROCKS
CROFT
CROFTS
CROMB
CROMBS
CROME
CROMED
CROMES
CRONE
CRONES
CRONET
CROOK
CROOKS
CROON
CROONS
CRORE
CRORES
CROSS
ACROSS
CROSSE
CROUP
CROUPE
CROUPS
CROUPY
CROUT
CROUTE
CROUTS
CROWD
CROWDS
CROWN
CROWNS
CROWS

SCROWS
CROZE
CROZES
CRUCK
CRUCKS
CRUDE
CRUDER
CRUDES
CRUEL
CRUELS
CRUET
CRUETS
CRUMB
CRUMBS
CRUMBY
CRUMP
SCRUMP
CRUMPS
CRUMPY
CRUSE
CRUSES
CRUSET
CRUST
CRUSTA
CRUSTS
CRUSTY
CRUVE
CRUVES
CRWTH
CRWTHS
CRYPT
CRYPTO
CRYPTS
CTENE
CTENES
CUBEB
CUBEBS
CUBIC
CUBICA
CUBICS
CUBIT
CUBITS
CUFFS
SCUFFS
CULET
CULETS
CULLS
SCULLS
CUMEC
CUMECS
CUMIN
CUMINS
CUPEL
CUPELS
CUPID
CUPIDS
CUPPA
CUPPAS
CURAT
CURATE
CURATS
CURER
CURERS
CURIA
CURIAE
CURIAS
CURIE
ECURIE
CURIES
CURIET

CURIO
CURIOS
CURRY
SCURRY
CURSE
CURSED
CURSER
CURSES
CURVE
CURVED
CURVES
CURVET
CURVY
SCURVY
CUSEC
CUSECS
CUTCH
SCUTCH
CUTCHA
CUTER
ACUTER
CUTES
ACUTES
SCUTES
CUTEST
CUTESY
CUTEY
CUTEYS
CUTIE
CUTIES
CUTIN
CUTINS
CUTTO
CUTTOE
CUVEE
CUVEES
CYCAD
CYCADS
CYCLE
CYCLED
CYCLER
CYCLES
CYCLO
CYCLOS
CYDER
CYDERS
CYMAR
CYMARS
CYNIC
CYNICS
CYTON
CYTONS
DACHA
DACHAS
DAGGA
DAGGAS
DAINE
SDAINE
DAINED
DAINES
DAINT
DAINTY
DAKER
DAKERS
DALLE
DALLES
DAMAN
DAMANS
DAMAR
DAMARS

DAMME
DAMMED
DAMMER
DANCE
DANCED
DANCER
DANCES
DANIO
DANIOS
DARAF
DARAFS
DARCY
DARCYS
DARGA
DARGAS
DARIC
DARICS
DARRE
DARRED
DARRES
DARZI
DARZIS
DATAL
DATALS
DATER
DATERS
DAUBE
DAUBED
DAUBER
DAUBES
DAULT
DAULTS
DAUNT
DAUNTS
DAVEN
DAVENS
DAVIT
DAVITS
DAWED
ADAWED
DAZER
DAZERS
DEALS
IDEALS
DEARE
DEARED
DEARER
DEARES
DEARN
DEARNS
DEATH
DEATHS
DEATHY
DEAVE
DEAVED
DEAVES
DEBAG
DEBAGS
DEBAR
DEBARK
DEBARS
DEBEL
DEBELS
DEBIT
DEBITS
DEBUG
DEBUGS
DEBUT
DEBUTS
DECAD

DECADE
DECADS
DECAL
DECALS
DECAY
DECAYS
DECKO
DECKOS
DECOR
DECORS
DECOY
DECOYS
DEEMS
ADEEMS
DEEVE
DEEVED
DEEVES
DEFAT
DEFATS
DEFER
DEFERS
DEGUM
DEGUMS
DEIGN
SDEIGN
DEIGNS
DEISM
DEISMS
DEIST
DEISTS
DEKKO
DEKKOS
DELAY
DELAYS
DELFT
DELFTS
DELPH
DELPHS
DELTA
DELTAS
DELVE
DELVED
DELVER
DELVES
DEMAN
DEMAND
DEMANS
DEMIT
DEMITS
DEMOB
DEMOBS
DEMON
DEMONS
DEMUR
DEMURE
DEMURS
DENAY
DENAYS
DENIM
DENIMS
DENSE
DENSER
DEPOT
DEPOTS
DEPTH
DEPTHS
DERAY
DERAYS
DERIG
DERIGS

DERMA
DERMAL
DERMAS
DERTH
DERTHS
DESSE
DESSES
DETER
DETERS
DEUCE
DEUCED
DEUCES
DEVEL
DEVELS
DEVIL
DEVILS
DEVOT
DEVOTE
DEVOTS
DEWAN
DEWANI
DEWANS
DEWAR
DEWARS
DHOBI
DHOBIS
DHOLE
DHOLES
DHOLL
DHOLLS
DHOTI
DHOTIS
DIAZO
DIAZOS
DICER
DICERS
DICHT
DICHTS
DICOT
DICOTS
DICTS
EDICTS
DIENE
DIENES
DIGHT
DIGHTS
DIGIT
DIGITS
DIKAS
DIKAST
DIKER
DIKERS
DILDO
DILDOE
DILDOS
DILLI
DILLIS
DIMER
DIMERS
DINAR
DINARS
DINER
DINERS
DINGE
DINGED
DINGER
DINGES
DINGEY
DINIC
DINICS

DIODE
DIODES
DIOTA
DIOTAS
DIPSO
DIPSOS
DIRGE
DIRGES
DIRKE
DIRKED
DIRKES
DISCO
DISCOS
DISME
DISMES
DITAL
DITALS
DITED
EDITED
DITTO
DITTOS
DIVAN
DIVANS
DIVER
DIVERS
DIVERT
DIVES
DIVEST
DIVOT
DIVOTS
DIWAN
DIWANS
DIXIE
DIXIES
DIZEN
DIZENS
DJINN
DJINNI
DODGE
DODGED
DODGER
DODGES
DOGIE
DOGIES
DOGMA
DOGMAS
DOHYO
DOHYOS
DOING
DOINGS
DOLCE
DOLCES
DOLMA
DOLMAN
DOLMAS
DOLOR
DOLORS
DONAH
DONAHS
DONEE
DONEES
DONGA
DONGAS
DONNE
DONNED
DONNEE
DONNES
DONOR
DONORS
DONUT

DONUTS
DOOLE
DOOLES
DOONA
DOONAS
DOORN
DOORNS
DOORS
ADOORS
DOPER
DOPERS
DORAD
DORADO
DORADS
DOREE
DOREES
DORSA
DORSAL
DORSE
DORSEL
DORSER
DORSES
DOSEH
DOSEHS
DOTER
DOTERS
DOUAR
DOUARS
DOUBT
DOUBTS
DOUCE
DOUCER
DOUCET
DOUGH
DOUGHS
DOUGHT
DOUGHY
DOUMA
DOUMAS
DOURA
DOURAS
DOUSE
DOUSED
DOUSER
DOUSES
DOVER
DOVERS
DOVIE
DOVIER
DOWAR
DOWARS
DOWEL
DOWELS
DOWER
DOWERS
DOWIE
DOWIER
DOWLE
DOWLES
DOWSE
DOWSED
DOWSER
DOWSES
DOWSET
DOYEN
DOYENS
DOZEN
DOZENS
DOZER
DOZERS

DRAFF
DRAFFS
DRAFFY
DRAFT
DRAFTS
DRAFTY
DRAIL
DRAILS
DRAIN
DRAINS
DRAKE
DRAKES
DRAMA
DRAMAS
DRANT
DRANTS
DRAPE
DRAPED
DRAPER
DRAPES
DRAPET
DRAWL
DRAWLS
DREAD
ADREAD
DREADS
DREAM
DREAMS
DREAMT
DREAMY
DREAR
DREARE
DREARS
DREARY
DRECK
DRECKS
DRECKY
DRERE
DRERES
DRESS
DRESSY
DRIER
DRIERS
DRIES
DRIEST
DRIFT
ADRIFT
DRIFTS
DRIFTY
DRILL
DRILLS
DRINK
DRINKS
DRIVE
DRIVEL
DRIVEN
DRIVER
DRIVES
DROIL
DROILS
DROIT
ADROIT
DROITS
DROLE
DROLER
DROLES
DROLL
DROLLS
DROLLY
DROME

DROMES
DRONE
DRONED
DRONES
DROOG
DROOGS
DROOK
DROOKS
DROOL
DROOLS
DROOP
DROOPS
DROOPY
DROPS
DROPSY
DROSS
DROSSY
DROUK
DROUKS
DROVE
DROVER
DROVES
DROWN
DROWNS
DROWS
DROWSE
DROWSY
DRUID
DRUIDS
DRUNK
DRUNKS
DRUPE
DRUPEL
DRUPES
DRUSE
DRUSES
DRYAD
DRYADS
DRYER
DRYERS
DSOBO
DSOBOS
DSOMO
DSOMOS
DUCAT
DUCATS
DUCES
EDUCES
DUCTS
EDUCTS
DUETT
DUETTI
DUETTO
DUETTS
DULIA
DULIAS
DULSE
DULSES
DUMBO
DUMBOS
DUNCE
DUNCES
DUOMO
DUOMOS
DUPER
DUPERS
DUPERY
DUPLE
DUPLET
DUPLEX

DURAL
DURALS
DURES
DURESS
DUROY
DUROYS
DURRA
DURRAS
DURUM
DURUMS
DUSTS
ADUSTS
DUVET
DUVETS
DWALE
DWALES
DWALM
DWALMS
DWANG
DWANGS
DWARF
DWARFS
DWAUM
DWAUMS
DWEEB
DWEEBS
DWELL
DWELLS
DWILE
DWILES
DWINE
DWINED
DWINES
DYING
DYINGS
EAGER
EAGERS
EAGLE
BEAGLE
TEAGLE
EAGLES
EAGLET
EAGRE
MEAGRE
EAGRES
EALES
VEALES
EANED
BEANED
LEANED
MEANED
PEANED
SEANED
WEANED
YEANED
EARDS
BEARDS
HEARDS
YEARDS
EARED
BEARED
DEARED
FEARED
GEARED
LEARED
NEARED
REARED
SEARED
WEARED
EARLS

PEARLS
EARLY
DEARLY
NEARLY
PEARLY
REARLY
YEARLY
EARNS
DEARNS
LEARNS
YEARNS
EARST
PEARST
EARTH
DEARTH
HEARTH
EARTHS
EARTHY
EASED
CEASED
LEASED
MEASED
PEASED
SEASED
TEASED
EASEL
TEASEL
WEASEL
EASELS
EASES
CEASES
LEASES
MEASES
PEASES
SEASES
TEASES
EASLE
MEASLE
EASLES
EASTS
BEASTS
FEASTS
HEASTS
LEASTS
REASTS
YEASTS
EATEN
BEATEN
NEATEN
EATER
BEATER
HEATER
NEATER
SEATER
EATERS
EATERY
EATHE
MEATHE
EAVES
DEAVES
HEAVES
LEAVES
REAVES
WEAVES
EBBED
KEBBED
NEBBED
WEBBED
ECADS
DECADS

ECHED
EECHED
LECHED
PECHED
ECHES
EECHES
LECHES
ECLAT
ECLATS
EDEMA
OEDEMA
EDEMAS
EDGED
HEDGED
KEDGED
SEDGED
WEDGED
EDGER
HEDGER
KEDGER
LEDGER
EDGERS
EDGES
HEDGES
KEDGES
LEDGES
SEDGES
WEDGES
EDICT
EDICTS
EDILE
AEDILE
SEDILE
EDILES
EDUCE
DEDUCE
REDUCE
SEDUCE
EDUCED
EDUCES
EDUCT
DEDUCT
EDUCTS
EERIE
FEERIE
PEERIE
EERIER
EEVEN
EEVENS
EFFED
JEFFED
REFFED
EGERS
LEGERS
EGEST
REGEST
EGESTA
EGESTS
EGGAR
BEGGAR
SEGGAR
EGGARS
EGGED
BEGGED
LEGGED
PEGGED
EGGER
LEGGER
EGGERS
EGGERY

EGRET
REGRET
EGRETS
EIDER
DEIDER
EIDERS
EIGHT
HEIGHT
KEIGHT
WEIGHT
EIGHTH
EIGHTS
EIGHTY
EIKON
EIKONS
EISEL
EISELL
EISELS
EJECT
DEJECT
REJECT
EJECTA
EJECTS
EKING
REKING
ELAND
ELANDS
ELATE
BELATE
DELATE
RELATE
VELATE
ELATED
ELATER
ELATES
ELBOW
ELBOWS
ELCHI
ELCHIS
ELDER
GELDER
MELDER
WELDER
ELDERS
ELDIN
ELDING
ELDINS
ELECT
SELECT
ELECTS
ELEMI
ELEMIS
ELFED
SELFED
ELFIN
ELFING
ELFINS
ELIAD
ELIADS
ELIDE
RELIDE
ELIDED
ELIDES
ELITE
PELITE
ELITES
ELOGE
ELOGES
ELOIN
ELOINS

ELOPE
DELOPE
ELOPED
ELOPER
ELOPES
ELPEE
ELPEES
ELSIN
ELSINS
ELUDE
DELUDE
ELUDED
ELUDER
ELUDES
ELUTE
ELUTED
ELUTES
ELVAN
ELVANS
ELVER
DELVER
ELVERS
ELVES
DELVES
HELVES
PELVES
SELVES
EMBAR
EMBARK
EMBARS
EMBAY
EMBAYS
EMBED
KEMBED
EMBEDS
EMBER
MEMBER
EMBERS
EMBOG
EMBOGS
EMBOW
EMBOWS
EMBUS
EMBUSY
EMCEE
EMCEED
EMCEES
EMEER
EMEERS
EMEND
EMENDS
EMITS
DEMITS
REMITS
EMMAS
LEMMAS
EMMER
EMMERS
EMMET
EMMETS
EMMEW
EMMEWS
EMOTE
DEMOTE
REMOTE
EMOTED
EMOTES
EMOVE
REMOVE
EMOVED

EMOVES
EMULE
AEMULE
EMULED
EMULES
EMURE
DEMURE
EMURED
EMURES
ENACT
ENACTS
ENARM
ENARMS
ENATE
SENATE
ENDED
BENDED
FENDED
HENDED
MENDED
PENDED
SENDED
TENDED
VENDED
WENDED
ENDEW
ENDEWS
ENDOW
ENDOWS
ENDUE
VENDUE
ENDUED
ENDUES
ENEMA
ENEMAS
ENEWS
RENEWS
ENIAC
ENIACS
ENJOY
ENJOYS
ENMEW
ENMEWS
ENNUI
ENNUIS
ENOKI
ENOKIS
ENROL
ENROLL
ENROLS
ENSEW
ENSEWS
ENSUE
ENSUED
ENSUES
ENTER
CENTER
RENTER
TENTER
VENTER
ENTERA
ENTERS
ENTIA
KENTIA
ENTRY
CENTRY
GENTRY
SENTRY
ENURE
TENURE

ENURED
ENURES
ENVOI
RENVOI
ENVOIS
ENVOY
LENVOY
RENVOY
ENVOYS
EORLS
CEORLS
EOSIN
EOSINS
EPACT
EPACTS
EPEES
TEPEES
EPHAH
EPHAHS
EPHOD
EPHODS
EPHOR
EPHORS
EPOCH
EPOCHA
EPOCHS
EPODE
EPODES
EPOPT
EPOPTS
EPRIS
EPRISE
EPROM
EPROMS
EQUAL
EQUALS
EQUID
EQUIDS
EQUIP
EQUIPE
EQUIPS
ERASE
ERASED
ERASER
ERASES
ERBIA
ERBIAS
ERECT
ERECTS
ERGON
ERGONS
ERGOT
ERGOTS
ERICA
ERICAS
ERICK
ERICKS
ERING
CERING
DERING
LERING
MERING
SERING
ERINGO
ERNED
CERNED
GERNED
KERNED
TERNED
ERNES

CERNES
GERNES
KERNES
TERNES
ERODE
ERODED
ERODES
ERRED
SERRED
ERROR
TERROR
ERRORS
ERSES
HERSES
MERSES
PERSES
VERSES
ERUCT
ERUCTS
ERUPT
ERUPTS
ERVEN
VERVEN
ESCOT
ESCOTS
ESILE
RESILE
ESILES
ESKAR
ESKARS
ESKER
ESKERS
ESSAY
ESSAYS
ESSES
CESSES
DESSES
FESSES
GESSES
JESSES
LESSES
MESSES
NESSES
SESSES
YESSES
ESTER
FESTER
JESTER
NESTER
PESTER
RESTER
TESTER
WESTER
YESTER
ZESTER
ESTERS
ESTOC
ESTOCS
ESTOP
ESTOPS
ESTRO
ESTROS
ETAGE
METAGE
ETAGES
ETAPE
ETAPES
ETHAL
LETHAL
ETHALS

ETHER
AETHER
HETHER
NETHER
PETHER
TETHER
WETHER
ETHERS
ETHIC
ETHICS
ETHYL
METHYL
ETHYLS
ETTIN
ETTINS
ETTLE
FETTLE
KETTLE
METTLE
NETTLE
PETTLE
SETTLE
ETTLED
ETTLES
ETUDE
ETUDES
ETWEE
ETWEES
EUGHS
HEUGHS
EUKED
YEUKED
EUPAD
EUPADS
EUSOL
EUSOLS
EVADE
EVADED
EVADER
EVADES
EVENS
EEVENS
SEVENS
EVENT
EVENTS
EVERT
REVERT
EVERTS
EVERY
REVERY
SEVERY
EVETS
REVETS
EVICT
EVICTS
EVILS
DEVILS
EVITE
LEVITE
EVITED
EVITES
EVOKE
REVOKE
EVOKED
EVOKER
EVOKES
EWERS
HEWERS
SEWERS
EWEST

FEWEST
NEWEST
EXACT
HEXACT
EXACTS
EXALT
EXALTS
EXCEL
EXCELS
EXEAT
EXEATS
EXEEM
EXEEMS
EXEME
LEXEME
EXEMED
EXEMES
EXERT
EXERTS
EXILE
EXILED
EXILES
EXINE
EXINES
EXIST
SEXIST
EXISTS
EXODE
EXODES
EXPAT
EXPATS
EXPEL
EXPELS
EXPOS
EXPOSE
EXTOL
EXTOLD
EXTOLS
EXTRA
EXTRAS
EXUDE
EXUDED
EXUDES
EXULT
EXULTS
EXURB
EXURBS
EYING
FEYING
HEYING
KEYING
EYRIE
EYRIES
FABLE
FABLED
FABLER
FABLES
FACER
FACERS
FACET
FACETE
FACETS
FACIA
FACIAL
FACIAS
FADER
FADERS
FADGE
FADGED
FADGES
FAGOT
FAGOTS
FAINE
FAINED
FAINER
FAINES
FAINT
FAINTS
FAINTY
FAITH
FAITHS
FAKER
FAKERS
FAKERY
FAKIR
FAKIRS
FALSE
FALSED
FALSER
FALSES
FANAL
FANALS
FANGO
FANGOS
FANON
FANONS
FARAD
FARADS
FARCE
FARCED
FARCES
FARCI
FARCIN
FARLE
FARLES
FARSE
FARSED
FARSES
FASCI
FASCIA
FASCIO
FATSO
FATSOS
FATWA
FATWAH
FATWAS
FAULT
FAULTS
FAULTY
FAUNA
FAUNAE
FAUNAL
FAUNAS
FAVEL
FAVELA
FAVELL
FAVOR
FAVORS
FAYNE
FAYNED
FAYNES
FAYRE
FAYRES
FEARE
FEARED
FEARES
FEARS
AFEARS
FEAST
FEASTS
FECHT
FECHTS
FEESE
FEESED
FEESES
FEEZE
FEEZED
FEEZES
FEIGN
FEIGNS
FEINT
FEINTS
FELID
FELIDS
FELLA
FELLAH
FELLAS
FELON
FELONS
FELONY
FEMAL
FEMALE
FEMALS
FEMME
FEMMES
FEMUR
FEMURS
FENCE
FENCED
FENCER
FENCES
FEOFF
FEOFFS
FERES
FEREST
FERMI
FERMIS
FESSE
FESSES
FESTA
FESTAL
FESTAS
FETOR
FETORS
FETTA
FETTAS
FETWA
FETWAS
FEUAR
FEUARS
FEVER
FEVERS
FIBER
FIBERS
FIBRE
FIBRED
FIBRES
FIBRO
FIBROS
FICHE
FICHES
FICHU
FICHUS
FIDGE
FIDGED
FIDGES
FIDGET
FIELD
AFIELD
FIELDS
FIEND
FIENDS
FIENT
FIENTS
FIERE
FIERES
FIFER
FIFERS
FIFTH
FIFTHS
FIGHT
FIGHTS
FILER
FILERS
FILET
FILETS
FILLE
FILLED
FILLER
FILLES
FILLET
FILOS
FILOSE
FILTH
FILTHS
FILTHY
FINAL
FINALE
FINALS
FINER
FINERS
FINERY
FINES
FINEST
FINIS
FINISH
FIORD
FIORDS
FIRER
FIRERS
FIRST
FIRSTS
FIRTH
FIRTHS
FITCH
FITCHE
FITCHY
FITTE
FITTED
FITTER
FITTES
FIVER
FIVERS
FIXER
FIXERS
FJORD
FJORDS
FLACK
FLACKS
FLAFF
FLAFFS
FLAGS
OFLAGS
FLAIL
FLAILS
FLAIR
FLAIRS
FLAKE
FLAKED
FLAKES
FLAME
AFLAME
FLAMED
FLAMEN
FLAMES
FLAMM
FLAMMS
FLANK
FLANKS
FLARE
FLARED
FLARES
FLASH
FLASHY
FLASK
FLASKS
FLAWN
FLAWNS
FLEAM
FLEAMS
FLECK
FLECKS
FLEER
FLEERS
FLEET
FLEETS
FLEME
FLEMES
FLESH
FLESHY
FLICK
FLICKS
FLIER
FLIERS
FLIES
FLIEST
FLIMP
FLIMPS
FLING
FLINGS
FLINT
FLINTS
FLINTY
FLIRT
FLIRTS
FLIRTY
FLISK
FLISKS
FLISKY
FLITE
FLITED
FLITES
FLOAT
AFLOAT
FLOATS
FLOATY
FLOCK
FLOCKS
FLONG
FLONGS
FLOOD
FLOODS
FLOOR
FLOORS
FLORA
FLORAE
FLORAL
FLORAS
FLOSS
FLOSSY
FLOTA
FLOTAS
FLOTE
FLOTEL
FLOTES
FLOUR
FLOURS
FLOURY
FLOUT
FLOUTS
FLUFF
FLUFFS
FLUFFY
FLUID
FLUIDS
FLUKE
FLUKED
FLUKES
FLUKEY
FLUME
FLUMES
FLUMP
FLUMPS
FLUNK
FLUNKS
FLUNKY
FLUOR
FLUORS
FLURR
FLURRS
FLURRY
FLUSH
FLUSHY
FLUTE
FLUTED
FLUTER
FLUTES
FLYER
FLYERS
FLYPE
FLYPED
FLYPES
FLYTE
FLYTED
FLYTES
FOEHN
FOEHNS
FOGEY
FOGEYS
FOGLE
FOGLES
FOIST
FOISTS
FOLIA
FOLIAR
FOLIE
FOLIES
FOLIO
FOLIOS
FOLKS
FOLKSY
FONDA
FONDAS
FORAY
FORAYS
FORBY
FORBYE
FORCE
FORCED
FORCER
FORCES
FOREL
FORELS
FORES
FOREST
FORGE
FORGED
FORGER
FORGES
FORGET
FORGO
FORGOT
FORME
FORMED
FORMER
FORMES
FORTE
FORTED
FORTES
FORTH
FORTHY
FORUM
FORUMS
FOSSA
FOSSAE
FOSSAS
FOSSE
FOSSED
FOSSES
FOUAT
FOUATS
FOUET
FOUETS
FOULE
FOULED
FOULER
FOULES
FOUND
FOUNDS
FOUNT
FOUNTS
FOUTH
FOUTHS
FOVEA
FOVEAE
FOVEAL
FOWTH
FOWTHS
FOYER
FOYERS
FOYLE
FOYLED
FOYLES
FOYNE
FOYNED
FOYNES
FRACT
FRACTS
FRAIL
FRAILS
FRAIM
FRAIMS
FRAME
FRAMED
FRAMER
FRAMES
FRANC
FRANCO
FRANCS
FRANK
FRANKS
FRATE
FRATER
FRAUD
FRAUDS
FREAK
FREAKS
FREAKY
FREER
FREERS
FREES
FREEST
FREET
AFREET
FREETS
FREETY
FREIT
FREITS
FREITY
FREMD
FREMDS
FREON
FREONS
FRERE
FRERES
FRESH
AFRESH
FRIAR
FRIARS
FRIARY
FRIER
FRIERS
FRILL
FRILLS
FRILLY
FRISK
FRISKA
FRISKS
FRISKY
FRIST
FRISTS
FRITH
FRITHS
FRITS
AFRITS
FRIZE
FRIZES
FRIZZ
FRIZZY
FROCK
FROCKS
FROND
FRONDS
FRONT
AFRONT
FRONTS
FRORE
FROREN
FRORN
FRORNE
FROST
FROSTS
FROSTY
FROTH
FROTHS
FROTHY
FROWN
FROWNS
FROWS
FROWST
FROWSY
FROZE
FROZEN
FRUIT
FRUITS
FRUITY
FRUMP
FRUMPS
FRUMPY
FRUST
FRUSTA
FRUSTS
FRYER
FRYERS
FUDGE
FUDGED
FUDGES
FUERO
FUEROS
FUGIE
FUGIES
FUGLE
FUGLED
FUGLES
FUGUE
FUGUES
FUMET
FUMETS
FUNDI
FUNDIE
FUNDIS
FURAL
FURALS
FURAN
FURANE
FURANS
FUROL
FUROLE
FUROLS
FUROR
FURORE
FURORS
FURZE
FURZES
FUSEE
FUSEES
FUSIL
FUSILE
FUSILS
FUTON
FUTONS
FUZEE
FUZEES
FYTTE
FYTTES
GABLE
GABLED
GABLES
GABLET
GADGE
GADGES
GADGET
GADJE
GADJES
GADSO
GADSOS
GAFFE
GAFFED
GAFFER
GAFFES

GAITT
GAITTS
GALAH
GALAHS
GALEA
GALEAE
GALEAS
GALLY
EGALLY
GALOP
GALOPS
GALUT
GALUTH
GALUTS
GAMAY
GAMAYS
GAMBA
GAMBAS
GAMBO
GAMBOL
GAMBOS
GAMES
GAMEST
GAMESY
GAMIC
AGAMIC
OGAMIC
GAMIN
GAMINE
GAMING
GAMINS
GAMMA
GAMMAS
GAMME
GAMMED
GAMMER
GAMMES
GAMUT
GAMUTS
GANJA
GANJAS
GAPER
GAPERS
GAPOS
IGAPOS
GARBE
GARBED
GARBES
GARBO
GARBOS
GARDA
GARDAI
GARRE
GARRED
GARRES
GARRET
GARTH
GARTHS
GARUM
GARUMS
GATES
AGATES
GAUGE
GAUGED
GAUGER
GAUGES
GAUJE
GAUJES
GAULT
GAULTS

GAUNT
GAUNTS
GAUZE
GAUZES
GAVEL
GAVELS
GAYAL
GAYALS
GAZAL
GAZALS
GAZED
AGAZED
GAZER
GAZERS
GAZON
GAZONS
GAZOO
GAZOON
GAZOOS
GEARE
GEARED
GEARES
GEBUR
GEBURS
GECKO
GECKOS
GEIST
AGEIST
GEISTS
GEMEL
GEMELS
GEMMA
GEMMAE
GEMMAN
GEMOT
GEMOTS
GENES
AGENES
GENET
GENETS
GENIE
GENIES
GENIP
GENIPS
GENOA
GENOAS
GENOM
GENOME
GENOMS
GENRE
GENRES
GENTS
AGENTS
GEODE
GEODES
GEOID
GEOIDS
GERAH
GERAHS
GERBE
GERBES
GERLE
GERLES
GERNE
GERNED
GERNES
GESSE
GESSED
GESSES
GESTE

GESTES
GESTS
EGESTS
GHAST
AGHAST
GHASTS
GHAUT
GHAUTS
GHAZI
GHAZIS
GHOST
GHOSTS
GHOSTY
GHOUL
GHOULS
GHYLL
GHYLLS
GIANT
GIANTS
GIBEL
GIBELS
GIBER
GIBERS
GIGOT
GIGOTS
GIGUE
GIGUES
GILAS
AGILAS
GILET
GILETS
GIMME
GIMMER
GIMMES
GINGS
AGINGS
GIPPO
GIPPOS
GIRON
GIRONS
GIRTH
GIRTHS
GISMO
GISMOS
GISTS
AGISTS
GIUST
GIUSTO
GIUSTS
GIVER
GIVERS
GIVES
OGIVES
GIZMO
GIZMOS
GLACE
GLACES
GLADE
GLADES
GLAIK
GLAIKS
GLAIR
GLAIRS
GLAIRY
GLAND
GLANDS
GLARE
GLARED
GLARES
GLASS

GLASSY
GLAUM
GLAUMS
GLAUR
GLAURS
GLAURY
GLAZE
GLAZED
GLAZEN
GLAZER
GLAZES
GLEAM
AGLEAM
GLEAMS
GLEAMY
GLEAN
GLEANS
GLEBE
GLEBES
GLEDE
GLEDES
GLEED
GLEEDS
GLEEK
GLEEKS
GLEET
GLEETS
GLEETY
GLENT
GLENTS
GLIDE
GLIDED
GLIDER
GLIDES
GLIFF
GLIFFS
GLIFT
GLIFTS
GLIKE
GLIKES
GLINT
GLINTS
GLISK
GLISKS
GLITZ
GLITZY
GLOAT
GLOATS
GLOBE
GLOBED
GLOBES
GLOGG
GLOGGS
GLOOM
GLOOMS
GLOOMY
GLOOP
GLOOPS
GLOOPY
GLOSS
GLOSSA
GLOSSY
GLOUT
GLOUTS
GLOVE
GLOVED
GLOVER
GLOVES
GLOZE
GLOZED

GLOZES
GLUER
GLUERS
GLUME
GLUMES
GLUON
GLUONS
GLYPH
GLYPHS
GNARL
GNARLS
GNARLY
GNARR
GNARRS
GNOME
GNOMES
GODET
GODETS
GODSO
GODSON
GODSOS
GOFER
GOFERS
GOING
AGOING
GOINGS
GOLEM
GOLEMS
GOLPE
GOLPES
GOMBO
GOMBOS
GOMPA
GOMPAS
GONAD
GONADS
GONER
GONERS
GOOLD
GOOLDS
GOOSE
GOOSED
GOOSES
GOOSEY
GOPAK
GOPAKS
GORAL
GORALS
GORGE
GORGED
GORGES
GORGET
GORSE
GORSES
GOSHT
GOSHTS
GOSSE
GOSSES
GOUGE
GOUGED
GOUGES
GOURA
GOURAS
GOURD
GOURDE
GOURDS
GOURDY
GOUTY
AGOUTY
GOWAN

GOWANS
GOWANY
GRAAL
GRAALS
GRACE
GRACED
GRACES
GRADE
GRADED
GRADER
GRADES
GRAFF
GRAFFS
GRAFT
GRAFTS
GRAIL
GRAILE
GRAILS
GRAIN
GRAINE
GRAINS
GRAINY
GRAIP
GRAIPS
GRAMA
GRAMAS
GRAME
GRAMES
GRAND
GRANDE
GRANDS
GRANT
GRANTS
GRAPE
GRAPED
GRAPES
GRAPEY
GRAPH
GRAPHS
GRASP
GRASPS
GRASS
GRASSY
GRATE
GRATED
GRATER
GRATES
GRAVE
GRAVED
GRAVEL
GRAVEN
GRAVER
GRAVES
GRAZE
GRAZED
GRAZER
GRAZES
GREAT
GREATS
GREBE
GREBES
GRECE
GRECES
GREED
AGREED
GREEDS
GREEDY
GREEN
GREENS
GREENY

GREES
AGREES
GREESE
GREET
GREETE
GREETS
GREGE
AGREGE
GREGO
GREGOS
GREIN
GREINS
GRESE
GRESES
GREVE
GREVES
GRICE
GRICER
GRICES
GRIDE
GRIDED
GRIDES
GRIEF
GRIEFS
GRIFF
GRIFFE
GRIFFS
GRIFT
GRIFTS
GRIKE
GRIKES
GRILL
GRILLE
GRILLS
GRIME
GRIMED
GRIMES
GRIND
GRINDS
GRIOT
GRIOTS
GRIPE
GRIPED
GRIPER
GRIPES
GRISE
AGRISE
GRISED
GRISES
GRIST
GRISTS
GRITH
GRITHS
GRIZE
AGRIZE
GRIZES
GROAN
GROANS
GROAT
GROATS
GROIN
GROINS
GROMA
GROMAS
GRONE
GRONED
GRONES
GROOF
GROOFS
GROOM

GROOMS
GROPE
GROPED
GROPER
GROPES
GROUF
GROUFS
GROUP
GROUPS
GROUPY
GROUT
GROUTS
GROUTY
GROVE
GROVEL
GROVES
GROVET
GROWL
GROWLS
GROWLY
GRUEL
GRUELS
GRUFE
GRUFES
GRUME
GRUMES
GRUMP
GRUMPH
GRUMPS
GRUMPY
GRUNT
GRUNTS
GRYCE
GRYCES
GRYDE
GRYDED
GRYDES
GRYKE
GRYKES
GRYPE
GRYPES
GUACO
GUACOS
GUANA
IGUANA
GUANAS
GUANO
GUANOS
GUARD
GUARDS
GUAVA
GUAVAS
GUEST
GUESTS
GUIDE
GUIDED
GUIDER
GUIDES
GUILD
GUILDS
GUILE
GUILED
GUILER
GUILES
GUILT
GUILTS
GUILTY
GUIMP
GUIMPS
GUIRO

GUIROS
GUISE
AGUISE
GUISED
GUISER
GUISES
GULAG
GULAGS
GULPH
GULPHS
GUMBO
GUMBOS
GUNGE
GUNGES
GURGE
GURGES
GUSLA
GUSLAR
GUSLAS
GUSLE
GUSLES
GUSLI
GUSLIS
GUSTO
GUSTOS
GUTTA
GUTTAE
GUTTAS
GUYLE
GUYLED
GUYLER
GUYLES
GUYOT
GUYOTS
GUYSE
GUYSES
GYELD
GYELDS
GYNAE
GYNAES
GYNIE
GYNIES
GYPPO
GYPPOS
GYRON
GYRONS
GYROS
GYROSE
HABIT
HABITS
HACEK
HACEKS
HACKS
CHACKS
SHACKS
THACKS
WHACKS
HADED
SHADED
HADES
SHADES
HADJI
HADJIS
HAFFS
CHAFFS
HAFTS
CHAFTS
SHAFTS
HAICK
HAICKS

HAINS
CHAINS
HAIRS
CHAIRS
HAIRST
HAJJI
HAJJIS
HAKAM
HAKAMS
HAKES
SHAKES
HAKIM
HAKIMS
HALAL
HALALS
HALED
SHALED
WHALED
HALER
THALER
WHALER
HALERS
HALES
SHALES
WHALES
HALEST
HALFA
HALFAS
HALLO
HALLOA
HALLOO
HALLOS
HALLOW
HALMA
HALMAS
HALMS
SHALMS
HALON
HALONS
HALSE
HALSED
HALSER
HALSES
HALVA
HALVAH
HALVAS
HALVE
HALVED
HALVER
HALVES
HAMAL
HAMALS
HAMED
SHAMED
HAMES
SHAMES
HAMMY
CHAMMY
SHAMMY
WHAMMY
HAMZA
HAMZAH
HAMZAS
HANAP
HANAPS
HANCE
CHANCE
HANCES
HANDS
SHANDS

HANDY
SHANDY
HANGS
BHANGS
PHANGS
WHANGS
HANKS
CHANKS
SHANKS
THANKS
HAOMA
HAOMAS
HAPPY
CHAPPY
HARAM
HARAMS
HARDS
CHARDS
SHARDS
HARED
CHARED
SHARED
HAREM
HAREMS
HARES
CHARES
PHARES
SHARES
WHARES
HARIM
HARIMS
HARKS
CHARKS
SHARKS
HARMS
CHARMS
HARNS
SHARNS
HAROS
PHAROS
HARPS
SHARPS
HARRY
CHARRY
GHARRY
HARTS
CHARTS
HASTE
CHASTE
HASTED
HASTEN
HASTES
HATCH
THATCH
HATER
HATERS
HAUGH
HAUGHS
HAUGHT
HAULD
HAULDS
HAULM
HAULMS
HAULS
HAULST
HAUNT
CHAUNT
HAUNTS
HAUSE
HAUSED

HAUSES
HAVEN
SHAVEN
HAVENS
HAVER
SHAVER
HAVERS
HAVES
SHAVES
HAVOC
HAVOCS
HAWED
CHAWED
THAWED
HAWMS
SHAWMS
HAWSE
HAWSED
HAWSER
HAWSES
HAYLE
HAYLES
HAZEL
GHAZEL
HAZELS
HAZER
HAZERS
HEALD
HEALDS
HEALS
SHEALS
WHEALS
HEAPS
CHEAPS
HEAPY
CHEAPY
HEARD
HEARDS
HEARE
WHEARE
HEARER
HEARES
HEARS
SHEARS
HEARSE
HEARSY
HEART
HEARTH
HEARTS
HEARTY
HEAST
HEASTE
HEASTS
HEATH
SHEATH
HEATHS
HEATHY
HEATS
CHEATS
WHEATS
HEAVE
SHEAVE
THEAVE
HEAVED
HEAVEN
HEAVER
HEAVES
HEBEN
HEBENS
HECHT

HECHTS
HECKS
CHECKS
HEDGE
HEDGED
HEDGER
HEDGES
HEELS
SHEELS
WHEELS
HEEZE
PHEEZE
WHEEZE
HEEZED
HEEZES
HEFTE
HEFTED
HEFTS
THEFTS
WHEFTS
HEIGH
HEIGHT
HEIRS
THEIRS
HEIST
THEIST
HEISTS
HEJAB
HEJABS
HEJRA
HEJRAS
HELLO
HELLOS
HELLS
SHELLS
HELMS
WHELMS
HELOT
HELOTS
HELPS
WHELPS
HELVE
SHELVE
HELVED
HELVES
HEMES
THEMES
HENCE
THENCE
WHENCE
HENDS
SHENDS
HENGE
HENGES
HENNA
HENNAS
HENRY
HENRYS
HEPAR
HEPARS
HERDS
SHERDS
HERMA
HERMAE
HERMS
THERMS
HEROE
HEROES
HERON
HERONS

HERRY
CHERRY
SHERRY
WHERRY
HERSE
HERSED
HERSES
HERYE
HERYED
HERYES
HESTS
CHESTS
HETES
THETES
HEUCH
SHEUCH
HEUCHS
HEUGH
SHEUGH
WHEUGH
HEUGHS
HEVEA
HEVEAS
HEWED
CHEWED
SHEWED
THEWED
WHEWED
HEWER
CHEWER
HEWERS
HEXAD
HEXADS
HEXES
RHEXES
HICKS
CHICKS
THICKS
HIDED
CHIDED
HIDER
CHIDER
HIDERS
HIDES
CHIDES
HIGHS
THIGHS
HIGHT
HIGHTH
HIGHTS
HIJAB
HIJABS
HIJRA
HIJRAH
HIJRAS
HIKER
HIKERS
HILLO
HILLOS
HILLS
CHILLS
SHILLS
THILLS
HILLY
CHILLY
WHILLY
HINGE
WHINGE
HINGED
HINGES

HINGS
THINGS
HINNY
SHINNY
WHINNY
HIPPO
SHIPPO
HIPPOS
HIPPY
CHIPPY
WHIPPY
HIRER
HIRERS
HIRES
SHIRES
HISTS
WHISTS
HITCH
HITCHY
HITHE
HITHER
HITHES
HIVED
CHIVED
HIVER
SHIVER
HIVERS
HIVES
CHIVES
SHIVES
HIZEN
HIZENS
HOARD
HOARDS
HOARS
HOARSE
HOAST
HOASTS
HOCKS
CHOCKS
SHOCKS
HODJA
KHODJA
HODJAS
HOERS
SHOERS
HOGAN
HOGANS
HOGEN
HOGENS
HOICK
HOICKS
HOISE
HOISED
HOISES
HOIST
HOISTS
HOKED
CHOKED
HOKES
CHOKES
HOKEY
CHOKEY
HOKUM
HOKUMS
HOLED
THOLED
HOLES
DHOLES
THOLES

WHOLES
HOLLA
HOLLAS
HOLLO
HOLLOA
HOLLOS
HOLLOW
HOLLY
WHOLLY
HOMER
HOMERS
HOMME
HOMMES
HOMOS
ZHOMOS
HONED
PHONED
HONER
PHONER
HONERS
HONES
PHONES
RHONES
HONEST
HONEY
PHONEY
HONEYS
HONGI
HONGIS
HONGS
THONGS
HONKY
SHONKY
HONOR
HONORS
HOOEY
PHOOEY
HOOEYS
HOOFS
CHOOFS
HOOKA
HOOKAH
HOOKAS
HOOKS
CHOOKS
SHOOKS
HOOLY
DHOOLY
HOOPS
WHOOPS
HOORD
HOORDS
HOOSH
WHOOSH
HOOTS
SHOOTS
WHOOTS
HOOVE
HOOVED
HOOVEN
HOOVER
HOOVES
HOPER
HOPERS
HOPPY
CHOPPY
SHOPPY
HORAL
CHORAL
HORDE

HORDED
HORDES
HORME
HORMES
HORNS
THORNS
HORNY
THORNY
HORSE
AHORSE
HORSED
HORSES
HORSEY
HORST
HORSTS
HOSEN
CHOSEN
HOSES
CHOSES
HOSTA
HOSTAS
HOSTS
GHOSTS
HOTEL
HOTELS
HOUFF
HOUFFS
HOUGH
CHOUGH
SHOUGH
THOUGH
HOUGHS
HOUND
HOUNDS
HOURI
HOURIS
HOUSE
CHOUSE
HOUSED
HOUSEL
HOUSES
HOUTS
CHOUTS
SHOUTS
HOVED
SHOVED
HOVEL
SHOVEL
HOVELS
HOVER
SHOVER
HOVERS
HOVES
SHOVES
HOWFF
HOWFFS
HOWLS
THOWLS
HOWRE
HOWRES
HUBBY
CHUBBY
HUCKS
CHUCKS
SHUCKS
HUFFS
CHUFFS
HUFFY
CHUFFY
HULES

SHULES
HULLO
HULLOS
HUMAN
HUMANE
HUMANS
HUMOR
HUMORS
HUMPH
HUMPHS
HUMPS
CHUMPS
THUMPS
HUMUS
HUMUSY
HUNKS
CHUNKS
HUNKY
CHUNKY
HUNTS
SHUNTS
HURLS
CHURLS
HURRA
DHURRA
HURRAH
HURRAS
HURRAY
HURST
HURSTS
HUTIA
HUTIAS
HUZZA
HUZZAS
HYDRA
HYDRAS
HYDRO
HYDROS
HYENA
HYENAS
HYING
SHYING
HYLEG
HYLEGS
HYLES
CHYLES
PHYLES
HYMEN
HYMENS
HYNDE
HYNDES
HYPER
HYPERS
HYPHA
HYPHAE
HYPHAL
HYSON
HYSONS
HYTHE
HYTHES
IAMBI
IAMBIC
ICERS
DICERS
RICERS
ICHED
MICHED
NICHED
RICHED
ICHES

FICHES
LICHES
MICHES
NICHES
RICHES
TICHES
WICHES
ICHOR
ICHORS
ICIER
DICIER
RICIER
ICING
DICING
RICING
TICING
VICING
ICINGS
ICKER
BICKER
DICKER
KICKER
LICKER
NICKER
PICKER
RICKER
SICKER
TICKER
WICKER
YICKER
ICKERS
ICTAL
RICTAL
ICTUS
RICTUS
IDEAL
IDEALS
IDIOM
IDIOMS
IDIOT
IDIOTS
IDLED
SIDLED
IDLER
IDLERS
IDLES
SIDLES
IDLEST
IDOLA
EIDOLA
IDYLL
IDYLLS
IGAPO
IGAPOS
IGLOO
IGLOOS
IHRAM
IHRAMS
IKONS
EIKONS
ILEUM
PILEUM
ILEUS
PILEUS
ILIUM
CILIUM
ILLTH
ILLTHS
IMAGE
IMAGED
IMAGES
IMAGO
IMAGOS
IMARI
IMARIS
IMAUM
IMAUMS
IMBAR
MIMBAR
IMBARK
IMBARS
IMBED
LIMBED
NIMBED
IMBEDS
IMBUE
IMBUED
IMBUES
IMIDE
IMIDES
IMINE
IMINES
IMMEW
IMMEWS
IMMIT
IMMITS
IMPED
GIMPED
LIMPED
PIMPED
IMPEDE
IMPEL
IMPELS
IMPIS
IMPISH
IMPLY
DIMPLY
JIMPLY
LIMPLY
PIMPLY
SIMPLY
IMPOT
IMPOTS
INANE
INANER
INARM
INARMS
INCLE
INCLES
INCUR
INCURS
INCUS
INCUSE
INDEW
INDEWS
INDIE
INDIES
INDOL
INDOLE
INDOLS
INDRI
INDRIS
INDUE
INDUED
INDUES
INFER
INFERE
INFERS
INGAN
FINGAN
INGANS
INGLE
BINGLE
DINGLE
GINGLE
JINGLE
KINGLE
LINGLE
MINGLE
PINGLE
SINGLE
TINGLE
INGLES
INGOT
LINGOT
INGOTS
INION
MINION
PINION
INKED
DINKED
FINKED
JINKED
KINKED
LINKED
OINKED
PINKED
RINKED
TINKED
WINKED
ZINKED
INKER
DINKER
JINKER
LINKER
PINKER
SINKER
TINKER
WINKER
INKERS
INKLE
KINKLE
TINKLE
WINKLE
INKLED
INKLES
INLAY
INLAYS
INLET
INLETS
INNED
BINNED
DINNED
FINNED
GINNED
LINNED
PINNED
SINNED
TINNED
INNER
DINNER
FINNER
GINNER
PINNER
SINNER
TINNER
WINNER
INNERS
INORB
INORBS
INPUT
INPUTS
INSET
INSETS
INTER
LINTER
MINTER
SINTER
TINTER
WINTER
INTERN
INTERS
INTRO
INTRON
INTROS
INULA
INULAS
INURE
INURED
INURES
INURN
INURNS
INWIT
INWITH
INWITS
IONIC
BIONIC
PIONIC
IOTAS
BIOTAS
DIOTAS
IPPON
IPPONS
IRADE
TIRADE
IRADES
IRATE
PIRATE
IRATER
IRKED
DIRKED
FIRKED
KIRKED
LIRKED
YIRKED
IROKO
IROKOS
IRONS
GIRONS
ISHES
BISHES
DISHES
FISHES
HISHES
KISHES
PISHES
WISHES
ISLED
AISLED
MISLED
ISLES
AISLES
LISLES
ISLET
ISLETS
ISSEI
ISSEIS
ISSUE
TISSUE
ISSUED
ISSUER
ISSUES
ISTLE
MISTLE
ISTLES
ITCHY
BITCHY
FITCHY
HITCHY
PITCHY
TITCHY
WITCHY
IXTLE
IXTLES
IZARD
LIZARD
RIZARD
VIZARD
WIZARD
IZARDS
IZZAT
IZZATS
JABOT
JABOTS
JACKS
JACKSY
JAGER
JAGERS
JAGIR
JAGIRS
JALAP
JALAPS
JAMBE
JAMBEE
JAMBER
JAMBES
JAMBO
JAMBOK
JAMBOS
JAMBU
JAMBUL
JAMBUS
JAPAN
JAPANS
JAPER
JAPERS
JARTA
JARTAS
JARUL
JARULS
JASEY
JASEYS
JASPE
JASPER
JASPES
JAUNT
JAUNTS
JAUNTY
JAVEL
JAVELS
JAWAN
JAWANS
JEBEL
DJEBEL
JEBELS
JEHAD
JEHADS
JELAB
JELABS
JELLO
JELLOS
JERID
JERIDS
JETON
JETONS
JEWEL
JEWELS
JHALA
JHALAS
JIBER
JIBERS
JIGOT
JIGOTS
JIHAD
JIHADS
JINNI
DJINNI
JIRGA
JIRGAS
JIVER
JIVERS
JNANA
JNANAS
JOCKO
JOCKOS
JODEL
JODELS
JOINT
JOINTS
JOIST
JOISTS
JOKER
JOKERS
JORAM
JORAMS
JORUM
JORUMS
JOTUN
JOTUNN
JOTUNS
JOUAL
JOUALS
JOULE
JOULED
JOULES
JOUST
JOUSTS
JOWAR
JOWARI
JOWARS
JUDGE
JUDGED
JUDGES
JUGAL
JUGALS
JUICE
JUICED
JUICER
JUICES
JULEP
JULEPS
JUMAR
JUMARS
JUMART
JUMBO
JUMBOS
JUNCO
JUNCOS
JUNTA
JUNTAS
JUNTO
JUNTOS
JUPON
JUPONS
JURAT
JURATS
JUROR
JURORS
KAAMA
KAAMAS
KABAB
KABABS
KABOB
KABOBS
KAHAL
KAHALS
KAIAK
KAIAKS
KAILS
SKAILS
KALIF
KALIFS
KALPA
KALPAK
KALPAS
KAMIK
KAMIKS
KANEH
KANEHS
KANGA
KANGAS
KANJI
KANJIS
KANZU
KANZUS
KAPOK
KAPOKS
KAPPA
KAPPAS
KAPUT
KAPUTT
KARAT
KARATE
KARATS
KARMA
KARMAS
KARRI
KARRIS
KARST
KARSTS
KARTS
SKARTS
KASHA
KASHAS
KATTI
KATTIS
KAUGH
KAUGHS
KAURI
KAURIS
KAVAS
KAVASS
KAYAK
KAYAKS
KAYLE
KAYLES
KAZOO
KAZOOS
KEBAB
KEBABS
KEBOB
KEBOBS
KECKS
KECKSY
KEDGE
KEDGED
KEDGER
KEDGES
KEEVE
KEEVES
KEFIR
KEFIRS
KELIM
KELIMS
KELLS
SKELLS
KELLY
SKELLY
KELPS
SKELPS
KEMBO
KEMBOS
KENAF
KENAFS
KENDO
KENDOS
KERNE
KERNED
KERNEL
KERNES
KERVE
KERVED
KERVES
KESAR
KESARS
KETCH
SKETCH
KEVEL
KEVELS
KHADI
KHADIS
KHAKI
KHAKIS
KHAYA
KHAYAS
KHEDA
KHEDAS
KHOJA
KHOJAS
KIANG
KIANGS
KIDDO
KIDDOS
KIDEL
KIDELS
KIERS
SKIERS
KIEVE
KIEVES
KIGHT
KIGHTS
KIKOI
KIKOIS
KILEY
KILEYS
KILIM
KILIMS
KILLS
SKILLS
KIMBO
AKIMBO
KIMBOS
KINAS
KINASE
KININ
KININS
KINKS
SKINKS
KIOSK
KIOSKS
KIPPA
KIPPAS
KIRRI
KIRRIS
KISAN
KISANS
KITED
SKITED
KITES
SKITES
KITHE
KITHED
KITHES
KLANG
KLANGS
KLOOF
KLOOFS
KNACK
KNACKS
KNACKY
KNARL
KNARLS
KNAVE
KNAVES
KNEAD
KNEADS
KNEEL
KNEELS
KNELL
KNELLS
KNIFE
KNIFED
KNIFES
KNIVE
KNIVED
KNIVES
KNOCK
KNOCKS
KNOLL
KNOLLS
KNOSP
KNOSPS
KNOUT
KNOUTS
KNOWE
KNOWER
KNOWES
KNOWN
KNOWNS
KNURL
KNURLS
KNURLY
KNURR
KNURRS
KOALA
KOALAS
KOBAN
KOBANG
KOBANS
KOFFS

SKOFFS
KOFTA
KOFTAS
KOINE
KOINES
KOKER
KOKERS
KOKRA
KOKRAS
KOKUM
KOKUMS
KOMBU
KOMBUS
KOORI
KOORIS
KOPJE
KOPJES
KOPPA
KOPPAS
KORMA
KORMAS
KOTOW
KOTOWS
KRAAL
KRAALS
KRAFT
KRAFTS
KRAIT
KRAITS
KRANG
KRANGS
KRANS
SKRANS
KRAUT
KRAUTS
KRENG
KRENGS
KRILL
KRILLS
KRONE
KRONEN
KRONER
KUDZU
KUDZUS
KUKRI
KUKRIS
KULAK
KULAKS
KULAN
KULANS
KURRE
KURRES
KURTA
KURTAS
KUTCH
KUTCHA
KWELA
KWELAS
KYANG
KYANGS
KYLIE
KYLIES
KYLIN
KYLINS
KYLOE
KYLOES
KYNDE
KYNDED
KYNDES
KYTES
SKYTES
KYTHE
KYTHED
KYTHES
LABDA
LABDAS
LABEL
LABELS
LABIA
LABIAL
LABOR
LABORS
LACED
PLACED
LACES
GLACES
PLACES
LACET
PLACET
LACETS
LACKS
BLACKS
CLACKS
FLACKS
PLACKS
SLACKS
LADED
BLADED
LADES
BLADES
CLADES
GLADES
SLADES
LADLE
LADLED
LADLES
LAGAN
LAGANS
LAGER
LAGERS
LAHAR
LAHARS
LAIDS
PLAIDS
LAIGH
LAIGHS
LAIKA
LAIKAS
LAIKS
GLAIKS
LAIRD
LAIRDS
LAIRS
FLAIRS
GLAIRS
LAIRY
GLAIRY
LAKED
FLAKED
SLAKED
LAKER
LAKERS
LAKES
FLAKES
SLAKES
LAKIN
LAKING
LAKINS
LAMAS
LLAMAS
LAMED
BLAMED
FLAMED
LAMES
BLAMES
CLAMES
FLAMES
LAMEST
LAMIA
LAMIAE
LAMIAS
LAMMY
CLAMMY
LAMPS
CLAMPS
LANCE
ELANCE
GLANCE
LANCED
LANCER
LANCES
LANCET
LANCH
BLANCH
FLANCH
PLANCH
LANDE
LANDED
LANDER
LANDES
LANDS
BLANDS
ELANDS
GLANDS
LANES
PLANES
SLANES
LANKS
BLANKS
CLANKS
FLANKS
PLANKS
LANKY
BLANKY
LANTS
PLANTS
SLANTS
LAPEL
LAPELS
LAPJE
LAPJES
LAPSE
ELAPSE
LAPSED
LAPSES
LARES
BLARES
FLARES
GLARES
LARGE
LARGEN
LARGER
LARGES
LARGO
LARGOS
LARUM
ALARUM
LARUMS
LARVA
LARVAE
LARVAL
LASER
FLASER
LASERS
LASSI
LASSIE
LASSIS
LASSO
LASSOS
LASSU
LASSUS
LASTS
BLASTS
CLASTS
LATCH
CLATCH
SLATCH
LATED
ALATED
ELATED
PLATED
SLATED
LATEN
PLATEN
LATENS
LATENT
LATER
BLATER
ELATER
PLATER
SLATER
LATHE
LATHED
LATHEE
LATHEN
LATHER
LATHES
LATHI
LATHIS
LATKE
LATKES
LAUCH
LAUCHS
LAUDS
BLAUDS
LAUGH
LAUGHS
LAUGHY
LAUND
LAUNDS
LAURA
LAURAS
LAVED
SLAVED
LAVER
CLAVER
SLAVER
LAVERS
LAVES
CLAVES
SLAVES
LAVRA
LAVRAS
LAWED
CLAWED
FLAWED
LAWIN
LAWING
LAWINS
LAWNS
FLAWNS
LAXES
FLAXES
LAXEST
LAYER
FLAYER
PLAYER
SLAYER
LAYERS
LAZAR
LAZARS
LAZED
BLAZED
GLAZED
LAZES
BLAZES
GLAZES
LEACH
BLEACH
PLEACH
LEACHY
LEADS
PLEADS
LEAKS
BLEAKS
LEAKY
BLEAKY
LEAMS
FLEAMS
GLEAMS
LEANS
CLEANS
GLEANS
LEARE
LEARED
LEARES
LEARN
LEARNS
LEARNT
LEARS
BLEARS
CLEARS
LEARY
BLEARY
LEASE
PLEASE
LEASED
LEASER
LEASES
LEAST
LEASTS
LEATS
BLEATS
CLEATS
PLEATS
LEAVE
CLEAVE
GLEAVE
SLEAVE
LEAVED
LEAVEN
LEAVER
LEAVES
LEAZE
SLEAZE
LEAZES
LEDGE
FLEDGE
GLEDGE
PLEDGE
SLEDGE
LEDGER
LEDGES
LEDGY
FLEDGY
LEDUM
LEDUMS
LEEAR
LEEARS
LEECH
FLEECH
SLEECH
LEEKS
CLEEKS
GLEEKS
SLEEKS
LEEPS
BLEEPS
CLEEPS
SLEEPS
LEERS
FLEERS
LEESE
LEESES
LEETS
FLEETS
GLEETS
SLEETS
LEFTS
CLEFTS
LEGER
LEGERS
LEGGE
ALEGGE
LEGGED
LEGGER
LEGGES
LEGIT
ELEGIT
LEMAN
LEMANS
LEMEL
LEMELS
LEMES
FLEMES
LEMMA
LEMMAS
LEMON
LEMONS
LEMONY
LEMUR
LEMURS
LENDS
BLENDS
LENTI
LENTIC
LENTIL
LENTO
LENTOR
LENTOS
LEONE
LEONES
LEPER
LEPERS
LEPRA
LEPRAS
LESBO
LESBOS
LETCH
FLETCH
LEUCH
CLEUCH
PLEUCH
LEUGH
CLEUGH
PLEUGH
LEVEE
LEVEED
LEVEES
LEVEL
LEVELS
LEVER
CLEVER
LEVERS
LEVIN
ALEVIN
LEVINS
LEVIS
CLEVIS
LEXES
FLEXES
ILEXES
ULEXES
LIANA
LIANAS
LIANE
LIANES
LIANG
LIANGS
LIARD
LIARDS
LIBEL
LIBELS
LIBER
LIBERO
LIBERS
LIBRA
LIBRAE
LIBRAS
LICHI
LICHIS
LICHT
LICHTS
LICIT
ELICIT
LICKS
CLICKS
FLICKS
SLICKS
LIEGE
LIEGER
LIEGES
LIENS
ALIENS
LIERS
FLIERS
PLIERS
LIEVE
LIEVER
LIFER
LIFERS
LIFTS
CLIFTS
GLIFTS
LIGAN
LIGAND
LIGANS
LIGER
LIGERS
LIGGE
LIGGED
LIGGEN
LIGGER
LIGGES
LIGHT
ALIGHT
BLIGHT
FLIGHT
PLIGHT
SLIGHT
LIGHTS
LIGNE
LIGNES
LIKEN
LIKENS
LIKER
LIKERS
LIKES
GLIKES
LIKIN
LIKING
LIKINS
LILAC
LILACS
LIMAX
CLIMAX
LIMBO
LIMBOS
LIMBS
CLIMBS
LIMED
SLIMED
LIMEN
LIMENS
LIMES
CLIMES
SLIMES
LIMEY
BLIMEY
LIMEYS
LIMIT
LIMITS
LIMMA
LIMMAS
LIMPS
BLIMPS
FLIMPS
LINAC
LINACS
LINCH
CLINCH
FLINCH
LINDS
BLINDS
LINED
ALINED
LINEN
LINENS
LINER
LINERS
LINES
ALINES
CLINES
LINGA
LINGAM
LINGAS
LINGO
LINGOT
LINGS
CLINGS
FLINGS
PLINGS
SLINGS
LINGY
CLINGY
LININ
LINING
LININS
LINKS
BLINKS
CLINKS
PLINKS
SLINKS
LINTS
CLINTS
FLINTS
GLINTS
LINTY
FLINTY
LIPID
LIPIDE
LIPIDS
LIPPY
SLIPPY
LISKS
FLISKS
GLISKS
LISLE
LISLES
LITED
FLITED
LITER
LITERS
LITES
BLITES
ELITES
FLITES
LITHE
BLITHE
LITHED
LITHER
LITHES
LITHO
LITHOS
LITRE
LITRES
LIVED
SLIVED
LIVEN
SLIVEN
LIVENS
LIVER
OLIVER
SLIVER
LIVERS
LIVERY
LIVES
OLIVES
SLIVES
LIVOR
LIVORS
LIVRE
LIVRES
LLAMA
LLAMAS
LLANO
LLANOS
LOAMS
CLOAMS
LOANS

SLOANS
LOATH
LOATHE
LOATHY
LOAVE
LOAVED
LOAVES
LOBBY
GLOBBY
SLOBBY
LOBED
GLOBED
LOBES
GLOBES
LOBOS
LOBOSE
LOCAL
LOCALE
LOCALS
LOCKS
BLOCKS
CLOCKS
FLOCKS
LOCUM
LOCUMS
LOCUS
LOCUST
LODEN
LODENS
LODGE
LODGED
LODGER
LODGES
LOGAN
SLOGAN
LOGANS
LOGES
ELOGES
LOGIA
ALOGIA
LOGIC
LOGICS
LOGIE
LOGIER
LOGIES
LOIDS
SLOIDS
LOINS
ELOINS
LOIPE
LOIPEN
LOKES
BLOKES
CLOKES
LOLOG
LOLOGS
LONER
LONERS
LONGA
LONGAN
LONGAS
LONGE
PLONGE
LONGED
LONGER
LONGES
LONGS
FLONGS
PLONGS
LOOFA

LOOFAH
LOOFAS
LOOFS
KLOOFS
LOOKS
PLOOKS
LOOMS
BLOOMS
GLOOMS
SLOOMS
LOOPS
BLOOPS
CLOOPS
GLOOPS
SLOOPS
LOOPY
GLOOPY
LOORD
LOORDS
LOOSE
LOOSED
LOOSEN
LOOSER
LOOSES
LOOTS
CLOOTS
SLOOTS
LOPED
ELOPED
SLOPED
LOPER
ELOPER
LOPERS
LOPES
ELOPES
SLOPES
LORAL
FLORAL
LORAN
LORANS
LOREL
LORELS
LORES
BLORES
LORIC
LORICA
LORICS
LOSED
CLOSED
LOSEL
LOSELS
LOSER
CLOSER
LOSERS
LOSES
CLOSES
ULOSES
LOSSY
FLOSSY
GLOSSY
LOTAH
LOTAHS
LOTAS
FLOTAS
LOTES
CLOTES
FLOTES
LOTTO
BLOTTO
LOTTOS

LOUGH
CLOUGH
PLOUGH
SLOUGH
LOUGHS
LOUND
LOUNDS
LOUPE
LOUPED
LOUPEN
LOUPES
LOURE
LOURED
LOURES
LOURS
CLOURS
FLOURS
LOURY
FLOURY
LOUSE
BLOUSE
FLOUSE
LOUSED
LOUSES
LOUTS
CLOUTS
FLOUTS
GLOUTS
LOVAT
LOVATS
LOVED
GLOVED
LOVER
CLOVER
GLOVER
PLOVER
LOVERS
LOVES
CLOVES
GLOVES
LOVEY
LOVEYS
LOWAN
LOWANS
LOWED
BLOWED
FLOWED
GLOWED
PLOWED
SLOWED
LOWER
BLOWER
FLOWER
GLOWER
SLOWER
LOWERS
LOWERY
LOWES
LOWEST
LOWLY
SLOWLY
LOWND
LOWNDS
LOWNE
LOWNED
LOWNES
LOWNS
CLOWNS
LOWSE
BLOWSE

LOWSER
LOWSES
LOZEN
LOZENS
LUBRA
LUBRAS
LUCKS
CLUCKS
PLUCKS
LUCKY
CLUCKY
PLUCKY
LUCRE
LUCRES
LUFFA
LUFFAS
LUFFS
BLUFFS
FLUFFS
PLUFFS
LUGER
LUGERS
LUMEN
LUMENS
LUMMY
PLUMMY
SLUMMY
LUMPS
CLUMPS
FLUMPS
GLUMPS
PLUMPS
SLUMPS
LUMPY
CLUMPY
GLUMPY
PLUMPY
SLUMPY
LUNAR
LUNARS
LUNARY
LUNCH
CLUNCH
LUNGE
BLUNGE
PLUNGE
LUNGED
LUNGES
LUNGI
LUNGIE
LUNGIS
LUNTS
BLUNTS
LUPIN
LUPINE
LUPINS
LURES
ALURES
LURGI
LURGIS
LURRY
FLURRY
SLURRY
LUSHY
FLUSHY
PLUSHY
SLUSHY
LUTED
ELUTED
FLUTED

LUTER
FLUTER
LUTERS
LUTES
ELUTES
FLUTES
LUXES
FLUXES
LYCEE
LYCEES
LYING
CLYING
FLYING
PLYING
LYINGS
LYMPH
LYMPHS
LYRIC
LYRICS
LYSIN
LYSINE
LYSING
LYSINS
LYSOL
LYSOLS
LYSSA
LYSSAS
LYTED
FLYTED
LYTES
FLYTES
LYTHE
LYTHES
LYTTA
LYTTAE
MACAW
MACAWS
MACER
MACERS
MACHO
MACHOS
MACKS
SMACKS
MACLE
MACLED
MACLES
MACON
MACONS
MACRO
MACRON
MACROS
MADAM
MADAME
MADAMS
MADGE
MADGES
MAFIA
MAFIAS
MAFIC
MAFICS
MAGES
IMAGES
MAGIC
MAGICS
MAGMA
MAGMAS
MAGOT
MAGOTS
MAHOE
MAHOES

MAHUA
MAHUAS
MAHWA
MAHWAS
MAIKO
MAIKOS
MAIKS
SMAIKS
MAILE
MAILED
MAILER
MAILES
MAIRE
MAIRES
MAISE
MAISES
MAIZE
MAIZES
MAJOR
MAJORS
MAKAR
MAKARS
MAKER
MAKERS
MALAR
MALARS
MALIC
MALICE
MALIK
MALIKS
MALIS
MALISM
MALIST
MALLS
SMALLS
MALMS
SMALMS
MALTS
SMALTS
MALVA
MALVAS
MAMBA
MAMBAS
MAMBO
MAMBOS
MAMEE
MAMEES
MAMMA
MAMMAE
MAMMAL
MAMMAS
MANEH
MANEHS
MANGA
MANGAL
MANGAS
MANGE
MANGED
MANGEL
MANGER
MANGES
MANGEY
MANIA
MANIAC
MANIAS
MANNA
MANNAS
MANOR
MANORS
MANSE

MANSES
MANTA
MANTAS
MANTO
MANTOS
MANUL
MANULS
MAPLE
MAPLES
MAQUI
MAQUIS
MARAE
MARAES
MARAH
MARAHS
MARGE
MARGES
MARID
MARIDS
MARLE
MARLED
MARLES
MARMS
SMARMS
MARON
MARONS
MAROR
MARORS
MARSH
MARSHY
MARTS
SMARTS
MASER
MASERS
MASON
MASONS
MASSA
MASSAS
MASSE
MASSED
MASSES
MATCH
SMATCH
MATED
AMATED
MATER
MATERS
MATES
AMATES
MATIN
MATING
MATINS
MATLO
MATLOS
MATLOW
MATTE
MATTED
MATTER
MATTES
MATZA
MATZAH
MATZAS
MATZO
MATZOH
MATZOS
MATZOT
MAUND
MAUNDS
MAUNDY
MAUVE

MAUVER
MAUVES
MAVEN
MAVENS
MAVIN
MAVINS
MAXIM
MAXIMA
MAXIMS
MAYBE
MAYBES
MAYOR
MAYORS
MAZED
AMAZED
MAZER
MAZERS
MAZES
AMAZES
MAZUT
MAZUTS
MBIRA
MBIRAS
MEANE
MEANED
MEANER
MEANES
MEARE
MEARES
MEASE
MEASED
MEASES
MEATH
SMEATH
MEATHE
MEATHS
MEDAL
MEDALS
MEDIA
MEDIAE
MEDIAL
MEDIAN
MEDIC
MEDICK
MEDICO
MEDICS
MEDLE
MEDLED
MEDLES
MEDLEY
MEERS
AMEERS
EMEERS
MEITH
MEITHS
MELEE
MELEES
MELIC
MELICS
MELIK
MELIKS
MELLS
SMELLS
MELON
MELONS
MELTS
SMELTS
MENDS
AMENDS
EMENDS

MENED
AMENED
OMENED
MENGE
MENGED
MENGES
MENSE
MENSED
MENSES
MENTA
AMENTA
OMENTA
MENTAL
MENTO
MENTOR
MENTOS
MEREL
MERELL
MERELS
MERELY
MERES
MEREST
MERGE
EMERGE
MERGED
MERGER
MERGES
MERIL
MERILS
MERIS
MERISM
MERIT
MERITS
MERLE
MERLES
MERSE
MERSES
MESEL
MESELS
MESES
EMESES
TMESES
MESON
MESONS
METAL
METALS
METER
METERS
METIC
EMETIC
METICS
METIF
METIFS
METOL
METOLS
METRE
METRED
METRES
METRO
METROS
MEUSE
SMEUSE
MEUSED
MEUSES
MEZZE
MEZZES
MEZZO
MEZZOS
MHORR
MHORRS

MIAOW
MIAOWS
MIASM
MIASMA
MIASMS
MIAUL
MIAULS
MICHE
MICHED
MICHER
MICHES
MICRO
MICRON
MICROS
MIDDY
SMIDDY
MIDGE
MIDGES
MIDGET
MIDST
AMIDST
MIDSTS
MIEVE
MIEVED
MIEVES
MIGHT
SMIGHT
MIGHTS
MIGHTY
MILER
SMILER
MILERS
MILES
SMILES
MILKO
MILKOS
MILLE
MILLED
MILLER
MILLES
MILLET
MILOR
MILORD
MILORS
MIMER
MIMERS
MIMIC
MIMICS
MINAR
MINARS
MINCE
MINCED
MINCER
MINCES
MINER
MINERS
MINES
AMINES
IMINES
MINGE
MINGED
MINGES
MINIM
MINIMA
MINIMS
MINIS
MINISH
MINKE
MINKES
MINOR
MINORS
MIRIN
MIRING
MIRINS
MIRKS
SMIRKS
MIRTH
MIRTHS
MISER
MISERE
MISERS
MISERY
MISES
AMISES
MISSA
MISSAE
MISSAL
MISSAW
MISSAY
MITER
SMITER
MITERS
MITES
SMITES
MITRE
MITRED
MITRES
MIXEN
MIXENS
MIXER
MIXERS
MIZEN
MIZENS
MNEME
MNEMES
MOBLE
MOBLED
MOBLES
MOCHA
MOCHAS
MOCKS
SMOCKS
MODAL
MODALS
MODEL
MODELS
MODEM
MODEMS
MODER
MODERN
MODERS
MODES
MODEST
MOGGY
SMOGGY
MOGUL
MOGULS
MOHEL
MOHELS
MOHUR
MOHURS
MOIRE
MOIRES
MOIST
MOISTS
MOKES
SMOKES
MOKOS
SMOKOS
MOLAR
MOLARS
MOLES
MOLEST
MOLLA
MOLLAH
MOLLAS
MOLTS
SMOLTS
MOMMA
MOMMAS
MONAD
MONADS
MONAL
MONALS
MONER
MONERA
MONERS
MONEY
MONEYS
MONOS
MONOSY
MONTE
MONTEM
MONTES
MONTH
MONTHS
MOOCH
SMOOCH
MOOLA
MOOLAH
MOOLAS
MOOLI
MOOLIS
MOORS
SMOORS
MOOTS
SMOOTS
MOOVE
AMOOVE
MOOVED
MOOVES
MOPED
MOPEDS
MOPER
MOPERS
MORAL
AMORAL
MORALE
MORALL
MORALS
MORAS
MORASS
MORAT
MORATS
MORAY
MORAYS
MOREL
MORELS
MORES
SMORES
MORIA
MORIAS
MORNE
MORNED
MORNES
MORON
MORONS
MORPH
MORPHO
MORPHS
MORRA
MORRAS
MORRO
MORROS
MORROW
MORSE
MORSEL
MORSES
MOSEY
MOSEYS
MOTED
EMOTED
MOTEL
MOTELS
MOTES
EMOTES
MOTET
MOTETS
MOTETT
MOTIF
MOTIFS
MOTOR
MOTORS
MOTORY
MOTTE
MOTTES
MOTZA
MOTZAS
MOUCH
SMOUCH
MOULD
MOULDS
MOULDY
MOULT
MOULTS
MOUND
MOUNDS
MOUNT
AMOUNT
MOUNTS
MOURN
MOURNS
MOUSE
SMOUSE
MOUSED
MOUSER
MOUSES
MOUSEY
MOUST
MOUSTS
MOUTH
MOUTHS
MOUTHY
MOVED
AMOVED
EMOVED
MOVER
MOVERS
MOVES
AMOVES
EMOVES
MOVIE
MOVIES
MOWER
MOWERS
MOWRA
MOWRAS
MOXIE
MOXIES
MOYLE
SMOYLE
MOYLED
MOYLES
MPRET
MPRETS
MUCIN
MUCINS
MUCOR
MUCORS
MUCRO
MUCROS
MUDGE
SMUDGE
MUDGED
MUDGER
MUDGES
MUDIR
MUDIRS
MUDRA
MUDRAS
MUFTI
MUFTIS
MUIST
MUISTS
MUJIK
MUJIKS
MULCT
MULCTS
MULES
EMULES
MULEY
MULEYS
MULGA
MULGAS
MULSE
MULSES
MUNGO
MUNGOS
MUNTU
MUNTUS
MURAL
MURALS
MURED
EMURED
MURES
EMURES
MURRA
MURRAM
MURRAS
MURRAY
MURRE
MURREN
MURRES
MURREY
MURRY
SMURRY
MURVA
MURVAS
MUSED
AMUSED
MUSER
AMUSER
MUSERS
MUSES
AMUSES
MUSET
MUSETS
MUSIC
MUSICS
MUSIT
MUSITS
MUSSE
MUSSED
MUSSEL
MUSSES
MUSTH
MUSTHS
MUTCH
SMUTCH
MUTES
MUTEST
MUTIS
MUTISM
MUTON
MUTONS
MVULE
MVULES
MYALL
MYALLS
MYNAH
MYNAHS
MYOMA
MYOMAS
MYOPE
MYOPES
MYRRH
MYRRHS
MYTHI
MYTHIC
NABLA
NABLAS
NABOB
NABOBS
NACHE
NACHES
NACHO
NACHOS
NACRE
NACRED
NACRES
NADIR
NADIRS
NAEVE
NAEVES
NAGGY
KNAGGY
SNAGGY
NAGOR
NAGORS
NAHAL
NAHALS
NAIAD
NAIADS
NAILS
SNAILS
NAIRA
NAIRAS
NAIVE
NAIVER
NAKED
SNAKED
NAKER
NAKERS
NALLA
NALLAH
NALLAS
NAMER
NAMERS
NANAS
ANANAS
JNANAS
NANCE
NANCES
NANDU
NANDUS
NANNA
NANNAS
NAPOO
NAPOOS
NAPPA
NAPPAS
NAPPE
NAPPED
NAPPER
NAPPES
NAPPY
SNAPPY
NARCO
NARCOS
NARES
SNARES
NARKS
SNARKS
NASAL
NASALS
NATCH
SNATCH
NAUNT
NAUNTS
NAVEL
NAVELS
NAVES
KNAVES
NAVEW
NAVEWS
NAWAB
NAWABS
NAZIR
NAZIRS
NEAFE
NEAFES
NEAPS
SNEAPS
NEARS
ANEARS
NEATH
ANEATH
SNEATH
UNEATH
NEBEK
NEBEKS
NEBEL
NEBELS
NECKS
SNECKS
NEELD
NEELDS
NEELE
NEELES
NEEMB
NEEMBS
NEESE
NEESED
NEESES
NEEZE
SNEEZE
NEEZED
NEEZES
NEIGH
NEIGHS
NEIVE
NEIVES
NELLY
SNELLY
NEPER
NEPERS
NEPIT
NEPITS
NERKA
NERKAS
NERVE
ENERVE
NERVED
NERVER
NERVES
NEUME
NEUMES
NEVEL
NEVELS
NEWED
ENEWED
NEWEL
NEWELL
NEWELS
NGAIO
NGAIOS
NGANA
NGANAS
NICAD
NICADS
NICHE
NICHED
NICHER
NICHES
NICKS
KNICKS
SNICKS
NICOL
NICOLS
NIDES
SNIDES
NIDOR
NIDORS
NIECE
NIECES
NIEVE
NIEVES
NIFES
KNIFES
NIFFS
SNIFFS
NIFFY
SNIFFY
NIFTY
SNIFTY
NIGER
NIGERS
NIGHT
ANIGHT
KNIGHT
NIGHTS
NIGHTY
NIHIL
NIHILS
NIKAU
NIKAUS
NINJA
NINJAS
NINON
NINONS
NINTH
NINTHS
NIPPY
SNIPPY
NISEI
NISEIS
NISSE
NISSES
NITER
UNITER
NITERS
NITERY
NITES
UNITES
NITON
NITONS
NITRE
NITRES
NITRY
NITRYL
NIXIE
NIXIES
NIZAM
NIZAMS
NOBBY
KNOBBY
SNOBBY
NOBLE
NOBLER
NOBLES
NOCKS
KNOCKS
NODAL
ANODAL
ENODAL
NODES
ANODES
NOINT
ANOINT
NOINTS
NOISE
NOISED
NOISES
NOLLS
KNOLLS
NOMAD
NOMADE
NOMADS
NOMADY
NOMES
GNOMES
NOMIC
ANOMIC
GNOMIC
NONCE
NONCES
NONET
NONETS
NOOKS
SNOOKS
NOOPS
SNOOPS
NOOSE
NOOSED
NOOSES
NOPAL
NOPALS
NORIA
NORIAS
NORMA

NORMAL
NORMAN
NORMAS
NORTH
NORTHS
NOSER
NOSERS
NOSES
ENOSES
GNOSES
NOSEY
NOSEYS
NOTCH
NOTCHY
NOTER
NOTERS
NOULD
NOULDE
NOULE
NOULES
NOVEL
NOVELS
NOVUM
NOVUMS
NOWAY
NOWAYS
NOWED
SNOWED
UNOWED
NOYAU
NOYAUS
NUBBY
KNUBBY
SNUBBY
NUBIA
NUBIAS
NUCHA
NUCHAE
NUCHAL
NUDES
NUDEST
NUDGE
SNUDGE
NUDGED
NUDGER
NUDGES
NUDIE
NUDIES
NUFFS
SNUFFS
NULLA
NULLAH
NULLAS
NURLS
KNURLS
NURRS
KNURRS
NURSE
NURSED
NURSER
NURSES
NYAFF
NYAFFS
NYALA
INYALA
NYALAS
NYLON
NYLONS
NYMPH
NYMPHO
NYMPHS
NYSSA
NYSSAS
OAKEN
SOAKEN
OAKER
SOAKER
OAKERS
OAKUM
OAKUMS
OARED
HOARED
ROARED
SOARED
OASTS
BOASTS
COASTS
HOASTS
ROASTS
TOASTS
OATER
BOATER
COATER
DOATER
OATERS
OAVES
LOAVES
OBANG
GOBANG
KOBANG
OBANGS
OBEAH
OBEAHS
OBESE
OBESER
OBIAS
COBIAS
OBITS
OOBITS
OBJET
OBJETS
OBOES
GOBOES
HOBOES
OCCAM
OCCAMS
OCCAMY
OCCUR
OCCURS
OCEAN
OCEANS
OCHER
TOCHER
OCHERS
OCHERY
OCHES
BOCHES
ROCHES
OCHRE
OCHREA
OCHRED
OCHRES
OCHREY
OCKER
COCKER
DOCKER
HOCKER
LOCKER
MOCKER
ROCKER
OCKERS
OCREA
OCREAE
OCTAD
OCTADS
OCTAL
OCTALS
OCTET
OCTETS
OCTETT
OCULI
LOCULI
ODALS
MODALS
ODDER
CODDER
DODDER
FODDER
NODDER
ODEON
ODEONS
ODEUM
ODEUMS
ODISM
IODISM
ODISMS
ODIST
CODIST
MODIST
ODISTS
ODIUM
PODIUM
SODIUM
ODIUMS
ODOUR
ODOURS
ODSOS
GODSOS
ODYLE
ODYLES
OFFAL
OFFALS
OFFED
BOFFED
COFFED
DOFFED
GOFFED
OFFER
COFFER
DOFFER
GOFFER
OFFERS
OFLAG
OFLAGS
OFTEN
SOFTEN
OGGIN
HOGGIN
NOGGIN
OGGINS
OGHAM
OGHAMS
OGIVE
OGIVES
OGLER
OGLERS
OGLES
BOGLES
FOGLES
OGRES
OGRESS
OILED
BOILED
COILED
DOILED
FOILED
MOILED
ROILED
SOILED
TOILED
OILER
BOILER
MOILER
TOILER
OILERS
OILERY
OINKS
BOINKS
OINTS
JOINTS
NOINTS
POINTS
OJIME
OJIMES
OKAPI
OKAPIS
OKAYS
TOKAYS
OKRAS
KOKRAS
OLDEN
BOLDEN
GOLDEN
HOLDEN
OLDENS
OLDER
BOLDER
COLDER
FOLDER
GOLDER
HOLDER
POLDER
SOLDER
OLDIE
OLDIES
OLEIN
SOLEIN
OLEINS
OLENT
DOLENT
OLEUM
OLEUMS
OLIOS
FOLIOS
POLIOS
OLIVE
SOLIVE
OLIVER
OLIVES
OLIVET
OLLAS
HOLLAS
MOLLAS
OLLAV
OLLAVS
OLOGY
OOLOGY
OLPES
GOLPES
OMASA
OMASAL
OMBRE
HOMBRE
SOMBRE
OMBRES
OMBUS
KOMBUS
OMEGA
OMEGAS
OMERS
COMERS
HOMERS
VOMERS
OMITS
VOMITS
OMLAH
OMLAHS
OMRAH
OMRAHS
ONCER
ONCERS
ONCES
BONCES
NONCES
PONCES
SONCES
ONELY
LONELY
ONERS
BONERS
GONERS
HONERS
LONERS
MONERS
TONERS
ONION
GONION
ONIONS
ONIONY
ONNED
CONNED
DONNED
FONNED
WONNED
ONSET
ONSETS
OOBIT
OOBITS
OOHED
BOOHED
OOMPH
OOMPHS
OOPED
COOPED
HOOPED
LOOPED
MOOPED
POOPED
ROOPED
SOOPED
OORIE
TOORIE
OORIER
OOSES
BOOSES
GOOSES
LOOSES
NOOSES
ROOSES
OOZED
BOOZED
OOZES
BOOZES
OPALS
COPALS
NOPALS
OPEPE
OPEPES
OPERA
OPERAS
OPINE
OPINED
OPINES
OPING
COPING
DOPING
HOPING
LOPING
MOPING
OOPING
ROPING
TOPING
OPIUM
OPIUMS
OPTER
COPTER
OPTERS
OPTIC
OPTICS
ORACH
ORACHE
ORALS
CORALS
GORALS
MORALS
ORANG
ORANGE
ORANGS
ORANT
VORANT
ORANTS
ORATE
BORATE
LORATE
ORATED
ORATES
ORBED
SORBED
ORBIT
ORBITA
ORBITS
ORBITY
ORCIN
ORCINE
ORCINS
ORDER
BORDER
ORDERS
OREAD
OREADS
ORGAN
ORGANA
ORGANS
ORGIA
GORGIA
ORGIAS
ORGUE
MORGUE
ORGUES
ORIBI
ORIBIS
ORIEL
ORIELS
ORLOP
ORLOPS
ORMER
DORMER
FORMER
WORMER
ORMERS
ORPIN
ORPINE
ORPINS
ORRIS
MORRIS
ORTHO
ORTHOS
ORVAL
ORVALS
OSHAC
OSHACS
OSIER
COSIER
HOSIER
NOSIER
OOSIER
POSIER
ROSIER
OSIERS
OSIERY
OSMIC
COSMIC
OSTIA
OSTIAL
OTARY
NOTARY
ROTARY
VOTARY
OTHER
BOTHER
FOTHER
LOTHER
MOTHER
POTHER
ROTHER
TOTHER
OTHERS
OTTAR
COTTAR
OTTARS
OTTER
COTTER
HOTTER
JOTTER
POTTER
ROTTER
TOTTER
OTTERS
OTTOS
LOTTOS
POTTOS
OUBIT
WOUBIT
OUBITS
OUCHT
OUCHTS
OUGHT
BOUGHT
DOUGHT
FOUGHT
MOUGHT
NOUGHT
ROUGHT
SOUGHT
OUGHTS
OUIJA
OUIJAS
OUNCE
BOUNCE
JOUNCE
POUNCE
ROUNCE
OUNCES
OUNDY
WOUNDY
OUPED
COUPED
LOUPED
MOUPED
POUPED
ROUPED
OUPHE
OUPHES
OURIE
POURIE
TOURIE
OURIER
OUSEL
HOUSEL
OUSELS
OUSTS
JOUSTS
MOUSTS
ROUSTS
OUTBY
OUTBYE
OUTED
DOUTED
HOUTED
LOUTED
POUTED
ROUTED
TOUTED
OUTER
COUTER
DOUTER
FOUTER
MOUTER
POUTER
ROUTER
SOUTER
TOUTER
OUTERS
OUTRE
FOUTRE
OUTRED
OUZEL
OUZELS
OVARY
COVARY
OVATE
BOVATE
OVATED
OVATES
OVENS
COVENS
OVERS
COVERS
DOVERS
HOVERS
LOVERS
MOVERS
ROVERS
OVERT
COVERT
OVINE
BOVINE
OVIST
OVISTS
OVOID
OVOIDS
OVULE
OVULES
OWCHE
OWCHES
OWING
BOWING
COWING
DOWING
JOWING
LOWING
MOWING
ROWING
SOWING
TOWING
VOWING
WOWING
OWLED
BOWLED
COWLED
FOWLED
GOWLED
HOWLED
JOWLED
SOWLED
YOWLED
OWLER
BOWLER
FOWLER
HOWLER
JOWLER
OWLERS
OWLERY
OWLET
HOWLET
OWLETS
OWNED
BOWNED
DOWNED
GOWNED
LOWNED
OWNER
DOWNER
OWNERS
OWRES
HOWRES
POWRES
OWRIE
COWRIE
OWRIER
OXERS
BOXERS
OXIDE
OXIDES
OXIME
OXIMES
OXLIP
OXLIPS
OXTER
OXTERS

OYERS
FOYERS
TOYERS
OZEKI
OZEKIS
OZONE
OZONES
PACED
SPACED
PACER
SPACER
PACERS
PACES
SPACES
PACEY
SPACEY
PACHA
PACHAK
PACHAS
PACTS
EPACTS
PADLE
PADLES
PADMA
PADMAS
PADRE
PADRES
PAEAN
PAEANS
PAEON
PAEONS
PAEONY
PAGAN
PAGANS
PAGER
PAGERS
PAGLE
PAGLES
PAGOD
PAGODA
PAGODS
PAGRI
PAGRIS
PAINS
SPAINS
PAINT
PAINTS
PAINTY
PAIRE
PAIRED
PAIRES
PAISA
PAISAS
PALAY
PALAYS
PALEA
PALEAE
PALED
OPALED
PALES
SPALES
PALEST
PALET
PALETS
PALKI
PALKIS
PALLA
PALLAE
PALLAH
PALLS
SPALLS
PAMPA
PAMPAS
PANCE
PANCES
PANDA
PANDAR
PANDAS
PANED
SPANED
PANEL
PANELS
PANES
SPANES
PANGA
PANGAS
PANGS
SPANGS
PANIC
PANICK
PANICS
PANIM
PANIMS
PANNE
PANNED
PANNES
PANTO
PANTON
PANTOS
PAPAW
PAPAWS
PAPER
PAPERS
PAPERY
PARCH
EPARCH
PARDI
PARDIE
PARED
SPARED
PAREO
PAREOS
PARER
SPARER
PARERS
PARES
SPARES
PAREU
PAREUS
PARGE
SPARGE
PARGED
PARGES
PARGET
PARKA
PARKAS
PARKI
PARKIE
PARKIN
PARKIS
PARKS
SPARKS
PARKY
SPARKY
PARLE
PARLED
PARLES
PARLEY
PAROL
PAROLE
PARRY
SPARRY
PARSE
SPARSE
PARSEC
PARSED
PARSER
PARSES
PARTI
PARTIM
PARTIS
PARTS
SPARTS
PASEO
PASEOS
PASHA
PASHAS
PASHM
PASHMS
PASSE
PASSED
PASSEE
PASSER
PASSES
PASTA
PASTAS
PASTE
PASTED
PASTEL
PASTER
PASTES
PATCH
PATCHY
PATEN
PATENS
PATENT
PATER
PATERA
PATERS
PATES
SPATES
PATIN
PATINA
PATINE
PATINS
PATIO
PATIOS
PATTE
PATTED
PATTEE
PATTEN
PATTER
PATTES
PAULS
SPAULS
PAUSE
PAUSED
PAUSER
PAUSES
PAVAN
PAVANE
PAVANS
PAVEN
PAVENS
PAVER
PAVERS
PAVIN
SPAVIN
PAVING
PAVINS
PAVIS
PAVISE
PAWAW
PAWAWS
PAWLS
SPAWLS
PAWNS
SPAWNS
PAYED
SPAYED
PAYEE
PAYEES
PAYER
PAYERS
PEACE
PEACED
PEACES
PEACH
PEACHY
PEAKS
SPEAKS
PEALS
SPEALS
PEANS
SPEANS
PEARE
PEARES
PEARL
PEARLS
PEARLY
PEARS
SPEARS
PEARST
PEASE
PEASED
PEASES
PEATS
SPEATS
PEAZE
PEAZED
PEAZES
PECAN
PECANS
PECKE
PECKED
PECKER
PECKES
PECKS
SPECKS
PEDAL
PEDALO
PEDALS
PEDRO
PEDROS
PEECE
PEECES
PEELS
SPEELS
PEEOY
PEEOYS
PEEPE
PEEPED
PEEPER
PEEPES
PEERS
SPEERS
PEEVE
PEEVED
PEEVER
PEEVES
PEISE
PEISED
PEISES
PEIZE
PEIZED
PEIZES
PEKAN
PEKANS
PEKOE
PEKOES
PELLS
SPELLS
PELMA
PELMAS
PELTA
PELTAE
PELTAS
PELTS
SPELTS
PENCE
SPENCE
PENCEL
PENCES
PENDS
SPENDS
UPENDS
PENED
OPENED
PENIE
PENIES
PENNA
PENNAE
PENNAL
PENNE
PENNED
PENNER
PENNES
PERAI
PERAIS
PERCE
PERCED
PERCEN
PERCES
PERDU
EPERDU
PERDUE
PERDUS
PERIL
PERILS
PERIS
PERISH
PERMS
SPERMS
PERSE
SPERSE
PERSES
PERST
SPERST
PERVE
PERVED
PERVES
PESTO
PESTOS
PETAL
PETALS
PETAR
PETARA
PETARD
PETARS
PETARY
PETER
PETERS
PETIT
PETITE
PETRE
PETREL
PETRES
PEWIT
PEWITS
PEYSE
PEYSED
PEYSES
PHAGE
PHAGES
PHANG
UPHANG
PHANGS
PHARE
PHARES
PHASE
PHASED
PHASES
PHEER
PHEERE
PHEERS
PHENE
SPHENE
PHENES
PHEON
PHEONS
PHESE
PHESED
PHESES
PHIAL
PHIALS
PHOCA
PHOCAE
PHOCAS
PHONE
PHONED
PHONER
PHONES
PHONEY
PHONY
APHONY
PHOTO
PHOTON
PHOTOS
PHYLA
PHYLAE
PHYLE
PHYLES
PIANO
PIANOS
PICAS
SPICAS
PICKS
SPICKS
PICOT
PICOTE
PICOTS
PICRA
PICRAS
PICUL
PICULS
PIECE
APIECE
PIECED
PIECEN
PIECER
PIECES
PIEND
PIENDS
PIERS
PIERST
PIETA
PIETAS
PIGHT
SPIGHT
YPIGHT
PIGHTS
PIKED
SPIKED
PIKER
PIKERS
PIKES
SPIKES
PIKUL
PIKULS
PILAU
PILAUS
PILAW
PILAWS
PILED
SPILED
PILER
PILERS
PILES
SPILES
PILLS
SPILLS
PILOT
PILOTS
PILOW
PILOWS
PINAS
SPINAS
PINED
OPINED
SPINED
PINES
OPINES
SPINES
PINGO
PINGOS
PINKO
PINKOS
PINKS
SPINKS
PINNA
PINNAE
PINNY
SPINNY
PINON
PINONS
PINOT
PINOTS
PINTA
PINTAS
PINTO
PINTOS
PIOYE
PIOYES
PIPAL
PIPALS
PIPER
PIPERS
PIPIT
PIPITS
PIPUL
PIPULS
PIQUE
PIQUED
PIQUES
PIQUET
PIRAI
PIRAIS
PISTE
PISTES
PITCH
PITCHY
PITON
PITONS
PITTA
PITTAS
PIUMS
OPIUMS
PIVOT
PIVOTS
PIXEL
PIXELS
PIXIE
PIXIES
PIZZA
PIZZAS
PLACE
PLACED
PLACER
PLACES
PLACET
PLACK
PLACKS
PLAGE
PLAGES
PLAID
UPLAID
PLAIDS
PLAIN
PLAINS
PLAINT
PLAIT
PLAITS
PLANE
PLANED
PLANER
PLANES
PLANET
PLANK
PLANKS
PLANT
PLANTA
PLANTS
PLASH
SPLASH
PLASHY
PLASM
PLASMA
PLASMS
PLAST
YPLAST
PLASTE
PLATE
PLATED
PLATEN
PLATER
PLATES
PLATS
SPLATS
PLAYA
PLAYAS
PLAYS
SPLAYS
UPLAYS
PLAZA
PLAZAS
PLEAD
UPLEAD
PLEADS
PLEAS
PLEASE
PLEAT
PLEATS
PLEON
PLEONS
PLICA
PLICAE
PLICAL
PLIER
PLIERS
PLING
PLINGS
PLINK
UPLINK
PLINKS
PLOAT
PLOATS
PLONG
PLONGD
PLONGE
PLONGS
PLONK
PLONKS
PLONKY
PLOOK
UPLOOK
PLOOKS
PLOUK
PLOUKS
PLUCK
PLUCKS
PLUCKY
PLUFF
PLUFFS
PLUFFY
PLUMB
PLUMBS
PLUME
PLUMED
PLUMES
PLUMP
PLUMPS
PLUMPY
PLUNK
PLUNKS
PLUSH
PLUSHY
POACH
POACHY
POAKA
POAKAS
POAKE
POAKES
PODAL
APODAL
PODGE
PODGES
PODIA
PODIAL
POGGE
POGGES

POILU
POILUS
POIND
POINDS
POINT
POINTE
POINTS
POINTY
POISE
POISED
POISER
POISES
POKAL
POKALS
POKER
POKERS
POKES
SPOKES
POKEY
POKEYS
POLAR
POLARS
POLER
POLERS
POLEY
POLEYN
POLEYS
POLIO
POLIOS
POLKA
POLKAS
POLYP
POLYPE
POLYPI
POLYPS
POMBE
POMBES
PONCE
PONCED
PONCES
PONCEY
PONEY
PONEYS
PONGA
PONGAS
PONGO
PONGOS
PONGY
SPONGY
POOFS
SPOOFS
POOJA
POOJAH
POOJAS
POOKA
POOKAS
POOKS
SPOOKS
POOLS
SPOOLS
POONS
SPOONS
POORI
POORIS
POORT
POORTS
POOTS
SPOOTS
POOVE
POOVES
POPPA
POPPAS
PORER
PORERS
PORES
SPORES
PORGE
PORGED
PORGES
PORNO
PORNOS
PORTA
PORTAL
PORTAS
PORTS
SPORTS
PORTY
SPORTY
POSER
POSERS
POSES
EPOSES
POSIT
POSITS
POSSE
POSSED
POSSER
POSSES
POSSET
POTCH
POTCHE
POTIN
POTING
POTINS
POTOO
POTOOS
POTTO
POTTOS
POTTY
SPOTTY
POUCH
POUCHY
POUKE
POUKES
POULE
POULES
POULP
POULPE
POULPS
POULT
POULTS
POUND
POUNDS
POUPE
POUPED
POUPES
POUTS
SPOUTS
POUTY
SPOUTY
POWAN
POWANS
POWER
POWERS
POWIN
POWINS
POWND
POWNDS
POWRE
POWRED
POWRES
POYNT
POYNTS
POYSE
POYSED
POYSES
PRAAM
PRAAMS
PRAHU
PRAHUS
PRANA
PRANAS
PRANG
SPRANG
PRANGS
PRANK
PRANKS
PRANKY
PRASE
PRASES
PRATE
UPRATE
PRATED
PRATER
PRATES
PRATS
SPRATS
PRATT
PRATTS
PRAWN
PRAWNS
PRAYS
SPRAYS
PREED
SPREED
PREEN
PREENS
PREES
SPREES
PREIF
PREIFE
PREIFS
PRENT
SPRENT
PRENTS
PRESE
PRESES
PRESET
PREST
UPREST
PRESTO
PRESTS
PREVE
PREVED
PREVES
PRIAL
PRIALS
PRICE
PRICED
PRICER
PRICES
PRICEY
PRICK
PRICKS
PRIDE
PRIDED
PRIDES
PRIEF
PRIEFE
PRIEFS
PRIER
PRIERS
PRIES
PRIEST
PRIGS
SPRIGS
PRILL
PRILLS
PRIMA
PRIMAL
PRIME
PRIMED
PRIMER
PRIMES
PRIMO
PRIMOS
PRIMP
PRIMPS
PRINK
PRINKS
PRINT
SPRINT
PRINTS
PRION
PRIONS
PRIOR
PRIORS
PRIORY
PRISE
EPRISE
UPRISE
PRISED
PRISER
PRISES
PRISM
PRISMS
PRISMY
PRIZE
PRIZED
PRIZER
PRIZES
PROBE
PROBED
PROBER
PROBES
PRODS
SPRODS
PROEM
PROEMS
PROGS
SPROGS
PROIN
PROINE
PROINS
PROKE
PROKED
PROKER
PROKES
PROLE
PROLED
PROLEG
PROLER
PROLES
PROLL
UPROLL
PROLLS
PROMO
PROMOS
PROMS
EPROMS
PRONE
PRONER
PRONES
PRONG
SPRONG
PRONGS
PRONK
PRONKS
PROOF
PROOFS
PRORE
PRORES
PROSE
UPROSE
PROSED
PROSER
PROSES
PROSO
PROSOS
PROUL
PROULS
PROVE
PROVED
PROVEN
PROVER
PROVES
PROWL
PROWLS
PROYN
PROYNE
PROYNS
PRUDE
PRUDES
PRUNE
PRUNED
PRUNER
PRUNES
PRUNT
PRUNTS
PRYER
SPRYER
PRYERS
PRYSE
PRYSED
PRYSES
PSALM
PSALMS
PSEUD
PSEUDO
PSEUDS
PSHAW
PSHAWS
PSION
PSIONS
PSORA
PSORAS
PSYCH
PSYCHE
PSYCHO
PSYCHS
PSYOP
PSYOPS
PUDDY
SPUDDY
PUDGE
PUDGES
PUDOR
PUDORS
PUGIL
PUGILS
PUKER
PUKERS
PULER
PULERS
PULES
SPULES
PULKA
PULKAS
PULSE
PULSED
PULSES
PULUS
OPULUS
PUMIE
PUMIES
PUNCE
PUNCED
PUNCES
PUNCH
PUNCHY
PUNGA
PUNGAS
PUNKA
PUNKAH
PUNKAS
PUNKS
SPUNKS
PUNTO
PUNTOS
PUPIL
PUPILS
PUREE
PUREED
PUREES
PURES
PUREST
PURGE
SPURGE
PURGED
PURGER
PURGES
PURIM
PURIMS
PURIN
PURINE
PURING
PURINS
PURIS
PURISM
PURIST
PURSE
PURSED
PURSER
PURSES
PURSEW
PUSES
OPUSES
PUSLE
PUSLED
PUSLES
PUTTI
PUTTIE
PUZEL
PUZELS
PYGAL
PYGALS
PYLON
PYLONS
PYRES
SPYRES
QANAT
QANATS
QIBLA
QIBLAS
QUACK
QUACKS
QUADS
SQUADS
QUAFF
QUAFFS
QUAIL
SQUAIL
QUAILS
QUAIR
QUAIRS
QUAKE
QUAKED
QUAKER
QUAKES
QUALM
QUALMS
QUALMY
QUANT
EQUANT
QUANTA
QUANTS
QUARE
SQUARE
QUARER
QUARK
QUARKS
QUART
QUARTE
QUARTO
QUARTS
QUARTZ
QUASH
SQUASH
QUATS
SQUATS
QUEAN
QUEANS
QUEEN
QUEENS
QUEENY
QUEER
QUEERS
QUELL
QUELLS
QUEME
QUEMED
QUEMES
QUENA
QUENAS
QUERN
QUERNS
QUEST
QUESTS
QUEUE
QUEUED
QUEUES
QUEYN
QUEYNS
QUICH
QUICHE
QUICK
QUICKS
QUIDS
EQUIDS
SQUIDS
QUIET
QUIETS
QUIFF
SQUIFF
QUIFFS
QUILL
SQUILL
QUILLS
QUILT
QUILTS
QUINA
QUINAS
QUINE
EQUINE
QUINES
QUINS
QUINSY
QUINT
SQUINT
QUINTA
QUINTE
QUINTS
QUIPO
QUIPOS
QUIPS
EQUIPS
QUIPU
QUIPUS
QUIRE
SQUIRE
QUIRED
QUIRES
QUIRK
QUIRKS
QUIRKY
QUIRT
SQUIRT
QUIRTS
QUIST
QUISTS
QUITE
QUITED
QUITES
QUITS
SQUITS
QUOIF
QUOIFS
QUOIN
QUOINS
QUOIT
QUOITS
QUOLL
QUOLLS
QUONK
QUONKS
QUOTA
QUOTAS
QUOTE
QUOTED
QUOTER
QUOTES
QUOTH
QUOTHA
QUYTE
QUYTED
QUYTES
RABAT
RABATO
RABATS
RABBI
RABBIN
RABBIS
RABBIT
RABIS
ARABIS
RACED
BRACED
GRACED
TRACED
RACER
BRACER
TRACER
RACERS
RACES
BRACES
GRACES
TRACES
RACHE
ORACHE
RACHES
RACKS
BRACKS
CRACKS
TRACKS
WRACKS
RACON
RACONS
RADAR
RADARS
RADGE
RADGER
RADIO
RADIOS
RADON
RADONS
RAFFS
DRAFFS
GRAFFS
RAFTS
CRAFTS
DRAFTS
GRAFTS
KRAFTS
RAGEE
DRAGEE
RAGEES
RAGER
RAGERS
RAGGY
CRAGGY
DRAGGY
RAIDS
BRAIDS
RAIKS
TRAIKS
RAILE
GRAILE
RAILED
RAILER
RAILES
RAILS
BRAILS
DRAILS
FRAILS
GRAILS
TRAILS
RAINE
GRAINE
RAINED
RAINES

RAINS
BRAINS
DRAINS
GRAINS
TRAINS
RAINY
BRAINY
GRAINY
RAIRD
BRAIRD
RAIRDS
RAISE
ARAISE
BRAISE
FRAISE
PRAISE
RAISED
RAISER
RAISES
RAITA
RAITAS
RAITS
KRAITS
TRAITS
RAJAH
RAJAHS
RAKED
BRAKED
CRAKED
RAKEE
RAKEES
RAKER
RAKERS
RAKERY
RAKES
BRAKES
CRAKES
DRAKES
RAKIS
RAKISH
RALLY
ORALLY
RALLYE
RAMEE
RAMEES
RAMEN
RAMENS
RAMIE
RAMIES
RAMIN
RAMINS
RAMPS
CRAMPS
TRAMPS
RANAS
PRANAS
RANCE
PRANCE
TRANCE
RANCED
RANCEL
RANCES
RANCH
BRANCH
CRANCH
RANCHO
RANDS
BRANDS
GRANDS
RANDY
BRANDY
RANEE
RANEES
RANGE
GRANGE
ORANGE
RANGED
RANGER
RANGES
RANKE
RANKED
RANKER
RANKES
RANKS
BRANKS
CRANKS
FRANKS
PRANKS
RANTS
CRANTS
DRANTS
GRANTS
ORANTS
TRANTS
RAPED
DRAPED
GRAPED
TRAPED
RAPER
DRAPER
RAPERS
RAPES
CRAPES
DRAPES
GRAPES
TRAPES
RAPHE
RAPHES
RAPID
RAPIDS
RASED
ERASED
RASES
BRASES
CRASES
ERASES
PRASES
RASPS
GRASPS
RASSE
WRASSE
RASSES
RATAN
RATANS
RATCH
CRATCH
FRATCH
RATED
CRATED
GRATED
ORATED
PRATED
RATEL
RATELS
RATER
CRATER
FRATER
GRATER
IRATER
KRATER
PRATER
RATERS
RATES
CRATES
GRATES
ORATES
PRATES
URATES
RATHE
RATHER
RATHS
WRATHS
RATIO
RATION
RATIOS
RATOO
RATOON
RATOOS
RATTY
BRATTY
RAVED
BRAVED
CRAVED
GRAVED
RAVEL
GRAVEL
TRAVEL
RAVELS
RAVEN
CRAVEN
GRAVEN
RAVENS
RAVER
BRAVER
CRAVER
GRAVER
RAVERS
RAVES
BRAVES
CRAVES
GRAVES
TRAVES
RAVIN
RAVINE
RAVING
RAVINS
RAWER
BRAWER
DRAWER
RAWLY
BRAWLY
CRAWLY
RAWNS
BRAWNS
PRAWNS
RAXES
PRAXES
RAYAH
RAYAHS
RAYED
BRAYED
FRAYED
GRAYED
PRAYED
RAYLE
GRAYLE
RAYLED
RAYLES
RAYLET
RAYNE
TRAYNE
RAYNES
RAYON
CRAYON
RAYONS
RAZED
BRAZED
CRAZED
GRAZED
RAZEE
RAZEED
RAZEES
RAZES
BRAZES
CRAZES
GRAZES
RAZOO
RAZOOS
RAZOR
RAZORS
REACH
AREACH
BREACH
CREACH
PREACH
REACT
REACTS
READS
AREADS
BREADS
DREADS
OREADS
TREADS
REAKS
BREAKS
CREAKS
FREAKS
WREAKS
REALM
REALMS
REALO
REALOS
REAME
REAMED
REAMER
REAMES
REAMS
BREAMS
CREAMS
DREAMS
REAMY
CREAMY
DREAMY
REARM
REARMS
REARS
DREARS
REAST
BREAST
REASTS
REASTY
REATA
REATAS
REATE
CREATE
REATES
REAVE
GREAVE
REAVER
REAVES
REBBE
REBBES
REBEC
REBECK
REBECS
REBEL
REBELS
REBID
REBIDS
REBIT
REBITE
REBUT
REBUTS
RECAL
RECALL
RECALS
RECAP
RECAPS
RECCE
RECCED
RECCES
RECCO
RECCOS
RECIT
RECITE
RECITS
RECKS
DRECKS
TRECKS
WRECKS
RECTA
RECTAL
RECTO
RECTOR
RECTOS
RECUR
RECURE
RECURS
REDAN
REDANS
REDES
AREDES
BREDES
REDIA
UREDIA
REDIAE
REDIAL
REDIP
REDIPS
REDOS
CREDOS
REECH
BREECH
REECHY
REEDE
REEDED
REEDEN
REEDER
REEDES
REEDS
BREEDS
CREEDS
GREEDS
REEDY
GREEDY
REEKS
BREEKS
CREEKS
REEKY
CREEKY
REELS
CREELS
REENS
GREENS
PREENS
TREENS
REEST
FREEST
REESTS
REESTY
REEVE
PREEVE
REEVED
REEVES
REFEL
REFELS
REFER
PREFER
REFERS
REFFO
REFFOS
REFIT
REFITS
REGAL
REGALE
REGALS
REGAR
REGARD
REGARS
REGGO
REGGOS
REGIE
REGIES
REGMA
BREGMA
REGOS
GREGOS
REGUR
REGURS
REIFS
PREIFS
REIGN
REIGNS
REINS
GREINS
REIRD
REIRDS
REIST
REISTS
REIVE
REIVER
REIVES
REJIG
REJIGS
RELAY
RELAYS
RELET
RELETS
RELIC
RELICS
RELICT
RELIE
RELIED
RELIEF
RELIER
RELIES
REMAN
REMAND
REMANS
REMEN
REMENS
REMIT
FREMIT
REMITS
REMIX
PREMIX
RENAY
RENAYS
RENDS
TRENDS
RENEW
RENEWS
RENEY
RENEYS
RENGA
RENGAS
RENIG
RENIGS
RENIN
RENINS
RENNE
BRENNE
FRENNE
RENNED
RENNES
RENNET
RENTE
RENTED
RENTER
RENTES
RENTS
PRENTS
REPAY
PREPAY
REPAYS
REPEL
REPELS
REPLA
REPLAN
REPLAY
REPOS
REPOSE
REPOST
REPOT
REPOTS
REPRO
REPROS
RERUN
RERUNS
RESAY
RESAYS
RESES
GRESES
PRESES
URESES
RESET
PRESET
RESETS
RESIN
RESINS
RESIT
RESITS
RESTS
CRESTS
PRESTS
TRESTS
WRESTS
RETCH
WRETCH
RETES
ARETES
RETIE
RETIED
RETIES
RETRO
RETROD
RETROS
REUSE
REUSED
REUSES
REVEL
REVELS
REVET
BREVET
REVETS
REVIE
REVIED
REVIES
REVIEW
REVUE
PREVUE
REVUES
REWTH
REWTHS
RHEUM
RHEUMS
RHEUMY
RHIME
RHIMES
RHINE
RHINES
RHINO
RHINOS
RHOMB
RHOMBI
RHOMBS
RHONE
RHONES
RHUMB
RHUMBA
RHUMBS
RHYME
RHYMED
RHYMER
RHYMES
RHYNE
RHYNES
RIALS
PRIALS
TRIALS
URIALS
RIANT
CRIANT
RIATA
RIATAS
RICED
PRICED
TRICED
RICER
GRICER
PRICER
RICERS
RICES
GRICES
PRICES
TRICES
RICEY
PRICEY
RICHT
FRICHT
RICHTS
RICIN
RICING
RICINS
RICKS
BRICKS
CRICKS
ERICKS
PRICKS
TRICKS
WRICKS
RIDER
ARIDER
RIDERS
RIDES
BRIDES
GRIDES
IRIDES
PRIDES
RIDGE
BRIDGE
FRIDGE
RIDGED
RIDGEL
RIDGER
RIDGES
RIELS
ARIELS
ORIELS
RIEVE
GRIEVE
PRIEVE
RIEVER
RIEVES
RIFFS
GRIFFS
RIFLE
TRIFLE
RIFLED
RIFLER
RIFLES
RIFTE
RIFTED
RIFTS
DRIFTS
GRIFTS
RIFTY
DRIFTY
RIGHT
ARIGHT
BRIGHT
FRIGHT
WRIGHT
RIGHTO
RIGHTS
RIGID
FRIGID
RIGIDS
RIGOL
RIGOLL
RIGOLS
RIGOR
RIGORS
RILLE
GRILLE
RILLED
RILLES
RILLET
RILLS
BRILLS

DRILLS
FRILLS
GRILLS
KRILLS
PRILLS
TRILLS
RIMED
CRIMED
GRIMED
PRIMED
RIMER
PRIMER
TRIMER
RIMERS
RIMES
CRIMES
GRIMES
PRIMES
RIMUS
PRIMUS
RINDS
GRINDS
RINES
BRINES
CRINES
TRINES
URINES
RINGS
BRINGS
WRINGS
RINKS
BRINKS
DRINKS
PRINKS
RINSE
RINSED
RINSER
RINSES
RIOTS
GRIOTS
RIPED
GRIPED
RIPEN
RIPENS
RIPER
GRIPER
RIPERS
RIPES
CRIPES
GRIPES
TRIPES
RIPEST
RISEN
ARISEN
RISER
PRISER
RISERS
RISES
ARISES
BRISES
CRISES
FRISES
GRISES
IRISES
KRISES
PRISES
RISHI
RISHIS
RISKS
BRISKS
FRISKS
RISKY
BRISKY
FRISKY
RISPS
CRISPS
RITES
TRITES
URITES
WRITES
RIVAL
RIVALS
RIVEL
DRIVEL
RIVELS
RIVEN
DRIVEN
RIVER
DRIVER
RIVERS
RIVERY
RIVES
DRIVES
RIVET
GRIVET
PRIVET
TRIVET
RIVETS
RIYAL
RIYALS
ROACH
BROACH
ROADS
BROADS
TROADS
ROANS
GROANS
ROAST
ROASTS
ROATE
ROATED
ROATES
ROBED
PROBED
ROBES
PROBES
ROBIN
ROBING
ROBINS
ROBLE
ROBLES
ROBOT
ROBOTS
ROCKS
BROCKS
CROCKS
FROCKS
TROCKS
RODED
ERODED
RODEO
RODEOS
RODES
ERODES
TRODES
ROGER
DROGER
ROGERS
ROGUE
BROGUE
DROGUE
ROGUED
ROGUES
ROILS
BROILS
DROILS
ROINS
GROINS
PROINS
ROIST
ROISTS
ROKED
BROKED
PROKED
TROKED
ROKER
BROKER
PROKER
ROKERS
ROKES
BROKES
PROKES
TROKES
ROLAG
ROLAGS
ROLES
DROLES
PROLES
ROLLS
DROLLS
PROLLS
TROLLS
ROMAL
ROMALS
ROMAN
ROMANS
ROMAS
AROMAS
GROMAS
ROMPS
TROMPS
RONDE
RONDEL
RONDES
RONDO
RONDOS
RONEO
RONEOS
RONES
CRONES
DRONES
GRONES
PRONES
TRONES
RONTE
RONTES
RONTS
FRONTS
ROODS
BROODS
ROOFS
GROOFS
PROOFS
ROOKS
BROOKS
CROOKS
DROOKS
ROOMS
BROOMS
GROOMS
VROOMS
ROOMY
BROOMY
ROONS
CROONS
ROOPS
DROOPS
TROOPS
ROOPY
DROOPY
ROOSA
ROOSAS
ROOSE
BROOSE
ROOSED
ROOSES
ROOST
ROOSTS
ROOTS
WROOTS
ROOTSY
ROPED
GROPED
TROPED
ROPER
GROPER
PROPER
ROPERS
ROPERY
ROPES
GROPES
TROPES
ROQUE
ROQUES
ROQUET
RORES
CRORES
PRORES
RORIE
RORIER
ROSED
PROSED
ROSES
BROSES
PROSES
UROSES
ROSET
GROSET
ROSETS
ROSETY
ROSIN
ROSING
ROSINS
ROSINY
ROSIT
PROSIT
ROSITS
ROSTS
FROSTS
ROTAL
CROTAL
ROTCH
CROTCH
ROTCHE
ROTOR
ROTORS
ROUGE
ROUGED
ROUGES
ROUGH
BROUGH
GROUGH
TROUGH
ROUGHS
ROUGHT
ROUGHY
ROULE
TROULE
ROULES
ROULS
PROULS
ROUND
AROUND
GROUND
ROUNDS
ROUPS
CROUPS
GROUPS
ROUPY
CROUPY
GROUPY
ROUSE
AROUSE
CROUSE
GROUSE
TROUSE
ROUSED
ROUSER
ROUSES
ROUST
ROUSTS
ROUTE
CROUTE
ROUTED
ROUTER
ROUTES
ROUTH
DROUTH
ROUTHS
ROUTS
CROUTS
GROUTS
TROUTS
ROVED
PROVED
ROVER
DROVER
PROVER
TROVER
ROVERS
ROVES
DROVES
GROVES
PROVES
ROWAN
ROWANS
ROWED
CROWED
TROWED
ROWEL
TROWEL
ROWELS
ROWEN
ROWENS
ROWER
GROWER
ROWERS
ROWME
ROWMES
ROWND
ROWNDS
ROWTH
GROWTH
ROWTHS
ROYAL
ROYALS
ROYNE
GROYNE
PROYNE
ROYNED
ROYNES
ROYST
ROYSTS
ROZET
ROZETS
ROZIT
ROZITS
RUANA
RUANAS
RUBIN
RUBINE
RUBINS
RUBLE
RUBLES
RUCHE
RUCHED
RUCHES
RUCKS
CRUCKS
TRUCKS
RUDDY
CRUDDY
RUDER
CRUDER
RUDERY
RUDES
CRUDES
PRUDES
RUDEST
RUDIE
RUDIES
RUFFE
RUFFED
RUFFES
RUGGY
DRUGGY
RUING
GRUING
TRUING
RUINGS
RULER
RULERS
RUMAL
BRUMAL
RUMALS
RUMBA
RUMBAS
RUMBO
RUMBOS
RUMEN
CRUMEN
RUMES
BRUMES
GRUMES
RUMLY
DRUMLY
GRUMLY
RUMMY
CRUMMY
RUMOR
RUMORS
RUMPS
CRUMPS
FRUMPS
GRUMPS
TRUMPS
RUMPY
CRUMPY
FRUMPY
GRUMPY
RUNCH
BRUNCH
CRUNCH
RUNED
PRUNED
RUNES
PRUNES
RUNTS
BRUNTS
GRUNTS
PRUNTS
RUPEE
RUPEES
RUPIA
RUPIAH
RUPIAS
RURAL
CRURAL
RURALS
RUSES
CRUSES
DRUSES
URUSES
RUSHY
BRUSHY
RUSMA
RUSMAS
RUSTS
BRUSTS
CRUSTS
FRUSTS
TRUSTS
RUSTY
CRUSTY
TRUSTY
RUTHS
TRUTHS
RUTIN
RUTINS
RYBAT
RYBATS
RYKES
GRYKES
RYMME
RYMMED
RYMMES
SABER
SABERS
SABIN
SABINS
SABLE
USABLE
SABLED
SABLES
SABOT
SABOTS
SABRA
SABRAS
SABRE
SABRED
SABRES
SACRA
SACRAL
SADHE
SADHES
SADHU
SADHUS
SADZA
SADZAS
SAFES
SAFEST
SAGER
USAGER
SAGES
USAGES
SAGEST
SAHIB
SAHIBA
SAHIBS
SAICE
SAICES
SAICK
SAICKS
SAIDS
SAIDST
SAIGA
SAIGAS
SAINE
SAINED
SAINT
SAINTS
SAITH
SAITHE
SAITHS
SAJOU
SAJOUS
SAKER
SAKERS
SAKIA
SAKIAS
SALAD
SALADE
SALADS
SALAL
SALALS
SALEP
SALEPS
SALET
SALETS
SALLE
SALLEE
SALLES
SALLET
SALMI
SALMIS
SALON
SALONS
SALOP
SALOPS
SALPA
SALPAE
SALPAS
SALSA
SALSAS
SALSE
SALSES
SALTO
SALTOS
SALUE
SALUED
SALUES
SALVE
SALVED
SALVER
SALVES
SALVO
SALVOR
SALVOS
SAMAN
SAMANS
SAMBA
TSAMBA
SAMBAL
SAMBAR
SAMBAS
SAMBO
SAMBOS
SAMEL
SAMELY
SAMFU
SAMFUS
SAMPI
SAMPIS
SANKO
SANKOS
SANSA
SANSAS
SAPAN
SAPANS
SAPOR
SAPORS
SAREE
SAREES
SARGE
SARGES
SARGO
SARGOS
SARIN
SARING
SARINS
SAROD
SARODS
SASIN
SASINE
SASINS
SASSE
SASSED
SASSES
SATAY
SATAYS
SATIN
ISATIN
SATING
SATINS
SATINY
SATYR
SATYRA
SATYRS
SAUBA
SAUBAS
SAUCE
SAUCED
SAUCER
SAUCES
SAUCH
SAUCHS
SAUGH
SAUGHS
SAULT
SAULTS

SAUNA
SAUNAS
SAUNT
SAUNTS
SAUTE
SAUTED
SAUTES
SAVER
SAVERS
SAVEY
SAVEYS
SAVIN
SAVINE
SAVING
SAVINS
SAVOR
SAVORS
SAVORY
SAVOY
SAVOYS
SAWAH
SAWAHS
SAWER
SAWERS
SAYER
SAYERS
SAYID
SAYIDS
SAYON
SAYONS
SCAFF
SCAFFS
SCAIL
SCAILS
SCALA
SCALAE
SCALAR
SCALD
SCALDS
SCALE
SCALED
SCALER
SCALES
SCALL
SCALLS
SCALP
SCALPS
SCAMP
SCAMPI
SCAMPS
SCANT
SCANTS
SCANTY
SCAPA
SCAPAS
SCAPE
ESCAPE
SCAPED
SCAPES
SCARE
SCARED
SCARER
SCARES
SCAREY
SCARF
SCARFS
SCARP
ESCARP
SCARPA
SCARPH
SCARPS
SCART
SCARTH
SCARTS
SCATH
SCATHE
SCATHS
SCATT
SCATTS
SCATTY
SCAUD
SCAUDS
SCAUP
SCAUPS
SCAUR
SCAURS
SCAURY
SCEAT
SCEATT
SCEND
ASCEND
SCENDS
SCENE
SCENED
SCENES
SCENT
ASCENT
SCENTS
SCHWA
SCHWAS
SCION
SCIONS
SCLIM
SCLIMS
SCOFF
SCOFFS
SCOLD
SCOLDS
SCONE
SCONES
SCOOG
SCOOGS
SCOOP
SCOOPS
SCOOT
SCOOTS
SCOPA
SCOPAE
SCOPAS
SCOPE
SCOPED
SCOPES
SCORE
SCORED
SCORER
SCORES
SCORN
SCORNS
SCOTS
ASCOTS
ESCOTS
SCOUG
SCOUGS
SCOUP
SCOUPS
SCOUR
SCOURS
SCOUT
SCOUTH
SCOUTS
SCOWL
SCOWLS
SCOWP
SCOWPS
SCRAB
SCRABS
SCRAE
SCRAES
SCRAG
SCRAGS
SCRAM
SCRAMB
SCRAMS
SCRAN
SCRANS
SCRAP
SCRAPE
SCRAPS
SCRAT
SCRATS
SCRAW
SCRAWL
SCRAWM
SCRAWS
SCRAY
SCRAYE
SCRAYS
SCREE
SCREED
SCREEN
SCREES
SCREW
SCREWS
SCREWY
SCRIM
SCRIMP
SCRIMS
SCRIP
SCRIPS
SCRIPT
SCROD
SCRODS
SCROG
SCROGS
SCROW
ESCROW
SCROWL
SCROWS
SCRUB
SCRUBS
SCRUM
SCRUMP
SCRUMS
SCUBA
SCUBAS
SCUDO
ESCUDO
SCUFF
SCUFFS
SCUFT
SCUFTS
SCULK
SCULKS
SCULL
SCULLE
SCULLS
SCULP
SCULPS
SCULPT
SCURF
SCURFS
SCURFY
SCUSE
SCUSED
SCUSES
SCUTA
SCUTAL
SCUTE
SCUTES
SCUZZ
SCUZZY
SDAYN
SDAYNS
SDEIN
SDEINS
SEAME
SEAMED
SEAMEN
SEAMER
SEAMES
SEARE
SEARED
SEARER
SEASE
SEASED
SEASES
SEAZE
SEAZED
SEAZES
SEBUM
SEBUMS
SECCO
SECCOS
SEDAN
SEDANS
SEDGE
SEDGED
SEDGES
SEDUM
SEDUMS
SEGAR
SEGARS
SEGNO
SEGNOS
SEGOL
SEGOLS
SEGUE
SEGUED
SEGUES
SEINE
SEINED
SEINER
SEINES
SEISE
SEISED
SEISES
SEISM
SEISMS
SEITY
ASEITY
SEIZE
SEIZED
SEIZER
SEIZES
SELAH
SELAHS
SELLA
SELLAE
SELLAS
SELLE
SELLER
SELLES
SELVA
SELVAS
SEMEE
SEMEED
SEMEN
SEMENS
SEMIE
SEMIES
SENNA
SENNAS
SENSE
SENSED
SENSES
SEPAD
SEPADS
SEPAL
SEPALS
SEPIA
SEPIAS
SEPOY
SEPOYS
SEPTA
SEPTAL
SERAC
SERACS
SERAI
SERAIL
SERAIS
SERES
SEREST
SERGE
SERGES
SERIF
SERIFS
SERIN
SERINE
SERING
SERINS
SERON
SERONS
SEROW
SEROWS
SERRA
SERRAE
SERRAN
SERRAS
SERRE
SERRED
SERRES
SERUM
SERUMS
SERVE
SERVED
SERVER
SERVES
SETON
SETONS
SEVEN
SEVENS
SEVER
SEVERE
SEVERS
SEVERY
SEWEL
SEWELS
SEWEN
SEWENS
SEWER
SEWERS
SEWIN
SEWING
SEWINS
SEXER
SEXERS
SEYEN
SEYENS
SHACK
SHACKO
SHACKS
SHADE
SHADED
SHADES
SHAFT
SHAFTS
SHAKE
ASHAKE
SHAKED
SHAKEN
SHAKER
SHAKES
SHAKO
SHAKOS
SHALE
SHALED
SHALES
SHALL
SHALLI
SHALM
SHALMS
SHAMA
SHAMAN
SHAMAS
SHAME
ASHAME
SHAMED
SHAMER
SHAMES
SHAND
SHANDS
SHANDY
SHANK
SHANKS
SHAPE
SHAPED
SHAPEN
SHAPER
SHAPES
SHARD
SHARDS
SHARE
SHARED
SHARER
SHARES
SHARK
SHARKS
SHARN
SHARNS
SHARNY
SHARP
SHARPS
SHAVE
SHAVED
SHAVEN
SHAVER
SHAVES
SHAWL
SHAWLS
SHAWM
SHAWMS
SHAWS
PSHAWS
SHAYA
SHAYAS
SHCHI
SHCHIS
SHEAF
SHEAFS
SHEAFY
SHEAL
SHEALS
SHEAR
SHEARS
SHEEL
SHEELS
SHEEN
SHEENS
SHEENY
SHEEP
SHEEPO
SHEEPY
SHEER
SHEERS
SHEET
SHEETS
SHEETY
SHEIK
SHEIKH
SHEIKS
SHELF
SHELFS
SHELFY
SHELL
SHELLS
SHELLY
SHEND
YSHEND
SHENDS
SHENT
YSHENT
SHEOL
SHEOLS
SHERD
SHERDS
SHETS
ASHETS
SHEVA
SHEVAS
SHIEL
SHIELD
SHIELS
SHIER
ASHIER
SHIERS
SHIES
SHIEST
SHIFT
SHIFTS
SHIFTY
SHILL
SHILLS
SHINE
ASHINE
SHINED
SHINER
SHINES
SHIRE
SHIRES
SHIRK
SHIRKS
SHIRR
SHIRRA
SHIRRS
SHIRT
SHIRTS
SHIRTY
SHITE
SHITED
SHITES
SHIVE
SHIVER
SHIVES
SHLEP
SHLEPS
SHMEK
SHMEKS
SHMOE
SHMOES
SHOAL
SHOALS
SHOALY
SHOAT
SHOATS
SHOCK
SHOCKS
SHOER
SHOERS
SHOGI
SHOGIS
SHOJI
SHOJIS
SHOLA
SHOLAS
SHOOK
SHOOKS
SHOOL
SHOOLE
SHOOLS
SHOOT
SHOOTS
SHORE
ASHORE
SHORED
SHORER
SHORES
SHORT
SHORTS
SHORTY
SHOTE
SHOTES
SHOTT
SHOTTE
SHOTTS
SHOUT
SHOUTS
SHOVE
SHOVED
SHOVEL
SHOVER
SHOVES
SHOYU
SHOYUS
SHRED
SHREDS
SHREW
SHREWD
SHREWS
SHROW
SHROWD
SHROWS
SHRUB
SHRUBS
SHRUG
SHRUGS
SHTUM
SHTUMM
SHTUP
SHTUPS
SHUCK
SHUCKS
SHULE
SHULED
SHULES
SHUNT
SHUNTS
SHURA
SHURAS
SHUTE
SHUTES
SHYER
SHYERS
SIBYL
SIBYLS
SICKO
SICKOS
SIDER
SIDERS
SIDES
ASIDES
SIDHA
SIDHAS
SIDLE
SIDLED
SIDLES
SIEGE
SIEGED
SIEGER
SIEGES
SIENT
SIENTS
SIETH
SIETHS
SIEVE
SIEVED
SIEVES
SIGHT
SIGHTS
SIGIL
SIGILS
SIGMA
SIGMAS
SILEN
SILENE
SILENI
SILENS
SILENT
SILER
SILERS
SILES
ESILES
SILVA
SILVAE
SILVAN
SILVAS
SIMAR
SIMARS
SIMUL
SIMULS
SINEW

SINEWS
SINEWY
SINGE
SINGED
SINGER
SINGES
SIREN
SIRENS
SIRIH
SIRIHS
SIROC
SIROCS
SIRUP
SIRUPS
SISAL
SISALS
SITAR
SITARS
SITHE
SITHED
SITHEN
SITHES
SIVER
SIVERS
SIXER
SIXERS
SIXTE
SIXTES
SIXTH
SIXTHS
SIZAR
SIZARS
SIZEL
SIZELS
SIZER
SIZERS
SKAIL
SKAILS
SKALD
SKALDS
SKANK
SKANKS
SKART
SKARTH
SKARTS
SKATE
SKATED
SKATER
SKATES
SKATT
SKATTS
SKEAN
SKEANS
SKEAR
SKEARS
SKEARY
SKEER
SKEERS
SKEERY
SKEET
SKEETS
SKEGG
SKEGGS
SKEIN
SKEINS
SKELF
SKELFS
SKELL
SKELLS
SKELLY

SKELM
SKELMS
SKELP
SKELPS
SKENE
SKENES
SKERS
ASKERS
ESKERS
SKIER
SKIERS
SKIES
ESKIES
SKIFF
SKIFFS
SKILL
SKILLS
SKILLY
SKIMP
SKIMPS
SKIMPY
SKINK
SKINKS
SKIRL
SKIRLS
SKIRR
SKIRRS
SKIRT
SKIRTS
SKITE
SKITED
SKITES
SKIVE
SKIVED
SKIVER
SKIVES
SKLIM
SKLIMS
SKOFF
SKOFFS
SKRAN
SKRANS
SKRIK
SKRIKS
SKULK
SKULKS
SKULL
SKULLS
SKUNK
SKUNKS
SKYER
SKYERS
SKYRE
SKYRED
SKYRES
SKYTE
SKYTED
SKYTES
SLACK
SLACKS
SLADE
SLADES
SLAKE
ASLAKE
SLAKED
SLAKES
SLANE
SLANES
SLANG
SLANGS

SLANGY
SLANT
ASLANT
SLANTS
SLATE
SLATED
SLATER
SLATES
SLAVE
SLAVED
SLAVER
SLAVES
SLAVEY
SLEEK
SLEEKS
SLEEKY
SLEEP
ASLEEP
SLEEPS
SLEEPY
SLEET
SLEETS
SLEETY
SLICE
SLICED
SLICER
SLICES
SLICK
SLICKS
SLIDE
SLIDED
SLIDER
SLIDES
SLIME
SLIMED
SLIMES
SLIMS
SLIMSY
SLING
ISLING
SLINGS
SLINK
SLINKS
SLINKY
SLIPE
SLIPES
SLIVE
SLIVED
SLIVEN
SLIVER
SLIVES
SLOAN
SLOANS
SLOID
SLOIDS
SLOOM
SLOOMS
SLOOMY
SLOOP
SLOOPS
SLOOT
SLOOTS
SLOPE
ASLOPE
SLOPED
SLOPES
SLOSH
SLOSHY
SLOTH
SLOTHS

SLOVE
SLOVEN
SLOYD
SLOYDS
SLUBB
SLUBBS
SLUBBY
SLUIT
SLUITS
SLUMP
SLUMPS
SLUMPY
SLURB
SLURBS
SLURP
SLURPS
SLUSE
SLUSES
SLUSH
SLUSHY
SLYPE
SLYPES
SMACK
SMACKS
SMAIK
SMAIKS
SMALL
SMALLS
SMALM
SMALMS
SMALMY
SMALT
SMALTI
SMALTO
SMALTS
SMARM
SMARMS
SMARMY
SMART
SMARTS
SMARTY
SMEAR
ASMEAR
SMEARS
SMEARY
SMEEK
SMEEKS
SMELL
SMELLS
SMELLY
SMELT
SMELTS
SMILE
SMILED
SMILER
SMILES
SMILET
SMIRK
SMIRKS
SMIRKY
SMIRR
SMIRRS
SMIRRY
SMITE
SMITER
SMITES
SMITH
SMITHS
SMITHY
SMOCK

SMOCKS
SMOKE
SMOKED
SMOKER
SMOKES
SMOKO
SMOKOS
SMOLT
SMOLTS
SMOOR
SMOORS
SMOOT
SMOOTH
SMOOTS
SMORE
SMORED
SMORES
SMOUT
SMOUTS
SMOWT
SMOWTS
SNACK
SNACKS
SNAFU
SNAFUS
SNAIL
SNAILS
SNAILY
SNAKE
SNAKED
SNAKES
SNARE
SNARED
SNARER
SNARES
SNARK
SNARKS
SNARL
SNARLS
SNARLY
SNATH
SNATHE
SNATHS
SNEAD
SNEADS
SNEAK
SNEAKS
SNEAKY
SNEAP
SNEAPS
SNECK
SNECKS
SNEER
SNEERS
SNEERY
SNEES
SNEESH
SNELL
SNELLS
SNELLY
SNICK
SNICKS
SNIDE
SNIDER
SNIDES
SNIFF
SNIFFS
SNIFFY
SNIFT
SNIFTS

SNIFTY
SNIPE
SNIPED
SNIPER
SNIPES
SNIRT
SNIRTS
SNOEK
SNOEKS
SNOKE
SNOKED
SNOKES
SNOOD
SNOODS
SNOOK
SNOOKS
SNOOL
SNOOLS
SNOOP
SNOOPS
SNOOPY
SNOOT
SNOOTS
SNOOTY
SNORE
SNORED
SNORER
SNORES
SNORT
SNORTS
SNORTY
SNOUT
SNOUTS
SNOUTY
SNOWK
SNOWKS
SNUFF
SNUFFS
SNUFFY
SOARE
SOARED
SOARER
SOARES
SOBER
SOBERS
SOCLE
SOCLES
SOFAR
SOFARS
SOFTA
SOFTAS
SOGER
SOGERS
SOKAH
SOKAHS
SOKEN
SOKENS
SOLAH
SOLAHS
SOLAN
SOLANO
SOLANS
SOLAR
SOLARS
SOLDE
SOLDER
SOLDES
SOLER
SOLERA
SOLERS

SOLID
SOLIDI
SOLIDS
SOLUM
SOLUMS
SOLVE
SOLVED
SOLVER
SOLVES
SOMAN
SOMANS
SONAR
SONARS
SONCE
SONCES
SONDE
SONDES
SONIC
SONICS
SONNE
SONNES
SONNET
SONSE
SONSES
SOOLE
SOOLED
SOOLES
SOOTE
SOOTED
SOOTES
SOOTH
SOOTHE
SOOTHS
SOPOR
SOPORS
SORAS
PSORAS
SOREE
SOREES
SOREL
SORELL
SORELS
SORELY
SORES
SOREST
SORGO
SORGOS
SORRA
SORRAS
SOUCE
SOUCED
SOUCES
SOUGH
SOUGHS
SOUGHT
SOUND
SOUNDS
SOURS
SOURSE
SOUSE
SOUSED
SOUSES
SOUTH
SOUTHS
SOWAR
SOWARS
SOWCE
SOWCED
SOWCES
SOWER

SOWERS
SOWFF
SOWFFS
SOWLE
SOWLED
SOWLES
SOWND
SOWNDS
SOWNE
SOWNES
SOWSE
SOWSED
SOWSES
SOWTH
SOWTHS
SOYLE
SOYLES
SPACE
SPACED
SPACER
SPACES
SPACEY
SPADE
SPADED
SPADER
SPADES
SPADO
SPADOS
SPAER
SPAERS
SPAHI
SPAHIS
SPAIN
SPAING
SPAINS
SPALD
SPALDS
SPALE
SPALES
SPALL
SPALLE
SPALLS
SPALT
SPALTS
SPANE
SPANED
SPANES
SPANG
SPANGS
SPANK
SPANKS
SPARE
SPARED
SPARER
SPARES
SPARK
SPARKE
SPARKS
SPARKY
SPARS
SPARSE
SPART
SPARTH
SPARTS
SPASM
SPASMS
SPATE
SPATES
SPAUL
SPAULD

SPAULS
SPAWL
SPAWLS
SPAWN
SPAWNS
SPAWNY
SPAYD
SPAYDS
SPEAK
SPEAKS
SPEAL
SPEALS
SPEAN
SPEANS
SPEAR
SPEARS
SPEARY
SPEAT
SPEATS
SPECK
SPECKS
SPECKY
SPEED
SPEEDO
SPEEDS
SPEEDY
SPEEL
SPEELS
SPEER
SPEERS
SPEIR
SPEIRS
SPELD
SPELDS
SPELK
SPELKS
SPELL
SPELLS
SPELT
SPELTS
SPEND
SPENDS
SPERM
SPERMS
SPIAL
ESPIAL
SPIALS
SPICA
SPICAE
SPICAS
SPICE
SPICED
SPICER
SPICES
SPICK
ASPICK
SPICKS
SPICS
ASPICS
SPIDE
SPIDER
SPIED
ESPIED
SPIEL
SPIELS
SPIES
ESPIES
SPIFF
SPIFFY
SPIKE

SPIKED
SPIKES
SPILE
SPILED
SPILES
SPILL
SPILLS
SPILT
SPILTH
SPINA
SPINAE
SPINAL
SPINAR
SPINAS
SPINE
ASPINE
SPINED
SPINEL
SPINES
SPINET
SPINK
SPINKS
SPIRE
ASPIRE
SPIREA
SPIRED
SPIRES
SPIRT
SPIRTS
SPITE
SPITED
SPITES
SPLAT
SPLATS
SPLAY
SPLAYS
SPLIT
SPLITS
SPODE
SPODES
SPOIL
SPOILS
SPOILT
SPOKE
SPOKEN
SPOKES
SPOOF
SPOOFS
SPOOK
SPOOKS
SPOOKY
SPOOL
SPOOLS
SPOOM
SPOOMS
SPOON
SPOONS
SPOONY
SPOOR
SPOORS
SPOOT
SPOOTS
SPORE
SPORES
SPORT
ASPORT
SPORTS
SPORTY
SPOSH
SPOSHY

SPOUT
ASPOUT
SPOUTS
SPOUTY
SPRAG
SPRAGS
SPRAT
SPRATS
SPRAY
SPRAYS
SPRED
SPREDD
SPREDS
SPREE
SPREED
SPREES
SPREW
SPREWS
SPRIG
SPRIGS
SPRIT
ESPRIT
SPRITE
SPRITS
SPROD
SPRODS
SPROG
SPROGS
SPRUE
SPRUES
SPRUG
SPRUGS
SPULE
SPULES
SPUME
SPUMED
SPUMES
SPUNK
SPUNKS
SPUNKY
SPURN
SPURNE
SPURNS
SPURT
SPURTS
SPYAL
SPYALS
SPYRE
SPYRES
SQUAB
SQUABS
SQUAD
SQUADS
SQUAT
ASQUAT
SQUATS
SQUAW
SQUAWK
SQUAWS
SQUEG
SQUEGS
SQUIB
SQUIBS
SQUID
SQUIDS
SQUIT
SQUITS
STACK
STACKS
STADE

STADES
STAFF
STAFFS
STAGE
STAGED
STAGER
STAGES
STAGEY
STAIG
STAIGS
STAIN
STAINS
STAIR
STAIRS
STAKE
STAKED
STAKES
STALE
STALED
STALER
STALES
STALK
STALKO
STALKS
STALKY
STALL
STALLS
STAMP
STAMPS
STAND
STANDS
STANE
STANED
STANES
STANG
STANGS
STANK
STANKS
STAPH
STAPHS
STARE
ASTARE
STARED
STARER
STARES
STARK
STARKS
STARN
STARNS
STARR
STARRS
STARRY
START
ASTART
STARTS
STATE
ESTATE
STATED
STATER
STATES
STAVE
STAVED
STAVES
STEAD
STEADS
STEADY
STEAK
STEAKS
STEAL
OSTEAL

STEALE
STEALS
STEALT
STEAM
STEAMS
STEAMY
STEAN
STEANE
STEANS
STEAR
STEARD
STEARE
STEARS
STEDD
STEDDE
STEDDS
STEDDY
STEDE
STEDED
STEDES
STEED
STEEDS
STEEDY
STEEK
STEEKS
STEEL
STEELD
STEELS
STEELY
STEEM
ESTEEM
STEEMS
STEEN
STEENS
STEEP
STEEPS
STEEPY
STEER
STEERS
STEERY
STEIL
STEILS
STEIN
STEINS
STELA
STELAE
STELAR
STELE
STELES
STELL
STELLS
STEME
STEMED
STEMES
STEND
STENDS
STENT
OSTENT
STENTS
STERE
STEREO
STERES
STERN
ASTERN
STERNA
STERNS
STICH
STICHS
STICK
STICKS

STICKY
STIFF
STIFFS
STILB
STILBS
STILE
STILED
STILES
STILET
STILL
STILLS
STILLY
STILT
STILTS
STILTY
STIME
STIMED
STIMES
STING
STINGO
STINGS
STINGY
STINK
STINKO
STINKS
STINT
STINTS
STINTY
STIPA
STIPAS
STIPE
STIPEL
STIPES
STIRE
STIRED
STIRES
STIRK
STIRKS
STIRP
STIRPS
STIVE
STIVED
STIVER
STIVES
STOAT
STOATS
STOCK
STOCKS
STOCKY
STOEP
STOEPS
STOIC
STOICS
STOIT
STOITS
STOKE
STOKED
STOKER
STOKES
STOLE
STOLED
STOLEN
STOLES
STOMA
STOMAL
STOMP
STOMPS
STOND
STONDS
STONE

ASTONE
STONED
STONEN
STONER
STONES
STONK
STONKS
STONN
STONNE
STONNS
STONY
ASTONY
STOOK
STOOKS
STOOL
STOOLS
STOOP
ASTOOP
STOOPE
STOOPS
STOOR
STOORS
STOPE
STOPED
STOPES
STOPS
ESTOPS
STORE
STORED
STORER
STORES
STOREY
STORK
STORKS
STORM
STORMS
STORMY
STOUN
STOUND
STOUNS
STOUP
STOUPS
STOUR
STOURS
STOURY
STOUT
STOUTH
STOUTS
STOVE
STOVED
STOVER
STOVES
STOWN
STOWND
STRAD
STRADS
STRAE
STRAES
STRAP
STRAPS
STRAW
STRAWN
STRAWS
STRAWY
STRAY
ASTRAY
ESTRAY
STRAYS
STREP
STREPS

STREW
STREWN
STREWS
STRIA
STRIAE
STRIG
STRIGA
STRIGS
STRIP
STRIPE
STRIPS
STRIPY
STROP
STROPS
STROW
STROWN
STROWS
STROY
STROYS
STRUM
ESTRUM
STRUMA
STRUMS
STRUT
ASTRUT
STRUTS
STUCK
STUCKS
STUFF
STUFFS
STUFFY
STULL
STULLS
STULM
STULMS
STUMP
STUMPS
STUMPY
STUNS
ASTUNS
STUNT
STUNTS
STUPA
STUPAS
STUPE
STUPED
STUPES
STURT
STURTS
STYLE
STYLED
STYLES
STYLET
STYLO
STYLOS
STYME
STYMED
STYMES
STYRE
STYRED
STYRES
STYTE
STYTED
STYTES
SUAVE
SUAVER
SUBAH
SUBAHS
SUBER
SUBERS

SUCRE
SUCRES
SUDOR
SUDORS
SUEDE
SUEDED
SUEDES
SUGAR
SUGARS
SUGARY
SUING
SUINGS
SUINT
SUINTS
SUITE
SUITED
SUITES
SUJEE
SUJEES
SULFA
SULFAS
SUMAC
SUMACH
SUMACS
SUMMA
SUMMAE
SUMMAR
SUMMAT
SUMPH
SUMPHS
SUNUP
SUNUPS
SUPER
SUPERB
SUPERS
SURAH
SURAHS
SURAT
SURATS
SURED
USURED
SURER
USURER
SURES
USURES
SUREST
SURGE
SURGED
SURGES
SURRA
SURRAS
SUSHI
SUSHIS
SUTOR
SUTORS
SUTRA
SUTRAS
SWAGE
SWAGED
SWAGES
SWAIN
SWAINS
SWALE
SWALED
SWALES
SWAMI
SWAMIS
SWAMP
SWAMPS
SWAMPY

SWANK
SWANKS
SWANKY
SWARD
USWARD
SWARDS
SWARDY
SWARF
SWARFS
SWARM
ASWARM
SWARMS
SWART
SWARTH
SWARTY
SWASH
SWASHY
SWATH
SWATHE
SWATHS
SWATHY
SWAYL
SWAYLS
SWEAL
SWEALS
SWEAR
SWEARD
SWEARS
SWEAT
SWEATS
SWEATY
SWEDE
SWEDES
SWEEL
SWEELS
SWEEP
SWEEPS
SWEEPY
SWEER
SWEERT
SWEET
SWEETS
SWEETY
SWEIR
SWEIRT
SWELL
SWELLS
SWELT
SWELTS
SWERF
SWERFS
SWIFT
SWIFTS
SWILL
SWILLS
SWING
ASWING
SWINGE
SWINGS
SWINGY
SWINK
SWINKS
SWIPE
SWIPED
SWIPER
SWIPES
SWIPEY
SWIRE
SWIRES
SWIRL

ASWIRL SWIRLS SWIRLY **SWISH** SWISHY **SWIVE** SWIVED SWIVEL SWIVES SWIVET **SWONE** SWONES **SWOON** ASWOON SWOONS **SWOOP** SWOOPS **SWORD** SWORDS **SWOUN** SWOUND SWOUNE SWOUNS **SYBBE** SYBBES **SYBIL** SYBILS **SYBOE** SYBOES **SYBOW** SYBOWS **SYCEE** SYCEES **SYLPH** SYLPHS SYLPHY **SYLVA** SYLVAE SYLVAN SYLVAS **SYMAR** SYMARS **SYNCH** SYNCHS **SYNOD** SYNODS **SYNTH** SYNTHS **SYRAH** SYRAHS **SYREN** SYRENS **SYRUP** SYRUPS SYRUPY **SYSOP** SYSOPS **SYTHE** SYTHES **SYVER** SYVERS **TABLA** TABLAS **TABLE** STABLE TABLED TABLES TABLET **TABOO** TABOOS

TABOR TABORS **TABUN** TABUNS **TACAN** TACANS **TACHE** TACHES **TACHO** TACHOS **TACKS** STACKS **TAFIA** TAFIAS **TAIGA** TAIGAS **TAINT** TAINTS **TAIRA** TAIRAS **TAKER** TAKERS **TAKES** STAKES **TAKHI** TAKHIS **TAKIN** TAKING TAKINS **TALAK** TALAKS **TALAQ** TALAQS **TALAR** TALARS **TALEA** TALEAE **TALER** STALER TALERS **TALES** STALES **TALKS** STALKS **TALKY** STALKY **TALMA** TALMAS **TALON** ETALON TALONS **TALPA** TALPAE TALPAS **TALUK** TALUKA TALUKS **TAMAL** TAMALE TAMALS **TAMER** TAMERS **TAMES** TAMEST **TAMIN** TAMINE TAMING TAMINS **TAMIS** TAMISE

TAMPS STAMPS **TANGA** TANGAS **TANGI** TANGIE TANGIS **TANGO** TANGOS **TANGS** STANGS **TANKA** TANKAS **TANKS** STANKS **TANNA** TANNAH TANNAS **TAPER** TAPERS **TAPES** ETAPES STAPES **TAPET** TAPETA TAPETI TAPETS **TAPIR** TAPIRS **TAPIS** TAPIST **TAPPA** TAPPAS **TARED** STARED **TARES** STARES **TARGE** TARGED TARGES TARGET **TARNS** STARNS **TAROC** TAROCS **TAROK** TAROKS **TAROT** TAROTS **TARRE** TARRED TARRES **TARRY** STARRY **TARSI** TARSIA **TARTS** STARTS **TASAR** TASARS **TASER** TASERS **TASSE** TASSEL TASSES TASSET **TASTE** TASTED TASTER TASTES

TATER STATER TATERS **TATES** STATES **TATIE** TATIES **TATOU** TATOUS **TATUS** STATUS **TAUBE** TAUBES **TAUNT** TAUNTS **TAUPE** TAUPES **TAVAH** TAVAHS **TAVER** TAVERN TAVERS TAVERT **TAWED** STAWED **TAWER** TAWERS TAWERY **TAWSE** TAWSES **TAXER** TAXERS **TAXOL** TAXOLS **TAXOR** TAXORS **TAYRA** TAYRAS **TAZZA** TAZZAS **TEADE** TEADES **TEADS** STEADS **TEAKS** STEAKS **TEALS** STEALS **TEAMS** STEAMS **TEARS** STEARS **TEASE** TEASED TEASEL TEASER TEASES **TEAZE** TEAZED TEAZEL TEAZES **TEDDY** STEDDY **TEELS** STEELS **TEEMS** STEEMS **TEEND** TEENDS **TEENE**

TEENED TEENES **TEENS** STEENS TEENSY **TEERS** STEERS **TEETH** TEETHE **TEILS** STEILS **TEIND** TEINDS **TELAE** STELAE **TELIA** TELIAL **TELLS** STELLS **TEMED** ITEMED STEMED **TEMES** STEMES **TEMPO** TEMPOS **TEMPT** TEMPTS **TEMSE** TEMSED TEMSES **TENCH** STENCH **TENDS** STENDS **TENES** CTENES **TENET** TENETS **TENIA** TENIAE TENIAS **TENNE** TENNER TENNES **TENNO** TENNOS **TENON** TENONS **TENOR** TENORS **TENSE** TENSED TENSER TENSES **TENTH** TENTHS **TENTS** STENTS **TENUE** TENUES **TEPAL** TEPALS **TEPEE** TEPEES **TERAI** TERAIS **TERCE** TERCEL TERCES

TERCET **TEREK** TEREKS **TERES** STERES **TERFE** TERFES **TERGA** TERGAL **TERNE** ETERNE TERNED TERNES **TERNS** STERNS **TERRA** TERRAE TERRAS **TERSE** TERSER **TESLA** TESLAS **TESTA** TESTAE **TESTE** TESTED TESTEE TESTER TESTES **TETRA** TETRAD TETRAS **TEWED** STEWED **TEWEL** TEWELS **TEWIT** TEWITS **THACK** THACKS **THAGI** THAGIS **THANA** THANAH THANAS **THANE** ETHANE THANES **THANK** THANKS **THECA** THECAE THECAL **THEEK** THEEKS **THEFT** THEFTS **THEGN** THEGNS **THEIC** THEICS **THEIR** THEIRS **THEME** THEMED THEMES **THEOW** THEOWS **THERE** THERES

THERM THERMS **THESE** THESES **THETA** THETAS **THETE** THETES **THICK** THICKO THICKS THICKY **THIGH** THIGHS **THILL** THILLS **THING** THINGS THINGY **THINK** THINKS **THIOL** THIOLS **THIRD** THIRDS **THIRL** THIRLS **THOFT** THOFTS **THOLE** THOLED THOLES **THONG** THONGS **THORN** THORNS THORNY **THORP** THORPE THORPS **THOWL** THOWLS **THRAW** THRAWN THRAWS **THREE** THREEP THREES **THRID** THRIDS **THROB** ATHROB THROBS **THROE** THROED THROES **THROW** THROWE THROWN THROWS **THRUM** THRUMS **THUJA** THUJAS **THUMB** THUMBS THUMBY **THUMP** THUMPS **THUYA**

THUYAS **THYME** THYMES **THYMI** THYMIC **TIARA** TIARAS **TIBIA** TIBIAE TIBIAL TIBIAS **TICAL** TICALS **TICKS** STICKS **TICKY** STICKY **TIFFS** STIFFS **TIGER** TIGERS TIGERY **TIGHT** TIGHTS **TIGON** TIGONS **TILDE** TILDES **TILED** STILED **TILER** TILERS TILERY **TILES** STILES **TILLS** STILLS **TILLY** STILLY **TILTH** TILTHS **TILTS** STILTS **TIMBO** TIMBOS **TIMED** STIMED **TIMER** TIMERS **TIMES** STIMES **TIMON** TIMONS **TINCT** TINCTS **TINEA** TINEAL TINEAS **TINGE** TINGED TINGES **TINGS** STINGS **TINKS** STINKS **TINTS** STINTS **TINTY** STINTY **TIRED**

STIRED **TIRES** STIRES **TITAN** TITANS **TITCH** STITCH TITCHY **TITER** TITERS **TITHE** TITHED TITHER TITHES **TITIS** OTITIS **TITLE** TITLED TITLER TITLES **TITRE** TITRES **TITUP** TITUPS TITUPY **TOAST** TOASTS TOASTY **TOAZE** TOAZED TOAZES **TOCKS** STOCKS **TODAY** TODAYS **TODDE** TODDED TODDES **TOGUE** TOGUES **TOILE** ETOILE TOILED TOILER TOILES TOILET **TOISE** TOISES **TOKAY** TOKAYS **TOKED** STOKED **TOKEN** TOKENS **TOKES** ATOKES STOKES **TOLED** STOLED **TOLES** STOLES **TOLLS** ATOLLS **TOMAN** TOMANS **TOMIA** TOMIAL **TONAL** ATONAL **TONDO**

TONDOS
TONED
ATONED
STONED
TONER
ATONER
STONER
TONERS
TONES
ATONES
STONES
TONGA
TONGAS
TONIC
ATONIC
TONICS
TONKS
STONKS
TONNE
STONNE
TONNES
TOOLS
STOOLS
TOOTH
TOOTHS
TOOTHY
TOOTS
TOOTSY
TOPED
STOPED
TOPEE
TOPEES
TOPEK
TOPEKS
TOPER
TOPERS
TOPES
STOPES
TOPIC
ATOPIC
TOPICS
TOQUE
TOQUES
TORAN
TORANA
TORANS
TORES
STORES
TORSE
TORSEL
TORSES
TORSK
TORSKS
TORSO
TORSOS
TORTE
TORTEN
TORTES
TOSES
PTOSES
TOTAL
TOTALS
TOTEM
TOTEMS
TOUCH
TOUCHE
TOUCHY
TOUGH
TOUGHS
TOUNS
STOUNS
TOURS
STOURS
TOUSE
TOUSED
TOUSER
TOUSES
TOUTS
STOUTS
TOUZE
TOUZED
TOUZES
TOWED
STOWED
TOWEL
TOWELS
TOWER
STOWER
TOWERS
TOWERY
TOWSE
TOWSED
TOWSER
TOWSES
TOWZE
TOWZED
TOWZES
TOXIN
TOXINS
TOYER
TOYERS
TOZIE
TOZIES
TRACE
TRACED
TRACER
TRACES
TRACK
TRACKS
TRACT
TRACTS
TRADE
TRADED
TRADER
TRADES
TRADS
STRADS
TRAGI
TRAGIC
TRAIK
STRAIK
TRAIKS
TRAIL
TRAILS
TRAIN
STRAIN
TRAINS
TRAIT
STRAIT
TRAITS
TRAMP
STRAMP
TRAMPS
TRANT
TRANTS
TRAPE
TRAPED
TRAPES
TRAPS
STRAPS
TRASH
TRASHY
TRASS
STRASS
TRATT
TRATTS
TRAVE
TRAVEL
TRAVES
TRAWL
TRAWLS
TRAYS
STRAYS
TREAD
TREADS
TREAT
TREATS
TREATY
TRECK
TRECKS
TREEN
TREENS
TREMA
TREMAS
TREND
TRENDS
TRENDY
TRESS
STRESS
TRESSY
TREST
TRESTS
TREWS
STREWS
TRIAD
TRIADS
TRIAL
ATRIAL
TRIALS
TRIBE
TRIBES
TRICE
TRICED
TRICES
TRICK
TRICKS
TRICKY
TRIDE
STRIDE
TRIER
ETRIER
TRIERS
TRIGS
STRIGS
TRIKE
STRIKE
TRIKED
TRIKES
TRILL
TRILLO
TRILLS
TRINE
TRINED
TRINES
TRIOR
TRIORS
TRIPE
STRIPE
TRIPES
TRIPEY
TRIPS
STRIPS
TRIPY
STRIPY
TRIST
TRISTE
TRITE
TRITER
TRITES
TROAD
TROADE
TROADS
TROAT
TROATS
TROCK
TROCKS
TRODE
STRODE
TRODES
TROKE
STROKE
TROKED
TROKES
TROLL
STROLL
TROLLS
TROLLY
TROMP
TROMPE
TROMPS
TRONA
TRONAS
TRONC
TRONCS
TRONE
TRONES
TROOP
TROOPS
TROPE
TROPED
TROPES
TROTH
TROTHS
TROUT
STROUT
TROUTS
TROUTY
TROWS
STROWS
TROYS
STROYS
TRUCE
TRUCES
TRUCK
STRUCK
TRUCKS
TRUES
TRUEST
TRULL
TRULLS
TRUMP
TRUMPS
TRUNK
TRUNKS
TRUST
TRUSTS
TRUSTY
TRUTH
TRUTHS
TRUTHY
TRYER
TRYERS
TRYST
TRYSTS
TSUBA
TSUBAS
TUART
TUARTS
TUATH
TUATHS
TUBBY
STUBBY
TUBER
TUBERS
TUCKS
STUCKS
TUFFE
TUFFES
TUFFET
TUFFS
STUFFS
TUGRA
TUGRAS
TUISM
TUISMS
TULIP
TULIPS
TULLE
TULLES
TUMOR
TUMORS
TUMPS
STUMPS
TUMPY
STUMPY
TUNER
TUNERS
TUNIC
TUNICS
TUPEK
TUPEKS
TUPIK
TUPIKS
TUQUE
TUQUES
TURBO
TURBOS
TURBOT
TURME
TURMES
TUTEE
TUTEES
TUTOR
TUTORS
TUTTI
TUTTIS
TWAIN
ATWAIN
TWAINS
TWANG
TWANGS
TWANGY
TWANK
TWANKS
TWEAK
TWEAKS
TWEED
TWEEDS
TWEEDY
TWEEL
ATWEEL
TWEELS
TWEELY
TWEER
TWEERS
TWEET
TWEETS
TWERP
TWERPS
TWICE
TWICER
TWIER
TWIERS
TWILL
TWILLS
TWILLY
TWILT
TWILTS
TWINE
TWINED
TWINER
TWINES
TWINK
TWINKS
TWIRE
TWIRED
TWIRES
TWIRL
TWIRLS
TWIRLY
TWIRP
TWIRPS
TWIST
TWISTS
TWISTY
TWITE
TWITES
TWOER
TWOERS
TWYER
TWYERE
TWYERS
TYING
STYING
TYLER
TYLERS
TYPIC
ETYPIC
TYPTO
TYPTOS
TYRAN
TYRANS
TYRANT
TYRED
STYRED
TYRES
STYRES
TYTHE
TYTHED
TYTHES
UDDER
DUDDER
JUDDER
MUDDER
PUDDER
RUDDER
SUDDER
UDDERS
UGGED
BUGGED
FUGGED
HUGGED
JUGGED
LUGGED
MUGGED
PUGGED
RUGGED
TUGGED
UHLAN
UHLANS
UHURU
UHURUS
UKASE
UKASES
ULCER
ULCERS
ULEMA
ULEMAS
ULMIN
ULMINS
ULNAR
ULNARE
ULTRA
ULTRAS
ULVAS
VULVAS
ULYIE
ULYIES
ULZIE
ULZIES
UMBEL
UMBELS
UMBER
CUMBER
DUMBER
LUMBER
NUMBER
UMBERS
UMBERY
UMBOS
BUMBOS
DUMBOS
GUMBOS
JUMBOS
RUMBOS
UMBRA
UMBRAE
UMBRAL
UMBRAS
UMBRE
UMBREL
UMBRES
UMIAK
UMIAKS
UMPTY
HUMPTY
NUMPTY
UNARM
UNARMS
UNBAG
UNBAGS
UNBAR
UNBARE
UNBARK
UNBARS
UNBED
SUNBED
UNBEDS
UNCAP
UNCAPE
UNCAPS
UNCES
BUNCES
DUNCES
OUNCES
PUNCES
UNCLE
NUNCLE
UNCLED
UNCLES
UNCLEW
UNCOS
BUNCOS
JUNCOS
UNCUS
JUNCUS
UNDAM
UNDAMS
UNDER
DUNDER
FUNDER
SUNDER
UNDERN
UNFIT
UNFITS
UNGAG
UNGAGS
UNGET
UNGETS
UNGOD
UNGODS
UNGUM
UNGUMS
UNHAT
SUNHAT
UNHATS
UNIFY
MUNIFY
UNION
BUNION
UNIONS
UNITE
DUNITE
GUNITE
MUNITE
UNITED
UNITER
UNITES
UNKED
BUNKED
DUNKED
FUNKED
JUNKED
UNKET
JUNKET
SUNKET
UNLAW
UNLAWS
UNLAY
UNLAYS
UNLET
RUNLET
UNLID
UNLIDS
UNLIT
SUNLIT
UNMAN
GUNMAN
UNMANS
UNMEW
UNMEWS
UNPAY
UNPAYS
UNPEG
UNPEGS
UNPEN
UNPENS
UNPENT
UNPIN
UNPINS
UNRED
UNREDY
UNRIG
RUNRIG
UNRIGS
UNRIP
UNRIPE
UNRIPS
UNSAY
UNSAYS
UNSET
SUNSET
UNSETS
UNSEW
UNSEWN
UNSEWS
UNTIE
AUNTIE
UNTIED
UNTIES
UNTIL
UNTILE
UNTIN
MUNTIN
UNTINS
UNWIT
UNWITS
UNWON
UNWONT
UNZIP
UNZIPS
UPEND
UPENDS
UPJET
UPJETS
UPLAY
UPLAYS
UPPED
CUPPED
DUPPED
HUPPED
PUPPED
SUPPED
TUPPED
UPPER
CUPPER
SUPPER
UPPERS
UPRUN
UPRUNS
UPSEE
UPSEES
UPSET
UPSETS
UPSEY
UPSEYS
UPTAK
UPTAKE
UPTAKS
UPTIE

UPTIED
UPTIES
URALI
OURALI
URALIS
URARI
CURARI
OURARI
URARIS
URATE
AURATE
CURATE
URATES
URBAN
TURBAN
URBANE
URENA
MURENA
URENAS
URGED
PURGED
SURGED
URGER
BURGER
PURGER
URGERS
URGES
GURGES
PURGES
SURGES
URIAL
BURIAL
URIALS
URINE
MURINE
PURINE
URINED
URINES
URITE
URITES
URMAN
URMANS
URNED
BURNED
GURNED
TURNED
URSON
URSONS
URUBU
URUBUS
URVAS
MURVAS
USAGE
USAGER
USAGES
USERS
MUSERS
USHER
GUSHER
HUSHER
LUSHER
MUSHER
PUSHER
RUSHER
USHERS
USING
BUSING
FUSING
MUSING
USNEA
USNEAS
USUAL
USUALS
USURE
USURED
USURER
USURES
USURP
USURPS
UTILE
FUTILE
RUTILE
SUTILE
UTTER
BUTTER
CUTTER
GUTTER
MUTTER
NUTTER
PUTTER
RUTTER
UTTERS
UVULA
UVULAE
UVULAR
UVULAS
VADED
EVADED
VADES
EVADES
VAGUE
VAGUED
VAGUER
VAGUES
VAILS
AVAILS
VAKIL
VAKILS
VALES
AVALES
VALET
VALETA
VALETE
VALETS
VALIS
VALISE
VALOR
VALORS
VALSE
VALSED
VALSES
VALUE
VALUED
VALUER
VALUES
VALVE
VALVED
VALVES
VAPOR
VAPORS
VARAN
VARANS
VAREC
VARECH
VARECS
VARNA
VARNAS
VARVE
VARVED
VARVEL
VARVES
VAULT
VAULTS
VAULTY
VAUNT
AVAUNT
VAUNTS
VAUNTY
VAUTE
VAUTED
VAUTES
VAWTE
VAWTED
VAWTES
VEALE
VEALER
VEALES
VEENA
VEENAS
VEGAN
VEGANS
VEGIE
VEGIES
VELAR
VELARS
VELDT
VELDTS
VENEY
VENEYS
VENGE
AVENGE
VENGED
VENGER
VENGES
VENIN
VENINS
VENOM
VENOMS
VENTS
EVENTS
VENUE
AVENUE
VENUES
VERGE
VERGED
VERGER
VERGES
VERSE
AVERSE
VERSED
VERSER
VERSES
VERSET
VERSO
VERSOS
VERST
VERSTS
VERTS
AVERTS
EVERTS
VERTU
VERTUE
VERTUS
VERVE
VERVEL
VERVEN
VERVES
VERVET
VESPA
VESPAS
VESTA
VESTAL
VESTAS
VETCH
KVETCH
VETCHY
VEXER
VEXERS
VEZIR
VEZIRS
VIAND
VIANDS
VICAR
VICARS
VICARY
VIDEO
VIDEOS
VIFDA
VIFDAS
VIGIA
VIGIAS
VIGIL
VIGILS
VIGOR
VIGORO
VIGORS
VILLA
VILLAN
VILLAR
VILLAS
VINCA
VINCAS
VINER
VINERS
VINERY
VINEW
VINEWS
VINYL
VINYLS
VIOLA
VIOLAS
VIPER
VIPERS
VIREO
VIREOS
VIRGA
VIRGAS
VIRGE
VIRGER
VIRGES
VIRTU
VIRTUE
VIRTUS
VISED
AVISED
VISES
AVISES
VISIE
VISIED
VISIER
VISIES
VISIT
VISITE
VISITS
VISNE
VISNES
VISON
VISONS
VISOR
VISORS
VISTA
VISTAL
VISTAS
VISTO
VISTOS
VITAL
AVITAL
VITALS
VITTA
VITTAE
VIVAT
VIVATS
VIVDA
VIVDAS
VIVER
VIVERS
VIXEN
VIXENS
VIZIR
VIZIRS
VIZOR
VIZORS
VOCAB
VOCABS
VOCAL
VOCALS
VODKA
VODKAS
VOGIE
VOGIER
VOGUE
VOGUED
VOGUER
VOGUES
VOGUEY
VOICE
VOICED
VOICER
VOICES
VOIDS
AVOIDS
OVOIDS
VOILE
VOILES
VOLAR
VOLARY
VOLET
VOLETS
VOLTE
VOLTES
VOLVA
VOLVAS
VOLVE
EVOLVE
VOLVED
VOLVES
VOMER
VOMERS
VOMIT
VOMITO
VOMITS
VOTER
VOTERS
VOUCH
AVOUCH
VOUGE
VOUGES
VOWED
AVOWED
VOWEL
VOWELS
VOWER
AVOWER
VOWERS
VOZHD
VOZHDS
VRAIC
VRAICS
VROOM
VROOMS
VROUW
VROUWS
VULVA
VULVAE
VULVAL
VULVAR
VULVAS
WACKE
WACKER
WACKES
WADDY
SWADDY
WADER
WADERS
WAFER
WAFERS
WAFERY
WAGED
SWAGED
WAGER
WAGERS
WAGES
SWAGES
WAGON
WAGONS
WAHOO
WAHOOS
WAIFT
WAIFTS
WAINS
SWAINS
TWAINS
WAIST
WAISTS
WAITE
TWAITE
WAITED
WAITER
WAITES
WAITS
AWAITS
WAIVE
WAIVED
WAIVER
WAIVES
WAKED
AWAKED
WAKEN
AWAKEN
WAKENS
WAKER
WAKERS
WAKES
AWAKES
WALED
SWALED
WALER
WALERS
WALES
DWALES
SWALES
WALIS
WALISE
WALLA
WALLAH
WALLAS
WANGS
DWANGS
TWANGS
WANKS
SWANKS
TWANKS
WANKY
SWANKY
WANZE
WANZED
WANZES
WARDS
AWARDS
SWARDS
WARMS
SWARMS
WARNS
AWARNS
WARRE
WARRED
WARREN
WARREY
WARTY
SWARTY
WASHY
SWASHY
WASTE
WASTED
WASTEL
WASTER
WASTES
WATAP
WATAPS
WATCH
AWATCH
SWATCH
WATER
WATERS
WATERY
WAUFF
WAUFFS
WAUGH
WAUGHS
WAUGHT
WAULK
WAULKS
WAURS
WAURST
WAVER
WAVERS
WAVERY
WAVEY
WAVEYS
WAXER
WAXERS
WAYED
SWAYED
WAZIR
WAZIRS
WEALD
WEALDS
WEALS
SWEALS
WEAMB
WEAMBS
WEARS
SWEARS
WEARY
AWEARY
WEAVE
WEAVED
WEAVER
WEAVES
WEBER
WEBERS
WECHT
WECHTS
WEDGE
WEDGED
WEDGES
WEEDS
TWEEDS
WEEDY
TWEEDY
WEEKE
WEEKES
WEELS
SWEELS
TWEELS
WEENY
SWEENY
TWEENY
WEEPS
SWEEPS
WEEPY
SWEEPY
WEEST
TWEEST
WEETE
WEETED
WEETEN
WEETER
WEETS
SWEETS
TWEETS
WEFTE
WEFTED
WEFTES
WEIGH
AWEIGH
WEIGHS
WEIGHT
WEIRD
WEIRDO
WEIRDS
WEISE
WEISED
WEISES
WEIZE
WEIZED
WEIZES
WELKE
WELKED
WELKES
WELLS
DWELLS
SWELLS
WELTS
SWELTS
WHACK
WHACKO
WHACKS
WHACKY
WHALE
WHALED
WHALER
WHALES
WHANG
WHANGS
WHARE
WHARES
WHARF
WHARFS
WHATS
WHATSO
WHAUP
WHAUPS
WHAUR
WHAURS
WHEAL
WHEALS
WHEAR
WHEARE
WHEAT
WHEATO
WHEEL
AWHEEL
WHEELS
WHEELY
WHEEN
WHEENS
WHEFT
WHEFTS
WHELK
WHELKS
WHELKY
WHELM
WHELMS
WHELP
WHELPS
WHERE
WHERES
WHIFF
WHIFFS
WHIFFY
WHIFT
WHIFTS
WHILE
AWHILE
WHILED
WHILES
WHIMS
WHIMSY
WHINE
WHINED
WHINER
WHINES
WHIRL
WHIRLS
WHIRLY
WHIRR
WHIRRS
WHIRRY
WHISH
WHISHT
WHISK
WHISKS
WHISKY
WHIST
WHISTS
WHITE
WHITED
WHITEN
WHITER

WHITES
WHITEY
WHOLE
WHOLES
WHOOP
WHOOPS
WHOOT
WHOOTS
WHORE
WHORED
WHORES
WHORL
WHORLS
WHORT
WHORTS
WICCA
WICCAN
WICCAS
WIDEN
WIDENS
WIDES
WIDEST
WIDOW
WIDOWS
WIDTH
WIDTHS
WIELD
WIELDS
WIELDY
WIFIE
WIFIES
WIGAN
WIGANS
WIGHT
TWIGHT
WIGHTS
WILES
DWILES
WILGA
WILGAS
WILJA
WILJAS
WILLS
SWILLS
TWILLS
WILLY
TWILLY
WILTS
TWILTS
WINCE
WINCED
WINCER
WINCES
WINCEY
WINED
DWINED
TWINED
WINES
DWINES
TWINES
WINGE
SWINGE
TWINGE
WINGED
WINGER
WINGES
WINGS
SWINGS
WINGY
SWINGY
WINKS
SWINKS
TWINKS
WINZE
WINZES
WIPED
SWIPED
WIPER
SWIPER
WIPERS
WIPES
SWIPES
WIRED
TWIRED
WIRER
WIRERS
WIRES
SWIRES
TWIRES
WISES
WISEST
WISTS
TWISTS
WITCH
SWITCH
TWITCH
WITCHY
WITES
TWITES
WITHE
WITHED
WITHER
WITHES
WIVED
SWIVED
WIVES
SWIVES
WIZEN
WIZENS
WODGE
WODGES
WOKEN
AWOKEN
WOLVE
WOLVED
WOLVER
WOLVES
WOMAN
WOMANS
WONGA
WONGAS
WONGI
WONGIS
WOODS
WOODSY
WOOER
WOOERS
WOOLD
WOOLDS
WOONS
SWOONS
WOOSH
SWOOSH
WORDS
SWORDS
WORLD
WORLDS
WORSE
WORSED
WORSEN
WORSER
WORSES
WORST
WORSTS
WORTH
WORTHS
WORTHY
WOULD
WOULDS
WOUND
SWOUND
WOUNDS
WOUNDY
WRACK
AWRACK
WRACKS
WRAST
WRASTS
WRATH
WRATHS
WRATHY
WRAWL
WRAWLS
WREAK
WREAKS
WRECK
WRECKS
WREST
WRESTS
WRICK
WRICKS
WRIER
OWRIER
WRIES
WRIEST
WRING
WRINGS
WRIST
WRISTS
WRISTY
WRITE
WRITER
WRITES
WROKE
YWROKE
WROKEN
WRONG
AWRONG
WRONGS
WROOT
WROOTS
WURST
WURSTS
WUSHU
WUSHUS
XEBEC
XEBECS
XENIA
XENIAL
XENIAS
XENON
XENONS
XYLEM
XYLEMS
XYLOL
XYLOLS
XYLYL
XYLYLS
YACCA
YACCAS
YACHT
YACHTS
YAFFS
NYAFFS
YAGER
YAGERS
YAHOO
YAHOOS
YAKKA
YAKKAS
YAKOW
YAKOWS
YAMEN
YAMENS
YANGS
KYANGS
YAPOK
YAPOKS
YAPON
YAPONS
YARFA
YARFAS
YARTA
YARTAS
YARTO
YARTOS
YCLED
CYCLED
YEALM
YEALMS
YEARD
YEARDS
YEARN
YEARNS
YEAST
YEASTS
YEASTY
YENTA
YENTAS
YERBA
YERBAS
YESES
CYESES
OYESES
YIELD
YIELDS
YLEMS
XYLEMS
YOBBO
YOBBOS
YODEL
YODELS
YODLE
YODLED
YODLER
YODLES
YOGIN
YOGINI
YOGINS
YOGIS
YOGISM
YOICK
YOICKS
YOJAN
YOJANA
YOJANS
YOKEL
YOKELS
YOUNG
YOUNGS
YOURT
YOURTS
YOUTH
YOUTHS
YOUTHY
YOWIE
YOWIES
YRNEH
YRNEHS
YUCCA
YUCCAS
YULAN
YULANS
YUPON
YUPONS
ZABRA
ZABRAS
ZAKAT
ZAKATS
ZAMAN
ZAMANG
ZAMANS
ZAMBO
ZAMBOS
ZAMIA
ZAMIAS
ZANJA
ZANJAS
ZANTE
ZANTES
ZANZE
ZANZES
ZEBEC
ZEBECK
ZEBECS
ZEBRA
ZEBRAS
ZEBUB
ZEBUBS
ZERDA
ZERDAS
ZHOMO
ZHOMOS
ZIBET
ZIBETS
ZIGAN
ZIGANS
ZIMBI
ZIMBIS
ZINCO
ZINCOS
ZINEB
ZINEBS
ZINKE
ZINKED
ZINKES
ZIPPO
ZIPPOS
ZIZEL
ZIZELS
ZLOTY
ZLOTYS
ZOCCO
ZOCCOS
ZOISM
ZOISMS
ZOIST
ZOISTS
ZOMBI
ZOMBIE
ZOMBIS
ZONAL
AZONAL
ZONDA
ZONDAS
ZONES
OZONES
ZOOEA
ZOOEAE
ZOOEAL
ZOOEAS
ZOOID
ZOOIDS
ZORIL
ZORILS
ZORRO
ZORROS
ZUPAN
ZUPANS
ZYMES
AZYMES

6-LETTER WORD HOOKS: extensible words only

ABATOR
ABATORS
ABAYAS
KABAYAS
ABDABS
HABDABS
ABDUCE
ABDUCED
ABDUCES
ABDUCT
ABDUCTS
ABELES
KABELES
ABELIA
ABELIAS
ABJECT
ABJECTS
ABJURE
ABJURED
ABJURER
ABJURES
ABLATE
ABLATED
ABLATES
ABLAUT
ABLAUTS
ABLETS
CABLETS
GABLETS
TABLETS
ABLING
CABLING
FABLING
SABLING
TABLING
ABOLLA
ABOLLAE
ABOLLAS
ABOUND
ABOUNDS
ABRADE
ABRADED
ABRADES
ABRAID
ABRAIDS
ABRAZO
ABRAZOS
ABREGE
ABREGES
ABROAD
ABROADS
ABRUPT
ABRUPTS
ABSEIL
ABSEILS
ABSENT
ABSENTS
ABSORB
ABSORBS
ABULIA
ABULIAS
ABUSER
ABUSERS
ABVOLT
ABVOLTS

ABYING
BABYING
ACACIA
ACACIAS
ACAJOU
ACAJOUS
ACANTH
ACANTHA
ACANTHS
ACARID
ACARIDS
ACATER
ACATERS
ACATES
VACATES
ACCEDE
ACCEDED
ACCEDER
ACCEDES
ACCEND
ACCENDS
ACCENT
ACCENTS
ACCEPT
ACCEPTS
ACCITE
ACCITED
ACCITES
ACCLOY
ACCLOYS
ACCOIL
ACCOILS
ACCORD
ACCORDS
ACCOST
ACCOSTS
ACCREW
ACCREWS
ACCRUE
ACCRUED
ACCRUES
ACCUSE
ACCUSED
ACCUSER
ACCUSES
ACEDIA
ACEDIAS
ACETAL
ACETALS
ACETYL
ACETYLS
ACHAGE
ACHAGES
ACHENE
ACHENES
ACHING
BACHING
CACHING
ACHINGS
ACHKAN
ACHKANS
ACKEES
HACKEES
ACKERS
BACKERS

DACKERS
HACKERS
LACKERS
PACKERS
RACKERS
SACKERS
TACKERS
WACKERS
YACKERS
ACKNOW
ACKNOWN
ACKNOWS
ACMITE
ACMITES
ACQUIT
ACQUITE
ACQUITS
ACTING
ACTINGS
ACTION
FACTION
PACTION
TACTION
ACTIONS
ACTIVE
FACTIVE
ACTORS
FACTORS
ACTUAL
FACTUAL
TACTUAL
ACTURE
FACTURE
ACTURES
ACUITY
VACUITY
ACUMEN
ACUMENS
ACUTES
ACUTEST
ADAGIO
ADAGIOS
ADDEEM
ADDEEMS
ADDEND
ADDENDA
ADDENDS
ADDERS
GADDERS
LADDERS
MADDERS
PADDERS
ADDICT
ADDICTS
ADDING
DADDING
GADDING
HADDING
MADDING
PADDING
WADDING
ADDLED
DADDLED
FADDLED
PADDLED

RADDLED
SADDLED
WADDLED
ADDLES
DADDLES
FADDLES
PADDLES
RADDLES
SADDLES
WADDLES
ADDOOM
ADDOOMS
ADDUCE
ADDUCED
ADDUCER
ADDUCES
ADDUCT
ADDUCTS
ADHERE
ADHERED
ADHERER
ADHERES
ADJOIN
ADJOINS
ADJOINT
ADJURE
ADJURED
ADJURES
ADJUST
ADJUSTS
ADLAND
ADLANDS
ADMIRE
ADMIRED
ADMIRER
ADMIRES
ADNOUN
ADNOUNS
ADORER
ADORERS
ADREAD
ADREADS
ADSORB
ADSORBS
ADVENE
ADVENED
ADVENES
ADVENT
ADVENTS
ADVERB
ADVERBS
ADVERT
ADVERTS
ADVICE
ADVICES
ADVISE
ADVISED
ADVISER
ADVISES
ADWARD
ADWARDS
AEDILE
AEDILES
AEMULE
AEMULED

AEMULES
AERATE
AERATED
AERATES
AERIAL
AERIALS
AERIES
FAERIES
AERIEST
AEROBE
AEROBES
AETHER
AETHERS
AFFAIR
AFFAIRE
AFFAIRS
AFFEAR
AFFEARD
AFFEARE
AFFEARS
AFFECT
AFFECTS
AFFEER
AFFEERS
AFFIES
BAFFIES
DAFFIES
TAFFIES
AFFINE
AFFINED
AFFINES
AFFIRM
AFFIRMS
AFFORD
AFFORDS
AFFRAP
AFFRAPS
AFFRAY
AFFRAYS
AFFRET
AFFRETS
AFGHAN
AFGHANS
AFREET
AFREETS
AFTERS
RAFTERS
WAFTERS
AGAMID
AGAMIDS
AGARIC
AGARICS
AGEING
AGEINGS
AGEISM
AGEISMS
AGEIST
AGEISTS
AGENDA
AGENDAS
AGENES
SAGENES
AGGERS
DAGGERS
GAGGERS

JAGGERS
LAGGERS
NAGGERS
SAGGERS
TAGGERS
YAGGERS
AGINGS
PAGINGS
RAGINGS
AGLETS
EAGLETS
HAGLETS
AGNAIL
AGNAILS
AGNAME
AGNAMED
AGNAMES
AGNATE
MAGNATE
AGNATES
AGNISE
AGNISED
AGNISES
AGNIZE
AGNIZED
AGNIZES
AGOGIC
AGOGICS
AGOUTA
AGOUTAS
AGOUTI
AGOUTIS
AGREGE
AGREGES
AGRISE
AGRISED
AGRISES
AGRIZE
AGRIZED
AGRIZES
AGRYZE
AGRYZED
AGRYZES
AGUISE
AGUISED
AGUISES
AGUIZE
AGUIZED
AGUIZES
AHIMSA
AHIMSAS
AIDERS
RAIDERS
AIDING
LAIDING
MAIDING
RAIDING
AIGLET
AIGLETS
AIKIDO
AIKIDOS
AILING
BAILING
FAILING
HAILING

JAILING
MAILING
NAILING
RAILING
SAILING
TAILING
VAILING
WAILING
AIMING
MAIMING
AIRGAP
AIRGAPS
AIRIER
HAIRIER
LAIRIER
VAIRIER
AIRILY
FAIRILY
AIRING
FAIRING
HAIRING
LAIRING
PAIRING
SAIRING
AIRINGS
AIRNED
CAIRNED
AIRWAY
FAIRWAY
AIRWAYS
AJOWAN
AJOWANS
AKEDAH
AKEDAHS
ALALIA
ALALIAS
ALANGS
LALANGS
ALARUM
ALARUMS
ALATED
PALATED
ALBATA
ALBATAS
ALBEDO
ALBEDOS
ALBERT
HALBERT
ALBERTS
ALBINO
ALBINOS
ALBITE
ALBITES
ALBUGO
ALBUGOS
ALCOVE
ALCOVES
ALDOSE
ALDOSES
ALDRIN
ALDRINS
ALEGAR
ALEGARS
ALEGGE
ALEGGED

ALEGGES
ALERCE
ALERCES
ALEVIN
ALEVINS
ALEXIA
ALEXIAS
ALEXIN
ALEXINS
ALGATE
ALGATES
ALIDAD
ALIDADE
ALIDADS
ALIGHT
ALIGHTS
ALIGNS
MALIGNS
ALINES
SALINES
VALINES
ALIPED
TALIPED
ALIPEDS
ALISMA
ALISMAS
ALIYAH
ALIYAHS
ALKALI
ALKALIS
ALKANE
ALKANES
ALKANET
ALKENE
ALKENES
ALKIES
TALKIES
ALKYNE
ALKYNES
ALLEES
MALLEES
SALLEES
ALLEGE
ALLEGED
ALLEGER
ALLEGES
ALLELE
ALLELES
ALLEYS
GALLEYS
VALLEYS
ALLICE
ALLICES
ALLIED
DALLIED
GALLIED
RALLIED
SALLIED
TALLIED
ALLIES
DALLIES
GALLIES
RALLIES
SALLIES
TALLIES

WALLIES
ALLIUM
BALLIUM
GALLIUM
PALLIUM
ALLIUMS
ALLONS
BALLONS
GALLONS
ALLOTS
BALLOTS
TALLOTS
ALLOWS
BALLOWS
CALLOWS
FALLOWS
GALLOWS
HALLOWS
MALLOWS
SALLOWS
TALLOWS
WALLOWS
ALLUDE
ALLUDED
ALLUDES
ALLURE
ALLURED
ALLURER
ALLURES
ALMAIN
ALMAINS
ALMOND
ALMONDS
ALMUCE
ALMUCES
ALNAGE
ALNAGER
ALNAGES
ALOGIA
ALOGIAS
ALPACA
ALPACAS
ALPEEN
ALPEENS
ALPINE
ALPINES
ALSIKE
ALSIKES
ALSOON
ALSOONE
ALTERN
SALTERN
ALTERNE
ALTERS
FALTERS
HALTERS
PALTERS
SALTERS
ALTEZA
ALTEZAS
ALTHEA
ALTHEAS
ALUDEL
ALUDELS
ALUMNA
ALUMNAE
AMADOU
AMADOUS
AMATOL
AMATOLS
AMAZON
AMAZONS
AMBAGE
AMBAGES
AMBERS
CAMBERS
JAMBERS
LAMBERS
TAMBERS
AMBITS
GAMBITS
AMBLED
GAMBLED
HAMBLED
RAMBLED
WAMBLED
AMBLER
GAMBLER
RAMBLER
AMBLERS
AMBLES
GAMBLES
HAMBLES
RAMBLES
WAMBLES
AMELIA
AMELIAS
AMENDE
AMENDED
AMENDER
AMENDES
AMENTA
RAMENTA
AMENTAL
AMENTS
LAMENTS
AMERCE
AMERCED
AMERCES
AMINES
FAMINES
GAMINES
TAMINES
AMISES
CAMISES
KAMISES
TAMISES
AMMONS
GAMMONS
MAMMONS
AMOEBA
AMOEBAE
AMOEBAS
AMOMUM
AMOMUMS
AMOOVE
AMOOVED
AMOOVES
AMORCE
AMORCES
AMORET
AMORETS
AMOUNT
AMOUNTS
AMPERE
AMPERES
AMPLER
SAMPLER
AMPULE
AMPULES
AMRITA
AMRITAS
AMTMAN
AMTMANS
AMULET
AMULETS
AMUSER
AMUSERS
AMUSES
CAMUSES
WAMUSES
AMYLUM
AMYLUMS
AMYTAL
AMYTALS
ANADEM
ANADEMS
ANALLY
BANALLY
ANALOG
ANALOGA
ANALOGS
ANALOGY
ANANAS
BANANAS
MANANAS
ANANKE
ANANKES
ANARCH
ANARCHS
ANARCHY
ANATTA
ANATTAS
ANATTO
ANATTOS
ANCHOR
ANCHORS
ANCOME
ANCOMES
ANEMIA
ANEMIAS
ANGELS
MANGELS
ANGERS
BANGERS
DANGERS
GANGERS
HANGERS
MANGERS
RANGERS
ANGICO
ANGICOS
ANGINA
ANGINAL
ANGINAS
ANGLED
BANGLED
CANGLED
DANGLED
FANGLED
JANGLED
MANGLED
TANGLED
WANGLED
ANGLER
DANGLER
JANGLER
MANGLER
TANGLER
WANGLER
ANGLERS
ANGLES
BANGLES
CANGLES
DANGLES
FANGLES
JANGLES
MANGLES
TANGLES
WANGLES
ANGORA
ANGORAS
ANICUT
ANICUTS
ANIMAL
ANIMALS
ANIONS
FANIONS
ANKERS
BANKERS
CANKERS
HANKERS
JANKERS
RANKERS
TANKERS
WANKERS
YANKERS
ANKLED
FANKLED
RANKLED
ANKLES
FANKLES
RANKLES
ANKLET
ANKLETS
ANLACE
ANLACES
ANLAGE
ANLAGEN
ANLAGES
ANNEAL
ANNEALS
ANNEXE
ANNEXED
ANNEXES
ANNOYS
TANNOYS
ANNUAL
ANNUALS
ANOINT
ANOINTS
ANOMIE
ANOMIES
ANONYM
ANONYMA
ANONYMS
ANORAK
ANORAKS
ANOXIA
ANOXIAS
ANSATE
ANSATED
ANSWER
ANSWERS
ANTARA
TANTARA
ANTARAS
ANTARS
CANTARS
KANTARS
ANTHEM
ANTHEMS
ANTHER
PANTHER
ANTHERS
ANTIAR
ANTIARS
ANTICK
ANTICKE
ANTING
BANTING
CANTING
DANTING
GANTING
KANTING
PANTING
RANTING
WANTING
ANTINGS
ANTLER
PANTLER
ANTLERS
ANTLIA
ANTLIAE
ANTRUM
TANTRUM
ANURIA
ANURIAS
ANYONE
ANYONES
ANYWAY
ANYWAYS
AORIST
AORISTS
AOUDAD
AOUDADS
APACHE
APACHES
APEDOM
APEDOMS
APERCU
APERCUS
APHTHA
NAPHTHA
APHTHAE
APISMS
PAPISMS
APLITE
APLITES
APLOMB
APLOMBS
APNOEA
APNOEAS
APOGEE
APOGEES
APOLLO
APOLLOS
APORIA
APORIAS
APOZEM
APOZEMS
APPAIR
APPAIRS
APPEAL
APPEALS
APPEAR
APPEARS
APPELS
LAPPELS
RAPPELS
APPEND
WAPPEND
APPENDS
APPLES
DAPPLES
SAPPLES
APPORT
RAPPORT
APPORTS
APPOSE
PAPPOSE
APPOSED
APPOSER
APPOSES
APRONS
NAPRONS
APTOTE
APTOTES
ARABIN
CARABIN
ARABINS
ARABIS
ARABISE
ARABLE
PARABLE
ARAISE
ARAISED
ARAISES
ARALIA
ARALIAS
ARAYSE
ARAYSED
ARAYSES
ARBORS
HARBORS
ARBOUR
HARBOUR
ARBOURS
ARBUTE
ARBUTES
ARCADE
ARCADED
ARCADES
ARCHED
MARCHED
PARCHED
ARCHER
MARCHER
ARCHERS
ARCHERY
ARCHES
LARCHES
MARCHES
PARCHES
ARCHEST
ARCHIL
ARCHILS
ARCHON
ARCHONS
ARCING
FARCING
ARCINGS
ARCSIN
ARCSINS
ARCTAN
ARCTANS
ARCTIC
ARCTICS
ARDOUR
ARDOURS
AREOLA
AREOLAE
AREOLAR
AREOLE
AREOLES
ARGALA
ARGALAS
ARGALI
ARGALIS
ARGAND
ARGANDS
ARGENT
MARGENT
ARGENTS
ARGHAN
ARGHANS
ARGONS
JARGONS
ARGUER
ARGUERS
ARGYLE
ARGYLES
ARIOSO
ARIOSOS
ARISTA
ARISTAE
ARISTAS
ARISTO
ARISTOS
ARKING
BARKING
CARKING
HARKING
LARKING
MARKING
NARKING
PARKING
SARKING
ARKITE
ARKITES
ARKOSE
ARKOSES
ARLING
CARLING
DARLING
HARLING
MARLING
PARLING
WARLING
ARMADA
ARMADAS
ARMFUL
HARMFUL
ARMFULS
ARMING
FARMING
HARMING
WARMING
ARMLET
ARMLETS
ARMOUR
ARMOURS
ARMOURY
ARMPIT
ARMPITS
ARMURE
ARMURES
ARNICA
ARNICAS
AROINT
AROINTS
AROLLA
AROLLAS
AROUSE
CAROUSE
AROUSED
AROUSER
AROUSES
AROYNT
AROYNTS
ARPENT
PARPENT
ARPENTS
ARRACK
BARRACK
CARRACK
ARRACKS
ARRANT
FARRANT
WARRANT
ARRAYS
WARRAYS
ARREAR
ARREARS
ARRECT
CARRECT
ARREST
ARRESTS
ARRETS
BARRETS
GARRETS
ARRIDE
ARRIDED
ARRIDES
ARRIVE
ARRIVED
ARRIVES
ARROBA
ARROBAS
ARROWS
BARROWS
FARROWS
HARROWS
MARROWS
NARROWS
TARROWS
YARROWS
ARROWY
MARROWY
ARROYO
ARROYOS
ARSHIN
ARSHINE
ARSHINS
ARSINE
ARSINES
ARSONS
PARSONS
ARTELS
CARTELS
MARTELS
ARTIER
TARTIER
WARTIER
ARTIES
PARTIES
ARTIEST
ARTIST
ARTISTE
ARTISTS

ASARUM
ASARUMS
ASCEND
ASCENDS
ASCENT
NASCENT
ASCENTS
ASCIAN
ASCIANS
ASCOTS
MASCOTS
ASEITY
GASEITY
ASHAME
ASHAMED
ASHAMES
ASHERY
FASHERY
WASHERY
ASHIER
CASHIER
HASHIER
MASHIER
WASHIER
ASHLAR
ASHLARS
ASHLER
ASHLERS
ASHRAM
ASHRAMA
ASHRAMS
ASKANT
ASKANTS
ASKARI
ASKARIS
ASKERS
MASKERS
TASKERS
ASKING
BASKING
CASKING
MASKING
TASKING
ASLAKE
ASLAKED
ASLAKES
ASPECT
ASPECTS
ASPERS
GASPERS
JASPERS
RASPERS
ASPERSE
ASPICK
ASPICKS
ASPINE
ASPINES
ASPIRE
ASPIRED
ASPIRES
ASPORT
ASPORTS
ASSAIL
VASSAIL
WASSAIL
ASSAILS
ASSART
ASSARTS
ASSENT
ASSENTS
ASSERT
ASSERTS
ASSETS
BASSETS
TASSETS
ASSIGN
ASSIGNS
ASSIST
BASSIST
ASSISTS
ASSIZE
ASSIZED
ASSIZER
ASSIZES
ASSOIL
ASSOILS
ASSORT
ASSORTS
ASSUME
ASSUMED
ASSUMES
ASSURE
ASSURED
ASSURER
ASSURES
ASTART
ASTARTS
ASTERN
EASTERN
PASTERN
ASTERS
BASTERS
CASTERS
FASTERS
GASTERS
LASTERS
MASTERS
PASTERS
RASTERS
TASTERS
WASTERS
ASTERT
ASTERTS
ASTHMA
ASTHMAS
ASTONE
ASTONED
ASTONES
ASTRAL
CASTRAL
ASTUTE
ASTUTER
ASYLUM
ASYLUMS
ATABAL
ATABALS
ATABEG
ATABEGS
ATABEK
ATABEKS
ATAMAN
ATAMANS
ATAXIA
ATAXIAS
ATLATL
ATLATLS
ATOCIA
ATOCIAS
ATOKES
MATOKES
ATONED
BATONED
ATONER
ATONERS
ATRIAL
PATRIAL
ATRIUM
NATRIUM
ATRIUMS
ATTACH
ATTACHE
ATTACK
ATTACKS
ATTAIN
ATTAINS
ATTAINT
ATTASK
ATTASKS
ATTASKT
ATTEND
ATTENDS
ATTENT
ATTENTS
ATTEST
FATTEST
WATTEST
ATTESTS
ATTIRE
ATTIRED
ATTIRES
ATTONE
ATTONES
ATTORN
ATTORNS
ATTRAP
ATTRAPS
ATTRIT
ATTRITE
ATTRITS
ATTUNE
ATTUNED
ATTUNES
AUBADE
AUBADES
AUCUBA
AUCUBAS
AUDILE
AUDILES
AUGERS
GAUGERS
SAUGERS
AUGHTS
NAUGHTS
WAUGHTS
AUGITE
AUGITES
AUGUST
AUGUSTE
AUGUSTS
AUKLET
AUKLETS
AULDER
CAULDER
AUMAIL
AUMAILS
AUNTER
DAUNTER
GAUNTER
HAUNTER
SAUNTER
TAUNTER
VAUNTER
AUNTERS
AUNTIE
JAUNTIE
AUNTIES
AUNTLY
GAUNTLY
AURATE
AURATED
AURATES
AURIST
AURISTS
AURORA
AURORAE
AURORAL
AURORAS
AUTEUR
HAUTEUR
AUTEURS
AUTHOR
AUTHORS
AUTISM
AUTISMS
AUTUMN
AUTUMNS
AUTUMNY
AVAILE
AVAILED
AVAILES
AVATAR
AVATARS
AVAUNT
AVAUNTS
AVENGE
AVENGED
AVENGER
AVENGES
AVENIR
AVENIRS
AVENUE
AVENUES
AVIATE
AVIATED
AVIATES
AVIDIN
AVIDINS
AVISES
MAVISES
PAVISES
AVOCET
AVOCETS
AVOSET
AVOSETS
AVOURE
AVOURES
AVOWAL
AVOWALS
AVOWER
AVOWERS
AVOYER
AVOYERS
AVULSE
AVULSED
AVULSES
AWAKEN
AWAKENS
AWARDS
VAWARDS
AWHAPE
AWHAPED
AWHAPES
AWHEEL
AWHEELS
AWMRIE
AWMRIES
AWNERS
DAWNERS
FAWNERS
PAWNERS
AWNIER
LAWNIER
TAWNIER
YAWNIER
AWNING
DAWNING
FAWNING
PAWNING
YAWNING
AWNINGS
AXILLA
MAXILLA
AXILLAE
AXILLAR
AYWORD
NAYWORD
AYWORDS
AZALEA
AZALEAS
AZIONE
AZIONES
AZOLLA
AZOLLAS
AZURES
RAZURES
BAAING
BAAINGS
BABACO
BABACOS
BABBLE
BABBLED
BABBLER
BABBLES
BABIES
BABIEST
BABLAH
BABLAHS
BABOON
BABOONS
BABOOS
BABOOSH
BACKER
BACKERS
BACKET
BACKETS
BACKRA
BACKRAS
BADDIE
BADDIES
BADGER
BADGERS
BAETYL
BAETYLS
BAFFLE
BAFFLED
BAFFLER
BAFFLES
BAGFUL
BAGFULS
BAGGIT
BAGGITS
BAGNIO
BAGNIOS
BAGUIO
BAGUIOS
BAGWIG
BAGWIGS
BAHADA
BAHADAS
BAILEE
BAILEES
BAILER
BAILERS
BAILEY
BAILEYS
BAILIE
BAILIES
BAILLI
BAILLIE
BAILLIS
BAILOR
BAILORS
BAININ
BAININS
BAITER
BAITERS
BAJADA
BAJADAS
BAJREE
BAJREES
BAKING
BAKINGS
BALATA
BALATAS
BALBOA
BALBOAS
BALEEN
BALEENS
BALKER
BALKERS
BALLAD
BALLADE
BALLADS
BALLAN
BALLANS
BALLANT
BALLAT
BALLATS
BALLET
BALLETS
BALLON
BALLONS
BALLOT
BALLOTS
BALLOW
BALLOWS
BALLUP
BALLUPS
BALSAM
BALSAMS
BALSAMY
BAMBOO
BAMBOOS
BAMMER
BAMMERS
BAMPOT
BAMPOTS
BANANA
BANANAS
BANDAR
BANDARS
BANDED
ABANDED
BANDIT
BANDITS
BANDOG
BANDOGS
BANGER
BANGERS
BANGLE
BANGLED
BANGLES
BANIAN
BANIANS
BANKER
BANKERS
BANKET
BANKETS
BANNER
BANNERS
BANTAM
BANTAMS
BANTER
BANTERS
BANYAN
BANYANS
BANZAI
BANZAIS
BAOBAB
BAOBABS
BARAZA
BARAZAS
BARBEL
BARBELS
BARBER
BARBERS
BARBET
BARBETS
BARBIE
BARBIES
BAREGE
BAREGES
BARGEE
BARGEES
BARGES
BARGEST
BARITE
BARITES
BARIUM
BARIUMS
BARKAN
BARKANS
BARKEN
BARKENS
BARKER
BARKERS
BARLEY
BARLEYS
BARNEY
BARNEYS
BAROCK
BAROCKS
BARONG
BARONGS
BARQUE
BARQUES
BARRAT
BARRATS
BARREL
BARRELS
BARRET
BARRETS
BARRIO
BARRIOS
BARROW
BARROWS
BARTER
BARTERS
BARTON
BARTONS
BARYON
BARYONS
BARYTA
BARYTAS
BASALT
BASALTS
BASHAW
BASHAWS
BASHED
ABASHED
BASHER
BASHERS
BASHES
ABASHES
BASING
ABASING
BASKET
BASKETS
BASNET
BASNETS
BASQUE
BASQUED
BASQUES
BASSES
BASSEST
BASSET
BASSETS
BASTER
BASTERS
BASTLE
BASTLES
BATATA
BATATAS
BATEAU
BATEAUX
BATHER
BATHERS
BATING
ABATING
BATLER
BATLERS
BATLET
BATLETS
BATOON
BATOONS
BATTEL
BATTELS
BATTEN
BATTENS
BATTER
BATTERO
BATTERS
BATTERY
BATTLE
BATTLED
BATTLER
BATTLES
BATTUE
BATTUES
BAUBLE

BAUBLES
BAUERA
BAUERAS
BAWBEE
BAWBEES
BAWBLE
BAWBLES
BAWLER
BAWLERS
BAWLEY
BAWLEYS
BAXTER
BAXTERS
BAYARD
BAYARDS
BAZAAR
BAZAARS
BEACON
BEACONS
BEADLE
BEADLES
BEAGLE
BEAGLED
BEAGLER
BEAGLES
BEAKER
BEAKERS
BEAMER
BEAMERS
BEANIE
BEANIES
BEARER
BEARERS
BEATER
BEATERS
BEAVER
BEAVERS
BEAVERY
BEBUNG
BEBUNGS
BECALL
BECALLS
BECALM
BECALMS
BECKET
BECKETS
BECKON
BECKONS
BECOME
BECOMES
BECURL
BECURLS
BEDAUB
BEDAUBS
BEDAZE
BEDAZED
BEDAZES
BEDBUG
BEDBUGS
BEDDER
BEDDERS
BEDECK
BEDECKS
BEDELL
BEDELLS
BEDLAM
BEDLAMS
BEDPAN
BEDPANS
BEDRAL
BEDRALS
BEDROP
BEDROPS
BEDROPT
BEDUCK
BEDUCKS
BEDUIN
BEDUINS
BEDUNG
BEDUNGS
BEDUST
BEDUSTS
BEEGAH
BEEGAHS
BEENAH
BEENAHS
BEEPER
BEEPERS
BEETLE
BEETLED
BEETLES
BEFALL
BEFALLS
BEFANA
BEFANAS
BEFLUM
BEFLUMS
BEFOAM
BEFOAMS
BEFOOL
BEFOOLS
BEFOUL
BEFOULS
BEGGAR
BEGGARS
BEGGARY
BEGIFT
BEGIFTS
BEGILD
BEGILDS
BEGIRD
BEGIRDS
BEGNAW
BEGNAWS
BEGUIN
BEGUINE
BEGUINS
BEGUNK
BEGUNKS
BEHAVE
BEHAVED
BEHAVES
BEHEAD
BEHEADS
BEHEST
BEHESTS
BEHIND
BEHINDS
BEHOLD
BEHOLDS
BEHOOF
BEHOOFS
BEHOTE
BEHOTES
BEHOVE
BEHOVED
BEHOVES
BEHOWL
BEHOWLS
BEIGEL
BEIGELS
BEJADE
BEJADED
BEJADES
BEJANT
BEJANTS
BELACE
BELACED
BELACES
BELATE
BELATED
BELATES
BELAUD
BELAUDS
BELDAM
BELDAME
BELDAMS
BELIEF
BELIEFS
BELIER
BELIERS
BELLOW
BELLOWS
BELONG
BELONGS
BELOVE
BELOVED
BELOVES
BELTER
BELTERS
BELUGA
BELUGAS
BEMAUL
BEMAULS
BEMEAN
BEMEANS
BEMEANT
BEMETE
BEMETED
BEMETES
BEMIRE
BEMIRED
BEMIRES
BEMOAN
BEMOANS
BEMOCK
BEMOCKS
BEMOIL
BEMOILS
BEMUSE
BEMUSED
BEMUSES
BENAME
BENAMED
BENAMES
BENDER
BENDERS
BENNET
BENNETS
BENUMB
BENUMBS
BENZAL
BENZALS
BENZIL
BENZILS
BENZOL
BENZOLE
BENZOLS
BENZYL
BENZYLS
BEPELT
BEPELTS
BEPUFF
BEPUFFS
BERATE
BERATED
BERATES
BERLEY
BERLEYS
BERLIN
BERLINE
BERLINS
BERRET
BERRETS
BERTHA
BERTHAS
BERTHE
BERTHED
BERTHES
BESEEM
BESEEMS
BESIDE
BESIDES
BESIGH
BESIGHS
BESING
BESINGS
BESMUT
BESMUTS
BESOIN
BESOINS
BESORT
BESORTS
BESPAT
BESPATE
BESPIT
BESPITS
BESPOT
BESPOTS
BESTAR
BESTARS
BESTIR
BESTIRS
BESTOW
BESTOWS
BESTUD
BESTUDS
BETAKE
BETAKEN
BETAKES
BETEEM
BETEEME
BETEEMS
BETHEL
BETHELS
BETIDE
BETIDED
BETIDES
BETIME
BETIMED
BETIMES
BETISE
BETISES
BETOIL
BETOILS
BETRAY
BETRAYS
BETRIM
BETRIMS
BETTED
ABETTED
BETTER
ABETTER
BETTERS
BETTOR
ABETTOR
BETTORS
BEURRE
BEURRES
BEWAIL
BEWAILS
BEWARE
BEWARED
BEWARES
BEWEEP
BEWEEPS
BEWRAY
BEWRAYS
BEYOND
BEYONDS
BEZANT
BEZANTS
BEZOAR
BEZOARS
BEZZLE
BEZZLED
BEZZLES
BHAGEE
BHAGEES
BHAJAN
BHAJANS
BHAJEE
BHAJEES
BHAKTI
BHAKTIS
BHARAL
BHARALS
BHINDI
BHINDIS
BHISTI
BHISTIS
BIBBER
BIBBERS
BICARB
BICARBS
BICKER
BICKERS
BICORN
BICORNE
BICORNS
BIDDEN
ABIDDEN
BIDDER
BIDDERS
BIDENT
BIDENTS
BIDING
ABIDING
BIDINGS
BIFFIN
BIFFING
BIFFINS
BIGGIE
BIGGIES
BIGGIN
BIGGING
BIGGINS
BIGWIG
BIGWIGS
BIKING
BIKINGS
BIKINI
BIKINIS
BILIAN
BILIANS
BILKER
BILKERS
BILLET
BILLETS
BILLIE
BILLIES
BILLON
BILLONS
BILLOW
BILLOWS
BILLOWY
BINDER
BINDERS
BINDERY
BINGER
BINGERS
BINGHI
BINGHIS
BINGLE
BINGLED
BINGLES
BIOGEN
BIOGENS
BIOGENY
BIONIC
BIONICS
BIOPIC
BIOPICS
BIOTIC
ABIOTIC
BIOTIN
BIOTINS
BIRDER
BIRDERS
BIRDIE
BIRDIED
BIRDIES
BIREME
BIREMES
BIRKIE
BIRKIER
BIRKIES
BIRLER
BIRLERS
BIRSLE
BIRSLED
BIRSLES
BISECT
BISECTS
BISHOP
BISHOPS
BISMAR
BISMARS
BISQUE
BISQUES
BISTER
BISTERS
BISTRE
BISTRED
BISTRES
BISTRO
BISTROS
BITING
BITINGS
BITMAP
BITMAPS
BITTER
BITTERN
BITTERS
BITTIE
BITTIER
BITTIES
BITTOR
BITTORS
BITTUR
BITTURS
BIZONE
BIZONES
BLAGUE
BLAGUES
BLANCO
BLANCOS
BLASTS
OBLASTS
BLAZER
BLAZERS
BLAZON
BLAZONS
BLENDE
BLENDED
BLENDER
BLENDES
BLIGHT
BLIGHTS
BLIGHTY
BLINTZ
BLINTZE
BLITHE
BLITHER
BLONDE
BLONDER
BLONDES
BLOTCH
BLOTCHY
BLOUSE
BLOUSED
BLOUSES
BLOWER
BLOWERS
BLOWIE
BLOWIER
BLOWIES
BLOWSE
BLOWSED
BLOWSES
BLOWZE
BLOWZED
BLOWZES
BLUDGE
BLUDGED
BLUDGER
BLUDGES
BLUDIE
BLUDIER
BLUING
BLUINGS
BLUNGE
BLUNGED
BLUNGER
BLUNGES
BOATEL
BOATELS
BOATER
BOATERS
BOATIE
BOATIES
BOBBIN
BOBBING
BOBBINS
BOBBLE
BOBBLED
BOBBLES
BOBCAT
BOBCATS
BOBWIG
BOBWIGS
BOCAGE
BOCAGES
BODACH
BODACHS
BODDLE
BODDLES
BODEGA
BODEGAS
BODGER
BODGERS
BODGIE
BODGIER
BODGIES
BODICE
BODICES
BODING
ABODING
BODINGS
BODKIN
BODKINS
BODRAG
BODRAGS
BOFFIN
BOFFING
BOFFINS
BOGGLE
BOGGLED
BOGGLER
BOGGLES
BOGOAK
BOGOAKS
BOGONG
BOGONGS
BOHUNK
BOHUNKS
BOILER
BOILERS
BOILERY
BOLDEN
BOLDENS
BOLERO
BOLEROS
BOLIDE
BOLIDES
BOLTER
BOLTERS
BOMBER
BOMBERS
BONBON
BONBONS
BONDER
BONDERS
BONDUC
BONDUCS
BONING
BONINGS
BONISM
BONISMS
BONIST

EBONIST
BONISTS
BONITO
BONITOS
BONNET
BONNETS
BONNIE
BONNIER
BONNIES
BONSAI
BONSAIS
BONXIE
BONXIES
BOOBOO
BOOBOOK
BOOBOOS
BOODIE
BOODIED
BOODIES
BOODLE
BOODLES
BOOGIE
BOOGIED
BOOGIES
BOOKIE
BOOKIER
BOOKIES
BOOMER
BOOMERS
BOORDE
BOORDES
BOORKA
BOORKAS
BOOTEE
BOOTEES
BOOZER
BOOZERS
BOPPER
BOPPERS
BORAGE
BORAGES
BORANE
BORANES
BORATE
BORATES
BORDAR
BORDARS
BORDEL
BORDELS
BORDER
BORDERS
BOREEN
BOREENS
BORIDE
BORIDES
BORING
BORINGS
BORREL
BORRELL
BORROW
BORROWS
BORSCH
BORSCHT
BORZOI
BORZOIS
BOSBOK
BOSBOKS
BOSCHE
BOSCHES
BOSKET
BOSKETS
BOSSES
BOSSEST
BOSTON
BOSTONS
BOTHAN
BOTHANS
BOTHER
BOTHERS
BOTHIE
BOTHIES
BOTTLE
BOTTLED
BOTTLER
BOTTLES
BOTTOM
BOTTOMS
BOUCHE
BOUCHEE
BOUCHES
BOUCLE
BOUCLES
BOUGET
BOUGETS
BOUGHT
ABOUGHT
BOUGHTS
BOUGIE
BOUGIES
BOULLE
BOULLES
BOUNCE
BOUNCED
BOUNCER
BOUNCES
BOUNDS
ABOUNDS
BOURNE
BOURNES
BOURSE
BOURSES
BOUTON
BOUTONS
BOVATE
OBOVATE
BOVATES
BOVINE
BOVINES
BOVVER
BOVVERS
BOWFIN
BOWFINS
BOWGET
BOWGETS
BOWING
BOWINGS
BOWLER
BOWLERS
BOWPOT
BOWPOTS
BOWSER
BOWSERS
BOWWOW
BOWWOWS
BOWYER
BOWYERS
BOXCAR
BOXCARS
BOXFUL
BOXFULS
BOXING
BOXINGS
BRACER
BRACERS
BRAIDE
BRAIDED
BRAIDER
BRAIDS
ABRAIDS
BRAIRD
BRAIRDS
BRAISE
BRAISED
BRAISES
BRAIZE
BRAIZES
BRANCH
BRANCHY
BRANLE
BRANLES
BRAVER
BRAVERY
BRAVES
BRAVEST
BRAYED
ABRAYED
BRAYER
BRAYERS
BRAZEN
BRAZENS
BRAZIL
BRAZILS
BREARE
BREARES
BREAST
ABREAST
BREASTS
BREATH
BREATHE
BREATHS
BREATHY
BREESE
BREESES
BREEZE
BREEZED
BREEZES
BREHON
BREHONS
BRENNE
BRENNES
BRETON
BRETONS
BREVET
BREVETE
BREVETS
BREWER
BREWERS
BREWERY
BRIBER
BRIBERS
BRIBERY
BRIDAL
BRIDALS
BRIDGE
ABRIDGE
BRIDGED
BRIDGES
BRIDIE
BRIDIES
BRIDLE
BRIDLED
BRIDLER
BRIDLES
BRIGUE
BRIGUED
BRIGUES
BROACH
ABROACH
BROADS
ABROADS
BROCHE
BROCHED
BROCHES
BROGAN
BROGANS
BROGUE
BROGUES
BROKER
BROKERS
BROKERY
BROLGA
BROLGAS
BRONCO
BRONCOS
BRONZE
BRONZED
BRONZEN
BRONZER
BRONZES
BROOSE
BROOSES
BROUGH
BROUGHS
BROUGHT
BROUZE
BROUZES
BROWSE
BROWSED
BROWSER
BROWSES
BROWST
BROWSTS
BRUISE
BRUISED
BRUISER
BRUISES
BRUNET
BRUNETS
BRUTER
BRUTERS
BUBBLE
BUBBLED
BUBBLES
BUCKER
BUCKERS
BUCKET
BUCKETS
BUCKIE
BUCKIES
BUCKLE
BUCKLED
BUCKLER
BUCKLES
BUCKRA
BUCKRAM
BUCKRAS
BUDDHA
BUDDHAS
BUDDLE
BUDDLED
BUDDLES
BUDGER
BUDGERO
BUDGERS
BUDGET
BUDGETS
BUDGIE
BUDGIES
BUFFER
BUFFERS
BUFFET
BUFFETS
BUGGAN
BUGGANE
BUGGANS
BUGGER
BUGGERS
BUGGERY
BUGGIN
BUGGING
BUGGINS
BUGLER
BUGLERS
BUGLET
BUGLETS
BUGONG
BUGONGS
BUKSHI
BUKSHIS
BULBEL
BULBELS
BULBIL
BULBILS
BULBUL
BULBULS
BULGER
BULGERS
BULGUR
BULGURS
BULKER
BULKERS
BULLER
BULLERS
BULLET
BULLETS
BUMBAG
BUMBAGS
BUMBLE
BUMBLED
BUMBLER
BUMBLES
BUMKIN
BUMKINS
BUMMEL
BUMMELS
BUMMER
BUMMERS
BUMMLE
BUMMLED
BUMMLES
BUMPER
BUMPERS
BUNDLE
BUNDLED
BUNDLES
BUNGEE
BUNGEES
BUNGEY
BUNGEYS
BUNGIE
BUNGIES
BUNGLE
BUNGLED
BUNGLER
BUNGLES
BUNION
BUNIONS
BUNJEE
BUNJEES
BUNJIE
BUNJIES
BUNKER
BUNKERS
BUNKUM
BUNKUMS
BUNNIA
BUNNIAS
BUNSEN
BUNSENS
BUNTAL
BUNTALS
BUNTER
BUNTERS
BUNYIP
BUNYIPS
BURBLE
BURBLED
BURBLER
BURBLES
BURBOT
BURBOTS
BURDEN
BURDENS
BURDIE
BURDIES
BUREAU
BUREAUS
BUREAUX
BURGEE
BURGEES
BURGER
BURGERS
BURGLE
BURGLED
BURGLES
BURGOO
BURGOOS
BURHEL
BURHELS
BURIAL
BURIALS
BURITI
BURITIS
BURLAP
BURLAPS
BURLER
BURLERS
BURLEY
BURLEYS
BURNER
BURNERS
BURNET
BURNETS
BURREL
BURRELL
BURRELS
BURROW
BURROWS
BURSAR
BURSARS
BURSARY
BURTON
BURTONS
BUSBOY
BUSBOYS
BUSHEL
BUSHELS
BUSIES
BUSIEST
BUSING
ABUSING
BUSINGS
BUSKER
BUSKERS
BUSKET
BUSKETS
BUSKIN
BUSKING
BUSKINS
BUSTEE
BUSTEES
BUSTER
BUSTERS
BUSTLE
BUSTLED
BUSTLER
BUSTLES
BUTANE
BUTANES
BUTENE
BUTENES
BUTLER
BUTLERS
BUTLERY
BUTTED
ABUTTED
BUTTER
ABUTTER
BUTTERS
BUTTERY
BUTTLE
BUTTLED
BUTTLES
BUTTON
BUTTONS
BUTTONY
BUZZER
BUZZERS
BYGONE
BYGONES
BYLINE
BYLINES
BYNAME
BYNAMES
BYPATH
BYPATHS
BYRLAW
BYRLAWS
BYRNIE
BYRNIES
BYROAD
BYROADS
BYROOM
BYROOMS
BYSSAL
ABYSSAL
BYWORD
BYWORDS
BYZANT
BYZANTS
CABALA
CABALAS
CABANA
CABANAS
CABBIE
CABBIES
CABLET
CABLETS
CABRIE
CABRIES
CABRIT
CABRITS
CACHET
CACHETS
CACHOU
CACHOUS
CACKLE
CACKLED
CACKLER
CACKLES
CACOON
CACOONS
CADDIE
CADDIED
CADDIES
CADDIS
CADDISH
CADEAU
CADEAUX
CADGER
CADGERS
CADUAC
CADUACS
CAESAR
CAESARS
CAFARD
CAFARDS
CAFILA
CAFILAS
CAFTAN
CAFTANS
CAGOUL
CAGOULE
CAGOULS
CAHIER
CAHIERS
CAILLE
CAILLES
CAIMAC
CAIMACS
CAIMAN
CAIMANS
CAIQUE
CAIQUES
CAJOLE
CAJOLED
CAJOLER
CAJOLES
CAKING
CAKINGS
CALCAR
CALCARS
CALICO
CALICOS
CALIGO
CALIGOS
CALIMA
CALIMAS
CALIPH
CALIPHS

CALKER
CALKERS
CALKIN
CALKING
CALKINS
CALLAN
CALLANS
CALLANT
CALLED
SCALLED
CALLER
CALLERS
CALLET
CALLETS
CALLOW
CALLOWS
CALPAC
CALPACK
CALPACS
CALQUE
CALQUED
CALQUES
CALTHA
CALTHAS
CALVER
CALVERS
CAMBER
CAMBERS
CAMBIA
CAMBIAL
CAMELS
SCAMELS
CAMERA
CAMERAE
CAMERAL
CAMERAS
CAMESE
CAMESES
CAMION
CAMIONS
CAMISE
CAMISES
CAMLET
CAMLETS
CAMOTE
CAMOTES
CAMPED
SCAMPED
CAMPER
SCAMPER
CAMPERS
CAMPLE
CAMPLED
CAMPLES
CANADA
CANADAS
CANAPE
CANAPES
CANARD
CANARDS
CANCAN
CANCANS
CANCEL
CANCELS
CANCER
CANCERS
CANDID
CANDIDA
CANDIE
CANDIED
CANDIES
CANDLE
CANDLED
CANDLES
CANDOR
CANDORS
CANFUL
CANFULS
CANGLE
CANGLED
CANGLES
CANGUE
CANGUES
CANINE
CANINES
CANING
CANINGS
CANKER
CANKERS
CANKERY
CANNED
SCANNED
CANNEL
CANNELS
CANNER
SCANNER
CANNERS
CANNERY
CANNON
CANNONS
CANTAR
CANTARS
CANTED
SCANTED
CANTER
SCANTER
CANTERS
CANTLE
SCANTLE
CANTLED
CANTLES
CANTLET
CANTON
CANTONS
CANTOR
CANTORS
CANULA
CANULAE
CANULAS
CANVAS
CANVASS
CANYON
CANYONS
CAPING
SCAPING
CAPITA
CAPITAL
CAPITAN
CAPLET
CAPLETS
CAPLIN
CAPLINS
CAPOTE
CAPOTES
CAPPER
CAPPERS
CAPRIC
CAPRICE
CAPRID
CAPRIDS
CAPSID
CAPSIDS
CAPTAN
CAPTANS
CAPTOR
CAPTORS
CARACK
CARACKS
CARACT
CARACTS
CARAFE
CARAFES
CARBON
CARBONS
CARBOY
CARBOYS
CARDER
CARDERS
CAREEN
CAREENS
CAREER
CAREERS
CAREME
CAREMES
CARERS
SCARERS
CARIBE
CARIBES
CARINA
OCARINA
CARINAE
CARINAS
CARING
SCARING
CARLOT
CARLOTS
CARNAL
CARNALS
CARNET
CARNETS
CARNEY
CARNEYS
CARPAL
CARPALS
CARPED
SCARPED
CARPEL
CARPELS
CARPER
SCARPER
CARPERS
CARPET
CARPETS
CARRAT
CARRATS
CARREL
CARRELL
CARRELS
CARROT
CARROTS
CARROTY
CARSEY
CARSEYS
CARTED
SCARTED
CARTEL
CARTELS
CARTER
CARTERS
CARTES
ECARTES
CARTON
CARTONS
CARVEL
CARVELS
CARVER
CARVERS
CARVERY
CARVES
SCARVES
CASBAH
CASBAHS
CASEIN
CASEINS
CASERN
CASERNE
CASERNS
CASHAW
CASHAWS
CASHEW
CASHEWS
CASING
CASINGS
CASINO
CASINOS
CASKET
CASKETS
CASQUE
CASQUES
CASSIA
CASSIAS
CASTER
CASTERS
CASTLE
CASTLED
CASTLES
CASTOR
CASTORS
CASTORY
CASUAL
CASUALS
CATALO
CATALOG
CATALOS
CATENA
CATENAE
CATENAS
CATERS
ACATERS
CATGUT
CATGUTS
CATION
CATIONS
CATKIN
CATKINS
CATNAP
CATNAPS
CATNEP
CATNEPS
CATNIP
CATNIPS
CATSUP
CATSUPS
CATTED
SCATTED
CAUDAL
ACAUDAL
CAUDLE
CAUDLED
CAUDLES
CAUKER
CAUKERS
CAUSER
CAUSERS
CAUSEY
CAUSEYS
CAUTEL
CAUTELS
CAUTER
CAUTERS
CAUTERY
CAVEAT
CAVEATS
CAVERN
CAVERNS
CAVIAR
CAVIARE
CAVIARS
CAVING
CAVINGS
CAVORT
CAVORTS
CAWING
CAWINGS
CAWKER
CAWKERS
CAYMAN
CAYMANS
CAYUSE
CAYUSES
CEDULA
CEDULAS
CELIAC
CELIACS
CELLAR
OCELLAR
CELLARS
CELLOS
CELLOSE
CEMBRA
CEMBRAS
CEMENT
CEMENTA
CEMENTS
CENOTE
CENOTES
CENSER
CENSERS
CENSOR
CENSORS
CENTAL
CENTALS
CENTER
CENTERS
CENTRA
CENTRAL
CENTRE
CENTRED
CENTRES
CENTUM
CENTUMS
CERATE
ACERATE
CERATED
CERATES
CEREAL
CEREALS
CERIPH
CERIPHS
CERISE
CERISES
CERITE
CERITES
CERIUM
CERIUMS
CERMET
CERMETS
CERNED
SCERNED
CERNES
SCERNES
CEROON
CEROONS
CEROUS
ACEROUS
CERUSE
CERUSES
CERVID
CERVIDS
CESIUM
CESIUMS
CESSER
CESSERS
CESTUI
CESTUIS
CESURA
CESURAE
CESURAL
CESURAS
CESURE
CESURES
CETANE
CETANES
CETYLS
ACETYLS
CHACMA
CHACMAS
CHADAR
CHADARS
CHADOR
CHADORS
CHAETA
CHAETAE
CHAFER
CHAFERS
CHAGAN
CHAGANS
CHAINE
CHAINED
CHAINES
CHAISE
CHAISES
CHAKRA
CHAKRAS
CHALAN
CHALANS
CHALET
CHALETS
CHANCE
CHANCED
CHANCEL
CHANCER
CHANCES
CHANCEY
CHANGE
CHANGED
CHANGER
CHANGES
CHAPEL
CHAPELS
CHAPES
CHAPESS
CHAPKA
CHAPKAS
CHARET
CHARETS
CHARGE
CHARGED
CHARGER
CHARGES
CHARKA
CHARKAS
CHARTA
CHARTAS
CHASER
CHASERS
CHASSE
CHASSES
CHASTE
CHASTEN
CHASTER
CHATON
CHATONS
CHATTA
CHATTAS
CHATTI
CHATTIS
CHAUFE
CHAUFED
CHAUFER
CHAUFES
CHAUFF
CHAUFFS
CHAUNT
CHAUNTS
CHAZAN
CHAZANS
CHEESE
CHEESED
CHEESES
CHEMIC
CHEMICS
CHENAR
CHENARS
CHENET
CHENETS
CHEQUE
CHEQUER
CHEQUES
CHERUB
CHERUBS
CHERUP
CHERUPS
CHESIL
CHESILS
CHETAH
CHETAHS
CHEVEN
CHEVENS
CHEVET
CHEVETS
CHEVIN
CHEVINS
CHEVRE
CHEVRES
CHEWER
CHEWERS
CHEWET
CHEWETS
CHEWIE
CHEWIER
CHEWIES
CHIACK
CHIACKS
CHIASM
CHIASMA
CHIASMI
CHIASMS
CHIBOL
CHIBOLS
CHICHA
CHICHAS
CHICHI
CHICHIS
CHICKS
TCHICKS
CHICLE
CHICLES
CHICON
CHICONS
CHIDER
CHIDERS
CHIELD
CHIELDS
CHIGOE
CHIGOES
CHIGRE
CHIGRES
CHIKOR
CHIKORS
CHILDE
CHILDED
CHILDER
CHILLI
CHILLIS
CHIMER
CHIMERA
CHIMERE
CHIMERS
CHINAR
CHINARS
CHINES
CHINESE
CHINTZ
CHINTZY
CHIRRE
CHIRRED
CHIRRES
CHISEL
CHISELS
CHITAL
CHITALS
CHITIN
CHITINS
CHITON
CHITONS
CHOANA
CHOANAE
CHOCHO
CHOCHOS
CHOCKO
CHOCKOS
CHOICE
CHOICER
CHOICES
CHOKER
CHOKERS
CHOKEY
CHOKEYS
CHOKRA

CHOKRAS
CHOKRI
CHOKRIS
CHOLER
CHOLERA
CHOLERS
CHOOSE
CHOOSER
CHOOSES
CHOOSEY
CHOPIN
CHOPINE
CHOPINS
CHORAL
CHORALE
CHORALS
CHORDA
CHORDAE
CHORDAL
CHOREA
CHOREAS
CHOREE
CHOREES
CHORIA
CHORIAL
CHOUGH
CHOUGHS
CHOUSE
CHOUSED
CHOUSES
CHOUTS
SCHOUTS
CHOWRI
CHOWRIS
CHRISM
CHRISMS
CHROMA
CHROMAS
CHROME
CHROMED
CHROMEL
CHROMES
CHROMO
CHROMOS
CHUKAR
CHUKARS
CHUKKA
CHUKKAS
CHUKOR
CHUKORS
CHURCH
CHURCHY
CHYACK
CHYACKS
CHYPRE
CHYPRES
CICADA
CICADAS
CICALA
CICALAS
CICERO
CICEROS
CICUTA
CICUTAS
CIERGE
CIERGES
CIGGIE
CIGGIES
CILICE
CILICES
CIMIER
CIMIERS
CINDER
CINDERS
CINDERY
CINEMA
CINEMAS
CINEOL
CINEOLE
CINEOLS
CINQUE
CINQUES
CIPHER
CIPHERS
CIRCAR
CIRCARS
CIRCLE
CIRCLED
CIRCLER
CIRCLES
CIRCLET
CIRCUS
CIRCUSY
CIRQUE
CIRQUES
CITHER
CITHERN
CITHERS
CITOLE
CITOLES
CITRIN
CITRINE
CITRINS
CITRON
CITRONS
CIVISM
CIVISMS
CLAMOR
CLAMORS
CLAQUE
CLAQUES
CLARET
CLARETS
CLAUSE
CLAUSES
CLAVER
CLAVERS
CLAVES
SCLAVES
CLAVIE
CLAVIER
CLAVIES
CLEANS
CLEANSE
CLEAVE
CLEAVED
CLEAVER
CLEAVES
CLEEVE
CLEEVES
CLEPED
YCLEPED
CLERIC
CLERICS
CLEUCH
CLEUCHS
CLEUGH
CLEUGHS
CLICHE
CLICHES
CLIENT
CLIENTS
CLIFFS
SCLIFFS
CLINIC
ACLINIC
CLINICS
CLIQUE
CLIQUES
CLIQUEY
CLITIC
CLITICS
CLIVIA
CLIVIAS
CLOACA
CLOACAE
CLOACAL
CLOCHE
CLOCHES
CLOQUE
CLOQUES
CLOSED
ECLOSED
CLOSER
CLOSERS
CLOSES
ECLOSES
CLOSEST
CLOSET
CLOSETS
CLOTHE
CLOTHED
CLOTHES
CLOUGH
CLOUGHS
CLOVER
CLOVERS
CLOVERY
CLUSIA
CLUSIAS
COAITA
COAITAS
COALER
COALERS
COARSE
COARSEN
COARSER
COATEE
COATEES
COATER
COATERS
COAXER
COAXERS
COBALT
COBALTS
COBBER
COBBERS
COBBLE
COBBLED
COBBLER
COBBLES
COBNUT
COBNUTS
COBURG
COBURGS
COBWEB
COBWEBS
COCCID
COCCIDS
COCKER
COCKERS
COCKET
COCKETS
COCKLE
COCKLED
COCKLES
COCOON
COCOONS
CODDER
CODDERS
CODDLE
CODDLED
CODDLES
CODGER
CODGERS
CODING
CODINGS
CODIST
CODISTS
CODLIN
CODLING
CODLINS
COELOM
COELOMS
COERCE
COERCED
COERCES
COEVAL
COEVALS
COFFED
SCOFFED
COFFEE
COFFEES
COFFER
SCOFFER
COFFERS
COFFIN
COFFING
COFFINS
COFFLE
COFFLES
COGGED
SCOGGED
COGGER
COGGERS
COGGIE
COGGIES
COGGLE
COGGLED
COGGLES
COHEIR
COHEIRS
COHERE
COHERED
COHERER
COHERES
COHORN
COHORNS
COHORT
COHORTS
COHUNE
COHUNES
COIGNE
COIGNED
COIGNES
COINER
COINERS
COJOIN
COJOINS
COLDER
SCOLDER
COLLAR
COLLARD
COLLARS
COLLET
COLLETS
COLLIE
COLLIED
COLLIER
COLLIES
COLLOP
SCOLLOP
COLLOPS
COLOBI
COLOBID
COLOUR
COLOURS
COLOURY
COLTER
COLTERS
COLUGO
COLUGOS
COLUMN
COLUMNS
COLURE
COLURES
COMARB
COMARBS
COMART
COMARTS
COMATE
COMATES
COMBAT
COMBATS
COMBER
COMBERS
COMBLE
COMBLES
COMEDO
COMEDOS
COMFIT
COMFITS
COMICE
COMICES
COMING
COMINGS
COMMER
COMMERE
COMMERS
COMMIE
COMMIES
COMMIT
COMMITS
COMMON
COMMONS
COMMOT
COMMOTE
COMMOTS
COMPEL
COMPELS
COMPER
COMPERE
COMPERS
COMPOS
COMPOSE
COMPOST
COMPOT
COMPOTE
COMPOTS
CONCHA
CONCHAE
CONCHAL
CONCHE
CONCHED
CONCHES
CONCUR
CONCURS
CONDER
CONDERS
CONDIE
CONDIES
CONDOM
CONDOMS
CONDOR
CONDORS
CONFAB
CONFABS
CONFER
CONFERS
CONFIT
CONFITS
CONGEE
CONGEED
CONGEES
CONGER
CONGERS
CONGES
CONGEST
CONGOU
CONGOUS
CONIMA
CONIMAS
CONINE
CONINES
CONJEE
CONJEED
CONJEES
CONKER
CONKERS
CONNER
CONNERS
CONOID
CONOIDS
CONSUL
CONSULS
CONSULT
CONTES
CONTEST
CONTRA
CONTRAS
CONTRAT
CONURE
CONURES
CONVEY
CONVEYS
CONVOY
CONVOYS
COOING
COOINGS
COOKER
COOKERS
COOKERY
COOKIE
COOKIES
COOLER
COOLERS
COOLIE
COOLIES
COOLTH
COOLTHS
COOMBE
COOMBES
COOPED
SCOOPED
COOPER
SCOOPER
COOPERS
COOPERY
COOSER
COOSERS
COOTIE
COOTIES
COPECK
COPECKS
COPIER
COPIERS
COPING
SCOPING
COPINGS
COPITA
COPITAS
COPPER
COPPERS
COPPERY
COPPIN
COPPING
COPPINS
COPPLE
COPPLES
COPTER
COPTERS
COPULA
SCOPULA
COPULAR
COPULAS
COQUET
COQUETS
CORBAN
CORBANS
CORBEL
CORBELS
CORBIE
CORBIES
CORDON
CORDONS
CORERS
SCORERS
CORING
SCORING
CORIUM
CORIUMS
CORKER
CORKERS
CORKIR
CORKIRS
CORMEL
CORMELS
CORNEA
CORNEAL
CORNEAS
CORNED
ACORNED
SCORNED
CORNEL
CORNELS
CORNER
SCORNER
CORNERS
CORNET
CORNETS
CORNETT
CORNUA
CORNUAL
CORONA
CORONAE
CORONAL
CORONAS
COROZO
COROZOS
CORPSE
CORPSED
CORPSES
CORRAL
CORRALS
CORRIE
CORRIES
CORSAC
CORSACS
CORSES
SCORSES
CORSET
CORSETS
CORVEE
CORVEES
CORVET
CORVETS
CORVID
CORVIDS
CORYMB
CORYMBS
CORYZA
CORYZAS
COSECH
COSECHS
COSHER
COSHERS
COSHERY
COSIER
COSIERS
COSIES
COSIEST
COSINE
COSINES
COSMEA
COSMEAS
COSSET
COSSETS
COSSIE
COSSIES
COSTAL
COSTALS
COSTER
COSTERS
COTEAU
COTEAUX
COTING
COTINGA
COTISE
COTISED
COTISES
COTTAR
COTTARS
COTTER
COTTERS
COTTID
COTTIDS
COTTON
COTTONS
COTTONY
COTWAL

COTWALS
COTYLE
COTYLES
COUCAL
COUCALS
COUCHE
COUCHED
COUCHEE
COUCHES
COUGAR
COUGARS
COULEE
COULEES
COUPED
SCOUPED
COUPEE
COUPEES
COUPER
COUPERS
COUPLE
COUPLED
COUPLER
COUPLES
COUPLET
COUPON
COUPONS
COURED
SCOURED
COURSE
SCOURSE
COURSED
COURSER
COURSES
COUSIN
COUSINS
COUTER
SCOUTER
COUTERS
COUTIL
COUTILS
COVENT
COVENTS
COVERT
COVERTS
COVING
COVINGS
COVYNE
COVYNES
COWAGE
COWAGES
COWARD
COWARDS
COWBOY
COWBOYS
COWLED
SCOWLED
COWPAT
COWPATS
COWPEA
COWPEAS
COWPED
SCOWPED
COWRIE
SCOWRIE
COWRIES
COYOTE
COYOTES
COZIER
COZIERS
COZIES

COZIEST
CRADLE
CRADLED
CRADLES
CRAGGY
SCRAGGY
CRAMES
CRAMESY
CRANCH
SCRANCH
CRANIA
CRANIAL
CRANNY
SCRANNY
CRAPES
SCRAPES
CRAPLE
CRAPLES
CRAPPY
SCRAPPY
CRATCH
SCRATCH
CRATER
CRATERS
CRATON
CRATONS
CRATUR
CRATURS
CRAVAT
CRAVATS
CRAVEN
CRAVENS
CRAVER
CRAVERS
CRAWLS
SCRAWLS
CRAWLY
SCRAWLY
CRAYER
CRAYERS
CRAYON
CRAYONS
CREACH
CREACHS
CREAGH
CREAGHS
CREAKS
SCREAKS
CREAKY
SCREAKY
CREAMS
SCREAMS
CREASE
CREASED
CREASER
CREASES
CREATE
OCREATE
CREATED
CREATES
CRECHE
CRECHES
CREDIT
CREDITS
CREEDS
SCREEDS
CREESE
CREESED
CREESES
CREESH

CREESHY
CREMOR
CREMORS
CRENEL
CRENELS
CREOLE
CREOLES
CREPON
CREPONS
CRESOL
CRESOLS
CRETIC
CRETICS
CRETIN
CRETINS
CREWED
SCREWED
CREWEL
CREWELS
CRIMPS
SCRIMPS
CRIMPY
SCRIMPY
CRINES
SCRINES
CRINGE
CRINGED
CRINGER
CRINGES
CRINUM
CRINUMS
CRISTA
CRISTAE
CRITIC
CRITICS
CROCHE
CROCHES
CROCHET
CRONET
CRONETS
CROOVE
CROOVES
CROSSE
CROSSED
CROSSER
CROSSES
CROTAL
SCROTAL
CROTALA
CROTALS
CROTON
CROTONS
CROUPE
CROUPED
CROUPER
CROUPES
CROUTE
CROUTES
CRUDES
CRUDEST
CRUISE
CRUISED
CRUISER
CRUISES
CRUIVE
CRUIVES
CRUMEN
CRUMENS
CRUMMY
SCRUMMY

CRUMPS
SCRUMPS
CRUMPY
SCRUMPY
CRUNCH
SCRUNCH
CRUNCHY
CRUSET
CRUSETS
CRUSIE
CRUSIES
CRUSTA
CRUSTAE
CRUSTAL
CRYING
SCRYING
CRYINGS
CRYPTO
CRYPTON
CRYPTOS
CUBAGE
CUBAGES
CUBICA
CUBICAL
CUBICAS
CUBISM
CUBISMS
CUBIST
CUBISTS
CUBOID
CUBOIDS
CUCKOO
CUCKOOS
CUDDEN
CUDDENS
CUDDIE
CUDDIES
CUDDIN
CUDDINS
CUDDLE
SCUDDLE
CUDDLED
CUDDLES
CUDGEL
CUDGELS
CUEIST
CUEISTS
CUESTA
CUESTAS
CUFFED
SCUFFED
CUFFIN
CUFFING
CUFFINS
CUFFLE
SCUFFLE
CUFFLED
CUFFLES
CUISSE
CUISSER
CUISSES
CUITER
CUITERS
CULLED
SCULLED
CULLER
SCULLER
CULLERS
CULLET
CULLETS

CULMEN
CULMENS
CULTER
CULTERS
CULVER
CULVERS
CULVERT
CUMBER
SCUMBER
CUMBERS
CUMMER
SCUMMER
CUMMERS
CUMMIN
CUMMINS
CUNNER
SCUNNER
CUNNERS
CUPFUL
CUPFULS
CUPOLA
CUPOLAR
CUPOLAS
CUPPER
SCUPPER
CUPPERS
CUPULE
CUPULES
CURARA
CURARAS
CURARE
CURARES
CURARI
CURARIS
CURATE
CURATED
CURATES
CURDLE
CURDLED
CURDLES
CURFEW
CURFEWS
CURIES
ECURIES
CURIET
CURIETS
CURIOS
CURIOSA
CURIUM
CURIUMS
CURLER
CURLERS
CURLEW
CURLEWS
CURPEL
CURPELS
CURRED
SCURRED
CURRIE
CURRIED
CURRIER
CURRIES
CURSER
CURSERS
CURSOR
CURSORS
CURSORY
CURTAL
CURTALS
CURVET

CURVETS
CUSHAT
CUSHATS
CUSHAW
CUSHAWS
CUSPID
CUSPIDS
CUSSER
CUSSERS
CUSTOM
CUSTOMS
CUTELY
ACUTELY
CUTEST
ACUTEST
CUTLER
CUTLERS
CUTLERY
CUTLET
CUTLETS
CUTTER
SCUTTER
CUTTERS
CUTTLE
SCUTTLE
CUTTLES
CUTTOE
CUTTOES
CUZZES
SCUZZES
CYANIN
CYANINE
CYANINS
CYBORG
CYBORGS
CYBRID
CYBRIDS
CYCLER
CYCLERS
CYCLIC
ACYCLIC
CYGNET
CYGNETS
CYMBAL
CYMBALO
CYMBALS
CYPHER
CYPHERS
CYPRID
CYPRIDS
CYSTID
CYSTIDS
CYTASE
CYTASES
CYTODE
CYTODES
CZAPKA
CZAPKAS
DABBER
DABBERS
DABBLE
DABBLED
DABBLER
DABBLES
DACITE
DACITES
DACKER
DACKERS
DACOIT
DACOITS

DACOITY
DACTYL
DACTYLS
DADDLE
DADDLED
DADDLES
DAEMON
DAEMONS
DAFTAR
DAFTARS
DAFTIE
DAFTIES
DAGABA
DAGABAS
DAGGER
DAGGERS
DAGGLE
DAGGLED
DAGGLES
DAGOBA
DAGOBAS
DAHLIA
DAHLIAS
DAIDLE
DAIDLED
DAIDLES
DAIKER
DAIKERS
DAIKON
DAIKONS
DAIMIO
DAIMIOS
DAIMON
DAIMONS
DAINED
SDAINED
DAINES
SDAINES
DAKOIT
DAKOITI
DAKOITS
DALLOP
DALLOPS
DALTON
DALTONS
DAMAGE
DAMAGED
DAMAGES
DAMASK
DAMASKS
DAMMAR
DAMMARS
DAMMER
DAMMERS
DAMPEN
DAMPENS
DAMPER
DAMPERS
DAMSEL
DAMSELS
DAMSON
DAMSONS
DANCER
DANCERS
DANDER
DANDERS
DANDLE
DANDLED
DANDLER
DANDLES

DANGER
DANGERS
DANGLE
DANGLED
DANGLER
DANGLES
DANTON
DANTONS
DAPHNE
DAPHNES
DAPPER
DAPPERS
DAPPLE
DAPPLED
DAPPLES
DARGLE
DARGLES
DARING
DARINGS
DARKEN
DARKENS
DARKEY
DARKEYS
DARKIE
DARKIES
DARKLE
DARKLED
DARKLES
DARNEL
DARNELS
DARNER
DARNERS
DARTER
DARTERS
DARTLE
DARTLED
DARTLES
DARTRE
DARTRES
DASHER
DASHERS
DASSIE
DASSIES
DATING
DATINGS
DATIVE
DATIVES
DATURA
DATURAS
DAUBER
DAUBERS
DAUBERY
DAUNER
DAUNERS
DAUTIE
DAUTIES
DAWDLE
DAWDLED
DAWDLER
DAWDLES
DAWING
ADAWING
DAWNER
DAWNERS
DAWTIE
DAWTIES
DAZZLE
DAZZLED
DAZZLER
DAZZLES

DEACON
DEACONS
DEADEN
DEADENS
DEADER
DEADERS
DEAFEN
DEAFENS
DEALER
DEALERS
DEANER
DEANERS
DEANERY
DEARES
DEAREST
DEARIE
DEARIES
DEARTH
DEARTHS
DEASIL
DEASILS
DEBARK
DEBARKS
DEBASE
DEBASED
DEBASER
DEBASES
DEBATE
DEBATED
DEBATER
DEBATES
DEBTEE
DEBTEES
DEBTOR
DEBTORS
DEBUNK
DEBUNKS
DECADE
DECADES
DECAFF
DECAFFS
DECAMP
DECAMPS
DECANE
DECANES
DECANT
DECANTS
DECARB
DECARBS
DECARE
DECARES
DECCIE
DECCIES
DECEIT
DECEITS
DECERN
DECERNS
DECIDE
DECIDED
DECIDER
DECIDES
DECIME
DECIMES
DECKER
DECKERS
DECKLE
DECKLED
DECKLES
DECOCT
DECOCTS
DECODE
DECODED
DECODER
DECODES
DECOKE
DECOKED
DECOKES
DECREE
DECREED
DECREES
DECREET
DECREW
DECREWS
DECTET
DECTETS
DEDUCE
DEDUCED
DEDUCES
DEDUCT
DEDUCTS
DEEJAY
DEEJAYS
DEEMED
ADEEMED
DEEPEN
DEEPENS
DEEPIE
DEEPIES
DEFACE
DEFACED
DEFACER
DEFACES
DEFAME
DEFAMED
DEFAMES
DEFAST
DEFASTE
DEFEAT
DEFEATS
DEFECT
DEFECTS
DEFEND
DEFENDS
DEFIER
DEFIERS
DEFILE
DEFILED
DEFILER
DEFILES
DEFINE
DEFINED
DEFINER
DEFINES
DEFORM
DEFORMS
DEFOUL
DEFOULS
DEFRAY
DEFRAYS
DEFUSE
DEFUSED
DEFUSES
DEFUZE
DEFUZED
DEFUZES
DEGOUT
DEGOUTS
DEGREE
DEGREES
DEGUST
DEGUSTS
DEHORN
DEHORNS
DEHORT
DEHORTS
DEIGNS
SDEIGNS
DEJECT
DEJECTA
DEJECTS
DELATE
DELATED
DELATES
DELETE
DELETED
DELETES
DELICE
DELICES
DELICT
DELICTS
DELOPE
DELOPED
DELOPES
DELUDE
DELUDED
DELUDER
DELUDES
DELUGE
DELUGED
DELUGES
DELVER
DELVERS
DEMAIN
DEMAINE
DEMAINS
DEMAND
DEMANDS
DEMARK
DEMARKS
DEMEAN
DEMEANE
DEMEANS
DEMENT
DEMENTI
DEMENTS
DEMISE
DEMISED
DEMISES
DEMIST
DEMISTS
DEMODE
DEMODED
DEMOTE
DEMOTED
DEMOTES
DEMURE
DEMURED
DEMURER
DEMURES
DENGUE
DENGUES
DENIAL
DENIALS
DENIER
DENIERS
DENNET
DENNETS
DENOTE
DENOTED
DENOTES
DENTAL
EDENTAL
DENTALS
DENTEL
DENTELS
DENTIL
DENTILS
DENTIN
DENTINE
DENTING
DENTINS
DENUDE
DENUDED
DENUDES
DEODAR
DEODARS
DEPART
DEPARTS
DEPEND
DEPENDS
DEPICT
DEPICTS
DEPLOY
DEPLOYS
DEPONE
DEPONED
DEPONES
DEPORT
DEPORTS
DEPOSE
DEPOSED
DEPOSER
DEPOSES
DEPUTE
DEPUTED
DEPUTES
DERAIL
DERAILS
DERATE
DERATED
DERATES
DERHAM
DERHAMS
DERIDE
DERIDED
DERIDER
DERIDES
DERIVE
DERIVED
DERIVES
DESALT
DESALTS
DESERT
DESERTS
DESIGN
DESIGNS
DESINE
DESINED
DESINES
DESIRE
DESIRED
DESIRER
DESIRES
DESIST
DESISTS
DESMAN
DESMANS
DESMID
DESMIDS
DESORB
DESORBS
DESPOT
DESPOTS
DESYNE
DESYNED
DESYNES
DETAIL
DETAILS
DETAIN
DETAINS
DETECT
DETECTS
DETENT
DETENTE
DETENTS
DETENU
DETENUE
DETENUS
DETEST
DETESTS
DETORT
DETORTS
DETOUR
DETOURS
DETUNE
DETUNED
DETUNES
DEUTON
DEUTONS
DEVALL
DEVALLS
DEVEST
DEVESTS
DEVICE
DEVICES
DEVISE
DEVISED
DEVISEE
DEVISER
DEVISES
DEVOIR
DEVOIRS
DEVOTE
DEVOTED
DEVOTEE
DEVOTES
DEVOUR
DEVOURS
DEVVEL
DEVVELS
DEWANI
DEWANIS
DEWITT
DEWITTS
DEWLAP
DEWLAPS
DEWLAPT
DEXTER
DEXTERS
DHARMA
ADHARMA
DHARMAS
DHARNA
DHARNAS
DHOOTI
DHOOTIS
DHURRA
DHURRAS
DIABLE
DIABLES
DIADEM
DIADEMS
DIALOG
DIALOGS
DIAPER
DIAPERS
DIAPIR
DIAPIRS
DIARCH
DIARCHY
DIATOM
DIATOMS
DIAXON
DIAXONS
DIBBER
DIBBERS
DIBBLE
DIBBLED
DIBBLER
DIBBLES
DICAST
DICASTS
DICING
DICINGS
DICKER
DICKERS
DICKEY
DICKEYS
DICKIE
DICKIER
DICKIES
DIDDER
DIDDERS
DIDDLE
DIDDLED
DIDDLER
DIDDLES
DIEDRE
DIEDRES
DIESEL
DIESELS
DIETER
DIETERS
DIFFER
DIFFERS
DIGEST
DIGESTS
DIGGER
DIGGERS
DIGLOT
DIGLOTS
DIKAST
DIKASTS
DIKKOP
DIKKOPS
DIKTAT
DIKTATS
DILATE
DILATED
DILATER
DILATES
DILDOE
DILDOES
DILUTE
DILUTED
DILUTEE
DILUTER
DILUTES
DIMBLE
DIMBLES
DIMMER
DIMMERS
DIMPLE
DIMPLED
DIMPLES
DIMWIT
DIMWITS
DINDLE
DINDLED
DINDLES
DINGER
DINGERS
DINGEY
DINGEYS
DINGLE
DINGLES
DINNER
DINNERS
DINNLE
DINNLED
DINNLES
DIOXAN
DIOXANE
DIOXANS
DIOXIN
DIOXINS
DIPLOE
DIPLOES
DIPLON
DIPLONS
DIPLONT
DIPOLE
DIPOLES
DIPPER
DIPPERS
DIRDAM
DIRDAMS
DIRDUM
DIRDUMS
DIRECT
DIRECTS
DIRHAM
DIRHAMS
DIRHEM
DIRHEMS
DIRIGE
DIRIGES
DIRNDL
DIRNDLS
DISARM
DISARMS
DISBAR
DISBARK
DISBARS
DISBUD
DISBUDS
DISCUS
DISCUSS
DISEUR
DISEURS
DISMAL
DISMALS
DISMAN
DISMANS
DISMAY
DISMAYD
DISMAYL
DISMAYS
DISOWN
DISOWNS
DISPEL
DISPELS
DISPLE
DISPLED
DISPLES
DISTIL
DISTILL
DISTILS
DISUSE
DISUSED
DISUSES
DITHER
DITHERS
DITHERY
DITING
EDITING
DITONE
DITONES
DITTAY
DITTAYS
DIVERS
DIVERSE
DIVERT
DIVERTS
DIVEST
DIVESTS
DIVIDE
DIVIDED
DIVIDER
DIVIDES
DIVINE
DIVINED
DIVINER
DIVINES
DIVING
DIVINGS
DIZAIN
DIZAINS
DJEBEL
DJEBELS
DOATER
DOATERS
DOBBER
DOBBERS
DOBBIE
DOBBIES
DOBBIN
DOBBING
DOBBINS
DOCENT
DOCENTS
DOCILE
DOCILER
DOCKEN
DOCKENS
DOCKER
DOCKERS
DOCKET
DOCKETS
DOCTOR
DOCTORS
DODDER
DODDERS
DODDERY
DODDLE
DODDLES
DODGER
DODGERS
DODGERY
DODKIN

DODKINS
DODMAN
DODMANS
DOFFER
DOFFERS
DOGATE
DOGATES
DOGGER
DOGGERS
DOGGERY
DOGGIE
DOGGIER
DOGGIES
DOLINA
DOLINAS
DOLINE
DOLINES
DOLLAR
DOLLARS
DOLLOP
DOLLOPS
DOLMAN
DOLMANS
DOLMEN
DOLMENS
DOLOUR
DOLOURS
DOMAIN
DOMAINS
DOMETT
DOMETTS
DOMINO
DOMINOS
DONATE
DONATED
DONATES
DONDER
DONDERS
DONGLE
DONGLES
DONING
DONINGS
DONJON
DONJONS
DONKEY
DONKEYS
DONNAT
DONNATS
DONNEE
DONNEES
DONNOT
DONNOTS
DONSIE
DONSIER
DONZEL
DONZELS
DOOCOT
DOOCOTS
DOODAD
DOODADS
DOODAH
DOODAHS
DOODLE
DOODLED
DOODLER
DOODLES
DOOKET
DOOKETS
DOOLIE
DOOLIES
DOPANT
DOPANTS
DOPING
DOPINGS
DOPPER
DOPPERS
DOPPIE
DOPPIES
DORADO
DORADOS
DORISE
DORISED
DORISES
DORIZE
DORIZED
DORIZES
DORMER
DORMERS
DORSAL
DORSALS
DORSEL
DORSELS
DORSER
DORSERS
DORTER
DORTERS
DOSAGE
DOSAGES
DOSSAL
DOSSALS
DOSSEL
DOSSELS
DOSSER
DOSSERS
DOSSIL
DOSSILS
DOTAGE
DOTAGES
DOTANT
DOTANTS
DOTARD
DOTARDS
DOTING
DOTINGS
DOTTLE
DOTTLED
DOTTLER
DOTTLES
DOUANE
DOUANES
DOUBLE
DOUBLED
DOUBLER
DOUBLES
DOUBLET
DOUCET
DOUCETS
DOUCHE
DOUCHED
DOUCHES
DOUGHT
DOUGHTY
DOUSER
DOUSERS
DOUTER
DOUTERS
DOWLNE
DOWLNES
DOWLNEY
DOWNER
DOWNERS
DOWSER
DOWSERS
DOWSET
DOWSETS
DOYLEY
DOYLEYS
DOZING
DOZINGS
DRACHM
DRACHMA
DRACHMS
DRAGEE
DRAGEES
DRAGON
DRAGONS
DRAPER
DRAPERS
DRAPERY
DRAPET
DRAPETS
DRAUNT
DRAUNTS
DRAWEE
DRAWEES
DRAWER
DRAWERS
DRAZEL
DRAZELS
DREADS
ADREADS
DREARE
DREARER
DREARES
DREDGE
DREDGED
DREDGER
DREDGES
DRIVEL
DRIVELS
DRIVER
DRIVERS
DROGER
DROGERS
DROGUE
DROGUES
DROGUET
DROICH
DROICHS
DROICHY
DROLES
DROLEST
DROMON
DROMOND
DROMONS
DRONGO
DRONGOS
DROOME
DROOMES
DROUTH
DROUTHS
DROUTHY
DROVER
DROVERS
DROWSE
DROWSED
DROWSES
DRUDGE
DRUDGED
DRUDGER
DRUDGES
DRUPEL
DRUPELS
DRYING
DRYINGS
DUALIN
DUALINS
DUBBIN
DUBBING
DUBBINS
DUCKER
DUCKERS
DUDDER
DUDDERS
DUDDERY
DUDDIE
DUDDIER
DUDEEN
DUDEENS
DUDISM
DUDISMS
DUELLO
DUELLOS
DUENDE
DUENDES
DUENNA
DUENNAS
DUETTO
DUETTOS
DUFFEL
DUFFELS
DUFFER
DUFFERS
DUFFLE
DUFFLES
DUGONG
DUGONGS
DUGOUT
DUGOUTS
DUIKER
DUIKERS
DUMDUM
DUMDUMS
DUMPER
DUMPERS
DUMPLE
DUMPLED
DUMPLES
DUNDER
DUNDERS
DUNITE
DUNITES
DUNKER
DUNKERS
DUNLIN
DUNLINS
DUPION
DUPIONS
DUPLET
DUPLETS
DURANT
DURANTS
DURBAR
DURBARS
DURDUM
DURDUMS
DURESS
DURESSE
DURGAN
DURGANS
DURIAN
DURIANS
DURION
DURIONS
DURRIE
DURRIES
DUSKEN
DUSKENS
DUSTED
ADUSTED
DUSTER
DUSTERS
DUYKER
DUYKERS
DYBBUK
DYBBUKS
DYEING
DYEINGS
DYNAMO
DYNAMOS
DYNAST
DYNASTS
DYNASTY
DYNODE
DYNODES
DYVOUR
DYVOURS
DYVOURY
DZEREN
DZERENS
EAGLES
BEAGLES
TEAGLES
EAGLET
EAGLETS
EAGRES
MEAGRES
EANING
BEANING
LEANING
MEANING
PEANING
SEANING
WEANING
YEANING
EARBOB
EARBOBS
EARCON
EARCONS
EARDED
BEARDED
YEARDED
EARFUL
FEARFUL
TEARFUL
EARFULS
EARING
BEARING
DEARING
FEARING
GEARING
HEARING
LEARING
MEARING
NEARING
REARING
SEARING
TEARING
WEARING
EARINGS
EARLAP
EARLAPS
EARNED
LEARNED
YEARNED
EARNER
LEARNER
YEARNER
EARNERS
EARTHS
DEARTHS
HEARTHS
EARWIG
EARWIGS
EASELS
TEASELS
WEASELS
EASING
CEASING
LEASING
MEASING
PEASING
SEASING
TEASING
EASLES
MEASLES
EASTED
FEASTED
REASTED
YEASTED
EASTER
FEASTER
EASTERN
EATAGE
EATAGES
EATCHE
EATCHES
EATERS
BEATERS
HEATERS
SEATERS
EATERY
PEATERY
EATHLY
DEATHLY
EATING
BEATING
FEATING
HEATING
SEATING
EATINGS
EBBING
KEBBING
NEBBING
WEBBING
ECARTE
ECARTES
ECBOLE
ECBOLES
ECHING
EECHING
LECHING
PECHING
ECHOER
ECHOERS
ECLAIR
ECLAIRS
ECLOSE
RECLOSE
ECLOSED
ECLOSES
ECONUT
ECONUTS
ECTYPE
ECTYPES
ECURIE
ECURIES
ECZEMA
ECZEMAS
EDDIES
NEDDIES
TEDDIES
EDDISH
REDDISH
EDEMAS
OEDEMAS
EDGERS
HEDGERS
KEDGERS
LEDGERS
EDGIER
HEDGIER
KEDGIER
LEDGIER
SEDGIER
WEDGIER
EDGING
HEDGING
KEDGING
WEDGING
EDGINGS
EDIBLE
EDIBLES
EDILES
AEDILES
EDITOR
EDITORS
EDUCED
DEDUCED
REDUCED
SEDUCED
EDUCES
DEDUCES
REDUCES
SEDUCES
EDUCTS
DEDUCTS
EECHED
LEECHED
REECHED
EECHES
BEECHES
KEECHES
LEECHES
REECHES
EELIER
SEELIER
EERIER
BEERIER
LEERIER
PEERIER
EFFACE
EFFACED
EFFACES
EFFECT
EFFECTS
EFFEIR
EFFEIRS
EFFERE
EFFERED
EFFERES
EFFING
JEFFING
REFFING
EFFORT
EFFORTS
EFFRAY
EFFRAYS
EFFUSE
EFFUSED
EFFUSES
EFTEST
DEFTEST
EGALLY
LEGALLY
REGALLY
EGENCE
REGENCE
EGENCES
EGENCY
REGENCY
EGESTS
REGESTS
EGGARS
BEGGARS
SEGGARS
EGGCUP
EGGCUPS
EGGERS
LEGGERS
EGGIER
LEGGIER
EGGING
BEGGING
LEGGING
PEGGING
EGGLER
EGGLERS
EGGNOG
EGGNOGS
EGISES
AEGISES
EGOISM
EGOISMS
EGOIST
EGOISTS
EGRESS
NEGRESS
REGRESS
EGRETS
REGRETS
EIGHTH
EIGHTHS
EIGHTS
HEIGHTS
WEIGHTS
EIGHTY
WEIGHTY
EIRACK
EIRACKS
EISELL
EISELLS
EITHER
NEITHER
EJECTA
DEJECTA
EJECTS
DEJECTS
REJECTS
ELANCE

ELANCED
ELANCES
ELANET
ELANETS
ELAPSE
DELAPSE
RELAPSE
ELAPSED
ELAPSES
ELATED
BELATED
DELATED
RELATED
VELATED
ELATER
RELATER
ELATERS
ELATES
BELATES
DELATES
RELATES
ELCHEE
ELCHEES
ELDERS
GELDERS
MELDERS
WELDERS
ELDING
GELDING
MELDING
WELDING
ELDINGS
ELECTS
SELECTS
ELEGIT
ELEGITS
ELENCH
ELENCHI
ELENCHS
ELEVEN
ELEVENS
ELEVON
ELEVONS
ELFING
SELFING
ELFISH
SELFISH
ELICIT
ELICITS
ELITES
PELITES
ELIXIR
ELIXIRS
ELOIGN
ELOIGNS
ELOPED
DELOPED
ELOPER
ELOPERS
ELOPES
DELOPES
ELSHIN
ELSHINS
ELTCHI
ELTCHIS
ELUANT
ELUANTS
ELUATE
ELUATES
ELUDED
DELUDED
ELUDER
DELUDER
ELUDERS
ELUDES
DELUDES
ELUENT
ELUENTS
ELUTOR
ELUTORS
ELUVIA
ELUVIAL
ELVERS
DELVERS
ELYTRA
ELYTRAL
EMBACE
EMBACES
EMBAIL
EMBAILS
EMBALE
EMBALED
EMBALES
EMBALL
EMBALLS
EMBALM
EMBALMS
EMBANK
EMBANKS
EMBARK
EMBARKS
EMBASE
EMBASED
EMBASES
EMBERS
MEMBERS
EMBLEM
EMBLEMA
EMBLEMS
EMBLIC
EMBLICS
EMBOIL
EMBOILS
EMBOLI
EMBOLIC
EMBRUE
EMBRUED
EMBRUES
EMBRYO
EMBRYON
EMBRYOS
EMERGE
DEMERGE
REMERGE
EMERGED
EMERGES
EMESES
NEMESES
EMESIS
NEMESIS
EMETIC
EMETICS
EMETIN
EMETINE
EMETINS
EMEUTE
EMEUTES
EMIGRE
EMIGRES
EMMOVE
EMMOVED
EMMOVES
EMOTED
DEMOTED
EMOTES
DEMOTES
REMOTES
EMOVED
REMOVED
EMOVES
REMOVES
EMPALE
EMPALED
EMPALES
EMPARE
EMPARED
EMPARES
EMPARL
EMPARLS
EMPART
EMPARTS
EMPIRE
EMPIRES
EMPLOY
EMPLOYS
EMPUSA
EMPUSAS
EMPUSE
EMPUSES
EMULED
AEMULED
EMULES
AEMULES
EMULGE
EMULGED
EMULGES
EMUNGE
EMUNGED
EMUNGES
EMURED
DEMURED
EMURES
DEMURES
LEMURES
ENABLE
TENABLE
ENABLED
ENABLER
ENABLES
ENAMEL
ENAMELS
ENAMOR
ENAMORS
ENCAGE
ENCAGED
ENCAGES
ENCALM
ENCALMS
ENCAMP
ENCAMPS
ENCASE
ENCASED
ENCASES
ENCAVE
ENCAVED
ENCAVES
ENCODE
ENCODED
ENCODES
ENCORE
ENCORED
ENCORES
ENCYST
ENCYSTS
ENDART
ENDARTS
ENDEAR
ENDEARS
ENDING
BENDING
FENDING
HENDING
LENDING
MENDING
PENDING
RENDING
SENDING
TENDING
VENDING
WENDING
ENDINGS
ENDITE
ENDITED
ENDITES
ENDIVE
ENDIVES
ENDUES
VENDUES
ENDURE
ENDURED
ENDURER
ENDURES
ENERVE
ENERVED
ENERVES
ENEWED
RENEWED
ENFACE
ENFACED
ENFACES
ENFANT
ENFANTS
ENFIRE
ENFIRED
ENFIRES
ENFOLD
PENFOLD
TENFOLD
ENFOLDS
ENFORM
ENFORMS
ENFREE
ENFREED
ENFREES
ENGAGE
ENGAGED
ENGAGER
ENGAGES
ENGAOL
ENGAOLS
ENGILD
ENGILDS
ENGINE
ENGINED
ENGINER
ENGINES
ENGIRD
ENGIRDS
ENGLUT
ENGLUTS
ENGOBE
ENGOBES
ENGORE
ENGORED
ENGORES
ENGRAM
ENGRAMS
ENGULF
ENGULFS
ENHALO
ENHALOS
ENIGMA
ENIGMAS
ENISLE
ENISLED
ENISLES
ENJAMB
ENJAMBS
ENJOIN
ENJOINS
ENLACE
ENLACED
ENLACES
ENLARD
ENLARDS
ENLINK
ENLINKS
ENLIST
ENLISTS
ENLOCK
GENLOCK
ENLOCKS
ENMOVE
ENMOVED
ENMOVES
ENNAGE
ENNAGES
ENNEAD
ENNEADS
ENNUYE
ENNUYED
ENOSES
KENOSES
ENOSIS
KENOSIS
ENOUGH
ENOUGHS
ENRACE
ENRACED
ENRACES
ENRAGE
ENRAGED
ENRAGES
ENRANK
ENRANKS
ENRING
ENRINGS
ENROBE
ENROBED
ENROBES
ENROLL
ENROLLS
ENROOT
ENROOTS
ENSATE
SENSATE
ENSEAL
ENSEALS
ENSEAM
ENSEAMS
ENSEAR
ENSEARS
ENSIGN
ENSIGNS
ENSILE
PENSILE
SENSILE
TENSILE
ENSILED
ENSILES
ENSOUL
ENSOULS
ENSURE
CENSURE
ENSURED
ENSURER
ENSURES
ENTAIL
VENTAIL
ENTAILS
ENTAME
ENTAMED
ENTAMES
ENTERA
ENTERAL
ENTERS
CENTERS
RENTERS
TENTERS
VENTERS
ENTETE
ENTETEE
ENTICE
PENTICE
ENTICED
ENTICER
ENTICES
ENTIRE
ENTIRES
ENTOIL
ENTOILS
ENTOMB
ENTOMBS
ENTRAP
ENTRAPS
ENTREE
ENTREES
ENURED
TENURED
ENURES
TENURES
ENVIER
ENVIERS
ENVIES
SENVIES
ENVOIS
RENVOIS
ENVOYS
LENVOYS
RENVOYS
ENWALL
ENWALLS
ENWIND
ENWINDS
ENWOMB
ENWOMBS
ENWRAP
ENWRAPS
ENZIAN
ENZIANS
ENZONE
ENZONED
ENZONES
ENZYME
ENZYMES
EOLITH
NEOLITH
EOLITHS
EONISM
PEONISM
EONISMS
EPARCH
EPARCHS
EPARCHY
EPAULE
EPAULES
EPAULET
EPEIRA
EPEIRAS
EPERDU
EPERDUE
EPHEBE
EPHEBES
EPHEBI
EPHEBIC
EPIGON
EPIGONE
EPIGONI
EPIGONS
EPILOG
EPILOGS
EPIMER
EPIMERS
EPIZOA
EPIZOAN
EPOCHA
EPOCHAL
EPOCHAS
EPONYM
EPONYMS
EPOPEE
EPOPEES
EPOSES
DEPOSES
REPOSES
EPRISE
REPRISE
EPUISE
EPUISEE
EQUANT
EQUANTS
EQUATE
EQUATED
EQUATES
EQUIPE
EQUIPES
ERASER
ERASERS
ERBIUM
TERBIUM
ERBIUMS
ERGATE
ERGATES
ERIACH
ERIACHS
ERINGO
ERINGOS
ERMINE
ERMINED
ERMINES
ERNING
CERNING
FERNING
GERNING
KERNING
TERNING
EROTIC
XEROTIC
EROTICA
EROTICS
ERRAND
ERRANDS
ERRANT
ERRANTS
ERRING
HERRING
SERRING
ERRINGS
ERRORS
TERRORS
ERYNGO
ERYNGOS
ESCAPE
ESCAPED
ESCAPEE
ESCAPER
ESCAPES
ESCARP
ESCARPS
ESCHAR
ESCHARS
ESCHEW
ESCHEWS
ESCORT
ESCORTS
ESCROC
ESCROCS
ESCROL
ESCROLL
ESCROLS
ESCROW
ESCROWS
ESCUDO
ESCUDOS
ESILES
RESILES
ESLOIN
ESLOINS
ESPADA
ESPADAS
ESPIAL
ESPIALS
ESPRIT
ESPRITS
ESSIVE
ESSIVES
ESSOIN
ESSOINS
ESTATE
GESTATE
RESTATE
TESTATE
ESTATED
ESTATES
ESTEEM
ESTEEMS
ESTERS
FESTERS
JESTERS
NESTERS

PESTERS
RESTERS
TESTERS
WESTERS
ZESTERS
ESTRAL
OESTRAL
VESTRAL
ESTRAY
ESTRAYS
ESTRUM
OESTRUM
ESTRUMS
ESTRUS
OESTRUS
ETAGES
METAGES
ETALON
ETALONS
ETCHED
FETCHED
LETCHED
RETCHED
ETCHER
ETCHERS
ETCHES
FETCHES
KETCHES
LETCHES
RETCHES
VETCHES
ETHANE
METHANE
ETHANES
ETHENE
ETHENES
ETHERS
AETHERS
PETHERS
TETHERS
WETHERS
ETHNIC
ETHNICS
ETHYLS
METHYLS
ETHYNE
ETHYNES
ETOILE
ETOILES
ETRIER
ETRIERS
ETTLED
FETTLED
METTLED
NETTLED
PETTLED
SETTLED
ETTLES
FETTLES
KETTLES
METTLES
NETTLES
PETTLES
SETTLES
ETYMON
ETYMONS
EUCAIN
EUCAINE
EUCAINS
EUCHRE
EUCHRED
EUCHRES
EUGHEN
LEUGHEN
EUKING
YEUKING
EUNUCH
EUNUCHS
EUOUAE
EUOUAES
EUPHON
EUPHONS
EUPHONY
EUREKA
HEUREKA
EUREKAS
EVADER
EVADERS
EVEJAR
EVEJARS
EVENER
EVENERS
EVERTS
REVERTS
EVINCE
EVINCED
EVINCES
EVITES
LEVITES
EVOKED
REVOKED
EVOKER
EVOKERS
EVOKES
REVOKES
EVOLUE
EVOLUES
EVOLVE
DEVOLVE
REVOLVE
EVOLVED
EVOLVER
EVOLVES
EVOVAE
EVOVAES
EVULSE
EVULSED
EVULSES
EVZONE
EVZONES
EXACTS
HEXACTS
EXAMEN
EXAMENS
EXARCH
HEXARCH
EXARCHS
EXARCHY
EXCAMB
EXCAMBS
EXCEED
EXCEEDS
EXCEPT
EXCEPTS
EXCIDE
EXCIDED
EXCIDES
EXCISE
EXCISED
EXCISES
EXCITE
EXCITED
EXCITER
EXCITES
EXCUSE
EXCUSED
EXCUSER
EXCUSES
EXEDRA
EXEDRAE
EXEMES
LEXEMES
EXEMPT
EXEMPTS
EXHALE
EXHALED
EXHALES
EXHORT
EXHORTS
EXHUME
EXHUMED
EXHUMER
EXHUMES
EXISTS
SEXISTS
EXOGEN
EXOGENS
EXONYM
EXONYMS
EXOPOD
EXOPODS
EXOTIC
EXOTICA
EXOTICS
EXPAND
EXPANDS
EXPECT
EXPECTS
EXPEND
EXPENDS
EXPERT
SEXPERT
EXPERTS
EXPIRE
EXPIRED
EXPIRES
EXPORT
EXPORTS
EXPOSE
EXPOSED
EXPOSER
EXPOSES
EXPUGN
EXPUGNS
EXSECT
EXSECTS
EXSERT
EXSERTS
EXTANT
SEXTANT
EXTEND
EXTENDS
EXTENT
EXTENTS
EXTERN
EXTERNE
EXTERNS
EXTINE
EXTINES
EXTIRP
EXTIRPS
EXTORT
EXTORTS
EYALET
EYALETS
EYEFUL
EYEFULS
EYELET
EYELETS
EYELID
EYELIDS
EYLIAD
EYLIADS
FABLER
FABLERS
FABRIC
FABRICS
FACADE
FACADES
FACETE
FACETED
FACIAL
FACIALS
FACING
FACINGS
FACTOR
FACTORS
FACTORY
FACTUM
FACTUMS
FACULA
FACULAE
FACULAR
FADDLE
FADDLED
FADDLES
FADEUR
FADEURS
FADING
FADINGS
FAERIE
FAERIES
FAGGOT
FAGGOTS
FAIBLE
FAIBLES
FAILLE
FAILLES
FAINES
FAINEST
FAITOR
FAITORS
FALCON
FALCONS
FALLAL
FALLALS
FALLER
FALLERS
FALLOW
FALLOWS
FALSER
FALSERS
FALSES
FALSEST
FALSIE
FALSIES
FALTER
FALTERS
FAMINE
FAMINES
FANDOM
FANDOMS
FANGLE
FANGLED
FANGLES
FANION
FANIONS
FANKLE
FANKLED
FANKLES
FANNEL
FANNELL
FANNELS
FANNER
FANNERS
FANTAD
FANTADS
FANTOD
FANTODS
FANTOM
FANTOMS
FAQUIR
FAQUIRS
FARCIN
FARCING
FARCINS
FARDEL
FARDELS
FARDEN
FARDENS
FARINA
FARINAS
FARMER
FARMERS
FARMERY
FARREN
FARRENS
FARROW
FARROWS
FASCIA
FASCIAL
FASCIAS
FASTEN
FASTENS
FASTER
FASTERS
FATHER
FATHERS
FATHOM
FATHOMS
FATSIA
FATSIAS
FATTEN
FATTENS
FATWAH
FATWAHS
FAUCET
FAUCETS
FAUTOR
FAUTORS
FAVELA
FAVELAS
FAVISM
FAVISMS
FAVOUR
FAVOURS
FAWNER
FAWNERS
FEAGUE
FEAGUED
FEAGUES
FEARED
AFEARED
FECULA
FECULAS
FEDORA
FEDORAS
FEEBLE
FEEBLED
FEEBLER
FEEBLES
FEEDER
FEEDERS
FEELER
FEELERS
FEERIE
FEERIES
FEERIN
FEERING
FEERINS
FEIJOA
FEIJOAS
FELINE
FELINES
FELLAH
FELLAHS
FELLER
FELLERS
FELLOE
FELLOES
FELLOW
FELLOWS
FELTER
FELTERS
FEMALE
FEMALES
FEMORA
FEMORAL
FENCER
FENCERS
FENDER
FENDERS
FENNEC
FENNECS
FENNEL
FENNELS
FERREL
FERRELS
FERRET
FERRETS
FERRETY
FERULA
FERULAS
FERULE
FERULES
FESCUE
FESCUES
FESTAL
FESTALS
FESTER
FESTERS
FETICH
FETICHE
FETTER
FETTERS
FETTLE
FETTLED
FETTLER
FETTLES
FEUTRE
FEUTRED
FEUTRES
FEWMET
FEWMETS
FEWTER
FEWTERS
FIACRE
FIACRES
FIANCE
FIANCEE
FIANCES
FIASCO
FIASCOS
FIAUNT
FIAUNTS
FIBBER
FIBBERS
FIBBERY
FIBRIL
FIBRILS
FIBRIN
FIBRINS
FIBROS
FIBROSE
FIBULA
FIBULAE
FIBULAR
FIBULAS
FICKLE
FICKLED
FICKLER
FICKLES
FICTOR
FICTORS
FIDDLE
FIDDLED
FIDDLER
FIDDLES
FIDDLEY
FIDGET
FIDGETS
FIDGETY
FIERCE
FIERCER
FIESTA
FIESTAS
FIGURE
FIGURED
FIGURES
FILFOT
FILFOTS
FILING
FILINGS
FILLER
FILLERS
FILLET
FILLETS
FILLIP
FILLIPS
FILTER
FILTERS
FIMBLE
FIMBLES
FINALE
FINALES
FINDER
FINDERS
FINEER
FINEERS
FINGAN
FINGANS
FINGER
FINGERS
FINIAL
FINIALS
FINING
FININGS
FINJAN
FINJANS
FINNAC
FINNACK
FINNACS
FINNAN
FINNANS
FINNER
FINNERS
FIORIN
FIORINS
FIPPLE
FIPPLES
FIRING
FIRINGS
FIRKIN
FIRKING
FIRKINS
FIRLOT
FIRLOTS
FIRMAN
FIRMANS
FIRMER
FIRMERS
FISCAL
FISCALS
FISGIG
FISGIGS
FISHER
FISHERS
FISHERY
FISSLE
FISSLED
FISSLES
FITCHE
FITCHEE
FITCHES
FITCHET
FITCHEW
FITTER
FITTERS
FITTES
FITTEST
FIXATE
FIXATED
FIXATES
FIXING
FIXINGS
FIXURE
FIXURES
FIZGIG
FIZGIGS
FIZZEN
FIZZENS
FIZZER
FIZZERS
FIZZLE
FIZZLED
FIZZLES
FLACON
FLACONS
FLAGON
FLAGONS

FLAMEN
FLAMENS
FLANGE
FLANGED
FLANGES
FLASER
FLASERS
FLAUNE
FLAUNES
FLAUNT
FLAUNTS
FLAUNTY
FLAVIN
FLAVINE
FLAVINS
FLAVOR
FLAVORS
FLAYER
FLAYERS
FLECHE
FLECHES
FLEDGE
FLEDGED
FLEDGES
FLEECE
FLEECED
FLEECER
FLEECES
FLENSE
FLENSED
FLENSES
FLEXOR
FLEXORS
FLIGHT
FLIGHTS
FLIGHTY
FLORET
FLORETS
FLORIN
FLORINS
FLOTEL
FLOTELS
FLOUSE
FLOUSED
FLOUSES
FLOWER
FLOWERS
FLOWERY
FLUATE
FLUATES
FLUENT
FLUENTS
FLUGEL
FLUGELS
FLUTER
FLUTERS
FLYING
FLYINGS
FLYWAY
FLYWAYS
FODDER
FODDERS
FOETOR
FOETORS
FOGGER
FOGGERS
FOGLES
FOGLESS
FOGRAM
FOGRAMS
FOIBLE
FOIBLES
FOISON
FOISONS
FOLATE
FOLATES
FOLDER
FOLDERS
FOLIOS
FOLIOSE
FOLKIE
FOLKIES
FOLLOW
FOLLOWS
FOMENT
FOMENTS
FONDLE
FONDLED
FONDLER
FONDLES
FONDUE
FONDUES
FOODIE
FOODIES
FOOTER
FOOTERS
FOOTIE
FOOTIER
FOOTIES
FOOTLE
FOOTLED
FOOTLES
FOOTRA
FOOTRAS
FOOZLE
FOOZLED
FOOZLER
FOOZLES
FORAGE
FORAGED
FORAGER
FORAGES
FORBAD
FORBADE
FORBID
FORBIDS
FORCAT
FORCATS
FORCER
FORCERS
FOREST
FORESTS
FORGER
FORGERS
FORGERY
FORGET
FORGETS
FORHOO
FORHOOS
FORHOW
FORHOWS
FORINT
FORINTS
FORKER
FORKERS
FORMAT
FORMATE
FORMATS
FORMER
FORMERS
FORMOL
FORMOLS
FORPET
FORPETS
FORPIT
FORPITS
FORRAY
FORRAYS
FORSAY
FORSAYS
FOSSIL
FOSSILS
FOSSOR
FOSSORS
FOSTER
FOSTERS
FOTHER
FOTHERS
FOUGHT
FOUGHTY
FOULES
FOULEST
FOURTH
FOURTHS
FOUSSA
FOUSSAS
FOUTER
FOUTERS
FOUTRA
FOUTRAS
FOUTRE
FOUTRED
FOUTRES
FOWLER
FOWLERS
FOXING
FOXINGS
FRAGOR
FRAGORS
FRAISE
FRAISED
FRAISES
FRAMER
FRAMERS
FRAPPE
FRAPPED
FRAPPEE
FRAPPES
FRATCH
FRATCHY
FRATER
FRATERS
FRATERY
FRAZIL
FRAZILS
FREETS
AFREETS
FREEZE
FREEZER
FREEZES
FREMIT
FREMITS
FRESCO
FRESCOS
FRIAND
FRIANDE
FRIANDS
FRICHT
FRICHTS
FRIDGE
FRIDGED
FRIDGES
FRIEND
FRIENDS
FRIEZE
FRIEZED
FRIEZES
FRIGHT
FRIGHTS
FRIGOT
FRIGOTS
FRIJOL
FRIJOLE
FRINGE
FRINGED
FRINGES
FRIPON
FRIPONS
FRISEE
FRISEES
FRISKA
FRISKAS
FRIVOL
FRIVOLS
FROISE
FROISES
FROLIC
FROLICS
FROWIE
FROWIER
FROWST
FROWSTS
FROWSTY
FRUICT
FRUICTS
FRYING
FRYINGS
FUCKER
FUCKERS
FUCOID
FUCOIDS
FUDDLE
FUDDLED
FUDDLER
FUDDLES
FUGATO
FUGATOS
FULFIL
FULFILL
FULFILS
FULGOR
FULGORS
FULHAM
FULHAMS
FULLAM
FULLAMS
FULLAN
FULLANS
FULLER
FULLERS
FULMAR
FULMARS
FUMADO
FUMADOS
FUMAGE
FUMAGES
FUMBLE
FUMBLED
FUMBLER
FUMBLES
FUNDER
FUNDERS
FUNDIE
FUNDIES
FUNKIA
FUNKIAS
FUNNEL
FUNNELS
FURANE
FURANES
FUREUR
FUREURS
FURFUR
FURFURS
FUROLE
FUROLES
FURORE
FURORES
FURROW
FURROWS
FURROWY
FUSAIN
FUSAINS
FUSION
FUSIONS
FUSSER
FUSSERS
FUSTET
FUSTETS
FUSTIC
FUSTICS
FUSTOC
FUSTOCS
FUTILE
FUTILER
FUTURE
FUTURES
FUZZLE
FUZZLED
FUZZLES
FYLFOT
FYLFOTS
GABBER
GABBERS
GABBLE
GABBLED
GABBLER
GABBLES
GABBRO
GABBROS
GABION
GABIONS
GABLET
GABLETS
GADDER
GADDERS
GADGET
GADGETS
GADGIE
GADGIES
GADOID
GADOIDS
GAFFER
GAFFERS
GAGAKU
GAGAKUS
GAGGER
GAGGERS
GAGGLE
GAGGLED
GAGGLES
GAINER
GAINERS
GAITER
GAITERS
GALAGE
GALAGES
GALAGO
GALAGOS
GALENA
GALENAS
GALERE
GALERES
GALIOT
GALIOTS
GALLET
GALLETS
GALLEY
GALLEYS
GALLON
GALLONS
GALLOP
GALLOPS
GALLOW
GALLOWS
GALOOT
GALOOTS
GALUTH
GALUTHS
GAMBET
GAMBETS
GAMBIR
GAMBIRS
GAMBIT
GAMBITS
GAMBLE
GAMBLED
GAMBLER
GAMBLES
GAMBOL
GAMBOLS
GAMETE
GAMETES
GAMINE
GAMINES
GAMING
GAMINGS
GAMMER
GAMMERS
GAMMON
GAMMONS
GANDER
GANDERS
GANGER
GANGERS
GANGUE
GANGUES
GANNET
GANNETS
GANOID
GANOIDS
GANOIN
GANOINE
GANOINS
GANSEY
GANSEYS
GAOLER
GAOLERS
GAPING
GAPINGS
GARAGE
GARAGED
GARAGES
GARBLE
GARBLED
GARBLER
GARBLES
GARCON
GARCONS
GARDEN
GARDENS
GARGET
GARGETS
GARGETY
GARGLE
GARGLED
GARGLES
GARIAL
GARIALS
GARJAN
GARJANS
GARLIC
GARLICS
GARNER
GARNERS
GARNET
GARNETS
GARRAN
GARRANS
GARRET
GARRETS
GARRON
GARRONS
GARROT
GARROTE
GARROTS
GARRYA
GARRYAS
GARTER
GARTERS
GARUDA
GARUDAS
GARVIE
GARVIES
GASBAG
GASBAGS
GASCON
GASCONS
GASKET
GASKETS
GASKIN
GASKINS
GASPER
GASPERS
GASSER
GASSERS
GASTER
GASTERS
GATEAU
GATEAUS
GATEAUX
GATHER
GATHERS
GATING
GATINGS
GAUCHE
GAUCHER
GAUCHO
GAUCHOS
GAUCIE
GAUCIER
GAUFER
GAUFERS
GAUFRE
GAUFRES
GAUGER
GAUGERS
GAUPER
GAUPERS
GAVAGE
GAVAGES
GAVIAL
GAVIALS
GAWKER
GAWKERS
GAWPER
GAWPERS
GAZEBO
GAZEBOS
GAZOON
GAZOONS
GAZUMP
GAZUMPS
GEEGAW
GEEGAWS
GEEZER
GEEZERS
GEISHA
GEISHAS
GEISTS
AGEISTS
GELADA
GELADAS
GELATI
GELATIN
GELDER
GELDERS
GENDER
GENDERS
GENERA
GENERAL
GENEVA
GENEVAS
GENNEL
GENNELS
GENNET
GENNETS
GENOME
GENOMES
GENTLE
GENTLED
GENTLER
GENTLES
GENTOO
GENTOOS
GEODES
GEODESY
GERBIL
GERBILS
GERENT
GERENTS
GERMAN
GERMANE
GERMANS
GERMEN
GERMENS
GERMIN
GERMING
GERMINS
GERUND

GERUNDS
GETTER
GETTERS
GEWGAW
GEWGAWS
GEYSER
GEYSERS
GHARRI
GHARRIS
GHAZAL
GHAZALS
GHAZEL
GHAZELS
GHERAO
GHERAOS
GHESSE
GHESSED
GHESSES
GHETTO
GHETTOS
GIAOUR
GIAOURS
GIBBER
GIBBERS
GIBBET
GIBBETS
GIBBON
GIBBONS
GIBLET
GIBLETS
GIDGEE
GIDGEES
GIDJEE
GIDJEES
GIGGIT
GIGGITS
GIGGLE
GIGGLED
GIGGLER
GIGGLES
GIGLET
GIGLETS
GIGLOT
GIGLOTS
GIGOLO
GIGOLOS
GILCUP
GILCUPS
GILDER
GILDERS
GILGAI
GILGAIS
GILGIE
GILGIES
GILLET
GILLETS
GILLIE
GILLIED
GILLIES
GILPEY
GILPEYS
GIMBAL
GIMBALS
GIMLET
GIMLETS
GIMMAL
GIMMALS
GIMMER
GIMMERS
GIMMOR
GIMMORS
GINGAL
GINGALL
GINGALS
GINGER
GINGERS
GINGERY
GINGLE
GINGLES
GINNEL
GINNELS
GINNER
AGINNER
GINNERS
GINNERY
GIPSEN
GIPSENS
GIRDER
GIRDERS
GIRDLE
GIRDLED
GIRDLER
GIRDLES
GIRKIN
GIRKINS
GIRLIE
GIRLIES
GIRNEL
GIRNELS
GIRNER
GIRNERS
GIRNIE
GIRNIER
GITANA
GITANAS
GITANO
GITANOS
GIVING
GIVINGS
GIZZEN
GIZZENS
GLAIVE
GLAIVED
GLAIVES
GLAMOR
GLAMORS
GLANCE
GLANCED
GLANCES
GLAZER
GLAZERS
GLEAVE
GLEAVES
GLEDGE
GLEDGED
GLEDGES
GLIDER
GLIDERS
GLIOMA
GLIOMAS
GLOBIN
GLOBING
GLOBINS
GLOIRE
GLOIRES
GLORIA
GLORIAS
GLOSSA
GLOSSAE
GLOSSAL
GLOSSAS
GLOVER
GLOVERS
GLOWER
GLOWERS
GLUTEN
GLUTENS
GLYCIN
GLYCINE
GLYCINS
GLYCOL
GLYCOLS
GNAWER
GNAWERS
GNOMON
GNOMONS
GOALIE
GOALIES
GOANNA
GOANNAS
GOATEE
GOATEED
GOATEES
GOBANG
GOBANGS
GOBBET
GOBBETS
GOBBLE
GOBBLED
GOBBLER
GOBBLES
GOBIID
GOBIIDS
GOBLET
GOBLETS
GOBLIN
GOBLINS
GODDAM
GODDAMN
GODDEN
GODDENS
GODOWN
GODOWNS
GODSON
GODSONS
GODWIT
GODWITS
GOFFER
GOFFERS
GOGGLE
GOGGLED
GOGGLER
GOGGLES
GOGLET
GOGLETS
GOITER
GOITERS
GOITRE
GOITRED
GOITRES
GOLDEN
GOLDENS
GOLFER
GOLFERS
GOLLAN
GOLLAND
GOLLANS
GOLLAR
GOLLARS
GOLLER
GOLLERS
GOLLOP
GOLLOPS
GOMBRO
GOMBROS
GOMOKU
GOMOKUS
GOMUTI
GOMUTIS
GOMUTO
GOMUTOS
GOOBER
GOOBERS
GOOGLE
GOOGLED
GOOGLES
GOOGOL
GOOGOLS
GOOLEY
GOOLEYS
GOOLIE
GOOLIES
GOONDA
GOONDAS
GOONEY
GOONEYS
GOOROO
GOOROOS
GOOSEY
GOOSEYS
GOPHER
GOPHERS
GOPURA
GOPURAM
GOPURAS
GORGET
GORGETS
GORGIA
GORGIAS
GORGIO
GORGIOS
GORGON
GORGONS
GORING
GORINGS
GOSLET
GOSLETS
GOSPEL
GOSPELS
GOSSAN
GOSSANS
GOSSIB
GOSSIBS
GOSSIP
GOSSIPS
GOSSIPY
GOURDE
GOURDES
GOUTTE
GOUTTES
GOVERN
GOVERNS
GOWFER
GOWFERS
GOWLAN
GOWLAND
GOWLANS
GOWPEN
GOWPENS
GOZZAN
GOZZANS
GRABEN
GRABENS
GRADER
GRADERS
GRADIN
GRADINE
GRADING
GRADINI
GRADINO
GRADINS
GRAILE
GRAILES
GRAINE
GRAINED
GRAINER
GRAINES
GRAITH
GRAITHS
GRAKLE
GRAKLES
GRAMAS
GRAMASH
GRAMMA
GRAMMAR
GRAMMAS
GRAMME
GRAMMES
GRANDE
GRANDEE
GRANDER
GRANGE
GRANGER
GRANGES
GRAPLE
GRAPLES
GRAPPA
GRAPPAS
GRASTE
AGRASTE
GRATER
GRATERS
GRATIN
GRATINE
GRATING
GRATINS
GRAVEL
GRAVELS
GRAVELY
GRAVER
GRAVERS
GRAVES
GRAVEST
GRAYLE
GRAYLES
GRAZER
GRAZERS
GREASE
GREASED
GREASER
GREASES
GREAVE
GREAVED
GREAVES
GREECE
GREECES
GREESE
GREESES
GREETE
GREETED
GREETER
GREETES
GRICER
GRICERS
GRIECE
GRIECED
GRIECES
GRIEVE
GRIEVED
GRIEVER
GRIEVES
GRIFFE
GRIFFES
GRIGRI
GRIGRIS
GRILLE
GRILLED
GRILLES
GRILSE
GRILSES
GRINGO
GRINGOS
GRIPER
GRIPERS
GRIPPE
GRIPPED
GRIPPER
GRIPPES
GRISED
AGRISED
GRISES
AGRISES
GRISON
GRISONS
GRIVET
GRIVETS
GRIZES
AGRIZES
GROCER
GROCERS
GROCERY
GROMET
GROMETS
GROOVE
GROOVED
GROOVER
GROOVES
GROPER
GROPERS
GROSER
GROSERS
GROSERT
GROSET
GROSETS
GROTTO
GROTTOS
GROUCH
GROUCHY
GROUGH
GROUGHS
GROUND
AGROUND
GROUNDS
GROUSE
GROUSED
GROUSER
GROUSES
GROVEL
GROVELS
GROVET
GROVETS
GROWER
GROWERS
GROWTH
GROWTHS
GROYNE
GROYNES
GRUDGE
GRUDGED
GRUDGES
GRUMPH
GRUMPHS
GRUNGE
GRUNGES
GRYFON
GRYFONS
GUANAS
IGUANAS
GUANGO
GUANGOS
GUBBAH
GUBBAHS
GUDDLE
GUDDLED
GUDDLES
GUENON
GUENONS
GUFFAW
GUFFAWS
GUFFIE
GUFFIES
GUGGLE
GUGGLED
GUGGLES
GUIDER
GUIDERS
GUIDON
GUIDONS
GUILER
GUILERS
GUINEA
GUINEAS
GUISED
AGUISED
GUISER
GUISERS
GUISES
AGUISES
GUITAR
GUITARS
GUIZER
GUIZERS
GULDEN
GULDENS
GULLER
GULLERS
GULLERY
GULLET
GULLETS
GULLEY
GULLEYS
GULPER
GULPERS
GUMNUT
GUMNUTS
GUNITE
GUNITES
GUNNEL
GUNNELS
GUNNER
GUNNERA
GUNNERS
GUNNERY
GUNSEL
GUNSELS
GUNTER
GUNTERS
GUNYAH
GUNYAHS
GURAMI
GURAMIS
GURGLE
GURGLED
GURGLES
GURJUN
GURJUNS
GURLET
GURLETS
GURNET
GURNETS
GURNEY
GURNEYS
GURRAH
GURRAHS
GUSHER
GUSHERS
GUSLAR
GUSLARS
GUSSET
GUSSETS
GUSSIE
GUSSIES
GUSTIE
GUSTIER
GUTFUL
GUTFULS
GUTROT
GUTROTS
GUTSER
GUTSERS
GUTTER
GUTTERS
GUTTLE
GUTTLED
GUTTLES
GUTZER
GUTZERS
GUYLER
GUYLERS
GUZZLE
GUZZLED
GUZZLER
GUZZLES
GYMBAL
GYMBALS
GYMMAL
GYMMALS
GYNNEY
GYNNEYS
GYPPIE
GYPPIES
GYPSUM
GYPSUMS
GYRATE
GYRATED
GYRATES
HABOOB
HABOOBS
HACHIS
RHACHIS

HACKED
CHACKED
WHACKED
HACKEE
HACKEES
HACKER
WHACKER
HACKERS
HACKERY
HACKLE
SHACKLE
HACKLED
HACKLER
HACKLES
HACKLET
HADDIE
HADDIES
HADING
SHADING
HADRON
HADRONS
HAEMIN
HAEMINS
HAFFET
HAFFETS
HAFFIT
HAFFITS
HAFTED
SHAFTED
HAGBUT
HAGBUTS
HAGDEN
HAGDENS
HAGDON
HAGDONS
HAGGED
SHAGGED
HAGGIS
HAGGISH
HAGGLE
HAGGLED
HAGGLER
HAGGLES
HAGLET
HAGLETS
HAIDUK
HAIDUKS
HAILER
HAILERS
HAINED
CHAINED
HAIQUE
HAIQUES
HAIRDO
HAIRDOS
HAIRED
CHAIRED
HAIRST
HAIRSTS
HALERS
THALERS
WHALERS
HALIDE
HALIDES
HALING
SHALING
WHALING
HALITE
HALITES
HALLAL

HALLALI
HALLALS
HALLAN
CHALLAN
HALLANS
HALLOA
HALLOAS
HALLOO
HALLOOS
HALLOW
SHALLOW
HALLOWS
HALOID
HALOIDS
HALSER
HALSERS
HALTER
HALTERS
HALVAH
HALVAHS
HALVER
HALVERS
HAMBLE
SHAMBLE
HAMBLED
HAMBLES
HAMING
SHAMING
HAMLET
CHAMLET
HAMLETS
HAMMAL
HAMMALS
HAMMAM
HAMMAMS
HAMMED
SHAMMED
WHAMMED
HAMMER
SHAMMER
HAMMERS
HAMPER
HAMPERS
HAMZAH
HAMZAHS
HANCES
CHANCES
HANDER
HANDERS
HANDLE
HANDLED
HANDLER
HANDLES
HANGAR
HANGARS
HANGED
CHANGED
PHANGED
WHANGED
HANGER
CHANGER
HANGERS
HANJAR
KHANJAR
HANJARS
HANKED
SHANKED
THANKED
HANKER
THANKER

HANKERS
HANKIE
HANKIES
HANSEL
HANSELS
HANSOM
HANSOMS
HANTLE
HANTLES
HAPPED
CHAPPED
WHAPPED
HAPPEN
HAPPENS
HAPTEN
HAPTENS
HAPTIC
HAPTICS
HARBOR
HARBORS
HARDEN
HARDENS
HAREEM
HAREEMS
HARELD
HARELDS
HARING
CHARING
SHARING
HARKED
CHARKED
SHARKED
HARKEN
HARKENS
HARLOT
HARLOTS
HARMAN
HARMANS
HARMED
CHARMED
HARMEL
HARMELS
HARMIN
HARMINE
HARMING
HARMINS
HARPED
SHARPED
HARPER
SHARPER
HARPERS
HARROW
HARROWS
HARTAL
HARTALS
HARTEN
HARTENS
HASHED
SHASHED
HASHES
SHASHES
HASLET
HASLETS
HASSAR
HASSARS
HASSLE
HASSLED
HASSLES
HASTED
GHASTED

HASTEN
CHASTEN
HASTENS
HATFUL
HATFULS
HATPEG
HATPEGS
HATPIN
HATPINS
HATRED
HATREDS
HATTED
CHATTED
HATTER
CHATTER
SHATTER
HATTERS
HAUGHT
HAUGHTY
HAULER
HAULERS
HAUNTS
CHAUNTS
HAUYNE
HAUYNES
HAVERS
SHAVERS
HAVING
SHAVING
HAVINGS
HAWING
CHAWING
THAWING
HAWKER
HAWKERS
HAWKEY
HAWKEYS
HAWKIE
HAWKIES
HAWSER
HAWSERS
HAYING
HAYINGS
HAYMOW
HAYMOWS
HAYSEL
HAYSELS
HAZARD
HAZARDS
HAZELS
GHAZELS
HAZING
HAZINGS
HEADER
HEADERS
HEALED
SHEALED
HEALER
HEALERS
HEALTH
HEALTHS
HEALTHY
HEARER
SHEARER
HEARERS
HEARSE
HEARSED
HEARSES
HEARTH
HEARTHS

HEASTE
HEASTES
HEATED
CHEATED
HEATER
CHEATER
THEATER
HEATERS
HEATHS
SHEATHS
HEATHY
SHEATHY
HEAUME
HEAUMES
HEAVED
SHEAVED
HEAVEN
HEAVENS
HEAVER
HEAVERS
HEAVES
SHEAVES
THEAVES
HEBONA
HEBONAS
HECKLE
HECKLED
HECKLER
HECKLES
HECTIC
HECTICS
HECTOR
HECTORS
HEDDLE
HEDDLED
HEDDLES
HEDGER
HEDGERS
HEEHAW
HEEHAWS
HEELED
SHEELED
WHEELED
HEELER
WHEELER
HEELERS
HEEZED
PHEEZED
WHEEZED
HEEZES
PHEEZES
WHEEZES
HEEZIE
HEEZIES
HEGIRA
HEGIRAS
HEIFER
HEIFERS
HEIGHT
AHEIGHT
HEIGHTS
HEISTS
THEISTS
HEJIRA
HEJIRAS
HELIUM
HELIUMS
HELLED
SHELLED
HELLER

SHELLER
HELLERS
HELMED
WHELMED
HELMET
HELMETS
HELPED
WHELPED
HELPER
HELPERS
HELVED
SHELVED
HELVES
SHELVES
THELVES
HEMINA
HEMINAS
HENNER
HENNERS
HENNERY
HENNIN
HENNING
HENNINS
HEPTAD
HEPTADS
HERALD
HERALDS
HERBAL
HERBALS
HERBAR
HERBARS
HERBARY
HERDEN
HERDENS
HERDIC
HERDICS
HEREAT
THEREAT
WHEREAT
HEREBY
THEREBY
WHEREBY
HEREIN
THEREIN
WHEREIN
HEREOF
THEREOF
WHEREOF
HEREON
THEREON
WHEREON
HERETO
THERETO
WHERETO
HERIOT
HERIOTS
HERMAE
THERMAE
HERMIT
HERMITS
HERNIA
HERNIAL
HERNIAS
HEROIC
HEROICS
HEROIN
HEROINE
HEROINS
HEROON
HEROONS

HETERO
HETEROS
HETHER
THETHER
WHETHER
HETMAN
HETMANS
HEUCHS
SHEUCHS
HEUGHS
SHEUGHS
WHEUGHS
HEWERS
CHEWERS
HEWING
CHEWING
SHEWING
WHEWING
HEWINGS
HEXACT
HEXACTS
HEXANE
HEXANES
HEXENE
HEXENES
HEXING
HEXINGS
HEXOSE
HEXOSES
HEYDAY
HEYDAYS
HICCUP
HICCUPS
HICCUPY
HICKEY
HICKEYS
HIDAGE
HIDAGES
HIDDEN
CHIDDEN
HIDDER
SHIDDER
WHIDDER
HIDDERS
HIDERS
CHIDERS
HIDING
CHIDING
HIDINGS
HIGGLE
HIGGLED
HIGGLER
HIGGLES
HIGHER
HIGHERS
HIGHTH
HIGHTHS
HIJACK
HIJACKS
HIJRAH
HIJRAHS
HILLED
CHILLED
SHILLED
HINDER
HINDERS
HINGED
WHINGED
HINGES
WHINGES

HIPPED
CHIPPED
SHIPPED
WHIPPED
HIPPER
CHIPPER
SHIPPER
WHIPPER
HIPPIE
CHIPPIE
HIPPIER
HIPPIES
HIPPOS
SHIPPOS
HIRAGE
HIRAGES
HIRING
HIRINGS
HIRPLE
HIRPLED
HIRPLES
HIRSEL
HIRSELS
HIRSLE
HIRSLED
HIRSLES
HISHED
WHISHED
HISHES
WHISHES
HISSED
WHISSED
HISSES
WHISSES
HISTED
WHISTED
HITHER
THITHER
WHITHER
HITHERS
HITTER
CHITTER
WHITTER
HITTERS
HIVERS
SHIVERS
HIVING
CHIVING
HIZZED
CHIZZED
WHIZZED
HIZZES
CHIZZES
PHIZZES
WHIZZES
HOARSE
HOARSEN
HOARSER
HOAXER
HOAXERS
HOBBIT
HOBBITS
HOBBLE
HOBBLED
HOBBLER
HOBBLES
HOBDAY
HOBDAYS
HOBJOB
HOBJOBS

HOBNOB
HOBNOBS
HOCKED
CHOCKED
SHOCKED
HOCKER
CHOCKER
SHOCKER
HOCKERS
HOCKEY
HOCKEYS
HODDEN
HODDENS
HODDLE
HODDLED
HODDLES
HODJAS
KHODJAS
HOEING
SHOEING
HOGGED
SHOGGED
HOGGER
HOGGERS
HOGGERY
HOGGET
HOGGETS
HOGGIN
HOGGING
HOGGINS
HOGTIE
HOGTIED
HOGTIES
HOIDEN
HOIDENS
HOKIER
CHOKIER
HOKING
CHOKING
HOLDER
HOLDERS
HOLIES
HOLIEST
HOLING
THOLING
HOLINGS
HOLISM
WHOLISM
HOLISMS
HOLIST
WHOLIST
HOLISTS
HOLLER
HOLLERS
HOLLOA
HOLLOAS
HOLLOW
HOLLOWS
HOLMIA
HOLMIAS
HOMAGE
HOMAGED
HOMAGER
HOMAGES
HOMBRE
HOMBRES
HOMELY
HOMELYN
HOMING
HOMINGS

HONCHO
HONCHOS
HONERS
PHONERS
HONEST
HONESTY
HONEYS
PHONEYS
HONIED
PHONIED
HONING
PHONING
HONKER
HONKERS
HONKIE
HONKIES
HONOUR
HONOURS
HOODIE
HOODIES
HOODOO
HOODOOS
HOOFED
CHOOFED
HOOFER
HOOFERS
HOOKAH
HOOKAHS
HOOKER
HOOKERS
HOOKEY
HOOKEYS
HOOLEY
HOOLEYS
HOOPED
WHOOPED
HOOPER
WHOOPER
HOOPERS
HOOPOE
HOOPOES
HOORAH
HOORAHS
HOORAY
HOORAYS
HOOTED
WHOOTED
HOOTER
SHOOTER
HOOTERS
HOOVER
HOOVERS
HOPDOG
HOPDOGS
HOPPED
CHOPPED
SHOPPED
WHOPPED
HOPPER
CHOPPER
SHOPPER
WHOPPER
HOPPERS
HOPPLE
HOPPLED
HOPPLES
HORKEY
HORKEYS
HORNED
THORNED

HORNER
HORNERS
HORNET
HORNETS
HORROR
HORRORS
HORSON
HORSONS
HOSIER
HOSIERS
HOSIERY
HOSTED
GHOSTED
HOSTEL
HOSTELS
HOTBED
HOTBEDS
HOTPOT
HOTPOTS
HOTTED
SHOTTED
HOTTER
HOTTERS
HOTTIE
HOTTIES
HOUDAH
HOUDAHS
HOUDAN
HOUDANS
HOUGHS
CHOUGHS
SHOUGHS
HOUSED
CHOUSED
HOUSEL
HOUSELS
HOUSES
CHOUSES
HOUTED
SHOUTED
HOVELS
SHOVELS
HOVERS
SHOVERS
HOVING
SHOVING
HOWDAH
HOWDAHS
HOWDIE
HOWDIES
HOWKER
HOWKERS
HOWLER
HOWLERS
HOWLET
HOWLETS
HOYDEN
HOYDENS
HUBBUB
HUBBUBS
HUCKLE
CHUCKLE
HUCKLES
HUDDLE
HUDDLED
HUDDLES
HUFFED
CHUFFED
HUGGED
CHUGGED

HUMANE
HUMANER
HUMBLE
HUMBLED
HUMBLER
HUMBLES
HUMBUG
HUMBUGS
HUMECT
HUMECTS
HUMHUM
HUMHUMS
HUMITE
HUMITES
HUMLIE
HUMLIES
HUMMED
CHUMMED
HUMMEL
HUMMELS
HUMMER
HUMMERS
HUMMUM
HUMMUMS
HUMOUR
HUMOURS
HUMPED
THUMPED
HUMPEN
HUMPENS
HUMPER
THUMPER
HUMPERS
HUNGER
HUNGERS
HUNGRY
AHUNGRY
HUNKER
HUNKERS
HUNTED
SHUNTED
HUNTER
CHUNTER
SHUNTER
HUNTERS
HUPPAH
CHUPPAH
HUPPAHS
HURDEN
HURDENS
HURDLE
HURDLED
HURDLER
HURDLES
HURLER
HURLERS
HURLEY
HURLEYS
HURRAH
HURRAHS
HURRAS
DHURRAS
HURRAY
HURRAYS
HURTER
HURTERS
HURTLE
HURTLED
HURTLES
HUSHED

SHUSHED
HUSHER
HUSHERS
HUSHES
SHUSHES
HUSKER
HUSKERS
HUSSAR
HUSSARS
HUSSIF
HUSSIFS
HUSTLE
HUSTLED
HUSTLER
HUSTLES
HUTTED
PHUTTED
HUZOOR
HUZOORS
HYAENA
HYAENAS
HYBRID
HYBRIDS
HYDRIA
HYDRIAE
HYDRIAS
HYDYNE
HYDYNES
HYLISM
HYLISMS
HYLIST
HYLISTS
HYMNAL
HYMNALS
HYPATE
HYPATES
HYPHEN
HYPHENS
HYPNIC
HYPNICS
HYPNUM
HYPNUMS
HYSSOP
HYSSOPS
IAMBIC
IAMBICS
IBICES
VIBICES
ICECAP
ICECAPS
ICHING
MICHING
NICHING
RICHING
ICICLE
ICICLES
ICIEST
DICIEST
RICIEST
ICINGS
DICINGS
ICKERS
BICKERS
DICKERS
KICKERS
LICKERS
NICKERS
PICKERS
RICKERS
TICKERS

WICKERS
YICKERS
ICKIER
DICKIER
PICKIER
IDEATE
IDEATED
IDEATES
IDLING
HIDLING
KIDLING
SIDLING
IFFIER
MIFFIER
NIFFIER
IGNARO
IGNAROS
IGNITE
LIGNITE
IGNITED
IGNITER
IGNITES
IGNORE
SIGNORE
IGNORED
IGNORER
IGNORES
IGUANA
IGUANAS
ILEXES
SILEXES
ILICES
CILICES
ILLIAD
ILLIADS
ILLIPE
ILLIPES
ILLITE
TILLITE
ILLITES
ILLUDE
ILLUDED
ILLUDES
ILLUME
ILLUMED
ILLUMES
ILLUPI
ILLUPIS
IMARET
IMARETS
IMBARK
IMBARKS
IMBARS
MIMBARS
IMBASE
IMBASED
IMBASES
IMBIBE
IMBIBED
IMBIBER
IMBIBES
IMBOSK
IMBOSKS
IMBRUE
IMBRUED
IMBRUES
IMMASK
IMMASKS
IMMUNE
IMMUNES

IMMURE
IMMURED
IMMURES
IMPACT
IMPACTS
IMPAIR
IMPAIRS
IMPALA
IMPALAS
IMPALE
IMPALED
IMPALES
IMPARK
IMPARKS
IMPARL
IMPARLS
IMPART
IMPARTS
IMPAVE
IMPAVED
IMPAVES
IMPAWN
IMPAWNS
IMPEDE
IMPEDED
IMPEDES
IMPEND
IMPENDS
IMPING
GIMPING
LIMPING
PIMPING
IMPINGE
IMPISH
WIMPISH
IMPLEX
SIMPLEX
IMPONE
IMPONED
IMPONES
IMPORT
IMPORTS
IMPOSE
IMPOSED
IMPOSER
IMPOSES
IMPOST
IMPOSTS
IMPROV
IMPROVE
IMPROVS
IMPUGN
IMPUGNS
IMPURE
IMPURER
IMPUTE
IMPUTED
IMPUTER
IMPUTES
INCAGE
INCAGED
INCAGES
INCASE
PINCASE
INCASED
INCASES
INCAVE
INCAVED
INCAVES
INCEDE

INCEDED
INCEDES
INCEPT
INCEPTS
INCEST
INCESTS
INCHED
CINCHED
FINCHED
PINCHED
WINCHED
INCHES
CINCHES
FINCHES
LINCHES
PINCHES
WINCHES
INCISE
INCISED
INCISES
INCITE
ZINCITE
INCITED
INCITER
INCITES
INCLIP
INCLIPS
INCOME
INCOMER
INCOMES
INCUSE
INCUSED
INCUSES
INDABA
INDABAS
INDART
INDARTS
INDENE
INDENES
INDENT
INDENTS
INDICT
INDICTS
INDIES
KINDIES
INDIGO
WINDIGO
INDIGOS
INDITE
INDITED
INDITER
INDITES
INDIUM
INDIUMS
INDOLE
INDOLES
INDOOR
INDOORS
INDUCE
INDUCED
INDUCER
INDUCES
INDUCT
INDUCTS
INDULT
INDULTS
INDUNA
INDUNAS
INFALL
INFALLS

INFAME
INFAMED
INFAMES
INFANT
INFANTA
INFANTE
INFANTS
INFARE
INFARES
INFECT
INFECTS
INFEFT
INFEFTS
INFEST
INFESTS
INFILL
INFILLS
INFLOW
INFLOWS
INFOLD
PINFOLD
INFOLDS
INFORM
INFORMS
INFULA
INFULAE
INFUSE
INFUSED
INFUSER
INFUSES
INGANS
FINGANS
INGATE
INGATES
INGENU
INGENUE
INGENUS
INGEST
INGESTA
INGESTS
INGINE
INGINES
INGLES
BINGLES
DINGLES
GINGLES
JINGLES
KINGLES
LINGLES
MINGLES
PINGLES
SINGLES
TINGLES
INGOES
DINGOES
JINGOES
LINGOES
PINGOES
INGOTS
LINGOTS
INGULF
INGULFS
INHALE
INHALED
INHALER
INHALES
INHAUL
INHAULS
INHERE
INHERED
INHERES
INHOOP
INHOOPS
INHUME
INHUMED
INHUMER
INHUMES
INISLE
INISLED
INISLES
INJECT
INJECTS
INJERA
INJERAS
INJURE
INJURED
INJURER
INJURES
INKERS
JINKERS
LINKERS
SINKERS
TINKERS
WINKERS
INKIER
DINKIER
KINKIER
PINKIER
SINKIER
ZINKIER
INKING
DINKING
FINKING
JINKING
KINKING
LINKING
OINKING
PINKING
RINKING
SINKING
TINKING
WINKING
ZINKING
INKLED
TINKLED
WINKLED
INKLES
KINKLES
TINKLES
WINKLES
INKPOT
INKPOTS
INLACE
INLACED
INLACES
INLAND
INLANDS
INLIER
INLIERS
INLOCK
INLOCKS
INMATE
INMATES
INNATE
PINNATE
INNERS
DINNERS
FINNERS
GINNERS
PINNERS
SINNERS
TINNERS
WINNERS
INNING
BINNING
DINNING
GINNING
LINNING
PINNING
RINNING
SINNING
TINNING
WINNING
INNINGS
INROAD
INROADS
INSANE
INSANER
INSEAM
INSEAMS
INSECT
INSECTS
INSEEM
INSEEMS
INSERT
INSERTS
INSHIP
KINSHIP
INSHIPS
INSIDE
INSIDER
INSIDES
INSIST
INSISTS
INSOLE
INSOLES
INSOUL
INSOULS
INSPAN
INSPANS
INSTAL
INSTALL
INSTALS
INSTAR
INSTARS
INSTEP
INSTEPS
INSTIL
INSTILL
INSTILS
INSULA
INSULAE
INSULAR
INSULAS
INSULT
INSULTS
INSURE
INSURED
INSURER
INSURES
INTAKE
INTAKES
INTEND
INTENDS
INTENT
INTENTS
INTERN
INTERNE
INTERNS
INTERS
LINTERS
MINTERS
SINTERS
TINTERS
WINTERS
INTIMA
INTIMAE
INTINE
INTINES
INTOMB
INTOMBS
INTONE
INTONED
INTONER
INTONES
INTRON
INTRONS
INTUIT
INTUITS
INTUSE
INTUSES
INULAS
INULASE
INULIN
INULINS
INVADE
INVADED
INVADER
INVADES
INVENT
INVENTS
INVERT
INVERTS
INVEST
INVESTS
INVITE
INVITED
INVITEE
INVITER
INVITES
INVOKE
INVOKED
INVOKES
INWALL
INWALLS
INWARD
INWARDS
INWICK
INWICKS
INWIND
INWINDS
INWORK
INWORKS
INWOVE
INWOVEN
INWRAP
INWRAPS
INYALA
INYALAS
IODATE
IODATES
IODIDE
IODIDES
IODINE
IODINES
IODISE
IODISED
IODISES
IODISM
IODISMS
IODIZE
IODIZED
IODIZES
IOLITE
IOLITES
IONISE
LIONISE
IONISED
IONISER
IONISES
IONIUM
IONIUMS
IONIZE
LIONIZE
IONIZED
IONIZER
IONIZES
IONONE
IONONES
IPECAC
IPECACS
IRADES
TIRADES
IREFUL
DIREFUL
IRENIC
EIRENIC
SIRENIC
IRENICS
IRITIS
MIRITIS
IRKING
DIRKING
FIRKING
KIRKING
LIRKING
YIRKING
IRONER
IRONERS
IRONIC
GIRONIC
IRRUPT
IRRUPTS
ISABEL
ISABELS
ISATIN
ISATINE
ISATINS
ISCHIA
ISCHIAL
ISLAND
ISLANDS
ISLING
AISLING
ISOBAR
ISOBARE
ISOBARS
ISOGON
ISOGONS
ISOHEL
ISOHELS
ISOMER
ISOMERE
ISOMERS
ISOPOD
ISOPODS
ISSUED
TISSUED
ISSUER
ISSUERS
ISSUES
TISSUES
ISTLES
MISTLES
ITALIC
ITALICS
ITCHED
BITCHED
DITCHED
HITCHED
MITCHED
PITCHED
WITCHED
ITCHES
AITCHES
BITCHES
DITCHES
FITCHES
HITCHES
MITCHES
PITCHES
TITCHES
WITCHES
IZARDS
LIZARDS
RIZARDS
VIZARDS
WIZARDS
IZZARD
DIZZARD
GIZZARD
IZZARDS
JABBER
JABBERS
JABBLE
JABBLED
JABBLES
JABIRU
JABIRUS
JACANA
JACANAS
JACKAL
JACKALS
JACKET
JACKETS
JAEGER
JAEGERS
JAGGER
JAGGERS
JAGGERY
JAGHIR
JAGHIRE
JAGHIRS
JAGUAR
JAGUARS
JAILER
JAILERS
JAILOR
JAILORS
JAMBEE
JAMBEES
JAMBER
JAMBERS
JAMBOK
SJAMBOK
JAMBOKS
JAMBUL
JAMBULS
JAMJAR
JAMJARS
JAMMER
JAMMERS
JAMPAN
JAMPANI
JAMPANS
JAMPOT
JAMPOTS
JANDAL
JANDALS
JANGLE
JANGLED
JANGLER
JANGLES
JANKER
JANKERS
JANSKY
JANSKYS
JAPING
JAPINGS
JARFUL
JARFULS
JARGON
JARGONS
JAROOL
JAROOLS
JARRAH
JARRAHS
JARVEY
JARVEYS
JARVIE
JARVIES
JASPER
JASPERS
JASPERY
JATAKA
JATAKAS
JAUNCE
JAUNCED
JAUNCES
JAUNSE
JAUNSED
JAUNSES
JAWARI
JAWARIS
JAWING
JAWINGS
JAZZER
JAZZERS
JEBELS
DJEBELS
JEELIE
JEELIED
JEELIES
JEERER
JEERERS
JEMIMA
JEMIMAS
JENNET
JENNETS
JERBIL
JERBILS
JERBOA
JERBOAS
JEREED
JEREEDS
JERKER
JERKERS
JERKIN
JERKING
JERKINS
JERQUE
JERQUED
JERQUER
JERQUES
JERSEY
JERSEYS
JESSIE
JESSIES
JESTEE
JESTEES
JESTER
JESTERS
JETSAM
JETSAMS
JETSOM
JETSOMS
JETSON
JETSONS
JETTON
JETTONS
JEZAIL
JEZAILS
JIBBAH
DJIBBAH
JIBBAHS
JIBBER
JIBBERS
JIGGER
JIGGERS
JIGGLE
JIGGLED
JIGGLES
JIGJIG
JIGJIGS
JIGSAW
JIGSAWS
JILGIE
JILGIES
JILLET
JILLETS
JIMJAM
JIMJAMS
JINGAL
JINGALS
JINGLE
JINGLED
JINGLER
JINGLES
JINGLET
JINKER
JINKERS
JIRBLE
JIRBLED
JIRBLES
JISSOM
JISSOMS
JITNEY
JITNEYS
JITTER
JITTERS
JITTERY
JOANNA
JOANNAS
JOBBER
JOBBERS
JOBBERY
JOBBIE
JOBBIES
JOCKEY
JOCKEYS

JOGGER
JOGGERS
JOGGLE
JOGGLED
JOGGLES
JOINER
JOINERS
JOINERY
JOJOBA
JOJOBAS
JOLLEY
JOLLEYS
JOLTER
JOLTERS
JORDAN
JORDANS
JOSEPH
JOSEPHS
JOSHER
JOSHERS
JOSKIN
JOSKINS
JOSSER
JOSSERS
JOSTLE
JOSTLED
JOSTLES
JOTTER
JOTTERS
JOTUNN
JOTUNNS
JOUNCE
JOUNCED
JOUNCES
JOURNO
JOURNOS
JOWARI
JOWARIS
JOWLER
JOWLERS
JUBBAH
JUBBAHS
JUDDER
JUDDERS
JUDOGI
JUDOGIS
JUDOKA
JUDOKAS
JUGFUL
JUGFULS
JUGGLE
JUGGLED
JUGGLER
JUGGLES
JUGLET
JUGLETS
JUICER
JUICERS
JUJUBE
JUJUBES
JUMART
JUMARTS
JUMBAL
JUMBALS
JUMBIE
JUMBIES
JUMBLE
JUMBLED
JUMBLER
JUMBLES
JUMPER
JUMPERS
JUNGLE
JUNGLES
JUNGLI
JUNGLIS
JUNIOR
JUNIORS
JUNKER
JUNKERS
JUNKET
JUNKETS
JUNKIE
JUNKIER
JUNKIES
JUPATI
JUPATIS
JURANT
JURANTS
JURIST
JURISTS
JUSTLE
JUSTLED
JUSTLES
KABALA
KABALAS
KABAYA
KABAYAS
KABELE
KABELES
KABUKI
KABUKIS
KACCHA
KACCHAS
KAFILA
KAFILAS
KAFTAN
KAFTANS
KAIKAI
KAIKAIS
KAISER
KAISERS
KAKAPO
KAKAPOS
KALIAN
KALIANS
KALIUM
KALIUMS
KALMIA
KALMIAS
KALONG
KALONGS
KALPAK
KALPAKS
KAMALA
KAMALAS
KAMELA
KAMELAS
KAMILA
KAMILAS
KAMSIN
KAMSINS
KANAKA
KANAKAS
KANGHA
KANGHAS
KANTAR
KANTARS
KANTEN
KANTENS
KANTHA
KANTHAS
KAOLIN
KAOLINE
KAOLINS
KARAIT
KARAITS
KARAKA
KARAKAS
KARATE
KARATES
KARITE
KARITES
KARSEY
KARSEYS
KARTER
KARTERS
KARYON
KARYONS
KASBAH
KASBAHS
KATANA
KATANAS
KATHAK
KATHAKS
KATION
KATIONS
KATIPO
KATIPOS
KEASAR
KEASARS
KEAVIE
KEAVIES
KEBBIE
KEBBIES
KEBELE
KEBELES
KEBLAH
KEBLAHS
KECKLE
KECKLED
KECKLES
KEDDAH
KEDDAHS
KEDGER
KEDGERS
KEEKER
KEEKERS
KEELER
KEELERS
KEELIE
KEELIES
KEENER
KEENERS
KEEPER
KEEPERS
KEFFEL
KEFFELS
KEKSYE
KEKSYES
KELOID
KELOIDS
KELPER
KELPERS
KELPIE
KELPIES
KELSON
KELSONS
KELTER
SKELTER
KELTERS
KELTIE
KELTIES
KELVIN
KELVINS
KEMPER
KEMPERS
KEMPLE
KEMPLES
KENNEL
KENNELS
KENNER
KENNERS
KENNET
KENNETS
KENTIA
KENTIAS
KEPHIR
KEPHIRS
KERNEL
KERNELS
KERRIA
KERRIAS
KERSEY
KERSEYS
KETONE
KETONES
KETOSE
KETOSES
KETTLE
KETTLES
KEYPAD
KEYPADS
KGOTLA
KGOTLAS
KHALAT
KHALATS
KHALIF
KHALIFA
KHALIFS
KHANGA
KHANGAS
KHANUM
KHANUMS
KHARIF
KHARIFS
KHILAT
KHILATS
KHILIM
KHILIMS
KHODJA
KHODJAS
KHURTA
KHURTAS
KIAUGH
KIAUGHS
KIBBLE
KIBBLED
KIBBLES
KIBLAH
KIBLAHS
KICKER
KICKERS
KIDDED
SKIDDED
KIDDER
SKIDDER
KIDDERS
KIDDLE
KIDDLES
KIDGIE
KIDGIER
KIDLET
KIDLETS
KIDNAP
KIDNAPS
KIDNEY
KIDNEYS
KIERIE
KIERIES
KIKUYU
KIKUYUS
KILERG
KILERGS
KILLED
SKILLED
KILLER
KILLERS
KILLUT
KILLUTS
KILTER
KILTERS
KILTIE
KILTIES
KIMCHI
KIMCHIS
KIMMER
SKIMMER
KIMMERS
KIMONO
OKIMONO
KIMONOS
KINASE
KINASES
KINCOB
KINCOBS
KINDER
KINDERS
KINDLE
KINDLED
KINDLER
KINDLES
KINEMA
KINEMAS
KINGLE
KINGLES
KINGLET
KINKED
SKINKED
KINKLE
KINKLES
KINONE
KINONES
KINRED
KINREDS
KIPPED
SKIPPED
KIPPER
SKIPPER
KIPPERS
KIRBEH
KIRBEHS
KIRPAN
KIRPANS
KIRTLE
KIRTLED
KIRTLES
KISHKE
KISHKES
KISMET
KISMETS
KISSEL
KISSELS
KISSER
KISSERS
KITING
SKITING
KITINGS
KITSCH
KITSCHY
KITTEN
KITTENS
KITTENY
KITTLE
SKITTLE
KITTLED
KITTLER
KITTLES
KITTUL
KITTULS
KLAXON
KLAXONS
KLEPHT
KLEPHTS
KLUDGE
KLUDGES
KNAWEL
KNAWELS
KNIGHT
KNIGHTS
KNOWER
KNOWERS
KOBANG
KOBANGS
KOBOLD
KOBOLDS
KONFYT
KONFYTS
KOODOO
KOODOOS
KOOKIE
KOOKIER
KOOLAH
KOOLAHS
KOPECK
KOPECKS
KOPPIE
KOPPIES
KORERO
KOREROS
KORKIR
KORKIRS
KORORA
KORORAS
KORUNA
KORUNAS
KOSHER
KOSHERS
KOTWAL
KOTWALS
KOULAN
KOULANS
KOWHAI
KOWHAIS
KOWTOW
KOWTOWS
KRAKEN
KRAKENS
KRATER
KRATERS
KREESE
KREESED
KREESES
KUMARA
KUMARAS
KUMARI
KUMARIS
KUMMEL
KUMMELS
KUNKAR
KUNKARS
KUNKUR
KUNKURS
KURGAN
KURGANS
KURVEY
KURVEYS
KWACHA
KWACHAS
KWANZA
KWANZAS
KYOGEN
KYOGENS
LAAGER
LAAGERS
LABIAL
LABIALS
LABLAB
LABLABS
LABOUR
LABOURS
LABRET
LABRETS
LABRID
LABRIDS
LACETS
PLACETS
LACIER
GLACIER
LACING
PLACING
LACINGS
LACKED
BLACKED
CLACKED
SLACKED
LACKER
BLACKER
CLACKER
FLACKER
SLACKER
LACKERS
LACKEY
LACKEYS
LACUNA
LACUNAE
LACUNAL
LACUNAR
LADDER
BLADDER
CLADDER
GLADDER
LADDERS
LADDERY
LADDIE
GLADDIE
LADDIES
LADING
LADINGS
LAGENA
LAGENAS
LAGGED
BLAGGED
CLAGGED
FLAGGED
SLAGGED
LAGGEN
LAGGENS
LAGGER
BLAGGER
LAGGERS
LAGGIN
LAGGING
LAGGINS
LAGOON
LAGOONS
LAGUNE
LAGUNES
LAIDED
PLAIDED
LAIKER
LAIKERS
LAIRED
GLAIRED
LAISSE
LAISSES
LAKIER
FLAKIER
LAKING
FLAKING
SLAKING
LALANG
LALANGS
LALDIE
LALDIES
LALLAN
LALLANS
LAMBDA
LAMBDAS
LAMBER
CLAMBER
LAMBERS
LAMBERT
LAMBIE
LAMBIES
LAMENT
LAMENTS
LAMINA
LAMINAE
LAMINAR
LAMING
BLAMING
FLAMING
LAMMED
CLAMMED
FLAMMED
SLAMMED
LAMMER
SLAMMER
LAMMERS
LAMMIE
LAMMIES
LAMPAD
LAMPADS
LAMPED
CLAMPED
LANCED
BLANCED
GLANCED
LANCER

LANCERS
LANCES
ELANCES
GLANCES
LANCET
LANCETS
LANDAU
LANDAUS
LANDER
BLANDER
SLANDER
LANDERS
LANDES
GLANDES
LANGER
CLANGER
SLANGER
LANGUE
LANGUED
LANGUES
LANGUET
LANGUR
LANGURS
LANKED
BLANKED
CLANKED
FLANKED
PLANKED
LANKER
BLANKER
FLANKER
LANKLY
BLANKLY
LANNER
PLANNER
LANNERS
LANUGO
LANUGOS
LAPDOG
LAPDOGS
LAPFUL
LAPFULS
LAPPED
CLAPPED
FLAPPED
PLAPPED
SLAPPED
LAPPEL
LAPPELS
LAPPER
CLAPPER
FLAPPER
SLAPPER
LAPPERS
LAPPET
LAPPETS
LAPPIE
LAPPIES
LAPSED
ELAPSED
LAPSES
ELAPSES
LAPTOP
LAPTOPS
LARDER
LARDERS
LARDON
LARDONS
LARGEN
LARGENS

LARGES
LARGESS
LARGEST
LARIAT
LARIATS
LARKER
LARKERS
LARRUP
LARRUPS
LARUMS
ALARUMS
LASCAR
LASCARS
LASERS
FLASERS
LASHED
CLASHED
FLASHED
PLASHED
SLASHED
LASHER
CLASHER
FLASHER
SLASHER
LASHERS
LASHES
BLASHES
CLASHES
FLASHES
PLASHES
SLASHES
LASING
LASINGS
LASKET
FLASKET
LASKETS
LASQUE
LASQUES
LASSES
CLASSES
GLASSES
LASSIE
LASSIES
LASSIS
CLASSIS
LASTED
BLASTED
LASTER
BLASTER
PLASTER
LASTERS
LATEEN
LATEENS
LATENS
PLATENS
LATEST
BLATEST
LATESTS
LATHEE
LATHEES
LATHER
BLATHER
SLATHER
LATHERS
LATHERY
LATRIA
LATRIAS
LATRON
LATRONS
LATTEN

FLATTEN
LATTENS
LATTER
BLATTER
CLATTER
FLATTER
PLATTER
SLATTER
LAUDED
BLAUDED
LAUDER
LAUDERS
LAUNCE
LAUNCED
LAUNCES
LAUNCH
FLAUNCH
LAUREL
LAURELS
LAVABO
LAVABOS
LAVAGE
LAVAGES
LAVEER
LAVEERS
LAVERS
CLAVERS
SLAVERS
LAVING
SLAVING
LAVISH
SLAVISH
LAVOLT
LAVOLTA
LAVOLTS
LAWING
CLAWING
FLAWING
LAWINGS
LAWYER
LAWYERS
LAXISM
LAXISMS
LAXIST
LAXISTS
LAYERS
FLAYERS
PLAYERS
SLAYERS
LAYING
ALAYING
CLAYING
FLAYING
PLAYING
SLAYING
LAYINGS
LAYOUT
LAYOUTS
LAZIER
GLAZIER
LAZING
BLAZING
GLAZING
LEADED
PLEADED
LEADEN
LEADENS
LEADER
PLEADER
LEADERS

LEAGUE
LEAGUED
LEAGUER
LEAGUES
LEAKER
BLEAKER
LEAKERS
LEAMED
GLEAMED
LEANED
CLEANED
GLEANED
LEANER
CLEANER
GLEANER
LEANLY
CLEANLY
LEAPER
LEAPERS
LEARED
BLEARED
CLEARED
LEASED
PLEASED
LEASER
PLEASER
LEASERS
LEASES
PLEASES
LEASOW
LEASOWE
LEASOWS
LEAVED
CLEAVED
SLEAVED
LEAVEN
LEAVENS
LEAVER
CLEAVER
LEAVERS
LEAVES
CLEAVES
GLEAVES
SLEAVES
LEAZES
SLEAZES
LEBBEK
LEBBEKS
LECHER
LECHERS
LECHERY
LECHES
FLECHES
LECHWE
LECHWES
LECTIN
LECTINS
LECTOR
ELECTOR
LECTORS
LEDDEN
LEDDENS
LEDGER
PLEDGER
SLEDGER
LEDGERS
LEDGES
FLEDGES
GLEDGES
PLEDGES

SLEDGES
LEEING
FLEEING
GLEEING
LEEPED
BLEEPED
CLEEPED
LEERED
FLEERED
LEEWAY
LEEWAYS
LEFTIE
LEFTIES
LEGATE
LEGATEE
LEGATES
LEGATO
LEGATOR
LEGATOS
LEGEND
LEGENDS
LEGGED
ALEGGED
FLEGGED
LEGGER
GLEGGER
LEGGERS
LEGGES
ALEGGES
LEGION
LEGIONS
LEGIST
ELEGIST
LEGISTS
LEGLAN
LEGLANS
LEGLEN
LEGLENS
LEGLET
LEGLETS
LEGLIN
LEGLINS
LEGUME
LEGUMES
LEIGER
LEIGERS
LEIPOA
LEIPOAS
LEMING
FLEMING
LENDER
BLENDER
SLENDER
LENDERS
LENGTH
ALENGTH
LENGTHS
LENGTHY
LENSES
FLENSES
LENTIL
LENTILS
LENTOR
LENTORS
LENVOY
LENVOYS
LEPTON
LEPTONS
LESION
LESIONS

LESSEE
LESSEES
LESSEN
LESSENS
LESSES
BLESSES
LESSON
LESSONS
LESSOR
PLESSOR
LESSORS
LETHEE
LETHEES
LETTED
BLETTED
LETTER
LETTERN
LETTERS
LETTRE
LETTRES
LEUCIN
LEUCINE
LEUCINS
LEVANT
LEVANTS
LEVINS
ALEVINS
LEVITE
LEVITES
LEXEME
LEXEMES
LIABLE
PLIABLE
LIAISE
LIAISED
LIAISES
LIBATE
LIBATED
LIBATES
LIBBED
GLIBBED
LIBBER
GLIBBER
LIBBERS
LIBERO
LIBEROS
LIBIDO
LIBIDOS
LIBKEN
LIBKENS
LICHEE
LICHEES
LICHEN
LICHENS
LICHES
CLICHES
LICKED
CLICKED
FLICKED
SLICKED
LICKER
CLICKER
FLICKER
SLICKER
LICKERS
LICTOR
LICTORS
LIDGER
LIDGERS
LIEGER

LIEGERS
LIERNE
LIERNES
LIFTED
CLIFTED
LIFTER
LIFTERS
LIGAND
LIGANDS
LIGASE
LIGASES
LIGATE
LIGATED
LIGATES
LIGGER
LIGGERS
LIGHTS
ALIGHTS
BLIGHTS
FLIGHTS
PLIGHTS
SLIGHTS
LIGNIN
LIGNINS
LIGNUM
LIGNUMS
LIGULA
LIGULAE
LIGULAR
LIGULAS
LIGULE
LIGULES
LIGURE
LIGURES
LIKING
LIKINGS
LIMAIL
LIMAILS
LIMBEC
LIMBECK
LIMBECS
LIMBED
CLIMBED
LIMBER
CLIMBER
LIMBERS
LIMIER
SLIMIER
LIMING
SLIMING
LIMINGS
LIMMER
GLIMMER
SLIMMER
LIMMERS
LIMNER
LIMNERS
LIMPED
FLIMPED
LIMPET
LIMPETS
LINAGE
LINAGES
LINDEN
LINDENS
LINGAM
LINGAMS
LINGEL
LINGELS
LINGER

CLINGER
FLINGER
SLINGER
LINGERS
LINGLE
LINGLES
LINGOT
LINGOTS
LINGUA
LINGUAE
LINGUAL
LINGUAS
LINHAY
LINHAYS
LINING
ALINING
LININGS
LINKED
BLINKED
CLINKED
PLINKED
LINKER
BLINKER
CLINKER
KLINKER
SLINKER
LINKERS
LINNED
BLINNED
LINNET
LINNETS
LINNEY
LINNEYS
LINSEY
LINSEYS
LINTEL
LINTELS
LINTER
SLINTER
LINTERS
LINTIE
LINTIER
LINTIES
LIONEL
LIONELS
LIONET
LIONETS
LIPASE
LIPASES
LIPIDE
LIPIDES
LIPOID
LIPOIDS
LIPPED
BLIPPED
CLIPPED
FLIPPED
SLIPPED
LIPPEN
LIPPENS
LIPPIE
CLIPPIE
LIPPIER
LIPPIES
LIQUID
LIQUIDS
LIQUOR
LIQUORS
LISPER
LISPERS

LISSES
BLISSES
LISSOM
LISSOME
LISTEL
LISTELS
LISTEN
GLISTEN
LISTENS
LISTER
BLISTER
GLISTER
LISTERS
LITCHI
LITCHIS
LITHER
BLITHER
SLITHER
LITHES
LITHEST
LITHIA
LITHIAS
LITING
FLITING
LITTER
CLITTER
FLITTER
GLITTER
SLITTER
LITTERS
LITTERY
LITTLE
LITTLER
LITTLES
LIVERS
CLIVERS
OLIVERS
SLIVERS
LIVING
SLIVING
LIVINGS
LIZARD
LIZARDS
LOADEN
LOADENS
LOADER
LOADERS
LOAFER
LOAFERS
LOATHE
LOATHED
LOATHER
LOATHES
LOBATE
GLOBATE
LOBBED
BLOBBED
LOBING
GLOBING
LOBINGS
LOBOSE
GLOBOSE
LOBULE
GLOBULE
LOBULES
LOCALE
LOCALES
LOCATE
LOCATED
LOCATES
LOCHAN
LOCHANS
LOCHIA
LOCHIAL
LOCKED
BLOCKED
CLOCKED
FLOCKED
LOCKER
BLOCKER
CLOCKER
LOCKERS
LOCKET
LOCKETS
LOCULE
LOCULES
LOCUST
LOCUSTA
LOCUSTS
LODGER
LODGERS
LOFTER
LOFTERS
LOGANS
SLOGANS
LOGGAT
LOGGATS
LOGGED
CLOGGED
FLOGGED
SLOGGED
LOGGER
CLOGGER
SLOGGER
LOGGERS
LOGGIA
LOGGIAS
LOGIES
ELOGIES
OLOGIES
LOGIEST
LOGLOG
LOGLOGS
LOITER
LOITERS
LOLIGO
LOLIGOS
LOLIUM
LOLIUMS
LOLLER
LOLLERS
LOLLOP
LOLLOPS
LOMENT
LOMENTA
LOMENTS
LONELY
ALONELY
LONGAN
LONGANS
LONGED
PLONGED
LONGES
PLONGES
LONGEST
LOOFAH
LOOFAHS
LOOKER
LOOKERS
LOOMED
BLOOMED
GLOOMED
SLOOMED
LOONIE
LOONIER
LOONIES
LOOPED
BLOOPED
GLOOPED
LOOPER
BLOOPER
LOOPERS
LOOSEN
LOOSENS
LOOSES
LOOSEST
LOOTER
LOOTERS
LOPERS
ELOPERS
LOPING
ELOPING
SLOPING
LOPPED
CLOPPED
FLOPPED
PLOPPED
SLOPPED
LOPPER
LOPPERS
LOQUAT
LOQUATS
LORCHA
LORCHAS
LORICA
LORICAE
LORIES
GLORIES
LORING
LORINGS
LORIOT
LORIOTS
LOSERS
CLOSERS
LOSING
CLOSING
LOSINGS
LOSSES
FLOSSES
GLOSSES
LOTION
LOTIONS
LOTTED
BLOTTED
CLOTTED
PLOTTED
SLOTTED
LOUDEN
LOUDENS
LOUGHS
CLOUGHS
PLOUGHS
SLOUGHS
LOUNGE
LOUNGED
LOUNGER
LOUNGES
LOURED
CLOURED
FLOURED
LOUSED
BLOUSED
FLOUSED
LOUSES
BLOUSES
FLOUSES
LOUTED
CLOUTED
FLOUTED
GLOUTED
LOUVER
LOUVERS
LOUVRE
LOUVRED
LOUVRES
LOVAGE
LOVAGES
LOVERS
CLOVERS
GLOVERS
PLOVERS
LOVING
GLOVING
LOVINGS
LOWBOY
LOWBOYS
LOWERS
BLOWERS
FLOWERS
GLOWERS
LOWERY
FLOWERY
LOWEST
SLOWEST
LOWING
BLOWING
FLOWING
GLOWING
PLOWING
SLOWING
LOWINGS
LOWNED
CLOWNED
LOWNES
LOWNESS
LOWSES
BLOWSES
LOWSEST
LOZELL
LOZELLS
LUBBER
BLUBBER
CLUBBER
SLUBBER
LUBBERS
LUCERN
LUCERNE
LUCERNS
LUCKIE
LUCKIER
LUCKIES
LUCUMA
LUCUMAS
LUCUMO
LUCUMOS
LUFFED
BLUFFED
FLUFFED
PLUFFED
LUGGED
GLUGGED
PLUGGED
SLUGGED
LUGGER
PLUGGER
SLUGGER
LUGGERS
LUGGIE
LUGGIES
LUGING
LUGINGS
LUMBER
CLUMBER
PLUMBER
SLUMBER
LUMBERS
LUMINA
ALUMINA
LUMINAL
LUMINE
LUMINED
LUMINES
LUMMOX
FLUMMOX
LUMPED
CLUMPED
FLUMPED
PLUMPED
SLUMPED
LUMPEN
PLUMPEN
LUMPER
CLUMPER
PLUMPER
LUMPERS
LUNATE
LUNATED
LUNGED
BLUNGED
PLUNGED
LUNGES
BLUNGES
PLUNGES
LUNGIE
LUNGIES
LUNKER
BLUNKER
PLUNKER
LUNKERS
LUNTED
BLUNTED
LUNULA
LUNULAE
LUNULAR
LUNULE
LUNULES
LUNYIE
LUNYIES
LUPINE
LUPINES
LURDAN
LURDANE
LURDANS
LURDEN
LURDENS
LURKER
LURKERS
LUSHED
BLUSHED
FLUSHED
SLUSHED
LUSHER
BLUSHER
FLUSHER
PLUSHER
LUSHERS
LUSHES
BLUSHES
FLUSHES
PLUSHES
SLUSHES
LUSHEST
LUSTER
BLUSTER
CLUSTER
FLUSTER
LUSTERS
LUSTRA
LUSTRAL
LUSTRE
LUSTRED
LUSTRES
LUTEAL
GLUTEAL
PLUTEAL
LUTEIN
LUTEINS
LUTERS
FLUTERS
LUTING
ELUTING
FLUTING
LUTINGS
LUTIST
FLUTIST
LUTISTS
LUTZES
KLUTZES
LUXATE
LUXATED
LUXATES
LUZERN
LUZERNS
LYCEUM
LYCEUMS
LYCHEE
LYCHEES
LYINGS
FLYINGS
LYNAGE
LYNAGES
LYRATE
LYRATED
LYRISM
LYRISMS
LYRIST
LYRISTS
LYSINE
LYSINES
LYTING
FLYTING
MACACO
MACACOS
MACHAN
MACHANS
MACKLE
MACKLED
MACKLES
MACOYA
MACOYAS
MACRON
MACRONS
MACULA
MACULAE
MACULAR
MACULE
MACULES
MADAME
MADAMED
MADCAP
MADCAPS
MADDEN
MADDENS
MADDER
MADDERS
MADRAS
MADRASA
MAELID
MAELIDS
MAENAD
MAENADS
MAFFIA
MAFFIAS
MAGGOT
MAGGOTS
MAGGOTY
MAGIAN
MAGIANS
MAGILP
MAGILPS
MAGISM
IMAGISM
MAGISMS
MAGNET
MAGNETO
MAGNETS
MAGNON
MAGNONS
MAGNUM
MAGNUMS
MAGPIE
MAGPIES
MAGUEY
MAGUEYS
MAHMAL
MAHMALS
MAHOUT
MAHOUTS
MAHSIR
MAHSIRS
MAIDAN
MAIDANS
MAIDEN
MAIDENS
MAIGRE
MAIGRES
MAILER
MAILERS
MAINOR
MAINORS
MAKING
MAKINGS
MALATE
MALATES
MALGRE
MALGRED
MALGRES
MALICE
MALICED
MALICES
MALIGN
MALIGNS
MALISM
MALISMS
MALKIN
MALKINS
MALLAM
MALLAMS
MALLED
SMALLED
MALLEE
MALLEES
MALLET
MALLETS
MALLOW
MALLOWS
MALMAG
MALMAGS
MALTHA
MALTHAS
MAMMAL
MAMMALS
MAMMEE
MAMMEES
MAMMER
MAMMERS
MAMMET
MAMMETS
MAMMON
MAMMONS
MAMZER
MAMZERS
MANAGE
MANAGED
MANAGER
MANAGES
MANANA
MANANAS
MANATI
MANATIS
MANCHE
MANCHES
MANCHET
MANDIR
MANDIRA
MANDIRS
MANDOM
MANDOMS
MANEGE
MANEGED
MANEGES
MANGAL
MANGALS
MANGEL
MANGELS
MANGER
MANGERS
MANGLE
MANGLED
MANGLER
MANGLES
MANIAC
MANIACS
MANILA
MANILAS
MANIOC
MANIOCS
MANITO
MANITOS
MANITOU

MANNER
MANNERS
MANOAO
MANOAOS
MANRED
MANREDS
MANTEL
MANTELS
MANTID
MANTIDS
MANTLE
MANTLED
MANTLES
MANTLET
MANTRA
MANTRAM
MANTRAP
MANTRAS
MANTUA
MANTUAS
MANUAL
MANUALS
MANUKA
MANUKAS
MANURE
MANURED
MANURER
MANURES
MAPPER
MAPPERS
MAPPERY
MARACA
MARACAS
MARAUD
MARAUDS
MARBLE
MARBLED
MARBLER
MARBLES
MARCEL
MARCELS
MARGAY
MARGAYS
MARGIN
MARGINS
MARINA
MARINAS
MARINE
MARINER
MARINES
MARKER
MARKERS
MARKET
MARKETS
MARKKA
MARKKAA
MARKKAS
MARLIN
MARLINE
MARLING
MARLINS
MARMOT
MARMOTS
MAROON
MAROONS
MARQUE
MARQUEE
MARQUES
MARRAM
MARRAMS
MARROW
MARROWS
MARROWY
MARRUM
MARRUMS
MARTED
SMARTED
MARTEL
MARTELS
MARTEN
SMARTEN
MARTENS
MARTIN
MARTING
MARTINI
MARTINS
MARTYR
MARTYRS
MARTYRY
MARVEL
MARVELS
MARVER
MARVERS
MASCLE
MASCLED
MASCLES
MASCON
MASCONS
MASCOT
MASCOTS
MASHED
SMASHED
MASHER
SMASHER
MASHERS
MASHES
SMASHES
MASHIE
MASHIER
MASHIES
MASHUA
MASHUAS
MASJID
MASJIDS
MASKER
MASKERS
MASLIN
MASLINS
MASQUE
MASQUER
MASQUES
MASSED
AMASSED
MASSES
AMASSES
MASSIF
MASSIFS
MASTER
MASTERS
MASTERY
MASTIC
MASTICH
MASTICS
MASULA
MASULAS
MATICO
MATICOS
MATING
AMATING
MATLOW
MATLOWS
MATOKE
MATOKES
MATRIC
MATRICE
MATRICS
MATRON
MATRONS
MATTER
SMATTER
MATTERS
MATTERY
MATTIE
MATTIES
MATURE
MATURED
MATURER
MATURES
MATZAH
MATZAHS
MATZOT
MATZOTH
MAUGRE
MAUGRED
MAUGRES
MAULVI
MAULVIS
MAUMET
MAUMETS
MAUVES
MAUVEST
MAUVIN
MAUVINE
MAUVINS
MAWKIN
MAWKINS
MAWMET
MAWMETS
MAXIMA
MAXIMAL
MAXIXE
MAXIXES
MAYDAY
MAYDAYS
MAYHEM
MAYHEMS
MAYING
MAYINGS
MAZARD
MAZARDS
MAZHBI
MAZHBIS
MAZING
AMAZING
MAZOUT
MAZOUTS
MAZUMA
MAZUMAS
MEADOW
MEADOWS
MEADOWY
MEAGRE
MEAGRER
MEAGRES
MEALER
MEALERS
MEALIE
MEALIER
MEALIES
MEANES
MEANEST
MEANIE
MEANIES
MEASLE
MEASLED
MEASLES
MEATHE
MEATHES
MEATHS
SMEATHS
MEAZEL
MEAZELS
MEDAKA
MEDAKAS
MEDDLE
MEDDLED
MEDDLER
MEDDLES
MEDIAL
MEDIALS
MEDIAN
MEDIANS
MEDIANT
MEDICK
MEDICKS
MEDICO
MEDICOS
MEDINA
MEDINAS
MEDIUM
MEDIUMS
MEDLAR
MEDLARS
MEDLEY
MEDLEYS
MEDUSA
MEDUSAE
MEDUSAN
MEDUSAS
MEEKEN
MEEKENS
MEEMIE
MEEMIES
MEGARA
MEGARAD
MEGASS
MEGASSE
MEGILP
MEGILPS
MEGOHM
MEGOHMS
MEGRIM
MEGRIMS
MEINEY
MEINEYS
MEINIE
MEINIES
MEISHI
MEISHIS
MELANO
MELANOS
MELDER
MELDERS
MELLAY
MELLAYS
MELLED
SMELLED
MELLOW
MELLOWS
MELLOWY
MELTED
SMELTED
MELTON
MELTONS
MEMBER
MEMBERS
MEMOIR
MEMOIRS
MENACE
MENACED
MENACER
MENACES
MENAGE
AMENAGE
MENAGED
MENAGES
MENDED
AMENDED
EMENDED
MENDER
AMENDER
MENDERS
MENEER
MENEERS
MENHIR
MENHIRS
MENIAL
MENIALS
MENING
AMENING
OMENING
MENTAL
AMENTAL
OMENTAL
MENTEE
MENTEES
MENTOR
MENTORS
MENTUM
AMENTUM
OMENTUM
MENYIE
MENYIES
MERCAT
MERCATS
MERCER
MERCERS
MERCERY
MERELL
MERELLS
MERGED
EMERGED
MERGER
MERGERS
MERGES
EMERGES
MERINO
MERINOS
MERISM
MERISMS
MERKIN
MERKINS
MERLIN
MERLING
MERLINS
MERLON
MERLONS
MEROME
MEROMES
MESAIL
MESAILS
MESCAL
MESCALS
MESETA
MESETAS
MESSAN
MESSANS
MESTEE
MESTEES
METAGE
METAGES
METATE
METATES
METEOR
METEORS
METHOD
METHODS
METHYL
METHYLS
METICS
EMETICS
METIER
METIERS
METOPE
METOPES
METRIC
METRICS
METTLE
METTLED
METTLES
MEUSES
SMEUSES
MEZAIL
MEZAILS
MEZUZA
MEZUZAH
MGANGA
MGANGAS
MIASMA
MIASMAL
MIASMAS
MICATE
EMICATE
MICATED
MICATES
MICHER
MICHERS
MICKEY
MICKEYS
MICKLE
MICKLES
MICRON
OMICRON
MICRONS
MIDAIR
MIDAIRS
MIDDAY
MIDDAYS
MIDDEN
MIDDENS
MIDDLE
MIDDLED
MIDDLES
MIDGET
MIDGETS
MIDRIB
MIDRIBS
MIDWAY
MIDWAYS
MIGHTS
SMIGHTS
MIGHTST
MIHRAB
MIHRABS
MIKADO
MIKADOS
MIKRON
MIKRONS
MILADI
MILADIS
MILAGE
MILAGES
MILDEN
MILDENS
MILDEW
MILDEWS
MILDEWY
MILERS
SMILERS
MILIEU
MILIEUS
MILIEUX
MILKER
MILKERS
MILLER
MILLERS
MILLET
MILLETS
MILORD
MILORDS
MILSEY
MILSEYS
MILTER
MILTERS
MIMBAR
MIMBARS
MIMOSA
MIMOSAS
MINBAR
MINBARS
MINCER
MINCERS
MINDER
MINDERS
MINGIN
MINGING
MINGLE
MINGLED
MINGLER
MINGLES
MINIMA
MINIMAL
MINIMAX
MINING
MININGS
MINION
MINIONS
MINIUM
MINIUMS
MINNIE
MINNIES
MINNOW
MINNOWS
MINTER
MINTERS
MINUET
MINUETS
MINUTE
MINUTED
MINUTER
MINUTES
MINYAN
MINYANS
MIOMBO
MIOMBOS
MIOTIC
MIOTICS
MIRAGE
MIRAGES
MIRITI
MIRITIS
MIRROR
MIRRORS
MISAIM
MISAIMS
MISCUE
MISCUED
MISCUES
MISERE
MISERES
MISFIT
MISFITS
MISHAP
MISHAPS
MISHAPT
MISHIT
MISHITS
MISHMI
MISHMIS
MISKEN
MISKENS
MISKENT
MISKEY
MISKEYS
MISLAY
MISLAYS
MISSAL
MISSALS
MISSAY
MISSAYS
MISSEE
MISSEEM
MISSEEN
MISSEES
MISSEL
MISSELS
MISSES
AMISSES
MISSET
MISSETS
MISSIS
MISSISH
MISTER
MISTERM
MISTERS
MISTERY
MISTLE
MISTLED
MISTLES
MISUSE
MISUSED
MISUSER
MISUSES
MITERS
SMITERS
MITHER
MITHERS
MITTEN
SMITTEN
MITTENS

MIZZEN
MIZZENS
MIZZLE
MIZZLED
MIZZLES
MNEMON
MNEMONS
MOANER
MOANERS
MOBBIE
MOBBIES
MOBBLE
MOBBLED
MOBBLES
MOBILE
MOBILES
MOCHIE
MOCHIER
MOCKED
SMOCKED
MOCKER
MOCKERS
MOCKERY
MOCOCK
MOCOCKS
MOCUCK
MOCUCKS
MODENA
MODENAS
MODERN
MODERNS
MODEST
MODESTY
MODIST
MODISTE
MODISTS
MODULE
MODULES
MOGGAN
MOGGANS
MOGGIE
MOGGIES
MOHAIR
MOHAIRS
MOHAWK
MOHAWKS
MOIDER
MOIDERS
MOILED
SMOILED
MOILER
MOILERS
MOISER
MOISERS
MOLEST
MOLESTS
MOLINE
MOLINES
MOLINET
MOLLAH
MOLLAHS
MOLLIE
MOLLIES
MOLOCH
MOLOCHS
MOLTEN
YMOLTEN
MOMENT
MOMENTA
MOMENTS
MOMMET
MOMMETS
MOMZER
MOMZERS
MONAUL
MONAULS
MONETH
MONETHS
MONGER
MONGERS
MONGERY
MONGOL
MONGOLS
MONIAL
MONIALS
MONISM
MONISMS
MONIST
MONISTS
MONKEY
MONKEYS
MONTEM
MONTEMS
MONTRE
MONTRES
MOOLAH
MOOLAHS
MOONER
MOONERS
MOORED
SMOORED
MOORVA
MOORVAS
MOOTED
SMOOTED
MOOTER
MOOTERS
MOOVED
AMOOVED
MOOVES
AMOOVES
MOPANE
MOPANES
MOPANI
MOPANIS
MOPOKE
MOPOKES
MOPPER
MOPPERS
MOPPET
MOPPETS
MORALE
MORALES
MORALL
MORALLS
MORALLY
MORASS
MORASSY
MOREEN
MOREENS
MORGAY
MORGAYS
MORGEN
MORGENS
MORGUE
MORGUES
MORION
MORIONS
MORKIN
MORKINS
MORNAY
MORNAYS
MOROSE
MOROSER
MORPHO
MORPHOS
MORROW
MORROWS
MORSEL
MORSELS
MORTAL
MORTALS
MORTAR
MORTARS
MORULA
MORULAE
MORULAR
MOSAIC
MOSAICS
MOSQUE
MOSQUES
MOSSIE
MOSSIER
MOSSIES
MOTETT
MOTETTS
MOTHER
SMOTHER
MOTHERS
MOTHERY
MOTILE
MOTILES
MOTION
EMOTION
MOTIONS
MOTIVE
EMOTIVE
MOTIVED
MOTIVES
MOTLEY
MOTLEYS
MOTMOT
MOTMOTS
MOTSER
MOTSERS
MOTTLE
MOTTLED
MOTTLES
MOTUCA
MOTUCAS
MOUJIK
MOUJIKS
MOULIN
MOULINS
MOUNTS
AMOUNTS
MOUSED
SMOUSED
MOUSER
SMOUSER
MOUSERS
MOUSERY
MOUSES
SMOUSES
MOUSIE
MOUSIER
MOUSIES
MOUSLE
MOUSLED
MOUSLES
MOUSME
MOUSMEE
MOUSMES
MOUSSE
MOUSSES
MOUTAN
MOUTANS
MOUTER
MOUTERS
MOUTON
MOUTONS
MOVING
AMOVING
EMOVING
MOWING
MOWINGS
MOYLED
SMOYLED
MOYLES
SMOYLES
MOZZIE
MOZZIES
MOZZLE
MOZZLES
MUCATE
MUCATES
MUCHEL
MUCHELL
MUCHELS
MUCKER
MUCKERS
MUCKLE
MUCKLES
MUCLUC
MUCLUCS
MUCOSA
MUCOSAE
MUDCAT
MUDCATS
MUDDER
MUDDERS
MUDDLE
MUDDLED
MUDDLER
MUDDLES
MUDGED
SMUDGED
MUDGER
SMUDGER
MUDGERS
MUDGES
SMUDGES
MUESLI
MUESLIS
MUFFIN
MUFFING
MUFFINS
MUFFLE
MUFFLED
MUFFLER
MUFFLES
MUFLON
MUFLONS
MUGFUL
MUGFULS
MUGGED
SMUGGED
MUGGEE
MUGGEES
MUGGER
SMUGGER
MUGGERS
MUKLUK
MUKLUKS
MULLAH
MULLAHS
MULLER
MULLERS
MULLET
MULLETS
MULLEY
MULLEYS
MULMUL
MULMULL
MULMULS
MULTUM
MULTUMS
MUMBLE
MUMBLED
MUMBLER
MUMBLES
MUMMER
MUMMERS
MUMMERY
MUMMIA
MUMMIAS
MUMPER
MUMPERS
MUNDIC
MUNDICS
MUNITE
MUNITED
MUNITES
MUNSHI
MUNSHIS
MUNTIN
MUNTING
MUNTINS
MURAGE
MURAGES
MURDER
MURDERS
MURENA
MURENAS
MURINE
MURINES
MURING
EMURING
MURLAN
MURLANS
MURLIN
MURLING
MURLINS
MURMUR
MURMURS
MURRAM
MURRAMS
MURRAY
MURRAYS
MURREN
MURRENS
MURREY
MURREYS
MURRHA
MURRHAS
MURRIN
MURRINE
MURRINS
MUSANG
MUSANGS
MUSCAT
MUSCATS
MUSCID
MUSCIDS
MUSCLE
MUSCLED
MUSCLES
MUSERS
AMUSERS
MUSEUM
MUSEUMS
MUSHER
MUSHERS
MUSING
AMUSING
MUSINGS
MUSIVE
AMUSIVE
MUSKEG
MUSKEGS
MUSKET
MUSKETS
MUSKLE
MUSKLES
MUSLIN
MUSLINS
MUSMON
MUSMONS
MUSROL
MUSROLS
MUSSEL
MUSSELS
MUSTEE
MUSTEES
MUSTER
MUSTERS
MUTANT
MUTANTS
MUTATE
MUTATED
MUTATES
MUTINE
MUTINED
MUTINES
MUTISM
MUTISMS
MUTTER
MUTTERS
MUTTON
MUTTONS
MUTTONY
MUTUCA
MUTUCAS
MUTULE
MUTULES
MUTUUM
MUTUUMS
MUZHIK
MUZHIKS
MUZZLE
MUZZLED
MUZZLER
MUZZLES
MYELIN
MYELINS
MYELON
MYELONS
MYGALE
MYGALES
MYOGEN
MYOGENS
MYOPIA
MYOPIAS
MYOPIC
MYOPICS
MYOSIN
MYOSINS
MYRIAD
MYRIADS
MYRTLE
MYRTLES
MYSTIC
MYSTICS
MZUNGU
MZUNGUS
NABBER
NABBERS
NACKET
NACKETS
NAGANA
NAGANAS
NAGARI
NAGARIS
NAGGED
SNAGGED
NAGGER
NAGGERS
NAILED
SNAILED
NAILER
NAILERS
NAILERY
NALLAH
NALLAHS
NAMING
NAMINGS
NANDOO
NANDOOS
NANISM
ONANISM
NANISMS
NANKIN
NANKINS
NAPALM
NAPALMS
NAPKIN
NAPKINS
NAPPED
KNAPPED
SNAPPED
NAPPER
KNAPPER
SNAPPER
NAPPERS
NAPRON
NAPRONS
NARDOO
NARDOOS
NARROW
NARROWS
NASARD
NASARDS
NASION
NASIONS
NASUTE
NASUTES
NATION
ENATION
NATIONS
NATIVE
NATIVES
NATRON
NATRONS
NATTER
NATTERS
NATTERY
NATURA
NATURAE
NATURAL
NATURE
NATURED
NATURES
NAUGHT
NAUGHTS
NAUGHTY
NAUSEA
NAUSEAS
NAUTIC
NAUTICS
NAVAID
NAVAIDS
NEAFFE
NEAFFES
NEAPED
SNEAPED
NEARED
ANEARED
UNEARED
NEATEN
UNEATEN
NEATENS
NEBBED
SNEBBED
NEBBUK
NEBBUKS
NEBECK
NEBECKS
NEBULA
NEBULAE
NEBULAR
NEBULAS
NEBULE
NEBULES
NECKED
SNECKED
NECTAR
NECTARS
NECTARY
NEEDER
NEEDERS
NEEDLE
NEEDLED
NEEDLER
NEEDLES
NEEZED
SNEEZED
NEEZES
SNEEZES
NEGATE
NEGATED
NEGATES
NEKTON
NEKTONS
NELSON
NELSONS
NEPETA
NEPETAS
NEPHEW
NEPHEWS
NEREID

NEREIDS
NERINE
NERINES
NERITE
NERITES
NEROLI
NEROLIS
NERVED
ENERVED
NERVER
NERVERS
NERVES
ENERVES
NESTER
NESTERS
NESTLE
NESTLED
NESTLES
NETFUL
NETFULS
NETTLE
NETTLED
NETTLES
NEURON
NEURONE
NEURONS
NEUTER
NEUTERS
NEWELL
NEWELLS
NEWING
ENEWING
NEWTON
NEWTONS
NHANDU
NHANDUS
NIACIN
NIACINS
NIBBED
SNIBBED
NIBBLE
NIBBLED
NIBBLER
NIBBLES
NICHER
NICHERS
NICKAR
NICKARS
NICKED
SNICKED
NICKEL
NICKELS
NICKER
KNICKER
SNICKER
NICKERS
NICKUM
NICKUMS
NIDGET
NIDGETS
NIDING
NIDINGS
NIELLO
NIELLOS
NIFFED
SNIFFED
NIFFER
SNIFFER
NIFFERS
NIGGER
SNIGGER
NIGGERS
NIGGERY
NIGGLE
SNIGGLE
NIGGLED
NIGGLER
NIGGLES
NIGHTS
KNIGHTS
NILGAI
NILGAIS
NILGAU
NILGAUS
NIMBLE
NIMBLER
NIMMER
NIMMERS
NINCOM
NINCOMS
NINCUM
NINCUMS
NIPPED
SNIPPED
NIPPER
SNIPPER
NIPPERS
NIPPLE
NIPPLED
NIPPLES
NIPTER
NIPTERS
NIRLIE
NIRLIER
NITERS
UNITERS
NITRYL
NITRYLS
NITWIT
NITWITS
NOBBLE
KNOBBLE
NOBBLED
NOBBLER
NOBBLES
NOBLES
NOBLEST
NOCAKE
NOCAKES
NOCENT
NOCENTS
NOCHEL
NOCHELS
NOCKED
KNOCKED
NOCKET
NOCKETS
NOCTUA
NOCTUAS
NODDED
SNODDED
NODDER
SNODDER
NODDERS
NODDLE
NODDLED
NODDLES
NODULE
NODULED
NODULES
NOESES
ANOESES
NOESIS
ANOESIS
NOETIC
ANOETIC
NOGGED
SNOGGED
NOGGIN
NOGGING
NOGGINS
NOINTS
ANOINTS
NOMADE
NOMADES
NOMINA
NOMINAL
NOMISM
NOMISMS
NONAGE
NONAGED
NONAGES
NONANE
NONANES
NOODLE
NOODLED
NOODLES
NOOKIE
NOOKIER
NOOKIES
NOONER
NOONERS
NORITE
NORITES
NORMAL
NORMALS
NORMAN
NORMANS
NORSEL
NORSELS
NOSEAN
NOSEANS
NOSHER
NOSHERS
NOSHERY
NOSIES
NOSIEST
NOSING
NOSINGS
NOSTOC
NOSTOCS
NOTATE
NOTATED
NOTATES
NOTICE
NOTICED
NOTICES
NOTION
NOTIONS
NOUGAT
NOUGATS
NOUGHT
NOUGHTS
NOUSLE
NOUSLED
NOUSLES
NOVENA
NOVENAS
NOVICE
NOVICES
NOYADE
NOYADES
NOZZER
NOZZERS
NOZZLE
NOZZLES
NUANCE
NUANCED
NUANCES
NUBBED
SNUBBED
NUBBIN
NUBBING
NUBBINS
NUBBLE
KNUBBLE
NUBBLED
NUBBLES
NUBBLY
KNUBBLY
NUCLEI
NUCLEIN
NUCULE
NUCULES
NUDGED
SNUDGED
NUDGER
NUDGERS
NUDGES
SNUDGES
NUDISM
NUDISMS
NUDIST
NUDISTS
NUDNIK
NUDNIKS
NUFFIN
NUFFINS
NUGGAR
NUGGARS
NUGGET
NUGGETS
NUGGETY
NULLAH
NULLAHS
NUMBAT
NUMBATS
NUMBER
NUMBERS
NUMDAH
NUMDAHS
NUMNAH
NUMNAHS
NUNCIO
NUNCIOS
NUNCLE
NUNCLES
NURDLE
NURDLED
NURDLES
NURHAG
NURHAGS
NURLED
KNURLED
NURSER
NURSERS
NURSERY
NURSLE
NURSLED
NURSLES
NUTATE
NUTATED
NUTATES
NUTLET
NUTLETS
NUTMEG
NUTMEGS
NUTRIA
NUTRIAS
NUTTER
NUTTERS
NUTTERY
NUZZER
NUZZERS
NUZZLE
SNUZZLE
NUZZLED
NUZZLES
NYALAS
INYALAS
NYANZA
NYANZAS
NYBBLE
NYBBLES
NYMPHO
NYMPHOS
OAKERS
SOAKERS
OARAGE
OARAGES
OARIER
HOARIER
ROARIER
OARING
HOARING
ROARING
SOARING
OATERS
BOATERS
COATERS
DOATERS
OBANGS
GOBANGS
KOBANGS
OBDURE
OBDURED
OBDURES
OBECHE
OBECHES
OBEISM
OBEISMS
OBEYER
OBEYERS
OBIISM
OBIISMS
OBJECT
OBJECTS
OBJURE
OBJURED
OBJURES
OBLAST
OBLASTS
OBLATE
OBLATES
OBLIGE
OBLIGED
OBLIGEE
OBLIGES
OBLONG
OBLONGS
OBOIST
OBOISTS
OBSIGN
OBSIGNS
OBTAIN
OBTAINS
OBTEND
OBTENDS
OBTEST
OBTESTS
OBTUND
OBTUNDS
OBTUSE
OBTUSER
OBVERT
OBVERTS
OCCULT
OCCULTS
OCELOT
OCELOTS
OCHERS
TOCHERS
OCHREA
OCHREAE
OCKERS
COCKERS
DOCKERS
HOCKERS
LOCKERS
MOCKERS
ROCKERS
OCTANE
OCTANES
OCTANT
OCTANTS
OCTAVE
OCTAVES
OCTAVO
OCTAVOS
OCTETT
OCTETTE
OCTETTS
OCTROI
OCTROIS
OCTUOR
OCTUORS
OCULAR
JOCULAR
LOCULAR
VOCULAR
OCULARS
OCULUS
LOCULUS
ODISMS
IODISMS
ODISTS
CODISTS
MODISTS
ODIUMS
SODIUMS
OECIST
OECISTS
OEDEMA
OEDEMAS
OEUVRE
OEUVRES
OFFCUT
OFFCUTS
OFFEND
OFFENDS
OFFERS
COFFERS
DOFFERS
GOFFERS
OFFICE
OFFICER
OFFICES
OFFING
BOFFING
COFFING
DOFFING
GOFFING
OFFINGS
OFFISH
TOFFISH
OFFPUT
OFFPUTS
OFFSET
OFFSETS
OGDOAD
OGDOADS
OGGINS
HOGGINS
NOGGINS
OGLING
OGLINGS
OHMAGE
OHMAGES
OIKIST
OIKISTS
OILCAN
OILCANS
OILERS
BOILERS
MOILERS
TOILERS
OILERY
BOILERY
OILIER
ROILIER
SOILIER
OILING
BOILING
COILING
FOILING
MOILING
ROILING
SOILING
TOILING
OILLET
OILLETS
OILNUT
OILNUTS
OINKED
BOINKED
OINTED
JOINTED
NOINTED
POINTED
OLDENS
BOLDENS
GOLDENS
OLDEST
BOLDEST
COLDEST
GOLDEST
OLDISH
COLDISH
GOLDISH
OLEATE
OLEATES
OLEFIN
OLEFINE
OLEFINS
OLFACT
OLFACTS
OLIVER
OLIVERS
OLIVES
SOLIVES
OLIVET
OLIVETS
OLLAMH
OLLAMHS
OMBRES
HOMBRES
SOMBRES
OMELET
OMELETS
OMENTA
LOMENTA
MOMENTA
TOMENTA
OMENTAL
OMERTA
OMERTAS
OMNIUM
OMNIUMS
ONAGER
ONAGERS
ONCOME
ONCOMES
ONCOST
ONCOSTS
ONDINE
ONDINES
ONDING
BONDING
FONDING
PONDING
ONDINGS
ONEYER
MONEYER
ONEYERS
ONEYRE
ONEYRES
ONFALL
ONFALLS
ONFLOW
ONFLOWS
ONNING
CONNING
DONNING
FONNING
KONNING
RONNING
WONNING
ONSIDE
ONSIDES
ONUSES
BONUSES
TONUSES
ONWARD
ONWARDS
ONYCHA
ONYCHAS
OOCYTE
OOCYTES
OODLES
BOODLES

DOODLES
NOODLES
POODLES
OOGAMY
ZOOGAMY
OOGENY
ZOOGENY
OOHING
BOOHING
OOIDAL
ZOOIDAL
OOLITE
ZOOLITE
OOLITES
OOLOGY
NOOLOGY
ZOOLOGY
OOLONG
OOLONGS
OOMIAC
OOMIACK
OOMIACS
OOMIAK
OOMIAKS
OOMPAH
OOMPAHS
OOPING
COOPING
HOOPING
LOOPING
MOOPING
POOPING
ROOPING
SOOPING
OORIAL
OORIALS
OORIER
MOORIER
OOSIER
GOOSIER
OOZIER
BOOZIER
WOOZIER
OOZILY
BOOZILY
WOOZILY
OOZING
BOOZING
OPAQUE
OPAQUED
OPAQUER
OPAQUES
OPCODE
OPCODES
OPENER
OPENERS
OPERON
OPERONS
OPHITE
OPHITES
OPIATE
OPIATED
OPIATES
OPPOSE
OPPOSED
OPPOSER
OPPOSES
OPPUGN
OPPUGNS
OPTANT

OPTANTS
OPTERS
COPTERS
OPTIMA
OPTIMAL
OPTIME
OPTIMES
OPTION
OPTIONS
OPUSES
MOPUSES
ORACHE
ORACHES
ORACLE
CORACLE
ORACLED
ORACLES
ORALLY
MORALLY
ORANGE
ORANGER
ORANGES
ORANGEY
ORARIA
ORARIAN
ORATES
BORATES
ORATOR
ORATORS
ORATORY
ORBING
SORBING
ORBITA
ORBITAL
ORBITAS
ORCEIN
ORCEINS
ORCHAT
ORCHATS
ORCHEL
ORCHELS
ORCHID
ORCHIDS
ORCHIL
ORCHILS
ORCINE
PORCINE
ORCINES
ORDAIN
ORDAINS
ORDEAL
ORDEALS
ORDERS
BORDERS
ORDURE
BORDURE
ORDURES
OREIDE
OREIDES
ORGASM
ORGASMS
ORGEAT
ORGEATS
ORGIAS
GORGIAS
ORGIAST
ORGIES
PORGIES
ORGONE
FORGONE

ORGONES
ORGUES
MORGUES
ORIENT
ORIENTS
ORIGAN
ORIGANE
ORIGANS
ORIGIN
ORIGINS
ORIOLE
ORIOLES
ORISON
ORISONS
ORMERS
DORMERS
FORMERS
WORMERS
ORMOLU
ORMOLUS
ORNATE
ORNATER
OROGEN
OROGENS
OROGENY
OROIDE
OROIDES
ORPHAN
ORPHANS
ORPINE
FORPINE
ORPINES
ORTHOS
PORTHOS
OSCULA
OSCULAR
OSCULE
OSCULES
OSIERS
COSIERS
HOSIERS
ROSIERS
OSIERY
HOSIERY
OSMATE
OSMATES
OSMIUM
OSMIUMS
OSMOSE
OSMOSED
OSMOSES
OSMUND
OSMUNDA
OSMUNDS
OSPREY
OSPREYS
OSSEIN
OSSEINS
OSTENT
OSTENTS
OSTLER
HOSTLER
OSTLERS
OTHERS
BOTHERS
FOTHERS
MOTHERS
POTHERS
ROTHERS
OTTARS

COTTARS
OTTAVA
OTTAVAS
OTTERS
COTTERS
HOTTERS
JOTTERS
POTTERS
ROTTERS
TOTTERS
OUBITS
WOUBITS
OUCHES
BOUCHES
COUCHES
DOUCHES
MOUCHES
POUCHES
TOUCHES
VOUCHES
OUGHLY
ROUGHLY
TOUGHLY
OUGHTS
BOUGHTS
NOUGHTS
OUGLIE
OUGLIED
OUGLIES
OULDER
BOULDER
FOULDER
MOULDER
POULDER
OULONG
OULONGS
OUNCES
BOUNCES
JOUNCES
POUNCES
ROUNCES
OUPING
COUPING
LOUPING
MOUPING
POUPING
ROUPING
OURALI
WOURALI
OURALIS
OURARI
OURARIS
OUREBI
OUREBIS
OURIER
COURIER
LOURIER
OUSELS
HOUSELS
OUSTED
JOUSTED
MOUSTED
ROUSTED
OUSTER
JOUSTER
ROUSTER
OUSTERS
OUTAGE
OUTAGES
OUTBAR

OUTBARS
OUTBID
OUTBIDS
OUTEAT
OUTEATS
OUTERS
COUTERS
DOUTERS
FOUTERS
MOUTERS
POUTERS
ROUTERS
SOUTERS
TOUTERS
OUTFIT
OUTFITS
OUTFLY
GOUTFLY
OUTGUN
OUTGUNS
OUTHER
COUTHER
MOUTHER
POUTHER
SOUTHER
OUTHIT
OUTHITS
OUTING
DOUTING
HOUTING
LOUTING
POUTING
ROUTING
TOUTING
OUTINGS
OUTJET
OUTJETS
OUTJUT
OUTJUTS
OUTLAW
OUTLAWS
OUTLAY
OUTLAYS
OUTLER
OUTLERS
OUTLET
OUTLETS
OUTLIE
OUTLIED
OUTLIER
OUTLIES
OUTMAN
OUTMANS
OUTPUT
OUTPUTS
OUTRAN
OUTRANK
OUTRED
FOUTRED
OUTREDS
OUTRUN
OUTRUNS
OUTSET
OUTSETS
OUTSIT
OUTSITS
OUTSUM
OUTSUMS
OUTTOP
OUTTOPS

OUTVIE
OUTVIED
OUTVIES
OUTWIN
OUTWIND
OUTWING
OUTWINS
OUTWIT
OUTWITH
OUTWITS
OUVERT
COUVERT
OUVERTE
OVATES
BOVATES
OVATOR
OVATORS
OVERED
COVERED
DOVERED
HOVERED
LOVERED
OVERGO
OVERGOT
OVERLY
LOVERLY
OVISAC
OVISACS
OWLERS
BOWLERS
FOWLERS
HOWLERS
JOWLERS
OWLETS
HOWLETS
OWLIER
JOWLIER
LOWLIER
OWLING
BOWLING
COWLING
FOWLING
GOWLING
HOWLING
JOWLING
SOWLING
YOWLING
OWNERS
DOWNERS
OWNING
BOWNING
DOWNING
GOWNING
LOWNING
OXFORD
OXFORDS
OXGANG
OXGANGS
OXGATE
OXGATES
OXHEAD
OXHEADS
OXLAND
OXLANDS
OXSLIP
OXSLIPS
OXTAIL
OXTAILS
OXYGEN
LOXYGEN

OXYGENS
OXYMEL
OXYMELS
OYESES
NOYESES
OYSTER
ROYSTER
OYSTERS
OZAENA
OZAENAS
PACERS
SPACERS
PACHAK
PACHAKS
PACIER
SPACIER
PACING
SPACING
PACKER
PACKERS
PACKET
PACKETS
PADANG
PADANGS
PADAUK
PADAUKS
PADDER
PADDERS
PADDLE
PADDLED
PADDLER
PADDLES
PADOUK
PADOUKS
PADSAW
PADSAWS
PAELLA
PAELLAS
PAGING
PAGINGS
PAGODA
PAGODAS
PAIDLE
PAIDLES
PAIGLE
PAIGLES
PAINED
SPAINED
PAINIM
PAINIMS
PAIOCK
PAIOCKE
PAIOCKS
PAJOCK
PAJOCKE
PAJOCKS
PAKEHA
PAKEHAS
PAKORA
PAKORAS
PALACE
PALACES
PALAGI
PALAGIS
PALAMA
PALAMAE
PALATE
PALATED
PALATES
PALING

PALINGS
PALKEE
PALKEES
PALLAH
PALLAHS
PALLED
SPALLED
PALLET
PALLETS
PALLIA
PALLIAL
PALLOR
PALLORS
PALMAR
PALMARY
PALMER
PALMERS
PALMIE
PALMIER
PALMIES
PALMIET
PALOLO
PALOLOS
PALTER
PALTERS
PAMPER
PAMPERO
PAMPERS
PANADA
PANADAS
PANAMA
PANAMAS
PANDAR
PANDARS
PANDER
PANDERS
PANDIT
PANDITS
PANFUL
PANFULS
PANGED
SPANGED
PANGEN
PANGENE
PANGENS
PANICK
PANICKS
PANICKY
PANING
SPANING
PANISC
PANISCS
PANISK
PANISKS
PANNED
SPANNED
PANTER
PANTERS
PANTON
PANTONS
PANTUN
PANTUNS
PANZER
PANZERS
PAPAIN
PAPAINS
PAPAYA
PAPAYAS
PAPISM
PAPISMS

PAPIST
PAPISTS
PAPULA
PAPULAE
PAPULAR
PAPULE
PAPULES
PARADE
PARADED
PARADES
PARAGE
PARAGES
PARAMO
PARAMOS
PARANG
PARANGS
PARAPH
PARAPHS
PARCEL
PARCELS
PARDAL
PARDALE
PARDALS
PARDON
PARDONS
PARENT
PARENTS
PARERS
SPARERS
PARGED
SPARGED
PARGES
SPARGES
PARGET
PARGETS
PARIAH
PARIAHS
PARIAL
PARIALS
PARING
SPARING
PARINGS
PARKED
SPARKED
PARKEE
PARKEES
PARKER
PARKERS
PARKIE
SPARKIE
PARKIER
PARKIES
PARKIN
PARKING
PARKINS
PARKIS
PARKISH
PARKLY
SPARKLY
PARLAY
PARLAYS
PARLEY
PARLEYS
PARLOR
PARLORS
PAROLE
PAROLED
PAROLEE
PAROLES
PARPEN
PARPEND
PARPENS
PARPENT
PARRAL
PARRALS
PARREL
PARRELS
PARROT
PARROTS
PARROTY
PARSEC
PARSECS
PARSER
SPARSER
PARSERS
PARSON
PARSONS
PARTAN
SPARTAN
PARTANS
PARTER
PARTERS
PARTON
PARTONS
PARURE
PARURES
PARVIS
PARVISE
PASCAL
PASCALS
PASEAR
PASEARS
PASHIM
PASHIMS
PASSER
PASSERS
PASTEL
PASTELS
PASTER
PASTERN
PASTERS
PASTIL
PASTILS
PASTOR
PASTORS
PATACA
PATACAS
PATENT
PATENTS
PATERA
PATERAE
PATHED
SPATHED
PATHIC
SPATHIC
PATHICS
PATINA
PATINAS
PATINE
PATINED
PATINES
PATROL
PATROLS
PATRON
PATRONS
PATTED
SPATTED
PATTEE
SPATTEE
PATTEN
PATTENS
PATTER
SPATTER
PATTERN
PATTERS
PATTLE
PATTLES
PATZER
PATZERS
PAUNCE
PAUNCES
PAUNCH
PAUNCHY
PAUPER
PAUPERS
PAUSER
PAUSERS
PAVAGE
PAVAGES
PAVANE
PAVANES
PAVING
PAVINGS
PAVINS
SPAVINS
PAVIOR
PAVIORS
PAVISE
PAVISES
PAVONE
PAVONES
PAWNCE
PAWNCES
PAWNED
SPAWNED
PAWNEE
PAWNEES
PAWNER
SPAWNER
PAWNERS
PAWPAW
PAWPAWS
PAYING
APAYING
SPAYING
PAYINGS
PAYNIM
PAYNIMS
PAYOLA
PAYOLAS
PEACOD
PEACODS
PEANED
SPEANED
PEANUT
PEANUTS
PEAPOD
PEAPODS
PEARCE
PEARCED
PEARCES
PEAVEY
PEAVEYS
PEBBLE
PEBBLED
PEBBLES
PECKED
SPECKED
PECKER
PECKERS
PECTIN
PECTINS
PEDALO
PEDALOS
PEDANT
PEDANTS
PEDDER
PEDDERS
PEDDLE
PEDDLED
PEDDLER
PEDDLES
PEDLAR
PEDLARS
PEDLARY
PEELED
SPEELED
PEELER
SPEELER
PEELERS
PEENGE
PEENGED
PEENGES
PEEPER
PEEPERS
PEEPUL
PEEPULS
PEERED
SPEERED
PEERIE
PEERIER
PEERIES
PEEVER
PEEVERS
PEEWEE
PEEWEES
PEEWIT
PEEWITS
PEINCT
PEINCTS
PELAGE
PELAGES
PELHAM
PELHAMS
PELITE
PELITES
PELLET
PELLETS
PELMET
PELMETS
PELOID
PELOIDS
PELOTA
PELOTAS
PELTAS
PELTAST
PELTER
SPELTER
PELTERS
PENCEL
PENCELS
PENCES
SPENCES
PENCIL
PENCILS
PENDED
UPENDED
PENFUL
PENFULS
PENING
OPENING
PENNAL
PENNALS
PENNER
PENNERS
PENNON
PENNONS
PENSEE
PENSEES
PENSEL
PENSELS
PENSIL
PENSILE
PENSILS
PENSUM
PENSUMS
PENTAD
PENTADS
PENTEL
PENTELS
PENULT
PENULTS
PEOPLE
PEOPLED
PEOPLES
PEPINO
PEPINOS
PEPLUM
PEPLUMS
PEPPER
PEPPERS
PEPPERY
PEPSIN
PEPSINE
PEPSINS
PEPTIC
PEPTICS
PERDUE
EPERDUE
PERDUES
PERIOD
PERIODS
PERKIN
PERKING
PERKINS
PERMIT
PERMITS
PERONE
PERONES
PERRON
PERRONS
PERSES
SPERSES
PERSON
PERSONA
PERSONS
PERSUE
PERSUED
PERSUES
PERUKE
PERUKED
PERUKES
PERUSE
PERUSED
PERUSER
PERUSES
PESADE
PESADES
PESANT
PESANTE
PESANTS
PESETA
PESETAS
PESEWA
PESEWAS
PESHWA
PESHWAS
PESTER
PESTERS
PESTLE
PESTLED
PESTLES
PETARA
PETARAS
PETARD
PETARDS
PETHER
PETHERS
PETREL
PETRELS
PETROL
PETROLS
PETTER
PETTERS
PETTLE
PETTLED
PETTLES
PEWTER
PEWTERS
PEYOTE
PEYOTES
PEZANT
PEZANTS
PHALLI
PHALLIC
PHALLIN
PHANGS
UPHANGS
PHASIC
APHASIC
PHEERE
PHEERES
PHEESE
PHEESED
PHEESES
PHEEZE
PHEEZED
PHEEZES
PHENES
SPHENES
PHENIC
SPHENIC
PHENOL
PHENOLS
PHENOM
PHENOMS
PHENYL
PHENYLS
PHESES
APHESES
PHIZOG
PHIZOGS
PHLEGM
PHLEGMS
PHLEGMY
PHLOEM
PHLOEMS
PHOBIA
PHOBIAS
PHOBIC
PHOBICS
PHOEBE
PHOEBES
PHONER
PHONERS
PHONEY
PHONEYS
PHONIC
APHONIC
PHONICS
PHONON
PHONONS
PHOTIC
APHOTIC
PHOTICS
PHOTON
PHOTONS
PHRASE
PHRASED
PHRASER
PHRASES
PHYLLO
PHYLLOS
PHYSIC
PHYSICS
PHYSIO
PHYSIOS
PHYTON
PHYTONS
PIAFFE
PIAFFED
PIAFFER
PIAFFES
PIAZZA
PIAZZAS
PICENE
EPICENE
PICENES
PICKER
SPICKER
PICKERS
PICKERY
PICKET
PICKETS
PICKLE
PICKLED
PICKLER
PICKLES
PICNIC
PICNICS
PICOTE
PICOTED
PICOTEE
PIDDLE
PIDDLED
PIDDLER
PIDDLES
PIDGIN
PIDGINS
PIECEN
PIECENS
PIECER
PIECERS
PIERCE
PIERCED
PIERCER
PIERCES
PIERID
PIERIDS
PIFFLE
PIFFLED
PIFFLER
PIFFLES
PIGEON
PIGEONS
PIGGIE
PIGGIER
PIGGIES
PIGGIN
PIGGING
PIGGINS
PIGHTS
SPIGHTS
PIGLET
PIGLETS
PIGNUT
PIGNUTS
PIGPEN
PIGPENS
PIKING
SPIKING
PILAFF
PILAFFS
PILFER
PILFERS
PILFERY
PILING
SPILING
PILINGS
PILLAR
PILLARS
PILLAU
PILLAUS
PILLED
SPILLED
PILLOW
PILLOWS
PILLOWY
PILULA
PILULAR
PILULAS
PILULE
PILULES
PIMENT
PIMENTO
PIMENTS
PIMPLE
PIMPLED
PIMPLES
PINATA
PINATAS
PINCER
PINCERS
PINDER
PINDERS
PINGER
PINGERS
PINGLE
PINGLED
PINGLER
PINGLES
PINIER
SPINIER
PINIES
PINIEST
PINING
OPINING
PINION
OPINION
PINIONS

PINITE
PINITES
PINKIE
PINKIER
PINKIES
PINNER
SPINNER
PINNERS
PINNET
SPINNET
PINNETS
PINNIE
PINNIES
PINOLE
PINOLES
PINTLE
PINTLES
PIOLET
PIOLETS
PIONER
PIONERS
PIONEY
PIONEYS
PIPAGE
PIPAGES
PIPING
PIPINGS
PIPKIN
PIPKINS
PIPPIN
PIPPING
PIPPINS
PIQUET
PIQUETS
PIRANA
PIRANAS
PIRATE
PIRATED
PIRATES
PIRAYA
PIRAYAS
PIRNIE
PIRNIES
PISTIL
PISTILS
PISTOL
PISTOLE
PISTOLS
PISTON
PISTONS
PITARA
PITARAH
PITARAS
PITIER
PITIERS
PITTED
SPITTED
PITTEN
SPITTEN
PITTER
SPITTER
PITTERS
PITURI
PITURIS
PIUPIU
PIUPIUS
PIZZLE
PIZZLES
PLACER
PLACERS
PLACET
PLACETS
PLACIT
PLACITA
PLACITS
PLAGUE
PLAGUED
PLAGUES
PLAGUEY
PLAICE
PLAICES
PLAINT
PLAINTS
PLANER
PLANERS
PLANET
PLANETS
PLANTA
PLANTAR
PLANTAS
PLAQUE
PLAQUES
PLASHY
SPLASHY
PLASMA
PLASMAS
PLASTE
PLASTER
PLATAN
PLATANE
PLATANS
PLATEN
PLATENS
PLATER
PLATERS
PLAYED
SPLAYED
PLAYER
PLAYERS
PLEADS
UPLEADS
PLEASE
PLEASED
PLEASER
PLEASES
PLEDGE
PLEDGED
PLEDGEE
PLEDGER
PLEDGES
PLEDGET
PLENTY
APLENTY
PLENUM
PLENUMS
PLEUCH
PLEUCHS
PLEUGH
PLEUGHS
PLEURA
PLEURAE
PLEURAL
PLEXOR
PLEXORS
PLIGHT
YPLIGHT
PLIGHTS
PLINKS
UPLINKS
PLINTH
PLINTHS
PLONGE
PLONGED
PLONGES
PLOOKS
UPLOOKS
PLOUGH
PLOUGHS
PLOVER
PLOVERS
PLOVERY
PLUNGE
PLUNGED
PLUNGER
PLUNGES
PLURAL
PLURALS
PLUTON
PLUTONS
PLYING
UPLYING
PNEUMA
PNEUMAS
POCHAY
POCHAYS
POCKET
POCKETS
PODITE
PODITES
PODIUM
SPODIUM
PODLEY
PODLEYS
PODSOL
PODSOLS
PODZOL
PODZOLS
POETIC
POETICS
POFFLE
POFFLES
POGROM
POGROMS
POINTE
POINTED
POINTEL
POINTER
POINTES
POISER
POISERS
POISON
POISONS
POKIES
POKIEST
POLDER
POLDERS
POLEYN
POLEYNS
POLICE
POLICED
POLICES
POLING
POLINGS
POLITE
POLITER
POLLAN
POLLANS
POLLEN
POLLENS
POLLENT
POLLER
POLLERS
POLYPE
POLYPES
POMACE
POMACES
POMADE
POMADED
POMADES
POMELO
POMELOS
POMMEL
POMMELE
POMMELS
POMPEY
POMPEYS
POMPOM
POMPOMS
POMPON
POMPONS
POMROY
POMROYS
PONCHO
PONCHOS
PONDER
PONDERS
PONDOK
PONDOKS
PONGED
SPONGED
PONGEE
PONGEES
PONGID
PONGIDS
PONTIE
PONTIES
PONTIL
PONTILE
PONTILS
PONTON
PONTONS
POODLE
POODLES
POOGYE
POOGYEE
POOGYES
POOJAH
POOJAHS
POOLED
SPOOLED
POONAC
POONACS
POONCE
POONCES
POORER
SPOORER
POORIS
POORISH
POOTER
POOTERS
POPJOY
POPJOYS
POPLAR
POPLARS
POPLIN
POPLINS
POPPER
POPPERS
POPPET
POPPETS
POPPIT
POPPITS
POPPLE
POPPLED
POPPLES
POPRIN
POPRINS
PORGIE
PORGIES
PORISM
PORISMS
PORKER
PORKERS
POROSE
POROSES
PORTAL
PORTALS
PORTED
SPORTED
PORTER
SPORTER
PORTERS
POSADA
POSADAS
POSEUR
POSEURS
POSHES
SPOSHES
POSHEST
POSIES
POSIEST
POSING
POSINGS
POSNET
POSNETS
POSSER
POSSERS
POSSES
POSSESS
POSSET
POSSETS
POSSIE
POSSIES
POSSUM
OPOSSUM
POSSUMS
POSTAL
POSTALS
POSTER
POSTERN
POSTERS
POSTIE
POSTIES
POSTIL
APOSTIL
POSTILS
POTAGE
POTAGER
POTAGES
POTASS
POTASSA
POTBOY
POTBOYS
POTCHE
POTCHED
POTCHER
POTCHES
POTEEN
POTEENS
POTENT
POTENTS
POTFUL
POTFULS
POTGUN
POTGUNS
POTHER
POTHERS
POTHERY
POTION
POTIONS
POTTED
SPOTTED
POTTER
SPOTTER
POTTERS
POTTERY
POTTLE
POTTLES
POUDER
POUDERS
POUDRE
POUDRES
POUFFE
POUFFED
POUFFES
POULPE
POULPES
POUNCE
POUNCED
POUNCES
POUNCET
POURER
POURERS
POURIE
POURIES
POUSSE
POUSSES
POUTED
SPOUTED
POUTER
SPOUTER
POUTERS
POWDER
POWDERS
POWDERY
POWNEY
POWNEYS
POWNIE
POWNIES
POWTER
POWTERS
POWWOW
POWWOWS
POYSON
POYSONS
PRAISE
UPRAISE
PRAISED
PRAISER
PRAISES
PRANCE
PRANCED
PRANCER
PRANCES
PRANCK
PRANCKE
PRANCKS
PRATED
UPRATED
PRATER
PRATERS
PRATES
UPRATES
PRATIE
PRATIES
PRAWLE
PRAWLES
PRAYED
SPRAYED
PRAYER
SPRAYER
PRAYERS
PREACE
PREACED
PREACES
PREACH
PREACHY
PREAMP
PREAMPS
PREASE
PREASED
PREASES
PRECIS
PRECISE
PRECUT
PRECUTS
PREEVE
PREEVED
PREEVES
PREFAB
PREFABS
PREFER
PREFERS
PREIFE
PREIFES
PRELIM
PRELIMS
PREMED
PREMEDS
PREMIE
PREMIER
PREMIES
PREPAY
PREPAYS
PRESET
PRESETS
PRESTO
PRESTOS
PRESTS
UPRESTS
PRETOR
PRETORS
PREVUE
PREVUED
PREVUES
PREWYN
PREWYNS
PRICER
PRICERS
PRIEFE
PRIEFES
PRIEST
PRIESTS
PRIEVE
PRIEVED
PRIEVES
PRIMER
PRIMERO
PRIMERS
PRINCE
PRINCED
PRINCES
PRINTS
SPRINTS
PRISER
PRISERS
PRISES
UPRISES
PRISON
PRISONS
PRIVET
PRIVETS
PRIZER
PRIZERS
PROBER
PROBERS
PROBIT
PROBITS
PROBITY
PROFIT
PROFITS
PROIGN
PROIGNS
PROINE
PROINED
PROINES
PROKER
PROKERS
PROLEG
PROLEGS
PROLER
PROLERS
PROLLS
UPROLLS
PROMPT
PROMPTS
PRONES
PRONEST
PROPEL
PROPELS
PROPER
PROPERS
PROPYL
PROPYLA
PROPYLS
PROSER
PROSERS
PROTEA
PROTEAN
PROTEAS
PROTON
PROTONS
PROTYL
PROTYLE
PROTYLS
PROVEN
PROVEND
PROVER
PROVERB
PROVERS
PROYNE
PROYNED
PROYNES
PRUINA
PRUINAS
PRUINE
PRUINES
PRUNER
PRUNERS
PRUSIK

PRUSIKS
PRYING
PRYINGS
PSOCID
PSOCIDS
PSYCHE
PSYCHED
PSYCHES
PSYCHO
PSYCHOS
PSYLLA
PSYLLAS
PSYWAR
PSYWARS
PTERIA
APTERIA
PTERIN
PTERINS
PTISAN
PTISANS
PUBLIC
PUBLICS
PUCKER
PUCKERS
PUCKERY
PUCKLE
PUCKLES
PUDDEN
PUDDENS
PUDDER
PUDDERS
PUDDLE
PUDDLED
PUDDLER
PUDDLES
PUEBLO
PUEBLOS
PUFFER
PUFFERS
PUFFERY
PUFFIN
PUFFING
PUFFINS
PUGGIE
PUGGIER
PUGGIES
PUGGLE
PUGGLED
PUGGLES
PUISNE
PUISNES
PUKEKO
PUKEKOS
PULING
PULINGS
PULKHA
PULKHAS
PULLER
PULLERS
PULLET
PULLETS
PULLEY
PULLEYS
PULPER
PULPERS
PULPIT
PULPITS
PULQUE
PULQUES
PULSAR
PULSARS
PULTAN
PULTANS
PULTON
PULTONS
PULTUN
PULTUNS
PULVER
PULVERS
PULVIL
PULVILS
PULWAR
PULWARS
PUMELO
PUMELOS
PUMICE
PUMICED
PUMICES
PUMMEL
PUMMELS
PUMPER
PUMPERS
PUNCTO
PUNCTOS
PUNDIT
PUNDITS
PUNKAH
PUNKAHS
PUNNER
PUNNERS
PUNNET
PUNNETS
PUNTEE
PUNTEES
PUNTER
PUNTERS
PUPATE
PUPATED
PUPATES
PUPPET
PUPPETS
PURDAH
PURDAHS
PURFLE
PURFLED
PURFLES
PURGER
PURGERS
PURGES
SPURGES
PURINE
PURINES
PURISM
PURISMS
PURIST
PURISTS
PURLER
PURLERS
PURLIN
PURLINE
PURLING
PURLINS
PURPIE
PURPIES
PURPLE
PURPLED
PURPLER
PURPLES
PURRED
SPURRED
PURSER
PURSERS
PURSEW
PURSEWS
PURSUE
PURSUED
PURSUER
PURSUES
PURVEY
PURVEYS
PUSHER
PUSHERS
PUSSEL
PUSSELS
PUSSER
PUSSERS
PUTEAL
PUTEALS
PUTELI
PUTELIS
PUTLOG
PUTLOGS
PUTTEE
PUTTEES
PUTTER
SPUTTER
PUTTERS
PUTTIE
PUTTIED
PUTTIER
PUTTIES
PUTURE
PUTURES
PUZZEL
PUZZELS
PUZZLE
PUZZLED
PUZZLER
PUZZLES
PYCNON
PYCNONS
PYEMIA
PYEMIAS
PYGARG
PYGARGS
PYONER
PYONERS
PYRENE
PYRENES
PYRITE
PYRITES
PYROPE
PYROPES
PYTHON
PYTHONS
PYURIA
PYURIAS
QASIDA
QASIDAS
QIGONG
QIGONGS
QINTAR
QINTARS
QIVIUT
QIVIUTS
QUAERE
QUAERED
QUAERES
QUAGGA
QUAGGAS
QUAHOG
QUAHOGS
QUAICH
QUAICHS
QUAIGH
QUAIGHS
QUAILS
SQUAILS
QUAKER
QUAKERS
QUANGO
QUANGOS
QUANTA
QUANTAL
QUANTS
EQUANTS
QUARER
SQUARER
QUARTE
QUARTER
QUARTES
QUARTET
QUARTO
QUARTOS
QUARTZ
QUARTZY
QUASAR
QUASARS
QUAVER
QUAVERS
QUAVERY
QUEACH
QUEACHY
QUEEST
QUEESTS
QUELCH
SQUELCH
QUELEA
QUELEAS
QUETHE
QUETHES
QUICHE
QUICHED
QUICHES
QUIDAM
QUIDAMS
QUIGHT
QUIGHTS
QUILLS
SQUILLS
QUINCE
QUINCES
QUINIE
QUINIES
QUINOA
QUINOAS
QUINOL
QUINOLS
QUINTA
QUINTAL
QUINTAN
QUINTAS
QUINTE
QUINTES
QUINTET
QUINTS
SQUINTS
QUINZE
QUINZES
QUIRED
SQUIRED
QUIRES
SQUIRES
QUIRTS
SQUIRTS
QUITCH
SQUITCH
QUIVER
AQUIVER
QUIVERS
QUIVERY
QUOIST
QUOISTS
QUOKKA
QUOKKAS
QUORUM
QUORUMS
QUOTER
QUOTERS
QUOTUM
QUOTUMS
QWERTY
QWERTYS
RABBET
DRABBET
RABBETS
RABBIN
RABBINS
RABBIT
FRABBIT
RABBITS
RABBITY
RABBLE
BRABBLE
DRABBLE
GRABBLE
PRABBLE
RABBLED
RABBLER
RABBLES
RACEME
RACEMED
RACEMES
RACERS
BRACERS
TRACERS
RACHES
BRACHES
ORACHES
RACHIS
ARACHIS
RACING
BRACING
GRACING
TRACING
RACINGS
RACISM
RACISMS
RACIST
RACISTS
RACKED
CRACKED
TRACKED
WRACKED
RACKER
CRACKER
TRACKER
RACKERS
RACKET
BRACKET
RACKETS
RACKETT
RACKETY
RACOON
RACOONS
RADDLE
RADDLED
RADDLES
RADIAL
RADIALE
RADIALS
RADIAN
RADIANS
RADIANT
RADIUM
RADIUMS
RADOME
RADOMES
RADULA
RADULAE
RADULAR
RAFALE
RAFALES
RAFFIA
RAFFIAS
RAFFLE
RAFFLED
RAFFLER
RAFFLES
RAFTED
CRAFTED
DRAFTED
GRAFTED
RAFTER
DRAFTER
GRAFTER
RAFTERS
RAGBAG
RAGBAGS
RAGEES
DRAGEES
RAGGED
BRAGGED
CRAGGED
DRAGGED
FRAGGED
RAGGEDY
RAGGEE
RAGGEES
RAGGLE
DRAGGLE
RAGGLED
RAGGLES
RAGING
RAGINGS
RAGINI
RAGINIS
RAGLAN
RAGLANS
RAGMAN
RAGMANS
RAGMEN
RAGMENT
RAGOUT
RAGOUTS
RAGTAG
RAGTAGS
RAGTOP
RAGTOPS
RAIDED
BRAIDED
RAIDER
BRAIDER
RAIDERS
RAIKED
TRAIKED
RAILED
BRAILED
DRAILED
TRAILED
RAILER
FRAILER
TRAILER
RAILERS
RAILES
GRAILES
RAILLY
FRAILLY
RAINED
BRAINED
DRAINED
GRAINED
TRAINED
RAINES
GRAINES
RAIRDS
BRAIRDS
RAISED
ARAISED
BRAISED
FRAISED
PRAISED
RAISER
PRAISER
RAISERS
RAISES
ARAISES
BRAISES
FRAISES
PRAISES
RAISIN
RAISING
RAISINS
RAIYAT
RAIYATS
RAKING
BRAKING
CRAKING
RAKINGS
RALLYE
RALLYES
RAMBLE
BRAMBLE
RAMBLED
RAMBLER
RAMBLES
RAMCAT
RAMCATS
RAMJET
RAMJETS
RAMMED
CRAMMED
DRAMMED
TRAMMED
RAMMER
CRAMMER
RAMMERS
RAMPED
CRAMPED
TRAMPED
RAMPER
TRAMPER
RAMPERS
RAMROD
RAMRODS
RAMSON
RAMSONS
RANCED
PRANCED
TRANCED
RANCEL
RANCELS
RANCES
PRANCES
TRANCES
RANCHO
RANCHOS
RANCOR
RANCORS
RANDAN
RANDANS
RANDED
BRANDED
RANDEM
RANDEMS
RANDIE
RANDIER
RANDIES
RANDOM
RANDOMS
RANDON
RANDONS
RANGED
PRANGED
RANGER
GRANGER
ORANGER
RANGERS
RANGES
GRANGES
ORANGES
RANKED
BRANKED
CRANKED
FRANKED
PRANKED
RANKER
FRANKER
RANKERS
RANKES
RANKEST
RANKLE
CRANKLE
PRANKLE
RANKLED
RANKLES
RANKLY
FRANKLY
RANSEL
RANSELS
RANSOM
TRANSOM
RANSOMS
RANTED
DRANTED
GRANTED
TRANTED
RANTER
GRANTER
TRANTER

RANTERS
RANULA
RANULAS
RANZEL
RANZELS
RAPERS
DRAPERS
RAPHIA
RAPHIAS
RAPIER
CRAPIER
DRAPIER
GRAPIER
RAPIERS
RAPINE
RAPINES
RAPING
DRAPING
GRAPING
TRAPING
RAPIST
RAPISTS
RAPPED
CRAPPED
DRAPPED
FRAPPED
TRAPPED
WRAPPED
RAPPEE
FRAPPEE
RAPPEES
RAPPEL
RAPPELS
RAPPER
TRAPPER
WRAPPER
RAPPERS
RAPTOR
RAPTORS
RASCAL
RASCALS
RASHED
BRASHED
CRASHED
TRASHED
RASHER
BRASHER
RASHERS
RASHES
BRASHES
CRASHES
TRASHES
RASHEST
RASING
ERASING
RASPED
GRASPED
RASPER
GRASPER
RASPERS
RASSES
BRASSES
FRASSES
GRASSES
TRASSES
WRASSES
RASTER
RASTERS
RASURE
ERASURE
RASURES
RATBAG
RATBAGS
RATERS
CRATERS
FRATERS
GRATERS
KRATERS
PRATERS
RATIFY
GRATIFY
RATINE
GRATINE
RATINES
RATING
CRATING
GRATING
ORATING
PRATING
RATINGS
RATION
ORATION
RATIONS
RATLIN
RATLINE
RATLING
RATLINS
RATOON
RATOONS
RATTAN
RATTANS
RATTED
DRATTED
PRATTED
RATTEN
RATTENS
RATTER
RATTERS
RATTERY
RATTLE
BRATTLE
PRATTLE
RATTLED
RATTLER
RATTLES
RATTON
RATTONS
RAUCLE
RAUCLER
RAUGHT
DRAUGHT
FRAUGHT
RAUNCH
BRAUNCH
CRAUNCH
GRAUNCH
RAUNCHY
RAUNGE
RAUNGED
RAUNGES
RAVAGE
RAVAGED
RAVAGER
RAVAGES
RAVELS
GRAVELS
TRAVELS
RAVENS
CRAVENS
RAVERS
CRAVERS
GRAVERS
RAVINE
RAVINED
RAVINES
RAVING
BRAVING
CRAVING
GRAVING
RAVINGS
RAWEST
BRAWEST
RAWING
DRAWING
RAWINGS
RAYING
BRAYING
FRAYING
GRAYING
PRAYING
RAYLES
GRAYLES
RAYLESS
RAYLET
RAYLETS
RAYNES
TRAYNES
RAYONS
CRAYONS
RAZING
BRAZING
CRAZING
GRAZING
RAZURE
RAZURES
RAZZIA
RAZZIAS
RAZZLE
FRAZZLE
RAZZLES
READER
DREADER
TREADER
READERS
REAKED
CREAKED
FREAKED
WREAKED
REAMED
BREAMED
CREAMED
DREAMED
REAMER
CREAMER
DREAMER
REAMERS
REAPER
REAPERS
REARER
DREARER
REARERS
REASON
TREASON
REASONS
REASTS
BREASTS
REATES
CREATES
REAVER
REAVERS
REAVES
GREAVES
REBACK
REBACKS
REBATE
REBATED
REBATER
REBATES
REBECK
REBECKS
REBIND
REBINDS
REBITE
REBITES
REBOIL
REBOILS
REBORE
REBORED
REBORES
REBORN
PREBORN
REBUFF
REBUFFS
REBUKE
REBUKED
REBUKER
REBUKES
RECALL
RECALLS
RECANT
RECANTS
RECAST
PRECAST
RECASTS
RECEDE
PRECEDE
RECEDED
RECEDES
RECEPT
PRECEPT
RECEPTS
RECESS
PRECESS
RECIPE
RECIPES
RECITE
RECITED
RECITER
RECITES
RECKED
TRECKED
WRECKED
RECKON
RECKONS
RECODE
RECODED
RECODES
RECOIL
RECOILS
RECOIN
RECOINS
RECORD
RECORDS
RECOUP
RECOUPS
RECTOR
ERECTOR
RECTORS
RECTORY
RECTUM
RECTUMS
RECULE
RECULED
RECULES
RECURE
RECURED
RECURES
RECUSE
RECUSED
RECUSES
REDACT
REDACTS
REDATE
PREDATE
REDATED
REDATES
REDBUD
REDBUDS
REDCAP
REDCAPS
REDDEN
REDDENS
REDDER
REDDERS
REDDLE
TREDDLE
REDDLED
REDDLES
REDEAL
REDEALS
REDEALT
REDEEM
REDEEMS
REDIAL
PREDIAL
REDIALS
REDING
AREDING
BREDING
REDLEG
REDLEGS
REDOWA
REDOWAS
REDRAW
REDRAWN
REDRAWS
REDTOP
REDTOPS
REDUCE
REDUCED
REDUCER
REDUCES
REDUIT
REDUITS
REEBOK
REEBOKS
REEDER
BREEDER
REEDERS
REEFER
REEFERS
REEKIE
REEKIER
REELER
REELERS
REEVED
PREEVED
REEVES
PREEVES
REFACE
PREFACE
REFACED
REFACES
REFECT
PREFECT
REFECTS
REFERS
PREFERS
REFILL
REFILLS
REFINE
REFINED
REFINER
REFINES
REFLAG
REFLAGS
REFLET
REFLETS
REFLOW
REFLOWS
REFOOT
REFOOTS
REFORM
PREFORM
REFORMS
REFUEL
REFUELS
REFUGE
REFUGED
REFUGEE
REFUGES
REFUND
REFUNDS
REFUSE
REFUSED
REFUSER
REFUSES
REFUTE
REFUTED
REFUTER
REFUTES
REGAIN
REGAINS
REGALE
GREGALE
REGALED
REGALES
REGARD
REGARDS
REGENT
REGENTS
REGEST
REGESTS
REGGAE
REGGAES
REGIME
REGIMEN
REGIMES
REGINA
REGINAE
REGINAL
REGINAS
REGION
REGIONS
REGIVE
REGIVEN
REGIVES
REGLET
REGLETS
REGRET
REGRETS
REGULA
REGULAE
REGULAR
REGULO
REGULOS
REHANG
REHANGS
REHEAR
REHEARD
REHEARS
REHEAT
PREHEAT
REHEATS
REHEEL
REHEELS
REINED
GREINED
REITER
REITERS
REIVER
REIVERS
REJECT
REJECTS
REJOIN
REJOINS
RELATE
PRELATE
RELATED
RELATER
RELATES
RELENT
RELENTS
RELICT
RELICTS
RELIEF
RELIEFS
RELIER
RELIERS
RELINE
RELINED
RELINES
RELIVE
RELIVED
RELIVER
RELIVES
RELOAD
RELOADS
RELUCT
RELUCTS
RELUME
RELUMED
RELUMES
REMADE
REMADES
REMAIN
REMAINS
REMAKE
REMAKES
REMAND
REMANDS
REMARK
REMARKS
REMBLE
TREMBLE
REMBLED
REMBLES
REMEAD
REMEADS
REMEDE
REMEDED
REMEDES
REMEID
REMEIDS
REMIND
REMINDS
REMINT
REMINTS
REMISE
PREMISE
REMISED
REMISES
REMISS
PREMISS
REMITS
FREMITS
REMORA
REMORAS
REMOTE
REMOTER
REMOTES
REMOVE
PREMOVE
REMOVED
REMOVER
REMOVES
REMUDA
REMUDAS
RENAME
RENAMED
RENAMES
RENDER
RENDERS
RENEGE
RENEGED
RENEGER
RENEGES
RENNED
GRENNED
RENNES
BRENNES
RENNET
RENNETS
RENNIN
RENNING
RENNINS
RENOWN
RENOWNS
RENTAL
TRENTAL
RENTALS
RENTED
PRENTED
RENTER
BRENTER
RENTERS
RENVOI
RENVOIS
RENVOY
RENVOYS
REOPEN
REOPENS
REPACK
PREPACK
REPACKS
REPAID
PREPAID
REPAIR
REPAIRS
REPAST

REPASTS
REPAYS
PREPAYS
REPEAL
REPEALS
REPEAT
REPEATS
REPENT
REPENTS
REPINE
REPINED
REPINER
REPINES
REPLAN
REPLANS
REPLANT
REPLAY
REPLAYS
REPONE
PREPONE
REPONED
REPONES
REPORT
REPORTS
REPOSE
PREPOSE
REPOSED
REPOSES
REPOST
REPOSTS
REPPED
PREPPED
REPUGN
REPUGNS
REPULP
REPULPS
REPURE
REPURED
REPURES
REPUTE
REPUTED
REPUTES
REQUIT
REQUITE
REQUITS
RERAIL
RERAILS
REREAD
REREADS
RESALE
RESALES
RESCUE
RESCUED
RESCUER
RESCUES
RESEAL
RESEALS
RESEAT
RESEATS
RESEAU
RESEAUS
RESEAUX
RESECT
RESECTS
RESEDA
RESEDAS
RESELL
RESELLS
RESENT
PRESENT
RESENTS
RESETS
PRESETS
RESHIP
RESHIPS
RESIDE
PRESIDE
RESIDED
RESIDER
RESIDES
RESIGN
RESIGNS
RESILE
RESILED
RESILES
RESIST
RESISTS
RESKEW
RESKEWS
RESKUE
RESKUED
RESKUES
RESOLE
RESOLED
RESOLES
RESORB
RESORBS
RESORT
RESORTS
RESTED
CRESTED
PRESTED
WRESTED
RESTEM
RESTEMS
RESTER
WRESTER
RESTERS
RESULT
RESULTS
RESUME
PRESUME
RESUMED
RESUMES
RETAIL
RETAILS
RETAIN
RETAINS
RETAKE
RETAKEN
RETAKER
RETAKES
RETAMA
RETAMAS
RETARD
RETARDS
RETELL
RETELLS
RETENE
RETENES
RETILE
RETILED
RETILES
RETIME
RETIMED
RETIMES
RETINA
RETINAE
RETINAL
RETINAS
RETIRE
RETIRED
RETIREE
RETIRER
RETIRES
RETOOL
RETOOLS
RETORT
RETORTS
RETOUR
RETOURS
RETREE
RETREES
RETRIM
RETRIMS
RETTED
ARETTED
FRETTED
RETUND
RETUNDS
RETUNE
RETUNED
RETUNES
RETURF
RETURFS
RETURN
RETURNS
REURGE
REURGED
REURGES
REVAMP
REVAMPS
REVEAL
REVEALS
REVERB
PREVERB
REVERBS
REVERE
REVERED
REVERER
REVERES
REVERS
REVERSE
REVERSI
REVERSO
REVERT
REVERTS
REVEST
REVESTS
REVETS
BREVETS
REVEUR
REVEURS
REVIEW
PREVIEW
REVIEWS
REVILE
REVILED
REVILER
REVILES
REVISE
PREVISE
REVISED
REVISER
REVISES
REVIVE
REVIVED
REVIVER
REVIVES
REVOKE
REVOKED
REVOKES
REVOLT
REVOLTS
REVUES
PREVUES
REWARD
REWARDS
REWIND
REWINDS
REWIRE
REWIRED
REWIRES
REWORD
REWORDS
REWORK
REWORKS
REWRAP
REWRAPS
REZONE
REZONED
REZONES
RHAPHE
RHAPHES
RHETOR
RHETORS
RHODIE
RHODIES
RHOMBI
RHOMBIC
RHUMBA
RHUMBAS
RHYMER
RHYMERS
RHYTHM
RHYTHMI
RHYTHMS
RIBALD
RIBALDS
RIBAND
RIBANDS
RIBAUD
RIBAUDS
RIBBED
CRIBBED
DRIBBED
RIBBON
RIBBONS
RIBBONY
RIBIBE
RIBIBES
RIBLET
DRIBLET
TRIBLET
RIBLETS
RIBOSE
RIBOSES
RICERS
GRICERS
PRICERS
RICHEN
RICHENS
RICHES
RICHEST
RICHTS
FRICHTS
RICIER
PRICIER
RICING
GRICING
PRICING
TRICING
RICKED
BRICKED
CRICKED
PRICKED
TRICKED
WRICKED
RICKER
PRICKER
TRICKER
RICKERS
RICKLE
BRICKLE
PRICKLE
TRICKLE
RICKLES
RICKLY
PRICKLY
TRICKLY
RIDDER
GRIDDER
RIDDERS
RIDDLE
GRIDDLE
RIDDLED
RIDDLER
RIDDLES
RIDENT
TRIDENT
RIDGED
BRIDGED
FRIDGED
RIDGEL
RIDGELS
RIDGER
RIDGERS
RIDGES
BRIDGES
FRIDGES
RIDGIL
RIDGILS
RIDING
BRIDING
GRIDING
PRIDING
RIDINGS
RIEVER
GRIEVER
RIEVERS
RIEVES
GRIEVES
PRIEVES
RIFFLE
RIFFLED
RIFFLER
RIFFLES
RIFLED
TRIFLED
RIFLER
TRIFLER
RIFLERS
RIFLES
TRIFLES
RIFTED
DRIFTED
GRIFTED
RIGGED
FRIGGED
GRIGGED
PRIGGED
TRIGGED
RIGGER
FRIGGER
PRIGGER
TRIGGER
RIGGERS
RIGHTO
RIGHTOS
RIGHTS
FRIGHTS
WRIGHTS
RIGLIN
RIGLING
RIGLINS
RIGOLL
RIGOLLS
RIGOUR
RIGOURS
RILLED
DRILLED
FRILLED
GRILLED
PRILLED
TRILLED
RILLES
GRILLES
RILLET
RILLETS
RIMERS
PRIMERS
TRIMERS
RIMIER
GRIMIER
RIMING
BRIMING
CRIMING
GRIMING
PRIMING
RIMMED
BRIMMED
PRIMMED
TRIMMED
RINDED
BRINDED
GRINDED
RINGED
CRINGED
FRINGED
WRINGED
RINGER
BRINGER
CRINGER
WRINGER
RINGERS
RINKED
PRINKED
RINSER
RINSERS
RIOTER
RIOTERS
RIPECK
RIPECKS
RIPERS
GRIPERS
RIPING
GRIPING
RIPPED
DRIPPED
GRIPPED
TRIPPED
RIPPER
FRIPPER
GRIPPER
TRIPPER
RIPPERS
RIPPLE
ARIPPLE
CRIPPLE
GRIPPLE
TRIPPLE
RIPPLED
RIPPLER
RIPPLES
RIPPLET
RIPRAP
RIPRAPS
RISERS
PRISERS
RISING
ARISING
GRISING
KRISING
PRISING
RISINGS
RISKED
BRISKED
FRISKED
RISKER
BRISKER
FRISKER
RISKERS
RISPED
CRISPED
RISQUE
RISQUES
RITTED
FRITTED
GRITTED
RITTER
CRITTER
FRITTER
GRITTER
RITTERS
RITUAL
RITUALS
RIVAGE
RIVAGES
RIVELS
DRIVELS
RIVERS
DRIVERS
RIVETS
GRIVETS
PRIVETS
TRIVETS
RIVING
DRIVING
RIVLIN
RIVLINS
RIZARD
RIZARDS
RIZZAR
RIZZARS
RIZZART
RIZZER
RIZZERS
RIZZOR
RIZZORS
ROADIE
ROADIES
ROAMER
ROAMERS
ROARER
ROARERS
ROARIE
ROARIER
ROATED
TROATED
ROBALO
ROBALOS
ROBBER
ROBBERS
ROBBERY
ROBING
PROBING
ROBINGS
ROBUST
ROBUSTA
ROCHES
BROCHES
CROCHES
TROCHES
ROCHET
CROCHET
ROCHETS
ROCKED
BROCKED
CROCKED
FROCKED
TROCKED
ROCKER
ROCKERS
ROCKERY
ROCKET
BROCKET
CROCKET
ROCKETS
ROCOCO
ROCOCOS
RODDED
BRODDED
PRODDED
RODENT
ERODENT
RODENTS
RODING
ERODING
RODINGS
ROEMER
ROEMERS
ROGERS
DROGERS
ROGUES
BROGUES
DROGUES
ROILED
BROILED
DROILED
ROINED
GROINED
PROINED
ROKERS
BROKERS
PROKERS
ROKING
BROKING
PROKING
TROKING
ROLFER

ROLFERS
ROLLED
DROLLED
PROLLED
TROLLED
ROLLER
DROLLER
PROLLER
TROLLER
ROLLERS
ROMAGE
ROMAGES
ROMPED
TROMPED
ROMPER
ROMPERS
RONDEL
RONDELS
RONYON
RONYONS
ROOFED
PROOFED
ROOFER
ROOFERS
ROOKED
BROOKED
CROOKED
DROOKED
ROOKIE
ROOKIES
ROOMED
BROOMED
GROOMED
VROOMED
ROOMER
ROOMERS
ROOMIE
ROOMIER
ROOMIES
ROOPED
DROOPED
TROOPED
ROOSES
BROOSES
ROOTED
WROOTED
ROOTER
ROOTERS
ROOTLE
ROOTLED
ROOTLES
ROOTLET
ROPERS
GROPERS
PROPERS
ROPING
GROPING
TROPING
ROPINGS
ROQUET
CROQUET
ROQUETS
RORTER
RORTERS
ROSACE
ROSACEA
ROSACES
ROSETS
GROSETS
ROSIER
CROSIER
PROSIER
ROSIERE
ROSIERS
ROSIES
ROSIEST
ROSILY
PROSILY
ROSING
PROSING
ROSSER
CROSSER
GROSSER
ROSSERS
ROSTED
FROSTED
ROSTER
ROSTERS
ROSTRA
ROSTRAL
ROSULA
ROSULAS
ROTATE
ROTATED
ROTATES
ROTCHE
ROTCHES
ROTGUT
ROTGUTS
ROTHER
BROTHER
ROTHERS
ROTOLO
ROTOLOS
ROTTAN
ROTTANS
ROTTED
TROTTED
ROTTEN
ROTTENS
ROTTER
TROTTER
ROTTERS
ROTULA
ROTULAS
ROTUND
OROTUND
ROTUNDA
ROTUNDS
ROUBLE
TROUBLE
ROUBLES
ROUCOU
ROUCOUS
ROUGHS
BROUGHS
GROUGHS
TROUGHS
ROUGHT
BROUGHT
DROUGHT
WROUGHT
ROUGHY
FROUGHY
ROULES
TROULES
ROUNCE
FROUNCE
TROUNCE
ROUNCES
ROUNDS
GROUNDS
ROUPED
CROUPED
GROUPED
TROUPED
ROUSED
AROUSED
GROUSED
ROUSER
AROUSER
GROUSER
TROUSER
ROUSERS
ROUSES
AROUSES
GROUSES
TROUSES
ROUTED
GROUTED
ROUTER
GROUTER
TROUTER
ROUTERS
ROUTES
CROUTES
ROUTHS
DROUTHS
ROVERS
DROVERS
PROVERS
TROVERS
ROVING
DROVING
PROVING
ROVINGS
ROWELS
TROWELS
ROWERS
GROWERS
ROWING
CROWING
GROWING
TROWING
ROWINGS
ROWTHS
GROWTHS
ROYNED
PROYNED
ROYNES
GROYNES
PROYNES
ROZZER
ROZZERS
RUBATO
RUBATOS
RUBBED
DRUBBED
GRUBBED
RUBBER
GRUBBER
RUBBERS
RUBBERY
RUBBLE
GRUBBLE
RUBBLES
RUBIES
RUBIEST
RUBINE
RUBINES
RUBOUT
RUBOUTS
RUBRIC
RUBRICS
RUCKED
TRUCKED
RUCKLE
BRUCKLE
TRUCKLE
RUCKLED
RUCKLES
RUCOLA
RUCOLAS
RUDDED
CRUDDED
RUDDER
RUDDERS
RUDDLE
CRUDDLE
RUDDLED
RUDDLES
RUDELY
CRUDELY
RUDERY
PRUDERY
RUDEST
CRUDEST
RUDISH
PRUDISH
RUEING
GRUEING
TRUEING
RUEINGS
RUELLE
RUELLES
RUFFIN
RUFFING
RUFFINS
RUFFLE
TRUFFLE
RUFFLED
RUFFLER
RUFFLES
RUGGED
DRUGGED
RUGGER
DRUGGER
RUGGERS
RUINER
RUINERS
RULING
RULINGS
RUMBLE
CRUMBLE
DRUMBLE
GRUMBLE
RUMBLED
RUMBLER
RUMBLES
RUMBLY
CRUMBLY
GRUMBLY
RUMKIN
RUMKINS
RUMMER
BRUMMER
DRUMMER
GRUMMER
RUMMERS
RUMOUR
RUMOURS
RUMPED
CRUMPED
FRUMPED
GRUMPED
TRUMPED
RUMPLE
CRUMPLE
FRUMPLE
RUMPLED
RUMPLES
RUNDLE
TRUNDLE
RUNDLED
RUNDLES
RUNDLET
RUNKLE
CRUNKLE
RUNKLED
RUNKLES
RUNLET
RUNLETS
RUNNEL
RUNNELS
RUNNER
RUNNERS
RUNNET
RUNNETS
RUNRIG
RUNRIGS
RUNTED
BRUNTED
GRUNTED
PRUNTED
RUNWAY
RUNWAYS
RUPIAH
RUPIAHS
RUSHED
BRUSHED
CRUSHED
FRUSHED
RUSHEE
RUSHEES
RUSHER
BRUSHER
CRUSHER
RUSHERS
RUSHES
BRUSHES
CRUSHES
FRUSHES
RUSSEL
RUSSELS
RUSSET
RUSSETS
RUSSETY
RUSSIA
RUSSIAS
RUSTED
CRUSTED
TRUSTED
RUSTIC
RUSTICS
RUSTLE
RUSTLED
RUSTLER
RUSTLES
RUSTRE
RUSTRED
RUSTRES
RUTILE
RUTILES
RUTTER
RUTTERS
RYOKAN
RYOKANS
RYPECK
RYPECKS
SABBAT
SABBATS
SABKHA
SABKHAH
SABKHAS
SABKHAT
SACHEM
SACHEMS
SACHET
SACHETS
SACKER
SACKERS
SACQUE
SACQUES
SADDEN
SADDENS
SADDHU
SADDHUS
SADDLE
SADDLED
SADDLER
SADDLES
SADISM
SADISMS
SADIST
SADISTS
SAETER
SAETERS
SAFARI
SAFARIS
SAGENE
SAGENES
SAGGAR
SAGGARD
SAGGARS
SAGGER
SAGGERS
SAGOIN
SAGOINS
SAGUIN
SAGUINS
SAHIBA
SAHIBAH
SAHIBAS
SAIKEI
SAIKEIS
SAILER
SAILERS
SAILOR
SAILORS
SAIQUE
SAIQUES
SAITHE
SAITHES
SAKIEH
SAKIEHS
SALAAM
SALAAMS
SALADE
SALADES
SALAMI
SALAMIS
SALINA
SALINAS
SALINE
SALINES
SALIVA
SALIVAL
SALIVAS
SALLAD
SALLADS
SALLAL
SALLALS
SALLEE
SALLEES
SALLET
SALLETS
SALLOW
SALLOWS
SALLOWY
SALMON
SALMONS
SALOON
SALOONS
SALOOP
SALOOPS
SALTER
PSALTER
SALTERN
SALTERS
SALUKI
SALUKIS
SALUTE
SALUTED
SALUTER
SALUTES
SALVER
SALVERS
SALVIA
SALVIAS
SALVOR
SALVORS
SAMAAN
SAMAANS
SAMARA
SAMARAS
SAMBAL
SAMBALS
SAMBAR
SAMBARS
SAMBAS
TSAMBAS
SAMBUR
SAMBURS
SAMEKH
SAMEKHS
SAMFOO
SAMFOOS
SAMIEL
SAMIELS
SAMITE
SAMITES
SAMITI
SAMITIS
SAMLET
SAMLETS
SAMLOR
SAMLORS
SAMOSA
SAMOSAS
SAMPAN
SAMPANS
SAMPLE
SAMPLED
SAMPLER
SAMPLES
SAMSHU
SAMSHUS
SANCAI
SANCAIS
SANCHO
SANCHOS
SANDAL
SANDALS
SANDER
SANDERS
SANDHI
SANDHIS
SANGAR
SANGARS
SANJAK
SANJAKS
SANNIE
SANNIES
SANNUP
SANNUPS
SANPAN
SANPANS
SANSEI
SANSEIS
SANTAL
SANTALS
SANTIR
SANTIRS
SANTON
SANTONS
SANTUR
SANTURS
SAPELE
SAPELES
SAPOTA
SAPOTAS
SAPPAN
SAPPANS
SAPPER
SAPPERS
SAPPLE
SAPPLED
SAPPLES
SARAPE
SARAPES
SARDEL
SARDELS
SARNEY
SARNEYS
SARNIE
SARNIES
SARONG
SARONGS
SARSEN
SARSENS
SARTOR
SARTORS
SASHAY
SASHAYS
SASINE
SASINES
SATARA
SATARAS
SATEEN
SATEENS

SATINS
ISATINS
SATIRE
SATIRES
SATORI
SATORIS
SATRAP
SATRAPS
SATRAPY
SATYRA
SATYRAL
SATYRAS
SAUCER
SAUCERS
SAUGER
SAUGERS
SAULGE
SAULGES
SAULIE
SAULIES
SAUREL
SAURELS
SAVAGE
SAVAGED
SAVAGER
SAVAGES
SAVANT
SAVANTS
SAVATE
SAVATES
SAVINE
SAVINES
SAVING
SAVINGS
SAVOUR
SAVOURS
SAVOURY
SAVVEY
SAVVEYS
SAWDER
SAWDERS
SAWING
SAWINGS
SAWNEY
SAWNEYS
SAWPIT
SAWPITS
SAWYER
SAWYERS
SAXAUL
SAXAULS
SAYING
SAYINGS
SAYYID
SAYYIDS
SAZHEN
SAZHENS
SCAITH
SCAITHS
SCALAR
SCALARS
SCALER
SCALERS
SCAMEL
SCAMELS
SCAMPI
SCAMPIS
SCAPED
ESCAPED
SCAPES
ESCAPES
SCARAB
SCARABS
SCARCE
SCARCER
SCARER
SCARERS
SCARPA
SCARPAS
SCARPH
SCARPHS
SCARPS
ESCARPS
SCARRE
SCARRED
SCARRES
SCARTH
SCARTHS
SCATHE
SCATHED
SCATHES
SCAZON
SCAZONS
SCENDS
ASCENDS
SCENTS
ASCENTS
SCERNE
SCERNED
SCERNES
SCHELM
SCHELMS
SCHEME
SCHEMED
SCHEMER
SCHEMES
SCHISM
SCHISMA
SCHISMS
SCHIST
SCHISTS
SCHIZO
SCHIZOS
SCHLEP
SCHLEPP
SCHLEPS
SCHOOL
SCHOOLE
SCHOOLS
SCHORL
SCHORLS
SCHOUT
SCHOUTS
SCHTIK
SCHTIKS
SCHUIT
SCHUITS
SCHUYT
SCHUYTS
SCILLA
SCILLAS
SCIROC
SCIROCS
SCLAFF
SCLAFFS
SCLATE
SCLATED
SCLATES
SCLAVE
SCLAVES
SCLERA
SCLERAL
SCLERAS
SCLERE
SCLERES
SCLIFF
SCLIFFS
SCONCE
ASCONCE
SCONCED
SCONCES
SCORER
SCORERS
SCORIA
SCORIAC
SCORIAE
SCORSE
SCORSED
SCORSER
SCORSES
SCOTER
SCOTERS
SCOTIA
SCOTIAS
SCOURS
SCOURSE
SCOUSE
SCOUSER
SCOUSES
SCOUTH
SCOUTHS
SCOWTH
SCOWTHS
SCRAMB
SCRAMBS
SCRAPE
SCRAPED
SCRAPER
SCRAPES
SCRAWL
SCRAWLS
SCRAWLY
SCRAWM
SCRAWMS
SCRAYE
SCRAYES
SCREAK
SCREAKS
SCREAKY
SCREAM
SCREAMS
SCREED
SCREEDS
SCREEN
SCREENS
SCRIBE
ASCRIBE
ESCRIBE
SCRIBED
SCRIBER
SCRIBES
SCRIKE
SCRIKED
SCRIKES
SCRIMP
SCRIMPS
SCRIMPY
SCRINE
SCRINES
SCRIPT
SCRIPTS
SCRIVE
SCRIVED
SCRIVES
SCROBE
SCROBES
SCROLL
ESCROLL
SCROLLS
SCROOP
SCROOPS
SCROTA
SCROTAL
SCROWL
SCROWLE
SCROWLS
SCROWS
ESCROWS
SCRUFF
SCRUFFS
SCRUFFY
SCRUMP
SCRUMPS
SCRUMPY
SCRUNT
SCRUNTS
SCRUNTY
SCRUTO
SCRUTOS
SCRUZE
SCRUZED
SCRUZES
SCRYER
SCRYERS
SCRYNE
SCRYNES
SCULLE
SCULLED
SCULLER
SCULLES
SCULPT
SCULPTS
SCUNGE
SCUNGED
SCUNGES
SCYTHE
SCYTHED
SCYTHER
SCYTHES
SDAINE
SDAINED
SDAINES
SDEIGN
SDEIGNE
SDEIGNS
SEABED
SEABEDS
SEAHOG
SEAHOGS
SEALCH
SEALCHS
SEALER
SEALERS
SEALERY
SEALGH
SEALGHS
SEAMER
SEAMERS
SEANCE
SEANCES
SEARAT
SEARATS
SEARCE
SEARCED
SEARCES
SEASON
SEASONS
SEATER
SEATERS
SEAWAY
SEAWAYS
SEBATE
SEBATES
SECANT
SECANTS
SECEDE
SECEDED
SECEDER
SECEDES
SECERN
SECERNS
SECKEL
SECKELS
SECKLE
SECKLES
SECOND
SECONDE
SECONDI
SECONDO
SECONDS
SECRET
SECRETA
SECRETE
SECRETS
SECTOR
SECTORS
SECURE
SECURED
SECURER
SECURES
SEDATE
SEDATED
SEDATER
SEDATES
SEDUCE
SEDUCED
SEDUCER
SEDUCES
SEEDER
SEEDERS
SEEING
SEEINGS
SEEKER
SEEKERS
SEEMER
SEEMERS
SEESAW
SEESAWS
SEETHE
SEETHED
SEETHER
SEETHES
SEGGAR
SEGGARS
SEGHOL
SEGHOLS
SEICHE
SEICHES
SEINER
SEINERS
SEISIN
SEISING
SEISINS
SEITEN
SEITENS
SEIZER
SEIZERS
SEIZIN
SEIZING
SEIZINS
SELECT
SELECTS
SELKIE
SELKIES
SELLER
SELLERS
SEMBLE
SEMBLED
SEMBLES
SEMEME
SEMEMES
SEMMIT
SEMMITS
SEMPLE
SEMPLER
SEMSEM
SEMSEMS
SENATE
SENATES
SENDAL
SENDALS
SENDER
SENDERS
SENEGA
SENEGAS
SENIOR
SENIORS
SENNET
SENNETS
SENNIT
SENNITS
SENSOR
SENSORS
SENSORY
SEPHEN
SEPHENS
SEPIUM
SEPIUMS
SEPSES
ASEPSES
SEPSIS
ASEPSIS
SEPTET
SEPTETS
SEPTIC
ASEPTIC
SEQUEL
SEQUELA
SEQUELS
SEQUIN
SEQUINS
SERAIL
SERAILS
SERANG
SERANGS
SERAPE
SERAPES
SERAPH
SERAPHS
SERDAB
SERDABS
SEREIN
SEREINS
SERENE
SERENED
SERENER
SERENES
SERIAL
SERIALS
SERINE
SERINES
SERING
SERINGA
SERIPH
SERIPHS
SERMON
SERMONS
SEROON
SEROONS
SEROSA
SEROSAE
SEROSAS
SERRAN
SERRANS
SERVAL
SERVALS
SERVER
SERVERS
SERVERY
SESAME
SESAMES
SESELI
SESELIS
SESTET
SESTETS
SESTETT
SESTON
SESTONS
SETTEE
SETTEES
SETTER
SETTERS
SETTLE
SETTLED
SETTLER
SETTLES
SETULE
SETULES
SEVERE
SEVERED
SEVERER
SEWAGE
SEWAGES
SEWING
SEWINGS
SEXISM
SEXISMS
SEXIST
SEXISTS
SEXPOT
SEXPOTS
SEXTAN
SEXTANS
SEXTANT
SEXTET
SEXTETS
SEXTETT
SEXTON
SEXTONS
SEXUAL
ASEXUAL
SHACKO
SHACKOS
SHADOW
SHADOWS
SHADOWY
SHADUF
SHADUFS
SHAIKH
SHAIKHS
SHAIRN
SHAIRNS
SHAKER
SHAKERS
SHALLI
SHALLIS
SHALOT
SHALOTS
SHAMAN
SHAMANS
SHAMBA
SHAMBAS
SHAMED
ASHAMED
SHAMER
SHAMERS
SHAMES
ASHAMES
SHAMOY
SHAMOYS
SHAPER
SHAPERS
SHARER
SHARERS
SHARIA
SHARIAS
SHARIAT
SHARIF
SHARIFS
SHAVER
SHAVERS
SHAVIE
SHAVIES
SHEATH
SHEATHE
SHEATHS
SHEATHY
SHEAVE
SHEAVED
SHEAVES
SHEEPO
SHEEPOS
SHEIKH
SHEIKHA
SHEIKHS
SHEILA
SHEILAS
SHEKEL
SHEKELS
SHELVE
SHELVED
SHELVES
SHENDS
YSHENDS
SHERIA
SHERIAS
SHERIAT
SHERIF
SHERIFF
SHERIFS

SHERPA
SHERPAS
SHEUCH
SHEUCHS
SHEUGH
SHEUGHS
SHEWEL
SHEWELS
SHIBAH
SHIBAHS
SHIELD
SHIELDS
SHIEST
ASHIEST
SHIKAR
SHIKARI
SHIKARS
SHIKSA
SHIKSAS
SHIKSE
SHIKSES
SHINER
SHINERS
SHINES
SHINESS
SHINNE
SHINNED
SHINNES
SHIPPO
SHIPPON
SHIPPOS
SHIRRA
SHIRRAS
SHIVAH
SHIVAHS
SHIVER
ASHIVER
SHIVERS
SHIVERY
SHIVOO
SHIVOOS
SHLOCK
SHLOCKS
SHMOCK
SHMOCKS
SHMUCK
SHMUCKS
SHODER
SHODERS
SHOFAR
SHOFARS
SHOGUN
SHOGUNS
SHOOLE
SHOOLED
SHOOLES
SHORAN
SHORANS
SHORER
SHORERS
SHOTTE
SHOTTED
SHOTTEN
SHOTTES
SHOUGH
SHOUGHS
SHOVEL
SHOVELS
SHOVER
SHOVERS
SHOWER
SHOWERS
SHOWERY
SHREEK
SHREEKS
SHREIK
SHREIKS
SHRIEK
SHRIEKS
SHRIFT
SHRIFTS
SHRIKE
SHRIKED
SHRIKES
SHRILL
SHRILLS
SHRILLY
SHRIMP
SHRIMPS
SHRIMPY
SHRINE
SHRINED
SHRINES
SHRINK
SHRINKS
SHRIVE
SHRIVED
SHRIVEL
SHRIVEN
SHRIVER
SHRIVES
SHROFF
SHROFFS
SHROUD
SHROUDS
SHROUDY
SHROVE
SHROVED
SHROVES
SHTCHI
SHTCHIS
SHTETL
SHTETLS
SHTICK
SHTICKS
SHTOOK
SHTOOKS
SHTUCK
SHTUCKS
SHUFTI
SHUFTIS
SIALON
SIALONS
SICKEN
SICKENS
SICKIE
SICKIES
SICKLE
SICKLED
SICKLES
SIDDHA
SIDDHAS
SIDDHI
SIDDHIS
SIDING
SIDINGS
SIEGER
SIEGERS
SIENNA
SIENNAS
SIERRA
SIERRAN
SIERRAS
SIESTA
SIESTAS
SIFAKA
SIFAKAS
SIFFLE
SIFFLED
SIFFLES
SIFTER
SIFTERS
SIGHER
SIGHERS
SIGNAL
SIGNALS
SIGNER
SIGNERS
SIGNET
SIGNETS
SIGNOR
SIGNORA
SIGNORE
SIGNORI
SIGNORS
SIGNORY
SILAGE
SILAGED
SILAGES
SILANE
SILANES
SILENE
SILENES
SILENT
SILENTS
SILICA
SILICAS
SILKEN
SILKENS
SILKIE
SILKIER
SILKIES
SILLER
SILLERS
SILVAN
SILVANS
SILVER
SILVERN
SILVERS
SILVERY
SIMIAN
SIMIANS
SIMILE
SIMILES
SIMKIN
SIMKINS
SIMMER
SIMMERS
SIMNEL
SIMNELS
SIMOOM
SIMOOMS
SIMOON
SIMOONS
SIMORG
SIMORGS
SIMPAI
SIMPAIS
SIMPER
SIMPERS
SIMPLE
SIMPLED
SIMPLER
SIMPLES
SIMPLEX
SIMURG
SIMURGH
SIMURGS
SINDON
SINDONS
SINGER
SINGERS
SINGLE
SINGLED
SINGLES
SINGLET
SINKER
SINKERS
SINNER
SINNERS
SINNET
SINNETS
SINTER
SINTERS
SINTERY
SIPHON
SIPHONS
SIPPER
SIPPERS
SIPPET
SIPPETS
SIPPLE
SIPPLED
SIPPLES
SIRCAR
SIRCARS
SIRDAR
SIRDARS
SIRKAR
SIRKARS
SIRRAH
SIRRAHS
SIRREE
SIRREES
SISKIN
SISKINS
SISSOO
SISSOOS
SISTER
SISTERS
SITCOM
SITCOMS
SITHEN
SITHENS
SITREP
SITREPS
SITTAR
SITTARS
SITTER
SITTERS
SITULA
SITULAE
SIXAIN
SIXAINE
SIXAINS
SIZING
SIZINGS
SIZISM
SIZISMS
SIZIST
SIZISTS
SIZZLE
SIZZLED
SIZZLER
SIZZLES
SKAITH
SKAITHS
SKARTH
SKARTHS
SKATER
SKATERS
SKELUM
SKELUMS
SKETCH
SKETCHY
SKEWER
SKEWERS
SKIBOB
SKIBOBS
SKIDOO
SKIDOOS
SKIING
SKIINGS
SKIVER
SKIVERS
SKIVIE
SKIVIER
SKLATE
SKLATED
SKLATES
SKLENT
ASKLENT
SKLENTS
SKLIFF
SKLIFFS
SKREEN
SKREENS
SKRIMP
SKRIMPS
SKRUMP
SKRUMPS
SKRYER
SKRYERS
SKYLAB
SKYLABS
SKYWAY
SKYWAYS
SLAIRG
SLAIRGS
SLAKED
ASLAKED
YSLAKED
SLAKES
ASLAKES
SLALOM
SLALOMS
SLATER
SLATERS
SLAVER
SLAVERS
SLAVERY
SLAVEY
SLAVEYS
SLAYER
SLAYERS
SLEAVE
SLEAVED
SLEAVES
SLEAZE
SLEAZES
SLEDGE
SLEDGED
SLEDGER
SLEDGES
SLEECH
SLEECHY
SLEEVE
SLEEVED
SLEEVER
SLEEVES
SLEIGH
SLEIGHS
SLEIGHT
SLEUTH
SLEUTHS
SLICER
SLICERS
SLIDER
SLIDERS
SLIGHT
SLIGHTS
SLIVER
SLIVERS
SLOGAN
SLOGANS
SLOKEN
SLOKENS
SLOUCH
SLOUCHY
SLOUGH
SLOUGHS
SLOUGHY
SLOVEN
SLOVENS
SLUDGE
SLUDGES
SLUICE
SLUICED
SLUICES
SMALTO
SMALTOS
SMEATH
SMEATHS
SMEETH
SMEETHS
SMEGMA
SMEGMAS
SMEUSE
SMEUSES
SMIGHT
SMIGHTS
SMILER
SMILERS
SMILET
SMILETS
SMITER
SMITERS
SMOILE
SMOILED
SMOILES
SMOKER
SMOKERS
SMOOTH
SMOOTHS
SMOUSE
SMOUSED
SMOUSER
SMOUSES
SMOYLE
SMOYLED
SMOYLES
SMUDGE
SMUDGED
SMUDGER
SMUDGES
SNARER
SNARERS
SNASTE
SNASTES
SNATCH
SNATCHY
SNATHE
SNATHES
SNEATH
SNEATHS
SNEBBE
SNEBBED
SNEBBES
SNEEZE
SNEEZED
SNEEZER
SNEEZES
SNIDES
SNIDEST
SNIPER
SNIPERS
SNIVEL
SNIVELS
SNOOZE
SNOOZED
SNOOZER
SNOOZES
SNORER
SNORERS
SNUBBE
SNUBBED
SNUBBER
SNUBBES
SNUDGE
SNUDGED
SNUDGES
SOAKER
SOAKERS
SOAPER
SOAPERS
SOAPIE
SOAPIER
SOAPIES
SOARER
SOARERS
SOBOLE
SOBOLES
SOCAGE
SOCAGER
SOCAGES
SOCCER
SOCCERS
SOCIAL
ASOCIAL
SOCIALS
SOCKET
SOCKETS
SODAIN
SODAINE
SODDEN
SODDENS
SODGER
SODGERS
SODIUM
SODIUMS
SOFFIT
SOFFITS
SOFTEN
SOFTENS
SOFTIE
SOFTIES
SOIGNE
SOIGNEE
SOIREE
SOIREES
SOLACE
SOLACED
SOLACES
SOLANO
SOLANOS
SOLDAN
SOLDANS
SOLDER
SOLDERS
SOLERA
SOLERAS
SOLION
SOLIONS
SOLITO
SOLITON
SOLIVE
SOLIVES
SOLLAR
SOLLARS
SOLLER
SOLLERS
SOLUTE
SOLUTES
SOLVER
SOLVERS
SOMBER
SOMBERS
SOMBRE
SOMBRED
SOMBRER
SOMBRES
SOMITE
SOMITES
SONANT
SONANTS
SONATA
SONATAS
SONERI
SONERIS
SONNET
SONNETS
SONSIE
SONSIER
SONTAG
SONTAGS
SOOGEE
SOOGEED
SOOGEES
SOOGIE
SOOGIED
SOOGIES
SOOJEY
SOOJEYS
SOOTHE
SOOTHED
SOOTHER
SOOTHES
SOPITE
SOPITED
SOPITES

SORAGE
SORAGES
SORBET
SORBETS
SORELL
SORELLS
SORGHO
SORGHOS
SORNER
SORNERS
SORREL
SORRELS
SORROW
SORROWS
SORTER
SORTERS
SORTIE
SORTIED
SORTIES
SOUARI
SOUARIS
SOUPER
SOUPERS
SOUPLE
SOUPLED
SOUPLES
SOURCE
SOURCED
SOURCES
SOURSE
SOURSES
SOUTAR
SOUTARS
SOUTER
SOUTERS
SOVIET
SOVIETS
SOVRAN
SOVRANS
SOWING
SOWINGS
SOWSSE
SOWSSED
SOWSSES
SOWTER
SOWTERS
SOZZLE
SOZZLED
SOZZLES
SPACER
SPACERS
SPADER
SPADERS
SPAHEE
SPAHEES
SPAING
SPAINGS
SPALLE
SPALLED
SPALLES
SPARER
SPARERS
SPARES
SPAREST
SPARGE
SPARGED
SPARGER
SPARGES
SPARID
SPARIDS
SPARKE
SPARKED
SPARKES
SPARRE
SPARRED
SPARRER
SPARRES
SPARSE
SPARSER
SPARTH
SPARTHE
SPARTHS
SPATHE
SPATHED
SPATHES
SPAULD
SPAULDS
SPAVIE
SPAVIES
SPAVIN
SPAVINS
SPAYAD
SPAYADS
SPECIE
SPECIES
SPEEDO
SPEEDOS
SPENCE
SPENCER
SPENCES
SPERRE
SPERRED
SPERRES
SPERSE
ASPERSE
SPERSED
SPERSES
SPEWER
SPEWERS
SPHAER
SPHAERE
SPHAERS
SPHEAR
SPHEARE
SPHEARS
SPHENE
SPHENES
SPHERE
SPHERED
SPHERES
SPIALS
ESPIALS
SPICER
SPICERS
SPICERY
SPICKS
ASPICKS
SPIDER
SPIDERS
SPIDERY
SPIGHT
SPIGHTS
SPIGOT
SPIGOTS
SPILTH
SPILTHS
SPINAR
SPINARS
SPINEL
SPINELS
SPINES
ASPINES
SPINET
SPINETS
SPIRAL
SPIRALS
SPIREA
SPIREAS
SPIRED
ASPIRED
SPIRES
ASPIRES
SPIRIC
SPIRICS
SPIRIT
SPIRITS
SPIRITY
SPITAL
SPITALS
SPLASH
SPLASHY
SPLEEN
SPLEENS
SPLEENY
SPLICE
SPLICED
SPLICER
SPLICES
SPLIFF
SPLIFFS
SPLINE
SPLINED
SPLINES
SPLINT
SPLINTS
SPLORE
SPLORES
SPONGE
SPONGED
SPONGER
SPONGES
SPORTS
ASPORTS
SPOUSE
ESPOUSE
SPOUSED
SPOUSES
SPRAIN
SPRAINS
SPRAINT
SPRAWL
ASPRAWL
SPRAWLS
SPRAWLY
SPREAD
ASPREAD
SPREADS
SPREDD
SPREDDE
SPREDDS
SPRING
SPRINGE
SPRINGS
SPRINGY
SPRINT
SPRINTS
SPRITE
SPRITES
SPRITS
ESPRITS
SPROUT
ASPROUT
SPROUTS
SPRUCE
SPRUCED
SPRUCER
SPRUCES
SPRUIK
SPRUIKS
SPRUIT
SPRUITS
SPULYE
SPULYED
SPULYES
SPUNGE
SPUNGES
SPURGE
SPURGES
SPURNE
SPURNED
SPURNER
SPURNES
SPYING
ESPYING
SPYINGS
SQUAIL
SQUAILS
SQUALL
SQUALLS
SQUALLY
SQUAMA
SQUAMAE
SQUAME
SQUAMES
SQUARE
SQUARED
SQUARER
SQUARES
SQUASH
SQUASHY
SQUAWK
SQUAWKS
SQUAWKY
SQUEAK
SQUEAKS
SQUEAKY
SQUEAL
SQUEALS
SQUIER
SQUIERS
SQUIFF
SQUIFFY
SQUILL
SQUILLA
SQUILLS
SQUINT
ASQUINT
SQUINTS
SQUIRE
ESQUIRE
SQUIRED
SQUIRES
SQUIRM
SQUIRMS
SQUIRMY
SQUIRR
SQUIRRS
SQUIRT
SQUIRTS
SQUISH
SQUISHY
STABLE
ASTABLE
STABLED
STABLER
STABLES
STACTE
STACTES
STADDA
STADDAS
STADIA
STADIAL
STADIAS
STAGER
STAGERS
STAGERY
STAITH
STAITHE
STAITHS
STALAG
STALAGS
STALES
STALEST
STAMEN
STAMENS
STANCE
STANCES
STANZA
STANZAS
STANZE
STANZES
STANZO
STANZOS
STAPLE
STAPLED
STAPLER
STAPLES
STARCH
STARCHY
STARER
STARERS
STARTS
ASTARTS
STARVE
STARVED
STARVES
STATED
ESTATED
STATER
STATERS
STATES
ESTATES
STATIC
ASTATIC
STATICE
STATICS
STATOR
STATORS
STATUA
STATUAS
STATUE
STATUED
STATUES
STAYER
STAYERS
STAYNE
STAYNED
STAYNES
STAYRE
STAYRES
STEALE
STEALED
STEALER
STEALES
STEALT
STEALTH
STEANE
STEANED
STEANES
STEARE
STEARED
STEARES
STEDDE
STEDDED
STEDDES
STEEMS
ESTEEMS
STEEVE
STEEVED
STEEVER
STEEVES
STEMME
STEMMED
STEMMER
STEMMES
STENCH
STENCHY
STENTS
OSTENTS
STEPPE
STEPPED
STEPPER
STEPPES
STEREO
STEREOS
STERNA
STERNAL
STEROL
STEROLS
STERVE
STERVED
STERVES
STEVEN
STEVENS
STEWER
STEWERS
STIEVE
STIEVER
STIFLE
STIFLED
STIFLER
STIFLES
STIGMA
STIGMAS
STIGME
STIGMES
STILET
STILETS
STIMIE
STIMIED
STIMIES
STINGO
STINGOS
STIPEL
STIPELS
STIRRA
STIRRAH
STIRRAS
STIRRE
STIRRED
STIRRER
STIRRES
STIVER
STIVERS
STODGE
STODGED
STODGER
STODGES
STOGEY
STOGEYS
STOGIE
STOGIES
STOKER
STOKERS
STOLON
STOLONS
STONED
ASTONED
STONER
STONERN
STONERS
STONES
ASTONES
STONNE
STONNED
STONNES
STOOGE
STOOGED
STOOGES
STOOPE
STOOPED
STOOPER
STOOPES
STORER
STORERS
STOREY
STOREYS
STORGE
STORGES
STOUND
ASTOUND
STOUNDS
STOUTH
STOUTHS
STOVER
ESTOVER
STOVERS
STOWER
STOWERS
STOWND
STOWNDS
STOWRE
STOWRES
STRAFE
STRAFED
STRAFES
STRAFF
STRAFFS
STRAIK
STRAIKS
STRAIN
STRAINS
STRAINT
STRAIT
STRAITS
STRAKE
STRAKES
STRAMP
STRAMPS
STRAND
ASTRAND
STRANDS
STRATH
STRATHS
STRAYS
ESTRAYS
STREAK
STREAKS
STREAKY
STREAM
STREAMS
STREAMY
STREEK
STREEKS
STREEL
STREELS
STREET
STREETS
STREETY
STRENE
STRENES
STRICH
ESTRICH
OSTRICH
STRICT
ASTRICT
STRIDE
ASTRIDE
STRIDES
STRIFE
STRIFES
STRIFT
STRIFTS
STRIGA
STRIGAE
STRIKE
STRIKER
STRIKES
STRING
STRINGS
STRINGY
STRIPE
STRIPED
STRIPES
STRIPEY
STRIVE
STRIVED
STRIVEN
STRIVER
STRIVES
STROAM
STROAMS
STROBE
STROBES
STROKE
STROKED
STROKEN
STROKER
STROKES
STROLL
STROLLS
STROMB
STROMBS
STROND
STRONDS
STROOK
STROOKE
STROUD
STROUDS
STROUP

STROUPS
STROUT
STROUTS
STRUMA
STRUMAE
STRUMS
ESTRUMS
STRUNT
STRUNTS
STUCCO
STUCCOS
STUDIO
STUDIOS
STUMER
STUMERS
STUPID
STUPIDS
STUPOR
STUPORS
STYLAR
ASTYLAR
STYLET
STYLETS
STYMIE
STYMIED
STYMIES
SUBACT
SUBACTS
SUBBIE
SUBBIES
SUBDEW
SUBDEWS
SUBDUE
SUBDUED
SUBDUER
SUBDUES
SUBFEU
SUBFEUS
SUBGUM
SUBGUMS
SUBLET
SUBLETS
SUBMIT
SUBMITS
SUBORN
SUBORNS
SUBSET
SUBSETS
SUBTIL
SUBTILE
SUBTLE
SUBTLER
SUBURB
SUBURBS
SUBWAY
SUBWAYS
SUCCAH
SUCCAHS
SUCCES
SUCCESS
SUCCOR
SUCCORS
SUCCORY
SUCCUS
SUCCUSS
SUCKEN
SUCKENS
SUCKER
SUCKERS
SUCKET

SUCKETS
SUCKLE
SUCKLED
SUCKLER
SUCKLES
SUDATE
SUDATED
SUDATES
SUDDEN
ASUDDEN
SUDDER
SUDDERS
SUDSER
SUDSERS
SUFFER
SUFFERS
SUITOR
SUITORS
SUKKAH
SUKKAHS
SULFUR
SULFURS
SULPHA
SULPHAS
SULTAN
SULTANA
SULTANS
SUMACH
SUMACHS
SUMMAR
SUMMARY
SUMMAT
SUMMATE
SUMMATS
SUMMER
SUMMERS
SUMMERY
SUMMIT
SUMMITS
SUMMON
SUMMONS
SUMPIT
SUMPITS
SUNBED
SUNBEDS
SUNBOW
SUNBOWS
SUNDAE
SUNDAES
SUNDER
ASUNDER
SUNDERS
SUNDEW
SUNDEWS
SUNDOG
SUNDOGS
SUNDRA
SUNDRAS
SUNDRI
SUNDRIS
SUNGAR
SUNGARS
SUNHAT
SUNHATS
SUNKET
SUNKETS
SUNKIE
SUNKIES
SUNRAY
SUNRAYS

SUNSET
SUNSETS
SUNTAN
SUNTANS
SUPAWN
SUPAWNS
SUPINE
SUPINES
SUPPER
SUPPERS
SUPPLE
SUPPLED
SUPPLER
SUPPLES
SURBED
SURBEDS
SURFER
SURFERS
SURFIE
SURFIER
SURFIES
SURING
USURING
SURREY
SURREYS
SURVEW
SURVEWE
SURVEWS
SURVEY
SURVEYS
SUSLIK
SUSLIKS
SUTLER
SUTLERS
SUTLERY
SUTTEE
SUTTEES
SUTTLE
SUTTLED
SUTTLES
SUTURE
SUTURED
SUTURES
SVELTE
SVELTER
SWARDS
USWARDS
SWARTH
SWARTHS
SWARTHY
SWARVE
SWARVED
SWARVES
SWATHE
SWATHED
SWATHES
SWAYER
SWAYERS
SWEARD
SWEARDS
SWERVE
SWERVED
SWERVER
SWERVES
SWEVEN
SWEVENS
SWINGE
SWINGED
SWINGER
SWINGES

SWIPER
SWIPERS
SWITCH
SWITCHY
SWIVEL
SWIVELS
SWIVET
SWIVETS
SWOUND
SWOUNDS
SWOUNE
SWOUNED
SWOUNES
SWOWND
SWOWNDS
SWOWNE
SWOWNES
SYLVAN
SYLVANS
SYLVIA
SYLVIAS
SYMBOL
SYMBOLE
SYMBOLS
SYNDET
SYNDETS
SYNDIC
SYNDICS
SYNROC
SYNROCS
SYNTAN
SYNTANS
SYPHER
SYPHERS
SYPHON
SYPHONS
SYSTEM
SYSTEMS
TABARD
TABARDS
TABBED
STABBED
TABERD
TABERDS
TABLED
STABLED
TABLES
STABLES
TABLET
TABLETS
TABOUR
TABOURS
TABRET
TABRETS
TABULA
TABULAE
TABULAR
TACKED
STACKED
TACKER
STACKER
TACKERS
TACKET
STACKET
TACKETS
TACKETY
TACKLE
TACKLED
TACKLER
TACKLES

TACTIC
ATACTIC
TACTICS
TADDIE
TADDIES
TAENIA
TAENIAE
TAENIAS
TAFFIA
TAFFIAS
TAGGED
STAGGED
TAGGEE
TAGGEES
TAGGER
STAGGER
TAGGERS
TAGRAG
TAGRAGS
TAGUAN
TAGUANS
TAHINA
TAHINAS
TAHINI
TAHINIS
TAHSIL
TAHSILS
TAIAHA
TAIAHAS
TAIGLE
TAIGLED
TAIGLES
TAILLE
TAILLES
TAILOR
TAILORS
TAILYE
TAILYES
TAIPAN
TAIPANS
TAIVER
TAIVERS
TAIVERT
TAJINE
TAJINES
TAKAHE
TAKAHES
TAKING
STAKING
TAKINGS
TALANT
TALANTS
TALBOT
TALBOTS
TALCUM
TALCUMS
TALENT
TALENTS
TALION
TALIONS
TALKED
STALKED
TALKER
STALKER
TALKERS
TALKIE
TALKIER
TALKIES
TALLAT
TALLATS

TALLET
TALLETS
TALLOT
TALLOTS
TALLOW
TALLOWS
TALLOWY
TALMUD
TALMUDS
TALONS
ETALONS
TALUKA
TALUKAS
TALWEG
TALWEGS
TAMALE
TAMALES
TAMANU
TAMANUS
TAMARA
TAMARAO
TAMARAS
TAMARAU
TAMARI
TAMARIN
TAMARIS
TAMBAC
TAMBACS
TAMBER
TAMBERS
TAMINE
TAMINES
TAMING
TAMINGS
TAMISE
TAMISES
TAMMAR
TAMMARS
TAMPED
STAMPED
TAMPER
STAMPER
TAMPERS
TAMPON
TAMPONS
TANDEM
TANDEMS
TANGED
STANGED
TANGIE
TANGIER
TANGIES
TANGLE
TANGLED
TANGLER
TANGLES
TANGUN
TANGUNS
TANIST
TANISTS
TANKER
TANKERS
TANKIA
TANKIAS
TANNAH
TANNAHS
TANNER
TANNERS
TANNERY
TANNIC

STANNIC
TANNIN
TANNING
TANNINS
TANNOY
TANNOYS
TANREC
TANRECS
TANTRA
TANTRAS
TAPETA
TAPETAL
TAPETI
TAPETIS
TAPIST
TAPISTS
TAPPED
STAPPED
TAPPER
TAPPERS
TAPPET
TAPPETS
TARAND
TARANDS
TARBOY
TARBOYS
TARCEL
TARCELS
TARGET
TARGETS
TARIFF
TARIFFS
TARING
STARING
TARINGS
TARMAC
TARMACS
TARPAN
TARPANS
TARPON
TARPONS
TARRED
STARRED
TARROW
TARROWS
TARSAL
TARSALS
TARSEL
TARSELS
TARSIA
TARSIAS
TARTAN
TARTANA
TARTANE
TARTANS
TARTAR
TARTARE
TARTARS
TARTER
STARTER
TARTLY
STARTLY
TASHED
STASHED
TASHES
STASHES
TASKER
TASKERS
TASLET
TASLETS

TASSEL
TASSELL
TASSELS
TASSET
TASSETS
TASSIE
TASSIES
TASTER
TASTERS
TATAMI
TATAMIS
TATERS
STATERS
TATLER
TATLERS
TATTER
TATTERS
TATTERY
TATTIE
TATTIER
TATTIES
TATTLE
TATTLED
TATTLER
TATTLES
TATTOO
TATTOOS
TATTOW
TATTOWS
TATUED
STATUED
TAUPIE
TAUPIES
TAUTEN
TAUTENS
TAUTOG
TAUTOGS
TAVERN
TAVERNA
TAVERNS
TAWING
STAWING
TAWINGS
TAWNEY
TAWNEYS
TAWPIE
TAWPIES
TAWTIE
TAWTIER
TAXIES
ATAXIES
TAXING
TAXINGS
TCHICK
TCHICKS
TEACUP
TEACUPS
TEAGLE
TEAGLED
TEAGLES
TEAMED
STEAMED
TEAMER
STEAMER
TEAMERS
TEAPOT
TEAPOTS
TEAPOY
TEAPOYS
TEARER

TEARERS
TEASEL
TEASELS
TEASER
TEASERS
TEAZEL
TEAZELS
TEAZLE
TEAZLED
TEAZLES
TEBBAD
TEBBADS
TECHNO
TECHNOS
TECKEL
TECKELS
TEDDED
STEDDED
TEDDER
TEDDERS
TEDDIE
TEDDIES
TEDIUM
TEDIUMS
TEEMED
STEEMED
TEEMER
TEEMERS
TEENED
STEENED
TEEPEE
TEEPEES
TEERED
STEERED
TEETER
TEETERS
TEETHE
TEETHED
TEETHES
TEGULA
TEGULAE
TEGULAR
TELEDU
TELEDUS
TELEGA
TELEGAS
TELESM
TELESMS
TELFER
TELFERS
TELLAR
STELLAR
TELLARS
TELLEN
TELLENS
TELLER
TELLERS
TELLIN
TELLING
TELLINS
TELSON
TELSONS
TEMPEH
TEMPEHS
TEMPER
TEMPERA
TEMPERS
TEMPLE
STEMPLE
TEMPLED

TEMPLES
TEMPLET
TENACE
TENACES
TENAIL
TENAILS
TENANT
TENANTS
TENDED
STENDED
TENDER
TENDERS
TENDON
TENDONS
TENDRE
TENDRES
TENNER
TENNERS
TENOUR
TENOURS
TENREC
TENRECS
TENSES
TENSEST
TENSON
TENSONS
TENSOR
TENSORS
TENTED
STENTED
TENTER
TENTERS
TENTIE
TENTIER
TENURE
TENURED
TENURES
TENUTO
TENUTOS
TENZON
TENZONS
TEPHRA
TEPHRAS
TERCEL
TERCELS
TERCET
TERCETS
TERCIO
TERCIOS
TEREDO
TEREDOS
TEREFA
TEREFAH
TERETE
TERETES
TERMER
TERMERS
TERMOR
TERMORS
TERNAL
ETERNAL
STERNAL
TERNED
STERNED
TERRET
TERRETS
TERRIT
TERRITS
TERROR
TERRORS

TERTIA
TERTIAL
TERTIAN
TERTIAS
TESTEE
TESTEES
TESTER
TESTERN
TESTERS
TESTON
TESTONS
TETHER
TETHERS
TETRAD
TETRADS
TETRYL
TETRYLS
TETTER
TETTERS
TEWART
TEWARTS
TEWHIT
TEWHITS
TEWING
STEWING
THAIRM
THAIRMS
THALER
THALERS
THALLI
THALLIC
THANAH
THANAHS
THANES
ETHANES
THANNA
THANNAH
THANNAS
THATCH
THATCHT
THAWER
THAWERS
THEAVE
THEAVES
THEINE
THEINES
THEISM
ATHEISM
THEISMS
THEIST
ATHEIST
THEISTS
THENAR
THENARS
THIBET
THIBETS
THIBLE
THIBLES
THICKO
THICKOS
THIEVE
THIEVED
THIEVES
THIRAM
THIRAMS
THIRST
ATHIRST
THIRSTS
THIRSTY
THIVEL

THIVELS
THORIA
THORIAS
THORON
THORONS
THORPE
THORPES
THOUGH
THOUGHT
THOWEL
THOWELS
THRALL
THRALLS
THRANG
THRANGS
THRAVE
THRAVES
THREAD
THREADS
THREADY
THREAP
THREAPS
THREAT
THREATS
THREEP
THREEPS
THRENE
THRENES
THRIFT
THRIFTS
THRIFTY
THRILL
ATHRILL
THRILLS
THRILLY
THRIST
THRISTS
THRISTY
THRIVE
THRIVED
THRIVEN
THRIVER
THRIVES
THROAT
THROATS
THROATY
THRONE
THRONED
THRONES
THRONG
THRONGS
THROWE
THROWER
THROWES
THRUST
THRUSTS
THUGGO
THUGGOS
THULIA
THULIAS
THWACK
THWACKS
THWART
ATHWART
THWARTS
THYMOL
THYMOLS
THYRSE
THYRSES
TIBIAL

STIBIAL
TICKED
STICKED
TICKEN
TICKENS
TICKER
STICKER
TICKERS
TICKET
TICKETS
TICKEY
TICKEYS
TICKLE
STICKLE
TICKLED
TICKLER
TICKLES
TIDBIT
TIDBITS
TIDDLE
TIDDLED
TIDDLER
TIDDLES
TIDDLEY
TIDIES
TIDIEST
TIDING
TIDINGS
TIEPIN
TIEPINS
TIERCE
TIERCED
TIERCEL
TIERCES
TIERCET
TIEROD
TIERODS
TIETAC
TIETACK
TIETACS
TIFFED
STIFFED
TIFFIN
TIFFING
TIFFINS
TIGLON
TIGLONS
TILING
STILING
TILINGS
TILLED
STILLED
TILLER
STILLER
TILLERS
TILTED
STILTED
TILTER
STILTER
TILTERS
TIMBAL
TIMBALE
TIMBALS
TIMBER
TIMBERS
TIMBRE
TIMBREL
TIMBRES
TIMING
STIMING

TIMINGS
TIMIST
TIMISTS
TINAJA
TINAJAS
TINCAL
TINCALS
TINDAL
TINDALS
TINDER
TINDERS
TINDERY
TINEID
TINEIDS
TINFUL
TINFULS
TINGED
STINGED
TINGLE
ATINGLE
TINGLED
TINGLER
TINGLES
TINIES
TINIEST
TINKER
STINKER
TINKERS
TINKLE
TINKLED
TINKLER
TINKLES
TINNER
TINNERS
TINNIE
TINNIER
TINNIES
TINPOT
TINPOTS
TINSEL
TINSELS
TINSEY
TINSEYS
TINTED
STINTED
TINTER
STINTER
TINTERS
TIPCAT
TIPCATS
TIPPER
TIPPERS
TIPPET
TIPPETS
TIPPLE
STIPPLE
TIPPLED
TIPPLER
TIPPLES
TIPTOE
TIPTOED
TIPTOES
TIPTOP
TIPTOPS
TIPULA
TIPULAS
TIRADE
TIRADES
TIRING
STIRING

TIRINGS
TIRRED
STIRRED
TIRRIT
TIRRITS
TISANE
TISANES
TISICK
TISICKS
TISSUE
TISSUED
TISSUES
TITBIT
TITBITS
TITFER
TITFERS
TITHER
TITHERS
TITIAN
TITIANS
TITLER
TITLERS
TITOKI
TITOKIS
TITTER
TITTERS
TITTLE
TITTLED
TITTLES
TITTUP
TITTUPS
TITTUPY
TITULE
TITULED
TITULES
TOCHER
TOCHERS
TOCKED
STOCKED
TOCSIN
TOCSINS
TODDLE
TODDLED
TODDLER
TODDLES
TOECAP
TOECAPS
TOERAG
TOERAGS
TOETOE
TOETOES
TOFFEE
TOFFEES
TOGATE
TOGATED
TOGGLE
TOGGLED
TOGGLES
TOILER
TOILERS
TOILES
ETOILES
TOILET
TOILETS
TOISON
TOISONS
TOITOI
TOITOIS
TOKING
STOKING

TOLING
TOLINGS
TOLLER
TOLLERS
TOLSEL
TOLSELS
TOLSEY
TOLSEYS
TOLTER
TOLTERS
TOLUOL
TOLUOLS
TOLZEY
TOLZEYS
TOMBAC
TOMBACS
TOMBAK
TOMBAKS
TOMBOC
TOMBOCS
TOMBOY
TOMBOYS
TOMCAT
TOMCATS
TOMPON
TOMPONS
TOMTIT
TOMTITS
TONEME
TONEMES
TONERS
ATONERS
STONERS
TONGUE
TONGUED
TONGUES
TONIER
STONIER
TONIES
ATONIES
STONIES
TONIEST
TONING
ATONING
STONING
TONINGS
TONITE
TONITES
TONKER
STONKER
TONKERS
TONLET
TONLETS
TONNAG
TONNAGE
TONNAGS
TONNES
STONNES
TONSIL
TONSILS
TONSOR
TONSORS
TOOART
TOOARTS
TOOLED
STOOLED
TOOLER
TOOLERS
TOORIE
TOORIES

TOOTER
TOOTERS
TOOTLE
TOOTLED
TOOTLES
TOPING
STOPING
TOPPED
STOPPED
TOPPER
STOPPER
TOPPERS
TOPPLE
STOPPLE
TOPPLED
TOPPLES
TORANA
TORANAS
TORERO
TOREROS
TOROID
TOROIDS
TORPID
TORPIDS
TORPOR
TORPORS
TORQUE
TORQUED
TORQUES
TORRET
TORRETS
TORSEL
TORSELS
TORULA
TORULAE
TORULI
TORULIN
TOSHER
TOSHERS
TOSSER
TOSSERS
TOSSES
STOSSES
TOTARA
TOTARAS
TOTTED
STOTTED
TOTTER
STOTTER
TOTTERS
TOTTERY
TOTTIE
TOTTIER
TOTTIES
TOUCAN
TOUCANS
TOUCHE
TOUCHED
TOUCHER
TOUCHES
TOUPEE
TOUPEES
TOUPET
TOUPETS
TOURER
TOURERS
TOURIE
TOURIES
TOUSER
TOUSERS
TOUSLE
TOUSLED
TOUSLES
TOUTER
STOUTER
TOUTERS
TOUTIE
TOUTIER
TOUZLE
TOUZLED
TOUZLES
TOWAGE
STOWAGE
TOWAGES
TOWARD
TOWARDS
TOWBAR
TOWBARS
TOWERS
STOWERS
TOWHEE
TOWHEES
TOWING
STOWING
TOWINGS
TOWMON
TOWMOND
TOWMONS
TOWMONT
TOWNEE
TOWNEES
TOWNIE
TOWNIER
TOWNIES
TOWSER
TOWSERS
TOXOID
TOXOIDS
TOYING
TOYINGS
TRACER
TRACERS
TRACERY
TRADER
TRADERS
TRAIKS
STRAIKS
TRAINS
STRAINS
TRAITS
STRAITS
TRAMPS
STRAMPS
TRANCE
TRANCED
TRANCES
TRANSE
TRANSES
TRAPAN
TRAPANS
TRAPPY
STRAPPY
TRAUMA
TRAUMAS
TRAVEL
TRAVELS
TRAYNE
TRAYNED
TRAYNES
TREBLE
TREBLED
TREBLES
TREMIE
TREMIES
TREMOR
TREMORS
TREPAN
TREPANG
TREPANS
TREVIS
TREVISS
TRIAGE
TRIAGES
TRICAR
TRICARS
TRICKS
TRICKSY
TRICOT
TRICOTS
TRIERS
ETRIERS
TRIFLE
TRIFLED
TRIFLER
TRIFLES
TRIGON
TRIGONS
TRIKES
STRIKES
TRILBY
TRILBYS
TRIMER
TRIMERS
TRIODE
TRIODES
TRIPES
STRIPES
TRIPEY
STRIPEY
TRIPLE
TRIPLED
TRIPLES
TRIPLET
TRIPLEX
TRIPOD
TRIPODS
TRIPODY
TRISUL
TRISULA
TRISULS
TRITES
TRITEST
TRITON
TRITONE
TRITONS
TRIUNE
TRIUNES
TRIVET
TRIVETS
TRIVIA
TRIVIAL
TROADE
TROADES
TROCAR
TROCARS
TROCHE
TROCHEE
TROCHES
TROGON
TROGONS
TROIKA
TROIKAS
TROKED
STROKED
TROKES
STROKES
TROLLS
STROLLS
TROMPE
TROMPED
TROMPES
TROPHI
TROPHIC
TROPHY
ATROPHY
TROPIC
TROPICS
TROTYL
TROTYLS
TROUGH
TROUGHS
TROULE
TROULED
TROULES
TROUPE
TROUPED
TROUPER
TROUPES
TROUSE
TROUSER
TROUSES
TROUTS
STROUTS
TROVER
TROVERS
TROWED
STROWED
TROWEL
TROWELS
TRUANT
TRUANTS
TRUDGE
TRUDGED
TRUDGEN
TRUDGER
TRUDGES
TRUISM
TRUISMS
TRYING
TRYINGS
TSAMBA
TSAMBAS
TSETSE
TSETSES
TSOTSI
TSOTSIS
TUBAGE
TUBAGES
TUBBED
STUBBED
TUBBER
TUBBERS
TUBFUL
TUBFULS
TUBING
TUBINGS
TUBULE
TUBULES
TUCHUN
TUCHUNS
TUCKER
TUCKERS
TUCKET
TUCKETS
TUFFET
TUFFETS
TUFTER
TUFTERS
TUGGER
TUGGERS
TUGHRA
TUGHRAS
TUGRIK
TUGRIKS
TUILLE
TUILLES
TULBAN
TULBANS
TULWAR
TULWARS
TUMBLE
STUMBLE
TUMBLED
TUMBLER
TUMBLES
TUMOUR
TUMOURS
TUMPED
STUMPED
TUMULT
TUMULTS
TUNDRA
TUNDRAS
TUNDUN
TUNDUNS
TUNING
TUNINGS
TUNNED
STUNNED
TUNNEL
TUNNELS
TUPELO
TUPELOS
TURACO
TURACOS
TURBAN
TURBAND
TURBANS
TURBANT
TURBIT
TURBITH
TURBITS
TURBOT
TURBOTS
TUREEN
TUREENS
TURGOR
TURGORS
TURION
TURIONS
TURKEY
TURKEYS
TURNER
TURNERS
TURNERY
TURNIP
TURNIPS
TURRET
TURRETS
TURTLE
TURTLED
TURTLER
TURTLES
TUSCHE
TUSCHES
TUSHIE
STUSHIE
TUSHIES
TUSKAR
TUSKARS
TUSKER
TUSKERS
TUSSAH
TUSSAHS
TUSSEH
TUSSEHS
TUSSER
TUSSERS
TUSSLE
TUSSLED
TUSSLES
TUTSAN
TUTSANS
TUXEDO
TUXEDOS
TUYERE
TUYERES
TWAITE
TWAITES
TWEEZE
TWEEZED
TWEEZES
TWELVE
TWELVES
TWICER
TWICERS
TWIGHT
TWIGHTS
TWINER
TWINERS
TWINGE
TWINGED
TWINGES
TWITCH
TWITCHY
TWYERE
TWYERES
TYCOON
TYCOONS
TYLOTE
TYLOTES
TYMBAL
TYMBALS
TYMPAN
TYMPANA
TYMPANI
TYMPANO
TYMPANS
TYMPANY
TYPHON
TYPHONS
TYPING
TYPINGS
TYPIST
TYPISTS
TYRANT
TYRANTS
TYSTIE
TYSTIES
TZETSE
TZETSES
UAKARI
OUAKARI
UAKARIS
UBERTY
PUBERTY
UBIETY
DUBIETY
UCKERS
BUCKERS
DUCKERS
FUCKERS
MUCKERS
PUCKERS
SUCKERS
TUCKERS
YUCKERS
UDDERS
DUDDERS
JUDDERS
MUDDERS
PUDDERS
RUDDERS
SUDDERS
UGGING
BUGGING
FUGGING
HUGGING
JUGGING
LUGGING
MUGGING
PUGGING
RUGGING
SUGGING
TUGGING
UGLIED
OUGLIED
UGLIES
OUGLIES
UGLIEST
UJAMAA
UJAMAAS
ULICON
ULICONS
ULIKON
ULIKONS
ULLAGE
FULLAGE
SULLAGE
ULLAGED
ULLAGES
ULLING
BULLING
CULLING
DULLING
FULLING
GULLING
HULLING
LULLING
MULLING
NULLING
PULLING
WULLING
ULLINGS
ULOSES
DULOSES
ULOSIS
DULOSIS
ULSTER
ULSTERS
ULTIMA
ULTIMAS
ULTION
ULTIONS
UMBERS
CUMBERS
LUMBERS
NUMBERS
UMBLES
BUMBLES
FUMBLES
HUMBLES
JUMBLES
MUMBLES
NUMBLES
RUMBLES
TUMBLES
UMBREL
TUMBREL
UMBRELS
UMBRIL
TUMBRIL
UMBRILS
UMLAUT
UMLAUTS
UMPIRE
UMPIRED
UMPIRES
UNABLE
TUNABLE
UNBARE
UNBARED
UNBARES
UNBARK
UNBARKS
UNBEAR
UNBEARS
UNBEDS
SUNBEDS
UNBELT
SUNBELT
UNBELTS
UNBEND
UNBENDS
UNBIND
UNBINDS
UNBITT
UNBITTS
UNBOLT
UNBOLTS
UNBONE
UNBONED
UNBONES
UNBOOT
UNBOOTS
UNBORN
UNBORNE
UNCAGE
UNCAGED
UNCAGES
UNCAPE
UNCAPED
UNCAPES
UNCART
UNCARTS
UNCASE
UNCASED
UNCASES
UNCATE
JUNCATE

UNCIAL
UNCIALS
UNCLES
NUNCLES
UNCLEW
UNCLEWS
UNCLOG
UNCLOGS
UNCOCK
UNCOCKS
UNCOIL
UNCOILS
UNCOLT
UNCOLTS
UNCOPE
UNCOPED
UNCOPES
UNCORD
UNCORDS
UNCORK
UNCORKS
UNCOWL
UNCOWLS
UNCURL
UNCURLS
UNDATE
UNDATED
UNDEAF
UNDEAFS
UNDECK
SUNDECK
UNDECKS
UNDERN
UNDERNS
UNDIES
CUNDIES
FUNDIES
GUNDIES
UNDINE
NUNDINE
UNDINES
UNDOCK
UNDOCKS
UNDOER
UNDOERS
UNDRAW
UNDRAWN
UNDRAWS
UNEASE
UNEASES
UNEDGE
UNEDGED
UNEDGES
UNFACT
UNFACTS
UNFAIR
FUNFAIR
UNFAIRS
UNFOLD
UNFOLDS
UNFOOL
UNFOOLS
UNFORM
UNFORMS
UNFREE
UNFREED
UNFURL
UNFURLS
UNGEAR
UNGEARS

UNGILD
UNGILDS
UNGIRD
UNGIRDS
UNGIRT
UNGIRTH
UNGLUE
UNGLUED
UNGLUES
UNGOWN
UNGOWNS
UNGULA
UNGULAE
UNGYVE
UNGYVED
UNGYVES
UNHAIR
UNHAIRS
UNHAND
UNHANDS
UNHANDY
UNHANG
UNHANGS
UNHASP
UNHASPS
UNHATS
SUNHATS
UNHEAD
UNHEADS
UNHEAL
UNHEALS
UNHELE
UNHELED
UNHELES
UNHELM
UNHELMS
UNHIVE
UNHIVED
UNHIVES
UNHOOD
NUNHOOD
UNHOODS
UNHOOK
UNHOOKS
UNHOOP
UNHOOPS
UNHUSK
UNHUSKS
UNIONS
BUNIONS
UNIPED
UNIPEDS
UNIPOD
UNIPODS
UNIQUE
UNIQUER
UNIQUES
UNISON
UNISONS
UNITED
MUNITED
UNITER
UNITERS
UNITES
DUNITES
GUNITES
MUNITES
UNKING
BUNKING
DUNKING

FUNKING
JUNKING
UNKINGS
UNKNIT
UNKNITS
UNKNOT
UNKNOTS
UNLACE
UNLACED
UNLACES
UNLADE
UNLADED
UNLADEN
UNLADES
UNLAST
UNLASTE
UNLEAD
UNLEADS
UNLESS
GUNLESS
SUNLESS
UNLIKE
SUNLIKE
UNLIKES
UNLIME
UNLIMED
UNLIMES
UNLINE
UNLINED
UNLINES
UNLINK
UNLINKS
UNLIVE
UNLIVED
UNLIVES
UNLOAD
UNLOADS
UNLOCK
GUNLOCK
UNLOCKS
UNLORD
UNLORDS
UNLOVE
UNLOVED
UNLOVES
UNMAKE
UNMAKES
UNMASK
UNMASKS
UNMOOR
UNMOORS
UNNAIL
UNNAILS
UNNEST
DUNNEST
UNNESTS
UNPACK
UNPACKS
UNPICK
UNPICKS
UNPLUG
UNPLUGS
UNPOPE
UNPOPED
UNPOPES
UNPRAY
UNPRAYS
UNPROP
UNPROPS
UNRAKE

UNRAKED
UNRAKES
UNREAD
UNREADY
UNREEL
UNREELS
UNREIN
UNREINS
UNREST
UNRESTS
UNRIGS
RUNRIGS
UNRIPE
UNRIPER
UNROBE
UNROBED
UNROBES
UNROLL
UNROLLS
UNROOF
SUNROOF
UNROOFS
UNROOT
UNROOTS
UNROPE
UNROPED
UNROPES
UNRULE
UNRULED
UNRULES
UNSAFE
UNSAFER
UNSEAL
UNSEALS
UNSEAM
UNSEAMS
UNSEAT
UNSEATS
UNSEEL
UNSEELS
UNSEEN
UNSEENS
UNSELF
UNSELFS
UNSETS
SUNSETS
UNSHED
DUNSHED
UNSHIP
GUNSHIP
NUNSHIP
UNSHIPS
UNSHOE
UNSHOED
UNSHOES
UNSHOT
GUNSHOT
UNSHUT
UNSHUTS
UNSNAP
UNSNAPS
UNSOUL
UNSOULS
UNSPAR
UNSPARS
UNSTEP
UNSTEPS
UNSTOP
UNSTOPS
UNSTOW

UNSTOWS
UNSUIT
SUNSUIT
UNSUITS
UNSURE
UNSURED
UNSURER
UNTACK
UNTACKS
UNTAME
UNTAMED
UNTAMES
UNTEAM
UNTEAMS
UNTENT
UNTENTS
UNTENTY
UNTHAW
UNTHAWS
UNTIES
AUNTIES
PUNTIES
UNTILE
UNTILED
UNTILES
UNTINS
MUNTINS
UNTOMB
UNTOMBS
UNTRIM
UNTRIMS
UNTRUE
UNTRUER
UNTUCK
UNTUCKS
UNTUNE
UNTUNED
UNTUNES
UNTURF
UNTURFS
UNTURN
UNTURNS
UNVAIL
UNVAILE
UNVAILS
UNVEIL
UNVEILS
UNWARE
UNWARES
UNWEAL
UNWEALS
UNWILL
UNWILLS
UNWIND
UNWINDS
UNWIRE
UNWIRED
UNWIRES
UNWISE
SUNWISE
UNWISER
UNWIVE
UNWIVED
UNWIVES
UNWORK
UNWORKS
UNWOVE
UNWOVEN
UNWRAP
UNWRAPS

UNYOKE
UNYOKED
UNYOKES
UPBEAR
UPBEARS
UPBIND
UPBINDS
UPBLOW
UPBLOWN
UPBLOWS
UPBOIL
UPBOILS
UPBRAY
UPBRAYS
UPCAST
UPCASTS
UPCOIL
UPCOILS
UPCOME
UPCOMES
UPCURL
UPCURLS
UPDATE
UPDATED
UPDATES
UPDRAG
UPDRAGS
UPDRAW
UPDRAWN
UPDRAWS
UPFILL
UPFILLS
UPFLOW
UPFLOWS
UPFURL
UPFURLS
UPGANG
UPGANGS
UPGAZE
UPGAZED
UPGAZES
UPGROW
UPGROWN
UPGROWS
UPHANG
UPHANGS
UPHAUD
UPHAUDS
UPHEAP
UPHEAPS
UPHILL
UPHILLS
UPHOLD
UPHOLDS
UPHROE
EUPHROE
UPHROES
UPHURL
UPHURLS
UPKEEP
UPKEEPS
UPKNIT
UPKNITS
UPLAND
UPLANDS
UPLEAD
UPLEADS
UPLEAN
UPLEANS
UPLEANT

UPLEAP
UPLEAPS
UPLEAPT
UPLIFT
UPLIFTS
UPLINK
UPLINKS
UPLOCK
UPLOCKS
UPLOOK
UPLOOKS
UPMAKE
UPMAKER
UPMAKES
UPPERS
CUPPERS
SUPPERS
UPPING
CUPPING
DUPPING
HUPPING
PUPPING
SUPPING
TUPPING
UPPINGS
UPRATE
UPRATED
UPRATES
UPREAR
UPREARS
UPREST
UPRESTS
UPRISE
UPRISEN
UPRISES
UPRIST
UPRISTS
UPROAR
UPROARS
UPROLL
UPROLLS
UPROOT
UPROOTS
UPSEND
UPSENDS
UPSHOT
UPSHOTS
UPSIDE
UPSIDES
UPSTAY
UPSTAYS
UPSWAY
UPSWAYS
UPTAKE
UPTAKEN
UPTAKES
UPTEAR
UPTEARS
UPTILT
UPTILTS
UPTOWN
UPTOWNS
UPTURN
UPTURNS
UPWAFT
UPWAFTS
UPWARD
UPWARDS
UPWELL
UPWELLS

UPWIND
UPWINDS
UPWRAP
UPWRAPS
URACIL
URACILS
URALIS
OURALIS
URANIN
URANINS
URANYL
URANYLS
URARIS
CURARIS
OURARIS
URATES
AURATES
CURATES
URBANE
URBANER
URCHIN
URCHINS
UREIDE
UREIDES
UREMIA
UREMIAS
URENAS
MURENAS
URETER
URETERS
URGENT
SURGENT
TURGENT
URGERS
BURGERS
PURGERS
URGING
PURGING
SURGING
URGINGS
URIALS
BURIALS
URINAL
URINALS
URINES
MURINES
PURINES
URNFUL
URNFULS
URNING
BURNING
GURNING
TURNING
URNINGS
UROPOD
UROPODS
URTEXT
URTEXTS
URTICA
URTICAS
USAGER
USAGERS
USANCE
USANCES
USEFUL
MUSEFUL
USHERS
GUSHERS
HUSHERS
LUSHERS

MUSHERS
PUSHERS
RUSHERS
USTION
USTIONS
USURER
USURERS
USURES
USURESS
USWARD
USWARDS
UTISES
CUTISES
UTMOST
OUTMOST
UTMOSTS
UTOPIA
UTOPIAN
UTOPIAS
UTTERS
BUTTERS
CUTTERS
GUTTERS
MUTTERS
NUTTERS
PUTTERS
RUTTERS
VACATE
VACATED
VACATES
VACUUM
VACUUMS
VADING
EVADING
VAGINA
VAGINAE
VAGINAL
VAGINAS
VAGUES
VAGUEST
VAHINE
VAHINES
VAILED
AVAILED
VAKEEL
VAKEELS
VALETA
VALETAS
VALETE
VALETED
VALETES
VALINE
VALINES
VALISE
VALISES
VALLAR
VALLARY
VALLEY
VALLEYS
VALLUM
VALLUMS
VALOUR
VALOURS
VALUER
VALUERS
VALUTA
VALUTAS
VAMOSE
VAMOSED
VAMOSES
VAMPER
VAMPERS
VANDAL
VANDALS
VANISH
EVANISH
VANNER
VANNERS
VAPOUR
VAPOURS
VAPOURY
VARECH
VARECHS
VARIER
VARIERS
VARIES
OVARIES
VARLET
VARLETS
VARROA
VARROAS
VARVEL
VARVELS
VASSAL
VASSALS
VATFUL
VATFULS
VATTER
VATTERS
VAUDOO
VAUDOOS
VAUNCE
VAUNCED
VAUNCES
VAUNTS
AVAUNTS
VAWARD
VAWARDS
VEALER
VEALERS
VECTOR
VECTORS
VEGGIE
VEGGIES
VELATE
VELATED
VELETA
VELETAS
VELLET
VELLETS
VELLON
VELLONS
VELLUM
VELLUMS
VELOUR
VELOURS
VELURE
VELURED
VELURES
VELVET
VELVETS
VELVETY
VENDEE
VENDEES
VENDER
VENDERS
VENDIS
VENDISS
VENDOR
VENDORS
VENDUE
VENDUES
VENEER
VENEERS
VENEWE
VENEWES
VENGED
AVENGED
VENGER
AVENGER
VENGERS
VENGES
AVENGES
VENIRE
VENIRES
VENITE
VENITES
VENNEL
VENNELS
VENTED
EVENTED
VENTER
EVENTER
VENTERS
VENTIL
VENTILS
VENTRE
AVENTRE
VENTRED
VENTRES
VENUES
AVENUES
VENULE
VENULES
VERBAL
VERBALS
VERBID
OVERBID
VERBIDS
VERDET
VERDETS
VERDIN
VERDINS
VERDIT
VERDITE
VERDITS
VERGER
VERGERS
VERISM
VERISMO
VERISMS
VERIST
VERISTS
VERMIL
VERMILS
VERMILY
VERMIN
VERMINS
VERMINY
VERREL
VERRELS
VERSAL
VERSALS
VERSER
VERSERS
VERSET
OVERSET
VERSETS
VERSIN
VERSINE
VERSING
VERSINS
VERTED
AVERTED
EVERTED
VERTUE
VERTUES
VERVEL
VERVELS
VERVEN
VERVENS
VERVET
VERVETS
VESICA
VESICAE
VESICAL
VESPER
VESPERS
VESSEL
VESSELS
VESTAL
VESTALS
VEXING
VEXINGS
VIATOR
AVIATOR
VIATORS
VIBIST
VIBISTS
VIBRIO
VIBRIOS
VICTIM
VICTIMS
VICTOR
EVICTOR
VICTORS
VICTORY
VICUNA
VICUNAS
VIDAME
VIDAMES
VIELLE
VIELLES
VIEWER
VIEWERS
VIGORO
VIGOROS
VIGOUR
VIGOURS
VIHARA
VIHARAS
VIKING
VIKINGS
VILLAN
VILLANS
VILLANY
VIMANA
VIMANAS
VIOLER
VIOLERS
VIOLET
VIOLETS
VIOLIN
VIOLINS
VIRAGO
VIRAGOS
VIRGER
VIRGERS
VIRGIN
VIRGINS
VIRINO
VIRINOS
VIRION
VIRIONS
VIROID
VIROIDS
VIROSE
VIROSES
VIRTUE
VIRTUES
VISAGE
VISAGED
VISAGES
VISCIN
VISCINS
VISCUM
VISCUMS
VISIER
VISIERS
VISILE
VISILES
VISING
AVISING
VISION
VISIONS
VISITE
VISITED
VISITEE
VISITER
VISITES
VISUAL
VISUALS
VITRIC
VITRICS
VITTLE
VITTLES
VIZARD
VIZARDS
VIZIER
VIZIERS
VIZSLA
VIZSLAS
VIZZIE
VIZZIED
VIZZIES
VOCULE
VOCULES
VOGUER
VOGUERS
VOICER
VOICERS
VOIDED
AVOIDED
VOIDEE
VOIDEES
VOIDER
VOIDERS
VOLANT
VOLANTE
VOLLEY
VOLLEYS
VOLOST
VOLOSTS
VOLUME
VOLUMED
VOLUMES
VOLUTE
EVOLUTE
VOLUTED
VOLUTES
VOLVED
EVOLVED
VOLVES
EVOLVES
VOMICA
VOMICAE
VOMICAS
VOMITO
VOMITOS
VOODOO
VOODOOS
VOTEEN
VOTEENS
VOUDOU
VOUDOUS
VOULGE
VOULGES
VOWERS
AVOWERS
VOWING
AVOWING
VOYAGE
VOYAGED
VOYAGER
VOYAGES
VOYEUR
VOYEURS
VULCAN
VULCANS
VULGAR
VULGARS
WABAIN
WABAINS
WABBLE
WABBLED
WABBLER
WABBLES
WABOOM
WABOOMS
WACKER
WACKERS
WADDIE
WADDIED
WADDIES
WADDLE
SWADDLE
TWADDLE
WADDLED
WADDLER
WADDLES
WADING
WADINGS
WADMAL
WADMALS
WADMOL
WADMOLL
WADMOLS
WADSET
WADSETS
WADSETT
WAFFLE
WAFFLED
WAFFLER
WAFFLES
WAFTER
WAFTERS
WAGGED
SWAGGED
WAGGLE
WAGGLED
WAGGLES
WAGGON
WAGGONS
WAGING
SWAGING
WAHINE
WAHINES
WAILER
WAILERS
WAITED
AWAITED
WAITER
WAITERS
WAITES
TWAITES
WAIVER
WAIVERS
WAKANE
WAKANES
WAKENS
AWAKENS
WAKIKI
WAKIKIS
WAKING
AWAKING
WAKINGS
WALIER
SWALIER
WALIES
WALIEST
WALING
SWALING
WALISE
WALISES
WALKER
WALKERS
WALLAH
WALLAHS
WALLER
WALLERS
WALLET
SWALLET
WALLETS
WALLIE
WALLIER
WALLIES
WALLOP
WALLOPS
WALLOW
SWALLOW
WALLOWS
WALNUT
WALNUTS
WAMBLE
WAMBLED
WAMBLES
WAMPEE
WAMPEES
WAMPUM
WAMPUMS
WANDER
WANDERS
WANDOO
WANDOOS
WANGAN
WANGANS
WANGLE
TWANGLE
WANGLED
WANGLER
WANGLES
WANGUN
WANGUNS
WANING
WANINGS
WANKED
SWANKED
WANKER
SWANKER
WANKERS
WANNED
SWANNED
WANTER
WANTERS
WANTON
WANTONS
WAPITI
WAPITIS
WAPPED
SWAPPED
WAPPER
SWAPPER
WAPPERS
WARBLE
WARBLED
WARBLER
WARBLES
WARDED
AWARDED
SWARDED
WARDEN
WARDENS
WARDER
WARDERS
WARDOG
WARDOGS
WARMED
SWARMED
WARMER
SWARMER
WARMERS
WARMTH
WARMTHS
WARNED
AWARNED
WARNER
WARNERS
WARPER
WARPERS
WARRAN
WARRAND
WARRANS
WARRANT
WARRAY
WARRAYS
WARREN
WARRENS
WARREY
WARREYS
WARSLE
WARSLED
WARSLES
WASHED
SWASHED
WASHER
SWASHER
WASHERS
WASHERY
WASHES
SWASHES

WASPIE
WASPIER
WASPIES
WASTEL
WASTELS
WASTER
WASTERS
WASTERY
WATTER
SWATTER
WATTLE
TWATTLE
WATTLED
WATTLES
WAUCHT
WAUCHTS
WAUGHT
WAUGHTS
WAUKER
WAUKERS
WAVIES
WAVIEST
WAVING
WAVINGS
WAXING
WAXINGS
WAYING
SWAYING
WAYLAY
WAYLAYS
WEAKEN
WEAKENS
WEALTH
WEALTHS
WEALTHY
WEANEL
WEANELS
WEANER
WEANERS
WEAPON
WEAPONS
WEARER
SWEARER
WEARERS
WEASEL
WEASELS
WEAVER
WEAVERS
WEAZEN
WEAZENS
WEDDER
WEDDERS
WEDELN
WEDELNS
WEDGIE
WEDGIER
WEDGIES
WEEDER
WEEDERS
WEEDERY
WEEING
SWEEING
WEEPER
SWEEPER
WEEPERS
WEEPIE
WEEPIER
WEEPIES
WEETED
SWEETED
TWEETED
WEETEN
SWEETEN
WEETER
SWEETER
TWEETER
WEEVER
WEEVERS
WEEVIL
WEEVILS
WEEVILY
WEIGHT
WEIGHTS
WEIGHTY
WEIRDO
WEIRDOS
WELDER
WELDERS
WELDOR
WELDORS
WELKIN
WELKING
WELKINS
WELLED
DWELLED
SWELLED
WELLIE
WELLIES
WELTED
SWELTED
WELTER
SWELTER
WELTERS
WESAND
WESANDS
WESTER
WESTERN
WESTERS
WETHER
WETHERS
WEZAND
WEZANDS
WHACKO
WHACKOS
WHALER
WHALERS
WHALERY
WHAMMO
WHAMMOS
WHARVE
WHARVES
WHEECH
WHEECHS
WHEELS
AWHEELS
WHEESH
WHEESHT
WHEEZE
WHEEZED
WHEEZES
WHENCE
WHENCES
WHERES
WHERESO
WHEUGH
WHEUGHS
WHIDAH
WHIDAHS
WHINER
WHINERS
WHINGE
WHINGED
WHINGER
WHINGES
WHISHT
WHISHTS
WHITEN
WHITENS
WHITES
WHITEST
WHITEY
WHITEYS
WHYDAH
WHYDAHS
WICCAN
WICCANS
WICKED
WICKEDS
WICKEN
WICKENS
WICKER
WICKERS
WICKET
WICKETS
WIDDLE
TWIDDLE
WIDDLED
WIDDLES
WIDGET
WIDGETS
WIDGIE
WIDGIES
WIENIE
WIENIES
WIGEON
WIGEONS
WIGGED
SWIGGED
TWIGGED
WIGGLE
WIGGLED
WIGGLER
WIGGLES
WIGHTS
TWIGHTS
WIGWAG
WIGWAGS
WIGWAM
WIGWAMS
WILDER
WILDERS
WILLED
SWILLED
TWILLED
WILLER
SWILLER
WILLERS
WILLET
WILLETS
WILLEY
WILLEYS
WILLIE
WILLIED
WILLIES
WILLOW
WILLOWS
WILLOWY
WILTED
TWILTED
WILTJA
WILTJAS
WIMBLE
WIMBLED
WIMBLES
WIMPLE
WIMPLED
WIMPLES
WINCER
WINCERS
WINCEY
WINCEYS
WINDAC
WINDACS
WINDER
WINDERS
WINDLE
DWINDLE
SWINDLE
WINDLES
WINDOW
WINDOWS
WINERY
SWINERY
WINGED
SWINGED
TWINGED
WINGER
SWINGER
WINGERS
WINGES
SWINGES
TWINGES
WINIER
TWINIER
WINING
DWINING
TWINING
WINKED
SWINKED
TWINKED
WINKER
WINKERS
WINKLE
TWINKLE
WINKLED
WINKLER
WINKLES
WINNER
WINNERS
WINNLE
WINNLES
WINNOW
WINNOWS
WINSEY
WINSEYS
WINTER
TWINTER
WINTERS
WINTERY
WINTLE
WINTLED
WINTLES
WIPERS
SWIPERS
WIPING
SWIPING
WIPINGS
WIPPEN
WIPPENS
WIRING
TWIRING
WIRINGS
WISARD
WISARDS
WISDOM
WISDOMS
WISENT
WISENTS
WISHED
SWISHED
WISHER
SWISHER
WISHERS
WISHES
SWISHES
WISKET
WISKETS
WISTED
TWISTED
WITCHY
SWITCHY
TWITCHY
WITGAT
WITGATS
WITHER
SWITHER
WITHERS
WITHIN
WITHING
WITTED
TWITTED
WITTER
TWITTER
WITTERS
WITTOL
WITTOLS
WIVERN
WIVERNS
WIVING
SWIVING
WIZARD
WIZARDS
WIZIER
WIZIERS
WOBBLE
WOBBLED
WOBBLER
WOBBLES
WOGGLE
WOGGLES
WOLFER
WOLFERS
WOLVER
WOLVERS
WOMBAT
WOMBATS
WOMERA
WOMERAS
WONDER
WONDERS
WONING
WONINGS
WOOBUT
WOOBUTS
WOODIE
WOODIER
WOODIES
WOOFER
WOOFERS
WOOING
WOOINGS
WOOLEN
WOOLENS
WOONED
SWOONED
WOOSEL
WOOSELL
WOOSELS
WOPPED
SWOPPED
WORDED
SWORDED
WORKER
WORKERS
WORMER
WORMERS
WORMERY
WORRAL
WORRALS
WORREL
WORRELS
WORRIT
WORRITS
WORSEN
WORSENS
WORTLE
WORTLES
WOTTED
SWOTTED
WOUBIT
WOUBITS
WOULDS
WOULDST
WOUNDS
SWOUNDS
WOWSER
WOWSERS
WRAITH
WRAITHS
WRASSE
WRASSES
WRAXLE
WRAXLED
WRAXLES
WREATH
WREATHE
WREATHS
WREATHY
WRETHE
WRETHED
WRETHES
WRIEST
OWRIEST
WRIGHT
WRIGHTS
WRITER
WRITERS
WRITHE
WRITHED
WRITHEN
WRITHES
WROATH
WROATHS
WUNNER
WUNNERS
WURLEY
WURLEYS
WUTHER
WUTHERS
WUZZLE
WUZZLED
WUZZLES
WYVERN
WYVERNS
XEROMA
XEROMAS
XYLENE
XYLENES
XYLOMA
XYLOMAS
XYLOSE
XYLOSES
XYSTER
XYSTERS
YABBER
YABBERS
YABBIE
YABBIES
YACKER
YACKERS
YAFFED
NYAFFED
YAFFLE
YAFFLES
YAGGER
YAGGERS
YAKKER
YAKKERS
YAMMER
YAMMERS
YANKER
YANKERS
YANKIE
YANKIES
YANQUI
YANQUIS
YAOURT
YAOURTS
YAPOCK
YAPOCKS
YAPPER
YAPPERS
YAPPIE
YAPPIER
YAPPIES
YAQONA
YAQONAS
YARPHA
YARPHAS
YARROW
YARROWS
YATTER
YATTERS
YAUPON
YAUPONS
YAWPER
YAWPERS
YELLOW
YELLOWS
YELLOWY
YELPER
YELPERS
YESTER
DYESTER
YESTERN
YICKER
YICKERS
YIKKER
YIKKERS
YIPPER
YIPPERS
YMPING
GYMPING
YNAMBU
YNAMBUS
YODLER
YODLERS
YOGINI
YOGINIS
YOGISM
YOGISMS
YOGURT
YOGURTS
YOJANA
YOJANAS
YOKING
YOKINGS
YONDER
YONDERS
YONKER
YONKERS
YOPPER
YOPPERS
YORKER
YORKERS
YORKIE
YORKIES
YOWLEY
YOWLEYS
YSHEND
YSHENDS
YTTRIA
YTTRIAS
YUCKER
YUCKERS
YUKATA
YUKATAS
YUMPIE
YUMPIES
YUPPIE
YUPPIES
ZABETA
ZABETAS
ZADDIK
TZADDIK
ZADDIKS
ZAFFER
ZAFFERS
ZAFFRE
ZAFFRES
ZAMANG
ZAMANGS
ZAMBUK
ZAMBUKS
ZANDER
ZANDERS
ZANIES
ZANIEST
ZAPPER
ZAPPERS
ZARAPE
ZARAPES
ZAREBA
ZAREBAS
ZARIBA
ZARIBAS
ZARNEC
ZARNECS
ZEALOT
ZEALOTS

ZEBECK
ZEBECKS
ZEBRAS
ZEBRASS
ZELANT
ZELANTS
ZENANA
ZENANAS
ZENDIK
ZENDIKS

ZENITH
ZENITHS
ZEPHYR
ZEPHYRS
ZEREBA
ZEREBAS
ZERIBA
ZERIBAS
ZESTER
ZESTERS

ZEUGMA
ZEUGMAS
ZIGZAG
ZIGZAGS
ZILLAH
ZILLAHS
ZIMMER
ZIMMERS
ZINGEL
ZINGELS

ZINGER
ZINGERS
ZINNIA
ZINNIAS
ZIPPER
ZIPPERS
ZIRCON
ZIRCONS
ZITHER
ZITHERN

ZITHERS
ZODIAC
ZODIACS
ZOMBIE
ZOMBIES
ZONATE
ZONATED
ZONING
ZONINGS
ZONULA

ZONULAE
ZONULAR
ZONULAS
ZONULE
ZONULES
ZONULET
ZONURE
ZONURES
ZOOZOO
ZOOZOOS

ZORINO
ZORINOS
ZOSTER
ZOSTERS
ZYGOMA
ZYGOMAS
ZYGOSE
ZYGOSES
ZYGOTE
ZYGOTES

ZYMASE
ZYMASES
ZYMITE
AZYMITE
ZYMITES
ZYMOME
ZYMOMES
ZYTHUM
ZYTHUMS

7-LETTER WORD HOOKS: extensible words only

ABACTOR
ABACTORS
ABALONE
ABALONES
ABANDON
ABANDONS
ABATURE
ABATURES
ABDOMEN
ABDOMENS
ABETTAL
ABETTALS
ABETTER
ABETTERS
ABETTOR
ABETTORS
ABIDING
ABIDINGS
ABIGAIL
ABIGAILS
ABILITY
LABILITY
ABJOINT
ABJOINTS
ABJURER
ABJURERS
ABLATOR
ABLATORS
ABOMASA
ABOMASAL
ABOULIA
ABOULIAS
ABREACT
ABREACTS
ABRIDGE
ABRIDGED
ABRIDGER
ABRIDGES
ABROOKE
ABROOKED
ABROOKES
ABSCIND
ABSCINDS
ABSCISE
ABSCISED
ABSCISES
ABSCISS
ABSCISSA
ABSCISSE
ABSCOND
ABSCONDS
ABSENCE
ABSENCES
ABSINTH

ABSINTHE
ABSINTHS
ABSOLVE
ABSOLVED
ABSOLVER
ABSOLVES
ABSTAIN
ABSTAINS
ABTHANE
ABTHANES
ABUSAGE
ABUSAGES
ABUSION
ABUSIONS
ABUTTAL
ABUTTALS
ABUTTER
ABUTTERS
ACADEME
ACADEMES
ACALEPH
ACALEPHE
ACALEPHS
ACANTHA
ACANTHAS
ACAPNIA
ACAPNIAS
ACATOUR
ACATOURS
ACCEDER
ACCEDERS
ACCIDIE
ACCIDIES
ACCINGE
ACCINGED
ACCINGES
ACCLAIM
ACCLAIMS
ACCOAST
ACCOASTS
ACCOMPT
ACCOMPTS
ACCOUNT
ACCOUNTS
ACCOURT
ACCOURTS
ACCRETE
ACCRETED
ACCRETES
ACCRUAL
ACCRUALS
ACCURSE
ACCURSED
ACCURSES

ACCUSAL
ACCUSALS
ACCUSER
ACCUSERS
ACERATE
LACERATE
MACERATE
ACETATE
ACETATES
ACETONE
ACETONES
ACHARYA
ACHARYAS
ACHENIA
ACHENIAL
ACHIEVE
ACHIEVED
ACHIEVER
ACHIEVES
ACKNOWN
ACKNOWNE
ACOLYTE
ACOLYTES
ACOLYTH
ACOLYTHS
ACONITE
TACONITE
ACONITES
ACOUCHI
ACOUCHIS
ACQUEST
ACQUESTS
ACQUIRE
ACQUIRED
ACQUIRES
ACQUIST
ACQUISTS
ACQUITE
ACQUITES
ACREAGE
ACREAGES
ACRIDIN
ACRIDINE
ACRIDINS
ACROBAT
ACROBATS
ACROGEN
ACROGENS
ACROMIA
ACROMIAL
ACRONYM
ACRONYMS
ACROTER
ACROTERS

ACRYLIC
ACRYLICS
ACTINIA
ACTINIAE
ACTINIAN
ACTINIAS
ACTINON
ACTINONS
ACTIONS
FACTIONS
PACTIONS
TACTIONS
ACTUATE
ACTUATED
ACTUATES
ACTURES
FACTURES
ACUSHLA
ACUSHLAS
ADAMANT
ADAMANTS
ADAPTER
ADAPTERS
ADAPTOR
ADAPTORS
ADDLING
DADDLING
FADDLING
PADDLING
RADDLING
SADDLING
WADDLING
ADDUCER
ADDUCERS
ADENINE
ADENINES
ADENOID
ADENOIDS
ADENOMA
ADENOMAS
ADERMIN
ADERMINS
ADHARMA
ADHARMAS
ADHERER
ADHERERS
ADHIBIT
ADHIBITS
ADJOINT
ADJOINTS
ADJOURN
ADJOURNS
ADJUDGE
ADJUDGED

ADJUDGES
ADJUNCT
ADJUNCTS
ADLANDS
BADLANDS
ADMIRAL
ADMIRALS
ADMIRER
ADMIRERS
ADONISE
ADONISED
ADONISES
ADONIZE
ADONIZED
ADONIZES
ADOPTER
ADOPTERS
ADRENAL
ADRENALS
ADULATE
RADULATE
ADULATED
ADULATES
ADVANCE
TADVANCE
ADVANCED
ADVANCES
ADVERSE
ADVERSER
ADVISER
ADVISERS
ADVISOR
ADVISORS
ADVISORY
AERATOR
AERATORS
AEROBIC
AEROBICS
AEROSOL
AEROSOLS
AFFAIRE
AFFAIRES
AFFEARE
AFFEARED
AFFEARES
AFFICHE
AFFICHES
AFFLICT
AFFLICTS
AFFOORD
AFFOORDS
AFFORCE
AFFORCED
AFFORCES

AFFRONT
AFFRONTE
AFFRONTS
AGACANT
AGACANTE
AGAMOID
AGAMOIDS
AGELAST
AGELASTS
AGELESS
WAGELESS
AGGRACE
AGGRACED
AGGRACES
AGGRADE
AGGRADED
AGGRADES
AGGRATE
AGGRATED
AGGRATES
AGILITY
VAGILITY
AGINNER
AGINNERS
AGISTER
MAGISTER
AGISTERS
AGISTOR
AGISTORS
AGITATE
AGITATED
AGITATES
AGITATO
AGITATOR
AGNATES
MAGNATES
AGNOMEN
AGNOMENS
AGNOSIA
AGNOSIAS
AGONISE
AGONISED
AGONISES
AGONIST
AGONISTS
AGONIZE
AGONIZED
AGONIZES
AGRAFFE
AGRAFFES
AIDANCE
AIDANCES
AIDLESS
MAIDLESS

AILANTO
AILANTOS
AILERON
TAILERON
AILERONS
AILETTE
AILETTES
AILMENT
BAILMENT
AILMENTS
AIRBASE
AIRBASES
AIRFLOW
AIRFLOWS
AIRFOIL
AIRFOILS
AIRHEAD
AIRHEADS
AIRHOLE
AIRHOLES
AIRIEST
HAIRIEST
LAIRIEST
VAIRIEST
AIRINGS
FAIRINGS
PAIRINGS
AIRLESS
HAIRLESS
AIRLIFT
AIRLIFTS
AIRLINE
HAIRLINE
AIRLINER
AIRLINES
AIRLOCK
AIRLOCKS
AIRMAIL
AIRMAILS
AIRPORT
AIRPORTS
AIRSHIP
AIRSHIPS
AIRSIDE
AIRSIDES
AIRSTOP
AIRSTOPS
AIRTIME
AIRTIMES
AIRWARD
AIRWARDS
AIRWAVE
AIRWAVES
AIRWAYS

FAIRWAYS
AISLING
AISLINGS
AJUTAGE
AJUTAGES
AKVAVIT
AKVAVITS
ALAMEDA
ALAMEDAS
ALAMODE
ALAMODES
ALANINE
ALANINES
ALANNAH
ALANNAHS
ALBERTS
HALBERTS
ALBUMEN
ALBUMENS
ALBUMIN
ALBUMINS
ALCAIDE
ALCAIDES
ALCALDE
ALCALDES
ALCAYDE
ALCAYDES
ALCAZAR
ALCAZARS
ALCHERA
ALCHERAS
ALCOHOL
ALCOHOLS
ALCORZA
ALCORZAS
ALECOST
ALECOSTS
ALEMBIC
ALEMBICS
ALEPINE
ALEPINES
ALERION
ALERIONS
ALEURON
ALEURONE
ALEURONS
ALFALFA
ALFALFAS
ALFAQUI
ALFAQUIS
ALFORJA
ALFORJAS
ALGEBRA
ALGEBRAS
ALGESIA
ALGESIAS
ALICANT
ALICANTS
ALIDADE
ALIDADES
ALIENEE
ALIENEES
ALIENOR
ALIENORS
ALIFORM
PALIFORM
ALIGNED
MALIGNED
ALIMENT
ALIMENTS
ALIMONY
PALIMONY
ALIPEDS
TALIPEDS
ALIZARI
ALIZARIN
ALIZARIS
ALKALIS
ALKALISE
ALKANET
ALKANETS
ALLAYER
ALLAYERS
ALLEDGE
ALLEDGED
ALLEDGES
ALLEGER
ALLEGERS
ALLEGGE
ALLEGGED
ALLEGGES
ALLEGRO
ALLEGROS
ALLHEAL
ALLHEALS
ALLISES
GALLISES
ALLIUMS
BALLIUMS
GALLIUMS
ALLNESS
TALLNESS
ALLONGE
ALLONGES
ALLONYM
ALLONYMS
ALLOWED
FALLOWED
GALLOWED
HALLOWED
SALLOWED
TALLOWED
WALLOWED
ALLSEED
ALLSEEDS
ALLURER
ALLURERS
ALLUVIA
ALLUVIAL
ALLYING
DALLYING
GALLYING
RALLYING
SALLYING
TALLYING
ALMANAC
ALMANACS
ALMIRAH
ALMIRAHS
ALMONER
ALMONERS
ALNAGER
ALNAGERS
ALODIUM
ALODIUMS
ALOETIC
ALOETICS
ALPHORN
ALPHORNS
ALTERED
FALTERED
HALTERED
PALTERED
ALTERNE
ALTERNES
ALTESSE
ALTESSES
ALTEZZA
ALTEZZAS
ALTHAEA
ALTHAEAS
ALTHORN
ALTHORNS
ALUMINA
ALUMINAS
ALUMIUM
ALUMIUMS
ALUNITE
ALUNITES
ALVEOLE
ALVEOLES
ALYSSUM
ALYSSUMS
AMALGAM
AMALGAMS
AMANITA
AMANITAS
AMARANT
AMARANTH
AMARANTS
AMASSES
CAMASSES
AMATEUR
AMATEURS
AMATION
AMATIONS
AMBERED
CAMBERED
AMBIENT
AMBIENTS
AMBLERS
GAMBLERS
RAMBLERS
AMBLING
GAMBLING
HAMBLING
LAMBLING
RAMBLING
WAMBLING
AMBLINGS
AMBONES
JAMBONES
AMBROID
AMBROIDS
AMENAGE
AMENAGED
AMENAGES
AMENDER
AMENDERS
AMENTIA
AMENTIAS
AMENTUM
RAMENTUM
AMILDAR
AMILDARS
AMMETER
AMMETERS
AMMIRAL
AMMIRALS
AMMONAL
AMMONALS
AMMONIA
AMMONIAC
AMMONIAS
AMNESIA
AMNESIAC
AMNESIAS
AMNESIC
AMNESICS
AMORISM
AMORISMS
AMORIST
AMORISTS
AMOROSA
AMOROSAS
AMOROSO
AMOROSOS
AMOSITE
AMOSITES
AMPHORA
AMPHORAE
AMPOULE
AMPOULES
AMPULLA
AMPULLAE
AMPUTEE
AMPUTEES
AMTRACK
AMTRACKS
AMYGDAL
AMYGDALA
AMYGDALE
AMYGDALS
AMYLASE
AMYLASES
AMYLENE
AMYLENES
AMYLOID
AMYLOIDS
ANAEMIA
ANAEMIAS
ANAGOGE
ANAGOGES
ANAGRAM
ANAGRAMS
ANALYSE
ANALYSED
ANALYSER
ANALYSES
ANALYST
ANALYSTS
ANALYZE
ANALYZED
ANALYZER
ANALYZES
ANAPEST
ANAPESTS
ANATASE
ANATASES
ANCIENT
ANCIENTS
ANDANTE
ANDANTES
ANDIRON
ANDIRONS
ANDROID
ANDROIDS
ANDVILE
ANDVILES
ANELACE
ANELACES
ANEMONE
ANEMONES
ANEROID
ANEROIDS
ANEURIN
ANEURINS
ANGEKOK
ANGEKOKS
ANGELIC
ANGELICA
ANGERED
DANGERED
ANGIOMA
ANGIOMAS
ANGLERS
DANGLERS
JANGLERS
MANGLERS
TANGLERS
WANGLERS
ANGLING
CANGLING
DANGLING
FANGLING
GANGLING
JANGLING
MANGLING
TANGLING
WANGLING
ANGLINGS
ANGLIST
ANGLISTS
ANGRIES
ANGRIEST
ANGUINE
SANGUINE
ANGUISH
LANGUISH
ANILINE
ANILINES
ANIMATE
ANIMATED
ANIMATER
ANIMATES
ANIMISM
ANIMISMS
ANIMIST
ANIMISTS
ANISEED
ANISEEDS
ANKLONG
ANKLONGS
ANKLUNG
ANKLUNGS
ANNATES
TANNATES
ANNATTA
ANNATTAS
ANNATTO
ANNATTOS
ANNELID
ANNELIDS
ANNICUT
ANNICUTS
ANNOYED
TANNOYED
ANNOYER
ANNOYERS
ANNULAR
CANNULAR
ANNULARS
ANNULET
ANNULETS
ANODISE
ANODISED
ANODISES
ANODIZE
ANODIZED
ANODIZES
ANODYNE
ANODYNES
ANONYMA
ANONYMAS
ANOSMIA
ANOSMIAS
ANTACID
ANTACIDS
ANTARAS
TANTARAS
ANTBEAR
ANTBEARS
ANTBIRD
ANTBIRDS
ANTEFIX
ANTEFIXA
ANTENNA
ANTENNAE
ANTENNAL
ANTENNAS
ANTHERS
PANTHERS
ANTICKE
ANTICKED
ANTIENT
ANTIENTS
ANTIGEN
ANTIGENS
ANTILOG
ANTILOGS
ANTILOGY
ANTINGS
BANTINGS
CANTINGS
PANTINGS
RANTINGS
WANTINGS
ANTIQUE
ANTIQUED
ANTIQUES
ANTLERS
PANTLERS
ANTLION
ANTLIONS
ANTONYM
ANTONYMS
ANTONYMY
APADANA
APADANAS
APAGOGE
APAGOGES
APANAGE
APANAGED
APANAGES
APATITE
APATITES
APEHOOD
APEHOODS
APEPSIA
APEPSIAS
APERIES
NAPERIES
APHAGIA
APHAGIAS
APHASIA
APHASIAC
APHASIAS
APHELIA
APHELIAN
APHIDES
RAPHIDES
APHONIA
APHONIAS
APLANAT
APLANATS
APLASIA
APLASIAS
APOCOPE
APOCOPES
APOPLEX
APOPLEXY
APOSTIL
APOSTILS
APOSTLE
APOSTLES
APOTHEM
APOTHEMS
APPARAT
APPARATS
APPAREL
APPARELS
APPEASE
APPEASED
APPEASER
APPEASES
APPERIL
APPERILL
APPERILS
APPLAUD
APPLAUDS
APPLIER
APPLIERS
APPOINT
APPOINTS
APPORTS
RAPPORTS
APPOSER
APPOSERS
APPRISE
APPRISED
APPRISER
APPRISES
APPRIZE
APPRIZED
APPRIZER
APPRIZES
APPROOF
APPROOFS
APPROVE
APPROVED
APPROVER
APPROVES
APPULSE
APPULSES
APRAXIA
APRAXIAS
APRICOT
APRICOTS
AQUAFER
AQUAFERS

AQUARIA
AQUARIAN
AQUATIC
AQUATICS
AQUAVIT
AQUAVITS
AQUIFER
AQUIFERS
AQUILON
AQUILONS
ARABICA
ARABICAS
ARABINS
CARABINS
ARABISE
ARABISED
ARABISES
ARABIZE
ARABIZED
ARABIZES
ARANEID
ARANEIDS
ARAROBA
ARAROBAS
ARBITER
ARBITERS
ARBLAST
ARBLASTS
ARBORET
ARBORETA
ARBORETS
ARBOURS
HARBOURS
ARCHERS
MARCHERS
ARCHING
MARCHING
PARCHING
ARCHIVE
ARCHIVED
ARCHIVES
ARCHLET
ARCHLETS
ARCHWAY
ARCHWAYS
ARCINGS
FARCINGS
ARCKING
ARCKINGS
ARCTIID
ARCTIIDS
ARCUATE
ARCUATED
ARDRIGH
ARDRIGHS
AREAWAY
AREAWAYS
AREFIED
RAREFIED
AREFIES
RAREFIES
ARGENTS
MARGENTS
ARGUSES
SARGUSES
ARGYRIA
ARGYRIAS
ARIETTA
ARIETTAS
ARIETTE
ARIETTES
ARISHES
GARISHES
MARISHES
PARISHES
ARMBAND
ARMBANDS
ARMHOLE
ARMHOLES
ARMIGER
ARMIGERO
ARMIGERS
ARMILLA
ARMILLAE
ARMILLAS
ARMLESS
HARMLESS
ARMLOCK
ARMLOCKS
ARMOIRE
ARMOIRES
ARNOTTO
ARNOTTOS
AROUSAL
CAROUSAL
AROUSALS
AROUSED
CAROUSED
AROUSER
CAROUSER
AROUSERS
AROUSES
CAROUSES
ARPENTS
PARPENTS
ARRACKS
BARRACKS
CARRACKS
ARRAIGN
DARRAIGN
ARRAIGNS
ARRANGE
ARRANGED
ARRANGER
ARRANGES
ARRASES
NARRASES
TARRASES
ARRAYAL
ARRAYALS
ARRAYED
WARRAYED
ARRAYER
ARRAYERS
ARREEDE
ARREEDES
ARRIAGE
CARRIAGE
MARRIAGE
ARRIAGES
ARRIERO
ARRIEROS
ARRIVAL
ARRIVALS
ARROWED
FARROWED
HARROWED
MARROWED
NARROWED
TARROWED
ARSENAL
ARSENALS
ARSENIC
ARSENICS
ARSHEEN
ARSHEENS
ARSHINE
ARSHINES
ARTICLE
PARTICLE
ARTICLED
ARTICLES
ARTIEST
TARTIEST
WARTIEST
ARTISAN
BARTISAN
PARTISAN
ARTISANS
ARTISTE
ARTISTES
ARTLESS
WARTLESS
ARTSIES
ARTSIEST
ARTWORK
PARTWORK
ARTWORKS
ARUGULA
ARUGULAS
ASCARID
ASCARIDS
ASCETIC
ASCETICS
ASCIDIA
ASCIDIAN
ASCRIBE
ASCRIBED
ASCRIBES
ASEPTIC
ASEPTICS
ASHIEST
HASHIEST
MASHIEST
WASHIEST
ASHRAMA
ASHRAMAS
ASINICO
ASINICOS
ASKANCE
ASKANCED
ASKANCES
ASPERGE
ASPERGED
ASPERGER
ASPERGES
ASPERSE
ASPERSED
ASPERSES
ASPHALT
ASPHALTS
ASPIRIN
ASPIRING
ASPIRINS
ASSAGAI
ASSAGAIS
ASSAILS
VASSAILS
WASSAILS
ASSAULT
ASSAULTS
ASSAYER
ASSAYERS
ASSEGAI
ASSEGAIS
ASSEVER
ASSEVERS
ASSHOLE
ASSHOLES
ASSIEGE
ASSIEGED
ASSIEGES
ASSISTS
BASSISTS
ASSIZER
ASSIZERS
ASSUAGE
ASSUAGED
ASSUAGES
ASSURED
ASSUREDS
ASSURER
ASSURERS
ASSWAGE
TASSWAGE
ASSWAGED
ASSWAGES
ASTABLE
TASTABLE
WASTABLE
ASTATKI
ASTATKIS
ASTEISM
ASTEISMS
ASTERIA
ASTERIAS
ASTERID
ASTERIDS
ASTHORE
ASTHORES
ASTILBE
ASTILBES
ASTOUND
ASTOUNDS
ASTRICT
ASTRICTS
ASTROID
ASTROIDS
ATABRIN
ATABRINS
ATAGHAN
YATAGHAN
ATAGHANS
ATALAYA
ATALAYAS
ATAVISM
ATAVISMS
ATEBRIN
ATEBRINS
ATELIER
ATELIERS
ATHANOR
ATHANORS
ATHEISE
ATHEISED
ATHEISES
ATHEISM
ATHEISMS
ATHEIST
ATHEISTS
ATHEIZE
ATHEIZED
ATHEIZES
ATHLETA
ATHLETAS
ATHLETE
ATHLETES
ATISHOO
ATISHOOS
ATOMISE
ATOMISED
ATOMISER
ATOMISES
ATOMISM
ATOMISMS
ATOMIST
ATOMISTS
ATOMIZE
ATOMIZED
ATOMIZER
ATOMIZES
ATONING
BATONING
ATRESIA
ATRESIAS
ATRIUMS
NATRIUMS
ATROPIA
ATROPIAS
ATROPIN
ATROPINE
ATROPINS
ATTACHE
ATTACHED
ATTACHES
ATTAINT
ATTAINTS
ATTEMPT
ATTEMPTS
ATTRACT
ATTRACTS
ATTRIST
ATTRISTS
ATTRITE
ATTRITED
ATTRITES
ATTUITE
ATTUITED
ATTUITES
AUBERGE
AUBERGES
AUCTION
AUCTIONS
AUDIBLE
AUDIBLES
AUDIENT
AUDIENTS
AUDITOR
AUDITORS
AUDITORY
AUFGABE
AUFGABES
AUGMENT
AUGMENTS
AUGURER
AUGURERS
AUGUSTE
AUGUSTER
AUGUSTES
AULDEST
CAULDEST
AULNAGE
AULNAGER
AULNAGES
AUNTERS
DAUNTERS
HAUNTERS
SAUNTERS
TAUNTERS
VAUNTERS
AUNTIES
JAUNTIES
AUREATE
LAUREATE
AURELIA
AURELIAN
AURELIAS
AUREOLA
AUREOLAS
AUREOLE
AUREOLED
AUREOLES
AURICLE
AURICLED
AURICLES
AUSPICE
AUSPICES
AUSTERE
AUSTERER
AUTEURS
HAUTEURS
AUTOCAR
AUTOCARP
AUTOCARS
AUTOCUE
AUTOCUES
AUTOMAT
AUTOMATA
AUTOMATE
AUTOMATS
AUTONYM
TAUTONYM
AUTONYMS
AUTOVAC
AUTOVACS
AUXETIC
AUXETICS
AVARICE
AVARICES
AVENGER
AVENGERS
AVENTRE
AVENTRED
AVENTRES
AVERAGE
AVERAGED
AVERAGES
AVIATOR
AVIATORS
AVIETTE
AVIETTES
AVIONIC
AVIONICS
AVOCADO
AVOCADOS
AWAKING
AWAKINGS
AWFULLY
LAWFULLY
AWLBIRD
AWLBIRDS
AWNIEST
LAWNIEST
TAWNIEST
YAWNIEST
AWNINGS
DAWNINGS
FAWNINGS
YAWNINGS
AXILLAE
MAXILLAE
AXILLAR
AXILLARY
AXINITE
AXINITES
AXOLOTL
AXOLOTLS
AYWORDS
NAYWORDS
AZIMUTH
AZIMUTHS
AZOTISE
AZOTISED
AZOTISES
AZOTIZE
AZOTIZED
AZOTIZES
AZULEJO
AZULEJOS
AZURINE
AZURINES
AZURITE
LAZURITE
AZURITES
AZYMITE
AZYMITES
BABASSU
BABASSUS
BABBITT
BABBITTS
BABBLER
BABBLERS
BABICHE
BABICHES
BABUCHE
BABUCHES
BABUDOM
BABUDOMS
BABUISM
BABUISMS
BACCARA
BACCARAS
BACCARAT
BACKBIT
BACKBITE
BACKHOE
BACKHOES
BACKING
BACKINGS
BACKLOG
BACKLOGS
BACKLOT
BACKLOTS
BACKPAY
BACKPAYS
BACKSAW
BACKSAWS
BACKSET
BACKSETS
BACKSEY

BACKSEYS
BACLAVA
BACLAVAS
BACONER
BACONERS
BACULUM
BACULUMS
BAFFLER
BAFFLERS
BAGARRE
BAGARRES
BAGASSE
BAGASSES
BAGGAGE
BAGGAGES
BAGGIES
BAGGIEST
BAGGING
BAGGINGS
BAGPIPE
BAGPIPER
BAGPIPES
BAILIFF
BAILIFFS
BAILLIE
BAILLIES
BAINITE
BAINITES
BAITING
BAITINGS
BAKLAVA
BAKLAVAS
BALADIN
BALADINE
BALADINS
BALANCE
BALANCED
BALANCER
BALANCES
BALDRIC
BALDRICK
BALDRICS
BALISTA
BALISTAE
BALISTAS
BALKING
BALKINGS
BALLADE
BALLADED
BALLADES
BALLANT
BALLANTS
BALLAST
BALLASTS
BALLING
BALLINGS
BALLIUM
BALLIUMS
BALLOON
BALLOONS
BALONEY
BALONEYS
BAMBINO
BAMBINOS
BANDAGE
BANDAGED
BANDAGES
BANDANA
BANDANAS
BANDEAU
BANDEAUX
BANDIES
BANDIEST
BANDING
ABANDING
BANDINGS
BANDOOK
BANDOOKS
BANDORA
BANDORAS
BANDORE
BANDORES
BANDROL
BANDROLS
BANDURA
BANDURAS
BANGING
BANGINGS
BANKING
BANKINGS
BANKSIA
BANKSIAS
BANNOCK
BANNOCKS
BANQUET
BANQUETS
BANSHEE
BANSHEES
BANTENG
BANTENGS
BANTING
BANTINGS
BAPTISE
BAPTISED
BAPTISES
BAPTISM
BAPTISMS
BAPTIST
BAPTISTS
BAPTIZE
BAPTIZED
BAPTIZES
BARACAN
BARACANS
BARBATE
BARBATED
BARBOLA
BARBOLAS
BARBULE
BARBULES
BARCHAN
BARCHANE
BARCHANS
BARGAIN
BARGAINS
BARGEES
BARGEESE
BARGEST
BARGESTS
BARILLA
BARILLAS
BARKHAN
BARKHANS
BARMAID
BARMAIDS
BARMKIN
BARMKINS
BAROCCO
BAROCCOS
BARONET
BARONETS
BARONNE
BARONNES
BAROQUE
BAROQUES
BARRACE
BARRACES
BARRACK
BARRACKS
BARRAGE
BARRAGES
BARRICO
BARRICOS
BARRIER
BARRIERS
BARRING
BARRINGS
BARWOOD
BARWOODS
BARYTON
BARYTONE
BARYTONS
BASCULE
BASCULES
BASEMEN
BASEMENT
BASENJI
BASENJIS
BASHING
ABASHING
BASHINGS
BASHLIK
BASHLIKS
BASIDIA
BASIDIAL
BASINET
BASINETS
BASOCHE
BASOCHES
BASSIST
BASSISTS
BASSOON
BASSOONS
BASTARD
BASTARDS
BASTARDY
BASTIDE
BASTIDES
BASTING
BASTINGS
BASTION
BASTIONS
BATABLE
ABATABLE
BATHTUB
BATHTUBS
BATISTE
BATISTES
BATTERO
BATTEROS
BATTILL
BATTILLS
BATTING
BATTINGS
BATTLER
BATTLERS
BATTUTA
BATTUTAS
BAUCHLE
BAUCHLED
BAUCHLES
BAUDRIC
BAUDRICK
BAUDRICS
BAUXITE
BAUXITES
BAWCOCK
BAWCOCKS
BAWDIES
BAWDIEST
BAWDKIN
BAWDKINS
BAWLING
BAWLINGS
BAYONET
BAYONETS
BAZOOKA
BAZOOKAS
BAZOUKI
BAZOUKIS
BEADING
BEADINGS
BEAGLER
BEAGLERS
BEAMING
BEAMINGS
BEAMLET
BEAMLETS
BEANBAG
BEANBAGS
BEARDIE
BEARDIES
BEARING
ABEARING
BEARINGS
BEASTIE
BEASTIES
BEATING
BEATINGS
BEATNIK
BEATNIKS
BEAUFET
BEAUFETS
BEAUFIN
BEAUFINS
BEBEERU
BEBEERUS
BECASSE
BECASSES
BECHARM
BECHARMS
BECLOUD
BECLOUDS
BEDAWIN
BEDAWINS
BEDDING
BEDDINGS
BEDERAL
BEDERALS
BEDEVIL
BEDEVILS
BEDIGHT
BEDIGHTS
BEDIZEN
BEDIZENS
BEDOUIN
BEDOUINS
BEDPOST
BEDPOSTS
BEDROCK
BEDROCKS
BEDROOM
BEDROOMS
BEDSIDE
BEDSIDES
BEDSORE
BEDSORES
BEDTICK
BEDTICKS
BEDTIME
BEDTIMES
BEDWARD
BEDWARDS
BEDWARF
BEDWARFS
BEEFALO
BEEFALOS
BEEHIVE
BEEHIVES
BEELINE
BEELINES
BEERAGE
BEERAGES
BEFFANA
BEFFANAS
BEGGING
BEGGINGS
BEGHARD
BEGHARDS
BEGINNE
BEGINNER
BEGINNES
BEGLOOM
BEGLOOMS
BEGONIA
BEGONIAS
BEGORRA
BEGORRAH
BEGRIME
BEGRIMED
BEGRIMES
BEGUILE
BEGUILED
BEGUILER
BEGUILES
BEGUINE
BEGUINES
BEHIGHT
BEHIGHTS
BEHOOVE
BEHOOVED
BEHOOVES
BEIGNET
BEIGNETS
BEJEWEL
BEJEWELS
BEKNAVE
BEKNAVED
BEKNAVES
BELABOR
BELABORS
BELCHER
BELCHERS
BELDAME
BELDAMES
BELGARD
BELGARDS
BELIEVE
BELIEVED
BELIEVER
BELIEVES
BELLHOP
BELLHOPS
BELOVED
BELOVEDS
BELTING
BFLTINGS
BELTWAY
BELTWAYS
BEMEDAL
BEMEDALS
BEMOUTH
BEMOUTHS
BENCHER
BENCHERS
BENDING
BENDINGS
BENDLET
BENDLETS
BENEFIC
BENEFICE
BENEFIT
BENEFITS
BENIGHT
BENIGHTS
BENISON
BENISONS
BENZENE
BENZENES
BENZINE
BENZINES
BENZOIN
BENZOINS
BENZOLE
BENZOLES
BENZOYL
BENZOYLS
BEPAINT
BEPAINTS
BEPEARL
BEPEARLS
BEPROSE
BEPROSED
BEPROSES
BEQUEST
BEQUESTS
BERCEAU
BERCEAUX
BEREAVE
BEREAVED
BEREAVEN
BEREAVES
BERGAMA
BERGAMAS
BERGERE
BERGERES
BERGYLT
BERGYLTS
BERLINE
BERLINES
BERSERK
BERSERKS
BESAINT
BESAINTS
BESEEKE
BESEEKES
BESHAME
BESHAMED
BESHAMES
BESHINE
BESHINES
BESHREW
BESHREWS
BESIEGE
BESIEGED
BESIEGER
BESIEGES
BESLAVE
BESLAVED
BESLAVER
BESLAVES
BESMEAR
BESMEARS
BESPEAK
BESPEAKS
BESPEED
BESPEEDS
BESPICE
BESPICED
BESPICES
BESPOKE
BESPOKEN
BESPORT
BESPORTS
BESPOUT
BESPOUTS
BESTAIN
BESTAINS
BESTEAD
BESTEADS
BESTIAL
BESTIALS
BESTICK
BESTICKS
BESTILL
BESTILLS
BESTORM
BESTORMS
BESTREW
BESTREWN
BESTREWS
BESTRID
BESTRIDE
BETAINE
BETAINES
BETEEME
BETEEMED
BETEEMES
BETHINK
BETHINKS
BETHUMB
BETHUMBS
BETHUMP
BETHUMPS
BETITLE
BETITLED
BETITLES
BETOKEN
BETOKENS
BETREAD
BETREADS
BETROTH
BETROTHS
BETTERS
ABETTERS
BETTING
ABETTING
BETTINGS
BETTORS
ABETTORS

BETWEEN
BETWEENS
BEWHORE
BEWHORED
BEWHORES
BEZIQUE
BEZIQUES
BHANGRA
BHANGRAS
BHISTEE
BHISTEES
BIASING
BIASINGS
BIBCOCK
BIBCOCKS
BIBELOT
BIBELOTS
BIBLIST
BIBLISTS
BICORNE
BICORNES
BICYCLE
BICYCLED
BICYCLES
BIDARKA
BIDARKAS
BIDDING
BIDDINGS
BIDINGS
ABIDINGS
BIFOCAL
BIFOCALS
BIGENER
BIGENERS
BIGFOOT
BIGFOOTS
BIGHORN
BIGHORNS
BIKEWAY
BIKEWAYS
BILIMBI
BILIMBIS
BILLING
BILLINGS
BILLION
BILLIONS
BILTONG
BILTONGS
BINDING
BINDINGS
BINOCLE
BINOCLES
BIOCIDE
BIOCIDES
BIOPHOR
BIOPHORE
BIOPHORS
BIOTITE
BIOTITES
BIOTYPE
BIOTYPES
BIPLANE
BIPLANES
BIRDING
BIRDINGS
BIRETTA
BIRETTAS
BIRKIES
BIRKIEST
BIRLING
BIRLINGS
BIRLINN
BIRLINNS
BIRYANI
BIRYANIS
BISCUIT
BISCUITS
BISCUITY
BISMUTH
BISMUTHS
BISTORT
BISTORTS
BITTERN
BITTERNS
BITTIES
BITTIEST
BITTOCK
BITTOCKS
BITTOUR
BITTOURS
BITUMEN
BITUMENS
BIVALVE
BIVALVES
BIVOUAC
BIVOUACS
BLABBER
BLABBERS
BLACKEN
BLACKENS
BLADDER
BLADDERS
BLADDERY
BLAGGER
BLAGGERS
BLANKET
BLANKETS
BLANKETY
BLARNEY
BLARNEYS
BLASTER
BLASTERS
BLATHER
BLATHERS
BLATTER
BLATTERS
BLAUBOK
BLAUBOKS
BLAWORT
BLAWORTS
BLEATER
BLEATERS
BLEEDER
BLEEDERS
BLEEPER
BLEEPERS
BLENDER
BLENDERS
BLESBOK
BLESBOKS
BLETHER
BLETHERS
BLEWART
BLEWARTS
BLINDER
BLINDERS
BLINKER
BLINKERS
BLINTZE
BLINTZES
BLISTER
BLISTERS
BLISTERY
BLITHER
BLITHERS
BLOATER
BLOATERS
BLOCKER
BLOCKERS
BLONDES
BLONDEST
BLOOMER
BLOOMERS
BLOOMERY
BLOOPER
BLOOPERS
BLOOSME
BLOOSMED
BLOOSMES
BLOSSOM
BLOSSOMS
BLOSSOMY
BLOTTER
BLOTTERS
BLOUBOK
BLOUBOKS
BLOUSON
BLOUSONS
BLOWGUN
BLOWGUNS
BLOWIES
BLOWIEST
BLOWJOB
BLOWJOBS
BLUBBER
BLUBBERS
BLUCHER
BLUCHERS
BLUDGER
BLUDGERS
BLUECAP
BLUECAPS
BLUEING
BLUEINGS
BLUETTE
BLUETTES
BLUFFER
BLUFFERS
BLUNDER
BLUNDERS
BLUNGER
BLUNGERS
BLUNKER
BLUNKERS
BLUSHER
BLUSHERS
BLUSHET
BLUSHETS
BLUSTER
BLUSTERS
BLUSTERY
BOARDER
BOARDERS
BOASTER
BOASTERS
BOATING
BOATINGS
BOBSLED
BOBSLEDS
BOBTAIL
BOBTAILS
BODGIES
BODGIEST
BODHRAN
BODHRANS
BODIKIN
BODIKINS
BOGBEAN
BOGBEANS
BOGGARD
BOGGARDS
BOGGART
BOGGARTS
BOGGLER
BOGGLERS
BOGLAND
BOGLANDS
BOGYISM
BOGYISMS
BOILING
BOILINGS
BOLIVAR
BOLIVARS
BOLLARD
BOLLARDS
BOLLOCK
BOLLOCKS
BOLONEY
BOLONEYS
BOLSHIE
BOLSHIER
BOLSHIES
BOLSTER
BOLSTERS
BOLTING
BOLTINGS
BOMBARD
BOMBARDS
BOMBAST
BOMBASTS
BOMBLET
BOMBLETS
BOMBORA
BOMBORAS
BONAMIA
BONAMIAS
BONANZA
BONANZAS
BONDAGE
BONDAGER
BONDAGES
BONDING
BONDINGS
BONESET
BONESETS
BONFIRE
BONFIRES
BONISTS
EBONISTS
BONNIES
BONNIEST
BOOBOOK
BOOBOOKS
BOOKIES
BOOKIEST
BOOKING
BOOKINGS
BOOKLET
BOOKLETS
BOOKSIE
BOOKSIER
BOOMING
BOOMINGS
BOOMLET
BOOMLETS
BOOSTER
BOOSTERS
BOOTLEG
BOOTLEGS
BORAZON
BORAZONS
BORDURE
BORDURES
BOREDOM
BOREDOMS
BORNITE
BORNITES
BORONIA
BORONIAS
BOROUGH
BOROUGHS
BORSCHT
BORSCHTS
BORSTAL
BORSTALL
BORSTALS
BOSCAGE
BOSCAGES
BOSKAGE
BOSKAGES
BOSQUET
BOSQUETS
BOTARGO
BOTARGOS
BOTCHER
BOTCHERS
BOTCHERY
BOTHOLE
BOTHOLES
BOTTEGA
BOTTEGAS
BOTTINE
BOTTINES
BOTTLER
BOTTLERS
BOUCHEE
BOUCHEES
BOUDOIR
BOUDOIRS
BOUILLI
BOUILLIS
BOULDER
BOULDERS
BOULTER
BOULTERS
BOUNCER
BOUNCERS
BOUNDED
ABOUNDED
BOUNDEN
YBOUNDEN
BOUNDER
BOUNDERS
BOUQUET
BOUQUETS
BOURBON
BOURBONS
BOURDER
BOURDERS
BOURDON
BOURDONS
BOURKHA
BOURKHAS
BOURLAW
BOURLAWS
BOURREE
BOURREES
BOUTADE
BOUTADES
BOWHEAD
BOWHEADS
BOWKNOT
BOWKNOTS
BOWLDER
BOWLDERS
BOWLFUL
BOWLFULS
BOWLINE
BOWLINES
BOWLING
BOWLINGS
BOWSHOT
BOWSHOTS
BOWYANG
BOWYANGS
BOXROOM
BOXROOMS
BOXWOOD
BOXWOODS
BOYCOTT
BOYCOTTS
BOYHOOD
BOYHOODS
BRABBLE
BRABBLED
BRABBLES
BRACHET
BRACHETS
BRACHIA
BRACHIAL
BRACKEN
BRACKENS
BRACKET
BRACKETS
BRADAWL
BRADAWLS
BRAIDED
ABRAIDED
BRAMBLE
BRAMBLED
BRAMBLES
BRANDER
BRANDERS
BRANGLE
BRANGLED
BRANGLES
BRANSLE
BRANSLES
BRANTLE
BRANTLES
BRASERO
BRASEROS
BRASHES
BRASHEST
BRASIER
BRASIERS
BRASSET
BRASSETS
BRASSIE
BRASSIER
BRASSIES
BRATTLE
BRATTLED
BRATTLES
BRAVADO
BRAVADOS
BRAVURA
BRAVURAS
BRAWLER
BRAWLERS
BRAYING
ABRAYING
BRAZIER
BRAZIERS
BREADTH
BREADTHS
BREAKER
BREAKERS
BREATHE
BREATHED
BREATHER
BREATHES
BRECCIA
BRECCIAS
BRECHAM
BRECHAMS
BREEDER
BREEDERS
BREVETE
BREVETED
BREVIER
BREVIERS
BREWAGE
BREWAGES
BREWING
BREWINGS
BREWPUB
BREWPUBS
BRICKIE
BRICKIER
BRICKIES
BRICOLE
BRICOLES
BRIDGED
ABRIDGED
BRIDGES
ABRIDGES
BRIDLER
BRIDLERS
BRIDOON
BRIDOONS
BRIGADE
BRIGADED
BRIGADES
BRIGAND
BRIGANDS
BRIMING
BRIMINGS
BRIMMER
BRIMMERS
BRINDLE
BRINDLED
BRINDLES
BRINGER
BRINGERS
BRINJAL
BRINJALS
BRIOCHE
BRIOCHES
BRIQUET

BRIQUETS
BRISKEN
BRISKENS
BRISKET
BRISKETS
BRISTLE
BRISTLED
BRISTLES
BRISURE
BRISURES
BRITSKA
BRITSKAS
BRITTLE
BRITTLER
BRITTLES
BRITZKA
BRITZKAS
BROADEN
BROADENS
BROCADE
BROCADED
BROCADES
BROCAGE
BROCAGES
BROCARD
BROCARDS
BROCHAN
BROCHANS
BROCKET
BROCKETS
BRODKIN
BRODKINS
BROIDER
BROIDERS
BROIDERY
BROILER
BROILERS
BROKAGE
BROKAGES
BROKING
BROKINGS
BROMATE
BROMATES
BROMIDE
BROMIDES
BROMINE
BROMINES
BROMISM
BROMISMS
BROMMER
BROMMERS
BRONCHI
BRONCHIA
BRONCHO
BRONCHOS
BRONZER
BRONZERS
BROODER
BROODERS
BROOKED
ABROOKED
BROTHEL
BROTHELS
BROTHER
BROTHERS
BROWNIE
BROWNIER
BROWNIES
BROWSER
BROWSERS
BRUCHID
BRUCHIDS
BRUCINE
BRUCINES
BRUCITE
BRUCITES
BRUHAHA
BRUHAHAS
BRUISER
BRUISERS
BRULYIE
BRULYIES
BRULZIE
BRULZIES
BRUMMER
BRUMMERS
BRUSHER
BRUSHERS
BRUSQUE
BRUSQUER
BRUTING
BRUTINGS
BRUXISM
BRUXISMS
BUBINGA
BUBINGAS
BUBUKLE
BUBUKLES
BUCCINA
BUCCINAS
BUCKEEN
BUCKEENS
BUCKING
BUCKINGS
BUCKLER
BUCKLERS
BUCKRAM
BUCKRAMS
BUCKSAW
BUCKSAWS
BUCOLIC
BUCOLICS
BUDDIES
BUDDIEST
BUDDING
BUDDINGS
BUDGERO
BUDGEROS
BUDGEROW
BUDWORM
BUDWORMS
BUFFING
BUFFINGS
BUFFOON
BUFFOONS
BUGABOO
BUGABOOS
BUGBANE
BUGBANES
BUGBEAR
BUGBEARS
BUGGANE
BUGGANES
BUGGIES
BUGGIEST
BUGGING
BUGGINGS
BUGWORT
BUGWORTS
BUILDER
BUILDERS
BUKSHEE
BUKSHEES
BULGHUR
BULGHURS
BULGINE
BULGINES
BULIMIA
BULIMIAS
BULIMIC
BULIMICS
BULLACE
BULLACES
BULLBAR
BULLBARS
BULLBAT
BULLBATS
BULLDOG
BULLDOGS
BULLIES
BULLIEST
BULLING
BULLINGS
BULLION
BULLIONS
BULLOCK
BULLOCKS
BULLOCKY
BULRUSH
BULRUSHY
BULWARK
BULWARKS
BUMBAZE
BUMBAZED
BUMBAZES
BUMBLER
BUMBLERS
BUMMOCK
BUMMOCKS
BUMPING
BUMPINGS
BUMPKIN
BUMPKINS
BUNDOOK
BUNDOOKS
BUNGLER
BUNGLERS
BUNRAKU
BUNRAKUS
BUNTING
BUNTINGS
BUOYAGE
BUOYAGES
BURBLER
BURBLERS
BURDOCK
BURDOCKS
BURETTE
BURETTES
BURGAGE
BURGAGES
BURGEON
BURGEONS
BURGHER
BURGHERS
BURGHUL
BURGHULS
BURGLAR
BURGLARS
BURGLARY
BURNING
BURNINGS
BURNOUS
BURNOUSE
BURRELL
BURRELLS
BURRHEL
BURRHELS
BURRITO
BURRITOS
BURSTER
BURSTERS
BURTHEN
BURTHENS
BURWEED
BURWEEDS
BUSGIRL
BUSGIRLS
BUSHIDO
BUSHIDOS
BUSHIES
BUSHIEST
BUSHING
BUSHINGS
BUSKING
BUSKINGS
BUSSING
BUSSINGS
BUSTARD
BUSTARDS
BUSTIER
BUSTIERS
BUSTING
BUSTINGS
BUSTLER
BUSTLERS
BUTANOL
BUTANOLS
BUTCHER
BUTCHERS
BUTCHERY
BUTCHES
BUTCHEST
BUTMENT
ABUTMENT
BUTMENTS
BUTTERS
ABUTTERS
BUTTING
ABUTTING
BUTTOCK
BUTTOCKS
BUVETTE
BUVETTES
BUYABLE
BUYABLES
BUZZARD
BUZZARDS
BUZZING
BUZZINGS
BYCOKET
BYCOKETS
BYPLACE
BYPLACES
BYWONER
BYWONERS
CABARET
CABARETS
CABBAGE
CABBAGED
CABBAGES
CABBALA
CABBALAS
CABINET
CABINETS
CABLING
CABLINGS
CABOOSE
CABOOSES
CACIQUE
CACIQUES
CACKLER
CACKLERS
CACODYL
CACODYLS
CACOLET
CACOLETS
CADAVER
CADAVERS
CADDICE
CADDICES
CADELLE
CADELLES
CADENCE
CADENCED
CADENCES
CADENZA
CADENZAS
CADMIUM
CADMIUMS
CAESIUM
CAESIUMS
CAESURA
CAESURAE
CAESURAL
CAESURAS
CAFFEIN
CAFFEINE
CAFFEINS
CAFFILA
CAFFILAS
CAGOULE
CAGOULES
CAISSON
CAISSONS
CAITIFF
CAITIFFS
CAITIVE
CAITIVES
CAJEPUT
CAJEPUTS
CAJOLER
CAJOLERS
CAJOLERY
CAJUPUT
CAJUPUTS
CALCINE
CALCINED
CALCINES
CALCITE
CALCITES
CALCIUM
CALCIUMS
CALDERA
CALDERAS
CALDRON
CALDRONS
CALIBER
CALIBERS
CALIBRE
CALIBRED
CALIBRES
CALICHE
CALICHES
CALICLE
CALICLES
CALIPEE
CALIPEES
CALIPER
CALIPERS
CALIVER
CALIVERS
CALLANT
CALLANTS
CALLING
CALLINGS
CALLUNA
CALLUNAS
CALMANT
CALMANTS
CALOMEL
CALOMELS
CALORIC
CALORICS
CALORIE
CALORIES
CALOTTE
CALOTTES
CALOYER
CALOYERS
CALPACK
CALPACKS
CALTRAP
CALTRAPS
CALTROP
CALTROPS
CALUMBA
CALUMBAS
CALUMET
CALUMETS
CALYCLE
CALYCLED
CALYCLES
CALYPSO
CALYPSOS
CALZONE
CALZONES
CAMAIEU
CAMAIEUX
CAMARON
CAMARONS
CAMBISM
CAMBISMS
CAMBIST
CAMBISTS
CAMBIUM
CAMBIUMS
CAMBOGE
CAMBOGES
CAMBREL
CAMBRELS
CAMBRIC
CAMBRICS
CAMELID
CAMELIDS
CAMELOT
CAMELOTS
CAMOGIE
CAMOGIES
CAMORRA
CAMORRAS
CAMPANA
CAMPANAS
CAMPERS
SCAMPERS
CAMPHOR
CAMPHORS
CAMPING
SCAMPING
CAMPION
CAMPIONS
CAMWOOD
CAMWOODS
CANAKIN
CANAKINS
CANASTA
CANASTAS
CANBANK
CANBANKS
CANDELA
CANDELAS
CANDENT
SCANDENT
CANDIDA
CANDIDAL
CANDIDAS
CANDOCK
CANDOCKS
CANDOUR
CANDOURS
CANELLA
CANELLAS
CANIKIN
CANIKINS
CANNACH
CANNACHS
CANNERS
SCANNERS
CANNING
SCANNING
CANNULA
CANNULAE
CANNULAR
CANNULAS
CANTALA
CANTALAS
CANTATA
CANTATAS
CANTATE
CANTATES
CANTDOG
CANTDOGS
CANTEEN
CANTEENS
CANTEST
SCANTEST
CANTHUS
ACANTHUS
CANTICO
CANTICOS
CANTICOY
CANTIER
SCANTIER
CANTINA
CANTINAS
CANTING
SCANTING
CANTINGS
CANTION
CANTIONS

CANTLED
SCANTLED
CANTLES
SCANTLES
CANTLET
CANTLETS
CANTRED
CANTREDS
CANTREF
CANTREFS
CANTRIP
CANTRIPS
CANZONA
CANZONAS
CANZONE
CANZONET
CAPABLE
CAPABLER
CAPELET
CAPELETS
CAPELIN
CAPELINE
CAPELINS
CAPERER
CAPERERS
CAPITAL
CAPITALS
CAPITAN
CAPITANI
CAPITANO
CAPITANS
CAPORAL
CAPORALS
CAPPING
CAPPINGS
CAPRATE
CAPRATES
CAPRICE
CAPRICES
CAPSIZE
CAPSIZED
CAPSIZES
CAPSTAN
CAPSTANS
CAPSULE
CAPSULES
CAPTAIN
CAPTAINS
CAPTION
CAPTIONS
CAPTIVE
CAPTIVED
CAPTIVES
CAPTURE
CAPTURED
CAPTURER
CAPTURES
CAPUCHE
CAPUCHES
CAPUERA
CAPUERAS
CARABAO
CARABAOS
CARABID
CARABIDS
CARABIN
CARABINE
CARABINS
CARACAL
CARACALS
CARACOL
CARACOLE
CARACOLS
CARACUL
CARACULS
CARAMEL
CARAMELS
CARANNA
CARANNAS
CARAUNA
CARAUNAS
CARAVAN
CARAVANS
CARAVEL
CARAVELS
CARAWAY
CARAWAYS
CARBIDE
CARBIDES
CARBINE
CARBINES
CARCAKE
CARCAKES
CARCASE
CARCASED
CARCASES
CARDECU
CARDECUE
CARDECUS
CARDIAC
CARDIACS
CARDOON
CARDOONS
CARFARE
CARFARES
CARIAMA
CARIAMAS
CARIBOU
CARIBOUS
CARIERE
CARIERES
CARINAS
OCARINAS
CARIOCA
CARIOCAS
CARIOLE
CARIOLES
CARIOUS
SCARIOUS
CARLINE
CARLINES
CARLING
CARLINGS
CARLOAD
CARLOADS
CARLOCK
CARLOCKS
CARMINE
CARMINES
CARNAGE
CARNAGES
CARNIES
CARNIEST
CAROCHE
CAROCHES
CAROMEL
CAROMELS
CAROTIN
CAROTINS
CAROUSE
CAROUSED
CAROUSEL
CAROUSER
CAROUSES
CARPARK
CARPARKS
CARPERS
SCARPERS
CARPING
SCARPING
CARPINGS
CARPORT
CARPORTS
CARRACK
CARRACKS
CARRACT
CARRACTS
CARRECT
CARRECTS
CARRELL
CARRELLS
CARRIER
SCARRIER
CARRIERS
CARRION
CARRIONS
CARTAGE
CARTAGES
CARTING
SCARTING
CARTOON
CARTOONS
CARTWAY
CARTWAYS
CARVING
CARVINGS
CASCADE
CASCADED
CASCADES
CASCARA
CASCARAS
CASEMEN
CASEMENT
CASERNE
CASERNES
CASHIER
CASHIERS
CASSATA
CASSATAS
CASSAVA
CASSAVAS
CASSINO
CASSINOS
CASSOCK
CASSOCKS
CASSONE
CASSONES
CASTING
CASTINGS
CASTOCK
CASTOCKS
CASUIST
CASUISTS
CATALOG
CATALOGS
CATALPA
CATALPAS
CATAPAN
CATAPANS
CATARRH
CATARRHS
CATASTA
CATASTAS
CATAWBA
CATAWBAS
CATBIRD
CATBIRDS
CATBOAT
CATBOATS
CATCALL
CATCALLS
CATCHER
CATCHERS
CATCHES
SCATCHES
CATCHUP
CATCHUPS
CATECHU
CATECHUS
CATELOG
CATELOGS
CATERAN
CATERANS
CATERER
CATERERS
CATHEAD
CATHEADS
CATHODE
CATHODES
CATHOLE
CATHOLES
CATHOOD
CATHOODS
CATLING
CATLINGS
CATMINT
CATMINTS
CATSKIN
CATSKINS
CATSUIT
CATSUITS
CATTABU
CATTABUS
CATTALO
CATTALOS
CATTERY
SCATTERY
CATTIER
SCATTIER
CATTIES
CATTIEST
CATTING
SCATTING
CATWORM
CATWORMS
CAUDATE
ACAUDATE
ECAUDATE
CAUDATED
CAUDRON
CAUDRONS
CAULINE
ACAULINE
CAULKER
CAULKERS
CAULOME
CAULOMES
CAUSTIC
CAUSTICS
CAUTION
CAUTIONS
CAVALLA
CAVALLAS
CAVIARE
CAVIARES
CAYENNE
CAYENNED
CAYENNES
CAZIQUE
CAZIQUES
CEASING
CEASINGS
CEDILLA
CEDILLAS
CEDRATE
CEDRATES
CEILIDH
CEILIDHS
CEILING
CEILINGS
CELADON
CELADONS
CELESTA
CELESTAS
CELESTE
CELESTES
CELLIST
CELLISTS
CELLOSE
CELLOSES
CELLULE
CELLULES
CEMBALO
CEMBALOS
CENACLE
CENACLES
CENSURE
CENSURED
CENSURES
CENTAGE
CENTAGES
CENTARE
CENTARES
CENTAUR
CENTAURS
CENTAURY
CENTAVO
CENTAVOS
CENTIME
CENTIMES
CENTIMO
CENTIMOS
CENTNER
CENTNERS
CENTRUM
CENTRUMS
CERAMAL
CERAMALS
CERAMIC
CERAMICS
CERASIN
CERASINS
CEREBRA
CEREBRAL
CERESIN
CERESINE
CERESINS
CERNING
SCERNING
CERUMEN
CERUMENS
CESSION
CESSIONS
CESSPIT
CESSPITS
CESTODE
CESTODES
CESTOID
CESTOIDS
CEVICHE
CEVICHES
CHABOUK
CHABOUKS
CHADDAR
CHADDARS
CHADDOR
CHADDORS
CHAFFER
CHAFFERS
CHAFFERY
CHAGRIN
CHAGRINS
CHALAZA
CHALAZAE
CHALAZAS
CHALCID
CHALCIDS
CHALDER
CHALDERS
CHALICE
CHALICED
CHALICES
CHALLAH
CHALLAHS
CHALLAN
CHALLANS
CHALLIE
CHALLIES
CHALONE
CHALONES
CHAMADE
CHAMADES
CHAMBER
CHAMBERS
CHAMFER
CHAMFERS
CHAMISE
CHAMISES
CHAMISO
CHAMISOS
CHAMLET
CHAMLETS
CHAMPAC
CHAMPACS
CHAMPAK
CHAMPAKS
CHANCEL
CHANCELS
CHANCER
CHANCERS
CHANCERY
CHANCRE
CHANCRES
CHANGER
CHANGERS
CHANNEL
CHANNELS
CHANNER
CHANNERS
CHANOYU
CHANOYUS
CHANSON
CHANSONS
CHANTER
CHANTERS
CHANTEY
CHANTEYS
CHANTIE
CHANTIES
CHANTOR
CHANTORS
CHAPATI
CHAPATIS
CHAPEAU
CHAPEAUX
CHAPLET
CHAPLETS
CHAPPAL
CHAPPALS
CHAPPED
SCHAPPED
CHAPPIE
CHAPPIER
CHAPPIES
CHAPTER
CHAPTERS
CHARADE
CHARADES
CHARGER
CHARGERS
CHARIOT
CHARIOTS
CHARISM
CHARISMA
CHARISMS
CHARKHA
CHARKHAS
CHARLEY
CHARLEYS
CHARLIE
CHARLIES
CHARMER
CHARMERS
CHARNEL
CHARNELS
CHARPIE
CHARPIES
CHARPOY
CHARPOYS
CHARQUI
CHARQUIS
CHARTER
CHARTERS
CHASING
CHASINGS
CHASTEN
CHASTENS
CHATEAU
CHATEAUX
CHATTEL
CHATTELS
CHATTER
CHATTERS
CHAUFER
CHAUFERS
CHAUMER
CHAUMERS
CHAUNCE
CHAUNCED
CHAUNCES

CHAUNGE
CHAUNGED
CHAUNGES
CHAUVIN
CHAUVINS
CHAYOTE
CHAYOTES
CHEAPEN
CHEAPENS
CHEAPIE
CHEAPIES
CHEATER
CHEATERS
CHEATERY
CHECHIA
CHECHIAS
CHECKER
CHECKERS
CHEEPER
CHEEPERS
CHEERER
CHEERERS
CHEERIO
CHEERIOS
CHEETAH
CHEETAHS
CHEKIST
CHEKISTS
CHELATE
CHELATED
CHELATES
CHELOID
CHELOIDS
CHELONE
CHELONES
CHEMISE
CHEMISES
CHEMISM
CHEMISMS
CHEMIST
CHEMISTS
CHEQUER
CHEQUERS
CHEROOT
CHEROOTS
CHERVIL
CHERVILS
CHESNUT
CHESNUTS
CHESSEL
CHESSELS
CHETNIK
CHETNIKS
CHEVRON
CHEVRONS
CHEVRONY
CHEWIES
CHEWIEST
CHEWINK
CHEWINKS
CHIASMA
CHIASMAS
CHIBOUK
CHIBOUKS
CHICANA
CHICANAS
CHICANE
CHICANED
CHICANER
CHICANES
CHICANO
CHICANOS
CHICKEN
CHICKENS
CHIDING
CHIDINGS
CHIEFER
CHIEFERY
CHIFFON
CHIFFONS
CHIGGER
CHIGGERS
CHIGNON
CHIGNONS
CHIKARA
CHIKARAS
CHIKHOR
CHIKHORS
CHILIAD
CHILIADS
CHILIOI
CHILIOIS
CHILLER
SCHILLER
CHILLERS
CHILLUM
CHILLUMS
CHIMERA
CHIMERAS
CHIMERE
CHIMERES
CHIMLEY
CHIMLEYS
CHIMNEY
CHIMNEYS
CHINDIT
CHINDITS
CHINKIE
CHINKIER
CHINKIES
CHINOOK
CHINOOKS
CHINWAG
CHINWAGS
CHIPPER
CHIPPERS
CHIPPIE
CHIPPIER
CHIPPIES
CHIRPER
CHIRPERS
CHIRRUP
CHIRRUPS
CHIRRUPY
CHITTER
CHITTERS
CHLORAL
CHLORALS
CHLORIN
CHLORINE
CHLORINS
CHOBDAR
CHOBDARS
CHOCTAW
CHOCTAWS
CHOICES
CHOICEST
CHOKIES
CHOKIEST
CHOLENT
CHOLENTS
CHOLERA
CHOLERAS
CHOLINE
CHOLINES
CHONDRE
CHONDRES
CHONDRI
CHONDRIN
CHOOKIE
CHOOKIES
CHOOSER
CHOOSERS
CHOPINE
CHOPINES
CHOPPER
CHOPPERS
CHORAGI
CHORAGIC
CHORALE
CHORALES
CHORDEE
CHORDEES
CHOREGI
CHOREGIC
CHORINE
CHORINES
CHORISM
CHORISMS
CHORIST
CHORISTS
CHORIZO
CHORIZOS
CHOROID
CHOROIDS
CHORTLE
CHORTLED
CHORTLES
CHOWDER
CHOWDERS
CHRISOM
CHRISOMS
CHROMEL
CHROMELS
CHRONIC
CHRONICS
CHRONON
CHRONONS
CHUCKIE
CHUCKIES
CHUCKLE
CHUCKLED
CHUCKLES
CHUDDAH
CHUDDAHS
CHUDDAR
CHUDDARS
CHUKKER
CHUKKERS
CHUMLEY
CHUMLEYS
CHUNDER
CHUNDERS
CHUNNEL
CHUNNELS
CHUNNER
CHUNNERS
CHUNTER
CHUNTERS
CHUPATI
CHUPATIS
CHUPPAH
CHUPPAHS
CHUTIST
CHUTISTS
CHUTNEY
CHUTNEYS
CICHLID
CICHLIDS
CIELING
CIELINGS
CILIATE
CILIATES
CINEAST
CINEASTE
CINEASTS
CINEOLE
CINEOLES
CINEREA
CINEREAL
CINEREAS
CINERIN
CINERINS
CIPOLIN
CIPOLINS
CIRCLER
CIRCLERS
CIRCLET
CIRCLETS
CIRCLIP
CIRCLIPS
CIRCUIT
CIRCUITS
CIRCUITY
CISSIES
CISSIEST
CISSOID
CISSOIDS
CISTERN
CISTERNA
CISTERNS
CISTRON
CISTRONS
CITADEL
CITADELS
CITHARA
CITHARAS
CITHERN
CITHERNS
CITIZEN
CITIZENS
CITRATE
CITRATES
CITRINE
CITRINES
CITTERN
CITTERNS
CLABBER
CLABBERS
CLACHAN
CLACHANS
CLACKER
CLACKERS
CLADDER
CLADDERS
CLADISM
CLADISMS
CLADIST
CLADISTS
CLADODE
CLADODES
CLAIMER
CLAIMERS
CLAMBER
CLAMBERS
CLAMOUR
CLAMOURS
CLAMPER
CLAMPERS
CLANGER
CLANGERS
CLANGOR
CLANGORS
CLAPNET
CLAPNETS
CLAPPER
CLAPPERS
CLARAIN
CLARAINS
CLARINO
CLARINOS
CLARION
CLARIONS
CLARKIA
CLARKIAS
CLASHER
CLASHERS
CLASPER
CLASPERS
CLASSIC
CLASSICS
CLASSIS
CLASSISM
CLASSIST
CLATTER
CLATTERS
CLATTERY
CLAUCHT
CLAUCHTS
CLAUGHT
CLAUGHTS
CLAVATE
CLAVATED
CLAVIER
CLAVIERS
CLAYPAN
CLAYPANS
CLEANER
CLEANERS
CLEANSE
CLEANSED
CLEANSER
CLEANSES
CLEARER
CLEARERS
CLEAVER
CLEAVERS
CLEEPED
YCLEEPED
CLERUCH
CLERUCHS
CLERUCHY
CLICKER
CLICKERS
CLICKET
CLICKETS
CLIMATE
CLIMATED
CLIMATES
CLIMBER
CLIMBERS
CLINGER
CLINGERS
CLINKER
CLINKERS
CLIPPER
CLIPPERS
CLIPPIE
CLIPPIES
CLITTER
CLITTERS
CLOBBER
CLOBBERS
CLOCKER
CLOCKERS
CLOGGER
CLOGGERS
CLOISON
CLOISONS
CLOSING
ECLOSING
CLOSINGS
CLOSURE
CLOSURED
CLOSURES
CLOTBUR
CLOTBURS
CLOTTER
CLOTTERS
CLOTURE
CLOTURED
CLOTURES
CLOUTER
CLOUTERS
CLOWDER
CLOWDERS
CLUBBER
CLUBBERS
CLUDGIE
CLUDGIES
CLUMBER
CLUMBERS
CLUMPER
CLUMPERS
CLUPEID
CLUPEIDS
CLUSTER
CLUSTERS
CLUSTERY
CLUTTER
CLUTTERS
CLYSTER
CLYSTERS
COACHEE
COACHEES
COACHER
COACHERS
COALISE
COALISED
COALISES
COALIZE
COALIZED
COALIZES
COALTAR
COALTARS
COAMING
COAMINGS
COARSEN
COARSENS
COASTER
COASTERS
COATING
COATINGS
COBBLER
COBBLERS
COBBLERY
COCAINE
COCAINES
COCHLEA
COCHLEAE
COCHLEAR
COCKADE
COCKADES
COCKEYE
COCKEYED
COCKEYES
COCKIES
COCKIEST
COCKNEY
COCKNEYS
COCKPIT
COCKPITS
COCONUT
COCONUTS
COCOPAN
COCOPANS
COCOTTE
COCOTTES
COCTION
COCTIONS
CODEINE
CODEINES
CODETTA
CODETTAS
CODICIL
CODICILS
CODILLA
CODILLAS
CODILLE
CODILLES
CODLING
CODLINGS
COEHORN
COEHORNS
COELIAC
COELIACS
COEQUAL
COEQUALS
COEXIST
COEXISTS
COFFERS
SCOFFERS
COFFING
SCOFFING
COFFRET
COFFRETS
COGENCE
COGENCES
COGENER
COGENERS
COGGING
SCOGGING
COGGINGS
COGNATE
COGNATES
COGNISE
COGNISED
COGNISES
COGNIZE
COGNIZED

COGNIZES
COHABIT
COHABITS
COHERER
COHERERS
COHIBIT
COHIBITS
COINAGE
COINAGES
COINING
COININGS
COITION
COITIONS
COLETIT
COLETITS
COLIBRI
COLIBRIS
COLLAGE
COLLAGEN
COLLAGES
COLLARD
COLLARDS
COLLATE
COLLATED
COLLATES
COLLECT
COLLECTS
COLLEEN
COLLEENS
COLLEGE
COLLEGER
COLLEGES
COLLIDE
COLLIDED
COLLIDER
COLLIDES
COLLIER
COLLIERS
COLLIERY
COLLING
COLLINGS
COLLOID
COLLOIDS
COLLOPS
SCOLLOPS
COLLUDE
COLLUDED
COLLUDER
COLLUDES
COLOGNE
COLOGNES
COLONEL
COLONELS
COLONIC
COLONICS
COLUMEL
COLUMELS
COMBINE
COMBINED
COMBINES
COMBING
COMBINGS
COMBLES
COMBLESS
COMBUST
COMBUSTS
COMFORT
COMFORTS
COMFREY
COMFREYS

COMMAND
COMMANDO
COMMANDS
COMMEND
COMMENDS
COMMENT
COMMENTS
COMMERE
COMMERES
COMMODE
COMMODES
COMMOTE
COMMOTES
COMMOVE
COMMOVED
COMMOVES
COMMUNE
COMMUNED
COMMUNES
COMMUTE
COMMUTED
COMMUTER
COMMUTES
COMPACT
COMPACTS
COMPAGE
COMPAGES
COMPARE
COMPARED
COMPARES
COMPART
COMPARTS
COMPEAR
COMPEARS
COMPEER
COMPEERS
COMPERE
COMPERED
COMPERES
COMPETE
COMPETED
COMPETES
COMPILE
COMPILED
COMPILER
COMPILES
COMPING
COMPINGS
COMPLIN
COMPLINE
COMPLINS
COMPLOT
COMPLOTS
COMPORT
COMPORTS
COMPOSE
COMPOSED
COMPOSER
COMPOSES
COMPOST
COMPOSTS
COMPOTE
COMPOTES
COMPTER
COMPTERS
COMPUTE
COMPUTED
COMPUTER
COMPUTES
COMRADE

COMRADES
CONACRE
CONACRED
CONACRES
CONARIA
CONARIAL
CONCAVE
CONCAVED
CONCAVES
CONCEAL
CONCEALS
CONCEDE
CONCEDED
CONCEDER
CONCEDES
CONCEIT
CONCEITS
CONCEITY
CONCENT
CONCENTS
CONCEPT
CONCEPTI
CONCEPTS
CONCERN
CONCERNS
CONCERT
CONCERTI
CONCERTO
CONCERTS
CONCHIE
CONCHIES
CONCISE
CONCISED
CONCISER
CONCISES
CONCOCT
CONCOCTS
CONCORD
CONCORDS
CONCREW
CONCREWS
CONDEMN
CONDEMNS
CONDOLE
CONDOLED
CONDOLES
CONDONE
CONDONED
CONDONES
CONDUCE
CONDUCED
CONDUCES
CONDUCT
CONDUCTI
CONDUCTS
CONDUIT
CONDUITS
CONDYLE
CONDYLES
CONFECT
CONFECTS
CONFIDE
CONFIDED
CONFIDER
CONFIDES
CONFINE
CONFINED
CONFINER
CONFINES
CONFIRM

CONFIRMS
CONFORM
CONFORMS
CONFUSE
CONFUSED
CONFUSES
CONFUTE
CONFUTED
CONFUTES
CONGEAL
CONGEALS
CONGEST
CONGESTS
CONGREE
CONGREED
CONGREES
CONGREET
CONGRUE
CONGRUED
CONGRUES
CONIDIA
CONIDIAL
CONIFER
CONIFERS
CONIINE
CONIINES
CONJECT
CONJECTS
CONJOIN
CONJOINS
CONJOINT
CONJURE
CONJURED
CONJURER
CONJURES
CONNECT
CONNECTS
CONNING
CONNINGS
CONNIVE
CONNIVED
CONNIVER
CONNIVES
CONNOTE
CONNOTED
CONNOTES
CONQUER
CONQUERS
CONSEIL
CONSEILS
CONSENT
CONSENTS
CONSIGN
CONSIGNS
CONSIST
CONSISTS
CONSOLE
CONSOLED
CONSOLER
CONSOLES
CONSORT
CONSORTS
CONSTER
CONSTERS
CONSULT
CONSULTA
CONSULTS
CONSUME
CONSUMED
CONSUMER

CONSUMES
CONTACT
CONTACTS
CONTAIN
CONTAINS
CONTECK
CONTECKS
CONTEMN
CONTEMNS
CONTEND
CONTENDS
CONTENT
CONTENTS
CONTEST
CONTESTS
CONTEXT
CONTEXTS
CONTORT
CONTORTS
CONTOUR
CONTOURS
CONTRAS
CONTRAST
CONTRAT
CONTRATE
CONTRATS
CONTROL
CONTROLE
CONTROLS
CONTUND
CONTUNDS
CONTUSE
CONTUSED
CONTUSES
CONVENE
CONVENED
CONVENER
CONVENES
CONVENT
CONVENTS
CONVERT
CONVERTS
CONVICT
CONVICTS
CONVIVE
CONVIVED
CONVIVES
CONVOKE
CONVOKED
CONVOKES
COOKOUT
COOKOUTS
COOLANT
COOLANTS
COONCAN
COONCANS
COONDOG
COONDOGS
COONTIE
COONTIES
COOPERS
SCOOPERS
COOPING
SCOOPING
COPAIBA
COPAIBAS
COPAIVA
COPAIVAS
COPEPOD
COPEPODS

COPILOT
COPILOTS
COPPICE
COPPICED
COPPICES
COPSHOP
COPSHOPS
COPULAS
SCOPULAS
COPYCAT
COPYCATS
COPYISM
COPYISMS
COPYIST
COPYISTS
COQUINA
COQUINAS
COQUITO
COQUITOS
CORACLE
CORACLES
CORANTO
CORANTOS
CORBEAU
CORBEAUS
CORBEIL
CORBEILS
CORDAGE
CORDAGES
CORDIAL
CORDIALS
CORDING
CORDINGS
CORDITE
CORDITES
CORDOBA
CORDOBAS
CORELLA
CORELLAS
CORIOUS
SCORIOUS
CORIVAL
CORIVALS
CORKAGE
CORKAGES
CORNAGE
CORNAGES
CORNERS
SCORNERS
CORNETT
CORNETTI
CORNETTO
CORNETTS
CORNICE
CORNICED
CORNICES
CORNING
SCORNING
CORNIST
CORNISTS
CORNROW
CORNROWS
CORNUTE
CORNUTED
CORNUTES
CORNUTO
CORNUTOS
COROLLA
COROLLAS
CORONAL

CORONALS
CORONER
CORONERS
CORONET
CORONETS
CORPORA
CORPORAL
CORPORAS
CORRADE
CORRADED
CORRADES
CORRECT
CORRECTS
CORRIDA
CORRIDAS
CORRODE
CORRODED
CORRODES
CORRUPT
CORRUPTS
CORSAGE
CORSAGES
CORSAIR
CORSAIRS
CORSIVE
CORSIVES
CORSLET
CORSLETS
CORSNED
CORSNEDS
CORTEGE
CORTEGES
CORYPHE
CORYPHEE
CORYPHES
COSINES
COSINESS
COSMISM
ACOSMISM
COSMISMS
COSMIST
ACOSMIST
COSMISTS
COSTARD
COSTARDS
COSTATE
ECOSTATE
COSTATED
COSTEAN
COSTEANS
COSTREL
COSTRELS
COSTUME
COSTUMED
COSTUMER
COSTUMES
COTERIE
COTERIES
COTHURN
COTHURNI
COTHURNS
COTINGA
COTINGAS
COTLAND
COTLANDS
COTTAGE
COTTAGED
COTTAGER
COTTAGES
COTTAGEY

COTTIER
COTTIERS
COTTISE
COTTISED
COTTISES
COTTOWN
COTTOWNS
COUCHEE
COUCHEES
COUGHER
COUGHERS
COUGUAR
COUGUARS
COULOIR
COULOIRS
COULOMB
COULOMBS
COULTER
COULTERS
COUNCIL
COUNCILS
COUNSEL
COUNSELS
COUNTER
COUNTERS
COUPING
SCOUPING
COUPLER
COUPLERS
COUPLET
COUPLETS
COUPURE
COUPURES
COURAGE
COURAGES
COURANT
COURANTE
COURANTS
COURIER
COURIERS
COURING
SCOURING
COURLAN
COURLANS
COURSED
SCOURSED
COURSER
COURSERS
COURSES
SCOURSES
COUTERS
SCOUTERS
COUTHER
SCOUTHER
COUTHIE
COUTHIER
COUTURE
COUTURES
COUVADE
COUVADES
COUVERT
COUVERTS
COVELET
COVELETS
COWBANE
COWBANES
COWBELL
COWBELLS
COWBIRD
COWBIRDS
COWGIRL
COWGIRLS
COWHAGE
COWHAGES
COWHAND
COWHANDS
COWHEEL
COWHEELS
COWHERB
COWHERBS
COWHERD
COWHERDS
COWHIDE
COWHIDED
COWHIDES
COWLICK
COWLICKS
COWLING
SCOWLING
COWLINGS
COWPING
SCOWPING
COWPOKE
COWPOKES
COWRIES
SCOWRIES
COWSHED
COWSHEDS
COWSLIP
COWSLIPS
COWTREE
COWTREES
COXCOMB
COXCOMBS
COZENER
COZENERS
CRABBED
SCRABBED
CRABBER
CRABBERS
CRACKER
CRACKERS
CRACKLE
CRACKLED
CRACKLES
CRAGGED
SCRAGGED
CRAMMED
SCRAMMED
CRAMMER
CRAMMERS
CRAMPET
CRAMPETS
CRAMPIT
CRAMPITS
CRAMPON
CRAMPONS
CRANAGE
CRANAGES
CRANIUM
CRANIUMS
CRANKLE
CRANKLED
CRANKLES
CRANNOG
CRANNOGS
CRAPPED
SCRAPPED
CRAVING
CRAVINGS
CRAWLED
SCRAWLED
CRAWLER
SCRAWLER
CRAWLERS
CRAZIES
CRAZIEST
CREAKED
SCREAKED
CREAMED
SCREAMED
CREAMER
SCREAMER
CREAMERS
CREAMERY
CREANCE
CREANCES
CREASER
CREASERS
CREATIN
CREATINE
CREATING
CREATINS
CREATOR
CREATORS
CREEPER
CREEPERS
CREEPIE
CREEPIER
CREEPIES
CREMATE
CREMATED
CREMATES
CREMONA
CREMONAS
CRENATE
CRENATED
CREOSOL
CREOSOLS
CRESSET
CRESSETS
CRESTON
CRESTONS
CRETISM
CRETISMS
CREVICE
CREVICES
CREWING
SCREWING
CRIBBLE
SCRIBBLE
CRIBBLED
CRIBBLES
CRICKET
CRICKETS
CRICOID
CRICOIDS
CRIMINA
CRIMINAL
CRIMMER
CRIMMERS
CRIMPED
SCRIMPED
CRIMPER
CRIMPERS
CRIMPLE
CRIMPLED
CRIMPLES
CRIMSON
CRIMSONS
CRINATE
CRINATED
CRINGER
CRINGERS
CRINGLE
CRINGLES
CRINITE
CRINITES
CRINKLE
CRINKLED
CRINKLES
CRINOID
CRINOIDS
CRIOLLO
CRIOLLOS
CRIPPLE
CRIPPLED
CRIPPLES
CRISPER
CRISPERS
CRISPIN
CRISPING
CRISPINS
CRITTER
CRITTERS
CRITTUR
CRITTURS
CROAKER
CROAKERS
CROCEIN
CROCEINS
CROCHET
CROCHETS
CROCKET
CROCKETS
CROFTER
CROFTERS
CROMACK
CROMACKS
CROMBIE
CROMBIES
CROODLE
CROODLED
CROODLES
CROONER
CROONERS
CROPFUL
CROPFULL
CROPFULS
CROPPER
CROPPERS
CROQUET
CROQUETS
CROSIER
CROSIERS
CROSSES
CROSSEST
CROTTLE
CROTTLES
CROUPER
CROUPERS
CROUPON
CROUPONS
CROUTON
CROUTONS
CROWBAR
CROWBARS
CROWDER
CROWDERS
CROWDIE
CROWDIES
CROWNER
CROWNERS
CROWNET
CROWNETS
CROZIER
CROZIERS
CRUBEEN
CRUBEENS
CRUCIAN
CRUCIANS
CRUDDLE
CRUDDLED
CRUDDLES
CRUISER
CRUISERS
CRUISIE
CRUISIES
CRULLER
CRULLERS
CRUMBLE
CRUMBLED
CRUMBLES
CRUMPED
SCRUMPED
CRUMPET
CRUMPETS
CRUMPLE
CRUMPLED
CRUMPLES
CRUNCHY
SCRUNCHY
CRUNKLE
CRUNKLED
CRUNKLES
CRUPPER
CRUPPERS
CRUSADE
CRUSADED
CRUSADER
CRUSADES
CRUSADO
CRUSADOS
CRUSHER
CRUSHERS
CRUSIAN
CRUSIANS
CRUZADO
CRUZADOS
CRYINGS
SCRYINGS
CRYOGEN
CRYOGENS
CRYOGENY
CRYONIC
CRYONICS
CRYPTON
CRYPTONS
CRYSTAL
CRYSTALS
CUBBING
CUBBINGS
CUBHOOD
CUBHOODS
CUBICLE
CUBICLES
CUCKOLD
CUCKOLDS
CUDBEAR
CUDBEARS
CUDDLED
SCUDDLED
CUDDLES
SCUDDLES
CUDWEED
CUDWEEDS
CUFFING
SCUFFING
CUFFLED
SCUFFLED
CUFFLES
SCUFFLES
CUISINE
CUISINES
CUISSER
CUISSERS
CUITTLE
CUITTLED
CUITTLES
CULCHIE
CULCHIES
CULICID
CULICIDS
CULLERS
SCULLERS
CULLING
SCULLING
CULLINGS
CULLION
SCULLION
CULLIONS
CULPRIT
CULPRITS
CULTISM
CULTISMS
CULTIST
CULTISTS
CULTURE
CULTURED
CULTURES
CULVERT
CULVERTS
CUMARIN
CUMARINS
CUMBERS
SCUMBERS
CUMMERS
SCUMMERS
CUMQUAT
CUMQUATS
CUMSHAW
CUMSHAWS
CUNETTE
CUNETTES
CUNNERS
SCUNNERS
CUNNING
CUNNINGS
CUPCAKE
CUPCAKES
CUPGALL
CUPGALLS
CUPHEAD
CUPHEADS
CUPPERS
SCUPPERS
CUPPING
CUPPINGS
CUPRITE
CUPRITES
CURACAO
CURACAOS
CURACOA
CURACOAS
CURARIS
CURARISE
CURATOR
CURATORS
CURATORY
CURCUMA
CURCUMAS
CURETTE
CURETTED
CURETTES
CURLING
CURLINGS
CURRACH
CURRACHS
CURRAGH
CURRAGHS
CURRANT
CURRANTS
CURRANTY
CURRENT
CURRENTS
CURRIED
SCURRIED
CURRIER
SCURRIER
CURRIERS
CURRIES
SCURRIES
CURRING
SCURRING
CURSING
CURSINGS
CURTAIL
CURTAILS
CURTAIN
CURTAINS
CURTANA
CURTANAS
CURTSEY
CURTSEYS
CURVATE
CURVATED
CURVIER
SCURVIER
CUSHION
CUSHIONS
CUSHIONY
CUSTARD
CUSTARDS
CUSTOCK
CUSTOCKS
CUSTREL
CUSTRELS
CUTAWAY
CUTAWAYS
CUTBACK
CUTBACKS
CUTCHES
SCUTCHES
CUTICLE
CUTICLES
CUTIKIN
CUTIKINS
CUTLINE
CUTLINES
CUTTERS

SCUTTERS
CUTTIES
CUTTIEST
CUTTING
CUTTINGS
CUTTLES
SCUTTLES
CUTWORK
CUTWORKS
CUTWORM
CUTWORMS
CUVETTE
CUVETTES
CYANATE
CYANATES
CYANIDE
CYANIDED
CYANIDES
CYANINE
CYANINES
CYANISE
CYANISED
CYANISES
CYANITE
CYANITES
CYANIZE
CYANIZED
CYANIZES
CYCLING
CYCLINGS
CYCLIST
CYCLISTS
CYCLOID
CYCLOIDS
CYCLONE
CYCLONES
CYMBALO
CYMBALOS
CYPRIAN
CYPRIANS
CYPSELA
CYPSELAE
CYSTINE
CYSTINES
CYSTOID
CYSTOIDS
CZARDOM
CZARDOMS
CZARINA
CZARINAS
CZARISM
CZARISMS
CZARIST
CZARISTS
DABBLER
DABBLERS
DABSTER
DABSTERS
DADDOCK
DADDOCKS
DAFFIES
DAFFIEST
DAFFING
DAFFINGS
DAGGING
DAGGINGS
DAGLOCK
DAGLOCKS
DAGWOOD
DAGWOODS
DAINING
SDAINING
DAKOITI
DAKOITIS
DALLIER
DALLIERS
DAMBROD
DAMBRODS
DAMOSEL
DAMOSELS
DAMOZEL
DAMOZELS
DAMPING
DAMPINGS
DANCING
DANCINGS
DANDIES
DANDIEST
DANDLER
DANDLERS
DANELAW
DANELAWS
DANGLER
DANGLERS
DANSEUR
DANSEURS
DAPHNID
DAPHNIDS
DAPSONE
DAPSONES
DAQUIRI
DAQUIRIS
DARIOLE
DARIOLES
DARLING
DARLINGS
DARNING
DARNINGS
DARRAIN
DARRAINE
DARRAINS
DARRAYN
DARRAYNS
DARSHAN
DARSHANS
DASHEEN
DASHEENS
DASHEKI
DASHEKIS
DASHIKI
DASHIKIS
DASTARD
DASTARDS
DASTARDY
DASYPOD
DASYPODS
DASYURE
DASYURES
DATARIA
DATARIAS
DAUBING
DAUBINGS
DAUNDER
DAUNDERS
DAUNTER
DAUNTERS
DAUNTON
DAUNTONS
DAUPHIN
DAUPHINE
DAUPHINS
DAVIDIA
DAVIDIAS
DAWCOCK
DAWCOCKS
DAWDLER
DAWDLERS
DAWNING
DAWNINGS
DAYMARK
DAYMARKS
DAYSTAR
DAYSTARS
DAYTALE
DAYTALER
DAYTALES
DAYTIME
DAYTIMES
DAZZLER
DAZZLERS
DEADPAN
DEADPANS
DEALING
DEALINGS
DEASIUL
DEASIULS
DEASOIL
DEASOILS
DEBACLE
DEBACLES
DEBASER
DEBASERS
DEBATER
DEBATERS
DEBBIES
DEBBIEST
DEBITOR
DEBITORS
DEBOUCH
DEBOUCHE
DEBRIDE
DEBRIDED
DEBRIDES
DEBRIEF
DEBRIEFS
DECAGON
DECAGONS
DECAPOD
DECAPODS
DECEASE
DECEASED
DECEASES
DECEIVE
DECEIVED
DECEIVER
DECEIVES
DECIARE
DECIARES
DECIBEL
DECIBELS
DECIDER
DECIDERS
DECIDUA
DECIDUAE
DECIDUAL
DECIDUAS
DECIMAL
DECIMALS
DECKING
DECKINGS
DECLAIM
DECLAIMS
DECLARE
DECLARED
DECLARER
DECLARES
DECLASS
DECLASSE
DECLINE
DECLINED
DECLINES
DECODER
DECODERS
DECOLOR
DECOLORS
DECORUM
DECORUMS
DECREET
DECREETS
DECRIAL
DECRIALS
DECRIER
DECRIERS
DECROWN
DECROWNS
DECRYPT
DECRYPTS
DECUMAN
DECUMANS
DECUPLE
DECUPLED
DECUPLES
DECURIA
DECURIAS
DECURVE
DECURVED
DECURVES
DEEMING
ADEEMING
DEERLET
DEERLETS
DEFACER
DEFACERS
DEFAULT
DEFAULTS
DEFENCE
DEFENCED
DEFENCES
DEFENSE
DEFENSES
DEFICIT
DEFICITS
DEFILER
DEFILERS
DEFINER
DEFINERS
DEFLATE
DEFLATED
DEFLATER
DEFLATES
DEFLECT
DEFLECTS
DEFORCE
DEFORCED
DEFORCES
DEFRAUD
DEFRAUDS
DEFROCK
DEFROCKS
DEFROST
DEFROSTS
DEFROZE
DEFROZEN
DEFUNCT
DEFUNCTS
DEGRADE
DEGRADED
DEGRADES
DEHISCE
DEHISCED
DEHISCES
DEICIDE
DEICIDES
DEICTIC
DEICTICS
DEIFIER
DEIFIERS
DEIGNED
SDEIGNED
DEISEAL
DEISEALS
DEJEUNE
DEJEUNER
DEJEUNES
DELAINE
DELAINES
DELAPSE
DELAPSED
DELAPSES
DELATOR
DELATORS
DELAYER
DELAYERS
DELIGHT
DELIGHTS
DELIMIT
DELIMITS
DELIVER
DELIVERS
DELIVERY
DELOUSE
DELOUSED
DELOUSES
DELTOID
DELTOIDS
DELUDER
DELUDERS
DEMAINE
DEMAINES
DEMAYNE
DEMAYNES
DEMEANE
DEMEANED
DEMEANES
DEMENTI
DEMENTIA
DEMENTIS
DEMERGE
DEMERGED
DEMERGER
DEMERGES
DEMERIT
DEMERITS
DEMERSE
DEMERSED
DEMERSES
DEMESNE
DEMESNES
DEMIGOD
DEMIGODS
DEMIREP
DEMIREPS
DEMOUNT
DEMOUNTS
DEMURES
DEMUREST
DENDRON
DENDRONS
DENIZEN
DENIZENS
DENTATE
EDENTATE
DENTATED
DENTINE
DENTINES
DENTIST
DENTISTS
DENTURE
DENTURES
DEODAND
DEODANDS
DEODATE
DEODATES
DEONTIC
DEONTICS
DEPAINT
DEPAINTS
DEPECHE
DEPECHES
DEPLANE
DEPLANED
DEPLANES
DEPLETE
DEPLETED
DEPLETES
DEPLORE
DEPLORED
DEPLORES
DEPLUME
DEPLUMED
DEPLUMES
DEPOSAL
DEPOSALS
DEPOSER
DEPOSERS
DEPOSIT
DEPOSITS
DEPRAVE
DEPRAVED
DEPRAVES
DEPRIVE
DEPRIVED
DEPRIVES
DEPSIDE
DEPSIDES
DERAIGN
DERAIGNS
DERANGE
DERANGED
DERANGES
DERIDER
DERIDERS
DERMOID
DERMOIDS
DERRICK
DERRICKS
DESCALE
DESCALED
DESCALES
DESCANT
DESCANTS
DESCEND
DESCENDS
DESCENT
DESCENTS
DESERVE
DESERVED
DESERVER
DESERVES
DESIRER
DESIRERS
DESKILL
DESKILLS
DESKTOP
DESKTOPS
DESMINE
DESMINES
DESMOID
DESMOIDS
DESPAIR
DESPAIRS
DESPISE
DESPISED
DESPISER
DESPISES
DESPITE
DESPITES
DESPOIL
DESPOILS
DESPOND
DESPONDS
DESSERT
DESSERTS
DESTINE
DESTINED
DESTINES
DESTROY
DESTROYS
DETENTE
DETENTES
DETENUE
DETENUES
DETERGE
DETERGED
DETERGES
DETINUE
DETINUES
DETRACT
DETRACTS
DETRAIN
DETRAINS
DETRUDE
DETRUDED
DETRUDES
DEVALUE
DEVALUED
DEVALUES
DEVELOP
DEVELOPE
DEVELOPS
DEVIANT
DEVIANTS
DEVIATE
DEVIATED
DEVIATES
DEVILET
DEVILETS
DEVISAL
DEVISALS
DEVISEE

DEVISEES
DEVISER
DEVISERS
DEVISOR
DEVISORS
DEVLING
DEVLINGS
DEVOICE
DEVOICED
DEVOICES
DEVOLVE
DEVOLVED
DEVOLVES
DEVOTEE
DEVOTEES
DEWATER
DEWATERS
DEXTRAN
DEXTRANS
DEXTRIN
DEXTRINE
DEXTRINS
DHARMAS
ADHARMAS
DHURRIE
DHURRIES
DIABASE
DIABASES
DIABOLO
DIABOLOS
DIADROM
DIADROMS
DIAGRAM
DIAGRAMS
DIAGRID
DIAGRIDS
DIALECT
DIALECTS
DIALIST
DIALISTS
DIALLER
DIALLERS
DIALYSE
DIALYSED
DIALYSER
DIALYSES
DIALYZE
DIALYZED
DIALYZER
DIALYZES
DIAMOND
DIAMONDS
DIAPASE
DIAPASES
DIARISE
DIARISED
DIARISES
DIARIST
DIARISTS
DIARIZE
DIARIZED
DIARIZES
DIASTER
DIASTERS
DIBBLER
DIBBLERS
DICHORD
DICHORDS
DICKIES
DICKIEST
DICTATE
DICTATED
DICTATES
DICTION
DICTIONS
DIDAKAI
DIDAKAIS
DIDAKEI
DIDAKEIS
DIDDIES
DIDDIEST
DIDDLER
DIDDLERS
DIDICOI
DIDICOIS
DIDICOY
DIDICOYS
DIEBACK
DIEBACKS
DIEDRAL
DIEDRALS
DIETINE
DIETINES
DIETIST
DIETISTS
DIFFUSE
DIFFUSED
DIFFUSER
DIFFUSES
DIGAMMA
DIGAMMAS
DIGGING
DIGGINGS
DIGITAL
DIGITALS
DIGLYPH
DIGLYPHS
DIGRAPH
DIGRAPHS
DIHEDRA
DIHEDRAL
DILATER
DILATERS
DILATOR
DILATORS
DILATORY
DILEMMA
DILEMMAS
DILLIES
DILLIEST
DILLING
DILLINGS
DILUENT
DILUENTS
DILUTEE
DILUTEES
DILUTER
DILUTERS
DILUTOR
DILUTORS
DILUVIA
DILUVIAL
DILUVIAN
DIMETER
DIMETERS
DIMORPH
DIMORPHS
DINETTE
DINETTES
DINGBAT
DINGBATS
DINGIES
DINGIEST
DINKIES
DINKIEST
DINMONT
DINMONTS
DIOCESE
DIOCESES
DIOPTER
DIOPTERS
DIOPTRE
DIOPTRES
DIORAMA
DIORAMAS
DIORISM
DIORISMS
DIORITE
DIORITES
DIOXANE
DIOXANES
DIOXIDE
DIOXIDES
DIPHONE
DIPHONES
DIPLOID
DIPLOIDY
DIPLOMA
DIPLOMAS
DIPLOMAT
DIPLONT
DIPLONTS
DIPNOAN
DIPNOANS
DIPPING
DIPPINGS
DIPTERA
DIPTERAL
DIPTERAN
DIPTERAS
DIPTYCH
DIPTYCHS
DIREMPT
DIREMPTS
DIRTIES
DIRTIEST
DISABLE
DISABLED
DISABLES
DISAVOW
DISAVOWS
DISBAND
DISBANDS
DISBARK
DISBARKS
DISCAGE
DISCAGED
DISCAGES
DISCANT
DISCANTS
DISCARD
DISCARDS
DISCASE
DISCASED
DISCASES
DISCEPT
DISCEPTS
DISCERN
DISCERNS
DISCERP
DISCERPS
DISCIDE
DISCIDED
DISCIDES
DISCOER
DISCOERS
DISCORD
DISCORDS
DISCURE
DISCURED
DISCURES
DISDAIN
DISDAINS
DISEASE
DISEASED
DISEASES
DISEDGE
DISEDGED
DISEDGES
DISEUSE
DISEUSES
DISFAME
DISFAMES
DISFORM
DISFORMS
DISGEST
DISGESTS
DISGOWN
DISGOWNS
DISGUST
DISGUSTS
DISHELM
DISHELMS
DISHFUL
DISHFULS
DISHING
DISHINGS
DISHOME
DISHOMED
DISHOMES
DISHORN
DISHORNS
DISJECT
DISJECTS
DISJOIN
DISJOINS
DISJOINT
DISJUNE
DISJUNES
DISLEAF
DISLEAFS
DISLIKE
DISLIKED
DISLIKEN
DISLIKES
DISLIMB
DISLIMBS
DISLIMN
DISLIMNS
DISLINK
DISLINKS
DISLOAD
DISLOADS
DISMASK
DISMASKS
DISMAST
DISMASTS
DISMAYL
DISMAYLS
DISNEST
DISNESTS
DISOBEY
DISOBEYS
DISPACE
DISPACED
DISPACES
DISPARK
DISPARKS
DISPART
DISPARTS
DISPEND
DISPENDS
DISPLAY
DISPLAYS
DISPONE
DISPONED
DISPONEE
DISPONER
DISPONES
DISPORT
DISPORTS
DISPOSE
DISPOSED
DISPOSER
DISPOSES
DISPOST
DISPOSTS
DISPRED
DISPREDS
DISPUTE
DISPUTED
DISPUTER
DISPUTES
DISRANK
DISRANKS
DISRATE
DISRATED
DISRATES
DISROBE
DISROBED
DISROBES
DISROOT
DISROOTS
DISRUPT
DISRUPTS
DISSEAT
DISSEATS
DISSECT
DISSECTS
DISSENT
DISSENTS
DISSERT
DISSERTS
DISTAFF
DISTAFFS
DISTAIN
DISTAINS
DISTEND
DISTENDS
DISTICH
DISTICHS
DISTILL
DISTILLS
DISTORT
DISTORTS
DISTUNE
DISTUNED
DISTUNES
DISTURB
DISTURBS
DISTYLE
DISTYLES
DISYOKE
DISYOKED
DISYOKES
DITCHER
DITCHERS
DIURNAL
DIURNALS
DIVERGE
DIVERGED
DIVERGES
DIVERSE
DIVERSED
DIVERSES
DIVIDER
DIVIDERS
DIVINER
DIVINERS
DIVINES
DIVINEST
DIVISOR
DIVISORS
DIVORCE
DIVORCED
DIVORCEE
DIVORCER
DIVORCES
DIVULGE
DIVULGED
DIVULGES
DIZZARD
DIZZARDS
DIZZIES
DIZZIEST
DJIBBAH
DJIBBAHS
DOATING
DOATINGS
DOCKAGE
DOCKAGES
DOCKING
DOCKINGS
DOCKISE
DOCKISED
DOCKISES
DOCKIZE
DOCKIZED
DOCKIZES
DOCQUET
DOCQUETS
DODDIES
DODDIEST
DODGING
DODGINGS
DOGBANE
DOGBANES
DOGBOLT
DOGBOLTS
DOGCART
DOGCARTS
DOGEATE
DOGEATES
DOGGIES
DOGGIEST
DOGGING
DOGGINGS
DOGGONE
DOGGONED
DOGGREL
DOGGRELS
DOGHOLE
DOGHOLES
DOGSHIP
DOGSHIPS
DOGSKIN
DOGSKINS
DOGSLED
DOGSLEDS
DOGTOWN
DOGTOWNS
DOGTROT
DOGTROTS
DOGVANE
DOGVANES
DOGWOOD
DOGWOODS
DOITKIN
DOITKINS
DOLLDOM
DOLLDOMS
DOLLIER
DOLLIERS
DOLPHIN
DOLPHINS
DOMICIL
DOMICILE
DOMICILS
DOMINEE
DOMINEER
DOMINEES
DOMINIE
DOMINIES
DONATOR
DONATORS
DONATORY
DONNISM
DONNISMS
DONSHIP
DONSHIPS
DOODLER
DOODLERS
DOORMAT
DOORMATS
DOORWAY
DOORWAYS
DOPATTA
DOPATTAS
DOPPING
DOPPINGS
DORHAWK
DORHAWKS
DORLACH
DORLACHS
DORMANT
DORMANTS
DORNICK
DORNICKS
DORTOUR
DORTOURS
DOSSIER
DOSSIERS
DOTTLES
DOTTLEST
DOTTREL
DOTTRELS
DOUBLER
DOUBLERS
DOUBLET
DOUBLETS

DOUBTER
DOUBTERS
DOUCEUR
DOUCEURS
DOUCINE
DOUCINES
DOULEIA
DOULEIAS
DOURINE
DOURINES
DOVECOT
DOVECOTS
DOVEKIE
DOVEKIES
DOVELET
DOVELETS
DOWAGER
DOWAGERS
DOWDIES
DOWDIEST
DOWNBOW
DOWNBOWS
DOYENNE
DOYENNES
DOZENTH
DOZENTHS
DRABBER
DRABBERS
DRABBET
DRABBETS
DRABBLE
DRABBLED
DRABBLER
DRABBLES
DRABLER
DRABLERS
DRACHMA
DRACHMAE
DRACHMAI
DRACHMAS
DRACONE
DRACONES
DRAFTEE
DRAFTEES
DRAFTER
DRAFTERS
DRAGGLE
DRAGGLED
DRAGGLES
DRAGNET
DRAGNETS
DRAGOON
DRAGOONS
DRAINER
DRAINERS
DRAPIER
DRAPIERS
DRAPPIE
DRAPPIES
DRASTIC
DRASTICS
DRAUGHT
DRAUGHTS
DRAUGHTY
DRAWBAR
DRAWBARS
DRAWING
DRAWINGS
DRAWLER
DRAWLERS
DRAYAGE
DRAYAGES
DREADED
ADREADED
DREADER
DREADERS
DREAMER
DREAMERS
DREAMERY
DREARES
DREAREST
DREDGER
DREDGERS
DRESSER
DRESSERS
DREVILL
DREVILLS
DRIBBER
DRIBBERS
DRIBBLE
DRIBBLED
DRIBBLER
DRIBBLES
DRIBBLET
DRIBLET
DRIBLETS
DRIFTER
DRIFTERS
DRILLER
DRILLERS
DRINKER
DRINKERS
DRIZZLE
DRIZZLED
DRIZZLES
DROGHER
DROGHERS
DROGUET
DROGUETS
DROLLER
DROLLERY
DROMOND
DROMONDS
DROPLET
DROPLETS
DROPPER
DROPPERS
DROPPLE
DROPPLES
DROSERA
DROSERAS
DROSTDY
DROSTDYS
DROUGHT
DROUGHTS
DROUGHTY
DROVING
DROVINGS
DROWNER
DROWNERS
DRUDGER
DRUDGERS
DRUDGERY
DRUGGER
DRUGGERS
DRUGGET
DRUGGETS
DRUGGIE
DRUGGIER
DRUGGIES
DRUMBLE
DRUMBLED
DRUMBLES
DRUMLIN
DRUMLINS
DRUMMER
DRUMMERS
DRYBEAT
DRYBEATS
DUALISM
DUALISMS
DUALIST
DUALISTS
DUBBING
DUBBINGS
DUCHESS
DUCHESSE
DUCKIES
DUCKIEST
DUCKING
DUCKINGS
DUDGEON
DUDGEONS
DUDHEEN
DUDHEENS
DUELLER
DUELLERS
DUFFING
DUFFINGS
DUKEDOM
DUKEDOMS
DULCIAN
DULCIANA
DULCIANS
DULCITE
DULCITES
DULCOSE
DULCOSES
DULLARD
DULLARDS
DUMAIST
DUMAISTS
DUMMIES
DUMMIEST
DUMPBIN
DUMPBINS
DUMPIES
DUMPIEST
DUNGEON
DUNGEONS
DUNNAGE
DUNNAGES
DUNNART
DUNNARTS
DUNNIES
DUNNIEST
DUNNING
DUNNINGS
DUNNITE
DUNNITES
DUNNOCK
DUNNOCKS
DUODENA
DUODENAL
DUOTONE
DUOTONES
DUPATTA
DUPATTAS
DURABLE
DURABLES
DURAMEN
DURAMENS
DURANCE
DURANCES
DURESSE
DURESSES
DURMAST
DURMASTS
DUSTBIN
DUSTBINS
DUSTING
ADUSTING
DUUMVIR
DUUMVIRI
DUUMVIRS
DUVETYN
DUVETYNE
DUVETYNS
DVANDVA
DVANDVAS
DVORNIK
DVORNIKS
DWELLER
DWELLERS
DWINDLE
DWINDLED
DWINDLES
DYELINE
DYELINES
DYESTER
DYESTERS
DYNAMIC
ADYNAMIC
DYNAMICS
DYSODIL
DYSODILE
DYSODILS
DYSPNEA
DYSPNEAL
DYSPNEAS
DYSURIA
DYSURIAS
EANLING
WEANLING
YEANLING
EANLINGS
EARACHE
EARACHES
EARDING
BEARDING
YEARDING
EARDROP
EARDROPS
EARDRUM
EARDRUMS
EARFLAP
EARFLAPS
EARINGS
BEARINGS
GEARINGS
HEARINGS
SEARINGS
WEARINGS
EARLDOM
EARLDOMS
EARLESS
FEARLESS
GEARLESS
TEARLESS
EARLIER
PEARLIER
EARLIES
PEARLIES
YEARLIES
EARLIEST
EARLOBE
EARLOBES
EARLOCK
EARLOCKS
EARMARK
EARMARKS
EARNERS
LEARNERS
YEARNERS
EARNEST
EARNESTS
EARNING
LEARNING
YEARNING
EARNINGS
EARPICK
EARPICKS
EARPLUG
EARPLUGS
EARRING
EARRINGS
EARSHOT
EARSHOTS
EASTING
FEASTING
REASTING
YEASTING
EASTINGS
EASTLIN
EASTLING
EASTLINS
EATABLE
BEATABLE
EATABLES
EATINGS
BEATINGS
HEATINGS
SEATINGS
EBAUCHE
EBAUCHES
EBBTIDE
EBBTIDES
EBONISE
EBONISED
EBONISES
EBONIST
EBONISTS
EBONITE
EBONITES
EBONIZE
EBONIZED
EBONIZES
EBRIATE
EBRIATED
ECBOLIC
ECBOLICS
ECHAPPE
ECHAPPES
ECHELON
ECHELONS
ECHIDNA
ECHIDNAS
ECHOISE
ECHOISED
ECHOISES
ECHOISM
ECHOISMS
ECHOIST
ECHOISTS
ECHOIZE
ECHOIZED
ECHOIZES
ECLIPSE
ECLIPSED
ECLIPSES
ECLOGUE
ECLOGUES
ECLOSED
RECLOSED
ECLOSES
RECLOSES
ECOCIDE
ECOCIDES
ECOLOGY
OECOLOGY
ECORCHE
ECORCHES
ECOTYPE
ECOTYPES
ECTHYMA
ECTHYMAS
ECTOPIA
ECTOPIAS
ECTOZOA
ECTOZOAN
ECUELLE
ECUELLES
ECURIES
DECURIES
EDEMATA
OEDEMATA
EDGIEST
HEDGIEST
KEDGIEST
LEDGIEST
SEDGIEST
WEDGIEST
EDGINGS
HEDGINGS
WEDGINGS
EDIFICE
EDIFICES
EDIFIER
EDIFIERS
EDITION
SEDITION
EDITIONS
EDUCATE
EDUCATED
EDUCATES
EDUCING
DEDUCING
REDUCING
SEDUCING
EDUCTOR
SEDUCTOR
EDUCTORS
EECHING
LEECHING
REECHING
EELFARE
EELFARES
EELIEST
SEELIEST
EELPOUT
EELPOUTS
EELWORM
EELWORMS
EERIEST
BEERIEST
LEERIEST
PEERIEST
EEVNING
EEVNINGS
EFFENDI
EFFENDIS
EFFORCE
EFFORCED
EFFORCES
EFFULGE
EFFULGED
EFFULGES
EGALITY
LEGALITY
REGALITY
EGENCES
REGENCES
EGGHEAD
EGGHEADS
EGGIEST
LEGGIEST
EGOTISE
EGOTISED
EGOTISES
EGOTISM
EGOTISMS
EGOTIST
EGOTISTS
EGOTIZE
EGOTIZED
EGOTIZES
EIDETIC
EIDETICS
EIGHTVO
EIGHTVOS
EILDING
EILDINGS
EJECTED
DEJECTED
REJECTED
EJECTOR
REJECTOR
EJECTORS
EKISTIC
EKISTICS
EKPWELE
EKPWELES
ELAPSED
DELAPSED
RELAPSED
ELAPSES
DELAPSES
RELAPSES
ELASTIC
GELASTIC
ELASTICS
ELASTIN
ELASTINS
ELATERS
RELATERS
ELATING
BELATING
DELATING
RELATING
ELATION

DELATION
GELATION
RELATION
ELATIONS
ELATIVE
RELATIVE
ELATIVES
ELDINGS
GELDINGS
WELDINGS
ELECTED
SELECTED
ELECTOR
SELECTOR
ELECTORS
ELECTRO
ELECTRON
ELECTROS
ELEGIAC
ELEGIACS
ELEGISE
ELEGISED
ELEGISES
ELEGIST
ELEGISTS
ELEGIZE
ELEGIZED
ELEGIZES
ELEMENT
ELEMENTS
ELEVATE
ELEVATED
ELEVATES
ELFHOOD
SELFHOOD
ELFHOODS
ELFLAND
ELFLANDS
ELISION
ELISIONS
ELITISM
ELITISMS
ELITIST
ELITISTS
ELLIPSE
ELLIPSES
ELLWAND
ELLWANDS
ELMWOOD
ELMWOODS
ELOCUTE
ELOCUTED
ELOCUTES
ELOGIST
ELOGISTS
ELOGIUM
ELOGIUMS
ELOINER
ELOINERS
ELOPING
DELOPING
ELUDERS
DELUDERS
ELUDING
DELUDING
ELUSION
DELUSION
ELUSIONS
ELUSIVE
DELUSIVE
ELUSORY
DELUSORY
ELUTION
ELUTIONS
ELUVIUM
ELUVIUMS
EMANATE
EMANATED
EMANATES
EMBATHE
EMBATHED
EMBATHES
EMBLAZE
EMBLAZED
EMBLAZES
EMBLOOM
EMBLOOMS
EMBOGUE
EMBOGUED
EMBOGUES
EMBOSOM
EMBOSOMS
EMBOUND
EMBOUNDS
EMBOWEL
EMBOWELS
EMBOWER
EMBOWERS
EMBRACE
EMBRACED
EMBRACER
EMBRACES
EMBRAID
EMBRAIDS
EMBRAVE
EMBRAVED
EMBRAVES
EMBREAD
EMBREADS
EMBREWE
EMBREWED
EMBREWES
EMBROIL
EMBROILS
EMBROWN
EMBROWNS
EMBRUTE
EMBRUTED
EMBRUTES
EMBRYON
EMBRYONS
EMERALD
EMERALDS
EMERGED
DEMERGED
REMERGED
EMERGES
DEMERGES
REMERGES
EMERSED
DEMERSED
EMETINE
EMETINES
EMICATE
EMICATED
EMICATES
EMIRATE
EMIRATES
EMITTED
DEMITTED
REMITTED
EMITTER
REMITTER
EMITTERS
EMONGES
EMONGEST
EMOTING
DEMOTING
EMOTION
DEMOTION
REMOTION
EMOTIONS
EMOVING
REMOVING
EMPAIRE
EMPAIRED
EMPAIRES
EMPANEL
EMPANELS
EMPERCE
EMPERCED
EMPERCES
EMPEROR
EMPERORS
EMPIRIC
EMPIRICS
EMPLACE
EMPLACED
EMPLACES
EMPLANE
EMPLANED
EMPLANES
EMPLUME
EMPLUMED
EMPLUMES
EMPOWER
EMPOWERS
EMPRESS
EMPRESSE
EMPRISE
EMPRISES
EMPTIER
EMPTIERS
EMPTIES
EMPTIEST
EMPTION
EMPTIONS
EMPYEMA
EMPYEMAS
EMULATE
EMULATED
EMULATES
EMULING
AEMULING
EMULSIN
EMULSINS
EMULSOR
EMULSORS
EMURING
DEMURING
ENABLER
ENABLERS
ENACTOR
ENACTORS
ENAMOUR
ENAMOURS
ENATION
VENATION
ENATIONS
ENCHAFE
ENCHAFED
ENCHAFES
ENCHAIN
ENCHAINS
ENCHANT
PENCHANT
ENCHANTS
ENCHARM
ENCHARMS
ENCHASE
ENCHASED
ENCHASES
ENCHEER
ENCHEERS
ENCLASP
ENCLASPS
ENCLAVE
ENCLAVED
ENCLAVES
ENCLOSE
ENCLOSED
ENCLOSER
ENCLOSES
ENCLOUD
ENCLOUDS
ENCRUST
ENCRUSTS
ENCRYPT
ENCRYPTS
ENDEMIC
ENDEMICS
ENDERON
ENDERONS
ENDGAME
ENDGAMES
ENDINGS
BENDINGS
LENDINGS
MENDINGS
SENDINGS
ENDIRON
ENDIRONS
ENDOGEN
ENDOGENS
ENDOGENY
ENDORSE
ENDORSED
ENDORSEE
ENDORSER
ENDORSES
ENDOWER
ENDOWERS
ENDSHIP
ENDSHIPS
ENDURER
ENDURERS
ENDWISE
BENDWISE
ENERGID
ENERGIDS
ENEWING
RENEWING
ENFELON
ENFELONS
ENFEOFF
ENFEOFFS
ENFLAME
ENFLAMED
ENFLAMES
ENFOLDS
PENFOLDS
ENFORCE
RENFORCE
ENFORCED
ENFORCER
ENFORCES
ENFRAME
ENFRAMED
ENFRAMES
ENFROZE
ENFROZEN
ENGAGER
ENGAGERS
ENGINER
ENGINERS
ENGINERY
ENGLOBE
ENGLOBED
ENGLOBES
ENGLOOM
ENGLOOMS
ENGORGE
ENGORGED
ENGORGES
ENGRACE
ENGRACED
ENGRACES
ENGRAFF
ENGRAFFS
ENGRAFT
ENGRAFTS
ENGRAIL
ENGRAILS
ENGRAIN
ENGRAINS
ENGRASP
ENGRASPS
ENGRAVE
ENGRAVED
ENGRAVEN
ENGRAVER
ENGRAVES
ENGUARD
ENGUARDS
ENGULPH
ENGULPHS
ENHANCE
ENHANCED
ENHANCER
ENHANCES
ENJOYER
ENJOYERS
ENLARGE
ENLARGED
ENLARGEN
ENLARGER
ENLARGES
ENLIGHT
PENLIGHT
ENLIGHTS
ENLIVEN
ENLIVENS
ENLOCKS
GENLOCKS
ENNOBLE
ENNOBLED
ENNOBLES
ENOUNCE
DENOUNCE
RENOUNCE
ENOUNCED
ENOUNCES
ENPLANE
ENPLANED
ENPLANES
ENPRINT
ENPRINTS
ENQUIRE
ENQUIRED
ENQUIRER
ENQUIRES
ENRANGE
ENRANGED
ENRANGES
ENRHEUM
ENRHEUMS
ENROUGH
ENROUGHS
ENROUND
ENROUNDS
ENSHELL
ENSHELLS
ENSLAVE
ENSLAVED
ENSLAVER
ENSLAVES
ENSNARE
ENSNARED
ENSNARES
ENSNARL
ENSNARLS
ENSTAMP
ENSTAMPS
ENSTEEP
ENSTEEPS
ENSTYLE
ENSTYLED
ENSTYLES
ENSURED
CENSURED
ENSURER
ENSURERS
ENSURES
CENSURES
ENSWEEP
ENSWEEPS
ENTAILS
VENTAILS
ENTAYLE
VENTAYLE
ENTAYLED
ENTAYLES
ENTENTE
ENTENTES
ENTERED
CENTERED
TENTERED
ENTERER
ENTERERS
ENTERIC
ENTERICS
ENTHRAL
ENTHRALL
ENTHRALS
ENTHUSE
ENTHUSED
ENTHUSES
ENTICED
PENTICED
ENTICER
ENTICERS
ENTICES
PENTICES
ENTITLE
ENTITLED
ENTITLES
ENTOMIC
PENTOMIC
ENTOZOA
ENTOZOAL
ENTRAIL
ENTRAILS
ENTRAIN
ENTRAINS
ENTRANT
ENTRANTS
ENTREAT
ENTREATS
ENTREATY
ENTRIES
CENTRIES
GENTRIES
SENTRIES
ENTRISM
CENTRISM
ENTRISMS
ENTRIST
CENTRIST
ENTRISTS
ENTRUST
ENTRUSTS
ENTWINE
ENTWINED
ENTWINES
ENTWIST
ENTWISTS
ENVAULT
ENVAULTS
ENVELOP
ENVELOPE
ENVELOPS
ENVENOM
ENVENOMS
ENVIRON
ENVIRONS
ENVYING
ENVYINGS
ENWHEEL
ENWHEELS
EOLITHS
NEOLITHS
EONISMS
PEONISMS
EPACRID
EPACRIDS
EPAGOGE
EPAGOGES
EPAULET
EPAULETS
EPEIRID
EPEIRIDS
EPERGNE
EPERGNES
EPHEDRA
EPHEDRAS
EPICARP
EPICARPS
EPICEDE
EPICEDES
EPICENE

EPICENES
EPICIER
EPICIERS
EPICISM
EPICISMS
EPICIST
EPICISTS
EPICURE
EPICURES
EPIDOTE
LEPIDOTE
EPIDOTES
EPIGONE
EPIGONES
EPIGRAM
EPIGRAMS
EPILATE
DEPILATE
EPILATED
EPILATES
EPISODE
EPISODES
EPISOME
EPISOMES
EPISTLE
EPISTLED
EPISTLER
EPISTLES
EPITAPH
EPITAPHS
EPITHEM
EPITHEMA
EPITHEMS
EPITHET
EPITHETS
EPITOME
EPITOMES
EPITOPE
EPITOPES
EPIZOAN
EPIZOANS
EPOXIDE
EPOXIDES
EPSILON
EPSILONS
EPURATE
DEPURATE
EPURATED
EPURATES
EQUATOR
EQUATORS
EQUINIA
EQUINIAS
ERASION
ERASIONS
ERASURE
ERASURES
ERATHEM
ERATHEMS
ERBIUMS
TERBIUMS
ERECTER
ERECTERS
ERECTOR
ERECTORS
EREMITE
EREMITES
EREPSIN
EREPSINS
ERINITE

ERINITES
ERISTIC
MERISTIC
VERISTIC
ERMELIN
ERMELINS
ERMINED
VERMINED
ERODENT
ERODENTS
ERODIUM
ERODIUMS
EROSION
EROSIONS
EROTEMA
EROTEMAS
EROTEME
EROTEMES
EROTICA
EROTICAL
EROTISM
EROTISMS
ERRATIC
ERRATICS
ERRHINE
ERRHINES
ERRINGS
HERRINGS
ERUDITE
ERUDITES
ESCALOP
ESCALOPE
ESCALOPS
ESCAPEE
ESCAPEES
ESCAPER
ESCAPERS
ESCHEAT
ESCHEATS
ESCOLAR
ESCOLARS
ESCRIBE
DESCRIBE
ESCRIBED
ESCRIBES
ESCROLL
ESCROLLS
ESCUAGE
ESCUAGES
ESLOYNE
ESLOYNED
ESLOYNES
ESPARTO
ESPARTOS
ESPOUSE
ESPOUSED
ESPOUSER
ESPOUSES
ESQUIRE
ESQUIRES
ESSAYER
ESSAYERS
ESSENCE
ESSENCES
ESSOYNE
ESSOYNES
ESTATED
GESTATED
RESTATED
ESTATES

GESTATES
RESTATES
ESTHETE
AESTHETE
ESTHETES
ESTIVAL
AESTIVAL
FESTIVAL
ESTOILE
ESTOILES
ESTOVER
ESTOVERS
ESTRADE
ESTRADES
ESTREAT
ESTREATS
ESTREPE
ESTREPED
ESTREPES
ESTROUS
OESTROUS
ESTRUMS
OESTRUMS
ETACISM
BETACISM
ETACISMS
ETAERIO
ETAERIOS
ETAGERE
ETAGERES
ETALAGE
ETALAGES
ETCHANT
ETCHANTS
ETCHING
FETCHING
KETCHING
LETCHING
RETCHING
ETCHINGS
ETHANES
METHANES
ETHANOL
METHANOL
ETHANOLS
ETHICAL
ETHICALS
ETIOLIN
ETIOLINS
ETOURDI
ETOURDIE
ETRENNE
ETRENNES
ETTLING
FETTLING
NETTLING
PETTLING
SETTLING
EUCAINE
EUCAINES
EUCLASE
EUCLASES
EUCRITE
EUCRITES
EUGENIA
EUGENIAS
EUGENIC
EUGENICS
EUGENOL
EUGENOLS

EUPHROE
EUPHROES
EUREKAS
HEUREKAS
EUSTYLE
EUSTYLES
EUTEXIA
EUTEXIAS
EVACUEE
EVACUEES
EVANGEL
EVANGELS
EVANGELY
EVASION
EVASIONS
EVENING
EVENINGS
EVENTER
EVENTERS
EVERTED
REVERTED
EVERTOR
EVERTORS
EVICTOR
EVICTORS
EVIDENT
EVIDENTS
EVIRATE
LEVIRATE
EVIRATED
EVIRATES
EVITATE
LEVITATE
EVITATED
EVITATES
EVOCATE
EVOCATED
EVOCATES
EVOKING
REVOKING
EVOLUTE
REVOLUTE
EVOLUTED
EVOLUTES
EVOLVED
DEVOLVED
REVOLVED
EVOLVER
REVOLVER
EVOLVERS
EVOLVES
DEVOLVES
REVOLVES
EXACTER
EXACTERS
EXACTOR
EXACTORS
EXAMINE
EXAMINED
EXAMINEE
EXAMINER
EXAMINES
EXAMPLE
EXAMPLED
EXAMPLES
EXCERPT
EXCERPTA
EXCERPTS
EXCHEAT
EXCHEATS

EXCITER
EXCITERS
EXCITON
EXCITONS
EXCITOR
EXCITORS
EXCLAIM
EXCLAIMS
EXCLAVE
EXCLAVES
EXCLUDE
EXCLUDED
EXCLUDEE
EXCLUDER
EXCLUDES
EXCRETA
EXCRETAL
EXCRETE
EXCRETED
EXCRETER
EXCRETES
EXCURSE
EXCURSED
EXCURSES
EXCUSAL
EXCUSALS
EXCUSER
EXCUSERS
EXECUTE
EXECUTED
EXECUTER
EXECUTES
EXEGETE
EXEGETES
EXEMPLA
EXEMPLAR
EXEMPLE
EXEMPLES
EXERGUE
EXERGUES
EXHAUST
EXHAUSTS
EXHEDRA
EXHEDRAE
EXHIBIT
EXHIBITS
EXHUMER
EXHUMERS
EXIGENT
EXIGENTS
EXOCARP
EXOCARPS
EXODERM
EXODERMS
EXODIST
EXODISTS
EXOMION
EXOMIONS
EXORDIA
EXORDIAL
EXPANSE
EXPANSES
EXPENSE
EXPENSES
EXPERTS
SEXPERTS
EXPIATE
EXPIATED
EXPIATES
EXPLAIN

EXPLAINS
EXPLANT
EXPLANTS
EXPLODE
EXPLODED
EXPLODER
EXPLODES
EXPLOIT
EXPLOITS
EXPLORE
EXPLORED
EXPLORER
EXPLORES
EXPOSAL
EXPOSALS
EXPOSER
EXPOSERS
EXPOUND
EXPOUNDS
EXPRESS
EXPRESSO
EXPULSE
EXPULSED
EXPULSES
EXPUNCT
EXPUNCTS
EXPUNGE
EXPUNGED
EXPUNGER
EXPUNGES
EXPURGE
EXPURGED
EXPURGES
EXSCIND
EXSCINDS
EXTERNE
EXTERNES
EXTRACT
EXTRACTS
EXTRAIT
EXTRAITS
EXTREAT
EXTREATS
EXTREME
EXTREMER
EXTREMES
EXTRUDE
EXTRUDED
EXTRUDER
EXTRUDES
EXUDATE
EXUDATES
EXURBIA
EXURBIAS
EYEBALL
EYEBALLS
EYEBOLT
EYEBOLTS
EYEBROW
EYEBROWS
EYEHOOK
EYEHOOKS
EYELIAD
EYELIADS
EYESORE
EYESORES
FABLIAU
FABLIAUX
FABLING
FABLINGS

FACONNE
FACONNES
FACTICE
FACTICES
FACTION
FACTIONS
FACTOID
FACTOIDS
FACTURE
FACTURES
FADAISE
FADAISES
FADDISM
FADDISMS
FADDIST
FADDISTS
FAGGING
FAGGINGS
FAHLORE
FAHLORES
FAIENCE
FAIENCES
FAILING
FAILINGS
FAILURE
FAILURES
FAIRING
FAIRINGS
FAIRWAY
FAIRWAYS
FAITOUR
FAITOURS
FALAFEL
FALAFELS
FALBALA
FALBALAS
FALCADE
FALCADES
FALCATE
FALCATED
FALCULA
FALCULAS
FALDAGE
FALDAGES
FALLING
FALLINGS
FALLOUT
FALLOUTS
FALSISM
FALSISMS
FANATIC
FANATICS
FANCIER
FANCIERS
FANCIES
FANCIEST
FANFARE
FANFARED
FANFARES
FANGLES
FANGLESS
FANNELL
FANNELLS
FANNING
FANNINGS
FANTAIL
FANTAILS
FANTASM
FANTASMS
FANTAST

FANTASTS
FANTEEG
FANTEEGS
FANZINE
FANZINES
FARADAY
FARADAYS
FARAWAY
FARAWAYS
FARCEUR
FARCEURS
FARCING
FARCINGS
FARDAGE
FARDAGES
FARDING
FARDINGS
FARMING
FARMINGS
FARRIER
FARRIERS
FARRIERY
FARRUCA
FARRUCAS
FARTHEL
FARTHELS
FARTLEK
FARTLEKS
FASCINE
FASCINES
FASCISM
FASCISMI
FASCISMO
FASCISMS
FASCIST
FASCISTA
FASCISTI
FASCISTS
FASHION
FASHIONS
FASTING
FASTINGS
FATIGUE
FATIGUED
FATIGUES
FATLING
FATLINGS
FATTIES
FATTIEST
FAUCHON
FAUCHONS
FAUNIST
FAUNISTS
FAVORER
FAVORERS
FAVRILE
FAVRILES
FAWNING
FAWNINGS
FAYENCE
FAYENCES
FAZENDA
FAZENDAS
FEARING
AFEARING
FEASTER
FEASTERS
FEATHER
FEATHERS
FEATHERY
FEATURE
FEATURED
FEATURES
FECHTER
FECHTERS
FEDARIE
FEDARIES
FEDAYEE
FEDAYEEN
FEDERAL
FEDERALS
FEEBLES
FEEBLEST
FEEDING
FEEDINGS
FEEDLOT
FEEDLOTS
FEELING
FEELINGS
FEERING
FEERINGS
FELAFEL
FELAFELS
FELICIA
FELICIAS
FELLATE
FELLATED
FELLATES
FELSITE
FELSITES
FELSPAR
FELSPARS
FELTING
FELTINGS
FELUCCA
FELUCCAS
FELWORT
FELWORTS
FEMITER
FEMITERS
FENCING
FENCINGS
FENITAR
FENITARS
FENLAND
FENLANDS
FENNIES
FENNIEST
FEOFFEE
FEOFFEES
FEOFFER
FEOFFERS
FEOFFOR
FEOFFORS
FERLIES
FERLIEST
FERMATA
FERMATAS
FERMENT
FERMENTS
FERMION
FERMIONS
FERMIUM
FERMIUMS
FERNING
FERNINGS
FERRATE
FERRATES
FERRITE
FERRITES
FERRUGO
FERRUGOS
FERRULE
FERRULES
FERTILE
FERTILER
FERVOUR
FERVOURS
FESTOON
FESTOONS
FETICHE
FETICHES
FETLOCK
FETLOCKS
FETTLER
FETTLERS
FEUDING
FEUDINGS
FEUDIST
FEUDISTS
FIANCEE
FIANCEES
FIBROID
FIBROIDS
FIBROIN
FIBROINS
FIBROMA
FIBROMAS
FIBROSE
FIBROSED
FIBROSES
FIBSTER
FIBSTERS
FICKLES
FICKLEST
FICTION
FICTIONS
FIDDLER
FIDDLERS
FIDDLEY
FIDDLEYS
FIDEISM
FIDEISMS
FIDEIST
FIDEISTS
FIEFDOM
FIEFDOMS
FIELDER
FIELDERS
FIFTEEN
FIFTEENS
FIGHTER
FIGHTERS
FIGMENT
FIGMENTS
FIGWORT
FIGWORTS
FILABEG
FILABEGS
FILACER
FILACERS
FILARIA
FILARIAL
FILARIAS
FILASSE
FILASSES
FILAZER
FILAZERS
FILBERD
FILBERDS
FILBERT
FILBERTS
FILCHER
FILCHERS
FILEMOT
FILEMOTS
FILIATE
FILIATED
FILIATES
FILIBEG
FILIBEGS
FILLING
FILLINGS
FILMDOM
FILMDOMS
FILMSET
FILMSETS
FIMBRIA
FIMBRIAE
FINAGLE
FINAGLED
FINAGLES
FINANCE
FINANCED
FINANCES
FINBACK
FINBACKS
FINDING
FINDINGS
FINDRAM
FINDRAMS
FINESSE
FINESSED
FINESSER
FINESSES
FINNACK
FINNACKS
FINNOCK
FINNOCKS
FIREARM
FIREARMS
FIREBUG
FIREBUGS
FIREDOG
FIREDOGS
FIREPAN
FIREPANS
FIREPOT
FIREPOTS
FIRRING
FIRRINGS
FISHEYE
FISHEYES
FISHGIG
FISHGIGS
FISHING
FISHINGS
FISSION
FISSIONS
FISSURE
FISSURED
FISSURES
FISTFUL
FISTFULS
FISTULA
FISTULAE
FISTULAR
FISTULAS
FITCHET
FITCHETS
FITCHEW
FITCHEWS
FITMENT
FITMENTS
FITTING
FITTINGS
FIVEPIN
FIVEPINS
FIXTURE
FIXTURES
FIZZGIG
FIZZGIGS
FIZZING
FIZZINGS
FLACKER
FLACKERS
FLACKET
FLACKETS
FLAFFER
FLAFFERS
FLAKIES
FLAKIEST
FLAMFEW
FLAMFEWS
FLAMING
FLAMINGO
FLANEUR
FLANEURS
FLANKER
FLANKERS
FLANNEL
FLANNELS
FLANNEN
FLANNENS
FLAPPER
FLAPPERS
FLASHER
FLASHERS
FLASHES
FLASHEST
FLASKET
FLASKETS
FLATBED
FLATBEDS
FLATLET
FLATLETS
FLATTEN
FLATTENS
FLATTER
FLATTERS
FLATTERY
FLAUGHT
FLAUGHTS
FLAVINE
FLAVINES
FLAVONE
FLAVONES
FLAVOUR
FLAVOURS
FLEAPIT
FLEAPITS
FLECKER
FLECKERS
FLEECER
FLEECERS
FLEERER
FLEERERS
FLESHER
FLESHERS
FLETTON
FLETTONS
FLEURET
FLEURETS
FLEURON
FLEURONS
FLEXION
FLEXIONS
FLEXURE
FLEXURES
FLICKER
FLICKERS
FLINDER
FLINDERS
FLINGER
FLINGERS
FLIPPER
FLIPPERS
FLITTER
FLITTERN
FLITTERS
FLIVVER
FLIVVERS
FLOATEL
FLOATELS
FLOATER
FLOATERS
FLOKATI
FLOKATIS
FLOORER
FLOORERS
FLOOSIE
FLOOSIES
FLOOZIE
FLOOZIES
FLORIST
FLORISTS
FLORUIT
FLORUITS
FLOTAGE
FLOTAGES
FLOTSAM
FLOTSAMS
FLOUNCE
FLOUNCED
FLOUNCES
FLOWAGE
FLOWAGES
FLUENCE
FLUENCES
FLUIDIC
FLUIDICS
FLUNKEY
FLUNKEYS
FLUSHER
FLUSHERS
FLUSHES
FLUSHEST
FLUSTER
FLUSTERS
FLUSTERY
FLUTINA
FLUTINAS
FLUTING
FLUTINGS
FLUTIST
FLUTISTS
FLUTTER
AFLUTTER
FLUTTERS
FLUXION
FLUXIONS
FLYBANE
FLYBANES
FLYBELT
FLYBELTS
FLYBLOW
FLYBLOWS
FLYBOAT
FLYBOATS
FLYBOOK
FLYBOOKS
FLYOVER
FLYOVERS
FLYTING
FLYTINGS
FLYTRAP
FLYTRAPS
FOAMING
FOAMINGS
FOGGAGE
FOGGAGES
FOGHORN
FOGHORNS
FOGYDOM
FOGYDOMS
FOGYISM
FOGYISMS
FOILING
FOILINGS
FOISTER
FOISTERS
FOLACIN
FOLACINS
FOLDING
FOLDINGS
FOLIAGE
FOLIAGED
FOLIAGES
FOLIATE
FOLIATED
FOLIATES
FOLIOLE
FOLIOLES
FOLKWAY
FOLKWAYS
FONDANT
FONDANTS
FONDLER
FONDLERS
FONTLET
FONTLETS
FOODISM
FOODISMS
FOOLING
FOOLINGS
FOOTAGE
FOOTAGES
FOOTBAR
FOOTBARS
FOOTBOY
FOOTBOYS
FOOTIES
FOOTIEST
FOOTING
FOOTINGS
FOOTLES
FOOTLESS
FOOTPAD
FOOTPADS
FOOTROT

FOOTROTS
FOOTWAY
FOOTWAYS
FOOZLER
FOOZLERS
FOPLING
FOPLINGS
FORAGER
FORAGERS
FORAYER
FORAYERS
FORBEAR
FORBEARS
FORBODE
FORBODES
FOREARM
FOREARMS
FORECAR
FORECARS
FOREGUT
FOREGUTS
FORELAY
FORELAYS
FORELEG
FORELEGS
FORELIE
FORELIES
FOREPAW
FOREPAWS
FORERUN
FORERUNS
FORESAY
FORESAYS
FORESEE
FORESEEN
FORESEES
FORETOP
FORETOPS
FOREVER
FOREVERS
FORFAIR
FORFAIRN
FORFAIRS
FORFEIT
FORFEITS
FORFEND
FORFENDS
FORGING
FORGINGS
FORGIVE
FORGIVEN
FORGIVES
FORHENT
FORHENTS
FORKFUL
FORKFULS
FORLANA
FORLANAS
FORLEND
FORLENDS
FORLESE
FORLESES
FORLORN
FORLORNS
FORMANT
FORMANTS
FORMATE
FORMATED
FORMATES
FORMING
FORMINGS
FORMULA
FORMULAE
FORMULAR
FORMULAS
FORPINE
FORPINED
FORPINES
FORSAKE
FORSAKEN
FORSAKES
FORSLOE
FORSLOED
FORSLOES
FORSLOW
FORSLOWS
FORTLET
FORTLETS
FORTUNE
FORTUNED
FORTUNES
FORWARD
FORWARDS
FORWARN
FORWARNS
FORZATI
SFORZATI
FORZATO
SFORZATO
FORZATOS
FOSSICK
FOSSICKS
FOSSULA
FOSSULAE
FOUDRIE
FOUDRIES
FOUETTE
FOUETTES
FOUGADE
FOUGADES
FOULARD
FOULARDS
FOULDER
FOULDERS
FOUMART
FOUMARTS
FOUNDER
FOUNDERS
FOURGON
FOURGONS
FOVEOLA
FOVEOLAE
FOVEOLAS
FOVEOLE
FOVEOLES
FOWLING
FOWLINGS
FOXHOLE
FOXHOLES
FOXSHIP
FOXSHIPS
FOXTROT
FOXTROTS
FRACTAL
FRACTALS
FRAGILE
FRAGILER
FRAMING
FRAMINGS
FRANION
FRANIONS
FRAUGHT
FRAUGHTS
FRAYING
FRAYINGS
FRAZZLE
FRAZZLED
FRAZZLES
FRECKLE
FRECKLED
FRECKLES
FREEBEE
FREEBEES
FREEBIE
FREEBIES
FREEDOM
FREEDOMS
FREESIA
FREESIAS
FREEWAY
FREEWAYS
FREEZER
FREEZERS
FREIGHT
FREIGHTS
FRESHEN
FRESHENS
FRESHER
FRESHERS
FRESHES
FRESHEST
FRESHET
FRESHETS
FRESNEL
FRESNELS
FRETSAW
FRETSAWS
FRIANDE
FRIANDES
FRIBBLE
FRIBBLED
FRIBBLER
FRIBBLES
FRIGATE
FRIGATES
FRIGGER
FRIGGERS
FRIJOLE
FRIJOLES
FRIPPER
FRIPPERS
FRIPPERY
FRISEUR
FRISEURS
FRISKER
FRISKERS
FRISKET
FRISKETS
FRISSON
FRISSONS
FRISURE
FRISURES
FRITTER
FRITTERS
FRITURE
FRITURES
FRIZZLE
FRIZZLED
FRIZZLES
FROGBIT
FROGBITS
FROGLET
FROGLETS
FRONTAL
FRONTALS
FRONTON
FRONTONS
FROUNCE
FROUNCED
FROUNCES
FROWARD
FROWARDS
FRUITER
FRUITERS
FRUITERY
FRUMPLE
FRUMPLED
FRUMPLES
FRUSTUM
FRUSTUMS
FUCHSIA
FUCHSIAS
FUCKING
FUCKINGS
FUDDLER
FUDDLERS
FUELLER
FUELLERS
FUGUIST
FUGUISTS
FULCRUM
FULCRUMS
FULFILL
FULFILLS
FULGOUR
FULGOURS
FULLAGE
FULLAGES
FULMINE
FULMINED
FULMINES
FULSOME
FULSOMER
FUMBLER
FUMBLERS
FUMETTE
FUMETTES
FUNDING
FUNDINGS
FUNERAL
FUNERALS
FUNFAIR
FUNFAIRS
FUNICLE
FUNICLES
FUNNIES
FUNNIEST
FUNSTER
FUNSTERS
FURCATE
FURCATED
FURCULA
FURCULAE
FURCULAR
FURFAIR
FURFAIRS
FURIOSO
FURIOSOS
FURLANA
FURLANAS
FURLONG
FURLONGS
FURNACE
FURNACED
FURNACES
FURRIER
FURRIERS
FURRIERY
FURRING
FURRINGS
FURTHER
FURTHERS
FURTIVE
FURTIVER
FUSAROL
FUSAROLE
FUSAROLS
FUSHION
FUSHIONS
FUSTIAN
FUSTIANS
FUTCHEL
FUTCHELS
FUTHARK
FUTHARKS
FUTHORC
FUTHORCS
FUTHORK
FUTHORKS
FUTTOCK
FUTTOCKS
GABBARD
GABBARDS
GABBART
GABBARTS
GABBLER
GABBLERS
GABELLE
GABELLER
GABELLES
GABFEST
GABFESTS
GADLING
GADLINGS
GADROON
GADROONS
GADWALL
GADWALLS
GAFFING
GAFFINGS
GAGSTER
GAGSTERS
GAHNITE
GAHNITES
GAINING
GAININGS
GAINSAY
GAINSAYS
GALABEA
GALABEAH
GALABEAS
GALABIA
GALABIAH
GALABIAS
GALANGA
GALANGAL
GALANGAS
GALATEA
GALATEAS
GALEATE
GALEATED
GALETTE
GALETTES
GALILEE
GALILEES
GALIPOT
GALIPOTS
GALLANT
GALLANTS
GALLATE
GALLATES
GALLEON
GALLEONS
GALLIOT
GALLIOTS
GALLISE
GALLISED
GALLISES
GALLIUM
GALLIUMS
GALLIZE
GALLIZED
GALLIZES
GALLNUT
GALLNUTS
GALLOON
GALLOONS
GALOCHE
GALOCHED
GALOCHES
GALOPIN
GALOPING
GALOPINS
GALUMPH
GALUMPHS
GAMBADO
GAMBADOS
GAMBIER
GAMBIERS
GAMBIST
GAMBISTS
GAMBLER
GAMBLERS
GAMBOGE
GAMBOGES
GAMBREL
GAMBRELS
GAMELAN
GAMELANS
GAMINES
GAMINESS
GAMMOCK
GAMMOCKS
GANGING
GANGINGS
GANGLIA
GANGLIAR
GANGREL
GANGRELS
GANGWAY
GANGWAYS
GANOINE
GANOINES
GANTLET
GANTLETS
GARBAGE
GARBAGES
GARBLER
GARBLERS
GARBOIL
GARBOILS
GARBURE
GARBURES
GARDANT
GARDANTS
GARIGUE
GARIGUES
GARLAND
GARLANDS
GARMENT
GARMENTS
GAROTTE
GAROTTED
GAROTTER
GAROTTES
GARPIKE
GARPIKES
GARROTE
GARROTED
GARROTES
GARVOCK
GARVOCKS
GASAHOL
GASAHOLS
GASOHOL
GASOHOLS
GASPING
GASPINGS
GASSING
GASSINGS
GASTRIN
GASTRINS
GATEWAY
GATEWAYS
GAUDGIE
GAUDGIES
GAUDIES
GAUDIEST
GAUFFER
GAUFFERS
GAUGING
GAUGINGS
GAULTER
GAULTERS
GAVOTTE
GAVOTTES
GAWKIES
GAWKIEST
GAZANIA
GAZANIAS
GAZELLE
GAZELLES
GAZETTE
GAZETTED
GAZETTES
GAZOOKA
GAZOOKAS
GEALOUS
GEALOUSY
GEARING
GEARINGS
GEEBUNG
GEEBUNGS
GEECHEE
GEECHEES
GELATIN
GELATINE
GELATINS
GELDING
GELDINGS

GEMMATE
GEMMATED
GEMMATES
GEMMULE
GEMMULES
GEMSBOK
GEMSBOKS
GENAPPE
GENAPPES
GENERAL
GENERALE
GENERALS
GENERIC
GENERICS
GENETIC
GENETICS
GENETTE
GENETTES
GENIPAP
GENIPAPS
GENISTA
GENISTAS
GENITAL
GENITALS
GENITOR
GENITORS
GENIZAH
GENIZAHS
GENLOCK
GENLOCKS
GENTIAN
GENTIANS
GENTILE
GENTILES
GENTLES
GENTLEST
GEOFACT
GEOFACTS
GEOMANT
GEOMANTS
GEORGIC
GEORGICS
GERBERA
GERBERAS
GERENUK
GERENUKS
GERMAIN
GERMAINE
GERMAINS
GESTALT
GESTALTS
GESTAPO
GESTAPOS
GESTATE
GESTATED
GESTATES
GESTURE
GESTURED
GESTURES
GETAWAY
GETAWAYS
GETTING
GETTINGS
GHARIAL
GHARIALS
GHERKIN
GHERKINS
GHILGAI
GHILGAIS
GHILLIE
GHILLIED
GHILLIES
GIDDIES
GIDDIEST
GIGGLER
GIGGLERS
GILBERT
GILBERTS
GILDING
GILDINGS
GILLION
GILLIONS
GILTCUP
GILTCUPS
GIMMICK
GIMMICKS
GIMMICKY
GINGALL
GINGALLS
GINGHAM
GINGHAMS
GINGILI
GINGILIS
GINNERS
AGINNERS
GINSENG
GINSENGS
GINSHOP
GINSHOPS
GIRAFFE
GIRAFFES
GIRASOL
GIRASOLE
GIRASOLS
GIRDING
GIRDINGS
GIRDLER
GIRDLERS
GIRLOND
GIRLONDS
GIROSOL
GIROSOLS
GISARME
GISARMES
GITTERN
GITTERNS
GIZZARD
GIZZARDS
GLACIAL
GLACIALS
GLACIER
GLACIERS
GLADDEN
GLADDENS
GLADDIE
GLADDIES
GLADDON
GLADDONS
GLAIRIN
GLAIRING
GLAIRINS
GLAMOUR
GLAMOURS
GLAZIER
GLAZIERS
GLAZING
GLAZINGS
GLEANER
GLEANERS
GLENOID
GLENOIDS
GLIADIN
GLIADINE
GLIADINS
GLIBBER
GLIBBERY
GLIDDER
GLIDDERY
GLIDING
GLIDINGS
GLIMMER
AGLIMMER
GLIMMERS
GLIMMERY
GLIMPSE
GLIMPSED
GLIMPSES
GLISTEN
GLISTENS
GLISTER
GLISTERS
GLITTER
AGLITTER
GLITTERS
GLITTERY
GLOATER
GLOATERS
GLOBATE
GLOBATED
GLOBOID
GLOBOIDS
GLOBOSE
GLOBOSES
GLOBULE
GLOBULES
GLOBULET
GLONOIN
GLONOINS
GLOSSER
GLOSSERS
GLOVING
GLOVINGS
GLOZING
GLOZINGS
GLUCINA
GLUCINAS
GLUCOSE
GLUCOSES
GLUTTON
GLUTTONS
GLUTTONY
GLYCINE
GLYCINES
GLYCOSE
GLYCOSES
GLYPTIC
GLYPTICS
GNASHER
GNASHERS
GNOCCHI
GNOCCHIS
GNOMIST
GNOMISTS
GNOSTIC
AGNOSTIC
GOBBLER
GOBBLERS
GOBURRA
GOBURRAS
GODETIA
GODETIAS
GODHEAD
GODHEADS
GODHOOD
GODHOODS
GODLING
GODLINGS
GODROON
GODROONS
GODSEND
GODSENDS
GODSHIP
GODSHIPS
GODWARD
GODWARDS
GOGGLER
GOGGLERS
GOLDEYE
GOLDEYES
GOLFING
GOLFINGS
GOLIARD
GOLIARDS
GOLIARDY
GOLLAND
GOLLANDS
GOMBEEN
GOMBEENS
GOMERAL
GOMERALS
GOMERIL
GOMERILS
GONDOLA
GONDOLAS
GONIDIA
GONIDIAL
GOODIES
GOODIEST
GOOSIES
GOOSIEST
GOPURAM
GOPURAMS
GORCOCK
GORCOCKS
GORCROW
GORCROWS
GORILLA
GORILLAS
GORMAND
GORMANDS
GORSEDD
GORSEDDS
GORSOON
GORSOONS
GOSHAWK
GOSHAWKS
GOSLING
GOSLINGS
GOSSOON
GOSSOONS
GOTHITE
GOTHITES
GOUACHE
GOUACHES
GOUGERE
GOUGERES
GOURAMI
GOURAMIS
GOURMET
GOURMETS
GOWLAND
GOWLANDS
GOWNBOY
GOWNBOYS
GRABBER
GRABBERS
GRABBLE
GRABBLED
GRABBLER
GRABBLES
GRACKLE
GRACKLES
GRADATE
GRADATED
GRADATES
GRADDAN
GRADDANS
GRADINE
GRADINES
GRADUAL
GRADUALS
GRAFTER
GRAFTERS
GRAINER
GRAINERS
GRAMARY
GRAMARYE
GRAMMAR
GRAMMARS
GRANDAD
GRANDADS
GRANDAM
GRANDAMS
GRANDEE
GRANDEES
GRANDMA
GRANDMAS
GRANDPA
GRANDPAS
GRANFER
GRANFERS
GRANGER
GRANGERS
GRANITA
GRANITAS
GRANITE
GRANITES
GRANNAM
GRANNAMS
GRANNIE
GRANNIED
GRANNIES
GRANOLA
GRANOLAS
GRANTEE
GRANTEES
GRANTER
GRANTERS
GRANTOR
GRANTORS
GRANULE
GRANULES
GRAPHIC
AGRAPHIC
GRAPHICS
GRAPNEL
GRAPNELS
GRAPPLE
GRAPPLED
GRAPPLES
GRASPER
GRASPERS
GRASSER
GRASSERS
GRASSUM
GRASSUMS
GRATINE
GRATINEE
GRATING
GRATINGS
GRAUPEL
GRAUPELS
GRAVING
GRAVINGS
GRAVURE
GRAVURES
GRAZIER
GRAZIERS
GRAZING
GRAZINGS
GREASER
GREASERS
GREATEN
GREATENS
GRECIAN
GRECIANS
GRECISE
GRECISED
GRECISES
GRECIZE
GRECIZED
GRECIZES
GRECQUE
GRECQUES
GREEING
AGREEING
GREENER
GREENERS
GREENERY
GREENIE
GREENIER
GREENIES
GREENTH
GREENTHS
GREETER
GREETERS
GREGALE
GREGALES
GREISEN
GREISENS
GREMIAL
GREMIALS
GREMLIN
GREMLINS
GRENADE
GRENADES
GREYHEN
GREYHENS
GREYING
GREYINGS
GRIBBLE
GRIBBLES
GRICING
GRICINGS
GRIDDER
GRIDDERS
GRIDDLE
GRIDDLES
GRIEVER
GRIEVERS
GRIFFIN
GRIFFINS
GRIFFON
GRIFFONS
GRIFTER
GRIFTERS
GRIMACE
GRIMACED
GRIMACES
GRINDER
GRINDERS
GRINDERY
GRINNER
GRINNERS
GRIPPER
GRIPPERS
GRIPPLE
GRIPPLES
GRISING
AGRISING
GRISKIN
GRISKINS
GRISTLE
GRISTLES
GRITTER
GRITTERS
GRIZZLE
GRIZZLED
GRIZZLER
GRIZZLES
GROANER
GROANERS
GROCKLE
GROCKLES
GROGRAM
GROGRAMS
GROMMET
GROMMETS
GROOVER
GROOVERS
GROSERT
GROSERTS
GROSSES
GROSSEST
GROUPER
GROUPERS
GROUPIE
GROUPIES
GROUSER
GROUSERS
GROUSES
GROUSEST
GROUTER
GROUTERS
GROWING
GROWINGS
GROWLER
GROWLERS
GROWLERY
GRUBBER
GRUBBERS
GRUBBLE
GRUBBLED
GRUBBLES
GRUMBLE
GRUMBLED
GRUMBLER
GRUMBLES
GRUMMET
GRUMMETS

GRUNION
GRUNIONS
GRUNTER
GRUNTERS
GRUNTLE
GRUNTLED
GRUNTLES
GRYPHON
GRYPHONS
GRYSBOK
GRYSBOKS
GUANACO
GUANACOS
GUANINE
GUANINES
GUARANA
GUARANAS
GUARANI
GUARANIS
GUARDEE
GUARDEES
GUAYULE
GUAYULES
GUDGEON
GUDGEONS
GUERDON
GUERDONS
GUEREZA
GUEREZAS
GUERITE
GUERITES
GUESSER
GUESSERS
GUESTEN
GUESTENS
GUICHET
GUICHETS
GUIDAGE
GUIDAGES
GUIDING
GUIDINGS
GUILDER
GUILDERS
GUIPURE
GUIPURES
GUISARD
GUISARDS
GUISING
AGUISING
GUISINGS
GUMBOIL
GUMBOILS
GUMBOOT
GUMBOOTS
GUMDROP
GUMDROPS
GUMMING
GUMMINGS
GUMMITE
GUMMITES
GUMSHOE
GUMSHOED
GUMSHOES
GUNBOAT
GUNBOATS
GUNFIRE
GUNFIRES
GUNLOCK
GUNLOCKS
GUNNAGE
GUNNAGES
GUNNERA
GUNNERAS
GUNNING
GUNNINGS
GUNPLAY
GUNPLAYS
GUNPORT
GUNPORTS
GUNROOM
GUNROOMS
GUNSHIP
GUNSHIPS
GUNSHOT
GUNSHOTS
GUNWALE
GUNWALES
GURNARD
GURNARDS
GURUDOM
GURUDOMS
GURUISM
GURUISMS
GUTCHER
GUTCHERS
GUTSFUL
GUTSFULS
GUTTATE
GUTTATED
GUTTATES
GUTTIES
GUTTIEST
GUZZLER
GUZZLERS
GWINIAD
GWINIADS
GWYNIAD
GWYNIADS
GYMNAST
GYMNASTS
GYROCAR
GYROCARS
HABITAT
HABITATS
HABITUE
HABITUES
HACHURE
HACHURED
HACHURES
HACKBUT
HACKBUTS
HACKERS
WHACKERS
HACKING
CHACKING
WHACKING
HACKINGS
HACKLED
SHACKLED
HACKLER
HACKLERS
HACKLES
SHACKLES
HACKLET
HACKLETS
HACKNEY
HACKNEYS
HADDOCK
SHADDOCK
HADDOCKS
HADROME
HADROMES
HAFFLIN
HAFFLINS
HAFNIUM
HAFNIUMS
HAFTING
SHAFTING
HAGBOLT
HAGBOLTS
HAGDOWN
HAGDOWNS
HAGGARD
HAGGARDS
HAGGING
SHAGGING
HAGGLER
HAGGLERS
HAHNIUM
HAHNIUMS
HAINING
CHAINING
HAININGS
HAIRCUT
HAIRCUTS
HAIRING
CHAIRING
HAIRNET
HAIRNETS
HAIRPIN
HAIRPINS
HALAVAH
HALAVAHS
HALBERD
HALBERDS
HALBERT
HALBERTS
HALCYON
HALCYONS
HALFLIN
HALFLING
HALFLINS
HALFWIT
HALFWITS
HALIBUT
HALIBUTS
HALIDOM
HALIDOMS
HALIMOT
HALIMOTE
HALIMOTS
HALLALI
HALLALIS
HALLANS
CHALLANS
HALLIAN
HALLIANS
HALLING
HALLINGS
HALLION
HALLIONS
HALLOWS
SHALLOWS
HALLWAY
HALLWAYS
HALLYON
HALLYONS
HALOGEN
HALOGENS
HALTING
HALTINGS
HALYARD
HALYARDS
HAMBLED
SHAMBLED
HAMBLES
SHAMBLES
HAMLETS
CHAMLETS
HAMMERS
SHAMMERS
HAMMING
SHAMMING
WHAMMING
HAMMOCK
HAMMOCKS
HAMPERS
CHAMPERS
HAMSTER
HAMSTERS
HANAPER
HANAPERS
HANDBAG
HANDBAGS
HANDCAR
HANDCARS
HANDCART
HANDFUL
HANDFULS
HANDGUN
HANDGUNS
HANDJAR
HANDJARS
HANDLER
CHANDLER
HANDLERS
HANDLES
HANDLESS
HANDOUT
HANDOUTS
HANDSAW
HANDSAWS
HANDSEL
HANDSELS
HANDSET
HANDSETS
HANGDOG
HANGDOGS
HANGERS
CHANGERS
HANGING
CHANGING
PHANGING
WHANGING
HANGINGS
HANGOUT
HANGOUTS
HANJARS
KHANJARS
HANKERS
THANKERS
HANKING
SHANKING
THANKING
HANUMAN
HANUMANS
HAPLESS
CHAPLESS
HAPLOID
HAPLOIDY
HAPPIER
CHAPPIER
HAPPIES
CHAPPIES
HAPPIEST
HAPPING
CHAPPING
WHAPPING
HARBOUR
HARBOURS
HARDOKE
HARDOKES
HARDTOP
HARDTOPS
HARICOT
HARICOTS
HARKING
CHARKING
SHARKING
HARLING
HARLINGS
HARMALA
HARMALAS
HARMFUL
CHARMFUL
HARMINE
HARMINES
HARMING
CHARMING
HARMOST
HARMOSTS
HARMOSTY
HAROSET
CHAROSET
HAROSETH
HAROSETS
HARPERS
SHARPERS
HARPIES
CHARPIES
SHARPIES
HARPING
SHARPING
HARPINGS
HARPIST
HARPISTS
HARPOON
HARPOONS
HARRIER
HARRIERS
HARRIES
GHARRIES
HARSHEN
HARSHENS
HARSLET
HARSLETS
HARVEST
HARVESTS
HASHING
SHASHING
HASSOCK
HASSOCKS
HASSOCKY
HASTATE
HASTATED
HASTENS
CHASTENS
HASTING
GHASTING
HASTINGS
HATBAND
HATBANDS
HATCHED
THATCHED
HATCHEL
HATCHELS
HATCHER
THATCHER
HATCHERS
HATCHERY
HATCHES
THATCHES
HATCHET
HATCHETS
HATCHETY
HATRACK
HATRACKS
HATTERS
CHATTERS
SHATTERS
HATTING
CHATTING
HATTINGS
HATTOCK
HATTOCKS
HAUBERK
HAUBERKS
HAULAGE
HAULAGES
HAULIER
HAULIERS
HAUNTED
CHAUNTED
HAUNTER
CHAUNTER
HAUNTERS
HAUTBOY
HAUTBOYS
HAUTEUR
HAUTEURS
HAVEOUR
HAVEOURS
HAVEREL
HAVERELS
HAVINGS
SHAVINGS
HAVIOUR
HAVIOURS
HAWBUCK
HAWBUCKS
HAWKBIT
HAWKBITS
HAWKING
HAWKINGS
HAYBAND
HAYBANDS
HAYCOCK
HAYCOCKS
HAYFORK
HAYFORKS
HAYLOFT
HAYLOFTS
HAYRICK
HAYRICKS
HAYRIDE
HAYRIDES
HAYSEED
HAYSEEDS
HAYWARD
HAYWARDS
HAYWIRE
HAYWIRES
HEADAGE
HEADAGES
HEADING
SHEADING
HEADINGS
HEADRIG
HEADRIGS
HEADSET
HEADSETS
HEADWAY
HEADWAYS
HEALING
SHEALING
HEALINGS
HEARERS
SHEARERS
HEARING
SHEARING
HEARINGS
HEARKEN
HEARKENS
HEARSAY
HEARSAYS
HEARTEN
HEARTENS
HEATERS
CHEATERS
THEATERS
HEATHEN
HEATHENS
HEATHER
HEATHERS
HEATHERY
HEATING
CHEATING
HEATINGS
HEAVIES
HEAVIEST
HEAVING
SHEAVING
HEAVINGS
HEBENON
HEBENONS
HECKLER
HECKLERS
HECTARE
HECTARES
HEDGING
HEDGINGS
HEDONIC
HEDONICS
HEELERS
WHEELERS
HEELING
SHEELING
WHEELING
HEELINGS
HEEZING
PHEEZING
WHEEZING
HEIRDOM
HEIRDOMS
HEISTER
HEISTERS
HELICON
HELICONS
HELIPAD
HELIPADS

HELLERS
SHELLERS
HELLIER
SHELLIER
HELLIERS
HELLING
SHELLING
HELLION
HELLIONS
HELMING
WHELMING
HELPING
WHELPING
HELPINGS
HELVING
SHELVING
HEMIOLA
HEMIOLAS
HEMIONE
HEMIONES
HEMLOCK
HEMLOCKS
HEMPIES
HEMPIEST
HENBANE
HENBANES
HENDING
SHENDING
HENNIES
HENNIEST
HENPECK
HENPECKS
HEPARIN
HEPARINS
HEPATIC
HEPATICS
HEPSTER
HEPSTERS
HEPTANE
HEPTANES
HERBAGE
HERBAGED
HERBAGES
HERBIST
HERBISTS
HERBLET
HERBLETS
HERDBOY
HERDBOYS
HERETIC
HERETICS
HERITOR
HERITORS
HERLING
HERLINGS
HEROINE
HEROINES
HEROISE
HEROISED
HEROISES
HEROISM
HEROISMS
HEROIZE
HEROIZED
HEROIZES
HERRIED
CHERRIED
HERRIES
CHERRIES
SHERRIES
WHERRIES
HERRING
HERRINGS
HERSALL
HERSALLS
HERSHIP
HERSHIPS
HESSIAN
HESSIANS
HETAERA
HETAERAE
HETAIRA
HETAIRAI
HETAIRAS
HEUREKA
HEUREKAS
HEURISM
HEURISMS
HEXAGON
HEXAGONS
HEXAPLA
HEXAPLAR
HEXAPLAS
HEXAPOD
HEXAPODS
HEXAPODY
HEYDUCK
HEYDUCKS
HIBACHI
HIBACHIS
HICATEE
HICATEES
HIDALGA
HIDALGAS
HIDALGO
HIDALGOS
HIDDERS
SHIDDERS
WHIDDERS
HIDEOUT
HIDEOUTS
HIDINGS
CHIDINGS
HIDLING
HIDLINGS
HIGGLER
HIGGLERS
HIGHBOY
HIGHBOYS
HIGHWAY
HIGHWAYS
HILDING
CHILDING
HILDINGS
HILLIER
CHILLIER
HILLING
CHILLING
SHILLING
HILLOCK
HILLOCKS
HILLOCKY
HILLTOP
HILLTOPS
HINDLEG
HINDLEGS
HINNIED
SHINNIED
WHINNIED
HINNIES
SHINNIES
WHINNIES
HIPPIER
CHIPPIER
WHIPPIER
HIPPIES
CHIPPIES
HIPPIEST
HIPPING
CHIPPING
SHIPPING
WHIPPING
HIPPINGS
HIPSTER
WHIPSTER
HIPSTERS
HIREAGE
HIREAGES
HIRLING
CHIRLING
THIRLING
WHIRLING
HIRLINGS
HIRUDIN
HIRUDINS
HISHING
WHISHING
HISSING
WHISSING
HISSINGS
HISTING
WHISTING
HISTONE
HISTONES
HISTRIO
HISTRION
HISTRIOS
HITCHER
HITCHERS
HITHERS
WHITHERS
HITTERS
CHITTERS
WHITTERS
HITTING
CHITTING
SHITTING
HIZZING
CHIZZING
WHIZZING
HOARDER
HOARDERS
HOARSEN
HOARSENS
HOATZIN
HOATZINS
HOBBLER
HOBBLERS
HOBNAIL
HOBNAILS
HOBODOM
HOBODOMS
HOBOISM
HOBOISMS
HOCKERS
SHOCKERS
HOCKING
CHOCKING
SHOCKING
HOEDOWN
HOEDOWNS
HOGBACK
HOGBACKS
HOGGING
SHOGGING
HOGGINGS
HOGHOOD
HOGHOODS
HOGWARD
HOGWARDS
HOGWEED
HOGWEEDS
HOISTER
HOISTERS
HOKIEST
CHOKIEST
HOLDING
HOLDINGS
HOLESOM
HOLESOME
HOLIBUT
HOLIBUTS
HOLIDAY
HOLIDAYS
HOLISMS
WHOLISMS
HOLISTS
WHOLISTS
HOLLAND
HOLLANDS
HOLMIUM
HOLMIUMS
HOLSTER
HOLSTERS
HOLYDAM
HOLYDAME
HOLYDAMS
HOMAGER
HOMAGERS
HOMELYN
HOMELYNS
HOMINID
HOMINIDS
HOMMOCK
HOMMOCKS
HOMOLOG
HOMOLOGS
HOMOLOGY
HOMONYM
HOMONYMS
HOMONYMY
HONEYED
PHONEYED
HOODLUM
HOODLUMS
HOOFING
CHOOFING
HOOFROT
HOOFROTS
HOOKIES
CHOOKIES
HOOKIEST
HOOLOCK
HOOLOCKS
HOOPERS
WHOOPERS
HOOPING
WHOOPING
HOOSGOW
HOOSGOWS
HOOSHED
WHOOSHED
HOOSHES
WHOOSHES
HOOTERS
SHOOTERS
HOOTING
SHOOTING
WHOOTING
HOPBIND
HOPBINDS
HOPBINE
HOPBINES
HOPEFUL
HOPEFULS
HOPLITE
HOPLITES
HOPPERS
CHOPPERS
SHOPPERS
WHOPPERS
HOPPIER
CHOPPIER
SHOPPIER
HOPPING
CHOPPING
SHOPPING
WHOPPING
HOPPINGS
HOPSACK
HOPSACKS
HORDEIN
HORDEINS
HORDING
CHORDING
HORDOCK
HORDOCKS
HORIZON
HORIZONS
HORMONE
HORMONES
HORNBUG
HORNBUGS
HORNFUL
HORNFULS
HORNIER
THORNIER
HORNING
THORNING
HORNINGS
HORNIST
HORNISTS
HORNITO
HORNITOS
HORNLET
HORNLETS
HORSING
HORSINGS
HOSANNA
HOSANNAS
HOSPICE
HOSPICES
HOSTAGE
HOSTAGES
HOSTING
GHOSTING
HOSTINGS
HOSTLER
HOSTLERS
HOTHEAD
HOTHEADS
HOTLINE
HOTLINES
HOTSHOT
HOTSHOTS
HOTTING
SHOTTING
HOTTINGS
HOUSING
CHOUSING
HOUSINGS
HOUTING
SHOUTING
HOUTINGS
HOWLING
HOWLINGS
HUANACO
HUANACOS
HUCKLES
CHUCKLES
HUFFIER
CHUFFIER
HUFFING
CHUFFING
HUFFKIN
HUFFKINS
HUGGING
CHUGGING
HUITAIN
HUITAINS
HUMBLES
HUMBLEST
HUMDRUM
HUMDRUMS
HUMERAL
HUMERALS
HUMIDOR
HUMIDORS
HUMMAUM
HUMMAUMS
HUMMING
CHUMMING
HUMMINGS
HUMMOCK
HUMMOCKS
HUMMOCKY
HUMOGEN
HUMOGENS
HUMPERS
THUMPERS
HUMPIES
HUMPIEST
HUMPING
CHUMPING
THUMPING
HUNDRED
HUNDREDS
HUNKIER
CHUNKIER
HUNKIES
HUNKIEST
HUNTERS
CHUNTERS
SHUNTERS
HUNTING
SHUNTING
HUNTINGS
HUPPAHS
CHUPPAHS
HURDLER
HURDLERS
HURLBAT
HURLBATS
HURLING
HURLINGS
HURRIES
DHURRIES
HURTLES
HURTLESS
HUSBAND
HUSBANDS
HUSHING
SHUSHING
HUSKIES
HUSKIEST
HUSKING
HUSKINGS
HUSTLER
HUSTLERS
HUTMENT
HUTMENTS
HUTTING
PHUTTING
SHUTTING
HUTTINGS
HUTZPAH
CHUTZPAH
HUTZPAHS
HYACINE
HYACINES
HYALINE
HYALINES
HYALITE
HYALITES
HYDATID
HYDATIDS
HYDRANT
HYDRANTH
HYDRANTS
HYDRATE
HYDRATED
HYDRATES
HYDRIDE
HYDRIDES
HYDROID
HYDROIDS
HYDROXY
HYDROXYL
HYGIENE
HYGIENES
HYLDING
HYLDINGS
HYLOIST
HYLOISTS
HYMENIA
HYMENIAL
HYMNIST
HYMNISTS
HYPERON
HYPERONS
HYPNONE
HYPNONES
HYPOGEA
HYPOGEAL
HYPOGEAN
HYPONYM
HYPONYMS
HYPONYMY
HYPOXIA
HYPOXIAS

IAMBIST
IAMBISTS
ICEBALL
ICEBALLS
ICEBERG
ICEBERGS
ICEBOAT
ICEBOATS
ICEPACK
ICEPACKS
ICHNITE
ICHNITES
ICKIEST
DICKIEST
PICKIEST
ICONISE
ICONISED
ICONISES
ICONIZE
ICONIZED
ICONIZES
ICTERIC
ICTERICS
ICTERID
ICTERIDS
ICTUSES
RICTUSES
IDLESSE
IDLESSES
IDOLISE
IDOLISED
IDOLISER
IDOLISES
IDOLISM
IDOLISMS
IDOLIST
IDOLISTS
IDOLIZE
IDOLIZED
IDOLIZER
IDOLIZES
IFFIEST
MIFFIEST
NIFFIEST
IGARAPE
IGARAPES
IGNEOUS
LIGNEOUS
IGNITER
IGNITERS
IGNITES
LIGNITES
IGNOBLE
IGNOBLER
IGNORER
IGNORERS
IGNORES
SIGNORES
IGUANID
IGUANIDS
IJTIHAD
IJTIHADS
IKEBANA
IKEBANAS
ILKADAY
ILKADAYS
ILLAPSE
ILLAPSED
ILLAPSES
ILLITES
TILLITES
ILLOGIC
ILLOGICS
ILLUVIA
ILLUVIAL
IMAGINE
IMAGINED
IMAGINER
IMAGINES
IMAGING
IMAGINGS
IMAGISM
IMAGISMS
IMAGIST
IMAGISTS
IMAMATE
IMAMATES
IMBATHE
IMBATHED
IMBATHES
IMBIBER
IMBIBERS
IMBOSOM
IMBOSOMS
IMBOWER
IMBOWERS
IMBROWN
IMBROWNS
IMBRUTE
IMBRUTED
IMBRUTES
IMBURSE
IMBURSED
IMBURSES
IMITANT
IMITANTS
IMITATE
IMITATED
IMITATES
IMMENSE
IMMENSER
IMMERGE
IMMERGED
IMMERGES
IMMERSE
IMMERSED
IMMERSES
IMPAINT
IMPAINTS
IMPANEL
IMPANELS
IMPASSE
IMPASSES
IMPASTE
IMPASTED
IMPASTES
IMPASTO
IMPASTOS
IMPEARL
IMPEARLS
IMPERIA
IMPERIAL
IMPERIL
IMPERILS
IMPINGE
IMPINGED
IMPINGES
IMPLANT
IMPLANTS
IMPLATE
IMPLATED
IMPLATES
IMPLEAD
IMPLEADS
IMPLETE
IMPLETED
IMPLETES
IMPLODE
IMPLODED
IMPLODES
IMPLORE
IMPLORED
IMPLORER
IMPLORES
IMPOSER
IMPOSERS
IMPOUND
IMPOUNDS
IMPREGN
IMPREGNS
IMPRESA
IMPRESAS
IMPRESE
IMPRESES
IMPRESS
IMPRESSE
IMPREST
IMPRESTS
IMPRINT
IMPRINTS
IMPROVE
IMPROVED
IMPROVER
IMPROVES
IMPULSE
IMPULSED
IMPULSES
IMPUTER
IMPUTERS
INBEING
INBEINGS
INBREAK
INBREAKS
INBREED
INBREEDS
INBRING
INBRINGS
INBURST
INBURSTS
INCASES
PINCASES
INCENSE
INCENSED
INCENSER
INCENSES
INCHASE
INCHASED
INCHASES
INCHING
CINCHING
PINCHING
WINCHING
INCHPIN
LINCHPIN
INCHPINS
INCISOR
INCISORS
INCISORY
INCITER
INCITERS
INCITES
ZINCITES
INCLASP
INCLASPS
INCLINE
INCLINED
INCLINES
INCLOSE
INCLOSED
INCLOSER
INCLOSES
INCLUDE
INCLUDED
INCLUDES
INCOMER
INCOMERS
INCONNU
INCONNUE
INCONNUS
INCRUST
INCRUSTS
INCURVE
INCURVED
INCURVES
INDEXER
INDEXERS
INDICAN
INDICANS
INDICANT
INDICIA
INDICIAL
INDIGOS
WINDIGOS
INDITER
INDITERS
INDORSE
INDORSED
INDORSES
INDOXYL
INDOXYLS
INDRAFT
INDRAFTS
INDUCER
INDUCERS
INDULGE
INDULGED
INDULGER
INDULGES
INDULIN
INDULINE
INDULINS
INDUSIA
INDUSIAL
INDWELL
INDWELLS
INEARTH
INEARTHS
INERTIA
INERTIAL
INERTIAS
INFANTA
INFANTAS
INFANTE
INFANTES
INFARCT
INFARCTS
INFERNO
INFERNOS
INFIDEL
INFIDELS
INFIELD
INFIELDS
INFIMUM
INFIMUMS
INFLAME
INFLAMED
INFLAMER
INFLAMES
INFLATE
INFLATED
INFLATES
INFLECT
INFLECTS
INFLICT
INFLICTS
INFOLDS
PINFOLDS
INFORCE
INFORCED
INFORCES
INFRACT
INFRACTS
INFUSER
INFUSERS
INGENER
INGENERS
INGENUE
INGENUES
INGLOBE
INGLOBED
INGLOBES
INGOING
INGOINGS
INGRAFT
INGRAFTS
INGRAIN
INGRAINS
INGRATE
INGRATES
INGROUP
INGROUPS
INGULPH
INGULPHS
INHABIT
INHABITS
INHALER
INHALERS
INHAUST
INHAUSTS
INHERCE
INHERCED
INHERCES
INHERIT
INHERITS
INHIBIT
INHIBITS
INHUMAN
INHUMANE
INHUMER
INHUMERS
INITIAL
INITIALS
INJOINT
INJOINTS
INJUNCT
INJUNCTS
INJURER
INJURERS
INKHORN
INKHORNS
INKIEST
DINKIEST
KINKIEST
PINKIEST
SINKIEST
ZINKIEST
INKLING
TINKLING
WINKLING
INKLINGS
INKSPOT
INKSPOTS
INKWELL
INKWELLS
INLAYER
INLAYERS
INNERVE
INNERVED
INNERVES
INNINGS
PINNINGS
TINNINGS
WINNINGS
INNYARD
INNYARDS
INQILAB
INQILABS
INQUERE
INQUERED
INQUERES
INQUEST
INQUESTS
INQUIET
INQUIETS
INQUIRE
INQUIRED
INQUIRER
INQUIRES
INSANIE
INSANIES
INSCAPE
INSCAPES
INSCULP
INSCULPS
INSCULPT
INSHELL
INSHELLS
INSHIPS
KINSHIPS
INSIDER
INSIDERS
INSIGHT
INSIGHTS
INSIGNE
INSIGNES
INSINEW
INSINEWS
INSNARE
INSNARED
INSNARES
INSPECT
INSPECTS
INSPIRE
INSPIRED
INSPIRER
INSPIRES
INSTALL
INSTALLS
INSTANT
INSTANTS
INSTATE
INSTATED
INSTATES
INSTILL
INSTILLS
INSULIN
INSULINS
INSURED
INSUREDS
INSURER
INSURERS
INSWING
INSWINGS
INTEGER
INTEGERS
INTENSE
INTENSER
INTERIM
INTERIMS
INTERNE
INTERNED
INTERNEE
INTERNES
INTERNET
INTHRAL
INTHRALL
INTHRALS
INTONER
INTONERS
INTRADA
INTRADAS
INTRANT
INTRANTS
INTREAT
INTREATS
INTROIT
INTROITS
INTRUDE
INTRUDED
INTRUDER
INTRUDES
INTRUST
INTRUSTS
INTWINE
INTWINED
INTWINES
INTWIST
INTWISTS
INULASE
INULASES
INVADER
INVADERS
INVALID
INVALIDS
INVEIGH
INVEIGHS
INVERSE
INVERSES
INVITEE
INVITEES
INVITER
INVITERS
INVOICE
INVOICED
INVOICES
INVOLVE
INVOLVED
INVOLVES
INWEAVE
INWEAVES

IODURET
IODURETS
IONISED
LIONISED
IONISER
IONISERS
IONISES
LIONISES
IONIZED
LIONIZED
IONIZER
IONIZERS
IONIZES
LIONIZES
IONOMER
IONOMERS
IPOMOEA
IPOMOEAS
IRIDIAN
VIRIDIAN
IRIDISE
IRIDISED
IRIDISES
IRIDIUM
IRIDIUMS
IRIDIZE
IRIDIZED
IRIDIZES
IRISATE
IRISATED
IRISATES
IRONING
IRONINGS
IRONISE
IRONISED
IRONISES
IRONIST
IRONISTS
IRONIZE
IRONIZED
IRONIZES
ISAGOGE
ISAGOGES
ISATINE
ISATINES
ISOBARE
ISOBARES
ISOBASE
ISOBASES
ISOBATH
ISOBATHS
ISOCHOR
ISOCHORE
ISOCHORS
ISODONT
ISODONTS
ISOGAMY
MISOGAMY
ISOGRAM
ISOGRAMS
ISOHYET
ISOHYETS
ISOKONT
ISOKONTS
ISOLATE
ISOLATED
ISOLATES
ISOLINE
ISOLINES
ISOMERE

ISOMERES
ISOSPIN
ISOSPINS
ISOTONE
ISOTONES
ISOTOPE
ISOTOPES
ISOTRON
ISOTRONS
ISOTYPE
ISOTYPES
ISSUING
TISSUING
ITACISM
ITACISMS
ITCHIER
BITCHIER
HITCHIER
PITCHIER
TITCHIER
WITCHIER
ITCHING
BITCHING
DITCHING
HITCHING
MITCHING
PITCHING
WITCHING
ITEMISE
ITEMISED
ITEMISES
ITEMIZE
ITEMIZED
ITEMIZES
ITERATE
LITERATE
ITERATED
ITERATES
IVORIST
IVORISTS
IVRESSE
IVRESSES
IZZARDS
DIZZARDS
GIZZARDS
JACAMAR
JACAMARS
JACINTH
JACINTHS
JACKDAW
JACKDAWS
JACKEEN
JACKEENS
JACKPOT
JACKPOTS
JACKSIE
JACKSIES
JACOBIN
JACOBINS
JACONET
JACONETS
JACUZZI
JACUZZIS
JADEITE
JADEITES
JAGHIRE
JAGHIRES
JALAPIN
JALAPINS
JALOUSE

JALOUSED
JALOUSES
JAMADAR
JAMADARS
JAMBEAU
JAMBEAUX
JAMBIER
JAMBIERS
JAMBIYA
JAMBIYAH
JAMBIYAS
JAMBOKS
SJAMBOKS
JAMBONE
JAMBONES
JAMBOOL
JAMBOOLS
JAMDANI
JAMDANIS
JAMPANI
JAMPANIS
JANGLER
JANGLERS
JANITOR
JANITORS
JANIZAR
JANIZARS
JANIZARY
JANNOCK
JANNOCKS
JANTIES
JANTIEST
JARGOON
JARGOONS
JARRING
JARRINGS
JASMINE
JASMINES
JAUNTIE
JAUNTIER
JAUNTIES
JAVELIN
JAVELINS
JAWBONE
JAWBONED
JAWBONES
JAWFALL
JAWFALLS
JAWHOLE
JAWHOLES
JAYWALK
JAYWALKS
JEALOUS
JEALOUSE
JEALOUSY
JEEPNEY
JEEPNEYS
JEERING
JEERINGS
JELLABA
DJELLABA
JELLABAS
JEMADAR
JEMADARS
JEMIDAR
JEMIDARS
JEMMIES
JEMMIEST
JEOFAIL
JEOFAILS

JEOPARD
JEOPARDS
JEOPARDY
JERKIES
JERKIEST
JERKING
JERKINGS
JERQUER
JERQUERS
JESTING
JESTINGS
JETFOIL
JETFOILS
JETTIES
JETTIEST
JIBBAHS
DJIBBAHS
JIBBING
JIBBINGS
JIGAJIG
JIGAJIGS
JIGAJOG
JIGAJOGS
JIGGING
JIGGINGS
JILLION
JILLIONS
JINGLER
JINGLERS
JINGLET
JINGLETS
JINJILI
JINJILIS
JIPYAPA
JIPYAPAS
JOBBING
JOBBINGS
JOGGING
JOGGINGS
JOGTROT
JOGTROTS
JOHNNIE
JOHNNIES
JOINDER
JOINDERS
JOINING
JOININGS
JOINTER
JOINTERS
JOLLIES
JOLLIEST
JOLLYER
JOLLYERS
JONQUIL
JONQUILS
JOTTING
JOTTINGS
JOURNAL
JOURNALS
JOURNEY
JOURNEYS
JOUSTER
JOUSTERS
JOYANCE
JOYANCES
JUBILEE
JUBILEES
JUDOIST
JUDOISTS
JUGGING

JUGGINGS
JUGGLER
JUGGLERS
JUGGLERY
JUGHEAD
JUGHEADS
JUGULAR
JUGULARS
JUKSKEI
JUKSKEIS
JUMBLER
JUMBLERS
JUMBUCK
JUMBUCKS
JUMELLE
JUMELLES
JUNCATE
JUNCATES
JUNIPER
JUNIPERS
JUNKIES
JUNKIEST
JUSSIVE
JUSSIVES
JUSTICE
JUSTICER
JUSTICES
JUVENAL
JUVENALS
KABADDI
KABADDIS
KABBALA
KABBALAH
KABBALAS
KACHERI
KACHERIS
KACHINA
KACHINAS
KAGOULE
KAGOULES
KAHAWAI
KAHAWAIS
KAINITE
KAINITES
KAJAWAH
KAJAWAHS
KAKODYL
KAKODYLS
KAMERAD
KAMERADS
KAMICHI
KAMICHIS
KAMPONG
KAMPONGS
KAMSEEN
KAMSEENS
KANTELA
KANTELAS
KANTELE
KANTELES
KAOLINE
KAOLINES
KARAISM
KARAISMS
KARAKUL
KARAKULS
KARAOKE
KARAOKES
KARTING
KARTINGS

KASHMIR
KASHMIRS
KASHRUT
KASHRUTH
KASHRUTS
KATHODE
KATHODES
KATORGA
KATORGAS
KATYDID
KATYDIDS
KAYOING
KAYOINGS
KEBBOCK
KEBBOCKS
KEBBUCK
KEBBUCKS
KEELAGE
KEELAGES
KEELING
KEELINGS
KEELSON
KEELSONS
KEENING
KEENINGS
KEEPING
KEEPINGS
KEEPNET
KEEPNETS
KEISTER
KEISTERS
KEITLOA
KEITLOAS
KELLAUT
KELLAUTS
KELLIES
SKELLIES
KELTERS
SKELTERS
KEMPING
KEMPINGS
KENNING
KENNINGS
KEPPING
SKEPPING
KERATIN
KERATINS
KERNING
KERNINGS
KERNITE
KERNITES
KEROGEN
KEROGENS
KERYGMA
KERYGMAS
KESTREL
KESTRELS
KETCHES
SKETCHES
KETCHUP
KETCHUPS
KEYHOLE
KEYHOLES
KEYLINE
KEYLINES
KEYNOTE
KEYNOTED
KEYNOTES
KEYWORD
KEYWORDS

KHADDAR
KHADDARS
KHALIFA
KHALIFAH
KHALIFAS
KHALIFAT
KHAMSIN
KHAMSINS
KHANATE
KHANATES
KHANJAR
KHANJARS
KHEDIVA
KHEDIVAL
KHEDIVAS
KHEDIVE
KHEDIVES
KHOTBAH
KHOTBAHS
KHOTBEH
KHOTBEHS
KHUTBAH
KHUTBAHS
KIBITKA
KIBITKAS
KIDDERS
SKIDDERS
KIDDIER
KIDDIERS
KIDDING
SKIDDING
KIDLING
KIDLINGS
KIDSKIN
KIDSKINS
KIKUMON
KIKUMONS
KILLCOW
KILLCOWS
KILLDEE
KILLDEER
KILLDEES
KILLICK
KILLICKS
KILLING
SKILLING
KILLINGS
KILLJOY
KILLJOYS
KILLOCK
KILLOCKS
KILOBAR
KILOBARS
KILOBIT
KILOBITS
KILOTON
KILOTONS
KIMMERS
SKIMMERS
KIMONOS
OKIMONOS
KINCHIN
KINCHINS
KINDLER
KINDLERS
KINDLES
KINDLESS
KINDRED
KINDREDS
KINESES

AKINESES
KINESIS
AKINESIS
KINETIC
KINETICS
KINFOLK
KINFOLKS
KINGCUP
KINGCUPS
KINGDOM
KINGDOMS
KINGLES
KINGLESS
KINGLET
KINGLETS
KINKING
SKINKING
KINLESS
SKINLESS
KINSHIP
KINSHIPS
KIPPAGE
KIPPAGES
KIPPERS
SKIPPERS
KIPPING
SKIPPING
KIRIMON
KIRIMONS
KIRKING
KIRKINGS
KIRKTON
KIRKTONS
KITCHEN
KITCHENS
KITENGE
KITENGES
KITHARA
KITHARAS
KITLING
KITLINGS
KITTLED
SKITTLED
KITTLES
SKITTLES
KITTLEST
KLAVIER
KLAVIERS
KLINKER
KLINKERS
KNACKER
KNACKERS
KNACKERY
KNAPPER
KNAPPERS
KNAPPLE
KNAPPLED
KNAPPLES
KNEADER
KNEADERS
KNEECAP
KNEECAPS
KNEELER
KNEELERS
KNEVELL
KNEVELLS
KNICKER
KNICKERS
KNIFING
KNIFINGS

KNITTER
KNITTERS
KNITTLE
KNITTLES
KNOBBER
KNOBBERS
KNOBBLE
KNOBBLED
KNOBBLES
KNOCKER
KNOCKERS
KNOTTER
KNOTTERS
KNOWHOW
KNOWHOWS
KNUBBLE
KNUBBLED
KNUBBLES
KNUCKLE
KNUCKLED
KNUCKLES
KOFTGAR
KOFTGARI
KOFTGARS
KOKANEE
KOKANEES
KOMATIK
KOMATIKS
KOUPREY
KOUPREYS
KREMLIN
KREMLINS
KRIMMER
KRIMMERS
KRULLER
KRULLERS
KRYPTON
KRYPTONS
KRYTRON
KRYTRONS
KUFIYAH
KUFIYAHS
KUMQUAT
KUMQUATS
KUNZITE
KUNZITES
KURSAAL
KURSAALS
KYANISE
KYANISED
KYANISES
KYANITE
KYANITES
KYANIZE
KYANIZED
KYANIZES
LABARUM
LABARUMS
LABELLA
FLABELLA
GLABELLA
LABIATE
LABIATES
LABROID
LABROIDS
LACINGS
PLACINGS
LACINIA
LACINIAE
LACKERS

CLACKERS
FLACKERS
SLACKERS
LACKING
BLACKING
CLACKING
SLACKING
LACQUER
LACQUERS
LACQUEY
LACQUEYS
LACTASE
LACTASES
LACTATE
LACTATED
LACTATES
LACTEAL
LACTEALS
LACTONE
LACTONES
LACTOSE
LACTOSES
LACUNAR
LACUNARS
LACUNARY
LADANUM
LADANUMS
LADDERS
BLADDERS
CLADDERS
LADDERY
BLADDERY
LADDIES
GLADDIES
LADRONE
LADRONES
LADYBUG
LADYBUGS
LADYCOW
LADYCOWS
LADYISM
LADYISMS
LADYKIN
LADYKINS
LAETARE
LAETARES
LAGGARD
LAGGARDS
LAGGERS
BLAGGERS
LAGGING
BLAGGING
CLAGGING
FLAGGING
SLAGGING
LAGGINGS
LAICISE
LAICISED
LAICISES
LAICIZE
LAICIZED
LAICIZES
LAIDING
PLAIDING
LAIRAGE
LAIRAGES
LAIRIER
GLAIRIER
LAIRING
GLAIRING

LAIRISE
LAIRISED
LAIRISES
LAIRIZE
LAIRIZED
LAIRIZES
LAKELET
LAKELETS
LAKIEST
FLAKIEST
LALLING
LALLINGS
LAMBADA
LAMBADAS
LAMBAST
LAMBASTE
LAMBASTS
LAMBERS
CLAMBERS
LAMBERT
BLANKEST
LAMBERTS
LAMBKIN
LAMBKINS
LAMELLA
LAMELLAE
LAMELLAR
LAMETER
LAMETERS
LAMIGER
LAMIGERS
LAMINAR
LAMINARY
LAMITER
LAMITERS
LAMMERS
SLAMMERS
LAMMING
CLAMMING
FLAMMING
SLAMMING
LAMMINGS
LAMPERN
LAMPERNS
LAMPERS
CLAMPERS
LAMPING
CLAMPING
LAMPINGS
LAMPION
LAMPIONS
LAMPOON
LAMPOONS
LAMPREY
LAMPREYS
LAMPUKA
LAMPUKAS
LAMPUKI
LAMPUKIS
LANCHED
BLANCHED
FLANCHED
PLANCHED
LANCHES
BLANCHES
FLANCHES
PLANCHES
LANCING
BLANCING
GLANCING
LANDERS

GLANDERS
SLANDERS
LANDING
LANDINGS
LANDLER
LANDLERS
LANEWAY
LANEWAYS
LANGAHA
LANGAHAS
LANGREL
LANGRELS
LANGUET
LANGUETS
LANGUOR
LANGUORS
LANIARD
LANIARDS
LANKEST
LANKING
BLANKING
CLANKING
FLANKING
PLANKING
LANNERS
PLANNERS
LANOLIN
LANOLINE
LANOLINS
LANTANA
LANTANAS
LANTERN
LANTERNS
LANYARD
LANYARDS
LAPPERS
CLAPPERS
FLAPPERS
SLAPPERS
LAPPING
CLAPPING
FLAPPING
PLAPPING
SLAPPING
LAPPINGS
LAPSANG
LAPSANGS
LAPSING
ELAPSING
LAPWING
LAPWINGS
LAPWORK
LAPWORKS
LARDOON
LARDOONS
LARGESS
LARGESSE
LARMIER
LARMIERS
LARVATE
LARVATED
LASAGNA
LASAGNAS
LASAGNE
LASAGNES
LASHERS
CLASHERS
FLASHERS
SLASHERS

LASHING
CLASHING
FLASHING
PLASHING
SLASHING
LASHINGS
LASHKAR
LASHKARS
LASKETS
FLASKETS
LASSOCK
LASSOCKS
LASTAGE
LASTAGES
LASTERS
BLASTERS
PLASTERS
LASTING
BLASTING
LASTINGS
LATCHED
CLATCHED
LATCHES
CLATCHES
SLATCHES
LATCHET
LATCHETS
LATENCE
LATENCES
LATERAL
LATERALS
LATHERS
BLATHERS
SLATHERS
LATHING
LATHINGS
LATITAT
LATITATS
LATRINE
LATRINES
LATTENS
FLATTENS
LATTICE
LATTICED
LATTICES
LAUDING
BLAUDING
LAUGHER
LAUGHERS
LAUNDER
LAUNDERS
LAUWINE
LAUWINES
LAVOLTA
LAVOLTAS
LAWLAND
LAWLANDS
LAWLESS
CLAWLESS
FLAWLESS
LAWSUIT
LAWSUITS
LAXATOR
LAXATORS
LAYAWAY
LAYAWAYS
LAYBACK
PLAYBACK
LAYBACKS
LAYETTE

LAYETTES
LAYLOCK
LAYLOCKS
LAYTIME
PLAYTIME
LAYTIMES
LAZARET
LAZARETS
LAZIEST
GLAZIEST
LEACHED
BLEACHED
PLEACHED
LEACHES
BLEACHES
PLEACHES
LEADERS
PLEADERS
LEADING
PLEADING
LEADINGS
LEAFAGE
LEAFAGES
LEAFBUD
LEAFBUDS
LEAFLET
LEAFLETS
LEAGUER
LEAGUERS
LEAKAGE
LEAKAGES
LEAMING
GLEAMING
LEANEST
CLEANEST
LEANING
CLEANING
GLEANING
LEANINGS
LEARIER
BLEARIER
LEARING
BLEARING
CLEARING
LEARNER
LEARNERS
LEASERS
PLEASERS
LEASING
PLEASING
LEASINGS
LEASOWE
LEASOWED
LEASOWES
LEASURE
PLEASURE
LEASURES
LEATHER
LEATHERN
LEATHERS
LEATHERY
LEAVERS
CLEAVERS
LEAVING
CLEAVING
SLEAVING
LEAVINGS
LECTERN
LECTERNS
LECTION

ELECTION
FLECTION
LECTIONS
LECTORS
ELECTORS
LECTURE
LECTURED
LECTURER
LECTURES
LECTURN
LECTURNS
LEDGERS
PLEDGERS
SLEDGERS
LEDGIER
FLEDGIER
LEECHED
FLEECHED
LEECHEE
LEECHEES
LEECHES
FLEECHES
SLEECHES
LEEPING
BLEEPING
CLEEPING
SLEEPING
LEERING
FLEERING
LEERINGS
LEEWARD
LEEWARDS
LEFTISM
LEFTISMS
LEFTIST
LEFTISTS
LEGATEE
LEGATEES
LEGATOR
LEGATORS
LEGGING
ALEGGING
FLEGGING
LEGGINGS
LEGGISM
LEGGISMS
LEGHORN
LEGHORNS
LEGISTS
ELEGISTS
LEGITIM
LEGITIMS
LEGROOM
LEGROOMS
LEGUMIN
LEGUMINS
LEGWEAR
LEGWEARS
LEGWORK
LEGWORKS
LEIDGER
LEIDGERS
LEISLER
LEISLERS
LEISTER
LEISTERS
LEISURE
LEISURED
LEISURES
LEKKING
LEKKINGS
LEMMING
CLEMMING
LEMMINGS
LEMPIRA
LEMPIRAS
LENDERS
BLENDERS
LENDING
BLENDING
LENDINGS
LENIENT
LENIENTS
LENTISK
LENTISKS
LEOPARD
LEOPARDS
LEOTARD
LEOTARDS
LEPTOME
LEPTOMES
LESBIAN
LESBIANS
LESSORS
PLESSORS
LETCHED
FLETCHED
LETCHES
FLETCHES
LETTERN
LETTERNS
LETTING
BLETTING
LETTINGS
LETTUCE
LETTUCES
LEUCINE
LEUCINES
LEUCITE
LEUCITES
LEUCOMA
LEUCOMAS
LEVATOR
ELEVATOR
LEVATORS
LEVERET
LEVERETS
LEWISIA
LEWISIAS
LEXICON
LEXICONS
LIAISON
LIAISONS
LIBBARD
LIBBARDS
LIBBING
GLIBBING
LIBELEE
LIBELEES
LIBELER
LIBELERS
LIBERAL
LIBERALS
LIBRATE
LIBRATED
LIBRATES
LICENCE
LICENCED
LICENCES
LICENSE
LICENSED
LICENSEE
LICENSER
LICENSES
LICHTER
FLICHTER
LICHWAY
LICHWAYS
LICKERS
CLICKERS
FLICKERS
SLICKERS
LICKING
CLICKING
FLICKING
SLICKING
LICKINGS
LIGGING
LIGGINGS
LIGHTED
ALIGHTED
BLIGHTED
FLIGHTED
PLIGHTED
SLIGHTED
LIGHTEN
LIGHTENS
LIGHTER
BLIGHTER
PLIGHTER
SLIGHTER
LIGHTERS
LIGHTLY
SLIGHTLY
LIGNAGE
LIGNAGES
LIGNITE
LIGNITES
LIGNOSE
LIGNOSES
LIGROIN
LIGROINS
LIMACEL
LIMACELS
LIMACON
LIMACONS
LIMBECK
LIMBECKS
LIMBERS
CLIMBERS
LIMBING
BLIMBING
CLIMBING
LIMEADE
LIMEADES
LIMEPIT
LIMEPITS
LIMIEST
SLIMIEST
LIMITED
LIMITEDS
LIMITER
LIMITERS
LIMMERS
GLIMMERS
SLIMMERS
LIMPING
FLIMPING
LIMPINGS
LIMPKIN
LIMPKINS
LINCHES
CLINCHES
FLINCHES
LINCHET
LINCHETS
LINDANE
LINDANES
LINEAGE
LINEAGES
LINEATE
LINEATED
LINGERS
CLINGERS
FLINGERS
SLINGERS
LINGIER
CLINGIER
LINGULA
LINGULAE
LINGULAR
LINGULAS
LINKAGE
LINKAGES
LINKBOY
LINKBOYS
LINKERS
BLINKERS
CLINKERS
KLINKERS
SLINKERS
LINKING
BLINKING
CLINKING
PLINKING
SLINKING
LINNING
BLINNING
LINOCUT
LINOCUTS
LINSANG
LINSANGS
LINSEED
LINSEEDS
LINTERS
SLINTERS
LINTIER
FLINTIER
LINTIES
LINTIEST
LIONCEL
LIONCELS
LIONISE
LIONISED
LIONISES
LIONISM
LIONISMS
LIONIZE
LIONIZED
LIONIZES
LIPPIER
SLIPPIER
LIPPIES
CLIPPIES
LIPPIEST
LIPPING
BLIPPING
CLIPPING
FLIPPING
SLIPPING
LIQUATE
LIQUATED
LIQUATES
LIQUEUR
LIQUEURS
LISPING
LISPINGS
LISPUND
LISPUNDS
LISTENS
GLISTENS
LISTERS
BLISTERS
GLISTERS
LISTING
LISTINGS
LITERAL
LITERALS
LITHATE
LITHATES
LITHELY
BLITHELY
LITHEST
BLITHEST
LITHITE
LITHITES
LITHIUM
LITHIUMS
LITTERS
CLITTERS
FLITTERS
GLITTERS
SLITTERS
LITTERY
GLITTERY
LITTLES
LITTLEST
LITTLIN
LITTLING
LITTLINS
LIVELOD
LIVELODS
LIVENER
LIVENERS
LIXIVIA
LIXIVIAL
LLANERO
LLANEROS
LOADING
LOADINGS
LOAFING
LOAFINGS
LOAMING
GLOAMING
LOANING
LOANINGS
LOATHER
LOATHERS
LOATHES
LOATHEST
LOBBING
BLOBBING
LOBBYER
LOBBYERS
LOBELET
LOBELETS
LOBELIA
LOBELIAS
LOBSTER
LOBSTERS
LOBULAR
GLOBULAR
LOBULES
GLOBULES
LOBWORM
LOBWORMS
LOCKAGE
BLOCKAGE
LOCKAGES
LOCKERS
BLOCKERS
CLOCKERS
LOCKFUL
LOCKFULS
LOCKING
BLOCKING
CLOCKING
FLOCKING
LOCKJAW
LOCKJAWS
LOCKOUT
LOCKOUTS
LOCKRAM
LOCKRAMS
LOCUSTA
LOCUSTAE
LODGING
LODGINGS
LOGANIA
LOGANIAS
LOGBOOK
LOGBOOKS
LOGGERS
CLOGGERS
SLOGGERS
LOGGING
CLOGGING
FLOGGING
SLOGGING
LOGGINGS
LOGICAL
ALOGICAL
LOGLINE
LOGLINES
LOGWOOD
LOGWOODS
LONGBOW
LONGBOWS
LONGING
PLONGING
LONGINGS
LOOBIES
LOOBIEST
LOOFFUL
LOOFFULS
LOOKISM
LOOKISMS
LOOKOUT
LOOKOUTS
LOOMING
BLOOMING
GLOOMING
SLOOMING
LOONIES
LOONIEST
LOONING
LOONINGS
LOOPERS
BLOOPERS
LOOPIER
GLOOPIER
LOOPING
BLOOPING
GLOOPING
LOOPINGS
LOOTING
LOOTINGS
LOPPING
CLOPPING
FLOPPING
PLOPPING
SLOPPING
LOPPINGS
LORDING
LORDINGS
LORDKIN
LORDKINS
LORETTE
LORETTES
LORGNON
LORGNONS
LORIMER
LORIMERS
LORINER
LORINERS
LORRELL
LORRELLS
LOSINGS
CLOSINGS
LOSSIER
FLOSSIER
GLOSSIER
LOTTING
BLOTTING
CLOTTING
PLOTTING
SLOTTING
LOUNDER
FLOUNDER
LOUNDERS
LOUNGER
LOUNGERS
LOURIER
FLOURIER
LOURING
CLOURING
FLOURING
LOURINGS
LOUSING
BLOUSING
FLOUSING
LOUTING
CLOUTING
FLOUTING
GLOUTING
LOVERED
CLOVERED
LOVINGS
GLOVINGS
LOWERED
FLOWERED
GLOWERED
LOWINGS
SLOWINGS
LOWLAND
LOWLANDS
LOWNESS
SLOWNESS
LOWNING
CLOWNING

LOWVELD
LOWVELDS
LOXYGEN
LOXYGENS
LOZENGE
LOZENGED
LOZENGES
LUBBARD
LUBBARDS
LUBBERS
BLUBBERS
CLUBBERS
SLUBBERS
LUCARNE
LUCARNES
LUCERNE
LUCERNES
LUCIFER
LUCIFERS
LUCIGEN
LUCIGENS
LUCKIER
CLUCKIER
PLUCKIER
LUCKIES
LUCKIEST
LUCKILY
PLUCKILY
LUDSHIP
LUDSHIPS
LUFFING
BLUFFING
FLUFFING
PLUFFING
LUGEING
LUGEINGS
LUGGAGE
LUGGAGES
LUGGERS
PLUGGERS
SLUGGERS
LUGGING
GLUGGING
PLUGGING
SLUGGING
LUGHOLE
LUGHOLES
LUGSAIL
LUGSAILS
LUGWORM
LUGWORMS
LULIBUB
LULIBUBS
LUMBAGO
PLUMBAGO
LUMBAGOS
LUMBANG
LUMBANGS
LUMBERS
CLUMBERS
PLUMBERS
SLUMBERS
LUMMIER
PLUMMIER
SLUMMIER
LUMPERS
CLUMPERS
PLUMPERS
LUMPIER
CLUMPIER
GLUMPIER
SLUMPIER
LUMPING
CLUMPING
FLUMPING
PLUMPING
SLUMPING
LUMPISH
GLUMPISH
PLUMPISH
LUMPKIN
LUMPKINS
LUNATIC
LUNATICS
LUNCHER
LUNCHERS
LUNCHES
CLUNCHES
LUNETTE
LUNETTES
LUNGFUL
LUNGFULS
LUNGING
BLUNGING
PLUNGING
LUNKERS
BLUNKERS
PLUNKERS
LUNTING
BLUNTING
LUPULIN
LUPULINE
LUPULINS
LURCHER
LURCHERS
LURDANE
LURDANES
LURKING
LURKINGS
LURRIES
FLURRIES
SLURRIES
LUSHERS
BLUSHERS
FLUSHERS
LUSHEST
FLUSHEST
PLUSHEST
LUSHIER
FLUSHIER
PLUSHIER
SLUSHIER
LUSHING
BLUSHING
FLUSHING
SLUSHING
LUSTERS
BLUSTERS
CLUSTERS
FLUSTERS
LUSTRUM
LUSTRUMS
LUTHERN
LUTHERNS
LUTHIER
LUTHIERS
LUTINGS
FLUTINGS
LUTISTS
FLUTISTS
LYCOPOD
LYCOPODS
LYDDITE
LYDDITES
LYMITER
LYMITERS
LYMPHAD
LYMPHADS
LYNCHET
LYNCHETS
LYOPHIL
LYOPHILE
LYRICON
LYRICONS
MACADAM
MACADAMS
MACAQUE
MACAQUES
MACHAIR
MACHAIRS
MACHETE
MACHETES
MACHINE
MACHINED
MACHINES
MACHREE
MACHREES
MACRAME
MACRAMES
MACRAMI
MACRAMIS
MADDOCK
MADDOCKS
MADLING
MADLINGS
MADOQUA
MADOQUAS
MADRASA
MADRASAH
MADRASAS
MADRONA
MADRONAS
MADRONE
MADRONES
MADRONO
MADRONOS
MADWORT
MADWORTS
MADZOON
MADZOONS
MAESTRO
MAESTROS
MAFFICK
MAFFICKS
MAFFLIN
MAFFLING
MAFFLINS
MAGALOG
MAGALOGS
MAGENTA
MAGENTAS
MAGISMS
IMAGISMS
MAGNATE
MAGNATES
MAGNETO
MAGNETON
MAGNETOS
MAHATMA
MAHATMAS
MAHONIA
MAHONIAS
MAHSEER
MAHSEERS
MAIDISM
MAIDISMS
MAILBAG
MAILBAGS
MAILING
MAILINGS
MAILLOT
MAILLOTS
MAILVAN
MAILVANS
MAIMING
MAIMINGS
MAINOUR
MAINOURS
MAINTOP
MAINTOPS
MAISTER
MAISTERS
MAJORAT
MAJORATS
MALACIA
MALACIAS
MALAISE
MALAISES
MALARIA
MALARIAL
MALARIAN
MALARIAS
MALEATE
MALEATES
MALEFIC
MALEFICE
MALICHO
MALICHOS
MALISON
MALISONS
MALLARD
MALLARDS
MALLING
SMALLING
MALMSEY
MALMSEYS
MALTASE
MALTASES
MALTING
MALTINGS
MALTOSE
MALTOSES
MAMELON
MAMELONS
MAMILLA
MAMILLAE
MAMILLAR
MAMMOCK
MAMMOCKS
MAMMOTH
MAMMOTHS
MANACLE
MANACLED
MANACLES
MANAGER
MANAGERS
MANAKIN
MANAKINS
MANATEE
MANATEES
MANCALA
MANCALAS
MANCHET
MANCHETS
MANDALA
MANDALAS
MANDATE
MANDATED
MANDATES
MANDIOC
MANDIOCA
MANDIOCS
MANDIRA
MANDIRAS
MANDOLA
MANDOLAS
MANDORA
MANDORAS
MANDREL
MANDRELS
MANDRIL
MANDRILL
MANDRILS
MANGLER
MANGLERS
MANGOLD
MANGOLDS
MANHOLE
MANHOLES
MANHOOD
MANHOODS
MANHUNT
MANHUNTS
MANIHOC
MANIHOCS
MANIKIN
MANIKINS
MANILLA
MANILLAS
MANILLE
MANILLES
MANIPLE
MANIPLES
MANITOU
MANITOUS
MANJACK
MANJACKS
MANKIND
MANKINDS
MANNITE
MANNITES
MANNOSE
MANNOSES
MANPACK
MANPACKS
MANRENT
MANRENTS
MANSARD
MANSARDS
MANSION
MANSIONS
MANTEAU
MANTEAUS
MANTEAUX
MANTEEL
MANTEELS
MANTLET
MANTLETS
MANTRAM
MANTRAMS
MANTRAP
MANTRAPS
MANUMEA
MANUMEAS
MANUMIT
MANUMITS
MANURER
MANURERS
MANYATA
MANYATAS
MAORMOR
MAORMORS
MAPPING
MAPPINGS
MAPPIST
MAPPISTS
MARABOU
MARABOUS
MARABOUT
MARBLER
MARBLERS
MARCHER
MARCHERS
MARCHES
MARCHESA
MARCHESE
MARCHESI
MARCONI
MARCONIS
MARDIES
MARDIEST
MAREMMA
MAREMMAS
MARGENT
MARGENTS
MARGOSA
MARGOSAS
MARIMBA
MARIMBAS
MARINER
MARINERA
MARINERS
MARKHOR
MARKHORS
MARKING
MARKINGS
MARLINE
MARLINES
MARLING
MARLINGS
MARMITE
MARMITES
MARMOSE
MARMOSES
MARMOSET
MARPLOT
MARPLOTS
MARQUEE
MARQUEES
MARQUES
MARQUESS
MARQUIS
MARQUISE
MARRIER
MARRIERS
MARSHAL
MARSHALS
MARTENS
SMARTENS
MARTEXT
MARTEXTS
MARTING
SMARTING
MARTINI
MARTINIS
MARTLET
MARTLETS
MARYBUD
MARYBUDS
MASCARA
MASCARAS
MASHERS
SMASHERS
MASHIES
MASHIEST
MASHING
SMASHING
MASHINGS
MASHLAM
MASHLAMS
MASHLIM
MASHLIMS
MASHLIN
MASHLINS
MASHLUM
MASHLUMS
MASQUER
MASQUERS
MASSAGE
MASSAGED
MASSAGES
MASSEUR
MASSEURS
MASSING
AMASSING
MASTABA
MASTABAS
MASTICH
MASTICHS
MASTIFF
MASTIFFS
MASTOID
MASTOIDS
MATADOR
MATADORA
MATADORE
MATADORS
MATCHED
SMATCHED
MATCHER
MATCHERS
MATCHES
SMATCHES
MATELOT
MATELOTE
MATELOTS
MATINEE
MATINEES
MATOOKE
MATOOKES
MATRICE
MATRICES
MATSURI
MATSURIS
MATTERS
SMATTERS
MATTING
MATTINGS
MATTOCK
MATTOCKS

MATTOID
MATTOIDS
MATURES
MATUREST
MATWEED
MATWEEDS
MATZOON
MATZOONS
MAULGRE
MAULGRED
MAULGRES
MAUNDER
MAUNDERS
MAUTHER
MAUTHERS
MAUVAIS
MAUVAISE
MAUVEIN
MAUVEINE
MAUVEINS
MAUVINE
MAUVINES
MAWSEED
MAWSEEDS
MAWTHER
MAWTHERS
MAXILLA
MAXILLAE
MAXIMIN
MAXIMINS
MAXWELL
MAXWELLS
MAYPOLE
MAYPOLES
MAYSTER
MAYSTERS
MAYWEED
MAYWEEDS
MAZURKA
MAZURKAS
MAZZARD
MAZZARDS
MEACOCK
MEACOCKS
MEAGRES
MEAGREST
MEALIES
MEALIEST
MEANDER
MEANDERS
MEANING
MEANINGS
MEARING
SMEARING
MEASURE
MEASURED
MEASURER
MEASURES
MECONIN
MECONINS
MEDACCA
MEDACCAS
MEDALET
MEDALETS
MEDDLER
MEDDLERS
MEDIANT
MEDIANTS
MEDIATE
MEDIATED

MEDIATES
MEDICAL
MEDICALS
MEDULLA
MEDULLAE
MEDULLAR
MEDULLAS
MEDUSAN
MEDUSANS
MEERCAT
MEERCATS
MEERKAT
MEERKATS
MEETING
MEETINGS
MEGABAR
MEGABARS
MEGABIT
MEGABITS
MEGAFOG
MEGAFOGS
MEGARAD
MEGARADS
MEGARON
MEGARONS
MEGASSE
MEGASSES
MEGATON
MEGATONS
MEIOSES
AMEIOSES
MEIOSIS
AMEIOSIS
MELANGE
MELANGES
MELANIN
MELANINS
MELILOT
MELILOTS
MELISMA
MELISMAS
MELLING
SMELLING
MELLITE
MELLITES
MELODIC
MELODICA
MELODICS
MELTING
SMELTING
MELTINGS
MELTITH
MELTITHS
MEMENTO
MEMENTOS
MENACER
MENACERS
MENAGED
AMENAGED
MENAGES
AMENAGES
MENDERS
AMENDERS
MENDING
AMENDING
EMENDING
MENDINGS
MENFOLK
MENFOLKS
MENORAH

MENORAHS
MENTHOL
MENTHOLS
MENTION
MENTIONS
MERCHET
MERCHETS
MERFOLK
MERFOLKS
MERGING
EMERGING
MERLING
MERLINGS
MERMAID
MERMAIDS
MERONYM
MERONYMS
MERONYMY
MERRIES
MERRIEST
MERSION
EMERSION
MERSIONS
MESCLUM
MESCLUMS
MESCLUN
MESCLUNS
MESHING
MESHINGS
MESQUIN
MESQUINE
MESQUIT
MESQUITE
MESQUITS
MESSAGE
MESSAGED
MESSAGES
MESSIAH
MESSIAHS
MESTIZA
MESTIZAS
MESTIZO
MESTIZOS
METAMER
METAMERE
METAMERS
METAYER
METAYERS
METAZOA
METAZOAN
METCAST
METCASTS
METHANE
METHANES
METHINK
METHINKS
METICAL
EMETICAL
METICALS
METISSE
METISSES
METONYM
METONYMS
METONYMY
METOPON
METOPONS
METRIST
METRISTS
MEZUZAH
MEZUZAHS

MICATED
EMICATED
MICATES
EMICATES
MICELLA
MICELLAE
MICELLAR
MICELLE
MICELLES
MICHING
MICHINGS
MICROBE
MICROBES
MICRONS
OMICRONS
MICTION
EMICTION
MICTIONS
MIDDIES
SMIDDIES
MIDIRON
MIDIRONS
MIDLAND
MIDLANDS
MIDMOST
AMIDMOST
MIDMOSTS
MIDNOON
MIDNOONS
MIDRIFF
MIDRIFFS
MIDSHIP
MIDSHIPS
MIDTERM
MIDTERMS
MIDWIFE
MIDWIFED
MIDWIFES
MIDWIVE
MIDWIVED
MIDWIVES
MIGRANT
EMIGRANT
MIGRANTS
MIGRATE
EMIGRATE
MIGRATED
MIGRATES
MILEAGE
MILEAGES
MILFOIL
MILFOILS
MILITAR
MILITARY
MILITIA
MILITIAS
MILKING
MILKINGS
MILLDAM
MILLDAMS
MILLIME
MILLIMES
MILLING
MILLINGS
MILLION
MILLIONS
MILLRUN
MILLRUNS
MIMMICK
MIMMICKS

MINARET
MINARETS
MINCING
MINCINGS
MINDING
MINDINGS
MINDSET
MINDSETS
MINEOLA
MINEOLAS
MINERAL
MINERALS
MINETTE
MINETTES
MINEVER
MINEVERS
MINGLER
MINGLERS
MINIATE
MINIATED
MINIATES
MINICAB
MINICABS
MINICAM
MINICAMS
MINIKIN
MINIKINS
MINIVER
MINIVERS
MINIVET
MINIVETS
MINNICK
MINNICKS
MINNOCK
MINNOCKS
MINSTER
MINSTERS
MINTAGE
MINTAGES
MINUEND
MINUENDS
MINUTES
MINUTEST
MINUTIA
MINUTIAE
MIRACLE
MIRACLES
MIRADOR
MIRADORS
MIRBANE
MIRBANES
MISCALL
MISCALLS
MISCAST
MISCASTS
MISDATE
MISDATED
MISDATES
MISDEAL
MISDEALS
MISDEALT
MISDEED
MISDEEDS
MISDEEM
MISDEEMS
MISDIAL
MISDIALS
MISDIET
MISDIETS
MISDOER

MISDOERS
MISDRAW
MISDRAWN
MISDRAWS
MISEASE
MISEASES
MISFALL
MISFALLS
MISFARE
MISFARED
MISFARES
MISFEED
MISFEEDS
MISFILE
MISFILED
MISFILES
MISFIRE
MISFIRED
MISFIRES
MISFORM
MISFORMS
MISGIVE
MISGIVEN
MISGIVES
MISHEAR
MISHEARD
MISHEARS
MISHMEE
MISHMEES
MISJOIN
MISJOINS
MISKNOW
MISKNOWN
MISKNOWS
MISLEAD
MISLEADS
MISLIKE
MISLIKED
MISLIKER
MISLIKES
MISLIVE
MISLIVED
MISLIVES
MISLUCK
MISLUCKS
MISMAKE
MISMAKES
MISMATE
MISMATED
MISMATES
MISNAME
MISNAMED
MISNAMES
MISPLAY
MISPLAYS
MISRATE
MISRATED
MISRATES
MISREAD
MISREADS
MISRULE
MISRULED
MISRULES
MISSEEM
MISSEEMS
MISSEND
MISSENDS
MISSIES
MISSIEST
MISSILE

EMISSILE
MISSILES
MISSING
AMISSING
MISSION
EMISSION
OMISSION
MISSIONS
MISSIVE
EMISSIVE
OMISSIVE
MISSIVES
MISSTEP
MISSTEPS
MISSUIT
MISSUITS
MISTAKE
MISTAKEN
MISTAKES
MISTELL
MISTELLS
MISTERM
MISTERMS
MISTICO
MISTICOS
MISTIME
MISTIMED
MISTIMES
MISTING
MISTINGS
MISTRAL
MISTRALS
MISTUNE
MISTUNED
MISTUNES
MISUSER
MISUSERS
MISWEEN
MISWEENS
MISWEND
MISWENDS
MISWORD
MISWORDS
MISYOKE
MISYOKED
MISYOKES
MITHERS
SMITHERS
MITOGEN
MITOGENS
MITOSES
AMITOSES
MITOSIS
AMITOSIS
MITOTIC
AMITOTIC
MITZVAH
MITZVAHS
MIXTION
MIXTIONS
MIXTURE
MIXTURES
MIZMAZE
MIZMAZES
MOBBING
MOBBINGS
MOBSTER
MOBSTERS
MOCHELL
MOCHELLS

MOCKAGE
MOCKAGES
MOCKING
SMOCKING
MOCKINGS
MODELER
MODELERS
MODELLO
MODELLOS
MODICUM
MODICUMS
MODISTE
MODISTES
MOELLON
MOELLONS
MOFETTE
MOFETTES
MOIDORE
MOIDORES
MOILING
SMOILING
MOINEAU
MOINEAUS
MOISTEN
MOISTENS
MOITHER
MOITHERS
MOLERAT
MOLERATS
MOLIMEN
MOLIMENS
MOLINET
MOLINETS
MOLLUSC
MOLLUSCS
MOLLUSK
MOLLUSKS
MONARCH
MONARCHS
MONARCHY
MONARDA
MONARDAS
MONAXON
MONAXONS
MONDAIN
MONDAINE
MONDAINS
MONEYER
MONEYERS
MONGREL
MONGRELS
MONIKER
MONIKERS
MONILIA
MONILIAS
MONITOR
MONITORS
MONITORY
MONOCLE
MONOCLED
MONOCLES
MONOCOT
MONOCOTS
MONOFIL
MONOFILS
MONOMER
MONOMERS
MONOPOD
MONOPODE
MONOPODS

MONSOON
MONSOONS
MONSTER
MONSTERA
MONSTERS
MONTAGE
MONTAGED
MONTAGES
MONTANT
MONTANTO
MONTANTS
MONTERO
MONTEROS
MONTURE
MONTURES
MOOCHED
SMOOCHED
MOOCHER
MOOCHERS
MOOCHES
SMOOCHES
MOODIES
MOODIEST
MOOKTAR
MOOKTARS
MOONEYE
MOONEYES
MOONIES
MOONIEST
MOONLET
MOONLETS
MOONSET
MOONSETS
MOORAGE
MOORAGES
MOORHEN
MOORHENS
MOORILL
MOORILLS
MOORING
SMOORING
MOORINGS
MOORLOG
MOORLOGS
MOOTING
SMOOTING
MOOTINGS
MOOVING
AMOOVING
MOPHEAD
MOPHEADS
MORAINE
MORAINES
MORCEAU
MORCEAUX
MORDANT
MORDANTS
MORDENT
MORDENTS
MORELLO
MORELLOS
MORICHE
MORICHES
MORISCO
MORISCOS
MORLING
MORLINGS
MORMAOR
MORMAORS
MORNING

MORNINGS
MOROCCO
MOROCCOS
MORPHEW
MORPHEWS
MORPHIA
MORPHIAS
MORRHUA
MORRHUAS
MORRICE
MORRICES
MORRION
MORRIONS
MORSURE
MORSURES
MORTICE
MORTICED
MORTICER
MORTICES
MORTISE
AMORTISE
MORTISED
MORTISER
MORTISES
MORWONG
MORWONGS
MOSHING
MOSHINGS
MOSSIES
MOSSIEST
MOTHERS
SMOTHERS
MOTHERY
SMOTHERY
MOTIONS
EMOTIONS
MOUCHED
SMOUCHED
MOUCHER
MOUCHERS
MOUCHES
SMOUCHES
MOUFLON
MOUFLONS
MOULAGE
MOULAGES
MOULDER
SMOULDER
MOULDERS
MOUNTED
AMOUNTED
MOUNTER
MOUNTERS
MOURNER
MOURNERS
MOUSAKA
MOUSAKAS
MOUSERS
SMOUSERS
MOUSIES
MOUSIEST
MOUSING
SMOUSING
MOUSINGS
MOUSMEE
MOUSMEES
MOUTHER
MOUTHERS
MOVABLE
MOVABLES

MOWBURN
MOWBURNS
MOWBURNT
MOYLING
SMOYLING
MOZETTA
MOZETTAS
MRIDANG
MRIDANGA
MRIDANGS
MUCHELL
MUCHELLS
MUCIGEN
MUCIGENS
MUDBATH
MUDBATHS
MUDDIES
MUDDIEST
MUDDLER
MUDDLERS
MUDFLAP
MUDFLAPS
MUDFLAT
MUDFLATS
MUDGERS
SMUDGERS
MUDGING
SMUDGING
MUDHOLE
MUDHOLES
MUDHOOK
MUDHOOKS
MUDIRIA
MUDIRIAS
MUDLARK
MUDLARKS
MUDPACK
MUDPACKS
MUDSCOW
MUDSCOWS
MUDWORT
MUDWORTS
MUEDDIN
MUEDDINS
MUEZZIN
MUEZZINS
MUFFLER
MUFFLERS
MUGGING
SMUGGING
MUGGINGS
MUGSHOT
MUGSHOTS
MUGWORT
MUGWORTS
MUGWUMP
MUGWUMPS
MUKHTAR
MUKHTARS
MULATTA
MULATTAS
MULATTO
MULATTOS
MULLEIN
MULLEINS
MULLION
MULLIONS
MULLOCK
MULLOCKS
MULMULL

MULMULLS
MULTURE
MULTURED
MULTURER
MULTURES
MUMBLER
MUMBLERS
MUMMING
MUMMINGS
MUMMOCK
MUMMOCKS
MUNCHER
MUNCHERS
MUNDANE
MUNDANER
MUNNION
MUNNIONS
MUNSTER
MUNSTERS
MUNTING
MUNTINGS
MUNTJAC
MUNTJACS
MUNTJAK
MUNTJAKS
MUONIUM
MUONIUMS
MURAENA
MURAENAS
MURGEON
MURGEONS
MURIATE
MURIATED
MURIATES
MURLAIN
MURLAINS
MURRAIN
MURRAINS
MURRION
MURRIONS
MURTHER
MURTHERS
MUSCONE
MUSCONES
MUSETTE
AMUSETTE
MUSETTES
MUSICAL
MUSICALE
MUSICALS
MUSIMON
MUSIMONS
MUSKONE
MUSKONES
MUSKRAT
MUSKRATS
MUSTANG
MUSTANGS
MUSTARD
MUSTARDS
MUTAGEN
MUTAGENS
MUTCHES
SMUTCHES
MUZZLER
MUZZLERS
MYALGIA
MYALGIAS
MYALISM
MYALISMS

MYCELIA
MYCELIAL
MYELOMA
MYELOMAS
MYLODON
MYLODONS
MYLODONT
MYNHEER
MYNHEERS
MYOGRAM
MYOGRAMS
MYOSOTE
MYOSOTES
MYOTUBE
MYOTUBES
MYRBANE
MYRBANES
MYRINGA
MYRINGAS
MYRRHOL
MYRRHOLS
MYTHISE
MYTHISED
MYTHISES
MYTHISM
MYTHISMS
MYTHIST
MYTHISTS
MYTHIZE
MYTHIZED
MYTHIZES
NAARTJE
NAARTJES
NACARAT
NACARATS
NACELLE
NACELLES
NACRITE
NACRITES
NAGAPIE
NAGAPIES
NAGGIER
KNAGGIER
SNAGGIER
NAGGING
SNAGGING
NAGMAAL
NAGMAALS
NAILERY
SNAILERY
NAILING
SNAILING
NAILINGS
NAIVETE
NAIVETES
NAMASTE
NAMASTES
NANDINE
NANDINES
NANISMS
ONANISMS
NANKEEN
NANKEENS
NAPHTHA
NAPHTHAS
NAPPERS
KNAPPERS
SNAPPERS
NAPPIER
SNAPPIER

NAPPIES
NAPPIEST
NAPPING
KNAPPING
SNAPPING
NARCEEN
NARCEENS
NARGILE
NARGILEH
NARGILES
NARRATE
NARRATED
NARRATES
NARTJIE
NARTJIES
NARWHAL
NARWHALS
NASHGAB
NASHGABS
NASTIES
NASTIEST
NATCHES
SNATCHES
NATIONS
ENATIONS
NATRIUM
NATRIUMS
NATURAL
NATURALS
NAVARCH
NAVARCHS
NAVARCHY
NAVARHO
NAVARHOS
NAVARIN
NAVARINS
NAVETTE
NAVETTES
NAYWARD
NAYWARDS
NAYWORD
NAYWORDS
NEAPING
SNEAPING
NEARING
ANEARING
NEBBICH
NEBBICHS
NEBBING
SNEBBING
NEBBISH
NEBBISHE
NECKING
SNECKING
NECKINGS
NECKLET
NECKLETS
NECKTIE
NECKTIES
NECROSE
NECROSED
NECROSES
NEEDLER
NEEDLERS
NEEDLES
NEEDLESS
NEEZING
SNEEZING
NEGLECT
NEGLECTS

NEGLIGE
NEGLIGEE
NEGLIGES
NEGROID
NEGROIDS
NELUMBO
NELUMBOS
NEMESIA
NEMESIAS
NEOLITH
NEOLITHS
NEONATE
NEONATES
NEPHRON
NEPHRONS
NERVATE
ENERVATE
NERVINE
NERVINES
NERVING
ENERVING
NERVULE
NERVULES
NERVURE
NERVURES
NESTFUL
NESTFULS
NESTING
NESTINGS
NETBALL
NETBALLS
NETSUKE
NETSUKES
NETTING
NETTINGS
NETWORK
NETWORKS
NEURINE
NEURINES
NEURISM
ANEURISM
NEURISMS
NEURITE
NEURITES
NEUROMA
NEUROMAS
NEURONE
NEURONES
NEUSTON
NEUSTONS
NEUTRAL
NEUTRALS
NEUTRON
NEUTRONS
NEWCOME
NEWCOMER
NEWSBOY
NEWSBOYS
NEWSIES
NEWSIEST
NIBBING
SNIBBING
NIBBLER
NIBBLERS
NIBLICK
NIBLICKS
NICKERS
KNICKERS
SNICKERS
NICKING
SNICKING
NICTATE
NICTATED
NICTATES
NIFFERS
SNIFFERS
NIFFIER
SNIFFIER
NIFFING
SNIFFING
NIFTIER
SNIFTIER
NIGELLA
NIGELLAS
NIGGARD
NIGGARDS
NIGGERS
SNIGGERS
NIGGLED
SNIGGLED
NIGGLER
SNIGGLER
NIGGLERS
NIGGLES
SNIGGLES
NIGHTED
KNIGHTED
NIGHTIE
NIGHTIES
NIGHTLY
KNIGHTLY
NIHONGA
NIHONGAS
NINEPIN
NINEPINS
NIOBATE
NIOBATES
NIOBITE
NIOBITES
NIOBIUM
NIOBIUMS
NIPPERS
SNIPPERS
NIPPIER
SNIPPIER
NIPPING
SNIPPING
NIRVANA
NIRVANAS
NITERIE
NITERIES
NITHING
NITHINGS
NITRATE
NITRATED
NITRATES
NITRIDE
NITRIDED
NITRIDES
NITRILE
NITRILES
NITRITE
NITRITES
NOBBIER
KNOBBIER
SNOBBIER
NOBBLED
KNOBBLED
NOBBLER
NOBBLERS
NOBBLES
KNOBBLES
NOCKING
KNOCKING
NOCTUID
NOCTUIDS
NOCTULE
NOCTULES
NOCTURN
NOCTURNE
NOCTURNS
NODDING
SNODDING
NODDINGS
NOGGING
SNOGGING
NOGGINGS
NOINTED
ANOINTED
NOMARCH
NOMARCHS
NOMARCHY
NOMBRIL
NOMBRILS
NOMINAL
NOMINALS
NOMINEE
NOMINEES
NONAGON
NONAGONS
NONETTE
NONETTES
NONETTO
NONETTOS
NONSUIT
NONSUITS
NONUPLE
NONUPLET
NOOKIES
NOOKIEST
NOONDAY
NOONDAYS
NOONING
NOONINGS
NORIMON
NORIMONS
NORLAND
NORLANDS
NORTENA
NORTENAS
NORTENO
NORTENOS
NORTHER
NORTHERN
NORTHERS
NORWARD
NORWARDS
NOSEBAG
NOSEBAGS
NOSEGAY
NOSEGAYS
NOSTRIL
NOSTRILS
NOSTRUM
NOSTRUMS
NOTABLE
NOTABLES
NOTAEUM
NOTAEUMS
NOTCHEL
NOTCHELS
NOTCHER
NOTCHERS
NOTELET
NOTELETS
NOTHING
NOTHINGS
NOTITIA
NOTITIAS
NOUMENA
NOUMENAL
NOURICE
NOURICES
NOURSLE
NOURSLED
NOURSLES
NOUSELL
NOUSELLS
NOVELLA
NOVELLAE
NOVELLAS
NOWHERE
NOWHERES
NOYANCE
NOYANCES
NUBBIER
KNUBBIER
SNUBBIER
NUBBING
SNUBBING
NUBBLED
KNUBBLED
NUBBLES
KNUBBLES
NUCLEIN
NUCLEINS
NUCLEON
NUCLEONS
NUCLIDE
NUCLIDES
NUDGING
SNUDGING
NULLING
NULLINGS
NUMERAL
NUMERALS
NUNATAK
NUNATAKS
NUNDINE
NUNDINES
NUNHOOD
NUNHOODS
NUNSHIP
NUNSHIPS
NUPTIAL
NUPTIALS
NURAGHI
NURAGHIC
NURLING
KNURLING
NURSING
NURSINGS
NURTURE
NURTURED
NURTURER
NURTURES
NUTCASE
NUTCASES
NUTGALL
NUTGALLS
NUTMEAL
NUTMEALS
NUTTING
NUTTINGS
NUTWOOD
NUTWOODS
NUZZLED
SNUZZLED
NUZZLES
SNUZZLES
NYLGHAU
NYLGHAUS
NYMPHAE
NYMPHAEA
NYMPHET
NYMPHETS
OAKLING
OAKLINGS
OARIEST
HOARIEST
ROARIEST
OARWEED
OARWEEDS
OATCAKE
OATCAKES
OATMEAL
OATMEALS
OBELION
OBELIONS
OBELISE
OBELISED
OBELISES
OBELISK
OBELISKS
OBELIZE
OBELIZED
OBELIZES
OBLIGEE
OBLIGEES
OBLIGOR
OBLIGORS
OBLIQUE
OBLIQUED
OBLIQUER
OBLIQUES
OBSCENE
OBSCENER
OBSCURE
OBSCURED
OBSCURER
OBSCURES
OBSERVE
OBSERVED
OBSERVER
OBSERVES
OBTRUDE
OBTRUDED
OBTRUDER
OBTRUDES
OBVERSE
OBVERSES
OBVIATE
OBVIATED
OBVIATES
OCARINA
OCARINAS
OCCIPUT
OCCIPUTS
OCCLUDE
OCCLUDED
OCCLUDER
OCCLUDES
OCEANID
OCEANIDS
OCHERED
TOCHERED
OCTAGON
OCTAGONS
OCTAPLA
OCTAPLAS
OCTETTE
OCTETTES
OCTOPOD
OCTOPODS
OCTOPUS
OCTOPUSH
OCTUPLE
OCTUPLED
OCTUPLES
OCTUPLET
OCULATE
LOCULATE
OCULATED
OCULIST
OCULISTS
ODALISK
ODALISKS
ODALLER
ODALLERS
ODDBALL
ODDBALLS
ODDMENT
ODDMENTS
ODORANT
ODORANTS
ODYLISM
ODYLISMS
ODYSSEY
ODYSSEYS
OENOMEL
OENOMELS
OERSTED
OERSTEDS
OESTRUM
OESTRUMS
OFFBEAT
OFFBEATS
OFFENCE
OFFENCES
OFFENSE
OFFENSES
OFFERED
COFFERED
GOFFERED
OFFEREE
OFFEREES
OFFERER
OFFERERS
OFFEROR
OFFERORS
OFFICER
OFFICERS
OFFLOAD
OFFLOADS
OFFSCUM
OFFSCUMS
OFFSIDE
OFFSIDER
OFFSIDES
OFFTAKE
OFFTAKES
OFTENER
SOFTENER
OILIEST
ROILIEST
SOILIEST
OILSKIN
OILSKINS
OINKING
BOINKING
OINTING
JOINTING
NOINTING
POINTING
OKIMONO
OKIMONOS
OLDENED
BOLDENED
GOLDENED
OLDNESS
BOLDNESS
COLDNESS
OLDSTER
OLDSTERS
OLEARIA
OLEARIAS
OLEFINE
OLEFINES
OLIGIST
OLIGISTS
OLIVINE
OLIVINES
OLOGIES
OOLOGIES
OLOROSO
DOLOROSO
OLOROSOS
OLYCOOK
OLYCOOKS
OLYKOEK
OLYKOEKS
OMENTUM
LOMENTUM
MOMENTUM
TOMENTUM
OMICRON
OMICRONS
OMITTER
OMITTERS
OMNIFIC
SOMNIFIC
ONANISM
ONANISMS
ONANIST
ONANISTS
ONCOGEN
ONCOGENE
ONCOGENS
ONDATRA
ONDATRAS
ONDINGS
BONDINGS
ONENESS
DONENESS
GONENESS
LONENESS
ONEYERS
MONEYERS
ONGOING
ONGOINGS

ONSTEAD
ONSTEADS
ONYCHIA
ONYCHIAS
OOGONIA
OOGONIAL
OOLAKAN
OOLAKANS
OOLITES
ZOOLITES
OOLITIC
ZOOLITIC
OOMIACK
OOMIACKS
OOPHYTE
ZOOPHYTE
OOPHYTES
OORIEST
MOORIEST
OOSIEST
GOOSIEST
OOSPORE
ZOOSPORE
OOSPORES
OOZIEST
BOOZIEST
WOOZIEST
OPALINE
OPALINES
OPAQUES
OPAQUEST
OPENING
OPENINGS
OPERAND
OPERANDS
OPERANT
OPERANTS
OPERATE
OPERATED
OPERATES
OPHIURA
OPHIURAN
OPHIURAS
OPINION
OPINIONS
OPORICE
OPORICES
OPOSSUM
OPOSSUMS
OPPIDAN
OPPIDANS
OPPOSER
OPPOSERS
OPSONIN
OPSONINS
OPUNTIA
OPUNTIAS
OPUSCLE
OPUSCLES
ORACLES
CORACLES
ORALISM
MORALISM
ORALISMS
ORALITY
MORALITY
ORANGER
ORANGERY
ORANGES
ORANGEST
ORARIAN
ORARIANS
ORARION
ORARIONS
ORARIUM
ORARIUMS
ORATION
ORATIONS
ORATORY
MORATORY
ORBITAL
ORBITALS
ORBITER
ORBITERS
ORCHARD
ORCHARDS
ORCINOL
ORCINOLS
ORDERED
BORDERED
ORDERER
BORDERER
ORDERERS
ORDINAL
ORDINALS
ORDINAR
ORDINARS
ORDINARY
ORDINEE
ORDINEES
ORDURES
BORDURES
OREGANO
OREGANOS
OREWEED
OREWEEDS
ORGANZA
ORGANZAS
ORGIAST
ORGIASTS
ORIFICE
ORIFICES
ORIGAMI
ORIGAMIS
ORIGANE
ORIGANES
OROLOGY
HOROLOGY
OROPESA
OROPESAS
ORPHREY
ORPHREYS
ORPINES
FORPINES
ORRISES
MORRISES
ORTOLAN
PORTOLAN
ORTOLANS
OSMIATE
OSMIATES
OSMOSES
COSMOSES
KOSMOSES
OSMUNDA
OSMUNDAS
OSSELET
OSSELETS
OSSETER
OSSETERS
OSSICLE
OSSICLES
OSTEOMA
OSTEOMAS
OSTIOLE
OSTIOLES
OSTLERS
HOSTLERS
OTALGIA
OTALGIAS
OTARIES
NOTARIES
ROTARIES
VOTARIES
OTOCYST
OTOCYSTS
OTOLITH
OTOLITHS
OTTERED
HOTTERED
POTTERED
TOTTERED
OTTOMAN
OTTOMANS
OUABAIN
OUABAINS
OUAKARI
OUAKARIS
OULAKAN
OULAKANS
OURALIS
WOURALIS
OURIEST
LOURIEST
OURSELF
YOURSELF
OUSTERS
JOUSTERS
ROUSTERS
OUSTING
JOUSTING
MOUSTING
ROUSTING
OUSTITI
OUSTITIS
OUTBACK
OUTBACKS
OUTBRAG
OUTBRAGS
OUTBURN
OUTBURNS
OUTBURNT
OUTCAST
OUTCASTE
OUTCASTS
OUTCOME
OUTCOMES
OUTCROP
OUTCROPS
OUTDARE
OUTDARED
OUTDARES
OUTDATE
OUTDATED
OUTDATES
OUTDOOR
OUTDOORS
OUTDURE
OUTDURED
OUTDURES
OUTEDGE
OUTEDGES
OUTFACE
OUTFACED
OUTFACES
OUTFALL
OUTFALLS
OUTFLOW
OUTFLOWN
OUTFLOWS
OUTFOOT
OUTFOOTS
OUTGATE
OUTGATES
OUTGIVE
OUTGIVEN
OUTGIVES
OUTGOER
OUTGOERS
OUTGROW
OUTGROWN
OUTGROWS
OUTHAUL
OUTHAULS
OUTHIRE
OUTHIRED
OUTHIRES
OUTHYRE
OUTHYRED
OUTHYRES
OUTINGS
HOUTINGS
POUTINGS
ROUTINGS
OUTJEST
OUTJESTS
OUTJUMP
OUTJUMPS
OUTLAND
OUTLANDS
OUTLAST
OUTLASTS
OUTLEAP
OUTLEAPS
OUTLEAPT
OUTLIER
OUTLIERS
OUTLINE
OUTLINED
OUTLINES
OUTLIVE
OUTLIVED
OUTLIVES
OUTLOOK
OUTLOOKS
OUTMODE
OUTMODED
OUTMODES
OUTMOVE
OUTMOVED
OUTMOVES
OUTNAME
OUTNAMED
OUTNAMES
OUTPACE
OUTPACED
OUTPACES
OUTPART
OUTPARTS
OUTPEEP
OUTPEEPS
OUTPEER
OUTPEERS
OUTPLAY
OUTPLAYS
OUTPORT
OUTPORTS
OUTPOST
OUTPOSTS
OUTPOUR
OUTPOURS
OUTPRAY
OUTPRAYS
OUTRACE
OUTRACED
OUTRACES
OUTRAGE
OUTRAGED
OUTRAGES
OUTRANK
OUTRANKS
OUTRATE
OUTRATED
OUTRATES
OUTRIDE
OUTRIDER
OUTRIDES
OUTROAR
OUTROARS
OUTROOP
OUTROOPS
OUTROOT
OUTROOTS
OUTROPE
OUTROPER
OUTROPES
OUTSAIL
OUTSAILS
OUTSELL
OUTSELLS
OUTSHOT
OUTSHOTS
OUTSIDE
OUTSIDER
OUTSIDES
OUTSIZE
OUTSIZED
OUTSIZES
OUTSOAR
OUTSOARS
OUTSOLE
OUTSOLES
OUTSPAN
OUTSPANS
OUTSTAY
OUTSTAYS
OUTSTEP
OUTSTEPS
OUTSWIM
OUTSWIMS
OUTTAKE
OUTTAKEN
OUTTAKES
OUTTALK
OUTTALKS
OUTTELL
OUTTELLS
OUTTURN
OUTTURNS
OUTVOTE
OUTVOTED
OUTVOTER
OUTVOTES
OUTWALK
OUTWALKS
OUTWARD
OUTWARDS
OUTWEAR
OUTWEARS
OUTWEARY
OUTWEED
GOUTWEED
OUTWEEDS
OUTWEEP
OUTWEEPS
OUTWELL
OUTWELLS
OUTWICK
OUTWICKS
OUTWIND
OUTWINDS
OUTWING
OUTWINGS
OUTWORK
OUTWORKS
OUVRAGE
OUVRAGES
OUVRIER
OUVRIERE
OUVRIERS
OVARIES
COVARIES
OVATION
NOVATION
OVATIONS
OVERACT
OVERACTS
OVERAGE
COVERAGE
OVERAGES
OVERALL
COVERALL
OVERALLS
OVERAWE
OVERAWED
OVERAWES
OVERBID
OVERBIDS
OVERBUY
OVERBUYS
OVERDYE
OVERDYED
OVERDYES
OVEREAT
OVEREATS
OVEREYE
OVEREYED
OVEREYES
OVERGET
OVERGETS
OVERHIT
OVERHITS
OVERING
COVERING
DOVERING
HOVERING
OVERJOY
OVERJOYS
OVERLAP
OVERLAPS
OVERLAY
OVERLAYS
OVERLIE
OVERLIER
OVERLIES
OVERMAN
OVERMANS
OVERNET
OVERNETS
OVERPAY
OVERPAYS
OVERRAN
OVERRANK
OVERRED
OVERREDS
OVERREN
OVERRENS
OVERRUN
OVERRUNS
OVERSEA
OVERSEAS
OVERSEE
OVERSEEN
OVERSEER
OVERSEES
OVERSET
OVERSETS
OVERSEW
OVERSEWN
OVERSEWS
OVERSOW
OVERSOWN
OVERSOWS
OVERTLY
COVERTLY
OVERTOP
OVERTOPS
OVERUSE
OVERUSED
OVERUSES
OVICIDE
OVICIDES
OVIDUCT
OVIDUCTS
OVULATE
OVULATED
OVULATES
OWLIEST
JOWLIEST
LOWLIEST
OWRELAY
OWRELAYS
OXALATE
OXALATES
OXAZINE
OXAZINES
OXBLOOD
OXBLOODS
OXIDANT
OXIDANTS
OXIDASE
OXIDASES
OXIDATE
OXIDATED
OXIDATES
OXIDISE
OXIDISED
OXIDISER
OXIDISES
OXIDIZE

OXIDIZED
OXIDIZER
OXIDIZES
OXONIUM
OXONIUMS
OXYGENS
LOXYGENS
OXYTONE
OXYTONES
OYSTERS
ROYSTERS
OZONISE
OZONISED
OZONISER
OZONISES
OZONIZE
OZONIZED
OZONIZER
OZONIZES
PABULUM
PABULUMS
PACHISI
PACHISIS
PACIEST
SPACIEST
PACKAGE
PACKAGED
PACKAGER
PACKAGES
PACKING
PACKINGS
PACKWAY
PACKWAYS
PACTION
PACTIONS
PADDING
PADDINGS
PADDLER
PADDLERS
PADDOCK
PADDOCKS
PADELLA
PADELLAS
PADLOCK
PADLOCKS
PAENULA
PAENULAE
PAENULAS
PAEONIC
PAEONICS
PAGEANT
PAGEANTS
PAGURID
PAGURIDS
PAILFUL
PAILFULS
PAILLON
PAILLONS
PAINING
SPAINING
PAINTER
PAINTERS
PAIOCKE
PAIOCKES
PAIRIAL
PAIRIALS
PAIRING
PAIRINGS
PAISANO
PAISANOS
PAISLEY
PAISLEYS
PAJOCKE
PAJOCKES
PAKAPOO
PAKAPOOS
PAKFONG
PAKFONGS
PAKTONG
PAKTONGS
PALABRA
PALABRAS
PALADIN
PALADINS
PALATAL
PALATALS
PALAVER
PALAVERS
PALETOT
PALETOTS
PALETTE
PALETTES
PALFREY
PALFREYS
PALLING
SPALLING
PALLONE
PALLONES
PALMATE
PALMATED
PALMFUL
PALMFULS
PALMIES
PALMIEST
PALMIET
PALMIETS
PALMIST
PALMISTS
PALMTOP
PALMTOPS
PALMYRA
PALMYRAS
PALOOKA
PALOOKAS
PALPATE
PALPATED
PALPATES
PALSIES
PALSIEST
PAMPERO
PAMPEROS
PANACEA
PANACEAN
PANACEAS
PANACHE
PANACHES
PANCAKE
PANCAKED
PANCAKES
PANDECT
PANDECTS
PANDOOR
PANDOORS
PANDORA
PANDORAS
PANDORE
PANDORES
PANDOUR
PANDOURS
PANDURA
PANDURAS
PANGENE
PANGENES
PANGING
SPANGING
PANGRAM
PANGRAMS
PANICLE
PANICLED
PANICLES
PANNAGE
PANNAGES
PANNICK
PANNICKS
PANNIER
PANNIERS
PANNING
SPANNING
PANNINGS
PANOCHA
PANOCHAS
PANTHER
PANTHERS
PANTILE
PANTILED
PANTILES
PANTINE
PANTINES
PANTING
PANTINGS
PANTLER
PANTLERS
PANTOUM
PANTOUMS
PAPERER
PAPERERS
PAPILIO
PAPILIOS
PAPILLA
PAPILLAE
PAPILLAR
PAPOOSE
PAPOOSES
PAPPIES
PAPPIEST
PAPRIKA
PAPRIKAS
PARABLE
SPARABLE
PARABLED
PARABLES
PARACME
PARACMES
PARADOX
PARADOXY
PARAFLE
PARAFLES
PARAGON
PARAGONS
PARANYM
PARANYMS
PARAPET
PARAPETS
PARASOL
PARASOLS
PARATHA
PARATHAS
PARAZOA
PARAZOAN
PARBOIL
PARBOILS
PARCHES
PARCHESI
PARDALE
PARDALES
PARDNER
PARDNERS
PAREIRA
PAREIRAS
PARELLA
PARELLAS
PARELLE
PARELLES
PARFAIT
PARFAITS
PARGANA
PARGANAS
PARGING
SPARGING
PARISON
PARISONS
PARITOR
PARITORS
PARKIER
SPARKIER
PARKIES
SPARKIES
PARKIEST
PARKING
SPARKING
PARKINGS
PARKISH
SPARKISH
PARKWAY
PARKWAYS
PARLING
SPARLING
PARLOUR
PARLOURS
PAROLEE
PAROLEES
PARONYM
PARONYMS
PARONYMY
PAROTID
PAROTIDS
PARPANE
PARPANES
PARPEND
PARPENDS
PARPENT
PARPENTS
PARQUET
PARQUETS
PARROCK
PARROCKS
PARSING
PARSINGS
PARSLEY
PARSLEYS
PARSNEP
PARSNEPS
PARSNIP
PARSNIPS
PARTAKE
PARTAKEN
PARTAKER
PARTAKES
PARTANS
SPARTANS
PARTIAL
PARTIALS
PARTING
PARTINGS
PARTITA
PARTITAS
PARTLET
PARTLETS
PARTNER
PARTNERS
PARTURE
PARTURES
PARVENU
PARVENUS
PARVISE
PARVISES
PASSADE
PASSADES
PASSADO
PASSADOS
PASSAGE
PASSAGED
PASSAGES
PASSING
PASSINGS
PASSION
PASSIONS
PASSIVE
PASSIVES
PASSKEY
PASSKEYS
PASSMEN
PASSMENT
PASSOUT
PASSOUTS
PASTERN
PASTERNS
PASTIES
PASTIEST
PASTIME
PASTIMES
PASTING
PASTINGS
PASTURE
PASTURED
PASTURES
PATAGIA
PATAGIAL
PATAMAR
PATAMARS
PATBALL
PATBALLS
PATCHER
PATCHERS
PATCHERY
PATELLA
PATELLAE
PATELLAR
PATELLAS
PATHWAY
PATHWAYS
PATIENT
PATIENTS
PATRIAL
PATRIALS
PATRICK
PATRICKS
PATRIOT
PATRIOTS
PATROON
PATROONS
PATTERN
PATTERNS
PATTERS
SPATTERS
PATTING
SPATTING
PATULIN
PATULINS
PAUSING
PAUSINGS
PAVIOUR
PAVIOURS
PAVLOVA
PAVLOVAS
PAWNERS
SPAWNERS
PAWNING
SPAWNING
PAXIUBA
PAXIUBAS
PAYBACK
PAYBACKS
PAYFONE
PAYFONES
PAYMENT
PAYMENTS
PAYROLL
PAYROLLS
PAYSAGE
PAYSAGES
PAYSLIP
PAYSLIPS
PEACHER
PEACHERS
PEACOCK
PEACOCKS
PEACOCKY
PEAFOWL
PEAFOWLS
PEAKING
SPEAKING
PEANING
SPEANING
PEARLER
PEARLERS
PEARLIN
PEARLING
PEARLINS
PEASANT
PEASANTS
PEASANTY
PEASCOD
PEASCODS
PEBRINE
PEBRINES
PECCAVI
PECCAVIS
PECKING
SPECKING
PECKINGS
PECTISE
PECTISED
PECTISES
PECTIZE
PECTIZED
PECTIZES
PECTOSE
PECTOSES
PECULIA
PECULIAR
PEDDLER
PEDDLERS
PEDICAB
PEDICABS
PEDICEL
PEDICELS
PEDICLE
PEDICLED
PEDICLES
PEDRAIL
PEDRAILS
PEDRERO
PEDREROS
PEEKABO
PEEKABOO
PEEKABOS
PEELERS
SPEELERS
PEELING
SPEELING
PEELINGS
PEERAGE
PEERAGES
PEERIES
PEERIEST
PEERING
SPEERING
PEGGING
PEGGINGS
PEISHWA
PEISHWAH
PEISHWAS
PELICAN
PELICANS
PELISSE
PELISSES
PELLACH
PELLACHS
PELLACK
PELLACKS
PELLOCK
PELLOCKS
PELORIA
PELORIAS
PELTAST
PELTASTS
PELTERS
SPELTERS
PELTING
PELTINGS
PEMICAN
PEMICANS
PENANCE
PENANCED
PENANCES
PENDANT
PENDANTS
PENDENT
PENDENTS
PENDING
SPENDING
UPENDING
PENFOLD
PENFOLDS
PENGUIN
PENGUINS
PENNANT
PENNANTS
PENNINE

PENNINES
PENSION
PENSIONS
PENTACT
PENTACTS
PENTANE
PENTANES
PENTENE
PENTENES
PENTHIA
PENTHIAS
PENTICE
PENTICED
PENTICES
PENTISE
PENTISED
PENTISES
PENTODE
PENTODES
PENTOSE
PENTOSES
PENUCHE
PENUCHES
PENUCHI
PENUCHIS
PEONAGE
PEONAGES
PEONISM
PEONISMS
PEPSINE
PEPSINES
PEPTIDE
PEPTIDES
PEPTISE
PEPTISED
PEPTISES
PEPTIZE
PEPTIZED
PEPTIZES
PEPTONE
PEPTONES
PERAEON
PERAEONS
PERCALE
PERCALES
PERCEPT
PERCEPTS
PERCHER
PERCHERS
PERCHERY
PERDURE
PERDURED
PERDURES
PEREGAL
PEREGALS
PEREIRA
PEREIRAS
PERFECT
PERFECTA
PERFECTI
PERFECTO
PERFECTS
PERFORM
PERFORMS
PERFUME
PERFUMED
PERFUMER
PERFUMES
PERFUSE
PERFUSED
PERFUSES
PERGOLA
PERGOLAS
PERIAPT
PERIAPTS
PERIDIA
PERIDIAL
PERIDOT
PERIDOTE
PERIDOTS
PERIGEE
PERIGEES
PERIGON
PERIGONE
PERIGONS
PERINEA
PERINEAL
PERIOST
PERIOSTS
PERIQUE
PERIQUES
PERIWIG
PERIWIGS
PERJURE
PERJURED
PERJURER
PERJURES
PERLITE
PERLITES
PERMUTE
PERMUTED
PERMUTES
PERPEND
PERPENDS
PERPENT
PERPENTS
PERRIER
PERRIERS
PERSICO
PERSICOS
PERSICOT
PERSING
SPERSING
PERSIST
PERSISTS
PERSONA
PERSONAE
PERSONAL
PERSONAS
PERTAIN
PERTAINS
PERTAKE
PERTAKEN
PERTAKES
PERTURB
PERTURBS
PERTUSE
PERTUSED
PERUSAL
PERUSALS
PERUSER
PERUSERS
PERVADE
PERVADED
PERVADES
PERVERT
PERVERTS
PESAUNT
PESAUNTS
PESSIMA
PESSIMAL
PETCOCK
PETCOCKS
PETIOLE
PETIOLED
PETIOLES
PETTIES
PETTIEST
PETTING
SPETTING
PETTINGS
PETUNIA
PETUNIAS
PFENNIG
PFENNIGE
PFENNIGS
PHAEISM
PHAEISMS
PHAETON
PHAETONS
PHALLIN
PHALLINS
PHANTOM
PHANTOMS
PHANTOMY
PHASMID
PHASMIDS
PHEAZAR
PHEAZARS
PHELLEM
PHELLEMS
PHENATE
PHENATES
PHILTER
PHILTERS
PHILTRE
PHILTRES
PHOBISM
PHOBISMS
PHOBIST
PHOBISTS
PHONATE
PHONATED
PHONATES
PHONEME
PHONEMES
PHONIES
APHONIES
PHONIEST
PHOTISM
PHOTISMS
PHRASER
PHRASERS
PIAFFER
PIAFFERS
PIANINO
PIANINOS
PIANISM
PIANISMS
PIANIST
PIANISTE
PIANISTS
PIARIST
APIARIST
PIARISTS
PIASTRE
PIASTRES
PIBROCH
PIBROCHS
PICADOR
PICADORS
PICAMAR
PICAMARS
PICCOLO
PICCOLOS
PICENES
EPICENES
PICKAXE
PICKAXES
PICKEER
PICKEERS
PICKING
PICKINGS
PICKLER
PICKLERS
PICKMAW
PICKMAWS
PICOTEE
PICOTEES
PICQUET
PICQUETS
PICRATE
PICRATES
PICRITE
PICRITES
PICTURE
PICTURED
PICTURES
PIDDLER
PIDDLERS
PIDDOCK
PIDDOCKS
PIDGEON
PIDGEONS
PIEBALD
PIEBALDS
PIERAGE
PIERAGES
PIERCER
PIERCERS
PIERROT
PIERROTS
PIETISM
PIETISMS
PIETIST
PIETISTS
PIFFERO
PIFFEROS
PIFFLER
PIFFLERS
PIGBOAT
PIGBOATS
PIGFEED
PIGFEEDS
PIGGIES
PIGGIEST
PIGGING
PIGGINGS
PIGHTED
SPIGHTED
PIGHTLE
PIGHTLES
PIGLING
PIGLINGS
PIGMEAT
PIGMEATS
PIGMENT
PIGMENTS
PIGSKIN
PIGSKINS
PIGSNEY
PIGSNEYS
PIGSNIE
PIGSNIES
PIGTAIL
PIGTAILS
PIGWEED
PIGWEEDS
PIKELET
SPIKELET
PIKELETS
PILCHER
PILCHERS
PILCORN
PILCORNS
PILCROW
PILCROWS
PILEATE
PILEATED
PILGRIM
PILGRIMS
PILINGS
SPILINGS
PILLAGE
SPILLAGE
PILLAGED
PILLAGER
PILLAGES
PILLING
SPILLING
PILLINGS
PILLION
PILLIONS
PILLOCK
PILLOCKS
PILSNER
PILSNERS
PIMENTO
PIMENTOS
PINBALL
PINBALLS
PINCASE
PINCASES
PINCHER
PINCHERS
PINDARI
PINDARIS
PINDOWN
PINDOWNS
PINFOLD
PINFOLDS
PINGLER
PINGLERS
PINGUIN
PINGUINS
PINHEAD
PINHEADS
PINHOLE
PINHOLES
PINIEST
SPINIEST
PINIONS
OPINIONS
PINKIES
PINKIEST
PINKING
PINKINGS
PINNACE
PINNACES
PINNATE
PINNATED
PINNERS
SPINNERS
PINNETS
SPINNETS
PINNIES
SPINNIES
PINNING
SPINNING
PINNINGS
PINNOCK
PINNOCKS
PINNULA
PINNULAS
PINNULE
PINNULES
PINOCLE
PINOCLES
PINTADO
PINTADOS
PINTAIL
PINTAILS
PIONEER
PIONEERS
PIONING
PIONINGS
PIPEFUL
PIPEFULS
PIPETTE
PIPETTED
PIPETTES
PIRAGUA
PIRAGUAS
PIRANHA
PIRANHAS
PIRATED
SPIRATED
PIROGUE
PIROGUES
PISCINA
PISCINAE
PISCINAS
PISCINE
PISCINES
PISMIRE
PISMIRES
PISSOIR
PISSOIRS
PISTOLE
PISTOLES
PISTOLET
PITAPAT
PITAPATS
PITARAH
PITARAHS
PITCHER
SPITCHER
PITCHERS
PITFALL
PITFALLS
PITHEAD
PITHEADS
PITPROP
PITPROPS
PITTERS
SPITTERS
PITTING
SPITTING
PITTINGS
PITTITE
PITTITES
PITUITA
PITUITAS
PITUITE
PITUITES
PIVOTER
PIVOTERS
PLACARD
PLACARDS
PLACATE
PLACATED
PLACATES
PLACCAT
PLACCATE
PLACCATS
PLACEBO
PLACEBOS
PLACING
PLACINGS
PLACKET
PLACKETS
PLAFOND
PLAFONDS
PLAGIUM
PLAGIUMS
PLAITER
PLAITERS
PLANNER
PLANNERS
PLANTER
PLANTERS
PLANULA
PLANULAE
PLANULAR
PLASHED
SPLASHED
PLASHES
SPLASHES
PLASHET
PLASHETS
PLASMID
PLASMIDS
PLASMIN
PLASMINS
PLASTER
PLASTERS
PLASTERY
PLASTIC
APLASTIC
PLASTICS
PLASTID
PLASTIDS
PLATANE
PLATANES
PLATEAU
PLATEAUS
PLATEAUX
PLATINA
PLATINAS
PLATING
PLATINGS
PLATOON
PLATOONS
PLATTED
SPLATTED
PLATTER
SPLATTER
PLATTERS
PLAUDIT
PLAUDITE

PLAUDITS
PLAYBOY
PLAYBOYS
PLAYING
SPLAYING
UPLAYING
PLAYLET
PLAYLETS
PLAYPEN
PLAYPENS
PLEADER
PLEADERS
PLEASER
PLEASERS
PLEATER
PLEATERS
PLECTRE
PLECTRES
PLEDGEE
PLEDGEES
PLEDGER
PLEDGERS
PLEDGET
PLEDGETS
PLEDGOR
PLEDGORS
PLENIPO
PLENIPOS
PLENIST
PLENISTS
PLEOPOD
PLEOPODS
PLEROMA
PLEROMAS
PLEROME
PLEROMES
PLESSOR
PLESSORS
PLEXURE
PLEXURES
PLICATE
PLICATED
PLICATES
PLISKIE
PLISKIES
PLODDER
PLODDERS
PLONKER
PLONKERS
PLOOKIE
PLOOKIER
PLOSION
PLOSIONS
PLOSIVE
PLOSIVES
PLOTTER
PLOTTERS
PLOTTIE
PLOTTIES
PLOUKIE
PLOUKIER
PLOUTER
PLOUTERS
PLOWTER
PLOWTERS
PLUCKER
PLUCKERS
PLUGGER
PLUGGERS
PLUMAGE
PLUMAGED
PLUMAGES
PLUMBER
PLUMBERS
PLUMBERY
PLUMBUM
PLUMBUMS
PLUMCOT
PLUMCOTS
PLUMIST
PLUMISTS
PLUMMET
PLUMMETS
PLUMPEN
PLUMPENS
PLUMPER
PLUMPERS
PLUMULA
PLUMULAE
PLUMULAR
PLUMULE
PLUMULES
PLUNDER
PLUNDERS
PLUNGER
PLUNGERS
PLUNKER
PLUNKERS
PLUSAGE
PLUSAGES
PLUSHES
PLUSHEST
PLUVIAL
PLUVIALS
PLYWOOD
PLYWOODS
POACHER
POACHERS
POCHARD
POCHARDS
POCHOIR
POCHOIRS
POCKARD
POCKARDS
POCKPIT
POCKPITS
PODAGRA
PODAGRAL
PODAGRAS
PODDIES
PODDIEST
PODESTA
PODESTAS
POETISE
POETISED
POETISES
POETIZE
POETIZED
POETIZES
POINDER
POINDERS
POINTEL
POINTELS
POINTER
POINTERS
POISSON
POISSONS
POITREL
POITRELS
POKEFUL
POKEFULS
POLACCA
POLACCAS
POLACRE
POLACRES
POLARON
POLARONS
POLECAT
POLECATS
POLEMIC
POLEMICS
POLENTA
POLENTAS
POLITIC
POLITICK
POLITICO
POLITICS
POLLACK
POLLACKS
POLLARD
POLLARDS
POLLING
POLLINGS
POLLOCK
POLLOCKS
POLLUTE
POLLUTED
POLLUTER
POLLUTES
POLOIST
POLOISTS
POLONIE
POLONIES
POLYGAM
POLYGAMS
POLYGAMY
POLYGON
POLYGONS
POLYGONY
POLYMER
POLYMERS
POLYMERY
POLYNIA
POLYNIAS
POLYNYA
POLYNYAS
POLYOMA
POLYOMAS
POLYPOD
POLYPODS
POLYPODY
POLYZOA
POLYZOAN
POMATUM
POMATUMS
POMEROY
POMEROYS
POMFRET
POMFRETS
POMPANO
POMPANOS
POMPELO
POMPELOS
POMPION
POMPIONS
POMPOON
POMPOONS
PONCEAU
PONCEAUS
PONCEAUX
PONDAGE
PONDAGES
PONGIER
SPONGIER
PONGING
SPONGING
PONIARD
PONIARDS
PONTAGE
PONTAGES
PONTIFF
PONTIFFS
PONTILE
PONTILES
PONTOON
SPONTOON
PONTOONS
POOFTAH
POOFTAHS
POOFTER
POOFTERS
POOGYEE
POOGYEES
POOKING
SPOOKING
POOLING
SPOOLING
POPADUM
POPADUMS
POPCORN
POPCORNS
POPEDOM
POPEDOMS
POPERIN
POPERINS
POPOVER
POPOVERS
POPPIES
POPPIEST
POPULAR
POPULARS
PORIFER
PORIFERS
PORKIES
PORKIEST
PORPESS
PORPESSE
PORRECT
PORRECTS
PORRIGO
PORRIGOS
PORTAGE
PORTAGES
PORTEND
PORTENDS
PORTENT
PORTENTS
PORTERS
SPORTERS
PORTESS
PORTESSE
PORTICO
PORTICOS
PORTIER
SPORTIER
PORTIERE
PORTING
SPORTING
PORTION
PORTIONS
PORTRAY
PORTRAYS
POSAUNE
POSAUNES
POSEUSE
POSEUSES
POSITON
POSITONS
POSSUMS
OPOSSUMS
POSTAGE
POSTAGES
POSTBAG
POSTBAGS
POSTEEN
POSTEENS
POSTERN
POSTERNS
POSTILS
APOSTILS
POSTING
POSTINGS
POSTURE
POSTURED
POSTURER
POSTURES
POTABLE
POTABLES
POTAGER
POTAGERS
POTASSA
POTASSAS
POTCHER
POTCHERS
POTENCE
POTENCES
POTHEEN
POTHEENS
POTHOLE
POTHOLED
POTHOLER
POTHOLES
POTHOOK
POTHOOKS
POTICHE
POTICHES
POTOROO
POTOROOS
POTSHOP
POTSHOPS
POTTAGE
POTTAGES
POTTERS
SPOTTERS
POTTIER
SPOTTIER
POTTIES
POTTIEST
POTTING
SPOTTING
POUFTAH
POUFTAHS
POUFTER
POUFTERS
POULARD
POULARDS
POULDER
POULDERS
POULDRE
POULDRES
POULTER
POULTERS
POUNCET
POUNCETS
POUNDAL
POUNDALS
POUNDER
POUNDERS
POURING
POURINGS
POURSEW
POURSEWS
POURSUE
POURSUED
POURSUES
POUSSIN
POUSSINS
POUTERS
SPOUTERS
POUTHER
POUTHERS
POUTIER
SPOUTIER
POUTING
SPOUTING
POUTINGS
PRABBLE
PRABBLES
PRACTIC
PRACTICE
PRACTICK
PRACTICS
PRAETOR
PRAETORS
PRAIRIE
PRAIRIED
PRAIRIES
PRAISED
UPRAISED
PRAISER
PRAISERS
PRAISES
UPRAISES
PRALINE
PRALINES
PRANCER
PRANCERS
PRANCKE
PRANCKED
PRANCKES
PRANKLE
PRANKLED
PRANKLES
PRATING
UPRATING
PRATINGS
PRATTLE
SPRATTLE
PRATTLED
PRATTLER
PRATTLES
PRAUNCE
PRAUNCED
PRAUNCES
PRAWLIN
PRAWLINS
PRAYERS
SPRAYERS
PRAYING
SPRAYING
PRAYINGS
PREASSE
PREASSED
PREASSES
PREBEND
PREBENDS
PRECAVA
PRECAVAE
PRECEDE
PRECEDED
PRECEDES
PRECEPT
PRECEPTS
PRECISE
PRECISED
PRECISER
PRECISES
PRECOOK
PRECOOKS
PRECOOL
PRECOOLS
PREDATE
PREDATED
PREDATES
PREDAWN
PREDAWNS
PREDIAL
PREDIALS
PREDICT
PREDICTS
PREDOOM
PREDOOMS
PREEING
SPREEING
PREEMIE
PREEMIES
PREFACE
PREFACED
PREFACES
PREFADE
PREFADED
PREFADES
PREFECT
PREFECTS
PREFORM
PREFORMS
PREHEAT
PREHEATS
PREHEND
PREHENDS
PRELATE
PRELATES
PRELECT
PRELECTS
PRELUDE
PRELUDED
PRELUDES
PRELUDI
PRELUDIO
PREMIER
PREMIERE
PREMIERS
PREMISE
PREMISED
PREMISES
PREMIUM
PREMIUMS
PREMOVE
PREMOVED
PREMOVES

PREPACK
PREPACKS
PREPARE
PREPARED
PREPARER
PREPARES
PREPONE
PREPONED
PREPONES
PREPOSE
PREPOSED
PREPOSES
PREPUCE
PREPUCES
PREQUEL
PREQUELS
PRESAGE
PRESAGED
PRESAGER
PRESAGES
PRESENT
PRESENTS
PRESIDE
PRESIDED
PRESIDES
PRESSER
PRESSERS
PRESSIE
PRESSIES
PRESUME
PRESUMED
PRESUMER
PRESUMES
PRETEND
PRETENDS
PRETEST
PRETESTS
PRETEXT
PRETEXTS
PRETZEL
PRETZELS
PREVAIL
PREVAILS
PREVENE
PREVENED
PREVENES
PREVENT
PREVENTS
PREVERB
PREVERBS
PREVIEW
PREVIEWS
PREVISE
PREVISED
PREVISES
PREWARM
PREWARMS
PREWARN
PREWARNS
PREZZIE
PREZZIES
PRIBBLE
PRIBBLES
PRICKER
PRICKERS
PRICKET
PRICKETS
PRICKLE
PRICKLED
PRICKLES

PRIGGED
SPRIGGED
PRIGGER
PRIGGERS
PRIGGERY
PRIMAGE
PRIMAGES
PRIMATE
PRIMATES
PRIMERO
PRIMEROS
PRIMEUR
PRIMEURS
PRIMINE
PRIMINES
PRIMING
PRIMINGS
PRIMMER
PRIMMERS
PRIMULA
PRIMULAS
PRINCES
PRINCESS
PRINTED
SPRINTED
PRINTER
SPRINTER
PRINTERS
PRISAGE
PRISAGES
PRISING
UPRISING
PRIVADO
PRIVADOS
PRIVATE
PRIVATES
PRIVIES
PRIVIEST
PROBAND
PROBANDS
PROBANG
PROBANGS
PROBATE
PROBATED
PROBATES
PROBLEM
PROBLEMS
PROCEED
PROCEEDS
PROCTOR
PROCTORS
PROCURE
PROCURED
PROCURER
PROCURES
PRODUCE
PRODUCED
PRODUCER
PRODUCES
PRODUCT
PRODUCTS
PROFANE
PROFANED
PROFANER
PROFANES
PROFFER
PROFFERS
PROFILE
PROFILED
PROFILER

PROFILES
PROFUSE
PROFUSER
PROGRAM
PROGRAMS
PROJECT
PROJECTS
PROLATE
PROLATED
PROLATES
PROLINE
PROLINES
PROLLED
UPROLLED
PROLLER
PROLLERS
PROLONG
PROLONGE
PROLONGS
PROMISE
PROMISED
PROMISEE
PROMISER
PROMISES
PROMMER
PROMMERS
PROMOTE
PROMOTED
PROMOTER
PROMOTES
PRONATE
PRONATED
PRONATES
PRONEUR
PRONEURS
PRONOTA
PRONOTAL
PRONOUN
PRONOUNS
PROOTIC
PROOTICS
PROPAGE
PROPAGED
PROPAGES
PROPALE
PROPALED
PROPALES
PROPANE
PROPANES
PROPEND
PROPENDS
PROPENE
PROPENES
PROPHET
PROPHETS
PROPINE
PROPINED
PROPINES
PROPONE
PROPONED
PROPONES
PROPOSE
PROPOSED
PROPOSER
PROPOSES
PRORATE
PRORATED
PRORATES
PROSING
PROSINGS

PROSPER
PROSPERS
PROTEAS
PROTEASE
PROTECT
PROTECTS
PROTEGE
PROTEGEE
PROTEGES
PROTEID
PROTEIDS
PROTEIN
PROTEINS
PROTEND
PROTENDS
PROTEST
PROTESTS
PROTHYL
PROTHYLE
PROTHYLS
PROTIST
PROTISTS
PROTIUM
PROTIUMS
PROTORE
PROTORES
PROTYLE
PROTYLES
PROULER
PROULERS
PROVAND
PROVANDS
PROVEND
PROVENDS
PROVERB
PROVERBS
PROVIDE
PROVIDED
PROVIDER
PROVIDES
PROVINE
PROVINED
PROVINES
PROVING
PROVINGS
PROVISO
PROVISOR
PROVISOS
PROVOKE
PROVOKED
PROVOKER
PROVOKES
PROVOST
PROVOSTS
PROWLER
PROWLERS
PRUNING
PRUNINGS
PRURIGO
PRURIGOS
PSALTER
PSALTERS
PSALTERY
PSCHENT
PSCHENTS
PSIONIC
PSIONICS
PSYCHIC
PSYCHICS
PSYLLID

PSYLLIDS
PTARMIC
PTARMICS
PTERYLA
PTERYLAE
PTYALIN
PTYALINS
PUCCOON
PUCCOONS
PUCELLE
PUCELLES
PUDDING
SPUDDING
PUDDINGS
PUDDINGY
PUDDLER
PUDDLERS
PUDDOCK
PUDDOCKS
PUDENDA
PUDENDAL
PUFFING
PUFFINGS
PUGGIES
PUGGIEST
PUGGING
PUGGINGS
PUGGREE
PUGGREES
PULDRON
PULDRONS
PULSATE
PULSATED
PULSATES
PULTOON
PULTOONS
PULTURE
PULTURES
PUMPION
PUMPIONS
PUMPKIN
PUMPKINS
PUNALUA
PUNALUAN
PUNALUAS
PUNCHER
PUNCHERS
PUNNING
PUNNINGS
PUNSTER
PUNSTERS
PUPARIA
PUPARIAL
PUPILAR
PUPILARY
PUPUNHA
PUPUNHAS
PURGING
PURGINGS
PURITAN
PURITANS
PURLIEU
PURLIEUS
PURLINE
PURLINES
PURLING
SPURLING
PURLINGS
PURLOIN
PURLOINS

PURPLES
PURPLEST
PURPORT
PURPORTS
PURPOSE
PURPOSED
PURPOSES
PURPURA
PURPURAS
PURPURE
PURPURES
PURRING
SPURRING
PURRINGS
PURSUAL
PURSUALS
PURSUER
PURSUERS
PURSUIT
PURSUITS
PURVIEW
PURVIEWS
PUSHROD
PUSHRODS
PUSTULE
PUSTULES
PUTCHER
PUTCHERS
PUTCHUK
PUTCHUKS
PUTLOCK
PUTLOCKS
PUTTERS
SPUTTERS
PUTTIER
PUTTIERS
PUTTING
PUTTINGS
PUTTOCK
PUTTOCKS
PUZZLER
PUZZLERS
PYAEMIA
PYAEMIAS
PYCNITE
PYCNITES
PYEBALD
PYEBALDS
PYGIDIA
PYGIDIAL
PYRALID
PYRALIDS
PYRAMID
PYRAMIDS
PYRETIC
APYRETIC
PYREXIA
APYREXIA
PYREXIAL
PYREXIAS
PYROGEN
PYROGENS
PYRRHIC
PYRRHICS
PYRROLE
PYRROLES
PYTHIUM
PYTHIUMS
QABALAH
QABALAHS

QUACKER
QUACKERS
QUACKERY
QUACKLE
QUACKLED
QUACKLES
QUADRAT
QUADRATE
QUADRATS
QUADRIC
QUADRICS
QUAFFER
QUAFFERS
QUAHAUG
QUAHAUGS
QUAILED
SQUAILED
QUAKING
QUAKINGS
QUALITY
EQUALITY
QUANNET
QUANNETS
QUANTIC
QUANTICS
QUAREST
SQUAREST
QUARREL
QUARRELS
QUARTAN
QUARTANS
QUARTER
QUARTERN
QUARTERS
QUARTET
QUARTETS
QUARTETT
QUARTIC
QUARTICS
QUASHED
SQUASHED
QUASHEE
QUASHEES
QUASHES
SQUASHES
QUASHIE
QUASHIES
QUASSIA
QUASSIAS
QUAYAGE
QUAYAGES
QUEENIE
QUEENIER
QUEENIES
QUELLER
QUELLERS
QUERIST
QUERISTS
QUESTER
QUESTERS
QUESTOR
QUESTORS
QUETZAL
QUETZALS
QUEUING
QUEUINGS
QUEYNIE
QUEYNIES
QUIBBLE
QUIBBLED

QUIBBLER
QUIBBLES
QUIBLIN
QUIBLINS
QUICKEN
QUICKENS
QUICKIE
QUICKIES
QUIDDIT
QUIDDITS
QUIDDITY
QUIDDLE
QUIDDLED
QUIDDLER
QUIDDLES
QUIESCE
QUIESCED
QUIESCES
QUIETEN
QUIETENS
QUIETER
QUIETERS
QUILLAI
QUILLAIS
QUILLET
QUILLETS
QUILLON
QUILLONS
QUILTER
QUILTERS
QUINCHE
QUINCHED
QUINCHES
QUINIES
SQUINIES
QUININE
QUININES
QUINNAT
QUINNATS
QUINOID
QUINOIDS
QUINONE
QUINONES
QUINTAL
QUINTALS
QUINTET
QUINTETS
QUINTETT
QUIPPED
EQUIPPED
QUIRING
SQUIRING
QUIRTED
SQUIRTED
QUITTAL
QUITTALS
QUITTER
QUITTERS
QUITTOR
QUITTORS
QUIZZER
QUIZZERS
QUIZZERY
QUIZZES
SQUIZZES
QUODLIN
QUODLINS
QUOITER
QUOITERS
RABANNA
RABANNAS
RABATTE
RABATTED
RABATTES
RABBETS
DRABBETS
RABBLED
BRABBLED
DRABBLED
GRABBLED
RABBLER
DRABBLER
GRABBLER
RABBLERS
RABBLES
BRABBLES
DRABBLES
GRABBLES
PRABBLES
RABBONI
RABBONIS
RACCOON
RACCOONS
RACEWAY
RACEWAYS
RACHIAL
BRACHIAL
RACINGS
TRACINGS
RACKERS
CRACKERS
TRACKERS
RACKETS
BRACKETS
RACKETT
RACKETTS
RACKING
CRACKING
FRACKING
TRACKING
WRACKING
RACKINGS
RACLOIR
RACLOIRS
RACQUET
RACQUETS
RADIANT
RADIANTS
RADIATA
RADIATAS
RADIATE
ERADIATE
RADIATED
RADIATES
RADICAL
RADICALS
RADICEL
RADICELS
RADICLE
RADICLES
RAFFISH
DRAFFISH
RAFFLER
RAFFLERS
RAFTERS
DRAFTERS
GRAFTERS
RAFTING
CRAFTING
DRAFTING
GRAFTING
RAGBOLT
RAGBOLTS
RAGGIER
CRAGGIER
DRAGGIER
RAGGIES
RAGGIEST
RAGGING
BRAGGING
DRAGGING
FRAGGING
RAGGINGS
RAGGLED
DRAGGLED
RAGGLES
DRAGGLES
RAGHEAD
RAGHEADS
RAGMENT
FRAGMENT
RAGMENTS
RAGTIME
RAGTIMER
RAGTIMES
RAGWEED
RAGWEEDS
RAGWORK
RAGWORKS
RAGWORM
RAGWORMS
RAGWORT
RAGWORTS
RAIDING
BRAIDING
RAIKING
TRAIKING
RAILBED
RAILBEDS
RAILERS
TRAILERS
RAILING
BRAILING
DRAILING
TRAILING
RAILINGS
RAILWAY
RAILWAYS
RAIMENT
RAIMENTS
RAINBOW
RAINBOWS
RAINBOWY
RAINIER
BRAINIER
GRAINIER
RAINING
BRAINING
DRAINING
GRAINING
TRAINING
RAISERS
PRAISERS
RAISING
ARAISING
BRAISING
FRAISING
PRAISING
RAISINGS
RAKSHAS
RAKSHASA
RALLIER
RALLIERS
RAMAKIN
RAMAKINS
RAMBLED
BRAMBLED
RAMBLER
RAMBLERS
RAMBLES
BRAMBLES
RAMEKIN
RAMEKINS
RAMMERS
CRAMMERS
RAMMING
CRAMMING
DRAMMING
TRAMMING
RAMPAGE
RAMPAGED
RAMPAGES
RAMPART
RAMPARTS
RAMPERS
TRAMPERS
RAMPICK
RAMPICKS
RAMPIKE
RAMPIKES
RAMPING
CRAMPING
TRAMPING
RAMPINGS
RAMPION
RAMPIONS
RAMPIRE
RAMPIRED
RAMPIRES
RANCHED
BRANCHED
CRANCHED
RANCHER
BRANCHER
RANCHERO
RANCHERS
RANCHES
BRANCHES
CRANCHES
TRANCHES
RANCING
PRANCING
TRANCING
RANCOUR
RANCOURS
RANDIES
BRANDIES
RANDIEST
RANDING
BRANDING
RANGERS
GRANGERS
RANGING
PRANGING
RANGOLI
RANGOLIS
RANKEST
FRANKEST
RANKING
BRANKING
CRANKING
FRANKING
PRANKING
RANKINGS
RANKLED
CRANKLED
PRANKLED
RANKLES
CRANKLES
PRANKLES
RANSACK
RANSACKS
RANSOMS
TRANSOMS
RANTERS
GRANTERS
TRANTERS
RANTING
DRANTING
GRANTING
TRANTING
RANTINGS
RAOULIA
RAOULIAS
RAPHIDE
RAPHIDES
RAPIERS
DRAPIERS
RAPLOCH
RAPLOCHS
RAPPERS
TRAPPERS
WRAPPERS
RAPPING
CRAPPING
DRAPPING
FRAPPING
TRAPPING
WRAPPING
RAPPINGS
RAPPORT
RAPPORTS
RAPTURE
RAPTURED
RAPTURES
RAREBIT
RAREBITS
RASCHEL
RASCHELS
RASHEST
BRASHEST
RASHING
BRASHING
CRASHING
TRASHING
RASPERS
GRASPERS
RASPING
GRASPING
RASPINGS
RASTRUM
RASTRUMS
RASURES
ERASURES
RATAFIA
RATAFIAS
RATCHES
CRATCHES
FRATCHES
RATCHET
BRATCHET
RATCHETS
RATFINK
RATFINKS
RATINGS
GRATINGS
PRATINGS
RATIONS
ORATIONS
RATLINE
RATLINES
RATLING
BRATLING
RATLINGS
RATPACK
BRATPACK
RATPACKS
RATTEEN
RATTEENS
RATTIER
BRATTIER
RATTING
PRATTING
RATTINGS
RATTISH
BRATTISH
RATTLED
BRATTLED
PRATTLED
RATTLER
PRATTLER
RATTLERS
RATTLES
BRATTLES
PRATTLES
RATTLIN
RATTLINE
RATTLING
RATTLINS
RAVAGER
RAVAGERS
RAVELIN
RAVELINS
RAVENED
CRAVENED
RAVENER
RAVENERS
RAVINGS
CRAVINGS
GRAVINGS
RAVIOLI
RAVIOLIS
RAWBONE
RAWBONED
RAWHEAD
RAWHEADS
RAWHIDE
RAWHIDES
RAWINGS
DRAWINGS
RAYLING
GRAYLING
RAZZLES
FRAZZLES
REACHED
AREACHED
BREACHED
PREACHED
REACHER
PREACHER
TREACHER
REACHERS
REACHES
AREACHES
BREACHES
PREACHES
REACTOR
REACTORS
READAPT
READAPTS
READERS
DREADERS
TREADERS
READIES
READIEST
READING
AREADING
BREADING
DREADING
TREADING
READINGS
READMIT
READMITS
READOPT
READOPTS
REAGENT
REAGENTS
REAKING
BREAKING
CREAKING
FREAKING
WREAKING
REALGAR
REALGARS
REALIGN
REALIGNS
REALISE
REALISED
REALISER
REALISES
REALISM
REALISMS
REALIST
REALISTS
REALIZE
REALIZED
REALIZER
REALIZES
REALLIE
REALLIED
REALLIES
REALLOT
REALLOTS
REALTIE
REALTIES
REALTOR
REALTORS
REAMEND
REAMENDS
REAMERS
CREAMERS
DREAMERS
REAMIER
CREAMIER
DREAMIER
REAMING
BREAMING
CREAMING
DREAMING
REARING

DREARING
REARISE
REARISEN
REARISES
REASONS
TREASONS
REASTED
BREASTED
REAVING
GREAVING
REAWAKE
REAWAKED
REAWAKEN
REAWAKES
REAWOKE
REAWOKEN
REBATER
REBATERS
REBIRTH
REBIRTHS
REBLOOM
REBLOOMS
REBOUND
REBOUNDS
REBRACE
REBRACED
REBRACES
REBUILD
REBUILDS
REBUKER
REBUKERS
RECEDED
PRECEDED
RECEDES
PRECEDES
RECEIPT
RECEIPTS
RECEIVE
RECEIVED
RECEIVER
RECEIVES
RECENSE
RECENSED
RECENSES
RECEPTS
PRECEPTS
RECHART
RECHARTS
RECHATE
RECHATES
RECHEAT
RECHEATS
RECHECK
RECHECKS
RECITAL
RECITALS
RECITER
RECITERS
RECKING
TRECKING
WRECKING
RECLAIM
RECLAIMS
RECLAME
RECLAMES
RECLIMB
RECLIMBS
RECLINE
RECLINED
RECLINER
RECLINES
RECLOSE
RECLOSED
RECLOSES
RECLUSE
RECLUSES
RECOUNT
RECOUNTS
RECOURE
RECOURED
RECOURES
RECOVER
RECOVERS
RECOVERY
RECOWER
RECOWERS
RECOYLE
RECOYLED
RECOYLES
RECRUIT
RECRUITS
RECTION
ERECTION
RECTIONS
RECTORS
ERECTORS
RECUILE
RECUILED
RECUILES
RECURVE
RECURVED
RECURVES
RECYCLE
RECYCLED
RECYCLES
REDATED
PREDATED
REDATES
PREDATES
REDBACK
REDBACKS
REDCOAT
REDCOATS
REDDING
REDDINGS
REDDLED
TREDDLED
REDDLES
TREDDLES
REDHEAD
REDHEADS
REDIALS
PREDIALS
REDNECK
REDNECKS
REDOUBT
REDOUBTS
REDOUND
REDOUNDS
REDPOLL
REDPOLLS
REDRAFT
REDRAFTS
REDRIVE
REDRIVEN
REDRIVES
REDROOT
REDROOTS
REDSKIN
REDSKINS
REDUCER
REDUCERS
REDWING
REDWINGS
REDWOOD
REDWOODS
REECHED
BREECHED
REECHES
BREECHES
REECHIE
REECHIER
REEDBED
REEDBEDS
REEDERS
BREEDERS
REEDIER
GREEDIER
REEDING
BREEDING
REEDINGS
REEFING
REEFINGS
REEKIER
CREEKIER
REEKING
GREEKING
REELING
REELINGS
REEVING
PREEVING
REFACED
PREFACED
REFACES
PREFACES
REFECTS
PREFECTS
REFEREE
REFEREED
REFEREES
REFINER
REFINERS
REFINERY
REFLATE
REFLATED
REFLATES
REFLECT
REFLECTS
REFLOAT
REFLOATS
REFORMS
PREFORMS
REFOUND
REFOUNDS
REFRACT
REFRACTS
REFRAIN
REFRAINS
REFRAME
REFRAMED
REFRAMES
REFROZE
REFROZEN
REFUGEE
REFUGEES
REFUSAL
REFUSALS
REFUSER
REFUSERS
REFUTAL
REFUTALS
REFUTER
REFUTERS
REGALES
GREGALES
REGALIA
REGALIAN
REGALIAS
REGATTA
REGATTAS
REGENCE
REGENCES
REGIMEN
REGIMENS
REGIMENT
REGMATA
BREGMATA
REGNANT
PREGNANT
REGORGE
REGORGED
REGORGES
REGRADE
REGRADED
REGRADES
REGRANT
REGRANTS
REGRATE
REGRATED
REGRATER
REGRATES
REGREDE
REGREDED
REGREDES
REGREET
REGREETS
REGRIND
REGRINDS
REGROUP
REGROUPS
REGULAR
REGULARS
REHEARS
REHEARSE
REHEATS
PREHEATS
REHOUSE
REHOUSED
REHOUSES
REINING
GREINING
REINTER
REINTERS
REISSUE
REISSUED
REISSUES
REJOICE
REJOICED
REJOICER
REJOICES
REJONEO
REJONEOS
REJOURN
REJOURNS
REJUDGE
PREJUDGE
REJUDGED
REJUDGES
RELACHE
RELACHES
RELAPSE
RELAPSED
RELAPSER
RELAPSES
RELATER
RELATERS
RELATES
PRELATES
RELATOR
RELATORS
RELAXIN
RELAXING
RELAXINS
RELEASE
RELEASED
RELEASEE
RELEASER
RELEASES
RELIEVE
RELIEVED
RELIEVER
RELIEVES
RELIEVO
RELIEVOS
RELIGHT
RELIGHTS
RELIQUE
RELIQUES
RELIVER
RELIVERS
REMANET
REMANETS
REMANIE
REMANIES
REMBLAI
REMBLAIS
REMBLED
TREMBLED
REMBLES
TREMBLES
REMERGE
REMERGED
REMERGES
REMISED
PREMISED
REMISES
PREMISES
REMIXED
PREMIXED
REMIXES
PREMIXES
REMNANT
REMNANTS
REMODEL
REMODELS
REMORSE
PREMORSE
REMORSES
REMOTES
REMOTEST
REMOULD
REMOULDS
REMOUNT
REMOUNTS
REMOVAL
REMOVALS
REMOVED
PREMOVED
REMOVER
REMOVERS
REMOVES
PREMOVES
REMUAGE
REMUAGES
REMUEUR
REMUEURS
RENAGUE
RENAGUED
RENAGUES
RENDING
TRENDING
RENEGER
RENEGERS
RENEGUE
RENEGUED
RENEGUER
RENEGUES
RENEWAL
RENEWALS
RENEWER
RENEWERS
RENNING
BRENNING
GRENNING
RENNINGS
RENTALS
TRENTALS
RENTIER
RENTIERS
RENTING
PRENTING
REORDER
PREORDER
REORDERS
REPACKS
PREPACKS
REPAINT
REPAINTS
REPAPER
REPAPERS
REPINER
REPINERS
REPIQUE
REPIQUED
REPIQUES
REPLACE
REPLACED
REPLACER
REPLACES
REPLANT
REPLANTS
REPLETE
REPLETED
REPLETES
REPLICA
REPLICAS
REPLIER
REPLIERS
REPOINT
REPOINTS
REPONED
PREPONED
REPONES
PREPONES
REPOSAL
REPOSALL
REPOSALS
REPOSED
PREPOSED
REPOSES
PREPOSES
REPOSIT
REPOSITS
REPPING
PREPPING
REPPINGS
REPRIME
REPRIMED
REPRIMES
REPRINT
REPRINTS
REPRISE
REPRISED
REPRISES
REPRIVE
REPRIVED
REPRIVES
REPRIZE
REPRIZED
REPRIZES
REPROOF
REPROOFS
REPROVE
REPROVED
REPROVER
REPROVES
REPRYVE
REPRYVED
REPRYVES
REPTILE
REPTILES
REPULSE
REPULSED
REPULSES
REPUNIT
REPUNITS
REQUERE
REQUERED
REQUERES
REQUEST
REQUESTS
REQUIEM
REQUIEMS
REQUIRE
REQUIRED
REQUIRER
REQUIRES
REQUITE
REQUITED
REQUITER
REQUITES
REQUOTE
REQUOTED
REQUOTES
REROUTE
REROUTED
REROUTES
RESCALE
RESCALED
RESCALES
RESCIND
PRESCIND
RESCINDS
RESCORE
RESCORED
RESCORES
RESCUER
RESCUERS
RESEIZE
RESEIZED

RESEIZES
RESENTS
PRESENTS
RESERVE
PRESERVE
RESERVED
RESERVES
RESHAPE
RESHAPED
RESHAPES
RESIANT
RESIANTS
RESIDED
PRESIDED
RESIDER
RESIDERS
RESIDES
PRESIDES
RESIDUA
RESIDUAL
RESIDUE
RESIDUES
RESINER
RESINERS
RESOLVE
RESOLVED
RESOLVER
RESOLVES
RESOUND
RESOUNDS
RESPEAK
RESPEAKS
RESPECT
RESPECTS
RESPELL
RESPELLS
RESPIRE
RESPIRED
RESPIRES
RESPITE
RESPITED
RESPITES
RESPOKE
RESPOKEN
RESPOND
RESPONDS
RESPRAY
RESPRAYS
RESTAFF
RESTAFFS
RESTAGE
RESTAGED
RESTAGES
RESTART
RESTARTS
RESTATE
RESTATED
RESTATES
RESTERS
WRESTERS
RESTING
CRESTING
PRESTING
WRESTING
RESTINGS
RESTOCK
RESTOCKS
RESTORE
RESTORED
RESTORER

RESTORES
RESTYLE
RESTYLED
RESTYLES
RESUMED
PRESUMED
RESUMES
PRESUMES
RESURGE
RESURGED
RESURGES
RETABLE
RETABLES
RETAKER
RETAKERS
RETCHED
WRETCHED
RETCHES
WRETCHES
RETHINK
RETHINKS
RETICLE
RETICLES
RETINOL
RETINOLS
RETINUE
RETINUES
RETIRAL
RETIRALS
RETIREE
RETIREES
RETIRER
RETIRERS
RETITLE
RETITLED
RETITLES
RETRACE
RETRACED
RETRACES
RETRACT
RETRACTS
RETRAIN
RETRAINS
RETRAIT
RETRAITE
RETRAITS
RETRAITT
RETRATE
RETRATED
RETRATES
RETREAD
RETREADS
RETREAT
RETREATS
RETRIAL
RETRIALS
RETSINA
RETSINAS
RETTING
ARETTING
FRETTING
REUNION
REUNIONS
REUNITE
REUNITED
REUNITES
REUTTER
REUTTERS
REVALUE
REVALUED

REVALUES
REVENGE
REVENGED
REVENGER
REVENGES
REVENUE
REVENUED
REVENUES
REVERBS
PREVERBS
REVERER
REVERERS
REVERIE
REVERIES
REVERSE
REVERSED
REVERSER
REVERSES
REVERSI
REVERSIS
REVERSO
REVERSOS
REVEUSE
REVEUSES
REVIEWS
PREVIEWS
REVILER
REVILERS
REVISAL
REVISALS
REVISED
PREVISED
REVISER
REVISERS
REVISES
PREVISES
TREVISES
REVISIT
REVISITS
REVISOR
REVISORS
REVISORY
REVIVAL
REVIVALS
REVIVER
REVIVERS
REVIVOR
REVIVORS
REVOLVE
REVOLVED
REVOLVER
REVOLVES
REWEIGH
REWEIGHS
REWRITE
REWRITES
REYNARD
REYNARDS
RHABDOM
RHABDOMS
RHENIUM
RHENIUMS
RHIZINE
RHIZINES
RHIZOID
RHIZOIDS
RHIZOME
RHIZOMES
RHODIUM
RHODIUMS

RHODORA
RHODORAS
RHOMBOI
RHOMBOID
RHUBARB
RHUBARBS
RHUBARBY
RHYMIST
RHYMISTS
RHYTHMI
RHYTHMIC
RHYTINA
RHYTINAS
RIBBAND
RIBBANDS
RIBBING
CRIBBING
DRIBBING
RIBBINGS
RIBCAGE
RIBCAGES
RIBIBLE
RIBIBLES
RIBLETS
DRIBLETS
TRIBLETS
RIBSTON
RIBSTONE
RIBSTONS
RIBWORK
CRIBWORK
RIBWORKS
RIBWORT
RIBWORTS
RICHTED
FRICHTED
RICIEST
PRICIEST
RICKERS
PRICKERS
TRICKERS
RICKETS
CRICKETS
PRICKETS
RICKING
BRICKING
CRICKING
PRICKING
TRICKING
WRICKING
RICKLES
PRICKLES
TRICKLES
RICKSHA
RICKSHAS
RICKSHAW
RICOTTA
RICOTTAS
RIDDERS
GRIDDERS
RIDDLER
RIDDLERS
RIDDLES
GRIDDLES
RIDGING
BRIDGING
FRIDGING
RIDGINGS
RIDOTTO
RIDOTTOS

RIEMPIE
RIEMPIES
RIEVERS
GRIEVERS
RIEVING
GRIEVING
PRIEVING
RIFFLER
RIFFLERS
RIFLERS
TRIFLERS
RIFLING
TRIFLING
RIFLINGS
RIFTIER
DRIFTIER
RIFTING
DRIFTING
GRIFTING
RIGGALD
RIGGALDS
RIGGERS
FRIGGERS
PRIGGERS
TRIGGERS
RIGGING
FRIGGING
GRIGGING
PRIGGING
TRIGGING
RIGGINGS
RIGGISH
PRIGGISH
RIGHTED
FRIGHTED
RIGHTEN
BRIGHTEN
FRIGHTEN
RIGHTENS
RIGHTER
BRIGHTER
RIGHTERS
RIGHTLY
BRIGHTLY
RIGIDER
FRIGIDER
RIGIDLY
FRIGIDLY
RIGLING
RIGLINGS
RILLING
DRILLING
FRILLING
GRILLING
PRILLING
TRILLING
RIMIEST
GRIMIEST
RIMLESS
BRIMLESS
RIMMING
BRIMMING
PRIMMING
TRIMMING
RIMMINGS
RINDING
GRINDING
RINGBIT
RINGBITS
RINGERS

BRINGERS
CRINGERS
WRINGERS
RINGGIT
RINGGITS
RINGING
BRINGING
CRINGING
FRINGING
WRINGING
RINGINGS
RINGLET
RINGLETS
RINGWAY
RINGWAYS
RINKING
DRINKING
PRINKING
RINNING
GRINNING
RINSING
RINSINGS
RIOTING
RIOTINGS
RIOTISE
RIOTISES
RIOTIZE
RIOTIZES
RIPIENO
RIPIENOS
RIPOSTE
RIPOSTED
RIPOSTES
RIPPERS
FRIPPERS
GRIPPERS
TRIPPERS
RIPPIER
DRIPPIER
GRIPPIER
RIPPIERS
RIPPING
DRIPPING
GRIPPING
TRIPPING
RIPPLED
CRIPPLED
TRIPPLED
RIPPLER
TRIPPLER
RIPPLERS
RIPPLES
CRIPPLES
GRIPPLES
TRIPPLES
RIPPLET
RIPPLETS
RIPTIDE
RIPTIDES
RISKERS
FRISKERS
RISKFUL
FRISKFUL
RISKIER
FRISKIER
RISKILY
FRISKILY
RISKING
BRISKING
FRISKING

RISOTTO
RISOTTOS
RISPING
CRISPING
RISPINGS
RISSOLE
RISSOLES
RITTERS
CRITTERS
FRITTERS
GRITTERS
RITTING
FRITTING
GRITTING
RIVERET
RIVERETS
RIVETER
RIVETERS
RIVIERA
RIVIERAS
RIVIERE
RIVIERES
RIVULET
RIVULETS
RIZZART
RIZZARTS
ROACHED
BROACHED
ROACHES
BROACHES
ROADING
ROADINGS
ROADWAY
BROADWAY
ROADWAYS
ROAMING
ROAMINGS
ROARING
ROARINGS
ROASTER
ROASTERS
ROATING
TROATING
ROBINIA
ROBINIAS
ROBOTIC
ROBOTICS
ROBUSTA
ROBUSTAS
ROCHETS
CROCHETS
ROCKERY
CROCKERY
ROCKETS
BROCKETS
CROCKETS
ROCKIER
ROCKIERS
ROCKING
CROCKING
FROCKING
TROCKING
ROCKINGS
ROCKLAY
ROCKLAYS
ROCQUET
ROCQUETS
RODDING
BRODDING
PRODDING

RODDINGS
RODENTS
BRODENTS
RODEWAY
RODEWAYS
RODSTER
RODSTERS
ROEBUCK
ROEBUCKS
ROGUISH
BROGUISH
ROILING
BROILING
DROILING
ROINING
GROINING
PROINING
ROISTER
ROISTERS
ROKELAY
ROKELAYS
ROLFING
ROLFINGS
ROLLERS
PROLLERS
TROLLERS
ROLLICK
ROLLICKS
ROLLING
DROLLING
PROLLING
TROLLING
ROLLINGS
ROLLMOP
ROLLMOPS
ROLLOCK
ROLLOCKS
ROLLOUT
ROLLOUTS
ROMAIKA
ROMAIKAS
ROMANCE
ROMANCED
ROMANCER
ROMANCES
ROMAUNT
ROMAUNTS
ROMNEYA
ROMNEYAS
ROMPING
TROMPING
RONDEAU
RONDEAUX
RONDINO
RONDINOS
RONDURE
RONDURES
RONTGEN
RONTGENS
ROOFING
PROOFING
ROOFINGS
ROOFTOP
ROOFTOPS
ROOINEK
ROOINEKS
ROOKING
BROOKING
CROOKING
DROOKING
ROOMFUL
ROOMFULS
ROOMIER
BROOMIER
ROOMIES
ROOMIEST
ROOMING
BROOMING
GROOMING
VROOMING
ROOPIER
DROOPIER
ROOPING
DROOPING
TROOPING
ROOSTER
ROOSTERS
ROOTAGE
ROOTAGES
ROOTIES
ROOTIEST
ROOTING
WROOTING
ROOTINGS
ROOTLES
ROOTLESS
ROOTLET
ROOTLETS
ROPEWAY
ROPEWAYS
ROQUETS
CROQUETS
RORQUAL
RORQUALS
ROSACEA
ROSACEAS
ROSAKER
ROSAKERS
ROSALIA
ROSALIAS
ROSEBAY
ROSEBAYS
ROSEBUD
ROSEBUDS
ROSEHIP
ROSEHIPS
ROSELLA
ROSELLAS
ROSELLE
ROSELLES
ROSEOLA
ROSEOLAS
ROSETTE
ROSETTED
ROSETTES
ROSIERE
ROSIERES
ROSIERS
CROSIERS
ROSIEST
PROSIEST
ROSOLIO
ROSOLIOS
ROSSERS
TROSSERS
ROSTING
FROSTING
ROSTRUM
ROSTRUMS
ROTATOR
ROTATORS
ROTATORY
ROTCHES
CROTCHES
ROTCHIE
ROTCHIES
ROTHERS
BROTHERS
ROTIFER
ROTIFERS
ROTTERS
TROTTERS
ROTTING
TROTTING
ROTUNDA
ROTUNDAS
ROUBLES
TROUBLES
ROUGHEN
ROUGHENS
ROUGHER
ROUGHERS
ROUGHIE
ROUGHIES
ROUILLE
ROUILLES
ROULADE
ROULADES
ROULEAU
ROULEAUS
ROULEAUX
ROUMING
ROUMINGS
ROUNCES
FROUNCES
TROUNCES
ROUNDED
GROUNDED
ROUNDEL
ROUNDELS
ROUNDER
GROUNDER
ROUNDERS
ROUNDLE
ROUNDLES
ROUNDLET
ROUPIER
CROUPIER
ROUPING
CROUPING
GROUPING
TROUPING
ROUSERS
AROUSERS
GROUSERS
TROUSERS
ROUSING
AROUSING
GROUSING
ROUSTER
ROUSTERS
ROUTERS
GROUTERS
TROUTERS
ROUTHIE
ROUTHIER
ROUTINE
ROUTINES
ROUTING
GROUTING
TROUTING
ROUTINGS
ROVINGS
DROVINGS
PROVINGS
ROWABLE
GROWABLE
ROWBOAT
ROWBOATS
ROWDIES
CROWDIES
ROWDIEST
ROWINGS
GROWINGS
ROWLOCK
ROWLOCKS
ROWNDED
DROWNDED
ROYALET
ROYALETS
ROYNING
PROYNING
ROYSTER
ROYSTERS
ROZELLE
ROZELLES
RUBBERS
GRUBBERS
RUBBING
DRUBBING
GRUBBING
RUBBINGS
RUBBISH
RUBBISHY
RUBBLES
GRUBBLES
RUBDOWN
RUBDOWNS
RUBELLA
RUBELLAN
RUBELLAS
RUBEOLA
RUBEOLAS
RUBICON
RUBICONS
RUCHING
RUCHINGS
RUCKING
TRUCKING
RUCKLED
TRUCKLED
RUCKLES
TRUCKLES
RUCTION
RUCTIONS
RUDDIER
CRUDDIER
RUDDIES
RUDDIEST
RUDDING
CRUDDING
RUDDLED
CRUDDLED
RUDDLES
CRUDDLES
RUDDOCK
RUDDOCKS
RUDERAL
RUDERALS
RUELLIA
RUELLIAS
RUFFIAN
RUFFIANS
RUFFLED
TRUFFLED
RUFFLER
RUFFLERS
RUFFLES
TRUFFLES
RUFIYAA
RUFIYAAS
RUGGERS
DRUGGERS
RUGGIER
DRUGGIER
RUGGING
DRUGGING
RUGGINGS
RUINATE
RUINATED
RUINATES
RUINING
RUININGS
RULLION
RULLIONS
RULLOCK
RULLOCKS
RUMBLED
CRUMBLED
DRUMBLED
GRUMBLED
RUMBLER
GRUMBLER
RUMBLERS
RUMBLES
CRUMBLES
DRUMBLES
GRUMBLES
RUMMAGE
RUMMAGED
RUMMAGER
RUMMAGES
RUMMERS
BRUMMERS
DRUMMERS
RUMMEST
GRUMMEST
RUMMIER
CRUMMIER
RUMMIES
CRUMMIES
RUMMIEST
RUMNESS
GRUMNESS
RUMPING
CRUMPING
FRUMPING
GRUMPING
TRUMPING
RUMPLED
CRUMPLED
FRUMPLED
RUMPLES
CRUMPLES
FRUMPLES
RUMPLESS
RUNAWAY
RUNAWAYS
RUNBACK
RUNBACKS
RUNCHES
BRUNCHES
CRUNCHES
RUNDALE
RUNDALES
RUNDLED
TRUNDLED
RUNDLES
TRUNDLES
RUNDLET
RUNDLETS
RUNDOWN
RUNDOWNS
RUNKLED
CRUNKLED
RUNKLES
CRUNKLES
RUNNING
RUNNINGS
RUNNION
TRUNNION
RUNNIONS
RUPTURE
RUPTURED
RUPTURES
RUSALKA
RUSALKAS
RUSHERS
BRUSHERS
CRUSHERS
RUSHIER
BRUSHIER
RUSHING
BRUSHING
CRUSHING
FRUSHING
RUSTIER
CRUSTIER
TRUSTIER
RUSTILY
CRUSTILY
TRUSTILY
RUSTING
BRUSTING
CRUSTING
TRUSTING
RUSTINGS
RUSTLER
RUSTLERS
RUSTLES
RUSTLESS
RUTHFUL
TRUTHFUL
RUTTING
RUTTINGS
RYBAULD
RYBAULDS
RYEPECK
RYEPECKS
SABATON
SABATONS
SABELLA
ISABELLA
SABELLAS
SABKHAH
SABKHAHS
SABKHAT
SABKHATS
SABREUR
SABREURS
SABURRA
SABURRAL
SABURRAS
SACATON
SACATONS
SACCADE
SACCADES
SACCULE
SACCULES
SACKAGE
SACKAGES
SACKBUT
SACKBUTS
SACKFUL
SACKFULS
SACKING
SACKINGS
SACRING
SACRINGS
SACRIST
SACRISTS
SACRISTY
SADDLER
SADDLERS
SADDLERY
SADIRON
SADIRONS
SAFARIS
SAFARIST
SAFFIAN
SAFFIANS
SAFFRON
SAFFRONS
SAFFRONY
SAFROLE
SAFROLES
SAGENES
SAGENESS
SAGGARD
SAGGARDS
SAGGING
SAGGINGS
SAGITTA
SAGITTAL
SAGITTAS
SAGOUIN
SAGOUINS
SAGUARO
SAGUAROS
SAHIBAH
SAHIBAHS
SAILING
SAILINGS
SAIMIRI
SAIMIRIS
SAKERET
SAKERETS
SAKIYEH
SAKIYEHS
SAKSAUL
SAKSAULS
SALAMON
SALAMONS
SALBAND
SALBANDS
SALCHOW
SALCHOWS
SALFERN
SALFERNS
SALICET

SALICETA
SALICETS
SALICIN
SALICINE
SALICINS
SALIENT
SALIENTS
SALIGOT
SALIGOTS
SALPIAN
SALPIANS
SALTANT
SALTANTS
SALTATE
SALTATED
SALTATES
SALTCAT
SALTCATS
SALTERN
SALTERNS
SALTERS
PSALTERS
SALTIER
SALTIERS
SALTING
SALTINGS
SALTIRE
SALTIRES
SALUTER
SALUTERS
SALVAGE
SALVAGED
SALVAGES
SALVETE
SALVETES
SALVING
SALVINGS
SAMADHI
SAMADHIS
SAMBUCA
SAMBUCAS
SAMISEN
SAMISENS
SAMOVAR
SAMOVARS
SAMPIRE
SAMPIRES
SAMPLER
SAMPLERS
SAMPLERY
SAMSARA
SAMSARAS
SAMSHOO
SAMSHOOS
SANCTUM
SANCTUMS
SANDBAG
SANDBAGS
SANDBOY
SANDBOYS
SANDING
SANDINGS
SANDPIT
SANDPITS
SANGOMA
SANGOMAS
SANGRIA
SANGRIAS
SANICLE
SANICLES

SANTOUR
SANTOURS
SAOUARI
SAOUARIS
SAPAJOU
SAPAJOUS
SAPHEAD
SAPHEADS
SAPHENA
SAPHENAS
SAPLING
SAPLINGS
SAPONIN
SAPONINS
SAPPHIC
SAPPHICS
SAPROBE
SAPROBES
SAPSAGO
SAPSAGOS
SAPWOOD
SAPWOODS
SARAFAN
SARAFANS
SARANGI
SARANGIS
SARCASM
SARCASMS
SARCODE
SARCODES
SARCOID
SARCOIDS
SARCOMA
SARCOMAS
SARDANA
SARDANAS
SARDINE
SARDINES
SARKING
SARKINGS
SARMENT
SARMENTA
SARMENTS
SARSDEN
SARSDENS
SARSNET
SARSNETS
SASHIMI
SASHIMIS
SATCHEL
SATCHELS
SATIATE
SATIATED
SATIATES
SATINET
SATINETS
SATSUMA
SATSUMAS
SATYRAL
SATYRALS
SATYRID
SATYRIDS
SAUNTER
SAUNTERS
SAURIAN
SAURIANS
SAUSAGE
SAUSAGES
SAUTOIR
SAUTOIRS

SAVAGER
SAVAGERY
SAVAGES
SAVAGEST
SAVANNA
SAVANNAH
SAVANNAS
SAVARIN
SAVARINS
SAVELOY
SAVELOYS
SAVIOUR
SAVIOURS
SAWBILL
SAWBILLS
SAWBUCK
SAWBUCKS
SAWDUST
SAWDUSTS
SAWDUSTY
SAWMILL
SAWMILLS
SAXHORN
SAXHORNS
SAZERAC
SAZERACS
SCABBLE
SCABBLED
SCABBLES
SCAFFIE
SCAFFIES
SCAGLIA
SCAGLIAS
SCALADE
ESCALADE
SCALADES
SCALADO
ESCALADO
SCALADOS
SCALDER
SCALDERS
SCALIER
ESCALIER
SCALING
SCALINGS
SCALLOP
ESCALLOP
SCALLOPS
SCALPEL
SCALPELS
SCALPER
SCALPERS
SCAMBLE
SCAMBLED
SCAMBLER
SCAMBLES
SCAMPER
SCAMPERS
SCAMPIS
SCAMPISH
SCANDAL
SCANDALS
SCANNER
SCANNERS
SCANTLE
SCANTLED
SCANTLES
SCAPING
ESCAPING
SCAPPLE

SCAPPLED
SCAPPLES
SCAPULA
SCAPULAE
SCAPULAR
SCAPULAS
SCARLET
SCARLETS
SCARPED
ESCARPED
SCARPER
SCARPERS
SCATOLE
SCATOLES
SCATTER
SCATTERS
SCATTERY
SCAUPER
SCAUPERS
SCAVAGE
SCAVAGER
SCAVAGES
SCEDULE
SCEDULED
SCEDULES
SCENDED
ASCENDED
SCEPTER
SCEPTERS
SCEPTIC
SCEPTICS
SCEPTRE
SCEPTRED
SCEPTRES
SCHANSE
SCHANSES
SCHANZE
SCHANZES
SCHAPPE
SCHAPPED
SCHAPPES
SCHEMER
SCHEMERS
SCHERZO
SCHERZOS
SCHISMA
SCHISMAS
SCHLEPP
SCHLEPPS
SCHLEPPY
SCHLICH
SCHLICHS
SCHLOCK
SCHLOCKS
SCHLOCKY
SCHMECK
SCHMECKS
SCHMOCK
SCHMOCKS
SCHMOOZ
SCHMOOZE
SCHMUCK
SCHMUCKS
SCHNOOK
SCHNOOKS
SCHNORR
SCHNORRS
SCHOLAR
SCHOLARS
SCHOOLE

SCHOOLED
SCHOOLES
SCHTICK
SCHTICKS
SCHTOOK
SCHTOOKS
SCHTUCK
SCHTUCKS
SCIARID
SCIARIDS
SCIATIC
SCIATICA
SCIENCE
SCIENCED
SCIENCES
SCISSEL
SCISSELS
SCISSIL
SCISSILE
SCISSILS
SCISSOR
SCISSORS
SCOFFER
SCOFFERS
SCOLDER
SCOLDERS
SCOLLOP
SCOLLOPS
SCOOPER
SCOOPERS
SCOOTER
SCOOTERS
SCOPULA
SCOPULAS
SCORING
SCORINGS
SCORNER
SCORNERS
SCORPER
SCORPERS
SCORSER
SCORSERS
SCOTOMA
SCOTOMAS
SCOURER
SCOURERS
SCOURGE
SCOURGED
SCOURGER
SCOURGES
SCOURIE
SCOURIES
SCOURSE
SCOURSED
SCOURSES
SCOUSER
SCOUSERS
SCOUTER
SCOUTERS
SCOWDER
SCOWDERS
SCOWRER
SCOWRERS
SCOWRIE
SCOWRIES
SCRAICH
SCRAICHS
SCRAIGH
SCRAIGHS
SCRAPER

SCRAPERS
SCRAPIE
SCRAPIES
SCRATCH
SCRATCHY
SCRAUCH
SCRAUCHS
SCRAUGH
SCRAUGHS
SCREECH
SCREECHY
SCREEVE
SCREEVED
SCREEVER
SCREEVES
SCREICH
SCREICHS
SCREIGH
SCREIGHS
SCREWER
SCREWERS
SCRIBED
ASCRIBED
ESCRIBED
SCRIBER
SCRIBERS
SCRIBES
ASCRIBES
ESCRIBES
SCRIECH
SCRIECHS
SCRIENE
SCRIENES
SCRIEVE
SCRIEVED
SCRIEVES
SCROLLS
ESCROLLS
SCROOGE
SCROOGED
SCROOGES
SCROTUM
SCROTUMS
SCROUGE
SCROUGED
SCROUGER
SCROUGES
SCROWLE
SCROWLED
SCROWLES
SCROYLE
SCROYLES
SCRUNCH
SCRUNCHY
SCRUPLE
SCRUPLED
SCRUPLER
SCRUPLES
SCRYING
SCRYINGS
SCUCHIN
SCUCHINS
SCUDDER
SCUDDERS
SCUDDLE
SCUDDLED
SCUDDLES
SCUDLER
SCUDLERS
SCUFFLE

SCUFFLED
SCUFFLER
SCUFFLES
SCULLER
SCULLERS
SCULLERY
SCULPIN
SCULPING
SCULPINS
SCUMBAG
SCUMBAGS
SCUMBER
SCUMBERS
SCUMBLE
SCUMBLED
SCUMBLES
SCUMMER
SCUMMERS
SCUNNER
SCUNNERS
SCUPPER
SCUPPERS
SCURRIL
SCURRILE
SCUTAGE
SCUTAGES
SCUTTER
SCUTTERS
SCUTTLE
SCUTTLED
SCUTTLER
SCUTTLES
SCYTALE
SCYTALES
SCYTHER
SCYTHERS
SDEIGNE
SDEIGNED
SDEIGNES
SEABANK
SEABANKS
SEABIRD
SEABIRDS
SEACOCK
SEACOCKS
SEAFOLK
SEAFOLKS
SEAFOOD
SEAFOODS
SEAFOWL
SEAFOWLS
SEAGULL
SEAGULLS
SEAHAWK
SEAHAWKS
SEAKALE
SEAKALES
SEALANT
SEALANTS
SEALINE
SEALINES
SEALING
SEALINGS
SEAMAID
SEAMAIDS
SEAMARK
SEAMARKS
SEAMSET
SEAMSETS
SEAPORT

SEAPORTS
SEARING
SEARINGS
SEASIDE
SEASIDES
SEASURE
SEASURES
SEATING
SEATINGS
SEAWARD
SEAWARDS
SEAWARE
SEAWARES
SEAWEED
SEAWEEDS
SEAWORM
SEAWORMS
SECEDER
SECEDERS
SECLUDE
SECLUDED
SECLUDES
SECONDE
SECONDED
SECONDEE
SECONDER
SECONDES
SECRETE
SECRETED
SECRETES
SECTION
SECTIONS
SECULAR
SECULARS
SECULUM
SECULUMS
SECURER
SECURERS
SECURES
SECUREST
SEDATES
SEDATEST
SEDUCER
SEDUCERS
SEEDBED
SEEDBEDS
SEEDING
SEEDINGS
SEEDLIP
SEEDLIPS
SEELING
SEELINGS
SEEMING
SEEMINGS
SEEPAGE
SEEPAGES
SEETHER
SEETHERS
SEGMENT
SEGMENTS
SEINING
SEININGS
SEISMIC
ASEISMIC
SEITIES
ASEITIES
SEIZING
SEIZINGS
SEIZURE
SEIZURES
SELFING
SELFINGS
SELFISM
SELFISMS
SELFIST
SELFISTS
SELTZER
SELTZERS
SELVAGE
SELVAGED
SELVAGEE
SELVAGES
SEMINAR
SEMINARS
SEMINARY
SEMIPED
SEMIPEDS
SEMITAR
SEMITARS
SENATOR
SENATORS
SENDING
SENDINGS
SENECIO
SENECIOS
SENSING
SENSINGS
SENSISM
SENSISMS
SENSIST
SENSISTS
SEPIOST
SEPIOSTS
SEPPUKU
SEPPUKUS
SEPTATE
ASEPTATE
SEPTIME
SEPTIMES
SEPTUOR
SEPTUORS
SEQUELA
SEQUELAE
SEQUENT
SEQUENTS
SEQUOIA
SEQUOIAS
SERAFIN
SERAFINS
SERENES
SERENEST
SERFAGE
SERFAGES
SERFDOM
SERFDOMS
SERIATE
SERIATED
SERIATES
SERICIN
SERICINS
SERICON
SERICONS
SERIEMA
SERIEMAS
SERINGA
SERINGAS
SERKALI
SERKALIS
SERPENT
SERPENTS
SERPULA
SERPULAE
SERRATE
SERRATED
SERRATES
SERUEWE
SERUEWED
SERUEWES
SERVANT
SERVANTS
SERVEWE
SERVEWED
SERVEWES
SERVICE
SERVICED
SERVICES
SERVILE
SERVILES
SERVING
SERVINGS
SESSION
SESSIONS
SESTETT
SESTETTE
SESTETTO
SESTETTS
SESTINA
SESTINAS
SESTINE
SESTINES
SETBACK
SETBACKS
SETLINE
SETLINES
SETTING
SETTINGS
SETTLER
SETTLERS
SETTLOR
SETTLORS
SETUALE
SETUALES
SETWALL
SETWALLS
SEVENTH
SEVENTHS
SEVERAL
SEVERALS
SEVRUGA
SEVRUGAS
SEXFOIL
SEXFOILS
SEXPERT
SEXPERTS
SEXTANT
SEXTANTS
SEXTETT
SEXTETTE
SEXTETTS
SEXTILE
SEXTILES
SEXTUOR
SEXTUORS
SEYSURE
SEYSURES
SFUMATO
SFUMATOS
SHABBLE
SHABBLES
SHACKLE
SHACKLED
SHACKLES
SHADING
SHADINGS
SHADOOF
SHADOOFS
SHAFTER
SHAFTERS
SHAITAN
SHAITANS
SHAKING
SHAKINGS
SHAKUDO
SHAKUDOS
SHALLON
SHALLONS
SHALLOP
SHALLOPS
SHALLOT
SHALLOTS
SHALLOW
SHALLOWS
SHALWAR
SHALWARS
SHAMBLE
SHAMBLED
SHAMBLES
SHAMING
ASHAMING
SHAMMER
SHAMMERS
SHAMPOO
SHAMPOOS
SHANTEY
SHANTEYS
SHAPING
SHAPINGS
SHARIAT
SHARIATS
SHARING
SHARINGS
SHARKER
SHARKERS
SHARPEN
SHARPENS
SHARPER
SHARPERS
SHARPIE
SHARPIES
SHASTER
SHASTERS
SHASTRA
SHASTRAS
SHATTER
SHATTERS
SHATTERY
SHAVING
SHAVINGS
SHAWLEY
SHAWLEYS
SHAWLIE
SHAWLIES
SHEARER
SHEARERS
SHEATHE
SHEATHED
SHEATHES
SHEBANG
SHEBANGS
SHEBEEN
SHEBEENS
SHEDDER
SHEDDERS
SHEHITA
SHEHITAH
SHEHITAS
SHEIKHA
SHEIKHAS
SHELLAC
SHELLACS
SHELLER
SHELLERS
SHELTER
SHELTERS
SHELTERY
SHELTIE
SHELTIES
SHERBET
SHERBETS
SHEREEF
SHEREEFS
SHERIAT
SHERIATS
SHERIFF
SHERIFFS
SHIATSU
SHIATSUS
SHIATZU
SHIATZUS
SHICKER
SHICKERS
SHICKSA
SHICKSAS
SHIDDER
SHIDDERS
SHIFTER
SHIFTERS
SHIKARI
SHIKARIS
SHIMAAL
SHIMAALS
SHIMMER
SHIMMERS
SHIMMERY
SHIMMEY
SHIMMEYS
SHINDIG
SHINDIGS
SHINGLE
SHINGLED
SHINGLER
SHINGLES
SHINIES
SHINIEST
SHIPFUL
SHIPFULS
SHIPLAP
SHIPLAPS
SHIPMEN
SHIPMENT
SHIPPEN
SHIPPENS
SHIPPER
SHIPPERS
SHIPPON
SHIPPONS
SHIPWAY
SHIPWAYS
SHIRKER
SHIRKERS
SHITTAH
SHITTAHS
SHITTIM
SHITTIMS
SHMALTZ
SHMALTZY
SHMOOSE
SHMOOSED
SHMOOSES
SHMOOZE
SHMOOZED
SHMOOZES
SHOCKER
SHOCKERS
SHOEING
SHOEINGS
SHOGGLE
SHOGGLED
SHOGGLES
SHONEEN
SHONEENS
SHOOGIE
SHOOGIED
SHOOGIES
SHOOGLE
SHOOGLED
SHOOGLES
SHOOTER
SHOOTERS
SHOPFUL
SHOPFULS
SHOPHAR
SHOPHARS
SHOPPER
SHOPPERS
SHORING
SHORINGS
SHORTEN
SHORTENS
SHORTIE
SHORTIES
SHOTGUN
SHOTGUNS
SHOTPUT
SHOTPUTS
SHOTTLE
SHOTTLES
SHOUTER
SHOUTERS
SHOWGHE
SHOWGHES
SHOWING
SHOWINGS
SHRIEVE
SHRIEVED
SHRIEVES
SHRIGHT
SHRIGHTS
SHRIVEL
SHRIVELS
SHRIVER
SHRIVERS
SHTETEL
SHTETELS
SHUCKER
SHUCKERS
SHUDDER
SHUDDERS
SHUDDERY
SHUFFLE
SHUFFLED
SHUFFLER
SHUFFLES
SHUNNER
SHUNNERS
SHUNTER
SHUNTERS
SHUTTER
SHUTTERS
SHUTTLE
SHUTTLED
SHUTTLES
SHYSTER
SHYSTERS
SIAMANG
SIAMANGS
SIAMESE
SIAMESED
SIAMESES
SIAMEZE
SIAMEZED
SIAMEZES
SIBLING
SIBLINGS
SIBSHIP
SIBSHIPS
SICKBED
SICKBEDS
SIDEARM
SIDEARMS
SIDEBAR
SIDEBARS
SIDECAR
SIDECARS
SIEVERT
SIEVERTS
SIFTING
SIFTINGS
SIGHTER
SIGHTERS
SIGMATE
SIGMATED
SIGMATES
SIGNAGE
SIGNAGES
SIGNING
SIGNINGS
SIGNIOR
SIGNIORS
SIGNORE
SIGNORES
SIGNORI
SIGNORIA
SILENCE
SILENCED
SILENCER
SILENCES
SILESIA
SILESIAS
SILICLE
SILICLES
SILICON
SILICONE
SILICONS
SILIQUA
SILIQUAS
SILIQUE
SILIQUES
SILKIES
SILKIEST

SILLIES
SILLIEST
SILLOCK
SILLOCKS
SILURID
SILURIDS
SIMARRE
SIMARRES
SIMILOR
SIMILORS
SIMITAR
SIMITARS
SIMPKIN
SIMPKINS
SIMPLER
SIMPLERS
SIMPLES
SIMPLEST
SIMULAR
SIMULARS
SIMURGH
SIMURGHS
SINCERE
SINCERER
SINDING
SINDINGS
SINGING
SINGINGS
SINGLET
SINGLETS
SINGULT
SINGULTS
SINKAGE
SINKAGES
SINKING
SINKINGS
SINOPIA
SINOPIAS
SINUATE
SINUATED
SIRGANG
SIRGANGS
SIRLOIN
SIRLOINS
SIRNAME
SIRNAMED
SIRNAMES
SIROCCO
SIROCCOS
SISSIES
SISSIEST
SITFAST
SITFASTS
SITTING
SITTINGS
SITUATE
SITUATED
SITUATES
SIXAINE
SIXAINES
SIXTEEN
SIXTEENS
SIZEISM
SIZEISMS
SIZEIST
SIZEISTS
SIZZLER
SIZZLERS
SJAMBOK
SJAMBOKS

SKATING
SKATINGS
SKATOLE
SKATOLES
SKEETER
SKEETERS
SKEGGER
SKEGGERS
SKELDER
SKELDERS
SKELLIE
SKELLIED
SKELLIER
SKELLIES
SKELLUM
SKELLUMS
SKELTER
SKELTERS
SKEPFUL
SKEPFULS
SKEPTIC
SKEPTICS
SKIDDER
SKIDDERS
SKIDPAN
SKIDPANS
SKIFFLE
SKIFFLES
SKILLET
SKILLETS
SKIMMER
SKIMMERS
SKIMMIA
SKIMMIAS
SKINFUL
SKINFULS
SKINKER
SKINKERS
SKINNER
SKINNERS
SKIPPER
SKIPPERS
SKIPPET
SKIPPETS
SKIRRET
SKIRRETS
SKIRTER
SKIRTERS
SKITTER
SKITTERS
SKITTLE
SKITTLED
SKITTLES
SKIVING
SKIVINGS
SKOLLIE
SKOLLIES
SKREIGH
SKREIGHS
SKRIECH
SKRIECHS
SKRIEGH
SKRIEGHS
SKUDLER
SKUDLERS
SKULKER
SKULKERS
SKULPIN
SKULPINS
SKUMMER

SKUMMERS
SKUTTLE
SKUTTLED
SKUTTLES
SKYHOOK
SKYHOOKS
SKYJACK
SKYJACKS
SKYLARK
SKYLARKS
SKYLINE
SKYLINES
SKYSAIL
SKYSAILS
SKYWARD
SKYWARDS
SLABBER
SLABBERS
SLABBERY
SLACKEN
SLACKENS
SLACKER
SLACKERS
SLADANG
SLADANGS
SLAKING
ASLAKING
SLAMMER
SLAMMERS
SLANDER
ISLANDER
SLANDERS
SLANGER
SLANGERS
SLAPPER
SLAPPERS
SLASHER
SLASHERS
SLATHER
SLATHERS
SLATING
SLATINGS
SLATTER
SLATTERN
SLATTERS
SLATTERY
SLEDGER
SLEDGERS
SLEEKEN
SLEEKENS
SLEEKER
SLEEKERS
SLEEPER
SLEEPERS
SLEEPERY
SLEEVER
SLEEVERS
SLEIGHT
SLEIGHTS
SLENTER
SLENTERS
SLICING
SLICINGS
SLICKEN
SLICKENS
SLICKER
SLICKERS
SLIDDER
SLIDDERS
SLIDDERY

SLIDING
SLIDINGS
SLIMMER
SLIMMERS
SLINGER
SLINGERS
SLINKER
SLINKERS
SLINTER
SLINTERS
SLIPPER
SLIPPERS
SLIPPERY
SLIPWAY
SLIPWAYS
SLITHER
SLITHERS
SLITHERY
SLITTER
SLITTERS
SLOBBER
SLOBBERS
SLOBBERY
SLOCKEN
SLOCKENS
SLOGGER
SLOGGERS
SLOTTER
SLOTTERS
SLOWING
SLOWINGS
SLUBBER
SLUBBERS
SLUGGER
SLUGGERS
SLUMBER
SLUMBERS
SLUMBERY
SLUMMER
SLUMMERS
SLURPER
SLURPERS
SMACKER
SMACKERS
SMARAGD
SMARAGDS
SMARTEN
SMARTENS
SMARTIE
SMARTIES
SMASHER
SMASHERS
SMATTER
SMATTERS
SMEDDUM
SMEDDUMS
SMELLER
SMELLERS
SMELTER
SMELTERS
SMELTERY
SMICKER
SMICKERS
SMICKET
SMICKETS
SMIDGEN
SMIDGENS
SMIDGIN
SMIDGINS
SMILING

SMILINGS
SMOKIES
SMOKIEST
SMOKING
SMOKINGS
SMOLDER
SMOLDERS
SMOTHER
SMOTHERS
SMOTHERY
SMOUSER
SMOUSERS
SMUDGER
SMUDGERS
SMUGGLE
SMUGGLED
SMUGGLER
SMUGGLES
SMYTRIE
SMYTRIES
SNABBLE
SNABBLED
SNABBLES
SNAFFLE
SNAFFLED
SNAFFLES
SNAPPER
SNAPPERS
SNARING
SNARINGS
SNARLER
SNARLERS
SNEAKER
SNEAKERS
SNEERER
SNEERERS
SNEEZER
SNEEZERS
SNICKER
SNICKERS
SNICKET
SNICKETS
SNIFFER
SNIFFERS
SNIFFLE
SNIFFLED
SNIFFLER
SNIFFLES
SNIFTER
SNIFTERS
SNIGGER
SNIGGERS
SNIGGLE
SNIGGLED
SNIGGLER
SNIGGLES
SNIPING
SNIPINGS
SNIPPER
SNIPPERS
SNIPPET
SNIPPETS
SNIPPETY
SNIRTLE
SNIRTLED
SNIRTLES
SNOOKER
SNOOKERS
SNOOPER
SNOOPERS

SNOOZER
SNOOZERS
SNOOZLE
SNOOZLED
SNOOZLES
SNORING
SNORINGS
SNORKEL
SNORKELS
SNORTER
SNORTERS
SNOTTER
SNOTTERS
SNOTTERY
SNOTTIE
SNOTTIER
SNOTTIES
SNOWCAP
SNOWCAPS
SNUBBER
SNUBBERS
SNUFFER
SNUFFERS
SNUFFLE
SNUFFLED
SNUFFLER
SNUFFLES
SNUGGER
SNUGGERY
SNUGGLE
SNUGGLED
SNUGGLES
SNUZZLE
SNUZZLED
SNUZZLES
SOAKAGE
SOAKAGES
SOAKING
SOAKINGS
SOAPIES
SOAPIEST
SOARING
SOARINGS
SOBBING
SOBBINGS
SOCAGER
SOCAGERS
SOCCAGE
SOCCAGES
SOCIATE
SOCIATES
SOCKEYE
SOCKEYES
SOGGING
SOGGINGS
SOILAGE
SOILAGES
SOILING
SOILINGS
SOILURE
SOILURES
SOJOURN
SOJOURNS
SOLANUM
SOLANUMS
SOLDADO
SOLDADOS
SOLDIER
SOLDIERS
SOLDIERY

SOLFEGE
SOLFEGES
SOLICIT
SOLICITS
SOLICITY
SOLIDUM
SOLIDUMS
SOLIPED
SOLIPEDS
SOLITON
SOLITONS
SOLOIST
SOLOISTS
SOLVATE
SOLVATED
SOLVATES
SOLVENT
SOLVENTS
SOMBRER
SOMBRERO
SOMBRES
SOMBREST
SOMEONE
SOMEONES
SOMEWAY
SOMEWAYS
SONANCE
SONANCES
SONDAGE
SONDAGES
SONDELI
SONDELIS
SONSHIP
SONSHIPS
SOOPING
SOOPINGS
SOOTHER
SOOTHERS
SOOTHES
SOOTHEST
SOPHISM
SOPHISMS
SOPHIST
SOPHISTS
SOPPING
SOPPINGS
SOPRANO
SOPRANOS
SORBATE
SORBATES
SORBENT
SORBENTS
SORBITE
SORBITES
SOREDIA
SOREDIAL
SOREHON
SOREHONS
SORGHUM
SORGHUMS
SORNING
SORNINGS
SOROBAN
SOROBANS
SOROCHE
SOROCHES
SORTING
SORTINGS
SOSSING
SOSSINGS

SOTTING
SOTTINGS
SOUBISE
SOUBISES
SOUFFLE
SOUFFLES
SOULDAN
SOULDANS
SOUMING
SOUMINGS
SOUNDER
SOUNDERS
SOUPCON
SOUPCONS
SOURING
SOURINGS
SOUROCK
SOUROCKS
SOURSOP
SOURSOPS
SOUSING
SOUSINGS
SOUSLIK
SOUSLIKS
SOUTANE
SOUTANES
SOUTHER
SOUTHERN
SOUTHERS
SOWBACK
SOWBACKS
SPACING
SPACINGS
SPADGER
SPADGERS
SPAIRGE
SPAIRGED
SPAIRGES
SPANCEL
SPANCELS
SPANGLE
SPANGLED
SPANGLER
SPANGLES
SPANGLET
SPANIEL
SPANIELS
SPANKER
SPANKERS
SPANNER
SPANNERS
SPARGER
SPARGERS
SPARKIE
SPARKIER
SPARKIES
SPARKLE
SPARKLED
SPARKLER
SPARKLES
SPARKLET
SPAROID
SPAROIDS
SPARRER
SPARRERS
SPARROW
SPARROWS
SPARTAN
SPARTANS
SPARTHE

SPARTHES
SPASTIC
SPASTICS
SPATTEE
SPATTEES
SPATTER
SPATTERS
SPATULA
SPATULAR
SPATULAS
SPATULE
SPATULES
SPAWNER
SPAWNERS
SPEAKER
SPEAKERS
SPECIAL
ESPECIAL
SPECIALS
SPECKLE
SPECKLED
SPECKLES
SPECTER
SPECTERS
SPECTRA
SPECTRAL
SPECTRE
SPECTRES
SPECULA
SPECULAR
SPEEDER
SPEEDERS
SPEELER
SPEELERS
SPELDER
SPELDERS
SPELDIN
SPELDING
SPELDINS
SPELLER
SPELLERS
SPELTER
SPELTERS
SPENCER
SPENCERS
SPENDER
SPENDERS
SPERSED
ASPERSED
SPERSES
ASPERSES
SPERTHE
SPERTHES
SPHAERE
SPHAERES
SPHEARE
SPHEARES
SPHERIC
ASPHERIC
SPHERICS
SPICATE
SPICATED
SPICULA
SPICULAR
SPICULAS
SPICULE
SPICULES
SPIELER
SPIELERS
SPIGNEL

SPIGNELS
SPILING
SPILINGS
SPILITE
SPILITES
SPILLER
SPILLERS
SPINDLE
SPINDLED
SPINDLES
SPINNER
SPINNERS
SPINNERY
SPINNET
SPINNETS
SPINNEY
SPINNEYS
SPINODE
SPINODES
SPINOUT
SPINOUTS
SPINULE
SPINULES
SPIRAEA
SPIRAEAS
SPIRANT
ASPIRANT
SPIRANTS
SPIREME
SPIREMES
SPIRING
ASPIRING
SPIRTLE
SPIRTLES
SPITTER
SPITTERS
SPITTLE
SPITTLES
SPLENIA
SPLENIAL
SPLICER
SPLICERS
SPLODGE
SPLODGED
SPLODGES
SPLOTCH
SPLOTCHY
SPLURGE
SPLURGED
SPLURGES
SPODIUM
SPODIUMS
SPOILER
SPOILERS
SPONDEE
SPONDEES
SPONDYL
SPONDYLS
SPONGER
SPONGERS
SPONGIN
SPONGING
SPONGINS
SPONSON
SPONSONS
SPONSOR
SPONSORS
SPOOFER
SPOOFERS
SPOOFERY

SPOOLER
SPOOLERS
SPOONEY
SPOONEYS
SPOORER
SPOORERS
SPORRAN
SPORRANS
SPORTED
ASPORTED
SPORTER
SPORTERS
SPORULE
SPORULES
SPOTTER
SPOTTERS
SPOUSAL
ESPOUSAL
SPOUSALS
SPOUSED
ESPOUSED
SPOUSES
ESPOUSES
SPOUTER
SPOUTERS
SPRAINT
SPRAINTS
SPRAYER
SPRAYERS
SPREAGH
SPREAGHS
SPREAZE
SPREAZED
SPREAZES
SPREDDE
SPREDDEN
SPREDDES
SPREEZE
SPREEZED
SPREEZES
SPRIGHT
SPRIGHTS
SPRINGE
SPRINGED
SPRINGER
SPRINGES
SPRUCES
SPRUCEST
SPULYIE
SPULYIED
SPULYIES
SPULZIE
SPULZIED
SPULZIES
SPUNKIE
SPUNKIER
SPUNKIES
SPURNER
SPURNERS
SPURRER
SPURRERS
SPURREY
SPURREYS
SPURTLE
SPURTLES
SPURWAY
SPURWAYS
SPUTNIK
SPUTNIKS
SPUTTER

SPUTTERS
SPUTTERY
SPYHOLE
SPYHOLES
SQUACCO
SQUACCOS
SQUALOR
SQUALORS
SQUARER
SQUARERS
SQUARES
SQUAREST
SQUEEZE
SQUEEZED
SQUEEZER
SQUEEZES
SQUELCH
SQUELCHY
SQUIDGE
SQUIDGED
SQUIDGES
SQUILLA
SQUILLAS
SQUIRES
ESQUIRES
SQUIRESS
SRADDHA
SRADDHAS
STABBER
STABBERS
STABILE
STABILES
STABLER
STABLERS
STABLES
STABLEST
STACKER
STACKERS
STACKET
STACKETS
STADDLE
STADDLES
STADIAL
STADIALS
STADIUM
STADIUMS
STAFFER
STAFFERS
STAGGER
STAGGERS
STAGING
STAGINGS
STAINER
STAINERS
STAITHE
STAITHES
STALKER
STALKERS
STAMINA
STAMINAS
STAMMEL
STAMMELS
STAMMER
STAMMERS
STAMPED
STAMPEDE
STAMPEDO
STAMPER
STAMPERS
STANDEE

STANDEES
STANDER
STANDERS
STANIEL
STANIELS
STANNEL
STANNELS
STANYEL
STANYELS
STAPLER
STAPLERS
STAPPLE
STAPPLES
STARDOM
STARDOMS
STARING
STARINGS
STARKEN
STARKENS
STARKER
STARKERS
STARLET
STARLETS
STARNIE
STARNIES
STARTED
ASTARTED
STARTER
STARTERS
STARTLE
STARTLED
STARTLER
STARTLES
STASHIE
STASHIES
STATICE
STATICES
STATING
ESTATING
STATION
STATIONS
STATISM
STATISMS
STATIST
STATISTS
STATURE
STATURED
STATURES
STATUTE
STATUTES
STEALER
STEALERS
STEALTH
STEALTHS
STEALTHY
STEAMER
STEAMERS
STEAMIE
STEAMIER
STEAMIES
STEARIN
STEARINE
STEARING
STEARINS
STEEMED
ESTEEMED
STEEPEN
STEEPENS
STEEPER
STEEPERS

STEEPLE
STEEPLED
STEEPLES
STEERER
STEERERS
STEEVES
STEEVEST
STEMBOK
STEMBOKS
STEMLET
STEMLETS
STEMMER
STEMMERS
STEMPEL
STEMPELS
STEMPLE
STEMPLES
STEMSON
STEMSONS
STENCIL
STENCILS
STENGAH
STENGAHS
STENTOR
STENTORS
STEPNEY
STEPNEYS
STEPPER
STEPPERS
STEPSON
STEPSONS
STERLET
STERLETS
STERNUM
STERNUMS
STEROID
ASTEROID
STEROIDS
STEWARD
STEWARDS
STEWING
STEWINGS
STEWPAN
STEWPANS
STEWPOT
STEWPOTS
STHENIC
ASTHENIC
STIBBLE
STIBBLER
STIBBLES
STIBINE
STIBINES
STIBIUM
STIBIUMS
STICKER
STICKERS
STICKLE
STICKLED
STICKLER
STICKLES
STIDDIE
STIDDIED
STIDDIES
STIFFEN
STIFFENS
STIFLER
STIFLERS
STILLER
STILLERS

STILTER
STILTERS
STINGER
STINGERS
STINKER
STINKERS
STINTER
STINTERS
STIPEND
STIPENDS
STIPPLE
STIPPLED
STIPPLER
STIPPLES
STIPULE
STIPULED
STIPULES
STIRRAH
STIRRAHS
STIRRER
STIRRERS
STIRRUP
STIRRUPS
STISHIE
STISHIES
STOCKER
STOCKERS
STODGER
STODGERS
STOITER
STOITERS
STOLLEN
STOLLENS
STOMACH
STOMACHS
STOMACHY
STOMATA
STOMATAL
STOMPER
STOMPERS
STONIED
ASTONIED
STONIES
ASTONIES
STONIEST
STONING
ASTONING
STONINGS
STONKER
STONKERS
STOOKER
STOOKERS
STOOLIE
STOOLIES
STOOPER
STOOPERS
STOPGAP
STOPGAPS
STOPING
STOPINGS
STOPOFF
STOPOFFS
STOPPED
ESTOPPED
STOPPER
STOPPERS
STOPPLE
STOPPLED
STOPPLES
STORAGE
STORAGES
STOTTER
STOTTERS
STOUNDS
ASTOUNDS
STOUTEN
STOUTENS
STOVERS
ESTOVERS
STOVING
STOVINGS
STOWAGE
STOWAGES
STOWING
STOWINGS
STRAINT
STRAINTS
STRANGE
ESTRANGE
STRANGER
STRAYED
ESTRAYED
STRAYER
STRAYERS
STRETCH
STRETCHY
STREWER
STREWERS
STRIATE
STRIATED
STRIATES
STRIDOR
STRIDORS
STRIGIL
STRIGILS
STRIKER
STRIKERS
STRIVER
STRIVERS
STRODLE
STRODLED
STRODLES
STROKER
STROKERS
STROOKE
STROOKEN
STROOKES
STROPHE
STROPHES
STROWER
STROWERS
STRUDEL
STRUDELS
STUBBLE
STUBBLED
STUBBLES
STUDDLE
STUDDLES
STUDENT
STUDENTS
STUDIER
STUDIERS
STUFFER
STUFFERS
STUMBLE
STUMBLED
STUMBLER
STUMBLES
STUMMEL
STUMMELS
STUMPER
STUMPERS
STUNNED
ASTUNNED
STUNNER
STUNNERS
STURMER
STURMERS
STUSHIE
STUSHIES
STUTTER
STUTTERS
STYLISE
STYLISED
STYLISES
STYLIST
STYLISTS
STYLITE
STYLITES
STYLIZE
STYLIZED
STYLIZES
STYLOID
STYLOIDS
STYPTIC
STYPTICS
STYRENE
STYRENES
SUASION
SUASIONS
SUBADAR
SUBADARS
SUBAREA
SUBAREAS
SUBATOM
SUBATOMS
SUBBASE
SUBBASES
SUBBING
SUBBINGS
SUBDEAN
SUBDEANS
SUBDUAL
SUBDUALS
SUBDUCE
SUBDUCED
SUBDUCES
SUBDUCT
SUBDUCTS
SUBDUER
SUBDUERS
SUBEDAR
SUBEDARS
SUBEDIT
SUBEDITS
SUBERIN
SUBERINS
SUBFUSC
SUBFUSCS
SUBFUSK
SUBFUSKS
SUBGOAL
SUBGOALS
SUBHEAD
SUBHEADS
SUBJECT
SUBJECTS
SUBJOIN
SUBJOINS
SUBLATE
SUBLATED
SUBLATES
SUBLIME
SUBLIMED
SUBLIMER
SUBLIMES
SUBPLOT
SUBPLOTS
SUBRING
SUBRINGS
SUBSERE
SUBSERES
SUBSIDE
SUBSIDED
SUBSIDES
SUBSIST
SUBSISTS
SUBSOIL
SUBSOILS
SUBSONG
SUBSONGS
SUBSUME
SUBSUMED
SUBSUMES
SUBTACK
SUBTACKS
SUBTEEN
SUBTEENS
SUBTEND
SUBTENDS
SUBTEXT
SUBTEXTS
SUBTILE
SUBTILER
SUBTYPE
SUBTYPES
SUBUNIT
SUBUNITS
SUBVERT
SUBVERTS
SUBZONE
SUBZONES
SUCCADE
SUCCADES
SUCCEED
SUCCEEDS
SUCCOUR
SUCCOURS
SUCCUBA
SUCCUBAE
SUCCUBAS
SUCCUMB
SUCCUMBS
SUCKING
SUCKINGS
SUCKLER
SUCKLERS
SUCRASE
SUCRASES
SUCRIER
SUCRIERS
SUCROSE
SUCROSES
SUCTION
SUCTIONS
SUFFETE
SUFFETES
SUFFICE
SUFFICED
SUFFICER
SUFFICES
SUFFUSE
SUFFUSED
SUFFUSES
SUGGEST
SUGGESTS
SUGGING
SUGGINGS
SUICIDE
SUICIDES
SUIDIAN
SUIDIANS
SUITING
SUITINGS
SULCATE
SULCATED
SULFATE
SULFATED
SULFATES
SULFIDE
SULFIDES
SULFITE
SULFITES
SULFONE
SULFONES
SULKIES
SULKIEST
SULLAGE
SULLAGES
SULPHUR
SULPHURS
SULPHURY
SULTANA
SULTANAS
SUMATRA
SUMATRAS
SUMMAND
SUMMANDS
SUMMATE
SUMMATED
SUMMATES
SUMMING
SUMMINGS
SUMMIST
SUMMISTS
SUMPTER
SUMPTERS
SUNBAKE
SUNBAKED
SUNBAKES
SUNBATH
SUNBATHE
SUNBATHS
SUNBEAM
SUNBEAMS
SUNBEAMY
SUNBELT
SUNBELTS
SUNBIRD
SUNBIRDS
SUNBURN
SUNBURNS
SUNBURNT
SUNDARI
SUNDARIS
SUNDECK
SUNDECKS
SUNDIAL
SUNDIALS
SUNDOWN
SUNDOWNS
SUNGLOW
SUNGLOWS
SUNLAMP
SUNLAMPS
SUNRISE
SUNRISES
SUNROOF
SUNROOFS
SUNSPOT
SUNSPOTS
SUNSUIT
SUNSUITS
SUNTRAP
SUNTRAPS
SUNWARD
SUNWARDS
SUPPAWN
SUPPAWNS
SUPPLES
SUPPLEST
SUPPORT
SUPPORTS
SUPPOSE
SUPPOSED
SUPPOSER
SUPPOSES
SUPREME
SUPREMER
SUPREMES
SUPREMO
SUPREMOS
SURAMIN
SURAMINS
SURANCE
SURANCES
SURBASE
SURBASED
SURBASES
SURBATE
SURBATED
SURBATES
SURCOAT
SURCOATS
SURFACE
SURFACED
SURFACER
SURFACES
SURFEIT
SURFEITS
SURFIES
SURFIEST
SURFING
SURFINGS
SURGEON
SURGEONS
SURGING
SURGINGS
SURLOIN
SURLOINS
SURMISE
SURMISED
SURMISER
SURMISES
SURNAME
SURNAMED
SURNAMES
SURTOUT
SURTOUTS
SURVEWE
SURVEWED
SURVEWES
SURVIEW
SURVIEWS
SURVIVE
SURVIVED
SURVIVES
SUSPECT
SUSPECTS
SUSPEND
SUSPENDS
SUSPENS
SUSPENSE
SUSPIRE
SUSPIRED
SUSPIRES
SUSTAIN
SUSTAINS
SWABBER
SWABBERS
SWADDLE
SWADDLED
SWADDLER
SWADDLES
SWAGGER
SWAGGERS
SWAGGIE
SWAGGIES
SWALING
SWALINGS
SWALLET
SWALLETS
SWALLOW
SWALLOWS
SWAMPER
SWAMPERS
SWANKER
SWANKERS
SWANKEY
SWANKEYS
SWANKIE
SWANKIER
SWANKIES
SWAPPER
SWAPPERS
SWARMER
SWARMERS
SWASHER
SWASHERS
SWATTER
SWATTERS
SWAYING
SWAYINGS
SWAZZLE
SWAZZLES
SWEARER
SWEARERS
SWEATER
SWEATERS
SWEENEY
SWEENEYS
SWEEPER
SWEEPERS
SWEETEN
SWEETENS
SWEETIE
SWEETIES
SWELLER
SWELLERS
SWELTER

SWELTERS
SWERVER
SWERVERS
SWIDDEN
SWIDDENS
SWIFTER
SWIFTERS
SWIGGER
SWIGGERS
SWILLER
SWILLERS
SWIMMER
SWIMMERS
SWINDGE
SWINDGED
SWINDGES
SWINDLE
SWINDLED
SWINDLER
SWINDLES
SWINGER
SWINGERS
SWINGLE
SWINGLED
SWINGLES
SWIPPLE
SWIPPLES
SWISHER
SWISHERS
SWISHES
SWISHEST
SWITHER
SWITHERS
SWIZZLE
SWIZZLED
SWIZZLES
SWOBBER
SWOBBERS
SWOPPER
SWOPPERS
SWORDER
SWORDERS
SWOTTER
SWOTTERS
SWOZZLE
SWOZZLES
SYENITE
SYENITES
SYLLABI
SYLLABIC
SYLPHID
SYLPHIDE
SYLPHIDS
SYLVINE
SYLVINES
SYLVITE
SYLVITES
SYMBOLE
SYMBOLES
SYMITAR
SYMITARE
SYMITARS
SYMPTOM
SYMPTOMS
SYNAPSE
SYNAPSES
SYNAPTE
SYNAPTES
SYNCARP
SYNCARPS
SYNCARPY
SYNCHRO
SYNCHROS
SYNCOPE
SYNCOPES
SYNDING
SYNDINGS
SYNERGY
ASYNERGY
SYNFUEL
SYNFUELS
SYNODAL
SYNODALS
SYNONYM
SYNONYMS
SYNONYMY
SYNOVIA
SYNOVIAL
SYNOVIAS
SYNTAGM
SYNTAGMA
SYNTAGMS
SYNTHON
SYNTHONS
SYRINGA
SYRINGAS
SYRINGE
SYRINGED
SYRINGES
SYRPHID
SYRPHIDS
SYSTOLE
ASYSTOLE
SYSTOLES
SYSTYLE
SYSTYLES
TABANID
TABANIDS
TABARET
TABARETS
TABBING
STABBING
TABETIC
TABETICS
TABINET
TABINETS
TABLEAU
TABLEAUX
TABLIER
TABLIERS
TABLING
STABLING
TABLINGS
TABLOID
TABLOIDS
TABLOIDY
TABORER
TABORERS
TABORET
TABORETS
TABORIN
TABORING
TABORINS
TABRERE
TABRERES
TACHISM
TACHISME
TACHISMS
TACHIST
TACHISTE
TACHISTS
TACHYON
TACHYONS
TACKERS
STACKERS
TACKETS
STACKETS
TACKIES
TACKIEST
TACKING
STACKING
TACKINGS
TACKLER
TACKLERS
TACTION
TACTIONS
TACTISM
TACTISMS
TADPOLE
TADPOLES
TAEDIUM
TAEDIUMS
TAFFETA
TAFFETAS
TAGGERS
STAGGERS
TAGGING
STAGGING
TAGGINGS
TAGMEME
TAGMEMES
TAILARD
TAILARDS
TAILING
TAILINGS
TAILLES
TAILLESS
TAILLIE
TAILLIES
TAILZIE
TAILZIES
TAKEOUT
TAKEOUTS
TALAUNT
TALAUNTS
TALAYOT
TALAYOTS
TALIPAT
TALIPATS
TALIPED
TALIPEDS
TALIPOT
TALIPOTS
TALKERS
STALKERS
TALKIER
STALKIER
TALKIES
TALKIEST
TALKING
STALKING
TALKINGS
TALLAGE
STALLAGE
TALLAGED
TALLAGES
TALLBOY
TALLBOYS
TALLENT
TALLENTS
TALLIER
TALLIERS
TALLITH
TALLITHS
TALOOKA
TALOOKAS
TAMANDU
TAMANDUA
TAMANDUS
TAMARAO
TAMARAOS
TAMARAU
TAMARAUS
TAMARIN
TAMARIND
TAMARINS
TAMARIS
TAMARISK
TAMASHA
TAMASHAS
TAMBOUR
TAMBOURA
TAMBOURS
TAMBURA
TAMBURAS
TAMPERS
STAMPERS
TAMPING
STAMPING
TAMPINGS
TAMPION
TAMPIONS
TANADAR
TANADARS
TANAGER
TANAGERS
TANAGRA
TANAGRAS
TANBARK
TANBARKS
TANDOOR
TANDOORI
TANDOORS
TANGELO
TANGELOS
TANGENT
TANGENTS
TANGHIN
TANGHINS
TANGIES
TANGIEST
TANGING
STANGING
TANGLER
TANGLERS
TANGRAM
TANGRAMS
TANIWHA
TANIWHAS
TANKAGE
TANKAGES
TANKARD
TANKARDS
TANKFUL
TANKFULS
TANKING
TANKINGS
TANLING
TANLINGS
TANNAGE
TANNAGES
TANNATE
STANNATE
TANNATES
TANNING
TANNINGS
TANTARA
TANTARAS
TANTRUM
TANTRUMS
TANYARD
TANYARDS
TAPERER
TAPERERS
TAPIOCA
TAPIOCAS
TAPPICE
TAPPICED
TAPPICES
TAPPING
STAPPING
TAPPINGS
TAPROOM
TAPROOMS
TAPROOT
TAPROOTS
TAPSTER
TAPSTERS
TARDIES
TARDIEST
TARINGS
STARINGS
TARRIER
STARRIER
TARRIERS
TARRIES
TARRIEST
TARRING
STARRING
TARRINGS
TARROCK
TARROCKS
TARSIER
TARSIERS
TARTANA
TARTANAS
TARTANE
TARTANED
TARTANES
TARTARE
TARTARES
TARTINE
TARTINES
TARTISH
STARTISH
TARTLET
TARTLETS
TARWEED
TARWEEDS
TASHING
STASHING
TASKING
TASKINGS
TASSELL
TASSELLS
TASSELLY
TASTING
TASTINGS
TATOUAY
TATOUAYS
TATTIES
TATTIEST
TATTING
TATTINGS
TATTLER
TATTLERS
TAUNTER
TAUNTERS
TAURINE
TAURINES
TAVERNA
TAVERNAS
TAWNIES
TAWNIEST
TAXICAB
TAXICABS
TAXIWAY
TAXIWAYS
TEACHER
TEACHERS
TEAMERS
STEAMERS
TEAMING
STEAMING
TEAMINGS
TEARING
STEARING
TEASING
TEASINGS
TEATIME
TEATIMES
TECHNIC
TECHNICS
TEDDIES
STEDDIES
TEDDING
STEDDING
TEEMING
STEEMING
TEENAGE
TEENAGED
TEENAGER
TEENING
STEENING
TEERING
STEERING
TEKTITE
TEKTITES
TELECOM
TELECOMS
TELEOST
TELEOSTS
TELETEX
TELETEXT
TELLING
STELLING
TELLINGS
TELPHER
TELPHERS
TEMBLOR
TEMBLORS
TEMPERA
TEMPERAS
TEMPEST
TEMPESTS
TEMPLAR
TEMPLARS
TEMPLES
STEMPLES
TEMPLET
TEMPLETS
TEMPTER
TEMPTERS
TEMPURA
TEMPURAS
TENCHES
STENCHES
TENDING
STENDING
TENDRIL
TENDRILS
TENDRON
TENDRONS
TENONER
TENONERS
TENSION
TENSIONS
TENTAGE
TENTAGES
TENTFUL
TENTFULS
TENTIGO
TENTIGOS
TENTING
STENTING
TENTINGS
TEQUILA
TEQUILAS
TERBIUM
TERBIUMS
TEREBRA
TEREBRAE
TEREBRAS
TERGITE
TERGITES
TERMITE
TERMITES
TERNING
STERNING
TERNION
TERNIONS
TERPENE
TERPENES
TERRACE
TERRACED
TERRACES
TERRAIN
TERRAINS
TERRANE
TERRANES
TERREEN
TERREENS
TERRENE
TERRENES
TERRIER
TERRIERS
TERRINE
TERRINES
TERSION
TERSIONS
TERTIAL
TERTIALS
TERTIAN
TERTIANS
TESSERA
TESSERAE
TESSERAL
TESTERN
TESTERNS
TESTING

TESTINGS
TESTOON
TESTOONS
TESTRIL
TESTRILL
TESTRILS
TESTUDO
TESTUDOS
TETANIC
TETANICS
TETRACT
TETRACTS
TETRODE
TETRODES
TEUCHAT
TEUCHATS
TEXTILE
TEXTILES
TEXTURE
TEXTURED
TEXTURES
THALAMI
THALAMIC
THALWEG
THALWEGS
THANAGE
THANAGES
THANKER
THANKERS
THANNAH
THANNAHS
THAWING
THAWINGS
THEATER
THEATERS
THEATRE
THEATRES
THEISMS
ATHEISMS
THEISTS
ATHEISTS
THEORBO
THEORBOS
THEOREM
THEOREMS
THEORIC
THEORICS
THERIAC
THERIACA
THERIACS
THERIAN
THERIANS
THERMAL
THERMALS
THIAMIN
THIAMINE
THIAMINS
THICKEN
THICKENS
THICKET
THICKETS
THICKETY
THIGGER
THIGGERS
THILLER
THILLERS
THIMBLE
THIMBLED
THIMBLES
THINKER

THINKERS
THINNER
THINNERS
THISTLE
THISTLES
THORITE
THORITES
THORIUM
THORIUMS
THOUGHT
THOUGHTS
THREAVE
THREAVES
THRIMSA
THRIMSAS
THRIVER
THRIVERS
THROMBI
THROMBIN
THROWER
THROWERS
THRUWAY
THRUWAYS
THRYMSA
THRYMSAS
THUGGEE
THUGGEES
THULITE
THULITES
THULIUM
THULIUMS
THUMPER
THUMPERS
THUNDER
THUNDERS
THUNDERY
THWAITE
THWAITES
THYLOSE
THYLOSES
THYMINE
THYMINES
THYROID
THYROIDS
TICKERS
STICKERS
TICKIES
STICKIES
TICKING
STICKING
TICKINGS
TICKLED
STICKLED
TICKLER
STICKLER
TICKLERS
TICKLES
STICKLES
TIDDIES
STIDDIES
TIDDIEST
TIDDLER
TIDDLERS
TIDDLEY
TIDDLEYS
TIDEWAY
TIDEWAYS
TIEBACK
TIEBACKS
TIERCEL

TIERCELS
TIERCET
TIERCETS
TIETACK
TIETACKS
TIFFING
STIFFING
TIFFINGS
TIGHTEN
TIGHTENS
TILAPIA
TILAPIAS
TILLAGE
STILLAGE
TILLAGES
TILLERS
STILLERS
TILLIER
STILLIER
TILLING
STILLING
TILLINGS
TILLITE
TILLITES
TILTERS
STILTERS
TILTING
STILTING
TILTINGS
TIMARAU
TIMARAUS
TIMBALE
TIMBALES
TIMBREL
TIMBRELS
TINAMOU
TINAMOUS
TINCHEL
TINCHELS
TINFOIL
TINFOILS
TINGING
STINGING
TINGLER
TINGLERS
TINHORN
TINHORNS
TINKERS
STINKERS
TINKING
STINKING
TINKLER
TINKLERS
TINNIES
TINNIEST
TINNING
TINNINGS
TINTACK
TINTACKS
TINTERS
STINTERS
TINTIER
STINTIER
TINTING
STINTING
TINTINGS
TINTYPE
TINTYPES
TINWARE
TINWARES

TIPPING
TIPPINGS
TIPPLED
STIPPLED
TIPPLER
STIPPLER
TIPPLERS
TIPPLES
STIPPLES
TIPSTER
TIPSTERS
TIRASSE
TIRASSES
TIRRING
STIRRING
TITANIS
TITANISM
TITCHES
STITCHES
TITHING
TITHINGS
TITLARK
TITLARKS
TITLING
TITLINGS
TITRATE
TITRATED
TITRATES
TITULAR
TITULARS
TITULARY
TOASTER
TOASTERS
TOASTIE
TOASTIES
TOBACCO
TOBACCOS
TOCCATA
STOCCATA
TOCCATAS
TOCKING
STOCKING
TODDLER
TODDLERS
TOECLIP
TOECLIPS
TOEHOLD
TOEHOLDS
TOENAIL
TOENAILS
TOFFIES
TOFFIEST
TOHEROA
TOHEROAS
TOHUNGA
TOHUNGAS
TOILING
TOILINGS
TOISECH
TOISECHS
TOKAMAK
TOKAMAKS
TOLLAGE
TOLLAGES
TOLLING
TOLLINGS
TOLUATE
TOLUATES
TOLUENE
TOLUENES

TOMBOLA
TOMBOLAS
TOMBOLO
TOMBOLOS
TOMFOOL
TOMFOOLS
TOMPION
TOMPIONS
TONDINO
TONDINOS
TONEPAD
TONEPADS
TONIEST
STONIEST
TONIGHT
TONIGHTS
TONINGS
STONINGS
TONKERS
STONKERS
TONKING
STONKING
TONNAGE
TONNAGES
TONNEAU
TONNEAUS
TONNEAUX
TONNELL
TONNELLS
TONSURE
TONSURED
TONSURES
TONTINE
TONTINER
TONTINES
TOOLBAG
TOOLBAGS
TOOLBAR
TOOLBARS
TOOLING
STOOLING
TOOLINGS
TOOLKIT
TOOLKITS
TOOTSIE
TOOTSIES
TOPARCH
TOPARCHS
TOPARCHY
TOPCOAT
TOPCOATS
TOPKNOT
TOPKNOTS
TOPLESS
STOPLESS
TOPLINE
TOPLINED
TOPLINER
TOPLINES
TOPMAST
TOPMASTS
TOPONYM
TOPONYMS
TOPONYMY
TOPPERS
STOPPERS
TOPPING
STOPPING
TOPPINGS
TOPPLED

STOPPLED
TOPPLES
STOPPLES
TOPSAIL
TOPSAILS
TOPSIDE
TOPSIDES
TOPSOIL
TOPSOILS
TOPSPIN
TOPSPINS
TORCHER
TORCHERE
TORCHERS
TORCHON
TORCHONS
TORDION
TORDIONS
TORGOCH
TORGOCHS
TORMENT
TORMENTA
TORMENTS
TORMINA
TORMINAL
TORNADE
TORNADES
TORNADO
TORNADOS
TORPEDO
TORPEDOS
TORRENT
TORRENTS
TORSADE
TORSADES
TORSION
TORSIONS
TORTONI
TORTONIS
TORTURE
TORTURED
TORTURER
TORTURES
TORULIN
TORULINS
TOSHACH
TOSHACHS
TOSSING
TOSSINGS
TOSSPOT
TOSSPOTS
TOSTADA
TOSTADAS
TOTIENT
TOTIENTS
TOTTERS
STOTTERS
TOTTIES
TOTTIEST
TOTTING
STOTTING
TOTTINGS
TOUCHER
TOUCHERS
TOUGHEN
TOUGHENS
TOUGHIE
TOUGHIES
TOURACO
TOURACOS

TOURING
TOURINGS
TOURISM
TOURISMS
TOURIST
TOURISTS
TOURISTY
TOURNEY
TOURNEYS
TOUSING
TOUSINGS
TOWAGES
STOWAGES
TOWBOAT
TOWBOATS
TOWINGS
STOWINGS
TOWLINE
TOWLINES
TOWMOND
TOWMONDS
TOWMONT
TOWMONTS
TOWNIES
TOWNIEST
TOWPATH
TOWPATHS
TOWROPE
TOWROPES
TOXEMIA
TOXEMIAS
TOYSHOP
TOYSHOPS
TRACHEA
TRACHEAE
TRACHEAL
TRACING
TRACINGS
TRACKER
TRACKERS
TRACTOR
TRACTORS
TRADING
TRADINGS
TRADUCE
TRADUCED
TRADUCER
TRADUCES
TRAFFIC
TRAFFICS
TRAGULE
TRAGULES
TRAIKED
STRAIKED
TRAILER
TRAILERS
TRAINED
STRAINED
TRAINEE
TRAINEES
TRAINER
STRAINER
TRAINERS
TRAIPSE
TRAIPSED
TRAIPSES
TRAITOR
TRAITORS
TRAJECT
TRAJECTS

TRAMCAR
TRAMCARS
TRAMMEL
STRAMMEL
TRAMMELS
TRAMPED
STRAMPED
TRAMPER
TRAMPERS
TRAMPET
TRAMPETS
TRAMPLE
TRAMPLED
TRAMPLER
TRAMPLES
TRAMWAY
TRAMWAYS
TRANCHE
TRANCHES
TRANCHET
TRANECT
TRANECTS
TRANGAM
TRANGAMS
TRANGLE
STRANGLE
TRANGLES
TRANKUM
TRANKUMS
TRANNIE
TRANNIES
TRANSIT
TRANSITS
TRANSOM
TRANSOMS
TRANTER
TRANTERS
TRAPEZE
TRAPEZED
TRAPEZES
TRAPPED
STRAPPED
TRAPPER
STRAPPER
TRAPPERS
TRASSES
STRASSES
TRAVAIL
TRAVAILS
TRAWLER
TRAWLERS
TRAYBIT
TRAYBITS
TRAYFUL
TRAYFULS
TREACLE
TREACLED
TREACLES
TREADER
TREADERS
TREADLE
TREADLED
TREADLER
TREADLES
TREAGUE
TREAGUES
TREASON
TREASONS
TREATER
TREATERS
TREDDLE
TREDDLED
TREDDLES
TREETOP
TREETOPS
TREFOIL
TREFOILS
TREHALA
TREHALAS
TREILLE
TREILLES
TREKKER
TREKKERS
TREMBLE
ATREMBLE
TREMBLED
TREMBLER
TREMBLES
TREMOLO
TREMOLOS
TRENAIL
TRENAILS
TRENISE
TRENISES
TRENTAL
TRENTALS
TREPANG
TREPANGS
TRESSED
STRESSED
TRESSEL
TRESSELS
TRESSES
STRESSES
TRESTLE
TRESTLES
TREYBIT
TREYBITS
TRIARCH
TRIARCHS
TRIARCHY
TRIATIC
TRIATICS
TRIAXON
TRIAXONS
TRIBADE
TRIBADES
TRIBBLE
TRIBBLES
TRIBLET
TRIBLETS
TRIBUNE
TRIBUNES
TRIBUTE
TRIBUTER
TRIBUTES
TRICKER
TRICKERS
TRICKERY
TRICKLE
STRICKLE
TRICKLED
TRICKLES
TRICKLET
TRICORN
TRICORNE
TRICORNS
TRIDARN
TRIDARNS
TRIDENT
STRIDENT
TRIDENTS
TRIDUUM
TRIDUUMS
TRIFFID
TRIFFIDS
TRIFFIDY
TRIFLER
TRIFLERS
TRIGGED
STRIGGED
TRIGGER
TRIGGERS
TRIGLOT
TRIGLOTS
TRIGRAM
TRIGRAMS
TRIKING
STRIKING
TRILITH
TRILITHS
TRILOBE
TRILOBED
TRILOBES
TRIMMER
TRIMMERS
TRIMTAB
TRIMTABS
TRINDLE
TRINDLED
TRINDLES
TRINGLE
TRINGLES
TRINKET
TRINKETS
TRINKUM
TRINKUMS
TRIOLET
TRIOLETS
TRIONYM
TRIONYMS
TRIPIER
STRIPIER
TRIPLET
TRIPLETS
TRIPOLI
TRIPOLIS
TRIPPED
STRIPPED
TRIPPER
STRIPPER
TRIPPERS
TRIPPERY
TRIPPET
TRIPPETS
TRIPPLE
TRIPPLED
TRIPPLER
TRIPPLES
TRIREME
TRIREMES
TRISECT
TRISECTS
TRISEME
TRISEMES
TRISHAW
TRISHAWS
TRISOME
TRISOMES
TRISULA
TRISULAS
TRITIDE
TRITIDES
TRITIUM
TRITIUMS
TRITONE
TRITONES
TRIUMPH
TRIUMPHS
TRIVIUM
TRIVIUMS
TRIZONE
TRIZONES
TROCHEE
TROCHEES
TROELIE
TROELIES
TROKING
STROKING
TROLLED
STROLLED
TROLLER
STROLLER
TROLLERS
TROLLEY
TROLLEYS
TROLLOP
TROLLOPS
TROLLOPY
TROMINO
TROMINOS
TROMMEL
TROMMELS
TROOLIE
TROOLIES
TROOPER
TROOPERS
TROPHIC
STROPHIC
TROPISM
ATROPISM
TROPISMS
TROPIST
TROPISTS
TROTTER
TROTTERS
TROUBLE
TROUBLED
TROUBLER
TROUBLES
TROUNCE
TROUNCED
TROUNCER
TROUNCES
TROUPER
TROUPERS
TROUSER
TROUSERS
TROUTER
TROUTERS
TROWING
STROWING
TRUCAGE
TRUCAGES
TRUCKER
TRUCKERS
TRUCKIE
TRUCKIES
TRUCKLE
TRUCKLED
TRUCKLER
TRUCKLES
TRUDGEN
TRUDGENS
TRUDGER
TRUDGERS
TRUFFLE
TRUFFLED
TRUFFLES
TRUMEAU
TRUMEAUX
TRUMPET
STRUMPET
TRUMPETS
TRUNDLE
TRUNDLED
TRUNDLER
TRUNDLES
TRUSSER
TRUSSERS
TRUSTEE
TRUSTEES
TRUSTER
TRUSTERS
TRYPSIN
TRYPSINS
TRYSAIL
TRYSAILS
TRYSTER
TRYSTERS
TSADDIK
TSADDIKS
TSADDIQ
TSADDIQS
TSARDOM
TSARDOMS
TSARINA
TSARINAS
TSARISM
TSARISMS
TSARIST
TSARISTS
TSIGANE
TSIGANES
TSUNAMI
TSUNAMIS
TUATARA
TUATARAS
TUBBIER
STUBBIER
TUBBING
STUBBING
TUBBINGS
TUBEFUL
TUBEFULS
TUBFAST
TUBFASTS
TUBULIN
TUBULINS
TUFTING
TUFTINGS
TUGBOAT
TUGBOATS
TUGGING
TUGGINGS
TUGHRIK
TUGHRIKS
TUILYIE
TUILYIED
TUILYIES
TUILZIE
TUILZIED
TUILZIES
TUITION
TUITIONS
TULCHAN
TULCHANS
TUMBLED
STUMBLED
TUMBLER
STUMBLER
TUMBLERS
TUMBLES
STUMBLES
TUMBREL
TUMBRELS
TUMBRIL
TUMBRILS
TUMESCE
TUMESCED
TUMESCES
TUMPIER
STUMPIER
TUMPING
STUMPING
TUMSHIE
TUMSHIES
TUMULAR
TUMULARY
TUNICIN
TUNICINS
TUNICLE
TUNICLES
TUNNAGE
TUNNAGES
TUNNING
STUNNING
TUNNINGS
TURACIN
TURACINS
TURBAND
TURBANDS
TURBANT
TURBANTS
TURBINE
TURBINED
TURBINES
TURBITH
TURBITHS
TURBOND
TURBONDS
TURDION
TURDIONS
TURFING
TURFINGS
TURFITE
TURFITES
TURMOIL
TURMOILS
TURNDUN
TURNDUNS
TURNING
TURNINGS
TURNKEY
TURNKEYS
TURNOFF
TURNOFFS
TURNOUT
TURNOUTS
TURPETH
TURPETHS
TURTLER
TURTLERS
TUSHIES
STUSHIES
TUSHKAR
TUSHKARS
TUSHKER
TUSHKERS
TUSKING
TUSKINGS
TUSSOCK
TUSSOCKS
TUSSOCKY
TUSSORE
TUSSORES
TUTANIA
TUTANIAS
TUTELAR
TUTELARS
TUTELARY
TUTENAG
TUTENAGS
TUTTING
TUTTINGS
TUTWORK
TUTWORKS
TWADDLE
TWADDLED
TWADDLER
TWADDLES
TWANGLE
TWANGLED
TWANGLES
TWANKAY
TWANKAYS
TWASOME
TWASOMES
TWATTLE
TWATTLED
TWATTLER
TWATTLES
TWEEDLE
TWEEDLED
TWEEDLER
TWEEDLES
TWEETER
TWEETERS
TWELFTH
TWELFTHS
TWIBILL
TWIBILLS
TWIDDLE
TWIDDLED
TWIDDLER
TWIDDLES
TWIGGER
TWIGGERS
TWINING
TWININGS
TWINKLE
TWINKLED
TWINKLER
TWINKLES
TWINSET
TWINSETS
TWINTER
TWINTERS
TWIRLER
TWIRLERS

TWISCAR
TWISCARS
TWISTER
TWISTERS
TWISTOR
TWISTORS
TWITTEN
TWITTENS
TWITTER
ATWITTER
TWITTERS
TWITTERY
TWIZZLE
TWIZZLED
TWIZZLES
TWOCCER
TWOCCERS
TWOSOME
TWOSOMES
TYCHISM
TYCHISMS
TYLOPOD
TYLOPODS
TYMPANA
TYMPANAL
TYMPANI
TYMPANIC
TYPHOID
TYPHOIDS
TYPHOON
TYPHOONS
TYPICAL
ATYPICAL
ETYPICAL
TYRANNE
TYRANNED
TYRANNES
TZADDIK
TZADDIKS
TZADDIQ
TZADDIQS
UAKARIS
OUAKARIS
UBEROUS
SUBEROUS
TUBEROUS
UDALLER
UDALLERS
UDDERED
JUDDERED
PUDDERED
UKELELE
UKELELES
UKULELE
UKULELES
ULICHON
ULICHONS
ULLAGES
FULLAGES
SULLAGES
ULLINGS
BULLINGS
CULLINGS
NULLINGS
ULULATE
ULULATED
ULULATES
UMBERED
CUMBERED
LUMBERED
NUMBERED
UMBRAGE
UMBRAGED
UMBRAGES
UMBRELS
TUMBRELS
UMBRERE
UMBRERES
UMBRILS
TUMBRILS
UMBROUS
CUMBROUS
UNALIST
UNALISTS
UNAWARE
UNAWARES
UNBAKED
SUNBAKED
UNBEGET
UNBEGETS
UNBEING
UNBEINGS
UNBELTS
SUNBELTS
UNBLIND
SUNBLIND
UNBLINDS
UNBLOCK
SUNBLOCK
UNBLOCKS
UNBOSOM
UNBOSOMS
UNBRACE
UNBRACED
UNBRACES
UNBROKE
UNBROKEN
UNBUILD
UNBUILDS
UNBURNT
SUNBURNT
UNCHAIN
UNCHAINS
UNCHARM
UNCHARMS
UNCHECK
UNCHECKS
UNCHILD
UNCHILDS
UNCLASP
UNCLASPS
UNCLOAK
UNCLOAKS
UNCLOSE
UNCLOSED
UNCLOSES
UNCLOUD
UNCLOUDS
UNCLOUDY
UNCOVER
UNCOVERS
UNCRATE
UNCRATED
UNCRATES
UNCROWN
UNCROWNS
UNCTION
FUNCTION
JUNCTION
UNCTIONS
UNCURSE
UNCURSED
UNCURSES
UNDECKS
SUNDECKS
UNDERDO
UNDERDOG
UNDIGHT
UNDIGHTS
UNDINES
NUNDINES
UNDOING
UNDOINGS
UNDRESS
SUNDRESS
UNEARTH
UNEARTHS
UNEQUAL
UNEQUALS
UNFAIRS
FUNFAIRS
UNFAITH
UNFAITHS
UNFROCK
UNFROCKS
UNFROZE
UNFROZEN
UNGIRTH
UNGIRTHS
UNGLOVE
UNGLOVED
UNGLOVES
UNGUARD
UNGUARDS
UNGUENT
UNGUENTS
UNHEART
UNHEARTS
UNHINGE
UNHINGED
UNHINGES
UNHOARD
UNHOARDS
UNHOODS
NUNHOODS
UNHORSE
UNHORSED
UNHORSES
UNHOUSE
GUNHOUSE
UNHOUSED
UNHOUSES
UNICORN
UNICORNS
UNIFIED
MUNIFIED
UNIFIER
UNIFIERS
UNIFIES
MUNIFIES
UNIFORM
UNIFORMS
UNIQUES
UNIQUEST
UNITARD
UNITARDS
UNITING
MUNITING
UNITINGS
UNITION
MUNITION
PUNITION
UNITIONS
UNITISE
UNITISED
UNITISES
UNITIVE
PUNITIVE
UNITIZE
UNITIZED
UNITIZES
UNJOINT
UNJOINTS
UNKNOWN
UNKNOWNS
UNLEARN
UNLEARNS
UNLEARNT
UNLOCKS
GUNLOCKS
UNLOOSE
UNLOOSED
UNLOOSEN
UNLOOSES
UNMOULD
UNMOULDS
UNMOUNT
UNMOUNTS
UNNERVE
UNNERVED
UNNERVES
UNNOBLE
UNNOBLED
UNNOBLES
UNORDER
UNORDERS
UNPAINT
UNPAINTS
UNPANEL
UNPANELS
UNPAPER
UNPAPERS
UNPLACE
UNPLACED
UNPLACES
UNPLAIT
UNPLAITS
UNPLUMB
UNPLUMBS
UNPLUME
UNPLUMED
UNPLUMES
UNPURSE
UNPURSED
UNPURSES
UNQUEEN
UNQUEENS
UNQUIET
UNQUIETS
UNQUOTE
UNQUOTED
UNQUOTES
UNRAVEL
UNRAVELS
UNREAVE
UNREAVED
UNREAVES
UNREEVE
UNREEVED
UNREEVES
UNRIGHT
UNRIGHTS
UNRIVET
UNRIVETS
UNROOFS
SUNROOFS
UNROOST
UNROOSTS
UNROUND
UNROUNDS
UNSAINT
UNSAINTS
UNSCALE
UNSCALED
UNSCALES
UNSCREW
UNSCREWS
UNSENSE
UNSENSED
UNSENSES
UNSHALE
UNSHALED
UNSHALES
UNSHAPE
UNSHAPED
UNSHAPEN
UNSHAPES
UNSHELL
UNSHELLS
UNSHIPS
GUNSHIPS
NUNSHIPS
UNSHOOT
UNSHOOTS
UNSHOUT
UNSHOUTS
UNSINEW
UNSINEWS
UNSLING
UNSLINGS
UNSNARL
UNSNARLS
UNSNECK
UNSNECKS
UNSPEAK
UNSPEAKS
UNSPELL
UNSPELLS
UNSPOKE
UNSPOKEN
UNSTACK
UNSTACKS
UNSTATE
UNSTATED
UNSTATES
UNSTEEL
UNSTEELS
UNSTICK
GUNSTICK
UNSTICKS
UNSTOCK
GUNSTOCK
UNSTOCKS
UNSTRAP
UNSTRAPS
UNSTRIP
UNSTRIPS
UNSUITS
SUNSUITS
UNSWEAR
UNSWEARS
UNTHINK
UNTHINKS
UNTRACE
UNTRACED
UNTRACES
UNTREAD
UNTREADS
UNTRUST
UNTRUSTS
UNTRUSTY
UNTRUTH
UNTRUTHS
UNTWINE
UNTWINED
UNTWINES
UNTWIST
UNTWISTS
UNTYING
UNTYINGS
UNVAILE
UNVAILED
UNVAILES
UNVISOR
UNVISORS
UNVOICE
UNVOICED
UNVOICES
UNWARIE
UNWARIER
UNWATER
UNWATERS
UNWATERY
UNWEAVE
UNWEAVES
UNWOMAN
UNWOMANS
UNWORTH
UNWORTHS
UNWORTHY
UNWRITE
UNWRITES
UPBRAID
UPBRAIDS
UPBREAK
UPBREAKS
UPBRING
UPBRINGS
UPBROKE
UPBROKEN
UPBUILD
UPBUILDS
UPBURST
UPBURSTS
UPCHEER
UPCHEERS
UPCHUCK
UPCHUCKS
UPCLIMB
UPCLIMBS
UPCLOSE
UPCLOSED
UPCLOSES
UPGOING
UPGOINGS
UPGRADE
UPGRADED
UPGRADER
UPGRADES
UPHEAVE
UPHEAVED
UPHEAVES
UPHOARD
UPHOARDS
UPHOIST
UPHOISTS
UPHOORD
UPHOORDS
UPHROES
EUPHROES
UPLYING
DUPLYING
UPMAKER
UPMAKERS
UPPINGS
CUPPINGS
UPRAISE
UPRAISED
UPRAISES
UPRIGHT
UPRIGHTS
UPRISAL
UPRISALS
UPROUSE
UPROUSED
UPROUSES
UPSHOOT
UPSHOOTS
UPSILON
UPSILONS
UPSPEAK
UPSPEAKS
UPSPEAR
UPSPEARS
UPSPOKE
UPSPOKEN
UPSTAGE
UPSTAGED
UPSTAGES
UPSTAIR
UPSTAIRS
UPSTAND
UPSTANDS
UPSTARE
UPSTARED
UPSTARES
UPSTART
UPSTARTS
UPSURGE
UPSURGED
UPSURGES
UPSWARM
UPSWARMS
UPSWEEP
UPSWEEPS
UPSWELL
UPSWELLS
UPSWING
UPSWINGS
UPTHROW
UPTHROWN
UPTHROWS
UPTRAIN
UPTRAINS
UPTREND
UPTRENDS
UPVALUE
UPVALUED
UPVALUES
UPWHIRL

UPWHIRLS
URAEMIA
URAEMIAS
URALITE
URALITES
URANIDE
URANIDES
URANISM
URANISMS
URANITE
URANITES
URANIUM
URANIUMS
UREDINE
UREDINES
URETHAN
URETHANE
URETHANS
URETHRA
URETHRAE
URETHRAL
URETHRAS
URGENCE
URGENCES
URGINGS
PURGINGS
SURGINGS
URICASE
URICASES
URIDINE
URIDINES
URINATE
URINATED
URINATES
URNINGS
BURNINGS
TURNINGS
URODELE
URODELES
UROLITH
UROLITHS
UROLOGY
OUROLOGY
UROMERE
UROMERES
UROSOME
UROSOMES
USHERED
HUSHERED
USUCAPT
USUCAPTS
USURPER
USURPERS
UTENSIL
UTENSILS
UTILISE
UTILISED
UTILISER
UTILISES
UTILITY
FUTILITY
UTILIZE
UTILIZED
UTILIZER
UTILIZES
UTOPIAN
UTOPIANS
UTOPIAS
UTOPIAST
UTOPISM
UTOPISMS
UTOPIST
UTOPISTS
UTRICLE
UTRICLES
UTTERED
BUTTERED
GUTTERED
MUTTERED
PUTTERED
UTTERER
MUTTERER
UTTERERS
VACANCE
VACANCES
VACATUR
VACATURS
VACCINE
VACCINES
VACUATE
EVACUATE
VACUATED
VACUATES
VACUIST
VACUISTS
VACUOLE
VACUOLES
VAGRANT
VAGRANTS
VAILING
AVAILING
VAIVODE
VAIVODES
VALANCE
VALANCED
VALANCES
VALENCE
VALENCES
VALIANT
VALIANTS
VALONEA
VALONEAS
VALONIA
VALONIAS
VALUATE
EVALUATE
VALUATED
VALUATES
VALVULA
VALVULAE
VALVULAR
VALVULE
VALVULES
VAMOOSE
VAMOOSED
VAMOOSES
VAMPING
VAMPINGS
VAMPIRE
VAMPIRED
VAMPIRES
VANDYKE
VANDYKED
VANDYKES
VANESSA
VANESSAS
VANILLA
VANILLAS
VANNING
VANNINGS
VANTAGE
VANTAGED
VANTAGES
VAQUERO
VAQUEROS
VAREUSE
VAREUSES
VARIANT
VARIANTS
VARIATE
VARIATED
VARIATES
VARICES
AVARICES
VARIOLA
VARIOLAR
VARIOLAS
VARIOLE
OVARIOLE
VARIOLES
VARIOUS
OVARIOUS
VARMENT
VARMENTS
VARMINT
VARMINTS
VARYING
VARYINGS
VASCULA
VASCULAR
VASSAIL
VASSAILS
VAULTER
VAULTERS
VAUNTED
AVAUNTED
VAUNTER
VAUNTERS
VAUNTERY
VAURIEN
VAURIENS
VEDALIA
VEDALIAS
VEDETTE
VEDETTES
VEERING
VEERINGS
VEGETAL
VEGETALS
VEHICLE
VEHICLES
VEILING
VEILINGS
VEINING
VEININGS
VEINLET
VEINLETS
VELIGER
VELIGERS
VELOUTE
VELOUTES
VENATOR
VENATORS
VENDACE
VENDACES
VENDAGE
VENDAGES
VENERER
VENERERS
VENGERS
AVENGERS
VENGING
AVENGING
VENISON
VENISONS
VENTAGE
VENTAGES
VENTAIL
AVENTAIL
VENTAILE
VENTAILS
VENTANA
VENTANAS
VENTERS
EVENTERS
VENTIGE
VENTIGES
VENTING
EVENTING
VENTINGS
VENTRAL
VENTRALS
VENTRED
AVENTRED
VENTRES
AVENTRES
VENTURE
AVENTURE
VENTURED
VENTURER
VENTURES
VENTURI
VENTURIS
VERANDA
VERANDAH
VERANDAS
VERBENA
VERBENAS
VERBIDS
OVERBIDS
VERBOSE
VERBOSER
VERDICT
VERDICTS
VERDITE
VERDITER
VERDITES
VERDURE
VERDURED
VERDURES
VERISMO
VERISMOS
VERMEIL
VERMEILS
VERMELL
VERMELLS
VERNIER
VERNIERS
VERONAL
VERONALS
VERRUCA
VERRUCAE
VERRUCAS
VERRUGA
VERRUGAS
VERSANT
VERSANTS
VERSETS
OVERSETS
VERSINE
VERSINES
VERSING
VERSINGS
VERSION
AVERSION
EVERSION
VERSIONS
VERTIGO
VERTIGOS
VERTING
AVERTING
EVERTING
VERVAIN
VERVAINS
VESICLE
VESICLES
VESSAIL
VESSAILS
VESTIGE
VESTIGES
VESTING
VESTINGS
VESTURE
VESTURED
VESTURER
VESTURES
VETCHES
KVETCHES
VETERAN
VETERANS
VETIVER
VETIVERS
VETKOEK
VETKOEKS
VETTURA
VETTURAS
VIADUCT
VIADUCTS
VIALFUL
VIALFULS
VIATORS
AVIATORS
VIBRATE
VIBRATED
VIBRATES
VIBRATO
VIBRATOR
VIBRATOS
VICEROY
VICEROYS
VICIATE
VICIATED
VICIATES
VICOMTE
VICOMTES
VICTORS
EVICTORS
VICTUAL
VICTUALS
VIDETTE
VIDETTES
VIDUAGE
VIDUAGES
VIEWING
VIEWINGS
VIHUELA
VIHUELAS
VILAYET
VILAYETS
VILIACO
VILIACOS
VILIAGO
VILIAGOS
VILLAGE
VILLAGER
VILLAGES
VILLAIN
VILLAINS
VILLAINY
VILLEIN
VILLEINS
VINASSE
VINASSES
VINEGAR
VINEGARS
VINEGARY
VINTAGE
VINTAGED
VINTAGER
VINTAGES
VINTNER
VINTNERS
VIOLATE
VIOLATED
VIOLATER
VIOLATES
VIOLENT
VIOLENTS
VIOLIST
VIOLISTS
VIOLONE
VIOLONES
VIRANDA
VIRANDAS
VIRANDO
VIRANDOS
VIRELAY
VIRELAYS
VIRETOT
VIRETOTS
VIRGATE
VIRGATES
VIRGULE
VIRGULES
VISCERA
VISCERAL
VISCOSE
VISCOSES
VISIBLE
VISIBLES
VISITEE
VISITEES
VISITER
VISITERS
VISITOR
VISITORS
VITAMIN
VITAMINE
VITAMINS
VITELLI
VITELLIN
VITIATE
VITIATED
VITIATES
VITRAGE
VITRAGES
VITRAIN
VITRAINS
VITREUM
VITREUMS
VITRINE
VITRINES
VITRIOL
VITRIOLS
VIVERRA
VIVERRAS
VOCABLE
EVOCABLE
VOCABLES
VOCODER
VOCODERS
VOGUING
VOGUINGS
VOICING
VOICINGS
VOIDING
AVOIDING
VOIDINGS
VOITURE
VOITURES
VOIVODE
VOIVODES
VOLANTE
VOLANTES
VOLPINO
VOLPINOS
VOLTAGE
VOLTAGES
VOLUSPA
VOLUSPAS
VOLUTED
EVOLUTED
VOLUTES
EVOLUTES
VOLUTIN
VOLUTINS
VOLVING
EVOLVING
VOUCHED
AVOUCHED
VOUCHEE
VOUCHEES
VOUCHER
VOUCHERS
VOUCHES
AVOUCHES
VOYAGER
VOYAGERS
VULGATE
EVULGATE
VULGATES
VULTURE
VULTURES
VULTURN
VULTURNS
WABBLER
WABBLERS
WABSTER
WABSTERS
WADDIES
SWADDIES
WADDING
WADDINGS
WADDLED
SWADDLED
TWADDLED
WADDLER
SWADDLER
TWADDLER
WADDLERS

WADDLES
SWADDLES
TWADDLES
WADMAAL
WADMAALS
WADMOLL
WADMOLLS
WADSETT
WADSETTS
WAFFLER
WAFFLERS
WAFTAGE
WAFTAGES
WAFTING
WAFTINGS
WAFTURE
WAFTURES
WAGERER
WAGERERS
WAGGING
SWAGGING
WAGONER
WAGONERS
WAGTAIL
WAGTAILS
WAILING
WAILINGS
WAINAGE
WAINAGES
WAINING
SWAINING
WAISTER
WAISTERS
WAITING
AWAITING
WAITINGS
WAIVODE
WAIVODES
WAIWODE
WAIWODES
WAKENED
AWAKENED
WAKENER
WAKENERS
WAKINGS
AWAKINGS
WALIEST
SWALIEST
WALKING
WALKINGS
WALKWAY
WALKWAYS
WALLABA
WALLABAS
WALLETS
SWALLETS
WALLIES
WALLIEST
WALLING
WALLINGS
WALLOWS
SWALLOWS
WALTZER
WALTZERS
WAMEFUL
WAMEFULS
WANGLED
TWANGLED
WANGLER
WANGLERS

WANGLES
TWANGLES
WANHOPE
WANHOPES
WANIGAN
WANIGANS
WANKERS
SWANKERS
WANKIER
SWANKIER
WANKING
SWANKING
WANNABE
WANNABEE
WANNABES
WANNING
SWANNING
WANTAGE
WANTAGES
WANTING
AWANTING
WANTINGS
WAPPERS
SWAPPERS
WAPPING
SWAPPING
WARATAH
WARATAHS
WARBLER
WARBLERS
WARDING
AWARDING
SWARDING
WARDINGS
WARDROP
WARDROPS
WARFARE
WARFARED
WARFARER
WARFARES
WARHEAD
WARHEADS
WARISON
WARISONS
WARLING
WARLINGS
WARLOCK
WARLOCKS
WARLORD
WARLORDS
WARMERS
SWARMERS
WARMING
SWARMING
WARMINGS
WARNING
AWARNING
WARNINGS
WARPATH
WARPATHS
WARPING
WARPINGS
WARRAND
WARRANDS
WARRANT
WARRANTS
WARRANTY
WARRIOR
WARRIORS
WARSHIP

WARSHIPS
WARTHOG
WARTHOGS
WARTIME
WARTIMES
WASHDAY
WASHDAYS
WASHERS
SWASHERS
WASHIER
SWASHIER
WASHING
SWASHING
WASHINGS
WASHOUT
WASHOUTS
WASHPOT
WASHPOTS
WASHRAG
WASHRAGS
WASHTUB
WASHTUBS
WASPIES
WASPIEST
WASSAIL
WASSAILS
WASTAGE
WASTAGES
WASTING
WASTINGS
WASTREL
WASTRELS
WATCHER
WATCHERS
WATCHES
SWATCHES
WATCHET
WATCHETS
WATERER
WATERERS
WATTAGE
WATTAGES
WATTLED
TWATTLED
WATTLES
TWATTLES
WAULING
WAULINGS
WAULKER
WAULKERS
WAVELET
WAVELETS
WAVERER
WAVERERS
WAVESON
WAVESONS
WAWLING
WAWLINGS
WAXBILL
WAXBILLS
WAXWING
WAXWINGS
WAXWORK
WAXWORKS
WAYBILL
WAYBILLS
WAYFARE
WAYFARED
WAYFARER
WAYFARES

WAYMARK
WAYMARKS
WAYMENT
WAYMENTS
WAYPOST
WAYPOSTS
WAYSIDE
WAYSIDES
WAYWODE
WAYWODES
WEARERS
SWEARERS
WEARIED
AWEARIED
WEARIES
WEARIEST
WEARING
SWEARING
WEARINGS
WEASAND
WEASANDS
WEATHER
WEATHERS
WEAVING
WEAVINGS
WEAZAND
WEAZANDS
WEBBING
WEBBINGS
WEBSTER
WEBSTERS
WEBWORM
WEBWORMS
WEDDING
WEDDINGS
WEDGIES
WEDGIEST
WEDGING
WEDGINGS
WEDLOCK
WEDLOCKS
WEEDIER
TWEEDIER
WEEDING
WEEDINGS
WEEKDAY
WEEKDAYS
WEEKEND
WEEKENDS
WEENIES
SWEENIES
TWEENIES
WEENIEST
WEEPERS
SWEEPERS
WEEPIER
SWEEPIER
WEEPIES
WEEPIEST
WEEPING
SWEEPING
WEEPINGS
WEETEST
SWEETEST
WEETING
SWEETING
TWEETING
WEFTAGE
WEFTAGES
WEIGELA

WEIGELAS
WEIGHER
WEIGHERS
WEIRDIE
WEIRDIES
WELCHER
WELCHERS
WELCOME
WELCOMED
WELCOMER
WELCOMES
WELDING
WELDINGS
WELFARE
WELFARES
WELLING
DWELLING
SWELLING
WELLINGS
WELSHER
WELSHERS
WELTERS
SWELTERS
WELTING
SWELTING
WENCHER
WENCHERS
WENDIGO
WENDIGOS
WERGILD
WERGILDS
WESTERN
WESTERNS
WESTING
WESTINGS
WESTLIN
WESTLINS
WETBACK
WETBACKS
WETLAND
WETLANDS
WETWARE
WETWARES
WHACKER
WHACKERS
WHAISLE
WHAISLED
WHAISLES
WHAIZLE
WHAIZLED
WHAIZLES
WHALING
WHALINGS
WHAMPLE
WHAMPLES
WHANGAM
WHANGAMS
WHANGEE
WHANGEES
WHATNOT
WHATNOTS
WHATSIT
WHATSITS
WHEEDLE
WHEEDLED
WHEEDLER
WHEEDLES
WHEELER
WHEELERS
WHEELIE

WHEELIER
WHEELIES
WHEENGE
WHEENGED
WHEENGES
WHEEPLE
WHEEPLED
WHEEPLES
WHEESHT
WHEESHTS
WHEEZLE
WHEEZLED
WHEEZLES
WHEMMLE
WHEMMLED
WHEMMLES
WHERRET
WHERRETS
WHETTER
WHETTERS
WHICKER
WHICKERS
WHIDDER
WHIDDERS
WHIFFER
WHIFFERS
WHIFFET
WHIFFETS
WHIFFLE
WHIFFLED
WHIFFLER
WHIFFLES
WHIMPER
WHIMPERS
WHIMPLE
WHIMPLED
WHIMPLES
WHIMSEY
WHIMSEYS
WHINGER
WHINGERS
WHINING
WHININGS
WHIPCAT
WHIPCATS
WHIPPER
WHIPPERS
WHIPPET
WHIPPETS
WHIPSAW
WHIPSAWS
WHIRLER
WHIRLERS
WHIRRET
WHIRRETS
WHIRTLE
WHIRTLES
WHISKER
WHISKERS
WHISKERY
WHISKET
WHISKETS
WHISKEY
WHISKEYS
WHISPER
WHISPERS
WHISPERY
WHISTLE
WHISTLED
WHISTLER

WHISTLES
WHITHER
WHITHERS
WHITIES
WHITIEST
WHITING
WHITINGS
WHITLOW
WHITLOWS
WHITRET
WHITRETS
WHITTAW
WHITTAWS
WHITTER
WHITTERS
WHITTLE
WHITTLED
WHITTLER
WHITTLES
WHIZZER
WHIZZERS
WHOLISM
WHOLISMS
WHOLIST
WHOLISTS
WHOMBLE
WHOMBLED
WHOMBLES
WHOMMLE
WHOMMLED
WHOMMLES
WHOOBUB
WHOOBUBS
WHOOPEE
WHOOPEES
WHOOPER
WHOOPERS
WHOPPER
WHOPPERS
WHUMMLE
WHUMMLED
WHUMMLES
WICKIUP
WICKIUPS
WIDDLED
TWIDDLED
WIDDLES
TWIDDLES
WIDENER
WIDENERS
WIDGEON
WIDGEONS
WIDOWER
WIDOWERS
WIELDER
WIELDERS
WIGGING
SWIGGING
TWIGGING
WIGGINGS
WIGGLER
WIGGLERS
WIGHTED
TWIGHTED
WILDCAT
WILDCATS
WILDING
WILDINGS
WILLERS
SWILLERS

WILLIES
TWILLIES
WILLING
SWILLING
TWILLING
WILTING
TWILTING
WIMBREL
WIMBRELS
WINCING
WINCINGS
WINDAGE
WINDAGES
WINDBAG
WINDBAGS
WINDGUN
WINDGUNS
WINDIGO
WINDIGOS
WINDING
WINDINGS
WINDLES
DWINDLES
SWINDLES
WINDLESS
WINDOCK
WINDOCKS
WINDORE
WINDORES
WINDROW
WINDROWS
WINGERS
SWINGERS
WINGIER
SWINGIER
WINGING
SWINGING
TWINGING
WINGLET
WINGLETS
WINIEST
TWINIEST
WINKING
SWINKING
TWINKING
WINKINGS
WINKLED
TWINKLED
WINKLER
TWINKLER
WINKLERS
WINKLES
TWINKLES
WINNING
TWINNING
WINNINGS
WINNOCK
WINNOCKS
WINSOME
WINSOMER
WINTERS
TWINTERS
WIPEOUT
WIPEOUTS
WIRETAP
WIRETAPS
WIREWAY
WIREWAYS
WISHERS
SWISHERS
WISHING
SWISHING
WISHINGS
WISSING
SWISSING
WISTING
TWISTING
WISTITI
WISTITIS
WITCHED
SWITCHED
TWITCHED
WITCHEN
WITCHENS
WITCHES
SWITCHES
TWITCHES
WITHERS
SWITHERS
WITHIES
WITHIEST
WITLING
WITLINGS
WITLOOF
WITLOOFS
WITTERS
TWITTERS
WITTING
TWITTING
WITTINGS
WITWALL
WITWALLS
WOBBLER
WOBBLERS
WOIWODE
WOIWODES
WOLFING
WOLFINGS
WOLFKIN
WOLFKINS
WOLFRAM
WOLFRAMS
WOLVING
WOLVINGS
WONNING
WONNINGS
WOODCUT
WOODCUTS
WOODIES
WOODIEST
WOODSIA
WOODSIAS
WOOFTER
WOOFTERS
WOOLDER
WOOLDERS
WOOLFAT
WOOLFATS
WOOLLEN
WOOLLENS
WOOLSEY
WOOLSEYS
WOOMERA
WOOMERAS
WOONING
SWOONING
WOORALI
WOORALIS
WOORARA
WOORARAS
WOOSELL
WOOSELLS
WOOSHED
SWOOSHED
WOOSHES
SWOOSHES
WOPPING
SWOPPING
WORDAGE
WORDAGES
WORDING
SWORDING
WORDINGS
WORKBAG
WORKBAGS
WORKDAY
WORKDAYS
WORKING
WORKINGS
WORKTOP
WORKTOPS
WORRIER
WORRIERS
WORSHIP
WORSHIPS
WORSTED
WORSTEDS
WOSBIRD
WOSBIRDS
WOTTING
SWOTTING
WOUNDED
SWOUNDED
WOUNDER
WOUNDERS
WOURALI
WOURALIS
WRANGLE
WRANGLED
WRANGLER
WRANGLES
WRAPPER
WRAPPERS
WREAKER
WREAKERS
WREATHE
WREATHED
WREATHEN
WREATHER
WREATHES
WRECKER
WRECKERS
WRESTER
WRESTERS
WRESTLE
WRESTLED
WRESTLER
WRESTLES
WRIGGLE
WRIGGLED
WRIGGLER
WRIGGLES
WRINGER
WRINGERS
WRINKLE
WRINKLED
WRINKLES
WRITING
WRITINGS
WRONGER
WRONGERS
WRYBILL
WRYBILLS
WRYNECK
WRYNECKS
XANTHAM
XANTHAMS
XANTHAN
XANTHANS
XANTHIN
XANTHINE
XANTHINS
XERAFIN
XERAFINS
XERASIA
XERASIAS
XYLENOL
XYLENOLS
XYLITOL
XYLITOLS
XYLOGEN
XYLOGENS
YACHTER
YACHTERS
YACHTIE
YACHTIES
YAFFING
NYAFFING
YAKHDAN
YAKHDANS
YAMULKA
YAMULKAS
YAPPIES
YAPPIEST
YAPSTER
YAPSTERS
YARDAGE
YARDAGES
YARDANG
YARDANGS
YASHMAK
YASHMAKS
YATAGAN
YATAGANS
YAWNING
YAWNINGS
YCLEEPE
YCLEEPED
YCLEEPES
YEALDON
YEALDONS
YEARNER
YEARNERS
YELLING
YELLINGS
YELLOCH
YELLOCHS
YELPING
YELPINGS
YESHIVA
YESHIVAH
YESHIVAS
YIELDER
YIELDERS
YOBBISM
YOBBISMS
YOGHURT
YOGHURTS
YOUNGTH
YOUNGTHS
YOUNKER
YOUNKERS
YOWLING
YOWLINGS
YPSILON
YPSILONS
YTTRIUM
YTTRIUMS
ZABTIEH
ZABTIEHS
ZADDIKS
TZADDIKS
ZAMARRA
ZAMARRAS
ZAMARRO
ZAMARROS
ZAMBUCK
ZAMBUCKS
ZAMOUSE
ZAMOUSES
ZANELLA
ZANELLAS
ZANJERO
ZANJEROS
ZANYISM
ZANYISMS
ZAPTIAH
ZAPTIAHS
ZAPTIEH
ZAPTIEHS
ZAREEBA
ZAREEBAS
ZARNICH
ZARNICHS
ZEALANT
ZEALANTS
ZEBRINA
ZEBRINAS
ZEBRULA
ZEBRULAS
ZEBRULE
ZEBRULES
ZELATOR
ZELATORS
ZEMSTVO
ZEMSTVOS
ZEOLITE
ZEOLITES
ZETETIC
ZETETICS
ZEUXITE
ZEUXITES
ZIGANKA
ZIGANKAS
ZILLION
ZILLIONS
ZIMOCCA
ZIMOCCAS
ZINCITE
ZINCITES
ZINCODE
ZINCODES
ZITHERN
ZITHERNS
ZIZANIA
ZIZANIAS
ZOCCOLO
ZOCCOLOS
ZOISITE
ZOISITES
ZONULET
ZONULETS
ZOOLITE
ZOOLITES
ZOOLITH
ZOOLITHS
ZOONITE
ZOONITES
ZOOTYPE
ZOOTYPES
ZORGITE
ZORGITES
ZORILLE
ZORILLES
ZORILLO
ZORILLOS
ZYGOSES
AZYGOSES
ZYMITES
AZYMITES
ZYMOGEN
ZYMOGENS
ZYMOTIC
ZYMOTICS

8-LETTER WORD HOOKS: extensible words only, except most -S inflections (see p200)

ABDICATE
ABDICATED
ABDOMINA
ABDOMINAL
ABERRATE
ABERRATED
ABNEGATE
ABNEGATED
ABORIGIN
ABORIGINE
ABROGATE
ABROGATED
ABSCISIN
ABSCISING
ABSCISSA
ABSCISSAE
ABSTERGE
ABSTERGED
ABSTRUSE
ABSTRUSER
ACANTHIN
ACANTHINE
ACCORAGE
ACCORAGED
ACCOUTRE
ACCOUTRED
ACERBATE
ACERBATED
ACIERATE
ACIERATED
ACONITES
TACONITES
ACTIONED
PACTIONED
ACTIVATE
ACTIVATED
ACTUALLY
TACTUALLY
ACUITIES
VACUITIES
ACULEATE
ACULEATED
ADUNCATE
ADUNCATED
ADVOCATE
ADVOCATED
AFFIANCE
AFFIANCED
AFFRONTE
AFFRONTED
AFFRONTEE
AFTEREYE
AFTEREYED
AGGRIEVE
AGGRIEVED
AGISTERS
MAGISTERS
AGNOMINA
AGNOMINAL
AILERONS
TAILERONS
AILMENTS
BAILMENTS
AIRINESS
HAIRINESS
AIRLINES
HAIRLINES
ALBITISE
ALBITISED
ALBITIZE
ALBITIZED
ALIENATE
ALIENATED
ALIGNING
MALIGNING
ALIZARIN
ALIZARINE
ALKALISE
ALKALISED
ALKALIZE
ALKALIZED
ALLELUIA
ALLELUIAH
ALLIANCE
DALLIANCE
ALLIGATE
ALLIGATED
ALLOCATE
ALLOCATED
ALLOWING
FALLOWING
GALLOWING
HALLOWING
SALLOWING
TALLOWING
WALLOWING
ALTERING
FALTERING
HALTERING
PALTERING
ALTERNAT
ALTERNATE
AMBLINGS
GAMBLINGS
LAMBLINGS
RAMBLINGS
WAMBLINGS
AMBROSIA
AMBROSIAL
AMBROSIAN
AMBULATE
AMBULATED
AMMONITE
MAMMONITE
AMORTISE
AMORTISED
AMORTIZE
AMORTIZED
AMPHORIC
CAMPHORIC
AMPUTATE
AMPUTATED
ANGELICA
ANGELICAL
ANGERING
DANGERING
ANGLINGS
DANGLINGS
JANGLINGS
TANGLINGS
WANGLINGS
ANGUIPED
ANGUIPEDE
ANGULATE
ANGULATED
ANKYLOSE
ANKYLOSED
ANNALISE
ANNALISED
ANNALIZE
ANNALIZED
ANNOTATE
ANNOTATED
ANNOUNCE
ANNOUNCED
ANNOUNCER
ANNOYING
TANNOYING
ANNULATE
CANNULATE
ANNULATED
ANTECEDE
ANTECEDED
ANTEDATE
ANTEDATED
ANTEFIXA
ANTEFIXAL
ANTICIZE
ANTICIZED
ANTIPOLE
RANTIPOLE
APHETISE
APHETISED
APHETIZE
APHETIZED
APHORISE
APHORISED
APHORISER
APHORIZE
APHORIZED
APHORIZER
APPANAGE
APPANAGED
APPETISE
APPETISED
APPETISER
APPETIZE
APPETIZED
APPETIZER
APPRAISE
APPRAISED
APPRAISER
APRICATE
APRICATED
AQUATINT
AQUATINTA
ARBOURED
HARBOURED
ARCHAISE
ARCHAISED
ARCHAISER
ARCHAIZE
ARCHAIZED
ARCHAIZER
AREFYING
RAREFYING
AREOLATE
AREOLATED
ARGUMENT
ARGUMENTA
ARILLATE
ARILLATED
AROUSALS
CAROUSALS
AROUSERS
CAROUSERS
AROUSING
CAROUSING
ARQUEBUS
HARQUEBUS
ARRAIGNS
DARRAIGNS
ARRAYING
WARRAYING
ARRIAGES
CARRIAGES
MARRIAGES
ARROGATE
ARROGATED
ARROWING
FARROWING
HARROWING
MARROWING
NARROWING
TARROWING
ARTICLES
PARTICLES
ARTIFICE
ARTIFICER
ARTINESS
TARTINESS
ARTISANS
BARTISANS
PARTISANS
ARTWORKS
PARTWORKS
ASEITIES
GASEITIES
ASHERIES
FASHERIES
WASHERIES
ASPERATE
ASPERATED
ASPEROUS
JASPEROUS
ASPHYXIA
ASPHYXIAL
ASPIRATE
ASPIRATED
ASSAILED
WASSAILED
ASSAILER
WASSAILER
ASSEMBLE
ASSEMBLED
ASSEMBLER
ASSONATE
ASSONATED
ASTRAGAL
ASTRAGALI
ASTRINGE
ASTRINGED
ASTRINGER
ATAGHANS
YATAGHANS
ATCHIEVE
ATCHIEVED
ATHETISE
ATHETISED
ATHETIZE
ATHETIZED
ATMOLYSE
ATMOLYSED
ATMOLYZE
ATMOLYZED
AUGUSTES
AUGUSTEST
AURICULA
AURICULAR
AURIFORM
TAURIFORM
AUTOLOGY
TAUTOLOGY
AUTOLYSE
AUTOLYSED
AUTOLYZE
AUTOLYZED
AUTOMATE
AUTOMATED
AUTONYMS
TAUTONYMS
AUTOTYPE
AUTOTYPED
AVENTAIL
AVENTAILE
AVIFAUNA
AVIFAUNAE
AXILLARY
MAXILLARY
AZURITES
LAZURITES
BACCHANT
BACCHANTE
BACILLAR
BACILLARY
BACKBITE
BACKBITER
BACKBONE
BACKBONED
BACKFIRE
BACKFIRED
BACKSLID
BACKSLIDE
BACTERIA
BACTERIAL
BACTERIAN
BALDPATE
BALDPATED
BALLADIN
BALLADINE
BALLADING
BALLISTA
BALLISTAE
BANALISE
BANALISED
BANALIZE
BANALIZED
BANDEROL
BANDEROLE
BARBECUE
BARBECUED
BARBEQUE
BARBEQUED
BARNACLE
BARNACLED
BARRETTE
BARRETTER
BASEMENT
ABASEMENT
BASHLESS
ABASHLESS
BASILICA
BASILICAL
BASILICAN
BATEMENT
ABATEMENT
BAUDRICK
BAUDRICKE
BECHANCE
BECHANCED
BEDABBLE
BEDABBLED
BEDAGGLE
BEDAGGLED
BEDAZZLE
BEDAZZLED
BEFRINGE
BEFRINGED
BEFUDDLE
BEFUDDLED
BEGRUDGE
BEGRUDGED
BELITTLE
BELITTLED
BEMUDDLE
BEMUDDLED
BEMUFFLE
BEMUFFLED
BENEFICE
BENEFICED
BEPRAISE
BEPRAISED
BERGAMAS
BERGAMASK
BLASTULA
BLASTULAE
BLASTULAR
BLOCKADE
BLOCKADED
BLOODIES
BLOODIEST
BODEMENT
ABODEMENT
BOLSHIES
BOLSHIEST
BOTANISE
BOTANISED
BOTANIZE
BOTANIZED
BOUNDING
ABOUNDING
BOUTONNE
BOUTONNEE
BRAIDING
ABRAIDING
BRANCHIA
BRANCHIAE
BRANCHIAL
BRASSIER
BRASSIERE
BRASSIES
BRASSIEST
BRATTICE
BRATTICED
BRETTICE
BRETTICED
BRICKIES
BRICKIEST
BRIDGING
ABRIDGING
BRITTLES
BRITTLEST
BROMELIA
BROMELIAD
BRONCHIA
BRONCHIAL
BROOKING
ABROOKING
BROWNIES
BROWNIEST
BUBBLIES
BUBBLIEST
BULGINES
BULGINESS
BULLDOZE
BULLDOZED
BULLDOZER
BUTMENTS
ABUTMENTS
CABALLER
CABALLERO
CALCANEA
CALCANEAL
CALCANEAN
CALCEATE
CALCEATED
CALCULAR
CALCULARY
CANALISE
CANALISED
CANALIZE
CANALIZED
CANEPHOR
CANEPHORA
CANEPHORE
CANONISE
CANONISED
CANONIZE

CANONIZED
CANOODLE
CANOODLED
CANTHARI
CANTHARID
CANTIEST
SCANTIEST
CANTLING
SCANTLING
CAPITULA
CAPITULAR
CAPONIER
CAPONIERE
CAPONISE
CAPONISED
CAPONIZE
CAPONIZED
CAPRICCI
CAPRICCIO
CAPRIOLE
CAPRIOLED
CAPSULAR
CAPSULARY
CARABINE
CARABINER
CARACOLE
CARACOLED
CARETAKE
CARETAKEN
CARETAKER
CARPINGS
SCARPINGS
CARTOUCH
CARTOUCHE
CASEMATE
CASEMATED
CASTELLA
CASTELLAN
CASTRATE
CASTRATED
CATALYSE
CATALYSED
CATALYSER
CATALYZE
CATALYZED
CATALYZER
CATENATE
CATENATED
CATHEDRA
CATHEDRAL
CATTIEST
SCATTIEST
CAVITATE
CAVITATED
CELLULAR
ACELLULAR
CENTINEL
CENTINELL
CENTUPLE
CENTUPLED
CERCARIA
CERCARIAE
CERCARIAN
CHAPERON
CHAPERONE
CHAPPIES
CHAPPIEST
CHAROSET
CHAROSETH
CHASTISE

CHASTISED
CHATTIES
CHATTIEST
CHERRIES
CHERRIEST
CHILLERS
SCHILLERS
CHILLIES
CHILLIEST
CHILLING
SCHILLING
CHINKIES
CHINKIEST
CHIPPIES
CHIPPIEST
CHITTIES
CHITTIEST
CHLORDAN
CHLORDANE
CHOCCIES
CHOCCIEST
CHORIAMB
CHORIAMBI
CHUMMIES
CHUMMIEST
CICERONE
CICERONED
CINCTURE
CINCTURED
CIRRIPED
CIRRIPEDE
CISTERNA
CISTERNAE
CIVILISE
CIVILISED
CIVILISER
CIVILIZE
CIVILIZED
CIVILIZER
CLAUSTRA
CLAUSTRAL
CLAUSULA
CLAUSULAE
CLAUSULAR
CLEEPING
YCLEEPING
CLITELLA
CLITELLAR
CLODPATE
CLODPATED
COALESCE
COALESCED
COALMINE
COALMINER
COGITATE
COGITATED
COGNOSCE
COGNOSCED
COHOBATE
COHOBATED
COIFFURE
COIFFURED
COINCIDE
COINCIDED
COINHERE
COINHERED
COLLAPSE
COLLAPSED
COLLEGIA
COLLEGIAL

COLLEGIAN
COLLOGUE
COLLOGUED
COLLOQUE
COLLOQUED
COLONISE
COLONISED
COLONIZE
COLONIZED
COMEDDLE
COMEDDLED
COMMENCE
COMMENCED
COMMERCE
COMMERCED
COMMERGE
COMMERGED
COMPESCE
COMPESCED
COMPLETE
COMPLETED
COMPLETER
COMPRISE
COMPRISED
COMPULSE
COMPULSED
CONCEIVE
CONCEIVED
CONCISES
CONCISEST
CONCLUDE
CONCLUDED
CONCOURS
CONCOURSE
CONCRETE
CONCRETED
CONDENSE
CONDENSED
CONDENSER
CONFERVA
CONFERVAE
CONFLATE
CONFLATED
CONFRONT
CONFRONTE
CONGLOBE
CONGLOBED
CONSERVE
CONSERVED
CONSERVER
CONSPIRE
CONSPIRED
CONSPIRER
CONSTATE
CONSTATED
CONSTRUE
CONSTRUED
CONSTRUER
CONTINUA
CONTINUAL
CONTINUE
CONTINUED
CONTINUER
CONTRIVE
CONTRIVED
CONTRIVER
CONVERGE
CONVERGED
CONVERSE
CONVERSED

CONVINCE
CONVINCED
CONVOLVE
CONVOLVED
CONVULSE
CONVULSED
COPULATE
SCOPULATE
COPULATED
COQUETTE
COQUETTED
CORONATE
CORONATED
CORVETTE
CORVETTED
COSMISMS
ACOSMISMS
COSMISTS
ACOSMISTS
COURSING
SCOURSING
CRABBING
SCRABBING
CRAGGIER
SCRAGGIER
CRAMMING
SCRAMMING
CRANCHED
SCRANCHED
CRANCHES
SCRANCHES
CRAPPIER
SCRAPPIER
CRAPPING
SCRAPPING
CRATCHES
SCRATCHES
CRAWLERS
SCRAWLERS
CRAWLIER
SCRAWLIER
CRAWLING
SCRAWLING
CREAKIER
SCREAKIER
CREAKING
SCREAKING
CREAMERS
SCREAMERS
CREAMING
SCREAMING
CREASOTE
CREASOTED
CREEPIES
CREEPIEST
CRENELLE
CRENELLED
CREOSOTE
CREOSOTED
CREVASSE
CREVASSED
CRIBBLED
SCRIBBLED
CRIBBLES
SCRIBBLES
CRIBELLA
CRIBELLAR
CRIMPIER
SCRIMPIER
CRIMPING

SCRIMPING
CRITIQUE
CRITIQUED
CROSSBIT
CROSSBITE
CRUMMIER
SCRUMMIER
CRUMMIES
CRUMMIEST
CRUMPING
SCRUMPING
CRUNCHED
SCRUNCHED
CRUNCHES
SCRUNCHES
CRUSTATE
CRUSTATED
CUDDLING
SCUDDLING
CUFFLING
SCUFFLING
CULLINGS
SCULLINGS
CULLIONS
SCULLIONS
CULTRATE
CULTRATED
CUMBERED
SCUMBERED
CUMULATE
CUMULATED
CURARISE
CURARISED
CURARIZE
CURARIZED
CURCUMIN
CURCUMINE
CURRIERS
SCURRIERS
CURRYING
SCURRYING
CURVIEST
SCURVIEST
CUSPIDOR
CUSPIDORE
CUTENESS
ACUTENESS
CUTINISE
CUTINISED
CUTINIZE
CUTINIZED
DAINTIES
DAINTIEST
DAMASKIN
DAMASKING
DANCETTE
DANCETTEE
DARRAIGN
DARRAIGNE
DARRAINE
DARRAINED
DEBOUCHE
DEBOUCHED
DEBUTANT
DEBUTANTE
DECEMVIR
DECEMVIRI
DECENNIA
DECENNIAL
DECIMATE

DECIMATED
DECLASSE
DECLASSED
DECLASSEE
DECORATE
DECORATED
DECOUPLE
DECOUPLED
DECREASE
DECREASED
DEDICATE
DEDICATED
DEDICATEE
DEFECATE
DEFECATED
DEFILADE
DEFILADED
DEGREASE
DEGREASED
DEIGNING
SDEIGNING
DELEGATE
DELEGATED
DELIBATE
DELIBATED
DEMONISE
DEMONISED
DEMONIZE
DEMONIZED
DENATURE
DENATURED
DENOTATE
DENOTATED
DENOUNCE
DENOUNCED
DENOUNCER
DENUDATE
DENUDATED
DEPILATE
DEPILATED
DEPURATE
DEPURATED
DEPUTISE
DEPUTISED
DEPUTIZE
DEPUTIZED
DEROGATE
DEROGATED
DESCRIBE
DESCRIBED
DESCRIBER
DESCRIVE
DESCRIVED
DESOLATE
DESOLATED
DESOLATER
DESPOTAT
DESPOTATE
DETHRONE
DETHRONED
DETHRONER
DETONATE
DETONATED
DETRAQUE
DETRAQUEE
DEVELOPE
DEVELOPED
DEVELOPER
DIAGNOSE
DIAGNOSED

DIALOGUE
DIALOGUED
DIARRHEA
DIARRHEAL
DICHASIA
DICHASIAL
DIDRACHM
DIDRACHMA
DIGITATE
DIGITATED
DIGITISE
DIGITISED
DIGITISER
DIGITIZE
DIGITIZED
DIGITIZER
DIMERISE
DIMERISED
DIMERIZE
DIMERIZED
DIPLOMAT
DIPLOMATE
DIRIGISM
DIRIGISME
DISABUSE
DISABUSED
DISAGREE
DISAGREED
DISBURSE
DISBURSED
DISCIPLE
DISCIPLED
DISCLOSE
DISCLOSED
DISCOURE
DISCOURED
DISCRETE
DISCRETER
DISGORGE
DISGORGED
DISGRACE
DISGRACED
DISGRACER
DISGRADE
DISGRADED
DISGUISE
DISGUISED
DISGUISER
DISHABLE
DISHABLED
DISHORSE
DISHORSED
DISHOUSE
DISHOUSED
DISINURE
DISINURED
DISLEAVE
DISLEAVED
DISLODGE
DISLODGED
DISPENCE
DISPENCED
DISPENSE
DISPENSED
DISPENSER
DISPERSE
DISPERSED
DISPERSER
DISPLACE
DISPLACED

DISPLODE
DISPLODED
DISPLUME
DISPLUMED
DISPONGE
DISPONGED
DISPRIZE
DISPRIZED
DISPROVE
DISPROVED
DISPROVEN
DISPUNGE
DISPUNGED
DISPURSE
DISPURSED
DISSEISE
DISSEISED
DISSEIZE
DISSEIZED
DISSERVE
DISSERVED
DISSOLVE
DISSOLVED
DISSUADE
DISSUADED
DISSUADER
DISTANCE
DISTANCED
DISTASTE
DISTASTED
DISTRAIT
DISTRAITE
DISUNITE
DISUNITED
DISVALUE
DISVALUED
DIVAGATE
DIVAGATED
DIVINISE
DIVINISED
DIVINIZE
DIVINIZED
DJELLABA
DJELLABAH
DOMICILE
DOMICILED
DOMINATE
DOMINATED
DOWNSIZE
DOWNSIZED
DREADING
ADREADING
DRICKSIE
DRICKSIER
DRUGGIES
DRUGGIEST
DUBITATE
DUBITATED
DYNAMISE
DYNAMISED
DYNAMITE
DYNAMITED
DYNAMITER
DYNAMIZE
DYNAMIZED
DYSPNOEA
DYSPNOEAL
DYSTOPIA
DYSTOPIAN
EANLINGS
WEANLINGS
YEANLINGS
EARLIEST
PEARLIEST
EARNINGS
LEARNINGS
YEARNINGS
EASELESS
CEASELESS
EASTINGS
BEASTINGS
FEASTINGS
EATERIES
PEATERIES
EBAUCHES
DEBAUCHES
EBIONISE
EBIONISED
EBIONIZE
EBIONIZED
ECAUDATE
DECAUDATE
ECCLESIA
ECCLESIAE
ECCLESIAL
ECHINATE
ECHINATED
ECLOSING
RECLOSING
ECSTASIS
ECSTASISE
ECUMENIC
OECUMENIC
EDGEWISE
WEDGEWISE
EDITIONS
SEDITIONS
EDUCIBLE
DEDUCIBLE
REDUCIBLE
EDUCTION
DEDUCTION
REDUCTION
SEDUCTION
EDUCTORS
SEDUCTORS
EERINESS
BEERINESS
EFFIERCE
EFFIERCED
EFFLUVIA
EFFLUVIAL
EGENCIES
REGENCIES
EGOMANIA
EGOMANIAC
EGRESSES
NEGRESSES
REGRESSES
EJECTING
DEJECTING
REJECTING
EJECTION
DEJECTION
REJECTION
EJECTIVE
REJECTIVE
EJECTORS
REJECTORS
ELAPSING
DELAPSING
RELAPSING
ELATEDLY
BELATEDLY
ELATIONS
DELATIONS
GELATIONS
RELATIONS
ELATIVES
RELATIVES
ELECTING
SELECTING
ELECTION
SELECTION
ELECTIVE
SELECTIVE
ELECTORS
SELECTORS
ELFHOODS
SELFHOODS
ELONGATE
ELONGATED
ELUSIONS
DELUSIONS
EMACIATE
EMACIATED
EMBATTLE
EMBATTLED
EMBEZZLE
EMBEZZLED
EMBEZZLER
EMENDATE
EMENDATED
EMERGING
DEMERGING
REMERGING
EMERSION
DEMERSION
EMIGRATE
REMIGRATE
EMIGRATED
EMISSION
DEMISSION
REMISSION
EMISSIVE
DEMISSIVE
REMISSIVE
EMITTERS
REMITTERS
EMITTING
DEMITTING
REMITTING
EMMARBLE
EMMARBLED
EMOTIONS
DEMOTIONS
REMOTIONS
EMPEOPLE
EMPEOPLED
EMPERISE
EMPERISED
EMPERIZE
EMPERIZED
EMPHASIS
EMPHASISE
EMPIERCE
EMPIERCED
EMPLONGE
EMPLONGED
EMPURPLE
EMPURPLED
EMULSIFY
DEMULSIFY
ENARCHES
MENARCHES
ENATIONS
VENATIONS
ENCHANTS
PENCHANTS
ENCHARGE
ENCHARGED
ENCIRCLE
ENCIRCLED
ENCLOTHE
ENCLOTHED
ENCRADLE
ENCRADLED
ENCREASE
ENCREASED
ENDAMAGE
ENDAMAGED
ENDOSTEA
ENDOSTEAL
ENERGISE
ENERGISED
ENERGIZE
ENERGIZED
ENERVATE
ENERVATED
ENFEEBLE
ENFEEBLED
ENFIERCE
ENFIERCED
ENFILADE
ENFILADED
ENFORCED
RENFORCED
ENFORCES
RENFORCES
ENGIRDLE
ENGIRDLED
ENGRIEVE
ENGRIEVED
ENGROOVE
ENGROOVED
ENHEARSE
ENHEARSED
ENKINDLE
ENKINDLED
ENLIGHTS
PENLIGHTS
ENLUMINE
ENLUMINED
ENOUNCED
DENOUNCED
RENOUNCED
ENOUNCES
DENOUNCES
RENOUNCES
ENRAUNGE
ENRAUNGED
ENSAMPLE
ENSAMPLED
ENSCONCE
ENSCONCED
ENSHEATH
ENSHEATHE
ENSHRINE
ENSHRINED
ENSILAGE
ENSILAGED
ENSPHERE
ENSPHERED
ENSURING
CENSURING
ENSWATHE
ENSWATHED
ENTANGLE
PENTANGLE
ENTANGLED
ENTAYLES
VENTAYLES
ENTERING
CENTERING
TENTERING
ENTHRONE
ENTHRONED
ENTICING
PENTICING
ENTRANCE
ENTRANCED
ENTRISMS
CENTRISMS
ENTRISTS
CENTRISTS
ENVEIGLE
ENVEIGLED
ENVELOPE
ENVELOPED
ENVISAGE
ENVISAGED
EOLIPILE
AEOLIPILE
EPHEMERA
EPHEMERAE
EPHEMERAL
EPICEDIA
EPICEDIAL
EPICEDIAN
EPILATED
DEPILATED
EPILATES
DEPILATES
EPILATOR
DEPILATOR
EPURATED
DEPURATED
EPURATES
DEPURATES
EQUALISE
EQUALISED
EQUALISER
EQUALIZE
EQUALIZED
EQUALIZER
EQUIPAGE
EQUIPAGED
ERADIATE
RERADIATE
ERADIATED
ERGOTISE
ERGOTISED
ERGOTIZE
ERGOTIZED
ERRORIST
TERRORIST
ERUCTATE
ERUCTATED
ERYTHEMA
ERYTHEMAL
ESCALADE
ESCALADED
ESCALATE
ESCALATED
ESCALOPE
ESCALOPED
ESCRIBED
DESCRIBED
ESCRIBES
DESCRIBES
ESOPHAGI
OESOPHAGI
ESOTERIC
ESOTERICA
ESQUIRES
ESQUIRESS
ESSONITE
HESSONITE
ESTATING
GESTATING
RESTATING
ESTHESIA
AESTHESIA
ESTHETES
AESTHETES
ESTIMATE
ESTIMATED
ESTIVATE
AESTIVATE
ESTIVATED
ESTRANGE
ESTRANGED
ESTRANGER
ESTROGEN
OESTROGEN
ESTRUSES
OESTRUSES
ETACISMS
BETACISMS
ETCHINGS
LETCHINGS
ETERNISE
ETERNISED
ETERNIZE
ETERNIZED
ETHANOLS
METHANOLS
ETHERISE
ETHERISED
ETHERIZE
ETHERIZED
ETHICISE
ETHICISED
ETHICIZE
ETHICIZED
ETHYLATE
METHYLATE
ETHYLATED
ETHYLENE
METHYLENE
ETIOLATE
PETIOLATE
ETIOLATED
ETIOLOGY
AETIOLOGY
ETRANGER
ETRANGERE
EUCALYPT
EUCALYPTI
EUCARYOT
EUCARYOTE
EUKARYOT
EUKARYOTE
EULOGISE
EULOGISED
EULOGIZE
EULOGIZED
EUPHUISE
EUPHUISED
EUPHUIZE
EUPHUIZED
EVACUATE
EVACUATED
EVALUATE
DEVALUATE
EVALUATED
EVANESCE
EVANESCED
EVERMORE
NEVERMORE
EVERSION
REVERSION
EVERTING
REVERTING
EVIDENCE
EVIDENCED
EVIRATES
LEVIRATES
EVITATED
LEVITATED
EVITATES
LEVITATES
EVOCABLE
REVOCABLE
EVOLVERS
REVOLVERS
EVOLVING
DEVOLVING
REVOLVING
EVULGATE
EVULGATED
EVULSION
REVULSION
EXANTHEM
EXANTHEMA
EXCAVATE
EXCAVATED
EXCHANGE
EXCHANGED
EXCHANGER
EXECRATE
EXECRATED
EXERCISE
EXERCISED
EXERCISER
EXHUMATE
EXHUMATED
EXIGEANT
EXIGEANTE
EXORCISE
EXORCISED
EXORCISER
EXORCIZE
EXORCIZED
EXORCIZER
EXPEDITE
EXPEDITED
EXPEDITER
EXTREMES
EXTREMEST

EXTRORSE
DEXTRORSE
EXUVIATE
EXUVIATED
FABULISE
FABULISED
FABULIZE
FABULIZED
FANFARON
FANFARONA
FARADISE
FARADISED
FARADIZE
FARADIZED
FASCIATE
FASCIATED
FASCICLE
FASCICLED
FASCISTI
FASCISTIC
FATIGATE
FATIGATED
FEDERATE
FEDERATED
FELLATIO
FELLATION
FEMINISE
FEMINISED
FEMINIZE
FEMINIZED
FENESTRA
FENESTRAL
FIBRILLA
FIBRILLAE
FIBRILLAR
FIGURANT
FIGURANTE
FILIGREE
FILIGREED
FILTRATE
FILTRATED
FINALISE
FINALISED
FINALIZE
FINALIZED
FISSIPED
FISSIPEDE
FLIMSIES
FLIMSIEST
FLOPPIES
FLOPPIEST
FLOURISH
FLOURISHY
FLUIDISE
FLUIDISED
FLUIDIZE
FLUIDIZED
FOCALISE
FOCALISED
FOCALIZE
FOCALIZED
FORAMINA
FORAMINAL
FOREBODE
FOREBODED
FOREBODER
FOREDATE
FOREDATED
FOREHAND
AFOREHAND
FOREKNOW
FOREKNOWN
FORENAME
FORENAMED
FORESAID
AFORESAID
FORESHEW
FORESHEWN
FORESHOW
FORESHOWN
FORESTAL
FORESTALL
FORETIME
AFORETIME
FORHAILE
FORHAILED
FORHOOIE
FORHOOIED
FORJUDGE
FORJUDGED
FORMULAR
FORMULARY
FORSPOKE
FORSPOKEN
FORWASTE
FORWASTED
FORZANDI
SFORZANDI
FORZANDO
SFORZANDO
FORZATOS
SFORZATOS
FRACTURE
FRACTURED
FREEBASE
FREEBASED
FRILLIES
FRILLIEST
FRONTAGE
FRONTAGER
FROSTBIT
FROSTBITE
FUMIGATE
FUMIGATED
FURFUROL
FURFUROLE
GAILLARD
GAILLARDE
GALLABEA
GALLABEAH
GALLABIA
GALLABIAH
GANGRENE
GANGRENED
GARAGIST
GARAGISTE
GARROTTE
GARROTTED
GARROTTER
GASTNESS
GASTNESSE
GASTRULA
GASTRULAE
GEFUFFLE
GEFUFFLED
GELASTIC
AGELASTIC
GEMINATE
GEMINATED
GENERATE
GENERATED
GHASTFUL
GHASTFULL
GLABELLA
GLABELLAE
GLABELLAR
GLACIATE
GLACIATED
GLISSADE
GLISSADED
GLOSSIES
GLOSSIEST
GLYCERIN
GLYCERINE
GRADUATE
GRADUATED
GRAFFITI
SGRAFFITI
GRAFFITO
SGRAFFITO
GRANULAR
GRANULARY
GREASIES
GREASIEST
GREENIES
GREENIEST
GRUESOME
GRUESOMER
GYMNASIA
GYMNASIAL
HACKINGS
WHACKINGS
HACKLING
SHACKLING
HADDOCKS
SHADDOCKS
HALLOWED
SHALLOWED
HAMBLING
SHAMBLING
HANDLERS
CHANDLERS
HANDSOME
HANDSOMER
HAPPIEST
CHAPPIEST
HARANGUE
HARANGUED
HARANGUER
HARDLINE
HARDLINER
HARMALIN
HARMALINE
HARMLESS
CHARMLESS
HARMONIC
HARMONICA
HAROSETH
CHAROSETH
HAROSETS
CHAROSETS
HARPINGS
SHARPINGS
HASTENED
CHASTENED
HASTENER
CHASTENER
HATCHERS
THATCHERS
HATCHING
THATCHING
HATTERED
CHATTERED
SHATTERED
HAUNTERS
CHAUNTERS
HAUNTING
CHAUNTING
HEADINGS
SHEADINGS
HEADLINE
HEADLINED
HEADLINER
HEALINGS
SHEALINGS
HEARINGS
SHEARINGS
HEARTIES
HEARTIEST
HEATHIER
SHEATHIER
HEATINGS
CHEATINGS
HEBETATE
HEBETATED
HEELINGS
WHEELINGS
HELLFIRE
SHELLFIRE
HEPATISE
HEPATISED
HEPATIZE
HEPATIZED
HERBARIA
HERBARIAN
HEREAWAY
THEREAWAY
HEREFROM
THEREFROM
WHEREFROM
HERENESS
THERENESS
WHERENESS
HEREUNTO
THEREUNTO
WHEREUNTO
HEREUPON
THEREUPON
WHEREUPON
HEREWITH
THEREWITH
WHEREWITH
HERRYING
CHERRYING
HESITATE
HESITATED
HIDLINGS
CHIDLINGS
HIERATIC
HIERATICA
HILLIEST
CHILLIEST
HINNYING
SHINNYING
WHINNYING
HIPPIEST
CHIPPIEST
WHIPPIEST
HIPPINGS
CHIPPINGS
SHIPPINGS
WHIPPINGS
HIPSTERS
WHIPSTERS
HIRLINGS
WHIRLINGS
HITHERED
WHITHERED
HOLESOME
WHOLESOME
HOLISTIC
WHOLISTIC
HONEYING
PHONEYING
HOOSHING
WHOOSHING
HOPPIEST
CHOPPIEST
SHOPPIEST
HOPPINGS
CHOPPINGS
SHOPPINGS
WHOPPINGS
HORNBILL
THORNBILL
HORNIEST
THORNIEST
HORNLESS
THORNLESS
HOROLOGE
HOROLOGER
HOROLOGY
CHOROLOGY
HOSPITAL
HOSPITALE
HOSTINGS
GHOSTINGS
HOUTINGS
SHOUTINGS
HOVELLED
SHOVELLED
HOVELLER
SHOVELLER
HUFFIEST
CHUFFIEST
HUMANISE
HUMANISED
HUMANIZE
HUMANIZED
HUMBLING
THUMBLING
HUNGERED
AHUNGERED
HUNKIEST
CHUNKIEST
HUNTINGS
SHUNTINGS
HUTZPAHS
CHUTZPAHS
HYDROZOA
HYDROZOAN
HYPODERM
HYPODERMA
HYPOGAEA
HYPOGAEAL
HYPOGAEAN
IDEALISE
IDEALISED
IDEALISER
IDEALIZE
IDEALIZED
IDEALIZER
IDEOGRAM
VIDEOGRAM
IFFINESS
MIFFINESS
ILLUMINE
ILLUMINED
ILLUMINER
IMITABLE
LIMITABLE
IMMINGLE
IMMINGLED
IMMODEST
IMMODESTY
IMMOLATE
IMMOLATED
IMMUNISE
IMMUNISED
IMMUNIZE
IMMUNIZED
IMPISHLY
WIMPISHLY
IMPLEDGE
IMPLEDGED
IMPLUNGE
IMPLUNGED
IMPOLITE
IMPOLITER
IMPRESSE
IMPRESSED
IMPURPLE
IMPURPLED
INCHOATE
INCHOATED
INCHPINS
LINCHPINS
INCORPSE
INCORPSED
INCREASE
INCREASED
INCREASER
INCUBATE
INCUBATED
INDAGATE
INDAGATED
INDICATE
VINDICATE
INDICATED
INDURATE
INDURATED
INFAMISE
INFAMISED
INFAMIZE
INFAMIZED
INFOLDED
PINFOLDED
INFRINGE
INFRINGED
INGROOVE
INGROOVED
INHEARSE
INHEARSED
INHUMATE
INHUMATED
INITIATE
INITIATED
INKINESS
PINKINESS
INKLINGS
TINKLINGS
INNATELY
PINNATELY
INNOVATE
INNOVATED
INSCONCE
INSCONCED
INSCRIBE
INSCRIBED
INSCRIBER
INSHRINE
INSHRINED
INSOLATE
INSOLATED
INSOMNIA
INSOMNIAC
INSPHERE
INSPHERED
INSTANCE
INSTANCED
INSULATE
INSULATED
INSWATHE
INSWATHED
INTERESS
INTERESSE
INTERVAL
INTERVALE
INTIMATE
INTIMATED
INTIMIST
INTIMISTE
INTITULE
INTITULED
INTONATE
INTONATED
INTRIGUE
INTRIGUED
INTRIGUER
INTUBATE
INTUBATED
INUNDATE
INUNDATED
INVEAGLE
INVEAGLED
INVEIGLE
INVEIGLED
INVEIGLER
INVERTIN
INVERTING
INVOLUTE
INVOLUTED
IONISING
LIONISING
IONIZING
LIONIZING
IREFULLY
DIREFULLY
IRENICON
EIRENICON
IRRIGATE
IRRIGATED
IRRITATE
IRRITATED
ITCHIEST
BITCHIEST
HITCHIEST
PITCHIEST
TITCHIEST
WITCHIEST

ITERATES
LITERATES
JACULATE
EJACULATE
JACULATED
JALOUSIE
JALOUSIED
JAMBOLAN
JAMBOLANA
JAUNDICE
JAUNDICED
JAUNTIES
JAUNTIEST
JEALOUSE
JEALOUSED
JELLABAS
DJELLABAS
JOINTURE
JOINTURED
JUBILATE
JUBILATED
JUGULATE
JUGULATED
JULIENNE
JULIENNED
JUMBOISE
JUMBOISED
JUMBOIZE
JUMBOIZED
KEFUFFLE
KEFUFFLED
KETCHING
SKETCHING
KEYSTONE
KEYSTONED
KHALIFAT
KHALIFATE
KHANSAMA
KHANSAMAH
KILLINGS
SKILLINGS
KIPPERED
SKIPPERED
KITTLING
SKITTLING
KLONDIKE
KLONDIKED
KLONDIKER
KLONDYKE
KLONDYKED
KLONDYKER
KREASOTE
KREASOTED
KREOSOTE
KREOSOTED
LABELLUM
FLABELLUM
LACERATE
LACERATED
LACKERED
FLACKERED
LADDERED
BLADDERED
LAGGINGS
FLAGGINGS
LAIRIEST
GLAIRIEST
LAMBASTE
LAMBASTED
LAMINATE
LAMINATED
LAMMINGS
SLAMMINGS
LANCHING
BLANCHING
FLANCHING
PLANCHING
LANDDROS
LANDDROST
LANGUAGE
LANGUAGED
LANKNESS
BLANKNESS
LAPIDATE
LAPIDATED
LAPPERED
CLAPPERED
LAPPINGS
CLAPPINGS
FLAPPINGS
LASHINGS
CLASHINGS
FLASHINGS
PLASHINGS
SLASHINGS
LASTINGS
BLASTINGS
LATCHING
CLATCHING
LATERITE
ELATERITE
LATHERED
BLATHERED
SLATHERED
LATITUDE
PLATITUDE
LAUGHTER
FLAUGHTER
SLAUGHTER
LAUNCHED
FLAUNCHED
LAUNCHES
FLAUNCHES
LAUREATE
LAUREATED
LAVATION
CLAVATION
LAVISHES
LAVISHEST
LAVISHLY
SLAVISHLY
LAYBACKS
PLAYBACKS
LAYTIMES
PLAYTIMES
LEACHING
BLEACHING
PLEACHING
LEADINGS
PLEADINGS
LEANINGS
CLEANINGS
GLEANINGS
LEANNESS
CLEANNESS
LEARIEST
BLEARIEST
LEASINGS
PLEASINGS
LEASURES
PLEASURES
LEAVINGS
CLEAVINGS
LECTIONS
ELECTIONS
FLECTIONS
LECTRESS
ELECTRESS
LEDGIEST
FLEDGIEST
LEECHING
FLEECHING
LEERINGS
FLEERINGS
LEGALISE
LEGALISED
LEGALIZE
LEGALIZED
LENDINGS
BLENDINGS
LETCHING
FLETCHING
LEVATORS
ELEVATORS
LEVERAGE
LEVERAGED
LEVIGATE
LEVIGATED
LEVITATE
LEVITATED
LIBERATE
LIBERATED
LICKINGS
CLICKINGS
SLICKINGS
LIGATURE
LIGATURED
LIGHTERS
BLIGHTERS
PLIGHTERS
LIGHTEST
SLIGHTEST
LIGHTFUL
PLIGHTFUL
LIGHTING
ALIGHTING
BLIGHTING
FLIGHTING
PLIGHTING
SLIGHTING
LIGHTISH
SLIGHTISH
LIMINESS
SLIMINESS
LINDWORM
BLINDWORM
LINGIEST
CLINGIEST
LINTIEST
FLINTIEST
LIPPIEST
SLIPPIEST
LIQUESCE
LIQUESCED
LISTENED
GLISTENED
LITERATI
LITERATIM
LITERATO
LITERATOR
LITIGATE
LITIGATED
LITTERED
CLITTERED
FLITTERED
GLITTERED
LOBULATE
LOBULATED
LOCALISE
LOCALISED
LOCALISER
LOCALIZE
LOCALIZED
LOCALIZER
LOCKAGES
BLOCKAGES
LOCOMOTE
LOCOMOTED
LOCUTION
ELOCUTION
LOCUTORY
ELOCUTORY
LODICULA
LODICULAE
LOGGINGS
FLOGGINGS
LOGICISE
LOGICISED
LOGICIZE
LOGICIZED
LONENESS
ALONENESS
LOOPHOLE
LOOPHOLED
LOOPIEST
GLOOPIEST
LORICATE
LORICATED
LOSSIEST
FLOSSIEST
GLOSSIEST
LOUNDERS
FLOUNDERS
LOURIEST
FLOURIEST
LOVELIES
LOVELIEST
LOWERIER
FLOWERIER
LOWERING
FLOWERING
GLOWERING
LUCKIEST
CLUCKIEST
PLUCKIEST
LUMBAGOS
PLUMBAGOS
LUMBERED
SLUMBERED
LUMBERER
SLUMBERER
LUMINOUS
ALUMINOUS
LUMMIEST
PLUMMIEST
SLUMMIEST
LUMMOXES
FLUMMOXES
LUMPIEST
CLUMPIEST
GLUMPIEST
SLUMPIEST
LUNULATE
LUNULATED
LUSHIEST
FLUSHIEST
PLUSHIEST
SLUSHIEST
LUSHNESS
FLUSHNESS
LUSTERED
BLUSTERED
CLUSTERED
FLUSTERED
LUSTRATE
FLUSTRATE
LUSTRATED
LUSTROUS
BLUSTROUS
MACARISE
MACARISED
MACARIZE
MACARIZED
MACARONI
MACARONIC
MACERATE
MACERATED
MACULATE
MACULATED
MADERISE
MADERISED
MADERIZE
MADERIZED
MADRASSA
MADRASSAH
MAGDALEN
MAGDALENE
MAGNESIA
MAGNESIAN
MAGNIFIC
MAGNIFICO
MAHARAJA
MAHARAJAH
MAINLINE
MAINLINED
MAINLINER
MALAXATE
MALAXATED
MALLEATE
MALLEATED
MAMILLAR
MAMILLARY
MAMMILLA
MAMMILLAE
MANDARIN
MANDARINE
MANDOLIN
MANDOLINE
MANICURE
MANICURED
MANIFEST
MANIFESTO
MANUBRIA
MANUBRIAL
MARGARIN
MARGARINE
MARINADE
MARINADED
MARINATE
MARINATED
MARSUPIA
MARSUPIAL
MASHINGS
SMASHINGS
MASSACRE
MASSACRED
MATACHIN
MATACHINA
MATACHINI
MATCHING
SMATCHING
MATTERED
SMATTERED
MATURATE
MATURATED
MAXIMISE
MAXIMISED
MAXIMIZE
MAXIMIZED
MAZEMENT
AMAZEMENT
MEDICATE
MEDICATED
MEDICINE
MEDICINED
MEDICINER
MEDITATE
MEDITATED
MEDULLAR
MEDULLARY
MELINITE
GMELINITE
MELODISE
MELODISED
MELODIZE
MELODIZED
MELTINGS
SMELTINGS
MEMORISE
MEMORISED
MEMORIZE
MEMORIZED
MENAGING
AMENAGING
MENSTRUA
MENSTRUAL
MEPHITIS
MEPHITISM
MERGENCE
EMERGENCE
MERSIONS
EMERSIONS
METALIZE
METALIZED
METHADON
METHADONE
MICATING
EMICATING
MICROCAR
MICROCARD
MICTIONS
EMICTIONS
MIDSHIPS
AMIDSHIPS
MIGRANTS
EMIGRANTS
MIGRATED
EMIGRATED
MIGRATES
EMIGRATES
MILITATE
MILITATED
MILLEPED
MILLEPEDE
MILLIPED
MILLIPEDE
MINIMISE
MINIMISED
MINIMIZE
MINIMIZED
MISCEGEN
MISCEGENE
MISGUIDE
MISGUIDED
MISGUIDER
MISJUDGE
MISJUDGED
MISLEEKE
MISLEEKED
MISMETRE
MISMETRED
MISPLACE
MISPLACED
MISPRISE
MISPRISED
MISPRIZE
MISPRIZED
MISQUOTE
MISQUOTED
MISROUTE
MISROUTED
MISSHAPE
MISSHAPED
MISSHAPEN
MISSIONS
EMISSIONS
OMISSIONS
MISSPOKE
MISSPOKEN
MISSTATE
MISSTATED
MISTITLE
MISTITLED
MITIGATE
MITIGATED
MOBILISE
MOBILISED
MOBILISER
MOBILIZE
MOBILIZED
MOBILIZER
MOCKINGS
SMOCKINGS
MODERATE
MODERATED
MODERATO
MODERATOR
MODULATE
MODULATED
MONETISE
MONETISED
MONETIZE
MONETIZED
MONOTONE
MONOTONED
MOOCHING
SMOOCHING
MORALISE
MORALISED
MORALISER

MORALISM
AMORALISM
MORALIST
AMORALIST
MORALIZE
MORALIZED
MORALIZER
MORNINGS
AMORNINGS
MOROSITY
AMOROSITY
MORTGAGE
MORTGAGED
MORTGAGEE
MORTGAGER
MORTISED
AMORTISED
MORTISES
AMORTISES
MOTHERED
SMOTHERED
MOTIONAL
EMOTIONAL
MOTIVATE
MOTIVATED
MOTORISE
MOTORISED
MOTORIZE
MOTORIZED
MOUCHING
SMOUCHING
MOULDERS
SMOULDERS
MOUNTING
AMOUNTING
MRIDANGA
MRIDANGAM
MULTIPED
MULTIPEDE
MURICATE
MURICATED
MUSCADIN
MUSCADINE
MUSETTES
AMUSETTES
MUSINGLY
AMUSINGLY
MUTILATE
MUTILATED
NAGGIEST
KNAGGIEST
SNAGGIEST
NAPPIEST
SNAPPIEST
NASALISE
NASALISED
NASALIZE
NASALIZED
NAUSEATE
NAUSEATED
NAVICULA
NAVICULAR
NAVIGATE
NAVIGATED
NEBBISHE
NEBBISHER
NEBULISE
NEBULISED
NEBULISER
NEBULIZE
NEBULIZED
NEBULIZER
NECKLACE
NECKLACED
NEGATIVE
NEGATIVED
NERVINES
NERVINESS
NEURISMS
ANEURISMS
NEVELLED
KNEVELLED
NICKERED
KNICKERED
SNICKERED
NICKNAME
NICKNAMED
NICOTIAN
NICOTIANA
NICOTINE
NICOTINED
NIFFIEST
SNIFFIEST
NIFTIEST
SNIFTIEST
NIGGERED
SNIGGERED
NIGGLERS
SNIGGLERS
NIGGLING
SNIGGLING
NIGROSIN
NIGROSINE
NIPPIEST
SNIPPIEST
NOBBIEST
KNOBBIEST
SNOBBIEST
NOBBLING
KNOBBLING
NODALISE
NODALISED
NODALIZE
NODALIZED
NOINTING
ANOINTING
NOMADISE
NOMADISED
NOMADIZE
NOMADIZED
NOMINATE
NOMINATED
NOSEDIVE
NOSEDIVED
NOTARISE
NOTARISED
NOTARIZE
NOTARIZED
NOVELISE
NOVELISED
NOVELISER
NOVELIZE
NOVELIZED
NOVELIZER
NUBBIEST
KNUBBIEST
SNUBBIEST
NUBBLIER
KNUBBLIER
NUBBLING
KNUBBLING
NUBECULA
NUBECULAE
NUCLEATE
ANUCLEATE
ENUCLEATE
NUCLEATED
NUISANCE
NUISANCER
NUMERATE
ENUMERATE
NUMERATED
NUMMULAR
NUMMULARY
NUZZLING
SNUZZLING
OBDURATE
OBDURATED
OBLIGATE
OBLIGATED
OBLIQUES
OBLIQUEST
OBSCURES
OBSCUREST
OBTURATE
OBTURATED
OBVOLUTE
OBVOLUTED
OCCUPATE
OCCUPATED
OCELLATE
LOCELLATE
OCELLATED
OCHERING
TOCHERING
OCULARLY
JOCULARLY
ODOGRAPH
HODOGRAPH
ODOMETER
HODOMETER
ODOMETRY
HODOMETRY
OENOLOGY
POENOLOGY
OENOPHIL
OENOPHILE
OENOPHILY
OFFERING
COFFERING
GOFFERING
OILERIES
BOILERIES
OILINESS
SOILINESS
OLDENING
BOLDENING
GOLDENING
OOGAMIES
ZOOGAMIES
OOGAMOUS
ZOOGAMOUS
OOGENIES
ZOOGENIES
OOLOGIES
NOOLOGIES
ZOOLOGIES
OOLOGIST
ZOOLOGIST
OOPHYTES
ZOOPHYTES
OOSPHERE
NOOSPHERE
OOSPORES
ZOOSPORES
OOZINESS
BOOZINESS
WOOZINESS
OPERCULA
OPERCULAR
OPPILATE
OPPILATED
OPTIMISE
OPTIMISED
OPTIMIZE
OPTIMIZED
ORALISMS
MORALISMS
ORDERERS
BORDERERS
ORDERING
BORDERING
ORDINATE
ORDINATED
ORECROWE
ORECROWED
ORGANISE
ORGANISED
ORGANISER
ORGANIZE
ORGANIZED
ORGANIZER
ORTHODOX
ORTHODOXY
ORTHOSES
PORTHOSES
ORTOLANS
PORTOLANS
OSCITATE
OSCITATED
OSCULATE
OSCULATED
OSIERIES
HOSIERIES
OTTERING
HOTTERING
POTTERING
TOTTERING
OUTBRAVE
OUTBRAVED
OUTBROKE
OUTBROKEN
OUTCASTE
OUTCASTED
OUTDANCE
OUTDANCED
OUTDOORS
OUTDOORSY
OUTDRIVE
OUTDRIVEN
OUTFLIES
GOUTFLIES
OUTGLARE
OUTGLARED
OUTPRICE
OUTPRICED
OUTPRIZE
OUTPRIZED
OUTSPOKE
OUTSPOKEN
OUTSTARE
OUTSTARED
OUTVALUE
OUTVALUED
OUTVOICE
OUTVOICED
OUTWEEDS
GOUTWEEDS
OVATIONS
NOVATIONS
OVERAGES
COVERAGES
OVERALLS
COVERALLS
OVERBLOW
OVERBLOWN
OVERCROW
OVERCROWD
OVERDOSE
OVERDOSED
OVERDRAW
OVERDRAWN
OVERFLOW
OVERFLOWN
OVERGIVE
OVERGIVEN
OVERGROW
OVERGROWN
OVERHALE
OVERHALED
OVERHEAR
OVERHEARD
OVERHYPE
OVERHYPED
OVERLADE
OVERLADED
OVERLADEN
OVERLIVE
OVERLIVED
OVERNAME
OVERNAMED
OVERRAKE
OVERRAKED
OVERRATE
OVERRATED
OVERRIDE
OVERRIDER
OVERRIPE
OVERRIPEN
OVERRULE
OVERRULED
OVERRULER
OVERSIZE
OVERSIZED
OVERSLIP
COVERSLIP
OVERTAKE
OVERTAKEN
OVERTIME
OVERTIMED
OVERTIMER
OVERTIRE
OVERTIRED
OVERTURE
COVERTURE
OVERTURED
PAGANISE
PAGANISED
PAGANIZE
PAGANIZED
PAGINATE
PAGINATED
PALESTRA
PALESTRAE
PALISADE
PALISADED
PALLIATE
PALLIATED
PALMIPED
PALMIPEDE
PANDEMIA
PANDEMIAN
PANNIKEL
PANNIKELL
PAPALISE
PAPALISED
PAPALIZE
PAPALIZED
PAPILLAR
PAPILLARY
PARABLES
SPARABLES
PARAFFIN
PARAFFINE
PARAFFINY
PARALYSE
PARALYSED
PARALYSER
PARALYZE
PARALYZED
PARALYZER
PARANOIA
PARANOIAC
PARKIEST
SPARKIEST
PAROCHIN
PAROCHINE
PAROEMIA
PAROEMIAC
PAROEMIAL
PASTICCI
PASTICCIO
PASTORAL
PASTORALE
PATHETIC
APATHETIC
PATRIATE
PATRIATED
PATTERED
SPATTERED
PEARLIES
PEARLIEST
PECULATE
SPECULATE
PECULATED
PEDICURE
PEDICURED
PEDIGREE
PEDIGREED
PEDIPALP
PEDIPALPI
PEJORATE
PEJORATED
PENALISE
PENALISED
PENALIZE
PENALIZED
PENDICLE
PENDICLER
PENTOSAN
PENTOSANE
PENUMBRA
PENUMBRAL
PERCEIVE
PERCEIVED
PERCEIVER
PERFECTO
PERFECTOR
PERIODIC
APERIODIC
PERMEATE
PERMEATED
PERORATE
PERORATED
PEROXIDE
PEROXIDED
PERSPIRE
PERSPIRED
PERSUADE
PERSUADED
PERSUADER
PERSWADE
PERSWADED
PERTNESS
APERTNESS
PERVERSE
PERVERSER
PERVIATE
PERVIATED
PETALOUS
APETALOUS
PETECHIA
PETECHIAE
PETECHIAL
PHALANGE
PHALANGER
PHANGING
UPHANGING
PHANTASM
PHANTASMA
PHOTOGEN
PHOTOGENE
PHOTOGENY
PIARISTS
APIARISTS
PIGHTING
SPIGHTING
PIKELETS
SPIKELETS
PILLAGES
SPILLAGES
PILLINGS
SPILLINGS
PINAFORE
PINAFORED
PINIONED
OPINIONED
PINNACLE
PINNACLED
PINNINGS
SPINNINGS
PINNIPED
PINNIPEDE
PIRLICUE
PIRLICUED
PISTOLET
EPISTOLET
PITTINGS
SPITTINGS
PLACEMEN

PLACEMENT
PLACENTA
PLACENTAE
PLACENTAL
PLASHIER
SPLASHIER
PLASHING
SPLASHING
PLATTERS
SPLATTERS
PLATTING
SPLATTING
PLEADING
UPLEADING
PLEASURE
PLEASURED
PLEASURER
PLEONAST
PLEONASTE
PLIGHTED
UPLIGHTED
PLIGHTER
UPLIGHTER
PLINKING
UPLINKING
POLARISE
POLARISED
POLARISER
POLARIZE
POLARIZED
POLARIZER
POLEMISE
POLEMISED
POLEMIZE
POLEMIZED
POLONISE
POLONISED
POLONIZE
POLONIZED
POLYARCH
POLYARCHY
POLYPHON
POLYPHONE
POLYPHONY
PONGIEST
SPONGIEST
PONTIFIC
PONTIFICE
PONTOONS
SPONTOONS
POPULATE
POPULATED
PORPOISE
PORPOISED
PORTABLE
SPORTABLE
PORTANCE
SPORTANCE
PORTIEST
SPORTIEST
PORTOLAN
PORTOLANI
PORTOLANO
POSTCAVA
POSTCAVAE
POSTCODE
POSTCODED
POSTDATE
POSTDATED
POSTPONE
POSTPONED
POSTPONER
POSTPOSE
POSTPOSED
POTTIEST
SPOTTIEST
POULTICE
POULTICED
POURTRAY
POURTRAYD
POUTIEST
SPOUTIEST
POUTINGS
SPOUTINGS
PRACTICE
PRACTICED
PRACTISE
PRACTISED
PRACTISER
PRAECAVA
PRAECAVAE
PRAISING
UPRAISING
PRATTLED
SPRATTLED
PRATTLES
SPRATTLES
PREAMBLE
PREAMBLED
PRECISES
PRECISEST
PRECLUDE
PRECLUDED
PREJUDGE
PREJUDGED
PRELATES
PRELATESS
PREMIERE
PREMIERED
PRENTICE
PRENTICED
PREPENSE
PREPENSED
PREPPIES
PREPPIEST
PRESBYTE
PRESBYTER
PRESERVE
PRESERVED
PRESERVER
PRESIDIA
PRESIDIAL
PRESSURE
PRESSURED
PRETERIT
PRETERITE
PRETTIES
PRETTIEST
PRIGGING
SPRIGGING
PRIMROSE
PRIMROSED
PRINCESS
PRINCESSE
PRINTERS
SPRINTERS
PRINTING
SPRINTING
PRIORITY
APRIORITY
PROCURES
PROCURESS
PRODNOSE
PRODNOSED
PRODROMI
PRODROMIC
PROGRADE
PROGRADED
PROLAMIN
PROLAMINE
PROLAPSE
PROLAPSED
PROLLING
UPROLLING
PROLOGUE
PROLOGUED
PROLONGE
PROLONGED
PROLONGER
PROMULGE
PROMULGED
PROROGUE
PROROGUED
PROTOZOA
PROTOZOAL
PROTOZOAN
PROTRUDE
PROTRUDED
PROVEDOR
PROVEDORE
PTERYGIA
PTERYGIAL
PTYALISE
PTYALISED
PTYALIZE
PTYALIZED
PUDDINGS
SPUDDINGS
PULVILLE
PULVILLED
PULVILLI
PULVILLIO
PUMICATE
PUMICATED
PUNCTATE
PUNCTATED
PUNCTURE
PUNCTURED
PUNCTURER
PUPILLAR
PUPILLARY
PURCHASE
PURCHASED
PURCHASER
PURLICUE
PURLICUED
PURLINGS
SPURLINGS
PURRINGS
SPURRINGS
PUTTERED
SPUTTERED
PYREXIAS
APYREXIAS
PYRITISE
PYRITISED
PYRITIZE
PYRITIZED
PYROLYSE
PYROLYSED
PYROLYZE
PYROLYZED
QUADRATE
QUADRATED
QUADRIGA
QUADRIGAE
QUAGMIRE
QUAGMIRED
QUAILING
SQUAILING
QUANTISE
QUANTISED
QUANTIZE
QUANTIZED
QUARTETT
QUARTETTE
QUARTETTI
QUARTETTO
QUASHING
SQUASHING
QUEENIES
QUEENIEST
QUELCHED
SQUELCHED
QUELCHES
SQUELCHES
QUINCHES
SQUINCHES
QUINTETT
QUINTETTE
QUINTETTI
QUINTETTO
QUIPPING
EQUIPPING
QUIRTING
SQUIRTING
QUITCHES
SQUITCHES
RABBLERS
DRABBLERS
GRABBLERS
RABBLING
BRABBLING
DRABBLING
GRABBLING
RACEMISE
RACEMISED
RACEMIZE
RACEMIZED
RACHISES
ARACHISES
RACHITIS
TRACHITIS
RACKETED
BRACKETED
RACKINGS
FRACKINGS
TRACKINGS
RADIATED
ERADIATED
RADIATES
ERADIATES
RADICATE
ERADICATE
RADICATED
RAFTSMAN
CRAFTSMAN
DRAFTSMAN
RAFTSMEN
CRAFTSMEN
DRAFTSMEN
RAGGIEST
CRAGGIEST
DRAGGIEST
RAGGLING
DRAGGLING
RAGMENTS
FRAGMENTS
RAINBAND
TRAINBAND
RAINIEST
BRAINIEST
GRAINIEST
RAINLESS
BRAINLESS
TRAINLESS
RAISINGS
PRAISINGS
RAMBLING
BRAMBLING
RAMPAUGE
RAMPAUGED
RAMPINGS
TRAMPINGS
RANCHERS
BRANCHERS
RANCHING
BRANCHING
CRANCHING
RANKINGS
PRANKINGS
RANKLING
CRANKLING
PRANKLING
RANKNESS
CRANKNESS
FRANKNESS
RAPESEED
GRAPESEED
RAPPINGS
TRAPPINGS
WRAPPINGS
RATCHETS
BRATCHETS
RATCHING
FRATCHING
RATIFIED
GRATIFIED
RATIFIER
GRATIFIER
RATIFIES
GRATIFIES
RATIONAL
RATIONALE
RATLINGS
BRATLINGS
RATTIEST
BRATTIEST
RATTLERS
PRATTLERS
RATTLING
BRATTLING
PRATTLING
RAUNCHED
BRAUNCHED
CRAUNCHED
GRAUNCHED
RAUNCHES
BRAUNCHES
CRAUNCHES
GRAUNCHES
RAVELLED
GRAVELLED
TRAVELLED
RAVENING
CRAVENING
RAVISHED
YRAVISHED
REACHERS
PREACHERS
TREACHERS
REACHING
AREACHING
BREACHING
PREACHING
READINGS
TREADINGS
READVISE
READVISED
REAEDIFY
REAEDIFYE
REAMIEST
CREAMIEST
DREAMIEST
REAROUSE
REAROUSED
REASSUME
REASSUMED
REASSURE
REASSURED
REASSURER
REASTING
BREASTING
RECEDING
PRECEDING
RECENTRE
RECENTRED
RECEPTOR
PRECEPTOR
RECESSED
PRECESSED
RECESSES
PRECESSES
RECHARGE
RECHARGED
RECISION
PRECISION
RECKLING
FRECKLING
RECLOTHE
RECLOTHED
RECOURSE
RECOURSED
RECREATE
RECREATED
RECTIONS
ERECTIONS
REDARGUE
REDARGUED
REDATING
PREDATING
REDDLING
TREDDLING
REDEFINE
PREDEFINE
REDEFINED
REDESIGN
PREDESIGN
REDIVIDE
REDIVIDED
REDOUBLE
REDOUBLED
REECHING
BREECHING
REEDIEST
GREEDIEST
REEDINGS
BREEDINGS
REEKIEST
CREEKIEST
REFACING
PREFACING
REFERRED
PREFERRED
REFIGURE
PREFIGURE
REFIGURED
REFORMED
PREFORMED
REFRINGE
REFRINGED
REGELATE
REGELATED
REGULATE
REGULATED
REGULISE
REGULISED
REGULIZE
REGULIZED
REHANDLE
REHANDLED
REHEARSE
REHEARSED
REHEARSER
REHEATED
PREHEATED
REILLUME
REILLUMED
REIMPOSE
REIMPOSED
REINFUSE
REINFUSED
REINSURE
REINSURED
REINSURER
REJUDGED
PREJUDGED
REJUDGES
PREJUDGES
REKINDLE
REKINDLED
RELATION
PRELATION
RELEGATE
RELEGATED
RELOCATE
RELOCATED
RELUMINE
RELUMINED
REMARQUE
REMARQUED
REMASTER
CREMASTER
REMBLING
TREMBLING
REMEDIAT
REMEDIATE
REMIGATE
REMIGATED
REMISING

PREMISING
REMIXING
PREMIXING
REMOTION
PREMOTION
REMOVING
PREMOVING
RENEGADE
RENEGADED
RENFORCE
RENFORCED
RENOUNCE
RENOUNCED
RENOUNCER
RENOVATE
RENOVATED
RENVERSE
RENVERSED
REOCCUPY
PREOCCUPY
REORDAIN
PREORDAIN
REORDERS
PREORDERS
REPACKED
PREPACKED
REPARTEE
REPARTEED
REPAYING
PREPAYING
REPEOPLE
REPEOPLED
REPERUSE
REPERUSED
REPHRASE
REPHRASED
REPONING
PREPONING
REPOSING
PREPOSING
REPREEVE
REPREEVED
REPRIEVE
REPRIEVED
REQUOYLE
REQUOYLED
REREVISE
REREVISED
RESALUTE
RESALUTED
RESCINDS
PRESCINDS
RESCRIPT
PRESCRIPT
RESELECT
PRESELECT
RESEMBLE
RESEMBLED
RESEMBLER
RESENTED
PRESENTED
RESENTER
PRESENTER
RESERVED
PRESERVED
RESERVES
PRESERVES
RESETTLE
RESETTLED
RESIDENT
PRESIDENT
RESIDING
PRESIDING
RESINISE
RESINISED
RESINIZE
RESINIZED
RESONATE
RESONATED
RESOURCE
RESOURCED
RESPONSE
RESPONSER
RESTLESS
CRESTLESS
RESTRING
RESTRINGE
RESUMING
PRESUMING
RETINOID
CRETINOID
RETINULA
RETINULAE
RETINULAR
RETRIEVE
RETRIEVED
RETRIEVER
REVETTED
BREVETTED
REVIEWED
PREVIEWED
REVISING
PREVISING
REVISION
PREVISION
RHYTHMIC
ARHYTHMIC
RIBWORKS
CRIBWORKS
RICERCAR
RICERCARE
RICHTING
FRICHTING
RICKYARD
BRICKYARD
RIDGINGS
BRIDGINGS
RIDICULE
RIDICULED
RIDICULER
RIFTIEST
DRIFTIEST
RIFTLESS
DRIFTLESS
RIGGINGS
FRIGGINGS
PRIGGINGS
RIGHTENS
BRIGHTENS
FRIGHTENS
RIGHTEST
BRIGHTEST
RIGHTFUL
FRIGHTFUL
RIGHTING
FRIGHTING
RIGIDEST
FRIGIDEST
RIGIDISE
RIGIDISED
RIGIDITY
FRIGIDITY
RIGIDIZE
RIGIDIZED
RIMMINGS
TRIMMINGS
RINGINGS
BRINGINGS
CRINGINGS
WRINGINGS
RINGSIDE
RINGSIDER
RIPPLERS
TRIPPLERS
RIPPLING
CRIPPLING
TRIPPLING
RISKIEST
FRISKIEST
RITORNEL
RITORNELL
RIVALISE
RIVALISED
RIVALIZE
RIVALIZED
RIVELLED
DRIVELLED
ROACHING
BROACHING
ROADSIDE
BROADSIDE
ROADWAYS
BROADWAYS
ROBOTISE
ROBOTISED
ROBOTIZE
ROBOTIZED
ROCKINGS
FROCKINGS
ROLLINGS
DROLLINGS
TROLLINGS
ROOFINGS
PROOFINGS
ROOFLESS
PROOFLESS
ROOMIEST
BROOMIEST
ROOPIEST
DROOPIEST
ROQUETED
CROQUETED
ROQUETTE
CROQUETTE
ROSINESS
PROSINESS
ROSTRATE
EROSTRATE
PROSTRATE
ROSTRATED
ROTAVATE
ROTAVATED
ROTOVATE
ROTOVATED
ROUNDERS
GROUNDERS
ROUNDING
GROUNDING
ROUPIEST
CROUPIEST
ROUTHIER
DROUTHIER
ROUTINGS
GROUTINGS
TROUTINGS
ROWELLED
TROWELLED
ROYALISE
ROYALISED
ROYALIZE
ROYALIZED
RUBBINGS
DRUBBINGS
RUCKLING
TRUCKLING
RUDDIEST
CRUDDIEST
RUDDLING
CRUDDLING
RUDENESS
CRUDENESS
RUDERIES
PRUDERIES
RUFFLING
TRUFFLING
RUGGIEST
DRUGGIEST
RUMBLERS
GRUMBLERS
RUMBLIER
CRUMBLIER
GRUMBLIER
RUMBLING
CRUMBLING
DRUMBLING
GRUMBLING
RUMINATE
RUMINATED
RUMMIEST
CRUMMIEST
RUMPLING
CRUMPLING
FRUMPLING
RUNKLING
CRUNKLING
RUNNIONS
TRUNNIONS
RURALISE
RURALISED
RURALIZE
RURALIZED
RUSHIEST
BRUSHIEST
RUSTIEST
CRUSTIEST
TRUSTIEST
RUSTLESS
CRUSTLESS
TRUSTLESS
RUTHLESS
TRUTHLESS
SABELLAS
ISABELLAS
SABOTAGE
SABOTAGED
SAFRANIN
SAFRANINE
SAGINATE
SAGINATED
SALIVATE
SALIVATED
SANDARAC
SANDARACH
SANGUINE
SANGUINED
SANITATE
SANITATED
SANITISE
SANITISED
SANITIZE
SANITIZED
SANNYASI
SANNYASIN
SAPPHIRE
SAPPHIRED
SARABAND
SARABANDE
SATIRISE
SATIRISED
SATIRIZE
SATIRIZED
SATURATE
SATURATED
SCALADES
ESCALADES
SCALLOPS
ESCALLOPS
SCANTIES
SCANTIEST
SCARPING
ESCARPING
SCAVENGE
SCAVENGED
SCAVENGER
SCELERAT
SCELERATE
SCENDING
ASCENDING
SCHEDULE
SCHEDULED
SCHEDULER
SCHMALTZ
SCHMALTZY
SCHMOOZE
SCHMOOZED
SCHNECKE
SCHNECKEN
SCIATICA
SCIATICAL
SCLEREID
SCLEREIDE
SCLEROSE
SCLEROSED
SCRABBLE
SCRABBLED
SCRABBLER
SCRAMBLE
SCRAMBLED
SCRAMBLER
SCRATTLE
SCRATTLED
SCRIBBLE
SCRIBBLED
SCRIBBLER
SCRIBING
ASCRIBING
ESCRIBING
SCRIGGLE
SCRIGGLED
SCROGGIE
SCROGGIER
SCROUNGE
SCROUNGED
SCROUNGER
SCROWDGE
SCROWDGED
SCURVIES
SCURVIEST
SCUTELLA
SCUTELLAR
SECRETIN
SECRETING
SELVEDGE
SELVEDGED
SEMINATE
SEMINATED
SEMUNCIA
SEMUNCIAE
SEMUNCIAL
SENSIBLE
SENSIBLER
SENSORIA
SENSORIAL
SENTENCE
SENTENCED
SENTENCER
SEPALOUS
ASEPALOUS
SEPARATE
SEPARATED
SEPTARIA
SEPTARIAN
SEPTUPLE
SEPTUPLED
SEPTUPLET
SEQUENCE
SEQUENCED
SEQUENCER
SERAPHIN
SERAPHINE
SERENADE
SERENADED
SERENADER
SEROTYPE
SEROTYPED
SEXTUPLE
SEXTUPLED
SEXTUPLET
SEXUALLY
ASEXUALLY
SHAMIANA
SHAMIANAH
SHAUCHLE
SHAUCHLED
SHECHITA
SHECHITAH
SHEENIES
SHEENIEST
SHENDING
YSHENDING
SHODDIES
SHODDIEST
SHOWCASE
SHOWCASED
SIBILATE
SIBILATED
SICKLIES
SICKLIEST
SIDELINE
SIDELINED
SIDERATE
SIDERATED
SIGHTSEE
SIGHTSEEN
SIGHTSEER
SIGNORIA
SIGNORIAL
SILICATE
SILICATED
SIMILISE
SIMILISED
SIMILIZE
SIMILIZED
SIMPLIST
SIMPLISTE
SIMULATE
SIMULATED
SINICISE
SINICISED
SINICIZE
SINICIZED
SIRENISE
SIRENISED
SIRENIZE
SIRENIZED
SKELLIES
SKELLIEST
SKILLIES
SKILLIEST
SLANDERS
ISLANDERS
SLIVOVIC
SLIVOVICA
SLUGHORN
SLUGHORNE
SMOULDER
ASMOULDER
SNEESHIN
SNEESHING
SNOTTIES
SNOTTIEST
SNOWSHOE
SNOWSHOED
SOBERISE
SOBERISED
SOBERIZE
SOBERIZED
SODOMISE
SODOMISED
SODOMIZE
SODOMIZED
SOLARISE
SOLARISED
SOLARIZE
SOLARIZED
SOLATION
ISOLATION
SOLECISE
SOLECISED
SOLECIZE
SOLECIZED
SOLFEGGI
SOLFEGGIO
SOLIDATE
SOLIDATED
SOMNIATE
SOMNIATED
SORORISE
SORORISED
SORORIZE

SORORIZED
SOUVLAKI
SOUVLAKIA
SPARKIES
SPARKIEST
SPARKLES
SPARKLESS
SPATLESE
SPATLESEN
SPECIATE
SPECIATED
SPECKLES
SPECKLESS
SPECTATE
SPECTATED
SPELDRIN
SPELDRING
SPERSING
ASPERSING
SPIRANTS
ASPIRANTS
SPIRATED
ASPIRATED
SPIRILLA
SPIRILLAR
SPLENIUM
ASPLENIUM
SPOLIATE
SPOLIATED
SPOONIES
SPOONIEST
SPORIDIA
SPORIDIAL
SPORTING
ASPORTING
SPOUSALS
ESPOUSALS
SPOUSING
ESPOUSING
SPRACKLE
SPRACKLED
SPRANGLE
SPRANGLED
SPRATTLE
SPRATTLED
SPREATHE
SPREATHED
SPREETHE
SPREETHED
SPRINGAL
SPRINGALD
SPRINKLE
SPRINKLED
SPRINKLER
SPUILZIE
SPUILZIED
SPUNKIES
SPUNKIEST
SPURRIES
SPURRIEST
SQUABBLE
SQUABBLED
SQUABBLER
SQUADRON
SQUADRONE
SQUATTLE
SQUATTLED
SQUEEGEE
SQUEEGEED
SQUIGGLE

SQUIGGLED
SQUILGEE
SQUILGEED
SQUIRESS
ESQUIRESS
STABLISH
ESTABLISH
STAGNATE
STAGNATED
STAMPEDE
STAMPEDED
STANCHES
STANCHEST
STARTING
ASTARTING
STEADIES
STEADIEST
STEAMIES
STEAMIEST
STEEMING
ESTEEMING
STELLATE
STELLATED
STEROIDS
ASTEROIDS
STICKIES
STICKIEST
STIPULAR
STIPULARY
STOCKADE
STOCKADED
STONYING
ASTONYING
STOPPAGE
ESTOPPAGE
STOPPING
ESTOPPING
STOUNDED
ASTOUNDED
STRADDLE
ASTRADDLE
STRADDLED
STRAGGLE
STRAGGLED
STRAGGLER
STRANGER
ESTRANGER
STRANGLE
STRANGLED
STRANGLER
STRAYING
ESTRAYING
STREIGNE
STREIGNED
STRELITZ
STRELITZI
STRICHES
ESTRICHES
OSTRICHES
STRICKLE
STRICKLED
STRIDDLE
STRIDDLED
STRINGED
ASTRINGED
STRINGER
ASTRINGER
STRINKLE
STRINKLED
STROBILA

STROBILAE
STRODDLE
STRODDLED
STRONGYL
STRONGYLE
STRONTIA
STRONTIAN
STRUGGLE
STRUGGLED
STRUGGLER
STUBBIES
STUBBIEST
STUMPIES
STUMPIEST
STUNNING
ASTUNNING
STUPRATE
STUPRATED
STURDIES
STURDIEST
SUBCOSTA
SUBCOSTAE
SUBCOSTAL
SUBERISE
SUBERISED
SUBERIZE
SUBERIZED
SUBITISE
SUBITISED
SUBITIZE
SUBITIZED
SUBLEASE
SUBLEASED
SUBLIMES
SUBLIMEST
SUBLUNAR
SUBLUNARY
SUBMERGE
SUBMERGED
SUBMERSE
SUBMERSED
SUBSERVE
SUBSERVED
SUBTITLE
SUBTITLED
SUBTOPIA
SUBTOPIAN
SUBTRUDE
SUBTRUDED
SUBVERSE
SUBVERSED
SUDAMINA
SUDAMINAL
SUFFLATE
SUFFLATED
SULPHATE
SULPHATED
SUNBATHE
SUNBATHED
SUNBATHER
SUPERATE
SUPERATED
SUPINATE
SUPINATED
SUPREMES
SUPREMEST
SURCEASE
SURCEASED
SURPLICE
SURPLICED

SURPRISE
SURPRISED
SURPRISER
SUSPENSE
SUSPENSER
SWANKIES
SWANKIEST
SYLLABLE
SYLLABLED
SYMMETRY
ASYMMETRY
SYMPODIA
SYMPODIAL
SYMPOSIA
SYMPOSIAC
SYMPOSIAL
SYNCYTIA
SYNCYTIAL
SYNDETIC
ASYNDETIC
SYNEDRIA
SYNEDRIAL
SYNOPSIS
SYNOPSISE
SYPHILIS
SYPHILISE
SYSTOLES
ASYSTOLES
TABLINGS
STABLINGS
TABOURIN
TABOURING
TABULATE
TABULATED
TACKINGS
STACKINGS
TAILGATE
TAILGATED
TAILGATER
TAILPIPE
TAILPIPED
TALKIEST
STALKIEST
TALKINGS
STALKINGS
TALLAGES
STALLAGES
TALLIATE
TALLIATED
TAMPINGS
STAMPINGS
TANNATES
STANNATES
TARANTAS
TARANTASS
TARRIEST
STARRIEST
TARRINGS
STARRINGS
TARTINES
TARTINESS
TAWDRIES
TAWDRIEST
TEAMINGS
STEAMINGS
TEGMENTA
TEGMENTAL
TELESTIC
TELESTICH
TELEVISE

TELEVISED
TELEVISER
TENTACLE
TENTACLED
TENTORIA
TENTORIAL
TESSELLA
TESSELLAE
TESSELLAR
TETANISE
TETANISED
TETANIZE
TETANIZED
THEISTIC
ATHEISTIC
THEMATIC
ATHEMATIC
THEOLOGY
ATHEOLOGY
THEORISE
THEORISED
THEORISER
THEORIZE
THEORIZED
THEORIZER
THEREFOR
THEREFORE
THERIACA
THERIACAL
THINGIES
THINGIEST
THIOPHEN
THIOPHENE
THRAPPLE
THRAPPLED
THROPPLE
THROPPLED
THROTTLE
THROTTLED
THROTTLER
THYROXIN
THYROXINE
TICKINGS
STICKINGS
TICKLERS
STICKLERS
TICKLING
STICKLING
TIDDLIES
TIDDLIEST
TIDIVATE
TIDIVATED
TILLAGES
STILLAGES
TILLIEST
STILLIEST
TILLINGS
STILLINGS
TILTINGS
STILTINGS
TINCTURE
TINCTURED
TINPLATE
TINPLATED
TINTIEST
STINTIEST
TINTINGS
STINTINGS
TINTLESS
STINTLESS

TIPPLERS
STIPPLERS
TIPPLING
STIPPLING
TITIVATE
TITIVATED
TITUBATE
TITUBATED
TOCCATAS
STOCCATAS
TOLERATE
TOLERATED
TONALITY
ATONALITY
TONELESS
STONELESS
TONICITY
ATONICITY
TOPPINGS
STOPPINGS
TOPPLING
STOPPLING
TORCHIER
TORCHIERE
TORQUATE
TORQUATED
TOTALISE
TOTALISED
TOTALISER
TOTALIZE
TOTALIZED
TOTALIZER
TRABEATE
TRABEATED
TRACHEID
TRACHEIDE
TRAIKING
STRAIKING
TRAINERS
STRAINERS
TRAINING
STRAINING
TRAMLINE
TRAMLINED
TRAMMELS
STRAMMELS
TRAMPING
STRAMPING
TRANGLES
STRANGLES
TRANSUDE
TRANSUDED
TRANSUME
TRANSUMED
TRAPEZIA
TRAPEZIAL
TRAPPERS
STRAPPERS
TRAPPIER
STRAPPIER
TRAPPING
STRAPPING
TRAUCHLE
TRAUCHLED
TRAVERSE
TRAVERSED
TRAVERSER
TREASURE
TREASURED
TREASURER

TRENDIES
TRENDIEST
TREPHINE
TREPHINED
TREPHINER
TRESSING
STRESSING
TRESSURE
TRESSURED
TRIANGLE
TRIANGLED
TRICHINA
TRICHINAE
TRICKLED
STRICKLED
TRICKLES
STRICKLES
TRICKLESS
TRICYCLE
TRICYCLED
TRICYCLER
TRIGGING
STRIGGING
TRIPIEST
STRIPIEST
TRIPLING
STRIPLING
TRIPLOID
TRIPLOIDY
TRIPPERS
STRIPPERS
TRIPPING
STRIPPING
TRITIATE
TRITIATED
TRITICAL
TRITICALE
TRIUMVIR
TRIUMVIRI
TRIUMVIRY
TRIVALVE
TRIVALVED
TROCHLEA
TROCHLEAR
TROLLERS
STROLLERS
TROLLING
STROLLING
TROPHIED
ATROPHIED
TROPHIES
ATROPHIES
TROPISMS
ATROPISMS
TROSSERS
STROSSERS
TROUTING
STROUTING
TRUMPETS
STRUMPETS
TRUNCATE
TRUNCATED
TRUSTIES
TRUSTIEST
TUBBIEST
STUBBIEST
TUBERCLE
TUBERCLED
TUBULATE
TUBULATED

TUMBLERS
STUMBLERS
TUMBLING
STUMBLING
TUMPIEST
STUMPIEST
TUNICATE
TUNICATED
TUNNINGS
STUNNINGS
TUTORISE
TUTORISED
TUTORIZE
TUTORIZED
TYRANNES
TYRANNESS
TYRANNIS
TYRANNISE
UBERTIES
PUBERTIES
UBIETIES
DUBIETIES
ULCERATE
ULCERATED
UMBERING
CUMBERING
LUMBERING
NUMBERING
UNBATHED
SUNBATHED
UNBEATEN
SUNBEATEN
UNBLINDS
SUNBLINDS
UNBLOCKS
SUNBLOCKS
UNBRIDLE
UNBRIDLED
UNBUCKLE
UNBUCKLED
UNBUNDLE
UNBUNDLED
UNBURNED
SUNBURNED
UNCHARGE
UNCHARGED
UNCINATE
RUNCINATE
UNCINATED
UNCLOTHE
UNCLOTHED
UNCOUPLE
UNCOUPLED
UNCREATE
UNCREATED
UNCTIONS
FUNCTIONS
JUNCTIONS
UNDAZZLE
UNDAZZLED

UNDERBIT
UNDERBITE
UNDERSAY
UNDERSAYE
UNDERSEA
UNDERSEAL
UNDERUSE
UNDERUSED
UNDOUBLE
UNDOUBLED
UNDULATE
UNDULATED
UNFOUGHT
GUNFOUGHT
UNGENTLY
PUNGENTLY
UNHEARSE
UNHEARSED
UNHOUSES
GUNHOUSES
UNIFYING
MUNIFYING
UNIONISE
UNIONISED
UNIONIZE
UNIONIZED
UNITIONS
MUNITIONS
PUNITIONS
UNMANTLE
UNMANTLED
UNMUFFLE
UNMUFFLED
UNMUZZLE
UNMUZZLED
UNPEOPLE
UNPEOPLED
UNPRAISE
UNPRAISED
UNRIDDLE
UNRIDDLED
UNRIDDLER
UNRUFFLE
UNRUFFLED
UNSADDLE
UNSADDLED
UNSETTLE
UNSETTLED
UNSLUICE
UNSLUICED
UNSPHERE
UNSPHERED
UNSTABLE
UNSTABLER
UNSTICKS
GUNSTICKS
UNSTOCKS
GUNSTOCKS
UNSTRUCK
SUNSTRUCK

UNSWATHE
UNSWATHED
UNTACKLE
UNTACKLED
UNTANGLE
UNTANGLED
UNTANNED
SUNTANNED
UNTHRONE
UNTHRONED
UNTIDIES
UNTIDIEST
URBANISE
URBANISED
URBANIZE
URBANIZED
UREDINIA
UREDINIAL
URGENTLY
TURGENTLY
UROPYGIA
UROPYGIAL
UROSCOPY
OUROSCOPY
URTICATE
URTICATED
USEFULLY
MUSEFULLY
USHERING
HUSHERING
UTTERERS
MUTTERERS
UTTERING
BUTTERING
GUTTERING
MUTTERING
PUTTERING
VACCINIA
VACCINIAL
VACUATED
EVACUATED
VACUATES
EVACUATES
VAGINATE
EVAGINATE
VAGINATED
VAGINULA
VAGINULAE
VALIDATE
VALIDATED
VALORISE
VALORISED
VALORIZE
VALORIZED
VALUATED
EVALUATED
VALUATES
EVALUATES
VAMBRACE
VAMBRACED

VANISHED
EVANISHED
VANISHES
EVANISHES
VAPORISE
VAPORISED
VAPORISER
VAPORIZE
VAPORIZED
VAPORIZER
VAPULATE
VAPULATED
VARIOLES
OVARIOLES
VASCULAR
AVASCULAR
VAUNTING
AVAUNTING
VEGETATE
VEGETATED
VELARISE
VELARISED
VELARIZE
VELARIZED
VENERATE
VENERATED
VENGEFUL
AVENGEFUL
VENTAILE
AVENTAILE
VENTAILS
AVENTAILS
VENTINGS
EVENTINGS
VENTRING
AVENTRING
VENTURES
AVENTURES
VERATRIN
VERATRINE
VERJUICE
VERJUICED
VERSIONS
AVERSIONS
EVERSIONS
VERTEBRA
VERTEBRAE
VERTEBRAL
VESICATE
VESICATED
VESICULA
VESICULAE
VESICULAR
VESTIGIA
VESTIGIAL
VIBRISSA
VIBRISSAE
VIDEOTEX
VIDEOTEXT
VIGILANT

VIGILANTE
VIGNETTE
VIGNETTED
VIGNETTER
VINCIBLE
EVINCIBLE
VIRTUOSI
VIRTUOSIC
VISAGIST
VISAGISTE
VITALISE
VITALISED
VITALISER
VITALIZE
VITALIZED
VITALIZER
VITELLIN
VITELLINE
VOCALISE
VOCALISED
VOCALISER
VOCALIZE
VOCALIZED
VOCALIZER
VOCATION
AVOCATION
EVOCATION
VOCATIVE
EVOCATIVE
VOIDABLE
AVOIDABLE
VOIDANCE
AVOIDANCE
VOLITATE
VOLITATED
VOLPLANE
VOLPLANED
VOLUTION
EVOLUTION
VOUCHING
AVOUCHING
VOUTSAFE
VOUTSAFED
VOWELISE
VOWELISED
VOWELIZE
VOWELIZED
VULGATES
EVULGATES
VULSELLA
VULSELLAE
WADDLERS
SWADDLERS
TWADDLERS
WADDLING
SWADDLING
TWADDLING
WAKENING
AWAKENING
WALLOWED

SWALLOWED
WALLOWER
SWALLOWER
WANGLING
TWANGLING
WANKIEST
SWANKIEST
WARDROBE
WARDROBER
WARFARIN
WARFARING
WARMINGS
SWARMINGS
WASHIEST
SWASHIEST
WASHINGS
SWASHINGS
WATTLING
TWATTLING
WEARINGS
SWEARINGS
WEEDIEST
TWEEDIEST
WEEPIEST
SWEEPIEST
WEEPINGS
SWEEPINGS
WELLINGS
DWELLINGS
SWELLINGS
WELTERED
SWELTERED
WHEELIES
WHEELIEST
WHEREFOR
WHEREFORE
WHIMSIES
WHIMSIEST
WHINNIES
WHINNIEST
WIDDLING
TWIDDLING
WIGHTING
TWIGHTING
WINDBLOW
WINDBLOWN
WINERIES
SWINERIES
WINGEING
SWINGEING
WINGIEST
SWINGIEST
WINKLERS
TWINKLERS
WINKLING
TWINKLING
WINNINGS
TWINNINGS
WIREDRAW
WIREDRAWN

WISHINGS
SWISHINGS
WITCHIER
SWITCHIER
TWITCHIER
WITCHING
SWITCHING
TWITCHING
WITHDRAW
WITHDRAWN
WITHERED
SWITHERED
WITTERED
TWITTERED
WITTINGS
TWITTINGS
WOBBLIES
WOBBLIEST
WOMANISE
WOMANISED
WOMANISER
WOMANIZE
WOMANIZED
WOMANIZER
WOOLLIES
WOOLLIEST
WOOSHING
SWOOSHING
WORDLESS
SWORDLESS
WORDPLAY
SWORDPLAY
WORMHOLE
WORMHOLED
WORTHIES
WORTHIEST
WOUNDING
SWOUNDING
XYLOIDIN
XYLOIDINE
YERSINIA
YERSINIAE
YESHIVOT
YESHIVOTH
ZADDIKIM
TZADDIKIM
ZAMINDAR
ZAMINDARI
ZAMINDARY
ZEMINDAR
ZEMINDARI
ZEMINDARY
ZONATION
OZONATION
ZOOGLOEA
ZOOGLOEAE
ZOOPHORI
ZOOPHORIC

BLOCKERS

Blockers are the opposites of hooks – they don't allow for the addition of a letter at the front or end of the word.

Lists of blockers of length two to six letters are given in the lists here. To 'unclutter' the five- and six-letter lists, so that you can focus on the more relevant blockers, all five- and six-letter words ending in -ED, -J, -S, -X, -Y and -Z have been excluded. It hardly seems necessary to indicate that words like BAKED, FALAJ, CHIPS, HELIX, DUMMY and TOPAZ are blockers! Removal of blockers like these from the lists should make it easier to concentrate on the remaining blockers.

2-LETTER WORD BLOCKERS

FY	MY	XU

3-LETTER WORD BLOCKERS

BEZ	FAB	FRY	KEX	NAE	PLY	RHY	SMA	VLY	ZEX
BIZ	FAP	GEY	KYE	NOH	POH	SAE	SOX	VOX	ZOA
BYS	FAX	GOT	LEU	NOX	PST	SAX	SWY	WHY	ZUZ
CLY	FEW	HEX	LOX	NTH	PUH	SAZ	TAJ	WOX	
COY	FEZ	HOX	LUZ	NYS	PYX	SEZ	THY	YEX	
CUZ	FIX	HUH	MAE	PAX	QIS	SIX	TUX	YOS	
DUX	FLY	IVY	MUX	PHS	RAX	SLY	TWP	ZAX	

4-LETTER WORD BLOCKERS

ABBS	BADS	BOHS	CELS	CUSS	DIMS	DUBS	EUGE	FIKY	FUNS
ABED	BAGS	BOKS	CEPS	CWMS	DINS	DUDS	EUOI	FILS	FURS
ABLY	BAMS	BONA	CHEZ	DABS	DISS	DUED	EVOE	FINS	FURY
ACHY	BANS	BOPS	CHIS	DADS	DIVS	DUES	EWKS	FITS	FUSC
ADRY	BAPS	BORS	CIGS	DAES	DIXY	DUGS	EYAS	FLED	GABS
AESC	BARS	BOSH	CITO	DAFT	DOBS	DULY	EYES	FLEX	GABY
AHEM	BATS	BOTS	CITS	DAGS	DOCS	DUOS	EYNE	FLIX	GAED
AHOY	BAYS	BOXY	CITY	DAHS	DODS	DUPS	EYRY	FLUX	GAES
AIAS	BEDS	BOYS	COAX	DAKS	DOEN	DUSH	FADS	FOBS	GAGA
AJAR	BEEN	BRRR	COBS	DAMS	DOGS	DUTY	FADY	FOCI	GAGS
AJEE	BEES	BUBO	CODS	DANS	DOGY	DYED	FAGS	FOEN	GALS
ALAE	BEGS	BUBS	COFT	DAPS	DOHS	DYES	FAHS	FOES	GAMY
ALBS	BELS	BUDS	COKY	DASH	DOMY	DZOS	FAIX	FOGS	GANE
ALEE	BENJ	BUGS	COLS	DEAF	DONS	EASY	FALX	FOGY	GAPS
ALIT	BENS	BUMS	COMS	DEBS	DOOS	EAUS	FANS	FOHS	GARE
ALSO	BEVY	BUNS	CONY	DEEK	DOPS	EBBS	FASH	FONE	GASH
AMOK	BIBS	BURY	COPY	DEFT	DOPY	ECHO	FAUX	FONS	GATS
ANEW	BIDS	BUSY	CORF	DEFY	DORY	ECOD	FAWS	FOPS	GAYS
ANOW	BIEN	BUYS	CORY	DELS	DOSH	ECUS	FEDS	FOUS	GAZY
APEX	BIGS	CAGY	COSH	DEMY	DOSS	EDDO	FEET	FOXY	GEDS
APTS	BINS	CAKY	COSS	DENY	DOST	EDHS	FEGS	FOYS	GEED
AREG	BIOS	CALX	COSY	DEUS	DOTH	EHED	FEIS	FOZY	GELS
AREW	BISH	CANY	COXY	DEWS	DOTS	ELMY	FENS	FRAE	GEMS
AROW	BLEW	CAPS	COZY	DEWY	DOTY	ELSE	FETS	FROM	GENS
AWRY	BOBS	CASH	CRUX	DEYS	DOWF	EMUS	FEUS	FUCI	GEOS
AYUS	BODS	CAUF	CUBS	DIBS	DOXY	EMYS	FEYS	FUDS	GETS
BAAS	BODY	CAVY	CUED	DIED	DOZY	ENOW	FIBS	FUGS	GHIS
BABY	BOGS	CAYS	CUES	DIES	DRAT	EOAN	FIDS	FUMS	GIBS
BADE	BOGY	CEES	CURT	DIGS	DREW	ESPY	FIGS	FUMY	GIDS

GIED GIEN GIES GIGS GINS GITS GIZZ GJUS GLEG GNUS GOAS GOBS GOBY GOES GOEY GOGO GORY GOVS GOYS GUBS GULY GUMS GUNS GUPS GURS GUVS GYMS GYNY GYRI HATH HAZY HEIL HELD HEMS HEPS HEPT HISN HIYA HOAX HOBS HODS HOLP HOLS HOLY HOMY HOSS HOYS HUED HUES HUGY HUIS HUNG HUPS HYED HYES

HYPS IBIS IDEM IDLY IGAD ILKA INIA INLY INRO IURE JABS JAGS JAKS JAMS JAPS JARS JASS JASY JAWS JAYS JAZY JEED JEES JESS JETS JEUX JEWS JIBS JIGS JINX JIZZ JOBS JOCO JOES JOGS JOKY JORS JOSH JOSS JOTS JOWS JOYS JUDS JUDY JUGS JURE JURY JUTS JYNX KAED KAES KAIS KANS KEAS KEBS

KEDS KEFS KENS KEPT KESH KETS KEYS KIFS KILD KINE KIRS KISH KISS KNEW KOAS KOBS KOND KOPS KOSS KOWS KRIS KYNE KYUS LACS LACY LANX LAVS LEAL LECH LEKE LEKS LEPS LEVA LEVY LEWD LIDS LIGS LINY LIRE LOBI LOCI LORN LOST LUDS LUVS LYES LYMS LYNX MAAS MACS MADE MADS MAGS MAKS MALS

MAND MANY MAPS MARY MATS MATY MAWS MAZY MEGS MELS METS MHOS MILS MINX MINY MIRY MIXT MIXY MIZZ MNAS MOAS MOBS MODS MOES MOLY MOMS MONY MOOI MOPY MOTS MOWN MOWS MOYS MOZZ MUCH MUDS NAIF NAIN NAMS NANS NAOI NAOS NAVY NAYS NEFS NEKS NEPS NESH NESS NETS NEVI NIDI NIDS NIED NIMS

NISI NIXY NODI NOES NOMS NOPE NOSH NOSY NOTT NOUS NOYS NUNS NYAS NYED OAKY OBIS ODDS ODEA OHMS ONST ONYX OPTS ORFS ORYX OYEZ PADS PALY PAMS PAPS PEDS PEGS PEPS PHEW PHIZ PHOS PIAS PIGS PIPS PIPY PIRS PISS PITY PIXY POAS POCO POKY POMS PONS PONY POOH POOS PORY POSY POWS PRUH

PSST PUBS PUGH PUGS PUIR PULY PUNS PUNY PUPS PUTS PUTZ PUYS PYES QATS QUEP RACA RAHS RAZZ RECS REFS REFT REHS RELY REMS RENY REVS RHOS RHUS RIPT ROED ROES ROKS ROKY ROPY ROUX RUBY RUCS RUNS RUTS RYAS RYES RYFE SABS SACS SAGS SAGY SAPS SASH SAWN SAWS SCRY SECO SECS SEEN SEES

SEGS SEIK SELD SELS SEPS SETS SEWN SEWS SEXY SEYS SHAT SHOD SIBS SICH SICS SIMS SINS SIPS SIRS SITS SIZY SKAS SKIS SKOL SKRY SOBS SOCS SODS SOGS SOHO SOHS SOLS SOME SOON SOPS SORI SOSS SOTS SOVS SOYS SPED SPRY STEY SUBS SUCH SUES SUKS SUMS SUNG SUNS SUPS SUQS SUSS SWIZ SWUM

SYED SYES TADS TAED TAES TAKS TAKY TALI TAMS TAUS TAXA TEDY TEES TEFS TEGS TELD TELS TELT THAE THAT THEY THIS THUS TICS TIDS TIDY TIGS TILS TINS TINY TIPT TITS TOBY TODS TODY TOED TOES TOEY TOGS TOLD TONS TORN TOWY TOYS TREZ TUGS TUNY TUPS TUTS TUZZ TWAS TWOS TYDE TYGS UGLY

UNCI UNDO UNIS UPGO UPSY UTAS UVAE UVAS VACS VAES VAGI VAIN VANS VATS VAUS VEES VETO VEXT VIAE VIAS VIBS VIDS VIMS VINS VIVO VIZY VOES VOLS VORS VUGS VUMS WADY WANY WARY WAVY WAWS WAXY WEBS WEDS WEMS WENS WERE WERT WETS WHOA WHOM WHOT WICH WIFE WILY WIRY WOES WOGS WOKS WONS

WOST WOWF WOWS WUDS WUSS WYCH WYES WYNS YAKS YALD YAPS YAUP YAWS YAWY YBET YEAH YECH YEPS YEWS YGOE YINS YIPS YMPT YOBS YOKS YOLD YOND YOWS YUAN YUGS YUKS YUKY YUNX YUPS YWIS ZAGS ZANY ZAPS ZEAS ZEDS ZEKS ZELS ZIGS ZIPS ZITE ZITI ZITS ZIZZ ZOOS

5-LETTER WORD BLOCKERS
(except words ending in -ED, -J, -S, -X, -Y, -Z)

ABACI ABACK ABAFT ABASH ABASK ABEAM ABLOW ABOIL ABORE ABOVE

ABRAM ABRIM ABUNE ACERB ACINI ACOCK ACOLD ACRID ADOWN ADRAD

ADSUM ADUNC ADYTA AECIA AESIR AFALD AFIRE AFOOT AFORE AFOUL

AGAIN AGAPE AGAST AGGRI AGLEE AGLOW AGONE AGOOD AGRIN AHEAD

AHEAP AHENT AHIGH AHIND AHINT AHOLD AHULL AIDOI AINEE AITCH

ALACK ALAND ALBEE ALEFT ALGAE ALGAL ALGID ALIKE ALIVE ALOFT

ALOHA ALONE ALOOF ALOUD ALOWE AMAIN AMNIA AMONG AMORT AMUCK

ANCON ANILE ANTAE APACE APAGE APAID APART APAYD APEAK APEEK

APERT APIAN APOOP APORT APTER AQUAE AREAL AREAR AREDD ARERE

ARIOT AROSE ASKEW ASTIR ASWIM ATILT ATRIP AULIC AULOI AURAE

AURAL
AUREI
AVAST
AVIAN
AWASH
AWAVE
AWEEL
AWORK
AXIAL
AXILE
AYELP
AYGRE
AYONT
AZOIC
AZURN
BAKEN
BANAL
BARER
BARIC
BASER
BASHO
BASSI
BASTA
BATCH
BEDAD
BEECH
BEGAD
BEGAN
BEGAT
BEGOT
BELCH
BELOW
BENCH
BESAT
BESAW
BIFID
BIGAE
BIRCH
BIVIA
BLAER
BLASE
BLIST
BLIVE
BLOWN
BLUER
BONZA
BOREL
BORIC
BOXEN
BRACH
BRAVA
BRAVI
BREEM
BREME
BRULE
BUCKO
BUFFA
BUFFI
BUFFO
BUILT
BURNT
BUTCH
BUXOM
BYSSI
CABRE
CACTI
CAESE
CAJUN
CALID
CANST

CAPUT
CARGO
CARPI
CECAL
CECUM
CERCI
CERIC
CESTI
CHAVE
CHERE
CHIAO
CHIMO
CHODE
CHOTA
CHYND
CILIA
CINCH
CINCT
CIPPI
CIRRI
CIVIL
CLASH
CLIPT
CLOMB
CLOZE
CLUNG
COMAE
COMAL
COOST
CORAM
CORNI
CORNO
COUDE
COULD
COURD
COXAE
COXAL
COYER
CRASH
CREPT
CRONK
CRUOR
CRUSH
CUFFO
CUING
CUISH
CULCH
CURCH
CURSI
CURST
DATUM
DAYNT
DEALT
DEDAL
DEERE
DEMIC
DEMPT
DIACT
DICTA
DIDST
DINGO
DIRER
DITCH
DOCHT
DOEST
DOETH
DOGGO
DOILT
DOLIA
DOMAL

DOTAL
DOWNA
DRANK
DRAVE
DRAWN
DRENT
DREST
DUCAL
DUING
DUMKA
DUNCH
DUNNO
DUNSH
DUOMI
DURST
DUTCH
DWELT
EHING
EIGNE
ELMEN
EMONG
ENLIT
ENORM
EROSE
ETYMA
EVHOE
EVOHE
EWHOW
FASTI
FATAL
FAUGH
FAURD
FAVER
FAYER
FECAL
FECIT
FEHME
FERAL
FERER
FETAL
FETCH
FETID
FEWER
FEYER
FILAR
FILCH
FINCH
FLITT
FLOSH
FLOWN
FLUNG
FOCAL
FORDO
FOUER
FRACK
FRATI
FRENA
FRUSH
FUGAL
FUNGI
FURTH
GAMER
GANCH
GARNI
GAYER
GEESE
GELID
GENAL
GENIC
GENII

GESSO
GEYAN
GEYER
GHEST
GIVEN
GLIAL
GLODE
GNASH
GNAWN
GOBBI
GOBBO
GOIER
GONIA
GONNA
GONZO
GOTTA
GOYIM
GROWN
GRUFF
GRYPT
GULAR
GULCH
GUMMA
GYRAL
HABLE
HADAL
HADST
HAIKU
HAITH
HANCH
HARSH
HASTA
HAULT
HAUTE
HEAME
HEMAL
HEWGH
HIANT
HILAR
HILCH
HILUM
HOING
HOKKU
HOOCH
HOTCH
HOTEN
HOVEN
HOWBE
HOWSO
HUGER
HUMIC
HUMID
HUNCH
HUTCH
HYLIC
HYOID
HYPNA
ICTIC
ILEAC
ILIAC
IMSHI
INAPT
INBYE
INCUT
INEPT
INERM
INERT
INFRA
INTIL
INTRA

INUST
IODIC
JEUNE
JINGO
JOKOL
JUGUM
JURAL
KACHA
KAING
KAMME
KEECH
KEMPT
KIDGE
KINDA
KNELT
KNISH
KRONA
KYDST
LABRA
LADEN
LAITH
LAMER
LARCH
LAWER
LAXER
LAZZI
LAZZO
LEANT
LEAPT
LEASH
LEFTE
LEGAL
LEISH
LEPID
LEPTA
LIART
LIVID
LOACH
LOAST
LOBAR
LOSEN
LOTIC
LOYAL
LUCID
LUDIC
LUMME
LURCH
LURID
LYART
LYNCH
MADID
MAIST
MANET
MANGO
MANIC
MARCH
MARIA
MAYST
MEANT
MEDII
MEINT
MENSH
MERER
MESAL
MESIC
MESNE
MESTO
MEYNT
MICRA
MIKRA

MILCH
MINAE
MISDO
MISGO
MITCH
MODII
MOLAL
MOLTO
MONDO
MOOSE
MOTEN
MOTTO
MUCID
MULCH
MULSH
MUNCH
MUSHA
MUTER
MYOID
NAEVI
NARRE
NATAL
NAVAL
NEGRO
NEIST
NEMPT
NEVER
NEWER
NGWEE
NICER
NIDAL
NIMBI
NITID
NIVAL
NOHOW
NOMEN
NOMOI
NOTAL
NOTUM
NOVAE
NOXAL
NUDER
NUGAE
NUMEN
NYING
OATEN
OBELI
OBIIT
OBOLI
OGMIC
OHMIC
OHONE
OIDIA
OLEIC
OLPAE
ORGIC
OSSIA
OUTDO
OUTGO
OVOLI
OVOLO
OWSEN
PACTA
PAISE
PAKKA
PALER
PALPI
PAOLI
PAOLO
PAPAL

PAVID
PAYSD
PEART
PENAL
PEPLA
PERCH
PIERT
PIEZO
PILCH
PILEA
PILEI
PILUM
PINCH
PLENA
PLESH
POOCH
PORAL
PORCH
POUPT
PRESA
PROUD
PUBIC
PUCKA
PUDIC
PUKKA
PULMO
PUPAE
PUPAL
PURER
PUTID
PUTTO
PYOID
PYRAL
QUALE
QUASI
QUAYD
QUOAD
RABIC
RABID
RADII
RAGDE
RAMAL
RARER
RASTA
RECTI
REDID
REJON
RELIT
RENAL
RERAN
RESAT
RHYTA
RIFER
RIMAE
RONNE
RORAL
RORIC
RORID
RUBAI
RUNIC
RYPER
SAFER
SAGUM
SAIST
SALIC
SAMEN
SANER
SAPID
SAYNE
SAYST

SCAND
SCAPI
SCENA
SCHMO
SCUDI
SEELD
SENSA
SENZA
SERAL
SERER
SERIC
SERVO
SESSA
SETAE
SHAKT
SHALT
SHASH
SHERE
SHEWN
SHONE
SHOON
SHOPE
SHORN
SHOWN
SHULN
SHUSH
SIELD
SIGLA
SINCE
SKINT
SKOAL
SLAID
SLAIN
SLASH
SLEER
SLEPT
SLIER
SLIPT
SLISH
SLUNG
SLUNK
SLYER
SMASH
SMOTE
SNASH
SNUCK
SNUSH
SOCKO
SODIC
SOLDI
SOLDO
SOPRA
SORAL
SORDA
SORDO
SORER
SOUCT
SPAKE
SPARD
SPENT
SPRAD
SPUTA
STAID
STASH
STEPT
STOAE
STOAI
STOLN
STONG
STOOD

STUMM
STUNG
STUNK
STURE
STYLI
SUCCI
SULCI
SURAL
SWACK
SWANG
SWAPT
SWARE
SWEPT
SWINE
SWITH
SWOLN
SWOPT
SWORE
SWORN
SWUNG
SYKER
TABID
TACET
TACIT
TAGMA
TAISH
TAKEN
TANTI
TANTO
TAPEN
TATIN
TAULD
TAWIE
TAXON
TAZZE
TEACH
TECTA
TELIC
TEMPI
TEPID
TEUCH
TEUGH
THAIM
THELF
THEMA
THIEF
THILK
THINE
THOLI
THOSE
THRAE
THREW
TICCA
TIDAL
TIKKA
TIMID
TONDI
TOPHI
TOPOI
TORCH
TORIC
TORII
TORSI
TOXIC
TREFA
TREIF
TRIFF
TRILD
TRUER
TUBAE

TUBAL
TUBAR
TUMID
TYNDE
TYPAL
ULNAE
UNAPT
UNBID
UNCUT
UNDEE
UNDID
UNDUE
UNDUG
UNETH
UNGOT
UNHIP
UNKID
UNMET
UNRID
UNSOD
UNWET
UPBYE
UPRAN
URAEI
URDEE
UREAL
UREDO
UREIC
URENT
URNAL
UTERI
UVEAL
VACUA
VAGAL
VAIRE
VALID
VAPID
VASAL
VATIC
VEHME
VELUM
VENAE
VENAL
VILDE
VILER
VILLI
VINAL
VIOLD
VIRAL
VIRID
VITAE
VIVID
VOILA
VOLAE
VOLTA
VOULU
VULGO
VYING
WACKO
WAIDE
WANLE
WANNA
WARST
WAXEN
WELCH
WELKT
WELSH
WENCH
WERSH
WHICH

WHILK
WHIPT
WHOSE
WHOSO
WIDER
WINCH
WINNA
WISER
WITAN
WOFUL
WOMEN
WOVEN
WOWEE
WOXEN
WRAPT
WRATE
WROTE
WROTH
WRUNG
WRYER
XERIC
XOANA
XYLIC
XYSTI
YARER
YAULD
YBORE
YCLAD
YCOND
YDRAD
YEVEN
YEWEN
YFERE
YINCE
YLIKE
YMOLT
YOGIC
YOKUL
YOURN
YRAPT
YRENT
YRIVD
YSAME
YTOST
ZAIRE
ZILCH
ZOEAE
ZOEAL
ZONAE
ZOPPO
ZOWIE
ZUZIM
ZYGAL
ZYGON
ZYMIC

6-LETTER WORD BLOCKERS (except words ending in -ED, -J, -S, -X, -Y, -Z)

ABATTU
ABEIGH
ABLAZE
ABLEST
ABLOOM
ABLUSH
ABOARD
ABORAL
ABORNE
ABSURD
ABURST
ACETIC
ACHIER
ACIDER
ACIDIC
ACKNEW
ACRAWL
ACULEI
ACUTER
ADNATE
ADRIFT
ADROIT
ADYTUM
AECIUM
AEFALD
AERIER
AFAWLD
AFEARD
AFFYDE
AFIELD
AFLAME
AFLOAT
AFRAID
AFRESH
AFRONT
AGAMIC
AGAPAE
AGHAST
AGILER
AGLEAM
AGOING
AGONIC
AGOROT
AGUISH
AHORSE
AIDANT
AIDFUL
AIKONA
AIRMAN
AIRMEN
AKIMBO
ALBEIT
ALDERN
ALEXIC
ALGOID
ALMOST
ALULAE
ALUMNI
ALVINE
AMBUSH
AMEBAE
AMEBIC
AMIDST
AMNION
AMORAL
ANCILE
ANCORA
ANEATH
ANEMIC
ANETIC
ANGOLA
ANIGHT
ANNULI
ANODAL
ANODIC
ANOMIC
ANOUGH
ANOXIC
ANYHOW
AORTAE
AORTAL
AORTIC
APEMAN
APEMEN
APICAL
APIECE
APODAL
APPAID
APPAYD
APTEST
APTING
ARCANA
ARCANE
ARCHEI
ARDENT
AREACH
ARGULI
ARGUTE
ARIDER
ARIGHT
ARILLI
ARIOSI
ARISEN
AROUND
ARRISH
ARTFUL
ASHAKE
ASHINE
ASHORE
ASLANT
ASLEEP
ASLOPE
ASMEAR
ASPOUT
ASQUAT
ASSOTT
ASTARE
ASTOOP
ASTRUT
ASWARM
ASWING
ASWIRL
ASWOON
ATAXIC
ATHROB
ATOKAL
ATOMIC
ATONAL
ATONIC
ATOPIC
ATWAIN
ATWEEL
ATWEEN
ATWIXT
AUBURN
AVANTI
AVERSE
AVIDER
AVITAL
AVOUCH
AWARER
AWATCH
AWEIGH
AWHILE
AWOKEN
AWRACK
AWRONG
AWSOME
AXEMAN
AXEMEN
AZONAL
AZONIC
AZOTIC
BABIER
BACCAE
BACULA
BADMAN
BADMEN
BAGMAN
BAGMEN
BALDER
BALING
BANING
BANISH
BARDIC
BAREST
BARFUL
BARING
BARISH
BARMAN
BARMEN
BARREN
BASEST
BASSER
BATMAN
BATMEN
BAYING
BEATEN
BECAME
BEDASH
BEDIDE
BEDRID
BEDYDE
BEFELD
BEFELL
BEFORE
BEGILT
BEGIRT
BEGONE
BEHALF
BEHELD
BELIKE
BELIVE
BEMATA
BENDEE
BENIGN
BEREFT
BESANG
BESEEN
BESTAD
BESUNG
BETING
BETOOK
BETROD
BEWENT
BEWEPT
BIAXAL
BIFOLD
BIFORM
BIGGER
BINATE
BINMAN
BINMEN
BIRKEN
BISSON
BITTEN
BIVIUM
BLAEST
BLAISE
BLAIZE
BLANCH
BLATER
BLEACH
BLENCH
BLOTTO
BLUEST
BLUIER
BLUISH
BOKING
BOLDER
BOLETI
BOLLEN
BONIER
BONZER
BOOING
BOREAL
BOSHTA
BOSKER
BOSSER
BOTONE
BOWMAN
BOWMEN
BOXIER
BOYING
BOYISH
BRAWER
BREACH
BREECH
BREGMA
BRIGHT
BROKEN
BROMIC
BROOCH
BRUMAL
BRUNCH
BRUTAL
BUCCAL
BULBAR
BULLAE
BUMALO
BURSAE
BURSAL
BUSIER
BUSMAN
BUSMEN
BUYING
BYKING
BYLIVE
CABMAN
CABMEN
CADENT
CAECAL
CAECUM
CAGIER
CAGING
CAKIER
CALAMI
CALASH
CALCIC
CALLID
CALMER
CAMASH
CAMSHO
CANIER
CANNAE
CANNOT
CANTHI
CARMAN
CARMEN
CAROLI
CARVEN
CATCHT
CATTLE
CAUDAD
CAUGHT
CAUSAE
CAUSAL
CAUSEN
CEDARN
CEDING
CELLAE
CENDRE
CERCAL
CERING
CERULE
CHEAPO
CHELAE
CHICER
CHINCH
CHIRAL
CHOLIC
CHORIC
CHOSEN
CHYLDE
CILIUM
CISTIC
CITING
CITRIC
CLATCH
CLECHE
CLENCH
CLEVER
CLINCH
CLONAL
CLONIC
CLOVEN
CLUING
CLUNCH
CLUTCH
CLYING
CLYPEI
CNIDAE
COBRIC
COCCAL
COGENT
COITAL
COKIER
COKING
COMODO
COMOSE
CONGII
CONING
COSING
COSMIC
COSTAE
COWING
COWISH
COWMAN
COWMEN
COXIER
COXING
COYEST
COZING
CRAMBO
CREANT
CREDAL
CRIANT
CRIBLE
CRIMEN
CRINAL
CRISSA
CROTCH
CROUCH
CROUSE
CRUDER
CRURAL
CRUTCH
CUBING
CUEING
CULTCH
CULTIC
CUMULI
CUNEAL
CUPMAN
CUPMEN
CUPRIC
CURIAE
CURING
CURSAL
CURTER
CURULE
CUTCHA
CYANIC
CYATHI
CYMOID
CYMOSE
CYSTIC
CYTISI
CYTOID
DAEDAL
DAEING
DAFTER
DAIMEN
DAMMIT
DANKER
DARKER
DAWISH
DAYGLO
DAZING
DEAFER
DEARER
DEAWIE
DEBILE
DEBOSH
DECANI
DECENT
DEEDER
DEEING
DEEPER
DEFFER
DEFTER
DEGAGE
DEIDER
DEIFIC
DENSER
DERING
DERMAL
DERMIC
DETACH
DEVOID
DEVOUT
DEWIER
DEWING
DIACID
DIAMYL
DICIER
DICTUM
DIKIER
DIKING
DINFUL
DINING
DINKER
DINKUM
DIREST
DISCAL
DISTAL
DITTIT
DJINNI
DOABLE
DOITIT
DOLENT
DOLING
DOLIUM
DOMIER
DOMING
DOPIER
DORMIE
DORSUM
DOSING
DOTIER
DOTISH
DOUCER
DOURER
DOVIER
DOVING
DOVISH
DOWIER
DOWING
DOZIER
DREAMT
DREICH
DRENCH
DRIEST
DRIVEN
DROLER
DROMIC
DROMOI
DRYISH
DUDISH
DUEFUL
DUETTI
DUKING
DULCET
DULLER
DUMBER
DUMOSE
DUNNER
DUPING
DURING
DUSKER
DYABLE
DYADIC
DYKIER
DYKING
EADISH
EASIER
EASSEL
EASSIL
ECHINI
ECHOIC
EFFETE
EGESTA
EIDENT
EIDOLA
EIKING
EKUELE
ELDEST
ELMIER
ELVISH
EMBOST
EMMESH
ENARCH
ENCASH
ENGILT
ENGIRT
ENLEVE
ENMESH
ENODAL
ENRAPT
ENRICH
EOTHEN
EPICAL
EPODIC
EQUINE
EREMIC
ERENOW
ERRATA
ETERNE
ETYMIC
ETYPIC
EURIPI
EWGHEN
EWKING
EXEUNT
EXILIC
EXODIC
EXONIC
EXTOLD
EYEING
FABBER
FACILE
FADIER
FAECAL
FAINER
FAIRER
FAKING
FALLEN
FAMING
FAMISH
FARAND
FARFET
FARING
FASCIO
FATTER
FAUCAL
FAUNAE
FAUNAL
FAVELL
FAVEST
FAVOSE
FAXING
FAYEST
FAYING
FAZING
FECIAL
FECUND
FEEING
FEHMIC
FELSIC
FENMAN
FENMEN
FEODAL
FEREST
FERIAL
FERINE
FERRIC
FERVID
FETIAL
FETING
FETISH
FEUDAL
FEUING
FEWEST
FEYEST
FEYING
FIFING
FIKIER
FIKING
FIKISH
FILIAL
FILMIC
FILOSE
FINEST
FINISH
FINITE
FINSKO
FISTIC
FITFUL
FIXIVE
FLAMBE

FLANCH FLAXEN FLEECH FLEMIT FLENCH FLETCH FLIEST FLINCH FLITCH FLOCCI FLORAE FLORAL FLORID FLOUSH FLUIER FLYEST FLYSCH FOEMAN FOEMEN FOETAL FOETID FOGASH FOGMAN FOGMEN FOLIAR FOLIUM FONDER FONTAL FORANE FORBYE FORDID FOREGO FORGAT FORGOT FORMAL FORMIC FORRAD FORREN FORRIT FOSSAE FOUEST FOULER FOVEAE FOVEAL FOXIER FOZIER FRAENA FRANCO FREEST FRENCH FRENNE FRENUM FRIGID FROREN FRORNE FROZEN FRUGAL FRUSTA FULCRA FULGID FULVID FUMIER FUMING FUNEST FUNGAL FURCAL FURDER FUSILE FUSING FYKING

GAGING GAGMAN GAGMEN GAIJIN GALANT GALEAE GALLIC GALORE GALOSH GAMASH GAMEST GAMIER GARDAI GARISH GASLIT GASMAN GASMEN GAUNCH GAYEST GAZIER GAZING GEASON GEDDIT GEEING GELATO GEMINI GEMMAE GEMMAN GEMMEN GENIAL GEODIC GESTIC GEYEST GIBING GIDDAP GIDDUP GIEING GIGMAN GIGMEN GILDEN GINGKO GINKGO GIUSTO GLAZEN GLITCH GLOBAL GLUIER GLUING GLUISH GLUTEI GNOMAE GNOMIC GOETIC GOIEST GOLDER GOLOSH GONION GOOIER GORIER GOTHIC GOTTEN GOWDER GOYISH GRAVEN GRAVID GRAYER GREIGE GREYER GRIPLE GRUING

GRUTCH GRYSIE GUNMAN GUNMEN GUTTAE GUYING GYBING GYLDEN GYMNIC GYRANT GYRING GYROSE GYVING HABILE HADDEN HAEING HAEMAL HAEMIC HAIKAI HAINCH HALEST HALFEN HAMATE HAMOSE HAMULI HARDER HARISH HATING HAULST HAUNCH HAWKIT HAZIER HEARIE HELIAC HELING HEMPEN HEPPER HETING HEYING HIEING HIEMAL HIKING HIPPIC HISPID HISTIE HOAING HODMAN HODMEN HOHING HOLDEN HOLIER HOLMIC HOLPEN HOMIER HOOROO HOOTCH HOOVEN HOPING HORRID HOSING HOWZAT HOXING HOYING HUDDEN HUDDUP HUGEST HUMERI HYDRIC HYEING HYETAL

HYMNIC HYPHAE HYPHAL HYPING HYPOID IBIDEM ICONIC IDLEST IDOLUM IMIDIC IMMANE IMMESH INANER INARCH INBENT INBORN INCAVI INCAVO INCUBI INCULT INDIGN INFELT INFERE INFIRM INGRAM INGRUM INLAID INMESH INMOST INRUSH INTACT INTIME INTIRE INTOWN INWITH INWORN IRATER IRIDAL IRIDIC IRITIC ITERUM ITSELF JACENT JADING JADISH JANTEE JEEING JEJUNA JEJUNE JEWING JIBING JIMPER JINNEE JIVING JOBING JOCOSE JOCUND JOKIER JOKING JOLING JOVIAL JOWING JOYFUL JOYING JUBATE JUGATE JUKING JUSTER JYMOLD KAEING

KAPUTT KARMIC KAWING KEIGHT KEPPIT KEYING KIBOSH KIRSCH KLOOCH KNITCH KOUROI KRONEN KRONER KRONOR KRONUR KUTCHA KVETCH KYBOSH LABARA LABILE LABIUM LABRUM LACTIC LAESIE LAICAL LAKISH LAMEST LAMIAE LAMISH LANATE LANOSE LARGER LARINE LAROID LARVAE LARVAL LATENT LATHEN LATISH LAWEST LAWFUL LAWMAN LAWMEN LAXEST LAYMAN LAYMEN LEARNT LEETLE LENGER LENTEN LENTIC LERING LESBIC LESSER LETHAL LEWDER LIBANT LIBRAE LIEDER LIEFER LIENAL LIEVER LIFULL LIGGEN LIMBIC LIMPER LIMPID LIMULI LINEAL LINEAR

LINIER LIPOMA LITHIC LITTEN LOBULI LOCULI LOGGIE LOGIER LOGION LOIPEN LOMING LONGER LOOING LOOSER LOOTEN LORATE LOTHER LOUCHE LOUDER LOUPEN LOUPIT LOWSER LOWSIT LUBRIC LUCENT LUCKEN LUETIC LUITEN LUMBAR LUPPEN LURING LUTTEN LYFULL LYSING LYTTAE MAAING MACING MADMAN MADMEN MAGLEV MAGYAR MAHZOR MAINER MALEIC MALIST MALLEI MAMMAE MANENT MANFUL MANQUE MANTIC MARISH MASING MATIER MATZOH MAUNNA MAUVER MAYEST MAYHAP MAZIER MEANER MEATAL MEDIAE MEEKER MEETER MENSAL MENSCH MEREST MERING MERMAN

MERMEN MESIAL MESIAN METING MEVING MEWING MIGNON MILDER MILKEN MIMING MIMMER MINIER MINISH MIRIER MIRING MIRKER MISDID MISLIT MISSAE MISSAW MISUST MITIER MITRAL MIXIER MIXING MNEMIC MODISH MODULI MODULO MONACT MONERA MOOING MOPIER MOPING MOPISH MORBID MORISH MORSAL MOSHAV MOSING MOTIER MOUGHT MOZING MUCOID MULISH MUONIC MURKER MUTEST MUTING MUTUAL MUXING MYSELF MYTHIC MYTHOI MYXOMA NAIANT NAIFER NAIVER NARIAL NARINE NASTIC NATANT NAUTCH NEANIC NEARER NEATER NEBISH NEFAST NERVAL NESHER

NETHER NEURAL NEWEST NEWISH NICEST NICISH NIELLI NIOBIC NIRLIT NITRIC NIXING NOBBUT NOBLER NODOSE NOGAKU NOSIER NOSTOI NOTING NOTOUR NOULDE NOUNAL NOWISE NOYING NUBILE NUCHAE NUCHAL NUDEST NUKING NUMINA NUTANT OAFISH OAKIER OBESER OBIING OBITAL OBITER OBTECT OCELLI OCHONE OCREAE OCTOPI ODDEST ODDISH OGAMIC OGIVAL OGRISH OIDIUM OILMAN OILMEN OMASAL OMASUM ONIRIC ONRUSH OPIOID OPTING ORBIER ORGANA OSCINE OSTEAL OSTIAL OSTIUM OTIOSE OUTATE OUTBYE OUTDID OUTSAT OUTWON OVERDO OVULAR OWLISH

OWRIER OXALIC PACTUM PALEAE PALEST PALIER PALISH PALLAE PALLID PALPAL PAPISH PAPYRI PARDIE PARISH PARTIM PASSEE PASSIM PAUSAL PAWING PEARST PEASON PECTEN PECTIC PEDATE PEEING PELTAE PELVIC PENIAL PENILE PENMAN PENMEN PENNAE PEPFUL PERAEA PERCEN PERDIE PEREIA PERFET PERISH PERITI PERTER PETITE PHAEIC PHATIC PHOCAE PHONAL PHYLAE PHYLUM PICINE PICRIC PIEING PIEMAN PIEMEN PIERST PILEUM PILOSE PINEAL PINETA PINKER PINNAE PINXIT PIONIC PIPIER PIRNIT PITHOI PITMAN PITMEN PLACID PLAGAL PLANAR

PLANCH PLEACH PLIANT PLICAE PLICAL PLISSE PLONGD PODIAL POKIER POKING POLISH POLYPI POMATO PONENT PONTAL PONTIC POOING POOKIT POPISH PORIER PORING POSHER POSIER POTASH POTATO POTING POTMAN POTMEN POUKIT POWWAW POXIER POXING PREMIA PRIMAL PRONER PRONTO PROSIT PSEUDO PSORIC PUDENT PUIRER PUKING PULIER PUNCTA PUNIER PUNISH PUREST PURING PUTRID PUTSCH PUTTEN PYCNIC PYEING PYKNIC PYNING PYXING QUAINT QUALIA QUATCH QUEINT QUENCH QUETCH QUINIC QUOOKE QUOTHA RABATO RACIAL RACIER RADGER RADISH

RAHING
RAKISH
RAMATE
RAMEAL
RAMOSE
RAMULI
RANCID
RANINE
RAREST
RARING
RATHER
RATITE
RAUCID
RAVISH
RAWISH
RAXING
REALER
REALIA
REBATO
RECENT
RECHIE
RECKAN
RECTAL
REDIAE
REDONE
REDREW
REEDEN
REGAVE
REGNAL
REHASH
REHUNG
REKING
RELAID
RELIDE
RELISH
REMOUD
REPAND
REPLUM
RESAID
RESOLD
RETIAL
RETOLD
RETOOK
RETRAL
RETROD
RETUSE
RHINAL
RHIZIC
RHODIC
RHOTIC
RHYTON
RICHER
RICTAL
RIDDEN
RIFEST
RILIER
RILING
RIMOSE
RIPEST
RODMAN
RODMEN
ROKIER
ROOPIT
ROPIER
RORIER
ROSCID
ROSEAL
ROTING
ROUPIT
RUBATI
RUBBET
RUBBIT
RUBIER
RUEFUL
RUGATE
RUGOSE
RULIER
RUMINA
RUSHEN
RUSINE
RYKING
SACCOI
SACRAL
SACRUM
SADDER
SAFEST
SAFING
SAGEST
SAGIER
SAIDST
SAIRER
SAKKOI
SALEWD
SALPAE
SAMIER
SANCTA
SANEST
SAPEGO
SAPFUL
SARING
SATANG
SATING
SATIVE
SAYEST
SBIRRI
SBIRRO
SCALAE
SCATCH
SCEATT
SCENIC
SCHEMA
SCIENT
SCOLIA
SCOPAE
SCORCH
SCOTCH
SCRYDE
SCUTAL
SCUTCH
SCUTUM
SCYPHI
SEAMAN
SEAMEN
SEARCH
SEARER
SECESH
SECUND
SEDENT
SEDILE
SEIKER
SEJANT
SELDOM
SELLAE
SEMEIA
SEMPER
SEMPRE
SENILE
SENSUM
SEPMAG
SEPTAL
SEPTUM
SEREST
SERRAE
SETOSE
SEXFID
SEXIER
SEXING
SHAKEN
SHALOM
SHAPEN
SHAVEN
SHOLOM
SHOULD
SHRANK
SHREWD
SHROWD
SHRUNK
SHTOOM
SHTUMM
SHYEST
SHYING
SHYISH
SIALIC
SICCAN
SICCAR
SICKER
SIDDUR
SILENI
SILING
SILVAE
SIMIAL
SINFUL
SINING
SIPING
SIRING
SISTRA
SITING
SIWASH
SIZIER
SKEIGH
SKOLIA
SKOOSH
SKYIER
SKYING
SKYISH
SKYMAN
SKYMEN
SLATCH
SLEEST
SLIEST
SLIVEN
SLOOSH
SLOWER
SLUING
SLYEST
SLYISH
SMALTI
SMATCH
SMEECH
SMIRCH
SMOOCH
SMOUCH
SMUTCH
SNEESH
SNIDER
SNITCH
SOAKEN
SOBEIT
SOCMAN
SOCMEN
SODAIC
SOEVER
SOFTER
SOLEIN
SOLEMN
SOLGEL
SOLIDI
SOLING
SOMATA
SOONER
SORDID
SOREST
SORING
SOUGHT
SOURER
SPEECH
SPERST
SPETCH
SPICAE
SPINAE
SPINAL
SPLOSH
SPOILT
SPOKEN
SPRACK
SPRAID
SPRANG
SPRENT
SPRONG
SPRUNG
SPRUSH
SPRYER
SPUING
SPUTUM
STALER
STALKO
STANCH
STANCK
STATAL
STATIM
STEARD
STEELD
STELAE
STELAR
STEMMA
STERIC
STEYER
STINKO
STITCH
STOLEN
STOLID
STOMAL
STONEN
STOUSH
STRATA
STRATI
STRAWN
STREWN
STRIAE
STRODE
STROMA
STRONG
STROVE
STROWN
STRUCK
STRUNG
STYING
SUABLE
SUAVER
SUBITO
SUBMAN
SUBMEN
SUBSEA
SULCAL
SULLEN
SUMMAE
SUNKEN
SUNLIT
SUPERB
SURBET
SUREST
SUTILE
SWATCH
SWEERT
SWEIRT
SWOOSH
SYEING
SYLVAE
SYNING
SYPING
SYRLYE
TAEING
TAISCH
TAKIER
TALEAE
TALLER
TALPAE
TAMEST
TAPING
TAPPIT
TARNAL
TAUGHT
TAURIC
TAUTER
TAUTIT
TAVERT
TAXMAN
TAXMEN
TEAING
TECTUM
TEDIER
TEEING
TEGMEN
TELIAL
TELIUM
TEMENE
TENIAE
TENSER
TERAPH
TERATA
TERBIC
TERGAL
TERGUM
TERRAE
TERSER
TESTAE
THECAE
THECAL
THENCE
THETCH
THETIC
THOLOI
THRASH
THRAWN
THRESH
THRICE
THROVE
THROWN
THRUSH
THYINE
THYMIC
THYRSI
TIBIAE
TICING
TIDIER
TIFOSI
TIFOSO
TINEAL
TINIER
TINING
TINMAN
TINMEN
TOEIER
TOEING
TOFORE
TOLUIC
TOMATO
TOMBIC
TOMIAL
TOMIUM
TONANT
TONISH
TOOMER
TOPMAN
TOPMEN
TOROSE
TORRID
TORTEN
TOSING
TOSSEN
TOTHER
TOTING
TOWIER
TOYISH
TOYMAN
TOYMEN
TOZING
TRAGIC
TRENCH
TREPID
TRIACT
TRIBAL
TRIFID
TRILLO
TRINAL
TRISTE
TRITER
TROCHI
TROPPO
TRUEST
TRUING
TUBATE
TUMULI
TUNIER
TURBID
TURFEN
TURGID
TUSSAL
TUTMAN
TUTMEN
TWEEST
TWILIT
TYEING
TYKISH
TYNING
UBIQUE
UGLIER
UGSOME
ULNARE
ULTIMO
UMBRAE
UMBRAL
UNBEEN
UNBENT
UNBORE
UNCINI
UNCLAD
UNCOOL
UNDEAD
UNDEAR
UNDONE
UNDREW
UNEATH
UNEVEN
UNFELT
UNFINE
UNFIRM
UNGAIN
UNGILT
UNGLAD
UNGORD
UNGUAL
UNHEWN
UNHUNG
UNHURT
UNIFIC
UNITAL
UNJUST
UNKENT
UNKEPT
UNKIND
UNLAID
UNLASH
UNLEAL
UNLICH
UNLOST
UNMADE
UNMARD
UNMEEK
UNMEET
UNMOWN
UNPAID
UNPENT
UNREAL
UNRENT
UNROVE
UNRUDE
UNSAID
UNSENT
UNSEWN
UNSHOD
UNSOFT
UNSOLD
UNSOWN
UNSPUN
UNSUNG
UNTOLD
UNTORN
UNTROD
UNWELL
UNWEPT
UNWISH
UNWIST
UNWONT
UNWORN
UPBEAT
UPBLEW
UPBORE
UPDREW
UPGONE
UPGREW
UPGUSH
UPHAND
UPHELD
UPHILD
UPHUNG
UPLAID
UPMOST
UPPISH
UPROSE
UPRUSH
UPRYST
UPSENT
UPTOOK
UPTORE
UPTORN
UPWENT
URACHI
URANIC
UREDIA
UREMIC
URETIC
URSINE
USABLE
UVULAE
UVULAR
VACANT
VADOSE
VAGILE
VAGROM
VAGUER
VAINER
VALVAL
VALVAR
VARSAL
VASTER
VATMAN
VATMEN
VEDUTA
VEDUTE
VEGETE
VEHMIC
VELOCE
VENIAL
VENOSE
VERIER
VERLIG
VERMAL
VERNAL
VIABLE
VICING
VIDUAL
VILEST
VILLAR
VINIER
VINING
VIRENT
VIRILE
VIRING
VISCID
VISIVE
VISTAL
VITTAE
VIVACE
VOGIER
VOLAGE
VOLING
VORAGO
VORANT
VORPAL
VOTING
VOTIVE
VULVAE
VULVAL
VULVAR
WABBIT
WAEFUL
WANDLE
WANIER
WANKLE
WANNEL
WANNER
WARIER
WARING
WARMAN
WARMEN
WASHEN
WAURST
WAVIER
WAXIER
WEAKER
WETTER
WEXING
WEYARD
WHATEN
WHATNA
WHATSO
WHEARE
WHILOM
WHILST
WHITER
WHOOSH
WIDEST
WIDISH
WILFUL
WILIER
WILING
WIRIER
WISEST
WISING
WITHAL
WITING
WOEFUL
WOODEN
WORSER
WOWFER
WOWING
WRENCH
WRETCH
WROKEN
WRYEST
WRYING
WYTING
XENIAL
XENIUM
XOANON
XYLOID
XYSTOI
YAKUZA
YAREST
YAWING
YBLENT
YBOUND
YBRENT
YCLEPT
YEDING
YEOMAN
YEOMEN
YEVING
YEXING
YIPPEE
YPIGHT
YPLAST
YSHENT
YTTRIC
YUKIER
YUKING
YWROKE
ZANIER
ZAPATA
ZELOSO
ZEROTH
ZIPTOP
ZOARIA
ZOETIC
ZONOID
ZOOEAE
ZOOEAL
ZOONAL
ZOONIC
ZUFOLI
ZUFOLO
ZYMOID

SECTION FIVE

ANAGRAMS

Introduction

The final substantial section contains all valid seven-letter and eight-letter words arranged in alphabetical order of their constituent letters.

Suppose you have the seven letters THORCES on your rack. You are convinced that there must be a valid 7-letter word there. Just arrange the letters in alphabetical order (CEHORST), then look for CEHORST in the following seven-letter lists, where it appears alphabetically ordered between CEHORSS and CEHORSU. You will find that there are six valid anagrams of your seven letters! Perhaps you have the seven letters CORLINE, and you cannot see a valid seven-letter word. Arrange the letters into alphabetical order (CEILNOR) and check the list here. Lo and behold! The list goes from CEILNOP to CEILNOS, confirming that there is no valid anagram of those seven letters.

The same theory applies to eight-letter words. All valid eight-letter words have been reduced to their alphabetically ordered forms, and these have then been themselves arranged into alphabetical order. What anagrams, if any, are there for the eight letters THROUCES? Easy! Put the letters into alphabetical order, check CEHORSTU in the eight-letter list, and find that SCOUTHER and TOUCHERS are both valid words!

The Seven-Letter Anagrams list contains over 26 000 words, and the Eight-Letter list has over 30 000 words. Happy anagram searching!

7-LETTER ANAGRAMS

AAAADNP APADANA
AAAALTY ATALAYA
AAABBCL CABBALA
AAABBKL KABBALA
AAABCCR BACCARA
AAABCIR ARABICA
AAABCLS CABALAS
AAABCLV BACLAVA
AAABCMR CARAMBA
AAABCNR BARACAN
AAABCNS CABANAS
AAABCOR CARABAO
AAABCTW CATAWBA
AAABDGS DAGABAS
AAABDHS BAHADAS
AAABDJS BAJADAS
AAABDLM LAMBADA
AAABDNN BANDANA
AAABEGL GALABEA
AAABFLL FALBALA
AAABGIL GALABIA
AAABHLQ QABALAH
AAABILX ABAXIAL
AAABKLS KABALAS
AAABKLV BAKLAVA
AAABKSY KABAYAS
AAABLLW WALLABA
AAABLPR PALABRA
AAABLST ALBATAS
ATABALS
BALATAS
AAABMOS ABOMASA
AAABMST MASTABA
AAABNNR RABANNA
AAABNNS BANANAS
AAABORR ARAROBA
AAABRSX ABRAXAS
AAABRSZ BARAZAS
BAZAARS
AAABSTT BATATAS
AAACCIS ACACIAS
AAACCLR CARACAL
AAACCRS CASCARA
AAACDLU ACAUDAL
AAACDMM MACADAM
AAACDNS CANADAS
AAACENP PANACEA
AAACGNT AGACANT
AAACHLZ CHALAZA
AAACHNT ACANTHA
AAACHRY ACHARYA
AAACILM MALACIA
AAACIMR CARIAMA
AAACINP ACAPNIA
AAACINR ACARIAN
AAACJMR JACAMAR
AAACJNS JACANAS
AAACLLV CAVALLA
AAACLMN ALMANAC
MANCALA
AAACLNT CANTALA
AAACLPS ALPACAS
AAACLPT CATALPA
AAACLRZ ALCAZAR
AAACMNP CAMPANA
AAACMRS MARACAS
MASCARA
AAACNNR CARANNA
AAACNPT CATAPAN
AAACNRT NACARAT
AAACNRU CARAUNA
AAACNRV CARAVAN
AAACNST CANASTA
AAACNTT CANTATA
AAACPST PATACAS
AAACRWY CARAWAY
AAACSST CASSATA
AAACSSV CASSAVA
AAACSTT CATASTA
AAADELM ALAMEDA
AAADFRY FARADAY
AAADHMR ADHARMA
AAADILX ADAXIAL
AAADIRT DATARIA
RADIATA
AAADJMR JAMADAR
AAADLMN MANDALA
AAADLMW WADMAAL
AAADMNT ADAMANT
AAADMRS ARMADAS
MADRASA
AAADNPS PANADAS
AAADNRS SARDANA
AAADNRT TANADAR
AAAEGLT GALATEA
AAAEGNP APANAGE
AAAEHLT ALTHAEA
AAAEIMN ANAEMIA
AAAELMP PALAMAE
AAAELSZ AZALEAS
AAAENST ANATASE
AAAERWY AREAWAY
AAAFFLL ALFALFA
AAAFIRT RATAFIA
AAAFNRS SARAFAN
AAAFRWY FARAWAY
AAAGGLN GALANGA
AAAGHIP APHAGIA
AAAGHLN LANGAHA
AAAGHNT ATAGHAN
AAAGHPR AGRAPHA
AAAGINZ GAZANIA
AAAGIPT PATAGIA
AAAGISS ASSAGAI
AAAGLMM AMALGAM
AAAGLMN NAGMAAL
AAAGLNO ANALOGA
AAAGLNS LASAGNA
AAAGLRS ARGALAS
AAAGMMT MAGMATA
AAAGMNR ANAGRAM
AAAGMNS SAGAMAN
AAAGMTT TAGMATA
AAAGNNS NAGANAS
AAAGNPR PARGANA
AAAGNRT TANAGRA
AAAGNRU GUARANA
AAAGNTY YATAGAN
AAAHHLV HALAVAH
AAAHIKW KAHAWAI
AAAHIPS APHASIA
AAAHIST TAIAHAS
AAAHJKW KAJAWAH
AAAHLMR HARMALA
AAAHLNN ALANNAH
AAAHMMT MAHATMA
AAAHMRS ASHRAMA
AAAHMST TAMASHA
AAAHPRT PARATHA
AAAHRTW WARATAH
AAAILLS ALALIAS
AAAILMR MALARIA
AAAILNX ANAXIAL
AAAILPS APLASIA
AAAILRS ARALIAS
AAAILRT TALARIA
AAAIMNT AMANITA
AAAIPRX APRAXIA
AAAIQRU AQUARIA
AAAISTX ATAXIAS
AAAJKST JATAKAS
AAAJMPS PAJAMAS
AAAJMSU UJAMAAS
AAAKKMR MARKKAA
AAAKKNS KANAKAS
AAAKKRS KARAKAS
AAAKLMS KAMALAS
AAAKNST KATANAS
AAALLPT PALATAL
AAALMSS SALAAMS
AAALNNT LANTANA
AAALNPT APLANAT
AAALRRY ARRAYAL
AAALWYY LAYAWAY
AAAMNNS MANANAS
AAAMNPS PANAMAS
AAAMNRT AMARANT
AAAMNSS SAMAANS
AAAMNST ATAMANS
AAAMNTY MANYATA
AAAMORT TAMARAO
AAAMPRT PATAMAR
AAAMRRZ ZAMARRA
AAAMRSS SAMARAS
SAMSARA
AAAMRST TAMARAS
AAAMRTU TAMARAU
AAANNSV SAVANNA
AAANNTT ANNATTA
AAANRST ANTARAS
AAANRTT TANTARA
TARTANA
AAANSTT ANATTAS
AAAOPRZ PARAZOA
AAAPPRT APPARAT
AAAPPSY PAPAYAS
AAAPRSS APSARAS
AAARSST SATARAS
AAARSTV AVATARS
AAARTTU TUATARA
AAARTXY ATARAXY
AABBBOS BAOBABS
AABBCEG CABBAGE
AABBCGY CABBAGY
AABBCOS BABACOS
AABBDGR GABBARD
AABBDHS HABDABS
AABBEGN BEANBAG
AABBELT BATABLE
AABBERT BARBATE
AABBGRT GABBART
AABBHLS BABLAHS
AABBLLS LABLABS
AABBLOR BARBOLA
AABBLOS BALBOAS
AABBSST SABBATS
AABBSSU BABASSU
AABCCEL ACCABLE
AABCCER BACCARE
AABCCET BACCATE
AABCCIR BRACCIA
AABCDIR CARABID
AABCEKR BACKARE
AABCELN BALANCE
AABCELP CAPABLE
PACABLE
AABCELT ACTABLE
AABCEMR MACABRE
AABCERR BARRACE
AABCERT ABREACT
CABARET
AABCHIR BRACHIA
AABCHMT AMBATCH
AABCHNR BARCHAN
AABCHOR ABROACH
AABCHSS CASBAHS
AABCILM CAMBIAL
AABCINR CARABIN
AABCIOP COPAIBA
AABCITX TAXICAB
AABCKLY LAYBACK
AABCKNN CANBANK
AABCKPY BACKPAY
PAYBACK
AABCKRR BARRACK
AABCKRS BACKRAS
AABCKSW BACKSAW
AABCLMU CALUMBA
AABCLSY SCYBALA
AABCMST TAMBACS
AABCMSU SAMBUCA
AABCORT ABACTOR
ACROBAT
AABCOTT CATBOAT
AABCRSS SCARABS
AABCSUU AUCUBAS
AABCTTU CATTABU
AABDDEN ABANDED
AABDDER ABRADED
AABDDIK KABADDI
AABDEFL FADABLE
AABDEGN BANDAGE
AABDEHS ABASHED
AABDEIS DIABASE
AABDELL BALLADE
AABDELT ABLATED
DATABLE
AABDEMN BEADMAN
AABDEMS SAMBAED
AABDENU BANDEAU
AABDERS ABRADES
AABDERY ABRAYED
AABDESU AUBADES
AABDGHN HANDBAG

AABDGMO	GAMBADO
AABDGNS	SANDBAG
AABDGOS	DAGOBAS
AABDHMS	BADMASH
AABDHNT	HATBAND
AABDHNY	HAYBAND
AABDHRS	BARDASH
AABDIIS	BASIDIA
AABDIKR	BIDARKA
AABDILN	BALADIN
AABDIMR	BARMAID
AABDINS	INDABAS
AABDINT	TABANID
AABDIOT	BIODATA
AABDIRS	ABRAIDS
AABDLLS	BALLADS
AABDLMS	LAMBDAS
AABDLNS	SALBAND
AABDLRW	BRADAWL
AABDMNR	ARMBAND
AABDNNO	ABANDON
AABDNOR	BANDORA
AABDNRS	BANDARS
AABDNRU	BANDURA
AABDORS	ABROADS
AABDORV	BRAVADO
AABDRRW	DRAWBAR
AABDRST	BASTARD
	TABARDS
AABDRSU	SUBADAR
AABDRSY	BAYARDS
AABDSTU	DATABUS
AABEELT	EATABLE
AABEEMO	AMOEBAE
AABEERZ	ZAREEBA
AABEFFL	AFFABLE
AABEFFN	BEFFANA
AABEFGU	AUFGABE
AABEFNS	BEFANAS
AABEGGG	BAGGAGE
AABEGGR	GARBAGE
AABEGLR	ALGEBRA
AABEGMR	BERGAMA
	MEGABAR
AABEGMS	AMBAGES
AABEGRR	BAGARRE
	BARRAGE
AABEGSS	BAGASSE
AABEGST	ATABEGS
AABEGSU	ABUSAGE
AABEHLT	HATABLE
AABEHNT	ABTHANE
AABEHRS	EARBASH
AABEHSS	ABASHES
AABEIKN	IKEBANA
AABEILM	AMABILE
	AMIABLE
AABEILS	ABELIAS
AABEILT	LABIATE
AABEIRS	AIRBASE
	ARABISE
AABEIRZ	ARABIZE
AABEJLL	JELLABA
AABEJMU	JAMBEAU
AABEKLM	MAKABLE
AABEKLT	TAKABLE
AABEKNS	SEABANK
AABEKST	ATABEKS
AABELLL	LABELLA
AABELLN	BALNEAL

AABELLO	ABOLLAE
AABELLS	SABELLA
	SALABLE
AABELMN	NAMABLE
AABELMT	TAMABLE
AABELNO	ABALONE
AABELNR	BANALER
AABELPP	PAPABLE
AABELPR	PARABLE
AABELPY	PAYABLE
AABELRT	RATABLE
AABELSS	BALASES
AABELST	ABLATES
	ASTABLE
AABELSV	SAVABLE
AABELSY	SAYABLE
AABELTT	ABETTAL
AABELTU	TABLEAU
	TABULAE
AABELTV	VATABLE
AABELTX	TAXABLE
AABEMNS	BASEMAN
AABEMOS	AMOEBAS
AABENNW	WANNABE
AABENRT	ANTBEAR
AABENTY	ABEYANT
AABERST	ABREAST
AABERSU	BAUERAS
	SUBAREA
AABERSZ	ZAREBAS
AABERTT	RABATTE
	TABARET
AABERTU	ABATURE
AABESTZ	ZABETAS
AABETUX	BATEAUX
AABFFLY	AFFABLY
AABFILU	FABLIAU
AABFLRU	FABULAR
AABGGRS	RAGBAGS
AABGGSS	GASBAGS
AABGHNR	BHANGRA
AABGHNS	GABNASH
	NASHGAB
AABGHSW	BAGWASH
AABGIIL	ABIGAIL
AABGILM	MAILBAG
AABGINR	BARGAIN
AABGINS	ABASING
	BAAINGS
AABGINT	ABATING
AABGRST	RATBAGS
AABHHIS	SAHIBAH
AABHHKS	SABKHAH
AABHHRU	BRUHAHA
AABHISS	SAHIBAS
AABHITT	HABITAT
AABHJNS	BHAJANS
AABHKNR	BARKHAN
AABHKSS	KASBAHS
	SABKHAS
AABHKST	SABKHAT
AABHLRS	BHARALS
AABHLTY	BATHYAL
AABHMSS	SHAMBAS
AABHSSW	BASHAWS
AABIILX	BIAXIAL
AABIJMY	JAMBIYA
AABIKNS	BANKSIA
AABILLR	BARILLA
AABILLS	LABIALS

AABILMN	BIMANAL
AABILMY	AMIABLY
AABILOU	ABOULIA
AABILRS	BASILAR
AABILST	BALISTA
AABILSU	ABULIAS
AABIMMR	MARIMBA
AABIMNO	BONAMIA
AABIMOS	ABOMASI
AABINNS	BANIANS
AABINOU	OUABAIN
AABINRS	ARABINS
AABINRT	ATABRIN
AABINST	ABSTAIN
AABINSW	WABAINS
AABINSZ	BANZAIS
AABIPUX	PAXIUBA
AABIRSZ	ZARIBAS
AABISTT	ABATTIS
AABKNRS	BARKANS
AABKNRT	TANBARK
AABKOOZ	BAZOOKA
AABLLNS	BALLANS
AABLLNT	BALLANT
AABLLNY	BANALLY
AABLLOS	ABOLLAS
AABLLPT	PATBALL
AABLLST	BALLAST
	BALLATS
AABLLSY	SALABLY
AABLLWY	WALLABY
AABLMRU	LABARUM
AABLMSS	BALSAMS
	SAMBALS
AABLMST	LAMBAST
AABLMSY	ABYSMAL
	BALSAMY
AABLNTT	BLATANT
AABLORT	ABLATOR
AABLOSV	LAVABOS
AABLPRU	PABULAR
AABLRST	ARBLAST
AABLRTU	TABULAR
AABLRTY	RATABLY
AABLSST	BASALTS
AABLSSY	ABYSSAL
AABLSTU	ABLAUTS
AABLTTU	ABUTTAL
AABLTXY	TAXABLY
AABMNOT	BOATMAN
AABMNST	BANTAMS
	BATSMAN
AABMORU	MARABOU
AABMRSS	SAMBARS
AABMRTU	TAMBURA
AABMSST	TSAMBAS
AABMSSY	AMBASSY
AABNNOZ	BONANZA
AABNNSY	BANYANS
AABNOST	SABATON
AABORRS	ARROBAS
AABORST	ABATORS
AABORSZ	ABRAZOS
AABOTTY	ATTABOY
AABQSUU	SUBAQUA
AABRRST	BARRATS
AABRRSU	SABURRA
AABRRUV	BRAVURA
AABRSTY	BARYTAS
AABSSSY	SASSABY

AABTTTU	BATTUTA
AACCDEM	MEDACCA
AACCDES	CASCADE
	SACCADE
AACCDIR	CARDIAC
AACCDIS	CICADAS
AACCDSU	CADUACS
AACCEKR	CARCAKE
AACCELO	CLOACAE
AACCENV	VACANCE
AACCERS	CARCASE
AACCEST	SACCATE
AACCHHK	KACHCHA
AACCHIN	CHICANA
AACCHIR	ARCHAIC
AACCHKS	KACCHAS
AACCHLN	CLACHAN
AACCHMP	CHAMPAC
AACCHMS	CHACMAS
AACCHNN	CANNACH
AACCILM	ACCLAIM
AACCILS	CICALAS
AACCIMS	CAIMACS
AACCIOR	CARIOCA
AACCITT	ATACTIC
AACCKLP	CALPACK
AACCKRR	CARRACK
AACCKRS	CARACKS
AACCLLO	CLOACAL
AACCLLT	CATCALL
AACCLOP	POLACCA
AACCLOR	CARACOL
AACCLPS	CALPACS
AACCLPT	PLACCAT
AACCLRS	CALCARS
AACCLRU	ACCRUAL
	CARACUL
AACCLSU	ACCUSAL
AACCMOS	MACACOS
AACCNNS	CANCANS
AACCNVY	VACANCY
AACCORU	CURACAO
	CURACOA
AACCOST	ACCOAST
AACCOTT	TOCCATA
AACCRRT	CARRACT
AACCRSS	CARCASS
AACCRST	CARACTS
AACDDEL	DECADAL
AACDDER	ARCADED
AACDDHR	CHADDAR
AACDDIN	CANDIDA
AACDEEM	ACADEME
AACDEFL	FALCADE
AACDEFS	FACADES
AACDEHM	CHAMADE
AACDEHR	CHARADE
AACDEHT	CATHEAD
AACDEII	AECIDIA
AACDEIL	ALCAIDE
AACDEIN	AIDANCE
AACDEIS	ACEDIAS
AACDELL	ALCALDE
AACDELN	CANDELA
	DECANAL
AACDELR	CALDERA
AACDELS	SCALADE
AACDELY	ALCAYDE
AACDEMY	ACADEMY
AACDENV	ADVANCE

AACDENZ CADENZA
AACDEPS SCAPAED
AACDERS ARCADES
AACDERV CADAVER
AACDETU CAUDATE
AACDETV VACATED
AACDEUX CADEAUX
AACDFIR FARADIC
AACDFRS CAFARDS
AACDHMR DRACHMA
AACDHNR HANDCAR
AACDHRS CHADARS
AACDIIS ASCIDIA
AACDILR RADICAL
AACDINT ANTACID
AACDINV VANADIC
AACDIOR ACAROID
AACDIRS ACARIDS
ASCARID
AACDJKW JACKDAW
AACDLNO CALANDO
AACDLNS SCANDAL
AACDLOR CARLOAD
AACDLOS SCALADO
AACDLPR PLACARD
AACDMPS MADCAPS
AACDNRS CADRANS
CANARDS
AACDOOV AVOCADO
AACDRSS CSARDAS
AACDRSZ CZARDAS
AACEEGR ACREAGE
AACEEHR EARACHE
AACEEHT CHAETAE
AACEELN ANELACE
AACEEMR CAMERAE
AACEENT CATENAE
AACEERT ACERATE
AACEETT ACETATE
AACEFLT FALCATE
AACEFLU FACULAE
AACEFMN FACEMAN
AACEFRR CARFARE
AACEFRS CARAFES
AACEGGR AGGRACE
AACEGHS ACHAGES
AACEGKP PACKAGE
AACEGKS SACKAGE
AACEGNR CARNAGE
CRANAGE
AACEGRT CARTAGE
AACEGSV SCAVAGE
AACEHIN ACHENIA
AACEHIR ARCHAEI
AACEHLP ACALEPH
AACEHLR ALCHERA
AACEHNO CHOANAE
AACEHNP PANACHE
AACEHNR ACHARNE
AACEHPP APPEACH
AACEHPS APACHES
AACEHPU CHAPEAU
AACEHRT TRACHEA
AACEHST ACHATES
AACEHTT ATTACHE
AACEHTU CHATEAU
AACEIMN ANAEMIC
AACEIMU CAMAIEU
AACEINR ACARINE
CARINAE

AACEIRV AVARICE
CAVIARE
AACEKNP PANCAKE
AACEKNS ASKANCE
AACEKOT OATCAKE
AACELLN CANELLA
AACELLS SACELLA
AACELLT LACTEAL
AACELMN MANACLE
AACELMR CAMERAL
CARAMEL
CERAMAL
AACELMU MACULAE
AACELNS ANLACES
AACELNU CANULAE
LACUNAE
AACELNV VALANCE
AACELPS PALACES
AACELPT PLACATE
AACELRV CARAVEL
AACELST ACETALS
LACTASE
AACELTT LACTATE
AACELTV CLAVATE
AACEMMR MACRAME
AACEMNS CASEMAN
AACEMNV CAVEMAN
AACEMPR PARACME
AACEMQU MACAQUE
AACEMRS CAMERAS
AACEMSS CAMASES
AACENPS CANAPES
AACENRT CATERAN
AACENST CATENAS
AACENTT CANTATE
AACENTY CYANATE
AACEORS ROSACEA
AACEPRT CAPRATE
AACEPRU CAPUERA
AACEPRV PRECAVA
AACERSS CAESARS
AACERST ACATERS
AACERSU CAESURA
AACERSZ SAZERAC
AACERTU ARCUATE
AACERWY RACEWAY
AACESTV CAVEATS
VACATES
AACETTU ACTUATE
AACETUV VACUATE
AACFFIL CAFFILA
AACFILS CAFILAS
FACIALS
FASCIAL
AACFILU FAUCIAL
AACFINT FANATIC
AACFISS FASCIAS
AACFLLU FALCULA
AACFLLY FALLACY
AACFLRT FRACTAL
AACFLRU FACULAR
AACFLTU FACTUAL
AACFNST CAFTANS
AACFRRU FARRUCA
AACGHNS CHAGANS
AACGILL GLACIAL
AACGILM MAGICAL
AACGILS SCAGLIA
AACGINT AGNATIC
AACGIRS AGARICS

AACGIRV AGRAVIC
AACGLOT CATALOG
AACGLOU COAGULA
AACGNOU GUANACO
AACHHKR CHARKHA
AACHHLL CHALLAH
AACHIKN KACHINA
AACHIKR CHIKARA
AACHILR RACHIAL
AACHILT CALATHI
AACHIMR MACHAIR
AACHIMS CHIASMA
AACHIPS APHASIC
AACHIPT CHAPATI
AACHIRS ARACHIS
AACHIRT CITHARA
AACHKMP CHAMPAK
AACHKNS ACHKANS
AACHKPS CHAPKAS
PACHAKS
AACHKRS CHAKRAS
CHARKAS
AACHKRT HATRACK
AACHKSW KWACHAS
AACHLLN CHALLAN
AACHLMS CHASMAL
AACHLNS CHALANS
AACHLPP CHAPPAL
AACHLPS PASCHAL
AACHLST CALTHAS
AACHLSU ACUSHLA
AACHMNP CHAPMAN
AACHMNS MACHANS
AACHNOP PANOCHA
AACHNOU HUANACO
AACHNPX PANCHAX
AACHNRS ANARCHS
AACHNRV NAVARCH
AACHNRY ANARCHY
AACHNST ACANTHS
AACHNSZ CHAZANS
AACHRRT CATARRH
AACHRST CHARTAS
AACHRWY ARCHWAY
AACHSSW CASHAWS
AACHSTT CHATTAS
AACIILN ANCILIA
LACINIA
AACIINP APICIAN
AACIINT ACTINIA
AACIITV VIATICA
AACIJLP JALAPIC
AACIKLR CLARKIA
AACIKNN CANAKIN
AACILMS CALIMAS
AACILNR CLARAIN
CRANIAL
AACILNT ACTINAL
ALICANT
AACILOS ASOCIAL
AACILOX COAXIAL
AACILPS SPACIAL
AACILPT CAPITAL
PLACITA
AACIMMR MACRAMI
AACIMNS CAIMANS
MANIACS
AACIMOR ACROMIA
AACIMPR PICAMAR
AACIMTY CYMATIA

AACINNT CANTINA
AACINOR CONARIA
OCARINA
AACINPT CAPITAN
CAPTAIN
AACINRS ARNICAS
CARINAS
AACINRZ CZARINA
AACINSS ASCIANS
SANCAIS
AACINST SATANIC
AACIOPT TAPIOCA
AACIOPV COPAIVA
AACIOST ATOCIAS
COAITAS
AACIQTU AQUATIC
AACIRSS ASCARIS
AACIRST CARITAS
AACIRSV CAVIARS
AACISSS CASSIAS
AACISTT ASTATIC
AACJKLS JACKALS
AACJKMN JACKMAN
MANJACK
AACJKSS JACKASS
AACJOSU ACAJOUS
AACKMNP MANPACK
PACKMAN
AACKMRT AMTRACK
AACKNRS RANSACK
AACKPRR CARPARK
AACKPRT RATPACK
AACKPSZ CZAPKAS
AACKPWY PACKWAY
AACKRRS ARRACKS
AACKSTT ATTACKS
AACLLNS CALLANS
AACLLNT CALLANT
AACLLNU CALLUNA
LACUNAL
AACLLOR CORALLA
AACLLSU CLAUSAL
AACLLVY CAVALLY
AACLMNO COALMAN
AACLMNT CALMANT
CLAMANT
AACLMRU MACULAR
AACLMSU CALAMUS
AACLNNU CANNULA
AACLNPY CLAYPAN
AACLNRS CARNALS
AACLNRU LACUNAR
AACLNSU CANULAS
AACLOPR CAPORAL
AACLOPT OCTAPLA
AACLORT COALTAR
CROTALA
AACLORZ ALCORZA
AACLOST CATALOS
COASTAL
AACLOTT CATTALO
AACLOTV OCTAVAL
AACLPRS CARPALS
AACLPRT CALTRAP
AACLPSS PASCALS
AACLPSU PASCUAL
SCAPULA
AACLRSS LASCARS
RASCALS
SCALARS

AACLRST	CASTRAL
AACLRVY	CALVARY
	CAVALRY
AACLSSU	CASUALS
AACLSTT	SALTCAT
AACLSUV	VASCULA
AACLTTU	TACTUAL
AACMNOR	CAMARON
AACMNRU	ARCANUM
AACMNSY	CAYMANS
AACMORR	CAMORRA
AACMORS	SARCOMA
AACMORT	MARCATO
AACMOSY	MACOYAS
AACMRRT	TRAMCAR
AACMRSS	SARCASM
AACMRST	RAMCATS
	TARMACS
AACNNOZ	CANZONA
AACNOST	SACATON
AACNPST	CAPSTAN
	CAPTANS
	CATNAPS
AACNRST	ARCTANS
	CANTARS
AACNRTU	CURTANA
AACNSSV	CANVASS
AACNSTU	ASCAUNT
AACORST	OSTRACA
AACORTU	ACATOUR
	AUTOCAR
AACOTUV	AUTOVAC
AACPRSS	SCARPAS
AACRRST	CARRATS
AACRRSU	CURARAS
AACRSTV	CRAVATS
AACRTTT	ATTRACT
AACRTUV	VACATUR
AACRTUY	ACTUARY
AACRTWY	CARTWAY
AACTUWY	CUTAWAY
AADDDEN	ADDENDA
AADDEGM	DAMAGED
AADDEIL	ALIDADE
AADDEMM	MADAMED
AADDENP	DEADPAN
AADDEPR	PARADED
AADDEPT	ADAPTED
AADDERS	ADREADS
AADDERW	AWARDED
AADDESX	ADDAXES
AADDGNR	GRADDAN
	GRANDAD
AADDHKR	KHADDAR
AADDHRS	SRADDHA
AADDIIK	DIDAKAI
AADDIIV	DAVIDIA
AADDILS	ALIDADS
AADDLNS	ADLANDS
AADDNVV	DVANDVA
AADDOSU	AOUDADS
AADDRST	DASTARD
AADDRSW	ADWARDS
AADDSST	STADDAS
AADEEFR	AFEARED
AADEEGH	HEADAGE
AADEEMT	EDEMATA
AADEENR	ANEARED
AADEERT	AERATED
AADEFFR	AFFEARD
AADEFGL	FALDAGE
AADEFGR	FARDAGE
AADEFIS	FADAISE
AADEFLU	AEFAULD
AADEFNZ	FAZENDA
AADEFTW	FATWAED
AADEGGR	AGGRADE
	GARAGED
AADEGHR	RAGHEAD
AADEGLS	GELADAS
AADEGMN	AGNAMED
	MANAGED
AADEGMR	MEGARAD
AADEGMS	DAMAGES
AADEGNS	AGENDAS
AADEGRT	GRADATE
AADEGRV	RAVAGED
AADEGRY	DRAYAGE
	YARDAGE
AADEGSV	SAVAGED
AADEHIR	AIRHEAD
AADEHKS	AKEDAHS
AADEHMN	HEADMAN
AADEHMS	ASHAMED
AADEHPS	SAPHEAD
AADEHPW	AWHAPED
AADEHRW	RAWHEAD
	WARHEAD
AADEHWY	HEADWAY
AADEIKK	KAIAKED
AADEILR	RADIALE
AADEILV	AVAILED
	VEDALIA
AADEIMS	SEAMAID
AADEINR	ARANEID
AADEINS	NAIADES
AADEIPS	DIAPASE
AADEIRS	ARAISED
AADEIRT	RADIATE
	TIARAED
AADEITV	AVIATED
AADEITW	AWAITED
AADEJMR	JEMADAR
AADEKKY	KAYAKED
AADEKLR	KRAALED
AADEKLS	ASLAKED
AADEKMR	KAMERAD
AADEKMS	MEDAKAS
AADELLP	PADELLA
AADELLY	ALLAYED
AADELMO	ALAMODE
AADELMR	ALARMED
AADELMX	MALAXED
AADELNR	ADRENAL
AADELNW	DANELAW
AADELPR	PARDALE
AADELPT	PALATED
AADELRU	RADULAE
AADELRY	ALREADY
AADELSS	SALADES
	SALSAED
AADELTU	ADULATE
AADELTY	DAYTALE
AADEMNO	ADENOMA
AADEMNS	ANADEMS
	MAENADS
AADEMNT	MANDATE
AADEMSS	AMASSED
AADENNT	ANDANTE
AADENRV	VERANDA
AADENRW	AWARNED
AADENST	ANSATED
AADENSW	WEASAND
AADENWZ	WEAZAND
AADEPRS	ASPREAD
	PARADES
AADEPRT	ADAPTER
	READAPT
AADEPSS	ESPADAS
	PASSADE
AADEPWW	PAWAWED
AADERRS	ARRASED
AADERRY	ARRAYED
AADERSW	SEAWARD
AADERSY	ARAYSED
AADERTU	AURATED
AADESSY	ASSAYED
AADFLTW	TWAFALD
AADFNRR	FARRAND
AADFNST	FANTADS
AADFRST	DAFTARS
AADGGHR	HAGGARD
AADGGLR	LAGGARD
AADGGRS	SAGGARD
AADGHIL	HIDALGA
AADGIMM	DIGAMMA
AADGIMO	AGAMOID
AADGIMR	DIAGRAM
AADGIMS	AGAMIDS
AADGINW	ADAWING
AADGIOS	ADAGIOS
AADGLLW	GADWALL
AADGLMY	AMYGDAL
AADGLNO	GONADAL
AADGLNR	GARLAND
AADGLNS	SLADANG
AADGLRU	GRADUAL
AADGMNR	GRANDAM
	GRANDMA
AADGMNS	GADSMAN
AADGMRS	SMARAGD
AADGNPR	GRANDPA
AADGNPS	PADANGS
AADGNRS	ARGANDS
AADGNRT	GARDANT
AADGNRY	YARDANG
AADGOPR	PODAGRA
AADGOPS	PAGODAS
AADGRSU	GARUDAS
AADHILS	DAHLIAS
AADHIMS	SAMADHI
AADHJNR	HANDJAR
AADHKNY	YAKHDAN
AADHLRY	HALYARD
AADHMRS	DHARMAS
AADHNRS	DARSHAN
	DHARNAS
AADHNSW	HANDSAW
AADHRSZ	HAZARDS
AADHRWY	HAYWARD
AADHSWY	WASHDAY
AADIILR	DIARIAL
AADIINR	DIARIAN
AADIIPS	ASPIDIA
AADIJMN	JAMDANI
AADIKLY	ILKADAY
AADILLO	ALODIAL
AADILMR	ADMIRAL
	AMILDAR
AADILNP	PALADIN
AADILNR	LANIARD
AADILPS	APSIDAL
AADILRS	RADIALS
AADILRT	TAILARD
AADILST	STADIAL
AADILTV	DATIVAL
AADILWY	WAYLAID
AADIMNR	MANDIRA
AADIMNS	MAIDANS
AADIMOR	DIORAMA
AADIMOT	DOMATIA
AADINRR	DARRAIN
AADINRS	RADIANS
AADINRT	INTRADA
	RADIANT
AADINRV	VIRANDA
AADINSV	NAVAIDS
AADIQSS	QASIDAS
AADIRRW	AIRWARD
AADIRSU	SUDARIA
AADISST	STADIAS
AADJLNS	JANDALS
AADKMRY	DAYMARK
AADKMSS	DAMASKS
AADKNRT	TANKARD
AADKPSU	PADAUKS
AADKRWW	AWKWARD
AADLLMR	MALLARD
AADLLNW	LAWLAND
AADLLPU	PALUDAL
AADLLSS	SALLADS
AADLMNN	LANDMAN
AADLMNO	MANDOLA
AADLMNU	LADANUM
AADLMPS	LAMPADS
AADLMSW	WADMALS
AADLNRY	LANYARD
AADLNSS	SANDALS
AADLNSU	LANDAUS
AADLNSV	VANDALS
AADLPPU	APPLAUD
AADLPRS	PARDALS
AADLRRU	RADULAR
AADMMRS	DAMMARS
AADMNNS	SANDMAN
AADMNOR	MADRONA
	MANDORA
	MONARDA
	ROADMAN
AADMNRS	MANSARD
AADMNRY	DRAYMAN
	YARDMAN
AADMNSY	DAYSMAN
AADMNTU	MUTANDA
	TAMANDU
AADMOQU	MADOQUA
AADMORT	MATADOR
AADMOSU	AMADOUS
AADMRSU	MARAUDS
AADMRSZ	MAZARDS
AADMRZZ	MAZZARD
AADMSYY	MAYDAYS
AADNNOT	NOTANDA
AADNNRS	RANDANS
AADNOPR	PANDORA
AADNORT	ONDATRA
AADNORY	ANYROAD
AADNPRS	PANDARS
AADNPRU	PANDURA
AADNRRW	WARRAND

AADNRRY	DARRAYN
AADNRSS	NASARDS
AADNRST	ASTRAND
	TARANDS
AADNRTY	TANYARD
AADNRVW	VANWARD
AADNRWY	NAYWARD
AADOPRR	PARADOR
AADOPRS	PARADOS
AADOPRT	ADAPTOR
AADOPRX	PARADOX
AADOPSS	PASSADO
	POSADAS
AADOPTT	DOPATTA
AADORWY	ROADWAY
AADOSTT	TOSTADA
AADPSSW	PADSAWS
AADPSSY	SPAYADS
AADPTTU	DUPATTA
AADQRTU	QUADRAT
AADRSTU	DATURAS
AADRSTY	DAYSTAR
AADRSVW	VAWARDS
AADRWWY	WAYWARD
AAEEFFR	AFFEARE
AAEEFGL	LEAFAGE
AAEEGKL	LEAKAGE
AAEEGLT	ETALAGE
	GALEATE
AAEEGMN	AMENAGE
AAEEGRV	AVERAGE
AAEEGST	EATAGES
AAEEHRT	HETAERA
AAEEINT	TAENIAE
AAEEKLS	SEAKALE
AAEEKRW	REAWAKE
AAEELMT	MALEATE
AAEELOR	AREOLAE
AAEELRT	LAETARE
AAEEMNT	EMANATE
	ENEMATA
	MANATEE
AAEEPPS	APPEASE
AAEEPRT	PATERAE
AAEERST	AERATES
AAEERSW	SEAWARE
AAEERTU	AUREATE
AAEERTX	EXARATE
AAEFFGR	AGRAFFE
AAEFFIR	AFFAIRE
AAEFFLL	FALAFEL
AAEFFNR	FANFARE
AAEFFRS	AFFEARS
AAEFFTT	TAFFETA
AAEFGTW	WAFTAGE
AAEFKLO	OAKLEAF
AAEFLPR	EARFLAP
	PARAFLE
AAEFLRS	RAFALES
AAEFLSV	FAVELAS
AAEFMRT	FERMATA
AAEFQRU	AQUAFER
AAEFRRW	WARFARE
AAEFRWY	WAYFARE
AAEGGLS	GALAGES
AAEGGNO	ANAGOGE
AAEGGOP	APAGOGE
AAEGGRS	GARAGES
AAEGGRT	AGGRATE
AAEGGSV	GAVAGES
AAEGHLU	HAULAGE
AAEGHNT	THANAGE
AAEGILR	LAIRAGE
	REGALIA
AAEGILS	ALGESIA
AAEGINP	NAGAPIE
AAEGINV	VAGINAE
AAEGINW	WAINAGE
AAEGIPR	IGARAPE
AAEGIRR	ARRIAGE
AAEGISS	ASSEGAI
AAEGITT	AGITATE
AAEGJTU	AJUTAGE
AAEGKNT	TANKAGE
AAEGKOS	SOAKAGE
AAEGLLR	GLAREAL
AAEGLLT	GALLATE
	TALLAGE
AAEGLMN	GAMELAN
AAEGLMT	GAMETAL
AAEGLNN	ANLAGEN
AAEGLNR	ALNAGER
AAEGLNS	ALNAGES
	ANLAGES
	GALENAS
	LAGENAS
	LASAGNE
AAEGLNU	AULNAGE
AAEGLOP	APOGEAL
AAEGLRR	REALGAR
AAEGLRS	ALEGARS
	LAAGERS
AAEGLST	AGELAST
	ALGATES
	LASTAGE
AAEGLSV	LAVAGES
	SALVAGE
AAEGMNR	MANAGER
AAEGMNS	AGNAMES
	MANAGES
	SAGAMEN
AAEGMNT	GATEMAN
	MAGENTA
	MAGNATE
AAEGMPR	RAMPAGE
AAEGMRT	REGMATA
AAEGMSS	MASSAGE
AAEGNNP	PANNAGE
AAEGNNT	TANNAGE
AAEGNOP	APOGEAN
AAEGNPT	PAGEANT
AAEGNRR	ARRANGE
AAEGNRT	TANAGER
AAEGNST	AGNATES
AAEGNTV	VANTAGE
AAEGNTW	WANTAGE
AAEGORS	OARAGES
AAEGPRR	PARERGA
AAEGPRS	PARAGES
AAEGPSS	PASSAGE
AAEGPSV	PAVAGES
AAEGPSY	PAYSAGE
AAEGQUY	QUAYAGE
AAEGRRV	RAVAGER
AAEGRST	AGRASTE
AAEGRSV	RAVAGES
	SAVAGER
AAEGRTT	REGATTA
AAEGSSU	ASSUAGE
	SAUSAGE
AAEGSSV	AVGASES
	SAVAGES
AAEGSSW	ASSWAGE
AAEGSTU	GATEAUS
AAEGSTW	WASTAGE
AAEGTTW	WATTAGE
AAEGTUX	GATEAUX
AAEGTWY	GATEWAY
	GETAWAY
AAEHHPT	APHTHAE
AAEHILP	APHELIA
AAEHIRT	HETAIRA
AAEHKNT	KHANATE
AAEHKPS	PAKEHAS
AAEHKST	TAKAHES
AAEHKSW	SEAHAWK
AAEHLLL	ALLHEAL
AAEHLPX	HEXAPLA
AAEHLRT	TREHALA
AAEHLST	ALTHEAS
AAEHLTT	ATHLETA
AAEHMSS	ASHAMES
AAEHMTT	THEMATA
AAEHNPR	HANAPER
AAEHNPS	SAPHENA
AAEHNSY	HYAENAS
AAEHPRZ	PHEAZAR
AAEHPSW	AWHAPES
AAEHRSY	HEARSAY
AAEHSTT	HASTATE
AAEILLX	AXILLAE
AAEILMN	LAMINAE
AAEILMS	AMELIAS
	MALAISE
AAEILNN	ALANINE
AAEILNO	AEOLIAN
AAEILNT	ANTLIAE
AAEILOR	OLEARIA
AAEILPX	EPAXIAL
AAEILRS	AERIALS
AAEILRU	AURELIA
AAEILRV	VELARIA
AAEILSS	ALIASES
AAEILSV	AVAILES
AAEILSX	ALEXIAS
AAEIMMT	IMAMATE
AAEIMNS	AMNESIA
	ANEMIAS
AAEIMNT	AMENTIA
	ANIMATE
AAEIMPY	PYAEMIA
AAEIMRU	URAEMIA
AAEIMTV	AMATIVE
AAEINNO	AEONIAN
AAEINST	TAENIAS
AAEIPPS	APEPSIA
AAEIPRR	PAREIRA
AAEIPRS	SPIRAEA
AAEIPRT	APTERIA
AAEIPTT	APATITE
AAEIRSS	ARAISES
AAEIRST	ARISTAE
	ASTERIA
	ATRESIA
AAEIRSX	XERASIA
AAEIRTT	ARIETTA
AAEIRTV	VARIATE
AAEIRVW	AIRWAVE
AAEISTT	SATIATE
AAEISTV	AVIATES
AAEISTX	ATAXIES
AAEJMST	MAATJES
AAEJNRT	NAARTJE
AAEKKOR	KARAOKE
AAEKLMS	KAMELAS
AAEKLNS	ALKANES
AAEKLNT	ALKANET
	KANTELA
AAEKLSS	ASLAKES
AAEKMNW	WAKEMAN
AAEKMRR	EARMARK
AAEKMRS	SEAMARK
AAEKNNS	ANANKES
AAEKNSW	AWAKENS
	WAKANES
AAEKPRT	PARTAKE
AAEKRSS	KEASARS
AAEKRST	KARATES
AAELLLM	LAMELLA
AAELLNZ	ZANELLA
AAELLPR	PARELLA
AAELLPS	PAELLAS
AAELLPT	PATELLA
AAELLRT	LATERAL
AAELLRY	ALLAYER
AAELMMT	LEMMATA
AAELMNT	AMENTAL
AAELMNU	ALUMNAE
AAELMOT	OATMEAL
AAELMPT	PALMATE
AAELMST	MALATES
	MALTASE
	TAMALES
AAELMSX	MALAXES
AAELMSY	AMYLASE
AAELNNS	ANNEALS
AAELNOV	VALONEA
AAELNPT	PLATANE
AAELNPU	PAENULA
AAELNRS	ARSENAL
AAELNST	SEALANT
AAELNSY	ANALYSE
AAELNTT	TETANAL
AAELNTZ	ZEALANT
AAELNWY	LANEWAY
AAELNYZ	ANALYZE
AAELORR	AREOLAR
AAELORU	AUREOLA
AAELOTX	OXALATE
AAELPPR	APPAREL
AAELPPS	APPEALS
AAELPPT	PALPATE
AAELPPU	PAPULAE
AAELPRS	EARLAPS
AAELPRT	APTERAL
AAELPRV	PALAVER
AAELPSS	PALASES
AAELPST	PALATES
AAELPTT	TAPETAL
AAELPTU	PLATEAU
AAELPTY	APETALY
AAELRTV	LARVATE
AAELRTZ	LAZARET
AAELRVY	ALVEARY
AAELSST	ATLASES
AAELSTT	SALTATE
AAELSTV	VALETAS
AAELSTZ	ALTEZAS
AAELSUX	ASEXUAL
AAELSWX	SEALWAX

AAELTUV VALUATE
AAELTVV VALVATE
AAELTZZ ALTEZZA
AAELWWY WELAWAY
AAEMMMR MAREMMA
AAEMMMT MAMMATE
AAEMMNU MANUMEA
AAEMMOT OMMATEA
AAEMNNT EMANANT
AAEMNPP PAMPEAN
AAEMNPS SPAEMAN
AAEMNPT PEATMAN
AAEMNRT RAMENTA
AAEMNRU MURAENA
AAEMNST NAMASTE
AAEMNTU MANTEAU
AAEMOTZ METAZOA
AAEMQSU SQUAMAE
AAEMRST AMEARST
RETAMAS
AAEMRTU AMATEUR
AAEMSSS AMASSES
AAENNNT ANTENNA
AAENNST ANNATES
AAENNSZ ZENANAS
AAENNTT TANNATE
AAENNTV VENTANA
AAENOPS APNOEAS
AAENOSZ OZAENAS
AAENPPR PARPANE
AAENPST ANAPEST
PEASANT
AAENPSV PAVANES
AAENPSX PANAXES
AAENPTT EPATANT
AAENRRT NARRATE
AAENRSS NARASES
AAENRST ANESTRA
AAENRTT TARTANE
AAENRTU NATURAE
TAUREAN
AAENRTV TAVERNA
AAENRUW UNAWARE
AAENRUZ AZUREAN
AAENSSU NAUSEAS
AAENSSV VANESSA
AAEORRT AERATOR
AAEORRU AURORAE
AAEPPRS APPEARS
AAEPPRT PARAPET
AAEPRSS PASEARS
SARAPES
AAEPRST PETARAS
AAEPRSZ ZARAPES
AAEPRTY PEATARY
AAERRRS ARREARS
AAERRRY ARRAYER
AAERRSS ARRASES
AAERRTT TARTARE
AAERSST SEARATS
AAERSSY ARAYSES
ASSAYER
AAERSTU AURATES
AAERSTW AWAREST
AAESSTV SAVATES
AAESSWY SEAWAYS
AAFFIMS MAFFIAS
AAFFINS SAFFIAN
AAFFIRS AFFAIRS
RAFFIAS

AAFFIST TAFFIAS
AAFFPRS AFFRAPS
AAFFRSY AFFRAYS
AAFGHNS AFGHANS
AAFGORR FARRAGO
AAFHIKL KHALIFA
AAFHLWY HALFWAY
AAFHSTW FATWAHS
AAFIILR FILARIA
AAFIJST FAJITAS
AAFIKLS KAFILAS
AAFIKSS SIFAKAS
AAFILNT FANTAIL
AAFILQU ALFAQUI
AAFINNT INFANTA
AAFINRS FARINAS
AAFIPRT PARFAIT
AAFIRSS SAFARIS
AAFIRUY RUFIYAA
AAFIRWY FAIRWAY
AAFISST FATSIAS
AAFJLLW JAWFALL
AAFJLOR ALFORJA
AAFKNST KAFTANS
AAFLLLS FALLALS
AAFLLTY FATALLY
AAFLMPR FRAMPAL
AAFLNOR FORLANA
AAFLNRU FURLANA
AAFLWYY FLYAWAY
AAFMNRT RAFTMAN
AAFMNST FANTASM
AAFNRRT FARRANT
AAFNSTT FANTAST
AAFNSTY FANTASY
AAGGILN GANGLIA
AAGGKSU GAGAKUS
AAGGLMO MAGALOG
AAGGLOS GALAGOS
AAGGMNS MGANGAS
AAGGNOY ANAGOGY
AAGGNWY GANGWAY
AAGGQSU QUAGGAS
AAGGRSS SAGGARS
AAGGRST RAGTAGS
TAGRAGS
AAGHILR GHARIAL
AAGHKNS KANGHAS
KHANGAS
AAGHLNT GNATHAL
AAGHLOS GASAHOL
AAGHLSZ GHAZALS
AAGHMNN HANGMAN
AAGHMNW WHANGAM
AAGHMRS GRAMASH
AAGHNRS ARGHANS
HANGARS
AAGHQUU QUAHAUG
AAGHRSW WASHRAG
AAGHSTY SAGATHY
AAGIKNW AWAKING
AAGIKNZ ZIGANKA
AAGILMY MYALGIA
AAGILNN ANGINAL
AAGILNO LOGANIA
AAGILNP PAGINAL
AAGILNS AGNAILS
AAGILNV AVALING
VAGINAL
AAGILNY ALAYING

AAGILOS ALOGIAS
AAGILOT OTALGIA
AAGILPS PALAGIS
AAGILRS ARGALIS
GARIALS
AAGILSV GAVIALS
AAGILTW WAGTAIL
AAGIMNO ANGIOMA
AAGIMNS MAGIANS
SIAMANG
AAGIMNT AMATING
AAGIMNZ AMAZING
AAGINNS ANGINAS
AAGINNW WANIGAN
AAGINOS AGNOSIA
AAGINPY APAYING
AAGINRR ARRAIGN
AAGINRS NAGARIS
SANGRIA
SARANGI
AAGINRT GRANITA
AAGINRU GUARANI
AAGINST AGAINST
GITANAS
AAGINSU IGUANAS
AAGINSV VAGINAS
AAGINSY GAINSAY
AAGINTY ANTIGAY
AAGIOTT AGITATO
AAGIPRS AIRGAPS
AAGIPRU PIRAGUA
AAGIRRY ARGYRIA
AAGISTT SAGITTA
AAGJNRS GARJANS
AAGJRSU JAGUARS
AAGKOOZ GAZOOKA
AAGKORT KATORGA
AAGLLNS LALANGS
AAGLLNT GALLANT
AAGLMMS MALMAGS
AAGLMNS MANGALS
AAGLNOR GRANOLA
AAGLNOS ANALOGS
AAGLNOY ANALOGY
AAGLNPS LAPSANG
AAGLNRS RAGLANS
AAGLNRU ANGULAR
AAGLRUU ARUGULA
AUGURAL
AAGLRVX GRAVLAX
AAGLSST STALAGS
AAGMMNS MAGSMAN
AAGMMRR GRAMMAR
AAGMMRS GRAMMAS
AAGMMTU GUMMATA
AAGMNNR GRANNAM
AAGMNOS SANGOMA
AAGMNPR PANGRAM
AAGMNPY PANGAMY
AAGMNRS RAGMANS
AAGMNRT TANGRAM
TRANGAM
AAGMNSW SWAGMAN
AAGMNSZ ZAMANGS
AAGMOPY APOGAMY
AAGMORS MARGOSA
AAGMOSU AGAMOUS
AAGMRRY GRAMARY
AAGMRSY MARGAYS
AAGNNOS GOANNAS

AAGNNSW WANGANS
AAGNOPR PARAGON
AAGNORS ANGORAS
AAGNORZ ORGANZA
AAGNPRS PARANGS
AAGNRRS GARRANS
AAGNRRY GRANARY
AAGNRSS SANGARS
AAGNRTV VAGRANT
AAGNSTU TAGUANS
AAGOPSS SAPSAGO
AAGORSU SAGUARO
AAGOSTU AGOUTAS
AAGPPRS GRAPPAS
AAGRRSY GARRYAS
AAHHLSV HALVAHS
AAHHMSZ HAMZAHS
AAHHNNT THANNAH
AAHHNPT NAPHTHA
AAHHNST THANAHS
AAHIIMT HIMATIA
AAHIKRT KITHARA
AAHILLL HALLALI
AAHILLN HALLIAN
AAHILMR ALMIRAH
AAHILMS SHIMAAL
AAHILMT THALAMI
AAHILNT THALIAN
AAHILSY ALIYAHS
AAHIMNO MAHONIA
AAHIMSS AHIMSAS
AAHINOP APHONIA
AAHINPR PIRANHA
AAHINST SHAITAN
TAHINAS
AAHINTW TANIWHA
AAHIPRS PARIAHS
RAPHIAS
AAHIPRT PITARAH
AAHIPTZ ZAPTIAH
AAHIRSS SHARIAS
AAHIRST SHARIAT
AAHIRSV VIHARAS
AAHJKNR KHANJAR
AAHJNRS HANJARS
AAHJRRS JARRAHS
AAHKKST KATHAKS
AAHKLRS LASHKAR
AAHKLST KHALATS
AAHKMSY YASHMAK
AAHKNST KANTHAS
AAHKRSS RAKSHAS
AAHLLLS HALLALS
AAHLLNS HALLANS
NALLAHS
AAHLLOS HALLOAS
AAHLLPS PALLAHS
AAHLLSW WALLAHS
AAHLLWY HALLWAY
AAHLMMS HAMMALS
MAHMALS
MASHLAM
AAHLMRS MARSHAL
AAHLMRU HAMULAR
AAHLMST MALTHAS
AAHLNPX PHALANX
AAHLNRW NARWHAL
AAHLPRS PHRASAL
AAHLPST ASPHALT
TAPLASH

AAHLRSS	ASHLARS
AAHLRST	HARTALS
AAHLRSW	SHALWAR
AAHMMMS	HAMMAMS
AAHMMNS	MASHMAN
AAHMNNU	HANUMAN
AAHMNRS	HARMANS
AAHMNSS	SHAMANS
AAHMNTX	XANTHAM
AAHMOPR	AMPHORA
AAHMQSU	QUAMASH
AAHMRSS	ASHRAMS
AAHMSST	ASTHMAS
AAHMSSU	MASHUAS
AAHMSTZ	MATZAHS
AAHNNOS	HOSANNA
AAHNNST	TANNAHS
	THANNAS
AAHNNTX	XANTHAN
AAHNORT	ATHANOR
AAHNORV	NAVARHO
AAHNRTX	ANTHRAX
AAHNRTY	RHATANY
AAHPPRS	PARAPHS
AAHPRSY	YARPHAS
AAHPRTW	WARPATH
AAHPTWY	PATHWAY
AAHRSSS	HASSARS
AAHRSST	SHASTRA
AAHRTTW	ATHWART
AAHSSSY	SASHAYS
AAIIKKS	KAIKAIS
AAIILMR	AIRMAIL
AAIILPR	PAIRIAL
AAIILPT	TILAPIA
AAIILRZ	ALIZARI
AAIINNZ	ANZIANI
AAIINZZ	ZIZANIA
AAIIRVV	VIVARIA
AAIJLNP	JALAPIN
AAIJMNP	JAMPANI
AAIJNRZ	JANIZAR
AAIJNST	TINAJAS
AAIJPPY	JIPYAPA
AAIJRSW	JAWARIS
AAIKLLS	ALKALIS
AAIKLMS	KALMIAS
	KAMILAS
AAIKLNS	KALIANS
AAIKMNN	MANAKIN
AAIKMNR	RAMAKIN
AAIKMOR	ROMAIKA
AAIKMRS	KARAISM
AAIKNST	TANKIAS
AAIKORU	OUAKARI
AAIKPPR	PAPRIKA
AAIKRSS	ASKARIS
AAIKRST	KARAITS
AAIKRSU	UAKARIS
AAIKSTT	ASTATKI
AAIKTVV	AKVAVIT
AAILLLP	PALLIAL
AAILLMM	MAMILLA
AAILLMN	MANILLA
AAILLMR	ARMILLA
AAILLMX	MAXILLA
AAILLNV	VANILLA
AAILLPP	PAPILLA
AAILLRX	AXILLAR
AAILLSV	SALIVAL
AAILLUV	ALLUVIA
AAILLXY	AXIALLY
AAILMMN	MAILMAN
AAILMMR	AMMIRAL
AAILMMS	MIASMAL
AAILMMX	MAXIMAL
AAILMNR	LAMINAR
	RAILMAN
AAILMNS	ALMAINS
	ANIMALS
	MANILAS
AAILMNT	MATINAL
AAILMNU	ALUMINA
AAILMNV	MAILVAN
AAILMPS	IMPALAS
AAILMRT	MARITAL
	MARTIAL
AAILMSS	ALISMAS
	SALAMIS
AAILMSU	AUMAILS
AAILNOT	AILANTO
AAILNOV	NOVALIA
	VALONIA
AAILNPS	SALPIAN
AAILNPT	PLATINA
AAILNRU	ULNARIA
AAILNRY	LANIARY
AAILNSS	SALINAS
AAILNSY	INYALAS
AAILNTV	VALIANT
AAILORS	ROSALIA
	SOLARIA
AAILORU	RAOULIA
AAILORV	VARIOLA
AAILOST	SOLATIA
AAILPPT	APPALTI
AAILPRS	PARIALS
AAILPRT	PARTIAL
	PATRIAL
AAILPST	SPATIAL
AAILPTT	TALIPAT
AAILPZZ	PALAZZI
AAILRRV	ARRIVAL
AAILRST	LARIATS
	LATRIAS
AAILRTV	TRAVAIL
AAILRWY	RAILWAY
AAILSSS	ASSAILS
AAILSSV	SALIVAS
	SALVIAS
	VASSAIL
AAILSSW	WASSAIL
AAILTTT	LATITAT
AAIMMNO	AMMONIA
AAIMMSS	MIASMAS
AAIMNNO	OMNIANA
AAIMNOS	ANOSMIA
AAIMNOT	AMATION
AAIMNRS	MARINAS
AAIMNRT	TAMARIN
AAIMNST	MANATIS
	STAMINA
AAIMNSV	VIMANAS
AAIMNTX	TAXIMAN
AAIMRST	AMRITAS
	TAMARIS
AAIMRSU	SAMURAI
AAIMRTU	TIMARAU
AAIMSST	STASIMA
AAIMSTT	TATAMIS
AAIMSTV	ATAVISM
AAIMSUV	MAUVAIS
AAINNRU	URANIAN
AAINNRV	NAVARIN
	NIRVANA
AAINOPS	PAISANO
AAINORR	ORARIAN
AAINORV	OVARIAN
AAINOSX	ANOXIAS
AAINPPS	PAPAINS
AAINPRS	PIRANAS
AAINPST	PATINAS
	PINATAS
	TAIPANS
AAINRST	ANTIARS
	ARTISAN
	TSARINA
AAINRSU	ANURIAS
	SAURIAN
AAINRSV	SAVARIN
AAINRTV	VARIANT
AAINRTW	ANTIWAR
AAINSTT	ATTAINS
AAINSTV	VANITAS
AAINTTT	ATTAINT
AAINTTU	TUTANIA
AAIOPRS	APORIAS
AAIOPRT	ATROPIA
AAIORSU	SAOUARI
AAIORTV	AVIATOR
AAIPPRS	APPAIRS
AAIPPRU	PUPARIA
AAIPPTT	PITAPAT
AAIPRST	PITARAS
AAIPRSY	PIRAYAS
AAIPRTT	PARTITA
AAIPSZZ	PIAZZAS
AAIQSSU	QUASSIA
AAIQTUV	AQUAVIT
AAIRSST	ARISTAS
	TARSIAS
AAIRSTT	STRIATA
AAIRSTY	RAIYATS
AAIRSWY	AIRWAYS
AAIRSZZ	RAZZIAS
AAITWXY	TAXIWAY
AAJJMRS	JAMJARS
AAJKLWY	JAYWALK
AAJKMNR	JARKMAN
AAJKNSS	SANJAKS
AAJMNPS	JAMPANS
AAJMNZZ	JAZZMAN
AAJMORT	MAJORAT
AAJMPSY	PYJAMAS
AAJNNOS	JOANNAS
AAJNOSW	AJOWANS
AAJNOSY	YOJANAS
AAJOPSU	SAPAJOU
AAKKLPS	KALPAKS
AAKKLRU	KARAKUL
AAKKMOT	TOKAMAK
AAKKMRS	MARKKAS
AAKKOPS	KAKAPOS
AAKKSUZ	ZAKUSKA
AAKLMPU	LAMPUKA
AAKLMRY	MALARKY
AAKLMUY	YAMULKA
AAKLNOO	OOLAKAN
AAKLNOU	OULAKAN
AAKLOOP	PALOOKA
AAKLOOT	TALOOKA
AAKLRSU	KURSAAL
	RUSALKA
AAKLSSU	SAKSAUL
AAKLSTU	TALUKAS
AAKLWWY	WALKWAY
AAKMMNR	MARKMAN
AAKMNSU	MANUKAS
AAKMOSU	MOUSAKA
AAKMRSU	KUMARAS
AAKMRUZ	MAZURKA
AAKMRWY	WAYMARK
AAKNNTU	NUNATAK
AAKNORS	ANORAKS
AAKNRST	KANTARS
AAKNSST	ASKANTS
AAKNSWZ	KWANZAS
AAKNTWY	TWANKAY
AAKOOPP	PAKAPOO
AAKOPRS	PAKORAS
AAKORST	OSTRAKA
AAKPRWY	PARKWAY
AAKRTUY	AUTARKY
AAKSSTT	ATTASKS
AAKSTTT	ATTASKT
AAKSTUY	YUKATAS
AALLLNS	LALLANS
AALLLSS	SALLALS
AALLMMS	MALLAMS
AALLMPU	AMPULLA
AALLNPU	PLANULA
AALLNSY	NASALLY
AALLORS	AROLLAS
AALLOSZ	AZOLLAS
AALLOTV	LAVOLTA
AALLPPY	PAPALLY
AALLRUY	AURALLY
AALLRVY	VALLARY
AALLSTT	ATLATLS
	TALLATS
AALLUVV	VALVULA
AALMMMS	MAMMALS
AALMMNO	AMMONAL
AALMMNT	MALTMAN
AALMNOS	SALAMON
AALMNOY	ANOMALY
AALMNPS	NAPALMS
AALMNSU	MANUALS
AALMORT	ALAMORT
AALMORY	MAYORAL
AALMOST	AMATOLS
AALMPRY	PALMARY
	PALMYRA
AALMPSS	PLASMAS
AALMRRU	RAMULAR
AALMRSU	ALARUMS
AALMSSU	MASULAS
AALMSTY	AMYTALS
AALMTTU	MULATTA
AALNNRU	ANNULAR
AALNNSU	ANNUALS
AALNPRT	PLANTAR
AALNPST	PLANTAS
	PLATANS
AALNPUU	PUNALUA
AALNQTU	QUANTAL
AALNRSU	RANULAS
AALNRTT	LATRANT
AALNRTU	NATURAL
AALNSST	SANTALS

AALNSTT	SALTANT
	TALANTS
AALNSTU	SULTANA
AALNSTY	ANALYST
AALNTTU	TALAUNT
AALOPPT	APPALTO
AALOPRS	PARASOL
AALOPSY	PAYOLAS
AALOPVV	PAVLOVA
AALOPZZ	PALAZZO
AALORRU	AURORAL
AALORSU	AROUSAL
AALORTX	LAXATOR
AALOSTT	SALTATO
AALOSVW	AVOWALS
AALOTTY	TALAYOT
AALPPRU	PAPULAR
AALPRRS	PARRALS
AALPRSW	ASPRAWL
AALPRSY	PARLAYS
AALPSTU	SPATULA
AALRSST	TARSALS
AALRSTU	AUSTRAL
AALRSTY	ASTYLAR
	SATYRAL
AALSSSV	VASSALS
AALSSTU	ASSAULT
AALSSUX	SAXAULS
AALSTUV	VALUTAS
AALSWYY	WAYLAYS
AAMMMRY	MAMMARY
AAMMNRT	MANTRAM
AAMMNST	AMTMANS
AAMMOTY	MYOMATA
AAMMRRS	MARRAMS
AAMMRST	RAMSTAM
	TAMMARS
AAMMSUZ	MAZUMAS
AAMNNOY	ANONYMA
AAMNOOS	MANOAOS
AAMNORS	OARSMAN
AAMNORT	AMORANT
AAMNOSZ	AMAZONS
AAMNOTY	ANATOMY
AAMNPRT	MANTRAP
	RAMPANT
AAMNPRY	PARANYM
AAMNPSS	PASSMAN
	SAMPANS
AAMNPST	TAPSMAN
AAMNPTY	TYMPANA
AAMNRST	ARTSMAN
	MANTRAS
AAMNSTU	MANTUAS
	TAMANUS
AAMOORS	AMOROSA
AAMOPRS	PARAMOS
AAMORRZ	ZAMARRO
AAMORSV	SAMOVAR
AAMORTY	AMATORY
AAMOSSS	SAMOSAS
AAMOSTT	STOMATA
AAMOTTU	AUTOMAT
AAMPRRT	RAMPART
AAMPSSY	AMPASSY
AAMRSST	MATRASS
AAMRSSU	ASARUMS
AAMRSTU	SUMATRA
	TRAUMAS
AAMRTWY	TRAMWAY
AAMSSTU	SATSUMA
AANNOTT	ANNATTO
AANNPSS	SANPANS
AANNSYZ	NYANZAS
AANOQSY	YAQONAS
AANORST	TORANAS
AANOSST	SONATAS
AANOSTT	ANATTOS
AANPPSS	SAPPANS
AANPRST	PARTANS
	SPARTAN
	TARPANS
	TRAPANS
AANPSST	PASSANT
AANQRTU	QUARTAN
AANRRSW	WARRANS
AANRRTW	WARRANT
AANRSTT	RATTANS
	TANTRAS
	TARTANS
AANRUWY	RUNAWAY
AANSSTV	SAVANTS
AANSSTZ	STANZAS
AANSTTT	STATANT
AANSTUV	AVAUNTS
AANSWYY	ANYWAYS
AAOORRW	WOORARA
AAOPSST	POTASSA
	SAPOTAS
AAORRSU	AURORAS
AAORRSV	VARROAS
AAORSTT	TOTARAS
AAOSTTV	OTTAVAS
AAOTTUY	TATOUAY
AAPPSWW	PAWPAWS
AAPRSST	SATRAPS
AAPRSTT	ATTRAPS
AAPRSTY	SATRAPY
AAQRSSU	QUASARS
AARRSTT	TARTARS
AARRSWY	WARRAYS
AARSSST	ASSARTS
AARSSTT	ASTARTS
AARSSTY	SATYRAS
AASSTTU	STATUAS
ABBBDEL	BABBLED
	BLABBED
ABBBELR	BABBLER
	BLABBER
	BRABBLE
ABBBELS	BABBLES
ABBBITT	BABBITT
ABBCDER	CRABBED
ABBCDES	SCABBED
ABBCEHI	BABICHE
ABBCEHU	BABUCHE
ABBCEIS	CABBIES
ABBCELR	CLABBER
ABBCELS	SCABBLE
ABBCERR	CRABBER
ABBCIKT	BACKBIT
ABBCIRS	BICARBS
ABBCOST	BOBCATS
ABBCRYY	CRYBABY
ABBDDEL	DABBLED
ABBDDER	DRABBED
ABBDEFR	FRABBED
ABBDEGL	GABBLED
ABBDEGR	GRABBED
ABBDEIT	TABBIED
ABBDEJL	JABBLED
ABBDELR	DABBLER
	DRABBLE
	RABBLED
ABBDELS	DABBLES
	SLABBED
ABBDELW	WABBLED
ABBDERR	DRABBER
ABBDERS	DABBERS
ABBDERT	DRABBET
ABBDEST	STABBED
	TEBBADS
ABBDESU	BEDAUBS
ABBDESW	SWABBED
ABBDGIN	DABBING
ABBDHIJ	DJIBBAH
ABBDILR	LIBBARD
ABBDINR	RIBBAND
ABBDITY	DABBITY
ABBDLRU	LUBBARD
ABBDMOR	BOMBARD
ABBDMOU	BABUDOM
ABBEESW	BAWBEES
ABBEFST	FABBEST
ABBEGIR	GABBIER
ABBEGLR	GABBLER
	GRABBLE
ABBEGLS	GABBLES
ABBEGNO	BOGBEAN
ABBEGNU	BUGBANE
ABBEGRR	GRABBER
ABBEGRS	GABBERS
ABBEGRU	BUGBEAR
ABBEHLS	SHABBLE
ABBEIRS	BARBIES
ABBEIST	BABIEST
	TABBIES
ABBEISY	YABBIES
ABBEJLS	JABBLES
ABBEJRS	JABBERS
ABBELMR	BRAMBLE
ABBELNS	SNABBLE
ABBELOR	BELABOR
ABBELPR	PRABBLE
ABBELRR	RABBLER
ABBELRS	BARBELS
	RABBLES
	SLABBER
ABBELRU	BARBULE
ABBELRW	WABBLER
ABBELSU	BAUBLES
ABBELSW	BAWBLES
	WABBLES
ABBELUY	BUYABLE
ABBEMUZ	BUMBAZE
ABBENRS	NABBERS
ABBEORS	EARBOBS
ABBERRS	BARBERS
ABBERST	BARBETS
	RABBETS
	STABBER
ABBERSW	SWABBER
ABBERSY	YABBERS
ABBESSU	SUBBASE
ABBFIRT	FRABBIT
ABBGGIN	GABBING
ABBGHSU	GUBBAHS
ABBGIJN	JABBING
ABBGINN	NABBING
ABBGINR	BARBING
ABBGINT	TABBING
ABBGINU	BUBINGA
ABBGINY	BABYING
ABBGMSU	BUMBAGS
ABBGOOU	BUGABOO
ABBGORS	GABBROS
ABBHIJS	JIBBAHS
ABBHISY	BABYISH
ABBHJSU	JUBBAHS
ABBHOOS	BABOOSH
	HABOOBS
ABBHRRU	RHUBARB
ABBHTTU	BATHTUB
ABBIIMN	BAMBINI
ABBILOR	BILOBAR
ABBILOT	BOBTAIL
ABBILSU	BUBALIS
ABBIMNO	BAMBINO
ABBIMSU	BABUISM
ABBINOR	RABBONI
ABBINRS	RABBINS
ABBIRST	RABBITS
ABBIRTY	RABBITY
ABBKLOU	BLAUBOK
ABBLLRU	BULLBAR
ABBLLTU	BULLBAT
ABBLMRY	BRAMBLY
ABBMOOR	BOMBORA
ABBMOOS	BAMBOOS
ABBMOST	BOMBAST
ABBNOOS	BABOONS
ABBORSS	ABSORBS
ABBQSUY	SQUABBY
ABCCCHI	BACCHIC
ABCCEIR	ACERBIC
	BRECCIA
ABCCEIS	BACCIES
	SEBACIC
ABCCEOS	BACCOES
ABCCHII	BACCHII
ABCCHTY	BYCATCH
ABCCILU	CUBICAL
ABCCIMR	CAMBRIC
ABCCINU	BUCCINA
ABCCIOR	BORACIC
	BRACCIO
ABCCISU	CUBICAS
ABCCKOW	BAWCOCK
ABCCKTU	CUTBACK
ABCCOOR	BAROCCO
ABCCOOT	TOBACCO
ABCCSUU	SUCCUBA
ABCDDEU	ABDUCED
ABCDEEH	BEACHED
ABCDEEL	BELACED
	DEBACLE
ABCDEHT	BATCHED
ABCDEHU	DEBAUCH
ABCDEIK	DIEBACK
ABCDEIN	CABINED
ABCDEIP	PEDICAB
ABCDEIR	CARBIDE
ABCDEKL	BLACKED
ABCDEKR	REDBACK
ABCDEOR	BROCADE
ABCDERS	DECARBS
ABCDERU	CUDBEAR
ABCDESU	ABDUCES
ABCDHIO	ICHABOD
ABCDHOR	CHOBDAR

ABCDHOS	BODACHS
ABCDIIS	DIBASIC
ABCDILR	BALDRIC
ABCDINS	ABSCIND
ABCDIRS	SCABRID
ABCDIRT	CATBIRD
ABCDIRU	BAUDRIC
ABCDISU	SUBACID
ABCDNOS	ABSCOND
ABCDOOR	CORDOBA
ABCDORR	BROCARD
ABCDSTU	ABDUCTS
ABCEEHS	BEACHES
ABCEEHU	EBAUCHE
ABCEELS	BELACES
ABCEEMR	EMBRACE
ABCEEMS	EMBACES
ABCEENS	ABSENCE
ABCEERR	ACERBER
	CEREBRA
	REBRACE
ABCEERU	BERCEAU
ABCEESS	BECASSE
ABCEESU	BECAUSE
ABCEGIR	RIBCAGE
ABCEGMO	CAMBOGE
ABCEGOR	BROCAGE
ABCEGOS	BOCAGES
	BOSCAGE
ABCEGSU	CUBAGES
ABCEHKO	BACKHOE
ABCEHLU	BAUCHLE
ABCEHMR	BECHARM
	BRECHAM
	CHAMBER
	CHAMBRE
ABCEHOS	BASOCHE
ABCEHRS	BRACHES
ABCEHRT	BRACHET
ABCEHST	BATCHES
ABCEIKT	TIEBACK
ABCEILL	ICEBALL
ABCEILM	ALEMBIC
	CEMBALI
ABCEILR	CALIBER
	CALIBRE
ABCEILT	CITABLE
ABCEIMO	AMOEBIC
ABCEINR	CARBINE
ABCEINT	CABINET
ABCEIOR	AEROBIC
ABCEIOT	ICEBOAT
ABCEIRS	ASCRIBE
	CABRIES
	CARBIES
	CARIBES
ABCEISS	ABSCISE
	SCABIES
ABCEITT	TABETIC
ABCEJST	ABJECTS
ABCEKLN	BLACKEN
ABCEKLR	BLACKER
ABCEKNR	BRACKEN
ABCEKRS	BACKERS
	REBACKS
ABCEKRT	BRACKET
ABCEKST	BACKETS
	BACKSET
	SETBACK
ABCEKSY	BACKSEY
ABCEKTW	WETBACK
ABCELLS	BECALLS
ABCELLU	BULLACE
ABCELMO	CEMBALO
ABCELMR	CAMBREL
	CLAMBER
ABCELMS	BECALMS
	SCAMBLE
ABCELOP	PLACEBO
ABCELOV	VOCABLE
ABCELPU	BLUECAP
ABCELPY	BYPLACE
ABCELRU	CURABLE
ABCELST	CABLETS
ABCELSU	BASCULE
ABCEMRS	CAMBERS
	CEMBRAS
ABCEMSX	EXCAMBS
ABCENOR	BACONER
ABCENOS	BEACONS
ABCENOW	COWBANE
ABCENRU	UNBRACE
ABCEOOS	CABOOSE
ABCEORU	CORBEAU
ABCERRS	BRACERS
ABCESSS	ABSCESS
ABCFIKN	FINBACK
ABCFILO	BIFOCAL
ABCFIRS	FABRICS
ABCFLOO	COBLOAF
ABCFNOS	CONFABS
ABCGHIN	BACHING
ABCGHKO	HOGBACK
ABCGIKN	BACKING
ABCGILN	CABLING
ABCGINR	BRACING
ABCGKLO	BACKLOG
ABCGMSU	SCUMBAG
ABCHHII	HIBACHI
ABCHIMT	BATHMIC
ABCHIOT	COHABIT
ABCHKOU	CHABOUK
ABCHKTU	HACKBUT
ABCHKUW	HAWBUCK
ABCHNOR	BROCHAN
ABCHNRU	BRAUNCH
ABCHNRY	BRANCHY
ABCIILL	BACILLI
ABCIILN	ALBINIC
ABCIILT	ALBITIC
ABCIIMN	MINICAB
ABCIIMS	IAMBICS
ABCIIOR	CIBORIA
ABCIIOT	ABIOTIC
ABCIJNO	JACOBIN
ABCILRS	SCRIBAL
ABCILTU	CUBITAL
ABCIMMS	CAMBISM
ABCIMMU	CAMBIUM
ABCIMST	CAMBIST
ABCINOT	BOTANIC
ABCIORR	BARRICO
ABCIORU	CARIBOU
ABCIOUV	BIVOUAC
ABCIRST	CABRITS
ABCIRTY	BARYTIC
ABCISSS	ABSCISS
ABCJOSU	JACOBUS
ABCKLLY	BLACKLY
ABCKLOT	BACKLOT
ABCKMRU	BUCKRAM
ABCKMUZ	ZAMBUCK
ABCKNNO	BANNOCK
ABCKNRU	RUNBACK
ABCKORS	BAROCKS
ABCKOSW	SOWBACK
ABCKOTU	OUTBACK
ABCKRSU	BUCKRAS
ABCKSTU	SACKBUT
	SUBTACK
ABCKSUW	BUCKSAW
	SAWBUCK
ABCLMNU	CLUBMAN
ABCLMOY	CYMBALO
ABCLMSY	CYMBALS
ABCLMUU	BACULUM
ABCLNOS	BLANCOS
ABCLNOY	BALCONY
ABCLOST	COBALTS
ABCMORS	COMARBS
ABCMOST	COMBATS
	TOMBACS
ABCMRSS	SCRAMBS
ABCNORS	CARBONS
	CORBANS
ABCORRW	CROWBAR
ABCORSX	BOXCARS
ABCORSY	CARBOYS
ABCSSTU	SUBACTS
ABDDDEL	BLADDED
ABDDEEJ	BEJADED
ABDDEER	BEARDED
	BREADED
ABDDEES	DEBASED
ABDDEET	DEBATED
ABDDEEZ	BEDAZED
ABDDEIN	ABIDDEN
	BANDIED
ABDDEIR	BRAIDED
ABDDEIS	BADDIES
ABDDELR	BLADDER
ABDDELU	BLAUDED
ABDDENR	BRANDED
ABDDEOR	ABORDED
	BOARDED
ABDDERW	BEDWARD
ABDDHIS	BADDISH
ABDDHSU	BUDDHAS
ABDDINS	DISBAND
ABDDLLO	ODDBALL
ABDDMOR	DAMBROD
ABDEEGL	BEAGLED
ABDEEHO	OBEAHED
ABDEEHS	BEHEADS
ABDEEHT	BEATHED
ABDEEHV	BEHAVED
ABDEEIR	BEADIER
	BEARDIE
ABDEEJS	BEJADES
ABDEELM	BELDAME
	BEMEDAL
	EMBALED
ABDEELN	ENABLED
ABDEELR	BEDERAL
	BLEARED
ABDEELS	BEADLES
ABDEELT	BELATED
	BLEATED
ABDEELY	BELAYED
	DYEABLE
ABDEEMN	BEADMEN
	BEDEMAN
	BENAMED
ABDEEMR	AMBERED
	BREAMED
	EMBREAD
ABDEEMS	EMBASED
ABDEEMY	EMBAYED
ABDEEMZ	BEMAZED
ABDEERS	DEBASER
	SABERED
ABDEERT	BERATED
	BETREAD
	DEBATER
	REBATED
ABDEERW	BEWARED
ABDEERY	BERAYED
ABDEESS	DEBASES
	SEABEDS
ABDEEST	BESTEAD
	DEBATES
ABDEESZ	BEDAZES
ABDEETT	ABETTED
ABDEFFL	BAFFLED
ABDEFLT	FLATBED
ABDEFLU	LEAFBUD
ABDEFOR	FORBADE
ABDEFRW	BEDWARF
ABDEFST	BEDFAST
ABDEGGL	BLAGGED
ABDEGGR	BRAGGED
ABDEGHR	BEGHARD
ABDEGIN	BEADING
ABDEGIR	ABRIDGE
	BRIGADE
ABDEGLM	GAMBLED
ABDEGLN	BANGLED
ABDEGLR	BELGARD
	GARBLED
ABDEGNO	BONDAGE
	DOGBANE
ABDEGOS	BODEGAS
ABDEGRS	BADGERS
ABDEHIT	HABITED
ABDEHLM	HAMBLED
ABDEHLR	HALBERD
ABDEHOW	BOWHEAD
ABDEHRS	BERDASH
	BRASHED
ABDEHRT	BREADTH
ABDEHSU	SUBHEAD
ABDEILP	BIPEDAL
	PIEBALD
ABDEILR	BRAILED
	RAILBED
	RIDABLE
ABDEILS	BALDIES
	DIABLES
	DISABLE
ABDEILT	LIBATED
ABDEILU	AUDIBLE
ABDEIMR	EMBRAID
ABDEIMS	IMBASED
ABDEINR	BANDIER
	BRAINED
ABDEINS	BANDIES
ABDEINW	BEDAWIN
ABDEIRR	BARDIER
	BRAIDER
	BRIARED

	RABIDER
ABDEIRS	BRAISED
	DARBIES
	SEABIRD
	SIDEBAR
ABDEIRT	TRIBADE
ABDEIRU	DAUBIER
ABDEIRW	BAWDIER
ABDEISS	BIASSED
ABDEIST	BASTIDE
ABDEISW	BAWDIES
ABDEJRU	ABJURED
ABDEKLN	BLANKED
ABDEKLU	BAULKED
ABDEKNR	BRANKED
ABDEKNU	UNBAKED
ABDEKRS	DEBARKS
ABDELMR	MARBLED
	RAMBLED
ABDELMS	BEDLAMS
	BELDAMS
ABDELMW	WAMBLED
ABDELMY	EMBAYLD
ABDELNR	BLANDER
ABDELOR	LABORED
ABDELOS	ALBEDOS
ABDELOT	BLOATED
ABDELOW	DOWABLE
ABDELPU	DUPABLE
ABDELPY	PYEBALD
ABDELRR	DRABLER
ABDELRS	BEDRALS
ABDELRU	DURABLE
ABDELRW	BRAWLED
	WARBLED
ABDELST	BALDEST
	BLASTED
	STABLED
ABDELSU	BELAUDS
ABDELTT	BATTLED
	BLATTED
ABDEMMO	MAMBOED
ABDEMNO	ABDOMEN
ABDEMRU	RUMBAED
ABDENOR	BANDORE
	BROADEN
ABDENOT	BATONED
ABDENOY	NAEBODY
ABDENPS	BEDPANS
ABDENRR	BRANDER
ABDENRU	UNBARED
ABDENRW	BRAWNED
ABDENSS	BADNESS
ABDENSU	SUBDEAN
ABDENTU	UNBATED
ABDEOOT	TABOOED
ABDEORR	BOARDER
	BROADER
ABDEORT	ABORTED
	TABORED
ABDEOST	BOASTED
ABDEOTU	BOUTADE
ABDEQSU	BASQUED
ABDERSS	SERDABS
ABDERST	DABSTER
	TABERDS
ABDERSU	DAUBERS
	SUBEDAR
ABDERSV	ADVERBS
ABDERTY	DRYBEAT
ABDERUY	DAUBERY
ABDETTU	ABUTTED
ABDGGIN	BADGING
ABDGGOR	BOGGARD
ABDGIIN	ABIDING
ABDGILN	BALDING
ABDGINN	BANDING
ABDGINO	ABODING
ABDGINR	BARDING
	BRIGAND
ABDGINT	DINGBAT
ABDGINU	DAUBING
ABDGINW	WINDBAG
ABDGLNO	BOGLAND
ABDGLUY	LADYBUG
ABDGNOS	BANDOGS
ABDGORS	BODRAGS
ABDHHOS	DOBHASH
ABDHIIT	ADHIBIT
ABDHILS	BALDISH
ABDHMOR	RHABDOM
ABDHMSU	BUDMASH
ABDHMTU	MUDBATH
ABDHNOR	BODHRAN
ABDHNSU	HUSBAND
ABDHOSY	HOBDAYS
ABDHRSU	BURDASH
	RHABDUS
ABDIKNW	BAWDKIN
ABDIKRS	DISBARK
ABDILMO	BIMODAL
ABDILOO	DIABOLO
ABDILOR	LABROID
ABDILOT	TABLOID
ABDILRS	BRIDALS
	LABRIDS
	RIBALDS
ABDILRW	AWLBIRD
ABDILRY	RABIDLY
ABDILUY	AUDIBLY
ABDILWY	BAWDILY
ABDIMNR	BIRDMAN
ABDIMOR	AMBROID
ABDINOR	INBOARD
ABDINRS	RIBANDS
ABDINRT	ANTBIRD
ABDINST	BANDITS
ABDIOSU	BADIOUS
ABDIPRU	UPBRAID
ABDIRRS	BRAIRDS
ABDIRSS	DISBARS
ABDIRSU	RIBAUDS
	SUBARID
ABDIRTY	TRIBADY
ABDKNOO	BANDOOK
ABDLLNY	BLANDLY
ABDLLOR	BOLLARD
ABDLNOR	BANDROL
ABDLORY	BROADLY
ABDLRUY	DURABLY
	RYBAULD
ABDLRYY	BYRLADY
ABDLSUU	SUBDUAL
ABDMNNO	BONDMAN
ABDMRUY	MARYBUD
ABDNOOR	ONBOARD
ABDNOPR	PROBAND
ABDNOSU	ABOUNDS
	BAUSOND
ABDNOSX	SANDBOX
ABDNOSY	SANDBOY
ABDNOYY	ANYBODY
ABDNRTU	TURBAND
ABDOORW	BARWOOD
ABDORRS	BORDARS
ABDORSS	ADSORBS
ABDORSY	BYROADS
ABDRRSU	DURBARS
ABDRSTU	BUSTARD
ABDRUZZ	BUZZARD
ABEEEGR	BEERAGE
ABEEELS	SEEABLE
ABEEERV	BEREAVE
ABEEFFL	EFFABLE
ABEEFLO	BEEFALO
ABEEFTU	BEAUFET
ABEEGHR	HERBAGE
ABEEGHS	BEEGAHS
	BHAGEES
ABEEGLL	GABELLE
ABEEGLR	BEAGLER
ABEEGLS	BEAGLES
ABEEGRR	GERBERA
ABEEGRS	ABREGES
	BAREGES
	BARGEES
ABEEGRU	AUBERGE
ABEEGRW	BREWAGE
ABEEHJS	BHAJEES
ABEEHMS	BESHAME
ABEEHMT	EMBATHE
ABEEHNN	HENBANE
ABEEHNS	BANSHEE
	BEENAHS
ABEEHNT	BENEATH
ABEEHRT	BREATHE
ABEEHSV	BEHAVES
ABEEIKR	BEAKIER
ABEEILS	BAILEES
ABEEIMR	BEAMIER
ABEEINS	BEANIES
ABEEINT	BETAINE
ABEEIRT	EBRIATE
ABEEIST	BEASTIE
ABEEJMS	JAMBEES
ABEEJRS	BAJREES
ABEEKLR	BLEAKER
ABEEKLS	KABELES
ABEEKNT	BETAKEN
ABEEKNV	BEKNAVE
ABEEKOP	PEEKABO
ABEEKPS	BESPAKE
	BESPEAK
ABEEKRR	BREAKER
ABEEKRS	BEAKERS
ABEEKST	BETAKES
ABEELLY	EYEBALL
ABEELMM	EMBLEMA
ABEELMS	EMBALES
ABEELMT	BEAMLET
ABEELMZ	EMBLAZE
ABEELNP	PLEBEAN
ABEELNR	ENABLER
ABEELNS	BALEENS
	ENABLES
ABEELNT	TENABLE
ABEELNU	NEBULAE
ABEELOR	EARLOBE
ABEELPR	BEPEARL
ABEELQU	EQUABLE
ABEELRR	BLEARER
	ERRABLE
ABEELRT	BLEATER
	RETABLE
ABEELST	BELATES
ABEELSU	SUEABLE
ABEELSV	BESLAVE
ABEEMNS	BASEMEN
	BEMEANS
	BENAMES
ABEEMNT	BEMEANT
ABEEMRS	BEAMERS
	BESMEAR
ABEEMRV	EMBRAVE
ABEEMSS	EMBASES
ABEEMST	EMBASTE
ABEENRV	VERBENA
ABEENRY	BEANERY
ABEEORS	AEROBES
ABEEPST	BESPATE
ABEERRS	BEARERS
	BREARES
ABEERRT	REBATER
	TABRERE
	TEREBRA
ABEERST	BEATERS
	BERATES
	REBATES
ABEERSV	BEAVERS
ABEERSW	BEWARES
ABEERSZ	ZEREBAS
ABEERTT	ABETTER
ABEERVY	BEAVERY
ABEESST	SEBATES
ABEESWX	BEESWAX
ABEFFIS	BAFFIES
ABEFFLR	BAFFLER
ABEFFLS	BAFFLES
ABEFFOT	OFFBEAT
ABEFGIL	FILABEG
ABEFGST	GABFEST
ABEFILN	FINABLE
ABEFILR	FRIABLE
ABEFILS	FAIBLES
ABEFILU	FIBULAE
ABEFILX	FIXABLE
ABEFINU	BEAUFIN
ABEFITY	BEATIFY
ABEFLLS	BEFALLS
ABEFLLU	BALEFUL
ABEFLLY	FLYABLE
ABEFLNU	BANEFUL
ABEFLNY	FLYBANE
ABEFLRS	FABLERS
ABEFMOS	BEFOAMS
ABEFORR	FORBEAR
ABEFPRS	PREFABS
ABEGGIR	BAGGIER
ABEGGIS	BAGGIES
ABEGGLR	BLAGGER
ABEGGMO	GAMBOGE
ABEGGNU	BUGGANE
ABEGGRS	BEGGARS
ABEGGRU	BURGAGE
ABEGGRY	BEGGARY
ABEGHNS	SHEBANG
ABEGIMN	BEAMING
ABEGIMR	GAMBIER
ABEGIMT	MEGABIT
ABEGINN	BEANING

ABEGINO	BEGONIA
ABEGINR	BEARING
ABEGINT	BEATING
ABEGINY	ABYEING
ABEGIPP	BAGPIPE
ABEGKOR	BROKAGE
ABEGKOS	BOSKAGE
ABEGLMR	GAMBLER
	GAMBREL
ABEGLMS	GAMBLES
ABEGLNR	BRANGLE
ABEGLNS	BANGLES
ABEGLOR	ALBERGO
ABEGLOT	GLOBATE
ABEGLRR	GARBLER
ABEGLRS	GARBLES
ABEGLST	GABLETS
ABEGLSU	BELUGAS
	BLAGUES
ABEGMOR	EMBARGO
ABEGMRU	UMBRAGE
ABEGMST	GAMBETS
ABEGNNT	BANTENG
ABEGNOS	NOSEBAG
ABEGNRS	BANGERS
	GRABENS
ABEGNSW	BEGNAWS
ABEGORR	BEGORRA
ABEGORS	BORAGES
ABEGORX	GEARBOX
ABEGOSZ	GAZEBOS
ABEGOTT	BOTTEGA
ABEGOUY	BUOYAGE
ABEGRRU	GARBURE
ABEGRST	BARGEST
ABEGSTU	TUBAGES
ABEHILR	HIRABLE
ABEHIMS	BEAMISH
ABEHIMT	IMBATHE
ABEHIRS	BEARISH
ABEHISU	BEAUISH
ABEHITU	HABITUE
ABEHITZ	ZABTIEH
ABEHKLS	KEBLAHS
ABEHKRU	HAUBERK
ABEHLMS	HAMBLES
	SHAMBLE
ABEHLNU	UNHABLE
ABEHLRS	HERBALS
ABEHLRT	BLATHER
	HALBERT
ABEHLSS	BLASHES
ABEHNOS	HEBONAS
ABEHRRS	BRASHER
	HERBARS
ABEHRRY	HERBARY
ABEHRSS	BASHERS
	BRASHES
ABEHRST	BATHERS
	BERTHAS
	BREATHS
ABEHRTY	BREATHY
ABEIILL	BAILLIE
ABEIILS	BAILIES
ABEIINT	BAINITE
ABEIJMR	JAMBIER
ABEIJNS	BASENJI
ABEIKLL	LIKABLE
ABEIKLR	BALKIER
ABEIKLS	SKIABLE
ABEIKNR	INBREAK
ABEIKNT	BEATNIK
ABEIKRR	BARKIER
	BRAKIER
ABEIKWY	BIKEWAY
ABEILLO	LOBELIA
ABEILLP	PLIABLE
ABEILLR	LIBERAL
ABEILLV	LIVABLE
ABEILMR	BALMIER
	MIRABLE
	REMBLAI
ABEILMS	EMBAILS
	LAMBIES
ABEILMT	LIMBATE
	TIMBALE
ABEILMX	MIXABLE
ABEILMY	BEAMILY
ABEILNP	BIPLANE
ABEILNS	LESBIAN
ABEILPT	PATIBLE
ABEILRS	BAILERS
ABEILRT	LIBRATE
	TABLIER
	TRIABLE
ABEILSS	ABSEILS
	ISABELS
	LABISES
ABEILST	ALBITES
	ASTILBE
	BESTIAL
	LIBATES
	STABILE
ABEILSW	BEWAILS
ABEILSY	BAILEYS
ABEILSZ	SIZABLE
ABEILVV	BIVALVE
ABEIMNR	MIRBANE
ABEIMNT	AMBIENT
ABEIMRR	BARMIER
ABEIMRS	AMBRIES
ABEIMSS	IMBASES
ABEINOT	NIOBATE
ABEINPT	BEPAINT
ABEINRT	ATEBRIN
ABEINRZ	ZEBRINA
ABEINST	BASINET
	BESAINT
	BESTAIN
ABEINTT	TABINET
ABEIORS	ISOBARE
ABEIOSS	ABIOSES
	ISOBASE
ABEIOST	BOATIES
ABEIOTV	OBVIATE
ABEIPST	BAPTISE
ABEIPTZ	BAPTIZE
ABEIRRR	BARRIER
ABEIRRS	BRASIER
ABEIRRT	ARBITER
	RAREBIT
ABEIRRW	WARBIER
ABEIRRZ	BIZARRE
	BRAZIER
ABEIRSS	BASSIER
	BRAISES
	BRASSIE
ABEIRST	BAITERS
	BARITES
ABEIRSX	BRAXIES
ABEIRSZ	BRAIZES
	ZERIBAS
ABEIRTT	BATTIER
	BIRETTA
ABEIRTV	VIBRATE
ABEIRUX	EXURBIA
ABEISSS	BIASSES
ABEISTT	BATISTE
ABEISUV	ABUSIVE
ABEITUX	BAUXITE
ABEJMNO	JAMBONE
ABEJMNS	ENJAMBS
ABEJMRS	JAMBERS
ABEJMUX	JAMBEUX
ABEJNOS	BANJOES
ABEJNOW	JAWBONE
ABEJNST	BEJANTS
ABEJORS	JERBOAS
ABEJRRU	ABJURER
ABEJRSU	ABJURES
ABEKLLY	BLEAKLY
ABEKLNR	BLANKER
ABEKLNT	BLANKET
ABEKLRS	BALKERS
ABEKMNS	EMBANKS
ABEKMRS	EMBARKS
ABEKNRS	BANKERS
	BARKENS
ABEKNST	BANKETS
ABEKNSU	SUNBAKE
ABEKOOR	ABROOKE
ABEKPRU	UPBREAK
ABEKRRS	BARKERS
ABEKSST	BASKETS
ABELLMN	BELLMAN
ABELLMS	EMBALLS
ABELLNT	NETBALL
ABELLOS	LOSABLE
ABELLOV	LOVABLE
	VOLABLE
ABELLRU	RUBELLA
	RULABLE
ABELLST	BALLETS
ABELLTU	BULLATE
ABELMMR	MEMBRAL
ABELMMS	EMBALMS
ABELMNT	BELTMAN
	LAMBENT
ABELMNU	ALBUMEN
ABELMOV	MOVABLE
ABELMRR	MARBLER
	RAMBLER
ABELMRS	AMBLERS
	LAMBERS
	MARBLES
	RAMBLES
ABELMRT	LAMBERT
ABELMSU	BEMAULS
ABELMSW	WAMBLES
ABELMTU	MUTABLE
ABELNOT	NOTABLE
ABELNOY	BALONEY
ABELNRS	BRANLES
	BRANSLE
ABELNRT	BRANTLE
ABELNRU	NEBULAR
ABELNRY	BLARNEY
ABELNSU	NEBULAS
ABELNSZ	BENZALS
ABELNTU	TUNABLE
ABELOPR	ROPABLE
ABELOPT	POTABLE
ABELORS	LABROSE
ABELORT	BLOATER
ABELORU	RUBEOLA
ABELORW	ROWABLE
ABELOSS	BOLASES
ABELOST	BOATELS
	OBLATES
ABELOSV	ABSOLVE
ABELOTW	TOWABLE
ABELPRU	PUBERAL
ABELQUY	EQUABLY
ABELRRS	BARRELS
ABELRRW	BRAWLER
	WARBLER
ABELRSS	BRALESS
ABELRST	ALBERTS
	BATLERS
	BLASTER
	LABRETS
	STABLER
ABELRSV	VERBALS
ABELRSW	BAWLERS
	WARBLES
ABELRSY	BARLEYS
ABELRSZ	BLAZERS
ABELRTT	BATTLER
	BLATTER
	BRATTLE
ABELRTW	BLEWART
ABELRUZ	ZEBRULA
ABELRVY	BRAVELY
ABELSST	BASTLES
	STABLES
ABELSTT	BATLETS
	BATTELS
	BATTLES
	BLATEST
	TABLETS
ABELSTU	SUBLATE
ABELSTY	BAETYLS
	BEASTLY
ABELSWY	BAWLEYS
ABELTWY	BELTWAY
ABEMMRS	BAMMERS
ABEMNOS	AMBONES
	BEMOANS
ABEMNOT	BOATMEN
ABEMNRY	BYREMAN
	MYRBANE
ABEMNST	BATSMEN
ABEMNSU	SUNBEAM
ABEMNSY	BYNAMES
ABEMORT	BROMATE
ABEMRST	TAMBERS
ABEMSSY	EMBASSY
ABENNOR	BARONNE
ABENNRS	BANNERS
ABENORS	BORANES
ABENORT	BARONET
	REBOANT
ABENORW	RAWBONE
ABENOTY	BAYONET
ABENQTU	BANQUET
ABENRRU	URBANER
ABENRST	BANTERS
ABENRSU	UNBARES
	UNBEARS
ABENRSY	BARNEYS

ABENRSZ	BRAZENS
ABENRUX	EXURBAN
ABENSST	ABSENTS
	BASNETS
ABENSTT	BATTENS
ABENSTU	BUTANES
	SUNBEAT
ABENSTZ	BEZANTS
ABEOOTV	OBOVATE
ABEOPRS	SAPROBE
ABEOPRT	PROBATE
ABEOQRU	BAROQUE
ABEORRS	ARBORES
	BRASERO
ABEORRT	ARBORET
	TABORER
ABEORST	BOASTER
	BOATERS
	BORATES
	SORBATE
ABEORSU	AEROBUS
ABEORSV	BRAVOES
ABEORSX	BORAXES
ABEORSY	ROSEBAY
ABEORSZ	BEZOARS
ABEORTT	ABETTOR
	BATTERO
	TABORET
ABEOSTV	BOVATES
ABEPRSU	UPBEARS
ABEQRSU	BARQUES
ABEQSSU	BASQUES
ABERRST	BARRETS
	BARTERS
ABERRSU	SABREUR
ABERRSY	BRAYERS
ABERRVY	BRAVERY
ABERSSS	BRASSES
ABERSST	BASTERS
	BESTARS
	BRASSET
	BREASTS
ABERSSU	ABUSERS
	SURBASE
ABERSSZ	ZEBRASS
ABERSTT	BATTERS
	TABRETS
ABERSTU	ARBUTES
	SURBATE
ABERSTV	BRAVEST
ABERSTW	BRAWEST
	WABSTER
ABERSTX	BAXTERS
ABERSTY	BARYTES
	BETRAYS
ABERSUU	BUREAUS
ABERSWY	BEWRAYS
ABERTTU	ABUTTER
ABERTTY	BATTERY
ABERUUX	BUREAUX
ABESSST	BASSEST
	BASSETS
ABESSSY	ABYSSES
ABESTTU	BATTUES
ABFFGIN	BAFFING
ABFFIIL	BAILIFF
ABFFLOU	BUFFALO
ABFGILN	FABLING
ABFGINR	BARFING
ABFGLSU	BAGFULS
ABFHIST	BATFISH
ABFHLSU	BASHFUL
ABFIILR	BIFILAR
ABFIIMR	FIMBRIA
ABFILRU	FIBULAR
ABFILSU	FIBULAS
ABFIMOR	FIBROMA
ABFLOTY	FLYBOAT
ABFOORT	FOOTBAR
ABFSTTU	TUBFAST
ABGGGIN	BAGGING
ABGGILY	BAGGILY
ABGGINN	BANGING
ABGGINR	BARGING
	GARBING
ABGGIST	BAGGITS
ABGGISW	BAGWIGS
ABGGNOS	GOBANGS
ABGGNSU	BUGGANS
ABGGORT	BOGGART
ABGHILN	BLAHING
ABGHINS	BASHING
ABGHINT	BATHING
ABGHLOT	HAGBOLT
ABGHLRU	BURGHAL
ABGHOTU	ABOUGHT
ABGHSTU	HAGBUTS
ABGIILN	BAILING
ABGIINS	BIASING
ABGIINT	BAITING
ABGIINZ	BAIZING
ABGIKLN	BALKING
ABGIKNN	BANKING
ABGIKNO	BOAKING
ABGIKNR	BARKING
	BRAKING
ABGIKNS	BAKINGS
	BASKING
ABGIKNU	BAUKING
ABGILLN	BALLING
ABGILMN	AMBLING
	BALMING
	BLAMING
	LAMBING
ABGILMS	GIMBALS
ABGILNR	BLARING
ABGILNS	SABLING
ABGILNT	TABLING
ABGILNW	BAWLING
ABGILNZ	BLAZING
ABGILOR	GARBOIL
ABGIMMN	BAMMING
ABGIMRS	GAMBIRS
ABGIMST	GAMBIST
	GAMBITS
ABGINNN	BANNING
ABGINNR	BARNING
ABGINNT	BANTING
ABGINOS	BAGNIOS
	GABIONS
ABGINOT	BOATING
ABGINRR	BARRING
ABGINRS	SABRING
ABGINRV	BRAVING
ABGINRY	BRAYING
ABGINRZ	BRAZING
ABGINSS	BASSING
ABGINST	BASTING
ABGINSU	ABUSING
ABGINTT	BATTING
ABGINTU	TABUING
ABGINTY	BAYTING
ABGIOPT	PIGBOAT
ABGIOSU	BAGUIOS
ABGKNOS	KOBANGS
ABGKOOS	BOGOAKS
ABGKORW	WORKBAG
ABGLMNU	LUMBANG
ABGLMOS	GAMBOLS
ABGLMOU	LUMBAGO
ABGLMSY	GYMBALS
ABGLOOT	TOOLBAG
ABGLORS	BROLGAS
ABGLORT	RAGBOLT
ABGLOSU	ALBUGOS
	SUBGOAL
ABGLRRU	BURGLAR
ABGNOPR	PROBANG
ABGNORS	BARONGS
	BROGANS
ABGNOTU	GUNBOAT
ABGNOWY	BOWYANG
ABGOORT	BOTARGO
ABGOPST	POSTBAG
ABGORRU	GOBURRA
ABGORTU	OUTBRAG
ABGOTTU	TUGBOAT
ABHHISS	SHIBAHS
ABHHKOT	KHOTBAH
ABHHKTU	KHUTBAH
ABHHSUY	HUSHABY
ABHIINT	INHABIT
ABHIKLS	BASHLIK
	KIBLAHS
ABHIKST	BHAKTIS
ABHIKTW	HAWKBIT
ABHILNO	HOBNAIL
ABHILOS	ABOLISH
ABHILTU	HALIBUT
ABHIMRS	MIHRABS
ABHIMSZ	MAZHBIS
ABHINST	ABSINTH
ABHIOPS	PHOBIAS
ABHIORS	BOARISH
ABHIOST	ISOBATH
ABHISTU	HABITUS
ABHKORU	BOURKHA
ABHKRSU	KURBASH
ABHLMSY	SHAMBLY
ABHLRTU	HURLBAT
ABHMNSU	BUSHMAN
ABHMRSU	RHUMBAS
ABHNOST	BOTHANS
ABHNSTU	SUNBATH
ABHORRS	HARBORS
ABHORRU	HARBOUR
ABHOTUY	HAUTBOY
ABHPSTY	BYPATHS
ABHRSTU	TARBUSH
ABHSTUW	WASHTUB
ABIIKKT	KIBITKA
ABIILLS	BAILLIS
ABIILMU	BULIMIA
ABIILNQ	INQILAB
ABIILNS	AIBLINS
	BILIANS
ABIILRY	BILIARY
ABIILST	STIBIAL
ABIILTY	ABILITY
ABIIMST	IAMBIST
ABIINNS	BAININS
ABIINOR	ROBINIA
ABIINRY	BIRYANI
ABIIOSS	ABIOSIS
ABIJLNR	BRINJAL
ABIJNOT	ABJOINT
ABIJRSU	JABIRUS
ABIKKSU	KABUKIS
ABIKLMN	LAMBKIN
ABIKLOR	KILOBAR
ABIKMNR	BARMKIN
ABIKMRS	IMBARKS
ABIKOUZ	BAZOUKI
ABIKRST	BRITSKA
ABIKRTZ	BRITZKA
ABILLMN	BILLMAN
ABILLMU	BALLIUM
ABILLMY	BALMILY
ABILLNP	PINBALL
ABILLPY	PLIABLY
ABILLSW	SAWBILL
ABILLSY	SYLLABI
ABILLTT	BATTILL
ABILLWX	WAXBILL
ABILLWY	WAYBILL
ABILMNU	ALBUMIN
ABILMOX	MAILBOX
ABILMST	TIMBALS
ABILNOS	ALBINOS
ABILNOT	BITONAL
ABILNOZ	BIZONAL
ABILNRY	BAIRNLY
ABILOPR	BIPOLAR
	PARBOIL
ABILORS	BAILORS
ABILORT	ORBITAL
ABILORV	BOLIVAR
ABILOTU	OBITUAL
ABILRRY	LIBRARY
ABILRSU	BURIALS
	RAILBUS
ABILRSZ	BRAZILS
ABIMMRS	MIMBARS
ABIMNRS	MINBARS
ABIMOSS	BIOMASS
ABIMPST	BAPTISM
	BITMAPS
ABIMRSS	BISMARS
ABIMRST	IMBRAST
ABIMRSU	BARIUMS
ABIMRTT	TRIMTAB
ABIMTTY	AMBITTY
ABINNSU	BUNNIAS
ABINOOR	BORONIA
ABINORT	TABORIN
ABINORW	RAINBOW
ABINOSS	BONSAIS
ABINOST	BASTION
	OBTAINS
ABINOSU	ABUSION
ABINRTV	VIBRANT
ABIORRS	BARRIOS
ABIORSS	ISOBARS
ABIORST	ORBITAS
ABIORTV	VIBRATO
ABIPSTT	BAPTIST
ABIRTTY	TRAYBIT
ABISSST	BASSIST
ABJJOOS	JOJOBAS
ABJKMOS	JAMBOKS

SJAMBOK
ABJLMOO JAMBOOL
ABJLMSU JAMBULS
JUMBALS
ABKLLNY BLANKLY
ABKLRUW BULWARK
ABKLSSY SKYLABS
ABKMNOO BOOKMAN
ABKMOST TOMBAKS
ABKMSUZ ZAMBUKS
ABKNRSU UNBARKS
ABKNRUU BUNRAKU
ABKOORS BOORKAS
ABLLLUY LULLABY
ABLLNOO BALLOON
ABLLNOS BALLONS
ABLLOPR PROBALL
ABLLORU LOBULAR
ABLLOST BALLOTS
ABLLOSW BALLOWS
ABLLOTY TALLBOY
ABLLPSU BALLUPS
ABLLRUY BULLARY
ABLMMOU BUMMALO
ABLMNOU UMBONAL
ABLMOOT TOMBOLA
ABLMOPS APLOMBS
ABLMOSY LAMBOYS
ABLMOVY MOVABLY
ABLMPUU PABULUM
ABLMSTY TYMBALS
ABLMTUY MUTABLY
ABLNOSZ BLAZONS
ABLNOTU BUTANOL
ABLNOTY NOTABLY
ABLNSTU BUNTALS
TULBANS
ABLNTUY TUNABLY
ABLOORS ROBALOS
ABLOORT TOOLBAR
ABLOORY OBOLARY
ABLOPYY PLAYBOY
ABLORST BORSTAL
ABLORSU LABOURS
ABLORTW BLAWORT
ABLORUW BOURLAW
ABLOSST OBLASTS
ABLOSTT TALBOTS
ABLOSTV ABVOLTS
ABLOSTX SALTBOX
ABLPRSU BURLAPS
ABLPSUY PLAYBUS
ABLRSWY BYRLAWS
ABLRTUU TUBULAR
ABMMNOS MOBSMAN
ABMNSTU NUMBATS
ABMNSUY YNAMBUS
ABMOOSW WABOOMS
ABMOPST BAMPOTS
ABMORTU TAMBOUR
ABMOSTU SUBATOM
ABMOSTW WOMBATS
ABMRSSU SAMBURS
ABNOORS SOROBAN
ABNOORZ BORAZON
ABNOOSS BASSOON
ABNOOST BATOONS
ABNORST BARTONS
ABNORSY BARYONS
ABNORTY BARYTON

ABNOSSU BONASUS
ABNOTUY BUOYANT
ABNRSTU TURBANS
ABNRTTU TURBANT
ABNSTYZ BYZANTS
ABOOPSX SOAPBOX
ABOORTW ROWBOAT
ABOOTTW TOWBOAT
ABORRSU ARBOURS
ABORRSW BARROWS
ABORSTU OUTBARS
ROBUSTA
RUBATOS
TABOURS
ABORSTW TOWBARS
ABORSTY TARBOYS
ABOSTUU AUTOBUS
ABPRSTU ABRUPTS
UPBRAST
ABPRSUY UPBRAYS
ABRRSSU BURSARS
ABRRSUY BURSARY
ABRRTUY TURBARY
ABRSTUU ARBUTUS
ABSSUWY SUBWAYS
ACCCILY ACYCLIC
ACCDDEE ACCEDED
ACCDDEI CADDICE
ACCDEEN CADENCE
ACCDEER ACCEDER
ACCDEES ACCEDES
ACCDEHK CHACKED
ACCDEHN CHANCED
ACCDEHO COACHED
ACCDEHT CATCHED
ACCDEII ACCIDIE
ACCDEIO ACCOIED
ACCDEIT ACCITED
ACCDEIU CADUCEI
ACCDEKL CACKLED
CLACKED
ACCDEKO COCKADE
ACCDEKR CRACKED
ACCDENS ACCENDS
ACCDENY CADENCY
ACCDEOT COACTED
ACCDEOY ACCOYED
ACCDERU ACCRUED
CARDECU
ACCDESU ACCUSED
SUCCADE
ACCDFIL FLACCID
ACCDHIL CHALCID
ACCDILS SCALDIC
ACCDIOT OCTADIC
ACCDKNO CANDOCK
ACCDKOW DAWCOCK
ACCDLOY ACCOYLD
CACODYL
ACCDORS ACCORDS
ACCEEHO COACHEE
ACCEELN CENACLE
ACCEENR CREANCE
ACCEERT ACCRETE
ACCEFIT FACTICE
ACCEFLU FELUCCA
ACCEGIN ACCINGE
ACCEGOS SOCCAGE
ACCEHHI CHECHIA
ACCEHIL CALICHE

CHALICE
ACCEHIM MACCHIE
ACCEHIN CHICANE
ACCEHLN CHANCEL
ACCEHLO COCHLEA
ACCEHNO CONCHAE
ACCEHNR CHANCER
CHANCRE
ACCEHNS CHANCES
ACCEHNT CATCHEN
ACCEHNU CHAUNCE
ACCEHNY CHANCEY
ACCEHOR CAROCHE
COACHER
ACCEHOS CHACOES
COACHES
ACCEHPU CAPUCHE
ACCEHRS CREACHS
ACCEHRT CATCHER
RECATCH
ACCEHST CACHETS
CATCHES
ACCEHTU CATECHU
ACCEHXY CACHEXY
ACCEIKP ICEPACK
ACCEILL CALICLE
ACCEILN CALCINE
ACCEILO COELIAC
ACCEILS CALICES
CELIACS
ACCEILT CALCITE
ACCEIMR CERAMIC
RACEMIC
ACCEINO COCAINE
OCEANIC
ACCEINV VACCINE
ACCEIPR CAPRICE
ACCEIPS ICECAPS
IPECACS
ACCEIPV PECCAVI
ACCEIQU CACIQUE
ACCEIRS CARICES
ACCEIRT CREATIC
ACCEIST ACCITES
ASCETIC
ACCEKLR CACKLER
CLACKER
CRACKLE
ACCEKLS CACKLES
ACCEKMO MEACOCK
ACCEKOP PEACOCK
ACCEKOS SEACOCK
ACCEKPU CUPCAKE
ACCEKRR CRACKER
ACCELLY CALYCLE
ACCELNO CONCEAL
ACCELNS CANCELS
ACCELOR CORACLE
ACCELOT CACOLET
ACCELSU SACCULE
ACCELSY CALYCES
ACCENOR CONACRE
ACCENOS ASCONCE
ACCENOV CONCAVE
ACCENPT PECCANT
ACCENRS CANCERS
ACCENST ACCENTS
ACCEOPY CACOEPY
ACCEPRY PECCARY
ACCEPST ACCEPTS

ACCERRS SCARCER
ACCERRT CARRECT
ACCERSU ACCRUES
ACCURSE
ACCUSER
ACCERSW ACCREWS
ACCESSU ACCUSES
ACCFIIP PACIFIC
ACCFILY CALCIFY
ACCGHIN CACHING
CHACING
ACCHHIS CHICHAS
ACCHHKU KUCHCHA
ACCHIKS CHIACKS
ACCHIMS CHASMIC
ACCHINO CHICANO
ACCHIOT CHAOTIC
ACCHIOU ACOUCHI
ACCHIRS SCRAICH
ACCHJSU JACCHUS
ACCHKOY HAYCOCK
ACCHKSY CHYACKS
ACCHLNO CONCHAL
ACCHLTU CLAUCHT
ACCHNRS SCRANCH
ACCHNRU CRAUNCH
ACCHOPU CAPOUCH
ACCHOSU CACHOUS
ACCHOTW CHOCTAW
ACCHOUY ACOUCHY
ACCHPTU CATCHUP
UPCATCH
ACCHRRU CURRACH
ACCHRST SCRATCH
ACCHRSU SCRAUCH
ACCHSSU SUCCAHS
ACCIILN ACLINIC
ACCIINT ACTINIC
ACCIIST ASCITIC
SCIATIC
ACCILLU CALCULI
ACCILMO COMICAL
ACCILMU CALCIUM
ACCILNO CONICAL
LACONIC
ACCILNY CYNICAL
ACCILOR CALORIC
ACCILOS ACCOILS
CALICOS
ACCILOV VOCALIC
ACCILRU CRUCIAL
ACCILRY ACRYLIC
ACCILSS CLASSIC
ACCILST CLASTIC
ACCILSU SACCULI
ACCIMOZ ZIMOCCA
ACCINNO CANONIC
ACCINOT CANTICO
ACCINRU CRUCIAN
ACCINSW WICCANS
ACCIOPR CAPROIC
ACCIORS SCORIAC
ACCIPRT PRACTIC
ACCIRRS CIRCARS
ACCIRST ARCTICS
ACCISTT TACTICS
ACCISTU CAUSTIC
CICUTAS
ACCKLOR CARLOCK
ACCKLRY CRACKLY

ACCKMOR	CROMACK
ACCKOSS	CASSOCK
ACCKOST	CASTOCK
ACCLOSU	COUCALS
ACCLOSY	ACCLOYS
ACCMOPT	ACCOMPT
	COMPACT
ACCMRUU	CURCUMA
ACCNNOO	COONCAN
ACCNOOP	COCOPAN
ACCNOOR	RACCOON
ACCNOOS	CACOONS
ACCNOTT	CONTACT
ACCNOTU	ACCOUNT
ACCOPTY	COPYCAT
ACCOQSU	SQUACCO
ACCORSS	CORCASS
	CORSACS
ACCORTU	ACCOURT
ACCOSST	ACCOSTS
ACCRSTU	ACCURST
ACDDDEI	CADDIED
ACDDDEL	CLADDED
ACDDDEU	ADDUCED
ACDDDKO	DADDOCK
ACDDEEF	DEFACED
ACDDEER	CEDARED
ACDDEES	DECADES
ACDDEEY	DECAYED
ACDDEIN	CANDIED
ACDDEIS	CADDIES
ACDDEIU	DECIDUA
ACDDELN	CANDLED
ACDDELO	CLADODE
ACDDELR	CLADDER
	CRADLED
ACDDELS	SCALDED
ACDDELU	CAUDLED
ACDDEMU	DUCDAME
ACDDEOP	DECAPOD
ACDDERU	ADDUCER
ACDDESU	ADDUCES
	SCAUDED
ACDDHHU	CHUDDAH
ACDDHIS	CADDISH
ACDDHKO	HADDOCK
ACDDHOR	CHADDOR
ACDDHRU	CHUDDAR
ACDDIRS	DISCARD
ACDDIST	ADDICTS
ACDDKMO	MADDOCK
ACDDKOP	PADDOCK
ACDDSSY	CADDYSS
ACDDSTU	ADDUCTS
ACDEEES	DECEASE
ACDEEFF	EFFACED
ACDEEFN	ENFACED
ACDEEFR	DEFACER
	REFACED
ACDEEFS	DEFACES
ACDEEFT	FACETED
ACDEEGL	GLACEED
ACDEEGN	ENCAGED
ACDEEHL	LEACHED
ACDEEHP	PEACHED
ACDEEHR	REACHED
ACDEEHT	CHEATED
ACDEEIR	DECIARE
ACDEEJT	DEJECTA
ACDEEKR	CREAKED
ACDEELL	CADELLE
ACDEELN	CLEANED
	ELANCED
	ENLACED
ACDEELR	CLEARED
	CREEDAL
	DECLARE
ACDEELS	DESCALE
ACDEELT	CLEATED
ACDEELV	CLEAVED
ACDEEMN	MENACED
ACDEEMR	AMERCED
	CREAMED
	RACEMED
ACDEENR	ENRACED
ACDEENS	DECANES
	ENCASED
ACDEENT	ENACTED
ACDEENV	ENCAVED
	VENDACE
ACDEEPR	CAPERED
	PEARCED
	PREACED
ACDEEPS	ESCAPED
ACDEERS	CREASED
	DECARES
	SEARCED
ACDEERT	CATERED
	CEDRATE
	CERATED
	CREATED
	REACTED
ACDEEST	TEDESCA
ACDEETU	EDUCATE
ACDEETX	EXACTED
ACDEFFH	CHAFFED
ACDEFFS	DECAFFS
ACDEFHU	CHAUFED
ACDEFIN	FANCIED
ACDEFIR	FARCIED
ACDEFRS	SCARFED
ACDEFRT	CRAFTED
	FRACTED
ACDEGGL	CLAGGED
ACDEGGR	CRAGGED
ACDEGHN	CHANGED
	GANCHED
ACDEGHR	CHARGED
ACDEGIN	INCAGED
ACDEGIR	CADGIER
ACDEGIS	DISCAGE
ACDEGKO	DOCKAGE
ACDEGLN	CANGLED
	CLANGED
	GLANCED
ACDEGNO	CONGAED
	DECAGON
ACDEGNU	UNCAGED
ACDEGOR	CARGOED
	CORDAGE
ACDEGRS	CADGERS
ACDEHHN	HANCHED
ACDEHHT	HATCHED
ACDEHIN	CHAINED
	ECHIDNA
ACDEHIP	EDAPHIC
ACDEHIR	CHAIRED
ACDEHIX	HEXADIC
ACDEHKL	CHALKED
	HACKLED
ACDEHKR	CHARKED
ACDEHKW	WHACKED
ACDEHLN	LANCHED
ACDEHLR	CHALDER
ACDEHLS	CLASHED
ACDEHLT	LATCHED
ACDEHMP	CHAMPED
ACDEHMR	CHARMED
	MARCHED
ACDEHMS	CHASMED
ACDEHMT	MATCHED
ACDEHNR	ENDARCH
	RANCHED
ACDEHNT	CHANTED
ACDEHOP	POACHED
ACDEHOR	CHORDAE
	ROACHED
ACDEHOT	CATHODE
ACDEHPP	CHAPPED
ACDEHPR	PARCHED
ACDEHPT	PATCHED
ACDEHPU	CUPHEAD
ACDEHRR	CHARRED
ACDEHRS	CRASHED
ACDEHRT	CHARTED
	RATCHED
ACDEHST	SCATHED
ACDEHTT	CHATTED
ACDEHTW	WATCHED
ACDEHTY	YACHTED
ACDEILL	CEDILLA
ACDEILM	CAMELID
	CLAIMED
	DECIMAL
	DECLAIM
	MALICED
	MEDICAL
ACDEILN	INLACED
ACDEILR	DECRIAL
	RADICEL
	RADICLE
ACDEILS	SCAILED
ACDEILT	CITADEL
	DELTAIC
	DIALECT
	EDICTAL
ACDEIMT	MICATED
ACDEIMY	MEDIACY
ACDEINO	OCEANID
ACDEINR	CAIRNED
	CARNIED
ACDEINS	CANDIES
	INCASED
ACDEINV	INCAVED
ACDEINY	CYANIDE
ACDEIPR	EPACRID
ACDEIPS	DISPACE
ACDEIRR	ACRIDER
	CARRIED
ACDEIRS	CARDIES
	DARCIES
	RADICES
	SIDECAR
ACDEIRU	DECURIA
ACDEISS	DISCASE
ACDEIST	ACIDEST
	DACITES
ACDEISV	ADVICES
ACDEITT	DICTATE
ACDEITY	EDACITY
ACDEJLO	CAJOLED
ACDEJNU	JAUNCED
ACDEKLM	MACKLED
ACDEKLN	CLANKED
ACDEKLO	CLOAKED
ACDEKLS	SLACKED
ACDEKLT	TACKLED
	TALCKED
ACDEKLU	CAULKED
ACDEKMS	SMACKED
ACDEKNR	CRANKED
ACDEKNS	SNACKED
ACDEKOR	CROAKED
ACDEKQU	QUACKED
ACDEKRS	DACKERS
ACDEKRT	TRACKED
ACDEKRW	WRACKED
ACDEKST	STACKED
ACDELLS	SCALLED
ACDELMM	CLAMMED
ACDELMP	CAMPLED
	CLAMPED
ACDELMS	MASCLED
ACDELNO	CELADON
ACDELNS	CALENDS
	CANDLES
ACDELNT	CANTLED
ACDELNU	LAUNCED
	UNLACED
ACDELOR	ORACLED
ACDELOS	SOLACED
ACDELOT	LOCATED
ACDELPP	CLAPPED
ACDELPS	CLASPED
	SCALPED
ACDELQU	CALQUED
ACDELRS	CRADLES
	SCALDER
ACDELRT	CLARTED
ACDELRU	CAULDER
ACDELRW	CRAWLED
ACDELSS	CLASSED
	DECLASS
ACDELST	CASTLED
	SCLATED
ACDELSU	CAUDLES
	CEDULAS
ACDELTT	CLATTED
ACDELTU	CLAUTED
ACDEMMR	CRAMMED
ACDEMNU	DECUMAN
ACDEMOR	CAROMED
	COMRADE
ACDEMPR	CRAMPED
ACDEMPS	DECAMPS
	SCAMPED
ACDENNS	SCANNED
ACDENNT	CANDENT
ACDENNU	NUANCED
ACDENOR	ACORNED
	DRACONE
ACDENOS	DEACONS
ACDENPR	PRANCED
ACDENPT	PANDECT
ACDENPU	UNCAPED
	UNPACED
ACDENRS	DANCERS
ACDENRT	CANTRED
	TRANCED
ACDENRU	DURANCE

	UNRACED
ACDENRY	ARDENCY
ACDENSS	ASCENDS
ACDENST	DECANTS
	DESCANT
	SCANTED
ACDENSU	UNCASED
ACDENTU	UNACTED
ACDENUV	VAUNCED
ACDEOPS	PEACODS
	PEASCOD
ACDEOPT	COAPTED
ACDEORR	CORRADE
ACDEORS	SARCODE
ACDEORT	CORDATE
	REDCOAT
ACDEOST	COASTED
ACDEOTT	CODETTA
ACDEOUV	COUVADE
ACDEPPR	CRAPPED
ACDEPRS	REDCAPS
	SCARPED
	SCRAPED
ACDEPSU	SCAUPED
ACDERRS	CARDERS
	SCARRED
ACDERST	REDACTS
	SCARTED
ACDERSU	CRUSADE
	SCAURED
ACDERTT	DETRACT
	TRACTED
ACDERTU	CURATED
	TRADUCE
ACDESTT	SCATTED
ACDFIIY	ACIDIFY
ACDFIOT	FACTOID
ACDGGIN	CADGING
ACDGINN	DANCING
ACDGINO	GONADIC
ACDGINR	CARDING
ACDGKLO	DAGLOCK
ACDGNOT	CANTDOG
ACDGORT	DOGCART
ACDHIIL	CHILIAD
ACDHIOP	PHACOID
ACDHIRY	DIARCHY
ACDHLOR	CHORDAL
	DORLACH
ACDHMRS	DRACHMS
ACDHNOW	COWHAND
ACDHOOT	CATHOOD
ACDHOPR	POCHARD
ACDHORR	ORCHARD
ACDHORS	CHADORS
ACDHRUY	DUARCHY
ACDHRYY	DYARCHY
ACDIIIN	INDICIA
ACDIINN	INDICAN
ACDIINO	CONIDIA
ACDIINR	ACRIDIN
ACDIIOS	ISODICA
ACDIIRS	CIDARIS
	SCIARID
ACDIIRT	ARCTIID
	TRIACID
	TRIADIC
ACDIITY	ACIDITY
ACDIKLS	SKALDIC
ACDILLO	CODILLA
ACDILMO	DOMICAL
ACDILMS	CLADISM
ACDILNO	NODICAL
ACDILNU	DULCIAN
ACDILOP	PLACOID
	PODALIC
ACDILOR	CORDIAL
ACDILOT	COTIDAL
ACDILPU	PALUDIC
ACDILST	CLADIST
ACDILTW	WILDCAT
ACDIMMU	CADMIUM
ACDIMNO	MANDIOC
	MONACID
	MONADIC
	NOMADIC
ACDIMNY	DYNAMIC
ACDINRU	IRACUND
ACDINST	DISCANT
ACDINSW	WINDACS
ACDIOPR	PARODIC
	PICADOR
ACDIORR	CORRIDA
ACDIORS	SARCOID
ACDIORT	ARCTOID
	CAROTID
ACDIOST	DACOITS
ACDIOSZ	ZODIACS
ACDIOTY	DACOITY
ACDIPRS	CAPRIDS
ACDIPSS	CAPSIDS
ACDIQRU	QUADRIC
ACDIRST	DRASTIC
ACDISST	DICASTS
ACDITUV	VIADUCT
ACDJNTU	ADJUNCT
ACDKLOP	PADLOCK
ACDKLSY	SKYCLAD
ACDKMOO	MOCKADO
ACDKMPU	MUDPACK
ACDKOPR	POCKARD
ACDLLOR	COLLARD
ACDLLUY	DUCALLY
ACDLNOR	CALDRON
ACDLNOT	COTLAND
ACDLOWY	LADYCOW
ACDLSTY	DACTYLS
ACDMMNO	COMMAND
ACDMOOW	CAMWOOD
ACDMORZ	CZARDOM
ACDMSTU	MUDCATS
ACDNOOR	CARDOON
ACDNORS	CANDORS
ACDNORU	CANDOUR
	CAUDRON
ACDORST	COSTARD
ACDORSU	CRUSADO
ACDORSW	COWARDS
ACDORUZ	CRUZADO
ACDRSTU	CUSTARD
ACDRSUU	CARDUUS
ACEEEPS	ESCAPEE
ACEEEUV	EVACUEE
ACEEFFS	EFFACES
ACEEFHN	ENCHAFE
ACEEFIN	FAIENCE
	FIANCEE
ACEEFMN	FACEMEN
ACEEFNS	ENFACES
ACEEFNY	FAYENCE
ACEEFPR	PREFACE
ACEEFRS	REFACES
ACEEGIL	ELEGIAC
ACEEGNR	ENGRACE
ACEEGNS	ENCAGES
ACEEGNT	CENTAGE
ACEEGSU	ESCUAGE
ACEEHHT	CHEETAH
ACEEHIP	CHEAPIE
ACEEHIT	HICATEE
	TEACHIE
ACEEHIV	ACHIEVE
ACEEHKS	HACKEES
ACEEHLR	RELACHE
ACEEHLS	LEACHES
ACEEHLT	CHELATE
ACEEHMP	EMPEACH
ACEEHMR	MACHREE
ACEEHMT	MACHETE
ACEEHNN	ENHANCE
ACEEHNP	CHEAPEN
ACEEHNS	ACHENES
	ENCHASE
ACEEHOR	OCHREAE
ACEEHPP	ECHAPPE
ACEEHPR	CHEAPER
	PEACHER
ACEEHPS	PEACHES
ACEEHRR	REACHER
ACEEHRS	REACHES
ACEEHRT	CHEATER
	HECTARE
	RECHATE
	RECHEAT
	TEACHER
ACEEHST	EATCHES
	ESCHEAT
	TEACHES
ACEEHTT	THECATE
ACEEHTX	EXCHEAT
ACEEILP	CALIPEE
ACEEIMT	EMICATE
ACEEINR	CINEREA
ACEEINU	EUCAINE
ACEEIRR	CARIERE
ACEEISV	VESICAE
ACEEJKN	JACKEEN
ACEEKNP	KNEECAP
ACEELLN	NACELLE
ACEELMP	EMPLACE
ACEELMR	RECLAME
ACEELNR	CLEANER
ACEELNS	CLEANSE
	ELANCES
	ENLACES
	SCALENE
ACEELNT	LATENCE
ACEELNV	ENCLAVE
	VALENCE
ACEELPR	PERCALE
	REPLACE
ACEELPT	CAPELET
ACEELRR	CLEARER
ACEELRS	ALERCES
	CEREALS
	RESCALE
ACEELRT	TREACLE
ACEELRU	CAERULE
ACEELRV	CLEAVER
ACEELST	CELESTA
ACEELSU	EUCLASE
ACEELSV	CLEAVES
ACEELVX	EXCLAVE
ACEEMNR	MENACER
ACEEMNS	CASEMEN
	MENACES
ACEEMNT	CEMENTA
ACEEMNV	CAVEMEN
ACEEMRR	CREAMER
ACEEMRS	AMERCES
	CAREMES
	RACEMES
ACEEMRT	CREMATE
	MEERCAT
ACEEMSS	CAMESES
ACEEMSZ	ECZEMAS
ACEENNP	PENANCE
ACEENNR	NARCEEN
ACEENNT	CANTEEN
ACEENNY	CAYENNE
ACEENOT	ACETONE
ACEENRS	CAREENS
	CASERNE
	ENRACES
ACEENRT	CENTARE
	CRENATE
ACEENSS	ENCASES
	SEANCES
ACEENST	CETANES
	TENACES
ACEENSV	ENCAVES
ACEENTU	CUNEATE
ACEEORS	ACEROSE
ACEEORT	OCREATE
ACEEOST	ACETOSE
	COATEES
ACEEOTV	EVOCATE
ACEEPRR	CAPERER
ACEEPRS	ESCAPER
	PEARCES
	PERCASE
	PREACES
ACEEPSS	ESCAPES
ACEERRS	CAREERS
	CREASER
ACEERRT	CATERER
	RETRACE
	TERRACE
ACEERSS	CREASES
	SEARCES
ACEERST	CERATES
	CREATES
	ECARTES
	SECRETA
ACEERSU	CESURAE
ACEERTX	EXACTER
	EXCRETA
ACEESSS	ASCESES
ACEESST	ECTASES
ACEFFHI	AFFICHE
ACEFFHR	CHAFFER
ACEFFIN	CAFFEIN
ACEFFIS	SCAFFIE
ACEFFOR	AFFORCE
ACEFFST	AFFECTS
ACEFGOT	GEOFACT
ACEFHMR	CHAMFER
ACEFHRS	CHAFERS
ACEFHRU	CHAUFER
ACEFHSU	CHAUFES

ACEFIIL FELICIA
ACEFILM MALEFIC
ACEFILR FILACER
ACEFINN FINANCE
ACEFINR FANCIER
ACEFINS FANCIES
FASCINE
FIANCES
ACEFIRS FARCIES
FIACRES
ACEFITV FACTIVE
ACEFITY ACETIFY
ACEFKLR FLACKER
ACEFKLT FLACKET
ACEFLRU CAREFUL
ACEFLSU FECULAS
ACEFNNO FACONNE
ACEFNRT CANTREF
ACEFNRU FURNACE
ACEFOPR PROFACE
ACEFORR FORECAR
ACEFOTU OUTFACE
ACEFRRT REFRACT
ACEFRRU FARCEUR
ACEFRSU SURFACE
ACEFRTU FACTURE
FURCATE
ACEFSTU FAUCETS
ACEGHLO GALOCHE
ACEGHNR CHANGER
ACEGHNS CHANGES
GANCHES
ACEGHNU CHAUNGE
ACEGHOU GOUACHE
ACEGHOW COWHAGE
ACEGHRR CHARGER
ACEGHRS CHARGES
CREAGHS
ACEGHRT GERTCHA
ACEGHRU GAUCHER
ACEGILL ELLAGIC
ACEGILN ANGELIC
ANGLICE
ACEGILP PELAGIC
ACEGILR GLACIER
GRACILE
ACEGIMO CAMOGIE
ACEGIMR GRIMACE
ACEGIMT GAMETIC
ACEGINO COINAGE
ACEGINP PEACING
ACEGINR GRECIAN
ACEGINS CEASING
INCAGES
ACEGINV VEGANIC
ACEGINY GYNECIA
ACEGINZ CEAZING
ACEGIRU GAUCIER
ACEGIRW GAWCIER
ACEGIST CAGIEST
ACEGKLO LOCKAGE
ACEGKLR GRACKLE
ACEGKMO MOCKAGE
ACEGKOR CORKAGE
ACEGLLO COLLAGE
ACEGLNO CONGEAL
ACEGLNR CLANGER
ACEGLNS CANGLES
GLANCES
ACEGLOT CATELOG
ACEGLOU CAGOULE
ACEGMOP COMPAGE
ACEGNOR ACROGEN
CORNAGE
ACEGNOT COGNATE
ACEGNSU CANGUES
UNCAGES
ACEGORS CARGOES
CORSAGE
SOCAGER
ACEGORU COURAGE
ACEGOSS SOCAGES
ACEGOSW COWAGES
ACEGOTT COTTAGE
ACEGRTU TRUCAGE
ACEGSTU SCUTAGE
ACEHHLT HATCHEL
ACEHHNS HANCHES
ACEHHRT HATCHER
ACEHHRU HACHURE
ACEHHRX HEXARCH
ACEHHST CHETAHS
HATCHES
ACEHHTT HATCHET
ACEHIKR KACHERI
ACEHILL CHALLIE
HELICAL
ACEHILR CHARLIE
ACEHILT ETHICAL
ACEHIMN MACHINE
ACEHIMP IMPEACH
ACEHIMR CHIMERA
ACEHIMS CHAMISE
ACEHINN ENCHAIN
ACEHINS CHAINES
INCHASE
ACEHINT CHANTIE
ACEHINY HYACINE
ACEHIPP CHAPPIE
ACEHIPR CHARPIE
ACEHIPT APHETIC
HEPATIC
ACEHIRR CHARIER
ACEHIRS CAHIERS
CASHIER
ERIACHS
ACEHIRT THERIAC
ACEHIRV ARCHIVE
ACEHISS CHAISES
ACEHIST ACHIEST
AITCHES
ACEHITY YACHTIE
ACEHKLR HACKLER
ACEHKLS HACKLES
SHACKLE
ACEHKLT HACKLET
ACEHKNY HACKNEY
ACEHKRS HACKERS
ACEHKRW WHACKER
ACEHKRY HACKERY
ACEHLLP PELLACH
ACEHLLS SHELLAC
ACEHLMT CHAMLET
ACEHLMY ALCHEMY
ACEHLNN CHANNEL
ACEHLNO CHALONE
ACEHLNR CHARNEL
LARCHEN
ACEHLNS LANCHES
ACEHLOP EPOCHAL
ACEHLOR CHOLERA
CHORALE
ACEHLOS LOACHES
OSCHEAL
ACEHLOT CATHOLE
ACEHLPS CHAPELS
ACEHLPT CHAPLET
ACEHLPY CHEAPLY
ACEHLRS CLASHER
LARCHES
RASCHEL
ACEHLRT ARCHLET
ACEHLRY CHARLEY
ACEHLSS CLASHES
SEALCHS
ACEHLST CHALETS
LATCHES
SATCHEL
ACEHLTT CHATTEL
LATCHET
ACEHMNP CHAPMEN
ACEHMNR ENCHARM
ACEHMNS MANCHES
ACEHMNT MANCHET
ACEHMRR CHARMER
MARCHER
ACEHMRS MARCHES
MESARCH
ACEHMRT MATCHER
REMATCH
ACEHMRU CHAUMER
ACEHMSS SACHEMS
ACEHMST MATCHES
ACEHMTY ECTHYMA
ACEHNNR CHANNER
ACEHNNT ENCHANT
ACEHNRR RANCHER
ACEHNRS CHENARS
RANCHES
ACEHNRT CHANTER
TRANCHE
ACEHNSS SCHANSE
ACEHNST CHASTEN
NATCHES
ACEHNSZ SCHANZE
ACEHNTT ETCHANT
ACEHNTU UNTEACH
ACEHNTY CHANTEY
ACEHOPR POACHER
ACEHOPS EPOCHAS
POACHES
ACEHORS CHOREAS
ORACHES
ROACHES
ACEHOSS CHAOSES
ACEHOTY CHAYOTE
ACEHPPS SCHAPPE
ACEHPRS EPARCHS
PARCHES
ACEHPRT CHAPTER
PATCHER
ACEHPRY EPARCHY
PREACHY
ACEHPSS CHAPESS
ACEHPST PATCHES
ACEHQUY QUEACHY
ACEHRRS ARCHERS
ACEHRRT CHARTER
RECHART
ACEHRRX XERARCH
ACEHRRY ARCHERY
ACEHRSS CHASERS
CRASHES
ESCHARS
ACEHRST ARCHEST
CHARETS
CHASTER
RATCHES
ACEHRSU ARCHEUS
ACEHRSV VARECHS
ACEHRSX EXARCHS
ACEHRSY HYRACES
ACEHRTT CHATTER
RATCHET
ACEHRTW WATCHER
ACEHRTY YACHTER
ACEHRXY EXARCHY
ACEHSSS CHASSES
ACEHSST SACHETS
SCATHES
ACEHSSW CASHEWS
ACEHSTW WATCHES
ACEHSTX HEXACTS
ACEHTTU TEUCHAT
ACEHTTW WATCHET
ACEIILM CIMELIA
ACEIILS LAICISE
ACEIILT CILIATE
ACEIILZ LAICIZE
ACEIITV CAITIVE
VICIATE
ACEIJKS JACKSIE
ACEIKLS SACLIKE
ACEIKLT CATLIKE
ACEIKNT ANTICKE
ACEIKOP PAIOCKE
ACEIKPR EARPICK
ACEIKPX PICKAXE
ACEIKRS EIRACKS
ACEIKRT TACKIER
ACEIKRW WACKIER
ACEIKSS SEASICK
ACEIKST CAKIEST
TACKIES
ACEIKTT TIETACK
ACEILLM LIMACEL
MICELLA
ACEILLS ALLICES
CAILLES
ACEILLX LEXICAL
ACEILMN CNEMIAL
MELANIC
ACEILMR CALMIER
CLAIMER
MIRACLE
RECLAIM
ACEILMS LIMACES
MALICES
ACEILMT CLIMATE
METICAL
ACEILMX EXCLAIM
ACEILMY MYCELIA
ACEILNP CAPELIN
PANICLE
PELICAN
ACEILNR CARLINE
ACEILNS INLACES
SANICLE
SCALENI
ACEILNU CAULINE

ACEILOR	CALORIE
	CARIOLE
	COALIER
	LORICAE
ACEILOS	COALISE
ACEILOT	ALOETIC
ACEILOZ	COALIZE
ACEILPR	CALIPER
	REPLICA
ACEILPS	PLAICES
	SPECIAL
ACEILPT	PLICATE
ACEILPU	PECULIA
ACEILRR	CERRIAL
ACEILRS	CLARIES
	ECLAIRS
	SCALIER
ACEILRT	ARTICLE
	RECITAL
	TALCIER
ACEILRU	AURICLE
ACEILRV	CALIVER
	CLAVIER
	VELARIC
ACEILRY	CLAYIER
ACEILSS	SALICES
ACEILST	ASTELIC
	ELASTIC
	LACIEST
	LATICES
	SALICET
ACEILSV	CLAVIES
	VESICAL
ACEILTT	LATTICE
	TACTILE
ACEIMNO	ENCOMIA
ACEIMNP	PEMICAN
ACEIMNR	CARMINE
ACEIMNS	AMNESIC
	CINEMAS
ACEIMNT	EMICANT
	NEMATIC
ACEIMOV	VOMICAE
ACEIMPR	CAMPIER
ACEIMPY	PYAEMIC
ACEIMRT	MATRICE
ACEIMRU	URAEMIC
ACEIMSS	CAMISES
ACEIMST	ACMITES
	ETACISM
	MICATES
	SEMATIC
ACEIMSU	CAESIUM
ACEINNP	PINNACE
ACEINNR	CANNIER
ACEINNS	CANINES
	NANCIES
ACEINNT	ANCIENT
ACEINNY	CYANINE
ACEINOP	PAEONIC
ACEINOS	ACINOSE
ACEINOT	ACONITE
	ANOETIC
ACEINPR	CAPRINE
ACEINPS	INSCAPE
	PINCASE
ACEINRR	CARNIER
ACEINRS	ARSENIC
	CARNIES
	CERASIN
ACEINRT	CANTIER
	CERTAIN
	CREATIN
	CRINATE
	NACRITE
ACEINSS	CASEINS
	INCASES
ACEINST	CANIEST
	CINEAST
ACEINSU	EUCAINS
ACEINSV	INCAVES
ACEINSY	CYANISE
ACEINTT	NICTATE
	TETANIC
ACEINTV	VENATIC
ACEINTX	INEXACT
ACEINTY	CYANITE
ACEINYZ	CYANIZE
ACEIOOZ	ZOOECIA
ACEIOPT	ECTOPIA
ACEIORS	ORACIES
	SCORIAE
ACEIORT	EROTICA
ACEIOST	SOCIATE
ACEIOTX	EXOTICA
ACEIPPR	EPICARP
ACEIPPT	TAPPICE
ACEIPRR	CRAPIER
ACEIPRS	EPACRIS
	SCRAPIE
	SPACIER
ACEIPRT	PARETIC
	PICRATE
ACEIPST	ASEPTIC
	PACIEST
	SPICATE
ACEIPSU	AUSPICE
ACEIPSZ	CAPIZES
	CAPSIZE
ACEIPTV	CAPTIVE
ACEIQRU	ACQUIRE
ACEIQSU	CAIQUES
ACEIQTU	ACQUITE
ACEIQUZ	CAZIQUE
ACEIRRR	CARRIER
ACEIRRS	CARRIES
	SCARIER
ACEIRRT	CIRRATE
	ERRATIC
ACEIRRZ	CRAZIER
ACEIRST	CRISTAE
	RACIEST
	STEARIC
ACEIRSU	SAUCIER
	URICASE
ACEIRSV	CARVIES
	VARICES
	VISCERA
ACEIRSZ	CRAZIES
ACEIRTT	CATTIER
	CITRATE
ACEISSS	ASCESIS
ACEISST	ASCITES
	ECTASIS
ACEISTT	CATTIES
	STATICE
	TIETACS
ACEITTV	CAVETTI
ACEITTX	EXTATIC
ACEITUX	AUXETIC
ACEJKMN	JACKMEN
ACEJKOP	PAJOCKE
ACEJKST	JACKETS
ACEJLOR	CAJOLER
ACEJLOS	CAJOLES
ACEJNOT	JACONET
ACEJNOY	JOYANCE
ACEJNSU	JAUNCES
ACEJNTU	JUNCATE
ACEJPTU	CAJEPUT
ACEJRTT	TRAJECT
ACEKKNR	KNACKER
ACEKLLP	PELLACK
ACEKLMS	MACKLES
ACEKLNR	CRANKLE
ACEKLNS	SLACKEN
ACEKLOR	EARLOCK
ACEKLPT	PLACKET
ACEKLQU	QUACKLE
ACEKLRS	CALKERS
	LACKERS
	SLACKER
ACEKLRT	TACKLER
ACEKLRU	CAULKER
ACEKLST	TACKLES
ACEKLSY	LACKEYS
ACEKMNP	PACKMEN
ACEKMRS	SMACKER
ACEKNOS	NOCAKES
ACEKNPR	PRANCKE
ACEKNRS	CANKERS
ACEKNRY	CANKERY
ACEKNST	NACKETS
ACEKORR	CROAKER
ACEKPPR	PREPACK
ACEKPRS	PACKERS
	REPACKS
ACEKPST	PACKETS
ACEKQRU	QUACKER
ACEKRRS	RACKERS
ACEKRRT	TRACKER
ACEKRSS	SACKERS
	SCREAKS
ACEKRST	RACKETS
	STACKER
	TACKERS
ACEKRSU	CAUKERS
ACEKRSW	CAWKERS
	WACKERS
ACEKRSY	SCREAKY
	YACKERS
ACEKRTT	RACKETT
ACEKRTY	RACKETY
ACEKSST	CASKETS
ACEKSTT	STACKET
	TACKETS
ACEKTTY	TACKETY
ACELLMO	CALOMEL
ACELLNU	NUCLEAL
ACELLNY	CLEANLY
ACELLOR	CORELLA
	OCELLAR
ACELLOS	LOCALES
ACELLOT	COLLATE
ACELLPS	SCALPEL
ACELLPY	CLYPEAL
ACELLRR	CARRELL
ACELLRS	CALLERS
	CELLARS
	RECALLS
	SCLERAL
ACELLRY	CLEARLY
ACELLST	CALLETS
ACELMNO	COALMEN
ACELMNS	ENCALMS
ACELMOR	CAROMEL
ACELMOT	CAMELOT
ACELMOU	CAULOME
	LEUCOMA
ACELMPR	CLAMPER
ACELMPS	CAMPLES
ACELMRS	MARCELS
ACELMRY	CAMELRY
ACELMSS	MASCLES
	MESCALS
	SCAMELS
ACELMST	CALMEST
	CAMLETS
ACELMSU	ALMUCES
	MACULES
ACELMTU	CALUMET
ACELNNS	CANNELS
ACELNNU	UNCLEAN
ACELNNY	LYNCEAN
ACELNOR	CORNEAL
ACELNOT	LACTONE
ACELNOZ	CALZONE
ACELNPS	ENCLASP
	SPANCEL
ACELNPT	CLAPNET
ACELNPU	UNPLACE
ACELNRS	LANCERS
	RANCELS
ACELNRT	CENTRAL
ACELNRU	LUCARNE
	NUCLEAR
	UNCLEAR
ACELNRY	LARCENY
ACELNST	CANTLES
	CENTALS
	LANCETS
	SCANTLE
ACELNSU	CENSUAL
	LAUNCES
	UNLACES
	UNSCALE
ACELNTT	CANTLET
ACELNTY	LATENCY
ACELNVY	VALENCY
ACELOPR	POLACRE
ACELOPS	ESCALOP
ACELOPT	POLECAT
ACELOQU	COEQUAL
ACELORS	CLAROES
	COALERS
	ESCOLAR
	ORACLES
ACELORY	CALOYER
ACELOSS	SOLACES
ACELOST	ALECOST
	LACTOSE
	LOCATES
	SCATOLE
	TALCOSE
ACELOSV	ALCOVES
	COEVALS
ACELOTT	CALOTTE
ACELOTU	OCULATE
ACELOTY	ACOLYTE
	COTYLAE

ACELOUV VACUOLE
ACELPPR CLAPPER
ACELPPS SCAPPLE
ACELPRS CARPELS
CLASPER
CRAPLES
PARCELS
PLACERS
SCALPER
ACELPRT PLECTRA
ACELPRY PRELACY
ACELPST CAPLETS
PLACETS
ACELPSU CAPSULE
SPECULA
UPSCALE
ACELPSY CYPSELA
ACELPTY ECTYPAL
ACELQRU LACQUER
ACELQSU CALQUES
CLAQUES
ACELQUY LACQUEY
ACELRRS CARRELS
ACELRRU RAUCLER
ACELRRW CRAWLER
ACELRSS SCALERS
SCLERAS
ACELRST CARTELS
CLARETS
SCARLET
TARCELS
ACELRSU CESURAL
SECULAR
ACELRSV CALVERS
CARVELS
CLAVERS
ACELRTT CLATTER
ACELRTY TREACLY
ACELSSS CLASSES
SACLESS
ACELSST CASTLES
SCLATES
ACELSSU CLAUSES
ACELSSV SCLAVES
ACELSTU CAUTELS
SULCATE
ACELSTY ACETYLS
SCYTALE
ACELSUU ACULEUS
ACELSUX EXCUSAL
ACELSXY CALYXES
ACELTUY ACUTELY
ACELTXY EXACTLY
ACEMMRR CRAMMER
ACEMNOR CREMONA
ROMANCE
ACEMNOS ANCOMES
ACEMNPS ENCAMPS
ACEMNSU ACUMENS
ACEMOPR COMPARE
COMPEAR
ACEMOPS POMACES
ACEMORS AMORCES
ACEMORU MORCEAU
ACEMOSS COSMEAS
ACEMOST CAMOTES
COMATES
ACEMOSU MUCOSAE
ACEMPRS CAMPERS
SCAMPER

ACEMPRT CRAMPET
ACEMPST CAMPEST
ACEMRSS SCREAMS
ACEMRST MERCATS
ACEMRSY CRAMESY
ACEMSSU CAMUSES
ACEMSTT METCAST
ACEMSTU MUCATES
ACENNOS ANCONES
SONANCE
ACENNOT CONNATE
ACENNOY NOYANCE
ACENNOZ CANZONE
ACENNRS CANNERS
SCANNER
ACENNRY CANNERY
ACENNST NASCENT
ACENNSU NUANCES
ACENNTY TENANCY
ACENOOR CORONAE
ACENOPT PATONCE
ACENOPU PONCEAU
ACENORS CARNOSE
COARSEN
CORNEAS
EARCONS
ACENORT ENACTOR
ACENOSS CASSONE
ACENOST COSTEAN
OCTANES
ACENOTT ATTONCE
ACENOTV CENTAVO
ACENPRR PRANCER
ACENPRS PRANCES
ACENPRU PRAUNCE
ACENPST CATNEPS
ACENPSU PAUNCES
UNCAPES
ACENPSW PAWNCES
ACENPTT PENTACT
ACENPTY PATENCY
ACENRSS ANCRESS
CASERNS
ACENRST CANTERS
CARNETS
NECTARS
RECANTS
SCANTER
TANRECS
TRANCES
ACENRSU SURANCE
ACENRSV CAVERNS
CRAVENS
ACENRSY CARNEYS
SCENARY
ACENRSZ ZARNECS
ACENRTT TRANECT
ACENRTU CENTAUR
UNCRATE
UNTRACE
ACENRTY ENCRATY
NECTARY
ACENSST ASCENTS
SECANTS
STANCES
ACENSSU UNCASES
USANCES
ACENSTT CANTEST
ACENSTU NUTCASE
ACENSUV VAUNCES

ACEOOPP APOCOPE
ACEOOTZ ECTOZOA
ACEOPRX EXOCARP
ACEOPST CAPOTES
SCOPATE
TOECAPS
ACEOPSW COWPEAS
ACEOPTU OUTPACE
ACEORRS COARSER
ACEORRT ACROTER
CREATOR
REACTOR
ACEORSS ROSACES
ACEORST COASTER
COATERS
ACEORSU ACEROUS
CAROUSE
ACEORSX COAXERS
ACEORTU OUTRACE
ACEORTV OVERACT
ACEORTX EXACTOR
ACEOSSU CASEOUS
ACEOSTT COSTATE
ACEOSTU ACETOUS
ACEOSTV AVOCETS
OCTAVES
ACEOTTV CAVETTO
ACEOTUU AUTOCUE
ACEOTUX COTEAUX
ACEPPRS CAPPERS
ACEPRRS CARPERS
SCARPER
SCRAPER
ACEPRSS ESCARPS
PARSECS
SCRAPES
SPACERS
ACEPRST CARPETS
PRECAST
SPECTRA
ACEPRSU APERCUS
SCAUPER
ACEPRTU CAPTURE
ACEPSST ASPECTS
ACEPSTU CUSPATE
TEACUPS
ACEQRTU RACQUET
ACEQSSU CASQUES
SACQUES
ACEQSTU ACQUEST
ACERRSS CRASSER
SCARERS
SCARRES
ACERRST CARTERS
CRATERS
TRACERS
ACERRSU CURARES
ACERRSV CARVERS
CRAVERS
ACERRSY CRAYERS
ACERRTT RETRACT
ACERRTY TRACERY
ACERRUV VERRUCA
ACERRVY CARVERY
ACERSST ACTRESS
CASTERS
RECASTS
ACERSSU ARCUSES
CAUSERS
CESURAS

SAUCERS
SUCRASE
ACERSSV SCARVES
ACERSSY CARSEYS
SCRAYES
ACERSTT SCATTER
ACERSTU ACTURES
CAUTERS
CRUSTAE
CURATES
ACERSTY SECTARY
ACERTTT TETRACT
ACERTTU CURTATE
ACERTTX EXTRACT
ACERTTY CATTERY
ACERTUV CURVATE
ACERTUY CAUTERY
ACESSTT STACTES
ACESSTU CAESTUS
CUESTAS
ACESSTY CYTASES
ECSTASY
ACESSUY CAUSEYS
CAYUSES
ACESTTU ACUTEST
SCUTATE
ACESTTY TESTACY
ACESTUY EUSTACY
ACFFHSU CHAUFFS
ACFFIIT CAITIFF
ACFFIKM MAFFICK
ACFFILT AFFLICT
ACFFIRT TRAFFIC
ACFFIRY FARCIFY
ACFFLSS SCLAFFS
ACFGHIN CHAFING
ACFGINR FARCING
ACFGINS FACINGS
ACFHIST CATFISH
ACFHISU FUCHSIA
ACFHLNU FLAUNCH
ACFHNOU FAUCHON
ACFHRTY FRATCHY
ACFIILN FINICAL
ACFIKNN FINNACK
ACFILNO FOLACIN
ACFILRY CLARIFY
ACFILSS FISCALS
ACFIMOR ACIFORM
ACFIMSS FASCISM
ACFINNS FINNACS
ACFINNY INFANCY
ACFINOT FACTION
ACFINRS FARCINS
ACFINRT FRANTIC
INFARCT
INFRACT
ACFINRY CARNIFY
ACFIOSS FIASCOS
ACFIPRY CAPRIFY
ACFIRSY SACRIFY
SCARIFY
ACFISST FASCIST
ACFKLSU SACKFUL
ACFLLOY FOCALLY
ACFLNOS FALCONS
FLACONS
ACFLNSU CANFULS
ACFLOST OLFACTS
ACFLRUU FURCULA

ACFLTTU TACTFUL
ACFLTUY FACULTY
ACFMSTU FACTUMS
ACFNSTU UNFACTS
ACFORST FACTORS
FORCATS
ACFORTY FACTORY
ACGGINR GRACING
ACGGIOS AGOGICS
ACGGRSY SCRAGGY
ACGHIKN HACKING
ACGHIMO OGHAMIC
ACGHINR ARCHING
CHAGRIN
CHARING
ACGHINS ACHINGS
CASHING
CHASING
ACGHINT GNATHIC
ACGHINW CHAWING
CHINWAG
ACGHIOR CHORAGI
ACGHIPR GRAPHIC
ACGHIRS SCRAIGH
ACGHLTU CLAUGHT
ACGHNRU GRAUNCH
ACGHOSU GAUCHOS
ACGHRRU CURRAGH
ACGHRSU SCRAUGH
ACGIILN ALGINIC
ACGIITU AUGITIC
ACGIJKN JACKING
ACGIKLN CALKING
LACKING
ACGIKNP PACKING
ACGIKNR ARCKING
CARKING
CRAKING
RACKING
ACGIKNS CAKINGS
CASKING
SACKING
ACGIKNT TACKING
ACGIKNV VACKING
ACGIKNY YACKING
ACGILLN CALLING
ACGILLO LOGICAL
ACGILMN CALMING
ACGILMY MYALGIC
ACGILNN LANCING
ACGILNO COALING
ACGILNP PLACING
ACGILNR CARLING
ACGILNS LACINGS
SCALING
ACGILNT CATLING
TALCING
ACGILNU CINGULA
GLUCINA
ACGILNV CALVING
ACGILNW CLAWING
ACGILNY CLAYING
ACGILOS CALIGOS
ACGILRS GARLICS
ACGIMMN CAMMING
ACGIMNO COAMING
ACGIMNP CAMPING
ACGIMNU CAUMING
ACGINNN CANNING
ACGINNR CRANING
RANCING
ACGINNS CANINGS
ACGINNT CANTING
ACGINOR ORGANIC
ACGINOS ANGICOS
ACGINOT COATING
COTINGA
ACGINOX COAXING
ACGINPP CAPPING
ACGINPR CARPING
ACGINPS SCAPING
SPACING
ACGINRS ARCINGS
RACINGS
SACRING
SCARING
ACGINRT CARTING
CRATING
TRACING
ACGINRV CARVING
CRAVING
ACGINRZ CRAZING
ACGINSS CASINGS
ACGINST ACTINGS
CASTING
ACGINSU CAUSING
SAUCING
ACGINSV CAVINGS
ACGINSW CAWINGS
ACGINTT CATTING
ACGIRST GASTRIC
ACGKMMO GAMMOCK
ACGKORV GARVOCK
ACGLLPU CUPGALL
ACGLNOR CLANGOR
ACGLOSU CAGOULS
ACGNNOR CRANNOG
ACGNOOT OCTAGON
ACGNORS GARCONS
ACGNOSS GASCONS
ACGORRY GYROCAR
ACGORSU COUGARS
ACGORUU COUGUAR
ACGSTTU CATGUTS
ACHHIRS RHACHIS
ACHHOST TOSHACH
ACHHPPU CHUPPAH
ACHHTTT THATCHT
ACHIIKM KAMICHI
ACHIILS ISCHIAL
ACHIIMS CHIASMI
ACHIIPS PACHISI
ACHIJKS HIJACKS
ACHIJNT JACINTH
ACHIKRS RICKSHA
ACHIKRY HAYRICK
ACHIKSS SHICKSA
ACHILLO LOCHIAL
ACHILLP PHALLIC
ACHILLS CHALLIS
ACHILLT THALLIC
ACHILMO MALICHO
ACHILOR CHORIAL
ACHILOS SCHOLIA
ACHILPS CALIPHS
ACHILRS ARCHILS
CARLISH
ACHILRY CHARILY
ACHILST CHITALS
ACHILSY CLAYISH
ACHILWY LICHWAY
ACHIMNO MANIHOC
ACHIMOS CHAMISO
CHAMOIS
ACHIMRS CHARISM
ACHIMSS CHIASMS
SCHISMA
ACHIMST MASTICH
TACHISM
ACHINNU UNCHAIN
ACHINOP APHONIC
ACHINOY ONYCHIA
ACHINPS SPINACH
ACHINRS CHINARS
ACHINRZ ZARNICH
ACHINTX XANTHIC
ACHINUV CHAUVIN
ACHIOPT APHOTIC
ACHIORT CHARIOT
HARICOT
ACHIPPS SAPPHIC
ACHIPST HAPTICS
PATHICS
SPATHIC
ACHIPTU CHUPATI
ACHIPTW WHIPCAT
ACHIQRU CHARQUI
ACHIQSU QUAICHS
ACHIRRT TRIARCH
ACHIRTU HAIRCUT
ACHIRTY CHARITY
ACHISSS CHASSIS
ACHISST SCAITHS
ACHISTT CATTISH
CHATTIS
TACHIST
ACHKKSU CHUKKAS
ACHKMMO HAMMOCK
ACHKOPS HOPSACK
ACHKORS CHOKRAS
ACHKOSS HASSOCK
SHACKOS
ACHKOSW WHACKOS
ACHKOTT HATTOCK
ACHKRSU CHUKARS
ACHKSTW THWACKS
ACHLLOO ALCOHOL
ACHLLOR CHLORAL
ACHLMSY CHLAMYS
ACHLMYY ALCHYMY
ACHLNOS LOCHANS
ACHLNOY HALCYON
ACHLNTU TULCHAN
UNLATCH
ACHLOPR RAPLOCH
ACHLOPT POTLACH
ACHLORS CHORALS
LORCHAS
SCHOLAR
ACHLORT TROCHAL
ACHLOSW SALCHOW
ACHLOTY ACOLYTH
ACHLPST SPLATCH
ACHLTUZ CHALUTZ
ACHMNOR MONARCH
NOMARCH
ACHMNRU UNCHARM
ACHMOPR CAMPHOR
ACHMORS CHROMAS
ACHMORZ MACHZOR
ACHMOST STOMACH
ACHMSSU SUMACHS
ACHMSUW CUMSHAW
ACHNNOS CHANSON
ACHNORS ANCHORS
ARCHONS
RANCHOS
ACHNORT CHANTOR
ACHNOSS SANCHOS
ACHNOST CHATONS
ACHNOSY ONYCHAS
ACHNOTY TACHYON
ACHNOUY CHANOYU
ACHNOVY ANCHOVY
ACHNPSS SCHNAPS
ACHNPUY PAUNCHY
ACHNRTY CHANTRY
ACHNRUY RAUNCHY
UNCHARY
ACHNSTU CANTHUS
CHAUNTS
STAUNCH
ACHNSTY SNATCHY
ACHOOST CAHOOTS
ACHOPRT TOPARCH
ACHOPRY CHARPOY
ACHOPSY POCHAYS
ACHORST ORCHATS
ACHORSU AUROCHS
ACHPRSS SCARPHS
ACHRSST SCARTHS
ACHRSTY STARCHY
ACHRSUU URACHUS
ACHSSTU CUSHATS
ACHSSTY STACHYS
ACHSSUW CUSHAWS
ACHSTUW WAUCHTS
ACHSTUY CYATHUS
ACIIKNN CANIKIN
ACIIKRS AIRSICK
ACIILMM MIMICAL
ACIILNR CLARINI
ACIILNS SALICIN
SINICAL
ACIILNV VICINAL
ACIILOV VILIACO
ACIILRY CILIARY
ACIILSS SILICAS
ACIILST ITALICS
ACIILSU ILIACUS
ACIILSV CLIVIAS
ACIILTY LAICITY
ACIIMMN MINICAM
ACIIMMS MIASMIC
ACIIMNR CRIMINA
ACIIMOT COMITIA
ACIIMST ISMATIC
ITACISM
ACIINNO ANIONIC
ACIINNS NIACINS
ACIINOS ASINICO
ACIINOV AVIONIC
ACIINPS PISCINA
ACIINTT TITANIC
ACIIPPR PRIAPIC
ACIIPRT PIRATIC
ACIIRST SATIRIC
ACIIRTT TRIATIC
ACIJUZZ JACUZZI
ACIKLNS CALKINS

ACIKLOR AIRLOCK
ACIKLTY TACKILY
ACIKMOO OOMIACK
ACIKMPR RAMPICK
ACIKMPW PICKMAW
ACIKNNP PANNICK
ACIKNPS PANICKS
ACIKNPY PANICKY
ACIKNRS NICKARS
ACIKNST CATKINS
CATSKIN
ACIKNTT TINTACK
ACIKOPS PAIOCKS
ACIKPRT PATRICK
ACIKPSS ASPICKS
ACIKRST KARSTIC
ACILLMS MISCALL
ACILLRY LYRICAL
ACILLSS SCILLAS
ACILMNO LIMACON
ACILMOT COMITAL
ACILMPS PLASMIC
ACILMSU MUSICAL
ACILNNY CANNILY
ACILNOR CLARINO
CLARION
ACILNOS OILCANS
ACILNOU INOCULA
ACILNOZ CALZONI
ACILNPS CAPLINS
INCLASP
ACILNPY PLIANCY
ACILNST TINCALS
ACILNSU UNCIALS
ACILNTU LUNATIC
ACILNUV VINCULA
ACILOPT OPTICAL
TOPICAL
ACILORR RACLOIR
ACILORV CORIVAL
ACILOSS SOCIALS
ACILOST STOICAL
ACILOTV VOLATIC
VOLTAIC
ACILOTX TOXICAL
ACILPST PLACITS
PLASTIC
ACILPSU SPICULA
ACILPTY TYPICAL
ACILRSU URACILS
ACILRTU CURTAIL
TRUCIAL
ACILRTY CLARITY
ACILRYZ CRAZILY
ACILSSS CLASSIS
ACILSSU CLUSIAS
ACILSUY SAUCILY
ACILTTY CATTILY
TACITLY
ACILTUV VICTUAL
ACIMNOP CAMPION
ACIMNOR MARCONI
ACIMNOS CAMIONS
CONIMAS
MANIOCS
MASONIC
ACIMNRU CRANIUM
CUMARIN
ACIMNTT CATMINT
ACIMOOS OOMIACS

ACIMOPT POTAMIC
ACIMOSS MOSAICS
ACIMOST MATICOS
SOMATIC
ACIMOSV VOMICAS
ACIMPRT CRAMPIT
PTARMIC
ACIMPRY PRIMACY
ACIMPSS SCAMPIS
SPASMIC
ACIMPST IMPACTS
ACIMRSS RACISMS
ACIMRST MATRICS
ACIMRSZ CZARISM
ACIMSST MASTICS
MISCAST
ACIMSTT TACTISM
ACINNOT ACTINON
CANTION
CONTAIN
ACINNOZ CANZONI
ACINNST STANNIC
ACINNSY CYANINS
ACINNTU ANNICUT
ACINOPT CAPTION
PACTION
ACINOQU COQUINA
ACINORR CARRION
ACINORS SARONIC
ACINORT CAROTIN
ACINOSS CAISSON
CASINOS
CASSINO
ACINOST ACTIONS
CATIONS
ACINOSU ACINOUS
ACINOSY SYCONIA
ACINOTT TACTION
ACINOTU AUCTION
CAUTION
ACINPRT CANTRIP
ACINPRY CYPRIAN
ACINPSS PANISCS
ACINPST CATNIPS
ACINQTU QUANTIC
ACINRSS ARCSINS
ACINRSU CRUSIAN
ACINRTT TANTRIC
ACINRTU CURTAIN
TURACIN
ACINSTU ANICUTS
NAUTICS
ACINSUV VICUNAS
ACIOPRS PROSAIC
ACIOPRT APRICOT
PAROTIC
PATRICO
ACIOPST COPITAS
ACIOPTT APTOTIC
ACIOPTY OPACITY
ACIORRS CORSAIR
ACIORSU CARIOUS
CURIOSA
ACIORTT RICOTTA
ACIOSST SCOTIAS
ACIOSSV OVISACS
ACIPRSY PISCARY
ACIPRVY PRIVACY
ACIPSST SPASTIC
ACIPSTT TIPCATS

ACIPTUY PAUCITY
ACIQRTU QUARTIC
ACIQSTU ACQUIST
ACQUITS
ACIRRSS SIRCARS
ACIRRST TRICARS
ACIRRSU CURARIS
ACIRSST RACISTS
SACRIST
ACIRSSU CUIRASS
ACIRSTT ASTRICT
ACIRSTU URTICAS
ACIRSTW TWISCAR
ACIRSTY SATYRIC
ACIRSTZ CZARIST
ACISSTT STATICS
ACISSTU CASUIST
ACISTTU CATSUIT
ACISTUV VACUIST
ACITUVY VACUITY
ACJKKSY SKYJACK
ACJKLOW LOCKJAW
ACJKNNO JANNOCK
ACJKOPS PAJOCKS
ACJKOPT JACKPOT
ACJLORU JOCULAR
ACJMNTU MUNTJAC
ACJPTUU CAJUPUT
ACKLLOP POLLACK
ACKLLOY LAYLOCK
ACKLLSY SLACKLY
ACKLMNO LOCKMAN
ACKLMOR ARMLOCK
LOCKRAM
ACKLNOU UNCLOAK
ACKLORW WARLOCK
ACKLORY ROCKLAY
ACKLOSS LASSOCK
ACKMMMO MAMMOCK
ACKMOTT MATTOCK
ACKNNOW ACKNOWN
ACKNOSW ACKNOWS
ACKNPRS PRANCKS
ACKNPSU UNPACKS
ACKNSTU UNSTACK
UNTACKS
ACKOPRR PARROCK
ACKOPSY YAPOCKS
ACKORRT TARROCK
ACLLLOY LOCALLY
ACLLOOR COROLLA
ACLLOPS SCALLOP
ACLLORS COLLARS
ACLLORU LOCULAR
ACLLOSU CALLOUS
ACLLOSW CALLOWS
ACLLOVY VOCALLY
ACLMNOO LOCOMAN
ACLMNUY CALUMNY
ACLMORS CLAMORS
ACLMORU CLAMOUR
ACLMSTU TALCUMS
ACLMSUU LUCUMAS
ACLMSUY MASCULY
ACLNOOR CORONAL
ACLNOOT COOLANT
ACLNOOV VOLCANO
ACLNORU CORNUAL
COURLAN
ACLNOUV UNVOCAL

ACLNPSU UNCLASP
ACLNRTU TRUNCAL
ACLNSTY SCANTLY
ACLNSUV VULCANS
ACLOPRT CALTROP
PROCTAL
ACLOPRU COPULAR
CUPOLAR
ACLOPSU COPULAS
CUPOLAS
SCOPULA
ACLOPSY CALYPSO
ACLOPTY POLYACT
ACLORRS CORRALS
ACLORST CARLOTS
CROTALS
SCROTAL
ACLORSU CAROLUS
OCULARS
OSCULAR
RUCOLAS
ACLORUV VOCULAR
ACLOSST COSTALS
ACLOSTU LOCUSTA
TALCOUS
ACLOSTW COTWALS
ACLPRTY CRYPTAL
ACLPRUU CUPULAR
ACLRSSW SCRAWLS
ACLRSSY CRASSLY
ACLRSTU CRUSTAL
CURTALS
ACLRSTY CRYSTAL
ACLRSWY SCRAWLY
ACLSSTU CUTLASS
ACMNOPR CRAMPON
ACMNOPY COMPANY
ACMNORS MACRONS
ACMNORY ACRONYM
ACMNOSS MASCONS
ACMNSTU SANCTUM
ACMOOST SCOTOMA
ACMOPRT COMPART
ACMOPSS COMPASS
ACMOPST COMPAST
ACMORST COMARTS
ACMORTW CATWORM
ACMOSST MASCOTS
ACMOSTT TOMCATS
ACMOSTU MOTUCAS
ACMQTUU CUMQUAT
ACMRSSW SCRAWMS
ACMSSTU MUSCATS
ACMSTUU MUTUCAS
ACMSUUV VACUUMS
ACNNNOS CANNONS
ACNNNUY UNCANNY
ACNNORY CANONRY
ACNNOST CANTONS
ACNNOSY CANYONS
SONANCY
ACNNRSY SCRANNY
ACNOOPS POONACS
ACNOORS CORONAS
RACOONS
ACNOORT CARTOON
CORANTO
ACNOPSW SNOWCAP
ACNORRS RANCORS
ACNORRU RANCOUR

ACNORST	CANTORS
	CARTONS
	CONTRAS
	CRATONS
ACNORSU	NACROUS
ACNORSY	CRAYONS
ACNORTT	CONTRAT
ACNORTU	COURANT
ACNOSSZ	SCAZONS
ACNOSTT	OCTANTS
ACNOSTU	CONATUS
	NOCTUAS
	TOUCANS
ACNPRSY	SYNCARP
ACNRRTU	CURRANT
ACNRSTU	UNCARTS
ACNRSUY	UNSCARY
ACNRSWY	SCRAWNY
ACNRTUY	TRUANCY
ACOOPRR	CORPORA
ACOOPSU	OPACOUS
ACOOPTT	TOPCOAT
ACOORTU	TOURACO
ACOOSTV	OCTAVOS
ACOPRRT	CARPORT
ACOPRST	CAPTORS
ACOPSTU	UPCOAST
ACOPSTW	COWPATS
ACORRST	CARROTS
	TROCARS
ACORRTT	TRACTOR
ACORRTU	CURATOR
ACORRTY	CARROTY
ACORSST	CASTORS
ACORSSU	SARCOUS
ACORSTT	COTTARS
ACORSTU	SURCOAT
	TURACOS
ACORSTV	CAVORTS
ACORSTY	CASTORY
ACORSUU	RAUCOUS
ACORSYZ	CORYZAS
ACOSTTU	OUTCAST
ACOSUUV	VACUOUS
ACPPRSY	SCRAPPY
ACPSSTU	CATSUPS
	UPCASTS
ACPSTUU	USUCAPT
ACRRSTU	CRATURS
ACRSTTU	TRACTUS
ADDDDEL	DADDLED
ADDDDOR	DODDARD
ADDDEER	DREADED
ADDDEFL	FADDLED
ADDDEGL	GLADDED
ADDDEIL	DAIDLED
ADDDEIS	DADDIES
ADDDEIW	WADDIED
ADDDELN	DANDLED
ADDDELP	PADDLED
ADDDELR	RADDLED
ADDDELS	DADDLES
	SADDLED
ADDDELW	DAWDLED
	WADDLED
ADDDENO	DEODAND
ADDDENS	ADDENDS
ADDDEQU	QUADDED
ADDDGIN	DADDING
ADDDOOS	DOODADS
ADDEEEM	ADEEMED
ADDEEFM	DEFAMED
ADDEEGR	DEGRADE
ADDEEHL	HEALDED
ADDEEHR	ADHERED
	REDHEAD
ADDEEIR	READIED
ADDEEIT	IDEATED
ADDEEKN	KNEADED
ADDEEKR	DAKERED
ADDEELM	MEDALED
ADDEELN	DELENDA
ADDEELP	PEDALED
	PLEADED
ADDEELT	DELATED
ADDEELY	DELAYED
ADDEEMN	AMENDED
ADDEEMR	DREAMED
ADDEEMS	ADDEEMS
ADDEENS	DEADENS
ADDEENV	ADVENED
	DAVENED
ADDEENY	DENAYED
ADDEEOT	DEODATE
ADDEERR	DkEADER
ADDEERS	DEADERS
ADDEERT	DERATED
	REDATED
ADDEERY	DERAYED
	YEARDED
ADDEEST	DEADEST
	SEDATED
	STEADED
ADDEEVW	ADVEWED
ADDEFIR	FADDIER
ADDEFLS	FADDLES
ADDEFLY	FADEDLY
ADDEFNU	UNFADED
ADDEFRT	DRAFTED
ADDEFRU	DEFRAUD
ADDEFRW	DWARFED
ADDEGGL	DAGGLED
ADDEGGR	DRAGGED
ADDEGHO	GODHEAD
ADDEGIL	GLADDIE
ADDEGIN	DEADING
ADDEGJU	ADJUDGE
ADDEGLN	DANGLED
	GLADDEN
ADDEGLR	GLADDER
ADDEGRS	GADDERS
ADDEGRU	GUARDED
ADDEHIR	DIHEDRA
ADDEHIS	HADDIES
ADDEHKS	KEDDAHS
ADDEHLN	HANDLED
ADDEHOR	HOARDED
ADDEHRS	SHARDED
ADDEIIK	DIDAKEI
ADDEIIS	DAISIED
ADDEILL	DALLIED
	DIALLED
ADDEILP	PLAIDED
ADDEILR	DIEDRAL
	DRAILED
ADDEILS	DAIDLES
	LADDIES
ADDEILT	DILATED
ADDEIMR	ADMIRED
	MARDIED
ADDEIMS	DIADEMS
ADDEIMX	ADMIXED
ADDEINO	ADENOID
ADDEINP	PANDIED
ADDEINR	DANDIER
	DRAINED
ADDEINS	DANDIES
	SDAINED
ADDEINU	UNAIDED
ADDEINV	INVADED
	VIDENDA
ADDEIOR	RADIOED
ADDEIOT	TOADIED
ADDEIOV	AVOIDED
ADDEIPS	PADDIES
ADDEIRR	ARRIDED
ADDEIRT	TARDIED
ADDEIST	TADDIES
ADDEISV	ADVISED
ADDEISW	WADDIES
ADDEITU	AUDITED
ADDEJLY	JADEDLY
ADDEJNU	UNJADED
ADDEJRU	ADJURED
ADDEKLR	DARKLED
ADDELLU	ALLUDED
	DUALLED
ADDELMW	DWALMED
ADDELNR	DANDLER
ADDELNS	DANDLES
ADDELNU	UNLADED
ADDELPP	DAPPLED
ADDELPR	PADDLER
ADDELPS	PADDLES
ADDELRS	LADDERS
	RADDLES
	SADDLER
ADDELRT	DARTLED
ADDELRW	DAWDLER
	DRAWLED
	WADDLER
ADDELRY	DREADLY
	LADDERY
ADDELSS	SADDLES
ADDELST	STADDLE
ADDELSW	DAWDLES
	SWADDLE
	WADDLES
ADDELTW	TWADDLE
ADDELYZ	DAZEDLY
ADDELZZ	DAZZLED
ADDEMMR	DRAMMED
ADDEMMW	DWAMMED
ADDEMNS	DEMANDS
	MADDENS
ADDEMNU	MAUNDED
ADDEMOP	POMADED
ADDEMRS	MADDERS
ADDEMST	MADDEST
ADDEMUW	DWAUMED
ADDENOR	ADORNED
ADDENOT	DONATED
	NODATED
ADDENOU	DUODENA
ADDENPU	PUDENDA
ADDENRS	DANDERS
ADDENRT	DRANTED
ADDENRU	DAUNDER
ADDENSS	SADDENS
ADDENSU	ASUDDEN
ADDENSY	SDAYNED
ADDENTU	DAUNTED
	UNDATED
ADDEOPT	ADOPTED
ADDEORS	DEODARS
ADDEPPR	DRAPPED
ADDEPRS	PADDERS
ADDEPTU	UPDATED
ADDERSS	ADDRESS
ADDERST	ADDREST
ADDERSW	SWARDED
ADDERSY	DRYADES
ADDERTT	DRATTED
ADDESST	SADDEST
ADDESTU	ADUSTED
	SUDATED
ADDFHIS	FADDISH
ADDFIMS	FADDISM
ADDFINY	DANDIFY
ADDFIST	FADDIST
ADDGGIN	GADDING
ADDGHIN	HADDING
ADDGIIR	DIAGRID
ADDGILN	ADDLING
ADDGIMN	MADDING
ADDGINO	DADOING
ADDGINP	PADDING
ADDGINU	DAUDING
ADDGINW	DAWDING
	WADDING
ADDGIOS	GADOIDS
ADDGLNO	GLADDON
ADDGMNO	GODDAMN
ADDGOOS	OGDOADS
ADDGOOW	DAGWOOD
ADDGORW	GODWARD
ADDGOSY	DOGDAYS
ADDHINP	DAPHNID
ADDHISS	SADDISH
	SIDDHAS
ADDHITY	HYDATID
ADDHOOS	DOODAHS
ADDHSSU	SADDHUS
ADDIINS	DISDAIN
ADDIKST	TSADDIK
ADDIKSZ	ZADDIKS
ADDIKTY	KATYDID
ADDIKTZ	TZADDIK
ADDILMN	MIDLAND
ADDILNY	DANDILY
ADDILOS	DISLOAD
ADDIMNO	DIAMOND
ADDIMOR	DIADROM
ADDIMRS	DIRDAMS
ADDIMSY	DISMAYD
	MIDDAYS
ADDINOR	ANDROID
ADDINRY	DIANDRY
ADDIPRS	DISPRAD
ADDIQST	TSADDIQ
ADDIQTZ	TZADDIQ
ADDIRZZ	DIZZARD
ADDLLRU	DULLARD
ADDLOOS	SOLDADO
ADDLTWY	TWADDLY
ADDMNOS	DODMANS
	ODDSMAN
ADDMOOS	ADDOOMS
ADDNNOR	DONNARD
ADDOORS	DORADOS

ADDOPSY	DASYPOD
ADDORST	DOTARDS
ADDQSUY	SQUADDY
ADEEEFY	FEDAYEE
ADEEEMN	DEMEANE
ADEEERR	ARREEDE
ADEEERX	EXEDRAE
ADEEESW	SEAWEED
ADEEFGU	FEAGUED
ADEEFHS	SHEAFED
ADEEFIR	AREFIED
	FEDARIE
ADEEFKR	FREAKED
ADEEFLR	FEDERAL
ADEEFLT	DEFLATE
ADEEFMS	DEFAMES
ADEEFNS	DEAFENS
ADEEFPR	PREFADE
ADEEFRT	DRAFTEE
ADEEFRW	WAFERED
ADEEFST	DEAFEST
	DEFASTE
	DEFEATS
	FEASTED
ADEEGGH	EGGHEAD
ADEEGGL	ALEGGED
ADEEGGN	ENGAGED
ADEEGLL	ALLEDGE
	ALLEGED
ADEEGLM	GLEAMED
ADEEGLN	GLEANED
ADEEGLR	REGALED
ADEEGLT	TEAGLED
ADEEGLU	LEAGUED
ADEEGMN	ENDGAME
	MANEGED
	MENAGED
ADEEGNR	ANGERED
	DERANGE
	ENRAGED
	GRANDEE
	GRENADE
ADEEGNT	AGENTED
	NEGATED
ADEEGNV	AVENGED
	VENDAGE
ADEEGOT	DOGEATE
	GOATEED
ADEEGRR	REGRADE
ADEEGRS	DRAGEES
	GREASED
ADEEGRU	GUARDEE
ADEEGRV	GREAVED
ADEEGRW	RAGWEED
	WAGERED
ADEEHIR	HEADIER
ADEEHLR	HEDERAL
ADEEHLS	LEASHED
	SHEALED
ADEEHLX	EXHALED
ADEEHMN	HEADMEN
ADEEHNN	HENNAED
ADEEHNS	DASHEEN
ADEEHNV	HAVENED
ADEEHPR	EPHEDRA
ADEEHRR	ADHERER
	REHEARD
ADEEHRS	ADHERES
	HEADERS
	HEARSED
	SHEARED
ADEEHRT	EARTHED
	HEARTED
ADEEHRV	HAVERED
ADEEHRX	EXHEDRA
ADEEHST	HEADSET
ADEEHSV	SHEAVED
ADEEHSY	HAYSEED
ADEEIJT	JADEITE
ADEEILM	LIMEADE
ADEEILN	ALIENED
	DELAINE
ADEEILR	LEADIER
ADEEILS	AEDILES
	DEISEAL
ADEEILY	EYELIAD
ADEEIMN	DEMAINE
ADEEIMT	MEDIATE
ADEEINN	ADENINE
ADEEINS	ANISEED
ADEEIRR	READIER
ADEEIRS	DEARIES
	READIES
ADEEIRW	WEARIED
ADEEISS	DISEASE
	SEASIDE
ADEEIST	IDEATES
ADEEITV	DEVIATE
ADEEJSY	DEEJAYS
ADEEKNR	KNEADER
	NAKEDER
ADEEKNS	SNEAKED
ADEEKNW	WAKENED
ADEEKRS	SKEARED
ADEEKRW	WREAKED
ADEEKTW	TWEAKED
ADEEKWY	WEEKDAY
ADEELLS	ALLSEED
ADEELLY	ALLEYED
ADEELMP	EMPALED
ADEELMR	EMERALD
ADEELMS	MEASLED
ADEELMT	MEDALET
	METALED
ADEELMU	AEMULED
ADEELMY	YEALMED
ADEELNP	DEPLANE
ADEELNR	LEARNED
ADEELNS	LEADENS
ADEELNT	EDENTAL
	LATENED
ADEELPR	PEARLED
	PLEADER
ADEELPS	DELAPSE
	ELAPSED
	PLEASED
ADEELPT	PLEATED
ADEELRS	DEALERS
	LEADERS
	REDEALS
ADEELRT	ALERTED
	ALTERED
	REDEALT
	RELATED
	TREADLE
ADEELRW	LEEWARD
ADEELRX	RELAXED
ADEELRY	DELAYER
	LAYERED
	RELAYED
ADEELST	DELATES
	STEALED
ADEELSV	SLEAVED
ADEELSW	SWEALED
ADEELTV	VALETED
	VELATED
ADEELTX	EXALTED
ADEELTZ	TEAZLED
ADEELUV	DEVALUE
ADEEMNR	AMENDER
	ENARMED
	MEANDER
	REAMEND
	RENAMED
ADEEMNS	AMENDES
	DEMEANS
ADEEMNT	ENTAMED
ADEEMNY	DEMAYNE
ADEEMOS	OEDEMAS
ADEEMPR	EMPARED
ADEEMRR	DREAMER
	REARMED
ADEEMRS	REMADES
	REMEADS
	SMEARED
ADEEMST	STEAMED
ADEEMSU	MEDUSAE
ADEEMSW	MAWSEED
ADEEMTW	MATWEED
ADEEMWY	MAYWEED
ADEENNS	ENNEADS
ADEENNX	ANNEXED
ADEENPS	SNEAPED
	SPEANED
ADEENRS	DEANERS
	ENDEARS
ADEENRU	UNEARED
ADEENRV	RAVENED
ADEENRY	DEANERY
	RENAYED
	YEARNED
ADEENST	STANDEE
	STEANED
ADEENSV	ADVENES
ADEENTT	DENTATE
ADEEORS	OREADES
ADEEORW	OARWEED
ADEEPPR	PAPERED
ADEEPRS	PREASED
	SPEARED
ADEEPRT	ADEPTER
	PREDATE
	TAPERED
ADEEPRV	DEPRAVE
	PERVADE
ADEEPSS	PESADES
ADEEQRU	QUAERED
ADEEQTU	EQUATED
ADEERRR	DREARER
ADEERRS	DREARES
	READERS
	REDSEAR
	REREADS
ADEERRT	RETREAD
	TREADER
ADEERRV	AVERRED
ADEERSS	RESEDAS
ADEERST	DEAREST
	DERATES
	ESTRADE
	REASTED
	REDATES
	SEDATER
	STEARED
	TASERED
ADEERSV	ADVERSE
	EVADERS
ADEERSW	DRAWEES
ADEERTT	ARETTED
	TREATED
ADEERTV	AVERTED
	TAVERED
ADEERTW	DEWATER
	TARWEED
	WATERED
ADEERVW	WAVERED
ADEESST	SEDATES
ADEESSY	ESSAYED
ADEESTT	ESTATED
ADEESTU	SAUTEED
ADEESTW	SWEATED
ADEESTY	YEASTED
ADEESVY	SAVEYED
ADEETUX	EXUDATE
ADEFFFL	FLAFFED
ADEFFGR	GRAFFED
ADEFFIN	AFFINED
ADEFFIP	PIAFFED
ADEFFIR	DAFFIER
ADEFFIS	DAFFIES
ADEFFIX	AFFIXED
ADEFFLM	MAFFLED
ADEFFLR	RAFFLED
ADEFFLW	WAFFLED
ADEFFNY	NYAFFED
ADEFFQU	QUAFFED
ADEFFST	STAFFED
ADEFFUW	WAUFFED
ADEFGGL	FLAGGED
ADEFGGR	FRAGGED
ADEFGLN	FANGLED
	FLANGED
ADEFGOR	FORAGED
ADEFGOT	FAGOTED
ADEFGOU	FOUGADE
ADEFGRT	GRAFTED
ADEFHIT	FAITHED
ADEFHLS	FLASHED
ADEFHRW	WHARFED
ADEFHST	SHAFTED
ADEFILL	FLAILED
ADEFILS	DISLEAF
ADEFIMN	INFAMED
ADEFIMS	DISFAME
ADEFINR	FRIANDE
ADEFINT	DEFIANT
	FAINTED
ADEFIRS	FRAISED
ADEFIST	DAFTIES
	FADIEST
ADEFITX	FIXATED
ADEFKLN	FANKLED
	FLANKED
ADEFKNR	FRANKED
ADEFLLN	ELFLAND
ADEFLMM	FLAMMED
ADEFLNN	FENLAND
ADEFLOT	FLOATED
ADEFLPP	FLAPPED
ADEFLRS	FARDELS

ADEFLRU	DAREFUL
ADEFLTT	FLATTED
ADEFLTU	DEFAULT
	FAULTED
ADEFMNU	UNFAMED
ADEFNRS	FARDENS
ADEFNSU	UNDEAFS
ADEFNUZ	UNFAZED
ADEFOOS	SEAFOOD
ADEFORS	FEDORAS
ADEFORV	FAVORED
ADEFORY	FEODARY
	FORAYED
ADEFPPR	FRAPPED
ADEFPRR	PREFARD
ADEFRRT	DRAFTER
	REDRAFT
ADEFRST	STRAFED
ADEFRSU	FADEURS
ADEFRSW	SWARFED
ADEFRSY	DEFRAYS
ADEFRUY	FEUDARY
ADEFSTT	DAFTEST
ADEGGGL	GAGGLED
ADEGGHL	HAGGLED
ADEGGHS	SHAGGED
ADEGGIR	DAGGIER
ADEGGIS	GADGIES
ADEGGIU	GAUDGIE
	GUIDAGE
ADEGGLR	DRAGGLE
	GARGLED
	RAGGLED
ADEGGLS	DAGGLES
	SLAGGED
ADEGGLW	WAGGLED
ADEGGNS	SNAGGED
ADEGGRS	DAGGERS
ADEGGRY	RAGGEDY
ADEGGST	GADGETS
	STAGGED
ADEGGSW	SWAGGED
ADEGHIN	HEADING
ADEGHIR	HEADRIG
ADEGHIS	HIDAGES
ADEGHJU	JUGHEAD
ADEGHLU	LAUGHED
ADEGHMO	HOMAGED
ADEGHNP	PHANGED
ADEGHNS	GNASHED
	HAGDENS
ADEGHNW	WHANGED
ADEGHPR	GRAPHED
ADEGHST	GHASTED
ADEGHUW	WAUGHED
ADEGILL	GALLIED
ADEGILN	ALIGNED
	DEALING
	LEADING
ADEGILO	GEOIDAL
ADEGILR	GLADIER
	GLAIRED
ADEGILS	SILAGED
ADEGILT	LIGATED
	TAIGLED
ADEGILV	GLAIVED
ADEGINR	AREDING
	DEARING
	DERAIGN
	EARDING
	GRADINE
	GRAINED
	READING
ADEGINS	AGNISED
ADEGINV	DEAVING
	EVADING
ADEGINW	WINDAGE
ADEGINY	YEADING
ADEGINZ	AGNIZED
ADEGIOT	GODETIA
ADEGIRS	AGRISED
ADEGIRU	GAUDIER
ADEGIRZ	AGRIZED
ADEGIST	AGISTED
ADEGISU	AGUISED
	GAUDIES
ADEGISV	VISAGED
ADEGIUV	VIDUAGE
ADEGIUZ	AGUIZED
ADEGJLN	JANGLED
ADEGLLU	ULLAGED
ADEGLMN	MANGLED
ADEGLMR	MALGRED
ADEGLMU	GLAUMED
ADEGLNN	ENDLANG
ADEGLNR	DANGLER
	GNARLED
ADEGLNS	DANGLES
	GLANDES
	SLANGED
ADEGLNT	TANGLED
ADEGLNU	LANGUED
ADEGLNW	WANGLED
ADEGLOP	GALOPED
ADEGLOT	GLOATED
ADEGLPU	PLAGUED
ADEGLRS	DARGLES
ADEGLRU	RAGULED
ADEGLRY	GRADELY
ADEGLSS	GLASSED
ADEGMNS	GADSMEN
ADEGMNU	GUDEMAN
ADEGMRU	MAUGRED
ADEGNNO	NONAGED
ADEGNNU	DUNNAGE
ADEGNOP	PONDAGE
ADEGNOR	GROANED
ADEGNOS	SONDAGE
ADEGNOT	TANGOED
ADEGNOV	DOGVANE
ADEGNOW	GOWANED
	WAGONED
ADEGNPR	PRANGED
ADEGNPS	SPANGED
ADEGNPU	UNPAGED
ADEGNRR	GNARRED
	GRANDER
ADEGNRS	DANGERS
	GANDERS
	GARDENS
ADEGNRT	DRAGNET
	GRANTED
ADEGNRU	ENGUARD
	RAUNGED
ADEGNST	STANGED
ADEGNTU	GAUNTED
ADEGNTW	TWANGED
ADEGNUW	UNWAGED
ADEGORW	DOWAGER
	WORDAGE
ADEGOSS	DOSAGES
ADEGOST	DOGATES
	DOTAGES
ADEGOTT	TOGATED
ADEGOVY	VOYAGED
ADEGPRS	GRASPED
	SPADGER
	SPARGED
ADEGPRU	UPGRADE
ADEGPUZ	UPGAZED
ADEGRRS	GRADERS
	REGARDS
ADEGRSS	GRASSED
ADEGRST	RADGEST
ADEGRSU	SUGARED
ADEGRTY	GYRATED
	TRAGEDY
ADEGRUU	AUGURED
ADEGRUY	GAUDERY
ADEGRYZ	AGRYZED
ADEGSSU	DEGAUSS
ADEHHOT	HOTHEAD
ADEHHSS	SHASHED
ADEHIKS	DASHEKI
ADEHIKV	KHEDIVA
ADEHILN	INHALED
ADEHILP	HELIPAD
ADEHILS	HALIDES
ADEHILY	HEADILY
ADEHINP	PINHEAD
ADEHINR	HANDIER
ADEHIPP	HAPPIED
ADEHIPR	RAPHIDE
ADEHIPS	APHIDES
ADEHIPT	PITHEAD
ADEHIRR	HARDIER
	HARRIED
ADEHIRS	SHADIER
ADEHIRW	RAWHIDE
ADEHIRY	HAYRIDE
	HYDRIAE
ADEHKNS	SHANKED
ADEHKNT	THANKED
ADEHKOR	HARDOKE
ADEHKOT	KATHODE
ADEHKRS	SHARKED
ADEHLLO	HALLOED
ADEHLLP	LAPHELD
ADEHLNR	HANDLER
ADEHLNS	HANDLES
	HANDSEL
ADEHLOS	SHOALED
ADEHLOT	LOATHED
ADEHLPS	PLASHED
ADEHLRS	HARELDS
	HERALDS
ADEHLSS	HASSLED
	SLASHED
ADEHLSW	SHAWLED
ADEHLTY	DEATHLY
ADEHMMS	SHAMMED
ADEHMMW	WHAMMED
ADEHMNR	HERDMAN
ADEHMOP	MOPHEAD
ADEHMOR	HADROME
ADEHMRS	DERHAMS
ADEHMSS	SMASHED
ADEHNPS	DAPHNES
ADEHNRS	HANDERS
	HARDENS
ADEHNRU	UNHEARD
ADEHNSS	SNASHED
ADEHNST	HANDSET
ADEHNSU	UNHEADS
ADEHNTU	HAUNTED
ADEHOOP	APEHOOD
ADEHOPX	HEXAPOD
ADEHORR	HOARDER
ADEHOST	HOASTED
ADEHOSX	OXHEADS
ADEHPPW	WHAPPED
ADEHPRS	PHRASED
	SHARPED
ADEHPST	HEPTADS
	SPATHED
ADEHPSW	PSHAWED
ADEHQSU	QUASHED
ADEHRRU	HURRAED
ADEHRSS	DASHERS
ADEHRST	DEARTHS
	HARDEST
	HATREDS
	THREADS
	TRASHED
ADEHRTW	WRATHED
ADEHRTY	HYDRATE
	THREADY
ADEHSST	STASHED
ADEHSSW	SWASHED
ADEHSTW	SWATHED
ADEHSYY	HEYDAYS
ADEHUZZ	HUZZAED
ADEIILR	DELIRIA
	IRIDEAL
ADEIILS	DAILIES
	LIAISED
	SEDILIA
ADEIINR	DENARII
ADEIIPR	PERIDIA
ADEIIRS	AIRSIDE
	DAIRIES
	DIARIES
	DIARISE
ADEIIRZ	DIARIZE
ADEIISS	DAISIES
ADEIJMR	JEMIDAR
ADEIKLN	KNAIDEL
ADEIKLS	SKAILED
ADEIKNS	KANDIES
ADEIKRS	DAIKERS
	DARKIES
ADEIKRT	TRAIKED
ADEILLR	DALLIER
	DIALLER
	RALLIED
ADEILLS	DALLIES
	DISLEAL
	LALDIES
	SALLIED
ADEILLT	TALLIED
ADEILLV	VIALLED
ADEILLY	IDEALLY
ADEILMM	DILEMMA
ADEILMP	IMPALED
	IMPLEAD
ADEILMS	MAELIDS
	MEDIALS
	MISDEAL
	MISLEAD
ADEILMU	MIAULED

ADEILNN	ANNELID
	LINDANE
ADEILNP	PLAINED
ADEILNS	DENIALS
	SNAILED
ADEILNU	ALIUNDE
	UNIDEAL
ADEILNV	ANDVILE
ADEILNX	INDEXAL
ADEILOR	DARIOLE
ADEILOS	DEASOIL
ADEILOU	DOULEIA
ADEILPP	APPLIED
ADEILPR	PEDRAIL
	PREDIAL
ADEILPS	ALIPEDS
	PAIDLES
	PALSIED
ADEILPT	PLAITED
	TALIPED
ADEILQU	QUAILED
ADEILRR	LARDIER
ADEILRS	DERAILS
	REDIALS
	SIDERAL
ADEILRT	DILATER
	TRAILED
ADEILRV	VALIDER
ADEILRY	READILY
ADEILSS	AIDLESS
	DEASILS
ADEILST	DETAILS
	DILATES
ADEILSU	AUDILES
	DEASIUL
ADEILSV	DEVISAL
ADEILSY	DIALYSE
	EYLIADS
ADEILYZ	DIALYZE
ADEIMMR	MERMAID
ADEIMMS	MISMADE
ADEIMNR	ADERMIN
	INARMED
ADEIMNS	DEMAINS
	MAIDENS
	MEDIANS
	MEDINAS
	SIDEMAN
ADEIMNT	MEDIANT
ADEIMNU	UNAIMED
ADEIMOW	MIAOWED
ADEIMPR	DAMPIER
ADEIMPV	IMPAVED
ADEIMRR	ADMIRER
	MARDIER
	MARRIED
ADEIMRS	ADMIRES
	MARDIES
	MISREAD
	SIDEARM
ADEIMRT	READMIT
ADEIMST	MISDATE
ADEIMSV	VIDAMES
ADEIMSX	ADMIXES
ADEIMTU	TAEDIUM
ADEIMTY	DAYTIME
ADEINNN	NANDINE
	NANNIED
ADEINOR	ANEROID
ADEINOS	ADONISE
	ANODISE
	SODAINE
ADEINOV	NAEVOID
ADEINOX	DIOXANE
ADEINOZ	ADONIZE
	ANODIZE
ADEINPR	PARDINE
ADEINPS	PANDIES
	PANSIED
	SPAINED
ADEINPT	DEPAINT
	PAINTED
	PATINED
ADEINRR	DRAINER
	RANDIER
ADEINRS	RANDIES
	SANDIER
	SARDINE
ADEINRT	DETRAIN
	TRAINED
ADEINRU	UNAIRED
	URANIDE
ADEINRV	INVADER
	RAVINED
ADEINSS	SDAINES
ADEINST	DETAINS
	INSTEAD
	SAINTED
	SATINED
	STAINED
ADEINSV	INVADES
ADEINSW	DEWANIS
ADEINTT	TAINTED
ADEINTU	AUDIENT
ADEINTV	DEVIANT
ADEINVV	NAVVIED
ADEIOPS	ADIPOSE
ADEIOPT	OPIATED
ADEIORS	ROADIES
	SOREDIA
ADEIORX	EXORDIA
ADEIOST	IODATES
	TOADIES
ADEIOSX	OXIDASE
ADEIOSZ	DIAZOES
ADEIOTX	OXIDATE
ADEIOVV	VAIVODE
ADEIOVW	WAIVODE
ADEIOWW	WAIWODE
ADEIPPR	DRAPPIE
	PREPAID
ADEIPPU	APPUIED
ADEIPRR	DRAPIER
	PARRIED
	RAPIDER
ADEIPRS	ASPIRED
	DESPAIR
	DIAPERS
	PRAISED
ADEIPRT	DIPTERA
	PARTIED
	PIRATED
ADEIPRV	VAPIDER
ADEIPSS	APSIDES
ADEIRRS	ARRIDES
	RAIDERS
ADEIRRT	TARDIER
	TARRIED
ADEIRRV	ARRIVED
ADEIRST	ARIDEST
	ASTERID
	ASTRIDE
	DIASTER
	DISRATE
	STAIDER
	STAIRED
	TARDIES
	TIRADES
ADEIRSU	RESIDUA
ADEIRSV	ADVISER
	VARDIES
ADEIRTT	ATTIRED
ADEIRTV	TARDIVE
ADEIRTY	DIETARY
ADEISSS	DASSIES
ADEISST	DISSEAT
	SAIDEST
ADEISSV	ADVISES
ADEISSZ	ASSIZED
ADEISTU	DAUTIES
ADEISTV	AVIDEST
	DATIVES
	VISTAED
ADEISTW	DAWTIES
	WAISTED
ADEISVV	SAVVIED
ADEISWY	WAYSIDE
ADEITWY	TIDEWAY
ADEJMOR	MAJORED
ADEJMRU	MUDEJAR
ADEJNSU	JAUNSED
ADEJNTU	JAUNTED
ADEJOPR	JEOPARD
ADEJRSU	ADJURES
ADEJSSU	JUDASES
ADEKKNS	SKANKED
ADEKLNP	PLANKED
ADEKLNR	RANKLED
ADEKLNS	KALENDS
ADEKLNY	NAKEDLY
ADEKLRS	DARKLES
ADEKLST	SKLATED
	STALKED
ADEKLSY	YSLAKED
ADEKLUW	WAULKED
ADEKMRS	DEMARKS
ADEKNPP	KNAPPED
ADEKNPR	PRANKED
ADEKNPS	SPANKED
ADEKNRR	KNARRED
ADEKNRS	DARKENS
ADEKNRU	UNRAKED
ADEKNST	DANKEST
ADEKNSU	UNASKED
ADEKNSW	SWANKED
ADEKNUW	UNWAKED
ADEKNVY	VANDYKE
ADEKPRS	SPARKED
ADEKPSY	KEYPADS
ADEKRST	DARKEST
	STARKED
ADEKRSY	DARKEYS
ADELLMS	SMALLED
ADELLMU	MEDULLA
ADELLNR	LANDLER
ADELLNW	ELLWAND
ADELLOR	ODALLER
ADELLOW	ALLOWED
ADELLOY	ALLOYED
ADELLPS	SPALLED
ADELLRU	ALLURED
	UDALLER
ADELLST	STALLED
ADELLSU	ALLUDES
	ALUDELS
ADELLSV	DEVALLS
ADELMMS	SLAMMED
	SMALMED
ADELMNN	LANDMEN
ADELMNR	MANDREL
ADELMNT	MANTLED
ADELMOR	EARLDOM
ADELMOS	DAMOSEL
ADELMOZ	DAMOZEL
ADELMPS	SAMPLED
ADELMRS	MEDLARS
ADELMSS	DAMSELS
ADELNNP	PLANNED
ADELNNU	UNLADEN
ADELNOR	LADRONE
ADELNOS	LOADENS
ADELNOT	TALONED
ADELNOY	YEALDON
ADELNPT	PLANTED
ADELNRS	DARNELS
	ENLARDS
	LANDERS
	SLANDER
	SNARLED
ADELNRU	LAUNDER
	LURDANE
	RUNDALE
ADELNRY	DEARNLY
ADELNSS	SENDALS
ADELNST	DENTALS
	SLANTED
ADELNSU	UNLADES
	UNLEADS
ADELNTU	LUNATED
	UNDEALT
ADELNTW	WETLAND
ADELNUW	UNLAWED
ADELOPR	LEOPARD
	PAROLED
ADELOPS	DEPOSAL
	PEDALOS
ADELOPT	PLOATED
	TADPOLE
ADELORS	LOADERS
	ORDEALS
	RELOADS
ADELORT	DELATOR
	LEOTARD
ADELORU	ROULADE
ADELOSS	ALDOSES
	LASSOED
ADELOST	SALTOED
ADELPPP	PLAPPED
ADELPPS	DAPPLES
	SAPPLED
	SLAPPED
ADELPRS	PEDLARS
ADELPRY	PEDLARY
ADELPST	SPALTED
	STAPLED
ADELPSU	UPLEADS
ADELPSW	DEWLAPS
	SPAWLED
ADELPSY	SPLAYED
ADELPTT	PLATTED

ADELPTW DEWLAPT
ADELPTY ADEPTLY
ADELRRS LARDERS
ADELRRU RUDERAL
ADELRRW DRAWLER
ADELRSS SARDELS
ADELRST DARTLES
ADELRSU LAUDERS
ADELRSW WARSLED
ADELRSZ DRAZELS
ADELRTT RATTLED
ADELRTW TRAWLED
ADELRTX DEXTRAL
ADELRTY LYRATED
ADELRWW WRAWLED
ADELRWX WRAXLED
ADELRZZ DAZZLER
ADELSST DESALTS
ADELSTT SLATTED
ADELSTU AULDEST
SALUTED
ADELSUV AVULSED
ADELSWY SWAYLED
ADELSZZ DAZZLES
ADELTTT TATTLED
ADELTTW WATTLED
ADELTUV VAULTED
ADELTUX LUXATED
ADELTWZ WALTZED
ADEMMRS DAMMERS
SMARMED
ADEMMRT TRAMMED
ADEMNNS SANDMEN
ADEMNNU MUNDANE
UNNAMED
ADEMNOR MADRONE
ROADMEN
ADEMNOS DAEMONS
MASONED
MODENAS
MONADES
NOMADES
ADEMNOW WOMANED
ADEMNPS DAMPENS
ADEMNRS MANREDS
RANDEMS
REMANDS
ADEMNRU DURAMEN
MANURED
MAUNDER
UNARMED
ADEMNRY DRAYMEN
YARDMEN
ADEMNSS DESMANS
MADNESS
ADEMNST TANDEMS
ADEMNSU MEDUSAN
SUDAMEN
ADEMNSY DAYSMEN
ADEMNTU UNMATED
UNTAMED
ADEMOOV AMOOVED
ADEMOPS APEDOMS
POMADES
ADEMORS RADOMES
ADEMOSV VAMOSED
ADEMOSW MEADOWS
ADEMOSY SOMEDAY
ADEMOWY MEADOWY
ADEMPRS DAMPERS
ADEMPRT TRAMPED
ADEMPSS SPASMED
ADEMPST DAMPEST
STAMPED
ADEMPSW SWAMPED
ADEMRRU EARDRUM
ADEMRST SMARTED
ADEMRSU REMUDAS
ADEMRSW SWARMED
ADEMRTU MATURED
ADEMSSU ASSUMED
MEDUSAS
ADEMTTU MUTATED
ADENNOY ANNOYED
ANODYNE
ADENNPS SPANNED
ADENNPT PENDANT
ADENNST STANDEN
ADENNSU DUENNAS
ADENNSW SWANNED
ADENNWY DEWANNY
ADENOOP NAPOOED
ADENOOZ ENDOZOA
ADENOPR APRONED
OPERAND
PADRONE
PANDORE
ADENOPS DAPSONE
ADENOPT TONEPAD
ADENORT TORNADE
ADENORU RONDEAU
ADENOST ASTONED
DONATES
ONSTEAD
ADENOSU DOUANES
ADENOSY NOYADES
ADENOTT NOTATED
ADENOTZ ZONATED
ADENPPR PARPEND
ADENPPS APPENDS
SNAPPED
ADENPPW WAPPEND
ADENPRR PARDNER
ADENPRS PANDERS
ADENPRU UNPARED
ADENPRW PRAWNED
PREDAWN
ADENPST PEDANTS
PENTADS
ADENPSW SPAWNED
ADENPSX EXPANDS
SPANDEX
ADENPSY DYSPNEA
ADENPUV UNPAVED
ADENQTU QUANTED
ADENRRS DARNERS
ERRANDS
SNARRED
ADENRRW REDRAWN
ADENRRY REYNARD
ADENRSS SANDERS
SARSDEN
ADENRST ENDARTS
STANDER
STARNED
ADENRSU ASUNDER
DANSEUR
DAUNERS
ADENRSW DAWNERS
WANDERS
WARDENS
ADENRSZ ZANDERS
ADENRTT TRANTED
ADENRTU DAUNTER
NATURED
UNRATED
UNTREAD
ADENRTV VERDANT
ADENRTX DEXTRAN
ADENRTY DENTARY
TRAYNED
TYRANED
ADENRUY UNREADY
ADENSSS SADNESS
ADENSSU SUNDAES
ADENSSW WESANDS
ADENSTT ATTENDS
ADENSTU SAUNTED
UNSATED
ADENSTV ADVENTS
ADENSTY STAYNED
ADENSUV UNSAVED
ADENSWY ENDWAYS
ADENSWZ WEZANDS
ADENTTU ATTUNED
NUTATED
TAUNTED
ADENTUV VAUNTED
ADENTUX UNTAXED
ADENUWY UNWAYED
ADEOORT ODORATE
ADEOPPS APPOSED
PEAPODS
ADEOPQU OPAQUED
ADEOPRR EARDROP
ADEOPRT ADOPTER
READOPT
ADEOPRV VAPORED
ADEOPSS SPADOES
ADEOPST PODESTA
ADEORRS ADORERS
DROSERA
ADEORRW ARROWED
ADEORST DOATERS
ROASTED
TORSADE
TROADES
ADEORSU AROUSED
ADEORSV SAVORED
ADEORSW REDOWAS
ADEORTT ROTATED
TROATED
ADEORTU OUTDARE
ADEORWY RODEWAY
ADEORYZ ZEDOARY
ADEOSTT TOASTED
ADEOTTU OUTDATE
ADEOWWY WAYWODE
ADEPPRS DAPPERS
ADEPPRT TRAPPED
ADEPPRW WRAPPED
ADEPPST STAPPED
ADEPPSW SWAPPED
ADEPPTU PUPATED
ADEPPUY APPUYED
ADEPRRS DRAPERS
SPARRED
ADEPRRY DRAPERY
ADEPRSS ADPRESS
SPADERS
SPREADS
ADEPRST DEPARTS
DRAPETS
PETARDS
ADEPRSY SPRAYED
ADEPRTT PRATTED
ADEPRTU UPRATED
ADEPSTT SPATTED
ADEPSTU UPDATES
ADEQRSU SQUARED
ADERRST DARTERS
DARTRES
RETARDS
STARRED
TRADERS
ADERRSW DRAWERS
REDRAWS
REWARDS
WARDERS
ADERSSU ASSURED
RUDASES
ADERSSW SAWDERS
SWEARDS
ADERSTT STARTED
TETRADS
ADERSTV ADVERTS
STARVED
ADERSTW STEWARD
STRAWED
WRASTED
ADERSTY STRAYED
ADERSUY DASYURE
ADERSVW DWARVES
SWARVED
ADERWWY WEYWARD
ADESSTU SUDATES
ADESSTW WADSETS
ADESTTU STATUED
ADESTTW SWATTED
WADSETT
ADFFGIN DAFFING
ADFFHNO OFFHAND
ADFFIST DISTAFF
ADFFLNO FANFOLD
ADFFLOO OFFLOAD
ADFFOOR AFFOORD
ADFFORS AFFORDS
ADFGGIN FADGING
ADFGINN FANDING
ADFGINR FARDING
ADFGINS FADINGS
ADFGLLU GLADFUL
ADFHLNU HANDFUL
ADFHOOS SHADOOF
ADFHSSU SHADUFS
ADFILLU FLUIDAL
ADFIMNR FINDRAM
ADFIMNY DAMNIFY
ADFINRS FRIANDS
ADFINRT INDRAFT
ADFIORS FORSAID
ADFLLYY LADYFLY
ADFLMOO DAMFOOL
ADFLMPU MUDFLAP
ADFLMTU MUDFLAT
ADFLNOP PLAFOND
ADFLNSY SANDFLY
ADFLORU FOULARD
ADFMNOS FANDOMS
ADFMOSU FUMADOS

ADFNNOT FONDANT
ADFNOST FANTODS
ADFOOPT FOOTPAD
ADFORRW FORWARD
FROWARD
ADGGGIN DAGGING
ADGGHNO HANGDOG
ADGGILN GADLING
ADGGILR RIGGALD
ADGGINN DANGING
ADGGINO GOADING
ADGGINR GRADING
NIGGARD
ADGGINU GAUDING
ADGHILO HIDALGO
ADGHINN HANDING
ADGHINS DASHING
SHADING
ADGHINU HAUDING
ADGHIPR DIGRAPH
ADGHIRR ARDRIGH
ADGHNNU HANDGUN
ADGHNOS HAGDONS
ADGHNOW HAGDOWN
ADGHORW HOGWARD
ADGHRTU DRAUGHT
ADGIILN DIALING
GLIADIN
LAIDING
ADGIILT DIGITAL
ADGIIMN MAIDING
ADGIINN DAINING
ADGIINO GONIDIA
ADGIINR GRADINI
RAIDING
ADGIINU IGUANID
ADGIINW GWINIAD
ADGIIPY PYGIDIA
ADGILLN LADLING
ADGILMN MADLING
ADGILNN LANDING
ADGILNO DIGONAL
LOADING
ADGILNR DARLING
LARDING
ADGILNS LADINGS
LIGANDS
ADGILNU LANGUID
LAUDING
ADGILOR GOLIARD
ADGILOS DIALOGS
ADGILSU GLADIUS
ADGILUY GAUDILY
ADGIMMN DAMMING
ADGIMNN DAMNING
ADGIMNP DAMPING
ADGIMNR MRIDANG
ADGINNR DARNING
NARDING
RANDING
ADGINNS SANDING
ADGINNT DANTING
ADGINNW DAWNING
ADGINOR ADORING
GRADINO
ROADING
ADGINOS GANOIDS
ADGINOT DOATING
ADGINPP DAPPING
ADGINPR DRAPING
ADGINPS SPADING
ADGINRR DARRING
ADGINRS DARINGS
GRADINS
ADGINRT DARTING
TRADING
ADGINRU DAURING
ADGINRW DRAWING
WARDING
ADGINRY YARDING
ADGINST DATINGS
ADGINSW WADINGS
ADGINTU DAUTING
ADGINTW DAWTING
ADGINWY GWYNIAD
ADGIPRU PAGURID
ADGIRSU GUISARD
ADGIRZZ GIZZARD
ADGLLNO GOLLAND
ADGLMNO MANGOLD
ADGLNOO GONDOLA
ADGLNOR GOLDARN
ADGLNOW GOWLAND
ADGLNOY DAYLONG
ADGLNRY GRANDLY
ADGLOPS LAPDOGS
ADGMNOO GOODMAN
ADGMNOR GORMAND
ADGNOOR DRAGOON
GADROON
ADGNOOS GOONDAS
ADGNORS DRAGONS
ADGNORU AGROUND
ADGNRRU GURNARD
ADGNRSU DURGANS
ADGNRUU UNGUARD
ADGORSW WARDOGS
ADGPRSU UPDRAGS
ADHHIRS HARDISH
ADHHISW WHIDAHS
ADHHOSU HOUDAHS
ADHHOSW HOWDAHS
ADHHSWY WHYDAHS
ADHIIJT IJTIHAD
ADHIIKS DASHIKI
ADHIIMS MAIDISH
ADHIKNS DANKISH
ADHIKRS DARKISH
ADHIKSU HAIDUKS
ADHILMO HALIDOM
ADHILNY HANDILY
ADHILOP HAPLOID
ADHILOS HALOIDS
ADHILOY HOLIDAY
HYALOID
ADHILRY HARDILY
ADHILSY LADYISH
SHADILY
ADHIMPS DAMPISH
PHASMID
ADHIMRS DIRHAMS
ADHINOT ANTHOID
ADHINPU DAUPHIN
ADHINSS SANDHIS
ADHIORS HAIRDOS
ADHIRSY HYDRIAS
ADHJKOS KHODJAS
ADHKORW DORHAWK
ADHKOSU SHAKUDO
ADHLLNO HOLLAND
ADHLMOY HOLYDAM
ADHLMPY LYMPHAD
ADHMNOO HOODMAN
MANHOOD
ADHMNSU NUMDAHS
ADHNNSU NHANDUS
UNHANDS
ADHNNUY UNHANDY
ADHNORS HADRONS
ADHNORU UNHOARD
ADHNOSU HOUDANS
ADHNOTU HANDOUT
ADHNRSY SHANDRY
ADHNRTY HYDRANT
ADHNRUY UNHARDY
ADHOORR RHODORA
ADHOPRT HARDTOP
ADHOPRU UPHOARD
ADHOSSW SHADOWS
ADHOSWY SHADOWY
ADHPRSU PURDAHS
ADHPSUU UPHAUDS
ADHRRSU DHURRAS
ADIIILR IRIDIAL
ADIIINR IRIDIAN
ADIIKOS AIKIDOS
ADIIKOT DAKOITI
ADIILLS ILLIADS
ADIILMS MILADIS
MISDIAL
MISLAID
ADIILNO LIANOID
ADIILNV INVALID
ADIILOS SIALOID
ADIILST DIALIST
ADIILUV DILUVIA
ADIIMMS MAIDISM
ADIIMOS DAIMIOS
ADIIMPV IMPAVID
ADIIMRS MIDAIRS
ADIIMRU MUDIRIA
ADIIMSS MISSAID
ADIINPR PINDARI
PRIDIAN
ADIINST DISTAIN
ADIINSU INDUSIA
SUIDIAN
ADIINSV AVIDINS
ADIINSZ DIZAINS
ADIIPRS DIAPIRS
ADIIPXY PYXIDIA
ADIIQRU DAQUIRI
ADIIRST DIARIST
ADIIRTY ARIDITY
ADIITVY AVIDITY
ADIJMSS MASJIDS
ADIJNOS ADJOINS
ADIJNOT ADJOINT
ADIKLNY LADYKIN
ADIKLOS ODALISK
ADIKLPS KLIPDAS
ADIKMNN MANKIND
ADIKMOS MIKADOS
ADIKMSS DISMASK
ADIKNOS DAIKONS
ADIKNPS KIDNAPS
SKIDPAN
ADIKNRS DISRANK
ADIKOST DAKOITS
ADIKPRS DISPARK
ADIKSST DIKASTS
ADIKSTT DIKTATS
ADILLMM MILLDAM
ADILLSY DISALLY
ADILLVY VALIDLY
ADILMNO MONDIAL
ADILMNR MANDRIL
ADILMNU MAUDLIN
ADILMOP DIPLOMA
ADILMOU ALODIUM
ADILMOY AMYLOID
ADILMPS PLASMID
ADILMSS DISMALS
ADILMSU DUALISM
ADILMSY DISMAYL
LADYISM
ADILNNS INLANDS
ADILNOR ORDINAL
ADILNOS DOLINAS
ADILNRS ALDRINS
ADILNRU DIURNAL
ADILNSS ISLANDS
ADILNST TINDALS
ADILNSU DUALINS
SUNDIAL
ADILOOV OVOIDAL
ADILOOZ ZOOIDAL
ADILOPR DIPOLAR
ADILORT DILATOR
ADILOTU OUTLAID
ADILPRY PYRALID
RAPIDLY
ADILPST PLASTID
ADILPSY DISPLAY
ADILPTU PLAUDIT
ADILPVY VAPIDLY
ADILQSU SQUALID
ADILRSZ LIZARDS
ADILRTY TARDILY
ADILSTU DUALIST
ADILSTY STAIDLY
ADILTUY DUALITY
ADIMNNO MONDAIN
ADIMNOS DAIMONS
DOMAINS
ADIMNRS MANDIRS
ADIMNSS DISMANS
ADIMNST MANTIDS
ADIMOOS ISODOMA
ADIMORR MIRADOR
ADIMOST DIATOMS
MASTOID
ADIMOTT MATTOID
ADIMPRY PYRAMID
ADIMQSU QUIDAMS
ADIMRSS DISARMS
ADIMRSU RADIUMS
ADIMRSW MISDRAW
ADIMRSY MYRIADS
ADIMSSS SADISMS
ADIMSST DISMAST
ADIMSSY DISMAYS
ADIMSTU DUMAIST
STADIUM
ADIMSWY MIDWAYS
ADINNOP DIPNOAN
ADINNOR ANDIRON
ADINNRS INNARDS
ADINNRW INDRAWN
ADINNRY INNYARD

ADINNSU INDUNAS
ADINOOP POINADO
ADINOPP OPPIDAN
ADINOPR PADRONI
PONIARD
ADINOPT PINTADO
ADINORR ORDINAR
ADINORS INROADS
ORDAINS
SADIRON
ADINORV VIRANDO
ADINOSX DIAXONS
DIOXANS
ADINOTX OXIDANT
ADINPST PANDITS
SANDPIT
ADINRRT TRIDARN
ADINRST INDARTS
ADINRSU DURIANS
SUNDARI
ADINRSW INWARDS
ADINRTU TRIDUAN
UNITARD
ADINSTT DISTANT
ADINSTU UNSTAID
ADINTTY DITTANY
ADIOOSW WOODSIA
ADIOPRS SPAROID
ADIOPRT PAROTID
ADIOPRV PRIVADO
ADIORST ASTROID
ADIORSU SAUROID
ADIORSV ADVISOR
ADIORTU AUDITOR
ADIOSVW DISAVOW
ADIPRSS SPARIDS
ADIPRST DISPART
ADIRRSS SIRDARS
ADIRRSZ RIZARDS
ADIRSSU SARDIUS
ADIRSSW WISARDS
ADIRSTY SATYRID
ADIRSUY DYSURIA
ADIRSVZ VIZARDS
ADIRSWZ WIZARDS
ADIRSZZ IZZARDS
ADISSST SADISTS
ADISSYY SAYYIDS
ADISTTY DITTAYS
ADJKOSU JUDOKAS
ADJNORS JORDANS
ADJNORU ADJOURN
ADJSSTU ADJUSTS
ADKKLOY KAKODYL
ADKLMRU MUDLARK
ADKOPSU PADOUKS
ADKORWY WORKDAY
ADKRSWY SKYWARD
ADLLMOW WADMOLL
ADLLMOY MODALLY
ADLLNOW LOWLAND
ADLLNOY NODALLY
ADLLOPR POLLARD
ADLLOPS DALLOPS
ADLLORS DOLLARS
ADLMNOS ALMONDS
DOLMANS
ADLMORU MODULAR
ADLMOSW WADMOLS
ADLMSTU TALMUDS
ADLNNOR NORLAND
ADLNOOR LARDOON
ADLNOPU POUNDAL
ADLNORS LARDONS
ADLNORU NODULAR
ADLNOSS SOLDANS
ADLNOST DALTONS
ADLNOSU SOULDAN
UNLOADS
ADLNOSX OXLANDS
ADLNOSY SYNODAL
ADLNOTU OUTLAND
ADLNPSU UPLANDS
ADLNRSU LURDANS
ADLNRUY LAUNDRY
ADLOPRU POULARD
ADLORRW WARLORD
ADLORSS DORSALS
ADLORSU SUDORAL
ADLOSSS DOSSALS
ADLPSSU SPAULDS
ADMMNOS MANDOMS
ADMMNSU SUMMAND
ADMNOOR MADRONO
ADMNOOW WOODMAN
ADMNOOZ MADZOON
ADMNOQU QUONDAM
ADMNORS RANDOMS
RODSMAN
ADMNORT DORMANT
MORDANT
ADMNOSS DAMSONS
ADMNOSU OSMUNDA
ADMNOSY DYNAMOS
ADMNSTU DUSTMAN
ADMOORT DOORMAT
ADMOPPU POPADUM
ADMORRS RAMRODS
ADMORST STARDOM
TSARDOM
ADMORTW MADWORT
ADMRSTU DURMAST
MUSTARD
ADNNOOS NANDOOS
ADNNOOY NOONDAY
ADNNORS RANDONS
ADNNORT DONNART
ADNNOST DANTONS
DONNATS
ADNNOSU ADNOUNS
ADNNOTU DAUNTON
ADNNRTU DUNNART
ADNNRUW UNDRAWN
ADNOOPR PANDOOR
ADNOORS NARDOOS
ADNOORT DONATOR
ODORANT
TANDOOR
TORNADO
ADNOOSW WANDOOS
ADNOPRS PARDONS
ADNOPRU PANDOUR
ADNOPRV PROVAND
ADNOPST DOPANTS
ADNORRW NORWARD
ADNORSW ONWARDS
ADNORTU ROTUNDA
ADNORWY NAYWORD
ADNOSTT DOTANTS
ADNOSTU ASTOUND
ADNPRUW UPDRAWN
ADNPSTU UPSTAND
ADNRSST STRANDS
ADNRSSU SUNDRAS
ADNRSTU DRAUNTS
DURANTS
TUNDRAS
ADNRSUW SUNWARD
UNDRAWS
ADNSSTY DYNASTS
ADNSTYY DYNASTY
ADOOPSU APODOUS
ADOOPSW SAPWOOD
ADOORWY DOORWAY
ADOOSUV VAUDOOS
ADOOWWX WOODWAX
ADOPRRW WARDROP
ADORRSU ARDOURS
ADORSTW TOWARDS
ADORSUU ARDUOUS
ADORSWY AYWORDS
ADORTUW OUTWARD
ADOUUVX VAUDOUX
ADPRSUW UPDRAWS
UPWARDS
ADRSSUW USWARDS
ADSSTUW SAWDUST
AEEEFLR EELFARE
AEEEGKL KEELAGE
AEEEGLT LEGATEE
AEEEGNT TEENAGE
AEEEGPR PEERAGE
AEEEGPS SEEPAGE
AEEEGRR EAGERER
AEEEGRT ETAGERE
AEEEILN ALIENEE
AEEELRS RELEASE
AEEELTV ELEVATE
AEEFFLL FELAFEL
AEEFFNS NEAFFES
AEEFFRS AFFEERS
AEEFGNT FANTEEG
AEEFGRS SERFAGE
AEEFGSU FEAGUES
AEEFGTW WEFTAGE
AEEFHRT FEATHER
TEREFAH
AEEFILR LEAFIER
AEEFILW ALEWIFE
AEEFIRS AREFIES
FAERIES
FREESIA
AEEFISW SEAWIFE
AEEFLLT FELLATE
LEAFLET
AEEFLMN ENFLAME
AEEFLMS FEMALES
AEEFLRT REFLATE
AEEFLRW WELFARE
AEEFLRY LEAFERY
AEEFLRZ ALFEREZ
AEEFLSU EASEFUL
AEEFLTX TELEFAX
AEEFMNR ENFRAME
FREEMAN
AEEFMRR REFRAME
AEEFMRT FERMATE
AEEFOTV FOVEATE
AEEFPPR FRAPPEE
AEEFRRT FERRATE
AEEFRST AFREETS
FEASTER
AEEFRTU FEATURE
AEEFRWY FREEWAY
AEEGGLL ALLEGGE
AEEGGLR GREGALE
AEEGGLS ALEGGES
AEEGGLT GATELEG
AEEGGNR ENGAGER
AEEGGNS ENGAGES
AEEGGOP EPAGOGE
AEEGGRS AGREGES
RAGGEES
REGGAES
AEEGGST TAGGEES
AEEGGSW GEEGAWS
AEEGHIR HIREAGE
AEEGHNW WHANGEE
AEEGILL GALILEE
AEEGILM MILEAGE
AEEGILN LINEAGE
AEEGILP EPIGEAL
AEEGILW WEIGELA
AEEGINP EPIGEAN
AEEGINR REGINAE
AEEGINU EUGENIA
AEEGIPR PIERAGE
AEEGISS AEGISES
ASSIEGE
AEEGJRS JAEGERS
AEEGLLR ALLEGER
AEEGLLS ALLEGES
AEEGLLZ GAZELLE
AEEGLMN GLEEMAN
MELANGE
AEEGLNR ENLARGE
GENERAL
GLEANER
AEEGLNT ELEGANT
AEEGLNV EVANGEL
AEEGLPR PEREGAL
AEEGLPS PELAGES
AEEGLRS GALERES
REGALES
AEEGLRU LEAGUER
REGULAE
AEEGLRW LEGWEAR
AEEGLRY EAGERLY
AEEGLSS AGELESS
ALGESES
AEEGLST EAGLETS
LEGATES
TEAGLES
TELEGAS
AEEGLSU LEAGUES
AEEGLSV GLEAVES
SELVAGE
AEEGLTT GALETTE
AEEGLTU TEGULAE
AEEGLTV VEGETAL
AEEGMMT GEMMATE
TAGMEME
AEEGMNR GERMANE
AEEGMNS MANEGES
MENAGES
AEEGMNT GATEMEN
AEEGMRR MEAGRER
AEEGMRS MEAGRES
AEEGMRU REMUAGE
AEEGMSS MEGASSE

Letters	Words
	MESSAGE
AEEGMST	GAMETES
	METAGES
AEEGNNP	PANGENE
AEEGNNR	ENRANGE
AEEGNNS	ENNAGES
AEEGNOP	PEONAGE
AEEGNPP	GENAPPE
AEEGNRS	ENRAGES
AEEGNRT	GRANTEE
	GREATEN
	REAGENT
AEEGNRU	RENAGUE
AEEGNRV	AVENGER
	ENGRAVE
AEEGNSS	SAGENES
	SENEGAS
AEEGNST	NEGATES
AEEGNSV	AVENGES
	GENEVAS
AEEGNTT	TENTAGE
AEEGNTV	VENTAGE
AEEGOPS	APOGEES
AEEGORV	OVERAGE
AEEGOST	GOATEES
AEEGPRS	ASPERGE
	PRESAGE
AEEGRRS	GREASER
AEEGRRT	GREATER
	REGRATE
AEEGRRW	WAGERER
AEEGRSS	GREASES
AEEGRST	ERGATES
	RESTAGE
AEEGRSV	GREAVES
AEEGRTU	TREAGUE
AEEGRUZ	GUEREZA
AEEGSSW	SEWAGES
AEEGSTT	GESTATE
	TAGETES
AEEGTTZ	GAZETTE
AEEHHNT	HEATHEN
AEEHHRT	HEATHER
AEEHHST	SHEATHE
AEEHHSW	HEEHAWS
AEEHIPR	HEAPIER
AEEHIRV	HEAVIER
AEEHIST	ATHEISE
AEEHISV	HEAVIES
AEEHITZ	ATHEIZE
AEEHKNR	HEARKEN
AEEHKNT	THANKEE
AEEHKRU	HEUREKA
AEEHLNT	LETHEAN
AEEHLRS	HEALERS
AEEHLRT	LEATHER
AEEHLRV	HAVEREL
AEEHLSS	LEASHES
AEEHLST	LATHEES
AEEHLSW	AWHEELS
AEEHLSX	EXHALES
AEEHLSY	EYELASH
AEEHLTT	ATHLETE
AEEHMNT	METHANE
AEEHMRS	HAREEMS
	MAHSEER
AEEHMRT	ERATHEM
	THERMAE
AEEHMST	MEATHES
AEEHMSU	HEAUMES
AEEHNPT	HEPTANE
	PHENATE
AEEHNRS	ARSHEEN
AEEHNRT	EARTHEN
	HEARTEN
AEEHNST	ETHANES
AEEHNSV	HEAVENS
AEEHNSX	HEXANES
AEEHNTW	WHEATEN
AEEHPRS	RESHAPE
	SPHAERE
	SPHEARE
AEEHPRT	PREHEAT
AEEHPSS	APHESES
	SPAHEES
AEEHPUV	UPHEAVE
AEEHQSU	QUASHEE
AEEHRRS	HEARERS
	REHEARS
	SHEARER
AEEHRSS	HEARSES
AEEHRST	AETHERS
	HEATERS
	REHEATS
AEEHRSV	HEAVERS
AEEHRSW	WHEREAS
AEEHRTT	THEATER
	THEATRE
	THEREAT
AEEHRTV	THREAVE
AEEHRTW	WEATHER
	WHEREAT
	WREATHE
AEEHSST	HEASTES
AEEHSSV	SHEAVES
AEEHSTV	THEAVES
AEEIIRS	AIERIES
AEEIKLR	LEAKIER
AEEIKPR	PEAKIER
AEEIKSV	KEAVIES
AEEILLR	REALLIE
AEEILMR	MEALIER
AEEILMS	MEALIES
AEEILNP	ALEPINE
AEEILNS	SEALINE
AEEILNT	LINEATE
AEEILPT	EPILATE
	PILEATE
AEEILRR	EARLIER
	LEARIER
AEEILRS	EARLIES
	REALISE
AEEILRT	ATELIER
	REALTIE
AEEILRV	LEAVIER
	VEALIER
AEEILRZ	REALIZE
AEEILTT	AILETTE
AEEILTV	ELATIVE
AEEIMNR	REMANIE
AEEIMNS	MEANIES
	NEMESIA
AEEIMNT	MATINEE
AEEIMNX	EXAMINE
AEEIMPR	EMPAIRE
AEEIMRR	REAMIER
AEEIMRS	SEAMIER
	SERIEMA
AEEIMRT	EMIRATE
	MEATIER
AEEIMSS	MISEASE
	SIAMESE
AEEIMST	STEAMIE
AEEIMSZ	SIAMEZE
AEEIMTT	TEATIME
AEEINPR	PERINEA
AEEINRT	RETINAE
	TRAINEE
AEEINST	ETESIAN
AEEINTV	NAIVETE
AEEINVW	INWEAVE
AEEIORT	ETAERIO
AEEIPRR	PEREIRA
AEEIPRS	APERIES
	EPEIRAS
AEEIPRT	PEATIER
AEEIPSV	PEAVIES
AEEIPTX	EXPIATE
AEEIRRR	ARRIERE
AEEIRRS	REARISE
AEEIRRT	TEARIER
AEEIRRW	WEARIER
AEEIRST	AERIEST
	SERIATE
AEEIRSW	WEARIES
AEEIRTT	ARIETTE
	ITERATE
AEEIRTV	EVIRATE
AEEISST	EASIEST
AEEISVV	EVASIVE
AEEITTV	AVIETTE
	EVITATE
AEEITUX	EUTEXIA
AEEIUVX	EXUVIAE
AEEJKSS	JAKESES
AEEJMSS	JAMESES
AEEJNST	SEJEANT
AEEJNTU	JAUNTEE
AEEJRSV	EVEJARS
AEEKKNO	KOKANEE
AEEKLLT	LAKELET
AEEKLMN	KEELMAN
AEEKLNS	ALKENES
AEEKLNT	KANTELE
AEEKLPS	PALKEES
AEEKLRS	LEAKERS
AEEKLSV	VAKEELS
AEEKMNS	KAMSEEN
AEEKMNW	WAKEMEN
AEEKMRS	REMAKES
AEEKMRT	MEERKAT
AEEKNNN	NANKEEN
AEEKNRS	SNEAKER
AEEKNRT	RETAKEN
AEEKNRW	WAKENER
AEEKNSW	WEAKENS
AEEKORW	REAWOKE
AEEKPRS	PARKEES
	RESPEAK
	SPEAKER
AEEKPRT	PERTAKE
AEEKRRT	RETAKER
AEEKRRW	WREAKER
AEEKRST	RETAKES
	SAKERET
AEEKRSU	EUREKAS
AEEKSSS	ASKESES
AEEKSTW	WEAKEST
AEELLLS	ALLELES
AEELLMS	MALLEES
AEELLOV	ALVEOLE
AEELLPR	PARELLE
AEELLSS	SALLEES
AEELMNP	EMPANEL
	EMPLANE
AEELMNR	REELMAN
AEELMNS	ENAMELS
AEELMNT	MANTEEL
AEELMNV	VELAMEN
AEELMNY	AMYLENE
AEELMPS	EMPALES
AEELMPX	EXAMPLE
	EXEMPLA
AEELMRS	MEALERS
AEELMRT	LAMETER
AEELMSS	MEASLES
AEELMSU	AEMULES
AEELMSZ	MEAZELS
AEELMTU	EMULATE
AEELNNP	ENPLANE
AEELNNR	LERNEAN
AEELNPS	ALPEENS
	SPELEAN
AEELNRR	LEARNER
AEELNRT	ALTERNE
	ENTERAL
	ETERNAL
AEELNRW	RENEWAL
AEELNSS	ENSEALS
AEELNST	ELANETS
	LATEENS
	LEANEST
AEELNSV	ENSLAVE
	LEAVENS
AEELNSW	WEANELS
AEELNTY	ENTAYLE
AEELOPR	PAROLEE
AEELORS	AREOLES
AEELORU	AUREOLE
AEELOST	OLEATES
AEELOSW	LEASOWE
AEELPRR	PEARLER
AEELPRS	LEAPERS
	PLEASER
	RELAPSE
	REPEALS
AEELPRT	PLEATER
	PRELATE
AEELPRU	PLEURAE
AEELPSS	ELAPSES
	PLEASES
	SAPELES
AEELPSU	EPAULES
AEELPTT	PALETTE
	PELTATE
AEELPTU	EPAULET
AEELQSU	QUELEAS
	SEQUELA
AEELRRT	ALERTER
	RELATER
AEELRSS	EARLESS
	LEASERS
	RESALES
	RESEALS
	SEALERS
AEELRST	ELATERS
	REALEST
	RELATES
	STEALER
AEELRSU	LEASURE

AEELRSV	LAVEERS
	LEAVERS
	REVEALS
	SEVERAL
	VEALERS
AEELRSX	RELAXES
AEELRSY	SEALERY
AEELRUV	REVALUE
AEELSST	ALTESSE
	STEALES
	TEASELS
AEELSSV	SLEAVES
AEELSSW	AWELESS
	WEASELS
AEELSSZ	SLEAZES
AEELSTU	ELUATES
	SETUALE
AEELSTV	SALVETE
	VALETES
	VELETAS
AEELSTX	LATEXES
AEELSTY	EYALETS
AEELSTZ	TEAZELS
	TEAZLES
AEELSWY	LEEWAYS
AEELTTY	LAYETTE
AEELTVW	WAVELET
AEEMMMS	MAMMEES
AEEMMPY	EMPYEMA
AEEMMRT	AMMETER
	METAMER
AEEMNNO	ANEMONE
AEEMNPS	SPAEMEN
AEEMNPT	PEATMEN
AEEMNRS	RENAMES
AEEMNRT	REMANET
AEEMNSS	ENSEAMS
AEEMNST	ENTAMES
	MEANEST
AEEMNSX	EXAMENS
AEEMOPT	METOPAE
AEEMORT	EROTEMA
AEEMOSW	AWESOME
	WAESOME
AEEMPRS	AMPERES
	EMPARES
AEEMPRT	TEMPERA
AEEMPSW	WAMPEES
AEEMPTU	AMPUTEE
AEEMQRU	MARQUEE
AEEMRRS	REAMERS
AEEMRSS	SEAMERS
AEEMRST	STEAMER
	TEAMERS
AEEMRSU	MEASURE
AEEMRTY	METAYER
AEEMSSS	SESAMES
AEEMSST	MESETAS
	SEAMSET
AEEMSTT	METATES
AEENNOT	NEONATE
AEENNPT	PENNATE
	PENTANE
AEENNRS	ENSNARE
AEENNRX	REANNEX
AEENNST	NEATENS
AEENNSX	ANNEXES
AEENNTU	UNEATEN
AEENOPR	PERAEON
AEENOSS	ANOESES
AEENOSU	AENEOUS
AEENPST	NEPETAS
	PENATES
	PESANTE
AEENPSW	PAWNEES
AEENPSX	EXPANSE
AEENRRS	EARNERS
AEENRRT	TERRANE
AEENRRV	RAVENER
AEENRRY	YEARNER
AEENRSS	ENSEARS
AEENRST	EARNEST
	EASTERN
	NEAREST
AEENRSW	WEANERS
AEENRTT	ENTREAT
	RATTEEN
	TERNATE
AEENRTV	AVENTRE
	NERVATE
	VETERAN
AEENRUV	UNREAVE
AEENSST	ENTASES
	SATEENS
	SENATES
	SENSATE
	STEANES
AEENSSU	UNEASES
AEENSSV	AVENSES
AEENSSW	WAENESS
AEENSTT	NEATEST
AEENSUV	AVENUES
AEENSWZ	WEAZENS
AEENTTV	NAVETTE
AEENUVW	UNWEAVE
AEEOPRT	OPERATE
AEEORRS	REAROSE
AEEORSS	SEROSAE
AEEORST	ROSEATE
AEEORSV	OVERSEA
AEEORTV	OVERATE
	OVEREAT
AEEORVW	OVERAWE
AEEOSUU	EUOUAES
AEEOSVV	EVOVAES
AEEPPRR	PAPERER
	PREPARE
	REPAPER
AEEPPRS	RAPPEES
AEEPRRS	REAPERS
AEEPRRT	TAPERER
AEEPRSS	ASPERSE
	PARESES
	PRAESES
	PREASES
	PREASSE
	SERAPES
AEEPRST	REPEATS
AEEPRSZ	SPREAZE
AEEPRTU	EPURATE
AEEPRTY	PEATERY
AEEPRTZ	TRAPEZE
AEEPSSS	ASEPSES
AEEPSST	PESETAS
AEEPSSW	PESEWAS
AEEPSTT	SEPTATE
	SPATTEE
AEEPSVY	PEAVEYS
AEEQRSU	QUAERES
AEEQSTU	EQUATES
AEERRRS	REARERS
AEERRSS	ERASERS
AEERRST	SERRATE
	TEARERS
AEERRSU	ERASURE
AEERRSV	REAVERS
AEERRSW	SWEARER
	WEARERS
AEERRTT	RETRATE
	RETREAT
	TREATER
AEERRTW	WATERER
AEERRVW	WAVERER
AEERSST	RESEATS
	SAETERS
	SEAREST
	SEATERS
	STEARES
	TEASERS
	TESSERA
AEERSSU	RESEAUS
	SEASURE
AEERSSV	ASSEVER
AEERSSY	ESSAYER
AEERSTT	ESTREAT
	RESTATE
AEERSTU	AUSTERE
AEERSTW	SWEATER
AEERSUV	VAREUSE
AEERSUX	RESEAUX
AEERSVW	WEAVERS
AEERTTX	EXTREAT
AEERTWW	WETWARE
AEESSSW	SEESAWS
AEESSTT	ESTATES
AEESSTU	SAUTEES
AEESSTX	TEXASES
AEESSUX	AUXESES
AEESTTT	TESTATE
AEFFFLR	FLAFFER
AEFFGIR	GIRAFFE
AEFFGNR	ENGRAFF
AEFFGRS	GAFFERS
AEFFGRU	GAUFFER
AEFFHST	HAFFETS
AEFFINS	AFFINES
AEFFIPR	PIAFFER
AEFFIPS	PIAFFES
AEFFIST	TAFFIES
AEFFISX	AFFIXES
AEFFKOP	OFFPEAK
AEFFKOT	OFFTAKE
AEFFLLY	FLYLEAF
AEFFLMW	FLAMFEW
AEFFLNS	SNAFFLE
AEFFLRR	RAFFLER
AEFFLRS	RAFFLES
AEFFLRU	FEARFUL
AEFFLRW	WAFFLER
AEFFLSW	WAFFLES
AEFFLSY	YAFFLES
AEFFLTU	FATEFUL
AEFFQRU	QUAFFER
AEFFRST	AFFRETS
	RESTAFF
	STAFFER
AEFFRSY	EFFRAYS
AEFFRSZ	ZAFFERS
	ZAFFRES
AEFFTTY	TAFFETY
AEFGGGO	FOGGAGE
AEFGGMO	MEGAFOG
AEFGGRY	FAGGERY
AEFGILN	FEALING
	FINAGLE
	LEAFING
AEFGILO	FOLIAGE
AEFGILR	FRAGILE
AEFGINR	FEARING
AEFGINT	FEATING
AEFGIRT	FRIGATE
AEFGIRU	REFUGIA
AEFGITU	FATIGUE
AEFGLLU	FULLAGE
AEFGLNS	FANGLES
	FLANGES
AEFGLOT	FLOTAGE
AEFGLOW	FLOWAGE
AEFGLRS	REFLAGS
AEFGLRU	RAGEFUL
AEFGLUZ	GAZEFUL
AEFGMSU	FUMAGES
AEFGNRR	GRANFER
AEFGNRT	ENGRAFT
AEFGOOT	FOOTAGE
AEFGORR	FORAGER
AEFGORS	FORAGES
AEFGORV	FORGAVE
AEFGRRT	GRAFTER
AEFGRSU	GAUFERS
	GAUFRES
AEFHLLS	FELLAHS
AEFHLOR	FAHLORE
AEFHLRS	FLASHER
AEFHLRT	FARTHEL
AEFHLRZ	FAHLERZ
AEFHLSS	FLASHES
AEFHLTU	HATEFUL
AEFHRRT	FARTHER
AEFHRST	FATHERS
	SHAFTER
AEFHRSY	FASHERY
AEFIILT	FILIATE
AEFIIRS	FAIRIES
AEFIJLO	JEOFAIL
AEFIJOS	FEIJOAS
AEFIKLR	FLAKIER
AEFIKLS	FLAKIES
AEFILLS	FAILLES
AEFILMN	FEMINAL
	INFLAME
AEFILMR	FLAMIER
AEFILNS	FINALES
AEFILNT	INFLATE
AEFILNU	INFULAE
AEFILNV	FLAVINE
AEFILOT	FOLIATE
AEFILPT	FLEAPIT
AEFILRR	FLARIER
	FRAILER
AEFILRU	FAILURE
AEFILRV	FAVRILE
AEFILRW	FLAWIER
AEFILRX	FLAXIER
AEFILRZ	FILAZER
AEFILSS	FALSIES
	FILASSE
AEFIMNR	FIREMAN
AEFIMNS	FAMINES
	INFAMES

AEFIMOR FOAMIER
AEFIMRR FIREARM
AEFIMRS MISFARE
AEFINNS FANNIES
AEFINNT INFANTE
AEFINNZ FANZINE
AEFINPR FIREPAN
AEFINRR REFRAIN
AEFINRS INFARES
SERAFIN
AEFINRT FAINTER
FENITAR
AEFINRX XERAFIN
AEFINST FAINEST
NAIFEST
AEFINTX ANTEFIX
AEFIQRU AQUIFER
AEFIRRR FARRIER
AEFIRSS FRAISES
AEFIRST FAIREST
AEFIRTT FATTIER
AEFISST FIESTAS
AEFISTT FATTIES
AEFISTX FIXATES
AEFKLNR FLANKER
AEFKLNS FANKLES
AEFKLOS SEAFOLK
AEFKLRT FARTLEK
AEFKLST FLASKET
AEFKLUW WAKEFUL
AEFKNRR FRANKER
AEFKORS FORSAKE
AEFLLNN FANNELL
FLANNEL
AEFLLOT FLOATEL
AEFLLRS FALLERS
AEFLLSY FALSELY
AEFLLTT FLATLET
AEFLLTU TALEFUL
AEFLLUZ ZEALFUL
AEFLMNS FLAMENS
AEFLMOR FEMORAL
AEFLMUW WAMEFUL
AEFLMUZ MAZEFUL
AEFLNNN FLANNEN
AEFLNNS FANNELS
AEFLNOV FLAVONE
AEFLNRS SALFERN
AEFLNRU FLANEUR
FRENULA
FUNERAL
AEFLNSU FLAUNES
AEFLNTT FLATTEN
AEFLOOV FOVEOLA
AEFLOPW PEAFOWL
AEFLORS LOAFERS
SAFROLE
AEFLORT FLOATER
FLOREAT
REFLOAT
AEFLORY FORELAY
AEFLOST FOLATES
AEFLOSW SEAFOWL
AEFLPPR FLAPPER
AEFLPRS FELSPAR
AEFLPRY PALFREY
AEFLRSS FALSERS
FLASERS
AEFLRST FALTERS
AEFLRSU EARFULS
FERULAS
REFUSAL
AEFLRSY FLAYERS
AEFLRTT FLATTER
AEFLRTU REFUTAL
TEARFUL
AEFLRZZ FRAZZLE
AEFLSST FALSEST
FESTALS
AEFLSTU FLUATES
SULFATE
AEFMNOR FORAMEN
FOREMAN
AEFMNRT RAFTMEN
AEFMNRU FRAENUM
AEFMORR FOREARM
AEFMORT FORMATE
AEFMRRS FARMERS
FRAMERS
AEFMRRY FARMERY
AEFNNRS FANNERS
AEFNNST ENFANTS
AEFNOPR PROFANE
AEFNOPY PAYFONE
AEFNORR FORERAN
AEFNRRS FARRENS
AEFNRSS FARNESS
AEFNRSU FURANES
UNSAFER
AEFNRSW FAWNERS
AEFNSST FASTENS
FATNESS
AEFNSTT FATTENS
AEFOPRW FOREPAW
AEFORRV FAVORER
OVERFAR
AEFORRY FORAYER
AEFORSW FORESAW
AEFORSY FORESAY
AEFOSST FATSOES
AEFOSTU FEATOUS
AEFPPRS FRAPPES
AEFRRST FRATERS
RAFTERS
AEFRRTY FRATERY
AEFRSSS FRASSES
AEFRSST FASTERS
STRAFES
AEFRSTW FRETSAW
WAFTERS
AEFRTUW WAFTURE
AEFSSTT FASTEST
AEFSSUV FAVUSES
AEFSTTT FATTEST
AEGGGLS GAGGLES
AEGGGLU LUGGAGE
AEGGGRS GAGGERS
AEGGHLR HAGGLER
AEGGHLS HAGGLES
AEGGHSW EGGWASH
AEGGIJR JAGGIER
AEGGILN GEALING
LIGNAGE
AEGGINR GEARING
NAGGIER
AEGGINS AGEINGS
SIGNAGE
AEGGIOS ISAGOGE
AEGGIRR RAGGIER
AEGGIRS RAGGIES
SAGGIER
AEGGIRT TAGGIER
AEGGIRU GARIGUE
AEGGISW SWAGGIE
AEGGJRS JAGGERS
AEGGJRY JAGGERY
AEGGLNO AGELONG
AEGGLNR GANGREL
AEGGLNS LAGGENS
AEGGLRS GARGLES
LAGGERS
RAGGLES
AEGGLSW WAGGLES
AEGGMNY YEGGMAN
AEGGMSS EGGMASS
AEGGNNU GUNNAGE
AEGGNRR GRANGER
AEGGNRS GANGERS
GRANGES
NAGGERS
AEGGNSU GANGUES
AEGGRRY RAGGERY
AEGGRSS AGGRESS
SAGGERS
SEGGARS
AEGGRST GAGSTER
GARGETS
STAGGER
TAGGERS
AEGGRSU GAUGERS
AEGGRSW SWAGGER
AEGGRSY YAGGERS
AEGGRTY GARGETY
AEGGRWY WAGGERY
AEGGSWW GEWGAWS
AEGHHIT AHEIGHT
AEGHIJR JAGHIRE
AEGHILN HEALING
AEGHILR LAIGHER
AEGHINP HEAPING
AEGHINR HEARING
AEGHINT GAHNITE
HEATING
AEGHINV HEAVING
AEGHINZ GENIZAH
AEGHIRS HEGIRAS
HIRAGES
AEGHISS GEISHAS
AEGHLNO HALOGEN
AEGHLNT ALENGTH
AEGHLRU LAUGHER
AEGHLSS SEALGHS
AEGHLST HAGLETS
AEGHLSZ GHAZELS
AEGHLTW THALWEG
AEGHMNN HANGMEN
AEGHMOR HOMAGER
AEGHMOS HOMAGES
OHMAGES
AEGHMSU MESHUGA
AEGHNOX HEXAGON
AEGHNRS GNASHER
HANGERS
REHANGS
AEGHNRU NURAGHE
AEGHNSS GNASHES
AEGHNST STENGAH
AEGHOPY HYPOGEA
AEGHORS GHERAOS
AEGHOSS SEAHOGS
AEGHOST HOSTAGE
AEGHPRS SPREAGH
AEGHPST HATPEGS
AEGHRST GATHERS
AEGIIMN IMAGINE
AEGIKLN LEAKING
LINKAGE
AEGIKLT GLAIKET
AEGIKNP PEAKING
AEGIKNR REAKING
AEGIKNS SINKAGE
AEGIKPP KIPPAGE
AEGIKPR GARPIKE
AEGIKRW GAWKIER
AEGIKSW GAWKIES
AEGILLL ILLEGAL
AEGILLN NIGELLA
AEGILLP PILLAGE
AEGILLS GALLIES
GALLISE
AEGILLT TILLAGE
AEGILLU LIGULAE
AEGILLV VILLAGE
AEGILLY AGILELY
AEGILLZ GALLIZE
AEGILMN LEAMING
MEALING
AEGILMR GREMIAL
LAMIGER
AEGILMS MILAGES
AEGILNN ANELING
EANLING
LEANING
NEALING
AEGILNP LEAPING
PEALING
PLEAING
AEGILNR ENGRAIL
LAERING
LEARING
NARGILE
REALIGN
REGINAL
AEGILNS LEASING
LINAGES
SEALING
AEGILNT ATINGLE
ELATING
GELATIN
GENITAL
AEGILNU LINGUAE
AEGILNV LEAVING
AEGILNY ALEYING
AEGILOS GOALIES
SOILAGE
AEGILOU EULOGIA
AEGILPS PAIGLES
AEGILRR GLARIER
AEGILRS GRAILES
AEGILRZ GLAZIER
AEGILSS ALGESIS
LIGASES
SILAGES
AEGILST AGILEST
AIGLETS
LIGATES
TAIGLES
AEGILSV GLAIVES
AEGILTU GLUTAEI
AEGILTY EGALITY

AEGIMMR	GAMMIER
AEGIMNN	AMENING
	MEANING
AEGIMNP	PIGMEAN
AEGIMNR	GERMAIN
	MANGIER
	MEARING
	REAMING
AEGIMNS	ENIGMAS
	GAMINES
	MEASING
	SEAMING
AEGIMNT	MINTAGE
	TEAMING
	TEGMINA
AEGIMOS	IMAGOES
AEGIMPR	EPIGRAM
	PRIMAGE
AEGIMPS	MAGPIES
AEGIMPT	PIGMEAT
AEGIMRR	ARMIGER
AEGIMRS	GISARME
	MAIGRES
	MIRAGES
AEGIMRT	MIGRATE
	RAGTIME
AEGIMRU	GAUMIER
AEGIMRY	IMAGERY
AEGIMSS	AGEISMS
AEGIMST	GAMIEST
	SIGMATE
AEGIMSV	MISGAVE
AEGINNO	GANOINE
AEGINNP	NEAPING
	PEANING
AEGINNR	AGINNER
	EARNING
	ENGRAIN
	GRANNIE
	NEARING
AEGINNS	SEANING
AEGINNT	ANTEING
	ANTIGEN
	GENTIAN
AEGINNU	ANGUINE
	GUANINE
AEGINNW	WEANING
AEGINNY	YEANING
AEGINOR	ORIGANE
AEGINOS	AGONIES
	AGONISE
AEGINOZ	AGONIZE
AEGINPP	GENIPAP
AEGINPR	REAPING
AEGINPS	PEASING
	SPAEING
AEGINPZ	PEAZING
AEGINRR	ANGRIER
	EARRING
	GRAINER
	RANGIER
	REARING
AEGINRS	ANGRIES
	EARINGS
	ERASING
	GAINERS
	GRAINES
	REGAINS
	REGINAS
	SEARING
	SERINGA
AEGINRT	GRANITE
	GRATINE
	INGRATE
	TANGIER
	TEARING
AEGINRV	REAVING
	VINEGAR
AEGINRW	WEARING
AEGINSS	AGNISES
	SEASING
AEGINST	EASTING
	EATINGS
	GAINEST
	GENISTA
	INGATES
	INGESTA
	SEATING
	TANGIES
	TEASING
	TSIGANE
AEGINSU	GUINEAS
AEGINSZ	AGNIZES
	SEAZING
AEGINTV	VINTAGE
AEGINTZ	TEAZING
AEGINVW	WEAVING
AEGIORT	GOATIER
AEGIPPR	GAPPIER
AEGIPPS	PIPAGES
AEGIPRR	GRAPIER
AEGIPRS	GASPIER
	PRISAGE
	SPAIRGE
AEGIRRZ	GRAZIER
AEGIRSS	AGRISES
	GASSIER
AEGIRST	AGISTER
	GAITERS
	STAGIER
	STRIGAE
	TRIAGES
AEGIRSV	GARVIES
	GRAVIES
	RIVAGES
AEGIRSW	EARWIGS
	GAWSIER
AEGIRSZ	AGRIZES
AEGIRTV	VIRGATE
	VITRAGE
AEGIRUZ	GAUZIER
AEGISST	AGEISTS
	SAGIEST
AEGISSU	AGUISES
AEGISSV	VISAGES
AEGISTU	AUGITES
AEGISTY	GASEITY
AEGISTZ	GAZIEST
AEGISUZ	AGUIZES
AEGISYZ	AZYGIES
AEGJLNR	JANGLER
AEGJLNS	JANGLES
AEGKKNO	ANGEKOK
AEGKLOU	KAGOULE
AEGKLRS	GRAKLES
AEGKMRY	KERYGMA
AEGKRSW	GAWKERS
AEGKSST	GASKETS
AEGLLLY	LEGALLY
AEGLLNO	ALLONGE
	GALLEON
AEGLLNR	LANGREL
AEGLLNS	LEGLANS
AEGLLOR	ALLEGRO
AEGLLOT	TOLLAGE
AEGLLRY	ALLERGY
	GALLERY
	LARGELY
	REGALLY
AEGLLST	GALLETS
AEGLLSU	SEAGULL
	SULLAGE
	ULLAGES
AEGLLSY	GALLEYS
AEGLLTU	GLUTEAL
AEGLMNR	MANGLER
AEGLMNS	MANGELS
	MANGLES
AEGLMOR	GOMERAL
AEGLMOU	MOULAGE
AEGLMPU	PLUMAGE
AEGLMRS	MALGRES
AEGLMRU	MAULGRE
AEGLMSY	MYGALES
AEGLNOS	ENGAOLS
AEGLNOT	TANGELO
AEGLNPR	GRAPNEL
AEGLNPS	SPANGLE
AEGLNRS	ANGLERS
	LARGENS
	SLANGER
AEGLNRT	TANGLER
	TRANGLE
AEGLNRU	GRANULE
AEGLNRW	WANGLER
	WRANGLE
AEGLNRY	ANGERLY
AEGLNSS	GLASSEN
AEGLNST	LANGEST
	TANGLES
AEGLNSU	ANGELUS
	LAGUNES
	LANGUES
AEGLNSW	WANGLES
AEGLNSY	LYNAGES
AEGLNTT	GANTLET
AEGLNTU	LANGUET
AEGLNTW	TWANGLE
AEGLNUU	UNGULAE
AEGLNUW	GUNWALE
AEGLOPR	PERGOLA
AEGLORS	GAOLERS
AEGLORT	GLOATER
	LEGATOR
AEGLOSS	GLOSSAE
AEGLOST	LEGATOS
AEGLOSU	GEALOUS
AEGLOSV	LOVAGES
AEGLOTV	VOLTAGE
AEGLPPR	GRAPPLE
AEGLPRS	GRAPLES
AEGLPRU	EARPLUG
	GRAUPEL
AEGLPSU	PLAGUES
	PLUSAGE
AEGLPUY	PLAGUEY
AEGLRRU	REGULAR
AEGLRSS	LARGESS
AEGLRST	LARGEST
AEGLRSV	GRAVELS
	VERGLAS
AEGLRSY	ARGYLES
	GRAYLES
AEGLRSZ	GLAZERS
AEGLRTU	GAULTER
	TEGULAR
	TRAGULE
AEGLRTY	GREATLY
AEGLRVY	GRAVELY
AEGLSSS	GLASSES
AEGLSSU	SAULGES
AEGLSTT	GESTALT
AEGLSTW	TALWEGS
AEGLTUV	VULGATE
AEGLUUY	GUAYULE
AEGLUVY	VAGUELY
AEGMMNS	MAGSMEN
AEGMMRS	GAMMERS
	GRAMMES
AEGMMRU	RUMMAGE
AEGMMSS	SMEGMAS
AEGMNNO	AGNOMEN
AEGMNOR	MEGARON
AEGMNOS	MANGOES
AEGMNOT	GEOMANT
	MAGNETO
	MEGATON
	MONTAGE
AEGMNPY	PYGMEAN
AEGMNRS	ENGRAMS
	GERMANS
	MANGERS
AEGMNRT	GARMENT
	MARGENT
	RAGMENT
AEGMNST	MAGNETS
AEGMNSW	SWAGMEN
AEGMNTU	AUGMENT
	MUTAGEN
AEGMOOR	MOORAGE
AEGMORS	ROMAGES
AEGMOSY	GAYSOME
AEGMOXY	EXOGAMY
AEGMRSU	MAUGRES
	MURAGES
AEGMSUY	MAGUEYS
AEGMSUZ	ZEUGMAS
AEGNNOS	NONAGES
AEGNNOT	TONNAGE
AEGNNPS	PANGENS
AEGNNRT	REGNANT
AEGNNRU	GUNNERA
AEGNNST	GANNETS
AEGNNTT	TANGENT
AEGNNTU	TUNNAGE
AEGNOOR	OREGANO
AEGNOPT	PONTAGE
AEGNORR	GROANER
	ORANGER
AEGNORS	ONAGERS
	ORANGES
AEGNORW	WAGONER
AEGNORY	ORANGEY
AEGNOSY	NOSEGAY
AEGNOWY	WAYGONE
AEGNPRS	ENGRASP
AEGNPRT	TREPANG
AEGNRRS	GARNERS
	RANGERS
AEGNRRT	GRANTER

	REGRANT
AEGNRSS	SERANGS
AEGNRST	ARGENTS
	GARNETS
	STRANGE
AEGNRSU	RAUNGES
	UNGEARS
AEGNRSW	GNAWERS
AEGNRTU	GAUNTER
AEGNSSY	GANSEYS
	GAYNESS
AEGNSTT	GESTANT
AEGNTTU	TUTENAG
AEGOORT	ROOTAGE
AEGOPPR	PROPAGE
AEGOPRT	PORTAGE
	POTAGER
AEGOPST	GESTAPO
	POSTAGE
	POTAGES
AEGOPTT	POTTAGE
AEGORRT	GARROTE
AEGORSS	SORAGES
AEGORST	ORGEATS
	STORAGE
	TOERAGS
AEGORTT	GAROTTE
AEGORTU	OUTRAGE
AEGORUV	OUVRAGE
AEGORVY	VOYAGER
AEGOSSU	GASEOUS
AEGOSTU	OUTAGES
AEGOSTW	STOWAGE
	TOWAGES
AEGOSTX	OXGATES
AEGOSVY	VOYAGES
AEGOTTU	OUTGATE
AEGOTTV	GAVOTTE
AEGOTUV	OUTGAVE
AEGPRRS	GRASPER
	SPARGER
AEGPRRY	GRAPERY
AEGPRSS	GASPERS
	SPARGES
AEGPRST	PARGETS
AEGPRSU	GAUPERS
AEGPRSW	GAWPERS
AEGPSSU	PEGASUS
AEGPSTU	UPSTAGE
AEGPSUZ	UPGAZES
AEGRRSS	GRASSER
AEGRRST	GARRETS
	GARTERS
	GRATERS
AEGRRSU	ARGUERS
AEGRRSV	GRAVERS
AEGRRSZ	GRAZERS
AEGRRUU	AUGURER
AEGRRUV	GRAVURE
	VERRUGA
AEGRSSS	GASSERS
	GRASSES
AEGRSST	GASTERS
	STAGERS
AEGRSSU	ARGUSES
	SAUGERS
	USAGERS
AEGRSTT	TARGETS
AEGRSTV	GRAVEST
AEGRSTY	GRAYEST
	GYRATES
	STAGERY
AEGRSUV	SEVRUGA
AEGRSYZ	AGRYZES
AEGSSSU	GAUSSES
AEGSTUU	AUGUSTE
AEGSTUV	VAGUEST
AEGTTTU	GUTTATE
AEHHIKS	SHEIKHA
AEHHIRS	HASHIER
AEHHIST	SHEHITA
AEHHLST	HEALTHS
AEHHLTY	HEALTHY
AEHHNRS	HARSHEN
AEHHPRS	RHAPHES
AEHHRRS	HARSHER
AEHHRST	HEARTHS
AEHHSSS	SHASHES
AEHHSST	SHEATHS
AEHHSTY	SHEATHY
AEHIILR	HAILIER
AEHIIRR	HAIRIER
AEHIJRS	HEJIRAS
AEHIKNS	HANKIES
AEHIKRS	SHAKIER
AEHIKSS	SAKIEHS
AEHIKSW	HAWKIES
AEHIKSY	SAKIYEH
AEHILMN	HELIMAN
AEHILMO	HEMIOLA
AEHILNR	HERNIAL
	INHALER
AEHILNS	INHALES
AEHILNY	HYALINE
AEHILOR	AIRHOLE
AEHILRS	HAILERS
	SHALIER
AEHILRT	LATHIER
AEHILRU	HAULIER
AEHILSS	SHEILAS
AEHILST	HALITES
AEHILSW	SHAWLIE
	WHAISLE
AEHILTT	LITHATE
AEHILTY	HYALITE
AEHILUV	VIHUELA
AEHILVY	HEAVILY
AEHILWZ	WHAIZLE
AEHIMMR	HAMMIER
AEHIMNR	HARMINE
AEHIMNS	HAEMINS
	HEMINAS
AEHIMNY	HYMENIA
AEHIMPS	PHAEISM
AEHIMRS	MASHIER
	MISHEAR
AEHIMSS	MASHIES
	MESSIAH
AEHIMST	ATHEISM
AEHINPR	HEPARIN
AEHINPS	INPHASE
AEHINPT	PENTHIA
AEHINRS	ARSHINE
	HERNIAS
AEHINRT	HAIRNET
	INEARTH
	THERIAN
AEHINSS	HESSIAN
AEHINSV	EVANISH
	VAHINES
AEHINSW	WAHINES
AEHIORR	HOARIER
AEHIPPR	HAPPIER
AEHIPPS	HAPPIES
AEHIPPT	EPITAPH
AEHIPRS	HARPIES
	SHARPIE
AEHIPSS	APHESIS
AEHIPSW	PEISHWA
AEHIPTZ	ZAPTIEH
AEHIQSU	HAIQUES
	QUASHIE
AEHIRRR	HARRIER
AEHIRRS	HARRIES
AEHIRSS	ARISHES
	SHERIAS
AEHIRST	HASTIER
	SHERIAT
AEHIRSV	ASHIVER
AEHIRSW	WASHIER
	WEARISH
AEHIRTW	THAWIER
AEHIRWY	HAYWIRE
AEHISST	ASHIEST
	SAITHES
	STASHIE
	TAISHES
AEHISSV	SHAVIES
AEHISTT	ATHEIST
	STAITHE
AEHISTZ	HAZIEST
AEHISVY	YESHIVA
AEHITTW	THWAITE
AEHJLOW	JAWHOLE
AEHKMSS	SAMEKHS
AEHKNRS	HANKERS
	HARKENS
AEHKNRT	THANKER
AEHKOSS	SHAKOES
AEHKRRS	SHARKER
AEHKRSS	SHAKERS
AEHKRSW	HAWKERS
AEHKSWY	HAWKEYS
AEHLLOV	HELLOVA
AEHLLRS	HERSALL
AEHLLUV	HELLUVA
AEHLLYZ	HAZELLY
AEHLMNO	MANHOLE
AEHLMNY	HYMENAL
AEHLMOR	ARMHOLE
AEHLMPS	PELHAMS
AEHLMPW	WHAMPLE
AEHLMRS	HARMELS
AEHLMRT	THERMAL
AEHLMRU	HUMERAL
AEHLMST	HAMLETS
AEHLNOS	ENHALOS
AEHLNOT	ETHANOL
AEHLNRT	ENTHRAL
AEHLNSS	HANSELS
AEHLNST	HANTLES
AEHLNSU	UNHEALS
	UNLEASH
	UNSHALE
AEHLORS	SHOALER
AEHLORT	LOATHER
AEHLOSS	ASSHOLE
AEHLOST	LOATHES
AEHLPRS	SPHERAL
AEHLPSS	HAPLESS
	PLASHES
AEHLPST	PLASHET
AEHLPSY	SHAPELY
AEHLRSS	ASHLERS
	HALSERS
	LASHERS
	SLASHER
AEHLRST	HALTERS
	HARSLET
	LATHERS
	SLATHER
	THALERS
AEHLRSU	HAULERS
AEHLRSV	HALVERS
AEHLRSW	WHALERS
AEHLRTY	EARTHLY
	HARTELY
	HEARTLY
	LATHERY
AEHLRWY	WHALERY
AEHLSSS	HASSLES
	SLASHES
AEHLSST	HASLETS
	HATLESS
AEHLSSY	HAYSELS
AEHLSTT	STEALTH
AEHLSTW	WEALTHS
AEHLSWY	SHAWLEY
AEHLTWY	WEALTHY
AEHMMNS	MASHMEN
AEHMMRS	HAMMERS
	SHAMMER
AEHMMSS	SHAMMES
AEHMMSY	MAYHEMS
AEHMNOR	MENORAH
AEHMNOS	HOSEMAN
AEHMNOT	NATHEMO
AEHMNOY	HAEMONY
AEHMNPY	NYMPHAE
AEHMNRU	HUMANER
AEHMNST	ANTHEMS
	HETMANS
AEHMOPT	APOTHEM
AEHMPRS	HAMPERS
AEHMPTY	EMPATHY
AEHMRSS	MARSHES
	MASHERS
	SHAMERS
	SMASHER
AEHMRST	HAMSTER
AEHMRTU	MAUTHER
AEHMRTW	MAWTHER
AEHMSSS	SMASHES
AEHMSST	SMEATHS
AEHMUZZ	MEZUZAH
AEHNNTU	UNNEATH
AEHNNWY	ANYWHEN
AEHNOPT	PHAETON
	PHONATE
AEHNOPW	WANHOPE
AEHNORS	HOARSEN
AEHNORT	ANOTHER
AEHNPPS	HAPPENS
AEHNPRS	SHARPEN
AEHNPRT	PANTHER
AEHNPST	HAPTENS
AEHNPSU	UNSHAPE
AEHNRSS	HARNESS
AEHNRST	ANTHERS
	HARTENS

THENARS
AEHNRTU HAUNTER
UNEARTH
UNHEART
URETHAN
AEHNRTX NARTHEX
AEHNSSS SNASHES
AEHNSST HASTENS
SNATHES
SNEATHS
AEHNSSZ SAZHENS
AEHNSTY SHANTEY
AEHNSUY HAUYNES
AEHNTTW WHATTEN
AEHOORT TOHEROA
AEHORRS HOARSER
AEHORST ASTHORE
EARSHOT
HAROSET
AEHORSX HOAXERS
AEHORUV HAVEOUR
AEHOSTU ATHEOUS
AEHPPRS PERHAPS
AEHPPSU UPHEAPS
AEHPRRS HARPERS
PHRASER
SHARPER
AEHPRSS PHRASES
SERAPHS
SHAPERS
SHERPAS
SPHAERS
SPHEARS
AEHPRST SPARTHE
TEPHRAS
THREAPS
AEHPRTY THERAPY
AEHPSST SPATHES
AEHPSSW PESHWAS
AEHPSTY HYPATES
AEHQSSU QUASHES
AEHRRSS RASHERS
SHARERS
AEHRRTU URETHRA
AEHRSST RASHEST
SHASTER
TRASHES
AEHRSSV SHAVERS
AEHRSSW HAWSERS
SWASHER
WASHERS
AEHRSTT HATTERS
RATHEST
SHATTER
THREATS
AEHRSTV HARVEST
THRAVES
AEHRSTW THAWERS
WREATHS
AEHRSVW WHARVES
AEHRSWY WASHERY
AEHRSXY HYRAXES
AEHRTUU HAUTEUR
AEHRTWY WREATHY
AEHSSST STASHES
AEHSSSW SWASHES
AEHSSTW SWATHES
AEHSTUX EXHAUST
AEIIKNT KAINITE
AEIIKSS SAIKEIS
AEIILLT TAILLIE
AEIILNN ANILINE
AEIILNR AIRLINE
AEIILNX EXILIAN
AEIILRR LAIRIER
AEIILRS LAIRISE
AEIILRZ LAIRIZE
AEIILSS LIAISES
SILESIA
AEIILST LAITIES
AEIILSW LEWISIA
AEIILTZ TAILZIE
AEIIMNT INTIMAE
MINIATE
AEIIMPR IMPERIA
AEIIMRT AIRTIME
AEIIMST AMITIES
ATIMIES
AEIIMTT IMITATE
AEIINNS ASININE
INSANIE
AEIINQU EQUINIA
AEIINRR RAINIER
AEIINRS SENARII
AEIINRT INERTIA
AEIINST ISATINE
AEIINSX SIXAINE
AEIINTX AXINITE
AEIIPRR PRAIRIE
AEIIRRV RIVIERA
VAIRIER
AEIIRST AIRIEST
IRISATE
AEIITTV VITIATE
AEIJLNV JAVELIN
AEIJLRS JAILERS
AEIJLSZ JEZAILS
AEIJMMR JAMMIER
AEIJMMS JEMIMAS
AEIJMNS JASMINE
AEIJNRS INJERAS
AEIJNRT JANTIER
NARTJIE
AEIJNST JANTIES
TAJINES
AEIJNTU JAUNTIE
AEIJRSV JARVIES
AEIJRZZ JAZZIER
AEIKLNO KAOLINE
AEIKLNR LANKIER
AEIKLNU UNALIKE
AEIKLOT KEITLOA
AEIKLRR LARKIER
AEIKLRS LAIKERS
SERKALI
AEIKLRT TALKIER
AEIKLRV KLAVIER
AEIKLRW WARLIKE
AEIKLSS ALSIKES
AEIKLST LAKIEST
TALKIES
AEIKMMS MISMAKE
AEIKMNP PIKEMAN
AEIKMNR MANKIER
RAMEKIN
AEIKMNS KINEMAS
AEIKMPR RAMPIKE
AEIKMRW MAWKIER
AEIKMSS KAMISES
AEIKMST MISTAKE
AEIKNRR NARKIER
AEIKNRS SNAKIER
AEIKNRT KERATIN
AEIKNRW WANKIER
AEIKNSS KINASES
AEIKNST INTAKES
KENTIAS
TANKIES
AEIKNSW SWANKIE
AEIKNSY KYANISE
YANKIES
AEIKNTY KYANITE
AEIKNYZ KYANIZE
AEIKOST OAKIEST
AEIKPRR PARKIER
AEIKPRS PARKIES
SPARKIE
AEIKPRW PAWKIER
AEIKQRU QUAKIER
AEIKRRS KERRIAS
SARKIER
AEIKRSS KAISERS
KARSIES
AEIKRST ARKITES
KARITES
AEIKRSZ KARZIES
AEIKSSS ASKESIS
AEIKSTT TAKIEST
AEILLMN MANILLE
AEILLNR RALLINE
AEILLOV ALVEOLI
AEILLPR PALLIER
AEILLPS ILLAPSE
AEILLRR RALLIER
AEILLRS RALLIES
AEILLRT LITERAL
TALLIER
AEILLRU RUELLIA
AEILLRW WALLIER
AEILLSS ALLISES
SALLIES
AEILLST TAILLES
TALLIES
AEILLSW WALLIES
AEILLUV ELUVIAL
AEILLVX VEXILLA
AEILMMN MAILMEN
AEILMMS LAMMIES
MELISMA
AEILMNN LINEMAN
MELANIN
AEILMNO MINEOLA
AEILMNP IMPANEL
MANIPLE
AEILMNR MANLIER
MARLINE
MINERAL
RAILMEN
AEILMNS ISLEMAN
MENIALS
SEMINAL
AEILMNT AILMENT
ALIMENT
AEILMOR LOAMIER
AEILMPR IMPEARL
LEMPIRA
PALMIER
AEILMPS IMPALES
PALMIES
AEILMPT IMPLATE
PALMIET
AEILMRR LARMIER
MARLIER
AEILMRS MAILERS
REALISM
AEILMRT LAMITER
MALTIER
AEILMSS AIMLESS
MESAILS
SAMIELS
SEISMAL
AEILMSZ MEZAILS
AEILMTY LAYTIME
MEATILY
AEILNNY INANELY
AEILNOP OPALINE
AEILNOR AILERON
ALERION
ALIENOR
AEILNOT ELATION
TOENAIL
AEILNPR PEARLIN
PLAINER
PRALINE
AEILNPS ALPINES
SPANIEL
SPLENIA
AEILNPT PANTILE
AEILNPX EXPLAIN
AEILNQU EQUINAL
AEILNRS NAILERS
AEILNRT ENTRAIL
LATRINE
RATLINE
RELIANT
RETINAL
TRENAIL
AEILNRV RAVELIN
AEILNRW LAWNIER
AEILNRX RELAXIN
AEILNRY INLAYER
NAILERY
AEILNSS SALINES
SILANES
AEILNST EASTLIN
ELASTIN
ENTAILS
SALIENT
SLAINTE
STANIEL
TENAILS
AEILNSU INSULAE
INULASE
AEILNSV ALEVINS
VALINES
AEILNSX ALEXINS
AEILNTU ALUNITE
AEILNTV VENTAIL
AEILNUV UNALIVE
UNVAILE
AEILNUW LAUWINE
AEILNVY NAIVELY
AEILOPR PELORIA
AEILOPS LEIPOAS
AEILORV VARIOLE
AEILOST ISOLATE
AEILOTV VIOLATE
AEILPPR APPERIL
APPLIER
ARIPPLE

AEILPPS	APPLIES
	LAPPIES
AEILPRS	PALSIER
	PARLIES
AEILPRT	PLAITER
	PLATIER
AEILPRV	PREVAIL
AEILPSS	ESPIALS
	LAPISES
	LIPASES
	PALSIES
AEILPST	APLITES
	PALIEST
	TALIPES
AEILPSY	PAISLEY
AEILQTU	LIQUATE
	TEQUILA
AEILRRS	RAILERS
	RERAILS
AEILRRT	RETIRAL
	RETRIAL
	TRAILER
AEILRSS	AIRLESS
	SAILERS
	SERAILS
	SERIALS
AEILRST	REALIST
	RETAILS
	SALTIER
	SALTIRE
	SLATIER
AEILRSV	REVISAL
AEILRSW	SWALIER
	WAILERS
AEILRTT	TERTIAL
AEILRTU	URALITE
AEILRTW	WALTIER
AEILRTY	IRATELY
	REALITY
AEILRVV	REVIVAL
AEILRVY	VIRELAY
AEILRWY	WEARILY
AEILSSS	LAISSES
	LASSIES
AEILSSU	SAULIES
AEILSSV	VALISES
	VESSAIL
AEILSSW	WALISES
AEILSTU	SITULAE
AEILSTV	ESTIVAL
AEILSTW	WALIEST
AEILSTY	TAILYES
AEILSTZ	LAZIEST
AEILTVY	VILAYET
AEILUVX	EXUVIAL
AEIMMMS	MAMMIES
AEIMMNS	MISNAME
AEIMMRS	RAMMIES
AEIMMRT	MARMITE
AEIMMST	MISMATE
	TAMMIES
AEIMMZZ	MIZMAZE
AEIMNNT	MANNITE
AEIMNOR	MORAINE
AEIMNOS	ANOMIES
AEIMNOU	MOINEAU
AEIMNRR	MARINER
AEIMNRS	MARINES
	REMAINS
	SEMINAR
	SIRNAME
AEIMNRT	MINARET
	RAIMENT
AEIMNRV	VERMIAN
AEIMNRW	WIREMAN
AEIMNSS	INSEAMS
	SAMISEN
AEIMNST	INMATES
	MAINEST
	MANTIES
	TAMINES
AEIMNTX	TAXIMEN
AEIMNTY	AMENITY
	ANYTIME
AEIMNUV	MAUVEIN
	MAUVINE
AEIMOOP	IPOMOEA
AEIMOPR	EMPORIA
AEIMORR	ARMOIRE
AEIMOST	AMOSITE
	ATOMIES
	ATOMISE
	OSMIATE
AEIMOTX	TOXEMIA
AEIMOTZ	ATOMIZE
AEIMPRR	RAMPIRE
AEIMPRS	IMPRESA
	SAMPIRE
AEIMPRT	PRIMATE
AEIMPRV	VAMPIRE
AEIMPSS	IMPASSE
	PESSIMA
AEIMPST	IMPASTE
	PASTIME
AEIMPSV	IMPAVES
AEIMPSW	MAPWISE
AEIMPSY	PYEMIAS
AEIMRRR	MARRIER
AEIMRRS	MARRIES
	SIMARRE
AEIMRSS	MASSIER
AEIMRST	IMARETS
	MAESTRI
	MAISTER
	MASTIER
	MISRATE
	SEMITAR
	SMARTIE
AEIMRSU	UREMIAS
AEIMRSW	AWMRIES
AEIMRTU	MURIATE
AEIMRTW	WARTIME
AEIMSSS	AMISSES
	MESSIAS
AEIMSST	ASTEISM
	SAMIEST
	SAMITES
	TAMISES
AEIMSSV	MASSIVE
	MAVISES
AEIMSSY	MYIASES
AEIMSTT	MATIEST
	MATTIES
AEIMSTZ	MAZIEST
	MESTIZA
AEIMSUV	AMUSIVE
AEIMSXX	MAXIXES
AEIMTYZ	AZYMITE
AEINNNS	NANNIES
AEINNOT	ENATION
AEINNPR	PANNIER
AEINNPT	PANTINE
	PINNATE
AEINNRS	INSANER
	INSNARE
AEINNRT	ENTRAIN
	TRANNIE
AEINNRU	ANEURIN
AEINNSS	SANNIES
	SIENNAS
AEINNST	INANEST
AEINNSZ	ENZIANS
AEINNTT	ANTIENT
AEINOPZ	EPIZOAN
AEINORS	ERASION
AEINORT	OTARINE
AEINOSS	ANOESIS
AEINOST	ATONIES
AEINOSV	EVASION
AEINOSZ	AZIONES
AEINOXZ	OXAZINE
AEINPPR	NAPPIER
AEINPPS	NAPPIES
AEINPRS	RAPINES
AEINPRT	PAINTER
	PERTAIN
	REPAINT
AEINPSS	ASPINES
	PANSIES
AEINPST	PANTIES
	PATINES
	SAPIENT
	SPINATE
AEINPTT	PATIENT
AEINPTU	PETUNIA
AEINPTY	PANEITY
AEINQTU	ANTIQUE
	QUINATE
AEINRRS	SIERRAN
	SNARIER
AEINRRT	RETRAIN
	TERRAIN
	TRAINER
AEINRSS	ARSINES
	SARNIES
AEINRST	ANESTRI
	NASTIER
	RATINES
	RESIANT
	RETAINS
	RETINAS
	RETSINA
	STAINER
	STARNIE
	STEARIN
AEINRSV	AVENIRS
	RAVINES
AEINRTT	INTREAT
	ITERANT
	NATTIER
	NITRATE
	TARTINE
	TERTIAN
AEINRTU	RUINATE
	TAURINE
	URANITE
	URINATE
AEINRTW	TAWNIER
	TINWARE
AEINRUV	VAURIEN
AEINRUW	UNWARIE
AEINRUZ	AZURINE
AEINRVV	VERVAIN
AEINRWY	YAWNIER
AEINSSS	SANSEIS
	SASINES
AEINSST	ENTASIS
	NASTIES
	SESTINA
	TANSIES
	TISANES
AEINSSV	SAVINES
	VINASSE
AEINSTT	INSTATE
	SATINET
AEINSTU	AUNTIES
	SINUATE
AEINSTV	NAIVEST
	NATIVES
	VAINEST
AEINSTW	AWNIEST
	TAWNIES
	WANIEST
	WANTIES
AEINSTZ	ZANIEST
AEINSVV	NAVVIES
AEINSWY	ANYWISE
AEINTVY	NAIVETY
AEINTXY	ANXIETY
AEIOPRS	SOAPIER
AEIOPSS	SOAPIES
AEIOPST	ATOPIES
	OPIATES
AEIOQSU	SEQUOIA
AEIORRR	ARRIERO
	ROARIER
AEIORST	OARIEST
	OTARIES
AEIORSV	OVARIES
AEIOSTT	OSTIATE
	TOASTIE
AEIOSTZ	AZOTISE
AEIOTZZ	AZOTIZE
AEIPPPR	PAPPIER
AEIPPPS	PAPPIES
AEIPPRS	APPRISE
	SAPPIER
AEIPPRT	PERIAPT
AEIPPRY	YAPPIER
AEIPPRZ	APPRIZE
	ZAPPIER
AEIPPSS	PASPIES
AEIPPSY	YAPPIES
AEIPRRS	PARRIES
	PRAISER
	RAPIERS
	RASPIER
	REPAIRS
AEIPRSS	ASPIRES
	PARESIS
	PRAISES
	SPIREAS
AEIPRST	PARTIES
	PASTIER
	PIASTRE
	PIRATES
	PRATIES
	TRAIPSE
AEIPRSU	SPURIAE
	UPRAISE

AEIPRSV	PARVISE
AEIPRSW	WASPIER
AEIPRTT	PARTITE
AEIPRTV	PRIVATE
AEIPRTW	WIRETAP
AEIPRXY	PYREXIA
AEIPSSS	ASEPSIS
AEIPSST	PASTIES
	PATSIES
	TAPISES
AEIPSSV	PASSIVE
	PAVISES
	SPAVIES
AEIPSSW	WASPIES
AEIPSTT	PATTIES
	TAPETIS
AEIPSTU	TAUPIES
AEIPSTW	TAWPIES
AEIPTXY	EPITAXY
AEIQRUV	AQUIVER
AEIQSSU	SAIQUES
AEIRRRT	TARRIER
AEIRRSS	ARRISES
	RAISERS
	SIERRAS
AEIRRST	ARTSIER
	SERRATI
	TARRIES
	TARSIER
AEIRRSV	ARRIVES
	VARIERS
AEIRRTT	RATTIER
	RETRAIT
	TARTIER
AEIRRTW	WARTIER
AEIRRTY	RETIARY
AEIRRVV	VIVERRA
AEIRSSS	SASSIER
AEIRSST	ARTSIES
	SAIREST
	SATIRES
	TIRASSE
AEIRSSU	SAURIES
AEIRSSZ	ASSIZER
AEIRSTT	ARTIEST
	ARTISTE
	ATTIRES
	IRATEST
	STRIATE
	TASTIER
	TERTIAS
AEIRSTV	TAIVERS
	VASTIER
AEIRSTW	WAISTER
	WAITERS
	WARIEST
AEIRSVW	WAIVERS
AEIRTTT	ATTRITE
	TATTIER
	TITRATE
AEIRTTV	TAIVERT
AEIRTTW	TAWTIER
AEIRTTX	EXTRAIT
AEIRTUY	AUREITY
AEIRTUZ	AZURITE
AEIRTVY	VARIETY
AEIRWWY	WIREWAY
AEISSST	SIESTAS
	TASSIES
AEISSSZ	ASSIZES
AEISSUV	SUASIVE
AEISSUX	AUXESIS
AEISSVV	SAVVIES
AEISTTT	TATTIES
AEISTTU	SITUATE
AEISTTV	STATIVE
AEISTTW	TWAITES
AEISTTY	SATIETY
AEISTVW	WAVIEST
AEISTWX	WAXIEST
AEITTTU	ATTUITE
AEITTTV	VITTATE
AEJKMNR	JARKMEN
AEJKNRS	JANKERS
AEJLNUV	JUVENAL
AEJLOSU	JALOUSE
	JEALOUS
AEJLOUZ	AZULEJO
AEJMMRS	JAMMERS
AEJMNZZ	JAZZMEN
AEJMRST	RAMJETS
AEJMSST	JETSAMS
AEJMSSY	JESSAMY
AEJMSTY	MAJESTY
AEJNNOS	JOANNES
AEJNORZ	ZANJERO
AEJNSST	JESSANT
AEJNSSU	JAUNSES
AEJPRSS	JASPERS
AEJPRSY	JASPERY
AEJRSVY	JARVEYS
AEJRSZZ	JAZZERS
AEKKNRS	KRAKENS
AEKKRSY	YAKKERS
AEKLLTU	KELLAUT
AEKLNPP	KNAPPLE
AEKLNPR	PRANKLE
AEKLNRS	RANKLES
AEKLNST	ANKLETS
	ASKLENT
	LANKEST
AEKLNSW	KNAWELS
AEKLNSY	ALKYNES
AEKLORY	ROKELAY
AEKLOST	SKATOLE
AEKLPRS	SPARKLE
AEKLRRS	LARKERS
AEKLRST	STALKER
	TALKERS
AEKLRSW	WALKERS
AEKLRUW	WAULKER
AEKLSST	LASKETS
	SKLATES
AEKLSTU	AUKLETS
AEKMMNR	MARKMEN
AEKMNOS	SOKEMAN
AEKMNSU	UNMAKES
AEKMOOT	MATOOKE
AEKMOST	MATOKES
AEKMPRU	UPMAKER
AEKMPSU	UPMAKES
AEKMRRS	MARKERS
	REMARKS
AEKMRSS	MASKERS
AEKMRST	MARKETS
AEKNNRS	ENRANKS
AEKNNST	KANTENS
AEKNNTU	UNTAKEN
AEKNPPR	KNAPPER
AEKNPRS	SPANKER
AEKNPSU	UNSPEAK
AEKNPTU	UPTAKEN
AEKNRRS	RANKERS
AEKNRSS	KRANSES
AEKNRST	RANKEST
	STARKEN
	TANKERS
AEKNRSU	UNRAKES
AEKNRSW	SWANKER
	WANKERS
AEKNRSY	YANKERS
AEKNRSZ	KRANZES
AEKNRVY	KNAVERY
AEKNSSU	ANKUSES
AEKNSWY	SWANKEY
AEKORRS	ROSAKER
AEKORSS	ARKOSES
	SOAKERS
AEKOTTU	OUTTAKE
	TAKEOUT
AEKPPSU	UPSPAKE
	UPSPEAK
AEKPRRS	PARKERS
AEKPRSS	SPARKES
AEKPSSY	PASSKEY
AEKPSTU	UPTAKES
AEKQRSU	QUAKERS
AEKQSSU	SQUEAKS
AEKQSUY	SQUEAKY
AEKRRST	KARTERS
	KRATERS
	STARKER
AEKRSST	SKATERS
	STRAKES
	STREAKS
	TASKERS
AEKRSSY	KARSEYS
AEKRSTY	STREAKY
AEKRSUW	WAUKERS
AEKSSSV	KVASSES
AELLMNU	LUMENAL
AELLMRS	SMALLER
AELLMST	MALLETS
AELLMSU	MALLEUS
AELLMSY	MELLAYS
	MESALLY
AELLMTY	METALLY
AELLMWX	MAXWELL
AELLNOP	PALLONE
AELLNOR	LLANERO
AELLNOV	NOVELLA
AELLNOY	ALONELY
AELLNPY	PENALLY
AELLNRT	ENTRALL
AELLNSS	ALLNESS
AELLNSW	ENWALLS
AELLNTT	TALLENT
AELLNUU	LUNULAE
AELLNVY	VENALLY
AELLORS	ROSELLA
AELLORT	REALLOT
AELLORV	OVERALL
AELLPPS	LAPPELS
AELLPRU	PLEURAL
AELLPSS	SPALLES
AELLPST	PALLETS
AELLPTU	PLUTEAL
AELLPTY	PLAYLET
AELLQUY	EQUALLY
AELLRRU	ALLURER
AELLRST	STELLAR
	TELLARS
AELLRSU	ALLURES
	LAURELS
AELLRSW	WALLERS
AELLRSY	RALLYES
AELLRTY	ALERTLY
	ELYTRAL
AELLSST	SALLETS
	TASSELL
AELLSSW	LAWLESS
AELLSTT	TALLEST
	TALLETS
AELLSTW	SETWALL
	SWALLET
	WALLETS
AELLSTY	STALELY
AELLSVY	VALLEYS
AELLTUU	ULULATE
AELLUVV	VALVULE
AELMMNO	MAMELON
AELMMNT	MALTMEN
AELMMOY	MYELOMA
AELMMRS	LAMMERS
	SLAMMER
AELMMRT	TRAMMEL
AELMMST	STAMMEL
AELMMSY	MALMSEY
AELMNNS	LENSMAN
AELMNOR	ALMONER
	NEMORAL
AELMNOS	MELANOS
AELMNOT	LOMENTA
	OMENTAL
	TELAMON
AELMNPR	LAMPERN
AELMNRU	NUMERAL
AELMNST	LAMENTS
	MANTELS
	MANTLES
AELMNSU	MENSUAL
AELMNTT	MANTLET
AELMNTU	NUTMEAL
AELMOPR	PLEROMA
AELMOPU	AMPOULE
AELMOPY	MAYPOLE
AELMORS	MORALES
AELMORT	MOLERAT
AELMORU	MORULAE
AELMORV	REMOVAL
AELMOST	MALTOSE
AELMOTT	MATELOT
AELMPRS	EMPARLS
	LAMPERS
	PALMERS
	SAMPLER
AELMPRT	TEMPLAR
	TRAMPLE
AELMPRY	LAMPREY
AELMPSS	SAMPLES
AELMPST	AMPLEST
AELMPSU	AMPULES
AELMPTU	PLUMATE
AELMRRS	MARRELS
AELMRSS	ARMLESS
AELMRST	ARMLETS
	MARTELS
AELMRSU	MAULERS
AELMRSV	MARVELS
AELMRTT	MARTLET

AELMSST SAMLETS
AELMSTU AMULETS
AELNNPR PLANNER
AELNNPS PENNALS
AELNNPU UNPANEL
AELNNRS ENSNARL
LANNERS
AELNNRT LANTERN
AELNNRU UNLEARN
AELNNST STANNEL
AELNNTU ANNULET
AELNOOS ALSOONE
AELNOPT POLENTA
AELNORS ORLEANS
AELNORU ALEURON
AELNORV VERONAL
AELNOST ETALONS
AELNOTV VOLANTE
AELNOUZ ZONULAE
AELNPPY PLAYPEN
AELNPRS PLANERS
REPLANS
AELNPRT PANTLER
PLANTER
REPLANT
AELNPRY PLENARY
AELNPSS NAPLESS
AELNPST PLANETS
PLATENS
AELNPSU UPLEANS
AELNPTU UPLEANT
AELNPTX EXPLANT
AELNPTY APLENTY
PENALTY
AELNQUU UNEQUAL
AELNRRS SNARLER
AELNRSS RANSELS
AELNRST ANTLERS
RENTALS
SALTERN
STERNAL
AELNRSZ RANZELS
AELNRTT TRENTAL
AELNRTU NEUTRAL
AELNRTV VENTRAL
AELNRUV UNRAVEL
AELNSSU SENSUAL
UNSEALS
AELNSSW AWNLESS
AELNSSX LAXNESS
AELNSTT LATTENS
TALENTS
AELNSTU ELUANTS
UNLASTE
AELNSTV LEVANTS
AELNSTY STANYEL
AELNSTZ ZELANTS
AELNSUW UNWEALS
AELNTUV ENVAULT
AELOORS AEROSOL
ROSEOLA
AELOPPR PROPALE
AELOPPX APOPLEX
AELOPRR PREORAL
AELOPRS PAROLES
REPOSAL
AELOPRT PROLATE
AELOPRV OVERLAP
AELOPST APOSTLE
PELOTAS

AELOPSX EXPOSAL
AELOPTT PALETOT
AELOPTU OUTLEAP
AELORRT REALTOR
RELATOR
AELORSS OARLESS
SOLERAS
AELORST OESTRAL
AELORTU TORULAE
AELORTV LEVATOR
AELORTY ROYALET
AELORTZ ZELATOR
AELORUU ROULEAU
AELORVY OVERLAY
AELORWY OWRELAY
AELOSSS LASSOES
AELOSSV SALVOES
AELOSSW LEASOWS
AELOSTV SOLVATE
AELOSTZ ZEALOTS
AELOSUZ ZEALOUS
AELOSVY SAVELOY
AELOTTU TOLUATE
AELOTUV OVULATE
AELOTVV VOLVATE
AELPPRS LAPPERS
RAPPELS
SLAPPER
AELPPRY REAPPLY
AELPPSS SAPPLES
AELPPST LAPPETS
STAPPLE
AELPPSU APPULSE
PAPULES
UPLEAPS
AELPPTU UPLEAPT
AELPQSU PLAQUES
AELPRRS PARRELS
AELPRST PALTERS
PLASTER
PLATERS
PSALTER
STAPLER
AELPRSU PERUSAL
SERPULA
AELPRSW PRAWLES
AELPRSY PARLEYS
PARSLEY
PLAYERS
REPLAYS
SPARELY
AELPRTT PARTLET
PLATTER
PRATTLE
AELPRTY PEARTLY
PRELATY
PTERYLA
AELPRUY EPULARY
AELPSSS SAPLESS
AELPSST PASTELS
STAPLES
AELPSTT PATTLES
PELTAST
AELPSTU PULSATE
PUTEALS
SPATULE
AELPUUV UPVALUE
AELQRRU QUARREL
AELQSSU LASQUES
SQUEALS

AELQTUZ QUETZAL
AELRRSU SURREAL
AELRRTT RATTLER
AELRRTW TRAWLER
AELRSST ARTLESS
LASTERS
SALTERS
SLATERS
TARSELS
AELRSSU SAURELS
AELRSSV SALVERS
SERVALS
SLAVERS
VERSALS
AELRSSW WARSLES
AELRSSY RAYLESS
SLAYERS
AELRSTT RATTLES
SLATTER
STARLET
STARTLE
TATLERS
AELRSTU SALUTER
AELRSTV TRAVELS
VARLETS
VESTRAL
AELRSTW WASTREL
AELRSTY RAYLETS
AELRSUV VALUERS
AELRSVV VARVELS
AELRSVY SLAVERY
AELRSWX WRAXLES
AELRSWY LAWYERS
AELRSZZ RAZZLES
AELRTTT TARTLET
TATTLER
AELRTTU TUTELAR
AELRTUV VAULTER
AELRTWZ WALTZER
AELSSST TASSELS
AELSSTT LATESTS
SALTEST
STALEST
TASLETS
AELSSTU SALUTES
TALUSES
AELSSTV VESTALS
AELSSTW WASTELS
AELSSTX TAXLESS
AELSSUV AVULSES
AELSSVY SLAVEYS
AELSSWY WAYLESS
AELSTTT TATTLES
AELSTTW WATTLES
AELSTTY STATELY
STYLATE
AELSTUX LUXATES
AELSTWZ WALTZES
AELSUVY SUAVELY
AELSWZZ SWAZZLE
AELTTTW TWATTLE
AELTTUX TEXTUAL
AELTUVV VULVATE
AEMMMRS MAMMERS
AEMMMST MAMMETS
AEMMNOT MOMENTA
AEMMNTU AMENTUM
AEMMORS MARMOSE
AEMMRRS RAMMERS
AEMMRST STAMMER

AEMMRSY YAMMERS
AEMMRSZ MAMZERS
AEMMSTU MAUMETS
SUMMATE
AEMMSTW MAWMETS
AEMNNOS MANNOSE
AEMNNOT MONTANE
AEMNNOU NOUMENA
AEMNNRS MANNERS
AEMNNRT MANRENT
REMNANT
AEMNNSW NEWSMAN
AEMNNTU UNMEANT
AEMNOPR REPOMAN
AEMNOPS MOPANES
AEMNOPZ ZAMPONE
AEMNORS ENAMORS
MOANERS
OARSMEN
AEMNORU ENAMOUR
NEUROMA
AEMNORV OVERMAN
AEMNORY ROMNEYA
AEMNOSS MONASES
AEMNOST MANTOES
AEMNOTT TOMENTA
AEMNOTU NOTAEUM
OUTNAME
AEMNPSS PASSMEN
AEMNPST ENSTAMP
TAPSMEN
AEMNPSU PNEUMAS
AEMNPTU PUTAMEN
AEMNPTY PAYMENT
AEMNRRU MANURER
AEMNRST ARTSMEN
MARTENS
SARMENT
SMARTEN
AEMNRSU MANURES
MURENAS
SURNAME
AEMNRTU TRUEMAN
AEMNRTV VARMENT
AEMNSSS MESSANS
AEMNSST STAMENS
AEMNSSU UNSEAMS
AEMNSTU UNTAMES
UNTEAMS
AEMNSTY AMNESTY
AEMNTWY WAYMENT
AEMOORW WOOMERA
AEMOOST OSTEOMA
AEMOOSV AMOOVES
VAMOOSE
AEMOPPR PAMPERO
AEMOPSZ APOZEMS
AEMORRS REMORAS
ROAMERS
AEMORRV OVERARM
AEMORST AMORETS
MAESTRO
OMERTAS
AEMORSU RAMEOUS
AEMORSW SEAWORM
WOMERAS
AEMORSX XEROMAS
AEMOSST OSMATES
AEMOSSV VAMOSES
AEMOSTW TWASOME

AEMOSUZ ZAMOUSE
AEMOSWY SOMEWAY
AEMOTTZ MOZETTA
AEMPPRS MAPPERS
PAMPERS
PREAMPS
AEMPPRY MAPPERY
AEMPRRS RAMPERS
AEMPRRT TRAMPER
AEMPRRW PREWARM
AEMPRST EMPARTS
STAMPER
TAMPERS
AEMPRSV REVAMPS
VAMPERS
AEMPRSW SWAMPER
AEMPRTT TRAMPET
AEMPRTU TEMPURA
AEMPSSU EMPUSAS
AEMPTTT ATTEMPT
AEMPTTU TAPETUM
AEMQRSU MARQUES
MASQUER
AEMQSSU MASQUES
SQUAMES
AEMRRRY REMARRY
AEMRRST SMARTER
AEMRRSU ARMURES
AEMRRSV MARVERS
AEMRRSW SWARMER
WARMERS
AEMRRTU ERRATUM
MATURER
AEMRSST MASTERS
STREAMS
AEMRSSU AMUSERS
MASSEUR
AEMRSTT MATTERS
SMATTER
AEMRSTU MATURES
STRUMAE
AEMRSTW WARMEST
AEMRSTY MASTERY
MAYSTER
STREAMY
AEMRTTX MARTEXT
AEMRTTY MATTERY
AEMRTUU TRUMEAU
AEMSSSU ASSUMES
AEMSSUW WAMUSES
AEMSSYZ ZYMASES
AEMSTTU MUTATES
AEMSTUV MAUVEST
AEMSTVZ ZEMSTVA
AENNNOS NONANES
AENNNPT PENNANT
AENNOPS PANNOSE
AENNORT NORTENA
AENNORY ANNOYER
AENNOSS NOSEANS
AENNOSV NOVENAS
AENNOSY ANYONES
AENNOTU TONNEAU
AENNPRS SPANNER
AENNQTU QUANNET
AENNRST TANNERS
AENNRSV VANNERS
AENNRTT ENTRANT
AENNRTV VERNANT
AENNRTY TANNERY
TYRANNE
AENNSSW WANNESS
AENNSTT TANNEST
TENANTS
AENNSTW WANNEST
AENOOTZ ENTOZOA
AENOPPR PROPANE
AENOPRS PERSONA
AENOPRT OPERANT
PRONATE
PROTEAN
AENOPSU POSAUNE
AENOPSV PAVONES
AENOPSW WEAPONS
AENORRT ORNATER
AENORRV OVERRAN
AENORSS REASONS
AENORST ATONERS
SENATOR
TREASON
AENORTV VENATOR
AENORXY ANOREXY
AENOSSS SEASONS
AENOSST ASTONES
AENOSTT ATTONES
NOTATES
AENOSTU SOUTANE
AENOSVW WAVESON
AENOUUV NOUVEAU
AENPPRS NAPPERS
PARPENS
PARSNEP
SNAPPER
AENPPRT PARPENT
AENPPRU UNPAPER
AENPRRT PARTNER
AENPRRW PREWARN
AENPRST ARPENTS
ENTRAPS
PANTERS
PARENTS
PASTERN
PERSANT
TREPANS
AENPRSW ENWRAPS
PAWNERS
SPAWNER
AENPRSZ PANZERS
AENPRTT PATTERN
REPTANT
AENPRUV PARVENU
AENPSST APTNESS
PATNESS
PESANTS
AENPSSY SYNAPSE
AENPSTT PATENTS
PATTENS
AENPSTU PEANUTS
PESAUNT
AENPSTW STEWPAN
AENPSTY SYNAPTE
AENPSTZ PEZANTS
AENQSTU EQUANTS
AENRRSS SERRANS
SNARERS
AENRRST ERRANTS
RANTERS
AENRRSW WARNERS
WARRENS
AENRRTT TRANTER
AENRRTY TERNARY
AENRSSS SARSENS
AENRSST SARSNET
TRANSES
AENRSSW ANSWERS
RAWNESS
AENRSSY SARNEYS
AENRSTT NATTERS
RATTENS
AENRSTU AUNTERS
NATURES
SAUNTER
AENRSTV SERVANT
TAVERNS
VERSANT
AENRSTW STRAWEN
WANTERS
AENRSTY TRAYNES
AENRSUW UNSWEAR
UNWARES
AENRTTU TAUNTER
AENRTTY NATTERY
AENRTUV VAUNTER
AENRTUW UNWATER
AENRUWY UNWEARY
AENSSST ASSENTS
SNASTES
AENSSTU NASUTES
UNSEATS
AENSSTX SEXTANS
AENSSTY STAYNES
AENSSTZ STANZES
AENSSWY SAWNEYS
AENSSXY SYNAXES
AENSTTT ATTENTS
AENSTTU ATTUNES
NUTATES
TAUTENS
TETANUS
UNSTATE
AENSTTX SEXTANT
AENSTUX UNTAXES
AENSTWY TAWNEYS
AENTTTU ATTUENT
AEOOPPS PAPOOSE
AEOOPRS OROPESA
AEOPPPS PAPPOSE
AEOPPRS APPOSER
AEOPPRV APPROVE
AEOPPSS APPOSES
AEOPQRU OPAQUER
AEOPQSU OPAQUES
AEOPRRT PRAETOR
PRORATE
AEOPRSS SOAPERS
AEOPRST ESPARTO
PROTEAS
SEAPORT
AEOPRTT PORTATE
AEOPRVY OVERPAY
AEOPRWY ROPEWAY
AEOPSSS PSOASES
AEOPSTT APTOTES
TEAPOTS
AEOPSTY TEAPOYS
AEOPSTZ TOPAZES
AEOQRTU EQUATOR
QUORATE
AEOQRUV VAQUERO
AEOQSUU AQUEOUS
AEORRRS ROARERS
AEORRSS SOARERS
AEORRST ROASTER
AEORRSU AROUSER
AEORSSS SAROSES
SEROSAS
AEORSSU AROUSES
AEORSTT ROTATES
TOASTER
AEORSUV AVOURES
AEORSVW AVOWERS
OVERSAW
AEORSVY AVOYERS
AEORTTU OUTRATE
AEORTUW OUTWEAR
AEORTVX OVERTAX
AEOSSTV AVOSETS
AEOSTTU OUTEATS
AEPPRRS RAPPERS
AEPPRRT TRAPPER
AEPPRRW WRAPPER
AEPPRSS APPRESS
SAPPERS
AEPPRST TAPPERS
AEPPRSU PAUPERS
UPSPEAR
AEPPRSW SWAPPER
WAPPERS
AEPPRSY PREPAYS
YAPPERS
AEPPRSZ ZAPPERS
AEPPSTT TAPPETS
AEPPSTU PUPATES
AEPQRTU PARQUET
AEPRRRS SPARRER
AEPRRSS PARSERS
RASPERS
SPARERS
SPARRES
SPARSER
AEPRRST PARTERS
PRATERS
AEPRRSU PARURES
UPREARS
AEPRRSW REWRAPS
WARPERS
AEPRRSY PRAYERS
RESPRAY
SPRAYER
AEPRRTU PARTURE
RAPTURE
AEPRRTY PETRARY
AEPRSSS PASSERS
AEPRSST PASTERS
REPASTS
SPAREST
AEPRSSU PAUSERS
AEPRSSY PESSARY
AEPRSTT PATTERS
SPATTER
TAPSTER
AEPRSTU PASTURE
UPRATES
UPSTARE
UPTEARS
AEPRSTY YAPSTER
AEPRSTZ PATZERS
AEPRSWY YAWPERS
AEPRSYY SPRAYEY
AEPRTXY APTERYX

AEPSSTU	PETASUS
AEPSTTU	UPSTATE
AEPSZZZ	PZAZZES
AEQRRSU	SQUARER
AEQRRTU	QUARTER
AEQRSSU	SQUARES
AEQRSTU	QUAREST
	QUARTES
AEQRSUV	QUAVERS
AEQRTTU	QUARTET
AEQRUVY	QUAVERY
AERRSST	ARRESTS
	RASTERS
	STARERS
AERRSSU	ASSURER
	RASURES
AERRSTT	RATTERS
	RESTART
	STARTER
AERRSTY	STRAYER
AERRSUZ	RAZURES
AERRSWY	WARREYS
AERRTTY	RATTERY
AERSSST	ASSERTS
	TRASSES
AERSSSU	ASSURES
	SARUSES
AERSSSW	WRASSES
AERSSTT	ASTERTS
	STARETS
	STATERS
	TASTERS
AERSSTV	STARVES
AERSSTW	WASTERS
AERSSTY	ESTRAYS
	STAYERS
	STAYRES
AERSSUV	VARUSES
AERSSVW	SWARVES
AERSSWY	SAWYERS
	SWAYERS
AERSTTT	STRETTA
	TARTEST
	TATTERS
AERSTTU	ASTUTER
	STATURE
AERSTTV	VATTERS
AERSTTW	SWATTER
	TEWARTS
AERSTTY	YATTERS
AERSTTZ	STARETZ
AERSTUU	AUTEURS
AERSTUY	ESTUARY
AERSTWY	WASTERY
AERTTTY	TATTERY
AERTTUV	VETTURA
AESSSTT	TASSETS
AESSTTT	ATTESTS
AESSTTU	STATUES
AESSTTV	VASTEST
AESSTUV	SUAVEST
AESSTUY	EUSTASY
AESSVVY	SAVVEYS
AESTTTU	STATUTE
	TAUTEST
AESTTTW	WATTEST
AFFFGIN	FAFFING
AFFGGIN	GAFFING
AFFGINN	NAFFING
AFFGINW	WAFFING

AFFGINY	AFFYING
	YAFFING
AFFGSUW	GUFFAWS
AFFHILN	HAFFLIN
AFFHIRS	RAFFISH
AFFHIST	HAFFITS
AFFILMN	MAFFLIN
AFFILPS	PILAFFS
AFFILSY	FALSIFY
AFFIMRS	AFFIRMS
AFFIMST	MASTIFF
AFFINRU	FUNFAIR
	RUFFIAN
AFFINTY	TIFFANY
AFFIORR	FORFAIR
AFFIRRU	FURFAIR
AFFIRST	TARIFFS
AFFNORS	SAFFRON
AFFNORT	AFFRONT
AFFRSST	STRAFFS
AFGGGIN	FAGGING
AFGGINN	FANGING
AFGGOST	FAGGOTS
AFGHHIS	HAGFISH
AFGHINS	FASHING
AFGHINT	HAFTING
AFGHIRS	GARFISH
AFGHLSU	GASHFUL
AFGHLTU	FLAUGHT
AFGHRTU	FRAUGHT
AFGIIKN	FAIKING
AFGIILN	FAILING
AFGIINN	FAINING
AFGIINR	FAIRING
AFGIINT	FIATING
AFGIINW	WAIFING
AFGIKLN	FLAKING
AFGILLN	FALLING
AFGILMN	FLAMING
AFGILNO	FOALING
	LOAFING
AFGILNR	FLARING
AFGILNS	FALSING
AFGILNT	FATLING
AFGILNU	GAINFUL
AFGILNW	FLAWING
AFGILNY	ANGLIFY
	FLAYING
AFGILRU	FIGURAL
AFGIMNO	FOAMING
AFGIMNR	FARMING
	FRAMING
AFGIMNY	MAGNIFY
AFGINNN	FANNING
AFGINNS	FINGANS
AFGINNW	FAWNING
AFGINNY	FAYNING
AFGINRR	FARRING
AFGINRS	FARSING
AFGINRT	FARTING
	INGRAFT
	RAFTING
AFGINRY	FRAYING
AFGINST	FASTING
AFGINTT	FATTING
AFGINTW	WAFTING
AFGIOTT	FAGOTTI
AFGIRTY	GRATIFY
AFGKNOP	PAKFONG
AFGKORT	KOFTGAR

AFGLLLY	GALLFLY
AFGLLUY	FUGALLY
AFGLNOS	FLAGONS
AFGLRYY	GRAYFLY
AFGMNOR	FROGMAN
AFGMORS	FOGRAMS
AFGOOTT	FAGOTTO
AFGORRS	FRAGORS
AFGOSTU	FUGATOS
AFHIIRS	FAIRISH
AFHIKLS	KHALIFS
AFHIKRS	KHARIFS
AFHIKUY	KUFIYAH
AFHILLN	HALFLIN
AFHILSS	FALSISH
AFHILTW	HALFWIT
AFHIMNU	HAFNIUM
AFHINOS	FASHION
AFHINTU	UNFAITH
AFHIRSS	SHARIFS
AFHISST	FASTISH
AFHISSW	SAWFISH
AFHISTT	FATTISH
AFHKORY	HAYFORK
AFHKRTU	FUTHARK
AFHLMRU	HARMFUL
AFHLMSU	FULHAMS
AFHLOOS	LOOFAHS
AFHLOTY	HAYLOFT
AFHLSTU	HATFULS
AFHMOST	FATHOMS
AFHOOPT	POOFTAH
AFHOPTU	POUFTAH
AFHORSS	SHOFARS
AFIILNS	FINIALS
AFIILOR	AIRFOIL
AFIILRT	AIRLIFT
AFIILRY	FAIRILY
AFIIMOS	MAFIOSI
AFIJNNS	FINJANS
AFIKLOT	FLOKATI
AFIKNRT	RATFINK
AFIKNSU	FUNKIAS
AFIKRSS	FRISKAS
AFILLMS	MISFALL
AFILLNS	INFALLS
AFILLNY	FINALLY
AFILLPT	PITFALL
AFILLPU	PAILFUL
AFILLRY	FRAILLY
AFILLUV	FLUVIAL
	VIALFUL
AFILLUW	WAILFUL
AFILMOR	ALIFORM
AFILMOY	FOAMILY
AFILMPY	AMPLIFY
AFILMSS	FALSISM
AFILNPU	PAINFUL
AFILNSV	FLAVINS
AFILNTU	FLUTINA
AFILNTY	FAINTLY
AFILORW	AIRFLOW
AFILQUY	QUALIFY
AFILRRY	FRIARLY
AFILRSZ	FRAZILS
AFILRTY	FRAILTY
AFILSSY	SALSIFY
AFILSTU	FISTULA
AFILSTY	FALSITY
AFIMNRS	FIRMANS

AFIMOOS	MAFIOSO
AFIMORV	AVIFORM
AFIMSSS	MASSIFS
AFIMSSV	FAVISMS
AFINNNS	FINNANS
AFINNOR	FRANION
AFINNOS	FANIONS
AFINNST	INFANTS
AFINRSU	UNFAIRS
AFINSSU	FUSAINS
AFINSTU	FAUNIST
	FIAUNTS
	FUSTIAN
	INFAUST
AFIORST	FAITORS
AFIORTU	FAITOUR
AFIORTZ	FORZATI
AFIQRSU	FAQUIRS
AFISSTT	SITFAST
AFISSTY	SATISFY
AFITTUY	FATUITY
AFJLRSU	JARFULS
AFKLNRY	FRANKLY
AFKLNTU	TANKFUL
AFKLOWY	FOLKWAY
AFLLMPU	PALMFUL
AFLLMSU	FULLAMS
AFLLNOS	ONFALLS
AFLLNSU	FULLANS
AFLLOOY	ALOOFLY
AFLLOSW	FALLOWS
AFLLOTU	FALLOUT
	OUTFALL
AFLLPSU	LAPFULS
AFLLPUY	PLAYFUL
AFLLUWY	AWFULLY
AFLMNOU	MOANFUL
AFLMORU	FORMULA
AFLMORW	WOLFRAM
AFLMOST	FLOTSAM
AFLMRSU	ARMFULS
	FULMARS
AFLMSTU	MASTFUL
AFLMSUU	FAMULUS
AFLNORT	FRONTAL
AFLNOTT	FLOTANT
AFLNPSU	PANFULS
AFLNRTU	RUNFLAT
AFLNSTU	FLAUNTS
AFLNTUY	FLAUNTY
AFLOOTW	WOOLFAT
AFLORSU	FUSAROL
AFLORSV	FLAVORS
AFLORUV	FLAVOUR
AFLORWW	WARWOLF
AFLOSSU	FOSSULA
AFLPRTY	FLYTRAP
AFLRTUY	TRAYFUL
AFLSTUV	VATFULS
AFLSWYY	FLYWAYS
AFMNOOT	FOOTMAN
AFMNORT	FORMANT
AFMNOST	FANTOMS
AFMNRSU	SURFMAN
AFMNRTU	TURFMAN
AFMOOSS	SAMFOOS
AFMORST	FARMOST
	FORMATS
AFMORTU	FOUMART
AFMOSTT	AFTMOST

AFMOSTU	SFUMATO
AFNORRW	FORWARN
AFNSSTU	SUNFAST
AFOOPPR	APPROOF
AFOORST	FOOTRAS
AFOORTZ	FORZATO
AFOOTWY	FOOTWAY
AFORRSW	FARROWS
AFORRSY	FORRAYS
AFORSSY	FORSAYS
AFORSTU	FAUTORS
	FOUTRAS
AFORSUV	FAVOURS
AFOSSSU	FOUSSAS
AFOSTUU	FATUOUS
AFPSTUW	UPWAFTS
AGGGGIN	GAGGING
AGGGHIN	HAGGING
AGGGIJN	JAGGING
AGGGILN	LAGGING
AGGGIMN	MAGGING
AGGGINN	GANGING
	NAGGING
AGGGINR	RAGGING
AGGGINS	SAGGING
AGGGINT	TAGGING
AGGGINU	GAUGING
AGGGINW	WAGGING
AGGGINZ	ZAGGING
AGGHHIS	HAGGISH
AGGHIIL	GHILGAI
AGGHIMN	GINGHAM
AGGHINN	HANGING
AGGHINS	GASHING
AGGHISW	WAGGISH
AGGIIJJ	JIGAJIG
AGGIILS	GILGAIS
AGGIIMN	IMAGING
AGGIINN	GAINING
AGGIINT	GAITING
AGGIJJO	JIGAJOG
AGGIKNW	GAWKING
AGGILLN	GALLING
	GINGALL
AGGILNN	ANGLING
AGGILNO	GAOLING
	GOALING
AGGILNR	GLARING
AGGILNS	GINGALS
	LAGGINS
AGGILNZ	GLAZING
AGGILOS	LOGGIAS
AGGIMMN	GAMMING
AGGIMNN	MANGING
AGGIMNS	GAMINGS
AGGIMNU	GAUMING
AGGINNP	PANGING
AGGINNR	RANGING
AGGINNT	GANTING
	TANGING
AGGINNW	GNAWING
AGGINPP	GAPPING
AGGINPR	GRAPING
	PARGING
AGGINPS	GAPINGS
	GASPING
	PAGINGS
AGGINPU	GAUPING
AGGINPW	GAWPING
AGGINRR	GARRING
AGGINRS	RAGINGS
	SIRGANG
AGGINRT	GRATING
	TARGING
AGGINRU	ARGUING
AGGINRV	GRAVING
AGGINRY	GRAYING
AGGINRZ	GRAZING
AGGINSS	GASSING
AGGINST	GASTING
	GATINGS
	STAGING
AGGINSW	SWAGING
AGGINUV	VAGUING
AGGIORS	GORGIAS
AGGISWW	WIGWAGS
AGGISZZ	ZIGZAGS
AGGLOST	LOGGATS
AGGMNOS	MOGGANS
AGGMORR	GROGRAM
AGGMOST	MAGGOTS
AGGMOTY	MAGGOTY
AGGNOSU	GUANGOS
AGGNOSW	WAGGONS
AGGNOSX	OXGANGS
AGGNPSU	UPGANGS
AGGNRSU	NUGGARS
AGGPRSY	PYGARGS
AGHHIMN	HIGHMAN
AGHHINS	HASHING
AGHHIWY	HIGHWAY
AGHHOSW	HOGWASH
AGHHTUY	HAUGHTY
AGHIILN	HAILING
AGHIINN	HAINING
AGHIINR	HAIRING
AGHIJRS	JAGHIRS
AGHIKNN	HANKING
AGHIKNR	HARKING
AGHIKNS	SHAKING
AGHIKNW	HAWKING
AGHIKSU	KIAUGHS
AGHILLN	HALLING
AGHILNO	HALOING
AGHILNR	HARLING
AGHILNS	HALSING
	LASHING
	SHALING
AGHILNT	HALTING
	LATHING
AGHILNU	HAULING
AGHILNV	HALVING
AGHILNW	WHALING
AGHILRS	LARGISH
AGHILRT	ALRIGHT
AGHILST	ALIGHTS
AGHIMMN	HAMMING
AGHIMNR	HARMING
AGHIMNS	MASHING
	SHAMING
AGHIMNW	HAWMING
AGHIMPS	GAMPISH
AGHINNO	NIHONGA
AGHINNT	TANGHIN
AGHINOR	HOARING
AGHINOX	HOAXING
AGHINPP	HAPPING
AGHINPR	HARPING
AGHINPS	HASPING
	PASHING
	PHASING
	SHAPING
AGHINPT	PATHING
AGHINRS	GARNISH
	RASHING
	SHARING
AGHINRU	NURAGHI
AGHINSS	SASHING
AGHINST	HASTING
	TASHING
AGHINSU	ANGUISH
	HAUSING
AGHINSV	HAVINGS
	SHAVING
AGHINSW	HAWSING
	WASHING
AGHINSY	HAYINGS
AGHINSZ	HAZINGS
AGHINTT	HATTING
	TATHING
AGHINTW	THAWING
AGHIOST	GOATISH
AGHIPSW	PIGWASH
AGHIQSU	QUAIGHS
AGHIRRS	GHARRIS
AGHIRST	GRAITHS
AGHIRSU	GUARISH
AGHKOSW	GOSHAWK
AGHLMPU	GALUMPH
AGHLNUY	NYLGHAU
AGHLOOS	GASOHOL
AGHLOSU	GOULASH
AGHLSTU	GALUTHS
AGHLSTY	GHASTLY
AGHNNSU	UNHANGS
AGHNOTU	HANGOUT
	TOHUNGA
AGHNPSU	UPHANGS
AGHNRST	THRANGS
AGHNRSU	NURHAGS
AGHNRUY	AHUNGRY
AGHNSTU	NAUGHTS
AGHNSUY	GUNYAHS
AGHNTUY	NAUGHTY
AGHOQSU	QUAHOGS
AGHORTW	WARTHOG
AGHPTUY	PAUGHTY
AGHRRSU	GURRAHS
AGHRSTU	TUGHRAS
AGHRSTY	GYTRASH
AGHSTUW	WAUGHTS
AGIIJLN	JAILING
AGIIKLN	LAIKING
AGIIKLT	GLAIKIT
AGIIKNP	PAIKING
AGIIKNR	RAIKING
AGIILMN	MAILING
AGIILNN	ALINING
	NAILING
AGIILNR	GLAIRIN
	LAIRING
	RAILING
AGIILNS	AISLING
	NILGAIS
	SAILING
AGIILNT	TAILING
AGIILNV	VAILING
AGIILNW	WAILING
AGIILOV	VILIAGO
AGIILPT	PIGTAIL
AGIILTY	AGILITY
AGIIMMN	MAIMING
AGIIMMS	IMAGISM
AGIIMNN	MAINING
AGIIMOR	ORIGAMI
AGIIMST	IMAGIST
AGIINNP	PAINING
AGIINNR	AIRNING
	INGRAIN
	RAINING
AGIINNS	SAINING
AGIINNW	WAINING
AGIINPR	PAIRING
AGIINRS	AIRINGS
	ARISING
	RAGINIS
	RAISING
	SAIRING
AGIINRT	AIRTING
	RAITING
AGIINSV	AVISING
	VISAING
AGIINTW	WAITING
AGIINTX	TAXIING
AGIINVV	VIVAING
AGIINVW	WAIVING
AGIINVZ	AVIZING
AGIJLNS	JINGALS
AGIJMMN	JAMMING
AGIJNPP	JAPPING
AGIJNPS	JAPINGS
AGIJNPU	JAUPING
AGIJNRR	JARRING
AGIJNSW	JAWINGS
AGIJNZZ	JAZZING
AGIJSSW	JIGSAWS
AGIKKNY	YAKKING
AGIKLNN	LANKING
AGIKLNO	OAKLING
AGIKLNR	LARKING
AGIKLNS	SLAKING
AGIKLNT	TALKING
AGIKLNW	WALKING
AGIKMNR	MARKING
AGIKMNS	MAKINGS
	MASKING
AGIKNNR	NARKING
	RANKING
AGIKNNS	SNAKING
AGIKNNT	KANTING
	TANKING
AGIKNNU	UNAKING
AGIKNNW	WANKING
AGIKNNY	YANKING
AGIKNOS	SOAKING
AGIKNOY	KAYOING
	OKAYING
AGIKNPR	PARKING
AGIKNQU	QUAKING
AGIKNRS	RAKINGS
	SARKING
AGIKNRT	KARTING
AGIKNSS	GASKINS
AGIKNST	SKATING
	STAKING
	TAKINGS
	TASKING
AGIKNSW	WAKINGS
AGIKNUW	WAUKING
AGILLLN	LALLING

AGILLMN MALLING
AGILLMU GALLIUM
AGILLNP PALLING
AGILLNU LINGUAL
LINGULA
AGILLNW WALLING
AGILLNY ALLYING
AGILLOR GORILLA
AGILLOT GALLIOT
AGILLRU LIGULAR
AGILLSU LIGULAS
LUGSAIL
AGILMMN LAMMING
AGILMMS GIMMALS
AGILMNO LOAMING
AGILMNP LAMPING
PALMING
AGILMNR MARLING
AGILMNS LINGAMS
MALIGNS
AGILMNT MALTING
AGILMNU MAULING
AGILMOS GLIOMAS
AGILMPS MAGILPS
AGILMPU PLAGIUM
AGILNNO LOANING
AGILNNP PLANING
AGILNNR LARNING
AGILNNS LINSANG
AGILNNT TANLING
AGILNOP GALOPIN
AGILNOR RANGOLI
AGILNOT ANTILOG
AGILNOV LOAVING
AGILNOZ LAZOING
AGILNPP LAPPING
PALPING
AGILNPR PARLING
AGILNPS LAPSING
PALINGS
SAPLING
AGILNPT PLATING
AGILNPW LAPWING
AGILNPY PLAYING
AGILNRT RATLING
AGILNRW WARLING
AGILNRY ANGRILY
NARGILY
RAYLING
AGILNSS LASINGS
SIGNALS
AGILNST ANGLIST
LASTING
SALTING
SLATING
STALING
AGILNSU LINGUAS
NILGAUS
SALUING
AGILNSV SALVING
SLAVING
VALSING
AGILNSW LAWINGS
SWALING
AGILNSY LAYINGS
SLAYING
AGILNTY GIANTLY
AGILNUV VALUING
AGILNUW WAULING
AGILNVV VALVING
AGILNWW WAWLING
AGILNWY YAWLING
AGILOPT GALIPOT
AGILORS GIRASOL
GLORIAS
AGILOST GALIOTS
SALIGOT
AGILRSS SLAIRGS
AGILSTY STAGILY
AGIMMNR RAMMING
AGIMMSS MAGISMS
AGIMNNN MANNING
AGIMNNO MOANING
AGIMNNR RINGMAN
AGIMNNS NAMINGS
AGIMNOR ROAMING
AGIMNOT MOATING
AGIMNOV AMOVING
AGIMNPP MAPPING
AGIMNPR RAMPING
AGIMNPT TAMPING
AGIMNPV VAMPING
AGIMNRR MARRING
AGIMNRS MARGINS
AGIMNRT MARTING
MIGRANT
AGIMNRW WARMING
AGIMNRY MYRINGA
AGIMNSS MASSING
AGIMNST MASTING
TAMINGS
AGIMNSU AMUSING
AGIMNSY MAYINGS
AGIMNTT MATTING
AGIMORS ISOGRAM
AGIMORU GOURAMI
AGIMOSY ISOGAMY
AGIMRRT TRIGRAM
AGIMRSU GURAMIS
AGIMRTY TRIGAMY
AGIMSST STIGMAS
AGIMSWW WIGWAMS
AGINNNP PANNING
AGINNNT TANNING
AGINNNV VANNING
AGINNNW WANNING
AGINNOS GANOINS
AGINNOT ATONING
AGINNPP NAPPING
AGINNPS SPANING
AGINNPT PANTING
AGINNPW PAWNING
AGINNRS SNARING
AGINNRT RANTING
AGINNRW WARNING
AGINNRY YARNING
AGINNST ANTINGS
STANING
AGINNSW AWNINGS
WANINGS
AGINNTW WANTING
AGINNWY YAWNING
AGINNWZ WANZING
AGINNYZ ZANYING
AGINOOO OOGONIA
AGINOPS SOAPING
AGINORR ROARING
AGINORS IGNAROS
ORIGANS
SIGNORA
SOARING
AGINORT ORATING
ROATING
AGINOSS SAGOINS
AGINOST AGONIST
GITANOS
AGINOSU SAGOUIN
AGINOTV OVATING
AGINOTZ TOAZING
AGINOVW AVOWING
AGINPPP PAPPING
AGINPPR PARPING
RAPPING
AGINPPS SAPPING
AGINPPT TAPPING
AGINPPW WAPPING
AGINPPY YAPPING
AGINPPZ ZAPPING
AGINPRS PARINGS
PARSING
RASPING
SPARING
AGINPRT PARTING
PRATING
TRAPING
AGINPRW WARPING
AGINPRY PRAYING
AGINPSS PASSING
SPAINGS
AGINPST PASTING
AGINPSU PAUSING
AGINPSV PAVINGS
AGINPSY PAYINGS
SPAYING
AGINPTT PATTING
AGINPTU TAPUING
AGINPWY YAWPING
AGINRRT TARRING
AGINRRW WARRING
AGINRST GASTRIN
GRATINS
RATINGS
STARING
TARINGS
AGINRSV RAVINGS
AGINRSW RAWINGS
AGINRSY SIGNARY
SYRINGA
AGINRTT RATTING
AGINRTY GIANTRY
AGINRUW WAURING
AGINRVY VARYING
AGINRWY RINGWAY
AGINRZZ RAZZING
AGINSSS ASSIGNS
SASSING
AGINSSU SAGUINS
AGINSSV SAVINGS
AGINSSW SAWINGS
AGINSSY SAYINGS
AGINSTT STATING
TASTING
AGINSTU SAUTING
AGINSTV STAVING
AGINSTW STAWING
TAWINGS
WASTING
AGINSTX TAXINGS
AGINSTY STAYING
AGINSVW WAVINGS
AGINSWX WAXINGS
AGINSWY SWAYING
AGINTTT TATTING
AGINTTU TATUING
TAUTING
AGINTTV VATTING
AGINTTW TAWTING
AGINTUV VAUTING
AGINTVW VAWTING
AGINTXY TAXYING
AGINTYZ TZIGANY
AGINVYZ AVYZING
AGINWWX WAXWING
AGIORST AGISTOR
ORGIAST
AGIORSU GIAOURS
AGIORSV VIRAGOS
AGIOSTU AGOUTIS
AGIRSTU GUITARS
AGIRTVY GRAVITY
AGISTTW WITGATS
AGISTUV VAGITUS
AGJLRUU JUGULAR
AGJNOOR JARGOON
AGJNORS JARGONS
AGKLNNO ANKLONG
AGKLNNU ANKLUNG
AGKLNOS KALONGS
AGKLOST KGOTLAS
AGKMNOP KAMPONG
AGKNOPT PAKTONG
AGKNRSU KURGANS
AGKORRW RAGWORK
AGLLNOO GALLOON
AGLLNOS GALLONS
GOLLANS
AGLLNTU GALLNUT
NUTGALL
AGLLOPS GALLOPS
AGLLORS GOLLARS
AGLLOSS GLOSSAL
AGLLOSW GALLOWS
AGLLOTT GLOTTAL
AGLLRYY GYRALLY
AGLMMSY GYMMALS
AGLMOPY POLYGAM
AGLMORS GLAMORS
AGLMORU GLAMOUR
AGLNNOS LONGANS
AGLNOOS LAGOONS
AGLNORU LANGUOR
AGLNOSS SLOGANS
AGLNOST ALONGST
AGLNOSU LANUGOS
AGLNOSW GOWLANS
AGLNPSY SPANGLY
AGLNPUY GUNPLAY
AGLNRSU LANGURS
AGLNTUY GAUNTLY
AGLOOPY APOLOGY
AGLOOST GALOOTS
AGLOSSS GLOSSAS
AGLOSUV VALGOUS
AGLRSSU GUSLARS
AGLRSUU ARGULUS
AGLRSUV VULGARS
AGMMNOS GAMMONS
AGMMNSU MAGNUMS
AGMMORY MYOGRAM
AGMNNOS MAGNONS

	SONGMAN
AGMNNOW	GOWNMAN
AGMNORU	ORGANUM
AGMNOST	AMONGST
AGMNSSU	MUSANGS
AGMNSTU	MUSTANG
AGMNSTY	GYMNAST
	SYNTAGM
AGMNSYY	SYNGAMY
AGMOOYZ	ZOOGAMY
AGMOPRR	PROGRAM
AGMOPRU	GOPURAM
AGMORRW	RAGWORM
AGMORSS	ORGASMS
AGMORSY	MORGAYS
AGMOSYZ	ZYGOMAS
AGMPRSU	GRAMPUS
AGMPSUZ	GAZUMPS
AGMRSSU	GRASSUM
AGNNNOO	NONAGON
AGNNOOR	ORGANON
AGNNOST	TONNAGS
AGNNSTU	TANGUNS
AGNNSUW	WANGUNS
AGNOOSZ	GAZOONS
AGNOQSU	QUANGOS
AGNORRS	GARRONS
AGNORRT	GRANTOR
AGNORSS	SARONGS
AGNOSSS	GOSSANS
AGNOSST	SONTAGS
AGNOSTU	NOUGATS
AGNOSZZ	GOZZANS
AGNRSSU	SUNGARS
AGNRTUY	GAUNTRY
AGOPPST	STOPGAP
AGOPRST	RAGTOPS
AGOPRSU	GOPURAS
AGORRST	GARROTS
AGORRTW	RAGWORT
AGORSTU	RAGOUTS
AGOSTTU	TAUTOGS
AGOSUYZ	AZYGOUS
AGSSTUU	AUGUSTS
AHHHISS	HASHISH
AHHIJRS	HIJRAHS
AHHIKSS	SHAIKHS
AHHIKSW	HAWKISH
AHHIMNU	HAHNIUM
AHHIPRS	RHAPHIS
AHHISSV	SHIVAHS
AHHISTT	SHITTAH
AHHKOOS	HOOKAHS
AHHLRSY	HARSHLY
AHHOORS	HOORAHS
AHHOPRS	SHOPHAR
AHHPPSU	HUPPAHS
AHHPTUZ	HUTZPAH
AHHRRSU	HURRAHS
AHIIKRS	SHIKARI
AHIILPS	SILPHIA
AHIILST	LITHIAS
AHIIMNT	THIAMIN
AHIIMSS	SASHIMI
AHIINPR	HAIRPIN
AHIINST	TAHINIS
AHIINTU	HUITAIN
AHIIPRS	AIRSHIP
AHIKLRS	LARKISH
AHIKLST	KHILATS
AHIKLSY	SHAKILY
AHIKMNS	KHAMSIN
AHIKMRS	KASHMIR
AHIKMSW	MAWKISH
AHIKNSS	SNAKISH
AHIKNSV	KNAVISH
AHIKOSW	KOWHAIS
AHIKPRS	PARKISH
AHIKRSS	SHIKARS
AHIKSSS	SHIKSAS
AHIKSST	SKAITHS
AHILLNO	HALLION
AHILLNP	PHALLIN
AHILLRT	ATHRILL
AHILLSS	SHALLIS
AHILLST	TALLISH
AHILLSZ	ZILLAHS
AHILLTT	TALLITH
AHILMMS	MASHLIM
AHILMMY	HAMMILY
AHILMNS	MASHLIN
AHILMOS	HOLMIAS
AHILMOT	HALIMOT
AHILMSU	ALUMISH
AHILNPS	PLANISH
AHILNRS	SHRINAL
AHILNRT	INTHRAL
AHILNSU	INHAULS
AHILNSY	LINHAYS
AHILORY	HOARILY
AHILPPS	SHIPLAP
AHILPPY	HAPPILY
AHILPSY	APISHLY
AHILSST	SALTISH
	TAHSILS
AHILSSV	SLAVISH
AHILSTU	HALITUS
	THULIAS
AHILSTY	HASTILY
AHIMMRS	RAMMISH
AHIMNNS	MANNISH
AHIMNNU	INHUMAN
AHIMNPS	SHIPMAN
AHIMNRS	HARMINS
AHIMOPR	MORPHIA
AHIMORS	MOHAIRS
AHIMPSS	MISHAPS
	PASHIMS
AHIMPST	MISHAPT
AHIMPSV	VAMPISH
AHIMPSW	WAMPISH
AHIMRSS	MAHSIRS
AHIMRST	THAIRMS
	THIRAMS
	THRIMSA
AHIMRSW	WARMISH
AHIMTUZ	AZIMUTH
AHIMTVZ	MITZVAH
AHINNSW	WANNISH
AHINNTX	XANTHIN
AHINORT	ORTHIAN
AHINOTZ	HOATZIN
AHINPST	HATPINS
AHINRSS	ARSHINS
	SHAIRNS
AHINRST	TARNISH
AHINRSU	UNHAIRS
AHINRSV	VARNISH
AHINRTY	RHYTINA
AHINSTU	INHAUST
AHIOOST	ATISHOO
AHIOPRU	OPHIURA
AHIOPXY	HYPOXIA
AHIORST	THORIAS
AHIORUV	HAVIOUR
AHIPRST	HARPIST
AHIPRSU	RUPIAHS
AHIPRSW	WARSHIP
AHIPSSW	WASPISH
AHIPSWW	WHIPSAW
AHIPSWY	SHIPWAY
AHIRRSS	SHIRRAS
	SIRRAHS
AHIRRST	STIRRAH
AHIRSST	HAIRSTS
AHIRSTT	ATHIRST
	RATTISH
	TARTISH
AHIRSTW	TRISHAW
	WRAITHS
AHISSTT	STAITHS
AHISSTU	SHIATSU
	THIASUS
AHISSTW	WHATSIS
AHISTTW	WHATSIT
AHISTUZ	SHIATZU
AHITTWW	WHITTAW
AHJOOPS	POOJAHS
AHKKSSU	SUKKAHS
AHKLOOS	KOOLAHS
AHKLPSU	PULKHAS
AHKMNSU	KHANUMS
AHKMORR	MARKHOR
AHKMOSW	MOHAWKS
AHKMRTU	MUKHTAR
AHKNPSU	PUNKAHS
AHKRSST	SKARTHS
AHKRSSU	KASHRUS
AHKRSTU	KASHRUT
	KHURTAS
	TUSHKAR
AHLLMOS	MOLLAHS
	OLLAMHS
AHLLMSU	MULLAHS
AHLLNOS	SHALLON
AHLLNOY	HALLYON
AHLLNSU	NULLAHS
AHLLOOS	HALLOOS
	HOLLOAS
AHLLOPS	SHALLOP
AHLLOST	SHALLOT
AHLLOSW	HALLOWS
	SHALLOW
AHLLOTY	LOATHLY
AHLLPSU	PHALLUS
AHLLPYY	APHYLLY
AHLLRST	THRALLS
AHLLSTU	THALLUS
AHLMMSU	MASHLUM
AHLMNPY	NYMPHAL
AHLMNSY	HYMNALS
AHLMNUY	HUMANLY
AHLMOOS	MOOLAHS
AHLMORU	HUMORAL
AHLMSTZ	SHMALTZ
AHLMSUU	HAMULUS
AHLNOPR	ALPHORN
AHLNORT	ALTHORN
AHLORST	HARLOTS
AHLOSST	SHALOTS
AHLOSTU	OUTLASH
AHLOTUU	OUTHAUL
AHLPRSY	SHARPLY
AHLPRUY	HYPURAL
AHLPSSU	SULPHAS
AHLPSSY	SPLASHY
AHMMMOT	MAMMOTH
AHMMMUU	HUMMAUM
AHMMOSW	WHAMMOS
AHMNNSU	NUMNAHS
AHMNNTU	MANHUNT
AHMNNUU	UNHUMAN
AHMNOPS	SHOPMAN
AHMNOPT	PHANTOM
AHMNORY	HARMONY
AHMNOSS	HANSOMS
AHMNOSW	SHOWMAN
AHMNRYY	HYMNARY
AHMOOPS	OOMPAHS
	SHAMPOO
AHMOOSS	SAMSHOO
AHMORRU	MORRHUA
AHMORST	HARMOST
AHMOSSY	SHAMOYS
AHMOSTU	MAHOUTS
AHMOSWY	HAYMOWS
AHMOTTZ	MATZOTH
AHMRRSU	MURRHAS
AHMRSTW	WARMTHS
AHMRSTY	THRYMSA
AHMSSSU	SAMSHUS
AHNOOPR	HARPOON
AHNOPRS	ORPHANS
AHNORSS	SHORANS
AHNORSX	SAXHORN
AHNOTTW	WHATNOT
AHNPPUU	PUPUNHA
AHNPPUY	UNHAPPY
AHNPRXY	PHARYNX
AHNPSSU	UNHASPS
AHNSSTU	SUNHATS
AHNSTUW	UNTHAWS
AHNSTUY	UNHASTY
AHOORSY	HOORAYS
AHOPRTY	ATROPHY
AHOPSTW	WASHPOT
AHOPTTW	TOWPATH
AHORRSW	HARROWS
AHORSTT	THROATS
AHORSTU	AUTHORS
AHORSTW	WROATHS
AHORTTY	THROATY
AHOSTUW	OUTWASH
	WASHOUT
AHPRRTY	PHRATRY
AHPRSST	SPARTHS
AHPSXYY	ASPHYXY
AHQSSUY	SQUASHY
AHRRSUY	HURRAYS
AHRSSSU	HUSSARS
AHRSSTT	STRATHS
AHRSSTW	SWARTHS
AHRSTTW	THWARTS
AHRSTWY	SWARTHY
AHRTUWY	THRUWAY
AHSSSTU	TUSSAHS
AIIILMT	MILITIA
AIIILNT	INITIAL
AIIILVX	LIXIVIA
AIIIMRS	SAIMIRI

AIIKKSW WAKIKIS
AIIKMMS SKIMMIA
AIIKMNN MANIKIN
AIIKRTT TRAIKIT
AIILLLP LAPILLI
AIILLMN LIMINAL
AIILLMS LIMAILS
AIILLNV VILLAIN
AIILLQU QUILLAI
AIILLUV ILLUVIA
AIILMMN MINIMAL
AIILMNO MONILIA
AIILMRS SIMILAR
AIILMRT MILITAR
AIILMRY MILIARY
AIILNOS LIAISON
AIILNPT PINTAIL
AIILNPU NAUPLII
AIILNTU NAUTILI
AIILNTY ANILITY
AIILOPP PAPILIO
AIILORV RAVIOLI
AIILQSU SILIQUA
AIILRTV TRIVIAL
VITRAIL
AIIMMNS ANIMISM
AIIMMNX MAXIMIN
MINIMAX
AIIMMSS MISAIMS
AIIMNOR AMORINI
AIIMNPS PAINIMS
PIANISM
AIIMNPT IMPAINT
TIMPANI
AIIMNRT MARTINI
AIIMNSS SIMIANS
AIIMNST ANIMIST
AIIMNTT IMITANT
AIIMNTU MINUTIA
AIIMNTV VITAMIN
AIIMPRS IMPAIRS
AIIMPSS SIMPAIS
AIIMRST SIMITAR
AIIMSST SAMITIS
AIIMSSY MYIASIS
AIINNOP PIANINO
AIINNSZ ZINNIAS
AIINNTY INANITY
AIINOPS SINOPIA
AIINOTT NOTITIA
AIINPRS ASPIRIN
AIINPST PIANIST
AIINRSS RAISINS
AIINRTV VITRAIN
AIINSST ISATINS
AIINSSX SIXAINS
AIINSTT TITANIS
TITIANS
AIINSTV NAIVIST
AIIPRST PIARIST
AIIPSTW WAPITIS
AIIPTTU PITUITA
AIJJMMS JIMJAMS
AIJLORS JAILORS
AIJLSTW WILTJAS
AIJLYZZ JAZZILY
AIJNORT JANITOR
AIJORSW JOWARIS
AIJPSTU JUPATIS
AIKKMOT KOMATIK

AIKKSUZ ZAKUSKI
AIKLLNY LANKILY
AIKLMMN MILKMAN
AIKLMNN LINKMAN
AIKLMNS MALKINS
AIKLMPU LAMPUKI
AIKLMSU KALIUMS
AIKLNOS KAOLINS
AIKLNSY SNAKILY
AIKLPWY PAWKILY
AIKLRTT TITLARK
AIKLSSU SALUKIS
AIKLSSY SKYSAIL
AIKMMSS IMMASKS
AIKMNNS KINSMAN
AIKMNSS KAMSINS
AIKMNSW MAWKINS
AIKMOOS OOMIAKS
AIKMPRS IMPARKS
AIKMRSU KUMARIS
AIKNNNS NANKINS
AIKNNPS NAPKINS
AIKNOST KATIONS
AIKNPRS KIRPANS
PARKINS
AIKNPSS PANISKS
AIKOPST KATIPOS
AIKORST TROIKAS
AIKRRSS SIRKARS
AIKRSST STRAIKS
AILLMNU LUMINAL
AILLMOT MAILLOT
AILLMPU PALLIUM
AILLMSU ALLIUMS
AILLMSW SAWMILL
AILLMSY MISALLY
AILLNNO LANOLIN
AILLNOP PAILLON
AILLNPY PLAINLY
AILLNST INSTALL
AILLNSV VILLANS
AILLNSW INWALLS
AILLNVY VILLANY
AILLPRS PILLARS
AILLPRU PILULAR
AILLPSU PILLAUS
PILULAS
AILLPUV PLUVIAL
AILLQSU SQUILLA
AILLRSU ARILLUS
AILLSTY SALTILY
AILLTVY VITALLY
AILLTWW WITWALL
AILMMOR IMMORAL
AILMMSS MALISMS
AILMMSY MYALISM
AILMMUU ALUMIUM
AILMNNO NOMINAL
AILMNOP LAMPION
AILMNOS MALISON
MONIALS
SOMNIAL
AILMNOY ALIMONY
AILMNPS PLASMIN
AILMNPT IMPLANT
AILMNRS MARLINS
AILMNRU MURLAIN
AILMNSS MASLINS
AILMOPT OPTIMAL
AILMORS ORALISM

AILMOST SOMITAL
AILMPRS IMPARLS
AILMPRU PRIMULA
AILMPST PALMIST
AILMPSY MISPLAY
AILMRST MISTRAL
AILMRSU SIMULAR
AILMSSS MISSALS
AILMSSX LAXISMS
AILMSSY MISLAYS
AILMSTU ULTIMAS
AILMSUV MAULVIS
AILNNOT ANTLION
AILNNPU PINNULA
AILNNSU UNNAILS
UNSLAIN
AILNOPY POLYNIA
AILNOQU AQUILON
AILNOSS SIALONS
AILNOST TALIONS
AILNOTU OUTLAIN
AILNPRW PRAWLIN
AILNPST PLAINTS
AILNPSX SALPINX
AILNPTU NUPTIAL
PATULIN
UNPLAIT
AILNPTY INAPTLY
PTYALIN
AILNQTU QUINTAL
AILNRST RATLINS
AILNRSU INSULAR
URINALS
AILNRTT RATTLIN
AILNSST INSTALS
AILNSSU INSULAS
AILNSSV SILVANS
AILNSTU UNALIST
AILNSTY NASTILY
SAINTLY
AILNSUV UNVAILS
AILNTTY NATTILY
AILNTUV UNVITAL
AILOORS OORIALS
AILOORW WOORALI
AILOPST APOSTIL
TOPSAIL
AILOPSY SOAPILY
AILOPTT TALIPOT
AILOPTV PIVOTAL
AILOQTU ALIQUOT
AILORSS SAILORS
AILORST TAILORS
AILORSU OURALIS
AILORTY ORALITY
AILORUW WOURALI
AILORUX UXORIAL
AILORVY OLIVARY
AILOSSS ASSOILS
AILOSTU OUTSAIL
AILOSTX OXTAILS
AILPPRU PUPILAR
AILPPSY PAYSLIP
AILPRSS SPIRALS
AILPRSU PARULIS
UPRISAL
AILPRSY PYRALIS
AILPSST PASTILS
SPITALS
AILPSTU TIPULAS

AILPSWY SLIPWAY
AILQSSU SQUAILS
AILQTTU QUITTAL
AILQTUY QUALITY
AILRRVY RIVALRY
AILRSTT STARLIT
AILRSTU RITUALS
TRISULA
AILRSTY TRYSAIL
AILRTTU TITULAR
AILRTUV VIRTUAL
VITULAR
AILSSTX LAXISTS
AILSSUV VISUALS
AILSSVY SYLVIAS
AILSSVZ VIZSLAS
AILSTTY TASTILY
AILSTUW LAWSUIT
AILTTTY TATTILY
AIMMMSU MUMMIAS
AIMMMUX MAXIMUM
AIMMNTU MANUMIT
AIMMORS AMORISM
AIMMOSS MIMOSAS
AIMMOST ATOMISM
AIMNNOS MANSION
ONANISM
AIMNNSS NANISMS
AIMNNSY MINYANS
AIMNOOR AMORINO
AIMNOPR RAMPION
AIMNOPS MOPANIS
AIMNOPT MAINTOP
TAMPION
TIMPANO
AIMNOPZ ZAMPONI
AIMNORS MAINORS
AIMNORT TORMINA
AIMNORU MAINOUR
AIMNOST MANITOS
STAMNOI
AIMNOTU MANITOU
TINAMOU
AIMNPSW IMPAWNS
AIMNPSY PAYNIMS
AIMNPTY TYMPANI
AIMNRRU MURRAIN
AIMNRST MARTINS
AIMNRSU SURAMIN
URANISM
AIMNRTU NATRIUM
AIMNRTV VARMINT
AIMNRUU URANIUM
AIMNSTT MATTINS
AIMNSTU TSUNAMI
AIMNSUV MAUVINS
AIMNSYZ ZANYISM
AIMOPST IMPASTO
AIMOPSY MYOPIAS
AIMORRU ORARIUM
AIMORST AMORIST
AIMORUZ ZOARIUM
AIMOSTT ATOMIST
AIMPPSS PAPISMS
AIMPPST MAPPIST
AIMPRRY PRIMARY
AIMPRST ARMPITS
IMPARTS
AIMPRSY PYRAMIS
AIMQRSU MARQUIS

AIMRSST TSARISM
AIMRSTU ATRIUMS
MATSURI
AIMRSTY MAISTRY
SYMITAR
AIMSSSY MISSAYS
AIMSSTT STATISM
AIMSSTU AUTISMS
AINNNST TANNINS
AINNOPS SAPONIN
AINNOSS NASIONS
AINNOST ANOINTS
NATIONS
ONANIST
AINNPSS INSPANS
AINNPTU UNPAINT
AINNQTU QUINNAT
QUINTAN
AINNRSU URANINS
AINNRTT INTRANT
AINNRTU URINANT
AINNSTT INSTANT
AINNSTU UNSAINT
AINNTUY ANNUITY
AINOOPR PRONAOI
AINOORR ORARION
AINOORT ORATION
AINOOTV OVATION
AINOPPT APPOINT
AINOPRS PARISON
SOPRANI
AINOPRT ATROPIN
AINOPSS PASSION
AINOPTU OPUNTIA
UTOPIAN
AINOQSU QUINOAS
AINORST AROINTS
RATIONS
AINORSW WARISON
AINORTX TRIAXON
AINOSSU SANIOUS
SUASION
AINOSTT STATION
AINOSUX ANXIOUS
AINOSVY SYNOVIA
AINPPRS PARSNIP
AINPQTU PIQUANT
AINPRSS SPINARS
SPRAINS
AINPRST SPIRANT
SPRAINT
AINPRSU PRUINAS
AINPRSW INWRAPS
AINPRTU PURITAN
UPTRAIN
AINPSST PTISANS
AINPSSV SPAVINS
AINQRST QINTARS
AINQRUY QUINARY
AINQSTU ASQUINT
QUINTAS
AINQSUY YANQUIS
AINRRTY TRINARY
AINRRUY URINARY
AINRSST INSTARS
SANTIRS
STRAINS
AINRSTT STRAINT
TRANSIT
AINRSTU NUTRIAS

AINRTUY UNITARY
AINSSTT TANISTS
AINSSTU ISSUANT
SUSTAIN
AINSSXY SYNAXIS
AINTTVY TANTIVY
AIOORSS ARIOSOS
AIOPRRT AIRPORT
PARITOR
AIOPRST AIRSTOP
PAROTIS
AIOPRSV PAVIORS
AIOPRTT PATRIOT
AIOPRTY TOPIARY
AIOPRUV PAVIOUR
AIOPSTU UTOPIAS
AIORRRW WARRIOR
AIORRSU OURARIS
AIORRTT TRAITOR
AIORRTX ORATRIX
AIORSST AORISTS
ARISTOS
SATORIS
AIORSSU SOUARIS
AIORSTU SAUTOIR
AIORSTV TRAVOIS
VIATORS
AIORSTY OSTIARY
AIORSUV SAVIOUR
VARIOUS
AIPPRRS RIPRAPS
AIPPSST PAPISTS
AIPRSST RAPISTS
AIPRSTU UPSTAIR
AIPRSUY PYURIAS
AIPRTVY PRAVITY
AIPSSTT TAPISTS
AIPSSTW SAWPITS
AIRRSST STIRRAS
AIRRSZZ RIZZARS
AIRRTZZ RIZZART
AIRSSSU RUSSIAS
AIRSSTT ARTISTS
SITTARS
STRAITS
TSARIST
AIRSSTU AURISTS
AIRSTTT ATTRIST
ATTRITS
AIRSTTY YTTRIAS
AIRSTVY VARSITY
AIRTUVX VITRAUX
AISSSST ASSISTS
AISSTTT STATIST
AISTTVY VASTITY
AISTUVY SUAVITY
AJKMNNU JUNKMAN
AJKMNTU MUNTJAK
AJKNSSY JANSKYS
AJLLRUY JURALLY
AJLNORU JOURNAL
AJLOORS JAROOLS
AJLOPPY JALOPPY
AJMNRUY JURYMAN
AJMOPST JAMPOTS
AJMRSTU JUMARTS
AJNRSTU JURANTS
AKKKORU ROKKAKU
AKKLRSY SKYLARK
AKKNRSU KUNKARS

AKKOQSU QUOKKAS
AKLNOSU KOULANS
AKLNOSX KLAXONS
AKLOPRW LAPWORK
AKLOSTW KOTWALS
AKLOTTU OUTTALK
AKLOTUW OUTWALK
AKLPRSY SPARKLY
AKLRSTY STARKLY
AKMNORW WORKMAN
AKMNRTU TRANKUM
AKMNSSU UNMASKS
AKMOORT MOOKTAR
AKMQTUU KUMQUAT
AKMRSTU MUSKRAT
AKNORSU KORUNAS
AKNORSY KARYONS
RYOKANS
AKNORTU OUTRANK
AKOOPRT PARTOOK
AKOORRS KORORAS
AKOOSTU ATOKOUS
AKORRTW ARTWORK
AKORWWX WAXWORK
AKQSSUW SQUAWKS
AKQSUWY SQUAWKY
AKRSSTU TUSKARS
AKSSWYY SKYWAYS
ALLLOYY LOYALLY
ALLMNOP POLLMAN
ALLMNOT TOLLMAN
ALLMNOY ALLONYM
ALLMORS MORALLS
ALLMORY MORALLY
ALLMOSS SLALOMS
ALLMOSW MALLOWS
ALLMPUU PLUMULA
ALLMSUV VALLUMS
ALLNOPS POLLANS
ALLNOTY TONALLY
ALLNRUU LUNULAR
ALLNSTY SLANTLY
ALLNTUU ULULANT
ALLOOPS APOLLOS
PALOLOS
ALLOOTX AXOLOTL
ALLOPRS PALLORS
ALLOPRY PAYROLL
ALLOPSW WALLOPS
ALLORSS SOLLARS
ALLORYY ROYALLY
ALLOSSW SALLOWS
ALLOSTT TALLOTS
ALLOSTV LAVOLTS
ALLOSTW TALLOWS
ALLOSWW SWALLOW
WALLOWS
ALLOSWY SALLOWY
ALLOTTY TOTALLY
ALLOTWY TALLOWY
ALLOTYY LOYALTY
ALLPRSU PLURALS
ALLPSSY PSYLLAS
ALLQSSU SQUALLS
ALLQSUY SQUALLY
ALLRRUY RURALLY
ALLRSTU LUSTRAL
ALLSUUY USUALLY
ALMMSUY AMYLUMS
ALMNNUY UNMANLY

ALMNOOP LAMPOON
ALMNOOT TOOLMAN
ALMNOOW WOOLMAN
ALMNORS NORMALS
ALMNORU UNMORAL
ALMNORY ALMONRY
ALMNOSS SALMONS
ALMNOSU MONAULS
SOLANUM
ALMNOWY WOMANLY
ALMNPSU SUNLAMP
ALMNRSU MURLANS
ALMNSUU ALUMNUS
ALMOOPY POLYOMA
ALMOPPT PALMTOP
ALMOPRT MARPLOT
ALMORRU MORULAR
ALMORSS SAMLORS
ALMORST MORTALS
ALMOSST SMALTOS
ALMOSTW MATLOWS
ALMOSXY XYLOMAS
ALMOTTU MULATTO
ALMRSTY SMARTLY
ALMRSUU RAMULUS
ALMRTUU TUMULAR
ALMSSUY ALYSSUM
ASYLUMS
ALMSTUU UMLAUTS
ALNNRSU UNSNARL
ALNNSUU ANNULUS
ALNOOPR POLARON
ALNOOPT PLATOON
ALNOORT ORTOLAN
ALNOOSS SALOONS
SOLANOS
ALNOPPY PANOPLY
ALNOPSS SPONSAL
ALNOPYY POLYNYA
ALNORST LATRONS
ALNORUY UNROYAL
ALNORUZ ZONULAR
ALNOSUZ ZONULAS
ALNPRUY PLANURY
ALNPSTU PULTANS
ALNPTUY UNAPTLY
ALNPTXY PLANXTY
ALNRSUY URANYLS
ALNSSTU SULTANS
ALNSSVY SYLVANS
ALNSTUW WALNUTS
ALNSUUU UNUSUAL
ALOOPSS SALOOPS
ALOOPYZ POLYZOA
ALOORRS SORORAL
ALOPPRS POPLARS
ALOPPRU POPULAR
ALOPPRY PROPYLA
ALOPPST LAPTOPS
ALOPRRS PARLORS
ALOPRRU PARLOUR
ALOPRST PATROLS
PORTALS
ALOPRSU PARLOUS
ALOPSST POSTALS
ALOPSSU SPOUSAL
ALOPSUV VOLUSPA
ALOPTUY OUTPLAY
ALOQRRU RORQUAL
ALOQRSU SQUALOR

ALOQSTU	LOQUATS
ALORRST	ROSTRAL
ALORRSW	WORRALS
ALORSSU	ROSULAS
ALORSSV	SALVORS
ALORSTU	ROTULAS
ALORSUV	VALOURS
ALORTYY	ROYALTY
ALOSTTU	OUTLAST
ALOSTUW	OUTLAWS
ALOSTUY	LAYOUTS
	OUTLAYS
ALPRRSU	LARRUPS
ALPRSSU	PULSARS
ALPRSSW	SPRAWLS
ALPRSUU	PURSUAL
ALPRSUW	PULWARS
ALPRSWY	SPRAWLY
ALRSTTY	STARTLY
ALRSTUU	SUTURAL
ALRSTUW	TULWARS
AMMMNOS	MAMMONS
AMMMOSU	AMOMUMS
AMMNOOR	MOORMAN
AMMNOOT	MOOTMAN
AMMNRUY	NUMMARY
AMMOORR	MAORMOR
	MORMAOR
AMMOPTU	POMATUM
AMMORST	MARMOTS
AMMPSUW	WAMPUMS
AMMRRSU	MARRUMS
	MURRAMS
AMMRSUY	SUMMARY
AMMSSTU	SUMMATS
AMNNOOX	MONAXON
AMNNORS	NORMANS
AMNNOSW	SNOWMAN
AMNNOSY	ANONYMS
AMNNOTT	MONTANT
AMNNOTY	ANTONYM
AMNNOUW	UNWOMAN
AMNOOPP	POMPANO
AMNOORS	MAROONS
AMNOOTT	OTTOMAN
AMNOOTZ	MATZOON
AMNOPRT	PORTMAN
AMNOPRY	PARONYM
AMNOPST	POSTMAN
	TAMPONS
	TOPSMAN
AMNOPTU	PANTOUM
AMNOPTY	TYMPANO
AMNORSS	RAMSONS
	RANSOMS
AMNORST	MATRONS
	TRANSOM
AMNORSY	MASONRY
	MORNAYS
AMNORTU	ROMAUNT
AMNOSST	STAMNOS
AMNOSTU	AMOUNTS
	MOUTANS
	OUTMANS
AMNOTUY	AUTONYM
AMNPSTY	TYMPANS
AMNPTYY	TYMPANY
AMNQTUU	QUANTUM
AMNRRUY	UNMARRY
AMNRSTU	UNSMART
AMNRTTU	TANTRUM
AMNSTTU	MUTANTS
AMNSTUU	AUTUMNS
AMNTUUY	AUTUMNY
AMOOORS	AMOROSO
AMOOPRT	TAPROOM
AMOORSU	AMOROUS
AMOORSV	MOORVAS
AMOPSTT	TOPMAST
AMORRST	MORTARS
AMORRSU	ARMOURS
AMORRSW	MARROWS
AMORRUY	ARMOURY
AMORRWY	MARROWY
AMORSST	MATROSS
	STROAMS
AMORSSY	MORASSY
AMOSTUW	OUTSWAM
AMOSTUZ	MAZOUTS
AMOSUYZ	AZYMOUS
AMPRSST	STRAMPS
AMPRSUW	UPSWARM
AMRRSTU	RASTRUM
AMRRSTY	MARTYRS
AMRRSUY	MURRAYS
AMRRTYY	MARTYRY
AMRSTTU	STRATUM
ANNOPRS	NAPRONS
ANNOPST	PANTONS
ANNOPTY	POYNANT
ANNORST	NATRONS
ANNOSST	SANTONS
	SONANTS
ANNOSTW	WANTONS
ANNOSTY	TANNOYS
ANNOTTY	TANTONY
ANNPSSU	SANNUPS
	UNSNAPS
ANNPSTU	PANTUNS
ANNRTYY	TYRANNY
ANNSSTU	SUNTANS
ANNSSTY	SYNTANS
ANOOPRS	PRONAOS
	SOPRANO
ANOOPRT	PATROON
	PRONOTA
ANOORST	RATOONS
ANOORTT	ARNOTTO
ANOPRRS	SPORRAN
ANOPRSS	PARSONS
ANOPRST	PARTONS
	PATRONS
	TARPONS
ANOPRTV	PROVANT
ANOPSTT	OPTANTS
ANOPSTU	OUTSPAN
ANOPSUY	YAUPONS
ANORRSW	NARROWS
ANORSSV	SOVRANS
ANORSTT	ATTORNS
	RATTONS
	ROTTANS
ANORSTU	ROUSANT
	SANTOUR
ANORSTY	AROYNTS
ANORSUU	ANUROUS
	URANOUS
ANORWWY	WAYWORN
ANOSSTZ	STANZOS
ANOSTTU	TOTANUS
ANPPSUW	SUPPAWN
ANPRSSU	UNSPARS
ANPRSTU	SUNTRAP
	UNSTRAP
ANPRSUW	UNWRAPS
ANPRSUY	UNPRAYS
ANPSSUW	SUPAWNS
ANRSSTU	SANTURS
ANRSSUY	SUNRAYS
ANRSTTU	TRUANTS
ANRSTTY	TYRANTS
ANRSUWY	RUNWAYS
ANSSTTU	TUTSANS
AOOPPRS	APROPOS
AOOPRTT	TAPROOT
AOORRST	ORATORS
AOORRSY	ARROYOS
AOORRTT	ROTATOR
AOORRTU	OUTROAR
AOORRTY	ORATORY
AOORSTT	TOOARTS
AOORSTU	OUTSOAR
AOORSTV	OVATORS
AOOSTTT	TATTOOS
AOOSTUZ	AZOTOUS
AOOTXYZ	ZOOTAXY
AOPPPSU	PAPPOUS
AOPPRRT	RAPPORT
AOPPRST	APPORTS
AOPRRST	PARROTS
	RAPTORS
AOPRRSU	UPROARS
AOPRRSW	SPARROW
AOPRRTY	PARROTY
	PORTRAY
AOPRSST	ASPORTS
	PASTORS
AOPRSTU	ASPROUT
AOPRSTW	POSTWAR
AOPRSUV	VAPOURS
AOPRTTU	OUTPART
AOPRTUY	OUTPRAY
AOPRUVY	VAPOURY
AOPSSTU	PASSOUT
AOPSTUY	AUTOPSY
AOPSTWY	WAYPOST
AOQRSTU	QUARTOS
AORRSST	SARTORS
AORRSTW	TARROWS
AORRSWY	SOWARRY
	YARROWS
AORSSST	ASSORTS
AORSSTT	STATORS
AORSSTU	SOUTARS
AORSSUV	SAVOURS
AORSSUY	OSSUARY
	SUASORY
AORSTUY	YAOURTS
AORSUVY	SAVOURY
AORTUVY	AVOUTRY
AOSTTTW	TATTOWS
AOSTTUY	OUTSTAY
APPRRUU	PURPURA
APPRSTY	STRAPPY
APPRSUW	UPWRAPS
APPRSUY	PAPYRUS
APRSSSU	SURPASS
APRSSWY	PSYWARS
APRSTTU	UPSTART
APRSTTY	TAPSTRY
APRSUWY	SPURWAY
APSSTUY	UPSTAYS
APSSUWY	UPSWAYS
AQRTUYZ	QUARTZY
AQSTTUY	SQUATTY
ARSSTTU	STRATUS
BBBDELO	BLOBBED
	BOBBLED
BBBDELU	BLUBBED
	BUBBLED
BBBEIOS	BOBBIES
BBBEIRS	BIBBERS
BBBEISU	BUBBIES
BBBELOS	BOBBLES
BBBELRU	BLUBBER
BBBELSU	BUBBLES
BBBEORY	BOBBERY
BBBGIIN	BIBBING
BBBGINO	BOBBING
BBBHIOS	BOBBISH
BBBHSUU	HUBBUBS
BBBINOS	BOBBINS
BBCCIKO	BIBCOCK
BBCDEIR	CRIBBED
BBCDELO	COBBLED
BBCDELU	CLUBBED
BBCEHIN	NEBBICH
BBCEILR	CRIBBLE
BBCEIOR	COBBIER
BBCEISU	CUBBIES
BBCEKKO	KEBBOCK
BBCEKKU	KEBBUCK
BBCELOR	CLOBBER
	COBBLER
BBCELOS	COBBLES
BBCELRU	CLUBBER
BBCEORS	COBBERS
BBCEOSW	COBWEBS
BBCGINO	COBBING
BBCGINU	CUBBING
BBCHISU	CUBBISH
BBCINOU	BUBONIC
BBCRSUY	SCRUBBY
BBDDEIL	DIBBLED
BBDDEIR	DRIBBED
BBDDERU	DRUBBED
BBDEEIR	DEBBIER
BBDEEIS	DEBBIES
BBDEEIT	EBBTIDE
BBDEELP	PEBBLED
BBDEENS	SNEBBED
BBDEFLU	FLUBBED
BBDEGIL	GLIBBED
BBDEGLO	GOBBLED
BBDEGRU	GRUBBED
BBDEGSU	BEDBUGS
BBDEHLO	HOBBLED
BBDEIIM	IMBIBED
BBDEIKL	KIBBLED
BBDEILN	NIBBLED
BBDEILO	BILOBED
	LOBBIED
BBDEILR	DIBBLER
	DRIBBLE
BBDEILS	DIBBLES
BBDEINS	SNIBBED
BBDEIOS	DOBBIES
BBDEIRR	DRIBBER
BBDEIRS	DIBBERS
BBDEKNO	KNOBBED

BBDELMO	MOBBLED
BBDELMU	BUMBLED
BBDELNO	NOBBLED
BBDELNU	NUBBLED
BBDELOS	BOBSLED
BBDELOW	WOBBLED
BBDELRU	BLURBED
	BURBLED
BBDELSU	SLUBBED
BBDENSU	SNUBBED
BBDEORS	DOBBERS
BBDEOSW	SWOBBED
BBDESTU	STUBBED
BBDGIIN	DIBBING
BBDGINO	DOBBING
BBDGINU	DUBBING
BBDILRY	DRIBBLY
BBDINOS	DOBBINS
BBDINSU	DUBBINS
BBDKSUY	DYBBUKS
BBEEERU	BEBEERU
BBEEIKS	KEBBIES
BBEEIRW	WEBBIER
BBEEKLS	LEBBEKS
BBEELPS	PEBBLES
BBEELSS	EBBLESS
BBEENSS	SNEBBES
BBEFILR	FRIBBLE
BBEFIRS	FIBBERS
BBEFIRU	FUBBIER
BBEFIRY	FIBBERY
BBEFRUY	FUBBERY
BBEGIKN	KEBBING
BBEGILR	GLIBBER
	GRIBBLE
BBEGINN	NEBBING
BBEGINW	WEBBING
BBEGIOS	GIBBOSE
BBEGIRS	GIBBERS
BBEGIST	GIBBETS
BBEGLOR	GOBBLER
BBEGLOS	GOBBLES
BBEGLRU	GRUBBLE
BBEGNSU	BEBUNGS
BBEGOST	GOBBETS
BBEGRRU	GRUBBER
BBEHINS	NEBBISH
BBEHIOS	HOBBIES
BBEHISU	HUBBIES
BBEHLOR	HOBBLER
BBEHLOS	HOBBLES
BBEHMTU	BETHUMB
BBEIILR	RIBIBLE
BBEIIMR	IMBIBER
BBEIIMS	IMBIBES
BBEIIRR	RIBBIER
BBEIIRS	RIBIBES
BBEIJOS	JOBBIES
BBEIJRS	JIBBERS
BBEIKLS	KIBBLES
BBEILNR	NIBBLER
BBEILNS	NIBBLES
BBEILOS	BILBOES
	LOBBIES
BBEILOT	BIBELOT
BBEILPR	PRIBBLE
BBEILQU	QUIBBLE
BBEILRS	LIBBERS
BBEILRT	TRIBBLE
BBEILST	STIBBLE
BBEILSY	YIBBLES
BBEIMOS	MOBBIES
BBEINOR	NOBBIER
BBEINRU	NUBBIER
BBEIOOS	BOOBIES
BBEIRRS	BRIBERS
BBEIRRY	BRIBERY
BBEIRTU	TUBBIER
BBEISSU	BUSBIES
	SUBBIES
BBEJORS	JOBBERS
BBEJORY	JOBBERY
BBEKLNO	KNOBBLE
BBEKLNU	KNUBBLE
BBEKLOS	BLESBOK
BBEKLUU	BUBUKLE
BBEKNOR	KNOBBER
BBEKNSU	NEBBUKS
BBELLSU	BULBELS
BBELMOS	MOBBLES
BBELMOT	BOMBLET
BBELMRU	BUMBLER
BBELMSU	BUMBLES
BBELNOR	NOBBLER
BBELNOS	NOBBLES
BBELNSU	NUBBLES
BBELNSY	NYBBLES
BBELORS	SLOBBER
BBELORW	WOBBLER
BBELORY	LOBBYER
BBELOSW	WOBBLES
BBELRRU	BURBLER
BBELRSU	BURBLES
	LUBBERS
	RUBBLES
	SLUBBER
BBELSTU	STUBBLE
BBEMNSU	BENUMBS
BBEMORS	BOMBERS
BBENOTW	BOWBENT
BBENRSU	SNUBBER
BBENSSU	SNUBBES
BBEOOSY	YOBBOES
BBEORRS	ROBBERS
BBEORRY	ROBBERY
BBEORSW	SWOBBER
BBEORYY	YOBBERY
BBEPRUW	BREWPUB
BBERRSU	RUBBERS
BBERRUY	RUBBERY
BBERSTU	TUBBERS
BBFGIIN	FIBBING
BBFGINO	FOBBING
BBFGINU	FUBBING
BBGGIIN	GIBBING
BBGGINO	GOBBING
BBGIIJN	JIBBING
BBGIILN	LIBBING
BBGIINN	NIBBING
BBGIINR	BRIBING
	RIBBING
BBGIJNO	JOBBING
BBGILNO	LOBBING
BBGILNU	BULBING
BBGIMNO	BOMBING
	MOBBING
BBGINNU	NUBBING
BBGINOO	BOOBING
BBGINOR	ROBBING
BBGINOS	GIBBONS
	SOBBING
BBGINRU	RUBBING
BBGINSU	GUBBINS
	SUBBING
BBGINTU	TUBBING
BBGIOSU	GIBBOUS
BBGIOSW	BOBWIGS
BBHHIOS	HOBBISH
BBHIMOS	MOBBISH
BBHIOST	HOBBITS
BBHIOSY	YOBBISH
BBHIRSU	RUBBISH
BBHISTU	TUBBISH
BBHJOOS	HOBJOBS
BBHNOOS	HOBNOBS
BBHOOUW	WHOOBUB
BBHRSUY	SHRUBBY
BBIIILM	BILIMBI
BBIILST	BIBLIST
BBIKOSS	SKIBOBS
BBIKTUZ	KIBBUTZ
BBILLSU	BULBILS
BBILLUU	LULIBUB
BBILNOY	NOBBILY
BBIMOSY	YOBBISM
BBINNSU	NUBBINS
BBINORS	RIBBONS
BBINORY	RIBBONY
BBJLOOW	BLOWJOB
BBKLNOY	KNOBBLY
BBKLNUY	KNUBBLY
BBKLOOU	BLOUBOK
BBKOOOO	BOOBOOK
BBKOOSS	BOSBOKS
BBLLSUU	BULBULS
BBLOSUU	BULBOUS
BBLSTUY	STUBBLY
BBNNOOS	BONBONS
BBNOORU	BOURBON
BBOOOOS	BOOBOOS
BBORSTU	BURBOTS
BBOSSUY	BUSBOYS
BBRSSUU	SUBURBS
BCCEIIS	BICCIES
BCCEILO	ECBOLIC
BCCEILU	CUBICLE
BCCEILY	BICYCLE
BCCILOU	BUCOLIC
BCCINOO	OBCONIC
BCCISUU	SUCCUBI
BCCMOOX	COXCOMB
BCCMSUU	SUCCUMB
BCDEEHL	BELCHED
BCDEEHN	BENCHED
BCDEEIL	DECIBEL
BCDEEKS	BEDECKS
BCDEHIR	BIRCHED
BCDEHIT	BITCHED
BCDEHNU	BUNCHED
BCDEHOR	BROCHED
BCDEHOT	BOTCHED
BCDEHOU	DEBOUCH
BCDEIIO	BIOCIDE
BCDEIKR	BRICKED
BCDEIKS	SICKBED
BCDEIKT	BEDTICK
BCDEILM	CLIMBED
BCDEILO	DOCIBLE
BCDEIOS	BODICES
BCDEIRS	SCRIBED
BCDEKLO	BLOCKED
BCDEKLU	BUCKLED
BCDEKOR	BEDROCK
	BROCKED
BCDEKSU	BEDUCKS
BCDELOU	BECLOUD
BCDEMOR	CROMBED
BCDEMRU	CRUMBED
BCDENOU	BOUNCED
	BUNCOED
BCDEORU	COURBED
BCDESUU	SUBDUCE
BCDHIOR	BICHORD
BCDHIRU	BRUCHID
BCDHOOU	CUBHOOD
BCDILOO	COLOBID
BCDIORW	COWBIRD
BCDIOSU	CUBOIDS
BCDIRSY	CYBRIDS
BCDKORU	BURDOCK
BCDNOSU	BONDUCS
BCDSTUU	SUBDUCT
BCEEEHN	BEECHEN
BCEEEHS	BEECHES
	BESEECH
BCEEFIN	BENEFIC
BCEEGIR	ICEBERG
BCEEHIP	EPHEBIC
BCEEHLR	BELCHER
BCEEHLS	BELCHES
BCEEHNR	BENCHER
BCEEHNS	BENCHES
BCEEHOS	OBECHES
BCEEHOU	BOUCHEE
BCEEIPS	BESPICE
BCEEIRS	ESCRIBE
BCEEKNS	NEBECKS
BCEEKNU	BUCKEEN
BCEEKRS	REBECKS
BCEEKST	BECKETS
BCEEKSZ	ZEBECKS
BCEELOS	ECBOLES
BCEEMOS	BECOMES
BCEENOS	OBSCENE
BCEENRU	CRUBEEN
BCEFIIS	SEBIFIC
BCEGIKN	BECKING
BCEHINR	BIRCHEN
BCEHINT	BENTHIC
BCEHIOR	BRIOCHE
BCEHIRS	BIRCHES
BCEHIST	BITCHES
BCEHITW	BEWITCH
BCEHLRU	BLUCHER
BCEHNSU	BUNCHES
BCEHORS	BROCHES
BCEHORT	BOTCHER
BCEHORW	COWHERB
BCEHOSS	BOSCHES
BCEHOST	BOTCHES
BCEHOSU	BOUCHES
BCEHRSU	CHERUBS
BCEHRTU	BUTCHER
BCEHSTU	BUTCHES
BCEIIKR	BRICKIE
BCEIISV	VIBICES
BCEIKLM	LIMBECK
BCEIKLR	BRICKLE
BCEIKNR	BRICKEN
BCEIKRS	BICKERS

BCEIKST	BESTICK
BCEIKSU	BUCKIES
BCEILMO	EMBOLIC
BCEILMR	CLIMBER
	RECLIMB
BCEILMS	EMBLICS
	LIMBECS
BCEILNO	BINOCLE
BCEILOR	BRICOLE
	CORBEIL
BCEIMNO	COMBINE
BCEIMOR	COMBIER
	CROMBIE
	MICROBE
BCEINOR	BICORNE
BCEINOZ	BENZOIC
BCEINRU	BRUCINE
BCEIORS	CORBIES
BCEIRRS	SCRIBER
BCEIRSS	SCRIBES
BCEIRSU	SUBERIC
BCEIRTU	BRUCITE
BCEISST	BISECTS
BCEJOST	OBJECTS
BCEJSTU	SUBJECT
BCEKLOR	BLOCKER
BCEKLRU	BRUCKLE
	BUCKLER
BCEKLSU	BUCKLES
BCEKMOS	BEMOCKS
BCEKNOS	BECKONS
BCEKORT	BROCKET
BCEKORU	ROEBUCK
BCEKOSU	BUCKOES
BCEKOTY	BYCOKET
BCEKRSU	BUCKERS
BCEKSTU	BESTUCK
	BUCKETS
BCELLOW	COWBELL
BCELMNU	CLUBMEN
BCELMOS	COMBLES
BCELMRU	CLUMBER
	CRUMBLE
BCELMSU	SCUMBLE
BCELORS	CORBELS
BCELOSU	BOUCLES
BCELRSU	BECURLS
BCELSSU	CUBLESS
BCEMNTU	CUMBENT
BCEMOOS	COOMBES
BCEMORS	COMBERS
BCEMRSU	CUMBERS
	SCUMBER
BCENORU	BOUNCER
BCENOSU	BOUNCES
BCEORSS	SCROBES
BCEORSU	OBSCURE
BCFSSUU	SUBFUSC
BCGIKNO	BOCKING
BCGIKNU	BUCKING
BCGIMNO	COMBING
BCGINNU	BUNCING
BCGINRU	CURBING
BCGORSU	COBURGS
BCGORSY	CYBORGS
BCHIIOT	COHIBIT
BCHIKOU	CHIBOUK
BCHIKSU	BUCKISH
BCHILOS	CHIBOLS
BCHIMOR	RHOMBIC
BCHINOR	BRONCHI
BCHIOPR	PIBROCH
BCHIOPS	PHOBICS
BCHLOTY	BLOTCHY
BCHNOOR	BRONCHO
BCHORST	BORSCHT
	BORTSCH
BCIIKLN	NIBLICK
BCIILMU	BULIMIC
BCIILOR	COLIBRI
BCIILSY	SIBYLIC
BCIINOS	BIONICS
BCIINOT	BIONTIC
BCIIOPS	BIOPICS
BCIISTU	BISCUIT
BCIKNOS	KINCOBS
BCIKORT	BROCKIT
BCIKOTT	BITTOCK
BCILMPU	PLUMBIC
	UPCLIMB
BCILPSU	PUBLICS
BCIMSSU	CUBISMS
BCINORS	BICORNS
BCINORU	RUBICON
BCINSUU	INCUBUS
BCIOORT	ROBOTIC
BCIORST	STROBIC
BCIOSTY	SYBOTIC
BCIRRSU	RUBRICS
BCIRTUY	BUTYRIC
BCISSTU	CUBISTS
BCISTUU	CUBITUS
BCJKMUU	JUMBUCK
BCKLLOO	BOLLOCK
BCKLLOU	BULLOCK
BCKLNOU	UNBLOCK
BCKMMOU	BUMMOCK
BCKMOSU	BUCKSOM
BCKOTTU	BUTTOCK
BCLMOOU	COULOMB
BCLMRUY	CRUMBLY
BCLOOSU	COLOBUS
	SUBCOOL
BCLORTU	CLOTBUR
BCMOOST	TOMBOCS
BCMORSY	CORYMBS
BCMOSTU	COMBUST
BCNOORS	BRONCOS
BCNOSTU	COBNUTS
BCOOSWY	COWBOYS
BCOOTTY	BOYCOTT
BDDDELU	BUDDLED
BDDDEOR	BRODDED
BDDEEER	REEDBED
BDDEEES	SEEDBED
BDDEEEW	BEDEWED
BDDEEIL	BIELDED
BDDEEIR	DEBRIDE
BDDEEIS	BEDSIDE
BDDEEIT	BETIDED
	DEBITED
BDDEELN	BLENDED
BDDEERS	BEDDERS
BDDEETU	DEBUTED
BDDEGIN	BEDDING
BDDEGIR	BRIDGED
BDDEGLU	BLUDGED
BDDEIIR	BIRDIED
BDDEIIS	BIDDIES
BDDEILN	BLINDED
BDDEILR	BRIDLED
BDDEILU	BUILDED
BDDEINR	BRINDED
BDDEIOO	BOODIED
BDDEIRS	BIDDERS
BDDEIRU	BUDDIER
BDDEISU	BUDDIES
BDDELNU	BUNDLED
BDDELOO	BLOODED
BDDELOS	BODDLES
BDDELOU	DOUBLED
BDDELSU	BUDDLES
BDDENOU	BOUNDED
BDDEOOR	BROODED
BDDEORU	OBDURED
BDDEOTU	DOUBTED
BDDERSU	REDBUDS
BDDESUU	SUBDUED
BDDGIIN	BIDDING
BDDGINU	BUDDING
BDDISSU	DISBUDS
BDEEEFL	FEEBLED
BDEEELL	DELEBLE
BDEEELP	BLEEPED
BDEEELR	BLEEDER
BDEEELT	BEETLED
BDEEEMN	BEDEMEN
BDEEEMT	BEMETED
BDEEEPS	BESPEED
BDEEERR	BREEDER
	BREERED
BDEEERZ	BREEZED
BDEEEST	DEBTEES
BDEEFIR	BRIEFED
	DEBRIEF
	FIBERED
BDEEGOR	BEGORED
BDEEHOV	BEHOVED
BDEEHRT	BERTHED
BDEEIKN	BEINKED
BDEEILL	BELLIED
	DELIBLE
	LIBELED
BDEEILS	EDIBLES
BDEEILV	BEDEVIL
BDEEIMR	BEMIRED
BDEEIMT	BEDTIME
	BETIMED
BDEEINR	BENDIER
	INBREED
BDEEINZ	BEDIZEN
BDEEIRR	BERRIED
	BRIERED
BDEEIRS	DERBIES
BDEEISS	BESIDES
BDEEIST	BETIDES
BDEEIVV	BEVVIED
BDEEJLS	DJEBELS
BDEEKMO	KEMBOED
BDEEKRU	REBUKED
BDEELLS	BEDELLS
BDEELMR	REMBLED
BDEELMS	SEMBLED
BDEELNR	BLENDER
BDEELNS	BLENDES
BDEELNT	BENDLET
BDEELOV	BELOVED
BDEELOW	ELBOWED
BDEELRT	TREBLED
BDEELSS	BLESSED
BDEELTT	BLETTED
BDEELZZ	BEZZLED
BDEEMOS	BESOMED
BDEEMOW	EMBOWED
BDEEMOX	EMBOXED
BDEEMRU	EMBRUED
	UMBERED
BDEEMSU	BEMUSED
BDEENOR	ENROBED
BDEENPR	PREBEND
BDEENRS	BENDERS
BDEEORR	REBORED
BDEEORS	BEDSORE
	SOBERED
BDEEORW	BOWERED
BDEEOSX	SEEDBOX
BDEERUW	BURWEED
BDEFFLU	BLUFFED
BDEFILR	FILBERD
BDEFLMU	FUMBLED
BDEFLOU	BODEFUL
BDEFOOR	FORBODE
BDEGGLO	BOGGLED
BDEGGOR	BROGGED
BDEGHIT	BEDIGHT
BDEGILN	BINGLED
BDEGILO	OBLIGED
BDEGILS	BEGILDS
BDEGINN	BENDING
BDEGINO	BOINGED
BDEGINR	BREDING
BDEGIOO	BOOGIED
BDEGIOR	BODGIER
BDEGIOS	BODGIES
BDEGIOT	BIGOTED
BDEGIRS	BEGIRDS
	BRIDGES
BDEGIRU	BRIGUED
BDEGISU	BUDGIES
BDEGLNU	BLUNGED
	BUNGLED
BDEGLRU	BLUDGER
	BURGLED
BDEGLSU	BLUDGES
BDEGNSU	BEDUNGS
BDEGORS	BODGERS
BDEGORU	BUDGERO
BDEGRSU	BUDGERS
BDEGSTU	BUDGETS
BDEHINS	BEHINDS
BDEHIRT	BIRTHED
BDEHLMU	HUMBLED
BDEHLOS	BEHOLDS
BDEHLSU	BLUSHED
BDEHMTU	THUMBED
BDEHORY	HERDBOY
BDEHOST	HOTBEDS
BDEHRSU	BRUSHED
BDEIIRS	BIRDIES
	BRIDIES
BDEIIVV	BIVVIED
BDEIJLR	JIRBLED
BDEIKLN	BLINKED
BDEIKMO	KIMBOED
BDEIKNO	BOINKED
BDEIKRS	BRISKED
BDEILLU	BULLIED
BDEILMS	DIMBLES
BDEILMW	WIMBLED
BDEILNN	BLINNED

BDEILNR BLINDER
BRINDLE
BDEILOP LOBIPED
BDEILOR BROILED
BDEILOS BOLIDES
BDEILOX BOLIXED
BDEILPP BLIPPED
BDEILRR BRIDLER
BDEILRS BIRSLED
BRIDLES
BDEILRT DRIBLET
BDEILRU BLUDIER
BUILDER
REBUILD
BDEILTZ BLITZED
BDEIMMR BRIMMED
BDEIMNR BIRDMEN
BDEIMOR BROMIDE
BDEIMRU IMBRUED
BDEIMTU BITUMED
BDEINOR INORBED
BDEINOU BEDOUIN
BDEINRS BINDERS
REBINDS
BDEINRY BINDERY
BDEINST BIDENTS
BDEINSU BEDUINS
BDEIOOS BOODIES
BDEIORR BROIDER
BDEIORS BORIDES
DISROBE
BDEIORT DEBITOR
ORBITED
BDEIORV OVERBID
BDEIORZ ZEBROID
BDEIOSY DISOBEY
BDEIRRS BIRDERS
BDEIRST BESTRID
BISTRED
BDEIRSU BRUISED
BURDIES
BDEIRSV VERBIDS
BDEIRTU BRUITED
BDEISSU SUBSIDE
BDEISTU BUISTED
SUBEDIT
BDEITUY DUBIETY
BDEJLMU JUMBLED
BDEJORU OBJURED
BDEKLNU BLUNKED
BDEKNOU BUNKOED
BDEKNSU DEBUNKS
BDEKOOR BROOKED
BDELMMU BUMMLED
MUMBLED
BDELMOO BLOOMED
BDELMPU PLUMBED
BDELMRU DRUMBLE
RUMBLED
BDELMTU TUMBLED
BDELNOR BLONDER
BDELNOS BLONDES
BOLDENS
BDELNRU BLUNDER
BDELNSU BUNDLES
BDELNTU BLUNTED
BDELOOP BLOOPED
BDELOOS BOODLES
BDELORS BORDELS
BDELORU BOULDER
DOUBLER
BDELORW BOWLDER
BDELOST BOLDEST
BDELOSU BLOUSED
DOUBLES
BDELOSW BLOWSED
BDELOTT BLOTTED
BOTTLED
BDELOTU BOULTED
DOUBLET
BDELOWZ BLOWZED
BDELRRU BLURRED
BDELRTU BLURTED
BDELSSU BUDLESS
BDELSTU BUSTLED
BDELSWY LEWDSBY
BDELTTU BUTTLED
BDEMNNO BONDMEN
BDEMNOU EMBOUND
BDEMOOR BEDROOM
BOREDOM
BROOMED
BDEMOOS BOSOMED
BDEMORS SOMBRED
BDEMSTU DUMBEST
BDENNOU BOUNDEN
UNBONED
BDENNSU UNBENDS
BDENORS BONDERS
BDENORU BOUNDER
REBOUND
UNROBED
BDENORW BROWNED
BDENORZ BRONZED
BDENOST OBTENDS
BDENOSY BEYONDS
BDENOUW UNBOWED
BDENOUX UNBOXED
BDENRSU BURDENS
BDENRTU BRUNTED
BDENSSU SUNBEDS
BDENSTU SUBTEND
BDENSUY SEBUNDY
BDEOORR BROODER
BDEOORS BOORDES
BDEOOST BOOSTED
BDEOPRS BEDROPS
BDEOPRT BEDROPT
BDEOPST BEDPOST
BDEORRS BORDERS
BDEORRU BORDURE
BOURDER
BDEORSS DESORBS
BDEORST DEBTORS
BDEORSU OBDURES
ROSEBUD
BDEORSW BROWSED
BDEORTU DOUBTER
OBTRUDE
OUTBRED
REDOUBT
BDERSSU SURBEDS
BDERSTU BURSTED
BDERSUU SUBDUER
BDERSUY RUDESBY
BDESSTU BEDUSTS
BESTUDS
BDESSUU SUBDUES
BDESSUW SUBDEWS
BDFIIOR FIBROID
BDFIISU FIDIBUS
BDFIORS FORBIDS
BDGGINO BODGING
BDGGINU BUDGING
BDGIINN BINDING
BDGIINR BIRDING
BRIDING
BDGIINS BIDINGS
BDGIIOO GOBIOID
BDGIIOS GOBIIDS
BDGILOO GLOBOID
BDGIMNU DUMBING
BDGINNO BONDING
BDGINNU BUNDING
BDGINOS BODINGS
BDGINOY BODYING
BDGLLOU BULLDOG
BDGLOOT DOGBOLT
BDHIINS BHINDIS
BDHINOP HOPBIND
BDHIOSU BUSHIDO
BDHIRSY HYBRIDS
BDHMOOO HOBODOM
BDHOOOY BOYHOOD
BDIIKNO BODIKIN
BDIILMS DISLIMB
BDIILOS LIBIDOS
BDIIMRS MIDRIBS
BDIISTT TIDBITS
BDIKNOR BRODKIN
BDIKNOS BODKINS
BDILLNY BLINDLY
BDILNNU UNBLIND
BDILNUU UNBUILD
BDILPUU UPBUILD
BDILRUY BUIRDLY
BDILTUY DIBUTYL
BDIMNPU DUMPBIN
BDINNOU INBOUND
BDINNSU UNBINDS
BDINOOR BRIDOON
BDINPSU UPBINDS
BDINRSU SUNBIRD
BDINSTU DUSTBIN
BDIOOOV OBOVOID
BDIOORU BOUDOIR
BDIORSW WOSBIRD
BDIOSSY BYSSOID
BDIOSTU OUTBIDS
BDIOSUU DUBIOUS
BDIRSTU DISTURB
BDISSUY SUBSIDY
BDKLOOS KOBOLDS
BDKNOOU BUNDOOK
BDLOOOX OXBLOOD
BDMORUW BUDWORM
BDNNOUU UNBOUND
BDNOORU BOURDON
BDNOOWW DOWNBOW
BDNOPUU UPBOUND
BDNORTU TURBOND
BDNORUW RUBDOWN
BDNOSTU OBTUNDS
BDOOOWX BOXWOOD
BDORSWY BYWORDS
BEEEEFR FREEBEE
BEEEEKS BESEEKE
BEEEEMT BETEEME
BEEEFIR BEEFIER
FREEBIE
BEEEFLR FEEBLER
BEEEFLS FEEBLES
BEEEFTW WEBFEET
BEEEGIS BESIEGE
BEEEGRR BERGERE
BEEEHIV BEEHIVE
BEEEHNS SHEBEEN
BEEEHPS EPHEBES
BEEEILL LIBELEE
BEEEILN BEELINE
BEEEILV BELIEVE
BEEEIRR BEERIER
BEEEJLW BEJEWEL
BEEEKLS KEBELES
BEEELPR BLEEPER
BEEELST BEETLES
BEEEMOS BEESOME
BEEEMRW EMBREWE
BEEEMSS BESEEMS
BEEEMST BEMETES
BETEEMS
BEEENNZ BENZENE
BEEENTW BETWEEN
BEEEPRS BEEPERS
BEEEPSW BEWEEPS
BEEERSS BREESES
BEEERSZ BREEZES
BEEERTV BREVETE
BEEFGIN BEEFING
BEEFILR FEBRILE
BEEFILS BELIEFS
BEEFINT BENEFIT
BEEFIRR BRIEFER
BEEFNRU FUNEBRE
BEEGGNU GEEBUNG
BEEGILL LEGIBLE
BEEGILO OBLIGEE
BEEGILS BEIGELS
BEEGILU BEGUILE
BEEGIMR BEGRIME
BEEGINN BEGINNE
BEEGINP BEEPING
BEEGINR BIGENER
BEEGINT BEETING
BEIGNET
BEEGINU BEGUINE
BEEGLNO ENGLOBE
BEEGMNO GOMBEEN
BEEGMOU EMBOGUE
BEEGNOS ENGOBES
BEEGNSU BUNGEES
BEEGNTU UNBEGET
BEEGRSU BURGEES
BEEHINS BESHINE
BEEHIRR HERBIER
BEEHIST BHISTEE
BEEHKSU BUKSHEE
BEEHLRT BLETHER
HERBLET
BEEHLST BETHELS
BEEHNNO HEBENON
BEEHNOS BESHONE
BEEHOOV BEHOOVE
BEEHOPS EPHEBOS
PHOEBES
BEEHORS HERBOSE
BEEHORW BEWHORE
BEEHOST BEHOTES
BEEHOSV BEHOVES
BEEHPSU EPHEBUS

BEEHRST BERTHES
SHERBET
BEEHRSW BESHREW
BEEHRTY THEREBY
BEEHRWY WHEREBY
BEEHSST BEHESTS
BEEHSTY BHEESTY
BEEIJLU JUBILEE
BEEILLR LIBELER
BEEILLS BELLIES
BEEILNR BERLINE
BEEILOS OBELISE
BEEILOZ OBELIZE
BEEILRS BELIERS
BEEILTT BETITLE
BEEIMRS BEMIRES
BIREMES
BEEIMST BETIMES
BEEINNS BENNIES
BEEINNZ BENZINE
BEEINOS EBONIES
EBONISE
BEEINOT EBONITE
BEEINOZ EBONIZE
BEEINPR PEBRINE
BEEINRT BENTIER
BEEINRZ ZEBRINE
BEEIORS EBRIOSE
BEEIQUZ BEZIQUE
BEEIRRS BERRIES
BEEIRRV BREVIER
BEEIRST REBITES
BEEIRTY EBRIETY
BEEISST BETISES
BEEISTT BETTIES
BEEISVV BEVVIES
BEEJNSU BUNJEES
BEEKNOT BETOKEN
BEEKOPS BESPOKE
BEEKORS REEBOKS
BEEKRRS BERSERK
BEEKRRU REBUKER
BEEKRSU REBUKES
BEELLMN BELLMEN
BEELLOT LOBELET
BEELMMS EMBLEMS
BEELMNT BELTMEN
BEELMOW EMBOWEL
BEELMRS REMBLES
BEELMRT TREMBLE
BEELMSS SEMBLES
BEELNNO ENNOBLE
BEELNOZ BENZOLE
BEELNSU NEBULES
BEELOSV BELOVES
BEELOTY EYEBOLT
BEELPST BEPELTS
BEELRST BELTERS
TREBLES
BEELRSY BERLEYS
BEELRUZ ZEBRULE
BEELSSS BLESSES
BEELSZZ BEZZLES
BEELTTU BLUETTE
BEEMMRS MEMBERS
BEEMNPT BENEMPT
BEEMNRY BYREMEN
BEEMORW EMBOWER
BEEMOSS MEBOSES
BEEMOSX EMBOXES
BEEMRRU UMBRERE
BEEMRSU EMBRUES
BEEMRTU EMBRUTE
BEEMSSU BEMUSES
BEENNRS BRENNES
BEENNST BENNETS
BEENORS BOREENS
ENROBES
BEENOST BONESET
BEENRRT BRENTER
BEENSTU BUTENES
SUBTEEN
BEEOOST BOOTEES
BEEOPRS BEPROSE
BEEORRS REBORES
SOBERER
BEEORRU BOURREE
BEEORSV OBSERVE
OBVERSE
VERBOSE
BEEORSY OBEYERS
BEEORWY EYEBROW
BEEOSST OBESEST
BEEPRRV PREVERB
BEEQSTU BEQUEST
BEERRST BERRETS
BEERRSU BEURRES
BEERRSV REVERBS
BEERRSW BREWERS
BEERRWY BREWERY
BEERSSU REBUSES
SUBSERE
BEERSTT BETTERS
BEERSTV BREVETS
BEERSTW BESTREW
WEBSTER
BEERTTU BURETTE
BEESSTU BUSTEES
BEETTUV BUVETTE
BEFFLRU BLUFFER
BEFFPSU BEPUFFS
BEFFRSU BUFFERS
REBUFFS
BEFFSTU BUFFETS
BEFGIIL FILIBEG
BEFGIRU FIREBUG
BEFGIST BEGIFTS
BEFHOOS BEHOOFS
BEFILMS FIMBLES
BEFILOS FOIBLES
BEFILPY PLEBIFY
BEFILRT FILBERT
BEFILRY BRIEFLY
BEFILSU FUSIBLE
BEFINOR BONFIRE
BEFIORS FIBROSE
BEFIORX FIREBOX
BEFIRST FIBSTER
BEFIRSU FUBSIER
BEFIRVY VERBIFY
BEFITUX TUBIFEX
BEFLLTY FLYBELT
BEFLMRU FUMBLER
BEFLMSU BEFLUMS
FUMBLES
BEFLOOS BEFOOLS
BEFLOSU BEFOULS
BEFLTUU TUBEFUL
BEFOORR FORBORE
BEFOOTW WEBFOOT
BEFSSUU SUBFEUS
BEGGGIN BEGGING
BEGGIIS BIGGIES
BEGGINO BEGOING
BEGGIOR BOGGIER
BEGGIRU BUGGIER
BEGGIST BIGGEST
BEGGISU BUGGIES
BEGGLOR BOGGLER
BEGGLOS BOGGLES
BEGGRSU BUGGERS
BEGGRUY BUGGERY
BEGHHIT BEHIGHT
BEGHINT BENIGHT
BEGHISS BESIGHS
BEGHITT BETIGHT
BEGHRRU BURGHER
BEGIILR BILGIER
BEGIINN INBEING
BEGIINS BINGIES
BEGIKMN KEMBING
BEGILLN BELLING
BEGILLY LEGIBLY
BEGILNO IGNOBLE
INGLOBE
BEGILNS BINGLES
BEGILNT BELTING
BEGILNU BLUEING
BULGINE
BEGILNY BELYING
BEGILOS OBLIGES
BEGILRS GERBILS
BEGILRT GILBERT
BEGILRU BULGIER
BEGILST GIBLETS
BEGINNU UNBEING
BEGINOS BIOGENS
BEGINOY BIOGENY
OBEYING
BEGINRR BRINGER
BEGINRS BINGERS
BEGINRW BREWING
BEGINSS BESINGS
BIGNESS
BEGINST BESTING
BEGINSU BEGUINS
BUNGIES
BEGINTT BETTING
BEGIOOS BOOGIES
BEGIOSU BOUGIES
BEGIRSU BRIGUES
RUGBIES
BEGISSU GIBUSES
BEGKMOS GEMSBOK
BEGKNSU BEGUNKS
BEGLLOU GLOBULE
BEGLMOO BEGLOOM
BEGLMRU GRUMBLE
BEGLNOS BELONGS
BEGLNRU BLUNGER
BUNGLER
BEGLNSU BLUNGES
BUNGLES
BEGLOOS GLOBOSE
BEGLOOT BOOTLEG
BEGLOST GOBLETS
BEGLOSU GLEBOUS
BEGLRSU BUGLERS
BULGERS
BURGLES
BEGLRTY BERGYLT
BEGLSTU BUGLETS
BEGNNUU UNBEGUN
BEGNORU BURGEON
BEGNOSY BYGONES
BEGNOTU UNBEGOT
BEGNSUY BUNGEYS
BEGOORS GOOBERS
BEGORSU BROGUES
BEGOSTU BOUGETS
BEGOSTW BOWGETS
BEGRRSU BURGERS
BEGRSSU BURGESS
BEHHKOT KHOTBEH
BEHIITX EXHIBIT
BEHIKNT BETHINK
BEHIKRS KIRBEHS
BEHILMS BLEMISH
BEHILMT THIMBLE
BEHILOS BOLSHIE
BEHILRT BLITHER
BEHILST THIBLES
BEHILSU HELIBUS
BEHINOP HOPBINE
BEHIOST BOTHIES
BEHIOTW HOWBEIT
BEHIRRT REBIRTH
BEHIRST HERBIST
BEHIRSU BUSHIER
BEHISSU BUSHIES
BEHISTT THIBETS
BEHLLOP BELLHOP
BEHLMOW WHOMBLE
BEHLMRU HUMBLER
BEHLMSU HUMBLES
BEHLOOT BOTHOLE
BEHLORT BROTHEL
BEHLOSW BEHOWLS
BEHLRRU BURRHEL
BEHLRSU BLUSHER
BURHELS
BEHLSSU BLUSHES
BUSHELS
BEHLSTU BLUSHET
BEHMNSU BUSHMEN
BEHMORS HOMBRES
BEHMOTU BEMOUTH
BEHMPTU BETHUMP
BEHNORS BREHONS
BEHNOST BENTHOS
BEHNRTU BURTHEN
BEHOORT THEORBO
BEHORRT BROTHER
BEHORST BOSHTER
BOTHERS
BEHORSU HERBOUS
BEHORTT BETROTH
BEHRRSU BRUSHER
BEHRSSU BRUSHES
BEIIKLR RIBLIKE
BEIIKRR BIRKIER
BEIIKRS BIRKIES
BEIILLS BILLIES
BEIILRS RISIBLE
BEIILSV VISIBLE
BEIINOT NIOBITE
BEIINRR BRINIER
BEIINST STIBINE
BEIIOTT BIOTITE
BEIIRRS BIRSIER

BEIIRST BITSIER
BEIIRTT BITTIER
BEIISTT BITTIES
BEIISVV BIVVIES
BEIJLRS JERBILS
JIRBLES
BEIJMSU JUMBIES
BEIJNSU BUNJIES
BEIKLNR BLINKER
BEIKLNS LIBKENS
BEIKLOS OBELISK
BEIKLRS BILKERS
BEIKLRU BULKIER
BEIKNRS BRISKEN
BEIKOOR BOOKIER
BEIKOOS BOOKIES
BOOKSIE
BEIKORS BOSKIER
BEIKRRS BRISKER
BEIKRST BRISKET
BEILLMN BILLMEN
BEILLRR BRILLER
BEILLRU BULLIER
BEILLST BESTILL
BILLETS
BEILLSU BULLIES
BEILMNR NIMBLER
BEILMOR EMBROIL
BEILMOS BEMOILS
EMBOILS
MOBILES
BEILMRS LIMBERS
BEILMRT TIMBREL
BEILMRW WIMBREL
BEILMSU SUBLIME
BEILMSW WIMBLES
BEILNOO OBELION
BEILNOW BOWLINE
BEILNRS BERLINS
BEILNSY BYLINES
BEILNSZ BENZILS
BEILNTZ BLINTZE
BEILOOR LOOBIER
BEILOOS LOOBIES
BEILOQU OBLIQUE
BEILORR BROILER
BEILORS BOILERS
LIBEROS
REBOILS
BEILORT TRILOBE
BEILORW BLOWIER
BEILORY BOILERY
BEILOST BETOILS
BEILOSW BLOWIES
BEILOSX BOLIXES
BEILRRS BIRLERS
BEILRRU BURLIER
BEILRSS BIRSLES
RIBLESS
BEILRST BLISTER
BRISTLE
RIBLETS
BEILRTT BRITTLE
TRIBLET
BEILRTU REBUILT
BEILRTY LIBERTY
BEILRUY BRULYIE
BEILRUZ BRULZIE
BEILSSS BLISSES
BEILSST BITLESS

BEILSTU BLUIEST
SUBTILE
BEILSTW BLEWITS
BEILSTZ BLITZES
BEIMMRR BRIMMER
BEIMNOR BROMINE
BEIMNTU BITUMEN
BEIMORW IMBOWER
BEIMOSS OBEISMS
BEIMOSZ ZOMBIES
BEIMPRU BUMPIER
BEIMRST BETRIMS
TIMBERS
TIMBRES
BEIMRSU ERBIUMS
IMBRUES
IMBURSE
BEIMRTU IMBRUTE
TERBIUM
BEINNOR BONNIER
BEINNOS BENISON
BONNIES
BEINNOZ BENZOIN
BEINNSU BUNNIES
BEINORT BORNITE
BEINORW BROWNIE
BEINOSS BESOINS
BEINOST BONIEST
EBONIST
BEINOSV BOVINES
BEINOSX BONXIES
BEINOSZ BIZONES
BEINOTT BOTTINE
BEINRSU RUBINES
SUBERIN
BEINRSY BYRNIES
BEINRTT BITTERN
BEINRTU BUNTIER
TRIBUNE
TURBINE
BEINSSY BYSSINE
BEIOORZ BOOZIER
BEIOOST BOOTIES
BEIOPTY BIOTYPE
BEIORRT ORBITER
BEIORSS BOSSIER
RIBOSES
BEIORST ORBIEST
SORBITE
BEIORSU BOUSIER
OUREBIS
BEIOSSU SOUBISE
BEIOSTT BOTTIES
BEIOSTX BOXIEST
BEIOSTY OBESITY
BEIPPSU BUPPIES
BEIPSST BESPITS
BEIPSSU PUBISES
BEIQRTU BRIQUET
BEIQSSU BISQUES
BEIRRRU BURRIER
BEIRRSU BRISURE
BRUISER
BEIRSST BESTIRS
BISTERS
BISTRES
BEIRSSU BRUISES
BEIRSTT BITTERS
BEIRSTU BUSTIER
RUBIEST

BEIRTTU TRIBUTE
BEIRTTY TREYBIT
BEIRTVY BREVITY
BEIRUZZ BUZZIER
BEISSTU BUSIEST
BEISTTU BUTTIES
BEITTWX BETWIXT
BEJJSUU JUJUBES
BEJLMRU JUMBLER
BEJLMSU JUMBLES
BEJLOSS JOBLESS
BEJORSU OBJURES
BEKLNRU BLUNKER
BEKLOOT BOOKLET
BEKLRSU BULKERS
BEKMNOO BOOKMEN
BEKMOST STEMBOK
BEKNNOW BEKNOWN
BEKNORS BONKERS
BEKNORU UNBROKE
BEKNRSU BUNKERS
BEKOPRU UPBROKE
BEKORRS BROKERS
BEKORRY BROKERY
BEKOSST BOSKETS
BEKRSSU BUSKERS
BEKSSTU BUSKETS
BELLORR BORRELL
BELLOSU BOULLES
LOBULES
SOLUBLE
BELLOSW BELLOWS
BELLOUV VOLUBLE
BELLRRU BURRELL
BELLRSU BULLERS
BELLSTU BULLETS
BELMMOO EMBLOOM
BELMMRU MUMBLER
BELMMSU BUMMELS
BUMMLES
MUMBLES
BELMNOS NOMBLES
BELMNOU NELUMBO
BELMNSU NUMBLES
BELMOOR BLOOMER
REBLOOM
BELMOOS BLOOSME
BELMOOT BOOMLET
BELMOPR PROBLEM
BELMORT TEMBLOR
BELMOSU EMBOLUS
BELMOSY SYMBOLE
BELMPRU PLUMBER
BELMRRU RUMBLER
BELMRSU LUMBERS
RUMBLES
SLUMBER
UMBRELS
BELMRTU TUMBLER
TUMBREL
BELMRTY TREMBLY
BELMSTU STUMBLE
TUMBLES
BELNNOU UNNOBLE
BELNNTU UNBLENT
BELNOOY BOLONEY
BELNOST NOBLEST
BELNOSZ BENZOLS
BELNOYZ BENZOYL
BELNRTU BLUNTER

BELNSSU UNBLESS
BELNSTU SUNBELT
UNBELTS
UNBLEST
BELNSYZ BENZYLS
BELOOPR BLOOPER
BELOORS BOLEROS
BELOOSS SOBOLES
BELOPSU PUEBLOS
BELORST BOLSTER
BOLTERS
LOBSTER
BELORSU ROUBLES
BELORSW BLOWERS
BOWLERS
BELORSY SOBERLY
BELORTT BLOTTER
BOTTLER
BELORTU BOULTER
TROUBLE
BELOSSU BLOUSES
BOLUSES
BELOSSW BLOWSES
BELOSTT BOTTLES
BELOSTU BOLETUS
BELOSWZ BLOWZES
BELRRSU BURLERS
BURRELS
BELRSTU BLUSTER
BUSTLER
BUTLERS
SUBTLER
BELRSUY BURLEYS
BELRTUY BUTLERY
BELSSTU BUSTLES
SUBLETS
BELSTTU BUTTLES
BELSTUU TUBULES
BEMMNOS MOBSMEN
BEMMOOS EMBOSOM
BEMMORR BROMMER
BEMMRRU BRUMMER
BEMMRSU BUMMERS
BEMNORW EMBROWN
BEMNORY EMBRYON
BEMNOST ENTOMBS
BEMNOSU UMBONES
BEMNOSW ENWOMBS
BEMNPTY BYNEMPT
BEMNRSU NUMBERS
BEMNSTU NUMBEST
BEMNTTU BUTMENT
BEMOORS BOOMERS
BEMORRS SOMBRER
BEMORSS SOMBERS
SOMBRES
BEMORST BESTORM
MOBSTER
BEMORSU UMBROSE
BEMORSY EMBRYOS
BEMORUX BUXOMER
BEMORWW WEBWORM
BEMOTUY MYOTUBE
BEMPRSU BUMPERS
BEMSSTU BESMUTS
BEMSSUU SUBSUME
BENNORU UNBORNE
BENNORW NEWBORN
BENNORZ BRONZEN
BENNOST BONNETS

BENNOSU	UNBONES
BENNSSU	BUNSENS
BENOPRR	PREBORN
BENOPRU	UPBORNE
BENORRW	BROWNER
BENORRZ	BRONZER
BENORST	BRETONS
	SORBENT
BENORSU	BOURNES
	UNROBES
BENORSZ	BRONZES
BENORWY	BYWONER
BENOSSU	BONUSES
BENOSUX	UNBOXES
BENOSUZ	SUBZONE
BENOSWY	NEWSBOY
BENRRSU	BURNERS
BENRSTU	BRUNETS
	BUNTERS
	BURNETS
	BURSTEN
BEOORSS	BROOSES
BEOORST	BOOSTER
BEOORSZ	BOOZERS
BEOPPRS	BOPPERS
BEOPRRS	PROBERS
BEOPRRV	PROVERB
BEOPRST	BESPORT
BEOPSST	BESPOTS
BEOPSTU	BESPOUT
BEOQSTU	BOSQUET
BEOQSUY	OBSEQUY
BEOQTUU	BOUQUET
BEORRSS	RESORBS
BEORRSW	BROWSER
BEORSST	BESORTS
	SORBETS
	STROBES
BEORSSU	BOURSES
BEORSSW	BOWSERS
	BROWSES
BEORSTT	BETTORS
BEORSTU	OBTUSER
BEORSTV	OBVERTS
BEORSUU	UBEROUS
BEORSUZ	BROUZES
	SUBZERO
BEORSVV	BOVVERS
BEORSWY	BOWYERS
BEORUVY	OVERBUY
BEOSSST	BOSSEST
BEOSSTT	OBTESTS
BEOSSTW	BESTOWS
BEPRRTU	PERTURB
BEPRTUY	PUBERTY
BEPSTUY	SUBTYPE
BEQRSUU	BRUSQUE
BERRSTU	BRUTERS
	BURSTER
BERSSTU	BUSTERS
BERSTTU	BUTTERS
BERSTUV	SUBVERT
BERSUZZ	BUZZERS
BERTTUY	BUTTERY
BESSSTU	SUBSETS
BESTTUX	SUBTEXT
BFFGIIN	BIFFING
BFFGINO	BOFFING
BFFGINU	BUFFING
BFFIINS	BIFFINS
BFFINOS	BOFFINS
BFFLLUY	BLUFFLY
BFFNOOU	BUFFOON
BFGIOOT	BIGFOOT
BFGIORT	FROGBIT
BFHILSU	LUBFISH
BFHIRSU	FURBISH
BFHISTU	TUBFISH
BFIILRS	FIBRILS
BFIINOR	FIBROIN
BFIINRS	FIBRINS
BFILMRU	BRIMFUL
BFIMOYZ	ZOMBIFY
BFINOSW	BOWFINS
BFIORSU	FIBROUS
BFIRTUY	BRUTIFY
BFKLOOU	BOOKFUL
BFKLOOY	FLYBOOK
BFKSSUU	SUBFUSK
BFLLOUW	BOWLFUL
BFLLOWY	BLOWFLY
	FLYBLOW
BFLOSUX	BOXFULS
BFLSTUU	TUBFULS
BFOOOTY	FOOTBOY
BGGGIIN	BIGGING
BGGGINO	BOGGING
BGGGINU	BUGGING
BGGHIIS	BIGGISH
BGGIILN	BILGING
BGGIINN	BINGING
BGGIINS	BIGGINS
BGGIISW	BIGWIGS
BGGILNO	GLOBING
BGGILNU	BUGLING
	BULGING
BGGINNO	BONGING
BGGINNU	BUNGING
BGGINOU	BOUGING
BGGINSU	BUGGINS
BGGNOOS	BOGONGS
BGGNOSU	BUGONGS
BGHHIOY	HIGHBOY
BGHIINS	BINGHIS
BGHILST	BLIGHTS
BGHILTY	BLIGHTY
BGHINOO	BOOHING
	HOBOING
BGHINOR	BIGHORN
BGHINSU	BUSHING
BGHLRUU	BULGHUR
	BURGHUL
BGHMSUU	HUMBUGS
BGHNORU	HORNBUG
BGHOORU	BOROUGH
BGHORSU	BROUGHS
BGHORTU	BROUGHT
BGHOSTU	BOUGHTS
BGIIKLN	BILKING
BGIIKNS	BIKINGS
BGIILLN	BILLING
BGIILMN	LIMBING
BGIILNO	BOILING
BGIILNR	BIRLING
BGIILNS	SIBLING
BGIIMNR	BRIMING
BGIIMNU	IMBUING
BGIINNN	BINNING
BGIINNR	BRINING
	INBRING
BGIINRR	BIRRING
BGIINRT	RINGBIT
BGIINST	BITINGS
BGIINTT	BITTING
BGIKLNU	BULKING
BGIKNNO	BONKING
BGIKNNU	BUNKING
BGIKNOO	BOOKING
BGIKNOR	BROKING
BGIKNRU	BURKING
BGIKNSU	BUSKING
BGILLNO	BOLLING
BGILLNU	BULLING
BGILMNO	MOBLING
BGILMOU	GUMBOIL
BGILNOS	GLOBINS
	GOBLINS
	LOBINGS
BGILNOT	BILTONG
	BOLTING
BGILNOW	BLOWING
	BOWLING
BGILNOY	IGNOBLY
BGILNRU	BURLING
BGILNSU	BLUINGS
BGILOOR	OBLIGOR
BGILOOY	BIOLOGY
BGILRSU	BUSGIRL
BGIMMNU	BUMMING
BGIMNNU	NUMBING
BGIMNOO	BOOMING
BGIMNOT	TOMBING
BGIMNOW	WOMBING
BGIMNPU	BUMPING
BGIMOSY	BOGYISM
BGINNOS	BONINGS
BGINNOU	BOUNING
BGINNOW	BOWNING
BGINNRU	BURNING
BGINNTU	BUNTING
BGINOOS	BOOSING
BGINOOT	BOOTING
BGINOOZ	BOOZING
BGINOPP	BOPPING
BGINOPR	PROBING
BGINORS	BORINGS
	ROBINGS
	SORBING
BGINOSS	BOSSING
	OBSIGNS
BGINOSU	BOUSING
BGINOSW	BOWINGS
	BOWSING
BGINOSX	BOXINGS
BGINOTT	BOTTING
BGINOUY	BUOYING
BGINPRU	BURPING
	UPBRING
BGINRRU	BURRING
BGINRSU	SUBRING
BGINRTU	BRUTING
BGINRUY	BURYING
	RUBYING
BGINSSU	BUSINGS
	BUSSING
BGINSTU	BUSTING
	TUBINGS
BGINSUY	BUSYING
BGINTTU	BUTTING
BGINUZZ	BUZZING
BGIORTY	BIGOTRY
BGIOSSS	GOSSIBS
BGKLOOO	LOGBOOK
BGKORSY	GRYSBOK
BGLMRUY	GRUMBLY
BGLNOOS	OBLONGS
BGLNOOW	LONGBOW
BGLNOUW	BLOWGUN
BGLOOSU	GLOBOUS
BGLOSSU	BUGLOSS
BGLRSUU	BULGURS
BGMOORS	GOMBROS
BGMOOTU	GUMBOOT
BGMSSUU	SUBGUMS
BGNOOWY	GOWNBOY
BGNOSSU	SUBSONG
BGOORSU	BURGOOS
BGORTUW	BUGWORT
BHIIINT	INHIBIT
BHIINRS	BRINISH
BHIIPSS	SIBSHIP
BHIISST	BHISTIS
BHIKOOS	BOOKISH
BHIKSSU	BUKSHIS
BHILLSU	BULLISH
BHILOTU	HOLIBUT
BHILPSU	PUBLISH
BHIMOOR	RHOMBOI
BHIMOOS	HOBOISM
BHIMOPS	PHOBISM
BHIMORT	THROMBI
BHIMSTU	BISMUTH
BHINRSU	BURNISH
BHIOOPR	BIOPHOR
BHIOORS	BOORISH
BHIOPSS	BISHOPS
BHIOPST	PHOBIST
BHIOSWZ	SHOWBIZ
BHIRSTU	BRUTISH
BHIRTTU	TURBITH
BHKNOSU	BOHUNKS
BHLRSUU	BULRUSH
BHMOORS	RHOMBOS
BHMORSU	RHOMBUS
BHMUUZZ	HUMBUZZ
BHOOSTW	BOWSHOT
BHOOSWX	SHOWBOX
BIIIKNS	BIKINIS
BIIKLOT	KILOBIT
BIILLNO	BILLION
BIILLOU	BOUILLI
BIILLTW	TWIBILL
BIILNNR	BIRLINN
BIILNQU	QUIBLIN
BIILOSU	BILIOUS
BIILSVY	VISIBLY
BIIMNOU	NIOBIUM
BIIMNSU	MINIBUS
BIIMOSS	OBIISMS
BIIMSTU	STIBIUM
BIINOST	BIOTINS
BIIORSV	VIBRIOS
BIIOSUV	BIVIOUS
BIIRSTU	BURITIS
BIISSTV	VIBISTS
BIISTTT	TITBITS
BIJNOSU	SUBJOIN
BIKLLUY	BULKILY
BIKLNOY	LINKBOY
BIKLRSY	BRISKLY

BIKMNPU	BUMPKIN
BIKMNSU	BUMKINS
BIKMOSS	IMBOSKS
BIKNSSU	BUSKINS
BIKORRW	RIBWORK
BILLNOS	BILLONS
BILLNOU	BULLION
BILLOOY	LOOBILY
BILLOSW	BILLOWS
BILLOUV	VOLUBIL
BILLOWY	BILLOWY
BILLRWY	WRYBILL
BILMNOR	NOMBRIL
BILMOSU	LIMBOUS
BILMPUY	BUMPILY
BILMRSU	UMBRILS
BILMRTU	TUMBRIL
BILMSUU	BULIMUS
BILNNOY	BONNILY
BILNTUU	TUBULIN
	UNBUILT
BILOOYZ	BOOZILY
BILOPSU	UPBOILS
BILOSSU	SUBSOIL
BILOSSY	BOSSILY
BILPTUU	UPBUILT
BILRSTY	BRISTLY
	TRILBYS
BILRTTY	BRITTLY
BILRTUY	TILBURY
BIMMOOS	IMBOSOM
	MIOMBOS
BIMMORS	BROMISM
BIMNORS	MISBORN
BIMNORW	IMBROWN
BIMNOSS	BONISMS
BIMNOST	INTOMBS
BIMNOSU	OMNIBUS
BIMRSUX	BRUXISM
BIMSSSU	SUBMISS
BIMSSTU	SUBMITS
BINNOSU	BUNIONS
BINOORS	BONSOIR
BINOOST	BONITOS
BINOOSU	NIOBOUS
BINORST	RIBSTON
BINOSST	BONISTS
BINPSUY	BUNYIPS
BINRSTU	INBURST
BINSTTU	UNBITTS
BINSTUU	SUBUNIT
BIOORSZ	BORZOIS
BIOOSST	OBOISTS
BIOOSUV	OBVIOUS
BIOPRST	PROBITS
BIOPRTY	PROBITY
BIORRTU	BURRITO
BIORRTW	RIBWORT
BIORSST	BISTROS
BIORSTT	BISTORT
	BITTORS
BIORSUU	RUBIOUS
BIORTTU	BITTOUR
BIOSTUW	WOUBITS
BIRSTTU	BITTURS
	TURBITS
BISSSTU	SUBSIST
BJNOORU	BONJOUR
BKMNSUU	BUNKUMS
BKNOOTW	BOWKNOT
BKNORSY	SKYBORN
BKOORWX	WORKBOX
BLLNTUY	BLUNTLY
BLLOSUU	LOBULUS
BLLOUVY	VOLUBLY
BLMMPUU	PLUMBUM
BLMNPUU	UNPLUMB
BLMOOOT	TOMBOLO
BLMOORW	LOBWORM
BLMOOSS	BLOSSOM
BLMOSSY	SYMBOLS
BLMRSUY	SLUMBRY
BLMSTUY	STUMBLY
BLNNOUW	UNBLOWN
BLNOOSU	BLOUSON
BLNOPUW	UPBLOWN
BLNOSTU	UNBOLTS
BLOOOTX	TOOLBOX
BLOOQUY	OBLOQUY
BLOOSWY	LOWBOYS
BLOPSTU	SUBPLOT
BLOPSUW	UPBLOWS
BMNOOSU	UNBOSOM
BMNORUW	MOWBURN
BMNOSTU	UNTOMBS
BMOOORX	BOXROOM
BMOORSY	BYROOMS
BMOOSTT	BOTTOMS
BMOOSTY	TOMBOYS
BMORSST	STROMBS
BMORSUU	BRUMOUS
	UMBROUS
BNNRSUU	SUNBURN
BNNRTUU	UNBURNT
BNOOSST	BOSTONS
BNOOSTU	BOUTONS
	UNBOOTS
BNOOTTY	BOTTONY
BNORSSU	SUBORNS
BNORSTU	BURTONS
BNORSUU	BURNOUS
BNORTUU	OUTBURN
BNOSSUW	SUNBOWS
BNOSTTU	BUTTONS
BNOTTUY	BUTTONY
BOOPSTW	BOWPOTS
BOOPSTX	POSTBOX
BOOPSTY	POTBOYS
BOORRSW	BORROWS
BOOSTUW	WOOBUTS
BOOSWWW	BOWWOWS
BOPSSTU	POSTBUS
BORRSUW	BURROWS
BORSSTW	BROWSTS
BORSTTU	TURBOTS
BORSTUU	RUBOUTS
BORSTXY	BOSTRYX
BPRSTUU	UPBURST
CCCDIOO	COCCOID
CCCDIOS	COCCIDS
CCCNOOT	CONCOCT
CCDEEER	RECCEED
CCDEEHK	CHECKED
CCDEEIO	ECOCIDE
CCDEEIR	RECCIED
CCDEEIS	DECCIES
CCDEEKL	CLECKED
CCDEENO	CONCEDE
CCDEENY	DECENCY
CCDEEOR	COERCED
CCDEESU	SUCCEED
CCDEHIN	CINCHED
CCDEHKO	CHOCKED
CCDEHKU	CHUCKED
CCDEHNO	CONCHED
CCDEHOU	COUCHED
CCDEIIT	DEICTIC
CCDEIKL	CLICKED
CCDEIKR	CRICKED
CCDEILR	CIRCLED
CCDEIMO	COMEDIC
CCDEIOS	CODICES
CCDEKLO	CLOCKED
	COCKLED
CCDEKLU	CLUCKED
CCDEKOR	CROCKED
CCDELOU	OCCLUDE
CCDENOO	CONCEDO
CCDENOS	SCONCED
CCDENOU	CONDUCE
CCDEOST	DECOCTS
CCDHIIL	CICHLID
CCDIILO	CODICIL
CCDIILU	CULICID
CCDIIOR	CRICOID
CCDILOY	CYCLOID
CCDKLOU	CUCKOLD
CCDNOOR	CONCORD
CCDNOTU	CONDUCT
CCEEGNO	COGENCE
CCEEHIV	CEVICHE
CCEEHKR	CHECKER
	RECHECK
CCEEHOR	ECORCHE
CCEEHOU	COUCHEE
CCEEHRS	CRECHES
	SCREECH
CCEEILN	LICENCE
CCEEINR	ECCRINE
CCEEINS	SCIENCE
CCEEIRS	RECCIES
CCEEIRV	CREVICE
CCEEKOY	COCKEYE
CCEELRY	RECYCLE
CCEENRY	RECENCY
CCEEORS	COERCES
CCEERSY	SECRECY
CCEFNOT	CONFECT
CCEGNOY	COGENCY
CCEHHIS	CHICHES
CCEHIKN	CHICKEN
CCEHIKU	CHUCKIE
CCEHILS	CHICLES
	CLICHES
CCEHILU	CULCHIE
CCEHIMS	CHEMICS
CCEHINO	CONCHIE
CCEHINS	CINCHES
CCEHINT	TECHNIC
CCEHIOR	CHOICER
	CHOREIC
CCEHIOS	CHOICES
CCEHIRS	SCREICH
	SCRIECH
CCEHIST	CHICEST
	HECTICS
CCEHKLU	CHUCKLE
CCEHKMS	SCHMECK
CCEHKNU	UNCHECK
CCEHKOR	CHOCKER
CCEHLOS	CLOCHES
CCEHLRU	CLERUCH
CCEHLSU	CLEUCHS
	CULCHES
CCEHNOS	CONCHES
CCEHORS	CROCHES
CCEHORT	CROCHET
CCEHOSS	COSECHS
CCEHOSU	COUCHES
CCEHRSU	CURCHES
CCEHSTU	CUTCHES
CCEIILS	CILICES
	ICICLES
CCEIIMS	CIMICES
CCEIIPS	PICCIES
CCEIIRT	ICTERIC
CCEIIST	CECITIS
CCEIKLR	CLICKER
CCEIKLT	CLICKET
CCEIKOR	COCKIER
CCEIKOS	COCKIES
CCEIKRT	CRICKET
CCEIKRY	CRICKEY
CCEILOT	COCTILE
CCEILRR	CIRCLER
CCEILRS	CIRCLES
	CLERICS
CCEILRT	CIRCLET
CCEILSU	CULICES
CCEILSY	CYLICES
CCEILTU	CUTICLE
CCEIMNO	MECONIC
CCEIMOS	COMICES
CCEIMOT	COMETIC
CCEIMST	SMECTIC
CCEINOR	CORNICE
	CROCEIN
CCEINOS	CONCISE
CCEINOT	CONCEIT
CCEINRT	CENTRIC
CCEIOPP	COPPICE
CCEIOPT	ECTOPIC
CCEIORS	CICEROS
CCEIORT	ORECTIC
CCEIOSS	CISCOES
CCEIPST	SCEPTIC
CCEIRST	CRETICS
CCEISSU	SUCCISE
CCEJNOT	CONJECT
CCEKLOR	CLOCKER
CCEKLOS	COCKLES
CCEKNOT	CONTECK
CCEKNOY	COCKNEY
CCEKOPS	COPECKS
CCEKOPT	PETCOCK
CCEKORS	COCKERS
CCEKORT	CROCKET
CCEKOST	COCKETS
CCELLOT	COLLECT
CCELNOY	CYCLONE
CCELNUY	LUCENCY
CCELRSY	CYCLERS
CCENNOR	CONCERN
CCENNOT	CONCENT
	CONNECT
CCENOPT	CONCEPT
CCENORT	CONCERT
CCENORW	CONCREW
CCENOSS	SCONCES
CCEOOTT	COCOTTE

CCEOPRT PERCOCT
CCEORRT CORRECT
CCEORSS ESCROCS
SOCCERS
CCEORTW TWOCCER
CCEOSSU SUCCOSE
CCESSSU SUCCESS
CCFIRUY CRUCIFY
CCFLOSU FLOCCUS
CCGHINO GNOCCHI
CCGIINS SICCING
CCGIKNO COCKING
CCGILNY CYCLING
CCGKOOR GORCOCK
CCHHIIS CHICHIS
CCHHIIT ICHTHIC
CCHHILS SCHLICH
CCHHOOS CHOCHOS
CCHHRUY CHURCHY
CCHIIST STICHIC
CCHIKST SCHTICK
TCHICKS
CCHILOR CHLORIC
CCHIMOR CHROMIC
CCHINOR CHRONIC
CCHINOS CHICONS
CCHINSU SCUCHIN
CCHIORY CHICORY
CCHIOTW COWITCH
CCHIPSU HICCUPS
CCHIPSY PSYCHIC
CCHIPUY HICCUPY
CCHIRST SCRITCH
CCHKLOS SCHLOCK
CCHKMOS SCHMOCK
CCHKMSU SCHMUCK
CCHKOOS CHOCKOS
CCHKOSY COCKSHY
CCHKPUU UPCHUCK
CCHKSTU SCHTUCK
CCHNRSU SCRUNCH
CCHNRUY CRUNCHY
CCIIILS SILICIC
CCIILNS CLINICS
CCIILPR CIRCLIP
CCIILST CLITICS
CCIINPS PICNICS
CCIIRST CRITICS
CCIIRTU CIRCUIT
CCIISTY SICCITY
CCIKLOW COWLICK
CCIKLOY COCKILY
COLICKY
CCIKOPT COCKPIT
CCILNOO COLONIC
CCILNOU COUNCIL
CCILOOP PICCOLO
CCILSTY CYCLIST
CCIMOTY MYCOTIC
CCINOOT COCTION
CCINORY CRYONIC
CCINOTV CONVICT
CCIOORS SIROCCO
CCIOPTU OCCIPUT
CCIORSS SCIROCS
CCIPRTY CRYPTIC
CCIRSUY CIRCUSY
CCKMOOS MOCOCKS
CCKMOSU MOCUCKS
CCKNOSU UNCOCKS
CCKOOSU CUCKOOS
CCKOSTU CUSTOCK
CCLMSUU MUCLUCS
CCLOOOZ ZOCCOLO
CCLOPSY CYCLOPS
CCLOSTU OCCULTS
CCMOOOR MOROCCO
CCNOOOS COCOONS
CCNOOPU PUCCOON
CCNOOTU COCONUT
CCNOPUY CONCUPY
CCNORSU CONCURS
CCNOSSU CONCUSS
CCOOORS ROCOCOS
CCORSSU SUCCORS
CCORSUU SUCCOUR
CCORSUY SUCCORY
CCOSSTU STUCCOS
CCOSSUU SUCCOUS
CCSSSUU SUCCUSS
CDDDEEI DECIDED
CDDDEEO DECODED
CDDDEEU DEDUCED
CDDDELO CLODDED
CODDLED
CDDDELU CUDDLED
CDDDERU CRUDDED
CDDDESU SCUDDED
CDDEEER DECREED
RECEDED
CDDEEES SECEDED
CDDEEII DEICIDE
CDDEEIN INCEDED
CDDEEIR DECIDER
DECRIED
CDDEEIS DECIDES
CDDEEIX EXCIDED
CDDEEKL DECKLED
CDDEEKO DECKOED
DECOKED
CDDEENO ENCODED
CDDEENS DESCEND
SCENDED
CDDEEOR DECODER
RECODED
CDDEEOS DECODES
CDDEEOY DECOYED
CDDEERU REDUCED
CDDEESU DEDUCES
SEDUCED
CDDEEUW CUDWEED
CDDEHIL CHILDED
CDDEHIN CHIDDEN
CDDEHIT DICHTED
DITCHED
CDDEHNU DUNCHED
CDDEHOU DOUCHED
CDDEIIS DISCIDE
CDDEINU INDUCED
CDDEIOS DISCOED
CDDEISU CUDDIES
CDDELOS CODDLES
SCOLDED
CDDELOU CLOUDED
CDDELRU CRUDDLE
CURDLED
CDDELSU CUDDLES
SCUDDLE
CDDENSU CUDDENS
CDDEORS CODDERS
CDDEORW CROWDED
CDDERSU SCUDDER
CDDESTU DEDUCTS
CDDGINO CODDING
CDDHIOR DICHORD
CDDIIIO DIDICOI
CDDIIOS DISCOID
CDDIIOY DIDICOY
CDDIIRU DRUIDIC
CDDIKOP PIDDOCK
CDDINSU CUDDINS
CDDIORS DISCORD
CDDKOPU PUDDOCK
CDDKORU RUDDOCK
CDEEEFL FLEECED
CDEEEFN DEFENCE
CDEEEHK CHEEKED
CDEEEHL LEECHED
CDEEEHP CHEEPED
DEPECHE
CDEEEHR CHEERED
REECHED
CDEEEHS CHEESED
CDEEEIP EPICEDE
CDEEEIV DECEIVE
CDEEEJT EJECTED
CDEEEKL CLEEKED
CDEEELP CLEEPED
CDEEELT ELECTED
CDEEEPR PRECEDE
CDEEERS CREESED
DECREES
RECEDES
SECEDER
CDEEERT DECREET
ERECTED
CDEEESS SECEDES
CDEEESX EXCEEDS
CDEEFHT FETCHED
CDEEFII EDIFICE
CDEEFKL FLECKED
CDEEFLT DEFLECT
CDEEFOR DEFORCE
CDEEFST DEFECTS
CDEEGIR GRIECED
CDEEGNO CONGEED
CDEEHIS DEHISCE
CDEEHIV CHEVIED
CDEEHKL HECKLED
CDEEHLT LETCHED
CDEEHLW WELCHED
CDEEHMS SCHEMED
CDEEHNW WENCHED
CDEEHOR CHORDEE
COHERED
OCHERED
CDEEHPR PERCHED
CDEEHRT RETCHED
CDEEHRU EUCHRED
CDEEHST CHESTED
CDEEIIT EIDETIC
CDEEILN DECLINE
CDEEILP PEDICEL
PEDICLE
CDEEILS DELICES
CDEEIMN ENDEMIC
CDEEIMS DECIMES
CDEEINO CODEINE
CDEEINR CEDRINE
CDEEINS INCEDES
CDEEINT ENTICED
CDEEINV EVINCED
CDEEIOS DIOCESE
CDEEIOV DEVOICE
CDEEIPR PIERCED
CDEEIPT PEDETIC
CDEEIRR DECRIER
CDEEIRS DECRIES
CDEEIRT RECITED
TIERCED
CDEEIST DECEITS
CDEEISV DEVICES
CDEEISX EXCIDES
EXCISED
CDEEITV EVICTED
CDEEITX EXCITED
CDEEJNO CONJEED
CDEEJST DEJECTS
CDEEKKL KECKLED
CDEEKLR CLERKED
CDEEKLS DECKLES
CDEEKNR REDNECK
CDEEKNS SNECKED
CDEEKOS DECOKES
CDEEKPS SPECKED
CDEEKRS DECKERS
CDEEKRT TRECKED
CDEEKRW WRECKED
CDEELMM CLEMMED
CDEELOS ECLOSED
CDEELPU CUPELED
DECUPLE
CDEELPY YCLEPED
CDEELRU RECULED
ULCERED
CDEELSU SCEDULE
SECLUDE
CDEELUX EXCLUDE
CDEENOR ENCORED
CDEENOS ENCODES
SECONDE
CDEENOZ COZENED
CDEENRS DECERNS
SCERNED
CDEENRT CENTRED
CREDENT
CDEENST DESCENT
SCENTED
CDEEOOY COOEYED
CDEEOPR COPERED
PROCEED
CDEEORS RECODES
CDEEORV COVERED
CDEEORW COWERED
CDEEOST CESTODE
TEDESCO
CDEEOTV COVETED
CDEERRU RECURED
REDUCER
CDEERSS SCREEDS
CDEERST CRESTED
CDEERSU RECUSED
REDUCES
RESCUED
SECURED
SEDUCER
CDEERSW DECREWS
SCREWED
CDEERTU ERUCTED
CDEERUV DECURVE

CDEESSU SEDUCES
CDEESSY ECDYSES
CDEESTT DECTETS
DETECTS
CDEESUX EXCUSED
CDEFFHU CHUFFED
CDEFFIL CLIFFED
CDEFFLU CUFFLED
CDEFFOS SCOFFED
CDEFFSU SCUFFED
CDEFHIL FILCHED
CDEFHIN FINCHED
CDEFHOO CHOOFED
CDEFIIT DEFICIT
CDEFIKL FICKLED
FLICKED
CDEFILT CLIFTED
CDEFINO CONFIDE
CDEFKLO FLOCKED
CDEFKOR DEFROCK
FROCKED
CDEFNTU DEFUNCT
CDEFOSU FOCUSED
CDEFRTU FRUCTED
CDEFSUU FUCUSED
CDEGGHU CHUGGED
CDEGGLO CLOGGED
COGGLED
CDEGGOS SCOGGED
CDEGGSU SCUGGED
CDEGHLU GULCHED
CDEGHOU COUGHED
CDEGIKN DECKING
CDEGILU CLUDGIE
CDEGINO COIGNED
CDEGINR CRINGED
CDEGINU EDUCING
CDEGIOR ERGODIC
CDEGLSU CUDGELS
CDEGNSU SCUNGED
CDEGOOS SCOOGED
CDEGORS CODGERS
CDEGOSU SCOUGED
CDEHHIL HILCHED
CDEHHIT HITCHED
CDEHHNU HUNCHED
CDEHHOT HOTCHED
CDEHHTU HUTCHED
CDEHIIL CEILIDH
CDEHIIV CHIVIED
CDEHIKN CHINKED
CDEHIKO HOICKED
CDEHIKR CHIRKED
CDEHIKT THICKED
CDEHILL CHILLED
CDEHILO CHELOID
HELCOID
CDEHILP DELPHIC
CDEHILR CHILDER
CHIRLED
CDEHILS CHIELDS
CDEHILT LICHTED
CDEHIMR CHIRMED
CDEHIMT MITCHED
CDEHINN CHINNED
CDEHINO HEDONIC
CDEHINP PINCHED
CDEHINW WINCHED
CDEHIOR CHOIRED
CDEHIOW COWHIDE

CDEHIPP CHIPPED
CDEHIPR CHIRPED
CDEHIPT PITCHED
CDEHIQU QUICHED
CDEHIRR CHIRRED
CDEHIRS CHIDERS
HERDICS
CDEHIRT CHIRTED
DITCHER
RICHTED
CDEHIST DITCHES
CDEHISU DUCHIES
CDEHITT CHITTED
CDEHITW WITCHED
CDEHIVV CHIVVED
CDEHIZZ CHIZZED
CDEHKOS SHOCKED
CDEHKSU SHUCKED
CDEHKUY HEYDUCK
CDEHLMU MULCHED
CDEHLNU LUNCHED
CDEHLNY LYNCHED
CDEHLOT CLOTHED
CDEHLRU LURCHED
CDEHMMU CHUMMED
CDEHMNU MUNCHED
CDEHMOO MOOCHED
CDEHMOP CHOMPED
CDEHMOR CHROMED
CDEHMOU MOUCHED
CDEHNOR CHONDRE
CDEHNOT NOTCHED
CDEHNPU PUNCHED
CDEHNRU CHUNDER
CHURNED
CDEHNSU DUNCHES
CDEHNSY SYNCHED
CDEHOPP CHOPPED
CDEHOPT POTCHED
CDEHOPU POUCHED
CDEHORT TORCHED
CDEHORW CHOWDER
COWHERD
CDEHOSU CHOUSED
DOUCHES
HOCUSED
CDEHOSW COWSHED
CDEHOTU TOUCHED
CDEHOUV VOUCHED
CDEHPSY PSYCHED
CDEHRRU CHURRED
CDEHRSU CRUSHED
CDEHSSU DUCHESS
CDEHSTU DUTCHES
CDEHSTY SCYTHED
CDEIIKR DICKIER
CDEIIKS DICKIES
CDEIIMR DIMERIC
CDEIINS INCISED
INDICES
CDEIINT IDENTIC
INCITED
CDEIIOR ERICOID
CDEIIOV OVICIDE
CDEIIRT DICTIER
ICTERID
CDEIIST DEISTIC
DICIEST
CDEIISU SUICIDE
CDEIJST DISJECT

CDEIKLN CLINKED
CDEIKLP PICKLED
CDEIKLS SICKLED
SLICKED
CDEIKLT TICKLED
CDEIKMS MEDICKS
CDEIKNS DICKENS
SNICKED
CDEIKNZ ZINCKED
CDEIKOS DOCKISE
CDEIKOY YOICKED
CDEIKOZ DOCKIZE
CDEIKPR PRICKED
CDEIKRR DERRICK
CDEIKRS DICKERS
SCRIKED
CDEIKRT TRICKED
CDEIKRU DUCKIER
CDEIKRW WRICKED
CDEIKST STICKED
CDEIKSU DUCKIES
CDEIKSW WICKEDS
CDEIKSY DICKEYS
CDEILLO CODILLE
COLLIDE
COLLIED
CDEILLU CULLIED
CDEILMO MELODIC
CDEILNU INCLUDE
NUCLIDE
CDEILOO OCELOID
CDEILOP POLICED
CDEILOR DOCILER
CDEILPP CLIPPED
CDEILPS SPLICED
CDEILPU CLUPEID
CDEILRU LUCIDER
CDEILST DELICTS
CDEILSU SLUICED
CDEILTU DUCTILE
DULCITE
CDEIMNO DEMONIC
CDEIMOR DORMICE
CDEIMOS MEDICOS
CDEIMOT DEMOTIC
CDEIMPR CRIMPED
CDEIMPU PUMICED
CDEIMSU MISCUED
CDEINOS CONDIES
SECONDI
CDEINOT CTENOID
DEONTIC
NOTICED
CDEINOU DOUCINE
CDEINOZ ZINCODE
CDEINPR PRINCED
CDEINRS CINDERS
DISCERN
RESCIND
CDEINRU INDUCER
CDEINRY CINDERY
CDEINSU CUNDIES
INCUDES
INCUSED
INDUCES
CDEINSX EXSCIND
CDEINTT TINCTED
CDEINTU UNCITED
CDEIOPR PERCOID
CDEIOPT PICOTED

CDEIORS DISCOER
CDEIORT CORDITE
CDEIORV DIVORCE
CDEIORW CROWDIE
CDEIOST CESTOID
COTISED
CDEIPRS CRISPED
DISCERP
CDEIPRT PREDICT
CDEIPST DEPICTS
DISCEPT
CDEIRRU CURDIER
CURRIED
CDEIRST CREDITS
DIRECTS
CDEIRSU CRUISED
DISCURE
CDEIRSV CERVIDS
SCRIVED
CDEIRTV VERDICT
CDEISST DISSECT
CDEISSY ECDYSIS
CDEITUX EXCUDIT
CDEJNOU JOUNCED
CDEKKNO KNOCKED
CDEKLNO CLONKED
CDEKLNU CLUNKED
CDEKLOW WEDLOCK
CDEKLPU PLUCKED
CDEKLRU RUCKLED
CDEKLSU SCULKED
SUCKLED
CDEKMOS SMOCKED
CDEKNOS DOCKENS
CDEKNRU DRUCKEN
CDEKNSU SUNDECK
UNDECKS
CDEKOOR CROOKED
CDEKORS DOCKERS
CDEKORT TROCKED
CDEKOST DOCKETS
STOCKED
CDEKRSU DUCKERS
CDEKRTU TRUCKED
CDELLOU COLLUDE
CDELLSU SCULLED
CDELMOP CLOMPED
CDELMPU CLUMPED
CDELMSU MUSCLED
CDELMTU MULCTED
CDELNOO CONDOLE
CDELNOU ENCLOUD
CDELNOW CLOWNED
CDELNOY CONDYLE
CDELOOR COLORED
CROODLE
DECOLOR
CDELOPP CLOPPED
CDELOPU COUPLED
CDELORS SCOLDER
CDELORU CLOURED
CDELORW CLOWDER
CDELOST COLDEST
CDELOSU DULCOSE
CDELOSW SCOWLED
CDELOTT CLOTTED
CDELOTU CLOUTED
CDELOUY DOUCELY
CDELPSU SCULPED
CDELRSU CURDLES

SCUDLER
CDELRUY CRUDELY
CDEMMNO COMMEND
CDEMMOO COMMODE
CDEMMSU SCUMMED
CDEMNNO CONDEMN
CDEMOOS COMEDOS
CDEMOPT COMPTED
CDEMORU DECORUM
CDEMPRU CRUMPED
CDENNOO CONDONE
CDENNOT CONTEND
CDENOOR CROONED
CDENOOS SECONDO
CDENOPU POUNCED
UNCOPED
CDENORS CONDERS
CORSNED
SCORNED
CDENORW CROWNED
DECROWN
CDENOSS SECONDS
CDENOST DOCENTS
CDENOTU COUNTED
CDENPUY PUDENCY
CDENRUU UNCURED
CDENRUY DUNCERY
CDEOOPP COPEPOD
CDEOOPS OPCODES
SCOOPED
CDEOOPT COOPTED
CDEOORR CORRODE
CDEOORV VOCODER
CDEOOST SCOOTED
CDEOOTV DOVECOT
CDEOPPR CROPPED
CDEOPRS CORPSED
CDEOPRU CROUPED
PRODUCE
CDEOPSU SCOUPED
CDEOPSW SCOWPED
CDEOQTU DOCQUET
CDEORRS RECORDS
CDEORRW CROWDER
CDEORSS CROSSED
SCORSED
CDEORSU COURSED
SCOURED
SOURCED
CDEORSW SCOWDER
CDEORTU COURTED
EDUCTOR
CDEORUU DOUCEUR
CDEOSSU ESCUDOS
CDEOSTU DOUCEST
DOUCETS
SCOUTED
CDEOSTY CYTODES
CDEPRSU SPRUCED
CDEPRTY DECRYPT
CDERRSU SCURRED
CDERSTU CRUDEST
CRUSTED
CDERSUZ SCRUZED
CDFHIOS CODFISH
CDFIILU FLUIDIC
CDFILUY DULCIFY
CDFIOOT OCTOFID
CDFIOSU FUCOIDS
CDGHIIN CHIDING
CDGIINO GONIDIC
CDGIINS DICINGS
DISCING
CDGIINT DICTING
CDGIKNO DOCKING
CDGIKNU DUCKING
CDGILNO CODLING
CDGINNO CONDIGN
CDGINOR CORDING
CDGINOS CODINGS
CDGINRU CURDING
CDGINTU DUCTING
CDGNOOO COONDOG
CDHIIMO DOCHMII
CDHIINT CHINDIT
CDHIIST DISTICH
CDHILLY CHILDLY
CDHILNU UNCHILD
CDHILOS COLDISH
CDHINOR CHONDRI
CDHIOOR CHOROID
OCHROID
CDHIORS DROICHS
ORCHIDS
CDHIORY DROICHY
CDHIPTY DIPTYCH
CDHKOOR HORDOCK
CDIIIOT IDIOTIC
CDIIJRU JURIDIC
CDIILLY IDYLLIC
CDIILMO DOMICIL
CDIINOR CRINOID
CDIINOT DICTION
CDIINOZ ZINCOID
CDIINST INDICTS
CDIIORS CIRSOID
CDIIOSS CISSOID
CDIIOTY IDIOTCY
CDIKNOR DORNICK
CDIKNOW WINDOCK
CDILLOO COLLOID
CDILLUY LUCIDLY
CDILNOS CODLINS
CDILOTU DULOTIC
CDIMMOU MODICUM
CDIMNOO MONODIC
CDIMNSU MUNDICS
CDIMOSU MUSCOID
CDIMSSU MUSCIDS
CDINOOS CONOIDS
CDINOOT ODONTIC
CDINOSY SYNODIC
CDINOTU CONDUIT
NOCTUID
CDINSSY SYNDICS
CDINSTU INDUCTS
CDIOOTT COTTOID
CDIOPSS PSOCIDS
CDIORSV CORVIDS
CDIOSST CODISTS
CDIOSTT COTTIDS
CDIOSTY CYSTOID
CDIOTUV OVIDUCT
CDIPRSY CYPRIDS
CDIPSSU CUSPIDS
CDIRSUY DYSURIC
CDIRTUY CRUDITY
CDISSSU DISCUSS
CDISSTY CYSTIDS
CDKNNOU DUNNOCK
CDKNOSU UNDOCKS
CDLNOUU UNCLOUD
CDLOOPY LYCOPOD
CDMMOOO COMMODO
CDMNOOS CONDOMS
CDMOSUW MUDSCOW
CDNNOTU CONTUND
CDNOORS CONDORS
CORDONS
CDNORSU UNCORDS
CDOOOPT OCTOPOD
CDOOOST DOOCOTS
CDOORRY CORRODY
CDOORST DOCTORS
CDOOTUW WOODCUT
CDOPRTU PRODUCT
CDOSTUY CUSTODY
CEEEEGH GEECHEE
CEEEEHL LEECHEE
CEEEFLR FLEECER
CEEEFLS FLEECES
CEEEGNR REGENCE
CEEEGNS EGENCES
CEEEGRS GREECES
CEEEHIR REECHIE
CEEEHKS KEECHES
CEEEHLS ELCHEES
LEECHES
CEEEHNR ENCHEER
CEEEHPR CHEEPER
CEEEHRR CHEERER
CEEEHRS REECHES
CEEEHSS CHEESES
CEEEINP EPICENE
CEEEIPR CREEPIE
CEEEIRV RECEIVE
CEEELLU ECUELLE
CEEELPY YCLEEPE
CEEELST CELESTE
CEEELSV CLEEVES
CEEEMPR EMPERCE
CEEENRS RECENSE
CEEENSS ESSENCE
CEEEPRR CREEPER
CEEERRT ERECTER
CEEERSS CREESES
CEEERST SECRETE
CEEERSV SCREEVE
CEEERTX EXCRETE
CEEETUX EXECUTE
CEEFFNO OFFENCE
CEEFFOR EFFORCE
CEEFFOS COFFEES
CEEFFST EFFECTS
CEEFHIR CHIEFER
CEEFHIT FETICHE
FITCHEE
CEEFHLS FLECHES
CEEFHRT FECHTER
CEEFHST FETCHES
CEEFINV VENEFIC
CEEFIRR FIERCER
CEEFKLR FLECKER
FRECKLE
CEEFLNU FLUENCE
CEEFLRT REFLECT
CEEFNNS FENNECS
CEEFNOR ENFORCE
CEEFNRS FENCERS
CEEFPRT PERFECT
PREFECT
CEEFRST REFECTS
CEEFSSU FESCUES
CEEGHIN EECHING
CEEGINR CREEING
ENERGIC
GENERIC
CEEGINT GENETIC
CEEGINU EUGENIC
CEEGIRS CIERGES
GRECISE
GRIECES
CEEGIRZ GRECIZE
CEEGKOS GECKOES
CEEGLLO COLLEGE
CEEGLNT NEGLECT
CEEGLOU ECLOGUE
CEEGNOR COGENER
CONGREE
CEEGNOS CONGEES
CEEGNRU URGENCE
CEEGNRY REGENCY
CEEGORT CORTEGE
CEEGQRU GRECQUE
CEEHHSW WHEECHS
CEEHILN ELENCHI
CEEHILS HELICES
LICHEES
CEEHILV VEHICLE
CEEHIMR CHIMERE
CEEHIMS CHEMISE
CEEHINR INHERCE
CEEHINS CHINESE
CEEHIOR CHEERIO
CEEHIOS ECHOISE
CEEHIOZ ECHOIZE
CEEHIRT ETHERIC
HERETIC
TECHIER
CEEHIRW CHEWIER
CEEHISS SEICHES
CEEHISV CHEVIES
CEEHISW CHEWIES
CEEHKLR HECKLER
CEEHKLS HECKLES
CEEHKNP HENPECK
CEEHKST KETCHES
CEEHLNO CHELONE
ECHELON
CEEHLNS ELENCHS
CEEHLNU LEUCHEN
CEEHLOW COWHEEL
CEEHLRS LECHERS
CEEHLRW WELCHER
CEEHLRY CHEERLY
LECHERY
CEEHLSS CHESSEL
CEEHLST LETCHES
CEEHLSW LECHWES
WELCHES
CEEHLSY LYCHEES
SLEECHY
CEEHMRS SCHEMER
CEEHMRT MERCHET
CEEHMSS SCHEMES
CEEHNPU PENUCHE
CEEHNRW WENCHER
CEEHNST CHENETS
TENCHES
CEEHNSV CHEVENS

CEEHNSW	WENCHES
	WHENCES
CEEHORR	COHERER
CEEHORS	CHOREES
	COHERES
	ECHOERS
CEEHORT	TROCHEE
CEEHOUV	VOUCHEE
CEEHPRR	PERCHER
CEEHPRS	PERCHES
CEEHPRU	UPCHEER
CEEHQRU	CHEQUER
CEEHQSU	CHEQUES
CEEHQUY	QUEECHY
CEEHRST	ETCHERS
	RETCHES
CEEHRSU	EUCHRES
CEEHRSV	CHEVRES
CEEHRSW	CHEWERS
CEEHRSY	CREESHY
CEEHRTU	TEUCHER
CEEHSSS	CHESSES
CEEHSSW	ESCHEWS
CEEHSTV	CHEVETS
	VETCHES
CEEHSTW	CHEWETS
CEEIINR	EIRENIC
CEEIIPR	EPICIER
CEEIJOR	REJOICE
CEEIKLT	CLEEKIT
CEEIKNT	NECKTIE
CEEIKPR	PICKEER
CEEILLM	MICELLE
CEEILNO	CINEOLE
CEEILNR	RECLINE
CEEILNS	LICENSE
	SELENIC
	SILENCE
CEEILNU	LEUCINE
CEEILPS	ECLIPSE
CEEILRT	RETICLE
	TIERCEL
CEEILRU	RECUILE
CEEILST	SECTILE
CEEILSV	VESICLE
CEEILTU	LEUCITE
CEEIMNT	CENTIME
CEEIMRS	MERCIES
CEEIMST	EMETICS
CEEINNS	INCENSE
CEEINOS	SENECIO
CEEINPR	PERCINE
CEEINPS	PICENES
	PIECENS
CEEINPT	PENTICE
CEEINRS	CERESIN
	SCRIENE
	SINCERE
CEEINRT	ENTERIC
	ENTICER
CEEINRV	CERVINE
CEEINST	ENTICES
CEEINSV	EVINCES
CEEIOPT	PICOTEE
CEEIORT	COTERIE
CEEIPRR	CREPIER
	PIERCER
CEEIPRS	PIECERS
	PIERCES
	PRECISE
	RECIPES
CEEIPRT	RECEIPT
CEEIPRU	EPICURE
CEEIPSS	SPECIES
CEEIPST	PECTISE
CEEIPTZ	PECTIZE
CEEIQSU	QUIESCE
CEEIRRT	RECITER
CEEIRSS	CERISES
CEEIRST	CERITES
	RECITES
	TIERCES
CEEIRSU	ECURIES
CEEIRSV	SCRIEVE
	SERVICE
CEEIRTT	TIERCET
CEEIRTU	EUCRITE
CEEIRTX	EXCITER
CEEISSX	EXCISES
CEEISTX	EXCITES
CEEITTZ	ZETETIC
CEEJNOS	CONJEES
CEEJORT	EJECTOR
CEEJRST	REJECTS
CEEKKLS	KECKLES
CEEKKSS	KECKSES
CEEKLNT	NECKLET
CEEKLPS	SPECKLE
CEEKLSS	SECKELS
	SECKLES
CEEKLST	TECKELS
CEEKOSS	COKESES
CEEKOSY	SOCKEYE
CEEKPRS	PECKERS
CEEKPRY	RYEPECK
CEEKRRW	WRECKER
CEELLLU	CELLULE
CEELLNO	COLLEEN
CEELLOS	CELLOSE
CEELLPU	PUCELLE
CEELMNT	CLEMENT
CEELMOT	TELECOM
CEELMOW	WELCOME
CEELNOS	ENCLOSE
CEELNPS	PENCELS
CEELNRS	CRENELS
CEELNRT	LECTERN
CEELNRU	LUCERNE
CEELORS	CREOLES
	RECLOSE
CEELORT	ELECTOR
	ELECTRO
CEELORY	RECOYLE
CEELOSS	ECLOSES
CEELOSU	COULEES
CEELOTU	ELOCUTE
CEELOTV	COVELET
CEELPRT	PLECTRE
	PRELECT
CEELRSS	SCLERES
CEELRST	TERCELS
CEELRSU	RECLUSE
	RECULES
CEELRSW	CREWELS
CEELRTU	LECTURE
CEELRTY	ERECTLY
CEELSST	SELECTS
CEELTTU	LETTUCE
CEEMMOR	COMMERE
CEEMNOW	NEWCOME
CEEMNRU	CERUMEN
CEEMNST	CEMENTS
CEEMOPR	COMPEER
	COMPERE
CEEMOPT	COMPETE
CEEMRRS	MERCERS
CEEMRRY	MERCERY
	REMERCY
CEEMRST	CERMETS
CEEMSTU	TUMESCE
CEEMSTY	MYCETES
CEENNOU	ENOUNCE
CEENNOV	CONVENE
CEENNRT	CENTNER
CEENOPT	POTENCE
CEENORS	ENCORES
	NECROSE
CEENORZ	COZENER
CEENOST	CENOTES
CEENPRS	SPENCER
CEENPSS	SPENCES
CEENRSS	CENSERS
	SCERNES
	SCREENS
	SECERNS
CEENRST	CENTERS
	CENTRES
	TENRECS
CEENRSU	CENSURE
CEENRSY	SCENERY
CEENTTU	CUNETTE
CEEOPST	PECTOSE
CEEOPSU	COUPEES
CEEOPTY	ECOTYPE
CEEORRS	RESCORE
CEEORRT	ERECTOR
CEEORRU	RECOURE
CEEORRV	RECOVER
CEEORRW	RECOWER
CEEORSU	CEREOUS
CEEORSV	CORVEES
CEEORTW	COWTREE
CEEOTTT	OCTETTE
CEEPPRT	PERCEPT
	PRECEPT
CEEPPRU	PREPUCE
CEEPRSS	PRECESS
CEEPRST	RECEPTS
	RESPECT
	SCEPTER
	SCEPTRE
	SPECTER
	SPECTRE
CEEPRTX	EXCERPT
CEEPSTX	EXCEPTS
	EXPECTS
CEEPSTY	ECTYPES
CEERRSU	RECURES
	RESCUER
	SECURER
CEERRSW	SCREWER
CEERRUV	RECURVE
CEERSSS	CESSERS
	CRESSES
CEERSST	CRESSET
	RESECTS
	SECRETS
CEERSSU	CERUSES
	CESURES
	RECUSES
	RESCUES
	SECURES
CEERSTT	TERCETS
CEERSUX	EXCURSE
	EXCUSER
CEERTTU	CURETTE
CEESSTX	EXSECTS
CEESSUX	EXCUSES
CEETTUV	CUVETTE
CEFFIOR	OFFICER
CEFFIOS	OFFICES
CEFFISU	SUFFICE
CEFFLOS	COFFLES
CEFFLSU	CUFFLES
	SCUFFLE
CEFFORS	COFFERS
	SCOFFER
CEFFORT	COFFRET
CEFFSTU	SUFFECT
CEFGINN	FENCING
CEFHILR	FILCHER
CEFHILS	FILCHES
CEFHILY	CHIEFLY
CEFHINS	FINCHES
CEFHIRY	CHIEFRY
CEFHIST	FITCHES
CEFHITT	FITCHET
CEFHITW	FITCHEW
CEFHLTU	FUTCHEL
CEFIILT	FICTILE
CEFIIOR	ORIFICE
CEFIITV	FICTIVE
CEFIKLR	FICKLER
	FLICKER
CEFIKLS	FICKLES
CEFILNT	INFLECT
CEFILNU	FUNICLE
CEFILRU	LUCIFER
CEFIMOR	COMFIER
CEFIMRY	MERCIFY
CEFINNO	CONFINE
CEFINOR	CONIFER
	INFORCE
CEFINST	INFECTS
CEFIPSY	SPECIFY
CEFIRSS	SFERICS
CEFIRTY	CERTIFY
	RECTIFY
CEFISSU	FICUSES
CEFKLOT	FETLOCK
CEFKLRY	FRECKLY
CEFKRSU	FUCKERS
CEFLNOU	FLOUNCE
CEFLNUY	FLUENCY
CEFMORY	COMFREY
CEFNORS	CONFERS
CEFNORU	FROUNCE
CEFNOSS	CONFESS
CEFNOST	CONFEST
CEFNOSU	CONFUSE
CEFNOTU	CONFUTE
CEFOPRS	FORCEPS
CEFORRS	FORCERS
CEFORRT	CROFTER
CEFORSS	FRESCOS
CEFORSU	REFOCUS
CEFOSSU	FOCUSES
CEFRSUW	CURFEWS
CEFSSUU	FUCUSES
CEGGHIR	CHIGGER

Letters	Words
CEGGIIS	CIGGIES
CEGGIKN	GECKING
CEGGIOR	GEORGIC
CEGGIOS	COGGIES
CEGGLOR	CLOGGER
CEGGLOS	COGGLES
CEGGORS	COGGERS
CEGGPSU	EGGCUPS
CEGHILN	LECHING
CEGHINO	ECHOING
CEGHINP	PECHING
CEGHINT	ETCHING
CEGHINW	CHEWING
CEGHIOR	CHOREGI
CEGHIOS	CHIGOES
CEGHIRS	CHIGRES
	SCREIGH
CEGHITU	GUICHET
CEGHLSU	CLEUGHS
	GULCHES
CEGHORU	COUGHER
CEGHRTU	GUTCHER
CEGIILN	CEILING
	CIELING
CEGIINP	PIECING
CEGIKKN	KECKING
CEGIKNN	NECKING
CEGIKNP	PECKING
CEGIKNR	RECKING
CEGIKRU	GUCKIER
CEGILNP	CLEPING
CEGILNR	CLINGER
	CRINGLE
CEGILNU	CLUEING
	LUCIGEN
CEGILNW	CLEWING
CEGILNY	GLYCINE
CEGIMNU	MUCIGEN
CEGINNR	CERNING
CEGINNS	CENSING
	SCENING
CEGINOS	COGNISE
	COIGNES
CEGINOZ	COGNIZE
CEGINPR	PERCING
CEGINRR	CRINGER
CEGINRS	CRINGES
CEGINRW	CREWING
CEGINSS	CESSING
CEGIRRS	GRICERS
CEGKLNO	GENLOCK
CEGKLOR	GROCKLE
CEGLNOO	COLOGNE
CEGLOOY	ECOLOGY
CEGLOSU	GLUCOSE
CEGLOSY	GLYCOSE
CEGNNOO	ONCOGEN
CEGNORS	CONGERS
CEGNORU	CONGRUE
CEGNORY	CRYOGEN
CEGNOST	CONGEST
CEGNRUY	URGENCY
CEGNSSU	SCUNGES
CEGNSTY	CYGNETS
CEGOORS	SCROOGE
CEGORRS	GROCERS
CEGORRY	GROCERY
CEGORSU	SCOURGE
	SCROUGE
CEHHILS	HILCHES
CEHHIRS	CHERISH
	SHRIECH
CEHHIRT	HITCHER
CEHHIST	HITCHES
CEHHNSU	HUNCHES
CEHHOOS	HOOCHES
CEHHOST	HOTCHES
	SHOCHET
CEHHSSU	SHEUCHS
CEHHSTU	HUTCHES
CEHIIKN	CHINKIE
CEHIINR	HIRCINE
CEHIINS	NICEISH
CEHIINT	ICHNITE
CEHIIPP	CHIPPIE
CEHIIRT	ITCHIER
	TICHIER
CEHIISV	CHIVIES
	VICHIES
CEHIKNT	CHETNIK
	KITCHEN
	THICKEN
CEHIKNW	CHEWINK
CEHIKOO	CHOOKIE
CEHIKOR	CHOKIER
CEHIKOS	CHOKIES
CEHIKPS	PECKISH
CEHIKRS	SHICKER
	SKRIECH
CEHIKRT	THICKER
CEHIKRW	WHICKER
CEHIKST	CHEKIST
CEHIKSY	HICKEYS
CEHIKTT	THICKET
CEHILLR	CHILLER
CEHILMY	CHIMLEY
CEHILNO	CHOLINE
	HELICON
CEHILNS	LICHENS
	LINCHES
CEHILNT	LINCHET
	TINCHEL
CEHILPR	PILCHER
CEHILPS	PILCHES
CEHILRT	LICHTER
CEHILRV	CHERVIL
CEHILSS	CHESILS
	CHISELS
CEHILST	ELTCHIS
CEHILSZ	ZILCHES
CEHILTY	LECYTHI
	TECHILY
CEHIMMS	CHEMISM
CEHIMNY	CHIMNEY
CEHIMOR	MOCHIER
	MORICHE
CEHIMOS	ECHOISM
CEHIMRS	CHIMERS
	MICHERS
CEHIMRT	THERMIC
CEHIMST	CHEMIST
	MITCHES
CEHINOP	CHOPINE
	PHOCINE
CEHINOR	CHORINE
CEHINOT	HENOTIC
CEHINOX	CHOENIX
CEHINPR	NEPHRIC
	PHRENIC
	PINCHER
CEHINPS	PINCHES
	SPHENIC
CEHINPU	PENUCHI
CEHINQU	QUINCHE
CEHINRS	NICHERS
	RICHENS
CEHINRT	CITHERN
CEHINST	ETHNICS
	STHENIC
CEHINSU	ECHINUS
CEHINSV	CHEVINS
CEHINSW	WINCHES
CEHINTW	WITCHEN
CEHIOPS	HOSPICE
CEHIOPT	POTICHE
CEHIORS	COHEIRS
	HEROICS
CEHIORT	ROTCHIE
	THEORIC
CEHIOST	ECHOIST
	TOISECH
CEHIOTU	COUTHIE
CEHIPPR	CHIPPER
CEHIPRR	CHIRPER
CEHIPRS	CERIPHS
	CIPHERS
	SPHERIC
CEHIPRT	PITCHER
CEHIPST	PITCHES
CEHIQSU	QUICHES
CEHIRRS	CHIRRES
CEHIRRT	RICHTER
CEHIRST	CITHERS
	ESTRICH
	RICHEST
CEHIRSU	CUSHIER
CEHIRSZ	SCHERZI
CEHIRTT	CHITTER
CEHISSU	CUISHES
CEHISTT	TITCHES
CEHISTW	WITCHES
CEHISZZ	CHIZZES
CEHKKRU	CHUKKER
CEHKLMO	HEMLOCK
CEHKLSU	HUCKLES
CEHKORS	CHOKERS
	HOCKERS
	SHOCKER
CEHKOSY	CHOKEYS
	HOCKEYS
CEHKPTU	KETCHUP
CEHKRSU	SHUCKER
CEHKSTU	KUTCHES
CEHKSTY	SKETCHY
CEHLLMO	MOCHELL
CEHLLMU	MUCHELL
CEHLLNS	SCHNELL
CEHLLOY	YELLOCH
CEHLMOR	CHROMEL
CEHLMSS	SCHELMS
CEHLMSU	MUCHELS
	MULCHES
CEHLMSZ	SCHMELZ
CEHLMUY	CHUMLEY
CEHLNNU	CHUNNEL
CEHLNOS	NOCHELS
CEHLNOT	CHOLENT
	NOTCHEL
CEHLNRU	LUNCHER
CEHLNSU	LUNCHES
CEHLNSY	LYNCHES
CEHLNTY	LYNCHET
CEHLOOS	SCHOOLE
CEHLORS	CHOLERS
	ORCHELS
CEHLORT	CHORTLE
CEHLOST	CLOTHES
CEHLPPS	SCHLEPP
CEHLPSS	SCHLEPS
CEHLPSU	PLEUCHS
CEHLQSU	SQUELCH
CEHLRRU	LURCHER
CEHLRSU	LURCHES
CEHMNRU	MUNCHER
CEHMNSU	MUNCHES
CEHMOOR	MOOCHER
CEHMOOS	MOOCHES
CEHMORS	CHROMES
CEHMORU	MOUCHER
CEHMOSS	SCHMOES
CEHMOSU	MOUCHES
CEHMSTU	HUMECTS
	MUTCHES
CEHNNRU	CHUNNER
CEHNOOR	COEHORN
CEHNORT	NOTCHER
CEHNORV	CHEVRON
CEHNOST	NOTCHES
	TECHNOS
CEHNOSU	COHUNES
CEHNPRU	PUNCHER
	UNPERCH
CEHNPST	PSCHENT
CEHNPSU	PUNCHES
CEHNRSU	RUNCHES
CEHNRTU	CHUNTER
CEHNSTU	CHESNUT
CEHNSTY	STENCHY
CEHNSUU	EUNUCHS
CEHNTUY	CHUTNEY
CEHOOPS	POOCHES
CEHOORS	CHOOSER
	SOROCHE
CEHOORT	CHEROOT
CEHOOSS	CHOOSES
CEHOOSY	CHOOSEY
CEHOPPR	CHOPPER
CEHOPRS	PORCHES
CEHOPRT	POTCHER
CEHOPRY	CORYPHE
CEHOPST	POTCHES
CEHOPSU	POUCHES
CEHORRT	TORCHER
CEHORSS	COSHERS
CEHORST	HECTORS
	ROCHETS
	ROTCHES
	TOCHERS
	TORCHES
	TROCHES
CEHORSU	CHOREUS
CEHORSY	COSHERY
CEHORSZ	SCHERZO
CEHORTU	COUTHER
	RETOUCH
	TOUCHER
CEHORTW	WOTCHER
CEHORUV	VOUCHER
CEHOSSU	CHOUSES
	HOCUSES

CEHOSTU TOUCHES
CEHOSUV VOUCHES
CEHPRSU CHERUPS
CEHPRSY CHYPRES
CYPHERS
CEHPRTU PUTCHER
CEHPSSY PSYCHES
CEHQSTU QUETSCH
CEHRRSU CRUSHER
CEHRSSU CRUSHES
CEHRSTT STRETCH
CEHRSTY SCYTHER
CEHSSTU TUSCHES
CEHSSTY SCYTHES
CEIIJRU JUICIER
CEIIKLS SICLIKE
CEIIKMS MICKIES
CEIIKNT KINETIC
CEIIKPR PICKIER
CEIIKQU QUICKIE
CEIIKSS SICKIES
CEIIKST EKISTIC
ICKIEST
TICKIES
CEIIKSW WICKIES
CEIILLS SILICLE
CEIILNN INCLINE
CEIILPP CLIPPIE
CEIILPT PELITIC
CEIILST ELICITS
CEIILTV LEVITIC
CEIIMMT MIMETIC
CEIIMNR CRIMINE
CEIIMNS MENISCI
CEIIMOT MEIOTIC
CEIIMPR EMPIRIC
CEIIMPS EPICISM
CEIIMRS CIMIERS
CEIIMSS SEISMIC
CEIIMTT TITMICE
CEIINNO CONIINE
INCONIE
CEIINNR CINERIN
CEIINOR ONEIRIC
CEIINOS ICONISE
CEIINOV INVOICE
CEIINOZ ICONIZE
CEIINPS PISCINE
CEIINRS IRENICS
SERICIN
SIRENIC
CEIINRT CITRINE
CRINITE
INCITER
NERITIC
CEIINRZ ZINCIER
CEIINSS ICINESS
INCISES
CEIINST INCITES
CEIINSU CUISINE
CEIINTZ CITIZEN
ZINCITE
CEIIOPZ EPIZOIC
CEIIPPR PIPERIC
CEIIPRR PRICIER
CEIIPRS SPICIER
CEIIPRT PICRITE
CEIIPST EPICIST
CEIIRSS CISSIER
CEIIRST ERISTIC
RICIEST
CEIIRSU CRUISIE
CEIISSS CISSIES
CEIISVV CIVVIES
CEIITUV UVEITIC
CEIJNST INJECTS
CEIJRSU JUICERS
CEIJSTU JUSTICE
CEIKKNR KNICKER
CEIKKRS KICKERS
CEIKLMS MICKLES
CEIKLNR CLINKER
CRINKLE
CEIKLNS NICKELS
SLICKEN
CEIKLPR PICKLER
PRICKLE
CEIKLPS PICKLES
CEIKLRS LICKERS
RICKLES
SLICKER
CEIKLRT TICKLER
TRICKLE
CEIKLRU LUCKIER
CEIKLSS SICKLES
CEIKLST STICKLE
TICKLES
CEIKLSU LUCKIES
CEIKLSY KYLICES
CEIKMRS SMICKER
CEIKMRU MUCKIER
CEIKMST SMICKET
CEIKMSY MICKEYS
CEIKNOT KENOTIC
CEIKNQU QUICKEN
CEIKNRS NICKERS
SNICKER
CEIKNSS SICKENS
CEIKNST SNICKET
TICKENS
CEIKNSW WICKENS
CEIKOOS COOKIES
CEIKOPR POCKIER
CEIKORR CORKIER
ROCKIER
CEIKOST COKIEST
CEIKPRR PRICKER
CEIKPRS PICKERS
RIPECKS
SPICKER
CEIKPRT PRICKET
CEIKPRY PICKERY
CEIKPST PICKETS
SKEPTIC
CEIKQRU QUICKER
CEIKRRS RICKERS
CEIKRRT TRICKER
CEIKRSS SCRIKES
CEIKRST RICKETS
STICKER
TICKERS
CEIKRSW WICKERS
CEIKRSY YICKERS
CEIKRTU TRUCKIE
CEIKRTY RICKETY
CEIKRUY YUCKIER
CEIKSST SICKEST
CEIKSTT TICKETS
CEIKSTW WICKETS
CEIKSTY TICKEYS
CEILLNO LIONCEL
CEILLNU NUCELLI
CEILLOR COLLIER
CEILLOS COLLIES
CEILLST CELLIST
CEILLSU CULLIES
CEILMOP COMPILE
POLEMIC
CEILMPR CRIMPLE
CEILNNU NUCLEIN
CEILNOP PINOCLE
CEILNOS CINEOLS
CONSEIL
INCLOSE
CEILNOT LECTION
CEILNOX LEXICON
CEILNPS PENCILS
SPLENIC
CEILNST CLIENTS
LECTINS
STENCIL
CEILNSU LEUCINS
CEILNTU CUTLINE
TUNICLE
CEILOOS COOLIES
CEILOPR PELORIC
CEILOPS POLICES
CEILOPT TOECLIP
CEILORS RECOILS
CEILORT CORTILE
CEILORU URCEOLI
CEILOSS OSSICLE
CEILOST CITOLES
CEILOTT COLETIT
CEILPPR CLIPPER
CRIPPLE
CEILPRS SPLICER
CEILPSS SPLICES
CEILPSU SPICULE
CEILQSU CLIQUES
CEILQUY CLIQUEY
CEILRRU CURLIER
CEILRSS SLICERS
CEILRST RELICTS
CEILRSV CLIVERS
CEILRSY CLERISY
CEILRTT CLITTER
CEILRTU UTRICLE
CEILSSS SCISSEL
CEILSSU SLUICES
CEILTTU CUITTLE
CEIMMOS COMMIES
CEIMMRR CRIMMER
CEIMNNO MECONIN
CEIMNOR INCOMER
CEIMNOS INCOMES
MESONIC
CEIMNOT CENTIMO
ENTOMIC
TONEMIC
CEIMNRS CREMSIN
MINCERS
CEIMNRU MINCEUR
NUMERIC
CEIMNYZ ENZYMIC
CEIMOOR COOMIER
CEIMOPT METOPIC
CEIMORR MORRICE
CEIMORT MORTICE
CEIMOTT TOTEMIC
CEIMOTV VICOMTE
CEIMOTX TOXEMIC
CEIMPRR CRIMPER
CEIMPRS SPERMIC
CEIMPSU PUMICES
CEIMRST CRETISM
METRICS
CEIMRSU CERIUMS
MURICES
CEIMSSU CESIUMS
MISCUES
CEINNOS CONINES
CEINNOV CONNIVE
CEINOOT COONTIE
CEINOPR PERICON
PONCIER
PORCINE
CEINOPT ENTOPIC
NEPOTIC
CEINORR CORNIER
CEINORS COINERS
CRINOSE
CRONIES
ORCEINS
ORCINES
RECOINS
SERICON
CEINORT RECTION
CEINORU COENURI
NOURICE
CEINORV CORVINE
CEINORY ORIENCY
CEINOSS CESSION
COSINES
CEINOST NOTICES
SECTION
CEINOSV NOVICES
CEINOTT ENTOTIC
TONETIC
CEINOTX EXCITON
CEINOUV UNVOICE
CEINOVV CONVIVE
CEINPRS PINCERS
PRINCES
CEINPRY CYPRINE
CEINPST INCEPTS
INSPECT
PECTINS
PEINCTS
CEINPTY PYCNITE
CEINQSU CINQUES
QUINCES
CEINRRU CURNIER
CEINRSS SCRINES
CEINRST CISTERN
CRETINS
CEINRSV CRIVENS
CEINRSW WINCERS
CEINRTT CITTERN
CEINRUV INCURVE
CEINSST INCESTS
INSECTS
CEINSSU INCUSES
CEINSTY CYSTINE
CEINSWY WINCEYS
CEINTTX EXTINCT
CEINVVY VIVENCY
CEIOOPR OPORICE
CEIOOST COOTIES
CEIOPPS COPPIES

CEIOPRS	COPIERS
	COPSIER
	PERSICO
CEIOPST	POETICS
CEIOPSU	PICEOUS
CEIORRS	CIRROSE
	CORRIES
	CROSIER
CEIORRU	COURIER
CEIORRZ	CROZIER
CEIORSS	COSIERS
CEIORST	EROTICS
	TERCIOS
CEIORSU	SCOURIE
CEIORSV	CORSIVE
	VOICERS
CEIORSW	COWRIES
	SCOWRIE
CEIORSZ	COZIERS
CEIORTT	COTTIER
CEIORTV	EVICTOR
CEIORTX	EXCITOR
	XEROTIC
CEIORVY	VICEROY
CEIOSSS	COSSIES
CEIOSST	COSIEST
	COTISES
	OECISTS
CEIOSSV	VISCOSE
CEIOSTT	COTTISE
CEIOSTV	COSTIVE
CEIOSTX	COEXIST
	COXIEST
	EXOTICS
CEIOSTY	SOCIETY
CEIOSTZ	COZIEST
CEIPPST	PEPTICS
CEIPQTU	PICQUET
CEIPRRS	CRISPER
	PRICERS
CEIPRSS	SPICERS
CEIPRST	TRICEPS
CEIPRSY	SPICERY
CEIPRTU	CUPRITE
	PICTURE
CEIPRTY	PYRETIC
CEIPRXY	PYREXIC
CEIPSSS	SCEPSIS
CEIPSST	CESSPIT
CEIQRSU	CIRQUES
CEIRRRU	CURRIER
CEIRRSU	CRUISER
	CURRIES
	SUCRIER
CEIRRTT	CRITTER
CEIRRTU	RECRUIT
CEIRRTX	RECTRIX
CEIRRUV	CURVIER
CEIRSSU	CRUISES
	CRUSIES
	CUISSER
CEIRSSV	SCRIVES
CEIRSTT	TRISECT
CEIRSTU	CUITERS
	CURIETS
	ICTERUS
CEIRSTW	TWICERS
CEIRSUV	CRUIVES
	CURSIVE
CEIRTTU	CUTTIER
CEIRTTX	TECTRIX
CEISSSU	CUISSES
CEISSTU	CESTUIS
	CUEISTS
	CUTISES
	ICTUSES
CEISTTU	CUTTIES
CEJKOSY	JOCKEYS
CEJNOOS	COJONES
CEJNORU	CONJURE
CEJNOSU	JOUNCES
	JUNCOES
CEJOPRT	PROJECT
CEKKLNU	KNUCKLE
CEKKNOR	KNOCKER
CEKKOPS	KOPECKS
CEKLLOP	PELLOCK
CEKLLRY	CLERKLY
CEKLMNO	LOCKMEN
CEKLMSU	MUCKLES
CEKLNOS	ENLOCKS
	SLOCKEN
CEKLNRU	CRUNKLE
CEKLORS	LOCKERS
CEKLOST	LOCKETS
CEKLPRU	PLUCKER
CEKLPSU	PUCKLES
CEKLRSU	RUCKLES
	SUCKLER
CEKLRTU	TRUCKLE
CEKLSSU	SUCKLES
CEKMORS	MOCKERS
CEKMORY	MOCKERY
CEKMRSU	MUCKERS
CEKNNSU	UNSNECK
CEKNOOV	CONVOKE
CEKNORR	CRONKER
CEKNORS	CONKERS
	RECKONS
CEKNORT	TROCKEN
CEKNOST	NOCKETS
CEKNRWY	WRYNECK
CEKNSSU	SUCKENS
CEKOOPR	PRECOOK
CEKOOPW	COWPOKE
CEKOORR	CROOKER
CEKOORS	COOKERS
CEKOORY	COOKERY
CEKOPST	POCKETS
CEKORRS	CORKERS
	ROCKERS
CEKORRY	ROCKERY
CEKORST	RESTOCK
	ROCKETS
	STOCKER
CEKOSST	SOCKETS
CEKPRSU	PUCKERS
CEKPRSY	RYPECKS
CEKPRUY	PUCKERY
CEKRRTU	TRUCKER
CEKRSSU	SUCKERS
CEKRSTU	TUCKERS
CEKRSUY	YUCKERS
CEKSSTU	SUCKETS
CEKSTTU	TUCKETS
CELLMOU	COLUMEL
CELLNOO	COLONEL
CELLORS	ESCROLL
CELLOST	COLLETS
CELLOSU	LOCULES
	OCELLUS
CELLOSY	CLOSELY
CELLRRU	CRULLER
CELLRSU	CRUELLS
	CULLERS
	SCULLER
CELLRUY	CRUELLY
CELLSSU	SCULLES
CELLSTU	CULLETS
CELMMSU	MESCLUM
CELMNOO	LOCOMEN
	MONOCLE
CELMNSU	CULMENS
	MESCLUN
CELMOOS	COELOMS
CELMOPS	COMPELS
CELMOPX	COMPLEX
CELMORS	CORMELS
CELMPRU	CLUMPER
	CRUMPLE
CELMSSU	MUSCLES
CELMSUU	SECULUM
CELMSUY	LYCEUMS
CELNNOU	NUCLEON
CELNNSU	NUNCLES
CELNOOS	COLONES
	CONSOLE
CELNORS	CORNELS
CELNOSU	COUNSEL
	UNCLOSE
CELNOTU	NOCTULE
CELNRSU	LUCERNS
CELNRTU	LECTURN
CELNSUU	NUCLEUS
	NUCULES
CELNSUW	UNCLEWS
CELOOPR	PRECOOL
CELOORS	COOLERS
	CREOSOL
CELOOST	COOLEST
	OCELOTS
CELOPPS	COPPLES
CELOPRU	COUPLER
CELOPSU	COUPLES
	OPUSCLE
	UPCLOSE
CELOPTU	COUPLET
	OCTUPLE
CELOQSU	CLOQUES
CELORSS	CLOSERS
	CRESOLS
	ESCROLS
CELORST	COLTERS
	CORSLET
	COSTREL
	LECTORS
CELORSU	CLOSURE
	COLURES
CELORSV	CLOVERS
CELORSW	SCROWLE
CELORSY	SCROYLE
CELORTT	CLOTTER
	CROTTLE
CELORTU	CLOTURE
	CLOUTER
	COULTER
CELORVY	CLOVERY
CELOSST	CLOSEST
	CLOSETS
CELOSSU	OSCULES
CELOSTY	COTYLES
CELOSUV	VOCULES
CELPRSU	CURPELS
	SCRUPLE
CELPSUU	CUPULES
CELPSUY	CLYPEUS
CELRRSU	CURLERS
CELRSTU	CLUSTER
	CULTERS
	CUSTREL
	CUTLERS
	RELUCTS
CELRSTY	CLYSTER
CELRSUV	CULVERS
CELRSUW	CURLEWS
CELRTTU	CLUTTER
CELRTUU	CULTURE
CELRTUV	CULVERT
CELRTUY	CRUELTY
	CUTLERY
CELSTTU	CUTLETS
	CUTTLES
	SCUTTLE
CEMMNOT	COMMENT
CEMMNOU	COMMUNE
CEMMOOT	COMMOTE
CEMMOOV	COMMOVE
CEMMORS	COMMERS
CEMMOTU	COMMUTE
CEMMRSU	CUMMERS
	SCUMMER
CEMNNOT	CONTEMN
CEMNOOP	COMPONE
CEMNOOS	ONCOMES
CEMNOOY	ECONOMY
CEMNOSU	CONSUME
	MUSCONE
CEMNRSU	CRUMENS
CEMNRTU	CENTRUM
CEMNSTU	CENTUMS
CEMOOPS	COMPOSE
CEMOOPT	COMPOTE
CEMOOTU	OUTCOME
CEMOPRS	COMPERS
CEMOPRT	COMPTER
CEMOPSU	UPCOMES
CEMOPTU	COMPUTE
CEMORRS	CREMORS
CEMOSSU	COMUSES
	MUSCOSE
CEMOSSY	MYCOSES
CEMOSTU	COSTUME
CEMPRRU	CRUMPER
CEMPRTU	CRUMPET
CEMRRUY	MERCURY
CEMRSTU	RECTUMS
CEMSSUU	MUCUSES
CENNOOT	CONNOTE
CENNORS	CONNERS
CENNOST	CONSENT
	NOCENTS
CENNOTT	CONTENT
CENNOTV	CONVENT
CENNRSU	CUNNERS
	SCUNNER
CENOOPS	POONCES
CENOORR	CORONER
	CROONER
CENOORS	CEROONS
CENOORT	CORONET

CENOPRS CREPONS
CENOPSU POUNCES
UNCOPES
CENOPSY SYNCOPE
CENOPTU POUNCET
CENOPTY POTENCY
CENOQRU CONQUER
CENORRS CORNERS
SCORNER
CENORRW CROWNER
CENORSS CENSORS
CENORST CONSTER
CORNETS
CRESTON
CRONETS
CENORSU CONURES
ROUNCES
CENORTT CORNETT
CENORTU CORNUTE
COUNTER
RECOUNT
TROUNCE
CENORTV CONVERT
CENORTW CROWNET
CENORUV UNCOVER
CENOSSY COYNESS
CENOSTT CONTEST
CENOSTU CONTUSE
ECONUTS
CENOSTV COVENTS
CENOSVY CONVEYS
COVYNES
CENOTTX CONTEXT
CENPRTY ENCRYPT
CENPTUX EXPUNCT
CENRRTU CURRENT
CENRSSY SCRYNES
CENRSTU ENCRUST
CENRSUU UNCURSE
CENRSUW UNSCREW
CENRTUY CENTURY
CENSSTY ENCYSTS
CEOOPRS COOPERS
SCOOPER
CEOOPRY COOPERY
CEOORSS COOSERS
CEOORST SCOOTER
CEOORSV CROOVES
CEOOSTY COYOTES
OOCYTES
CEOPPRR CROPPER
CEOPPRS COPPERS
CEOPPRY COPPERY
CEOPRRS SCORPER
CEOPRRT PORRECT
CEOPRRU CROUPER
PROCURE
CEOPRSS CORPSES
PROCESS
CEOPRST COPTERS
CEOPRSU COUPERS
CROUPES
RECOUPS
CEOPRTT PROTECT
CEOPRUU COUPURE
CEOQRTU CROQUET
ROCQUET
CEOQSTU COQUETS
CEORRSS CROSSER
RECROSS
SCORERS
SCORSER
CEORRST RECTORS
CEORRSU COURSER
CRUORES
SCOURER
CEORRSW SCOWRER
CEORRSY SORCERY
CEORRTY RECTORY
CEORSSS CROSSES
SCORSES
CEORSST CORSETS
COSTERS
ESCORTS
SCOTERS
SECTORS
CEORSSU COURSES
SCOURSE
SCOUSER
SOURCES
SUCROSE
CEORSSW ESCROWS
CEORSTT COTTERS
CEORSTU COUTERS
CROUTES
SCOUTER
CEORSTV CORVETS
COVERTS
VECTORS
CEORTUU COUTURE
CEORTUV COUVERT
CEOSSST COSSETS
CEOSSSU SCOUSES
CEOSSSY SYCOSES
CEOSTTT OCTETTS
CEOSTTU CUTTOES
CEPPRRU CRUPPER
CEPPRSU CUPPERS
SCUPPER
CEPRRSU SPRUCER
CEPRSSU PERCUSS
SPRUCES
CEPRSSY CYPRESS
CEPRSTU PRECUTS
CEPRSTY SCEPTRY
CEPSSTU SUSPECT
CERRSSU CURSERS
CERRSSY SCRYERS
CERSSSU CUSSERS
CERSSTU CRUSETS
CERSSUZ SCRUZES
CERSTTU CURTEST
CUTTERS
SCUTTER
CERSTUV CURVETS
CERSTUY CURTESY
CURTSEY
CESSUZZ SCUZZES
CFFGINO COFFING
CFFGINU CUFFING
CFFHINO CHIFFON
CFFIIRT TRIFFIC
CFFILSS SCLIFFS
CFFINOS COFFINS
CFFINSU CUFFINS
CFFMOSU OFFSCUM
CFFOSTU OFFCUTS
CFFRSSU SCRUFFS
CFFRSUY SCRUFFY
CFGIINO COIFING
CFGIKNU FUCKING
CFGINOR FORCING
CFHILYY CHYLIFY
CFHIMYY CHYMIFY
CFHIOSW COWFISH
CFHIRST FRICHTS
CFHORTU FUTHORC
CFIIIMR MIRIFIC
CFIIIVV VIVIFIC
CFIIKNY FINICKY
CFIILNT INFLICT
CFIIMNO OMNIFIC
CFIINOT FICTION
CFIINOY ICONIFY
CFIINYZ ZINCIFY
CFIIOSS OSSIFIC
CFIKNNO FINNOCK
CFIKOSS FOSSICK
CFILORS FROLICS
CFILORU FLUORIC
CFIMNOR CONFIRM
CFIMOST COMFITS
CFINOST CONFITS
CFIORST FICTORS
CFIORSY SCORIFY
CFIRSTU FRUICTS
CFISSTU FUSTICS
CFKLLOU LOCKFUL
CFKNORU UNFROCK
CFKOTTU FUTTOCK
CFLMRUU FULCRUM
CFLNORY CORNFLY
CFLNOUX CONFLUX
CFLNOUY FLOUNCY
CFLOPRU CROPFUL
CFLPSUU CUPFULS
CFMNOOR CONFORM
CFMOORT COMFORT
CFOSSTU FUSTOCS
CFOSSUU FUSCOUS
CGGGINO COGGING
CGGIINR GRICING
CGGORSY SCROGGY
CGHHOSU CHOUGHS
CGHIIMN CHIMING
MICHING
CGHIINN CHINING
INCHING
NICHING
CGHIINR RICHING
CGHIINT ITCHING
CGHIINV CHIVING
CGHIKNO CHOKING
HOCKING
CGHILPY GLYPHIC
CGHINNO CHIGNON
CGHINOR OCHRING
CGHINOS COSHING
CGHINRU RUCHING
CGHINSU CHUSING
CGHIOSY GOYISCH
CGHLOSU CLOUGHS
CGHOORT TORGOCH
CGHORUY GROUCHY
CGIIJNU JUICING
CGIIKKN KICKING
CGIIKLN LICKING
CGIIKMM GIMMICK
CGIIKNN NICKING
CGIIKNP PICKING
CGIIKNR RICKING
CGIIKNS SICKING
CGIIKNT TICKING
CGIIKNW WICKING
CGIILLO ILLOGIC
CGIILNO COILING
CGIILNP CLIPING
CGIILNS SLICING
CGIIMNN MINCING
CGIIMNR CRIMING
CGIINNO COINING
CGIINNR CRINING
CGIINNW WINCING
CGIINNZ ZINCING
CGIINOR GIRONIC
CGIINOV VOICING
CGIINPR PRICING
CGIINPS SPICING
CGIINRT TRICING
CGIKLNO CLOKING
LOCKING
CGIKMNO MOCKING
CGIKMNU MUCKING
CGIKNNO CONKING
NOCKING
CGIKNOO COOKING
CGIKNOR CORKING
ROCKING
CGIKNOS SOCKING
CGIKNOT TOCKING
CGIKNOY YOCKING
CGIKNPU KINGCUP
CGIKNRU RUCKING
CGIKNSU SUCKING
CGIKNTU TUCKING
CGIKNUY YUCKING
CGILLNO COLLING
CGILLNU CULLING
CGILMNU CULMING
CGILNNO CLONING
CGILNNU UNCLING
CGILNOO COOLING
CGILNOS CLOSING
CGILNOT COLTING
CGILNOW COWLING
CGILNOY CLOYING
CGILNPY CLYPING
CGILNRU CURLING
CGILNSY GLYCINS
CGILORW COWGIRL
CGILOTT GLOTTIC
CGILPSU GILCUPS
CGILPTU GILTCUP
CGILPTY GLYPTIC
CGIMNOO COOMING
CGIMNOP COMPING
CGIMNOR CROMING
CGIMNOS COMINGS
CGINNNO CONNING
CGINNNU CUNNING
CGINNOP PONCING
CGINNOR CORNING
CGINNOS CONSIGN
CGINNPU PUNCING
CGINNSY SYNCING
CGINOOP COOPING
CGINOOS COOINGS
CGINOPP COPPING
CGINOPS COPINGS
COPSING

SCOPING
CGINOPU COUPING
CGINOPW COWPING
CGINOPY COPYING
CGINORS SCORING
CGINORU COURING
CGINORW CROWING
CGINORY GYRONIC
CGINOST COSTING
GNOSTIC
CGINOSU CONGIUS
SOUCING
CGINOSV COVINGS
CGINOSW SOWCING
CGINPPU CUPPING
CGINRRU CURRING
CGINRSU CURSING
CGINRSY CRYINGS
SCRYING
CGINRUV CURVING
CGINSSU CUSSING
SCUSING
CGINTTU CUTTING
CGIOOOS GIOCOSO
CGIOTYZ ZYGOTIC
CGKLNOU GUNLOCK
CGLLOSY GLYCOLS
CGLNOSU UNCLOGS
CGLOOSU COLUGOS
CGNOOSU CONGOUS
CGOORRW GORCROW
CHHIKOR CHIKHOR
CHHINOR RHONCHI
CHHINTU UNHITCH
CHHIRST SHRITCH
CHHISST SHTCHIS
CHHISTY ICHTHYS
CHHNOOS HONCHOS
CHHRTTU THRUTCH
CHIIILO CHILIOI
CHIIKMS KIMCHIS
CHIIKNN KINCHIN
CHIIKSS SICKISH
CHIILLS CHILLIS
CHIILST LITCHIS
CHIIMSU ISCHIUM
CHIINNP INCHPIN
CHIINST CHITINS
CHIIOPT OPHITIC
CHIIOST STICHOI
CHIKLLO HILLOCK
CHIKLTY THICKLY
CHIKNOO CHINOOK
CHIKORS CHIKORS
CHOKRIS
CHIKORY HICKORY
CHIKOST THICKOS
CHIKPSU PUCKISH
CHIKSST SCHTIKS
SHTICKS
CHIKSTY KITSCHY
CHILLMU CHILLUM
CHILLTY LICHTLY
CHILNOR CHLORIN
CHILNOU ULICHON
CHILNSY LYCHNIS
CHILOOS COOLISH
CHILORS ORCHILS
CHILOST COLTISH
CHILSTU CULTISH

CHIMNPY NYMPHIC
CHIMOPR MORPHIC
CHIMORS CHORISM
CHRISOM
CHIMRRY MYRRHIC
CHIMRSS CHRISMS
CHIMSSS SCHISMS
CHIMSTY TYCHISM
CHINOOR CHORION
CHINOPS CHOPINS
PHONICS
CHINOST CHITONS
CHINOSU CUSHION
CHINPSY HYPNICS
CHINQSU SQUINCH
CHINRSU URCHINS
CHINTUW UNWITCH
CHINTYZ CHINTZY
CHIOOPR POCHOIR
CHIOORS ISOCHOR
CHIOORZ CHORIZO
CHIOPRT TROPHIC
CHIOPST PHOTICS
CHIOPXY HYPOXIC
CHIORST CHORIST
OSTRICH
CHIORSW CHOWRIS
CHIOSST STICHOS
CHIOSSZ SCHIZOS
CHIPRRU CHIRRUP
CHIPRRY PYRRHIC
CHIPSSY PHYSICS
CHIQSTU SQUITCH
CHIRRSU CURRISH
CHIRSTY CHRISTY
CHISSST SCHISTS
CHISSTU SCHUITS
CHISTTU CHUTIST
CHISTWY SWITCHY
CHITTWY TWITCHY
CHKLOOO HOOLOCK
CHKLOOT KLOOTCH
CHKLOSS SHLOCKS
CHKMMOO HOMMOCK
CHKMMOU HUMMOCK
CHKMOSS SHMOCKS
CHKMSSU SHMUCKS
CHKNOOS SCHNOOK
CHKOOST SCHTOOK
CHKORSU CHUKORS
CHKPTUU PUTCHUK
CHKSSTU SHTUCKS
CHLMOOS MOLOCHS
CHLOOSS SCHOOLS
CHLOOST COOLTHS
CHLOPST SPLOTCH
CHLORSS SCHORLS
CHLORTY CHOLTRY
CHLOSSS SCHLOSS
CHLOSUY SLOUCHY
CHMOORS CHROMOS
CHMOOST SCHTOOM
CHMOOSZ SCHMOOZ
CHMOSUY CHYMOUS
CHNNOOR CHRONON
CHNNOSU NONSUCH
CHNOOPS PONCHOS
CHNOORS COHORNS
CHNOORT TORCHON
CHNORRS SCHNORR

CHNORSY SYNCHRO
CHNORTU COTHURN
CHNOTUU UNCOUTH
CHNSTUU TUCHUNS
CHOOPPS COPSHOP
CHOORST COHORTS
CHOORSU OCHROUS
CHOPSSY PSYCHOS
CHORSTU TROCHUS
CHOSSTU SCHOUTS
SCOUTHS
CHOSSTW SCOWTHS
CHPSSUY SCYPHUS
CHRRSUU CHURRUS
CHSSTUY SCHUYTS
CIIILLT ILLICIT
CIIILNV INCIVIL
CIIIMNR CRIMINI
CIIINPT INCIPIT
CIIKKLL KILLICK
CIIKMMM MIMMICK
CIIKMNN MINNICK
CIIKNSW INWICKS
CIIKNTU CUTIKIN
CIIKPUW WICKIUP
CIIKSST TISICKS
CIIKSTT STICKIT
CIILLTY LICITLY
CIILLVY CIVILLY
CIILNOP CIPOLIN
CIILNOS SILICON
CIILNPS INCLIPS
CIILNUV UNCIVIL
CIILOOT OOLITIC
CIILOPT POLITIC
CIILORT CORTILI
CIILOST COLITIS
SOLICIT
CIILPSY SPICILY
CIILSSS SCISSIL
CIIMMRY MIMICRY
CIIMNNO NIMONIC
CIIMNOT MICTION
CIIMOST MIOTICS
MISTICO
SOMITIC
CIIMOTT MITOTIC
CIIMOTV MOTIVIC
CIIMSSV CIVISMS
CIIMSTV VICTIMS
CIINNTU TUNICIN
CIINOOT COITION
CIINOPS PSIONIC
CIINORS INCISOR
CIINPRS CRISPIN
CIINQTU QUINTIC
CIINRST CITRINS
CIINSSV VISCINS
CIINTUY UNICITY
CIIORST SORITIC
CIIOSUV VICIOUS
CIIPRSS SPIRICS
CIIPRTY PYRITIC
CIIRSTV VITRICS
CIIRTVX VICTRIX
CIJNNOO CONJOIN
CIJNNTU INJUNCT
CIJNOOS COJOINS
CIKKLLO KILLOCK
CIKLLOP PILLOCK

CIKLLOR ROLLICK
CIKLLOS SILLOCK
CIKLLOW KILLCOW
CIKLLSY SLICKLY
CIKLLUY LUCKILY
CIKLMSU MISLUCK
CIKLMSY SMICKLY
CIKLNOS INLOCKS
CIKLNRY CRINKLY
CIKLOPZ ZIPLOCK
CIKLORY ROCKILY
CIKLPRY PRICKLY
CIKLQUY QUICKLY
CIKLRTY TRICKLY
CIKLSTU LUSTICK
CIKMNNO MINNOCK
CIKMNSU NICKUMS
CIKNNOP PINNOCK
CIKNNOW WINNOCK
CIKNPSU UNPICKS
CIKNSTU UNSTICK
CIKOPPT POCKPIT
CIKORRS CORKIRS
CIKOTUW OUTWICK
CIKRSTY TRICKSY
CILLNOS COLLINS
CILLNOU CULLION
CILLOOR CRIOLLO
CILLOPY POLLICY
CILMNOP COMPLIN
CILMSTU CULTISM
CILNOOR ORCINOL
CILNOOS CLOISON
SCOLION
CILNOPR PILCORN
CILNORY LYRICON
CILNOSU ULICONS
UNCOILS
CILNOTU LINOCUT
CILNOXY XYLONIC
CILNPSU INSCULP
SCULPIN
CILNPTU UNCLIPT
CILNSTU LINCTUS
CILOOPT COPILOT
CILOORU COULOIR
CILOOSS COLOSSI
CILOOST SCIOLTO
CILOPRW PILCROW
CILOPRY PYLORIC
CILOPSU UPCOILS
CILOPSW COWSLIP
CILORST LICTORS
CILOSTU COUTILS
OCULIST
CILPRSY CRISPLY
CILPRTU CULPRIT
CILRRSU SCURRIL
CILRSUU SURCULI
CILSTTU CULTIST
CIMMNSU CUMMINS
CIMMOSS COSMISM
CIMMOST COMMITS
CIMNNOS NINCOMS
CIMNNSU NINCUMS
CIMNOOR MORONIC
OMICRON
CIMNORS CRIMSON
MICRONS
CIMNRSU CRINUMS

CIMOORS	MORISCO
CIMOOST	OSMOTIC
CIMOPSY	COPYISM
	MISCOPY
	MYOPICS
CIMORSU	CORIUMS
CIMOSST	COSMIST
	SITCOMS
CIMOSSY	MYCOSIS
CIMOTYZ	ZYMOTIC
CIMPRSS	SCRIMPS
CIMPRSY	SCRIMPY
CIMRSSU	CRISSUM
CIMRSUU	CURIUMS
CIMSSTY	MYSTICS
CIMSSUV	VISCUMS
CINNNOU	INCONNU
CINNORU	UNICORN
CINNOSU	NUNCIOS
CINNOTU	UNCTION
CINNSUU	UNCINUS
CINOOPS	OPSONIC
CINOORS	CORONIS
CINOPPS	COPPINS
CINOPRX	PRINCOX
CINORRT	TRICORN
CINORSS	INCROSS
CINORST	CISTRON
	CITRONS
	CORNIST
CINORSZ	ZIRCONS
CINORTU	RUCTION
CINOSST	CONSIST
	TOCSINS
CINOSSU	COUSINS
CINOSTU	SUCTION
CINOSUZ	ZINCOUS
CINRSTU	INCRUST
CIOOPRT	PORTICO
	PROOTIC
CIOOPSU	COPIOUS
CIOOQTU	COQUITO
CIOORST	OCTROIS
CIOORSU	CORIOUS
CIOPRST	TROPICS
CIOPSTY	COPYIST
CIOQRSU	CROQUIS
CIORRSU	CIRROUS
CIORSSS	SCISSOR
CIORSTT	TRICOTS
CIORSTU	CITROUS
CIORSTV	VICTORS
CIORSUU	CURIOUS
CIORTVY	VICTORY
CIOSSSY	SYCOSIS
CIOSSUV	VISCOUS
CIPRSST	SCRIPTS
CIPRSSU	PRUSSIC
CIPRTTY	TRYPTIC
CIPSTTY	STYPTIC
CIRRTTU	CRITTUR
CIRSSTU	RUSTICS
CIRTUVY	CURVITY
CISSTUY	CYTISUS
CJNORUY	CONJURY
CKKLNUY	KNUCKLY
CKLLMOU	MULLOCK
CKLLOOP	POLLOCK
CKLLOOR	ROLLOCK
CKLLORU	RULLOCK
CKLNOSU	UNLOCKS
CKLNUUY	UNLUCKY
CKLOOOY	OLYCOOK
CKLOORW	ROWLOCK
CKLOOTU	LOCKOUT
CKLOPSU	UPLOCKS
CKLOPTU	PUTLOCK
CKMMMOU	MUMMOCK
CKNORSU	UNCORKS
CKNOSTU	UNSTOCK
CKNSTUU	UNSTUCK
	UNTUCKS
CKOOOTU	COOKOUT
CKOORSU	SOUROCK
CKOPTTU	PUTTOCK
CKORTUW	CUTWORK
CKOSSTU	TUSSOCK
CLLMOSU	MOLLUSC
CLLOOPS	COLLOPS
	SCOLLOP
CLLORSS	SCROLLS
CLLOSUU	LOCULUS
CLMNOSU	COLUMNS
CLMOOPT	COMPLOT
CLMOPTU	PLUMCOT
CLMOSUU	LUCUMOS
	OSCULUM
CLMSUUU	CUMULUS
CLNOORT	CONTROL
CLNOOSS	CONSOLS
CLNOSSU	CONSULS
CLNOSTU	CONSULT
	UNCOLTS
CLNOSUW	UNCOWLS
CLNRSUU	UNCURLS
CLOORSU	COLOURS
CLOORUY	COLOURY
CLORSSW	SCROWLS
CLORSSY	CROSSLY
CLORSUY	CORYLUS
CLORTUY	COURTLY
CLOSSTU	LOCUSTS
CLPRSUU	UPCURLS
CLPSSTU	SCULPTS
CMMNOOS	COMMONS
CMMOOST	COMMOTS
CMMRSUY	SCRUMMY
CMNOOOT	MONOCOT
CMNOOPY	COMPONY
CMNPTUU	PUNCTUM
CMOOPRT	COMPORT
CMOOPST	COMPOST
	COMPOTS
CMOORSU	CORMOUS
CMOOSTY	SCOTOMY
CMORSTU	SCROTUM
CMORTUW	CUTWORM
CMOSSTU	CUSTOMS
CMPRSSU	SCRUMPS
CMPRSUY	SCRUMPY
CNNOPSY	PYCNONS
CNNORTU	NOCTURN
CNNORUW	UNCROWN
CNOOPPR	POPCORN
CNOOPRU	CROUPON
CNOOPSU	COUPONS
	SOUPCON
CNOORRW	CORNROW
CNOORST	CONSORT
	CROTONS
CNOORTT	CONTORT
CNOORTU	CONTOUR
	CORNUTO
	CROUTON
CNOOSST	NOSTOCS
	ONCOSTS
CNOOSTT	COTTONS
CNOOSTY	TYCOONS
CNOOSUU	NOCUOUS
CNOOSVY	CONVOYS
CNOOTTW	COTTOWN
CNOOTTY	COTTONY
CNOPRTY	CRYPTON
CNOPSTU	PUNCTOS
CNORSSU	UNCROSS
CNORSSY	SYNROCS
CNORTUY	COUNTRY
CNRSSTU	SCRUNTS
CNRSTUY	SCRUNTY
COOORSZ	COROZOS
COOPRRT	PROCTOR
COOPRSS	SCROOPS
COOPRTU	OUTCROP
COOPSTU	OCTOPUS
COORSTU	OCTUORS
COORSUU	ROUCOUS
COOSTTY	OTOCYST
COPRRTU	CORRUPT
COPRSTY	CRYPTOS
COPRSUU	CUPROUS
CORRSSU	CURSORS
CORRSUY	CURSORY
CORSSTU	SCRUTOS
DDDDEIL	DIDDLED
DDDEEGR	DREDGED
DDDEEHL	HEDDLED
DDDEEIR	DERIDED
DDDEELM	MEDDLED
DDDEELP	PEDDLED
DDDEELR	REDDLED
DDDEELS	SLEDDED
DDDEELU	DELUDED
DDDEEMO	DEMODED
DDDEENS	SNEDDED
DDDEENU	DENUDED
DDDEERU	UDDERED
DDDEEST	STEDDED
DDDEFIL	FIDDLED
DDDEFLU	FUDDLED
DDDEGII	GIDDIED
DDDEGLU	GUDDLED
DDDEGRU	DRUDGED
DDDEHIW	WHIDDED
DDDEHLO	HODDLED
DDDEHLU	HUDDLED
DDDEHTU	THUDDED
DDDEIIK	KIDDIED
DDDEIIR	DIDDIER
DDDEIIS	DIDDIES
DDDEIIV	DIVIDED
DDDEIKS	SKIDDED
DDDEILM	MIDDLED
DDDEILN	DINDLED
DDDEILP	PIDDLED
DDDEILR	DIDDLER
	RIDDLED
DDDEILS	DIDDLES
DDDEILT	TIDDLED
DDDEILW	WIDDLED
DDDEIMU	MUDDIED
DDDEIOR	DODDIER
DDDEIOS	DODDIES
DDDEIRS	DIDDERS
DDDEIRU	DUDDIER
	RUDDIED
DDDELMU	MUDDLED
DDDELNO	NODDLED
DDDELOO	DOODLED
DDDELOP	PLODDED
DDDELOS	DODDLES
DDDELOT	TODDLED
DDDELPU	PUDDLED
DDDELRU	RUDDLED
DDDENOS	SNODDED
DDDEOPR	PRODDED
DDDEOQU	QUODDED
DDDEORS	DODDERS
DDDEORY	DODDERY
DDDEPSU	SPUDDED
DDDERSU	DUDDERS
DDDERUY	DUDDERY
DDDESTU	STUDDED
DDDGINO	DODDING
DDEEEIR	DEEDIER
DDEEELN	NEEDLED
DDEEELT	DELETED
DDEEEMN	EMENDED
DDEEEMR	REMEDED
DDEEENT	TEENDED
DDEEENW	ENDEWED
DDEEEPS	SPEEDED
DDEEEST	DEEDEST
	STEEDED
DDEEESX	DESEXED
DDEEFGL	FLEDGED
DDEEFII	DEIFIED
	EDIFIED
DDEEFIL	DEFILED
	FIELDED
DDEEFIN	DEFINED
DDEEFLU	DEEDFUL
DDEEFNS	DEFENDS
DDEEFSU	DEFUSED
DDEEFUZ	DEFUZED
DDEEGGL	GLEDGED
DDEEGIN	DEEDING
	DEIGNED
DDEEGIS	DISEDGE
DDEEGLP	PLEDGED
DDEEGLS	SLEDGED
DDEEGLU	DELUGED
DDEEGNU	UNEDGED
DDEEGRR	DREDGER
DDEEGRS	DREDGES
DDEEHLS	HEDDLES
DDEEHNU	DUDHEEN
DDEEHRS	SHEDDER
DDEEILS	SLEIDED
DDEEILV	DEVILED
DDEEILW	WIELDED
DDEEILY	DEEDILY
	YIELDED
DDEEIMP	IMPEDED
DDEEIMS	DEMISED
	MISDEED
DDEEINS	DESINED
	NEDDIES
	SDEINED
DDEEINT	ENDITED
	TEINDED

DDEEINW INDEWED
WIDENED
DDEEINX INDEXED
DDEEINZ DIZENED
DDEEIOV VIDEOED
DDEEIPR PREDIED
DDEEIPS DEPSIDE
DDEEIRR DERIDER
REDDIER
RIDERED
DDEEIRS DERIDES
DESIRED
DIEDRES
RESIDED
DDEEIRV DERIVED
DDEEIRW WEIRDED
DDEEIST DEIDEST
TEDDIES
DDEEISV DEVISED
DDEEKKO DEKKOED
DDEELLU DUELLED
DDEELLW DWELLED
DDEELMO MODELED
DDEELMR MEDDLER
DDEELMS MEDDLES
DDEELNO OLDENED
DDEELNS LEDDENS
DDEELOP DELOPED
DDEELPR PEDDLER
DDEELPS PEDDLES
SPELDED
DDEELRS REDDLES
DDEELRT TREDDLE
DDEELRU DELUDER
DDEELSU DELUDES
DDEEMMO MODEMED
DDEEMOT DEMOTED
DDEEMRU DEMURED
DDEENOP DEPONED
DDEENOT DENOTED
DDEENOW ENDOWED
DDEENOZ DOZENED
DDEENPS DEPENDS
DDEENPU UPENDED
DDEENRS REDDENS
DDEENRT TRENDED
DDEENRU ENDURED
DDEENST STENDED
DDEENSU DENUDES
DUDEENS
DUENDES
DDEENSY DESYNED
DDEENTU DETUNED
DDEEOPS DEPOSED
DDEEORR ORDERED
DDEEORV DOVERED
DDEEORW DOWERED
DDEEOTV DEVOTED
DDEEOTX DETOXED
DDEEPRS PEDDERS
SPREDDE
DDEEPTU DEPUTED
DDEERRS REDDERS
DDEERSS DRESSED
DDEERST REDDEST
TEDDERS
DDEERSW WEDDERS
DDEERTU DETRUDE
DDEESST STEDDES
DDEETTU DUETTED

DDEFGIR FRIDGED
DDEFILR FIDDLER
DDEFILS FIDDLES
DDEFILY FIDDLEY
DDEFIRT DRIFTED
DDEFLNO FONDLED
DDEFLOO FLOODED
DDEFLRU FUDDLER
DDEFLSU FUDDLES
DDEFNOR FRONDED
DDEFNOU FOUNDED
DDEFORS FODDERS
DDEGGRU DRUGGED
GRUDGED
DDEGHIT DIGHTED
DDEGIIR GIDDIER
DDEGIIS GIDDIES
DDEGILR GIRDLED
GLIDDER
GRIDDLE
DDEGIMO DEMIGOD
DDEGINR GRINDED
REDDING
DDEGINT TEDDING
DDEGINW WEDDING
DDEGINY EDDYING
DDEGIOR DODGIER
DDEGIRR GRIDDER
DDEGLOS DOGSLED
DDEGLSU GUDDLES
DDEGMOS DODGEMS
DDEGMSU SMUDGED
DDEGNOS GODDENS
GODSEND
DDEGNOU DUDGEON
DDEGNSU SNUDGED
DDEGORS DODGERS
GORSEDD
DDEGORY DODGERY
DDEGOSS GODDESS
DDEGOST STODGED
DDEGRRU DRUDGER
DDEGRSU DRUDGES
DDEGRTU TRUDGED
DDEHIRS HIDDERS
REDDISH
SHIDDER
DDEHIRT THIRDED
DDEHIRW WHIDDER
DDEHIRY HYDRIDE
DDEHLOS HODDLES
DDEHLRU HURDLED
DDEHLSU HUDDLES
DDEHNOS HODDENS
DDEHNOU HOUNDED
DDEHNRU HUNDRED
DDEHNSU DUNSHED
DDEHRSU SHUDDER
DDEHRSY SHREDDY
DDEIIKR KIDDIER
DDEIIKS KIDDIES
DDEIIMS MIDDIES
DDEIINT INDITED
DDEIINV DIVINED
DDEIIOS IODIDES
IODISED
DDEIIOX DIOXIDE
DDEIIOZ IODIZED
DDEIIRT DIRTIED
TIDDIER

DDEIIRV DIVIDER
DDEIIST STIDDIE
TIDDIES
DDEIISV DIVIDES
DDEIISW WIDDIES
DDEIITT DITTIED
DDEIIZZ DIZZIED
DDEIKLN KINDLED
DDEIKLS KIDDLES
DDEIKNR KINDRED
DDEIKRS KIDDERS
SKIDDER
DDEILLO DOLLIED
DDEILLR DRILLED
DDEILLU ILLUDED
DDEILMP DIMPLED
DDEILMS MIDDLES
DDEILNN DINNLED
DDEILNS DINDLES
SLIDDEN
DDEILNW DWINDLE
DDEILOR DROILED
DDEILOS DILDOES
DDEILOT DELTOID
DDEILPR PIDDLER
DDEILPS DISPLED
PIDDLES
DDEILPU DUPLIED
DDEILQU QUIDDLE
DDEILRR RIDDLER
DDEILRS RIDDLES
SLIDDER
DDEILRT TIDDLER
DDEILST TIDDLES
DDEILSW WIDDLES
DDEILTU DILUTED
DDEILTW TWIDDLE
DDEILTY LYDDITE
TIDDLEY
DDEIMMU DUMMIED
DDEIMNS MIDDENS
DDEIMNU MUEDDIN
DDEIMOO MOODIED
DDEIMOR DERMOID
DDEIMOS DESMOID
DDEIMRU MUDDIER
DDEIMSS DESMIDS
DDEIMST MIDDEST
DDEIMSU DEDIMUS
MUDDIES
DDEINOP POINDED
DDEINOS NODDIES
DDEINOT DENTOID
DDEINPS DISPEND
DDEINRU UNDRIED
DDEINST DISTEND
DDEINSW SWIDDEN
DDEIOPR PODDIER
DDEIOPS PODDIES
DDEIORS DORISED
SODDIER
DDEIORV OVERDID
DDEIORW DOWDIER
DDEIORZ DORIZED
DDEIOST TODDIES
DDEIOSW DOWDIES
DDEIOTT DITTOED
DDEIOWW WIDOWED
DDEIPPR DRIPPED
DDEIPRS DISPRED

DDEIPSU PUDDIES
DDEIRRS RIDDERS
DDEIRRU RUDDIER
DDEIRSU RUDDIES
DDEISSU DISUSED
DDEISTU STUDIED
DDEJRSU JUDDERS
DDEKMOU DUKEDOM
DDEKOOR DROOKED
DDEKORU DROUKED
DDELLOR DROLLED
DDELMOU MOULDED
DDELMPU DUMPLED
DDELMRU MUDDLER
DDELMSU MUDDLES
DDELNOO NOODLED
DDELNOS NODDLES
DDELNOU LOUNDED
NODULED
DDELNOW LOWNDED
DDELNRU NURDLED
RUNDLED
DDELOOR DOODLER
DROOLED
DDELOOS DOODLES
DDELOOW WOOLDED
DDELOPR PLODDER
DDELORT TODDLER
DDELORW WORLDED
DDELOST TODDLES
DDELOTT DOTTLED
DDELPRU PUDDLER
DDELPSU PUDDLES
DDELRSU RUDDLES
DDELSTU STUDDLE
DDEMMRU DRUMMED
DDEMMSU SMEDDUM
DDEMNOS ODDSMEN
DDEMNOT ODDMENT
DDEMNOU MOUNDED
DDEMRSU MUDDERS
DDENNOR DENDRON
DONNERD
DDENOOS SNOODED
DDENOPS DESPOND
DDENOPU POUNDED
DDENOPW POWNDED
DDENORS DONDERS
NODDERS
SNODDER
DDENORT TRODDEN
DDENORU REDOUND
ROUNDED
UNDERDO
DDENORW DROWNED
ROWNDED
WONDRED
DDENOSS ODDNESS
SODDENS
DDENOSU SOUNDED
DDENOSW SOWNDED
DDENOSY DYNODES
DDENOUW WOUNDED
DDENPSU PUDDENS
DDENRSU DUNDERS
DDENSTU STUDDEN
DDEOOPR DROOPED
DDEOORU ODOURED
DDEOORW REDWOOD
DDEOPPR DROPPED

Letters	Words
DDEORSW	DROWSED
	SWORDED
DDEPRSS	SPREDDS
DDEPRSU	PUDDERS
DDERRSU	RUDDERS
DDERSSU	SUDDERS
DDGGINO	DODGING
	GODDING
DDGHINO	HODDING
DDGHOOO	GODHOOD
DDGIIKN	KIDDING
DDGIILY	GIDDILY
DDGIINR	RIDDING
DDGIMNU	MUDDING
DDGINNO	NODDING
DDGINOP	PODDING
DDGINOR	RODDING
DDGINOS	SODDING
DDGINOT	TODDING
DDGINPU	PUDDING
DDGINRU	RUDDING
DDGINUW	WUDDING
DDGOOOW	DOGWOOD
DDHIISS	SIDDHIS
DDHIKSU	KIDDUSH
DDHIORY	HYDROID
DDIILOP	DIPLOID
DDIIQTU	QUIDDIT
DDIKNOS	DODKINS
DDILMUY	MUDDILY
DDILNRS	DIRNDLS
DDILOSY	DYSODIL
DDILOWY	DOWDILY
DDILRUY	RUDDILY
DDILTWY	TWIDDLY
DDIMRSU	DIRDUMS
DDIMSSU	DUDISMS
DDINOST	SNODDIT
DDIORTU	TURDOID
DDLLMOO	DOLLDOM
DDMMSUU	DUMDUMS
DDMNOOR	DROMOND
DDMRSUU	DURDUMS
DDORSTY	DROSTDY
DEEEEMX	EXEEMED
DEEEFFR	EFFERED
DEEEFLR	FLEERED
DEEEFLT	FLEETED
DEEEFNR	ENFREED
DEEEFNS	DEFENSE
DEEEFRS	FEEDERS
DEEEFRV	FEVERED
DEEEGKL	GLEEKED
DEEEGLP	PLEDGEE
DEEEGLT	GLEETED
DEEEGMR	DEMERGE
	EMERGED
DEEEGNP	PEENGED
DEEEGNR	GREENED
	RENEGED
DEEEGRR	REGREDE
DEEEGRS	DEGREES
DEEEGRT	DETERGE
	GREETED
DEEEGST	EGESTED
DEEEHKT	THEEKED
DEEEHLS	SHEELED
DEEEHLW	WHEEDLE
	WHEELED
DEEEHNS	SHEENED
DEEEHPS	PHEESED
DEEEHPZ	PHEEZED
DEEEHRS	SHEERED
DEEEHST	SEETHED
	SHEETED
DEEEHTT	TEETHED
DEEEHWZ	WHEEZED
DEEEIJL	JEELIED
DEEEIMR	EMERIED
DEEEINR	NEEDIER
DEEEIPS	DEEPIES
DEEEIRR	REEDIER
DEEEIRS	SEEDIER
DEEEIRW	WEEDIER
DEEEISV	DEVISEE
DEEEJNU	DEJEUNE
DEEEJRS	JEREEDS
DEEEKLN	KNEELED
DEEEKLS	SLEEKED
DEEEKMS	SMEEKED
DEEEKNW	WEEKEND
DEEEKRS	KREESED
	SKEERED
DEEELMS	MESELED
DEEELNR	NEEDLER
DEEELNS	NEEDLES
DEEELPS	SPEELED
DEEELPT	DEPLETE
DEEELRT	DEERLET
DEEELRV	LEVERED
DEEELST	DELETES
	SLEETED
	STEELED
DEEELSV	SLEEVED
DEEELSW	SWEELED
DEEELTW	TWEEDLE
	TWEELED
DEEELTX	TELEXED
DEEEMMW	EMMEWED
DEEEMNS	DEMESNE
DEEEMNW	ENMEWED
DEEEMRS	DEMERSE
	EMERSED
	REDEEMS
	REMEDES
DEEEMRT	METERED
DEEEMST	STEEMED
DEEENPR	PREENED
DEEENPS	DEEPENS
DEEENQU	QUEENED
DEEENRS	NEEDERS
	SERENED
	SNEERED
DEEENRT	ENTERED
DEEENRV	ENERVED
DEEENRW	RENEWED
DEEENRY	RENEYED
DEEENST	STEENED
DEEENSV	VENDEES
DEEENSW	ENSEWED
DEEENSZ	SNEEZED
DEEENTT	DETENTE
DEEENTU	DETENUE
DEEENTV	EVENTED
DEEEORW	OREWEED
DEEEOTV	DEVOTEE
DEEEPRS	SPEEDER
	SPEERED
DEEEPRT	PETERED
DEEEPRU	EPERDUE
DEEEPRV	PREEVED
DEEEPSS	PEDESES
DEEEPST	DEEPEST
	STEEPED
DEEEQRU	QUEERED
DEEERRS	REEDERS
DEEERRV	REVERED
DEEERSS	SEEDERS
DEEERST	REESTED
	STEERED
DEEERSV	DESERVE
	SEVERED
DEEERSW	SEWERED
	SWEERED
	WEEDERS
DEEERTV	EVERTED
DEEERTW	TWEERED
DEEERTX	EXERTED
DEEERWY	WEEDERY
DEEESSX	DESEXES
DEEESTV	STEEVED
DEEESTW	SWEETED
DEEETTV	VEDETTE
DEEETTW	TWEETED
DEEETWZ	TWEEZED
DEEFFFO	FEOFFED
DEEFFIN	EFFENDI
DEEFFOR	OFFERED
DEEFFST	DEFFEST
DEEFFSU	EFFUSED
DEEFGGL	FLEGGED
DEEFGIN	FEEDING
	FEIGNED
DEEFGIP	PIGFEED
DEEFGLS	FLEDGES
DEEFGRU	REFUGED
DEEFHLS	FLESHED
	SHELFED
DEEFHLU	HEEDFUL
DEEFHRS	FRESHED
DEEFIIR	DEIFIER
	EDIFIER
	REIFIED
DEEFIIS	DEIFIES
	EDIFIES
DEEFILN	ENFILED
DEEFILR	DEFILER
	FERLIED
	FIELDER
DEEFILS	DEFILES
DEEFIMS	MISFEED
DEEFINR	DEFINER
	ENFIRED
	FENDIER
	REFINED
DEEFINS	DEFINES
DEEFINT	FEINTED
DEEFINX	ENFIXED
DEEFIRR	FERRIED
DEEFIRS	DEFIERS
DEEFIRT	FETIDER
DEEFIRZ	FRIEZED
DEEFLLU	FUELLED
DEEFLNS	FLENSED
DEEFLNU	NEEDFUL
DEEFLOT	FEEDLOT
DEEFLTT	FETTLED
DEEFMOR	FREEDOM
DEEFNRS	FENDERS
DEEFNRU	UNFREED
DEEFNUU	UNFEUED
DEEFORV	OVERFED
DEEFORZ	DEFROZE
DEEFRSU	REFUSED
DEEFRSW	SWERFED
DEEFRTT	FRETTED
DEEFRTU	FEUTRED
	REFUTED
DEEFSSU	DEFUSES
DEEFSTT	DEFTEST
DEEFSUZ	DEFUZES
DEEGGIS	GIDGEES
DEEGGLS	GLEDGES
DEEGHIN	HEEDING
	NEIGHED
DEEGHIR	HEDGIER
DEEGHIW	WEIGHED
DEEGHOW	HOGWEED
DEEGHRS	HEDGERS
DEEGHSS	GHESSED
DEEGIJS	GIDJEES
DEEGIKR	KEDGIER
DEEGILN	DELEING
DEEGILR	GELIDER
	LEDGIER
	LEIDGER
DEEGIMN	DEEMING
DEEGINN	ENGINED
	NEEDING
DEEGINR	DREEING
	ENERGID
	GREINED
	REEDING
	REIGNED
DEEGINS	SDEIGNE
	SEEDING
DEEGINV	DEEVING
DEEGINW	WEEDING
DEEGINY	YEEDING
DEEGIPW	PIGWEED
DEEGIRS	SEDGIER
DEEGIRV	DIVERGE
	GRIEVED
DEEGIRW	WEDGIER
DEEGIST	EDGIEST
DEEGISW	WEDGIES
DEEGJRU	REJUDGE
DEEGKRS	KEDGERS
DEEGLMU	EMULGED
DEEGLNS	LEGENDS
DEEGLNT	GENTLED
	GLENTED
DEEGLOY	GOLDEYE
DEEGLPR	PLEDGER
DEEGLPS	PLEDGES
DEEGLPT	PLEDGET
DEEGLRS	GELDERS
	LEDGERS
	REDLEGS
	SLEDGER
DEEGLSS	SLEDGES
DEEGLSU	DELUGES
DEEGMNU	EMUNGED
	GUDEMEN
DEEGNNO	ENDOGEN
DEEGNNR	GRENNED
DEEGNOR	ENGORED
DEEGNRS	GENDERS
DEEGNSU	DENGUES
	UNEDGES

DEEGOOS SOOGEED
DEEGORR ROGERED
DEEGOSY GEODESY
DEEGOTU OUTEDGE
DEEGRRU REURGED
DEEGSSU GUESSED
DEEGSTU GUESTED
DEEHIKV KHEDIVE
DEEHILS SHIELED
DEEHILT LETHIED
DEEHINR INHERED
DEEHIRR HERRIED
DEEHIST HEISTED
DEEHITV THIEVED
DEEHKLW WHELKED
DEEHLLO HELLOED
DEEHLLS SHELLED
DEEHLMW WHELMED
DEEHLNU UNHELED
DEEHLOV HOVELED
DEEHLPW WHELPED
DEEHLSV SHELVED
DEEHLSW WELSHED
DEEHMNR HERDMEN
DEEHMNS MENSHED
DEEHMRU RHEUMED
DEEHMUX EXHUMED
DEEHNOY HONEYED
DEEHNPR PREHEND
DEEHNRS HERDENS
DEEHNUY UNHEEDY
DEEHORV HOVERED
DEEHPRS SPHERED
DEEHRSS HERDESS
DEEHRSU USHERED
DEEHRSW SHREWED
DEEHRTW WRETHED
DEEHTTW WHETTED
DEEIINT DIETINE
DEEIIPR EPEIRID
DEEIIRW WEIRDIE
DEEIIST DEITIES
DEEIJLL JELLIED
DEEIJMM JEMMIED
DEEIJTT JETTIED
DEEIKLL KILLDEE
DEEIKLN LIKENED
DEEIKNS ENSKIED
DEEIKOV DOVEKIE
DEEILNO ELOINED
DEEILNR RELINED
DEEILNS ENISLED
ENSILED
LINSEED
DEEILNV LIVENED
DEEILNY DYELINE
NEEDILY
DEEILPR REPLIED
DEEILPS SEEDLIP
SPIELED
DEEILRS RESILED
DEEILRT RETILED
DEEILRV DELIVER
RELIVED
REVILED
DEEILRW WIELDER
DEEILRY YIELDER
DEEILSS DIESELS
IDLESSE
DEEILSY EYELIDS
SEEDILY
DEEILTU DILUTEE
DEEILTV DEVILET
DEEIMMS MISDEEM
DEEIMMW IMMEWED
DEEIMNO DOMINEE
DEEIMNR ERMINED
DEEIMNS DESMINE
SIDEMEN
DEEIMNT DEMENTI
DEEIMPR DEMIREP
DEEIMPS IMPEDES
SEMIPED
DEEIMPT EMPTIED
DEEIMRS REMEIDS
REMISED
DEEIMRT DEMERIT
DIMETER
MERITED
MITERED
RETIMED
DEEIMRX REMIXED
DEEIMSS DEMISES
DEEIMTT EMITTED
DEEINNP PENNIED
DEEINNS INDENES
DEEINNT DENTINE
DEEINNU ENNUIED
DEEINNZ DENIZEN
DEEINOR ORDINEE
DEEINPR REPINED
RIPENED
DEEINRR DERNIER
NERDIER
DEEINRS DENIERS
NEREIDS
RESINED
DEEINRU UREDINE
DEEINRW WIDENER
DEEINRX INDEXER
DEEINSS DESINES
DEEINST DESTINE
ENDITES
STEINED
DEEINSV ENDIVES
DEEINSW ENDWISE
SINEWED
DEEINSX INDEXES
DEEINTT DINETTE
DEEINTU DETINUE
DEEINTV EVIDENT
DEEINVW VINEWED
DEEINVX INVEXED
DEEINWZ WIZENED
DEEIOPS EPISODE
POESIED
DEEIOPT EPIDOTE
DEEIOPX EPOXIDE
DEEIORS OREIDES
OSIERED
DEEIOSV VOIDEES
DEEIPPT PEPTIDE
DEEIPRS PREDIES
PRESIDE
SPEIRED
DEEIPRT TEPIDER
DEEIPRV DEPRIVE
PRIEVED
DEEIPRX EXPIRED
DEEIPSS DESPISE
PEDESIS
DEEIPST DESPITE
DEEIQRU QUERIED
DEEIQTU QUIETED
DEEIRRS DERRIES
DESIRER
RESIDER
SERRIED
DEEIRRT RETIRED
RETRIED
TIREDER
DEEIRRV REDRIVE
RIVERED
DEEIRRW REWIRED
WEIRDER
DEEIRSS DESIRES
RESIDES
DEEIRST DIETERS
REISTED
DEEIRSU RESIDUE
UREIDES
DEEIRSV DERIVES
DEVISER
DIVERSE
REVISED
DEEIRTU ERUDITE
DEEIRTV RIVETED
VERDITE
DEEIRVV REVIVED
DEEISSU DISEUSE
DEEISSV DEVISES
DEEISTT TEDIEST
DEEISTW DEWIEST
DEEISTX EXISTED
DEEITTV VIDETTE
DEEJNOY ENJOYED
DEEJQRU JERQUED
DEEKKRT TREKKED
DEEKLLN KNELLED
DEEKLPS SKELPED
DEEKLRS SKELDER
DEEKNOT TOKENED
DEEKORV REVOKED
DEEKPPS SKEPPED
DEEKPRU PERUKED
DEEKRRS SKERRED
DEEKRSU RESKUED
DEELLMS SMELLED
DEELLNS SNELLED
DEELLPS SPELLED
DEELLQU QUELLED
DEELLRU DUELLER
DEELLRW DWELLER
DEELLRY ELDERLY
DEELLST STELLED
DEELLSW SWELLED
DEELMNO LEMONED
DEELMOR MODELER
REMODEL
DEELMPT TEMPLED
DEELMPU DEPLUME
DEELMRS MELDERS
DEELMRU RELUMED
DEELMST SMELTED
DEELMSY MEDLEYS
DEELMTT METTLED
DEELNRS LENDERS
SLENDER
DEELNSS ENDLESS
DEELNST DENTELS
NESTLED
DEELNSW WEDELNS
DEELNSY DENSELY
DEELNTT NETTLED
DEELOPP PEOPLED
DEELOPR DEPLORE
DEELOPS DELOPES
DEELOPV DEVELOP
DEELOPX EXPLODE
DEELORS RESOLED
DEELORU URODELE
DEELORV LOVERED
DEELORW LOWERED
DEELOSU DELOUSE
DEELOTV DOVELET
DEELOTW TOWELED
DEELOVV DEVOLVE
EVOLVED
DEELPRS SPELDER
DEELPRU PRELUDE
DEELPST PESTLED
DEELPTT PETTLED
DEELRRU RULERED
DEELRSU ELUDERS
DEELRSV DELVERS
DEELRSW WELDERS
DEELRUV VELURED
DEELSTT SETTLED
DEELSTU TELEDUS
DEELSTW LEWDEST
SWELTED
DEELSUV EVULSED
DEELSVV DEVVELS
DEELTUX EXULTED
DEELVXY VEXEDLY
DEEMMOV EMMOVED
DEEMMST STEMMED
DEEMNOV ENMOVED
VENOMED
DEEMNOY MONEYED
DEEMNRS MENDERS
DEEMNST DEMENTS
DEEMNTU UNMETED
DEEMNUW UNMEWED
DEEMORS EMERODS
DEEMORV REMOVED
DEEMORX EXODERM
DEEMOSS DEMOSES
DEEMOST DEMOTES
DEEMOSY MOSEYED
DEEMPRS PREMEDS
DEEMPTT TEMPTED
DEEMRRU DEMURER
DEEMRSU DEMURES
RESUMED
DEENNOR ENDERON
DEENNOS DONNEES
DEENNOT TENONED
DEENNOY DOYENNE
DEENNOZ ENZONED
DEENNPT PENDENT
DEENNST DENNETS
STENNED
DEENNTZ TENDENZ
DEENNUY ENNUYED
DEENOOR RONEOED
DEENOPR REPONED
DEENOPS DEPONES
SPONDEE
DEENOPT PENTODE

DEENORS	ENDORSE
DEENORT	ERODENT
DEENORW	ENDOWER
DEENORZ	REZONED
DEENOST	DENOTES
DEENPPR	PERPEND
DEENPRS	SPENDER
DEENPRT	PRENTED
	PRETEND
DEENPSX	EXPENDS
DEENRRS	RENDERS
DEENRRU	ENDURER
DEENRSS	REDNESS
	SENDERS
DEENRST	STERNED
	TENDERS
	TENDRES
DEENRSU	ENDURES
	ENSURED
DEENRSV	VENDERS
DEENRSZ	DZERENS
DEENRTU	DENTURE
	RETUNED
	TENURED
DEENRTV	VENTRED
DEENSST	DENSEST
DEENSSY	DESYNES
DEENSTT	DETENTS
	STENTED
DEENSTU	DETENUS
	DETUNES
DEENSTX	EXTENDS
DEENSUV	VENDUES
DEENSUW	UNSEWED
DEENSUX	UNSEXED
DEENUVX	UNVEXED
DEEOPRR	PEDRERO
DEEOPRS	DEPOSER
	REPOSED
DEEOPRW	POWERED
DEEOPSS	DEPOSES
	SPEEDOS
DEEOPSX	EXPOSED
	PODEXES
DEEORRR	ORDERER
	REORDER
DEEORRS	REREDOS
DEEORRV	OVERRED
	REDROVE
DEEORST	OERSTED
	ROSETED
	TEREDOS
DEEORTT	OTTERED
	TETRODE
DEEORTW	TOWERED
DEEORTX	OXTERED
DEEORTZ	ROZETED
DEEORUV	OVERDUE
DEEORVY	OVERDYE
DEEOSTV	DEVOTES
DEEOSTX	DETOXES
DEEOTUW	OUTWEED
DEEPPPR	PREPPED
DEEPPST	STEPPED
DEEPRRS	SPERRED
DEEPRRU	PERDURE
	REPURED
DEEPRSS	DEPRESS
	PRESSED
	SPERSED
DEEPRST	PRESTED
DEEPRSU	PERDUES
	PERSUED
	PERUSED
DEEPRTU	ERUPTED
	REPUTED
DEEPRUV	PREVUED
DEEPSTU	DEPUTES
DEEQSTU	QUESTED
DEERRSS	DRESSER
	REDRESS
DEERRUV	VERDURE
DEERSSS	DRESSES
DEERSST	DESERTS
	DESSERT
	TRESSED
DEERSSU	DURESSE
DEERSTV	STERVED
	VERDETS
DEERSTW	STREWED
	WRESTED
DEERSTX	DEXTERS
DEERSTY	DYESTER
DEERSVW	SWERVED
DEERTTU	UTTERED
DEERTUX	EXTRUDE
DEESSTT	DETESTS
DEESSTV	DEVESTS
DEESTTT	STETTED
DEFFFLU	FLUFFED
DEFFHIW	WHIFFED
DEFFHOU	HOUFFED
DEFFHOW	HOWFFED
DEFFIKS	SKIFFED
DEFFILP	PIFFLED
DEFFILR	RIFFLED
DEFFILS	SIFFLED
DEFFIMO	FIEFDOM
DEFFINS	SNIFFED
DEFFIOS	OFFSIDE
DEFFIRS	DIFFERS
DEFFIST	STIFFED
DEFFISU	DIFFUSE
DEFFKOS	SKOFFED
DEFFLMU	MUFFLED
DEFFLPU	PLUFFED
DEFFLRU	RUFFLED
DEFFLSU	DUFFELS
	DUFFLES
DEFFNOR	FORFEND
DEFFNOS	OFFENDS
DEFFNSU	SNUFFED
DEFFOPU	POUFFED
DEFFORS	DOFFERS
DEFFOSW	SOWFFED
DEFFRSU	DUFFERS
DEFFSTU	DUFFEST
	STUFFED
DEFGGIR	FRIGGED
DEFGGLO	FLOGGED
DEFGGOR	FROGGED
DEFGINN	FENDING
DEFGINR	FRINGED
DEFGINU	FEUDING
DEFGINY	DEFYING
DEFGIOR	FIREDOG
DEFGIRS	FRIDGES
DEFGIRT	GRIFTED
DEFGIRU	FIGURED
DEFGIST	FIDGETS
DEFGITY	FIDGETY
DEFGRTU	GRUFTED
DEFHIRS	REDFISH
DEFHIST	SHIFTED
DEFHLOO	ELFHOOD
DEFHLSU	FLUSHED
DEFHORT	FROTHED
DEFHRSU	FRUSHED
DEFIILN	INFIDEL
	INFIELD
DEFIIMS	FIDEISM
DEFIIMW	MIDWIFE
DEFIINU	UNIFIED
DEFIINX	INFIXED
DEFIIST	FIDEIST
DEFIKLS	FLISKED
DEFIKRS	FRISKED
DEFILLO	FOLLIED
DEFILLR	FRILLED
DEFILMP	FLIMPED
DEFILNR	FLINDER
DEFILNU	UNFILDE
	UNFILED
DEFILOO	FOLIOED
DEFILPP	FLIPPED
DEFILRT	FLIRTED
	TRIFLED
DEFILRU	DIREFUL
DEFILSS	FISSLED
DEFILST	STIFLED
DEFILSU	SULFIDE
DEFILTT	FLITTED
DEFILXY	FIXEDLY
DEFILZZ	FIZZLED
DEFIMOR	DEIFORM
DEFINRS	FINDERS
	FRIENDS
DEFINRU	UNFIRED
DEFINST	SNIFTED
DEFINSU	FUNDIES
	INFUSED
DEFINSY	DENSIFY
DEFINUX	UNFIXED
DEFINUY	UNDEIFY
DEFIOOS	FOODIES
DEFIOQU	QUOIFED
DEFIORU	FOUDRIE
DEFIOST	FOISTED
DEFIPRY	PERFIDY
DEFIRRT	DRIFTER
DEFIRST	FRISTED
DEFIRTT	FRITTED
DEFIRTU	FRUITED
DEFIRZZ	FRIZZED
DEFISTU	FEUDIST
DEFISTW	SWIFTED
DEFKLNU	FLUNKED
DEFLLOU	DOLEFUL
DEFLLUW	DEWFULL
DEFLMPU	FLUMPED
DEFLNOO	ONEFOLD
DEFLNOP	PENFOLD
DEFLNOR	FONDLER
	FORLEND
DEFLNOS	ENFOLDS
	FONDLES
DEFLNOT	TENFOLD
DEFLNRU	DERNFUL
DEFLOOR	FLOORED
DEFLOOT	FOOTLED
DEFLOOZ	FOOZLED
DEFLOPP	FLOPPED
DEFLORS	FOLDERS
DEFLORU	FLOURED
	FOULDER
DEFLOSS	FLOSSED
DEFLOSU	DEFOULS
	FLOUSED
DEFLOTU	FLOUTED
DEFLPRU	PURFLED
DEFLRRU	FLURRED
DEFLRUU	DUREFUL
DEFLUZZ	FUZZLED
DEFMNUU	UNFUMED
DEFMORS	DEFORMS
	SERFDOM
DEFMPRU	FRUMPED
DEFNOOR	FORDONE
DEFNORT	FRONTED
DEFNORU	FOUNDER
	REFOUND
DEFNORW	FROWNED
DEFNOST	FONDEST
DEFNOSU	FONDUES
DEFNRSU	FUNDERS
	REFUNDS
DEFOOPR	PROOFED
DEFOOPS	SPOOFED
DEFOORS	FORDOES
DEFORST	DEFROST
	FROSTED
DEFORTU	FOUTRED
DEGGGIL	GIGGLED
DEGGGIR	GRIGGED
DEGGGLO	GOGGLED
DEGGGLU	GLUGGED
	GUGGLED
DEGGGOR	GROGGED
DEGGHIL	HIGGLED
DEGGHIN	HEDGING
DEGGHIW	WHIGGED
DEGGHOS	SHOGGED
DEGGIJL	JIGGLED
DEGGIKN	KEDGING
DEGGILN	GELDING
	NIGGLED
DEGGILW	WIGGLED
DEGGINS	EDGINGS
	SNIGGED
DEGGINW	WEDGING
DEGGIOR	DOGGIER
DEGGIOS	DOGGIES
DEGGIPR	PRIGGED
DEGGIRS	DIGGERS
DEGGIRT	TRIGGED
DEGGIRU	DRUGGIE
DEGGISW	SWIGGED
DEGGITW	TWIGGED
DEGGJLO	JOGGLED
DEGGJLU	JUGGLED
DEGGKSU	SKUGGED
DEGGLOO	GOOGLED
DEGGLOR	DOGGREL
DEGGLOS	SLOGGED
DEGGLOT	TOGGLED
DEGGLPU	PLUGGED
	PUGGLED
DEGGLRU	GURGLED
DEGGLSU	SLUGGED
DEGGMSU	SMUGGED

DEGGNOO	DOGGONE
DEGGNOS	SNOGGED
DEGGNOU	GUDGEON
DEGGNSU	SNUGGED
DEGGOPR	PROGGED
DEGGORS	DOGGERS
DEGGORT	TROGGED
DEGGORY	DOGGERY
DEGGOSS	DOGGESS
DEGGRRU	DRUGGER
DEGGRSU	GRUDGES
DEGGRTU	DRUGGET
DEGHHOU	HOUGHED
DEGHILN	HINDLEG
DEGHILT	DELIGHT
	LIGHTED
DEGHINN	HENDING
DEGHINR	HERDING
DEGHINT	NIGHTED
DEGHINW	WHINGED
DEGHIOT	HOGTIED
DEGHIPT	PIGHTED
DEGHIRT	GIRTHED
	RIGHTED
DEGHIST	SIGHTED
DEGHITW	WIGHTED
DEGHLOO	DOGHOLE
DEGHNOT	THONGED
DEGHORR	DROGHER
DEGHORU	ROUGHED
DEGHOST	GHOSTED
DEGHOSU	SOUGHED
DEGIIKR	KIDGIER
DEGIILL	GILLIED
DEGIILN	EILDING
	ELIDING
DEGIINR	DINGIER
DEGIINS	DINGIES
DEGIINT	DIETING
	EDITING
	IGNITED
DEGIIPS	GIPSIED
DEGIIRR	RIDGIER
	RIGIDER
DEGIIRS	DIRIGES
DEGIISW	WIDGIES
DEGIJLN	JINGLED
DEGIKLO	GODLIKE
DEGILLR	GRILLED
DEGILLU	GULLIED
DEGILLY	GELIDLY
DEGILMN	MEDLING
	MELDING
	MINGLED
DEGILNN	LENDING
DEGILNO	GLENOID
DEGILNP	PINGLED
DEGILNS	DINGLES
	ELDINGS
	ENGILDS
	SINGLED
DEGILNT	GLINTED
	TINGLED
DEGILNU	ELUDING
	INDULGE
DEGILNV	DELVING
	DEVLING
DEGILNW	WELDING
DEGILOR	GLORIED
	GODLIER
	GOLDIER
DEGILOU	OUGLIED
DEGILRR	GIRDLER
DEGILRS	GILDERS
	GIRDLES
	GLIDERS
	GRISLED
	LIDGERS
	RIDGELS
DEGILRU	GUILDER
DEGILRW	WERGILD
DEGILUV	DIVULGE
DEGIMNN	MENDING
DEGIMNS	SMIDGEN
DEGIMPU	GUIMPED
DEGIMST	MIDGETS
DEGINNN	DENNING
DEGINNP	PENDING
DEGINNR	GRINNED
	RENDING
DEGINNS	ENDINGS
	SENDING
DEGINNT	DENTING
	TENDING
DEGINNU	ENDUING
DEGINNV	VENDING
DEGINNW	WENDING
DEGINNY	DENYING
DEGINOP	PIDGEON
DEGINOR	ERODING
	GROINED
	IGNORED
	NEGROID
	REDOING
DEGINOS	DINGOES
DEGINOW	WENDIGO
	WIDGEON
	WONGIED
DEGINRR	GRINDER
	REGRIND
DEGINRS	DINGERS
	ENGIRDS
DEGINRU	DUNGIER
DEGINRW	REDWING
	WRINGED
DEGINRY	YERDING
DEGINSS	DESIGNS
	SDEIGNS
DEGINST	NIDGETS
	STEDING
	STINGED
DEGINSU	GUNDIES
	SUEDING
DEGINSW	SWINDGE
	SWINGED
DEGINSY	DINGEYS
	DYEINGS
DEGINTW	TWINGED
DEGINUX	EXUDING
DEGIOOR	GOODIER
DEGIOOS	GOODIES
	SOOGIED
DEGIOPR	PODGIER
DEGIORR	GRODIER
DEGIORT	GOITRED
DEGIPPR	GRIPPED
DEGIPRU	PUDGIER
DEGIPSY	GYPSIED
DEGIQSU	SQUIDGE
DEGIRRS	GIRDERS
	RIDGERS
DEGIRRU	DURGIER
DEGIRSS	DIGRESS
DEGIRSU	GUIDERS
DEGIRTT	GRITTED
DEGISST	DIGESTS
	DISGEST
DEGISTU	GIUSTED
DEGISTW	WIDGETS
DEGKLSU	KLUDGES
DEGLMMO	GLOMMED
DEGLMOO	GLOOMED
DEGLMOU	MOGULED
DEGLNNO	ENDLONG
DEGLNOP	PLONGED
DEGLNOS	DONGLES
	GOLDENS
DEGLNOU	LOUNGED
DEGLNPU	PLUNGED
DEGLNSU	GULDENS
DEGLNUU	UNGLUED
	UNGULED
DEGLOOP	GLOOPED
DEGLOPR	PLEDGOR
DEGLOPS	SPLODGE
DEGLORS	LODGERS
DEGLORW	GROWLED
DEGLOSS	GLOSSED
	GODLESS
DEGLOST	GOLDEST
DEGLOTU	GLOUTED
DEGLSSU	SLUDGES
DEGLTTU	GLUTTED
	GUTTLED
DEGLUZZ	GUZZLED
DEGMNOO	GOODMEN
DEGMOOR	GROOMED
DEGMPRU	GRUMPED
DEGMRSU	MUDGERS
	SMUDGER
DEGMSSU	SMUDGES
DEGNNOU	DUNGEON
DEGNOPR	PRONGED
DEGNOPS	SPONGED
DEGNORU	GUERDON
	UNDERGO
	UNGORED
DEGNORW	WRONGED
DEGNOTU	TONGUED
DEGNRSU	GERUNDS
	NUDGERS
DEGNRTU	GRUNTED
	TRUDGEN
DEGNRUU	UNURGED
DEGNSSU	SNUDGES
DEGNUVY	UNGYVED
DEGOORV	GROOVED
DEGOOST	STOOGED
DEGOPRU	GROUPED
DEGORRS	DROGERS
DEGORSS	GROSSED
	SODGERS
DEGORST	STODGER
DEGORSU	DROGUES
	GOURDES
	GROUSED
DEGORTU	DROGUET
	GROUTED
DEGOSST	STODGES
DEGOSTU	DEGOUTS
DEGOSTW	GOWDEST
DEGRRTU	TRUDGER
DEGRSTU	TRUDGES
DEGSSTU	DEGUSTS
DEHHISW	WHISHED
DEHHMPU	HUMPHED
DEHHOOS	HOOSHED
DEHHSSU	SHUSHED
DEHIINN	HINNIED
DEHIIPS	PIEDISH
DEHIIRS	DISHIER
DEHIKRS	SHIRKED
	SHRIKED
DEHIKSW	WHISKED
DEHILLO	HILLOED
DEHILLS	SHILLED
DEHILMS	DISHELM
DEHILNP	DELPHIN
DEHILPR	HIRPLED
DEHILRS	HIRSLED
DEHILRT	THIRLED
DEHILRW	WHIRLED
DEHILSS	SHIELDS
DEHILTY	DIETHYL
DEHIMMS	SHIMMED
DEHIMMW	WHIMMED
DEHIMNU	INHUMED
DEHIMOR	HEIRDOM
DEHIMOS	DISHOME
DEHIMOT	ETHMOID
DEHIMRS	DIRHEMS
DEHIMRU	HUMIDER
DEHIMST	SMITHED
DEHINNS	SHINNED
DEHINNT	THINNED
DEHINOP	DIPHONE
	PHONIED
DEHINOR	HORDEIN
DEHINOS	HOIDENS
DEHINPS	ENDSHIP
DEHINRS	HINDERS
	SHRINED
DEHINRU	UNHIRED
DEHINUV	UNHIVED
DEHIOOS	HOODIES
DEHIORS	RHODIES
DEHIORT	THEROID
DEHIOST	HOISTED
DEHIOSU	HIDEOUS
DEHIOSV	DOVEISH
DEHIOSW	HOWDIES
DEHIOTU	HIDEOUT
DEHIPPS	SHIPPED
DEHIPPW	WHIPPED
DEHIRRS	SHIRRED
DEHIRRU	DHURRIE
	HURRIED
DEHIRRW	WHIRRED
DEHIRST	DITHERS
	SHIRTED
DEHIRSU	HURDIES
DEHIRSV	DERVISH
	SHRIVED
DEHIRTV	THRIVED
DEHIRTW	WRITHED
DEHIRTY	DITHERY
DEHISSW	SWISHED
	WHISSED
DEHISTT	SHITTED
DEHISTW	WHISTED

DEHISVV SHIVVED
DEHIWZZ WHIZZED
DEHLLOO HOLLOED
DEHLLOU HULLOED
DEHLMOU MUDHOLE
DEHLMSU MULSHED
DEHLOOS SHOOLED
DEHLOOT TOEHOLD
DEHLOPP HOPPLED
DEHLORS HOLDERS
DEHLORW WHORLED
DEHLOSS SLOSHED
DEHLOST SLOTHED
DEHLRRU HURDLER
DEHLRSU HURDLES
DEHLRTU HURTLED
DEHLSSU SLUSHED
DEHLSTU HUSTLED
DEHMNOO HOODMEN
DEHMORU HUMORED
DEHMOST METHODS
DEHMOTU MOUTHED
DEHMPTU THUMPED
DEHNNSU SHUNNED
DEHNOOR HONORED
DEHNOOW HOEDOWN
DEHNOPU UNHOPED
DEHNORS DEHORNS
DEHNORT NORTHED
THONDER
THORNED
THRONED
DEHNOSU UNSHOED
DEHNOSY HOYDENS
DEHNOTZ DOZENTH
DEHNRSU HURDENS
DEHNRTU THUNDER
DEHNSSU DUNSHES
SNUSHED
DEHNSSY YSHENDS
DEHNSTU SHUNTED
DEHNSYY HYDYNES
DEHOOPT PHOTOED
DEHOOPW WHOOPED
DEHOOST SOOTHED
DEHOOSW WOOSHED
DEHOOTT TOOTHED
DEHOOTW WHOOTED
DEHOPPS SHOPPED
DEHOPPW WHOPPED
DEHORSS SHODERS
DEHORST DEHORTS
SHORTED
DEHORSV SHROVED
DEHORSW SHROWED
DEHORTT TROTHED
DEHORTW WORTHED
DEHOSTT SHOTTED
DEHOSTU SHOUTED
SOUTHED
DEHOSTW SOWTHED
DEHPTTU PHUTTED
DEIIIRS IRIDISE
DEIIIRZ IRIDIZE
DEIIJMM JIMMIED
DEIIKLS DISLIKE
DEIIKNR DINKIER
DEIIKNS DINKIES
KINDIES
DEIIKST DIKIEST
DEIILLR DILLIER
DEIILLS DILLIES
DEIILLW WILLIED
DEIILMP IMPLIED
DEIILMT DELIMIT
LIMITED
DEIILNS INISLED
DEIILOS DOILIES
IDOLISE
DEIILOZ IDOLIZE
DEIILPS LIPIDES
DEIILRV LIVIDER
DEIIMMX IMMIXED
DEIIMNO DOMINIE
DEIIMRT TIMIDER
DEIIMST MISDIET
STIMIED
DEIIMSZ MIDSIZE
DEIIMVW MIDWIVE
DEIINOS IODINES
IONISED
DEIINOT EDITION
TENIOID
DEIINOZ IONIZED
DEIINRR RINDIER
DEIINRS INSIDER
DEIINRT INDITER
NITRIDE
DEIINRU URIDINE
DEIINRV DIVINER
DEIINRW WINDIER
DEIINSS INSIDES
DEIINST INDITES
TINEIDS
DEIINSV DIVINES
DEIINTV INVITED
DEIIORT DIORITE
DEIIORV IVORIED
DEIIOSS IODISES
DEIIOSX OXIDISE
DEIIOSZ IODIZES
DEIIOXZ OXIDIZE
DEIIPPR DIPPIER
DEIIPRS PIERIDS
DEIIPRT RIPTIDE
DEIIRRT DIRTIER
DEIIRST DIRTIES
DITSIER
DEIIRTT TRITIDE
DEIIRTZ DITZIER
DEIIRVV VIVIDER
DEIIRZZ DIZZIER
DEIISTT DIETIST
DITTIES
TIDIEST
DEIISTV VISITED
DEIISVV DIVVIES
DEIISZZ DIZZIES
DEIIVZZ VIZZIED
DEIJLLO JOLLIED
DEIJNOR JOINDER
DEIJNOT JOINTED
DEIJNRU INJURED
DEIJNSU DISJUNE
DEIJOST JOISTED
DEIJTTU JUTTIED
DEIKKNS SKINKED
DEIKLLS DESKILL
SKILLED
DEIKLNP PLINKED
DEIKLNR KINDLER
DEIKLNS KINDLES
DEIKLNT TINKLED
DEIKLNW WINKLED
DEIKLOR RODLIKE
DEIKLOS KELOIDS
DEIKLRS SKIRLED
DEIKLRT KIRTLED
DEIKLST KIDLETS
DEIKLTT KITTLED
DEIKMMS SKIMMED
DEIKMPS SKIMPED
DEIKMRS SMIRKED
DEIKNNS SKINNED
DEIKNOV INVOKED
DEIKNPR PRINKED
DEIKNRR DRINKER
DEIKNRS KINDERS
KINREDS
REDSKIN
DEIKNST DINKEST
KINDEST
DEIKNSW SWINKED
DEIKNSY KIDNEYS
DEIKNSZ ZENDIKS
DEIKNTT KNITTED
DEIKNTW TWINKED
DEIKORR DORKIER
DEIKOSY DISYOKE
DEIKPPS SKIPPED
DEIKQRU QUIRKED
DEIKRRS SKIRRED
DEIKRST SKIRTED
DEIKRSU DUIKERS
DUSKIER
DEIKSTY DYKIEST
DEILLMO MODELLI
DEILLMU ILLUMED
DEILLNW INDWELL
DEILLOR DOLLIER
DEILLOS DOLLIES
DEILLOV LIVELOD
DEILLPR PRILLED
DEILLPS SPILLED
DEILLQU QUILLED
DEILLRR DRILLER
DEILLRT TRILLED
DEILLRU DULLIER
DEILLRV DREVILL
DEILLSS LIDLESS
DEILLST STILLED
DEILLSU ILLUDES
SULLIED
DEILLSW SWILLED
DEILLTW TWILLED
DEILMMP PLIMMED
DEILMMS SLIMMED
DEILMNS MILDENS
DEILMNU LUMINED
UNLIMED
DEILMOP IMPLODE
DEILMOS SMOILED
DEILMOY MYELOID
DEILMPP PIMPLED
DEILMPS DIMPLES
SIMPLED
DEILMPW WIMPLED
DEILMST MILDEST
MISTLED
DEILMSW MILDEWS
DEILMWY MILDEWY
DEILMXY MIXEDLY
DEILMZZ MIZZLED
DEILNNS DINNLES
LINDENS
DEILNNU UNLINED
DEILNOO EIDOLON
DEILNOS DOLINES
INDOLES
SONDELI
DEILNOT LENTOID
DEILNOU UNOILED
DEILNPP NIPPLED
DEILNPS SPELDIN
SPINDLE
SPLINED
DEILNRT TENDRIL
TRINDLE
DEILNST DENTILS
DEILNSW SWINDLE
WINDLES
DEILNSY SNIDELY
DEILNTU DILUENT
UNTILED
DEILNTW INDWELT
WINTLED
DEILNUV UNLIVED
DEILOOS DOOLIES
DEILOPS DESPOIL
DIPLOES
DIPOLES
PELOIDS
SOLIPED
SPOILED
DEILOPT PILOTED
DEILORS SOLDIER
SOLIDER
DEILORT DOILTER
DEILOSY DOYLIES
DEILOTU OUTLIED
DEILPPR RIPPLED
DEILPPS SIPPLED
SLIPPED
DEILPPT TIPPLED
DEILPPU UPPILED
DEILPRT TRIPLED
DEILPRU PRELUDI
DEILPSS DISPELS
DISPLES
DEILPSU DUPLIES
DEILPTY TEPIDLY
DEILQTU QUILTED
DEILRRU LURIDER
DEILRSS SLIDERS
DEILRSV DRIVELS
DEILRSW SWIRLED
WILDERS
DEILRTU DILUTER
DEILRTW TWIRLED
DEILRTY TIREDLY
DEILRVY DEVILRY
DEILRWY WEIRDLY
DEILRWZ WRIZLED
DEILRZZ DRIZZLE
DEILSTT STILTED
DEILSTU DILUTES
DEILSTW WILDEST
DEILSTY DISTYLE
DEILSZZ SIZZLED
DEILTTT TITTLED

DEILTTU TITULED
DEILTTW TWILTED
DEIMMMU MUMMIED
DEIMMOT TOMMIED
DEIMMPR PRIMMED
DEIMMRS DIMMERS
DEIMMRT MIDTERM
TRIMMED
DEIMMRU DUMMIER
IMMURED
DEIMMST DIMMEST
DEIMMSU DUMMIES
MEDIUMS
DEIMNNU MINUEND
DEIMNOP IMPONED
DEIMNOR MINORED
DEIMNOS MISDONE
DEIMNPS IMPENDS
DEIMNRS MINDERS
REMINDS
DEIMNRU UNRIMED
DEIMNSS DIMNESS
MISSEND
DEIMNST MINDSET
DEIMNSW MISWEND
DEIMNTU MINUTED
MUNITED
MUTINED
DEIMNUX UNMIXED
DEIMOOR DOOMIER
MOIDORE
MOODIER
DEIMOOS MOODIES
DEIMOPS IMPOSED
DEIMORS MISDOER
MOIDERS
DEIMORU ERODIUM
DEIMOSS MISDOES
DEIMOST DOMIEST
MODISTE
MOISTED
DEIMOTT OMITTED
DEIMOTV MOTIVED
VOMITED
DEIMPPR PRIMPED
DEIMPRT DIREMPT
DEIMPRU DUMPIER
UMPIRED
DEIMPSU DUMPIES
DEIMPTU IMPUTED
DEIMRRS SMIRRED
DEIMRSW MISDREW
DEIMRUU UREDIUM
DEIMSST DEMISTS
DEIMSSU MISUSED
DEIMSTT SMITTED
DEIMSTU MUISTED
TEDIUMS
DEIMSTY STYMIED
DEINNNU NUNDINE
DEINNOO ONIONED
DEINNOP PINNOED
DEINNOR ENDIRON
DEINNOS ONDINES
DEINNOT INTONED
NOINTED
DEINNRS DINNERS
DEINNRU DUNNIER
INURNED
DEINNST DENTINS
INDENTS
INTENDS
DEINNSU DUNNIES
UNDINES
DEINNSW ENWINDS
DEINNTU DUNNITE
DEINNTW TWINNED
DEINOPR POINDER
PROINED
DEINOPS DISPONE
SPINODE
DEINOPT POINTED
DEINOQU QUOINED
DEINORR DRONIER
DEINORS DONSIER
INDORSE
ROSINED
DEINORU DOURINE
DEINORW DOWNIER
WINDORE
DEINOSS ONSIDES
DEINOST DITONES
STONIED
DEINPPS SNIPPED
DEINPRS PINDERS
DEINPRT PRINTED
DEINPST STIPEND
DEINPSU UNIPEDS
UNSPIDE
UNSPIED
DEINPUW UNWIPED
DEINRST TINDERS
DEINRSU INSURED
DEINRSV VERDINS
DEINRSW REWINDS
WINDERS
DEINRTT TRIDENT
DEINRTU INTRUDE
TURDINE
UNTIRED
UNTRIDE
UNTRIED
DEINRTX DEXTRIN
DEINRTY TINDERY
DEINRUW UNWIRED
DEINSST DISNEST
DISSENT
SNIDEST
DEINSSV VENDISS
DEINSSW WINDSES
DEINSTT DENTIST
DISTENT
STINTED
DEINSTU DISTUNE
DUNITES
DEINSTY DENSITY
DESTINY
DEINSUZ UNSIZED
DEINUVW UNWIVED
DEIOORS OROIDES
DEIOORW WOODIER
DEIOOST OSTEOID
DEIOOSW WOODIES
DEIOOVV VOIVODE
DEIOOWW WOIWODE
DEIOPPP POPPIED
DEIOPPS DOPPIES
DEIOPRS PERIODS
DEIOPRT DIOPTER
DIOPTRE
PERIDOT
PROTEID
DEIOPRV PROVIDE
DEIOPSS DISPOSE
DEIOPST DEPOSIT
DOPIEST
PODITES
POSITED
SOPITED
TOPSIDE
DEIOPSV VESPOID
DEIOPTT TIPTOED
DEIOPTV PIVOTED
DEIOQTU QUOITED
DEIORRT DORTIER
DEIORRW ROWDIER
WORDIER
WORRIED
DEIORSS DORISES
DOSSIER
DEIORST EDITORS
ROISTED
ROSITED
SORTIED
STEROID
STORIED
TIBRODS
TRIODES
DEIORSV DEVISOR
DEVOIRS
VISORED
VOIDERS
DEIORSW DOWRIES
ROWDIES
WEIRDOS
DEIORSZ DORIZES
DEIORTT DOTTIER
DEIORTU ETOURDI
IODURET
OUTRIDE
DEIORTZ ROZITED
DEIORVZ VIZORED
DEIORWW WIDOWER
DEIOSTT DOTIEST
STOITED
DEIOSTU OUTSIDE
TEDIOUS
DEIOSTV DOVIEST
DEIOSTW DOWIEST
DEIOSTX EXODIST
DEIOSTZ DOZIEST
DEIOSUV DEVIOUS
DEIOTUV OUTVIED
DEIPPPU PUPPIED
DEIPPQU QUIPPED
DEIPPRS DIPPERS
DEIPPRT TRIPPED
DEIPPSU DUPPIES
DEIPRSS SPIDERS
DEIPRST SPIRTED
STRIPED
DEIPRSU PUDSIER
SIRUPED
DEIPRSY SPIDERY
DEIPSSU UPSIDES
DEIPSTT SPITTED
DEIPSTU DISPUTE
DEIPSXY PYXIDES
DEIPTTU PUTTIED
TITUPED
DEIQRSU SQUIRED
DEIQRTU QUIRTED
DEIQTTU QUITTED
DEIQUZZ QUIZZED
DEIRRST STIRRED
DEIRRSU DRUSIER
DURRIES
DEIRRSV DRIVERS
DEIRRUX DRUXIER
DEIRSST DISSERT
STRIDES
DEIRSSU DISEURS
SUDSIER
DEIRSTU DUSTIER
REDUITS
STUDIER
DEIRSTV DIVERTS
STRIVED
VERDITS
DEISSST DESISTS
DEISSSU DISUSES
DEISSTU STUDIES
TISSUED
DEISSTV DIVESTS
DEISTTW DEWITTS
TWISTED
DEISWZZ SWIZZED
DEITTTW TWITTED
DEJLOST JOSTLED
DEJLSTU JUSTLED
DEJOSTU JOUSTED
DEKKLSU SKULKED
DEKKNSU SKUNKED
DEKLLNO KNOLLED
DEKLNOP PLONKED
DEKLNPU PLUNKED
DEKLNRU KNURLED
RUNKLED
DEKLRSU SKUDLER
DEKNNRU DRUNKEN
DEKNOOS SNOOKED
DEKNOPR PRONKED
DEKNOQU QUONKED
DEKNOSW SNOWKED
DEKNOSY DONKEYS
DEKNOTT KNOTTED
DEKNOTU KNOUTED
DEKNOUY UNYOKED
DEKNPSU SPUNKED
DEKNRRU DRUNKER
DEKNRSU DUNKERS
DEKNRTU TRUNKED
DEKNSSU DUSKENS
DEKOOPS SPOOKED
DEKOOST DOOKETS
STOOKED
DEKOOTW KOTOWED
DEKOPST DESKTOP
DEKORST STROKED
DEKORWY KEYWORD
DEKOSSU KUDOSES
DEKRSUY DUYKERS
DEKSSTU DUSKEST
DELLMOO MODELLO
DELLOOW WOOLLED
DELLOPR PROLLED
REDPOLL
DELLORR DROLLER
DELLORT TROLLED
DELLOSU DUELLOS

DELLOVW	LOWVELD
DELLSTU	DULLEST
DELMMSU	SLUMMED
DELMNOS	DOLMENS
DELMOOS	SLOOMED
DELMOOW	ELMWOOD
DELMORS	SMOLDER
DELMORU	MOULDER
	REMOULD
DELMOSU	MODULES
	MOUSLED
DELMOSY	SMOYLED
DELMOTT	MOTTLED
DELMOTU	MOULTED
DELMOUV	VOLUMED
DELMPPU	PLUMPED
DELMPRU	RUMPLED
DELMPSU	DUMPLES
	SLUMPED
DELMUZZ	MUZZLED
DELNOOS	NOODLES
	SNOOLED
DELNORS	RONDELS
DELNORT	ENTROLD
DELNORU	LOUNDER
	ROUNDEL
	ROUNDLE
DELNOSS	OLDNESS
DELNOSU	LOUDENS
	NODULES
	NOUSLED
DELNOSW	DOWLNES
DELNOSZ	DONZELS
DELNOTY	NOTEDLY
DELNOUV	UNLOVED
DELNOWY	DOWLNEY
DELNPRU	PLUNDER
DELNRSU	LURDENS
	NURDLES
	NURSLED
	RUNDLES
DELNRTU	RUNDLET
	TRUNDLE
DELNRUU	UNRULED
DELNSSU	DULNESS
DELNUWY	UNWELDY
DELNUZZ	NUZZLED
DELOOPP	PLEOPOD
DELOOPS	POODLES
	SPOOLED
DELOORT	ROOTLED
DELOORW	WOOLDER
DELOOST	STOOLED
DELOOTT	TOOTLED
DELOPPP	PLOPPED
	POPPLED
DELOPPR	DROPPLE
DELOPPS	SLOPPED
DELOPPT	TOPPLED
DELOPRS	POLDERS
DELOPRT	DROPLET
DELOPRU	POULDER
	POULDRE
	PROULED
DELOPRW	PROWLED
DELOPSU	SOUPLED
DELOPSY	DEPLOYS
	PODLEYS
DELOPTT	PLOTTED
DELORRY	ORDERLY
DELORSS	DORSELS
	RODLESS
	SOLDERS
DELORST	DROLEST
	OLDSTER
	STRODLE
DELORSW	WELDORS
DELORSY	YODLERS
DELORTT	DOTTLER
	DOTTREL
DELORTU	TROULED
DELORUV	LOUVRED
DELOSSS	DOSSELS
DELOSSU	DULOSES
DELOSTT	DOTTLES
	SLOTTED
DELOSTU	LOUDEST
	OULDEST
	TOUSLED
DELOSYY	DOYLEYS
DELOSZZ	SOZZLED
DELOTUV	VOLUTED
DELOTUZ	TOUZLED
DELPPRU	PURPLED
DELPPSU	SUPPLED
DELPRSU	DRUPELS
	SLURPED
DELPSSU	PLUSSED
DELPSTU	DUPLETS
DELPSUY	SPULYED
DELPUZZ	PUZZLED
DELRRSU	SLURRED
DELRSTU	LUSTRED
	RUSTLED
	STRUDEL
DELRTTU	TURTLED
DELSSTU	TUSSLED
DELSTTU	SUTTLED
DELUWZZ	WUZZLED
DEMMRRU	DRUMMER
DEMMSTU	STUMMED
DEMNOOR	MORENDO
DEMNOOW	WOODMEN
DEMNORS	MODERNS
	RODSMEN
DEMNORT	MORDENT
DEMNORU	MOURNED
DEMNORY	DEMONRY
DEMNOST	ENDMOST
DEMNOTU	DEMOUNT
	MOUNTED
DEMNOUV	UNMOVED
DEMNSTU	DUSTMEN
DEMOOPP	POPEDOM
DEMOOPR	PREDOOM
DEMOOPS	SPOOMED
DEMOORS	DROOMES
	SMOORED
DEMOORT	MOTORED
DEMOORV	VROOMED
DEMOOSS	OSMOSED
DEMOOST	SMOOTED
DEMOOTT	MOTTOED
DEMOOTU	OUTMODE
DEMOPRT	TROMPED
DEMOPST	STOMPED
DEMORRS	DORMERS
DEMORRU	RUMORED
DEMORST	STORMED
DEMOSSU	SMOUSED
DEMOSTT	DOMETTS
DEMOSTU	MOUSTED
	SMOUTED
DEMOSTY	MODESTY
DEMPRSU	DUMPERS
DEMPRTU	TRUMPED
DEMPSTU	STUMPED
DEMRRSU	MURDERS
	SMURRED
DEMSTTU	SMUTTED
DENNORT	DONNERT
	TENDRON
DENNORU	ENROUND
DENNOST	STONNED
	TENDONS
DENNOTU	UNNOTED
	UNTONED
DENNOUW	ENWOUND
	UNOWNED
DENNOUZ	UNZONED
DENNRSU	UNDERNS
DENNSTU	DUNNEST
	STUNNED
DENNTUU	UNTUNED
DENOOPS	SNOOPED
	SPOONED
DENOOST	SNOOTED
	STOODEN
DENOOSW	SWOONED
DENOOSZ	SNOOZED
DENOOTU	DUOTONE
	OUTDONE
DENOOUW	UNWOOED
DENOPPR	PROPEND
DENOPPU	UNPOPED
DENOPRS	PONDERS
	RESPOND
DENOPRT	PORTEND
	PROTEND
DENOPRU	POUNDER
	UNROPED
DENOPRV	PROVEND
DENOPRY	PROYNED
DENOPSU	UNPOSED
DENOPTY	POYNTED
DENOPUX	EXPOUND
DENORRU	RONDURE
	ROUNDER
	UNORDER
DENORRW	DROWNER
DENORST	RODENTS
	SNORTED
DENORSU	RESOUND
	SOUNDER
	UNDOERS
DENORSV	VENDORS
DENORSW	DOWNERS
	WONDERS
DENORSY	YONDERS
DENORUW	REWOUND
	WOUNDER
DENOSTT	SNOTTED
DENOSTU	DEUTONS
	SNOUTED
DENOSUW	SWOUNED
DENPRSU	SPURNED
DENPRTU	PRUDENT
	PRUNTED
	UPTREND
DENPSSU	SUSPEND
	UPSENDS
DENRSSU	SUNDERS
	UNDRESS
DENRSSY	DRYNESS
DENRSTU	RETUNDS
DENRSUU	UNSURED
DENSSTY	SYNDETS
DENSSUW	SUNDEWS
DENSTTU	STUDENT
	STUNTED
DENTUVY	DUVETYN
DEOOPPS	OPPOSED
DEOOPRS	SPOORED
DEOOPRT	TORPEDO
	TROOPED
DEOOPST	STOOPED
DEOOPSW	SWOOPED
DEOOPSX	EXOPODS
DEOORRT	REDROOT
DEOORST	ROOSTED
DEOORTU	OUTRODE
DEOORTW	WROOTED
DEOOSTT	TOOTSED
DEOOSTU	OUTDOES
DEOPPPR	PROPPED
DEOPPQU	QUOPPED
DEOPPRR	DROPPER
DEOPPRS	DOPPERS
DEOPPST	STOPPED
DEOPPSW	SWOPPED
DEOPRRU	PROUDER
DEOPRST	DEPORTS
	REDTOPS
	SPORTED
DEOPRSU	POUDERS
	POUDRES
DEOPRSW	POWDERS
DEOPRTU	TROUPED
DEOPRWY	POWDERY
DEOPSST	DESPOTS
DEOPSSU	SPOUSED
DEOPSTT	SPOTTED
DEOPSTU	SPOUTED
DEOPTTY	TYPTOED
DEOQRTU	TORQUED
DEORRSS	DORSERS
DEORRST	DORTERS
	RODSTER
DEORRSU	ORDURES
DEORRSV	DROVERS
DEORRSW	REWORDS
	SWORDER
DEORSSS	DOSSERS
	DROSSES
DEORSSU	DOUSERS
DEORSSW	DOWSERS
	DROWSES
DEORSTT	DETORTS
DEORSTU	DETOURS
	DOUREST
	DOUTERS
	OUTREDS
	ROUSTED
DEORSTW	STROWED
	WORSTED
DEORSTY	DESTROY
	ROYSTED
	STROYED
DEORSUV	DEVOURS
DEORTTT	TROTTED

DEORTTU	TUTORED
DEORTUU	OUTDURE
DEOSSSW	SOWSSED
DEOSSTW	DOWSETS
DEOSSYY	ODYSSEY
DEOSTTT	STOTTED
DEOSTTU	DUETTOS
	TESTUDO
DEOSTTW	SWOTTED
DEOSTUU	DUTEOUS
DEOSTUX	TUXEDOS
DEPRRSU	SPURRED
DEPRRUY	PRUDERY
DEPRSTU	SPURTED
DEPRSUU	PURSUED
	USURPED
DEPRSUY	SYRUPED
DERRSTU	RUSTRED
DERSSSU	SUDSERS
DERSSTU	DUSTERS
	TRUSSED
DERSTTU	STURTED
	TRUSTED
DERSTTY	TRYSTED
DERSTUU	SUTURED
DFFGINO	DOFFING
DFFGINU	DUFFING
DFFIIMR	MIDRIFF
DFFIIRT	TRIFFID
DFFIMOR	DIFFORM
DFFLOOU	FOODFUL
DFGGIIN	FIDGING
DFGGINU	FUDGING
DFGHIOS	DOGFISH
DFGIINN	FINDING
DFGIINY	DIGNIFY
DFGILNO	FOLDING
DFGINNO	FONDING
DFGINNU	FUNDING
DFGINOR	FORDING
DFGINOU	FUNGOID
DFGMOOY	FOGYDOM
DFHILSU	DISHFUL
DFHIMSU	MUDFISH
DFILMMO	FILMDOM
DFILMNU	MINDFUL
DFILNOP	PINFOLD
DFILNOS	INFOLDS
DFILOSX	SIXFOLD
DFILOTW	TWIFOLD
DFILTUU	DUTIFUL
DFIMNUY	MUNDIFY
DFIMOOS	FOODISM
DFIMORS	DISFORM
DFLMOOU	DOOMFUL
DFLNOSU	UNFOLDS
DFLOOTW	TWOFOLD
DFLOPRY	DROPFLY
DFLOTWY	TWYFOLD
DFNNOUU	UNFOUND
DFNORUY	FOUNDRY
DFOORSX	OXFORDS
DGGGIIN	DIGGING
DGGGINO	DOGGING
DGGHIOS	DOGGISH
DGGIILN	GILDING
	GLIDING
DGGIINN	DINGING
DGGIINR	GIRDING
	GRIDING
	RIDGING
DGGIINU	GUIDING
DGGIJNU	JUDGING
DGGILNO	GODLING
	LODGING
DGGIMNU	MUDGING
DGGINNO	DONGING
DGGINNU	DUNGING
	NUDGING
DGGINRY	GRYDING
DGGNOSU	DUGONGS
DGHHOOO	HOGHOOD
DGHIILN	HIDLING
	HILDING
DGHIINS	DISHING
	HIDINGS
	SHINDIG
DGHILNO	HOLDING
DGHILNY	HYLDING
DGHILOS	GOLDISH
DGHILPY	DIGLYPH
DGHINOO	HOODING
DGHINOR	HORDING
DGHINSU	DUSHING
DGHINTU	UNDIGHT
DGHIOOS	GOODISH
DGHIOPS	DOGSHIP
	GODSHIP
DGHOOPS	HOPDOGS
DGHORTU	DROUGHT
DGHOTUY	DOUGHTY
DGIIKLN	KIDLING
DGIIKNN	DINKING
	KINDING
DGIIKNR	DIRKING
DGIIKNS	DISKING
DGIILLN	DILLING
DGIILNO	LOIDING
DGIILNR	DIRLING
DGIILNS	SIDLING
	SLIDING
DGIILNW	WILDING
DGIILRS	RIDGILS
DGIILRY	RIGIDLY
DGIIMMN	DIMMING
DGIIMNN	MINDING
DGIIMNS	SMIDGIN
DGIIMOP	PIGMOID
DGIIMOS	SIGMOID
DGIINNN	DINNING
DGIINNR	RINDING
DGIINNS	NIDINGS
	SINDING
DGIINNT	DINTING
	TINDING
DGIINNU	INDUING
DGIINNW	DWINING
	WINDING
DGIINOS	INDIGOS
DGIINOV	VOIDING
DGIINOW	WINDIGO
DGIINPP	DIPPING
DGIINPR	PRIDING
DGIINPS	PIDGINS
DGIINPU	PINGUID
DGIINRS	RIDINGS
DGIINRT	DIRTING
DGIINRV	DRIVING
DGIINRY	YIRDING
DGIINSS	DISSING
	SIDINGS
DGIINST	TIDINGS
DGIINSV	DIVINGS
DGIINTT	DITTING
DGIINTY	DIGNITY
	TIDYING
DGIIORT	TIGROID
DGIJOSU	JUDOGIS
DGIKMNO	KINGDOM
DGIKNNU	DUNKING
DGIKNNY	KYNDING
DGIKNOO	DOOKING
DGIKNOS	DOGSKIN
DGIKNSU	DUSKING
DGILLNO	DOLLING
DGILLNU	DULLING
DGILLOY	GODLILY
DGILMNO	MOLDING
DGILNOR	GIRLOND
	LORDING
DGILNOY	YODLING
DGILNSU	UNGILDS
DGILNYY	DYINGLY
DGILOST	DIGLOTS
DGILRUY	GUILDRY
DGIMNOO	DOOMING
DGIMNPU	DUMPING
DGIMOPY	PYGMOID
DGINNNO	DONNING
DGINNNU	DUNNING
DGINNOP	PONDING
DGINNOR	DRONING
DGINNOS	DONINGS
	ONDINGS
DGINNOU	UNDOING
DGINNOW	DOWNING
DGINNSY	SYNDING
DGINNTU	DUNTING
	TUNDING
DGINNUW	WINDGUN
DGINNUY	UNDYING
DGINOOW	WOODING
DGINOPP	DOPPING
DGINOPS	DOPINGS
	PONGIDS
DGINORR	DORRING
DGINORS	RODINGS
DGINORT	DORTING
DGINORV	DROVING
DGINORW	WORDING
DGINOSS	DOSSING
DGINOST	DOTINGS
DGINOSU	DOUSING
	GUIDONS
DGINOSW	DISGOWN
	DOWSING
DGINOSZ	DOZINGS
DGINOTT	DOTTING
DGINOTU	DOUTING
DGINPPU	DUPPING
DGINRSU	UNGIRDS
DGINRSY	DRYINGS
DGINSSU	SUDSING
DGINSTU	DUSTING
DGIOPRY	PRODIGY
DGIOSTW	GODWITS
DGIQSUY	SQUIDGY
DGISSTU	DISGUST
DGLNOUY	UNGODLY
DGLOOOW	LOGWOOD
DGLOPSY	SPLODGY
DGLOSYY	DYSLOGY
DGMOPRU	GUMDROP
DGMORUU	GURUDOM
DGNOOOR	GODROON
DGNOORS	DRONGOS
DGNOOSS	GODSONS
DGNOOSW	GODOWNS
DGNOOTW	DOGTOWN
DGNORSU	GROUNDS
DGNOSSU	SUNDOGS
DGOORTT	DOGTROT
DGOSTUU	DUGOUTS
DHIILNS	HIDLINS
DHIILOT	LITHOID
DHIILSW	WILDISH
DHIIMMS	DIMMISH
DHIIMNO	HOMINID
DHIIMPS	MIDSHIP
DHIINRU	HIRUDIN
DHIIOPX	XIPHOID
DHIIORZ	RHIZOID
DHIIOST	HISTOID
DHIKSSU	DUSKISH
DHILLOS	DOLLISH
DHILLSU	DULLISH
DHILMUY	HUMIDLY
DHILNOP	DOLPHIN
DHILOST	DOLTISH
DHILOSU	LOUDISH
DHILPSU	LUDSHIP
DHILPSY	SYLPHID
DHILRTY	THIRDLY
DHIMOPR	DIMORPH
DHIMORU	HUMIDOR
	RHODIUM
DHIMPSU	DUMPISH
DHINNOS	DONNISH
DHINNSU	DUNNISH
DHINOPS	DONSHIP
DHINOPY	HYPNOID
DHINORS	DISHORN
	DRONISH
DHIOOST	DHOOTIS
DHIOPTY	TYPHOID
DHIORSW	WORDISH
DHIORTY	THYROID
DHIPRSU	PRUDISH
DHIPRSY	SYRPHID
DHKMOOU	MUDHOOK
DHKORSY	DROSHKY
DHLMOOU	HOODLUM
DHLOPSU	UPHOLDS
DHMMRUU	HUMDRUM
DHMNOYY	HYMNODY
DHNNOOU	NUNHOOD
DHNOOSU	UNHOODS
DHOOOOS	HOODOOS
DHOOPRU	UPHOORD
DHOORSU	RHODOUS
DHOPRSU	PUSHROD
DHORSSU	SHROUDS
DHORSTU	DROUTHS
DHORSUY	HYDROUS
	SHROUDY
DHORTUY	DROUTHY
DHORXYY	HYDROXY
DIIIMRU	IRIDIUM
DIIIMSV	DIVISIM
DIIINPS	INSIPID

DIIJNOS DISJOIN
DIIKKNS KIDSKIN
DIIKLNS DISLINK
DIIKNOT DOITKIN
DIILLST DISTILL
DIILLVY LIVIDLY
DIILMNS DISLIMN
DIILMOO MODIOLI
DIILMOS IDOLISM
DIILMTY TIMIDLY
DIILNNU INDULIN
DIILNWY WINDILY
DIILOPS LIPOIDS
DIILOST IDOLIST
DIILQSU LIQUIDS
DIILRSU SILURID
DIILRTY DIRTILY
DIILSST DISTILS
DIILVVY VIVIDLY
DIILYZZ DIZZILY
DIIMNOR MIDIRON
DIIMNSU INDIUMS
DIIMORS DIORISM
DIIMOSS IODISMS
DIIMSSS DISMISS
DIIMSTW DIMWITS
DIIMSUV VIDIMUS
DIINNOT TONDINI
DIINNSW INWINDS
DIINOQU QUINOID
DIINORS SORDINI
DIINOSX DIOXINS
DIIOPRS SPIROID
DIIORSV DIVISOR
VIROIDS
DIITUVY VIDUITY
DIJOSTU JUDOIST
DIKKOPS DIKKOPS
DIKLNOR LORDKIN
DIKLSUY DUSKILY
DIKNNSU NUDNIKS
DIKNORV DVORNIK
DIKOORT DROOKIT
DIKOOSS SKIDOOS
DIKORTU DROUKIT
DILLOSY SOLIDLY
DILLPSY PSYLLID
DILLRUY LURIDLY
DILMNRU DRUMLIN
DILMOOY MOODILY
DILMORS MILORDS
DILMOST MISTOLD
DILMOSU SOLIDUM
DILMOSY ODYLISM
DILMTUY TUMIDLY
DILNNSU DUNLINS
DILNOOS OODLINS
DILNOPS DIPLONS
DILNOPT DIPLONT
DILNOQU QUODLIN
DILNORT INTROLD
DILNOSU UNSOLID
DILNOXY INDOXYL
DILNPSU LISPUND
DILNPSY SPINDLY
DILNSTU INDULTS
DILORTU DILUTOR
DILORWY ROWDILY
WORDILY
DILOSSS DOSSILS
DILOSSU DULOSIS
SOLIDUS
DILOSTY STYLOID
DILRYZZ DRIZZLY
DILSTUY DUSTILY
DIMMOST MIDMOST
DIMNNOO MIDNOON
DIMNNOS DONNISM
DIMNNOT DINMONT
DIMNOOS DOMINOS
DIMNOPU IMPOUND
DIMNSSU NUDISMS
DIMOPSU SPODIUM
DIMORSW MISWORD
DIMOSST MODISTS
DIMOSSU SODIUMS
DIMOSSW WISDOMS
DIMRTUU TRIDUUM
DIMRUUV DUUMVIR
DINNOOR RONDINO
DINNOOT TONDINO
DINNOPW PINDOWN
DINNOSS SINDONS
DINNOUW INWOUND
DINNSUW UNWINDS
DINOORS INDOORS
SORDINO
DINOORT TORDION
DINOOST ISODONT
DINOPSU DUPIONS
UNIPODS
DINORSU DURIONS
DINORTU TURDION
DINORWW WINDROW
DINOSSW DISOWNS
DINOSWW WINDOWS
DINOTUW OUTWIND
DINPSTU PUNDITS
DINPSUW UPWINDS
DINRSSU SUNDRIS
DINSSTU NUDISTS
DIOOPSS ISOPODS
DIOORST DISROOT
TOROIDS
DIOORTT RIDOTTO
DIOOSTX TOXOIDS
DIOPRST DISPORT
TORPIDS
TRIPODS
DIOPRTY TRIPODY
DIOPSST DISPOST
DIORRST STRIDOR
DIORSTT DISTORT
DIOSSTU STUDIOS
DIOSUUV VIDUOUS
DIPRSTU DISRUPT
DIPSSTU STUPIDS
DIRSTUY SURDITY
DJNNOOS DONJONS
DKNNRUU UNDRUNK
DKNOOPS PONDOKS
DKOOOOS KOODOOS
DKOOOSZ ODZOOKS
DLLOOPS DOLLOPS
DLLORWY WORLDLY
DLMNOOY MYLODON
DLMNOUU UNMOULD
DLMOSUU MODULUS
DLNOPRU PULDRON
DLNOPSY SPONDYL
DLNORSU UNLORDS
DLNORUY ROUNDLY
DLNOSUY SOUNDLY
DLOOPPY POLYPOD
DLOOPSS PODSOLS
DLOOPSZ PODZOLS
DLOOPTY TYLOPOD
DLOOPUY DUOPOLY
DLOOPWY PLYWOOD
DLOORSU DOLOURS
DLOOSTU OUTSOLD
DLOOTTU OUTTOLD
DLOPRUY PROUDLY
DLOSTUW WOULDST
DMNOOOP MONOPOD
DMNOORS DROMONS
DMNOOTW TOWMOND
DMNOSSU OSMUNDS
DMORTUW MUDWORT
DNNOOST DONNOTS
DNNORUU UNROUND
DNNORUW RUNDOWN
DNNOSUU UNSOUND
DNNOSUW SUNDOWN
DNNOUUW UNWOUND
DNNRTUU TURNDUN
DNNSTUU TUNDUNS
DNOORTU OROTUND
DNOOTUW NUTWOOD
DNOPUUW UPWOUND
DNORSST STRONDS
DNORSTU ROTUNDS
DNOSSTU STOUNDS
DNOSSTW STOWNDS
DNOSSUW SWOUNDS
DNOSSWW SWOWNDS
DOOOOSV VOODOOS
DOOORSU ODOROUS
DOOORTU OUTDOOR
DOOPRSU UROPODS
DOOPRSY PROSODY
DOOPSTU UPSTOOD
DOORRTU DORTOUR
DOOSUUV VOUDOUS
DORSSTU STROUDS
DORSUVY DYVOURS
DORUVYY DYVOURY
EEEEFRR REFEREE
EEEEGTX EXEGETE
EEEENTT ENTETEE
EEEEPST TEEPEES
EEEEPSW PEEWEES
EEEFFFO FEOFFEE
EEEFFOR OFFEREE
EEEFFRS EFFERES
EEEFGRU REFUGEE
EEEFHRS SHEREEF
EEEFIRS FEERIES
EEEFLRR FLEERER
EEEFLRS FEELERS
EEEFLRT FLEETER
EEEFMNR FREEMEN
EEEFNRS ENFREES
EEEFORS FORESEE
EEEFRRS REEFERS
EEEFRRZ FREEZER
EEEFRSZ FREEZES
EEEGHNW WHEENGE
EEEGIKR GEEKIER
EEEGILS ELEGIES
ELEGISE
EEEGILZ ELEGIZE
EEEGINP EPIGENE
EEEGINR GREENIE
EEEGIPR PERIGEE
EEEGLMN GLEEMEN
EEEGLNT GENTEEL
EEEGMRR REMERGE
EEEGMRS EMERGES
EEEGNPR EPERGNE
EEEGNPS PEENGES
EEEGNRR GREENER
RENEGER
EEEGNRS RENEGES
EEEGNRU RENEGUE
EEEGNRV REVENGE
EEEGNSS GENESES
EEEGNTT GENETTE
EEEGRRT GREETER
REGREET
EEEGRSS GREESES
EEEGRST GREETES
EEEGRSZ GEEZERS
EEEGRUX EXERGUE
EEEHILW WHEELIE
EEEHISZ HEEZIES
EEEHLNW ENWHEEL
EEEHLPW WHEEPLE
EEEHLRS HEELERS
REHEELS
EEEHLRW WHEELER
EEEHLST LETHEES
EEEHLWZ WHEEZLE
EEEHNST ETHENES
EEEHNSX HEXENES
EEEHPRS PHEERES
EEEHPSS PHEESES
EEEHPSZ PHEEZES
EEEHRRS SHEERER
EEEHRST SEETHER
EEEHSST SEETHES
EEEHSTT ESTHETE
TEETHES
EEEHSWZ WHEEZES
EEEIJLS JEELIES
EEEIKLS KEELIES
EEEIKRR REEKIER
EEEILRR LEERIER
EEEILRS SEELIER
EEEILRV RELIEVE
EEEILST EELIEST
EEEIMMS MEEMIES
EEEIMNS ENEMIES
EEEIMNT EMETINE
EEEIMPR PREEMIE
EEEIMRS EMERIES
EEEIMRT EREMITE
EEEINQU QUEENIE
EEEINRT TEENIER
EEEINRW WEENIER
EEEINSW WEENIES
EEEIPRR PEERIER
EEEIPRS PEERIES
SEEPIER
EEEIPRW WEEPIER
EEEIPSU EPUISEE
EEEIPSW WEEPIES
EEEIRRT RETIREE
EEEIRRV REVERIE
EEEIRST EERIEST

EEEIRSV VEERIES
EEEIRSZ RESEIZE
EEEISTW SWEETIE
EEEJNPY JEEPNEY
EEEJPRS JEEPERS
EEEJRRS JEERERS
EEEJSST JESTEES
EEEKKRS KEEKERS
EEEKLLU UKELELE
EEEKLMN KEELMEN
EEEKLNR KNEELER
EEEKLNS SLEEKEN
EEEKLPW EKPWELE
EEEKLRS KEELERS
SLEEKER
EEEKMNS MEEKENS
EEEKMST MEEKEST
EEEKNPT KEEPNET
EEEKNRS KEENERS
EEEKNST KEENEST
EEEKPRS KEEPERS
EEEKRSS KREESES
SEEKERS
EEEKRST SKEETER
EEELMNR REELMEN
EEELMNT ELEMENT
EEELMPX EXEMPLE
EEELMSX LEXEMES
EEELNST STELENE
EEELNSV ELEVENS
EEELPRS PEELERS
SLEEPER
SPEELER
EEELPRT REPLETE
EEELPST STEEPLE
EEELRRS REELERS
EEELRSV SLEEVER
EEELRTV LEVERET
EEELSSS LESSEES
EEELSST TELESES
EEELSSV SLEEVES
EEELSSY EYELESS
EEELSTX TELEXES
EEELSTY EYELETS
EEELTTX TELETEX
EEEMMSS SEMEMES
EEEMNRS MENEERS
EEEMNSS NEMESES
EEEMNST MENTEES
EEEMORT EROTEME
EEEMRSS SEEMERS
EEEMRST TEEMERS
EEEMRTX EXTREME
EEEMSST ESTEEMS
MESTEES
EEEMSTT MEETEST
EEEMSTU EMEUTES
EEENNPT PENTENE
EEENNRT ETRENNE
EEENNTT ENTENTE
EEENPRT TERPENE
EEENPRV PREVENE
EEENPSS PENSEES
EEENPST ENSTEEP
STEEPEN
EEENPSW ENSWEEP
EEENPSX EXPENSE
EEENRRS SERENER
SNEERER
EEENRRT ENTERER
TERREEN
TERRENE
EEENRRV VENERER
EEENRRW RENEWER
EEENRSS SERENES
EEENRST ENTREES
RETENES
EEENRSV ENERVES
EVENERS
VENEERS
EEENRSZ SNEEZER
EEENRTV EVENTER
EEENRTX EXTERNE
EEENRUV REVENUE
UNREEVE
EEENSSZ SNEEZES
EEENSTV EVENEST
EEENSTW SWEETEN
EEENSTX EXTENSE
EEENSVW VENEWES
EEENSWY SWEENEY
EEEOPPS EPOPEES
EEEORSV OVERSEE
EEEORSY EYESORE
EEEORVY OVEREYE
EEEPPRS PEEPERS
EEEPRSS PEERESS
EEEPRST ESTREPE
STEEPER
EEEPRSV PEEVERS
PREEVES
EEEPRSW SWEEPER
WEEPERS
EEEPRSZ SPREEZE
EEEQRRU QUEERER
REQUERE
EEEQSUZ SQUEEZE
EEERRRV REVERER
EEERRST RETREES
STEERER
EEERRSV RESERVE
REVERES
REVERSE
SEVERER
EEERSSS SEERESS
EEERSTT TEETERS
TERETES
EEERSTV STEEVER
EEERSTW SWEETER
EEERSUV REVEUSE
EEERSUW SERUEWE
EEERSVW SERVEWE
WEEVERS
EEERTTW TWEETER
EEESSTT SETTEES
TESTEES
EEESSTV STEEVES
EEESTTW WEETEST
EEESTWZ TWEEZES
EEFFFNO ENFEOFF
EEFFFOR FEOFFER
EEFFGLU EFFULGE
EEFFINT FIFTEEN
EEFFIRS EFFEIRS
EEFFKLS KEFFELS
EEFFNOS OFFENSE
EEFFORR OFFERER
EEFFOST TOFFEES
EEFFSSU EFFUSES
EEFFSTU SUFFETE
EEFGILN FEELING
FLEEING
EEFGINR FEERING
FREEING
REEFING
EEFGINS FEESING
EEFGINZ FEEZING
EEFGLLU GLEEFUL
EEFGLOR FORELEG
EEFGLOS SOLFEGE
EEFGRSU REFUGES
EEFHIRS HEIFERS
EEFHIRT HEFTIER
EEFHISY FISHEYE
EEFHLNS ENFLESH
EEFHLRS FLESHER
HERSELF
EEFHLSS FLESHES
EEFHNRS FRESHEN
EEFHORT THEREOF
EEFHORW WHEREOF
EEFHRRS FRESHER
REFRESH
EEFHRSS FRESHES
EEFHRST FRESHET
EEFIIRR FIERIER
EEFIIRS REIFIES
EEFILLS FELLIES
EEFILLX FLEXILE
EEFILNO OLEFINE
EEFILNS FELINES
EEFILOR FORELIE
EEFILRR FERLIER
EEFILRS FERLIES
RELIEFS
EEFILRT FELTIER
FERTILE
EEFILST FELSITE
LEFTIES
LIEFEST
EEFIMNR FIREMEN
EEFIMRT FEMITER
EEFINNR FENNIER
EEFINNS FENNIES
EEFINRR FERNIER
REFINER
EEFINRS ENFIRES
FEERINS
FINEERS
REFINES
EEFINRT FEINTER
EEFINSS FINESSE
EEFINSX ENFIXES
EEFIPRS PREIFES
PRIEFES
EEFIRRS FERRIES
EEFIRRT FERRITE
EEFIRSS FRISEES
EEFIRSZ FRIEZES
EEFISTV FESTIVE
EEFLLOS FELLOES
EEFLLRS FELLERS
EEFLLRU FUELLER
EEFLLST FELLEST
EEFLLTY FLEETLY
EEFLMTU TEEMFUL
EEFLNNO ENFELON
EEFLNNS FENNELS
EEFLNOS ONESELF
EEFLNRS FRESNEL
EEFLNSS FLENSES
EEFLOOV FOVEOLE
EEFLORS FORLESE
EEFLRRS FERRELS
EEFLRRU FERRULE
EEFLRST FELTERS
REFLETS
TELFERS
EEFLRSU FERULES
REFUELS
EEFLRTT FETTLER
EEFLRTU FLEURET
EEFLRUX FLEXURE
EEFLSTT FETTLES
EEFLSUY EYEFULS
EEFMNOR FOREMEN
EEFMNRT FERMENT
EEFMOTT MOFETTE
EEFMPRU PERFUME
EEFMSTW FEWMETS
EEFMTTU FUMETTE
EEFNORT OFTENER
EEFNORZ ENFROZE
EEFNRRY FERNERY
EEFNRTV FERVENT
EEFNSSW FEWNESS
EEFORRV FOREVER
EEFORRZ REFROZE
EEFOTTU FOUETTE
EEFPRRS PREFERS
EEFPRSU PERFUSE
EEFRRST FERRETS
EEFRRSU REFUSER
EEFRRTU REFUTER
EEFRRTY FERRETY
EEFRSST FESTERS
EEFRSSU REFUSES
EEFRSTT FETTERS
EEFRSTU FEUTRES
REFUTES
EEFRSTW FEWTERS
EEFSSTU FETUSES
EEGGGLR GLEGGER
EEGGHTU THUGGEE
EEGGILN GLEEING
NEGLIGE
EEGGILR LEGGIER
EEGGINR GREEING
EEGGIPS PEGGIES
EEGGIST EGGIEST
EEGGISV VEGGIES
EEGGKRS SKEGGER
EEGGLRS EGGLERS
LEGGERS
EEGGMNY YEGGMEN
EEGGMSU MUGGEES
EEGGNOR ENGORGE
EEGGNOY GEOGENY
EEGGORR REGORGE
EEGGORU GOUGERE
EEGGPRU PUGGREE
EEGHILN HEELING
EEGHINT THEEING
EEGHINY HYGIENE
EEGHINZ HEEZING
EEGHIRW REWEIGH
WEIGHER
EEGHLNU LEUGHEN
EEGHNRT GREENTH
EEGHNRY GREYHEN

EEGHRTU TEUGHER
EEGHSSS GHESSES
EEGIIRS GRIESIE
EEGIJLN JEELING
EEGIJNR JEERING
EEGIKKN KEEKING
EEGIKLN KEELING
EEGIKNN KEENING
KNEEING
EEGIKNP KEEPING
PEEKING
EEGIKNR REEKING
EEGIKNS SEEKING
EEGIKNT KITENGE
EEGILLS GELLIES
EEGILNP LEEPING
PEELING
EEGILNR LEERING
REELING
EEGILNS LEESING
SEELING
EEGILNT GENTILE
EEGILOS ELOGIES
EEGILRS LEIGERS
LIEGERS
EEGILRV VELIGER
EEGILST ELEGIST
ELEGITS
EEGIMMR GEMMIER
IMMERGE
EEGIMNR MEERING
REGIMEN
EEGIMNS SEEMING
EEGIMNT MEETING
TEEMING
EEGIMNX EXEMING
EEGIMRS EMIGRES
REGIMES
REMIGES
EEGINNP PEENING
EEGINNR ENGINER
INGENER
EEGINNS ENGINES
NEESING
SNEEING
EEGINNT TEENING
EEGINNU GENUINE
INGENUE
EEGINNV EEVNING
EVENING
EEGINNW ENEWING
WEENING
EEGINNZ NEEZING
EEGINOP EPIGONE
EEGINOS SOIGNEE
EEGINPP PEEPING
EEGINPR PEERING
PREEING
EEGINPS SEEPING
EEGINPV PEEVING
EEGINPW WEEPING
EEGINRS GREISEN
EEGINRT GENTIER
INTEGER
TEERING
TREEING
EEGINRV REEVING
REGIVEN
VEERING
EEGINSS GENESIS
SEEINGS
EEGINSW SEEWING
SWEEING
EEGINTV VENTIGE
EEGINTW WEETING
EEGINTX EXIGENT
EEGIOST EGOTISE
GOETIES
EEGIOTZ EGOTIZE
EEGIRRV GRIEVER
EEGIRSS SIEGERS
EEGIRSV GRIEVES
REGIVES
EEGIRTT TERGITE
EEGIRTU GUERITE
EEGISTV VESTIGE
EEGKNOR KEROGEN
EEGKNRU GERENUK
EEGLLNS LEGLENS
EEGLLSS LEGLESS
EEGLLST LEGLETS
EEGLMMU GEMMULE
EEGLMSU EMULGES
LEGUMES
EEGLNNS GENNELS
EEGLNOR ERELONG
EEGLNOU EUGENOL
EEGLNOZ LOZENGE
EEGLNRT GENTLER
EEGLNRY GREENLY
EEGLNST GENTLES
LENGEST
EEGLRST REGLETS
EEGLRTY TELERGY
EEGMMRY GEMMERY
EEGMNOS EMONGES
GENOMES
EEGMNRS GERMENS
EEGMNST SEGMENT
EEGMNSU EMUNGES
EEGMRRS MERGERS
EEGNNST GENNETS
EEGNOPS PONGEES
EEGNORS ENGORES
NEGROES
EEGNOSX EXOGENS
EEGNPUX EXPUNGE
EEGNRSS NEGRESS
EEGNRST GERENTS
REGENTS
EEGNRSV VENGERS
EEGNSSU GENUSES
NEGUSES
EEGNSTU GUESTEN
EEGOOPY POOGYEE
EEGOOSS SOOGEES
EEGOPRT PROTEGE
EEGORTV OVERGET
EEGOSSS GESSOES
EEGPRUX EXPURGE
EEGRRSS REGRESS
EEGRRST REGRETS
EEGRRSU RESURGE
REURGES
EEGRRSV VERGERS
EEGRSST REGESTS
EEGRSSU GUESSER
EEGRSSY GEYSERS
EEGRSTT GETTERS
EEGRSTU GESTURE
EEGRSTY GREYEST
EEGSSSU GUESSES
EEHHRTT THETHER
EEHHRTW WHETHER
EEHHSTW WHEESHT
EEHILLR HELLIER
EEHILMN HELIMEN
EEHILPS EPHELIS
EEHILRS LEISHER
EEHILRW WHILERE
EEHILST SHELTIE
EEHILSX HELIXES
EEHIMMS MISHMEE
EEHIMNO HEMIONE
EEHIMPR HEMPIER
EEHIMPS HEMPIES
EEHIMPT EPITHEM
EEHIMRS MESHIER
EEHINNR HENNIER
EEHINNS HENNIES
EEHINOR HEROINE
EEHINRR ERRHINE
EEHINRS HENRIES
INHERES
EEHINRT NEITHER
THEREIN
EEHINRW WHEREIN
EEHINST THEINES
EEHIORS HEROISE
EEHIORZ HEROIZE
EEHIPRT PRITHEE
EEHIPSV PEEVISH
EEHIPTT EPITHET
EEHIRRS HERRIES
EEHIRSS HEIRESS
HERISSE
EEHIRST HEISTER
EEHIRSV SHRIEVE
EEHIRTW THEWIER
EEHIRWY WHEYIER
EEHISTV THIEVES
EEHKLOY KEYHOLE
EEHKLSS SHEKELS
EEHKOOY EYEHOOK
EEHKRSS SHREEKS
EEHLLMP PHELLEM
EEHLLNS ENSHELL
EEHLLRS HELLERS
SHELLER
EEHLMMW WHEMMLE
EEHLMST HELMETS
EEHLNSU UNHELES
EEHLPRS HELPERS
EEHLPRT TELPHER
EEHLPSS PLESHES
EEHLRST SHELTER
EEHLRSW WELSHER
EEHLRSY SHEERLY
EEHLSSU HUELESS
EEHLSSV SHELVES
EEHLSSW SHEWELS
WELSHES
EEHLSTT SHTETEL
EEHLSTV THELVES
EEHMNOP PHONEME
EEHMNOS HOSEMEN
EEHMNRU ENRHEUM
EEHMNRY MYNHEER
EEHMNSS MENSHES
EEHMORT THEOREM
EEHMPST TEMPEHS
EEHMRUX EXHUMER
EEHMSST SMEETHS
EEHMSUX EXHUMES
EEHNNOS SHONEEN
EEHNNRS HENNERS
EEHNNRY HENNERY
EEHNOPT POTHEEN
EEHNORT THEREON
EEHNORW NOWHERE
WHEREON
EEHNPSS SEPHENS
SPHENES
EEHNPSW NEPHEWS
EEHNRST THRENES
EEHNSST NESHEST
EEHNSTU ENTHUSE
EEHNSTV SEVENTH
EEHNSTY ETHYNES
EEHOOPW WHOOPEE
EEHOPRU EUPHROE
EEHOPSS SHEEPOS
EEHORST HETEROS
EEHORSU REHOUSE
EEHORSW WHERESO
EEHORTT THERETO
EEHORTW WHERETO
EEHORVW HOWEVER
WHOEVER
EEHOSST ETHOSES
EEHOSSX HEXOSES
EEHOSTW TOWHEES
EEHPPST HEPPEST
EEHPRSS SPHERES
EEHPRST HEPSTER
PETHERS
SPERTHE
THREEPS
EEHPRTY PRYTHEE
EEHQSTU QUETHES
EEHRRSW WERSHER
EEHRRTW WHERRET
EEHRSSU RUSHEES
EEHRSTT TETHERS
EEHRSTW WETHERS
WRETHES
EEHRSTZ HERTZES
EEHRTTW WHETTER
EEHRVWY WHYEVER
EEIIKRS KIERIES
EEIILRV VEILIER
EEIIMNS MEINIES
EEIIMPR RIEMPIE
EEIIMRT EMERITI
EEIIMST ITEMISE
EEIIMTZ ITEMIZE
EEIINRT ERINITE
NITERIE
EEIINRV VEINIER
EEIINSW WIENIES
EEIINTV INVITEE
EEIIPST PIETIES
EEIIRRV RIVIERE
EEIIRVW VIEWIER
EEIISST SEITIES
EEIISTV VISITEE
EEIJKRR JERKIER
EEIJKRS JERKIES
EEIJLLS JELLIES
EEIJMMR JEMMIER

EEIJMMS JEMMIES
EEIJNNS JENNIES
EEIJRRS JERRIES
EEIJRTT JETTIER
EEIJSSS JESSIES
EEIJSTT JETTIES
EEIKLLS KELLIES
SKELLIE
EEIKLNY KEYLINE
EEIKLPS KELPIES
EEIKLPT PIKELET
EEIKLSS SELKIES
EEIKLST KELTIES
SLEEKIT
EEIKMNP PIKEMEN
EEIKNRT KERNITE
EEIKNSS ENSKIES
KINESES
EEIKPRR PERKIER
EEIKPRS PESKIER
EEIKRST KEISTER
EEIKRSY SKIEYER
EEIKSST SEIKEST
EEIKSTT STEEKIT
EEIKTTT TEKTITE
EEILLMT MELLITE
EEILLNS NELLIES
EEILLPS ELLIPSE
EEILLRS LEISLER
EEILLRT TREILLE
EEILLRV EVILLER
EEILLSS EISELLS
EEILLST TELLIES
EEILLSV VIELLES
EEILLSW WELLIES
EEILMNN LINEMEN
EEILMNR ERMELIN
EEILMNS ISLEMEN
EEILMPT IMPLETE
EEILMRV VERMEIL
EEILMST ELMIEST
EEILNNO LEONINE
EEILNNT LENIENT
EEILNNV ENLIVEN
EEILNOR ELOINER
EEILNPS PENSILE
EEILNRS LIERNES
RELINES
EEILNRV LIVENER
EEILNSS ENISLES
ENSILES
SENSILE
SILENES
EEILNST SETLINE
TENSILE
EEILNTT ENTITLE
EEILNTV VEINLET
EEILOPT PETIOLE
EEILORT TROELIE
EEILORV OVERLIE
RELIEVO
EEILOST ESTOILE
ETOILES
EEILOTZ ZEOLITE
EEILPRR REPLIER
EEILPRS REPLIES
SPIELER
EEILPRT PERLITE
REPTILE
EEILPRU PUERILE
EEILPSS PELISSE
EEILPST EPISTLE
PELITES
EEILQRU RELIQUE
EEILRRS RELIERS
EEILRRV RELIVER
REVILER
EEILRSS RESILES
EEILRST LEISTER
RETILES
STERILE
EEILRSU LEISURE
EEILRSV RELIVES
REVILES
SERVILE
EEILRTT RETITLE
EEILSSS SESELIS
SESSILE
EEILSST TELESIS
TIELESS
EEILSSU ILEUSES
EEILSSW LEWISES
EEILSSX LEXISES
SILEXES
EEILSTV LEVITES
LIEVEST
EEILSTX SEXTILE
EEILSUV ELUSIVE
EEILSVW WEEVILS
EEILSZZ LEZZIES
EEILTTX TEXTILE
EEILVWY WEEVILY
EEIMMNS IMMENSE
EEIMMRS IMMERSE
EEIMMSS MIMESES
MISSEEM
EEIMNNO NOMINEE
EEIMNNT EMINENT
EEIMNOS SEMEION
EEIMNRS ERMINES
EEIMNRV MINEVER
EEIMNRW WIREMEN
EEIMNSS INSEEMS
MISSEEN
NEMESIS
SIEMENS
EEIMNST EMETINS
EEIMNSW MISWEEN
EEIMNSY MEINEYS
MENYIES
EEIMNTT MINETTE
EEIMOPS EPISOME
EEIMOPT EPITOME
EEIMORS ISOMERE
EEIMOSS MEIOSES
EEIMOTV EMOTIVE
EEIMPRR PREMIER
REPRIME
EEIMPRS EMPIRES
EMPRISE
EPIMERS
IMPRESE
PREMIES
PREMISE
SPIREME
EEIMPRT EMPTIER
EEIMPST EMPTIES
SEPTIME
EEIMQRU REQUIEM
EEIMRRR MERRIER
EEIMRRS MERRIES
EEIMRRT TRIREME
EEIMRSS MESSIER
MISERES
REMISES
EEIMRST METIERS
RETIMES
TREMIES
TRISEME
EEIMRSX REMIXES
EEIMRTT EMITTER
TERMITE
EEIMSSS MISSEES
SEMISES
EEIMSST METISSE
EEINNNP PENNINE
EEINNPS PENNIES
EEINNRS NERINES
EEINNRT INTERNE
EEINNRU NEURINE
EEINNRV ENRIVEN
INNERVE
NERVINE
EEINNRW WENNIER
EEINNST INTENSE
TENNIES
EEINNTW ENTWINE
EEINOPR PEREION
PIONEER
EEINOPS PEONIES
EEINPPS PEPSINE
EEINPRR REPINER
EEINPRS EREPSIN
REPINES
EEINPRT INEPTER
EEINPRZ PRENZIE
EEINPSS PENISES
EEINPST PENTISE
EEINPSV PENSIVE
VESPINE
EEINQRU ENQUIRE
INQUERE
EEINQTU QUIETEN
EEINQUY QUEYNIE
EEINRRS RESINER
EEINRRT INERTER
REINTER
RENTIER
TERRINE
EEINRRV NERVIER
VERNIER
EEINRSS SEINERS
SEREINS
SERINES
EEINRST ENTIRES
ENTRIES
NERITES
TRENISE
EEINRSV ENVIERS
INVERSE
VENIRES
VERSINE
EEINRSW NEWSIER
EEINRTT NETTIER
TENTIER
EEINRTU NEURITE
RETINUE
REUNITE
UTERINE
EEINSST SEITENS
SESTINE
EEINSSV SENVIES
EEINSSW NEWSIES
EEINSTV TENSIVE
VENITES
EEINSTX EXTINES
SIXTEEN
EEINSTY SYENITE
EEIOPPT EPITOPE
EEIOPSS POESIES
EEIOPST POETISE
EEIOPSX EPOXIES
EEIOPTZ POETIZE
EEIORRS ROSIERE
EEIORSS SOIREES
EEIORSV EROSIVE
EEIOSST ISOETES
EEIOSTT TOEIEST
EEIPPPR PEPPIER
EEIPPST PEPTISE
EEIPPTT PIPETTE
EEIPPTZ PEPTIZE
EEIPQRU PERIQUE
REPIQUE
EEIPQSU EQUIPES
EEIPRRR PERRIER
EEIPRRS PERRIES
REPRISE
RESPIRE
EEIPRRV REPRIVE
EEIPRRZ REPRIZE
EEIPRSS PRESSIE
EEIPRST RESPITE
EEIPRSV PREVISE
PRIEVES
EEIPRSW SPEWIER
EEIPRSX EXPIRES
PREXIES
EEIPRTT PETTIER
EEIPRVW PREVIEW
EEIPRZZ PREZZIE
EEIPSTT PETTIES
EEIPSTW PEEWITS
EEIQRRU REQUIRE
EEIQRSU ESQUIRE
QUERIES
EEIQRTU QUIETER
REQUITE
EEIRRRT RETIRER
TERRIER
EEIRRSS SERRIES
SIRREES
EEIRRST ETRIERS
REITERS
RESTIER
RETIRES
RETRIES
TERRIES
EEIRRSV REIVERS
REVERSI
REVISER
RIEVERS
EEIRRSW REWIRES
EEIRRTV RIVERET
RIVETER
EEIRRTW REWRITE
EEIRRVV REVIVER
EEIRSSU REISSUE
EEIRSSV IVRESSE
REVISES

EEIRSSZ	SEIZERS
EEIRSTT	TESTIER
EEIRSTU	SUETIER
EEIRSTV	RESTIVE
	SIEVERT
	STIEVER
	VERIEST
EEIRSTW	STEWIER
EEIRSTZ	ZESTIER
EEIRSUZ	SEIZURE
EEIRSVV	REVIVES
EEIRSVW	REVIEWS
	VIEWERS
EEIRTVV	VETIVER
EEISSSV	ESSIVES
EEISSTX	SEXIEST
EEISTVX	VITEXES
EEITUXZ	ZEUXITE
EEJKRRS	JERKERS
EEJLLMU	JUMELLE
EEJLRWY	JEWELRY
EEJNNST	JENNETS
EEJNOOR	REJONEO
EEJNORS	REJONES
EEJNORY	ENJOYER
EEJPRRU	PERJURE
EEJQRRU	JERQUER
EEJQRSU	JERQUES
EEJRSST	JESTERS
EEJRSSY	JERSEYS
EEKKOTV	VETKOEK
EEKKRRT	TREKKER
EEKKSSY	KEKSYES
EEKLLNV	KNEVELL
EEKLLSY	SLEEKLY
EEKLLUU	UKULELE
EEKLMPS	KEMPLES
EEKLNNS	KENNELS
EEKLNOS	KEELSON
EEKLNRS	KERNELS
EEKLPRS	KELPERS
EEKLRST	KELTERS
	KESTREL
	SKELTER
EEKLSSY	KEYLESS
EEKLSTT	KETTLES
EEKMNOS	SOKEMEN
EEKMPRS	KEMPERS
EEKNNRS	KENNERS
EEKNNST	KENNETS
EEKNOSS	KENOSES
EEKNOST	KETONES
EEKNOTY	KEYNOTE
EEKNRSS	SKREENS
EEKNSTU	NETSUKE
EEKOPRS	RESPOKE
EEKORSV	EVOKERS
	REVOKES
EEKOSSS	SEKOSES
EEKOSST	KETOSES
EEKPPSU	UPKEEPS
EEKPRSU	PERUKES
EEKRSST	STREEKS
EEKRSSU	RESKUES
EEKRSSW	RESKEWS
	SKEWERS
EEKRSSY	KERSEYS
EEKSSTW	SKEWEST
EELLMRS	MERELLS
	SMELLER
EELLMRV	VERMELL
EELLNOV	NOVELLE
EELLNRS	SNELLER
EELLNST	TELLENS
EELLNSW	NEWELLS
EELLORS	ROSELLE
EELLORZ	ROZELLE
EELLPRS	RESPELL
	SPELLER
EELLPST	PELLETS
EELLQRU	QUELLER
EELLRSS	RESELLS
	SELLERS
EELLRST	RETELLS
	TELLERS
EELLRSU	RUELLES
EELLRSW	SWELLER
EELLSTV	VELLETS
EELMMOP	POMMELE
EELMMPU	EMPLUME
EELMNNS	LENSMEN
EELMNOO	OENOMEL
EELMOPR	PLEROME
EELMOPT	LEPTOME
EELMORW	EELWORM
EELMOST	OMELETS
EELMPRS	SEMPLER
EELMPST	PELMETS
	STEMPEL
	STEMPLE
	TEMPLES
EELMPTT	TEMPLET
EELMRST	SMELTER
EELMRSU	LEMURES
	RELUMES
EELMSST	TELESMS
EELMSTT	METTLES
	STEMLET
EELNNSV	VENNELS
EELNOPV	ENVELOP
EELNOSV	ELEVONS
EELNOSY	ESLOYNE
EELNOTT	NOTELET
EELNOTU	TOLUENE
EELNPSS	PENSELS
	SPLEENS
EELNPST	PENTELS
EELNPSY	SPLEENY
EELNQUY	QUEENLY
EELNRST	RELENTS
	SLENTER
EELNRSU	UNREELS
EELNRTT	LETTERN
EELNRUV	NERVULE
EELNSSS	LESSENS
EELNSST	NESTLES
EELNSSU	UNSEELS
EELNSTT	NETTLES
EELNSTU	ELUENTS
	UNSTEEL
EELNSTY	ENSTYLE
	TENSELY
EELNSUV	VENULES
EELNSXY	XYLENES
EELNTTU	LUNETTE
EELOPPS	PEOPLES
EELOPRS	ELOPERS
	LEPROSE
EELOPRX	EXPLORE
EELOPSS	ELOPSES
EELOPTU	EELPOUT
EELORSS	RESOLES
EELORSV	RESOLVE
EELORTT	LORETTE
EELORVV	EVOLVER
	REVOLVE
EELOSSS	LOESSES
EELOSST	OSSELET
	TELOSES
	TOELESS
EELOSTT	TELEOST
EELOSUV	EVOLUES
EELOSVV	EVOLVES
EELOTUV	EVOLUTE
	VELOUTE
EELPPRX	PERPLEX
EELPPSU	PEEPULS
EELPQRU	PREQUEL
EELPRST	PELTERS
	PETRELS
	RESPELT
	SPELTER
EELPRSU	REPULSE
EELPRSY	SLEEPRY
	YELPERS
EELPRTZ	PRETZEL
EELPRUX	PLEXURE
EELPRVY	REPLEVY
EELPSST	PESTLES
EELPSTT	PETTLES
EELPSTY	STEEPLY
EELPSUX	EXPULSE
EELQRUY	QUEERLY
EELQSSU	SEQUELS
EELRRSV	VERRELS
EELRRVY	REVELRY
EELRSST	STREELS
	TRESSEL
EELRSSU	RULESSE
EELRSTT	LETTERS
	LETTRES
	SETTLER
	STERLET
	TRESTLE
EELRSTV	SVELTER
EELRSTW	SWELTER
	WELTERS
	WRESTLE
EELRSTY	RESTYLE
	TERSELY
EELRSTZ	SELTZER
EELRSUV	VELURES
EELRSVV	VERVELS
EELSSSU	USELESS
EELSSSV	VESSELS
EELSSSX	SEXLESS
EELSSTT	SETTLES
EELSSTU	SETULES
EELSSUV	EVULSES
EELSTUY	EUSTYLE
EELSTVV	VELVETS
EELSTVW	TWELVES
EELSTWY	SWEETLY
EELTVVY	VELVETY
EEMMNOT	MEMENTO
EEMMORS	MEROMES
EEMMOSU	MOUSMEE
EEMMOSV	EMMOVES
EEMMRST	STEMMER
EEMMSSS	SEMSEMS
EEMMSST	STEMMES
EEMNNOV	ENVENOM
EEMNNSW	NEWSMEN
EEMNOOS	SOMEONE
EEMNOOY	MOONEYE
EEMNOPR	REPOMEN
EEMNORS	MOREENS
EEMNORV	OVERMEN
EEMNORY	MONEYER
EEMNOST	TEMENOS
	TONEMES
EEMNOSV	ENMOVES
EEMNPTU	UMPTEEN
EEMNRTU	TRUEMEN
EEMNSYZ	ENZYMES
EEMOOSW	WOESOME
EEMOPRR	EMPEROR
EEMOPRT	TEMPORE
EEMOPRV	PREMOVE
EEMOPRW	EMPOWER
EEMOPST	METOPES
EEMORRS	REMORSE
	ROEMERS
EEMORRT	REMOTER
EEMORRU	UROMERE
EEMORRV	REMOVER
EEMORST	METEORS
	REMOTES
EEMORSV	REMOVES
EEMPRRT	PRETERM
EEMPRSS	EMPRESS
EEMPRST	TEMPERS
EEMPRSU	PRESUME
	SUPREME
EEMPRTT	TEMPTER
EEMPRTU	PERMUTE
EEMPSSU	EMPUSES
EEMPSTT	TEMPEST
EEMPSTX	EXEMPTS
EEMRRST	TERMERS
EEMRRUU	REMUEUR
EEMRSST	RESTEMS
EEMRSSU	RESUMES
EEMRSUX	MUREXES
EEMSSSU	SMEUSES
EEMSSTU	MUSTEES
EEMSTTU	MUSETTE
EENNORT	ENTERON
	TENONER
EENNORU	NEURONE
EENNOSS	ONENESS
EENNOSZ	ENZONES
EENNOTT	NONETTE
EENNOTY	NEOTENY
EENNPRS	PENNERS
EENNQUU	UNQUEEN
EENNRST	RENNETS
	TENNERS
EENNRUV	UNNERVE
EENNSST	SENNETS
EENNSSU	UNSEENS
	UNSENSE
EENNSSW	NEWNESS
EENOPPR	PREPONE
	PROPENE
EENOPPT	PEPTONE
EENOPRS	OPENERS
	PERONES
	REOPENS
	REPONES

EENOPST OPENEST
PENTOSE
POSTEEN
POTEENS
EENORRV OVERREN
EENORSY ONEYERS
ONEYRES
EENORSZ REZONES
EENORTV OVERNET
EENOSSY ESSOYNE
NOYESES
EENOSTV VENTOSE
VOTEENS
EENOSTW TOWNEES
EENOSVZ EVZONES
EENPPRT PERPENT
EENPRST PRESENT
REPENTS
SERPENT
EENPRSY PYRENES
EENPRTV PREVENT
EENPSTU PUNTEES
EENPSTW ENSWEPT
EENPSTY STEPNEY
EENQSTU SEQUENT
EENRRST RENTERS
STERNER
EENRRSU ENSURER
EENRRSV NERVERS
EENRRUV NERVURE
EENRSST NESTERS
RESENTS
STRENES
EENRSSU ENSURES
EENRSTT TENTERS
TESTERN
EENRSTU NEUTERS
RETUNES
TENURES
TUREENS
EENRSTV VENTERS
VENTRES
EENRSTW WESTERN
EENRSTX EXTERNS
EENRSTY STYRENE
YESTERN
EENRSVV VERVENS
EENRTUV VENTURE
EENSSST SETNESS
EENSSSY SYNESES
EENSSTT TENSEST
EENSSTV STEVENS
EENSSTW WETNESS
EENSSUV VENUSES
EENSSUX UNSEXES
EENSSVW SWEVENS
EENSTTX EXTENTS
EENSTTY TEENTSY
EENSTUW UNSWEET
EENSTVY SEVENTY
EEOOPRS OPEROSE
EEOOSTT TOETOES
EEOPPRS PREPOSE
EEOPPTU OUTPEEP
EEOPRRV REPROVE
EEOPRSS REPOSES
EEOPRSX EXPOSER
EEOPRTT TREETOP
EEOPRTU OUTPEER
EEOPSSS SPEOSES
EEOPSST POETESS
EEOPSSU ESPOUSE
POSEUSE
EEOPSSX EXPOSES
EEOPSTU TOUPEES
EEOPSTY PEYOTES
EEOPTUW OUTWEEP
EEOQRTU REQUOTE
EEORRST RESTORE
EEORRSV REVERSO
EEORRTU REROUTE
EEORRTV EVERTOR
EEORRTW REWROTE
EEORSST OSSETER
STEREOS
EEORSSX SOREXES
XEROSES
EEORSTT ROSETTE
EEORSTV ESTOVER
OVERSET
EEORSTX XEROTES
EEORSTY ESOTERY
EEORSUV OEUVRES
OVERUSE
EEORSVW OVERSEW
EEORTUV OUVERTE
EEPPPRS PEPPERS
EEPPPRY PEPPERY
EEPPRST STEPPER
EEPPSST STEPPES
EEPPSUW UPSWEEP
EEPPSUY EUPEPSY
EEPRRSS PRESSER
REPRESS
SPERRES
EEPRRSU PERUSER
REPURES
EEPRRTV PERVERT
EEPRRVY REPRYVE
EEPRSSS PRESSES
SPERSES
EEPRSST PESTERS
PRESETS
EEPRSSU PERSUES
PERUSES
EEPRSSV VESPERS
EEPRSSW SPEWERS
EEPRSSX EXPRESS
EEPRSTT PERTEST
PETTERS
PRETEST
EEPRSTU PERTUSE
REPUTES
EEPRSTW PEWTERS
EEPRSTX EXPERTS
SEXPERT
EEPRSUV PREVUES
EEPRTTX PRETEXT
EEPSSTT SEPTETS
EEPSTTU PUTTEES
EEPSTTY TYPESET
EEQRRUY EQUERRY
EEQRSTU QUESTER
REQUEST
EEQSSTU QUEESTS
EEQSUYZ SQUEEZY
EERRSST RESTERS
EERRSSV SERVERS
VERSERS
EERRSTT TERRETS
EERRSTU URETERS
EERRSTV REVERTS
EERRSTW STREWER
WRESTER
EERRSUV REVEURS
EERRSVW SWERVER
EERRSVY SERVERY
EERRTTU REUTTER
UTTERER
EERRTTY RETTERY
EERSSST TRESSES
EERSSTT SETTERS
STREETS
TERSEST
TESTERS
EERSSTV REVESTS
STERVES
VERSETS
EERSSTW STEWERS
WESTERS
EERSSTX EXSERTS
EERSSTZ ZESTERS
EERSSUY SEYSURE
EERSSVW SWERVES
EERSTTT STRETTE
TETTERS
EERSTTU TRUSTEE
EERSTTY STREETY
EERSTUV VERSUTE
VERTUES
VESTURE
EERSTUY TUYERES
EERSTVV VERVETS
EERSTWY TWYERES
EERSUVW SURVEWE
EERTTUX TEXTURE
EESSSTT SESTETS
TSETSES
EESSTTT SESTETT
EESSTTU SUTTEES
EESSTTX SEXTETS
EESSTTY STEYEST
EESSTTZ TZETSES
EESTTTW WETTEST
EESTTTX SEXTETT
EFFFIRU FUFFIER
EFFFOOR FEOFFOR
EFFGIJN JEFFING
EFFGINR REFFING
EFFGIRS GRIFFES
EFFGISU GUFFIES
EFFGORS GOFFERS
EFFGRRU GRUFFER
EFFHILW WHIFFLE
EFFHIRS SHERIFF
EFFHIRU HUFFIER
EFFHIRW WHIFFER
EFFHITW WHIFFET
EFFHLSU SHUFFLE
EFFIIJS JIFFIES
EFFIIMR MIFFIER
EFFIINR NIFFIER
EFFIIST FIFTIES
IFFIEST
EFFIKLS SKIFFLE
EFFILLU LIFEFUL
EFFILNS SNIFFLE
EFFILPR PIFFLER
EFFILPS PIFFLES
EFFILRR RIFFLER
EFFILRS RIFFLES
EFFILRY FIREFLY
EFFILSS SIFFLES
EFFINRS NIFFERS
SNIFFER
EFFINST INFEFTS
STIFFEN
EFFIOPR PIFFERO
EFFIORT FORFEIT
TOFFIER
EFFIOST TOFFIES
EFFIPRU PUFFIER
EFFIRRT TRIFFER
EFFIRST RESTIFF
STIFFER
EFFLMRU MUFFLER
EFFLMSU MUFFLES
EFFLNSU SNUFFLE
EFFLOPS POFFLES
EFFLOSU SOUFFLE
EFFLRRU RUFFLER
EFFLRSU RUFFLES
EFFLRTU FRETFUL
TRUFFLE
EFFNRSU SNUFFER
EFFNRUU UNRUFFE
EFFOORR OFFEROR
EFFOPRR PROFFER
EFFOPSU POUFFES
EFFORST EFFORTS
EFFOSST OFFSETS
EFFPRSU PUFFERS
EFFPRUY PUFFERY
EFFRSSU SUFFERS
EFFRSTU STUFFER
EFFSSUU SUFFUSE
EFFSTTU TUFFETS
EFGGIOR FOGGIER
EFGGIRR FRIGGER
EFGGIRU FUGGIER
EFGGIRY FIGGERY
EFGGORS FOGGERS
EFGHIMS GEMFISH
EFGHINT HEFTING
EFGHIRT FIGHTER
FREIGHT
EFGILLN FELLING
EFGILMN FLEMING
EFGILNR FLINGER
EFGILNS SELFING
EFGILNT FELTING
EFGILNX FLEXING
EFGILNY FLEYING
EFGILRU GULFIER
EFGIMNT FIGMENT
EFGINNP PFENNIG
EFGINNR FERNING
EFGINOR FOREIGN
EFGINRS FINGERS
FRINGES
EFGINRU GUNFIRE
EFGINTT FETTING
EFGINTW WEFTING
EFGIOOR GOOFIER
EFGIORV FORGIVE
EFGIRRT GRIFTER
EFGIRSU FIGURES
EFGLLSU FLUGELS
EFGLNSU ENGULFS
EFGLNTU FULGENT

EFGLORS	GOLFERS
EFGLORT	FROGLET
EFGLOSS	FOGLESS
EFGMNOR	FROGMEN
EFGNOOR	FORGONE
EFGOORS	FORGOES
EFGORRS	FORGERS
EFGORRU	FERRUGO
EFGORRY	FORGERY
EFGORST	FORGETS
EFGORSW	GOWFERS
EFGORTU	FOREGUT
EFHIINS	FINEISH
EFHIIRS	FISHIER
EFHIJSW	JEWFISH
EFHILMS	FLEMISH
	HIMSELF
EFHILSS	SELFISH
EFHILST	LEFTISH
EFHILTY	HEFTILY
EFHINNS	FENNISH
EFHIRSS	FISHERS
	SERFISH
	SHERIFS
EFHIRST	SHIFTER
EFHIRSY	FISHERY
EFHISUW	HUSWIFE
EFHLLPU	HELPFUL
EFHLLSY	FLESHLY
EFHLNSU	UNFLESH
EFHLOOX	FOXHOLE
EFHLOPU	HOPEFUL
EFHLOSS	FLOSHES
EFHLRSU	FLUSHER
EFHLRSY	FRESHLY
EFHLSSU	FLUSHES
EFHLSTY	THYSELF
EFHLTTW	TWELFTH
EFHNORT	FORHENT
EFHOORS	HOOFERS
EFHORST	FOTHERS
EFHRRTU	FURTHER
EFHRSSU	FRUSHES
EFIIKST	FIKIEST
EFIILLS	FILLIES
EFIILMR	FILMIER
EFIILMS	MISFILE
EFIILRT	FITLIER
EFIILRY	FIERILY
EFIILSS	FISSILE
EFIIMRS	MISFIRE
EFIINNR	FINNIER
EFIINPV	FIVEPIN
EFIINRT	NIFTIER
EFIINRU	UNIFIER
EFIINSU	UNIFIES
EFIINSX	INFIXES
EFIIRRR	FIRRIER
EFIIRRT	RIFTIER
EFIIRST	FISTIER
EFIIRZZ	FIZZIER
EFIISSV	FISSIVE
EFIJLLY	JELLIFY
EFIJLOR	FRIJOLE
EFIJLOT	JETFOIL
EFIKLOS	FOLKIES
EFIKLRU	FLUKIER
EFIKNRU	FUNKIER
EFIKORR	FORKIER
EFIKRRS	FRISKER
EFIKRST	FRISKET
EFILLMS	MISFELL
EFILLOO	FOLIOLE
EFILLOS	FOLLIES
EFILLRS	FILLERS
	REFILLS
EFILLST	FILLETS
EFILLUW	WILEFUL
EFILMNU	FULMINE
EFILMOT	FILEMOT
EFILMSS	SELFISM
EFILMST	FILMSET
	LEFTISM
EFILNOS	OLEFINS
EFILNOX	FLEXION
EFILNSS	FINLESS
EFILOOS	FLOOSIE
	FOLIOSE
EFILOOZ	FLOOZIE
EFILOPR	PROFILE
EFILORR	FLORIER
EFILORT	LOFTIER
	TREFOIL
EFILOSX	SEXFOIL
EFILPPR	FLIPPER
EFILPPS	FIPPLES
EFILPPU	PIPEFUL
EFILPRS	PILFERS
EFILPRY	PILFERY
EFILQUY	LIQUEFY
EFILRRS	RIFLERS
EFILRRT	TRIFLER
EFILRST	FILTERS
	LIFTERS
	STIFLER
	TRIFLES
EFILRTT	FLITTER
EFILRTU	FLUTIER
	FUTILER
EFILRVV	FLIVVER
EFILRZZ	FRIZZLE
EFILSSS	FISSLES
EFILSST	SELFIST
	STIFLES
EFILSTT	LEFTIST
EFILSTU	FLUIEST
	SULFITE
EFILSZZ	FIZZLES
EFILUVX	FLUXIVE
EFIMMRU	FERMIUM
EFIMNOR	FERMION
EFIMNTT	FITMENT
EFIMOST	FOMITES
EFIMRRS	FIRMERS
EFIMRST	FIRMEST
	FREMITS
EFIMSTU	FUMIEST
EFIMTTU	FUMETTI
EFINNOR	INFERNO
EFINNRS	FINNERS
EFINNRU	FUNNIER
EFINNSU	FUNNIES
EFINOPR	PORPINE
EFINRST	SNIFTER
EFINRSU	INFUSER
EFINRUY	REUNIFY
EFINSST	FITNESS
	INFESTS
EFINSSU	INFUSES
EFINSUX	UNFIXES
EFINSZZ	FIZZENS
EFIOOPR	POOFIER
EFIOORR	ROOFIER
EFIOORT	FOOTIER
EFIOORW	WOOFIER
EFIOOST	FOOTIES
EFIOPRR	PORIFER
EFIOPRT	FIREPOT
EFIORRT	ROTIFER
EFIORRW	FROWIER
EFIORSS	FROISES
EFIORST	FOISTER
	FORTIES
EFIOSST	SOFTIES
EFIOSTX	FOXIEST
EFIOSTZ	FOZIEST
EFIPPRR	FRIPPER
EFIPRTY	PETRIFY
EFIRRRU	FURRIER
EFIRRSU	FRISEUR
	FRISURE
	SURFIER
EFIRRTT	FRITTER
EFIRRTU	FRITURE
	FRUITER
	TURFIER
EFIRRTY	TERRIFY
EFIRRUZ	FURZIER
EFIRSST	SIFTERS
	STRIFES
EFIRSSU	FISSURE
	FUSSIER
	SURFIES
EFIRSTT	FITTERS
	TITFERS
EFIRSTU	FUSTIER
	SURFEIT
EFIRSTW	SWIFTER
EFIRSUX	FIXURES
EFIRSVY	VERSIFY
EFIRSZZ	FIZZERS
	FRIZZES
EFIRTTU	TUFTIER
	TURFITE
EFIRTUV	FURTIVE
EFIRTUX	FIXTURE
EFIRUZZ	FUZZIER
EFISTTT	FITTEST
EFISTTY	TESTIFY
EFJLSTU	JESTFUL
EFKLMNO	MENFOLK
EFKLMOR	MERFOLK
EFKLNUY	FLUNKEY
EFKLOPU	POKEFUL
EFKLPSU	SKEPFUL
EFKORRS	FORKERS
EFLLOST	FLOTELS
EFLLOSW	FELLOWS
EFLLRSU	FULLERS
EFLLSTU	FULLEST
EFLMOSU	FULSOME
EFLMPRU	FRUMPLE
EFLMSUU	MUSEFUL
EFLNNSU	FUNNELS
EFLNORT	FORLENT
EFLNORU	FLEURON
EFLNORY	FELONRY
EFLNOSU	SULFONE
EFLNOTT	FLETTON
	FONTLET
EFLNPSU	PENFULS
EFLNSSU	FULNESS
	UNSELFS
EFLNSTU	FLUENTS
	NESTFUL
	NETFULS
EFLNSUY	SYNFUEL
EFLNTTU	TENTFUL
EFLNTUU	TUNEFUL
EFLOORR	FLOORER
	FORLORE
EFLOORS	FORSLOE
EFLOORY	FOOLERY
EFLOORZ	FOOZLER
EFLOOST	FOOTLES
EFLOOSZ	FOOZLES
EFLORRS	ROLFERS
EFLORST	FLORETS
	LOFTERS
EFLORSU	FUROLES
	OURSELF
EFLORSW	FLOWERS
	FOWLERS
	REFLOWS
	WOLFERS
EFLORSX	FLEXORS
EFLORTT	FORTLET
EFLORTW	FELWORT
EFLORVY	FLYOVER
	OVERFLY
EFLORWW	WERWOLF
EFLORWY	FLOWERY
EFLOSSS	FLOSSES
EFLOSSU	FLOUSES
EFLOSTU	FOULEST
EFLOTUW	OUTFLEW
EFLPRSU	PURFLES
EFLPRUY	PREYFUL
EFLPSTU	PESTFUL
EFLRSTU	FLUSTER
	FLUTERS
	RESTFUL
EFLRTTU	FLUTTER
EFLSTUZ	ZESTFUL
EFLSUZZ	FUZZLES
EFMNOOT	FOOTMEN
EFMNORS	ENFORMS
EFMNOST	FOMENTS
EFMNRSU	SURFMEN
EFMNRTU	TURFMEN
EFMOORZ	ZOEFORM
EFMOPRR	PERFORM
	PREFORM
EFMOPRT	POMFRET
EFMORRS	FORMERS
	REFORMS
EFMOTTU	FUMETTO
EFMPRUY	PERFUMY
EFMRTUY	FURMETY
EFNNORT	FORNENT
EFNNOTU	UNOFTEN
EFNOOST	FESTOON
EFNORRU	FORERUN
EFNORTU	FORTUNE
EFNORTW	FORWENT
EFNORUZ	UNFROZE
EFNOSST	SOFTENS
EFNRSTU	FUNSTER
EFOOPRR	REPROOF
EFOOPRS	SPOOFER

EFOOPRT FORETOP
POOFTER
EFOORRS ROOFERS
EFOORST FOETORS
FOOTERS
REFOOTS
EFOORSW WOOFERS
EFOORTW WOOFTER
EFOPPRY FOPPERY
EFOPRSS PROFESS
EFOPRST FORPETS
EFOPRSU PROFUSE
EFOPRTU POUFTER
EFOPRTY TORPEFY
EFORRSU FERROUS
FURORES
EFORRTY TORREFY
EFORRUV FERVOUR
EFORSST FORESTS
FOSTERS
EFORSSU FOURSES
EFORSTU FOUTERS
FOUTRES
EFOSSTT SOFTEST
EFOSTWW WOWFEST
EFPRTUY PUTREFY
EFPSTUY STUPEFY
EFRRSSU SURFERS
EFRRSTU RETURFS
EFRRSUU FUREURS
EFRSSSU FUSSERS
EFRSTTU TUFTERS
EFRSTUU FUTURES
EFSSTTU FUSTETS
EGGGILN LEGGING
EGGGILR GIGGLER
EGGGILS GIGGLES
EGGGINP PEGGING
EGGGLOR GOGGLER
EGGGLOS GOGGLES
EGGGLSU GUGGLES
EGGGNOS EGGNOGS
EGGHILR HIGGLER
EGGHILS HIGGLES
EGGHINP PEGHING
EGGHIRT THIGGER
EGGHLOS SHOGGLE
EGGHORS HOGGERS
EGGHORY HOGGERY
EGGHOST HOGGETS
EGGIILS GILGIES
EGGIINS SIEGING
EGGIIPR PIGGIER
EGGIIPS PIGGIES
EGGIJLS JIGGLES
EGGIJRS JIGGERS
EGGILLN GELLING
EGGILMS LEGGISM
EGGILNN LENGING
EGGILNR NIGGLER
EGGILNS GINGLES
NIGGLES
SNIGGLE
EGGILNU LUGEING
EGGILNY GLEYING
EGGILRS LIGGERS
EGGILRW WIGGLER
WRIGGLE
EGGILST GIGLETS
EGGILSU LUGGIES
EGGILSW WIGGLES
EGGIMMN GEMMING
EGGIMNN MENGING
EGGIMNR GERMING
MERGING
EGGIMOS MOGGIES
EGGIMRU MUGGIER
EGGINNR GERNING
EGGINNS GINSENG
EGGINNV VENGING
EGGINRS GINGERS
NIGGERS
SNIGGER
EGGINRU GRUEING
GUNGIER
EGGINRV VERGING
EGGINRW GREWING
EGGINRY GINGERY
GREYING
NIGGERY
EGGINSS GESSING
EGGINTT GETTING
EGGINTW TWIGGEN
EGGIORS SOGGIER
EGGIPRR PRIGGER
EGGIPRU PUGGIER
EGGIPRY PIGGERY
EGGIPSU PUGGIES
EGGIRRS RIGGERS
EGGIRRT TRIGGER
EGGIRRU RUGGIER
EGGIRSW SWIGGER
EGGIRTW TWIGGER
EGGIRUV VUGGIER
EGGIRWY WIGGERY
EGGJLOS JOGGLES
EGGJLRU JUGGLER
EGGJLSU JUGGLES
EGGJORS JOGGERS
EGGLMSU SMUGGLE
EGGLNSU SNUGGLE
EGGLOOS GOOGLES
EGGLOOY GEOLOGY
EGGLORS LOGGERS
SLOGGER
EGGLOST GOGLETS
TOGGLES
EGGLOSW WOGGLES
EGGLPRU PLUGGER
EGGLPSU PUGGLES
EGGLRSU GURGLES
LUGGERS
SLUGGER
EGGMRSU MUGGERS
SMUGGER
EGGNOOY GEOGONY
EGGNRSU GRUNGES
SNUGGER
EGGNSTU NUGGETS
EGGNTUY NUGGETY
EGGORST GORGETS
EGGORTY TOGGERY
EGGPRUY PUGGERY
EGGRRSU RUGGERS
EGGRSTU TUGGERS
EGGSSTU SUGGEST
EGHHIMN HIGHMEN
EGHHIRS HIGHERS
EGHHIST EIGHTHS
HEIGHTS
HIGHEST
EGHHOSW SHOWGHE
EGHHSSU SHEUGHS
EGHHSUW WHEUGHS
EGHIILL GHILLIE
EGHIINR HEIRING
EGHIINT NIGHTIE
EGHIINV INVEIGH
EGHIKNR GHERKIN
EGHIKRS SKREIGH
SKRIEGH
EGHILLN HELLING
EGHILMN HELMING
EGHILNP HELPING
EGHILNR HERLING
EGHILNS SHINGLE
EGHILNT ENLIGHT
LIGHTEN
EGHILNV HELVING
EGHILPT PIGHTLE
EGHILRT LIGHTER
RELIGHT
EGHILSS SLEIGHS
EGHILST SLEIGHT
EGHIMMN HEMMING
EGHIMNS MESHING
EGHIMNT THEMING
EGHIMPT EMPIGHT
EGHINNN HENNING
EGHINNT HENTING
EGHINNU UNHINGE
EGHINOS SHOEING
EGHINPS HESPING
PHESING
EGHINRR HERRING
EGHINRT RIGHTEN
EGHINRW WHINGER
EGHINRY HERYING
EGHINST NIGHEST
EGHINSW HEWINGS
SHEWING
WHINGES
EGHINSX HEXINGS
EGHINTT TIGHTEN
EGHINWW WHEWING
EGHIOOS SHOOGIE
EGHIORS OGREISH
EGHIORU ROUGHIE
EGHIOST HOGTIES
EGHIOTT GOTHITE
EGHIOTU TOUGHIE
EGHIOTV EIGHTVO
EGHIRRT RIGHTER
EGHIRSS SIGHERS
EGHIRST SIGHTER
EGHIRSU GUSHIER
EGHIRSY GREYISH
EGHIRTT TIGHTER
EGHISTW WEIGHTS
EGHITWY WEIGHTY
EGHLLOU LUGHOLE
EGHLMPS PHLEGMS
EGHLMPY PHLEGMY
EGHLNOR LEGHORN
EGHLNPU ENGULPH
EGHLNST LENGTHS
EGHLNTY LENGTHY
EGHLOOS SHOOGLE
EGHLOSS SEGHOLS
EGHLPSU PLEUGHS
EGHMMOS MEGOHMS
EGHMNOU HUMOGEN
EGHMOSU GUMSHOE
EGHNORU ENROUGH
ROUGHEN
EGHNOSU ENOUGHS
EGHNOTU TOUGHEN
EGHNRSU HUNGERS
EGHOPRS GOPHERS
EGHORRU ROUGHER
EGHORTU TOUGHER
EGHOSTT GHETTOS
EGHOSUU HUGEOUS
EGHRSSU GUSHERS
EGHRTUY THEURGY
EGIIJLS JILGIES
EGIIKLW WIGLIKE
EGIILLS GILLIES
EGIILMT LEGITIM
EGIILNR LEIRING
LINGIER
EGIILNS SEILING
EGIILNT LIGNITE
EGIILNV VEILING
EGIILNX EXILING
EGIILPS GILPIES
EGIILRS GIRLIES
EGIIMNN MEINING
EGIIMNP IMPINGE
EGIIMNR MINGIER
EGIIMNT ITEMING
EGIIMNV MIEVING
EGIIMPR GIMPIER
EGIIMPS PIGMIES
EGIIMRR GRIMIER
EGIIMSV MISGIVE
EGIINNP PEINING
EGIINNR GINNIER
REINING
EGIINNS INGINES
INSIGNE
SEINING
EGIINNV VEINING
EGIINOP EPIGONI
EGIINPS PEISING
PIGSNIE
EGIINPZ PEIZING
EGIINRR GIRNIER
EGIINRT IGNITER
TIERING
TIGRINE
EGIINRV REIVING
RIEVING
EGIINRW WEIRING
WINGIER
EGIINRZ ZINGIER
EGIINSS SEISING
EGIINST IGNITES
EGIINSV SIEVING
VISEING
EGIINSW WEISING
EGIINSZ SEIZING
EGIINTV EVITING
EGIINTX EXITING
EGIINVW VIEWING
EGIINWZ WEIZING
EGIIPPS GIPPIES
EGIIPRW PERIWIG
EGIIPSS GIPSIES
EGIJKNR JERKING

EGIJLLN JELLING
EGIJLNR JINGLER
EGIJLNS JINGLES
EGIJLNT JINGLET
EGIJNOS JINGOES
EGIJNST JESTING
EGIJNTT JETTING
EGIKKLN LEKKING
EGIKLNS KINGLES
EGIKLNT KINGLET
EGIKLNW WELKING
EGIKLRS KILERGS
EGIKMNP KEMPING
EGIKNNN KENNING
EGIKNNR KERNING
EGIKNNT KENTING
EGIKNOV EVOKING
EGIKNPP KEPPING
EGIKNPR PERKING
EGIKNRV KERVING
EGIKNRY YERKING
EGIKNST KESTING
EGIKNSW SKEWING
EGIKNSY YESKING
EGIKNUY YEUKING
EGILLMN MELLING
EGILLNO LOGLINE
EGILLNS LEGLINS
LINGELS
LINGLES
SELLING
EGILLNT TELLING
EGILLNW WELLING
EGILLNY YELLING
EGILLOS GOLLIES
EGILLRS GRILLES
EGILLST GILLETS
EGILLSU GULLIES
LIGULES
EGILMMN LEMMING
EGILMMR GLIMMER
EGILMNR GREMLIN
MERLING
MINGLER
EGILMNS MINGLES
EGILMNT MELTING
EGILMNU EMULING
LEGUMIN
EGILMNW MEWLING
EGILMNY YELMING
EGILMOR GOMERIL
EGILMOU ELOGIUM
EGILMPS GLIMPSE
MEGILPS
EGILMST GIMLETS
EGILNNS GINNELS
EGILNOP ELOPING
EGILNOS ELOIGNS
LEGIONS
LIGNOSE
LINGOES
EGILNOT LENTIGO
EGILNPP LEPPING
EGILNPR PINGLER
EGILNPS PINGLES
SPIGNEL
EGILNPT PELTING
EGILNPY YELPING
EGILNRS GIRNELS
LINGERS
SLINGER
EGILNRT RINGLET
TINGLER
TRINGLE
EGILNRY RELYING
EGILNSS SINGLES
EGILNST GLISTEN
LESTING
SINGLET
TINGLES
EGILNSU LUNGIES
SLUEING
EGILNSW SLEWING
SWINGLE
EGILNSZ ZINGELS
EGILNTT ETTLING
LETTING
EGILNTU ELUTING
EGILNTW WELTING
WINGLET
EGILNVY LEVYING
EGILOOS GOOLIES
OLOGIES
EGILOPS EPILOGS
EGILORS GLOIRES
GLORIES
EGILOSS GLIOSES
EGILOST ELOGIST
LOGIEST
EGILOSU OUGLIES
EGILPPR GRIPPLE
EGILPST PIGLETS
EGILPSY GILPEYS
EGILRRU GURLIER
EGILRSS GRILSES
EGILRST GLISTER
GRISTLE
EGILRSU GUILERS
LIGURES
LURGIES
EGILRSY GREISLY
GRIESLY
GRISELY
EGILRTT GLITTER
EGILRTY TIGERLY
EGILRUV VIRGULE
EGILRZZ GRIZZLE
EGILSST LEGISTS
EGILSSW WIGLESS
EGILSTU GLUIEST
UGLIEST
EGILSTZ GLITZES
EGIMMRR GRIMMER
EGIMMRS GIMMERS
MEGRIMS
EGIMMRU GUMMIER
EGIMMTU GUMMITE
EGIMNNN NEMNING
EGIMNNO OMENING
EGIMNNR RINGMEN
EGIMNNS MENSING
EGIMNOS MISGONE
EGIMNOT EMOTING
MITOGEN
EGIMNOV EMOVING
EGIMNOW MEOWING
EGIMNPR IMPREGN
PERMING
EGIMNPT PIGMENT
TEMPING
EGIMNQU QUEMING
EGIMNRS GERMINS
EGIMNRT METRING
TERMING
EGIMNRU EMURING
EGIMNSS MESSING
EGIMNST STEMING
TEMSING
EGIMNSU MEUSING
EGIMNSW MEWSING
EGIMORR GORMIER
EGIMOSS EGOISMS
MISGOES
EGIMOST EGOTISM
EGIMPSY PYGMIES
EGIMSST STIGMES
EGINNNP PENNING
EGINNNR RENNING
EGINNNY YENNING
EGINNOP OPENING
EGINNPU PENGUIN
EGINNRR GRINNER
EGINNRS ENRINGS
GINNERS
EGINNRT RENTING
RINGENT
TERNING
EGINNRU ENURING
EGINNRV NERVING
EGINNRY GINNERY
RENYING
EGINNSS ENSIGNS
SENSING
EGINNST NESTING
SENTING
TENSING
EGINNSU ENSUING
GUNNIES
INGENUS
EGINNSW NEWSING
EGINNSY GYNNIES
EGINNTT NETTING
TENTING
EGINNTV VENTING
EGINNVY ENVYING
EGINOPR PERIGON
PONGIER
EGINOPS EPIGONS
PIGEONS
PINGOES
EGINORR IGNORER
EGINORS ERINGOS
IGNORES
REGIONS
SIGNORE
EGINORT GENITOR
EGINORV OVERING
EGINORZ ZEROING
EGINOSU IGNEOUS
EGINOSW WIGEONS
EGINOSY ISOGENY
EGINOTT TENTIGO
EGINOTV VETOING
EGINPPP PEPPING
EGINPPR REPPING
EGINPPS PIGPENS
EGINPRS PERSING
PINGERS
SPRINGE
EGINPRU PUERING
EGINPRV PERVING
PREVING
EGINPRY PREYING
EGINPSS GIPSENS
EGINPSU SPUEING
EGINPSW SPEWING
EGINPSY ESPYING
PEYSING
PIGSNEY
EGINPTT PETTING
EGINPYY EPIGYNY
EGINQUU QUEUING
EGINRRS ERRINGS
GIRNERS
RINGERS
SERRING
EGINRRW WRINGER
EGINRSS INGRESS
RESIGNS
SIGNERS
SINGERS
EGINRST RESTING
STINGER
EGINRSU REUSING
RUEINGS
SIGNEUR
EGINRSV SERVING
VERSING
EGINRSW SWINGER
WINGERS
EGINRSY SYRINGE
EGINRSZ ZINGERS
EGINRTT GITTERN
RETTING
EGINRTU TRUEING
EGINRTV VERTING
EGINRTY RETYING
EGINRVV REVVING
EGINRVY REVYING
EGINSST INGESTS
SIGNETS
EGINSSW SEWINGS
SWINGES
EGINSTT SETTING
TESTING
EGINSTU GUNITES
EGINSTV VESTING
EGINSTW STEWING
TWINGES
WESTING
EGINSTZ ZESTING
EGINSVX VEXINGS
EGINSWY SWEYING
EGINSZZ GIZZENS
EGINTTV VETTING
EGINTTW WETTING
EGIOOPR GOOPIER
EGIOORS GOOSIER
EGIOOSS GOOSIES
SOOGIES
EGIOOST GOOIEST
EGIOPRS PORGIES
SERPIGO
EGIOPRU GROUPIE
PIROGUE
EGIORRS GORSIER
EGIORST GOITERS
GOITRES
GORIEST
EGIORTU GOUTIER

EGIORTV	VERTIGO
EGIORTZ	ZORGITE
EGIORUV	VOGUIER
EGIOSST	EGOISTS
	STOGIES
EGIOSTT	EGOTIST
EGIOSTV	VOGIEST
EGIOTUV	OUTGIVE
EGIPPRR	GRIPPER
EGIPPRS	GRIPPES
EGIPPSU	GUPPIES
EGIPPSY	GYPPIES
EGIPRRS	GRIPERS
EGIPRUU	GUIPURE
EGIPSSY	GYPSIES
EGIRRSU	GURRIES
	SURGIER
EGIRRSV	VIRGERS
EGIRRTT	GRITTER
EGIRSST	TIGRESS
EGIRSSU	GUISERS
EGIRSTU	GUSTIER
	GUTSIER
EGIRSTV	GRIVETS
EGIRSUZ	GUIZERS
EGIRTTU	GUTTIER
EGISSSU	GUSSIES
EGISTTU	GUTTIES
EGJLNSU	JUNGLES
EGJLSTU	JUGLETS
EGKLORW	LEGWORK
EGKMSSU	MUSKEGS
EGKNOSY	KYOGENS
EGLLORS	GOLLERS
EGLLRSU	GULLERS
EGLLRUY	GULLERY
EGLLSTU	GULLETS
EGLLSUY	GULLEYS
EGLMMRU	GLUMMER
EGLMNOO	ENGLOOM
EGLMNOR	MONGREL
EGLMOOR	LEGROOM
EGLNNSU	GUNNELS
EGLNOOY	NEOLOGY
EGLNOPS	PLONGES
EGLNORU	LOUNGER
EGLNOST	LONGEST
EGLNOSU	LOUNGES
EGLNOUV	UNGLOVE
EGLNOXY	LOXYGEN
	XYLOGEN
EGLNOYZ	LOZENGY
EGLNPRU	PLUNGER
EGLNPSU	PLUNGES
EGLNRTU	GRUNTLE
EGLNSSU	GUNLESS
	GUNSELS
EGLNSTU	ENGLUTS
	GLUTENS
EGLNSUU	UNGLUES
EGLOOSY	GOOLEYS
EGLOPRS	PROLEGS
EGLOPSS	GOSPELS
EGLORRW	GROWLER
EGLORSS	GLOSSER
EGLORSU	REGULOS
EGLORSV	GLOVERS
	GROVELS
EGLORSW	GLOWERS
EGLOSSS	GLOSSES
EGLOSST	GOSLETS
EGLOSUV	VOULGES
EGLPRSU	GULPERS
	SPLURGE
EGLRSTU	GURLETS
EGLRSUU	REGULUS
EGLRSUY	GUYLERS
EGLRSYY	GRYESLY
	GRYSELY
EGLRUZZ	GUZZLER
EGLSSTU	GUTLESS
EGLSTTU	GUTTLES
EGLSTUU	GLUTEUS
EGLSUZZ	GUZZLES
EGMMORT	GROMMET
EGMMRRU	GRUMMER
EGMMRTU	GRUMMET
EGMNNOS	SONGMEN
EGMNNOW	GOWNMEN
EGMNORS	MONGERS
	MORGENS
EGMNORU	MURGEON
EGMNORY	MONGERY
EGMNOST	EMONGST
EGMNOSY	MYOGENS
EGMNOYZ	ZYMOGEN
EGMNSTU	NUTMEGS
EGMORST	GROMETS
EGMORSU	GRUMOSE
	MORGUES
EGMORTU	GOURMET
EGNNORT	RONTGEN
EGNNOSU	GUENONS
EGNNPTU	PUNGENT
EGNNRSU	GUNNERS
EGNNRUY	GUNNERY
EGNNSYY	GYNNEYS
EGNNTUU	UNGUENT
EGNOOPS	PONGOES
EGNOORS	ORGONES
	OROGENS
EGNOORY	OROGENY
EGNOOST	GENTOOS
EGNOOSY	GOONEYS
EGNOOTU	OUTGONE
EGNOOYZ	ZOOGENY
EGNOPRS	SPONGER
EGNOPRY	PROGENY
	PYROGEN
EGNOPSS	SPONGES
EGNOPSW	GOWPENS
EGNORRW	WRONGER
EGNORSS	ENGROSS
EGNORSU	SURGEON
EGNORSV	GOVERNS
EGNORSY	ERYNGOS
	GROYNES
EGNORUY	YOUNGER
EGNOSSY	GONYSES
EGNOSTU	TONGUES
EGNOSXY	OXYGENS
EGNPRSU	REPUGNS
EGNPSSU	SPUNGES
EGNPSUX	EXPUGNS
EGNRRTU	GRUNTER
EGNRSTU	GUNTERS
	GURNETS
	SURGENT
EGNRSUY	GURNEYS
EGNRSYY	SYNERGY
EGNRTTU	GRUTTEN
	TURGENT
EGNSUVY	UNGYVES
EGOOPSY	POOGYES
EGOORRV	GROOVER
EGOORSV	GROOVES
EGOORSY	GOOSERY
EGOORTU	OUTGOER
EGOORTV	OVERGOT
EGOOSST	STOOGES
EGOOSSY	GOOSEYS
EGOOSTU	OUTGOES
EGOPRRS	GROPERS
EGOPRRU	GROUPER
	REGROUP
EGORRSS	GROSERS
	GROSSER
EGORRST	GROSERT
EGORRSU	GROUSER
EGORRSW	GROWERS
EGORRTU	GROUTER
EGORRUY	ROGUERY
EGORSSS	GROSSES
EGORSST	GROSETS
	STORGES
EGORSSU	GROUSES
EGORSTV	GROVETS
EGORSUV	VOGUERS
EGORTUW	OUTGREW
EGOSSTY	STOGEYS
EGOSSYZ	ZYGOSES
EGOSTTU	GOUTTES
EGOSTYZ	ZYGOTES
EGPRRSU	PURGERS
EGPRSSU	SPURGES
EGPRSUU	UPSURGE
EGRRSUY	SURGERY
EGRSSTU	GUTSERS
EGRSSUY	GYRUSES
EGRSTTU	GUTTERS
EGRSTUZ	GUTZERS
EGSSSTU	GUSSETS
EHHIKSS	SHEIKHS
EHHILLS	HELLISH
EHHIPRS	HERSHIP
EHHIRST	HITHERS
EHHIRSU	HUSHIER
EHHIRTT	THITHER
EHHIRTW	WHITHER
EHHISSW	WHISHES
EHHISWY	WHEYISH
EHHNPSY	HYPHENS
EHHOOSS	HOOSHES
EHHORTT	THOTHER
EHHRSSU	HUSHERS
EHHSSSU	SHUSHES
EHIILLR	HILLIER
EHIILTT	LITHITE
EHIIMSS	MEISHIS
EHIINNS	HINNIES
EHIINRS	SHINIER
EHIINRT	INHERIT
EHIINRW	WHINIER
EHIINRZ	RHIZINE
EHIINSS	SHINIES
EHIIPPR	HIPPIER
EHIIPPS	HIPPIES
EHIIPRT	PITHIER
EHIIRST	HIRSTIE
EHIIRTW	WHITIER
	WITHIER
EHIISST	STISHIE
EHIISTW	WHITIES
	WITHIES
EHIJNNO	JOHNNIE
EHIKKSS	KISHKES
EHIKLRU	HULKIER
EHIKMNT	METHINK
EHIKNOS	HONKIES
EHIKNRS	KERNISH
EHIKNRT	RETHINK
	THINKER
EHIKNRU	HUNKIER
EHIKNSS	KNISHES
EHIKNSU	HUNKIES
EHIKOOR	HOOKIER
EHIKOOS	HOOKIES
EHIKOST	HOKIEST
EHIKPRS	KEPHIRS
EHIKRRS	SHIRKER
EHIKRSS	SHREIKS
	SHRIEKS
	SHRIKES
EHIKRSU	HUSKIER
EHIKRSW	WHISKER
EHIKSSS	SHIKSES
EHIKSSU	HUSKIES
EHIKSTW	WHISKET
EHIKSWY	WHISKEY
EHILLMN	HILLMEN
EHILLNO	HELLION
EHILLNS	INSHELL
EHILLOS	HOLLIES
EHILLRS	RELLISH
EHILLRT	THILLER
EHILLRU	HULLIER
EHILLTY	LITHELY
EHILMPW	WHIMPLE
EHILMSU	HELIUMS
	HUMLIES
EHILMTT	MELTITH
EHILMUW	UMWHILE
EHILNOP	PINHOLE
EHILNOT	HOTLINE
	NEOLITH
EHILNPS	PLENISH
EHILNSS	ELSHINS
EHILOOR	HOOLIER
EHILOPT	HOPLITE
EHILOSS	ISOHELS
EHILOST	EOLITHS
	HOLIEST
	HOSTILE
EHILPRS	HIRPLES
EHILPRT	PHILTER
	PHILTRE
EHILRRW	WHIRLER
EHILRSS	HIRSELS
	HIRSLES
EHILRST	SLITHER
EHILRSU	HURLIES
	LUSHIER
EHILRSV	SHRIVEL
EHILRTU	LUTHIER
EHILRTW	WHIRTLE
EHILSSS	SLISHES
EHILSTT	LISTETH
	LITHEST
	THISTLE
EHILSTV	THIVELS

EHILSTW	WHISTLE
EHILTTU	THULITE
EHILTTW	WHITTLE
EHILTWY	WHITELY
EHIMMRS	SHIMMER
EHIMMSY	SHIMMEY
EHIMNPS	SHIPMEN
EHIMNRS	MENHIRS
EHIMNRU	INHUMER
	RHENIUM
EHIMNSU	INHUMES
EHIMNTY	THYMINE
EHIMORS	HEROISM
	MOREISH
EHIMORT	MOITHER
	MOTHIER
EHIMORZ	RHIZOME
EHIMOST	HOMIEST
EHIMPRU	HUMPIER
EHIMPRW	WHIMPER
EHIMPSU	HUMPIES
EHIMRST	HERMITS
	MITHERS
EHIMRSU	HEURISM
	MUSHIER
EHIMRTY	THYMIER
EHIMSST	THEISMS
EHIMSTU	HUMITES
	TUMSHIE
EHIMSTY	MYTHISE
EHIMSWY	WHIMSEY
EHIMTYZ	MYTHIZE
EHINNNS	HENNINS
EHINNRT	THINNER
EHINNSS	SHINNES
EHINNSW	WENNISH
EHINOPR	PHONIER
EHINOPS	PHONIES
EHINOPX	PHOENIX
EHINORR	HORNIER
EHINORS	HEROINS
	INSHORE
EHINOST	HISTONE
EHINOSU	HEINOUS
EHINPPS	SHIPPEN
EHINPSS	HIPNESS
EHINRSS	SHINERS
	SHRINES
EHINRSV	SHRIVEN
EHINRSW	WHINERS
EHINRTV	THRIVEN
EHINRTW	WRITHEN
EHINRTZ	ZITHERN
EHINSSS	SHINESS
EHINSST	SITHENS
EHINSTW	WHITENS
EHINSTZ	ZENITHS
EHINSUV	UNHIVES
EHIOPPR	HOPPIER
EHIOPRS	ROSEHIP
EHIOPST	ETHIOPS
	OPHITES
EHIORRS	HORSIER
EHIORRT	HERITOR
EHIORSS	HOSIERS
EHIORST	HERIOTS
	HOISTER
	SHORTIE
	TOSHIER
EHIORSW	SHOWIER

EHIORSY	HOSIERY
EHIORTT	THORITE
EHIORTU	OUTHIRE
	ROUTHIE
EHIORTV	OVERHIT
EHIOSTT	HOTTIES
EHIOSTY	ISOHYET
EHIPPRS	SHIPPER
EHIPPRW	WHIPPER
EHIPPST	HIPPEST
EHIPPTW	WHIPPET
EHIPRSS	RESHIPS
	SERIPHS
EHIPRST	HIPSTER
EHIPRSU	PUSHIER
EHIPRSW	WHISPER
EHIPSTT	PETTISH
EHIPSZZ	PHIZZES
EHIRRSS	SHERRIS
EHIRRSU	HURRIES
	RUSHIER
EHIRRSV	SHRIVER
EHIRRTV	THRIVER
EHIRRTW	WHIRRET
EHIRSSV	SHIVERS
	SHRIVES
EHIRSSW	SWISHER
	WISHERS
EHIRSTT	HITTERS
	TITHERS
EHIRSTU	HIRSUTE
EHIRSTV	THRIVES
EHIRSTW	SWITHER
	WITHERS
	WRITHES
EHIRSTZ	ZITHERS
EHIRSVY	SHIVERY
EHIRTTW	WHITRET
	WHITTER
EHIRWZZ	WHIZZER
EHISSSU	HUSSIES
EHISSSW	SWISHES
	WHISSES
EHISSTT	THEISTS
EHISSTU	STUSHIE
	TUSHIES
EHISTTW	TEWHITS
	WETTISH
	WHITEST
EHISTWY	WHITEYS
EHISUZZ	HUZZIES
EHISWZZ	WHIZZES
EHJOPSS	JOSEPHS
EHJORSS	JOSHERS
EHKLNOS	LOKSHEN
EHKLPST	KLEPHTS
EHKNORS	HONKERS
EHKNRSU	HUNKERS
EHKNSSU	HUNKSES
EHKOORS	HOOKERS
EHKOOSY	HOOKEYS
EHKORSS	KOSHERS
EHKORSW	HOWKERS
EHKORSY	HORKEYS
EHKRSSU	HUSKERS
EHKRSTU	TUSHKER
EHLLNSU	UNSHELL
EHLLOOS	HOLLOES
EHLLORS	HOLLERS
EHLMMOW	WHOMMLE

EHLMMSU	HUMMELS
EHLMMUW	WHUMMLE
EHLMNOT	MENTHOL
EHLMNOY	HOMELYN
EHLMNSU	UNHELMS
EHLMOOS	HOLESOM
EHLMOPS	PHLOEMS
EHLMSSU	MULSHES
EHLMSTY	METHYLS
EHLNOPS	PHENOLS
EHLNORT	HORNLET
EHLNPSY	PHENYLS
EHLNRTU	LUTHERN
EHLNTTY	TENTHLY
EHLOOPT	POTHOLE
EHLOOSS	SHOOLES
EHLOOSY	HOOLEYS
EHLOPPS	HOPPLES
EHLOPSX	PHLOXES
EHLOPSY	SPYHOLE
EHLORST	HOLSTER
	HOSTLER
EHLORSW	HOWLERS
EHLORTY	HELOTRY
EHLOSSS	SLOSHES
EHLOSST	HOSTELS
EHLOSSU	HOUSELS
EHLOSSV	SHOVELS
EHLOSTT	LOTHEST
	SHOTTLE
EHLOSTW	HOWLETS
	THOWELS
EHLOSTY	THYLOSE
EHLPRSU	PLUSHER
EHLPSSU	PLUSHES
EHLRRSU	HURLERS
EHLRSSU	LUSHERS
EHLRSTU	HURTLES
	HUSTLER
EHLRSUY	HURLEYS
EHLSSSU	SLUSHES
EHLSSTT	SHTETLS
EHLSSTU	HUSTLES
	LUSHEST
	SLEUTHS
EHLSTTU	SHUTTLE
EHMMRSU	HUMMERS
EHMNOOR	HORMONE
	MOORHEN
EHMNOPS	PHENOMS
	SHOPMEN
EHMNOST	MONETHS
EHMNOSW	SHOWMEN
EHMNPSU	HUMPENS
EHMNPTY	NYMPHET
EHMNTTU	HUTMENT
EHMOOSS	SHMOOSE
EHMOOSW	SOMEHOW
EHMOOSZ	SHMOOZE
EHMOPRW	MORPHEW
EHMORST	MOTHERS
	SMOTHER
EHMORTU	MOUTHER
EHMORTY	MOTHERY
EHMOSWY	SOMEWHY
EHMPRSU	HUMPERS
EHMPRTU	THUMPER
EHMRRSY	RHYMERS
EHMRRTU	MURTHER
EHMRSSU	MUSHERS

EHMRSUU	HUMERUS
EHMSSUU	HUMUSES
EHNNOPR	NEPHRON
EHNNOPY	HYPNONE
EHNNRSU	SHUNNER
EHNNSTU	UNSHENT
EHNNSUW	UNSHEWN
EHNOORS	HEROONS
	ONSHORE
	SOREHON
EHNOPRS	PHONERS
EHNOPRY	HYPERON
EHNOPSU	EUPHONS
EHNOPSY	PHONEYS
EHNOPUY	EUPHONY
EHNORRS	HORNERS
EHNORRT	HORRENT
	NORTHER
EHNORRY	HERONRY
EHNORSS	NOSHERS
EHNORST	HORNETS
	SHORTEN
	THRENOS
	THRONES
EHNORSU	UNHORSE
EHNORSY	NOSHERY
EHNOSST	HOTNESS
EHNOSSU	UNSHOES
EHNOSTT	SHOTTEN
EHNOSTY	HONESTY
EHNOSUU	UNHOUSE
EHNPRSY	PHRENSY
EHNRSTU	HUNTERS
	SHUNTER
	UNHERST
EHNRTWY	WRYTHEN
EHNSSSU	SNUSHES
EHNSSSY	SHYNESS
EHOOOPS	HOOPOES
EHOOPRS	HOOPERS
EHOOPRW	WHOOPER
EHOOPTY	OOPHYTE
EHOORST	HOOTERS
	SHOOTER
	SOOTHER
EHOORSV	HOOVERS
EHOOSST	SOOTHES
EHOOSSW	WOOSHES
EHOPPRS	HOPPERS
	SHOPPER
EHOPPRT	PROPHET
EHOPPRW	WHOPPER
EHOPRRY	ORPHREY
EHOPRST	POTHERS
	STROPHE
	THORPES
EHOPRSU	UPHROES
EHOPRTU	POUTHER
EHOPRTY	POTHERY
EHOPRUY	EUPHORY
EHOPSSS	SPOSHES
EHOPSST	POSHEST
EHORRSS	SHORERS
EHORRST	RHETORS
	ROTHERS
	SHORTER
EHORRTW	THROWER
EHORSST	TOSHERS
EHORSSV	SHOVERS
	SHROVES

EHORSSW SHOWERS
EHORSTT HOTTERS
EHORSTU SHOUTER
SOUTHER
EHORSTW THROWES
EHORSTX EXHORTS
EHORSWY SHOWERY
EHORTUY OUTHYRE
EHOSSST HOSTESS
EHOSSTT SHOTTES
EHOSTTT HOTTEST
EHOTTTW WOTTETH
EHPRSSU PUSHERS
EHPRSSY SYPHERS
EHPRSYZ ZEPHYRS
EHPRTTU TURPETH
EHPRTUW UPTHREW
EHRRSSU RUSHERS
EHRRSTU HURTERS
EHRSSTY SHYSTER
THYRSES
EHRSTTU SHUTTER
EHRSTTW STREWTH
EHRSTUW WUTHERS
EHRSTUY TUSHERY
EHRTTTY THRETTY
EHSSSTU TUSSEHS
EIIILRV RILIEVI
EIIILST ILEITIS
EIIINPR RIPIENI
EIIJMMS JIMMIES
EIIJMPR JIMPIER
EIIKKNR KINKIER
EIIKLLP LIPLIKE
EIIKLMR MILKIER
EIIKLMS MISLIKE
EIIKLPS PLISKIE
EIIKLRS SILKIER
EIIKLSS SILKIES
EIIKLST KILTIES
EIIKNPR PINKIER
EIIKNPS PINKIES
EIIKNRS SINKIER
EIIKNRZ ZINKIER
EIIKNSS KINESIS
EIIKNST INKIEST
EIIKPRS SPIKIER
EIIKPSS PISKIES
EIIKRRS RISKIER
EIIKRSV SKIVIER
EIIKSTT KITTIES
EIILLMM MILLIME
EIILLMT LIMELIT
EIILLNV VILLEIN
EIILLPS ILLIPES
EIILLRS SILLIER
EIILLRT TILLIER
EIILLSS SILLIES
EIILLST ILLITES
EIILLSW WILLIES
EIILLTT TILLITE
EIILLTV VITELLI
EIILMNV MILVINE
EIILMPR IMPERIL
EIILMPS IMPLIES
EIILMPT LIMEPIT
EIILMRR MIRLIER
EIILMRS MILREIS
SLIMIER
EIILMRT LIMITER

EIILMSS MISSILE
SIMILES
EIILMST ELITISM
LIMIEST
LIMITES
EIILMSU MILIEUS
EIILMSV MISLIVE
EIILMUX MILIEUX
EIILNNS LINNIES
EIILNOS ELISION
ISOLINE
LIONISE
EIILNOT ETIOLIN
EIILNOV OLIVINE
EIILNOZ LIONIZE
EIILNPS SPLENII
EIILNRR NIRLIER
EIILNRS INLIERS
EIILNRT LINTIER
NITRILE
EIILNSS INISLES
EIILNST LINIEST
LINTIES
EIILORR ROILIER
EIILORS SOILIER
EIILORV RILIEVO
EIILOST IOLITES
OILIEST
EIILPPR LIPPIER
EIILPPS LIPPIES
EIILPST SPILITE
EIILQSU SILIQUE
EIILRST RILIEST
SILTIER
EIILRSX ELIXIRS
EIILSSV VISILES
EIILSTT ELITIST
EIILSTU UTILISE
EIILSTW WILIEST
EIILTUY TUILYIE
EIILTUZ TUILZIE
UTILIZE
EIILTXY EXILITY
EIIMMRS MIMSIER
EIIMMSS MIMESIS
EIIMMST MISTIME
EIIMMSX IMMIXES
EIIMNNS MINNIES
EIIMNPR PRIMINE
EIIMNRT INTERIM
MINTIER
TERMINI
EIIMNRV MINIVER
EIIMNST MINIEST
EIIMNTV MINIVET
EIIMNTY NIMIETY
EIIMOSS MEIOSIS
EIIMPRS PISMIRE
PRIMSIE
EIIMPRW WIMPIER
EIIMPST PIETISM
EIIMPTY IMPIETY
EIIMRSS MISSIER
EIIMRST MIRIEST
MISTIER
RIMIEST
EIIMSSS MISSIES
EIIMSST STIMIES
EIIMSSV MISSIVE
EIIMSSZ SIZEISM

EIIMSTT MITIEST
EIIMSTX MIXIEST
EIINNNP NINEPIN
EIINNNS NINNIES
EIINNPS PINNIES
EIINNQU QUININE
EIINNRT TINNIER
EIINNST INTINES
TINNIES
EIINNSW INSINEW
EIINNTV INVENIT
EIINNTW INTWINE
EIINOPR RIPIENO
EIINOPS PIONIES
EIINORS IONISER
IRONIES
IRONISE
NOISIER
EIINORZ IONIZER
IRONIZE
EIINOSS IONISES
EIINOSZ IONIZES
EIINPPR NIPPIER
EIINPRS INSPIRE
PIRNIES
SNIPIER
SPINIER
EIINPST PINIEST
PINITES
TIEPINS
EIINQRU INQUIRE
EIINQSU QUINIES
EIINQTU INQUIET
EIINRTT NITRITE
NITTIER
TINTIER
EIINRTV INVITER
VITRINE
EIINRTW TWINIER
EIINSSS SEISINS
EIINSSZ SEIZINS
EIINSTT SITTINE
TINIEST
EIINSTU UNITIES
UNITISE
EIINSTV INVITES
VINIEST
EIINSTW WINIEST
EIINTUV UNITIVE
EIINTUZ UNITIZE
EIIORST RIOTISE
EIIORSV IVORIES
EIIORTZ RIOTIZE
EIIOSTZ ZOISITE
EIIPPPR PIPPIER
EIIPPRR RIPPIER
EIIPPRT TIPPIER
EIIPPRZ ZIPPIER
EIIPPST PIPIEST
EIIPPSY YIPPIES
EIIPRRS SPIRIER
EIIPRRT TRIPIER
EIIPRRV PRIVIER
EIIPRST PITIERS
TIPSIER
EIIPRSV PRIVIES
EIIPRSW SWIPIER
WISPIER
EIIPSTT PIETIST
EIIPTTT PITTITE

EIIPTTU PITUITE
EIIRRTZ RITZIER
EIIRSSS SISSIER
EIIRSSV VISIERS
EIIRSTV REVISIT
STIVIER
VISITER
EIIRSTW WIRIEST
EIIRSVZ VIZIERS
EIIRSWZ WIZIERS
EIIRTTW WITTIER
EIISSSS SISSIES
EIISSTV VISITES
EIISSTX SIXTIES
EIISSTZ SIZEIST
SIZIEST
EIISTTT TITTIES
EIISTUV UVEITIS
EIISTZZ TIZZIES
EIISVZZ VIZZIES
EIJKKSU JUKSKEI
EIJKNPR PERJINK
PREJINK
EIJKNRS JERKINS
JINKERS
EIJKNRU JUNKIER
EIJKNSU JUNKIES
EIJKOST JOKIEST
EIJLLNY INJELLY
EIJLLOR JOLLIER
EIJLLOS JOLLIES
EIJLLST JILLETS
EIJLORT JOLTIER
EIJLORW JOWLIER
EIJMPRU JUMPIER
EIJMPST JIMPEST
EIJNNOS ENJOINS
EIJNORS JOINERS
REJOINS
EIJNORT JOINTER
EIJNORY JOINERY
EIJNOST JONTIES
EIJNPRU JUNIPER
EIJNRRU INJURER
EIJNRSU INJURES
EIJNSTY JITNEYS
EIJRSTT JITTERS
EIJRTTY JITTERY
EIJSSUV JUSSIVE
EIJSTTU JUTTIES
EIKKLNR KLINKER
EIKKLNS KINKLES
EIKKNRS SKINKER
EIKKOOR KOOKIER
EIKKRSY YIKKERS
EIKKRUY YUKKIER
EIKLLNW INKWELL
EIKLLOS SKOLLIE
EIKLLRS KILLERS
EIKLLST SKILLET
EIKLMMN MILKMEN
EIKLMNN LINKMEN
EIKLMNR KREMLIN
EIKLMRS MILKERS
EIKLNNS ENLINKS
EIKLNRS LINKERS
SLINKER
EIKLNRT TINKLER
EIKLNRW WINKLER
WRINKLE

EIKLNSS KINLESS
SILKENS
EIKLNST LENTISK
TINKLES
EIKLNSU SUNLIKE
UNLIKES
EIKLNSV KELVINS
EIKLNSW WELKINS
WINKLES
EIKLNSY SKYLINE
EIKLNTT KNITTLE
EIKLNTU NUTLIKE
EIKLNTW TWINKLE
EIKLOOP PLOOKIE
EIKLOPU PLOUKIE
EIKLORY YOLKIER
EIKLOTY TOYLIKE
EIKLPRY PERKILY
EIKLPSY PESKILY
EIKLRST KILTERS
KIRTLES
EIKLRSU SULKIER
EIKLRTT KITTLER
EIKLSSS KISSELS
EIKLSSU SULKIES
EIKLSTT KITTLES
SKITTLE
EIKMMRR KRIMMER
EIKMMRS KIMMERS
SKIMMER
EIKMNNS KINSMEN
EIKMNOR MONIKER
EIKMNRS MERKINS
EIKMNSS MISKENS
EIKMNST MISKENT
EIKMNSW MISKNEW
EIKMORS IRKSOME
SMOKIER
EIKMOSS SMOKIES
EIKMOSY MISYOKE
EIKMRRU MURKIER
EIKMRSS KIRMESS
EIKMRST MIRKEST
EIKMRSU MUSKIER
EIKMSST KISMETS
EIKMSSY MISKEYS
EIKNNOS KINONES
EIKNNRS SKINNER
EIKNOOR NOOKIER
ROOINEK
EIKNOOS NOOKIES
EIKNOPS PINKOES
EIKNORW WONKIER
EIKNOSS KENOSIS
EIKNOSV INVOKES
EIKNPRS PERKINS
EIKNPST PINKEST
EIKNPSU SPUNKIE
EIKNRSS SINKERS
EIKNRST SKINTER
STINKER
TINKERS
EIKNRSW WINKERS
EIKNRTT KNITTER
TRINKET
EIKNSSU SUNKIES
EIKNSTT KITTENS
EIKNTTY KITTENY
EIKNTUZ KUNZITE
EIKOORS ROOKIES

EIKOPPS KOPPIES
EIKOPRR PORKIER
EIKOPRS PORKIES
EIKOPST POKIEST
EIKORST ROKIEST
EIKORSY YORKIES
EIKOSST KETOSIS
EIKPPRS KIPPERS
SKIPPER
EIKPPST SKIPPET
EIKPRSY SPIKERY
EIKPSSS SKEPSIS
EIKRRSS RISKERS
EIKRRST SKIRRET
SKIRTER
STRIKER
EIKRSSS KISSERS
EIKRSST STRIKES
EIKRSSV SKIVERS
EIKRSTT SKITTER
EIKRSTU TURKIES
TUSKIER
EIKSSTW WISKETS
EIKSSTY SKYIEST
EIKSTUY YUKIEST
EILLLOS LOLLIES
EILLMNU MULLEIN
EILLMOS MOLLIES
EILLMOT MELILOT
EILLMOU MOUILLE
EILLMRS MILLERS
EILLMST MILLETS
MISTELL
EILLMSU ILLUMES
EILLNNP PENNILL
EILLNOS LIONELS
NIELLOS
EILLNSS ILLNESS
EILLNST LENTILS
LINTELS
TELLINS
EILLOPS POLLIES
EILLORU ROUILLE
EILLORW LOWLIER
EILLORZ ZORILLE
EILLOST OILLETS
EILLOSV VILLOSE
EILLOSW WOLLIES
EILLPRS SPILLER
EILLPSS LIPLESS
EILLPSU PILULES
EILLQTU QUILLET
EILLRSS SILLERS
EILLRST RILLETS
STILLER
TILLERS
TRELLIS
EILLRSW SWILLER
WILLERS
EILLRTT LITTLER
EILLSST LISTELS
EILLSSU SULLIES
EILLSTT LITTLES
EILLSTU TUILLES
EILLSTW WILLEST
WILLETS
EILLSWY WILLEYS
EILMMNO MOLIMEN
EILMMRS LIMMERS
SLIMMER

EILMMRU LUMMIER
EILMNOS MOLINES
EILMNOT MOLINET
EILMNRS LIMNERS
MERLINS
EILMNSS SIMNELS
EILMNSU EMULSIN
LUMINES
UNLIMES
EILMNSY MYELINS
EILMOOS MOOLIES
EILMOPR IMPLORE
EILMORR LORIMER
EILMORS MOILERS
EILMORT MOTLIER
EILMOSS LIMOSES
LISSOME
SMOILES
EILMOST MOTILES
EILMPPS PIMPLES
EILMPPU PLUMPIE
EILMPRS PRELIMS
SIMPLER
EILMPRU LUMPIER
PLUMIER
EILMPRY PRIMELY
EILMPSS SIMPLES
EILMPST LIMPEST
LIMPETS
EILMPSU IMPULSE
EILMPSW WIMPLES
EILMPSX SIMPLEX
EILMPTY EMPTILY
EILMRRU MURLIER
EILMRRY MERRILY
EILMRSS RIMLESS
SMILERS
EILMRST MILTERS
EILMRSU MISRULE
EILMRSV VERMILS
EILMRSY MISERLY
EILMRTY LYMITER
EILMRVY VERMILY
EILMSSS MISSELS
EILMSST MISTLES
SMILETS
EILMSSU MUESLIS
EILMSSY MESSILY
MILSEYS
EILMSTT SMITTLE
EILMSTZ MILTZES
EILMSZZ MIZZLES
EILMUUV ELUVIUM
EILNNPU PINNULE
EILNNST LINNETS
EILNNSU UNLINES
EILNNSW WINNLES
EILNNSY LINNEYS
EILNOOP POLONIE
EILNOOR LOONIER
EILNOOS LOONIES
EILNOOV VIOLONE
EILNOPP PLENIPO
EILNOPR PROLINE
EILNOPS EPSILON
PINOLES
EILNOPT POINTEL
PONTILE
TOPLINE
EILNORR LORINER

EILNORS NEROLIS
EILNORT RETINOL
EILNOSS ESLOINS
INSOLES
LESIONS
LIONESS
EILNOST ENTOILS
LIONETS
ONLIEST
EILNOSU ELUSION
EILNOTU ELUTION
OUTLINE
EILNOTV VIOLENT
EILNOTW TOWLINE
EILNOVV INVOLVE
EILNPPS LIPPENS
NIPPLES
EILNPRS PILSNER
EILNPRU PURLINE
EILNPSS PENSILS
SPINELS
SPLINES
EILNPST PINTLES
PLENIST
EILNPSU LUPINES
SPINULE
EILNPTY INEPTLY
EILNPUV VULPINE
EILNRST LINTERS
SLINTER
SNIRTLE
EILNRSV SILVERN
EILNRTY INERTLY
EILNRVY NERVILY
EILNSSS SINLESS
EILNSST ENLISTS
LISTENS
SILENTS
TINSELS
EILNSSU INSULSE
SILENUS
EILNSSV SNIVELS
EILNSSY LINSEYS
LYSINES
EILNSTU LUTEINS
UNTILES
UTENSIL
EILNSTV VENTILS
EILNSTW WESTLIN
WINTLES
EILNSUV UNLIVES
UNVEILS
EILNSUY LUNYIES
EILNSVY SYLVINE
EILNVXY VIXENLY
EILOOPR LOOPIER
EILOORS ORIOLES
EILOORT TROOLIE
EILOOST OOLITES
OSTIOLE
STOOLIE
EILOOTZ ZOOLITE
EILOPRS SLOPIER
SPOILER
EILOPRT POITREL
POLITER
EILOPST PIOLETS
PISTOLE
EILOPSU PILEOUS
EILOPSV PLOSIVE

EILOPTT	PLOTTIE
EILOPTX	EXPLOIT
EILORRS	LORRIES
EILORRU	LOURIER
EILORSS	LORISES
	LOSSIER
	RISSOLE
EILORST	LOITERS
	TOILERS
EILORSU	LOUSIER
	SOILURE
EILORSV	OLIVERS
	VIOLERS
EILORTT	TORTILE
	TRIOLET
EILORTU	OUTLIER
EILOSSV	SOLIVES
EILOSTT	LITOTES
	TOILETS
EILOSTU	OUTLIES
EILOSTV	OLIVETS
	VIOLETS
EILOSTW	OWLIEST
EILOTUV	OUTLIVE
EILPPRR	RIPPLER
EILPPRS	RIPPLES
	SLIPPER
EILPPRT	RIPPLET
	TIPPLER
	TRIPPLE
EILPPRU	PULPIER
EILPPSS	PIPLESS
	SIPPLES
EILPPST	STIPPLE
	TIPPLES
EILPPSW	SWIPPLE
EILPRSS	LISPERS
EILPRST	SPIRTLE
	TRIPLES
EILPRTT	TRIPLET
EILPRTX	TRIPLEX
EILPRUU	PURLIEU
EILPSST	STIPELS
EILPSTT	SPITTLE
EILPSTU	PULIEST
	PUTELIS
	STIPULE
EILPSUY	SPULYIE
EILPSUZ	SPULZIE
EILPSZZ	PIZZLES
EILPTTY	PETTILY
EILQRTU	QUILTER
EILQRUU	LIQUEUR
EILQTUY	QUIETLY
EILRRSU	LURRIES
	SURLIER
EILRRTW	TWIRLER
EILRSST	LISTERS
EILRSSV	SILVERS
	SLIVERS
EILRSTT	LITTERS
	SLITTER
	STILTER
	TESTRIL
	TILTERS
	TITLERS
EILRSTU	LUSTIER
	RULIEST
	RUTILES
EILRSUW	WURLIES
EILRSVY	SILVERY
EILRSZZ	SIZZLER
EILRTTY	LITTERY
	TRITELY
EILRTUV	RIVULET
EILSSTT	STILETS
EILSSTW	WITLESS
EILSSTY	STYLISE
EILSSVW	SWIVELS
EILSSZZ	SIZZLES
EILSTTT	TITTLES
EILSTTU	TITULES
EILSTTV	VITTLES
EILSTTY	STYLITE
	TESTILY
EILSTVY	SYLVITE
EILSTYZ	STYLIZE
EILSWZZ	SWIZZLE
EILTWZZ	TWIZZLE
EIMMMOS	MOMMIES
EIMMMST	MIMMEST
EIMMMSU	MUMMIES
EIMMNRS	NIMMERS
EIMMNSU	IMMUNES
EIMMOPS	POMMIES
EIMMORS	MEMOIRS
EIMMOST	TOMMIES
EIMMPRR	PRIMMER
EIMMPRU	PREMIUM
EIMMRRT	TRIMMER
EIMMRRU	RUMMIER
EIMMRSS	MERISMS
	SIMMERS
EIMMRST	MISTERM
EIMMRSU	IMMURES
	MUMSIER
	RUMMIES
EIMMRSW	SWIMMER
EIMMRSZ	ZIMMERS
EIMMRUY	YUMMIER
EIMMSST	SEMMITS
EIMMSTU	TUMMIES
EIMMSTZ	TZIMMES
EIMNNOT	MENTION
EIMNOOR	IONOMER
	MOONIER
EIMNOOS	MOONIES
	NOISOME
EIMNOOT	EMOTION
EIMNOOX	EXOMION
EIMNOPS	IMPONES
	PEONISM
EIMNOPT	EMPTION
	PIMENTO
EIMNORS	MERINOS
	MERSION
EIMNOSS	EONISMS
EIMNOST	MOISTEN
EIMNOSW	WINSOME
EIMNOTY	OMNEITY
	OMNIETY
EIMNPST	PIMENTS
EIMNPTU	PINETUM
EIMNQSU	MESQUIN
EIMNRRU	MURRINE
EIMNRST	ENTRISM
	MINSTER
	MINTERS
	REMINTS
EIMNRSU	MURINES
	NEURISM
EIMNRSV	VERMINS
EIMNRTU	MINUTER
EIMNRVY	VERMINY
EIMNSSS	SENSISM
EIMNSST	MISSENT
EIMNSSU	MINUSES
EIMNSTT	MITTENS
	SMITTEN
EIMNSTU	MINUETS
	MINUTES
	MISTUNE
	MUNITES
	MUTINES
EIMNSTW	MISWENT
EIMNSZZ	MIZZENS
EIMNUZZ	MUEZZIN
EIMOORR	MOORIER
	ROOMIER
EIMOORS	ROOMIES
EIMOPPR	MOPPIER
	POMPIER
EIMOPRR	PRIMERO
EIMOPRS	IMPOSER
	PROMISE
EIMOPRV	IMPROVE
EIMOPSS	IMPOSES
	MOPSIES
EIMOPST	MOPIEST
	OPTIMES
EIMORRW	WORMIER
EIMORSS	ISOMERS
	MOISERS
	MOSSIER
EIMORST	EROTISM
	MOISTER
	MORTISE
	TRISOME
EIMORSU	MOUSIER
EIMORSV	VERISMO
EIMORTT	MOTTIER
	OMITTER
EIMOSSS	MOSSIES
EIMOSST	MITOSES
	SOMITES
EIMOSSU	MOUSIES
EIMOSTT	MOTIEST
	TITMOSE
EIMOSTU	TIMEOUS
EIMOSTV	MOTIVES
EIMOSTZ	MESTIZO
EIMOSZZ	MOZZIES
EIMPRRS	PRIMERS
EIMPRRU	IMPURER
	PRIMEUR
EIMPRSS	IMPRESS
	PREMISS
	SIMPERS
EIMPRST	IMPREST
	PERMITS
EIMPRSU	RUMPIES
	SPUMIER
	UMPIRES
EIMPRTU	IMPUTER
	TUMPIER
EIMPSST	MISSTEP
EIMPSSU	SEPIUMS
EIMPSTU	IMPETUS
	IMPUTES
EIMPSUY	YUMPIES
EIMQSTU	MESQUIT
EIMRRST	RETRIMS
	TRIMERS
EIMRRSU	MURRIES
EIMRSST	MISTERS
	SMITERS
EIMRSSU	MISUSER
	MUSSIER
	SURMISE
EIMRSSV	VERISMS
EIMRSTT	METRIST
EIMRSTU	MUSTIER
EIMRSTY	MISTERY
	SMYTRIE
EIMRTUV	VITREUM
EIMRTUX	MIXTURE
EIMRUZZ	MUZZIER
EIMSSST	MISSETS
EIMSSSU	MISUSES
EIMSSSX	SEXISMS
EIMSSTY	STYMIES
EIMSTYZ	ZYMITES
EINNNOS	NONNIES
EINNNRS	RENNINS
EINNOOS	IONONES
EINNOPS	PENSION
EINNOQU	QUINONE
EINNORT	INTONER
	TERNION
EINNORU	NOUNIER
	REUNION
EINNORV	ENVIRON
EINNOSS	SONNIES
EINNOST	INTONES
	TENSION
EINNOSV	VENISON
EINNOTT	NONETTI
	TONTINE
EINNOVW	INWOVEN
EINNPRS	PINNERS
	SPINNER
EINNPRT	ENPRINT
EINNPST	PINNETS
	SPINNET
	TENPINS
EINNPSY	SPINNEY
EINNRRU	RUNNIER
EINNRSS	SINNERS
EINNRST	INTERNS
	TINNERS
EINNRSU	SUNNIER
	UNREINS
	UNRISEN
EINNRSW	WINNERS
EINNRTV	VINTNER
EINNRUV	UNRIVEN
EINNSST	SENNITS
	SINNETS
EINNSSY	SINSYNE
EINNSTT	INTENTS
EINNSTU	TUNNIES
EINNSTV	INVENTS
EINNSUW	UNSINEW
EINNTUW	UNTWINE
EINOOPZ	EPIZOON
EINOORS	EROSION
EINOOST	ISOTONE
EINOOSZ	OZONISE
EINOOTZ	ZOONITE
EINOOZZ	OZONIZE

EINOPPR	POPERIN
	PROPINE
EINOPPS	PEPINOS
EINOPRS	ORPINES
	PIONERS
	PROINES
EINOPRT	POINTER
	PROTEIN
	PTERION
	REPOINT
EINOPRV	PROVINE
EINOPSS	SPINOSE
EINOPST	POINTES
	PONTIES
EINOPSW	POWNIES
EINOPSY	PIONEYS
EINOQUX	EQUINOX
EINORRS	IRONERS
EINORSS	ORNISES
	SENIORS
	SONERIS
	SONSIER
EINORST	NORITES
	ORIENTS
	STONIER
	TERSION
	TRIONES
EINORSU	URINOSE
EINORSV	RENVOIS
	VERSION
EINORSW	SNOWIER
EINORTT	TRITONE
EINORTU	ROUTINE
EINORTW	TOWNIER
EINORTZ	TRIZONE
EINOSSS	ESSOINS
	OSSEINS
	SESSION
EINOSST	NOSIEST
	SONTIES
	STONIES
EINOSSU	SINUOSE
EINOSTT	SNOTTIE
	TONIEST
	TONITES
EINOSTW	TOWNIES
EINOSUV	ENVIOUS
	NIVEOUS
	VEINOUS
EINOTTT	TOTIENT
EINPPRS	NIPPERS
	SNIPPER
EINPPSS	PEPSINS
EINPPST	SNIPPET
EINPPSW	WIPPENS
EINPRRT	PRINTER
	REPRINT
EINPRRU	UNRIPER
EINPRSS	SNIPERS
EINPRST	NIPTERS
	PTERINS
EINPRSU	PRUINES
	PURINES
	UPRISEN
EINPRTU	REPUNIT
EINPSST	INSTEPS
	SPINETS
EINPSSU	PUISNES
	SUPINES
EINPSTT	SPITTEN
EINPSTU	PUNIEST
	PUNTIES
EINPTTY	TINTYPE
EINQRUU	UNIQUER
EINQRUY	ENQUIRY
EINQSSU	SEQUINS
EINQSTU	INQUEST
	QUINTES
EINQSUU	UNIQUES
EINQSUZ	QUINZES
EINQTTU	QUINTET
EINQTUU	UNQUIET
EINRRSS	RINSERS
EINRRSU	INSURER
	RUINERS
EINRRTU	RUNTIER
EINRSST	INSERTS
	SINTERS
EINRSSU	INSURES
	SUNRISE
EINRSSV	VERSINS
EINRSTT	ENTRIST
	STINTER
	TINTERS
EINRSTU	TRIUNES
	UNITERS
EINRSTV	INVERTS
	STRIVEN
EINRSTW	TWINERS
	WINTERS
EINRSTY	SINTERY
EINRSUW	UNWIRES
	UNWISER
EINRSVW	WIVERNS
EINRSWY	SWINERY
EINRTTU	NUTTIER
EINRTTW	TWINTER
	WRITTEN
EINRTUV	UNRIVET
	VENTURI
EINRTUW	UNWRITE
EINRTWY	WINTERY
EINSSST	SENSIST
EINSSSU	SINUSES
EINSSSY	SYNESIS
EINSSTU	INTUSES
EINSSTV	INVESTS
EINSSTW	WISENTS
	WITNESS
EINSSTY	TINSEYS
EINSSUW	SUNWISE
EINSSWY	WINSEYS
EINSTTU	TUNIEST
EINSTTW	ENTWIST
	TWINSET
EINSTTY	TENSITY
EINSUVW	UNWIVES
EINTTTW	TWITTEN
EINTTUY	TENUITY
EIOOPRR	ROOPIER
EIOOPRV	POOVIER
EIOOPST	ISOTOPE
EIOORRT	ROOTIER
EIOORST	OORIEST
	ROOTIES
	SOOTIER
	TOORIES
EIOORWZ	WOOZIER
EIOOSST	OOSIEST
EIOOSTT	TOOTSIE
EIOOSTZ	OOZIEST
EIOPPPR	POPPIER
EIOPPPS	POPPIES
EIOPPRS	SOPPIER
EIOPPSS	POPSIES
EIOPRRS	PROSIER
EIOPRRT	PIERROT
	PORTIER
EIOPRRU	ROUPIER
EIOPRSS	POISERS
EIOPRST	PERIOST
	PORIEST
	REPOSIT
	RIPOSTE
	ROPIEST
EIOPRSU	POURIES
	SOUPIER
EIOPRSX	PROXIES
EIOPRTT	POTTIER
EIOPRTU	POUTIER
EIOPRTV	PIVOTER
EIOPSSS	POSSIES
EIOPSST	POSIEST
	POSTIES
	SEPIOST
	SOPITES
EIOPSTT	POTTIES
	TIPTOES
EIOPSTU	PITEOUS
EIOPSTX	POXIEST
EIOPSTY	ISOTYPE
EIOPSZZ	POZZIES
EIOPTUW	WIPEOUT
EIOQRTU	QUOITER
EIORRRS	SORRIER
EIORRRT	RORTIER
EIORRRW	WORRIER
EIORRSS	ORRISES
	ROSIERS
EIORRST	RIOTERS
	ROISTER
	RORIEST
EIORRSV	REVISOR
EIORRSW	WORRIES
EIORRUV	OUVRIER
EIORRVV	REVIVOR
EIORSST	ROSIEST
	SORITES
	SORTIES
	STORIES
	TOSSIER
EIORSSU	SERIOUS
EIORSSV	VIROSES
EIORSSX	XEROSIS
EIORSTT	STOITER
EIORSTU	OURIEST
	TOURIES
	TOUSIER
EIORSTV	TORSIVE
EIORSTW	OWRIEST
	TOWSIER
EIORTTT	TOTTIER
EIORTTU	TOUTIER
EIORTTV	TORTIVE
	VIRETOT
EIORTUV	VOITURE
EIORTUZ	TOUZIER
EIORTWZ	TOWZIER
EIOSSTV	SOVIETS
	STOVIES
EIOSTTT	TOTTIES
EIOSTTU	TOUSTIE
EIOSTTW	TOWIEST
EIOSTUV	OUTVIES
EIOSTUZ	OUTSIZE
EIPPPSU	PUPPIES
EIPPRRS	RIPPERS
EIPPRRT	TRIPPER
EIPPRSS	SIPPERS
EIPPRST	TIPPERS
EIPPRSU	PURPIES
EIPPRSY	YIPPERS
EIPPRSZ	ZIPPERS
EIPPRTT	TRIPPET
EIPPSST	SIPPETS
EIPPSTT	TIPPETS
EIPPSUY	YUPPIES
EIPQSTU	PIQUETS
EIPRRSS	PRISERS
EIPRRSU	PURSIER
EIPRRSZ	PRIZERS
EIPRRTU	PURTIER
EIPRRTY	TRIPERY
EIPRRUV	UPRIVER
EIPRSST	ESPRITS
	PERSIST
	PRIESTS
	SITREPS
	SPRITES
	STIRPES
	STRIPES
	TRIPSES
EIPRSSU	SUSPIRE
	UPRISES
EIPRSSW	SWIPERS
EIPRSTT	PITTERS
	SPITTER
	TIPSTER
EIPRSTU	PERITUS
	PUIREST
EIPRSTV	PRIVETS
EIPRSTX	EXTIRPS
EIPRSTY	PYRITES
	STRIPEY
EIPRSUU	EURIPUS
EIPRTTU	PUTTIER
EIPRUVW	PURVIEW
EIPSSSU	PUSSIES
EIPSSTZ	SPITZES
EIPSTTU	PUTTIES
EIQRSSU	RISQUES
	SQUIERS
	SQUIRES
EIQRSTU	QUERIST
	REQUITS
EIQRSUV	QUIVERS
EIQRTTU	QUITTER
EIQRUVY	QUIVERY
EIQRUZZ	QUIZZER
EIQSTUU	QUIETUS
EIQSUZZ	QUIZZES
EIRRRST	STIRRER
EIRRSST	STIRRES
EIRRSTT	RITTERS
	TERRITS
EIRRSTU	RUSTIER
EIRRSTV	STRIVER
EIRRSTW	WRITERS
EIRRSZZ	RIZZERS
EIRRTTU	RUTTIER

EIRSSST RESISTS
SISTERS
EIRSSSU ISSUERS
RISUSES
EIRSSTT SITTERS
EIRSSTV STIVERS
STRIVES
TREVISS
VERISTS
EIRSSUU USURIES
EIRSSUV VIRUSES
EIRSTTT STRETTI
TITTERS
TRITEST
EIRSTTU TERTIUS
EIRSTTV TRIVETS
EIRSTTW TWISTER
WITTERS
EIRSTUV VIRTUES
EIRSUVV SURVIVE
EIRSUVW SURVIEW
EIRTTTW TWITTER
EISSSTU TISSUES
EISSSTW SWITSES
EISSSTX SEXISTS
EISSTTY TYSTIES
EISSTUV TUSSIVE
EISSTVW SWIVETS
EISSWZZ SWIZZES
EISTTTU TUTTIES
EJJMNUU JEJUNUM
EJKMNNU JUNKMEN
EJKNRSU JUNKERS
EJKNSTU JUNKETS
EJKOORY JOOKERY
EJKORUY JOUKERY
EJLLORY JOLLYER
EJLLOSY JOLLEYS
EJLORST JOLTERS
EJLORSW JOWLERS
EJLOSST JOSTLES
EJLOSSY JOYLESS
EJLSSTU JUSTLES
EJMNRUY JURYMEN
EJMOSST JETSOMS
EJMPRSU JUMPERS
EJNORRU REJOURN
EJNORUY JOURNEY
EJNOSST JETSONS
EJNOSTT JETTONS
EJOORVY OVERJOY
EJOOSSY SOOJEYS
EJORSSS JOSSERS
EJORSTT JOTTERS
EJORSTU JOUSTER
EJOSTTU OUTJEST
OUTJETS
EJPRRUY PERJURY
EJSSTTU JUSTEST
EKKLOOY OLYKOEK
EKKLRSU SKULKER
EKKOPSU PUKEKOS
EKLLMSU SKELLUM
EKLLRRU KRULLER
EKLMMSU KUMMELS
EKLMSSU MUSKLES
SKELUMS
EKLNOPR PLONKER
EKLNORS SNORKEL
EKLNOSS KELSONS
SLOKENS
EKLNPRU PLUNKER
EKLNRSU LUNKERS
RUNKLES
EKLNSST SKLENTS
EKLOORS LOOKERS
EKLRRSU LURKERS
EKLSTTU SKUTTLE
EKLSTUZ KLUTZES
EKMMRSU SKUMMER
EKMNORW WORKMEN
EKMNORY MONKERY
EKMNOSU MUSKONE
EKMNOSY MONKEYS
EKMNPTU UNKEMPT
EKMOOPS MOPOKES
EKMORSS SMOKERS
EKMRSTU MURKEST
EKMSSTU MUSKETS
EKNNOST NEKTONS
EKNOORS SNOOKER
EKNOPSU UNSPOKE
EKNORST STONKER
STROKEN
TONKERS
EKNORSW KNOWERS
EKNORSY YONKERS
EKNORTT KNOTTER
EKNORTW NETWORK
EKNORUY YOUNKER
EKNOSUY UNYOKES
EKNRTUY TURNKEY
EKNSSTU SUNKETS
EKOOPRT PERTOOK
EKOOPRV PROVOKE
EKOORRS KOREROS
EKOORRY ROOKERY
EKOORST STOOKER
STROOKE
EKOPPSU UPSPOKE
EKOPRRS PORKERS
PROKERS
EKOPRUY KOUPREY
EKORRST STROKER
EKORRSW REWORKS
WORKERS
EKORRSY YORKERS
EKORSST STOKERS
STROKES
EKPPSUU SEPPUKU
EKPRSSY KRYPSES
EKRRSSY SKRYERS
EKRSSTU TUSKERS
EKRSTUY TURKEYS
EKRSUVY KURVEYS
ELLLORR LORRELL
ELLLORS LOLLERS
ELLLOSZ LOZELLS
ELLMNOO MOELLON
ELLMNOP POLLMEN
ELLMNOT TOLLMEN
ELLMOOR MORELLO
ELLMOSW MELLOWS
ELLMOWY MELLOWY
ELLMPUU PLUMULE
ELLMRSU MULLERS
ELLMSTU MULLETS
ELLMSUV VELLUMS
ELLMSUY MULLEYS
ELLNNOT TONNELL
ELLNOOW WOOLLEN
ELLNOPS POLLENS
ELLNOPT POLLENT
ELLNORS ENROLLS
ELLNOST STOLLEN
ELLNOSU NOUSELL
ELLNOSV VELLONS
ELLNOSW SWOLLEN
ELLNOXY XYLENOL
ELLNPSU UNSPELL
ELLNSUU LUNULES
ELLOOSW WOOSELL
ELLOOSY LOOSELY
ELLOPRR PROLLER
ELLOPRS POLLERS
ELLOPTU POLLUTE
ELLORRS ROLLERS
ELLORRT TROLLER
ELLORSS SOLLERS
SORELLS
ELLORST TOLLERS
ELLORTY TROLLEY
ELLORVY LOVERLY
ELLOSST TOLSELS
ELLOSTU OUTSELL
ELLOSVY VOLLEYS
ELLOSWY YELLOWS
ELLOTTU OUTTELL
ELLOTUW OUTWELL
ELLOVWY VOWELLY
ELLOWYY YELLOWY
ELLPRSU PULLERS
ELLPSTU PULLETS
ELLPSUW UPSWELL
UPWELLS
ELLPSUY PULLEYS
ELMMOPS POMMELS
ELMMORT TROMMEL
ELMMPSU PUMMELS
ELMMPTU PLUMMET
ELMMRSU SLUMMER
ELMMSTU STUMMEL
ELMNOOT MOONLET
TOOLMEN
ELMNOOW WOOLMEN
ELMNORS MERLONS
ELMNOST LOMENTS
MELTONS
ELMNOSY MYELONS
ELMNOTU MOULTEN
ELMNOTY YMOLTEN
ELMNPPU PLUMPEN
ELMNPSU PLENUMS
ELMNPUU UNPLUME
ELMOOPP POMPELO
ELMOOPS POMELOS
ELMOORT TREMOLO
ELMOPRY POLYMER
ELMOPSU PLUMOSE
PUMELOS
ELMOPSY EMPLOYS
ELMORSS MORSELS
ELMORSU EMULSOR
ELMOSST MOLESTS
ELMOSSU MOUSLES
ELMOSSY SMOYLES
ELMOSTT MOTTLES
ELMOSTY MOTLEYS
ELMOSUU EMULOUS
ELMOSUV VOLUMES
ELMOSXY OXYMELS
ELMOSZZ MOZZLES
ELMPPRU PLUMPER
ELMPPSU PEPLUMS
ELMPRSU LUMPERS
RUMPLES
ELMPRUY PLUMERY
ELMRSTY MYRTLES
ELMRTUU MULTURE
ELMRTUY ELYTRUM
ELMRUZZ MUZZLER
ELMSSSU MUSSELS
SUMLESS
ELMSTUU MUTULES
ELMSUZZ MUZZLES
ELNNOPU NONUPLE
ELNNOSS NELSONS
ELNNRSU RUNNELS
ELNNSTU TUNNELS
ELNOOSS LOOSENS
ELNOOSU UNLOOSE
ELNOOSW WOOLENS
ELNOOSZ SNOOZLE
ELNOPRU PLEURON
ELNOPRY PRONELY
ELNOPST LEPTONS
ELNOPSY POLEYNS
ELNOPTU OPULENT
ELNORSS NORSELS
ELNORST LENTORS
ELNORSU NOURSLE
ELNORTY ELYTRON
ELNOSSS LESSONS
SONLESS
ELNOSST TELSONS
ELNOSSU ENSOULS
NOUSLES
ELNOSSV SLOVENS
ELNOSSW LOWNESS
ELNOSTT TONLETS
ELNOSTU LENTOUS
ELNOSTV SOLVENT
ELNOSUV UNLOVES
ELNOSUZ ZONULES
ELNOSVY LENVOYS
ELNOSZZ NOZZLES
ELNOTUZ ZONULET
ELNOTVY NOVELTY
ELNPSTU PENULTS
ELNRSSU NURSLES
ELNRSTU RUNLETS
ELNRSTY STERNLY
ELNRSUU UNRULES
ELNRSUZ LUZERNS
ELNSSSU SUNLESS
ELNSSSY SLYNESS
ELNSTTU NUTLETS
ELNSUZZ NUZZLES
SNUZZLE
ELOOPRS LOOPERS
SPOOLER
ELOORST LOOTERS
RETOOLS
ROOTLES
TOOLERS
ELOORTT ROOTLET
ELOOSST LOOSEST
LOTOSES
ELOOSSW WOOSELS
ELOOSTT TOOTLES

ELOOSTU	OUTSOLE
ELOOSWY	WOOLSEY
ELOPPPS	POPPLES
ELOPPRS	LOPPERS
	PROPELS
ELOPPST	STOPPLE
	TOPPLES
ELOPPSU	POULPES
ELOPPSY	POLYPES
ELOPRRS	PROLERS
ELOPRRU	PROULER
ELOPRRW	PROWLER
ELOPRRY	PYRROLE
ELOPRSS	PLESSOR
	SPLORES
ELOPRST	PETROLS
ELOPRSU	LEPROUS
	PELORUS
	PERLOUS
	SPORULE
ELOPRSV	PLOVERS
ELOPRSX	PLEXORS
ELOPRSY	LEPROSY
ELOPRTT	PLOTTER
ELOPRTU	PLOUTER
	POULTER
ELOPRTW	PLOWTER
ELOPRTY	PROTYLE
ELOPRVY	OVERPLY
	PLOVERY
ELOPSST	TOPLESS
ELOPSSU	SOUPLES
ELOPSTT	POTTLES
ELOPSTU	TUPELOS
ELORRSS	SORRELS
ELORRSW	WORRELS
ELORSSS	LESSORS
ELORSST	OSTLERS
	STEROLS
	TORSELS
ELORSSV	SOLVERS
ELORSTT	SETTLOR
	SLOTTER
	TOLTERS
ELORSTU	ELUTORS
	OUTLERS
	TROULES
ELORSTV	REVOLTS
ELORSTW	TROWELS
	WORTLES
ELORSUV	LOUVERS
	LOUVRES
	VELOURS
ELORSUY	ELUSORY
ELORSVW	WOLVERS
ELORTTY	LOTTERY
ELORTVY	OVERTLY
ELOSSTU	LOTUSES
	SOLUTES
	TOUSLES
ELOSSTW	LOWSEST
	SLOWEST
ELOSSTY	SYSTOLE
	TOLSEYS
	TOYLESS
	TYLOSES
ELOSSXY	XYLOSES
ELOSSZZ	SOZZLES
ELOSTTU	OUTLETS
ELOSTTY	TYLOTES
ELOSTUU	LUTEOUS
ELOSTUV	VOLUTES
ELOSTUZ	TOUZLES
ELOSTYZ	TOLZEYS
ELOSWYY	YOWLEYS
ELOSWZZ	SWOZZLE
ELPPRRU	PURPLER
ELPPRSU	PULPERS
	PURPLES
	REPULPS
	SUPPLER
ELPPSSU	SUPPLES
ELPQSUU	PULQUES
ELPRRSU	PURLERS
	SLURPER
ELPRSTU	SPURTLE
ELPRSUV	PULVERS
ELPRTUU	PULTURE
ELPRUZZ	PUZZLER
ELPSSSU	PLUSSES
	PUSSELS
ELPSSUU	LUPUSES
ELPSSUY	SPULYES
ELPSTUU	PLUTEUS
	PUSTULE
ELPSUZZ	PUZZELS
	PUZZLES
ELRRSTU	RUSTLER
ELRRTTU	TURTLER
ELRSSSU	RUSSELS
ELRSSTU	LUSTERS
	LUSTRES
	RESULTS
	RUSTLES
	SUTLERS
	ULSTERS
ELRSTTU	TURTLES
ELRSTTY	TETRYLS
ELRSTUY	SUTLERY
ELRSTWY	SWELTRY
ELRSUWY	WURLEYS
ELRTTUY	UTTERLY
ELRTUUV	VULTURE
ELSSSTU	TUSSLES
ELSSTTU	SUTTLES
ELSSTTY	STYLETS
ELSSTYY	SYSTYLE
ELSUWZZ	WUZZLES
EMMMOST	MOMMETS
EMMMRSU	MUMMERS
EMMMRUY	MUMMERY
EMMNNOS	MNEMONS
EMMNOOR	MONOMER
	MOORMEN
EMMNOOT	MOOTMEN
EMMNORY	MERONYM
EMMNOST	MOMENTS
	MONTEMS
EMMNOTU	OMENTUM
EMMNOTY	METONYM
EMMOPRR	PROMMER
EMMORSZ	MOMZERS
EMMOSSU	MOUSMES
EMMOSYZ	ZYMOMES
EMMPRSU	MUMPERS
EMMRRSU	RUMMERS
EMMRSSU	SUMMERS
EMMRSTU	RUMMEST
EMMRSUY	SUMMERY
EMMSSUU	MUSEUMS
EMNNOOR	MONERON
EMNNOSW	SNOWMEN
EMNOOPT	METOPON
EMNOORS	MOONERS
EMNOORT	MONTERO
EMNOOSS	MONOSES
EMNOOST	MOONSET
EMNOOSY	NOYSOME
EMNOOTY	ENOMOTY
EMNOPRT	PORTMEN
EMNOPST	POSTMEN
	TOPSMEN
EMNOPSY	EPONYMS
EMNORRU	MOURNER
EMNORSS	SERMONS
EMNORST	MENTORS
	MONSTER
	MONTRES
EMNORTT	TORMENT
EMNORTU	MONTURE
	MOUNTER
	REMOUNT
EMNOSST	STEMSON
EMNOSTU	UNSMOTE
EMNOSTY	ETYMONS
EMNOSXY	EXONYMS
EMNPSSU	PENSUMS
EMNRRSU	MURRENS
EMNRSSU	RUMNESS
EMNRSTU	MUNSTER
	STERNUM
EMOOPRT	PROMOTE
EMOOPRY	POMEROY
EMOORRS	MOROSER
	ROOMERS
EMOORST	MOOTERS
EMOORSU	UROSOME
EMOOSSS	OSMOSES
EMOOSTT	MOOTEST
	MOTTOES
	TOOMEST
EMOOSTW	TWOSOME
EMOOSTY	MYOSOTE
	TOYSOME
EMOOTUV	OUTMOVE
EMOPPRS	MOPPERS
EMOPPST	MOPPETS
EMOPPSY	POMPEYS
EMOPRRS	ROMPERS
EMOPRST	STOMPER
	TROMPES
EMOPRSU	SUPREMO
EMOPSSU	MOPUSES
EMOPSSY	MYOPSES
EMOQSSU	MOSQUES
EMORRST	TERMORS
	TREMORS
EMORRSU	MORSURE
EMORRSW	WORMERS
EMORRWY	WORMERY
EMORSST	MOTSERS
EMORSSU	MOUSERS
	SMOUSER
EMORSTU	MOUTERS
	OESTRUM
EMORSUY	MOUSERY
EMOSSSU	MOUSSES
	SMOUSES
EMOSSYZ	ZYMOSES
EMOSTTT	MOTETTS
EMOSTVZ	ZEMSTVO
EMPPRSU	PUMPERS
EMPRSTU	STUMPER
	SUMPTER
EMPRTTU	TRUMPET
EMRRSTU	STURMER
EMRRSUY	MURREYS
EMRSSTU	ESTRUMS
	MUSTERS
	STUMERS
EMRSTTU	MUTTERS
EMRSTYY	MYSTERY
EMSSSTY	SYSTEMS
ENNNOPS	PENNONS
ENNNRUY	NUNNERY
ENNOORS	NOONERS
ENNOORT	NORTENO
ENNOOTT	NONETTO
ENNORST	STONERN
ENNORSU	NEURONS
ENNORSW	RENOWNS
ENNORTU	NEUTRON
ENNOSST	SONNETS
	STONNES
	TENSONS
ENNOSSW	NOWNESS
ENNOSTU	NEUSTON
ENNOSTW	NEWTONS
ENNOSTZ	TENZONS
ENNOUVW	UNWOVEN
ENNPRSU	PUNNERS
ENNPSTU	PUNNETS
	UNSPENT
ENNRRSU	RUNNERS
ENNRSTU	RUNNETS
	STUNNER
ENNRSUW	WUNNERS
ENNSSTU	UNNESTS
ENNSTTU	UNTENTS
ENNSTUU	UNTUNES
ENNTTUY	UNTENTY
ENOOPPR	PROPONE
ENOOPRS	OPERONS
	SNOOPER
ENOOPSY	SPOONEY
ENOORSS	SEROONS
ENOORST	ENROOTS
ENOORSU	ONEROUS
ENOORSZ	SNOOZER
ENOOSST	SOONEST
ENOOSSZ	SNOOZES
ENOOSTT	TESTOON
ENOOSTU	UNSOOTE
ENOOTXY	OXYTONE
ENOPPSU	UNPOPES
ENOPRRS	PERRONS
ENOPRRU	PRONEUR
ENOPRSS	PERSONS
ENOPRST	POSTERN
	PRONEST
ENOPRSU	UNROPES
ENOPRSY	PROYNES
	PYONERS
ENOPRTT	PORTENT
ENOPRTY	ENTROPY
ENOPSST	POSNETS
	STEPSON
ENOPSTT	POTENTS
ENOPSWY	POWNEYS
ENOQTUU	UNQUOTE

ENORRSS	SNORERS
	SORNERS
ENORRST	SNORTER
ENORRTT	TORRENT
ENORRUV	OVERRUN
ENORSSS	SENSORS
ENORSST	STONERS
	TENSORS
ENORSSW	WORSENS
ENORSSY	SENSORY
ENORSTT	ROTTENS
	SNOTTER
	STENTOR
ENORSTU	TENOURS
	TONSURE
ENORSTY	TYRONES
ENORSUV	NERVOUS
ENORSUW	UNSWORE
ENORSUZ	ZONURES
ENORSVY	RENVOYS
ENORSZZ	NOZZERS
ENORTUW	UNWROTE
ENORTUY	TOURNEY
ENOSSST	SESTONS
ENOSSTT	OSTENTS
	TESTONS
ENOSSTU	OUTNESS
	TONUSES
ENOSSTW	TWONESS
ENOSSTX	SEXTONS
ENOSSUW	SWOUNES
ENOSSWW	SWOWNES
ENOSTTU	STOUTEN
	TENUTOS
ENOSTUU	TENUOUS
ENOTTUW	OUTWENT
ENPRRSU	PRUNERS
	SPURNER
ENPRSSU	SPURNES
ENPRSTU	PUNSTER
	PUNTERS
ENPRSUU	UNPURSE
ENPRSWY	PREWYNS
ENPSSSU	SUSPENS
ENPSSTU	UNSTEPS
ENPSTTU	STUPENT
ENPSTUW	UNSWEPT
ENRRSSU	NURSERS
ENRRSTU	RETURNS
	TURNERS
ENRRSUU	UNSURER
ENRRSUY	NURSERY
ENRRTUU	NURTURE
	UNTRUER
ENRRTUY	TURNERY
ENRSSTU	UNRESTS
ENRSSWY	WRYNESS
ENRSTTU	ENTRUST
	NUTTERS
ENRSUZZ	NUZZERS
ENRSVWY	WYVERNS
ENRTTUY	NUTTERY
ENSSSTU	SUNSETS
EOOOPRS	OOSPORE
EOOPPRS	OPPOSER
	PROPOSE
EOOPPRV	POPOVER
EOOPPSS	OPPOSES
EOOPRRS	SPOORER
EOOPRRT	PROTORE
	TROOPER
EOOPRSS	POROSES
EOOPRST	POOREST
	POOTERS
	STOOPER
EOOPRTU	OUTROPE
EOOPRTV	OVERTOP
EOOPRTW	TOWROPE
EOOPRVY	POOVERY
EOOPRYZ	ZOOPERY
EOOPSST	STOOPES
EOOPTYZ	ZOOTYPE
EOORRST	ROOSTER
	ROOTERS
	TOREROS
EOORSSS	SOROSES
EOORSTT	TOOTERS
EOORSVW	OVERSOW
EOORTUW	OUTWORE
EOOSSSU	OSSEOUS
EOOSSTT	TOOTSES
EOOSTWZ	WOOTZES
EOOTTUV	OUTVOTE
EOPPPRS	POPPERS
EOPPPST	POPPETS
EOPPRRS	PROPERS
	PROSPER
EOPPRSS	OPPRESS
	PORPESS
EOPPRST	STOPPER
	TOPPERS
EOPPRSU	PURPOSE
EOPPRSW	SWOPPER
EOPPRSY	PYROPES
	YOPPERS
EOPPSSU	SUPPOSE
EOPRRSS	PRESSOR
	PROSERS
EOPRRST	PORTERS
	PRETORS
	REPORTS
	SPORTER
EOPRRSU	POURERS
EOPRRSV	PROVERS
EOPRRTU	TROUPER
EOPRSSS	POSSERS
EOPRSST	PORTESS
	POSTERS
	PRESTOS
	REPOSTS
EOPRSSU	POSEURS
	SEROPUS
	SOUPERS
EOPRSSW	PROWESS
EOPRSSY	OSPREYS
	PYROSES
EOPRSTT	POTTERS
	PROTEST
	SPOTTER
EOPRSTU	PETROUS
	POSTURE
	POUTERS
	PROTEUS
	SEPTUOR
	SPOUTER
	TROUPES
EOPRSTW	POWTERS
EOPRSTX	EXPORTS
EOPRSUU	POURSUE
	UPROUSE
EOPRSUW	POURSEW
EOPRTTY	POTTERY
EOPRTUY	EUTROPY
EOPRTVY	POVERTY
EOPSSSS	POSSESS
EOPSSST	POSSETS
EOPSSSU	POUSSES
	SPOUSES
EOPSSTX	SEXPOTS
EOPSTTU	OUTSTEP
	TOUPETS
EOPSTTW	STEWPOT
EOPTTUW	OUTWEPT
EOQRSTU	QUESTOR
	QUOTERS
	ROQUETS
	TORQUES
EORRRST	RORTERS
	TERRORS
EORRSSS	ROSSERS
EORRSST	RESORTS
	ROSTERS
	SORTERS
	STORERS
EORRSSU	ROUSERS
EORRSTT	RETORTS
	ROTTERS
	TORRETS
EORRSTU	RETOURS
	ROUSTER
	ROUTERS
	TOURERS
	TROUSER
EORRSTV	TROVERS
EORRSTW	STROWER
EORRSTY	ROYSTER
EORRSZZ	ROZZERS
EORRTTT	TROTTER
EORRTTU	TORTURE
	TROUTER
EORSSST	TOSSERS
EORSSSU	SOURSES
EORSSTU	ESTROUS
	OESTRUS
	OUSTERS
	SOUREST
	SOUTERS
	TOUSERS
	TROUSES
	TUSSORE
EORSSTV	STOVERS
	VOTRESS
EORSSTW	SOWTERS
	STOWERS
	STOWRES
	TOWSERS
EORSSTY	OYSTERS
	STOREYS
EORSSTZ	ZOSTERS
EORSSWW	WOWSERS
EORSTTT	STOTTER
	STRETTO
	TOTTERS
EORSTTU	STOUTER
	TOUTERS
EORSTTW	SWOTTER
EORSTTX	EXTORTS
EORSTTY	ROSETTY
EORSTUX	SEXTUOR
EORSUVY	VOYEURS
EORTTTY	TOTTERY
EOSSSST	STOSSES
EOSSSSW	SOWSSES
EOSSTTU	OUTSETS
EOSTTTW	WOTTEST
EPPPSTU	PUPPETS
EPPRRTU	PRERUPT
EPPRRUU	PURPURE
EPPRSSU	SUPPERS
EPPSTUW	UPSWEPT
EPRRRSU	SPURRER
EPRRSSU	PURSERS
EPRRSUU	PURSUER
	USURPER
EPRRSUY	SPURREY
EPRRTUU	RUPTURE
EPRSSSU	PUSSERS
EPRSSTU	UPRESTS
EPRSSTY	SPRYEST
EPRSSUU	PURSUES
EPRSSUW	PURSEWS
EPRSTTU	PUTTERS
	SPUTTER
EPRSTUU	PUTURES
EPRSUVY	PURVEYS
EQRSTWY	QWERTYS
ERRSSTU	RUSTRES
	TRUSSER
ERRSSUU	USURERS
ERRSSUY	SURREYS
ERRSTTU	RUTTERS
	TRUSTER
	TURRETS
ERRSTTY	TRYSTER
ERSSSTU	RUSSETS
	TRUSSES
	TUSSERS
ERSSSUU	USURESS
ERSSTTU	TUTRESS
ERSSTUU	SUTURES
ERSSTUY	RUSSETY
ERSSTXY	XYSTERS
ERSSUVW	SURVEWS
ERSSUVY	SURVEYS
ERSTTTU	STUTTER
ERSTTUX	URTEXTS
FFFGINU	FUFFING
FFGGINO	GOFFING
FFGHINU	HUFFING
FFGIIMN	MIFFING
FFGIINN	NIFFING
FFGIINR	GRIFFIN
FFGIINT	TIFFING
FFGILNU	LUFFING
FFGIMNU	MUFFING
FFGINOR	GRIFFON
FFGINOS	OFFINGS
FFGINPU	PUFFING
FFGINRU	RUFFING
FFGLRUY	GRUFFLY
FFHHISU	HUFFISH
FFHIISY	FISHIFY
FFHIKNU	HUFFKIN
FFHILSU	FISHFUL
FFHILTY	FIFTHLY
FFHILUY	HUFFILY
FFHIMSU	MUFFISH
FFHIOST	TOFFISH
FFHORSS	SHROFFS
FFIILMY	MIFFILY

FFIINST TIFFINS
FFIISUZ ZIFFIUS
FFIKLSS SKLIFFS
FFILLLU FULFILL
FFILLSU FULFILS
FFILOST FILFOTS
FFILOUZ ZUFFOLI
FFILPSS SPLIFFS
FFILPUY PUFFILY
FFILRTY FRITFLY
FFILSTU FISTFUL
FFILSTY STIFFLY
FFIMNSU MUFFINS
FFINNSU NUFFINS
FFINOPT PONTIFF
FFINPSU PUFFINS
FFINRSU RUFFINS
FFIORTY FORTIFY
FFIOSST SOFFITS
FFIQSUY SQUIFFY
FFIRTUY FRUTIFY
FFKLORU FORKFUL
FFLLOOU LOOFFUL
FFLNSUY SNUFFLY
FFLOOUZ ZUFFOLO
FFLOSTY FYLFOTS
FFNORTU TURNOFF
FFOOPST STOPOFF
FFOPSTU OFFPUTS
FFRRSUU FURFURS
FGGGIIN FIGGING
FGGGINO FOGGING
FGGGINU FUGGING
FGGHIIS FISHGIG
FGGIINT GIFTING
FGGIISS FISGIGS
FGGIISZ FIZGIGS
FGGIIZZ FIZZGIG
FGGILNO GOLFING
FGGILNU FUGLING
GULFING
FGGILOY FOGGILY
FGGINOO GOOFING
FGGINOR FORGING
FGGINOW GOWFING
FGHIINS FISHING
FGHILST FLIGHTS
FGHILSU SIGHFUL
FGHILTY FLIGHTY
FGHIMNU HUMFING
FGHINOO HOOFING
FGHINOU HOUFING
FGHINOW HOWFING
FGHIOSY FOGYISH
FGHIRST FRIGHTS
FGHNOOR FOGHORN
FGHORUY FROUGHY
FGHOTUY FOUGHTY
FGIIKNN FINKING
KNIFING
FGIIKNR FIRKING
FGIIKNS FISKING
FGIILLN FILLING
FGIILMN FILMING
FGIILNO FOILING
FGIILNR RIFLING
FGIILNS FILINGS
FGIILNT FLITING
LIFTING
FGIILNX FLIXING

FGIILNY LIGNIFY
FGIIMNR FIRMING
FGIINNO FOINING
FGIINNS FININGS
FGIINRR FIRRING
FGIINRS FIRINGS
FGIINRT RIFTING
FGIINRY NIGRIFY
FGIINRZ FRIZING
FGIINST FISTING
SIFTING
FGIINSX FIXINGS
FGIINSY SIGNIFY
FGIINTT FITTING
TIFTING
FGIINZZ FIZZING
FGIKLNU FLUKING
FGIKNNU FUNKING
FGIKNOR FORKING
FGILLNU FULLING
FGILNOO FOOLING
FGILNOP FOPLING
FGILNOR ROLFING
FGILNOT LOFTING
FGILNOU FOULING
FGILNOW FLOWING
FOWLING
WOLFING
FGILNOY FOYLING
FGILNPY FLYPING
FGILNRU FURLING
FGILNSU INGULFS
FGILNSY FLYINGS
FGILNTU FLUTING
FGILNTY FLYTING
FGILNUX FLUXING
FGILOOY GOOFILY
FGILORY GLORIFY
FGIMNOR FORMING
FGIMOSY FOGYISM
FGINNNO FONNING
FGINNNU FUNNING
FGINNOY FOYNING
FGINOOR ROOFING
FGINOOT FOOTING
FGINOOW WOOFING
FGINOPU POUFING
FGINORT FORTING
FGINOST SOFTING
FGINOSW SOWFING
FGINOSX FOXINGS
FGINRRU FURRING
FGINRSU SURFING
FGINRSY FRYINGS
FGINRTU TURFING
FGINSSU FUSSING
FGINSTU FUSTING
FGINTTU TUFTING
FGINUZZ FUZZING
FGIORST FRIGOTS
FGIORTW FIGWORT
FGISTUU FUGUIST
FGJLSUU JUGFULS
FGLLNUU LUNGFUL
FGLMSUU MUGFULS
FGLNORU FURLONG
FGLNOSU SONGFUL
FGLNPUU UPFLUNG
FGLOOUY UFOLOGY
FGLORSU FULGORS

FGLORUU FULGOUR
FGLOTUY GOUTFLY
FGLSTUU GUSTFUL
GUTFULS
GUTSFUL
FGNOORU FOURGON
FGNORSY GRYFONS
FGNOSUU FUNGOUS
FHIILMS FILMISH
FHIINPS PINFISH
FHILLSU FULLISH
FHILOOS FOOLISH
FHILOSW WOLFISH
FHILPSU SHIPFUL
FHILPTU PITHFUL
FHILSUW WISHFUL
FHINOSU FUSHION
FHINRSU FURNISH
FHINSSU SUNFISH
FHIOOST OOFTISH
FHIOPPS FOPPISH
FHIOPSX FOXSHIP
FHIORRY HORRIFY
FHIOSST SOFTISH
FHIPPSU PUPFISH
FHIRSST SHRIFTS
FHIRSTT THRIFTS
FHIRTTY THRIFTY
FHIRTUY THURIFY
FHISSSU HUSSIFS
FHISSTU SHUFTIS
FHKORTU FUTHORK
FHLNORU HORNFUL
FHLNSUU UNFLUSH
FHLOOSY SHOOFLY
FHLOPSU SHOPFUL
FHLPSUU PUSHFUL
FHLRTUU HURTFUL
RUTHFUL
FHOOORS FORHOOS
FHOOORT HOOFROT
FHOOOTT HOTFOOT
FHOORSW FORHOWS
FHORSTU FOURTHS
FIIIKNN FINIKIN
FIIKNRS FIRKINS
FIIKNYZ ZINKIFY
FIILLMO MILFOIL
FIILLNS INFILLS
FIILLPS FILLIPS
FIILLSU FUSILLI
FIILNOT TINFOIL
FIILNTY NIFTILY
FIILPTU PITIFUL
FIIMMNU INFIMUM
FIIMSST MISFITS
FIINORS FIORINS
FIINOSS FISSION
FIINRTY NITRIFY
FIIPSTY TIPSIFY
FIIRTVY VITRIFY
FIJLLOY JOLLIFY
FIJSTUY JUSTIFY
FIKKLNO KINFOLK
FIKLLSU SKILFUL
FIKLNOW WOLFKIN
FIKLNSU SKINFUL
FIKLRSU RISKFUL
FIKNNOS FINNSKO
FILLLUW WILLFUL

FILLMOY MOLLIFY
FILLNUY NULLIFY
FILLOTU TOILFUL
FILLOTY LOFTILY
FILLPSU UPFILLS
FILLSTU LISTFUL
FILMNOO MONOFIL
FILMSTU MISTFUL
FILNNUY FUNNILY
FILNORS FLORINS
FILNOSW INFLOWS
FILNOUX FLUXION
FILNSTU TINFULS
FILNTUY UNFITLY
FILOOTW WITLOOF
FILORST FIRLOTS
FLORIST
FILORSV FRIVOLS
FILORTU FLORUIT
FILORTY TRIFOLY
FILOSSS FOSSILS
FILPPUY PULPIFY
FILPSTU UPLIFTS
FILRSTY FIRSTLY
FILRYZZ FRIZZLY
FILSSUY FUSSILY
FILSTTU FLUTIST
FILSTUW WISTFUL
FILSTUY FUSTILY
FILSTWY SWIFTLY
FILUYZZ FUZZILY
FIMMMUY MUMMIFY
FIMMORS MISFORM
FIMNORS INFORMS
FIMNORU UNIFORM
FIMOORV OVIFORM
FIMORRT TRIFORM
FIMORTY MORTIFY
FIMRTUY FURMITY
FIMSTYY MYSTIFY
FINOOSS FOISONS
FINOPRS FRIPONS
FINOPTY PONTIFY
FINORSS FRISSON
FINORST FORINTS
FINOSSU FUSIONS
FIOORSU FURIOSO
FIOPRST FORPITS
PROFITS
FIOPRSY PROSIFY
FIOPSTX POSTFIX
FIORSUU FURIOUS
FIOSTTU OUTFITS
FIPPUYY YUPPIFY
FIRSSTT STRIFTS
FKLORUW WORKFUL
FKNOSTY KONFYTS
FKOOORS FORSOOK
FLLOOSW FOLLOWS
FLLOPTU PLOTFUL
TOPFULL
FLLOSUU SOULFUL
FLLOUWY WOFULLY
FLLSTUU LUSTFUL
FLMMOUX FLUMMOX
FLMNOOU MOUFLON
FLMNOSU MUFLONS
FLMOOOT TOMFOOL
FLMOORS FORMOLS
FLMOORU ROOMFUL

FLNOORR FORLORN
FLNOOSU UNFOOLS
FLNOOSW ONFLOWS
FLNRSUU UNFURLS
URNFULS
FLOORSW FORSLOW
FLOOTUW OUTFLOW
FLOPSTU POTFULS
FLOPSUW UPFLOWS
FLOSUUV FULVOUS
FLPRSUU UPFURLS
FLRSSUU SULFURS
FMNORSU UNFORMS
FMRSTUU FRUSTUM
FNNNUUY UNFUNNY
FNNOORT FRONTON
FNOORRW FORWORN
FNOORSU SUNROOF
UNROOFS
FNOPRTU UPFRONT
FNRSTUU UNTURFS
FNSTTUU UNSTUFT
FOOOPRT ROOFTOP
FOOORTT FOOTROT
FOOOTTU OUTFOOT
FOORSSS FOSSORS
FOORTTX FOXTROT
FORRSUW FURROWS
FORRUWY FURROWY
FORSSTW FROWSTS
FORSTWY FROWSTY
GGGGIIN GIGGING
GGGHINO HOGGING
GGGHINU HUGGING
GGGIIJN JIGGING
GGGIILN LIGGING
GGGIINP PIGGING
GGGIINR RIGGING
GGGIINT TIGGING
GGGIINW WIGGING
GGGIINZ ZIGGING
GGGIIST GIGGITS
GGGIJNO JOGGING
GGGIJNU JUGGING
GGGILNO LOGGING
GGGILNU LUGGING
GGGIMNU MUGGING
GGGINNO GONGING
NOGGING
GGGINOR GORGING
GGGINOS SOGGING
GGGINOT TOGGING
GGGINOU GOUGING
GGGINPU PUGGING
GGGINRU RUGGING
GGGINSU SUGGING
GGGINTU TUGGING
GGHHIIN HIGHING
GGHHIOS HOGGISH
GGHIIJS JIGGISH
GGHIINN HINGING
NIGHING
GGHIINS SIGHING
GGHIIPS PIGGISH
GGHIIRS RIGGISH
GGHIITT THIGGIT
GGHIMSU MUGGISH
GGHINNO HONGING
GGHINOS HOGGINS
GGHINSU GUSHING

GGHIPSU PUGGISH
GGHLOSY SHOGGLY
GGHORSU GROUGHS
GGHOSTU THUGGOS
GGIIILN GINGILI
GGIIJJS JIGJIGS
GGIIKNN KINGING
GGIILLN GILLING
GGIILNP PIGLING
GGIILNR RIGLING
GGIILNU GUILING
GGIIMNN MINGING
GGIIMNP GIMPING
GGIIMNR GRIMING
GGIINNN GINNING
GGIINNO INGOING
GGIINNP PINGING
GGIINNR GIRNING
RINGING
GGIINNS SIGNING
SINGING
GGIINNT TINGING
GGIINNW WINGING
GGIINNZ ZINGING
GGIINPR GRIPING
GGIINPS PIGGINS
GGIINRS GRISING
GGIINRT GIRTING
RINGGIT
GGIINSU GUISING
GGIINSV GIVINGS
GGIIRRS GRIGRIS
GGIJNSU JUGGINS
GGILLNU GULLING
GGILNNO LONGING
GGILNNU LUNGING
GGILNOS GOSLING
OGLINGS
GGILNOV GLOVING
GGILNOW GLOWING
GOWLING
GGILNOZ GLOZING
GGILNPU GULPING
GGILNRU GURLING
GGILNSU LUGINGS
GGILNUY GUYLING
UGLYING
GGILOOS GIGOLOS
GGILOST GIGLOTS
GGILOSY SOGGILY
GGILRWY WRIGGLY
GGIMMNU GUMMING
GGIMNOR GORMING
GGIMNPU GUMPING
GGIMNPY GYMPING
GGIMNSU MUGGINS
GGINNNU GUNNING
GGINNOO ONGOING
GGINNOP PONGING
GGINNOR GRONING
GGINNOS NOGGINS
GGINNOT TONGING
GGINNOW GOWNING
GGINNRU GURNING
GGINOOP POGOING
GGINOOS GOOSING
GGINOPR GORPING
GROPING
PORGING
GGINOPU UPGOING

GGINOQS QIGONGS
GGINORS GORINGS
GRINGOS
GGINORU ROGUING
ROUGING
GGINORW GROWING
GGINOUV VOGUING
GGINPPY GYPPING
GGINPRU PURGING
GGINRSU SURGING
URGINGS
GGINSTU GUSTING
GUTSING
GGINTTU GUTTING
GGIOORS GORGIOS
GGIPRSY SPRIGGY
GGLLOOS LOGLOGS
GGLOOOS GOOGOLS
GGNOORS GORGONS
GHHHIIS HIGHISH
GHHHIST HIGHTHS
GHHIINS HISHING
GHHINSU HUSHING
GHHIRST SHRIGHT
GHHORTU THROUGH
GHHOSSU SHOUGHS
GHHOTTU THOUGHT
GHIIKNO HOIKING
GHIIKNT KITHING
GHIILLN HILLING
GHIILNR HIRLING
GHIILNT HILTING
LITHING
GHIILNW WHILING
GHIILRS GIRLISH
GHIINNS SHINING
GHIINNT HINTING
NITHING
GHIINNW WHINING
GHIINOS HOISING
GHIINPP HIPPING
GHIINPS PISHING
GHIINPT PITHING
GHIINRS HIRINGS
GHIINSS HISSING
GHIINST HISTING
INSIGHT
SHITING
SITHING
GHIINSW WISHING
GHIINTT HITTING
TITHING
GHIINTW WHITING
WITHING
GHIINZZ HIZZING
GHIIRST TIGRISH
GHIJNOS JOSHING
GHIKLNU HULKING
GHIKNNO HONKING
GHIKNOO HOOKING
GHIKNOW HOWKING
GHIKNST KNIGHTS
GHIKNSU HUSKING
GHIKNTY KYTHING
GHIKRTU TUGHRIK
GHILLNU HULLING
GHILLSU GULLISH
GHILLTY LIGHTLY
GHILNOS HOLINGS
LONGISH

GHILNOT THOLING
GHILNOW HOWLING
GHILNPU INGULPH
GHILNRU HURLING
GHILNSU LUSHING
SHULING
GHILNSY SHINGLY
GHILNTY NIGHTLY
GHILPST PLIGHTS
GHILPTY YPLIGHT
GHILRTY RIGHTLY
GHILSST SLIGHTS
GHILSTY SIGHTLY
GHILTTY TIGHTLY
GHILTWY WIGHTLY
GHIMMNU HUMMING
GHIMNNY HYMNING
GHIMNOS GNOMISH
HOMINGS
MOSHING
GHIMNPU HUMPING
GHIMNRY RHYMING
GHIMNSU MUSHING
GHIMRSU SIMURGH
GHIMSST SMIGHTS
GHIMSTT MIGHTST
GHINNOP PHONING
GHINNOR HORNING
GHINNOS NOSHING
GHINNOT NOTHING
GHINNTU HUNTING
GHINOOP HOOPING
GHINOOS SHOOING
GHINOOT HOOTING
GHINOOV HOOVING
GHINOPP HOPPING
GHINOPS GINSHOP
POSHING
GHINORS HORSING
SHORING
GHINORW WHORING
GHINOST HOSTING
TOSHING
GHINOSU HOUSING
GHINOSV SHOVING
GHINOSW SHOWING
GHINOTT HOTTING
TONIGHT
GHINOTU HOUTING
THOUING
GHINPPU HUPPING
GHINPPY HYPPING
GHINPSU GUNSHIP
PUSHING
GHINRSU RUSHING
GHINRTU HURTING
UNGIRTH
UNRIGHT
GHINSTU TUSHING
UNSIGHT
GHINTTU HUTTING
GHINTTY TYTHING
GHIOPSZ PHIZOGS
GHIORST RIGHTOS
GHIORSU ROGUISH
GHIOSUV VOGUISH
GHIPRST SPRIGHT
GHIPRTU UPRIGHT
GHIPSST SPIGHTS
GHIPTTU UPTIGHT

GHIQSTU	QUIGHTS
GHIRSTW	WRIGHTS
GHISTTW	TWIGHTS
GHLMOOO	HOMOLOG
GHLOOSY	SHOOGLY
GHLOPSU	PLOUGHS
GHLORUY	ROUGHLY
GHLOSSU	SLOUGHS
GHLOSTY	GHOSTLY
GHLOSUY	SLOUGHY
GHLOTUY	TOUGHLY
GHMORSU	SORGHUM
GHMOSTU	MUGSHOT
GHMPRSU	GRUMPHS
GHNOPRY	GRYPHON
GHNORST	THRONGS
GHNORUU	UNROUGH
GHNOSSU	SHOGUNS
GHNOSTU	GUNSHOT
	NOUGHTS
	SHOTGUN
GHNOTUY	YOUNGTH
GHOOOSW	HOOSGOW
GHOORSS	SORGHOS
GHORSTU	TROUGHS
GHORSTW	GROWTHS
GHORTUW	WROUGHT
GHORTUY	YOGHURT
GHOSTUU	OUTGUSH
GIIJKNN	JINKING
GIIJLNT	JILTING
GIIJNNO	JOINING
GIIJNNX	JINXING
GIIKKNN	KINKING
GIIKKNR	KIRKING
GIIKLLN	KILLING
GIIKLMN	MILKING
GIIKLNN	INKLING
	KILNING
	LINKING
GIIKLNR	LIRKING
GIIKLNS	LIKINGS
	SILKING
GIIKLNT	KILTING
	KITLING
GIIKNNO	OINKING
GIIKNNP	PINKING
GIIKNNR	RINKING
GIIKNNS	SINKING
GIIKNNT	TINKING
GIIKNNV	KNIVING
GIIKNNW	WINKING
GIIKNNZ	ZINKING
GIIKNPP	KIPPING
GIIKNPS	PIGSKIN
	SPIKING
GIIKNRS	GIRKINS
	GRISKIN
	KRISING
	RISKING
GIIKNRT	TRIKING
GIIKNRY	YIRKING
GIIKNSS	KISSING
	SKIINGS
GIIKNST	KISTING
	KITINGS
	SKITING
GIIKNSV	SKIVING
	VIKINGS
GIIKNTT	KITTING
GIILLLN	LILLING
GIILLMN	MILLING
GIILLNN	NILLING
GIILLNO	GILLION
GIILLNP	PILLING
GIILLNR	RILLING
GIILLNT	LILTING
	TILLING
GIILLNW	WILLING
GIILMNN	LIMNING
GIILMNO	MOILING
GIILMNP	LIMPING
GIILMNS	LIMINGS
	SLIMING
	SMILING
GIILMNT	MILTING
GIILMPR	PILGRIM
GIILMRY	GRIMILY
GIILNNN	LINNING
GIILNNR	NIRLING
GIILNNS	LIGNINS
	LININGS
GIILNNY	INLYING
GIILNOR	LIGROIN
	ROILING
GIILNOS	SILOING
	SOILING
GIILNOT	TOILING
GIILNPP	LIPPING
GIILNPS	LISPING
	PILINGS
	SPILING
GIILNRS	RIGLINS
GIILNRT	TIRLING
GIILNST	LISTING
	SILTING
	STILING
	TILINGS
GIILNSV	LIVINGS
	SLIVING
GIILNTT	TILTING
	TITLING
GIILNTW	WILTING
	WITLING
GIILOSS	GLIOSIS
GIILOST	OLIGIST
GIILRST	STRIGIL
GIIMMNN	NIMMING
GIIMMNR	RIMMING
GIIMNNS	MININGS
GIIMNNT	MINTING
GIIMNPP	PIMPING
GIIMNPR	PRIMING
GIIMNRT	MITRING
GIIMNRV	MIRVING
GIIMNSS	MISSING
GIIMNST	MISTING
	SMITING
	STIMING
	TIMINGS
GIINNNP	PINNING
GIINNNR	RINNING
GIINNNS	INNINGS
	SINNING
GIINNNT	TINNING
GIINNNW	WINNING
GIINNOP	OPINING
	PIONING
GIINNOR	IRONING
	ROINING
GIINNOS	NOISING
GIINNOT	OINTING
GIINNPP	NIPPING
GIINNPS	SNIPING
GIINNPU	PINGUIN
GIINNRS	RINSING
GIINNRT	TRINING
GIINNRU	INURING
	RUINING
	URINING
GIINNSW	INSWING
GIINNTT	TINTING
GIINNTU	UNITING
GIINNTV	VINTING
GIINNTW	TWINING
GIINOPS	POISING
GIINORS	ORIGINS
	SIGNIOR
	SIGNORI
GIINORT	RIOTING
GIINOSY	YOGINIS
GIINPPP	PIPPING
GIINPPR	RIPPING
GIINPPS	PIPINGS
	SIPPING
GIINPPT	TIPPING
GIINPPY	YIPPING
GIINPPZ	ZIPPING
GIINPQU	PIQUING
GIINPRS	PRISING
	RISPING
	SPIRING
GIINPRZ	PRIZING
GIINPSS	PISSING
GIINPST	SPITING
GIINPSW	SWIPING
	WIPINGS
	WISPING
GIINPTT	PITTING
GIINPTY	PITYING
GIINQRU	QUIRING
GIINQTU	QUITING
GIINRRS	SIRRING
GIINRRT	TIRRING
GIINRSS	RISINGS
GIINRST	STIRING
	TIRINGS
GIINRSV	VIRGINS
GIINRSW	WIRINGS
GIINRTT	RITTING
GIINRTW	TWIRING
	WRITING
GIINSST	SISTING
GIINSSU	ISSUING
GIINSSW	WISSING
GIINSSZ	SIZINGS
GIINSTT	SITTING
GIINSTU	SUITING
GIINSTV	STIVING
GIINSTW	WISTING
GIINSVW	SWIVING
GIINTTT	TITTING
GIINTTW	WITTING
GIINVYZ	VIZYING
GIINZZZ	ZIZZING
GIJKNNU	JUNKING
GIJKNOO	JOOKING
GIJKNOU	JOUKING
GIJLLNO	JOLLING
GIJLNOT	JOLTING
GIJLNOU	JOULING
GIJLNOW	JOWLING
GIJLNSU	JUNGLIS
GIJMNPU	JUMPING
GIJNOTT	JOTTING
GIJNSTU	JUSTING
GIJNTTU	JUTTING
GIKKNNO	KONKING
GIKKNOO	KOOKING
GIKKNOY	YOKKING
GIKLNOO	LOOKING
GIKLNOP	POLKING
GIKLNRU	LURKING
GIKLNSU	LUSKING
	SULKING
GIKMNOS	SMOKING
GIKMNSU	MUSKING
GIKNNNO	KONNING
GIKNNOP	PONKING
GIKNNOS	SNOKING
GIKNNOT	TONKING
GIKNNOW	KNOWING
GIKNNOZ	ZONKING
GIKNNSU	UNKINGS
GIKNOOP	POOKING
GIKNOOR	ROOKING
GIKNOPR	PROKING
GIKNOPU	POUKING
GIKNORT	TROKING
GIKNORW	WORKING
GIKNORY	YORKING
GIKNOST	STOKING
GIKNOSY	YOKINGS
GIKNOTU	TOUKING
GIKNOUY	YOUKING
GIKNRSY	SKRYING
	SKYRING
GIKNSTU	TUSKING
GIKNSTY	SKYTING
GIKRSTU	TUGRIKS
GILLLNO	LOLLING
GILLLNU	LULLING
GILLMNU	MULLING
GILLNNU	NULLING
GILLNOP	POLLING
GILLNOR	ROLLING
GILLNOT	TOLLING
GILLNPU	PULLING
GILLNSU	ULLINGS
GILLNUW	WULLING
GILLNYY	LYINGLY
GILLOOS	LOLIGOS
GILLORS	RIGOLLS
GILMNOO	LOOMING
	MOOLING
GILMNOR	MORLING
GILMNOT	MOLTING
GILMNOY	MOYLING
GILMNPU	LUMPING
	PLUMING
GILMNRU	MURLING
GILMNSU	LIGNUMS
GILNNOO	GLONOIN
	LOONING
GILNNOU	LOUNING
GILNNOW	LOWNING
GILNNRU	NURLING
GILNNSU	UNSLING
GILNNTU	LUNTING
GILNNUV	VULNING

GILNOOP LOOPING
POOLING
GILNOOS LOOSING
SOLOING
SOOLING
GILNOOT LOOTING
TOOLING
GILNOPP LOPPING
GILNOPR PROLING
GILNOPS POLINGS
SLOPING
GILNOPT POLTING
GILNOPU LOUPING
GILNOPW PLOWING
GILNORS LORINGS
GILNORU LOURING
GILNOSS LOSINGS
GILNOST LINGOTS
TIGLONS
TOLINGS
GILNOSU LOUSING
GILNOSV LOVINGS
SOLVING
GILNOSW LOWINGS
LOWSING
SLOWING
SOWLING
GILNOTT LOTTING
GILNOTU LOUTING
GILNOTW LOWTING
GILNOVV VOLVING
GILNOVW WOLVING
GILNOWY YOWLING
GILNPPU PULPING
GILNPRU PURLING
GILNPSU PLUSING
PULINGS
PULSING
PUSLING
GILNPUY UPLYING
GILNRSU RULINGS
GILNSTU LUSTING
LUTINGS
SINGULT
GILNSTY STYLING
GILNVYY VYINGLY
GILOORS GIROSOL
GILORTT TRIGLOT
GILORTY TRILOGY
GILOSTT GLOTTIS
GILRSTY GRISTLY
GILRTUY LITURGY
GILRYZZ GRIZZLY
GIMMMNU MUMMING
GIMMNPU MUMPING
GIMMNRY RYMMING
GIMMNSU SUMMING
GIMMNUV VUMMING
GIMMORS GIMMORS
GIMNNOO MOONING
GIMNNOR MORNING
GIMNNTU MUNTING
GIMNOOP MOOPING
GIMNOOR MOORING
ROOMING
GIMNOOS SOOMING
GIMNOOT MOOTING
TOOMING
GIMNOOV MOOVING
GIMNOOZ ZOOMING

GIMNOPP MOPPING
GIMNOPR ROMPING
GIMNOPU MOUPING
GIMNOPY YOMPING
GIMNORS SMORING
GIMNORU ROUMING
GIMNORW WORMING
GIMNOSS MOSSING
GIMNOST GNOMIST
GIMNOSU MOUSING
SOUMING
GIMNOSW MOWINGS
SOWMING
GIMNPPU PUMPING
GIMNPRU RUMPING
GIMNPSU IMPUGNS
SPUMING
GIMNPTU TUMPING
GIMNPUY YUMPING
GIMNSSU MUSINGS
MUSSING
GIMNSTU MUSTING
GIMNSTY STYMING
GIMORSS SIMORGS
GIMOSSY YOGISMS
GIMOSTU GOMUTIS
GIMRSSU SIMURGS
GIMRSUU GURUISM
GINNNOO NOONING
GINNNOR RONNING
GINNNOW WONNING
GINNNPU PUNNING
GINNNRU RUNNING
GINNNSU SUNNING
GINNNTU TUNNING
GINNOOS NOOSING
GINNOOW WOONING
GINNOPS SPONGIN
GINNOPY PONYING
GINNORS SNORING
SORNING
GINNORU GRUNION
GINNORW INGROWN
GINNORY ROYNING
GINNOSS NOSINGS
GINNOST STONING
TONINGS
GINNOSW SNOWING
WONINGS
GINNOSZ ZONINGS
GINNOTW WONTING
GINNPRU PRUNING
GINNPTU PUNTING
GINNRSU NURSING
URNINGS
GINNRTU TURNING
GINNSTU TUNINGS
GINNTTU NUTTING
GINNTUY UNTYING
GINOOPP POOPING
GINOOPR ROOPING
GINOOPS SOOPING
GINOOPT POOTING
GINOORS ROOSING
GINOORT ROOTING
GINOOSS ISOGONS
GINOOST SOOTING
GINOOSW WOOINGS
GINOOTT TOOTING
GINOPPP POPPING

GINOPPS SOPPING
GINOPPT TOPPING
GINOPPU POUPING
GINOPPW WOPPING
GINOPRS PROIGNS
PROSING
ROPINGS
GINOPRT PORTING
TROPING
GINOPRU INGROUP
POURING
ROUPING
GINOPRV PROVING
GINOPRW POWRING
GINOPSS POSINGS
POSSING
GINOPST POSTING
STOPING
GINOPSY POYSING
GINOPTT POTTING
GINOPTU POUTING
GINOQTU QUOTING
GINORRT RORTING
GINORRV VORRING
GINORSS GRISONS
INGROSS
SIGNORS
GINORST ROSTING
SORTING
STORING
TRIGONS
GINORSU ROUSING
SOURING
GINORSV ROVINGS
GINORSW ROWINGS
WORSING
GINORSY ROSYING
SIGNORY
GINORTT ROTTING
GINORTU ROUTING
TOURING
GINORTW ROWTING
TROWING
GINOSSS SOSSING
GINOSST STINGOS
TOSSING
GINOSSU SOUSING
GINOSSW SOWINGS
SOWSING
GINOSTT SOTTING
GINOSTU OUSTING
OUTINGS
TOUSING
GINOSTV STOVING
GINOSTW STOWING
TOWINGS
TOWSING
GINOSTY TOYINGS
GINOTTT TOTTING
GINOTTU TOUTING
GINOTTW TOWTING
WOTTING
GINOTUW OUTWING
GINOTUZ TOUZING
GINOTWZ TOWZING
GINPPPU PUPPING
GINPPSU SUPPING
UPPINGS
GINPPTU TUPPING
GINPRRU PURRING

GINPRSS SPRINGS
GINPRSU PURSING
GINPRSY PRYINGS
PRYSING
SPRINGY
GINPSSY SPYINGS
GINPSTU PIGNUTS
STUPING
GINPSTY TYPINGS
GINPSUW UPSWING
GINPTTU PUTTING
GINPTUY UPTYING
GINQTUY QUYTING
GINRRSU RUNRIGS
GINRSST STRINGS
GINRSTU RUSTING
GINRSTY STRINGY
STYRING
TRYINGS
GINRSUU USURING
GINRTTU RUTTING
GINSSSU SUSSING
GINSTTU TUTSING
GINSTTY STYTING
GINTTTU TUTTING
GIOOPRR PORRIGO
GIOORSV VIGOROS
GIOPRRU PRURIGO
GIOPSSS GOSSIPS
GIOPSST SPIGOTS
GIOPSSY GOSSIPY
GIORRSU RIGOURS
GIORSUV VIGOURS
GIOSSYZ ZYGOSIS
GISWWYY WYSIWYG
GJNOOSU GOUJONS
GJNRSUU GURJUNS
GJOORTT JOGTROT
GKMOOSU GOMOKUS
GLLOOPS GOLLOPS
GLMNOOS MONGOLS
GLMOOOR MOORLOG
GLMOOYY MYOLOGY
GLMORUW LUGWORM
GLNNOOR LORGNON
GLNNSUU UNSLUNG
GLNOOOS OOLONGS
GLNOOOY NOOLOGY
GLNOOPR PROLONG
GLNOOPY POLYGON
GLNOOSU OULONGS
GLNORWY WRONGLY
GLNOSUW SUNGLOW
GLNOTTU GLUTTON
GLNOUYY YOUNGLY
GLNPSUU UNPLUGS
GLOOORY OROLOGY
GLOOOTY OTOLOGY
GLOOOYZ ZOOLOGY
GLOORUY UROLOGY
GLOPSTU PUTLOGS
GLORSSY GROSSLY
GLPRSUY SPLURGY
GMMOSUU GUMMOUS
GMMPUUW MUGWUMP
GMNNOOS GNOMONS
GMNOORU GUNROOM
GMNOORW MORWONG
GMNSTUU GUMNUTS
GMNSUUZ MZUNGUS

GMOOPRS POGROMS
GMOOSTU GOMUTOS
GMORSUU GRUMOUS
GMORTUW MUGWORT
GMPSSUY GYPSUMS
GMRUYYZ ZYMURGY
GNNORUW UNGROWN
GNNORYY GYRONNY
GNNOSUW UNGOWNS
GNNRUUW UNWRUNG
GNOOORS GORSOON
GNOOOSS GOSSOON
GNOOOYZ ZOOGONY
GNOORST TROGONS
GNOPPSU OPPUGNS
GNOPRTU GUNPORT
GNOPRUW UPGROWN
GNOPSTU POTGUNS
GNOSTUU OUTGUNS
GOOOORS GOOROOS
GOORSTT GROTTOS
GOORTUW OUTGROW
GOPRSUW UPGROWS
GORRSTU TURGORS
GORSTTU GUTROTS
ROTGUTS
GORSTUY YOGURTS
HHIIPPS HIPPISH
HHIISTW WHITISH
HHIMRTY RHYTHMI
HHINORS HORNISH
HHIORSW WHORISH
HHIOSTT HOTTISH
HHISSTW WHISHTS
HHMMSUU HUMHUMS
HHMRSTY RHYTHMS
HHOOSTT HOTSHOT
HIIIKRS RIKISHI
HIIJKNS HIJINKS
HIIKLMS KHILIMS
HIIKNPS KINSHIP
PINKISH
HIILMTU LITHIUM
HIILPST SHILPIT
HIILPTY PITHILY
HIILRTT TRILITH
HIIMMSS MISHMIS
HIIMPSW WIMPISH
HIIMSSS MISSISH
HIIMSST MISHITS
HIIMSTT SHITTIM
HIINORS ROINISH
HIINPSS INSHIPS
HIINSSW SWINISH
HIIOPRZ RHIZOPI
HIIORST HISTRIO
HIISTTT TITTISH
HIKLSSU LUSKISH
HIKLSUY HUSKILY
HIKMNOS MONKISH
HIKMRSU MURKISH
HIKMSUZ MUZHIKS
HIKNNOR INKHORN
HIKNNTU UNTHINK
HIKNRSS SHRINKS
HIKOORS ROOKISH
HILLOPT HILLTOP
HILLOPY LYOPHIL
HILLPSU UPHILLS
HILLRSS SHRILLS

HILLRST THRILLS
HILLRSY SHRILLY
HILLRTY THRILLY
HILMMOU HOLMIUM
HILMOPS LOMPISH
PHLOMIS
HILMOSS HOLISMS
HILMOSW WHOLISM
HILMPSU LUMPISH
HILMSSY HYLISMS
HILMSUY MUSHILY
HILMTUU THULIUM
HILNNTY NINTHLY
HILNPST PLINTHS
HILOOTT OTOLITH
HILOOTZ ZOOLITH
HILORTU UROLITH
HILOSST HOLISTS
HILOSSW SLOWISH
HILOSTU LOUTISH
HILOSTW WHOLIST
HILOSTY HYLOIST
HILOSVW WOLVISH
HILOSWY SHOWILY
HILOTWW WHITLOW
HILPRUW UPWHIRL
HILPSST SPILTHS
HILSSTY HYLISTS
STYLISH
HILSTTY THISTLY
HILSTXY SIXTHLY
HIMMPSU MUMPISH
HIMMRSU RUMMISH
HIMMSTY MYTHISM
HIMNOOS MOONISH
HIMNSSU MUNSHIS
HIMNSTY HYMNIST
HIMOORS MOORISH
HIMOPRS ROMPISH
HIMOPSS SOPHISM
HIMOPST PHOTISM
HIMORTU THORIUM
HIMOTTY TIMOTHY
HIMPRSS SHRIMPS
HIMPRSY SHRIMPY
HIMPRTU TRIUMPH
HIMPTUY PYTHIUM
HIMRSTY RHYMIST
HIMSSTU ISTHMUS
HIMSTTY MYTHIST
HINNNSU NUNNISH
HINNORT TINHORN
HINNOST TONNISH
HINNPSU NUNSHIP
HINOOPS INHOOPS
HINOORT HORNITO
HINOORZ HORIZON
HINOOST INSOOTH
HINOPPS SHIPPON
HINOPSS SIPHONS
SONSHIP
HINORST HORNIST
HINORSU NOURISH
HINORSY ROYNISH
HINOSSW SNOWISH
HINOSTW TOWNISH
HINPSSU UNSHIPS
HINPTUW UNWHIPT
HINRSTU RUNTISH
HIOOPRS POORISH

HIOOSSV SHIVOOS
HIOPPPS POPPISH
HIOPPSS SHIPPOS
HIOPRSW WORSHIP
HIOPSST SOPHIST
HIOPSSY PHYSIOS
HIOPSTU UPHOIST
HIORSSU SOURISH
HIORSTY HISTORY
HIOSSTT SOTTISH
HIOSTTU OUTHITS
HIOTTUW OUTWITH
WITHOUT
HIQSSUY SQUISHY
HIRSSTT THIRSTS
THRISTS
HIRSTTU RUTTISH
HIRSTTY THIRSTY
THRISTY
HKKLOOZ KOLKHOZ
HKKOOSY SKYHOOK
HKNOOSU UNHOOKS
HKNOOWW KNOWHOW
HKNSSUU UNHUSKS
HKOOOPT POTHOOK
HKOOSST SHTOOKS
HKORSWY WORKSHY
HLLOOSW HOLLOWS
HLLOPSY PHYLLOS
HLMNOTY MONTHLY
HLMNPYY NYMPHLY
HLMORRY MYRRHOL
HLMOSTY THYMOLS
HLOOSTY SOOTHLY
HLOPRTY PROTHYL
HLORSTY SHORTLY
HLOTUYY YOUTHLY
HLPRSUU SULPHUR
UPHURLS
HMMMSUU HUMMUMS
HMMNOOY HOMONYM
HMMOOSU HOUMMOS
HMMRTUY THRUMMY
HMNOPSY NYMPHOS
HMNOPYY HYPONYM
HMNPSUY HYPNUMS
HMOOPRS MORPHOS
HMOOSST SMOOTHS
HMORSUU HUMOURS
HMSTUYZ ZYTHUMS
HNNOOPS PHONONS
HNNORSU UNSHORN
HNNOSTY SYNTHON
HNNOSUW UNSHOWN
HNOOPST PHOTONS
HNOOPSU UNHOOPS
HNOOPTY TYPHOON
HNOORSS HORSONS
HNOORST THORONS
HNOORSU HONOURS
HNOOSTU UNSHOOT
HNOPSSY SYPHONS
HNOPSTY PHYTONS
PYTHONS
TYPHONS
HNORTUW UNWORTH
HNOSTUU UNSHOUT
HNRTTUU UNTRUTH
HNSSTUU UNSHUTS
HOOPPST POTSHOP

HOOPRST PORTHOS
HOOPSTT HOTPOTS
HOOPSTU UPSHOOT
HOOPSTY TOYSHOP
HOORRRS HORRORS
HOORRST ORTHROS
HOORSUZ HUZOORS
HOOSTTU OUTSHOT
HOPRTUW UPTHROW
HOPSSSY HYSSOPS
HOPSSTU UPSHOTS
HOPSTTU SHOTPUT
HOPSTUY TYPHOUS
HORSTUU OUTRUSH
HOSSTTU STOUTHS
HRSSTTU THRUSTS
HRSSTUY THYRSUS
IIIJJLN JINJILI
IIIKMNN MINIKIN
IIIMRST MIRITIS
IIISTTW WISTITI
IIJLLNO JILLION
IIJMNOS MISJOIN
IIJNNOT INJOINT
IIKLLMY MILKILY
IIKLLSY SILKILY
IIKLMNP LIMPKIN
IIKLNOS OILSKIN
IIKLPSY SPIKILY
IIKLRSY RISKILY
IIKMNOR KIRIMON
IIKMNPS SIMPKIN
IIKMNSS SIMKINS
IIKNPPS PIPKINS
IIKNSSS SISKINS
IIKOSST OIKISTS
IIKOSTT TITOKIS
IILLLSY SILLILY
IILLMNO MILLION
IILLMSY SLIMILY
IILLNOP PILLION
IILLNOZ ZILLION
IILLNST INSTILL
IILLNTT LITTLIN
IILLPSU ILLUPIS
IILMNOS LIONISM
IILMORS SIMILOR
IILMOSS LIMOSIS
IILMSTU STIMULI
IILMSTY MISTILY
IILNNSU INSULIN
INULINS
IILNORS SIRLOIN
IILNOSV VIOLINS
IILNOSY NOISILY
IILNPPY NIPPILY
IILNPUV PULVINI
IILNRSV RIVLINS
IILNSST INSTILS
IILOPRT TRIPOLI
IILOPST PILOTIS
IILORTV VITRIOL
IILOSTV VIOLIST
IILPRVY PRIVILY
IILPSST PISTILS
IILPSTY TIPSILY
IILTTUY UTILITY
IILTTWY WITTILY
IIMMMNU MINIMUM
IIMMNSU MINIMUS

	MINIUMS
IIMNNOS	MINIONS
IIMNOSS	MISSION
IIMNOSU	IONIUMS
	NIMIOUS
IIMNOTX	MIXTION
IIMNPRT	IMPRINT
IIMOPSU	IMPIOUS
IIMOSST	MITOSIS
IIMOSSU	SIMIOUS
IIMRTTU	TRITIUM
IIMRTUV	TRIVIUM
IIMSSSZ	SIZISMS
IIMSSTT	TIMISTS
IIMSSTU	MISSUIT
IINNOOP	OPINION
IINNOPS	PINIONS
IINNOTU	UNITION
IINOPSS	ISOSPIN
	SINOPIS
IINORST	IRONIST
IINORSV	VIRINOS
	VIRIONS
IINORTT	INTROIT
IINOSSV	VISIONS
IINOSUV	INVIOUS
IINOTTU	TUITION
IINPPPS	PIPPINS
IINQRUY	INQUIRY
IINRTTY	TRINITY
IINSSST	INSISTS
IINSTTU	INTUITS
IINSTTW	INTWIST
	NITWITS
IIOOSTT	TOITOIS
IIOPRSS	PISSOIR
IIORSSV	VIROSIS
IIORSTV	IVORIST
	VISITOR
IIOSTTU	OUSTITI
IIPPSUU	PIUPIUS
IIPRSST	SPIRITS
	TRIPSIS
IIPRSTU	PITURIS
IIPRSTY	SPIRITY
IIPRTVY	PRIVITY
IIQSTUV	QIVIUTS
IIRRSTT	TIRRITS
IISSSTZ	SIZISTS
IJKLLOY	KILLJOY
IJKMOSU	MOUJIKS
IJKNOSS	JOSKINS
IJLLLOY	JOLLILY
IJLLOTY	JOLLITY
IJLMPUY	JUMPILY
IJLNOQU	JONQUIL
IJLNOTY	JOINTLY
IJMOSSS	JISSOMS
IJNNOTU	UNJOINT
IJNORSU	JUNIORS
IJRSSTU	JURISTS
IKKMNOU	KIKUMON
IKKNORT	KIRKTON
IKKORRS	KORKIRS
IKKSUUY	KIKUYUS
IKLLSTU	KILLUTS
IKLLSUY	SULKILY
IKLMNPU	LUMPKIN
IKLMOOS	LOOKISM
IKLMOSY	SMOKILY
IKLMRUY	MURKILY
IKLMSUY	MUSKILY
IKLNNSU	UNLINKS
IKLNOOS	SKOLION
IKLNOOT	KILOTON
IKLNOSU	ULIKONS
IKLNPSU	SKULPIN
	UPLINKS
IKLNRWY	WRINKLY
IKLOOTT	TOOLKIT
IKLOSSU	SOUSLIK
IKLSSSU	SUSLIKS
IKLSTTU	KITTULS
IKMNOOO	OKIMONO
IKMNOOS	KIMONOS
IKMNORS	MIKRONS
	MORKINS
IKMNOSW	MISKNOW
IKMNPPU	PUMPKIN
IKMNRSU	RUMKINS
IKMNRTU	TRINKUM
IKMOOST	MISTOOK
IKMOSSU	KOUMISS
IKMPRSS	SKRIMPS
IKNNPTU	UNPINKT
IKNNSTU	UNKNITS
IKNOOST	ISOKONT
IKNOPST	INKPOTS
	INKSPOT
IKNORSW	INWORKS
IKNPSTU	SPUTNIK
	UPKNITS
IKPRSSU	PRUSIKS
	SPRUIKS
IKPRSSY	KRYPSIS
ILLLOWY	LOWLILY
ILLMNOU	MULLION
ILLMNRU	MILLRUN
ILLMOOR	MOORILL
ILLMOSU	LOLIUMS
ILLMPUY	LUMPILY
ILLMSUU	LIMULUS
ILLNOQU	QUILLON
ILLNORU	RULLION
ILLNPUU	LUPULIN
ILLNSUW	UNWILLS
ILLNTUY	NULLITY
ILLOORZ	ZORILLO
ILLOPRY	PILLORY
ILLOPSW	PILLOWS
ILLOPWY	PILLOWY
ILLOSUV	VILLOUS
ILLOSUY	LOUSILY
ILLOSWW	WILLOWS
ILLOTXY	XYLITOL
ILLOUVV	VOLVULI
ILLOWWY	WILLOWY
ILLPPUY	PULPILY
ILLPSUV	PULVILS
ILLQSSU	SQUILLS
ILLRSUY	SURLILY
ILLSTUY	LUSTILY
ILMMRUY	RUMMILY
ILMMSUU	MIMULUS
ILMNOOT	MOONLIT
ILMNOSU	MOULINS
ILMNRSU	MURLINS
ILMNSSU	MUSLINS
ILMOORY	ROOMILY
ILMOOSS	MOLOSSI
ILMORTU	TURMOIL
ILMOSTY	MOISTLY
ILMPSTU	PLUMIST
ILMRSSY	LYRISMS
ILMSTUY	MUSTILY
ILMUYZZ	MUZZILY
ILNNSUY	SUNNILY
ILNOOPS	PLOSION
ILNOOPV	VOLPINO
ILNOOSS	SOLIONS
ILNOOST	LOTIONS
	SOLITON
ILNOPPS	POPLINS
ILNOPRU	PURLOIN
ILNOPST	PONTILS
ILNOPSU	UPSILON
ILNOPSY	YPSILON
ILNOQSU	QUINOLS
ILNORST	NOSTRIL
ILNORSU	SURLOIN
ILNORTU	TORULIN
ILNOSST	TONSILS
ILNOSSU	INSOULS
ILNOSTU	OILNUTS
	ULTIONS
ILNOSTY	STONILY
ILNOSWY	SNOWILY
ILNOTUV	VOLUTIN
ILNPRSU	PURLINS
ILNPSST	SPLINTS
ILNPSTU	UNSPILT
ILNRSTY	NITRYLS
ILNSSTU	INSULTS
ILNTTUY	NUTTILY
ILOOORS	ROSOLIO
ILOOPST	POLOIST
	TOPSOIL
ILOORST	LORIOTS
ILOORTY	OLITORY
ILOOSST	SOLOIST
ILOOSTY	SOOTILY
ILOOWYZ	WOOZILY
ILOPPSY	SOPPILY
ILOPRSY	PROSILY
ILOPSST	PISTOLS
	POSTILS
ILOPSSX	OXSLIPS
ILOPSTT	SPOTLIT
ILOPSUY	PIOUSLY
ILOQRSU	LIQUORS
ILORRSY	SORRILY
ILOSSTY	TOSSILY
	TYLOSIS
ILOSTTW	WITTOLS
ILPPSTU	PULPITS
ILPSTTU	UPTILTS
ILRSSTU	TRISULS
ILRSSTY	LYRISTS
ILRSTUY	RUSTILY
ILSSTTU	LUTISTS
ILSSTTY	STYLIST
IMMNOSS	MONISMS
	NOMISMS
IMMNOSU	MUSIMON
	OMNIUMS
IMMNOUU	MUONIUM
IMMOOSS	SIMOOMS
IMMOPTU	OPTIMUM
IMMOSSU	OSMIUMS
IMMSSTU	MUTISMS
	SUMMIST
	SUMMITS
IMNNNOU	MUNNION
IMNNOOR	NORIMON
IMNNOSW	MINNOWS
IMNNSTU	MUNTINS
IMNOOPP	POMPION
IMNOOPT	TOMPION
IMNOORR	MORRION
IMNOORS	MORIONS
IMNOORT	MONITOR
	TROMINO
IMNOOSS	MONOSIS
	SIMOONS
IMNOOST	MOTIONS
IMNOOSU	OMINOUS
IMNOOSY	ISONOMY
IMNOOUX	OXONIUM
IMNOPPU	PUMPION
IMNORRU	MURRION
IMNORTY	TRIONYM
IMNOSST	MONISTS
IMNOSSY	MYOSINS
IMNOSVY	VISNOMY
IMNRRSU	MURRINS
IMNRSTU	UNTRIMS
IMOOPRX	PROXIMO
IMOOSSS	OSMOSIS
IMOOSSU	OSMIOUS
IMOOSTV	VOMITOS
IMOPRSS	PORISMS
IMOPRST	IMPORTS
	TROPISM
IMOPRSV	IMPROVS
IMOPRTU	PROTIUM
IMOPSST	IMPOSTS
IMOPSTU	UTOPISM
IMORRRS	MIRRORS
IMORSTU	TOURISM
IMORSTY	TRISOMY
IMOSSYZ	ZYMOSIS
IMOSTTT	TOMTITS
IMOSTUV	VOMITUS
IMOSTUW	OUTSWIM
IMPRSSU	PURISMS
IMPSSTU	SUMPITS
IMQRSSU	SQUIRMS
IMQRSUY	SQUIRMY
IMRSSTU	SISTRUM
	TRISMUS
	TRUISMS
IMRTTUY	YTTRIUM
INNNORU	RUNNION
INNOOPS	OPSONIN
INNOOST	NOTIONS
INNORST	INTRONS
INNOSSU	UNISONS
INNOSTU	NONSUIT
INNOSWW	WINNOWS
INNQSUY	SQUINNY
INOOPRT	PORTION
INOOPSS	POISONS
	POISSON
INOOPST	OPTIONS
	POSITON
	POTIONS
INOORSS	ORISONS
INOORST	ISOTRON
	NITROSO
	TORSION

INOORSZ ZORINOS
INOORTT TORTONI
INOOSST TOISONS
INOOSUX NOXIOUS
INOPPRS POPRINS
INOPPST TOPSPIN
INOPRSS PRISONS
INOPSST PISTONS
INOPSSU POUSSIN
SPINOUS
INOPSTT TINPOTS
INOPSTU SPINOUT
INORSTT TRITONS
INORSTU NITROUS
TURIONS
INORSUU RUINOUS
URINOUS
INORSUV UNVISOR
INOSSTU USTIONS
INOSSUU SINUOUS
INOSTUW OUTWINS
INPRSST SPRINTS
INPRSTU TURNIPS
UNSTRIP
INPRSTY TRYPSIN
INQSSTU SQUINTS
INRSTTU INTRUST
INSSTUU SUNSUIT
UNSUITS
INSTTUW UNTWIST
INTTUWY UNWITTY
IOOPRSS POROSIS
IOOPRSV PROVISO
IOOPSTY ISOTOPY
IOORSSS SOROSIS
IOORSTT RISOTTO
IOORSTU RIOTOUS
IOOSSSS SISSOOS
IOPPPRT PITPROP
IOPPPST POPPITS
IOPPRST RIPSTOP
IOPPSTT TIPTOPS
IOPRSSY PYROSIS
IOPRSTT PROTIST
TROPIST
IOPSTTU UTOPIST
IOQRTTU QUITTOR
IOQSSTU QUOISTS
IORRSTW WORRITS
IORRSZZ RIZZORS
IORRTTX TORTRIX
IORSSTU SUITORS
TSOURIS
IORSTTU TOURIST
IORSTTW TWISTOR
IOSSSTT TSOTSIS
IOSSTTU OUTSITS
IOSTTUW OUTWITS
IPRRSTU IRRUPTS
STIRRUP
IPRSSTU PURISTS
SPRUITS
UPRISTS
IPRSTUU PURSUIT
IPSSSTY STYPSIS
IPSSTTY TYPISTS
IPSTTTU TITTUPS
IPTTTUY TITTUPY
IQRRSSU SQUIRRS
IQRSSTU SQUIRTS
JMOPTUU OUTJUMP
JNNOSTU JOTUNNS
JNOORSU JOURNOS
SOJOURN
JOOPPSY POPJOYS
JOSTTUU OUTJUTS
KKLMSUU MUKLUKS
KKNRSUU KUNKURS
KLLMOSU MOLLUSK
KLOOOTU LOOKOUT
OUTLOOK
KLOOPSU UPLOOKS
KMPRSSU SKRUMPS
KNNNOUW UNKNOWN
KNNOSTU UNKNOTS
KNOOPTT TOPKNOT
KNOPRTY KRYPTON
KNORRTY KRYTRON
KNORSUW UNWORKS
KOOOTTU OUTTOOK
KOOPRTW WORKTOP
KOORTUW OUTWORK
KOOSSUU SOUKOUS
KOOSTWW KOWTOWS
KORTTUW TUTWORK
LLLMMUU MULMULL
LLLOOPS LOLLOPS
LLMMSUU MULMULS
LLMOOPR ROLLMOP
LLMPPUY PLUMPLY
LLNORSU UNROLLS
LLOOPRT TROLLOP
LLOORTU ROLLOUT
LLOOSTU TOLUOLS
LLOPRSU UPROLLS
LLORSST STROLLS
LMMSTUU MULTUMS
LMOORSU ORMOLUS
LMOOSTY TOYLSOM
LMOPSUU PLUMOUS
LMORSSU MUSROLS
LMRSTUU LUSTRUM
LMSTTUU TUMULTS
LMSTUUU TUMULUS
LNNOPSU NONPLUS
LNOOPTU PULTOON
LNOOSST STOLONS
LNOPSTU PLUTONS
PULTONS
LNOSSUU UNSOULS
LNPSTUU PULTUNS
LNRTUUV VULTURN
LNRTUUY UNTRULY
LOOORS OLOROSO
LOOORST ROTOLOS
LOOSSTV VOLOSTS
LOPPRSY PROPYLS
LOPPSUU PULPOUS
LOPPSUY POLYPUS
LOPRSTY PROTYLS
LOPRSUY PYLORUS
LOPRTUY POULTRY
LORSTTY TROTYLS
LORSTUU TORULUS
LOSTTUY STOUTLY
LPRSSUU SURPLUS
MMNOSSU MUSMONS
SUMMONS
MMOOPPS POMPOMS
MMOOSTT MOTMOTS
MMOPSTY SYMPTOM
MMRRSUU MURMURS
MMSTUUU MUTUUMS
MNNOOOS MONSOON
MNNOSYY SYNONYM
MNNOTUU UNMOUNT
MNOOOPP POMPOON
MNOOOYZ ZOONOMY
MNOOPPS POMPONS
MNOOPST TOMPONS
MNOOPTY TOPONYM
MNOORSU UNMOORS
MNOOSTU MOUTONS
MNOOSTW TOWMONS
MNOOSUY ONYMOUS
MNOOTTW TOWMONT
MNORSTU NOSTRUM
MNOSTTU MUTTONS
MNOTTUY MUTTONY
MOOOTYZ ZOOTOMY
MOOPPSU POMPOUS
MOOPRSY POMROYS
MOOPSSU OPOSSUM
MOOPSTT TOPMOST
MOORRSW MORROWS
MOOSTTU OUTMOST
MOPPRST PROMPTS
MOPSSSU POSSUMS
MOPSSUU SPUMOUS
MOQRSUU QUORUMS
MOQSTUU QUOTUMS
MORRSTU ROSTRUM
MORRSUU RUMOURS
MORSTUU TUMOURS
MOSSTTU UTMOSTS
MOSSTUU OUTSUMS
MOSTUUW OUTSWUM
NNNSUUY UNSUNNY
NNOOOPT PONTOON
NNOOPRU PRONOUN
NNOOPSS SPONSON
NNOOPST PONTONS
NNOORSY RONYONS
NNORSUW UNSWORN
NNOSSUY UNSONSY
NNOSTYY SYNTONY
NNRSTUU UNTURNS
NOOPRSS SPONSOR
NOOPRST PROTONS
NOOPSSY POYSONS
NOORSST TONSORS
NOORSTU UNROOST
UNROOTS
NOORTUW OUTWORN
NOPPRSU UNPROPS
NOPSSTU SUNSPOT
UNSTOPS
NOPSTUW UPTOWNS
NORSTUU OUTRUNS
NORTTUU OUTTURN
TURNOUT
NOSSTUW UNSTOWS
NPRSTUU UPTURNS
NRSSTTU STRUNTS
NRSSTUU STURNUS
UNTRUSS
NRSTTUU UNTRUST
OOOOPRT POTOROO
OOOOSZZ ZOOZOOS
OOOPRTU OUTROOP
OOORTTU OUTROOT
OOPRRST TORPORS
OOPRSSU SOURSOP
OOPRSTU PORTOUS
UPROOTS
OOPRSTV PROVOST
OOPRTTU OUTPORT
OOPRTUU OUTPOUR
OOPSSTT TOSSPOT
OOPSTTU OUTPOST
OUTTOPS
OOPSWWW POWWOWS
OORRSSW SORROWS
OORSTUU ROUTOUS
OPPRRTU PURPORT
OPPRSTU SUPPORT
OPPRSTY STROPPY
OPPRSUY PYROPUS
OPRSSTU SPROUTS
STROUPS
STUPORS
OPSTTUU OUTPUTS
ORSSTTU STROUTS
ORSSUUU USUROUS
ORSTTUU SURTOUT

8-LETTER ANAGRAMS

AAAACCRR	CARACARA
AAAACJRR	JARARACA
AAAACNRS	ANASARCA
AAAADMTV	AMADAVAT
AAAADNPS	APADANAS
AAAADTVV	AVADAVAT
AAAAHJMR	MAHARAJA
AAAAIMPR	ARAPAIMA
AAAAIRTX	ATARAXIA
AAAAJKRR	JARARAKA
AAAAKKMT	TAKAMAKA
AAAAKKNT	KATAKANA
AAAALSTY	ATALAYAS
AAAAMMTT	MATAMATA
AAAARRSS	SASARARA
AAABBCLS	CABBALAS
AAABBELT	ABATABLE
AAABBHKL	KABBALAH
AAABBILT	ABBATIAL
AAABBKLS	KABBALAS
AAABCCRS	BACCARAS
AAABCCRT	BACCARAT
AAABCHLS	CALABASH
AAABCHMU	MACAHUBA
AAABCINT	ANABATIC
AAABCIRS	ARABICAS
AAABCLSV	BACLAVAS
AAABCNRR	BARRACAN
	BARRANCA
AAABCNRS	BARACANS
AAABCNRU	CARNAUBA
AAABCORS	CARABAOS
AAABCPRY	CAPYBARA
AAABCSTW	CATAWBAS
AAABDEST	DATABASE
AAABDKNT	DATABANK
AAABDLMS	LAMBADAS
AAABDNNN	BANDANNA
AAABDNNS	BANDANAS
AAABDNRS	SARABAND
AAABDNRT	ABRADANT
AAABEGHL	GALABEAH
AAABEGLL	GALLABEA
AAABEGLS	GALABEAS
AAABEHNR	HABANERA
AAABEHRT	BARATHEA
AAABEMPR	PARABEMA
AAABENSS	ANABASES
AAABFLLS	FALBALAS
AAABGHIL	GALABIAH
AAABGILL	GALLABIA
AAABGILS	GALABIAS
AAABGLOR	ALGAROBA
AAABGMNQ	MBAQANGA
AAABGRTU	RUTABAGA
AAABHLQS	QABALAHS
AAABILTT	BATTALIA
AAABINSS	ANABASIS
AAABIPSS	PIASSABA
AAABKLSV	BAKLAVAS
AAABKPSS	BAASSKAP
AAABLLSW	WALLABAS
AAABLMOS	ABOMASAL
AAABLOPR	PARABOLA
AAABLPRS	PALABRAS
AAABMSST	MASTABAS
AAABNNRS	RABANNAS
AAABORRS	ARAROBAS
AAACCELN	CALCANEA
AAACCEPR	CARAPACE
AAACCILR	CALCARIA
AAACCIMM	CAIMACAM
AAACCLRS	CARACALS
AAACCRSS	CASCARAS
AAACCRTT	CATARACT
AAACDEIM	ACADEMIA
AAACDEQU	AQUACADE
AAACDETU	ACAUDATE
AAACDILR	CALDARIA
AAACDINR	ACARIDAN
AAACDKLY	LACKADAY
AAACDMMS	MACADAMS
AAACDNNO	ANACONDA
AAACDNRS	SANDARAC
AAACDOTV	ADVOCAAT
AAACEGNT	AGACANTE
AAACEGTU	AGUACATE
AAACEHIN	ACHAENIA
AAACEHLT	CALATHEA
AAACEHLZ	CHALAZAE
AAACELNT	ANALECTA
AAACELST	CATALASE
AAACENNP	PANACEAN
AAACENPS	PANACEAS
AAACEPRV	PRAECAVA
AAACGINT	CAATINGA
AAACGLSW	SCALAWAG
AAACGMNP	CAMPAGNA
AAACHILZ	CHALAZIA
AAACHIPS	APHASIAC
AAACHLNR	ANARCHAL
AAACHLSZ	CHALAZAS
AAACHNST	ACANTHAS
AAACHRSY	ACHARYAS
AAACILMN	MANIACAL
AAACILMR	CALAMARI
AAACILMS	MALACIAS
AAACILRV	CALVARIA
AAACILSY	CALISAYA
AAACIMRS	CARIAMAS
AAACINPS	ACAPNIAS
AAACINTV	CAVATINA
AAACIPSU	SAPUCAIA
AAACIRRS	SACRARIA
AAACIRTX	ATARAXIC
AAACJMRS	JACAMARS
AAACKMRT	TAMARACK
AAACLLSV	CAVALLAS
AAACLMNS	ALMANACS
	MANCALAS
AAACLMRY	CALAMARY
AAACLNST	CANTALAS
AAACLPST	CATALPAS
AAACLRST	ALCATRAS
AAACLRSZ	ALCAZARS
AAACMNPS	CAMPANAS
AAACMRSS	MACASSAR
	MASCARAS
AAACMRSU	AMARACUS
AAACNNRS	CARANNAS
AAACNPST	CATAPANS
AAACNRST	NACARATS
AAACNRSU	CARAUNAS
AAACNRSV	CARAVANS
AAACNSST	CANASTAS
AAACNSTT	CANTATAS
AAACRRWY	CARRAWAY
AAACRSWY	CARAWAYS
AAACSSST	CASSATAS
AAACSSSV	CASSAVAS
AAACSSTT	CATASTAS
AAACSTWY	CASTAWAY
AAADEGNP	APANAGED
AAADELMS	ALAMEDAS
	SALAAMED
AAADENTV	VANADATE
AAADEPRT	TAPADERA
AAADFRSY	FARADAYS
AAADGIMM	GAMMADIA
AAADGLMY	AMYGDALA
AAADHMRS	ADHARMAS
	MADRASAH
AAADHNRT	THANADAR
AAADIILR	RADIALIA
AAADILRU	ADULARIA
AAADIMNY	ADYNAMIA
AAADIRST	DATARIAS
	RADIATAS
AAADJMRS	JAMADARS
AAADKLMN	KALAMDAN
AAADKRRV	AARDVARK
AAADLMNQ	QALAMDAN
AAADLMNS	MANDALAS
AAADLMSW	WADMAALS
AAADMNST	ADAMANTS
AAADMNTU	TAMANDUA
AAADMORT	MATADORA
AAADMRSS	MADRASAS
	MADRASSA
AAADNRSS	SARDANAS
AAADNRST	TANADARS
AAAEGISS	ASSEGAAI
AAAEGLMX	MALAXAGE
AAAEGLRT	ALTARAGE
AAAEGLST	GALATEAS
AAAEGNPP	APPANAGE
AAAEGNPS	APANAGES
AAAEGRST	GASTRAEA
AAAEHLST	ALTHAEAS
AAAEHMNT	ANATHEMA
AAAEHNPS	ANAPHASE
AAAEIMNS	ANAEMIAS
AAAEKKRT	KARATEKA
AAAEKTWY	TAKEAWAY
AAAELMMN	ANALEMMA
AAAELMPT	PALAMATE
AAAELMTX	MALAXATE
AAAELRTV	LAVATERA
AAAENNSS	ANANASES
AAAENOPR	PARANOEA
AAAENPRV	PARAVANE
AAAENPST	ANAPAEST
AAAENSST	ANATASES
AAAEPRST	SEPARATA
AAAERSWY	AREAWAYS
AAAERTWY	TEARAWAY
AAAFFLLS	ALFALFAS
AAAFINST	FANTASIA
AAAFINUV	AVIFAUNA
AAAFIRST	RATAFIAS
AAAFNRSS	SARAFANS
AAAFRSWY	FARAWAYS
AAAGGLLN	GALANGAL
AAAGGLNS	GALANGAS
AAAGGLOP	GALAPAGO
AAAGHINR	HIRAGANA
AAAGHIPR	AGRAPHIA
AAAGHIPS	APHAGIAS
AAAGHLNS	LANGAHAS
AAAGHNST	ATAGHANS
AAAGHNTY	YATAGHAN
AAAGILPT	PATAGIAL
AAAGILRT	ALIGARTA
AAAGIMMT	GAMMATIA
AAAGINRR	AGRARIAN
AAAGINSZ	GAZANIAS
AAAGISSS	ASSAGAIS
AAAGLMMS	AMALGAMS
AAAGLMNS	NAGMAALS
AAAGLNSS	LASAGNAS
AAAGLRRW	WARRAGAL
AAAGLRST	ASTRAGAL
AAAGMNRS	ANAGRAMS
AAAGMPRR	PARAGRAM
AAAGNOPR	ARAPONGA
AAAGNPRS	PARASANG
	PARGANAS
AAAGNPRU	ARAPUNGA
AAAGNRST	TANAGRAS
AAAGNRSU	GUARANAS
AAAGNSTY	YATAGANS
AAAHHLSV	HALAVAHS
AAAHIKSW	KAHAWAIS
AAAHIMNR	MAHARANI
AAAHIMNS	SHAMIANA
AAAHIMRT	HAMARTIA
AAAHINPR	RAPHANIA
AAAHIPSS	APHASIAS
AAAHJKSW	KAJAWAHS
AAAHKMNS	KHANSAMA
AAAHKRSS	RAKSHASA
AAAHLMRS	HARMALAS
AAAHLNNS	ALANNAHS
AAAHMMST	MAHATMAS
AAAHMNRT	AMARANTH
AAAHMRSS	ASHRAMAS
AAAHMSST	TAMASHAS
AAAHNNSV	SAVANNAH
AAAHNOPR	ANAPHORA
AAAHNSTY	ATHANASY
AAAHPRST	PARATHAS
AAAHRSTW	WARATAHS
AAAHTTWY	THATAWAY
AAAIINPR	APIARIAN
AAAIKKMM	KAIMAKAM
AAAILLMR	MALARIAL
AAAILLPT	PALATIAL
AAAILMNR	MALARIAN
AAAILMRS	MALARIAS
AAAILMSV	MALVASIA
AAAILNRU	AULARIAN
AAAILPRV	PARAVAIL
AAAILPSS	APLASIAS
AAAILRST	SALARIAT

AAAIMMQQ	QAIMAQAM
AAAIMMST	MIASMATA
AAAIMNST	AMANITAS
AAAINNRR	RANARIAN
AAAINOPR	PARANOIA
AAAINQRU	AQUARIAN
AAAIPRSX	APRAXIAS
AAAIPSSV	PIASSAVA
AAAKKTZZ	KAZATZKA
AAAKMNRS	NAMASKAR
AAAKOSWY	SOAKAWAY
AAALLPRX	PARALLAX
AAALLPST	PALATALS
AAALNNPT	PLATANNA
AAALNNST	LANTANAS
AAALNPRT	RATAPLAN
AAALNPST	APLANATS
AAALNRTT	TARLATAN
AAALPRST	SATRAPAL
AAALRRSY	ARRAYALS
AAALSWYY	LAYAWAYS
AAAMNOPR	PANORAMA
AAAMNRRY	YARRAMAN
AAAMNRST	AMARANTS
AAAMNSTY	MANYATAS
AAAMNTTY	MANYATTA
AAAMORST	TAMARAOS
AAAMOTTU	AUTOMATA
AAAMPRST	PATAMARS
AAAMRRSZ	ZAMARRAS
AAAMRSSS	SAMSARAS
AAAMRSTU	TAMARAUS
AAAMRTTU	TRAUMATA
AAAMRTZZ	RAZMATAZ
AAANNSSV	SAVANNAS
AAANNSTT	ANNATTAS
AAANOPRZ	PARAZOAN
AAANORSY	SAYONARA
AAANPRTV	PARAVANT
AAANQTUU	AQUANAUT
AAANRSTT	TANTARAS
	TARANTAS
	TARTANAS
AAAORSWY	SOARAWAY
AAAPPRST	APPARATS
AAAPQRTU	PARAQUAT
AAARSTTU	TUATARAS
AAASTWYY	STAYAWAY
AABBBDEK	KABABBED
AABBCDEG	CABBAGED
AABBCDKN	BACKBAND
AABBCDRS	SCABBARD
AABBCEGS	CABBAGES
AABBCEIS	ABBACIES
AABBCEKR	BAREBACK
AABBCEKT	BACKBEAT
AABBCINR	BARBICAN
AABBCIRR	BARBARIC
AABBCIST	SABBATIC
AABBCORS	BARBASCO
AABBDENS	BASEBAND
AABBDERT	BARBATED
AABBDGRS	GABBARDS
AABBEELR	BEARABLE
AABBEELT	BEATABLE
AABBEGNS	BEANBAGS
AABBEILL	BAILABLE
AABBEKLN	BANKABLE
AABBELLM	BLAMABLE
AABBELLS	BASEBALL
AABBELRY	BEARABLY
AABBEORT	BAREBOAT
AABBGRST	GABBARTS
AABBHKSU	BABUSHKA
AABBIILL	BILABIAL
AABBILRT	BARBITAL
AABBIRSU	BABIRUSA
AABBLLMY	BLAMABLY
AABBLORS	BARBOLAS
AABBLSSU	SUBBASAL
AABBMMOZ	ZAMBOMBA
AABBSSSU	BABASSUS
AABCCCHI	BACCHIAC
AABCCEHK	BACKACHE
AABCCELS	CASCABEL
AABCCERT	BRACCATE
AABCCHIN	BACCHIAN
AABCCHIS	BISCACHA
AABCCHIZ	BIZCACHA
AABCCHKT	BACKCHAT
AABCCHNT	BACCHANT
AABCCINN	CANNABIC
AABCCKKP	BACKPACK
AABCCKLP	BLACKCAP
AABCCKLW	CLAWBACK
AABCCMOT	CATACOMB
AABCDEIN	ABIDANCE
AABCDEIT	ABDICATE
AABCDELL	CABALLED
AABCDELN	BALANCED
AABCDHKN	BACKHAND
AABCDHKR	HARDBACK
AABCDIIS	DIABASIC
AABCDINT	ABDICANT
AABCDIRS	CARABIDS
AABCDKLN	BACKLAND
AABCDKRW	BACKWARD
	DRAWBACK
AABCDKRY	BACKYARD
AABCDNRR	BRANCARD
AABCEENY	ABEYANCE
AABCEERS	SCARABEE
AABCEERT	ACERBATE
AABCEGOT	CABOTAGE
AABCEHNR	BARCHANE
AABCEILM	AMICABLE
AABCEIMN	AMBIANCE
AABCEINR	CARABINE
AABCEIRT	BACTERIA
AABCEKLM	CLAMBAKE
AABCEKLR	LACEBARK
AABCELLP	PLACABLE
AABCELLR	CABALLER
AABCELLS	SCALABLE
AABCELNR	BALANCER
	BARNACLE
AABCELNS	BALANCES
AABCELOR	ALBACORE
AABCELPR	CAPABLER
AABCELRT	BRACTEAL
AABCELWY	CABLEWAY
AABCEMRV	VAMBRACE
AABCENYY	ABEYANCY
AABCEORT	BOATRACE
AABCERRS	BARRACES
AABCERST	ABREACTS
	CABARETS
AABCERTT	CABRETTA
AABCESSU	ABACUSES
AABCFIIL	BIFACIAL
AABCFKLL	BACKFALL
AABCFKLT	FLATBACK
AABCFKST	FASTBACK
AABCHILR	BRACHIAL
AABCHINR	BRANCHIA
AABCHKLS	BACKLASH
AABCHKRS	SHABRACK
AABCHKSW	BACKWASH
AABCHLOO	COOLABAH
AABCHMRY	CHAMBRAY
AABCHNRS	BARCHANS
AABCIILS	BASILICA
AABCIKLT	TAILBACK
AABCILLR	BACILLAR
AABCILMS	BALSAMIC
	CABALISM
AABCILMY	AMICABLY
AABCILNN	CANNIBAL
AABCILNO	ANABOLIC
AABCILST	BASALTIC
	CABALIST
AABCINNN	CANNABIN
AABCINNR	CINNABAR
AABCINNS	CANNABIS
AABCINRS	CARABINS
AABCINSU	BANAUSIC
AABCIOPS	COPAIBAS
AABCIRSS	BRASSICA
AABCISSS	ABSCISSA
AABCISTX	TAXICABS
AABCKKLT	TALKBACK
AABCKLNO	LOANBACK
AABCKLPY	PLAYBACK
AABCKLSY	LAYBACKS
AABCKNNS	CANBANKS
AABCKPRT	BRATPACK
AABCKPSY	BACKPAYS
	PAYBACKS
AABCKRRS	BARRACKS
AABCKSSW	BACKSAWS
AABCKSWY	SWAYBACK
AABCLLLO	COALBALL
AABCLLLY	BALLCLAY
AABCLLPY	PLACABLY
AABCLMSU	CALUMBAS
AABCLNUU	CUNABULA
AABCLRRY	CARBARYL
AABCMSSU	SAMBUCAS
AABCNORR	BARRANCO
AABCORST	ABACTORS
	ACROBATS
AABCOSTT	CATBOATS
AABCRSTT	ABSTRACT
AABCSTTU	CATTABUS
AABDDEGN	BANDAGED
AABDDEHN	HEADBAND
AABDDEIR	ABRAIDED
AABDDELL	BALLADED
AABDDENR	BRANDADE
AABDDESS	BADASSED
AABDDIKS	KABADDIS
AABDDLNS	BADLANDS
AABDDMOR	DAMBOARD
AABDEEHL	BEHEADAL
AABDEELR	READABLE
AABDEELT	DATEABLE
	DEALBATE
AABDEELV	EVADABLE
AABDEERY	BAYADERE
AABDEGIN	BADINAGE
AABDEGIR	BIGARADE
AABDEGLR	GRADABLE
AABDEGNS	BANDAGES
AABDEHHI	DAHABIEH
AABDEHKR	HARDBAKE
AABDEHMR	HARDBEAM
AABDEILN	BALADINE
AABDEIOU	ABOIDEAU
AABDEIRS	ARABISED
AABDEIRZ	ARABIZED
AABDEISS	DIABASES
AABDEJLL	DJELLABA
AABDEJNX	BANJAXED
AABDEKRY	DAYBREAK
AABDELLS	BALLADES
AABDELLT	BALLATED
AABDELLU	LAUDABLE
AABDELMN	DAMNABLE
AABDELMS	BALSAMED
AABDELOR	ADORABLE
AABDELPR	PARABLED
AABDELPT	BALDPATE
AABDELRS	BASELARD
AABDELRT	TRADABLE
AABDELRW	DRAWABLE
AABDELRY	READABLY
AABDELSW	SAWBLADE
AABDEMNS	BEADSMAN
AABDENTU	UNABATED
AABDENUX	BANDEAUX
AABDENVW	WAVEBAND
AABDEORS	SEABOARD
AABDEORT	TEABOARD
AABDERRT	TABERDAR
AABDERRW	BEARWARD
AABDERTT	RABATTED
AABDERTV	VARTABED
AABDERWY	WAYBREAD
AABDESSS	BADASSES
AABDFHLN	FAHLBAND
AABDGHNS	HANDBAGS
AABDGINN	ABANDING
AABDGINR	ABRADING
AABDGMOS	GAMBADOS
AABDGNOV	VAGABOND
AABDGNSS	SANDBAGS
AABDGORR	GARBOARD
AABDGOTU	GADABOUT
AABDHLLR	HARDBALL
AABDHNST	HATBANDS
AABDHNSY	HAYBANDS
AABDHRSU	SUBAHDAR
AABDIILS	BASIDIAL
AABDIKRS	BIDARKAS
AABDILLN	BALLADIN
AABDILNS	BALADINS
AABDIMNO	ABDOMINA
AABDIMNR	MADBRAIN
AABDIMRS	BARMAIDS
AABDINNR	RAINBAND
AABDINST	TABANIDS
AABDKNNS	SANDBANK
AABDLLRY	BALLADRY
AABDLLUY	LAUDABLY
AABDLMNU	LABDANUM
AABDLMNY	DAMNABLY
AABDLNPT	PLATBAND
AABDLNSS	SALBANDS
AABDLORR	LARBOARD
AABDLORY	ADORABLY

AABDLRSW	BRADAWLS
AABDMNNS	BANDSMAN
AABDMNNY	BANDYMAN
AABDMNRS	ARMBANDS
AABDNNOS	ABANDONS
AABDNNTU	ABUNDANT
AABDNORS	BANDORAS
AABDNRRY	BARNYARD
AABDNRSU	BANDURAS
AABDORSV	BRAVADOS
AABDORWY	BROADWAY
	WAYBOARD
AABDRRSS	BRASSARD
AABDRRSW	DRAWBARS
AABDRSST	BASTARDS
AABDRSSU	SUBADARS
AABDRSTY	BASTARDY
AABEEGKR	BREAKAGE
AABEEGNT	ABNEGATE
AABEEHLL	HEALABLE
AABEEHLT	HATEABLE
AABEEHMR	HARAMBEE
AABEEKLM	MAKEABLE
AABEEKLT	TAKEABLE
AABEEKMT	BAKEMEAT
	MAKEBATE
AABEEKRW	BAKEWARE
AABEELLS	LEASABLE
	SALEABLE
AABEELMN	AMENABLE
	NAMEABLE
AABEELMT	TAMEABLE
AABEELPT	TAPEABLE
AABEELRS	ERASABLE
AABEELRT	RATEABLE
	TEARABLE
AABEELRW	WEARABLE
AABEELST	EATABLES
AABEEMPR	ABAMPERE
AABEENNW	WANNABEE
AABEENOR	ANAEROBE
AABEERRT	ABERRATE
AABEERSZ	ZAREEBAS
AABEERTT	TRABEATE
AABEFFNS	BEFFANAS
AABEFGSU	AUFGABES
AABEFLLL	FLABELLA
AABEFLMU	FLAMBEAU
AABEGGGS	BAGGAGES
AABEGGRS	GARBAGES
AABEGHLN	HANGABLE
AABEGHNR	BERGHAAN
AABEGILN	GAINABLE
AABEGINR	ABEARING
AABEGLLL	GLABELLA
AABEGLRS	ALGEBRAS
AABEGLRT	GLABRATE
AABEGLRU	ARGUABLE
AABEGMNR	BARGEMAN
AABEGMNY	MANGABEY
AABEGMRS	BERGAMAS
	MEGABARS
AABEGMRT	BREGMATA
AABEGMTT	GAMBETTA
AABEGNOR	BARONAGE
AABEGORT	ABROGATE
AABEGOST	SABOTAGE
AABEGRRS	BAGARRES
	BARRAGES
AABEGSSS	BAGASSES
AABEGSSU	ABUSAGES
AABEHIRR	HERBARIA
AABEHKLS	SHAKABLE
AABEHLMS	SHAMABLE
AABEHLOT	OATHABLE
AABEHLPS	SHAPABLE
AABEHLPT	ALPHABET
AABEHLRW	WARHABLE
AABEHLSW	WASHABLE
AABEHNST	ABTHANES
AABEIKNS	IKEBANAS
AABEILLM	MAILABLE
AABEILLS	ISABELLA
	SAILABLE
AABEILNR	INARABLE
AABEILNS	BANALISE
AABEILNZ	BANALIZE
AABEILRS	RAISABLE
AABEILRV	VARIABLE
AABEILST	BALISTAE
	LABIATES
	SATIABLE
AABEILTV	ABLATIVE
AABEINOZ	ZABAIONE
AABEINRT	RABATINE
AABEINST	BASANITE
AABEIOTU	ABOITEAU
AABEIRSS	AIRBASES
	ARABISES
AABEIRSV	ABRASIVE
AABEIRSZ	ARABIZES
AABEIRTU	AUBRETIA
	AUBRIETA
AABEJLLS	JELLABAS
AABEJMUX	JAMBEAUX
AABEJNSX	BANJAXES
AABEKLLT	TALKABLE
AABEKLLW	WALKABLE
AABEKMNR	BRAKEMAN
AABEKNSS	SEABANKS
AABEKPRR	PARBREAK
AABEKRRS	BARESARK
AABELLMT	MEATBALL
AABELLNO	LOANABLE
AABELLPP	PALPABLE
AABELLPS	LAPSABLE
AABELLPY	PLAYABLE
AABELLSS	SABELLAS
AABELLSV	SALVABLE
AABELLSY	SALEABLY
AABELLUV	VALUABLE
AABELMNY	AMENABLY
AABELMST	BLASTEMA
	LAMBASTE
AABELMSU	AMUSABLE
AABELMTU	AMBULATE
AABELNNT	TANNABLE
AABELNOS	ABALONES
AABELNPS	ANABLEPS
AABELNPT	PANTABLE
AABELNRY	BALNEARY
AABELNST	BANALEST
AABELOPR	PARABOLE
AABELORR	ARBOREAL
AABELOSV	LAVABOES
AABELOVW	AVOWABLE
AABELPPT	TAPPABLE
AABELPRS	PARABLES
	SPARABLE
AABELPSS	PASSABLE
AABELRST	ARBALEST
AABELRTY	BETRAYAL
	RATEABLY
AABELSTT	ABETTALS
	STATABLE
	TASTABLE
AABELSTW	WASTABLE
AABELTTU	TABULATE
AABELTUX	TABLEAUX
AABENNSW	WANNABES
AABENRRT	ABERRANT
AABENRST	ANTBEARS
	RATSBANE
AABEORRT	ARBORETA
AABEORST	RABATOES
AABERSSU	SUBAREAS
AABERSTT	RABATTES
	TABARETS
AABERSTU	ABATURES
AABESZZZ	BAZAZZES
AABFILUX	FABLIAUX
AABFLLST	FASTBALL
AABFLOTT	FALTBOAT
	FLATBOAT
AABGGNOT	TABOGGAN
AABGGRRT	BRAGGART
AABGHINS	ABASHING
AABGHNRS	BHANGRAS
AABGHNSS	NASHGABS
AABGIILS	ABIGAILS
AABGILMS	MAILBAGS
AABGILNT	ABLATING
AABGIMNS	SAMBAING
AABGINRS	BARGAINS
AABGINRY	ABRAYING
AABGLLLO	GOALBALL
AABGLLRY	BALLYRAG
AABGLMNU	GALBANUM
AABGLRUY	ARGUABLY
AABGMORR	BAROGRAM
AABGNORZ	GARBANZO
AABHHISS	SAHIBAHS
AABHHKSS	SABKHAHS
AABHHORU	BROUHAHA
AABHHRSU	BRUHAHAS
AABHIINU	BAUHINIA
AABHIJMY	JAMBIYAH
AABHILTU	HABITUAL
AABHINST	HABITANS
AABHINTT	HABITANT
AABHIRST	TABASHIR
AABHISTT	HABITATS
AABHKNRS	BARKHANS
AABHKSST	SABKHATS
AABHLLSW	WASHBALL
AABHNOTU	AUTOBAHN
AABHQSSU	SQUABASH
AABHRRSU	SURBAHAR
AABIJMSY	JAMBIYAS
AABIKNSS	BANKSIAS
AABILLLY	LABIALLY
AABILLRS	BARILLAS
AABILLST	BALLISTA
AABILMNS	BAILSMAN
AABILMNU	BIMANUAL
AABILNNU	BIANNUAL
AABILNOR	BARONIAL
AABILNOT	ABLATION
AABILNRU	BINAURAL
AABILNTY	BANALITY
AABILOSU	ABOULIAS
AABILOTT	BOATTAIL
AABILRRT	ARBITRAL
AABILRST	ARBALIST
AABILRVY	VARIABLY
AABILSST	BALISTAS
AABIMMRS	MARIMBAS
AABIMNNO	BONAMANI
AABIMNOS	BONAMIAS
AABIMNRU	MANUBRIA
AABIMORS	AMBROSIA
AABIMRSU	SIMARUBA
AABINNPR	BRAINPAN
AABINORS	ABRASION
AABINOSU	OUABAINS
AABINRST	ATABRINS
	BARTISAN
AABINRTZ	BARTIZAN
AABINSST	ABSTAINS
AABIORRS	SORBARIA
AABIORTT	ABATTOIR
AABIOSSY	BIOASSAY
AABIPSUX	PAXIUBAS
AABIRTUY	RUBAIYAT
AABJLMNO	JAMBOLAN
AABKLLPR	BALLPARK
AABKMNNS	BANKSMAN
AABKNRST	TANBARKS
AABKOOSZ	BAZOOKAS
AABKOPRS	SOAPBARK
AABLLMOR	BALMORAL
AABLLNST	BALLANTS
AABLLPPY	PALPABLY
AABLLPST	PATBALLS
AABLLSST	BALLASTS
AABLLSTU	BLASTULA
AABLLUVY	VALUABLY
AABLMNOR	ABNORMAL
AABLMNTU	AMBULANT
AABLMRSU	LABARUMS
AABLMSST	LAMBASTS
AABLNTTT	BLATTANT
AABLORST	ABLATORS
AABLOTUY	LAYABOUT
AABLPSSY	PASSABLY
AABLRRSU	SABURRAL
AABLRSST	ARBLASTS
AABLRSUU	SUBAURAL
AABLSTTU	ABUTTALS
AABMMOSU	ABOMASUM
AABMNNOO	BONAMANO
AABMNOTW	BATWOMAN
AABMNRTU	RAMBUTAN
AABMORSU	MARABOUS
AABMORTU	MARABOUT
	TAMBOURA
AABMOSSU	ABOMASUS
AABMRSTU	TAMBURAS
AABNNOST	ABSONANT
AABNNOSZ	BONANZAS
AABNOSST	SABATONS
AABORRRT	BARRATOR
AABORSTT	BAROSTAT
AABRRRTY	BARRATRY
AABRRSST	BRASSART
AABRRSSU	SABURRAS
AABRRSUV	BRAVURAS
AABSTTTU	BATTUTAS
AACCCDIS	SACCADIC
AACCCHHU	CACHUCHA

AACCCRUY ACCURACY
AACCDDES CASCADED
AACCDEIM ACADEMIC
AACCDELO ACCOLADE
AACCDEMS MEDACCAS
AACCDENU CADUCEAN
AACCDERR RACECARD
AACCDERS CARCASED
AACCDESS CASCADES
SACCADES
AACCDHIR CHARACID
AACCDIRS CARDIACS
AACCDOVY ADVOCACY
AACCEELT CALCEATE
AACCEENT CETACEAN
AACCEFLO COALFACE
AACCEGOR ACCORAGE
AACCEGRU CARUCAGE
AACCEHIX CACHEXIA
AACCEILN CALCANEI
AACCEIRR CERCARIA
AACCEKRS CARCAKES
AACCELOR CARACOLE
AACCELPT PLACCATE
AACCELRR CARCERAL
AACCENRT CARCANET
AACCENSV VACANCES
AACCERSS CARCASES
AACCERTU ACCURATE
CARUCATE
AACCFGOO CACAFOGO
AACCFILR FARCICAL
AACCGILT GALACTIC
AACCHILL CAILLACH
AACCHILP PACHALIC
AACCHINR ANARCHIC
CHARACIN
AACCHINS CHICANAS
AACCHISV VISCACHA
AACCHIVZ VIZCACHA
AACCHLNS CLACHANS
AACCHLOR CHARCOAL
AACCHLOT CACHALOT
AACCHLRS CLARSACH
AACCHMNO COACHMAN
AACCHMPS CHAMPACS
AACCHNNS CANNACHS
AACCHNOR CORANACH
AACCIINV VACCINIA
AACCIIST SCIATICA
AACCILMS ACCLAIMS
AACCILNV VACCINAL
AACCILRU ACICULAR
AACCILTT TACTICAL
AACCIORS CARIOCAS
AACCIORU CARIACOU
AACCIPTY CAPACITY
AACCIRTY CARYATIC
AACCJKRW CRACKJAW
AACCJORU CARCAJOU
CARJACOU
AACCKLPS CALPACKS
AACCKORT COATRACK
AACCKRRS CARRACKS
AACCLLRU CALCULAR
AACCLLST CATCALLS
AACCLMNY CLAMANCY
AACCLOPS POLACCAS
AACCLORS CARACOLS
AACCLPRS CALCSPAR
AACCLPST PLACCATS
AACCLRSU ACCRUALS
CARACULS
SACCULAR
AACCLSSU ACCUSALS
AACCORSU CURACAOS
CURACOAS
AACCOSST ACCOASTS
AACCOSTT STACCATO
STOCCATA
TOCCATAS
AACCRRST CARRACTS
AACDDEIL DAEDALIC
AACDDENV ADVANCED
AACDDETU CAUDATED
AACDDHRS CHADDARS
AACDDILN CANDIDAL
AACDDINS CANDIDAS
AACDEEHH HEADACHE
AACDEEHR AREACHED
HEADRACE
AACDEEHS HEADCASE
AACDEELS ESCALADE
AACDEEMS ACADEMES
AACDEEPS ESCAPADE
AACDEEST ESTACADE
AACDEETU ECAUDATE
AACDEFHR HARDFACE
AACDEFLS FALCADES
AACDEFLT FALCATED
AACDEGGR AGGRACED
AACDEGKP PACKAGED
AACDEGMR DECAGRAM
AACDEHHY HEADACHY
AACDEHIN HACIENDA
AACDEHLN CHALANED
AACDEHLP CEPHALAD
AACDEHMR DRACHMAE
AACDEHMS CHAMADES
AACDEHRS CHARADES
AACDEHRT CATHEDRA
AACDEHST CATHEADS
AACDEHTT ATTACHED
AACDEILS ALCAIDES
SIDALCEA
AACDEIMN MAENADIC
AACDEIMS CAMISADE
AACDEINR CANARIED
RADIANCE
AACDEINS AIDANCES
AACDEIRT RADICATE
AACDEJNT ADJACENT
AACDEKNP PANCAKED
AACDEKNS ASKANCED
AACDEKTT ATTACKED
AACDELLS ALCALDES
AACDELMN MANACLED
AACDELNR CALENDAR
LANDRACE
AACDELNS CANDELAS
AACDELNV VALANCED
AACDELOS ESCALADO
AACDELPT PLACATED
AACDELRS CALDERAS
AACDELSS SCALADES
AACDELSY ALCAYDES
AACDELTT LACTATED
AACDELTV CLAVATED
AACDENSV ADVANCES
CANVASED
AACDENSZ CADENZAS
AACDENTU ADUNCATE
AACDENTV TADVANCE
AACDEOPS ESCAPADO
AACDEOTU AUTOCADE
AACDEOTV ADVOCATE
AACDEPRS SCARPAED
AACDEQUY ADEQUACY
AACDERST CADASTRE
AACDERSV CADAVERS
AACDERTU ARCUATED
AACDETTU ACTUATED
AACDETUV VACUATED
AACDGINR ARCADING
CARANGID
CARDIGAN
AACDHHKR HARDHACK
AACDHIIS DICHASIA
AACDHILL CHILLADA
AACDHILR DIARCHAL
AACDHIMR DRACHMAI
AACDHINP HANDICAP
AACDHINR ARACHNID
AACDHKRT HARDTACK
AACDHLNP HANDCLAP
AACDHLOT CATHODAL
AACDHLRY CHARLADY
AACDHMMR DRAMMACH
AACDHMRS DRACHMAS
AACDHNRS HANDCARS
AACDHNRT HANDCART
AACDHPRS CRASHPAD
AACDIINS ASCIDIAN
AACDILLP PALLADIC
AACDILMT DALMATIC
AACDILMU CALADIUM
AACDILNO DIACONAL
AACDILNR CARDINAL
AACDILNU DULCIANA
AACDILOZ ZODIACAL
AACDILRR RAILCARD
AACDILRS RADICALS
AACDIMNO MANDIOCA
AACDIMNY ADYNAMIC
AACDIMOS CAMISADO
AACDIMRT DRAMATIC
AACDINRT RADICANT
TRIDACNA
AACDINRY RADIANCY
AACDINST ANTACIDS
AACDIOTU AUTACOID
AACDIRSS ASCARIDS
AACDIRTY CARYATID
AACDITUY AUDACITY
AACDJKSW JACKDAWS
AACDJQRU JACQUARD
AACDKLLN LACKLAND
AACDLNSS SCANDALS
AACDLORS CARLOADS
AACDLORT CARTLOAD
AACDLOSS SCALADOS
AACDLPRS PLACARDS
AACDLRTY DACTYLAR
AACDMMOR CARDAMOM
AACDMMRU CARDAMUM
AACDMNNO MANCANDO
AACDMNOR CARDAMON
AACDOOSV AVOCADOS
AACDORRT CARTROAD
AACEEFIT FACETIAE
AACEEFLP PALEFACE
AACEEGIR ACIERAGE
AGACERIE
AACEEGLR CLEARAGE
AACEEGLV CLEAVAGE
AACEEGRS ACREAGES
AACEEHLP ACALEPHE
AACEEHLT LEACHATE
AACEEHRS AREACHES
EARACHES
AACEEHRT TRACHEAE
AACEEIMT EMACIATE
AACEEINN ENCAENIA
AACEEIRT ACIERATE
AACEEKRT CARETAKE
AACEELNS ANELACES
AACEELRT LACERATE
AACEELST ESCALATE
AACEELTU ACULEATE
AACEEMRT MACERATE
RACEMATE
AACEEMST CASEMATE
AACEENNT CATENANE
AACEENTT CATENATE
AACEEPRV PRECAVAE
AACEEPSS SEASCAPE
AACEERSU CAESURAE
AACEERTV ACERVATE
AACEESTT ACETATES
AACEETUV EVACUATE
AACEETVX EXCAVATE
AACEFFIN AFFIANCE
AACEFHLP HALFPACE
AACEFIST FASCIATE
AACEFRRS CARFARES
AACEFRST SEACRAFT
AACEFRSX CARFAXES
AACEFRTT ARTEFACT
AACEGGRS AGGRACES
AACEGHNT CHANTAGE
AACEGILN ANGELICA
AACEGILT GLACIATE
AACEGINR CANAIGRE
AACEGINY GYNAECIA
AACEGIOP APOGAEIC
AACEGIRR CARRIAGE
AACEGIRV VICARAGE
AACEGKPR PACKAGER
AACEGKPS PACKAGES
AACEGKRT TRACKAGE
AACEGKSS SACKAGES
AACEGLNY LANCEGAY
AACEGNRS CARNAGES
CRANAGES
AACEGRST CARTAGES
AACEGRSV SCAVAGER
AACEGSSV SCAVAGES
AACEHILL ACHILLEA
HELIACAL
AACEHILN ACHENIAL
AACEHILP PHACELIA
AACEHIMR CHIMAERA
AACEHIMT HAEMATIC
AACEHIRS ARCHAISE
AACEHIRT THERIACA
AACEHIRZ ARCHAIZE
AACEHLNT CALANTHE
AACEHLNU EULACHAN
AACEHLPS ACALEPHS
AACEHLRS ALCHERAS

AACEHLRT	TRACHEAL
AACEHLRX	EXARCHAL
AACEHLSS	CALASHES
AACEHLST	ALCAHEST
AACEHMNP	CAMPHANE
AACEHMRS	MARCHESA
AACEHMSS	CAMASHES
AACEHMST	SCHEMATA
AACEHNPS	PANACHES
AACEHPRT	RACEPATH
AACEHPUX	CHAPEAUX
AACEHRSS	CHARASES
AACEHRSU	ARCHAEUS
AACEHRTT	REATTACH
AACEHSTT	ATTACHES
AACEHTUX	CHATEAUX
AACEIILN	LACINIAE
AACEIINT	ACTINIAE
AACEIKMT	KAMACITE
AACEILLM	CAMELLIA
AACEILLN	ALLIANCE
	CANAILLE
AACEILMN	ANALCIME
	CALAMINE
AACEILMT	CALAMITE
AACEILNS	CANALISE
AACEILNT	ANALCITE
	LAITANCE
AACEILNU	ACAULINE
AACEILNV	VALIANCE
AACEILNZ	CANALIZE
AACEILOP	ALOPECIA
AACEILRT	TAILRACE
AACEILRV	CAVALIER
AACEILST	SALICETA
AACEIMNS	AMNESIAC
AACEIMRS	MACARISE
	MESARAIC
AACEIMRZ	MACARIZE
AACEIMTT	CATAMITE
AACEIMUX	CAMAIEUX
AACEINRS	CANARIES
AACEINRT	CARINATE
AACEINRV	VARIANCE
AACEINST	ESTANCIA
AACEIOPR	CAPOEIRA
AACEIPPS	PAPACIES
AACEIPRS	AIRSPACE
AACEIPRT	APRICATE
AACEIPSS	CAPIASES
AACEIPTT	APATETIC
	CAPITATE
AACEIRSV	AVARICES
	CAVIARES
AACEIRTV	VICARATE
AACEITTV	ACTIVATE
	CAVITATE
AACEJLTU	JACULATE
AACEKKLW	CAKEWALK
AACEKNPS	PANCAKES
AACEKNSS	ASKANCES
AACEKOST	OATCAKES
AACEKRTT	ATTACKER
AACELLMR	MARCELLA
AACELLNS	CANELLAS
AACELLOT	ALLOCATE
AACELLST	CASTELLA
	LACTEALS
AACELLTY	ALLEYCAT
AACELMNP	PLACEMAN
AACELMNS	MANACLES
AACELMRS	CARAMELS
	CERAMALS
AACELMTU	MACULATE
AACELNNU	CANNULAE
AACELNOR	LECANORA
AACELNPR	PARLANCE
AACELNPT	PLACENTA
AACELNRT	LACERANT
AACELNRY	ARCANELY
AACELNST	ANALECTS
AACELNSV	VALANCES
AACELNTU	LACUNATE
	TENACULA
AACELOST	CATALOES
AACELOSU	ACAULOSE
AACELPST	PLACATES
AACELPSU	SCAPULAE
AACELRSU	CAESURAL
AACELRSV	CARAVELS
AACELRWY	CLEARWAY
AACELSST	LACTASES
AACELSTT	LACTATES
AACELSTY	CATALYSE
AACELTTY	CATTLEYA
AACELTYZ	CATALYZE
AACEMMRS	MACRAMES
AACEMNOR	AMORANCE
AACEMNPS	SPACEMAN
AACEMNST	CAMSTANE
AACEMPRS	PARACMES
AACEMQSU	MACAQUES
AACEMRSS	MASSACRE
AACEMSSS	CAMASSES
AACENOTU	OCEANAUT
AACENPRS	PANCREAS
AACENPST	PASTANCE
AACENPSU	SAUCEPAN
AACENRST	CANASTER
	CATERANS
AACENRTT	REACTANT
AACENRTY	CATENARY
AACENRVZ	CZAREVNA
AACENSSV	CANVASES
AACENSTT	CANTATES
	CASTANET
AACENSTY	CYANATES
AACENTUV	EVACUANT
AACEOPRT	CAPROATE
AACEORSS	ROSACEAS
AACEORSU	ARACEOUS
AACEOSST	SEACOAST
AACEPRST	CAPRATES
AACEPRSU	CAPUERAS
AACERSSS	RASCASSE
AACERSSU	CAESURAS
AACERSSZ	SAZERACS
AACERSTT	CASTRATE
AACERSWY	RACEWAYS
AACERTTT	TRACTATE
AACESSSV	CAVASSES
AACESSTT	SCEATTAS
AACESTTU	ACTUATES
AACESTUV	VACUATES
AACESUWY	CAUSEWAY
AACFFILS	CAFFILAS
AACFGRST	CRAGFAST
AACFHMST	CAMSHAFT
AACFILLY	FACIALLY
AACFILOS	FASCIOLA
AACFINST	FANATICS
AACFIRRT	AIRCRAFT
AACFIRTT	ARTIFACT
AACFISST	FASCISTA
AACFJKLP	FLAPJACK
AACFLLSU	FALCULAS
AACFLRST	FRACTALS
AACFRRSU	FARRUCAS
AACGGINO	ANAGOGIC
AACGGIOP	APAGOGIC
AACGHIPR	AGRAPHIC
AACGHIRR	CHIRAGRA
AACGHLLO	AGALLOCH
AACGHNOR	CHARANGO
AACGHOPZ	GAZPACHO
AACGHORU	GUACHARO
AACGIIMN	MAGICIAN
AACGIINR	GARCINIA
AACGILLO	ALOGICAL
AACGILLS	GLACIALS
AACGILLU	ALGUACIL
AACGILNO	ANALOGIC
AACGILNV	GALVANIC
AACGILOX	COXALGIA
AACGILRT	TRAGICAL
AACGILSS	SCAGLIAS
AACGIMMT	MAGMATIC
AACGIMNN	MANGANIC
AACGIMNP	CAMPAIGN
	PANGAMIC
AACGIMOP	APOGAMIC
AACGIMRR	MARGARIC
AACGIMUU	GUAIACUM
AACGINOT	CONTAGIA
AACGINPS	SCAPAING
AACGINTV	VACATING
AACGISTY	SAGACITY
AACGLMOU	GLAUCOMA
AACGLOST	CATALOGS
AACGMNRS	CRAGSMAN
AACGNOSU	GUANACOS
AACGNRVY	VAGRANCY
AACHHIKR	KACHAHRI
AACHHKRS	CHARKHAS
AACHHLLS	CHALLAHS
AACHHTWY	HATCHWAY
AACHIIMR	MARIACHI
AACHIKNR	CHINKARA
AACHIKNS	KACHINAS
AACHIKRS	CHIKARAS
AACHILLP	CALIPHAL
AACHILLR	RACHILLA
AACHILMS	CHAMISAL
AACHILMT	THALAMIC
AACHILNP	CHAPLAIN
AACHILPS	CALIPASH
AACHILRV	ARCHIVAL
AACHIMNN	CHAINMAN
AACHIMNP	CHINAMPA
AACHIMNR	CHAIRMAN
AACHIMNS	SHAMANIC
AACHIMNT	MATACHIN
AACHIMRR	ARMCHAIR
AACHIMRS	ARCHAISM
	CHARISMA
	MACHAIRS
AACHIMSS	CHIASMAS
AACHIMST	CATHISMA
AACHINNT	ACANTHIN
AACHINRT	CANTHARI
AACHINSW	CHAINSAW
AACHIPST	CHAPATIS
AACHIPTT	CHAPATTI
AACHIRST	ARCHAIST
	CITHARAS
AACHIRTX	TAXIARCH
AACHKMPS	CHAMPAKS
AACHKPSS	SCHAPSKA
AACHKRST	HATRACKS
AACHKSTY	HAYSTACK
AACHLLNS	CHALLANS
AACHLMNO	MONACHAL
AACHLMOS	CHLOASMA
AACHLORT	THORACAL
AACHLPPS	CHAPPALS
AACHLSSU	ACUSHLAS
AACHLSTU	CALATHUS
AACHMMNR	MARCHMAN
AACHMNNR	RANCHMAN
AACHMNTW	WATCHMAN
AACHMNUY	NAUMACHY
AACHMORT	ACHROMAT
	TRACHOMA
AACHMPRT	CHAMPART
AACHMPRY	PHARMACY
AACHNOPS	PANOCHAS
AACHNOSU	HUANACOS
AACHNPRS	SARPANCH
AACHNRST	TRASHCAN
AACHNRSV	NAVARCHS
AACHNRVY	NAVARCHY
AACHNSTU	ACANTHUS
AACHOPPR	APPROACH
AACHORTU	RACAHOUT
AACHOTTU	TACAHOUT
AACHRRST	CATARRHS
AACHRSWY	ARCHWAYS
AACHRTUY	AUTARCHY
AACIILMN	ANIMALIC
AACIILMO	MAIOLICA
AACIILRV	VICARIAL
AACIIMNT	ANIMATIC
AACIINNT	ACTINIAN
AACIINPR	PICARIAN
AACIINPT	CAPITANI
AACIINST	ACTINIAS
AACIJLMO	MAJOLICA
AACIJNOP	JAPONICA
AACIKLMS	MAILSACK
AACIKLRS	CLARKIAS
AACIKMNW	MACKINAW
AACIKNNS	CANAKINS
AACIKRTU	AUTARKIC
AACILLMR	LACRIMAL
AACILLMT	CLIMATAL
AACILLPY	APICALLY
AACILLRY	RACIALLY
AACILMNT	CALAMINT
	CLAIMANT
AACILMOR	ACROMIAL
AACILMOT	ATOMICAL
AACILMTY	CALAMITY
AACILNOR	CONARIAL
AACILNRS	CLARAINS
AACILNRV	CARNIVAL
AACILNST	ALICANTS
AACILNTU	NAUTICAL
AACILNTY	ANALYTIC
AACILNUV	NAVICULA
AACILNVY	VALIANCY

AACILPRU	PIACULAR
AACILPST	APLASTIC
	CAPITALS
AACILPSZ	CAPSIZAL
AACILPTU	CAPITULA
AACILPTY	ATYPICAL
AACILQRU	ACQUIRAL
AACILRTY	ALACRITY
AACILRUU	AURICULA
AACILSTT	STATICAL
AACILSTY	SALACITY
AACIMMNO	AMMONIAC
AACIMMRS	MACARISM
	MACRAMIS
	MARASMIC
AACIMNOR	MACARONI
	MAROCAIN
AACIMNOT	ANATOMIC
AACIMORT	AROMATIC
AACIMPRS	PICAMARS
AACINNST	CANTINAS
AACINOPR	PARANOIC
AACINOPT	CAPITANO
	PACATION
AACINORS	OCARINAS
AACINORT	RAINCOAT
AACINOTV	VACATION
AACINPST	CAPITANS
	CAPTAINS
AACINPTY	CAPITAYN
AACINQTU	ACQUAINT
AACINRST	ARCANIST
AACINRSZ	CZARINAS
AACINSTZ	STANZAIC
AACIOPST	TAPIOCAS
AACIOPSV	COPAIVAS
AACIPRTY	RAPACITY
AACIQSTU	AQUATICS
AACIRRTT	TARTARIC
AACIRSTT	CASTRATI
AACIRSTZ	CZARITSA
AACJKLPS	SLAPJACK
AACJKMNS	MANJACKS
AACJKOOR	JACKAROO
AACKKNPS	KNAPSACK
AACKLNPS	KNAPSCAL
AACKLOWY	LOCKAWAY
AACKMNPS	MANPACKS
AACKMNRT	TRACKMAN
AACKMNST	TACKSMAN
AACKMRST	AMTRACKS
AACKNRSS	RANSACKS
AACKORWY	ROCKAWAY
AACKPRRS	CARPARKS
AACKPRST	RATPACKS
AACKPSWY	PACKWAYS
AACKRTWY	TRACKWAY
AACLLMMU	MACALLUM
AACLLMRY	LACRYMAL
AACLLNRY	CARNALLY
AACLLNST	CALLANTS
AACLLNSU	CALLUNAS
AACLLRRY	CARRYALL
AACLLRSY	RASCALLY
AACLLSUU	CLAUSULA
AACLLSUY	CASUALLY
	CAUSALLY
AACLLTUY	ACTUALLY
AACLMNNS	CLANSMAN
AACLMNSS	CLASSMAN
AACLMNST	CALMANTS
AACLMRRU	MACRURAL
AACLNNOT	CANTONAL
AACLNNRU	CANNULAR
AACLNNSU	CANNULAS
AACLNOPR	COPLANAR
AACLNOTT	OCTANTAL
AACLNPSY	CLAYPANS
AACLNRSU	LACUNARS
AACLNRUY	LACUNARY
AACLNTVY	VACANTLY
AACLOOPT	TAPACOLO
AACLOPRS	CAPORALS
AACLOPST	OCTAPLAS
AACLOPTU	TAPACULO
AACLORRU	ORACULAR
AACLORST	COALTARS
AACLORSU	CAROUSAL
AACLORSZ	ALCORZAS
AACLORUV	VACUOLAR
AACLOSTT	CATTALOS
AACLPPRT	CLAPTRAP
AACLPRST	CALTRAPS
AACLPRSU	CAPSULAR
	SCAPULAR
AACLPRTY	CALYPTRA
AACLPSSU	SCAPULAS
AACLPTTU	CATAPULT
AACLRSTU	CLAUSTRA
AACLRSUV	VASCULAR
AACLSSTT	SALTCATS
AACLSTTY	CATALYST
AACLSTUY	CASUALTY
AACMNOOR	MACAROON
AACMNORS	CAMARONS
	MASCARON
AACMNPRY	RAMPANCY
AACMORRS	CAMORRAS
AACMORSS	SARCOMAS
AACMRRST	TRAMCARS
AACMRSSS	SARCASMS
AACNNOSZ	CANZONAS
AACNOSST	SACATONS
AACNPSST	CAPSTANS
AACNRSTT	TRANSACT
AACNRSTU	CURTANAS
AACOORTX	TOXOCARA
AACOPRSU	ACARPOUS
AACOPRTU	AUTOCARP
AACOPSTV	POSTCAVA
AACORRTV	VARACTOR
AACORSTT	CASTRATO
AACORSTU	ACATOURS
	AUTOCARS
AACORTTU	ACTUATOR
	AUTOCRAT
AACOSTUV	AUTOVACS
AACRSTTT	ATTRACTS
AACRSTUV	VACATURS
AACRSTWY	CARTWAYS
AACSTUWY	CUTAWAYS
AADDDEEH	DEADHEAD
AADDDEER	ADREADED
AADDDERW	ADWARDED
AADDDGNR	GRANDDAD
AADDEGGR	AGGRADED
AADDEGRT	GRADATED
AADDEHHR	HARDHEAD
AADDEHLN	HEADLAND
AADDEHMN	HANDMADE
AADDEHRZ	HAZARDED
AADDEILN	DEDALIAN
AADDEILS	ALIDADES
AADDEIRT	RADIATED
AADDEKMS	DAMASKED
AADDELTU	ADULATED
AADDEMNT	MANDATED
AADDEMRU	MARAUDED
AADDEMRY	DAYDREAM
AADDENPR	PANDARED
AADDENPS	DEADPANS
AADDGNRS	GRADDANS
	GRANDADS
AADDGNRU	GRADUAND
AADDHHRS	SHRADDHA
AADDHIMN	HANDMAID
AADDHKRS	KHADDARS
AADDHRSS	SRADDHAS
AADDIIKS	DIDAKAIS
AADDIISV	DAVIDIAS
AADDILNO	DIANODAL
AADDKMMO	MOKADDAM
AADDLLNY	LANDLADY
AADDLNRW	LANDWARD
AADDLNRY	YARDLAND
AADDMMQU	MUQADDAM
AADDNRST	STANDARD
AADDNRWY	YARDWAND
AADDNSVV	DVANDVAS
AADDRSST	DASTARDS
AADDRSTY	DASTARDY
AADEEFFR	AFFEARED
AADEEGHR	HEADGEAR
AADEEGHS	HEADAGES
AADEEGLR	LAAGERED
AADEEGLT	GALEATED
AADEEGMN	AMENAGED
	ENDAMAGE
AADEEGRV	AVERAGED
AADEEHMT	MEATHEAD
AADEEIRT	ERADIATE
AADEEIRW	AWEARIED
AADEEKNW	AWAKENED
AADEEKRW	REAWAKED
AADEELNN	ANNEALED
AADEELPP	APPEALED
AADEELTV	ALVEATED
AADEEMNT	EMANATED
AADEEMOT	OEDEMATA
AADEEMRR	DEMERARA
AADEENPT	TAPENADE
AADEENTT	ANTEDATE
AADEEPPR	APPEARED
AADEEPPS	APPEASED
AADEEPRS	PASEARED
AADEEQTU	ADEQUATE
AADEFFLT	AFFLATED
AADEFFNR	FANFARED
AADEFFRY	AFFRAYED
AADEFGLS	FALDAGES
AADEFGRS	FARDAGES
AADEFHLT	FLATHEAD
AADEFHST	HEADFAST
AADEFHTW	FATWAHED
AADEFIRS	FARADISE
	SAFARIED
AADEFIRZ	FARADIZE
AADEFISS	FADAISES
AADEFLLR	FALDERAL
AADEFLRY	DEFRAYAL
AADEFLTT	FALDETTA
AADEFNSZ	FAZENDAS
AADEFRRW	WARFARED
AADEFRWY	WAYFARED
AADEGGRS	AGGRADES
AADEGGRT	AGGRATED
AADEGGRU	GUARDAGE
AADEGHLN	DANELAGH
AADEGHRS	RAGHEADS
	RHAGADES
AADEGILL	DIALLAGE
AADEGILT	GLADIATE
AADEGINR	AREADING
	DRAINAGE
	GARDENIA
AADEGINT	INDAGATE
AADEGITT	AGITATED
AADEGITV	DIVAGATE
AADEGJTU	ADJUTAGE
AADEGLLT	TALLAGED
AADEGLMN	MAGDALEN
AADEGLMY	AMYGDALE
AADEGLNS	SELADANG
AADEGLSV	SALVAGED
AADEGMPR	RAMPAGED
AADEGMRS	MEGARADS
AADEGMSS	MASSAGED
AADEGNRR	ARRANGED
AADEGNTV	VANTAGED
AADEGPSS	PASSAGED
AADEGRST	GRADATES
AADEGRSV	SAVEGARD
AADEGRSY	DRAYAGES
	YARDAGES
AADEGRTU	GRADUATE
AADEGSSU	ASSUAGED
AADEGSSW	ASSWAGED
AADEHHOR	HOARHEAD
AADEHILR	HEADRAIL
	RAILHEAD
AADEHIRR	DIARRHEA
AADEHIRS	AIRHEADS
AADEHKMR	HEADMARK
AADEHLLL	HALALLED
AADEHLLO	HALLOAED
AADEHLMP	HEADLAMP
AADEHLNR	ANHEDRAL
AADEHLRS	ASHLARED
AADEHMNS	HEADSMAN
AADEHMST	MASTHEAD
AADEHNPS	SANDHEAP
AADEHNRV	VERANDAH
AADEHPPR	PARAPHED
AADEHPSS	SAPHEADS
AADEHRRW	HARDWARE
AADEHRSS	HARASSED
AADEHRSW	RAWHEADS
	WARHEADS
AADEHSSY	SASHAYED
AADEHSTT	HASTATED
AADEHSWY	HEADWAYS
AADEILMS	MALADIES
AADEILMU	AUMAILED
AADEILNT	DENTALIA
AADEILPR	PRAEDIAL
AADEILPS	PALISADE
AADEILPT	LAPIDATE
AADEILRS	SALARIED
AADEILSS	ASSAILED
AADEILSV	VEDALIAS

AADEILTV	VALIDATE
AADEIMNN	AMANDINE
AADEIMNP	PANDEMIA
AADEIMNR	MARINADE
AADEIMNT	ANIMATED
	DIAMANTE
AADEIMPZ	DIAZEPAM
AADEIMRV	MARAVEDI
AADEIMSS	SEAMAIDS
AADEIMST	DIASTEMA
AADEINRR	DARRAINE
AADEINRS	ARANEIDS
AADEINRT	DENTARIA
	RAINDATE
AADEINTT	ATTAINED
AADEIPPR	APPAIRED
AADEIPRS	PARADISE
AADEIPSS	DIAPASES
AADEIPSU	DIAPAUSE
AADEIPTV	ADAPTIVE
AADEIRST	DATARIES
	RADIATES
AADEIRTV	VARIATED
AADEISST	DIASTASE
AADEISTT	SATIATED
AADEITVW	VIEWDATA
AADEJMPY	PYJAMAED
AADEJMRS	JEMADARS
AADEJNNP	JAPANNED
AADEKLLN	LAKELAND
AADEKLNR	KALENDAR
AADEKMNR	MANDRAKE
AADEKMRS	KAMERADS
AADEKNST	ASKANTED
AADEKSTT	ATTASKED
AADELLPP	APPALLED
AADELLPS	PADELLAS
AADELLRT	DATALLER
AADELLWY	WELLADAY
AADELMNP	NAPALMED
AADELMNR	ALDERMAN
	MALANDER
AADELMNS	DALESMAN
	LEADSMAN
AADELMOS	ALAMODES
AADELMPT	PALMATED
AADELMRU	ALARUMED
AADELMYZ	AMAZEDLY
AADELNRS	ADRENALS
AADELNST	EASTLAND
AADELNSW	DANELAWS
AADELNSY	ANALYSED
AADELNYZ	ANALYZED
AADELPPT	PALPATED
AADELPRS	PARDALES
AADELPRY	PARLAYED
AADELRSY	SALEYARD
AADELRTU	RADULATE
AADELRTV	LARVATED
AADELRTY	DAYTALER
AADELSTT	SALTATED
AADELSTU	ADULATES
AADELSTY	DAYTALES
AADELTUV	VALUATED
AADEMNOS	ADENOMAS
AADEMNPS	SPADEMAN
AADEMNST	MANDATES
AADEMNUZ	UNAMAZED
AADEMORT	MATADORE
AADEMRRU	MARAUDER
AADEMRSS	MADRASES
AADEMSSS	ADMASSES
AADENNST	ANDANTES
AADENRRT	NARRATED
AADENRRW	WARRANED
AADENRSV	VERANDAS
AADENRTT	TARTANED
AADENSSW	WEASANDS
AADENSWZ	WEAZANDS
AADENTUV	AVAUNTED
AADEOPRT	TAPADERO
AADEOPST	ADESPOTA
AADEORRT	AERODART
AADEPRST	ADAPTERS
	READAPTS
AADEPSSS	PASSADES
AADEQRTU	QUADRATE
AADERRRW	REARWARD
AADERRWY	WARRAYED
AADERSST	ASSARTED
AADERSSW	SEAWARDS
AADERSTT	ASTARTED
AADERSTW	EASTWARD
	RADWASTE
AADFGNNO	FANDANGO
AADFGRSU	SAUFGARD
AADFHNST	HANDFAST
AADFIINT	INTIFADA
AADFIMRS	FARADISM
AADFINRU	UNAFRAID
AADFLLLN	LANDFALL
AADFLORW	AARDWOLF
AADFLOTX	TOADFLAX
AADFLOWY	FOLDAWAY
AADFMRRY	FARMYARD
AADGGHRS	HAGGARDS
AADGGIMN	DAMAGING
AADGGLNN	GANGLAND
AADGGLRS	LAGGARDS
AADGGRSS	SAGGARDS
AADGGRST	STAGGARD
AADGHILS	HIDALGAS
AADGHIPR	DIAGRAPH
AADGHRTU	HATGUARD
AADGIINS	GAINSAID
AADGILLR	GAILLARD
	GALLIARD
AADGILMR	MADRIGAL
AADGILNO	DIAGONAL
	GONADIAL
AADGILNS	SALADING
AADGIMMN	MADAMING
AADGIMMS	DIGAMMAS
AADGIMNR	MRIDANGA
AADGIMOS	AGAMOIDS
AADGIMPR	PARADIGM
AADGIMRS	DIAGRAMS
AADGIMRT	GRADATIM
AADGINPR	PARADING
AADGINPT	ADAPTING
AADGINRR	DARRAIGN
AADGINRU	GUARDIAN
AADGINRW	AWARDING
AADGIQRU	QUADRIGA
AADGLLSW	GADWALLS
AADGLMOR	MALGRADO
AADGLMSY	AMYGDALS
AADGLNRS	GARLANDS
AADGLNSS	SLADANGS
AADGLOPR	PODAGRAL
AADGLRSU	GRADUALS
AADGMNOR	DRAGOMAN
AADGMNOS	GOADSMAN
AADGMNRS	DRAGSMAN
	GRANDAMS
	GRANDMAS
AADGMRSS	SMARAGDS
AADGNNQU	QUANDANG
AADGNPRS	GRANDPAS
AADGNRST	GARDANTS
AADGNRSY	YARDANGS
AADGNRTU	GUARDANT
AADGNRUV	VANGUARD
AADGOPRS	PODAGRAS
AADGRRUW	GURDWARA
AADHHIPS	PADISHAH
AADHIINP	APHIDIAN
AADHILLR	HALLIARD
AADHILNR	HANDRAIL
AADHILRV	HAVILDAR
AADHIMSS	SAMADHIS
AADHINRR	HARRIDAN
AADHJNRS	HANDJARS
AADHKNSY	YAKHDANS
AADHLMOY	DALMAHOY
AADHLNPY	HANDPLAY
AADHLNSW	WASHLAND
AADHLRSY	HALYARDS
AADHMNNY	HANDYMAN
AADHMNOU	OMADHAUN
AADHNRSS	DARSHANS
AADHNSSW	HANDSAWS
AADHNSTT	HATSTAND
AADHRRTW	THRAWARD
AADHRRYZ	HAZARDRY
AADHRSWY	HAYWARDS
AADHSSWY	WASHDAYS
AADIJMNS	JAMDANIS
AADIKLLO	ALKALOID
AADIKLLR	KILLADAR
AADIKLRY	KAILYARD
AADIKLSY	ILKADAYS
AADIKMNS	DAMASKIN
AADILLLO	ALLODIAL
AADILLNR	LANDRAIL
AADILLPR	PALLIARD
AADILLRS	SILLADAR
AADILLRY	RADIALLY
AADILMNN	MAINLAND
AADILMNO	DOMAINAL
	DOMANIAL
AADILMNP	PLAIDMAN
AADILMRS	ADMIRALS
	AMILDARS
AADILNOR	ORDALIAN
AADILNPR	PRANDIAL
AADILNPS	PALADINS
AADILNRS	LANIARDS
AADILNTT	DILATANT
AADILOPS	PALISADO
AADILORR	RAILROAD
AADILPRS	PARDALIS
AADILPRY	LAPIDARY
AADILRRS	RISALDAR
AADILRST	TAILARDS
AADILSST	STADIALS
AADIMNNR	MANDARIN
AADIMNRS	MANDIRAS
AADIMNRT	TAMARIND
AADIMNRY	DAIRYMAN
	MAINYARD
AADIMNRZ	ZAMINDAR
AADIMNSS	DAMASSIN
AADIMNSU	SUDAMINA
AADIMNUV	VANADIUM
AADIMORS	DIORAMAS
AADIMSTZ	SAMIZDAT
AADINNOT	ADNATION
AADINOPR	PARANOID
AADINOPS	DIAPASON
AADINOPT	ADAPTION
AADINRRS	DARRAINS
AADINRRW	AIRDRAWN
AADINRST	INTRADAS
	RADIANTS
AADINRSV	VIRANDAS
AADIOPRS	DIASPORA
AADIORRT	RADIATOR
AADIPSUY	UPADAISY
AADIRRSW	AIRWARDS
AADIRRSY	DISARRAY
AADJNTTU	ADJUTANT
AADJNTUV	ADJUVANT
AADKLMNR	LANDMARK
AADKLNPR	PARKLAND
AADKLRTU	TALUKDAR
AADKMNRS	DARKMANS
AADKMRSY	DAYMARKS
AADKNRST	TANKARDS
AADKORWY	WORKADAY
AADKPRRW	PARKWARD
AADLLMRS	MALLARDS
AADLLNSW	LAWLANDS
AADLMNNS	LANDSMAN
AADLMNOR	MANDORLA
AADLMNOS	MANDOLAS
AADLMNSS	LANDMASS
AADLMNSU	LADANUMS
AADLMNUU	LAUDANUM
AADLNOPR	PARLANDO
AADLNOPS	SOAPLAND
AADLNOST	SALTANDO
AADLNRSY	LANYARDS
AADLORST	LOADSTAR
AADLORTU	ADULATOR
AADLPPRW	WALDRAPP
AADLPPSU	APPLAUDS
AADMMNOW	MADWOMAN
AADMMNSU	MANDAMUS
AADMNORS	MADRONAS
	MANDORAS
	MONARDAS
	ROADSMAN
AADMNORT	MANDATOR
AADMNRSS	MANSARDS
AADMNSTU	TAMANDUS
AADMOPPP	PAPPADOM
AADMOQSU	MADOQUAS
AADMORRT	TRAMROAD
AADMORST	MATADORS
AADMRSZZ	MAZZARDS
AADNOPRS	PANDORAS
AADNORST	ONDATRAS
AADNORTY	DONATARY
AADNOSUV	VANADOUS
AADNOSWY	NOWADAYS
AADNPRSU	PANDURAS
AADNQRSU	QUADRANS
AADNQRTU	QUADRANT
AADNQRUY	QUANDARY

AADNRRSW WARRANDS
AADNRRSY DARRAYNS
AADNRSTY TANYARDS
AADNRSWY NAYWARDS
AADOPPRR PARADROP
AADOPRST ADAPTORS
AADOPRXY PARADOXY
AADOPSSS PASSADOS
AADOPSTT DOPATTAS
AADOPSUY PADUASOY
AADORSVY SAVOYARD
AADORSWY ROADWAYS
AADOSSTT TOSTADAS
AADPSTTU DUPATTAS
AADQRSTU QUADRATS
AADRSSTY DAYSTARS
AAEEEHRT HETAERAE
AAEEFFRS AFFEARES
AAEEFGLS LEAFAGES
AAEEFRRS SEAFARER
AAEEGILN ALIENAGE
AAEEGILP EPIGAEAL
AAEEGINP EPIGAEAN
AAEEGKLS LEAKAGES
AAEEGLLN ENALLAGE
AAEEGLST ETALAGES
AAEEGMNS AMENAGES
AAEEGMPR AMPERAGE
AAEEGMTY METAYAGE
AAEEGNRS SANGAREE
AAEEGRST STEARAGE
AAEEGRSV AVERAGES
AAEEGRTW WATERAGE
AAEEHIMR HAEREMAI
AAEEHPRT HEARTPEA
AAEEHRTW WHEATEAR
AAEEHRWY HEREAWAY
AAEEILNT ALIENATE
AAEEINTT TAENIATE
AAEEJMNP JAMPANEE
AAEEKLSS SEAKALES
AAEEKLTW LATEWAKE
AAEEKMNS NAMESAKE
AAEEKNRW REAWAKEN
AAEEKPRT PARAKEET
AAEEKPSS SEASPEAK
AAEEKQSU SEAQUAKE
AAEEKRSW REAWAKES
AAEELLLM LAMELLAE
AAEELLMT MALLEATE
AAEELLPT PATELLAE
AAEELMST MALEATES
AAEELNNR ANNEALER
LERNAEAN
AAEELNPS SEAPLANE
SPELAEAN
AAEELNPU PAENULAE
AAEELORT AREOLATE
AAEELRST LAETARES
AAEELRTU LAUREATE
AAEELSST ELASTASE
AAEELTUV EVALUATE
AAEELVWY WAYLEAVE
AAEEMNPT NAMETAPE
AAEEMNST EMANATES
MANATEES
AAEEMPRS PARAMESE
AAEENNNT ANTENNAE
AAEENPRT PARANETE
AAEENRRS ARRASENE

AAEENRST ARSENATE
SERENATA
AAEENRTT ANTEATER
AAEENSTU NAUSEATE
AAEEPPRR APPEARER
RAPPAREE
REAPPEAR
AAEEPPRS APPEASER
AAEEPPSS APPEASES
AAEEPRST ASPERATE
SEPARATE
AAEEPSTT ASEPTATE
AAEERRWW REWAREWA
AAEERSSW SEAWARES
AAEERSTT STEARATE
AAEERSTW SEAWATER
AAEERSWX EARWAXES
AAEFFGRS AGRAFFES
AAEFFGST STAFFAGE
AAEFFIRS AFFAIRES
AAEFFLLS FALAFELS
AAEFFLPR PARAFFLE
AAEFFNRS FANFARES
AAEFFSTT TAFFETAS
AAEFGHRW WHARFAGE
AAEFGINR AFEARING
AAEFGITT FATIGATE
AAEFGLLL FLAGELLA
AAEFGLOT FLOATAGE
AAEFGRTU FRAUTAGE
AAEFGSTW WAFTAGES
AAEFILTY FAYALITE
AAEFIMRR AIRFRAME
AAEFINNT FAINEANT
AAEFINTX ANTEFIXA
AAEFLMTT FLATMATE
AAEFLPRS EARFLAPS
PARAFLES
AAEFLRTW FLATWARE
AAEFMRST FERMATAS
AAEFQRSU AQUAFERS
AAEFRRRW WARFARER
AAEFRRSW WARFARES
AAEFRRWY WAYFARER
AAEFRSWY WAYFARES
AAEGGINR GRAINAGE
AAEGGIOT AGIOTAGE
AAEGGLNR LANGRAGE
AAEGGLNU LANGUAGE
AAEGGNOS ANAGOGES
AAEGGNOW WAGONAGE
AAEGGNRY GARGANEY
AAEGGOPR PARAGOGE
AAEGGOPS APAGOGES
AAEGGRST AGGRATES
AAEGHLNP PHALANGE
AAEGHLSU HAULAGES
AAEGHMRX HEXAGRAM
AAEGHMSS GAMASHES
AAEGHNRU HARANGUE
AAEGHNST THANAGES
AAEGHOPY HYPOGAEA
AAEGILLR GALLERIA
AAEGILLT ALLIGATE
AAEGILNP PELAGIAN
AAEGILNR REGALIAN
AAEGILNT AGENTIAL
ALGINATE
AAEGILRS GASALIER
LAIRAGES

REGALIAS
AAEGILSS ALGESIAS
AAEGILSX GALAXIES
AAEGILTT TAILGATE
AAEGIMNO EGOMANIA
AAEGIMNP PIGMAEAN
AAEGIMNS MAGNESIA
AAEGIMNZ MAGAZINE
AAEGIMRR MARRIAGE
AAEGIMRT GEMATRIA
MARITAGE
AAEGINNR ANEARING
AAEGINPS NAGAPIES
PAGANISE
AAEGINPT PAGINATE
AAEGINPZ PAGANIZE
AAEGINRS ANGARIES
AAEGINRT AERATING
AAEGINST SAGINATE
AAEGINSW WAINAGES
AAEGINTV NAVIGATE
VAGINATE
AAEGIPRS IGARAPES
AAEGIPRU PERIAGUA
AAEGIRRS ARRIAGES
AAEGIRSV VAGARIES
AAEGISSS ASSEGAIS
AAEGISTT AGITATES
AAEGIVWY GIVEAWAY
AAEGJSTU AJUTAGES
AAEGKNST TANKAGES
AAEGKOSS SOAKAGES
AAEGLLMS SMALLAGE
AAEGLLPR PELLAGRA
AAEGLLSS GALLEASS
AAEGLLST GALLATES
STALLAGE
TALLAGES
AAEGLLTU GLUTAEAL
AAEGLMNS GAMELANS
AAEGLMNV GAVELMAN
AAEGLNOU ANALOGUE
AAEGLNPP LAGNAPPE
AAEGLNPT PLANTAGE
AAEGLNRS ALNAGERS
AAEGLNRU AULNAGER
AAEGLNSS LASAGNES
AAEGLNSU AULNAGES
AAEGLNTU ANGULATE
AAEGLOSV AASVOGEL
AAEGLRRS REALGARS
RESALGAR
AAEGLRRW WARRAGLE
AAEGLRST AGRESTAL
AAEGLRTY LEGATARY
AAEGLSST AGELASTS
LASTAGES
AAEGLSSV SALVAGES
AAEGLSVY SAVAGELY
AAEGLTUV VAULTAGE
AAEGMMNR ENGRAMMA
AAEGMNPY PYGMAEAN
AAEGMNRS MANAGERS
AAEGMNRV GRAVAMEN
AAEGMNST MAGENTAS
MAGNATES
AAEGMORR AEROGRAM
AAEGMORS SAGAMORE
AAEGMPRS RAMPAGES
AAEGMPRU RAMPAUGE

AAEGMRRV MARGRAVE
AAEGMRRY GRAMARYE
AAEGMRTU AGERATUM
AAEGMSSS MASSAGES
AAEGMTTW MEGAWATT
AAEGNNOP NEOPAGAN
AAEGNNPS PANNAGES
AAEGNNST TANNAGES
AAEGNPST PAGEANTS
AAEGNRRR ARRANGER
AAEGNRRS ARRANGES
AAEGNRST STARAGEN
TANAGERS
AAEGNRTU RUNAGATE
AAEGNSTT STAGNATE
AAEGNSTV VANTAGES
AAEGNSTW WANTAGES
AAEGNTUV VAUNTAGE
AAEGORRT ARROGATE
AAEGORTT AEGROTAT
AAEGPPRW WRAPPAGE
AAEGPSSS PASSAGES
AAEGPSSY PAYSAGES
AAEGQSUY QUAYAGES
AAEGRRSV RAVAGERS
AAEGRSTT REGATTAS
AAEGRSVY SAVAGERY
AAEGSSSU ASSUAGES
SAUSAGES
AAEGSSSW ASSWAGES
AAEGSSTV SAVAGEST
AAEGSSTW TASSWAGE
WASTAGES
AAEGSTTW WATTAGES
AAEGSTWY GATEWAYS
GETAWAYS
AAEHIIRT HETAIRAI
HETAIRIA
AAEHILMN HIELAMAN
AAEHILNP APHELIAN
AAEHILNT ANTHELIA
AAEHILPR PARHELIA
AAEHIMNT ANTHEMIA
HAEMATIN
AAEHINPT APHANITE
AAEHINST ASTHENIA
AAEHIPST APATHIES
AAEHIRST HETAIRAS
AAEHKLST ALKAHEST
AAEHKMRY HAYMAKER
AAEHKNST KHANATES
AAEHKSSW SEAHAWKS
AAEHLLLS ALLHEALS
AAEHLMNT METHANAL
AAEHLMNW WHALEMAN
AAEHLMSY SEALYHAM
AAEHLMTU HAMULATE
AAEHLNTX EXHALANT
AAEHLPRX HEXAPLAR
AAEHLPSX HEXAPLAS
AAEHLPUV UPHEAVAL
AAEHLRST TREHALAS
AAEHLRTT THEATRAL
AAEHLSTT ATHLETAS
AAEHMNPY NYMPHAEA
AAEHMNRS SHAREMAN
SHEARMAN
AAEHMNRT EARTHMAN
AAEHMOPR AMPHORAE
AAEHMORT ATHEROMA

AAEHNPRS HANAPERS
AAEHNPSS SAPHENAS
AAEHNPST PHEASANT
AAEHNPSY SYNAPHEA
AAEHNTTX XANTHATE
AAEHPRSZ PHEAZARS
AAEHRRSS HARASSER
AAEHRSSS HARASSES
AAEHRSSY HEARSAYS
AAEHRTWX EARTHWAX
AAEIIKNS AKINESIA
AAEIIMRV VIRAEMIA
AAEIIPRS APIARIES
AAEIIRSV AVIARIES
AAEIKKMZ KAMIKAZE
AAEIKLLN ALKALINE
AAEIKLLS ALKALIES
ALKALISE
AAEIKLLZ ALKALIZE
AAEIKMRR KRAMERIA
AAEILLLU ALLELUIA
AAEILLMM MAMILLAE
AAEILLMR ARMILLAE
AAEILLMX MAXILLAE
AAEILLPP PAPILLAE
AAEILLPT PALLIATE
AAEILLRT ARILLATE
AAEILLRY AERIALLY
AAEILLTT TALLIATE
AAEILLTV ALLATIVE
AAEILMNT ALAIMENT
LAMINATE
AAEILMNV VELAMINA
AAEILMRT MATERIAL
AAEILMSS MALAISES
AAEILNNS ALANINES
ANNALISE
AAEILNNZ ANNALIZE
AAEILNPR AIRPLANE
AAEILNPT PALATINE
AAEILNRU AURELIAN
AAEILNRV VALERIAN
AAEILNSS NASALISE
AAEILNSZ NASALIZE
AAEILNTT ANTLIATE
AAEILNTV AVENTAIL
AAEILORS OLEARIAS
AAEILPPS PAPALISE
AAEILPPZ PAPALIZE
AAEILPRT PARIETAL
AAEILPST STAPELIA
AAEILRRT ARTERIAL
AAEILRSS ASSAILER
SALARIES
AAEILRSU AURELIAS
AAEILRTV VARIETAL
AAEILSTV AESTIVAL
SALIVATE
AAEILSTX SAXATILE
AAEILTVX LAXATIVE
AAEIMMST IMAMATES
AAEIMNOT METANOIA
AAEIMNPR PEARMAIN
AAEIMNPT IMPANATE
AAEIMNRR MARINERA
AAEIMNRT ANIMATER
MARINATE
AAEIMNRZ MAZARINE
AAEIMNSS AMNESIAS
AAEIMNST AMENTIAS
ANIMATES
AAEIMOPR PAROEMIA
AAEIMOTX TOXAEMIA
AAEIMPSY PYAEMIAS
AAEIMRSU URAEMIAS
AAEIMSUV MAUVAISE
AAEINNTT ANTENATI
AAEINORT AERATION
AAEINORX ANOREXIA
AAEINPRS PANARIES
AAEINRRW RAINWEAR
AAEINRST ANTISERA
ARTESIAN
RESINATA
AAEINRTT REATTAIN
AAEINRTU INAURATE
AAEINRTZ ATRAZINE
AAEINSTT ASTATINE
SANITATE
TANAISTE
AAEINSTV SANATIVE
AAEINTTT TITANATE
AAEIPPRS APPRAISE
AAEIPPSS APEPSIAS
AAEIPRRS PAREIRAS
AAEIPRSS SPIRAEAS
AAEIPRST ASPIRATE
PARASITE
SEPTARIA
AAEIPRTT PATRIATE
AAEIPRTZ TRAPEZIA
AAEIPRXY APYREXIA
AAEIPSTT APATITES
AAEIRRRT TERRARIA
AAEIRSST ASTERIAS
ATRESIAS
AAEIRSSX XERASIAS
AAEIRSTT ARIETTAS
ARISTATE
AAEIRSTV VARIATES
AAEIRSVW AIRWAVES
AAEIRTTZ ZARATITE
AAEISSTT SATIATES
AAEITTVX TAXATIVE
AAEJLNOP JALAPENO
AAEJNNPR JAPANNER
AAEJNRST NAARTJES
AAEJNRTZ JAZERANT
AAEJRSSW SWARAJES
AAEKKORS KARAOKES
AAEKLMRY MALARKEY
AAEKLNRS LARNAKES
AAEKLNST ALKANETS
KANTELAS
AAEKMRRS EARMARKS
AAEKMRSS SEAMARKS
AAEKNPRT PARTAKEN
AAEKORTY AKARYOTE
AAEKPRRT PARTAKER
AAEKPRST PARTAKES
AAEKSSSV KAVASSES
VAKASSES
AAELLLMR LAMELLAR
AAELLLPR PARALLEL
AAELLMPU AMPULLAE
AAELLNPU PLANULAE
AAELLNSZ ZANELLAS
AAELLORV ALVEOLAR
AAELLPRS PARELLAS
AAELLPRT PATELLAR
AAELLPST PATELLAS
AAELLRST LATERALS
AAELLRSY ALLAYERS
AAELLUVV VALVULAE
AAELLWWY WELLAWAY
AAELLWYY ALLEYWAY
AAELMMNO MELANOMA
AAELMMTU MALAMUTE
AAELMNOT MALONATE
AAELMNPT PLATEMAN
AAELMNRT MATERNAL
AAELMNSS SALESMAN
AAELMNST TALESMAN
AAELMNSW WEALSMAN
AAELMNSY SEAMANLY
AAELMOST OATMEALS
AAELMPRT MALAPERT
AAELMPRX EXAMPLAR
AAELMPSS LAMPASES
LAMPASSE
AAELMPST PLATEASM
AAELMPTV VAMPLATE
AAELMPTY PLAYMATE
AAELMRSY LAMASERY
AAELMRTT MALTREAT
AAELMSST MALTASES
AAELMSSY AMYLASES
AAELNNNT ANTENNAL
AAELNNOT NEONATAL
AAELNNTU ANNULATE
AAELNOSS SEASONAL
AAELNOSV VALONEAS
AAELNPRS PRENASAL
AAELNPRT PARENTAL
PATERNAL
PRENATAL
AAELNPRW WARPLANE
AAELNPST PLATANES
PLEASANT
AAELNPSU PAENULAS
AAELNRSS ARSENALS
AAELNRSY ANALYSER
AAELNRTT ALTERANT
ALTERNAT
AAELNRTX RELAXANT
AAELNRYZ ANALYZER
AAELNSST SEALANTS
AAELNSSV ENVASSAL
AAELNSSY ANALYSES
AAELNSTZ ZEALANTS
AAELNSWY LANEWAYS
AAELNSYZ ANALYZES
AAELORSU AUREOLAS
AAELORTY ALEATORY
AAELOSTX OXALATES
AAELPPRS APPARELS
AAELPPST PALPATES
AAELPPSU APPLAUSE
AAELPRST PALESTRA
AAELPRSV PALAVERS
AAELPRSY PARALYSE
AAELPRTT TETRAPLA
AAELPRYZ PARALYZE
AAELPSTU PLATEAUS
AAELPSTV PALSTAVE
AAELPTUV VAPULATE
AAELPTUX PLATEAUX
AAELRSTZ LAZARETS
AAELRTUV VELATURA
AAELRUZZ ZARZUELA
AAELRWYY WAYLAYER
AAELSSTT SALTATES
AAELSTUV VALUATES
AAELSTZZ ALTEZZAS
AAEMMMRS MAREMMAS
AAEMMNRT ARMAMENT
AAEMMNSU MANUMEAS
AAEMMSTT STEMMATA
AAEMNOSW SEAWOMAN
AAEMNOTZ METAZOAN
AAEMNPRS SPEARMAN
AAEMNPRT PARAMENT
AAEMNRST SARMENTA
SEMANTRA
AAEMNRSU MURAENAS
AAEMNRTT ATRAMENT
AAEMNRTW WATERMAN
AAEMNSST NAMASTES
AAEMNSTU MANTEAUS
AAEMNTUX MANTEAUX
AAEMORTT AMARETTO
TERATOMA
AAEMORTX XEROMATA
AAEMOSTT STEATOMA
AAEMOTTU AUTOMATE
AAEMPPSS PAMPASES
AAEMPTTU AMPUTATE
AAEMQSTU SQUAMATE
AAEMRRTU ARMATURE
AAEMRSTU AMATEURS
AAEMRTTU MATURATE
AAENNNST ANTENNAS
AAENNOTT ANNOTATE
AAENNSTT STANNATE
TANNATES
AAENNSTU NAUSEANT
AAENNSTV VENTANAS
AAENORRU AUROREAN
AAENORST ANOESTRA
AAENORSU ARANEOUS
AAENORTU AERONAUT
AAENOSST ASSONATE
AAENPPRS PARPANES
AAENPPRT APPARENT
TRAPPEAN
AAENPRTY PRYTANEA
AAENPSST ANAPESTS
PEASANTS
AAENPSTT ANTEPAST
AAENPSTY PEASANTY
AAENRRSS NARRASES
AAENRRST NARRATES
AAENRSTT TARTANES
AAENRSTV TAVERNAS
TSAREVNA
AAENRSUW UNAWARES
AAENSSSV VANESSAS
AAENTTTT ATTENTAT
AAEOPSTT APOSTATE
AAEORRST AERATORS
AAEORSTT AEROSTAT
AAEORTTV ROTAVATE
AAEPPRST PARAPETS
AAEPPSTT APPESTAT
AAEPSWXX PAXWAXES
AAEPSZZZ PAZAZZES
AAERRRSY ARRAYERS
AAERRSST TARRASES
AAERRSTT TARTARES
AAERRTTT TARTRATE

AAERSSSY ASSAYERS
AAERSTTU SATURATE
AAERTWWY WATERWAY
AAFFILRT TAFFRAIL
AAFFINPR PARAFFIN
AAFFINSS SAFFIANS
AAFFLPST PALSTAFF
AAFFLSTU AFFLATUS
AAFFNNOR FANFARON
AAFGILNO GOLFIANA
AAFGINTW FATWAING
AAFGLLNU LANGLAUF
AAFGLNRT FLAGRANT
AAFGNRRT FRAGRANT
AAFHHIKL KHALIFAH
AAFHIKLS KHALIFAS
AAFHIKLT KHALIFAT
KHILAFAT
AAFHIRST AIRSHAFT
AAFHRSUU HAUSFRAU
AAFIILLM FAMILIAL
AAFIILLR FILARIAL
AAFIILMR FAMILIAR
AAFIILRS FILARIAS
AAFIINST FISTIANA
AAFIKLLY ALKALIFY
AAFILLNR RAINFALL
AAFILLUV AVAILFUL
AAFILMST FATALISM
AAFILNST FANTAILS
AAFILOPR PARAFOIL
AAFILQSU ALFAQUIS
AAFILSTT FATALIST
AAFILTTY FATALITY
AAFIMNOR FORAMINA
AAFINNRS SAFRANIN
AAFINNST INFANTAS
AAFINRRW WARFARIN
AAFINSTU FAUSTIAN
AAFIPRST PARFAITS
AAFIRSST SAFARIST
AAFIRSUY RUFIYAAS
AAFIRSWY FAIRWAYS
AAFJLLSW JAWFALLS
AAFJLORS ALFORJAS
AAFLLPRT PRATFALL
AAFLLPST SPATFALL
AAFLMORV LAVAFORM
AAFLNORS FORLANAS
SAFRONAL
AAFLNOTT FLOATANT
AAFLNRSU FURLANAS
AAFLSTWY FLATWAYS
AAFMNRST RAFTSMAN
AAFMNSST FANTASMS
AAFNPPRT FRAPPANT
AAFNSSTT FANTASTS
AAGGGINR GARAGING
AAGGILNR GANGLIAR
AAGGIMNN MANAGING
AAGGIMNR MARAGING
AAGGINRV RAVAGING
AAGGINSV SAVAGING
AAGGIRST GARAGIST
AAGGITTW GIGAWATT
AAGGLLLY LALLYGAG
AAGGLMOS MAGALOGS
AAGGMNNS GANGSMAN
AAGGNSWY GANGWAYS
AAGHHINS SHANGHAI
AAGHILNN HANGNAIL
AAGHILPY HYPALGIA
AAGHILRS GHARIALS
HARIGALS
AAGHIMNS ASHAMING
AAGHIMRT TAGHAIRM
AAGHINPS PAGANISH
AAGHINPW AWHAPING
AAGHIPRR AIRGRAPH
AAGHIRSV VAGARISH
AAGHKMNY GYMKHANA
AAGHLNPY ANAGLYPH
AAGHLOSS GASAHOLS
AAGHMNOY MAHOGANY
AAGHMNSW WHANGAMS
AAGHNOPR AGRAPHON
AAGHOPPR APOGRAPH
AAGHQSUU QUAHAUGS
AAGHRRTU ARRAUGHT
AAGHRSSW WASHRAGS
AAGIIKKN KAIAKING
AAGIILMN IMAGINAL
AAGIILNS ALIASING
AAGIILNV AVAILING
AAGIIMST ASTIGMIA
AAGIINRS ARAISING
AAGIINTV AVIATING
AAGIINTW AWAITING
AAGIKKNY KAYAKING
AAGIKLNO KAOLIANG
AAGIKLNR KRAALING
AAGIKLNS ASLAKING
AAGIKMRS SKIAGRAM
AAGIKNSW AWAKINGS
AAGIKNSZ ZIGANKAS
AAGILLNY ALLAYING
AAGILLSS GALLIASS
AAGILLTV GALLIVAT
AAGILLUZ ALGUAZIL
AAGILMMR MAILGRAM
AAGILMNO MAGNOLIA
AAGILMNR ALARMING
MARGINAL
AAGILMNX MALAXING
AAGILMOT GLIOMATA
AAGILMSY MYALGIAS
AAGILNOS LOGANIAS
AAGILNOT GALTONIA
AAGILNPT PALATING
AAGILNRR LARRIGAN
AAGILNSS SALSAING
AAGILNUV VAGINULA
AAGILOOP APOLOGIA
AAGILOST OTALGIAS
AAGILPRY PLAGIARY
AAGILRRW WARRIGAL
AAGILSTT SAGITTAL
AAGILSTW WAGTAILS
AAGIMMRR MARIGRAM
AAGIMNNO AGNOMINA
AAGIMNOS ANGIOMAS
AAGIMNPS PAGANISM
AAGIMNRR MARGARIN
AAGIMNSS AMASSING
SIAMANGS
AAGIMNSY GYMNASIA
AAGIMPTU PATAGIUM
AAGIMSSV SAVAGISM
AAGIMSTT STIGMATA
AAGINNNY NANNYGAI
AAGINNOT AGNATION
AAGINNRW AWARNING
AAGINNSW WANIGANS
AAGINNSY SYNANGIA
AAGINNTV VAGINANT
AAGINNTW AWANTING
AAGINOSS AGNOSIAS
AAGINPPY APPAYING
AAGINPRU PAGURIAN
AAGINPWW PAWAWING
AAGINRRS ARRAIGNS
AAGINRRY ARRAYING
AAGINRSS SANGRIAS
SARANGIS
AAGINRST GRANITAS
AAGINRSU GUARANIS
AAGINRSY ARAYSING
AAGINSST ASSIGNAT
AAGINSSU GAUSSIAN
AAGINSSY ASSAYING
GAINSAYS
AAGIORTT AGITATOR
AAGIPRSU PIRAGUAS
AAGIRRSY ARGYRIAS
AAGIRSTV GRAVITAS
STRAVAIG
AAGISSTT SAGITTAS
AAGKNOOR KANGAROO
AAGKOOSZ GAZOOKAS
AAGKORST KATORGAS
AAGLLMOY ALLOGAMY
AAGLLNOO LAGOONAL
AAGLLNRY LARYNGAL
AAGLLNST GALLANTS
AAGLLOPY POLYGALA
AAGLMNSS GLASSMAN
AAGLNNOO ANALOGON
AAGLNORS GRANOLAS
AAGLNPSS LAPSANGS
AAGLNQUU AQUALUNG
AAGLNRRU GRANULAR
AAGLOPRY PARALOGY
AAGLRRUW WARRAGUL
AAGLRSTU GASTRULA
AAGLRSUU ARUGULAS
AAGMMRRS GRAMMARS
AAGMNNOR NANOGRAM
AAGMNNRS GRANNAMS
AAGMNOPZ ZAMPOGNA
AAGMNORT MARTAGON
AAGMNOSS SANGOMAS
AAGMNPRS PANGRAMS
AAGMNRST TANGRAMS
TRANGAMS
AAGMNRTU ARMGAUNT
AAGMNSSW SWAGSMAN
AAGMNSTY SYNTAGMA
AAGMORSS MARGOSAS
AAGMOTUY AUTOGAMY
AAGMOTYZ ZYGOMATA
AAGMRSST MATGRASS
AAGNNSTT STAGNANT
AAGNOPRS PARAGONS
AAGNOPRT TRAGOPAN
AAGNORRT ARROGANT
TARRAGON
AAGNORSZ ORGANZAS
AAGNORTU ARGONAUT
AAGNRSTV VAGRANTS
AAGNRTUY GUARANTY
AAGNRTYZ ZYGANTRA
AAGOPSSS SAPSAGOS
AAGORSSS SARGASSO
AAGORSSU SAGUAROS
AAGRSSTU SASTRUGA
AAGRSTUZ ZASTRUGA
AAHHKMRS HASHMARK
AAHHMMSS SHAMMASH
AAHHNNST THANNAHS
AAHHNPST NAPHTHAS
AAHIIKRT TARAKIHI
AAHIJPRS RAJASHIP
AAHIKLPS PASHALIK
AAHIKRST KITHARAS
AAHILLLS HALLALIS
AAHILLNS HALLIANS
AAHILMNR HARMALIN
AAHILMRS ALMIRAHS
AAHILMSS SHIMAALS
AAHILNNT INHALANT
AAHILNOT HALATION
AAHILPSY PHYSALIA
AAHIMNOS MAHONIAS
AAHIMNPS PASHMINA
AAHINOPS APHONIAS
AAHINPRS PIRANHAS
AAHINRTU HAURIANT
AAHINSST SHAITANS
AAHINSTW TANIWHAS
AAHIPRST PITARAHS
AAHIPSTZ ZAPTIAHS
AAHIPSXY ASPHYXIA
AAHIRSST SHARIATS
AAHJKNRS KHANJARS
AAHKLLMR HALLMARK
AAHKLRSS LASHKARS
AAHKMOTW TOMAHAWK
AAHKMSSY YASHMAKS
AAHKRSSW SAWSHARK
AAHLLLOO HALLALOO
AAHLLOPT ALLOPATH
AAHLLSWY HALLWAYS
AAHLMMSS MASHLAMS
AAHLMOOS MASOOLAH
AAHLMRSS MARSHALS
AAHLMSTU THALAMUS
AAHLNRSW NARWHALS
AAHLPSST ASPHALTS
AAHLRSSW SHALWARS
AAHMNNSU HANUMANS
AAHMNORT MARATHON
AAHMNOST HOASTMAN
AAHMNOTX XANTHOMA
AAHMNPST PHANTASM
AAHMNRST TRASHMAN
AAHMNSTX XANTHAMS
AAHMRSST STRAMASH
AAHNNOSS HOSANNAS
AAHNNSTX XANTHANS
AAHNORST ATHANORS
AAHNORSV NAVARHOS
AAHNPSTY PHANTASY
AAHOPRTU AUTOHARP
AAHPRSTW WARPATHS
AAHPSTWY PATHWAYS
AAHRRTTW THRAWART
AAHRSSST SHASTRAS
AAIIILMR MILIARIA
AAIIIMNR NIRAMIAI
AAIIKKNN KINAKINA

AAIILMNS	MAINSAIL
AAIILMRS	AIRMAILS
AAIILNRZ	ALIZARIN
AAIILNUX	UNIAXIAL
AAIILPRR	RIPARIAL
AAIILPRS	PAIRIALS
AAIILPST	TILAPIAS
AAIILRSZ	ALIZARIS
AAIILRTX	TRIAXIAL
AAIILRUX	AUXILIAR
AAIILTXY	AXIALITY
AAIIMNNT	MAINTAIN
AAIIMNPX	PANMIXIA
AAIINOTV	AVIATION
AAIINPRR	RIPARIAN
AAIINPZZ	PIAZZIAN
AAIINRST	INTARSIA
AAIINSZZ	ZIZANIAS
AAIIOPST	APOSITIA
AAIIORTZ	ZOIATRIA
AAIIPRST	APIARIST
AAIIRSTV	AVIARIST
AAIIRSTW	WISTARIA
AAIIRTVX	AVIATRIX
AAIJLNPS	JALAPINS
AAIJMNPS	JAMPANIS
AAIJNRSZ	JANIZARS
AAIJNRYZ	JANIZARY
AAIJPPSY	JIPYAPAS
AAIKKNOS	SKOKIAAN
AAIKLNST	NASTALIK
AAIKMNNS	MANAKINS
AAIKMNOY	YAKIMONA
AAIKMNRS	RAMAKINS
AAIKMNST	ANTIMASK
AAIKMORS	ROMAIKAS
AAIKMRSS	KARAISMS
AAIKMRST	TAMARISK
AAIKNNTT	ANTITANK
AAIKORSU	OUAKARIS
AAIKPPRS	PAPRIKAS
AAIKSSTT	ASTATKIS
AAIKSSTV	SVASTIKA
AAIKSSTW	SWASTIKA
AAIKSTVV	AKVAVITS
AAILLLUV	ALLUVIAL
AAILLMMM	MAMMILLA
AAILLMMR	MAMILLAR
AAILLMNS	MANILLAS
AAILLMNT	MANTILLA
AAILLMNY	ANIMALLY
AAILLMRS	ARMILLAS
AAILLNOV	VALLONIA
AAILLNSV	VANILLAS
AAILLPPR	PAPILLAR
AAILLRRY	ARILLARY
AAILLRXY	AXILLARY
AAILMMRS	ALARMISM
	AMMIRALS
AAILMNNT	LAMANTIN
AAILMNOP	PALAMINO
AAILMNOR	MANORIAL
	MORAINAL
AAILMNOX	MONAXIAL
AAILMNPS	PANISLAM
AAILMNRU	MANURIAL
AAILMNRY	LAMINARY
AAILMNST	TALISMAN
AAILMNSU	ALUMINAS
AAILMNSV	MAILVANS
	NAVALISM
AAILMOPT	LIPOMATA
AAILMORR	ARMORIAL
AAILMPPS	PAPALISM
AAILMPRT	PRIMATAL
AAILMRST	ALARMIST
	ALASTRIM
AAILMTTU	ULTIMATA
AAILNNOT	NATIONAL
AAILNNPT	PLAINANT
	PLANTAIN
AAILNNRU	LUNARIAN
AAILNNST	ANNALIST
	SANTALIN
AAILNOPS	SALOPIAN
AAILNOPT	TALAPOIN
AAILNORT	NOTARIAL
	RATIONAL
AAILNOST	AILANTOS
AAILNOSV	VALONIAS
AAILNOTV	LAVATION
AAILNPRU	PLANURIA
AAILNPSS	SALPIANS
AAILNPST	PLATINAS
AAILNQTU	ALIQUANT
AAILNSSY	ANALYSIS
AAILNSTV	VALIANTS
AAILNSTY	NASALITY
AAILNTTT	LATITANT
AAILNTTY	NATALITY
AAILORRS	RASORIAL
AAILORRV	VARIOLAR
AAILORSS	ROSALIAS
AAILORSU	RAOULIAS
AAILORSV	VARIOLAS
AAILPPRU	PUPARIAL
AAILPPST	PAPALIST
AAILPRST	PARTIALS
	PATRIALS
	TRIAPSAL
AAILPSTT	TALIPATS
AAILQRSU	SQUARIAL
AAILRRSV	ARRIVALS
AAILRSTV	TRAVAILS
AAILRSVY	SALIVARY
AAILRSWY	RAILWAYS
AAILSSSV	VASSAILS
AAILSSSW	WASSAILS
AAILSSTY	STAYSAIL
AAILSTTT	LATITATS
AAIMMNOS	AMMONIAS
AAIMMNST	MAINMAST
AAIMMRSU	SAMARIUM
AAIMNORT	ANIMATOR
	MONTARIA
	TAMANOIR
AAIMNORW	AIRWOMAN
AAIMNOSS	ANOSMIAS
AAIMNOST	AMATIONS
AAIMNPRZ	MARZIPAN
AAIMNPTU	PUTAMINA
AAIMNRRT	TRIMARAN
AAIMNRRU	RANARIUM
AAIMNRST	TAMARINS
AAIMNSST	MANTISSA
	SATANISM
	STAMINAS
AAIMNSTU	AMIANTUS
AAIMNSTY	MAINSTAY
AAIMOPRS	MARIPOSA
AAIMPRST	PASTRAMI
AAIMPRSU	MARSUPIA
AAIMQRUU	AQUARIUM
AAIMRRSY	MISARRAY
AAIMRRTY	MARTYRIA
AAIMRSTU	TIMARAUS
AAIMSSTV	ATAVISMS
AAINNOPV	PAVONIAN
AAINNOST	SONATINA
AAINNOTT	NATATION
AAINNRSV	NAVARINS
	NIRVANAS
AAINNRTU	NUTARIAN
AAINNSST	NAISSANT
AAINNSSY	SANNYASI
AAINOPSS	PAISANOS
AAINORRS	ORARIANS
	ROSARIAN
AAINOTTX	TAXATION
AAINPRST	ASPIRANT
	PARTISAN
AAINPRTZ	PARTIZAN
AAINQRTU	QUATRAIN
AAINQTTU	AQUATINT
AAINRRSS	SARRASIN
AAINRRSZ	SARRAZIN
AAINRSST	ARTISANS
	TSARINAS
AAINRSSU	SAURIANS
AAINRSSV	SAVARINS
AAINRSTV	VARIANTS
AAINRSTY	SANITARY
AAINSSSS	ASSASSIN
AAINSTTT	ANTISTAT
	ATTAINTS
AAINSTTU	TUTANIAS
AAINSTTY	SATANITY
AAIOPRRT	TROPARIA
AAIOPRST	ATROPIAS
AAIOPRSU	PAROUSIA
AAIOPSTU	AUTOPSIA
AAIORSSU	SAOUARIS
AAIORSTV	AVIATORS
AAIORTUZ	AZOTURIA
AAIPPSTT	PITAPATS
AAIPRSSX	SPARAXIS
AAIPRSTT	PARTITAS
AAIQRSTU	AQUARIST
AAIQSSSU	QUASSIAS
AAIQSTUV	AQUAVITS
AAIRSSTT	TSARITSA
AAIRSTWY	STAIRWAY
AAISTWXY	TAXIWAYS
AAJKLSWY	JAYWALKS
AAJMMORR	MARJORAM
AAJMORST	MAJORATS
AAJOPSSU	SAPAJOUS
AAKKLRSU	KARAKULS
AAKKMOST	TOKAMAKS
AAKLMPSU	LAMPUKAS
AAKLMRUY	YARMULKA
AAKLMSUY	YAMULKAS
AAKLNOOS	OOLAKANS
AAKLNOSU	OULAKANS
AAKLOOPS	PALOOKAS
AAKLOOST	TALOOKAS
AAKLPRTY	KALYPTRA
AAKLRSSU	KURSAALS
	RUSALKAS
AAKLSSSU	SAKSAULS
AAKLSWWY	WALKWAYS
AAKMMNRS	MARKSMAN
AAKMOSSU	MOUSAKAS
	MOUSSAKA
AAKMRSUZ	MAZURKAS
AAKMRSWY	WAYMARKS
AAKNNSTU	NUNATAKS
AAKNSTWY	TWANKAYS
AAKOOPPS	PAKAPOOS
AAKPRSWY	PARKWAYS
AALLLSTY	LAYSTALL
AALLMNST	STALLMAN
AALLMNTY	TALLYMAN
AALLMNUY	MANUALLY
AALLMSST	SMALLSAT
AALLNNUY	ANNUALLY
AALLNPRU	PLANULAR
AALLNRTY	TARNALLY
AALLOORW	WALLAROO
AALLORSU	ALLOSAUR
AALLOSTV	LAVOLTAS
AALLPRST	PLASTRAL
AALLRUVV	VALVULAR
AALMMNOS	AMMONALS
AALMNORT	MATRONAL
AALMNORU	MONAURAL
AALMNOSS	SALAMONS
AALMNOWY	LAYWOMAN
AALMNPTY	TYMPANAL
AALMNTTU	TANTALUM
AALMNTUU	AUTUMNAL
AALMOOSS	MASSOOLA
AALMOPSX	AXOPLASM
AALMOSTT	STOMATAL
AALMOTXY	XYLOMATA
AALMPPSU	PASPALUM
AALMPRSY	PALMYRAS
AALMPSTY	PLATYSMA
AALMQSUU	SQUAMULA
AALMSTTU	MULATTAS
AALNNOPT	PANTALON
AALNNPUU	PUNALUAN
AALNNRSU	ANNULARS
AALNNTUU	LUNANAUT
AALNOPRT	PATRONAL
AALNPSUU	PUNALUAS
AALNRRTY	ARRANTLY
AALNRSTU	NATURALS
AALNSSTT	SALTANTS
AALNSSTU	SULTANAS
AALNSSTY	ANALYSTS
AALNSTTU	TALAUNTS
	TANTALUS
AALOPPRV	APPROVAL
AALOPRSS	PARASOLS
AALOPRST	PASTORAL
AALOPSVV	PAVLOVAS
AALORSSU	AROUSALS
AALORSTX	LAXATORS
AALORTUV	VALUATOR
AALORTVY	LAVATORY
AALOSTTY	TALAYOTS
AALPRSTU	PASTURAL
	SPATULAR
AALPSSTU	SPATULAS
AALRRTTY	TARTARLY
AALRSSTY	SATYRALS
AALRSSVY	VASSALRY
AALRSTTW	STALWART
AALRSTUY	SALUTARY

AALSSSTU ASSAULTS
AAMMNPRS RAMPSMAN
AAMMNRST MANTRAMS
AAMMOTXY MYXOMATA
AAMMRSSU MARASMUS
AAMNNOSY ANONYMAS
AAMNPRST MANTRAPS
AAMNPRSY PARANYMS
AAMNQSUW SQUAWMAN
AAMOORSS AMOROSAS
AAMOPRRU PARAMOUR
AAMORRSZ ZAMARROS
AAMORSSV SAMOVARS
AAMORSTT STROMATA
AAMOSTTU AUTOMATS
AAMPRRST RAMPARTS
AAMRSSST SMARTASS
AAMRSSTU SUMATRAS
AAMRSTWY TRAMWAYS
AAMSSSTU SATSUMAS
AANNOSST ASSONANT
AANNOSTT ANNATTOS
AANNRSTY STANNARY
AANOOPPX OPOPANAX
AANOOPRZ PARAZOON
AANOPRTY ANATROPY
AANORRRT NARRATOR
AANORSTY SANATORY
AANORTTY NATATORY
AANPRSST SPARTANS
AANQRSTU QUARTANS
AANRRSTW WARRANTS
AANRRTTY TARTANRY
AANRRTWY WARRANTY
AANRSTTU SATURANT
AANRSUWY RUNAWAYS
AAOORRSW WOORARAS
AAOPSSST POTASSAS
AAOPSSTY APOSTASY
AAORSSTT STAROSTA
AAORSUVV VAVASOUR
AAORSVVY VAVASORY
AAOSTTUY TATOUAYS
AAOSTWWY STOWAWAY
AARSTTUY STATUARY
ABBBCDEO CABOBBED
ABBBDEEK KEBABBED
ABBBDEEL BEDABBLE
ABBBDEKO KABOBBED
ABBBDELR BRABBLED
ABBBEILR BABBLIER
ABBBELRS BABBLERS
BLABBERS
BRABBLES
ABBBGILN BABBLING
BLABBING
ABBBISTT BABBITTS
ABBBOSTU SUBABBOT
ABBCDELS SCABBLED
ABBCDERS SCRABBED
ABBCDKNO BACKBOND
ABBCEERU BARBECUE
ABBCEGIR CRIBBAGE
ABBCEHIS BABICHES
ABBCEHOU BABOUCHE
ABBCEHSU BABUCHES
ABBCEHTU BATHCUBE
ABBCEIKT BACKBITE
ABBCEILR BARBICEL
ABBCEIRR CRABBIER
ABBCEIRS SCABBIER
ABBCEKLU BLUEBACK
ABBCEKNO BACKBONE
ABBCEKNU BUCKBEAN
ABBCELLU CLUBABLE
ABBCELRS CLABBERS
SCRABBLE
ABBCELRU CURBABLE
ABBCELSS SCABBLES
ABBCERRS CRABBERS
ABBCGINR CRABBING
ABBCGINS SCABBING
ABBCGIOR GABBROIC
ABBCIILL BIBLICAL
ABBCIINR RABBINIC
ABBCIKRT BRICKBAT
ABBCILRY CRABBILY
ABBCKLOY BLACKBOY
ABBDDEEL BEDDABLE
ABBDDEEU BEDAUBED
ABBDDEIL BIDDABLE
ABBDDELR DRABBLED
ABBDEEJR JABBERED
ABBDEERR BARBERED
ABBDEERT RABBETED
ABBDEERY YABBERED
ABBDEGLR GRABBLED
ABBDEIRR DRABBIER
ABBDEIRT RABBITED
ABBDELMO BABELDOM
ABBDELMR BRAMBLED
ABBDELNS SNABBLED
ABBDELRR DRABBLER
ABBDELRS DABBLERS
DRABBLES
ABBDEMUZ BUMBAZED
ABBDENRU UNBARBED
ABBDEORS ABSORBED
ABBDEQSU SQUABBED
ABBDERRS DRABBERS
ABBDERST DRABBEST
DRABBETS
ABBDFOOY BABYFOOD
ABBDGILN DABBLING
ABBDGINR DRABBING
ABBDGIOR GABBROID
ABBDHIJS DJIBBAHS
ABBDHIRS DRABBISH
ABBDHIRT BIRDBATH
ABBDHOOY BABYHOOD
ABBDILNO BAILBOND
ABBDILRS LIBBARDS
ABBDINRS RIBBANDS
ABBDLRSU LUBBARDS
ABBDMORS BOMBARDS
ABBDMOSU BABUDOMS
ABBDNORW BROWBAND
ABBEEINR BEARBINE
ABBEEJRR JABBERER
ABBEEJRS BEJABERS
ABBEENOR BAREBONE
ABBEEQRU BARBEQUE
ABBEERTT BARBETTE
ABBEESSS ABBESSES
ABBEFILR FLABBIER
ABBEGIST GABBIEST
ABBEGLRR GRABBLER
ABBEGLRS GABBLERS
GRABBLES
ABBEGNOS BOGBEANS
ABBEGNSU BUGBANES
ABBEGRRS GRABBERS
ABBEGRSU BUGBEARS
ABBEHILS BABELISH
ABBEHIRS SHABBIER
ABBEHLSS SHABBLES
ABBEHORT BATHROBE
ABBEILMS BABELISM
ABBEILNU BUBALINE
ABBEILOT BILOBATE
ABBEILRS SLABBIER
ABBEILST BISTABLE
ABBEINTT TABBINET
ABBEIRRT RABBITER
ABBEISSW SWABBIES
ABBEKLOO BOOKABLE
ABBELMRS BRAMBLES
ABBELNSS SNABBLES
ABBELOPR PROBABLE
ABBELORS BELABORS
ABBELORU BELABOUR
ABBELPRS PRABBLES
ABBELQSU SQUABBLE
ABBELRRS RABBLERS
ABBELRSS SLABBERS
ABBELRSU BARBULES
ABBELRSW WABBLERS
ABBELRSY SLABBERY
ABBELSUY BUYABLES
ABBEMOOR AEROBOMB
ABBEMOSX BOMBAXES
ABBEMSUZ BUMBAZES
ABBEORRS ABSORBER
REABSORB
ABBEORTW BROWBEAT
ABBEQRSU SQUABBER
ABBERRRY BARBERRY
ABBERRYY BAYBERRY
ABBERSST STABBERS
ABBERSSW SWABBERS
ABBESSSU SUBBASES
ABBFGINR FRABBING
ABBFILLY FLABBILY
ABBGGILN GABBLING
ABBGGINR GRABBING
ABBGIJLN JABBLING
ABBGILNR RABBLING
ABBGILNS SLABBING
ABBGILNU BAUBLING
ABBGILNW WABBLING
ABBGINST STABBING
ABBGINSU BUBINGAS
ABBGINSW SWABBING
ABBGINTY TABBYING
ABBGOOSU BUGABOOS
ABBHIIMS BIMBASHI
ABBHILSY SHABBILY
ABBHRRSU RHUBARBS
ABBHRRUY RHUBARBY
ABBHSTTU BATHTUBS
ABBIINOT BIBATION
ABBILLOT BOATBILL
ABBILLSU SILLABUB
ABBILOST BIOBLAST
BOBTAILS
ABBIMNOS BAMBINOS
ABBIMSSU BABUISMS
ABBINORS RABBONIS
ABBINORX BRAINBOX
ABBIRRTY RABBITRY
ABBIRSUU SUBURBIA
ABBKLOSU BLAUBOKS
ABBLLLOW BLOWBALL
ABBLLRSU BULLBARS
ABBLLSTU BULLBATS
ABBLLSUY SYLLABUB
ABBLOPRY PROBABLY
ABBMOORS BOMBORAS
ABBMOSST BOMBASTS
ABBNRSUU SUBURBAN
ABBOSSTY BOBSTAYS
ABCCDEHO CABOCHED
ABCCDHIK DABCHICK
ABCCEEHN BECHANCE
ABCCEELP PECCABLE
ABCCEEOR CABOCEER
ABCCEILY CELIBACY
ABCCEIRS BRECCIAS
ABCCEIRT BACTERIC
ABCCEKMO COMEBACK
ABCCESUU SUCCUBAE
ABCCHISU BACCHIUS
ABCCHNOO CABOCHON
ABCCIKKK KICKBACK
ABCCIKKP PICKBACK
ABCCIKOR ABRICOCK
ABCCILOR CARBOLIC
ABCCILOT COBALTIC
ABCCIMRS CAMBRICS
ABCCINOR CARBONIC
ABCCINSU BUCCINAS
ABCCKLLO BALLCOCK
ABCCKLOX CLACKBOX
ABCCKOOT COCKBOAT
ABCCKOSW BAWCOCKS
ABCCKSTU CUTBACKS
ABCCOORS BAROCCOS
ABCCOOST TOBACCOS
ABCCSSUU SUCCUBAS
ABCDDEER DECARBED
ABCDDEOR BROCADED
ABCDDETU ABDUCTED
ABCDEEFK FEEDBACK
ABCDEEHL BLEACHED
ABCDEEHR BERDACHE
BREACHED
ABCDEEJT ABJECTED
ABCDEEKR REBACKED
ABCDEELL BECALLED
ABCDEELM BECALMED
ABCDEELS DEBACLES
ABCDEELU EDUCABLE
ABCDEEMR CAMBERED
EMBRACED
ABCDEEMX EXCAMBED
ABCDEENO BEACONED
ABCDEERR REBRACED
ABCDEETU ABDUCTEE
ABCDEGIR BIRDCAGE
CAGEBIRD
ABCDEHLN BLANCHED
ABCDEHLU BAUCHLED
ABCDEHNR BRANCHED
ABCDEHOR BROACHED
ABCDEHOS CABOSHED
ABCDEIIT DIABETIC
ABCDEIKS BACKSIDE
DIEBACKS
ABCDEILR CALIBRED
ABCDEIPS PEDICABS

ABCDEIRS	ASCRIBED
	CARBIDES
ABCDEISS	ABSCISED
ABCDEKLO	BLOCKADE
ABCDEKLV	BACKVELD
ABCDEKNN	NECKBAND
ABCDEKNU	UNBACKED
ABCDEKRS	REDBACKS
ABCDELMS	SCAMBLED
ABCDELNO	BLANCOED
ABCDELOO	CABOODLE
ABCDEMOT	COMBATED
ABCDEMRS	SCRAMBED
ABCDENRU	UNBRACED
ABCDENTU	ABDUCENT
ABCDEORS	BROCADES
ABCDERSU	CUDBEARS
ABCDESTU	SUBACTED
ABCDGINU	ABDUCING
ABCDHKLO	HOLDBACK
ABCDHORS	CHOBDARS
ABCDIILO	BIOCIDAL
	DIABOLIC
ABCDIIMY	CYMBIDIA
ABCDIIRT	TRIBADIC
ABCDIKLR	BALDRICK
ABCDIKLS	BACKSLID
ABCDIKRU	BAUDRICK
ABCDILLR	BIRDCALL
ABCDILOU	CUBOIDAL
ABCDILRS	BALDRICS
ABCDINSS	ABSCINDS
ABCDIRST	CATBIRDS
ABCDIRSU	BAUDRICS
	SUBACRID
ABCDKNOW	BACKDOWN
ABCDKOPR	BACKDROP
ABCDKORW	BACKWORD
ABCDLLNU	CLUBLAND
ABCDNOSS	ABSCONDS
ABCDOORS	CORDOBAS
ABCDOPRU	CUPBOARD
ABCDORRS	BROCARDS
ABCDORTU	ABDUCTOR
ABCDORUY	OBDURACY
ABCEEEFK	BEEFCAKE
ABCEEFNT	BENEFACT
ABCEEHIR	BEACHIER
ABCEEHLM	BECHAMEL
ABCEEHLN	ALEBENCH
ABCEEHLR	BLEACHER
ABCEEHLS	BLEACHES
ABCEEHLW	CHEWABLE
ABCEEHRS	BREACHES
ABCEEHSU	EBAUCHES
ABCEEILT	CELIBATE
	CITEABLE
ABCEEIMN	AMBIENCE
ABCEELOV	EVOCABLE
ABCEELRR	CEREBRAL
ABCEELRT	BRACELET
ABCEEMRR	EMBRACER
ABCEEMRS	EMBRACES
ABCEENRT	CABERNET
ABCEENSS	ABSENCES
ABCEERRS	REBRACES
ABCEERST	ACERBEST
ABCEERUX	BERCEAUX
ABCEESSS	BECASSES
ABCEFIIT	BEATIFIC
ABCEFIKL	BACKFILE
ABCEFIKR	BACKFIRE
ABCEFINO	BONIFACE
ABCEGHIN	BEACHING
ABCEGILN	BELACING
ABCEGIMN	EMBACING
ABCEGIRS	RIBCAGES
ABCEGKLL	BLACKLEG
ABCEGKLO	BLOCKAGE
ABCEGKMU	MEGABUCK
ABCEGKOR	BROCKAGE
ABCEGMOS	CAMBOGES
ABCEGNOR	BONGRACE
ABCEGORS	BROCAGES
ABCEGOSS	BOSCAGES
ABCEHITT	BATHETIC
ABCEHKOS	BACKHOES
ABCEHKTW	BETHWACK
ABCEHLNS	BLANCHES
ABCEHLOR	BACHELOR
ABCEHLSU	BAUCHLES
	CHASUBLE
ABCEHLTU	LEACHTUB
ABCEHMOT	HECATOMB
ABCEHMRS	BECHARMS
	BRECHAMS
	CHAMBERS
ABCEHNRR	BRANCHER
ABCEHNRS	BRANCHES
ABCEHOOT	COHOBATE
ABCEHOPU	PABOUCHE
ABCEHORR	BROACHER
ABCEHORS	BROACHES
ABCEHORU	BAROUCHE
ABCEHOSS	BASOCHES
ABCEHRST	BRACHETS
ABCEHRTT	BRATCHET
ABCEIKKL	KICKABLE
ABCEIKLR	CRABLIKE
ABCEIKST	TIEBACKS
ABCEILLR	CRIBELLA
ABCEILLS	ICEBALLS
ABCEILLT	BALLETIC
ABCEILMS	ALEMBICS
ABCEILNN	BINNACLE
ABCEILNU	BACULINE
ABCEILOR	ALBICORE
	CABRIOLE
ABCEILOS	SOCIABLE
ABCEILRS	CALIBERS
	CALIBRES
ABCEILTT	BITTACLE
ABCEILTU	BACULITE
ABCEIMST	BETACISM
ABCEINOO	COENOBIA
ABCEINRS	CARBINES
ABCEINST	CABINETS
ABCEINTU	INCUBATE
ABCEIORS	AEROBICS
ABCEIORT	BORACITE
ABCEIOST	ICEBOATS
ABCEIRRT	CRIBRATE
ABCEIRSS	ASCRIBES
ABCEIRSW	CRABWISE
ABCEIRTT	BRATTICE
ABCEIRTY	ACERBITY
ABCEISSS	ABSCISES
	ABSCISSE
ABCEISST	ASBESTIC
ABCEISTT	TABETICS
ABCEJLTY	ABJECTLY
ABCEKKRU	BUCKRAKE
ABCEKKSW	SKEWBACK
ABCEKLLO	LOCKABLE
ABCEKLMO	MOCKABLE
ABCEKLNS	BLACKENS
ABCEKLOO	COOKABLE
ABCEKLPU	PALEBUCK
ABCEKLST	BLACKEST
ABCEKNRS	BRACKENS
ABCEKOOS	BOOKCASE
	CASEBOOK
ABCEKRST	BRACKETS
ABCEKSST	BACKSETS
	SETBACKS
ABCEKSSY	BACKSEYS
ABCEKSTW	WETBACKS
ABCELLPU	CULPABLE
ABCELLSU	BUCELLAS
	BULLACES
ABCELMNY	LAMBENCY
ABCELMOS	CEMBALOS
ABCELMRS	CAMBRELS
	CLAMBERS
	SCAMBLER
	SCRAMBLE
ABCELMSS	SCAMBLES
ABCELNOT	BALCONET
ABCELNUU	NUBECULA
ABCELOOT	BOOTLACE
ABCELOPS	PLACEBOS
ABCELORT	BROCATEL
ABCELOST	OBSTACLE
ABCELOSV	VOCABLES
ABCELOTU	BLUECOAT
ABCELPSU	BLUECAPS
ABCELPSY	BYPLACES
ABCELRSW	BESCRAWL
ABCELRTT	BRACTLET
ABCELSSU	BASCULES
ABCEMORS	CRAMBOES
ABCENORS	BACONERS
ABCENOSW	COWBANES
ABCENOUY	BUOYANCE
ABCENRSU	UNBRACES
ABCENTUX	EXCUBANT
ABCEOOSS	CABOOSES
ABCEORSU	CORBEAUS
ABCEOSUX	SAUCEBOX
ABCERRTU	CARBURET
ABCERTUU	CUBATURE
ABCESSTU	SUBCASTE
ABCESTUU	SUBACUTE
ABCFIKLL	BACKFILL
ABCFIKLT	BACKLIFT
	LIFTBACK
ABCFIKNS	FINBACKS
ABCFILOS	BIFOCALS
ABCFKLLU	FULLBACK
ABCFKOST	SOFTBACK
ABCGGIMO	GAMBOGIC
ABCGHINT	BATCHING
ABCGHKOS	HOGBACKS
ABCGIINN	CABINING
ABCGIKLN	BLACKING
ABCGIKNS	BACKINGS
ABCGILNS	CABLINGS
ABCGKLOS	BACKLOGS
ABCGLNOX	CLANGBOX
ABCGMSSU	SCUMBAGS
ABCHHIIS	HIBACHIS
ABCHIIPS	BIPHASIC
ABCHIKLS	BLACKISH
ABCHIKRS	BRACKISH
ABCHILMO	CHOLIAMB
ABCHILOO	COOLIBAH
ABCHIMOR	CHORIAMB
ABCHIMRU	BRACHIUM
ABCHINOR	BRONCHIA
ABCHIOOR	BORACHIO
ABCHIOST	COHABITS
ABCHIRRT	TRIBRACH
ABCHKLOT	HACKBOLT
ABCHKMPU	HUMPBACK
ABCHKOOP	CHAPBOOK
ABCHKOSU	CHABOUKS
ABCHKSTU	HACKBUTS
ABCHKSUW	HAWBUCKS
ABCHMOTX	MATCHBOX
ABCHNORS	BROCHANS
ABCHOTWX	WATCHBOX
ABCIIMNS	MINICABS
ABCIINOT	CIBATION
ABCIINSS	ABSCISIN
ABCIIORS	ISOBARIC
ABCIIRST	TRIBASIC
ABCIISTY	BASICITY
ABCIITUX	BAUXITIC
ABCIJNOS	JACOBINS
ABCIKKLL	KICKBALL
ABCIKLST	BACKLIST
ABCIKNPS	BACKSPIN
ABCILLRU	LUBRICAL
ABCILLSU	BACILLUS
ABCILLSY	SYLLABIC
ABCILMMO	CIMBALOM
ABCILMSU	SUBCLAIM
ABCILNPU	PUBLICAN
ABCILOOR	COOLIBAR
ABCILOSY	SOCIABLY
ABCILRRU	RUBRICAL
ABCIMMSS	CAMBISMS
ABCIMMSU	CAMBIUMS
ABCIMORR	MICROBAR
ABCIMRTU	UMBRATIC
ABCIMSST	CAMBISTS
ABCINORU	CONURBIA
ABCINRVY	VIBRANCY
ABCIORRS	BARRICOS
ABCIORSU	CARIBOUS
ABCIOSSU	SCABIOUS
ABCIOSUV	BIVOUACS
ABCIRSTT	ABSTRICT
ABCJKOOT	JACKBOOT
ABCKKORW	BACKWORK
ABCKLLOS	BALLOCKS
ABCKLOPT	BLACKTOP
ABCKLOST	BACKLOTS
ABCKLOSW	SLOWBACK
ABCKLOTU	BLACKOUT
ABCKMOOR	BACKROOM
ABCKMORR	BROCKRAM
ABCKMOSS	MOSSBACK
ABCKMOST	BACKMOST
ABCKMRSU	BUCKRAMS
ABCKMSUZ	ZAMBUCKS
ABCKNNOS	BANNOCKS
ABCKNRSU	RUNBACKS
ABCKNRTU	TURNBACK
ABCKOORU	BUCKAROO

ABCKOPST	BACKSTOP
ABCKORUY	BUCKAYRO
ABCKOSSW	SOWBACKS
ABCKOSTU	OUTBACKS
ABCKSSTU	SACKBUTS
	SUBTACKS
ABCKSSUW	BUCKSAWS
	SAWBUCKS
ABCLLNOR	CORNBALL
ABCLLPUY	CULPABLY
ABCLMOOO	COLOBOMA
ABCLMOSY	CYMBALOS
ABCLMSUU	BACULUMS
ABCLMSUY	SCYBALUM
ABCLNORY	CARBONYL
ABCLORXY	CARBOXYL
ABCLOSUV	SUBVOCAL
ABCLSSSU	SUBCLASS
ABCLSUUU	SUBUCULA
ABCMOORT	MOBOCRAT
ABCNNORU	CONURBAN
ABCNORTY	CORYBANT
ABCNOUYY	BUOYANCY
ABCORRSS	CROSSBAR
ABCORRSW	CROWBARS
ABCORRTU	TURBOCAR
ABCORSSU	SCABROUS
ABCOSSTU	SUBCOSTA
ABCOSTTU	COTTABUS
ABCRSTTU	SUBTRACT
ABDDDEEM	BEMADDED
ABDDDEET	ADDEBTED
ABDDEEEH	BEHEADED
ABDDEEGG	DEBAGGED
ABDDEEGR	BADGERED
ABDDEEHS	BEDASHED
ABDDEEKR	DEBARKED
ABDDEELU	BELAUDED
ABDDEERR	DEBARRED
ABDDEEST	BEDSTEAD
	BESTADDE
ABDDEGIR	ABRIDGED
	BRIGADED
ABDDEHMO	HEBDOMAD
ABDDEHOY	HOBDAYED
ABDDEILS	DISABLED
ABDDEILU	BUDDLEIA
ABDDEINR	BRANDIED
ABDDEINS	SIDEBAND
ABDDEIRR	BRAIRDED
ABDDELRS	BLADDERS
ABDDELRY	BLADDERY
ABDDENNU	UNBANDED
ABDDENOU	ABOUNDED
ABDDEORS	ADSORBED
ABDDERSW	BEDWARDS
ABDDGILN	BLADDING
ABDDHIOR	RHABDOID
ABDDILMO	LAMBDOID
ABDDILRY	LADYBIRD
ABDDIMNO	BONDMAID
ABDDINSS	DISBANDS
ABDDIRRY	YARDBIRD
ABDDLLOS	ODDBALLS
ABDDMORS	DAMBRODS
ABDEEEFN	BEDEAFEN
ABDEEEMN	BEMEANED
ABDEEERV	BEAVERED
	BEREAVED
ABDEEFIT	TABEFIED
ABDEEFLM	FLAMBEED
ABDEEFMO	BEFOAMED
ABDEEGGL	BEDAGGLE
ABDEEGGR	BEGGARED
ABDEEGHR	HERBAGED
ABDEEGNW	BEGNAWED
ABDEEGRU	BEDEGUAR
ABDEEHMS	BESHAMED
ABDEEHMT	EMBATHED
ABDEEHNO	BONEHEAD
ABDEEHRT	BREATHED
ABDEEHSS	BEDASHES
ABDEEHST	BETHESDA
ABDEEHTT	BEHATTED
ABDEEILM	EMBAILED
ABDEEILN	DENIABLE
ABDEEILR	RIDEABLE
ABDEEILS	ABSEILED
ABDEEILT	DELIBATE
ABDEEILW	BEWAILED
ABDEEIRS	BEARDIES
ABDEEIRT	EBRIATED
ABDEEIST	BEADIEST
	DIABETES
ABDEEITU	BEAUTIED
ABDEEJMN	ENJAMBED
ABDEEKMN	EMBANKED
ABDEEKMR	BEDMAKER
	EMBARKED
ABDEEKNR	BARKENED
	BEDARKEN
ABDEEKNV	BEKNAVED
ABDEELLL	LABELLED
ABDEELLM	EMBALLED
ABDEELLT	BALLETED
ABDEELLW	WELDABLE
ABDEELMM	EMBALMED
ABDEELMS	BELDAMES
	BEMEDALS
ABDEELMU	BEMAULED
ABDEELMZ	EMBLAZED
ABDEELNT	BANDELET
ABDEELRS	BEDERALS
ABDEELRZ	BLAZERED
ABDEELSV	BESLAVED
ABDEELTT	BATTELED
	TABLETED
ABDEELZZ	BEDAZZLE
ABDEEMNO	BEMOANED
ABDEEMNS	BEADSMEN
	BEDESMAN
ABDEEMRR	EMBARRED
ABDEEMRS	EMBREADS
ABDEEMRV	EMBRAVED
ABDEENNR	BANNERED
ABDEENRT	BANTERED
ABDEENRZ	BRAZENED
ABDEENST	ABSENTED
ABDEENTT	BATTENED
ABDEEPRS	BESPREAD
ABDEEPTT	BEPATTED
ABDEERRT	BARTERED
ABDEERRY	RYEBREAD
ABDEERSS	DEBASERS
ABDEERST	BETREADS
	BREASTED
	DEBATERS
ABDEERTT	BATTERED
	DRABETTE
ABDEERTY	BETRAYED
ABDEERWY	BEWRAYED
ABDEESST	BASSETED
	BESTEADS
ABDEFLLO	FOLDABLE
ABDEFLNU	FUNDABLE
	UNFABLED
ABDEFLOR	FORDABLE
ABDEFLST	FLATBEDS
ABDEFLSU	LEAFBUDS
ABDEFNRU	FABURDEN
ABDEFRSW	BEDWARFS
ABDEGGIL	DIGGABLE
ABDEGGNU	UNBAGGED
ABDEGHRS	BEGHARDS
ABDEGIJN	BEJADING
ABDEGILN	BLINDAGE
ABDEGILU	GUIDABLE
ABDEGIMT	GAMBITED
ABDEGINO	GABIONED
ABDEGINR	BEARDING
	BREADING
ABDEGINS	BEADINGS
	DEBASING
ABDEGINT	DEBATING
ABDEGINZ	BEDAZING
ABDEGIRR	ABRIDGER
ABDEGIRS	ABRIDGES
	BRIGADES
ABDEGLNR	BRANGLED
ABDEGLOT	GLOBATED
ABDEGLRS	BELGARDS
ABDEGLRY	BADGERLY
ABDEGMRU	UMBRAGED
ABDEGNOR	BONDAGER
ABDEGNOS	BONDAGES
	DOGBANES
ABDEGOPR	PEGBOARD
ABDEGRSU	SUBGRADE
ABDEHILL	BILLHEAD
ABDEHILS	DISHABLE
ABDEHIMT	IMBATHED
ABDEHINS	BANISHED
ABDEHITU	HABITUDE
ABDEHKLU	BULKHEAD
ABDEHLLN	HANDBELL
ABDEHLLU	BULLHEAD
ABDEHLMS	SHAMBLED
ABDEHLOT	BOLTHEAD
ABDEHLRS	HALBERDS
ABDEHMRU	RHUMBAED
ABDEHMSU	AMBUSHED
ABDEHNTU	UNBATHED
ABDEHORR	ABHORRED
	HARBORED
ABDEHOSW	BESHADOW
	BOWHEADS
ABDEHRST	BREADTHS
ABDEHSSU	SUBHEADS
ABDEIIRT	DIATRIBE
ABDEIKMR	IMBARKED
ABDEIKNU	BAUDEKIN
ABDEILMN	MANDIBLE
ABDEILNR	BILANDER
ABDEILNT	BIDENTAL
ABDEILNY	DENIABLY
ABDEILOV	VOIDABLE
ABDEILPS	PIEBALDS
ABDEILRS	RAILBEDS
ABDEILRT	LIBRATED
ABDEILRV	DRIVABLE
ABDEILRY	DIABLERY
ABDEILSS	DISABLES
ABDEILSU	AUDIBLES
ABDEILTU	DUTIABLE
ABDEIMNR	BRIDEMAN
ABDEIMOO	AMOEBOID
ABDEIMOR	AMBEROID
ABDEIMRR	IMBARRED
ABDEIMRS	EMBRAIDS
ABDEINOR	DEBONAIR
ABDEINOT	OBTAINED
ABDEINRS	BRANDIES
	BRANDISE
ABDEINST	BANDIEST
ABDEINSU	UNBIASED
ABDEINSW	BEDAWINS
ABDEINTU	UNBAITED
ABDEIOTV	OBVIATED
ABDEIPST	BAPTISED
ABDEIPTZ	BAPTIZED
ABDEIRSS	SEABIRDS
	SIDEBARS
ABDEIRST	BARDIEST
	BRAIDEST
	RABIDEST
	TRIBADES
ABDEIRSW	BAWDRIES
	DAWBRIES
ABDEIRTV	VIBRATED
ABDEISST	BASTIDES
ABDEISSU	DISABUSE
ABDEISTU	DAUBIEST
ABDEISTW	BAWDIEST
ABDEITTU	DUBITATE
ABDEJNOW	JAWBONED
ABDEKLSW	SKEWBALD
ABDEKNNU	UNBANKED
ABDEKNRU	UNBARKED
ABDEKNSU	SUNBAKED
ABDEKOOR	ABROOKED
ABDEKORY	KEYBOARD
ABDELLOT	BALLOTED
ABDELMNU	UNBLAMED
ABDELNOR	BANDEROL
ABDELNOZ	BLAZONED
ABDELNRY	BYLANDER
ABDELNSS	BALDNESS
ABDELNST	BLANDEST
ABDELORU	LABOURED
ABDELOSV	ABSOLVED
ABDELPSY	PYEBALDS
ABDELRRS	DRABLERS
ABDELRSU	DURABLES
ABDELRTT	BRATTLED
ABDELSTU	SUBLATED
ABDEMNNS	BANDSMEN
ABDEMNNY	BANDYMEN
ABDEMNOS	ABDOMENS
ABDEMRTU	DRUMBEAT
	UMBRATED
ABDENNOS	NOSEBAND
ABDENOOT	BATOONED
ABDENORS	BANDORES
	BROADENS
ABDENORW	RAWBONED
ABDENORY	BONEYARD
ABDENOTW	DOWNBEAT
ABDENRRS	BRANDERS
ABDENRRU	UNBARRED
ABDENRSS	DRABNESS

ABDENRST BANDSTER
ABDENRTU BREADNUT
TURBANED
ABDENSSU SUBDEANS
ABDENTTU DEBUTANT
ABDEOPRT PROBATED
ABDEORRS BOARDERS
ABDEORRU ARBOURED
ABDEORRW WARDROBE
ABDEORST BROADEST
ABDEORSW SOWBREAD
ABDEORTU OBDURATE
TABOURED
ABDEOSTU BOUTADES
ABDEPRUY UPBRAYED
ABDEPSSY BYPASSED
ABDERRSU ABSURDER
ABDERSST DABSTERS
ABDERSSU SUBEDARS
SURBASED
ABDERSTU SURBATED
ABDERSTW BEDSTRAW
ABDERSTY DRYBEATS
ABDFLOOT FOLDBOAT
ABDGGORS BOGGARDS
ABDGHINR HANGBIRD
ABDGIINR BRAIDING
ABDGIINS ABIDINGS
ABDGILNR BARDLING
ABDGILNU BLAUDING
ABDGIMRU GUIMBARD
ABDGINNR BRANDING
ABDGINNS BANDINGS
ABDGINNY BANDYING
ABDGINOR ABORDING
BOARDING
ABDGINRS BRIGANDS
ABDGINST DINGBATS
ABDGINSU DAUBINGS
ABDGINSW WINDBAGS
ABDGLNOS BOGLANDS
ABDGLOOR LOGBOARD
ABDGLSUY LADYBUGS
ABDHHSSU SHADBUSH
ABDHIIST ADHIBITS
DISHABIT
ABDHILLN HANDBILL
ABDHILNS BLANDISH
ABDHINRS BRANDISH
ABDHIORS BROADISH
ABDHIPRS BARDSHIP
ABDHIRTY BIRTHDAY
ABDHKNOO HANDBOOK
ABDHLORW BLOWHARD
ABDHLOSW SHADBLOW
ABDHMORS RHABDOMS
ABDHMOTU BADMOUTH
ABDHMSTU MUDBATHS
ABDHNORS BODHRANS
ABDHNSSU HUSBANDS
ABDIILLR BILLIARD
ABDIIMNR MIDBRAIN
ABDIIMSU BASIDIUM
ABDIINOS OBSIDIAN
ABDIINTT BANDITTI
ABDIIRTY RABIDITY
ABDIKLNR BLINKARD
ABDIKNSW BAWDKINS
ABDIKRSS DISBARKS
ABDILOOS DIABOLOS

ABDILORS LABROIDS
ABDILOST BLASTOID
TABLOIDS
ABDILOTY TABLOIDY
ABDILRRY RIBALDRY
ABDILRSW AWLBIRDS
ABDILRZZ BLIZZARD
ABDILSTU SUBTIDAL
ABDIMORS AMBROIDS
ABDINOTY ANTIBODY
ABDINRST ANTBIRDS
ABDINRTY BANDITRY
ABDIOSUU SUBAUDIO
ABDIPRSU UPBRAIDS
ABDIRRUY RIBAUDRY
ABDKLNOO BOOKLAND
ABDKNOOS BANDOOKS
ABDLLNOS SLOBLAND
ABDLLORS BOLLARDS
ABDLNORS BANDROLS
ABDLRSUU SUBDURAL
ABDLRSUY ABSURDLY
RYBAULDS
ABDLSSUU SUBDUALS
ABDLSTUU SUBADULT
ABDMNNOS BONDSMAN
ABDMNOUW MAWBOUND
ABDMOOPR MOPBOARD
ABDMRSUY MARYBUDS
ABDNOPRS PROBANDS
ABDNORSU BAUDRONS
ABDNORUY BOUNDARY
ABDNOSSY SANDBOYS
ABDNRSTU TURBANDS
ABDOORSW BARWOODS
ABDOORTU OUTBOARD
ABDOOSSW BASSWOOD
ABDRSSTU BUSTARDS
ABDRSUZZ BUZZARDS
ABEEEFRS FREEBASE
ABEEEGRS BARGEESE
BEERAGES
ABEEEGRV BEVERAGE
ABEEEHTT HEBETATE
ABEEENRT TENEBRAE
ABEEENRV BEREAVEN
ABEEENST ABSENTEE
ABEEERRT TEREBRAE
ABEEERSV BEREAVES
ABEEFFTU BEAUFFET
ABEEFILS FEASIBLE
ABEEFIST TABEFIES
ABEEFLLL FELLABLE
ABEEFLLN BEFALLEN
ABEEFLOS BEEFALOS
ABEEFORR FOREBEAR
ABEEFSTU BEAUFETS
ABEEGHRS HERBAGES
ABEEGHRT BERTHAGE
ABEEGINR BAREGINE
BERGENIA
ABEEGIRV VERBIAGE
ABEEGLLR GABELLER
ABEEGLLS GABELLES
ABEEGLRS BEAGLERS
ABEEGLTT GETTABLE
ABEEGMNR BARGEMEN
ABEEGMTY MEGABYTE
ABEEGOSZ GAZEBOES
ABEEGRRS GERBERAS

ABEEGRST ABSTERGE
ABEEGRSU AUBERGES
ABEEGRSW BREWAGES
ABEEGTTU BAGUETTE
ABEEHILR HIREABLE
ABEEHINT THEBAINE
ABEEHLLP HELPABLE
ABEEHLLR BEERHALL
HAREBELL
ABEEHLSV BEHALVES
ABEEHMSS BESHAMES
ABEEHMST EMBATHES
ABEEHNNS HENBANES
ABEEHNPP BEHAPPEN
ABEEHNSS BANSHEES
ABEEHNTT HEBETANT
ABEEHQTU BEQUEATH
ABEEHRRT BREATHER
ABEEHRST BREATHES
HARTBEES
ABEEIKLL LIKEABLE
ABEEIKRS BAKERIES
ABEEIKST BEAKIEST
ABEEILLR RELIABLE
ABEEILLV LEVIABLE
LIVEABLE
ABEEILMS BELAMIES
ABEEILNP PLEBEIAN
ABEEILNU BANLIEUE
ABEEILNV ENVIABLE
ABEEILPX EXPIABLE
ABEEILRR BLEARIER
ABEEILRT LIBERATE
ABEEILST SEABLITE
ABEEILSV EVASIBLE
ABEEILSZ SEIZABLE
SIZEABLE
ABEEILTV EVITABLE
ABEEILVW VIEWABLE
ABEEIMRT AMBERITE
ABEEIMST BEAMIEST
ABEEINST BETAINES
ABEEINTY AYENBITE
ABEEIPRS BEPRAISE
ABEEIRTT BATTERIE
ABEEIRTV BREVIATE
ABEEISST BEASTIES
ABEEISSV ABESSIVE
ABEEISTU BEAUTIES
ABEEITUX BEAUXITE
ABEEJMOR JAMBOREE
ABEEKLOT KEELBOAT
ABEEKLST BLEAKEST
ABEEKMNR BRAKEMEN
EMBANKER
ABEEKNSV BEKNAVES
ABEEKOOP PEEKABOO
ABEEKOPS PEEKABOS
ABEEKPSS BESPEAKS
ABEEKRRS BREAKERS
ABEEKRST BESTREAK
ABEELLLS SELLABLE
ABEELLLT TELLABLE
ABEELLOT BALLOTEE
ABEELLOV LOVEABLE
ABEELLSY EYEBALLS
ABEELLTT LETTABLE
ABEELMMR EMBALMER
EMMARBLE
ABEELMOV MOVEABLE

ABEELMPR PREAMBLE
ABEELMRT ATREMBLE
ABEELMSS ASSEMBLE
BEAMLESS
ABEELMST BEAMLETS
ABEELMSZ EMBLAZES
ABEELMTT EMBATTLE
ABEELNOP BEANPOLE
OPENABLE
ABEELNRS ENABLERS
ABEELNRT RENTABLE
ABEELNTU TUNEABLE
ABEELOPR OPERABLE
ROPEABLE
ABEELOPS POSEABLE
ABEELORS EARLOBES
ABEELORX EXORABLE
ABEELPRS BEPEARLS
ABEELRST BLEAREST
BLEATERS
RETABLES
ABEELRSU REUSABLE
ABEELRSV BESLAVER
ABEELRTT BATTELER
ABEELRTU BATELEUR
BLEUATRE
ABEELSSS BASELESS
ABEELSST BATELESS
ABEELSSU SUBLEASE
ABEELSSV BESLAVES
ABEELSTT TESTABLE
ABEEMMNR MEMBRANE
ABEEMMRU BUMMAREE
ABEEMNOR BEMOANER
ABEEMNST BASEMENT
ABEEMNTT ABETMENT
BATEMENT
ABEEMRSS BESMEARS
ABEEMRSV EMBRAVES
ABEENNRT BANNERET
ABEENNRU EBURNEAN
ABEENNTU UNBEATEN
ABEENORS SEABORNE
ABEENOTZ BENZOATE
ABEENRRR BARRENER
ABEENRRT BANTERER
ABEENRSS BARENESS
ABEENRSV VERBENAS
ABEENSSS BASENESS
ABEEORRV OVERBEAR
ABEEORST REBATOES
ABEEORTV OVERBEAT
ABEEPRRY PEABERRY
ABEERRRT BARTERER
ABEERRST REBATERS
TABRERES
TEREBRAS
ABEERRTT BARRETTE
ABEERRTV VERTEBRA
ABEERRTY BETRAYER
TEABERRY
ABEERSTT ABETTERS
ABEERSTU SUBERATE
ABEESZZZ BEZAZZES
ABEFFLRS BAFFLERS
ABEFFOST OFFBEATS
ABEFGILS FILABEGS
ABEFGLLR BERGFALL
ABEFGSST GABFESTS
ABEFHILS FISHABLE

ABEFHOOT HOOFBEAT
ABEFIIMR FIMBRIAE
ABEFILLL FALLIBLE
ABEFILLM FILMABLE
ABEFILLR FIREBALL
ABEFILLT LIFTABLE
ABEFILOT LIFEBOAT
ABEFILRS BARFLIES
ABEFILSU FABULISE
ABEFILSY FEASIBLY
ABEFILUZ FABULIZE
ABEFINSU BEAUFINS
ABEFIRRT FIREBRAT
ABEFITUY BEAUTIFY
ABEFLLMU BLAMEFUL
ABEFLLTU TABLEFUL
ABEFLMOR FORMABLE
ABEFLNRU FUNEBRAL
ABEFLNSY FLYBANES
ABEFMRSU SUBFRAME
ABEFOORT BAREFOOT
ABEFORRS FORBEARS
ABEGGHLU HUGGABLE
ABEGGILN BEAGLING
ABEGGIST BAGGIEST
ABEGGLLU LUGGABLE
ABEGGLRS BLAGGERS
ABEGGLRY BEGGARLY
ABEGGMOS GAMBOGES
ABEGGNSU BUGGANES
ABEGGRSU BURGAGES
ABEGHILP PHILABEG
ABEGHILR ALBERGHI
ABEGHINO OBEAHING
ABEGHINT BEATHING
ABEGHINV BEHAVING
ABEGHNSS SHEBANGS
ABEGHORR BEGORRAH
ABEGHRRY HAGBERRY
ABEGHRST BARGHEST
ABEGIIMS BIGAMIES
ABEGIKNR BREAKING
ABEGIKNT BETAKING
ABEGILMN EMBALING
ABEGILNN ENABLING
ABEGILNR BLEARING
ABEGILNS SINGABLE
ABEGILNT BELATING
BLEATING
TANGIBLE
ABEGILNY BELAYING
ABEGILOT OBLIGATE
ABEGIMNN BENAMING
ABEGIMNR BREAMING
ABEGIMNS BEAMINGS
EMBASING
ABEGIMNY EMBAYING
ABEGIMRS GAMBIERS
ABEGIMST MEGABITS
ABEGIMUX GIAMBEUX
ABEGINOR ABORIGEN
ABEGINOS BEGONIAS
ABEGINRS BEARINGS
SABERING
ABEGINRT BERATING
REBATING
ABEGINRW BEWARING
ABEGINRY BERAYING
ABEGINST BEATINGS
ABEGINTT ABETTING

ABEGINTW WINGBEAT
ABEGIOSS BIOGASES
ABEGIPPR BAGPIPER
ABEGIPPS BAGPIPES
ABEGKORS BROKAGES
GROSBEAK
ABEGKOSS BOSKAGES
ABEGLLLU GULLABLE
ABEGLLOR BARGELLO
ABEGLMRS GAMBLERS
GAMBRELS
ABEGLNRS BRANGLES
ABEGLORW GROWABLE
ABEGLRRS GARBLERS
ABEGLRUU BLAGUEUR
ABEGLSTU GUSTABLE
ABEGMNOS GAMBESON
ABEGMORT BERGAMOT
ABEGMRSU UMBRAGES
ABEGNNST BANTENGS
ABEGNOSS NOSEBAGS
ABEGNRST BANGSTER
ABEGNRTU BURGANET
ABEGNSTU SUBAGENT
ABEGOORS BARGOOSE
ABEGOSTT BOTTEGAS
ABEGOSUY BUOYAGES
ABEGRRSU GARBURES
ABEGRRUV BURGRAVE
ABEGRSST BARGESTS
ABEGSSTU SUBSTAGE
ABEHILLR HAIRBELL
ABEHILNR HIBERNAL
ABEHILRS BLASHIER
ABEHILTT TITHABLE
ABEHIMOS OBEAHISM
ABEHIMST IMBATHES
ABEHINSS BANISHES
ABEHINST ABSINTHE
ABEHIOPU EUPHOBIA
ABEHIORV BEHAVIOR
ABEHIRRS BRASHIER
ABEHISTU HABITUES
ABEHISTZ ZABTIEHS
ABEHJORS JOBSHARE
ABEHKLLW HAWKBELL
ABEHKNOR HORNBEAK
ABEHKRSU HAUBERKS
ABEHLLRT BETHRALL
ABEHLMMU HUMMABLE
ABEHLMSS SHAMBLES
ABEHLNOT BENTHOAL
ABEHLOTY HYLOBATE
ABEHLRST BLATHERS
HALBERTS
ABEHLSSS BASHLESS
ABEHMNOR HORNBEAM
ABEHMOOR REHOBOAM
ABEHMSSU AMBUSHES
ABEHNSTU SUNBATHE
ABEHORRR ABHORRER
HARBORER
ABEHORST BATHORSE
ABEHOSST BATHOSES
ABEHOSTX HATBOXES
ABEHOSXY HAYBOXES
ABEHRSST BRASHEST
ABEIILLS BAILLIES
ABEIILMT IMITABLE
ABEIILNN BIENNIAL

ABEIILNV INVIABLE
ABEIILPT PITIABLE
ABEIILRR LIBRAIRE
ABEIILRS BISERIAL
ABEIILST ALBITISE
SIBILATE
ABEIILTV VITIABLE
ABEIILTZ ALBITIZE
ABEIINRR BRAINIER
ABEIINRS BINARIES
ABEIINST BAINITES
ABEIJLTU JUBILATE
ABEIJMNN BENJAMIN
ABEIJMRS JAMBIERS
ABEIJNSS BASENJIS
ABEIKLLN BALKLINE
LINKABLE
ABEIKLNS BLANKIES
ABEIKLSS KISSABLE
ABEIKLST BALKIEST
ABEIKNRR BRANKIER
ABEIKNRS BEARSKIN
INBREAKS
ABEIKNST BEATNIKS
ABEIKRST BARKIEST
BRAKIEST
BREASKIT
ABEIKSWY BIKEWAYS
ABEILLLT TILLABLE
ABEILLLW WILLABLE
ABEILLMM LIMBMEAL
ABEILLNT LIBELANT
ABEILLOS ISOLABLE
LOBELIAS
ABEILLOV VIOLABLE
ABEILLQU LIQUABLE
ABEILLRR BRAILLER
ABEILLRS BALLSIER
LIBERALS
ABEILLRY BERYLLIA
RELIABLY
ABEILLST BASTILLE
ABEILLTT TILTABLE
ABEILMNS BAILSMEN
ABEILMNT BAILMENT
ABEILMOR BROMELIA
ABEILMRR MARBLIER
ABEILMRS REMBLAIS
ABEILMRW WAMBLIER
ABEILMSS MISSABLE
ABEILMST BALMIEST
TIMBALES
ABEILNNW WINNABLE
ABEILNOP OPINABLE
ABEILNPS BIPLANES
ABEILNPT PINTABLE
ABEILNRS RINSABLE
ABEILNRU RUINABLE
ABEILNSS ALBINESS
LESBIANS
ABEILNST INSTABLE
ABEILNSU SABULINE
ABEILNTV BIVALENT
ABEILNUV UNVIABLE
ABEILNVY ENVIABLY
ABEILPPT TIPPABLE
ABEILPRT PARTIBLE
ABEILPRZ PRIZABLE
ABEILPSS PASSIBLE
ABEILPST EPIBLAST

ABEILRRU REBURIAL
ABEILRRW BRAWLIER
ABEILRST LIBRATES
TABLIERS
ABEILRTW WRITABLE
ABEILSST ASTILBES
BESTIALS
STABILES
ABEILSSU ISSUABLE
SUASIBLE
ABEILSTU SUITABLE
ABEILSTY BEASTILY
ABEILSUX BISEXUAL
ABEILSVV BIVALVES
ABEIMNRS MIRBANES
ABEIMNST AMBIENTS
ABEIMRST BARMIEST
ABEIMRSU AUMBRIES
ABEIMRTV AMBIVERT
VERBATIM
ABEIMSSU IAMBUSES
ABEINNOS BESONIAN
ABEINNOZ BEZONIAN
ABEINNRR BRANNIER
ABEINNRU INURBANE
ABEINORR AIRBORNE
ABEINORS BARONIES
ABEINORT BARITONE
OBTAINER
ABEINOST BOTANIES
BOTANISE
NIOBATES
OBEISANT
ABEINOTZ BOTANIZE
ABEINPST BEPAINTS
ABEINQSU BASQUINE
ABEINRRW BRAWNIER
ABEINRST ATEBRINS
BANISTER
ABEINRSU ANBURIES
URBANISE
ABEINRSZ ZEBRINAS
ABEINRTU BRAUNITE
URBANITE
ABEINRUZ URBANIZE
ABEINSST BASINETS
BASSINET
BESAINTS
BESTAINS
ABEINSSU UNBIASES
ABEINSTT TABINETS
ABEINTTU INTUBATE
ABEIORSS ISOBARES
ABEIORST SABOTIER
ABEIORTV ABORTIVE
ABEIOSSS ISOBASES
ABEIOSTV OBVIATES
ABEIPSST BAPTISES
ABEIPSTZ BAPTIZES
ABEIRRRS BARRIERS
ABEIRRSS BRASIERS
BRASSIER
ABEIRRST ARBITERS
RAREBITS
ABEIRRSZ BRAZIERS
ABEIRRTT BRATTIER
ABEIRRVY BREVIARY
ABEIRSSS BRASSIES
ABEIRSTT BIRETTAS
ABEIRSTV VIBRATES

ABEIRSTW WARBIEST
ABEIRSTY BESTIARY
SYBARITE
ABEIRSUX EXURBIAS
ABEIRTTY YTTERBIA
ABEISSST BASSIEST
ABEISSTT BATISTES
ABEISTTT BATTIEST
ABEISTUX BAUXITES
ABEISZZZ BIZAZZES
ABEITTTU TITUBATE
ABEJKLOU KABELJOU
ABEJLMPU JUMPABLE
ABEJMNOS JAMBONES
ABEJMOOR JEROBOAM
ABEJNOSW JAWBONES
ABEJOSWX JAWBOXES
ABEJRRSU ABJURERS
ABEKLMOS SMOKABLE
ABEKLNOW KNOWABLE
ABEKLNRY BANKERLY
ABEKLNST BLANKEST
BLANKETS
ABEKLNTY BLANKETY
ABEKLORW WORKABLE
ABEKLRSS BARKLESS
ABEKMNNS BANKSMEN
ABEKNSSU SUNBAKES
ABEKNSSY SNEAKSBY
ABEKOORS ABROOKES
ABEKOORY YEARBOOK
ABEKORTU OUTBREAK
ABEKPRSU UPBREAKS
ABEKRSTY BASKETRY
ABELLLMU LABELLUM
ABELLLOR ROLLABLE
ABELLLOT TOLLABLE
ABELLLSY SYLLABLE
ABELLMOR OMBRELLA
ABELLMRU UMBELLAR
UMBRELLA
ABELLNOS BONSELLA
ABELLNOT BALLONET
ABELLNRU RUBELLAN
ABELLNST NETBALLS
ABELLOSV SOLVABLE
ABELLOTU LOBULATE
ABELLRSU RUBELLAS
ABELLRVY VERBALLY
ABELMNNO NOBLEMAN
ABELMNOZ EMBLAZON
ABELMNST SEMBLANT
ABELMNSU ALBUMENS
ABELMOOT MOOTABLE
ABELMOSV MOVABLES
ABELMOVY MOVEABLY
ABELMPTU PLUMBATE
ABELMRRS MARBLERS
RAMBLERS
ABELMRST LAMBERTS
ABELMSSY ASSEMBLY
ABELNNOR BANNEROL
ABELNNRU RUNNABLE
ABELNORZ BLAZONER
ABELNOST NEOBLAST
NOTABLES
ABELNOSY BALONEYS
ABELNQTU BLANQUET
ABELNRSS BRANSLES
ABELNRST BRANTLES

ABELNRSY BLARNEYS
ABELNRUY URBANELY
ABELNRYZ BRAZENLY
ABELNSTU UNSTABLE
ABELNSTY ABSENTLY
ABELNSUU UNUSABLE
ABELOPRT PORTABLE
ABELOPRU POURABLE
ABELOPRV PROVABLE
ABELOPST POTABLES
ABELOPTT TABLETOP
ABELOQTU QUOTABLE
ABELORRU LABOURER
ABELORST BLOATERS
SORTABLE
STORABLE
ABELORSU RUBEOLAS
ABELORSV ABSOLVER
ABELOSSU SABULOSE
ABELOSSV ABSOLVES
ABELOSTU ABSOLUTE
ABELOSTW BESTOWAL
ABELPRTU PUBERTAL
ABELQSUU SUBEQUAL
ABELRRSW BRAWLERS
WARBLERS
ABELRRTU BARRULET
ABELRSST BLASTERS
STABLERS
ABELRSSY LABRYSES
ABELRSTT BATTLERS
BLATTERS
BRATTLES
ABELRSTU BALUSTER
ABELRSTW BLEWARTS
ABELRSUZ ZEBRULAS
ABELRTTU BURLETTA
REBUTTAL
ABELSSTT STABLEST
ABELSSTU SUBLATES
ABELSTUU SUBULATE
ABELSTWY BELTWAYS
ABELTTUU TUBULATE
ABEMMNOO MOONBEAM
ABEMNOTU UMBONATE
ABEMNOTW BATWOMEN
ABEMNPRU PENUMBRA
ABEMNRSY MYRBANES
ABEMNSSU SUNBEAMS
ABEMNSUY SUNBEAMY
ABEMNTTU ABUTMENT
ABEMORRS EMBRASOR
ABEMORST BROMATES
ABEMORSU AMBEROUS
ABEMORTZ BAROMETZ
ABENNORS BARONNES
ABENOPSU SUBPOENA
ABENORSS BARONESS
ABENORST BARONETS
ABENORTT BETATRON
ABENORTV BEVATRON
ABENORTY BARYTONE
ABENOSSW SAWBONES
ABENOSTY BAYONETS
ABENQSTU BANQUETS
ABENRRYZ BRAZENRY
ABENRSTU UNBRASTE
URBANEST
ABEOPRSS SAPROBES
ABEOPRST PROBATES

ABEOQRSU BAROQUES
ABEORRSS BRASEROS
ABEORRST ARBORETS
TABORERS
ABEORSST BOASTERS
SORBATES
ABEORSSY ROSEBAYS
ABEORSTT ABETTORS
BATTEROS
TABORETS
ABEORSTU SABOTEUR
ABEORTTU OBTURATE
TABOURET
ABEORTUV OUTBRAVE
ABEOSSST ASBESTOS
ABEOSTUV SUBOVATE
ABEPRRTU ABRUPTER
ABEPSSSY BYPASSES
ABEQRSUU ARQUEBUS
ABERRSSU SABREURS
ABERRTYY TAYBERRY
ABERRWXY WAXBERRY
ABERSSST BRASSETS
ABERSSSU SURBASES
ABERSSTU ABSTRUSE
SURBATES
ABERSSTW WABSTERS
ABERSTTU ABUTTERS
ABERTTUY BUTYRATE
ABESSTTU SUBSTATE
ABFFGILN BAFFLING
ABFFIILS BAILIFFS
ABFFLLPU PUFFBALL
ABFFNOTU BOUFFANT
ABFGILNS FABLINGS
ABFGLLOO GOOFBALL
ABFGORUU FAUBOURG
ABFHIIST BAITFISH
ABFHILLS FISHBALL
ABFHIORS BOARFISH
ABFIILLR FIBRILLA
ABFILLLY FALLIBLY
ABFILNSU BASINFUL
ABFILSTU FABULIST
ABFIMORS FIBROMAS
ABFJORSU FRABJOUS
ABFKLLOR KORFBALL
ABFLLOOT FOOTBALL
ABFLLOST SOFTBALL
ABFLOSTU BOASTFUL
ABFLOSTY FLYBOATS
ABFLOSUU FABULOUS
ABFNORTU TURBOFAN
ABFOORST FOOTBARS
ABFSSTTU TUBFASTS
ABGGGILN BLAGGING
ABGGGINR BRAGGING
ABGGGINS BAGGINGS
ABGGIJNN JINGBANG
ABGGILMN GAMBLING
ABGGILNR GARBLING
ABGGINNS BANGINGS
ABGGNOOT TOBOGGAN
ABGGORST BOGGARTS
ABGHHILL HIGHBALL
ABGHIINT HABITING
ABGHILMN HAMBLING
ABGHINRS BRASHING
ABGHINSS BASHINGS
ABGHINWZ WHIZBANG

ABGHIOPR BIOGRAPH
ABGHLOST HAGBOLTS
ABGHMORU BROUGHAM
ABGIILNR BRAILING
ABGIILNS SAIBLING
ABGIILNT LIBATING
ABGIILOT OBLIGATI
ABGIIMNS IMBASING
ABGIIMST BIGAMIST
ABGIINNO BIGNONIA
ABGIINNR BRAINING
ABGIINOR ABORIGIN
ABGIINRS BRAISING
ABGIINSS BIASINGS
BIASSING
ABGIINST BAITINGS
ABGIJNRU ABJURING
ABGIKLNN BLANKING
ABGIKLNS BALKINGS
ABGIKLNU BAULKING
ABGIKNNR BRANKING
ABGIKNNS BANKINGS
ABGILLMN LAMBLING
ABGILLNS BALLINGS
ABGILMNR MARBLING
RAMBLING
ABGILMNS AMBLINGS
ABGILMNW WAMBLING
ABGILNNT BANTLING
ABGILNOR LABORING
ABGILNOT BLOATING
OBLIGANT
ABGILNRT BRATLING
ABGILNRW BRAWLING
WARBLING
ABGILNST BLASTING
STABLING
TABLINGS
ABGILNSW BAWLINGS
ABGILNTT BATTLING
BLATTING
ABGILNTY TANGIBLY
ABGILOOT OBLIGATO
ABGILORS GARBOILS
ABGILORW BRIGALOW
ABGIMMNO MAMBOING
ABGIMNRU RUMBAING
ABGIMOSU BIGAMOUS
SUBIMAGO
ABGIMSST GAMBISTS
ABGINNOR ABORNING
ABGINNOT BATONING
ABGINNRU UNBARING
ABGINNRX BANXRING
ABGINNST BANTINGS
ABGINOOT TABOOING
ABGINORT ABORTING
TABORING
ABGINOST BOASTING
BOATINGS
BOSTANGI
ABGINRRS BARRINGS
ABGINRST BRASTING
ABGINSST BASTINGS
ABGINSTT BATTINGS
ABGINSTW BATSWING
ABGINTTU ABUTTING
ABGIOPST PIGBOATS
ABGKORSW WORKBAGS
ABGLLLOY GLOBALLY

ABGLLORU GLOBULAR
ABGLLRUY BULLYRAG
ABGLMNSU LUMBANGS
ABGLMOPU PLUMBAGO
ABGLMOSU LUMBAGOS
ABGLNOOT LONGBOAT
ABGLNOUW BUNGALOW
ABGLOOST TOOLBAGS
ABGLOOTY BATOLOGY
ABGLORST RAGBOLTS
ABGLORSU GLABROUS
ABGLOSSU SUBGOALS
ABGLRRSU BURGLARS
ABGLRRUY BURGLARY
ABGMNOOR GAMBROON
ABGNOPRS PROBANGS
ABGNORSU OSNABURG
ABGNOSTU GUNBOATS
ABGNOSWY BOWYANGS
ABGOORST BOTARGOS
ABGOPSST POSTBAGS
ABGORRSU GOBURRAS
ABGORSTU OUTBRAGS
ABGOSTTU TUGBOATS
ABHHKOST KHOTBAHS
ABHHKSTU KHUTBAHS
ABHHRSTU HATBRUSH
ABHIINRS BRAINISH
ABHIINST INHABITS
ABHIIORZ RHIZOBIA
ABHIKLOR KOHLRABI
ABHIKLSS BASHLIKS
ABHIKSTW HAWKBITS
ABHILLPT PITHBALL
ABHILNOS HOBNAILS
ABHILNOT BIATHLON
ABHILOPS BASOPHIL
ABHILRTW WHIRLBAT
ABHILSST STABLISH
ABHILSTU HALIBUTS
ABHIMMST BATHMISM
ABHINSST ABSINTHS
ABHIOSST ISOBATHS
ABHIOSTU HAUTBOIS
ABHIRSTT BRATTISH
ABHKLSUW BUSHWALK
ABHKORSU BOURKHAS
KOURBASH
ABHLLMOT MOTHBALL
ABHLLOOY BALLYHOO
ABHLORTW WHORLBAT
ABHLOSWW WASHBOWL
ABHLPSUY SUBPHYLA
ABHLRSTU HURLBATS
ABHLSSTU SALTBUSH
ABHMNOTY BOTHYMAN
ABHMNSUU SUBHUMAN
ABHMOORT BATHROOM
ABHNSSTU SUNBATHS
ABHOORST TARBOOSH
ABHOOSTW SHOWBOAT
ABHORRSU HARBOURS
ABHORSTU TARBOUSH
ABHOSTUY HAUTBOYS
ABHSSTUW WASHTUBS
ABIIINRY BIRIYANI
ABIIKKST KIBITKAS
ABIIKLSS BASILISK
ABIILLMR MILLIBAR
ABIILLTY LABILITY

ABIILMNO BINOMIAL
ABIILMNS ALBINISM
ABIILMSU BULIMIAS
ABIILNOT LIBATION
ABIILNQS INQILABS
ABIILNRZ BRAZILIN
ABIILNST SIBILANT
ABIILPTY PITIABLY
ABIIMNOT AMBITION
ABIIMSST IAMBISTS
ABIINORS ROBINIAS
ABIINRSY BIRYANIS
ABIIRSSV VIBRISSA
ABIJLNRS BRINJALS
ABIJLNTU JUBILANT
ABIJNOOT JOBATION
ABIJNOST ABJOINTS
BANJOIST
ABIKLMNS LAMBKINS
LAMBSKIN
ABIKLNRY BYRLAKIN
ABIKLORS KILOBARS
ABIKMNNR BRINKMAN
ABIKMNRS BARMKINS
ABIKNORR IRONBARK
ABIKOSUZ BAZOUKIS
ABIKRSST BRITSKAS
ABIKRSTZ BRITZKAS
BRITZSKA
ABILLLPY PLAYBILL
ABILLMSU BALLIUMS
ABILLNPS PINBALLS
ABILLOVY VIOLABLY
ABILLRTY TRIBALLY
ABILLSSW SAWBILLS
ABILLSTT BATTILLS
ABILLSWX WAXBILLS
ABILLSWY WAYBILLS
ABILMNOU OLIBANUM
ABILMNSU ALBUMINS
ABILMOPS BIOPLASM
ABILMOTU BUMALOTI
ABILNOOT LOBATION
OBLATION
ABILNORU UNILOBAR
ABILNOTU ABLUTION
ABUTILON
ABILNRTU TRIBUNAL
TURBINAL
ABILOPRS PARBOILS
ABILOPST BIOPLAST
ABILORST ORBITALS
STROBILA
ABILORSV BOLIVARS
ABILORTY LIBATORY
ABILPSSY PASSIBLY
ABILRSSY BRASSILY
ABILRSUV SUBVIRAL
ABILSSUY ISSUABLY
ABILSTUY SUITABLY
ABIMMNOO MAINBOOM
ABIMNOSU BIMANOUS
ABIMNRTU TAMBURIN
ABIMORSU BIRAMOUS
ABIMPSST BAPTISMS
ABIMRSST STRABISM
ABIMRSTT TRIMTABS
ABINOORS BORONIAS
ABINOORT ABORTION
ABINORST TABORINS

ABINORSW RAINBOWS
ABINORTU TABOURIN
ABINORWY RAINBOWY
ABINOSST BASTIONS
ABINOSSU ABUSIONS
ABINOSTT BOTANIST
ABINRTUY URBANITY
ABINTTTU TITUBANT
ABIOPRSU BIPAROUS
ABIOPSTU SUBTOPIA
ABIORRST ARBORIST
ABIORRTV VIBRATOR
ABIORSTV VIBRATOS
ABIORTUY OBITUARY
ABIPSSTT BAPTISTS
ABIRRSTU AIRBURST
ABIRSSUZ SUBSIZAR
ABIRSTTY TRAYBITS
ABISSSST BASSISTS
ABJKMOSS SJAMBOKS
ABJLMOOS JAMBOOLS
ABKKMOOR BOOKMARK
ABKLLNOR BANKROLL
ABKLOOPY PLAYBOOK
ABKLRSUW BULWARKS
ABKNOPST STOPBANK
ABKNPRTU BANKRUPT
ABKNRSUU BUNRAKUS
ABKOORTW WORKBOAT
ABKOOSTT KOTTABOS
ABLLMOOR BALLROOM
ABLLMOPW BLOWLAMP
ABLLNOOS BALLOONS
ABLLNOSW SNOWBALL
ABLLORST BORSTALL
ABLLOSTY TALLBOYS
ABLLRTUY BRUTALLY
ABLLSSUY SYLLABUS
ABLMNRUU ALBURNUM
LABURNUM
ABLMOOST TOMBOLAS
ABLMOSTY MYOBLAST
ABLMPSUU PABULUMS
ABLNORYZ BLAZONRY
ABLNOSTU BUTANOLS
ABLNOSUZ SUBZONAL
ABLNRSUU SUBLUNAR
ABLNSUUY UNUSABLY
ABLOORST TOOLBARS
ABLOORTY OBLATORY
ABLOOSTT BOOTLAST
ABLOOSTZ ZOOBLAST
ABLOPRSU SUBPOLAR
ABLOPRVY PROVABLY
ABLOPSUU PABULOUS
ABLOPSYY PLAYBOYS
ABLOQTUY QUOTABLY
ABLORSST BORSTALS
ABLORSSU SUBSOLAR
ABLORSTW BLAWORTS
ABLORSUW BOURLAWS
ABLOSSUU SABULOUS
ABLOSTTU SUBTOTAL
ABLPRTUY ABRUPTLY
ABMNTTUY BUTTYMAN
ABMORSTU TAMBOURS
ABMOSSTU SUBATOMS
ABNOORRT ROBORANT
ABNOORSS SOROBANS
ABNOORSZ BORAZONS

ABNOOSSS BASSOONS
ABNORSTY BARYTONS
ABNORTUU RUNABOUT
ABNOSSSU BONASSUS
ABNRSTTU TURBANTS
ABOORRSU ARBOROUS
ABOORSTW ROWBOATS
ABOOSTTW TOWBOATS
ABORSSTU ROBUSTAS
ACCCDIIO COCCIDIA
ACCCENPY PECCANCY
ACCCFIIL CALCIFIC
ACCCHILO COLCHICA
ACCCIIPR CAPRICCI
ACCCILLY CYCLICAL
ACCDDEEN ACCENDED
CADENCED
ACCDDEIS CADDICES
ACCDDEOR ACCORDED
ACCDDIIT DIDACTIC
ACCDEENS CADENCES
ACCDEENT ACCENTED
ACCDEEPT ACCEPTED
ACCDEERS ACCEDERS
ACCDEERT ACCRETED
ACCDEERU CARDECUE
ACCDEERW ACCREWED
ACCDEESS ACCESSED
ACCDEGIN ACCEDING
ACCINGED
ACCDEHIK CHIACKED
ACCDEHIL CHALICED
ACCDEHIN CHICANED
ACCDEHKY CHYACKED
ACCDEHLT CLATCHED
ACCDEHNR CRANCHED
ACCDEHNU CHAUNCED
ACCDEIIS ACCIDIES
ACCDEILN CALCINED
ACCDEILU CAUDICLE
ACCDEILY DELICACY
ACCDEINT ACCIDENT
ACCDEIRT ACCREDIT
ACCDEISU CAUDICES
ACCDEKLR CRACKLED
ACCDEKOS COCKADES
ACCDELLY CALYCLED
ACCDELOY ACCLOYED
ACCDENOR CONACRED
ACCDENOV CONCAVED
ACCDEORR ACCORDER
ACCDEOST ACCOSTED
ACCDERSU ACCURSED
CARDECUS
ACCDESSU SUCCADES
ACCDESUU CADUCEUS
CAUCUSED
ACCDGHOO COACHDOG
ACCDHIIR DIARCHIC
ACCDHILS CHALCIDS
ACCDHIMO DOCHMIAC
ACCDHIOT CATHODIC
ACCDHLOR CLOCHARD
ACCDIIST DICASTIC
ACCDIITY DICACITY
ACCDILOY CALYCOID
ACCDILTY DACTYLIC
ACCDINOR CANCROID
DRACONIC
ACCDIOOR CORACOID

ACCDIORS SARCODIC
ACCDIOST STICCADO
ACCDITUY CADUCITY
ACCDKNOS CANDOCKS
ACCDKOSW DAWCOCKS
ACCDLOSY CACODYLS
ACCDOOST STOCCADO
ACCDOOXY CACODOXY
ACCDOSUU CADUCOUS
ACCEEHIT HICCATEE
ACCEEHLO COCHLEAE
ACCEEHOS COACHEES
ACCEEHRT CETERACH
ACCEEHST SEECATCH
ACCEEILR CELERIAC
ACCEEILS ECCLESIA
ACCEEKLN NECKLACE
ACCEELNR CLARENCE
ACCEELNS CENACLES
ACCEELOS COALESCE
ACCEELRT CALCRETE
ACCEENNS NASCENCE
ACCEENPR CREPANCE
ACCEENRS CREANCES
ACCEENST ACESCENT
ACCEEORT CROCEATE
ACCEEPRT ACCEPTER
ACCEERST ACCRETES
ACCEESSS ACCESSES
ACCEFFIY EFFICACY
ACCEFILS FASCICLE
ACCEFIST FACTICES
ACCEFLSU FELUCCAS
ACCEGINS ACCINGES
ACCEGKMO GAMECOCK
ACCEGOSS SOCCAGES
ACCEHHIS CHECHIAS
ACCEHHKO CHECHAKO
ACCEHIKP CHICKPEA
ACCEHILM ALCHEMIC
CHEMICAL
ACCEHILP CEPHALIC
ACCEHILS CALICHES
CHALICES
ACCEHILT HECTICAL
ACCEHIMN MECHANIC
ACCEHIMS SACHEMIC
ACCEHINO ANECHOIC
ACCEHINR CHANCIER
CHICANER
ACCEHINS CHICANES
ACCEHIOS COACHIES
ACCEHIRT CATCHIER
ACCEHLNS CHANCELS
ACCEHLOR COCHLEAR
ACCEHLOT CATECHOL
ACCEHLST CLATCHES
ACCEHMNO COACHMEN
ACCEHNNO CHACONNE
ACCEHNNY CYNANCHE
ACCEHNOR CHARNECO
ENCROACH
ACCEHNOT CONCHATE
ACCEHNRS CHANCERS
CHANCRES
CRANCHES
ACCEHNRY CHANCERY
ACCEHNSU CHAUNCES
ACCEHOPT CACHEPOT
ACCEHORS CAROCHES
COACHERS
ACCEHPSU CAPUCHES
ACCEHRST CATCHERS
CRATCHES
ACCEHSST SCATCHES
ACCEHSTU CATECHUS
ACCEIIST CAECITIS
ACCEIKPS ICEPACKS
ACCEILLN CANCELLI
ACCEILLR CLERICAL
ACCEILLS CALICLES
ACCEILLU CAULICLE
ACCEILLV CLAVICLE
ACCEILNS CALCINES
SCENICAL
ACCEILNT CANTICLE
ACCEILNV CLAVECIN
ACCEILNY CALYCINE
ACCEILOS CALICOES
COELIACS
ACCEILRV CERVICAL
ACCEILST CALCITES
ACCEIMOS OCCAMIES
ACCEIMRS CERAMICS
ACCEINNR CANCRINE
ACCEINOS COCAINES
ACCEINSV VACCINES
ACCEINTU CUNEATIC
ACCEIOPR CECROPIA
ACCEIOTV COACTIVE
ACCEIPRS CAPRICES
ACCEIPRT PRACTICE
ACCEIPSV PECCAVIS
ACCEIQSU CACIQUES
ACCEIRRR RICERCAR
ACCEIRSU CURACIES
ACCEIRTU CRUCIATE
ACCEISST ASCETICS
ACCEISTT ECSTATIC
ACCEKLNR CRACKNEL
ACCEKLRS CACKLERS
CLACKERS
CRACKLES
ACCEKMOS MEACOCKS
ACCEKOPS PEACOCKS
ACCEKOPY PEACOCKY
ACCEKOSS SEACOCKS
ACCEKPSU CUPCAKES
ACCEKRRS CRACKERS
ACCELLSY CALYCLES
ACCELLUY CALYCULE
ACCELMNY CYCLAMEN
ACCELNOS CONCEALS
ACCELNOV CONCLAVE
ACCELNRU CARUNCLE
ACCELORS CORACLES
ACCELOST CACOLETS
ACCELRSY SCARCELY
ACCELSSU SACCULES
ACCELWYY CYCLEWAY
ACCENNSY NASCENCY
ACCENORR CORNACRE
ACCENORS CONACRES
ACCENORT ACCENTOR
ACCENOST COSECANT
ACCENOSU CONCAUSE
ACCENOSV CONCAVES
ACCEOPRT ACCEPTOR
ACCEOPTU OCCUPATE
ACCEORSS ARCCOSES
ACCEORST ECTOSARC
ACCEORTU ACCOUTER
ACCOUTRE
ACCEOSSS SACCOSES
ACCERRST CARRECTS
ACCERSST SCARCEST
ACCERSSU ACCURSES
ACCUSERS
ACCESSTU CACTUSES
ACCESSUU CAUCUSES
ACCFHLTY CATCHFLY
ACCFIILT LACTIFIC
ACCFLNOO CONFOCAL
ACCFOORT COFACTOR
ACCGHIKN CHACKING
ACCGHINN CHANCING
ACCGHINO COACHING
ACCGHINT CATCHING
ACCGHIOR CHORAGIC
ACCGIINT ACCITING
ACCGIKLN CACKLING
CLACKING
ACCGIKMR GIMCRACK
ACCGIKNR CRACKING
ACCGINOT COACTING
ACCGINOY ACCOYING
ACCGINRU ACCRUING
ACCGINSU ACCUSING
ACCGLOOY CACOLOGY
ACCHHITT CHITCHAT
ACCHHMOS CAMSHOCH
ACCHIIRT RACHITIC
ACCHIIST CHIASTIC
ACCHILNO CHALONIC
ACCHILOR ORICHALC
ACCHILOT CATHOLIC
ACCHINNO CINCHONA
ACCHINOS CHICANOS
ACCHINPU CAPUCHIN
ACCHIORT THORACIC
TROCHAIC
ACCHIOSU ACOUCHIS
ACCHIRRT CARRITCH
ACCHIRSS SCRAICHS
ACCHKLOR CHARLOCK
ACCHKOSY HAYCOCKS
ACCHLOOT CACHOLOT
ACCHLSTU CLAUCHTS
ACCHMORS CASCHROM
ACCHNNUY UNCHANCY
ACCHNOOR CORONACH
ACCHNOTU COUCHANT
ACCHORTU CARTOUCH
ACCHOSTW CHOCTAWS
ACCHPSTU CATCHUPS
ACCHRRSU CURRACHS
ACCHRSSU SCRAUCHS
ACCHRSTY SCRATCHY
ACCIIIOT OITICICA
ACCIILLN CLINICAL
ACCIILMT CLIMATIC
ACCIILRT CRITICAL
ACCIIMNN CINNAMIC
ACCIINNO ANICONIC
ACCIINNP PICCANIN
ACCIINOT ACONITIC
ACCIIPST PASTICCI
ACCIIRTX CICATRIX
ACCIJKMR JIMCRACK
ACCIKLOT COCKTAIL
ACCIKNST CANSTICK
ACCIKOPR APRICOCK
ACCIKPRT PRACTICK
ACCILLUY CALYCULI
ACCILMOS COSMICAL
ACCILMOX CACOMIXL
ACCILMSU CALCIUMS
ACCILNOT CICLATON
ACCILNOV VOLCANIC
ACCILNUV VULCANIC
ACCILORS CALORICS
ACCILORT CORTICAL
ACCILPRY CAPRYLIC
ACCILRRU CIRCULAR
ACCILRSY ACRYLICS
ACCILSSS CLASSICS
ACCIMNOS MOCCASIN
ACCIMNTU CANTICUM
ACCIMORR MICROCAR
ACCIMORU COUMARIC
ACCIMOSZ ZIMOCCAS
ACCIMPSU CAPSICUM
ACCINOOS OCCASION
ACCINOOT COACTION
ACCINORT NARCOTIC
ACCINORV CAVICORN
ACCINOST CANTICOS
ACCINOTY CANTICOY
CYANOTIC
ACCINRSU CRUCIANS
ACCIOPST SPICCATO
ACCIORST ACROSTIC
ACCIORSY ISOCRACY
ACCIOSTT STICCATO
ACCIOSTU ACOUSTIC
ACCIPRST PRACTICS
ACCIRSTY SCARCITY
ACCISSTU CAUSTICS
ACCKKRSU RUCKSACK
ACCKLORS CARLOCKS
ACCKMMRU CRUMMACK
ACCKMORS CROMACKS
ACCKOOOT COCKATOO
ACCKOPRT CRACKPOT
ACCKOSSS CASSOCKS
ACCKOSST CASTOCKS
ACCLLOSU OCCLUSAL
ACCLLSUU CALCULUS
ACCLSSUU SACCULUS
ACCMOPST ACCOMPTS
COMPACTS
ACCMOSTU ACCUSTOM
ACCMRSUU CURCUMAS
ACCNNOOS COONCANS
ACCNOOPS COCOPANS
ACCNOORS RACCOONS
ACCNOOTU COCOANUT
ACCNOPTU OCCUPANT
ACCNORTT CONTRACT
ACCNOSTT CONTACTS
ACCNOSTU ACCOUNTS
ACCOPSTY COPYCATS
ACCOQSSU SQUACCOS
ACCORRTY CARRYCOT
ACCORSTU ACCOURTS
ACDDDEIT ADDICTED
ACDDDETU ADDUCTED
ACDDDKOS DADDOCKS
ACDDEEES DECEASED
ACDDEEHT DETACHED

ACDDEEIT DEDICATE
ACDDEEIU DECIDUAE
ACDDEEKR DACKERED
ACDDEELR DECLARED
ACDDEELS DESCALED
ACDDEEMP DECAMPED
ACDDEENR CREDENDA
ACDDEENS ASCENDED
ACDDEENT DECADENT
DECANTED
ACDDEERT REDACTED
ACDDEETU EDUCATED
ACDDEGIS DISCAGED
ACDDEHIK DICKHEAD
ACDDEIIL DEICIDAL
ACDDEIIM MEDICAID
ACDDEILU DECIDUAL
ACDDEINR CANDIDER
RIDDANCE
ACDDEINT DEDICANT
ACDDEINY CYANIDED
ACDDEIPS DISPACED
ACDDEISS CADDISES
DISCASED
ACDDEISU DECIDUAS
ACDDEITT DICTATED
ACDDEKLO DEADLOCK
ACDDEKOR RADDOCKE
ACDDELOS CLADODES
ACDDELRS CLADDERS
ACDDENTU ADDUCENT
ACDDEOPS DECAPODS
ACDDEORR CORRADED
ACDDEORW COWARDED
ACDDERSU ADDUCERS
CRUSADED
ACDDERTU TRADUCED
ACDDGILN CLADDING
ACDDGINU ADDUCING
ACDDGINY CADDYING
ACDDHHSU CHUDDAHS
ACDDHIIO DIADOCHI
ACDDHIMR DIDRACHM
ACDDHKOS HADDOCKS
SHADDOCK
ACDDHORS CHADDORS
ACDDHRSU CHUDDARS
ACDDIIOR CARDIOID
ACDDILNY CANDIDLY
ACDDILTY DIDACTYL
ACDDINNU UNCANDID
ACDDINSY DISCANDY
ACDDIRSS DISCARDS
ACDDKLNO DOCKLAND
ACDDKMOS MADDOCKS
ACDDKOPS PADDOCKS
ACDDKORY DOCKYARD
ACDDORTU ADDUCTOR
ACDEEEFT DEFECATE
ACDEEEKS SEEDCAKE
ACDEEEMR REEDMACE
ACDEEENR CAREENED
ACDEEENT ANTECEDE
ACDEEERR CAREERED
ACDEEERS DECREASE
ACDEEESS DECEASES
SEEDCASE
ACDEEFFT AFFECTED
ACDEEFHN ENCHAFED
ACDEEFIL CALEFIED
ACDEEFIN DEFIANCE
ACDEEFPR PREFACED
ACDEEFRS DEFACERS
FRESCADE
ACDEEFRY FEDERACY
ACDEEGLY DELEGACY
ACDEEGNR ENGRACED
ACDEEHIV ACHIEVED
ACDEEHLP PLEACHED
ACDEEHLT CHELATED
ACDEEHMR DEMARCHE
ACDEEHNN ENHANCED
ACDEEHNR ENARCHED
ACDEEHNS ENCASHED
ENCHASED
ACDEEHPR PREACHED
ACDEEHRS SEARCHED
ACDEEHSS CHASSEED
ACDEEHST DETACHES
ACDEEIIP EPICEDIA
ACDEEILT DELICATE
ACDEEIMR MEDICARE
ACDEEIMT DECIMATE
EMICATED
MEDICATE
ACDEEINN DECENNIA
ENNEADIC
ACDEEINR DERACINE
ACDEEINU AUDIENCE
ACDEEINV DEVIANCE
ACDEEIPS DISPEACE
ACDEEIRS DECIARES
ACDEEJKT JACKETED
ACDEEKLR LACKERED
ACDEEKLY LACKEYED
ACDEEKNR CANKERED
ACDEEKPR REPACKED
ACDEEKPT PACKETED
ACDEEKRS SCREAKED
ACDEEKRT RACKETED
ACDEELLR CELLARED
RECALLED
ACDEELLS CADELLES
ACDEELMN ENCALMED
ACDEELMP EMPLACED
ACDEELNR CALENDER
ENCRADLE
ACDEELNS CLEANSED
ACDEELNT LANCETED
ACDEELNV ENCLAVED
ACDEELPR REPLACED
ACDEELRR DECLARER
ACDEELRS DECLARES
RESCALED
ACDEELRT CLARETED
DECRETAL
TREACLED
ACDEELRV CALVERED
CLAVERED
ACDEELSS DECLASSE
DESCALES
ACDEEMNP ENCAMPED
ACDEEMRS SCREAMED
ACDEEMRT CREMATED
ACDEENNP PENANCED
ACDEENNT TENDANCE
ACDEENNY CAYENNED
ACDEENOT ANECDOTE
ACDEENRS ASCENDER
REASCEND
ACDEENRT CANTERED
CRENATED
DECANTER
NECTARED
RECANTED
ACDEENRV CAVERNED
CRAVENED
ACDEENRY CARNEYED
ACDEENRZ CREDENZA
ACDEENSV VENDACES
ACDEENTT DANCETTE
ACDEEOPS PEASECOD
ACDEEORT DECORATE
ACDEEOTV EVOCATED
ACDEEPPR RECAPPED
ACDEEPRS ESCARPED
ACDEEPRT CARPETED
ACDEEPST ASPECTED
ACDEERRS SCAREDER
ACDEERRT CRATERED
RETRACED
TERRACED
ACDEERSS CARESSED
ACDEERST CEDRATES
ACDEESTU EDUCATES
ACDEESUX CAUDEXES
ACDEFFHU CHAUFFED
ACDEFFLS SCLAFFED
ACDEFFOR AFFORCED
ACDEFGIN DEFACING
ACDEFHLN FLANCHED
ACDEFIIL DEIFICAL
ACDEFIIP PACIFIED
ACDEFILN CANFIELD
ACDEFILR FRICADEL
ACDEFINN FINANCED
ACDEFLOT OLFACTED
ACDEFNRU FURNACED
ACDEFORT FACTORED
ACDEFOTU OUTFACED
ACDEFRSU SURFACED
ACDEFRTU FURCATED
ACDEGGRS SCRAGGED
ACDEGHLO GALOCHED
ACDEGHNU CHAUNGED
GAUNCHED
ACDEGIIL ALGICIDE
ACDEGIKM MAGICKED
ACDEGIMR DECIGRAM
GRIMACED
ACDEGINU GUIDANCE
ACDEGINY DECAYING
ACDEGIRS DISGRACE
ACDEGISS DISCAGES
ACDEGIST CADGIEST
ACDEGKOS DOCKAGES
ACDEGLOU CLOUDAGE
ACDEGNOS DECAGONS
ACDEGNRU UNGRACED
ACDEGORS CORDAGES
ACDEGOTT COTTAGED
ACDEHHIN HAINCHED
ACDEHHNU HAUNCHED
ACDEHHRU HACHURED
ACDEHHTT THATCHED
ACDEHIIP APHICIDE
ACDEHIJK HIJACKED
ACDEHILR HERALDIC
ACDEHILT DITHECAL
ACDEHIMN MACHINED
ACDEHIMS SCHIEDAM
ACDEHINR INARCHED
ACDEHINS ECHIDNAS
INCHASED
ACDEHIRS RACHIDES
ACDEHIRT THRIDACE
TRACHEID
ACDEHIRV ARCHIVED
ACDEHIST SCAITHED
ACDEHISU CHIAUSED
ACDEHKLO HEADLOCK
ACDEHKLS SHACKLED
ACDEHKNU UNHACKED
ACDEHKOV HAVOCKED
ACDEHKRU ARCHDUKE
ACDEHKTW THWACKED
ACDEHLNP PLANCHED
ACDEHLNR CHANDLER
ACDEHLNU LAUNCHED
ACDEHLRS CHALDERS
ACDEHMST SMATCHED
ACDEHNOR ANCHORED
RONDACHE
ACDEHNPU PAUNCHED
ACDEHNRU RAUNCHED
ACDEHNST SNATCHED
STANCHED
ACDEHNSU UNCASHED
ACDEHNTU CHAUNTED
ACDEHORT CHORDATE
ACDEHORW COWHEARD
ACDEHOST CATHODES
ACDEHOUV AVOUCHED
ACDEHPPS SCHAPPED
ACDEHPRS SCARPHED
ACDEHPRU UPCHEARD
ACDEHPST DESPATCH
ACDEHPSU CUPHEADS
ACDEHQTU QUATCHED
ACDEHRST STARCHED
ACDEHTUW WAUCHTED
ACDEIILS LAICISED
ACDEIILZ LAICIZED
ACDEIIMU AECIDIUM
ACDEIINR ACRIDINE
ACDEIINS SCIAENID
ACDEIINT ACTINIDE
DIACTINE
INDICATE
ACDEIINU INDUCIAE
ACDEIITV CAVITIED
VATICIDE
VICIATED
ACDEIJNU JAUNDICE
ACDEIKNP PANICKED
ACDEIKNT ANTICKED
ACDEILLM MEDALLIC
ACDEILLN DECLINAL
ACDEILLS CEDILLAS
ACDEILLV CAVILLED
ACDEILMO CAMELOID
MELODICA
ACDEILMS CAMELIDS
DECIMALS
DECLAIMS
MEDICALS
ACDEILMT CLIMATED
MALEDICT
ACDEILMX CLIMAXED
ACDEILNP PANICLED

ACDEILOS	COALISED
ACDEILOZ	COALIZED
ACDEILPR	PLACIDER
ACDEILPS	DISPLACE
ACDEILPT	PLICATED
ACDEILRS	DECRIALS
	RADICELS
	RADICLES
ACDEILRT	ARTICLED
ACDEILRU	AURICLED
	RADICULE
ACDEILST	CITADELS
	DIALECTS
ACDEILTT	LATTICED
ACDEIMNO	COMEDIAN
	DAEMONIC
	DEMONIAC
ACDEIMNP	PANDEMIC
ACDEIMPT	IMPACTED
ACDEIMRT	DERMATIC
	TIMECARD
ACDEINNR	CRANNIED
ACDEINOP	CANOPIED
ACDEINOS	DIOCESAN
	OCEANIDS
ACDEINOT	ACTIONED
ACDEINOV	VOIDANCE
ACDEINPT	PEDANTIC
	PENTADIC
ACDEINRR	RANCIDER
ACDEINRT	CRINATED
	DICENTRA
ACDEINSS	ACIDNESS
ACDEINST	DISTANCE
ACDEINSY	CYANIDES
	CYANISED
ACDEINTT	NICTATED
ACDEINVY	DEVIANCY
ACDEINYZ	CYANIZED
ACDEIOPS	DIASCOPE
ACDEIORS	IDOCRASE
ACDEIORT	CERATOID
ACDEIORV	COVARIED
ACDEIOSS	ACIDOSES
ACDEIOSU	EDACIOUS
ACDEIPPT	TAPPICED
ACDEIPRS	EPACRIDS
ACDEIPSS	DISPACES
	SPADICES
ACDEIPST	SPICATED
ACDEIPSZ	CAPSIZED
ACDEIPTV	CAPTIVED
ACDEIQRU	ACQUIRED
ACDEIRSS	SIDECARS
ACDEIRST	ACRIDEST
ACDEIRSU	DECURIAS
ACDEIRTT	TETRACID
	TETRADIC
ACDEISSS	DISCASES
ACDEISTT	DICTATES
ACDEKLNR	CRANKLED
ACDEKLQU	QUACKLED
ACDEKNPR	PRANCKED
ACDEKNPU	UNPACKED
ACDEKNRU	UNRACKED
ACDEKNTU	UNTACKED
ACDEKOST	STOCKADE
ACDELLNU	UNCALLED
ACDELLOR	CAROLLED
	COLLARED
ACDELLOT	COLLATED
ACDELMOR	CLAMORED
ACDELMSU	MUSCADEL
ACDELNOO	CANOODLE
ACDELNOR	COLANDER
ACDELNOS	CELADONS
ACDELNPU	UNPLACED
ACDELNRY	CALENDRY
ACDELNST	SCANTLED
ACDELNSU	UNSCALED
ACDELOPT	CLODPATE
ACDELOPU	CUPOLAED
ACDELORV	OVERCLAD
ACDELOTU	OCULATED
ACDELPPS	SCAPPLED
ACDELRSS	SCALDERS
ACDELRSW	SCRAWLED
ACDELRSY	SACREDLY
ACDELSTU	CAULDEST
	SULCATED
ACDEMMRS	SCRAMMED
ACDEMNOR	ROMANCED
ACDEMNSU	DECUMANS
ACDEMOPR	COMPADRE
	COMPARED
ACDEMORS	COMRADES
ACDEMORT	DEMOCRAT
ACDEMRSW	SCRAWMED
ACDEMUUV	VACUUMED
ACDENNNO	CANNONED
ACDENNOR	ORDNANCE
ACDENNOT	CANTONED
ACDENNST	SCANDENT
ACDENOPR	ENDOCARP
ACDENORS	DRACONES
	ENDOSARC
ACDENORT	CARTONED
ACDENORY	CRAYONED
	DEACONRY
ACDENOSY	CYANOSED
ACDENOTU	OUTDANCE
	UNCOATED
ACDENPPU	UNCAPPED
ACDENPRU	PRAUNCED
ACDENPST	PANDECTS
ACDENRST	CANTREDS
ACDENRSU	DURANCES
ACDENRTU	UNCARTED
	UNCRATED
	UNDERACT
	UNTRACED
ACDENRVY	VERDANCY
ACDENSST	DESCANTS
ACDENSUU	UNCAUSED
ACDENTTY	DANCETTY
ACDEOPRU	CROUPADE
ACDEOPRY	COPYREAD
ACDEOPSS	PEASCODS
ACDEOPTT	CAPOTTED
ACDEOPTU	OUTPACED
ACDEORRS	CORRADES
ACDEORRT	REDACTOR
ACDEORSS	SARCODES
ACDEORST	REDCOATS
ACDEORSU	CAROUSED
ACDEORTU	EDUCATOR
	OUTRACED
ACDEORTV	CAVORTED
ACDEOSTT	CODETTAS
	COSTATED
ACDEOSUV	COUVADES
ACDEPPRS	SCRAPPED
ACDEPRTU	CAPTURED
ACDEQTUU	AQUEDUCT
ACDERRSU	CRUSADER
ACDERRTU	TRADUCER
ACDERSSU	CRUSADES
ACDERSTT	DETRACTS
	SCRATTED
ACDERSTU	TRADUCES
ACDERTUV	CURVATED
ACDFFHNU	HANDCUFF
ACDFFIRT	DIFFRACT
ACDFFLOS	SCAFFOLD
ACDFIILU	FIDUCIAL
ACDFILOU	FUCOIDAL
ACDFIOST	FACTOIDS
ACDGHOTW	WATCHDOG
ACDGIILO	DIALOGIC
ACDGILNN	CANDLING
ACDGILNR	CRADLING
ACDGILNS	SCALDING
ACDGILNU	CAUDLING
ACDGIMOT	DOGMATIC
ACDGINNS	DANCINGS
ACDGINNY	CANDYING
ACDGINSU	SCAUDING
ACDGIOPR	PODAGRIC
ACDGKLOS	DAGLOCKS
ACDGNOST	CANTDOGS
ACDGORST	DOGCARTS
ACDHIILS	CHILIADS
ACDHIINT	TACHINID
ACDHIKOR	CHOKIDAR
ACDHILPR	PILCHARD
ACDHILPS	CLAPDISH
ACDHINOR	HADRONIC
	RHODANIC
ACDHINRY	DINARCHY
ACDHINSW	SANDWICH
ACDHIOPS	SCAPHOID
ACDHIORY	HYRACOID
ACDHIPST	DISPATCH
ACDHLNOR	CHALDRON
	CHLORDAN
	CHONDRAL
ACDHLORS	DORLACHS
ACDHMORU	MOUCHARD
ACDHNORW	CHAWDRON
ACDHNOSW	COWHANDS
ACDHOOST	CATHOODS
ACDHOOTW	WOODCHAT
ACDHOPRS	POCHARDS
ACDHORRS	ORCHARDS
ACDHORSY	DYSCHROA
ACDIIILN	INDICIAL
ACDIIIPR	DIAPIRIC
ACDIIJLU	JUDICIAL
ACDIILMS	DISCLAIM
ACDIILNO	CONIDIAL
ACDIILNS	SCALDINI
ACDIILSU	SUICIDAL
ACDIILTY	CALIDITY
	DIALYTIC
ACDIIMNO	DAIMONIC
ACDIIMOR	CORMIDIA
	DIORAMIC
ACDIIMOT	DIATOMIC
ACDIIMSU	ASCIDIUM
ACDIINNS	INDICANS
ACDIINNT	INDICANT
ACDIINOP	PINACOID
ACDIINOT	ACTINOID
	DIATONIC
ACDIINPY	PYCNIDIA
ACDIINRS	ACRIDINS
ACDIIOSS	ACIDOSIS
ACDIIRSS	SCIARIDS
ACDIIRST	ARCTIIDS
	CARDITIS
ACDIIRTY	ACRIDITY
ACDIISST	SADISTIC
ACDIKMOO	COOKMAID
ACDIKRRY	RICKYARD
ACDILLOS	CODILLAS
ACDILLOU	CAUDILLO
	LODICULA
ACDILLPY	PLACIDLY
ACDILMOR	DROMICAL
ACDILMSS	CLADISMS
ACDILNOO	CONOIDAL
ACDILNOS	SCALDINO
ACDILNSU	DULCIANS
ACDILNSY	SYNDICAL
ACDILNUU	NUDICAUL
ACDILOPY	POLYACID
ACDILORS	CORDIALS
ACDILOUV	OVIDUCAL
ACDILPSU	CUSPIDAL
ACDILSST	CLADISTS
ACDILSTW	WILDCATS
ACDIMMSU	CADMIUMS
ACDIMNOO	MONOACID
ACDIMNOS	MANDIOCS
ACDIMNSU	MUSCADIN
	SCANDIUM
ACDIMNSY	DYNAMICS
ACDIMOSY	DOCIMASY
ACDINOPS	SPONDAIC
ACDINORS	SARDONIC
ACDINORT	TORNADIC
ACDINORW	CORDWAIN
ACDINSST	DISCANTS
ACDINSTY	DYNASTIC
ACDINTUY	ADUNCITY
ACDIOPRS	PICADORS
	SPORADIC
ACDIORRS	CORRIDAS
ACDIORSS	SARCOIDS
ACDIORTT	DICTATOR
ACDIOSTY	DYSTOCIA
ACDIPRST	ADSCRIPT
ACDIQRSU	QUADRICS
ACDIRSST	DRASTICS
ACDIRSTT	DISTRACT
ACDISTUV	VIADUCTS
ACDJNSTU	ADJUNCTS
ACDKLOPS	PADLOCKS
ACDKMMOR	DRAMMOCK
ACDKMPSU	MUDPACKS
ACDKOPRS	POCKARDS
ACDLLORS	COLLARDS
ACDLNNOR	CORNLAND
ACDLNOPR	CROPLAND
ACDLNORS	CALDRONS
ACDLNORU	CAULDRON
ACDLNORY	CONDYLAR
ACDLNOST	COTLANDS
ACDLOORT	DOCTORAL
ACDLORWY	COWARDLY

ACDLOSWY	LADYCOWS
ACDMMNOO	COMMANDO
ACDMMNOS	COMMANDS
ACDMNORY	DORMANCY
	MORDANCY
ACDMOOPR	MACROPOD
ACDMOOSW	CAMWOODS
ACDMORSZ	CZARDOMS
ACDNOORR	RONCADOR
ACDNOORS	CARDOONS
ACDNOORV	CORDOVAN
ACDNOOTU	DUCATOON
ACDNORRW	WARDCORN
ACDNORSU	CANDOURS
	CAUDRONS
ACDNOSTW	DOWNCAST
ACDNOSUU	ADUNCOUS
ACDOOPPR	PODOCARP
ACDOOPTY	OCTAPODY
ACDOORST	OSTRACOD
	SCORDATO
ACDOPRST	POSTCARD
ACDORRWY	COWARDRY
ACDORSST	COSTARDS
ACDORSSU	CRUSADOS
ACDORSUZ	CRUZADOS
ACDRSSTU	CUSTARDS
ACDRSTTU	DUSTCART
ACEEEFRR	CAREFREE
ACEEEGLN	ELEGANCE
ACEEEGRS	CARGEESE
ACEEEIPR	EARPIECE
ACEEEKNT	NECKATEE
ACEEELMR	CAMELEER
ACEEENRS	ENCREASE
ACEEENSV	EVANESCE
ACEEEPSS	ESCAPEES
ACEEERRT	RECREATE
ACEEERTT	ETCETERA
ACEEERTX	EXECRATE
ACEEESUV	EVACUEES
ACEEFFIN	CAFFEINE
ACEEFFRT	AFFECTER
ACEEFHNS	ENCHAFES
ACEEFILM	MALEFICE
ACEEFILS	CALEFIES
ACEEFINS	FAIENCES
	FIANCEES
ACEEFKOR	ECOFREAK
ACEEFLPU	PEACEFUL
ACEEFLSS	FACELESS
ACEEFNSY	FAYENCES
ACEEFPRS	PREFACES
ACEEFPRT	PERFECTA
	PRAEFECT
ACEEFRSU	FARCEUSE
ACEEGHNR	ENCHARGE
ACEEGHNX	EXCHANGE
ACEEGHRR	RECHARGE
ACEEGILS	ELEGIACS
	LEGACIES
ACEEGINS	AGENCIES
ACEEGKNR	NECKGEAR
ACEEGKRW	WRECKAGE
ACEEGLNY	ELEGANCY
ACEEGLPU	PUCELAGE
ACEEGNOZ	COZENAGE
ACEEGNRS	ENGRACES
ACEEGNRY	REAGENCY
ACEEGNST	CENTAGES
ACEEGNSV	SCAVENGE
ACEEGORR	RACEGOER
ACEEGORV	COVERAGE
ACEEGSSU	ESCUAGES
ACEEHHST	CHEETAHS
ACEEHILR	LEACHIER
ACEEHINT	ECHINATE
ACEEHIPR	PEACHIER
ACEEHIPS	CHEAPIES
ACEEHIPT	PETECHIA
ACEEHIRV	ACHIEVER
	CHIVAREE
ACEEHIST	HICATEES
ACEEHISV	ACHIEVES
ACEEHITV	ATCHIEVE
ACEEHKNS	SKEECHAN
ACEEHKTT	HACKETTE
ACEEHLMP	EMPLEACH
ACEEHLOS	SHOELACE
ACEEHLPS	PLEACHES
ACEEHLRS	RELACHES
ACEEHLSS	LACHESES
ACEEHLST	CHELATES
ACEEHLSW	ESCHEWAL
ACEEHLTV	CHEVALET
ACEEHMNP	CAMPHENE
ACEEHMNR	MENARCHE
ACEEHMRS	CASHMERE
	MACHREES
	MARCHESE
ACEEHMST	MACHETES
ACEEHNNR	ENHANCER
ACEEHNNS	ENHANCES
ACEEHNPS	CHEAPENS
ACEEHNRS	ENARCHES
ACEEHNRV	REVANCHE
ACEEHNSS	ENCASHES
	ENCHASES
ACEEHORT	OCHREATE
ACEEHPPS	ECHAPPES
ACEEHPRR	PREACHER
ACEEHPRS	PEACHERS
	PREACHES
ACEEHPRT	ETHERCAP
ACEEHPST	CHEAPEST
ACEEHQSU	QUEACHES
ACEEHRRS	REACHERS
	RESEARCH
	SEARCHER
ACEEHRRT	TREACHER
ACEEHRSS	SEARCHES
ACEEHRST	CHEATERS
	HECTARES
	RECHATES
	RECHEATS
	TEACHERS
ACEEHRTT	CATHETER
ACEEHRTY	CHEATERY
ACEEHSST	ESCHEATS
ACEEHSTX	CATHEXES
	EXCHEATS
ACEEIKNP	PEACENIK
ACEEIKRR	CREAKIER
ACEEILLM	MICELLAE
ACEEILMN	CAMELINE
ACEEILMT	EMETICAL
ACEEILNP	CAPELINE
ACEEILNR	CINEREAL
	RELIANCE
ACEEILNS	SALIENCE
ACEEILPS	CALIPEES
	ESPECIAL
ACEEILRS	ESCALIER
ACEEILRV	RECEIVAL
ACEEIMOT	ACOEMETI
ACEEIMRR	CREAMIER
	REARMICE
ACEEIMRS	CASIMERE
	RACEMISE
ACEEIMRT	CEMITARE
ACEEIMRZ	RACEMIZE
ACEEIMST	EMICATES
ACEEINNR	NARCEINE
ACEEINPS	SAPIENCE
ACEEINPT	PATIENCE
ACEEINRS	CINEREAS
	INCREASE
	RESIANCE
ACEEINRT	CENTIARE
	CREATINE
	INCREATE
	ITERANCE
ACEEINST	CINEASTE
ACEEINSU	EUCAINES
ACEEINTV	ENACTIVE
ACEEINTX	EXITANCE
ACEEIPST	SPECIATE
ACEEIRRS	CARIERES
	CREASIER
ACEEIRSU	CAUSERIE
ACEEIRSW	WISEACRE
ACEEIRTV	CREATIVE
	REACTIVE
ACEEISTV	VESICATE
ACEEJKNS	JACKEENS
ACEEKLMR	MACKEREL
ACEEKLRW	EELWRACK
ACEEKMPT	EMPACKET
ACEEKNPS	KNEECAPS
ACEEKNRW	NECKWEAR
ACEEKRRT	RACKETER
ACEELLNS	NACELLES
ACEELLNT	LANCELET
ACEELLOT	OCELLATE
ACEELLPT	CAPELLET
ACEELLRR	CELLARER
ACEELLRT	CELLARET
ACEELMNO	CAMELEON
ACEELMNP	PLACEMEN
ACEELMPS	EMPLACES
ACEELMRS	RECLAMES
	SCLEREMA
ACEELNPT	PENTACLE
ACEELNRR	LARCENER
ACEELNRS	CLEANERS
	CLEANSER
ACEELNRU	CERULEAN
ACEELNSS	CLEANSES
ACEELNST	CLEANEST
	LATENCES
ACEELNSU	NUCLEASE
ACEELNSV	ENCLAVES
	VALENCES
ACEELNTT	TENTACLE
ACEELNTU	NUCLEATE
ACEELOPS	ESCALOPE
ACEELORS	ESCAROLE
ACEELORT	RELOCATE
ACEELOSV	VOCALESE
ACEELPRR	REPLACER
ACEELPRS	PERCALES
	REPLACES
ACEELPST	CAPELETS
ACEELPSY	CYPSELAE
ACEELPTU	PECULATE
ACEELPTY	CLYPEATE
ACEELRRS	CLEARERS
ACEELRSS	CARELESS
	RESCALES
ACEELRST	CLEAREST
	SCELERAT
	TREACLES
ACEELRSV	CLEAVERS
ACEELRTT	RACLETTE
ACEELRTU	ULCERATE
ACEELRTV	CERVELAT
ACEELRTX	EXCRETAL
ACEELSST	CELESTAS
ACEELSSU	EUCLASES
ACEELSTT	TELECAST
ACEELSVX	EXCLAVES
ACEEMNNS	SCENEMAN
ACEEMNOT	MECONATE
ACEEMNPS	SPACEMEN
ACEEMNRS	MENACERS
ACEEMNST	CASEMENT
ACEEMOPR	CAMPOREE
ACEEMOPT	COPEMATE
ACEEMORS	RACEMOSE
ACEEMORV	OVERCAME
ACEEMRRS	CREAMERS
	SCREAMER
ACEEMRRY	CREAMERY
ACEEMRST	CREMATES
	MEERCATS
ACEENNPS	PENANCES
ACEENNRS	NARCEENS
ACEENNRT	ENTRANCE
ACEENNST	CANTEENS
ACEENNSY	CAYENNES
ACEENORT	CAROTENE
ACEENOST	ACETONES
	NOTECASE
ACEENPRR	PARCENER
ACEENPRT	PERCEANT
ACEENRRT	RECANTER
	RECREANT
ACEENRSS	CASERNES
ACEENRST	CENTARES
	REASCENT
	SARCENET
ACEENRTU	ENACTURE
	UNCREATE
ACEEORST	CREASOTE
ACEEOSTT	ECOSTATE
ACEEOSTV	EVOCATES
ACEEPRRS	CAPERERS
ACEEPRSS	ESCAPERS
ACEEPRTT	ETTERCAP
ACEEPRTU	PERACUTE
ACEEPRTX	EXCERPTA
ACEEPSSU	AUCEPSES
ACEEPSTT	SPECTATE
ACEERRSS	CREASERS
ACEERRST	CATERERS
	RETRACES
	TERRACES
ACEERRSU	ECRASEUR
ACEERRTU	CREATURE
ACEERRUV	VERRUCAE

ACEERSSS	CARESSES
ACEERSST	CATERESS
	CERASTES
ACEERSSU	SURCEASE
ACEERSSV	CREVASSE
ACEERSTX	EXACTERS
ACEERTTU	ERUCTATE
ACEESSST	ECSTASES
ACEESSTT	CASSETTE
ACEESTTX	EXACTEST
ACEFFGIN	EFFACING
ACEFFHIS	AFFICHES
ACEFFHRS	CHAFFERS
ACEFFHRU	CHAUFFER
ACEFFHRY	CHAFFERY
ACEFFIMS	CAFFEISM
ACEFFINS	CAFFEINS
ACEFFISS	SCAFFIES
ACEFFORS	AFFORCES
ACEFGINN	ENFACING
ACEFGINR	REFACING
ACEFGINT	FACETING
ACEFGLRU	GRACEFUL
ACEFGOST	GEOFACTS
ACEFHLNS	FLANCHES
ACEFHMRS	CHAMFERS
ACEFHORU	FAROUCHE
ACEFHRST	FRATCHES
ACEFHRSU	CHAUFERS
ACEFIILS	FELICIAS
ACEFIIPR	PACIFIER
ACEFIIPS	PACIFIES
ACEFIIRT	ARTIFICE
ACEFILLY	FACILELY
ACEFILOP	EPIFOCAL
ACEFILOS	FASCIOLE
	FOCALISE
ACEFILOZ	FOCALIZE
ACEFILRS	FILACERS
ACEFIMPR	CAMPFIRE
ACEFINNS	FINANCES
ACEFINRS	FANCIERS
ACEFINRX	CARNIFEX
ACEFINSS	FASCINES
ACEFINST	FANCIEST
ACEFIOSS	FIASCOES
ACEFIRRT	CRAFTIER
ACEFIRTT	TRIFECTA
ACEFIRTY	FERACITY
ACEFISST	FACTISES
ACEFKLRS	FLACKERS
ACEFKLST	FLACKETS
ACEFLLSS	CALFLESS
ACEFLMNO	FLAMENCO
ACEFLNOR	FALCONER
ACEFLNOT	CONFLATE
	FALCONET
ACEFLNRY	CRANEFLY
ACEFLORS	ALFRESCO
ACEFLRTU	FULCRATE
ACEFLRUU	FURCULAE
ACEFMNOO	MOONFACE
ACEFNNOS	FACONNES
ACEFNORV	CONFERVA
ACEFNPRT	PENCRAFT
ACEFNRST	CANTREFS
ACEFNRSU	FURNACES
ACEFOOPT	FOOTPACE
ACEFOPST	POSTFACE
ACEFORRS	FORECARS
ACEFORST	FORECAST
ACEFORSX	CARFOXES
ACEFOSTU	OUTFACES
ACEFRRST	REFRACTS
ACEFRRSU	FARCEURS
	SURFACER
ACEFRRTU	FRACTURE
ACEFRSSU	SURFACES
ACEFRSTU	FACTURES
ACEGGILN	CAGELING
	GLACEING
ACEGGILR	CLAGGIER
ACEGGINN	ENCAGING
ACEGGIOP	EPAGOGIC
ACEGGIRR	CRAGGIER
ACEGHILN	LEACHING
ACEGHILT	LICHGATE
ACEGHINP	PEACHING
ACEGHINR	REACHING
ACEGHINT	CHEATING
	TEACHING
ACEGHLOS	GALOCHES
ACEGHLRS	SCHLAGER
ACEGHLRU	RUGELACH
ACEGHLTY	LYCHGATE
ACEGHMMU	CHUMMAGE
ACEGHMOR	ECHOGRAM
	GRAMOCHE
ACEGHNRS	CHANGERS
ACEGHNRU	UNCHARGE
ACEGHNSU	CHAUNGES
	GAUNCHES
ACEGHOSU	GOUACHES
ACEGHOSW	COWHAGES
ACEGHRRS	CHARGERS
ACEGHRTU	RECAUGHT
ACEGHSTU	GAUCHEST
ACEGIIMP	EPIGAMIC
ACEGIINV	VICINAGE
ACEGIKNR	CREAKING
ACEGILLO	COLLEGIA
ACEGILLR	ALLERGIC
ACEGILMU	MUCILAGE
ACEGILNN	CLEANING
	ELANCING
	ENLACING
ACEGILNR	CLEARING
ACEGILNT	CLEATING
ACEGILNV	CLEAVING
ACEGILNW	LACEWING
ACEGILOS	CALIGOES
ACEGILRS	GLACIERS
ACEGILRV	CLAVIGER
ACEGILRY	GLYCERIA
ACEGILSS	GLACISES
ACEGILST	GELASTIC
ACEGIMMT	TAGMEMIC
ACEGIMNN	MENACING
ACEGIMNR	AMERCING
	CREAMING
ACEGIMNT	MAGNETIC
ACEGIMOS	CAMOGIES
ACEGIMOX	EXOGAMIC
ACEGIMRS	GRIMACES
ACEGIMTY	MEGACITY
ACEGINNO	CANOEING
ACEGINNR	ENRACING
ACEGINNS	ENCASING
ACEGINNT	ENACTING
ACEGINNV	ENCAVING
ACEGINOS	COINAGES
ACEGINOY	GYNOECIA
ACEGINPR	CAPERING
	PEARCING
	PREACING
ACEGINPS	ESCAPING
ACEGINRS	CREASING
	GRECIANS
	SEARCING
ACEGINRT	CATERING
	CITRANGE
	CREATING
	REACTING
ACEGINSS	CAGINESS
	CEASINGS
ACEGINTX	EXACTING
ACEGIOTT	COGITATE
ACEGIPRS	SPAGERIC
ACEGIRST	AGRESTIC
ACEGISTU	GAUCIEST
ACEGISTW	GAWCIEST
ACEGKLOS	LOCKAGES
ACEGKLOV	GAVELOCK
ACEGKLRS	GRACKLES
ACEGKMOS	MOCKAGES
ACEGKORS	CORKAGES
ACEGKORW	CAGEWORK
ACEGKRTU	TRUCKAGE
ACEGLLNO	COLLAGEN
ACEGLLOS	COLLAGES
ACEGLNOS	CONGEALS
ACEGLNRS	CLANGERS
ACEGLOST	CATELOGS
ACEGLOSU	CAGOULES
ACEGMNOY	GEOMANCY
ACEGMNRS	CRAGSMEN
ACEGMOPS	COMPAGES
ACEGMORS	SCARMOGE
ACEGMRRY	GRAMERCY
ACEGNNOY	CYANOGEN
ACEGNNTY	TANGENCY
ACEGNORS	ACROGENS
	CORNAGES
ACEGNOST	COGNATES
ACEGNSSY	CAGYNESS
ACEGOORS	CARGOOSE
ACEGOPRY	GEOCARPY
ACEGORSS	CORSAGES
	SOCAGERS
ACEGORST	ESCARGOT
ACEGORSU	COURAGES
ACEGORTT	COTTAGER
ACEGORTY	CATEGORY
ACEGOSTT	COTTAGES
ACEGOTTY	COTTAGEY
ACEGRSTU	TRUCAGES
ACEGSSTU	SCUTAGES
ACEHHINS	HAINCHES
ACEHHIRR	HIERARCH
ACEHHIST	SHECHITA
ACEHHLST	HATCHELS
ACEHHLSU	SHAUCHLE
ACEHHMNN	HENCHMAN
ACEHHNRT	ETHNARCH
ACEHHNSU	HAUNCHES
ACEHHPRT	HEPTARCH
ACEHHRST	HATCHERS
ACEHHRSU	HACHURES
ACEHHRTT	THATCHER
ACEHHRTY	HATCHERY
	THEARCHY
ACEHHSTT	HATCHETS
	THATCHES
ACEHHTTY	HATCHETY
ACEHIIMS	ISCHEMIA
ACEHIIRT	HIERATIC
ACEHIJKR	HIJACKER
ACEHIKLP	KEPHALIC
ACEHIKLR	CHALKIER
	HACKLIER
ACEHIKLW	LICHWAKE
ACEHIKRS	KACHERIS
ACEHIKRW	WHACKIER
ACEHILLS	CHALLIES
ACEHILLT	HELLICAT
ACEHILMN	INCHMEAL
ACEHILMO	CHOLEMIA
ACEHILMP	IMPLEACH
ACEHILMS	CAMELISH
ACEHILNP	CEPHALIN
ACEHILNT	CHAINLET
	CHATLINE
	ETHNICAL
ACEHILOR	HALICORE
	HEROICAL
ACEHILPR	PARHELIC
ACEHILRS	CHARLIES
ACEHILST	ETHICALS
ACEHILTT	ATHLETIC
	THETICAL
ACEHIMMS	CHAMMIES
ACEHIMNN	CHAINMEN
ACEHIMNP	CAMPHINE
ACEHIMNR	CHAIRMEN
ACEHIMNS	MACHINES
ACEHIMNU	ACHENIUM
ACEHIMPR	CAMPHIRE
ACEHIMPT	EMPATHIC
	EMPHATIC
ACEHIMRS	CHASMIER
	CHIMERAS
	MARCHESI
ACEHIMRT	RHEMATIC
ACEHIMSS	CHAMISES
ACEHIMST	MISTEACH
	TACHISME
ACEHIMTT	THEMATIC
ACEHINNS	ENCHAINS
ACEHINOT	INCHOATE
ACEHINRS	INARCHES
ACEHINRV	VACHERIN
ACEHINSS	INCHASES
ACEHINST	ASTHENIC
	CHANTIES
ACEHINSY	HYACINES
	SYNECHIA
ACEHIOPR	POACHIER
ACEHIOST	TOISEACH
ACEHIPPR	CHAPPIER
ACEHIPPS	CHAPPIES
ACEHIPRS	ASPHERIC
	CHARPIES
	PARCHESI
	SERAPHIC
ACEHIPRT	CHAPITER
	PATCHIER
	PHREATIC
ACEHIPST	HEPATICS
	PASTICHE
ACEHIPTT	PATHETIC

ACEHIPTW	WHITECAP
ACEHIRSS	CASHIERS
	RACHISES
ACEHIRST	CHARIEST
	THERIACS
ACEHIRSU	EUCHARIS
ACEHIRSV	ARCHIVES
ACEHIRSW	ARCHWISE
ACEHIRTT	CHATTIER
	THEATRIC
ACEHISST	CHASTISE
	TAISCHES
ACEHISSU	CHIAUSES
ACEHISTT	CHATTIES
	TACHISTE
ACEHISTX	CATHEXIS
ACEHISTY	YACHTIES
ACEHKLOV	HAVELOCK
ACEHKLPR	KREPLACH
ACEHKLRS	HACKLERS
ACEHKLSS	SHACKLES
ACEHKLST	HACKLETS
ACEHKLTY	LATCHKEY
ACEHKMPU	MUCKHEAP
ACEHKNSY	HACKNEYS
ACEHKOSS	SHACKOES
ACEHKOSW	WHACKOES
ACEHKOTU	TUCKAHOE
ACEHKRSW	WHACKERS
ACEHKRTW	THWACKER
ACEHLLMO	MALLECHO
ACEHLLOR	ORCHELLA
ACEHLLPS	PELLACHS
ACEHLLSS	SHELLACS
ACEHLLSU	HALLUCES
ACEHLMOT	CHAMELOT
ACEHLMST	CHAMLETS
ACEHLNNS	CHANNELS
ACEHLNOS	CHALONES
ACEHLNOU	EULACHON
ACEHLNPS	PLANCHES
ACEHLNPT	PLANCHET
ACEHLNRS	CHARNELS
ACEHLNRU	LAUNCHER
	RELAUNCH
ACEHLNST	STANCHEL
ACEHLNSU	LAUNCHES
ACEHLORS	CHOLERAS
	CHORALES
ACEHLORT	CHELATOR
	CHLORATE
	TROCHLEA
ACEHLORU	LEACHOUR
ACEHLOST	CATHOLES
	ESCHALOT
ACEHLPRT	CHAPTREL
ACEHLPRY	CHAPELRY
ACEHLPSS	CHAPLESS
ACEHLPST	CHAPLETS
ACEHLRSS	CLASHERS
	RASCHELS
ACEHLRST	ARCHLETS
ACEHLRSY	CHARLEYS
ACEHLRTU	ARCHLUTE
	TRAUCHLE
ACEHLSSS	CASHLESS
ACEHLSST	SATCHELS
	SLATCHES
ACEHLSTT	CHATTELS
	LATCHETS
ACEHLSTY	CHASTELY
ACEHMMNR	MARCHMEN
ACEHMNNR	RANCHMEN
ACEHMNRS	ENCHARMS
ACEHMNRT	MERCHANT
ACEHMNSS	CHESSMAN
ACEHMNST	MANCHETS
ACEHMNTW	WATCHMEN
ACEHMORT	CHROMATE
ACEHMPRS	CHAMPERS
ACEHMRRS	CHARMERS
	MARCHERS
ACEHMRST	MATCHERS
ACEHMRSU	CHAUMERS
ACEHMSST	SMATCHES
ACEHMSTU	MUSTACHE
ACEHMSTY	ECTHYMAS
ACEHNNOP	PANCHEON
ACEHNNPT	PENCHANT
ACEHNNRS	CHANNERS
ACEHNNST	ENCHANTS
ACEHNOPR	CANEPHOR
	CHAPERON
ACEHNOPT	CENOTAPH
ACEHNORR	RANCHERO
ACEHNORT	ANCHORET
ACEHNPRT	PENTARCH
ACEHNPRU	UNPREACH
ACEHNPSU	PAUNCHES
ACEHNRRS	RANCHERS
ACEHNRSS	ARCHNESS
ACEHNRST	CHANTERS
	SNATCHER
	STANCHER
	TRANCHES
ACEHNRSU	RAUNCHES
ACEHNRTT	TRANCHET
ACEHNRTU	CHAUNTER
ACEHNSSS	SCHANSES
ACEHNSST	CHASTENS
	SNATCHES
	STANCHES
ACEHNSSZ	SCHANZES
ACEHNSTT	ETCHANTS
ACEHNSTU	NAUTCHES
	UNCHASTE
ACEHNSTY	CHANTEYS
ACEHNSTZ	SCHANTZE
ACEHOPRR	REPROACH
ACEHOPRS	POACHERS
ACEHORRS	HORSECAR
ACEHORRV	OVERARCH
ACEHORST	CHAROSET
	THORACES
ACEHORTT	THEOCRAT
ACEHORTU	OUTREACH
ACEHOSSW	SHOWCASE
ACEHOSTU	CATHOUSE
	SOUTACHE
ACEHOSTY	CHAYOTES
ACEHOSUV	AVOUCHES
ACEHPPSS	CHAPPESS
	SCHAPPES
ACEHPRST	CHAPTERS
	PATCHERS
ACEHPRSU	PURCHASE
ACEHPRTY	PATCHERY
	PETCHARY
ACEHQSTU	QUATCHES
ACEHRRST	CHARTERS
	RECHARTS
	STARCHER
ACEHRRTT	TETRARCH
ACEHRSST	STARCHES
ACEHRSSU	CHASSEUR
ACEHRSTT	CHATTERS
	RATCHETS
ACEHRSTW	WATCHERS
ACEHRSTY	YACHTERS
ACEHRTTY	TRACHYTE
ACEHSSSU	CHAUSSES
ACEHSSTT	CHASTEST
ACEHSSTW	SWATCHES
ACEHSTTU	CATHETUS
	TEUCHATS
ACEHSTTW	WATCHETS
ACEHTTUZ	ZUCHETTA
ACEIILMN	LIMACINE
ACEIILNR	IRENICAL
ACEIILNS	SALICINE
ACEIILSS	LAICISES
ACEIILST	CILIATES
	SILICATE
ACEIILSZ	LAICIZES
ACEIIMRV	VIRAEMIC
ACEIIMSS	ASEISMIC
ACEIIMTU	MAIEUTIC
ACEIINPS	PISCINAE
ACEIINRS	RIANCIES
ACEIINST	CANITIES
ACEIINTV	INACTIVE
ACEIINTZ	ANTICIZE
ACEIIPRS	PIRACIES
ACEIIRRT	CRITERIA
ACEIIRSV	VICARIES
ACEIISTU	ACUITIES
ACEIISTV	CAITIVES
	CAVITIES
	VICIATES
ACEIITTV	VITICETA
ACEIJKSS	JACKSIES
ACEIJMST	MAJESTIC
ACEIJNRR	JERRICAN
ACEIKKNR	KNACKIER
ACEIKLRT	TALCKIER
ACEIKLRY	CREAKILY
ACEIKMNN	NICKNAME
ACEIKMRV	MAVERICK
ACEIKNPS	CAPESKIN
ACEIKNRR	CRANKIER
ACEIKOPS	PAIOCKES
ACEIKORR	CROAKIER
ACEIKPRS	EARPICKS
ACEIKPSX	PICKAXES
ACEIKRRV	VRAICKER
ACEIKSTT	TACKIEST
	TIETACKS
ACEIKSTW	WACKIEST
ACEILLLT	CLITELLA
ACEILLMR	MICELLAR
	MILLRACE
ACEILLMS	LIMACELS
ACEILLMT	METALLIC
ACEILLMY	MYCELIAL
ACEILLNT	CLIENTAL
ACEILLOP	CALLIOPE
ACEILLOR	ROCAILLE
ACEILLOS	LOCALISE
ACEILLOT	TEOCALLI
ACEILLOZ	LOCALIZE
ACEILLPR	CALLIPER
ACEILLPS	ALLSPICE
ACEILLPY	EPICALLY
ACEILLRV	CAVILLER
ACEILMMO	CAMOMILE
ACEILMMR	CLAMMIER
ACEILMNN	CLINAMEN
ACEILMNO	COALMINE
ACEILMNP	MANCIPLE
ACEILMNS	MESCALIN
ACEILMOS	CAMISOLE
ACEILMPS	MISPLACE
ACEILMPT	PELMATIC
ACEILMRS	CLAIMERS
	MIRACLES
	RECLAIMS
ACEILMRT	METRICAL
ACEILMST	CALMIEST
	CLEMATIS
	CLIMATES
	METICALS
ACEILMSU	MUSICALE
ACEILMSX	CLIMAXES
	EXCLAIMS
ACEILMTU	AMULETIC
ACEILNNP	PANNICLE
	PINNACLE
ACEILNNR	ENCRINAL
ACEILNOR	ACROLEIN
	CREOLIAN
	LONICERA
ACEILNPS	CAPELINS
	PANICLES
	PELICANS
ACEILNPT	PECTINAL
	PLANETIC
ACEILNRS	CARLINES
ACEILNRT	CLARINET
ACEILNSS	SANICLES
ACEILNSU	AESCULIN
	LUNACIES
ACEILNSY	SALIENCY
ACEILOPR	CAPRIOLE
ACEILOPT	POETICAL
ACEILORR	CARRIOLE
ACEILORS	CALORIES
	CARIOLES
ACEILORT	EROTICAL
	LORICATE
ACEILORV	ARVICOLE
ACEILOSS	COALISES
ACEILOST	ALOETICS
	COALIEST
	SOCIETAL
ACEILOSV	VOCALISE
ACEILOSZ	COALIZES
ACEILOTV	LOCATIVE
ACEILOVZ	VOCALIZE
ACEILPPY	PIPECLAY
ACEILPRS	CALIPERS
	REPLICAS
	SPIRACLE
ACEILPRT	PARTICLE
	PRELATIC
ACEILPRU	PECULIAR
ACEILPSS	SLIPCASE
	SPECIALS
ACEILPST	PLICATES
ACEILPTY	ETYPICAL
ACEILPXY	EPICALYX

ACEILRRT CLARTIER
ACEILRRW CRAWLIER
ACEILRSS CLASSIER
ACEILRST ALTRICES
ARTICLES
RECITALS
SELICTAR
ACEILRSU AURICLES
ACEILRSV CALIVERS
CLAVIERS
VISCERAL
ACEILRTT TRACTILE
ACEILRTV VERTICAL
ACEILRTY LITERACY
ACEILSST ELASTICS
SALICETS
SCALIEST
ACEILSTT LATTICES
TALCIEST
ACEILSTY CLAYIEST
ACEILSUV VESICULA
ACEILTVY ACTIVELY
ACEIMMNP PEMMICAN
ACEIMMOS SEMICOMA
ACEIMMRS RACEMISM
ACEIMNOR CORAMINE
ACEIMNPS PEMICANS
ACEIMNRS CARMINES
ACEIMNRU MANICURE
ACEIMNSS AMNESICS
ACEIMNST SEMANTIC
ACEIMNSU SEMUNCIA
ACEIMNSY SYCAMINE
ACEIMOPT POEMATIC
ACEIMOTX TOXAEMIC
ACEIMOTZ METAZOIC
ACEIMPRR CRAMPIER
MERICARP
ACEIMPSS ESCAPISM
ACEIMPST CAMPIEST
CAMPSITE
ACEIMPTU PUMICATE
ACEIMRST CERAMIST
MATRICES
ACEIMRTT TREMATIC
ACEIMRTU MURICATE
ACEIMSST ETACISMS
ACEIMSSU CAESIUMS
ACEINNOS CANONISE
ACEINNOT ENACTION
ACEINNOZ CANONIZE
ACEINNPS PINNACES
ACEINNRS CRANNIES
ACEINNST ANCIENTS
CANNIEST
INSTANCE
ACEINNSU NUISANCE
ACEINNSY CYANINES
ACEINNTU UNCINATE
ACEINOPR APOCRINE
CAPONIER
PROCAINE
ACEINOPS CANOPIES
CAPONISE
PAEONICS
ACEINOPZ CAPONIZE
ACEINORS SCENARIO
ACEINORT ANORETIC
CREATION
REACTION

ACEINORV VERONICA
ACEINORX ANOREXIC
ACEINOST ACONITES
CANOEIST
ACEINOTT TACONITE
ACEINOTV CONATIVE
ACEINOTX EXACTION
ACEINPSS INSCAPES
PINCASES
ACEINPTT PITTANCE
ACEINPUY PICAYUNE
ACEINRRU CURARINE
ACEINRRY CINERARY
ACEINRSS ARSENICS
CERASINS
RACINESS
ACEINRST CANISTER
CARNIEST
CISTERNA
CREATINS
NACRITES
SCANTIER
ACEINRTT INTERACT
ACEINRTV NAVICERT
ACEINRTX XERANTIC
ACEINRVY VICENARY
ACEINSST CINEASTS
SCANTIES
ACEINSSU ISSUANCE
ACEINSSY CYANISES
ACEINSTT CANTIEST
NICTATES
TETANICS
ACEINSTV CISTVAEN
VESICANT
ACEINSTY CYANITES
ACEINSYZ CYANIZES
ACEINTTU TUNICATE
ACEINTTX EXCITANT
ACEINTTY TENACITY
ACEINTUV UNACTIVE
ACEIOPRT OPERATIC
ACEIOPST ECTOPIAS
ACEIORSV COVARIES
VARICOSE
ACEIOSST SOCIATES
ACEIOSSU CAESIOUS
ACEIOSTT OSCITATE
ACEIOTVV VOCATIVE
ACEIPPRR CRAPPIER
PERICARP
ACEIPPRS EPICARPS
ACEIPPST TAPPICES
ACEIPRRS PERISARC
ACEIPRSS SCRAPIES
ACEIPRST CRAPIEST
CRISPATE
PICRATES
PRACTISE
ACEIPRTV PRACTIVE
ACEIPRTY APYRETIC
ACEIPSST ASEPTICS
ESCAPIST
SPACIEST
ACEIPSSU AUSPICES
ACEIPSSZ CAPSIZES
ACEIPSTV CAPTIVES
ACEIQRSU ACQUIRES
ACEIQSTU ACQUITES
ACEIQSUZ CAZIQUES

ACEIRRRS CARRIERS
SCARRIER
ACEIRRST ERRATICS
ACEIRRSU CURARISE
ACEIRRSW AIRSCREW
ACEIRRTT RETRAICT
ACEIRRTX CREATRIX
ACEIRRTY RETIRACY
ACEIRRUZ CURARIZE
ACEIRSST SCARIEST
ACEIRSSU SCAURIES
URICASES
ACEIRSSV VICARESS
ACEIRSTT CITRATES
CRISTATE
SCATTIER
ACEIRSTU SURICATE
ACEIRSTZ CRAZIEST
ACEIRTTU URTICATE
ACEIRTTV TRACTIVE
ACEIRTUV CURATIVE
ACEIRTVY VERACITY
ACEISSSS CASSISES
ACEISSST ECSTASIS
ACEISSSU SAUCISSE
ACEISSTT STATICES
ACEISSTU SAUCIEST
SUITCASE
ACEISTTT CATTIEST
ACEISTTU EUSTATIC
ACEISTTW SCAWTITE
ACEISTUX AUXETICS
ACEJKOOR JACKEROO
ACEJKOPS PAJOCKES
ACEJLORS CAJOLERS
ACEJLORY CAJOLERY
ACEJMRST SCRAMJET
ACEJNNOO JONCANOE
ACEJNOST JACONETS
ACEJNOSY JOYANCES
ACEJNRRY JERRYCAN
ACEJNSTU JUNCATES
ACEJPSTU CAJEPUTS
ACEJRSTT TRAJECTS
ACEKKNRS KNACKERS
ACEKKNRY KNACKERY
ACEKLLPS PELLACKS
ACEKLNRS CRANKLES
ACEKLNSS SLACKENS
ACEKLNTU UNTACKLE
ACEKLORS EARLOCKS
ACEKLORV LAVEROCK
ACEKLPRS SPRACKLE
ACEKLPST PLACKETS
ACEKLQSU QUACKLES
ACEKLRSS SLACKERS
ACEKLRST TACKLERS
ACEKLRSU CAULKERS
ACEKLSSS SACKLESS
ACEKLSST SLACKEST
ACEKMNRT TRACKMEN
ACEKMNST TACKSMEN
ACEKMRSS SMACKERS
ACEKNNOW ACKNOWNE
ACEKNPRS PRANCKES
ACEKNPRU UNPACKER
ACEKOORT CARETOOK
ACEKOORW COOKWARE
ACEKOPRW CAPEWORK
ACEKORRS CROAKERS

ACEKORRV OVERRACK
ACEKORSW CASEWORK
ACEKPPRS PREPACKS
ACEKPSSY SKYSCAPE
ACEKQRSU QUACKERS
ACEKQRUY QUACKERY
ACEKRRST TRACKERS
ACEKRRTY RACKETRY
ACEKRSST STACKERS
ACEKRSTT RACKETTS
ACEKRSTU RUCKSEAT
ACEKSSTT STACKETS
ACEKSSUW WAESUCKS
ACELLLRU CELLULAR
ACELLMOS CALOMELS
ACELLMSU SACELLUM
ACELLNRU NUCELLAR
ACELLOPS COLLAPSE
ESCALLOP
ACELLORR CAROLLER
ACELLORS CORELLAS
ACELLORV COVERALL
OVERCALL
ACELLORW CALLOWER
ACELLOST COLLATES
ACELLOSW COLESLAW
ACELLOTU LOCULATE
ACELLPSS SCALPELS
ACELLRRS CARRELLS
ACELLRTY RECTALLY
ACELLSSU CALLUSES
ACELLSSW CLAWLESS
ACELLSTU SCUTELLA
ACELLTWY CETYWALL
ACELMMOU MAMELUCO
ACELMNNS CLANSMEN
ACELMNOR AMELCORN
ACELMNRU CRUMENAL
ACELMNSS CALMNESS
CLASSMEN
ACELMOPT COMPLEAT
ACELMORS CAROMELS
SCLEROMA
ACELMORY CLAYMORE
ACELMOST CAMELOTS
MOLECAST
ACELMOSU CAULOMES
LEUCOMAS
MACULOSE
ACELMPRS CLAMPERS
ACELMPSY ECLAMPSY
ACELMSSU LACMUSES
ACELMSTU CALUMETS
MUSCATEL
ACELMSUU SAECULUM
ACELMTUU CUMULATE
ACELNNRS SCRANNEL
ACELNORV NOVERCAL
ACELNOST LACTONES
ACELNOSU LACUNOSE
ACELNOSZ CALZONES
ACELNOTV COVALENT
ACELNOVY CONVEYAL
ACELNPSS ENCLASPS
SPANCELS
ACELNPST CLAPNETS
ACELNPSU UNPLACES
ACELNRSU LUCARNES
ACELNRVY CRAVENLY
ACELNSST SCANTLES

ACELNSSU	SCALENUS
	UNSCALES
ACELNSTT	CANTLETS
ACELNSTY	SECANTLY
ACELOPPU	POPULACE
ACELOPRS	PARCLOSE
	POLACRES
ACELOPRT	PECTORAL
ACELOPRU	OPERCULA
ACELOPSS	ESCALOPS
ACELOPST	POLECATS
ACELOPTU	COPULATE
ACELOPTY	CALOTYPE
ACELOQSU	COEQUALS
ACELORRT	RECTORAL
ACELORSS	ESCOLARS
	LACROSSE
ACELORST	SECTORAL
ACELORSU	CAROUSEL
ACELORSY	CALOYERS
	COARSELY
ACELOSST	ALECOSTS
	COATLESS
	LACTOSES
	SCATOLES
ACELOSTT	CALOTTES
ACELOSTU	LACTEOUS
	LOCUSTAE
	OSCULATE
ACELOSTY	ACOLYTES
ACELOSUV	VACUOLES
ACELPPRS	CLAPPERS
	SCRAPPLE
ACELPPSS	SCAPPLES
ACELPRSS	CLASPERS
	SCALPERS
ACELPRST	SCEPTRAL
	SPECTRAL
ACELPRSU	SPECULAR
ACELPSSU	CAPSULES
ACELPTUU	CUPULATE
ACELPTUY	EUCALYPT
ACELQRSU	LACQUERS
ACELQRUU	CLAQUEUR
ACELQSUY	LACQUEYS
ACELRRSW	CRAWLERS
	SCRAWLER
ACELRSSS	SCARLESS
ACELRSST	SCARLETS
ACELRSSU	SECULARS
ACELRSTT	CLATTERS
	SCRATTLE
ACELRSTU	RAUCLEST
ACELRTTU	CULTRATE
ACELRTTY	CLATTERY
ACELSSTT	TACTLESS
ACELSSTY	SCYTALES
ACELSSUX	EXCUSALS
ACEMMOTY	MYCETOMA
ACEMMRRS	CRAMMERS
ACEMNORR	ROMANCER
ACEMNORS	CREMONAS
	ROMANCES
ACEMNOST	CAMSTONE
ACEMNPSS	CAMPNESS
ACEMNRUY	NUMERACY
ACEMNSSU	MANCUSES
ACEMOORS	ACROSOME
ACEMOOST	COMATOSE
ACEMOPRS	COMPARES
	COMPEARS
	MESOCARP
ACEMORRT	CREMATOR
ACEMORSY	SYCAMORE
ACEMORTY	COMETARY
ACEMORUX	MORCEAUX
ACEMPRSS	SCAMPERS
ACEMPRST	CRAMPETS
ACEMPSSU	CAMPUSES
ACEMSSTT	METCASTS
ACENNNOU	ANNOUNCE
ACENNOSS	CANONESS
	SONANCES
ACENNOSY	NOYANCES
ACENNOTT	COTENANT
ACENNOTV	COVENANT
ACENNOTZ	CANZONET
ACENNPRY	PERNANCY
ACENNRSS	SCANNERS
ACENNSUY	SEACUNNY
ACENOORT	CORONATE
ACENOOTZ	ECTOZOAN
ACENOPRT	PORTANCE
ACENOPST	CAPSTONE
ACENOPSU	PONCEAUS
ACENOPUX	PONCEAUX
ACENOQTU	COTQUEAN
ACENORRW	CAREWORN
ACENORSS	COARSENS
	NARCOSES
ACENORST	ANCESTOR
	ENACTORS
	SORTANCE
ACENORSU	CARNEOUS
	NACREOUS
ACENORTT	CONTRATE
ACENORTU	COURANTE
	OUTRANCE
ACENORUY	EUCARYON
ACENOSSS	CASSONES
ACENOSST	CONTESSA
	COSTEANS
ACENOSSV	CAVESSON
ACENOSSY	CYANOSES
ACENOSTT	CONSTATE
ACENOSTV	CENTAVOS
ACENOTTU	TOUCANET
ACENPRRS	PRANCERS
ACENPRSU	ENCARPUS
	PRAUNCES
ACENPSTT	PENTACTS
ACENPTTU	PUNCTATE
ACENRSST	CRANTSES
ACENRSSU	SURANCES
ACENRSTT	TRANECTS
	TRANSECT
ACENRSTU	CENTAURS
	RECUSANT
	UNCRATES
	UNTRACES
ACENRSTY	ANCESTRY
ACENRTTU	TRUNCATE
ACENRTUY	CENTAURY
	CYANURET
ACENSSTT	SCANTEST
ACENSSTU	NUTCASES
ACENSSTW	NEWSCAST
ACEOOPPS	APOCOPES
ACEOOPSU	POACEOUS
ACEOORTV	EVOCATOR
	OVERCOAT
ACEOPPRS	COPPERAS
ACEOPRRT	RECAPTOR
ACEOPRSX	EXOCARPS
ACEOPRTT	ATTERCOP
ACEOPSTU	OUTPACES
ACEORRST	ACROTERS
	CREATORS
	REACTORS
ACEORRSU	CAROUSER
ACEORRTT	RETROACT
ACEORRVW	OVERCRAW
ACEORSST	COARSEST
	COASTERS
ACEORSSU	CAROUSES
ACEORSTT	SECTATOR
ACEORSTU	OUTRACES
ACEORSTV	OVERACTS
	OVERCAST
ACEORSTX	EXACTORS
ACEORTUY	EUCARYOT
ACEOSTTU	OUTCASTE
ACEOSTUU	AUTOCUES
ACEPRRSS	SCARPERS
	SCRAPERS
ACEPRRTU	CAPTURER
ACEPRSSU	SCAUPERS
ACEPRSTU	CAPTURES
	PRESCUTA
ACEPSTTY	TYPECAST
ACEQRSTU	RACQUETS
ACEQSSTU	ACQUESTS
ACERRSTT	RETRACTS
ACERRSUV	VERRUCAS
ACERSSST	CRASSEST
ACERSSSU	SUCRASES
ACERSSTT	SCATTERS
ACERSTTT	TETRACTS
ACERSTTU	CRUSTATE
ACERSTTX	EXTRACTS
ACERSTTY	SCATTERY
ACFFGHIN	CHAFFING
ACFFHNOR	CHAFFRON
ACFFIILO	OFFICIAL
ACFFIIST	CAITIFFS
ACFFIKMS	MAFFICKS
ACFFILNU	FANCIFUL
ACFFILST	AFFLICTS
ACFFIRST	TRAFFICS
ACFFLOSW	SCOFFLAW
ACFGHINU	CHAUFING
ACFGIIMN	MAGNIFIC
ACFGIIPR	CAPRIFIG
ACFGIKNR	FRACKING
ACFGINNY	FANCYING
ACFGINRS	FARCINGS
	SCARFING
ACFGINRT	CRAFTING
	FRACTING
ACFGITUY	FUGACITY
ACFGKNOP	PACKFONG
ACFGLNOR	CORNFLAG
ACFHHINW	HAWFINCH
ACFHILNO	FALCHION
ACFHILNU	FAULCHIN
ACFHILOS	COALFISH
ACFHINOU	FAUCHION
ACFHIRSS	SCARFISH
ACFHIRSW	CRAWFISH
ACFHIRSY	CRAYFISH
ACFHISSU	FUCHSIAS
ACFHLMRU	CHARMFUL
ACFHLTUW	WATCHFUL
ACFHMNOR	CHAMFRON
ACFHNOSU	FAUCHONS
ACFIILST	FISTICAL
ACFIILSV	SALVIFIC
ACFIILTY	FACILITY
ACFIIMPS	PACIFISM
ACFIIMSS	FASCISMI
ACFIIPST	PACIFIST
ACFIISST	FASCISTI
ACFIKLNS	CALFSKIN
ACFIKNNS	FINNACKS
ACFILLSY	FISCALLY
ACFILNOR	FORNICAL
ACFILNOS	FOLACINS
ACFILORT	TRIFOCAL
ACFILRTY	CRAFTILY
ACFILSSY	CLASSIFY
ACFIMNRU	FRANCIUM
ACFIMOSS	FASCISMO
ACFIMSSS	FASCISMS
ACFINORT	FRACTION
ACFINOST	FACTIONS
ACFINRST	INFARCTS
	INFRACTS
ACFINSTY	SANCTIFY
ACFIOSTU	FACTIOUS
ACFIRTUY	FURACITY
ACFISSST	FASCISTS
ACFKLORS	FORSLACK
ACFKLOST	LOCKFAST
ACFKLRUW	WRACKFUL
ACFKLSSU	SACKFULS
ACFKOSTT	FATSTOCK
ACFLMNOO	MOONCALF
ACFLNORY	FALCONRY
ACFLOOPS	FOOLSCAP
ACFLORSU	SCROFULA
ACFLRRUU	FURCULAR
ACFMOTTU	FACTOTUM
ACFNRSTU	FRUCTANS
ACGGGILN	CLAGGING
ACGGHINN	CHANGING
	GANCHING
ACGGHINR	CHARGING
ACGGIINN	INCAGING
ACGGIINT	GIGANTIC
ACGGIIOS	ISAGOGIC
ACGGILNN	CANGLING
	CLANGING
	GLANCING
ACGGINNO	CONGAING
ACGGINNU	UNCAGING
ACGGINOR	CARGOING
ACGGIOOR	CORAGGIO
ACGGLNOU	GLUCAGON
ACGGLRSY	SCRAGGLY
ACGHHIJK	HIGHJACK
ACGHHINN	HANCHING
ACGHHINT	HATCHING
ACGHIINN	CHAINING
ACGHIINR	CHAIRING
ACGHIKLN	CHALKING
	HACKLING
ACGHIKNR	CHARKING
ACGHIKNS	HACKINGS
ACGHIKNW	WHACKING
ACGHILNN	LANCHING

ACGHILNS CLASHING
ACGHILNT LATCHING
ACGHILNU LAUCHING
ACGHILNY ACHINGLY
ACGHILOR OLIGARCH
ACGHIMNP CHAMPING
ACGHIMNR CHARMING
MARCHING
ACGHIMNT MATCHING
ACGHINNR RANCHING
ACGHINNT CHANTING
ACGHINNU UNACHING
ACGHINOP POACHING
ACGHINOR ROACHING
ACGHINPP CHAPPING
ACGHINPR PARCHING
ACGHINPT NIGHTCAP
PATCHING
ACGHINRR CHARRING
ACGHINRS CHAGRINS
CRASHING
ACGHINRT CHARTING
RATCHING
ACGHINRU CHURINGA
NURAGHIC
ACGHINSS CHASINGS
ACGHINST SCATHING
ACGHINSW CHINWAGS
ACGHINTT CHATTING
ACGHINTW WATCHING
ACGHINTY YACHTING
ACGHIPRS GRAPHICS
ACGHIQTU ACQUIGHT
ACGHIRSS SCRAIGHS
ACGHLLOR GRALLOCH
ACGHLOOY CHAOLOGY
ACGHLSTU CLAUGHTS
ACGHNTUU UNCAUGHT
ACGHORSU CHORAGUS
ACGHPTUU UPCAUGHT
ACGHRRSU CURRAGHS
ACGHRSSU SCRAUGHS
ACGIILMN CLAIMING
MALICING
ACGIILNN INLACING
ACGIILNO LOGICIAN
ACGIILNS SCAILING
ACGIIMNT MICATING
ACGIIMOS ISOGAMIC
ACGIIMST SIGMATIC
ACGIINNS INCASING
ACGIINNV INCAVING
ACGIINRT GRANITIC
ACGIIPRS SPAGIRIC
ACGIJJKO JICKAJOG
ACGIJLNO CAJOLING
ACGIJNNU JAUNCING
ACGIKLMN MACKLING
ACGIKLNN CLANKING
ACGIKLNO CLOAKING
ACGIKLNS SLACKING
ACGIKLNT TACKLING
TALCKING
ACGIKLNU CAULKING
ACGIKLRY GARLICKY
ACGIKMNS SMACKING
ACGIKNNR CRANKING
ACGIKNNS SNACKING
ACGIKNOR CROAKING
ACGIKNPS PACKINGS
ACGIKNQU QUACKING
ACGIKNRS ARCKINGS
RACKINGS
ACGIKNRT TRACKING
ACGIKNRW WRACKING
ACGIKNSS SACKINGS
ACGIKNST STACKING
TACKINGS
ACGIKPRS GRIPSACK
ACGILLNS CALLINGS
ACGILMMN CLAMMING
ACGILMNP CAMPLING
CLAMPING
ACGILNNT CANTLING
ACGILNNU LAUNCING
UNLACING
ACGILNOR ORACLING
ACGILNOS SOLACING
ACGILNOT LOCATING
ACGILNPP CLAPPING
ACGILNPS CLASPING
PLACINGS
SCALPING
ACGILNQU CALQUING
ACGILNRS CARLINGS
ACGILNRT CLARTING
ACGILNRW CRAWLING
ACGILNSS CLASSING
SCALINGS
ACGILNST CASTLING
CATLINGS
SCLATING
ACGILNSU GLUCINAS
ACGILNTT CLATTING
ACGILNTU CLAUTING
ACGILRSU SURGICAL
ACGIMMNR CRAMMING
ACGIMNOR CAROMING
ACGIMNOS COAMINGS
ACGIMNPR CRAMPING
ACGIMNPS SCAMPING
ACGIMNSY GYMNASIC
SYNGAMIC
ACGIMORS ORGASMIC
ACGINNNS SCANNING
ACGINNNU NUANCING
ACGINNPR PRANCING
ACGINNPU UNCAPING
ACGINNRT TRANCING
ACGINNRU UNCARING
ACGINNRY CARNYING
ACGINNST CANTINGS
SCANTING
ACGINNSU UNCASING
ACGINNUV VAUNCING
ACGINOPT COAPTING
ACGINORY CONGIARY
ACGINOST AGNOSTIC
COASTING
COATINGS
COTINGAS
ACGINPPR CRAPPING
ACGINPPS CAPPINGS
ACGINPRS CARPINGS
SCARPING
SCRAPING
ACGINPSS SPACINGS
ACGINPSU SCAUPING
ACGINRRS SCARRING
ACGINRRY CARRYING
ACGINRSS SACRINGS
ACGINRST SCARTING
TRACINGS
ACGINRSU SCAURING
ACGINRSV CARVINGS
CRAVINGS
ACGINRTT TRACTING
ACGINRTU CURATING
ACGINSST CASTINGS
ACGINSTT SCATTING
ACGIOORS GRACIOSO
ACGIORST ORGASTIC
ACGIORSU GRACIOUS
ACGIPRSY SPAGYRIC
ACGJLNOU CONJUGAL
ACGKMMOS GAMMOCKS
ACGKORSV GARVOCKS
ACGLLPSU CUPGALLS
ACGLMOUU COAGULUM
ACGLNORS CLANGORS
ACGLNORU CLANGOUR
ACGLOSUU GLAUCOUS
ACGLSSTU CUTGLASS
ACGNNOOT CONTANGO
ACGNNORS CRANNOGS
ACGNOOST OCTAGONS
ACGNORST CONGRATS
ACGORRSY GYROCARS
ACGORSSW COWGRASS
ACGORSUU COUGUARS
ACGPPSUU SCUPPAUG
ACHHILPT PHTHALIC
ACHHINTW WHINCHAT
ACHHINTY HYACINTH
ACHHIPPR HIPPARCH
ACHHLMOS MASHLOCH
ACHHLNOR RHONCHAL
ACHHLPRY PHYLARCH
ACHHLSUY SHAUCHLY
ACHHNTTU NUTHATCH
UNTHATCH
ACHHOSST TOSHACHS
ACHHPPSU CHUPPAHS
ACHHPTUZ CHUTZPAH
ACHIIKMS KAMICHIS
ACHIILMS CHILIASM
ACHIILST CHILIAST
ACHIINRT TRICHINA
ACHIIPSS PACHISIS
ACHIIRST RACHITIS
ACHIIRSU ISCHURIA
ACHIJKPW WHIPJACK
ACHIJNST JACINTHS
ACHIKKNS KNACKISH
ACHIKKSW KICKSHAW
ACHIKLLW HICKWALL
ACHIKLPT CHALKPIT
ACHIKNOP PACHINKO
ACHIKRSS RICKSHAS
ACHIKRSW RICKSHAW
ACHIKRSY HAYRICKS
ACHIKSSS SHICKSAS
ACHILLOR ORCHILLA
ACHILLRT CLITHRAL
ACHILMOP OMPHALIC
ACHILMOS MALICHOS
ACHILMRS CHRISMAL
ACHILMTY MYTHICAL
ACHILNNS CLANNISH
ACHILNOO HOOLICAN
ACHILNOS LICHANOS
ACHILNPS CLANSHIP
ACHILOPR RHOPALIC
ACHILORT ACROLITH
ACHILPSY PHYSICAL
ACHILPTY PATCHILY
ACHILRUY CHYLURIA
ACHILRVY CHIVALRY
ACHILSWY LICHWAYS
ACHIMMOS MACHISMO
ACHIMMST MISMATCH
ACHIMNNW WINCHMAN
ACHIMNOP CHAMPION
ACHIMNOR CHOIRMAN
HARMONIC
ACHIMNOS MANIHOCS
ACHIMNPT PITCHMAN
ACHIMOPR AMPHORIC
ACHIMOSS CHAMISOS
ISOCHASM
ACHIMPSS SCAMPISH
ACHIMRSS CHARISMS
ACHIMRST CHARTISM
ACHIMSSS SCHISMAS
ACHIMSST MASTICHS
TACHISMS
ACHIMSSU CHIASMUS
ACHINNOP PANCHION
ACHINNSU UNCHAINS
ACHINOPR PAROCHIN
ACHINORT ANORTHIC
ACHINOSY ONYCHIAS
ACHINOTZ HOACTZIN
ACHINRSZ ZARNICHS
ACHINSUV CHAUVINS
ACHIORSS COARSISH
ACHIORST CHARIOTS
HARICOTS
ACHIORTV TOVARICH
ACHIPPSS SAPPHICS
ACHIPRRT PARRITCH
ACHIPSTU CHUPATIS
ACHIPSTW WHIPCATS
ACHIPTTU CHUPATTI
ACHIQRSU CHARQUIS
ACHIRRST TRIARCHS
ACHIRRTY TRIARCHY
ACHIRSTT CHARTIST
STRAICHT
ACHIRSTU HAIRCUTS
ACHISSTT TACHISTS
ACHISTTY CHASTITY
ACHKMMOS HAMMOCKS
ACHKMORS SHAMROCK
ACHKNNUU NUNCHAKU
ACHKNOOT CANTHOOK
ACHKOPSS HOPSACKS
ACHKOSSS HASSOCKS
ACHKOSSY HASSOCKY
ACHKOSTT HATTOCKS
ACHLLOOS ALCOHOLS
ACHLLORS CHLORALS
ACHLLORY CHORALLY
ACHLMSTZ SCHMALTZ
ACHLNOOU OULACHON
ACHLNOSY HALCYONS
ACHLNSTU TULCHANS
ACHLOPRS RAPLOCHS
ACHLOPRT CALTHROP
ACHLOPRY POLYARCH

ACHLOPTT POTLATCH
ACHLORSS SCHOLARS
ACHLOSSW SALCHOWS
ACHLOSTY ACOLYTHS
ACHLOTWX WAXCLOTH
ACHMNORS MONARCHS
NOMARCHS
ACHMNORY MONARCHY
NOMARCHY
ACHMNRSU UNCHARMS
ACHMNRTU TRUCHMAN
ACHMOPRS CAMPHORS
ACHMORTU OUTMARCH
ACHMOSST STOMACHS
ACHMOSTY STOMACHY
ACHMOTTU OUTMATCH
ACHMSSUW CUMSHAWS
ACHNNORU UNANCHOR
ACHNNOSS CHANSONS
ACHNORST CHANTORS
ACHNOSTY TACHYONS
ACHNOSUY CHANOYUS
ACHNPPSS SCHNAPPS
ACHNRSTU UNSTARCH
ACHNRSYY SYNARCHY
ACHNRTUY CHAUNTRY
ACHOORTY CHAYROOT
ACHOPRST TOPARCHS
ACHOPRSY CHARPOYS
ACHOPRTY TOPARCHY
ACHOTTUW OUTWATCH
ACHRSTTU STRAUCHT
ACIIILMN INIMICAL
ACIIILNV CIVILIAN
ACIIKNNN CANNIKIN
ACIIKNNS CANIKINS
ACIIKPRT PAITRICK
ACIILLSU SILICULA
ACIILLTV VILLATIC
ACIILMNR CRIMINAL
ACIILNOR IRONICAL
ACIILNOT TALIONIC
ACIILNPT PLATINIC
ACIILNSS SALICINS
ACIILOSV VILIACOS
ACIILRTT TRITICAL
ACIILRTU URALITIC
ACIILSST SILASTIC
ACIILSTV SILVATIC
ACIIMMNS MINICAMS
ACIIMNOR MORAINIC
ACIIMNOS SIMONIAC
ACIIMNOT AMNIOTIC
ACIIMNST ACTINISM
ACIIMNSU MUSICIAN
ACIIMNTU ACTINIUM
ACIIMNTY IMITANCY
INTIMACY
MINACITY
ACIIMOTT AMITOTIC
ACIIMPRT PRIMATIC
ACIIMPRV VAMPIRIC
ACIIMRST SCIMITAR
ACIIMRTU MURIATIC
ACIIMSST ITACISMS
ACIIMSTV ACTIVISM
ACIIMTUV VIATICUM
ACIINNOT INACTION
NICOTIAN
ACIINNQU CINQUAIN

ACIINNTT INCITANT
ACIINNTY CANINITY
ACIINOPT OPTICIAN
ACIINORZ ZIRCONIA
ACIINOSS ASINICOS
ACIINOSV AVIONICS
ACIINOTT CITATION
ACIINPSS PISCINAS
ACIINRSS NARCISSI
ACIINRSU URANISCI
ACIINRTU URANITIC
ACIIOPST APOSITIC
ACIIORST AORISTIC
ACIIORTV VICTORIA
ACIIPPST PAPISTIC
ACIIRSTT ARTISTIC
TRIATICS
ACIISTTU AUTISTIC
ACIISTTV ACTIVIST
ACIITTVY ACTIVITY
ACIITVVY VIVACITY
ACIJKKPS SKIPJACK
ACIJKSTW STICKJAW
ACIJSUZZ JACUZZIS
ACIKLMST MALSTICK
ACIKLNRY CRANKILY
ACIKLORS AIRLOCKS
ACIKLORY CROAKILY
ACIKMOOS OOMIACKS
ACIKMPRS RAMPICKS
ACIKMPST MAPSTICK
ACIKMPSW PICKMAWS
ACIKNNPS PANNICKS
ACIKNSST CATSKINS
ACIKNSTT TINTACKS
ACIKPRST PATRICKS
ACILLLOP POLLICAL
ACILLMMY CLAMMILY
ACILLMOS LOCALISM
ACILLMSS MISCALLS
ACILLNOO COLONIAL
ACILLNOR CARILLON
ACILLNOS SCALLION
ACILLOQU COQUILLA
ACILLORT CLITORAL
ACILLORY COLLYRIA
ACILLOST LOCALIST
ACILLOSY SOCIALLY
ACILLOTY LOCALITY
ACILMNOP COMPLAIN
ACILMNOS LACONISM
LIMACONS
ACILMOOS SCOLIOMA
ACILMOPR PROCLAIM
ACILMOPT COMPITAL
ACILMOSV VOCALISM
ACILMPTU PLACITUM
ACILMSSS CLASSISM
ACILMSSU MUSICALS
ACILMSTY MYSTICAL
ACILMTUY ULTIMACY
ACILNOOT LOCATION
ACILNOOV VOCALION
ACILNOPS SALPICON
ACILNOPT PLATONIC
ACILNORS CLARINOS
CLARIONS
ACILNORT CONTRAIL
ACILNOSU UNSOCIAL
ACILNOUV UNIVOCAL

ACILNPSS INCLASPS
SCALPINS
ACILNRSU CISLUNAR
ACILNRUY CULINARY
URANYLIC
ACILNSTU LUNATICS
SULTANIC
ACILNSTY SCANTILY
ACILOPRT TROPICAL
ACILORRS RACLOIRS
ACILORRV CORRIVAL
ACILORST CALORIST
ACILORSV CORIVALS
ACILORTV VORTICAL
ACILORYZ ZIRCALOY
ACILOSTV VOCALIST
ACILOTVY VOCALITY
ACILPRSU SPICULAR
ACILPRTU PICTURAL
ACILPSST PLASTICS
ACILPSSU SPICULAS
ACILRSTU CURTAILS
RUSTICAL
ACILRTUV CULTIVAR
CURVITAL
ACILSSST CLASSIST
ACILSTUV VICTUALS
ACILSTVY SYLVATIC
ACIMMOSS ACOSMISM
ACIMMTUY CYMATIUM
ACIMNNNO CINNAMON
ACIMNOOR ACROMION
ACIMNOPS CAMPIONS
ACIMNORS MARCONIS
ACIMNORT ROMANTIC
ACIMNORU CONARIUM
COUMARIN
ACIMNORY ACRIMONY
ACIMNOSS MOCASSIN
ACIMNOST MONASTIC
ACIMNOTU ACONITUM
ACIMNPTY TYMPANIC
ACIMNRSU CRANIUMS
CUMARINS
ACIMNSTT CATMINTS
ACIMOOST SCOTOMIA
ACIMORST ACROTISM
ACIMORSY CRAMOISY
ACIMOSST ACOSMIST
MASSICOT
ACIMOSTT MASTICOT
STOMATIC
ACIMPRST CRAMPITS
PTARMICS
ACIMRRSY MISCARRY
ACIMRSSZ CZARISMS
ACIMSSST MISCASTS
ACIMSSTT TACTISMS
ACINNOOT CONATION
INTONACO
ACINNORR NARICORN
ACINNOSS SCANSION
ACINNOST ACTINONS
CANONIST
CANTIONS
CONTAINS
SANCTION
ACINNOTU CONTINUA
ACINNRTY TYRANNIC
ACINNSTU ANNICUTS

ACINNSTY INSTANCY
ACINOOPR PICAROON
ACINOOTV VOCATION
ACINOPPT PANOPTIC
ACINOPRS PARSONIC
ACINOPST CAPTIONS
PACTIONS
ACINOQSU COQUINAS
ACINORRS CARRIONS
ACINORRT CONTRAIR
ACINORSS NARCOSIS
ACINORST CANTORIS
CAROTINS
ACINORTT TRACTION
ACINOSSS CAISSONS
CASSINOS
ACINOSSY CYANOSIS
ACINOSTT OSCITANT
TACTIONS
ACINOSTU ANTICOUS
AUCTIONS
CAUTIONS
ACINOSTW WAINSCOT
ACINOSWX COXSWAIN
ACINOTTX TOXICANT
ACINPQUY PIQUANCY
ACINPRST CANTRIPS
ACINPRSY CYPRIANS
ACINPSTY SYNAPTIC
ACINQSTU QUANTICS
ACINRSSU CRUSIANS
ACINRSTU CURTAINS
SATURNIC
TURACINS
ACINRTTU TACITURN
URTICANT
ACINSTTY SANCTITY
SCANTITY
ACINSTYY SYNCYTIA
ACIOOPST SCOTOPIA
ACIOOTYZ ZOOCYTIA
ACIOPRST APRICOTS
PISCATOR
ACIOPRTT PROTATIC
ACIOPRTY POTICARY
ACIOPSST POTASSIC
ACIOPSSU SPACIOUS
ACIOPSTU CAPTIOUS
ACIOPTTU AUTOPTIC
ACIORRSS CORSAIRS
ACIORSSU SCARIOUS
ACIORSTT RICOTTAS
ACIORTTY ATROCITY
CITATORY
ACIORTVY VORACITY
ACIOSTUU CAUTIOUS
ACIPRRUU PIRARUCU
ACIPSSST SPASTICS
ACIQRSTU QUARTICS
ACIQSSTU ACQUISTS
ACIRRTTX TRACTRIX
ACIRRTUX CURATRIX
ACIRSSST SACRISTS
ACIRSSTT ASTRICTS
ACIRSSTW TWISCARS
ACIRSSTY SACRISTY
ACIRSSTZ CZARISTS
ACISSSTU CASUISTS
ACISSTTU CATSUITS
ACISSTUV VACUISTS

ACISTTUY ASTUCITY
ACJKKSSY SKYJACKS
ACJKLOSW LOCKJAWS
ACJKNNOS JANNOCKS
ACJKOPST JACKPOTS
ACJMNSTU MUNTJACS
ACJPSTUU CAJUPUTS
ACKKMOPR POCKMARK
ACKKORRW RACKWORK
ACKLLOPS POLLACKS
ACKLLOSY LAYLOCKS
ACKLLPSU SKULLCAP
ACKLMNOS LOCKSMAN
ACKLMORS ARMLOCKS
LOCKRAMS
ACKLNOSU UNCLOAKS
ACKLOOPW WOOLPACK
ACKLOOSW WOOLSACK
ACKLORSW WARLOCKS
ACKLORSY ROCKLAYS
ACKLOSSS LASSOCKS
ACKMMMOS MAMMOCKS
ACKMNOST STOCKMAN
ACKMNRTU TRUCKMAN
ACKMOSTT MATTOCKS
ACKNSSTU UNSTACKS
ACKOPRRS PARROCKS
ACKOPRRT TRAPROCK
ACKORRST TARROCKS
ACKORSTW CATWORKS
ACLLLNOY CLONALLY
ACLLMNOU COLUMNAL
ACLLMORU CORALLUM
ACLLOORS COROLLAS
ACLLOORT COLLATOR
ACLLOOSS COLOSSAL
ACLLOPSS SCALLOPS
ACLLORUY OCULARLY
ACLLRTUU CULTURAL
ACLMMNOU COMMUNAL
ACLMNOOO COOLAMON
ACLMNORU COLUMNAR
ACLMNORY NORMALCY
ACLMORSU CLAMOURS
ACLMORTU CROTALUM
ACLMPRSU SCALPRUM
ACLMRSUU MUSCULAR
ACLMSUUV VASCULUM
ACLNOORS CORONALS
ACLNOORT COLORANT
ACLNOOST COOLANTS
ACLNOPSY SYNCOPAL
ACLNORSU CONSULAR
COURLANS
ACLNORTU CALUTRON
ACLNOSTU CONSULTA
OSCULANT
ACLNPSSU UNCLASPS
ACLNPTUU PUNCTUAL
ACLNSSUY UNCLASSY
ACLOOPRR CORPORAL
ACLOPRST CALTROPS
ACLOPRXY XYLOCARP
ACLOPSSU SCOPULAS
ACLOPSSY CALYPSOS
ACLOPSUU OPUSCULA
ACLORRTU TORCULAR
ACLOSSTU OUTCLASS
ACLRSSTY CRYSTALS
ACMMNOSY SCAMMONY
ACMMNOYY MYOMANCY
ACMNOOPR MONOCARP
ACMNOORR CROMORNA
ACMNOORT MONOCRAT
ACMNOOYZ ZOOMANCY
ACMNOPRS CRAMPONS
ACMNORSY ACRONYMS
ACMNSSTU SANCTUMS
ACMOOPRS COPROSMA
ACMOOSST SCOTOMAS
ACMOPRST COMPARTS
ACMORSTW CATWORMS
WORMCAST
ACMORSTY COSTMARY
ACMQSTUU CUMQUATS
ACNNNORY CANNONRY
ACNNOSTT CONSTANT
ACNOOORT OCTAROON
ACNOORRY CORONARY
ACNOORST CARTOONS
CORANTOS
OSTRACON
ACNOORSU CANOROUS
ACNOORTY OCTONARY
ACNOPSSW SNOWCAPS
ACNORRSU RANCOURS
ACNORRTY CONTRARY
ACNORSTT CONTRAST
CONTRATS
ACNORSTU COURANTS
ACNORTTU TURNCOAT
ACNORTUY NOCTUARY
ACNPRSSY SYNCARPS
ACNPRSUY SPRAUNCY
ACNPRSYY SYNCARPY
ACNRRSTU CURRANTS
ACNRRTUY CURRANTY
ACOOPRRS CORPORAS
ACOOPSTT TOPCOATS
ACOORSTU TOURACOS
ACOPRRST CARPORTS
ACOPRRTT PROTRACT
ACORRSTT TRACTORS
ACORRSTU CURATORS
ACORRTUY CURATORY
ACORSSTU SURCOATS
ACORSSUW CURASSOW
ACORSSWY CROSSWAY
ACORSTTY CRYOSTAT
ACOSSTTU OUTCASTS
ACPSSTUU USUCAPTS
ADDDEEEM ADDEEMED
ADDDEEEN DEADENED
ADDDEEGR DEGRADED
ADDDEEIM DIADEMED
ADDDEELR LADDERED
ADDDEEMN DEMANDED
MADDENED
ADDDEENR DANDERED
REDDENDA
ADDDEENS SADDENED
ADDDEEPS SEPADDED
ADDDEGJU ADJUDGED
ADDDELSW SWADDLED
ADDDELTW TWADDLED
ADDDEMNU ADDENDUM
ADDDEMOO ADDOOMED
ADDDENOS DEODANDS
ADDDENRU DEUDDARN
ADDDEORS ADDORSED
ADDDGILN DADDLING
ADDEEEFN DEAFENED
ADDEEEFT DEFEATED
ADDEEEJY DEEJAYED
ADDEEELN LEADENED
ADDEEEMN DEMEANED
ADDEEEMR REMEADED
ADDEEENR DEADENER
ENDEARED
ADDEEFIL DEFILADE
ADDEEFIM MADEFIED
ADDEEFLT DEFLATED
ADDEEFNU UNDEAFED
ADDEEFPR PREFADED
ADDEEFRY DEFRAYED
ADDEEFTT DEFATTED
ADDEEGLL ALLEDGED
ADDEEGLN DANEGELD
ADDEEGNR DANGERED
DERANGED
GARDENED
ADDEEGRR REGARDED
REGRADED
ADDEEGRS DEGRADES
ADDEEGSS DEGASSED
ADDEEHLR HERALDED
ADDEEHLY ALDEHYDE
ADDEEHNR HARDENED
ADDEEHNU UNHEADED
ADDEEHRS REDHEADS
ADDEEHRT THREADED
ADDEEIKR DAIKERED
ADDEEILN DEADLINE
ADDEEILR DEADLIER
DERAILED
REDIALED
ADDEEILT DETAILED
ADDEEIMT MEDIATED
ADDEEINT DETAINED
ADDEEIPR DIAPERED
ADDEEISS DISEASED
ADDEEIST STEADIED
ADDEEITV DEVIATED
ADDEEKMR DEMARKED
ADDEEKNR DARKENED
ADDEELLM MEDALLED
ADDEELLP PEDALLED
ADDEELLV DEVALLED
ADDEELNO LOADENED
ADDEELNP DEPLANED
ADDEELNR ENLARDED
ADDEELNU UNLEADED
ADDEELOR RELOADED
ADDEELPS DELAPSED
ADDEELRT TREADLED
ADDEELST DESALTED
ADDEELUV DEVALUED
ADDEEMNN DEMANNED
ADDEEMNP DAMPENED
ADDEEMNR DAMNEDER
DEMANDER
REMANDED
ADDEENPP APPENDED
ADDEENPR PANDERED
ADDEENPX EXPANDED
ADDEENRR DARNEDER
ADDEENRT ENDARTED
ADDEENRU DAUNERED
ADDEENRW DAWNERED
WANDERED
WARDENED
ADDEENSS DEADNESS
ADDEENTT ATTENDED
DENTATED
ADDEENTU DENUDATE
ADDEEOST DEODATES
ADDEEPRT DEPARTED
PREDATED
ADDEEPRV DEPRAVED
PERVADED
ADDEERRS DREADERS
ADDEERRT RETARDED
ADDEERRW REWARDED
WARDERED
ADDEERSW SAWDERED
ADDEERTV ADVERTED
ADDEFFOR AFFORDED
ADDEFIIL LADIFIED
ADDEFILY LADYFIED
ADDEFIST FADDIEST
ADDEFLRU DREADFUL
ADDEFRSU DEFRAUDS
ADDEGGLR DRAGGLED
ADDEGHOS GODHEADS
ADDEGILS GLADDIES
ADDEGINR DREADING
ADDEGIRS DISGRADE
ADDEGJSU ADJUDGES
ADDEGLNS GLADDENS
ADDEGLST GLADDEST
ADDEGNRU UNGRADED
ADDEGPRU UPGRADED
ADDEHHIN HINDHEAD
ADDEHILR DIHEDRAL
ADDEHMRU DRUMHEAD
ADDEHNNU UNHANDED
ADDEHNSU UNDASHED
UNSHADED
ADDEHORW HEADWORD
ADDEHOSW SHADOWED
ADDEHPRU PURDAHED
ADDEHRTY HYDRATED
ADDEIIKS DIDAKEIS
ADDEIIRS DIARISED
ADDEIIRZ DIARIZED
ADDEIITV ADDITIVE
ADDEIJNO ADJOINED
ADDEILNS ISLANDED
LANDSIDE
ADDEILNT TIDELAND
ADDEILRS DIEDRALS
ADDEILSY DIALYSED
ADDEILYZ DIALYZED
ADDEIMOS SODAMIDE
ADDEIMRS DISARMED
MISDREAD
ADDEIMST MISDATED
ADDEIMSY DISMAYED
ADDEIMTT ADMITTED
ADDEINOR ORDAINED
ADDEINOS ADENOIDS
ADONISED
ANODISED
ADDEINOZ ADONIZED
ANODIZED
ADDEINRT INDARTED
ADDEINST DANDIEST
ADDEIOPR PARODIED
ADDEIORS ROADSIDE
SIDEROAD

ADDEIOTX	OXIDATED
ADDEIPPR	DIDAPPER
ADDEIPRS	DISPREAD
ADDEIPSS	DIPSADES
ADDEIQSU	SQUADDIE
ADDEIRST	DISRATED
ADDEIRSW	SIDEWARD
ADDEIRVZ	VIZARDED
ADDEISSU	DISSUADE
ADDEISSW	SWADDIES
ADDEJSTU	ADJUSTED
ADDEKNVY	VANDYKED
ADDELLOR	DOLLARED
ADDELMOS	DOLMADES
ADDELNOU	DUODENAL
	UNLOADED
ADDELNPU	PUDENDAL
ADDELNRS	DANDLERS
ADDELNSU	UNSADDLE
ADDELPRS	PADDLERS
ADDELRSS	SADDLERS
ADDELRST	STRADDLE
ADDELRSW	DAWDLERS
	SWADDLER
	WADDLERS
ADDELRSY	SADDLERY
ADDELRTW	TWADDLER
ADDELSST	STADDLES
ADDELSSW	SWADDLES
ADDELSTW	TWADDLES
ADDEMMNU	UNDAMMED
ADDEMNNU	UNDAMNED
ADDEMNPU	UNDAMPED
ADDENNOT	DANTONED
ADDENOPR	PARDONED
ADDENORU	UNADORED
ADDENPRU	UNDRAPED
ADDENRST	STRANDED
ADDENRSU	DAUNDERS
ADDENRTU	DRAUNTED
	UNTRADED
ADDENRUW	UNWARDED
ADDEORTU	OUTDARED
ADDEOTTU	OUTDATED
ADDEPRSU	SUPERADD
ADDFFILO	DAFFODIL
ADDFFINR	DANDRIFF
ADDFFNRU	DANDRUFF
ADDFGILN	FADDLING
ADDFIMSS	FADDISMS
ADDFISST	FADDISTS
ADDGGILN	GLADDING
ADDGIILN	DAIDLING
ADDGIIRS	DIAGRIDS
ADDGILNN	DANDLING
ADDGILNP	PADDLING
ADDGILNR	RADDLING
ADDGILNS	SADDLING
ADDGILNW	DAWDLING
	WADDLING
ADDGINPS	PADDINGS
ADDGINQU	QUADDING
ADDGINSW	WADDINGS
ADDGINWY	WADDYING
ADDGLNOS	GLADDONS
ADDGMRUU	MUDGUARD
ADDGOOSW	DAGWOODS
ADDGORSW	GODWARDS
ADDHHLNO	HANDHOLD
ADDHIMOO	MAIDHOOD
ADDHINPS	DAPHNIDS
ADDHINRW	HINDWARD
ADDHINSY	DANDYISH
ADDHIOTY	HYDATOID
ADDHISTY	HYDATIDS
ADDHLOOY	LADYHOOD
ADDHOORW	HARDWOOD
ADDIIKMZ	ZADDIKIM
ADDIILUV	DIVIDUAL
ADDIINOT	ADDITION
ADDIINSS	DISDAINS
ADDIINTV	DIVIDANT
ADDIKSST	TSADDIKS
ADDIKSTY	KATYDIDS
ADDIKSTZ	TZADDIKS
ADDILLNW	WILDLAND
ADDILMNS	MIDLANDS
ADDILNNW	LANDWIND
ADDILOSS	DISLOADS
ADDIMNOS	DIAMONDS
ADDIMNSY	DANDYISM
ADDIMORS	DIADROMS
ADDINNOR	ORDINAND
ADDINORS	ANDROIDS
	DISADORN
ADDINQUY	QUIDDANY
ADDINRWW	WINDWARD
ADDIQSST	TSADDIQS
ADDIQSTZ	TZADDIQS
ADDIRSZZ	DIZZARDS
ADDKNRRU	DRUNKARD
ADDLLNOR	LANDLORD
ADDLLRSU	DULLARDS
ADDLNNOW	DOWNLAND
ADDLNOOW	DOWNLOAD
	WOODLAND
ADDLNORS	LANDDROS
ADDLOOSS	SOLDADOS
ADDMOOSY	DOOMSDAY
ADDNOPWY	PANDOWDY
ADDNORWW	DOWNWARD
ADDOORWW	WOODWARD
ADDOORWY	WOODYARD
ADDOPSSY	DASYPODS
ADEEEFFR	AFFEERED
ADEEEFNY	FEDAYEEN
ADEEEFRT	FEDERATE
ADEEEGLT	DELEGATE
ADEEEGNR	RENEGADE
ADEEEGNT	TEENAGED
ADEEEGPS	GAPESEED
ADEEEGRS	DEGREASE
ADEEEHHW	HEEHAWED
ADEEEHRT	REHEATED
ADEEEHRX	EXHEDRAE
ADEEEHSY	EYESHADE
ADEEEINT	DETAINEE
ADEEEKNW	WEAKENED
ADEEELNS	ENSEALED
ADEEELNV	LEAVENED
ADEEELPR	REPEALED
ADEEELRS	RELEASED
	RESEALED
ADEEELRV	LAVEERED
	REVEALED
ADEEELST	TEASELED
ADEEELSW	WEASELED
ADEEELTV	ELEVATED
ADEEELTZ	TEAZELED
ADEEEMNS	DEMEANES
	ENSEAMED
ADEEEMNT	EMENDATE
ADEEEMRU	EMERAUDE
ADEEENNT	NEATENED
ADEEENRS	ENSEARED
	SERENADE
ADEEENTT	ATTENDEE
	EDENTATE
ADEEENWZ	WEAZENED
ADEEEPRS	RAPESEED
ADEEEPRT	REPEATED
ADEEERRS	ARREEDES
ADEEERST	RESEATED
ADEEESSW	SEAWEEDS
	SEESAWED
ADEEFFIR	EFFRAIDE
ADEEFHNR	FREEHAND
ADEEFHOR	FOREHEAD
ADEEFHRT	FATHERED
ADEEFILN	ENFILADE
ADEEFIMS	MADEFIES
ADEEFINR	FREDAINE
ADEEFIOR	FOEDARIE
ADEEFIRR	RAREFIED
ADEEFIRS	FEDARIES
ADEEFIRY	REAEDIFY
ADEEFLLT	FELLATED
ADEEFLMN	ENFLAMED
ADEEFLOR	FREELOAD
ADEEFLRR	DEFERRAL
ADEEFLRS	FEDERALS
ADEEFLRT	DEFLATER
	FALTERED
	REFLATED
ADEEFLSS	FADELESS
ADEEFLST	DEFLATES
ADEEFMNR	ENFRAMED
	FREEDMAN
ADEEFMRR	REFRAMED
ADEEFNRU	UNFEARED
ADEEFNSS	DEAFNESS
ADEEFNST	FASTENED
ADEEFNTT	FATTENED
ADEEFORR	FOREREAD
ADEEFORT	FOREDATE
ADEEFPRS	PREFADES
ADEEFRRT	RAFTERED
ADEEFRRY	DEFRAYER
	FEDERARY
ADEEFRST	DRAFTEES
ADEEFRTU	FEATURED
ADEEGGHS	EGGHEADS
ADEEGGLL	ALLEGGED
ADEEGGRR	RAGGEDER
ADEEGHOR	GHERAOED
ADEEGHRT	GATHERED
ADEEGIMN	ADEEMING
ADEEGINR	REGAINED
ADEEGIRS	DISAGREE
ADEEGISS	ASSIEGED
ADEEGLLS	ALLEDGES
ADEEGLLT	GALLETED
ADEEGLNO	ENGAOLED
ADEEGLNR	ENLARGED
	LARGENED
ADEEGLNT	DANEGELT
ADEEGLSV	SELVAGED
ADEEGMMT	GEMMATED
ADEEGMNR	GENDARME
ADEEGMNS	ENDGAMES
ADEEGMNY	MEGADYNE
ADEEGMOP	MEGAPODE
ADEEGMOS	MEGADOSE
ADEEGMSS	MESSAGED
ADEEGNNR	ENDANGER
	ENRANGED
ADEEGNNV	VENDANGE
ADEEGNOR	RENEGADO
ADEEGNRR	GARDENER
	GARNERED
ADEEGNRS	DERANGES
	GRANDEES
	GRENADES
ADEEGNRU	DUNGAREE
	RENAGUED
	UNGEARED
ADEEGNRV	ENGRAVED
ADEEGNSS	AGEDNESS
ADEEGNSV	VENDAGES
ADEEGORT	DEROGATE
ADEEGOST	DOGEATES
ADEEGOTW	GOATWEED
ADEEGPRS	ASPERGED
	PRESAGED
ADEEGPRT	PARGETED
ADEEGRRR	REGARDER
ADEEGRRS	REGRADES
ADEEGRRT	GARRETED
	GARTERED
	REGRATED
ADEEGRRU	REDARGUE
ADEEGRSS	DRESSAGE
ADEEGRST	RESTAGED
ADEEGRSU	GUARDEES
ADEEGRSW	RAGWEEDS
ADEEGRTT	TARGETED
ADEEGSSS	DEGASSES
ADEEGSTT	GESTATED
ADEEGSWY	EDGEWAYS
ADEEGTTZ	GAZETTED
ADEEHHRS	REHASHED
ADEEHHST	SHEATHED
ADEEHILN	HEADLINE
ADEEHILS	DEISHEAL
ADEEHIRT	DEATHIER
ADEEHISS	EADISHES
ADEEHIST	ATHEISED
	HEADIEST
ADEEHISV	ADHESIVE
ADEEHITZ	ATHEIZED
ADEEHKNR	HANKERED
	HARKENED
ADEEHKWW	HAWKWEED
ADEEHLLW	WELLHEAD
ADEEHLNO	ENHALOED
ADEEHLNR	REHANDLE
ADEEHLNU	UNHEALED
ADEEHLRS	ASHLERED
ADEEHLRT	HALTERED
	LATHERED
ADEEHLSS	HEADLESS
ADEEHMMR	HAMMERED
ADEEHMNN	MENHADEN
ADEEHMNS	HEADSMEN
ADEEHMNT	ANTHEMED
ADEEHMPR	HAMPERED
ADEEHNOT	HEADNOTE
ADEEHNPP	HAPPENED
ADEEHNRR	HARDENER
ADEEHNRT	ADHERENT

HARTENED
THREADEN
ADEEHNSS DASHEENS
ADEEHNST HASTENED
ADEEHNTU UNHEATED
ADEEHOPR HEADROPE
ADEEHORS SOREHEAD
ADEEHORV OVERHEAD
ADEEHPPU UPHEAPED
ADEEHPRS EPHEDRAS
RESHAPED
ADEEHPUV UPHEAVED
ADEEHRRS ADHERERS
REDSHARE
ADEEHRRT THREADER
ADEEHRST HEADREST
ADEEHRSW WASHERED
ADEEHRTT HATTERED
THREATED
ADEEHRTW WREATHED
ADEEHSST HEADSETS
ADEEHSSY HAYSEEDS
ADEEIILS IDEALISE
ADEEIILZ IDEALIZE
ADEEIITV IDEATIVE
ADEEIJMR JEREMIAD
ADEEIJRS JADERIES
ADEEIJST JADEITES
ADEEIKLS LAKESIDE
ADEEILLN LEADLINE
ADEEILLO OEILLADE
ADEEILLR REALLIED
ADEEILMN ENDEMIAL
ADEEILMR REMEDIAL
ADEEILMS LIMEADES
ADEEILMV MEDIEVAL
ADEEILNS DELAINES
ADEEILNT ENTAILED
LINEATED
ADEEILPR PEDALIER
ADEEILPT DEPILATE
EPILATED
PILEATED
ADEEILRR DERAILER
RERAILED
ADEEILRS REALISED
SIDEREAL
ADEEILRT RETAILED
ADEEILRZ REALIZED
ADEEILSS DEISEALS
ADEEILST LEADIEST
ADEEILSV DISLEAVE
ADEEILSY EYELIADS
ADEEIMNR REMAINED
ADEEIMNS DEMAINES
INSEAMED
ADEEIMNT DEMENTIA
ADEEIMNX EXAMINED
ADEEIMPR EMPAIRED
ADEEIMRR DREAMIER
ADEEIMRS MADERISE
ADEEIMRT DIAMETER
REMEDIAT
ADEEIMRZ MADERIZE
ADEEIMSS SIAMESED
ADEEIMST MEDIATES
ADEEIMSZ SIAMEZED
ADEEIMTT MEDITATE
ADEEINNS ADENINES
ANDESINE
ADEEINPR PINDAREE
ADEEINPT DIAPENTE
ADEEINRS ARSENIDE
DENARIES
DRAISENE
NEARSIDE
ADEEINRT DETAINER
RETAINED
ADEEINSS ANISEEDS
ADEEINST ANDESITE
ADEEIPRR REPAIRED
ADEEIPRS AIRSPEED
ADEEIPTX EXPIATED
ADEEIRRR DREARIER
ADEEIRST READIEST
SERIATED
SIDERATE
STEADIER
ADEEIRSV READVISE
ADEEIRTT ITERATED
ADEEIRTV DERIVATE
EVIRATED
TAIVERED
ADEEISSS DISEASES
SEASIDES
ADEEISST STEADIES
ADEEISSV ADESSIVE
ADEEISTV DEVIATES
SEDATIVE
ADEEITTV EVITATED
ADEEITVW TIDEWAVE
ADEEKMRR REMARKED
ADEEKMRT MARKETED
ADEEKNNR ENRANKED
ADEEKNPW KNAPWEED
ADEEKNRS KNEADERS
ADEEKNST NAKEDEST
ADEEKQSU SQUEAKED
ADEEKRST STREAKED
ADEEKSWY WEEKDAYS
ADEELLLP LAPELLED
ADEELLMT METALLED
ADEELLMU MEDULLAE
ADEELLNP PANELLED
ADEELLNW ENWALLED
ADEELLNY LEADENLY
ADEELLPR PEDALLER
PREDELLA
ADEELLPT PALLETED
PETALLED
ADEELLQU EQUALLED
ADEELLRS SARDELLE
ADEELLRT TELLARED
ADEELLRV RAVELLED
ADEELLSS ALLSEEDS
LEADLESS
ADEELLTY ELATEDLY
ADEELMNO LEMONADE
ADEELMNP EMPLANED
ADEELMNR ALDERMEN
ADEELMNS DALESMEN
EMENDALS
LEADSMEN
ADEELMNT LAMENTED
ADEELMOS SOMEDEAL
ADEELMPR EMPARLED
ADEELMPX EXAMPLED
ADEELMRS DEMERSAL
EMERALDS
ADEELMST MEDALETS
ADEELMTU EMULATED
ADEELNNP ENPLANED
ADEELNNU UNANELED
ADEELNOR OLEANDER
ADEELNPS DEPLANES
ADEELNPU UPLEANED
ADEELNRT ANTLERED
ADEELNRV LAVENDER
ADEELNSU UNLEASED
UNSEALED
ADEELNSV ENSLAVED
ADEELNTT TALENTED
ADEELNTU UNELATED
ADEELNTV LEVANTED
ADEELNTY ENTAYLED
ADEELOPS PEDALOES
ADEELORU AUREOLED
ADEELORV OVERLADE
ADEELOST DESOLATE
ADEELOSW LEASOWED
ADEELPPR LAPPERED
ADEELPPT LAPPETED
ADEELPPU UPLEAPED
ADEELPRS PLEADERS
RELAPSED
ADEELPRT PALTERED
ADEELPRY PARLEYED
REPLAYED
ADEELPSS DELAPSES
ADEELPST PEDESTAL
ADEELPTY PEDATELY
ADEELQSU SQUEALED
ADEELRRR LARDERER
ADEELRRT TREADLER
ADEELRST TREADLES
ADEELRSV SLAVERED
ADEELRSW LEEWARDS
ADEELRSY DELAYERS
ADEELRTV TRAVELED
ADEELRUV REVALUED
ADEELSST DATELESS
TASSELED
ADEELSTY SEDATELY
ADEELSUV DEVALUES
ADEEMMMR MAMMERED
ADEEMMRY YAMMERED
ADEEMMSS MESDAMES
ADEEMMXY MYXEDEMA
ADEEMNNR MANNERED
REMANNED
ADEEMNOR DEMEANOR
ENAMORED
ADEEMNOT NEMATODE
ADEEMNPS SPADEMEN
ADEEMNRS AMENDERS
MEANDERS
REAMENDS
ADEEMNSS SEEDSMAN
ADEEMNST STAMENED
ADEEMNSU UNSEAMED
ADEEMNSY DEMAYNES
ADEEMNTU UNTEAMED
ADEEMNTW METEWAND
ADEEMORS SEADROME
ADEEMORT MODERATE
ADEEMPPR PAMPERED
ADEEMPRT EMPARTED
TAMPERED
ADEEMPRV REVAMPED
ADEEMPST STAMPEDE
STEPDAME
ADEEMRRS DREAMERS
ADEEMRRV MARVERED
ADEEMRRY DREAMERY
ADEEMRST MASTERED
STREAMED
ADEEMRSU MEASURED
ADEEMRTT MATTERED
ADEEMRTY METEYARD
ADEEMSSW MAWSEEDS
ADEEMSTW MATWEEDS
ADEEMSWY MAYWEEDS
ADEENNRS ENSNARED
ADEENNRU UNEARNED
ADEENNTT TENANTED
ADEENNUW UNWEANED
ADEENNUY UNYEANED
ADEENOPW WEAPONED
ADEENORS REASONED
ADEENORV ENDEAVOR
ADEENORY AERODYNE
ADEENOSS SEASONED
ADEENOST ENDOSTEA
ADEENOTT DENOTATE
DETONATE
ADEENPRT PARENTED
ADEENPRU UNREAPED
ADEENPRX EXPANDER
ADEENPTT PATENTED
PATTENED
ADEENRRW WANDERER
ADEENRSS DEARNESS
ADEENRSU UNDERSEA
ADEENRSW ANSWERED
ADEENRTT ATTENDER
NATTERED
RATTENED
ADEENRTU DENATURE
ADEENRTV AVENTRED
ADEENRUV UNREAVED
ADEENSST ASSENTED
STANDEES
ADEENSSU DANSEUSE
ADEENSTU UNSEATED
ADEENTTU TAUTENED
ADEENTTV VENDETTA
ADEEOPRR PADERERO
ADEEOPRT OPERATED
ADEEORRV OVERREAD
ADEEORSW OARWEEDS
ADEEORVW OVERAWED
ADEEPPRR DAPPERER
PREPARED
ADEEPPRW WAPPERED
ADEEPRRS SPREADER
ADEEPRRT DEPARTER
ADEEPRRU UPREARED
ADEEPRSS ASPERSED
PREASSED
REPASSED
ADEEPRST PEDERAST
PREDATES
REPASTED
TRAPESED
ADEEPRSU PERSUADE
ADEEPRSV DEPRAVES
PERVADES
ADEEPRSW PERSWADE
ADEEPRSZ SPREAZED
ADEEPRTT PATTERED

ADEEPRTU	DEPURATE
	EPURATED
ADEEPRTZ	TRAPEZED
ADEEPSST	STAPEDES
ADEEPSTT	ADEPTEST
ADEEPSWY	SPEEDWAY
ADEEQRTU	DETRAQUE
ADEEQRUV	QUAVERED
ADEERRRT	RETARDER
ADEERRRW	REREWARD
	REWARDER
ADEERRST	ARRESTED
	DREAREST
	RETREADS
	SERRATED
	TREADERS
ADEERRSV	ADVERSER
ADEERRTT	RETRATED
ADEERRTW	REDWATER
ADEERRWY	WARREYED
ADEERSST	ASSERTED
	ESTRADES
ADEERSTT	ASTERTED
	RESTATED
ADEERSTW	DEWATERS
	TARWEEDS
	WASTERED
ADEERSTY	ESTRAYED
ADEERTTT	TATTERED
ADEERTTY	YATTERED
ADEERTWW	WARTWEED
ADEERVYY	EVERYDAY
ADEESSSS	ASSESSED
ADEESSTT	SEDATEST
ADEESTTT	ATTESTED
ADEESTUX	EXUDATES
ADEESVVY	SAVVEYED
ADEFFGUW	GUFFAWED
ADEFFIMR	AFFIRMED
ADEFFIRR	DRAFFIER
ADEFFIRT	TARIFFED
ADEFFIST	DAFFIEST
ADEFFLNS	SNAFFLED
ADEFFRST	STRAFFED
ADEFGGOT	FAGGOTED
ADEFGIIS	GASIFIED
ADEFGILN	FINAGLED
ADEFGILO	FOLIAGED
ADEFGILS	GADFLIES
	GASFIELD
ADEFGIMN	DEFAMING
ADEFGIRT	DRIFTAGE
ADEFGIRU	ARGUFIED
ADEFGITU	FATIGUED
ADEFGLOT	GATEFOLD
ADEFGLRU	FELDGRAU
ADEFGNOR	FRONDAGE
ADEFGOSU	FOUGADES
ADEFHILS	DEALFISH
ADEFHILY	HAYFIELD
ADEFHIMS	FAMISHED
ADEFHKOR	FORKHEAD
ADEFHLTU	DEATHFUL
ADEFHMOT	FATHOMED
ADEFHNOR	FOREHAND
ADEFHOST	SOFTHEAD
ADEFIILR	AIRFIELD
ADEFIILS	LADIFIES
	SALIFIED
ADEFIILT	FILIATED
ADEFIIMR	RAMIFIED
ADEFIINS	SANIFIED
ADEFIIRT	RATIFIED
ADEFIIRU	AURIFIED
ADEFILMN	INFLAMED
ADEFILNR	FILANDER
ADEFILNT	INFLATED
ADEFILOR	FORELAID
ADEFILOT	FOLIATED
ADEFILSS	DISLEAFS
ADEFILSY	LADYFIES
ADEFIMPR	FIREDAMP
ADEFIMRS	MISFARED
ADEFIMSS	DISFAMES
ADEFINRR	INFRARED
ADEFINRS	FRIANDES
ADEFINRU	UNFAIRED
ADEFINYZ	DENAZIFY
ADEFIORS	FORESAID
ADEFIRRT	DRAFTIER
ADEFLLLU	LADLEFUL
ADEFLLNS	ELFLANDS
ADEFLLOW	FALLOWED
ADEFLLUY	FEUDALLY
ADEFLMRU	DREAMFUL
ADEFLNNS	FENLANDS
ADEFLNOR	FORELAND
ADEFLNRU	DEARNFUL
ADEFLNTU	FLAUNTED
ADEFLNUU	UNFEUDAL
ADEFLNUW	UNFLAWED
ADEFLORT	DEFLATOR
ADEFLORV	FLAVORED
ADEFLPRS	FELDSPAR
ADEFLPSU	SPADEFUL
ADEFLRTU	TRADEFUL
ADEFLRTW	LEFTWARD
ADEFLRZZ	FRAZZLED
ADEFLSTU	DEFAULTS
	SULFATED
ADEFMNRU	UNFRAMED
ADEFMORT	FORMATED
ADEFMOSU	FAMOUSED
	FUMADOES
ADEFNNNU	UNFANNED
ADEFNOPR	PROFANED
ADEFNSST	DAFTNESS
ADEFOOSS	SEAFOODS
ADEFORRR	FORRADER
ADEFORRW	FARROWED
	FOREWARD
ADEFORRY	FORRAYED
ADEFORUV	FAVOURED
ADEFPTUW	UPWAFTED
ADEFRRST	DRAFTERS
	REDRAFTS
ADEFSSTT	STEDFAST
ADEGGGNU	UNGAGGED
ADEGGIRR	DRAGGIER
ADEGGIST	DAGGIEST
ADEGGISU	GAUDGIES
	GUIDAGES
ADEGGJLY	JAGGEDLY
ADEGGLRS	DRAGGLES
ADEGGLRY	RAGGEDLY
ADEGGMOY	DEMAGOGY
ADEGGNOW	WAGGONED
ADEGGNUU	UNGAUGED
ADEGGOPY	PEDAGOGY
ADEGGPRS	SPRAGGED
ADEGGRTY	GADGETRY
ADEGHHOS	HOGSHEAD
ADEGHILN	HEALDING
ADEGHILT	ALIGHTED
ADEGHINR	ADHERING
	HEADRING
ADEGHINS	HEADINGS
	SHEADING
ADEGHIRS	GARISHED
	HEADRIGS
ADEGHIRT	GRAITHED
ADEGHJSU	JUGHEADS
ADEGHLNO	HEADLONG
ADEGHLOS	GALOSHED
ADEGHNNU	UNHANGED
ADEGHNRT	THRANGED
ADEGHOOP	PAGEHOOD
ADEGHORT	GOATHERD
ADEGHRTU	DAUGHTER
ADEGHTUW	WAUGHTED
ADEGIILN	GLIADINE
ADEGIILP	DIPLEGIA
ADEGIIMN	IMAGINED
ADEGIIMS	DIGAMIES
ADEGIINT	IDEATING
ADEGIITT	DIGITATE
ADEGIJSW	JIGSAWED
ADEGIKNN	KNEADING
ADEGIKNR	DAKERING
ADEGILLO	GLADIOLE
ADEGILLP	PILLAGED
ADEGILLR	GRILLADE
ADEGILLS	GALLISED
ADEGILLZ	GALLIZED
ADEGILMN	MALIGNED
	MEDALING
ADEGILNO	GALENOID
ADEGILNP	PEDALING
	PLEADING
ADEGILNR	DANGLIER
	DEARLING
	DRAGLINE
ADEGILNS	DEALINGS
	LEADINGS
	SIGNALED
ADEGILNT	DELATING
ADEGILNY	DELAYING
ADEGILOS	GOLIASED
ADEGILOU	DIALOGUE
ADEGILRS	SLAIRGED
ADEGILSS	GLISSADE
ADEGILST	GLADIEST
ADEGILSV	DISGAVEL
ADEGIMNN	AMENDING
ADEGIMNR	DREAMING
	MARGINED
ADEGIMOR	IDEOGRAM
ADEGIMRT	MIGRATED
ADEGIMST	SIGMATED
ADEGINNR	GRANNIED
ADEGINNV	ADVENING
	DAVENING
ADEGINNY	DENAYING
ADEGINOR	ORGANDIE
ADEGINOS	AGONISED
	DIAGNOSE
ADEGINOZ	AGONIZED
ADEGINPU	ANGUIPED
ADEGINRR	DREARING
ADEGINRS	DERAIGNS
	GRADINES
	READINGS
ADEGINRT	DERATING
	GRADIENT
	REDATING
	TREADING
ADEGINRY	DERAYING
	READYING
	YEARDING
ADEGINSS	ASSIGNED
ADEGINST	SEDATING
	STEADING
ADEGINSW	WINDAGES
ADEGINTV	VINTAGED
ADEGINVW	ADVEWING
ADEGINYZ	ZYGAENID
ADEGIORT	ERGATOID
ADEGIOST	GODETIAS
ADEGIPRS	SPAIRGED
ADEGIRWY	RIDGEWAY
ADEGISSU	DISUSAGE
ADEGISTU	GAUDIEST
ADEGISUV	VIDUAGES
ADEGJNOR	JARGONED
ADEGKLOY	DEKALOGY
ADEGLLNU	GLANDULE
	UNGALLED
ADEGLLOP	GALLOPED
ADEGLLOR	GOLLARED
ADEGLLOW	GALLOWED
ADEGLMOR	GLAMORED
ADEGLMOS	GLADSOME
ADEGLMPU	PLUMAGED
ADEGLMRU	MAULGRED
ADEGLMUY	AMYGDULE
ADEGLNOY	GONDELAY
ADEGLNPS	SPANGLED
ADEGLNRS	DANGLERS
	GLANDERS
ADEGLNRW	WRANGLED
ADEGLNSS	GLADNESS
ADEGLNTW	TWANGLED
ADEGLNUZ	UNGLAZED
ADEGLOPP	GALOPPED
ADEGLPPR	GRAPPLED
ADEGMMNO	GAMMONED
ADEGMMRU	RUMMAGED
ADEGMNOS	GOADSMEN
ADEGMNOT	MONTAGED
ADEGMNOY	ENDOGAMY
ADEGMNRS	DRAGSMEN
ADEGMORS	ORGASMED
ADEGMORW	WORDGAME
ADEGMPUZ	GAZUMPED
ADEGNNOR	ANDROGEN
	DRAGONNE
ADEGNNPU	UNPANGED
ADEGNNSU	DUNNAGES
ADEGNOPS	PONDAGES
ADEGNOPU	POUNDAGE
ADEGNORT	DRAGONET
ADEGNOSS	SONDAGES
ADEGNOSV	DOGVANES
ADEGNPUY	PYENGADU
ADEGNRRU	GRANDEUR
ADEGNRST	DRAGNETS
	GRANDEST
ADEGNRSU	ENGUARDS
ADEGNRUU	UNARGUED
ADEGNRUZ	GAZUNDER

UNGRAZED
ADEGOORY GOODYEAR
ADEGOPPR PROPAGED
ADEGOPRR PROGRADE
ADEGORRT GARROTED
ADEGORST GOADSTER
ADEGORSW DOWAGERS
WORDAGES
ADEGORTT GAROTTED
ADEGORTU OUTRAGED
RAGOUTED
ADEGPRRU UPGRADER
ADEGPRSS SPADGERS
ADEGPRSU UPGRADES
ADEGPSTU UPSTAGED
ADEGRRST DRAGSTER
ADEGRSSU GRADUSES
ADEGTTTU GUTTATED
ADEHHIPR RHAPHIDE
ADEHHIPS HEADSHIP
ADEHHIST SHITHEAD
ADEHHNTU HEADHUNT
ADEHHOOR HOORAHED
ADEHHOST HEADSHOT
HOTHEADS
ADEHHRRU HURRAHED
ADEHHRST THRASHED
ADEHIITZ THIAZIDE
ADEHIKLV KHEDIVAL
ADEHIKNS SKINHEAD
ADEHIKSS DASHEKIS
ADEHIKST SKAITHED
ADEHIKSV KHEDIVAS
ADEHILLP PHIALLED
PILLHEAD
ADEHILNR HARDLINE
ADEHILNU UNHAILED
ADEHILPS HELIPADS
ADEHILSV LAVISHED
ADEHILSW WHAISLED
ADEHILWZ WHAIZLED
ADEHIMRS MISHEARD
ADEHIMRY HYDREMIA
ADEHINOP DIAPHONE
ADEHINOS ADHESION
ADEHINPS DEANSHIP
PINHEADS
ADEHINPU DAUPHINE
ADEHINRU UNHAIRED
ADEHINSS SHANDIES
ADEHINST HANDIEST
ADEHINSV VANISHED
ADEHIOTT ATHETOID
ADEHIPRS RAPHIDES
ADEHIPSS PISSHEAD
ADEHIPST PITHEADS
SIDEPATH
ADEHIRSS RADISHES
ADEHIRST HAIRSTED
HARDIEST
ADEHIRSV RAVISHED
ADEHIRSW RAWHIDES
ADEHIRSY HAYRIDES
ADEHIRVW HIVEWARD
ADEHISST SHADIEST
ADEHJLOT JOLTHEAD
ADEHKLNU LUNKHEAD
ADEHKNRS REDSHANK
ADEHKNSU UNSHAKED
ADEHKORS HARDOKES
ADEHKORW HEADWORK
ADEHKOST KATHODES
ADEHLLOO HALLOOED
HOLLOAED
ADEHLLOW HALLOWED
ADEHLLRT THRALLED
ADEHLLRW HELLWARD
ADEHLMNO HOMELAND
ADEHLMOY HOLYDAME
ADEHLNRS HANDLERS
ADEHLNSS HANDLESS
HANDSELS
ADEHLNST SHETLAND
ADEHLNSU UNHALSED
UNLASHED
UNSHALED
ADEHLOPS ASPHODEL
PHOLADES
ADEHLPSS SPLASHED
ADEHLRRY HERALDRY
ADEHMNNY HANDYMEN
ADEHMNOS HANDSOME
ADEHMNOT METHADON
THANEDOM
ADEHMNRS HERDSMAN
ADEHMNRU UNHARMED
ADEHMNSU UNSHAMED
ADEHMOOP OOMPAHED
ADEHMOOR HEADROOM
ADEHMOPS MOPHEADS
ADEHMORS HADROMES
ADEHMORW HOMEWARD
ADEHMOST HEADMOST
ADEHMOSU MADHOUSE
ADEHMOSY SHAMOYED
ADEHNOPR ORPHANED
ADEHNOPT PHONATED
ADEHNORV HANDOVER
OVERHAND
ADEHNOSS SANDSHOE
ADEHNOSU SEAHOUND
ADEHNPSU UNHASPED
UNSHAPED
ADEHNPTU UNPATHED
ADEHNRSS HARDNESS
ADEHNRSU UNSHARED
ADEHNRSW SWANHERD
ADEHNRTU UNTHREAD
ADEHNSST HANDSETS
ADEHNSSU SUNSHADE
UNSASHED
ADEHNSUV UNSHAVED
ADEHNSUW UNWASHED
ADEHNTTU UNHATTED
ADEHNTUW UNTHAWED
ADEHOOPS APEHOODS
ADEHOORW HAREWOOD
ADEHOORY HOORAYED
ADEHOPRS RHAPSODE
ADEHOPST POTASHED
ADEHOPSX HEXAPODS
ADEHOPXY HEXAPODY
ADEHORRS HOARDERS
ADEHORRW HARROWED
ADEHORSW SHADOWER
ADEHORTT THROATED
ADEHORTU AUTHORED
ADEHQSSU SQUASHED
ADEHRRUY HURRAYED
ADEHRSTY HYDRATES
ADEHRTTW THWARTED
ADEIILMN LIMNAEID
ADEIILMS IDEALISM
MILADIES
ADEIILPR PERIDIAL
ADEIILRS LAIRISED
ADEIILRZ LAIRIZED
ADEIILST IDEALIST
ADEIILTV DILATIVE
ADEIILTY IDEALITY
ADEIIMMS MISAIMED
ADEIIMNN INDAMINE
ADEIIMNR MERIDIAN
ADEIIMNT MINIATED
ADEIIMPR IMPAIRED
ADEIIMTT IMITATED
ADEIINNS SANIDINE
ADEIINOT IDEATION
TAENIOID
ADEIINRS DRAISINE
ADEIINRT DAINTIER
ADEIINRU UREDINIA
ADEIINST ADENITIS
DAINTIES
ADEIINUV INDUVIAE
ADEIIPRR PERRADII
PRAIRIED
ADEIIPRS PRESIDIA
ADEIIPST STAPEDII
ADEIIRSS AIRSIDES
DIARISES
ADEIIRST IRISATED
ADEIIRSZ DIARIZES
ADEIITTV TIDIVATE
VITIATED
ADEIITUV AUDITIVE
ADEIJMRS JEMIDARS
ADEIKLLO KELOIDAL
ADEIKLLY LADYLIKE
ADEIKLSW SIDEWALK
ADEIKMMS IMMASKED
ADEIKMPR IMPARKED
ADEIKMRT TIDEMARK
ADEIKNSY KYANISED
ADEIKNYZ KYANIZED
ADEIKORT KERATOID
ADEIKRST STRAIKED
ADEILLMY MEDIALLY
ADEILLNU UNALLIED
ADEILLNW INWALLED
ADEILLOR ARILLODE
ADEILLPR PALLIDER
ADEILLPS ILLAPSED
SPADILLE
ADEILLRS DALLIERS
DIALLERS
ADEILLRT TRIALLED
ADEILLRV RIVALLED
ADEILLSW SIDEWALL
ADEILMMS DILEMMAS
ADEILMNP PLAIDMEN
ADEILMNU UNMAILED
ADEILMNY MAIDENLY
ADEILMOS DAMOISEL
ADEILMPP PALMIPED
ADEILMPR IMPARLED
ADEILMPS IMPLEADS
MISPLEAD
ADEILMPT IMPLATED
ADEILMRY DREAMILY
ADEILMSS MAIDLESS
MISDEALS
MISLEADS
ADEILMST MEDALIST
MISDEALT
ADEILMSY DYSMELIA
ADEILNNR INLANDER
ADEILNNS ANNELIDS
LINDANES
ADEILNNU UNNAILED
ADEILNOP PALINODE
ADEILNOS NODALISE
ADEILNOT DELATION
ADEILNOZ NODALIZE
ADEILNPT PANTILED
ADEILNPU PALUDINE
ADEILNRS ISLANDER
ADEILNSU UNSAILED
ADEILNSV ANDVILES
ADEILNTU UNTAILED
ADEILNTV DIVALENT
ADEILNUV UNVAILED
ADEILOPS EPISODAL
OPALISED
SEPALOID
ADEILOPT PETALOID
ADEILOPZ OPALIZED
ADEILOQU ODALIQUE
ADEILORS DARIOLES
SOLIDARE
SOREDIAL
ADEILORT IDOLATER
TAILORED
ADEILORV OVERLAID
ADEILORX EXORDIAL
ADEILOSS ASSOILED
DEASOILS
ADEILOST DIASTOLE
ISOLATED
SODALITE
SOLIDATE
ADEILOSU DOULEIAS
ADEILOTT DATOLITE
ADEILOTV DOVETAIL
VIOLATED
ADEILPPP PEDIPALP
ADEILPRS PEDRAILS
PREDIALS
ADEILPRT DIPTERAL
TRIPEDAL
ADEILPRU EPIDURAL
ADEILPRV DEPRIVAL
ADEILPSS DESPISAL
ADEILPST TALIPEDS
ADEILPTU PLAUDITE
ADEILQSU SQUAILED
ADEILQTU LIQUATED
ADEILRRY DREARILY
ADEILRST DILATERS
LARDIEST
ADEILRSU RESIDUAL
ADEILRSY DIALYSER
ADEILRTT DETRITAL
ADEILRTY DIELYTRA
ADEILRVY VARIEDLY
ADEILRYZ DIALYZER
ADEILSSU DEASIULS
ADEILSSV DEVISALS
ADEILSSY DIALYSES
ADEILSTV VALIDEST

Letters	Words
ADEILSTY	DIASTYLE
	STEADILY
ADEILSUV	DISVALUE
ADEILSXY	DYSLEXIA
ADEILSYZ	DIALYZES
ADEILTTU	ALTITUDE
	LATITUDE
ADEIMMNS	MISNAMED
ADEIMMNU	UNMAIMED
ADEIMMRS	MERMAIDS
ADEIMMST	MISMATED
ADEIMNNO	DEMONIAN
	MONDAINE
ADEIMNOP	DOPAMINE
ADEIMNOS	NOMADIES
	NOMADISE
ADEIMNOT	DOMINATE
	NEMATOID
ADEIMNOZ	NOMADIZE
ADEIMNPW	IMPAWNED
ADEIMNRR	MANRIDER
ADEIMNRS	ADERMINS
	SIRNAMED
ADEIMNRY	DAIRYMEN
ADEIMNRZ	ZEMINDAR
ADEIMNSS	SIDESMAN
ADEIMNST	MEDIANTS
	TIDESMAN
ADEIMNSU	MAUNDIES
ADEIMNSY	DYNAMISE
ADEIMNTY	DYNAMITE
ADEIMNYZ	DYNAMIZE
ADEIMORR	AIRDROME
ADEIMORT	MEDIATOR
ADEIMOSS	SESAMOID
ADEIMOST	ATOMISED
ADEIMOTZ	ATOMIZED
ADEIMPRR	RAMPIRED
ADEIMPRT	IMPARTED
ADEIMPRV	VAMPIRED
ADEIMPST	DAMPIEST
	IMPASTED
ADEIMRRS	ADMIRERS
	DISARMER
ADEIMRSS	MISREADS
	SIDEARMS
ADEIMRST	MARDIEST
	MISRATED
	READMITS
ADEIMRTU	MURIATED
ADEIMSST	MISDATES
ADEIMSTU	TAEDIUMS
ADEIMSTY	DAYTIMES
ADEINNNS	NANDINES
ADEINNOT	ANOINTED
	ANTINODE
ADEINNPT	PINNATED
ADEINNPU	UNPAINED
ADEINNRS	INSNARED
ADEINNRZ	RENDZINA
ADEINNSU	UNSAINED
ADEINNSX	DISANNEX
ADEINNTU	INUNDATE
ADEINOPT	ANTIPODE
ADEINORR	ORDAINER
	REORDAIN
ADEINORS	ANEROIDS
	DONARIES
ADEINORT	AROINTED
	DERATION
	ORDINATE
	RATIONED
ADEINORU	DOUANIER
ADEINOSS	ADONISES
	ANODISES
ADEINOST	ASTONIED
	SEDATION
ADEINOSX	DIOXANES
ADEINOSZ	ADONIZES
	ANODIZES
ADEINOTT	ANTIDOTE
	TETANOID
ADEINOTV	DONATIVE
ADEINPPX	APPENDIX
ADEINPRS	SPRAINED
ADEINPRT	DIPTERAN
ADEINPRU	UNPAIRED
	UNREPAID
ADEINPST	DEPAINTS
ADEINPSV	SPAVINED
ADEINQTU	ANTIQUED
ADEINRRS	DRAINERS
	SERRANID
ADEINRSS	ARIDNESS
	SARDINES
ADEINRST	DETRAINS
	RANDIEST
	STRAINED
ADEINRSU	DENARIUS
	UNRAISED
	URANIDES
ADEINRSV	INVADERS
	SANDIVER
ADEINRSY	SYNEDRIA
ADEINRTT	NITRATED
ADEINRTU	DATURINE
	INDURATE
	RUINATED
	URINATED
ADEINRUV	UNVARIED
ADEINRVY	VINEYARD
ADEINSST	SANDIEST
ADEINSSV	AVIDNESS
ADEINSSW	WINDASES
ADEINSTT	INSTATED
ADEINSTU	AUDIENTS
	SINUATED
ADEINSTV	DEVIANTS
ADEINSTY	DESYATIN
ADEIOPRS	DIASPORE
	PARODIES
ADEIOPRV	OVERPAID
ADEIOPST	DIOPTASE
ADEIOPTV	ADOPTIVE
ADEIORRT	ADROITER
ADEIORST	ASTEROID
ADEIORTT	TERATOID
ADEIORTV	DEVIATOR
ADEIOSSX	OXIDASES
ADEIOSTX	OXIDATES
ADEIOSTZ	AZOTISED
ADEIOSVV	VAIVODES
ADEIOSVW	WAIVODES
ADEIOSWW	WAIWODES
ADEIOTZZ	AZOTIZED
ADEIPPRS	APPRISED
	DRAPPIES
ADEIPPRZ	APPRIZED
ADEIPRRS	DRAPIERS
ADEIPRSS	DESPAIRS
ADEIPRST	DIPTERAS
	RAPIDEST
	SPIRATED
	TARSIPED
	TRAIPSED
ADEIPRSU	UPRAISED
ADEIPRTU	EUPATRID
ADEIPSTV	VAPIDEST
ADEIPTTU	APTITUDE
ADEIQRRU	QUARRIED
ADEIQSUY	QUAYSIDE
ADEIRRSW	SWARDIER
ADEIRRTW	TAWDRIER
ADEIRRWW	WIREDRAW
ADEIRRZZ	RIZZARED
ADEIRSST	ASTERIDS
	DIASTERS
	DISASTER
	DISRATES
ADEIRSSU	RADIUSES
	SUDARIES
ADEIRSSV	ADVISERS
ADEIRSTT	STRAITED
	STRIATED
	TARDIEST
ADEIRSTW	TAWDRIES
ADEIRTTT	ATTRITED
	TITRATED
ADEIRVWY	DRIVEWAY
ADEISSST	ASSISTED
	DISSEATS
ADEISSTT	DISTASTE
	STAIDEST
ADEISSWY	SIDEWAYS
	WAYSIDES
ADEISTTU	SITUATED
ADEISTWY	TIDEWAYS
ADEITTTU	ATTITUDE
	ATTUITED
ADEJLOSU	JALOUSED
ADEJMRRU	JUMARRED
ADEJOPRS	JEOPARDS
ADEJOPRY	JEOPARDY
ADEJRSTU	ADJUSTER
	READJUST
ADEKLMRY	MARKEDLY
ADEKLNOX	KLAXONED
ADEKLNPP	KNAPPLED
ADEKLNPR	PRANKLED
ADEKLNSU	UNSLAKED
ADEKLPRS	SPARKLED
ADEKMNRU	UNMARKED
ADEKMNSU	UNMASKED
ADEKMORS	DARKSOME
ADEKNNSS	DANKNESS
ADEKNRSS	DARKNESS
ADEKNSVY	VANDYKES
ADEKQSUW	SQUAWKED
ADELLMOR	MORALLED
ADELLMOS	SLALOMED
ADELLMRU	MEDULLAR
ADELLMSU	MEDULLAS
ADELLNNU	ANNULLED
ADELLNPS	SPENDALL
ADELLNRS	LANDLERS
ADELLNSS	LANDLESS
ADELLNSW	ELLWANDS
	WALLSEND
ADELLNUW	UNWALLED
ADELLOPW	WALLOPED
ADELLORS	ODALLERS
ADELLOSW	SALLOWED
ADELLOTT	ALLOTTED
	TOTALLED
ADELLOTV	LAVOLTED
ADELLOTW	TALLOWED
ADELLOWW	WALLOWED
ADELLQSU	SQUALLED
ADELLRSU	UDALLERS
ADELLTUU	ULULATED
ADELMNNS	LANDSMEN
ADELMNOS	LODESMAN
ADELMNRS	MANDRELS
ADELMOOW	WOODMEAL
ADELMORS	EARLDOMS
ADELMOSS	DAMOSELS
ADELMOSZ	DAMOZELS
ADELMOTU	MODULATE
ADELMPRT	TRAMPLED
ADELMRRU	DEMURRAL
ADELMSUY	AMUSEDLY
ADELMTUU	UMLAUTED
ADELNNNU	UNNANELD
ADELNNOT	LENTANDO
ADELNOPR	PONDERAL
ADELNORS	LADRONES
	SOLANDER
ADELNORU	UNLOADER
	URODELAN
ADELNORV	OVERLAND
	RONDAVEL
ADELNOSY	YEALDONS
ADELNPRS	SPANDREL
ADELNPRU	PENDULAR
	UNDERLAP
	UPLANDER
ADELNPRY	PANDERLY
ADELNPSY	DYSPNEAL
ADELNPUY	UNPLAYED
ADELNRSS	SLANDERS
ADELNRSU	LAUNDERS
	LURDANES
	RUNDALES
ADELNRTY	ARDENTLY
ADELNRUY	UNDERLAY
ADELNSTU	UNSALTED
ADELNSTW	WETLANDS
ADELNTUU	UNDULATE
ADELNUUV	UNVALUED
ADELNUZZ	UNDAZZLE
ADELOORV	OVERLOAD
ADELOOWW	WOODWALE
ADELOPPR	PROPALED
ADELOPRS	LEOPARDS
ADELOPRT	PROLATED
ADELOPSS	DEPOSALS
ADELOPST	TADPOLES
ADELOPSU	PALUDOSE
ADELOPSY	SEPALODY
ADELOPTY	PETALODY
ADELORRV	OVERLARD
ADELORSS	ROADLESS
ADELORST	DELATORS
	LEOTARDS
	LODESTAR
ADELORSU	ROULADES
ADELOSSW	DOWLASES
ADELOSTV	SOLVATED
ADELOTUV	OVULATED
ADELOTUW	OUTLAWED

ADELOVWY	AVOWEDLY
ADELPPRY	DAPPERLY
ADELPRRU	LARRUPED
ADELPRSW	SPRAWLED
ADELPRTT	PRATTLED
ADELPSTT	SPLATTED
ADELPSTU	PULSATED
ADELPUUV	UPVALUED
ADELRRSU	RUDERALS
ADELRRSW	DRAWLERS
ADELRRTU	ULTRARED
ADELRSTT	STARTLED
ADELRSZZ	DAZZLERS
ADELRTUY	ADULTERY
ADELSTTY	STATEDLY
ADELTTTW	TWATTLED
ADEMMNOW	MADWOMEN
ADEMMSTU	SUMMATED
ADEMNNNU	UNMANNED
ADEMNNOU	UNMOANED
ADEMNNRU	MUNDANER
	UNDERMAN
ADEMNOOR	MAROONED
ADEMNOPR	POMANDER
ADEMNOPT	TAMPONED
ADEMNORS	MADRONES
	RANSOMED
	ROADSMEN
ADEMNOTU	AMOUNTED
	OUTNAMED
ADEMNPSS	DAMPNESS
ADEMNRRU	UNDERARM
	UNMARRED
ADEMNRSU	DURAMENS
	MAUNDERS
	SURNAMED
ADEMNRTU	UNDREAMT
ADEMNRUW	UNWARMED
ADEMNSSU	MEDUSANS
ADEMNSUU	UNAMUSED
ADEMOORT	MODERATO
ADEMOOSV	VAMOOSED
ADEMOPST	STAMPEDO
ADEMORRT	MORTARED
ADEMORRU	ARMOURED
ADEMORRW	MARROWED
ADEMORST	STROAMED
ADEMORTW	WARDMOTE
ADEMPRST	STRAMPED
ADEMRRSU	EARDRUMS
ADEMRRTY	MARTYRED
ADENNNTU	UNTANNED
ADENNOSY	ANODYNES
ADENNOTU	UNATONED
ADENNOTW	WANTONED
ADENNOTY	TANNOYED
ADENNPST	PENDANTS
ADENNRRU	UNDERRAN
ADENNRTY	TYRANNED
ADENNRUW	UNWARNED
ADENNSTU	ASTUNNED
ADENNTUW	UNWANTED
ADENOOPS	EPANODOS
ADENOORT	RATOONED
ADENOORW	WANDEROO
ADENOPRR	PARDONER
ADENOPRS	OPERANDS
	PANDORES
ADENOPRT	PRONATED
ADENOPRX	EXPANDOR
ADENOPSS	DAPSONES
	SPADONES
ADENOPST	TONEPADS
ADENOPSU	UNSOAPED
ADENOPSY	DYSPNOEA
ADENORRW	NARROWED
ADENORST	TORNADES
ADENORTT	ATTORNED
ADENORTY	AROYNTED
ADENORUX	RONDEAUX
ADENOSST	ONSTEADS
ADENOTUY	AUTODYNE
ADENOUVW	UNAVOWED
ADENPPRS	PARPENDS
ADENPPSU	UNSAPPED
ADENPPTU	UNTAPPED
ADENPRRS	PARDNERS
ADENPRSU	UNSPARED
ADENPRSW	PREDAWNS
ADENPRTU	DEPURANT
ADENPRTY	PEDANTRY
ADENPRUW	UNWARPED
ADENPRUY	UNDERPAY
	UNPRAYED
ADENPSSY	DYSPNEAS
ADENQRSU	SQUANDER
ADENRRSY	REYNARDS
ADENRRTU	UNTARRED
ADENRRWY	WARDENRY
ADENRSSS	SARSDENS
ADENRSST	STANDERS
ADENRSSU	DANSEURS
ADENRSTU	DAUNTERS
	TRANSUDE
	UNTREADS
ADENRSTX	DEXTRANS
ADENRSUY	UNDERSAY
ADENRTTU	TRUANTED
ADENRTTY	TYRANTED
ADENRUWY	UNDERWAY
ADENSTTU	UNSTATED
	UNTASTED
ADENSTUW	UNWASTED
ADENSTUY	UNSTAYED
	UNSTEADY
ADENSUWY	UNSWAYED
ADEOOPSS	APODOSES
ADEOORRT	TOREADOR
ADEOOTTT	TATTOOED
ADEOPPRV	APPROVED
ADEOPRRS	EARDROPS
ADEOPRRT	PARROTED
	PREDATOR
	PRORATED
ADEOPRRU	UPROARED
ADEOPRST	ADOPTERS
	ASPORTED
	READOPTS
ADEOPRTT	TETRAPOD
ADEOPRUV	VAPOURED
ADEOPSST	PODESTAS
ADEOPSTT	DESPOTAT
	POSTDATE
ADEORRSS	DROSERAS
ADEORRST	ROADSTER
ADEORRTW	TARROWED
ADEORRVW	OVERDRAW
ADEORSST	ASSORTED
	TORSADES
ADEORSTU	OUTDARES
ADEORSTX	EXTRADOS
ADEORSUV	SAVOURED
ADEORSWY	RODEWAYS
ADEORTTU	OUTRATED
ADEOSSTT	ASSOTTED
ADEOSTTU	OUTDATES
ADEOSWWY	WAYWODES
ADEOTTTW	TATTOWED
ADEPPRST	STRAPPED
ADEPRRTU	RAPTURED
ADEPRSTU	PASTURED
	UPSTARED
ADEPSTUY	UPSTAYED
ADEPSUWY	UPSWAYED
ADEQSTTU	SQUATTED
ADERRSSW	WARDRESS
ADERRSTT	REDSTART
ADERSSSU	ASSUREDS
ADERSSTW	STEWARDS
ADERSSUY	DASYURES
ADERSTTU	STATURED
ADERSTUX	SURTAXED
ADERSTWW	WESTWARD
ADESSTTW	WADSETTS
ADFFGIIR	GIRAFFID
ADFFGINS	DAFFINGS
ADFFHIRS	DRAFFISH
ADFFISST	DISTAFFS
ADFFLOOS	OFFLOADS
ADFFLRUU	FRAUDFUL
ADFFNOST	STANDOFF
ADFFOORS	AFFOORDS
ADFGINNU	UNFADING
ADFGINRS	FARDINGS
ADFGINRT	DRAFTING
ADFGINRW	DWARFING
ADFHIOST	TOADFISH
ADFHIRSW	DWARFISH
ADFHLNSU	HANDFULS
ADFHLOST	HOLDFAST
ADFHOOSS	SHADOOFS
ADFIILPY	LAPIDIFY
ADFILLLN	LANDFILL
ADFILLMN	FILMLAND
ADFILLNW	WINDFALL
ADFILMNO	MANIFOLD
ADFIMNRS	FINDRAMS
ADFIMORY	FAIRYDOM
ADFIMRSW	DWARFISM
ADFINORZ	FORZANDI
ADFINRST	INDRAFTS
ADFIORSV	DISFAVOR
ADFKLLNO	FOLKLAND
ADFLLNOW	DOWNFALL
ADFLMNOR	LANDFORM
ADFLMNOY	MANYFOLD
ADFLMOPR	FRAMPOLD
ADFLMPSU	MUDFLAPS
ADFLMSTU	MUDFLATS
ADFLNOPS	PLAFONDS
ADFLOOWY	FLOODWAY
ADFLORSU	FOULARDS
ADFMRSTU	STUDFARM
ADFNNOST	FONDANTS
ADFNOORZ	FORZANDO
ADFOOPST	FOOTPADS
ADFORRSW	FORWARDS
	FROWARDS
ADGGGILN	DAGGLING
ADGGGINR	DRAGGING
ADGGGINS	DAGGINGS
ADGGHNOS	HANGDOGS
ADGGILNN	DANGLING
ADGGILNS	GADLINGS
ADGGILRS	RIGGALDS
ADGGINRS	NIGGARDS
ADGGINRU	GUARDING
ADGGLRSU	SLUGGARD
ADGHHILN	HIGHLAND
ADGHHIOR	HIGHROAD
ADGHILNN	HANDLING
ADGHILOS	HIDALGOS
ADGHILPY	DIAGLYPH
ADGHILTY	DAYLIGHT
ADGHINOR	HOARDING
ADGHINPR	HANDGRIP
ADGHINSS	SHADINGS
ADGHIPRS	DIGRAPHS
ADGHIRRS	ARDRIGHS
ADGHITTW	TIGHTWAD
ADGHLNNO	LONGHAND
ADGHNNSU	HANDGUNS
ADGHNOSW	HAGDOWNS
ADGHOOPR	ODOGRAPH
ADGHORSW	HOGWARDS
ADGHPSYY	DYSPHAGY
ADGHRSTU	DRAUGHTS
ADGHRTUY	DRAUGHTY
ADGIILLN	DIALLING
ADGIILLO	GLADIOLI
ADGIILNO	GONIDIAL
ADGIILNP	PLAIDING
ADGIILNR	DRAILING
ADGIILNS	GLIADINS
ADGIILNT	DILATING
ADGIILPY	PYGIDIAL
ADGIILST	DIGITALS
ADGIILTY	ALGIDITY
ADGIIMNR	ADMIRING
ADGIIMNX	ADMIXING
ADGIIMST	DIGAMIST
ADGIINNR	DRAINING
ADGIINNS	SDAINING
ADGIINNV	INVADING
ADGIINNY	DIGYNIAN
ADGIINOR	RADIOING
ADGIINOV	AVOIDING
ADGIINRR	ARRIDING
ADGIINRY	DAIRYING
ADGIINSU	IGUANIDS
ADGIINSV	ADVISING
ADGIINSW	GWINIADS
ADGIINTU	AUDITING
ADGIJNRU	ADJURING
ADGIKLNR	DARKLING
ADGILLNU	ALLUDING
	DUALLING
ADGILLNW	WINDGALL
ADGILLNY	DALLYING
ADGILMNS	MADLINGS
ADGILMNW	DWALMING
ADGILMOR	MARIGOLD
ADGILNNS	LANDINGS
	SANDLING
ADGILNNU	UNLADING
ADGILNOS	LOADINGS
ADGILNPP	DAPPLING
ADGILNRS	DARLINGS
ADGILNRT	DARTLING
ADGILNRW	DRAWLING

ADGILNRY	DARINGLY
ADGILNZZ	DAZZLING
ADGILOOS	SOLIDAGO
ADGILOPR	PRODIGAL
ADGILORS	GOLIARDS
ADGILORY	GOLIARDY
	GYROIDAL
ADGIMMNR	DRAMMING
ADGIMMNW	DWAMMING
ADGIMNNU	MAUNDING
ADGIMNOP	POMADING
ADGIMNPS	DAMPINGS
ADGIMNRS	MRIDANGS
ADGIMNRY	MARDYING
ADGIMNUW	DWAUMING
ADGIMOSU	DIGAMOUS
ADGINNOR	ADORNING
ADGINNOT	DONATING
ADGINNPY	PANDYING
ADGINNRS	DARNINGS
ADGINNRT	DRANTING
ADGINNSS	SANDINGS
ADGINNST	STANDING
ADGINNSW	DAWNINGS
ADGINNSY	SDAYNING
ADGINNTU	DAUNTING
ADGINOOP	POIGNADO
ADGINOOR	RIGADOON
ADGINOPT	ADOPTING
ADGINORS	ROADINGS
ADGINOST	DOATINGS
ADGINOTY	TOADYING
ADGINPPR	DRAPPING
ADGINPTU	UPDATING
ADGINRST	TRADINGS
ADGINRSW	DRAWINGS
	SWARDING
	WARDINGS
ADGINRTY	TARDYING
ADGINSTU	ADUSTING
	SUDATING
ADGINSWY	GWYNIADS
ADGIPRSU	PAGURIDS
ADGIRSSU	GUISARDS
ADGIRSZZ	GIZZARDS
ADGKOOSZ	GADZOOKS
ADGLLNOS	GOLLANDS
ADGLMNOS	MANGOLDS
ADGLNOOS	GONDOLAS
ADGLNOSW	GOWLANDS
ADGLOORY	GARDYLOO
ADGMNORS	GORMANDS
ADGMNORU	GOURMAND
ADGNNOQU	QUANDONG
ADGNNORS	GRANDSON
ADGNNRYY	GYNANDRY
ADGNOORS	DRAGOONS
	GADROONS
ADGNRRSU	GURNARDS
ADGNRSUU	UNGUARDS
ADGOOPRS	GOSPODAR
ADGOPRSU	PODARGUS
ADGORTUU	OUTGUARD
ADHHIPRS	HARDSHIP
ADHHNRTY	HYDRANTH
ADHIIJST	IJTIHADS
ADHIIKSS	DASHIKIS
ADHIINOP	OPHIDIAN
ADHIINRW	WHINIARD
ADHILLMO	HOLLIDAM
ADHILLNS	SANDHILL
ADHILLOP	PHALLOID
ADHILLOT	THALLOID
ADHILMOO	HOMALOID
ADHILMOS	HALIDOMS
ADHILNST	HANDLIST
ADHILOPS	SHIPLOAD
ADHILOPY	HAPLOIDY
ADHILOSY	HOLIDAYS
ADHILPSY	LADYSHIP
ADHIMNOS	ADMONISH
ADHIMNOU	HUMANOID
ADHIMOPP	AMPHIPOD
ADHIMPSS	PHASMIDS
ADHIMRTY	MYRIADTH
ADHINPSU	DAUPHINS
ADHINRWY	WHINYARD
ADHINSST	STANDISH
ADHINSTU	DIANTHUS
ADHIOSTY	TOADYISH
ADHIPRSW	WARDSHIP
ADHIPRSY	SHIPYARD
ADHIPSTY	DISPATHY
ADHIRTWW	WITHDRAW
ADHKNORW	HANDWORK
ADHKORSW	DORHAWKS
ADHKOSSU	SHAKUDOS
ADHLLNOS	HOLLANDS
ADHLMORT	THRALDOM
ADHLMOSY	HOLYDAMS
ADHLMPSY	LYMPHADS
ADHLNORW	WALDHORN
ADHMNOOS	MANHOODS
ADHNNOOR	HONORAND
ADHNORSU	UNHOARDS
ADHNOSTU	HANDOUTS
	THOUSAND
ADHNOSUW	UNSHADOW
ADHNRSTY	HYDRANTS
ADHOOPRS	HOSPODAR
ADHOORRS	RHODORAS
ADHOORSW	ROADSHOW
ADHOORYZ	HYDROZOA
ADHOPRST	HARDTOPS
	POTSHARD
ADHOPRSU	UPHOARDS
ADHOPRSY	RHAPSODY
ADHORSTU	TOADRUSH
ADHORSWY	SHOWYARD
ADHPSTYY	DYSPATHY
ADIIINRV	VIRIDIAN
ADIIIQRU	DAIQUIRI
ADIIKLMM	MILKMAID
ADIIKLST	TAILSKID
ADIIKNOP	PINAKOID
ADIIKNST	ANTISKID
ADIIKOST	DAKOITIS
ADIILLMR	MILLIARD
ADIILLNY	IDYLLIAN
ADIILLOR	ARILLOID
ADIILLUV	DILUVIAL
ADIILMSS	MISDIALS
ADIILNOT	DILATION
ADIILNSU	INDUSIAL
ADIILNSV	INVALIDS
ADIILNSW	WINDSAIL
ADIILNTY	DAINTILY
ADIILNUV	DILUVIAN
	INDUVIAL
ADIILOPP	DIPLOPIA
ADIILRST	DISTRAIL
ADIILSST	DIALISTS
ADIILSSY	DIALYSIS
ADIILTVY	VALIDITY
ADIIMMSS	MAIDISMS
ADIIMPSU	ASPIDIUM
ADIIMRSU	MUDIRIAS
ADIINNOT	NIDATION
ADIINOTU	AUDITION
ADIINPRS	PINDARIS
ADIINRST	DISTRAIN
ADIINSST	DISTAINS
ADIINSSU	SUIDIANS
ADIIOPRS	SPORIDIA
ADIIOPRT	TAPIROID
ADIIORST	TARSIOID
ADIIPRTU	TRIPUDIA
ADIIPRTY	RAPIDITY
ADIIPSTY	SAPIDITY
ADIIPTVY	VAPIDITY
ADIIQRSU	DAQUIRIS
ADIIRSST	DIARISTS
ADIIRSTT	DISTRAIT
	TRIADIST
ADIJNOST	ADJOINTS
ADIKKRRW	KIRKWARD
ADIKKRRY	KIRKYARD
ADIKLNPS	LANDSKIP
ADIKLNSY	LADYKINS
ADIKLOSS	ODALISKS
ADIKMNNS	MANKINDS
ADIKMSSS	DISMASKS
ADIKNNNU	DUNNAKIN
ADIKNNST	INKSTAND
ADIKNPSS	SKIDPANS
ADIKNRSS	DISRANKS
ADIKNRST	STINKARD
ADIKPRSS	DISPARKS
ADILLLPY	PALLIDLY
ADILLMMS	MILLDAMS
ADILLMNR	MANDRILL
ADILLMOU	ALLODIUM
ADILLMOV	VILLADOM
ADILLMSY	DISMALLY
ADILLNPS	LANDSLIP
ADILLOOP	POLOIDAL
ADILLOPS	SPADILLO
ADILLOSW	DISALLOW
ADILLOSY	DISLOYAL
ADILLRWY	WILLYARD
ADILLSTY	DISTALLY
ADILMMOS	MODALISM
ADILMNNO	MANDOLIN
ADILMNOS	SALMONID
ADILMNRS	MANDRILS
ADILMOOR	MODIOLAR
ADILMOPS	DIPLOMAS
ADILMOPT	DIPLOMAT
ADILMOPY	OLYMPIAD
ADILMORU	ORDALIUM
ADILMOST	MODALIST
ADILMOSU	ALODIUMS
ADILMOSY	AMYLOIDS
ADILMOTY	MODALITY
ADILMPSS	PLASMIDS
ADILMPSU	PALUDISM
ADILMSSU	DUALISMS
ADILMSSY	DISMAYLS
	LADYISMS
ADILNNNU	NUNDINAL
ADILNNSU	DISANNUL
ADILNOOR	DOORNAIL
ADILNOOV	VINDALOO
ADILNOPY	PALINODY
ADILNORS	ORDINALS
ADILNOTY	NODALITY
ADILNPRS	SPANDRIL
ADILNPST	DISPLANT
ADILNRSU	DIURNALS
ADILNRWY	INWARDLY
ADILNSSU	SUNDIALS
ADILNSSW	WINDLASS
ADILOOPZ	DIPLOZOA
ADILOORT	TOROIDAL
ADILOPRT	TRIPODAL
ADILOPSS	DISPOSAL
ADILOQSU	SQUALOID
ADILORST	DILATORS
ADILORSY	SOLIDARY
ADILORTY	ADROITLY
	DILATORY
	IDOLATRY
ADILOSTY	SODALITY
ADILPPSY	DISAPPLY
ADILPRSY	PYRALIDS
ADILPSST	PLASTIDS
ADILPSSY	DISPLAYS
ADILPSTU	PLAUDITS
ADILRTWY	TAWDRILY
ADILRWYZ	WIZARDLY
ADILSSTU	DUALISTS
ADIMMNOO	AMMONOID
ADIMMNOS	MONADISM
	NOMADISM
ADIMMNSY	DYNAMISM
ADIMMOST	AMIDMOST
ADIMMOTU	DOMATIUM
ADIMNNOS	MONDAINS
ADIMNNOT	DOMINANT
ADIMNOOR	MAINDOOR
ADIMNOST	DONATISM
	SAINTDOM
ADIMNOWW	WIDOWMAN
ADIMNRSW	MISDRAWN
ADIMNRSY	MISANDRY
ADIMNSTY	DYNAMIST
ADIMOPRY	MYRIAPOD
ADIMOPSY	SYMPODIA
ADIMORRS	MIRADORS
ADIMOSST	MASTOIDS
ADIMOSTT	MATTOIDS
ADIMOSTY	TOADYISM
ADIMPRSY	PYRAMIDS
ADIMRSSW	MISDRAWS
ADIMRSUU	SUDARIUM
ADIMSSST	DISMASTS
ADIMSSTU	DUMAISTS
	STADIUMS
ADINNNTU	INUNDANT
ADINNOOT	DONATION
	NODATION
ADINNOPS	DIPNOANS
ADINNORS	ANDIRONS
ADINNORT	ORDINANT
ADINNOTU	NUDATION
ADINNRSY	INNYARDS
ADINOOPS	ISOPODAN
ADINOOPT	ADOPTION
ADINOORT	TANDOORI
ADINOOTT	DOTATION

ADINOPPS OPPIDANS
ADINOPRR RAINDROP
ADINOPRS PONIARDS
ADINOPST PINTADOS
ADINORRS ORDINARS
ADINORRY ORDINARY
ADINORSS SADIRONS
ADINORST INTRADOS
ADINORSU DINOSAUR
ADINORSV VIRANDOS
ADINORTU DURATION
ADINOSTU SUDATION
ADINOSTX OXIDANTS
ADINOSTY DYSTONIA
ADINPSST SANDPITS
ADINRRST TRIDARNS
ADINRSSU SUNDARIS
ADINRSTU UNITARDS
ADINRUVZ UNVIZARD
ADIOOPSS APODOSIS
ADIOOSSW WOODSIAS
ADIOPRSS SPAROIDS
ADIOPRST PARODIST
PAROTIDS
ADIOPRSV PRIVADOS
ADIOPRTY PODIATRY
ADIOPSTY DYSTOPIA
ADIORRTT TRADITOR
ADIORSST ASTROIDS
ADIORSSV ADVISORS
ADIORSTT STRADIOT
ADIORSTU AUDITORS
ADIORSVY ADVISORY
ADIORTUY AUDITORY
ADIOSSVW DISAVOWS
ADIPRRTU PURTRAID
ADIPRSST DISPARTS
ADIRRWYZ WIZARDRY
ADIRSSTY SATYRIDS
ADIRSSUY DYSURIAS
ADJNORSU ADJOURNS
ADJORSTU ADJUSTOR
ADKKLOSY KAKODYLS
ADKLMRSU MUDLARKS
ADKLOORW WOODLARK
WORKLOAD
ADKMOORR DARKROOM
ADKNORTU OUTDRANK
ADKNRSTU STUNKARD
ADKORSWY WORKDAYS
ADKRSSWY SKYWARDS
ADLLLOOY DOOLALLY
ADLLMOSW WADMOLLS
ADLLNOSW LOWLANDS
ADLLOPRS POLLARDS
ADLLORSY DORSALLY
ADLMNOOR MOORLAND
ADLMNORY RANDOMLY
ADLMNOSS MOSSLAND
ADLMOORU MALODOUR
ADLMOPRW MOLDWARP
ADLMOPSY PSALMODY
ADLNNORS NORLANDS
ADLNNOTW TOWNLAND
ADLNNTUU UNDULANT
ADLNOORS LARDOONS
ADLNOPRT PORTLAND
ADLNOPRU PAULDRON
ADLNOPSU POUNDALS
ADLNOPWY DOWNPLAY
ADLNORWY ONWARDLY
ADLNOSSU SOULDANS
ADLNOSSY SYNODALS
ADLNOSTU OUTLANDS
ADLOORWW WOOLWARD
ADLOPRSU POULARDS
ADLOPRWY WORDPLAY
ADLOPSUU PALUDOUS
ADLOQSUW OLDSQUAW
ADLORRSW WARLORDS
ADLORTWY TOWARDLY
ADLPRUWY UPWARDLY
ADMMNOOS DOOMSMAN
ADMMNSSU SUMMANDS
ADMMNTUU MUTANDUM
ADMNNORY MONANDRY
ADMNNOSU SOUNDMAN
ADMNNOTU NOTANDUM
ADMNOOOT ODONTOMA
ADMNOORS DOORSMAN
MADRONOS
ADMNOOST MASTODON
ADMNOOSW WOODSMAN
ADMNOOSZ MADZOONS
ADMNORST DORMANTS
MORDANTS
ADMNORSW SANDWORM
SWORDMAN
ADMNOSSU OSMUNDAS
ADMNPPSU SANDPUMP
ADMOORRW WARDROOM
ADMOORST DOORMATS
ADMOPPPU POPPADUM
ADMOPPSU POPADUMS
ADMORSST STARDOMS
TSARDOMS
ADMORSTW MADWORTS
ADMRSSTU DURMASTS
MUSTARDS
ADNNOOSY NOONDAYS
ADNNORTY DYNATRON
ADNNOSTU DAUNTONS
ADNNRSTU DUNNARTS
ADNOOPRS PANDOORS
SPADROON
ADNOOQRU QUADROON
ADNOORST DONATORS
ODORANTS
TANDOORS
TORNADOS
ADNOORTY DONATORY
ADNOOSVW ADVOWSON
ADNOPRSU PANDOURS
ADNOPRSV PROVANDS
ADNOQRSU SQUADRON
ADNORRSW NORWARDS
ADNORSTU ROTUNDAS
ADNORSTW SANDWORT
ADNORSWY NAYWORDS
ADNORSXY SARDONYX
ADNORTUW UNTOWARD
ADNORWWY WANWORDY
ADNOSSTU ASTOUNDS
ADNOSTTU OUTSTAND
ADNPSSTU UPSTANDS
ADNRSSUW SUNWARDS
ADOOPRRT TRAPDOOR
ADOOPRSU SAUROPOD
ADOOPSSW SAPWOODS
ADOORSWY DOORWAYS
ADOPRRSW WARDROPS
ADOPRSSW PASSWORD
ADOPSSSU SOAPSUDS
ADORRSTU DARTROUS
ADORSTUW OUTWARDS
ADORSTUY SUDATORY
ADORTUVY ADVOUTRY
ADPRRTUY PURTRAYD
ADRSSTTU STARDUST
ADSSSTUW SAWDUSTS
ADSSTUWY SAWDUSTY
AEEEELRS RELEASEE
AEEEFLRS EELFARES
AEEEFRTY AFTEREYE
AEEEGKLS KEELAGES
AEEEGLLS LEGALESE
AEEEGLNR GENERALE
AEEEGLRT EGLATERE
REGELATE
RELEGATE
AEEEGLRV LEVERAGE
AEEEGLST LEGATEES
AEEEGLSV SELVAGEE
AEEEGNRT GENERATE
RENEGATE
TEENAGER
AEEEGPRS PEERAGES
AEEEGPSS SEEPAGES
AEEEGRST EAGEREST
ETAGERES
STEERAGE
AEEEGRSW SEWERAGE
AEEEGTTV VEGETATE
AEEEHLRT ETHEREAL
AEEEHMPR EPHEMERA
AEEEHNRS ENHEARSE
AEEEHRRS REHEARSE
AEEEHRRT REHEATER
AEEEHSTT AESTHETE
AEEEILNS ALIENEES
AEEEIMNX EXAMINEE
AEEEIRST EATERIES
AEEEJNTT JEANETTE
AEEEKKPS KEEPSAKE
AEEEKMSS KAMEESES
AEEEKMSZ KAMEEZES
AEEEKNRW WEAKENER
AEEELLST TELESALE
AEEELNRV VENEREAL
AEEELNST SELENATE
AEEELPRR REPEALER
AEEELQSU SEQUELAE
AEEELRRS RELEASER
AEEELRRV REVEALER
AEEELRSS RELEASES
AEEELRST TEASELER
AEEELRSW WEASELER
AEEELSSS EASELESS
AEEELSTV ELEVATES
AEEEMMRT METAMERE
AEEEMNST EASEMENT
AEEEMPRS PERMEASE
AEEEMPRT PERMEATE
AEEENNRV VENEREAN
AEEENPTT PATENTEE
AEEENRST SERENATE
AEEENRTT ENTERATE
AEEENRTV ENERVATE
VENERATE
AEEEPRRT REPARTEE
REPEATER
AEEEPSTW SWEETPEA
AEEERRST ARRESTEE
AEEERSST TESSERAE
AEEFFLLS FELAFELS
AEEFFLRT TAFFEREL
AEEFFNRT AFFERENT
AEEFGILR FILAGREE
AEEFGIRR FERRIAGE
AEEFGIRS FEGARIES
AEEFGLSU FUSELAGE
AEEFGNST FANTEEGS
AEEFGRSS SERFAGES
AEEFGSTW WEFTAGES
AEEFHIRS SHEAFIER
AEEFHLLS SELFHEAL
AEEFHRST FEATHERS
AEEFHRTY FEATHERY
AEEFIINR INFERIAE
AEEFIKLL LEAFLIKE
AEEFIKRR FREAKIER
AEEFIKRS FAKERIES
AEEFIKRW WAKERIFE
AEEFILMN FILENAME
AEEFILNR FLANERIE
AEEFILRS SERAFILE
AEEFILRT FRAILTEE
AEEFILST FEALTIES
LEAFIEST
AEEFIPSW SPAEWIFE
AEEFIRRS RAREFIES
AEEFIRSS FREESIAS
AEEFISST SAFETIES
AEEFKMNT FAKEMENT
AEEFKOPR FOREPEAK
AEEFLLMR FEMERALL
AEEFLLMT FLAMELET
AEEFLLNV EVENFALL
AEEFLLRW FAREWELL
AEEFLLSS LEAFLESS
AEEFLLST FELLATES
LEAFLETS
AEEFLMNS ENFLAMES
AEEFLMOS FLEASOME
AEEFLMSS FAMELESS
AEEFLNRU FUNEREAL
AEEFLOOV FOVEOLAE
AEEFLORV OVERLEAF
AEEFLRRR REFERRAL
AEEFLRSS FEARLESS
AEEFLRST REFLATES
AEEFLRSW WELFARES
AEEFMNOR FOREMEAN
FORENAME
AEEFMNRS ENFRAMES
AEEFMORS FEARSOME
AEEFMRRS REFRAMES
AEEFMRTY FEMETARY
AEEFNRST FASTENER
FENESTRA
AEEFNRTT FATTENER
AEEFNSSS SAFENESS
AEEFOSTU FEATEOUS
AEEFRRST FERRATES
AEEFRSST FEASTERS
AEEFRSTU FEATURES
AEEFRSWY FREEWAYS
AEEFTTUV FAUVETTE
AEEGGHIW WEIGHAGE
AEEGGINR AGREEING

AEEGGIRV AGGRIEVE
AEEGGLLS ALLEGGES
AEEGGLOU AEGLOGUE
AEEGGLRS GREGALES
AEEGGNNR GANGRENE
AEEGGNOS GASOGENE
AEEGGNOZ GAZOGENE
AEEGGNRS ENGAGERS
AEEGGOPS EPAGOGES
AEEGGPRU PUGGAREE
AEEGHIRS HIREAGES
AEEGHIRT HERITAGE
AEEGHLOT HELOTAGE
AEEGHLRS SHEARLEG
AEEGHLRW RAGWHEEL
AEEGHMPR GRAPHEME
AEEGHNRS SHAGREEN
AEEGHNSW WHANGEES
AEEGHRRT GATHERER
REGATHER
AEEGIINR AEGIRINE
AEEGIIRT AEGIRITE
AEEGIIST GAIETIES
AEEGILLS GALILEES
LEGALISE
AEEGILLZ LEGALIZE
AEEGILMN LIEGEMAN
AEEGILMR GLEAMIER
AEEGILMS MILEAGES
AEEGILNR ALGERINE
AEEGILNS ENSILAGE
LINEAGES
AEEGILNT GALENITE
GELATINE
LEGATINE
AEEGILNV INVEAGLE
AEEGILPR PERIGEAL
AEEGILRS GASELIER
AEEGILST ELEGIAST
AEEGILSW WEIGELAS
AEEGILTV LEVIGATE
AEEGIMNR GERMAINE
AEEGIMNT GEMINATE
AEEGIMRS GAMESIER
AEEGIMRT EMIGRATE
REMIGATE
AEEGINPR PERIGEAN
AEEGINRR REGAINER
AEEGINRS GESNERIA
AEEGINRT GRATINEE
AEEGINRZ RAZEEING
AEEGINSS ASSIGNEE
AEEGINST SAGENITE
AEEGINSU EUGENIAS
AEEGINSV ENVISAGE
AEEGINTV AGENTIVE
NEGATIVE
AEEGINTX EXIGEANT
AEEGIPQU EQUIPAGE
AEEGIPRS PIERAGES
AEEGIRRS GREASIER
AEEGIRSS GREASIES
AEEGIRTT AIGRETTE
AEEGIRTV ERGATIVE
AEEGISSS ASSIEGES
AEEGLLNR ALLERGEN
AEEGLLRS ALLEGERS
AEEGLLSZ GAZELLES
AEEGLMNS MELANGES
AEEGLMNV GAVELMEN

AEEGLMRT TELEGRAM
AEEGLMRY MEAGRELY
AEEGLNNR ENLARGEN
AEEGLNNT ENTANGLE
AEEGLNOS GASOLENE
AEEGLNOT ELONGATE
AEEGLNRR ENLARGER
AEEGLNRS ENLARGES
GENERALS
GLEANERS
AEEGLNSV EVANGELS
AEEGLNVY EVANGELY
AEEGLOST SEGOLATE
AEEGLPRS PEREGALS
AEEGLRSS EELGRASS
GEARLESS
LARGESSE
AEEGLRSU LEAGUERS
AEEGLRSW LEGWEARS
AEEGLRTU REGULATE
AEEGLRUX EXERGUAL
AEEGLSST GATELESS
AEEGLSSV SELVAGES
AEEGLSSW WAGELESS
AEEGLSSY EYEGLASS
AEEGLSTT GALETTES
AEEGLSTV VEGETALS
AEEGLTTU TUTELAGE
AEEGLTUV EVULGATE
AEEGMMOS GAMESOME
AEEGMMST GEMMATES
TAGMEMES
AEEGMNOR ARGEMONE
AEEGMNRS AGREMENS
AEEGMNRT AGREMENT
AEEGMNSS GAMENESS
MAGNESES
AEEGMNTT TEGMENTA
AEEGMNTZ GAZEMENT
AEEGMOST SOMEGATE
AEEGMRST GAMESTER
MEAGREST
AEEGMRSU REMUAGES
AEEGMSSS MEGASSES
MESSAGES
AEEGMSSU MESSUAGE
AEEGNNNO ENNEAGON
AEEGNNPS PANGENES
AEEGNNRS ENRANGES
AEEGNNRT GENERANT
AEEGNNRU ENRAUNGE
AEEGNNRV ENGRAVEN
AEEGNOPS PEONAGES
AEEGNPPS GENAPPES
AEEGNRRT ETRANGER
AEEGNRRV ENGRAVER
AEEGNRST ESTRANGE
GRANTEES
GREATENS
REAGENTS
SEGREANT
SERGEANT
STERNAGE
AEEGNRSU RENAGUES
AEEGNRSV AVENGERS
ENGRAVES
AEEGNRTU GAUNTREE
AEEGNSSS SAGENESS
AEEGNSTT TENTAGES
AEEGNSTV VENTAGES

AEEGNTTV VEGETANT
AEEGOPRV OVERPAGE
AEEGOPSS SAPEGOES
AEEGORSV OVERAGES
AEEGORVV OVERGAVE
AEEGOSTX GEOTAXES
AEEGPRRS ASPERGER
PRESAGER
AEEGPRRT PARGETER
AEEGPRSS ASPERGES
PRESAGES
AEEGRRRT REGRATER
AEEGRRSS GREASERS
AEEGRRST REGRATES
AEEGRRSW WAGERERS
AEEGRSST RESTAGES
AEEGRSTT GREATEST
AEEGRSTU TREAGUES
AEEGRSTW STREWAGE
AEEGRSUZ GUEREZAS
AEEGSSTT GESTATES
AEEGSTTZ GAZETTES
AEEHHHSS HASHEESH
AEEHHIRT HEATHIER
AEEHHNST ENSHEATH
HEATHENS
AEEHHOOP PAHOEHOE
AEEHHRSS REHASHES
AEEHHRST HEATHERS
AEEHHRTY HEATHERY
AEEHHSST SHEATHES
AEEHIKRS SHIKAREE
AEEHILNP ELAPHINE
AEEHILRS SHIRALEE
AEEHILRT ETHERIAL
AEEHIMPT EPITHEMA
AEEHINRS INHEARSE
AEEHINRT ATHERINE
AEEHIPST APHETISE
HEAPIEST
HEPATISE
AEEHIPTT HEPATITE
AEEHIPTZ APHETIZE
HEPATIZE
AEEHIRRS HEARSIER
AEEHIRRT EARTHIER
HEARTIER
AEEHIRSS ASHERIES
AEEHIRST HEARTIES
AEEHIRSV SHIVAREE
AEEHISST ATHEISES
ESTHESIA
AEEHISTT ATHETISE
HESITATE
AEEHISTV HEAVIEST
AEEHISTZ ATHEIZES
AEEHITTZ ATHETIZE
AEEHKLLR RAKEHELL
AEEHKLLU KEELHAUL
AEEHKNRS HEARKENS
AEEHKRSU HEUREKAS
AEEHLLSS SEASHELL
AEEHLMNW WHALEMEN
WHEELMAN
AEEHLMNY HYMENEAL
AEEHLMOS HEALSOME
AEEHLMPT HELPMATE
AEEHLNOS ENHALOES
AEEHLNPT ELEPHANT
AEEHLNRT LEATHERN

AEEHLNSS HALENESS
AEEHLNVY HEAVENLY
AEEHLORS ARSEHOLE
AEEHLORV OVERHALE
AEEHLPST PLEASETH
AEEHLPTT TELEPATH
AEEHLRST HALTERES
LEATHERS
AEEHLRSV HAVERELS
AEEHLRTT HEARTLET
AEEHLRTY LEATHERY
AEEHLSST HATELESS
AEEHLSTT ATHLETES
AEEHLTTY ETHYLATE
AEEHMMRR HAMMERER
AEEHMNNY HYMENEAN
AEEHMNRS SHAREMEN
SHEARMEN
AEEHMNRT EARTHMEN
AEEHMNST METHANES
AEEHMNTX EXANTHEM
AEEHMPSS EMPHASES
AEEHMRSS MAHSEERS
AEEHMRST ERATHEMS
AEEHMRTY ERYTHEMA
AEEHMSST MATHESES
AEEHMTUX EXHUMATE
AEEHNNSS SNEESHAN
AEEHNNTX XANTHENE
AEEHNOPR EARPHONE
AEEHNPST HEPTANES
PHENATES
STEPHANE
AEEHNRSS ARSHEENS
AEEHNRST HASTENER
HEARTENS
AEEHNRSU UNHEARSE
AEEHNRTT HATERENT
THREATEN
AEEHNRTU URETHANE
AEEHNRTW WATERHEN
WREATHEN
AEEHNRWY ANYWHERE
AEEHNSST ANTHESES
AEEHNSTU UNEATHES
AEEHNSTW ENSWATHE
AEEHORRV OVERHEAR
AEEHORSS SEAHORSE
SEASHORE
AEEHORTV OVERHEAT
AEEHPRRS REPHRASE
AEEHPRSS RESHAPES
SPHAERES
SPHEARES
AEEHPRST PREHEATS
SPREATHE
AEEHPSUV UPHEAVES
AEEHQSSU QUASHEES
AEEHRRSS SHEARERS
AEEHRRTU URETHRAE
AEEHRRTW WREATHER
AEEHRSTT THEATERS
THEATRES
AEEHRSTV THREAVES
AEEHRSTW WEATHERS
WREATHES
AEEHRTVW WHATEVER
AEEHSTTW SAWTEETH
AEEIIMRT METAIRIE
AEEIISST ASEITIES

AEEIKKLW	LIKEWAKE
AEEIKLMU	LEUKEMIA
AEEIKLPT	TAPELIKE
AEEIKLRW	WEAKLIER
AEEIKLST	LEAKIEST
AEEIKLVW	WAVELIKE
AEEIKMMR	MERIMAKE
AEEIKMNT	KETAMINE
AEEIKNRS	SNEAKIER
AEEIKNRT	ANKERITE
	KREATINE
AEEIKNSS	AKINESES
AEEIKPST	PEAKIEST
AEEIKRRS	RAKERIES
	SKEARIER
AEEILLNT	TENAILLE
AEEILLRS	REALLIES
AEEILLST	LEALTIES
AEEILLVX	LIVEAXLE
AEEILMMN	MELAMINE
AEEILMMT	MEALTIME
AEEILMNT	MELANITE
AEEILMRS	ALMERIES
	MEASLIER
AEEILMRT	EREMITAL
	MATERIEL
	REALTIME
AEEILMST	MEALIEST
AEEILMSV	MALVESIE
AEEILMTZ	METALIZE
AEEILNNS	SELENIAN
AEEILNPR	PERINEAL
AEEILNPS	ALEPINES
	PENALISE
	SEPALINE
AEEILNPT	PETALINE
	TAPELINE
AEEILNPZ	PENALIZE
AEEILNRT	ELATERIN
	ENTAILER
	TREENAIL
AEEILNSS	SEALINES
AEEILNTV	ELVANITE
	VENTAILE
AEEILORT	AEROLITE
AEEILOTT	ETIOLATE
AEEILPRR	PEARLIER
AEEILPRS	ESPALIER
	PEARLIES
AEEILPRT	PEARLITE
AEEILPST	EPILATES
AEEILPSW	PALEWISE
AEEILQSU	EQUALISE
AEEILQUX	EXEQUIAL
AEEILQUZ	EQUALIZE
AEEILRRS	REALISER
AEEILRRT	RETAILER
AEEILRRZ	REALIZER
AEEILRSS	REALISES
AEEILRST	ATELIERS
	EARLIEST
	LEARIEST
	REALTIES
AEEILRSV	VELARISE
AEEILRSY	YEARLIES
AEEILRSZ	REALIZES
	SLEAZIER
AEEILRTT	LATERITE
	LITERATE
AEEILRTV	LEVIRATE
	RELATIVE
AEEILRVW	LIVEWARE
	REVIEWAL
AEEILRVZ	VELARIZE
AEEILSST	ASTELIES
AEEILSTT	AILETTES
AEEILSTV	ELATIVES
	LEAVIEST
	VEALIEST
AEEILSVW	ALEWIVES
AEEILTTV	LEVITATE
AEEIMMNT	MEANTIME
AEEIMNRS	REMANIES
AEEIMNRX	EXAMINER
AEEIMNSS	NEMESIAS
AEEIMNST	MATINEES
	SEMINATE
AEEIMNSX	EXAMINES
AEEIMNUV	MAUVEINE
AEEIMOSS	AMEIOSES
AEEIMPRS	EMPAIRES
AEEIMRRS	SMEARIER
AEEIMRSS	SERIEMAS
AEEIMRST	EMIRATES
	REAMIEST
	STEAMIER
AEEIMRTV	VIAMETER
AEEIMSSS	MISEASES
	SIAMESES
AEEIMSST	SEAMIEST
	STEAMIES
AEEIMSSZ	SIAMEZES
AEEIMSTT	ESTIMATE
	ETATISME
	MEATIEST
	TEATIMES
AEEIMSTW	TEAMWISE
AEEINNRS	ANSERINE
AEEINOPS	PAEONIES
AEEINPRS	NAPERIES
AEEINPRT	APERIENT
AEEINPTT	PIANETTE
AEEINRRS	REARISEN
AEEINRRT	RETAINER
AEEINRSS	SENARIES
AEEINRST	ARSENITE
	RESINATE
	STEARINE
	TRAINEES
AEEINRSU	UNEASIER
AEEINSSS	EASINESS
AEEINSSV	VAINESSE
AEEINSTT	ANISETTE
	TETANIES
	TETANISE
AEEINSTV	NAIVETES
AEEINSVW	INWEAVES
AEEINTTZ	TETANIZE
AEEIOOPP	EPOPOEIA
AEEIORST	ETAERIOS
AEEIPPSS	APEPSIES
AEEIPPST	APPETISE
AEEIPPSU	EUPEPSIA
AEEIPPTT	APPETITE
AEEIPPTZ	APPETIZE
AEEIPRRR	REPAIRER
AEEIPRRS	PEREIRAS
	SPEARIER
AEEIPRST	PETARIES
AEEIPRTV	PERVIATE
AEEIPSST	EPITASES
AEEIPSTT	PEATIEST
AEEIPSTX	EXPIATES
AEEIQRSU	QUEASIER
AEEIQRUZ	QUEAZIER
AEEIQSTU	EQUISETA
AEEIRRSS	REARISES
AEEIRRST	ARTERIES
	REASTIER
AEEIRRTT	RETRAITE
AEEIRRTW	WATERIER
AEEIRSST	SERIATES
AEEIRSTT	ARIETTES
	ITERATES
	TEARIEST
	TREATIES
	TREATISE
AEEIRSTV	EVIRATES
AEEIRSTW	SWEATIER
	TAWERIES
	WEARIEST
AEEIRSTY	YEASTIER
AEEIRSVV	AVERSIVE
AEEISSTX	EXTASIES
AEEISSVW	SEAWIVES
AEEISTTT	ETATISTE
	STEATITE
AEEISTTV	AVIETTES
	ESTIVATE
	EVITATES
AEEISTUX	EUTAXIES
	EUTEXIAS
AEEITTUX	EUTAXITE
AEEITUVX	EXUVIATE
AEEJLNPT	JETPLANE
AEEJLOSU	JEALOUSE
AEEJNRST	SERJEANT
AEEJOPRT	PEJORATE
AEEKKLWY	LYKEWAKE
AEEKKNOS	KOKANEES
AEEKKPSY	KEEPSAKY
AEEKLLST	LAKELETS
	SKELETAL
AEEKLMRT	TELEMARK
AEEKLMSS	MAKELESS
AEEKLNST	KANTELES
AEEKLSSW	WAKELESS
AEEKLSTY	EYESTALK
AEEKMNSS	KAMSEENS
AEEKMORV	MAKEOVER
AEEKMRRR	REMARKER
AEEKMRRT	MARKETER
AEEKMRST	MEERKATS
AEEKNNNS	NANKEENS
AEEKNORW	REAWOKEN
AEEKNPRT	PERTAKEN
AEEKNPSU	SNEAKEUP
AEEKNPSW	NEWSPEAK
AEEKNRSS	SNEAKERS
AEEKNRSW	WAKENERS
AEEKNSSW	WEAKNESS
AEEKORRV	OVERRAKE
AEEKORST	KERATOSE
	KREASOTE
AEEKORTV	OVERTAKE
	TAKEOVER
AEEKPRSS	RESPEAKS
	SPEAKERS
AEEKPRST	PERTAKES
AEEKQRSU	SQUEAKER
AEEKRRST	RETAKERS
	STREAKER
AEEKRRSW	WREAKERS
AEEKRSST	SAKERETS
AEELLLTT	TELLTALE
AEELLMMS	MAMSELLE
AEELLNOV	NOVELLAE
AEELLOSV	ALVEOLES
AEELLOTT	ALLOTTEE
AEELLPRS	PARELLES
AEELLPTT	PLATELET
AEELLPTY	TELEPLAY
AEELLRRT	TERRELLA
AEELLSST	SATELLES
	TESSELLA
AEELLSSZ	ZEALLESS
AEELLSTT	STELLATE
AEELLSWY	WEASELLY
AEELLTVV	VALVELET
AEELMMTU	MALEMUTE
AEELMNPS	EMPANELS
	EMPLANES
	ENSAMPLE
AEELMNPT	PLATEMEN
AEELMNSS	LAMENESS
	MANELESS
	NAMELESS
	SALESMEN
AEELMNST	MANTEELS
	STEELMAN
	TALESMEN
AEELMNSW	WEALSMEN
AEELMNSY	AMYLENES
AEELMNTT	MANTELET
AEELMNTV	LAVEMENT
AEELMOTT	MATELOTE
AEELMPRX	EXEMPLAR
AEELMPRY	EMPYREAL
AEELMPSX	EXAMPLES
AEELMPTT	PALMETTE
	TEMPLATE
AEELMRST	LAMETERS
AEELMSSS	SEAMLESS
AEELMSST	MATELESS
	MEATLESS
	TAMELESS
AEELMSTU	EMULATES
AEELNNPS	ENPLANES
AEELNNRT	LANNERET
AEELNNSS	LEANNESS
AEELNOPR	PERONEAL
AEELNOPT	ANTELOPE
AEELNORU	ALEURONE
AEELNPPS	SPALPEEN
AEELNPSS	PALENESS
AEELNQSU	SQUALENE
AEELNRRS	LEARNERS
AEELNRSS	REALNESS
AEELNRST	ALTERNES
AEELNRSV	ENSLAVER
AEELNRSW	RENEWALS
AEELNRTV	LEVANTER
	RELEVANT
AEELNRTX	EXTERNAL
AEELNSST	LATENESS
AEELNSSV	ENSLAVES
	VANELESS
AEELNSTY	ENTAYLES
AEELNTUV	EVENTUAL
AEELNTVY	VENTAYLE

AEELOPRS	PAROLEES
AEELOPRV	OVERLEAP
AEELORRS	RELEASOR
AEELORST	OLEASTER
AEELORSU	AUREOLES
AEELORTT	TOLERATE
AEELORTV	ELEVATOR
AEELORTW	TOLEWARE
AEELOSSW	LEASOWES
AEELOTTT	TEETOTAL
AEELPRRS	PEARLERS
	RELAPSER
AEELPRRT	PALTERER
AEELPRSS	PLEASERS
	RELAPSES
AEELPRST	PLEATERS
	PRELATES
AEELPRSU	PLEASURE
	SERPULAE
AEELPRSV	VESPERAL
AEELPRTY	PTERYLAE
AEELPSST	SPATLESE
	TAPELESS
AEELPSTT	PALETTES
AEELPSTU	EPAULETS
AEELPSTV	SEPTLEVA
AEELQRSU	SQUEALER
AEELRRST	RELATERS
AEELRRSV	REVERSAL
	SLAVERER
AEELRRTU	URETERAL
AEELRRTV	TRAVELER
AEELRSST	STEALERS
	TEARLESS
	TESSERAL
AEELRSSU	LEASURES
AEELRSSV	SEVERALS
AEELRSSW	WARELESS
AEELRSTT	ALERTEST
AEELRSTU	RESALUTE
AEELRSTY	EASTERLY
AEELRSUV	REVALUES
AEELRSVY	AVERSELY
AEELSSST	ALTESSES
	SATELESS
	SEATLESS
AEELSSTU	SETUALES
AEELSSTV	SALVETES
AEELSSVW	WAVELESS
AEELSTTY	LAYETTES
AEELSTVW	WAVELETS
AEEMMNRS	MERESMAN
AEEMMNTZ	MAZEMENT
AEEMMPSY	EMPYEMAS
AEEMMRST	AMMETERS
	METAMERS
AEEMMSST	MESSMATE
AEEMNNOS	ANEMONES
AEEMNNRT	REMANENT
AEEMNNSS	MEANNESS
AEEMNORV	OVERNAME
AEEMNORZ	ARMOZEEN
AEEMNOSW	SEAWOMEN
AEEMNPRS	SPEARMEN
AEEMNPRT	PETERMAN
AEEMNPRY	EMPYREAN
AEEMNPTV	PAVEMENT
AEEMNRST	REMANETS
AEEMNRSW	MENSWEAR
AEEMNRTU	NUMERATE
AEEMNRTV	AVERMENT
AEEMNRTW	WATERMEN
AEEMNRUV	MANEUVER
AEEMNRVY	EVERYMAN
AEEMNSSS	SAMENESS
AEEMNSST	TAMENESS
AEEMNSTU	MANSUETE
AEEMORST	EROTEMAS
AEEMPPRR	PAMPERER
AEEMPRRT	TAMPERER
AEEMPRST	TEMPERAS
AEEMPRTT	ATTEMPER
AEEMPSTU	AMPUTEES
AEEMQRRU	REMARQUE
AEEMQRSU	MARQUEES
AEEMQTTU	MAQUETTE
AEEMRRST	REMASTER
	STREAMER
AEEMRRSU	MEASURER
AEEMRSST	MASSETER
	SEAMSTER
	STEAMERS
AEEMRSSU	MEASURES
	REASSUME
AEEMRSTT	TEAMSTER
AEEMRSTY	METAYERS
AEEMSSST	SEAMSETS
AEEMSSSU	MASSEUSE
AEEMSSTU	MEATUSES
AEEMSTTU	AMUSETTE
AEENNOST	NEONATES
AEENNPST	PENTANES
AEENNRSS	ENSNARES
	NEARNESS
AEENNRTU	ENAUNTER
AEENNRTV	REVENANT
AEENNRUX	ANNEXURE
AEENNSSS	SANENESS
AEENNSST	NEATNESS
AEENOPRS	PERAEONS
	PERSONAE
AEENORRS	REASONER
AEENORSS	SEASONER
AEENORST	RESONATE
AEENORTV	OVERNEAT
	RENOVATE
AEENORVW	OVENWARE
AEENOTTU	OUTEATEN
AEENPPTT	APPETENT
AEENPQTU	PETANQUE
AEENPSSX	EXPANSES
AEENRRRW	WARRENER
AEENRRSS	RARENESS
AEENRRST	TERRANES
AEENRRSV	RAVENERS
AEENRRSW	ANSWERER
	REANSWER
AEENRRSY	YEARNERS
AEENRRTT	NATTERER
AEENRRTV	TAVERNER
AEENRSSS	SEARNESS
AEENRSST	ASSENTER
	EARNESTS
	SARSENET
AEENRSSX	XERANSES
AEENRSTT	ENTREATS
	RATTEENS
AEENRSTV	AVENTRES
	VETERANS
AEENRSUV	UNREAVES
AEENRTTV	ANTEVERT
AEENRTTX	EXTERNAT
AEENRTTY	ENTREATY
AEENRTUV	AVENTURE
AEENSTTV	NAVETTES
AEENSUVW	UNWEAVES
AEEOPRRT	PATERERO
	PERORATE
AEEOPRST	OPERATES
	PROTEASE
AEEOPRTT	OPERETTA
AEEORRSU	REAROUSE
AEEORRSW	SOWARREE
AEEORRTV	OVERRATE
AEEORRVW	OVERWEAR
AEEORRVY	OVERYEAR
AEEORSSV	OVERSEAS
AEEORSTV	OVEREATS
AEEORSVW	OVERAWES
AEEPPRRR	PREPARER
AEEPPRRS	PAPERERS
	PREPARES
	REPAPERS
AEEPRRRT	PARTERRE
AEEPRRST	TAPERERS
AEEPRRTT	PATTERER
AEEPRRTU	APERTURE
AEEPRSSS	ASPERSES
	PREASSES
	REPASSES
AEEPRSST	TRAPESES
AEEPRSSZ	SPREAZES
AEEPRSTU	EPURATES
	SUPERATE
AEEPRSTZ	TRAPEZES
AEEPSSTT	SPATTEES
AEEQRRUV	QUAVERER
AEERRRST	ARRESTER
	REARREST
AEERRSST	ASSERTER
	REASSERT
	SERRATES
	TERRASES
AEERRSSU	ERASURES
	REASSURE
AEERRSSW	SWEARERS
AEERRSTT	RETRATES
	RETREATS
	TREATERS
AEERRSTU	AUSTERER
	TREASURE
AEERRSTV	TRAVERSE
AEERRSTW	WATERERS
AEERRSVW	WAVERERS
AEERSSSS	REASSESS
AEERSSSU	SEASURES
AEERSSSV	ASSEVERS
AEERSSSY	ESSAYERS
AEERSSTT	ESTREATS
	RESTATES
AEERSSTW	SWEATERS
AEERSSTZ	ERSATZES
AEERSSUU	URAEUSES
AEERSSUV	VAREUSES
AEERSTTT	ATTESTER
AEERSTTX	EXTREATS
AEERSTWW	WETWARES
AEERTTTZ	TERZETTA
AEERVWYY	EVERYWAY
AEESSSSS	ASSESSES
AEFFFLRS	FLAFFERS
AEFFGIRS	GIRAFFES
AEFFGNRS	ENGRAFFS
AEFFGRSU	GAUFFERS
	SUFFRAGE
AEFFHIKY	KAFFIYEH
AEFFILRW	WAFFLIER
AEFFILUV	EFFLUVIA
AEFFIMRR	AFFIRMER
	REAFFIRM
AEFFIPRS	PIAFFERS
AEFFKLRU	FREAKFUL
AEFFKOST	OFFTAKES
AEFFLMSW	FLAMFEWS
AEFFLNSS	SNAFFLES
AEFFLNTU	AFFLUENT
AEFFLRRS	RAFFLERS
AEFFLRSW	WAFFLERS
AEFFLSTU	FEASTFUL
	SUFFLATE
AEFFLSUX	AFFLUXES
AEFFMRSU	EARMUFFS
AEFFNNSS	NAFFNESS
AEFFNORT	AFFRONTE
AEFFORST	AFFOREST
AEFFQRSU	QUAFFERS
AEFFRSST	RESTAFFS
	STAFFERS
AEFGGGOS	FOGGAGES
AEFGGILR	FLAGGIER
AEFGGINU	FEAGUING
AEFGGMOS	MEGAFOGS
AEFGHINR	HANGFIRE
AEFGHINS	SHEAFING
AEFGHOSS	FOGASHES
AEFGHTTU	FUGHETTA
AEFGIIRS	GASIFIER
AEFGIISS	GASIFIES
AEFGIKNR	FREAKING
AEFGILNS	FINAGLES
AEFGILOS	FOLIAGES
AEFGILRR	FRAGILER
AEFGIMTU	FUMIGATE
AEFGINRW	WAFERING
AEFGINRY	AREFYING
AEFGINST	FEASTING
AEFGINTU	FANTIGUE
AEFGIRRU	ARGUFIER
AEFGIRST	FRIGATES
AEFGIRSU	ARGUFIES
AEFGIRTU	FIGURATE
	FRUITAGE
AEFGISTU	FATIGUES
AEFGLLOP	FLAGPOLE
AEFGLLSU	FULLAGES
AEFGLMNU	FUGLEMAN
AEFGLNSS	FANGLESS
AEFGLORW	GAREFOWL
AEFGLOST	FLOTAGES
AEFGLOSW	FLOWAGES
AEFGLRTU	GRATEFUL
AEFGMNOR	FORGEMAN
AEFGMNRT	FRAGMENT
AEFGNNOT	FONTANGE
AEFGNORT	FRONTAGE
AEFGNRRS	GRANFERS
AEFGNRST	ENGRAFTS
AEFGOOPT	FOOTPAGE
AEFGOORT	FOOTGEAR
AEFGOOST	FOOTAGES

AEFGORRS FORAGERS
AEFGORTT FROTTAGE
AEFGOSSU FOUGASSE
AEFGRRST GRAFTERS
AEFHIKRS FREAKISH
AEFHIKSW WEAKFISH
AEFHILLN FELLAHIN
AEFHILLT TEFILLAH
AEFHILOR FORHAILE
AEFHILOX HEXAFOIL
AEFHILRS FLASHIER
AEFHIMSS FAMISHES
AEFHLMSU SHAMEFUL
AEFHLORS FAHLORES
AEFHLRSS FLASHERS
AEFHLRST FARTHELS
AEFHLRTY FATHERLY
AEFHLSST FLASHEST
AEFHMNRS FRESHMAN
AEFHNRSW FERNSHAW
AEFHRSST SHAFTERS
AEFHRSTT FARTHEST
AEFIILMS FAMILIES
AEFIILNS FINALISE
AEFIILNZ FINALIZE
AEFIILSS SALIFIES
AEFIILST FILIATES
AEFIIMNS INFAMIES
INFAMISE
AEFIIMNZ INFAMIZE
AEFIIMRS RAMIFIES
AEFIINRT FAINTIER
AEFIINSS SANIFIES
AEFIINST FAINITES
AEFIIPRT APERITIF
AEFIIRRS FRIARIES
AEFIIRRT RATIFIER
AEFIIRST RATIFIES
AEFIIRSU AURIFIES
AEFIITVX FIXATIVE
AEFIJLOS JEOFAILS
AEFIKLST FLAKIEST
AEFIKMRR FIREMARK
AEFIKRUW WAUKRIFE
AEFILLOT FELLATIO
AEFILMNR INFLAMER
RIFLEMAN
AEFILMNS FLAMINES
INFLAMES
MISFALNE
AEFILMNT FILAMENT
AEFILMST FLAMIEST
AEFILMSY MAYFLIES
AEFILMTY FEMALITY
AEFILNNR INFERNAL
AEFILNOR FORELAIN
AEFILNOT OLEFIANT
AEFILNPS LIFESPAN
AEFILNRU FRAULEIN
AEFILNST INFLATES
AEFILNSV FLAVINES
AEFILOOR AEROFOIL
AEFILORS FORESAIL
AEFILORT FLOATIER
AEFILOST FOLIATES
AEFILPPR FLAPPIER
AEFILPST FLEAPITS
AEFILRST FLARIEST
FRAILEST
AEFILRSU FAILURES
AEFILRSV FAVRILES
AEFILRSZ FILAZERS
AEFILRTT FILTRATE
AEFILRTU FAULTIER
FILATURE
AEFILRUW WEARIFUL
AEFILSSS FILASSES
AEFILSTU FISTULAE
AEFILSTV FESTIVAL
AEFILSTW FLATWISE
FLAWIEST
AEFILSTX FLAXIEST
AEFILTUU FAUTEUIL
AEFIMMMR MAMMIFER
AEFIMNST MANIFEST
AEFIMORR AERIFORM
AEFIMORT FORMIATE
AEFIMOST FOAMIEST
AEFIMRRS FIREARMS
AEFIMRRW FIRMWARE
AEFIMRSS MISFARES
AEFINNSS FAINNESS
AEFINNST INFANTES
AEFINNSZ FANZINES
AEFINOPR PINAFORE
AEFINORS FARINOSE
AEFINPRS FIREPANS
AEFINRRS REFRAINS
AEFINRRU UNFAIRER
AEFINRRZ FRANZIER
AEFINRSS FAIRNESS
SANSERIF
SERAFINS
AEFINRST FENITARS
AEFINRSX XERAFINS
AEFINSTT FAINTEST
AEFIORTV FAVORITE
AEFIQRSU AQUIFERS
AEFIRRRS FARRIERS
AEFIRRRY FARRIERY
AEFIRRST FRATRIES
AEFIRSTW WASTRIFE
AEFIRTUX FIXATURE
AEFISTTT FATTIEST
AEFKLMRY FLYMAKER
AEFKLNRS FLANKERS
AEFKLOSS SEAFOLKS
AEFKLRST FARTLEKS
AEFKLRUW WREAKFUL
AEFKLSST FLASKETS
AEFKLSTT TALKFEST
AEFKNORS FORSAKEN
AEFKNRST FRANKEST
AEFKOPRS FORSPEAK
AEFKORRW WORKFARE
AEFKORSS FORSAKES
AEFLLMMU FLAMMULE
AEFLLNNS FANNELLS
FLANNELS
AEFLLNNU UNFALLEN
AEFLLORV OVERFALL
AEFLLORW FALLOWER
AEFLLOST FLOATELS
AEFLLPRT PRATFELL
AEFLLPTU PLATEFUL
AEFLLRUW AWFULLER
AEFLLRUX FLEXURAL
AEFLLSSW FLAWLESS
AEFLLSTT FLATLETS
AEFLLSTY FESTALLY
AEFLMNOT MATFELON
AEFLMORU FORMULAE
FUMAROLE
AEFLMOSS FOAMLESS
AEFLMPRR FRAMPLER
AEFLMSUW WAMEFULS
AEFLNNNS FLANNENS
AEFLNNOT FONTANEL
AEFLNOPR FOREPLAN
AEFLNOPT PANTOFLE
AEFLNORS FARNESOL
AEFLNOSV FLAVONES
AEFLNRSS SALFERNS
AEFLNRSU FLANEURS
FUNERALS
AEFLNRTU FLAUNTER
AEFLNSST FLATNESS
AEFLNSTT FLATTENS
AEFLNSUY UNSAFELY
AEFLOOSV FOVEOLAS
AEFLOPRT TERAFLOP
AEFLOPRY FOREPLAY
AEFLOPSW PEAFOWLS
AEFLORSS SAFROLES
AEFLORST FLOATERS
FORESTAL
REFLOATS
AEFLORSU FUSAROLE
AEFLORSY FORELAYS
AEFLORTW FLEAWORT
AEFLOSSU FOSSULAE
AEFLOSSW SEAFOWLS
AEFLOSTT FALSETTO
AEFLPPRS FLAPPERS
AEFLPPRY FLYPAPER
AEFLPRSS FELSPARS
AEFLPRSY PALFREYS
AEFLPSUU PAUSEFUL
AEFLRSSU REFUSALS
AEFLRSTT FATTRELS
FLATTERS
AEFLRSTU REFUTALS
AEFLRSZZ FRAZZLES
AEFLRTTU AFLUTTER
AEFLRTTY FLATTERY
AEFLSSTU FLATUSES
SULFATES
AEFLSTTT FLATTEST
AEFLSTTU TASTEFUL
AEFLSTUW WASTEFUL
AEFMNRRY FERRYMAN
AEFMNRST RAFTSMEN
AEFMORRS FOREARMS
AEFMORRT REFORMAT
AEFMORST FOREMAST
FORMATES
AEFMORVW WAVEFORM
AEFMOSSU FAMOUSES
AEFNNSTU UNFASTEN
AEFNOPRR PROFANER
AEFNOPRS PROFANES
AEFNOPSY PAYFONES
AEFNORRW FOREWARN
AEFNORST SEAFRONT
AEFNRRST TRANSFER
AEFNRRUY FUNERARY
AEFNSSST FASTNESS
AEFNSSTU UNSAFEST
AEFNSTUY UNSAFETY
AEFOORTW FOOTWEAR
AEFOPRRT FOREPART
AEFOPRST FOREPAST
AEFOPRSW FOREPAWS
AEFORRSV FAVORERS
AEFORRSW FORSWEAR
AEFORRSY FORAYERS
AEFORRUV FAVOURER
AEFORRWY FORWEARY
AEFORSSY FORESAYS
AEFORSTW FORWASTE
SOFTWARE
AEFORSTY FORESTAY
AEFOSTUU FEATUOUS
AEFOSTUV VOUTSAFE
AEFPRSST PRESSFAT
AEFRSSTW FRETSAWS
AEFRSTUW WAFTURES
AEGGGILN ALEGGING
AEGGGINN ENGAGING
AEGGGLSU LUGGAGES
AEGGHIRS SHAGGIER
AEGGHISS HAGGISES
AEGGHLRS HAGGLERS
AEGGHMSU MESHUGGA
AEGGHOPY GEOPHAGY
AEGGHORU ROUGHAGE
AEGGIJST JAGGIEST
AEGGIKNR KNAGGIER
AEGGILLN ALLEGING
AEGGILLR GRILLAGE
AEGGILMN GLEAMING
AEGGILNN GLEANING
AEGGILNR GANGLIER
REGALING
AEGGILNS LIGNAGES
AEGGILNT TEAGLING
AEGGILNU LEAGUING
AEGGILRS SLAGGIER
AEGGILRW WAGGLIER
AEGGIMNN MANEGING
MENAGING
AEGGIMRT GREGATIM
AEGGINNR ANGERING
ENRAGING
AEGGINNT AGENTING
NEGATING
AEGGINNV AVENGING
AEGGINRS GEARINGS
GREASING
SNAGGIER
AEGGINRV GREAVING
AEGGINRW WAGERING
AEGGINSS SIGNAGES
AEGGINST NAGGIEST
AEGGIOPR ARPEGGIO
GEROPIGA
AEGGIOSS ISAGOGES
AEGGIQRU QUAGGIER
AEGGIRRU GARRIGUE
AEGGIRST RAGGIEST
AEGGIRSU GARIGUES
AEGGIRWY EARWIGGY
AEGGISST SAGGIEST
AEGGISSW SWAGGIES
AEGGISTT TAGGIEST
AEGGLNRS GANGRELS
AEGGLORY GARGOYLE
AEGGLRST STRAGGLE
AEGGMNNS GANGSMEN
AEGGMORR ERGOGRAM

AEGGMORT	MORTGAGE
AEGGNNSU	GUNNAGES
AEGGNORV	OVERGANG
AEGGNORW	WAGGONER
AEGGNRRS	GRANGERS
AEGGNRST	GANGSTER
AEGGOPRU	GROUPAGE
AEGGRSST	GAGSTERS
	STAGGERS
AEGGRSSW	SWAGGERS
AEGHIJRS	JAGHIRES
AEGHILLM	MEGILLAH
AEGHILLS	SHIGELLA
AEGHILMT	MEGALITH
AEGHILNR	NARGHILE
	NARGILEH
AEGHILNS	HEALINGS
	LEASHING
	SHEALING
AEGHILNT	ATHELING
AEGHILNX	EXHALING
AEGHILPS	SHAGPILE
AEGHILRT	LITHARGE
	THIRLAGE
AEGHILRU	LAUGHIER
AEGHILST	LAIGHEST
AEGHIMPS	MAGESHIP
AEGHINNT	NAETHING
AEGHINNV	HAVENING
AEGHINRS	HEARINGS
	HEARSING
	SHEARING
AEGHINRT	EARTHING
	HEARTING
	INGATHER
AEGHINRV	HAVERING
AEGHINST	GAHNITES
	HEATINGS
AEGHINSV	HEAVINGS
	SHEAVING
AEGHINSZ	GENIZAHS
AEGHINTT	GNATHITE
AEGHIOPS	ESOPHAGI
AEGHIPPR	EPIGRAPH
AEGHIPRT	GRAPHITE
AEGHIRRS	GHARRIES
AEGHIRSS	GARISHES
AEGHLNOS	HALOGENS
AEGHLOPY	HYPOGEAL
AEGHLOSS	GALOSHES
AEGHLOTX	HEXAGLOT
AEGHLRSU	LAUGHERS
AEGHLRTU	LAUGHTER
AEGHLRTY	LETHARGY
AEGHLSTW	THALWEGS
AEGHMNOP	PHENOGAM
AEGHMOPT	APOTHEGM
AEGHMORS	HOMAGERS
AEGHNNST	HANGNEST
AEGHNOPT	HEPTAGON
	PATHOGEN
AEGHNOPY	HYPOGEAN
AEGHNORV	HANGOVER
	OVERHANG
AEGHNOSX	HEXAGONS
AEGHNPSW	SPANGHEW
AEGHNRSS	GNASHERS
AEGHNSST	STENGAHS
AEGHOPPR	PROPHAGE
AEGHOPPY	APOPHYGE
AEGHOPXY	EXOPHAGY
AEGHORST	SHORTAGE
AEGHOSST	HOSTAGES
AEGHPRSS	SPREAGHS
AEGHPRTU	UPGATHER
AEGIILLU	AIGUILLE
AEGIILMR	REMIGIAL
AEGIILNN	ALIENING
AEGIILNR	GAINLIER
AEGIILRR	GLAIRIER
AEGIILTT	LITIGATE
AEGIIMNR	IMAGINER
	MIGRAINE
AEGIIMNS	IMAGINES
AEGIIMTT	MITIGATE
AEGIINNN	NENNIGAI
AEGIINNR	ARGININE
AEGIINRR	GRAINIER
AEGIIRRT	IRRIGATE
AEGIISTV	VESTIGIA
AEGIJLNR	JANGLIER
AEGIKLNS	LINKAGES
AEGIKLNW	WEAKLING
AEGIKMNR	REMAKING
AEGIKNNS	SNEAKING
AEGIKNNW	WAKENING
AEGIKNPS	SPEAKING
AEGIKNRS	SKEARING
AEGIKNRT	RETAKING
AEGIKNRW	WREAKING
AEGIKNSS	SINKAGES
AEGIKNTW	TWEAKING
AEGIKPPS	KIPPAGES
AEGIKPRS	GARPIKES
AEGIKSTW	GAWKIEST
AEGILLMS	LEGALISM
AEGILLNS	NIGELLAS
AEGILLNU	LINGULAE
AEGILLNY	GENIALLY
AEGILLPR	PILLAGER
AEGILLPS	PILLAGES
	SPILLAGE
AEGILLRU	GUERILLA
AEGILLRV	VILLAGER
AEGILLSS	GALLISES
AEGILLST	LEGALIST
	STILLAGE
	TILLAGES
AEGILLSV	VILLAGES
AEGILLSZ	GALLIZES
AEGILLTU	LIGULATE
AEGILLTY	LEGALITY
AEGILMMR	AGLIMMER
	LAMMIGER
AEGILMNP	EMPALING
AEGILMNR	GERMINAL
	MALIGNER
	MALINGER
AEGILMNS	MEASLING
AEGILMNT	LIGAMENT
	METALING
AEGILMNU	AEMULING
AEGILMNY	YEALMING
AEGILMRS	GREMIALS
	LAMIGERS
	REGALISM
AEGILMRX	LEXIGRAM
AEGILNNR	LEARNING
AEGILNNS	EANLINGS
	LEANINGS
AEGILNNT	GANTLINE
	LATENING
AEGILNNU	UNGENIAL
AEGILNNW	WEANLING
AEGILNNY	YEANLING
AEGILNOR	GERANIOL
	REGIONAL
AEGILNOS	GASOLINE
AEGILNOT	GELATION
	LEGATION
AEGILNPR	PEARLING
AEGILNPS	ELAPSING
	PLEASING
AEGILNPT	PLEATING
AEGILNRR	GNARLIER
AEGILNRS	ENGRAILS
	NARGILES
	REALIGNS
	SALERING
	SANGLIER
	SIGNALER
	SLANGIER
AEGILNRT	ALERTING
	ALTERING
	INTEGRAL
	RELATING
	TANGLIER
	TRIANGLE
AEGILNRX	RELAXING
AEGILNRY	LAYERING
	RELAYING
	YEARLING
AEGILNSS	GAINLESS
	GLASSINE
	LEASINGS
	SEALINGS
AEGILNST	EASTLING
	GELATINS
	GENITALS
	STEALING
AEGILNSV	LEAVINGS
	SLEAVING
AEGILNSW	SWEALING
AEGILNTV	VALETING
AEGILNTX	EXALTING
AEGILNTZ	TEAZLING
AEGILNUV	VAGINULE
AEGILOPS	SPOILAGE
AEGILOPT	PILOTAGE
AEGILORS	GASOLIER
	GIRASOLE
	SERAGLIO
AEGILOSS	GOLIASES
	SOILAGES
AEGILOST	OTALGIES
AEGILPPS	SLIPPAGE
AEGILPPU	PUPILAGE
AEGILPRU	PLAGUIER
AEGILRRU	GLAURIER
AEGILRSS	GLASSIER
AEGILRST	GLARIEST
	REGALIST
AEGILRSY	GREASILY
AEGILRSZ	GLAZIERS
AEGILRTT	AGLITTER
AEGILRTU	LIGATURE
AEGILRTY	REGALITY
AEGILSTZ	GLAZIEST
AEGIMMST	GAMMIEST
AEGIMNNR	ENARMING
	RENAMING
AEGIMNNS	MEANINGS
AEGIMNNT	ENTAMING
AEGIMNPR	EMPARING
AEGIMNRR	REARMING
AEGIMNRS	GERMAINS
	SMEARING
AEGIMNRT	EMIGRANT
AEGIMNRU	GERANIUM
	MAUNGIER
AEGIMNSS	GAMINESS
AEGIMNST	MANGIEST
	MINTAGES
	STEAMING
	TEAMINGS
AEGIMNSV	VEGANISM
AEGIMOOS	OOGAMIES
AEGIMORR	ARMIGERO
AEGIMORS	GORAMIES
AEGIMORW	WAGMOIRE
AEGIMPRS	EPIGRAMS
	PRIMAGES
AEGIMPRU	UMPIRAGE
AEGIMPST	PIGMEATS
AEGIMQRU	QUAGMIRE
AEGIMRRS	ARMIGERS
AEGIMRRT	RAGTIMER
AEGIMRSS	GISARMES
AEGIMRST	MAGISTER
	MIGRATES
	RAGTIMES
	STERIGMA
AEGIMSST	SIGMATES
AEGIMSSU	MISUSAGE
AEGIMSTU	GAUMIEST
AEGINNNX	ANNEXING
AEGINNOS	GANOINES
AEGINNOT	NEGATION
AEGINNPS	SNEAPING
	SPEANING
AEGINNRS	AGINNERS
	EARNINGS
	ENGRAINS
	GRANNIES
AEGINNRV	RAVENING
AEGINNRY	RENAYING
	YEARNING
AEGINNST	ANTIGENS
	GENTIANS
	STEANING
AEGINNSU	GUANINES
	SANGUINE
AEGINORS	IGNAROES
	ORGANISE
	ORIGANES
AEGINORZ	ORGANIZE
AEGINOSS	AGONISES
AEGINOSZ	AGONIZES
AEGINPPR	PAPERING
AEGINPPS	GENIPAPS
AEGINPRS	PREASING
	SPEARING
AEGINPRT	TAPERING
AEGINPRY	REPAYING
AEGINQTU	EQUATING
AEGINRRS	EARRINGS
	GRAINERS
AEGINRRV	AVERRING
AEGINRSS	REASSIGN
	SEARINGS

	SERINGAS
AEGINRST	ANGRIEST
	ASTRINGE
	GANISTER
	GANTRIES
	GRANITES
	INGRATES
	RANGIEST
	REASTING
	STEARING
	TASERING
AEGINRSV	VINEGARS
AEGINRSW	SWEARING
	WEARINGS
AEGINRSY	RESAYING
AEGINRTT	ARETTING
	TREATING
AEGINRTV	AVERTING
	TAVERING
	VINTAGER
AEGINRTW	TWANGIER
	WATERING
AEGINRVW	WAVERING
AEGINRVY	VINEGARY
AEGINRWY	WEARYING
AEGINSST	EASTINGS
	GENISTAS
	GIANTESS
	SEATINGS
	TEASINGS
	TSIGANES
AEGINSSY	ESSAYING
AEGINSTT	ESTATING
	TANGIEST
AEGINSTU	SAUTEING
AEGINSTV	VINTAGES
AEGINSTW	SWEATING
AEGINSTY	YEASTING
AEGINSVW	WEAVINGS
AEGINSVY	SAVEYING
AEGIOPRR	PROGERIA
AEGIORSS	ARGOSIES
AEGIORSV	VIRAGOES
AEGIOSTT	GOATIEST
AEGIOSTU	AGOUTIES
AEGIOSTX	GEOTAXIS
AEGIPPRT	GRIPTAPE
AEGIPPST	GAPPIEST
AEGIPRSS	PRISAGES
	SPAIRGES
AEGIPRST	GRAPIEST
AEGIPRTY	PTERYGIA
AEGIPSST	GASPIEST
AEGIQRSU	SQUIRAGE
AEGIRRSS	GRASSIER
AEGIRRSU	SUGARIER
AEGIRRSZ	GRAZIERS
AEGIRRTY	ARGYRITE
AEGIRSST	AGISTERS
AEGIRSTT	STRIGATE
AEGIRSTV	VIRGATES
	VITRAGES
AEGIRSUU	AUGURIES
AEGISSST	GASSIEST
AEGISSTT	STAGIEST
AEGISSTW	GAWSIEST
AEGISTUZ	GAUZIEST
AEGJLNRS	JANGLERS
AEGJLTUU	JUGULATE
AEGKKKNO	ANGEKKOK
AEGKKNOS	ANGEKOKS
AEGKLOSU	KAGOULES
AEGKMNRU	GUNMAKER
AEGKMRSY	KERYGMAS
AEGLLLMU	GLUMELLA
AEGLLNOS	ALLONGES
	GALLEONS
AEGLLNOV	LONGEVAL
AEGLLNPS	LANGSPEL
AEGLLNRS	LANGRELS
AEGLLOPR	GALLOPER
AEGLLORS	ALLEGROS
AEGLLORV	OVERGALL
AEGLLORY	ALLEGORY
AEGLLOSS	GOALLESS
AEGLLOST	TOLLAGES
AEGLLRVY	GRAVELLY
AEGLLSSU	GALLUSES
	SEAGULLS
	SULLAGES
AEGLMNNO	MANGONEL
AEGLMNRS	MANGLERS
AEGLMNSS	GLASSMEN
AEGLMNTU	GUNMETAL
AEGLMORS	GOMERALS
AEGLMOSU	MOULAGES
AEGLMOTV	MEGAVOLT
AEGLMPSU	PLUMAGES
AEGLMRSU	MAULGRES
AEGLMSSU	GAUMLESS
AEGLNNPT	PLANGENT
AEGLNNTU	UNTANGLE
AEGLNOPT	GANTLOPE
AEGLNORY	YEARLONG
AEGLNOST	TANGELOS
AEGLNPRS	GRAPNELS
	SPANGLER
	SPRANGLE
AEGLNPSS	PANGLESS
	SPANGLES
AEGLNPST	SPANGLET
AEGLNRRW	WRANGLER
AEGLNRSS	SLANGERS
AEGLNRST	STRANGLE
	TANGLERS
	TRANGLES
AEGLNRSU	GRANULES
AEGLNRSW	WANGLERS
	WRANGLES
AEGLNRSY	LARYNGES
AEGLNRUY	GUNLAYER
AEGLNSTT	GANTLETS
AEGLNSTU	LANGUETS
AEGLNSTW	TWANGLES
AEGLNSUW	GUNWALES
AEGLNTTU	GAUNTLET
AEGLNTUU	UNGULATE
AEGLOOOZ	ZOOGLOEA
AEGLOOPU	APOLOGUE
AEGLOORY	AEROLOGY
AEGLOPRS	PERGOLAS
AEGLORST	GLOATERS
	LEGATORS
AEGLORSU	GLAREOUS
AEGLORTU	OUTGLARE
AEGLORTV	TRAVELOG
AEGLORTW	WATERLOG
AEGLORTY	GEOLATRY
AEGLOSSW	GALOWSES
AEGLOSTV	VOLTAGES
AEGLOSUY	GEALOUSY
AEGLPPRS	GRAPPLES
AEGLPRSU	EARPLUGS
	GRAUPELS
AEGLPSSU	PLUSAGES
	PLUSSAGE
AEGLRRSU	REGULARS
AEGLRRUV	VULGARER
AEGLRSTU	GAULTERS
	GESTURAL
	TRAGULES
AEGLRTUY	ARGUTELY
AEGLSSTT	GESTALTS
AEGLSSUV	VALGUSES
AEGLSTUU	GLUTAEUS
AEGLSTUV	VULGATES
AEGLSUUY	GUAYULES
AEGMMNOR	GAMMONER
AEGMMRRU	RUMMAGER
AEGMMRSU	RUMMAGES
AEGMNNOS	AGNOMENS
AEGMNNOT	MAGNETON
AEGMNORS	MEGARONS
AEGMNORV	MANGROVE
AEGMNOST	GEOMANTS
	MAGNETOS
	MEGATONS
	MONTAGES
AEGMNOSX	MAGNOXES
AEGMNOXY	XENOGAMY
AEGMNRST	GARMENTS
	MARGENTS
	RAGMENTS
AEGMNRTU	ARGUMENT
AEGMNSSW	SWAGSMEN
AEGMNSSY	GAMYNESS
AEGMNSTU	AUGMENTS
	MUTAGENS
AEGMOORS	MOORAGES
AEGMOPRW	GAPEWORM
AEGMORSS	GOSSAMER
AEGMPSTU	STUMPAGE
AEGNNOPT	PENTAGON
AEGNNORT	NEGATRON
AEGNNOST	TONNAGES
AEGNNPRT	PREGNANT
AEGNNRSU	GUNNERAS
AEGNNRTY	GANNETRY
AEGNNSTT	TANGENTS
AEGNNSTU	TUNNAGES
AEGNOORS	OREGANOS
AEGNOPRR	PARERGON
AEGNOPST	PONTAGES
AEGNORRS	GROANERS
AEGNORRY	ORANGERY
AEGNORST	ORANGEST
	RAGSTONE
	STONERAG
AEGNORSW	WAGONERS
AEGNORTT	TETRAGON
AEGNORTY	NEGATORY
AEGNORUV	VARGUENO
AEGNOSSY	NOSEGAYS
AEGNOTUY	AUTOGENY
AEGNPRSS	ENGRASPS
AEGNPRST	TREPANGS
AEGNPRYY	PANEGYRY
AEGNRRST	GRANTERS
	REGRANTS
	STRANGER
AEGNRSTU	STRAUNGE
AEGNRSYY	ASYNERGY
AEGNSSST	GASTNESS
AEGNSSSY	SYNGASES
AEGNSTTU	GAUNTEST
	TUTENAGS
AEGOORST	ROOTAGES
AEGOORSV	VORAGOES
AEGOOSWY	WAYGOOSE
AEGOPPRS	PROPAGES
AEGOPPST	STOPPAGE
AEGOPPSU	SUPPEAGO
AEGOPRST	PORTAGES
	POTAGERS
AEGOPRTU	PORTAGUE
AEGOPSST	GESTAPOS
	POSTAGES
AEGOPSSU	SPOUSAGE
AEGOPSTT	GATEPOST
	POTTAGES
AEGORRRT	REGRATOR
AEGORRST	GARROTES
AEGORRTT	GAROTTER
	GARROTTE
AEGORSSS	SARGOSES
AEGORSST	STORAGES
AEGORSTT	GAROTTES
AEGORSTU	OUTRAGES
AEGORSUV	OUVRAGES
AEGORSVY	VOYAGERS
AEGORTTU	TUTORAGE
AEGORUVY	VOYAGEUR
AEGOSSTW	STOWAGES
AEGOSSYZ	AZYGOSES
AEGOSTTU	OUTGATES
AEGOSTTV	GAVOTTES
AEGPRRSS	GRASPERS
	SPARGERS
AEGPSSTU	UPSTAGES
AEGPSSUU	GAUPUSES
AEGPSSUW	GAWPUSES
AEGQRTUU	TRUQUAGE
AEGRRSSS	GRASSERS
AEGRRSUU	AUGURERS
AEGRRSUV	GRAVURES
	VERRUGAS
AEGRSSSU	SARGUSES
AEGRSSUV	SEVRUGAS
AEGRSTTY	STRATEGY
AEGRSTUU	AUGUSTER
AEGSSTUU	AUGUSTES
AEGSTTTU	GUTTATES
AEHHHIST	SHEHITAH
AEHHIKSS	SHEIKHAS
AEHHIMTW	HAMEWITH
AEHHIPSW	PEISHWAH
AEHHISST	HASHIEST
	SHEHITAS
AEHHISVY	YESHIVAH
AEHHLNTU	UNHEALTH
AEHHNRSS	HARSHENS
AEHHNRSW	HERNSHAW
AEHHORST	HAROSETH
AEHHRRST	THRASHER
AEHHRSST	HARSHEST
	THRASHES
AEHIIKLR	HAIRLIKE
AEHIIKRT	TERAKIHI
AEHIIKST	SHIITAKE
AEHIILMO	HEMIOLIA

AEHIILNR HAIRLINE
AEHIILST HAILIEST
AEHIIMNT THIAMINE
AEHIIMOP HEMIOPIA
AEHIINNT IANTHINE
AEHIINTZ THIAZINE
AEHIIRST HAIRIEST
AEHIKKLW HAWKLIKE
AEHIKLLT LATHLIKE
AEHIKLNP KEPHALIN
AEHIKNSS SNEAKISH
AEHIKSST SHAKIEST
AEHIKSSY SAKIYEHS
AEHILLNT THALLINE
AEHILMNY HYMENIAL
AEHILMOS HEMIOLAS
AEHILMOT HALIMOTE
AEHILMSW LIMEWASH
AEHILNOP APHELION
AEHILNRS INHALERS
AEHILNRU INHAULER
AEHILNSY HYALINES
AEHILNTX ANTHELIX
AEHILNTZ ZENITHAL
AEHILORS AIRHOLES
SHOALIER
AEHILORT AEROLITH
LOATHIER
AEHILPRS PLASHIER
AEHILRSS HAIRLESS
AEHILRSU HAULIERS
AEHILRSV LAVISHER
SHRIEVAL
AEHILRTY HEARTILY
AEHILSST SHALIEST
AEHILSSV LAVISHES
AEHILSSW SHAWLIES
WHAISLES
AEHILSTT LATHIEST
LITHATES
AEHILSTY HYALITES
AEHILSUV VIHUELAS
AEHILSWZ WHAIZLES
AEHIMMSS SHAMMIES
AEHIMMST HAMMIEST
AEHIMMSW WHAMMIES
AEHIMNNU INHUMANE
AEHIMNRS HARMINES
SHIREMAN
AEHIMNSS SHAMISEN
AEHIMNSU HUMANISE
AEHIMNTU INHUMATE
AEHIMNUZ HUMANIZE
AEHIMPRS SAMPHIRE
SERAPHIM
AEHIMPRT TERAPHIM
AEHIMPRX XERAPHIM
AEHIMPSS EMPHASIS
MISSHAPE
PHAEISMS
AEHIMPST MATESHIP
SHIPMATE
AEHIMRRS MARSHIER
AEHIMRSS MARISHES
MISHEARS
AEHIMSSS MESSIAHS
AEHIMSST ATHEISMS
MASHIEST
MATHESIS
AEHINNSS SHANNIES

AEHINNTX XANTHEIN
XANTHINE
AEHINOPS APHONIES
AEHINOPU EUPHONIA
AEHINPRS HEPARINS
PARISHEN
SERAPHIN
AEHINPRT PERIANTH
AEHINPST PENTHIAS
THESPIAN
AEHINRRS SHARNIER
AEHINRSS ARSHINES
AEHINRST HAIRNETS
INEARTHS
THERIANS
AEHINRSV ENRAVISH
VANISHER
AEHINRSW SHERWANI
AEHINRTU HAURIENT
AEHINRTW TARWHINE
AEHINSSS HESSIANS
AEHINSST ANTHESIS
SHANTIES
AEHINSSV VANISHES
AEHINSSZ HAZINESS
AEHINSTT HESITANT
AEHINSTW INSWATHE
AEHINTTT ANTITHET
AEHIOPRS APHORISE
AEHIOPRU EUPHORIA
AEHIOPRZ APHORIZE
AEHIORRV OVERHAIR
AEHIORST HOARIEST
AEHIORTU THIOUREA
AEHIPPRS PAPISHER
SAPPHIRE
AEHIPPSS PAPISHES
AEHIPPST EPITAPHS
HAPPIEST
PEATSHIP
AEHIPRRS PHRASIER
AEHIPRRT RATHRIPE
AEHIPRSS PARISHES
SHARPIES
AEHIPRTT THREAPIT
AEHIPSSW PEISHWAS
AEHIPSTZ ZAPTIEHS
AEHIPSWW WASHWIPE
AEHIQSSU QUASHIES
AEHIRRRS HARRIERS
AEHIRRSS ARRISHES
AEHIRRST TRASHIER
AEHIRRSV RAVISHER
AEHIRRTW WRATHIER
AEHIRSST SHERIATS
AEHIRSSV RAVISHES
AEHIRSSW SWASHIER
AEHIRSTU THESAURI
AEHIRSTW SWATHIER
WATERISH
AEHIRSTY HYSTERIA
AEHIRSWY HAYWIRES
AEHISSST STASHIES
AEHISSSW SIWASHES
AEHISSSY ESSAYISH
AEHISSTT ATHEISTS
HASTIEST
STAITHES
AEHISSTU HIATUSES
AEHISSTW WASHIEST

AEHISSVY YESHIVAS
AEHISTTW THAWIEST
THWAITES
AEHJLOSW JAWHOLES
AEHJNNOS JOHANNES
AEHKMOPW MOPEHAWK
AEHKNNSU UNSHAKEN
AEHKNRST THANKERS
AEHKNSWW NEWSHAWK
AEHKRRSS SHARKERS
AEHLLLTY LETHALLY
AEHLLMOP LAMPHOLE
AEHLLNRT ENTHRALL
AEHLLRSS HERSALLS
AEHLMMNS HELMSMAN
AEHLMNOS MANHOLES
AEHLMNOT METHANOL
AEHLMNUY HUMANELY
AEHLMORS ARMHOLES
AEHLMPPT PAMPHLET
AEHLMPSW WHAMPLES
AEHLMRSS HARMLESS
AEHLMRST THERMALS
AEHLMRSU HUMERALS
AEHLNOST ETHANOLS
AEHLNPRS SHRAPNEL
AEHLNPTY ENTHALPY
AEHLNRST ENTHRALS
AEHLNSST NATHLESS
AEHLNSSU UNLASHES
UNSHALES
AEHLNSTY NAYTHLES
AEHLNTUZ HAZELNUT
AEHLOPRT PLETHORA
AEHLORST LOATHERS
AEHLORSY HOARSELY
AEHLORUV OVERHAUL
AEHLOSSS ASSHOLES
AEHLOSST SHOALEST
AEHLOSTT LOATHEST
AEHLPPRT THRAPPLE
AEHLPRSS SPLASHER
AEHLPSSS SPLASHES
AEHLPSST PATHLESS
PLASHETS
AEHLPSTU SULPHATE
AEHLRRTU URETHRAL
AEHLRSSS SLASHERS
AEHLRSST HARSLETS
SLATHERS
AEHLSSTT STEALTHS
AEHLSSTW THAWLESS
AEHLSSWY SHAWLEYS
AEHLSTTY STEALTHY
AEHMMRSS SHAMMERS
AEHMNNPY NYMPHEAN
AEHMNOPR MORPHEAN
AEHMNORS HORSEMAN
MENORAHS
SHOREMAN
AEHMNOST HOASTMEN
AEHMNOSU HOUSEMAN
AEHMNPRU PREHUMAN
AEHMNRST TRASHMEN
AEHMNSTU HUMANEST
AEHMOPRT METAPHOR
AEHMOPST APOTHEMS
AEHMOSTW SOMEWHAT
AEHMPRST HAMPSTER
AEHMRSSS SMASHERS

AEHMRSST HAMSTERS
AEHMRSTU MAUTHERS
AEHMRSTW MAWTHERS
AEHMSSSU SHAMUSES
AEHMSTTY AMETHYST
AEHMSUZZ MEZUZAHS
AEHNNPRU NENUPHAR
AEHNNPSU UNSHAPEN
AEHNNSUV UNSHAVEN
AEHNNSUW UNWASHEN
AEHNOOPT HANEPOOT
AEHNOPRT HAPTERON
AEHNOPST PHAETONS
PHONATES
STANHOPE
AEHNOPSW WANHOPES
AEHNOPXY XENOPHYA
AEHNOQTU HAQUETON
AEHNORSS HOARSENS
AEHNPRSS SHARPENS
AEHNPRST PANTHERS
AEHNPSSU UNSHAPES
AEHNRSSS RASHNESS
AEHNRSTU HAUNTERS
UNEARTHS
UNHEARTS
URETHANS
AEHNSSTT THATNESS
AEHNSSTW WHATNESS
AEHNSSTY SHANTEYS
AEHNSTUW UNSWATHE
AEHOORST TOHEROAS
AEHOPPRS PROPHASE
AEHOPRSS PHAROSES
AEHOPRST POTSHARE
AEHOPSST PATHOSES
POTASHES
SPATHOSE
AEHOPSTT HEATSPOT
AEHOQRUU HUAQUERO
AEHORRSV OVERRASH
AEHORRSW WARHORSE
AEHORSST ASTHORES
EARSHOTS
HAROSETS
HOARSEST
AEHORSSW SAWHORSE
AEHORSTT RHEOSTAT
AEHORSTX THORAXES
AEHORSUV HAVEOURS
AEHORSVW OVERWASH
AEHORSWY HORSEWAY
AEHPRRSS PHRASERS
SHARPERS
AEHPRSST SHARPEST
SPARTHES
AEHPRSUX HARUSPEX
AEHPRSUY EUPHRASY
AEHQRSSU SQUASHER
AEHQSSSU SQUASHES
AEHRRSTU URETHRAS
AEHRRSTY TRASHERY
AEHRRTTW THWARTER
AEHRSSST SHASTERS
AEHRSSSW SWASHERS
AEHRSSTT SHATTERS
AEHRSSTV HARVESTS
AEHRSTTY SHATTERY
AEHRSTUU HAUTEURS
AEHSSTUX EXHAUSTS

AEIIINTT INITIATE
AEIIIRRT RETIARII
AEIIKLNT KALINITE
AEIIKNRS KAISERIN
AEIIKNSS AKINESIS
AEIIKNST KAINITES
AEIIKRTY TERIYAKI
AEIILLMR MILLIARE
AEIILLRS RAILLIES
AEIILLST TAILLIES
AEIILLTV ILLATIVE
AEIILMNN MAINLINE
AEIILMNS ALIENISM
AEIILMPR IMPERIAL
AEIILMTT MILITATE
AEIILNNS ANILINES
AEIILNQU AQUILINE
AEIILNRR AIRLINER
AEIILNRS AIRLINES
SNAILIER
AEIILNRT INERTIAL
AEIILNST ALIENIST
LITANIES
AEIILPPT TAILPIPE
AEIILPRT LIPARITE
AEIILRSS LAIRISES
AEIILRST LAIRIEST
LISTERIA
AEIILRSV RIVALISE
AEIILRSZ LAIRIZES
AEIILRTT LITERATI
AEIILRVZ RIVALIZE
AEIILSSS SILESIAS
AEIILSSW LEWISIAS
AEIILSTV VITALISE
AEIILSTX LAXITIES
AEIILSTZ TAILZIES
AEIILTVZ VITALIZE
AEIIMMRT MARITIME
AEIIMMSX MAXIMISE
AEIIMMXZ MAXIMIZE
AEIIMNST MINIATES
AEIIMNSZ SIMAZINE
AEIIMNTT INTIMATE
AEIIMNTU MINUTIAE
AEIIMNTV VITAMINE
AEIIMOSS AMEIOSIS
AEIIMPRR IMPAIRER
AEIIMRST AIRTIMES
SERIATIM
AEIIMSTT IMITATES
AEIINNRS SIRENIAN
AEIINNSS INSANIES
AEIINNTV INNATIVE
AEIINPRT PAINTIER
AEIINPST PIANISTE
AEIINQSU EQUINIAS
AEIINRRV RIVERAIN
AEIINRSS AIRINESS
AEIINRST INERTIAS
RAINIEST
AEIINRSY YERSINIA
AEIINSST ISATINES
SANITIES
SANITISE
AEIINSSX SIXAINES
AEIINSTV VANITIES
AEIINSTX AXINITES
AEIINSTZ SANITIZE
AEIINSVV INVASIVE

AEIINTTT TITANITE
AEIINTTU UINTAITE
AEIIPRRS PRAIRIES
AEIIPRST PARITIES
AEIIPRSW PAIRWISE
AEIIPRTZ TRAPEZII
AEIIPRZZ PIZZERIA
AEIIPSST EPITASIS
AEIIRRST RARITIES
AEIIRRSV RIVIERAS
AEIIRRTT IRRITATE
AEIIRSSS SIRIASES
AEIIRSST IRISATES
SATIRISE
AEIIRSTV VAIRIEST
AEIIRSTW WISTERIA
AEIIRSTZ SATIRIZE
AEIIRSVV VIVARIES
AEIIRTTT TRITIATE
AEIIRTVZ VIZIRATE
AEIISTTV VITIATES
AEIISTVZ IZVESTIA
AEIITTTV TITIVATE
AEIITTVV VITATIVE
AEIJLMSS MAJLISES
AEIJLNSV JAVELINS
AEIJLOPS JALOPIES
AEIJLOSU JALOUSIE
AEIJMMST JAMMIEST
AEIJMNSS JASMINES
AEIJNRST NARTJIES
AEIJNRTU JAUNTIER
AEIJNSTT JANTIEST
AEIJNSTU JAUNTIES
AEIJORST JAROSITE
AEIJPSSS JASPISES
AEIJSTZZ JAZZIEST
AEIKKLLW LIKEWALK
AEIKKLPR PARKLIKE
AEIKKMNO KAKIEMON
AEIKLLSS KILLASES
AEIKLNNP PANNIKEL
AEIKLNOS KAOLINES
AEIKLNSS SEALSKIN
AEIKLNST LANKIEST
AEIKLNSW SWANLIKE
AEIKLNSY SNEAKILY
AEIKLOST KEITLOAS
AEIKLPRT TRAPLIKE
AEIKLPSS KALPISES
AEIKLRSS SERKALIS
AEIKLRST LARKIEST
STALKIER
STARLIKE
AEIKLRSV KLAVIERS
AEIKLRTW WARTLIKE
AEIKLSSS SAIKLESS
AEIKLSTT TALKIEST
AEIKMMSS MISMAKES
AEIKMNRS RAMEKINS
AEIKMNST MANKIEST
MISTAKEN
AEIKMPRS RAMPIKES
AEIKMPSS MISSPEAK
AEIKMSST MISTAKES
AEIKMSTW MAWKIEST
AEIKNPRR PRANKIER
AEIKNRST KERATINS
NARKIEST
AEIKNRSW SWANKIER

AEIKNRTW KNITWEAR
AEIKNSST SNAKIEST
AEIKNSSW SWANKIES
AEIKNSSY KYANISES
AEIKNSTV KISTVAEN
AEIKNSTW WANKIEST
AEIKNSTY KYANITES
AEIKNSYZ KYANIZES
AEIKPRRS SPARKIER
AEIKPRSS SPARKIES
AEIKPRST PARKIEST
AEIKPSTW PAWKIEST
AEIKQSTU QUAKIEST
AEIKRSST ASTERISK
SARKIEST
AEILLLMO MALLEOLI
AEILLLNY LINEALLY
AEILLMNS MANILLES
AEILLMSY MESIALLY
AEILLNNO LANOLINE
AEILLNNS NAINSELL
AEILLNNU UNLINEAL
AEILLNOR ALLERION
AEILLNPS SPLENIAL
AEILLNQU QUINELLA
AEILLNRY LINEARLY
AEILLNSS NAILLESS
SENSILLA
AEILLNVY VENIALLY
AEILLOTV VOLATILE
AEILLPPR APPERILL
AEILLPSS ILLAPSES
AEILLPST PALLIEST
PASTILLE
AEILLQTU TEQUILLA
AEILLRRS RALLIERS
AEILLRRY RAILLERY
AEILLRSS RAILLESS
AEILLRST LITERALS
TALLIERS
AEILLRSU RUELLIAS
AEILLRSY SERIALLY
AEILLRTU TAILLEUR
AEILLSSS SAILLESS
AEILLSST TAILLESS
AEILLSTW WALLIEST
AEILLSUV ALLUSIVE
AEILLSYZ SLEAZILY
AEILLTUZ LAZULITE
AEILMMNS MELANISM
AEILMMNY IMMANELY
AEILMMOR MEMORIAL
AEILMMOT IMMOLATE
AEILMMRT TRILEMMA
AEILMMSS MELISMAS
AEILMNNO MINNEOLA
AEILMNNP IMPANNEL
AEILMNNS LINESMAN
MELANINS
AEILMNOS LAMINOSE
MINEOLAS
SEMOLINA
AEILMNPS IMPANELS
MANIPLES
AEILMNRS MARLINES
MINERALS
AEILMNRT TERMINAL
TRAMLINE
AEILMNRU LEMURIAN
AEILMNSS ISLESMAN

AEILMNST AILMENTS
ALIMENTS
MANLIEST
AEILMOPR PROEMIAL
AEILMORS MORALISE
AEILMORZ MORALIZE
AEILMOST LOAMIEST
AEILMPRS IMPEARLS
LEMPIRAS
AEILMPRV PRIMEVAL
AEILMPSS PESSIMAL
AEILMPST IMPLATES
PALMIEST
PALMIETS
PETALISM
SEPTIMAL
AEILMPTY PLAYTIME
AEILMQRU QUALMIER
AEILMRRS LARMIERS
AEILMRSS REALISMS
AEILMRST LAMITERS
MARLIEST
AEILMRSY SMEARILY
AEILMRTT REMITTAL
AEILMRUV VELARIUM
AEILMSSX SMILAXES
AEILMSTT MALTIEST
METALIST
SMALTITE
AEILMSTU SIMULATE
AEILMSTY LAYTIMES
STEAMILY
AEILMTTU MUTILATE
ULTIMATE
AEILNNOS SOLANINE
AEILNNRT INTERNAL
AEILNNSY INSANELY
AEILNNTY INNATELY
AEILNOPS OPALINES
AEILNOPT ANTIPOLE
AEILNOPU POULAINE
AEILNORS AILERONS
ALERIONS
ALIENORS
AEILNORT ORIENTAL
RELATION
TAILERON
AEILNORV OVERLAIN
AEILNOST ELATIONS
INSOLATE
TOENAILS
AEILNOTT TONALITE
AEILNPRS PEARLINS
PRALINES
AEILNPRT TRIPLANE
AEILNPSS PAINLESS
SPANIELS
AEILNPST PANTILES
PLAINEST
AEILNPSX EXPLAINS
AEILNPTT TINPLATE
AEILNRRS SNARLIER
AEILNRSS RAINLESS
AEILNRST ENTRAILS
LATRINES
RATLINES
TRENAILS
AEILNRSU LUNARIES
AEILNRSV RAVELINS
AEILNRSX RELAXINS

AEILNRSY	INLAYERS
	SNAILERY
AEILNRTT	RATTLINE
AEILNRTU	AUNTLIER
	RETINULA
	TENURIAL
AEILNRTV	INTERVAL
AEILNRTY	INTERLAY
AEILNSST	EASTLINS
	ELASTINS
	SALIENTS
	STANIELS
AEILNSSU	INULASES
AEILNSSZ	LAZINESS
AEILNSTU	ALUNITES
	INSULATE
AEILNSTV	VENTAILS
AEILNSTW	LAWNIEST
AEILNSUV	UNVAILES
AEILNSUW	LAUWINES
AEILNSUY	UNEASILY
AEILNTVY	NATIVELY
	VENALITY
AEILNUVV	UNIVALVE
AEILOORV	OVARIOLE
AEILOPPT	OPPILATE
AEILOPRS	PELORIAS
	POLARISE
AEILOPRT	EPILATOR
	PETIOLAR
AEILOPRZ	POLARIZE
AEILOPST	SPOLIATE
AEILORSS	SOLARISE
AEILORST	SOTERIAL
AEILORSV	OVERSAIL
	VALORISE
	VARIOLES
	VOLARIES
AEILORSY	ROYALISE
AEILORSZ	SOLARIZE
AEILORTT	LITERATO
AEILORTV	VIOLATER
AEILORVZ	VALORIZE
AEILORYZ	ROYALIZE
AEILOSST	ISOLATES
AEILOSSX	OXALISES
AEILOSTT	TOTALISE
AEILOSTV	VIOLATES
AEILOTTV	VOLITATE
AEILOTTZ	TOTALIZE
AEILPPQU	APPLIQUE
AEILPPRS	APPERILS
	APPLIERS
AEILPRRS	REPRISAL
AEILPRRT	PALTRIER
AEILPRST	PILASTER
	PLAISTER
	PLAITERS
AEILPRSV	PREVAILS
AEILPRSW	SLIPWARE
AEILPRXY	PYREXIAL
AEILPSST	PALSIEST
AEILPSSY	PAISLEYS
AEILPSTT	PLATIEST
AEILPSTY	PTYALISE
AEILPSUV	PLAUSIVE
AEILPTYZ	PTYALIZE
AEILQRSU	SQUAILER
AEILQRTU	QUARTILE
	REQUITAL
AEILQSTU	LIQUATES
	TEQUILAS
AEILQSUY	QUEASILY
AEILQTUY	EQUALITY
AEILRRST	RETIRALS
	RETRIALS
	TRAILERS
AEILRRSU	RURALISE
AEILRRTT	RATTLIER
AEILRRTY	LITERARY
AEILRRUZ	RURALIZE
AEILRSST	REALISTS
	SALTIERS
	SALTIRES
	SLAISTER
AEILRSSV	REVISALS
	RIVALESS
AEILRSTT	TERTIALS
AEILRSTU	URALITES
AEILRSVV	REVIVALS
AEILRSVY	VIRELAYS
AEILRTTY	ALTERITY
AEILRTUZ	LAZURITE
AEILRTVV	TRIVALVE
AEILRTXZ	ZELATRIX
AEILSSSV	VESSAILS
AEILSSTT	SALTIEST
	SLATIEST
AEILSSTW	SWALIEST
AEILSTTW	WALTIEST
AEILSTVY	VILAYETS
AEIMMMRZ	MAMZERIM
AEIMMNNT	IMMANENT
AEIMMNOT	AMMONITE
AEIMMNSS	MISNAMES
AEIMMPRS	SPAMMIER
AEIMMPST	PSAMMITE
AEIMMRRS	SMARMIER
AEIMMRST	MARMITES
AEIMMRTU	IMMATURE
AEIMMSST	MISMATES
AEIMMSZZ	MIZMAZES
AEIMNNOT	NOMINATE
AEIMNNRS	REINSMAN
AEIMNNST	MANNITES
AEIMNOPT	PTOMAINE
AEIMNORS	MORAINES
AEIMNORW	AIRWOMEN
AEIMNORZ	ARMOZINE
AEIMNOST	SOMNIATE
AEIMNOSU	MOINEAUS
AEIMNOSW	WOMANISE
AEIMNOTZ	MONAZITE
AEIMNOWZ	WOMANIZE
AEIMNPRT	TRIPEMAN
AEIMNPRZ	PRIZEMAN
AEIMNQRU	RAMEQUIN
AEIMNRRS	MARINERS
AEIMNRRV	RIVERMAN
AEIMNRSS	SEMINARS
	SIRNAMES
AEIMNRST	MINARETS
	RAIMENTS
AEIMNRSU	ANEURISM
AEIMNRSY	SEMINARY
AEIMNRTT	MARTINET
AEIMNRTU	RUMINATE
AEIMNRTW	WARIMENT
AEIMNRTY	TYRAMINE
AEIMNSSS	SAMISENS
AEIMNSST	MANTISES
	MATINESS
AEIMNSSU	ANIMUSES
AEIMNSSZ	MAZINESS
AEIMNSUV	MAUVEINS
	MAUVINES
AEIMNTTU	MATUTINE
AEIMNTVZ	VIZAMENT
AEIMOOPS	IPOMOEAS
AEIMOPSX	APOMIXES
AEIMOPTT	OPTIMATE
AEIMORRS	ARMOIRES
	ARMORIES
AEIMORST	AMORTISE
	ATOMISER
AEIMORTT	AMORETTI
AEIMORTZ	AMORTIZE
	ATOMIZER
AEIMOSST	AMITOSES
	AMOSITES
	ATOMISES
	OSMIATES
AEIMOSTX	TOXEMIAS
AEIMOSTZ	ATOMIZES
AEIMOTTV	MOTIVATE
AEIMPRRS	RAMPIRES
AEIMPRRT	IMPARTER
AEIMPRSS	IMPRESAS
	SAMPIRES
AEIMPRST	APTERISM
	PRIMATES
AEIMPRSV	VAMPIRES
AEIMPRSW	SWAMPIER
AEIMPRTU	APTERIUM
AEIMPSSS	IMPASSES
AEIMPSST	IMPASTES
	PASTIMES
AEIMQRSU	MARQUISE
AEIMRRRS	MARRIERS
AEIMRRSS	SIMARRES
AEIMRSST	ASTERISM
	MAISTERS
	MISRATES
	SEMITARS
	SMARTIES
AEIMRSSY	EMISSARY
AEIMRSTT	MISTREAT
	TERATISM
AEIMRSTU	MURIATES
	SEMITAUR
AEIMRSTW	WARTIMES
AEIMRSTX	MATRIXES
AEIMRSTY	SYMITARE
AEIMRSWW	SWIMWEAR
AEIMSSST	ASTEISMS
	MASSIEST
AEIMSSTT	MASTIEST
	MISSTATE
AEIMSSTZ	MESTIZAS
AEIMSTYZ	AZYMITES
AEIMTTUV	MUTATIVE
AEINNNOX	ANNEXION
AEINNOPV	PAVONINE
AEINNORS	RAISONNE
AEINNORT	ANOINTER
	INORNATE
AEINNOST	ENATIONS
AEINNOTT	INTONATE
AEINNOTV	INNOVATE
	VENATION
AEINNPRS	PANNIERS
AEINNPST	PANTINES
AEINNRRT	INERRANT
AEINNRSS	INSNARES
AEINNRST	ENTRAINS
	TRANNIES
AEINNRSU	ANEURINS
	UNARISEN
AEINNRSW	SWANNIER
AEINNSST	INSANEST
AEINNSSV	VAINNESS
AEINNSSZ	ZANINESS
AEINNSTT	ANTIENTS
	STANNITE
AEINNTUV	UNNATIVE
AEINOPPT	ANTIPOPE
AEINOPRT	ATROPINE
AEINOPST	SAPONITE
AEINOPSZ	EPIZOANS
AEINOPTZ	TOPAZINE
AEINOQTU	EQUATION
AEINORRT	ANTERIOR
AEINORRW	IRONWARE
AEINORSS	ERASIONS
	SENSORIA
AEINORST	ANOESTRI
	ARSONITE
	NOTARIES
	NOTARISE
	ROSINATE
AEINORSV	AVERSION
AEINORTT	TENTORIA
AEINORTZ	NOTARIZE
AEINOSST	ASSIENTO
	ASTONIES
AEINOSSV	EVASIONS
AEINOSSX	SAXONIES
AEINOSTV	STOVAINE
AEINOSTX	SAXONITE
AEINOSXZ	OXAZINES
AEINOTVX	VEXATION
AEINPPRS	SNAPPIER
AEINPPST	NAPPIEST
AEINPRRT	TERRAPIN
AEINPRRU	UNREPAIR
AEINPRST	PAINTERS
	PANTRIES
	PERTAINS
	PINASTER
	PRISTANE
	REPAINTS
AEINPRSU	UNPRAISE
AEINPRSW	SPAWNIER
AEINPRTT	TRIPTANE
AEINPRTU	PAINTURE
AEINPRTX	EXPIRANT
AEINPSST	STEAPSIN
AEINPSTT	PATIENTS
AEINPSTU	PETUNIAS
	SUPINATE
AEINPSTY	EPINASTY
AEINPTTY	ANTITYPE
AEINQRTU	QUAINTER
AEINQSTU	ANTIQUES
	QUANTISE
AEINQTTU	EQUITANT
AEINQTUZ	QUANTIZE
AEINRRST	RESTRAIN
	RETRAINS
	STRAINER

	TERRAINS
	TRAINERS
	TRANSIRE
AEINRRTV	VERATRIN
AEINRRTW	INTERWAR
AEINRRUW	UNWARIER
AEINRSST	ARTINESS
	RESIANTS
	RETSINAS
	SNARIEST
	STAINERS
	STARNIES
	STEARINS
AEINRSSU	SENARIUS
AEINRSSW	WARINESS
AEINRSSX	XERANSIS
AEINRSTT	INTREATS
	NITRATES
	STRAITEN
	TARTINES
	TERTIANS
AEINRSTU	RUINATES
	TAURINES
	URANITES
	URINATES
AEINRSTW	TINWARES
AEINRSUV	VAURIENS
AEINRSUZ	AZURINES
	SUZERAIN
AEINRSVV	VERVAINS
AEINRSZZ	SNAZZIER
AEINRTTU	TAINTURE
AEINRTUV	VAUNTIER
AEINSSST	SAINTESS
	SESTINAS
AEINSSSV	VINASSES
AEINSSTT	INSTATES
	NASTIEST
	SATINETS
	TITANESS
AEINSSVW	WAVINESS
AEINSSWX	WAXINESS
AEINSTTT	NATTIEST
AEINSTTV	TASTEVIN
AEINSTTW	TAWNIEST
AEINSTUV	SUIVANTE
AEINSTWY	YAWNIEST
AEINSUVV	VESUVIAN
AEINTTUU	AUTUNITE
AEIOPPST	APPOSITE
AEIOPRRT	PRIORATE
AEIOPRSV	VAPORISE
AEIOPRTX	EXPIATOR
AEIOPRVZ	VAPORIZE
AEIOPSST	SOAPIEST
AEIOPTTV	OPTATIVE
AEIOQSSU	SEQUOIAS
AEIORRRS	ARRIEROS
AEIORRSS	ROSARIES
AEIORRST	ROARIEST
	ROTARIES
AEIORSSV	SAVORIES
AEIORSTV	VOTARIES
AEIORSVW	AVOWRIES
AEIORTTV	ROTATIVE
AEIOSSTT	TOASTIES
AEIOSSTZ	AZOTISES
AEIOSTZZ	AZOTIZES
AEIPPPST	PAPPIEST
AEIPPRRS	APPRISER
AEIPPRRT	TRAPPIER
AEIPPRRZ	APPRIZER
AEIPPRSS	APPRISES
AEIPPRST	PERIAPTS
AEIPPRSZ	APPRIZES
AEIPPSST	SAPPIEST
AEIPPSTY	YAPPIEST
AEIPPSTZ	ZAPPIEST
AEIPQRTU	PRATIQUE
AEIPRRRS	SPARRIER
AEIPRRSS	PRAISERS
AEIPRRSY	SPRAYIER
AEIPRSST	PASTRIES
	PIASTRES
	RASPIEST
	TRAIPSES
AEIPRSSU	UPRAISES
AEIPRSSV	PARVISES
AEIPRSTV	PRIVATES
AEIPRSTW	WIRETAPS
AEIPRSTY	ASPERITY
AEIPRSVY	VESPIARY
AEIPRSXY	PYREXIAS
AEIPSSST	PASTISES
AEIPSSSV	PASSIVES
AEIPSSTT	PASTIEST
AEIPSSTW	WASPIEST
AEIPSZZZ	PIZAZZES
AEIPTTUV	PUTATIVE
AEIQRRRU	QUARRIER
AEIQRRSU	QUARRIES
AEIQRRTU	QUARTIER
AEIRRRST	STARRIER
	TARRIERS
AEIRRSST	TARSIERS
AEIRRSSY	SISERARY
AEIRRSTT	RETRAITS
	STRAITER
	TARRIEST
AEIRRSTW	STRAWIER
AEIRRSVV	VIVERRAS
AEIRRTTT	RETRAITT
AEIRRTTY	TERTIARY
AEIRRVWY	RIVERWAY
AEIRSSST	TIRASSES
AEIRSSSZ	ASSIZERS
AEIRSSTT	ARTISTES
	ARTSIEST
	STRIATES
AEIRSSTV	TRAVISES
AEIRSSTW	WAISTERS
	WAITRESS
	WASTRIES
AEIRSTTT	ATTRITES
	RATTIEST
	TARTIEST
	TITRATES
AEIRSTTW	WARTIEST
AEIRSTTX	EXTRAITS
AEIRSTUZ	AZURITES
AEIRSTVY	VESTIARY
AEIRSWWY	WAYWISER
	WIREWAYS
AEIRTTTW	ATWITTER
AEISSSST	SASSIEST
AEISSSTW	TISWASES
AEISSSTY	ESSAYIST
AEISSTTT	TASTIEST
AEISSTTU	SITUATES
AEISSTTV	VASTIEST
AEISSTWZ	TIZWASES
AEISTTTT	TATTIEST
AEISTTTU	ATTUITES
AEISTTTW	TAWTIEST
AEJLNSUV	JUVENALS
AEJLOSSU	JALOUSES
AEJLOSUY	JEALOUSY
AEJLOSUZ	AZULEJOS
AEJNORSZ	ZANJEROS
AEKKLLWY	LYKEWALK
AEKKMNOO	KAKEMONO
AEKKOSSS	SAKKOSES
AEKLLSTU	KELLAUTS
AEKLMRUW	LUKEWARM
AEKLMRUY	YARMULKE
AEKLNNSS	LANKNESS
AEKLNOSY	ANKYLOSE
AEKLNPPS	KNAPPLES
AEKLNPRS	PRANKLES
AEKLOPTY	KALOTYPE
AEKLORSY	ROKELAYS
AEKLORTV	OVERTALK
AEKLOSST	SKATOLES
	STALKOES
AEKLPRRS	SPARKLER
AEKLPRSS	SPARKLES
AEKLPRST	SPARKLET
AEKLRSST	STALKERS
AEKLRSUW	WAULKERS
AEKMMNRS	MARKSMEN
AEKMNRSU	UNMASKER
AEKMOOST	MATOOKES
AEKMOPRT	TOPMAKER
AEKMORTW	TEAMWORK
	WORKMATE
AEKMPRRV	VERKRAMP
AEKMPRSU	UPMAKERS
AEKNNRSS	RANKNESS
AEKNORRV	OVERRANK
AEKNORUY	EUKARYON
AEKNOTTU	OUTTAKEN
AEKNPPRS	KNAPPERS
AEKNPRSS	SPANKERS
AEKNPSSU	UNSPEAKS
AEKNRSST	STARKENS
AEKNRSSW	SWANKERS
AEKNRSTZ	KRANTZES
AEKNSSTW	SWANKEST
AEKNSSWY	SWANKEYS
AEKOPSTU	OUTSPEAK
	SPEAKOUT
AEKORRSS	ROSAKERS
AEKORRWW	WORKWEAR
AEKORSSS	KAROSSES
AEKORSTV	OVERTASK
AEKORTUY	EUKARYOT
AEKOSTTU	OUTTAKES
	TAKEOUTS
AEKPPSSU	UPSPEAKS
AEKPSSSY	PASSKEYS
AEKQRSUW	SQUAWKER
AEKRRSST	STARKERS
AEKRSSTT	STARKEST
AELLLORY	LOYALLER
AELLLRTU	TELLURAL
AELLLSUV	VULSELLA
AELLMNOZ	MANZELLO
AELLMNST	STALLMEN
AELLMNTY	MENTALLY
	TALLYMEN
AELLMORR	MORALLER
AELLMORT	MARTELLO
AELLMOTY	TOMALLEY
AELLMPUU	PLUMULAE
AELLMRSY	MERSALYL
AELLMSST	SMALLEST
AELLMSWX	MAXWELLS
AELLNOPS	PALLONES
AELLNOPV	VOLPLANE
AELLNORS	LLANEROS
AELLNOSV	NOVELLAS
AELLNOWW	ENWALLOW
AELLNPRU	PRUNELLA
AELLNPSS	PLANLESS
AELLNPTT	PLANTLET
AELLNPTU	PLANTULE
AELLNRUY	NEURALLY
	UNREALLY
AELLNRVY	VERNALLY
AELLNSST	TALLNESS
AELLNSTT	TALLENTS
AELLNTTY	LATENTLY
AELLNTUU	LUNULATE
AELLOPRS	REPOSALL
AELLOPRW	WALLOPER
AELLORRY	ROYALLER
AELLORSS	ROSELLAS
AELLORST	REALLOTS
AELLORSV	OVERALLS
AELLORSW	SALLOWER
AELLORWW	WALLOWER
AELLOSUV	ALVEOLUS
AELLPSTY	PLAYLETS
AELLQRSU	SQUALLER
AELLRRSU	ALLURERS
AELLRRTY	RETRALLY
AELLRTTY	LATTERLY
AELLRTVY	TREVALLY
AELLRWYY	LAWYERLY
AELLSSST	SALTLESS
	TASSELLS
AELLSSTW	SETWALLS
	SWALLETS
AELLSSTY	TASSELLY
AELLSTUU	ULULATES
AELLSUVV	VALVULES
AELLSUXY	SEXUALLY
AELMMNOS	MAMELONS
AELMMORW	MEALWORM
AELMMOSY	MYELOMAS
AELMMRSS	SLAMMERS
AELMMRST	STRAMMEL
	TRAMMELS
AELMMSST	STAMMELS
AELMMSSY	MALMSEYS
AELMNNOU	NOUMENAL
AELMNNRY	MANNERLY
AELMNNTU	UNMANTLE
AELMNOPS	NEOPLASM
	PLEONASM
AELMNORS	ALMONERS
AELMNOST	SALMONET
AELMNOSU	MELANOUS
AELMNOWY	LAYWOMEN
AELMNOYY	YEOMANLY
AELMNPRS	LAMPERNS
AELMNRSU	MENSURAL
	NUMERALS
AELMNSTT	MANTLETS
AELMNSTU	NUTMEALS

AELMOOPT	OMOPLATE
AELMOORS	SALEROOM
AELMOPRR	PREMOLAR
AELMOPRS	PLEROMAS
AELMOPRT	PROMETAL
	TEMPORAL
AELMOPSU	AMPOULES
AELMOPSX	EXOPLASM
AELMOPSY	MAYPOLES
	PLAYSOME
AELMOPTT	METAPLOT
	PALMETTO
AELMORST	MOLERATS
AELMORSU	RAMULOSE
AELMORSV	REMOVALS
AELMORTU	EMULATOR
AELMOSSS	MOLASSES
AELMOSST	MALTOSES
AELMOSTT	MATELOTS
AELMOSTY	ATMOLYSE
AELMOTVZ	MAZELTOV
AELMOTYZ	ATMOLYZE
AELMPRRT	TRAMPLER
AELMPRSS	SAMPLERS
AELMPRST	TEMPLARS
	TRAMPLES
AELMPRSY	LAMPREYS
	SAMPLERY
AELMPSUX	AMPLEXUS
AELMQSUU	SQUAMULE
AELMRSTT	MALTSTER
	MARTLETS
AELMRSTY	MASTERLY
AELMRTUY	MATURELY
AELMSSST	MASTLESS
AELNNNPU	UNPANNEL
AELNNOOP	NAPOLEON
AELNNOOX	NALOXONE
AELNNORU	NEURONAL
AELNNOSU	ANNULOSE
AELNNPRS	PLANNERS
AELNNPSU	UNPANELS
AELNNRSS	ENSNARLS
AELNNRST	LANTERNS
AELNNRSU	UNLEARNS
AELNNRTU	UNLEARNT
AELNNSST	STANNELS
AELNNSTU	ANNULETS
AELNOOTZ	ENTOZOAL
AELNOPRS	PERSONAL
	PSORALEN
AELNOPST	LAPSTONE
	PLEONAST
	POLENTAS
AELNORSU	ALEURONS
AELNORSV	VERONALS
AELNORTT	TETRONAL
	TOLERANT
AELNORTU	OUTLEARN
AELNORTY	ORNATELY
AELNOSTV	VOLANTES
AELNPPSY	PLAYPENS
	SPYPLANE
AELNPRST	PANTLERS
	PLANTERS
	REPLANTS
AELNPRSU	PURSLANE
	SUPERNAL
AELNPRTY	PLENARTY
AELNPSSS	SPANLESS
AELNPSSU	SPANSULE
AELNPSTX	EXPLANTS
AELNPTTU	PETULANT
AELNPTTY	PATENTLY
AELNQSUU	UNEQUALS
AELNRRSS	SNARLERS
AELNRRTY	ERRANTLY
AELNRRUV	NERVULAR
AELNRSST	SALTERNS
AELNRSTT	SLATTERN
	TRENTALS
AELNRSTU	NEUTRALS
AELNRSTV	VENTRALS
AELNRSUV	UNRAVELS
AELNRSVY	SYLVANER
AELNRSXY	LARYNXES
AELNRUWY	UNWARELY
AELNSSST	SALTNESS
AELNSSTY	STANYELS
AELNSTUV	ENVAULTS
AELNSUUX	UNSEXUAL
AELNTTUX	EXULTANT
AELOOPRZ	ZOOPERAL
AELOORSS	AEROSOLS
	ROSEOLAS
AELOORTZ	ZOOLATER
AELOPPRS	PROLAPSE
	PROPALES
	SAPROPEL
AELOPPSU	PAPULOSE
AELOPPTU	POPULATE
AELOPPXY	APOPLEXY
AELOPQUY	OPAQUELY
AELOPRRV	REPROVAL
AELOPRSS	REPOSALS
AELOPRST	PETROSAL
	PROLATES
AELOPRSU	LEAPROUS
AELOPRSV	OVERLAPS
AELOPRVY	OVERPLAY
AELOPSSS	SOAPLESS
AELOPSST	APOSTLES
AELOPSSU	ESPOUSAL
	SEPALOUS
AELOPSSX	EXPOSALS
AELOPSTT	PALETOTS
AELOPSTU	OUTLEAPS
	PETALOUS
AELOPTTU	OUTLEAPT
AELORRST	REALTORS
	RELATORS
AELORSTU	ROSULATE
AELORSTV	LEVATORS
AELORSTY	ROYALETS
AELORSTZ	ZELATORS
AELORSUU	ROULEAUS
AELORSVY	OVERLAYS
AELORSWY	OWRELAYS
AELORTTV	VARLETTO
AELORTYZ	ZEALOTRY
AELORUUX	ROULEAUX
AELOSSTV	SOLVATES
AELOSSTY	ASYSTOLE
AELOSSVY	SAVELOYS
AELOSTTU	TOLUATES
AELOSTTW	WASTELOT
AELOSTUV	OVULATES
AELOSTUY	AUTOLYSE
AELOTUUV	OUTVALUE
AELOTUYZ	AUTOLYZE
AELPPRSS	SLAPPERS
AELPPSST	STAPPLES
AELPPSSU	APPULSES
AELPRRSW	SPRAWLER
AELPRRTT	PRATTLER
AELPRSST	PLASTERS
	PSALTERS
	STAPLERS
AELPRSSU	PERUSALS
AELPRSSY	PARSLEYS
	SPARSELY
AELPRSTT	PARTLETS
	PLATTERS
	PRATTLES
	SPLATTER
	SPRATTLE
AELPRSTU	APLUSTRE
AELPRSTY	PLASTERY
	PSALTERY
AELPSSSS	PASSLESS
AELPSSSU	LAPSUSES
AELPSSTT	PELTASTS
AELPSSTU	PULSATES
	SPATULES
AELPSUUV	UPVALUES
AELQRRSU	QUARRELS
AELQRSUY	SQUARELY
AELQSTTU	SQUATTLE
AELQSTUZ	QUETZALS
AELRRSTT	RATTLERS
	STARTLER
AELRRSTW	TRAWLERS
AELRRTVY	VARLETRY
AELRSSST	STARLESS
AELRSSTT	SLATTERS
	STARLETS
	STARTLES
AELRSSTU	SALUTERS
AELRSSTW	WARTLESS
	WASTRELS
AELRSSUW	WALRUSES
AELRSTTT	TARTLETS
	TATTLERS
AELRSTTU	LUSTRATE
	TUTELARS
AELRSTTY	SLATTERY
AELRSTUV	VAULTERS
	VESTURAL
AELRSTWZ	WALTZERS
AELRSUVY	SURVEYAL
AELRTTTW	TWATTLER
AELRTTUX	TEXTURAL
AELRTTUY	TUTELARY
AELSSSTU	SALTUSES
AELSSSTY	STAYLESS
AELSSWZZ	SWAZZLES
AELSTTTW	TWATTLES
AELSTTUY	ASTUTELY
AEMMMOTU	OMMATEUM
AEMMMRTY	MAMMETRY
AEMMNNOY	MONEYMAN
AEMMNPRS	RAMPSMEN
AEMMNRRY	MERRYMAN
AEMMNRTU	RAMENTUM
AEMMORSS	MARMOSES
AEMMORST	MARMOSET
AEMMRSST	STAMMERS
AEMMRTUY	MAUMETRY
AEMMRTWY	MAWMETRY
AEMMSSTU	SUMMATES
AEMMSSUW	WAMMUSES
AEMNNOPW	PENWOMAN
AEMNNORT	ORNAMENT
AEMNNOSS	MANNOSES
AEMNNRST	MANRENTS
	REMNANTS
AEMNOORR	MAROONER
AEMNOORT	ANTEROOM
AEMNOORY	AERONOMY
AEMNOOTZ	METAZOON
AEMNOPRS	PROSEMAN
AEMNOPRT	EMPATRON
AEMNOPRW	MANPOWER
AEMNORRS	RANSOMER
AEMNORST	MONSTERA
	STOREMAN
AEMNORSU	ENAMOURS
	NEUROMAS
AEMNORSV	OVERMANS
	OVERSMAN
AEMNORSY	ROMNEYAS
AEMNORTT	TORMENTA
AEMNORTU	ROUTEMAN
AEMNORTY	MONETARY
AEMNORYY	YEOMANRY
AEMNOSTU	NOTAEUMS
	OUTNAMES
	SEAMOUNT
AEMNPRSS	PRESSMAN
AEMNPRSU	SUPERMAN
AEMNPSST	ENSTAMPS
	PASSMENT
AEMNPSTY	PAYMENTS
AEMNQSUW	SQUAWMEN
AEMNRRSU	MANURERS
AEMNRRUY	NUMERARY
AEMNRSST	SARMENTS
	SMARTENS
AEMNRSSU	SURNAMES
AEMNRSSW	WARMNESS
AEMNRSTU	ANESTRUM
	MENSTRUA
	TRANSUME
AEMNRSTV	VARMENTS
AEMNRSTW	TRANSMEW
	TREWSMAN
AEMNRSUY	ANEURYSM
AEMNSTWY	WAYMENTS
AEMOOPST	POMATOES
AEMOORSW	WOOMERAS
AEMOORTT	AMORETTO
AEMOOSST	MAESTOSO
	OSTEOMAS
AEMOOSSV	VAMOOSES
AEMOOSTT	TOMATOES
AEMOOSTU	AUTOSOME
AEMOOTTY	TOMATOEY
AEMOPPRS	PAMPEROS
AEMOPRTW	POMWATER
	TAPEWORM
AEMOQSSU	SQUAMOSE
AEMORRRU	ARMOURER
AEMORRST	REARMOST
AEMORRSY	ROSEMARY
AEMORSSS	MORASSES
AEMORSST	MAESTROS
AEMORSSW	SEAWORMS
AEMORSSY	MAYORESS
AEMORSTV	OVERMAST
AEMORSVW	OVERSWAM

AEMORTTU TAUTOMER
AEMOSSTT EASTMOST
AEMOSSTW TWASOMES
AEMOSSUZ ZAMOUSES
AEMOSSWY SOMEWAYS
AEMOSTTZ MOZETTAS
AEMOTTZZ MOZZETTA
AEMPRRST TRAMPERS
AEMPRRSW PREWARMS
AEMPRRSY SPERMARY
AEMPRSST STAMPERS
AEMPRSSW SWAMPERS
AEMPRSTT TRAMPETS
AEMPRSTU TEMPURAS
UPSTREAM
AEMPSSUW MAWPUSES
WAMPUSES
AEMPSTTT ATTEMPTS
AEMQRSSU MARQUESS
MASQUERS
AEMRRSSW SWARMERS
AEMRRTUV VERATRUM
AEMRSSSU MASSEURS
AEMRSSTT MATTRESS
SMARTEST
SMATTERS
AEMRSSTY MAYSTERS
AEMRSTTU MATUREST
TESTAMUR
AEMRSTTX MARTEXTS
AEMRTUUX TRUMEAUX
AEMSTTTU TESTATUM
AENNNPST PENNANTS
AENNNTTU UNTENANT
AENNOPRT PATRONNE
AENNOPST PENTOSAN
AENNOPUW UNWEAPON
AENNORST NORTENAS
RESONANT
AENNORSU UNREASON
AENNORSY ANNOYERS
AENNORTW WANTONER
AENNORVY NOVENARY
AENNOSSU UNSEASON
AENNOSTU TONNEAUS
AENNOTUX TONNEAUX
AENNPRSS SPANNERS
AENNPSSU PANNUSES
AENNQSTU QUANNETS
AENNRSTT ENTRANTS
AENNRSTY TYRANNES
AENNRSWY SWANNERY
AENNRTTY TENANTRY
AENOOPST TEASPOON
AENOORRT RATOONER
AENOPPRS PROPANES
AENOPRSS PERSONAS
RESPONSA
AENOPRST OPERANTS
PRONATES
AENOPRTT PATENTOR
AENOPRWY WEAPONRY
AENOPSSU POSAUNES
AENORRRW NARROWER
AENORRST ANTRORSE
AENORSST ASSENTOR
SENATORS
TREASONS
AENORSTT ORNATEST
AENORSTV VENATORS
AENORSTW STONERAW
AENORSUV RAVENOUS
AENORTTX TETRAXON
AENORTTY ATTORNEY
AENOSSTU SOUTANES
AENOSSTZ STANZOES
AENOSSUU NAUSEOUS
AENOSSVW WAVESONS
AENPPRSS PARSNEPS
SNAPPERS
AENPPRST PARPENTS
AENPPRSU UNPAPERS
AENPRRST PARTNERS
AENPRRSW PREWARNS
AENPRSST PASTERNS
AENPRSSW SPAWNERS
AENPRSTT PATTERNS
TRANSEPT
AENPRSTU PERSAUNT
AENPRSUV PARVENUS
AENPSSSY SYNAPSES
AENPSSTU PESAUNTS
AENPSSTW STEWPANS
WASPNEST
AENPSSTY SYNAPTES
AENPSSTZ SPETSNAZ
AENPSTZZ SPETZNAZ
AENQRRTU QUARTERN
AENQSTTU QUESTANT
AENRRRTY ERRANTRY
AENRRSTT TRANTERS
AENRSSST SARSNETS
AENRSSTT TARTNESS
AENRSSTU ANESTRUS
SAUNTERS
AENRSSTV SERVANTS
VERSANTS
AENRSSUW UNSWEARS
AENRSTTU TAUNTERS
AENRSTUV VAUNTERS
AENRSTUW UNWATERS
AENRSTWY STERNWAY
AENRTUVY VAUNTERY
AENRTUWY UNWATERY
AENSSSTV VASTNESS
AENSSSTW WASTNESS
AENSSTTU TAUTNESS
UNSTATES
AENSSTTX SEXTANTS
AENSSTXY SYNTAXES
AEOOPPPS PAPPOOSE
AEOOPPSS PAPOOSES
AEOOPRRT OPERATOR
AEOOPRSS OROPESAS
AEOOPSTT POTATOES
AEOORRST SORORATE
AEOORTTT TATTOOER
AEOORTTV ROTOVATE
AEOPPRRV APPROVER
AEOPPRSS APPOSERS
AEOPPRSV APPROVES
AEOPQRTU PAROQUET
AEOPQSTU OPAQUEST
AEOPRRRT PARROTER
AEOPRRST PRAETORS
PRORATES
AEOPRRTV OVERPART
AEOPRRUV VAPOURER
AEOPRRVW WRAPOVER
AEOPRSST ESPARTOS
PORTASES
PROTASES
SEAPORTS
AEOPRSSU ASPEROUS
AEOPRSSV OVERPASS
AEOPRSTT PROSTATE
AEOPRSTU APTEROUS
AEOPRSTV OVERPAST
AEOPRSVY OVERPAYS
AEOPRSWY ROPEWAYS
AEOPRTWX WATERPOX
AEOPSSST POTASSES
AEOPTTUY AUTOTYPE
AEOQRSTU EQUATORS
QUAESTOR
AEOQRSUV VAQUEROS
AEOQRTTU TORQUATE
AEOQRTUZ QUATORZE
AEORRRST ARRESTOR
AEORRSST ASSERTOR
ASSORTER
ORATRESS
ROASTERS
AEORRSSU AROUSERS
AEORRSTT ROSTRATE
AEORRTUV AVOUTRER
AEORRTZZ TERRAZZO
AEORSSSS ASSESSOR
AEORSSTT STRATOSE
TOASTERS
AEORSSTV VOTARESS
AEORSSTX STORAXES
AEORSTTT ATTESTOR
TESTATOR
AEORSTTU OUTRATES
OUTSTARE
AEORSTUW OUTSWEAR
OUTWEARS
AEORSTVY OVERSTAY
AEORSUVW WAVEROUS
AEORSVWY OVERSWAY
AEORTUWY OUTWEARY
AEORTVXY VEXATORY
AEPPPSSU PAPPUSES
AEPPRRST STRAPPER
TRAPPERS
AEPPRRSW WRAPPERS
AEPPRSSU UPSPEARS
AEPPRSSW SWAPPERS
AEPQRSTU PARQUETS
AEPRRRSS SPARRERS
AEPRRSSY RESPRAYS
SPRAYERS
AEPRRSTU PARTURES
RAPTURES
AEPRSSST SPARSEST
TRESPASS
AEPRSSTT SPATTERS
TAPSTERS
AEPRSSTU PASTURES
UPSTARES
AEPRSSTY YAPSTERS
AEPRSTTU STUPRATE
AEPRSTTY TAPESTRY
AEPRSTUX SUPERTAX
AEPRTUVY PYRUVATE
AEPSSSSU PASSUSES
AEQRRSSU SQUARERS
AEQRRSTU QUARTERS
AEQRSSTU SQUAREST
AEQRSTTU QUARTETS
SQUATTER
AEQRSTUZ QUARTZES
AEQRTTTU QUARTETT
AERRSSSU ASSURERS
AERRSSTT RESTARTS
STARTERS
AERRSSTU SERRATUS
AERRSSTY STRAYERS
AERRSTUY TREASURY
AERSSSST STRASSES
AERSSSTY SATYRESS
AERSSTTU STATURES
AERSSTTW SWATTERS
AERSSTUX SURTAXES
AERSSTXY STYRAXES
AERSTTUV VETTURAS
AERSTTVY TRAVESTY
AERTTUXY TEXTUARY
AESSSTTU STATUSES
AESSTTTU ASTUTEST
STATUTES
AFFFFINN NIFFNAFF
AFFFGILN FLAFFING
AFFGGINR GRAFFING
AFFGGINS GAFFINGS
AFFGHIRT AFFRIGHT
AFFGIINP PIAFFING
AFFGIINX AFFIXING
AFFGIIRT GRAFFITI
AFFGILMN MAFFLING
AFFGILNR RAFFLING
AFFGILNW WAFFLING
AFFGIMRS MISGRAFF
AFFGINNY NYAFFING
AFFGINQU QUAFFING
AFFGINST STAFFING
AFFGINUW WAUFFING
AFFGIORT GRAFFITO
AFFHILNS HAFFLINS
AFFHILST FLATFISH
AFFHILTU FAITHFUL
AFFIINTY AFFINITY
AFFILMNS MAFFLINS
AFFILSUX SUFFIXAL
AFFIMSST MASTIFFS
AFFINORR FORFAIRN
AFFINOSU AFFUSION
AFFINRSU FUNFAIRS
RUFFIANS
AFFIORRS FORFAIRS
AFFIPSTT TIPSTAFF
AFFIRRSU FURFAIRS
AFFLLOOT FOOTFALL
AFFLLTUU FAULTFUL
AFFLOOOT FOALFOOT
AFFLORTU FORFAULT
AFFLRRUU FURFURAL
AFFNORSS SAFFRONS
AFFNORST AFFRONTS
AFFNORSY SAFFRONY
AFFNRRUU FURFURAN
AFGGGILN FLAGGING
AFGGGINR FRAGGING
AFGGGINS FAGGINGS
AFGGILNN FANGLING
FLANGING
AFGGINOR FORAGING
AFGGINOT FAGOTING
AFGGINRT GRAFTING

AFGHIINT FAITHING
AFGHILLN HALFLING
AFGHILNS FLASHING
AFGHILNT FANLIGHT
AFGHILPS FLAGSHIP
AFGHINRT FARTHING
AFGHINRW WHARFING
AFGHINST SHAFTING
AFGHIOST GOATFISH
AFGHLLUU LAUGHFUL
AFGHLNSU FLASHGUN
AFGHLSTU FLAUGHTS
GHASTFUL
AFGHRSTU FRAUGHTS
AFGIILLN FLAILING
AFGIILNS FAILINGS
AFGIIMNN INFAMING
AFGIINNT FAINTING
AFGIINRS FAIRINGS
FRAISING
AFGIINTX FIXATING
AFGIKLNN FANKLING
FLANKING
AFGIKNNR FRANKING
AFGIKORT KOFTGARI
AFGILLNS FALLINGS
AFGILLNT FLATLING
AFGILMMN FLAMMING
AFGILMNO FLAMINGO
AFGILNOS LOAFINGS
AFGILNOT FLOATING
AFGILNPP FLAPPING
AFGILNST FATLINGS
AFGILNTT FLATTING
AFGILNTU FAULTING
AFGILORW GAIRFOWL
AFGILSSY GLASSIFY
AFGIMNOS FOAMINGS
AFGIMNRS FARMINGS
FRAMINGS
AFGIMNTU FUMIGANT
AFGIMORS GASIFORM
AFGIMRST MISGRAFT
AFGINNNS FANNINGS
AFGINNSW FAWNINGS
AFGINORV FAVORING
AFGINORY FORAYING
AFGINPPR FRAPPING
AFGINRST INGRAFTS
STRAFING
AFGINRSW SWARFING
AFGINRSY FRAYINGS
AFGINRTU FIGURANT
AFGINSST FASTINGS
AFGINSTW WAFTINGS
AFGINSUY SANGUIFY
AFGKNOPS PAKFONGS
AFGKORST KOFTGARS
AFGLLNOT FLATLONG
AFGLLRUU FULGURAL
AFGLLRUY FRUGALLY
AFGLLSSU GLASSFUL
AFGLLSTU GASTFULL
AFGLNNOO GONFALON
AFGLNORU GROANFUL
AFGLNOUW WAGONFUL
AFGNNNOO GONFANON
AFGOORTZ ZOOGRAFT
AFHIILRS FRAILISH
AFHIILSS SAILFISH
AFHIIMST MISFAITH
AFHIINST FAINTISH
AFHIKSUY KUFIYAHS
AFHILLNS HALFLINS
AFHILLSW WALLFISH
AFHILLSY FLASHILY
AFHILSST SALTFISH
AFHILSTT FLATTISH
AFHILSTW HALFWITS
AFHIMNST MANSHIFT
AFHIMNSU HAFNIUMS
AFHINOSS FASHIONS
AFHINSTU UNFAITHS
AFHIOSSU FASHIOUS
AFHIRSST STARFISH
AFHKLNTU THANKFUL
AFHKORSX FOXSHARK
AFHKORSY HAYFORKS
AFHKRSTU FUTHARKS
AFHLLOTU LOATHFUL
AFHLOSTU OUTFLASH
AFHLOSTY HAYLOFTS
AFHLRTUW WRATHFUL
AFHNOOST FANTOOSH
AFHOOPST POOFTAHS
AFHOOPTT FOOTPATH
AFHOPSTU POUFTAHS
AFIIKMRS FAKIRISM
AFIILLLY FILIALLY
AFIILLNU UNFILIAL
AFIILMMS FAMILISM
AFIILMNS FINALISM
AFIILNRU UNIFILAR
AFIILNST FINALIST
AFIILNTY FINALITY
AFIILORS AIRFOILS
AFIILRST AIRLIFTS
AFIIMRSY FAIRYISM
AFIINNOS SAINFOIN
SINFONIA
AFIINOTX FIXATION
AFIIORRT TRIFORIA
AFIKLNNR FRANKLIN
AFIKLORT FORKTAIL
AFIKLOST FLOKATIS
AFIKNRST RATFINKS
AFIKRSTY KARSTIFY
AFILLLOT FLOTILLA
AFILLMSS MISFALLS
AFILLNPU PLAINFUL
AFILLPST PITFALLS
AFILLPSU PAILFULS
AFILLSUV VIALFULS
AFILLTUY FAULTILY
AFILMNOR FORMALIN
INFORMAL
AFILMOPR PALIFORM
AFILMSSS FALSISMS
AFILNORT FLATIRON
INFLATOR
AFILNPPT FLIPPANT
AFILNRUY UNFAIRLY
AFILNSTU FLUTINAS
INFLATUS
AFILORSW AIRFLOWS
AFILORTY FILATORY
AFILRSTU FISTULAR
AFILSSTU FISTULAS
AFILSTTU FLAUTIST
AFIMMNOR MANIFORM
AFIMMORR RAMIFORM
AFIMNOPR NAPIFORM
AFIMNORR RANIFORM
AFIMNORT NATIFORM
AFIMNOSU INFAMOUS
AFIMORRU AURIFORM
AFIMORRV VARIFORM
AFIMORSV VASIFORM
AFINNORS FRANIONS
AFINNOTU FOUNTAIN
AFINNRTY INFANTRY
AFINOPSY SAPONIFY
AFINQTUY QUANTIFY
AFINRSTX TRANSFIX
AFINSSTU FAUNISTS
FUSTIANS
AFIORSTU FAITOURS
AFIORSTZ SFORZATI
AFIRSTTY STRATIFY
AFISSSTT SITFASTS
AFKLNOTU OUTFLANK
AFKLNPRU PRANKFUL
AFKLNSTU TANKFULS
AFKLOSWY FOLKWAYS
AFKMOORT FOOTMARK
AFLLLORY FLORALLY
AFLLLUWY LAWFULLY
AFLLMNUY MANFULLY
AFLLMORY FORMALLY
AFLLMPSU PALMFULS
AFLLNOSW SNOWFALL
AFLLNUUW UNLAWFUL
AFLLOSTU FALLOUTS
OUTFALLS
AFLLRTUY ARTFULLY
AFLLSTUW WASTFULL
AFLMNORU UNFORMAL
AFLMOPRT PLATFORM
AFLMORRU FORMULAR
AFLMORSU FORMULAS
AFLMORSW WOLFRAMS
AFLMORTU FOULMART
AFLMORTW FLATWORM
AFLMOSST FLOTSAMS
AFLMOSUY FAMOUSLY
AFLNOPRU APRONFUL
AFLNORST FRONTALS
AFLNRTUU UNARTFUL
AFLNTUUV VAUNTFUL
AFLNTUUY UNFAULTY
AFLOOSTW WOOLFATS
AFLORSSU FUSAROLS
AFLORSUV FLAVOURS
AFLOSTUU FLATUOUS
AFLPRSTY FLYTRAPS
AFLRSTTU STARTFUL
AFLRSTUY TRAYFULS
AFMNNORT FRONTMAN
AFMNORST FORMANTS
AFMOOPRR PROFORMA
AFMORSTU FOUMARTS
AFMORTUY FUMATORY
AFMOSSTU SFUMATOS
AFNORRSW FORWARNS
AFOOPPRS APPROOFS
AFOOPRRT RATPROOF
AFOORSTZ FORZATOS
SFORZATO
AFOOSTWY FOOTWAYS
AFORSTTW FORSWATT
AFOSSTUU FASTUOUS
AGGGGILN GAGGLING
AGGGHILN HAGGLING
AGGGHINS SHAGGING
AGGGILNN GANGLING
AGGGILNR GARGLING
RAGGLING
AGGGILNS LAGGINGS
SLAGGING
AGGGILNW WAGGLING
AGGGINNS GANGINGS
SNAGGING
AGGGINRS RAGGINGS
AGGGINSS SAGGINGS
AGGGINST STAGGING
TAGGINGS
AGGGINSU GAUGINGS
AGGGINSW SWAGGING
AGGGIYZZ ZIGZAGGY
AGGHIILS GHILGAIS
AGGHILNU LAUGHING
AGGHILST GASLIGHT
AGGHILSY SHAGGILY
AGGHIMNO HOMAGING
AGGHIMNS GINGHAMS
AGGHINNP PHANGING
AGGHINNS GNASHING
HANGINGS
AGGHINNW WHANGING
AGGHINPR GRAPHING
AGGHINST GHASTING
AGGHINUW WAUGHING
AGGIIJJS JIGAJIGS
AGGIILNN ALIGNING
AGGIILNR GLAIRING
AGGIILNS SILAGING
AGGIILNT LIGATING
TAIGLING
AGGIILNV GINGIVAL
AGGIIMNS IMAGINGS
AGGIINNR GRAINING
AGGIINNS AGNISING
GAININGS
AGGIINNZ AGNIZING
AGGIINRS AGRISING
AGGIINRZ AGRIZING
AGGIINST AGISTING
AGGIINSU AGUISING
AGGIINUZ AGUIZING
AGGIJJOS JIGAJOGS
AGGIJLNN JANGLING
AGGILLNS GINGALLS
AGGILLNU ULLAGING
AGGILLNY GALLYING
AGGILMNN MANGLING
AGGILMNO GLOAMING
AGGILMNR MALGRING
AGGILMNU GLAUMING
AGGILNNO GANGLION
AGGILNNR GNARLING
AGGILNNS ANGLINGS
SLANGING
AGGILNNT GNATLING
TANGLING
AGGILNNW WANGLING
AGGILNOP GALOPING
AGGILNOT GLOATING
GOATLING
AGGILNPU PLAGUING
AGGILNPY GAPINGLY

AGGILNRY	GRAYLING
	RAGINGLY
AGGILNSS	GLASSING
AGGILNSZ	GLAZINGS
AGGIMNRU	MAUGRING
AGGINNOR	GROANING
AGGINNOT	TANGOING
AGGINNOW	WAGONING
AGGINNPR	PRANGING
AGGINNPS	SPANGING
AGGINNRR	GNARRING
AGGINNRT	GRANTING
AGGINNRU	RAUNGING
AGGINNST	STANGING
AGGINNTU	GAUNTING
AGGINNTW	TWANGING
AGGINOVY	VOYAGING
AGGINPRS	GRASPING
	SPARGING
AGGINPSS	GASPINGS
AGGINPUZ	UPGAZING
AGGINRSS	GRASSING
	SIRGANGS
AGGINRST	GRATINGS
AGGINRSU	SUGARING
AGGINRSV	GRAVINGS
AGGINRSZ	GRAZINGS
AGGINRTY	GYRATING
AGGINRUU	AUGURING
AGGINRYZ	AGRYZING
AGGINSSS	GASSINGS
AGGINSST	STAGINGS
AGGIRTUZ	ZIGGURAT
AGGKLNNU	ANGKLUNG
AGGLLLOY	LOLLYGAG
AGGLLOOY	ALGOLOGY
AGGLMOOR	LOGOGRAM
AGGLOORY	AGROLOGY
AGGLRSTY	STRAGGLY
AGGMORRS	GROGRAMS
AGGNUWZZ	ZUGZWANG
AGHHIILT	HIGHTAIL
AGHHINSS	SHASHING
AGHHISWY	HIGHWAYS
AGHHLOTU	ALTHOUGH
AGHIILNN	INHALING
AGHIINNS	HAININGS
AGHIIPRR	HAIRGRIP
AGHIIRTT	AIRTIGHT
AGHIJNRT	NIGHTJAR
AGHIKNNS	SHANKING
AGHIKNNT	THANKING
AGHIKNRS	SHARKING
AGHIKNSS	SHAKINGS
AGHIKNSW	HAWKINGS
AGHILLNO	HALLOING
AGHILLNS	HALLINGS
AGHILLNT	ALLNIGHT
AGHILMTY	ALMIGHTY
AGHILNOO	HOOLIGAN
AGHILNOS	SHOALING
AGHILNOT	LOATHING
AGHILNPS	PLASHING
AGHILNRS	HARLINGS
	RINGHALS
AGHILNRY	NARGHILY
AGHILNSS	HASSLING
	LASHINGS
	SLANGISH
	SLASHING
AGHILNST	HALTINGS
	LATHINGS
AGHILNSU	LANGUISH
AGHILNSW	SHAWLING
	WHALINGS
AGHILRSY	GARISHLY
AGHILRTY	GRAITHLY
AGHILSUY	AGUISHLY
AGHIMMNS	SHAMMING
AGHIMMNW	WHAMMING
AGHIMNSS	MASHINGS
	SMASHING
AGHIMNTY	THINGAMY
AGHIMPRU	GRAPHIUM
AGHINNOS	NIHONGAS
AGHINNSS	SNASHING
AGHINNST	TANGHINS
AGHINNTU	HAUNTING
AGHINNTY	ANYTHING
AGHINOST	HOASTING
AGHINPPW	WHAPPING
AGHINPPY	HAPPYING
AGHINPRS	HARPINGS
	PHRASING
	SHARPING
AGHINPSS	SHAPINGS
AGHINPSW	PSHAWING
AGHINQSU	QUASHING
AGHINRRU	HURRAING
AGHINRRY	HARRYING
AGHINRSS	SHARINGS
AGHINRST	TRASHING
AGHINRTW	THRAWING
	WRATHING
AGHINSST	HASTINGS
	STASHING
AGHINSSV	SHAVINGS
AGHINSSW	SWASHING
	WASHINGS
AGHINSTT	HATTINGS
AGHINSTW	SWATHING
	THAWINGS
AGHINUZZ	HUZZAING
AGHIPRRT	TRIGRAPH
AGHIRSTT	STRAIGHT
AGHISSTW	SIGHTSAW
AGHKOSSW	GOSHAWKS
AGHLLMPU	GALLUMPH
AGHLMOOR	HOLOGRAM
AGHLMPSU	GALUMPHS
AGHLNOSU	SHOGUNAL
AGHLNSUY	NYLGHAUS
AGHLOOSS	GASOHOLS
AGHMMOOY	HOMOGAMY
AGHMNPSU	SPHAGNUM
AGHMOOPY	OMOPHAGY
AGHMOPRY	MYOGRAPH
AGHNNSTU	SHANTUNG
AGHNOORS	SHAGROON
AGHNOSTU	HANGOUTS
	TOHUNGAS
AGHNPRSY	SYNGRAPH
AGHNTTUU	UNTAUGHT
AGHOOPYZ	ZOOPHAGY
AGHOPSSW	SWAGSHOP
AGHORSTW	WARTHOGS
AGHRSTTU	STRAUGHT
AGIIILNS	LIAISING
AGIIINNS	INSIGNIA
AGIIKLNS	SKAILING
AGIIKNRT	TRAIKING
AGIILLOV	VILLAGIO
	VILLIAGO
AGIILMNP	IMPALING
AGIILMNS	MAILINGS
	MISALIGN
AGIILMNU	MIAULING
AGIILNNP	PLAINING
AGIILNNS	NAILINGS
	SNAILING
AGIILNNU	INGUINAL
AGIILNNY	INLAYING
AGIILNOR	ORIGINAL
AGIILNOT	INTAGLIO
	LIGATION
	TAGLIONI
AGIILNOX	GLOXINIA
AGIILNPT	PLAITING
AGIILNQU	QUAILING
AGIILNRS	GLAIRINS
	RAILINGS
AGIILNRT	RINGTAIL
	TRAILING
AGIILNRV	VIRGINAL
AGIILNSS	AISLINGS
	SAILINGS
AGIILNST	TAILINGS
AGIILNSW	WAILINGS
AGIILNTT	LITIGANT
AGIILNTV	VIGILANT
AGIILORU	OLIGURIA
AGIILOSV	VILIAGOS
AGIILPST	PIGTAILS
AGIILTVY	VAGILITY
AGIIMMNS	MAIMINGS
AGIIMMSS	IMAGISMS
AGIIMNNR	INARMING
AGIIMNOW	MIAOWING
AGIIMNPV	IMPAVING
AGIIMNSS	AMISSING
AGIIMNST	GIANTISM
AGIIMNTT	MITIGANT
AGIIMORS	ORIGAMIS
AGIIMSST	IMAGISTS
AGIINNPS	SPAINING
AGIINNPT	PAINTING
AGIINNRS	INGRAINS
AGIINNRT	TRAINING
AGIINNRV	RAVINING
AGIINNST	SAINTING
	SATINING
	STAINING
AGIINNSW	SWAINING
AGIINNTT	TAINTING
AGIINOPT	OPIATING
AGIINORS	SIGNORIA
AGIINORT	RIGATONI
AGIINPRS	ASPIRING
	PAIRINGS
	PRAISING
AGIINPRT	PIRATING
AGIINRRV	ARRIVING
AGIINRSS	RAISINGS
AGIINRTT	ATTIRING
AGIINSSZ	ASSIZING
AGIINSTV	VISTAING
AGIINSTW	WAITINGS
AGIISSTV	VISAGIST
AGIJMNOR	MAJORING
AGIJNNSU	JAUNSING
AGIJNNTT	TJANTING
AGIJNNTU	JAUNTING
AGIJNRRS	JARRINGS
AGIKKNNS	SKANKING
AGIKLMOR	KILOGRAM
AGIKLNNP	PLANKING
AGIKLNNR	RANKLING
AGIKLNOS	OAKLINGS
AGIKLNST	SKLATING
	STALKING
	TALKINGS
AGIKLNSW	WALKINGS
AGIKLNTY	TAKINGLY
AGIKLNUW	WAULKING
AGIKLORY	KILOGRAY
AGIKMNNU	UNMAKING
AGIKMNPU	UPMAKING
AGIKMNRS	MARKINGS
AGIKNNPP	KNAPPING
AGIKNNPR	PRANKING
AGIKNNPS	SPANKING
AGIKNNRR	KNARRING
AGIKNNRS	RANKINGS
AGIKNNRU	UNRAKING
AGIKNNST	TANKINGS
AGIKNNSW	SWANKING
AGIKNOSS	SOAKINGS
AGIKNOST	GOATSKIN
AGIKNOSY	KAYOINGS
AGIKNPRS	PARKINGS
	SPARKING
AGIKNPTU	UPTAKING
AGIKNQSU	QUAKINGS
AGIKNRSS	SARKINGS
AGIKNRST	KARTINGS
	STARKING
AGIKNSST	SKATINGS
	TASKINGS
AGILLLNS	LALLINGS
AGILLMNS	SMALLING
AGILLMNU	MULLIGAN
AGILLMNY	MALIGNLY
AGILLMSU	GALLIUMS
AGILLNOW	ALLOWING
AGILLNOY	ALLOYING
AGILLNPS	SPALLING
AGILLNRU	ALLURING
	LINGULAR
AGILLNRY	NARGILLY
	RALLYING
AGILLNST	STALLING
AGILLNSU	LINGULAS
AGILLNSW	WALLINGS
AGILLNSY	SALLYING
	SIGNALLY
	SLANGILY
AGILLNTY	TALLYING
AGILLOOR	GILLAROO
AGILLOPT	GALLIPOT
AGILLORS	GORILLAS
AGILLOST	GALLIOTS
AGILLPRY	PLAYGIRL
AGILLPUY	PLAGUILY
AGILLSSU	LUGSAILS
AGILLSSY	GLASSILY
AGILMMNS	LAMMINGS
	SLAMMING
	SMALMING
AGILMNNT	MANTLING
AGILMNPS	LAMPINGS

SAMPLING
AGILMNQU QUALMING
AGILMNRS MARLINGS
AGILMNST MALTINGS
AGILMOPR LIPOGRAM
AGILMORS ALGORISM
AGILMPSU PLAGIUMS
AGILNNNP PLANNING
AGILNNOP PANGOLIN
AGILNNOS LOANINGS
AGILNNPT PLANTING
AGILNNRS SNARLING
AGILNNSS LINSANGS
AGILNNST SLANTING
TANLINGS
AGILNNUW UNLAWING
AGILNNUY UNGAINLY
UNLAYING
AGILNOOO OOGONIAL
AGILNOOS ISOGONAL
AGILNOPR PAROLING
AGILNOPS GALOPINS
AGILNOPT PLOATING
AGILNORS RANGOLIS
AGILNORT TRIGONAL
AGILNOSS GLOSSINA
LASSOING
AGILNOST ANTILOGS
SALTOING
AGILNOTY ANTILOGY
AGILNPPP PLAPPING
AGILNPPS LAPPINGS
SAPPLING
SLAPPING
AGILNPPY APPLYING
AGILNPRS SPARLING
SPRINGAL
AGILNPSS SAPLINGS
AGILNPST PLATINGS
SPALTING
STAPLING
AGILNPSW LAPWINGS
SPAWLING
AGILNPSY PALSYING
SPLAYING
AGILNPTT PLATTING
AGILNPUY UPLAYING
AGILNRST RATLINGS
STARLING
AGILNRSU SINGULAR
AGILNRSW WARLINGS
WARSLING
AGILNRTT RATTLING
AGILNRTW TRAWLING
AGILNRVY RAVINGLY
AGILNRWW WRAWLING
AGILNRWX WRAXLING
AGILNSST ANGLISTS
LASTINGS
SALTINGS
SLATINGS
AGILNSSV SALVINGS
AGILNSSW SWALINGS
AGILNSTT SLATTING
AGILNSTU SALUTING
AGILNSUV AVULSING
AGILNSUW WAULINGS
AGILNSVY SAVINGLY
AGILNSWW WAWLINGS
AGILNSWY SWAYLING
AGILNTTT TATTLING
AGILNTTW WATTLING
AGILNTUV VAULTING
AGILNTUX LUXATING
AGILNTWZ WALTZING
AGILOORS GLORIOSA
AGILOOXY AXIOLOGY
AGILOPST GALIPOTS
AGILORSS GIRASOLS
AGILOSST SALIGOTS
AGILSYYZ SYZYGIAL
AGIMMNRS SMARMING
AGIMMNRT TRAMMING
AGIMMOSY MISOGAMY
AGIMNNOS MASONING
AGIMNNOW WOMANING
AGIMNNRU MANURING
UNARMING
AGIMNNTU UNTAMING
AGIMNOOV AMOOVING
AGIMNORS ORGANISM
ROAMINGS
AGIMNORU ORIGANUM
AGIMNORY AGRIMONY
AGIMNOSV VAMOSING
AGIMNPPS MAPPINGS
AGIMNPRS RAMPINGS
AGIMNPRT TRAMPING
AGIMNPSS SPASMING
AGIMNPST STAMPING
TAMPINGS
AGIMNPSV VAMPINGS
AGIMNPSW SWAMPING
AGIMNRRY MARRYING
AGIMNRST MIGRANTS
SMARTING
AGIMNRSW SWARMING
WARMINGS
AGIMNRSY MYRINGAS
AGIMNRTU MATURING
AGIMNSSU ASSUMING
AGIMNSTT MATTINGS
AGIMNTTU MUTATING
AGIMORRT MIGRATOR
AGIMORSS ISOGRAMS
AGIMORSU GOURAMIS
AGIMQRUY QUAGMIRY
AGIMRRST TRIGRAMS
AGINNNNY NANNYING
AGINNNOY ANNOYING
AGINNNPS PANNINGS
SPANNING
AGINNNST TANNINGS
AGINNNSV VANNINGS
AGINNNSW SWANNING
AGINNOOP NAPOOING
AGINNOPR APRONING
AGINNOPT POIGNANT
AGINNORT IGNORANT
AGINNOST ASTONING
AGINNOTT NOTATING
AGINNPPS SNAPPING
AGINNPRW PRAWNING
AGINNPST PANTINGS
AGINNPSW SPAWNING
WINGSPAN
AGINNPUY UNPAYING
AGINNQTU QUANTING
AGINNRRS SNARRING
AGINNRSS SNARINGS
AGINNRST RANTINGS
STARNING
AGINNRSW WARNINGS
AGINNRTT TRANTING
AGINNRTU NATURING
AGINNRTY TRAYNING
TYRANING
AGINNSTU SAUNTING
UNSATING
AGINNSTW WANTINGS
AGINNSTY STAYNING
AGINNSUY UNSAYING
AGINNSWY YAWNINGS
AGINNTTU ATTUNING
NUTATING
TAUNTING
AGINNTUV VAUNTING
AGINNTUX UNTAXING
AGINNVVY NAVVYING
AGINOORT ROGATION
AGINOPPS APPOSING
AGINOPQU OPAQUING
AGINOPRV VAPORING
AGINORRS GARRISON
ROARINGS
AGINORRW ARROWING
AGINORSS ASSIGNOR
SOARINGS
AGINORST ORGANIST
ROASTING
AGINORSU AROUSING
AGINORSV SAVORING
AGINORTT ROTATING
TROATING
AGINORTV GRAVITON
AGINORTY GYRATION
ORGANITY
AGINOSST AGONISTS
AGINOSSU SAGOUINS
AGINOSTT TANGOIST
TOASTING
AGINPPRS RAPPINGS
AGINPPRT TRAPPING
AGINPPRW WRAPPING
AGINPPST STAPPING
TAPPINGS
AGINPPSW SWAPPING
AGINPPTU PUPATING
AGINPPUY APPUYING
AGINPRRS SPARRING
AGINPRRY PARRYING
AGINPRSS PARSINGS
RASPINGS
AGINPRST PARTINGS
PRATINGS
AGINPRSW WARPINGS
AGINPRSY PRAYINGS
SPRAYING
AGINPRTT PRATTING
AGINPRTU UPRATING
AGINPRTY PARTYING
AGINPSSS PASSINGS
AGINPSST PASTINGS
AGINPSSU PAUSINGS
AGINPSTT SPATTING
AGINQRSU SQUARING
AGINRRST STARRING
TARRINGS
AGINRRTY TARRYING
AGINRSST GASTRINS
STARINGS
AGINRSSU ASSURING
AGINRSSY SYRINGAS
AGINRSTT RATTINGS
STARTING
AGINRSTV STARVING
AGINRSTW STRAWING
WRASTING
AGINRSTY STRAYING
AGINRSVW SWARVING
AGINRSVY VARYINGS
AGINRSWY RINGWAYS
AGINSSTT TASTINGS
AGINSSTW WASTINGS
AGINSSWY SWAYINGS
AGINSTTT TATTINGS
AGINSTTW SWATTING
AGINSVVY SAVVYING
AGINSWWX WAXWINGS
AGIOORSU ORAGIOUS
AGIOORSZ GRAZIOSO
AGIOORTU AUTOGIRO
AGIOPPRT AGITPROP
AGIOPRUY UROPYGIA
AGIORRTT GRATTOIR
AGIORSST AGISTORS
ORGIASTS
AGIRSSTU SASTRUGI
AGIRSTUZ ZASTRUGI
AGIRTTUY GRATUITY
AGJLRSUU JUGULARS
AGJNOORS JARGOONS
AGJNOPST JOGPANTS
AGKLNNOS ANKLONGS
AGKLNNSU ANKLUNGS
AGKMMORY KYMOGRAM
AGKMNOPS KAMPONGS
AGKNOPST PAKTONGS
AGKORRSW RAGWORKS
AGLLLNOW LONGWALL
AGLLMOPW GLOWLAMP
AGLLNOOS GALLOONS
AGLLNSTU GALLNUTS
NUTGALLS
AGLLRUVY VULGARLY
AGLMOOTY ATMOLOGY
AGLMOPSY POLYGAMS
AGLMOPYY POLYGAMY
AGLMORSU GLAMOURS
AGLNORSU LANGUORS
AGLNOSST GLASNOST
AGLNOSWY LONGWAYS
AGLNPSUY GUNPLAYS
AGLNRUUV UNVULGAR
AGLNSSSU SUNGLASS
AGLNSTUY YGLAUNST
AGLOOPST GOALPOST
AGLOOTUY AUTOLOGY
AGLOPRSS LOPGRASS
AGLORSSY GLOSSARY
AGLPSSSY SPYGLASS
AGLRTTUU GUTTURAL
AGLSTUUY AUGUSTLY
AGMMNOOR MONOGRAM
NOMOGRAM
AGMMNOOY MONOGAMY
AGMMOORT TOMOGRAM
AGMMORSY MYOGRAMS
AGMNNOSW GOWNSMAN
AGMNOOPR PORNOMAG

AGMNOORS	SONOGRAM
AGMNOORY	AGRONOMY
AGMNORST	ANGSTROM
AGMNSSTU	MUSTANGS
AGMNSSTY	GYMNASTS
	SYNTAGMS
AGMOOOSU	OOGAMOUS
AGMOOPRY	POROGAMY
AGMOPRRS	PROGRAMS
AGMOPRSU	GOPURAMS
AGMORRSW	RAGWORMS
AGMRSSSU	GRASSUMS
AGNNNOOS	NONAGONS
AGNNOOPT	POONTANG
AGNNOQTU	QUANTONG
AGNORRST	GRANTORS
AGNORTUY	NUGATORY
AGNPPRSU	UPSPRANG
AGOORRTY	ROGATORY
AGOORTUY	AUTOGYRO
AGOPPSST	STOPGAPS
AGORRSST	GROSSART
	ROTGRASS
AGORRSTW	RAGWORTS
AGORRTYY	GYRATORY
AGORSTTY	GYROSTAT
AHHIKLSS	SHASHLIK
AHHILNPT	PHTHALIN
AHHILOST	HAILSHOT
AHHILPSW	WHIPLASH
AHHIMMSS	MISHMASH
AHHIMNSU	HAHNIUMS
AHHIPRSS	SHARPISH
AHHISSTT	SHITTAHS
AHHKRSTU	KASHRUTH
AHHLMRTY	RHYTHMAL
AHHLNOPT	NAPHTHOL
AHHMPRRU	HARRUMPH
AHHNORTW	HAWTHORN
AHHOPRSS	SHOPHARS
AHHOPSTU	APHTHOUS
AHHPSTUZ	HUTZPAHS
AHIIKRSS	SHIKARIS
AHIILNPS	PLAINISH
AHIILOST	HALIOTIS
AHIILPTW	WHIPTAIL
AHIILRTY	HILARITY
AHIIMNOT	HIMATION
AHIIMNST	ISTHMIAN
	THIAMINS
AHIIMSSS	SASHIMIS
AHIINOPT	PHOTINIA
AHIINPRS	HAIRPINS
AHIINPST	ANTISHIP
AHIINSST	SAINTISH
AHIINSSW	SWAINISH
AHIINSTU	HUITAINS
AHIIOPST	HOSPITIA
AHIIPRSS	AIRSHIPS
AHIKLNRS	RINKHALS
AHIKLRSY	RAKISHLY
AHIKMNSS	KHAMSINS
AHIKMRSS	KASHMIRS
AHIKNPRS	PRANKISH
AHIKPRSS	SPARKISH
AHILLMOU	HALLOUMI
AHILLMPS	PHALLISM
AHILLMSS	SMALLISH
AHILLMTU	THALLIUM
AHILLNOS	HALLIONS
AHILLNPS	PHALLINS
AHILLNRT	INTHRALL
AHILLNTW	WANTHILL
AHILLSTT	TALLITHS
AHILLSVY	LAVISHLY
AHILMMSS	MASHLIMS
AHILMNSS	MASHLINS
AHILMOPT	PHILAMOT
AHILMOST	HALIMOTS
AHILMQSU	QUALMISH
AHILNOPS	SIPHONAL
AHILNOPT	OLIPHANT
AHILNORT	HORNTAIL
AHILNRST	INTHRALS
AHILOPST	HOSPITAL
AHILOSTU	HALITOUS
AHILPPSS	SHIPLAPS
AHILPSSY	PHYSALIS
AHILRSTY	TRASHILY
AHILRTWY	WRATHILY
AHIMMNSU	HUMANISM
AHIMMORZ	MAHZORIM
AHIMMOSV	MOSHAVIM
AHIMNOST	HOISTMAN
AHIMNOSW	WOMANISH
AHIMNSTU	HUMANIST
AHIMNTUY	HUMANITY
AHIMOPRS	APHORISM
	MORPHIAS
AHIMOPST	OPSIMATH
AHIMPPSS	SAPPHISM
AHIMPRST	TRAMPISH
AHIMRSST	SMARTISH
	THRIMSAS
AHIMSTUZ	AZIMUTHS
AHIMSTVZ	MITZVAHS
AHINNNSY	NANNYISH
AHINNOPT	ANTIPHON
AHINNSTX	XANTHINS
AHINOPRU	OPHIURAN
AHINORST	TRAHISON
AHINOSST	ASTONISH
AHINOSTZ	HOATZINS
AHINPPSS	SNAPPISH
AHINPRST	TRANSHIP
AHINQSUV	VANQUISH
AHINRSTY	RHYTINAS
AHINSSTU	INHAUSTS
AHIOOPPT	PHOTOPIA
AHIOOSST	ATISHOOS
AHIOPRST	APHORIST
AHIOPRSU	OPHIURAS
AHIOPSXY	HYPOXIAS
AHIORSTV	TOVARISH
AHIORSUV	HAVIOURS
AHIOSTWY	HOISTWAY
AHIPPSST	SAPPHIST
AHIPRSST	HARPISTS
AHIPRSSW	WARSHIPS
AHIPSSWW	WHIPSAWS
AHIPSSWY	SHIPWAYS
AHIQRSSU	SQUARISH
AHIRRSST	STIRRAHS
AHIRSSTT	STARTISH
AHIRSSTW	TRISHAWS
AHISSSTU	SHIATSUS
AHISSTTW	WHATSITS
AHISSTUZ	SHIATZUS
AHISTTWW	WHITTAWS
AHKMORRS	MARKHORS
AHKMRSTU	MUKHTARS
AHKNOTUY	THANKYOU
AHKRSSTU	KASHRUTS
	TUSHKARS
AHLLNOOS	SHALLOON
AHLLNOSS	SHALLONS
AHLLNOSY	HALLYONS
AHLLNOUW	UNHALLOW
AHLLOPSS	SHALLOPS
AHLLOSST	SHALLOTS
AHLLOSSW	SHALLOWS
AHLLOSTU	THALLOUS
AHLLPRYY	PHYLLARY
AHLMMOPY	LYMPHOMA
AHLMMSSU	MASHLUMS
AHLMNOOR	HORMONAL
AHLMOOPS	OMPHALOS
AHLMOPTY	POLYMATH
AHLMSTYZ	SHMALTZY
AHLNNORT	LANTHORN
AHLNOPRS	ALPHORNS
AHLNORST	ALTHORNS
AHLOPSST	SLAPSHOT
AHLORRTY	HARLOTRY
AHLOSTUU	OUTHAULS
AHLRSTUY	LATHYRUS
AHLRTTWY	THWARTLY
AHMMMOST	MAMMOTHS
AHMMMSUU	HUMMAUMS
AHMNNSTU	HUNTSMAN
	MANHUNTS
AHMNOPST	PHANTOMS
AHMNOPTY	PHANTOMY
AHMOOPSS	SHAMPOOS
AHMOORSW	WASHROOM
AHMOOSSS	SAMSHOOS
AHMORRST	SHORTARM
AHMORRSU	MORRHUAS
AHMORSST	HARMOSTS
AHMORSTY	HARMOSTY
AHMORTTW	TAMWORTH
AHMOSTTW	MOSTWHAT
AHMPSTYY	SYMPATHY
AHMQSSUU	MUSQUASH
AHMRSSTY	THRYMSAS
AHNNSTYY	SYNANTHY
AHNOOPRS	HARPOONS
AHNOOPSU	APHONOUS
AHNOORRY	HONORARY
AHNOPPSW	PAWNSHOP
AHNOPPSY	PANSOPHY
AHNOPSST	SNAPSHOT
AHNORSSX	SAXHORNS
AHNORTWW	WANWORTH
AHNOSTTW	WHATNOTS
AHNOSTUX	XANTHOUS
AHNPPSUU	PUPUNHAS
AHOOPTYZ	ZOOPATHY
AHOOSSTY	SOOTHSAY
AHOOSTTW	SAWTOOTH
AHOPSSTW	WASHPOTS
AHOPSTTW	TOWPATHS
AHOPSTUW	SOUTHPAW
AHOSSTUW	WASHOUTS
AHOSSTUY	SOUTHSAY
AHRSTUWY	THRUWAYS
AIIILLVX	LIXIVIAL
AIIILMST	MILITIAS
AIIILNST	INITIALS
AIIILRVZ	VIZIRIAL
AIIIMRSS	SAIMIRIS
AIIIRSSS	SIRIASIS
AIIJKMOT	KOMITAJI
AIIJNRTX	JANITRIX
AIIKKSUY	SUKIYAKI
AIIKLLST	SILKTAIL
AIIKLNRR	LARRIKIN
AIIKMMSS	SKIMMIAS
AIIKMNNN	MANNIKIN
AIIKMNNS	MANIKINS
AIIKNNNP	PANNIKIN
AIIKORTY	YAKITORI
AIIKTTZZ	TZATZIKI
AIILLLMT	MILLTAIL
AIILLLUV	ILLUVIAL
AIILLMRY	MILLIARY
AIILLNNV	VANILLIN
AIILLNOP	POLLINIA
AIILLNOT	ILLATION
AIILLNSV	VILLAINS
AIILLNVY	VILLAINY
AIILLPRS	SLIPRAIL
	SPIRILLA
AIILLQSU	QUILLAIS
AIILLWWW	WILLIWAW
AIILMNOS	MONILIAS
AIILMNOT	LIMATION
	MILTONIA
AIILMNPS	ALPINISM
AIILMNPT	PALMITIN
AIILMNTT	MILITANT
AIILMPUV	IMPLUVIA
AIILMRST	MISTRIAL
	TRIALISM
AIILMRTY	LIMITARY
	MILITARY
AIILMSTV	VITALISM
AIILNOPV	PAVILION
AIILNOSS	LIAISONS
AIILNOSV	VISIONAL
AIILNPST	ALPINIST
	PINTAILS
	TAILSPIN
AIILNSTY	SALINITY
AIILOPPS	PAPILIOS
AIILORSV	RAVIOLIS
AIILQSSU	SILIQUAS
AIILRSTT	TRIALIST
AIILRTTY	TRIALITY
AIILRTVY	RIVALITY
AIILSTTV	VITALIST
AIILTTVY	VITALITY
AIIMMNNY	MINYANIM
AIIMMNSS	ANIMISMS
AIIMMNSX	MAXIMINS
AIIMMNTY	IMMANITY
AIIMMSTX	MAXIMIST
AIIMNNOS	INSOMNIA
AIIMNPSS	PIANISMS
	SINAPISM
AIIMNPST	IMPAINTS
AIIMNPSX	PANMIXIS
AIIMNRST	MARTINIS
AIIMNSST	ANIMISTS
	SAINTISM
	SAMNITIS
AIIMNSTT	IMITANTS
	TITANISM
AIIMNSTV	NATIVISM
	VITAMINS

AIIMNTTU TITANIUM
AIIMOPSX APOMIXIS
AIIMORTT IMITATOR
TIMARIOT
AIIMOSST AMITOSIS
AIIMPPRS PRIAPISM
AIIMPRTY IMPARITY
AIIMRSST SIMITARS
AIIMRSTU TIRAMISU
AIIMRUVV VIVARIUM
AIIMSSTT MASTITIS
AIINNOPS PIANINOS
AIINNOSV INVASION
AIINNQTU QUINTAIN
AIINNSTY INSANITY
AIINOOSV AVOISION
AIINOPSS SINOPIAS
AIINORTT ANTIRIOT
TRITONIA
AIINOSTT NOTITIAS
AIINPRSS ASPIRINS
AIINPSST PIANISTS
AIINRRTT IRRITANT
AIINRSTV VITRAINS
AIINSTTV NATIVIST
VISITANT
AIINTTVY NATIVITY
AIIORRST SARTORII
AIIORSTT AORTITIS
AIIORSTV OVARITIS
AIIORTTV VITIATOR
AIIPRRST AIRSTRIP
AIIPRSST PIARISTS
AIIPRVVY VIVIPARY
AIIPSTTU PITUITAS
AIIRSSTT SATIRIST
AIISSSTY SYSSITIA
AIJKKNOU KINKAJOU
AIJLLOOR JILLAROO
AIJLLOVY JOVIALLY
AIJLNTUY JAUNTILY
AIJMORTY MAJORITY
AIJNOPPY POPINJAY
AIJNORST JANITORS
AIKKMOST KOMATIKS
AIKKNOTY KANTIKOY
AIKKRTUZ ZIKKURAT
AIKLLLMW WALKMILL
AIKLLMRR RILLMARK
AIKLLMUW WAUKMILL
AIKLMPSU LAMPUKIS
AIKLMPTU KALUMPIT
AIKLNPST LANTSKIP
AIKLOSUV SOUVLAKI
AIKLOTTW KILOWATT
AIKLRSTT TITLARKS
AIKLSSSY SKYSAILS
AIKMMNOO MAKIMONO
AIKMORSS KOMISSAR
AIKNNOOS NAINSOOK
AIKNNSSW SWANSKIN
AIKNORST SKIATRON
AIKNORTY KARYOTIN
AIKNOSTT STOTINKA
AIKRSSTY SATYRISK
AILLLNOO LINALOOL
AILLMMSY SMALMILY
AILLMNQU QUILLMAN
AILLMOST MAILLOTS
MISALLOT
AILLMOTY MOLALITY
AILLMPRY PRIMALLY
AILLMSSW SAWMILLS
AILLMUUV ALLUVIUM
AILLNNOS LANOLINS
AILLNOPP PAPILLON
AILLNOPS PAILLONS
AILLNOST STALLION
AILLNOSU ALLUSION
AILLNOUV ALLUVION
AILLNPTY PLIANTLY
AILLNSST INSTALLS
AILLOQTU TOQUILLA
AILLORSY SAILORLY
AILLORTT LITTORAL
TORTILLA
AILLOSTY LOYALIST
AILLPPRU PUPILLAR
AILLPPSU SUPPLIAL
AILLPRSY SPIRALLY
AILLPRTY PALTRILY
AILLPSUV PLUVIALS
AILLPSWY SPILLWAY
AILLQSSU SQUILLAS
AILLRSTY RALLYIST
AILLRTUY RITUALLY
AILLRTWY WILLYART
AILLSTWW WITWALLS
AILLSUVY VISUALLY
AILMMNOO MONOMIAL
AILMMNUU ALUMINUM
AILMMOOR MAILROOM
AILMMORS MORALISM
AILMMORT IMMORTAL
AILMMRSY SMARMILY
AILMMSSY MYALISMS
AILMMSTU SUMMITAL
AILMMSUU ALUMIUMS
AILMNNOS NOMINALS
AILMNNOT MANNITOL
AILMNNTU LUMINANT
AILMNOOP PALOMINO
AILMNOOR MONORAIL
AILMNOOS MOONSAIL
AILMNOOT MOTIONAL
AILMNOPR PROLAMIN
AILMNOPS LAMPIONS
AILMNOPT PILOTMAN
AILMNOPY PALIMONY
AILMNORT TORMINAL
AILMNOSS MALISONS
AILMNPSS PLASMINS
AILMNPST IMPLANTS
AILMNPTU PLATINUM
AILMNRSU MURLAINS
AILMNRUY LUMINARY
AILMNSTU SIMULANT
AILMOORS SAILROOM
AILMOORT MOTORAIL
MOTORIAL
AILMOPRX PROXIMAL
AILMORSS ORALISMS
SOLARISM
AILMORST MORALIST
AILMORSU SOLARIUM
AILMORSY ROYALISM
AILMORTY MOLARITY
MORALITY
AILMOSTU SOLATIUM
AILMOSTV VOLTAISM
AILMPPSY MISAPPLY
AILMPRSU PRIMULAS
AILMPSST PALMISTS
PSALMIST
AILMPSSY MISPLAYS
AILMPSTY PTYALISM
AILMRRSU RURALISM
AILMRSST MISTRALS
AILMRSSU SIMULARS
SURMISAL
AILMRSTU ALTRUISM
MURALIST
ULTRAISM
AILNNOOT NOTIONAL
AILNNOST ANTLIONS
AILNNOSU UNISONAL
AILNNOTU LUNATION
AILNNPSU PINNULAS
AILNNPTU UNPLIANT
AILNOOPT OPTIONAL
AILNOOST SOLATION
AILNOPRU UNIPOLAR
AILNOPSY POLYNIAS
AILNOPTY PONYTAIL
AILNOQSU AQUILONS
AILNORTZ TRIZONAL
AILNOSSS SASSOLIN
AILNOSUV AVULSION
AILNOSVY SYNOVIAL
AILNOTTV VOLITANT
AILNOTTY TONALITY
AILNOTUX LUXATION
AILNPPSY SNAPPILY
AILNPRSU PURSLAIN
AILNPRSW PRAWLINS
AILNPRUV PULVINAR
AILNPSTU NUPTIALS
PATULINS
UNPLAITS
AILNPSTY PTYALINS
AILNPSUU NAUPLIUS
AILNPTTU TULIPANT
AILNQRTU TRANQUIL
AILNQSTU QUINTALS
AILNQTUY QUAINTLY
AILNRSTT RATTLINS
AILNRSTU LUNARIST
AILNRTTU RUTILANT
AILNRUWY UNWARILY
AILNSSTU STUNSAIL
UNALISTS
AILNSTTU LUTANIST
AILNSTUU NAUTILUS
AILOOPRT TROOPIAL
AILOORRS SORORIAL
AILOORST ISOLATOR
AILOORSW WOORALIS
AILOORTV VIOLATOR
AILOPRRV PROVIRAL
AILOPRSU PLIOSAUR
AILOPRTU TROUPIAL
AILOPRTY POLARITY
AILOPRUY POLYURIA
AILOPSST APOSTILS
TOPSAILS
AILOPSTT TALIPOTS
AILORSST SOLARIST
AILORSTU SUTORIAL
AILORSTY ROYALIST
SOLITARY
AILORSUW WOURALIS
AILORTTU TUTORIAL
AILORTUV OUTRIVAL
AILOSSTU OUTSAILS
AILOTTTY TOTALITY
AILPPRUY PUPILARY
AILPPSSY PAYSLIPS
AILPRSSU UPRISALS
AILPRSTU STIPULAR
AILPSSWY SLIPWAYS
AILPSTUY PLAYSUIT
AILQSTTU QUITTALS
AILRRSTU RURALIST
AILRRSTY STARRILY
AILRRTUY RURALITY
AILRSSTU TRISULAS
AILRSSTY TRYSAILS
AILRSTTU ALTRUIST
TITULARS
ULTRAIST
AILRSTTY STRAITLY
AILRSUVV SURVIVAL
AILRTTUY TITULARY
AILSSTUW LAWSUITS
AIMMMNOU AMMONIUM
AIMMNORT MORTMAIN
AIMMNSTU MANUMITS
AIMMORSS AMORISMS
AIMMOSST ATOMISMS
SOMATISM
AIMMOSSU MIASMOUS
AIMMRRSY MISMARRY
AIMMRSUU MASURIUM
AIMNNOSS MANSIONS
ONANISMS
AIMNNOTU MOUNTAIN
AIMNNOTY ANTIMONY
ANTINOMY
AIMNNRTU RUMINANT
AIMNOOOZ ZOONOMIA
AIMNOOTY MYOTONIA
AIMNOPRS RAMPIONS
AIMNOPST MAINTOPS
TAMPIONS
AIMNOQRU MAROQUIN
AIMNORSU MAINOURS
AIMNORTY MINATORY
AIMNOSST STASIMON
AIMNOSTU MANITOUS
TINAMOUS
AIMNOTTU MUTATION
AIMNPRYY PAYNIMRY
AIMNPSTU SUMPITAN
AIMNRRSU MURRAINS
AIMNRSSU SURAMINS
URANISMS
AIMNRSTT TRANSMIT
AIMNRSTU NATRIUMS
NATURISM
AIMNRSTV VARMINTS
AIMNRSUU URANIUMS
AIMNSSTU TSUNAMIS
AIMNSSYZ ZANYISMS
AIMOPRSS PROSAISM
AIMOPRST ATROPISM
AIMOPSST IMPASTOS
AIMOPSSY SYMPOSIA
AIMORRST ARMORIST
AIMORRSU ORARIUMS
ROSARIUM

AIMORRUV VARIORUM
AIMORSST AMORISTS
AIMORSSU OSSARIUM
AIMOSSTT ATOMISTS
SOMATIST
AIMPPRUU PUPARIUM
AIMPPSST MAPPISTS
AIMPRSTY PARTYISM
AIMRSSST TSARISMS
AIMRSSTU MATSURIS
AIMRSSTY SYMITARS
AIMRSTTU STRIATUM
AIMRTTUY MATURITY
AIMSSSTT STATISMS
AINNNOST SANTONIN
AINNOOTT NOTATION
AINNOOTV NOVATION
AINNOOTZ ZONATION
AINNOPSS SAPONINS
AINNOSST ONANISTS
AINNOTTU NUTATION
AINNPSTU UNPAINTS
AINNQSTU QUINNATS
AINNRSTT INTRANTS
AINNRSTU INSURANT
AINNRSTY TYRANNIS
AINNSSTT INSTANTS
AINNSSTU UNSAINTS
AINNSTTY NYSTATIN
AINOOPTT POTATION
AINOORRS ORARIONS
AINOORST ORATIONS
AINOORTT ROTATION
AINOOSTT OSTINATO
AINOOSTV OVATIONS
AINOOTTV OTTAVINO
AINOPPRT PARPOINT
AINOPPST APPOINTS
AINOPPTU PUPATION
AINOPRSS PARISONS
AINOPRST ATROPINS
AINOPRTV PROVIANT
AINOPSSS PASSIONS
AINOPSTT POSTNATI
AINOPSTU OPUNTIAS
UTOPIANS
AINOPSTW SWAPTION
AINOQRSU NARQUOIS
AINORRSW WARRISON
AINORRTU URINATOR
AINORSST ARSONIST
AINORSSW WARISONS
AINORSTT STRONTIA
AINORSTU SUTORIAN
AINORSTX TRIAXONS
AINORTVY VANITORY
AINOSSSU SUASIONS
AINOSSTT STATIONS
AINOSSVY SYNOVIAS
AINOSTTU TITANOUS
AINPPRSS PARSNIPS
AINPPRTT TRIPPANT
AINPRSST SPIRANTS
SPRAINTS
AINPRSTU PURITANS
UPTRAINS
AINPSSSY SYNAPSIS
AINPSSTU PUISSANT
AINQTTUY QUANTITY
AINRSSTT STRAINTS
TRANSITS
AINRSTTU ANTIRUST
NATURIST
AINRSTTY TANISTRY
AINSSSTU SUSTAINS
AIOOORRT ORATORIO
AIOORSUV OVARIOUS
AIOPRRST AIRPORTS
PARITORS
AIOPRRTT PORTRAIT
AIOPRSST AIRSTOPS
PROSAIST
PROTASIS
AIOPRSTT PATRIOTS
AIOPRSUV PAVIOURS
AIOPSTTU UTOPIAST
AIORRRSW WARRIORS
AIORRSTT TRAITORS
AIORRSTV VARISTOR
AIORRTWY RYOTWARI
AIORSSTU SAUTOIRS
AIORSSUV SAVIOURS
AIORSTTV VOTARIST
AIORSTUV VIRTUOSA
AIOSSSTY ISOSTASY
AIPPRSTY PAPISTRY
AIPRSSTU UPSTAIRS
AIPRSSTY SPARSITY
AIRRSTTY ARTISTRY
AIRRSTZZ RIZZARTS
AIRSSSTT TSARISTS
AIRSSTTT ATTRISTS
AISSSTTT STATISTS
AJKMNSTU MUNTJAKS
AJKNNOOU JUNKANOO
AJLNORSU JOURNALS
AJMRSTUY JURYMAST
AJORRTUY JURATORY
AKKLRSSY SKYLARKS
AKLLMRUY MULLARKY
AKLMNOOW MOONWALK
AKLNNOPT PLANKTON
AKLOPRSW LAPWORKS
AKLOSTTU OUTTALKS
AKLOSTUW OUTWALKS
AKLPRRSU LARKSPUR
AKMMNOOR MONOMARK
AKMNRSTU TRANKUMS
AKMOORST MOOKTARS
AKMOPRST POSTMARK
AKMQSTUU KUMQUATS
AKMRSSTU MUSKRATS
AKNOORST OSTRAKON
AKNOOUYZ YOKOZUNA
AKNOPSTW SWANKPOT
AKNORSTU OUTRANKS
AKOPRRTW PARTWORK
AKORRSTW ARTWORKS
AKORSWWX WAXWORKS
ALLLPRUY PLURALLY
ALLMNORY NORMALLY
ALLMNOSY ALLONYMS
ALLMOPSX SMALLPOX
ALLMORTY MORTALLY
ALLMOUWY MULLOWAY
ALLMPRUU PLUMULAR
ALLMTUUY MUTUALLY
ALLNORSS LASSLORN
ALLOOSTX AXOLOTLS
ALLOPRSY PAYROLLS
ALLOPSTY POSTALLY
ALLORSST ALLSORTS
ALLORTWW WALLWORT
ALLOSSWW SWALLOWS
ALLRUUVY UVULARLY
ALMMNRUU NUMMULAR
ALMMORTW MALTWORM
ALMNOOPS LAMPOONS
ALMNORTY MATRONLY
ALMNOSSU SOLANUMS
ALMNPSSU SUNLAMPS
ALMOOPRY PLAYROOM
ALMOOPSY POLYOMAS
ALMOPPST LAMPPOST
PALMTOPS
ALMOPRST MARPLOTS
ALMORSUU RAMULOUS
ALMOSTTU MULATTOS
ALMPSSTY SYMPLAST
ALMRTUUY TUMULARY
ALMSSSUY ALYSSUMS
ALNNOOPR NONPOLAR
ALNNOTWY WANTONLY
ALNNRSSU UNSNARLS
ALNOOPPR PROPANOL
ALNOOPRS POLARONS
ALNOOPRT PORTOLAN
PRONOTAL
ALNOOPST PLATOONS
ALNOOPXY POLYAXON
ALNOOPYZ POLYZOAN
ALNOORST ORTOLANS
ALNOPRST PLASTRON
ALNOPRTU PORTULAN
ALNOPSYY POLYNYAS
ALNORRWY NARROWLY
ALNORSVY SOVRANLY
ALNPPSTU SUPPLANT
ALNRRTUU NURTURAL
ALOOPPRS PROPOSAL
ALOOPRST POSTORAL
ALOOPRTU UPROOTAL
ALOORSUV VALOROUS
ALOORTYZ ZOOLATRY
ALOPPRSU POPULARS
ALOPPRYY POLYPARY
ALOPPSSU SUPPOSAL
ALOPPSUU PAPULOUS
ALOPRRSU PARLOURS
SPORULAR
ALOPRSTT PORTLAST
ALOPRSTU POSTURAL
PULSATOR
ALOPRSTY PASTORLY
ALOPSSSU SPOUSALS
ALOPSSUV VOLUSPAS
ALOPSTUU PATULOUS
ALOPSTUY OUTPLAYS
ALOQRRSU RORQUALS
ALOQRSSU SQUALORS
ALORRSUY SURROYAL
ALORSTTW SALTWORT
ALORSUVY SAVOURLY
ALORTUWY OUTLAWRY
ALOSSTTU OUTLASTS
ALPPSTUY PLATYPUS
ALPRSSUU PURSUALS
ALPRSTUU PUSTULAR
AMMNOORT MOTORMAN
AMMNPTUY TYMPANUM
AMMOORRS MAORMORS
MORMAORS
AMMOPSTU POMATUMS
AMNNOOSX MONAXONS
AMNNOOTT MONTANTO
AMNNORSW MANSWORN
AMNNORSY MANSONRY
AMNNOSTT MONTANTS
AMNNOSTW TOWNSMAN
AMNNOSTY ANTONYMS
AMNNOSUW UNWOMANS
AMNNOTTU MOUNTANT
AMNNOTYY ANTONYMY
AMNNPSTU PUNTSMAN
AMNNSTTU STUNTMAN
AMNOOPPS POMPANOS
AMNOOSTT OTTOMANS
AMNOOSTZ MATZOONS
AMNOOTUY AUTONOMY
AMNOOTWY TOYWOMAN
AMNOOTXY TAXONOMY
AMNOPRSY PARONYMS
AMNOPRYY PARONYMY
AMNOPSTU PANTOUMS
AMNORSST TRANSOMS
AMNORSTU ROMAUNTS
AMNOSTUY AUTONYMS
AMNOTTUY TAUTONYM
AMNRSTTU TANTRUMS
AMOOORSS AMOROSOS
AMOOPRST TAPROOMS
AMOORRTY MORATORY
AMOORSTZ SMORZATO
AMOORTWY MOTORWAY
AMOOSSTU ASTOMOUS
AMOOTTUY AUTOTOMY
AMOPRRST MARSPORT
AMOPRSXY PAROXYSM
AMOPSSTT TOPMASTS
AMOQSSUU SQUAMOUS
AMORRTUY MORTUARY
AMORSTTU OUTSMART
AMORTTUY MUTATORY
AMPRSSUW UPSWARMS
AMRRSSTU RASTRUMS
ANNOORST SONORANT
ANNOSSTU STANNOUS
ANNPRSUY SPUNYARN
ANOOPRRT PRONATOR
ANOOPRSS SOPRANOS
ANOOPRST PATROONS
ANOORSTT ARNOTTOS
ANOORSUU ANOUROUS
ANOPPPRT PROPPANT
ANOPRRSS SPORRANS
ANOPRSTU STROUPAN
ANOPRTTU TRAPUNTO
ANOPSSTU OUTSPANS
ANOQRSSU SQUARSON
ANORSSTU SANTOURS
ANORSTVY SOVRANTY
ANPPSSUW SUPPAWNS
ANPRSSTU SUNTRAPS
UNSTRAPS
ANPRSTUU PURSUANT
ANRRTTUY TRUANTRY
ANRSSTYY SYNASTRY
AOOOPRST SOAPROOT
AOOOPRTZ PROTOZOA
AOOPPRSY APOSPORY

AOOPRSSU SAPOROUS
AOOPRSTT TAPROOTS
AOOPRSTU ATROPOUS
AOOPRSTW SOAPWORT
AOOPRSUV VAPOROUS
AOOPRTTY POTATORY
AOORRSTT ROTATORS
AOORRSTU OUTROARS
AOORRTTY ROTATORY
AOORSSTU OUTSOARS
AOORSSUV SAVOROUS
AOPPRRST RAPPORTS
AOPPRSST PASSPORT
AOPRRRTY PARROTRY
AOPRRSSW SPARROWS
AOPRRSTY PORTRAYS
AOPRRTUY POURTRAY
AOPRSSTT STARSPOT
AOPRSTTU OUTPARTS
AOPRSTTY PYROSTAT
AOPRSTUY OUTPRAYS
AOPSSSTU PASSOUTS
AOPSSTWY WAYPOSTS
AORRSTTW STARWORT
AORRTTWW WARTWORT
AORSSTTU STRATOUS
AORSSTTY STAROSTY
AOSSTTUY OUTSTAYS
APPRRSUU PURPURAS
APRSSTTU UPSTARTS
APRSSUWY SPURWAYS
BBBCEOWY COBWEBBY
BBBDEEKO KEBOBBED
BBBDEEOR BEROBBED
BBBEILOR BOBBLIER
BBBEILRU BUBBLIER
BBBEILSU BUBBLIES
BBBEINOT BOBBINET
BBBELRSU BLUBBERS
BBBGILNO BLOBBING
BOBBLING
BBBGILNU BLUBBING
BUBBLING
BBBHNOOY HOBNOBBY
BBBHOOUU HUBBUBOO
BBCCIKOS BIBCOCKS
BBCDEILR CRIBBLED
BBCDERSU SCRUBBED
BBCDIMOY BOMBYCID
BBCEHINS NEBBICHS
BBCEHIRU CHUBBIER
BBCEILRS CRIBBLES
SCRIBBLE
BBCEILRU CLUBBIER
BBCEIOST COBBIEST
BBCEKKOS KEBBOCKS
BBCEKKSU KEBBUCKS
BBCEKLUU BLUEBUCK
BBCELORS CLOBBERS
COBBLERS
BBCELORY COBBLERY
BBCELRSU CLUBBERS
BBCEMNOU BUNCOMBE
BBCERRSU SCRUBBER
BBCGIINR CRIBBING
BBCGILNO COBBLING
BBCGILNU CLUBBING
BBCGINSU CUBBINGS
BBCHILSU CLUBBISH
BBCHKOOS BOSCHBOK

BBCILMSU CLUBBISM
BBCILRSY SCRIBBLY
BBCILSTU CLUBBIST
BBDDEEMO DEMOBBED
BBDDEILR DRIBBLED
BBDDENUU UNDUBBED
BBDEEGIR GIBBERED
BBDEEGIT GIBBETED
BBDEEIJR JIBBERED
BBDEEIST DEBBIEST
EBBTIDES
BBDEEMNU BENUMBED
BBDEENUW UNWEBBED
BBDEEOPP BEBOPPED
BBDEERRU RUBBERED
BBDEERSU SUBBREED
BBDEFILR FRIBBLED
BBDEGLRU GRUBBLED
BBDEHORT THROBBED
BBDEHRSU SHRUBBED
BBDEILLN BELLBIND
BBDEILQU QUIBBLED
BBDEILRR DRIBBLER
BBDEILRS DIBBLERS
DRIBBLES
BBDEILRT DRIBBLET
BBDEILRU BLUEBIRD
BBDEINOR RIBBONED
BBDEINRU UNRIBBED
BBDEIQSU SQUIBBED
BBDEIRRS DRIBBERS
BBDEKLNO KNOBBLED
BBDEKLNU KNUBBLED
BBDELOSS BOBSLEDS
BBDELSTU STUBBLED
BBDENRUU UNRUBBED
BBDGIILN DIBBLING
BBDGIINR DRIBBING
BBDGINRU DRUBBING
BBDGINSU DUBBINGS
BBDOSUYY BUSYBODY
BBEEEMSX BEMBEXES
BBEEERSU BEBEERUS
BBEEHINS NEBBISHE
BBEEHLOW BOBWHEEL
BBEEIIRR BERIBERI
BBEEILPR PEBBLIER
PLEBBIER
BBEEIMSX BEMBIXES
BBEEIMTT BIMBETTE
BBEEIRRS BERBERIS
BBEEISTW WEBBIEST
BBEELLLU BLUEBELL
BBEFILRR FRIBBLER
BBEFILRS FRIBBLES
BBEFISTU FUBBIEST
BBEGIIST GIBBSITE
BBEGILNP PEBBLING
BBEGILOR GLOBBIER
BBEGILRS GRIBBLES
BBEGILRY GLIBBERY
BBEGILST GLIBBEST
BBEGINNS SNEBBING
BBEGINSW WEBBINGS
BBEGIRRU GRUBBIER
BBEGLORS GOBBLERS
BBEGLRSU GRUBBLES
BBEGRRSU GRUBBERS
BBEHLORS HOBBLERS
BBEHMSTU BETHUMBS

BBEIILRS RIBIBLES
BBEIIMRS IMBIBERS
BBEIIRST RIBBIEST
BBEIKNOR KNOBBIER
BBEIKNRU KNUBBIER
BBEILLNO BONIBELL
BBEILNRS NIBBLERS
BBEILNRU NUBBLIER
BBEILORS SLOBBIER
BBEILORW WOBBLIER
BBEILOST BIBELOTS
BBEILOSW WOBBLIES
BBEILPRS PRIBBLES
BBEILQRU QUIBBLER
BBEILQSU QUIBBLES
BBEILRRU RUBBLIER
BBEILRRY BILBERRY
BBEILRST STIBBLER
TRIBBLES
BBEILRSU SLUBBIER
BBEILSST STIBBLES
BBEIMOST BOMBSITE
BBEIMRSU BRUMBIES
BBEINORS SNOBBIER
BBEINOST NOBBIEST
BBEINRSU SNUBBIER
BBEINSTU NUBBIEST
BBEIRSTU STUBBIER
SUBTRIBE
BBEISSTU STUBBIES
BBEISTTU TUBBIEST
BBEKLNOS KNOBBLES
BBEKLNSU KNUBBLES
BBEKLOSS BLESBOKS
BBEKLSUU BUBUKLES
BBEKNOOT BONTEBOK
BBEKNORS KNOBBERS
BBELLRUY LUBBERLY
BBELMOST BOMBLETS
BBELMRSU BUMBLERS
BBELNORS NOBBLERS
BBELORSS SLOBBERS
BBELORSW WOBBLERS
BBELORSY LOBBYERS
SLOBBERY
BBELRRSU BURBLERS
BBELRSSU SLUBBERS
BBELSSTU STUBBLES
BBENORSY SNOBBERY
BBENRSSU SNUBBERS
BBEORSSW SWOBBERS
BBEPRSUW BREWPUBS
BBFGILNU FLUBBING
BBGGIILN GLIBBING
BBGGILNO GOBBLING
BBGGINRU GRUBBING
BBGHILNO HOBBLING
BBGIIIMN IMBIBING
BBGIIJNS JIBBINGS
BBGIIKLN KIBBLING
BBGIILMN BLIMBING
BBGIILNN NIBBLING
BBGIINNS SNIBBING
BBGIINRS RIBBINGS
BBGIJNOS JOBBINGS
BBGILMNO MOBBLING
BBGILMNU BUMBLING
BBGILNNO NOBBLING
BBGILNNU NUBBLING
BBGILNOW WOBBLING

BBGILNOY LOBBYING
BBGILNRU BLURBING
BURBLING
BBGILNSU SLUBBING
BBGIMNOS MOBBINGS
BBGINNSU SNUBBING
BBGINOSS SOBBINGS
BBGINOSW SWOBBING
BBGINRSU RUBBINGS
BBGINSSU SUBBINGS
BBGINSTU STUBBING
TUBBINGS
BBHILOSS SLOBBISH
BBHIMOSY HOBBYISM
BBHINOSS SNOBBISH
BBHINSSU SNUBBISH
BBHIOOSY BOOBYISH
BBHIORTY HOBBITRY
BBHIOSTY HOBBYIST
BBHIRSUY RUBBISHY
BBHOOSUW WHOOBUBS
BBHRSSUU SUBSHRUB
BBIIILMS BILIMBIS
BBIILSST BIBLISTS
BBIKLLOO BILLBOOK
BBIKLNOO BOBOLINK
BBILLOYY BILLYBOY
BBILLSUU LULIBUBS
BBILOSTY LOBBYIST
BBILOSUU BIBULOUS
BBIMNOSS SNOBBISM
BBIMOOSY BOOBYISM
BBIMOSSY YOBBISMS
BBINORRY RIBBONRY
BBJLOOSW BLOWJOBS
BBKLOOSU BLOUBOKS
BBKOOOOS BOOBOOKS
BBNOORSU BOURBONS
BBNORSTU STUBBORN
BCCDEILY BICYCLED
BCCDHIKO DOBCHICK
BCCDIKOR COCKBIRD
BCCEEIRR CEREBRIC
BCCEHIRU CHERUBIC
BCCEIIIS CICISBEI
BCCEIILO LIBECCIO
BCCEIIOS CICISBEO
BCCEILOS ECBOLICS
BCCEILRU CRUCIBLE
BCCEILSU CUBICLES
BCCEILSY BICYCLES
BCCEMRUU CUCUMBER
BCCIIMOR MICROBIC
BCCIISTU CUBISTIC
BCCILMOU COLUMBIC
BCCILOOR BROCCOLI
BCCILOSU BUCOLICS
BCCIRTUU CUCURBIT
BCCMOOSX COXCOMBS
BCCMSSUU SUCCUMBS
BCCSSUUU SUCCUBUS
BCDDEEEK BEDECKED
BCDDEEKU BEDUCKED
BCDDEHIL CHILDBED
BCDDESUU SUBDUCED
BCDEEEHR BREECHED
BCDEEHLN BLENCHED
BCDEEHNR BEDRENCH
BCDEEHOU DEBOUCHE
BCDEEIKR BICKERED

BCDEEILR CREDIBLE
BCDEEILS DECIBELS
BCDEEILU EDUCIBLE
BCDEEINT BENEDICT
BCDEEIPS BESPICED
BCDEEIRS DESCRIBE
ESCRIBED
BCDEEIST BISECTED
BCDEEJOT OBJECTED
BCDEEKMO BEMOCKED
BCDEEKNO BECKONED
BCDEEKTU BUCKETED
BCDEELOR CORBELED
BCDEELRU BECURLED
BCDEEMRU CUMBERED
BCDEEORV BEDCOVER
BCDEEOTT OBTECTED
BCDEHINS DISBENCH
BCDEHLOT BLOTCHED
BCDEHOOR BROOCHED
BCDEIIOS BIOCIDES
BCDEIITU DECUBITI
BCDEIKRR REDBRICK
BCDEIKSS SICKBEDS
BCDEIKST BEDTICKS
BCDEILRY CREDIBLY
BCDEIMNO COMBINED
BCDEINOU ICEBOUND
BCDEKOOO CODEBOOK
BCDEKORS BEDROCKS
BCDEKOSS BEDSOCKS
BCDELMRU CRUMBLED
BCDELMSU SCUMBLED
BCDELOSU BECLOUDS
BCDEMNOU UNCOMBED
BCDENRUU UNCURBED
BCDEORSU OBSCURED
BCDESSUU SUBDUCES
BCDHIRSU BRUCHIDS
BCDHOOSU CUBHOODS
BCDHORSU SUBCHORD
BCDIIMOR BROMIDIC
BCDIIPSU BICUSPID
BCDIKLLU DUCKBILL
BCDILMOY MOLYBDIC
BCDILORU COLUBRID
BCDIMORS SCOMBRID
BCDINRUU RUBICUND
BCDIORSW COWBIRDS
BCDKORSU BURDOCKS
BCDSSTUU SUBDUCTS
BCEEEFIN BENEFICE
BCEEEFKN NECKBEEF
BCEEEHRS BREECHES
BCEEENRS BESCREEN
BCEEERSU BERCEUSE
BCEEFILN FENCIBLE
BCEEGIRS ICEBERGS
BCEEHKSU BUCKSHEE
BCEEHLNS BLENCHES
BCEEHLRS BELCHERS
BCEEHNRS BENCHERS
BCEEHNRU UNBREECH
BCEEHOSU BOUCHEES
BCEEIILM IMBECILE
BCEEINOT CENOBITE
BCEEIOSX ICEBOXES
BCEEIPSS BESPICES
BICEPSES
BCEEIRSS ESCRIBES
BCEEIRTT BRETTICE
BCEEKNSU BUCKEENS
BCEELLOT BELLCOTE
BCEELOOR BORECOLE
BCEELRTU TUBERCLE
BCEEMNRU ENCUMBER
BCEEMRRU CEREBRUM
CUMBERER
BCEENORS OBSCENER
BCEENRSU CRUBEENS
BCEERSTU SUBERECT
BCEFFIIR FEBRIFIC
BCEFHISU SUBCHIEF
BCEFILOR FORCIBLE
BCEGHILN BELCHING
BCEGHINN BENCHING
BCEGIINO BIOGENIC
BCEGIMNO BECOMING
BCEGLNOO CONGLOBE
BCEHIIRT BITCHIER
BCEHIMRS BESMIRCH
BCEHIMRU CHERUBIM
BCEHINRU BUNCHIER
CHERUBIN
BCEHIORS BRIOCHES
BCEHIORT BOTCHIER
BCEHIRST BRITCHES
BCEHIRTY BITCHERY
BCEHLOST BLOTCHES
BCEHLRSU BLUCHERS
BCEHMSTU BESMUTCH
BCEHNRSU BRUNCHES
BCEHOORS BROOCHES
BCEHORRU BROCHURE
BCEHORSS BORSCHES
BCEHORST BOTCHERS
BCEHORSW COWHERBS
BCEHORTY BOTCHERY
BCEHRSTU BUTCHERS
BCEHRTUY BUTCHERY
BCEHSTTU BUTCHEST
BCEIIKLN ICEBLINK
BCEIIKRR BRICKIER
BCEIIKRS BRICKIES
BCEIILMS MISCIBLE
BCEIILNV VINCIBLE
BCEIIMRS IMBRICES
BCEIINRS INSCRIBE
BCEIKLMS LIMBECKS
BCEIKLOO BOOKLICE
BCEIKLOR BLOCKIER
BCEIKSST BESTICKS
BCEILMRS CLIMBERS
RECLIMBS
BCEILNOS BINOCLES
BCEILNRU RUNCIBLE
BCEILORS BRICOLES
CORBEILS
BCEILOTU TUBICOLE
BCEILPRU REPUBLIC
BCEIMNOS COMBINES
BCEIMORS CROMBIES
MICROBES
BCEIMOST COMBIEST
BCEIMOSW COMBWISE
BCEIMRRU CRUMBIER
BCEINORS BICORNES
BCEINORU BOUNCIER
BCEINOVX BICONVEX
BCEINRSU BRUCINES
BCEIOOPS BIOSCOPE
BCEIORRS CRIBROSE
BCEIORST BISECTOR
BCEIRRSS SCRIBERS
BCEIRSTU BRUCITES
BCEJOORT OBJECTOR
BCEJSSTU SUBJECTS
BCEKLNOT BLONCKET
BCEKLNUU UNBUCKLE
BCEKLORS BLOCKERS
BCEKLRSU BUCKLERS
BCEKMSTU STEMBUCK
BCEKOORU BUCKEROO
BCEKORST BROCKETS
BCEKORSU ROEBUCKS
BCEKOSTY BYCOKETS
BCELLOSW COWBELLS
BCELMOSS COMBLESS
BCELMRSU CLUMBERS
CRUMBLES
BCELMSSU SCUMBLES
BCELORTU CLOTEBUR
BCELRSSU CURBLESS
BCEMRSSU SCUMBERS
BCENORSU BOUNCERS
BCEORRSU OBSCURER
BCEORRWY COWBERRY
BCEORSSU OBSCURES
BCFIIMOR MORBIFIC
BCFIIORT FIBROTIC
BCFILORY FORCIBLY
BCFIMORU CUBIFORM
BCFSSSUU SUBFUSCS
BCGHIINR BIRCHING
BCGHIINT BITCHING
BCGHINNU BUNCHING
BCGHINOR BROCHING
BCGHINOT BOTCHING
BCGHINTU BUTCHING
BCGIIKNR BRICKING
BCGIILMN CLIMBING
BCGIINRS SCRIBING
BCGIKLNO BLOCKING
BCGIKLNU BUCKLING
BCGIKNSU BUCKINGS
BCGIMNOR CROMBING
BCGIMNOS COMBINGS
BCGIMNRU CRUMBING
BCGINNOU BOUNCING
BUNCOING
BCGINORU COURBING
BCHIILTY BITCHILY
BCHIIOST COHIBITS
BCHIISSU HIBISCUS
BCHIKLOS BLOCKISH
BCHIKOSU CHIBOUKS
BCHIOORY CHOIRBOY
BCHIOPRS PIBROCHS
BCHKNORU BUCKHORN
BCHKOSTU BUCKSHOT
BCHLRSUU CLUBRUSH
BCHNOORS BRONCHOS
BCHNORSU BRONCHUS
BCHORSST BORSCHTS
BCIIILMU UMBILICI
BCIIKLNS NIBLICKS
BCIILLSY SIBYLLIC
BCIILMRU LUMBRICI
BCIILMSU BULIMICS
BCIILORS COLIBRIS
BCIIMNOO BIONOMIC
BCIIMORU CIBORIUM
BCIIMRSS SCRIBISM
BCIINORV VIBRONIC
BCIIORST SORBITIC
BCIISSTU BISCUITS
BCIISTUY BISCUITY
BCIKKNSU BUCKSKIN
BCIKLOOT BOOTLICK
BCIKORRW CRIBWORK
BCIKOSTT BITTOCKS
BCILLPUY PUBLICLY
BCILMOSY SYMBOLIC
BCILMPSU UPCLIMBS
BCILNOUY BOUNCILY
BCIMORSU MICROBUS
BCINORSU RUBICONS
BCINOSSU SUBSONIC
BCINOSTU SUBTONIC
BCINOSUU INCUBOUS
BCIOORST ROBOTICS
BCIORRSU CRIBROUS
BCIORSST CROSSBIT
BCJKMSUU JUMBUCKS
BCKKOOOO COOKBOOK
BCKLLOOS BOLLOCKS
BCKLLOSU BULLOCKS
BCKLLOUY BULLOCKY
BCKLNOSU SUNBLOCK
UNBLOCKS
BCKMMOSU BUMMOCKS
BCKOOOPY COPYBOOK
BCKOSTTU BUTTOCKS
BCLMOORU CLUBROOM
BCLMOOSU COULOMBS
BCLOORTU CLUBROOT
BCLORSTU CLOTBURS
BCMORSUU CUMBROUS
BCMOSSTU COMBUSTS
BCOORSSW CROSSBOW
BCOOSTTY BOYCOTTS
BCORSTTU OBSTRUCT
BCRSSTUU SUBCRUST
BDDDEEEM EMBEDDED
BDDDEEIM IMBEDDED
BDDDEEIR DEBRIDED
BDDDEEMU BEMUDDED
BDDDEENU UNBEDDED
BDDDENUU UNBUDDED
BDDEEELL DEBELLED
BDDEEERS REEDBEDS
BDDEEESS SEEDBEDS
BDDEEFLU BEFUDDLE
BDDEEGGU DEBUGGED
BDDEEGIL BEGILDED
BDDEEGIR BEGIRDED
BDDEEGNU BEDUNGED
BDDEEGTU BUDGETED
BDDEEHOS DEBOSHED
BDDEEIMM BEDIMMED
BDDEEIMO EMBODIED
BDDEEINR REBIDDEN
BDDEEINT INDEBTED
BDDEEINW BINDWEED
BDDEEIRS BIRDSEED
DEBRIDES
BDDEEISS BEDSIDES
BDDEEKNU DEBUNKED
BDDEELMU BEMUDDLE
BDDEELNO BOLDENED

BDDEENNU UNBENDED
BDDEENOT OBTENDED
BDDEENRU BURDENED
BDDEEORR BORDERED
BDDEEORS DESORBED
BDDEEOSS DEBOSSED
BDDEESSU DEBUSSED
BDDEESTU BEDUSTED
BDDEESUW SUBDEWED
BDDEGINS BEDDINGS
BDDEIIMO IMBODIED
BDDEILNR BRINDLED
BDDEILOO BLOODIED
BDDEINNU UNBIDDEN
BDDEINOU UNBODIED
BDDEINRU UNDERBID
BDDEIORS DISORBED
DISROBED
BDDEIOWY WIDEBODY
BDDEISSU SUBSIDED
BDDEISTU BUDDIEST
BDDELMRU DRUMBLED
BDDENOTU OBTUNDED
BDDEORTU OBTRUDED
BDDGIINS BIDDINGS
BDDGILNU BUDDLING
BDDGINOR BRODDING
BDDGINSU BUDDINGS
BDDGOOSY DOGSBODY
BDDHIIRY DIHYBRID
BDDINOOW WOODBIND
BDDINPUU PUDIBUND
BDEEEEMS BESEEMED
BDEEEEMT BETEEMED
BDEEEGIS BESIEGED
BDEEEGMM BEGEMMED
BDEEEGNO EDGEBONE
BDEEEGRU BUDGEREE
BDEEEHTU HEBETUDE
BDEEEILV BELIEVED
BDEEEINS BENISEED
BDEEELLR REBELLED
BDEEELLV BEVELLED
BDEEELMM EMBLEMED
BDEEELPT BEPELTED
BDEEELRS BLEEDERS
BDEEELUW BLUEWEED
BDEEEMMR MEMBERED
BDEEEMNS BEDESMEN
BDEEEMRW EMBREWED
BDEEENTT BENETTED
BDEEEPSS BESPEEDS
BDEEERRS BREEDERS
BDEEERRV REVERBED
BDEEERTT BETTERED
BDEEERTV BREVETED
BDEEETTW BEWETTED
BDEEFFPU BEPUFFED
BDEEFFRU BUFFERED
REBUFFED
BDEEFFTU BUFFETED
BDEEFGGO BEFOGGED
BDEEFGIT BEGIFTED
BDEEFILR BELFRIED
BDEEFINN BEFINNED
BDEEFINR BEFRIEND
BDEEFIRS DEBRIEFS
BDEEFIRU RUBEFIED
BDEEFITT BEFITTED
BDEEFLOO BEFOOLED

BDEEFLOU BEFOULED
BDEEFOOR FOREBODE
BDEEFSUU SUBFEUED
BDEEGGIW BEWIGGED
BDEEGGMO EMBOGGED
BDEEGGNU UNBEGGED
BDEEGGRU BEGRUDGE
BUGGERED
BDEEGHIS BESIGHED
BDEEGILN BLEEDING
BDEEGILU BEGUILED
BDEEGIMR BEGRIMED
BDEEGINR BREEDING
BDEEGINW BEDEWING
BDEEGINY BEDYEING
BDEEGKNU BEGUNKED
BDEEGLNO BELONGED
ENGLOBED
BDEEGMOU EMBOGUED
BDEEHLNO BEHOLDEN
BDEEHLOR BEHOLDER
BDEEHLOW BEHOWLED
BDEEHOOV BEHOOVED
BDEEHORT BOTHERED
BDEEHORW BEWHORED
BDEEHOSS DEBOSHES
BDEEIILN INEDIBLE
BDEEIILR BIELDIER
BDEEIIPT BEPITIED
BDEEIKRS KERBSIDE
BDEEIKSS BEKISSED
BDEEILLL LIBELLED
BDEEILLT BILLETED
BDEEILLU ELUDIBLE
BDEEILMO BEMOILED
EMBOILED
BDEEILMR LIMBERED
BDEEILNV VENDIBLE
BDEEILOR ERODIBLE
REBOILED
BDEEILOS OBELISED
BDEEILOT BETOILED
BDEEILOZ OBELIZED
BDEEILRW BEWILDER
BDEEILSV BEDEVILS
BDEEILTT BETITLED
BDEEIMNR BRIDEMEN
BDEEIMOS EMBODIES
BDEEIMRT TIMBERED
BDEEIMST BEDTIMES
BDEEIMSU EMBUSIED
BDEEINOS EBONISED
BDEEINOT OBEDIENT
BDEEINOZ EBONIZED
BDEEINRS INBREEDS
BDEEINST BENDIEST
BDEEINSW BENDWISE
BDEEINSZ BEDIZENS
BDEEIORU BOUDERIE
BDEEIRRU REBURIED
BDEEIRST BESTRIDE
BDEEISTU BESUITED
BDEEKNRU BUNKERED
BDEEKORR BROKERED
BDEELLOW BELLOWED
BOWELLED
BDEELLRU BULLERED
BDEELLRY REDBELLY
BDEELMNO EMBOLDEN
BDEELMOR REBELDOM

BDEELMPU BEPLUMED
BDEELMRT TREMBLED
BDEELMRU LUMBERED
BDEELNNO ENNOBLED
BDEELNRS BLENDERS
BDEELNST BENDLETS
BDEELNTU UNBELTED
BDEELORU REDOUBLE
BDEELOSU BESOULED
BDEELOSV BELOVEDS
BDEELRTU BUTLERED
BDEEMNOT BODEMENT
ENTOMBED
BDEEMNOW ENWOMBED
BDEEMNRU NUMBERED
BDEEMORR EMBORDER
BDEEMORS SOMBERED
BDEEMOSS EMBOSSED
BDEEMPRU BUMPERED
BDEEMRTU EMBRUTED
BDEEMSSU EMBUSSED
BDEENNOT BONNETED
BDEENOUY UNOBEYED
BDEENPRS PREBENDS
BDEEOPRS BEPROSED
BDEEOPRW BEPOWDER
BDEEORRR BORDERER
BDEEORRS RESORBED
BDEEORSS BEDSORES
BDEEORST BESORTED
BESTRODE
BDEEORSV OBSERVED
BDEEORTU OUTBREED
BDEEORTV OBVERTED
BDEEOSSS DEBOSSES
OBSESSED
BDEEOSST BETOSSED
BDEEOSTT BESOTTED
OBTESTED
BDEEOSTW BESTOWED
BDEERSUW BURWEEDS
BDEERTTU BUTTERED
REBUTTED
BDEESSSU DEBUSSES
BDEFIIRU RUBIFIED
BDEFILRS FILBERDS
BDEFILSU SUBFIELD
BDEFINRR FERNBIRD
BDEFIORS FIBROSED
BDEFOORS FORBODES
BDEGHILT BLIGHTED
BDEGHIRT BEDRIGHT
BDEGHIST BEDIGHTS
BDEGIILN BIELDING
BDEGIINT BETIDING
DEBITING
BDEGILNN BLENDING
BDEGILNO INGLOBED
BDEGINNS BENDINGS
BDEGINOS OBSIGNED
BDEGINTU DEBUTING
BDEGIOST BODGIEST
BDEGLMRU GRUMBLED
BDEGLNOU BLUDGEON
BDEGLRSU BLUDGERS
BDEGORRY DOGBERRY
BDEGORSU BUDGEROS
BDEGORUW BUDGEROW
BDEHIKOS KIBOSHED
BDEHILMT THIMBLED

BDEHIOPS BISHOPED
BDEHKOSY KYBOSHED
BDEHLMOW WHOMBLED
BDEHLSUV BUSHVELD
BDEHORSY HERDBOYS
BDEIIKLR BIRDLIKE
BDEIIKTZ KIBITZED
BDEIILRU BLUIDIER
BDEIILTY DEBILITY
BDEIIMOS IMBODIES
BDEIKMOS IMBOSKED
BDEIKNOR BRODEKIN
BDEIKNSU BUSKINED
BDEILLMU BDELLIUM
BDEILLOW BILLOWED
BDEILLOX BOLLIXED
BDEILMOS SEMIBOLD
BDEILMSU SUBLIMED
BDEILNOU UNILOBED
BDEILNOY BODYLINE
BDEILNRS BLINDERS
BRINDLES
BDEILNRU UNBRIDLE
BDEILNST BLINDEST
BDEILNVY VENDIBLY
BDEILOOR BLOODIER
BDEILOOS BLOODIES
BDEILOPU UPBOILED
BDEILOQU OBLIQUED
BDEILORT TRILOBED
BDEILORV LOVEBIRD
BDEILOSS BODILESS
BDEILOSW DISBOWEL
BDEILRRS BRIDLERS
BDEILRST BRISTLED
DRIBLETS
BDEILRSU BUILDERS
REBUILDS
BDEILSTU BLUDIEST
BDEIMNOT INTOMBED
BDEIMNSU NIMBUSED
BDEIMNUU UNIMBUED
BDEIMORR IMBORDER
BDEIMORS BROMIDES
BDEIMORY EMBRYOID
BDEIMOSS IMBOSSED
BDEIMRSU IMBURSED
BDEIMRTU IMBRUTED
BDEINOOS NOBODIES
BDEINOOW WOODBINE
BDEINOSU BEDOUINS
BDEINRSU BURNSIDE
BDEINRTU TURBINED
UNDERBIT
BDEINRUU UNBURIED
BDEINTTU UNBITTED
BDEIOORR BROODIER
BDEIORRS BROIDERS
BDEIORRY BROIDERY
BDEIORSS DISROBES
BDEIORST DEBITORS
BDEIORSV OVERBIDS
BDEIOSSY DISOBEYS
BDEIOSUX SUBOXIDE
BDEIRSSU DISBURSE
BDEISSSU SUBSIDES
BDEISSTU SUBEDITS
BDEKNOOU UNBOOKED
BDELLOOR BORDELLO
DOORBELL

BDELLOUZ BULLDOZE
BDELMOOS BLOOSMED
BDELMRSU DRUMBLES
BDELMRUU DELUBRUM
BDELMSTU STUMBLED
BDELNNOU UNNOBLED
BDELNNUU UNBUNDLE
BDELNOSS BOLDNESS
BDELNOST BLONDEST
BDELNOTU UNBOLTED
BDELNOUU UNDOUBLE
BDELNOUW UNBLOWED
BDELNRSU BLUNDERS
BDELOORV OVERBOLD
BDELORSU BOULDERS
DOUBLERS
BDELORSW BOWLDERS
BDELORTU TROUBLED
BDELOSTU DOUBLETS
BDELPSUU SUBDUPLE
BDEMNNOS BONDSMEN
BDEMNOSU EMBOUNDS
BDEMNOTU UNTOMBED
BDEMNSSU DUMBNESS
BDEMOORS BEDROOMS
BOREDOMS
BDEMOOSY SOMEBODY
BDEMOOTT BOTTOMED
BDEMSSUU SUBSUMED
BDENNOUY YBOUNDEN
BDENNRUU UNBURDEN
UNBURNED
BDENOOTU UNBOOTED
BDENOOTW BENTWOOD
BDENORSU BOUNDERS
REBOUNDS
SUBORNED
BDENOTTU BUTTONED
BDENRSUU UNBRUSED
BDENRUUY UNDERBUY
BDENSSTU SUBTENDS
BDEOORRS BROODERS
BDEOORRW BORROWED
BDEOOTUX OUTBOXED
BDEOPSST BEDPOSTS
BDEORRSU BORDURES
BOURDERS
SUBORDER
BDEORRTU OBTRUDER
BDEORRUW BURROWED
BDEORSSU ROSEBUDS
BDEORSTU DOUBTERS
OBTRUDES
REDOUBTS
BDERSSUU SUBDUERS
BDERSTUU SUBTRUDE
BDFFIPRU PUFFBIRD
BDFGNOOU FOGBOUND
BDFIIORS FIBROIDS
BDFILLLO BILLFOLD
BDFINORU UNFORBID
BDFINRUU FURIBUND
BDFIRRSU SURFBIRD
BDFLOTUU DOUBTFUL
BDGGIINR BRIDGING
BDGGILNU BLUDGING
BDGIILNN BLINDING
BDGIILNR BRIDLING
BDGIILNU BUILDING
BDGIINNS BINDINGS
BDGIINRS BIRDINGS
BDGIINRW BIRDWING
BDGILNNU BUNDLING
BDGILNOO BLOODING
BDGILNOU DOUBLING
BDGILOOS GLOBOIDS
BDGINNOS BONDINGS
BDGINNOU BOUNDING
UNBODING
BDGINOOR BROODING
BDGINOOY BOODYING
BDGINORS BIRDSONG
SONGBIRD
BDGINORU OBDURING
BDGINOTU DOUBTING
BDGINSUU SUBDUING
BDGLLOSU BULLDOGS
BDGLOOST DOGBOLTS
BDGNRUUY BURGUNDY
BDHIIPRW WHIPBIRD
BDHIMOOR RHOMBOID
BDHIMORT BIRTHDOM
BDHIMSUU SUBHUMID
BDHINOPS HOPBINDS
BDHIORST BIRDSHOT
BDHIOSSU BUSHIDOS
BDHMOOOS HOBODOMS
BDHNRSUU UNSHRUBD
BDHOOOSY BOYHOODS
BDIIINRS BRINDISI
BDIIKNOS BODIKINS
BDIILMSS DISLIMBS
BDIILOQU OBLIQUID
BDIIMRUU RUBIDIUM
BDIKNORS BRODKINS
BDILLOOY BLOODILY
BDILMORY MORBIDLY
BDILNNSU SUNBLIND
UNBLINDS
BDILNOWW WINDBLOW
BDILNPRU PURBLIND
BDILNSUU UNBUILDS
BDILPSUU UPBUILDS
BDILRTUY TURBIDLY
BDIMNORU MORIBUND
BDIMNPSU DUMPBINS
BDIMOOSS DISBOSOM
BDIMOSTU MISDOUBT
BDINNRUW WINDBURN
BDINOORS BRIDOONS
BDINORSW SNOWBIRD
BDINRSSU SUNBIRDS
BDINRTUU UNTURBID
BDINSSTU DUSTBINS
BDIOORSU BOUDOIRS
BDIOORTY BOTRYOID
BDIORSSW WOSBIRDS
BDIOSTUY BODYSUIT
BDIRSSTU DISTURBS
BDKNOOOR DOORKNOB
BDKNOOSU BUNDOOKS
BDKOOORW WORDBOOK
BDKOORWY BODYWORK
BDKOOSTU STUDBOOK
BDLLSTUU BULLDUST
BDLNOOOU DOUBLOON
BDLNOOUY UNBLOODY
BDLNOOWW BLOWDOWN
BDLOOOSX OXBLOODS
BDMOORRS SMORBROD
BDMORSUW BUDWORMS
BDNNOOTU BUNODONT
BDNOORSU BOURDONS
BDNOOSWW DOWNBOWS
BDNOOTUU OUTBOUND
BDNORSTU TURBONDS
BDNORSUW RUBDOWNS
BDOOOSWX BOXWOODS
BDORUWZZ BUZZWORD
BEEEEFLN ENFEEBLE
BEEEEFRS FREEBEES
BEEEEKSS BESEEKES
BEEEEMST BETEEMES
BEEEENRT TEREBENE
BEEEENRZ EBENEZER
BEEEFIRS FREEBIES
BEEEFIST BEEFIEST
BEEEFLSS FEBLESSE
BEEEFLST FEEBLEST
BEEEGILN BELEEING
BEEEGINS BESEEING
BEEEGIRS BESIEGER
BEEEGISS BESIEGES
BEEEGRRS BERGERES
BEEEGRTT BEGETTER
BEEEHIST BHEESTIE
BEEEHISV BEEHIVES
BEEEHLRT HERBELET
BEEEHLWW WEBWHEEL
BEEEHNSS SHEBEENS
BEEEILLL LIBELLEE
BEEEILLS LIBELEES
BEEEILNS BEELINES
BEEEILRV BELIEVER
BEEEILSV BELIEVES
BEEEINST EBENISTE
BEEEIRRZ BREEZIER
BEEEIRST BEERIEST
BEEEJLSW BEJEWELS
BEEELLRR REBELLER
BEEELLRT BELLETER
BEEELLRV BEVELLER
BEEELMNS ENSEMBLE
BEEELMRS RESEMBLE
BEEELMSY BESEEMLY
BEEELMZZ EMBEZZLE
BEEELPRS BLEEPERS
BEEEMMRR REMEMBER
BEEEMNSU UNBESEEM
BEEEMRSW EMBREWES
BEEENNSZ BENZENES
BEEENSST SEBESTEN
BEEENSTW BETWEENS
BEEEPPPR BEPEPPER
BEEEPRST BEPESTER
BEEERSST BRETESSE
BEEERSTT BESETTER
BEEESSST TSESSEBE
BEEFFLMU BEMUFFLE
BEEFGILN FEEBLING
BEEFGINR BEFRINGE
BEEFHILS FEEBLISH
BEEFILLT LIFEBELT
BEEFILLX FLEXIBLE
BEEFILNU UNBELIEF
BEEFILRS BELFRIES
BEEFINST BENEFITS
BEEFIRST BRIEFEST
BEEFIRSU RUBEFIES
BEEFLORW BEFLOWER
BEEFNORR FREEBORN
BEEFNRTU UNBEREFT
BEEGGNSU GEEBUNGS
BEEGHLMR BERGMEHL
BEEGIILL ELIGIBLE
BEEGIILX EXIGIBLE
BEEGILLR GERBILLE
BEEGILNP BLEEPING
BEEGILNT BEETLING
BEEGILOS OBLIGEES
BEEGILRU BEGUILER
BEEGILSU BEGUILES
BEEGIMNT BEMETING
BEEGIMRS BEGRIMES
BEEGINNR BEGINNER
BENIGNER
BEEGINNS BEGINNES
BEEGINRR BREERING
BEEGINRS BIGENERS
BEEGINRZ BREEZING
BEEGINST BEIGNETS
BEEGINSU BEGUINES
BEEGINSW BEESWING
BEEGKLUY KEYBUGLE
BEEGLNOR BELONGER
BEEGLNOS ENGLOBES
BEEGMNOS GOMBEENS
BEEGMOSU EMBOGUES
BEEGMRSU SUBMERGE
BEEGNOOW WOBEGONE
BEEGNOTT BEGOTTEN
BEEGNRSU SUBGENRE
BEEGNSTU UNBEGETS
BEEHHMOT BEHEMOTH
BEEHINSS BESHINES
NEBISHES
BEEHIRST HERBIEST
BEEHISST BHISTEES
BEEHKSSU BUKSHEES
BEEHLOOR BOREHOLE
BEEHLOVY BEHOVELY
BEEHLRSS HERBLESS
BEEHLRST BLETHERS
HERBLETS
BEEHNNOS HEBENONS
BEEHNOOP NEOPHOBE
BEEHNRRT BRETHREN
BEEHOOSV BEHOOVES
BEEHORSW BEWHORES
BEEHRSST SHERBETS
BEEHRSSW BESHREWS
BEEIILNZ ZIBELINE
BEEIINOS EBIONISE
BEEIINOZ EBIONIZE
BEEIINRT BENITIER
BEEIIPST BEPITIES
BEEIIRRR BRIERIER
BEEIIRSS IBERISES
BEEIISTU UBIETIES
BEEIJLSU JUBILEES
BEEIJSTU BEJESUIT
BEEIKLTU TUBELIKE
BEEIKSSS BEKISSES
BEEILLLR LIBELLER
BEEILLNO LOBELINE
BEEILLRS LIBELERS
BEEILLTT BELITTLE
BEEILMOS EMBOLIES
BEEILMPR PERIBLEM
BEEILNNS BLENNIES

BEEILNRS BERLINES
BEEILNSS SENSIBLE
BEEILNST STILBENE
TENSIBLE
BEEILNSU NEBULISE
BEEILNUZ NEBULIZE
BEEILOSS OBELISES
BEEILOSZ OBELIZES
BEEILOTV LOVEBITE
BEEILRRT TERRIBLE
BEEILRSU BLUESIER
BEEILRYZ BREEZILY
BEEILSTT BETITLES
BEEIMRRU UMBRIERE
BEEIMRTT EMBITTER
BEEIMSSU EMBUSIES
BEEINNSS BEINNESS
BEEINNSZ BENZINES
BEEINORT TENEBRIO
BEEINOSS EBONISES
BEEINOST BETONIES
EBONITES
BEEINOSZ EBONIZES
BEEINPRS PEBRINES
BEEINRSS NEBRISES
BEEINRTT REBITTEN
BEEINSTT BENTIEST
BEEIOQSU OBSEQUIE
BEEIORSS SOBERISE
BEEIORSW BOWERIES
BEEIORSZ SOBERIZE
BEEIORTV OVERBITE
BEEIQSUZ BEZIQUES
BEEIRRSU REBURIES
BEEIRRSV BREVIERS
BEEIRRTT BITTERER
BEEIRSSU SUBERISE
BEEIRSSW BREWISES
BEEIRSTU UBERTIES
BEEIRSUZ SUBERIZE
BEEKMOPR PEMBROKE
BEEKNOPS BESPOKEN
BEEKNOST BETOKENS
STEENBOK
BEEKRRSS BERSERKS
BEEKRRSU REBUKERS
BEELLORW BELLOWER
REBELLOW
BEELLOST LOBELETS
BEELMMOP BEPOMMEL
BEELMNNO NOBLEMEN
BEELMOSW EMBOWELS
BEELMRRT TREMBLER
BEELMRRU LUMBERER
BEELMRST TREMBLES
BEELNNOS ENNOBLES
BEELNOSS BONELESS
NOBLESSE
BEELNOSU BLUENOSE
BEELNOSZ BENZOLES
BEELNSSU BLUENESS
BEELNTUY BUTYLENE
BEELOOST OBSOLETE
BEELOQRU BRELOQUE
BEELORVW OVERBLEW
BEELOSTW STEELBOW
BEELOSTY EYEBOLTS
BEELPRUV BUPLEVER
BEELRSSV VERBLESS
BEELRSUZ ZEBRULES
BEELSSTU TUBELESS
BEELSTTU BLUETTES
BEEMNRRU NUMBERER
RENUMBER
BEEMOPRT OBTEMPER
BEEMORRS SOMBERER
BEEMORSS EMBOSSER
BEEMORSW EMBOWERS
BEEMOSSS EMBOSSES
BEEMQSUU EMBUSQUE
BEEMRRSU UMBRERES
BEEMRSSU SUBMERSE
BEEMRSTU EMBRUTES
BEEMRTTU UMBRETTE
BEEMRTUZ ZERUMBET
BEEMSSSU EMBUSSES
BEENORTU BOUNTREE
BEENORTV VERBOTEN
BEENOSST BONESETS
BEENOSTU TUBENOSE
BEENPRST BESPRENT
BEENRSTT BRENTEST
BEENRSTW BESTREWN
BEENRTTU BRUNETTE
BEENSSTU SUBTEENS
SUBTENSE
BEEOORRT BOORTREE
BEEOORRV OVERBORE
BEEOORTT BEETROOT
BEEOPRSS BEPROSES
BEEORRSU BOURREES
BEEORRSV OBSERVER
VERBOSER
BEEORRTU BOURTREE
BEEORSST SOBEREST
BEEORSSU SUBEROSE
BEEORSSV OBSERVES
OBVERSES
BEEORSTU TUBEROSE
BEEORSTW BESTOWER
BEEORSWY EYEBROWS
BEEOSSSS OBSESSES
BEEOSSST BETOSSES
BEEPRRSU SUPERBER
BEEPRRSV PREVERBS
BEEPRSTY PRESBYTE
BEEQSSTU BEQUESTS
BEERRSTW BREWSTER
BEERRTTU REBUTTER
BEERSSSU SUBSERES
BEERSSTW BESTREWS
WEBSTERS
BEERSSUV SUBSERVE
SUBVERSE
BEERSTTU BURETTES
BEESTTUV BUVETTES
BEFFLRSU BLUFFERS
BEFFLSTU BLUFFEST
BEFGIILL FILLIBEG
BEFGIILS FILIBEGS
BEFGIINR BRIEFING
BEFGIRSU FIREBUGS
BEFHILSU BLUEFISH
BEFHIRSU BUSHFIRE
BEFIIRSU RUBIFIES
BEFILLXY FLEXIBLY
BEFILMOR FORELIMB
BEFILOST BOTFLIES
BEFILOUY LIFEBUOY
BEFILRST FILBERTS
BEFINORS BONFIRES
BEFIORSS FIBROSES
BEFIORTT FOREBITT
BEFIRSST FIBSTERS
BEFISSTU FUBSIEST
BEFLLLUY BELLYFUL
BEFLLSTY FLYBELTS
BEFLMRSU FUMBLERS
BEFLORUW FURBELOW
BEFLSTUU TUBEFULS
BEFNOORR FORBORNE
BEFNOSSY FYNBOSES
BEFORRXY FOXBERRY
BEGGGINS BEGGINGS
BEGGIINN BINGEING
BEGGIOST BOGGIEST
BEGGISTU BUGGIEST
BEGGLORS BOGGLERS
BEGGOOOS GOOSEGOB
BEGHHIST BEHIGHTS
BEGHIILP PHILIBEG
BEGHILRT BLIGHTER
THERBLIG
BEGHINOR NEIGHBOR
BEGHINOT BEHOTING
BEGHINOV BEHOVING
BEGHINRT BERTHING
BRIGHTEN
BEGHINST BENIGHTS
BEGHIRRT BRIGHTER
BEGHLNOU BUNGHOLE
BEGHNOTU BOUGHTEN
BEGHOSTU BESOUGHT
BEGHOSUU BUGHOUSE
BEGHRRSU BURGHERS
BEGIIISS SIGISBEI
BEGIILLN LIBELING
BEGIILLY ELIGIBLY
BEGIILST BILGIEST
BEGIIMNR BEMIRING
BEGIIMNT BETIMING
BEGIINNS INBEINGS
BEGIINRT REBITING
BEGIINRZ ZINGIBER
BEGIIOSS SIGISBEO
BEGIKMNO KEMBOING
BEGIKNRU REBUKING
BEGILLLU GULLIBLE
BEGILLNU BULLGINE
BEGILLNY BELLYING
BEGILMNR REMBLING
BEGILMNS SEMBLING
BEGILNNY BENIGNLY
BEGILNOR IGNOBLER
BEGILNOS INGLOBES
BEGILNOV BELOVING
BEGILNOW ELBOWING
BEGILNRT TREBLING
BEGILNSS BLESSING
GLIBNESS
BEGILNST BELTINGS
BEGILNSU BLUEINGS
BULGINES
BEGILNTT BLETTING
BEGILNUW BLUEWING
BEGILNZZ BEZZLING
BEGILRST GILBERTS
BEGILSTU BULGIEST
BEGIMNOS BESOMING
BEGIMNOW EMBOWING
BEGIMNOX EMBOXING
BEGIMNRU EMBRUING
UMBERING
BEGIMNSU BEMUSING
BEGIMOST MISBEGOT
BEGIMOSY BOGEYISM
BEGINNNR BRENNING
BEGINNNU UNBENIGN
BEGINNOR ENROBING
RINGBONE
BEGINNSU UNBEINGS
BEGINOOS BESOGNIO
BEGINORR REBORING
BEGINORS SOBERING
BEGINORW BOWERING
BEGINRRS BRINGERS
BEGINRRY BERRYING
BEGINRSW BREWINGS
BEGINSTT BETTINGS
BEGKMOSS GEMSBOKS
BEGLLOSU GLOBULES
BEGLLOTU GLOBULET
BEGLMOOS BEGLOOMS
BEGLMRRU GRUMBLER
BEGLMRSU GRUMBLES
BEGLNOUW BLUEGOWN
BEGLNRSU BLUNGERS
BUNGLERS
BEGLOOSS GLOBOSES
BEGLOOST BOOTLEGS
BEGLRSTY BERGYLTS
BEGNOORU BOURGEON
BEGNORSU BURGEONS
BEGNORTU BURGONET
BEGNSSUU SUBGENUS
BEHHKOST KHOTBEHS
BEHIISTX EXHIBITS
BEHIKLOS BLOKEISH
BEHIKNST BETHINKS
BEHIKOSS KIBOSHES
BEHILLOS SHOEBILL
BEHILLTY BLITHELY
BEHILMRW WHIMBREL
BEHILMST THIMBLES
BEHILNPY BIPHENYL
BEHILORR HORRIBLE
BEHILORS BOLSHIER
BEHILOSS BOLSHIES
BEHILRST BLITHERS
BEHILRTU THURIBLE
BEHILSTT BLITHEST
BEHIMNOO BONHOMIE
BEHIMRTU THUMBIER
BEHINNOS SHINBONE
BEHINOPS HOPBINES
BEHINOSW WISHBONE
BEHIOOPR BIOPHORE
BEHIRRST REBIRTHS
BEHIRRSU BRUSHIER
BEHIRSST HERBISTS
BEHIRSSU HUBRISES
BEHIRSSY HYBRISES
BEHISSTU BUSHIEST
BEHKOSSY KYBOSHES
BEHLLOOT BOLTHOLE
BEHLLOOW BLOWHOLE
BEHLLOPS BELLHOPS
BEHLLPSU BELLPUSH
BEHLMOSW WHOMBLES
BEHLMSTU HUMBLEST

BEHLOOPY	HYPOBOLE
	LYOPHOBE
BEHLOOST	BOTHOLES
BEHLORST	BROTHELS
BEHLOSSU	SLOEBUSH
BEHLRRSU	BURRHELS
BEHLRSSU	BLUSHERS
BEHLSSTU	BLUSHETS
BEHMNOTY	BOTHYMEN
BEHMOOOX	HOMEOBOX
BEHMOSTU	BEMOUTHS
BEHMPSTU	BETHUMPS
BEHNNOUY	HONEYBUN
BEHNRSTU	BURTHENS
BEHOOOST	BOOTHOSE
BEHOORST	THEORBOS
BEHOOSUY	HOUSEBOY
BEHORRST	BROTHERS
BEHORSSU	ROSEBUSH
BEHORSTT	BETROTHS
BEHRRSSU	BRUSHERS
BEIIIKMN	MINIBIKE
BEIIKRST	BIRKIEST
BEIIKRTZ	KIBITZER
BEIIKSTZ	KIBITZES
BEIILMMO	IMMOBILE
BEIILMOS	MOBILISE
BEIILMOZ	MOBILIZE
BEIILMSU	BULIMIES
BEIILNRS	RINSIBLE
BEIILOPR	PERIBOLI
BEIILRST	TRILBIES
BEIILRTT	LIBRETTI
BEIILRUZ	BRUILZIE
BEIILSSV	VISIBLES
BEIILSTT	STILBITE
BEIIMNNR	RENMINBI
BEIIMNOS	EBIONISM
BEIIMRTT	IMBITTER
BEIINORS	BRIONIES
BEIINOST	NIOBITES
BEIINRST	BRINIEST
BEIINSST	STIBINES
BEIINSTT	STIBNITE
BEIIOPSS	BIOPSIES
BEIIORST	ORBITIES
BEIIOSTT	BIOTITES
BEIIRSST	BIRSIEST
BEIISSTT	BITSIEST
BEIISSTU	SUBITISE
BEIISTTT	BITTIEST
BEIISTUZ	SUBITIZE
BEIJLMRU	JUMBLIER
BEIJMOSU	JUMBOISE
BEIJMOUZ	JUMBOIZE
BEIJNORW	BIJWONER
BEIKLMOW	WOMBLIKE
BEIKLNRS	BLINKERS
BEIKLOSS	OBELISKS
BEIKLOTY	KILOBYTE
BEIKLSTU	BULKIEST
BEIKMNNR	BRINKMEN
BEIKNRRY	INKBERRY
BEIKNRSS	BRISKENS
BEIKOORS	BOOKSIER
BEIKOORT	BROOKITE
BEIKOOST	BOOKIEST
BEIKOSST	BOSKIEST
BEIKRSST	BRISKEST
	BRISKETS
BEILLMSS	LIMBLESS
BEILLMSU	SEMIBULL
BEILLNTU	BULLETIN
BEILLORS	BROLLIES
BEILLOSU	LIBELOUS
BEILLOSX	BOLLIXES
BEILLRST	BRILLEST
BEILLSST	BESTILLS
BEILLSTU	BULLIEST
BEILMMOS	EMBOLISM
BEILMNOR	BROMELIN
BEILMNOU	NOBELIUM
BEILMNRU	UNLIMBER
BEILMNST	NIMBLEST
BEILMNUU	NEBULIUM
BEILMOOR	BLOOMIER
BEILMORS	EMBROILS
BEILMPTU	PLUMBITE
BEILMRRU	RUMBLIER
BEILMRSS	BRIMLESS
BEILMRST	TIMBRELS
BEILMRSU	SUBLIMER
BEILMRSW	WIMBRELS
BEILMSSU	SUBLIMES
BEILNNTU	BUNTLINE
BEILNOOS	OBELIONS
BEILNOPS	BONSPIEL
BEILNOSW	BOWLINES
BEILNOVY	BOVINELY
BEILNSSY	SENSIBLY
BEILNSTZ	BLINTZES
BEILOORV	OVERBOIL
BEILOOST	LOOBIEST
BEILOPPW	BLOWPIPE
BEILOPSS	POSSIBLE
BEILOQRU	OBLIQUER
BEILOQSU	OBLIQUES
BEILORRS	BROILERS
BEILORST	STROBILE
	TRILOBES
BEILORSW	BLOWSIER
BEILORTT	BLOTTIER
	LIBRETTO
BEILORWZ	BLOWZIER
BEILOSSY	BIOLYSES
BEILOSTW	BLOWIEST
BEILRRTT	BRITTLER
BEILRRTY	TERRIBLY
BEILRSST	BLISTERS
	BRISTLES
BEILRSTT	BRITTLES
	TRIBLETS
BEILRSTU	BURLIEST
	SUBTILER
BEILRSTY	BLISTERY
BEILRSUY	BRULYIES
BEILRSUZ	BRULZIES
BEILRTTY	BITTERLY
BEILSTTU	SUBTITLE
BEIMMRRS	BRIMMERS
BEIMNORS	BROMINES
BEIMNSSU	NIMBUSES
BEIMNSTU	BITUMENS
BEIMOORR	BROOMIER
BEIMOORS	RIBOSOME
BEIMORRV	OVERBRIM
BEIMORSW	IMBOWERS
BEIMORTY	BIOMETRY
BEIMORYZ	RIBOZYME
BEIMOSSS	IMBOSSES
BEIMPSTU	BUMPIEST
BEIMRSSU	IMBURSES
BEIMRSTU	IMBRUTES
	RESUBMIT
	TERBIUMS
BEINNOSS	BENISONS
	BONINESS
BEINNOST	BONNIEST
BEINNOSZ	BENZOINS
BEINNRYZ	ZEBRINNY
BEINORRW	BROWNIER
BEINORRZ	BRONZIER
BEINORST	BORNITES
	RIBSTONE
BEINORSW	BROWNIES
BEINORSY	BRYONIES
BEINORTZ	BRONZITE
BEINOSST	EBONISTS
BEINOSSX	BOXINESS
BEINOSTT	BOTTINES
BEINOSTU	BOUNTIES
BEINRRSY	NISBERRY
BEINRSSU	SUBERINS
BEINRSTT	BITTERNS
BEINRSTU	TRIBUNES
	TURBINES
BEINRSUU	UNBURIES
BEINSSSU	BUSINESS
BEINSTTU	BUNTIEST
BEIOORST	ROBOTISE
BEIOORTZ	ROBOTIZE
BEIOOSSV	OVIBOSES
BEIOOSTZ	BOOZIEST
BEIOPSTY	BIOTYPES
BEIOQTUU	BOUTIQUE
BEIORRST	ORBITERS
BEIORRSU	BOURSIER
BEIORRSW	BROWSIER
BEIORRTU	ROBURITE
BEIORSST	SORBITES
BEIORSTY	SOBRIETY
BEIOSSST	BOSSIEST
BEIOSSSU	SOUBISES
BEIOSSTU	BOUSIEST
BEIOTTZZ	BOZZETTI
BEIQRSTU	BRIQUETS
BEIRRSSU	BRISURES
	BRUISERS
BEIRRSTU	BURRIEST
BEIRRTTU	TRIBUTER
BEIRSSTU	BUSTIERS
BEIRSTTU	TRIBUTES
BEIRSTTY	TREYBITS
BEISSTTU	BUSTIEST
BEISTUZZ	BUZZIEST
BEJKOOST	JESTBOOK
BEJLMRSU	JUMBLERS
BEJORTTU	TURBOJET
BEKLNORY	BROKENLY
BEKLNRSU	BLUNKERS
BEKLOOOR	BOOKLORE
BEKLOORT	BROOKLET
BEKLOOSS	BOOKLESS
BEKLOOST	BOOKLETS
BEKLORUV	OVERBULK
BEKMOOPS	SPEKBOOM
BEKMOSST	STEMBOKS
BEKNNORU	UNBROKEN
BEKNOOOT	NOTEBOOK
BEKNOPRU	UPBROKEN
BEKOOORV	OVERBOOK
BEKOORST	BOOKREST
BEKOORTU	OUTBROKE
BEKOOTTX	TEXTBOOK
BELLMORT	MORTBELL
BELLMORU	UMBRELLO
BELLMRUY	LUMBERLY
BELLNOSU	BULLNOSE
BELLNTUY	TUNBELLY
BELLORTW	BELLWORT
BELLRRSU	BURRELLS
BELMMOOS	EMBLOOMS
BELMMRSU	MUMBLERS
BELMNOSU	NELUMBOS
BELMOORS	BLOOMERS
	REBLOOMS
BELMOORY	BLOOMERY
BELMOOSS	BLOOSMES
BELMOOST	BOOMLETS
BELMOPRS	PROBLEMS
BELMORST	TEMBLORS
BELMORSY	SOMBRELY
BELMORUW	RUMBELOW
BELMOSST	TOMBLESS
BELMOSSY	SYMBOLES
BELMPRSU	PLUMBERS
BELMPRUY	PLUMBERY
BELMRRSU	RUMBLERS
BELMRRUY	MULBERRY
BELMRSSU	SLUMBERS
BELMRSTU	STUMBLER
	TUMBLERS
	TUMBRELS
BELMRSUY	SLUMBERY
BELMSSTU	STUMBLES
BELNNOSU	UNNOBLES
BELNOOSY	BOLONEYS
BELNOSUU	NEBULOUS
BELNOSYZ	BENZOYLS
BELNSSTU	SUNBELTS
BELNSTTU	BLUNTEST
BELNSTUU	UNSUBTLE
BELOOPRS	BLOOPERS
BELOORSW	ROSEBOWL
BELOORVW	OVERBLOW
BELOOSST	BOOTLESS
BELOOTUV	OBVOLUTE
BELORRTU	TROUBLER
BELORSST	BOLSTERS
	LOBSTERS
BELORSSW	BROWLESS
BELORSTT	BLOTTERS
	BOTTLERS
BELORSTU	BOULTERS
	TROUBLES
BELOSTUY	OBTUSELY
BELPRSUY	SUPERBLY
BELRSSTU	BLUSTERS
	BUSTLERS
BELRSTUY	BLUSTERY
BELSSTTU	SUBTLEST
BELSSTUY	SUBSTYLE
BELSTTUY	SUBTLETY
BEMMOOSS	EMBOSOMS
BEMMORRS	BROMMERS
BEMMRRSU	BRUMMERS
BEMNNSSU	NUMBNESS
BEMNOORT	TROMBONE
BEMNORSW	EMBROWNS
BEMNORSY	EMBRYONS

BEMNSTTU BUTMENTS
BEMNTTUY BUTTYMEN
BEMOORRS SOMBRERO
BEMORSST BESTORMS
MOBSTERS
SOMBREST
BEMORSSU MORBUSES
BEMORSWW WEBWORMS
BEMOSTUX BUXOMEST
BEMOSTUY MYOTUBES
BEMSSSUU SUBSUMES
BENNNOTU UNBONNET
BENNOOTU BOUTONNE
BENORRSU SUBORNER
BENORRSZ BRONZERS
BENORRUV OVERBURN
BENORSST SORBENTS
BENORSTU RUBSTONE
BENORSTW BESTROWN
BROWNEST
BENORSUU BURNOUSE
BENORSWY BYWONERS
BENORTTU REBUTTON
BENOSSUZ SUBZONES
BENOSSWY NEWSBOYS
BENRRSUY SUNBERRY
BENSSSUY BUSYNESS
BEOORRRW BORROWER
REBORROW
BEOORRVW OVERBROW
BEOORSST BOOSTERS
BEOORSTY BOTRYOSE
BEOOSTUX OUTBOXES
BEOOTTZZ BOZZETTO
BEOPRRSV PROVERBS
BEOPRSST BESPORTS
BEOPSSTU BESPOUTS
BEOQSSTU BOSQUETS
BEOQSTUU BOUQUETS
BEORRSSW BROWSERS
BEORRSTU ROBUSTER
BEORSSSU SORBUSES
BEORSSUU SUBEROUS
BEORSTUU TUBEROUS
BEORSUVY OVERBUSY
OVERBUYS
BEOSSTTU OBTUSEST
BEPRRSTU PERTURBS
BEPSSTUY SUBTYPES
BEQRRSUU BRUSQUER
BERRSSTU BURSTERS
BERRSTUU SURREBUT
BERSSTTU BUTTRESS
BERSSTUV SUBVERST
SUBVERTS
BESSSSUY BYSSUSES
BESSTTUX SUBTEXTS
BFFGILNU BLUFFING
BFFGINSU BUFFINGS
BFFNOOSU BUFFOONS
BFFNOSUX SNUFFBOX
BFGILMNU FUMBLING
BFGIOOST BIGFOOTS
BFGIORST FROGBITS
BFGLLORU BULLFROG
BFHILOSW BLOWFISH
BFHLLSUU BLUSHFUL
BFIINORS FIBROINS
BFIIORSS FIBROSIS
BFILLSSU BLISSFUL
BFIMNORU NUBIFORM
BFIMORTU TUBIFORM
BFINORYZ BRONZIFY
BFIORSTT FROSTBIT
BFKLOOSY FLYBOOKS
BFKSSSUU SUBFUSKS
BFLLOSUW BOWLFULS
BFLLOSWY FLYBLOWS
BFLOORSU SUBFLOOR
BFOOOSTY FOOTBOYS
BGGGILNO BOGGLING
BGGGINOR BROGGING
BGGGINSU BUGGINGS
BGGIILNN BINGLING
BGGIILNO OBLIGING
BGGIILNY GIBINGLY
BGGIINNO BOINGING
BGGIINNR BRINGING
BGGIINRU BRIGUING
BGGILNNU BLUNGING
BUNGLING
BGGILNRU BURGLING
BGGINOOT TOBOGGIN
BGHHIORW HIGHBROW
BGHHIOSY HIGHBOYS
BGHIINRT BIRTHING
BGHILMNU HUMBLING
BGHILNSU BLUSHING
BGHILRTY BRIGHTLY
BGHIMNTU THUMBING
BGHIMOTU BIGMOUTH
BGHINORS BIGHORNS
BGHINRSU BRUSHING
BGHINSSU BUSHINGS
BGHIORSU BROGUISH
BGHLRSUU BULGHURS
BURGHULS
BGHNORSU HORNBUGS
BGHNOTUU UNBOUGHT
BGHOOPTU BOUGHPOT
BGHOORSU BOROUGHS
BGIIJLNR JIRBLING
BGIIKLNN BLINKING
BGIIKMNO KIMBOING
BGIIKNNO BOINKING
BGIIKNRS BRISKING
BGIILLNS BILLINGS
BGIILMNW WIMBLING
BGIILNNN BLINNING
BGIILNOR BROILING
BGIILNOS BOILINGS
BGIILNOX BOLIXING
BGIILNPP BLIPPING
BGIILNRS BIRLINGS
BIRSLING
BRISLING
BGIILNSS SIBLINGS
BGIILNTZ BLITZING
BGIIMMNR BRIMMING
BGIIMNRS BRIMINGS
BGIIMNRU IMBRUING
BGIINNOR INORBING
BGIINNRS INBRINGS
BGIINORT ORBITING
BGIINRST RINGBITS
BGIINRSU BRUISING
BGIINRTU BRUITING
BGIINSTU BUISTING
BGIINVVY BIVVYING
BGIJLMNU JUMBLING
BGIJNORU OBJURING
BGIKLNNU BLUNKING
BGIKNNOU BUNKOING
BGIKNOOR BROOKING
BGIKNOOS BOOKINGS
BGIKNORS BROKINGS
BGIKNSSU BUSKINGS
BGILLNOU GLOBULIN
BGILLNSU BULLINGS
BGILLNUY BULLYING
BGILMMNU BUMMLING
MUMBLING
BGILMNOO BLOOMING
BGILMNPU PLUMBING
BGILMNRU RUMBLING
BGILMNTU TUMBLING
BGILMORY GORBLIMY
BGILMOSU GUMBOILS
BGILNNOS SNOBLING
BGILNNTU BLUNTING
BGILNOOP BLOOPING
BGILNORY BORINGLY
BGILNOST BILTONGS
BOLTINGS
BGILNOSU BLOUSING
BGILNOSW BOWLINGS
BGILNOTT BLOTTING
BOTTLING
BGILNOTU BOULTING
BGILNRRU BLURRING
BGILNRTU BLURTING
BGILNSTU BUSTLING
BGILNTTU BUTTLING
BGILOORS OBLIGORS
BGILRSSU BUSGIRLS
BGIMNOOR BROOMING
BGIMNOOS BOOMINGS
BOSOMING
BGIMNORS SOMBRING
BGIMNPSU BUMPINGS
BGIMOSSY BOGYISMS
BGINNNOU UNBONING
BGINNORU UNROBING
BGINNORW BROWNING
BGINNORZ BRONZING
BGINNOUX UNBOXING
BGINNRSU BURNINGS
BGINNRTU BRUNTING
BGINNSTU BUNTINGS
BGINOOST BOOSTING
BGINORSW BROWSING
BGINPRSU UPBRINGS
BGINRSSU SUBRINGS
BGINRSTU BRUSTING
BRUTINGS
BURSTING
BGINSSSU BUSSINGS
BGINSSTU BUSTINGS
BGINSUZZ BUZZINGS
BGKLOOOS LOGBOOKS
BGKNOOOS SONGBOOK
BGKORSSY GRYSBOKS
BGLNOOSW LONGBOWS
BGLNOSUW BLOWGUNS
BGLOORYY BRYOLOGY
BGMOOSTU GUMBOOTS
BGNOOSWY GOWNBOYS
BGNOSSSU SUBSONGS
BGOPRSUU SUBGROUP
BGORSTUW BUGWORTS
BHIIINST INHIBITS
BHIIKRSS BRISKISH
BHIILMPS BLIMPISH
BHIIMRST MISBIRTH
BHIIOPRT PROHIBIT
BHIIPSSS SIBSHIPS
BHIKLLOO BILLHOOK
BHILLNOR HORNBILL
BHILLPUW BULLWHIP
BHILLSTU BULLSHIT
BHILNSTU BLUNTISH
BHILORRY HORRIBLY
BHILOSTU HOLIBUTS
BHILOSYY BOYISHLY
BHIMNORT THROMBIN
BHIMOOPR BIOMORPH
BHIMOOSS HOBOISMS
BHIMOPSS PHOBISMS
BHIMSSTU BISMUTHS
BHINOPSU UNBISHOP
BHINORSW BROWNISH
BHIOOPRS BIOPHORS
BHIOPSST PHOBISTS
BHIRSTTU TURBITHS
BHKNOOOR HORNBOOK
BHKOOOPS BOOKSHOP
BHLOOOTT TOLBOOTH
BHLRSUUY BULRUSHY
BHMNTTUU THUMBNUT
BHMOPTTU THUMBPOT
BHMORSTU THROMBUS
BHNOSSUW SNOWBUSH
BHOOSSTW BOWSHOTS
BIIKLOST KILOBITS
BIIKNOOT BOOTIKIN
BIILLMOR MORBILLI
BIILLNOS BILLIONS
BIILLOSU BOUILLIS
BIILLSTW TWIBILLS
BIILMOTY MOBILITY
BIILNNRS BIRLINNS
BIILNOOV OBLIVION
BIILNOTY NOBILITY
BIILNQSU QUIBLINS
BIILNTUY NUBILITY
BIILORST STROBILI
BIILOSSU SIBILOUS
BIILOSSY BIOLYSIS
BIILSTTW WITBLITS
BIIMMNSY NIMBYISM
BIIMMOSZ ZOMBIISM
BIIMNOSU NIOBIUMS
BIIMSSTU STIBIUMS
BIINRSTU BURINIST
BIIQTUUY UBIQUITY
BIIRSSTU BURSITIS
BIJNOSSU SUBJOINS
BIKLNOSY LINKBOYS
BIKMNPSU BUMPKINS
BIKOOUUZ BOUZOUKI
BIKORRSW RIBWORKS
BILLMSUY BULLYISM
BILLNOOU BOUILLON
BILLNOSU BULLIONS
BILLRSWY WRYBILLS
BILMMPSU PLUMBISM
BILMNORS NOMBRILS
BILMOSTU BOTULISM
BILMRSTU TUMBRILS
BILNOSUU NUBILOUS

BILNSTUU TUBULINS
BILOORST SORBITOL
BILOPSSY POSSIBLY
BILORSST BRISTOLS
BILOSSSU SUBSOILS
BIMMOOSS IMBOSOMS
BIMMORSS BROMISMS
BIMNORSW IMBROWNS
BIMNOSTY SYMBIONT
BIMNRRUU MUIRBURN
BIMNRUUV VIBURNUM
BIMOSSTY SYBOTISM
BIMRSSUX BRUXISMS
BINOORST ISOBRONT
BINORSST RIBSTONS
BINRSSTU INBURSTS
BINSSTUU SUBUNITS
BIOPRRSU SUBPRIOR
BIOPRSTW BOWSPRIT
BIORRSTU BURRITOS
BIORRSTW RIBWORTS
BIORSSTT BISTORTS
BIORSTTU BITTOURS
BIORSTUY BISTOURY
BIOSTTUY OBTUSITY
BIRSSTTU SUBTRIST
BISSSSTU SUBSISTS
BKKOOORW BOOKWORK
WORKBOOK
BKMOOORW BOOKWORM
BKMOORUZ ZOMBORUK
BKNOOSTW BOWKNOTS
BLLLLOOY LOBLOLLY
BLMMPSUU PLUMBUMS
BLMNPSUU UNPLUMBS
BLMOOOST TOMBOLOS
BLMOOOTY LOBOTOMY
BLMOORSW LOBWORMS
BLMOOSSS BLOSSOMS
BLMOOSSY BLOSSOMY
BLMOPSUU PLUMBOUS
BLNOOSSU BLOUSONS
BLOOSSTY SLYBOOTS
BLOPSSTU SUBPLOTS
BLORSTUY ROBUSTLY
BLOSTUUU TUBULOUS
BMNOOSSU UNBOSOMS
BMNORSUW MOWBURNS
BMNORTUW MOWBURNT
BMOOORSX BOXROOMS
BMOORSSU SOMBROUS
BMOORTTY BOTTOMRY
BMORSSTU STROMBUS
BNNOTTUU UNBUTTON
BNNRSSUU SUNBURNS
BNNRSTUU SUNBURNT
BNOOOSTW SNOWBOOT
BNOOOSUY SONOBUOY
BNOORTUW BROWNOUT
BNORRUUW UNBURROW
BNORSTUU OUTBURNS
BNORTTUU OUTBURNT
BNRSSTUU SUNBURST
BORSTTUU OUTBURST
BPRSSTUU UPBURSTS
CCCDIILY DICYCLIC
CCCEEILT ECLECTIC
CCCEGOSY COCCYGES
CCCEHIOR CHOCCIER
CCCEHIOS CHOCCIES

CCCEIIRT ECCRITIC
CCCEILNY ENCYCLIC
CCCEILUY EUCYCLIC
CCCHIORY CHICCORY
CCCIINSU SUCCINIC
CCCILNOY CYCLONIC
CCCILOPY CYCLOPIC
CCCINSTU SUCCINCT
CCCIOORS SCIROCCO
CCCNOOST CONCOCTS
CCDDEENO CONCEDED
CCDDEEOT DECOCTED
CCDDELOU OCCLUDED
CCDDENOU CONDUCED
CCDEEENR CREDENCE
CCDEEHIL CLICHEED
CCDEEHLN CLENCHED
CCDEEILN LICENCED
CCDEEINS SCIENCED
CCDEEIOP CODPIECE
CCDEEIOS ECOCIDES
CCDEEKOR COCKERED
CCDEEKOY COCKEYED
CCDEELRY RECYCLED
CCDEENOR CONCEDER
CCDEENOS CONCEDES
CCDEESSU SUCCEEDS
CCDEHHRU CHURCHED
CCDEHIKT TCHICKED
CCDEHILN CLINCHED
CCDEHIPU HICCUPED
CCDEHKLU CHUCKLED
CCDEHLTU CLUTCHED
DECLUTCH
CCDEHNRU CRUNCHED
CCDEHORS SCORCHED
CCDEHORT CROTCHED
CCDEHORU CROUCHED
CCDEHOST SCOTCHED
CCDEHRTU CRUTCHED
CCDEHSTU SCUTCHED
CCDEIILO CLEIDOIC
CCDEIINO COINCIDE
CCDEIIRT CRICETID
CCDEIIST DEICTICS
CCDEILOS SCOLECID
CCDEINOR CORNICED
CCDEINOS CONCISED
CCDEINOT OCCIDENT
CCDEIOPP COPPICED
CCDEIOPU OCCUPIED
CCDEKNOU UNCOCKED
CCDELNOU CONCLUDE
CCDELORU OCCLUDER
CCDELOSU OCCLUDES
CCDELOTU OCCULTED
CCDENOOO COCOONED
CCDENOSU CONDUCES
CCDEORRU OCCURRED
CCDEORSU SUCCORED
CCDEOSTU STUCCOED
CCDHIIKP DIPCHICK
CCDHIILO CICHLOID
CCDHIILS CICHLIDS
CCDHIIOR DICHROIC
CCDHINOO CONCHOID
CCDIILOS CODICILS
CCDIILSU CULICIDS
CCDIINOO CONOIDIC
CCDIINOS SCINCOID

CCDIINST DISCINCT
CCDIIORS CRICOIDS
CCDIIORT DICROTIC
CCDILOSY CYCLOIDS
CCDINOTU CONDUCTI
CCDKLOSU CUCKOLDS
CCDKOOOW WOODCOCK
CCDNOORS CONCORDS
CCDNOSTU CONDUCTS
CCEEGINR RECCEING
CCEEGNOS COGENCES
CCEEHINZ ZECCHINE
CCEEHISV CEVICHES
CCEEHKNS SCHNECKE
CCEEHKRS CHECKERS
RECHECKS
CCEEHLNS CLENCHES
CCEEHORS ECORCHES
CCEEHOSU COUCHEES
CCEEHRSY SCREECHY
CCEEIILS CICELIES
CCEEIIST CECITIES
CCEEILNR ENCIRCLE
CCEEILNS LICENCES
CCEEILNT ELENCTIC
CCEEILPY EPICYCLE
CCEEILRT ELECTRIC
CCEEIMNU ECUMENIC
CCEEINOR CICERONE
CCEEINOV CONCEIVE
CCEEINSS SCIENCES
CCEEIORV COERCIVE
CCEEIPSS SPECCIES
CCEEIRSS ECCRISES
CCEEIRSV CERVICES
CRESCIVE
CREVICES
CCEEITTU EUTECTIC
CCEEKLOR COCKEREL
CCEEKOSY COCKEYES
CCEELMNY CLEMENCY
CCEELOSS SCOLECES
CCEELRSY RECYCLES
CCEEMMNO COMMENCE
CCEEMMOR COMMERCE
CCEEMOPS COMPESCE
CCEENNOS ENSCONCE
CCEENORT CONCRETE
CCEENRST CRESCENT
CCEFIIPS SPECIFIC
CCEFIRRU CRUCIFER
CCEFLLOU FLOCCULE
CCEFLOOS FLOCCOSE
CCEFNOST CONFECTS
CCEGHIKN CHECKING
CCEGHIOR CHOREGIC
CCEGIKLN CLECKING
CCEGILOO ECOLOGIC
CCEGILRY GLYCERIC
CCEGINNO CONGENIC
CCEGINOR COERCING
CCEGINRY RECCYING
CCEGNOOS COGNOSCE
CCEHHINS CHINCHES
CCEHHRSU CHURCHES
CCEHIIMR CHIMERIC
CCEHIIMS ISCHEMIC
CCEHIINZ ZECCHINI
CCEHIKNS CHICKENS
CCEHIKSU CHUCKIES

CCEHILNR CLINCHER
CCEHILNS CLINCHES
CCEHILOR CHOLERIC
CCEHILOY CHOICELY
CCEHILSU CULCHIES
CCEHINOR CORNICHE
ENCHORIC
CCEHINOS CONCHIES
CCEHINOZ ZECCHINO
CCEHINST TECHNICS
CCEHIORT RICOCHET
CCEHIOST CHOICEST
CCEHIRSS SCREICHS
SCRIECHS
CCEHKLSU CHUCKLES
CCEHKMSS SCHMECKS
CCEHKNSU UNCHECKS
CCEHKOTU CHECKOUT
CCEHLMOR CROMLECH
CCEHLNNU UNCLENCH
CCEHLNSU CLUNCHES
CCEHLRSU CLERUCHS
CCEHLRUY CLERUCHY
CCEHLSTU CLUTCHES
CULTCHES
CCEHNRSU CRUNCHES
CCEHORRS SCORCHER
CCEHORSS SCORCHES
CCEHORST CROCHETS
CROTCHES
CCEHORSU CROUCHES
CCEHORTT CROTCHET
CCEHOSST SCOTCHES
CCEHRSTU CRUTCHES
SCUTCHER
CCEHRTUY CUTCHERY
CCEHSSTU SCUTCHES
CCEIIKLN NICKELIC
CCEIILNT ENCLITIC
CCEIILNU CULICINE
CCEIILOR LICORICE
CCEIILPT ECLIPTIC
CCEIILST SCILICET
CCEIILTU LEUCITIC
CCEIINNR ENCRINIC
CCEIINOR CICERONI
CCEIIRRT CIRCITER
CCEIIRSS ECCRISIS
CCEIIRST ICTERICS
CCEIIRTT RECTITIC
CCEIIRTU EUCRITIC
CCEIKLRS CLICKERS
CCEIKLRU CLUCKIER
CCEIKLST CLICKETS
CCEIKORS COCKSIER
CCEIKOST COCKIEST
CCEIKRST CRICKETS
CCEILMOO COELOMIC
CCEILMOP COMPLICE
CCEILNOR CORNICLE
CCEILNUY UNICYCLE
CCEILOSS SCOLICES
CCEILRRS CIRCLERS
CCEILRRU CURRICLE
CCEILRST CIRCLETS
CCEILRSY CRESYLIC
CCEILRTY TRICYCLE
CCEILRUU CURLICUE
CCEILSTU CUTICLES
CCEIMNOO ECONOMIC

	ONCOMICE
CCEIMOST	COSMETIC
CCEIMRRU	MERCURIC
CCEINNOS	INSCONCE
CCEINNOV	CONVINCE
CCEINOOR	COERCION
CCEINOPT	CONCEPTI
CCEINORS	CONCISER
	CORNICES
	CROCEINS
CCEINORT	CONCERTI
	NECROTIC
CCEINOSS	CONCISES
CCEINOST	CONCEITS
CCEINOTT	CONCETTI
	TECTONIC
CCEINOTY	CONCEITY
CCEINPRT	PRECINCT
CCEINRTU	CINCTURE
CCEINSTY	SYNECTIC
CCEIOORT	CROCOITE
CCEIOOTX	ECOTOXIC
CCEIOOTZ	ECTOZOIC
CCEIOPPS	COPPICES
CCEIOPRT	ECTROPIC
CCEIOPRU	OCCUPIER
CCEIOPSU	OCCUPIES
CCEIORST	CORTICES
CCEIPSST	SCEPTICS
CCEIRSSU	CIRCUSES
CCEJNOST	CONJECTS
CCEKLORS	CLOCKERS
CCEKNOST	CONTECKS
CCEKNOSY	COCKNEYS
CCEKOPST	PETCOCKS
CCEKORRY	CROCKERY
CCEKORST	CROCKETS
CCEKORSU	COCKSURE
CCELLOST	COLLECTS
CCELMOPT	COMPLECT
CCELNOSY	CYCLONES
CCELOPSY	CYCLOPES
CCELOSSY	CYCLOSES
CCELSSUY	CYCLUSES
CCENNORS	CONCERNS
CCENNOST	CONCENTS
	CONNECTS
CCENOORT	CONCERTO
CCENOOTT	CONCETTO
CCENOPST	CONCEPTS
CCENORST	CONCERTS
CCENORSW	CONCREWS
CCENORTY	CORNETCY
CCENRRUY	CURRENCY
CCEOOORR	COROCORE
CCEOORSU	CROCEOUS
CCEOOSTT	COCOTTES
CCEOPRUY	REOCCUPY
CCEORRST	CORRECTS
CCEORSSU	CROCUSES
CCEORSTU	STUCCOER
CCEORSTW	TWOCCERS
CCESSSUU	CUSCUSES
CCFIINOR	CORNIFIC
CCFIIRUX	CRUCIFIX
CCFIKNOY	COCKNIFY
CCFILLOU	FLOCCULI
CCFILNOT	CONFLICT
CCFKLOOT	COCKLOFT
CCFLOOOO	LOCOFOCO
CCGHHIOU	HICCOUGH
CCGHIINN	CINCHING
CCGHIKNO	CHOCKING
CCGHIKNU	CHUCKING
CCGHINNO	CONCHING
CCGHINOS	GNOCCHIS
CCGHINOU	COUCHING
CCGIIKLN	CLICKING
CCGIIKNR	CRICKING
CCGIILNR	CIRCLING
CCGIKLNO	CLOCKING
	COCKLING
CCGIKLNU	CLUCKING
CCGIKNOR	CROCKING
CCGILLOY	GLYCOLIC
CCGILNOY	GLYCONIC
CCGILNSY	CYCLINGS
CCGILOSU	GLUCOSIC
CCGINNOS	SCONCING
CCGINOTW	TWOCCING
CCGKOORS	GORCOCKS
CCHHIITY	ICHTHYIC
CCHHILSS	SCHLICHS
CCHHINOT	CHTHONIC
CCHHLRUY	CHURCHLY
CCHHNRUU	UNCHURCH
CCHIINUZ	ZUCCHINI
CCHIIORT	ORCHITIC
CCHIKMPU	CHIPMUCK
CCHIKSST	SCHTICKS
CCHINORS	CHRONICS
CCHINOSU	SCUCHION
CCHINSSU	SCUCHINS
CCHIPSSY	PSYCHICS
CCHKLOSS	SCHLOCKS
CCHKLOSY	SCHLOCKY
CCHKMOSS	SCHMOCKS
CCHKMSSU	SCHMUCKS
CCHKOOST	COCKSHOT
CCHKOPTU	PUTCHOCK
CCHKOSTU	COCKSHUT
CCHKPSUU	UPCHUCKS
CCHKSSTU	SCHTUCKS
CCHLNTUU	UNCLUTCH
CCHNRSUY	SCRUNCHY
CCIIKNPY	PICNICKY
CCIILPRS	CIRCLIPS
CCIIMNSY	CYNICISM
CCIINNSU	CICINNUS
CCIINORZ	ZIRCONIC
CCIIRSTU	CIRCUITS
CCIIRTUY	CIRCUITY
CCIKKLOP	LOCKPICK
	PICKLOCK
CCIKLOSW	COWLICKS
CCIKNOPR	PRINCOCK
CCIKOPST	COCKPITS
CCILNOOS	COLONICS
CCILNOSU	COUNCILS
CCILNSUY	SUCCINYL
CCILOOPS	PICCOLOS
CCILORUU	CURCULIO
CCILOSSY	CYCLOSIS
CCILSSTY	CYCLISTS
CCIMNRUU	CURCUMIN
CCINOOST	COCTIONS
CCINOPRT	PROCINCT
CCINOPSY	SYNCOPIC
CCINORSY	CRYONICS
CCINOSTV	CONVICTS
CCIOOPST	SCOTOPIC
CCIOORSS	SIROCCOS
CCIOOTXY	OXYTOCIC
CCIOPSTU	OCCIPUTS
CCIRSSUY	CIRCUSSY
CCJNNOTU	CONJUNCT
CCKKLMUU	MUCKLUCK
CCKMMORU	CRUMMOCK
CCKMOOOR	MOORCOCK
CCKNORTU	TURNCOCK
CCKOOPST	STOPCOCK
CCKOPRSU	COCKSPUR
CCKOSSTU	CUSTOCKS
CCLLOTUY	OCCULTLY
CCLMOOPU	COCOPLUM
CCLNOOOR	CONCOLOR
CCLOOOSZ	ZOCCOLOS
CCLOORSU	OCCLUSOR
CCMOOORS	MOROCCOS
CCNOOPSU	PUCCOONS
CCNOORSU	CONCOURS
CCNOOSTU	COCONUTS
CCOOOORR	COROCORO
CCOOSSUU	COUSCOUS
CCOOTTUU	TUCOTUCO
CCORSSTU	CROSSCUT
CCORSSUU	SUCCOURS
CCOTTUUU	TUCUTUCO
CCRSUUUU	SURUCUCU
CDDDEETU	DEDUCTED
CDDDEIIS	DISCIDED
CDDDELRU	CRUDDLED
CDDDELSU	SCUDDLED
CDDDIIOY	DIDDICOY
CDDEEEEX	EXCEEDED
CDDEEEFN	DEFENCED
CDDEEEFT	DEFECTED
CDDEEEIV	DECEIVED
CDDEEEJT	DEJECTED
CDDEEENR	DECERNED
CDDEEENT	DECEDENT
CDDEEEPR	PRECEDED
CDDEEERS	SCREEDED
CDDEEERW	DECREWED
CDDEEETT	DETECTED
CDDEEFOR	DEFORCED
CDDEEHIS	DEHISCED
CDDEEHIT	CHEDDITE
CDDEEHNR	DRENCHED
CDDEEIIS	DEICIDES
CDDEEIKR	DICKERED
CDDEEILN	DECLINED
CDDEEILP	PEDICLED
CDDEEINR	CINDERED
CDDEEIOV	DEVOICED
CDDEEIPT	DEPICTED
CDDEEIRS	DECIDERS
	DESCRIED
CDDEEIRT	CREDITED
	DIRECTED
CDDEEKNU	UNDECKED
CDDEEKOT	DOCKETED
CDDEEKUW	DUCKWEED
CDDEELMO	COMEDDLE
CDDEELPU	DECUPLED
CDDEELSU	SCEDULED
	SECLUDED
CDDEELUX	EXCLUDED
CDDEELUY	DEUCEDLY
CDDEENOS	SECONDED
CDDEENSS	DESCENDS
CDDEEORR	RECORDED
CDDEEORS	DECODERS
CDDEERUV	DECURVED
CDDEESUW	CUDWEEDS
CDDEFIIO	CODIFIED
CDDEFINO	CONFIDED
CDDEGIIN	DECIDING
CDDEGINO	DECODING
CDDEGINU	DEDUCING
CDDEHIOW	COWHIDED
CDDEHISU	CHUDDIES
CDDEIINT	INDICTED
CDDEIISS	DISCIDES
CDDEIKOS	DOCKISED
	DOCKSIDE
CDDEIKOZ	DOCKIZED
CDDEILLO	COLLIDED
CDDEILNU	INCLUDED
CDDEILOR	CLODDIER
CDDEILRU	CUDDLIER
CDDEINTU	INDUCTED
CDDEIORV	DIVORCED
CDDEIRRU	CRUDDIER
CDDEIRSU	DISCURED
CDDEKNOU	UNDOCKED
CDDELLOU	COLLUDED
CDDELNOO	CONDOLED
CDDELOOR	CROODLED
CDDELRSU	CRUDDLES
CDDELSSU	SCUDDLES
CDDEMNOU	DUNCEDOM
CDDENNOO	CONDONED
CDDENOOR	CORDONED
CDDENORU	UNCORDED
CDDEOORR	CORRODED
CDDEOORT	DOCTORED
CDDEOPRU	PRODUCED
CDDERSSU	SCUDDERS
CDDGHILO	GODCHILD
CDDGILNO	CLODDING
	CODDLING
CDDGILNU	CUDDLING
CDDGINRU	CRUDDING
CDDGINSU	SCUDDING
CDDHIIRY	DIHYDRIC
CDDHILOS	CLODDISH
CDDHIORS	DICHORDS
CDDIIIOS	DIDICOIS
CDDIIOSY	DIDICOYS
CDDIISTY	DYTISCID
CDDIKOPS	PIDDOCKS
CDDIORSS	DISCORDS
CDDKOPSU	PUDDOCKS
CDDKORSU	RUDDOCKS
CDDMMOUU	MOCUDDUM
CDDOOORW	CORDWOOD
CDEEEFFT	EFFECTED
CDEEEFHL	FLEECHED
CDEEEFNS	DEFENCES
CDEEEFRT	REFECTED
CDEEEHHW	WHEECHED
CDEEEHLR	LECHERED
CDEEEHMS	SMEECHED
CDEEEHPS	DEPECHES
	SPEECHED
CDEEEHRS	CREESHED
CDEEEHST	TEDESCHE
CDEEEHSW	ESCHEWED
CDEEEINP	PIECENED

CDEEEINV	EVIDENCE
CDEEEIPS	EPICEDES
CDEEEIRV	DECEIVER
	RECEIVED
CDEEEISV	DECEIVES
CDEEEJRT	REJECTED
CDEEEKNW	NECKWEED
CDEEELLX	EXCELLED
CDEEELOS	COLESEED
CDEEELPY	YCLEEPED
CDEEELST	DESELECT
	SELECTED
CDEEELUX	EXCLUDEE
CDEEEMNT	CEMENTED
CDEEEMPR	EMPERCED
CDEEENNT	TENDENCE
CDEEENOS	SECONDEE
CDEEENRS	RECENSED
	SCREENED
	SECERNED
CDEEENRT	CENTERED
	DECENTER
CDEEEPRS	PRECEDES
CDEEEPTX	EXCEPTED
	EXPECTED
CDEEERRS	SCREEDER
CDEEERSS	RECESSED
	SECEDERS
CDEEERST	DECREETS
	RESECTED
	SECRETED
CDEEERSV	SCREEVED
CDEEERTX	EXCRETED
CDEEESTX	EXSECTED
CDEEETUX	EXECUTED
CDEEFFOR	COFFERED
	EFFORCED
CDEEFHLN	FLENCHED
CDEEFHLT	FLETCHED
CDEEFIIL	ICEFIELD
CDEEFIIS	EDIFICES
CDEEFIIT	FETICIDE
CDEEFINT	INFECTED
CDEEFKLR	FRECKLED
CDEEFKOR	FOREDECK
CDEEFLST	DEFLECTS
CDEEFNNU	UNFENCED
CDEEFNOR	ENFORCED
CDEEFORS	DEFORCES
	FRESCOED
CDEEFORT	DEFECTOR
CDEEGIIR	REGICIDE
CDEEGINO	GENOCIDE
CDEEGINR	RECEDING
CDEEGINS	SECEDING
CDEEGIOS	GEODESIC
CDEEGIOT	GEODETIC
CDEEGIRS	GRECISED
CDEEGIRZ	GRECIZED
CDEEGNOR	CONGREED
CDEEHHSU	SHEUCHED
CDEEHHTT	THETCHED
CDEEHIKL	HELIDECK
CDEEHILN	LICHENED
CDEEHILP	CHELIPED
CDEEHINR	ENRICHED
	INHERCED
	NICHERED
	RICHENED
CDEEHIOS	ECHOISED
CDEEHIOZ	ECHOIZED
CDEEHIPR	CIPHERED
	DECIPHER
CDEEHIRR	CHERRIED
	DREICHER
CDEEHISS	DEHISCES
CDEEHIST	TEDESCHI
CDEEHITW	ITCHWEED
CDEEHKST	SKETCHED
CDEEHKTV	KVETCHED
CDEEHLMO	LEECHDOM
CDEEHLQU	QUELCHED
CDEEHLSU	SCHEDULE
CDEEHMTU	HUMECTED
CDEEHNQU	QUENCHED
CDEEHNRR	DRENCHER
CDEEHNRS	DRENCHES
CDEEHNRT	TRENCHED
CDEEHNRW	WRENCHED
CDEEHNST	STENCHED
CDEEHNUW	UNCHEWED
CDEEHORS	CHORDEES
	COSHERED
CDEEHORT	HECTORED
	TOCHERED
CDEEHPRU	CHERUPED
CDEEHPRY	CYPHERED
CDEEHQTU	QUETCHED
CDEEHRTW	WRETCHED
CDEEHSSU	DUCHESSE
CDEEIILT	ELICITED
CDEEIIMN	MEDICINE
CDEEIIMP	EPIDEMIC
CDEEIINT	INDICTEE
CDEEIIST	EIDETICS
CDEEIISV	DECISIVE
CDEEIITT	DIETETIC
CDEEIJNT	INJECTED
CDEEIJOR	REJOICED
CDEEIKLN	NICKELED
CDEEIKMY	MICKEYED
CDEEIKNR	NICKERED
CDEEIKNS	SICKENED
CDEEIKNV	INVECKED
CDEEIKPT	PICKETED
CDEEIKRR	DRECKIER
CDEEIKRW	WICKEDER
	WICKERED
CDEEIKRY	YICKERED
CDEEIKTT	TICKETED
CDEEILNP	PENDICLE
CDEEILNR	RECLINED
CDEEILNS	DECLINES
	LICENSED
	SILENCED
CDEEILNT	DENTICLE
CDEEILNU	NUCLEIDE
CDEEILOR	RECOILED
CDEEILPS	ECLIPSED
	PEDICELS
	PEDICLES
CDEEILRS	SCLEREID
CDEEILRT	DERELICT
CDEEILRU	RECUILED
CDEEIMNR	ENDERMIC
CDEEIMNS	ENDEMICS
CDEEIMOR	MEDIOCRE
CDEEIMOS	COMEDIES
CDEEIMPR	PREMEDIC
CDEEIMRS	MISCREED
CDEEIMRV	DECEMVIR
CDEEINNS	INCENSED
CDEEINNT	INDECENT
CDEEINOR	RECOINED
CDEEINOS	CODEINES
CDEEINPR	PINCERED
CDEEINPS	DISPENCE
CDEEINPT	DEPEINCT
	INCEPTED
	PEINCTED
	PENTICED
CDEEINTU	INDUCTEE
CDEEINTV	INVECTED
CDEEIORV	DIVORCEE
CDEEIOSS	DIOCESES
CDEEIOSV	DEVOICES
CDEEIPRS	PRECISED
CDEEIPRT	DECREPIT
	DEPICTER
CDEEIPRU	PEDICURE
CDEEIPST	PECTISED
CDEEIPTZ	PECTIZED
CDEEIQSU	QUIESCED
CDEEIRRS	DECRIERS
CDEEIRRT	DIRECTER
	REDIRECT
CDEEIRSS	DESCRIES
CDEEIRST	DISCREET
	DISCRETE
CDEEIRSU	DECURIES
CDEEIRSV	DESCRIVE
	SCRIEVED
	SERVICED
CDEEIRTU	CUITERED
CDEEJKOY	JOCKEYED
CDEEKLNO	ENLOCKED
CDEEKLPS	SPECKLED
CDEEKMRU	MUCKERED
CDEEKNOR	RECKONED
CDEEKNRS	REDNECKS
CDEEKNRU	UNRECKED
CDEEKOPT	POCKETED
CDEEKORT	ROCKETED
CDEEKORW	ROCKWEED
CDEEKOST	SOCKETED
CDEEKPRU	PUCKERED
CDEEKRSU	SUCKERED
CDEEKRTU	TUCKERED
CDEELLPU	CUPELLED
CDEELMOW	WELCOMED
CDEELNOS	ENCLOSED
CDEELNPU	PEDUNCLE
CDEELNTY	DECENTLY
CDEELNUW	UNCLEWED
CDEELOOW	LOCOWEED
CDEELOPU	DECOUPLE
CDEELORS	RECLOSED
CDEELORV	CLOVERED
CDEELORY	RECOYLED
CDEELOST	CLOSETED
CDEELOTU	ELOCUTED
CDEELPRU	PRECLUDE
CDEELPSU	DECUPLES
CDEELRTU	LECTURED
	RELUCTED
CDEELRUX	EXCLUDER
CDEELSSU	SCEDULES
	SECLUDES
CDEELSUX	EXCLUDES
CDEEMOPR	COMPERED
CDEEMOPT	COMPETED
CDEEMORT	ECTODERM
CDEEMSTU	TUMESCED
CDEENNOS	CONDENSE
CDEENNOU	DENOUNCE
	ENOUNCED
CDEENNOV	CONVENED
CDEENNPY	PENDENCY
CDEENNTU	UNDECENT
CDEENNTY	TENDENCY
CDEENORR	CORNERED
CDEENORS	CENSORED
	NECROSED
	SECONDER
CDEENORT	CENTRODE
CDEENOSS	SECONDES
CDEENOTX	COEXTEND
CDEENOVX	CONVEXED
CDEENOVY	CONVEYED
CDEENPRU	PRUDENCE
CDEENRSU	CENSURED
CDEENRUV	VERECUND
CDEENSST	DESCENTS
CDEENSSU	CENSUSED
CDEENSTY	ENCYSTED
CDEEOOPR	COOPERED
CDEEOPPR	COPPERED
CDEEOPRS	PROCEEDS
CDEEOPRU	RECOUPED
CDEEORRR	RECORDER
CDEEORRS	RESCORED
CDEEORRU	RECOURED
CDEEORST	CORSETED
	ESCORTED
	SECTORED
CDEEORTT	DETECTOR
CDEEORTV	CORVETED
	VECTORED
CDEEOSST	CESTODES
	COSSETED
CDEEOSTT	ESCOTTED
CDEEPRST	SCEPTRED
CDEERRRU	RECURRED
CDEERRSU	REDUCERS
CDEERRUV	RECURVED
CDEERSSU	SEDUCERS
CDEERSUV	DECURVES
CDEERSUX	EXCURSED
CDEERTTU	CURETTED
CDEERTUV	CURVETED
CDEFFINO	COFFINED
CDEFFISU	SUFFICED
CDEFFLSU	SCUFFLED
CDEFHILN	FLINCHED
CDEFHIMO	CHIEFDOM
CDEFHIRT	FRICHTED
CDEFIIIL	FILICIDE
CDEFIIIT	CITIFIED
CDEFIIOR	CODIFIER
CDEFIIOS	CODIFIES
CDEFIIST	DEFICITS
CDEFIITY	CITYFIED
CDEFINNO	CONFINED
CDEFINNU	INFECUND
CDEFINOR	CONFIDER
	INFORCED
CDEFINOS	CONFIDES
CDEFINOX	CONFIXED
CDEFKORS	DEFROCKS
CDEFLNOU	FLOUNCED

CDEFLORY FORCEDLY
CDEFNORU FROUNCED
UNFORCED
CDEFNOSU CONFUSED
CDEFNOTU CONFUTED
CDEFNSTU DEFUNCTS
CDEFOSSU FOCUSSED
CDEGHORU GROUCHED
CDEGHRTU GRUTCHED
CDEGIINN INCEDING
CDEGIINX EXCIDING
CDEGIKNO DECKOING
DECOKING
CDEGIKNS DECKINGS
CDEGILSU CLUDGIES
CDEGINNO ENCODING
CDEGINNS SCENDING
CDEGINOR RECODING
CDEGINOS COGNISED
CDEGINOY DECOYING
CDEGINOZ COGNIZED
CDEGINRU REDUCING
CDEGINRY DECRYING
CDEGINSU SEDUCING
CDEGINSY DYSGENIC
CDEGNORU CONGRUED
CDEGOORS SCROOGED
CDEGORSU SCOURGED
SCROUGED
CDEGORSW SCROWDGE
CDEHIILO HELICOID
CDEHIILS CEILIDHS
CDEHIIMO HOMICIDE
CDEHIIMR CHIMERID
CDEHIINO ECHINOID
CDEHIIVV CHIVVIED
CDEHIKOS HOICKSED
CDEHIKRW HERDWICK
CDEHILMR MERCHILD
CDEHILNR CHILDREN
CDEHILOR CHLORIDE
CDEHILOS CHELOIDS
CDEHILRT ELDRITCH
CDEHIMOT METHODIC
CDEHIMRS SMIRCHED
CDEHINNR INDRENCH
CDEHINOS HEDONICS
CDEHINQU QUINCHED
CDEHINST SNITCHED
CDEHIOOR OCHIDORE
CDEHIOSW COWHIDES
CDEHIOTY THEODICY
CDEHIQTU QUITCHED
CDEHIRST DITCHERS
CDEHISTT STITCHED
CDEHISTW SWITCHED
CDEHITTW TWITCHED
CDEHKLSU SHELDUCK
CDEHKSUY HEYDUCKS
CDEHLOOS DESCHOOL
SCHOOLED
CDEHLORT CHORTLED
CDEHLOSU SLOUCHED
CDEHMOOS SMOOCHED
CDEHMOSU SMOUCHED
CDEHMSTU SMUTCHED
CDEHNOOP CHENOPOD
CDEHNORS CHONDRES
CDEHNRSU CHUNDERS
CDEHOORR RHEOCORD
CDEHORSU CHORUSED
CDEHORSW CHOWDERS
COWHERDS
CDEHOSSU HOCUSSED
CDEHOSSW COWSHEDS
CDEHSSSU SCHUSSED
CDEIIILS SILICIDE
CDEIIIMT MITICIDE
CDEIIIOS IDIOCIES
CDEIIIRV VIRICIDE
CDEIIITV VITICIDE
CDEIIKKS SIDEKICK
CDEIIKLS SICKLIED
CDEIIKMM MIMICKED
CDEIIKNR CIDERKIN
CDEIIKNW INWICKED
CDEIIKRS DRICKSIE
CDEIIKRT DICKTIER
CDEIIKST DICKIEST
STICKIED
CDEIILMO DOMICILE
CDEIILNN INCLINED
CDEIILNO INDOCILE
CDEIILOT IDIOLECT
CDEIILPS DISCIPLE
CDEIILPU PEDICULI
PULICIDE
CDEIILRU RIDICULE
CDEIIMOS DIOECISM
CDEIIMRT DIMETRIC
CDEIINNT INCIDENT
CDEIINOS DECISION
ICONISED
CDEIINOV INVOICED
CDEIINOZ ICONIZED
CDEIINRT INDIRECT
CDEIIOPR PERIODIC
CDEIIOPS EPISODIC
CDEIIOPT EPIDOTIC
CDEIIOSV OVICIDES
CDEIIPRR CIRRIPED
CDEIIRST ICTERIDS
CDEIIRTU DIURETIC
CDEIIRUV VIRUCIDE
CDEIISSU SUICIDES
CDEIISTT DICTIEST
CDEIJNOO COJOINED
CDEIJSST DISJECTS
CDEIKLNO INLOCKED
CDEIKLNR CRINKLED
CDEIKLNU UNLICKED
CDEIKLOS SIDELOCK
CDEIKLPR PRICKLED
CDEIKLRT TRICKLED
CDEIKLST STICKLED
CDEIKLWY WICKEDLY
CDEIKMSU MUSICKED
CDEIKNPU UNPICKED
CDEIKNTU TUNICKED
CDEIKOSS DOCKISES
CDEIKOSY YOICKSED
CDEIKOSZ DOCKIZES
CDEIKRRS DERRICKS
CDEIKSTU DUCKIEST
CDEILLOR COLLIDER
CDEILLOS CODILLES
COLLIDES
CDEILLOU LODICULE
CDEILLPU PELLUCID
CDEILMMS SCLIMMED
CDEILMOP COMPILED
COMPLIED
CDEILMOS MELODICS
CDEILMPR CRIMPLED
CDEILMRU DULCIMER
CDEILMSY DYSMELIC
CDEILNOS INCLOSED
CDEILNOU UNCOILED
CDEILNRY CYLINDER
CDEILNSU INCLUDES
NUCLIDES
UNSLICED
CDEILOOW WOODLICE
CDEILOPS SCOPELID
CDEILOPU CLUPEOID
UPCOILED
CDEILORS SCLEROID
CDEILORU CLOUDIER
CDEILORV COVERLID
CDEILOSS DISCLOSE
CDEILOST DOCILEST
CDEILPPR CRIPPLED
CDEILPSU CLUPEIDS
CDEILRTY DIRECTLY
CDEILSTU DULCITES
LUCIDEST
CDEILSXY DYSLEXIC
CDEILTTU CUITTLED
CDEIMMOX COMMIXED
CDEIMOOW WOODMICE
CDEIMORT MORTICED
CDEIMOST DOMESTIC
CDEIMPRS SCRIMPED
CDEINNOU UNCOINED
CDEINNOV CONNIVED
CDEINOOZ ENDOZOIC
CDEINORR CORDINER
CDEINORS CONSIDER
CDEINORT CENTROID
DOCTRINE
CDEINORU DECURION
CDEINOST DEONTICS
CDEINOSU DOUCINES
CDEINOSZ ZINCODES
CDEINOTU EDUCTION
CDEINOUV UNVOICED
CDEINOVV CONVIVED
CDEINPRS PRESCIND
CDEINPRU UNPRICED
CDEINPSY DYSPNEIC
CDEINRRU INCURRED
CDEINRSS DISCERNS
RESCINDS
CDEINRSU INDUCERS
CDEINRUV INCURVED
CDEINSSX EXSCINDS
CDEINSTY SYNDETIC
CDEIOORS CORODIES
CDEIOPRT DEPICTOR
CDEIOPST DESPOTIC
CDEIORRT CREDITOR
DIRECTOR
CDEIORRV DIVORCER
CDEIORSS DISCOERS
CDEIORST CORDITES
CDEIORSU DISCOURE
CDEIORSV DISCOVER
DIVORCES
CDEIORSW CROWDIES
CDEIORSY DECISORY
CDEIORTU OUTCRIED
CDEIOSST CESTOIDS
CDEIOSTT COTTISED
CDEIPRSS DISCERPS
CDEIPRST PREDICTS
SCRIPTED
CDEIPRSY CYPRIDES
CDEIPRTU PICTURED
CDEIPSST DISCEPTS
CDEIRRSU SCURRIED
CDEIRSSU DISCURES
CDEIRSTU CRUDITES
CURDIEST
CURTSIED
CDEIRSTV VERDICTS
CDEISSST DISSECTS
CDEISSSU DISCUSES
CDEJNORU CONJURED
CDEKKLNU KNUCKLED
CDEKLMOR CLERKDOM
CDEKLMOU DUCKMOLE
CDEKLNOU UNLOCKED
CDEKLNRU CRUNKLED
CDEKLOPU UPLOCKED
CDEKLORY YELDROCK
CDEKLOSW WEDLOCKS
CDEKLRTU TRUCKLED
CDEKNOOU UNCOOKED
CDEKNOOV CONVOKED
CDEKNORU UNCORKED
CDEKNSSU SUNDECKS
CDEKNSUU UNSUCKED
CDEKNTUU UNTUCKED
CDELLNUU UNCULLED
CDELLOOP CLODPOLE
CDELLORS SCROLLED
CDELLORU COLLUDER
CDELLOSU COLLUDES
CDELLOTU CLOUDLET
CDELMNOO MONOCLED
CDELMNOU COLUMNED
CDELMPRU CRUMPLED
CDELNOOS CONDOLES
CONSOLED
CDELNOSS COLDNESS
CDELNOSU ENCLOUDS
UNCLOSED
CDELNOSY CONDYLES
SECONDLY
CDELNOTU UNCOLTED
CDELNOUW UNCOWLED
CDELNRUU UNCURLED
CDELOORS CROODLES
DECOLORS
CDELOORU COLOURED
DECOLOUR
CDELOPSU UPCLOSED
CDELOPTU OCTUPLED
CDELORSS CORDLESS
SCOLDERS
CDELORSU CLOSURED
CDELORSW CLOWDERS
SCROWLED
CDELORTU CLOTURED
CDELOSSU DULCOSES
CDELOSTU LOCUSTED
CDELPRSU SCRUPLED
CDELPRUU UPCURLED
CDELPSTU SCULPTED
CDELRSSU SCUDLERS

CDELRSUY CURSEDLY
CDELRTUU CULTURED
CDELSSTU DUCTLESS
CDELSTTU SCUTTLED
CDEMMNOO COMMONED
CDEMMNOS COMMENDS
CDEMMNOU COMMUNED
CDEMMOOS COMMODES
CDEMMOOV COMMOVED
CDEMMOTU COMMUTED
CDEMMRSU SCRUMMED
CDEMNNOS CONDEMNS
CDEMNOOW COMEDOWN
CDEMNOSU CONSUMED
CDEMNOTU DOCUMENT
CDEMNSUU SECUNDUM
CDEMOOPS COMPOSED
CDEMOPTU COMPUTED
CDEMORSU DECORUMS
CDEMOSTU COSTUMED
CUSTOMED
CDEMPRSU SCRUMPED
CDENNOOS CONDONES
CDENNOOT CONNOTED
CDENNOST CONTENDS
CDENNOUY UNCOYNED
CDENOORT CREODONT
CDENOOST SECODONT
CDENOOTT COTTONED
CDENOOVY CONVOYED
CDENORSS CORSNEDS
CDENORSW DECROWNS
CDENORTU CORNUTED
TROUNCED
CDENOSTU CONTUSED
CDENRSUU UNCURSED
CDENRTUU UNDERCUT
CDENRUUV UNCURVED
CDEOOPPS COPEPODS
CDEOOPRS SCROOPED
CDEOOPST POSTCODE
CDEOORRS CORRODES
CDEOORSU DECOROUS
CDEOORSV VOCODERS
CDEOOSTV DOVECOTS
CDEOPRRU PROCURED
PRODUCER
CDEOPRSU PRODUCES
CDEOQSTU DOCQUETS
CDEORRSW CROWDERS
CDEORSST DOCTRESS
CDEORSSU SCOURSED
CDEORSSW SCOWDERS
CDEORSTU EDUCTORS
SEDUCTOR
CDEORSUU DOUCEURS
CDEOSSTU CUSTODES
CDEPRSTY DECRYPTS
CDEPRUUV UPCURVED
CDERSTTU DESTRUCT
CDFIILSU FLUIDICS
CDFIKMNU MINDFUCK
CDFIKORS DISFROCK
CDFNNOOU CONFOUND
CDGHIILN CHILDING
CDGHIINS CHIDINGS
CDGHIINT DICHTING
DITCHING
CDGHINNU DUNCHING
CDGHINOR CHORDING

CDGHINOU DOUCHING
CDGIINNU INDUCING
CDGIINOS DISCOING
CDGIKLNU DUCKLING
CDGIKLOR GRIDLOCK
CDGIKNOS DOCKINGS
CDGIKNSU DUCKINGS
CDGILNOS CODLINGS
SCOLDING
CDGILNOU CLOUDING
CDGILNRU CURDLING
CDGINORS CORDINGS
CDGINORW CROWDING
CDGNOOOS COONDOGS
CDHHIILS CHILDISH
CDHIILTW TWICHILD
CDHIINST CHINDITS
CDHIIOOR CHORIOID
CDHIIORT HIDROTIC
TRICHOID
CDHIIOSZ SCHIZOID
CDHIISST DISTICHS
CDHILNSU UNCHILDS
CDHILOOP CHILOPOD
CDHILOOS DOLICHOS
CDHIMOSU DOCHMIUS
CDHINNOR CHONDRIN
CDHIOOPW WOODCHIP
CDHIOORS CHOROIDS
CDHIOORT TROCHOID
CDHIOPRW WHIPCORD
CDHIOPRY HYDROPIC
CDHIOPSY PSYCHOID
CDHIORRT TRICHORD
CDHIOSUV DISVOUCH
CDHIPSTY DIPTYCHS
CDHKOORS HORDOCKS
CDHLOOPY COPYHOLD
CDHNORSU CHONDRUS
CDHOORRU UROCHORD
CDIIIMNU INDICIUM
CDIIIORT DIORITIC
CDIIKPST DIPSTICK
CDIILMOS DOMICILS
CDIILOTY DOCILITY
CDIILTUY LUCIDITY
CDIIMNOU CONIDIUM
ONCIDIUM
CDIINOOS ISODICON
ONISCOID
CDIINORS CRINOIDS
CDIINOST DICTIONS
CDIINPRY CYPRINID
CDIINSTT DISTINCT
CDIIOORS SORICOID
CDIIOPRT DIOPTRIC
CDIIORSU SCIUROID
CDIIOSSS CISSOIDS
CDIIPTUY CUPIDITY
PUDICITY
CDIIRSTT DISTRICT
CDIJNSTU DISJUNCT
CDIKKNOW KICKDOWN
CDIKNORS DORNICKS
CDIKNOSW WINDOCKS
WINDSOCK
CDILLOOS COLLOIDS
CDILLOTU DULCITOL
CDILLOUY CLOUDILY
CDILOOPS PODSOLIC

CDILOORS DISCOLOR
CDILOORT LORDOTIC
CDILOOTY COTYLOID
CDILOSST DISCLOST
CDILOSTY SCOLYTID
CDIMMOSU MODICUMS
CDIMOORT MICRODOT
CDINNQUU QUIDNUNC
CDINOOOR CORONOID
CDINORSW DISCROWN
CDINORTU INDUCTOR
CDINOSTU CONDUITS
DISCOUNT
NOCTUIDS
CDINOSTY DYSTONIC
CDIOOPRS PROSODIC
CDIOORRR CORRIDOR
CDIOPRSU CUSPIDOR
CDIOSSTY CYSTOIDS
CDIOSTUV OVIDUCTS
CDJLNOUY JOCUNDLY
CDKMMORU DRUMMOCK
CDKNNOSU DUNNOCKS
CDKOOORW CORKWOOD
CDLLLOOP CLODPOLL
CDLNOSUU UNCLOUDS
CDLNOUUY UNCLOUDY
CDLOOPSY LYCOPODS
CDLOORTY DOCTORLY
CDLOOSTU OUTSCOLD
CDMNOOPU COMPOUND
CDMNORUU CORUNDUM
CDMOSSUW MUDSCOWS
CDNNOOOT CONODONT
CDNNOSTU CONTUNDS
CDOOOPST OCTOPODS
CDOORRUY CORDUROY
CDOOSTUW WOODCUTS
CDOPRSTU PRODUCTS
CDORSSUW CUSSWORD
CEEEEGHS GEECHEES
CEEEEHLS LEECHEES
CEEEELST SELECTEE
CEEEEPRS PRECEESE
CEEEFFIR EFFIERCE
CEEEFFRT EFFECTER
CEEEFHLS FLEECHES
CEEEFILR FLEECIER
CEEEFINR ENFIERCE
CEEEFLRS FLEECERS
CEEEFNOR CONFEREE
CEEEGIMN EMCEEING
CEEEGINS EGENCIES
CEEEGINX EXIGENCE
CEEEGITX EXEGETIC
CEEEGMNR MERGENCE
CEEEGNRS REGENCES
CEEEGNRV VERGENCE
CEEEHIKR CHEEKIER
CEEEHIRR CHEERIER
REECHIER
CEEEHIRS CHEESIER
CEEEHLRV CHEVEREL
CEEEHLSS SLEECHES
CEEEHMSS SMEECHES
CEEEHNNP PENNEECH
CEEEHNRS ENCHEERS
CEEEHPRS CHEEPERS
CEEEHPSS SPEECHES
CEEEHRRS CHEERERS

CEEEHRSS CREESHES
SECESHER
CEEEHRSW ESCHEWER
CEEEHRVY CHEVERYE
CEEEHSSS SECESHES
CEEEIJTV EJECTIVE
CEEEIKRR CREEKIER
CEEEILNN LENIENCE
CEEEILNS LICENSEE
CEEEILNT TELECINE
CEEEILRS CELERIES
CEEEILRT ERECTILE
CEEEILTV CLEVEITE
ELECTIVE
CEEEIMNN EMINENCE
CEEEIMPR EMPIERCE
CEEEIMRR REREMICE
CEEEINNT ENCEINTE
CEEEINPR PIECENER
CEEEINPS EPICENES
CEEEINRS CERESINE
CEEEINSS ESNECIES
CEEEIPRR CREEPIER
CREPERIE
CEEEIPRS CREEPIES
CEEEIPRV PERCEIVE
CEEEIRRV RECEIVER
CEEEIRSV RECEIVES
CEEEIRSX EXERCISE
CEEEIRTV ERECTIVE
CEEEJRRT REJECTER
CEEEKNNP PENNEECK
CEEELLNR CRENELLE
CEEELLSU ECUELLES
CEEELPSY YCLEEPES
CEEELRRV CLEVERER
CEEELRST RESELECT
CEEELRTT ELECTRET
TERCELET
CEEELSST CELESTES
CEEEMNNS SCENEMEN
CEEEMNRT CEMENTER
CEREMENT
CEEEMPRS EMPERCES
CEEEMRTY CEMETERY
CEEENNPT TENPENCE
CEEENNST SENTENCE
CEEENPRS PRESENCE
CEEENPRT PRETENCE
CEEENQSU SEQUENCE
CEEENRRS SCREENER
CEEENRRT RECENTER
RECENTRE
CEEENRSS RECENSES
CEEENSSS ESSENCES
CEEENSST CENTESES
CEEEPRRS CREEPERS
CEEEPRTX EXPECTER
CEEERRST ERECTERS
CEEERRSV SCREEVER
CEEERRTX EXCRETER
CEEERSSS RECESSES
CEEERSST SECRETES
SESTERCE
CEEERSSU CEREUSES
CEEERSSV SCREEVES
CEEERSTX EXCRETES
CEEERTTV CREVETTE
CEEERTUX EXECUTER
CEEESSSX EXCESSES

CEEESTUX	EXECUTES
CEEFFNOS	OFFENCES
CEEFFORS	EFFORCES
CEEFFORT	EFFECTOR
CEEFGILN	FLEECING
CEEFHIKR	KERCHIEF
CEEFHIRY	CHIEFERY
CEEFHISS	CHIEFESS
CEEFHIST	CHIEFEST
	FETICHES
CEEFHLNS	FLENCHES
CEEFHLRT	FLETCHER
CEEFHLRU	CHEERFUL
CEEFHLST	FLETCHES
CEEFHRST	FECHTERS
CEEFIINT	INFICETE
CEEFILRT	TELFERIC
CEEFILRY	FIERCELY
CEEFINPP	FIPPENCE
CEEFINRT	FRENETIC
CEEFIPRT	PERFECTI
CEEFIRST	FIERCEST
CEEFKLRS	FLECKERS
	FRECKLES
CEEFKLSS	FECKLESS
CEEFLNOR	FLORENCE
CEEFLNSU	FLUENCES
CEEFLNTU	FECULENT
CEEFLRST	REFLECTS
CEEFNORR	CONFRERE
	ENFORCER
	RENFORCE
CEEFNORS	ENFORCES
CEEFNRVY	FERVENCY
CEEFOPRR	PERFORCE
CEEFOPRT	PERFECTO
CEEFORRS	FRESCOER
CEEFORSS	FRESCOES
CEEFPRST	PERFECTS
	PREFECTS
CEEGHIKN	CHEEKING
CEEGHILN	LEECHING
CEEGHINP	CHEEPING
CEEGHINR	CHEERING
	REECHING
CEEGHINS	CHEESING
CEEGHLOW	COGWHEEL
CEEGIJNT	EJECTING
CEEGIKLN	CLEEKING
CEEGILNP	CLEEPING
CEEGILNT	ELECTING
CEEGILOT	ECLOGITE
CEEGILRS	CLERGIES
CEEGILRT	TELERGIC
CEEGIMNS	MISCEGEN
CEEGINOO	COOEEING
CEEGINOR	EROGENIC
CEEGINPR	CREEPING
CEEGINRS	CREESING
	GENERICS
CEEGINRT	ERECTING
	GENTRICE
CEEGINST	GENETICS
CEEGINSU	EUGENICS
CEEGINXY	EXIGENCY
CEEGIORX	EXOERGIC
CEEGIRSS	GRECISES
CEEGIRSZ	GRECIZES
CEEGLLOR	COLLEGER
CEEGLLOS	COLLEGES
CEEGLNST	NEGLECTS
CEEGLOSU	ECLOGUES
CEEGMMOR	COMMERGE
CEEGNNOO	ONCOGENE
CEEGNNOR	CONGENER
CEEGNNPU	PUNGENCE
CEEGNORS	COGENERS
	CONGREES
CEEGNORT	CONGREET
	COREGENT
CEEGNORV	CONVERGE
CEEGNOTY	ECTOGENY
CEEGNRSU	URGENCES
CEEGNRVY	VERGENCY
CEEGORST	CORTEGES
CEEGQRSU	GRECQUES
CEEHHMNN	HENCHMEN
CEEHHSTT	THETCHES
CEEHIIST	ETHICISE
CEEHIITZ	ETHICIZE
CEEHIKLY	CHEEKILY
CEEHIKNW	CHEEWINK
CEEHILLN	CHENILLE
CEEHILLV	CHEVILLE
CEEHILRT	TELECHIR
CEEHILRV	CHEVERIL
CEEHILRW	CLERIHEW
CEEHILRY	CHEERILY
CEEHILSV	VEHICLES
CEEHILSW	SWELCHIE
CEEHIMMS	CHEMMIES
CEEHIMRS	CHIMERES
CEEHIMRT	HERMETIC
CEEHIMSS	CHEMISES
CEEHINOR	COINHERE
CEEHINPR	ENCIPHER
CEEHINPT	PHENETIC
CEEHINRS	ENRICHES
	INHERCES
CEEHINST	SITHENCE
CEEHINSX	CHENIXES
CEEHINTT	ENTHETIC
CEEHIORS	CHEERIOS
CEEHIOSS	ECHOISES
CEEHIOSV	COHESIVE
CEEHIOSZ	ECHOIZES
CEEHIPRT	HERPETIC
CEEHIRRR	CHERRIER
CEEHIRRS	CHERRIES
CEEHIRRT	CHERTIER
CEEHIRSS	RICHESSE
CEEHIRST	CHESTIER
	HERETICS
CEEHIRTT	TETCHIER
CEEHIRTU	HEURETIC
CEEHIRTV	VETCHIER
CEEHISTT	TECHIEST
CEEHISTW	CHEWIEST
CEEHKLRS	HECKLERS
CEEHKNPS	HENPECKS
CEEHKRST	SKETCHER
CEEHKRTV	KVETCHER
CEEHKSST	SKETCHES
CEEHKSTV	KVETCHES
CEEHLNOS	CHELONES
	ECHELONS
CEEHLNOT	ENCLOTHE
CEEHLNPU	PENUCHLE
CEEHLNSU	ELENCHUS
CEEHLORT	RECLOTHE
CEEHLOSS	ECHOLESS
CEEHLOSW	COWHEELS
CEEHLQSU	QUELCHES
CEEHLRSW	WELCHERS
CEEHLSSS	CHESSELS
CEEHMNOR	CHROMENE
CEEHMNSS	CHESSMEN
	MENSCHES
CEEHMORT	COMETHER
CEEHMRSS	SCHEMERS
CEEHMRST	MERCHETS
CEEHNNOW	NOWHENCE
CEEHNNRT	ENTRENCH
CEEHNORT	COHERENT
CEEHNORV	CHEVERON
CEEHNPSU	PENUCHES
CEEHNQRU	QUENCHER
CEEHNQSU	QUENCHES
CEEHNRRT	RETRENCH
	TRENCHER
CEEHNRST	TRENCHES
CEEHNRSW	WENCHERS
	WRENCHES
CEEHNSST	STENCHES
CEEHOPRY	CORYPHEE
CEEHOPTT	POCHETTE
CEEHORRS	COHERERS
	COSHERER
CEEHORRT	HECTORER
	TORCHERE
CEEHORSS	ORCHESES
CEEHORST	TROCHEES
CEEHOSUV	VOUCHEES
CEEHPRRS	PERCHERS
CEEHPRRY	PERCHERY
CEEHPRSU	UPCHEERS
CEEHPSST	SPETCHES
CEEHQRSU	CHEQUERS
CEEHQSTU	QUETCHES
CEEHRSTW	WRETCHES
CEEHRTTU	TEUCHTER
CEEHSTTU	TEUCHEST
CEEIIMPR	EPIMERIC
CEEIIMRT	EREMITIC
CEEIINRT	ICTERINE
CEEIINST	NICETIES
CEEIINVV	EVINCIVE
CEEIIPRS	EPICIERS
CEEIIRST	SERICITE
CEEIJNOT	EJECTION
CEEIJORR	REJOICER
CEEIJORS	REJOICES
CEEIJRUV	VERJUICE
CEEIKKSS	KECKSIES
CEEIKLNN	NECKLINE
CEEIKLPR	PICKEREL
CEEIKNRS	SICKENER
CEEIKNST	NECKTIES
CEEIKPRS	PICKEERS
	SPECKIER
CEEIKPRT	PICKETER
CEEILLLP	PELLICLE
CEEILLMS	MICELLES
CEEILLNT	LENTICEL
	LENTICLE
CEEILMOR	COMELIER
CEEILMPS	SEMPLICE
CEEILNNT	CENTINEL
CEEILNNY	LENIENCY
CEEILNOS	CINEOLES
CEEILNOT	COTELINE
	ELECTION
CEEILNOV	VIOLENCE
CEEILNPX	CINEPLEX
CEEILNRR	RECLINER
CEEILNRS	LICENSER
	RECLINES
	SILENCER
CEEILNRU	CERULEIN
CEEILNRV	VERNICLE
CEEILNSS	ENCLISES
	LICENSES
	SILENCES
CEEILNSU	LEUCINES
CEEILORR	RECOILER
CEEILOSS	SOLECISE
CEEILOSZ	SOLECIZE
CEEILPSS	ECLIPSES
CEEILQSU	LIQUESCE
CEEILRST	RETICLES
	SCLERITE
	TIERCELS
CEEILRSU	CISELEUR
	CISELURE
	RECUILES
CEEILRSV	VERSICLE
CEEILRTU	RETICULE
CEEILRTY	CELERITY
CEEILSSV	CLEVISES
	VESICLES
	VICELESS
CEEILSTT	TELESTIC
	TESTICLE
CEEILSTU	LEUCITES
CEEIMMPY	EMPYEMIC
CEEIMMRS	MESMERIC
CEEIMNNY	EMINENCY
CEEIMNPS	SPECIMEN
CEEIMNST	CENTIMES
CEEIMORT	METEORIC
CEEIMSTT	SMECTITE
CEEINNOT	NEOTENIC
CEEINNRS	INCENSER
CEEINNRT	INCENTRE
CEEINNSS	INCENSES
	NICENESS
CEEINNST	NESCIENT
CEEINORR	ENCIERRO
CEEINORT	ERECTION
	NEOTERIC
CEEINORV	OVERNICE
CEEINORX	EXOCRINE
CEEINOSS	SENECIOS
CEEINOST	ICESTONE
	SEICENTO
CEEINOTV	EVECTION
CEEINPRT	PRENTICE
CEEINPST	PECTINES
	PENTICES
CEEINPSX	SIXPENCE
CEEINRRS	SINCERER
CEEINRSS	CERESINS
	SCRIENES
CEEINRST	CENTRIES
	ENTERICS
	ENTICERS
	SCIENTER
	SECRETIN
CEEINRSU	INSECURE
	SINECURE

CEEINRTT	RETICENT
CEEINRTU	CEINTURE
	ENURETIC
CEEINSST	CENTESIS
CEEINSTY	CYSTEINE
CEEIOPPR	PERICOPE
CEEIOPPS	EPISCOPE
CEEIOPST	ECTOPIES
	PICOTEES
CEEIORST	COTERIES
	ESOTERIC
CEEIORSX	EXORCISE
CEEIORTT	EROTETIC
CEEIORTX	EXOTERIC
CEEIORXZ	EXORCIZE
CEEIOSTV	COVETISE
CEEIPPRT	PRECEPIT
CEEIPPTU	EUPEPTIC
CEEIPRRS	PIERCERS
	PRECISER
CEEIPRSS	PRECISES
CEEIPRST	CREPIEST
	RECEIPTS
CEEIPRSU	EPICURES
CEEIPSST	PECTISES
CEEIPSTZ	PECTIZES
CEEIQSSU	QUIESCES
CEEIRRSS	CERRISES
CEEIRRST	RECITERS
CEEIRRSW	SCREWIER
CEEIRRTU	URETERIC
CEEIRSSV	SCRIEVES
	SERVICES
CEEIRSTT	TIERCETS
CEEIRSTU	CERUSITE
	CUTESIER
	EUCRITES
CEEIRSTV	VERTICES
CEEIRSTX	EXCITERS
CEEIRSVX	CERVIXES
CEEISSST	CITESSES
CEEISTTZ	ZETETICS
CEEISUVX	EXCUSIVE
CEEJKOTT	JOCKETTE
CEEJORRT	REJECTOR
CEEJORST	EJECTORS
CEEKKNPS	KENSPECK
CEEKLNST	NECKLETS
CEEKLPSS	SPECKLES
CEEKLRSS	CLERKESS
	RECKLESS
CEEKNORR	RECKONER
CEEKNRSU	SUCKENER
CEEKORRT	CORKTREE
	ROCKETER
CEEKOSSY	SOCKEYES
CEEKOSTT	SOCKETTE
CEEKPRSY	RYEPECKS
CEEKRRSW	WRECKERS
CEELLLSU	CELLULES
CEELLMOU	MOLECULE
CEELLNOS	COLLEENS
CEELLNOU	NUCLEOLE
CEELLORT	RECOLLET
CEELLOSS	CELLOSES
CEELLPSU	PUCELLES
CEELLRRU	CRUELLER
CEELLRVY	CLEVERLY
CEELLSSU	CLUELESS
CEELMOPT	COMPLETE
CEELMORW	WELCOMER
CEELMOST	TELECOMS
CEELMOSW	WELCOMES
CEELMRTU	ELECTRUM
CEELNNOP	PENONCEL
CEELNOPU	OPULENCE
CEELNORS	ENCLOSER
CEELNORT	ELECTRON
CEELNORU	ENCOLURE
CEELNOSS	ENCLOSES
CEELNPTU	CENTUPLE
CEELNRST	LECTERNS
CEELNRSU	LUCERNES
CEELNRTU	RELUCENT
CEELNRTY	RECENTLY
CEELNSTU	ESCULENT
CEELORSS	CORELESS
	RECLOSES
	SCLEROSE
CEELORST	CORSELET
	ELECTORS
	ELECTROS
	SELECTOR
CEELORSY	RECOYLES
CEELORTV	COVERLET
CEELOSSU	COLEUSES
CEELOSTU	ELOCUTES
CEELOSTV	COVELETS
CEELPRST	PLECTRES
	PRELECTS
CEELRRTU	LECTURER
CEELRSST	LECTRESS
CEELRSSU	CURELESS
	RECLUSES
CEELRSTU	LECTURES
CEELRSTY	SECRETLY
CEELRSUY	SECURELY
CEELSTTU	LETTUCES
CEEMMNTU	CEMENTUM
CEEMMORS	COMMERES
CEEMNORR	CREMORNE
CEEMNORW	NEWCOMER
CEEMNORY	CEREMONY
CEEMNOYZ	COENZYME
CEEMNRSU	CERUMENS
CEEMOORV	OVERCOME
CEEMOORW	OWRECOME
CEEMOPRS	COMPEERS
	COMPERES
CEEMOPST	COMPETES
CEEMOSSS	COSMESES
CEEMSSTU	TUMESCES
CEENNORT	CRETONNE
CEENNORU	RENOUNCE
CEENNORV	CONVENER
CEENNOST	CENTONES
CEENNOSU	ENOUNCES
CEENNOSV	CONVENES
CEENNRST	CENTNERS
CEENOPST	POTENCES
CEENOPTW	TWOPENCE
CEENORSS	NECROSES
CEENORSV	CONSERVE
	CONVERSE
CEENORSZ	COZENERS
CEENORTT	TRECENTO
CEENORVY	CONVEYER
	RECONVEY
CEENOSVX	CONVEXES
CEENPPTU	TUPPENCE
CEENPRSS	SPENCERS
CEENPSSU	SUSPENCE
CEENRSSU	CENSURES
CEENRSTU	UNSECRET
CEENSSSU	CENSUSES
CEENSSTU	CUTENESS
CEENSTTU	CUNETTES
CEEOORRW	ORECROWE
CEEOORST	CREOSOTE
CEEOPRRT	RECEPTOR
CEEOPRTX	EXCEPTOR
CEEOPRTY	CEROTYPE
CEEOPSST	PECTOSES
CEEOPSTY	ECOTYPES
CEEOQTTU	COQUETTE
CEEORRRS	SORCERER
CEEORRSS	RESCORES
CEEORRST	ERECTORS
CEEORRSU	RECOURES
	RECOURSE
	RESOURCE
CEEORRSV	RECOVERS
CEEORRSW	RECOWERS
CEEORRVY	RECOVERY
CEEORSTW	COWTREES
CEEORSTX	CORTEXES
CEEORTTV	CORVETTE
CEEORTUX	EXECUTOR
CEEOSSST	CESTOSES
CEEOSTTT	OCTETTES
CEEPPRST	PERCEPTS
	PRECEPTS
CEEPPRSU	PREPUCES
CEEPRRSU	PRECURSE
CEEPRSST	RESPECTS
	SCEPTERS
	SCEPTRES
	SPECTERS
	SPECTRES
CEEPRSTX	EXCERPTS
CEERRSST	RECTRESS
CEERRSSU	RESCUERS
	SECURERS
CEERRSSW	SCREWERS
CEERRSUV	RECURVES
CEERRTUZ	CREUTZER
CEERSSST	CRESSETS
CEERSSTU	SECUREST
CEERSSTW	SETSCREW
CEERSSUX	EXCURSES
	EXCUSERS
CEERSTTU	CURETTES
CEERTUXY	EXECUTRY
CEESTTUV	CUVETTES
CEFFHIRU	CHUFFIER
CEFFIILR	CLIFFIER
CEFFIORS	OFFICERS
CEFFIORU	COIFFEUR
	COIFFURE
CEFFIRSU	SUFFICER
CEFFISSU	SUFFICES
CEFFLORU	FORCEFUL
CEFFLRSU	SCUFFLER
CEFFLSSU	SCUFFLES
CEFFORSS	SCOFFERS
CEFFORST	COFFRETS
CEFGHINT	FECHTING
	FETCHING
CEFGIKLN	FLECKING
CEFGINNS	FENCINGS
CEFGLNUY	FULGENCY
CEFHIIMS	MISCHIEF
CEFHILNR	FLINCHER
CEFHILNS	FLINCHES
CEFHILRS	FILCHERS
CEFHILRT	FLICHTER
CEFHILST	FLITCHES
CEFHINSU	FUCHSINE
CEFHISTT	FITCHETS
CEFHISTU	FUCHSITE
CEFHISTW	FITCHEWS
CEFHLSSY	FLYSCHES
CEFHLSTU	CHESTFUL
	FUTCHELS
CEFIIIST	CITIFIES
CEFIILRT	CLIFTIER
CEFIILST	FELSITIC
CEFIILTY	FELICITY
CEFIIOPR	OPIFICER
CEFIIORS	ORIFICES
CEFIIPRT	PETRIFIC
CEFIIRRT	FERRITIC
	TERRIFIC
CEFIISTY	CITYFIES
CEFIKLOR	FIRELOCK
CEFIKLRS	FLICKERS
CEFIKLST	FICKLEST
CEFILLLO	FOLLICLE
CEFILMRU	CRIMEFUL
	MERCIFUL
CEFILNOT	FLECTION
CEFILNST	INFLECTS
CEFILNSU	FUNICLES
CEFILOUV	VOICEFUL
CEFILRSU	LUCIFERS
CEFIMOST	COMFIEST
CEFINNOR	CONFINER
CEFINNOS	CONFINES
CEFINORS	CONIFERS
	FORENSIC
	FORINSEC
	FORNICES
	INFORCES
CEFINORT	INFECTOR
CEFINOSX	CONFIXES
CEFINOTT	CONFETTI
CEFIOPRS	FORCIPES
CEFIORTY	FEROCITY
CEFIRRSU	SCURFIER
CEFIRSTU	FRUTICES
CEFIRTUV	FRUCTIVE
CEFKLLOS	ELFLOCKS
CEFKLOOR	FORELOCK
CEFKLOST	FETLOCKS
CEFKLRUW	WRECKFUL
CEFLLOSU	FLOSCULE
CEFLNOSU	FLOUNCES
CEFLNRUU	FURUNCLE
CEFLNSTU	SCENTFUL
CEFMORSY	COMFREYS
CEFNORSU	FROUNCES
CEFNOSSU	CONFUSES
CEFNOSTU	CONFUTES
CEFORRST	CROFTERS
CEFORSTU	FRUCTOSE
CEFOSSSU	FOCUSSES
CEGGHIRS	CHIGGERS
CEGGILOO	GEOLOGIC
CEGGILOR	CLOGGIER
	COGGLIER

CEGGILRS SCRIGGLE
CEGGINNO CONGEING
CEGGINOO GEOGONIC
CEGGIORS GEORGICS
SCROGGIE
CEGGLNOY GLYCOGEN
CEGGLORS CLOGGERS
CEGHHINT HECHTING
CEGHIINY HYGIENIC
CEGHIKLN HECKLING
CEGHIKNT KETCHING
CEGHILNT LETCHING
CEGHILNW WELCHING
CEGHILST GLITCHES
CEGHIMNS SCHEMING
CEGHINNW WENCHING
CEGHINOR COHERING
OCHERING
CEGHINPR PERCHING
CEGHINRT RETCHING
CEGHINRU EUCHRING
CEGHINST CHESTING
ETCHINGS
CEGHINVY CHEVYING
CEGHIRSS SCREIGHS
CEGHIRTU THEURGIC
CEGHISTU GUICHETS
CEGHMRUY CHEMURGY
CEGHNORS GROSCHEN
CEGHORSU CHOREGUS
COUGHERS
GROUCHES
CEGHRSTU GRUTCHES
GUTCHERS
CEGIILNR CLINGIER
CEGIILNS CEILINGS
CIELINGS
CEGIILNT GENTILIC
CEGIILOP EPILOGIC
CEGIILOS LOGICISE
CEGIILOZ LOGICIZE
CEGIINNT ENTICING
CEGIINNV EVINCING
CEGIINPR PIERCING
CEGIINRT RECITING
CEGIINSS GNEISSIC
CEGIINSX EXCISING
CEGIINTV EVICTING
CEGIINTX EXCITING
CEGIIOST EGOISTIC
CEGIJLOU LOGJUICE
CEGIKKLN KECKLING
CEGIKLNR CLERKING
RECKLING
CEGIKNNS NECKINGS
SNECKING
CEGIKNPS PECKINGS
SPECKING
CEGIKNRT TRECKING
CEGIKNRW WRECKING
CEGIKSTU GUCKIEST
CEGILMMN CLEMMING
CEGILNOO NEOLOGIC
CEGILNOS ECLOSING
CEGILNPU CUPELING
CEGILNRS CLINGERS
CRINGLES
CEGILNRU RECULING
ULCERING
CEGILNRY GLYCERIN
CEGILNSU LUCIGENS
CEGILNSY GLYCINES
CEGILNTU CULTIGEN
CEGIMNOY MYOGENIC
CEGIMNSU MUCIGENS
CEGIMNUY GYNECIUM
CEGINNOR ENCORING
CEGINNOZ COZENING
CEGINNRS SCERNING
CEGINNRT CENTRING
CEGINNST SCENTING
CEGINNSY ENSIGNCY
CEGINOOP GEOPONIC
CEGINOOR OROGENIC
CEGINOOY COOEYING
CEGINOOZ ZOOGENIC
CEGINOPR COPERING
CEGINOPY PYOGENIC
CEGINORT GERONTIC
CEGINORV COVERING
CEGINORW COWERING
CEGINOSS COGNISES
CEGINOSZ COGNIZES
CEGINOTV COVETING
CEGINRRS CRINGERS
CEGINRRU RECURING
CEGINRST CRESTING
CEGINRSU RECUSING
RESCUING
SCUNGIER
SECURING
CEGINRSW SCREWING
CEGINRSY SYNERGIC
CEGINRTU ERUCTING
CEGINSUX EXCUSING
CEGIRSTU SCUTIGER
CEGKLNOS GENLOCKS
CEGKLORS GROCKLES
CEGLLOOU COLLOGUE
CEGLLORY GLYCEROL
CEGLLRYY GLYCERYL
CEGLNOOS COLOGNES
CEGLNOTY COGENTLY
CEGLOOOY OECOLOGY
CEGLOOTY CETOLOGY
CEGLOSSU GLUCOSES
CEGLOSSY GLYCOSES
CEGMNNOO COGNOMEN
CEGNNOOS ONCOGENS
CEGNNPUY PUNGENCY
CEGNOOTY GONOCYTE
CEGNORSS CONGRESS
CEGNORSU CONGRUES
SCROUNGE
CEGNORSY CRYOGENS
CEGNORYY CRYOGENY
CEGNOSST CONGESTS
CEGOORSS SCROOGES
CEGORRSU SCOURGER
SCROUGER
CEGORSSU SCOURGES
SCROUGES
CEHHIIRT HITCHIER
CEHHINPY HYPHENIC
CEHHIRST HITCHERS
CEHHNORU HURCHEON
CEHHOOST HOOTCHES
CEHHOPTY HYPOTHEC
CEHIIKNR CHINKIER
CEHIIKNS CHINKIES
CEHIILLR CHILLIER
CEHIILLS CHILLIES
CEHIILMO HEMIOLIC
CEHIILNN LICHENIN
CEHIILNT LECITHIN
CEHIILOT EOLITHIC
CEHIIMOP HEMIOPIC
CEHIIMOS ISOCHEIM
ISOCHIME
CEHIIMPT MEPHITIC
CEHIIMST ETHICISM
CEHIINST ICHNITES
CEHIIPPR CHIPPIER
CEHIIPPS CHIPPIES
CEHIIPRR CHIRPIER
CEHIIPRT PITCHIER
CEHIIRST CHRISTIE
CEHIIRTT CHITTIER
TITCHIER
TRICHITE
CEHIIRTW WITCHIER
CEHIISTT CHITTIES
ETHICIST
ITCHIEST
THEISTIC
TICHIEST
CEHIISVV CHIVVIES
CEHIKLPT KLEPHTIC
CEHIKLRS CLERKISH
CEHIKLSU SUCHLIKE
CEHIKMOS HOMESICK
CEHIKNRU CHUNKIER
CEHIKNST CHETNIKS
KITCHENS
KNITCHES
THICKENS
CEHIKNSW CHEWINKS
CEHIKOOS CHOOKIES
CEHIKOSS HOICKSES
CEHIKOST CHOKIEST
THICKOES
CEHIKRSS KIRSCHES
SHICKERS
SKRIECHS
CEHIKRSW WHICKERS
CEHIKSST CHEKISTS
KITSCHES
CEHIKSTT THICKEST
THICKETS
THICKSET
CEHIKTTY THICKETY
CEHILLRS CHILLERS
SCHILLER
CEHILLST CHILLEST
CEHILMMS SCHIMMEL
CEHILMSY CHIMLEYS
CEHILMTY METHYLIC
CEHILNOP PHENOLIC
PINOCHLE
CEHILNOR CHLORINE
CEHILNOS CHOLINES
HELICONS
CEHILNPY PHENYLIC
CEHILNSS CHINLESS
CEHILNST LINCHETS
TINCHELS
CEHILORT CHLORITE
CLOTHIER
CEHILORY HEROICLY
CEHILPRS PILCHERS
CEHILPTY PHYLETIC
CEHILRSV CHERVILS
CEHILSTT LICHTEST
CEHILSTW SWITCHEL
CEHILTTY TETCHILY
CEHIMMRU CHUMMIER
CEHIMMSS CHEMISMS
CEHIMMSU CHUMMIES
CEHIMNNW WINCHMEN
CEHIMNOP PHONEMIC
CEHIMNOR CHOIRMEN
CEHIMNPT PITCHMEN
CEHIMNSY CHIMNEYS
CEHIMOOT HOMEOTIC
CEHIMORS MORICHES
CEHIMORT CHROMITE
TRICHOME
CEHIMOSS ECHOISMS
CEHIMOST MOCHIEST
CEHIMRSS SMIRCHES
CEHIMSST CHEMISTS
CEHINNRT INTRENCH
CEHINOOS COHESION
CEHINOPS CHOPINES
CEHINOPT PHONETIC
CEHINOPU EUPHONIC
CEHINORS CHORINES
CEHINORT NOTCHIER
CEHINORU UNHEROIC
CEHINOSY HYOSCINE
CEHINOTY ONYCHITE
CEHINPRS PINCHERS
CEHINPRU PUNCHIER
UNCIPHER
CEHINPSU PENUCHIS
CEHINQSU QUINCHES
CEHINRSS RICHNESS
CEHINRST CHRISTEN
CITHERNS
SNITCHER
CEHINRTU RUTHENIC
CEHINSST SNITCHES
CEHINSTW WITCHENS
CEHINSTZ CHINTZES
CEHIOORS CHOOSIER
ISOCHORE
CEHIOPPR CHOPPIER
CEHIOPRS SOPHERIC
CEHIOPRU EUPHORIC
POUCHIER
CEHIOPSS HOSPICES
CEHIOPST POSTICHE
POTICHES
CEHIORRT RHETORIC
TORCHIER
CEHIORSS CHORISES
ORCHESIS
ORCHISES
CEHIORST ROTCHIES
THEORICS
CEHIORSW CHOWRIES
CEHIORTT TROCHITE
CEHIORTU COUTHIER
TOUCHIER
CEHIOSST ECHOISTS
TOISECHS
CEHIPPRS CHIPPERS
CEHIPRRS CHIRPERS
CEHIPRSS SPHERICS
CEHIPRST PITCHERS

	SPITCHER
CEHIQSTU	QUITCHES
CEHIRSST	STRICHES
CEHIRSTT	CHITTERS
	RICHTEST
	STITCHER
CEHIRSTY	HYSTERIC
CEHIRTTW	TWITCHER
CEHIRTWY	WITCHERY
CEHISSTT	STITCHES
CEHISSTU	CUSHIEST
CEHISSTW	SWITCHES
CEHISSUW	SUCHWISE
CEHISTTW	TWITCHES
CEHKKRSU	CHUKKERS
CEHKLLOS	SKELLOCH
CEHKLMOS	HEMLOCKS
CEHKLOOS	KLOOCHES
CEHKLORS	SHERLOCK
CEHKNPUY	KEYPUNCH
CEHKORSS	SHOCKERS
CEHKPSTU	KETCHUPS
CEHKRSSU	SHUCKERS
CEHKRSTU	HUCKSTER
CEHLLMOS	MOCHELLS
CEHLLMSU	MUCHELLS
	SCHELLUM
CEHLLOSY	YELLOCHS
CEHLLOUY	LOUCHELY
CEHLMNOU	HOMUNCLE
CEHLMORS	CHROMELS
CEHLMSUY	CHUMLEYS
CEHLNNOU	LUNCHEON
CEHLNNSU	CHUNNELS
CEHLNOST	CHOLENTS
	NOTCHELS
CEHLNOTU	UNCLOTHE
CEHLNRSU	LUNCHERS
CEHLNSTY	LYNCHETS
CEHLOOSS	SCHOOLES
CEHLORST	CHORTLES
CEHLORSU	SLOUCHER
CEHLORTY	HECTORLY
CEHLOSSU	SLOUCHES
CEHLOSTU	SELCOUTH
CEHLPPSS	SCHLEPPS
CEHLPPSY	SCHLEPPY
CEHLQSUY	SQUELCHY
CEHLRRSU	LURCHERS
CEHLSTUY	LECYTHUS
CEHMNRSU	MUNCHERS
CEHMNRTU	TRUCHMEN
CEHMNSSU	MUCHNESS
CEHMOORS	MOOCHERS
CEHMOOSS	SMOOCHES
CEHMOOSZ	SCHMOOZE
CEHMORSU	MOUCHERS
CEHMORUV	OVERMUCH
CEHMOSSU	SMOUCHES
CEHMSSTU	SMUTCHES
CEHNNNOU	NUNCHEON
CEHNNOPU	PUNCHEON
CEHNNOSU	NONESUCH
	UNCHOSEN
CEHNNRSU	CHUNNERS
CEHNOORS	COEHORNS
	SCHOONER
CEHNOPTU	PUTCHEON
CEHNORST	NOTCHERS
CEHNORSV	CHEVRONS
CEHNORTU	CHOUNTER
CEHNORVY	CHEVRONY
CEHNPRSU	PUNCHERS
CEHNPSST	PSCHENTS
CEHNRSTU	CHUNTERS
CEHNSSSU	SUCHNESS
CEHNSSTU	CHESNUTS
CEHNSTTU	CHESTNUT
CEHNSTUY	CHUTNEYS
CEHOOORZ	ZOOCHORE
CEHOORSS	CHOOSERS
	SOROCHES
CEHOORST	CHEROOTS
CEHOORSU	OCHEROUS
	OCHREOUS
CEHOOSUW	COWHOUSE
CEHOPPRS	CHOPPERS
CEHOPPRY	PROPHECY
CEHOPRST	POTCHERS
CEHOPRSY	CORYPHES
CEHORRST	TORCHERS
CEHORSSU	CHORUSES
CEHORSSZ	SCHERZOS
CEHORSTU	SCOUTHER
	TOUCHERS
CEHORSTW	SCOWTHER
CEHORSUV	VOUCHERS
CEHOSSSU	HOCUSSES
CEHOSTTU	COUTHEST
CEHOTTUZ	ZUCHETTO
CEHPRSTU	PUTCHERS
CEHPSSTU	PUTSCHES
CEHRRSSU	CRUSHERS
CEHRSSTY	SCYTHERS
CEHRSTTY	STRETCHY
CEHSSSSU	SCHUSSES
CEIIILSV	CIVILISE
CEIIILVZ	CIVILIZE
CEIIIMNT	CIMINITE
CEIIINSS	SINICISE
CEIIINSV	INCISIVE
CEIIINSZ	SINICIZE
CEIIJSTU	JUICIEST
CEIIKLMR	LIMERICK
CEIIKLRS	SICKLIER
CEIIKLRT	TICKLIER
CEIIKLSS	SICKLIES
CEIIKMMR	MIMICKER
CEIIKNRZ	ZINCKIER
CEIIKNSS	KINESICS
CEIIKNST	KINETICS
CEIIKPST	PICKIEST
CEIIKQSU	QUICKIES
CEIIKRRT	TRICKIER
CEIIKRST	STICKIER
CEIIKSST	EKISTICS
	STICKIES
CEIILLMT	MELLITIC
CEIILLOP	POLLICIE
CEIILLPT	ELLIPTIC
CEIILLSS	SILICLES
CEIILLSU	SILICULE
CEIILMNT	LIMNETIC
CEIILMOT	CIMOLITE
CEIILNNS	INCLINES
CEIILNOS	ISOCLINE
	SILICONE
CEIILNQU	CLINIQUE
CEIILNSS	ENCLISIS
CEIILOPP	EPIPLOIC
	EPIPOLIC
CEIILOPS	POLICIES
CEIILORT	ELICITOR
CEIILOTZ	ZEOLITIC
CEIILPPS	CLIPPIES
CEIILPRT	PERLITIC
CEIILPRU	PIRLICUE
CEIILPTX	EXPLICIT
CEIILPTY	PYELITIC
CEIILQRU	CLIQUIER
CEIILRSU	SLUICIER
CEIILRTV	VERTICIL
CEIILSSS	SCISSILE
CEIIMNOT	EMICTION
CEIIMOPT	EPITOMIC
CEIIMORS	ISOMERIC
CEIIMOST	COMITIES
	SEMIOTIC
CEIIMPRR	CRIMPIER
CEIIMPRS	EMPIRICS
CEIIMPSS	EPICISMS
CEIIMRRT	TRIMERIC
CEIIMRST	MERISTIC
	TRISEMIC
CEIINNOP	NEPIONIC
CEIINNOR	IRENICON
CEIINNOS	CONIINES
	OSCININE
CEIINNOT	NICOTINE
CEIINNRS	CINERINS
CEIINNRT	INTRINCE
CEIINNST	INSCIENT
CEIINOPS	EPINOSIC
CEIINOPT	EPITONIC
CEIINORS	RECISION
	SORICINE
CEIINOSS	ICONISES
CEIINOSV	INVOICES
CEIINOSX	EXCISION
CEIINOSZ	ICONIZES
CEIINOTV	EVICTION
CEIINPSS	PISCINES
CEIINRSS	SERICINS
CEIINRST	CITRINES
	CRINITES
	INCITERS
CEIINRSU	INCISURE
	SCIURINE
CEIINRTU	NEURITIC
CEIINSSU	CUISINES
CEIINSTU	CUTINISE
CEIINSTY	CYTISINE
	SYENITIC
CEIINSTZ	CITIZENS
	ZINCIEST
	ZINCITES
CEIINTUZ	CUTINIZE
CEIIOPRS	IRISCOPE
CEIIOPRT	PERIOTIC
CEIIOPTT	PICOTITE
CEIIOSTV	SOVIETIC
CEIIPRRS	CRISPIER
CEIIPRST	PICRITES
	PRICIEST
CEIIPSST	EPICISTS
	SPICIEST
CEIIQRTU	CRITIQUE
CEIIRSSU	CRUISIES
CEIIRSTT	RECTITIS
CEIIRSTV	VERISTIC
CEIISSST	CISSIEST
CEIISTVV	VIVISECT
CEIJNORT	INJECTOR
CEIJNOUV	CUNJEVOI
CEIJRSTU	JUSTICER
CEIJSSTU	JUSTICES
CEIKKNRS	KNICKERS
CEIKKRRS	SKERRICK
CEIKLNPS	SPICKNEL
CEIKLNRS	CLINKERS
	CRINKLES
CEIKLNSS	SLICKENS
CEIKLOSV	LOVESICK
CEIKLPRS	PICKLERS
	PRICKLES
CEIKLPRU	PLUCKIER
CEIKLRSS	SLICKERS
CEIKLRST	STICKLER
	STRICKLE
	TICKLERS
	TRICKLES
CEIKLRSY	SICKERLY
CEIKLRTT	TRICKLET
CEIKLSST	SLICKEST
	STICKLES
CEIKLSTU	LUCKIEST
CEIKMNOR	MONICKER
CEIKMOPT	IMPOCKET
CEIKMORS	OCKERISM
CEIKMRSS	SMICKERS
CEIKMRSU	MUSICKER
CEIKMSST	SMICKETS
CEIKMSTU	MUCKIEST
CEIKNNSU	INSUCKEN
CEIKNOTY	CYTOKINE
CEIKNQSU	QUICKENS
CEIKNRSS	SNICKERS
CEIKNRST	STRICKEN
CEIKNRSU	UNSICKER
CEIKNSSS	SICKNESS
CEIKNSST	SNICKETS
CEIKOPST	POCKIEST
CEIKORRS	ROCKIERS
CEIKORST	CORKIEST
	ROCKIEST
	STOCKIER
CEIKOSSY	YOICKSES
CEIKPRRS	PRICKERS
CEIKPRST	PRICKETS
CEIKPSST	SKEPTICS
	SPICKEST
CEIKQSTU	QUICKEST
	QUICKSET
CEIKRRST	TRICKERS
CEIKRRTY	TRICKERY
CEIKRSST	STICKERS
CEIKRSTU	TRUCKIES
CEIKRTTY	RICKETTY
CEIKSTUY	YUCKIEST
CEILLNOS	LIONCELS
CEILLNOU	NUCLEOLI
CEILLOPS	POLLICES
CEILLOQU	COQUILLE
CEILLORS	COLLIERS
	ORSELLIC
CEILLORY	COLLIERY
CEILLOTU	COUTILLE
CEILLRTU	TELLURIC
CEILLSST	CELLISTS
CEILLSSU	CULLISES

CEILMMUY	MYCELIUM
CEILMNOP	COMPLINE
CEILMNOT	MONTICLE
CEILMOPR	COMPILER
	COMPLIER
CEILMOPS	COMPILES
	COMPLIES
	POLEMICS
CEILMOSS	SOLECISM
CEILMOSU	COLISEUM
CEILMPRS	CRIMPLES
CEILMPRU	CLUMPIER
CEILMPUU	PECULIUM
CEILMRSU	CLUMSIER
	MUSCLIER
CEILMTUU	LUTECIUM
CEILNNOT	CONTLINE
CEILNNSU	NUCLEINS
CEILNNSY	SYNCLINE
CEILNOOS	COLONIES
	COLONISE
	ECLOSION
CEILNOOZ	COLONIZE
CEILNOPR	PERCOLIN
	REPLICON
CEILNOPS	PINOCLES
CEILNOPT	LEPTONIC
CEILNORS	INCLOSER
	LICENSOR
CEILNOSS	CONSEILS
	INCLOSES
CEILNOST	LECTIONS
CEILNOSX	LEXICONS
CEILNPRY	PRINCELY
CEILNRTU	LINCTURE
CEILNRUV	CULVERIN
CEILNSST	STENCILS
CEILNSTU	CUTLINES
	TUNICLES
CEILNSUU	UNSLUICE
CEILOPRT	PETROLIC
CEILOPRV	PROCLIVE
CEILOPST	TOECLIPS
CEILOPTU	EPULOTIC
	POULTICE
CEILOPTY	EPICOTYL
CEILORST	CLOISTER
	COISTREL
	COSTLIER
	CREOLIST
CEILORTT	CLOTTIER
CEILORTY	CRYOLITE
CEILOSSS	OSSICLES
CEILOSST	SOLECIST
	SOLSTICE
CEILOSSU	COULISSE
CEILOSTT	COLETITS
CEILOTVY	VELOCITY
CEILPPRS	CLIPPERS
	CRIPPLES
CEILPRSS	SPLICERS
CEILPRSU	SURPLICE
CEILPRUU	PURLICUE
CEILPSSU	SPICULES
CEILRRSU	SCURRILE
CEILRSTT	CLITTERS
CEILRSTU	CURLIEST
	UTRICLES
CEILSSSS	SCISSELS
CEILSTTU	CUITTLES
CEIMMNNO	MNEMONIC
CEIMMNOU	ENCOMIUM
	MECONIUM
CEIMMORT	RECOMMIT
CEIMMOSX	COMMIXES
CEIMMRRS	CRIMMERS
CEIMMRRU	CRUMMIER
CEIMMRSU	CRUMMIES
	SCUMMIER
CEIMMRSY	MERYCISM
CEIMNNOO	ENCOMION
CEIMNNOS	MECONINS
CEIMNNOY	NEOMYCIN
CEIMNOPT	PENTOMIC
CEIMNOPY	EPONYMIC
CEIMNORS	CREMOSIN
	INCOMERS
	SERMONIC
CEIMNORT	INTERCOM
CEIMNOST	CENTIMOS
CEIMNRST	CENTRISM
CEIMNSSU	MENISCUS
CEIMOOST	COOMIEST
CEIMOOUZ	ZOOECIUM
CEIMOPRS	COMPRISE
CEIMORRS	MORRICES
CEIMORRT	MORTICER
CEIMORST	MORTICES
CEIMORSX	EXORCISM
CEIMORSY	ISOCRYME
CEIMORTY	EMICTORY
CEIMOSSS	COSMESIS
CEIMOSTV	VICOMTES
CEIMPRRS	CRIMPERS
CEIMPRRU	CRUMPIER
CEIMRRSU	SCRIMURE
CEIMRRTU	TURMERIC
CEIMRSST	CRETISMS
CEIMSSTY	SYSTEMIC
CEINNNOT	INNOCENT
CEINNNOU	INCONNUE
CEINNORS	INCENSOR
CEINNORU	NEURONIC
CEINNORV	CONNIVER
CEINNOSV	CONNIVES
CEINNOTU	CONTINUE
CEINOOST	COONTIES
CEINOOTZ	ENTOZOIC
	ENZOOTIC
CEINOPPR	CORNPIPE
CEINOPRS	CONSPIRE
	INCORPSE
CEINOPRT	INCEPTOR
CEINOPRV	PROVINCE
CEINOPST	PONCIEST
CEINOPTT	ENTOPTIC
CEINOPTU	UNPOETIC
CEINORRS	RESORCIN
CEINORRT	TRICORNE
CEINORSS	NECROSIS
	SERICONS
CEINORST	CORNIEST
	RECTIONS
CEINORSU	NOURICES
	ROUNCIES
CEINORTT	CONTRITE
	CORNETTI
CEINORTU	NEUROTIC
CEINORTV	CONTRIVE
CEINOSSS	CESSIONS
	COSINESS
CEINOSST	SECTIONS
CEINOSSX	COXINESS
CEINOSTT	CENTOIST
	STENOTIC
CEINOSTU	COUNTIES
CEINOSTX	EXCITONS
CEINOSTY	CYTOSINE
CEINOSUV	UNVOICES
CEINOSVV	CONVIVES
CEINPRSS	PRINCESS
CEINPSST	INSPECTS
CEINPSTY	PYCNITES
CEINRSST	CISTERNS
CEINRSTT	CENTRIST
	CITTERNS
CEINRSTU	CURNIEST
CEINRSUV	INCURVES
CEINRSVV	CRIVVENS
CEINRTTU	INTERCUT
	TINCTURE
CEINSSTY	CYSTINES
CEIOOPRS	OPORICES
CEIOOTUV	OUTVOICE
CEIOOTXX	EXOTOXIC
CEIOPPRS	CROPPIES
CEIOPPSY	EPISCOPY
CEIOPRRU	CROUPIER
CEIOPRSS	PERSICOS
CEIOPRST	PERSICOT
CEIOPRSU	PRECIOUS
CEIOPRTU	EUTROPIC
	OUTPRICE
CEIOPSST	COPSIEST
CEIOPSSU	SPECIOUS
CEIORRSS	CROSIERS
CEIORRSU	COURIERS
CEIORRSZ	CROZIERS
CEIORRTU	COURTIER
CEIORRUZ	CRUZEIRO
CEIORSST	CROSSTIE
CEIORSSU	SCOURIES
CEIORSSV	CORSIVES
CEIORSSW	SCOWRIES
CEIORSSX	SIXSCORE
CEIORSTT	COTTIERS
CEIORSTU	CITREOUS
	OUTCRIES
CEIORSTV	EVICTORS
	VORTICES
CEIORSTX	EXCITORS
	EXORCIST
CEIORSVY	VICEROYS
CEIORTTU	TOREUTIC
CEIOSSSV	VISCOSES
CEIOSSTT	COTTISES
CEIOSSTU	COITUSES
CEIOSSTX	COEXISTS
CEIPQSTU	PICQUETS
CEIPRRSS	CRISPERS
CEIPRRST	RESCRIPT
CEIPRSST	CRISPEST
CEIPRSTU	CREPITUS
	CUPRITES
	PICTURES
	PIECRUST
CEIPSSST	CESSPITS
CEIRRRSU	CURRIERS
	SCURRIER
CEIRRSSU	CRUISERS
	SCURRIES
	SUCRIERS
CEIRRSTT	CRITTERS
	RESTRICT
	STRICTER
CEIRRSTU	CRUSTIER
	RECRUITS
CEIRRSUV	SCURVIER
CEIRSSSU	CUISSERS
	SCISSURE
CEIRSSTT	TRISECTS
CEIRSSTU	CITRUSES
	CURTSIES
	RICTUSES
CEIRSSTV	VICTRESS
CEIRSSUV	SCURVIES
CEIRSTTU	TUTRICES
CEIRSTUV	CURVIEST
CEIRSTUY	SECURITY
CEIRSUZZ	SCUZZIER
CEISSSSU	CISSUSES
CEISSSTU	CISTUSES
CEISTTTU	CUTTIEST
CEJLOOSY	JOCOSELY
CEJNORRU	CONJURER
CEJNORSU	CONJURES
CEJNRTUU	JUNCTURE
CEJNSSUU	JUNCUSES
CEJOPRST	PROJECTS
CEKKLNSU	KNUCKLES
CEKKNORS	KNOCKERS
CEKLLOOV	LOVELOCK
CEKLLOPS	PELLOCKS
CEKLLSSU	LUCKLESS
CEKLMNOS	LOCKSMEN
CEKLNOSS	SLOCKENS
CEKLNOST	STENLOCK
CEKLNRSU	CRUNKLES
CEKLOORV	OVERLOCK
CEKLOPST	LOCKSTEP
CEKLPRSU	PLUCKERS
CEKLRRTU	TRUCKLER
CEKLRSSU	SUCKLERS
CEKLRSTU	TRUCKLES
CEKMNOST	STOCKMEN
CEKMNRTU	TRUCKMEN
CEKNNSSU	UNSNECKS
CEKNOOSV	CONVOKES
CEKNOPST	PENSTOCK
CEKNORST	CRONKEST
CEKNORTU	COKERNUT
CEKNOSTU	UNSOCKET
CEKNRSWY	WRYNECKS
CEKOOORV	OVERCOOK
CEKOOPRS	PRECOOKS
CEKOOPSW	COWPOKES
CEKOORST	CROOKEST
CEKOPRST	SPROCKET
CEKORRTY	ROCKETRY
CEKORSST	RESTOCKS
	STOCKERS
CEKRRSTU	TRUCKERS
CEKRSSUU	RUCKUSES
CELLMOSU	COLUMELS
CELLNOOS	COLONELS
CELLNSUU	NUCELLUS
CELLNTUU	LUCULENT
CELLOOQU	COLLOQUE
CELLORSS	ESCROLLS
CELLOSSY	CLOYLESS

CELLRRSU CRULLERS
CELLRSSU SCULLERS
CELLRSUY SCULLERY
CELMMSSU MESCLUMS
CELMNOOS MONOCLES
CELMNOTY CLOYMENT
CELMNOUY UNCOMELY
CELMNSSU MESCLUNS
CELMNTUU MUCULENT
CELMOOOT LOCOMOTE
CELMOOSY CLOYSOME
CELMOPSU COMPULSE
CELMOPSY SYMPLOCE
CELMOSUU CUMULOSE
CELMPRSU CLUMPERS
CRUMPLES
CELMPRTU PLECTRUM
CELMPSUU SPECULUM
CELMSSUU SECULUMS
CELNNOSU NUCLEONS
CELNNOTY NOCENTLY
CELNNOUV UNCLOVEN
CELNOORS CONSOLER
CELNOORT CONTROLE
CELNOORU ENCOLOUR
CELNOOSS CONSOLES
COOLNESS
CELNOOVV CONVOLVE
CELNOPRT PLECTRON
CELNOPUU UNCOUPLE
CELNORTW CROWNLET
CELNORWY CLOWNERY
CELNOSSU CLONUSES
COUNSELS
UNCLOSES
CELNOSTU NOCTULES
CELNOSUV CONVULSE
CELNOSVY SOLVENCY
CELNOVXY CONVEXLY
CELNPTUU PUNCTULE
CELNRSTU LECTURNS
CELOOPRS PRECOOLS
CELOOPSS CESSPOOL
CELOORRU COLOURER
CELOORSS CREOSOLS
CELOORTW COLEWORT
CELOORVY OVERCLOY
CELOPRSU COUPLERS
CELOPSSU OPUSCLES
UPCLOSES
CELOPSTU COUPLETS
OCTUPLES
CELOPSUU OPUSCULE
CELOPTTU OCTUPLET
CELORSST CORSLETS
COSTRELS
CROSSLET
CELORSSU CLOSURES
SCLEROUS
CELORSSW SCROWLES
CELORSSY SCROYLES
CELORSTT CLOTTERS
CROTTLES
CELORSTU CLOTURES
CLOUTERS
COULTERS
CELORSTY COYSTREL
CELORSUU ULCEROUS
URCEOLUS
CELORSUY CROUSELY

CELORTTU COURTLET
CELORTVY COVERTLY
CELOSTTU CULOTTES
CELPRRSU SCRUPLER
CELPRSSU SCRUPLES
CELPRSUY SPRUCELY
CELRSSTU CLUSTERS
CUSTRELS
CELRSSTY CLYSTERS
CELRSTTU CLUTTERS
SCUTTLER
CELRSTUU CULTURES
CELRSTUV CULVERTS
CELRSTUY CLUSTERY
CELSSTTU SCUTTLES
CELSSTUU CULTUSES
CEMMNOOR COMMONER
CEMMNOOS CONSOMME
CEMMNOOY COMMONEY
CEMMNOST COMMENTS
CEMMNOSU COMMUNES
CEMMOOST COMMOTES
CEMMOOSV COMMOVES
CEMMORTU COMMUTER
CEMMOSTU COMMUTES
CEMMRSSU SCUMMERS
CEMNNOST CONTEMNS
CEMNOORR CROMORNE
CEMNOOTY MONOCYTE
CEMNOPTT CONTEMPT
CEMNORSU CONSUMER
MUCRONES
CEMNOSSU CONSUMES
MUSCONES
CEMNRSTU CENTRUMS
CEMOOPRS COMPOSER
CEMOOPSS COMPOSES
CEMOOPST COMPOTES
CEMOORSY SYCOMORE
CEMOOSSS COSMOSES
CEMOOSTU OUTCOMES
CEMOOSTY CYTOSOME
CEMOPRSS COMPRESS
CEMOPRST COMPTERS
CEMOPRTU COMPUTER
CEMOPSTU COMPUTES
CEMORSSU CORMUSES
CEMORSTU COSTUMER
CUSTOMER
CEMOSSTU COSTUMES
CEMPRSTU CRUMPEST
CRUMPETS
SPECTRUM
CENNOORV CONVENOR
CENNOOST CONNOTES
CENNORRT CORNRENT
CENNORTU NOCTURNE
CENNOSST CONSENTS
CENNOSTT CONTENTS
CENNOSTV CONVENTS
CENNRSSU SCUNNERS
CENOOOTZ ECTOZOON
CENOORRS CORONERS
CROONERS
CENOORST CORONETS
CENOORSU CORNEOUS
CENOORTT CORNETTO
CENOORVY CONVEYOR
CENOPRSY NECROPSY
CENOPSSY PYCNOSES

SYNCOPES
CENOPSTU POUNCETS
CENOQRSU CONQUERS
CENOQSTU CONQUEST
CENORRSS SCORNERS
CENORRSW CROWNERS
CENORRTU TROUNCER
CENORSST CONSTERS
CRESTONS
CENORSTT CORNETTS
CENORSTU CONSTRUE
CORNUTES
COUNTERS
RECOUNTS
TROUNCES
CENORSTV CONVERTS
CENORSTW CROWNETS
CENORSUU CERNUOUS
COENURUS
CENORSUV UNCOVERS
CENORSUY CYNOSURE
CENOSSTT CONTESTS
CENOSSTU CONTUSES
COUNTESS
CENOSTTX CONTEXTS
CENPRSTY ENCRYPTS
CENPRTUU PUNCTURE
CENPSTUX EXPUNCTS
CENRRSTU CURRENTS
CENRSSTU CURTNESS
ENCRUSTS
CENRSSUU UNCURSES
CENRSSUW UNSCREWS
CEOOOPST OTOSCOPE
CEOOPRRV OVERCROP
CEOOPRSS SCOOPERS
CEOOPSWX COWPOXES
CEOORRVW OVERCROW
CEOORSST SCOOTERS
CEOOSTUV COVETOUS
CEOPPRRS CROPPERS
CEOPPRST PROSPECT
CEOPRRRU PROCURER
CEOPRRSS SCORPERS
CEOPRRST PORRECTS
CEOPRRSU CROUPERS
PROCURES
CEOPRSTT PROTECTS
CEOPRSTW SCREWTOP
CEOPRSUU COUPURES
CUPREOUS
CEOQRSTU CROQUETS
ROCQUETS
CEOQRTUY COQUETRY
CEORRSSS SCORSERS
CEORRSSU COURSERS
SCOURERS
CEORRSSW SCOWRERS
CEORRSTY CORSETRY
CEORSSST CROSSEST
CEORSSSU SCOURSES
SCOUSERS
SUCROSES
CEORSSTU SCOUTERS
CEORSSUV CORVUSES
CEORSTUU COUTURES
CEORSTUV COUVERTS
CEORSTUY COURTESY
CEOSSSTU COSTUSES
CEOSSTTU COTTUSES

CEPPRRSU CRUPPERS
CEPPRSSU SCUPPERS
CEPPRTUU UPPERCUT
CEPRSSTU SPRUCEST
CEPRSSUY CYPRUSES
CEPRSTUU CUTPURSE
CEPSSSTU SUSPECTS
CERSSSUU RUSCUSES
CERSSTTU SCUTTERS
CERSSTUY CURTSEYS
CERSSUUX EXCURSUS
CFFGHINU CHUFFING
CFFGILNU CUFFLING
CFFGINOS SCOFFING
CFFGINSU SCUFFING
CFFHINOS CHIFFONS
CFFIRTUY FRUCTIFY
CFFMOSSU OFFSCUMS
CFGHIILN FILCHING
CFGHINOO CHOOFING
CFGIIKLN FICKLING
FLICKING
CFGIKLNO FLOCKING
CFGIKNOR FROCKING
CFGIKNSU FUCKINGS
CFGINORT CROFTING
CFGINOSU FOCUSING
CFHIINOO FINOCHIO
CFHIIORR HORRIFIC
CFHIKORS ROCKFISH
CFHILPTY FLYPITCH
CFHIMOSS SCOMFISH
CFHIMSSU SCUMFISH
CFHLOPUU POUCHFUL
CFHORSTU FUTHORCS
CFIIILSY SILICIFY
CFIIKNYZ ZINCKIFY
CFIILNST INFLICTS
CFIILNUU FUNICULI
CFIILOPR PROLIFIC
CFIILPSU PULSIFIC
CFIIMNOS SOMNIFIC
CFIIMORT MORTIFIC
CFIINOPT PONTIFIC
CFIINORT FRICTION
CFIINOST FICTIONS
CFIKLSTU STICKFUL
CFIKNNOS FINNOCKS
CFIKOSSS FOSSICKS
CFIKPSTU PUCKFIST
CFILMOOR COLIFORM
CFILRSUU SULFURIC
CFIMNOOR CONIFORM
CFIMNORS CONFIRMS
CFIMNORU UNCIFORM
CFINNOTU FUNCTION
CFKLLOSU LOCKFULS
CFKNORSU UNFROCKS
CFKOSTTU FUTTOCKS
CFLLOPRU CROPFULL
CFLMRSUU FULCRUMS
CFLNOORT CORNLOFT
CFLNORSU SCORNFUL
CFLOOPSU SCOOPFUL
CFLOPRSU CROPFULS
CFMNOORS CONFORMS
CFMOORST COMFORTS
CFNNOORT CONFRONT
CFOOORTW CROWFOOT
CFRSTUUU USUFRUCT

Letters	Words
CGGGHINU	CHUGGING
CGGGILNO	CLOGGING
	COGGLING
CGGGINOS	COGGINGS
	SCOGGING
CGGGINSU	SCUGGING
CGGHILNU	GULCHING
CGGHINOU	COUGHING
CGGIILNN	CLINGING
CGGIINNO	COIGNING
CGGIINNR	CRINGING
CGGIINRS	GRICINGS
CGGILRSY	SCRIGGLY
CGGINNSU	SCUNGING
CGGINOOS	SCOOGING
CGGINOSU	SCOUGING
CGHHIILN	HILCHING
CGHHIINT	HITCHING
CGHHINNU	HUNCHING
CGHHINOT	HOTCHING
CGHHINTU	HUTCHING
CGHIIKNN	CHINKING
CGHIIKNO	HOICKING
CGHIIKNR	CHIRKING
CGHIIKNT	THICKING
CGHIILLN	CHILLING
CGHIILNR	CHIRLING
CGHIILNT	LICHTING
CGHIIMNR	CHIRMING
CGHIIMNS	MICHINGS
CGHIIMNT	MITCHING
CGHIINNN	CHINNING
CGHIINNP	PINCHING
CGHIINNW	WINCHING
CGHIINOR	CHOIRING
CGHIINPP	CHIPPING
CGHIINPR	CHIRPING
CGHIINPT	PITCHING
CGHIINQU	QUICHING
CGHIINRR	CHIRRING
CGHIINRT	CHIRTING
	RICHTING
CGHIINTT	CHITTING
CGHIINTW	WITCHING
CGHIINVV	CHIVVING
CGHIINVY	CHIVYING
CGHIINZZ	CHIZZING
CGHIKNNU	CHUNKING
CGHIKNOS	SHOCKING
CGHIKNSU	SHUCKING
CGHILMNU	MULCHING
CGHILNNU	LUNCHING
CGHILNNY	LYNCHING
CGHILNOT	CLOTHING
CGHILNRU	LURCHING
CGHIMMNU	CHUMMING
CGHIMNNU	MUNCHING
CGHIMNOO	MOOCHING
CGHIMNOP	CHOMPING
CGHIMNOR	CHROMING
CGHIMNOU	MOUCHING
CGHIMNPU	CHUMPING
CGHIMPSY	SPHYGMIC
CGHINNOS	CHIGNONS
CGHINNOT	NOTCHING
CGHINNPU	PUNCHING
CGHINNRU	CHURNING
CGHINNSY	SYNCHING
CGHINOOS	CHOOSING
CGHINOPP	CHOPPING
CGHINOPT	POTCHING
CGHINOPU	POUCHING
CGHINORT	TORCHING
CGHINOSU	CHOUSING
	HOCUSING
CGHINOTU	TOUCHING
CGHINOUV	VOUCHING
CGHINPSY	PSYCHING
CGHINPTU	PINCHGUT
CGHINRRU	CHURRING
CGHINRSU	CRUSHING
	RUCHINGS
CGHINSTY	SCYTHING
CGHNOOSU	SOUCHONG
CGHOORST	TORGOCHS
CGIIILNT	LIGNITIC
CGIIINNS	INCISING
CGIIINNT	INCITING
CGIIKLNN	CLINKING
CGIIKLNP	PICKLING
CGIIKLNS	LICKINGS
	SLICKING
CGIIKLNT	TICKLING
CGIIKMMS	GIMMICKS
CGIIKMMY	GIMMICKY
CGIIKNNS	SNICKING
CGIIKNNZ	ZINCKING
CGIIKNOY	YOICKING
CGIIKNPR	PRICKING
CGIIKNPS	PICKINGS
CGIIKNRS	SCRIKING
CGIIKNRT	TRICKING
CGIIKNRW	WRICKING
CGIIKNST	STICKING
	TICKINGS
CGIILLOS	ILLOGICS
CGIILMOS	LOGICISM
CGIILNOP	POLICING
CGIILNPP	CLIPPING
CGIILNPS	SPLICING
CGIILNSS	SLICINGS
CGIILNSU	SLUICING
CGIILOST	LOGICIST
	LOGISTIC
CGIILRTU	LITURGIC
CGIIMNNO	INCOMING
CGIIMNNS	MINCINGS
CGIIMNPR	CRIMPING
CGIIMNPU	PUMICING
CGIIMNSU	MISCUING
CGIINNOS	COININGS
CGIINNOT	NOTICING
CGIINNPR	PRINCING
CGIINNSU	INCUSING
CGIINNSW	WINCINGS
CGIINNTT	TINCTING
CGIINOOS	ISOGONIC
CGIINOPT	PICOTING
CGIINORT	TRIGONIC
CGIINOST	COTISING
CGIINOSV	VOICINGS
CGIINPRS	CRISPING
CGIINRSU	CRUISING
CGIINRSV	SCRIVING
CGIJNNOU	JOUNCING
CGIKKNNO	KNOCKING
CGIKLNNO	CLONKING
CGIKLNNU	CLUNKING
CGIKLNOR	ROCKLING
CGIKLNPU	PLUCKING
CGIKLNRU	RUCKLING
CGIKLNSU	SCULKING
	SUCKLING
CGIKMNOS	MOCKINGS
	SMOCKING
CGIKNOOR	CROOKING
CGIKNORS	ROCKINGS
CGIKNORT	TROCKING
CGIKNOST	STOCKING
CGIKNPSU	KINGCUPS
CGIKNRTU	TRUCKING
CGIKNSSU	SUCKINGS
CGIKNSTU	GUNSTICK
CGILLNOS	COLLINGS
CGILLNOY	COLLYING
CGILLNSU	CULLINGS
	SCULLING
CGILLNUY	CULLYING
CGILMNOP	CLOMPING
CGILMNPU	CLUMPING
CGILMNSU	MUSCLING
CGILMNTU	MULCTING
CGILMNUU	CINGULUM
	GLUCINUM
CGILNNOW	CLOWNING
CGILNOOR	COLORING
CGILNOOY	COOINGLY
CGILNOPP	CLOPPING
CGILNOPU	COUPLING
CGILNORU	CLOURING
CGILNOSS	CLOSINGS
CGILNOSW	COWLINGS
	SCOWLING
CGILNOTT	CLOTTING
CGILNOTU	CLOUTING
CGILNPSU	SCULPING
CGILNRSU	CURLINGS
CGILOORU	UROLOGIC
CGILORSW	COWGIRLS
CGILPSTU	GILTCUPS
CGILPSTY	GLYPTICS
CGIMMNSU	SCUMMING
CGIMNNOO	GNOMONIC
	ONCOMING
CGIMNOPS	COMPINGS
CGIMNOPT	COMPTING
CGIMNOPU	UPCOMING
CGIMNPRU	CRUMPING
CGIMRRUY	MICRURGY
CGINNNOS	CONNINGS
CGINNNSU	CUNNINGS
CGINNOOR	CROONING
CGINNOPU	POUNCING
	UNCOPING
CGINNORS	SCORNING
CGINNORW	CROWNING
CGINNOSS	CONSIGNS
CGINNOTU	COUNTING
CGINOOPS	SCOOPING
CGINOOPT	COOPTING
CGINOOST	SCOOTING
CGINOOTV	COGNOVIT
CGINOPPR	CROPPING
CGINOPRS	CORPSING
CGINOPRU	CROUPING
CGINOPSU	SCOUPING
CGINOPSW	SCOWPING
CGINORSS	CROSSING
	SCORINGS
	SCORSING
CGINORSU	COURSING
	SCOURING
	SOURCING
CGINORTU	COURTING
CGINOSTU	SCOUTING
CGINPPSU	CUPPINGS
CGINPRSU	SPRUCING
CGINRRSU	SCURRING
CGINRRUY	CURRYING
CGINRSSU	CURSINGS
CGINRSSY	SCRYINGS
CGINRSTU	CRUSTING
CGINRSUZ	SCRUZING
CGINSTTU	CUTTINGS
CGKLNOSU	GUNLOCKS
CGKNOSTU	GUNSTOCK
CGLLOSYY	GLYCOSYL
CGLMOOYY	MYCOLOGY
CGLNOOOY	ONCOLOGY
CGLOOOTY	TOCOLOGY
CGLOOTYY	CYTOLOGY
CGMNNOOR	MONGCORN
CGMNNORU	MUNGCORN
CGOORRSW	GORCROWS
CHHIIKST	THICKISH
CHHIILTY	HITCHILY
CHHIIPST	PHTHISIC
CHHIKORS	CHIKHORS
CHHILRSU	CHURLISH
CHHIMRTY	RHYTHMIC
CHHNORSU	RHONCHUS
CHHOOPTT	HOTCHPOT
CHIIILOS	CHILIOIS
CHIIKLST	TICKLISH
CHIIKNNS	KINCHINS
CHIIKRST	TRICKISH
CHIILLLY	CHILLILY
CHIILMSY	HYLICISM
CHIILNNP	LINCHPIN
CHIILOST	HOLISTIC
CHIILPRY	CHIRPILY
CHIILQSU	CLIQUISH
CHIILSTY	HYLICIST
CHIIMPRU	PICHURIM
CHIINNPS	INCHPINS
CHIINOPS	SIPHONIC
CHIINORT	ORNITHIC
CHIIORSS	CHORISIS
CHIIORST	HISTORIC
	ORCHITIS
CHIIPPRU	HIPPURIC
CHIIRSTT	TRISTICH
CHIKLLOS	HILLOCKS
CHIKLLOY	HILLOCKY
CHIKMNNU	MUNCHKIN
CHIKMNPU	CHIPMUNK
CHIKMNTU	MUTCHKIN
CHIKNNOP	PHINNOCK
CHIKNOOS	CHINOOKS
CHIKOPTY	KYPHOTIC
CHIKORST	TROCHISK
CHIKPSYY	PHYSICKY
CHILLMSU	CHILLUMS
CHILLOOT	OILCLOTH
CHILMOPS	COMPLISH
CHILMOSU	SCHOLIUM
CHILNNPY	LYNCHPIN
CHILNOOS	SCHOLION
CHILNORS	CHLORINS
CHILNOSU	ULICHONS

CHILNOSW CLOWNISH
CHILOOOZ HOLOZOIC
CHILOOPT HOLOPTIC
CHILOTUY TOUCHILY
CHIMMORU CHROMIUM
CHIMNOOR HORMONIC
CHIMNOSU INSOMUCH
CHIMNOUY ONYCHIUM
CHIMOORU MOUCHOIR
CHIMORSS CHORISMS
CHRISOMS
CHIMORST CHRISTOM
CHIMPSSY PSYCHISM
CHIMSSTY TYCHISMS
CHINOORT ORTHICON
CHINOPTY HYPNOTIC
PYTHONIC
TYPHONIC
CHINORTU COTHURNI
CHINOSSU CUSHIONS
CHINOSTZ SCHIZONT
CHINOSUY CUSHIONY
CHINSTTU UNSTITCH
CHIOOPPT PHOTOPIC
CHIOOPRS POCHOIRS
CHIOORSS ISOCHORS
CHIOORSU ICHOROUS
CHIOORSZ CHORIZOS
CHIOORTT ORTHOTIC
CHIOPRST STROPHIC
CHIOPSTY HYPOCIST
CHIORSSS CROSSISH
CHIORSST CHORISTS
CHIPRRSU CHIRRUPS
CHIPRRSY PYRRHICS
CHIPRRUY CHIRRUPY
CHIPRTTY TRIPTYCH
CHIPSSTY PSYCHIST
CHIRRSSU SCIRRHUS
CHISSTTU CHUTISTS
CHKLOOOS HOOLOCKS
CHKMMOOS HOMMOCKS
CHKMMOSU HUMMOCKS
CHKMMOUY HUMMOCKY
CHKNOOSS SCHNOOKS
CHKNORSU CORNHUSK
CHKOOSST SCHTOOKS
CHKPSTUU PUTCHUKS
CHLNOOOP COLOPHON
CHLOORSU CHLOROUS
CHLOPSTY SPLOTCHY
CHLORTUY CHOULTRY
CHMNOORT CORNMOTH
CHMNORRU CRUMHORN
CHNNOORS CHRONONS
CHNOORST TORCHONS
CHNORRSS SCHNORRS
CHNORSSY SYNCHROS
CHNORSTU COTHURNS
CHOOORYZ ZOOCHORY
CHOOPPSS COPSHOPS
CHOOPSTU OCTOPUSH
CIIIKNTU CUITIKIN
CIIILMPT IMPLICIT
CIIILMSU SILICIUM
CIIILPST SPILITIC
CIIILSTV CIVILIST
CIIILTVY CIVILITY
CIIIMNSV INCIVISM
CIIINNOS INCISION

CIIINTVY VICINITY
CIIJRSTU JURISTIC
CIIKKLLS KILLICKS
CIIKLLSY SICKLILY
CIIKLOPT POLITICK
CIIKLPST LIPSTICK
CIIKLRTY TRICKILY
CIIKLSTY STICKILY
CIIKMMMS MIMMICKS
CIIKMNNS MINNICKS
CIIKNOOT COOTIKIN
CIIKNSTU CUTIKINS
CIIKPSUW WICKIUPS
CIILLNOP POLLINIC
CIILMOPY IMPOLICY
CIILMOSS SCIOLISM
CIILMQSU CLIQUISM
CIILMRSY LYRICISM
CIILNOOT NOCTILIO
CIILNOPS CIPOLINS
PSILOCIN
CIILNOSS SILICONS
CIILOOPT POLITICO
CIILOOTZ ZOOLITIC
CIILOPPT POPLITIC
CIILOPST POLITICS
PSILOTIC
CIILORST CLITORIS
COISTRIL
CIILOSST SCIOLIST
SOLICITS
CIILOSTY SOLICITY
CIILOSVV SLIVOVIC
CIILRSTY LYRICIST
CIILRTUU UTRICULI
CIILSSSS SCISSILS
CIIMNOOS ISONOMIC
CIIMNOST MICTIONS
MONISTIC
NOMISTIC
CIIMORST TRISOMIC
CIIMOSST MISTICOS
STOICISM
CIIMRSTY MYRISTIC
CIINNSTT INSTINCT
CIINNSTU TUNICINS
CIINOOST COITIONS
ISOTONIC
CIINOOTZ ZOONITIC
CIINOPSS PSIONICS
CIINOPSU OPINICUS
CIINORSS INCISORS
CIINORSY INCISORY
CIINOSSS SCISSION
CIINOSTT STICTION
CIINOTTY TONICITY
CIINPRSS CRISPINS
CIINPSTU SINCIPUT
CIIOOPST ISOTOPIC
CIIOPRST PORISTIC
CIIOQTUX QUIXOTIC
CIIORRWW WIRRICOW
CIIOTTXY TOXICITY
CIIPRRTU PRURITIC
CIIPRSTU PURISTIC
CIIRSTTU TRUISTIC
CIISSTTY CYSTITIS
CIJNNOOS CONJOINS
CIJNNOOT CONJOINT
CIJNNOTU JUNCTION

CIJNNSTU INJUNCTS
CIJOOSTY JOCOSITY
CIKKLLOS KILLOCKS
CIKLLOPR KILLCROP
CIKLLOPS PILLOCKS
CIKLLORS ROLLICKS
CIKLLOSS SILLOCKS
CIKLLOSW KILLCOWS
CIKLLPUY PLUCKILY
CIKLMSSU MISLUCKS
CIKLNOST LINSTOCK
CIKLOSTY STOCKILY
CIKMNNOS MINNOCKS
CIKMOORS SICKROOM
CIKMOPST MOPSTICK
CIKNNOOS COONSKIN
CIKNNOPS PINNOCKS
CIKNNOSW WINNOCKS
CIKNSSTU UNSTICKS
CIKOPPST POCKPITS
CIKOSSTT STOCKIST
CIKOSTUW OUTWICKS
CILLMNOR CORNMILL
CILLMSUY CLUMSILY
CULLYISM
CILLNOOT COTILLON
CILLNORS INSCROLL
CILLNOSU CULLIONS
SCULLION
CILLOOOT OCOTILLO
CILLOORS CRIOLLOS
CILMNOPS COMPLINS
CILMNOPU PULMONIC
CILMNOUU INOCULUM
CILMNUUV VINCULUM
CILMOORS MISCOLOR
CILMOPSY OLYMPICS
CILMPRSY SCRIMPLY
CILMPSUU SPICULUM
CILMSSTU CULTISMS
CILNOORS ORCINOLS
CILNOORU UNICOLOR
CILNOOSS CLOISONS
CILNOOST COLONIST
CILNOOTU LOCUTION
CILNOPRS PILCORNS
CILNOPTU PLUTONIC
CILNORSY LYRICONS
CILNOSTU LINOCUTS
CILNOSUY COUSINLY
CILNPSSU INSCULPS
SCULPINS
CILNPSTU INSCULPT
CILOOPST COPILOTS
CILOOPYZ POLYZOIC
CILOORRT TRICOLOR
CILOORST CORTISOL
CILOORSU COULOIRS
CILOOSSU SCIOLOUS
CILOPPRY PROPYLIC
CILOPRSW PILCROWS
CILOPSSW COWSLIPS
CILORSTY COYSTRIL
CILOSSTU OCULISTS
CILOSSTY SYSTOLIC
CILOSSUU LUSCIOUS
CILPRSTU CULPRITS
CILPSSTU SCULPSIT
CILRSTTY STRICTLY
CILRSTUY CRUSTILY

CILRSUVY SCURVILY
CILSSTTU CULTISTS
CIMMOSSS COSMISMS
CIMNOOOZ ZOONOMIC
CIMNOORS OMICRONS
CIMNOORU CORONIUM
CIMNOPRT COMPRINT
CIMNORSS CRIMSONS
CIMNORSY CRONYISM
CIMNOSTU MISCOUNT
CIMNOSUY SYCONIUM
CIMOOOTZ ZOOTOMIC
CIMOORSS MORISCOS
CIMOPSSY COPYISMS
CIMOSSST COSMISTS
CIMOSTUU MUTICOUS
CIMOSTUY MUCOSITY
CIMOSTYZ ZYMOTICS
CINNNOSU INCONNUS
CINNOOSS SCOINSON
CINNOOST SCONTION
CINNOOTU CONTINUO
CINNORSU UNICORNS
CINNOSTU UNCTIONS
CINNOSTY SYNTONIC
CINNQUUX QUINCUNX
CINOOOTZ ZOONOTIC
CINOOPRS SCORPION
CINOOPRT PROTONIC
CINOOSUV COVINOUS
CINOOTXY OXYTOCIN
CINOPSSY PYCNOSIS
CINOPSTY SYNOPTIC
CINORRST TRICORNS
CINORSST CISTRONS
CORNISTS
CINORSTT CONTRIST
CINORSTU RUCTIONS
CINORSUY COUSINRY
CINOSSST CONSISTS
CINOSSTU SUCTIONS
CINOSTUV VISCOUNT
CINRSSTU INCRUSTS
CINRSTTU INSTRUCT
CINRSTUY SCRUTINY
CIOOPRST PORTICOS
PROOTICS
CIOOPTYZ ZOOTYPIC
CIOOQSTU COQUITOS
CIOORRWW WORRICOW
CIOORSSU SCORIOUS
CIOOSSTU STOCIOUS
CIOPSSTY COPYISTS
CIORRSTU CURSITOR
CIORSSSS SCISSORS
CIPPRRUU PURPURIC
CIPSSTTY STYPTICS
CIRRSTTU CRITTURS
CJNOORRU CONJUROR
CJRSUUUU SUCURUJU
CKKNOOTU KNOCKOUT
CKKOORRW ROCKWORK
CKLLMOSU MULLOCKS
CKLLOOPS POLLOCKS
CKLLOORS ROLLOCKS
CKLLORSU RULLOCKS
CKLMMOSU SLUMMOCK
CKLOOOSY OLYCOOKS
CKLOORSW ROWLOCKS
CKLOOSTU LOCKOUTS

CKLOPSTU	PUTLOCKS
CKMMMOSU	MUMMOCKS
CKMNOOOR	MOONROCK
CKMOOOOR	COOKROOM
CKNOSSTU	UNSTOCKS
CKNRSTUU	UNSTRUCK
CKOOOSTU	COOKOUTS
CKOOPSTT	STOCKPOT
CKOORSSU	SOUROCKS
CKOPSTTU	PUTTOCKS
CKORSTUW	CUTWORKS
CKOSSSTU	TUSSOCKS
CKOSSTUY	TUSSOCKY
CLLMOSSU	MOLLUSCS
CLLOOPSS	SCOLLOPS
CLLOOQUY	COLLOQUY
CLMMNOOY	COMMONLY
CLMOOOTY	COLOTOMY
CLMOOPST	COMPLOTS
CLMOPSTU	PLUMCOTS
CLNOORST	CONTROLS
CLNOORTU	CONTROUL
	COUNTROL
CLNOSSTU	CONSULTS
CLNOSTUY	UNCOSTLY
CLOOOPRT	PROTOCOL
CLOORTUY	LOCUTORY
CLOOSSSU	COLOSSUS
CLOPRSTU	SCULPTOR
CLRSSUUU	SURCULUS
CMMNNOOU	UNCOMMON
CMNOOOST	MONOCOTS
CMNOOOTY	ONCOTOMY
CMNOORRW	CORNWORM
CMNOPSTU	CONSUMPT
CMOOPRST	COMPORTS
CMOOPSST	COMPOSTS
CMOPRSUX	SCRUMPOX
CMORSSTU	SCROTUMS
CMORSTUW	CUTWORMS
CNNOOORT	CONTORNO
CNNORSTU	NOCTURNS
CNNORSUW	UNCROWNS
CNOOOORT	OCTOROON
CNOOPPRS	POPCORNS
CNOOPRSU	CROUPONS
CNOOPSSU	SOUPCONS
CNOORRSW	CORNROWS
CNOORRTY	CRYOTRON
CNOORSST	CONSORTS
CNOORSTT	CONTORTS
CNOORSTU	CONTOURS
	CORNUTOS
	CROUTONS
	OUTSCORN
CNOOSTTW	COTTOWNS
CNOPRSTY	CRYPTONS
CNOSTUUU	UNCTUOUS
COOOPSYZ	ZOOSCOPY
COOPRRST	PROCTORS
COOPRSTU	OUTCROPS
COOPRSUU	CROUPOUS
COOPRSUY	UROSCOPY
COORRWWY	WORRYCOW
COORSSTU	OUTCROSS
COOSSTTY	OTOCYSTS
COPRRSTU	CORRUPTS
DDDDEEIR	DIDDERED
DDDDEEOR	DODDERED
DDDEEEFN	DEFENDED
DDDEEENP	DEPENDED
DDDEEENR	REDDENED
DDDEEENU	UNDEEDED
DDDEEERW	WEDDERED
DDDEEFOR	FODDERED
DDDEEGIS	DISEDGED
DDDEEHRS	SHREDDED
DDDEEIST	STEDDIED
DDDEEJRU	JUDDERED
DDDEELRT	TREDDLED
DDDEENOR	DONDERED
	REDDENDO
DDDEENOS	SODDENED
DDDEENUW	UNWEDDED
DDDEEORR	DODDERER
DDDEEPRU	PUDDERED
DDDEERTU	DETRUDED
DDDEGNOU	UNGODDED
DDDEHIRT	THRIDDED
DDDEIIMS	SMIDDIED
DDDEIINV	DIVIDEND
DDDEIIST	DIDDIEST
	STIDDIED
DDDEILNU	UNLIDDED
DDDEILNW	DWINDLED
DDDEILQU	QUIDDLED
DDDEILRS	DIDDLERS
DDDEILTW	TWIDDLED
DDDEIMOS	DISMODED
DDDEINOR	DENDROID
DDDEINRU	UNDERDID
DDDEIOST	DODDIEST
DDDEIQSU	SQUIDDED
DDDEISTU	DUDDIEST
DDDENORW	DROWNDED
DDDGIILN	DIDDLING
DDDIIOOR	DORIDOID
DDEEEEMR	REDEEMED
DDEEEENP	DEEPENED
DDEEEFLX	DEFLEXED
DDEEEFNR	DEFENDER
DDEEEFRR	DEFERRED
DDEEEGLR	LEDGERED
DDEEEGMR	DEMERGED
DDEEEGNR	DEGENDER
	GENDERED
DDEEEGRR	REGREDED
DDEEEGRT	DETERGED
DDEEEHLW	WHEEDLED
DDEEEHNU	UNHEEDED
DDEEEIMR	REMEDIED
	REMEIDED
DDEEEIST	DEEDIEST
	STEEDIED
DDEEELLV	DEVELLED
DDEEELNW	WEDELNED
DDEEELPT	DEPLETED
DDEEELSS	DEEDLESS
DDEEELTW	TWEEDLED
DDEEEMNT	DEMENTED
DDEEEMRS	DEMERSED
DDEEENNU	UNNEEDED
DDEEENPX	EXPENDED
DDEEENRR	RENDERED
DDEEENRT	TENDERED
DDEEENSU	UNSEEDED
DDEEENTX	EXTENDED
DDEEENUW	UNWEEDED
DDEEERRT	DETERRED
DDEEERST	DESERTED
DDEEERSV	DESERVED
DDEEESTT	DETESTED
DDEEESTV	DEVESTED
DDEEFFIR	DIFFERED
DDEEFFNO	OFFENDED
DDEEFGIT	FIDGETED
DDEEFINR	FRIENDED
DDEEFINU	UNDEFIDE
	UNDEFIED
DDEEFLNO	ENFOLDED
DDEEFLOU	DEFOULED
DDEEFMOR	DEFORMED
DDEEFNRU	REFUNDED
	UNDERFED
DDEEFORR	FODDERER
DDEEGGIR	DERIGGED
DDEEGGOR	DOGGEDER
DDEEGHNU	UNHEDGED
DDEEGILN	ENGILDED
DDEEGINR	ENRIDGED
DDEEGINS	DESIGNED
	SDEIGNED
DDEEGIRV	DIVERGED
DDEEGISS	DISEDGES
DDEEGIST	DIGESTED
DDEEGJRU	REJUDGED
DDEEGLNO	GOLDENED
DDEEGMMU	DEGUMMED
DDEEGOPS	GODSPEED
DDEEGRRS	DREDGERS
DDEEGSTU	DEGUSTED
DDEEHILS	SHIELDED
DDEEHINR	HINDERED
DDEEHIRT	DITHERED
DDEEHISS	EDDISHES
DDEEHNOR	DEHORNED
DDEEHNSU	DUDHEENS
DDEEHORT	DEHORTED
DDEEHRRS	SHREDDER
DDEEHRSS	SHEDDERS
DDEEIINT	INEDITED
DDEEIIRV	REDIVIDE
DDEEILLV	DEVILLED
DDEEILMN	MILDENED
DDEEILMW	MILDEWED
DDEEILRW	WILDERED
DDEEIMNP	IMPENDED
DDEEIMNR	REMINDED
DDEEIMOR	MOIDERED
DDEEIMSS	MISDEEDS
DDEEIMST	DEMISTED
DDEEIMTT	DEMITTED
DDEEINNR	DINNERED
DDEEINNT	INDENTED
	INTENDED
DDEEINRT	DENDRITE
DDEEINST	DESTINED
DDEEINTU	UNEDITED
DDEEIOPR	PERIODED
DDEEIPPR	REDIPPED
DDEEIPRS	PRESIDED
DDEEIPRV	DEPRIVED
DDEEIPSS	DEPSIDES
	DESPISED
DDEEIRRS	DERIDERS
DDEEIRST	REDDIEST
DDEEIRSV	DIVERSED
DDEEIRTV	DIVERTED
DDEEISST	DESISTED
	STEDDIES
DDEEISTV	DIVESTED
DDEEITTW	DEWITTED
DDEEJLLO	JODELLED
DDEEKNSU	DUSKENED
DDEELLMO	MODELLED
DDEELLOW	DOWELLED
DDEELLOY	YODELLED
DDEELMPU	DEPLUMED
DDEELMRS	MEDDLERS
DDEELNOU	LOUDENED
DDEELOPR	DEPLORED
	POLDERED
DDEELOPX	EXPLODED
DDEELOPY	DEPLOYED
DDEELORS	SOLDERED
DDEELOSU	DELOUSED
DDEELOVV	DEVOLVED
DDEELPRS	PEDDLERS
DDEELPRU	PRELUDED
DDEELRST	TREDDLES
DDEELRSU	DELUDERS
DDEEMNOR	ENDODERM
DDEEMRRU	DEMURRED
	MURDERED
DDEENNOR	DONNERED
DDEENNOY	ENDODYNE
DDEENNTU	UNTENDED
DDEENOPR	PERDENDO
	PONDERED
DDEENOPW	PONDWEED
DDEENORS	ENDORSED
DDEENORW	WONDERED
DDEENOSS	ENDOSSED
DDEENPRS	SPREDDEN
DDEENRSU	SUNDERED
DDEENRTU	RETUNDED
DDEEOPRT	DEPORTED
DDEEOPRW	POWDERED
DDEEORRW	REWORDED
DDEEORTT	DETORTED
DDEEORTU	DETOURED
DDEEORUV	DEVOURED
DDEEORVY	OVERDYED
DDEEPRRU	PERDURED
DDEEPRSS	SPREDDES
DDEERRUV	VERDURED
DDEERSTU	DETRUDES
DDEERTUX	EXTRUDED
DDEFFISU	DIFFUSED
DDEFIIIN	NIDIFIED
DDEFIILM	MIDFIELD
DDEFIILR	FIDDLIER
DDEFIIMO	MODIFIED
DDEFIIMW	MIDWIFED
DDEFILNO	INFOLDED
DDEFILRS	FIDDLERS
DDEFILSY	FIDDLEYS
DDEFLNOU	UNFOLDED
DDEFLRSU	FUDDLERS
DDEFLRUU	UDDERFUL
DDEFNNUU	UNFUNDED
DDEGGINR	DREDGING
DDEGGLOY	DOGGEDLY
DDEGGNOO	DOGGONED
DDEGHILN	HEDDLING
DDEGHINS	SHEDDING
DDEGIINR	DERIDING
DDEGIIST	GIDDIEST
DDEGILMN	MEDDLING
DDEGILNP	PEDDLING

DDEGILNR REDDLING
DDEGILNS SLEDDING
DDEGILNU DELUDING
INDULGED
UNGILDED
DDEGILOS DISLODGE
DDEGILRS GRIDDLES
DDEGILRY GLIDDERY
DDEGILST GLIDDEST
DDEGILUV DIVULGED
DDEGIMOS DEMIGODS
DDEGINNS SNEDDING
DDEGINNU DENUDING
DDEGINRS REDDINGS
DDEGINRU UNGIRDED
DDEGINST STEDDING
DDEGINSW SWINDGED
WEDDINGS
DDEGINUU UNGUIDED
DDEGIOST DODGIEST
DDEGIQSU SQUIDGED
DDEGIRRS GRIDDERS
DDEGLOPS SPLODGED
DDEGLOSS DOGSLEDS
DDEGNORU GROUNDED
UNDERDOG
DDEGNOSS GODSENDS
DDEGNOSU DUDGEONS
DDEGORSS GORSEDDS
DDEGRRSU DRUDGERS
DDEGRRUY DRUDGERY
DDEHILNY HIDDENLY
DDEHILOO IDLEHOOD
DDEHIMOS DISHOMED
DDEHINNU UNHIDDEN
DDEHINOR DIHEDRON
DDEHIORS SHODDIER
DDEHIOSS SHODDIES
DDEHIRSS SHIDDERS
DDEHIRSW WHIDDERS
DDEHIRSY HYDRIDES
DDEHNOOU UNHOODED
DDEHNPUU UPHUDDEN
DDEHNRSU HUNDREDS
DDEHOOOO HOODOOED
DDEHOOSW WOODSHED
DDEHORSU SHROUDED
DDEHRSSU SHUDDERS
DDEHRSUY SHUDDERY
DDEIIIRS IRIDISED
DDEIIIRZ IRIDIZED
DDEIIKLS DISLIKED
DDEIIKRS KIDDIERS
DDEIILNR DIELDRIN
DDEIILOS IDOLISED
DDEIILOZ IDOLIZED
DDEIILRT TIDDLIER
DDEIILST TIDDLIES
DDEIIMSS SMIDDIES
DDEIIMVW MIDWIVED
DDEIINRT NITRIDED
DDEIINTU UNTIDIED
DDEIIOPS DIOPSIDE
DIPODIES
DDEIIOST ODDITIES
DDEIIOSX DIOXIDES
OXIDISED
DDEIIOXZ OXIDIZED
DDEIIRSV DIVIDERS
DDEIIRUV REDUVIID

DDEIISST STIDDIES
DDEIISTT TIDDIEST
DDEIKNRS KINDREDS
DDEIKOSY DISYOKED
DDEIKRSS SKIDDERS
DDEILMOP IMPLODED
DDEILMOV DEVILDOM
DDEILMSU MUDSLIDE
DDEILNPS SPINDLED
SPLENDID
DDEILNRT TRINDLED
DDEILNRU UNRIDDLE
DDEILNSW DWINDLES
SWINDLED
DDEILOPS DISPLODE
LOPSIDED
DDEILOST DELTOIDS
DDEILOSY DYSODILE
DDEILPRS PIDDLERS
DDEILPRU PUDDLIER
DDEILQRU QUIDDLER
DDEILQSU QUIDDLES
DDEILRRS RIDDLERS
DDEILRSS SLIDDERS
DDEILRST STRIDDLE
TIDDLERS
DDEILRSY SLIDDERY
DDEILRTW TWIDDLER
DDEILRZZ DRIZZLED
DDEILSTW TWIDDLES
DDEILSTY LYDDITES
TIDDLEYS
DDEIMMNU UNDIMMED
DDEIMNNU UNMINDED
DDEIMNSU MUEDDINS
DDEIMNUV VIDENDUM
DDEIMORS DERMOIDS
DDEIMOSS DESMOIDS
DDEIMOSU MEDUSOID
DDEIMSTU MUDDIEST
DDEINNRU UNRIDDEN
DDEINNTU UNDINTED
DDEINOPS DISPONED
DDEINORS INDORSED
DDEINOSW DISENDOW
DISOWNED
DOWNSIDE
DDEINOWW WINDOWED
DDEINPPU UNDIPPED
DDEINPSS DISPENDS
DDEINRST STRIDDEN
DDEINRTU INTRUDED
DDEINSST DISTENDS
DDEINSSW SWIDDENS
DDEINSTU DISTUNED
DDEIOPRS DROPSIED
DDEIOPRV PROVIDED
DDEIOPSS DISPOSED
DDEIOPST PODDIEST
DDEIORRS DISORDER
SORDIDER
DDEIOSST SODDIEST
DDEIOSTW DOWDIEST
DDEIPRSS DISPREDS
DDEIPRSU SPUDDIER
DDEIPSTU DISPUTED
DDEIRSSU DRUIDESS
DDEIRSTU RUDDIEST
STURDIED
DDEKMOSU DUKEDOMS

DDELLNUU UNDULLED
DDELMRSU MUDDLERS
DDELNORU UNLORDED
DDELNRTU TRUNDLED
DDELNSUY SUDDENLY
DDELOORS DOODLERS
DDELOPRS PLODDERS
DDELORST STRODDLE
STRODLED
TODDLERS
DDELOSYY DYSODYLE
DDELPRSU PUDDLERS
DDELSSTU STUDDLES
DDEMMSSU SMEDDUMS
DDEMNOOU UNDOOMED
DDEMNOST ODDMENTS
DDEMNOUU DUODENUM
DDEMNPUU PUDENDUM
DDEMOOTU OUTMODED
DDENNORS DENDRONS
DDENNOSU UNSODDEN
DDENOOUW UNWOODED
DDENOPSS DESPONDS
DDENORSU REDOUNDS
DDENORTU ROTUNDED
DDENORUW UNWORDED
DDENOSST SNODDEST
DDENOSTU STOUNDED
DDENOSTW STOWNDED
DDENOSUW SWOUNDED
DDENOTTU DONUTTED
DDENSTUY SUDDENTY
DDEOOOOV VOODOOED
DDEOORSW REDWOODS
DDEOORWW ROWDEDOW
DDEOOUUV VOUDOUED
DDEORTUU OUTDURED
DDFGIILN FIDDLING
DDFGILNU FUDDLING
DDFIIOSU FIDDIOUS
DDFMNOUU DUMFOUND
DDGGIINY GIDDYING
DDGGILNU GUDDLING
DDGGINOS DODGINGS
DDGGINRU DRUDGING
DDGHIINW WHIDDING
DDGHILNO HODDLING
DDGHILNU HUDDLING
DDGHINTU THUDDING
DDGHOOOS GODHOODS
DDGIIINV DIVIDING
DDGIIKNS SKIDDING
DDGIIKNY KIDDYING
DDGIILMN MIDDLING
DDGIILNN DINDLING
DDGIILNP PIDDLING
DDGIILNR RIDDLING
DDGIILNT TIDDLING
DDGIILNW WIDDLING
DDGILMNU MUDDLING
DDGILNNO NODDLING
DDGILNOO DOODLING
DDGILNOP PLODDING
DDGILNOT TODDLING
DDGILNPU PUDDLING
DDGILNRU RUDDLING
DDGIMNUY MUDDYING
DDGIMRSU DRUDGISM
DDGINNOS NODDINGS
SNODDING

DDGINOPR PRODDING
DDGINOQU QUODDING
DDGINORS RODDINGS
DDGINPSU PUDDINGS
SPUDDING
DDGINPUY PUDDINGY
DDGINRUY RUDDYING
DDGINSTU STUDDING
DDGOOOSW DOGWOODS
DDHILOSY SHODDILY
DDHIORSY HYDROIDS
DDHIOSWY DOWDYISH
DDHLLOOO DOLLHOOD
DDIIIIVV DIVIDIVI
DDIILOPY DIPLOIDY
DDIIMMUY DIDYMIUM
DDIIMRSU DRUIDISM
SIDDURIM
DDIINOPU DUPONDII
DDIIQSTU QUIDDITS
DDIIQTUY QUIDDITY
DDILOOWW WILDWOOD
DDILORSY SORDIDLY
DDILOSSY DYSODILS
DDIMOSUY DIDYMOUS
DDIMOSWY DOWDYISM
DDINNOWW DOWNWIND
DDINOOOT ODONTOID
DDINOOWW WOODWIND
DDLLMOOS DOLLDOMS
DDLMORSU DOLDRUMS
DDMNOORS DROMONDS
DDOORWWY ROWDYDOW
DDORSSTY DROSTDYS
DEEEEFRR REFEREED
DEEEEFRZ DEFREEZE
DEEEEGKR KEDGEREE
DEEEEHLR REHEELED
DEEEEKMN MEEKENED
DEEEELTY EYELETED
DEEEEMRR REDEEMER
DEEEEMST ESTEEMED
DEEEENRV VENEERED
DEEEERTT TEETERED
DEEEFFIR EFFEIRED
DEEEFINR FINEERED
NEEDFIRE
REDEFINE
DEEEFIPT TEPEFIED
DEEEFIRW FIREWEED
DEEEFLLR REFELLED
DEEEFLPT DEEPFELT
DEEEFLRT FELTERED
TELFERED
DEEEFLRX REFLEXED
DEEEFLSX DEFLEXES
DEEEFMNR FREEDMEN
DEEEFNRT DEFERENT
DEEEFNSS DEFENSES
DEEEFNST ENFESTED
DEEEFORV OVERFEED
DEEEFRRR DEFERRER
REFERRED
DEEEFRRT FERRETED
DEEEFRST FESTERED
DEEEFRTT FETTERED
DEEEFRTW FEWTERED
DEEEGHNW WHEENGED
DEEEGILS ELEGISED
DEEEGILZ ELEGIZED

DEEEGIPR PEDIGREE
DEEEGIRR GREEDIER
DEEEGISS DIEGESES
DEEEGISW EDGEWISE
DEEEGLPS PLEDGEES
DEEEGLSS EDGELESS
DEEEGLSV SELVEDGE
DEEEGMRR DEMERGER
REMERGED
DEEEGMRS DEMERGES
DEEEGNNR ENGENDER
DEEEGNRU RENEGUED
DEEEGNRV REVENGED
DEEEGRRS REGREDES
DEEEGRST DETERGES
DEEEGRTT GETTERED
DEEEHHSW WHEESHED
DEEEHKRS SHREEKED
DEEEHLMT HELMETED
DEEEHLPW WHEEPLED
DEEEHLRW WHEEDLER
DEEEHLSS HEEDLESS
DEEEHLSW WHEEDLES
DEEEHLWZ WHEEZLED
DEEEHMMS EMMESHED
DEEEHMNS ENMESHED
DEEEHRTT TETHERED
DEEEIKLS SEEDLIKE
DEEEILNR NEEDLIER
DEEEILNS SELENIDE
DEEEILRV RELIEVED
DEEEILTV DELETIVE
DEEEILVW WEEVILED
DEEEIMNS INSEEMED
DEEEIMRS REMEDIES
DEEEINRR REINDEER
DEEEINRS NEREIDES
DEEEINST NEEDIEST
DEEEINSX ENDEIXES
DEEEINTV EVENTIDE
DEEEIPRS SPEEDIER
DEEEIPTX EXPEDITE
DEEEIRRR DERRIERE
DEEEIRSS DIERESES
DEEEIRST REEDIEST
DEEEIRSZ RESEIZED
DEEEIRTW TWEEDIER
DEEEIRVW REVIEWED
DEEEISST SEEDIEST
STEEDIES
DEEEISSV DEVISEES
DEEEISTW WEEDIEST
DEEEJLLW JEWELLED
DEEEJNRU DEJEUNER
DEEEJNSU DEJEUNES
DEEEKNSW WEEKENDS
DEEEKOPW POKEWEED
DEEEKRST STREEKED
DEEEKRSW RESKEWED
SKEWERED
DEEELLLV LEVELLED
DEEELLNT DENTELLE
DEEELLNV NEVELLED
DEEELLNW NEWELLED
DEEELLPR REPELLED
DEEELLPT PELLETED
DEEELLPX EXPELLED
DEEELLRT TELLERED
DEEELLRV REVELLED
DEEELMOS SOMEDELE

DEEELNPU UNPEELED
DEEELNRS NEEDLERS
DEEELNRT RELENTED
DEEELNRU UNREELED
DEEELNSS LESSENED
NEEDLESS
SELDSEEN
DEEELNSU UNSEELED
DEEELOPV DEVELOPE
DEEELPRT PELTERED
REPLETED
DEEELPST DEPLETES
STEEPLED
DEEELRSS REDELESS
DEEELRST DEERLETS
STREELED
DEEELRTT LETTERED
DEEELRTW TWEEDLER
WELTERED
DEEELSSS SEEDLESS
DEEELSSW WEEDLESS
DEEELSTW TWEEDLES
DEEELTVV VELVETED
DEEEMNNT NEEDMENT
DEEEMNSS DEMESNES
SEEDSMEN
DEEEMPRT TEMPERED
DEEEMPTX EXEMPTED
DEEEMRRU MURDEREE
DEEEMRSS DEMERSES
DEEEMRST DEEMSTER
DEEENNRT ENTENDER
DEEENNUW UNWEENED
DEEENOPR REOPENED
DEEENORS ENDORSEE
DEEENPRT REPENTED
REPETEND
DEEENPRU UNPEERED
DEEENPRV PREVENED
DEEENPRX EXPENDER
DEEENPSS DEEPNESS
DEEENRRR RENDERER
DEEENRRT TENDERER
DEEENRRV REVEREND
DEEENRST RESENTED
DEEENRTT TENTERED
DEEENRTU NEUTERED
DEEENRTX EXTENDER
DEEENRUV REVENUED
UNREEVED
DEEENSSS SEEDNESS
DEEENSTT DETENTES
DEEENSTU DETENUES
DEEENSTX DENTEXES
DEEENSUV VENDEUSE
DEEEOPRR PEDERERO
DEEEOPRT DEPORTEE
DEEEORSW OREWEEDS
DEEEORVY OVEREYED
DEEEOSTV DEVOTEES
DEEEPPPR PEPPERED
DEEEPRSS SPEEDERS
DEEEPRST ESTREPED
PESTERED
DEEEPRSZ SPREEZED
DEEEPRTX EXPERTED
DEEEQRRU REQUERED
DEEEQSUZ SQUEEZED
DEEERRRV VERDERER
DEEERRST DESERTER

DEEERRSV DESERVER
RESERVED
REVERSED
DEEERRTV REVERTED
DEEERSSV DESERVES
DEEERSTT RESETTED
SETTERED
STREETED
DEEERSTV REVESTED
DEEERSTW WESTERED
DEEERSTX EXSERTED
DEEERSUW SERUEWED
DEEERSVW SERVEWED
DEEERTTT TETTERED
DEEERTTV REVETTED
DEEESTTU SUEDETTE
DEEESTTV VEDETTES
DEEFFGLU EFFULGED
DEEFFGOR GOFFERED
DEEFFINR NIFFERED
DEEFFINS EFFENDIS
DEEFFINT INFEFTED
DEEFFNOR OFFENDER
REOFFEND
DEEFFRSU SUFFERED
DEEFGILR FLEDGIER
DEEFGINR FINGERED
DEEFGINS FEEDINGS
DEEFGIPS PIGFEEDS
DEEFGIUW GUDEWIFE
DEEFGLNU ENGULFED
DEEFGLOO FEELGOOD
DEEFGLUW GULFWEED
DEEFHIMU HUMEFIED
DEEFHINT HINDFEET
DEEFHLOR FREEHOLD
DEEFHLRS FELDSHER
DEEFHORT FOTHERED
DEEFIILN FEDELINI
LENIFIED
DEEFIINT DEFINITE
DEEFIIRS DEIFIERS
EDIFIERS
FIRESIDE
DEEFIIRV VERIFIED
DEEFILLR REFILLED
DEEFILLT FILLETED
DEEFILMS MEDFLIES
DEEFILNX INFLEXED
DEEFILPR PILFERED
DEEFILRS DEFILERS
FIELDERS
DEEFILRT FILTERED
DEEFIMSS MISFEEDS
DEEFIMTU TUMEFIED
DEEFINRR INFERRED
DEEFINRS DEFINERS
DEEFINRZ FRENZIED
DEEFINSS FINESSED
DEEFINST FENDIEST
INFESTED
DEEFIORS FORESIDE
DEEFIORT FOETIDER
DEEFIPRX PREFIXED
DEEFIRRV FERVIDER
DEEFIRTT REFITTED
DEEFISTT FETIDEST
DEEFLLNU UNFELLED
DEEFLNOR FORELEND
DEEFLNSU UNSELFED

DEEFLNTU DEFLUENT
DEEFLORW DEFLOWER
FLOWERED
REFLOWED
DEEFLOST FEEDLOTS
DEEFLPSU SPEEDFUL
DEEFLRUX REFLUXED
DEEFMNOR ENFORMED
DEEFMNOT FOMENTED
DEEFMORR DEFORMER
REFORMED
DEEFMORS FREEDOMS
DEEFMPRU PERFUMED
DEEFNORZ DEFROZEN
DEEFNOST SOFTENED
DEEFNRRU REFUNDER
DEEFNSST DEFTNESS
DEEFOORT REFOOTED
DEEFORST DEFOREST
FORESTED
FOSTERED
DEEFORTU FOUTERED
DEEFPRSU PERFUSED
DEEFRRTU RETURFED
DEEGGHHO HEDGEHOG
DEEGGHIP HEDGEPIG
DEEGGIJR JIGGERED
REJIGGED
DEEGGINR GINGERED
NIGGERED
RENIGGED
DEEGGIRR DREGGIER
DEEGGLOR DOGGEREL
DEEGGNOR ENGORGED
DEEGGNPU UNPEGGED
DEEGGORR REGORGED
DEEGGQSU SQUEGGED
DEEGGRRU RUGGEDER
DEEGHHIR HIGHERED
DEEGHHSU SHEUGHED
DEEGHHUW WHEUGHED
DEEGHILS SLEIGHED
DEEGHIST HEDGIEST
DEEGHITW WEIGHTED
DEEGHNRU HUNGERED
DEEGHOPR GOPHERED
DEEGHOPS SHEEPDOG
DEEGHORW HEDGEROW
DEEGHOSW HOGWEEDS
DEEGHOTT DOGTEETH
DEEGIINN INDIGENE
DEEGIISS DIEGESIS
DEEGIKST KEDGIEST
DEEGILMO LIEGEDOM
DEEGILMP IMPLEDGE
DEEGILMT GIMLETED
DEEGILNN NEEDLING
DEEGILNO ELOIGNED
LEGIONED
DEEGILNR ENGIRDLE
LINGERED
REEDLING
DEEGILNS SEEDLING
DEEGILNT DELETING
DEEGILRS LEIDGERS
DEEGILRW WEREGILD
DEEGILRY GREEDILY
DEEGILST GELIDEST
LEDGIEST
DEEGIMMR IMMERGED

DEEGIMNN	EMENDING
DEEGIMNR	REMEDING
DEEGIMRU	DEMIURGE
DEEGINNR	ENRINGED
DEEGINNS	ENSIGNED
DEEGINNT	TEENDING
DEEGINNW	ENDEWING
DEEGINOP	PIGEONED
DEEGINPS	SPEEDING
DEEGINRS	DESIGNER
	ENERGIDS
	REDESIGN
	REEDINGS
	RESIGNED
DEEGINSS	DINGESES
	EDGINESS
	SDEIGNES
	SEEDINGS
DEEGINST	INGESTED
	SIGNETED
	STEEDING
DEEGINSW	WEEDINGS
DEEGINSX	DESEXING
DEEGINZZ	GIZZENED
DEEGIOST	EGOTISED
DEEGIOTZ	EGOTIZED
DEEGIPSW	PIGWEEDS
DEEGIRST	DIGESTER
	ESTRIDGE
DEEGIRSU	GUDESIRE
DEEGIRSV	DIVERGES
DEEGISST	SEDGIEST
DEEGISTW	WEDGIEST
DEEGJPRU	PREJUDGE
DEEGJRSU	REJUDGES
DEEGLLOR	GOLLERED
DEEGLLRU	GRUELLED
DEEGLLUY	GULLEYED
DEEGLNOR	GOLDENER
DEEGLNOU	ENGOULED
DEEGLNOZ	LOZENGED
DEEGLNRY	LEGENDRY
DEEGLOPR	PLEDGEOR
DEEGLOPS	DOGSLEEP
DEEGLORV	GROVELED
DEEGLORW	GLOWERED
DEEGLOSY	GOLDEYES
DEEGLPRS	PLEDGERS
DEEGLPST	PLEDGETS
DEEGLRSS	SLEDGERS
DEEGMNRU	DUNGMERE
DEEGNNOS	ENDOGENS
DEEGNNOY	ENDOGENY
DEEGNORV	GOVERNED
DEEGNPRU	REPUGNED
DEEGNPUX	EXPUGNED
	EXPUNGED
DEEGOSTU	OUTEDGES
DEEGOTUW	GOUTWEED
DEEGPRUX	EXPURGED
DEEGRRSU	RESURGED
DEEGRSTU	GESTURED
DEEGRTTU	GUTTERED
DEEGSSTU	GUSSETED
DEEHHIRT	HITHERED
DEEHHNPY	HYPHENED
DEEHHPRS	SHEPHERD
DEEHHRST	THRESHED
DEEHHRSU	HUSHERED
DEEHIKRS	SHREIKED
	SHRIEKED
DEEHIKSV	KHEDIVES
DEEHILNS	ENSHIELD
DEEHILRS	RELISHED
	SHIELDER
DEEHILSV	DISHEVEL
DEEHIMMS	IMMESHED
DEEHIMNS	INMESHED
DEEHIMRT	MITHERED
DEEHINRR	HINDERER
DEEHINRS	DRISHEEN
DEEHINST	DISTHENE
DEEHINTW	WHITENED
DEEHIORS	HEROISED
DEEHIORZ	HEROIZED
DEEHIPRS	HESPERID
	PERISHED
DEEHIRRS	REDSHIRE
DEEHIRRT	DITHERER
DEEHIRSV	SHIVERED
	SHRIEVED
DEEHIRSW	SHREWDIE
DEEHIRTW	WITHERED
DEEHIRTY	HEREDITY
DEEHKNOS	KEESHOND
DEEHKNRU	HUNKERED
DEEHKORS	KOSHERED
DEEHLLOR	HOLLERED
DEEHLLOV	HOVELLED
DEEHLMMW	WHEMMLED
DEEHLMNU	UNHELMED
DEEHLMSW	WELDMESH
DEEHLNPU	UNHELPED
DEEHLORV	OVERHELD
	VERDELHO
DEEHLPPS	SHLEPPED
DEEHLSTU	SLEUTHED
DEEHMNRS	HERDSMEN
DEEHMORT	MOTHERED
DEEHNOPY	PHONEYED
DEEHNORR	DEERHORN
	DEHORNER
DEEHNORT	DETHRONE
	THRENODE
DEEHNPRS	PREHENDS
DEEHNSTU	ENTHUSED
DEEHOORV	HOOVERED
DEEHOPRT	POTHERED
DEEHORRT	DEHORTER
DEEHORSU	REHOUSED
DEEHORSW	SHOWERED
DEEHORTT	HOTTERED
DEEHORTX	EXHORTED
DEEHPRSY	SYPHERED
DEEHRRSW	SHREWDER
DEEHRTUW	WUTHERED
DEEIILNS	SIDELINE
DEEIILRV	LIVERIED
DEEIILRW	WIELDIER
DEEIIMRS	DIMERISE
DEEIIMRZ	DIMERIZE
DEEIIMST	ITEMISED
DEEIIMTZ	ITEMIZED
DEEIINST	DIETINES
DEEIINSX	ENDEIXIS
DEEIIPRS	EPEIRIDS
DEEIIRSS	DIERESIS
DEEIIRST	SIDERITE
DEEIIRSV	DERISIVE
DEEIIRSW	WEIRDIES
DEEIISSS	DISSEISE
DEEIISSW	SIDEWISE
DEEIISSZ	DISSEIZE
DEEIJNNO	ENJOINED
DEEIJNOR	REJOINED
DEEIJRTT	JITTERED
DEEIKKRY	YIKKERED
DEEIKLLR	KILLDEER
DEEIKLLS	KILLDEES
	SKELLIED
DEEIKLNN	ENKINDLE
	ENLINKED
DEEIKLNR	REKINDLE
DEEIKLNS	SILKENED
DEEIKLOV	DOVELIKE
DEEIKLSW	SILKWEED
DEEIKMSY	MISKEYED
DEEIKNRS	DEERSKIN
DEEIKNRT	TINKERED
DEEIKNTT	KITTENED
DEEIKOSV	DOVEKIES
DEEIKPPR	KIPPERED
DEEIKRSU	DUKERIES
DEEIKRSV	SKIVERED
DEEIKSTT	DISKETTE
DEEILLMP	IMPELLED
	MILLEPED
DEEILLNO	NIELLOED
DEEILLOR	ORIELLED
DEEILLPR	PERILLED
DEEILLRT	TILLERED
	TREDILLE
DEEILLRV	RIVELLED
DEEILLWY	WILLEYED
DEEILMOS	MELODIES
	MELODISE
DEEILMOZ	MELODIZE
DEEILMPT	IMPLETED
DEEILNOS	ESLOINED
DEEILNOT	DELETION
	ENTOILED
DEEILNPP	LIPPENED
DEEILNRU	UNDERLIE
DEEILNSS	IDLENESS
	LINSEEDS
DEEILNST	ENLISTED
	LINTSEED
	LISTENED
	TINSELED
DEEILNSY	DYELINES
DEEILNTT	ENTITLED
DEEILNUV	UNVEILED
DEEILOPT	LEPIDOTE
	PETIOLED
DEEILORT	DOLERITE
	LOITERED
DEEILOTT	TOILETED
DEEILPSS	SEEDLIPS
DEEILPST	EPISTLED
DEEILPSU	EPULIDES
DEEILPSY	SPEEDILY
DEEILRSU	LEISURED
DEEILRSV	DELIVERS
	DESILVER
	SILVERED
	SLIVERED
DEEILRSW	WIELDERS
DEEILRSY	YIELDERS
DEEILRTT	LITTERED
	RETITLED
DEEILRVY	DELIVERY
DEEILSSS	IDLESSES
DEEILSST	TIDELESS
DEEILSSV	DEVILESS
DEEILSTU	DILUTEES
DEEILSTV	DEVILETS
DEEILSUV	DELUSIVE
DEEILTUY	YULETIDE
DEEIMMNS	ENDEMISM
DEEIMMRS	IMMERSED
	SIMMERED
DEEIMMSS	MISDEEMS
DEEIMNOR	DOMINEER
DEEIMNOS	DEMONISE
	DOMINEES
DEEIMNOZ	DEMONIZE
DEEIMNPT	PEDIMENT
DEEIMNRR	REMINDER
DEEIMNRT	REMINTED
DEEIMNRV	VERMINED
DEEIMNSS	DESMINES
	SIDESMEN
DEEIMNST	DEMENTIS
	SEDIMENT
	TIDESMEN
DEEIMNTT	MITTENED
DEEIMOST	TEDISOME
DEEIMPRR	PERIDERM
	REPRIMED
DEEIMPRS	DEMIREPS
	PREMISED
	SIMPERED
DEEIMPRX	PREMIXED
DEEIMPSS	SEMIPEDS
DEEIMRSS	DERMISES
DEEIMRST	DEMERITS
	DEMISTER
	DIMETERS
	MISTERED
DEEIMRTT	REMITTED
DEEIMSSU	MEDIUSES
DEEINNRS	SINNERED
DEEINNRT	INDENTER
	INTENDER
	INTERNED
DEEINNRU	UNREINED
DEEINNRV	INNERVED
DEEINNST	DENTINES
	DESINENT
DEEINNSZ	DENIZENS
DEEINNTV	INVENTED
DEEINNTW	ENTWINED
DEEINNUV	UNENVIED
DEEINOPS	DISPONEE
DEEINORS	ORDINEES
DEEINORT	ORIENTED
DEEINOST	SIDENOTE
DEEINOSV	NOSEDIVE
DEEINPPR	NIPPERED
DEEINPSS	DISPENSE
	PIEDNESS
DEEINPST	PENTISED
DEEINPSU	UNESPIED
DEEINQRU	ENQUIRED
	INQUERED
DEEINQSU	SEQUINED
DEEINRRT	INTERRED
	TRENDIER
DEEINRRV	REDRIVEN
DEEINRST	INSERTED

NERDIEST
RESIDENT
SINTERED
TRENDIES
DEEINRSU UREDINES
DEEINRSW WIDENERS
DEEINRSX INDEXERS
DEEINRTU REUNITED
DEEINRTV INVERTED
DEEINRTW WINTERED
DEEINRTX DEXTRINE
DEEINSST DESTINES
DEEINSSV VENDISES
DEEINSSW DEWINESS
WIDENESS
DEEINSTT DINETTES
DEEINSTU DETINUES
DEEINSTV EVIDENTS
INVESTED
DEEINSUZ UNSEIZED
DEEINTUV DUVETINE
DEEINUVW UNVIEWED
DEEIOPRT PERIDOTE
DEEIOPRX PEROXIDE
DEEIOPSS EPISODES
DEEIOPST EPIDOTES
POETISED
DEEIOPSX EPOXIDES
DEEIOPTZ POETIZED
DEEIORRV OVERRIDE
DEEIORSV OVERSIDE
DEEIORTU ETOURDIE
DEEIOTVX VIDEOTEX
DEEIPPQU EQUIPPED
DEEIPPRZ ZIPPERED
DEEIPPST PEPTIDES
PEPTISED
DEEIPPTT PIPETTED
DEEIPPTZ PEPTIZED
DEEIPQRU REPIQUED
DEEIPQTU PIQUETED
DEEIPRRS REPRISED
RESPIRED
DEEIPRRT TREPIDER
DEEIPRRV REPRIVED
DEEIPRRZ REPRIZED
DEEIPRSS DESPISER
DISPERSE
PRESIDES
DEEIPRST PRIESTED
RESPITED
DEEIPRSU DUPERIES
DEEIPRSV DEPRIVES
PREVISED
DEEIPRTT PITTERED
PRETTIED
DEEIPRTX EXTIRPED
DEEIPSSS DESPISES
DEEIPSST DESPITES
SIDESTEP
DEEIPSTT TEPIDEST
DEEIPSTU DEPUTIES
DEPUTISE
DEEIPTUZ DEPUTIZE
DEEIQRRU REQUIRED
DEEIQRTU REQUITED
DEEIQRUV QUIVERED
DEEIQTUU QUIETUDE
DEEIRRSS DERRISES
DESIRERS
DRESSIER
RESIDERS
DEEIRRST DESTRIER
DEEIRRSU RUDERIES
DEEIRRSV REDRIVES
DEEIRRTV VERDITER
DEEIRRWW WIREDREW
DEEIRRZZ RIZZERED
DEEIRSST EDITRESS
RESISTED
SISTERED
DEEIRSSU DIURESES
REISSUED
RESIDUES
DEEIRSSV DEVISERS
DISSERVE
DISSEVER
DIVERSES
DEEIRSTT TIREDEST
DEEIRSTU ERUDITES
SURETIED
DEEIRSTV VERDITES
DEEIRSTW WEIRDEST
DEEIRTTT TITTERED
DEEIRTTV RIVETTED
DEEIRTTW WITTERED
DEEISSSU DISEUSES
DEEISTTV VIDETTES
DEEJKNTU JUNKETED
DEEJPRRU PERJURED
DEEJPTTU UPJETTED
DEEKLNOS SLOKENED
DEEKLNST SKLENTED
DEEKLRSS SKELDERS
DEEKMNOY MONKEYED
DEEKNNNU UNKENNED
DEEKNOTW KNOTWEED
DEEKNOTY KEYNOTED
DEEKORRW REWORKED
DEEKRUVY KURVEYED
DEELLMOR MODELLER
DEELLMOW MELLOWED
DEELLNOP POLLENED
DEELLNOR ENROLLED
DEELLORW ROWELLED
DEELLORY YODELLER
DEELLOTW TOWELLED
DEELLOTX EXTOLLED
DEELLOVW VOWELLED
DEELLOVY VOLLEYED
DEELLOWY YELLOWED
DEELLPUW UPWELLED
DEELLRSU DUELLERS
DEELLRSW DWELLERS
DEELLSSW WELDLESS
DEELLSUX DUXELLES
DEELMMPU EMPLUMED
DEELMNOO MELODEON
DEELMNOS LODESMEN
DEELMNTU UNMELTED
DEELMNTW WELDMENT
DEELMOOS DOLESOME
DEELMOPR EMPOLDER
DEELMOPY EMPLOYED
DEELMORS MODELERS
REMODELS
DEELMOST MOLESTED
DEELMOSU DUELSOME
DEELMPSU DEPLUMES
DEELMRUY DEMURELY
DEELNNTU TUNNELED
DEELNOOS LOOSENED
DEELNORT REDOLENT
DEELNORV OVERLEND
DEELNOSS LESSONED
DEELNOSU ENSOULED
DEELNOSY ESLOYNED
DEELNPRS RESPLEND
DEELNRTU UNDERLET
DEELNRTY TENDERLY
DEELNSSW LEWDNESS
DEELNSTY ENSTYLED
DEELOORT RETOOLED
DEELOPPR LOPPERED
DEELOPRS DEPLORES
DEELOPRX EXPLODER
EXPLORED
DEELOPRY REDEPLOY
DEELOPSV DEVELOPS
DEELOPSX EXPLODES
DEELORRS SOLDERER
DEELORSU URODELES
DEELORSV RESOLVED
DEELORTT DOTTEREL
TOLTERED
DEELORTV REVOLTED
DEELORTY DELETORY
DEELORUV LOUVERED
DEELORVV REVOLVED
DEELOSSU DELOUSES
DEELOSTV DOVELETS
DEELOSVV DEVOLVES
DEELOTUV EVOLUTED
DEELPPRU REPULPED
DEELPRSS SPELDERS
DEELPRSU PRELUDES
REPULSED
DEELPRTU DRUPELET
DEELPRUV PULVERED
DEELPRUX DUPLEXER
DEELPSUX DUPLEXES
EXPULSED
DEELPTTY PETTEDLY
DEELRSTU LUSTERED
RESULTED
ULSTERED
DEELRSTW LEWDSTER
WRESTLED
DEELRSTY RESTYLED
DEEMMORS MESODERM
DEEMMRRU DUMMERER
DEEMMRSU SUMMERED
DEEMNNRU UNDERMEN
DEEMNNTU TENENDUM
DEEMNOOS MOONSEED
DEEMNOQU QUEENDOM
DEEMNORR MODERNER
DEEMNORS SERMONED
DEEMNORT ENTODERM
DEEMNOSS DEMONESS
ENMOSSED
DEEMOORT ODOMETER
DEEMOPPY POMPEYED
DEEMOPRV PREMOVED
DEEMOPST DEEPMOST
DEEMOQRU QUEERDOM
DEEMORRT TREMORED
DEEMORST MODESTER
DEEMORSW WORMSEED
DEEMORSX EXODERMS
DEEMORTU MOUTERED
UDOMETER
DEEMPRST DEMPSTER
DEEMPRSU PRESUMED
DEEMPRTU PERMUTED
DEEMRRRU DEMURRER
MURDERER
DEEMRSTU DEMUREST
MUSTERED
DEEMRTTU MUTTERED
DEEMSSTY SYSTEMED
DEENNNOP PENNONED
DEENNNPU UNPENNED
DEENNOPT DEPONENT
DEENNOPU UNOPENED
DEENNORS ENDERONS
DEENNORW RENOWNED
DEENNOSS DONENESS
DEENNOST SONNETED
DEENNOSY DOYENNES
DEENNPST PENDENTS
DEENNRTU UNTENDER
DEENNRUV UNNERVED
DEENNSSU NUDENESS
UNSENSED
DEENNSTU UNNESTED
DEENNTTU UNNETTED
UNTENTED
DEENNTUV UNVENTED
DEENOORT ENROOTED
DEENOORV OVERDONE
DEENOORW WOODENER
DEENOPPR PREPONED
DEENOPRR PONDERER
DEENOPSS SPONDEES
DEENOPST PENTODES
DEENORRS ENDORSER
DEENORRW WONDERER
DEENORSS ENDORSES
DEENORST ERODENTS
DEENORSW ENDOWERS
WORSENED
DEENORTU DEUTERON
DEENOSSS ENDOSSES
DEENOSST STENOSED
DEENPPRS PERPENDS
DEENPRSS SPENDERS
DEENPRST PRETENDS
DEENRRSU ENDURERS
SUNDERER
DEENRRTU RETURNED
DEENRSSU RUDENESS
DEENRSTU DENTURES
SEDERUNT
UNDERSET
UNDESERT
DEENRSUU UNDERUSE
DEENRSUV UNVERSED
DEENRTUV VENTURED
DEENSSSY SYNDESES
DEENSTTU UNTESTED
DEENTTUV UNVETTED
DEENTTUW UNWETTED
DEENTUVY DUVETYNE
DEEOORRV OVERDOER
OVERRODE
DEEOORSV OVERDOES
OVERDOSE
DEEOPPRS PREPOSED
DEEOPPST ESTOPPED

DEEOPRRR	PREORDER
DEEOPRRS	PEDREROS
DEEOPRRT	REPORTED
DEEOPRRV	REPROVED
DEEOPRSS	DEPOSERS
DEEOPRST	POSTERED
	REEDSTOP
	REPOSTED
DEEOPRTT	POTTERED
	REPOTTED
DEEOPRTW	POWTERED
DEEOPRTX	EXPORTED
DEEOPRUZ	DOUZEPER
DEEOPSST	POSSETED
DEEOPSSU	ESPOUSED
DEEOQRTU	REQUOTED
	ROQUETED
DEEORRRS	ORDERERS
	REORDERS
DEEORRRV	VERDEROR
DEEORRST	RESORTED
	RESTORED
	ROSTERED
DEEORRSV	OVERREDS
DEEORRTT	RETORTED
DEEORRTU	REROUTED
	RETOURED
DEEORRUV	DEVOURER
DEEORRVW	OVERDREW
DEEORSST	OERSTEDS
DEEORSTT	ROSETTED
	TETRODES
DEEORSTX	DEXTROSE
DEEORSTY	STOREYED
DEEORSUV	OVERUSED
DEEORSVY	OVERDYES
DEEORTTT	TOTTERED
DEEORTTX	EXTORTED
DEEORTUV	DEVOUTER
DEEOSSUX	EXODUSES
DEEOSTUW	OUTWEEDS
DEEOSTUX	TUXEDOES
DEEPPRSU	SUPPERED
DEEPRRSU	PERDURES
DEEPRRVY	REPRYVED
DEEPRSTU	PERTUSED
DEEPRSUW	PURSEWED
DEEPRSUY	PSEUDERY
DEEPRTTU	PUTTERED
DEEPRUVY	PURVEYED
DEERRSSS	DRESSERS
DEERRSUV	VERDURES
DEERRTTU	TURRETED
DEERRTUX	EXTRUDER
DEERSSST	DESSERTS
	STRESSED
DEERSSSU	DURESSES
DEERSSTU	RUSSETED
DEERSSTY	DYESTEPS
DEERSSUV	SUVERSED
DEERSTUV	VESTURED
DEERSTUX	EXTRUDES
DEERSUVW	SURVEWED
DEERSUVY	SURVEYED
DEERTTUX	TEXTURED
DEFFHILW	WHIFFLED
DEFFHLSU	SHUFFLED
DEFFHORS	SHROFFED
DEFFILNS	SNIFFLED
DEFFILOV	FIVEFOLD
DEFFIMOS	FIEFDOMS
DEFFIORS	OFFSIDER
DEFFIOSS	OFFSIDES
DEFFIRSU	DIFFUSER
DEFFISSU	DIFFUSES
DEFFISUX	SUFFIXED
DEFFLNSU	SNUFFLED
DEFFLRTU	TRUFFLED
DEFFNORS	FORFENDS
DEFFSSUU	SUFFUSED
DEFFSTUY	DYESTUFF
DEFGGILN	FLEDGING
DEFGHILT	FLIGHTED
DEFGHIRT	FRIGHTED
DEFGIILN	DEFILING
	FIELDING
DEFGIILU	UGLIFIED
DEFGIINN	DEFINING
DEFGIINY	DEIFYING
	EDIFYING
DEFGIIRR	FRIGIDER
DEFGILNU	INGULFED
DEFGILTY	GIFTEDLY
DEFGINSU	DEFUSING
	FEUDINGS
DEFGINTU	UNGIFTED
DEFGINUZ	DEFUZING
DEFGIOOW	GOODWIFE
DEFGIORS	FIREDOGS
DEFGJORU	FORJUDGE
DEFGMOOY	FOGEYDOM
DEFGNORU	UNFORGED
DEFGOOSX	DOGFOXES
DEFHIIMU	HUMIFIED
DEFHIINS	FIENDISH
	FINISHED
DEFHILLO	LIFEHOLD
DEFHILSS	DISFLESH
DEFHINSU	UNFISHED
DEFHIOOW	WIFEHOOD
DEFHLOOS	ELFHOODS
	SELFHOOD
DEFHLOSU	FLOUSHED
DEFHOOOR	FORHOOED
DEFHOORS	SERFHOOD
DEFHOORW	FORHOWED
DEFIIILV	VILIFIED
DEFIIIMN	MINIFIED
DEFIIINS	NIDIFIES
DEFIIIVV	VIVIFIED
DEFIILLN	INFILLED
DEFIILLO	OILFIELD
DEFIILLP	FILLIPED
DEFIILLW	WILDLIFE
DEFIILMS	MISFIELD
	MISFILED
DEFIILNS	INFIDELS
	INFIELDS
DEFIILRW	WILDFIRE
DEFIILSU	FLUIDISE
DEFIILTY	FIDELITY
DEFIILUZ	FLUIDIZE
DEFIIMNO	OMNIFIED
DEFIIMNU	MUNIFIED
DEFIIMOR	MODIFIER
DEFIIMOS	MODIFIES
DEFIIMRS	MISFIRED
DEFIIMSS	FIDEISMS
DEFIIMSW	MIDWIFES
DEFIINOT	NOTIFIED
DEFIINTU	FINITUDE
DEFIINTY	IDENTIFY
DEFIIOSS	OSSIFIED
DEFIIOTV	VIDEOFIT
DEFIIPRU	PURIFIED
DEFIIPSS	FISSIPED
DEFIIPTY	TYPIFIED
DEFIIRRT	DRIFTIER
DEFIISST	FIDEISTS
DEFILLNU	UNFILLED
DEFILLPU	UPFILLED
DEFILMNU	FULMINED
	UNFILMED
DEFILNNO	NINEFOLD
DEFILNRS	FLINDERS
DEFILNRU	UNRIFLED
	URNFIELD
DEFILNRY	FRIENDLY
DEFILOPR	PROFILED
DEFILORR	FLORIDER
DEFILORU	FLUORIDE
DEFILOTU	OUTFIELD
DEFILPRU	PRIDEFUL
DEFILPTU	UPLIFTED
DEFILRRU	FLURRIED
DEFILRVY	FERVIDLY
DEFILRZZ	FRIZZLED
DEFILSSU	SULFIDES
DEFIMNOR	INFORMED
DEFIMORY	REMODIFY
DEFIMRRU	DRUMFIRE
DEFINNRU	REINFUND
	UNFRIEND
DEFINOPR	FORPINED
DEFINORW	FOREWIND
DEFINSTU	UNSIFTED
DEFINTTU	UNFITTED
DEFIOORW	FIREWOOD
DEFIOPRT	PROFITED
DEFIORSU	FOUDRIES
DEFIOTXY	DETOXIFY
DEFIRRST	DRIFTERS
DEFIRSSU	FISSURED
DEFISSTU	FEUDISTS
DEFKLORY	FORKEDLY
DEFLLOOR	FOLDEROL
DEFLLOOW	FOLLOWED
DEFLMPRU	FRUMPLED
DEFLNOOU	UNFOOLED
DEFLNOPS	PENFOLDS
DEFLNORS	FONDLERS
	FORLENDS
DEFLNORU	FLOUNDER
	UNFOLDER
DEFLNRUU	UNFURLED
DEFLNSSU	FUNDLESS
DEFLOORS	FORSLOED
DEFLOORT	FORETOLD
DEFLOORV	OVERFOLD
DEFLOOSS	FOODLESS
DEFLOPUW	UPFLOWED
DEFLORSU	FOULDERS
DEFLPRUU	UPFURLED
DEFLRSUU	SULFURED
DEFMNORU	UNFORMED
DEFMOOOR	FOREDOOM
DEFMORSS	SERFDOMS
DEFNNORT	FRONDENT
DEFNNOSS	FONDNESS
DEFNOOPS	SPOONFED
DEFNOORS	FRONDOSE
DEFNOORU	UNROOFED
DEFNOORV	OVERFOND
DEFNOOTU	UNFOOTED
DEFNOPRS	FORSPEND
DEFNORRU	FRONDEUR
DEFNORSU	FOUNDERS
	REFOUNDS
DEFNORTU	FORTUNED
DEFNORUV	OVERFUND
DEFNOSSW	DOWFNESS
DEFNRRUU	UNDERFUR
	UNFURRED
DEFNRTUU	UNTURFED
DEFOORRW	FOREWORD
DEFOOTUX	OUTFOXED
DEFORRUW	FURROWED
DEFORSST	DEFROSTS
DEFORSTW	FROWSTED
DEGGGIIT	GIGGITED
DEGGGILN	GLEDGING
DEGGHINS	HEDGINGS
DEGGHLOS	SHOGGLED
DEGGHRSU	SHRUGGED
DEGGIINN	DEIGNING
DEGGILNP	PLEDGING
DEGGILNS	GELDINGS
	SLEDGING
	SNIGGLED
DEGGILNU	DELUGING
DEGGILRW	WRIGGLED
DEGGINNU	UNEDGING
DEGGINRU	UNRIGGED
DEGGINSW	WEDGINGS
DEGGINUW	UNWIGGED
DEGGIORS	DISGORGE
DEGGIOST	DOGGIEST
DEGGIPRS	SPRIGGED
DEGGIRRU	DRUGGIER
DEGGIRST	STRIGGED
DEGGIRSU	DRUGGIES
DEGGLMSU	SMUGGLED
DEGGLNSU	SNUGGLED
DEGGLORS	DOGGRELS
DEGGLRUY	RUGGEDLY
DEGGNORU	UNGORGED
DEGGNOSU	GUDGEONS
DEGGRRSU	DRUGGERS
DEGGRSTU	DRUGGETS
DEGHIILL	GHILLIED
DEGHIINS	DINGHIES
DEGHIKNT	KNIGHTED
DEGHILNS	HINDLEGS
	SHINGLED
DEGHILOU	OUGHLIED
DEGHILPT	PLIGHTED
DEGHILST	DELIGHTS
	SLIGHTED
DEGHINNS	SHENDING
DEGHINNU	UNHINGED
DEGHIOOS	SHOOGIED
DEGHIOPS	DOGESHIP
DEGHIORU	DOUGHIER
DEGHIPST	DESPIGHT
	SPIGHTED
DEGHIQTU	QUIGHTED
DEGHITTW	TWIGHTED
DEGHLNOR	HORNGELD
DEGHLOOS	DOGHOLES
	GOLOSHED

SHOOGLED
DEGHLOPU PLOUGHED
DEGHLOSU SLOUGHED
DEGHMOSU GUMSHOED
DEGHMPRU GRUMPHED
DEGHNORT THRONGED
DEGHNORY HYDROGEN
DEGHORRS DROGHERS
DEGHPSUU UPGUSHED
DEGIIIRS RIGIDISE
DEGIIIRZ RIGIDIZE
DEGIIIST DIGITISE
DEGIIITZ DIGITIZE
DEGIIKST KIDGIEST
DEGIILNR GRIDELIN
DEGIILNS EILDINGS
SIDELING
DEGIILNT DILIGENT
DEGIILNV DEVILING
DEGIILNW WIELDING
DEGIILNY YIELDING
DEGIILTY GELIDITY
DEGIIMNP IMPEDING
IMPINGED
DEGIIMNS DEMISING
DEGIIMSU MISGUIDE
DEGIINNR NIDERING
DEGIINNS DESINING
SDEINING
DEGIINNT ENDITING
INDIGENT
TEINDING
DEGIINNW INDEWING
WIDENING
DEGIINNX INDEXING
DEGIINNZ DIZENING
DEGIINOS INDIGOES
DEGIINOV VIDEOING
DEGIINRS DESIRING
RESIDING
RINGSIDE
DEGIINRT DIRIGENT
DEGIINRV DERIVING
VIRGINED
DEGIINRW WEIRDING
DEGIINST DINGIEST
INDIGEST
DEGIINSV DEVISING
DEGIIRST RIDGIEST
RIGIDEST
DEGIISSU DISGUISE
DEGIJMSU MISJUDGE
DEGIKKNO DEKKOING
DEGIKLNU DUKELING
DEGIKNNU UNKINGED
DEGILLNU DUELLING
DEGILLNW DWELLING
DEGILMNO MODELING
DEGILMPS GLIMPSED
DEGILNNO OLDENING
DEGILNNS LENDINGS
DEGILNOP DELOPING
DIPLOGEN
DEGILNOS GLENOIDS
SIDELONG
DEGILNPS SPELDING
DEGILNRU INDULGER
DEGILNRY YELDRING
DEGILNSU INDULGES
DEGILNSV DEVLINGS
DEGILNSW SWINGLED
WELDINGS
DEGILNWY WINGEDLY
DEGILOOR GOODLIER
DEGILOOY IDEOLOGY
DEGILOST GODLIEST
GOLDIEST
DEGILOSZ GOLDSIZE
DEGILPSU PULSIDGE
DEGILRRS GIRDLERS
DEGILRSU GUILDERS
SLUDGIER
DEGILRSW WERGILDS
DEGILRZZ GRIZZLED
DEGILSUV DIVULGES
DEGIMMNO MODEMING
DEGIMNNS MENDINGS
DEGIMNOS SMIDGEON
DEGIMNOT DEMOTING
DEGIMNPU IMPUGNED
DEGIMNRU DEMURING
DEGIMNSS SMIDGENS
DEGIMOOT GOODTIME
DEGIMOOY GEOMYOID
DEGIMRSU SMUDGIER
DEGINNNU UNENDING
DEGINNOP DEPONING
DEGINNOT DENOTING
DEGINNOW ENDOWING
DEGINNOZ DOZENING
DEGINNPS SPENDING
DEGINNPU UPENDING
DEGINNRT TRENDING
DEGINNRU ENDURING
UNRINGED
DEGINNSS SENDINGS
DEGINNST STENDING
DEGINNSU UNSIGNED
DEGINNSY DESYNING
DEGINNTU DETUNING
UNTINGED
DEGINNUW UNWINGED
DEGINOPR PROIGNED
DEGINOPS DEPOSING
DISPONGE
PIDGEONS
DEGINORR ORDERING
DEGINORS NEGROIDS
DEGINORU GUERIDON
DEGINORV DOVERING
DEGINORW DOWERING
DEGINOSW WENDIGOS
WIDGEONS
DEGINOTV DEVOTING
DEGINOTX DETOXING
DEGINPRS SPRINGED
DEGINPRY PREDYING
DEGINPSU DISPUNGE
DEGINPTU DEPUTING
DEGINRRS GRINDERS
REGRINDS
DEGINRRY GRINDERY
DEGINRSS DRESSING
DEGINRST STRINGED
DEGINRSW REDWINGS
DEGINRSY SYNERGID
SYRINGED
DEGINSSU DINGUSES
DEGINSSW SWINDGES
DEGINSTU DUNGIEST
DEGINTTU DUETTING
DEGIOORS GOODSIRE
DEGIOOST GOODIEST
DEGIOPRR PORRIDGE
DEGIOPSS GOSSIPED
DEGIOPST PODGIEST
DEGIORRU GOURDIER
DEGIORST GRODIEST
STODGIER
DEGIPSTU PUDGIEST
DEGIQSSU SQUIDGES
DEGIRSTU DURGIEST
DEGISSST DISGESTS
DEGJMNTU JUDGMENT
DEGLLNOY GOLDENLY
DEGLLOOP GOLLOPED
DEGLLOSS GOLDLESS
DEGLMNOT LODGMENT
DEGLMOOY DEMOLOGY
DEGLNOUV UNGLOVED
DEGLNRTU GRUNTLED
DEGLOOPY PEDOLOGY
DEGLOOUU DUOLOGUE
DEGLOPRS PLEDGORS
DEGLOPSS SPLODGES
DEGLPRSU SPLURGED
DEGMMNUU UNGUMMED
DEGMRSSU SMUDGERS
DEGNNORU GROUNDEN
DEGNNOSU DUNGEONS
DEGNNOUW UNGOWNED
DEGNOORS DRONGOES
DEGNOOSS GOODNESS
DEGNOOST STEGODON
DEGNOPPU OPPUGNED
DEGNORRU GROUNDER
REGROUND
DEGNORSU GUERDONS
DEGNORTU TRUDGEON
DEGNORUU UNROUGED
DEGNORYY GYRODYNE
DEGNPRUU UNPURGED
DEGNRSTU TRUDGENS
DEGORSST STODGERS
DEGORSTU DROGUETS
DEGPRSUU UPSURGED
DEGRRSTU TRUDGERS
DEHHILTW WITHHELD
DEHHISTW WHISHTED
DEHHMRTY RHYTHMED
DEHHOOSW WHOOSHED
DEHIILLS HILLSIDE
DEHIILLW WHILLIED
DEHIILSV DEVILISH
DEHIIMMS SHIMMIED
DEHIIMNS MINISHED
DEHIIMRU MUDIRIEH
DEHIIMST DITHEISM
SMITHIED
DEHIINNS SHINNIED
DEHIINNW WHINNIED
DEHIINSS SHINDIES
DEHIIRRW WHIRRIED
DEHIIRST DISHERIT
DEHIISST DISHIEST
DEHIISTT DITHEIST
STITHIED
DEHIJMNO DEMIJOHN
DEHIKMOS SHEIKDOM
DEHIKPSU DUKESHIP
DEHILLOP PHELLOID
DEHILLRS SHRILLED
DEHILLRT THRILLED
DEHILMOS DEMOLISH
DEHILMPW WHIMPLED
DEHILMSS DISHELMS
DEHILMTY DIMETHYL
DEHILNOR INHOLDER
DEHILNPY DIPHENYL
DEHILOOR HELIODOR
DEHILOOS DHOOLIES
DEHILOPS POLISHED
DEHILPSU SULPHIDE
DEHILPSY SYLPHIDE
DEHILRTW WRITHLED
DEHILSTW WHISTLED
DEHILTTW WHITTLED
DEHIMNOS HEDONISM
DEHIMORS HEIRDOMS
DEHIMOSS DISHOMES
DEHIMPRS SHRIMPED
DEHIMPSY DEMYSHIP
DEHIMSTU HUMIDEST
DEHIMSTY MYTHISED
DEHIMTYZ MYTHIZED
DEHINOOP INHOOPED
DEHINOPR NEPHROID
DEHINOPS DIPHONES
SIPHONED
SPHENOID
DEHINORS HORDEINS
DEHINOST HEDONIST
DEHINPSS ENDSHIPS
DEHINPSU PUNISHED
DEHINSUW UNWISHED
DEHIOOVW WIVEHOOD
DEHIOPRS SPHEROID
DEHIOPRT TROPHIED
DEHIORRR HORRIDER
DEHIORSS DISHORSE
HIDROSES
DEHIORTU OUTHIRED
DEHIORTW WORTHIED
DEHIORTY THYREOID
DEHIOSSU DISHOUSE
DEHIOSSW SIDESHOW
DEHIOSTU HIDEOUTS
DEHIPSSU PSEUDISH
DEHIQSSU SQUISHED
DEHIRRSU DHURRIES
DEHIRSTT THIRSTED
THRISTED
DEHIRTWW WITHDREW
DEHKLNOU ELKHOUND
DEHKNOOU UNHOOKED
DEHKNSUU UNHUSKED
DEHKOOSS SKOOSHED
DEHLLOOW HOLLOWED
DEHLLOPY PHYLLODE
DEHLMMOW WHOMMLED
DEHLMMUW WHUMMLED
DEHLMORY HYDROMEL
DEHLMOSU MUDHOLES
DEHLNOOW DOWNHOLE
DEHLOOOW WOODHOLE
DEHLOOPT POTHOLED
DEHLOORV HOLDOVER
OVERHOLD
DEHLOOSS HOODLESS
SLOOSHED

DEHLOOST	TOEHOLDS
DEHLOOSW	WOOLSHED
DEHLOPRU	UPHOLDER
DEHLOPSS	SPLOSHED
DEHLORSU	SHOULDER
DEHLPRUU	UPHURLED
DEHLRRSU	HURDLERS
DEHLRSWY	SHREWDLY
DEHLSTTU	SHUTTLED
DEHMMRTU	THRUMMED
DEHMNOOY	HOMODYNE
DEHMNRUY	UNRHYMED
DEHMOORW	WHOREDOM
DEHMOOSS	SHMOOSED
DEHMOOST	SMOOTHED
DEHMOOSZ	SHMOOZED
DEHMOPRY	HYPODERM
DEHMORUU	HUMOURED
DEHNNTUU	UNHUNTED
DEHNOOPU	UNHOOPED
DEHNOORU	HONOURED
DEHNOOSW	HOEDOWNS
DEHNOPSY	SYPHONED
DEHNORSU	ENSHROUD
	UNHORSED
DEHNORSY	ENHYDROS
DEHNORTY	THRENODY
DEHNOSTZ	DOZENTHS
DEHNOSUU	UNHOUSED
DEHNRSTU	THUNDERS
DEHNRTUY	THUNDERY
DEHOOOPP	POPEHOOD
DEHOOPRT	THEROPOD
DEHOOSSW	SWOOSHED
DEHOPRST	POTSHERD
DEHORRST	REDSHORT
DEHORTUY	OUTHYRED
DEHOSSTU	STOUSHED
DEHPPSTU	SHTUPPED
DEHPRSSU	SPRUSHED
DEHPRSUU	UPRUSHED
DEHRRSTU	DRUTHERS
DEHRSTTU	THRUSTED
DEIIIMST	DIMITIES
DEIIINSV	DIVINISE
DEIIINVZ	DIVINIZE
DEIIIRSS	IRIDISES
DEIIIRSZ	IRIDIZES
DEIIIRTV	VIRIDITE
DEIIISVV	DIVISIVE
DEIIKLMS	MISLIKED
DEIIKLNR	KINDLIER
DEIIKLNS	DISLIKEN
DEIIKLNV	DEVILKIN
DEIIKLSS	DISLIKES
DEIIKNST	DINKIEST
DEIIKSVV	SKIVVIED
DEIILLMP	MILLIPED
DEIILLMT	TIDEMILL
DEIILLST	DILLIEST
DEIILMPR	DIMPLIER
DEIILMRU	DELIRIUM
DEIILMST	DELIMITS
	LIMITEDS
DEIILMSV	DEVILISM
	MISLIVED
DEIILNNU	INDULINE
DEIILNOS	LIONISED
DEIILNOZ	LIONIZED
DEIILNPV	VILIPEND

DEIILNVY	DIVINELY
DEIILOPS	PLOIDIES
DEIILORS	IDOLISER
DEIILORZ	IDOLIZER
DEIILOSS	IDOLISES
DEIILOSZ	IDOLIZES
DEIILPRT	TRIPLIED
DEIILPSS	SIDESLIP
DEIILRST	REDISTIL
DEIILSTU	UTILISED
DEIILSTV	LIVIDEST
DEIILTUY	TUILYIED
DEIILTUZ	TUILZIED
	UTILIZED
DEIIMMRS	DIMERISM
DEIIMMST	MISTIMED
DEIIMMTT	IMMITTED
DEIIMNOS	DOMINIES
DEIIMNRT	DIRIMENT
DEIIMNTU	MUTINIED
DEIIMNUV	VENIDIUM
DEIIMPRU	PERIDIUM
DEIIMSST	MISDIETS
DEIIMSTT	TIMIDEST
DEIIMSVW	MIDWIVES
DEIINNOP	PINIONED
DEIINNPP	PINNIPED
DEIINNTW	INTWINED
DEIINNUV	UNDIVINE
DEIINORS	DERISION
	IRONISED
	RESINOID
DEIINORT	RETINOID
DEIINORZ	IRONIZED
DEIINOST	EDITIONS
	SEDITION
DEIINOSV	VISIONED
DEIINPPW	WINDPIPE
DEIINPRS	INSPIRED
DEIINPRT	INTREPID
DEIINPRY	PYRIDINE
DEIINPTU	UNPITIED
DEIINQRU	INQUIRED
DEIINQSU	QUINSIED
	SQUINIED
DEIINRSS	INDRISES
	INSIDERS
DEIINRST	DISINTER
	INDITERS
	NITRIDES
	RINDIEST
DEIINRSU	DISINURE
	URIDINES
DEIINRSV	DIVINERS
DEIINRTU	UNTIDIER
DEIINSST	INSISTED
	TIDINESS
DEIINSTU	DISUNITE
	NUDITIES
	UNITISED
	UNTIDIES
DEIINSTV	DIVINEST
DEIINSTW	WINDIEST
DEIINTTU	INTUITED
DEIINTTY	IDENTITY
DEIINTUZ	UNITIZED
DEIIOPRS	PRESIDIO
DEIIOPRT	DIPTEROI
DEIIOPZZ	PEZIZOID
DEIIORST	DIORITES

DEIIORSX	OXIDISER
DEIIORTX	TRIOXIDE
DEIIORTY	IODYRITE
DEIIORXZ	OXIDIZER
DEIIOSSX	OXIDISES
DEIIOSXZ	OXIDIZES
DEIIPPRR	DRIPPIER
DEIIPPST	DIPPIEST
DEIIPRST	RIPTIDES
	SPIRITED
DEIIPRSZ	DISPRIZE
DEIIPTTY	TEPIDITY
DEIIQSTU	DISQUIET
DEIIRSSU	DIURESIS
DEIIRSTT	DIRTIEST
	TRITIDES
DEIISSTT	DIETISTS
	DITSIEST
DEIISTTZ	DITZIEST
DEIISTVV	VIVIDEST
DEIISTZZ	DIZZIEST
DEIJNORS	JOINDERS
DEIJNSSU	DISJUNES
DEIKKLNO	KLONDIKE
DEIKLLSS	DESKILLS
DEIKLMMS	SKLIMMED
DEIKLMNU	UNMILKED
DEIKLNNU	UNLINKED
DEIKLNRS	KINDLERS
DEIKLNRW	WRINKLED
DEIKLNSS	KINDLESS
DEIKLNTW	TWINKLED
DEIKLSSS	DISKLESS
DEIKLSTT	SKITTLED
DEIKMOSY	MISYOKED
DEIKMPRS	SKRIMPED
DEIKNNPU	UNPINKED
DEIKNNRU	UNKINDER
DEIKNNSS	KINDNESS
DEIKNORV	OVERKIND
DEIKNORW	INWORKED
DEIKNRRS	DRINKERS
DEIKNRSS	REDSKINS
DEIKNSSU	UNKISSED
DEIKORSS	DROSKIES
DEIKORST	DORKIEST
DEIKOSSY	DISYOKES
DEIKPRSU	PRUSIKED
	SPRUIKED
DEIKRRSU	SKURRIED
DEIKRSVY	SKYDIVER
DEIKSSTU	DUSKIEST
DEILLMNU	UNMILLED
DEILLNSW	INDWELLS
DEILLNTU	UNTILLED
DEILLNUW	UNWILLED
DEILLOOV	LIVELOOD
DEILLOPW	PILLOWED
DEILLORR	LORDLIER
DEILLORS	DOLLIERS
DEILLOSV	LIVELODS
DEILLOWW	WILLOWED
DEILLRRS	DRILLERS
DEILLRSV	DREVILLS
DEILLSTU	DUELLIST
	DULLIEST
DEILMNOO	MELODION
DEILMNSS	MILDNESS
	MINDLESS
DEILMNSU	MUSLINED

DEILMOOT	DOLOMITE
DEILMOPR	IMPLORED
	IMPOLDER
DEILMOPS	IMPLODES
DEILMORU	LEMUROID
	MOULDIER
DEILMOST	MELODIST
DEILMOSU	EMULSOID
DEILMPPU	PLUMIPED
DEILMPSU	DISPLUME
	IMPULSED
DEILMPTU	MULTIPED
DEILMRRU	DRUMLIER
DEILMRSU	MISRULED
DEILMSSY	DEMISSLY
DEILNNOT	INDOLENT
DEILNOOS	SOLENOID
DEILNOPT	TOPLINED
DEILNORS	DISENROL
DEILNOSS	SONDELIS
DEILNOSU	DELUSION
	INSOULED
	UNSOILED
DEILNOTU	OUTLINED
DEILNOVV	INVOLVED
DEILNPRS	SPELDRIN
DEILNPRU	UNDERLIP
DEILNPSS	SPELDINS
	SPINDLES
DEILNPST	SPLINTED
DEILNRSS	RINDLESS
DEILNRST	SNIRTLED
	TENDRILS
	TRINDLES
DEILNRSW	SWINDLER
DEILNRTY	TRENDILY
DEILNSSV	VILDNESS
DEILNSSW	SWINDLES
	WILDNESS
	WINDLESS
DEILNSTU	DILUENTS
	INSULTED
	UNLISTED
DEILNTTU	UNTITLED
DEILNTUY	UNITEDLY
DEILNUWY	UNWIELDY
DEILOOPS	POOLSIDE
DEILOOPW	WOODPILE
DEILOPPY	POLYPIDE
DEILOPRU	PRELUDIO
DEILOPSS	DESPOILS
	SOLIPEDS
DEILOQRU	LIQUORED
DEILORSS	SOLDIERS
DEILORST	STOLIDER
DEILORSU	SOULDIER
DEILORSY	SOLDIERY
DEILOSST	SOLIDEST
DEILOSSV	DISSOLVE
DEILOSTT	DOILTEST
DEILOSTU	SOLITUDE
DEILOTUV	OUTLIVED
DEILPPRT	TRIPPLED
DEILPPST	STIPPLED
DEILPPSU	SUPPLIED
DEILPPTU	PULPITED
DEILPSTT	SPLITTED
DEILPSTU	STIPULED
DEILPSUY	SPULYIED
DEILPSUZ	SPULZIED

DEILPTTU	UPTILTED
DEILRSTU	DILUTERS
	LURIDEST
DEILRSVY	DIVERSLY
DEILRSZZ	DRIZZLES
DEILRTVY	DEVILTRY
DEILSSTY	DISTYLES
	STYLISED
DEILSTUY	SEDULITY
DEILSTYZ	STYLIZED
DEILSWZZ	SWIZZLED
DEILTWZZ	TWIZZLED
DEIMMNOS	DEMONISM
DEIMMOST	IMMODEST
DEIMMPST	MISDEMPT
DEIMMRST	MIDTERMS
DEIMMSTU	DUMMIEST
DEIMNNOS	MISDONNE
DEIMNNOU	UNMONIED
DEIMNNSU	MINUENDS
DEIMNOOS	DOMINOES
	MONODIES
DEIMNOOT	DEMOTION
	MOTIONED
DEIMNOOX	MONOXIDE
DEIMNOPT	PIEDMONT
DEIMNORT	DORMIENT
DEIMNOST	DEMONIST
DEIMNOTW	DOWNTIME
DEIMNOWW	WIDOWMEN
DEIMNPRU	UNPRIMED
DEIMNPSS	MISSPEND
DEIMNPTU	IMPUDENT
DEIMNRTU	RUDIMENT
DEIMNSSS	MISSENDS
DEIMNSST	MINDSETS
DEIMNSSU	UNMISSED
DEIMNSSW	MISWENDS
DEIMNSTU	MISTUNED
DEIMOORS	MOIDORES
DEIMOOSS	SODOMIES
	SODOMISE
DEIMOOST	DOOMIEST
	MOODIEST
	SODOMITE
DEIMOOSZ	SODOMIZE
DEIMOPRS	PROMISED
DEIMOPRT	IMPORTED
DEIMOPRV	IMPROVED
DEIMORRR	MIRRORED
DEIMORRS	MISORDER
	MORRISED
DEIMORSS	MISDOERS
DEIMORST	MORTISED
DEIMORSU	DIMEROUS
	ERODIUMS
	SOREDIUM
DEIMORUX	EXORDIUM
DEIMOSST	MODISTES
DEIMOSTT	DEMOTIST
DEIMPRST	DIREMPTS
DEIMPSTU	DUMPIEST
DEIMQRSU	SQUIRMED
DEIMRSSU	SURMISED
DEIMRSUU	RESIDUUM
DEINNNOU	INNUENDO
DEINNNPU	UNPINNED
DEINNNSU	NUNDINES
DEINNNTU	UNTINNED
DEINNOOT	NOONTIDE
DEINNORS	ENDIRONS
DEINNORU	UNIRONED
DEINNOWW	WINNOWED
DEINNPRU	UNDERPIN
DEINNRUU	UNINURED
DEINNRUV	UNDRIVEN
DEINNSTU	DUNNIEST
	DUNNITES
DEINNTUW	UNTWINED
DEINOOPS	POISONED
DEINOOPW	PINEWOOD
DEINOOSZ	OZONISED
DEINOOTV	DEVOTION
DEINOOZZ	OZONIZED
DEINOPPR	PROPINED
DEINOPPW	DOWNPIPE
DEINOPRS	DISPONER
	POINDERS
	PRISONED
DEINOPRV	PROVINED
DEINOPRY	PYRENOID
DEINOPSS	DISPONES
	DOPINESS
	SPINODES
DEINOPSU	UNPOISED
DEINOPTW	DEWPOINT
DEINORSS	INDORSES
DEINORST	DRONIEST
DEINORSU	DOURINES
	SOURDINE
DEINORSW	DISOWNER
	WINDORES
	WINDROSE
DEINORTT	INTORTED
DEINORVW	OVERWIND
DEINOSST	DONSIEST
DEINOSSV	VOIDNESS
DEINOSSZ	DOZINESS
DEINOSTW	DOWNIEST
DEINOSWZ	DOWNSIZE
DEINOTTU	DUETTINO
DEINPPRU	UNRIPPED
DEINPPUZ	UNZIPPED
DEINPRST	SPRINTED
DEINPRTU	TURNIPED
DEINPRUZ	UNPRIZED
DEINPSST	STIPENDS
DEINQSTU	SQUINTED
DEINRRTU	INTRUDER
DEINRSSU	INSUREDS
	SUNDRIES
DEINRSTT	STRIDENT
	TRIDENTS
DEINRSTU	INTRUDES
DEINRSTX	DEXTRINS
DEINRTUW	UNDERWIT
DEINSSST	DISNESTS
	DISSENTS
DEINSSSY	SYNDESIS
DEINSSTT	DENTISTS
DEINSSTU	DISTUNES
DEINSTUU	UNSUITED
DEINTTUW	UNWITTED
DEIOOPRR	DROOPIER
DEIOORSW	WOODSIER
DEIOOSTW	WOODIEST
DEIOOSVV	VOIVODES
DEIOOSWW	WOIWODES
DEIOPRRV	PROVIDER
DEIOPRSS	DISPOSER
	DROPSIES
DEIOPRST	DIOPTERS
	DIOPTRES
	DIPTEROS
	PERIDOTS
	PROTEIDS
	RIPOSTED
DEIOPRSV	DISPROVE
	PROVIDES
DEIOPRSW	DROPWISE
DEIOPSSS	DISPOSES
DEIOPSST	DEPOSITS
	TOPSIDES
DEIORRRT	TORRIDER
DEIORRSS	DROSSIER
DEIORRSW	DROWSIER
DEIORRSY	DERISORY
DEIORRTU	OUTRIDER
DEIORRTW	WORRITED
DEIORRZZ	RIZZORED
DEIORSSS	DOSSIERS
DEIORSST	STEROIDS
DEIORSSU	DESIROUS
DEIORSSV	DEVISORS
DEIORSTT	DORTIEST
DEIORSTU	IODURETS
	OUTRIDES
	OUTSIDER
	SUITORED
DEIORSTW	ROWDIEST
	WORDIEST
DEIORSWW	WIDOWERS
DEIORTUV	OUTDRIVE
DEIOSSTU	OUTSIDES
DEIOSSTX	EXODISTS
DEIOSTTT	DOTTIEST
DEIOSTUZ	OUTSIZED
DEIPPRST	STRIPPED
DEIPPTTU	TITUPPED
DEIPRRTU	IRRUPTED
	PUTRIDER
DEIPRSSU	DISPURSE
	SUSPIRED
DEIPRSTU	DISPUTER
	STUPIDER
DEIPSSTU	DISPUTES
	PUDSIEST
DEIPTTTU	TITTUPED
DEIQRRSU	SQUIRRED
DEIQRSTU	SQUIRTED
DEIRRSTU	STURDIER
DEIRSSST	DISSERTS
	DISTRESS
DEIRSSTU	DIESTRUS
	DRUSIEST
	STUDIERS
	STURDIES
DEIRSSUY	DYSURIES
DEIRSTTU	DETRITUS
DEIRSTUX	DRUXIEST
DEIRSUVV	SURVIVED
DEISSSTU	SUDSIEST
DEISSTTU	DUSTIEST
DEISTTTU	DUETTIST
DEJLOOOR	JORDELOO
DEJOOPPY	POPJOYED
DEKKLNOY	KLONDYKE
DEKLNOOU	UNLOOKED
DEKLOOPU	UPLOOKED
DEKLRSSU	SKUDLERS
DEKLSTTU	SKUTTLED
DEKMPRSU	SKRUMPED
DEKNORUW	UNWORKED
DEKNRSTU	DRUNKEST
DEKNRSUY	UNDERSKY
DEKNSSSU	DUSKNESS
DEKOOPRV	PROVOKED
DEKOOTWW	KOWTOWED
DEKOPSST	DESKTOPS
DEKORSWY	KEYWORDS
DELLLOOP	LOLLOPED
DELLMOOS	MODELLOS
DELLMOSW	SWELLDOM
DELLNOPU	UNPOLLED
DELLNORU	UNROLLED
DELLNORW	ROWNDELL
DELLNPUU	UNPULLED
DELLNSSU	DULLNESS
DELLOPRS	REDPOLLS
DELLOPRU	UPROLLED
DELLOPTU	POLLUTED
DELLORRY	DROLLERY
DELLORSS	LORDLESS
DELLORST	DROLLEST
	STROLLED
DELLOSVW	LOWVELDS
DELLOTUW	OUTDWELL
DELMNOOV	NOVELDOM
DELMNORY	MODERNLY
DELMNOSU	UNSELDOM
DELMNOTW	MELTDOWN
DELMNPUU	PENDULUM
	UNPLUMED
DELMOOSW	ELMWOODS
DELMORSS	SMOLDERS
DELMORSU	MOULDERS
	REMOULDS
	SMOULDER
DELMOSTY	MODESTLY
DELMRTUU	MULTURED
DELMTTUU	TUMULTED
DELNOOSU	NODULOSE
	UNLOOSED
DELNOOSZ	SNOOZLED
DELNOOWY	WOODENLY
DELNOPPU	UNLOPPED
DELNOPRS	SPLENDOR
DELNORSU	LOUNDERS
	NOURSLED
	ROUNDELS
	ROUNDLES
	UNSOLDER
DELNORTU	ROUNDLET
DELNORYY	YONDERLY
DELNOSSU	LOUDNESS
DELNOSUU	UNDULOSE
	UNSOULED
DELNOSUV	UNSOLVED
DELNPRSU	PLUNDERS
DELNRRTU	TRUNDLER
DELNRSTU	RUNDLETS
	TRUNDLES
DELNSUZZ	SNUZZLED
DELOOPPS	PLEOPODS
DELOORRV	OVERLORD
DELOORRW	WORDLORE
DELOORSS	LORDOSES
DELOORSV	OVERSOLD
DELOORSW	WOOLDERS
DELOORTY	ROOTEDLY

DELOORUV OVERLOUD
DELOOSSW WOODLESS
DELOPPRS DROPPLES
DELOPPST STOPPLED
DELOPRST DROPLETS
DELOPRSU POULDERS
POULDRES
DELOPSTU POSTLUDE
DELORSST OLDSTERS
STRODLES
DELORSSW WORDLESS
DELORSTT DOTTRELS
DELORSUY DELUSORY
DELOSSUU SEDULOUS
DELOSTTT DOTTLEST
DELOTTUW OUTDWELT
DELOTUVY DEVOUTLY
DELRSSTU STRUDELS
DELSSSTU DUSTLESS
DEMMNOOU MONOMODE
DEMMNOOS DOOMSMEN
DEMMNOSU SUMMONED
DEMMNSUU UNSUMMED
DEMMRRSU DRUMMERS
DEMMRRUU MURMURED
DEMMRSTU STRUMMED
DEMNNOSU SOUNDMEN
DEMNOOOP MONOPODE
DEMNOOPT TOMPONED
DEMNOORS DOORSMEN
DEMNOORU UNMOORED
DEMNOOSW WOODSMEN
DEMNORST MORDENTS
DEMNORSW SWORDMEN
DEMNORSY SYNDROME
DEMNORUW UNWORMED
DEMNOSTU DEMOUNTS
MUDSTONE
DEMOOPPS POPEDOMS
DEMOOPRR PRODROME
DEMOOPRS PREDOOMS
DEMOOPRT PROMOTED
DEMOORST DOOMSTER
DEMOORSU DORMOUSE
DEMOORTY ODOMETRY
DEMOOSTU OUTMODES
DEMOOTUV OUTMOVED
DEMOPPRT PROMPTED
DEMOPSSU POSSUMED
DEMORRUU RUMOURED
DENNNSUU UNSUNNED
DENNOOOZ ENDOZOON
DENNORST TENDRONS
DENNORSU ENROUNDS
DENNOTUW UNWONTED
DENNPRUU UNPRUNED
DENNRRUU UNDERRUN
DENNRTUU UNTURNED
DENOOOTW WOODNOTE
DENOOOVW OVENWOOD
DENOOPPR PROPONED
DENOOPRS PRODNOSE
DENOOPSY POYSONED
DENOORTU UNROOTED
DENOOSSW WOODNESS
DENOOSTU DUOTONES
DENOPPRS PROPENDS
DENOPRSS RESPONDS
DENOPRST PORTENDS
PROTENDS

DENOPRSU POUNDERS
DENOPRSV PROVENDS
DENOPRUV UNPROVED
DENOPSTU OUTSPEND
UNPOSTED
DENOPSTW STEWPOND
DENOPSUX EXPOUNDS
DENOQTUU UNQUOTED
DENORRSU RONDURES
ROUNDERS
UNORDERS
DENORRSW DROWNERS
DENORRTU ROTUNDER
DENORRUU ROUNDURE
DENORSSU DOURNESS
RESOUNDS
SOUNDERS
DENORSTU ROUNDEST
TONSURED
UNSORTED
DENORSUU UNROUSED
UNSOURED
DENORSUW WOUNDERS
DENORTTU UNROTTED
DENORTUW UNDERTOW
DENOSSTU SOUNDEST
DENOSTUW UNSTOWED
DENOTUUV UNDEVOUT
DENPRSTU UPTRENDS
DENPRSUU UNPURSED
DENPRTUU UPTURNED
DENPSSSU SUSPENDS
DENRRTUU NURTURED
DENRSSSU SUNDRESS
DENRSTTU STRUNTED
DENSSTTU STUDENTS
DENSTUVY DUVETYNS
DEOOORSW ROSEWOOD
DEOOOSWW WOODWOSE
DEOOPPRS PROPOSED
DEOOPPRT PTEROPOD
DEOOPRRV PROVEDOR
DEOOPRST DOORSTEP
TORPEDOS
DEOOPRTU UPROOTED
DEOOPWWW POWWOWED
DEOORRST REDROOTS
DEOORRSW SORROWED
DEOORRVW OVERWORD
DEOORRWW OWREWORD
DEOORTUV OUTDROVE
DEOOTTUV OUTVOTED
DEOPPRRS DROPPERS
DEOPPRST STROPPED
DEOPPRSU PURPOSED
DEOPPSSU SUPPOSED
DEOPRRTU PROTRUDE
DEOPRSTU POSTURED
PROUDEST
SPROUTED
DEOPRSUU POURSUED
UPROUSED
DEORRSST RODSTERS
DEORRSSW SWORDERS
DEORRTTU TORTURED
DEORSSTW WORSTEDS
DEORSSTY DESTROYS
DEORSTTU STROUTED
DEORSTUU OUTDURES
DEORSTUV OVERDUST

DEORSTUX DEXTROUS
DEOSSSYY ODYSSEYS
DEOSSTTU TESTUDOS
DEPPSSYY DYSPEPSY
DEPRRTUU RUPTURED
DEQRSUUY SURQUEDY
DERSTTTU STRUTTED
DFFGINSU DUFFINGS
DFFIILUY FLUIDIFY
DFFIIMRS MIDRIFFS
DFFIIRST TRIFFIDS
DFFIIRTY TRIFFIDY
DFFLOORU FOURFOLD
DFFOORUW WOODRUFF
DFGGHIOT DOGFIGHT
DFGGIINR FRIDGING
DFGHILOS GOLDFISH
DFGIIIRY RIGIDIFY
DFGIILRY FRIGIDLY
DFGIINNS FINDINGS
DFGIINRT DRIFTING
DFGILNNO FONDLING
DFGILNOO FLOODING
DFGILNOS FOLDINGS
DFGINNOU FOUNDING
DFGINNSU FUNDINGS
DFGINOOR FORDOING
DFGMOOSY FOGYDOMS
DFHIIMUY HUMIDIFY
DFHILSSU DISHFULS
DFHIMRSU DRUMFISH
DFHINOOT HINDFOOT
DFHLOOOT FOOTHOLD
DFHNOOUX FOXHOUND
DFIIINVY DIVINIFY
DFIILMTU MULTIFID
DFIILOSY SOLIDIFY
DFIILTUY FLUIDITY
DFIINPRT DRIFTPIN
DFIKNOOS SKINFOOD
DFILLOOT FLOODLIT
DFILLORY FLORIDLY
DFILLOWW WILDFOWL
DFILMMOS FILMDOMS
DFILNOPS PINFOLDS
DFIMOOOR IODOFORM
DFIMOOSS FOODISMS
DFIMORSS DISFORMS
DFINRSUW WINDSURF
DFIOOPRS DISPROOF
DFLNOOWW DOWNFLOW
DFLOPRUU PROUDFUL
DFNOOPRU PROFOUND
DFOOOORW WOODROOF
DFOOOSTW SOFTWOOD
DGGGIINS DIGGINGS
DGGGINOS DOGGINGS
DGGGINRU DRUGGING
GRUDGING
DGGHIINT DIGHTING
DGGIILNR GIRDLING
RIDGLING
DGGIILNS GILDINGS
GLIDINGS
DGGIINNR GRINDING
DGGIINNW WINGDING
DGGIINRS GIRDINGS
RIDGINGS
DGGIINSU GUIDINGS
DGGILNOS GODLINGS

LODGINGS
DGGIMNSU SMUDGING
DGGINNSU SNUDGING
DGGINOST STODGING
DGGINRTU TRUDGING
DGGIRSTU DRUGGIST
DGHHOOOS HOGHOODS
DGHIILNS HIDLINGS
HILDINGS
DGHIIMNT MIDNIGHT
DGHIIMST MISDIGHT
DGHIINNW HINDWING
DGHIINPS SPHINGID
DGHIINRT THIRDING
DGHIINSS DISHINGS
SHINDIGS
DGHIISST DISSIGHT
DGHIKNOO KINGHOOD
DGHILNOS HOLDINGS
DGHILNRU HURDLING
DGHILNSY HYLDINGS
DGHILOOR GIRLHOOD
DGHILPSY DIGLYPHS
DGHINNOU HOUNDING
DGHINNSU DUNSHING
DGHINSTU UNDIGHTS
DGHIOORS DROOGISH
DGHIOPSS DOGSHIPS
GODSHIPS
DGHNOTUU DOUGHNUT
DGHOOOTT DOGTOOTH
DGHORSTU DROUGHTS
DGHORTUY DROUGHTY
DGIIIMRS DIRIGISM
DGIIINNT INDITING
DGIIINNV DIVINING
DGIIINOS IODISING
DGIIINOZ IODIZING
DGIIIRTY RIGIDITY
DGIIKLNN KINDLING
DGIIKLNS KIDLINGS
DGIIKNNR DRINKING
DGIILLNR DRILLING
DGIILLNS DILLINGS
DGIILLNU ILLUDING
DGIILLOU LIGULOID
DGIILMNP DIMPLING
DGIILNNN DINNLING
DGIILNOR DROILING
DGIILNOS DISLOIGN
DGIILNPS DISPLING
DGIILNSS SLIDINGS
DGIILNSW WILDINGS
DGIILNTU DILUTING
DGIIMNNS MINDINGS
DGIIMNOS MISDOING
DGIIMNOU GONIDIUM
DGIIMNSS SMIDGINS
DGIIMPUY PYGIDIUM
DGIINNOP POINDING
DGIINNRW WINDRING
DGIINNSS SINDINGS
DGIINNSW WINDINGS
DGIINORR GRIDIRON
DGIINORS DORISING
DGIINORZ DORIZING
DGIINOSV VOIDINGS
DGIINOSW WINDIGOS
DGIINOTT DITTOING
DGIINOWW WIDOWING

DGIINPPR	DRIPPING
DGIINPPS	DIPPINGS
DGIINRST	STRIDING
DGIINRTY	DIRTYING
DGIINSSU	DISUSING
DGIINTTY	DITTYING
DGIINYZZ	DIZZYING
DGIKLOOY	KIDOLOGY
DGIKMNOS	KINGDOMS
DGIKNOOR	DROOKING
DGIKNOOW	KINGWOOD
DGIKNORU	DROUKING
DGIKNOSS	DOGSKINS
DGILLNOR	DROLLING
	LORDLING
DGILLNOY	DOLLYING
DGILLOOW	GOODWILL
DGILMNOU	MOULDING
DGILMNPU	DUMPLING
DGILMSUY	SMUDGILY
DGILNNOO	NOODLING
DGILNNOU	LOUNDING
DGILNNOW	LOWNDING
DGILNNRU	NURDLING
DGILNOOR	DROOLING
DGILNOOW	WOOLDING
DGILNORS	GIRLONDS
	LORDINGS
DGILNORY	YOLDRING
DGILNOTY	DOTINGLY
DGILNPUY	DUPLYING
DGILOOTW	GILTWOOD
DGILOPSU	SOLPUGID
DGILOSTY	STODGILY
DGILRTUY	TURGIDLY
DGIMMNRU	DRUMMING
DGIMMNUY	DUMMYING
DGIMNNOU	MOUNDING
DGIMNOOY	MOODYING
DGINNNSU	DUNNINGS
DGINNOOS	SNOODING
DGINNOPU	POUNDING
DGINNOPW	POWNDING
DGINNORU	ROUNDING
DGINNORW	DROWNING
	ROWNDING
DGINNOSU	SOUNDING
	UNDOINGS
DGINNOSW	SOWNDING
DGINNOUW	WOUNDING
DGINNSSY	SYNDINGS
DGINNSUW	WINDGUNS
DGINOOPR	DROOPING
DGINOOPS	SPONGOID
DGINOOTU	OUTDOING
DGINOPPR	DROPPING
DGINOPPS	DOPPINGS
DGINORSV	DROVINGS
DGINORSW	DROWSING
	SWORDING
	WORDINGS
DGINOSSW	DISGOWNS
DGINOSUY	DIGYNOUS
DGINSTUY	STUDYING
DGISSSTU	DISGUSTS
DGLOOOPY	PODOLOGY
DGLOOOSW	LOGWOODS
DGLOOOSY	DOSOLOGY
DGLOOOXY	DOXOLOGY
DGMOPRSU	GUMDROPS
DGMOPSYY	GYPSYDOM
DGMORSUU	GURUDOMS
DGNNORUU	UNGROUND
DGNOOORS	GODROONS
DGNOOSTW	DOGTOWNS
DGNOOTYZ	ZYGODONT
DGOORSTT	DOGTROTS
DHHILOTW	WITHHOLD
DHIIIMNS	DIMINISH
DHIIIOST	HISTIOID
	IDIOTISH
DHIILOSS	SOLIDISH
DHIIMNOO	HOMINOID
DHIIMNOS	HOMINIDS
DHIIMPSS	MIDSHIPS
DHIIMTUY	HUMIDITY
DHIINPSW	WINDSHIP
DHIINRSU	HIRUDINS
DHIINTWW	WITHWIND
DHIIOPRU	OPHIURID
DHIIORSS	HIDROSIS
DHIIORSZ	RHIZOIDS
DHIKNOOW	HOODWINK
DHIKORSY	HYDROSKI
DHILLNOW	DOWNHILL
DHILLOPY	PHYLLOID
DHILLORS	DROLLISH
DHILLOST	TOLLDISH
DHILMOPY	LYMPHOID
DHILMOSY	MODISHLY
DHILNOPS	DOLPHINS
DHILOPRS	LORDSHIP
DHILOPSS	SLIPSHOD
DHILORRY	HORRIDLY
DHILPSSU	LUDSHIPS
DHILPSSY	SYLPHIDS
DHIMNOST	HINDMOST
DHIMNOSU	UNMODISH
DHIMOOOY	OMOHYOID
DHIMOOSS	MISSHOOD
DHIMOPPY	HIPPYDOM
DHIMOPRS	DIMORPHS
DHIMORSU	HUMIDORS
	RHODIUMS
DHINOORS	DISHONOR
DHINOPSS	DONSHIPS
DHINORSS	DISHORNS
DHINORSU	ROUNDISH
DHIOOPRZ	RHIZOPOD
DHIOPRSU	PROUDISH
DHIOPSTY	TYPHOIDS
DHIORSTY	THYROIDS
	THYRSOID
DHIORSWY	ROWDYISH
DHIPRSSY	SYRPHIDS
DHJOPRSU	JODHPURS
DHKMNOOO	MONKHOOD
DHKMOOSU	MUDHOOKS
DHLLOPYY	PHYLLODY
DHLMOOSU	HOODLUMS
DHLOOORT	ROOTHOLD
DHLORXYY	HYDROXYL
DHLOSSTU	SHOULDST
DHMMRSUU	HUMDRUMS
DHMNOOOT	HOMODONT
DHMOOPPU	PUMPHOOD
DHMORTUY	DRYMOUTH
DHNNOOSU	NUNHOODS
DHNOOSWW	SHOWDOWN
DHNORSUU	UNSHROUD
DHNORSUW	DOWNRUSH
DHNOSTUW	SHUTDOWN
DHOOOPRT	ORTHOPOD
DHOOORTX	ORTHODOX
DHOOPRSU	UPHOORDS
DHOORSUW	WOODRUSH
DHOPRSSU	PUSHRODS
DHOPRSYY	HYDROPSY
DIIIKMNS	MINIDISK
DIIILLQU	ILLIQUID
DIIILTVY	LIVIDITY
DIIIMOST	IDIOTISM
DIIIMRSU	IRIDIUMS
DIIIMTTY	TIMIDITY
DIIINOSV	DIVISION
DIIINTVY	DIVINITY
DIIIPRST	DISPIRIT
DIIIRTVY	VIRIDITY
DIIITVVY	VIVIDITY
DIIJNOSS	DISJOINS
DIIJNOST	DISJOINT
DIIKKNSS	KIDSKINS
DIIKLLNY	KINDLILY
DIIKLNSS	DISLINKS
DIIKNOST	DOITKINS
DIILLMNR	MILLRIND
DIILLMNW	WINDMILL
DIILLMPY	LIMPIDLY
DIILLQUY	LIQUIDLY
DIILLSST	DISTILLS
DIILLSTY	IDYLLIST
DIILMNSS	DISLIMNS
DIILMOSS	IDOLISMS
	SOLIDISM
DIILMOTY	MYTILOID
DIILMUUV	DILUVIUM
DIILNNSU	INDULINS
DIILNOTU	DILUTION
DIILNOUV	DILUVION
DIILNOXY	XYLOIDIN
DIILNTUY	UNTIDILY
DIILOPRT	TRIPLOID
DIILOPSY	YPSILOID
DIILORSU	SILUROID
DIILOSST	IDOLISTS
	SOLIDIST
DIILOSTY	SOLIDITY
DIILQSUU	LIQUIDUS
DIILRSSU	SILURIDS
DIIMNNOO	DOMINION
DIIMNNSU	UNDINISM
DIIMNORS	MIDIRONS
DIIMNSUU	INDUSIUM
DIIMOPRS	PRISMOID
DIIMORSS	DIORISMS
DIIMPUXY	PYXIDIUM
DIIMRUUV	DUUMVIRI
DIIMTTUY	TUMIDITY
DIINNOSU	DISUNION
DIINOQSU	QUINOIDS
DIINOSSU	SINUSOID
DIINSTUY	DISUNITY
DIIOPRTY	PITYROID
DIIORSSV	DIVISORS
DIJOSSTU	JUDOISTS
DIKLMOOW	MILKWOOD
DIKLNNUY	UNKINDLY
DIKLNORS	LORDKINS
DIKLRUUU	DURUKULI
DIKNOOSW	WOODSKIN
DIKNORSV	DVORNIKS
DIKNORTU	OUTDRINK
DIKOOSTU	DITOKOUS
DILLMNOP	MILLPOND
DILLOSTY	STOLIDLY
DILLPSSY	PSYLLIDS
DILMNOOS	SMILODON
DILMNORW	LINDWORM
DILMNRSU	DRUMLINS
DILMOOSU	MODIOLUS
DILMOSSU	SOLIDUMS
DILMOSSY	ODYLISMS
DILNOPST	DIPLONTS
DILNOPSU	LISPOUND
DILNOQSU	QUODLINS
DILNOSXY	INDOXYLS
DILNOUWY	WOUNDILY
DILNPSSU	LISPUNDS
DILOOPPY	POLYPOID
DILOOPRY	DROOPILY
DILOORSS	LORDOSIS
DILOOSUY	ODIOUSLY
DILOOTUV	VOLUTOID
DILOPRTY	TORPIDLY
DILORRTY	TORRIDLY
DILORSTU	DILUTORS
DILORSWY	DROWSILY
DILOSSTY	STYLOIDS
DILPRTUY	PUTRIDLY
DILPSTUY	STUPIDLY
DILRSTUY	STURDILY
DIMMNORY	MYRMIDON
DIMMOOSU	ISODOMUM
DIMMOSST	MIDMOSTS
DIMNNOOS	MIDNOONS
DIMNNOSS	DONNISMS
DIMNNOST	DINMONTS
DIMNOOOS	ISODOMON
DIMNOOST	MONODIST
DIMNOPSU	IMPOUNDS
DIMNOSTU	DISMOUNT
DIMNOSUW	UNWISDOM
DIMOOPRR	PRODROMI
DIMOOPRY	MYRIOPOD
DIMOORTW	MODIWORT
DIMOPRSU	MISPROUD
DIMOPSSU	SPODIUMS
DIMORSSW	MISWORDS
DIMORSWY	ROWDYISM
DIMOSTUY	DUMOSITY
DIMRSTUU	TRIDUUMS
DIMRSUUV	DUUMVIRS
DINNOORS	RONDINOS
DINNOOST	TONDINOS
DINNOPSW	PINDOWNS
DINOOORW	IRONWOOD
DINOOPSU	DIPNOOUS
DINOORST	TORDIONS
DINOORSU	NIDOROUS
DINOOSST	ISODONTS
DINOOSTT	ODONTIST
DINOOSTY	NODOSITY
DINORSTU	STURNOID
	TURDIONS
DINORSWW	WINDROWS
DINOSTUW	OUTWINDS
DINPRTUY	PUNDITRY
DINRSTUY	INDUSTRY
DIOOPRRT	PRODITOR
DIOOPRRV	PROVIDOR

DIOORSST DISROOTS
DIOORSTT RIDOTTOS
DIOPRSST DISPORTS
DIOPSSST DISPOSTS
DIORRSST STRIDORS
DIORSSTT DISTORTS
DIOSSTUU STUDIOUS
DIPRSSTU DISRUPTS
DIRSSTTU DISTRUST
DKNORTUU OUTDRUNK
DKOOORWW WOODWORK
DKORSTUW STUDWORK
DLLMORSU SLUMLORD
DLLNORUY UNLORDLY
DLMNOOSY MYLODONS
DLMNOOTY MYLODONT
DLMNOSUU UNMOULDS
DLMORSUY SMOULDRY
DLNOOPRU POULDRON
DLNOOSUU NODULOUS
DLNOPRSU PULDRONS
DLNOPSSY SPONDYLS
DLNORTUY ROTUNDLY
DLNOSUUU UNDULOUS
DLOOOORS DOLOROSO
DLOOORSU DOLOROUS
DLOOPPSY POLYPODS
DLOOPPUW PULPWOOD
DLOOPPYY POLYPODY
DLOOPSTY TYLOPODS
DLOOPSWY PLYWOODS
DMNNOOOT MONODONT
DMNOOOPS MONOPODS
DMNOOSTW DOWNMOST
TOWMONDS
DMOOORWW WOODWORM
WORMWOOD
DMOPPPUU PUPPODUM
DMOPPPUY PUPPYDOM
DMORSTUW MUDWORTS
DMPPPUUY MUDPUPPY
DNNOOPRU PUNDONOR
DNNORSUU UNROUNDS
DNNORSUW RUNDOWNS
DNNORTUW DOWNTURN
DNNOSSUW SUNDOWNS
DNNRSTUU TURNDUNS
DNOOPPRU PROPOUND
DNOOPRSW SNOWDROP
DNOOPRUW DOWNPOUR
DNOORSUW WONDROUS
DNOOSTUW NUTWOODS
DNOOSTWW STOWDOWN
DNOOTUUW OUTWOUND
DNOPRSSU SUNDROPS
DNORRSUU SURROUND
DNORSSUY UNDROSSY
DOOOPRST DOORPOST
DOORSTOP
DOOORSTU OUTDOORS
DOOOSTTU OUTSTOOD
DOOPSWWY POWSOWDY
DOORRSTU DORTOURS
DOORRSUU ORDUROUS
DOORSSUU SUDOROUS
EEEEFNRZ ENFREEZE
EEEEFRRS REFEREES
EEEEFRRZ REFREEZE
EEEEGGRR GREEGREE
EEEEGQSU SQUEEGEE
EEEEGSSX EXEGESES
EEEEGSTX EXEGETES
EEEELLPX EXPELLEE
EEEELMST TELESEME
EEEELNSV SLEEVEEN
EEEENRRV VENEERER
EEEEPPSW PEESWEEP
EEEEPRRV REPREEVE
EEEEPTTW PEETWEET
EEEFFFOS FEOFFEES
EEEFFLOR FOREFEEL
EEEFFLTY EFFETELY
EEEFFNRT EFFERENT
EEEFFORS OFFEREES
EEEFFORT FOREFEET
EEEFFRVW FEVERFEW
EEEFGRSU REFUGEES
EEEFHRSS SHEREEFS
EEEFIPRR REPRIEFE
EEEFIPST TEPEFIES
EEEFIRRT FREETIER
EEEFLRRS FLEERERS
EEEFLRSX REFLEXES
EEEFLSST FEETLESS
EEEFLSTT FLEETEST
EEEFNNPY PENNYFEE
EEEFNORS FORESEEN
EEEFNRRT REFERENT
EEEFNRSS FREENESS
EEEFNRTT ENFETTER
EEEFNRUZ UNFREEZE
EEEFORRV OVERFREE
EEEFORSS FORESEES
EEEFRRRT FERRETER
EEEFRRSZ FREEZERS
EEEGGILN NEGLIGEE
EEEGGIRS EGGERIES
EEEGHINT EIGHTEEN
EEEGHLRS SHEERLEG
EEEGHNSW WHEENGES
EEEGIKST GEEKIEST
EEEGILMN LIEGEMEN
EEEGILNV ENVEIGLE
LEVEEING
EEEGILPS ESPIEGLE
EEEGILRT GLEETIER
EEEGILSS ELEGISES
EEEGILSZ ELEGIZES
EEEGIMNX EXEEMING
EEEGINNR ENGINEER
EEEGINRR GREENIER
EEEGINRS ENERGIES
ENERGISE
GREENIES
EEEGINRV ENGRIEVE
EEEGINRZ ENERGIZE
EEEGIPRS PERIGEES
EEEGISSX EXEGESIS
EEEGISTV EGESTIVE
EEEGITVV VEGETIVE
EEEGLMOS GLEESOME
EEEGLNRT GREENLET
EEEGMNRT EMERGENT
EEEGMNRU MERENGUE
EEEGMORT GEOMETER
EEEGMRRS REMERGES
EEEGNNRS SENGREEN
EEEGNPRS EPERGNES
EEEGNRRS GREENERS
RENEGERS
EEEGNRRU RENEGUER
EEEGNRRV REVENGER
EEEGNRRY GREENERY
EEEGNRST GREENEST
EEEGNRSU RENEGUES
EEEGNRSV REVENGES
EEEGNSTT GENETTES
EEEGOPRT PROTEGEE
EEEGRRST GREETERS
REGREETS
EEEGRSSS EGRESSES
EEEGRSUX EXERGUES
EEEHHSSW WHEESHES
EEEHILRW EREWHILE
WHEELIER
EEEHILSW WHEELIES
EEEHINRS SHEENIER
EEEHINSS SHEENIES
EEEHIPRS SHEEPIER
EEEHIRSS HERESIES
EEEHIRST ETHERISE
SHEETIER
EEEHIRTZ ETHERIZE
EEEHIRWZ WHEEZIER
EEEHKLNO KNEEHOLE
EEEHLMNW WHEELMEN
EEEHLMPT HELPMEET
EEEHLNSW ENWHEELS
EEEHLNTV ELEVENTH
EEEHLNTY ETHYLENE
EEEHLNXY HEXYLENE
EEEHLOPW WEEPHOLE
EEEHLPSW WHEEPLES
EEEHLRSW WHEELERS
EEEHLSWZ WHEEZLES
EEEHMMSS EMMESHES
EEEHMNSS ENMESHES
EEEHMNTV VEHEMENT
EEEHNNPT NEPENTHE
EEEHNNQU HENEQUEN
EEEHNPRS ENSPHERE
EEEHNRSS HERENESS
EEEHNRVW WHENEVER
EEEHNSSS SNEESHES
EEEHORST SHOETREE
EEEHPRST SPREETHE
EEEHRRVW WHEREVER
EEEHRSST SEETHERS
SHEEREST
EEEHSSTT ESTHETES
EEEIKLMS MISLEEKE
EEEIKLRS SKEELIER
SLEEKIER
EEEIKLSW WEEKLIES
EEEIKRRS SKEERIER
EEEIKRST REEKIEST
EEEILLRV REVEILLE
EEEILMRS SEEMLIER
EEEILNNO EOLIENNE
EEEILNPR PELERINE
EEEILNRY EYELINER
EEEILNST SELENITE
EEEILPRS SLEEPIER
EEEILRRV RELIEVER
EEEILRST LEERIEST
SLEETIER
STEELIER
EEEILRSV RELIEVES
EEEILRSZ SLEEZIER
EEEILSST SEELIEST
EEEILSSW ELSEWISE
EEEILSTV TELEVISE
EEEILTVW TELEVIEW
EEEIMNRU MEUNIERE
EEEIMNST EMETINES
EEEIMPRR PREMIERE
EEEIMPRS EMPERIES
EMPERISE
PREEMIES
EEEIMPRZ EMPERIZE
EEEIMRRS MISERERE
EEEIMRST EREMITES
EEEIMRTT REMITTEE
EEEINNNT NINETEEN
EEEINNRT INTERNEE
EEEINQRU QUEENIER
EEEINQSU QUEENIES
EEEINQTU QUEENITE
EEEINRRS SNEERIER
EEEINRSS EERINESS
EEEINRST ETERNISE
TEENSIER
EEEINRSV VENERIES
EEEINRSZ SNEEZIER
EEEINRTT REINETTE
TEENTIER
EEEINRTZ ETERNIZE
EEEINSSW SWEENIES
EEEINSTT TEENIEST
EEEINSTW TWEENIES
WEENIEST
EEEINTUX EUXENITE
EEEIPRRV REPRIEVE
EEEIPRST PEERIEST
STEEPIER
EEEIPRSW SWEEPIER
EEEIPSST SEEPIEST
EEEIPSTW WEEPIEST
EEEIQSUX EXEQUIES
EEEIRRST REESTIER
RETIREES
EEEIRRSV REREVISE
REVERIES
EEEIRRTV RETRIEVE
EEEIRRVW REVIEWER
EEEIRSST STEERIES
EEEIRSSV SEVERIES
EEEIRSSZ RESEIZES
EEEIRTVX EXERTIVE
EEEISSTW SWEETIES
EEEJLLRW JEWELLER
EEEJNPSY JEEPNEYS
EEEKLLSU UKELELES
EEEKLNNR ENKERNEL
EEEKLNRS KNEELERS
EEEKLNSS SLEEKENS
EEEKLPSW EKPWELES
EEEKLRSS SLEEKERS
EEEKLSST SLEEKEST
EEEKMNSS MEEKNESS
EEEKMRSS KERMESSE
EEEKNNSS KEENNESS
EEEKNORS KEROSENE
EEEKNORV OVERKNEE
EEEKNPST KEEPNETS
EEEKOPRV OVERKEEP
EEEKRSST SKEETERS
EEELLLRV LEVELLER
EEELLLSW SEWELLEL
EEELLNQU QUENELLE

EEELLPRR	REPELLER
EEELLRRT	RETELLER
EEELLRRV	REVELLER
EEELMNST	ELEMENTS
	STEELMEN
EEELMOPP	EMPEOPLE
EEELMOPY	EMPLOYEE
EEELMORT	TELOMERE
EEELMOTT	OMELETTE
EEELMPSX	EXEMPLES
EEELMRTU	MULETEER
EEELMSSS	SEEMLESS
EEELMSST	TEEMLESS
EEELNOPV	ENVELOPE
EEELNOSV	NOVELESE
EEELNQTU	QUEENLET
EEELNRSW	NEWSREEL
EEELNRSY	SERENELY
EEELNRTV	NERVELET
EEELOPPR	REPEOPLE
EEELORST	SLOETREE
EEELPRSS	PEERLESS
	SLEEPERS
	SPEELERS
EEELPRST	REPLETES
EEELPRSY	SLEEPERY
EEELPSST	STEEPLES
EEELRRTT	LETTERER
EEELRSST	TREELESS
EEELRSSV	SLEEVERS
EEELRSTT	RESETTLE
EEELRSTV	LEVERETS
	VERSELET
EEELRSVY	SEVERELY
EEELRTVV	VELVERET
EEELSSTW	WEETLESS
EEELSTVY	STEEVELY
EEELTTTX	TELETEXT
EEEMMNRS	MERESMEN
EEEMMRUZ	MEZEREUM
EEEMNNTT	TENEMENT
EEEMNORZ	MEZEREON
EEEMNPRT	PETERMEN
EEEMNRST	ENTREMES
EEEMNRVY	EVERYMEN
EEEMNSST	MEETNESS
EEEMORRV	EVERMORE
EEEMORST	EROTEMES
	STEREOME
EEEMORTV	OVERTEEM
EEEMPRRT	TEMPERER
EEEMPRSS	EMPRESSE
EEEMPSSY	EMPYESES
EEEMRRTX	EXTREMER
EEEMRSST	SEMESTER
EEEMRSTX	EXTREMES
EEENNOPR	NEOPRENE
EEENNPST	PENTENES
EEENNRST	ETRENNES
EEENNRUV	UNEVENER
EEENNSSV	EVENNESS
EEENNSTT	ENTENTES
EEENOPRR	REOPENER
EEENORSV	OVERSEEN
EEENORVW	OVERWEEN
EEENORVY	EVERYONE
EEENPPRS	PREPENSE
EEENPRRT	REPENTER
EEENPRST	PRETENSE
	TERPENES
EEENPRSV	PREVENES
EEENPSST	ENSTEEPS
	STEEPENS
EEENPSSW	ENSWEEPS
EEENPSSX	EXPENSES
EEENRRSS	SNEERERS
EEENRRST	ENTERERS
	RESENTER
	TERREENS
	TERRENES
EEENRRSV	RENVERSE
	VENERERS
EEENRRSW	RENEWERS
EEENRRTU	RETURNEE
EEENRRTV	REVERENT
EEENRSST	SERENEST
EEENRSSU	ENURESES
EEENRSSZ	SNEEZERS
EEENRSTV	EVENTERS
EEENRSTX	EXTERNES
EEENRSTY	YESTREEN
EEENRSUV	REVENUES
	UNREEVES
EEENSSTW	SWEETENS
	TWEENESS
EEENSSWY	SWEENEYS
EEEOPRRV	OVERPEER
EEEORRSV	OVERSEER
EEEORSST	EROTESES
EEEORSSV	OVERSEES
EEEORSSY	EYESORES
EEEORSVY	OVEREYES
EEEPPPRR	PEPPERER
EEEPRRST	PESTERER
EEEPRRSU	REPERUSE
EEEPRRSV	PERVERSE
	PRESERVE
EEEPRRTW	PEWTERER
EEEPRSST	ESTREPES
	STEEPERS
EEEPRSSW	SWEEPERS
EEEPRSSZ	SPREEZES
EEEPSSTT	STEEPEST
EEEPSTTT	SEPTETTE
EEEQRRSU	REQUERES
EEEQRRUV	VERQUERE
EEEQRSTU	QUEEREST
EEEQRSUZ	SQUEEZER
EEEQSSUZ	SQUEEZES
EEERRRSV	REVERERS
	REVERSER
EEERRSST	STEERERS
EEERRSSV	RESERVES
	REVERSES
EEERRSTT	RESETTER
EEERSSTV	SEVEREST
EEERSSUV	REVEUSES
EEERSSUW	SERUEWES
EEERSSVW	SERVEWES
EEERSTTW	TWEETERS
EEERSTVX	VERTEXES
EEERSTWZ	TWEEZERS
EEESSTTT	SESTETTE
EEESSTTV	STEEVEST
EEESSTTW	SWEETEST
EEESTTTX	SEXTETTE
EEFFFGLU	GEFUFFLE
EEFFFKLU	KEFUFFLE
EEFFFNOS	ENFEOFFS
EEFFFORS	FEOFFERS
EEFFGIIS	EFFIGIES
EEFFGINR	EFFERING
EEFFGIRR	GREFFIER
EEFFGLSU	EFFULGES
EEFFHIKY	KEFFIYEH
EEFFINST	FIFTEENS
EEFFISUV	EFFUSIVE
EEFFLNTU	EFFLUENT
EEFFLORT	FOREFELT
EEFFLSUX	EFFLUXES
EEFFNOSS	OFFENSES
EEFFORRS	OFFERERS
EEFFORSX	FORFEXES
EEFFRRSU	SUFFERER
EEFFSSTU	SUFFETES
EEFGIILR	FILIGREE
EEFGILNR	FLEERING
EEFGILNS	FEELINGS
EEFGILNT	FLEETING
EEFGINNP	PFENNIGE
EEFGINRR	REFRINGE
EEFGINRS	FEERINGS
	REEFINGS
EEFGINRV	FEVERING
EEFGINRZ	FREEZING
EEFGIRRU	REFIGURE
EEFGLMNU	FUGLEMEN
EEFGLNRY	GREENFLY
EEFGLNUV	VENGEFUL
EEFGLORS	FORELEGS
EEFGLOSS	SOLFEGES
EEFGMNOR	FORGEMEN
EEFGNOOR	FOREGONE
EEFGOORR	FOREGOER
EEFGOORS	FOREGOES
EEFHILLR	HELLFIRE
EEFHILRS	FLESHIER
	SHELFIER
EEFHIMSU	HUMEFIES
EEFHIRSV	FEVERISH
EEFHIRTY	ETHERIFY
EEFHISST	FETISHES
EEFHISSY	FISHEYES
EEFHISTT	HEFTIEST
EEFHLLWY	FLYWHEEL
EEFHLMOT	HOMEFELT
EEFHLMST	THEMSELF
EEFHLRSS	FLESHERS
EEFHMNRS	FRESHMEN
EEFHMORR	HEREFROM
EEFHNORT	FOREHENT
EEFHNRSS	FRESHENS
EEFHORRT	THEREFOR
EEFHORRW	WHEREFOR
EEFHORSW	FORESHEW
EEFHRRSS	FRESHERS
EEFHRSST	FRESHEST
	FRESHETS
EEFIIKLL	LIFELIKE
EEFIIKLW	WIFELIKE
EEFIIKRS	FIKERIES
EEFIILLN	LIFELINE
EEFIILMT	LIFETIME
EEFIILNS	LENIFIES
EEFIILRW	WIFELIER
EEFIIMNN	FEMININE
EEFIIMNS	FEMINISE
EEFIIMNZ	FEMINIZE
EEFIINRS	FINERIES
EEFIIRRT	FREITIER
EEFIIRRV	VERIFIER
EEFIIRST	FEISTIER
	FERITIES
	FIERIEST
EEFIIRSV	VERIFIES
EEFIKLRS	SERFLIKE
EEFIKNNP	PENKNIFE
EEFILLMT	TELEFILM
EEFILLSS	LIFELESS
EEFILMNR	RIFLEMEN
EEFILMOS	LIFESOME
EEFILMST	FISTMELE
EEFILNOS	FELONIES
	OLEFINES
EEFILNSS	FINELESS
EEFILNUV	NIEVEFUL
EEFILORS	FORELIES
EEFILPRR	PILFERER
EEFILRRT	FERTILER
EEFILRSS	FIRELESS
EEFILRST	FERLIEST
EEFILRSU	FUSILEER
EEFILSST	FELSITES
EEFILSSW	WIFELESS
EEFILSTT	FELTIEST
EEFIMORT	FORETIME
EEFIMRST	FEMITERS
EEFIMSTU	TUMEFIES
EEFINNSS	FINENESS
EEFINNST	FENNIEST
EEFINORV	OVERFINE
EEFINRRS	REFINERS
EEFINRRY	REFINERY
EEFINRSS	FINESSER
	RIFENESS
EEFINRST	FERNIEST
EEFINRSU	REINFUSE
EEFINRSZ	FRENZIES
EEFINSSS	FINESSES
EEFINSTT	FEINTEST
EEFIORSX	ORIFEXES
EEFIPRSX	PREFIXES
EEFIRRST	FERRITES
EEFIRRTT	FRETTIER
EEFIRSTT	FRISETTE
EEFIRSTY	ESTERIFY
EEFKNORW	FOREKNEW
EEFLLNSS	FELLNESS
EEFLLORT	FORETELL
EEFLLORV	OVERFELL
EEFLLRSU	FUELLERS
EEFLLRXY	REFLEXLY
EEFLLSSS	SELFLESS
EEFLMNSU	MENSEFUL
EEFLMORU	FUMEROLE
EEFLNNOS	ENFELONS
EEFLNORT	FORELENT
EEFLNORW	ENFLOWER
EEFLNOST	FELSTONE
EEFLNRSS	FRESNELS
EEFLNRTU	REFLUENT
EEFLNSSS	SELFNESS
EEFLNSSU	SENSEFUL
EEFLNTUV	EVENTFUL
EEFLOOSV	FOVEOLES
EEFLOPTT	POLTFEET
EEFLORRW	FLOWERER
	REFLOWER
EEFLORSS	FORLESES
EEFLORTV	LEFTOVER

EEFLORTW	FLOWERET
EEFLORVW	OVERFLEW
EEFLORWW	WEREWOLF
EEFLOSUX	FLEXUOSE
EEFLRRSU	FERRULES
EEFLRSTT	FETTLERS
EEFLRSTU	FLEURETS
EEFLRSUX	FLEXURES
	REFLUXES
EEFMNORT	FOMENTER
EEFMNRRY	FERRYMEN
EEFMNRST	FERMENTS
EEFMORRR	REFORMER
EEFMOSTT	MOFETTES
EEFMPRRU	PERFUMER
EEFMPRSU	PERFUMES
EEFMSTTU	FUMETTES
EEFNNORS	ENFROSEN
EEFNNORZ	ENFROZEN
EEFNORRZ	REFROZEN
EEFNORST	ENFOREST
	SOFTENER
EEFNORTU	FOURTEEN
EEFNORTW	FOREWENT
EEFNOSTT	OFTENEST
EEFNQRTU	FREQUENT
EEFNRTTU	UNFETTER
EEFOORRT	ROOFTREE
EEFORRST	FORESTER
	FOSTERER
	REFOREST
EEFORRSU	FERREOUS
EEFORRSV	FOREVERS
EEFORRTY	FERETORY
EEFORSUV	FEVEROUS
EEFOSSTT	FOSSETTE
EEFOSSTU	FOETUSES
EEFOSTTU	FOUETTES
EEFPRSSU	PERFUSES
EEFRRSSU	REFUSERS
EEFRRSTU	REFUTERS
EEGGGLST	GLEGGEST
EEGGHLLS	EGGSHELL
EEGGHLOR	HOGGEREL
EEGGHMSU	MESHUGGE
EEGGHSTU	THUGGEES
EEGGIJRR	REJIGGER
EEGGIKLN	GLEEKING
EEGGIKNR	GREEKING
EEGGILNR	LEGERING
EEGGILNS	NEGLIGES
EEGGILNT	GLEETING
EEGGILST	LEGGIEST
EEGGIMNR	EMERGING
EEGGINNP	PEENGING
EEGGINNR	GREENING
	RENEGING
EEGGINRS	GREESING
EEGGINRT	GREETING
EEGGINST	EGESTING
EEGGINSU	SEGUEING
EEGGKRSS	SKEGGERS
EEGGLOOR	GEOLOGER
EEGGNORS	ENGORGES
EEGGORRS	REGORGES
EEGGORSU	GOUGERES
EEGGPRRS	PREGGERS
EEGGPRSU	PUGGREES
EEGGQRSU	SQUEGGER
EEGHHINT	HEIGHTEN

EEGHIIST	EIGHTIES
EEGHIKNT	THEEKING
EEGHIKRS	SKEIGHER
EEGHILNS	HEELINGS
	SHEELING
EEGHILNW	WHEELING
EEGHILRS	SLEIGHER
EEGHINNS	SHEENING
EEGHINPS	PHEESING
EEGHINPT	PHENGITE
EEGHINPZ	PHEEZING
EEGHINRS	GREENISH
	SHEERING
EEGHINST	SEETHING
	SHEETING
EEGHINSY	HYGIENES
EEGHINTT	TEETHING
EEGHINWZ	WHEEZING
EEGHIOTT	GOETHITE
EEGHIRSW	REWEIGHS
	WEIGHERS
EEGHISST	SIGHTSEE
EEGHISTY	EYESIGHT
EEGHLNNT	LENGTHEN
EEGHMNOY	HEGEMONY
EEGHNNRU	ENHUNGER
EEGHNOOP	GEOPHONE
EEGHNOPS	PHOSGENE
EEGHNOPY	HYPOGENE
EEGHNRST	GREENTHS
EEGHNRSY	GREYHENS
EEGHNSSU	HUGENESS
EEGHOPTY	GEOPHYTE
EEGHORTT	TOGETHER
EEGHOSTT	GHETTOES
EEGHSTTU	TEUGHEST
EEGIILNR	LINGERIE
EEGIILNV	INVEIGLE
EEGIIMNS	GEMINIES
EEGIINTV	GENITIVE
EEGIIOST	EGOITIES
EEGIJLNY	JEELYING
EEGIJNRS	JEERINGS
EEGIKLNN	KNEELING
EEGIKLNS	KEELINGS
	SLEEKING
EEGIKLOT	EKLOGITE
EEGIKMNS	SMEEKING
EEGIKNNS	KEENINGS
EEGIKNPS	KEEPINGS
EEGIKNRS	KREESING
	SKEERING
EEGIKNST	KITENGES
	STEEKING
EEGILNOR	ELOIGNER
EEGILNPS	PEELINGS
	SLEEPING
	SPEELING
EEGILNRR	LINGERER
EEGILNRS	LEERINGS
	REELINGS
EEGILNRU	REGULINE
EEGILNRV	LEVERING
EEGILNSS	SEELINGS
EEGILNST	GENTILES
	SLEETING
	STEELING
EEGILNSV	SLEEVING
EEGILNSW	SWEELING
EEGILNTW	TWEELING

EEGILNTX	TELEXING
EEGILOPU	EPILOGUE
EEGILOSS	GELOSIES
EEGILOSU	EULOGIES
	EULOGISE
EEGILOUZ	EULOGIZE
EEGILQSU	SQUILGEE
EEGILRSU	REGULISE
EEGILRSV	VELIGERS
EEGILRTV	VERLIGTE
EEGILRTY	LEGERITY
EEGILRUZ	REGULIZE
EEGILSST	ELEGISTS
EEGIMMNW	EMMEWING
EEGIMMRS	IMMERGES
EEGIMMST	GEMMIEST
EEGIMNNS	MENINGES
EEGIMNNW	ENMEWING
EEGIMNRS	REGIMENS
EEGIMNRT	METERING
	REGIMENT
EEGIMNRU	MERINGUE
EEGIMNRY	EMERYING
EEGIMNSS	SEEMINGS
EEGIMNST	MEETINGS
	STEEMING
EEGIMNSU	EUGENISM
EEGINNPR	PREENING
EEGINNQU	QUEENING
EEGINNRS	ENGINERS
	INGENERS
	SERENING
	SNEERING
EEGINNRT	ENTERING
EEGINNRV	ENERVING
EEGINNRW	RENEWING
EEGINNRY	ENGINERY
	RENEYING
EEGINNST	STEENING
EEGINNSU	INGENUES
	UNSEEING
EEGINNSV	EEVNINGS
	EVENINGS
EEGINNSW	ENSEWING
EEGINNSZ	SNEEZING
EEGINNTV	EVENTING
EEGINOOS	OOGENIES
EEGINOPR	PERIGONE
EEGINOPS	EPIGONES
EEGINORR	ERIGERON
EEGINORS	ERINGOES
EEGINORV	VIROGENE
EEGINOST	EGESTION
EEGINPRS	SPEERING
	SPREEING
EEGINPRT	PETERING
EEGINPRU	PUREEING
EEGINPRV	PREEVING
EEGINPST	STEEPING
EEGINPSW	SWEEPING
	WEEPINGS
EEGINQRU	QUEERING
EEGINQUU	QUEUEING
EEGINRRS	RESIGNER
EEGINRRV	REVERING
EEGINRSS	GREISENS
EEGINRST	GENTRIES
	INTEGERS
	REESTING
	STEERING

	STREIGNE
EEGINRSU	SEIGNEUR
EEGINRSV	SEVERING
	VEERINGS
EEGINRSW	SEWERING
EEGINRTU	GENITURE
EEGINRTV	EVERTING
EEGINRTW	TWEERING
EEGINRTX	EXERTING
	GENETRIX
EEGINSSS	GNEISSES
EEGINSSU	GENIUSES
EEGINSTT	GENTIEST
EEGINSTU	EUGENIST
EEGINSTV	STEEVING
	VENTIGES
EEGINSTW	SWEETING
EEGINSTX	EXIGENTS
EEGINTTV	VIGNETTE
EEGINTTW	TWEETING
EEGINTUX	TEGUEXIN
EEGINTWZ	TWEEZING
EEGIOPSU	EPIGEOUS
EEGIORST	ERGOTISE
EEGIORTZ	ERGOTIZE
EEGIORVV	OVERGIVE
EEGIOSST	EGOTISES
EEGIOSTZ	EGOTIZES
EEGIPRST	PRESTIGE
EEGIRRST	REGISTER
EEGIRRSV	GRIEVERS
EEGIRSTT	GRISETTE
	TERGITES
EEGIRSTU	GUERITES
EEGISSTV	VESTIGES
EEGJORSU	GOUJEERS
EEGKNORS	KEROGENS
EEGKNRSU	GERENUKS
EEGLMMSU	GEMMULES
EEGLMNOP	EMPLONGE
EEGLMNTU	EMULGENT
EEGLMOSS	GLOSSEME
EEGLNNTU	UNGENTLE
EEGLNOPY	POLYGENE
EEGLNOSU	EUGENOLS
EEGLNOSZ	LOZENGES
EEGLNOTY	TELEGONY
EEGLNSTT	GENTLEST
EEGLORRV	GROVELER
EEGMMOSU	GEMMEOUS
EEGMNOST	EMONGEST
	GEMSTONE
EEGMNSST	SEGMENTS
EEGMNTTU	TEGUMENT
EEGMORSU	GRUESOME
EEGMORTY	GEOMETRY
EEGNNORT	ROENTGEN
EEGNNOSS	GONENESS
EEGNNOSV	EVENSONG
EEGNOORV	ENGROOVE
	OVERGONE
EEGNOOST	OSTEOGEN
EEGNOPTY	GENOTYPE
EEGNORST	ESTROGEN
EEGNORSU	GENEROUS
EEGNORSY	ERYNGOES
EEGNPRUX	EXPUNGER
EEGNPSUX	EXPUNGES
EEGNRSSY	GREYNESS
EEGNRSUY	GUERNSEY

EEGNSSTU GUESTENS
EEGOOPSY POOGYEES
EEGOORSV OVERGOES
EEGOPRST PROTEGES
EEGOPRSU SUPEREGO
EEGORRST OSTREGER
EEGORRVW OVERGREW
EEGORSSS OGRESSES
EEGORSTU UROSTEGE
EEGORSTV OVERGETS
EEGPRSUX EXPURGES
EEGRRSSU RESURGES
EEGRSSSU GUESSERS
EEGRSSTU GESTURES
EEHHIPSS SHEEPISH
EEHHIRTW HEREWITH
EEHHLRST THRESHEL
EEHHRRST THRESHER
EEHHRSST THRESHES
EEHHSSTW WHEESHTS
EEHIIKLV HIVELIKE
EEHIKLMO HOMELIKE
EEHIKLRW WHELKIER
EEHIKRRS SHRIEKER
EEHILLMS SHLEMIEL
EEHILLNP HELPLINE
EEHILLRS HELLIERS
SHELLIER
EEHILMNU HELENIUM
EEHILMOR HOMELIER
EEHILNOP NEOPHILE
EEHILORT HOTELIER
EEHILOSS HELIOSES
EEHILRSS HEIRLESS
RELISHES
EEHILRSV SHELVIER
EEHILSST LEISHEST
SHELTIES
EEHILSSV HIVELESS
EEHILWYZ WHEEZILY
EEHIMMSS IMMESHES
MISHMEES
EEHIMNOS HEMIONES
EEHIMNRS SHIREMEN
EEHIMNSS INMESHES
EEHIMPRS EMPERISH
EEHIMPST EPITHEMS
HEMPIEST
EEHIMQUV VEHMIQUE
EEHIMRRU RHEUMIER
EEHIMRST ERETHISM
ETHERISM
EEHIMRTT THERMITE
EEHIMSST MESHIEST
EEHINNQU HENEQUIN
EEHINNRS ENSHRINE
EEHINNRT INHERENT
EEHINNSS SNEESHIN
EEHINNST HENNIEST
EEHINORS HEROINES
EEHINORT ETHERION
EEHINPRS INSPHERE
EEHINPRT NEPHRITE
PREHNITE
TREPHINE
EEHINRRS ERRHINES
EEHINRTT THIRTEEN
EEHINRTW WHITENER
EEHIOPPS HOSEPIPE
EEHIORSS HEROISES

EEHIORST ISOTHERE
THEORIES
THEORISE
EEHIORSZ HEROIZES
EEHIORTZ THEORIZE
EEHIPPST PSEPHITE
EEHIPPTY EPIPHYTE
EEHIPRRS PERISHER
SPHERIER
EEHIPRSS PERISHES
EEHIPRST TREESHIP
EEHIPRTT PERTHITE
TEPHRITE
THREEPIT
EEHIPSST STEEPISH
EEHIPSTT EPITHETS
EEHIPSUU EUPHUISE
EEHIPUUZ EUPHUIZE
EEHIQRSU QUEERISH
EEHIRRSS SHERRIES
EEHIRRSV SHIVERER
EEHIRRSW WHERRIES
EEHIRSST HEISTERS
EEHIRSSV SHRIEVES
EEHIRSSX RHEXISES
EEHIRSTT ETHERIST
EEHIRTVY THIEVERY
EEHISSTW SWEETISH
EEHISTTW THEWIEST
EEHISTWY WHEYIEST
EEHKLOSY KEYHOLES
EEHKOOSY EYEHOOKS
EEHLLMPS PHELLEMS
EEHLLMSS HELMLESS
EEHLLNSS ENSHELLS
EEHLLORV HOVELLER
EEHLLPSS HELPLESS
EEHLLRSS SHELLERS
EEHLMMNS HELMSMEN
EEHLMMSW WHEMMLES
EEHLMOOS HOLESOME
EEHLMOSS HOMELESS
EEHLNOTT TELETHON
EEHLOPSS HOPELESS
EEHLORST HOSTELER
EEHLORSV SHOVELER
EEHLOSSS SHOELESS
EEHLPPRS SHLEPPER
EEHLPRST TELPHERS
EEHLPRSU SPHERULE
EEHLRSST SHELTERS
EEHLRSSW WELSHERS
EEHLRSTY SHELTERY
EEHLSSTT SHTETELS
EEHLSSTW THEWLESS
EEHMMOPR MORPHEME
EEHMMORT OHMMETER
EEHMNOOS MOONSHEE
EEHMNOPS PHONEMES
EEHMNORS HORSEMEN
SHOREMEN
EEHMNOSU HOUSEMEN
EEHMNOSW SOMEWHEN
EEHMNRSU ENRHEUMS
EEHMNRSY MYNHEERS
EEHMOORT RHEOTOME
EEHMOOSS HOMEOSES
EEHMORST THEOREMS
EEHMORVW WHOMEVER
EEHMRSUX EXHUMERS

EEHMSSTY METHYSES
EEHNNORT ENTHRONE
EEHNNOSS SHONEENS
EEHNNPPU UNHEPPEN
EEHNNSSS NESHNESS
EEHNNSTU UNNETHES
EEHNOPRU HEREUPON
EEHNOPST POSHTEEN
POTHEENS
EEHNOPTY HYPNOTEE
NEOPHYTE
EEHNORST HONESTER
EEHNORSW HERONSEW
NOWHERES
EEHNORTU HEREUNTO
EEHNORTV OVERHENT
EEHNPRSU UNSPHERE
EEHNRTTU UNTETHER
EEHNSSTU ENTHUSES
EEHNSSTV SEVENTHS
EEHOOPRS OOSPHERE
EEHOOPSW WHOOPEES
EEHOORSV OVERSHOE
EEHOPRSU EUPHROES
EEHOPRVY OVERHYPE
EEHORRTX EXHORTER
EEHORSSU REHOUSES
EEHORSVW WHOSEVER
EEHORTTU THEREOUT
EEHORTUW WHEREOUT
EEHPRSST HEPSTERS
SPERTHES
EEHPRSTY PHYSETER
EEHRRSTW WHERRETS
EEHRSSSU RHESUSES
USHERESS
EEHRSSTW WERSHEST
EEHRSTTW WHETTERS
EEIIKLLR LIKELIER
EEIIKLPP PIPELIKE
EEIIKLSW LIKEWISE
EEIILLMM MILLIEME
EEIILLMT MELILITE
EEIILLOP EOLIPILE
EEIILLRV LIVELIER
EEIILMNT ILMENITE
MELINITE
EEIILMRT TIMELIER
EEIILMSS EMISSILE
EEIILNPP PIPELINE
EEIILNST LENITIES
EEIILNTV LENITIVE
EEIILORS OILERIES
EEIILRST TILERIES
EEIILRSV LIVERIES
EEIILSTV LEVITIES
VEILIEST
EEIILSTW LEWISITE
EEIIMMTT MIMETITE
EEIIMNOT MEIONITE
EEIIMNST ENMITIES
EEIIMOST MOIETIES
EEIIMPRS RIEMPIES
EEIIMRSS MISERIES
EEIIMSST ITEMISES
EEIIMSSV EMISSIVE
EEIIMSTZ ITEMIZES
EEIINNST NINETIES
EEIINORT ERIONITE
EEIINPPR PIPERINE

EEIINPRS PINERIES
EEIINPRV VIPERINE
EEIINRRV RIVERINE
EEIINRSS RESINISE
SIRENISE
EEIINRST ERINITES
NITERIES
EEIINRSV VINERIES
EEIINRSW WINERIES
EEIINRSZ RESINIZE
SIRENIZE
EEIINRTT INTERTIE
RETINITE
EEIINSSV INESSIVE
EEIINSTT ENTITIES
EEIINSTV INVITEES
VEINIEST
EEIIORSS OSIERIES
EEIIPRSX EXPIRIES
EEIIPRTT EPITRITE
EEIIQSTU EQUITIES
EEIIQTUV QUIETIVE
EEIIRRSV RIVIERES
EEIIRRTV TIRRIVEE
EEIIRSTV VERITIES
EEIISSTV VISITEES
EEIISTVW VIEWIEST
EEIJKRST JERKIEST
EEIJLMSS MEJLISES
EEIJLNNU JULIENNE
EEIJLNRT JETLINER
EEIJLNUV JUVENILE
EEIJMMST JEMMIEST
EEIJNNOR ENJOINER
EEIJSTTT JETTIEST
EEIKLLRS SKELLIER
EEIKLLRY KYRIELLE
EEIKLLSS SKELLIES
EEIKLNSS LIKENESS
EEIKLNST NESTLIKE
EEIKLNSY KEYLINES
EEIKLORS ROSELIKE
EEIKLORT LORIKEET
EEIKLPST PIKELETS
SPIKELET
EEIKLRST TRISKELE
EEIKMRSS KERMISES
EEIKNORS KEROSINE
EEIKNRRT TINKERER
EEIKNRST KERNITES
EEIKOQUV EQUIVOKE
EEIKPPRR KIPPERER
EEIKPRST PERKIEST
EEIKPSST PESKIEST
EEIKRRSS SKERRIES
EEIKRSST KEISTERS
EEIKSSTY SKIEYEST
EEIKSTTT TEKTITES
EEILLMPR IMPELLER
EEILLMRS SMELLIER
EEILLMRU REILLUME
EEILLMST MELLITES
EEILLNOR LONELIER
EEILLNSY SENILELY
EEILLNVV VENVILLE
EEILLORS ORSEILLE
EEILLORV LOVELIER
EEILLOSV LOVELIES
EEILLPSS ELLIPSES
EEILLPSY SLEEPILY

EEILLRSS LEISLERS
EEILLRST TREILLES
EEILLSSV VEILLESS
EEILLSTV EVILLEST
EEILLTVY VELLEITY
EEILLVWY WEEVILLY
EEILMNNS LINESMEN
EEILMNNU ENLUMINE
EEILMNOP PEMOLINE
EEILMNRS ERMELINS
EEILMNRU LEMURINE
RELUMINE
EEILMNSS ISLESMEN
EEILMNSU SELENIUM
SEMILUNE
EEILMOPS POLEMISE
EEILMOPZ POLEMIZE
EEILMORT MOTELIER
EEILMOST MESOLITE
MISLETOE
EEILMPST IMPLETES
EEILMPSX IMPLEXES
EEILMRST TERMLIES
EEILMRSV VERMEILS
EEILMSST TIMELESS
EEILMSUV EMULSIVE
EEILNNST LENIENTS
SENTINEL
EEILNNSV ENLIVENS
EEILNOPR LEPORINE
EEILNORS ELOINERS
EEILNOST NOSELITE
EEILNOSV NOVELISE
EEILNOVZ NOVELIZE
EEILNPPZ ZEPPELIN
EEILNPRS PILSENER
EEILNPRU PERILUNE
EEILNPRV REPLEVIN
EEILNPST PLENTIES
EEILNRSS REINLESS
EEILNRST LISTENER
SILENTER
EEILNRSV LIVENERS
EEILNRTT NETTLIER
EEILNRTY ENTIRELY
LIENTERY
EEILNRUV UNVEILER
EEILNSST SETLINES
EEILNSSV EVILNESS
VILENESS
EEILNSTT ENTITLES
EEILNSTV VEINLETS
EEILOPRS PELORIES
EEILOPST PETIOLES
EEILORRT LOITERER
EEILORRV OVERLIER
EEILORRW LOWERIER
EEILORST LITEROSE
TROELIES
EEILORSV OVERLIES
RELIEVOS
VOLERIES
EEILORSW OWLERIES
EEILORVV OVERLIVE
OVERVEIL
EEILOSST ESTOILES
EEILOSTW OWELTIES
EEILOSTZ ZEOLITES
EEILOSVW VOWELISE
EEILOTTT TOILETTE

EEILOVWZ VOWELIZE
EEILPPSS PIPELESS
EEILPPSY EPILEPSY
EEILPRRS REPLIERS
EEILPRSS SPIELERS
EEILPRST EPISTLER
PELTRIES
PERLITES
REPTILES
EEILPSSS PELISSES
EEILPSST EPISTLES
EEILPSSU EPULISES
EEILPSSV PELVISES
EEILPSTY EPISTYLE
EEILQRSU RELIQUES
EEILRRSV RELIVERS
REVILERS
EEILRSST LEISTERS
RITELESS
TIRELESS
EEILRSSU LEISURES
EEILRSSV SERVILES
EEILRSSW WIRELESS
EEILRSTT RETITLES
EEILSSTW WITELESS
EEILSSTX SEXTILES
EEILSSVW VIEWLESS
EEILSTTX TEXTILES
EEILSTVY STIEVELY
EEIMMNRS IMMENSER
EEIMMORS MEMORIES
MEMORISE
EEIMMORZ MEMORIZE
EEIMMOST SOMETIME
EEIMMRSS IMMERSES
EEIMMRST MERISTEM
MIMESTER
MISMETRE
EEIMMRSU EUMERISM
EEIMMSSS MISSEEMS
EEIMNNOS NOMINEES
EEIMNNRS REINSMEN
EEIMNOPS EPISEMON
EEIMNORS EMERSION
EEIMNORT TIMONEER
EEIMNORV VOMERINE
EEIMNOST MONETISE
SEMITONE
EEIMNOTX XENOTIME
EEIMNOTZ MONETIZE
EEIMNPRT TRIPEMEN
EEIMNPRU PERINEUM
EEIMNPRZ PRIZEMEN
EEIMNPST SEPIMENT
EEIMNQSU MESQUINE
EEIMNRRT TERMINER
EEIMNRRV RIVERMEN
EEIMNRSV MINEVERS
EEIMNRTU MUTINEER
EEIMNRTV VIREMENT
EEIMNSSW MISWEENS
EEIMNSTT MINETTES
EEIMOPRS PROMISEE
REIMPOSE
EEIMOPSS EPISOMES
EEIMOPST EPITOMES
EPSOMITE
EEIMORSS ISOMERES
EEIMORST TIRESOME
EEIMORTV OVERTIME

EEIMORTX OXIMETER
EEIMOSSW SOMEWISE
EEIMOSSX EXOMISES
EEIMPPRS EPISPERM
EEIMPRRS PREMIERS
REPRIMES
SIMPERER
EEIMPRSS EMPRISES
IMPRESES
IMPRESSE
MESPRISE
PREMISES
SPIREMES
EEIMPRST EMPTIERS
EEIMPRSX PREMIXES
EEIMPRSZ MESPRIZE
EEIMPSST SEPTIMES
EEIMPSSY EMPYESIS
EEIMPSTT EMPTIEST
EEIMQRSU REQUIEMS
EEIMQSTU MESQUITE
EEIMRRST MERRIEST
TRIREMES
EEIMRRTT REMITTER
TRIMETER
EEIMRSST TRISEMES
EEIMRSTT EMITTERS
TERMITES
EEIMRSTU EMERITUS
EEIMRTTY TEMERITY
EEIMSSST MESSIEST
METISSES
EEINNNPS PENNINES
EEINNPTT PENITENT
EEINNRST INTENSER
INTERNES
EEINNRSU NEURINES
EEINNRSV INNERVES
NERVINES
EEINNRTT INTERNET
RENITENT
EEINNRUX XENURINE
EEINNSST TENNISES
EEINNSTT SENTIENT
EEINNSTW ENTWINES
WENNIEST
EEINOPPR PEPERINO
PEPERONI
EEINOPRS ISOPRENE
PIONEERS
EEINORRT REORIENT
EEINORSS ESSOINER
EEINORST SEROTINE
EEINORSV EVERSION
EEINORTT TENORITE
EEINORTX EXERTION
EEINOSST ESSONITE
EEINOSTT NOISETTE
TEOSINTE
EEINPPSS PEPSINES
EEINPRRS REPINERS
EEINPRSS EREPSINS
RIPENESS
EEINPRSU PENURIES
RESUPINE
EEINPRTX INEXPERT
EEINPSST PENTISES
EEINPSTT INEPTEST
SPINETTE
EEINQRRU ENQUIRER

EEINQRSU ENQUIRES
INQUERES
SQUIREEN
EEINQSTU QUIETENS
EEINQSUY QUEYNIES
EEINRRSS RESINERS
EEINRRST INSERTER
REINSERT
REINTERS
RENTIERS
TERRINES
EEINRRSU REINSURE
EEINRRSV VERNIERS
EEINRRTV INVERTER
EEINRRTX INTERREX
EEINRSST INTERESS
SENTRIES
TRENISES
EEINRSSU ENURESIS
EEINRSSV INVERSES
VERSINES
EEINRSTT INERTEST
INTEREST
STERNITE
EEINRSTU ESURIENT
NEURITES
RETINUES
REUNITES
EEINRSTV NERVIEST
REINVEST
SERVIENT
SIRVENTE
EEINRSTX INTERSEX
EEINRSTY SERENITY
EEINRSUV UNIVERSE
EEINRSWW NEWSWIRE
EEINRTTY ENTIRETY
ETERNITY
EEINSSST SESTINES
EEINSSSW WISENESS
EEINSSSX SEXINESS
EEINSSTW NEWSIEST
EEINSSTX SIXTEENS
EEINSSTY SYENITES
EEINSTTT NETTIEST
TENTIEST
EEINSTTW TENTWISE
TWENTIES
EEINSTTX EXISTENT
EEIOPPRS EPISPORE
POPERIES
EEIOPPST EPITOPES
EEIOPRRS ROPERIES
EEIOPRRT PORTIERE
EEIOPRRV OVERRIPE
EEIOPRST POETRIES
EEIOPSST POETISES
EEIOPSTZ POETIZES
EEIORRRS ORRERIES
EEIORRSS ROSERIES
ROSIERES
EEIORRTV OVERTIRE
EEIORRTW TOWERIER
EEIORRTX EXTERIOR
EEIORRUV OUVRIERE
EEIORSST EROTESIS
EEIORSSX OREXISES
EEIORSVW OVERWISE
EEIORSVZ OVERSIZE
EEIORVVW OVERVIEW

EEIORVWW	WIREWOVE
EEIPPPRR	PREPPIER
EEIPPPRS	PREPPIES
EEIPPPST	PEPPIEST
EEIPPRRS	PERSPIRE
EEIPPRTY	PERIPETY
EEIPPSST	PEPTISES
EEIPPSTT	PIPETTES
EEIPPSTZ	PEPTIZES
EEIPQRSU	PERIQUES
	REPIQUES
EEIPRRRS	PERRIERS
EEIPRRSS	REPRISES
	RESPIRES
EEIPRRSV	REPRIVES
EEIPRRSZ	REPRIZES
EEIPRRTT	PRETERIT
	PRETTIER
EEIPRSSS	PRESSIES
EEIPRSST	RESPITES
EEIPRSSV	PREVISES
EEIPRSTT	PRETTIES
EEIPRSTY	PERSEITY
EEIPRSVW	PREVIEWS
EEIPRSZZ	PREZZIES
EEIPRTUV	ERUPTIVE
EEIPSSSS	SPEISSES
EEIPSSTW	SPEWIEST
	STEPWISE
EEIPSTTT	PETTIEST
EEIQRRRU	REQUIRER
EEIQRRSU	REQUIRES
EEIQRRTU	REQUITER
EEIQRRUV	VERQUIRE
EEIQRSSU	ESQUIRES
EEIQRSTU	QUIETERS
	REQUITES
EEIQRSTW	QWERTIES
EEIQRTUY	QUEERITY
EEIQSSSU	ESQUISSE
EEIQSTTU	QUIETEST
EEIRRRST	RETIRERS
	TERRIERS
EEIRRSST	TRESSIER
EEIRRSSV	REVERSIS
	REVISERS
EEIRRSTV	REVERIST
	RIVERETS
	RIVETERS
EEIRRSTW	REWRITES
EEIRRSVV	REVIVERS
EEIRRTTT	TITTERER
EEIRSSSU	REISSUES
EEIRSSSV	IVRESSES
EEIRSSTT	RESTIEST
EEIRSSTU	SURETIES
EEIRSSTV	SIEVERTS
	TREVISES
	VESTRIES
EEIRSSUZ	SEIZURES
EEIRSTVV	VETIVERS
EEIRSTVY	SEVERITY
EEIRTTTZ	TERZETTI
EEISSTTT	TESTIEST
EEISSTTU	SUETIEST
EEISSTTV	STIEVEST
EEISSTTW	STEWIEST
EEISSTTZ	ZESTIEST
EEISTTTX	TETTIXES
EEISTUXZ	ZEUXITES
EEJJLNUY	JEJUNELY
EEJKMOOS	JOKESOME
EEJLLMSU	JUMELLES
EEJLLORY	JOLLEYER
EEJLPSTU	PULSEJET
EEJNOORS	REJONEOS
EEJNORSY	ENJOYERS
EEJPRRRU	PERJURER
EEJPRRSU	PERJURES
EEJPRSTU	SUPERJET
EEJQRRSU	JERQUERS
EEKKORWW	WORKWEEK
EEKKOSTV	VETKOEKS
EEKKRRST	TREKKERS
EEKLLNRY	KERNELLY
EEKLLNSV	KNEVELLS
EEKLLSUU	UKULELES
EEKLNNNU	UNKENNEL
EEKLNOSS	KEELSONS
EEKLNOST	SKELETON
EEKLNOSV	VELSKOEN
EEKLRSST	KESTRELS
	SKELTERS
EEKNOPRS	RESPOKEN
EEKNOSTY	KEYNOTES
	KEYSTONE
EEKNSSSW	SKEWNESS
EEKNSSTU	NETSUKES
EEKOORST	KREOSOTE
EEKOPRTV	OVERKEPT
EEKORSTV	OVERKEST
EEKRRTUZ	KREUTZER
EELLMORW	MELLOWER
EELLMPTU	PLUMELET
EELLMRSS	SMELLERS
EELLMRSV	VERMELLS
EELLNORR	ENROLLER
EELLNOUV	NOUVELLE
EELLNPRU	PRUNELLE
EELLNRSU	SULLENER
EELLNSST	SNELLEST
EELLNSSW	WELLNESS
EELLNSTU	ENTELLUS
EELLOPSS	ELLOPSES
EELLORSS	ROSELLES
EELLORST	SOLLERET
EELLORSV	OVERSELL
EELLORSZ	ROZELLES
EELLORTX	EXTOLLER
EELLORVY	VOLLEYER
EELLORWY	YELLOWER
EELLOSSV	LOVELESS
EELLOSUV	LEVULOSE
EELLPRSS	RESPELLS
	SPELLERS
EELLQRSU	QUELLERS
EELLRSSU	RULELESS
EELLRSSW	SWELLERS
EELLSSTU	TELLUSES
EELLSSTW	SWELLEST
EELMMPSU	EMPLUMES
EELMMPUX	EXEMPLUM
EELMNOOS	LONESOME
	OENOMELS
EELMNORS	SOLEMNER
EELMNSUY	UNSEEMLY
EELMNTTU	TEMULENT
EELMNTUY	UNMEETLY
EELMOOSV	LOVESOME
EELMOPRS	PLEROMES
EELMOPRY	EMPLOYER
EELMOPST	LEPTOMES
EELMOPSY	POLYSEME
EELMORST	MOLESTER
EELMORSW	EELWORMS
EELMORTY	MOTLEYER
	REMOTELY
EELMOSSV	MOVELESS
EELMOTVW	TWELVEMO
EELMPPRU	EMPURPLE
EELMPSST	SEMPLEST
	STEMPELS
	STEMPLES
EELMPSTT	TEMPLETS
EELMRRTU	MURRELET
EELMRSST	SMELTERS
	TERMLESS
EELMRSTY	SMELTERY
EELMRTUX	LUXMETER
EELMSSST	STEMLESS
EELMSSTT	STEMLETS
EELNNOSS	LONENESS
EELNNRTU	TUNNELER
EELNNUVY	UNEVENLY
EELNOORS	LOOSENER
EELNOPPU	UNPEOPLE
EELNOPRT	PETRONEL
EELNOPSV	ENVELOPS
EELNOPTY	POLYTENE
EELNOQTU	ELOQUENT
EELNORST	ENTRESOL
EELNORTT	TELETRON
EELNORTV	OVERLENT
EELNOSSS	NOSELESS
	SOLENESS
EELNOSST	NOTELESS
	TONELESS
EELNOSSU	SELENOUS
EELNOSSY	ESLOYNES
EELNOSSZ	ZONELESS
EELNOSTT	NOTELETS
EELNOSTU	TOLUENES
EELNOTVV	EVOLVENT
EELNRSST	SLENTERS
EELNRSTT	LETTERNS
EELNRSUV	NERVULES
EELNSSSW	NEWSLESS
EELNSSTT	TENTLESS
EELNSSTU	TUNELESS
	UNSTEELS
EELNSSTY	ENSTYLES
EELNSSUV	UNSELVES
EELNSTTU	LUNETTES
	UNSETTLE
EELOPPSS	PEPLOSES
EELOPPST	ESTOPPEL
EELOPRRX	EXPLORER
EELOPRSX	EXPLORES
EELOPRTT	TELEPORT
EELOPSTU	EELPOUTS
	OUTSLEEP
EELOQRUY	REQUOYLE
EELORRSV	RESOLVER
EELORRTV	REVOLTER
EELORRUV	OVERRULE
EELORRVV	REVOLVER
EELORSSS	ROSELESS
EELORSSV	RESOLVES
EELORSTT	LORETTES
EELORSTU	RESOLUTE
EELORSVV	EVOLVERS
	REVOLVES
EELORTTU	ROULETTE
EELORTUV	REVOLUTE
EELOSSST	OSSELETS
EELOSSSU	SOLEUSES
EELOSSTT	TELEOSTS
EELOSSTU	SETULOSE
EELOSSTV	VOTELESS
EELOSTTX	SEXTOLET
EELOSTUV	EVOLUTES
	VELOUTES
EELPPSSU	PEPLUSES
EELPPSTU	SEPTUPLE
EELPQRSU	PREQUELS
EELPRSST	SPELTERS
EELPRSSU	REPULSES
EELPRSTZ	PRETZELS
EELPRSUX	PLEXURES
EELPRTXY	EXPERTLY
EELPSSUX	EXPULSES
	PLEXUSES
EELPSTUX	SEXTUPLE
EELRRSTW	WRESTLER
EELRSSST	RESTLESS
	TRESSELS
EELRSSTT	SETTLERS
	STERLETS
	TRESTLES
EELRSSTW	SWELTERS
	WRESTLES
EELRSSTY	RESTYLES
	TYRELESS
EELRSSTZ	SELTZERS
EELRSTWY	WESTERLY
EELSSTTV	SVELTEST
EELSSTTX	TEXTLESS
EELSSTUY	EUSTYLES
EEMMNNOY	MONEYMEN
EEMMNOOP	MENOPOME
EEMMNOST	MEMENTOS
EEMMNOTV	MOVEMENT
EEMMNRRY	MERRYMEN
EEMMOORS	MEROSOME
EEMMOSSU	MOUSMEES
EEMMRSST	STEMMERS
EEMNNOPW	PENWOMEN
EEMNNOSV	ENVENOMS
EEMNOOSS	SOMEONES
EEMNOOSY	MOONEYES
EEMNOPRS	PROSEMEN
EEMNORRS	SERMONER
EEMNORST	SERMONET
	STOREMEN
EEMNORSU	MOUNSEER
EEMNORSV	OVERSMEN
EEMNORSY	MONEYERS
EEMNORTU	ROUTEMEN
EEMNPRSS	PRESSMEN
EEMNPRSU	SUPERMEN
EEMNPRTU	ERUMPENT
	UNTEMPER
EEMNRSTU	MUENSTER
EEMNRSTW	TREWSMEN
EEMNSSTU	MUTENESS
	TENESMUS
EEMNSTTV	VESTMENT
EEMOORRV	MOREOVER
EEMOORTT	ROOMETTE
EEMOOSSX	EXOSMOSE

EEMOPRRS	EMPERORS
	PREMORSE
EEMOPRSV	PREMOVES
EEMOPRSW	EMPOWERS
EEMOQTTU	MOQUETTE
EEMORRSS	REMORSES
EEMORRSU	UROMERES
EEMORRSV	REMOVERS
EEMORRTU	MOUTERER
	OUTREMER
EEMORSST	SOMERSET
EEMORSTT	REMOTEST
EEMORSTU	TEMEROUS
EEMOTTTU	TEETOTUM
EEMPRRSU	PRESUMER
	SUPREMER
EEMPRSST	SEMPSTER
EEMPRSSU	PRESUMES
	SUPREMES
EEMPRSTT	TEMPTERS
EEMPRSTU	PERMUTES
EEMPSSTT	TEMPESTS
EEMPSSTY	EMPTYSES
EEMRRSTU	MUSTERER
EEMRRSUU	REMUEURS
EEMRRTTU	MUTTERER
EEMSSTTU	MUSETTES
EENNNOSS	NONSENSE
EENNNPTY	TENPENNY
EENNOORT	ROTENONE
EENNOPSS	OPENNESS
EENNOPTX	EXPONENT
EENNORRW	RENOWNER
EENNORST	TENONERS
EENNORSU	NEURONES
EENNOSTT	NONETTES
EENNQSUU	UNQUEENS
EENNRSUV	UNNERVES
EENNSSSU	UNSENSES
EENNSSTX	NEXTNESS
EENOORST	ROESTONE
EENOORTV	OVERTONE
EENOPPRS	PREPONES
	PROPENES
	PROPENSE
EENOPPST	PEPTONES
EENOPRSS	RESPONSE
EENOPRST	PROTENSE
EENOPRSU	PERONEUS
EENOPRTT	ENTREPOT
EENOPRXY	PYROXENE
EENOPSST	PENTOSES
	POSTEENS
EENORRSV	OVERRENS
EENORRTT	ROTTENER
EENORSSS	SORENESS
EENORSSU	NEUROSES
EENORSTT	ONSETTER
EENORSTV	OVERNETS
EENORSTX	EXTENSOR
EENORSVW	OVERSEWN
EENORTVW	OVERWENT
EENOSSST	STENOSES
EENOSSSY	ESSOYNES
EENPPRST	PERPENTS
EENPRSST	PERTNESS
	PRESENTS
	SERPENTS
EENPRSSU	PURENESS
EENPRSTT	STREPENT
EENPRSTV	PREVENTS
EENPSSSU	SUSPENSE
EENPSSTY	STEPNEYS
EENPSTTU	PETUNTSE
EENPTTUZ	PETUNTZE
EENQSSTU	SEQUENTS
EENRRRTU	RETURNER
EENRRSSU	ENSURERS
EENRRSTV	RENVERST
EENRRSUV	NERVURES
EENRRTUV	VENTURER
EENRSSSU	SURENESS
EENRSSTT	STERNEST
	TESTERNS
EENRSSTU	TRUENESS
EENRSSTW	WESTERNS
EENRSSTY	STYRENES
EENRSTUV	VENTURES
EEOOPRST	PROTEOSE
EEOOPRSX	EXOSPORE
EEOOPRTZ	ZOETROPE
EEOORRVW	OVERWORE
EEOPPRSS	PORPESSE
	PREPOSES
EEOPPSTU	OUTPEEPS
EEOPRRRT	REPORTER
EEOPRRRV	REPROVER
EEOPRRSU	REPOSURE
EEOPRRSV	REPROVES
EEOPRRTT	POTTERER
EEOPRRTX	EXPORTER
EEOPRSSS	ESPRESSO
EEOPRSST	PORTESSE
EEOPRSSU	ESPOUSER
	REPOUSSE
EEOPRSSX	EXPOSERS
	EXPRESSO
EEOPRSTT	TREETOPS
EEOPRSTU	OUTPEERS
EEOPRSTV	OVERSTEP
EEOPRSTY	SEROTYPE
EEOPRSUX	EXPOSURE
EEOPSSSU	ESPOUSES
	POSEUSES
EEOPSSTW	SWEETSOP
EEOPSTUW	OUTWEEPS
EEOQRSTU	REQUOTES
EEOQRTTU	ROQUETTE
EEORRRST	RESORTER
	RESTORER
	RETRORSE
EEORRRTT	RETORTER
EEORRSST	RESTORES
EEORRSSV	REVERSOS
EEORRSTU	REROUTES
EEORRSTV	EVERTORS
EEORRSTX	EXTRORSE
EEORRTTT	TOTTERER
EEORRTUV	OVERTURE
	TROUVERE
EEORSSST	OSSETERS
EEORSSTT	ROSETTES
EEORSSTV	ESTOVERS
	OVERSETS
EEORSSUV	OVERUSES
EEORSSVW	OVERSEWS
EEORSTVX	VORTEXES
EEORTTTZ	TERZETTO
EEOSSSVW	VOWESSES
EEOSSTTT	SESTETTO
EEPPRSST	STEPPERS
EEPPSSUW	UPSWEEPS
EEPQRRUU	PERRUQUE
EEPRRSSS	PRESSERS
EEPRRSSU	PERUSERS
	PRESSURE
EEPRRSTV	PERVERTS
EEPRRSVY	REPRYVES
EEPRSSTT	PRETESTS
EEPRSSTX	SEXPERTS
EEPRSTTU	UPSETTER
EEPRSTTX	PRETEXTS
EEQRSSTU	QUESTERS
	REQUESTS
EERRSSTU	TRESSURE
EERRSSTW	STREWERS
	WRESTERS
EERRSSVW	SWERVERS
EERRSTTU	REUTTERS
	UTTERERS
EERRSTUV	VESTURER
EERRSTVY	REVESTRY
EERRSUVY	RESURVEY
EERSSSST	STRESSES
EERSSSTU	ESTRUSES
EERSSSUY	SEYSURES
EERSSTTU	TRUSTEES
EERSSTUV	VESTURES
EERSSUVW	SURVEWES
EERSTTTU	UTTEREST
EERSTTUX	TEXTURES
EESSSTTT	SESTETTS
EESSTTTX	SEXTETTS
EFFFGINO	FEOFFING
EFFFILRU	FLUFFIER
EFFFISTU	FUFFIEST
EFFFOORS	FEOFFORS
EFFGILRU	GRIEFFUL
EFFGINOR	OFFERING
EFFGINSU	EFFUSING
EFFGRSTU	GRUFFEST
EFFHIIRW	WHIFFIER
EFFHIISW	FISHWIFE
EFFHIITT	FIFTIETH
EFFHILRW	WHIFFLER
EFFHILSW	WHIFFLES
EFFHIRSS	SHERIFFS
EFFHIRSW	WHIFFERS
EFFHISTU	HUFFIEST
EFFHISTW	WHIFFETS
EFFHLRSU	SHUFFLER
EFFHLSSU	SHUFFLES
EFFHOORS	OFFSHORE
EFFIIMST	MIFFIEST
EFFIINRS	SNIFFIER
EFFIINSS	IFFINESS
EFFIINST	NIFFIEST
EFFIIPRS	SPIFFIER
EFFIKLSS	SKIFFLES
EFFILNRS	SNIFFLER
EFFILNSS	SNIFFLES
EFFILORT	FORELIFT
EFFILPRS	PIFFLERS
EFFILPRU	PLUFFIER
EFFILRRS	RIFFLERS
EFFILRSU	SIFFLEUR
EFFINOSU	EFFUSION
EFFINRSS	SNIFFERS
EFFINRSU	SNUFFIER
EFFINSST	STIFFENS
EFFIOPRS	PIFFEROS
EFFIORST	FORFEITS
EFFIOSTT	TOFFIEST
EFFIPSTU	PUFFIEST
EFFIQRSU	SQUIFFER
EFFIRSTT	TRIFFEST
EFFIRSTU	STUFFIER
EFFISSTT	STIFFEST
EFFISSUX	SUFFIXES
EFFLMNUU	UNMUFFLE
EFFLMRSU	MUFFLERS
EFFLNRSU	SNUFFLER
EFFLNRUU	UNRUFFLE
EFFLNSSU	SNUFFLES
EFFLOSSU	SOUFFLES
EFFLRRSU	RUFFLERS
EFFLRSTU	TRUFFLES
EFFNRSSU	SNUFFERS
EFFOOORT	FOREFOOT
EFFOORRS	OFFERORS
EFFOPRRS	PROFFERS
EFFORRUV	OVERRUFF
EFFRSSTU	STUFFERS
EFFSSSUU	SUFFUSES
EFGGGILN	FLEGGING
EFGGIINN	FEIGNING
EFGGILOS	SOLFEGGI
EFGGINRU	REFUGING
EFGGIORR	FROGGIER
EFGGIOST	FOGGIEST
EFGGIRRS	FRIGGERS
EFGGISTU	FUGGIEST
EFGGORRY	FROGGERY
EFGHILNS	FLESHING
	SHELFING
EFGHINRS	FRESHING
EFGHINRT	FRIGHTEN
EFGHIOSY	FOGEYISH
EFGHIRST	FIGHTERS
	FREIGHTS
EFGHNOTU	FOUGHTEN
EFGIILNU	FIGULINE
EFGIILSU	UGLIFIES
EFGIIMNS	MISFEIGN
EFGIINNR	ENFIRING
	INFRINGE
	REFINING
EFGIINNT	FEINTING
EFGIINNX	ENFIXING
EFGIINRR	FRINGIER
EFGIINRU	FIGURINE
EFGIINRY	REIFYING
EFGIINRZ	FRIEZING
EFGIITUV	FUGITIVE
EFGIKNOR	FOREKING
EFGILLNO	LIFELONG
EFGILLNU	FUELLING
EFGILLUU	GUILEFUL
EFGILMOR	FILMGOER
EFGILNNS	FLENSING
EFGILNOR	FLORIGEN
EFGILNRS	FLINGERS
EFGILNRY	FERLYING
EFGILNSS	SELFINGS
EFGILNST	FELTINGS
EFGILNTT	FETTLING
EFGILSTU	GULFIEST
EFGIMNST	FIGMENTS
EFGIMOSY	FOGEYISM
EFGIMRUU	REFUGIUM

EFGINNNP	PFENNING
EFGINNPS	PFENNIGS
EFGINNRS	FERNINGS
EFGINORV	FORGIVEN
EFGINORW	FOREWING
EFGINPUY	PINGUEFY
EFGINRRY	FERRYING
EFGINRSU	GUNFIRES
	REFUSING
EFGINRSW	SWERFING
EFGINRTT	FRETTING
EFGINRTU	FEUTRING
	REFUTING
EFGINRTY	GENTRIFY
EFGIOOST	GOOFIEST
EFGIOPTT	PETTIFOG
EFGIORSV	FORGIVES
EFGIRRST	GRIFTERS
EFGLOOVX	FOXGLOVE
EFGLORST	FROGLETS
EFGLRSUU	SURGEFUL
EFGLSSTU	SLUGFEST
EFGNOSST	SONGFEST
EFGNSSUU	FUNGUSES
EFGORRSU	FERRUGOS
EFGORSTU	FOREGUTS
EFHHIRSS	FRESHISH
EFHIILRT	FILTHIER
EFHIILST	TILEFISH
EFHIIMSU	HUMIFIES
EFHIINRS	FINISHER
EFHIINSS	FINISHES
EFHIIPPS	PIPEFISH
EFHIIPRS	FIRESHIP
EFHIIRST	SHIFTIER
EFHIISST	FISHIEST
EFHILRSU	FLUSHIER
EFHILTWY	WHITEFLY
EFHIOOOR	FORHOOIE
EFHIOPRS	FORESHIP
EFHIORRT	FROTHIER
EFHIORSS	ROSEFISH
EFHIORSV	OVERFISH
EFHIORTT	FORTIETH
EFHIPRSS	SERFSHIP
EFHIPRSU	FURPHIES
EFHIRRTU	THURIFER
EFHIRSST	SHIFTERS
EFHISSTU	SHUFTIES
EFHKLNOU	FUNKHOLE
EFHLLLSU	SHELLFUL
EFHLNORS	HORNFELS
EFHLOOSS	HOOFLESS
EFHLOOSX	FOXHOLES
EFHLOPSU	HOPEFULS
EFHLORSY	HORSEFLY
EFHLOSSU	FLOUSHES
EFHLOSUU	HOUSEFUL
EFHLOSUY	HOUSEFLY
EFHLRSSU	FLUSHERS
EFHLSSTU	FLUSHEST
EFHLSTTW	TWELFTHS
EFHNORST	FORHENTS
EFHOORSW	FORESHOW
EFHORRTY	FROTHERY
EFHRRSTU	FURTHERS
EFHRSTTU	FURTHEST
EFIIILRV	VILIFIER
EFIIILSV	VILIFIES
EFIIIMNS	MINIFIES
EFIIINNT	INFINITE
EFIIIRVV	VIVIFIER
EFIIISTX	FIXITIES
EFIIISVV	VIVIFIES
EFIIKLRS	FLISKIER
EFIIKRRS	FRISKIER
EFIILLNT	TEFILLIN
EFIILLRR	FRILLIER
EFIILLRS	FRILLIES
EFIILMRS	FLIMSIER
EFIILMSS	FLIMSIES
	MISFILES
EFIILMST	FILMIEST
EFIILNRT	FLINTIER
EFIILNTY	FELINITY
	FINITELY
EFIILOQU	FILIOQUE
EFIILRRT	FLIRTIER
EFIILRSU	FUSILIER
EFIILSTT	FITLIEST
EFIIMMNS	FEMINISM
EFIIMNOS	FISNOMIE
	OMNIFIES
EFIIMNRR	INFIRMER
EFIIMNST	FEMINIST
EFIIMNSU	MUNIFIES
EFIIMNTY	FEMINITY
EFIIMRSS	MISFIRES
EFIINNST	FINNIEST
EFIINORR	INFERIOR
EFIINORT	NOTIFIER
EFIINOST	NOTIFIES
EFIINPSV	FIVEPINS
EFIINPSX	SPINIFEX
EFIINRRT	FERRITIN
EFIINRST	SNIFTIER
EFIINRSU	UNIFIERS
EFIINRSY	RESINIFY
EFIINSTT	NIFTIEST
EFIINSUV	INFUSIVE
EFIIOSSS	OSSIFIES
EFIIPRRU	PURIFIER
EFIIPRST	SPITFIRE
EFIIPRSU	PURIFIES
EFIIPRTY	TYPIFIER
EFIIPSTY	TYPIFIES
EFIIRRST	FIRRIEST
EFIIRRTU	FRUITIER
EFIIRRZZ	FRIZZIER
EFIIRSTT	RIFTIEST
EFIIRTUV	FRUITIVE
EFIIRVVY	REVIVIFY
EFIISSTT	FISTIEST
EFIISTZZ	FIZZIEST
EFIJLORS	FRIJOLES
EFIJLOST	JETFOILS
EFIKLNSU	FLUNKIES
EFIKLOOR	ROOFLIKE
EFIKLORS	FOLKSIER
EFIKLSTU	FLUKIEST
EFIKNNOS	FINNESKO
EFIKNORS	FORESKIN
EFIKNRSU	REFUSNIK
EFIKNSTU	FUNKIEST
EFIKORRW	FIREWORK
EFIKORST	FORKIEST
EFIKRRSS	FRISKERS
EFIKRSST	FRISKETS
EFILLLNU	FLUELLIN
EFILLMSU	SMILEFUL
EFILLOOS	FOLIOLES
EFILLORV	OVERFILL
EFILLRUY	IREFULLY
EFILLSTY	STELLIFY
EFILLTUY	FUTILELY
EFILMNSU	FULMINES
EFILMOST	FILEMOTS
EFILMRSS	FIRMLESS
EFILMSSS	SELFISMS
EFILMSST	FILMSETS
	LEFTISMS
EFILMSUY	EMULSIFY
EFILNNTU	INFLUENT
EFILNORU	FLUORINE
EFILNOSU	NOISEFUL
EFILNOSX	FLEXIONS
EFILNRTT	FLITTERN
EFILNSUX	INFLUXES
EFILNUWY	UNWIFELY
EFILOOSS	FLOOSIES
EFILOOSZ	FLOOZIES
EFILOPPR	FLOPPIER
EFILOPPS	FLOPPIES
EFILOPRR	PROFILER
EFILOPRS	PROFILES
EFILORRU	FLOURIER
EFILORSS	FLOSSIER
EFILORST	FLORIEST
	TREFOILS
EFILORTU	FLUORITE
EFILOSSX	SEXFOILS
EFILOSTT	LOFTIEST
EFILOSTU	OUTFLIES
EFILPPRS	FLIPPERS
EFILPPST	FLIPPEST
EFILPPSU	PIPEFULS
EFILPRTU	UPLIFTER
EFILPSTU	SPITEFUL
EFILRRST	TRIFLERS
EFILRRSU	FLURRIES
EFILRSST	RIFTLESS
	STIFLERS
EFILRSTT	FLITTERS
EFILRSTW	FEWTRILS
EFILRSVV	FLIVVERS
EFILRSZZ	FRIZZLES
EFILRTTU	FRUITLET
EFILSSST	SELFISTS
EFILSSTT	LEFTISTS
EFILSSTU	SULFITES
EFILSTTU	FLUTIEST
	FUTILEST
EFILSTTW	SWIFTLET
EFIMMRSU	FERMIUMS
EFIMNORR	INFORMER
	REINFORM
	RENIFORM
EFIMNORS	ENSIFORM
	FERMIONS
EFIMNRSS	FIRMNESS
EFIMNSTT	FITMENTS
EFIMORRT	RETIFORM
EFIMORRW	FIREWORM
EFIMORST	SETIFORM
EFIMOSTT	OFTTIMES
EFIMPRRU	FRUMPIER
EFIMRSTU	FREMITUS
EFINNORS	INFERNOS
EFINNSTU	FUNNIEST
EFINOPRS	FORPINES
EFINOPTX	PONTIFEX
EFINORRT	FRONTIER
EFINORSU	REFUSION
EFINOSSX	FOXINESS
EFINOSSZ	FOZINESS
EFINRSST	SNIFTERS
EFINRSSU	INFUSERS
EFINRTTU	UNFITTER
EFIOOPST	POOFIEST
EFIOORST	ROOFIEST
EFIOOSTT	FOOTIEST
EFIOOSTW	WOOFIEST
EFIOPRRS	PORIFERS
EFIOPRRT	PROFITER
EFIOPRST	FIREPOTS
EFIORRST	FROSTIER
	ROTIFERS
EFIORRSW	FROWSIER
EFIORRTT	RETROFIT
EFIORRWZ	FROWZIER
EFIORSST	FOISTERS
EFIORSTU	FOUSTIER
EFIORSTW	FROWIEST
EFIPPRRS	FRIPPERS
EFIPPRRY	FRIPPERY
EFIPRRUY	REPURIFY
EFIPRTTY	PRETTIFY
EFIRRRSU	FURRIERS
EFIRRRUY	FURRIERY
EFIRRSSU	FRISEURS
	FRISURES
EFIRRSTT	FRITTERS
EFIRRSTU	FRITURES
	FRUITERS
	FURRIEST
EFIRRTUV	FURTIVER
EFIRRTUY	FRUITERY
EFIRSSSU	FISSURES
EFIRSSTU	SURFEITS
	SURFIEST
EFIRSSTW	SWIFTERS
EFIRSTTU	TURFIEST
	TURFITES
EFIRSTUX	FIXTURES
EFIRSTUZ	FURZIEST
EFISSSTU	FUSSIEST
EFISSTTU	FUSTIEST
EFISSTTW	SWIFTEST
EFISTTTU	TUFTIEST
EFISTUZZ	FUZZIEST
EFKLLOOR	FOLKLORE
EFKLMNOS	MENFOLKS
EFKLMORS	MERFOLKS
EFKLNSUY	FLUNKEYS
EFKLOPSU	POKEFULS
EFKLORUW	FLUEWORK
EFKLPSSU	SKEPFULS
EFKNOORW	FOREKNOW
EFKOOPRS	FORSPOKE
EFKORRTW	FRETWORK
EFLLLOOW	WOOLFELL
EFLLLOWY	FELLOWLY
EFLLLPSU	SPELLFUL
EFLLNSSU	FULLNESS
EFLLNTUY	FLUENTLY
EFLLOORW	FOLLOWER
EFLLOOTW	FOOTWELL
EFLLORUV	OVERFULL
EFLLOUWY	WOEFULLY
EFLLRUUY	RUEFULLY

EFLLSUUY USEFULLY
EFLMMRUY FLUMMERY
EFLMNRUU FRENULUM
EFLMORRY FORMERLY
EFLMORSS FORMLESS
EFLMORSU FULSOMER
EFLMPRSU FRUMPLES
EFLNOOSU FELONOUS
EFLNORSU FLEURONS
EFLNORTT FRONTLET
EFLNOSSU FOULNESS
SULFONES
EFLNOSTT FLETTONS
FONTLETS
EFLNOSTY STONEFLY
EFLNSSTU NESTFULS
EFLNSSUY SYNFUELS
EFLNSTTU TENTFULS
EFLNSUUU UNUSEFUL
EFLOORRS FLOORERS
EFLOORSS FORSLOES
ROOFLESS
EFLOORSW FORESLOW
EFLOORSZ FOOZLERS
EFLOORTU FOOTRULE
EFLOORVW OVERFLOW
EFLOOSST FOOTLESS
EFLOPRUW POWERFUL
EFLORRUY RYEFLOUR
EFLORSTT FORTLETS
EFLORSTW FELWORTS
EFLORSUY YOURSELF
EFLORSVY FLYOVERS
EFLOSUUX FLEXUOUS
EFLPRSSU PRESSFUL
EFLPRSUU PURSEFUL
EFLRSSTU FLUSTERS
EFLRSTTU FLUTTERS
EFLRSTUU FRUSTULE
EFLRSTUY FLUSTERY
EFMNNORT FRONTMEN
EFMNORTY FROMENTY
EFMNRTUY FRUMENTY
FURMENTY
EFMOORST FOREMOST
EFMOORSU FOURSOME
EFMOPRRS PERFORMS
PREFORMS
EFMOPRST POMFRETS
EFNNOOOR FORENOON
EFNNORST FORNENST
EFNNORUZ UNFROZEN
EFNOOOTT FOOTNOTE
EFNOOPRT PENTROOF
EFNOOSST EFTSOONS
FESTOONS
EFNOPRST FORSPENT
EFNORRST RENFORST
EFNORRSU FORERUNS
EFNORSTU FORTUNES
EFNOSSST SOFTNESS
EFNRSSTU FUNSTERS
EFOOORST FOOTSORE
EFOOPRRS REPROOFS
EFOOPRSS SPOOFERS
EFOOPRST FORETOPS
POOFTERS
EFOOPRSY SPOOFERY
EFOOPSTT FOOTSTEP
EFOORRSW FORSWORE
EFOORSTT FOOTREST
EFOORSTW WOOFTERS
EFOOSTUX OUTFOXES
EFOPRRSU PROFUSER
EFOPRSTU POUFTERS
EFORRSST FORTRESS
EFORRSTW FROWSTER
EFORRSTY FORESTRY
EFORRSUV FERVOURS
EFORRTTU FROTTEUR
EFORSSST FOSTRESS
EGGGIILR GIGGLIER
EGGGILNS LEGGINGS
EGGGILOR GOGGLIER
EGGGILRS GIGGLERS
EGGGINPS PEGGINGS
EGGGIORR GROGGIER
EGGGLORS GOGGLERS
EGGGNNOR RONGGENG
EGGGOOOS GOOSEGOG
EGGGORRY GROGGERY
EGGHIINN NEIGHING
EGGHIINW WEIGHING
EGGHILRS HIGGLERS
EGGHINSS GHESSING
EGGHIRST THIGGERS
EGGHLOSS SHOGGLES
EGGHRTUY THUGGERY
EGGIIJLR JIGGLIER
EGGIILNR NIGGLIER
EGGIILRW WIGGLIER
EGGIINNN ENGINING
EGGIINNR GREINING
REIGNING
EGGIINNS SINGEING
EGGIINNT TINGEING
EGGIINNW WINGEING
EGGIINRV GRIEVING
REGIVING
EGGIIPST PIGGIEST
EGGIIRTW TWIGGIER
EGGIKNOS GINGKOES
GINKGOES
EGGILLNY GINGELLY
EGGILMNU EMULGING
EGGILMSS LEGGISMS
EGGILNNO LONGEING
EGGILNNT GENTLING
GLENTING
EGGILNNU LUNGEING
EGGILNRS NIGGLERS
SNIGGLER
EGGILNRU GRUELING
EGGILNRY GINGERLY
EGGILNSS SNIGGLES
EGGILNSU LUGEINGS
EGGILOOS GOOGLIES
EGGILQSU SQUIGGLE
EGGILRRW WRIGGLER
EGGILRSW WIGGLERS
WRIGGLES
EGGIMNNU EMUNGING
EGGIMORS SMOGGIER
EGGIMSTU MUGGIEST
EGGINNNR GRENNING
EGGINNOR ENGORING
EGGINNSS GINSENGS
EGGINORR GORGERIN
ROGERING
EGGINOUV VOGUEING
EGGINRRU GRUNGIER
REURGING
EGGINRSS GRESSING
SNIGGERS
EGGINRSY GREYINGS
EGGINSSU GUESSING
EGGINSTT GETTINGS
EGGINSTU GUESTING
GUNGIEST
EGGIOSST SOGGIEST
EGGIPRRS PRIGGERS
EGGIPRRY PRIGGERY
EGGIPSTU PUGGIEST
EGGIRRST TRIGGERS
EGGIRSSW SWIGGERS
EGGIRSTT TRIGGEST
EGGIRSTU RUGGIEST
STUGGIER
EGGIRSTW TWIGGERS
EGGISTUV VUGGIEST
EGGJLRSU JUGGLERS
EGGJLRUY JUGGLERY
EGGLMOOY GEMOLOGY
EGGLMRSU SMUGGLER
EGGLMSSU SMUGGLES
EGGLNSSU SNUGGLES
EGGLORSS SLOGGERS
EGGLORUY GURGOYLE
EGGLPRSU PLUGGERS
EGGLRSSU SLUGGERS
EGGLRSTU STRUGGLE
EGGMNTUY NUTMEGGY
EGGMSSTU SMUGGEST
EGGNOOST GEOGNOST
EGGNOOSY GEOGNOSY
EGGNORST GONGSTER
EGGNRSUY SNUGGERY
EGGNSSTU SNUGGEST
EGGOORSU GORGEOUS
EGGSSSTU SUGGESTS
EGHHILTY EIGHTHLY
EGHHINSS HIGHNESS
EGHHOSSW SHOWGHES
EGHIILLS GHILLIES
EGHIILNR HIRELING
EGHIILNS SHEILING
SHIELING
EGHIIMRT MIGHTIER
EGHIINNR INHERING
EGHIINRT THINGIER
EGHIINST HEISTING
NIGHTIES
THINGIES
EGHIINSV INVEIGHS
EGHIINTV THIEVING
EGHIIRST TIGERISH
EGHIKNRS GHERKINS
EGHIKRSS SKREIGHS
SKRIEGHS
EGHILLNO HELLOING
EGHILLNS SHELLING
EGHILMNW WHELMING
EGHILNNU UNHELING
EGHILNOV HOVELING
EGHILNPS HELPINGS
EGHILNPT PENLIGHT
EGHILNPW WHELPING
EGHILNRS HERLINGS
SHINGLER
EGHILNSS SHINGLES
EGHILNST ENLIGHTS
LIGHTENS
EGHILNSV SHELVING
EGHILNSW WELSHING
EGHILNUW GLUHWEIN
EGHILORT REGOLITH
EGHILOSU OUGHLIES
EGHILPRT PLIGHTER
EGHILPST PIGHTLES
EGHILRST LIGHTERS
RELIGHTS
SLIGHTER
EGHILSST SLEIGHTS
EGHILSTT LIGHTEST
EGHIMNNS MENSHING
EGHIMNSS MESHINGS
EGHIMNUX EXHUMING
EGHIMPRU GRUMPHIE
EGHIMSTT MIGHTEST
EGHINNOY HONEYING
EGHINNSS NIGHNESS
EGHINNST SENNIGHT
EGHINNSU UNHINGES
EGHINORT THROEING
EGHINORV HOVERING
EGHINOSS SHOEINGS
EGHINOST HISTOGEN
EGHINOSU GINHOUSE
EGHINPRS SPHERING
EGHINPSS SPHINGES
EGHINQTU QUETHING
EGHINRRS HERRINGS
EGHINRRU HUNGRIER
EGHINRRY HERRYING
EGHINRST RIGHTENS
EGHINRSU USHERING
EGHINRSW SHREWING
WHINGERS
EGHINRTW WRETHING
EGHINSTT SHETTING
TIGHTENS
EGHINTTW WHETTING
EGHIOOSS SHOOGIES
EGHIOPSU PISHOGUE
EGHIORST GHOSTIER
EGHIORSU ROUGHIES
EGHIOSTT GOTHITES
EGHIOSTU TOUGHIES
EGHIOSTV EIGHTVOS
EGHIOTUW OUTWEIGH
EGHIQRTU REQUIGHT
EGHIRRST RIGHTERS
EGHIRRUY HIERURGY
EGHIRSST SIGHTERS
EGHIRSTT RIGHTEST
STREIGHT
EGHISSTU GUSHIEST
EGHISTTT TIGHTEST
EGHLLOSU LUGHOLES
EGHLMNOP PHLEGMON
EGHLNORS LEGHORNS
EGHLNPSU ENGULPHS
EGHLNRUY HUNGERLY
EGHLOOOR HOROLOGE
EGHLOORY RHEOLOGY
EGHLOOSS GOLOSHES
SHOOGLES
EGHLOOTY ETHOLOGY
THEOLOGY
EGHLOPRU PLOUGHER

EGHMNOOY	HOMOGENY
EGHMNORS	GEMSHORN
EGHMNOSU	HUMOGENS
EGHMOPUY	HYPOGEUM
EGHMOSSU	GUMSHOES
EGHNOOPT	PHOTOGEN
EGHNOOTY	THEOGONY
EGHNORSU	ENROUGHS
	ROUGHENS
EGHNORUV	OVERHUNG
EGHNOSTU	TOUGHENS
EGHNOSUU	GUNHOUSE
EGHNRSTT	STRENGTH
EGHOOOSW	HOOSEGOW
EGHORRSU	ROUGHERS
EGHORRTW	REGROWTH
EGHORSTU	ROUGHEST
EGHOSTTU	TOUGHEST
EGHPSSUU	UPGUSHES
EGIIINSV	VISIEING
EGIIJLNR	JINGLIER
EGIIKLLO	KILLOGIE
EGIIKLNN	LIKENING
EGIIKLNR	KINGLIER
EGIILMMN	IMMINGLE
EGIILMST	LEGITIMS
EGIILNNO	ELOINING
EGIILNNR	RELINING
EGIILNNS	ENISLING
	ENSILING
EGIILNNU	LINGUINE
EGIILNNV	LIVENING
EGIILNOR	RELIGION
EGIILNPS	SPIELING
EGIILNRS	RESILING
EGIILNRT	GIRTLINE
	RETILING
	TINGLIER
	TIRELING
EGIILNRV	RELIVING
	REVILING
EGIILNST	LIGNITES
	LINGIEST
EGIILNSV	VEILINGS
EGIILNSW	WISELING
EGIILRRS	GRISLIER
EGIILRTU	GUILTIER
EGIILRTZ	GLITZIER
EGIIMMNW	IMMEWING
EGIIMNNU	INGENIUM
EGIIMNOS	IGNOMIES
EGIIMNPS	IMPINGES
EGIIMNRS	REMISING
EGIIMNRT	MERITING
	MITERING
	RETIMING
EGIIMNRX	REMIXING
EGIIMNST	MINGIEST
EGIIMNSV	MISGIVEN
EGIIMNTT	EMITTING
EGIIMOPT	IMPETIGO
EGIIMORR	GRIMOIRE
EGIIMPST	GIMPIEST
EGIIMRST	GRIMIEST
	TIGERISM
EGIIMSSV	MISGIVES
EGIINNPR	REPINING
	RIPENING
EGIINNRS	RESINING
EGIINNSS	INSIGNES
	SEININGS
EGIINNST	GINNIEST
	STEINING
EGIINNSV	VEININGS
EGIINNSW	SINEWING
EGIINNVW	VINEWING
EGIINNWZ	WIZENING
EGIINOPR	PEIGNOIR
EGIINORS	SEIGNIOR
EGIINPRS	SPEIRING
EGIINPRV	PRIEVING
EGIINPRX	EXPIRING
EGIINPSS	PIGSNIES
EGIINQTU	QUIETING
EGIINRRT	RETIRING
EGIINRRW	REWIRING
EGIINRST	GIRNIEST
	IGNITERS
	REISTING
	STINGIER
	STRIGINE
EGIINRSU	SIGNIEUR
EGIINRSV	REVISING
EGIINRSW	RINGWISE
	SWINGIER
EGIINRTU	INTRIGUE
EGIINRTV	RIVETING
EGIINRTX	GENITRIX
EGIINRVV	REVIVING
EGIINSSZ	SEIZINGS
EGIINSTW	WINGIEST
EGIINSTX	EXISTING
EGIINSTZ	ZINGIEST
EGIINSVW	VIEWINGS
EGIIPPRR	GRIPPIER
EGIIPRSW	PERIWIGS
EGIIPSST	PIGSTIES
EGIIRRTT	GRITTIER
EGIITUXY	EXIGUITY
EGIJKNRS	JERKINGS
EGIJLLNY	JELLYING
EGIJLNRS	JINGLERS
EGIJLNRU	JUNGLIER
EGIJLNST	JINGLETS
EGIJMMNY	JEMMYING
EGIJNNOY	ENJOYING
EGIJNQRU	JERQUING
EGIJNSST	JESTINGS
EGIJNTTY	JETTYING
EGIKKLNS	LEKKINGS
EGIKKNRT	TREKKING
EGIKLLNN	KNELLING
EGIKLNOS	SONGLIKE
EGIKLNPS	SKELPING
EGIKLNSS	KINGLESS
EGIKLNST	KINGLETS
EGIKMNPS	KEMPINGS
EGIKNNNS	KENNINGS
EGIKNNOT	TOKENING
EGIKNNRS	KERNINGS
EGIKNNSY	ENSKYING
EGIKNORV	OVERKING
	REVOKING
EGIKNPPS	SKEPPING
EGIKNRRS	SKERRING
EGIKNRSU	RESKUING
EGILLMNS	SMELLING
EGILLNNS	SNELLING
EGILLNOS	LOGLINES
EGILLNOV	LIVELONG
EGILLNPS	SPELLING
EGILLNQU	QUELLING
EGILLNST	STELLING
	TELLINGS
EGILLNSW	SWELLING
	WELLINGS
EGILLNSY	YELLINGS
EGILLNTU	GLUTELIN
EGILLOOR	GLORIOLE
EGILMMNS	LEMMINGS
EGILMMRS	GLIMMERS
EGILMMRY	GLIMMERY
EGILMNNO	LEMONING
EGILMNPU	IMPLUNGE
EGILMNRS	GREMLINS
	MERLINGS
	MINGLERS
EGILMNRU	RELUMING
EGILMNST	MELTINGS
	SMELTING
EGILMNSU	LEGUMINS
EGILMOOR	GLOOMIER
EGILMORS	GOMERILS
EGILMOSU	ELOGIUMS
EGILMOUU	EULOGIUM
EGILMPRU	GLUMPIER
EGILMPSS	GLIMPSES
EGILNNST	NESTLING
EGILNNTT	NETTLING
EGILNOPP	PEOPLING
	POPELING
EGILNORS	RESOLING
EGILNORW	LOWERING
EGILNOSS	LIGNOSES
EGILNOSU	LIGNEOUS
EGILNOSW	LONGWISE
EGILNOTW	TOWELING
EGILNOVV	EVOLVING
EGILNPRS	PINGLERS
	SPERLING
	SPRINGLE
EGILNPRY	REPLYING
EGILNPSS	SPIGNELS
EGILNPST	PELTINGS
	PESTLING
EGILNPSY	YELPINGS
EGILNPTT	PETTLING
EGILNRRU	RULERING
EGILNRRY	ERRINGLY
EGILNRSS	RINGLESS
	SLINGERS
EGILNRST	LINGSTER
	RINGLETS
	STERLING
	TINGLERS
	TRINGLES
EGILNRSW	NEWSGIRL
EGILNRUV	VELURING
EGILNSSS	SIGNLESS
EGILNSST	GLISTENS
	SINGLETS
EGILNSSU	UGLINESS
EGILNSSW	SWINGLES
	WINGLESS
EGILNSTT	LETTINGS
	SETTLING
EGILNSTW	SWELTING
	WINGLETS
EGILNSUV	EVULSING
EGILNTUX	EXULTING
EGILNVXY	VEXINGLY
EGILOOOS	OOLOGIES
EGILOOPR	GLOOPIER
EGILOORR	GROOLIER
EGILOOSU	ISOLOGUE
EGILOOTY	ETIOLOGY
EGILORRW	GROWLIER
EGILORSS	GLOSSIER
EGILORTY	GYROLITE
EGILOSSS	GLOSSIES
EGILOSST	ELOGISTS
EGILOSTU	EULOGIST
EGILPPRS	GRIPPLES
EGILRRZZ	GRIZZLER
EGILRSST	GLISTERS
	GRISTLES
EGILRSTT	GLITTERS
EGILRSTU	GURLIEST
EGILRSUV	VIRGULES
EGILRSZZ	GRIZZLES
EGILRTTY	GLITTERY
EGIMMNOV	EMMOVING
EGIMMNST	STEMMING
EGIMMRST	GRIMMEST
EGIMMSTU	GUMMIEST
	GUMMITES
EGIMNNNO	MIGNONNE
EGIMNNOV	ENMOVING
	VENOMING
EGIMNNUW	UNMEWING
EGIMNORS	NEGROISM
EGIMNORV	REMOVING
EGIMNOST	MITOGENS
EGIMNOSU	GEMINOUS
EGIMNOSY	MOSEYING
EGIMNPRS	IMPREGNS
EGIMNPRU	IMPUGNER
EGIMNPST	PIGMENTS
EGIMNPTT	TEMPTING
EGIMNPTY	EMPTYING
EGIMNRSS	GRIMNESS
EGIMNRSU	RESUMING
EGIMNRUY	ERYNGIUM
EGIMORST	ERGOTISM
	GORMIEST
EGIMOSST	EGOTISMS
EGIMOSTW	TWIGSOME
EGIMPRRU	GRUMPIER
EGINNNOT	TENONING
EGINNNOZ	ENZONING
EGINNNRS	RENNINGS
EGINNNST	STENNING
EGINNNUY	ENNUYING
EGINNOOR	RONEOING
EGINNOPR	REPONING
EGINNOPS	OPENINGS
EGINNORT	NITROGEN
EGINNORV	VIGNERON
EGINNORZ	REZONING
EGINNPRT	PRENTING
EGINNPSU	PENGUINS
EGINNRRS	GRINNERS
EGINNRRU	UNERRING
EGINNRST	STERNING
EGINNRSU	ENSURING
EGINNRTU	RETUNING
EGINNRTV	VENTRING
EGINNSSS	SENSINGS
EGINNSST	NESTINGS
EGINNSTT	NETTINGS

STENTING
TENTINGS
EGINNSTV VENTINGS
EGINNSUW UNSEWING
EGINNSUX UNSEXING
EGINNSVY ENVYINGS
EGINOORV INGROOVE
EGINOPRS PERIGONS
REPOSING
SPONGIER
EGINOPRW POWERING
EGINOPRY PIGEONRY
EGINOPST PONGIEST
EGINOPSX EXPOSING
EGINOPSY POESYING
EGINORRS IGNORERS
EGINORSS GORINESS
SIGNORES
EGINORST GENITORS
ROSETING
EGINORSY SEIGNORY
EGINORTT OTTERING
EGINORTU OUTREIGN
ROUTEING
EGINORTW TOWERING
EGINORTX OXTERING
EGINORTZ ROZETING
EGINORVW OVERWING
EGINOSTT TENTIGOS
EGINOTUV OUTGIVEN
EGINPPPR PREPPING
EGINPPRS REPPINGS
EGINPPST STEPPING
EGINPRRS SPERRING
SPRINGER
EGINPRRU REPURING
EGINPRSS PRESSING
SPERSING
SPRINGES
EGINPRST PRESTING
EGINPRSU PERSUING
PERUSING
EGINPRTU ERUPTING
REPUTING
EGINPRUV PREVUING
EGINPRYY PERIGYNY
EGINPSSY PIGSNEYS
EGINPSTT PETTINGS
SPETTING
EGINQRUY QUERYING
EGINQSTU QUESTING
EGINQSUU QUEUINGS
EGINRRST RESTRING
RINGSTER
STRINGER
EGINRRSW WRINGERS
EGINRRSY SERRYING
EGINRRTY RETRYING
EGINRSST RESTINGS
STINGERS
TRESSING
TRIGNESS
EGINRSSV SERVINGS
VERSINGS
EGINRSSW SWINGERS
EGINRSSY SYRINGES
EGINRSTT GITTERNS
EGINRSTV STERVING
EGINRSTW STREWING
WRESTING
EGINRSVW SWERVING
EGINRTTU UTTERING
EGINSSTT SETTINGS
TESTINGS
EGINSSTV VESTINGS
EGINSSTW STEWINGS
WESTINGS
EGINSTTT STETTING
EGIOOPST GOOPIEST
EGIOORRV GROOVIER
EGIOOSST GOOSIEST
EGIOPRSU GROUPIES
PIROGUES
EGIOPRTU PORTIGUE
EGIORRTT GROTTIER
EGIORRTU GROUTIER
EGIORSST GORSIEST
STRIGOSE
EGIORSSU GRISEOUS
EGIORSTU GOUSTIER
EGIORSTV VERTIGOS
EGIORSTY OYSTRIGE
EGIORSTZ ZORGITES
EGIORSUV GRIEVOUS
EGIOSSTT EGOTISTS
EGIOSTTU GOUTIEST
EGIOSTUV OUTGIVES
VOGUIEST
EGIOSUUX EXIGUOUS
EGIPPRRS GRIPPERS
EGIPRSUU GUIPURES
EGIRRSTT GRITTERS
EGIRRSTY REGISTRY
EGIRSSTU SURGIEST
EGIRSTTT GRITTEST
EGISSTTU GUSTIEST
GUTSIEST
EGISSYYZ SYZYGIES
EGISTTTU GUTTIEST
EGJLNORU JONGLEUR
EGJLNOTU JELUTONG
EGKLORSW LEGWORKS
EGLLMORW GROMWELL
EGLLOOPY PELOLOGY
EGLMMSTU GLUMMEST
EGLMNOOS ENGLOOMS
LONGSOME
EGLMNOOY MENOLOGY
EGLMNORS MONGRELS
EGLMNSSU GLUMNESS
EGLMOORS LEGROOMS
EGLMOPRU PROMULGE
EGLMORSS GORMLESS
EGLNNOOR LONGERON
EGLNNOSS LONGNESS
EGLNNTUY UNGENTLY
EGLNOOOY OENOLOGY
EGLNOOPR PROLONGE
EGLNOOPY PENOLOGY
EGLNOORV OVERLONG
EGLNOPYY POLYGENY
EGLNORSU LOUNGERS
EGLNORUU LONGUEUR
EGLNOSSS SONGLESS
EGLNOSUV UNGLOVES
EGLNOSXY LOXYGENS
XYLOGENS
EGLNPRSU PLUNGERS
EGLNRSTU GRUNTLES
EGLNRTUY URGENTLY
EGLOOORY OREOLOGY
EGLOOPRU PROLOGUE
EGLOOPTY LOGOTYPE
EGLOORSY SEROLOGY
EGLOOSXY SEXOLOGY
EGLOPRTU GROUPLET
EGLORRSW GROWLERS
EGLORRWY GROWLERY
EGLORSSS GLOSSERS
EGLORSUU RUGULOSE
EGLORSUY RUGOSELY
EGLPRSSU SPLURGES
EGLRSUZZ GUZZLERS
EGLSSUUV VULGUSES
EGMMORST GROMMETS
EGMMOSSU GUMMOSES
EGMMRSTU GRUMMEST
GRUMMETS
EGMNNOOY MONOGENY
NOMOGENY
EGMNNOSW GOWNSMEN
EGMNOOOS MONGOOSE
EGMNOORY MEROGONY
EGMNOOSU MUNGOOSE
EGMNORSU MURGEONS
EGMNOSYZ ZYMOGENS
EGMNRSSU GRUMNESS
EGMNSSSU SMUGNESS
EGMORSTU GOURMETS
EGNNOOTY ONTOGENY
EGNNORST RONTGENS
EGNNOSTU GUNSTONE
EGNNOTTU UNGOTTEN
EGNNSSSU SNUGNESS
EGNNSTTU TUNGSTEN
EGNNSTUU UNGUENTS
EGNOORRV GOVERNOR
EGNOPPRU OPPUGNER
EGNOPRSS SPONGERS
EGNOPRSY PYROGENS
EGNORRST STRONGER
EGNORRSW WRONGERS
EGNORSST SONGSTER
EGNORSSU SURGEONS
EGNORSTT TONGSTER
EGNORSTU STURGEON
EGNORSTW WRONGEST
EGNOSTUY YOUNGEST
EGNPRSUU SUPERGUN
EGNRRSTU GRUNTERS
RESTRUNG
EGOOPRRU PROROGUE
EGOORRSV GROOVERS
EGOORRVW OVERGROW
EGOORSTT GROTTOES
EGOORSTU OUTGOERS
EGOPRRSS PROGRESS
EGOPRRSU GROUPERS
REGROUPS
EGOPSSUY GYPSEOUS
EGORRSST GROSERTS
EGORRSSU GROUSERS
EGORRSTU GROUTERS
EGORSSST GROSSEST
EGORSSTU GROUSEST
EGPRSSUU UPSURGES
EHHIIPRS HEIRSHIP
EHHIISTV THIEVISH
EHHILMNT HELMINTH
EHHILOST SHITHOLE
EHHINOPT THIOPHEN
EHHIOPRS HEROSHIP
EHHIORTT HITHERTO
EHHIPRSS HERSHIPS
EHHIPSST PHTHISES
EHHIRSSW SHREWISH
EHHIRSTW WHITHERS
EHHISSTU HUSHIEST
EHHLOOST SHOTHOLE
EHHNOORS SHOEHORN
EHHOOPST THEOSOPH
EHHOOSSW WHOOSHES
EHHOOSTU HOTHOUSE
EHHORSTU SHOUTHER
EHHRSSTU THRUSHES
EHIIKLPT PITHLIKE
EHIIKLPW WHIPLIKE
EHIIKSSW WHISKIES
EHIILLST HILLIEST
EHIILLSW WHILLIES
EHIILMOS HOMILIES
EHIILOSS HELIOSIS
EHIILRRW WHIRLIER
EHIILRSV LIVERISH
EHIILSTT LITHITES
EHIIMMRW WHIMMIER
EHIIMMSS SHIMMIES
EHIIMNOS HOMINIES
EHIIMNSS MINISHES
EHIIMPST MEPHITIS
EHIIMRSW WHIMSIER
EHIIMSST SMITHIES
EHIIMSSW WHIMSIES
EHIINNOS INHESION
EHIINNQU HENIQUIN
EHIINNRS INSHRINE
EHIINNRW WHINNIER
EHIINNSS SHINNIES
EHIINNSW WHINNIES
EHIINRRT HIRRIENT
EHIINRST INHERITS
EHIINRSZ RHIZINES
EHIINSST SHINIEST
SHINTIES
EHIINSTW WHINIEST
EHIINSVX VIXENISH
EHIIPPRW WHIPPIER
EHIIPPST HIPPIEST
EHIIPRSV VIPERISH
EHIIPSTT PITHIEST
EHIIRRST SHIRTIER
EHIIRRSW WHIRRIES
EHIIRRTX HERITRIX
EHIIRSSU HUISSIER
EHIIRSSW SWISHIER
EHIIRSTT SHITTIER
THIRTIES
EHIISSST STISHIES
EHIISSTT STITHIES
EHIISTTW WHITIEST
WITHIEST
EHIISTTX SIXTIETH
EHIJNNOS JOHNNIES
EHIKLNOS SINKHOLE
EHIKLOSY YOKELISH
EHIKLOTY LEKYTHOI
EHIKLRSU RUSHLIKE
EHIKLSTU HULKIEST
EHIKMNST METHINKS
EHIKNORS SHONKIER

EHIKNRRS	SHRINKER
EHIKNRST	RETHINKS
	THINKERS
EHIKNSTU	HUNKIEST
EHIKOOST	HOOKIEST
EHIKOPRS	POKERISH
EHIKRRSS	SHIRKERS
EHIKRSSW	WHISKERS
EHIKRSWY	WHISKERY
EHIKSSTU	HUSKIEST
EHIKSSTW	WHISKETS
EHIKSSWY	WHISKEYS
EHILLLMO	MOLEHILL
EHILLMOY	HOMELILY
EHILLNOS	HELLIONS
EHILLNSS	INSHELLS
EHILLOPY	LYOPHILE
EHILLPTY	PHYLLITE
EHILLRRS	SHRILLER
EHILLRRT	THRILLER
EHILLRST	THILLERS
EHILLRTY	LITHERLY
EHILLSSW	SWELLISH
EHILLSTU	HULLIEST
EHILMOOR	HEIRLOOM
EHILMOST	HELOTISM
EHILMPSW	WHIMPLES
EHILMPSY	SYMPHILE
EHILMQUU	UMQUHILE
EHILMSTT	MELTITHS
EHILNOOP	OENOPHIL
EHILNOPS	PINHOLES
EHILNORU	UNHOLIER
EHILNOSS	HOLINESS
EHILNOST	HOTLINES
	NEOLITHS
EHILNOSV	NOVELISH
EHILNOTX	XENOLITH
EHILNSWY	NEWISHLY
EHILOOPZ	ZOOPHILE
EHILOOST	HOOLIEST
EHILOPRS	PILHORSE
	POLISHER
EHILOPRT	HELIPORT
EHILOPSS	POLISHES
EHILOPST	HELISTOP
	HOPLITES
	ISOPLETH
EHILORSS	SLOSHIER
EHILORTY	RHYOLITE
EHILPRST	PHILTERS
	PHILTRES
EHILPRSU	PLUSHIER
EHILPRSY	SYLPHIER
EHILPSSS	SHIPLESS
EHILPSST	PITHLESS
	THLIPSES
EHILPSTU	SULPHITE
EHILRRSW	WHIRLERS
EHILRSST	SLITHERS
	THRISSEL
EHILRSSU	SLUSHIER
EHILRSSV	SHRIVELS
EHILRSTT	THRISTLE
EHILRSTU	LUTHIERS
EHILRSTW	WHIRTLES
	WHISTLER
EHILRSTY	SLITHERY
EHILRTTW	WHITTLER
EHILRTTY	TRIETHYL
EHILSSTT	THISTLES
EHILSSTU	LUSHIEST
EHILSSTW	WHISTLES
EHILSTTU	THULITES
EHILSTTW	WHITTLES
EHIMMNUY	HYMENIUM
EHIMMRSS	SHIMMERS
EHIMMRSY	SHIMMERY
EHIMMSSY	SHIMMEYS
EHIMNOPR	MORPHINE
EHIMNORT	THERMION
EHIMNOST	HOISTMEN
EHIMNOSU	HEMIONUS
EHIMNOTT	MONTEITH
EHIMNPRS	PHRENISM
EHIMNPST	SHIPMENT
EHIMNRRU	MURRHINE
EHIMNRRY	MYRRHINE
EHIMNRSU	INHUMERS
	RHENIUMS
EHIMNSTY	THYMINES
EHIMOOSS	HOMEOSIS
EHIMOOST	SMOOTHIE
EHIMOPRS	SOPHERIM
EHIMOPSS	PHIMOSES
EHIMORSS	HEROISMS
EHIMORST	ISOTHERM
	MOITHERS
EHIMORSZ	RHIZOMES
EHIMORTU	MOUTHIER
EHIMOSTT	MOTHIEST
EHIMPPSS	PSEPHISM
EHIMPRRS	SHRIMPER
EHIMPRSU	MURPHIES
EHIMPRSW	WHIMPERS
EHIMPSTU	HUMPIEST
	HUMPTIES
	TUMPHIES
EHIMPSUU	EUPHUISM
EHIMPTTU	UMPTIETH
EHIMRSST	SMITHERS
EHIMRSSU	HEURISMS
EHIMRSTY	SMITHERY
EHIMSSTU	MUSHIEST
	TUMSHIES
EHIMSSTY	METHYSIS
	MYTHISES
EHIMSSWY	WHIMSEYS
EHIMSTTY	THYMIEST
EHIMSTYZ	MYTHIZES
EHINNRST	THINNERS
EHINNSST	THINNESS
EHINNSSU	SUNSHINE
EHINNSTT	THINNEST
EHINOPPR	HORNPIPE
EHINOPRT	TRIPHONE
EHINOPST	PHONIEST
	SIPHONET
EHINORRT	THORNIER
EHINORSS	HERISSON
EHINORST	HORNIEST
EHINOSST	HISTONES
EHINOSTU	OUTSHINE
EHINPPSS	SHIPPENS
EHINPRSU	PUNISHER
EHINPSSU	PUNISHES
EHINPSSX	SPHINXES
EHINRSSU	INRUSHES
EHINRSTZ	ZITHERNS
EHINSSST	THISNESS
EHINSSUW	UNWISHES
EHIOOPSW	WHOOPSIE
EHIOORTT	TOOTHIER
EHIOOSST	STOOSHIE
EHIOPPPS	POPESHIP
EHIOPPRS	SHOPPIER
EHIOPPST	HOPPIEST
	POETSHIP
EHIOPRSS	ROSEHIPS
	SPOSHIER
EHIOPRST	TROPHIES
EHIOPTTW	WHITEPOT
EHIORRST	HERITORS
EHIORRTU	ROUTHIER
EHIORRTW	WORTHIER
EHIORSST	HOISTERS
	HORSIEST
	HOSTRIES
	SHORTIES
EHIORSTT	THEORIST
	THORITES
EHIORSTU	OUTHIRES
EHIORSTV	OVERHITS
EHIORSTW	WORTHIES
EHIORTUY	YOUTHIER
EHIORTWZ	HOWITZER
EHIOSSTT	TOSHIEST
EHIOSSTW	SHOWIEST
EHIOSSTY	ISOHYETS
EHIOSTVY	YESHIVOT
EHIPPRSS	SHIPPERS
EHIPPRSW	WHIPPERS
EHIPPSSU	HIPPUSES
EHIPPSTW	WHIPPETS
EHIPQSUY	PHYSIQUE
EHIPRSST	HIPSTERS
	THRIPSES
EHIPRSSW	WHISPERS
EHIPRSTW	WHIPSTER
EHIPRSWY	WHISPERY
EHIPSSTU	PUSHIEST
EHIPSTUU	EUPHUIST
EHIQSSSU	SQUISHES
EHIRRSSV	SHRIVERS
EHIRRSTT	THIRSTER
EHIRRSTV	THRIVERS
EHIRRSTW	WHIRRETS
EHIRRTTU	TRUTHIER
EHIRSSSW	SWISHERS
EHIRSSTU	RUSHIEST
EHIRSSTW	SWITHERS
EHIRSTTW	WHITRETS
	WHITSTER
	WHITTERS
EHIRSWZZ	WHIZZERS
EHIRTTTW	WHITTRET
EHISSSTU	STUSHIES
EHISSSTW	SWISHEST
EHISSTUW	THUSWISE
EHISSUVW	HUSWIVES
EHKLOSTY	LEKYTHOS
EHKMOORW	HOMEWORK
EHKMORSU	HUMORESK
EHKNNRSU	SHRUNKEN
EHKOOSSS	SKOOSHES
EHKOPSSY	KYPHOSES
EHKRSSTU	TUSHKERS
EHLLMOPY	PHYLLOME
EHLLNSSU	UNSHELLS
EHLLNSTU	NUTSHELL
EHLLOOOP	LOOPHOLE
EHLLOORW	HOLLOWER
EHLMMOSW	WHOMMLES
EHLMMSUW	WHUMMLES
EHLMNOST	MENTHOLS
EHLMNOSY	HOMELYNS
EHLMNOTU	MOLEHUNT
EHLMNOUY	UNHOMELY
EHLMOORW	WORMHOLE
EHLMORTY	MOTHERLY
EHLNNOPU	UNHOLPEN
EHLNOPSU	SULPHONE
EHLNORSS	HORNLESS
EHLNORST	HORNLETS
EHLNOSTY	HONESTLY
EHLNRSTU	LUTHERNS
EHLNSSSU	LUSHNESS
	SHUNLESS
EHLOOPRT	PORTHOLE
	POTHOLER
EHLOOPST	POTHOLES
EHLOOPTY	HOLOTYPE
EHLOOSSS	SLOOSHES
EHLOPPRT	THROPPLE
EHLOPRTY	PROTHYLE
EHLOPSSS	SPLOSHES
EHLOPSSY	SPYHOLES
EHLORSST	HOLSTERS
	HOSTLERS
EHLORSTT	THROSTLE
EHLORSTY	HOSTELRY
EHLORTTT	THROTTLE
EHLOSSTT	SHOTTLES
EHLOSSTW	THOWLESS
EHLOSSTY	THYLOSES
EHLPSSTU	PLUSHEST
EHLRSSTU	HURTLESS
	HUSTLERS
	RUTHLESS
EHLSSTTU	SHUTTLES
EHMMRRTU	THRUMMER
EHMMSSUU	HUMMUSES
EHMNNSTU	HUNTSMEN
EHMNOORS	HORMONES
	MOORHENS
EHMNOOST	SMOOTHEN
EHMNOOTY	THEONOMY
EHMNOPSU	HOMESPUN
EHMNPRYY	HYPERNYM
EHMNPSTY	NYMPHETS
EHMNSTTU	HUTMENTS
EHMOOOTZ	ZOOTHOME
EHMOOPTY	HOMOTYPE
EHMOORST	SMOOTHER
EHMOOSSS	SHMOOSES
EHMOOSSZ	SHMOOZES
EHMOPRSW	MORPHEWS
EHMORSST	SMOTHERS
EHMORSTU	MOUTHERS
EHMORSTY	SMOTHERY
EHMORTUV	VERMOUTH
EHMOSSUU	HOUMUSES
EHMOTUZZ	MEZUZOTH
EHMPRSTU	THUMPERS
EHMRRSTU	MURTHERS
EHMRTUYY	EURYTHMY
EHNNOPRS	NEPHRONS
EHNNOPSY	HYPNONES
EHNNORRT	NORTHERN
EHNNORTU	UNTHRONE

EHNNOSTU	UNHONEST
EHNNRSSU	SHUNNERS
EHNOOPTY	HONEYPOT
EHNOORRU	HONOURER
EHNOORSS	SOREHONS
EHNOORSW	WHORESON
EHNOORTW	HONEWORT
EHNOOSSW	SNOWSHOE
EHNOOSTU	OUTSHONE
EHNOPRSY	HYPERONS
EHNOPSSS	POSHNESS
EHNOPSSY	HYPNOSES
EHNORRST	NORTHERS
EHNORSST	SHORTENS
EHNORSSU	ONRUSHES
	UNHORSES
EHNORSTT	THORNSET
EHNORSTU	SOUTHERN
EHNOSSUU	UNHOUSES
EHNOSTUU	NUTHOUSE
EHNRSSTU	HUNTRESS
	SHUNTERS
EHNSSSTU	THUSNESS
EHOOPRSW	WHOOPERS
EHOOPRTY	ORTHOEPY
EHOOPSTU	HOUSETOP
	POTHOUSE
EHOOPSTY	OOPHYTES
EHOOPTYZ	ZOOPHYTE
EHOORSST	ORTHOSES
	SHOOTERS
	SOOTHERS
EHOORSTV	OVERSHOT
EHOOSSSW	SWOOSHES
EHOOSSTT	SOOTHEST
EHOOSTUU	OUTHOUSE
EHOPPRSS	SHOPPERS
EHOPPRST	PROPHETS
EHOPPRSW	WHOPPERS
EHOPPRSY	PROPHESY
EHOPRRSY	ORPHREYS
EHOPRSST	STROPHES
EHOPRSTU	POUTHERS
EHOPRSTY	TROPHESY
EHOPRTUY	EUTROPHY
EHOPSSTY	PHYTOSES
EHORRSTW	THROWERS
EHORSSTT	SHORTEST
EHORSSTU	SHOUTERS
	SOUTHERS
EHORSTUY	OUTHYRES
EHOSSSTU	STOUSHES
EHPRSSSU	SPRUSHES
EHPRSSUU	UPRUSHES
EHPRSTTU	TURPETHS
EHPSSTUY	TYPHUSES
EHRRSTTU	THRUSTER
EHRSSSTY	SHYSTERS
EHRSSTTU	SHUTTERS
EIIILMSS	SIMILISE
EIIILMSZ	SIMILIZE
EIIILPPR	LIRIPIPE
EIIIMMNS	MINIMISE
EIIIMMNZ	MINIMIZE
EIIIRRTV	TIRRIVIE
EIIIRSST	IRITISES
EIIJKNRT	JIRKINET
EIIJMPST	JIMPIEST
EIIJNRSU	INJURIES
EIIKKLLM	MILKLIKE
EIIKKNST	KINKIEST
EIIKLLMN	LIMEKILN
EIIKLLNO	LIONLIKE
EIIKLLRS	SKILLIER
EIIKLLSS	SKILLIES
EIIKLMRS	MISLIKER
EIIKLMSS	MISLIKES
EIIKLMST	MILKIEST
EIIKLNRS	SLINKIER
EIIKLNRT	TINKLIER
EIIKLPSS	PLISKIES
EIIKLRTT	KITTLIER
EIIKLSST	SILKIEST
EIIKMPRS	SKIMPIER
EIIKMRRS	SMIRKIER
EIIKNNRS	SKINNIER
EIIKNNSS	INKINESS
EIIKNNSW	WINESKIN
EIIKNPST	PINKIEST
EIIKNSST	SINKIEST
EIIKNSTZ	ZINKIEST
EIIKPPRS	SKIPPIER
EIIKPSST	SPIKIEST
EIIKQRRU	QUIRKIER
EIIKRSST	RISKIEST
EIIKSSTV	SKIVIEST
EIIKSSVV	SKIVVIES
EIILLLVY	LIVELILY
EIILLMMR	MILLIREM
EIILLMMS	MILLIMES
EIILLMNR	MILLINER
EIILLMNS	SLIMLINE
EIILLMNU	ILLUMINE
EIILLNST	NIELLIST
EIILLNSU	SUILLINE
EIILLNSV	VILLEINS
EIILLNTV	VITELLIN
EIILLPSS	ELLIPSIS
EIILLRST	STILLIER
EIILLSST	SILLIEST
EIILLSTT	TILLIEST
	TILLITES
EIILLSTW	TWILLIES
EIILLSUV	ILLUSIVE
EIILMNNT	LINIMENT
EIILMNOT	LIMONITE
EIILMNSS	LIMINESS
EIILMOPT	IMPOLITE
EIILMPPR	PIMPLIER
EIILMPRS	IMPERILS
EIILMPST	LIMEPITS
EIILMRSS	SLIMSIER
EIILMRST	LIMITERS
	MIRLIEST
EIILMRZZ	MIZZLIER
EIILMSSS	MISSILES
EIILMSST	ELITISMS
	SLIMIEST
EIILMSSV	MISLIVES
EIILMSTT	MISTITLE
EIILMSTY	MYELITIS
EIILNNOT	LENITION
EIILNOSS	ELISIONS
	ISOLINES
	LIONISES
	OILINESS
EIILNOST	ETIOLINS
EIILNOSV	OLIVINES
EIILNOSZ	LIONIZES
EIILNOTT	TOILINET
EIILNQTU	QUINTILE
EIILNRST	NIRLIEST
	NITRILES
EIILNSSW	WILINESS
EIILNSTT	LINTIEST
EIILNSTY	SENILITY
EIILNSVY	SYLVIINE
EIILNTTU	INTITULE
EIILNTUV	VITULINE
EIILOPST	PISOLITE
	POLITIES
EIILORST	ROILIEST
EIILORTT	TROILITE
EIILOSST	SOILIEST
EIILOTVV	VOLITIVE
EIILPPRR	RIPPLIER
EIILPPRS	SLIPPIER
EIILPPST	LIPPIEST
EIILPRST	TRIPLIES
EIILPRSU	PLURISIE
EIILPSST	PITILESS
	SPILITES
EIILPSTY	PYELITIS
EIILPSUZ	SPUILZIE
EIILQSSU	SILIQUES
EIILRRSW	SWIRLIER
EIILRRTW	TWIRLIER
EIILRSTT	STILTIER
EIILRSTU	UTILISER
EIILRTUZ	UTILIZER
EIILSSTT	ELITISTS
	SILTIEST
EIILSSTU	ULITISES
	UTILISES
EIILSTUY	TUILYIES
EIILSTUZ	TUILZIES
	UTILIZES
EIIMMNNO	MENOMINI
EIIMMNNT	IMMINENT
	MINIMENT
EIIMMNSU	IMMUNISE
EIIMMNTU	IMMINUTE
EIIMMNUZ	IMMUNIZE
EIIMMPRU	IMPERIUM
EIIMMRSW	SWIMMIER
EIIMMSSS	SEISMISM
EIIMMSST	MIMSIEST
	MISTIMES
EIIMNOPT	PIMIENTO
EIIMNOSS	EMISSION
	SIMONIES
EIIMNOSV	VISNOMIE
EIIMNOTV	MONITIVE
EIIMNPRS	PRIMINES
EIIMNRSS	MIRINESS
EIIMNRST	INTERIMS
	MINISTER
EIIMNRSV	MINIVERS
EIIMNRTT	INTERMIT
EIIMNRTX	INTERMIX
EIIMNSTT	MINTIEST
EIIMNSTU	MUTINIES
EIIMNSTV	MINIVETS
EIIMOPRX	MIREPOIX
EIIMOPST	OPTIMISE
EIIMOPTZ	OPTIMIZE
EIIMOSSV	OMISSIVE
EIIMOSTY	MOYITIES
EIIMOSUX	EXIMIOUS
EIIMOTVV	VOMITIVE
EIIMPRSS	MISPRISE
	PISMIRES
EIIMPRSZ	MISPRIZE
EIIMPSST	PIETISMS
EIIMPSTW	WIMPIEST
EIIMQSTU	QUIETISM
EIIMRRRS	SMIRRIER
EIIMRSTT	METRITIS
EIIMRSTW	MISWRITE
EIIMSSSS	MISSISES
EIIMSSST	MISSIEST
EIIMSSSV	MISSIVES
EIIMSSSZ	SIZEISMS
EIIMSSTT	MISTIEST
EIINNNPS	NINEPINS
EIINNOSU	UNIONISE
EIINNOSV	ENVISION
EIINNOUZ	UNIONIZE
EIINNPSS	SPINNIES
EIINNQSU	QUININES
EIINNRTV	INVERTIN
EIINNSST	TININESS
EIINNSSW	INSINEWS
EIINNSTT	TINNIEST
EIINNSTW	INTWINES
EIINOPRS	RIPIENOS
EIINOPRT	POINTIER
EIINOPST	SINOPITE
EIINOPTT	PETITION
EIINORRT	INTERIOR
EIINORSS	IONISERS
	IRONISES
EIINORSV	REVISION
	VISIONER
EIINORSZ	IONIZERS
	IRONIZES
EIINOSST	NOISIEST
EIINOSTV	NOVITIES
EIINPPRS	SNIPPIER
EIINPPST	NIPPIEST
EIINPRRS	INSPIRER
EIINPRSS	INSPIRES
EIINPRST	PRISTINE
EIINPSST	SNIPIEST
	SPINIEST
EIINPTUV	PUNITIVE
EIINQRRU	INQUIRER
EIINQRSU	INQUIRES
EIINQSSU	QUINSIES
	SQUINIES
EIINQSTU	INQUIETS
EIINQTUY	EQUINITY
	INEQUITY
EIINRRTW	WINTRIER
EIINRSST	SINISTER
EIINRSSW	WIRINESS
EIINRSTT	NITRITES
	STINTIER
EIINRSTU	NEURITIS
EIINRSTV	INVITERS
	VINTRIES
	VITRINES
EIINSSSZ	SIZINESS
EIINSSTU	UNITISES
EIINSTTT	NITTIEST
	TINTIEST
EIINSTTW	TWINIEST
EIINSTUZ	UNITIZES
EIIOPRRS	PRIORIES
EIIOPSTV	POSITIVE

EIIORRST RIOTRIES
EIIORSST RIOTISES
EIIORSTZ RIOTIZES
EIIOSSTT OSTEITIS
OTITISES
EIIOSSTZ ZOISITES
EIIOTTTV TOTITIVE
EIIPPPST PIPPIEST
EIIPPRRS RIPPIERS
EIIPPSTT TIPPIEST
EIIPPSTZ ZIPPIEST
EIIPRRSS PRISSIER
EIIPRRST STRIPIER
EIIPRRTW TRIPWIRE
EIIPRSST SPIRIEST
EIIPRSTT RISPETTI
TRIPIEST
EIIPRSTU PURITIES
EIIPRSTV PRIVIEST
EIIPRSTY PYRITISE
EIIPRSVV SPIVVIER
EIIPRTYZ PYRITIZE
EIIPSSTT PIETISTS
STIPITES
TIPSIEST
EIIPSSTW SWIPIEST
WISPIEST
EIIPSTTT PITTITES
EIIPSTTU PITUITES
EIIQSTTU QUIETIST
EIIRRSTW WRISTIER
EIIRSSTV REVISITS
VISITERS
EIIRSTTU UTERITIS
EIIRSTTW TWISTIER
EIIRSTTZ RITZIEST
EIISSSST SISSIEST
EIISSSTZ SIZEISTS
EIISSTTV STIVIEST
EIISTTTW WITTIEST
EIJJNTUY JEJUNITY
EIJKKSSU JUKSKEIS
EIJKNSTU JUNKIEST
EIJLLOST JOLLIEST
EIJLOSTT JOLTIEST
EIJLOSTW JOWLIEST
EIJMNPSS JIMPNESS
EIJMPSTU JUMPIEST
EIJNORST JOINTERS
EIJNORTU JOINTURE
EIJNOSTT JETTISON
EIJNPRSU JUNIPERS
EIJNRRSU INJURERS
EIJSSSUV JUSSIVES
EIKKLNRS KLINKERS
EIKKNRSS SKINKERS
EIKKOOST KOOKIEST
EIKKSTUY YUKKIEST
EIKLLMSS MILKLESS
EIKLLNSW INKWELLS
EIKLLNUY UNLIKELY
EIKLLORV OVERKILL
EIKLLOSS SKOLLIES
EIKLLSSS SKILLESS
EIKLLSST SKILLETS
EIKLMNOS MOLESKIN
EIKLMNRS KREMLINS
EIKLNOOR OERLIKON
EIKLNOPR PLONKIER
EIKLNOSW SNOWLIKE

EIKLNPRS SPRINKLE
EIKLNRRU KNURLIER
EIKLNRSS SLINKERS
EIKLNRST LINKSTER
STRINKLE
TINKLERS
EIKLNRSW WINKLERS
WRINKLES
EIKLNRTW TWINKLER
EIKLNSSS SKINLESS
EIKLNSST LENTISKS
EIKLNSSY SKYLINES
EIKLNSTT KNITTLES
EIKLNSTW TWINKLES
EIKLOOPR PLOOKIER
EIKLOORT ROOTLIKE
EIKLOPRU PLOUKIER
EIKLOPRW PILEWORK
EIKLOSTY YOLKIEST
EIKLSSTT SKITTLES
EIKLSSTU SULKIEST
EIKLSTTT KITTLEST
EIKMMRRS KRIMMERS
EIKMMRSS SKIMMERS
EIKMNORS MONIKERS
EIKMNOST TOKENISM
EIKMNOSU MOUSEKIN
EIKMOPSS MISSPOKE
EIKMOSST SMOKIEST
EIKMOSSY MISYOKES
EIKMRSTU MURKIEST
EIKMSSSU KUMISSES
EIKMSSTU MUSKIEST
EIKNNOST INKSTONE
EIKNNPSS PINKNESS
EIKNNRSS SKINNERS
EIKNOORS ROOINEKS
EIKNOOST NOOKIEST
EIKNORTT KNOTTIER
EIKNOSTW WONKIEST
EIKNPRSU SPUNKIER
EIKNPRTU TURNPIKE
EIKNPSSU SPUNKIES
EIKNRRTU RETURNIK
EIKNRSST STINKERS
EIKNRSTT KNITTERS
TRINKETS
EIKNSSSU UNKISSES
EIKNSSTT SKINTEST
EIKNSTUZ KUNZITES
EIKOOPRS SPOOKIER
EIKOPPRW PIPEWORK
EIKOPRST PORKIEST
EIKOPRSV OVERSKIP
EIKORRWW WIREWORK
EIKPPRSS SKIPPERS
EIKPPSST SKIPPETS
EIKPRRSU SPRUIKER
EIKRRSST SKIRRETS
SKIRTERS
STRIKERS
EIKRRSSU SKURRIES
EIKRSSTT SKITTERS
EIKRSSTU TURKISES
EIKSSTTU TUSKIEST
EILLLOVY LOVELILY
EILLLPUV PULVILLE
EILLMNOU LINOLEUM
EILLMNQU QUILLMEN
EILLMNSU MULLEINS

EILLMOPS PLIMSOLE
EILLMOST MELILOTS
EILLMPSS MISSPELL
PSELLISM
EILLMPTU MULTIPLE
EILLMSST MISTELLS
EILLMUVX VEXILLUM
EILLNOPY EPYLLION
EILLNOST STELLION
EILLNOTU LUTEOLIN
EILLNPUU LUPULINE
EILLNSTY SILENTLY
TINSELLY
EILLNSVY SNIVELLY
EILLNUVY UNLIVELY
EILLOORW WOOLLIER
EILLOOSW WOOLLIES
EILLOPTY POLITELY
EILLORST TRILLOES
TROLLIES
EILLORSU ROUILLES
EILLORSZ ZORILLES
EILLOSSS SOILLESS
EILLOSST TOILLESS
EILLOSTW LOWLIEST
EILLPRSS SPILLERS
EILLQSTU QUILLETS
EILLRSST STILLERS
EILLRSSW SWILLERS
EILLRSTT TESTRILL
EILLRSVY SILVERLY
EILLSSST LISTLESS
EILLSSTT STILLEST
EILLSTTT LITTLEST
EILLSTUV VITELLUS
EILMMNOS MOLIMENS
EILMMPRU PLUMMIER
EILMMRSS SLIMMERS
EILMMRSU SLUMMIER
EILMMSST SLIMMEST
EILMMSTU LUMMIEST
EILMNOPT PILOTMEN
EILMNOST MOLINETS
EILMNOSU EMULSION
EILMNOSV NOVELISM
EILMNOTU MOULINET
EILMNOTY MYLONITE
EILMNPSS LIMPNESS
EILMNPSU SPLENIUM
EILMNRST MINSTREL
EILMNSSS SLIMNESS
EILMNSSU EMULSINS
EILMNSTU MUSLINET
EILMNTUY MINUTELY
UNTIMELY
EILMOOPS LIPOSOME
EILMOORS SLOOMIER
EILMOOST TOILSOME
EILMOPRR IMPLORER
EILMOPRS IMPLORES
PELORISM
EILMOPST POLEMIST
EILMORRS LORIMERS
EILMOSTT MOTLIEST
EILMPPRU IMPURPLE
EILMPRSS SIMPLERS
EILMPRSU SLUMPIER
EILMPRUY IMPURELY
EILMPSST MISSPELT
SIMPLEST

EILMPSSU IMPULSES
EILMPSTU LUMPIEST
PLUMIEST
EILMRSSU MISRULES
EILMRSSY REMISSLY
EILMRSTU MURLIEST
EILMRSTY LYMITERS
EILMSSTU LITMUSES
EILMSUUV ELUVIUMS
EILMTTUU LUTETIUM
EILMTTUY MULTEITY
EILNNOST INSOLENT
EILNNOSW SNOWLINE
EILNNOTV VINOLENT
EILNNPSU PINNULES
EILNNTTY INTENTLY
EILNOOPP EPIPLOON
EILNOOPS POLONIES
POLONISE
EILNOOPZ POLONIZE
EILNOOST LOONIEST
OILSTONE
EILNOOSV VIOLONES
EILNOPPS PLENIPOS
EILNOPPY POLYPINE
EILNOPRS PROLINES
EILNOPRT TOPLINER
EILNOPRU NEUROPIL
EILNOPSS EPSILONS
EILNOPST POINTELS
PONTILES
TOPLINES
EILNOPTU UNPOLITE
EILNORRS LORINERS
EILNORRT RITORNEL
EILNORST RETINOLS
EILNORTT TROTLINE
EILNORTW TOWNLIER
EILNOSSU ELUSIONS
EILNOSSW LEWISSON
EILNOSTU ELUTIONS
OUTLINES
EILNOSTV NOVELIST
VIOLENTS
EILNOSTW TOWLINES
EILNOSUV EVULSION
EILNOSVV INVOLVES
EILNOTUV INVOLUTE
EILNOTXY XYLONITE
EILNOTYZ ZYLONITE
EILNPRSS PILSNERS
EILNPRST SPLINTER
EILNPRSU PURLINES
EILNPSST PLENISTS
EILNPSSU SPINULES
SPLENIUS
EILNPSUY SUPINELY
EILNQUUY UNIQUELY
EILNRRUU UNRULIER
EILNRSST SLINTERS
SNIRTLES
EILNRSTU INSULTER
LUSTRINE
EILNRSTY TINSELRY
EILNRTUV VIRULENT
EILNRTWY WINTERLY
EILNSSTT TINTLESS
EILNSSTU UTENSILS
EILNSSTW WESTLINS
EILNSSVY SYLVINES

EILNSTTU LUTENIST
EILNSUWY UNWISELY
EILOOPRR POORLIER
EILOOPST LOOPIEST
EILOOPTZ ZOPILOTE
EILOORST TROOLIES
EILOORTV OVERTOIL
EILOOSST OSTIOLES
STOOLIES
EILOOSTZ ZOOLITES
EILOPPPR POPPLIER
EILOPPRS SLOPPIER
EILOPPTY POLYPITE
EILOPRRT PORTLIER
EILOPRSS SPOILERS
EILOPRST POITRELS
EILOPRSU PERILOUS
EILOPRSV OVERSLIP
EILOPRTW PILEWORT
EILOPSSS PSILOSES
EILOPSST PISTOLES
PTILOSES
SLOPIEST
EILOPSSV PLOSIVES
EILOPSTT PISTOLET
PLOTTIES
POLITEST
EILOPSTX EXPLOITS
EILOPSUV PLUVIOSE
EILORRTU ULTERIOR
EILORSSS RISSOLES
EILORSSU SOILURES
EILORSTT TRIOLETS
EILORSTU LOURIEST
OUTLIERS
EILORSZZ SOZZLIER
EILORTTY TOILETRY
EILOSSST LOSSIEST
EILOSSTU LOUSIEST
EILOSTTT STILETTO
EILOSTUV OUTLIVES
SOLUTIVE
EILPPPRY PREPPILY
EILPPRRS RIPPLERS
EILPPRRT TRIPPLER
EILPPRSS SLIPPERS
EILPPRST RIPPLETS
STIPPLER
TIPPLERS
TRIPPLES
EILPPRSU PERIPLUS
SUPPLIER
EILPPRSY SLIPPERY
EILPPRTU PULPITER
EILPPSST STIPPLES
EILPPSSU SUPPLIES
EILPPSSW SWIPPLES
EILPPSTU PULPIEST
EILPRSST SPIRTLES
EILPRSTT SPLITTER
TRIPLETS
EILPRSTY PRIESTLY
SPRITELY
EILPRSUU PURLIEUS
EILPRSUY PLEURISY
EILPRTTY PRETTILY
EILPSSTT SPITTLES
EILPSSTU STIPULES
EILPSSUY SPULYIES
EILPSSUZ SPULZIES
EILQRRSU SQUIRREL
EILQRSTU QUILTERS
EILQRSUU LIQUEURS
EILQRSUY SQUIRELY
EILQSTUU LUSTIQUE
EILRRSSU SLURRIES
EILRRSTU SULTRIER
EILRRSTW TWIRLERS
EILRRTWY WRITERLY
EILRSSST STIRLESS
EILRSSTT SLITTERS
STILTERS
TESTRILS
EILRSSTU SURLIEST
EILRSSTY SISTERLY
EILRSSZZ SIZZLERS
EILRSTTU SURTITLE
EILRSTTW WRISTLET
EILRSTTZ STRELITZ
EILRSTUV RIVULETS
EILRSUUX LUXURIES
EILSSSTY STYLISES
EILSSTTU LUSTIEST
EILSSTTY STYLITES
EILSSTUU LITUUSES
EILSSTVY SYLVITES
EILSSTYZ STYLIZES
EILSSWZZ SWIZZLES
EILSTWZZ TWIZZLES
EIMMMNOT IMMOMENT
EIMMMORZ MOMZERIM
EIMMNNOT MONIMENT
EIMMNNTU MUNIMENT
EIMMNORS MISNOMER
EIMMOPRU EMPORIUM
EIMMOPST METOPISM
EIMMOSTT TOTEMISM
EIMMPRRS PRIMMERS
EIMMPRST PRIMMEST
EIMMPRSU PREMIUMS
EIMMPSSU PESSIMUM
EIMMRRST TRIMMERS
EIMMRSST MISTERMS
EIMMRSSW SWIMMERS
EIMMRSTT TRIMMEST
EIMMRSTU RUMMIEST
EIMMSSTU MUMSIEST
EIMMSTUY YUMMIEST
EIMNNOOT NOONTIME
EIMNNOPT IMPONENT
EIMNNOST MENTIONS
EIMNNOTT OINTMENT
EIMNNOUY EUONYMIN
EIMNOOPS EMPOISON
EIMNOORS IONOMERS
MOONRISE
EIMNOORT REMOTION
EIMNOORV OMNIVORE
EIMNOOSS MONOSIES
EIMNOOST EMOTIONS
MOONIEST
EIMNOOSX EXOMIONS
EIMNOPRT ORPIMENT
EIMNOPSS PEONISMS
EIMNOPST EMPTIONS
NEPOTISM
PIMENTOS
EIMNOPTT IMPOTENT
EIMNORSS MERSIONS
EIMNORSU INERMOUS
MONSIEUR
EIMNORSW WINSOMER
EIMNORTY ENORMITY
EIMNOSST MOISTENS
EIMNPRSS PRIMNESS
EIMNPSST MISSPENT
EIMNPSTU NUMPTIES
EIMNRSST ENTRISMS
MINSTERS
TRIMNESS
EIMNRSSU NEURISMS
EIMNRSTU TERMINUS
EIMNRSTY ENTRYISM
MISENTRY
EIMNSSSS SENSISMS
EIMNSSTU MISTUNES
EIMNSTTU MINUTEST
EIMNSUZZ MUEZZINS
EIMOORST MOORIEST
MOTORISE
ROOMIEST
EIMOORTZ MOTORIZE
EIMOPPRR IMPROPER
EIMOPPST MOPPIEST
EIMOPRRS PRIMEROS
PRIMROSE
PROMISER
EIMOPRRT IMPORTER
REIMPORT
EIMOPRRV IMPROVER
EIMOPRSS IMPOSERS
PROMISES
EIMOPRST IMPOSTER
EIMOPRSV IMPROVES
EIMOPRUU EUROPIUM
EIMOPSTY PEYOTISM
EIMOQSTU MISQUOTE
EIMORRSS MORRISES
EIMORRST MORTISER
STORMIER
EIMORRTT REMITTOR
EIMORRWW WIREWORM
EIMORSST EROTISMS
MORTISES
TRISOMES
EIMORSSV VERISMOS
EIMORSTT OMITTERS
EIMORSTU MISROUTE
MOISTURE
EIMORSTW MISWROTE
WORMIEST
EIMORSTY ISOMETRY
EIMORSVW OVERSWIM
EIMOSSST MOSSIEST
EIMOSSTT MOISTEST
EIMOSSTU MOUSIEST
EIMOSSTZ MESTIZOS
EIMOSTTT MOTTIEST
TOTEMIST
EIMOSTTU TITMOUSE
EIMPRRSU PRIMEURS
EIMPRSST IMPRESTS
EIMPRSSU PRIMUSES
EIMPRSTU IMPUREST
IMPUTERS
STUMPIER
EIMPSSST MISSTEPS
EIMPSSTU SPUMIEST
STUMPIES
EIMPSSTY EMPTYSIS
EIMPSTTU TUMPIEST
EIMQSSTU MESQUITS
EIMQSTUY MYSTIQUE
EIMRRRSU SMURRIER
EIMRRSSU SURMISER
EIMRSSST MISTRESS
EIMRSSSU MISUSERS
SURMISES
EIMRSSTT METRISTS
EIMRSSTY SMYTRIES
EIMRSSUU MIURUSES
EIMRSTTU SMUTTIER
EIMRSTUV VITREUMS
EIMRSTUX MIXTURES
EIMSSSSU MISSUSES
EIMSSSTU MUSSIEST
EIMSSTTU MUSTIEST
EIMSTUZZ MUZZIEST
EINNOOTX NEOTOXIN
EINNOPSS PENSIONS
EINNOQSU QUINONES
EINNORST INTONERS
TERNIONS
EINNORSU REUNIONS
EINNORSV ENVIRONS
EINNORTT TONTINER
EINNORTU NEUTRINO
EINNORTV INVENTOR
NOVERINT
EINNORWW WINNOWER
EINNOSSS NOSINESS
EINNOSST TENSIONS
EINNOSSV VENISONS
EINNOSTT TINSTONE
TONTINES
EINNOSTU NOUNIEST
EINNPRSS SPINNERS
EINNPRST ENPRINTS
EINNPRSY SPINNERY
EINNPSST SPINNETS
EINNPSSU PUNINESS
EINNPSSY SPINNEYS
EINNPSXY SIXPENNY
EINNRSTU RUNNIEST
STURNINE
EINNRSTV VINTNERS
EINNRTTU NUTRIENT
EINNSSTU SUNNIEST
EINNSSUW UNSINEWS
EINNSTUW UNTWINES
EINOOPRS POISONER
SNOOPIER
SPOONIER
EINOOPSS SPOONIES
EINOORSS EROSIONS
EINOORST SNOOTIER
EINOORSZ OZONISER
SNOOZIER
EINOORZZ OZONIZER
EINOOSST ISOTONES
EINOOSSZ OOZINESS
OZONISES
EINOOSTZ ZOONITES
EINOOSZZ OZONIZES
EINOOTXX EXOTOXIN
EINOPPRS POPERINS
PROPINES
EINOPRRS PRISONER
EINOPRSS PORINESS
PRESSION

	ROPINESS
EINOPRST	POINTERS
	PROTEINS
	REPOINTS
EINOPRSU	PRUINOSE
EINOPRSV	OVERSPIN
	PROVINES
EINOPRTU	ERUPTION
EINOPSTT	NEPOTIST
EINOQSTU	QUESTION
EINOQTTU	QUOTIENT
EINORRST	INTRORSE
	SNORTIER
EINORRTV	INVERTOR
EINORSSS	ROSINESS
EINORSST	TERSIONS
EINORSSU	NEUROSIS
	RESINOUS
EINORSSV	VERSIONS
EINORSTT	SNOTTIER
	TENORIST
	TRITONES
EINORSTU	ROUTINES
	SNOUTIER
EINORSTV	INVESTOR
EINORSTY	TYROSINE
EINORSTZ	TRIZONES
EINORSUV	SOUVENIR
EINORTTU	RITENUTO
EINOSSSS	SESSIONS
EINOSSST	SONSIEST
	STENOSIS
EINOSSTT	SNOTTIES
	STONIEST
EINOSSTW	SNOWIEST
EINOSTTT	TOTIENTS
EINOSTTW	TOWNIEST
EINOSTUU	TENUIOUS
EINOSTVY	VENOSITY
EINPPRSS	SNIPPERS
EINPPSST	SNIPPETS
EINPPSTY	SNIPPETY
EINPRRST	PRINTERS
	REPRINTS
	SPRINTER
EINPRRTU	PRURIENT
EINPRSST	SPINSTER
EINPRSTU	REPUNITS
	UNPRIEST
	UNRIPEST
EINPRTTU	INPUTTER
EINPSTTX	SPINTEXT
EINPSTTY	TINTYPES
EINQRSTU	SQUINTER
EINQSSTU	INQUESTS
EINQSTTU	QUINTETS
EINQSTUU	UNIQUEST
	UNQUIETS
EINQTTTU	QUINTETT
EINRRSSU	INSURERS
EINRSSST	INSTRESS
EINRSSSU	SUNRISES
EINRSSTT	ENTRISTS
	STINTERS
EINRSSXY	SYRINXES
EINRSTTU	RUNTIEST
EINRSTTW	TWINTERS
EINRSTTY	ENTRYIST
EINRSTUV	UNRIVETS
	VENTURIS
EINRSTUW	UNWRITES
EINRTUUV	UNVIRTUE
EINSSSST	SENSISTS
EINSSTTW	ENTWISTS
	TWINSETS
EINSSTUW	UNWISEST
EINSSTUX	UNSEXIST
EINSSTXY	SYNTEXIS
EINSTTTU	NUTTIEST
EINSTTTW	TWITTENS
EIOOPPRS	PORPOISE
EIOOPPST	OPPOSITE
EIOOPRST	PORTOISE
	ROOPIEST
EIOOPSST	ISOTOPES
EIOOPSTV	POOVIEST
EIOORRSS	SORORISE
EIOORRST	ROOTSIER
EIOORRSZ	SORORIZE
EIOORSTT	ROOTIEST
	TORTOISE
EIOOSSTT	SOOTIEST
	TOOTSIES
EIOOSTWZ	WOOZIEST
EIOPPPST	POPPIEST
EIOPPRTW	PIPEWORT
EIOPPSST	SOPPIEST
EIOPRRSS	PRIORESS
EIOPRRST	PIERROTS
	SPORTIER
EIOPRRSU	SUPERIOR
EIOPRRTV	OVERTRIP
EIOPRSST	PERIOSTS
	PROSIEST
	REPOSITS
	RIPOSTES
	TRIPOSES
EIOPRSTT	PORTIEST
	RISPETTO
	SPOTTIER
EIOPRSTU	ROUPIEST
	SPOUTIER
EIOPRSTV	PIVOTERS
	SPORTIVE
EIOPRSUV	PERVIOUS
	PREVIOUS
	VIPEROUS
EIOPRTTT	TRIPTOTE
EIOPRTTY	PETITORY
EIOPRTUZ	OUTPRIZE
EIOPSSST	SEPIOSTS
EIOPSSTU	SOUPIEST
EIOPSSTY	ISOTYPES
EIOPSTTT	POTTIEST
EIOPSTTU	POUTIEST
EIOPSTTY	PEYOTIST
EIOPSTUW	WIPEOUTS
EIOQRSTU	QUOITERS
EIORRRST	ERRORIST
EIORRRSW	WORRIERS
EIORRRTU	ROTURIER
EIORRSST	RESISTOR
	ROISTERS
	SORRIEST
EIORRSSV	REVISORS
EIORRSTT	RORTIEST
EIORRSTU	STOURIER
EIORRSTV	SERVITOR
EIORRSUV	OUVRIERS
EIORRSVV	REVIVORS
EIORRSVY	REVISORY
EIORRTTU	TROUTIER
EIORSSTT	STOITERS
EIORSSTY	SEROSITY
EIORSTTU	TUTORISE
EIORSTTV	VIRETOTS
EIORSTUV	VIRTUOSE
	VITREOUS
	VOITURES
EIORTTUZ	TUTORIZE
EIOSSSTT	TOSSIEST
EIOSSTTU	TOUSIEST
EIOSSTTW	TOWSIEST
EIOSSTUZ	OUTSIZES
EIOSTTTT	TOTTIEST
EIOSTTTU	TOUTIEST
EIOSTTUZ	TOUZIEST
EIOSTTWZ	TOWZIEST
EIPPRRST	STRIPPER
	TRIPPERS
EIPPRRTY	TRIPPERY
EIPPRSTT	TRIPPETS
EIPQRSTU	QUIPSTER
EIPRRRSU	SPURRIER
EIPRRSSU	SPURRIES
	SURPRISE
EIPRRSTZ	SPRITZER
EIPRSSST	PERSISTS
EIPRSSSU	SUSPIRES
EIPRSSTT	SPITTERS
	TIPSTERS
EIPRSSTU	PURSIEST
EIPRSTTU	PURTIEST
	PUTTIERS
EIPRSUVW	PURVIEWS
EIPRSVVY	SPIVVERY
EIPSSTXY	PTYXISES
EIQRRSTU	SQUIRTER
EIQRSSSU	SQUIRESS
EIQRSSTU	QUERISTS
EIQRSTTU	QUITTERS
EIQRSUZZ	QUIZZERS
EIQRUYZZ	QUIZZERY
EIQSSUZZ	SQUIZZES
EIRRRSST	STIRRERS
EIRRSSTV	STRIVERS
EIRRSTTU	TRUSTIER
EIRSSSTU	SUITRESS
	TSURISES
EIRSSTTU	RUSTIEST
	TRUSTIES
EIRSSTTW	TWISTERS
EIRSSUVV	SURVIVES
EIRSSUVW	SURVIEWS
EIRSTTTU	RUTTIEST
EIRSTTTW	TWITTERS
EIRSTTUX	TUTRIXES
EIRTTTWY	TWITTERY
EIRTTUWZ	WURTZITE
EISSSSTU	TUSSISES
EJLLORSY	JOLLYERS
EJLOPSTU	PULSOJET
EJMOPRUV	OVERJUMP
EJNORRSU	REJOURNS
EJNORSUY	JOURNEYS
EJNRSTUU	UNJUSTER
EJNSSSTU	JUSTNESS
EJOORSVY	OVERJOYS
EJORSSTU	JOUSTERS
EJOSSTTU	OUTJESTS
EKKLOOSY	OLYKOEKS
EKKLRSSU	SKULKERS
EKKMORSY	KROMESKY
EKLLMSSU	SKELLUMS
EKLLOSSY	KYLLOSES
EKLLRRSU	KRULLERS
EKLNOOOR	ONLOOKER
EKLNOPRS	PLONKERS
EKLNORSS	SNORKELS
EKLNOSST	KNOTLESS
EKLNPRSU	PLUNKERS
EKLOOORV	OVERLOOK
EKLOOPSW	SLOWPOKE
EKLORSSW	WORKLESS
EKLSSSTU	TUSKLESS
EKLSSTTU	SKUTTLES
EKMMORSU	MURKSOME
EKMMRSSU	SKUMMERS
EKMNOSSU	MUSKONES
EKMOOPRR	MOREPORK
EKMOORSW	WORKSOME
EKMOOSSS	KOSMOSES
EKMRSTUY	MUSKETRY
EKNNOPSU	UNSPOKEN
EKNOOPRW	OPENWORK
EKNOORSS	SNOOKERS
EKNOORST	STROOKEN
EKNOPPSU	UPSPOKEN
EKNORSST	STONKERS
EKNORSTT	KNOTTERS
EKNORSTW	NETWORKS
EKNORSUY	YOUNKERS
EKNRSTUY	TURNKEYS
EKOOORTV	OVERTOOK
EKOOPRRV	PROVOKER
EKOOPRRW	ROPEWORK
EKOOPRSV	PROVOKES
EKOOPRSY	SPOOKERY
EKOOPSTU	OUTSPOKE
EKOORRVW	OVERWORK
EKOORSST	STOOKERS
	STROOKES
EKOPRSTU	UPSTROKE
EKOPRSUY	KOUPREYS
EKORRSST	STROKERS
EKORRUVY	KURVEYOR
EKORSSTU	KURTOSES
EKPPSSUU	SEPPUKUS
ELLLMOWY	MELLOWLY
ELLLNSUY	SULLENLY
ELLLORRS	LORRELLS
ELLMNOOS	MOELLONS
ELLMNOSY	SOLEMNLY
ELLMNOTY	MOLTENLY
ELLMNPUY	LUMPENLY
ELLMOORS	MORELLOS
ELLMPSUU	PLUMULES
ELLNNOST	TONNELLS
ELLNNSSU	NULLNESS
ELLNOORV	LOVELORN
ELLNOOSW	WOOLLENS
ELLNOPRU	PRUNELLO
ELLNOSST	STOLLENS
ELLNOSSU	NOUSELLS
ELLNOSVY	SLOVENLY
ELLNOSXY	XYLENOLS
ELLNOUVY	UNLOVELY
ELLNPSSU	UNSPELLS
ELLOOSSW	WOOSELLS
ELLOPRRS	PROLLERS

ELLOPRST	POLLSTER
ELLOPRTU	POLLUTER
ELLOPRUV	PULLOVER
ELLOPSST	PLOTLESS
ELLOPSTU	POLLUTES
ELLORRST	STROLLER
	TROLLERS
ELLORSTY	TROLLEYS
ELLOSSSU	SOULLESS
ELLOSSTU	OUTSELLS
ELLOSTTU	OUTTELLS
ELLOSTUW	OUTSWELL
	OUTWELLS
ELLPPSUY	SUPPLELY
ELLPSSUW	UPSWELLS
ELLSSSTU	LUSTLESS
ELMMNOTU	LOMENTUM
ELMMNOTY	MOMENTLY
ELMMORST	TROMMELS
ELMMOSUX	LUMMOXES
ELMMPSTU	PLUMMETS
ELMMRSSU	SLUMMERS
ELMMRSTU	STRUMMEL
ELMMRSUY	SUMMERLY
ELMMSSTU	STUMMELS
ELMNNOSU	UNSOLEMN
ELMNOOOP	MONOPOLE
ELMNOOSS	MOONLESS
ELMNOOST	MOONLETS
ELMNOPSU	PULMONES
ELMNPPSU	PLUMPENS
ELMNPSUU	UNPLUMES
ELMNUUZZ	UNMUZZLE
ELMOOPPS	POMPELOS
ELMOOPSY	POLYSOME
ELMOORST	TREMOLOS
ELMOORSY	MOROSELY
ELMOOSSY	LYSOSOME
ELMOPRSY	POLYMERS
ELMOPRTY	METOPRYL
ELMOPRYY	POLYMERY
ELMOPSYY	POLYSEMY
ELMORSSU	EMULSORS
ELMOSYYZ	LYSOZYME
ELMPPRSU	PLUMPERS
ELMPPSTU	PLUMPEST
ELMPRSSU	RUMPLESS
ELMRRTUU	MULTURER
ELMRSTUU	MULTURES
ELMRSUZZ	MUZZLERS
ELNNOOSU	UNLOOSEN
ELNNOPTU	NONUPLET
ELNOOSST	SOLONETS
ELNOOSSU	UNLOOSES
ELNOOSSZ	SNOOZLES
ELNOOSTZ	SOLONETZ
ELNOPTTY	POTENTLY
ELNORSSU	NOURSLES
ELNORSTU	TURNSOLE
ELNORSVY	SLOVENRY
ELNORTTY	ROTTENLY
ELNOSSSW	SLOWNESS
	SNOWLESS
ELNOSSTV	SOLVENTS
ELNOSSTW	TOWNLESS
	WONTLESS
ELNOSTUZ	ZONULETS
ELNPPSUU	UNSUPPLE
ELNPRTUU	PURULENT
ELNSSUZZ	SNUZZLES

ELOOPRSS	SPOOLERS
ELOOPRSU	SUPERLOO
ELOOPRUW	OWERLOUP
ELOOPSSS	SESSPOOL
ELOORSST	ROOTLESS
ELOORSTT	ROOTLETS
ELOORSTU	TORULOSE
ELOORSUV	OVERSOUL
ELOOSSST	SOOTLESS
ELOOSSTU	OUTSOLES
ELOOSSWY	WOOLSEYS
ELOOSVVX	VOLVOXES
ELOPPRRY	PROPERLY
ELOPPSST	STOPPLES
ELOPRRSU	PROULERS
ELOPRRSW	PROWLERS
ELOPRRSY	PYRROLES
ELOPRRTY	PORTERLY
ELOPRSSS	PLESSORS
ELOPRSSU	SPORULES
ELOPRSTT	PLOTTERS
ELOPRSTU	PLOUTERS
	POULTERS
ELOPRSTW	PLOWTERS
ELOPRSTY	PROSTYLE
	PROTYLES
ELOPRSUV	OVERPLUS
ELOPRSYY	PYROLYSE
ELOPRXYY	PYROXYLE
ELOPRYYZ	PYROLYZE
ELOPSSST	SPOTLESS
	STOPLESS
ELOPSSUU	OPULUSES
ELOPSTTU	OUTSLEPT
ELORSSTT	SETTLORS
	SLOTTERS
ELORSTUY	SOUTERLY
	UROSTYLE
ELORTTTU	TROUTLET
ELOSSSTY	SYSTOLES
ELOSSTUU	SETULOUS
ELOSSWZZ	SWOZZLES
ELPPRSTU	PURPLEST
ELPPSSTU	SUPPLEST
ELPRRSSU	SLURPERS
ELPRSSSU	SPURLESS
ELPRSSTU	SPURTLES
ELPRSTTU	SPLUTTER
ELPRSTUU	PULTURES
ELPRSUZZ	PUZZLERS
ELPSSTUU	PUSTULES
ELRRSSTU	RUSTLERS
ELRRSTTU	TURTLERS
ELRSSSTU	RUSTLESS
ELRSTTUY	SLUTTERY
ELRSTUUV	VULTURES
ELSSSTUY	STYLUSES
ELSSSTYY	SYSTYLES
EMMMNOTU	MOMENTUM
EMMNNOTU	MONUMENT
EMMNOORS	MONOMERS
EMMNOORT	MOTORMEN
EMMNORSU	SUMMONER
EMMNORSY	MERONYMS
EMMNORYY	MERONYMY
EMMNOSTY	METONYMS
EMMNOTTU	TOMENTUM
EMMNOTYY	METONYMY
EMMOOORS	ROOMSOME
EMMOPRRS	PROMMERS

EMMOPTTY	POMMETTY
EMMRRRUU	MURMURER
	REMURMUR
EMMRSTYY	SYMMETRY
EMNNNOOU	NOUMENON
EMNNOOOT	MONOTONE
EMNNOSTW	TOWNSMEN
EMNNPSTU	PUNTSMEN
EMNNSTTU	STUNTMEN
EMNOOPST	METOPONS
EMNOOPTY	MONOTYPE
EMNOORST	MESOTRON
	MONTEROS
EMNOORSU	ENORMOUS
	NEMOROUS
EMNOORSW	NEWSROOM
EMNOORTY	NOOMETRY
EMNOOSST	MOONSETS
EMNOOSUV	VENOMOUS
EMNOOTTY	TENOTOMY
EMNOOTUV	OUTVENOM
EMNOOTWY	TOYWOMEN
EMNORRSU	MOURNERS
EMNORSST	MONSTERS
EMNORSTT	SORTMENT
	TORMENTS
EMNORSTU	MONTURES
	MOUNTERS
	REMOUNTS
EMNORSUU	NUMEROUS
EMNOSSST	STEMSONS
EMNOSUUY	EUONYMUS
EMNRSSTU	MUNSTERS
	STERNUMS
EMOOPRRT	PROMOTER
EMOOPRST	PROMOTES
EMOOPRSY	POMEROYS
	PYROSOME
EMOOPRSZ	ZOOSPERM
EMOOPSSU	ESPUMOSO
EMOORSST	MOROSEST
EMOORSSU	UROSOMES
EMOORTYZ	ZOOMETRY
EMOOSSTW	TWOSOMES
EMOOSSTY	MYOSOTES
EMOOSTUV	OUTMOVES
EMOPPRRT	PROMPTER
EMOPRSST	STOMPERS
EMOPRSSU	SPERMOUS
	SUPREMOS
EMORRRUU	RUMOURER
EMORRSSU	MORSURES
EMORSSSU	SMOUSERS
EMORSSTU	OESTRUMS
	STRUMOSE
EMORSUVW	OVERSWUM
EMOSSTTW	WESTMOST
EMOSSTVZ	ZEMSTVOS
EMPRRTUY	TRUMPERY
EMPRSSTU	STUMPERS
	SUMPTERS
EMPRSSUU	RUMPUSES
EMPRSTTU	STRUMPET
	TRUMPETS
EMRRSSTU	STURMERS
ENNOOORT	TENOROON
ENNOOOTZ	ENTOZOON
ENNOOPPT	OPPONENT
ENNOORST	NORTENOS
ENNOOSTT	NONETTOS

ENNOPRSU	UNPERSON
ENNOPRUV	UNPROVEN
ENNOPTWY	TWOPENNY
ENNORSST	STERNSON
ENNORSTU	NEUTRONS
ENNORTTU	UNROTTEN
ENNOSSTU	NEUSTONS
	SUNSTONE
ENNPPTUY	TUPPENNY
ENNRSSTU	STUNNERS
ENOOOSSZ	ZOONOSES
ENOOPPRS	PROPONES
ENOOPPST	POSTPONE
ENOOPRSS	POORNESS
	SNOOPERS
ENOOPSSY	SPOONEYS
ENOOPSTT	POTSTONE
ENOORRVW	OVERWORN
ENOORSSZ	SNOOZERS
ENOORSVW	OVERSOWN
ENOOSSTT	TESTOONS
ENOOSTXY	OXYTONES
ENOPPRRU	UNPROPER
ENOPRRSU	PRONEURS
ENOPRSST	POSTERNS
ENOPRSTT	PORTENTS
ENOPRTUW	UPTOWNER
ENOPSSST	STEPSONS
ENOPSSSY	SYNOPSES
ENOPSTTU	OUTSPENT
ENOQSTUU	UNQUOTES
ENORRSST	SNORTERS
ENORRSTT	TORRENTS
ENORRSUV	OVERRUNS
ENORRTUU	TOURNURE
ENORRTUV	OVERTURN
	TURNOVER
ENORSSSU	SOURNESS
ENORSSTT	SNOTTERS
	STENTORS
ENORSSTU	TONSURES
ENORSTTU	STENTOUR
ENORSTTY	SNOTTERY
ENORSTUV	VENTROUS
ENORSTUY	TOURNEYS
ENOSSSUU	SENSUOUS
ENOSSTTU	STOUTENS
ENPRRSSU	SPURNERS
ENPRSSSY	SPRYNESS
ENPRSSTU	PUNSTERS
ENPRSSUU	PRUNUSES
	UNPURSES
ENPRTTUY	UNPRETTY
ENRRRTUU	NURTURER
ENRRSTUU	NURTURES
ENRSSTTU	ENTRUSTS
ENRSSTUU	UNSUREST
ENRSTTUU	UNTRUEST
EOOOPRSS	OOSPORES
	SOPOROSE
EOOOPRSZ	ZOOSPORE
EOOOPRTZ	ZOOTROPE
EOOPPRRS	PROPOSER
EOOPPRSS	OPPOSERS
	PROPOSES
EOOPPRSV	POPOVERS
EOOPPSST	POSTPOSE
EOOPPTTY	TOPOTYPE
EOOPRRSS	SPOORERS
EOOPRRST	PROTORES

	TROOPERS
EOOPRRTU	OUTROPER
	UPROOTER
EOOPRSST	STOOPERS
EOOPRSTU	OUTROPES
	PORTEOUS
EOOPRSTV	OVERPOST
	OVERTOPS
	STOPOVER
EOOPRSTW	TOWROPES
EOOPRTUW	OUTPOWER
EOOPSTYZ	ZOOTYPES
EOORRRSW	SORROWER
EOORRSST	ROOSTERS
EOORSSTU	OESTROUS
EOORSSVW	OVERSOWS
EOORSTUW	OUTSWORE
EOORTTUV	OUTVOTER
EOOSTTUV	OUTVOTES
EOPPRRSS	PROSPERS
EOPPRRTY	PROPERTY
EOPPRSST	STOPPERS
EOPPRSSU	PURPOSES
	SUPPOSER
EOPPRSSW	SWOPPERS
EOPPSSSU	SUPPOSES
EOPRRSST	PORTRESS
	SPORTERS
EOPRRSTU	POSTURER
	TROUPERS
EOPRRUVY	PURVEYOR
EOPRSSTT	PROTESTS
	SPOTTERS
EOPRSSTU	POSTURES
	SEPTUORS
	SPOUTERS
EOPRSSUU	POURSUES
	UPROUSES
EOPRSSUW	POURSEWS
EOPSSTTU	OUTSTEPS
EOPSSTTW	STEWPOTS
EOQRSSTU	QUESTORS
EORRRTTU	TORTURER
EORRSSST	STRESSOR
	TROSSERS
EORRSSTU	ROUSTERS
	TROUSERS
EORRSSTW	STROWERS
	TROWSERS
EORRSSTY	ROYSTERS
EORRSTTT	TROTTERS
EORRSTTU	TORTURES
	TROUTERS
EORRSUVY	SURVEYOR
EORRTUUV	TROUVEUR
EORSSSTU	TUSSORES
EORSSTTT	STOTTERS
EORSSTTU	TUTORESS
EORSSTTW	SWOTTERS
EORSSTUX	SEXTUORS
EORSTTUW	OUTWREST
EORSTUUV	VERTUOUS
EOSSTTTU	STOUTEST
EPPPRTUY	PUPPETRY
EPPRRSUU	PURPURES
EPPRSSSU	SUPPRESS
EPPRSSUY	SUPERSPY
EPRRRSSU	SPURRERS
EPRRSSUU	PURSUERS
	USURPERS
EPRRSSUY	SPURREYS
EPRRSTUU	RUPTURES
EPRSSTTU	SPUTTERS
EPRSTTUY	SPUTTERY
EQRRTUUU	TRUQUEUR
ERRSSSTU	TRUSSERS
ERRSSTTU	TRUSTERS
ERRSSTTY	TRYSTERS
ERRSTTTU	STRUTTER
ERSSTTTU	STUTTERS
FFFGILNU	FLUFFING
FFFMOOTU	FOOTMUFF
FFGGIILN	GLIFFING
FFGHIINW	WHIFFING
FFGHINOU	HOUFFING
FFGHINOW	HOWFFING
FFGHIRSU	GRUFFISH
FFGIIKNS	SKIFFING
FFGIILNP	PIFFLING
FFGIILNR	RIFFLING
FFGIILNS	SIFFLING
FFGIINNS	SNIFFING
FFGIINPS	SPIFFING
FFGIINRS	GRIFFINS
FFGIINST	STIFFING
	TIFFINGS
FFGIKNOS	SKOFFING
FFGILMNU	MUFFLING
FFGILNPU	PLUFFING
FFGILNRU	RUFFLING
FFGINNSU	SNUFFING
FFGINOPU	POUFFING
FFGINORS	GRIFFONS
FFGINOSW	SOWFFING
FFGINPSU	PUFFINGS
FFGINSTU	STUFFING
FFHIISST	STIFFISH
FFHIISTY	FIFTYISH
FFHIKNSU	HUFFKINS
FFHIOPSS	SPOFFISH
FFHIRSSU	SURFFISH
FFHOOOST	OFFSHOOT
FFIILMOR	FILIFORM
FFIILNSY	SNIFFILY
FFIILNTY	FLINTIFY
FFIINOOS	SOFFIONI
FFIKLRSU	FRISKFUL
FFILLLSU	FULFILLS
FFILLTUY	FITFULLY
FFILRTUU	FRUITFUL
FFILSSTU	FISTFULS
FFILSTUY	STUFFILY
FFIMORSU	FUSIFORM
FFINOPRT	OFFPRINT
FFINOPST	PONTIFFS
FFKLORSU	FORKFULS
FFLLOOSU	LOOFFULS
FFLMNOOU	MOUFFLON
FFLNOTUU	FOUNTFUL
FFLORRUU	FURFUROL
FFNORSTU	TURNOFFS
FFNSTUUY	UNSTUFFY
FFOOPSST	STOPOFFS
FGGGIINR	FRIGGING
FGGGILNO	FLOGGING
FGGGINOR	FROGGING
FGGHIINT	FIGHTING
FGGHIISS	FISHGIGS
FGGHINTU	GUNFIGHT
FGGIILNN	FLINGING
FGGIINNR	FRINGING
FGGIINRT	GRIFTING
FGGIINRU	FIGURING
FGGIISZZ	FIZZGIGS
FGGILNOR	FROGLING
FGGILNOS	GOLFINGS
FGGINOOR	FORGOING
FGGINORS	FORGINGS
FGHIIKNS	KINGFISH
FGHIINSS	FISHINGS
FGHIINST	SHIFTING
FGHILLTU	LIGHTFUL
FGHILMTU	MIGHTFUL
FGHILNSU	FLUSHING
FGHILRTU	RIGHTFUL
FGHINORT	FROTHING
FGHINRSU	FRUSHING
FGHIOPST	GIFTSHOP
FGHIOTTU	OUTFIGHT
FGHLORUU	FURLOUGH
FGHNOORS	FOGHORNS
FGHNOTUU	UNFOUGHT
FGIIINNX	INFIXING
FGIIKLNS	FLISKING
FGIIKNNS	KNIFINGS
FGIIKNRS	FRISKING
FGIILLNR	FRILLING
FGIILLNS	FILLINGS
FGIILMNP	FLIMPING
FGIILNOO	FOLIOING
FGIILNOS	FOILINGS
FGIILNPP	FLIPPING
FGIILNRS	RIFLINGS
FGIILNRT	FLIRTING
	TRIFLING
FGIILNSS	FISSLING
FGIILNST	STIFLING
FGIILNTT	FLITTING
FGIILNZZ	FIZZLING
FGIINNST	SNIFTING
FGIINNSU	INFUSING
FGIINNUX	UNFIXING
FGIINNUY	UNIFYING
FGIINOQU	QUOIFING
FGIINOST	FOISTING
FGIINRRS	FIRRINGS
FGIINRST	FRISTING
FGIINRTT	FRITTING
FGIINRTU	FRUITING
FGIINRZZ	FRIZZING
FGIINSST	SIFTINGS
FGIINSTT	FITTINGS
FGIINSTW	SWIFTING
FGIINSZZ	FIZZINGS
FGIIRSTU	FIGURIST
FGIKLNNU	FLUNKING
FGILLNOW	WOLFLING
FGILLNOY	FOLLYING
FGILMNPU	FLUMPING
FGILNNTU	GUNFLINT
FGILNOOR	FLOORING
FGILNOOS	FOOLINGS
FGILNOOT	FOOTLING
FGILNOOZ	FOOZLING
FGILNOPP	FLOPPING
FGILNOPS	FOPLINGS
FGILNORS	ROLFINGS
FGILNORU	FLOURING
FGILNOSS	FLOSSING
FGILNOST	SOFTLING
FGILNOSU	FLOUSING
FGILNOSW	FOWLINGS
	WOLFINGS
FGILNOTU	FLOUTING
	OUTFLING
FGILNPRU	PURFLING
FGILNRRU	FLURRING
FGILNSTU	FLUTINGS
FGILNSTY	FLYTINGS
FGILNUZZ	FUZZLING
FGIMNORS	FORMINGS
FGIMNPRU	FRUMPING
FGIMOSSY	FOGYISMS
FGINNORT	FRONTING
FGINNORW	FROWNING
FGINOOPR	PROOFING
FGINOOPS	SPOOFING
FGINOORS	ROOFINGS
FGINOOST	FOOTINGS
FGINORST	FROSTING
FGINORTU	FOUTRING
FGINRRSU	FURRINGS
FGINRSSU	SURFINGS
FGINRSTU	TURFINGS
FGINSTTU	TUFTINGS
FGIORSTW	FIGWORTS
FGISSTUU	FUGUISTS
FGLLMOOU	GLOOMFUL
FGLLNSUU	LUNGFULS
FGLNORSU	FURLONGS
FGLNORUW	WRONGFUL
FGLOOOST	FOOTSLOG
FGLORSUU	FULGOURS
FGLSSTUU	GUTSFULS
FGNOORSU	FOURGONS
FGNOORTU	UNFORGOT
FHHOORST	SHOFROTH
FHIIKLMS	MILKFISH
FHIIKNSS	FISHSKIN
FHIILLTY	FILTHILY
FHIILRST	FLIRTISH
FHIILSTY	SHIFTILY
FHIKLLLO	HILLFOLK
FHIKMNOS	MONKFISH
FHIKNORT	FORTHINK
FHILLOOT	FOOTHILL
FHILMPSU	LUMPFISH
FHILMRTU	MIRTHFUL
FHILORSU	FLOURISH
FHILORTY	FROTHILY
FHILPSSU	SHIPFULS
FHIMPRSU	FRUMPISH
FHINOSSU	FUSHIONS
FHINRTTU	UNTHRIFT
FHIOOPTT	PHOTOFIT
FHIOPSSX	FOXSHIPS
FHIORSTY	FORTYISH
FHKORSTU	FUTHORKS
FHLLLOTU	LOTHFULL
FHLLOSTU	SLOTHFUL
FHLMOTUU	MOUTHFUL
FHLNORSU	HORNFULS
FHLOOSTU	SOOTHFUL
FHLOOTTU	TOOTHFUL
FHLOPSSU	SHOPFULS
FHLORTTU	TROTHFUL
FHLORTUW	WORTHFUL
FHLORTUY	FOURTHLY
FHLOSTUU	OUTFLUSH
FHLOTUUY	YOUTHFUL

FHLRTTUU TRUTHFUL
FHOOORST FORSOOTH
HOOFROTS
FIIINNTY INFINITY
FIIKLRSY FRISKILY
FIILLMOS MILFOILS
FIILLMSY FLIMSILY
FIILLMTU MULTIFIL
FIILLNTY FLINTILY
FIILMNRY INFIRMLY
FIILMOPR PILIFORM
FIILMPSY SIMPLIFY
FIILNOST TINFOILS
FIILTTUY FUTILITY
FIIMMNSU INFIMUMS
FIIMOPRS PISIFORM
FIIMOSTY MOISTIFY
FIINNOSU INFUSION
FIINORTU FRUITION
FIINOSSS FISSIONS
FIINTUXY UNFIXITY
FIIQUYZZ QUIZZIFY
FIKKLNOS KINFOLKS
KINSFOLK
FIKLLLSU SKILLFUL
FIKLNOSW WOLFKINS
WOLFSKIN
FIKLNSSU SKINFULS
FIKNORSW FORSWINK
FILLLUWY WILFULLY
FILLNSUY SINFULLY
SULFINYL
FILLNUUW UNWILFUL
FILLOPPY FLOPPILY
FILLOPSU SPOILFUL
FILMNOOS MONOFILS
FILMOPRS SLIPFORM
FILMORRY LYRIFORM
FILMOSSU MOFUSSIL
FILNOSUX FLUXIONS
FILOOSTW WITLOOFS
FILORSST FLORISTS
FILORSTU FLORUITS
FILORSTY FROSTILY
FILRSTTU TRISTFUL
FILSSTTU FLUTISTS
FILSTTUY STULTIFY
FIMMNOOR OMNIFORM
FIMMORRU MURIFORM
FIMMORSS MISFORMS
FIMNORSU UNIFORMS
FIMOPRRY PYRIFORM
FIMORTUY FUMITORY
FIMOSTUY FUMOSITY
FIMRSTUU FUTURISM
FINORSSS FRISSONS
FINORSUY INFUSORY
FIOORSSU FURIOSOS
FIORTTUY FORTUITY
FIRSTTUU FUTURIST
FIRTTUUY FUTURITY
FJLLOUYY JOYFULLY
FJLNOUUY UNJOYFUL
FKKLOORW WORKFOLK
FKKOORTW KOFTWORK
FKLMOOOT FOLKMOOT
FKLNRTUU TRUNKFUL
FKMOORRW FORMWORK
FKNORSUW FORSWUNK
FKOOORTW FOOTWORK

FLLOOPUW UPFOLLOW
FLMNOOSU MOUFLONS
FLMNORUU MOURNFUL
FLMOOORW MOORFOWL
FLMOOOST TOMFOOLS
FLMOORSU ROOMFULS
FLMORSTU STORMFUL
FLNOOPSU SPOONFUL
FLNOORRS FORLORNS
FLNOOSTU SNOOTFUL
FLNOOTUW OUTFLOWN
FLOOOPTT POLTFOOT
FLOOPTTY TOPLOFTY
FLOORSSW FORSLOWS
FLOOSTUW OUTFLOWS
FLOPRSTU SPORTFUL
FLORTTUU TROUTFUL
FLRSTTUU TRUSTFUL
FMNOOOOR MOONROOF
FMRSSTUU FRUSTUMS
FNNOOORT FRONTOON
FNNOORST FRONTONS
FNOOORTW FOOTWORN
FNOOPRSU SUNPROOF
FNOORRSW FORSWORN
FNOORSSU SUNROOFS
FNOORTUW OUTFROWN
FOOOPRST ROOFTOPS
FOOOPSTT FOOTPOST
FOOORSTT FOOTROTS
FOOOSTTU OUTFOOTS
FOORSTTX FOXTROTS
GGGGIILN GIGGLING
GGGGIINR GRIGGING
GGGGILNO GOGGLING
GGGGILNU GLUGGING
GUGGLING
GGGGINOR GROGGING
GGGHIILN HIGGLING
GGGHIINT THIGGING
GGGHIINW WHIGGING
GGGHINOS HOGGINGS
SHOGGING
GGGIIJLN JIGGLING
GGGIIJNS JIGGINGS
GGGIILNN NIGGLING
GGGIILNS LIGGINGS
GGGIILNW WIGGLING
GGGIINNS SNIGGING
GGGIINPR PRIGGING
GGGIINPS PIGGINGS
GGGIINRS RIGGINGS
GGGIINRT TRIGGING
GGGIINSW SWIGGING
WIGGINGS
GGGIINTW TWIGGING
GGGIJLNO JOGGLING
GGGIJLNU JUGGLING
GGGIJNOS JOGGINGS
GGGIJNSU JUGGINGS
GGGIKNSU SKUGGING
GGGILNOO GOOGLING
GGGILNOS LOGGINGS
SLOGGING
GGGILNOT TOGGLING
GGGILNPU PLUGGING
PUGGLING
GGGILNRU GURGLING
GGGILNSU SLUGGING
GGGIMNSU MUGGINGS

SMUGGING
GGGINNOS NOGGINGS
SNOGGING
GGGINNSU SNUGGING
GGGINOPR PROGGING
GGGINORT TROGGING
GGGINOSS SOGGINGS
GGGINPSU PUGGINGS
GGGINRSU RUGGINGS
GGGINSSU SUGGINGS
GGGINSTU TUGGINGS
GGHHIINT HIGHTING
GGHHINOU HOUGHING
GGHIILNT LIGHTING
GGHIINPT PIGHTING
GGHIINRT GIRTHING
RIGHTING
GGHIINST SIGHTING
GGHIINTW WIGHTING
GGHIIPRS PRIGGISH
GGHILSSU SLUGGISH
GGHIMSTU THUGGISM
GGHINORU ROUGHING
GGHINOST GHOSTING
GGHINOSU SOUGHING
GGHINOTY HOGTYING
GGIIILNS GINGILIS
GGIIINNT IGNITING
GGIIJLNN JINGLING
GGIIKLNN KINGLING
GGIILLNR GRILLING
GGIILLNY GILLYING
GGIILMNN MINGLING
GGIILMNY GINGLYMI
GGIILNNP PINGLING
GGIILNNS SINGLING
SLINGING
GGIILNNT GLINTING
TINGLING
GGIILNPS PIGLINGS
GGIILNRS RIGLINGS
GGIIMNOS MISGOING
GGIIMNPU GUIMPING
GGIIMPRS PRIGGISM
GGIINNNR GRINNING
GGIINNOR GROINING
IGNORING
GGIINNOS INGOINGS
GGIINNOW WONGIING
GGIINNRS RINGINGS
GGIINNRW WRINGING
GGIINNSS SIGNINGS
SINGINGS
GGIINNST STINGING
GGIINNSW SWINGING
GGIINNTW TWINGING
GGIINNUV UNGIVING
GGIINPPR GRIPPING
GGIINPSY GIPSYING
GGIINRST RINGGITS
GGIINRTT GRITTING
GGIINSSU GUISINGS
GGIINSTU GIUSTING
GGIIRRSS GRISGRIS
GGILLNUY GULLYING
GGILLOOW GOLLIWOG
GGILMMNO GLOMMING
GGILMNOO GLOOMING
GGILNNOP PLONGING
GGILNNOS LONGINGS

GGILNNOU LOUNGING
GGILNNPU PLUNGING
GGILNNUU UNGLUING
GGILNOOP GLOOPING
GGILNORW GROWLING
GGILNORY GLORYING
GGILNOSS GLOSSING
GOSLINGS
GGILNOSV GLOVINGS
GGILNOSZ GLOZINGS
GGILNOTU GLOUTING
GGILNTTU GLUTTING
GUTTLING
GGILNUZZ GUZZLING
GGILQSUY SQUIGGLY
GGIMMNSU GUMMINGS
GGIMNOOR GROOMING
GGIMNPRU GRUMPING
GGINNNSU GUNNINGS
GGINNOOS ONGOINGS
GGINNOPR PRONGING
GGINNOPS SPONGING
GGINNORW WRONGING
GGINNOSS SINGSONG
GGINNOTU TONGUING
GGINNRTU GRUNTING
GGINNUVY UNGYVING
GGINOORV GROOVING
GGINOOST STOOGING
GGINOOTU OUTGOING
GGINOPRS PROGGINS
GGINOPRU GROUPING
GGINOPSU UPGOINGS
GGINORSS GROSSING
GGINORSU GROUSING
GGINORSW GROWINGS
GGINORTU GROUTING
GGINOSUV VOGUINGS
GGINPRSU PURGINGS
GGINPSYY GYPSYING
GGINRSSU SURGINGS
GGLLOOWY GOLLYWOG
GHHIILST LIGHTISH
GHHIINSW WHISHING
GHHIIRST RIGHTISH
GHHIISTT TIGHTISH
GHHILOSU GHOULISH
GHHIMNPU HUMPHING
GHHIMOST HIGHMOST
GHHINOOS HOOSHING
GHHINSSU SHUSHING
GHHIORSU ROUGHISH
GHHIOSTU TOUGHISH
GHHIRSST SHRIGHTS
GHHOORTU THOROUGH
GHHOSTTU THOUGHTS
GHIIJNOS JINGOISH
GHIIKNNT THINKING
GHIIKNPS KINGSHIP
GHIIKNRS SHIRKING
SHRIKING
GHIIKNSW WHISKING
GHIILLNO HILLOING
GHIILLNS SHILLING
GHIILMST MISLIGHT
GHIILMTY MIGHTILY
GHIILNPR HIRPLING
GHIILNRS HIRLINGS
HIRSLING
GHIILNRT THIRLING

GHIILNRW	WHIRLING
GHIILNST	TINGLISH
GHIILNTW	WHITLING
GHIILTTW	TWILIGHT
GHIIMMNS	SHIMMING
GHIIMMNW	WHIMMING
GHIIMNNU	INHUMING
GHIIMNST	SMITHING
GHIINNNS	SHINNING
GHIINNNT	THINNING
GHIINNNY	HINNYING
GHIINNRS	SHRINING
GHIINNST	NITHINGS
GHIINNSW	WHININGS
GHIINNUV	UNHIVING
GHIINOST	HOISTING
GHIINPPS	HIPPINGS
	SHIPPING
GHIINPPW	WHIPPING
GHIINRRS	SHIRRING
GHIINRRW	WHIRRING
GHIINRST	SHIRTING
GHIINRSV	SHRIVING
GHIINRTV	THRIVING
GHIINRTW	WRITHING
GHIINSSS	HISSINGS
GHIINSST	INSIGHTS
GHIINSSW	SWISHING
	WHISSING
	WISHINGS
GHIINSTT	SHITTING
	TITHINGS
GHIINSTW	WHISTING
	WHITINGS
GHIINSVV	SHIVVING
GHIINWZZ	WHIZZING
GHIIORSV	VIGORISH
GHIIRSTT	RIGHTIST
GHIKLNTY	KNIGHTLY
GHIKLSTY	SKYLIGHT
GHIKNNTU	UNKNIGHT
GHIKNSSU	HUSKINGS
GHIKRSTU	TUGHRIKS
GHILLNOO	HOLLOING
GHILLNOU	HULLOING
GHILLOTW	LOWLIGHT
GHILLSTY	SLIGHTLY
GHILMNSU	MULSHING
GHILMPSU	GLUMPISH
GHILNOOS	SHOOLING
GHILNOPP	HOPPLING
GHILNOPS	LONGSHIP
GHILNOPY	HOPINGLY
GHILNOSS	SLOSHING
GHILNOST	SLOTHING
GHILNOSU	HOUSLING
GHILNOSW	HOWLINGS
GHILNPSU	INGULPHS
GHILNRSU	HURLINGS
GHILNRTU	HURTLING
GHILNRUY	HUNGRILY
GHILNSSU	SLUSHING
GHILNSTU	HUSTLING
	SUNLIGHT
GHILORSW	SHOWGIRL
GHILPRTY	TRIGLYPH
GHIMMNSU	HUMMINGS
GHIMNOPR	MORPHING
GHIMNOPU	GUMPHION
GHIMNORU	HUMORING
GHIMNOSS	MOSHINGS
GHIMNOTU	MOUTHING
GHIMNPTU	THUMPING
GHIMNSTU	GUNSMITH
GHIMRSSU	SIMURGHS
GHINNNSU	SHUNNING
GHINNOOR	HONORING
GHINNOPY	PHONYING
GHINNORS	HORNINGS
GHINNORT	NORTHING
	THORNING
	THRONING
GHINNOST	NOTHINGS
GHINNSSU	SNUSHING
GHINNSTU	HUNTINGS
	SHUNTING
GHINOOPT	PHOTOING
GHINOOPW	WHOOPING
GHINOOST	SHOOTING
	SOOTHING
GHINOOSW	WOOSHING
GHINOOTT	TOOTHING
GHINOOTW	WHOOTING
GHINOPPS	HOPPINGS
	SHOPPING
GHINOPPW	WHOPPING
GHINOPSS	GINSHOPS
GHINORSS	HORSINGS
	SHORINGS
GHINORST	SHORTING
GHINORSV	SHROVING
GHINORSW	SHROWING
GHINORTT	TROTHING
GHINORTW	INGROWTH
	THROWING
	WORTHING
GHINOSST	HOSTINGS
GHINOSSU	HOUSINGS
GHINOSSW	SHOWINGS
GHINOSTT	HOTTINGS
	SHOTTING
	TONIGHTS
GHINOSTU	HOUTINGS
	SHOUTING
	SOUTHING
GHINOSTW	SOWTHING
GHINOSUY	YOUNGISH
GHINOTTU	OUTNIGHT
GHINPSSU	GUNSHIPS
GHINPTTU	PHUTTING
GHINRRUY	HURRYING
GHINRSTU	UNGIRTHS
	UNRIGHTS
GHINSSTU	HUSTINGS
GHINSTTU	HUTTINGS
	SHUTTING
GHIORTTU	OUTRIGHT
GHIOSTTU	OUTSIGHT
GHIPRSST	SPRIGHTS
GHIPRSTU	UPRIGHTS
GHIPRSUU	GURUSHIP
GHLMOOOS	HOMOLOGS
GHLMOOOY	HOMOLOGY
GHLNNOOR	LONGHORN
GHLNOORU	HOURLONG
GHLNORSU	SLUGHORN
GHLNOTYY	YONGTHLY
GHLOOORY	HOROLOGY
GHLORTUU	TURLOUGH
GHMORSSU	SORGHUMS
GHMOSSTU	MUGSHOTS
GHMPSSUY	SPHYGMUS
GHNOPRSY	GRYPHONS
GHNOPYYY	HYPOGYNY
GHNOSSTU	GUNSHOTS
	SHOTGUNS
GHNOSTUU	UNSOUGHT
GHNOSTUY	YOUNGTHS
GHOOOSSW	HOOSGOWS
GHOORTUY	YOGHOURT
GHOPRTUW	UPGROWTH
GHORSTUY	YOGHURTS
GIIILMNT	LIMITING
GIIILNNS	INISLING
GIIILNNU	LINGUINI
GIIILOTV	VITILIGO
GIIIMMNX	IMMIXING
GIIINNOS	IONISING
GIIINNOT	IGNITION
GIIINNOZ	IONIZING
GIIINNTV	INVITING
GIIINSTV	VISITING
GIIJMMNY	JIMMYING
GIIJMNOS	JINGOISM
GIIJNNOS	JOININGS
GIIJNNOT	JOINTING
GIIJNNRU	INJURING
GIIJNOST	JINGOIST
	JOISTING
GIIKKLNP	KINGKLIP
GIIKKNNS	SKINKING
GIIKKNRS	KIRKINGS
GIIKLLNS	KILLINGS
	SKILLING
GIIKLMNS	MILKINGS
GIIKLNNP	PLINKING
GIIKLNNS	INKLINGS
	SLINKING
GIIKLNNT	TINKLING
GIIKLNNW	WINKLING
GIIKLNRS	SKIRLING
GIIKLNST	KITLINGS
GIIKLNTT	KITTLING
GIIKMMNS	SKIMMING
GIIKMNPS	SKIMPING
GIIKMNRS	SMIRKING
GIIKNNNS	SKINNING
GIIKNNOV	INVOKING
GIIKNNPR	PRINKING
GIIKNNPS	PINKINGS
GIIKNNSS	SINKINGS
GIIKNNST	STINKING
GIIKNNSW	SWINKING
	WINKINGS
GIIKNNTT	KNITTING
GIIKNNTW	TWINKING
GIIKNPPS	SKIPPING
GIIKNPSS	PIGSKINS
GIIKNQRU	QUIRKING
GIIKNRRS	SKIRRING
GIIKNRSS	GRISKINS
GIIKNRST	SKIRTING
	STRIKING
GIIKNSSV	SKIVINGS
GIILLMNS	MILLINGS
GIILLMNU	ILLUMING
GIILLNOS	GILLIONS
GIILLNPR	PRILLING
GIILLNPS	PILLINGS
	SPILLING
GIILLNQU	QUILLING
GIILLNRT	TRILLING
GIILLNST	STILLING
	TILLINGS
GIILLNSW	SWILLING
GIILLNTT	LITTLING
GIILLNTW	TWILLING
GIILLNWY	WILLYING
GIILLOPW	POLLIWIG
GIILLPSW	PIGSWILL
GIILLTUY	GUILTILY
GIILLTYZ	GLITZILY
GIILMMNP	PLIMMING
GIILMMNS	SLIMMING
GIILMNNU	LUMINING
	UNLIMING
GIILMNOS	SMOILING
GIILMNPS	LIMPINGS
	SIMPLING
GIILMNPW	WIMPLING
GIILMNPY	IMPLYING
GIILMNSS	SMILINGS
GIILMNST	MISTLING
GIILMNZZ	MIZZLING
GIILMPRS	PILGRIMS
GIILMPSU	PUGILISM
GIILNNNU	UNLINING
GIILNNPP	NIPPLING
GIILNNPS	SPLINING
GIILNNTU	UNTILING
GIILNNTW	TWINLING
	WINTLING
GIILNNUV	UNLIVING
GIILNOPS	SPOILING
GIILNOPT	PILOTING
GIILNORS	LIGROINS
GIILNOSS	SOILINGS
GIILNOST	TOILINGS
GIILNPPR	RIPPLING
GIILNPPS	SIPPLING
	SLIPPING
GIILNPPT	TIPPLING
GIILNPRS	SPIRLING
GIILNPRT	TRIPLING
GIILNPSS	LISPINGS
	SPILINGS
GIILNQSU	QUISLING
GIILNQTU	QUILTING
GIILNRSW	SWIRLING
GIILNRTW	TWIRLING
GIILNRVY	VIRGINLY
GIILNSST	LISTINGS
GIILNSTT	SLITTING
	STILTING
	TILTINGS
	TITLINGS
GIILNSTU	LINGUIST
GIILNSTW	WITLINGS
GIILNSTY	STINGILY
GIILNSZZ	SIZZLING
GIILNTTT	TITTLING
GIILNTTU	TITULING
GIILNTTW	TWILTING
GIILOSST	OLIGISTS
GIILPSTU	PUGILIST
GIILRSST	STRIGILS
GIIMMNPR	PRIMMING
GIIMMNRS	RIMMINGS
GIIMMNRT	TRIMMING
GIIMMNRU	IMMURING

GIIMMNSW SWIMMING
GIIMNNOP IMPONING
GIIMNNOR MINORING
GIIMNNOY IGNOMINY
GIIMNNTU MINUTING
MUNITING
MUTINING
GIIMNOPS IMPOSING
GIIMNOST MOISTING
GIIMNOTT OMITTING
GIIMNOTV MOTIVING
VOMITING
GIIMNPPR PRIMPING
GIIMNPRS PRIMINGS
GIIMNPRU UMPIRING
GIIMNPTU IMPUTING
GIIMNRRS SMIRRING
GIIMNSST MISTINGS
GIIMNSSU MISUSING
GIIMNSSW SWINGISM
GIIMNSTT SMITTING
GIIMNSTU MUISTING
GIIMNSTY STIMYING
GIIMORRS RIGORISM
GIINNNOO ONIONING
GIINNNOT INTONING
NOINTING
GIINNNPS PINNINGS
SPINNING
GIINNNRU INURNING
GIINNNST TINNINGS
GIINNNSW WINNINGS
GIINNNTW TWINNING
GIINNOPR PROINING
GIINNOPS PIONINGS
GIINNOPT POINTING
GIINNOQU QUOINING
GIINNORS IRONINGS
NIGROSIN
ROSINING
GIINNORT IGNITRON
GIINNPPS SNIPPING
GIINNPRT PRINTING
GIINNPSS SNIPINGS
GIINNPSU PINGUINS
GIINNRSS RINSINGS
GIINNRSU INSURING
RUININGS
GIINNRTU UNTIRING
GIINNRUW UNWIRING
GIINNSSW INSWINGS
GIINNSTT STINTING
TINTINGS
GIINNSTU UNITINGS
GIINNSTW TWININGS
GIINNUVW UNWIVING
GIINOPST POSITING
SOPITING
GIINOPTV PIVOTING
GIINOQTU QUOITING
GIINORSS SIGNIORS
GIINORST RIOTINGS
ROISTING
ROSITING
GIINORSV VISORING
GIINORTZ ROZITING
GIINORVZ VIZORING
GIINOSTT STOITING
GIINPPQU QUIPPING
GIINPPRT TRIPPING
GIINPPST TIPPINGS
GIINPRSS RISPINGS
GIINPRST SPIRTING
STRIPING
GIINPRSU SIRUPING
UPRISING
GIINPSTT PITTINGS
SPITTING
GIINPTTU TITUPING
GIINQRSU SQUIRING
GIINQRTU QUIRTING
GIINQTTU QUITTING
GIINQUZZ QUIZZING
GIINRRST STIRRING
GIINRSTV STRIVING
GIINRSTW WRITINGS
GIINSSSW SWISSING
GIINSSTT SITTINGS
GIINSSTU SUITINGS
TISSUING
GIINSTTW TWISTING
WITTINGS
GIINSWZZ SWIZZING
GIINTTTW TWITTING
GIIORRST RIGORIST
GIIPRSTZ SPRITZIG
GIJKLNOY JOKINGLY
GIJLLNOY JOLLYING
GIJLNOST JOSTLING
GIJLNSTU JUSTLING
GIJNOSTT JOTTINGS
GIJNOSTU JOUSTING
GIJNTTUY JUTTYING
GIKKLNSU SKULKING
GIKKNNSU SKUNKING
GIKLLNNO KNOLLING
GIKLNNOP PLONKING
GIKLNNPU PLUNKING
GIKLNNRU KNURLING
RUNKLING
GIKLNNUY UNKINGLY
GIKLNOPR PORKLING
GIKLNRSU LURKINGS
GIKLORRW WORKGIRL
GIKMNOSS SMOKINGS
GIKNNOOS SNOOKING
GIKNNOPR PRONKING
GIKNNOQU QUONKING
GIKNNOST STONKING
GIKNNOSW SNOWKING
GIKNNOTT KNOTTING
GIKNNOTU KNOUTING
GIKNNOUY UNYOKING
GIKNNPSU SPUNKING
GIKNNRTU TRUNKING
GIKNOOPS SPOOKING
GIKNOOST STOOKING
GIKNOOTW KOTOWING
GIKNOPST KINGPOST
GIKNORRW RINGWORK
GIKNORST STROKING
GIKNORSW WORKINGS
GIKNSSTU TUSKINGS
GILLMOOY GLOOMILY
GILLNNSU NULLINGS
GILLNOPR PROLLING
GILLNOPS POLLINGS
GILLNORS ROLLINGS
GILLNORT TROLLING
GILLNOST TOLLINGS
GILLNOSY LOSINGLY
GILLNOVY LOVINGLY
GILLNPUY PULINGLY
GILLNSUY SULLYING
GILLOOPW POLLIWOG
GILLOPWY POLLYWIG
GILLORVY GILLYVOR
GILLOSSY GLOSSILY
GILMMNSU SLUMMING
GILMMTUY MULTIGYM
GILMNOOS SLOOMING
GILMNOPY MOPINGLY
GILMNORS MORLINGS
GILMNORT MORTLING
GILMNOSS MOSLINGS
GILMNOSU MOUSLING
GILMNOSY SMOYLING
GILMNOTT MOTTLING
GILMNOTU MOULTING
GILMNOUV VOLUMING
GILMNOVY MOVINGLY
GILMNPPU PLUMPING
GILMNPRU RUMPLING
GILMNPSU SLUMPING
GILMNSUY MUSINGLY
GILMNUZZ MUZZLING
GILMOOSY MISOLOGY
GILMPRUY GRUMPILY
GILNNOOS GLONOINS
LOONINGS
SNOOLING
GILNNOSU NOUSLING
GILNNOTW TOWNLING
GILNNOUV UNLOVING
GILNNRSU NURSLING
GILNNSSU UNSLINGS
GILNNUZZ NUZZLING
GILNOOPS LOOPINGS
SPOOLING
GILNOORT ROOTLING
GILNOOST LOOTINGS
STOOLING
TOOLINGS
GILNOOTT TOOTLING
GILNOOVY VINOLOGY
GILNOOWY WOOINGLY
GILNOPPP PLOPPING
POPPLING
GILNOPPS LOPPINGS
SLOPPING
GILNOPPT TOPPLING
GILNOPRU PROULING
GILNOPRW PROWLING
GILNOPSU SOUPLING
GILNOPSY POSINGLY
SPONGILY
GILNOPTT PLOTTING
GILNORSU LOURINGS
GILNORTU TROULING
GILNORVY ROVINGLY
GILNOSSW SLOWINGS
GILNOSTT SLOTTING
GILNOSTU TOUSLING
GILNOSVW WOLVINGS
GILNOSWY YOWLINGS
GILNOSZZ SOZZLING
GILNOTUY OUTLYING
GILNOTUZ TOUZLING
GILNPPRU PURPLING
GILNPPSU SUPPLING
GILNPRSU PURLINGS
SLURPING
SPURLING
GILNPRYY PRYINGLY
GILNPSSU PLUSSING
GILNPUZZ PUZZLING
GILNRRSU SLURRING
GILNRSTU LUSTRING
RUSTLING
GILNRTTU TURTLING
GILNRTYY TRYINGLY
GILNSSTU SINGULTS
TUSSLING
GILNSTTU SUTTLING
GILNTUUY UNGUILTY
GILNUWZZ WUZZLING
GILOOORS ROSOGLIO
GILOOOST OOLOGIST
GILOORSS GIROSOLS
GILOORSU GLORIOUS
GILOORVY VIROLOGY
GILOOSSS ISOGLOSS
GILOOSTY SITOLOGY
GILORSTT TRIGLOTS
GILOSTUY GULOSITY
GIMMMNSU MUMMINGS
GIMMMNUY MUMMYING
GIMMNOTY TOMMYING
GIMMNSSU SUMMINGS
GIMMNSTU STUMMING
GIMMOSSU GUMMOSIS
GIMNNORS MORNINGS
GIMNNORU MOURNING
GIMNNOTU MOUNTING
GIMNNOUV UNMOVING
GIMNNSTU MUNTINGS
GIMNOOOU OOGONIUM
GIMNOOPS SPOOMING
GIMNOORS MOORINGS
SMOORING
GIMNOORT MOTORING
GIMNOORV VROOMING
GIMNOOSS OSMOSING
GIMNOOST MOOTINGS
SMOOTING
GIMNOPRT TROMPING
GIMNOPST STOMPING
GIMNOPTU GUMPTION
GIMNORRU RUMORING
GIMNORRW RINGWORM
GIMNORST STORMING
GIMNORSU ROUMINGS
GIMNOSST GNOMISTS
GIMNOSSU MOUSINGS
SMOUSING
SOUMINGS
GIMNOSTU MOUSTING
SMOUTING
GIMNOSYY MISOGYNY
GIMNPRTU TRUMPING
GIMNPSTU STUMPING
GIMNRRSU SMURRING
GIMNSTTU SMUTTING
GIMPSSYY GYPSYISM
GIMRSSUU GURUISMS
GINNNOOS NOONINGS
GINNNOST STONNING
GINNNOSW WONNINGS
GINNNPSU PUNNINGS
GINNNRSU RUNNINGS

GINNNSTU	STUNNING
	TUNNINGS
GINNNTUU	UNTUNING
GINNOOPS	SNOOPING
	SPOONING
GINNOOST	SNOOTING
GINNOOSW	SWOONING
GINNOOSZ	SNOOZING
GINNOPPU	UNPOPING
GINNOPRU	UNROPING
GINNOPRY	PROYNING
GINNOPSS	SPONGINS
	SPONSING
GINNOPSY	PYONINGS
GINNOPTU	GUNPOINT
GINNOPTY	POYNTING
GINNORSS	SNORINGS
	SORNINGS
GINNORST	SNORTING
GINNORSU	GRUNIONS
GINNOSST	STONINGS
GINNOSTT	SNOTTING
GINNOSTU	SNOUTING
	STOUNING
GINNOSTY	STONYING
GINNOSUW	SWOUNING
GINNPRSU	PRUNINGS
	SPURNING
GINNRSSU	NURSINGS
GINNRSTU	TURNINGS
	UNSTRING
GINNSTTU	NUTTINGS
	STUNTING
GINNSTUY	UNTYINGS
GINOOPPS	OPPOSING
GINOOPRS	SPOORING
GINOOPRT	TROOPING
GINOOPSS	SOOPINGS
GINOOPST	STOOPING
GINOOPSW	SWOOPING
GINOORST	ROOSTING
	ROOTINGS
GINOORTW	WROOTING
GINOOSTT	TOOTSING
GINOPPPR	PROPPING
GINOPPQU	QUOPPING
GINOPPSS	SOPPINGS
GINOPPST	STOPPING
	TOPPINGS
GINOPPSW	SWOPPING
GINOPRSS	PROSINGS
GINOPRST	SPORTING
GINOPRSU	INGROUPS
	POURINGS
GINOPRSV	PROVINGS
GINOPRTU	TROUPING
GINOPSST	POSTINGS
	SIGNPOST
	STOPINGS
GINOPSSU	SPOUSING
GINOPSTT	SPOTTING
GINOPSTU	POUTINGS
	SPOUTING
GINOPTTY	TYPTOING
GINORRWY	WORRYING
GINORSST	SORTINGS
GINORSSU	SOURINGS
GINORSTU	ROUSTING
	ROUTINGS
	TOURINGS
GINORSTW	STROWING
	WORSTING
GINORSTY	ROYSTING
	STORYING
	STROYING
GINORTTT	TROTTING
GINORTTU	TROUTING
	TUTORING
GINOSSSS	SOSSINGS
GINOSSST	TOSSINGS
GINOSSSU	SOUSINGS
GINOSSSW	SOWSSING
GINOSSTT	SOTTINGS
GINOSSTU	TOUSINGS
GINOSSTV	STOVINGS
GINOSSTW	STOWINGS
GINOSTTT	STOTTING
	TOTTINGS
GINOSTTW	SWOTTING
GINOSTUW	OUTSWING
	OUTWINGS
GINOTUVY	OUTVYING
GINPPPUY	PUPPYING
GINPPRSU	UPSPRING
GINPRRSU	PURRINGS
	SPURRING
GINPRSTU	SPURTING
GINPRSUU	PURSUING
	USURPING
GINPRSUY	SYRUPING
GINPSSUW	UPSWINGS
GINPSTTU	PUTTINGS
GINPTTUY	PUTTYING
GINRSSTU	RUSTINGS
	TRUSSING
GINRSTTU	RUTTINGS
	STURTING
	TRUSTING
GINRSTTY	TRYSTING
GINRSTUU	SUTURING
GINSTTTU	TUTTINGS
GIOOPRRS	PORRIGOS
GIOORRSU	RIGOROUS
GIOORSTU	GOITROUS
GIOORSUV	VIGOROUS
GIOPRRSU	PRURIGOS
GIOPRSSY	GOSSIPRY
GIOPRSTU	GROUPIST
GIORSTUY	RUGOSITY
GJOORSTT	JOGTROTS
GKLOOOTY	TOKOLOGY
GLLOOPTY	POLYGLOT
GLLOOPWY	POLLYWOG
GLLOOXYY	XYLOLOGY
GLMNOOOT	MONOGLOT
GLMNOOOY	MONOLOGY
	NOMOLOGY
GLMNRTUU	NGULTRUM
GLMOOOPY	POMOLOGY
GLMOOORS	MOORLOGS
GLMOOYYZ	ZYMOLOGY
GLMORSUW	LUGWORMS
GLNNOORS	LORGNONS
GLNOOOSY	NOSOLOGY
GLNOOOTY	ONTOLOGY
GLNOOPRS	PROLONGS
GLNOOPSY	POLYGONS
GLNOOPYY	POLYGONY
GLNOPYYY	POLYGYNY
GLNORSTY	STRONGLY
	STRONGYL
GLNORTUW	LUNGWORT
GLNOSSUW	SUNGLOWS
GLNOSTTU	GLUTTONS
GLNOTTUY	GLUTTONY
GLOOOPSY	POSOLOGY
GLOOOPTY	OPTOLOGY
	TOPOLOGY
GLOOORUY	OUROLOGY
GLOOPSSY	GOSSYPOL
GLOOPTYY	TYPOLOGY
GLOORSUU	ORGULOUS
GMMPSUUW	MUGWUMPS
GMNNOOOY	MONOGONY
GMNNOOYY	MONOGYNY
GMNOORSU	GUNROOMS
GMNOORSW	MORWONGS
GMORSTUW	MUGWORTS
GNNPRSUU	UNSPRUNG
GNNRSTUU	UNSTRUNG
GNOOORSS	GORSOONS
GNOOOSSS	GOSSOONS
GNOORSUW	WRONGOUS
GNOORTUW	OUTGROWN
GNOPRSTU	GUNPORTS
GNPPRSUU	UPSPRUNG
GOORSTUW	OUTGROWS
GOORTTUW	GOUTWORT
HHIILOPT	THIOPHIL
HHIINNST	THINNISH
HHIIPSST	PHTHISIS
HHILPSSY	SYLPHISH
HHIMNPSY	NYMPHISH
HHIMPSSU	SUMPHISH
HHINOOSW	NOHOWISH
HHIORSST	SHORTISH
HHKKSSUU	KHUSKHUS
HHMRSTUY	RHYTHMUS
HHOOPPRS	PHOSPHOR
HHOOSSTT	HOTSHOTS
HIIILMNS	NIHILISM
HIIILNST	NIHILIST
HIIILNTY	NIHILITY
HIIINRST	RHINITIS
HIIKMNST	MISTHINK
HIIKMRSS	SKIRMISH
HIIKNPSS	KINSHIPS
HIIKOPRS	PIROSHKI
HIIKOPRZ	PIROZHKI
HIIKQRSU	QUIRKISH
HIIKSSTT	SKITTISH
HIILMMSS	SLIMMISH
HIILMOST	HOMILIST
HIILMPSU	SILPHIUM
HIILMPSY	IMPISHLY
HIILMSTU	LITHIUMS
HIILMSWY	WHIMSILY
HIILMTUY	HUMILITY
HIILPSST	THLIPSIS
HIILPSSY	SYPHILIS
HIILRSTT	TRILITHS
HIILRSTY	SHIRTILY
HIILSSTT	STILTISH
HIIMNSTT	TINSMITH
HIIMOPSS	PHIMOSIS
HIIMSSTT	SHITTIMS
HIINORST	HISTRION
HIINPSTW	TWINSHIP
HIIORSST	HISTRIOS
HIIPPQSU	QUIPPISH
HIKMNSUU	MINSHUKU
HIKNNORS	INKHORNS
HIKNNSTU	UNTHINKS
HIKNOTTU	OUTTHINK
HIKOOPSS	SPOOKISH
HIKOPSSY	KYPHOSIS
HILLMSUY	MULISHLY
HILLNOUY	UNHOLILY
HILLOPST	HILLTOPS
HILMMOSU	HOLMIUMS
HILMNOOT	MONOLITH
HILMOOPT	PHILOMOT
HILMOPSY	MOPISHLY
HILMOSSW	WHOLISMS
HILMPPSU	PLUMPISH
HILMPSYY	SYMPHILY
HILMSTUU	THULIUMS
HILNOPSU	UNPOLISH
HILNOSTY	TONISHLY
HILOOPYZ	ZOOPHILY
HILOOSTT	OTOLITHS
HILOOSTZ	ZOOLITHS
HILOOTTY	TOOTHILY
HILOPPSY	POPISHLY
HILORSTU	UROLITHS
HILORTWY	WORTHILY
HILOSSTW	WHOLISTS
HILOSSTY	HYLOISTS
	THYLOSIS
HILOSTWW	WHITLOWS
HILOSTYY	TOYISHLY
HILPPRSU	PURPLISH
HILPPSUY	UPPISHLY
HILPRSUW	UPWHIRLS
HILSSTTU	SLUTTISH
HIMMOPRU	PHORMIUM
HIMMSSTY	MYTHISMS
HIMNOPRX	PHORMINX
HIMNOPSY	PHISNOMY
HIMNSSTY	HYMNISTS
HIMOOPRS	ISOMORPH
HIMOPRSW	SHIPWORM
HIMOPRWW	WHIPWORM
HIMOPSSS	SOPHISMS
HIMOPSST	PHOTISMS
HIMORSTU	HUMORIST
	THORIUMS
HIMOTTVZ	MITZVOTH
HIMPRSTU	TRIUMPHS
HIMPSTUY	PYTHIUMS
HIMRSSTY	RHYMISTS
HIMSSTTY	MYTHISTS
HINNORST	TINHORNS
HINNPSSU	NUNSHIPS
HINNSSUY	SUNSHINY
HINOORST	HORNITOS
HINOORSZ	HORIZONS
HINOPPSS	SHIPPONS
HINOPSSS	SONSHIPS
HINOPSSY	HYPNOSIS
HINOPSTW	TOWNSHIP
HINORSST	HORNISTS
HINORTXY	THYROXIN
HIOOOPRZ	ZOOPHORI
HIOOPRTT	POORTITH
HIOORSST	ORTHOSIS
HIOOSSTT	SHOOTIST
HIOPRSSW	WORSHIPS
HIOPRSUZ	RHIZOPUS
HIOPSSST	SOPHISTS

HIOPSSTU UPHOISTS
HIOPSSTY PHYTOSIS
HIORRSSY SORRYISH
HIOSSTTU STOUTISH
HIPPPSUY PUPPYISH
HIPSUYZZ ZIZYPHUS
HKKOOSSY SKYHOOKS
HKMNORRU KRUMHORN
HKNOORRW HORNWORK
HKNOOSWW KNOWHOWS
HKOOOPST POTHOOKS
HKOOPRSW WORKSHOP
HLLLOOWY HOLLOWLY
HLLMNOOU MONOHULL
HLLOPPRY PROPHYLL
HLMOOSTY SMOOTHLY
HLMORRSY MYRRHOLS
HLNOOPPY POLYPHON
HLOPRSTY PROTHYLS
HLPRSSUU SULPHURS
HLPRSUUY SULPHURY
HMMNOOSY HOMONYMS
HMMNOOYY HOMONYMY
HMMOORSU MUSHROOM
HMMRSTUU HUMSTRUM
HMNOOOST MOONSHOT
HMNOOOTY HOMOTONY
HMNOORRW HORNWORM
HMNOOSTU UNSMOOTH
HMNOPSYY HYPONYMS
SYMPHONY
HMNOPYYY HYPONYMY
HMOOOPRZ ZOOMORPH
HMOOORSW SHOWROOM
HMOOPTYY HOMOTYPY
HMOORSUU HUMOROUS
HNNOSSTY SYNTHONS
HNOOOOPR OOPHORON
HNOOPRSW SHOPWORN
HNOOPSTY TYPHOONS
HNOORRTW HORNWORT
HNOORSTU SOUTHRON
HNOOSSTU UNSHOOTS
HNOPRTUW UPTHROWN
HNORSTUW UNWORTHS
HNORTUWY UNWORTHY
HNOSSTUU UNSHOUTS
HNRSTTUU UNTRUTHS
HOOOSTTU OUTSHOOT
HOOPPSST POTSHOPS
HOOPPSTY PHOTOPSY
HOOPRRST PORTHORS
HOOPSSTU UPSHOOTS
HOOPSSTY TOYSHOPS
HOORTTUW OUTWORTH
HOOSSTTU OUTSHOTS
HOPPRRYY PORPHYRY
HOPRRSUY PYRRHOUS
HOPRSTUW UPTHROWS
HOPSSTTU SHOTPUTS
HPRSTTUU UPTHRUST
IIIJJLNS JINJILIS
IIIKLNPS SPILIKIN
IIIKMNNS MINIKINS
IIILLMNP MINIPILL
IIILLMNU ILLINIUM
IIILLNOS ILLISION
IIILMRSV VIRILISM
IIILMUVX LIXIVIUM
IIILRTVY VIRILITY
IIIMMMNS MINIMISM
IIIMMNST INTIMISM
MINIMIST
IIIMMPRS IMPRIMIS
IIIMNSTT INTIMIST
IIIMNTTY INTIMITY
IIINORRS IRRISION
IIINPRST INSPIRIT
IIINQTUY INIQUITY
IIINSSTU SINUITIS
IIIOSTTU OUISTITI
IIISSTTW WISTITIS
IIJLLNOS JILLIONS
IIJMNOSS MISJOINS
IIJNNOST INJOINTS
IIJNNSTU NINJITSU
IIKLLNOS SKILLION
IIKLMNPS LIMPKINS
IIKLMPSY SKIMPILY
IIKLNOSS OILSKINS
IIKLQRUY QUIRKILY
IIKMNORS KIRIMONS
IIKMNPSS SIMPKINS
IIKNOSTT STOTINKI
IILLLPUV PULVILLI
IILLMNOS MILLIONS
IILLMRTU TRILLIUM
IILLMUUV ILLUVIUM
IILLNOOR ORILLION
IILLNOPS PILLIONS
IILLNORT TRILLION
IILLNOST STILLION
IILLNOSU ILLUSION
IILLNOSZ ZILLIONS
IILLNSST INSTILLS
IILLNSTT LITTLINS
IILLOPUV PULVILIO
IILMMPSS SIMPLISM
IILMMSUU SIMULIUM
IILMNORT MIRLITON
IILMNOSS LIONISMS
IILMNSTU LUMINIST
IILMORSS SIMILORS
IILMORST TROILISM
IILMOTTY MOTILITY
IILMPSST SIMPLIST
IILMRSSY MISSILRY
IILNNOOT NOLITION
IILNNSSU INSULINS
IILNOOST INOSITOL
IILNOOTV VOLITION
IILNORSS SIRLOINS
IILOOPPR LIRIPOOP
IILOPRST TRIPOLIS
IILOPSSS PSILOSIS
IILOPSST PTILOSIS
IILOPSTY PILOSITY
IILORSTT TROILIST
IILORSTV VITRIOLS
IILOSSTV VIOLISTS
IILRSSTU SILURIST
IILSTUUV UVULITIS
IILSTUVV VULVITIS
IIMMNTUY IMMUNITY
IIMMOPST OPTIMISM
IIMMOPSU OPIUMISM
IIMMSTTU MITTIMUS
IIMNNOOT MONITION
IIMNNOSU UNIONISM
IIMNNOTU MUNITION
IIMNOOSS OMISSION
IIMNOPRS IMPRISON
IIMNOPST MISPOINT
IIMNORTT INTROMIT
IIMNORTY MINORITY
IIMNOSSS MISSIONS
IIMNOSST SIMONIST
IIMNOSTX MIXTIONS
IIMNPRST IMPRINTS
MISPRINT
IIMNPTUY IMPUNITY
IIMNRSTY MINISTRY
IIMOPSTT OPTIMIST
IIMOSSTY MYOSITIS
IIMOTTVY MOTIVITY
IIMPRTUY IMPURITY
IIMRRTUV TRIUMVIR
IIMRSTTU TRITIUMS
IIMRSTUV TRIVIUMS
IIMSSSTU MISSUITS
IIMSSTUW SWIMSUIT
IINNOOPS OPINIONS
IINNOPPT PINPOINT
IINNOPTU PUNITION
IINNOSTU INUSTION
UNIONIST
UNITIONS
IINNPSST TINSNIPS
IINNSTTU TINNITUS
IINOOPST POSITION
IINOPSSS ISOSPINS
IINORSST IRONISTS
IINORSTT INTROITS
IINOSTTU TUITIONS
IINOSTVY VINOSITY
IINRTTUY TRIUNITY
IINSSTTW INTWISTS
IIOOPSTV OVIPOSIT
IIOOSTTY OTIOSITY
IIOPRRTY PRIORITY
IIOPRSSS PISSOIRS
IIORRRSY IRRISORY
IIORSSTV IVORISTS
VISITORS
IIORSTUV VIRTUOSI
IIOSSTTU OUSTITIS
IIPRSSTU SPIRITUS
IJKLLOSY KILLJOYS
IJLNOQSU JONQUILS
IJNNOSTU UNJOINTS
IJNNSTUU NINJUTSU
IKKLNORW LINKWORK
IKKLNOSY KOLINSKY
IKKMNOSU KIKUMONS
IKKNORST KIRKTONS
IKKORSSY SIKORSKY
IKLLOOTV KILOVOLT
IKLLOSSY KYLLOSIS
IKLMNPSU LUMPKINS
IKLMOOSS LOOKISMS
IKLMORSW SILKWORM
IKLMORTW MILKWORT
IKLNOOST KILOTONS
IKLNOPST SLIPKNOT
IKLNPSSU SKULPINS
IKLOOPSY SPOOKILY
IKLOOSTT TOOLKITS
IKLOSSSU SOUSLIKS
IKMNNOSW MISKNOWN
IKMNOOOS OKIMONOS
IKMNOSSW MISKNOWS
IKMNPPSU PUMPKINS
IKMNRSTU TRINKUMS
IKNNOPSY PONYSKIN
IKNNRSTU TURNSKIN
IKNOOPRT PINKROOT
IKNOORRW IRONWORK
IKNOOSST ISOKONTS
IKNOPSST INKSPOTS
IKNOPSTW TOWNSKIP
IKNPSSTU SPUTNIKS
IKORSSTU KURTOSIS
ILLLMOPS PLIMSOLL
ILLLMPPU PULPMILL
ILLLOOPP LOLLIPOP
ILLMNOSU MULLIONS
ILLMNRSU MILLRUNS
ILLMOORS MOORILLS
ILLMOPRW PILLWORM
ILLMOSSY LISSOMLY
ILLMPTUY MULTIPLY
ILLNOQSU QUILLONS
ILLNORSU RULLIONS
ILLNPSUU LUPULINS
ILLOOPRW POORWILL
ILLOORSZ ZORILLOS
ILLOPPSS SLIPSLOP
ILLOPPSY SLOPPILY
ILLOPRTW PILLWORT
ILLOPRXY PROLIXLY
ILLORSTU TROLLIUS
ILLORSUY ILLUSORY
ILLOSTXY XYLITOLS
ILLOTTWY WITTOLLY
ILLRSTUY SULTRILY
ILMNOOPS POLONISM
ILMNOOPU POLONIUM
ILMNOSUU LUMINOUS
ILMOPPSU POPULISM
ILMORSTU TURMOILS
ILMORSTY STORMILY
ILMOSTUV VOLUMIST
ILMOSTUY TIMOUSLY
ILMPPTUU PULPITUM
ILMPSSTU PLUMISTS
ILMPSTUY STUMPILY
ILMSSTUU STIMULUS
ILMSTTUY SMUTTILY
ILNOOPSS PLOSIONS
ILNOOPSV VOLPINOS
ILNOOPSY SPOONILY
ILNOOSST SOLITONS
ILNOOSTU SOLUTION
ILNOOSTY SNOOTILY
ILNOOTUV VOLUTION
ILNOPRSU PURLOINS
ILNOPSSU UPSILONS
ILNOPSSW SNOWSLIP
ILNOPSSY YPSILONS
ILNOPSTU UNSPOILT
ILNORSST NOSTRILS
ILNORSSU SURLOINS
ILNORSTU TORULINS
ILNORSTY NITROSYL
ILNORTXY NITROXYL
ILNOSSTW STOWLINS
ILNOSTTY SNOTTILY
ILNOSTUV VOLUTINS
ILNPSUUV PULVINUS
ILOOORSS ROSOLIOS

ILOOPPRS PROPOLIS
ILOOPSST POLOISTS
TOPSOILS
ILOORSTU RISOLUTO
ILOOSSST SOLOISTS
ILOPPSTU POPULIST
ILOPRSTY SPORTILY
ILOPSTTY SPOTTILY
ILOPSUUV PLUVIOUS
ILOQRTUU LOQUITUR
ILPPRTUY PULPITRY
ILRSTTUY TRUSTILY
ILRSTUUX LUXURIST
ILSSSTTY STYLISTS
IMMNOSSU MUSIMONS
IMMNOSUU MUONIUMS
IMMOORTU MOTORIUM
IMMRSTUY SUMMITRY
IMMSSSTU SUMMISTS
IMNNNOSU MUNNIONS
IMNNOORS NORIMONS
IMNNOOTT MONOTINT
IMNNOSUU NUMINOUS
IMNOOPPS POMPIONS
IMNOOPST TOMPIONS
IMNOOPSU OPSONIUM
IMNOORRS MORRIONS
IMNOORST MONITORS
TROMINOS
IMNOORTY MONITORY
IMNOORVY OMNIVORY
IMNOOSUX OXONIUMS
IMNOPPSU PUMPIONS
IMNORRSU MURRIONS
IMNORSTY TRIONYMS
IMNOSTUU MUTINOUS
IMNRSTUU UNTRUISM
IMOOPRRS PROMISOR
IMOOPRST IMPOSTOR
IMOOQSTU MOSQUITO
IMOORSTT MOTORIST
IMOORSTU SUMOTORI
TIMOROUS
IMOORSTY MOROSITY
IMOORTVY VOMITORY
IMOOSSTY MYOSOTIS
IMOPRRSY PRIMROSY
IMOPRSST TROPISMS
IMOPRSTU PROTIUMS
IMOPSSTU UTOPISMS
IMORSSTU TOURISMS
IMORSTTU TUTORISM
IMOSSTUW OUTSWIMS
IMPPPSUY PUPPYISM
IMRSSTTU MISTRUST
IMRSSTTY MISTRYST
IMRSTTUY YTTRIUMS
INNNORSU RUNNIONS
INNNORTU TRUNNION
INNNOSTY SYNTONIN
INNOOPSS OPSONINS
SPONSION
INNOOPSU UNPOISON
INNOORST NOTORNIS
INNOPRSU UNPRISON
INNOSSTU NONSUITS
INOOOSSZ ZOONOSIS
INOOOTXZ ZOOTOXIN
INOOPRST PORTIONS
POSITRON
SORPTION
INOOPSSS POISSONS
INOOPSST POSITONS
INOOPSTT SPITTOON
INOOPTTU OUTPOINT
INOORSST ISOTRONS
TORSIONS
INOORSTT TORTONIS
INOORSTY SONORITY
INOPPSST TOPSPINS
INOPRTUY PUNITORY
INOPSSSU POUSSINS
INOPSSSY SYNOPSIS
INOPSSTU SPINOUTS
INORSSUV UNVISORS
INPPRRUU PURPURIN
INPRSSTU UNSTRIPS
INPRSSTY TRYPSINS
INPRSTTU TURNSPIT
INRSSTTU INTRUSTS
INSSSTUU SUNSUITS
INSSTTUW UNTWISTS
IOOPRRSV PROVISOR
IOOPRSSV PROVISOS
IOOPRSSY ISOSPORY
IOOPRSTY ISOTROPY
POROSITY
IOORRSTY SORORITY
IOORRTTT TROTTOIR
IOORSSTT RISOTTOS
IOORSSUV VOUSSOIR
IOORSTTU TORTIOUS
IOORSTUV VIRTUOSO
IOORSUUX UXORIOUS
IOOSSTTU STOTIOUS
IOPPPRST PITPROPS
IOPRRSUV PROVIRUS
IOPRSSTT PROTISTS
TROPISTS
IOPRSSUU SPURIOUS
IOPRSTTU OUTSTRIP
IOPRSTUU POURSUIT
IOPRSTUY PYRITOUS
IOPRSUVX POXVIRUS
IOPSSTTU UTOPISTS
IOQRSTTU QUITTORS
IOQRTUXY QUIXOTRY
IORRSUVV SURVIVOR
IORSSTTU TOURISTS
IORSSTTW TWISTORS
IORSSUUU USURIOUS
IORSTTUY TOURISTY
YTTRIOUS
IORSTUUV VIRTUOUS
IPRRSSTU STIRRUPS
IPRRSTUU PRURITUS
IPRSSTUU PURSUITS
JLNSTUUY UNJUSTLY
JLOOSUYY JOYOUSLY
JMOPSTUU OUTJUMPS
JNNOORRU NONJUROR
JNOORSSU SOJOURNS
JNOOSUUY UNJOYOUS
KKNOORTW KNOTWORK
KKOOSSUU KOUSKOUS
KLLMNSUU NUMSKULL
KLLMOSSU MOLLUSKS
KLNORSTY KLYSTRON
KLOOORWW WOOLWORK
KLOOOSTU LOOKOUTS
OUTLOOKS
KLOOPRSW SLOPWORK
KMOOORRW WORKROOM
KNNNOSUW UNKNOWNS
KNOOPSTT TOPKNOTS
KNOPRSTY KRYPTONS
KNORRSTY KRYTRONS
KOOPRSTW WORKTOPS
KOORSTUW OUTWORKS
KORSTTUW TUTWORKS
LLLMMSUU MULMULLS
LLMOOPRS ROLLMOPS
LLOOPRST TROLLOPS
LLOOPRTY TROLLOPY
LLOORSTU ROLLOUTS
LLOSUUVV VOLVULUS
LMNOOOPY MONOPOLY
LMNOOPYY POLYONYM
LMOOOORT TOOLROOM
LMOOPSYY POLYSOMY
LMOORSWW SLOWWORM
LMOOSSSU MOLOSSUS
LMOPPRTY PROMPTLY
LMRSSTUU LUSTRUMS
LNOOOPRT POLTROON
LNOOOPYZ POLYZOON
LNOOPPRY PROPYLON
LNOOPSTU PULTOONS
LNRSTUUV VULTURNS
LOOOORSS OLOROSOS
LOOPPSUU POPULOUS
LOOPPSUY POLYPOUS
LORSSTUU LUSTROUS
MMOPSSTY SYMPTOMS
MNNOOOSS MONSOONS
MNNOOOTY MONOTONY
MNNOSSYY SYNONYMS
MNNOSTUU UNMOUNTS
MNNOSYYY SYNONYMY
MNOOOPPS POMPOONS
MNOOORTW MOONWORT
MNOOORXY OXYMORON
MNOOPRTU PRONOTUM
MNOOPSTY TOPONYMS
MNOOPTYY TOPONYMY
MNOOSTTW TOWMONTS
MNORSSTU NOSTRUMS
MNORSTUU SURMOUNT
MOOOPRRT PROMOTOR
MOOORRTW TOMORROW
MOOPSSSU OPOSSUMS
MOORRSUU RUMOROUS
MOORSTUU TUMOROUS
MOORSTUY UROSTOMY
MORRSSTU ROSTRUMS
MORSSTUU STRUMOUS
MSSTTUUU TSUTSUMU
NNOOOPST PONTOONS
SPONTOON
NNOOPRSU PRONOUNS
NNOOPSSS SPONSONS
NOOOPPRS PROSOPON
NOOORSSU SONOROUS
NOOPRSSS SPONSORS
NOORSSTU UNROOSTS
NOORSTUW OUTSWORN
NOPSSSTU SUNSPOTS
NORSTTUU OUTTURNS
TURNOUTS
NRSSTTUU UNTRUSTS
NRSTTUUY UNTRUSTY
OOOOPRST POTOROOS
OOOPRSSU SOPOROUS
OOOPRSTU OUTROOPS
OOORSTTU OUTROOTS
OOPRSSSU SOURSOPS
OOPRSSTV PROVOSTS
OOPRSTTU OUTPORTS
OUTSPORT
OOPRSTUU OUTPOURS
OOPSSSTT TOSSPOTS
OOPSSTTU OUTPOSTS
OORSTTUU TORTUOUS
OPPRRSTU PURPORTS
OPPRSSTU SUPPORTS
OPRSSSUU SOURPUSS
ORSSTTUU SURTOUTS
RRSSSUUU SUSURRUS